Poetry Criticism

Guide to Gale Literary Criticism Series

For criticism on	Consult these Gale series
Authors now living or who died after December 31, 1999	***CONTEMPORARY LITERARY CRITICISM (CLC)***
Authors who died between 1900 and 1999	***TWENTIETH-CENTURY LITERARY CRITICISM (TCLC)***
Authors who died between 1800 and 1899	***NINETEENTH-CENTURY LITERATURE CRITICISM (NCLC)***
Authors who died between 1400 and 1799	***LITERATURE CRITICISM FROM 1400 TO 1800 (LC)*** ***SHAKESPEAREAN CRITICISM (SC)***
Authors who died before 1400	***CLASSICAL AND MEDIEVAL LITERATURE CRITICISM (CMLC)***
Authors of books for children and young adults	***CHILDREN'S LITERATURE REVIEW (CLR)***
Dramatists	***DRAMA CRITICISM (DC)***
Poets	***POETRY CRITICISM (PC)***
Short story writers	***SHORT STORY CRITICISM (SSC)***
Black writers of the past two hundred years	***BLACK LITERATURE CRITICISM (BLC)*** ***BLACK LITERATURE CRITICISM SUPPLEMENT (BLCS)***
Hispanic writers of the late nineteenth and twentieth centuries	***HISPANIC LITERATURE CRITICISM (HLC)*** ***HISPANIC LITERATURE CRITICISM SUPPLEMENT (HLCS)***
Native North American writers and orators of the eighteenth, nineteenth, and twentieth centuries	***NATIVE NORTH AMERICAN LITERATURE (NNAL)***
Major authors from the Renaissance to the present	***WORLD LITERATURE CRITICISM, 1500 TO THE PRESENT (WLC)*** ***WORLD LITERATURE CRITICISM SUPPLEMENT (WLCS)***

ISSN 1052-4851

Poetry Criticism

Excerpts from Criticism of the works of the Most Significant and Widely Studied Poets of World Literature

Volume 28

Anna Sheets Nesbitt and Susan Salas
Editors

GALE GROUP

Detroit
New York
San Francisco
London
Boston
Woodbridge, CT

STAFF

Janet Witalec, *Managing Editor, Literature Product*
Anna Sheets Nesbitt, Susan Salas, *Editors*
Mark W. Scott, *Publisher, Literature Product*

Jennifer Baise, Laura Wisner-Broyles, *Editors*
Rebecca J. Blanchard, Vince Cousino, Jenny Cromie, Justin Karr, Linda Pavlovski, Debra A. Wells, *Assistant Editors*
Patti A. Tippett, Timothy J. White *Technical Training Specialists*
Kathleen Lopez Nolan, Lynn M. Spampinato, *Managing Editors*
Susan M. Trosky, *Content Director*

Maria L. Franklin, *Permissions Manager*
Edna Hedblad, Kimberly F. Smilay, *Permissions Specialists*
Erin Bealmear, Sandy Gore, Keryl Stanley, *Permissions Assistants*

Victoria B. Cariappa, *Research Manager*
Andrew Guy Malonis, Barbara McNeil, Gary J. Oudersluys, Maureen Richards, Cheryl L. Warnock, *Research Specialists*
Tamara C. Nott, Tracie A. Richardson, *Research Associates*
Scott Floyd, Timothy Lehnerer, Ron Morelli *Research Assistants*

Dorothy Maki, *Manufacturing Manager*
Stacy Melson, *Buyer*

Mary Beth Trimper, *Composition Manager*
Evi Seoud, *Assistant Production Director*
Carolyn Fischer, Gary Leach, *Composition Specialists*

Randy Bassett, *Image Database Supervisor*
Robert Duncan, *Imaging Specialist*
Mike Logusz, *Graphic Artist*
Pamela A. Reed, *Imaging Coordinator*

Library of Congress Catalog Card Number 88-641014
ISBN 0-7876-3076-4
ISSN 1052-4851
Printed in the United States of America

10 9 8 7 6 5 4 3 2 1

Contents

Preface vii

Acknowledgments xi

Wendell Berry 1934-? 1

Robert Bridges 1844-1930 46

G. K. Chesterton 1874-1936 92

Hans Magnus Enzenberger 1929- 132

William Meredith 1919- 169

James Merrill 1926-1995 218

Michael Ondaatje 1943- 290

Dorothy Parker 1893-1967 343

Gary Soto 1952- 368

Literary Criticism Series Cumulative Author Index 407

PC Cumulative Nationality Index 479

PC Cumulative Title Index 481

Preface

Poetry Criticism (***PC***) presents significant criticism of the world's greatest poets and provides supplementary biographical and bibliographical material to guide the interested reader to a greater understanding of the genre and its creators. Although major poets and literary movements are covered in such Gale Literary Criticism series as *Contemporary Literary Criticism* (*CLC*), *Twentieth-Century Literary Criticism* (*TCLC*), *Nineteenth-Century Literature Criticism* (*NCLC*), *Literature Criticism from 1400 to 1800* (*LC*), and *Classical and Medieval Literature Criticism* (*CMLC*), ***PC*** offers more focused attention on poetry than is possible in the broader, survey-oriented entries on writers in these Gale series. Students, teachers, librarians, and researchers will find that the generous excerpts and supplementary material provided by ***PC*** supply them with the vital information needed to write a term paper on poetic technique, to examine a poet's most prominent themes, or to lead a poetry discussion group.

Scope of the Series

PC is designed to serve as an introduction to major poets of all eras and nationalities. Since these authors have inspired a great deal of relevant critical material, ***PC*** is necessarily selective, and the editors have chosen the most important published criticism to aid readers and students in their research. Each author entry presents a historical survey of the critical response to that author's work. The length of an entry is intended to reflect the amount of critical attention the author has received from critics writing in English and from foreign critics in translation. Every attempt has been made to identify and include the most significant essays on each author's work. In order to provide these important critical pieces, the editors sometimes reprint essays that have appeared elsewhere in Gale's Literary Criticism Series. Such duplication, however, never exceeds twenty percent of a ***PC*** volume.

Organization of the Book

Each *PC* entry consists of the following elements:

- The **Author Heading** cites the name under which the author most commonly wrote, followed by birth and death dates. Also located here are any name variations under which an author wrote, including transliterated forms for authors whose native languages use nonroman alphabets. If the author wrote consistently under a pseudonym, the pseudonym will be listed in the author heading and the author's actual name given in parenthesis on the first line of the biographical and critical introduction. Uncertain birth or death dates are indicated by question marks. Single-work entries are preceded by the title of the work and its date of publication.

- The **Introduction** contains background information that introduces the reader to the author and the critical debates surrounding his or her work.

- A **Portrait of the Author** is included when available.

- The list of **Principal Works** is ordered chronologically by date of first publication and lists the most important works by the author. The first section comprises poetry collections and book-length poems. The second section gives information on other major works by the author. For foreign authors, the editors have provided original foreign-language publication information and have selected what are considered the best and most complete English-language editions of their works.

- Reprinted **Criticism** is arranged chronologically in each entry to provide a useful perspective on changes in critical evaluation over time. All individual titles of poems and poetry collections by the author featured in the entry are printed in boldface type. The critic's name and the date of composition or publication of the critical work are given at the beginning of each piece of criticism. Unsigned criticism is preceded by the title of the source in which it appeared. Footnotes are reprinted at the end of each essay or excerpt. In the case of excerpted criticism, only those footnotes that pertain to the excerpted texts are included.

- Critical essays are prefaced by brief **Annotations** explicating each piece.

- A complete **Bibliographical Citation** of the original essay or book precedes each piece of criticism.

- An annotated bibliography of **Further Reading** appears at the end of each entry and suggests resources for additional study. In some cases, significant essays for which the editors could not obtain reprint rights are included here. Boxed material following the further reading list provides references to other biographical and critical sources on the author in series published by Gale.

Cumulative Indexes

A **Cumulative Author Index** lists all of the authors that appear in a wide variety of reference sources published by the Gale Group, including *PC*. A complete list of these sources is found facing the first page of the Author Index. The index also includes birth and death dates and cross references between pseudonyms and actual names.

A **Cumulative Nationality Index** lists all authors featured in *PC* by nationality, followed by the number of the *PC* volume in which their entry appears.

A **Cumulative Title Index** lists in alphabetical order all individual poems, book-length poems, and collection titles contained in the *PC* series. Titles of poetry collections and separately published poems are printed in italics, while titles of individual poems are printed in roman type with quotation marks. Each title is followed by the author's last name and corresponding volume and page numbers where commentary on the work is located. English-language translations of original foreign-language titles are cross-referenced to the foreign titles so that all references to discussion of a work are combined in one listing.

Citing *Poetry Criticism*

When writing papers, students who quote directly from any volume in the Literary Criticism Series may use the following general format to footnote reprinted criticism. The first example pertains to material drawn from periodicals, the second to material reprinted from books.

Sylvia Kasey Marks, "A Brief Glance at George Eliot's *The Spanish Gypsy,*" *Victorian Poetry* 20, no. 2 (Summer 1983), 184-90; reprinted in *Poetry Criticism,* vol. 20, ed. Carol T. Gaffke (Detroit: The Gale Group, 1998), 128-31.

Linden Peach, "Man, Nature and Wordsworth: American Versions," *British Influence on the Birth of American Literature,* (Macmillan Press Ltd., 1982), 29-57; reprinted in *Poetry Criticism,* vol. 20, ed. Carol T. Gaffke (Detroit: The Gale Group, 1998), 37-40.

Suggestions are Welcome

Readers who wish to suggest new features, topics, or authors to appear in future volumes, or who have other suggestions or comments are cordially invited to call, write, or fax the Managing Editor:

Managing Editor, Literary Criticism Series
The Gale Group
27500 Drake Road
Farmington Hills, MI 48331-3535
1-800-347-4253 (GALE)
Fax: 248-699-8054

Acknowledgments

The editors wish to thank the copyright holders of the excerpted criticism included in this volume and the permissions managers of many book and magazine publishing companies for assisting us in securing reproduction rights. We are also grateful to the staffs of the Detroit Public Library, the Library of Congress, the University of Detroit Mercy Library, Wayne State University Purdy/Kresge Library Complex, and the University of Michigan Libraries for making their resources available to us. Following is a list of the copyright holders who have granted us permission to reproduce material in this volume of *PC*. Every effort has been made to trace copyright, but if omissions have been made, please let us know.

COPYRIGHTED EXCERPTS IN *PC*, VOLUME 28, WERE REPRODUCED FROM THE FOLLOWING PERIODICALS:

American Book Review, v. 4, July-August, 1982. © 1982 by *The American Book Review*. Reproduced by permission.—***American Poetry***, v. 7, Spring, 1990. Reproduced by permission.—***The Americas Review***, v. 17, Spring, 1989. Arte Público Press—University of Houston. Reproduced by permission.—***Books in Canada***, v. 13, December, 1984, for "On the Brink" by Lucille King-Edwards. Reproduced by permission of the author.—***The Canadian Forum***, v. 687, March, 1979 for "II: Poems for People who Don't Read Poems" by Pamela McCallum; v. LXIV, January, 1985 for "Coming Through" by Sam Solecki. Both reproduced by permission of the respective authors.—***Canadian Literature***, n. 36, Spring, 1968 for "Controlling the Jungle" by Douglas Barbour; n. 112, Spring, 1987 for "A Note on Ondaatje's 'Peter': A Creative Myth" by Gillian Jarding-Russell; n. 137, Summer, 1993 for "Narrative in Michael Ondaatje's 'The Man with Seven Toes'" by Ray Wilton. All reproduced by permission of the respective authors.—***Canadian Poetry***, n. 6, Spring-Summer, 1982. Reproduced by permission.—***The Chesterton Review***, v. II, Spring-Summer, 1976 for "Chesterton and T. S. Eliot" by Russell Kirk; v. VI, Fall-Winter, 1979-80 for "Chesterton as Satirist" by David J. Dooley. © 1976, 1979-80 *The Chesterton Review*. Both reproduced by permission of the respective authors.—***Contemporary Literature***, v. XXI, Autumn, 1980. Reproduced by permission.—***Contemporary Poetry***, v, IV, 1982 for "Monsters Wrapped in Silk: James Merrill's Country of a Thousand Years of Peace" by J. D. McClatchy. © *Contemporary Poetry* 1982. Reproduced by permission of the author.—***The Dalhousie Review***, v. 44, Summer, 1964. Reproduced by permission of the publisher.—***Discurso Literario***, v. 5, Autumn, 1987. Reproduced by permission.—***Essays in Literature***, v. 23, Spring, 1996. Copyright 1996 by Western Illinois University. Reproduced by permission.—***German Life & Letters***, v. XXI, October, 1967. Reproduced by permission of Blackwell Publishers.—***Germanic Notes***, v. 22, 1991. Reproduced by permission.—***The Iowa Review***, v. 25, Spring-Summer, 1992 for "The Childhood Worries, Or Why I Became a Writer" by Gary Soto. Copyright © 1992 by The University of Iowa. All rights reserved. Reproduced by permission of the author and Bookstop Literary Agency.—***Journal of Modern Literature***, v. 2, September, 1971. © Temple University 1971. Reproduced by permission.—***Latin American Literary Review***, v. XVIII, January-June, 1990. Reproduced by permission.—***The Literary Review***, v. 31, Spring, 1988 for "Moving the Dark to Wholeness: The Elegies of Wendell Berry" by Jeffrey Alan Triggs. Copyright © 1988 by Fairleigh Dickinson University. Reproduced by permission of the author.—***MLN***, v. 97, April 3, 1982. © 1982 by The Johns Hopkins University Press. All rights reserved. Reproduced by permission.—***Modern Poetry Studies***, v. XI, 1982. Copyright 1982 by Media Study, Inc. Reproduced by permission.—***The Nation***, New York, v. 230, May 3, 1980. © 1980 *The Nation* magazine/ The Nation Company, Inc. Reproduced by permission.—***The New York Herald Tribune***, v. 4, July 15, 1928. Copyright 1928, 1956 by The New York Times Company. Reproduced by permission.—***The New York Review of Books***, v. X, April 11, 1968; v. XLII, May 11, 1995. Copyright © 1968, 1995 Nyrev, Inc. Both reproduced with permission from *The New York Review of Books*.—***The New York Times Book Review***, September 21, 1975. Copyright © 1975 by The New York Times Company. Reproduced by permission./ March 27, 1927; July 1, 1928; June 14, 1931; August 23, 1931; December 13, 1936. Copyright 1927, renewed 1955; copyright 1928, renewed 1956; copyright 1931, renewed 1959; copyright 1936, renewed 1964 by The New York Times Company. All reproduced by permission.—***Northwest Review***, n. XXI, 1983. Copyright © 1983 by Northwest Review. Reproduced by permission.—***Parnassus: Poetry in Review***, v. 8, Fall-Winter, 1979 for "I Can Hear You Now" by Peter Cooley; v. 9, Spring- Summer, 1981 for "Drowning as One of the Fine Arts" by Paul West. Copyright © 1979, 1981 Poetry in Review Foundation, NY. Both reproduced by permission of the respective authors.—***Renascence***, v. XXIII, Spring, 1971. © copyright, 1971, Marquette University Press. Reproduced by permission.—***Revista Chicano-Riqueña***, v. XI, Summer, 1983. Arte Público Press—University of Houston. Reproduced by permission.—***South Atlantic Bulletin***, v. XXXIX, May, 1974. Copyright © 1974 by the South Atlantic Modern Language Association. Reproduced by permission.—***Southwest Review***, v. 67, Winter, 1981. © 1981 Southern Methodist University. Reproduced by permission.—***Studies in Canadian Literature***, v. 8, 1983 for "'I Send You a Picture,' Ondaatje's Portrait of Billy the Kid" by Judith Owens. Copyright by the author. Reproduced by permission of the editors.—***Studies in the Literary Imagination***, v. XX-

VII, Fall, 1994. Copyright 1994 Department of English, Georgia State University. Reproduced by permission.—***The Times Literary Supplement***, June 25, 1931; n. 4045, October 10, 1980; n. 4816, July 21, 1995. Copyright The Times Supplements Limited 1931, 1980, 1995. All reproduced from *The Times Literary Supplement* by permission.—***The University of Mississippi Studies in English***, v. V, 1984-87. Copyright © 1984-87 The University of Mississippi. Reproduced by permission.—***Thought***, v. LXVI, June, 1991. Copyright © 1991 by Fordham University Press. Reproduced by permission of Fordham University Press, New York.

COPYRIGHTED EXCERPTS IN *PC*, VOLUME 28, WERE REPRODUCED FROM THE FOLLOWING BOOKS:

Barbour, Douglas. From ***Michael Ondaatje***. Twayne Publishers, 1993. Copyright © 1993 by Twayne Publishers. All rights reserved.—Collier, Michael. From a forward to ***Effort at Speech: New and Selected Poems***. By William Meredith. TriQuarterly Books, 1997. Copyright © 1997 by Michael Collier. Reproduced by permission.—de Selincourt, Ernest. From ***Oxford Lectures on Poetry***. Oxford University Press/Clarendon Press, 1934. Reprinted by Books for Libraries Press, Inc., 1967. Reproduced by permission of Oxford University Press.—Demetz, Peter. From "Hans Magnus Enzensberger," in ***Postwar German Literature.*** Pegasus, 1970.—Ehrenpreis, Irvin. From "Merrill" in ***Poetries of America: Essays on the Relation of Character in Style***. Edited by Daniel Albright. University of Virginia Press, 1989. Copyright © 1989 by the Rector of Visitors of the University of Virginia. Reproduced by permission.—Ganz, Robin. From ***Updating the Literary West***. Copyright © 1997, Western Literature Association. Reproduced by permission.—Howard, Richard. From ***Alone with America: The Art of Poetry in the United States Since 1950***. Thames and London, 1965. Reproduced by permission.—Johnson, William C. From "Tangible Mystery in the Poetry of Wendell Berry" in ***Wendell Berry***. Edited by Paul Merchant. Confluence Press, Inc., 1991. Copyright © 1991 by Confluence Press, Inc.—Kalstone, Davis. From "Transparent Things" in ***Modern Critical Views: James Merrill***. Edited by David Bloom. Chelsea House Publishers, 1985. Copyright © 1985 by Chelsea House Publishers. Reproduced by permission.—Kinney, Arthur F. From ***Dorothy Parker, Revised***. Twayne Publishers. 1998. Copyright © 1998 by Twayne Publishers. All rights reserved.—Labrie, Ross. From ***James Merrill***. Twayne, 1982. Copyright © 1982 by G.K. Hall & Company. All rights reserved.—Mason, Michael Tomasek. From "Poetry and Masculinity on the Anglo/Chicano Border: Gary Soto, Robert Frost, and Robert Hass" in ***The Calvinist Roots of the Modern Era***. Alilki Barnstone, Robert Tomasek Mason, and Carol J. Singley, eds. © 1997 University Press of New England. All rights reserved. Reproduced by permission.—Moffett, Judith. From ***James Merrill: An Introduction to the Poetry***. Copyright © 1984 Columbia University Press. All rights reserved. Reproduced by permission.—Ondaatje, Michael with Jon Pearce. From ***Twelve Voices: Interviews with Canadian Poets***. Borealis Press 1980. Copyright © Borealis Press Limited. All rights reserved. Reproduced by permission.—Rotella, Guy. From ***Three Contemporary Poets of New England: William Meredith, Philip Booth and Peter Davison***. Twayne, 1983. Copyright © 1983 by G. K. Hall. All rights reserved.—Stanford, Donald E. From ***In the Classic Mode: The Achievement of Robert Bridges***. Associated University Presses, 1978. © 1978 by Associated University Presses. Reproduced by permission.—Taylor, Henry. From ***Compulsory Essays on Recent American Poets***. Louisiana State University Press, 1992. Copyright © 1992 by Louisiana State University Press. All rights reserved. Reproduced by permission.—Williams, Charles. From ***Poetry at Present***. The Clarendon Press, 1930. Reproduced by permission of Oxford University Press.—Yenser, Stephen. From ***The Consuming Myth: The Works of James Merrill***. Harvard University Press, 1987. Copyright © 1987 by the President of Harvard College. All rights reserved. Reproduced by permission.

PHOTOGRAPHS APPEARING IN *PC*, VOLUME 28, WERE RECEIVED FROM THE FOLLOWING SOURCES:

Berry, Wendell, photograph by James Baker Hall. Reproduced by permission of James Baker Hall.—Bridges, Robert, photograph. AP/Wide World Photos. Reproduced by permission.—Chesterton, G. K., photograph. Archive Photos, Inc. Reproduced by permission.—Enzensberger, Hans Magnus, photograph by Miriam Berkley. Reproduced by permission of Miriam Berkley.—Meredith, William, photograph. AP/Wide World Photos. Reproduced by permission.—Merrill, James, photograph. AP/Wide World Photos. Reproduced by permission.—Ondaatje, Michael, photograph by Thomas Victor. Reproduced by permission of the Estate of Thomas Victor.—Parker, Dorothy, 1933, photograph. AP/Wide World Photos. Reproduced by permission.—Soto, Gary, photograph by M. L. Marinelli. Chronicle Books.

Wendell Berry
1934-

American poet, novelist, short story writer, essayist, and translator.

INTRODUCTION

In his poetry and prose, Berry documents the rural lifestyle of his native Kentucky. He often draws upon his experiences as a farmer to illustrate the dangers of disrupting the natural life cycle and to lament the passing of provincial American traditions. Like Henry David Thoreau, with whom he has been compared, Berry is also regarded for his pragmatic and even-tempered approach to environmental and ecological issues.

BIOGRAPHICAL INFORMATION

The son of an attorney, Berry was born and raised in a rural area of Kentucky. He attended college at the University of Kentucky, receiving his graduate degree in 1957. After a few years teaching at Georgetown College, he received a Wallace Stegner fellowship for fiction in 1958-1959. In 1961 he was the recipient of a Guggenheim Fellowship, which took him to Italy and France. After briefly holding a teaching position at New York University, he followed the five previous generations of his family and began farming in Port Royal, Kentucky. It was not long before he rejected modern agricultural methods and farm machinery in favor of more traditional and conservational means; this concern for the land is a defining theme of his poetry and prose. He began teaching at the University of Kentucky in 1964, eventually resigning his position to work on his farm full-time. He now works as a contributing editor for *New Farm Magazine,* a periodical devoted to small farming.

MAJOR WORKS

In his verse, Berry utilizes conventional stylistic techniques to demonstrate how the ordering and healing qualities of nature should be allowed to function in human life. In such volumes as *The Broken Ground, Openings, Farming: A Handbook,* and *Collected Poems, 1957-1982,* he often adopts an elegiac tone to convey his agrarian values and appreciation of traditional moral concerns. Furthermore, he explores recurring themes such as the beauty of the countryside, the turning of the seasons, the routines of the farm, the importance of marriage, the cycle of life, and the dynamics of the family. In his collections *Sabbath* and *Sabbaths, 1987-90,* Berry underscores the spiritual connection between man and the wilderness, perceiving nature as a place of meditation and rebirth for man.

CRITICAL RECEPTION

Although a few reviewers deem Berry's poetry antiquated and moralistic, most applaud his versatility and praise him for his appreciation of nature and ecological concerns. His poetry and prose appeals to a variety of readers, including environmentalists, but scholars often debate his emphasis on the relationship between "culture" and "agriculture." Some commentators classify Berry as a regionalist poet, in the sense that his work is deeply rooted in the concerns and cadences of his native Kentucky; however, his interest in ecological conservation and familial values are universal and topical themes. Berry is considered an eloquent and influential voice in twentieth-century American poetry.

PRINCIPAL WORKS

Poetry

The Broken Ground 1964
Openings 1968
Farming: A Handbook 1970
A Country of Marriage 1973
Clearing 1977
Collected Poems: 1957-1982 1985
Sabbaths 1987
Sabbaths: 1987-1990 1992
Entries 1994
Selected Poems 1998
Timbered Choir: The Sabbath Poems, 1979-1997 1998

Other Major Works

Nathan Coulter (novel) 1960
A Place on Earth (novel) 1967
The Long-Legged House (essays) 1969
The Hidden Wound (essays) 1970
The Unforeseen Wilderness: An Essay on Kentucky's Red River Gorge (essays) 1971
A Continuous Harmony: Essays Cultural and Agricultural (essays) 1972
The Memory of Old Jack (novel) 1974
The Unsettling of America: Culture and Agriculture (essays) 1977
Recollected Essays: 1965-1990 (essays) 1981
Standing by Words (essays) 1983
Wild Birds (short stories) 1986
Home Economics (essays) 1987
Remembering (novel) 1988
Harlan Hubbard: Life and Work (criticism) 1990
What are People For? (essays) 1990
Fidelity (short stories) 1992
Sex, Economy, Freedom & Community (essays) 1993
Watch with Me (short stories) 1994
Another Turn of the Crank (essays) 1995
Two More Stories of the Port Williams Membership (short stories) 1997

CRITICISM

Robert Collins (essay date 1982)

SOURCE: "A More Mingled Music: Wendell Berry's Ambivalent View of Language," in *Modern Poetry Studies,* Vol. XI, Nos. 1-2, 1982, pp. 35-56.

[*In the following essay, Collins asserts that Berry's poetry and prose stresses the importance of poetry in a technological world.*]

Ever since the appearance of ***The Broken Ground*** in 1964,[1] Wendell Berry has devoted a considerable portion of his work to the continuing evaluation of language and the function of art, especially poetry. Again and again in his prose, Berry emphasizes the importance of language, not only for the man of letters, but for every individual living in an increasingly technological world. His essay "In Defense of Literacy"[2] lampoons those American universities which have begun to teach language and literature as specialities. To teach our language and literature as such, according to Berry, is to submit to the assumption "that literacy is no more than an ornament" (*CH,* p. 170); but for Wendell Berry, literacy, far from being a mere ornament, is a necessity:

> We will understand the world, and preserve ourselves and our values in it, only insofar as we have a language that is alert and responsive to it, and careful of it. [*CH,* p. 171]

Literacy is all the more important today because in our culture, we no longer have a vital and coherent oral tradition as primitive peoples and folk societies had; yet we are constantly bombarded by a kind of language, what Berry calls "prepared, public language" (*CH,* p. 171), which is trying to compel us to do something, usually, in his words, "to buy or believe somebody else's line of goods" (*CH,* p. 171). In Berry's view, our only defense against such a use of language as power is to know a better language, that is, we must know our literature, for "The only defense against the worst is a knowledge of the best" (*CH,* p. 172).

For Wendell Berry, the abuse of language is largely responsible for the cultural, physical, and spiritual wasteland in which Americans are living today. In *The Long-Legged House,*[3] Berry acknowledges both the importance of language—"men fight when arguments fail" (*LLH,* p. 68)—and the way in which Americans have abused language. Our future is in jeopardy because we have lost our idealism, and ideals are the only real guides to the future. That loss of idealism has resulted in a loss of reality, for "Each is the measure and corrective of the other" (*LLH,* p. 48). While Berry views the constant migration of Americans from one part of the country to another or from part of a city to another as partly to blame for our loss of idealism, a cause just as significant is the abuse of language:

> Much of the blame for the erosion of our idealism must be laid to the government, because the language of ideals has been so grossly misused by the propagandists. [*LLH,* p. 51]

Again and again, Berry notes how our language has deteriorated, largely because of the wide gap between what governments, churches, businesses, and individuals say and what they do, what he calls "a radical disconnection between our words and our deeds" (*CH,* p. 128).

Berry doesn't confine himself, however, to commenting upon the importance and the abuse of the everyday language we speak and write or upon the prepared, public speech of politicians. He also has much to say about poetry, about its importance and its abuse. Berry derives one of his definitions of poetry from Thoreau: "Poetry is nothing but healthy speech" (*CH,* p. 14). He borrows another one of his definitions from R. H. Blyth: "Poetry is not the words written in a book, but the mode of activity of the mind of the poet" (*CH,* p. 15). For Berry, at least in his essays, as for Thoreau and Blyth, poetry, in addition to being the sacred tie which binds all things, is a power which can help to change the world insofar as it is "conducive to the health of the speaker, giving him a true and vigorous relation to the world" (*CH,* p. 14).

While poetry could be one of the most important means of restoring life and health to the world, of making the wasteland bloom, the poetry of this century, according to Berry, has failed to do so. It "has suffered from the schism in the modern consciousness. It has been turned back upon itself, fragmented, obscured in its function. . . . It has often seemed to lack wholeness and wisdom" (*CH,* p. 15). Berry finds hope, however, in the work of a number of contemporaries, most notably Denise Levertov, Gary Snyder, and A. R. Ammons, in whose poetry he finds "a sustained attentiveness to nature and to the relation between man and nature" (*CH,* p. 1). Their poetry appeals to him particularly because it is not turned self-consciously back upon itself, but rather toward the external world. "It seeks to give us a sense of our proper place in the scheme of things" (*CH,* p. 16).

Of all the poets of this century, however, Berry most admires William Carlos Williams, primarily because Williams' poems are so much concerned with the importance of place:

> His poems and stories and essays record the lifelong practice, the unceasingly labor of keeping responsibly conscious of where he was. He knew, as few white Americans have ever known, that a man has not meaningfully arrived in his place in body until he has arrived in spirit as well. [*CH,* pp. 56-57]

Berry also admires Williams for his insistence upon the concrete ("No ideas but in things") and for his insistence upon the necessity and usefulness of poetry. What Berry finds in Williams as well as in the work of the other poets mentioned above is, again, a power which moves toward the world and toward "a new pertinence of speech" (*CH,* p. 35).

As we have seen, for Wendell Berry, poetry, more than the words written on a page, is a power which has a good deal more to do with the way a person lives than with anything he might write. This definition, suggesting a kind of poetry other than that which takes the form of language, is the first hint in Berry's work of a growing ambivalence about the value and power of language, especially poetry. As we might expect, the view of language and poetry which we find in Berry's poems is both similar to and different from that which we find in his essays. At least early in his career in his essays and his poems, poetry is one of the most important means of restoring a world laid waste by men and of ushering in a new era in which there would be new contact between people and the earth; yet, at the same time, we can observe a paradoxical development in his poetry which increasingly emphasizes the importance of silence and increasingly stresses that poetry is not the words written in a book, but "the mode of activity of the mind of the poet."

A number of poems from ***The Broken Ground,*** Berry's first volume of poetry, demonstrate the way in which Berry, at least early in his career, values song, especially human son. In **"A Man Walking and Singing,"** he admires the ability of people to sing not in spite of but because of their knowledge of death, the oppressive climate in which they live. In keeping with what he says in his essays about the importance of place to his own writing, we can observe in this poem how the stuff of the world, what the speaker sees and hears, becomes part of his song, his footsteps, in a phrase Williams no doubt would have admired, "beating the measure of his song" (***BG,*** p. 29). Berry further underscores the importance of human song here by the way he contrasts it with "the mockingbird's crooked / arrogant notes" (***BG,*** p. 30). The man in the poem sings not in spite of but almost because of his awareness of death while the bird sings "as though no flight / or dying could equal him / at his momentary song." Not only is there a kind of triumph in human singing, but the poem also suggests that it is song which separates men from beasts, an idea which figures prominently in Berry's later work, significantly enough in almost the opposite way.

In **"To Go By Singing,"** a poem similar to the one we have just discussed, again Berry emphasizes the importance of human song. Here the singer who walks the street is "a rag of a man, with his game foot and bum's clothes" (***BG,*** p. 44). Still, the speaker admires him, for he is not the stereotyped, panhandling wino. He sings neither for love nor money, "his hands / aren't even held out." This man "sings / by profession," and, because of the religious connotations song has in other poems in ***The Broken Ground,*** most notably in **"Canticle,"** we must understand "profession" not only as a man's calling or occupation, but also as his declaration or avowal of faith in life.

In the second stanza of the poem, Berry juxtaposes singing with the noise and movement of the city:

> To hear him, you'd think the engines
> would all stop, and the flower vendor would stand
> with his hands full of flowers and not move.

The suggestion is that the man's singing goes largely unnoticed, even though the speaker finds it extraordinary; yet he also finds something admirable in the fact that the man sings even though no one listens to him, that "there's no special occasion or place / for his singing." The parallels we might draw here between the nature of this man's singing and the function of poetry would seem to be significantly at odds with what Berry says in his essays about poetry. There, in addition to the necessity and usefulness of poetry, he emphasizes the importance of writing out of a deep awareness of place.

Here, however, if we allow that when Berry writes about song he also means poetry, the suggestion would seem to be that poetry derives its importance and its strength precisely because there is no special occasion or place for it, that it thrives and somehow is admirable because it lacks an occasion or an audience or a home. Furthermore, even the usefulness of poetry appears to be in quesstion here, for, aside from its importance to the man in the poem as his way of going, his singing has little impact upon the world: "His song doesn't impede the morning / or change it, except by freely adding itself." If only implicitly, the power of poetry to change the world would appear to be in doubt.

How can we account for this discrepancy? A number of plausible explanations suggest themselves. First, perhaps we should not draw the connection between song and poetry so readily, a weak explanation, I think, in light of the title of the poem, which suggests, more than a walk through city streets, a way of life, and also in light of the way Berry views song in other poems in the collection as a kind of human design which makes the parallel with poetry unavoidable. Second, Berry wrote the poem earlier than most of his essays which discuss poetry, before he had returned to settle in Kentucky and, perhaps, before he had consciously formulated his view of the function of language, a plausible explanation when we realize as we shall see that Berry's view of the function of language and poetry as he expresses it in his poems, though it has changed and developed, remains ambivalent as recently as ***A Part,***[4] his latest collection. Third, Berry is talking about the only kind of song possible in the city where it is impossible to sing out of strong sense of place, a kind of song which he finds admirable, but inferior to poetry rooted in place, a possible but unlikely explanation, given Berry's admiration for the author of *Paterson.* Fourth, the poem suggests that Berry has doubts about the function of poetry and about his own poetry having any effect upon the world, an idea which appears significantly in ***Clearing,***[5] his sixth collection. A combination of these last three explanations, with reservations about the third, helps to account for the view of song this poem expresses.

Two other poems in ***The Broken Ground*** in which Berry asserts the importance of song are **"An Architecture"** and **"A Music."** In each, he further suggests in different ways that song functions as a kind of design which can provide order and meaning. In the former poem, it is the song of a bird opening "Like a room . . . among the noises / of motors and breakfasts" (***BG,*** p. 36). The obvious suggestion here is that the bird's singing creates the world in which it lives: "Around / him his singing is entire." Again, the parallel between the power of the bird's song and hence the power of poetry to create order and meaning, and even a world in which one can live, are all but obvious. Song is an architecture, both a plan or vision and the enactment of that vision. Rather than being created out of an awareness of place, the song, or poem, creates the place in which one lives, although one could argue that the bird's song certainly originates in the place in which it is sung.

In the latter poem, the song is that of a blind mandolin player whom the speaker employs by proffering a coin. The song of the mandolin player, like the song of the man in **"To Go By Singing,"** becomes all the more significant because of the place in which he plays—the subway station where all is transient. Here again, song is a unifying principle. It connects the speaker with the mandolin player and each of them with the place. And again, perhaps because of the nature of the place or perhaps because of Berry's view of song at this point in his life, the music of the mandolin player clearly supercedes the place in which it is played. "Nothing was here before he came," the speaker tells us, and "The tunnel is the resonance / and meaning of what he plays" (***BG,*** p. 43). The tunnel enriches and intensifies the music, but it is supplementary, not its source. The speaker further emphasizes the value of human song when he declares in the last line of the fourth stanza: "It's his music, not the place, I go by."

The importance of music as a human design and as a means of perception is underscored in the last two stanzas, where the speaker calls the blind man's mandolin, "the lantern of his world," where "his fingers make their *pattern* on the wires" (my emphasis). Berry suggests, as he does in **"A Man Walking and Singing,"** that song is a kind of triumph, for it takes shape in an alien clime, in a twofold darkness. In fact, the song lights up the stranger to the city and to the darkness of the subway. The song becomes a means of perception: "This is not the pursuing becomes a means of perception: "This is not the pursuing rhythm / of a blind cane pecking in the sun, / but is a singing in a dark place." That Berry finds human song all the more important in the city is borne out by the last phrase of the poem, for the metro and the city are symbolically dark places in Berry's scheme of things. It is borne out as well by the generally negative view of the city which Berry expresses in ***The Broken Ground*** and by the way in which he admires how nature, that is, anything living, manages to hang on there despite waste and ruin.

Nevertheless, Wendell Berry does not always view song in such a positive light in ***The Broken Ground.*** In **"Canticle,"** for example, he distinguishes between different kinds of song of which humans are capable. Here he values the concrete song of the coal merchant over the abstract, spiritual music of the moribund priests, precisely because the former consists of the stuff of this world:

> He mentions the daily and several colors of the world.
> His song is part of a singing into which the trees
> move, and fill themselves with all their living
> and their sounds. Dirt and offal assail the dead
> with music, and they vanish out of their bodies
>
> (***BG,*** p. 39).

This distinction makes the title of the poem all the more significant, for it provides insight into Berry's sense of the sacred and it emphasizes what Berry believes the proper focus of religion should be—the things of this world, not of the next.

Probably the most ambivalent poem about the value of song in this collection is **"Nine Verses of the Same Song,"** a group of loosely connected lyrics of which a number are concerned with song, speech, and the possibility of perfection in a finite world. Here Berry distinguishes not only between the different kinds of song of which humans are capable, but also between human song and the song of the world, between the world as humans know it and the world as it is. In the first section, Berry presents these themes in only seven lines. The ear, he tells us, is finely attuned "to the extravagant music / of yellow pears ripening . . . as if the world / were perfect" (***BG***, p. 19); but the ear also hears the sound of a cicada bursting its shell, breaking in upon that extravagant music. The distinction is between two kinds of music which humans are capable of hearing: the ideal, perfect music which the ear prefers; and the real, imperfect music which the ear cannot avoid. Berry's suggestion appears to be that in order to have perfection, humans must ignore reality, or at least pay attention only to certain parts of it, but the image of the whirring cicada in the last line suggests that the real will always break in upon and destroy that illusion of perfection.

Section two, which appears to be little more than a loose collection of images, distinguishes between human music and the music of the world. Here the human music, consisting of trumpets on a phonograph, which "hold the globed gold light / belling in the mirror's corridor / time out of time" (***BG***, p. 20), is juxtaposed with "the morning-red cockerel's / burnished crowing." Whereas the former is a human design which gives the illusion of stopping time, the latter is "counter-measure / to clocktick," that is, to another man-made, artificial way of measuring time. The crowing is heard by the quiet man of stanza one not merely with the ears, but "loud / in the quick of his wrist." The trumpets, like the yellow pears of section one, produce an extravagant, ideal music which contrasts with the sparer music of the cock, a kind of music of which the man is capable because it flows in his own veins. It is the real stuff of the world and as such it does not seek to impede the flow of time as human music does.

One other section of the poem is pertinent here. In section four, Berry juxtaposes two kinds of music in order to show which is most appropriate for humans. Here music is clearly analogous with speech. The two kinds of music are that which is all flesh and that which strives to be all soul. Berry finds both kinds unsatisfactory:

> it is a more mingled music
> we are fated to
> a speech breaking categories
> to confront its objects
>
> (***BG,*** p. 22).

This part of **"Nine Verses of the Same Song,"** along with **"The Apple Tree,"** in addition to suggesting the fundamental importance of music and speech, also provides a definition of poetry which applies to Berry's own work. Poetry is, first of all, in a definition Williams would have liked, "a speech breaking categories / to confront its objects," a speech which turns us toward the things of this world. Furthermore, as Berry asserts in **"The Apple Tree,"** a poem which John Ditsky has admired for its congruence of subject and form,[6] it is a kind of necessary or an essential prose. As Ditsky has observed:

> The tree becomes "poem"—though the word is not used—because of the way it "stands up, emphatic" among"accidents" and establishes its "necessity."[7]

Poetry, then, like the tree, which is "a major Fact or statement of nature,"[8] should endeavor to be a major human design, a major statement which stands against the background of all other kinds of utterance. It should be as rooted in its place as the tree in the poem is, and, while its growth or composition should be casual, the form it achieves should be unalterable and necessary.

In ***Openings***[9] and ***Findings***,[10] Berry's subsequent two collections, music, language, and poetry are not especially important as subject matter, although one of the **"Window Poems"** from ***Openings*** further hints at that ambivalence about the value of language and poetry which we have seen the seeds of the ***The Broken Ground***. There, in section fifteen, in one of his many poems in which he writes admiringly about a tree, Berry asserts how a person's perceptions of the world and his language, his way of expressing and sometimes of discovering those perceptions, are subordinate to the world, represented here by a sycamore tree. The speaker makes us aware that the tree is independent of human perception, that perception can distort and even falsify reality, and that language can come between him and the objects he seeks to know. He wants to see the sycamore "beyond his glances," and "to know it beyond words" (**O,** p. 50) while he denies any part that imagination, and therefore art and poetry, might play in creating the tree and ultimately the world in which he lives: "It is not by imagining / its whiteness comes."

Berry brings this hint of a diminishment in his estimation of the power of language more to the fore in his fourth collection, ***Farming: A Hand Book.***[11] In this volume, just as in ***The Broken Ground***, language, most often, takes the form of song, although at times Berry contrasts the mere language of which humans are capable with the song the world sings. In **"The Silence,"** for example, in answering his central question "What must a man do to be at home in the world?" (***FHB***, p. 23) Berry indicates that it is necessary for a person to efface himself before the world to be at home here. That effacement involves abandoning all human designs, words as well as thoughts, which stand between him and reality in favor of a mystical communing with nature:

> There must be times when he is here
> as though absent, gone beyond words into the woven
> shadows
> of the grass.

In the silence which follows, he becomes one with the world through a kind of death in which

> his bones fade beyond thought
> into the shadows that grow out of the ground
> so that the furrow he opens in the earth
> opens in his bones.

Having abandoned all human design, he begins to hear the song of the earth.

Berry repeats the same idea in slightly different fashion in two other poems in ***Farming: A Hand Book*—"A Letter"** and **"Meditation in the Spring Rain."** In the former, a poem dedicated to writers Ed McClanahan and Gurney Norman about a trip Berry made to visit them in California, Berry acknowledges the bond which language creates between people and between people and the earth: "our bond is speech / grown out of native ground / and langhter grown out of speech, / surpassing all ends" (***FHB***, p. 103). At the same time, he emphasizes how speech pales before the things of this world, here a blue flower in the woods:

> Speech can never fathom
> the flower's silence. Enough
> to honor it, and to live
> in my place beside it. I know
> it holds in its throat a sweet
> brief moisture of welcome
>
> (***FHB,*** p. 104)

The failure of speech to capture reality or even to free it through knowledge is further emphasized in **"Meditation in the Spring Rain."** As the poem begins, the speaker describes how in April in a light rain he climbed up a hill to drink of the water flowing there. Atop the hill, he undergoes an experience similar to that which Wordsworth describes in the Snowden episode toward the end of *The Prelude,* and he is left with a similar dilemma, although the experience in Berry's poem is much less apocalyptic. Awed by the scene before him, the speaker declares: "The thickets . . . send up their praise / at dawn" (***FHB***, p. 105). Immediately, however, he feels compelled to examine what he has said. The question which arises in the poem as a result is a gloss upon the entire body of Berry's poetry:

> Was that what I meant—I meant
> my words to have the heft and grace, the flight
> and weight of the very hill, its life
> rising—or was it some old exultation
> that abides with me?

The speaker, like Wordsworth on Snowden, is unsure whether what he is feeling and experiencing results from the external scene or from something within him, which leads him eventually to question in its entirety the value of language.

Before he does that, however, he embarks upon what appears to be a long digression to recount the story of crazy old Mrs. Gaines who stood one day "atop a fence in Port Royal, Kentucky, / singing: 'One Lord, one Faith, and one / Cornbread'." Most of the time, the speaker tells us, Mrs. Gaines was allowed to roam about town freely; but occasionally, when she became wild, the townspeople put her in a cage which was nearly as big as her room in which they had constructed it. One day, however, Mrs. Gaines wandered farther away than she ordinarily did and the town had difficulty finding her.

While this anecdote demonstrates the way in which Berry uses folk materials in his poetry, he seems to dwell on it out of all proportion to its importance in the poem; but what Mrs. Gaines teaches the speaker is the importance of going beyond what is normally accepted and known. That is the one way that people can be truly free: "For her, to be free / was only to be lost" (***FHB,*** p. 106). Berry sees a similarity between himself and Mrs. Gaines, realizing that in order to be free, to go beyond what he knows, he must relinquish all human designs, even language itself. For Berry to be free, he must be not crazy but silent, although he is aware that such a step would surely suggest madness to his public, his colleagues, and his contemporaries:

> For I too am perhaps a little mad
> standing here wet in the drizzle, listening
> to the clashing syllables of the water. Surely
> there is a great Word being put together here.

Unlike Wordsworth, who denies apocalypse, Berry denies the self.

In **"Meditation in the Spring Rain,"** more emphatically than in any previous poem, Berry contrasts the language of men with the song of the world, to the detriment of the former. In order to hear the assembly of the great Word, he must become silent, and give up his own language which intrudes between him and reality. Paradoxically, that silence and the fact that the speaker begins to hear the great Word restore his confidence in his own ability to speak, so that he is able to declare again without the doubts which plagued him earlier: "The thickets, I say, send up their praise / at dawn!"

The process has been a complex one. In order to affirm the world and the value of his affirmation of it, Berry has had to question that affirmation, to relinquish the very language in which he made it, so that he could be certain that he was speaking accurately and not imposing upon reality "some old exultation" from within. This process, involving as it does the abnegation of human vision and human design, is similar if not identical to the effacement of the self through a descent into darkness evident in Berry's first two collections. The abnegation of a language which limits the way in which the speaker might know reality leaves him with a feeling of oneness with the world:

> For a time there I turned away from the words I knew,
> and was lost.
> For a time I was lost and free, speechless
> in the multitudinous assembling of his Word
>
> (***FHB,*** p. 107).

In his fifth volume of poetry, Wendell Berry names that place where humans arrive having sailed beyond the utmost bounds of human thought. It is, as he calls the collection, the country of marriage.[12] Just as in Tennyson's poem, that place is fully and permanently reached only in death, but one can occasionally arrive there in life as Berry does through his marriage to his wife and to the land.

In one poem in this volume, Berry views human song almost as favorably as he does in the early poetry. In **"Zero,"** despite the severity of the weather, the speaker tells us that "the wren's at home / in the cubic acre of his song" (***COM***, p. 10). Here, Berry clearly intends us to understand song as analogous to human design, for like songs, the farm buildings in the poem, each a kind of human design, "stand up around their lives" against the cold; and the speaker also tells us that like the wren he has "a persistent music" in him. Here, however, song is not the sturdy structure that it was in **"An Architecture."** Rather it is "a flimsy enclosure," little more than a hope in the midst of winter "that says the warmer days / will come." That song remains important nonetheless, because, just as in **"A Man Walking and Singing,"** it is sung in the face of death. It is a singing "not to dread the end." The speaker here finds the zero-degree weather appealing because it brings the end, "the climate we sing in," more to the fore. It creates an environment "in which nothing lives by chance / but only by choosing to and by knowing how" (***COM***, p. 11), which stresses the importance of human vision and will.

Virtually every other poem in ***The Country of Marriage*** which deals with song as a kind of human design either emphasizes its limitations or subordinates it to the song of the world. **"The Strangers,"** for example, while it emphasizes the importance of vision in a world where men *do* act by design and the value of language which grows out of a deep awareness of place, suggests as well that language, rather than creating a bond between people, divides them. As the poem begins, the speaker hears the voices of lost travelers trying to find their way calling out to him. They are lost because they have ceased to know the country directly. They know it only through language: "For them, places have changed / into their names and vanished" (***COM***, p. 37). The speaker further realizes that the travelers will not understand his language because it grows out of a deep relationship with the land which has vanished for them. His is a speech which "is conversant with its trees / and stones." The language he speaks is that of a native of the place. Because their lives and languages are so different even though they appear to speak the same tongue, he realizes that they are lost to one another because the travelers will not be able to understand him.

Three other poems in ***The Country of Marriage***, **"The Silence," "A Song Sparrow Singing in the Fall,"** and **"Song,"** express the superiority of the world to any human expression of it, the limitations of language, the intrusive nature of language, and the necessity of going beyond language in order to be one with the world. More importantly, they suggest for the first time an idea which Berry elaborates in ***Clearing***, his sixth collection, that he is about to abandon poetry altogether for the joy and peace of full communion with the world. **"The Silence,"** a different poem from the poem of the same title in ***Farming: A Hand Book,*** is reminiscent in theme if not in tone of Williams' "Portrait of a Lady." It expresses the poet's dissatisfaction with his inability to stand silent before the world. As the poem begins, the speaker laments the way in which he prefers his own words to the song of the world, "Though the air is full of singing" (***COM***, p. 25). More concretely, he is upset by the way he "hungers for the sweet of speech" even though real fruit is readily available. The distinction between the world and the human view of it is rendered all the more forcefully in contrast between the way in which Berry characterizes the utterance the world makes, that is as song, and that of which humans are capable, mere words or speech. Human utterance, however, is not only inferior to the song of the world. It is also a temptation and a distraction which turns human attention away from reality:

> Though the beech is golden
> I cannot stand beside it
> mute, but must say
> "It is golden," while the leaves
> stir and fall with a sound
> that is not a name.

The speaker further suggests that hope for the world lies not in poetry, not in the creation of a new speech as Berry has suggested earlier, but rather in silence:

> Let me say
> and not mourn: the world
> lives in the death of speech
> and sings there.

Berry repeats the same idea in **"A Song Sparrow Singing in the Fall"** where he declares that he will abandon all other singing and "go / into the silence / of his songs" (***COM***, p. 20), so that he might hear the song of the world more clearly; and in **"Song,"** where the speaker perceives the finite nature of poetry, that he tells his love "in rhyme / In a sentence that must end" (***COM***, p. 46). The latter poem, however, while it too emphasizes the inferiority of language to the world, suggests as well that something about the world compels men to speak and that language, and presumably poetry, will be around as long as the world is. Also, implicit in the poem is the idea that our preoccupation with words might in some way be responsible for the world's demise:

> We will speak on until
> The flowers fall, and the birds
> With their bright songs depart.
> Then we will go without art,
> Without measure, or words.

The above passage illustrates as well as any of Berry's poems his ambivalence about language, since, as I've suggested above, it can be read either positively or negatively.

The value of human song and ultimately of language and poetry continues to be a ccentral concern in ***Clearing***, Berry's sixth collection of poems, as the titles of two of the poems suggest, **"Work Song"** and **"Reverdure."** (The title of the latter is drawn from the French *"reverdier"* meaning to grow green again, but also suggesting a kind of old French song signaling the return of spring.) In this volume, while Berry's attitude toward human song is more positive in some poems than it has been in the two previous collections, he remains at best ambivalent, for, where he is negative, he is more so than in any previous poem, suggesting for the first time the real possibility that he is on the verge of abandoning poetry altogether. Moreover, here old-fashioned, hard work replaces song and the creation of a new kind of speech as Berry's hope and means for restoring a world laid waste by men.

"History," the first poem in the collection, while it expresses the superiority of the world to all human design including song, suggests, nevertheless, that human song can have value as long as it grows out of and remains deeply rooted in a place on earth. In the first section of the poem in late autumn after the crops have been harvested, the speaker in the third year of living in that locale sets out on a walk which takes him beyond all human design:

> Beyond the farthest tracks
> of any domestic beast
> my walk led me, and into
> a place for which I knew
> no names. I went by paths
> that bespoke intelligence
> and memory I did not know
>
> (*C*, p. 3).

There he tries to become familiar with the place, not through language, but by "Learning / the landmarks and the ways / of the land." Once again, abandoning his own designs enables the speaker to begin to discover the designs of nature. He finds himself close to song precisely because he went into the place "wordless and gay as a deer."

In secton two of **"History,"** the speaker informs us that he returned many times to the place he ventured to in section one until he came "with a sharp eye / and the price of land" (*C*, p. 4) and purchased it. Once he becomes its "owner," he recognizes the wide gap between any ideal vision of the place he might have had on that first day and the real condition of the land whose history has almost ruined it irreparably. His journey, then, to be fully and truly in that place is mental as much as it is physical. He must perceive the difference between the ideal and the real, between vision and the enactment of vision; and he must be attentive to the history of the place in order to make that farm which he intends to be his "art of being here" (*C*, p. 5). Berry concludes section two declaring that until his song arrives in that place "to learn its words," his art "is but the hope of song." These last lines suggest not only the importance of place to song and poetry, but also the importance of song and poetry to the enactment of his vision and ultimately to the place itself, for farming is his art as much as poetry is.

Ultimately what Berry is aiming for, as we discover in section three, is union with the place, but he desires more than a physical union. He recognizes that he is already united with the place physically:

> All the lives this place
> has had, I have. I eat
> my history day by day.
> Bird, butterfly, and flower
> pass through the seasons
> of my flesh.

While that union is important, he desires as well a more mystical union, a union of mind as well as body, so he prays that "what is in the flesh, / . . . be brought to mind" (*C*, p. 6).

The process of **"History"** is a familiar one for Berry. Vision not rooted in reality is renounced by the speaker's act of turning toward the world, here as elsewhere the earth. That attention to reality produces a new, adjusted vision, one which is more in harmony with things as they are. That new vision is more firmly rooted in reality and is constantly readjusted to bring it more and more into harmony with the earth as the speaker learns more about it.

With **"Work Song,"** however, Berry's attitude toward language becomes more ambivalant. In section two, entitled **"A Vision,"** he foresees with delight the real possibility of song which is truly rooted in place: "Families will be singing in the fields / In their voices they will hear a music / rise out of the ground" (*C*, p. 32). In the following section, however, he expresses fears about the genuine nature of his words, and suggests the possibility that he is about to cease composing poetry altogether. As section three begins, the speaker tells us that "an ancient passion" singing in his veins beneath speech has brought him to his place, presumably the farm he has been writing about in previous poems. That passion has led him beyond speech and beyond books

> to stand in this hillside field
> in October wind, critical
> and solitary, like a horse dumbly
> approving of the grass
>
> (*C*, p. 33).

He wonders whether that passion is leading him away from books and speech because some days he stands "empty as a tree / whose birds and leaves have gone" (*C*, p. 34), lines which are reminiscent of those quoted above from **"Song"** about the lasting quality of language. He wonders further whether that condition might become permanent so that

> one day my poems may pass
> through my mind unwritten
> like the freshening of a stream
> in the hills, holding the light
> only while they pass, shaping
> only what they pass through,
> source and destination

the same. I am afraid
some days, that only vanity
keeps me at my words

(*C*, p. 33).

In sections four and five of **"Work Song,"** Berry writes of the way in which different kinds of language have troubled him. The first in section four is a private, illusory language which attempts to seduce him away from the laborious life he has chosen to a life of ease; but Berry realizes that he must not believe in such "miraculous deliverances," for they are not to be. The second in section five is a public language of lies which "finally drives us / to silence" (*C*, p. 35). This kind of language has caused him to turn more and more toward the world. "We are," Berry writes, "a people who must decline or perish." We should understand "decline" not only in its generally understood meanings, to diminish or refuse, but also in many of its secondary meanings, to turn or bend aside (presumably from the designs we seek to impose upon the world), to decay, to reject, to bend, lean, or slope downward as well as in its grammatical sense—to display the inflected forms of a noun, pronoun, or adjective in a fixed order. The language that would result from such "declining" would be uttered by humans who have fixed their attention upon the world, who have acknowledged limitation, and whose speech originates in a place on earth.

Thus, Berry rejects both kinds of illusory language, not so much now for another language, but for work, that value which is replacing speech in his scheme of things: "I work to renew a ruined place / that no life be hostage of my comfort" (*C*, p. 36). The song that results from that labor, "a work song / and an earth song," is the kind of singing which grows out of a close connection with a place, but it is hardly a kind of speech which can change the world. The work rather than the song effects change, although the song like the stream in the passage quoted above from **"A Vision"** is instrumental in shaping the mind it passes through to prepare it and discipline it for the work at hand.

In concluding **"Reverdure,"** the last poem in ***Clearing***, Berry repeats the idea expressed in the second section of "**Work Song**" that he may be on the verge of abandoning poetry altogether. Words for him seem to have become little more than a means of getting through the winter when he can do little to enact his vision in the actual. With the return of spring, he tells us: "It is time again I made an end to words / for a while—for this time, / or for all time. Any end my last" (*C*, p. 52). Once again, the poet views books and words as obstacles. They focus upon the past and the future and distract him from the song of the world which is in the air in spring.

This would seem to be the natural conclusion for a man who defines poetry as "the mode of activity of the mind of the poet" and for whom poetry has always been more important as a means of discovery and discipline than as an end in itself, especially since in his later work in more than a few places Berry has expressed the idea that language is more of an obstacle than a conduit. At the same time, it is curiously at odds with what he says in other places about the importance of language, not to mention with his own reliance upon language, attested to by the vast amount of written work he has produced in a variety of forms since 1960. Clearly, some signs indicate that Berry is not yet ready to abandon song altogether, not the least of which is the appearance of a new collection of poems in 1980 entitled ***A Part***.

Song continues to be a central concern in ***A Part***; yet, while the ambivalence of previous collections is present here too, it is not as pronounced as it has been in the two volumes immediately preceding this one, nor is there any hint that Berry is thinking about abandoning poetry altogether. In places, he still feels the weight of his own words and continues to suggest that it is language which keeps him from hearing the song of the world, for example in **"An Autumn Burning,"** where he has gone out to burn what he has written:

After the passing
of that light, there is sunlight
on the ash, in the distance singing
of crickets and of birds. I turn,
unburdened, to life beyond words

(***AP***, p. 37).

Yet in **"To What Listens,"** nature's beauty, though shadowed by death, compels him to sing: "Its songs and loves throb / in my head till like the wren / I sing—to what listens—again" (***AP***, p. 14). And in **"Creation Myth,"** Berry asserts the importance of language, here a single word spoken to a man lost in the woods which "laid the field out clear / . . . and placed / the map of it in his head" (***AP***, p. 45). The accommodation about language and song which ***A Part*** suggests Berry has reached is a result, perhaps, of his finally beginning to hear the song of the world, the great word being assembled. In **"Seventeen Years,"** for example, he describes the cyclical return of locusts: "The light is filled / with the song the ground exhales / once in seventeen years" (***AP***, p. 13). The lines above and others like them in this collection suggest that Berry has ceased talking about listening and working in his poetry and actually begun to render what he has heard and done. He concludes **"Horses,"** the final poem in ***A Part*** describing his labor:

This work of love rhymes
living and dead. A dance
is what this plodding is.
A song, whatever is said

(***AP***, p. 89).

Thus, Wendell Berry's view of language is characterized by conflict. From his deep faith in language, especially poetry, early in his career, as a way of changing people and the world for the better, through his later ambivalence about language and poetry in contrast with the song of the world, through his musings out loud about abandoning poetry altogether, he appears to have reached an accommodation about language which enables him, though he still questions the value and efficacy of words, "By division" to speak "out of wonder" (***AP***, p. 4).

Notes

1. Wendell Berry, *The Broken Ground* (New York: Harcourt and World, 1964). Hereafter abbreviated *BG.*
2. Wendell Berry, "In Defense of Literacy," *A Continuous Harmony: Essays Cultural and Agricultural* (New York: Harcourt Brace Jovanovich, 1970), pp. 169-173. Hereafter abbreviated *CH.*
3. Wendell Berry, *The Long-Legged House* (New York: Harcourt Brace and World, 1965). Hereafter abbreviated *LLH.*
4. Wendell Berry, *A Part* (San Francisco: North Point Press, 1980). Hereafter Abbreviated *AP.*
5. Wendell Berry, *Clearing* (New York: Harcourt Brace Jovanovich, 1977). Hereafter abbreviated *C.*
6. John Ditsky, "Wendell Berry: Homage to the Apple Tree," *Modern Poetry Studies,* 2 (1971), p. 9.
7. Ditsky, p. 9.
8. Ditsky, p. 9.
9. Wendell Berry, *Openings* (New York: Harcourt, Brace and World, 1968). Hereafter abbreviated *O.*
10. Wendell Berry, *Findings* (The Prairie Press, 1969).
11. Wendell Berry, *Farming: A Hand Book* (New York: Harcourt Brace Jovanovich, 1973). Hereafter abbreviated *FHB.*
12. Wendell Berry, *The Country of Marriage* (New York: Harcourt Brace Jovanovich, 1973). Hereafter abbreviated *COM.*

John T. Hiers (essay date 1984-1987)

SOURCE: "Wendell Berry: Love Poet," in *The University of Mississippi Studies in English,* Vol. V, 1984-1987, pp. 100-09.

[*In the following essay, Hiers asserts that Berry "both inherits and creates an agrarian ethos which sustains poetic visions of love unique among contemporary poets" and compares his poetry with that of Theodore Roethke and Anne Sexton.*]

Wendell Berry—poet, novelist, essayist—has produced an impressive canon since his first novel, *Nathan Coulter,* appeared in 1960. In two decades he has published three novels, several volumes of verse, and five volumes of essays. Two interrelated themes unify all of his mature work: man's proper relationship with the land and, a corollary, his harmonious relationship with his neighbors. These concerns place Berry squarely in the agrarian tradition of Southern literature, a position he finds both intellectually satisfying and aesthetically essential. Unlike many of his agrarian predecessors, however, Berry actually farms as well as writes and teaches.

Although Berry is a former Guggenheim fellow, a former Rockefeller Foundation fellow, the recipient of two prizes from *Poetry Magazine* and an award from the National Institute of Arts and Letters, he has not attracted widespread critical and scholarly attention. The few scholars with critical interest in Berry have concentrated on his regional agrarianism, his traditional moral values, and his direct pastoral mode, but they have failed to appreciate him as love poet of considerable distinction. One critic, John Hicks, finds marriage in Berry's novels "to be ideally a merging of the solitary selves, an act of healing, and a partial reconciliation with nature," yet Hicks limits himself to Berry's fiction and fails to find there much "passion, intensity, or personal encounter" in these novels' "farm marriages."[1] Nevertheless, much of Berry's love poetry does reveal a moving, if understated conjugal passion and controlled intensity.

Indeed, Wendell Berry's agrarianism makes him a love poet. Other modern American poets associated with agrarian perspectives and values—Ransom, Tate, Warren, Frost, for instance—certainly have composed love poetry; yet, none can be classified so easily as a love poet in any traditional, limited sense. But Berry's brand of agrarianism—far more convincing, far less stylized and academic than in his predecessors—naturally and organically evolves into constrained paeans of love. At times as exuberant as Theodore Roethke, at times as intensely intimate as Anne Sexton, Berry both inherits and creates an agrarian ethos which sustains poetic visions of love unique among contemporary poets. That is, Berry as love poet is a celebrant of procreative marriage. His seventh generation farm near Port Royal, Kentucky, is both metaphorically and literally a country of marriage, the title of one of his most mature books of verse.

Berry's world picture is one of microcosmic analogies based on man's unity with the land, and, consequently, with his wife and his creator. Harmony with nature both creates and reflects a continuous harmony with others, and man is husband to the land as he is husband to his wife. In his essay, "The Likenesses of Atonement (At-one-ment)," Berry explains the philosophical tenets of his unifying system of metaphors and analogies:

> Living in our speech, though no longer in our consciousness, is an ancient system of analogies that clarifies a series of mutually defining and sustaining unities: of farmer and field, of husband and wife, of the world and God. The language both of our literature and of our everyday speech is full of references and allusions to this expansive metaphor of farming and marriage and worship. A man planting a crop is like a man making love to his wife, and vice versa: he is a husband or a husbandman. A man praying is like a lover, or he is like a plant in a field waiting for rain. As husbandman, a man is both the steward and the likeness of God, the greater husbandman.[2]

This poet of agrarian harmonies and natural pieties can be no other than a love poet as well. What makes Berry's voice as love poet unique today is his complete, unabashed adherence to this ancient system of belief. Paradoxically, his voice sounds authentic and even original because it is so old-fashioned, didactic, and moralistic.

Agrarian imagery to describe sexual love, however, is hardly unique even in modern verse. Theodore Roethke, in such brilliant poems as "I Knew a Woman," gives perhaps the most striking examples:

> She was the sickle; I, poor I, the rake,
> Coming behind her for her pretty sake
> (But what prodigious mowing we did make).
>
> (12-14)[3]

Yet, Roethke's occasional use of this kind of agrarian metaphor in his love poetry ultimately is a celebration of the self through the ephemeral harmony of one soul with another. In Whitmanesque ecstasy he announces in "Words for the Wind" that "Being myself, I sing / The soul's immediate joy" and concludes:

> I kiss her moving mouth,
> Her sweet hilarious skin;
> She breaks my breath in half;
> She frolicks like a beast;
> And I dance round and round,
> A fond and foolish man,
> And see and suffer myself
> In another being at last.
>
> (105-112)

For Roethke, sexual love harmonizes individuals in their separate, doomed quests to defeat time. Berry's celebrations of sexuality unify individual souls with the natural order, redefining the individual's defeat by time as essentially a source of meaning and life. Death becomes a source of life metaphorically and analogously, for Berry, because it is a literal source witnessed almost daily on his farm.

Berry thus appropriates the Renaissance metaphor of death as sexuality. "What I am learning to give you is my death," he says to his wife in **"The Country of Marriage,"** "to set you free of me, and me from myself / into the dark and the new light."[4] Dark brings new light as death brings new life; hence, Berry presents sex primarily as procreative. But, again, his use of death as a sexual metaphor is more than merely quaint because it is, in Berry's world, more of a physical than a metaphysical figure. As a love poet Berry has indeed schooled himself on John Donne and similar company, but he has basically schooled himself on the ways of nature on his Port Royal farm.

As Berry generalizes in **"Enriching the Earth,"** death is never an end in itself in the natural world: "After death, willing or not, the body serves, / entering the earth. And so what was heaviest / and most mute is at last raised up into song" (17-19).[5] Sexual death, according to Berry's system of analogies, yields a similar song for similar reasons. It both mirrors a natural process of procreation and is one itself. More than two people are harmonized in Berry's hymns to marriage; a world is unified.

The unforgivable sin, for Berry, then, is to make a waste of death. He invariably associates violence and loneliness and despair with this kind of waste. In **"The Morning News,"** for example, he states that

> It is man, the inventor of cold violence,
> death as waste, who has made himself lonely
> among creatures, and set himself aside from
> creation, so that he cannot labor
> in the light of the sun with hope,
> or sit at peace in the shade of any tree.
>
> (***FAH,*** 11-16)

Analogously, sexual death as an end in itself brings disharmony, loneliness, alienation.

The farmer-lover-narrator of **"Air and Fire,"** borne away from the country of marriage by jetliner, composite symbol of modern technological and mechanistic society, is at once tempted by selfish, lustful passion:

> Having risen from my native land,
> I find myself smiled at by beautiful women,
> making me long for a whole life
> to devote to each one, making love to
> her in some house, in some way of sleeping sleeping
> and waking I would make only for her.
>
> (***FAH,*** 5-10)

Here Berry presents a traditional temptation scene, replete with an angel-temptor who satanically offers complete release from individual responsibility to wife, home, and farm. But the bonds of marriage paradoxically offer truer freedom ("I give you what is unbounded," Berry declares in **"The Country of Marriage"**). Meaningful love doesn't grow in *some* way, in *some* house; it is cultivated and nourished in the mind as well as in the flesh. "Like rest after a sleepless night," concludes the narrator, "my old love comes on me in midair" (***FAH***, 22-23).

But it would be erroneous to consider such a conclusion to be only the puritanical prudishness of an eastern Kentucky farm boy. His kind of love anchors his lustful mind in midair because it is also of the flesh. In **"Earth and Fire,"** a companion piece to **"Air and Fire,"** Berry sings love's ecstasy in lyrical harmonies worthy of Roethke or Anne Sexton. Here pain and joy are unified by passion and gusto:

> In this woman the earth speaks.
> Her words open in me, cells of light
> flashing in my body, and make a song
> that I follow toward her out of my need.
> The pain I have given her I wear
> like another skin, tender, the air
> around me flashing with thorns.
> And yet such joy as I have given her
> sings in me and is part of her song.
> The winds of her knees shake me

like a flame. I have risen up from her,
time and again, a new man.

(*FAH,* 1-12)

Renewal of life comes because this sexuality is of the earth, not of the air. The lovers are in harmony with time because they creatively participate in the cyclical order of nature. This poet measures time not by the swaying of a woman's body, but by the rushing of wind and the flashing of light.

Berry's ecstatic sensuality, though often as lyrical, stands outside of the modern tradition of love poetry as exemplified by the later Yeats or Roethke or Sexton. It especially contrasts to the sensuality of Sexton, who in many ways was Roethke's heir to the Bacchanalian muse. In "Barefoot," for instance, Sexton echoes Roethke's trumpeting of selfhood through orgiastic release:

The surf's a narcotic, calling out,
I am, I am, I am
all night long, Barefoot,
I drum up and down your back
In the morning I run from door to door
of the cabin playing *chase me.*
Now you grab me by the ankles,
Now you work your way up the legs
and come to pierce me at my hunger mark.

(25-33)[6]

Berry could never describe sexual union as a game, although he, too, revels in such climactic moments. For sexual union is but an extended metaphor of other Thoreauvian harmonies in his Kentucky Walden; it is, in short, a mode of participation in all of creation and, therefore, an act of joyful reverence.

But there are no more Waldens in the New England of Anne Sexton. Like her predecessor Roethke, she quickly plunges from zeniths of sensuality into labyrinths of remorse and loneliness. In "You All Know the Story of the Other Women," she sarcastically begins by shattering the Walden myth:

It's a little Walden.
She is private in her breathbed
as his body takes off and flies,
flies straight as an arrow.
But it's a bad translation.
Daylight is nobody's friend.

(1-6)

Creative, harmonious unions of lovers reflect only the heat of momentary passions. They are not analogies of natural order and design; they only intensify the desperate need for them in a world which can no longer accept them.

Sexton often perceives and dramatizes modern marriage as an artificial sham, an illusion of self-transcendence and self-definition. As a poetic metaphor or analogy it is useless because it is dead as a conventional sacrament. Even in her series of poems "Eighteen Days Without You," one is suspicious of the selfhood attained through sexual passion. Here the narrator remembers how it once was, how

you come and take my blood cup
and link me together and take my brine.
We are bare. We are stripped to the bone
and we swim in tandem and go up and up
the river, the identical river called Mine
and we enter together. No one's alone.

("December 11th," 7-12)

The irony is that she is alone even as she recalls this climactic moment of complete union. More often than not, Sexton's theme is the unassuaged hunger of love which is only intensified by these memories.

The true Sexton, in short, may be found in such a poem as "The Ballad of the Lonely Masturbator." There are few poems of greater intimacy and forlorn alienation in modern American verse. Here may be the inevitable, final lamentation of the kind of Romantic solipsism which Roethke and Sexton ultimately manifest as love poets. It is a tradition, a side of Romanticism completely rejected by Berry, whose agrarian world view is often and nebulously labeled "Romantic." Paradoxically, the opening lines of Sexton's poem easily might be confused with several of Berry's: "The end of the affair is always death. / She's my workshop." The similarity ends with the refrain, which closes each stanza with Euripidean pathos: "At night, alone, I marry the bed." In this instance, Sexton, like Berry, employs death as a sexual metaphor; but her irony is overwhelming and terrifying. The self-fulfillment of this affair (one recalls the Whitmanesque declarations of self in "Barefoot" and other poems) is finally masturbatory—with no affirmation of meaning, no possibility of rebirth, only introspective anguish. "All is an interminable chain of longing," writes Robert Frost.[7] Anne Sexton would agree.

Wendell Berry, although much taken with Frost's agrarian positions in such poems as "Build Soil," would not. If Roethke and Sexton are so far the erq's supreme strophic voices of solipsistic sensuality, Berry is emerging as an antistrophic singer of the timeless harmonies of marriage—marriage not as a social convention so much as a pantheistic sacrament. Although he is not Christian in any narrow denominational or theological sense, he nevertheless considers marriage as sacramental because it is a means to greater natural harmony and piety, a mode of creativity analogous to natural and, ultimately, to divine creativity.

Berry's **"An Anniversary"** epitomizes his poetic vision of marriage and of sexual love. Along with **"The Country of Marriage,"** it stands as one of the modern age's boldest poetic visions of marriage as sacramental. At a time when marriage as a social institution is becoming anachronistic, Berry dares to center a complete agrarian ethos upon it. And he succeeds, partly from refusing to be strident as he cuts across the modern American grain with affirmations from the past. **"An Anniversary"** is a complementary descriptive statement for all **"The Country of Marriage"** dramatizes. An anniversary of love and commitment, a marking of time, becomes a window on all time through the seasonal fruition, decay, and rebirth of all life in "The household / Of the woods":

> The fields and woods prepare
> The burden of their seed
> Out of time's wound, the old
> Richness of the fall. Their deed
> Is renewal
>
> (***CM,*** 6-10)

The love of man and woman has similar harvest, achieves definition through change that is forever orderly and predictable, at least from an agrarian vantage point.

Berry quietly, reverentially telescopes from nature in general to the particular celebrants of this anniversary:

> Love binds us to this term
> With its yes that is crying
> In our marrow to confirm
> Life that only lives by dying.
> Lovers live by the moon
> Whose dark and light are one,
> Changing without rest.
> The root struts from the seed
> In the earth's dark—harvest
> And feast at the edge of sleep.
> Darkened we are carried
> Out of need, deep
> In the country we have married.
>
> (***CM,*** 18-30)

Because these lovers are married to a country as well as to one another, they are carried away from need. In contrast, the lovers of Anne Sexton's poems, whose desires are confirmed only by their own voices, have their needs intensified even while they harvest the fruits of their love.

Lovers in the poetry of both Berry and Sexton live by the moon, but for different reasons. On the one hand, the narrator of Sexton's "Moon Song, Woman Song" declares: "I am alive at night. / I am dead in the morning." On the other hand, the married couple in **"An Anniversary"** is unified with both the night and the day, for dark and light give definition to each other as fall and winter define spring. Speer Morgan cogently says: "The statement 'Lovers live by the moon' implies the conjunction of both the woman's cycle and the farmer's labor with that of the moon; more important, the moon symbolizes the dark and light continually at work in one perfect circle: its essence is the 'changing without rest,' which suggests the joy of love-making itself as well as the pang of sorrow that the lovers . . . may feel in the face of transience."[8] This momentary regret of Berry's lovers is quickly assuaged by the dark itself, for it carries them out of need. Sexton's characters find no such solace. Feasting in the dark, they but hunger in the day.

Even when Sexton employs the agrarian images of planting and harvesting, she is consciously the poet of the moment rather than of the seasons. In "Us," another of her Roethke-like ecstasies, she concludes with a veritable fury of passion:

> Oh then
> I stood up in my gold skin
> and I beat down the psalms
> and I beat down the clothes
> and you undid the bridle
> and you undid the reins
> and I undid the buttons
> the bones, the confusions,
> the New England postcards,
> the January ten o'clock night,
> and we rose up like wheat,
> acre after acre of gold,
> and we harvested,
> we harvested.
>
> (20-33)

There can be no country of marriage for Sexton because there are no meaningful traditions left on which to found such a country. The traditions of New England are only post-card mementoes; the lyrics of the Psalms are now discordant. One can no longer return to the remnants of the past, as does Robert Frost's urban quester in "Directive," to "Drink and be whole again beyond confusion."[9] One can only throw off confusion, like clothes, as an act of the will. Sexual fulfillment is better than no fulfillment at all. When the time comes to face the reality of such uninhibited abandonment ("Let's face it, I have been momentary," concludes the narrator of "For My Lover, Returning to His Wife"), then at least the moment has been luxurious. Confusion inevitably, often pathetically, returns; one must wear clothes again. But the harvest has been golden, if short-lived.

Berry, of course, would find this kind of harvest to be not only too ephemeral, but also illusory. He would classify it as the fruition of "ignorant love." As he rather whimsically states in **"The Mad Farmer Manifesto: The First Amendment"**:

> And I declare myself free
> from ignorant love. You easy lovers
> and forgivers of mankind, stand back!
> I will love you at a distance,
> and not because you deserve it.
> My love must be discriminate
> or fail to bear its weight.
>
> (***CM,*** 21-27)

Discriminating love is harmonizing love; it is passion without lust, pleasure without hedonism. It is, in the final analysis, participation in the seminal processes of all plantings and all harvests and thus a consummation of all time.

Notes

1. John Hicks, "Berry's Husband to the World: A Place on Earth," *American Literature,* 51 (1979), 251-252.
2. In *A Continuous Harmony: Essays Cultural and Agricultural* (New York, 1972), pp. 159-160.

3. My text is *The Collected Poems of Theodore Roethke* (Garden City, 1961).
4. My text is *The Country of Marriage* (New York, 1973), hereafter cited with abbreviation *CM.*
5. My text is *Farming: A Handbook* (New York, 1970), hereafter cited with abbreviation *FAH.*
6. My text is *Love Poems* (Boston, 1969).
7. See "Escapist—Never," *The Poetry of Robert Frost,* ed. Edward Connery Lathem (New York, 1967), p. 421.
8. "Wendell Berry: A Fatal Singing," *Southern Review* 10 (1974), 876.
9. *The Poetry of Robert Frost,* p. 379.

Jeffery Alan Triggs (essay date 1988)

SOURCE: "Moving the Dark to Wholeness: The Elegies of Wendell Berry," in *The Literary Review,* Vol. 31, No. 3, Spring, 1988, pp. 279-92.

[*In the following essay, Triggs underscores the importance of Berry's elegiac verse.*]

With each year, Wendell Berry claims a more significant position among contemporary American poets. From his common beginnings as one of a generation of poets trained in the precepts of the New Criticism, he has pursued his own "path," as he calls it, with uncommon intellectual rigor and poetic sensitivity. In our age of weak religious faith, many poets, faced with death and the threat of nuclear devastation, have fallen into sterility or despair. Berry, however, over the course of his career, has come to terms with death and made its acceptance central to his philosophy of affirmation. For him, acceptance of death makes possible human love, fidelity, and the perpetuation of the community of men on earth.

Like so many poets of his generation, Berry has developed as an artist by escaping the ubiquitous enchantment of *Understanding Poetry.* Under the influence of Brooks and Warren, Berry began his career writing individual, "well-made" lyrics that emphasized paradox and irony, and drew for inspiration from the Elizabethans by way of Yeats and T.S. Eliot. A former Kentucky farm boy "exiled" to the freshman writing department of New York University, Berry found in the new critical approach a distancing irony to protect his sensibility from the city's hostile, alien environment:

In the empty lot—a place
not natural, but wild—among
the trash of human absence,
the slough and shamble
of the city's seasons, a few
old locusts bloom.

—**"The Wild,"** ***Poems*** (19)

Berry has never "outgrown" the theme of the evils of the modern, industrial world, but he was not content for long to express himself in the manner of **"The Wild."**

In 1964, Berry made the most important move of his career, when he returned to Kentucky to teach and bought a small farm near Port Royal, where his family had lived for generations. Indeed, his activities as a farmer have come gradually to dominate his life and work. Since his return home, urban imagery has faded almost completely from Berry's writing. Increasingly, he has come to emphasize history and place, seeking roots, and a refusal to separate literature from life's larger concerns. Berry has made himself the kind of poet, at once vatic and sane, who finds the creation of good literature inseparable from the creation of a good life. He has practiced and written about the spiritual discipline of the farmer's life. Such marriage to the land and fidelity to a place in the world involve, necessarily, the acceptance of death as part of accepting one's place in what he calls the "system of systems" (*Standing by Words* 46). It is, for Berry, the condition of our salvation

. . . . . .

Berry's elegies are vital to his work because they provide focus for his typical themes, such as his recurring metaphors that link past and future generations through their common working of the land. In **"The Current,"** for instance, a complex poem about "marriage" to a place and the subtle relations of the generations involved in that place, the marriage is made by a man's "having put his hand into the ground / seeding there what he hopes will outlast him." The man thus becomes the "descendant" of all those who once worked this land, even the "old tribespeople" bending

in the sun, digging with sticks, the forest opening
to receive their hills of corn, squash, and beans,
their lodges and graves, and closing again.

He is part of the "current" of their lives and the life of the land that flows

to him through the earth
flows past him, and he sees one descended from him,
a young man who has reached into the ground,
his hand held in the dark as by a hand.

(119)

The hope of the nurturer against the impermanence of mortal life lies in this mystical connection *through the land* with the generations gone and to come. What remains, permanent in its cycles, is the land itself, the natural order.

As early as ***The Broken Ground*** (1964), farming has provided Berry with the central metaphor of the life and death cycle, though in the early poetry his use of the metaphor is tentative. The **"Elegy"** for his paternal grandfather, Pryor Thomas Berry, shows Berry working toward his characteristic vein. The poem considers death, implicitly at least, in terms of farming and the seasonal death and rebirth of the crops. The title of this volume is a complex pun suggesting at once burial, the plowing up of fields for planting, and even the breaking of new "literary ground" as Berry's first book of poems. The poem's imagery, however, is still relatively abstract in a manner typical of the late fifties and early sixties. For instance, the conversational free verse and the delicate touches of surreal imagery are reminiscent of the early Robert Bly:

> All day our eyes could find no resting place.
> Over a flood of snow sight came back
> Empty to the mind. The sun
> In a shutter of clouds, light
> Staggered down the fall of snow.
> All circling surfaces of earth were white.
> No shape or shadow moved the flight
> Of winter birds. Snow held the earth its silence.
> We could pick no birdsong from the wind.
> At nightfall our father turned his eyes away.
> It was the storm of silence shook out his ghost.
>
> —***Poems*** (3)

This poem, despite its beauty, is conventionally lyrical in its emphasis on local effects of imagery, the heated expression of syntactically disconnected personal impressions. The snowy landscape offers the poem whatever unity it can, as well as the ironic contrast of its "light" with the "darkness" of the death it shrouds:

> he only wakes
> Who is unshapen in a night of snow.
> His shadow in the shadow of the earth
> Moves the dark to wholeness.
>
> —***Poems*** (3)

Here is an embryonic form of the light/dark paradox so important in much of Berry's poetry about death, suggesting mystery beyond human comprehension and hinting at the possibility of some form of resurrection. As the **"Elegy"** progresses, the farm metaphor takes shape, though fitfully and by hints. Berry speaks, for instance, of adorning "the shuck of him / With flowers as for a bridal" (4). The word "shuck," used here for the body, suggests a pod or husk containing the seeds of future life.

Indeed, there is something of the traditional elegy here, with funeral "strewings," burning lamps, even what seems an appropriate response of nature to the event, the snowstorm. The language has a proprietous, at times even a quaint stateliness ("Snow held the earth its silence"), suggesting an acquaintance with Elizabethan habits of diction and syntax. And there is also the implication that death shall bring forth sweetness and new life, like Virgil's golden bees that swarmed from the bodies of eight sacrificed cattle (see Speer Morgan 869). The landscape, however, is not Arcadian. It is the farm country that in increasing detail will take on a dominant role in Berry's poetry, as in his life. This setting emerges in the bleak winter landscape and the "winter rain" that "breaks the corners / Of our father's house, quickens / On the downslope to noise" (***Poems*** 4). On a metaphorical level, the ethos of farming is suggested by the "shuck" of the body and in one of the final lines: "The church heals our father in" (5). The word "heal," with its implications of restoration and cure, going back to the Germanic "hailaz," meaning whole, implies some hope of a resurrection. More specifically, "healing in" is a farming and gardening expression meaning to lay a plant in contact with the earth from which it will gain some sustenance before actual planting. Although the hope in **"Elegy"** is still only implicit, the language of farming, inaugurated here, leads Berry to increasingly firm assertions of such hope.

. . . . .

Berry's second book of poems, ***Openings*** (1969), greatly expands the consideration of death in terms of farming. Again the title puns on what might be "openings" for planting, for graves, and for literary development. A set of **"Three Elegiac Poems"** for Harry Erdman Perry, Berry's maternal grandfather, develops the metaphor suggested in the Pryor Berry elegy. The first poem takes the form of a prayer that Perry be freed into death from "hospital and doctor, / the manners and odors of strange places, / the dispassionate skills of experts," from all the torture chamber apparatus of modern medical technology with its "tubes and needles" and "public corridors" (49). If the hospital offers "the possibility of life without / possibility of joy, let him give it up" (50). Natural death, to Berry, is the joyous and preferred ending of a life. Thus the speaker asks that Perry be allowed "to die in one of the old rooms / of his living, no stranger near him," and that

> the final
> time and light of his life's place be
> last seen before his eyes' slow
> opening in the earth.

This way, the dying man, "like one familiar with the way," will go into the "furrowed" hill over which he lived and help sustain the land's future. Explicitly here, the "furrows" of planting are equated with the "furrow" of the grave.

The second poem in the set shifts from the subjunctive of the first poem's "prayer" to the dramatic present tense, using the speaker's personal point of view to describe the scene of the old man's dying.

> I stand at the cistern in front of the old barn
> in the darkness, in the dead of winter,
> the night strangely warm, the wind blowing,
> rattling an unlatched door.
> I draw the cold water up out of the ground, and drink.
> At the house the light is still waiting.
> An old man I've loved all my life is dying
> in his bed there. He is going
> slowly down from himself.
> In final obedience to his life, he follows
> his body out of our knowing.
> Only his hands, quiet on the sheet, keep
> a painful resemblance to what they no longer are.
>
> (50)

The poem interestingly contrasts the "normal" activity of the speaker drinking well water near the farm with the extraordinary event taking place "at the house." But though the event is extraordinary, nature does not go sympathetically awry as it would in a classical elegy; the death is ordained and natural: "In final obedience to his life, he follows / his body out of our knowing." Death is a mysterious but natural metamorphosis, after which the dying man simply and quietly passes "out of our knowing." What disturbs the speaker is not so much the act of dying as the "painful resemblance" of the hands "to what they no longer are," that is, the living flesh.

The third poem, with its tone of praising acceptance, corresponds to the "apotheosis" of the classical elegy:

> He goes free of the earth.
> The sun of his last day sets
> clear in the sweetness of his liberty.
> The earth recovers from his dying,
> the hallow of his life remaining
> in all his death leaves.
> Radiances know him. Grown lighter
> than breath, he is set free
> in our remembering. Grown brighter
> than vision, he goes dark
> into the life of the hill
> that holds his peace.
> He's hidden among all that is,
> and cannot be lost.
>
> (51)

This is Berry in one of his more mystical moments, and yet his claims for "apotheosis" are still cautious, tempered with the realism of farm life. Though the dead man has "grown brighter / than vision," he still must go paradoxically "dark / into the life of the hill / that holds his peace." This paradox may not satisfy the orthodox yearnings of a critic like Richard Pevear for a resurrection in Christ, but it does offer Berry consolation; because the dead man is "hidden among all that is," he "cannot be lost." The corn of wheat that falls into the ground and dies may bring forth much fruit.

The elegies in ***Openings***, though they make extensive use of realistic farm imagery, do not yet effect a completely natural combination of theme and material. The Arcadian echoes are still somewhat artificial and obtrusive. More important, the philosophy implicit in Berry's metaphor of seasonal death and resurrection has not yet been fully worked out and integrated into his expression. Though sometimes concerned with subjects addressed more effectively in his prose, the more speculative, theoretical poems of the 1970s, such as **"A Current"** and **"At a Country Funeral,"** have enabled Berry to practice and perfect the technique of the philosophical elegy.

. . . . .

In his most recent book, Berry has written the best elegiac poetry of his career. ***The Wheel*** (1982) refers by its title to the "Wheel of Life" of eastern religion, Berry's favorite theme of the recurring life cycle and the cyclical notion of time. In an epigraph to the book, Berry quotes Sir Albert Howard, author of *The Soil and Health: A Study of Organic Agriculture:*

> It needs a more refined perception to recognize throughout this stupendous wealth of varying shapes and forms the principle of stability. Yet the principle dominates. It dominates by means of an ever-recurring cycle . . . repeating itself silently and ceaselessly. . . . This cycle is constituted of the successive and repeated processes of birth, growth, maturity, death, and decay.
>
> An eastern religion calls this cycle the Wheel of Life and no better name could be given to it. The revolutions of this Wheel never falter and are perfect. Death supersedes life and life rises again from what is dead and decayed. (231)

Berry divides ***The Wheel*** into six parts, as it were, six different spokes. The first part consists of three elegies for his friend Owen Flood. The second part includes a series of his poems reckoning Berry's desolation, the contemplation of one "well acquainted now / among the dead" (246). The third part is made up of four love poems to Berry's wife, Tanya, written in Berry's characteristically elegiac tone. The fourth part, addressing what Berry calls "The Gift of Gravity," consists of two longer poems on the transience of human life, with the river as the overriding metaphor. In the fifth part, a group of six poems, the metaphor shifts to the Wheel of Life as a "dance" including both the dead and the new and future generations. The sixth part contains a single poem, **"In Rain,"** in which Berry considers the "path I follow" and the serene, accepting "marriage to place."

Easily the most powerful poems in ***The Wheel*** are those written in memory of Owen Flood, **"Requiem," "Elegy,"** and **"Rising."** The most formal of these, corresponding to the rhetorical first section of the **"Three Elegiac Poems"** for Harry Erdman Perry, is **"Requiem."** But this formality of tone acts in a kind of counterpoint to the firm, informal image of the farmer at his work:

> We will see no more
> the mown grass fallen behind him
> on the still ridges before night,
> or hear him laughing in the crop rows,
> of know the order of this delight.

Whatever incongruity exists here is typical of the risk-taking in Berry's more mature work. Even the most "literary" poems grow naturally now from Berry's experience of the world and aim at fidelity to that world and the community of men. These are a farmer's elegies, and they celebrate a way of life Berry has loved as much as they lament the passing from that life of his loved ones:

> Though the green fields are my delight,
> elegy is my fate. I have come to be
> survivor of many and of much
> that I love . . .
> * * * *
> I have left the safe shore
> where magnificence of art
> could suffice my heart.

With an almost Yeatsean austerity, the poem reaches out to the world to rhyme the particular and the cosmic, one man's fate and the fate of all into the acceptance of life and place in the world which alone promises serenity:

In the day of his work
when the grace of the world
was upon him, he made his way,
not turning back or looking aside,
light in his stride.
Now may the grace of death
be upon him, his spirit blessed
in the deep song of the world
and the stars turning, the seasons
returning, and long rest.

(233)

Berry's **"Requiem"** ends with a wide, spindrift, cosmic gaze that fixes the subject's life and death in the perspective of eternity.

The **"Elegy"** that follows, however, is a deeply personal, interior poem that does not yield up its human point of view. Ironically enough, the poem, cast in the form of a Dantean narrative, makes large claims in terms of literary antecedents. It begins with the typical Berry paradox that

To be at home on its native ground
the mind must go down below its horizon,
descend below the lightfall
on ridge and steep and valley floor
to receive the lives of the dead. It must wake
in their sleep, who wake in its dreams.

This stanza sets off an extended dream vision that forms the basis of the narrative. Berry is walking "on the rock road between / creek and woods in the fall of the year." He hears first "the cries / of little birds" and only "then the beat of old footsteps." At the moment of mystical vision, as Berry puts it,

my sight was changed.
I passed through the lens of darkness
as through a furrow, and the dead
gathered to meet me.

It is interesting to see again the old metaphor of the grave as a furrow in farming. In the dream vision of **"Elegy,"** however, the speaker is able to cross into the world of the dead and talk with them in the manner of a Homeric hero or Dante. Of course, this literary device has many antecedents (apart from the classical epics, one might instance Dante Gabriel Rossetti's "Willowwood" sonnets and T.S. Eliot's encounter with the "dead master" in "Little Gidding"). But Berry's poem exercises this tradition with wonderful naturalness and daring simplicity. The dead whom the speaker meets are not symbols or allegorical figures, but members of his family and close friends who "wonder at the lines in my face, / the white hairs sprinkled on my head." There are first of all his grandparents, "a tall old man leaning / upon a cane . . . knowledge of long labor in his eyes," and "an old woman, a saver / of little things, whose lonely grief / was the first I knew" (234). They are followed by others of Berry's "teachers . . . who once bore / the substance of our common ground." Berry describes their dread as having been somehow transfigured: "Their eyes, having grieved all grief, were clear."

At this point, the beginning of the poem's second part, Berry recognizes his old friend Owen Flood, who died in the early spring of 1974, "standing aside, alone, / weariness in his shoulders, his eyes / bewildered yet with the newness / of his death." Handing him a "clod of earth" from "a certain well-known field," Berry begins a restrained colloquial dialogue with the dead man that laces the remainder of the narrative. The clod of earth is a sort of talisman enabling the conversation, like the blood in Homer's *Odyssey.* But Berry's is an appropriately homely talisman, and similarly the language is simple and natural, touching with a kind of philosophical humor on the subject of death:

"Wendell, this is not a place
for you and me." And then he grinned;
we recognized his stubbornness—
it was his principle to doubt
all ease of satisfaction.
"The crops are in the barn," I said,
"the morning frost has come to the fields,
and I have turned back to accept,
if I can, what none of us could prevent."

Couched in this homely conversation of two farmers is the essence of Berry's philosophy of death: acceptance of it as part of the natural scheme of things. Interestingly, language of the poem, unlike the more forthright statements of Berry's prose, confesses some doubt ("if I can . . . ") about the possibility of acceptance, the human frailty of the poet confronting what is ultimately unknowable. Berry's doubt is "answered" not with abstract assertion, but the felt experience of the narrative. Owen Flood, Berry's old mentor, appears now to have

cast off
his own confusion, and assumed
for one last time, in one last kindness,
the duty of the older man.

(235)

This "duty" is to demonstrate for Berry, as he once demonstrated the techniques and joys of nurture, the equally natural acceptance of one's fate in death. To this end, Flood and Berry do what Dante, through the mouth of Francesca, suggested was so painful: recall their happy times in time of sadness. Yet, as Owen Flood will demonstrate, the time of death need not be one of unmitigated sadness. Indeed, the mood of the poem remains serene rather than miserable.

We stood on a height,
woods above us, and below
on the half-moved slope we saw ourselves
as we once were: a young man mowing,
a boy grubbing with an axe.

. . . . .

We made it [the old field] new in the heat haze
of that midsummer: he, proud

of the ground intelligence clarified,
and I, proud in his praise.
"I wish," I said, "that we could be
back in that good time again."
"We are back there again, today
and always. Where else would we be?"
He smiled, looked at me, and I knew
it was my mind he led me through.

(236)

The larger memory of mankind consists in the interlinking memories of the generations, in the connections that we make and maintain with past and future. This theme, so prominent in Berry's writings, is once more poignantly suggested here. And how typical of Berry that it should involve the memory of daily work, the kind of thing some people would consider "drudgery." But it is with such "drudgery" that "we enact and understand our oneness with the Creation" (*The Unsettling of America* 138). The narrative continues now with a number of episodes like this, as Owen Flood moves Berry

through all the fields of our lives,
preparations, plantings, harvests,
crews joking at the row ends,
the water jug passing like a kiss.
He spoke of our history passing through us,
the way our families' generations
overlap, the great teaching
coming down by deed of companionship . . .

The encounter with and contemplation of death is actually the contemplation of life itself, of which death is an inevitable part. Berry tells us that Owen Flood's "passion" was "to be true / to the condition of the Fall— / to live by the sweat of his face, to eat / his bread, assured that the cost was paid" (237). This is Berry's highest compliment.

The fifth section of the poem deals with "the time of [Owen Flood's] pain," when in spite of "the sweet world" about him, "his strength failed / before the light." In one of the most moving passages, Berry for the first time senses mortal weakness in a man whose strength he had always taken for granted:

Again, in the sun
of his last harvest, I heard him say:
"Do you want to take this row,
and let me get out of your way?"
I saw the world ahead of him then
for the first time, and I saw it
as he already had seen it,
himself gone from it. It was a sight
I could not see and not weep.

This sudden, often untimely fading of strength that lies at the center of our wondering about death is perhaps, to the human imagination, its most tragic quality. Berry the philosopher knows what to say next about it, but Berry, the poet in the grip of his vision, cannot help pausing to weep for the tragedy of the human condition. Owen Flood himself does not weep. In the sixth section offers yet another touching vignette of the two men together, looking over the fields and seeing

the years of care that place wore,
for his story lay upon it, a bloom,
a blessing.

(238)

It is the summer's end, and their conversation turns to "death and obligation, / the brevity of things and men" (238-39). At this moment of heavily moving words and heavy thoughts, Owen Flood is not bitter, but filled with the wonder of nature and of life:

We hushed.
And then that man who bore his death
in him, and knew it, quietly said:
"Well. It's a fascinating world,
after all."

We are a long way here from the literary posturings of **"A Man Walking and Singing."** Owen Flood delivers his farmerly words with a perfect naturalness and simplicity. Indeed, the whole poem moves us with the sort of difficult simplicity that we find only in the mature works of certain masters; it is Berry's version of a *Heiligedankgesang*.

In the very hour he died, I told him,
before he knew his death, the thought
of years to come had moved me
like a call. I thought of healing,
health, friendship going on,
the generations gathering, our good times
reaching one best time of all.

(239)

In the final sections of the poem, they return among the dead, and Berry has a vision of the essential unity in life *and* death of all the generations, even those to come.

Again the host of the dead
encircled us, as in a dance.
And I was aware now of the unborn
moving among them.

Berry's "teacher" speaks one more time, reminding him that "joy contains, survives its cost." And as he speaks, it is Berry's "gift" to hear the "song in the Creation":

In its changes and returns
his life was passing into life.
That moment, earth and song and mind,
the living and the dead, were one.

(240)

At the end, Owen Flood, "completed in his rest," drops the earth Berry had given him, and waves the living man, "inheritor of what I mourned, . . . back toward the light of day."

Berry's haunting by Owen Flood is not yet over, however. There is another poem in the sequence entitled **"Rising"** that is dedicated to Owen Flood's son Kevin. The poem offers a more detailed memory of Owen Flood in his prime as Berry's model of a farmer. Again, this poem does not suppress narrative. It begins with an anecdote of a young Berry working with Owen Flood in the harvest after having rather foolishly "danced until nearly / time to get up." The harvest does not wait for young men with hangovers, however, and Berry must work "half lame / with weariness . . . dizzy, half blind, bitter / with sweat in the hot light." Owen Flood, however, taking "no notice" of Berry's distress, goes on ahead, "assuming / that I would follow," and leading Berry

> through long rows
> of misery, moving like a dancer
> ahead of me, so elated
> he was, and able, filled
> with desire for the ground's growth.

As Berry puts it, "my own head / uttered his judgment, even / his laughter" (241). Owen Flood's only comment is gentle and laconic: "That social life don't get / down the row, does it, boy." The anecdote springs to life, full voiced and full of a kind of joy, the way our pleasant memories of the dead may spring to life again once we have come to terms with the primal tragedy of their death. Berry has done this through the visionary meeting of **"Elegy,"** and now Owen Flood may live again in his memories, which may be a gift, as the dedication of **"Rising"** suggests, to the future generation.

The anecdote also engages the theme of generations subtly linked by the human activity of living and working together in one place. This activity represents in microcosm the heritage of the land itself, always an important element of Berry's writing. From Owen Flood, Berry learns to work not "by will" but "by desire," making what might seem an "ordeal" into "order / and grace, ideal and real." The conjuction of Berry's "awkward boyhood" with "the time of [Owen Flood's] mastery," troubles the younger man "to become / what I had not thought to be." Thus the disciplines of the system of systems are "made, remembered, taught, learned, and practiced" (*Standing by Words* 47), passing from one generation to the next. Owen Flood teaches Berry the role of the "cyclical" man at home and in place, the nurturer who stands in opposition to the constant "traveler," the exploiter of the land:

> The boy must learn the man
> whose life does not travel
> along any road, toward
> any other place,
> but is a journey back and forth
> in rows, and in the rounds
> of years. His journey's end
> is no place of ease, but the farm
> itself, the place day labor
> starts form, journeys in,
> returns to: the fields
> whose past and potency are one.
>
> (242)

In such a way, time past and time future may indeed both be contained in time present; and one may indeed experience the paradoxical joy of fidelity, those "moments when what we have chosen and what we desire are the same" (*The Unsettling of America* 122). In *The Unsettling of America,* Berry quotes with approval Thomas Hardy's poem about the farmer, the "man harrowing clods" who "will go onward the same / Though Dynasties pass" (14); here he eulogizes Owen Flood in similar terms:

> The man at dawn
> in spring of the year,
> going to the fields,
> visionary of seed and desire,
> is timeless as a star.
>
> (242-43)

These lines form the emotional center of Berry's poem, and perhaps his work as a whole. Here Berry's gaze rises from the particular toward the universal, "personal at the beginning and religious at the end" (*Standing by Words* 50-51). And this movement of his vision suggests why what we have seen is "not the story of a life," but "the story of lives, knit together / overlapping in succession, rising / again from grave after grave." But the memories of living men are the keepers of this mystery, this "severe gift" we "keep / as part of ourselves" when "like graves, we heal over." As Berry puts it:

> There is a grave, too, in each
> survivor. By it, the dead one lives.
> He enters us, a broken blade,
> sharp, clear as a lens or mirror.
> And he comes into us helpless, tender
> as the newborn enter the world.

In such a way, "the dead become the intelligence of life" (243).

Berry ends his poem **"Rising"** with as deeply felt an "apotheosis" as we are likely to encounter in contemporary American poetry, and in it he sums up much of his attitude toward death and life. The mature version of Berry's song of death transforms itself into a song of life, "rhyming" flesh with flesh and generation with generation.

> But if a man's life
> continues in another man,
> then the flesh will rhyme
> its part in immortal song.
> By absence, he comes again.
> There is a kinship of the fields
> that gives to the living the breath
> of the dead. The earth
> opened in the spring, opens
> in all springs. Nameless,
> ancient, many lived, we reach
> through ages with the seed.
>
> (244)

This is an attitude which has been hard won, offering neither glibness of orthodoxy nor glibness of despair. It is an attitude proprietous and secure in man's place in the system of systems and the ultimate mystery surrounding it. The earth that opened one spring for Owen Flood opens in all springs to embrace the dead and to bring forth new life. Owen Flood's death was, as Berry would have his own, the good death of a farmer, a nurturer "reaching through ages."

Notes

Berry, Wendell. *Collected Poems: 1957-1982.* San Francisco: North Point Press, 1985.

———. Letter to the author. 19 April 1986.

———. *Recollected Essays: 1965-1980.* San Francisco: North Point Press, 1981.

———. *Standing by Words.* San Francisco: North Point Press, 1983.

———. *The Unsettling of America: Culture and Agriculture.* San Francisco: Sierra Club Books, 1977.

Morgan, Speer. "Wendell Berry: A Fatal Singing." *The Southern Review* 10.4 (October 1974): 865-77.

Pevear, Richard. "On the Prose of Wendell Berry." *The Hudson Review* 35.2 (Summer 1982): 341-47.

David E. Gamble (essay date 1988)

SOURCE: "Wendell Berry: The Mad Farmer and Wilderness," in *The Kentucky Review,* Vol. VIII, No. 2, Summer, 1988, pp. 40-52.

[*In the following essay, Gamble explores the relationship between wilderness and agriculture in Berry's poetry.*]

Wendell Berry envisions a moral agriculture that transforms the farmer from the enemy of wilderness to its most devoted guardian. This is one of Berry's most paradoxical themes, for traditionally the farmer's role has always been to destroy the wilderness; he clears away the forest with its vegetable and animal life to plant the crops and produce the agricultural abundance that makes civilization possible. Further, anyone with a rural background knows that farmers traditionally seem stubbornly blind to the virtues of the wild.[1] On a farm, wildlife is most often seen as a pest, and nature in general as an obstacle to be removed. Yet in both his poetry and his prose, Berry argues that all enlightened farmers must find room on their farms for wild areas, and that these pockets of wilderness must be tended as carefully in their own way as any cultivated field.

On this point, Berry calls for more than simply a change in agricultural practice; his work demands a revolution in thought about agriculture that would extend the responsibility of the farmer beyond his fields and into the wilderness. His rationale for this extension of agricultural responsibility is based on a religious experience of the wild that he believes must inform the daily practice of farming. Wilderness reminds the farmer that not only the fertility of his fields and the health of his animals, but his own life as well, ultimately rest on natural cycles of life that are beyond his control, that are wild. Berry associates these wild cycles of life with Creation, with God, and thus argues farming above all other human activities must be practiced as a religious rite; the farmer in his daily chores enacts his awe, humility, respect, and love for the Creation he is given to use, but never to destroy.

Berry's "Mad Farmer" poems contain his boldest expression of the ideal relationship between wilderness and agriculture. Some parts of these poems are typical examples of the influence of Chinese poetry and the Taoist philosophy of nature on Berry's work;[2] like the ancient Taoist mystics, Berry emphasizes the need to make human actions contribute to the natural order:

> Wanting the seed to grow,
> my hand is one with the light.
>
> . . . . .
>
> Eating the fruit,
> my body is one with the earth.[3]

But more characteristic of this series of poems is an iconoclastic voice reminiscent of Nietzsche's philosophical "madman" from *The Gay Science.* Where Nietzsche's prophet announces that nihilism has created a new age in thought and culture, Berry's mad farmer boldly states the essentials of a new agriculture which defies the conventions and platitudes of agribusiness. Like Nietzsche's mad philosopher who "lit a lantern in the bright morning hours,"[4] the mad farmer accepts that few will see the need for the ideas he espouses, and even celebrates the confusion he causes in the agricultural establishment. In **"The Contrariness of the Mad Farmer,"** Berry writes:

> If contrariness is my
> inheritance and destiny, so be it. If it is my mission
> to go in at exits and come out at entrances, so be it.
>
> (121)

Even Nietzsche's proclamation that "God is dead"[5] is repeated by Berry, though qualified by the mad farmer's deliberately contrary behavior:

> When they said "I know that my Redeemer liveth,"
> I told them, "He's dead." And when they told me,
> "God is dead," I answered, "He goes fishing
> everyday in the Kentucky River. I see Him often."
>
> (121)

Where his neighbors farm by the advice of "experts" from the university and the state, the mad farmer plants by the stars; instead of fertilizer, he chants incantations. He has no sense of propriety or property:

> He plowed the churchyard, the
> minister's wife, three graveyards
> and a golf course. In a parking lot
> he planted a forest of little pines.
>
> (120)

He laughs at funerals, prays at revels, and, in general, refuses to cooperate.

The purpose behind the mad farmer's deliberate provocation of his neighbors is that "Going against men," he tells us, "I have heard at times a deep harmony" (121). He is contrary only to the ways of man, whom he sees as a spoiler and desecrater of life; following the ways of nature, he claims to be a preserver and sanctifier of life. The harmony he hears results from his making his farm operate within, rather than against, the natural processes of Creation.

Berry's mad farmer is a revolutionary driven by a poetic vision of the true calling of farmers: to care not just for their crops but for all natural life; to love not just their property but the earth which endures beyond all property. He rebels against the city, where Creation is paved over and forgotten:

> As my first blow against it [the city] I would not stay.
> As my second, I learned to live without it.
> As my third, I went back one day and saw
> that my departure had left a little hole
> where some of its strength was flowing out,
> and I heard the earth singing beneath the street.
>
> (123)

He rebels against a system of production that not only systematically destroys Creation, but the dignity of human life as well:

> Love the quick profit, the annual raise,
> vacation with pay. Want more
> of everything ready-made . . . [and]
> Your mind will be punched in a card
> and shut away in a little drawer.
> When they want you to buy something
> they will call you. When they want you
> to die for profit they will let you know.
>
> (151)

He rebels against the abstractions and numbers modern economics uses to justify destruction and waste:

> It is *ignorant* money I declare
> myself free from, money fat
> and dreaming in its sums, driving
> us into the streets of absence,
> stranding the pasture trees
> in the deserted language of banks.
>
> (154, author's emphasis)

To the mad farmer, it is those who lead lives dependent on an exploitive system whose only value is profit at any cost who are truly mad. It is they who do not value life, and it is they who might ultimately destroy it. Declaring himself free from a system which he sees as the enemy of the living world, his advice to all is at least not to cooperate: "everyday do something/that won't compute" (151). To the farmer, his advice is more specific and more radical:

> Plant sequoias.
> Say that your main crop is the forest
> that you did not plant,
> that you will never live to harvest.
> Say that the leaves are harvested
> when they have rotted into the mold.
> Call that profit.
>
> (151)

The farmer must reckon profit not in terms of what he can sell, but in terms of what is good for the life Creation has placed under his care. Profit must be not only what is good for the farmer, but also what is good for the forest, the stream, the insect, the bird, the mammal, the microbe, and even the humus. He must remember that "the real products of any year's work are the farmer's mind / and the cropland itself" (131). He must remember that his real goals are to "Make the human race a better head. Make the world / a better piece of ground" (131).

It follows that the satisfactions of such a farmer cannot be measured in terms of business, but ony by the standards of husbandry, of care. Thus, it is not surprising to hear Berry celebrating a good, productive farm:

> Growing weather; enough rain;
> the cow's udder tight with milk;
> the peach tree bent with its yield.
>
> . . . . .
>
> the ground, new worked, moist
> and yielding underfoot, the feet
> comfortable in it as roots.
>
> (132)

But is it surprising, at least from the point of view of tradition, to hear him celebrating the wildlife on his poetic farm; the satisfactions of the mad farmer also include:

> dear tracks in the wet path,
> the deer sprung from them, gone on;
> live streams, live shiftings
> of the sun in the summer woods;
>
> . . . . .
>
> fox tracks in snow, the impact
> lightness upon lightness,
> unendingly silent.
>
> (134)

What would be nuisances to most farmers—the deer that eat the corn before it is harvested, the fox that raids the hen house—are presented here as not only having a legitimate place on a farm, but also as having a right to a share of the fruits of the farmer's labor. Berry suggests the farmer should be as pleased by his healthy deer herd as he is by his own livestock, as glad to provide for the fox as he is for his hens. His satisfactions, and therefore also his responsibilities, extend beyond what he actually cultivates. He must also help the natural plant and animal life of his farm to flourish even in the midst of his fields.

To some readers, this must seem an astonishing portrayal of the relationship between farming and nature; to some farmers, it must surely seem like "mad" farming indeed. But it is not merely a romantic fantasy; Berry has both practical and philosophical reasons for describing his poetic farmer in such unusual terms. In *The Unsettling of America,* his most detailed study of culture and agriculture in America, he contends in defense of wilderness that "Only by preserving areas where nature's processes are undisturbed can we preserve an accurate sense of the impact of civilization upon its natural sources," and endorses the idea that "farmers should pattern the maintenance of their fields after the forest floor, for the forces of growth and forces of decay are in balance there" (UA 30).

Berry here follows the lead of Aldo Leopold in arguing that wilderness provides a standard of normality against which we must measure our impact on nature; wilderness represents nature in self-renewing, self-sustaining health, and to keep the land that we develop healthy we must use wilderness as a reference point by which to judge our actions, and correct them when they go awry.[6] For much the same reason, Berry argues that each farm must have its own wild areas as models for healthy use. The farmer must try to imitate in his cultivated fields the processes which kept the land healthy and productive when it was wild. He maintains that only in this way can farmland remain naturally fertile; the wilderness is a model for "kindly use" (UA 30), the sort of use that the long-term survival of life demands.

But the practical reasons for the farmer to preserve wilderness on his farm are limited. It is fairly easy to see the connection between the fertility of fields and the creation of humus on the forest floor; seeing the farmer's need for foxes and deer is more difficult. At this point, Berry shifts his argument to a more philosophical level. There is no immediate need for the farm to have foxes; nevertheless, they should be there, as should all the plants and animals native to the area. There is a deeper reason for preserving wilderness, and it is a religious one. Berry claims that "We need what other ages would have called sacred groves," to help keep us "properly humble in our use of the world" (UA 30).

The farmer's use of land and life must be inspired by a religious sense of their value as parts of Creation; our relationship to the land under our care must be that of respect to a work of God. Though we must use the divine Creation to live well, we must use it in ways that do not diminish it: "To live, we must daily break the body and shed the blood of Creation. When we do this knowingly, lovingly, skillfully, reverently, it is a sacrament. When we do it ignorantly, greedily, clumsily, destructively, it is a desecration" (*GGL* 281). Wasting *any* part of Creation is, to Berry, a sacrilege. We must respect all of Creation, and so we must preserve all of the wild whether it is convenient to do so or not. We must survive, but not at the expense of forgetting that we are but parts of a larger Creation. We must remember that the land and its creatures, even the predators who lower our profit margins, are as much a divine gift as are our very lives.

Only one of Berry's books, *The Unforeseen Wilderness,* is devoted solely to wilderness and its spiritual values. Like many contemporary books devoted to the subject of wilderness, it is both a general plea for mercy towards wild areas and creatures, and an attempt to save a particular wilderness from destruction. Just as other contemporary American writers, such as Edward Abbey in *Desert Solitaire* and Colin Fletcher in *The Man Who Walked Through Time,* wrote in the late 1960s to try to save the Southwest from the apparently insatiable lust of government agencies for building dams, Berry writes in the early 1970s to save Kentucky's Red River Gorge from industrial recreation and "flood control." His argument here focuses exclusively on the "higher" values of peace, serenity, solitude, beauty, and harmony with nature which will be destroyed if the Gorge is dammed and its wilderness lost forever.

In *The Unforeseen Wilderness,* Berry's relationship to the land is not his usual one of the resident, "mad" farmer-poet, nor does he play the role of agricultural critic; in the wilderness, he, like Thoreau, is a sojourner in nature, a visitor who in his temporary stay uses the land only as the inspiration for philosophical meditation. He recounts for us several trips into the Gorge, the most interesting of which is the story of a solo hiking trip. The narrative begins with Berry, usually so fastidious about his responsibilities to home, farm, and society, making a mad dash for the back-country. Leaving some of his work as a professor at the University of Kentucky unfinished, and his home and farm far behind, he races down the Kentucky Parkway at sixty to seventy miles per hour towards the small area of the Red River Gorge that remains undeveloped. Here he will spend two days in solitude, wandering through the woods and along the streams which are very nearly the sole remnants of wild Kentucky.

At first, Berry has difficulty adjusting to the natural area he worked so desperately to reach. When he finally gets to a campsite, he feels restless, disoriented, and melancholy. But much like Thoreau's initial loneliness at Walden Pond, which he recognized as "a slight insanity,"[7] Berry is not deeply disturbed by this particular anxiety. He is familiar with it, and understands its sources. He knows, for example, that his "mind is still keyed to 70 mph" (*UW* 39). His senses and thought processes have difficulty making the transition from modern speeds to the natural pace of the wild: "We seem to grant to our high-speed roads . . . the rather thoughtless assumption that people can change places as rapidly as their bodies can be transported. That, as my own experience keeps proving to me, is not true" (*UW* 38). It is simply going to take some time to slow down enough for him to appreciate the world he has come to, to see it as something more than a blur from a highway, something alive and intricate and unique.

To see this wilderness, Berry knows he must experience the "uneasy awareness of severed connections, of being cut off from all familiar places and of being a stranger where I am" (*UW* 40). He must leave behind his daily routines, chores, habits, and responsibilities; for a while, he must voluntarily isolate himself from the human world in which he is comfortable. His wife, family, job, farm, and poetry are all out of reach for a few days, and he feels their loss. Everything that ordinarily occupies his time and attention is absent, and at first there is nothing to take their place. But, like Thoreau, he knows that it is but a matter of time before his senses, nerves, and thoughts will adjust themselves from the human pace of highway, career, and responsibility to the luxuriant, free, timeless natural world he has come to. It is to experience this very adjustment, and its attending insights, that he has come to the wild.

Berry has come to the Gorge to remind himself of the meaning of Creation, and of the small part the human world plays in the larger natural processes of the universe:

> I have come here to enact . . . the loneliness and humbleness of my kind. I must see in my flimsy shelter, pitched here for two nights, the transience of capitals and cathedrals. In growing used to being in this place, I will have to accept a humbler and truer view of myself than I usually have. (*UW* 42)

It is an experience Berry thinks necessary to both his own sanity and that of his species. Buffered by civilization, by a world we have created for our own comfort and convenience, we can be consumed by self-importance; we forget that there is more to life on earth than the human species. This self-importance in turn breeds overconfidence, and we begin to believe we have the right, because we have the power, to do anything we like to the natural world that surrounds and sustains civilization. In other words, we become careless with life, both natural and human, and begin to treat it as though it were cheap, infinite, indestructible. It is a sequence of attitudes such as this that Berry sees behind such ideas as the damming and ruining of a natural wonder such as the Gorge.

But Berry has not come to the Red River wilderness to rail at modern, industrial civilization. He has come alone, and does not expect to speak to anyone during his stay. He has come to reenact an ancient rite of self-purification; he has come to the wilderness to seek wisdom. He compares himself to Indian braves who once ventured into the wild to find themselves, to learn their names, and to understand their place in the world (*UW* 67). By temporarily escaping from the human world, Berry, too, hopes to put his life and his society into a larger, more natural perspective. Aware that he is human and thus prey to the same confusions as the engineers, politicians, and economists who cannot see why the Gorge should not be destroyed in the name of recreation or cheap power, he has come to make sure his own soul is in order.

As a farmer, Berry, too, is a user of nature; although he believes that all farms should have room for the wild, he also knows that the farmer has no choice but to alter nature on most of his land. What must not be forgotten in this interference is that there are considerations other than economic ones; Berry is in the wilderness to remind himself of the natural limitations of human knowledge and action. For example, as a successful breeder of one or two species of domestic animals, he faces the temptation of being too satisfied with himself, of succumbing to the illusion that he has mastered nature. A wilderness that effortlessly breeds a thousand species of animals, birds, and plants in perfect health with no help or interference from man is the perfect spiritual antidote. Struggling to maintain the fertility of his fields, a wealth wasted by his ancestors, he sees the primeval forest building soil through cycles of life, death, decay, and new life, cycles far longer than a man's life and thus far beyond his control. Finally, Berry contends that any man who has experienced the power of the river that carved the Gorge out of solid rock, or even that of a trickle of water that sculpts a channel for itself through a rock face, realizes that the idea of man holding back that water and using it as he pleases is a ludicrous, dangerous illusion.

For Berry, the Gorge is a holy place, as Walden Pond was for Thoreau, as the Sierras were for John Muir. Indeed, he shares with many American nature writers this sense of religious awe at wilderness as a place where the solitude and silence of creation is undisturbed, where God's handiwork is left in pure form. As Roderick Nash points out in *Wilderness and the American Mind,* "Romantics and Transcendentalists sensed the unity of the natural world and related it to the presence and reflection of divinity." In doing so, they gave nature a higher value; it was no longer simply raw material to be shaped by human desire. Rather, Nash argues that writers like Thoreau, Muir, George Perkins Marsh, and even the more scientific Leopold all "manifested a belief in the sanctity of all life."[8] What Berry does is to take this religious sense that he shares with literary tradition, and apply it to the practical occupation of farming, making it the basis for his view of the environmental responsibilities of farmers. The wilderness taught Thoreau and Muir about God; the Red River wilderness teaches Berry not only about God, but about how to farm as well.

Rightly understood, the wilderness experience is a humbling one. It reminds Berry that a successful farm, like a successful society, exists within the margins of the natural world, and a successful life is one that endures within the natural conditions that sustain life, rather than altering them at the expense of all life, present and future.

> The time he stays in the wilderness is a time spent in touch with a nonhuman world that is mysterious to him. From the flowers to the stars he sees little or nothing that men have made. He spends time not as a master of the world but as a dweller in it—which is, after all, his true condition. And he should emerge from his experience somewhat changed—less eager to cash in on his birthright, aware that men are *part* of what they destroy. (*UW* 66, author's emphasis)

When Berry leaves the Gorge, his perspective on human life and activity is restored. The natural pace of the wilderness cured the anxiety he felt as a modern man too much in a hurry to really see the world around him, and the vast intricacy of the natural life of the wilderness reminded him of his place in the natural order of things.

The wild Gorge of the Red River restored Berry's mental and physical health, much as Mat Feltner's faith in nature is restored by his perception of the wildness on his farm in Berry's major novel, *A Place on Earth.* Throughout this novel, Mat Feltner is haunted by the death of his son, which seems to negate the care and love Feltner has invested in his land; what is the point of husbandry, of restoring a farm's fertility, if there is no heir to carry on the work? Feltner stubbornly continues to fulfill his responsibilities to the land and his community: he takes over the deteriorating farm of his drunken counsin, Roger Merchant; he alone maintains a vigil over the body of his friend, Ernest Finley, an unfortunate veteran who has committed suicide; he is there when his son's widow gives birth to his grandson. But he is merely going through the motions; his life seems hollow and unhappy until one day he has to retrieve a new-born calf from the woods on his farm. His sense of the kinship of all life is rekindled when he perceives the trace of wildness, of the free, natural instinct to flourish with or without men, even in his own domestic animals. He "finds the calf curled up in some long grass in a patch of sumac. . . . obeying like its mother an instinct still wild in it."[9] Seeing this wildness brings Mat back to his senses; leaving the calf hidden for the moment, he continues on through the woods, observing the process whereby the wild vegetation reclaims spent cropland. The wildness seems to put both human sorrow and joy into perspective once more:

> He feels the great restfulness of that place. . . . [and] feels the difference between that restful order and his own constant struggle to maintain and regulate his clearings. Although the meanings of those clearings and his devotion to them remain firm in his mind, he knows without sorrow that they will end, the order he has made and kept in them will be overthrown, the effortless order of the wilderness will return.[10]

Like his fictional farmer, Berry's faith in the natural order is restored by the wilderness, and he returns to his civilized life and his farm with new energy and insight, calmed by "the recognition and acceptance of one's human limits, by acknowledging one's dependence on powers beyond human reach" (*UW* 68). He leaves the wilderness, like Mat Feltner, a better man than when he entered.

Thus the wilderness has both practical and moral lessons not only for the life of the farm, but for the life of the farmer as well. It reminds us that food, cultivated or not, ultimately comes from natural processes beyond human actions, that nature itself is a manifestation of God and must be respected as such, and that the meaning even of an individual human life must ultimately be found in its place in the natural order of life. Although this view of farming and nature is so different from modern agriculture that is must seem to man more like madness than sense, Berry insists that the truth of the matter is that agriculture, as well as human life in general, must exist within nature's economy, rather than at the expense of it. Because agriculture ultimately depends on the process of wilderness, Berry can tell farmers to plant sequoias, and to claim that the forest they will never see is their main crop. It is an investment in the future, a willingness to give back as well as to take from the natural world. It is why the satisfactions of the mad farmer include the bounty of his well-kept fields, the deer who live in his woods, and a stream kept clear and pure out of his respect for it.

To the farmer, the meaning of the wilderness, of the sacred grove, is that he must care for life in its entirety—the forest as much as the fields, the wildlife as much as his herds, the children of tomorrow as much as the children of today. The farmer who does otherwise is simply one more cog in the exploitive machinery of modern business, another person who profits from the land by taking as much from it as possible, and keeping as much of it as possible. Berry's farmer, in contrast, measures profit in the restored health and life of the land. He knows the wild creatures of his farm have as much right to be there as he does, and are as deserving of his care as the animals he owns. The forest he plants and tends not only provides the wilderness virtues of peace and solitude, but also shows him how to use his land and produces fertile soil for the next generation. Farming as a mere business cannot help but destroy the land it exploits; farming as an occupation informed by a religious sense of humility and wonder enhances the land it uses, and preserves both the natural and the human. The future will decide which kind of farming is mad and which is not, but for Wendell Berry "mad farming" is a moral obligation of the present, and must be practiced both in his writing and in his farming.

Notes

1. A recent study on the geographic distribution of ecological awareness finds that agricultural states tend to be low on the scale of concern for conservation. Berry's home state of Kentucky ranked "very low," as did many states in the South and Midwest. See "Conservation Cartography," *Sierra* 71 (March/April 1986): 11.

2. Berry discusses his debt to Chinese poetry and thought in *The Long-Legged House* (New York: Harcourt, Brace and World, 1969), 142. Further references to Berry's prose works will be by page numbers in parentheses using the following abbreviations: GGL: *The Gift of Good Land* (San Francisco: North Point Press, 1981); UA: *The Unsettling of America* (San Francisco: Sierra, 1977); and UW: *The Unforeseen Wilderness* (Lexington: University Press of Kentucky, 1971).

3. *Collected Poems* (San Francisco: North Point Press, 1985), 130. All references to Berry's poetry will be to this edition, and will be indicated simply by page numbers in parentheses.

4. Friedrich Nietzsche, *The Gay Science,* trans. Walter Kaufmann (New York: Random House, 1974), 181.

5. Nietzsche, 181.

6. See "Wilderness" or "Wildlife in American Culture" in Aldo Leopold's *A Sand County Almanac* (New York: Oxford University Press, 1949).

7. Henry David Thoreau, *Walden* (New York: New American Library, 1960), 92.

8. Roderick Nash, *Wilderness and the American Mind* (New Haven: Yale University Press, 1967), 194.

9. *A Place on Earth* (San Francisco: North Point Press, 1983), 314.

10. Ibid., 317.

William C. Johnson (essay date 1991)

SOURCE: "Tangible Mystery in the Poetry of Wendell Berry," in *Wendell Berry,* edited by Paul Merchant, Confluence Press, 1991, pp. 184-90.

[*In the following essay, Johnson contends that Berry's poetry affirms the sacred in the land, creature, and community, offering the reader "an ecology centered in spirit."*]

Wendell Berry's writing affirms the intimate partnership between earth and spirit, a bond whose roots are at once biblical—"The earth is full of the goodness of the Lord" (Psalm 33)—and practical, since Berry writes out of, and back to, his long experience of working a Kentucky farm. He is sensitive to the world's body, the deep reserves of meaning growing from the earth into the human mind, heart, and community. His poetry enjoins mystery through a ritual of loving observation, in which work and play are part of the earth and its (human and non-human) creatures. The meaning of ritual can be felt and understood as living energy informed and bounded by sacred mystery.

The bond between creature and place is sacred. Earth gives life; tradition teaches habits of responsibility for life. But as Berry has reminded us, "the great disaster of human history" has been "the conceptual division between the holy and the world" (*A Continuous Harmony* 6), so that, in turn, "the history of our time has been to a considerable extent a movement of the center of consciousness away from home" (*The Unsettling of America* 53).

Berry's poetry offers a counter-challenge to this disembodied "intelligence." In testifying to the indwelling presence of the sacred in land, creature, and community, Berry offers us an ecology centered in spirit. We sense this spirit in an early poem, **"The Sycamore"**:

> It is a fact, sublime, mystical and unassailable.
> In all the country there is no other like it.
> I recognize in it a principle, an indwelling
> the same as itself, and greater, that I would be ruled
> by.
> I see that it stands in its place, and feeds upon it,
> and is fed upon, and is native, and maker.
>
> (***Collected Poems*** 65)

The sycamore embodies a polarity of fact and presence. "An indwelling / the same as itself, and greater" articulates the interpenetration of flesh and energy in a tangible, yet mysterious way. What dwells within all living things is at once concrete and mystical, the self and the self's ruler. As it feeds in its place, and in turn is fed upon, the tree is "native, and maker." In Berry, the biblical idea of losing the self to find it, extends to all creation: " . . . moved / by what moves / all else, you move" (***Collected Poems*** 145).

To be ruled in this way is to enter the life of the other, to be keenly aware of its intricate subtlety, to respect its nature as other, as we see in another early poem, **"The Snake"**:

> At the end of October
> I found on the floor of the woods
> a small snake whose back
> was patterned with the dark
> of the dead leaves he lay on.
> His body was thickened with a mouse
> or small bird. He was cold,
> so stuporous with his full belly
> and the fall air that he hardly
> troubled to flicker his tongue.
> I held him a long time, thinking
> of the perfection of the dark
> marking on his back, the death
> that swelled in him, his living cold.
> Now the cold of him stays
> in my hand, and I think of him
> lying below the frost,
> big with death to nourish him
> during a long sleep.
>
> (***Collected Poems*** 58)

The poem locates the snake in its native place. The speaker's reverence is clear, but does not overcome or replace our sense of the snake's presence: "I held him a long time, thinking. . . . " Language is the mental "niche" through which we enter the snake's life. "The perfection of the dark" completes this life. The snake is part of its place, and part of the food-chain enters the snake, dying to warm it. The phrase "his living cold" plays on the mingling of death-in-life, for the snake embodies cold in three senses: it is cold-blooded; it is warmed by what has died and become cold; and the memory of its cold, in the poet's hand, kindles his thought. If every biology is a counter-physics, then Berry's ecology is ultimately, though never exclusively, meta-physics. We will all one day enter the "long sleep" of death, as food for something else, but in this at least our lives will not have been wasted. We live, breathe, and die in partnership.

In its domestic and natural reference, Berry's diction is simple, but never simplistic. His words reflect a direct encounter with place, thing, and creature. His line is supple, but not consciously rhetorical; his syntax graceful, at times almost biblical, but austere in its adherence to "necessary things" (***Collected Poems*** 128). He has the directness and immediacy of Williams, the historical perspicacity of Pound, the colloquial freshness of Frost. But the deeper "sources" of his work are not literary. They are rooted firmly in land, family, and community, in the mysterious, transactional relations in and through which we dwell. One inevitably thinks of Berry-like images to describe this: raking, haying, birthing, scattering seed. But the meaning of such acts transcends sociology or soil-chemistry. The will to live responsibly hinges on an ever-deepening relation between earth and spirit, often expressed in a language of dwelling. In some of Berry's best poems, this quality of dwelling becomes mysteriously accessible. He has a gift for bringing what is unseen into knowable, if never containable, presence, as in **"To the Unseeable Animal."**

Being, whose flesh dissolves
at our glance, knower
of the secret sums and measures,
you are always here,
dwelling in the oldest sycamores,
visiting the faithful springs
when they are dark and the foxes
have crept to their edges.
I have come upon pools
in streams, places overgrown
with the woods' shadow,
where I knew you had rested,
watching the little fish
hang still in the flow;
as I approached they seemed
particles of your clear mind
disappearing among the rocks.
I have waked deep in the woods
in the early morning, sure
that while I slept
your gaze passed over me.
That we do not know you
is your perfection
and our hope. The darkness
keeps us near you.

(***Collected Poems*** 140-1)

The "Being" the poem addresses is at once generic—generative of all beings—and specific. "Flesh dissolves" into a presence, not a thing, but is felt nonetheless as something near. Spirit in Berry's poems is never abstract, but present in the tacit pre-dispositions of sense, the interior, unseen energies of place and creature. The poem makes it clear why Berry's diction remains aptly general rather than strictly visual. He avoids what Coleridge called "the despotism of the eye" through an attentiveness to inner form, the felt life, the "clear mind" of other beings, their places. For an instant, we see through the unseen animal's eyes, as it watches the fishes suspended in the current like "particles," not of our own abstraction (the atom), but of the co-mingling of beast and stream, the "clear mind." The language is not sharply visual, but deeply visionary.

In his timeless conservatism, Berry is radical. In an uncivilized time, he writes of subjects as old as civilization itself, keeping early traditions alive not merely by writing *about* them, but by learning *from* them, through the active life of work and the contemplative enjoyment of its fruits. Not surprisingly, one of his favorite images is the seed, as in these lines from **"The Man Born to Farming"**:

What miraculous seed has he swallowed
that the unending sentence of his love flows out of his mouth
like a vine clinging in the sunlight, and like water
descending in the dark?

(***Collected Poems*** 103)

The "sentence" of the farmer's love is labor, its literal and figurative fruits. Unless words grow from authentic labor with the earth, transforming what Thoreau called this "cubic foot of flesh" (for flesh is sustained, Antaeus-like, by the earth), no seed will sprout. Clear expression springs not from rational concept, but from subtle purpose:

. . . the seed doesn't swell
in its husk by reason, but loves
itself, obeys light which is its
own thought and argues the leaf in secret.

(***Collected Poems*** 32)

The seed is the germ of inborn mystery—a crisp, bonelike ovum we can hold in our hand. It is a microcosm of creation itself, enacting the original unity as it unfolds: tendril, cotyledon, stem, leaf, fruit. Its growth enjoins earth and light in plant-form (homologically as root and blossom) as it enters the intricate alchemy of temperature, moisture, and soil, the metamorphoses that articulate our mystery. For we too are seeds, each with our chance to root:

But our memory of ourselves, hard earned
is one of the land's seeds, as a seed
is the memory of the life of its kind in its place,
to pass on into life the knowledge
of what has died.

(***Collected Poems*** 159)

And memory lives in the marriage of people to the earth and to each other. Indeed, Berry offers a vision of marriage as the central ritual within biological and human communities, something we must undertake out of a respect for mystery. The spouse is the "way" and the "place," marriage a journey into and by means of mystery, a mutual quest for the country of marriage:

You are the known way leading always to the unknown,
and you are the known place to which the unknown is always
leading me back.

(***Collected Poems*** 147)

Mystery is not the absurdity of a chance universe, but the ineffable, living presence-in-commitment opening outward into family, household, nature, and cosmos—back to the divine name. Fear, uncertainty, and the inevitability of death bring us back to refuge and renewal in bonds of love and work, bonds increasingly tenuous in a society that severs not only male and female, but work and home. To be so divided "reduces our largeness, our mystery, to a petty and sickly comprehensibility" (*Home Economics* 141). Berry reminds men and women alike that gender is but the biological expression of Being itself, both natural and spiritual, and as such must not be used as a weapon or an enticement, but humbly respected as a powerful manifestation of life itself, human, natural, and metaphysical.

Berry's poems do not often appear in popular, academic anthologies. His pastoralism, his traditional diction, the absence of psychologism, all bespeak a poetic mode currently unpopular. Berry is suspect because he is not, in the conventional sense of the term, a humanist poet. He does not explore the freedom of the isolate human self. In Berry's poems, humanity finds and expresses meaning not through a life apart, but as "a part." The numinous resides not in the cloying confines of ego or in the shortcircuitings of failed relationships, but in the intricate web of creation itself, experienced from a finite, local perspective. We discover freedom through responsible action for the whole, as but one form of being in the scale of creation. Hence the profound significance of restraint, both formal and conceptual, in Berry's work—his deeply felt, and deeply intelligent, response to the necessary limits of a life in its place.

Berry's imagination, then, is *embodied,* expressed through local intelligence and practice. Unlike many of his contemporaries, he does not break out of experience to "language itself," the infinitely regressive complexities of disembodied meaning: since the idea of language for itself, severed from the living world, would violate the web of creation. To write (or read) in this way, is tantamount to studying animals in a zoo, or farming by computer. Berry's language springs from, and back to, experience in the body of the earth household, the ancient "body politic." He reminds us that poetic as well as biological form exercises restraint, to preserve its own integrity and that of others, to respond adequately and responsibility to its superior subject, life—which in Berry is ultimately though never exclusively spiritual. Any meanings are possible, but only certain meanings are responsible, hence finally meaningful. Through his attunement to what is greater than human, Berry offers us healing. Hearing his voice, we enter the dance of creation, joining hands with unknown partners in a ring circling past and future:

> When you meet, and hold love
> in your arms, regardless of all,
> the unknown will dance away from you
> toward the horizon of light.
> Our names will flutter
> on these hills like little fires.

(***Collected Poems*** 264)

Stephen Whited (essay date 1994)

SOURCE: "On Devotion to the 'Communal Order': Wendell Berry's record of Fidelity, Interdependence, and Love," in *Studies in the Literary Imagination,* Vol. XXVII, No. 2, Fall, 1994, pp. 9-28.

[*In the following essay, Whited views Berry's work as a repudiation of consumer culture in favor of an appreciation and understanding of a value system based on spiritual, communal, and familial concerns.*]

> For with the Lord there is steadfast love,
> and with him is plenteous redemption.—Psalm 130

From my first reading of Wendell Berry's polemical essay *The Unsettling of America* (1978) and on through his other essays, fiction, and poems, I have been amused by the contradiction between my admiration for Berry's precise observation of the nature of things and observations by critics who object to his work as anachronistic, romantic, sentimental, naive, elitist, or merely foolish. Often in my classes, I have been surprised by non-traditional students with families and careers who read his work and are offended by its "negative" tone or by what they perceive to be an easy dismissal of the truths and values they claim to live by. In both cases, readers' problems with Berry's ideas are more complicated than merely misreading or philosophical disagreements; they are better explained in Berry's own terms as a cultural forgetfulness brought on by the consumer values of an industrial economy.

Defining "values" is, of course, a task complicated by the relativistic values by which we presently live. Nevertheless, I suggest that whatever understanding of "value" one seeks it must, to be of use, transcend the philosophical fashion of the day or that of any particular historical moment, as much as it is possible to do so within an ethos free of agrarian or communal traditions. Wendell Berry himself laments the loss of traditional farming techniques, but he counsels a return not so much to an agrarian past as to a knowledge of the *values* that preserved and redeemed those who experienced our past. In that knowledge lay the communal wisdom of the culture. If the knowledge of such values restores to our use some values of our past, so much the better. Berry's work, particularly the prose fiction and narrative poetry, is primarily a record of, or a witness to, the existence of such values. In a noisy culture that proclaims its own fragmentation and imminent collapse, Berry offers the welcomed sensitivity of one who takes "a journey from the sound of public voices to the sound of a private quiet voice rising falteringly out of the roots of my mind, that I listened carefully in the silence to hear." Berry's work records "a journey from the abstract collective life of the university and the city into the intimate country of my own life" (*Recollected Essays* 63). What one learns from this "intimate country" is the measure of its worth to those who manage to use it appropriately and to those who know their place in it; that is to say, Berry escapes the false "collective" individuality of our urban, consumer-driven culture and moves into an intimate, responsible communion with those whose past, present, and future define him. For this reason, Berry's writing places value not on a literal or historical return, which is impossible, but on the restoration of a traditional understanding that measures value by a mutual interdependence and by fidelity to place, to community, and to family.

Traditional views are unpopular among trend setters, pundits, and academic specialists because such views eschew acquisition, abstraction, or progressive fashions. As Berry writes:

> Contemporaneity, in the sense of being "up with the times," is of no value. Wakefulness to experience—as well as to instruction and example—is another matter. But what we call the modern world is not necessarily, and not often, the real world, and there is no virtue in being up-to-date in it. It is a false world, based upon economies and values and desires that are fantastical—a world in which millions of people have lost any idea of the materials, the disciplines, the restraints, and the work necessary to support human life, and have thus become dangerous to their own lives and to the possibility of life. The job now is to get back to that perennial and substantial world in which we really do live, in which the foundations of our life will be visible to us, and in which we can accept our responsibilities again within the conditions of necessity and mystery. (*Standing by Words* 13)

This criticism does not lament the loss of a simpler past nor does it call for an unachievable utopian solution; Berry assumes the existence of the world "we really do live in" as it is evident in nature. In this formulation, our redemption, which also implies our survival, is contingent upon our ability to heed "instruction and example." We witness and learn from the practical solutions to and the consequences of *particular actions conducted over the years* with the knowledge of a particular place, rather than from theories predicting the future or from the specialists and experts of the present.

> "If we fail to see that we live in the same world that Homer lived in," Berry says, "then we not only misunderstand Homer; we misunderstand ourselves. The past is our definition. We may strive, with good reason, to escape it, or to escape what is bad in it, but we will escape it only by adding something better to it." (*Standing by Words* 14)

Critics and reviewers of Berry's polemical essays often complain that Berry argues for traditional ideals which, while attractive, are impossible to realize in our "modern world." After all, such critics ask, who wants to return to the drudgery of the farm, and who could afford to farm on the small scale Berry recommends, even if it were a desirable alternative to modern life? Some critics of Berry's fiction find Berry's farming "membership," lovingly catalogued in four novels and two collections of short stories, lacking in verisimilitude because of its "quaint" views, its lack of passion and "real life" concerns, its "unbelievably simple lives" and problems.

Charles Hudson complains of *Recollected Essays* that "Berry's prescription for our malaise is an apolitical one, implying that by a multiplication of the separate efforts of disciplined individuals, all could come right again." Hudson blames what he views as an "apolitical" stance on Berry's disillusionment with a nineteen-sixties styled activism combined with a failed "back-to-the-land movement." Furthermore, he finds that Berry's return to the farm "sheds no light on the process by which the wholeness of work might be restored," and in any event it would require changes that could result in "cataclysmic social and economic upheaval." Besides, Hudson claims, Berry's experiences unwittingly demonstrate "how terribly difficult it is for a single family in our society to live on a small farm using hand and horse labor" (222).

Where Hudson finds unpersuasive Berry's prescription for disciplined behavior on the land, other unsympathetic critics find his interest in the knowledge and proper use of land inadequately focused because of his promoting agricultural use over ecological autonomy. In a review generally favoring the agrarian message but critical of the form, Peter Stitt complains about ***Collected Poems*** that for Berry,

> Ideas are comforting to this writer, a way by which the wilderness may be tamed. In their absence, nature is likely to take over, and then anything could happen. Thus Wendell Berry, in his poems, always maintains intellectual control over his raw materials, rarely letting the real world have its head in passages of pure descriptive beauty. This seems a loss and a contradiction, for a man who loves the land so deeply to treat it in such a highhanded way. (638).

While the inanimate should have a greater voice, Stitt insists, the inarticulate should not have so much voice. Examining Berry's poem **"Boone,"** Stitt criticizes the poet's failure to allow the "hunter and trapper" to speak in his own language; instead, readers hear the language of "a professor, considering his vocabulary and the analytic nature of his thinking." In perhaps his most disturbing criticism, Stitt finds Berry's prose "pedestrian" because of "such old-fashioned stuff":

> Among his essays is the collection *Standing by Words*, described on the jacket of ***Collected Poems*** as "an exploration of language as a source of confusion and a means to clarity." One does not have to be a card-carrying semiotician to recognize that such old-fashioned stuff barely touches upon the real nature of language. (638)

Concerning **"Boone,"** Stitt's complaint ignores pastoral traditions, but his criticism of Berry's use of language reveals a qualitative distinction too easily made by most contemporary theorists, in this case a direct opposition, between the specialists in semiotics who understand language and the language of a trapper who works in his wilderness home, between analytical thought and a hunter's practical skill and knowledge, between the new and the old-fashioned, between "the real nature of language" and some illiterate alternative. Since for many theorists "language" is a socially determined, self-reflexive form of communication, an attempt to get at truth or even to be truthful may be considered by them suspect, and one can easily detect a tone of condescension in critical dismissals of Berry's attempts to get at the "truth."

Condescension of a related sort is expressed in Bruce Bawer's *New Criterion* review of *Fidelity* where he faults Berry's most recent collection of short stories for the absence of contemporary perplexity and anguish. For Bawer,

Berry's characters are neither sufficiently confused by life's complexity nor appropriately "dysfunctional." Bawer argues, "Here and elsewhere, Berry demonstrates an unwarranted degree of faith in the innate goodness of country people." He also suggests that Berry's philosophy "makes no allowance for certain ways of thinking and feeling and loving; he seems unwilling to accept that the human family is full of differences, that they make life more interesting, and that it is in cities, not rural areas, that these differences tend to be most tolerated" (77). Whatever connection one might make between cities and civilization, it is problematic to assume that the tolerance of social differences in cities is inspired by an enlightened view of community rather than by the anonymity of the crowd made possible by overcrowding, indifference, loneliness, and isolation.

Yet even writers who praise Berry's work often fall into an unwitting, at times self-serving, apologetic for what they perceive as urban values. Gregory McNamee, in an otherwise sensible if partisan look at what he calls Berry's "Politics of Agriculture," concludes by outlining similarities between the essays in *I'll Take My Stand* by the Agrarians of the nineteen-thirties and the views Berry espouses in his recent work. Yet Berry's politically incorrect resemblance to "the neo-Confederate twelve Southerners" worries McNamee into making several curious qualifications. He finds that Berry's *Hidden Wound* (among other things, a tribute to slaves who were owned by his forebears and to Nick Watkins and Georgie Ashby, African-Americans who worked for Berry's father) "forces a distance between Berry and those who yearn for the stars and bars." He suggests that "the Faulknerian farm world of the Nashville scholars can barely be found today, even in Possum Run, Alabama, or Blytheville, Arkansas." And to the Agrarian charge that "the culture of the soil is the best and most sensitive of all vocations and that therefore it should have the economic preference and enlist the maximum number of workers," McNamee dismisses the view for having lost its currency in our time: "Yet we have seen the disregard in which small farmers are now held by the government they once sustained, the decline of the freeholding class to less than two percent of the nation's population. The times have changed, and the agrarian ideal has long since lost the day." Moreover, McNamee goes on to praise Berry because the poet "indulges nostalgia little, and his work remains properly forward-looking" (100).

McNamee's views diverge from Berry's argument for the creation of "a communal order of memory, insight, value, work, conviviality, reverence, aspiration" (*Unsettling of America* 43). McNamee correctly notes that Berry never confuses "agrarian ideas" and "too much fondness for a supposed Golden Age," but while McNamee's warning against looking to the future, to "theories of progress—Marxian, Comtean, Spencerian—[that] are bankrupt," is sensibly urged in Berry's own work, Berry logically cannot be simultaneously skeptical of theories of progress and also be, as McNamee suggests, "properly forward-looking." By his own definition, McNamee's term "forward-looking" posits a faith in "a great literary and political tradition" to which Berry would probably refuse to subscribe even if anyone could define what this combination would entail or what influence it might have on the future. Berry in fact has argued:

> In my judgment intelligence never goes whole hog for anything public, especially political movements. Across the whole range of politics now (and I suppose always) you find people willing to act on the assumption that there is some simple abstraction that will explain and solve the problems of the world, and who go direct from the discovery of the abstraction to the forming of an organization to promote it. In my opinion those people are all about equally dangerous, and I don't believe anything they say. (*Continuous Harmony* 51)

Berry, eyes focused on the present life around him, seeks practical solutions through the accumulated experience of past actions and informed deliberation. In that sense, literary tradition has merit, and perhaps the foolishness of political solutions acts as corrective. As Berry says of the construction of the "longlegged house":

> This dependence on the old materials determined to a considerable extent the shape of the new house, for we would shorten or lengthen the dimensions as we went along in accordance with the lengths of the old boards. And so the new house was a true descendant of the old, as the old in its time was the descendant of one still older. (*Recollected Essays* 58)

To be sure, Berry's care and attention for farming, community, and tradition suggest a "proper" concern with what is to come after him, but the value of any "forward-looking" views Berry might adopt are ones which he measures by his present obligations. "What we owe the future / is not a new start," Berry says in **"A Country Funeral,"** "for we can only begin / with what has happened. We owe the future / the past, the long knowledge / that is the potency of time to come" (***Collected Poems*** 159). In his essay "Discipline and Hope," Berry recalls that the "Twelve Southerners of *I'll Take My Stand*" developed in their Introduction a "'Statement of Principles' in which they declared for the agrarian way of life as opposed to the industrial" (179). The book has been ignored as "an act of sentimental allegiance to a lost cause," but, Berry continues, one can now "say that the cause for which the Twelve Southerners spoke in their Introduction was not a lost but a threatened cause: the cause of human culture" (*Recollected Essays* 180). Just what is Wendell Berry's "threatened cause" and why is it so difficult for many thoughtful readers fully to grasp its meaning?

The critical debate over the merit and social significance of Berry's literary thought requires reflection on the differences between traditions of the past, informed by rural and agrarian needs, and values of the present, the products of urban and industrial desire. Because of our fashionable nihilism and angst, however, the apparent dichotomy between the country, as depicted in Berry's essays, fiction, and poems, and the city, as depicted in other writers' contemporary fiction and poetry, has often been reduced by critics to a matter of Berry's disagreement with the modern "lifestyle" and the "diverse" arrangements we now refer to as cities and families. While the catchword "diversity" denotes a much praised virtue in our time, it is often used as a euphemism for our failure to care about one another as human beings bound by our place within the natural order of work, play, birth, and death. Out of respect for some vaguely defined ethnic, social, gender, political, or national identity, we create self-esteem and establish a cult of individuality, both of which are based on exclusions and differences. This arrangement inspires competing groups, for the values that inform the actions of these groups are always subject to the whims and wishes of each group. A fundamental difference, then, between those who value Berry's ideas and those who find fault with them must be identified by one's defining "community," specifically, how it develops, how it prospers, and how it continues. The term *community,* of course, bears no special relationship to rural life, though traditionally that is where "community" has been nurtured.

Many writers have addressed the issue of "community" in recent years. Some academic observers seek answers in various social science models that look toward the future for the promise of some predicted evolutionary development. The lessons of the past are offered, if at all, as cautionary tales. Generally speaking, it is not incorrect to assert that the value of the past in much current academic discussions of culture is ignored or dismissed as ideologically determined, as impossible to recover, as an embarrassment, or, at the very least, as an example of unenlightened thinking, perhaps even barbarism. Such negative opinion aside, the problem of reclaiming past ideas and values is an absorbing pursuit for those who, like Berry, believe that history can in fact be understood and that "community" can endure from one generation to the next.

Throughout history, most people have experienced their lives with only the slightest knowledge of, or interest in, their distant ancestry. This suggests among other things that whatever exchanges occurred between the generations of a family, they were not confined to the sort of political and territorial values epic poets and historians generally celebrate. Without titles and power, the lineage of common families expresses itself chiefly in the practical resources for survival passed down between generations; for example, the cultural significance of what has passed for the more humble kinds of information—the skills of tilling, growing, harvesting, conserving, salting, canning, and so forth—is expressed in the continuing experience and wisdom that has preserved them. Because this kind of information was passed down in the experiences, songs, stories, and practical knowledge of work done by hand, even long forgotten or only vaguely remembered ancestors speak to present families just as present-day families will speak to the progeny they will never know.

Berry displays the importance of these vital connections between generations in all of his literary work, believing that a knowledge of the cultural exchange that preserves the lives of generations is central to one's understanding his definition of "community." A fashionable assumption of our time that what is learned from the previous generation may be unquestioned conformity grounds itself in the belief that each generation must find its own way in a new world. However, experience suggests that the values and commitments that the younger generation express must have their origins in the elders' experience. Despite an apparent paradox, even disagreement (mediated by love) must be recognized as a significant connection. In recent poems about his father, Berry includes reference to political disagreements and arguments; nevertheless, as he has said elsewhere, "My father was the first, and the most passionate and comprehensive, of my teachers" (*Hidden Wound* 72). Although his father practiced law in the county seat, New Castle, Berry says, "He kept the farmer's passion that sees beyond the market values into the intricacy and beauty of the lives of things, and that hungers to preserve and enrich the land" (*Hidden Wound* 71). In the age-old way, the elder contrived to keep the lessons of the farm before the younger to convey the traditions and values of farm work that are "worthy of the best of a man's attention and care" (*Hidden Wound* 72).

Berry illustrates the manner in which significant traditions are exchanged between generations to preserve community by way of a private, accurate language in poem and story. In poem XII of **"In Extremis: Poems about my Father,"** the narrator recounts what he learned from the father:

> He kept in mind, alive,
> The idea of the dead:
> "A steer should graze and thrive
> Wherever he lowers his head."
> He said his father's saying.
> We were standing on the hill
> To watch the cattle grazing
> As the gray evening fell.
> "Look. See that this is good,
> And then you won't forget."
> I saw it as he said,
> And I have not forgot.
>
> (***Entries*** 77-78)

Such "hearing" and "seeing" are possible only when people are quiet or still enough in one place to hear and to see, thereby creating the memory that makes hearing and seeing possible for the next generation.

The exchange between kinsmen of what constitutes the "good" is best conducted within the love for a specific place, and one would assume that modern technology would enhance this exchange by extending the lives of people by means of the recording devices we enjoy: "I know the panic of that wish to save / the vital knowledge of the old times, handed down" (***Entries*** 9). But Berry offers an important qualification about the language of tradition in **"The Record,"** for the voice of an old man on a tape-recording preserves nothing of the man's life. Preservation occurs only when "his voice / speaking out of lives long dead, their minds / speaking in his own" are now passed on in similar fashion by those in the present with the memory of this life lived in this particular place. A tape machine merely provides an excuse to stop listening, or to defer listening, causing one to suffer the illusion that the voice is now permanent, always present. The poet insists on more attention to the moment:

Stay and listen
until he dies or you die, for death
is in this, and grief is in it. Live here
as one who knows these things. Stay, if you live;
listen and answer. Listen to the next one
like him, if there is to be one. Be
the next one like him, if you must;
stay and wait.

(***Entries*** 10)

To stay in one place implies a recognition of value and a commitment, which must come first. Such commitment to a place then makes listening possible, for to understand what is said, or to "live here / as one who knows these things," suggests a physical experience with the natural concerns of the place and a deeper knowledge caused by that experience. Even as one hears what is told him, he must also see it around him in context. But the phrase "if you live" invites mystery into the lesson. While one hears in the expression the hope for a long life, it also points to the biblical notions of "living" in the spirit, which, though never commanded, always implies the qualification, "if you are able": "But blessed are your eyes, for they see: and your ears, for they hear. For verily I say unto you, That many prophets and righteous men have desired to see those things which ye see, and have not seen them; and to hear those thing which ye hear, and have not heard them" (Matthew 13:16-17). In such grace one will "listen to the next one / like him, if there is to be one" or "Be / the next one like him, if you must." The first phrase, "if there is to be one," dark with foreboding, passes into the second phrase, "if you must," hopeful with responsibility for those who follow, who "stay and wait." The poem continues its instruction:

Tell your children. Tell them
to tell their children. As you depart
toward the coming light, turn back
and speak, as the creek steps downward
over the rocks, saying the same changing thing
in the same place as it goes.

(***Entries*** 10)

Whatever notion from the past is preserved, it must assume its place in the present moment. It is impossible to bring back the past or to resurrect some nostalgic memory of the past, but this understanding of time is relevant to the consideration of the future, as well. They who plan for the future without any consideration for the values of the past ignore their moral responsibility for the implementation of their plans and the consequences of their theory. They ignore the arrogance implied by their assumption that some complete and radical break with the past, even if it were possible, excuses all responsibility for the social costs of displacement, for the loss of meaningful work to industrial models of productivity, or for the disintegrating rural communities. These problems, to name but a few, are passed off as evolutionary changes, the price of social progress.

Berry illustrates this dilemma by narrating the experience of a farmer who must take care when planning for the use or improvement of land; experience (both witnessed and imparted) provides the necessary knowledge of the place, as the hope for future use should determine its value. To reveal the symbiotic relationship between the past, the present, and the future, Berry discusses the irresponsible use of the hillside farms of his region of Kentucky. He says that "it is no longer possible to imagine how this country looked in the beginning, before the white people drove their plows into it"; soil erosion has so altered the landscape that, "It is as though I walk knee-deep in its absence" (*Recollected Essays* 91). At once the topsoil disappears because of poor management, an ignorance of the needs of the place, or indifference to (or lack of imagination for) what future value the place represents. Although one cannot ameliorate the destructive errors of the past, if he cares for the life of his progeny he has no choice but to consider the demands nature will make on him.

Berry explains natural demands this way: "[I]t is the business of natural processes to produce consequences, and the first law of ecology is that justice is *always* done—though not necessarily to those who deserve it. Ecological justice, in fact, falls most often on later generations, or on the people who live downwind or downstream" (*Recollected Essays* 247). This cause and effect relationship is, of course, true both literally and figuratively for one's neighbors and one's progeny, but to understand Berry's view is very difficult when industrial consumption is officially defended as merely the way things must be. At their peril, industrial consumers discount the accounting of nature by forgetting or ignoring "consequences," and such knowledge is not easily discovered or recovered. It is gained by a fidelity to a particular place and to the forces that shape both the observer and the place. The knowledge of this relationship between the place and the forces that shape it then becomes the example by which those following will act. This insight lies at the heart of Berry's view of the world.

In one of his earliest collections of poems, ***The Broken Ground*** (1964), Berry outlines the various relations between the demands of a place and the human and natural forces that shape it. He says in **"Elegy"**: "Below the hill / The river bears the rain away, that cut / His fields their shape and stood them dry." But even in the silence of death, the father still speaks to his progeny in the place where he worked and in their memory of what he taught them. This relationship occurs because:

Water wearing the earth
Is the shape of the earth,
The river flattening in its bends.

Their mingling held
Ponderable in his words—
Knowledge polished on a stone.

(***Collected Poems*** 4)

In this passage, Berry illustrates the paradoxical nature of the forces that act and are acted upon. While water exerts a powerful force, it is itself shaped by the banks and river bottoms that it in turn shapes. The influence of its force is also in direct relation to the shape of the land. In some places it runs rough and quick, in others smooth and slow. Nevertheless, it eventually worries at the bank, ever widening at the bends, and sometimes after flood, leaves behind shoals for drinking troughs. Draining itself along the watershed to the rivers and to the oceans, it takes with it both the debris of Nature's process and the manmade refuse that pollutes it.

Berry's metaphor also reveals the symbiotic nature of all human endeavor. Each generation molded by its preset circumstances also shapes the life around it. Berry describes this effect in his first novel *Nathan Coulter.* While walking with his grandfather on property long cared for by his family, Nathan says: "When we got to grandpa's place we stopped to drink at the spring":

> "That's a good vein of water," he said. "Nobody ever knew it to go dry."
>
> I thought of the spring running there all that time, while the Indians hunted the country and while our people came and took the land away from them and cleared it; and still running while Grandpa's grandfather and his father got old and died. And running while Grandpa drank its water and waited his turn. When I thought of it that way I knew I was waiting my turn too. But that didn't seem real. It was too far away to think about. And I saw how it would have been unreal to Grandpa for so long, and how it must have grieved him when it had finally come close enough to be known.
>
> In a way the spring was like him, a part of his land; I couldn't divide the spring from the notch it had cut in the hill. Grandpa had owned his land and worked on it and taken his pride from it for so long that we knew him, and he knew himself, in the same way that we knew the spring. His life couldn't be divided from the days he'd spent at work in his fields. (*Nathan Coulter* 179-80)

A meaningful example set by the elders offers the next generation the confidence and authority by which it acts. As Margaret Feltner tells her grandson Andy Catlett, who is about to go off to college, "'Listen. There are some of us here who love you mighty well and respect you and think you're fine. There may be times when you'll need to think of that'" (*Remembering* 64). This speech assumes the memory of the examples and actions that represent the life of the child; but, more importantly, Andy has the satisfaction of possessing the shared memories that join him to the previous generations while such shared memory acts as an example to him. Difficult decisions are then made by the propriety of the shared knowledge made available to him.

Drawing from his own experiences (see *Recollected Essays* 76 and *Hidden Wound* 71), Berry illustrates this kind of exchanged value between generations throughout his fiction. In *Remembering,* Andy Catlett recalls his father's decision to return to the farm. After college, Wheeler Catlett "had been invited by the about-to-be-elected congressman from his district, Forrest Franklin, to go to Washington with him as his secretary. Wheeler accepted, on the condition that he would be permitted to attend law school as well" (67). Since he had conducted his business and his studies with distinction, "Franklin assumed, along with virtually every teacher Wheeler had ever had, that Wheeler's destiny was to be that of thousands of gifted country boys since the dawn of the republic, and before: college and then a profession and then a job in the city" (67). But Wheeler resisted the "opportunity that so many have taken."

Andy interprets his father's decision to return to Kentucky as a measure of the values he inherited from his own father. Berry writes:

> Andy knows how firmly ruled and how unendingly fascinated his father has been by that imagining of cattle on good grass. It was a vision, finally, given the terrian and nature of their place, of a community well founded and long lasting. Wheeler held himself answerable to that, he still holds himself answerable to it, and in choosing it he gave it to his children as a possible choice. (*Remembering* 69)

The power of this vision is offered to Andy by the voice and experience of Wheeler: "'It can inspire you, Andy,' he said. 'It can keep you awake at night. It doesn't matter whether you've got a manure fork in your hand or a library in your head'" (69). Wheeler instructs his son to look at the walnut grove near the spring where the cattle come to drink. In thinly veiled autobiography (see *Recollected Essays* 92), Berry establishes the scene that forms the basis of Andy's values:

> The cattle crowd around in to the little stone basin, hardly bigger than a washtub, that has never been dry, even in the terrible drouth of 1930; they drink in great slow swallows, their breath riffling the surface of the water, and then drift back out under the trees. Andy and Wheeler can hear the grass tearing as they graze.
>
> "If that won't move a man, what will move him? It's like a woman. It'll keep you awake at night."
>
> Andy is old enough to be told that loving a place is like loving a woman, but Wheeler does not trust him yet to know what he is seeing. He trusts it to come to him later, if he can get it into his mind.
>
> "Look," he says. And as if to summon Andy's mind back from wherever it may be wandering, for Andy's mind can always be supposed to be wandering, Wheeler takes hold of his shoulder and grips it hard. "Look. See what it is, and you'll always remember it." (69)

In this passage from *Remembering,* Berry's concern is with the exchange of information, the acceptance of it, and the enduring memory of this connection between people.

But the success of this exchange depends on the combined knowledge of the father and son—one who listened to his father and one who listens to his—prepared by the physical experience with the place they have shared. The grip of the father's hand reinforces word and memory. This sharing also joins their present concerns and aspirations. As Berry says about "the particular terms of my allegiance to my native place," there also comes "a deep estrangement from it. Going day after day about the work of my little farm, I began to have a sense of the thousands of acts, properly honored and understood generation after generation, that are necessary to surround a man with a culture sufficient to his life in a given place" (*Hidden Wound* 87). The ritualistic nature of these acts has a humbling effect, for he sees and feels his responsibility to the place as reflected in a larger relationship with Nature. And by his care and work, he joins in a membership with those who have given attention to the place, which comforts him with "the sense of familiarity [that] finally crests in ritual—exactly as work rhythms build into *songs*—which tends not only to protect the individual's sense of himself in relation to the place, but to protect the place as well" (*Hidden Wound* 88).

Such intimate observation also defines the rural "community" that Berry characterizes in novels, poems, and essays. Berry's characters live in a "communal order," taking their example from what Berry calls the "Great Economy"; that is to say, they live "under the necessity of making [their] little human economy within it, according to its terms, the smaller wheel turning in sympathy with the greater, receiving its being and its motion from it (*Home Economics* 72). And by this participation, one observes that as a hierarchy the "Great Economy" "is not the 'sum of its parts' but a *membership* of parts inextricably joined to each other, indebted to each other, receiving significance and worth from each other and from the whole" (72-73). In Berry's definition of a healthy community, the use of this practical knowledge of a larger, natural order *necessarily* informs the social order of healthy communities.

Throughout his writing, Berry has consistently defined the elements of community as an "understanding of our need to help and comfort each other" (*Hidden Wound* 137), as a "community of interest—a common dependence on a common life and a common ground" (*Home Economics* 192), as "a locally understood interdependence of local people, local culture, local economy, and local nature" (*Sex, Economy, Freedom, and Community* 120), all of which imply a communal membership that he has experienced first hand. It is important to note that Berry offers no theory on the subject; he supports his ideas with practical experience and with his own intimate knowledge of past experiences that define the "Great Economy" of Port Royal, Kentucky, where he has lived and farmed during the last thirty years.

To illustrate the values of the "Great Economy," Berry follows the example of the ancients by offering stories that at once exhibit and celebrate the knowledge of community. Yet as Berry says in various ways, the astonishing thing is that such ideas must be presented anew because of our cultural forgetfulness brought on by the distraction of an industrial economy. For that reason, his fiction is sometimes as polemical as his essays. In *Remembering,* Berry brings the story of his Port William membership up to the present with Andy Catlett's experience of temptation and redemption. Because of haste and impatience, Andy mangles his right hand in the machinery of a picker while helping Elton Penn's son Jack bring in his first corn crop. Berry writes: "The picker became fouled as it had been doing off and on all afternoon, and Andy stopped to clear it, leaving it running" (13). His fellow workers, neighbors, kinsmen, and friends, free him from the machine and take him to the hospital. Before the surgery, Andy's wife Flora "smiled and picked up his left hand in hers and patted it. She seemed still to be living in that other time, before. 'What have you done to yourself?"' Andy replies symbolically: "'I've ruined my hand"' (15).

This intimate exchange is one of many memories that Andy recalls while he briefly travels away from his rural home. During all the action excepting the conclusion of the novel, he is in San Francisco, having just left an agricultural conference held in the Midwest, to speak at a college. He evades the college representative at the airport and then wanders about the city with his memories. "A man could go so far from home, [Andy] thinks, that his own name would become unspeakable by him, unanswerable by anyone, so that if he dared to speak it, it would escape him utterly, a bird out an open window, leaving him untongued in some boundless amplitude of mere absence" (5). In Berry's work, such "absence" represents more than personal depression, loneliness, or angst; instead, Andy has briefly lost track of the communal relations that define him even to himself. For the urban culture around him, for his lost hand, for his soul adrift, "absence" signifies a spiritual separation redeemed only by forgiveness.

The origins of such separation are revealed in Andy's disgust with the recent Midwest conference. Among the first memories that haunt him, he reflects on the deeply felt outrage of his improvised speech, inspired by his indignation at such discussion panel titles as "Suggestable Parameters" and "Ontology and Epistemology of Agriculture." Recklessly and spontaneously, he ignores his prepared speech and speaks his mind:

> "What we have heard discussed here this morning," he said, "is an agriculture of the mind. No farmer is here. No farmer has been mentioned. No one who has spoken this morning has worked a day on an actual farm in twenty years, and the reason for that is that none of the speakers *wants* to work on a farm or be a farmer. The real interest of this meeting is in the academic careerism and the politics and the business of agriculture, and I daresay that most people here, like the first speaker, are proud to have escaped the life and work of farmers, whom they do not admire.
>
> "This room," he said, "it's an image of the minds of the professional careerists of agriculture—a room without windows, filled with artificial light and artificial air, where everything reducible has been reduced to numbers, and the rest ignored. Nothing that you are talking

about, and influencing by your talk, is present here, or can be seen from here." (23)

His anger builds, and he tells his listeners of the hardship his grandparents suffered in 1906 when Marce and Dorie Catlett learned that their "crop had lacked $3.57 of paying the warehouse commission on its own sale" (24). Andy says, "'I think that bill came out of a room like this . . . where a family's life work can be converted to numbers and to somebody else's profit, but the family cannot be seen and its suffering cannot be felt.'" What is there to feel? Andy remembers a detail:

> On the back of the bill, in some moment of desperation, Dorie Catlett had written, "Oh, Lord, whatever is to become of us?" And then, beneath, as if to correct what she had written already, she wrote: "Out of the depths have I cried unto thee, O Lord." (*Remembering* 25)

In his next breath, Andy turns from Dorie Catlett's stoic supplication from Psalm 130 to a judgment upon all that our industrial economy owes the communities it has ruined and the displacements it devised in the name of economic progress:

> "I say damn your systems and your numbers and your ideas. I speak for Dorie Catlett and Marce Catlett. I speak for Mat and Margaret Feltner, for Jack Beechum, for Jarrat and Burley Coulter, for Nathan Coulter and Hannah, for Danny and Lyda Branch, for Martin and Arthur Rowanberry, for Elton and Mary and Jack Penn." (25)

Andy's heartfelt speech metaphorically outlines both what has been lost and what is threatened in the industrial society and in his own family. Andy has lost the use of his "best reason" because his difficult adjustment to this new life, fragmented and irresponsible, has strained the ties between his family and his local community.

In grief and shame over leaving Flora in the middle of an unresolved argument, he wanders around the city, finally stopping to gaze at the ocean from the pier; he is lonely, anonymous, invisible, confused. But the pull of responsibility is strong, and like Frost's lonely observer of the property held by the absentee owner whose "house is in the village," he returns by habit of mind to his responsibilities and those who need him. While looking out over the water and later, while returning home by plane, he remembers the experiences of his family, examples that have defined what he was before the accident: we see how the Beechums joined with the Feltners, the Feltners with the Catletts; we learn how the Penns came to join these families, and how the Rowanberrys were related by a marriage in 1824 to the Coulters. His recollections of familiar details reinforce the sense of responsibility to his past that can save him. As Berry says in ***Sabbaths***:

> The burden of absence grows, and I pay
> daily the grief I owe to love
> for women and men, days and trees
> I will not know again. Pray
> for the world's light thus borne away.
>
> (81)

This poem represents "light" in a metaphor not unlike that used by Christ: "While ye have light, believe in the light, that ye may be the children of light" (John 12:36). As a reference both to Christ's presence and example, as well as to a spiritual truth that binds Christ and the disciples to each other, the "light" exists and is experienced in this life on earth. For the children of light who believe, which is to say who maintain faith and fidelity to things seen and unseen, this light recognized in its rightful place in the order of things can preserve them. Berry warns, however, that this optimistic view of "light" does not posit a dualism separating body and soul, because we are "living souls" existing within the limits of God's creation and because "all our acts have a supreme significance" (*Sex, Economy, Freedom & Community* 110).

To discover "supreme significance," Berry's short fiction in *Wild Birds: Six Stories of the Port William Membership* (1986) and *Fidelity* (1992) records the actions of a community of families joined by what he refers to as "membership," as "parts inextricably joined." These are complex relationships, and in these stories he carefully fills in the gaps left by his novels and reveals details of the kinship and social membership that bind the Catletts, Feltners, and Coulters to their Port William farms and to themselves. Many of the stories in *Wild Birds* describe the life and thoughts of Wheeler Catlett (Andy's father) and his various debts to Uncle Peach (Wheeler's uncle and alcoholic brother to Dorie Catlett), to Mat Feltner (his father-in-law), to Uncle Jack Beechum (brother to Mat's mother), to Elton and Mary Penn (beloved friends; Elton is like a son to Uncle Jack; a valued teacher to Andy), to Burley Coulter (a distant cousin), to Danny Branch (Burley's illegitimate son). Although Wheeler is a driving force behind the safety and maintenance of this clan, he recognizes in his love a duty more than a debt. When Elton Penn expresses his gratitude for Wheeler's help with the purchase of Uncle Jack's farm, Wheeler objects: "It's not accountable, because we're dealing in goods and services that we didn't make, that can't exist at all except as gifts" (72). This kind of interdependence, unexplainable in the language of business or law, is revealed only in the practical language of use, service, and tradition. In another story where Wheeler attempts to write about the difference between "price" and "value," he discovers that "A fidelity older than his fidelity to word and page began to work on him" (116). He puts the essay aside and plans the construction of "a shed to be built onto his feed barn. . . . His thoughts leapt from his speech to its sources in place and memory, the generations of his kin and kind" (117).

The stories in *Fidelity* demonstrate the means by which these families keep faith with one another and preserve their "sources in place and memory." To instruct him in the ways that forgiveness makes fidelity possible, Andy's grandmother Margaret Feltner relates how Thad Coulter, cousin to Dave Coulter (Burley's father), shot and killed Ben Feltner, Mat's father, Andy's great-grandfather. Thad had found his life's work lost because of his son's default on a loan secured by a mortgage on his farm; the loan had been made to set his son up in business, a complicated and unwise arrangement between agriculture and consumer capitalism not unlike that described in Wordsworth's "Michael." In grief and drunkenness and near madness, Thad mistakes Ben's reserve for a refusal to help, so he kills "the best friend I ever had." Despite this tragedy, Mat Feltner's daughter Bess will marry Wheeler Catlett, though his father Marce Catlett was a first cousin of Thad Coulter's (58). The tragedy, however, has less impact on their lives than the good work of the community and its farms.

Andy notes that "Though Coulters still abound in Port William, no Feltner of the name is left." In *A Place on Earth* (1983), we learn how Mat's life is again altered by violence when his only son, Virgil, is killed during the second World War. Virgil's wife Hannah gives birth to a daughter and several years later marries Nathan Coulter, Thad Coulter's kinsman. In **"The Bringer of Water,"** a one-act verse drama published in ***Farming: A Handbook***, Berry describes this second union of Feltners and Coulters during the summer of 1948. As Andy says, "My grandfather made a peace here that has joined many who would otherwise have been divided. I am the child of his forgiveness" (*Fidelity* 59).

In *Remembering,* however, Andy suffers from the loss of the memory of his debt to the work and love of those who lived before him. As natural forces have consequences, so have psychological forces. Andy's self-destructive behavior suggests the fate of those cut off from their past and kin. Returning by plane toward the east, he recounts how in self-pity and forgetfulness he tolerated petty arguments, how an egoistic forgetfulness discounts duty, honor, and mutual concerns between members of a family and of a community. By his remembering present and past events that involve his family and friends, interspersed with his own praying and the repetition of his grandmother Catlett's use of Psalm 130, he regains access to the grace of Flora's forgiveness: "He is praying to remain in time until what he owes is paid" (115). What he considered a dissatisfaction with Flora he now sees is a disaffection with himself. In the midst of his confusion, Flora had offered wise advice:

> "Do you know what you need?" she said to him one day.
> "What?"
> "Forgiveness. And I want to forgive you. All of us do. And you need more than ours. But you must forgive yourself."
> She was crying, and he pitied her. And he knew she had told the truth, and it made him furious.
>
> (35)

Berry holds out hope for Andy in the phrase "he pitied her." That tiny gesture of feeling, though still enveloped in his anger, exists because of the long habit of their mutual concern. For Berry, this marriage is the embodiment of a "generous enclosure—a household welcoming to neighbors and friends; a garden open to weather, between woods and the road": and it survives its private turmoil by the memory of community animated by "a marriage bond that would bind a woman and a man not only to each other, but to the community of marriage . . . a grievous, joyous human bond, endlessly renewable and renewing, again and again rejoining memory and passion and hope" (*Recollected Essays* 299). Andy's pity, inspired by the mutual love that allows Flora's forgiveness, suggests the existence of a bond of duty that will get him through this crisis, which, in his short fiction, Berry defines, among other things, two indispensable features of such bonds: first, a mutual need shared by members, modeled on Nature, and, second, the faith with the people and a fidelity to the values that make this bond possible.

In one of the stories included in *Wild Birds,* Burley Coulter has come to his attorney and kinsman Wheeler Catlett to claim kinship with his illegitimate son Danny Branch by making him the beneficiary of his will. Wheeler assumes that the property would go to Burley's nephew Nathan Coulter, but Burley has brought Nathan and his wife Hannah with him to support his decision. To explain his motives, Burley tells them that regret or the concern to "make it right" has little to do with what binds people together. Burley says:

> "I ain't saying we don't have to know what we ought to have been and ought to be, but we oughtn't to let that stand between us. That ain't the way we are. The way we are, we are members of each other. All of us. Everything. The difference ain't in who is a member and who is not, but in who knows it and who don't. What has been here, not what ought to have been, is what I have to claim." (136-37)

Burley's sentiment is Christian in origin; judgment is reserved for God, in order that relations between people of the present and the past can be preserved through love, forgiveness, and acceptance. This is, of course, what churches mean by "membership": not some exclusive sectarian distinction but an inclusive vow of interdependence between and among all members (see Romans 12:4-5, I Corinthians 12:12 and 26, Ephesians 4:15-16, Colossians 3:12-15). Despite the cynic's belief that this ideal is too difficult to observe in our time, such dismissal is no judgment against its veracity. Berry's country people are not impossibly good; they represent the good people, however few that may be, who know, in Wheeler's words, that "we're dealing in goods and services that we didn't make, that can't exist at all except as gifts. . . . The life of a neighborhood is a gift" (*Wild Birds* 72). They may represent ideals, but they are not impossible examples to follow. They may share with one another unusual grace, frugality, goodwill, and harmony, values that define productive agrarian communities, but they also know life's pain, poverty, social discord, loss, and death: Andy's tragic accident, the loss of one's children to the lure of urban wealth, the suicide of Margaret Feltner's brother Earnest, Uncle Peach's alcoholism, the murder of Ben Feltner, the loss of Virgil Feltner and Tom Coulter to the war. Port William represents no paradise; however, the gift of their lives together is available for the taking if one will accept it, if one can recognize its presence. Of course, with the competition for material goods and services, the cult of wealth and power, the faith in infinite economic progression, this distinction advances precisely the kind of instruction that contemporary critics refuse to countenance. One need only think of the critical derision meted out to novels openly didactic. To write fiction that presumes to illustrate goodness as a corrective to evil is so rare that some critics and reviewers refuse to recognize it as a record of values; indeed, for Berry to name the collection of stories *Fidelity* is for some readers not enough. For others, perhaps, it is too much.

I accept Berry at his word and attempt to read his fiction the way we have traditionally read "narrative poetry." Berry says, "Narrative poetry records, contemplates, hands down the actions of the past. Poetry has a responsibility to remember and to preserve and reveal the truth about these actions. But it also has a complementary responsibility . . . to help to preserve and to clarify the possibility of *responsible* action" (*Standing by Words* 19). This is a good explanation for a major concern in Berry's writing: we need to recover "the possibility of responsible action" wherever it is required to restore "order" to the local culture. By Berry's definition, "The word 'order,' as used here, clearly refers to the possibility of responsible action, the possibility of good works" (*Standing by Words* 19). Berry measures the quality of life by one's attempt to perfect through good work the whole person: "There are actions worthy of the patience and work of whole lives—actions, even, that no whole life can complete—that involve the lives of people in the lives of places and communities" (*Standing by Words* 21). The focus of this sentiment is on "place," but this proposition makes no demand for a return to the past or to the farm, nor does it suggest any foolish desire that the future and cities cease to be considered. While Berry's characters express his experiences with rural life and propose values that have traditionally informed it, one assumes that like the ancient Hebrew God's commandments these values apply wherever one goes, whether urban or rural, at home or in exile.

To the extent that we assume these problems relate only to farming, we measure how far we are from any understanding of Berry's ideas. These problems cannot be solved by the specialists or the futurists or the scientists because they involve the understanding of the heart, which is written in a language not easily reconciled with the economics of contemporary commerce and industrial capitalism. When Clara Petit refuses to honor the last wishes of her dead father, Jack Beechum, that Elton and Mary Penn receive his land at lower than market value, Wheeler complains that she and her banker husband "were playing a different game than any that Old Jack had ever played, and living in a different world from the one that he had lived in." A letter found in Uncle Jack's notebook, obviously in his hand, is judged to have no legal validity; it makes no moral. claim on his daughter because it "was written in a language the Pettits did not speak" (*Wild Birds* 51). Or, when Detective Kyle Bode is sent to discover what became of Burley Coulter who was taken from his deathbed at the hospital, he discovers a family of country people who talk respectfully of Burley's memory. He will not learn of Danny Branch's last kindness to his father, for these people are bound by stories he does not belong to; "It was not his conversation he was in; he could hardly think by what right he was in it" (*Fidelity* 182).

To recover such conversations and their knowledge and to use them even in our urban settings present a difficult task, for such recovery and use implements the practical acts of communal order like responsibility, forgiveness, fidelity, and redemption. It means giving up the notion that something else, somewhere else, and someone else always promise something better. It means recognizing a life's existence as a "witness" to what goodness can in fact survive in the world. And it means recognizing and valuing this witness as part of the accumulated vision of ancestors who also witnessed the redemptive practices that can preserve family, community, and Nature. Redemption is close at hand, and Berry's work is devoted to its revelation, for, like Andy, "He sees that he lives in eternity as he lives in time, and nothing is lost" (*Remembering* 123). Mat Feltner tells Andy about once "chop[ping] out a field of tall corn" in unbearable heat with Old Jack Beechum and how at the end of the rows they "hung their sweated clothes on willows" and "sank themselves in the cool stream up to their noses":

> "Well sir," Mat says, "it made that hard day good. I thought of all the times I'd worked in that field, hurrying to get through, to get to a better place, and it had been there all the time. I can't say I've always lived by what I learned that day—I wish I had—but I've never forgot."
>
> "What?" Andy says.
>
> "That it was there all the time."
>
> "What?"
>
> "Redemption," Mat says, and laughs. "A little flowing stream." (*Remembering* 58-59).

John R. Knott (essay date 1996)

SOURCE: "Into the Woods with Wendell Berry," in *Essays in Literature,* Vol. 23, No. 1, Spring, 1996, pp. 124-40.

[*In the following essay, Knot examines the role of wilderness in Berry's work.*]

Wendell Berry commands attention as a passionate and eloquent defender of sustainable agriculture on a human scale, a morally as well as economically viable farming that implies respect for the land, for family and community, and for the wisdom embodied in local culture. Through his fiction, his poetry (including ***Farming: A Handbook***), and especially collections of essays such as *The Unsettling of America* and *The Gift of Good Land,*

Berry has become widely known as a persuasive defender of life and work rooted in a particular, rural place (in his case a hill farm in Henry County, Kentucky) and as a trenchant critic of agribusiness and of what he would call the industrial as opposed to the natural economy. Yet one of the most striking things about Berry's work is his attraction to wilderness, particularly in the form of the forests from which the cleared fields of the farmer were wrested and to which he imagines them eventually returning.

Berry resists the common tendency to oppose nature and culture, the wild and the domestic, and finds meaning and health in their interaction. In his later essays, beginning at least with *A Continuous Harmony* (1970), Berry stresses the interdependency of nature and culture and urges a life based upon achieving a harmony between these apparent opposites. In "The Body and the Earth," published in *The Unsettling of America* (1977), he faults modern travellers for transforming the wilderness into "scenery" and forgetting that it "still circumscribe[s] civilization and persist[s] in domesticity" (*Recollected Essays* 273). Such a claim reverses the familiar perspective that assumes human dominion over the natural world, to suggest that wilderness contains civilization and continues to be felt within the space claimed by it; it implies that we should recognize that we are still part of a dominant natural order.

Berry's insistence that the civilized and the domestic depend upon wilderness reflects deeply held beliefs about both the health of the farm and the health of the spirit. If the farm is to last and to thrive, the wilderness must survive within it (*Recollected Essays* 313). In the most practical sense, this means recognizing that fertility is linked to the natural processes of growth and decay that the wilderness exemplifies. One must look to the woods to know how to preserve the fields, an insight Berry attributes to the English agriculturalist Sir Albert Howard but has made thoroughly his own. Berry also urges the importance of preserving a part of the actual forest within the farm as a "sacred grove," "a place where the Creation is let alone, to serve as instruction, example, refuge" (*Recollected Essays* 314).

In some of his more recent essays, particularly "Getting Along with Nature" and "Preserving Wildness" in *Home Economics* (1987), Berry insists even more strongly on what he calls there "the indivisibility of wildness and domesticity" (*Home Economics* 139), partly in an effort to stake out a middle ground between the "nature extremists," who assume that natural good is human good, and the "technology extremists," who would manipulate nature to serve their particular sense of human good. Berry can accept the argument for setting aside public places of "absolute wilderness" (Edward Abbey's term) but is more interested in the small pieces of wilderness found on farms or in corners of cities which he views as sacred groves "where one can go to learn and be restored" (*Home Economics* 17). Even margins, such as fence rows or streamsides, are valuable "freeholds of wilderness" (*Home Economics* 151) that help to create a "landscape of harmony," preferable to the "landscape of monoculture," in which the wild and the domesticated co-exist. One finds a growing concern about the survival of wilderness in Berry's later writing (expressed in "Preserving Wildness"), a concern that wilderness has become dependent upon human forbearance, but this only intensifies his conviction that one must find ways of valuing and preserving the wild in daily, domestic life. As what Berry calls "our native wilderness" comes to seem more vulnerable, his advocacy of living in harmony with it has become more urgent: "I am betting my life that such a harmony is possible" (*Home Economics* 138).

What interests me here is the persistent and vivid presence of wilderness in Berry's work, not as an alternative to or escape from ordinary life but as a source of illumination, order, peace, and joy that helps one to understand and sustain and finally to leave this life. Berry invites his reader to go into the woods with him over and over in his work, presenting this act variously as journey, pilgrimage, mediation and worship. My concern is with what woods (and, more broadly, wilderness) come to mean for him and why engagement with them assumes such fundamental importance in his writing. What does it mean to go into the woods with Wendell Berry? How does he reconcile, or attempt to reconcile, claims of wildness and of domesticity that many have found in conflict? How can he embrace the values he associates with agrarian life and still yield in so many ways to the attraction of wild nature?

Wilderness can take many forms for Berry, including an empty lot in which a few locust trees attract warblers and tanagers, "woods birds . . . wild as leaves" (**"The Wild,"** ***Collected Poems*** 19-20), and the "teeming wilderness in the topsoil" (*Home Economics* 11).[1] It can become a metaphoric way of referring to elements of human nature, as in "The Body and the Earth," where one form of wilderness is the instinctual sexuality that Berry sees as a vital component of marriage. In the early autobiographical essays Berry collected as *The Long-Legged House* (1969), wilderness can mean the Kentucky River beside which he writes, "the power and mystery of it" as it rises in flood (101); the natural setting of the Camp, the family "wilderness place" that he knew from childhood and to which he returned with his wife Tania the summer after their marriage; and, especially, the woods of the "native hill" to which he climbs from the fields he farms. In these essays and in his early poetry Berry began to articulate a sense of the nature of wilderness and of the ways humans have dealt with it and can find their place in relation to it, introducing themes that would recur and deepen throughout his work.

One of the most distinctive aspects of Berry's wilderness is its historical dimension. For him the land is haunted by "the ghost of the old forest / that stood here when we came" (**"Planting Trees,"** ***Collected Poems*** 155) and that has largely vanished through acts of exploitation and negligence. The "we" here represents the white settlers and their vanguard the long hunters, Daniel Boone among them, who came over the mountains from Virginia lured by the prospect of abundant game and fertile land and their by now numerous descendants, including Berry himself. Berry can imagine the wonder of discovery, when the long hunter emerging from his "unknown track" first sees the new country opening out beneath him: "from the height / he saw a place green as welcome / on whose still water the sky lay white" (**"The Long Hunter,"** ***Collected Poems*** 168). The early settlers of **"July, 1773"** find at a crowded salt lick an "upwelling / and abounding" of herds so astonishing that it seems a "holy vision" (***Collected Poems*** 221). Yet the scene turns foreboding as young Sam Adams shoots into a herd of buffalo (he "could not let it be") and stampedes them, at great risk to himself and his uncle. The act serves as an image of violation (they have been warned to respect the hunting ground of the Shawanoes), implying the future cost of white settlement. Berry assumes that the land is pristine to this point, undamaged by the activities of native tribes. The wonder of the unspoiled land is inseparable for him from a consciousness of the violence that has been done to it and to its original inhabitants, what he sees as the "burden" of its history. The effort to reconnect himself to his native place and the history of his famly in it that Berry describes in *The Long-Legged House* is painful; he recognizes the progress brought by settlement as dooming what he values most: "the life and health of the earth, the peacefulness of human communities and households" (179). He deals with the pain of loss by working to heal land damaged by abusive farming, and by finding a way of relating to the natural world with respect and humility. Berry's way will not be the destructive "way of the frontiersman" but the "way of Thoreau, who went to the natural places to become quiet in them, to learn from them, to be restored by them" (42). Ultimately, he salves the pain by imagining a wilderness so durable and encompassing that it will outlast human efforts to domesticate it.

To justify what he calls the "way of Thoreau" Berry must find in wild nature a mystery and natural goodness uncompromised by the occupation of white settlers bent on dominating it. When he hears pileated woodpeckers from a canoe, he imagines these birds of "big trees and big woods" as speaking "out of our past" (107), evoking for him by their wild cries a time before the power boating and strip mining that he inveighs against in other parts of *The Long-Legged House*. He finds vestiges of this time in the tall open groves that he sees scattered on the slopes of the river valley, "as if in a profound interior withheld from the ceaseless drone of engines, a fragment of the great quietness that two centuries ago lay upon the whole valley" (33). Berry must edit out the noise of engines, from traffic on the road as well as power boats on the river, to suggest the silence with which he invariably associates inviting natural places. Here these are groves of "solemn beauty" with "delicate flowers and mosses and ferns" on the woodland floor. In them one seems to enter a zone of quiet, which is as much a meditative as a physical state. The "voice" of these groves for Berry is the wood thrush, "whose notes, without replacing the quiet, flow into it from some hidden perch" (33). If one responds to such charged "quiet" with a meditative quiet of one's own, and with sufficient attentiveness, the woods will reveal its creatures. What Berry describes here and elsewhere in *The Long-Legged House* is a state of awareness that he comes to recognize as a condition of the knowledge and restoration of the spirit that he associates with Thoreau.[2]

Such an emphasis upon respectful awareness is not uncommon among writers who focus on human relationships with the natural world. One can find it in different forms in the writing of Annie Dillard and Barry Lopez, among others. What is unusual is Berry's pained consciousness of the damaging effects of human presence and his effort to recover a vision of the natural order that preceded this damage, an undisturbed wilderness (the "old forest") that he associates with the time prior to white settlement. This can never be an untroubled vision for Berry, as his poem **"The Dream"** suggests. There he describes a dream of taking away roads and fences and machines and restoring the great trees of the "first forest" ("I glimpse the country as it was" [***Collected Poems*** 64]), that turns bitter as he is unable to stop the "flowing in" of a human history of inevitable ruin. Berry can find fragments of the "great quietness" of the natural world of two hundred years ago, as his experience of the old groves of *The Long-Legged House* suggests, but his appreciation of these remnants is colored by deep nostalgia and a tragic sense of what has been lost. In one of his earliest published poems Berry pictures Daniel Boone in old age recognizing the elusiveness of the vision he pursued: "We held a country in our minds / which, unpossessed, allowed / the encroachment of our dreams" (**"Boone,"** ***Collected Poems*** 8). To possess the land is to destroy those qualities that made it so alluring in prospect.

Berry gives his wilderness a future as well as a past, by imagining it as resilient and vigorous enough to heal itself and ultimately efface the signs of human occupation. He finds hope in the recuperative powers of the natural world that he has observed around him. If the effects of bad farming practices are apparent, in eroded slopes and the silting and frequent flooding of the river, so are the failures of the farmers responsible for them to sustain their enterprise. Where the land has been abandoned, the woods returns: "The wild is flowing back like a tide" (*The Long-Legged House* 90). Berry frequently suggests the fragility of the farmer's hold on his land, sometimes in images of the scrub growth that overruns neglected fields, the "snarls and veils / of honeysuckle, tangles / of grape and bittersweet" (**"The Clearing,"** ***Collected Poems*** 180). In the short run, Berry the farmer views his own clearing of such fields as restoring their health by making them productive again. He takes pleasure in sowing the seeds that will result in a rich pasture of clover and grass and identifies with the succession of those who farm the land with a sense of how it should be used. Yet when he takes a longer view, he can identify with the grandfather of **"The Handing Down,"** who knows that "there's a wildness / waiting for him to go," and that eventually "the woods take back the land" (***Collected Poems*** 44) as the big trees return. In a striking late poem published in ***Sabbaths, 1987-90*** ("I walk in openings / That when I'm dead will close" [44]), Berry describes himself stopping his mower blade to spare the seedling trees invading his meadow, by this gesture affirming the larger natural order to which he submits. This perspective, which accepts oak and ash and hickory as "The genius of this place," enables him to value clearing and farming the land without devaluing wildness, as Jefferson and Crèvecoeur did in their visions of an agrarian America. Berry's confidence that the big trees will indeed return could scarcely be more unlike the fatalism with which Faulkner shows the Big Woods of *Go Down Moses* inexorably giving way to cotton fields.

Berry can accept the natural process by which the trees return as the ultimate healing of the land because he views human works as impermanent; the inevitable return of the woods offers a lesson in humility. One measure of Berry's sensitivity to the history of interaction with the land is his fascination with the signs of former human activity: old housesites or stonework in streams, overgrown wagon tracks, flowers planted by some farm wife that persist after the farm itself is gone. In *The Long-Legged House* he imagines the country as "a kind of palimpsest scrawled over with the comings and goings of people, the erasure of time already in process even as the marks of passage are put down" (185). This powerful image of human transience seems particularly appropriate to Berry's rural Kentucky, or to Frost's New England with its cellar holes and stone walls meandering through the woods. It seems less apt to urban America. One would find it harder to believe in the "erasure of time" in Manhattan or Los Angeles. While Berry is capable of picturing the forest returning to "the waste places of the cities" and "wild herds" on the highways (**"Window Poems,"** ***Collected Poems*** 83), such apocalyptic imaginings seem more natural and warranted in the extended fantasy of the collapse of urban civilization of Walker Percy's *Love in the Ruins,* where one sees vines engulfing the A and P and breaking through the pavement of the interstate.

The autobiographical essays of *The Long-Legged House* are most effective as a record of how Berry comes to appreciate what it means for him to be a "placed" person, rather than the kind of displaced person he finds more typical of modern America. In these essays one discovers how to live "within rather than upon the life of the place," "to belong as the thrushes and the herons and the muskrats belonged, to be altogether at home here" (150). This process grows out of Berry's earlier experience of returning periodically to enjoy the solitude and sense of freedom the place made possible; it is inseparable from the experience of restoring and then rebuilding the Camp, and of settling into his marriage there. It involves, crucially, learning the "power of silence" and of attentiveness and establishing the sense of trust, like that demanded by a marriage, that grows out of his commitment to make his life in the place. Then, with familiarity and trust and attentiveness, "the mind goes free of abstractions, and renews itself in the presence of creation" (160). The kind of seeing that this state makes possible has the character of a sudden revelation granted an initiate: "the details rise up out of the whole and become visible" (160), as a hawk stoops into a clearing and a wood drake swims out of his hiding place. In Berry's writing such experiences inevitably take on a religious coloration. He speaks of his "devotion" to the place, of his "holy days," of being born there in spirit as well as in body.

Berry recognizes that the kinds of questions he asks about the nature of the place and how he should live in it are religious because they acknowledge the limits of his understanding, at the same time distancing him from the tendency of the organized religion he knows to thrive on what he regards as "a destructive schism between body and soul, Heaven and earth" (199). Such questions are for him "an enactment of humility" (199), acknowledging and honoring the mystery he finds in the created world. To ask them and to use religious language in describing his experience is a way of rejecting and transcending the assumptions of orthodox religion, as his insistence that he belongs to the place is a way of rejecting or at least displacing the language of property ownership and the history of violence that he sees possession of the land as having entailed. What Berry offers in describing his most intimate and profound experiences of the natural world is a distinctive kind of spirituality. Its implications emerge most fully from the meditation on the experience of entering the woods that he describes near the end of **"A Native Hill."**

Berry represents himself as leaving the landmarks of civilization (barn, old roads, cow paths) to enter the "timelessness" of a wild place, here woods with large trunks rising free of undergrowth, not the great beech trees of the old forest but a reminder of them. They offer qualities Berry characteristically associates with woods: dignity, serenity, order, joy. He describes the delight of finding the floor of these woods covered with bluebells one spring morning. The image, with the sense of "joyful surprise" associated with the discovery, prints itself on the memory like Wordsworth's daffodils, and serves as a reminder that the world is "blessed" beyond his understanding. Berry's delight in spring woodland flowers, with their delicate beauty and their proof of the annual renewal of life, recurs throughout his work as a sign of the blessedness of the natural world. In a relatively recent poem the "saving loveliness" of "bloodroot, / Twinleaf, and rue anemone" offers an assurance of permanence despite "human wrong" (***Sabbaths*** 44-45). As he enters the woods, or "re-enter[s]" as he puts it, Berry imagines himself as moving out of the space and time of human domination of the natural world, out of the conditions of modern life, into a prior state: "One has come into the presence of mystery. . . . one has come back under the spell of a primitive awe, wordless and humble" (205). Berry describes himself at one point as a "pilgrim" coming to a "holy place." His primitivism is qualified by the sense that the presence he encounters is "the presence of creation," where he finds the "perfect interfusion of life and design" (201). Berry can enter the woods so humbly and reverentially, in other words, because he finds divinity in the order and peacefulness and beauty he discovers there.

His way of representing his experience of the woods recalls the negative way of Christian mysticism: "only there can a man encounter the silence and darkness of his own absence" (207). Henry Vaughan's "The Night" describes the soul retreating from the "loud" daytime world to discover God's "deep, but dazzling darkness" (Vaughan 289-90). The silence and darkness that Berry associates with the experience of the woods, here and repeatedly in his work, suggest the necessity of emptying the mind and disengaging oneself from the preoccupations of ordinary, daily life as preparation for this experience. Yet for Berry this process leads not to the mystic's sense of transcendence of this world and spiritual union with God but to a greatly heightened awareness of natural phenomena and a sense of harmony with the world to which they belong:

> As its sounds come into his hearing, and its lights and colors come into his vision, and its odors come into his nostrils, then he may come into *its* presence as he never has before, and he will arrive in his place and want to remain. His life will grow out of the ground like the other lives of the place, and take its place among them. (207)

One is transformed by entering the silence and darkness of the woods, "born again" as Berry puts it. At this stage of his career, such a rebirth means to understand and embrace the condition of being rooted in one's native place and, as we have seen, to develop the capacity to live "within" it. To live in the sense of immersing oneself fully in the present moment and experiencing a heightened sensuous awareness. The promise of such a life is for Berry something like the "great peacefulness" he sees in the lives of wild creatures, wood ducks dozing in the sun or a flock of cedar waxwings eating wild grapes: "though they have no Sundays, their days are full of sabbaths" (211). The term, which becomes richly symbolic in Berry's later poetry, embodies here a yearning to enter a state of rest and freedom from anxious thought authorized by the natural order of creation.

Berry's most sustained meditation on wilderness can be found in *The Unforeseen Wilderness,* the collection of essays on Kentucky's Red River Gorge that he published with photographs by his friend Gene Meatyard in 1971 and reissued in 1991.[3] This remarkable and insufficiently known work transcends its occasion, the eventually successful struggle to prevent the damming of the river. Berry describes the process of discovering the Red River country, through backpacking and canoeing trips over a period of several years, as "one of the landmarks of my life" (60).[4] The essays register his growing appreciation of the place as he passes from his initial unease and sense of "strangeness" to a familiarity that makes possible the feeling of surrendering to a place grown friendly in the solitary walk with which the book ends. Berry's sense of coming to find his own place in the landscape recalls the process he describes in *The Long-Legged House,* but this experience differs in that it involves the "ancient fear of the unknown" and the "essential loneliness" that he associates with going alone into "big woods" (29). The place itself, although marked by traces of human use in most of its parts, comes closer to what Berry calls "the creation in its pure state," his most fundamental definition of wilderness.

By giving a detailed record of his own observations and reactions, and interweaving these with meditations on others he regards as having treated the land well (the original Indian occupants, Daniel Boone and the Long Hunters, a family presently farming in the Gorge), Berry establishes a pattern of respectful use against which he can judge those who have abused the land in the past (miners and farmers out for quick profit) or who would abuse it in the future (the Corps of Engineers and developers selling the promise of recreation). He begins, in "A Country of Edges," by tracing his initial descent into the Gorge in March, through an abundance of spring wildflowers and the omnipresent sound of falling water, conveying a sense of the overwhelming freshness of the landscape and of the power and "residual mystery" (6) of the always changing river as it continues to sculpt its banks. As with the woods of his native hill, Berry establishes a sense of humility before a natural order that offers more than one can comprehend "in one human lifetime" (6). In the account of a June canoe trip on the river with which he ends the essay, he dislocates the reader's normal time sense, moving from a description of idling on the river and becoming intimately acquainted with its features to a meditation on the huge boulders that have fallen into the river and in their "silence and endurance" (9) prompt thoughts of the generations (Indian and white) that have paddled around them. This leisurely introduction, establishing a sense of the presence of the place and setting out the beginnings of his own journey of discovery, establishes a context for Berry's attack on the Corps of Engineers and other past and potential exploiters of the Red River country in his second essay, "The One-Inch Journey."

By returning to the legend of John Swift wandering in the Kentucky mountains in the mid-eighteenth century in search of silver, Berry links those who would dam the river and open the area to development with a history of abuse that includes mining, logging, and destructive farming practices. This is a history driven by the expectation of quick profit and oblivious to what Berry sees as the real life of the place, with its complex cycles of growth and decay. An unnamed family returned from the city to an ancestral farm in the bottomlands of the Gorge provides Berry with a countervailing example of how to live on the land. He offers a romantic vision of the isolated farmhouse on the edge of the woods at the foot of a great cliff: "the quiet of the wilderness rises over it like the loving gray cliff face. . . . [the house] seems somehow to have assumed the musing inwardness of the stone that towers over it" (25). We learn nothing of the house itself except that it "has over the years been cleansed of all unnecessary sounds," as if moving into the silence of the wild country that surrounds it. To create such a vision Berry must erase the normal signs of human occupancy of the land, blurring the boundary between natural and domesticated spaces. The potential flooding of this bottomland, with the consequent destruction of this idealized family's house and fields, becomes an emblem of the public logic of a kind of development that will destroy its natural purity.

In a subsequent essay Berry offers another kind of romantic vision that complements this one, prompted by seeing a crude hut with "D. boon" carved on a plank that has become a spectacle for tourists and is now surrounded by a chain-link fence and littered with trash. Upon entering the one grove of virgin forest left in the Red River country, Berry offers his own reconstruction of a hut Boone might have had in a cave overlooking such a place, in a time of "vast rich unspoiled distances quietly peopled by scattered Indian tribes" as well as by "buffalo and bear and panther and wolf":

> Imagine a man dressed in skins coming silently down off the ridge and along the cliff face into the shelter of the rock house. Imagine his silence that is unbroken as he enters, crawling, a small hut that is only a negligible detail among the stone rubble of the cave floor, as unobtrusive there as the nest of an animal or bird, and as he livens the banked embers of a fire on the stone hearth, adding wood, and holds out his chilled hands before the blaze. Imagine him roasting his supper meat on a stick over a fire while the night falls and the darkness and the wind enclose the hollow. Imagine him sitting on there, miles and months from words, staring into the fire, letting its warmth deepen in him until finally he sleeps. Imagine his sleep. (71-72)

This remarkable vision embodies a yearning for a natural world "in its pure state," not a world without humans but a world of primitive simplicity that admits no sense of a division between man and nature, a world before any human destruction. Berry virtually effaces the hut, making it "negligible," "unobtrusive" as the dwelling of a creature. The withdrawal from words, with the thought processes and human interactions language implies, suggests the recovery of a simpler state of consciousness that makes possible the perfect harmony of human figure and setting that the scene suggests. One could imagine other Boones: the colonizer who led settlers through the Cumberland Gap and founded Boonsborough, the legendary Indian fighter, the land speculator.[5] But what clearly matters to Berry here is the elemental character of the scene, with the solitary hunter absorbed by the silence and vastness of the primal wilderness rather than disrupting it, as John Swift and his successors would.

Berry opposes another kind of figure to those he accuses of exploitation, one who typifies for him the kind of seeing that leads to understanding and appreciation of the land, the "photographic artist." The immediate contrast in this case is with the tourist photographer interested only in preconceived, "postcard" pictures. Berry's rendering of the "quest" of the true photographer obviously draws upon his exposure to Gene Meatyard's methods and his black and white photographs of the Gorge. Just as obviously, it reflects his own sense of how he approaches the natural world as a writer. The photographer must have the humility to efface himself and must be open to the unexpected in order to "draw deeper into the presence, and into the mystery, of what is underfoot and overhead and all around" (29). He enters the darkness of the shadowy woods, and of his own uncertainty, in order to see: "Among the dark trees . . . there appears suddenly the tree of light" (28). Such moments have the character of revelations granted by the place, manifestations of grace. Berry comments in the foreword to the 1991 edition that the darkness in some of Meatyard's pictures, all of which involve the play of light and shadow, is not simply shadow but "the darkness of elemental mystery, the original condition in which we can see the light" (xii). A belief in the mysteriousness of the natural world, best symbolized by such darkness, is fundamental to Berry's sense of the spiritual character of the journey of the photographer and of anyone who would discover this world. This is not a journey to be measured by our usual notions of space and time, Berry suggests, but "a journey of one inch, very arduous and humbling and joyful, by which we arrive at the ground at our feet, and learn to be at home" (30).

In the central essay in the collection, "An Entrance to the Woods," Berry presents a solo trip into the Gorge as a paradigmatic encounter with wilderness. The process of entry begins with an acute sense of dislocation as Berry absorbs the shock of his sudden transition from freeway speed to foot speed and from his usual places and human relationships to the solitude of a campsite by a creek at the bottom of the Gorge. The emotional fallout of this dislocation is melancholy, the result of cutting himself off from the familiar and stripping away his "human facade," to enter the wilderness "naked," with no more than he can carry. Berry stresses the elemental nature of the experience, seeing himself as reduced to the "loneliness and humbleness" of unaccommodated man, and gives it the character of a religious quest. He must lose his normal identity ("I will be absorbed into the being of this place, invisible as a squirrel in his nest" [36]) and undergo "a kind of death" (38), in order to experience the spiritual rebirth that he seeks.

To enter the wilderness with Berry is to experience a sense of "nonhuman time" that makes human history seem insubstantial and to be haunted by the ephemeral presences of those who have preceded him in the place: Indians, Long Hunters, loggers, and farmers who have left only chimney stones and flowers marking a vanished dooryard. Berry's sensitivity to such ghosts is a further source of melancholy, but he appears to need to identify with them, particularly with the Indians and Long Hunters of the time prior to human settlement. To describe his tent as a "flimsy shelter" and picture himself as like a squirrel in his nest suggests a desire to recover something resembling the condition he attributes to Boone in his imagined hut, the solitary human figure blending into the vast surrounding wilderness. To perform this act of recovery, Berry must overcome or at least limit his awareness of the civilization he has temporarily left, symbolized by the highway noise audible from most parts of the Gorge. He does this in part by imagining wilderness as the enveloping element in which humans live, "encased in civilization," an inescapable primal nature that is "beautiful, dangerous, abundant, oblivious of us, mysterious, never to be conquered or controlled or second-guessed, or known more than a little" (37). Such a view attributes extraordinary power and resilience as well as romance to wild nature and minimizes the effects of human activity on it, more apparent today than when Berry wrote. He imagines an airplane, its engines or instruments failing, entering the sphere of the wilderness "where nothing is foreseeable" and "the power and the knowledge of humans counts for nothing" (36). This image of the fallibility of human technology is part of a broader attack on the machinery of industrial society that runs through Berry's writing. It focuses on the vulnerability of the machine—airplanes do crash in remote areas—rather than on its use to extend human power, as by minimizing the effect of distance and making the remote accessible. Berry must diminish the sense of a controlling human presence to sustain the view of wilderness he offers here. He recognizes that the Gorge is in fact an "island of wilderness" and a threatened one at that, but he would make it an emblem of a fundamental reality that should serve as a check on human pretension.

In the narrative he constructs of his day of hiking in the Gorge, Berry shows himself becoming progressively more attuned to the place, to its quietness and the movements of its creatures, and losing his sense of difference from it. When he climbs to a high, sunny rock to get out of the morning cold of the hollow, he delights in the sensations and in the freedom of being "afoot in the woods," although the roar of the highway as he looks out over the country triggers a meditation on the way engine noise has displaced natural silence on the continent; this modulates into a denunciation of the destructiveness of the American economy with an allusion to the war in Vietnam. Such a swerve into a more insistently didactic mode interrupts the flow of the narrative and reminds the reader of the society and the preoccupations Berry is trying to escape by coming to this wilderness place. The essay recovers its momentum as Berry shows himself regaining his calm and a measure of hopefulness by recalling his absence from human society and resuming his walk. He follows a more promising direction back into the woods, then off the trail and down a small branch of the creek, eventually picking his way from rock to rock "through a green tunnel" of overhanging vegetation. It is in this departure from the predictability of the trail, while sitting still to watch fish in a clear pool enveloped by a "grand deep autumn quiet," that Berry has the sense of having "come into the heart of the woods" (44). The process he describes is one of joining his own quiet of mind with the quiet of his surroundings. When he returns to his camp, his sense of union with the place is so complete that the sounds of the creek move through his mind "as they move through the valley, unimpeded and clear" (44). Achieving this union, and the peacefulness it affords, requires slowing the body and emptying the mind and stripping away all vestiges of the desire to control and exploit that he associates with the history of white settlement. Berry defines his role as if in opposition to that of his self-assertive predecessors, effacing himself in acts of submission to show an alternative to the way of dominion: "I move in the landscape as one of its details" (42).

The remaining two essays, "The Unforeseen Wilderness" and "The Journey's End," describe a deepening sense of harmony with the place and of the kinds of revelations this offers. Berry pictures himself as a "student" of wilderness, alert to its continuing lessons: that it changes continuously, as much process as place; that in such a place one is wiser to proceed without particular expectations; that here one is continuously being surprised, by a "rare flame azalea in bloom" revealed by a turn in the path or a little dell where several streams meet under great hemlocks and beeches (49). Berry takes such chance pleasures as blessings, evidence of an ongoing, divine work of creation that he increasingly opposes to what he sees as the human work of destruction. Berry acknowledges the religious turn of his thought in the final essay, recognizing that he is "celebrating the morning of the seventh day" and finding the creation good: "This is a great Work, this is a great Work" (71). He moves here from the sense of quiet and harmony he described earlier to a reverential joyousness in the "intelligence" of natural processes set in motion at the beginning of the world and continuing without regard to human action or understanding.

Berry ends *The Unforeseen Wilderness* with an account of a solo hike in December in an unfamiliar part of the Gorge in which he sees himself as abandoning any sense of control or direction. "Since I have no destination that I know, where I am going is always where I am. When I come to good resting places, I rest. I rest whether I am tired or not because the places are good. Each one is an arrival. I am where I have been going" (73). He experiences arrivals of a kind that Boone, chasing his dream of a promised land, never could ("There are no arrivals"). The journey can end because Berry recognizes that the destination does not matter, only the ease he feels wherever he chooses to pause and the process of yielding before "the mysteries of growth and renewal and change" (74), a yielding symbolized for him by the actual loss of his map among the fallen leaves of the Gorge. The image of the map rotting along with the leaves becomes the vehicle of an epiphany for Berry, a "cleansing vision" of the tragic inadequacy of human knowledge. He has reached the point where he can be guided by his responses to what he understands as a divine order embodied in the natural world rather than by the design of the mapmaker. Berry leaves the reader with a sense that the dominant presence is the earth, however man may abuse it, the creation that "bears triumphantly on from the fulfillment of catastrophe to the fulfillment of hepatica blossoms." His optimistic belief in the resilience of the earth, imagined here by the annual reappearance of one of the most delicate of spring woodland flowers, overcomes the sense of ruin and loss that has threatened the peace and reassurance he has sought in his solitary excursion.

The transformation that Berry describes in *The Unforeseen Wilderness* depends upon a radical separation from habitual physical and social environments that is unusual for him, but it is continuous with the process of recovery that he represents in the essays of *The Long-Legged House,* and it embodies attitudes toward wilderness that he elaborates in his poetry and, to a lesser extent, in his fiction. Berry typically places the climactic scenes of his novels in the woods, associated with peace and revelation and often with death: the beech grove in which Mat Feltner finally accepts the death of his son in *A Place on Earth* ("Into the Woods" 313-17); the familiar woods in which Jack Beechum can find a repose and awareness that enable him to let go and accept his own death in *The Memory of Old Jack* (190-92); the deep woods in whcih Andy Catlett experiences a dream vision that enables him to accept the loss of his arm and return to productive communal life in Berry's latest novel, *Remembering* (120-24). In the poetry, the peacefulness that Berry associates with the woods of *The Long-Legged House* and *The Unforeseen Wilderness* often appears as a capacity for healing. In **"A Standing Ground,"** for example, he pictures himself escaping anxiety and the fury of argument by climbing up "into the healing shadow of the woods" (***Collected Poems*** 116).

Berry associates this restorative peace of the woods with stillness and solitude and often with a sense of mystery in the poetry, and he explores more fully than in the essays the state of being that accompanies harmony with the natural world. This involves a movement beyond ordinary speech and thought, into silence and darkness, is a form of absence.[6] To be "at home in the world," Berry suggests in the first of two poems entitled **"The Silence,"** one must withdraw "beyond words into the woven shadows / of the grass and the flighty darkness / of leaves shaking in the wind"; it must be as though "his bones fade beyond thought" (***Collected Poems*** 111). Then one can hear "the silence / of the tongues of the dead tribesmen" and the "songs" of the natural world. Withdrawing from speech and entering the darkness becomes an enabling act, a way of escaping the forms of human consciousness associated with language and of attaining the desired harmony with the natural world. In **"Woods"** he suggests the paradoxical nature of this state: "Though I am silent / There is singing around me / Though I am dark / There is vision around me" (***Collected Poems*** 205). This singing can be the song of birds and insects, actual sounds of the woods, but more often it appears in the poetry as a generalized song of the earth, music heard in the mind that expresses the dynamism of the created and creating world: "Let the great song come / that sways the branches, that weaves / The nest of the vireo" (**"From the Crest,"** ***Collected Poems*** 194).

In the poetry darkness comes to symbolize a yielding to the ways of the earth and, finally, to a death understood as part of the cyclical rhythm of nature. It can be the darkness of the woods Berry describes in *The Unforeseen Wilderness* but also a more generalized "dark / of the earth" that suggests the mysteriousness of natural processes.[7] To "Learn the darkness," as a voice urges in **"Song in a Year of Catastrophe"** (***Collected Poems*** 117), is to "Put your hands / Into the earth. Live close / to the ground" but also to accept the death the earth "requires." Serving the dark means serving the earth, not only by tilling the ground but by entering it at death (**"Enriching the Earth,"** ***Collected Poems*** 110). One ultimately "bow[s] / to the mystery" by accepting one's life as "a patient willing descent into the grass" (**"The Wish to Be Generous,"** ***Collected Poems*** 114).

The later poetry collected in ***Sabbaths*** and ***Sabbaths, 1987-90*** is particularly interesting for my purposes, because it shows the act of entering the woods taking on a more overtly religious significance. Berry had described himself as a "pilgrim" entering a "holy place" in the final essay of *The Long-Legged House.* In ***Sabbaths*** he imagines an alternative religion associated not only with meditation but with participation in what he perceives as the joyful song of the created world. The Sunday church bell of the town sends him in a contrary direction, to resume "the standing Sabbath / Of the woods" (***Sabbaths*** 7):

> I go in pilgrimage
> Across an old fenced boundary
> To wildness without age
> Where, in their long dominion
> The trees have been left free.
>
> (11)

The woods function as a place where the mind can find rest and the promise of renewal as in the early essays, but the sense of mystery associated with the place has become more explicitly religious: "Miracle and parable / Exceeding thought" (8). Entering the woods has become a ritual activity, Berry's Sunday morning walk, and depends upon the recognition that it is "Your Sabbath, Lord, that keeps us by / Your will, not ours" (8). Berry now sees this entrance as a matter of coming "with song" into the "Presence" of God, understood as "shaping the seasons of His wild will" (82). The surprising adjective ("wild") links God with wilderness in its unpredictable ("unforeseen") character. The grove itself has become a natural church, a "high, restful sanctuary" (15) that Berry describes as a "columned room" where "trees like great saints stand in time, / Eternal in their patience" (74). In the final poem of ***Sabbaths*** the return of the great trees ("Slowly, slowly, they return") suggests that divinity is to be found in the world, not in some supernatural event: "They are the advent they await." The trees become for Berry "Apostles of the living light" saying a benediction "Over the living and the dead" (95), thus displacing the saints of orthodox Christianity as dispensers of blessings. In ***Farming: A Handbook*** Berry had imagined the god he "always expected / To appear at the woods edge, beckoning" as a "great relisher of the world" (**"The Satisfactions of the Mad Farmer,"** 63). The liturgical imagery-with which he ends ***Sabbaths*** makes a much stronger statement about the immanence of the Christian God in a sanctified natural world.

The worshipful mood that Berry establishes in ***Sabbaths*** has nothing to do with anticipation of a Christian heaven.

Rather, the sanctuary of the woods "keeps the memory of Paradise" (15). Entering this sanctuary becomes a way of recapturing, at least briefly, a sense of the innocence and vibrance of an unblemished, seemingly timeless nature "where the world is being made" (39) in the continuous process of creation that Berry had evoked in the final essay of *The Unforeseen Wilderness.* One's mind may "move with the leaves" and "live as the light lives" (39) if one enters in a properly detached and receptive state. Berry uses familiar imagery of song, derived here as often in his poetry from the birdsong of the woods, to suggest a state of harmony with the being of nature: "Sabbath economy / In which all thought is song, / All labor is dance" (63). The difference in ***Sabbaths*** is that the song of the earth has become psalmic praise of the Creator.[8] Berry's epigraph from Isaiah, from a passage referring to the rejoicing of the fir trees and the cedars of Lebanon, establishes the celebratory tone of the collection: "The whole earth is at rest and is / quiet: they break forth into singing" (Isa. 14:7). In several poems in ***Sabbaths*** Berry introduces a new optimism about the promise of a "healed harmony" of woods and field, wild and domesticated space, made possible by what he calls "loving work" (15). Field and woods rejoicing together "Rejoin the primal Sabbath's hymn" (14). Such poems offer a lyrical counterpoint to Berry's argument for reconciling the wild and the domestic in such late essays as "Getting Along with Nature."

The forest is "mostly dark" in Berry's earlier poetry and in the essays of *The Unforeseen Wilderness,* something one has to "stay brave enough" to keep entering, whether this is the actual forest with its mysteries and uncertainties or the wilderness of instinct upon which marriage depends (see **"In the Country of Marriage,"** ***Collected Poems*** 146-47). In ***Sabbaths*** the pull of the forest has become stronger and the woods seem mostly light, a place where one finds "Heavenly work of light and wind and leaf," set off against the "peopled dark / Of our unraveling century" (15). The final poem of the book concludes with an image of fall as "brightened leaves": we are pleased / To walk on radiance, amazed. / O light come down to earth, be praised!" (96). Berry had ended *The Long-Legged House* with an image of himself lying in newly fallen leaves, accepting the idea of the body's "long shudder into humus" (113). The calm embrace of mortality Berry arrives at in that work gives way in ***Sabbaths*** to joyful celebration of fall, with the change signalled by the "brightened" leaves welcomed as a manifestation of the splendor of the natural world and of the divinity that pervades and orders it.

If the hopefulness and the religious affirmations of ***Sabbaths*** distinguish this book from Berry's previous work, the poems that it and its sequel collect nonetheless reiterate and deepen themes that we have seen in the early essays and poetry. They show more clearly than ever the importance for Berry of preserving wild places within the human order, sacred groves that can function as places of meditation and of spiritual solace and renewal. And as reminders of the mysteriousness of the natural order and the limitations of human understanding and capacity. To go into the woods with Berry requires an intense awareness of the natural world and its processes, a respect grounded in humility and awe that can become a form of worship, and a willingness to submit to an order that transcends human works and preoccupations, ultimately by accepting the naturalness of death. Berry represents what he calls the "effortless order of wilderness" (*A Place on Earth*317) as always evolving and always "unforeseen": "I go amazed / Into the maze of a design / That mind can follow but not know" (***Sabbaths*** 47-48). He would have us amazed as we go into the woods, continually surprised and humbled, and at the same time drawn by the confidence that only here can one find the kind of design that explains and satisfies.

Notes

1. In "Preserving Wildness" Berry characterizes the fertile topsoil as "a dark wilderness, ultimately unknowable, teeming with wildlife" (*Home Economics* 140).
2. Scott Slovic discusses *The Long-Legged House* as a "celebration of watchfulness." *Seeking Awareness,* ch. 5.
3. See Gamble for a discussion of the lessons of the experience Berry describes in *The Unforeseen Wilderness.*
4. All quotations are from the revised edition, *The Unforeseen Wilderness* (San Francisco, 1991).
5. See Faragher's recent biography for an excellent reconstruction of the life and analysis of the growth of the legend. Berry draws upon an episode, reported in John Filson's *The Adventures of Col. Daniel Boone,* in which Boone remained in Kentucky by himself while his brother went back to Virginia for supplies. In his early poem "Boone," Berry presents a more complex image of Boone in old age, removed to Missouri, reflecting on the elusiveness of the dreams that brought him over the mountains in the first place: "The search / withholds the joy from what is found. . . . / There are no arrivals" (*Collected Poems* 10).
6. See Collins (35-36) for a suggestive discussion of the strain of skepticism about language, as opposed to the "song of the world," that runs through Berry's poetry.
7. Lang discusses Berry's use of metaphors of song and silence in the poetry and his use of darkness (and silence) to express the numinous, invoking Rudolph Otto's *The Idea of the Holy.*
8. The climactic scene of Berry's novel *Remembering,* published the year after *Sabbaths,* offers a similar vision of the psalmic praise of the created world:

   The light's music resounds and shines in the air and over the countryside, drawing everything into the infinite, sensed but mysterious pattern of its harmony. From every tree and leaf, grass blade, stone, bird, and beast, it is answered and again answers in return. The creatures sing back their names. But more than their names. They sing their being. (122)

FURTHER READING

Criticism

Berry, Wendell. "The Art of Place." *New Perspectives Quarterly* 9, No. 2 (Spring 1992): 29-34.

The poet emphasizes the relationship between culture and agriculture in his work.

Carruth, Hayden. "Human Authenticity in the Age of Massive, Multiplying Error." *Parnassus* 13, No. 2 (Spring-Summer 1986): 140-43.

Explores Berry's philosophical concerns.

Decker, William. "'Practice Resurrection': The Poesis of Wendell Berry." *NDQ* 55, No. 4 (Fall 1987): 170-84.

Surveys the major themes of Berry's verse.

Fields, Kenneth. "The Hunter's Trail: Poems by Wendell Berry." *The Iowa Review* 1, No. 1 (Winter 1970): 90-100.

Considers Berry's poetic themes limited and repetitive.

Lang, John. "'Close Mystery': Wendell Berry's Poetry of Incarnation." *Renascence* XXXV, No. 4 (Summer 1983): 258-68.

Analyzes Berry's treatment of nature in his poetry.

Merchant, Paul, ed. *Wendell Berry.* Lewiston, Idaho: Confluence Press, 1991, 223 p.

Collection of critical essays.

Murphy, Patrick D. "Penance or Perception: Spirituality and Land in the Poetry of Gary Snyder and Wendell Berry." In *Earthly Words: Essays on Contemporary American Nature and Environmental Writers,* edited by John Cooley, pp. 237-49. Ann Arbor: The University of Michigan Press, 1994.

Compares the poetic interests of Berry and Gary Snyder, particularly man's relationship to the land.

Additional coverage of Berry's life and career is contained in the following sources published by the Gale Group: *Authors in the News,* Vol. 1; *Contemporary Authors,* Vols. 73-76; *Contemporary Authors New Revision Series,* Vols. 50, 73; *Contemporary Literature Criticism,* Vols. 4, 6, 8, 27, 46; *DISCovering Authors Modules—Poetry; Dictionary of Literary Biography; Major 20th-Century Writers.*

Robert Bridges
1844-1930

English poet, dramatist, and critic.

INTRODUCTION

Having initially trained and worked as a physician, Bridges ultimately became prominent in English letters during the late Victorian and early twentieth century as a writer of lyrical verse. The English poet A. E. Housman described the lyrics in Bridges's famous collection, *The Shorter Poems* (1890-94), as universally excellent. While Bridges experimented with prosody and free verse, he is generally regarded as a classicist. His investigation into eighteenth-century classical forms culminated in *The Testament of Beauty* (1929), a long philosophical poem considered by many to be his masterpiece. Bridges served as England's poet laureate from 1913 until his death in 1930.

BIOGRAPHICAL INFORMATION

Bridges was born into a family of small landowners in Walmer, Kent. This port town and its famous resident, the Duke of Wellington, would be featured in some of the poet's lyrics. Bridges received his education at Eton and then at Oxford, where he befriended the poet Gerard Manley Hopkins. Hopkins's experiments with an unusual type of meter he called "sprung rhythm" mirrored Bridges's own, somewhat more conservative attempts at "stress prosody," which he used in such well-known poems as "On a Dead Child" and "London Snow."

Bridges did not embark on his poetic career immediately. His first impulse was to train as a cleric in the Church of England, but in 1869 he opted instead to enroll in medical school. After graduation in 1874, Bridges became a physician at St. Bartholomew's Hospital in London and later worked at the Hospital for Sick Children. Bridges retired from medicine in 1881 after becoming seriously ill with pneumonia. He moved with his mother to Yattendon, Berkshire, where he met and married Monica Waterhouse. While in Yattendon, from 1882 to 1904, Bridges wrote some of his most popular short lyrics as well as his narrative poem, *Eros and Psyche* (1885). In 1907 he moved back to Oxford with his family and into Boar's Hill—a house that he had designed himself. In 1914 when England entered World War I, Bridges felt it was his duty as newly appointed poet laureate to contribute to the war effort through his writing. His war poems were collected in *October and Other Poems, with Occasional Verses on the War* (1920). After his daughter Margaret died from a pro-

longed illness in 1926, Bridges tried to cope with his grief by embarking on a long philosophical work. The resulting *Testament of Beauty* was to be his final poetic work before his death in 1930.

MAJOR WORKS

Although Bridges wrote several long poems, he is perhaps best known for his shorter works. His sonnet sequence, *The Growth of Love* (1876), reveals Bridges's facility for the Italian and English sonnet forms and, indeed, are clearly influenced by the sonnets of Shakespeare and John Milton. The publication of *The Shorter Poems* (1890-94), selected from the best of Bridges's lyric poems up to that date, marks the summit of his growing fame as a poet. In addition to those written in irregularly stressed syllables, Bridges's lyrics also include many written in more conventional metric forms. The subjects of these short poems include the nostalgia of childhood, elegies on death, reflections on love, meditations on religious issues, and—what was of particular interest to Bridges—the nature of beauty and the beauty of the natural world. Bridges's collection of war poems, *October and Other Poems,* reflects the prolonged and unexpected course of World War I as well as the poet's concerns about his son, Edward, who was stationed at the western front. Accordingly, the earlier war poems are stirringly patriotic, while the later poems depict the appalling conditions of trench warfare. Bridges's *New Verse* (1925) offers examples of his interest in classical Greek and Latin poetry; several of the poems in this collection are experiments in what he described as classical, "neo-Miltonic syllabics." Bridges's final work of poetry, *The Testament of Beauty,* consists of over 4,000 lines and is divided into four books. It has been described by critic Donald E. Stanford as a "spiritual autobiography depicting the development of a poet's sense of beauty, his response to beauty wherever he finds it."

CRITICAL RECEPTION

Bridges's poetry received little notice before 1912 when a collection of his poetry was published by Oxford University Press and garnered praise from critics and public alike. Critics of the mid-twentieth century, however, did not hold him in high regard. Some described him as a minor poet; others criticized his conservative, Victorian values. The subject matter of Bridges's poetry has also been condemned as trivial or empty; scholars have argued that it focuses on the prettiness of nature and the details of prosody rather than delving into more important topics. More recently, critics have commended Bridges for his experimentation with verse form and have praised him for his skill as a poetic technician. Most critics are united in assessing Bridges's final poem, *The Testament of Beauty,* as a masterpiece of both form and content.

PRINCIPAL WORKS

Poetry

Poems 1873
The Growth of Love 1876
Poems by the Author of 'The Growth of Love' 1879
Poems 1884
Eros and Psyche 1885
Shorter Poems 1890-94
The Humours of the Court 1893
October and Other Poems, with Occasional Verses on the War 1920
New Verse 1925
The Testament of Beauty 1929

Other Major Works

Prometheus the Firegiver (drama) 1883
John Keats, A Critical Essay (essay) 1895
Poems of Gerard Manley Hopkins (editor) 1918
Three Friends (memoirs) 1932

CRITICISM

The Nation (review date 1913)

SOURCE: "An Oxford Poet," in *The Nation,* Vol. 96, No. 2482, January 23, 1913, pp. 83-84.

[*In the following review of the* Poetical Works of Robert Bridges, *the poet's verse is positively described as "slow-moving" and underscored with a "dreamy languor."*]

Outside of Oxford, where he now resides as a retired physician, Mr. Bridges has, we believe, never attained anything like popularity, and in this country he has scarcely been known except as a shadowy name. Yet his reputation has been spreading quietly among the refined for many years, and this cheap and attractive volume of his poems from the Oxford University Press will no doubt introduce him to many new readers.

It is not difficult to explain the exclusiveness, so to speak, of Mr. Bridges's fame. The fact is, his work falls between two stools. On the one hand, it has neither the swiftness of motion, the immediate impressiveness, the narrative zest, and facile emotionalism, which go to make up the style which is popularly and rather naïvely admired as "creative"; nor the esoteric intricacy and obscurity which commonly pass for profound. Lacking these qualities, it misses the great body of readers of verse. On the other hand, it does not quite hit such an audience as Matthew Arnold satisfied: it is intellectual without touching to the quick the deeper beliefs and doubts of the age; it is highly self-critical without being heavily freighted with thought. That is the negative count against Mr. Bridges, stated, perhaps, with a certain over-emphasis. In his favor he has great refinement, now and then a sober but exquisite sense of beauty, a kind of chaste sincerity with the Muse, an appealing modesty of self-confession.

In ***Eros and Psyche*** Mr. Bridges has employed with great dexterity the seven-line stanza which James Thomson adopted for his "City of Dreadful Night." It is slow-moving form, more lyric and reflective than narrative, but suits the relishing restraint with which the poet retells the beautiful old story of Apuleius. Anything more different from the light, almost breathless flow of William Morris's version of the tale could scarcely be conceived. At a first reading Morris will captivate where Bridges merely pleases, but it is not so sure that a second or third reading would leave the victory so absolutely to the earlier poet.

We cannot now criticise the sonnets and lyrics in detail, and from the studies of classical prosody we turn with abhorrent eyes. The space needed for such analysis may better be given to quoting at length one of the poems, **"Indolence,"** which exhibits a certain dreamy languor latent here and there in Mr. Bridges's verse, and which associates him most intimately with the romance of Oxford:

We left the city when the summer day
Had verged already on its hot decline,
And charmed Indolence in languor lay
In her gay gardens, 'neath her towers divine;
"Farewell," we said, "dear city of youth and dream!"
And in our boat we stepped and took the stream.
All through that idle afternoon we strayed
Upon our proposed travel well begun.
As loitering by the woodland's dreamy shade,
Past shallow islets floating in the sun,
Or searching down the banks for rarer flowers
We lingered out the pleasurable hours.
Till when that loveliest came, which mowers home
Turns from their longest labor, as we steered
Along a straitened channel flecked with foam.
We lost our landscape wide, and slowly neared
An ancient bridge, that like a blind wall lay
Low on its buried vaults to block the way.
Then soon the narrow tunnels broader showed,
Where with its arches three it sucked the mass
Of water, that in swirl thereunder flowed,
Or stood piled at the piers waiting to pass;
And pulling for the middle span, we drew
The tender blades aboard and floated through.
But past the bridge what change we found below!
The stream, that all day long had laughed and played
Betwixt the happy shires, ran dark and slow,
And with its easy flood no murmur made:
And weeds spread on its surface, and about
The stagnant margin reared their stout heads out.
Upon the left high elms, with giant wood
Skirting the water-meadows, interwove
Their slumbrous crowns, o'ershadowing where they stood
The floor and heavy pillars of the grove:
And in the shade, through reeds and sedges dank,
A footpath led along the moated bank.
Across, all down the right, an old brick wall,
Above and o'er the channel, red did lean;
Here buttressed up, and bulging there tofall
Tufted with grass and plants and lichen green;
And crumbling to the flood, which at its base
Slid gently nor disturbed its mirrored face.
Sheer on the wall the houses rose, their backs
All windowless, neglected and awry,
With tottering coigns, and crooked chimney stacks;
And here and there an unused door, set high
Above the fragments of its mouldering stair,
With rail and broken step led out on air.
Beyond, deserted wharves and vacant sheds,
With empty boats and barges moored along,
And rafts half-sunken, fringed with weedy shreds,
And sodden beams, once soaked to season strong.
No sight of man, nor sight of life, no stroke,
No voice the somnolence and silence broke.
Then I who rowed leant on my oar, whose drip
Fell without sparkle, and I rowed no more;
And he that steered moved neither hand nor lip,
But turned his wondering eye from shore to shore;
And our trim boat let her swift motion die,
Between the dim reflections floating by.

Alan Porter (review date 1929)

SOURCE: "The Spirit of Man," in *The Spectator,* Vol. 5288, November 2, 1929, pp. 635-36.

[*In the following review of* The Testament of Beauty, *Porter asserts that the poem reflects Bridges's belief that humanity and nature are "interdependent" and that they are "linked" together by beauty.*]

The Testament of Beauty is, I think, the greatest English poem of our time. It is a poem not of romance but of "high argument," Dr. Bridges' essay *de rerum natura.* If it seems to lack heat and variety of fancy, to be too austere for popularity, the reason lies mainly in its seriousness and philosophic import. To Schopenhauer *interest* as an aim in writing was fatal to *beauty;* and Dr. Bridges himself professes the aristocratic attitude—he writes for the few, he does not invite the applause of democracy. The poem is fittingly dedicated "To The King."

From the beginning of the first canto we are aware of the high ground from which the poet speaks. He echoes both Milton and Dante, and sets himself in their company:—

"'Twas late in my long journey, when I had clomb to where
the path was narrowing and the company few,
a glow of childlike wonder enthral'd me, as if my sense
had come to a new birth purified, my mind enrapt
re-awakening to a fresh initiation of life;
with like surprise of joy as any man may know
who rambling wide hath turn'd, resting on some hill-top
to view the plain he has left, and see'th it now out-spredd,
mapp'd at his feet, a landscape so by beauty estranged
he scarce will ken familiar haunts, nor his own home,
maybe, where far it lieth, small as a faded thought."

The scene out-spread for Dr. Bridges is the life of man, his intercourse with nature, the beauty he bears in him and finds truly given in the objective world around him. The first tenet of Dr. Bridges' belief is that beauty is neither imposed on nature by man nor exhibited by nature apart from man: the two are interdependent and beauty is a real influence linking them together.

It is in the Platonic image of man as a charioteer, governing two restive horses, that Dr. Bridges finds his satisfying symbol. The two horses are the dynamic of all human attainment: they are Selfhood and Breed, individualism and sex, or, at their greatest, courage and love. These two give to human life all its lustre and poignancy; they give it also its risk and danger. As Selfhood ungoverned or predominant becomes savagery and conquest—yet does not lose the aura of its nobility—so Breed ungoverned becomes passion without meaning. Where the two impulses have shown themselves unmanageable they have called out revenge against themselves; thus two "Essene Wars" have arisen, one against Selfhood, one against Breed. Nor are these wars unnatural:—

> "in man's eternal quest of happiness,
> contempt of fleshly pleasure is as near to his spirit
> as is the love of it to his animal nature."

None the less, these wars are not the principles of reconcilement. The beauty of life depends, not on a despotic subjugation of these horses, least of all upon killing them, but on their easy and ordered governance. Selfhood in especial has excited revenge against itself in our own days.

> "Nay, some I have seen will choose a beehive for their sign
> and gloss their soul-delusion with a muddled thought,
> picturing a skep of straw, the beekeeper's device,
> a millowner's workshop, for totem of their tribe;
> Not knowing the high goal of our great endeavour
> is spiritual attainment, individual worth,
> at all cost to be sought and at all cost pursued,
> to be won at all cost and at all cost assured."

In this way Dr. Bridges regards political Socialism as the enemy of personality, the attempt to abolish the first dynamic of man's spirit.

The charioteer, the ηγεμονιόν or principle of control, is the individual Ethic:—

> "If Duty hold us long, now as in the old adage,
> Pleasure may follow after, taking like second rank
> in Plato's myth, as I twist it: wherein we traced
> Duty from Selfhood of individual life
> growing to reach communion with life eternal;
> while in the younger horse was pleasure intensified
> by love, until it issueth in the Love of God."

This duty is no imposition from outside, no social obligation; it is the law of man's instinct, his own humanity, finding through the reason its free, harmonious and pleasurable fulfilment. The greatest excellence is the excellence which comes easiest.

This is the outline of Dr. Bridges' argument. There has been no opportunity to notice or illustrate the incidental beauty of his poem. Over the whole of it there is an air of serenity and deep cultivation of mind; idiom and cadence are perfectly matched with substance; we feel ourselves in the presence of a true poetic comprehension of human history. The argument itself will have suggested the limitations of the poem. Dr. Bridges has by no means the imaginative reach of Dante: he cannot include as much of fantasy in logical structure. There is a lack, too, of responsiveness to concrete men, to men everywhere and anywhere. Dr. Bridges' individualism denies him the perception of communal solidarity, and he preserves the distance between the *exceptional man* and the *herd.* In two ways, therefore, the poem is more austere than the greatest poetry. Nevertheless, ***The Testament of Beauty*** is a superb witness to "man's mounting spirit"; original without strain, profuse in deep intuitions, fresh, clear and beautiful.

Eda Lou Walton (review date 1930)

SOURCE: "The Testament of Beauty," in *The Nation,* Vol. 130, No. 3371, February 12, 1930, pp. 193-96.

[*In the following review of* The Testament of Beauty, *Walton describes the poem as Bridges's attempt to reevaluate his beliefs in beauty and human spirituality in the face of a society that has changed dramatically since his youth.*]

Robert Bridges, Poet Laureate of England, was born in 1844; he has lived, therefore, through three literary periods and has seen three well-defined shifts of scene. As a young man he must have been influenced by all that concerned Alfred Tennyson in his poetical epitomizing of the Victorian Age: its religious doubt and insecure faith, its attempt at fortification against the scientific revolution, its moral primness and ugly industrialism. Later he endured the nineties, fin de siècle, a period of pessimism and sensualism whose main dogmas were Impressionism and Art for Art's Sake; and at last he came upon the contemporary scene: he saw Science conquer, and a new Psychology begin to question even the integrity of the thinking mind; he saw Industrialism in complete command of human lives, and, worst of all, he lived to watch a war blot out all evidence of spiritual progress. He has continued after that war to observe a disillusioned group of men who have never known youth or idealism. Now, in the face of all this evidence against faith and hope, he has had the courage to publish, in his eighty-sixth year, his ***Testament of Beauty***, a long poem comparable in its purpose of teaching and prophesying to Wordsworth's Prelude and Excursion.

In this poem Mr. Bridges rededicates himself to the creed announced in 1876 in his ***Growth of Love***:

> I will be what God made me, nor protest
> Against the bent of genius in my time,
> That science of my friends robs all the best,
> While I love beauty and was born to rhyme.

The Testament of Beauty is not a protest; it is an argument and, to Mr. Bridges, a proof that Beauty will prevail, that all forces work toward a greater spirituality in men and toward a consequent greater Art; it is indeed a survey of the past with intent to force the conclusion that man's moral and aesthetic progress is one and the same, and that this progress points necessarily toward a conventional morality and religion. The compulsion toward religion remains important to his argument, but the religious emotion is lost through the author's attempt to use such modern abstractions as Force, Mind, Law, when he means God. If Mr. Bridges's argument remains unconvincing in view of the discoveries of history, science, anthropology, and psychology, if the proof is based upon an ephemeral idealism with which we today have little patience, this may not necessarily condemn the poem as poetry. Many a poet has gone badly astray in manipulating argument. But since, with the exception of the gracefully medieval tone of the Introduction, poetry here is freighted much too heavily with argument and philosophical jargon; since, indeed, most of ***The Testament of Beauty*** cannot be called poetry at all—even in its ineptly applied literary echoes of earlier poets, its pallid allegory, archaisms, inversions, and rhetoric—but is rather a prose tract cast into verse, we may consider its logic and its argument rather than its poetic quality. Doubtless Mr. Bridges himself realizes something of the difference between the technique of this, his latest work, and the quality of those delicate and charming lyrics by which he is most likely to be remembered; doubtless he would lead his readers to a consideration of his thought, for he has, in his ***Testament***, taken the tone of an instructor.

The Testament of Beauty is divided into an Introduction announcing that the poem is to be a Vision, and then into three parts, Selfhood, Breed, and Ethick. The Vision becomes in the second part much less allegorical and much more argumentative than the Introduction leads us to expect. The symbols are the two horses and their charioteer as employed in the apocalyptic imagery:

> The Vision of the Seer is Truth's Apocalypse,
> yet needeth for our aid a true interpreter.
> The names of the two horses are *Selfhood* and *Breed,*
> the charioteer is *Reason.*

Selfhood, the first horse, is the Ego, the selfishness in human beings, but this force may and does grow more altruistic:

> Selfhood is fundamental
> and universal in all individual Being,
> and that thru Motherhood it came in animals
> to altruistic feeling and thence after in men
> rose to spiritual affection.

Breed, on the other hand, is the instinct to propagate and is defined as follows:

> Now *Breed*
> is to the race as *Selfhood* to the individual;
> and these two prime Instincts as they differ in purpose
> are independent each from other, and separate
> as are organic tracts in animal body
> whereby they function; and tho' Breed is needful alike
> to plants and animals, yet its apparatus
> is found in animals of more special kind;
> and since race-propagation might have been assured
> without differentiation of sex, we are elect to guess
> nature's intention from its full effect in man:

Breed, too, develops toward a higher spirituality:

> Breed then together with Selfhood steppeth in pair,
> for as Self grew thru' Reason from animal rage
> to vice of war and gluttony, but meanwhile uprose
> thru' motherly yearning to profounder affection,
> So Breed, from like degrading brutality at heart,
> distilleth in the altruism of spiritual love
> to be the sublimest passion of humanity,
> with parallel corruption;

The evolution of both Selfhood and Breed toward higher spirituality may be brought about through Reason, which, in turn, develops its special science of individual and social Ethick. But before this satisfactory sublimation may be reached, the poet is put to some difficulties of argument and proof which should detain us.

The chief difficulty in proving the growth of Selfhood toward altruism is war. How can war be considered as a step toward progress? How is Mr. Bridges to explain this latest catastrophe, if we have progressed very far toward spiritual evaluation?

> And of War she (*Reason*) would say: it ranketh with
> those things
> that are like unto virtue, but not virtue itself:
> rather, in the conscience of spiritual beauty, a vice
> that needeth expert horsemanship to curb, yet being
> nativ in the sinew of selfhood, the life of things,
> the pride of animals, and virtue of savagery,
> so long as men be savage such it remaineth.

A statement meaning, I take it, that man is still savage.

Under Breed Mr. Bridges is forced into a discussion uncongenial to him concerning sex and marriage and the changing attitudes toward these. After a brief history of nations who have been ruined through immorality, and a brief history of marriage from its lower forms of polygamy and polyandry, he makes this statement:

> Now 'tis a backsliding and treason against nature
> when women will unsex their own ideal of Love,
> and ignorantly aiming to be in all things as man,
> would make love as men make it—tho' Sappho did
> thatt,
> who rare among women for manly mastery of art,
> A Nonsuch of her kind, exceeded by default,
> nondescript, and for lack of the true feminine
> borrow'd effeminacy of men, the incontinents,
> who, ranking with gluttons in Aristotle's book,
> made a lascivious pleasure of their Lesbian loves;

Women, the poet concludes, are made not to be artists but rather to be mothers; as artists they can only ape men or ape Sappho, but as mothers they are unique and unexcelled. As for the history of marriage it proves the supremacy of monogamy, and he clinches his argument with this final analogy:

> Refusal of christian marriage is, as 'twer in art
> to impugn the credit of the most beautiful things
> because there are so few of them, and hold it folly
> to aim at excellence where so few can succeed.

With these problems decided upon, Mr. Bridges can conclude that the boundary between Matter and Mind will became fixed, that terrestrial life will evolve toward conscience, and finally, that through personal prayer:

Reason (say I) wil rise to awareness of its rank
in the Ring of Existence, where man looketh up
to the first cause of all; and wil itself decree
and order discreetly the attitude of the soul
seeking self-realization in the vision of God

and

The attraction of this motion (*this evolution*) is our
consience of it,
our love of wisdom and of beauty; and the attitude
of those attracted wil be joyful obedience
with reverence to'rd the omnificent Creator
and First Cause, whose Being is thatt beauty and wisdom
which is apprehended only and only approach'd
by right understanding of his creation, and found
in that habit of faith which some thinkers have styled
The Life of Reason.

And it is to this Life of Reason the poet would persuade us. This heavily documented argument is offered as proof of the evolution of all baser instincts toward a higher spirituality. If he persuades us more directly through the one or two more exalted lyrical passages in the Introduction and in the closing Vision of a Sunset throughout the world, then this is nothing more than a statement that Poetry is not a vehicle, save indirectly, for teachings or philosophy, but may persuade only by the stirring of the emotions, a truth which Mr. Bridges regretfully acknowledges in closing:

Verily by Beauty it is that we come at Wisdom,
yet not by Reason at Beauty: and now with many words
pleasing myself betimes I am fearing lest in the end
I play the tedious orator who maundereth on
for lack of heart to make an end of his nothings.
Wherefor as when a runner who hath run his round
handeth his staff away, and is glad of his rest,
here break I off, knowing the goal was not for me
the while I ran on telling of what cannot be told.

Charles Williams (essay date 1930)

SOURCE: "Robert Bridges," in his *Poetry at Present,* The Clarendon Press, 1930, pp. 18-29.

[*In the following excerpt, Williams praises Bridges's lyric poetry, asserting that it succeeds in communicating both the ideals and physical existence of such abstractions as beauty and joy.*]

Of the fourteen laureates from—and including—Dryden, if we take him as the first, some five (if we include Southey) have been notable poets. With the exception of Dryden himself and of Wordsworth none of them has been a greater than Mr. Robert Bridges. Tennyson is not to be considered a greater, for his verbal achievement is no finer, and his philosophic (if the two can be divided) is very definitely less. None of them has contributed a greater mass of lyric beauty to our literature.

It may very well be held that Mr. Bridges is not only a lyric poet; he has written dramas, a sonnet-sequence, a long narrative poem, and of the volume ***New Poems*** at least four are more in the nature of philosophic poems than of lyric. But as his lyric verse is more popular, so also it contains so much of intellect that attention may, in such a short tribute as this, be very well concentrated upon it.

Mr. Bridges has been said, by various good judges, to be our greatest lyric poet since Shelley. He was born twenty-two years after Shelley died. But the poetic difference between him and Shelley is immense. There remains something not quite unfair in Matthew Arnold's famous description—'an ineffectual angel beating in the void his luminous wings in vain'. The angel may, merely by virtue of his being an angel, be not entirely ineffectual; the void may be rather an abyss of poetic ether. But Shelley, of all our poets, seems peculiarly unattached to the earth—except in *Œdipus in Thebes* and a few fragments—and peculiarly impatient of intellectual study. A philosophy is to be found in him, but it is not convincing in its poetic intensity. Reason interprets that inspiration too feebly; abstractions become more abstract and aerial and walk less certainly upon our earth.

Mr. Bridges's poetry produces exactly the opposite effect. It is perhaps not without significance that he abandoned a medical career for poetry. For the Laureate is one of the very few living poets who when they speak of abstractions seem to speak of living and significant things. To speak of Beauty, with that capital B, has become almost the defining habit of the minor poet. Mr. de la Mare has dreamed of her, Mr. Abercrombie has cried to her, each convincingly. But neither of these poets has spoken with more assured quietness or with more certain knowledge than Mr. Bridges; neither of them more persuades the reader of the real existence of that Beauty.

And what is true of Beauty is true also of those other abstractions—Virtue, Honour, Truth. What has given to Mr. Bridges's verse this singular prerogative?

Two things—which are indeed one: the concrete instances of these abstractions which he has given us in so many places, and the general quality of his verse.

To give examples of the first would necessitate continued and lengthy quotation. They are to be found in every anthology; they include the famous **'London Snow'**, **'Asian Birds'** and such poems.

But it is not beauty—of landscape or human figure or great poetry or other art, 'the Virgilian muse' or 'the gaiety of Mozart'—that furnishes the chief hidden theme of this verse, nor is it beauty (merely so undefined) that is its peculiar quality. It is rather beauty in restraint; still more it is the strength of beauty in restraint; or, to press it one farther step, it is the consciousness of the strength of beauty in restraint. Dull as the phrase is, and unworthy to approach the high loveliness of this Muse, all four terms could be justified.

The deliberate act by which Mr. Bridges laid aside the profession of medicine for (what to him must have seemed) the equally arduous profession of poetry was a symbol of his general approach to poetry in all its ways. The deliberate and learned interest which he has taken in the manners and habits of prosody, in the Society for Pure English, in hand-writing and phonetics, continue to express that approach. His mind seems to know all the time what it is doing; it judges seriously, if lightly; it is aware of its rejections as well as of its acceptances, even when those rejections appear so natural that almost any other poet would have forgotten them altogether, or perhaps been hardly aware that they existed. Joy, for example, which, in so many poets, seems but an accident of their mood, is here a conscious choice, almost a duty, and even, sometimes, an effort. That some of the finest of his lyrics rise into an attitude of pure delight is no contradiction of this; rather, it is its reward. 'Man's duty is to be happy,' said Dr. Johnson; Mr. Bridges's verse might almost be said to have fulfilled that duty after many a conflict and in spite of many an adversary. That it had an original leaning that way is to say no more than that Mr. Hardy's has had a leaning towards a thwarted happiness or Mr. Kipling's towards a fatalistic morality. But Mr. Bridges omits the consideration of evil fortune less than Hardy omits the consideration of good fortune. 'The master Reason' rides always on the right hand of his Muse when she goes through the cruel habitations of the earth, and directs her attentive glance not only to them but also to the satisfying stars. That the stars have been by now a little touched by the literary taint makes the metaphor only the more just. For a great deal of the happiness in this poetry arises from the recollection of great art.

> Days that the thought of grief refuse,
> Days that are one with human art,
> Worthy of the Virgilian muse,
> Fit for the gaiety of Mozart—

these are the terms in which he praises the 'brighter days' of the sea in one poem; and in another (*Dejection*) he warns his soul, revolving hopeless strife,

> Pointing at hindrance, and the bare
> Painful escapes of fitful life
> O soul, be patient: thou shalt find
> A little matter mend all this;
> Some strain of music to thy mind,
> Some praise for skill not spent amiss.

But this too, since literature nowadays is never unselfconscious, accentuates the inward and retired deliberation of this admirable verse. However frequent, however exact, the delight in external things may be, it is within that such delight justifies itself by reason and virtue.

This deliberation accentuates the momentary nature of Joy which is in certain of the lyrics so intensely expressed.

> Haste on, my joys! your treasure lies
> In swift, unceasing flight.
> O haste, for while your beauty flies
> I seize your full delight.

Poets enough have lamented a fugitive joy; not many have realized, as Mr. Bridges has done, that such a flight is indeed (in our present mode of being) of its very nature—that, without it, Joy apparently could not be at all. To such a dogma speculation can offer objections enough; it is, beyond all speculation, confirmed by experience. And it is from profound experience that this verse arises. In a great poem (No. 13 of the ***Shorter Poems,*** Book III) the gospel, and almost the mysticism, of Joy is expressed.

> Joy, sweetest lifeborn joy, where dost thou dwell?
> Upon the formless moments of our being
> Flitting, to mock the ear that heareth well,
> To escape the trainèd eye that strains in seeing,
> Or home in our creations, to withstand
> Black-wingèd death, that slays the making hand?
> The making mind, that must untimely perish
> Amidst its work which time may not destroy,
> The beauteous forms which man shall love to cherish,
> The glorious songs that combat earth's annoy?
> Thou dost dwell here, I know, divinest Joy:
> But they who built thy towers fair and strong,
> Of all that toil, feel most of care and wrong.
> Sense is so tender, O and hope so high,
> That common pleasures mock their hope and sense;
> And swifter than doth lightning from the sky
> The ecstasy they pine for flashes hence,
> Leaving the darkness and the woe immense,
> Wherewith it seems no thread of life was woven,
> Nor doth the track remain where once 'twas cloven.
> And heaven and all the stable elements
> That guard God's purpose mock us, though the mind
> Be spent in searching: for his old intents
> We see were never for our joy designed:
> They shine as doth the bright sun on the blind,
> Or like his pensioned stars, that hymn above
> His praise, but not toward us, that God is Love.
> For who so well hath wooed the maiden hours
> As quite to have won the worth of their rich show,
> To rob the night of mystery, or the flowers
> Of their sweet delicacy ere they go?
> Nay, even the dear occasion when we know,
> We miss the joy, and on the gliding day
> The special glories float and pass away.
> Only life's common plod: still to repair
> The body and the thing which perisheth:
> The soil, the smutch, the toil and ache and wear,
> The grinding enginry of blood and breath,
> Pain's random darts, the heartless spade of death;
> All is but grief, and heavily we call
> On the last terror for the end of all.
> Then comes the happy moment: not a stir
> In any tree, no portent in the sky:
> The morn doth neither hasten nor defer,

The morrow hath no name to call it by,
But life and joy are one,—we know not why,—
As though our very blood long breathless lain
Had tasted of the breath of God again.
And having tasted it I speak of it,
And praise him thinking how I trembled then
When his touch strengthened me, as now I sit
In wonder, reaching out beyond my ken,
Reaching to turn the day back, and my pen
Urging to tell a tale which told would seem
The witless phantasy of them that dream.
But O most blessèd truth, for truth thou art,
Abide thou with me till my life shall end.
Divinity hath surely touched my heart;
I have possessed more joy than earth can lend:
I may attain what time shall never spend.
Only let not my duller days destroy
The memory of thy witness and my joy.

But Joy, so desired, so experienced, so hoped, is not his only subject, or rather it has another name, and that name was given it in the title of his early sonnet-sequence, ***The Growth of Love***. Within that sequence are contained many implicit or explicit declarations of his temperament, his will, and his aim: for example, the lines—

Nor surer am I water hath the skill
To quench my thirst

is almost a definition, by its sound and simile, of his own verse—so cool, so simple, is it. So also the fifteenth sonnet may be quoted here because it seems to describe so well the sort of mind which the reader may conjecture lies behind that verse.

Who builds a ship must first lay down the keel
Of health, whereto the ribs of mirth are wed:
And knit, with beams and knees of strength, a bed
For decks of purity, her floor and ceil.
Upon her masts, Adventure, Pride, and Zeal,
To fortune's wind the sails of purpose spread:
And at the prow make figured maidenhead
O'erride the seas and answer to the wheel.
And let him deep in memory's hold have stor'd
Water of Helicon: and let him fit
The needle that doth true with heaven accord:
Then bid her crew, love, diligence and wit
With justice, courage, temperance come aboard,
And at her helm the master reason sit.

Love, diligence, wit, justice, courage, temperance, reason—these are the qualities Mr. Bridges praises and recommends to the young adventurer. They are, transmuted into poetry, the qualities of his verse; they are the analysed elements of its beauty as it praises Beauty. They are the method of his experience, and the things his genius chooses to experience are selected by them. Besides great art, a few things are pre-eminent in his poetic knowledge—the English landscape, man in society, Hellenism, solitude, piety. These things, communicated by those virtuous Pleiades named above, cause a profound and still delight. But it is a delight which may require a certain similarity of temperament or a certain prolonged discipline before it can be accepted, especially from a reader used to more violent effects. Violence attends on the steps of a number of our poets, and, so long as it is only allowed to act at its master's bidding, even violence may have its work to do. But it is an uncertain slave, and one whom Mr. Bridges would never spend a farthing to buy or shelter.

One of the best examples of his peculiar strength is in one of the finest love poems of the last century. **'Awake, my heart, to be loved: awake, awake'—**

Awake, the land is scattered with light, and see,
Uncanopied sleep is flying from field and tree:
And blossoming boughs of April in laughter shake;
Awake, O heart, to be loved, awake, awake!

The stanza is carried on its wide and awakening vowels. How many poets have welcomed morning in their love-songs, but never before had we seen how, in that world which is neither wholly mental nor wholly actual, being poetry's, never before had we known that sleep fled being uncanopied, nor how, among the new shadows, light is flung over the land, nor felt all this as a simile of awakening and hastening love. 'Uncanopied' is one of the most unusual epithets Mr. Bridges's temperance allows him; as a general rule his adjectives are as near the expected as a poet's could be. But they are always there to do their business, never from mere idleness or the needs of the line. 'Sunny hair', 'stout roots', 'branchèd trees', 'red roofs', 'whirling snow', 'delicious notes', these descriptions are there precisely because it is those separate facts which make beautiful whatever it is we see.

His diction, his feeling for words, is a part of his whole 'duteous chastity'; their potentiality in his verse is that rather of putting off their secular inheritance than expressing it. They mean what they say; that they mean no more than they say is a part of their exquisite simplicity. They are therefore peculiarly fit to convey those landscapes which are so distinct a part of this verse, the visions of 'England in the peace and delight of her glory'. No month of all the year is alien, nor is it easy to say that any month is a more welcome guest to this full-hearted host than any other.

But 'uncanopied sleep' has to fly from our minds yet more completely than in a recognition of the just diction of passionate love or sensitive country-side if we are to appreciate Mr. Bridges's verse properly. It is a marvellous training for the ear. This is no place to discuss his classical prosody, his book on Milton's prosody, or his scazons; they would form a too specialist dispute. But poem after poem in the ***Shorter Poems*** contains the most delicate rhythms, the most exquisite play of pauses, stresses, and variations. His sonnets, for a gross example, are not poems more or less accommodated to fourteen lines; they are sonnets. In them, perhaps more evidently than in the lyrics, the various long traditions of English verse are to be recognized. It is an additional pleasure to discern, for example, how the metaphysical note sounds in Mr. Bridges's own peculiar harmony; how, instead of that manner issuing in a complex and heightened darkness, it becomes a quiet and heightened lucidity. It is a quiet which is almost too profound for most of us to reach or trust. One sonnet begins

> For beauty being the best of all we know,

and it is in the implicit challenge offered by such a line to all the easy talk and cheap professions of beauty which go so much abroad in the world that Mr. Bridges's admirers find their own admiration challenged. It will not do, for all its quietness, to take this verse too lightly. It satisfies but it also inquires; its repose is as militant as (it is known) Mr. Bridges can, on occasion, be. No poetry of our day is less pretentious in its doctrine; none is more profoundly doctrinal in its very being. Beauty and love and joy and the rest are here certainly states of existence, but they are also virtues. If the poetry goes often in silver, it is the silver of a natural sanctity, the reward of a persevering and industrious faith. It is as if the genius of Mr. Bridges had determined to know all things in beauty, and as if beauty, here discovered and there imposed, had at last reconciled him to all things.

> Ah heavenly joy! But who hath ever heard,
> Who hath seen joy, or who shall ever find
> Joy's language? There is neither speech nor word;
> Nought but itself to teach it to mankind.

Well, perhaps not. But this voice at least might persuade many minds to be still and wait for the full revelation.

The Times Literary Supplement (review date 1931)

SOURCE: "Bridges's Shorter Poems," in *The Times Literary Supplement,* No. 1534, June 25, 1931, p. 505.

[*In the following review of Bridges's* Shorter Poems, *the poet is seen as responsible for keeping alive the heritage of a rapidly changing English Countryside.*]

Tasteful as is the form in which these poems are printed, another half-inch of width and height would have given us a sister-volume to ***The Testament of Beauty*** in its original and most popular dress. The type might then have been slightly larger, and there would have been more scope for thoughtful placing of the lyrics on the page. How much, in our impression of a lyric, depends on the printing, on the spacing even! The more fragile its structure the greater the risk of loss. A pretty trifle like **"Gay Robin"** loses step by being cut in two at the fourth line of the stanza, and without its step, what is it? Several poems immediately afterwards give their last stanza to a fresh page. These are small drawbacks, which work of classic soundness will surmount; but why should it have to surmount anything? Let us mention, while complaining, that we have noticed a misprint on page 202, a bad one, and that the second stop in the first poem is in the wrong place.

Perhaps the most striking quality of these lyrics is their versatility of mood and manner; an exquisite scrupulousness of workmanship rules everywhere; here are all the flowers of the garden in all their shapes. This conscious fashioning is un-English and accounts for the long coolness of the public towards them. The English attitude to poetry is that it must be central and natural: as Keats said, it must be as leaves to the tree, or not at all. For Bridges action came first, and poetry would have remained his pastime if he could have lived as he would. In a sense it always was a pastime, and for that very reason only worth doing if done supremely well. Take, for an example, one of his worst:—

> Sometimes when my lady sits by me
> My rapture's so great, that I tear
> My mind from the thought that she's nigh me,
> And strive to forget that she's there.
> And sometimes when she is away
> Her absence so sorely does try me,
> That I shut to my eyes, and assay
> To think she is there sitting by me.

As a poem of passion, this totally fails; its success, if it succeeds, is its revolving melody, its rhythmical invention; there is perhaps just enough feeling in it to carry that; it is a plaything of the Muse. And everywhere the beauty of craft in Bridges is an attainment in the second degree, like an English gentleman's good horsemanship, who never becomes part of his horse, as the base Indian does. The music of words was his delight, his strict and constant meditation, but his self and soul are in the English life, the English countryside, the attachments, the tendernesses, the endurances, which have nowhere in the world been more closely knit nor based on wider cognizance of the truth we set out from and the truth we seek. Poetry is his second nature; but he loves it so deeply that his life becomes essentially the poet's life; he does not, like Shakespeare, finish his last play and retire with a sigh of relief to the country, to the hares and the deer; he lives in the country because the Muses live there and there the converse he delights in will sustain him to the end.

So the prevailing charm of his lyrics is their personal intimacy with rural England, and the spirit of the life that is lived there, a life differently realized, of course, by different individuals, and yet sustained by a unity of purpose, of which the very trees are aware. He voices those sweet and sober feelings which to Englishmen and Englishwomen are "both law and impulse," making the best of their instinct and endeavour articulate to them: and, first of all, that deep sanity which chooses happiness:—

> Riding adown the country lanes
> One day in spring,
> Heavy at heart with all the pains
> Of man's imagining:—
> The mist was not yet melted quite
> Into the sky:
> The small round sun was dazzling white,
> The merry larks sang high.
> Deep in the sunny vale a burn

Ran with the lane,
O'erhung with ivy, moss and fern
It laugh'd in joyful strain.
So fair it was, so sweet and bright,
The jocund Spring
Awoke in me the old delight
Of man's imagining,
Riding adown the country lanes:
The larks sang high.—
O heart! for all thy griefs and pains
Thou shalt be loth to die.

This, and so much else, has become articulate in Bridges, because a final awareness is forced on us. We realize that if our peculiar heritage, our contribution to the world, is to live and hold, it must part with the old unconsciousness, must be prized, preserved. Its foundations are the English home and the English home is in the country. Bridges revives the debonair freshness of early England by an act of the will. His lyrics are written, not sung. How could they be sung, when, from his hilltop, the poet was watching the slow transformation of the Oxford he loved, first into a Surbiton, then into a Coventry?

The lovely city, thronging tower and spire,
The mind of the wide landscape, dreaming deep,
Grey-silvery in the vale.

The one hope, he realizes, of saving this, or anything, is to see and to define its worth. His work, in its perfect chiselling, always deliberate however light, is a sign of the threat that hangs over us all; its clearness protests against the encroaching fog; its quietness repudiates the senseless clamour. The delicate precision of his language and his lilt is the voice of the awakened spirit of modern times, warning us that beauty is the most precious of all our possessions and that, unless we resolve to keep her, she is lost. Such indeed is the beauty we actually find in these poems of his, a beauty kept by resolve.

Eda Lou Walton (review date 1931)

SOURCE: "The Shorter Poems of Robert Bridges," in *New York Times Book Review,* August 23, 1931, p. 5.

[*In the following review of* The Shorter Poems of Robert Bridges, *Walton contends that while Bridges was not an innovative poet, he was in fact "a marvelous technician," especially in regard to the short, lyric form.*]

Robert Bridges was born in the Victorian age, the period given over to moral rectitude and to the polishing of English manners and English verse. One feels that he went to school to Tennyson, the master craftsman. He lived through the somewhat decadent and very rebellious '90s, but he joined none of the movements that rated Tennyson and Queen Victoria as out of date. He became neither esthete, pessimist nor catholic, for his spirit was profoundly British, and, despite his amazing facility in all the dainty French verse forms, he remained essentially English in his choice of material for poetry. The twentieth century found him still the lutanist faithful to his theme of delicate and remote beauty, the decorous pursuit of which was a poet's only objective. Finally, just before his death, he summed up his platonic idealism in the ***Testament of Beauty.*** In this long scholarly poem he was hard beset to fit into the scheme of his theory of man's continuous development toward perfection the hard reality of the World War. Only the superb technique always at his command saved him and made his final accomplishment possible. And always, despite the maturity and thoughtful philosophy of the longer poems, Bridges is to be most remembered as a writer of perfect lyrics. Therefore this collection of shorter poems, arranged by the poet himself before his death and published posthumously, is a valuable addition to his various volumes.

Gone are the days—or so it seems now—when beauty in the conventional poetic sense is the absorption of the poet; gone are the days when delicate songs are woven and rewoven around mild melancholy and vague wistfulness with a dreamy delight. Moonlight and roses have, all too definitely, ceased to hold our hearts. And Robert Bridges is likely to be the last of the singers who walk in gardens of the violet and the lily, the last for some time to come—unless one includes as novitiates here the horde of sprouting young academicians who have returned in verse writing to the practice of simplicity and the perfect phrase to state the slight emotion. But, though Bridges's poetry be of another world and may not greatly move us, it is the traditional stuff of all poetry, the song which we have learned to recognize as the cry of the tremulous heart.

Bridges is, above everything else, a marvelous technician. He is complete master of every known lyric form—not one of them escapes him. He could give lessons to any living poet, and probably does so by means of his own finely wrought examples. The range of his accomplishment was great. And yet with all of this artistic perfection he made no innovations, added almost nothing to the forms of verse known nor to the scope of subject matter recognized as proper to poetry.

The phrase "pure poetry" is much bandied about and means, in reality, nothing clear; but if we take it to mean poetry whose very essence is of the traditional spirit, form and subject matter of most good poetry in the past, then Bridges's lyrics are the purest of pure poetry. Every nuance, every rhythm, every gentle mood is here. No overwhelming passions tear this poet's mind apart; passions would be, for so disciplined an artist, a little vulgar; but tenderness, sweet melancholy, reminiscent delight—these are given. Robert Bridges has spent his life finding them all out, these more subtle shades of meaning, these less blatant heroisms, these fanciful little intensities. And perfection is here, absolute perfection in form—and that is, in itself, no mean thing. It will prevail when innovations that are imperfect fail. Robert Bridges's poetry will always delight the lovers of excellent verse. Like Tennyson, he wrote, in his very last years, several new lyrics of much the same tenor as those of his youth:

So 'tis with me; the time hath
clear'd,
Not dull'd, my loving: I can see
Love's passing esctasies endear'd
In aspects of eternity:
I am like a miser—I can say
That, having hoarded all my
gold,
I must grow richer every day
And die possess'd of wealth un-
told.

E. De Selincourt (essay date 1934)

SOURCE: "Robert Bridges," in his *Oxford Lectures on Poetry,* Oxford University Press, 1934 (and reprinted by Books for Libraries Press, Inc., 1967), pp. 207-32.

[*In the following essay, De Selincourt describes the central theme in Bridges's poetry as the beauty of nature and compares Bridges's treatment of this theme with that of other poets such as Keats, Browning, and Swinburne.*]

Only a few months before his death Mr. Bridges bequeathed to us his ***Testament of Beauty.*** That great poem was, as he said, 'the intimate echo' of his life; it reflected his alert interest in the intellectual movement of his time, his deep knowledge and love of nature and the arts, his lyrical ecstasy, his pregnant humour, his fastidious taste—all that went to make up his lofty, distinguished personality. No revelation of the poetic mind, so complete and so illuminating, had appeared since Wordsworth's *Prelude.* The warmth of its reception surprised no less than delighted him, for he had never been widely popular. Though he had written a sonnet sequence, a long narrative poem, a series of masques, a sheaf of lyrics, matched by no living poet, the number of his readers had borne no relation to the value of his achievement. ***The Testament of Beauty*** won him many fresh admirers, and the reading of it sent them back to those earlier poems of his which they had neglected; they found in them the same genius for the creation of beauty, the same unswerving faith in its power 'to soothe the cares and lift the thoughts of man'. More than forty years before he made his Testament, Mr. Bridges had given clear expression to that faith:

For beauty being the best of all we know
Sums up the unsearchable and secret aims
Of nature, and on joys whose earthly names
Were never told can form and sense bestow;
And man hath sped his instinct to outgo
The step of science; and against her shames
Imagination stakes out heavenly claims,
Building a tower above the head of woe.

The spirit which prompted these lines was with him from the beginning. From infancy he was 'a nursling of great Nature's beauty'. As a child, though he loved companionship, his most memorable hours were passed alone in his father's garden and orchard, in the cornfields and on the downs beyond, and on the sea-shore at their feet. They were hours of unclouded happiness. He seems never to have known that discipline of fear which was so potent an influence on Wordsworth's education. The Kentish sea can be tempestuous enough, yet to this light-hearted boy 'his wrath was mirth, his wail was glee':

He from his dim enchanted caves
With shuddering roar and onrush wild
Fell down in sacrificial waves
At feet of his exulting child.

With an early glad response to nature went that instinctive feeling for the beauty of language which marks the poet, a feeling which affects a sensitive child quite apart from any intellectual understanding of the words, and springs rather from a love of rhythm and cadence for their own sakes, the sense of music in perhaps its subtlest form. At the age of eleven his eyes were opened to poetry by the reading of Ovid's *Elegiacs;* and soon afterwards he began to write verse himself. But a passion for poetry, not uncommon in boyhood, went in him with an abnormally keen critical sense, and a sturdy independence of judgement. He was scornful of facile or sloppy sentiment, or of phrasing either uncouth or merely elegant. In his last year at Eton, whilst he had already acquired a love of the great Greek poets, he was reading Shakespeare for the first time, was deep in Milton and Shelley, and carried a copy of Keats in his pocket. Nothing would satisfy him but the best. A young enthusiast for letters generally likes to swim on the crest of current fashion. But though Tennyson was the rage, and Browning had already won the suffrages of superior persons, the young Bridges was repelled by the *Idylls of the King,* and Browning, save in *Saul,* left him cold.[1] And this same severity with which he viewed the masters of his day made him dissatisfied with his own crude attempts at verse, so that for the time he almost gave up writing. He demanded from poetry, whether his own or another's, not merely the overflow of emotion, still less moral edification, but a flawless beauty of form and language.

This attitude was confirmed by his eager discussions on poetic first principles with his school friend Dolben, a boy who though some three years younger than himself was already marked by his fellows as a poet with a future. Dolben held uncompromisingly to the doctrine of poetic inspiration; he only wrote when he had some deeply felt emotion to express, and he could appreciate no poem, however perfect its artistry, unless it voiced his own emotions. 'What led *me* to poetry', Mr. Bridges tells us, 'was the inexhaustible satisfaction of form, the magic of speech, lying, as it seemed to me, in the masterly control of the material; it was an art which I hoped to learn. An instinctive rightness is essential, but, given that, I did not suppose that the poet's emotions were in any way better than mine, nor mine than another's: there is a point in art where these two ways merge and unite, but in apprenticehood they are the opposite approaches.' And, indeed, we may add that *until* they have merged there is no poetry, but merely formless or inarticulate emotion on the one hand,

and poetic exercises on the other. But of the two approaches Dolben's was unquestionably the more fraught with peril. Every one admits that to become a painter, a sculptor, a musician, a man must live laborious days; for each of these artists works in a medium whose technical difficulties are obvious enough. But because the medium of poetry is language, with which we all, from childhood, have some rough and ready acquaintance, there is a common tendency to ignore the technique in a poet's art, and to succumb to the fallacy that from a true poetic feeling poetry must result. But the gift of poetic vision is distinct from that difficult art by which alone it can be communicated. Poetry can only spring from what has been called 'the magical interaction of technical effort with imaginative insight'. And all technique, though it comes to one man more easily than to another, has to be acquired. Bridges resolved to acquire it. In his youth, doubtless, he under-rated both the rarity and the intensity of true poetic experience; yet he was only over-emphasizing a truth often lost sight of, viz. that the poet's power to move us lies primarily not in his depth of thought or feeling, but in his command over a language which compels us to enter into his experience, whatever it may be, and make it our own. And if there was a touch of boyish arrogance in his opinion that the poet's emotions were no better than his, Bridges did not fall into the kindred error of regarding poetry merely in the light of musical expression, which demands a beauty of form and sound, but regards as irrelevant the quality of the experience recorded in it. 'An instinctive rightness was essential': in this phrase spoke the relentless critic of all that loose thinking, vague observation, unreal sentimentality, which have often passed for poetry. His study of the great masters, with their 'instinctive rightness', had saved him from that.

Approaching poetry, then, as an art which must be learned, and conscious of his own immaturity, Bridges did not grudge a long apprenticehood. He inflicted no *Juvenilia* upon the world. He was nearly thirty when he published, in 1873, his first slender volume, and almost all its contents belonged to the previous year. It was followed, three years later, by a sheaf of twenty-four sonnets, and in 1879, after another three years, by a second slim book of lyrics.

He was now thirty-five years of age. Since leaving Eton he had spent four crowded, deeply formative years at Oxford, whence he took with him

> Bright memories of young poetic pleasure
> In free companionship, the loving stress
> Of all life beauty lull'd in studious leisure.

After Oxford he had widened his outlook by continental travel, then settled down to undergo a medical training at St. Bartholomew's, where he acted as casualty surgeon, and later served as assistant physician at the Great Northern and Children's Hospitals. There is plenty of evidence that he threw himself with energy into his work as a doctor, and he never lost his keen interest in the development of medical science; but poetry, then as ever, was his chief solace and delight. Among the earliest lines that he thought worthy of preservation is a lovely little poem wherein he tells how, after a day's toil, he returned home to commune with his divine mistress:

> Long are the hours the sun is above,
> But when evening comes I go home to my love.
>
> . . . . .
>
> Aching and hot as my tired eyes be,
> She is all that I wish to see.
> And in my wearied and toil-dinned ear,
> She says all things that I wish to hear.
>
> . . . . .
>
> And so I sit here night by night,
> In rest and enjoyment of love's delight.
> But a knock at the door, a step on the stair
> Will startle, alas, my love from her chair.
>
> . . . . .
>
> And he wonders, my guest, usurping her throne,
> That I sit so much by myself alone.

As his mind slowly matured in rich contact with the world of men and books, and his mastery of the technique of his art came more nearly to satisfy his own scrupulous taste, the call of the Muse grew ever more insistent. The publication, in 1880, of his third volume of Lyrics, only a year after the second, is proof of the rapidity with which poetry was gaining its hold upon him; the nature of its contents show that claim to have become irresistible. This was his *annus mirabilis.* Delicately phrased expression of poetic moods, both light and solemn, are to be found throughout the first two volumes, but they impress us more often with their exquisite craftsmanship than with their imaginative intensity: in the third volume, whilst the art is brought to an even finer distinction, there is a new spirit, the ecstasy of passion, the vital experience of poetry as not merely a loved pastime, but a terrible joy, an uncontrollable force within, driving he knew not whither.

> O my vague desires!
> Ye lambent flames of the soul, her offspring fires:
> That are my soul herself in pangs sublime
> Rising and flying to heaven before her time.

So opens the volume, and there follow deeply felt responses of the soul to nature in her different moods, **'To a Dead Child'**, that most poignant of all his lyrics,

> Perfect little body, without fault or stain on thee,

and also the most thrilling of his love poems:

> Awake, my heart, to be loved, awake, awake!
> The darkness silvers away, the morn doth break,
> It leaps in the sky: unrisen lustres slake
> The o'ertaken moon. Awake, O heart, awake!

But most significant of all is his address to 'sweetest lifeborn Joy', a poem which, like Shelley's *Hymn to Intellectual Beauty,* is at once a confession of his faith, a record of his own experience in the quest of his ideal, and a solemn dedication of his powers to its pursuit.

Pondering on the elusiveness of true joy in the life of man, he is overcome by the contrast between that joy in beauty which finds an abiding home in the creations of man's art, and the lot of the artist who creates it. For those only are capable of creating beauty who are themselves most susceptible to pain. The very loftiness of their aim brings sorrow upon them, their acute sensitiveness makes them intolerant of what most men account pleasure; the ideal joy for which they hunger seems destined for higher beings than they, and for a world far different from that in which it is their fate to labour: and even when they are rewarded with a fitful glimpse of it there is always something that they cannot capture: it vanishes, and they are left with a sense of irrecoverable loss:

For who so well hath wooed the maiden hours
As quite to have won the worth of their rich show,
To rob the night of mystery, or the flowers
Of their sweet delicacy ere they go?
Nay, even the dear occasion when we know,
We miss the joy, and on the gliding day
The special glories float and pass away.
Only life's common plod: still to repair
The body and the thing which perisheth:
The soil, the smutch, the toil and ache and wear,
The grinding enginry of blood and breath,
Pain's random darts, the heartless spade of death;
All is but grief, and heavily we call
On the last terror for the end of all.

Yet, in this veritable Slough of Despond, comes, as it were by miracle, the sudden vision, and he vows a lifelong surrender to its service:

Then comes the happy moment: not a stir
In any tree, no portent in the sky:
The morn doth neither hasten nor defer,
The morrow hath no name to call it by,
But life and joy are one,—we know not why,—
As though our very blood long breathless lain
Had tasted of the breath of God again.
And having tasted it I speak of it,
And praise him thinking how I trembled then
When his touch strengthened me, as now I sit
In wonder, reaching out beyond my ken,
Reaching to turn the day back, and my pen
Urging to tell a tale which told would seem
The witless phantasy of them that dream.
But O most blessèd truth, for truth thou art,
Abide thou with me till my life shall end.
Divinity hath surely touched my heart;
I have possessed more joy than earth can lend:
I may attain what time shall never spend.
Only let not my duller days destroy
The memory of thy witness and my joy.

Bridges was not unfaithful to the heavenly vision. Two years after writing this poem he left London, and gave up medical practice that he might devote himself wholly to his art. He had found his vocation.

I will be what God made me, nor protest
Against the bent of genius in my time,
That science of my friends robs all the best,
While I love beauty, and was born to rhyme.
Be they our mighty men, and let me dwell
In shadow among the mighty shades of old,
With love's forsaken palace for my cell;
Whence I look forth and all the world behold,
And say, These better days, in best things worse,
This bastardy of time's magnificence,
Will mend in fashion and throw off the curse,
To crown new love with higher excellence.
Curs'd tho' I be to live my life alone,
My toil is for man's joy, his joy my own.

For the rest of his life his 'toil is for man's joy'. The next volume of lyrics opens with a fresh resolve to live and work in the spirit of his creed:

I love all beauteous things,
I seek and adore them;
God hath no better praise,
And man in his hasty days
Is honoured for them.
I too will something make
And joy in the making;
Altho' to-morrow it seem
Like the empty words of a dream
Remembered on waking.

The songs that follow are all triumphant variations on the theme of the joy that lives in beauty—in the beauty of nature, and of each season as it passes, in the beauty of love satisfied, in the consciousness of experience daily enriched. No book of poems so entirely happy in tone had appeared since Blake's *Songs of Innocence,* and not a few of their number are touched with something of Blake's own moving simplicity:

The idle life I lead
Is like a pleasant sleep,
Wherein I rest and heed
The dreams that by me sweep.
And still of all my dreams
In turn so swiftly past,
Each in its fancy seems
A nobler than the last.
And every eve I say,
Noting my step in bliss,
That I have known no day
In all my life like this.

Henceforth he will so order his life that he 'may walk with the feet of joy in idleness'. But this term 'idleness', so often a reproach, in Bridges barely conceals a protest against what is commonly called business, 'with its sick hurry, its divided aims'; it denotes, indeed, a high virtue; it is but another name for a glad unity of purpose, and an unflagging devotion to that Muse who

In nuptial sacrament of thought and sense
Hallowest for toil the hours of indolence.

In point of fact, the ten years 1881-90, of which these 'idle' songs are the scant but precious gleaning, produced a rich harvest, and were, except perhaps for those last years which gave us ***The Testament of Beauty***, the most strenuous in Bridges's whole career. Freed from the claims of an exacting profession he now turned to the composition of longer works: *Prometheus,* a masque, appeared in 1883, ***Eros and Psyche*** in 1885, and before the end of the decade some half-dozen plays.

Prometheus must have been conceived and in part written in the previous year; for that exultant ode, **'O my vague desires'**, which had come first in the lyrical volume of 1880, was clearly written for its place in *Prometheus,* and voices the inspiration of the one book no less than of the other. The 'heavenly flame' which *Prometheus* brought for the comfort of man was no mere alleviation of physical distress: it betokens the emancipation of his whole being from that crushing tyranny of circumstance which checks the soul's flight:

> My heart, my heart is freed.
> Now can I sing: I loose a shaft from my bow,
> A song from my heart to heaven, and watch it speed.
> It revels in the air, and straight to its goal doth go.

If *Prometheus* can thus be associated in spirit with the third volume of lyrics, as clearly does ***Eros and Psyche*** breathe the atmosphere of the fourth. That 'loveliest vision far of all Olympus' faded hierarchy' , which shadows forth the fortunes of the soul in her quest for love, and the glad issue of their union in the birth to Psyche of a daughter Hedone,

> whom in our noble English Joy we call,

had a significance to Bridges that I need not labour. Nor did Bridges labour it. Telling the story for its own sweet sake, he is content to follow the original prose version of Apuleius, but, as he justly says, with a gentler handling of motive and a substitution of Hellenic feeling for Latin vulgarity. There is no more delightful long narrative poem in our language. Morris had included the tale of Psyche in his *Earthly Paradise;* but Morris's rendering, fine as it is, seems heavy and mannered beside the swift movement and exquisite grace of Bridges. The metre he uses is his own development from the rhyme royal, and he handles it through all its 365 stanzas with a delicacy and lightness that never fails. The natural ease with which the poem flows on its course seems all the more remarkable when we note its elaborately careful structure, with its division into twelve books apportioned to the twelve months of the year, and one stanza allotted to each day of the month. Yet his story fits into the scheme as though no other had been possible. If the young Keats could rejoice in the story of Psyche as a 'blessing melodiously given' him by the sententious Mrs. Tighe, we can well imagine with what ecstasy he would have 'ramped' through Bridges's poem. For another such narrative as the***Eros and Psyche*** one would gladly sacrifice some of the dramas. For Bridges had little of the dramatic gift, and though all his plays have a high distinction of style and diction, in them alone he fell below himself. But without dramatic genius a poet may excel in the masque, if only he have the lyric and narrative gifts, a true sense of decorative design, and an instinctive sympathy with the spirit of the 'lovely mythology of Greece'. Here, indeed, Bridges was at home, and in *Achilles in Scyros* and still more in his later masque *Demeter* he achieves a beauty which only *Comus* has surpassed. And to *Demeter* indeed, one might apply not inaptly the words in which Wootton praised *Comus:* 'wherein I should much commend the tragical part, if the lyrical did not ravish me with a certain Doric delicacy in your songs and odes: *ipsa mollities'.*

It is on his lyrics, along with***Eros and Psyche*** and ***The Testament of Beauty***, that Bridges's fame rests secure. Other lyrists may have reached greater imaginative heights, or struck a more ardent note of passion: none has produced a large body of verse more varied in music and design and yet so faultless in taste and workmanship. There is nothing freakish or mannered about his language; in poetry as in music Bridges 'loved the purer style', and his diction has the limpidity and ease of the best classical writing. In their form, too, and their melody they are in the line of that great tradition, to which, as he thought, his contemporaries had shown too scant respect. 'At the present', he wrote in the preface to his first volume, 'men seem to affect to have outgrown the rules of art'; such merit as his own poems mihgt possess he attributed to the fact the he 'turned to the great masters, and attempted to work in their manner'. It was probably his love for old music that led him for many of his models to that purest period of English song, when 'music and sweet poesy agreed, as sister with the brother'. The delicately cadenced Elizabethan and Carolingian rhythms he has made his own:

> Haste on, my joys! your treasure lies
> In swift, unceasing flight.
> O haste: for while your beauty flies
> I seize your full delight:

this might have been set to an air by Dowland, or Byrd, or Campion. In others, such as **'O Love, my muse'**, or **'Love on my heart from heaven fell,'** or **'Vivamus,'** he has caught the triumphant lilt of the seventeenth century. Like so many of his great predecessors, Milton, Shelley, Keats, he sat early at the feet of Spenser, that master of dreamy processional music:

> Let the priests go before, arrayed in white,
> And let the dark-stoled minstrels follow slow,
> Next they that bear her, honoured on this night,
> And then the maidens, in a double row,
> Each singing soft and low,
> And each on high a torch upstaying:
> Unto her lover lead her forth with light,
> With music, and with singing, and with praying.

In the sonnets there is often an unmistakable echo of Shakespeare:

> They that in play can do the thing they would,
> Having an instinct throned in reason's place,—
> And every perfect action hath the grace
> Of indolence or thoughtless hardihood—
> These are the best:

at times there is a touch of Milton:

Is old forgot? or do ye count for nought
What the Greek did and what the Florentine?

and the debt to Milton, though seldom more than an undercurrent in his verse, grew in depth and strength as Bridges developed his own individual harmonies. His music does not hark back only to the sixteenth and seventeenth centuries. In that late elegy **'Recollections of Solitude'**, as he calls to mind his own early love for Keats, his impassioned address to the muse recalls the tones in which Keats in *Endymion* had invoked his beloved moon-goddess:

O mighty Muse, wooer of virgin thought,
Beside thy charm all else counteth as nought;
The revelation of thy smile doth make
Him whom thou lovest reckless for thy sake;
Earthborn of suffering, thou knowest well
To call thine own, and with enamouring spell
Feedest the stolen powers of godlike youth
On dear imagination's only truth,

. . . . .

The only enchantress of the earth that art
To cheer his day and staunch man's bleeding heart.

In all this there is no imitation: the singing robes of his great forebears have fallen to him as his lawful heritage, and he wears them with a dignity and grace that is his own.

Yet though Bridges could often thus express himself within the limits of the great tradition, he loved, almost from the first, to explore the possibilities of new rhythms, whenever the subtleties of his own thought and feeling called for a more individual music.

The rhythmical beauty of verse lies in its subtle variation from a strict metrical basis, in its avoidance, by the shifting or resolution of its normal stresses, of a regularity which would soon become intolerably monotonous. Its aim is thus to achieve the greatest elasticity of movement compatible with a strict sense of form. The art of the poet consists in his power to do this, and to do it in such a way as to create a music not only beautiful in itself, but peculiarly expressive of the emotion he has to convey, just as the musical composer may take a melody and express his moods in the variations he plays upon it. But the poet's difficulty is greater than the musician's, in that the syllables of his words, which are the equivalent in poetry of the musician's notes, are not mere notes in a scale, but are essential parts of the intellectual symbols which convey his thought. In the desire to develop as far as possible this affinity of the music of verse to its intellectual and emotional content, Gerard Manley Hopkins, an Oxford friend of Bridges, started, about the year 1877, on a series of experiments in what he called counterpointed rhythms, and in the imposition of onerhythm upon another. Bridges, for all his deep-rooted sense of tradition, saw his art as a living thing with infinite capacity for growth, and he followed these experiments with an eager interest. Hopkins aimed, said Bridges, 'at an unattainable perfection, as if words, each with its two-fold value in sense and sound, could be arranged like so many gems, so as to compose a whole expression of thought in which the force of grammar and the beauty of rhythm absolutely correspond.' But like many another pioneer, Hopkins had not patience or judgment equal to his adventurous spirit. By eccentricity and extravagance he wrecked both his meaning and his music. His rhythmical variations are often so bold that his whole metrical scheme is lost in chaos; more often still, in forcing his language to fit his rhythmical purpose, his meaning becomes impenetrably obscure. Intermittent flashes of real beauty light up his poetry, but it lacks that lucidity and perfect sense of form which the true lyric demands. Yet it was, undoubtedly, the admiring but critical study of Hopkins's brilliant, wayward verse that gave Bridges the initial stimulus towards metrical adventure; and where Hopkins failed, he, with his finer ear and infallible taste, achieved some of his most signal successes.

The first triumphant example of his variation of rhythm to suggest the dominant emotion is to be found in an early sonnet. The effect of occasional anapaests to give lightness to lines whose predominant movement is iambic, was, of course, no new discovery. So Florizel to Perdita:

when you do dance, I wish you
A wave o' the sea, that you might ever do
Nothing but that.

Bridges carries this suggestion to its farthest limits, and by the introduction of anapaests in the proportion of one in four into an iambic groundwork gives to his poem the soaring flight of a bird:

I would be a bird, and straight on wings I arise,
And carry purpose up to the ends of the air:
In calm and storm my sails I feather, and where
By freezing cliffs the unransom'd wreckage lies:
Or, strutting on hot meridian banks, surprise
The silence: over plains in the moonlight bare
I chase my shadow, and perch where no bird dare
In tree-tops torn by fiercest winds of the skies.
Póor símple bírds, fóolish bírds! then I crý,
Ye pretty pictures of delight, unstir'd
By the only joy of *knowing* that ye fly;
Ye are nót what ye are, but rather, sum'd in a word,
The alphabet of a God's idea, and *I*
Who master it, *I* am the only bird.

In his later poetry Bridges developed, with even greater skill and subtlety, this correspondence of rhythmical suggestion with sense. But rhythm cannot be isolated from other metrical values. To a fundamental sense of rhythm the true artist must add a nice feeling for the musical quality of separate vowels and consonants and of their combinations, for alliteration, assonance and rhyme, and for the infinitely variable quantity of different syllables; and he must have the gift of subordinating such technical minutiae to one emotional purpose. In all this Bridges was a master. It would be hard to rival the exquisite effect with which in this perfect lyric internal rhymes are introduced, and the various vowel sounds manipulated:

Wanton with long delay the gay spring leaping cometh;
The blackthorn starreth now his bough on the eve of May:
All day in the sweet box-tree the bee for pleasure hummeth:
The cuckoo sends afloat his note on the air all day.
Now dewy nights again and rain in gentle shower
At root of tree and flower have quenched the winter's drouth:
On high the hot sun smiles, and banks of cloud uptower
In bulging heads that crowd for miles the dazzling south.

Browning, too, a master of facile rhyming, loved to introduce quickly recurrent internal rhymes, but their effect on his verse has been justly, if somewhat profanely, compared to a hiccough. In Bridges they add a tender sweetness to the melody. Swinburne was a master of all metrical devices, but he so rioted in his own facility that he never knew when to stop; and as a consequence, what delights us for a stanza or two becomes, before his poem is out, a merely tedious *tour de force*. In Bridges there is always a consummate control of the material; there is never a line too much, nor a note that cloys. Thus you will have observed in this lyric that the same scheme of internal rhyming is not carried uniformly through the poem. After its regular recurrence in the first five lines there comes a change, and in the last three, extra rhymes are still thrown in, but upon another plan, the middle of the sixth line echoing the end-rhyme of the fifth and seventh, whilst the seventh and eighth lines are given the cross rhymes—smiles cloud, crowd miles. This is the finest artistry; but it is not merely artistry—it is expression: it is like the spirit of April set to its own enchanting tune.

In his poems of nature Bridges brought to perfection his characteristic beauties of rhythm and melody. The 'landscape lure of rural England' was irresistible to him. He is among the finest poet-painters of our lovely varied countryside, making it live to the eye by his exact images and at the same time to our emotions by his delicately modulated music. How inevitably, in these two stanzas, is the contrast felt between the moods evoked by the melancholy English Channel as he knew it at the home of his childhood, and by the river which haunted his dreams at Eton and at Oxford.

I stand on the cliff and watch the veiled sun paling
A silver field afar in the mournful sea,
The scourge of the surf, and plaintive gulls sailing
At ease on the gale that smites the shuddering lea:
Whose smile severe and chaste
June never hath stirred to vanity, nor age defaced.
In lofty thought strive, O spirit, for ever:
In courage and strength pursue thine own endeavour.

. . . . .

But far away, I think, in the Thames valley,
The silent river glides by flowery banks:
And birds sing sweetly in branches that arch an alley
Of cloistered trees, moss-grown in their ancient ranks:
Where if a light air stray,
'Tis laden with hum of bees and scent of may.
Love and peace be thine, O spirit, for ever:
Serve thy sweet desire: despise endeavour.

A still finer example of musical invention is his rendering of the spirit of the wide wind-swept downs, achieved by a deft use of rhythms of his own devising, enforced by subtle melodic effects of vowel and consonant, such as the reiteration of the broad *o* sound at the beginning of the poem:

O bold majestic downs, smooth, fair and lonely;
O still solitude, only matched in the skies:
Perilous in steep places,
Soft in the level races,
Where sweeping in phantom silence the cloudland flies;
With lovely undulation of fall and rise;
Entrenched with thickets thorned,
By delicate miniature dainty flowers adorned!

Perhaps the masterpiece in this kind is **'London Snow'**. The whole landscape is painted in language which might have been chosen simply for its exact portrayal of the scene to the mind's eye, yet it has throughout a haunting music which, as exactly, conveys the emotional atmosphere. The slow movement of the verse, with its double endings and reiterated present participles, renders unerringly the slow, ceaseless, wavering fall of heavy snowflakes, whilst everywhere the poet fits rhythm and melody to the thought and feeling of the moment, whether he is recalling the silence, the mystery, or the muffled sounds; the fresh excited delight of the schoolboy, or the more sober joy that lifts the jaded toiler above his cares, to drink in the strange beauty that is about him:

When men were all asleep the snow came flying,
In large white flakes falling on the city brown,
Stealthily and perpetually settling and loosely lying,
Hushing the latest traffic of the drowsy town;
Deadening, muffling, stifling its murmurs failing;
Lazily and incessantly floating down and down:
Silently sifting and veiling road, roof and railing;
Hiding difference, making unevenness even,
Into angles and crevices softly drifting and sailing.
All night it fell, and when full inches seven
It lay in the depth of its uncompacted lightness,
The clouds blew off from a high and frosty heaven;
And all woke earlier for the unaccustomed brightness
Of the winter dawning, the strange unheavenly glare:
The eye marvelled—marvelled at the dazzling whiteness;
The ear hearkened to the stillness of the solemn air;
No sound of wheel rumbling nor of foot falling,
And the busy morning cries came thin and spare.
Then boys I heard, as they went to school, calling,
They gathered up the crystal manna to freeze
Their tongues with tasting, their hands with snowballing;
Or rioted in a drift, plunging up to the knees;
Or peering up from under the white-mossed wonder,

'O look at the trees!' they cried, 'O look at the trees!'
With lessened load a few carts creak and blunder,
Following along the white deserted way,
A country company long dispersed asunder:
When now already the sun, in pale display
Standing by Paul's high dome, spread forth below
His sparkling beams, and awoke the stir of the day.
For now doors open, and war is waged with the snow;
And trains of sombre men, past tale of number,
Tread long brown paths, as toward their toil they go:
But even for them awhile no cares encumber
Their minds diverted; the daily word is unspoken,
The daily thoughts of labour and sorrow slumber
At the sight of the beauty that greets them, for the charm they
have broken.

It is worth noting that one of the happiest effects in the poem, the break in the rhythm to express the school-boys' delight, was clearly suggested by a line from Hopkins—'Look at the stars! Look, look up at the skies!'

It was inevitable that Bridges, who in such verses had added new rhythms to English poetry, should wish to discover how far the prosody of those Greeks, whom he loved so deeply, could be applied to our verse; and under the influence of his friend Stone he spent some years in the attempt to naturalize the classical hexameter and pentameter. This attempt was, perhaps, his only metrical failure, and it had, I believe, a really unfortunate effect on his reputation. For it has led a large public, ignoring both his former triumphs and his latest developments, to speak of him as though he were a metrical crank rather than a true poet with the lively and proper interest of an artist in his art. To me these experiments are proof enough that the hexameter, as a medium for wholly serious thought and feeling, is not suited to the English tongue, for where Bridges failed who will succeed? In our language the accent is fixed by our natural speech, whilst quantity, though some syllables are clearly short and others as clearly long, is as a whole infinitely variable: hence, in our verse, accent must always take precedence of quantity. The hexameter and pentameter, on the other hand, are essentially metres in which quantity takes precedence of accent; with the result that in English you only get the true feeling of the hexameter when accent and quantity coincide. Now though one or two such lines may produce a pleasing effect, a succession of them produces a rhythm so marked as to become a monotonous sing-song; whereas in lines in which accent and quantity fall apart, the result is either a loss of rhythm altogether, or the substitution of another rhythm which bears no relation with the normal line, so that the rhythmical structure falls to pieces. The infallible test of good verse is to read it without thinking of its rhythm, simply with the object of giving the fullest force to its meaning. If it is good verse the rhythm will take care of itself, and the better you read it with a view to the sense, the more beautiful will be the rhythmical effect. Everywhere is this true, say, of Shakespeare or of Milton, everywhere of Bridges, except in his hexameters and pentameters. In these, if you read to bring out the metre you have often to violate not only the meaning but even the natural English accentuation; if you read for the meaning you often lose all sense of the metre, and though the line may have a beautiful rhythm of its own it is not the rhythm which we expect and which he has aimed at producing.

But if he was unsuccessful with the hexameter and pentameter, in certain of the more lyrical Greek measures he combined accent and quantity with entrancing effect. For sheer melody it would be hard to excel the song of the oceanides in *Demeter*:

Gay and lovely is earth, man's decorate dwelling;
With fresh beauty ever varying hour to hour;

and only a little less delightful is the ode in the last act,

O that the earth, or only this fair isle wer' ours.

In his later years Bridges gave up direct classical experiment, a proof that he was dissatisfied with the result, and turning back for metrical inspiration to Milton, greatest of all English metrists, evolved that lovely measure which will always be associated with his name—a measure not perhaps primarily lyrical, though capable of voicing the choicest lyrical feeling. But if Milton was here his master, no one can read ***The Testament of Beauty*** and earlier poems written in the same metre, without realizing that some of the many rhythms that find a home in it owe their presence to what Bridges had learnt from his experiments in classical prosody:

Thus ever at every season in every hour and place
visions await the soul on wide ocean or shore
mountain forest or garden in wind and floating cloud
in busy murmur of bees or blithe carol of birds:
nor is it memoried thought only nor pleasured sense
that holds us, nor whate'er Reason sits puzzling out
of light or atom, as if—say, the Rainbow's beauty
lay in our skill to fray the Sun's white-tissued ray
to unravel and measure off the gaudy threads thereof:
It is a deeper thrill, the joy that lovers learn
taking divine instruction from each other's eyes,
the Truth that all men feel gazing upon the skies
in constellated night—O God the Father of Heaven!
'when I arose and saw the dawn, I sighed for thee'.

And what is the content of these lyrics? They are, at their best, simply a record of the richest moments of one to whom life, no less than poetry, was a fine art. When they stray from his intimate experience they are seldom happy. Bridges's one attempt at the idyll of humble life is as feeble as any of Tennyson's, his few incursions into the weird or the romantic are hardly more successful. He had little of that dramatic sympathy which enables a man to project himself into moods and conditions of life other than his own. Still less is he one of those world-poets who descend into the arena of blood and tears and snatch a victory for their mistress Beauty out of the agony of human conflict, or draw inspiration even from the chaffering of the market place. Browning, for all his idealism, found

Somehow the proper goal for wisdom was the ground
And not the sky—so slid sagaciously betimes

> Down heaven's baluster ropes, to reach the mob of mimes
> And mummers:

Bridges slid down no baluster ropes; his graceful, retired muse

> will not leave her love
> to mix with men: her art
> is all to strive above
> the crowd, or stand apart;

and though he, too, sought wisdom on the ground of solid earth, for there is nothing of 'the ineffectual angel' about him, it was on a plot of his own careful choosing, where he could 'build a heaven in hell's despite'. This limitation of his range he frankly admits. To those masters of song whose flight is more daring than his own he has paid glowing tribute:

> Thrice happy he the rare
> Prometheus, who can play
> With hidden things, and lay
> New realms of nature bare;
> Whose venturous step has trod
> Hell underfoot, and won
> A crown from man and God
> For all that he has done.

To this, the highest gift of all, he lays no claims, but he is 'content, denied the best, in choosing right'. He 'will be what God made' him, the ardent votary of beauty, the perfect revealer of English landscape in her most delicate moods, as he has felt them, of human love as he has known it, at its rarest and most refined, of the sober joys of wrapt contemplation.

His poems of love are eminently characteristic of his art. By reason alike of depth and sincerity of feeling and of flawless execution he is among the finest of our love poets; but here again his range is strictly confined. There is nothing in him of the cross currents of love, of impossible longings, of tragic despair, of the pangs of mad desire, 'enjoyed no sooner but despised straight'. The physical basis of all love is not slighted, but the love he pictures is not Eros, the merely physical, with his soft unchristened smile, and with his

> shameless will and power immense,
> In secret sensuous innocence.

How is it, he asks Eros, that for all your beauty of limb your face is wholly expressionless, so that none cares to look upon it? The countenance into which he loves to gaze reflects the mind and heart; it is at once 'a mark and a lodestar'. A more perfect sequence of lyrics hymning the course of a true love that runs smooth could nowhere be found than in Bridges's shorter poems. They range from early trifles wherein the young man, fancy-free, sports with an emotion he has not yet experienced, through **'Wooing'**, where first the emotion has become serious, to the bright dawn of passion in **'Awake, my heart, to be loved'**, and to love's triumphant fulfilment in **'O my joy'**; and so, through many a poem which marks an anniversary, or some special stage in love's progress, such as that exquisite mature reflection upon the days of early love:

> His little spring, that sweet we found,
> So deep in summer floods is drowned,
> I wonder, bathed in joy complete,
> How love so young could be so sweet;

on to **'Vivamus'**:

> When thou didst give thy love to me,
> Asking no more of gods or men
> I vow'd I would contented be,
> If Fate should grant us summers ten.
> But now that twice the term is sped,
> And ever young my heart and gay,
> I fear the words that then I said,
> And turn my face from Fate away.
> To bid thee happily good-bye
> I have no hope that I can see,
> No way that I shall bravely die,
> Unless I give my life for thee.

And from **'Vivamus'** it is but a step to that last spiritual **'Vision'** when, at the close of more than forty years, he finds that

> time has cleared
> Not dulled my loving: I can see
> Love's passing ecstacies endeared
> In aspects of Eternity.

The poems of Bridges have been criticized as lacking passion, and if by passion is meant uncontrolled excitement, the charge is just enough. But 'the gods approve the depth and not the tumult of the soul', and among the gods is Apollo, the god of song. The love which Bridges hymns is that

> Whereby the lips in wonder reconcile
> Passion with peace, and show desire at rest.

And this is, on the whole, typical of his attitude to life. Clear vision seemed to him to call for calm. There is nothing revolutionary about him; the noisy and the blustering repel him: beauty to him lies in order and discipline. In life, as in his art, he is the true aristocrat. He knew that moral sanity, though it may not inspire poetry, is yet an indispensable element in it. In an age which, revolting from the complacent righteousness of the Victorian, affected to extol incontinent freedom, he pays tribute to the 'duteous heart'. But convinced no less than Wordsworth that it is by the deep power of joy that we see into the life of things, he conceives of joy itself as a duty, no less than of duty as a joy. To experience this joy is to fulfil our destiny; to reveal it is the prime glory of the artist. Bridges is not blind to the darker elements in life, and in his poem **'Nightingales'** has re-echoed, in music as immortal as Shelley's, the cry that 'our sweetest songs are those that tell of saddest thought'; yet, he holds that the very act of turning sorrow into song is itself an act of joy, and hence that the true artist must perforce know happiness.

Bridges is the aristocrat also in his lofty gift of selection. He is the victim of no optimistic delusions. He has studied nature and human life too closely not to admit their 'mean ugly brutish obscene clumsy irrelevances'; but man, the highest product of nature, is endowed with consciousness and judgment, and of what good is judgement if it does not choose the best? Nowadays, it seems, to revel in the ugly is accounted to a man for strength and realism. But beauty is as real as ugliness, and to Bridges more noteworthy. And so, where he 'holds up the mirror to Nature, She, seeing her face therein, shall not be ashamed'. And of his own moods those which he chiefly delights to celebrate are the most worthy, i.e. the happiest. Only seldom does his song re-echo the plangent notes of his **'Nightingales'**; he is for the most part content to lead, in accents of a hardly less piercing sweetness, 'the innumerable choir of day', who 'welcome the dawn'. He is essentially the poet of joy, rather than of sorrow, of attainment rather than of unsatisfied longing. He has himself, indeed, felt the growing-pains of melancholy, but he declines to make easy poetic capital out of them. That *Dejection* which is, after all, a mere dip in the buoyant flight of youth, he sees in its true perspective:

> Wherefore to-night so full of care,
> My soul, revolving hopeless strife,
> Pointing at hindrance, and the bare
> Painful escapes of fitful life?
>
> . . . . .
>
> O soul, be patient: thou shalt find
> A little matter mend all this;
> Some strain of music to thy mind,
> Some praise for skill not spent amiss.

He has known too that deeper self-wrought distress of manhood, to which of all men the poet, with his high hopes and keen sensibilities, is most subject; but this he repudiates as a form of morbid egoism, a denial of his whole creed:

> Fool, thou that hast impossibly desired
> And now impatiently despairest, see
> How nought is changed; Joy's wisdom is attired
> Splendid for others' eyes if not for thee:
> Not love or beauty or youth from earth is fled:
> If they delite thee not, 'tis thou art dead.

'Not love or beauty or youth from earth is fled'; in the poetry of Robert Bridges they find immortal voice. And we in this place can hardly forget how increasingly throughout his life he sought and found them in Oxford:

> The lovely city, thronging tower and spire,
> The mind of the wide landscape, dreaming deep,
> Grey-silvery in the vale; a shrine where keep
> Memorial hopes their pale celestial fire:
> Like man's immortal conscience of desire,
> The spirit that watcheth in me ev'n in my sleep.

He is in a special sense Oxford's poet, both in what he owed her and what, so richly, he repaid. None better than he has expressed the quiet charm of her countryside, none has distilled into a finer fragrance her essential spirit. And like a true son, the praise he most coveted was that which might fall from the lips of those who acknowledge the same loving allegiance. In one of his sonnets, addressing his own poems, he asks them, in the humility of genius, how they can ever hope to win a general welcome, and then he adds:

> Should others ask you this, say then I yearn'd
> To write you such as once, when I was young,
> Finding I should have loved and thereto turn'd.
> 'Twere something yet to live again among
> The gentle youth beloved, and where I learn'd
> My art, be there remember'd for my song.

May we not affirm, to-day, that that 'something' has been granted him?

Notes

1. Robert Bridges's incapacity to warm to Browning's poetry was lifelong, as the following incident, reported to me by Dr. F. Madan, puts beyond all doubt. 'A few weeks after the publication of *The Spirit of Man,* an anthology, I happened to meet him just between the South Gate of the Bodleian Quadrangle and the North Gate of the Radcliffe Camera enclosure, and ventured to ask him why he had not included a single line of Browning in his book. He replied that several friends had been "at him" about it, and some had pressed him at least to include *Rabbi Ben Ezra,* if nothing else. To account for his refusal he told me that it always seemed to him that one line was wanting in most of his poems, namely

   "With one hand slap his thigh, with one *pat God*".'

Joseph Warren Beach (essay date 1936)

SOURCE: "Victorian Afterglow," in his *The Concept of Nature in Nineteenth-Century English Poetry,* Macmillan Company, 1936 (and reprinted by Pageant Book Company, 1956), pp. 522-46.

[*In the following excerpt, Beach observes that Bridges's poetry reflects his training as a physician as well as his conservative Victorian background.*]

It is Robert Bridges who has the most to say of nature, and who, most persistently, develops the Meredithian view of the evolution of man's spiritual life out of natural instinct itself. Bridges was a trained physician; his philosophical poems are full of scientific lore; they are written with a mild, genial idiosyncrasy of thought and expression which makes them highly interesting reading. But these ***Poems in Classical Prosody*** and ***The Testament of Beauty*** (likewise in classical metres)—in which his theories are mainly developed—are poetry in form only—and that outlandish and irritating; the complacent Toryism of his sentiment given him in our day a curiously antediluvian air; and—what is more important for our purpose—he has failed to make a more than plausible synthesis of his evolutionary positivism and his religious-platonic cult of Eternal Essences.

As for his evolutionary positivism, this is displayed at length in the first and second of the ***Poems in Classical Prosody.*** The main problem here is to reconcile the goodness of nature with man's adverse judgments on her; and his argument might seem like an answer to Hardy's in "The Mother Mourns." The point is, simply, that man's moral ideal, by virtue of which he condemns so much in nature, is itself born of her and to be credited to her; it is a result of the process of natural selection.

And I see man's discontent as witness asserting
His moral ideal, that, born of Nature, is heir to
Her children's titles, which nought may cancel or impugn;
Not wer' of all her works man least, but ranking among them
Highly or ev'n as best, he wrongs himself to imagine
His soul foe to her aim, or from her sanction an outlaw.[1]

. . . . .

My parable may serve. What wisdom man hath attain'd to
Came to him of Nature's goodwill throu' tardy selection:
Should her teaching accuse herself and her method impugn,
I may share with her the reproach of approving as artist
Far other ideals than what seem needful in action.[2]

More explicit in its reference to the means by which man's higher nature has been developed is **"To Robert Burns"** in ***Later Poems.*** Here Bridges states more clearly than Wordsworth the doctrine of the ministry of pleasure.

For Nature did not idly spend
Pleasure: she ruled it should attend
On every act that doth amend
Our life's condition:
'Tis therefore not well-being's end,
But its fruition.

Pleasures attend the fulfilment of instinct, and Bridges tells us quite categorically what the instincts are, and which one of them has most conduced to the development of the soul in man.

But Instinct in the beasts that live
Is of three kinds; (Nature did give
To man three shakings in her sieve)—
The first is Racial,
The second Self-preservative,
The third is Social.
Without the first no race could be,
So 'tis the strongest of the three;
Nay, of such forceful tyranny
'Tis hard to attune it,
Because 'twas never made to agree
To serve the unit.
Art will not picture it, its name
In common talk is utter shame:
And yet hath Reason learn'd to tame
Its conflagration
Into a sacramental flame
Of consecration.
Those hundred thousand years, ah me!
Of budding soul! What slow degree,
With aim so dim, so true! We see,
Now that we know them,
Our humble cave-folk ancestry,
How much we owe them

The reader can fancy how the Victorian poet applies the moral to Robert Burns, and with what graceful openmindedness he pronounces on the erring Scotch poet his "friendly sentence."

But it is not till **"The Testament of Love"** (1929) that Bridges formally attacks his problem on all fronts; and his argument comes with a strange effect of archaism in the age of Aldous Huxley and T. S. Eliot. Since Mr. Bridges left express instructions that the reproduction of extracts from this poem was not to be allowed, the best I can do is to give a bald abstract of his discussion. In his introduction he declares, like any Romantic, his faith in the order of nature and its goodness. He has no hesitation in ascribing purpose to nature like a seventeenth-century theologian. He then proceeds to state, with all the vigor of a Meredith, and with far more detail of specification, that all man's higher faculties and intellectual constructions—emotion, imagination, ethics, art, the logic of science, philosophical dialectic, mathematics—have been evolved from inanimate nature. Even man's independent will cannot "separate him off from the impercipient." And conscience is "a natural flower-bud on its vigorous plant specialized to a function."

The second book treats of "selfhood,"—which corresponds to the Self-preservative Instinct of the Burns poem. In this book, which is otherwise largely devoted to a defense of war as based in natural instinct and full of benefits to the spirit, Bridges shows how the self-preservative impulse gives rise to parental instinct, which is the main root of man's "purest affection and of all compassion." In the third book he takes up "Breed," which corresponds to the dominant Racial Instinct. This he regards as, even more than Selfhood, the root of man's spiritual life.

In the fourth book, entitled "Ethick," Bridges traces moral obligation in man back to the "determin'd habit of electrons," with which it is essentially identical, except that in man Necessity has become "conscient." He considers how the positive Ought of lower orders of nature is transformed into the Ought Not of man's moral code, by which at times he is obliged to "oppose the bidding of instinct." He shows that religion and duty are one, and that consequently the compulsions of necessity lead by natural stages to identification of self with God.

Thus Bridges arrives, in the end, at a kind of mystical platonic deism suggestive of some of the eighteenth-century nature-poets. There is often a vagueness in his definitions that enables him to pass so airily from the natural to the spiritual. This is felt particularly in his rather confused concept of beauty, which in man becomes spiritualized, "as in its primal essence it must be conceived." One feels that it is the force of his religious sentiment that makes him wish to graft on to Meredith's genetic, positivistic and utilitarian account of the spirit, the platonic notion of Eternal Essences. These platonic essences he makes equivalent, in the popular manner, with "ideas"; and such "innate" ideas are hard to reconcile with evolutionism.

In the second book, he definitely adopts the platonic system, which he interprets in the modern "idealistic" way as implying that "all existence is expression of Mind." Plato's doctrine, he says, flourishes proudly in the schools because "the absurdity of indefinable forms is less than the denial of existence to thought." He thinks it necessary, however, to find a more unassailable term to take the place of the platonic Ideas, and in so doing introduces a vicious ambiguity into his thought. These Ideas he renames Influences; they are "supreme efficient causes of the thoughts of men." Of all these "occult influences" the most important and fundamental is Beauty, which leads man straight to the wisdom of God.

It is a far cry from a natural influence, which may be observed and studied in action, to an eternal Essence, an abstract entity little subject to empirical control, of the sort that flourishes so rankly in the garden of poetical theology. Something might have been done with a definition of beauty based in observable pleasure and pain; this might have been carried over with some plausibility, in the utilitarian manner, into the realm of social life and social morality. But Bridges abandoned too readily the fruitful concept of pleasure to soar on the filmy wings of an elusive and obliging beauty. It is thus that his scientific intentions were betrayed by the loyalty he felt he owed to poetry.

Notes

1. Robert Bridges, *Poems in Classical Prosody,* Epistle I, lines 212-217. Quoted, by kind permission of the publishers, from *The Poetical Works of Robert Bridges,* Oxford University Press, 1912.
2. *Ibid.,* Epistle II, 418-422. This, and the following passage from "To Robert Burns", quoted, by kind permission of the Oxford University Press, from *The Poetical Works of Robert Bridges.*

Cornelius Weygandt (essay date 1937)

SOURCE: "The Old Main Line," in his *The Time of Yeats: English Poetry of To-Day Against an American Background,* D. Appleton-Century Company, Inc., 1937 (and reissued by Russell & Russell, 1969), pp. 67-120.

[*In the following excerpt, Weygandt describes Bridges as a talented but nevertheless minor poet whose works can best be understood and appreciated after four or more readings.*]

There has never been any general acceptance of Robert Bridges (1844-1930) by the reading public. That is a lot which has fallen to few poets. There has not been even any large acceptance of him by that smaller reading public which cares for poetry. That is a lot which has fallen to fellows of his no better poets, but of less severe and bare a style. Bridges was made laureate at the wish of the poets of England, a large number of whom felt that he was the man for the place. Those of the public who were at all interested, whether in England or America or the Colonies, were willing to agree that the poets should know, that since such men as Yeats and Newbolt, Stephen Phillips and Binyon, had said that Bridges was the proper choice, that he was the proper choice.

Certainly Bridges looked the part. Certainly he had the dignity and position and traditions that made him a worthy representative of the English poets of his time. Certainly he had been an influence, technically, on many of the younger generation of poets. Certainly he had written in all the accredited forms of English poetry, and always worthily. And, certainly, he had to his credit an accomplishment in lyric poetry, narrow in range, but of impeccable artistry, and of a new beauty. No one else had caught just those aspects of English countryside and English life that are to be found in **"There is a hill beside the silver Thames," "Spring goeth all in white," "The Winnowers," "Nightingales," "The South Wind,"** and the two odes to spring, **"Invitation to the Country"** and **"Reply."**

These best poems of Bridges do not yield all that is in them on first acquaintance. There is, indeed, little of his writing that does. Nor is he to be appreciated on a second reading, or on a third. It requires rereading after rereading, in different moods, and at intervals, before his full significance makes itself apparent. He had no way with him, no irresistible felicities, no sudden bursts of music. He, himself, knew well his limitations, and he was candid in owning them. He confessed to "sluggish blood," that to him was denied "the best," that his "sense" was "hard," his style "so worn and bare." And yet he knew, as every true poet knows, that there was worth in what he had written.

Bridges was born on the Isle of Thanet, close by the meeting place of the great estuary of the Thames and the Channel. It was, he says, on

> a stony, breaking beach
> My childhood chanced and chose to be.

He knew sea and shore, inheriting with this knowledge that interest in ships that has been part of the Englishman from Anglo-Saxon times. He went the usual way of boys of his class, to Eton, further up the Thames, and then to Oxford, where the Thames is a little river indeed. The Thames was more to him, I think, than the sea, though the sea was much to him. It is the sight of the sea over the downs that lends spaciousness to **"The Downs."** It is the roar of the sea, reproduced in its sonorous rhythms, that gives such distinction to **"The Voice of Nature."** The sea is in **"The Cliff-Top," "A Poppy," "A Passer-By,"** and in a score poems else, but it can hardly, in the nature of things, be made an intimate in the close and familiar way a river can.

"Elegy," that takes place as the first poem of his ***Shorter Poems*** (1890), is inspired by the Thames. The river is named and described in loving detail in **"There is a hill beside the silver Thames."** This poem is a very symbol of southern England, a cross-section of the Thames valley. It catches the look and feel and atmosphere of this old, old countryside. So much of Bridges is, indeed, the picturing of the countryside of southern England that you would say to an outlander overseas who wished to know what rural England was like: "Read Robert Bridges and you will know. Read **'There is a hill beside the silver Thames.'** Read **'The Windmill.'** Read **'The Winnowers.'** Read **'The Garden in September.'** Read **'North Wind in October.'**"

And if you would know what the English code is, read **"Founders' Day. A Secular Ode on the Ninth Jubilee of Eton College"**:

> Now learn, love, have, do, be the best;
> Each in one thing excel the rest;
> Strive; and hold fast this truth of heaven—
> To him that hath shall more be given.

It is not often that Bridges is so forthright as this. Not that he would deceive anybody as to what he felt and believed about things, but that he was by nature reticent and restrained, and that he held it bad form for a gentleman to give himself away. Say a third of what you feel and believe about things, and leave it to the understanding of that other fellow, your reader, to multiply your statement into what its underlying feeling and thought would have it be. This is a dangerous practice for a poet. So many people expect poetry to be emotional, sentimental, romantic, extreme, that the poet who soft-pedals all he has to say is often hardly heard.

The best things in Bridges, too, are often hidden away. **"Eclogue I,"** for instance, that stands first in ***New Poems*** (1899), does not open very interestingly. Two old friends meet, literary fellows both, in Somerset, and reminisce. They exchange rhymes. You read along with a rather languid interest. You are off guard, and you may easily pass over the rare beauty of a passage like this:

> But if you have seen a village all red and old
> In cherry-orchards a-sprinkle with white and gold,
> By a hawthorn seated, or witchelm flowering high,
> A gay breeze making riot in the waving rye!

The picture you can hardly miss, but all is so quietly presented that you are not sufficiently quickened emotionally to realize to the full what color and movement there is in the passage. "A gay breeze making riot in the waving rye" is one of the most exactly descriptive lines in all English poetry. The irregularity of the accent pulls the line this way and that as the wind pulls a field of rye.

As you read "**There is a hill beside the silver Thames**," you expect it to continue to be what it starts out to be, a poem descriptive of landscape. You like its onset, stately for all its apparent simplicity. You like, more mildly, its second and third and fourth and fifth stanzas. Then, in the sixth stanza, you meet a human figure, a fisherman, who quickens your interest as the human figure always does. In the seventh stanza you meet a more memorable human:

> a slow figure 'neath the trees,
> In ancient-fashioned smock, with tottering care
> Upon a staff propping his weary knees.

If ever there was what George Moore calls "pure poetry" it is to be found in **"Spring goeth all in white."** Here is no moralizing, no comment of any kind by the poet, hardly any sense even of the personality of the poet. It is an almost completely objective poem, about hawthorne-time, which has never been better done:

> Spring goeth all in white,
> Crowned with milk-white may:
> In fleecy flocks of light
> O'er heaven the white clouds stray.

What a contrast this poem presents to the famous "Loveliest of trees the cherry now" of A. E. Housman! There is not so much of the spring, objectively, in the twelve lines of that poem as in the eight lines of Bridges, but how much more of the sharpness and sweetness of spring, how much more of youth and time and change. It is, perhaps, unjust to criticize a poem for not possessing what is outside of its intention, and there are poems of Bridges that have their own burden of the brevity of all good things. Yet it is fair to point out that Bridges lacks poignancy, that his poetry has been, most of it, by intention, a poetry without passion. By this I mean, not only without the passion of love, but without passionate feeling of any sort. What he lacks because of his "sluggish blood" is a real shortcoming to his poetry. That poetry has been, from the beginning, an old man's poetry. It is no less true poetry for this, but it is of a more restricted appeal because of this.

Years ago when I was reading Bridges I wondered if it might not be with my attitude toward him somewhat as it had been with my attitude in early life toward Milton. Milton had been a household book in the home of my youth. When my mother thought I was not being taught to "parse" properly in school she taught me to "parse," in her way, in *Paradise Lost*. To this day I know its opening lines as I know the opening lines of Cæsar's *Gallic Wars*. I had to study *Comus* as part of the required reading for admission to college, and it did not in those days become more to me than a thing I had to study. In college my teacher of literature was unsympathetic to Milton. At thirty, as a teacher of English literature, it became my duty to write college entrance examinations in English. I had to reread "Lycidas," "L'Allegro," and "Il Penseroso" to write questions on them. Even under such forbidding conditions the beauty of Milton could not escape me. The scales fell from my eyes. It was the bells at evening:

Swinging slow with sullen roar
Over some wide-watered shore

that began the loosening of the scales. From that day on I have been able to see for myself that Milton is the great poet all the English-speaking peoples declare him to be.

I thought, those years ago when I was reading Bridges and could not see him for more than a minor poet: "Perhaps the scales will suddenly fall from my eyes as they did when I was reading Milton, and I shall see Bridges as Binyon sees him, or Newbolt, or Yeats." I have to confess that the scales have not fallen. I can still see Bridges only as a minor poet.

You cannot say that Bridges, for all his predilection for the little things of the countryside, has wholly avoided great themes. He has retold the story of Psyche and Eros in narrative verse; he has written after the manner of Milton on Prometheus and Demeter; and he has attempted plays on Achilles, and Ulysses, and Nero. There is no bad work in ***Eros and Psyche*** (1885), *Prometheus the Firegiver* (1883), *Demeter* (1904), *Nero Part I* (1885), *Achilles in Scyros* (1890), *The Return of Ulysses* (1890), and *Nero Part II* (1894). Nor, save in *Nero Part I,* is there any writing which stands out against the sky. There are touches of tragic power here, too, closet drama though it is. "This play," he tells us, "was not intended for the stage, as the rest of my plays are." It is hard to believe that the rest of his plays were intended for the stage, for they are all just as untheatrical as the plays of Stephen Phillips, say, are theatrical. Phillips built up the third part of his *Ulysses* (1902) on his kinsman's *Return of Ulysses,* and one wonders if it was not the elder poet's handling of Nero that suggested him to the younger as material out of which he could make "good theater."

There are passages to mark in narrative, masques, and plays, but there are not passages that impress themselves, willy-nilly, on your memory, so that you can no more forget them than you can the names of your children. Yet that is the way of truly great passages, they will not out of mind, and even of passages of rhetorical effectiveness less than great.

Eros and Psyche has a suavity and ease of progression rather unusual in Bridges. The verse of most of his poems, good as much of it is, is apt to be a little stiff, as if it fell none too easily from his pen. One wonders why he did not try narrative oftener. There is **"Screaming Tarn,"** of course, good in a way, but conventional in make-up and tone. There is an approach to narrative, too, now and then, in the eclogues, but Bridges is, on the whole, a purely lyrical poet. You can dismiss all else than the lyrics, and you have left that by which he stands or falls.

The sonnet sequence, ***The Growth of Love*** (1889), is not a sequence in the sense that *Astrophel and Stella* or *Modern Love* is a sequence. It does not tell the story of a love, but records moments in the progress of a love, many of which have nothing to do with the feeling of the lover toward the lady of his choice. ***The Growth of Love*** is the first book of Bridges I owned. I bought it, in the Mosher reprint (1893), back in the nineties. That I have lived with it longest of my books of Bridges is why, perhaps, there are more marked passages in it than in any other of his books on my shelves. And yet that is not, I think, the only reason. There is more concern with his art in ***The Growth of Love*** than elsewhere in his writing, a subject on which he feels more strongly, perhaps, than on any other, and there is more speculation in it on the whys and wherefores of things than in any other of his poems.

In the very first sonnet there is an arresting four lines and a half:

They that in play can do the thing they would
Having an instinct throned in reason's place,
And every perfect action hath the grace
Of indolence or thoughtless hardihood—
These are the best.

There speaks the English amateur clearly and distinctly. Poet or sportsman, either one, would like us to believe that such is the way he attains, such is the origin of his "perfect actions." Bridges hardly puts himself among such "best." Indeed, he owns how hard he had to strive before he cast his chains, and became "Master of the art which for thy sake I serve." And yet one feels that he half-claims to attain both ways, by instinct, and by a hard-won and perfected art.

Bridges has said nothing more memorable than a half-dozen things he says here.

The very names of things belov'd are dear,
And sounds will gather beauty from their sense

we recognize as true from our own experience before we read on to his third line and find the concrete illustration that justifies his statement. In Sonnet 8 he lays down his credo about "beauty being the best of all we know." Again and again, in this sequence, and elsewhere, he repeats this belief, as again and again he returns to the expression of an aristocratic code of life. He likes:

an ancient house where state
From noble ancestry is handed on,

or any other like "relic of old splendour." He hates the "down-levelling of Socialism," and he frankly confesses his joy in the privilege that gives him:

My Japanese paintings, my fair blue Cheney, Hellenic
Statues and Caroline silver, my beautiful Aldines.

But I am running on beyond ***The Growth of Love***. Here Bridges tells us that "This world is unto God a work of art." Here he puts his feeling "So poor's the best that longest life can do." Here he laments "The perpetuity which all things lack." Here he writes down his realization of how lonely Adam was in Paradise "Before God of His pity fashion'd Eve." That is, I think, his greatest line, a line it is not an exaggeration to call Miltonic. If there were a hundred such in Bridges one might build up for him a claim to be a major poet.

There are not many "readings of life" in Bridges. There is, though, a definite philosophy that remained fairly constant through all the long years that he wrote. Like all men, he had in youth a quarrel with things as they are, "that old feud," he calls it, " 'Twixt things and me," but it passed quickly. At fifty-five he could write, in ***New Poems*** (1899):

> All my joys my hope excel,
> All my work hath prosper'd well,
> All my songs have happy been.

All three of these statements are given to few men to make, but of Bridges all three are true, the first and second completely true, and the third only a very little too sweeping. There are moments of unhappiness now and then in the poems, but even these are all but all passed before the poem comes to a close. It is rare in life for realization of joy to exceed man's hope of joy, and rarer, perhaps, that all a man's work has "prospered well," and rarest, perhaps, that a poet is able to say, "all my songs have happy been," which, indeed, Bridges can say with less qualification than any other English poet of his time.

It is not because Bridges has shut his eyes to ugliness and pain and wrong that he sees beauty and joy triumphant in life. In *Prometheus the Firegiver* he acknowledges:

> For many things there be upon this earth
> Unblest and fallen from beauty, to mislead
> Man's mind, and in a shadow justify
> The evil thoughts and deeds that work his ill.

He was a physician, with experience in London hospitals, and he had been brought face to face with things as they are. It was, I think, because what is beautiful or happy moved him so deeply that ugly and painful and unhappy things had little chance to register in his heart. The joy and delight in beauty filled his heart to the exclusion of all else. A fortunate lot in life and a temperament that responded intuitively to all that was happy and beautiful undoubtedly contributed to his optimism and to his discovery of so much beauty everywhere.

Happiness and beauty were very closely affiliated in his mind. It was the happy things in life and art that he found beautiful. "For howso'er man hug his care," he declared, "The best of his art is gay." And yet, with such an experience of the rich happiness of human things, Bridges can claim:

> Divinity hath surely touched my heart;
> I have possessed more joy than earth can lend.

The mood in which he so felt was, however, a rare one. Commoner was that he expressed in **"Dejection,"** in which he worked himself from a state of care to a height at which he could write:

> I praise my days for all they bring,
> Yet are they only not enough.

For many years Bridges lived the life of a country gentleman in the hills near Oxford. He made journeys to the Continent, Italy leaving more impress on his art than any other country, but only a slight impress at that. He came to America in 1925 on the foundation for visiting artists of the University of Michigan. He did not find much happiness or beauty in America. He was at home only in that sheltered life of England he celebrated in those two odes, **"Invitation to the Country"** and **"Reply,"** in Book II of ***The Shorter Poems***. **"Reply"** evidently tells us how Bridges found delight in his London days, before he knew well-being at Yattendon or Boar's Hill. Terence, Plato, and Socrates, he reads, who crown:

> the mind supreme,
> And her delights divine.

In **"Invitation to the Country,"** Bridges tells us:

> And country life I praise,
> And lead, because I find
> The philosophic mind
> Can take no middle ways;
> She will not leave her love
> To mix with men, her art
> Is all to strive above
> The crowd, or stand apart.

You can easily put your finger on the objects that stir him to such ecstasies. He has a long poem, **"A song of my heart,"** in which he enumerates what things of the country most delight him. In other poems he tells us of his love for the little out-of-the-way hamlets in the downs. It was his greatest art to picture bits of the countryside; a village; a stretch of mountainside; a tree; a bird; a team, ploughing, against the sky. It is trees that stirred him most. Of a score of such descriptions I quote two, one of a willow, and the other of a larch:

> The woodland willow stands a lonely bush
> Of nebulous gold.

That is much in little, and so is this:

> The larch thinneth her spire
> To lay the ways of the wood with cloth of gold.

It must be in the Lake County that Bridges found Dunstone Hill, on

> The purple mountain-side, where all
> The dewy night the meteors fall.

It was in his own hill country about Oxford, though, that he saw the team, ploughing, against the sky. These pictures, in which Bridges most often attained, are larger than miniatures, but they suggest the work of the miniaturist. They are exquisitely done. Though in the approved tradition, they are wholly his own. They are not, however, great poetry. Nor are they, relatively to great poetry, as important as the miniature-like novels of Jane Austen to the epical novels of Hardy. They are of the best of minor poetry, the rigidly artistic work of a man who would have life—I use his own words—

> all as this day,
> Simple, enjoyment calm in its excess,
> With not a grief to cloud, and not a ray
> Of passion overhot my peace to oppress;
> With no ambition to reproach delay,
> Nor rapture to disturb its happiness.

Hoxie Neale Fairchild (essay date 1962)

SOURCE: "Old Wine, New Bottles," in his *Religious Trends in English Poetry,* Columbia University Press, 1962, pp. 13-36.

[*In the following excerpt, Fairchild characterizes Bridges as a "noble bore" whose poetry reflects a central concern for preserving Victorian values and beliefs.*]

How highly we value the conservative art of Robert Bridges depends on our readiness to admire serene, high-minded, eloquently incantatory poetry which does very little to stretch our experience in any fresh direction. Within the whole period of this volume, he is doubtless the best poet of his well-bred, inky-blooded kind. In a few poems like **"A Passer-by"** ("Whither, O splendid ship"), **"London Snow," "Nightingales"** and **"My delight and thy delight"** he transcends his kind and touches the verge of greatness. On the whole, however, it seems to me that Bridges is a noble bore, and that Yvor Winters grows extravagant in asserting, "It is harder to imitate Bridges than it is to imitate Pound or Eliot, as it is harder to appreciate him, because Bridges is a finer poet and a saner man; he knows more than they, and to meet him on his own ground we must know more than to meet them."[1] But Winters' characteristic emphasis on sanity and knowledge suggests that he is thinking primarily of what he would call Bridges' "paraphrasable content"—a criterion which the poet himself, despite his genuine concern for aesthetic values, would consider valid for criticism of his work.

In approaching Bridges from this point of view we must ask ourselves at the outset what we are to do with ***The Testament of Beauty***, which appeared nine years after the terminal date of this study. A point-by-point analysis would run to many more pages than the substance of the poem is worth; but there is no reason why Bridges should reappear in Volume VI, and it seems unfair to ignore the work in which he offered the garnered wisdom of his long life. In the ***Testament,*** also, he says what he means explicitly, whereas the short lyrics, though basically rhetorical and not at all "difficult" in the modern sense, tend toward a more decorative and noncommital eloquence. The most practical solution will be to dip into the ***Testament*** for illustrations of ideas which are less explicitly adumbrated in the poems of our period. To do so is justified by the fact that Bridges' view of life seems to have undergone no marked change during the course of his career.

First, however, we should remind ourselves that Bridges' conservatism was mildly disheveled by crotchets concerning pure English, spelling reform, calligraphy, and prosody—the hobbies of a man so sure of his essential normality that he can safely cultivate a few personal eccentricities. His metrical experiments, which owed something to his classical studies and something to his friend Hopkins, were useful to Edwardian and Georgian literary liberals who wanted to cultivate more flexible rhythms, though the really radical innovators cannot have learned much from him. When we call him "Victorian," furthermore, we should recognize that he was less deeply indebted to any particular Victorian poet than to the more classical side of Keats and Shelley, to the nonmetaphysical seventeenth-century lyrical poets, to the Elizabethan madrigalists, and (chiefly in content) to Spenser. Yet his romantic impulses, like Arnold's, are curbed by a rather thin-blooded dread of agitation; he enjoys his personal feelings within norms established by the classical humanism which he imbibed at Eton and Oxford. Unlike Watson, with whom he otherwise had much in common, he does not attack contemporary society head on. He would serve his fellows, but in the way of Shelley's skylark—"Like a poet, hidden / In the light of thought." His ablest friends have given their devotion to science,

> While I love beauty, and was born to rhyme.
> Be they our mighty men, and let me dwell
> In shadow among the mighty shades of old,
> With love's forsaken palace for my cell;
> Whence I look forth and all the world behold.
>
> . . . . .
>
> Curs'd tho' I be to live my life alone,
> My toil is for man's joy, his joy my own.[2]

The Testament of Beauty, so well-informed concerning modern psychology and other current intellectual trends, shows that he has all along "looked forth" through the windows of beauty's cell with sharp perceptive eyes.

In schoolboy days at Eton Bridges identified love's palace with Holy Church: he was a devout young Puseyite who intended to become a priest. This phase was brief, but throughout his life Bridges thought himself a Christian and would have rejected the charge that religion for him was merely a matter of morality touched with emotion. The emotion, at least, was the emotion of a poet: it sought images, and those images were frequently derived from the Christian faith. He not only collected, edited, and translated hymns but wrote some of his own.

Under close inspection, however, Bridges' religion reveals ambiguities. A very minor poem, but for our purposes a suggestive one, is **"Founder's Day. A Secular Ode on the Ninth Jubilee of Eton College."** Although "secular" is used in the sense of "memorial," the main body of the poem does not purport to be religious. It opens, however, with the prayer:

Christ and his Mother, heavenly maid,
Mary, in whose fair name was laid
Eton's corner, bless our youth
With truth, and purity, mother of truth!

And at the close Bridges, this time without mentioning Christ and Mary, says that Eton's royal and sainted founder

biddeth a prayer to bless his youth
With truth, and purity, mother of truth.[3]

Allowance must be made for the occasion: a poet who wrote on Founder's Day in the vein of Charles Wesley would be called an infernal bounder. One feels, however, that Bridges has solved the ceremonial problem in a way congenial with his natural way of thinking. He seems to agree with Arnold's dictum:

God's wisdom and God's goodness!—Ay, but fools
Mis-define these till God knows them no more.
Wisdom and goodness, they are God![4]

The concluding lines of Bridges' poem mean all that the opening lines mean; there is merely a slight difference in flavor. Christ and his Mother, truth and purity, are interchangeable pairs of terms. But reality can be ascribed only to the second pair: Christ and his Mother function as venerable symbols of the Platonically real ethical abstractions. As images, however, they acquire an illusion of reality from what they symbolize. If we believe in truth and purity as eternal values, we are entitled to talk as if we believed in Christ and even in the Virgin Birth. Mary may be called the Mother of God *because* purity is the mother of truth.

Although this subordination of religion to ethics would have astonished a medieval realist, in modern times it has often been called "Christian Platonism." In this peculiar sense the term is obviously applicable to Bridges. In the ***Testament*** and in many shorter poems he shuttles back and forth between the traditional language of Platonism and the traditional language of Christianity. The reader need not be burdened with examples which he can so easily find for himself. Weary as he may be of the threadbare quip about the Holy Roman Empire, he may sometimes wonder to what extent Bridges' Christian Platonism is either genuinely Christian or genuinely Platonic.

Since his mind is more ethical than religious, his Platonism is more authentic than his Christianity. Yet one feels that his Platonic aspiration toward the great eternal ideas has been considerably refracted by Shelley's softer, vaguer "desire of the moth for the star." "Ah heavenly joy!" cries Bridges. We do not know what it may be, but beyond all that is best in nature and in art we dimly feel,

Writ in the expectancy of starry skies,
The faith which gloweth in our fleeting fires,
The aim of all the good that here we prize.

But elsewhere he associates this faith not with intuitive wisdom but with painful illusions from which he would gladly be released:

Could I but control
These vague desires, these leaping flames of the soul:
Could I but quench the fire: ah! could I stay
My soul that flieth, alas, and dieth away![5]

In modern times, however, Plato has been so persistently associated with this sort of *Schwärmerei* that it may seem unduly pedantic to insist upon the distinction.

But Bridges can also be a down-to-earth British empiricist whose experience as a physician has acquainted him with a good many hard facts. This side of his nature, although his poetry tries to transcend it, interferes with his attempt to glorify Platonic love, a subject to which he devoted a series of sixty-nine sonnets and not a few other poems. The subject appeals both to his prudery and to his yearning for "heavenly joy." In the ***Testament*** he declares that "God's worshipper / looking on any beauty falleth straightway in love." This love consumes all earthliness and gives "some initiat foretaste / of that mystic rapture, the consummation of which / is the absorption of Selfhood in the Being of God." This he would gladly believe, but unfortunately he knows better. As he says in the thirty-fifth of the ***Growth of Love*** sonnets, although

All earthly beauty hath one cause and proof,
To lead the pilgrim soul to beauty above,
Yet lieth the greater bliss so far aloof,
That few there be are wean'd from earthly love,

. . . . .

Nor e'en 'twixt night and day to heaven aspire:
So true it is that what the eye seeth not
But slow is loved, and loved is soon forgot.

He is much too sensible to be able to get rid of the notion that love of a beautiful woman has something to do with sex. Once, indeed, he tries a quite different sublimation—the idea that "bodily communion is a sacrament."[6] This thought is not Platonic, but in its precarious way Christian.

It is true that in ***The Testament of Beauty*** Bridges is not attempting to be purely Platonic. His main purpose is to authenticate the Platonic ideas for the modern world by showing that they are the flowers which burgeon by scientifically respectable processes from nature and from man's instincts as they actually exist. His Platonism includes a strong incongruous admixture of Aristotle and of the early Santayana. On the one hand, however, the poem is too obviously a piece of wishful mythmaking to be accepted as a contribution to a scientific philosophy; and on the other hand Reason, Love, Beauty, and the other great Platonic absolutes lose much of their quasi-religious potency when we are compelled to think of them as the emergent products of evolution. They become submerged in that world of time and space and matter which the Platonist seeks to transcend.

There is abundant evidence of Bridges' awareness of the ethical and aesthetic values of Christianity, but his conception of its specifically religious values is elusive. He has no taste for formal theology, confessing himself unable to imagine

> how Saint Thomas, with all his honesty and keen thought,
> toiling to found an irrefragable system
> of metaphysic, ethic, and theologic truth,
> should with open eyes have accepted for main premiss
> the myth of a divine fiasco, on which to assure
> the wisdom of God.

His distaste for "priestcraft" equals that of an eighteenth-century deist, but like Shaftesbury he believes that we should be amused rather than angered by the absurdities of creed-bound cults:

> The wise will live by Faith,
> faith in the order of Nature and that her order is good.
> 'Twer scepticism in them to cherish make-believe,
> creeds and precise focusings of the unsearchable:
> at such things they may smile.

To identify this faith with Stoicism would perhaps be to focus the unsearchable too precisely. Another passage, however, defines faith as

> reverence to'ard the omnificent Creator
> and First Cause, whose Being is that beauty and wisdom
> which is to be apprehended only and only approach'd
> by right understanding of his creation.

Such faith, Bridges adds, has nothing to do with superstition, though superstition may include its primitive germ.[7] Here again we are reminded of Shaftesbury's blend of aesthetico-ethical Platonism, Stoical nature-religion, and the sentimentalized Deism which points forward to romantic pantheism.

Bridges describes prayer as "the heav'n-breathing foliage of faith"—faith in the sense of the preceding paragraph. He thinks it unfortunate that philosophy

> in dread of superstition gave religion away
> to priests and monks, who rich in their monopoly
> furbish and trim the old idols.

For *true* prayer is "sovran to bind character, concentrate Will, / and purify intention." Hence it would have high pragmatic value even if its only effect were to develop the Greek sort of self-knowledge. There is an art of prayer: one should study its techniques and practise them. Prayer of communal worship is inferior to private contemplative prayer, but it gives the individual a sense of kinship with his fellows, "and its humility is the robe of intellect." Thus public worship helps us to understand the meaning of "the Communion of Saints."[8] As for the saints in Heaven rather than those in the parish church of Yattendon, Bridges wonders whether they have been wholly freed from the happy pangs of earthly love, and whether they have forgotten the fragrance of springtime and the glories of Greek sculpture and Florentine painting. He would prefer a negative answer to both questions. On *Septuagesima,* a fine winter Sunday, in preference to attending church

> I give a blessing to parson and people
> Across the fields as away I go.[9]

The more of Bridges we read, the more astonishing it appears that his personal loyalty, his literary taste, and his sense of editorial strategy should have been responsible for the present fame of Gerard Manley Hopkins. Of course the fact is greatly to Bridges' credit. It does not, however, imply that he had much sympathy with his friend's religion. He detested the Jesuits; he disapproved of Catholicism; he could share Hopkins' belief in the barest Christian fundamentals only by interpreting it in the light of his own private religion. In the 1918 Preface, his examples of Hopkins' "occasional affectation in metaphor"—they include the closing lines of *God's Grandeur*—are described as "mostly efforts to force emotion into theological or sectarian channels." He sees the same influence in "the exaggerated Marianism of some pieces, or the naked encounter of sensualism and asceticism which hurts the 'Golden Echo.'"[10] He shrinks from Hopkins' sensuousness, cannot understand his asceticism, and is especially bewildered and distressed when the two are combined.

On the whole, then, one feels that the eloquent piety of the concluding lines of the ***Testament*** is less revelatory of Bridges' working beliefs than is an earlier passage in which he says that spiritual growth depends on "good disposition" and "right education." These form

> The Habit Of Virtue: and thus a child well-bred
> in good environment, so soon as he is aware
> of personality, will know and think himself
> a virtuous being and instinctivly, in the proud
> realization of Self common to all animals,
> becometh to be his own ideal, a such-a-one
> as would Will and Do this (saith he) and never do
> thatt.[11]

Whatever else Bridges may or may not have believed in, he assuredly believed in what Samuel Butler calls "the Higher Grundyism"—the code of an English gentleman, "well-bred in good environment" and full of "proud realization of Self," who knows that certain things are done and certain things *not* done. But for the traditional ends of poetry this "habit of virtue" requires an elevating rationalization, and Bridges, as we have seen, found one that served the purpose.

Notes

1. *In Defense of Reason,* p. 101.
2. *Poetical Works,* p. 218.
3. *Ibid.,* p. 313.
4. *Religious Trends,* IV, 496. The italics are Arnold's.
5. *Poetical Works,* pp. 219, 264.
6. *Poetical Works,* p. 204; *The Testament of Beauty,* pp. 77, 97.

7. *The Testament of Beauty,* pp. 28, 31, 169-70.
8. *Ibid.,* pp. 171-76 *passim.*
9. *Poetical Works,* pp. 219, 341.
10. *The Poems of Gerard Manley Hopkins,* p. 204. See also *The Testament of Beauty,* p. 144.
11. *Testament,* p. 151.

Robert Beum (essay date 1964)

SOURCE: "Profundity Revisited: Bridges and His Critics," in *The Dalhousie Review,* Vol. 44, No. 2, Summer 1964, pp. 172-79.

[*In the following essay, Beum argues against the modern opinion that Bridges's poetry is merely concerned with "flowers" and meter rather than with serious and complicated ideas.*]

"The fact is that Bridges' poetry is a curious combination of consummate style, pure formal beauty, and a complete lack of profundity of thought".[1] This scarcely intelligible comment from one of the Kunitz and Haycraft dictionaries is representative of the kind of sentiment one is likely to hear whenever Bridges' name crops up. We make legends about the authors we never read, as well as about those we do. The Bridges legend is two stories. In one of them he is a late-Victorian flowers poet, one of the mob of laureates who write with ease lyrically descriptive verse, a Palgrave darling goldenly diffuse; in the other he is a leisured classicist who cares more for metres than for flowers, an unfeeling prosodist, indeed a tinkerer as mechanical as Poe but lacking even Poe's boldness and atmosphere. The two stories merge without ever cancelling each other out. Here is a writer—Tory, laureate, pastoral, austere but not sensationally austere—best left to legend and the literary dictionary and Ciardi's parodies.

It is true enough that for the modernist sensibility—which is to say, for nearly all sophisticated readers today—an appreciation of Bridges (as of Wordsworth or Coventry Patmore) entails a psychological and intellectual metamorphosis of such grand proportions as to resemble a religious conversion. But perhaps no great harm would ensue.

A logical first step towards such an adventurous increase in catholicity is perhaps to concede that Bridges is not, after all, completely unprofound, even in his short poems (about ***The Testament of Beauty*** and the keen and massively informed essays there can be no question). Modern taste in poetry is infected with nothing so much as with mere depth-hunting; and modern taste defines depth in its own way. Thus, experience of anxiety and ambivalence is deep; experience of delicacy, tenderness, or serenity is not. In any case, profundity is impossible except in the presence of conspicuous intellectualism (leading to an allusive, elusive, elliptical idiom) or of vast vistas of social, historical, or topographical consciousness and the attendant agonies and ecstasies. But the nature of things does not change. Profundity may, but need not and often does not, exist in a context of great issues or panoramas, or of ratiocinative complexity, which is apparently what Kunitz and Haycraft mean when they attach that connotatively damning prepositional phrase: "profundity *of thought*". The simplest things—a change of season, a London snow, a garden, a loving compliment—are profoundly important because they are essential to life or to a thoroughly civilized life, or because they involve us in long reverberating delight and sorrow. The rendering of the qualities of thought and feeling they evoke in a human sensibility in such a way as to make an experience realizable in the imagination is in itself no unprofound achievement. A poem is not an idea, although it may make use of an idea; its proper challenge is aesthetic, not forensic; it is an experience, not a nut to crack in order to tear out the meat. Dialectic, the free debate of ideas in the pursuit of truth and the satisfaction of our curiosity and our need for intellectual stimulation, is one thing; poetry, like music and painting and the dance, exists to satisfy other needs and interests. Homer "roared in the pines"—but in precise hexameters. The art-for-art's-sake people are wrong in a better way than the hyper-cerebral people who in their insatiable historicism and ideation, in their mania for "forces", "currents", "movements", and "directions", have been anathematized by the Muse—usually without their knowing it, since a good number of them teach literature at the universities, usually with great assurance. In the eyes of the rhythmless and phone-deaf idea-monger, it is not only Bridges but almost the whole tradition of the world's poetry that must seem a "magnificent emptiness".

All of us want profundity in verse; profundity "of thought"—in the narrow but now fashionable sense of intellectuality of reference, or of explicit conceptual complexity—is a matter of taste, a possible but not an essential ingredient of poetic excellence. **"The Canonization"** is more intellectual but no more profound than **"Fortunatus Nimium"**:

To dream as I may
And awake when I will
With the song of the birds
And the sun on the hill.
Or death—were it death—
To what should I awake
Who loved in my home
All life for its sake?

If we continue to hold intellectuality an important criterion, the least we can do is to see to it that Bridges' space in the anthologies grows; if erudition, critical intelligence, or intrinsic merit, rather than historical importance, were made a primary standard, both he and Coventry Patmore would run to longer selections than Tennyson. Any number of pieces from the ***Collected Poems*** will serve to demonstrate the absurdity of the legend. Let us take **"Eros,"** a poem Bridges wrote in 1899; it has not been thoroughly looked into elsewhere,[2] and is not well known, though it is one of the great short poems in our language and is fairly well anthologized. Here is the poem:

Why hast thou nothing in thy face?
Thou idol of the human race,
Thou tyrant of the human heart,
The flower of lovely youth that art;
Yea, and that standest in thy youth
An image of eternal Truth,
With thy exuberant flesh so fair
That only Pheidias might compare,
Ere from his chaste marmoreal form
Time had decayed the colours warm;
Like to his gods in thy proud dress,
Thy starry sheen of nakedness.
Surely thy body is thy mind,
For in thy face is nought to find,
Only thy soft unchristen'd smile,
That shadows neither love nor guile,
But shameless will and power immense,
In secret sensuous innocence.
O king of joy, what is thy thought?
I dream thou knowest it is nought,
And wouldst in darkness come, but thou
Makest the light where'er thou go.
Ah yet no victim of thy grace,
None who e'er long'd for thy embrace,
Hath cared to look upon thy face.

Guérard's statement that the theme is "the insufficiency of the Greek ideal of love"[3] will not quite serve: it is a bit too narrow. There were a number of Greek ideals of love, and as many Eroses to represent them. The restriction of Eros to symbolize only physical and romantic passion is a modern revision; and Bridges was no dilettante classicist. The Eros here is undoubtedly a god of sensuous experience generally, as well as of sexual passion in particular. Nothing in the poem itself seems to limit us to sex; and the fact that Bridges' attitude is so inclusive, embracing the ambivalence of our relationship with the god, leads one to feel that the god himself may well be meant to symbolize a similarly wide range of experience. He is both "tyrant" and "idol": idol, because we deify sensuous and sexual experience; tyrant, because of the god's stranglehold—because in our more animal preoccupations we have to sacrifice rationality and spirituality, and, paradoxically, we are always rebelling (more or less unsuccessfully) against that sacrifice. The real theme of the poem is much like that of Yeats's "Sailing to Byzantium": the inadequacy of merely sensual music for the needs and complexities of a rich and mature personality. To have civilization, reason and restraint must prevail. Agape and Apollo, as well as Aphrodite and Eros, are worthy of our devotions. Bridges' criticism is from the point of view of the Aristotelian mean and of Apollonian and Christian love. The criticism from the Mean is the more distinct: the superiority of Christian to pagan love is strongly intimated only in the phrase "unchristened smile." "Unchristened" here, by the way, is the perfect word: it emphasizes both the antiquity and the innocence of Eros.

Part of the poem's charm is that Bridges' critique is put in the most charitable manner compatible with a firm moral attitude. The point of view is far from anything like a barren Puritanism. After all, Eros is a "king of joy", even "An image of eternal Truth" (a phrase delicately ironic but also literal). In sensuous beauty are the beginnings of heavenly beauty, and Bridges' own worship was a worship of Beauty—though as a means to the highest evolution of mind and soul, not as an end in itself. The contemplation of physical beauty gives rise to an awareness of the existence—and, vaguely, intimations of the quality—of heavenly beauty. This is the aesthetic of Bridges' epic:

Beauty is the highest of all those occult influences,
the quality of appearances that thru' the sense
wakeneth spiritual emotion in the mind of man
But think not Aphrodite therefore disesteem'd
for rout of her worshippers, nor sensuous Beauty
torn from her royal throne, who is herself mother
of heavenly Love.

Here is a Platonism in which physical beauty and profane love are by no means denigrated. But, for that matter, even the most elementary and nontranscendent sensuous experience is in itself far from evil: evil, in the form of imbalance or incompleteness, comes about only when we make of Eros an idol and a tyrant. Bridges' attitude is simply the traditional wisdom: Eros is both king of joy and tyrant; he is essential, and yet he has to be kept in his place.

Several of the poem's lines are appropriately difficult: I say appropriately, because the poem's difficulty, and in places almost orphic quality, is beautifully consonant with both the complexity of attitude and the dark god's patronage of "secret sensuous innocence". The memorable first line of the second stanza, "Surely thy body is thy mind", is an instance of successful ambiguity: Eros is mindless, and is as preoccupied with his body as Narcissus was with his. The opening lines of the third stanza are perhaps the most difficult, and yet once again much of their power depends on their density, and the power continues the presence of the god's power:

O king of joy, what is thy thought?
I dream thou knowest it is nought,
And wouldst in darkness come, but thou
Makest the light where'er thou go.

If the god has any thought at all, it is only a certain minimal apprehension of his own mindlessness, and this leads him to wish to appear to his devotees only in darkness, that is, in the absence of reflection, where he can best work his "shameless will." And yet he makes "the light" wherever he goes: sensuous and sexual experience are inevitable, and (if controlled) good in themselves, and are good in that they lead to a higher good; this is one of the few instances in English poetry in which light, traditionally an image of mind, spirit, truth, or divinity, becomes a metaphor of sense experience. Still, sensuality palls: excess, and time, bring reaction. One hears that other music, looks for those "Monuments of unageing intellect." Bridges' indictment reaches its climax at the point of greatest rhetorical prominence, at the very end of the poem:

Ah yet no victim of thy grace,
None who e'er long'd for thy embrace,
Hath cared to look upon thy face.

Part of the poem's effectiveness lies in a feature so obvious that one forgets to credit it: personification has never been more successful; and the continual direct address makes it even more dramatic. Certainly one feels that the poem arose from some large encounter, that Bridges has seen a statue or painting of an Eros, and has fallen into reverie and cast it in the strong form of address. As is the case with nearly all his work, we know nothing of the circumstances of his conception and composition of the piece. From the mention of Pheidias in

> With thy exuberant flesh so fair,
> That ony Pheidias might compare,

one might assume that Bridges has in mind an Eros of that sculptor. But no Pheidian Eros is known. These lines only express Bridges' notion that a consummate articulation of the god would require the greatest of plastic artists. One thing is certain: the Eros is not the mere Cupid the god became in much Hellenistic and Roman art. If Bridges was struck by a particular Eros, it must have been the massive Eros Centrocelle or the Eros Borghese. Those are the only ones extant that have the lofty beauty and the physical dimensions to have served as models for such language as "power immense" and "king of joy".

Here is no meretricious metric. The octosyllabic couplet is perfectly suited to the matter. Its simplicity, together with the regularity of the metre, is felt as an embodiment of the moral control that informs the poem at every point. The lines are of uniform length: there is no rapturous lyricism or other kinetic quality that might call for the expansions and contractions of varying lengths of line. The rhymes are strong: weaker ones, or the dying fall of feminine rhyme, would be at odds with the rational and masculine attitude. Yet though the poem is not metrically ambitious, there is one really splendid felicity of rhythm; it is a commonly encountered license, but works here with uncommon force. In the seventh line, "With thy exuberant flesh so fair," the Latin word introduces an extra syllable into the pattern. A very light syllable, it is meant to be elided (but not ignored or unnaturally slurred); it creates a moment of unexpected and delightful freedom. It is an instance of the thing to be found so often in Bridges, and indeed in traditional English verse generally, a tiny metrical variation creating an effect of great beauty. The extra syllable breaks and yet preserves the iambic meter, and because it is such a slight syllable, we race over it, and the speed thereby gained heightens the effect of freedom still more, an effect that matches the sense of the word "exuberant" and makes it evocative. The word refers, of course, to the god's joy and pride in his flesh, but thanks to the buoyant effect which the word creates in the metre, it also-suggests the physical fact of Eros's wings. We get, out of this modest rhythmic freedom, not only an aesthetic quality in the medium which corresponds to the idea being expressed and which makes that idea vivid, but also, the connotation of a visual image.

The rhyme words themselves have that inevitability which every English poet strives for. Bridges' rhymes not infrequently, it seems to me, do little more than add a melodic, but sometimes trivial, ornamentation to his poems. Here, however, they are words that earn their emphasis. The very first couplet juxtaposes two thematic words. Even the phrase "that art" in the second couplet justifies its archaism and quasi-redundancy. Its intrinsic dignity and the emphasis it gives to the conception of "all lovely youth" are indispensable; and the phrase continues the universality of "human race" and "human heart" in the preceding lines. In the sixth couplet the rhyme is again strikingly active:

> Like to his gods in thy proud dress,
> Thy starry sheen of nakedness.

The metaphor of nakedness as dress is fresh and apt; it makes us feel the god's pride in his nudity, as one feels pride in a fine cloth. The first couplet of the final stanza has a tension which is derived from the powerful opposition of the rhyme words:

> O king of joy, what is thy thought?
> I dream thou knowest it is nought.

By the time we reach this couplet, we have become so thoroughly impressed with the god's mindlessness that we could expect no other rhyme than the one we find.

But the triumph of the rhyme is at the end. The poem closes with a triplet instead of the expected couplet; the rhyme is the same as the poem's opening rhyme, and the final image is the same as the image of the first line—the face of the god. The surprise of a triplet emphasizes the emptiness of the face, "the animality of love which it is sometimes difficult for the idealist to accept", as Rosenthal and Smith put it. And of course the structure of the poem has now come full cycle.

And yet we will not see that **"Eros"** is no more profound than **"Fortunatus Nimium"** or **"Nightingales."** One almost thinks that civilization will have taken some new turn or be about to take it before we will again distinguish profundity from the critical intelligence or from what is simply, as in Donne or Hopkins or Eliot, a stylistic novelty, a sportive idiom. Spenser's epic and Shakespeare's seventy-third sonnet and Wordsworth's most famous sonnet to sleep are profound without being ingenious or richly textured. Bridges' mode is that sort of mode. Donne and Hopkins often seem deeper than they are, simply because the textures of their poems are difficult and announce their difficulty proudly. Once one has solved their diction, syntax, allusion, and conceit, the substance—the poetic wisdom—turns out to be at about the same level as that of a good many other poems—by Spenser or Wordsworth or Bridges, whose quieter surfaces deceive us.

Notes

1. *Twentieth-Century Authors: A Biographical Dictionary of Modern Literature,* ed. Stanley J. Kunitz and Howard Haycraft (New York: H. W. Wilson Co., 1942).

2. The most perceptive and most detailed commentary on the poem is that by M. L. Rosenthal and A. J. M. Smith in *Exploring Poetry* (New York: Macmillan, 1955), pp. 183-184. Yvor Winters, however, Bridges' lonely champion among major modern critics, was the first to call attention to the poem's excellence (*In Defense of Reason,* 1937).
3. Albert Joseph Guérard, *Robert Bridges: A Study of Traditionalism in Poetry* (Cambridge: Harvard University Press, 1942).

Donald E. Stanford (essay date 1971)

SOURCE: "Robert Bridges and the Free Verse Rebellion," in *Journal of Modern Literature,* Vol. 2, No. 1, September 1971, pp. 19-32.

[*In the following essay, Stanford suggests that while Bridges was actively interested in the free verse movement of much younger poets such as Amy Lowell and Ezra Pound, the older poet nevertheless held to the traditional belief that the subjects of poems should be weighty matters rather than "trivial" items, such as a wheelbarrow, which interested the younger poets.*]

It is not generally recognized that Robert Bridges was (in his own way) involved in the free verse rebellion of the 1910s and 1920s. Although he was seventy years old in 1914 when one of the most important volumes of the new movement, *Des Imagistes,* appeared, he was still keenly aware of what was going on among the younger poets of his time, and like them, he had become dissatisfied with conventional rhythms based on the iambic foot. In this year he wrote "My own opinion is that, especially in the present condition of English verse, all methodical experiments are of value, and that a competent experiment is of value even though it may not please."[1] The Printer's Note to ***The Tapestry,*** published privately in 1925, carries this statement:

> Mr. Bridges has generously authorized the printing of the following complete collection up to the present date of all his "New Verse" described by him as 'Neo-miltonic syllabics' and offered as his considered contribution to the Free Verse controversy.[2]

A year before he had written to R. C. Trevelyan, "People are now running after 'free verse.' I say that this stuff is free verse."[3] "This stuff" refers to six of the eleven syllabic poems that were to appear in ***The Tapestry*** with particular reference to **"Come se Quando"**[4] which Trevelyan had praised in an article in the *New Statesman.*[5] And in January, 1926, he wrote again to Trevelyan, "I agree with the Free versifiers that the old humdrum is worn out: but I am quite orthodox in believing that freedom must be within prosody not without it."[6]

As the Ezra Pound and T. S. Eliot revolution began to dominate the literary scene in the later twenties and down to the present time, Bridges' milder and more refined experiments have been overlooked by most critics. Yet a history of the twentieth century experimental movement in Anglo-American poetry should not completely disregard Bridges' later work. It is the purpose of this brief article to summarize the history of Bridges' revolt against conventional metres and to discuss in some detail the dozen poems he offered as his contribution to the free verse controversy.

Bridges' work in non-conventional prosody may be classified as experiments in (1) accentual verse; (2) classical metres; (3) Neo-Miltonic syllabics; (4) the "loose alexandrines" of ***The Testament of Beauty.*** His interest in accentual verse (that is, verse in which each line has a predetermined number of accented syllables and an indeterminate number of unaccented syllables) began early in his career and received its final theoretical formulation in the 1921 edition of *Milton's Prosody.*[7] Accentual verse has a long and distinguished history. Among its chief practitioners in the nineteenth century were, besides Bridges, Coleridge and Hopkins. Bridges wrote some of his finest poems in the metre, including **"The Nightingales."**[8] Two of the poems in ***New Verse*** are in accentual metres, **"To Francis Jammes"** and **"Melancholy."** They were completed as late as 1921.

Bridges' composition of poems in classical metres probably began as early as 1898,[9] the year in which William Johnson Stone's essay "Classical Metres in English Verse" was privately printed. Stone advanced three major propositions: that successful poems in English in classical metres were possible; that to date no one had succeeded in writing such poems; and that one reason for this failure was that no one had correctly formulated the rules for quantity in English. Stone then formulated his own theories. Bridges was impressed by Stone's essay, and when the author died shortly after the publication of his essay, Bridges reprinted it in his 1901 edition of *Milton's Prosody* with this comment: "Mr. Stone was a convinced advocate for the introduction of classical rules of prosody into English. Upon the advisability or even the possibility of their introduction I do not myself express an opinion."[10] The introduction is dated 1901, and it is evident that Bridges had not yet completed poems in classical metres which satisfied him. He continued his efforts, however, and in 1903 published ***Now in Wintry Delights***[11] with an explanatory note at the end which begins "This poem is written according to the laws for English quantity suggested by William Stone " The poem itself, which is sub-titled "Epistle to L.M." [Lionel Muirhead] begins:

> Now in wintry delights, and long fireside meditation
> 'Twixt studies and routine paying due court to the Muses,
> My solace in solitude, when broken roads barricade me
> Mudbound, unvisited for months with my merry children
> Grateful t'ward Providence, and heeding a slander against me
> Less than a rheum, think of me to-day, dear Lionel,

and take
This letter as some account of Will Stone's versification.

Now in Wintry Delights appears to be the first written of Bridges' published poems in quantitative verse. His final selection of classical poems in his ***Collected Poems*** (Oxford, 1953) runs to sixty-four pages. They deserve more detailed study than they have yet received.

The first of the dozen poems in Neo-Miltonic syllabics which Bridges offered as his contribution to the free verse controversy was entitled **"The Flowering Tree"** and was written in November 1913,[12] and the second poem **"Noel: Christmas Eve, 1913"** was composed a few days later. **"In der Fremde"** was also written in 1913.[13] **"The Western Front"** is undated but was written sometime during World War I. The **"Epitaph: Hubert Hastings Parry"** printed in ***The Tapestry*** from the monument in Gloucester Cathedral, but not included in the ***New Verse*** reprint, is dated 1920. The other seven poems of this group were all composed in 1921.

Bridges' last experiment in non-conventional prosody was ***The Testament of Beauty,*** begun on Christmas day 1924,[14] and completed in 1929. Bridges himself described the metre as "loose alexandrines." Each line (with a very few exceptions) is composed of twelve syllables, with a varying number of accents. The rhythms of this poem appear to be the final development of the poet's experiments in Neo-Miltonic syllabics.

I return to the main subject of this paper, the poems in Neo-Miltonic syllabics which (with the one exception noted) appeared in ***The Tapestry*** as Bridges' contribution to the free verse controversy. Their metre is explained by Bridges in a brief article written December 1923,[15] entitled "'New Verse'/Explanation of the Prosody of My Late Syllabic 'Free Verse'."[16] The article is written in a condensed style; it is difficult to summarize a summary, but the gist of it appears to be this: Bridges, in his study of Milton's prosody, had discovered that Milton had "freed" every foot in his line except the last foot in which he allowed extra-metrical syllables. Bridges went a step further and "freed" every foot in the line and allowed no extra-metrical syllables. Thus, Bridges had a line with a definite number of syllables but an indeterminate number of accents and quantities. Bridges chose to make his line twelve syllables in length. Lines which appear to have more than twelve syllables can be reduced to twelve by elision. By Milton's "freeing the feet" Bridges meant that "there was no place in which any one syllable was necessarily long or short, accented or unaccented, heavy or light." After a great deal of careful technical analysis, Bridges came out with a line that was restricted only by syllable count. As he said, "It was plainly the freest of free verse, there being no speech-rhythm which it would not admit."[17]

Bridges also defends and explains his prosody in a note to the first printing of **"Poor Poll."** The poem, dated June 3, 1921, is probably the first poem written and printed in the Neo-Miltonic twelve syllable line without a caesural break and is therefore the first poem in what was later to become the "loose alexandrine" line of ***The Testament of Beauty.*** Bridges comments on his earlier experiments in the twelve syllable line printed as two lines of sixes to indicate the caesural break and then discusses his employment in**"Poor Poll"** of the line without a hemistich or with the hemistich optional. His note, in part, reads:

> To make the hemistich optional, as I have done, is no innovation: Milton would always have had it so; but this liberty when extended to my development of his system gives a result as new and as rich as the earlier experiments gave. The value of it is the consequent freedom of the diction; no syllable encounters any metrical demand that interferes with its inflexional value as part of the spoken phrase in which it occurs.[18]

As we have seen, the poems of ***The Tapestry*** are in two categories: (1) Those with lines having a strong caesural break in the middle. They were composed as alexandrines, but are printed in sixes[19] with each line broken in the center:

> A frosty Christmas Eve
> when the stars were shining

(2) A twelve syllable line without a caesural break and printed thus:

> These tapestries have hung fading around my hall.

This line (which became ***The Testament of Beauty*** line) was suggested by similar verses in Milton's "Nativity Ode" and *Samson Agonistes:*

> Or grovling soild thir crested helmets in the dust.

Of this type of line Bridges wrote: "The characteristic of Milton's twelve-syllable line is his neglect of this casual break, and he makes a verse which has a strong unity in itself, and no tendency to break up."[20]

So much for the prosody of the poems. What of their content?

"Come se quando" has received more favorable comment than any other of the Neo-Miltonic poems.[21] The title was suggested by Mrs. Bridges who, on reading the first draft, was struck by the numerous Dantean similes introduced by "as if when," "like as when" and similar phrases. "There are too many 'come se quandos'" she is reported to have said.[22] "Come se quando" and the more frequent "come cosi" are introductory phrases for similes in the *Divinia Commedia.* Bridges committed the error of substituting *si* for *se* and the title was not corrected until recent printings of the ***Collected Poems.***[23]

The poem is primarily a meditation on the threat to culture and civilization when the passions overcome reason—the same theme (or tenor) as **"Low Barometer"** which was composed about the same time. The vehicle is a dream-vision-parable. The narrator, falling asleep at night, sees first "the epiphany of a seraphic figure" of heroic beauty, with a face like a portrait by Giorgione:

> as if Nature had deign'd to take back from man's hand
> some work of her own as art had refashioned it.

This epiphany of the Greek-Christian ideal of heroic beauty which "all that looked on loved and many worshipp'd" is blotted out by passion and fear—the "fear of God." And here we have one of the many Dantean similes commented on by Mrs. Bridges:

> I saw its smoky shadow of dread;
> and as a vast Plutonian mountain that burieth
> its feet in molten lava and its high peak in heaven,
> whenever it hath decoy'd some dark voyaging storm
> to lave its granite shoulders, dischargeth the flood
> in a thousand torrents o'er its flanks to the plain
> and all the land is vocal with the swirl and gush
> of the hurrying waters, so suddenly in this folk
> a flood of troublous passion arose and mock'd control.

A poet-prophet figure next appears—the familiar alienated intellectual—who has fled the city to live in wilderness caves. He makes an impassioned appeal to Themis, the goddess of Justice, to unveil her eyes and to weigh in her scales on the one side her "Codes of Justice Duty and Awe," her "penal interdicts" together with the tables of her Law, and on the other side Mercy, Love, human thought, and suffering, "All tears from Adam's tears unto the tears of Christ." If mercy, love, and the experiences of suffering humanity are not enough to outweigh the codes of justice, duty, and law, then the poet tells Justice to bind up her eyes again. He will no more contend, but admit that confusion is the Final Cause. The address to Themis runs for over one hundred and thirty lines and there are several fundamental metaphysical questions raised and unanswered such as the origin and destiny of man and the efficacy of reason in a universe which seems to be largely governed by blind chance. The poet-prophet is, of course, not the spokesman for Robert Bridges who characterizes his plea as the "outrageous despair the self pity of mankind." Bridges is obviously more impressed by the figure of heroic beauty which preceded that of the poet.

The poet-prophet figure, having disburdened his heart "to the wilderness and silent sky" is suddenly overwhelmed with "a stream of natural feeling," memories of home and friends. Repenting his abandonment of his people, he returns to the market place of the city and, like an Old Testament prophet, preaches with "strong words of his chasten'd humanity." The people, rising against him, drive him from the city and are about to kill him when the mob is stopped by the sudden appearance of "a white-robed throng that came moving with solemn peace." This "choral convoy" takes the poet into its protection where, after receiving extreme unction, the poet dies. The body is carried in procession "with dirge and shriving prayer" by the priestly host to be buried within a church where it will await the second coming of Christ. The narrator is awakened by the sound of the funeral dirge and by the night wind which returns us to the opening lines of the poem, perhaps the best poetry of the entire Neo-Miltonic series:

> How thickly the far fields of heaven are strewn with stars!
> Tho' the open eye of day shendeth them with its glare
> yet, if no cloudy wind curtain them nor low mist
> of earth blindfold us, soon as Night in grey mantle
> wrappeth all else, they appear in their optimacy
> from under the ocean or behind the high mountains
> climbing in spacious ranks upon the stark-black void:
> Ev'n so in our mind's night burn far beacons of thought
> and the infinite architecture of our darkness,
> the dim essence and being of our mortalities,
> is sparkled with fair fire-flecks of eternity
> whose measure we know not nor the wealth of their rays.

Of the line "And the infinite architecture of our darkness" Bridges wrote to Trevelyan that it "seems to me one of the most beautiful of the many free rhythms—I have found it one of the lines that first converts the reader."[24]

"Come se Quando," written three years before the first lines of ***The Testament of Beauty,*** may be considered a preliminary exercise for the longer poem. The prosodic structure—"loose alexandrines"—is the same as that of the longer poem and several of the philosophical ideas in **"Come se Quando"** are given more extensive treatment in the ***Testament.*** With the exception of the opening lines quoted above, the diction of the earlier poem tends to be stereotyped and the rhythms rather flat. However, Bridges was developing a medium which according to Yvor Winters (referring to a passage in ***The Testament of Beauty,*** IV, 270-338) is "a new kind of poetry, which, however restricted its possibilities, is nevertheless an enrichment of our experience."[25]

"Poor Poll," as we have seen, is the first of the poems in the new twelve syllable line. In his "Metrical Elucidations" published in the first edition of the poem, Bridges explains that the "poem is privately printed for a few friends who wish to examine the pretensions of the experiment." He goes on to say that he deliberately chose a subject on a low plane and furthermore that he introduced quotations from foreign languages "to illustrate how certain well-established and unmistakably alien forms blend comfortably" within the new medium. **"Poor Poll"** incidentally was being composed at the same time as *The Waste Land* and both Bridges and Eliot were looking for a "carry all" medium which would blend excerpts from foreign languages as well as diction from "high" and "low" styles. Bridges found his medium in an adaptation of certain lines from Milton. Eliot found his in an adaptation of the method of Ezra Pound's early *Cantos.*

The vehicle of **"Poor Poll"** is, as Bridges has stated, on a low plane, but the tenor is not. It is, in fact, the same as that of *The Waste Land,* the destruction of the culture of

Western civilization. The poem starts with an incident observed by the poet. A parrot calls loudly for food, but when the pan of "sop" is given him by the cook, the bird surprises the poet by deftly gathering the food in its beak and scattering in on the lawn. Then it "summoned with loud cry the little garden birds / to take their feast." This incident leads to a meditation involving a number of ideas: the depth of the source of man's benevolence if benevolence can also be found in birds, the possibility that instinct is a better guide to moral behavior than reason, and the ability of the wild bird to adapt to an English domestic life and to mimic languages he cannot understand. In its instinctive desire for the unknown life of the tropics of which it had been robbed by a British sailor, the bird becomes

—a very figure and image of man's soul on earth
the almighty cosmic Will fidgeting in a trap—.

In appearance the parrot in "the impeccable spruceness" of his "grey-feather'd poll" might qualify for membership in the House of Lords or the Athenaeum Club for it has the "simulation of profoundest wisdom." But, the poet continues, in actuality the parrot is not wise but more like an "idle and puzzle-headed" monk in an unfurnished cell who will die in the peace that passes Understanding because he lacks Understanding. The parrot is next asked if he would willingly exchange his present pale, sedentary life with that of the tropical paradise from which he was captured—a monkey's paradise where he would be in constant danger of sudden death. The parrot cannot answer because he cannot understand the question. In fact, there can be no real communication between poet and parrot for the parrot lacks understanding and a sense of values:

I am writing verses to you & grieve that you sh[d] be
absolument incapable de les comprendre,
Tu, Polle, nescis ista nec potes scire:—
Alas! lambic, scazon and alexandrine,
spondee or choriamb, all is alike to you—

The parrot is, by implication, similar to the British public of the 1920s, the parents

of a new race of beings the unhallow'd offspring
of them who shall have quite dismember'd & destroy'd
our temple of Christian faith & fair Hellenic art
just as that monkey would, poor Polly, have done for you.

Poll is also the victim of the new "monkey's paradise" which would destroy Bridges' ideals: Christian faith and Hellenic art. The final lines link the poem thematically with **"Come se Quando."**

"The Tapestry" is a sequel to **"Poor Poll."** It begins with a brief account of a young lord who ordered his steward to turn his ancient tapestries to the wall. The mythological scenes, he believed, were out of date for the young, whereas the backs of the tapestries gave "more colour and less solemnity" to the hall for the feast which followed. The incident is a fable which gives the poet an opportunity to discuss the correct relationship between man and beauty, principally the beauties of nature. There follows an eloquent passage on his awareness from infancy to old age of natural beauty which includes a fine description of the dawn of the day on which he composed his poem:

Then looked I forth and lo! The Elysian fields of Dawn!
and there in naked peace my dumb expectancy
mirror'd above the hills, a pageant like music
heard in imagination or the silence of dreams.
What if I had not seen the cloths of Night take hue
soft-tinged as of brown bear-skin on green opal spread
which still persisting through shift imperceptible
grew to an incandescent copper on a pale light-blue!
Then one flame-yellow streak pierced thru' the molten bronze
with lilac freak'd above, where fiëry in red mist
the orb with slow surprise surged, till his whole blank blaze
dispell'd from out his path all colour—and Day began.

It was, he goes on to say, the gradual awareness of beauty that helped savage primitive man to become civilized. Then, returning to the tapestries with their faces to the wall:

I prop so far my slight fable with argument
to lay malison and ban on the upstart leprous clan
who wrong Nature's beauty turning her face about.

He has returned to the principal theme of his preceding poem on the parrot. He concludes with the statement that a full appreciation of beauty requires a study of both the back and the front of the tapestry—that is, of the ugly as well as of the beautiful.

In 1917 Bridges resided for a time in Merton College while repairs were being made on Chilswell House. **"The College Garden,"** although written in 1921, refers to the garden at Merton College during that year. The pensive philosopher mentioned in the poem is F. H. Bradley.[26] The theme is in the first line: "The infinitude of Life is in the Heart of Man," an infinitude that includes good—the good life being primarily the creation and contemplation of beauty by means of the imagination. But it also includes evil as manifested in the blood lust of hunting and on the battlefields of World War I. Thoughts of the turmoil of the war sharpen the contrast with the too peaceful garden of Merton College—deserted of students and empty except for himself, the pensive philosopher, and an aged gardener.

The poem ends with an excellent passage depicting the state of mind of the seventy-three year old poet:

I lie, like one who hath wander'd all his summer morn
among the heathery hills and hath come down at noon
in a breathless valley upon a mountain-brook
and for animal recreation of hot fatigue
hath stripp'd his body naked to lie down and taste
the play of the cool water on all his limbs and flesh

and lying in a pebbly shallow beneath the sky
supine and motionless feeleth each ripple pass
until his thought is merged in the flow of the stream
as it cometh upon him and lappeth him there
stark as a white corpse that stranded upon the stones
blocketh and for a moment delayeth the current
ere it can pass to pay its thin tribute of salt
into the choking storage of the quenchless sea.

Of **"The Psalm"** Bridges wrote to Trevelyan December 16, 1924, "The shortest of my six poems—attempt at an idyllic effect—was printed last year in *The Queen* with an ornamental border etc!! The Editor was (or seemed to be) enthusiastic about it—tho' he had no chance of scanning it.—Why should it be scanned?—*No one* ever scanned Milton."[27] The occasion of the poem is the sound of a Huguenot psalm sung by village folk in an English church and overheard by Bridges while he was pleasantly talking with a friend in a meadow. As in **"The College Garden,"** a peaceful scene is interrupted by thought of strife and suffering. Bridges appears to be quite conscious of the fact that his own life in contrast with that of the world at large has been relatively tranquil and idyllic. The substance of the poem is a meditation on the sufferings of the French protestants during the sixteenth, seventeenth, and eighteenth centuries and an expression of admiration for their endurance. An earlier poem **"The Summer-House on the Mound"** ends with a reference to the religious quarrels in England:

that old outlaw,
The Roman wolf, scratches with privy paw.

In both poems Bridges is clearly on the side of the protestants.

"Kate's Mother," which Trevelyan described as "a perfect short story, and a beautiful poem too," is, like **"Poor Poll,"** an experiment in the new metre as a "carry all" medium suitable for a wide range of subjects. Bridges wrote to Trevelyan, "I chose the subject as a simplest childish narrative for test of the metre—and the general liking for it proves I think that the metre can carry the highest and lowest business in juxtaposition without embarrassment or bathos: and that is the desideratum in English versification which I wished to supply. You will have observed that such a line as e.g. 'For difficulty and roughness and scorch of the way' which might be out of Dante's Inferno, does not show."[28]

The poem begins with a description of the house, windmill, fields, and the sea near the village of Walmer, Kent, with grounds overlooking the Channel where Bridges spent the first years of his childhood, the same place as that so beautifully depicted in **"The Summer-House on the Mound."** On a July afternoon the child, his elder sister, and their nurse Kate pay a visit to Kate's mother—a brief journey that was to the boy an adventure, for he was going beyond the Windmill into new territory. Also, this was "the first visit of compliment that ever I paid." The visit is also a journey into a new dimension of childhood experience—an awareness of human affliction and courage foreshadowed by the lines:

For difficulty and roughness and scorch of the way
then a great Bible-thought came on me: I was going
like the Israelites of old in the desert of Sin.

They arrive at the straw thatched cottage of Kate's mother with its typical country garden of sweet william, mint and jasmin and its interior which was full of surprises to the boy—a lofty clock picturing upon its face a full rigg'd ship and a huge copper warming-pan, but the greatest wonder of all is the old woman herself:

the wrinkles innumerable of her sallow skin
her thin voice and the trembling of her patient face
as there she swayed incessantly on her rocking-chair
like the ship in the clock: she had sprung into my ken
wholly to enthrall me, a fresh nucleus of life-surprise
such as I knew must hold mystery and could reveal:
for I had observed strange movement of her cotton skirt
and as she sat with one knee across the other, I saw
how her right foot in the air was all a-tremble and jerked
in little restless kicks: so when we sat to feast
about the table spredd with tea and cottage cakes
whenever her eye was off me I watched her furtively
to make myself assured of all the manner and truth
of this new thing, and ere we were sent out to play
(that so Kate might awhile chat with her mother alone)
I knew the SHAKING PALSY.

All of this is quite Wordsworthian and, as an initiation into evil, a mild performance indeed when we think for example of the Nick Adams stories of Hemingway. Nevertheless, the poem has a few charming though very minor passages.

The epitaph on Hubert Hastings Parry dated 1920 and written for his monument in Gloucester Cathedral was printed in ***The Tapestry*** but, to the best of my knowledge, not reprinted elsewhere. I therefore quote it in full:

From boyhood's eager play call'd by the English Muse
Her fine scholar to be than her Master's compeer
A spirit elect whom no unworthy thought might wrong
Nor any fear touch thee joyously o'er life's waves
Navigating thy soul into her holy haven
Long these familiar walls shall re-echo thy song
And this stone remember thy bounteous gaiety
Thy honour and thy grace and the love of thy friends.

The remaining Neo-Miltonic poems were written and printed in lines of six syllables each (with the exception of the 6+5 syllable lines of **"Cheddar Pinks"**). The first of these, **"The Flowering Tree,"** is on one of Bridges' favorite subjects—his response to beauty (and in this poem beauty's response to him). The poet falls asleep in the sun and dreams that he is covered by a flowering tree. He says that, unlike Endymion who slept by moonlight,

would I sleep in the sun
Neath the trees divinely

with day's azure above
When my love of Beauty
is met by beauty's love.

"Noel: Christmas Eve, 1913" was written by the recently appointed poet laureate for King George V who sent it to *The Times* of London where it was published December 24, 1913. During a walk on a frosty Christmas Eve the poet listens to the church bells:

And from many a village
in the water'd valley
Distant music reach'd me
peals of bells aringing:
The constellated sounds
ran sprinkling on earth's floor
As the dark vault above
with stars was spangled o'er.

The use of the words *water'd* and *sprinkling* together with *constellated* and *stars* achieves a very lovely effect of the sound of distant scattered music reinforced with his reference to the first Christmas in the next stanza when the shepherds

marveling could not tell
Whether it were angels
or the bright stars singing.

In the third stanza the poet blesses the village folk ringing the church bells and in the concluding stanza states what the music meant to him:

But to me heard afar
it was starry music
Angels' song, comforting
as the comfort of Christ.

Rhythm, imagery, and sound achieve a mood of serenity which makes this poem, Bridges' first as Laureate, one of his loveliest minor achievements. **"In Der Fremde"** because of its rhymes could be mistaken for accentual syllabic verse although Bridges considers it to be in Neo-Miltonic syllabics. **"The West Front"** is of little value and was not reprinted in ***The Tapestry.*** **"Cheddar Pinks,"** a very slight but charming performance, is on a theme we have discussed before—the ageing poet is reading Homer in his peaceful garden while the world struggles about him. He has a moment of very mild remorse:

Then felt I like to one
indulging in sin

but the remorse is easily dispelled as he busies himself composing his pleasant verses.

Three years after writing the last of this group of poems, Bridges began his major work, ***The Testament of Beauty,*** in which he continued his experiment with the twelve syllable line. The poem was published on his eighty-fifth birthday. Any serious history of the revolution in poetic technique in the twentieth century should take his work into account. Logan Pearsall Smith said of him, "He grew old learning many things, and he was always eager to consider, and often to welcome, promising experiments and new notions."[29] His daughter, Elizabeth Daryush, wrote: "As regards his general attitude, he was at once conservative and democratic, aesthetic and rational. Besides fighting to preserve the traditional and characteristic beauties of our language from the dangers of slovenly and meaningless degradation, and from all confusion and ugliness, whether of thought or sound, he was at the same time a keen experimenter, and no one was more ready to appreciate and encourage all natural and healthy developments of the national genius."[30]

How free was Bridges' "free verse"? To what extent did he actually participate in the movement which almost engulfed the poetry of the 1920s? The answer is suggested by Elizabeth Daryush's comment. He was "a keen experimenter" who at the same time wished to preserve "the traditional and characteristic beauties of our language." Robert Beum has said that Bridges' experiments resulted in "free verse which has taken one stride toward regular traditional verse."[31] Sister Mary Berg in her exhaustive statistical analysis of the Neo-Miltonic poems concluded that Bridges himself thought these poems to be regular traditional verse that has taken one step toward free verse.[32] My own opinion is that by "freeing" all the feet of his twelve syllable line, Bridges *theoretically* had a medium which could absorb any rhythmical or non-rhythmical matter, but the poet in practice preferred a rising disyllabic metre which Sister Mary describes as "a pervasive, though relaxed, iambic movement."[33] These iambic characteristics became stronger (as Sister Mary has demonstrated) in ***The Testament of Beauty.*** The rhythms of the Neo-Miltonic poems—those which Bridges offered as his contribution to the free verse movement—are considerably less relaxed (I believe) than those found in the poetry of Sandburg and Amy Lowell, but looser than the rapid cadences of the best free verse poems of Williams, Stevens, Pound, and H. D. As far as subject matter is concerned, Bridges, as we have seen, did not follow the suggestions of Pound, Williams, and others that any subject, no matter how trivial, (a bathtub—a wheelbarrow), is suitable for "modern verse." In his choice of themes and images Bridges usually maintained the decorum of the traditional classical poet.

Notes

1. *Ibant Obscuri* (Oxford, 1916), p. 142. Bridges indicates on p. 147 that the passage quoted was written in 1914 or earlier.
2. London, 1925. Printed by F. W. and S. M. at 41 Bedford Square. Limited to 150 copies. It contains the following poems: "The Flowering Tree," "Noel: Christmas Eve (1913)," "In der Fremde," "Epitaph: Hubert Hastings Parry," "Cheddar Pinks," "Poor Poll," "The Tapestry," "Kate's Mother," "The College Garden," "The Psalm," and "Come si Quando." It omits "The West Front" which Bridges in his *October and Other Poems* (London, 1920) described as being also in Neo-Miltonic syllabics. Thus twelve poems were written in this form. The

last seven in the above list were reprinted in *New Verse* (London, 1925).

3. *XXI Letters:* a correspondence between Robert Bridges and R. C. Trevelyan on *New Verse* and *The Testament of Beauty* (Stanford Dingley: The Mill House Press, 1955) p. 3. This volume was limited to 68 copies.
4. First published in *The London Mercury,* November, 1924.
5. "Prosody and the Poet Laureate," *The New Statesman,* XXIV (December 13, 1924), 296-298.
6. *XXI Letters,* p. 8.
7. *Milton's Prosody/with a chapter on/Accentual Verse/and/Notes/by/Robert Bridges* (Oxford University Press, 1921).
8. See Albert Guerard's scansion of this poem in his *Robert Bridges* (Harvard University Press, 1942), pp. 276-77.
9. We have the authority of Mrs. Bridges for this date. See Guerard, *Robert Bridges,* p. 27.
10. William Johnson Stone, *Milton's Prosody by Robert Bridges and Classical Metres in English Verse* (Oxford, 1901), p. iv.
11. *Now in Wintry Delights* (Oxford, The Daniel Press, 1903). There is a six page commentary by Bridges on the technique of the poem which, to the best of my knowledge, has never been reprinted.
12. See "'New Verse' / Explanation of the Prosody of My Late Syllabic 'Free Verse'" in Bridges *Collected Essays,* No. 15 (London, 1933), p. 88.
13. According to the prefatory note in the original edition of *October and Other Poems* (London, 1920).
14. See the note of M.M.B. (Mrs. Bridges) in *Collected Essays,* No. 15, p. 86.
15. *Ibid.*
16. *Collected Essays,* No. 15, London, 1933, pp. 87-91.
17. *Ibid.,* p. 90.
18. *Poor Poll,* Privately printed at the Oxford University Press, 1923.
19. "Cheddar Pinks," however is printed in lines of 6+5 because the poem "came to him that way." *Collected Essays,* No. 15, p. 90.
20. *Milton's Prosody* (London, 1921), p. 60.
21. See John Sparrow, *Robert Bridges,* (Oxford University Press, 1955), p. 165; Edward Thompson, *Robert Bridges* (Oxford University Press, 1944), pp. 100-101; R. C. Trevelyan, "Prosody and the Poet Laureate," *The New Statesman,* XXIV (December 13, 1924), 296-298; R. C. Trevelyan, *XXI Letters, passim.*
22. Thompson, *Bridges,* p. 100.
23. *Ibid.*
24. *XXI Letters,* p. 4.
25. Yvor Winters, *Forms of Discovery* (Chicago: Alan Swallow, 1967), p. 203.
26. Sparrow, *Bridges,* p. 165.
27. *XXI Letters,* p. 4. A remarkable statement from the author of *Milton's Prosody*!
28. *XXI Letters,* p. 7.
29. *S.P.E.* Tract, No. XXXV, Oxford, 1931, p. 481
30. *Ibid.,* p. 503.
31. "Syllabic Verse in English," *Prairie Schooner* XXXI (Fall, 1957), p. 265.
32. Sister Mary Gretchen Berg, *The Prosodic Structure of Robert Bridges' "Neo-Miltonic Syllabics"* (Washington, D.C., 1962), p. xliv.
33. *Ibid.,* p. 79.

Donald E. Stanford (essay date 1978)

SOURCE: "The Traditionalist Poet," in his *In the Classic Mode: The Achievement of Robert Bridges,* Associated University Presses, 1978, pp. 19-79.

[In the following excerpt, Stanford examines Bridges's shorter poems, sonnets, and philosophical poems, and concludes that these works display a complexity and attention to poetic craft that is missing in the works of other poets of his era.]

Bridges's collection of ***Shorter Poems*** (1890)[1] established his reputation as one of the great lyric poets in English. Of this book A. E. Housman said that no volume of English verse had ever attained such perfection and anthologists of the future would have immense difficulty in making a selection.[2] In this first collection of the ***Shorter Poems*** there were a few experiments in accentual meters, and later Bridges wrote poems in classical prosody and in neo-Miltonic syllabics. These experiments and Bridges's explanations of them are important contributions to the theory and history of English prosody, and they resulted in a few beautiful poems that will be discussed in a later chapter. But the bulk of Bridges's lyric poetry is in what Bridges called common or running meter or "old style." It may be more precisely referred to as *accentual syllabic verse.* The accentual syllabic line (usually with an iambic movement), in which the rhythm is measured by a predetermined number of syllables and accents, has been the most common and the most successful meter in English since the sixteenth century. In the hands of a master such as Bridges this meter is capable of the most sensitive and subtle effects, obtained by various means but particularly by the skillful substitution of one kind of foot for another, by the use of light extrametrical syllables, and by the careful handling of quantity in relation to accent. Bridges unfortunately grew tired of it in later years—but not until he had achieved a body of poetry of great range and delicacy of feeling. Some of these metrical achievements will be noted in the discussion of individual poems.

Landscape Painting.[3] Although I consider Bridges's poetry to be primarily classical for reasons given in the Introduction, it must be admitted that he had a romantic poet's love of rural England—of the Kentish Downs remembered from childhood, of the South Downs in the area around his Berkshire home at Yattendon, of Oxford and its environs, and of the moors and the sea. He wrote a handful of astonishingly lovely poems depicting landscapes (often seasonal), rivers and streams, woods and fields. His images are precise and his sound effects subtle; usually the tone is serene and low-pitched. He seldom gives way to the kind of rhetoric one finds in Shelley's "Ode to the West Wind." Streams, brooks, rivers inspire some of his loveliest writing. **"There is a hill beside the silver Thames"** is one of the best. The focus of the poem is on a caverned pool beneath the hill described in the first stanza:

> Swift from the sweltering pasturage he flows:
> His stream, alert to seek the pleasant shade,
> Pictures his gentle purpose, as he goes
> Straight to the caverned pool his toil has made.
> His winter floods lay bare
> The stout roots in the air:
> His summer streams are cool, when they have played
> Among their fibrous hair.
> A rushy island guards the sacred bower,
> And hides it from the meadow, where in peace
> The lazy cows wrench many a scented flower,
> Robbing the golden market of the bees.

To this "purple pool" where nothing grows an occasional angler comes and sometimes

> a slow figure 'neath the trees
> In ancient-fashioned smock, with tottering cane.

Otherwise the poet who wishes solitude is safe to bathe in the stream or arrange his love trysts there. Because he cherishes his solitude, he wishes to keep the location of his retreat a secret. This is a perfectly simple poem in praise of retreat to the beauties and the solitude of nature—without power or depth but successful as a quiet tone poem.

There is a similar theme of retreat in the elegy **"Clear and gentle stream,"** in which the stream symbolizes the nostalgia for lost youth,

> Clear and gentle stream!
> Known and loved so long,
> That has heard the song
> And the idle dream
> Of my boyish day;

together with the mature poet's love of rural peace,

> Many an afternoon
> Of the summer day
> Dreaming here I lay;
> And I know how soon,
> Idly at its hour,
> First the deep bell hums
> From the minster tower,
> And then evening comes,
> Creeping up the glade.

These lovely verses open all editions of ***Shorter Poems***.

In **"Indolence,"** a river also is the center of interest, and there is just a hint of allegorical significance. The poet and his companion leave the city by boat late in the afternoon of a hot summer's day to drift idly downstream

> Past shallow islets floating in the sun,
> Or searching down the banks for rarer flowers
> We lingered out the pleasurable hours.

Toward evening they pass beneath an ancient bridge into a completely different world of calm and stagnant waters lined with crumbling walls, deserted wharfs, and vacant sheds—a world of absolute death:

> Then I who rowed leant on my oar, whose drip
> Fell without sparkling, and I rowed no more.

Sea, clouds, downs, and moors are described in a number of poems,[4] of which **"The Downs"** (admired by Hopkins) is probably the best. It is discussed in the chapter on accentual verse. **"Who has not walked"** is one of the loveliest poems of this group. As the poet looks across the Channel from Kent,

> The snow-white clouds he northward chased
> Break into phalanx, line, and band:
> All one way to the south they haste,
> The south, their pleasant fatherland.
> From distant hills their shadows creep,
> Arrive in turn and mount the lea,
> And flit across the downs, and leap
> Sheer off the cliff upon the sea;
> And sail and sail far out of sight.
> But still I watch their fleecy trains,
> That piling all the south with light,
> Dapple in France the fertile plains.

A few poems are devoted to seasonal landscape.[5] The best of these, **"The storm is over,"** is considered in the chapter on accentual verse. These seasonal poems are usually purely descriptive, without symbolism or even the suggestion of ulterior meaning, and are therefore slight though often charming. From **"April 1885"**:

> Wanton with long delay the gay spring leaping cometh;
> The blackthorn starreth now his bough on the eve of May:
> All day in the sweet box-tree the bee for pleasure hummeth:
> The cuckoo sends afloat his note on the air all day.

Response to Nature. Of the descriptive poems confined to a single scene (rather than a landscape),[6] the best and most famous is the accentual **"London Snow"** discussed in a later chapter. **"The Garden in September"**

> Where tomtits, hanging from the drooping heads
> Of giant sunflowers, peck the nutty seeds;
> And in the feathery aster bees on wing
> Seize and set free the honied flowers,
> Till thousand stars leap with their visiting,

with the Keatsian attention to sensuous detail is typical. The inversion of the third foot in the last line quoted is particularly felicitous.

There is an impressive group of poems that may present considerable descriptive detail, but in the depth of feeling aroused in response to beauty in nature they go beyond mere description and often suggest religious, aesthetic, ethical, or metaphysical concepts.[7] A few of these poems (such as **"I love all beauteous things"**) are simple statements of the poet's response to beauty without descriptive detail.

Bridges wrote several eclogues in the classical manner with obvious affinities with Theocritus, Bion, and Virgil. **"Eclogue I: The Months"** is taken up mainly with the poet's response to beauty in nature as it appears in the change of seasons. The change of seasons implies some consideration of the ravages of time, and Bridges makes the point, repeated in **"Elegy": The Summer-House on the Mound"** and elsewhere, that the poet can gain a temporary victory over time by evoking the experiences of the past:

> "The passion as I please
> Of that past day I can to-day recall."

The dialogue between the poets Basil and Edward begins on a rocky hill overlooking the vales of Somerset and the sea:

> As there in happy indolence they lay
> And drank the sun, while round the breezy height
> Beneath their feet rabbit and listless ewe
> Nibbled the scented herb and grass at will.

They recall that twelve years ago they had held a friendly competition, each poet composing alternate verses praising the months of the year. Each poet now recites from memory the verses composed by his friend, thus successfully reliving the past in the present and reaffirming that

> Man hath with man on earth no holier bond
> Than that the Muse weaves with her dreamy thread.

They are, in fact, doing more than salvaging the immediate past of the last dozen years. They are evoking the experiences of centuries ago:

> Like those Sicilian swains, whose doric tongue
> After two thousand years is ever young,—
> *Sweet the pine's murmur, and, shepherd, sweet thy pipe,—*
> Or that which gentle Virgil, yet unripe,
> Of Tityrus sang under the spreading beech
> And gave to rustic clowns immortal speech,

and they are reaffirming the immortality of the muse that is operating in Greek, Roman, and modern times—

> But these were men when good Victoria reigned,
> Poets themselves, who without shepherd gear
> Each of his native fancy sang the year.

This poem has considerably more substance than those previously discussed. Although the form of the eclogue is derived from the ancients and the diction occasionally reminds us of Keats, the poem is more than pastiche. In fact, these echoes of the past in form and style are appropriate to a major theme of the poem—the power of poetic inspiration that manifests itself throughout time, in the Victorian period as well as in the Romantic period and in the classical era.

Another traditional form, the ode, is effectively employed in the two odes to spring. The poem is concerned with what one would call today two life-styles, one based on the country,

> And country life I praise,
> And lead, because I find
> The philosophic mind
> Can take no middle ways;
> She will not leave her love
> To mix with men, her art
> Is all to strive above
> The crowd, or stand apart,

the other on the city. **"Spring Ode I"** is an invitation to the country. **"Spring Ode II"** is a reply from a city man who accepts the invitation. Both men are fundamentally hedonistic. The first finds his joy in the simple unambitious rural life:

> For Nature can delight
> Fancies unoccupied
> With ecstasies so sweet
> As none can even guess,
> Who walk not with the feet
> Of joy in idleness.

The second finds his pleasure in the city in good company, music, literature, and philosophy:

> Or if grave study suit
> The yet unwearied brain,
> Plato can teach again
> And Socrates dispute;
> Till fancy in a dream
> Confront their souls with mine,
> Crowning the mind supreme,
> And her delights divine.

The life-style of Bridges himself was a combination of the best of both worlds.

"The birds that sing on Autumn eves" is worthy of an Elizabethan song writer of the caliber of Campion. The poem is clearly allegorical. The song of the birds in spring represents the enthusiasms and vitality of youthful poets, the songs of autumn the mastery of the mature poet:

> Their notes thro' all the jocund spring
> Were mixed in merry musicking:
> They sang for love the whole day long,
> But now their love is all for song.
> Now each hath perfected his lay

To praise the year that hastes away:
They sit on boughs apart, and vie
In single songs and rich reply.

The unusual inversion of the second and third feet in the line "Now eách háth perfécted his láy," which strongly modulates but does not break the rhythm, is worthy of Campion himself. Bird song is also the direct inspiration of **"Larks"** and **"Asian Birds"**:

How the delicious notes
come bubbling from their throats!
Full and sweet how they are shed
like round pearls from a thread!

Similarly, the pinks in his garden are the subjects of two minor but pleasant poems, **"Cheddar Pinks"** in neo-Miltonic syllabics and **"The pinks along my garden walks."**

In **"Late Spring Evening"** Bridges is attempting a major poem. The first stanza is an address to the "Virgin-mother"—who seems to be a kind of nature goddess, a manifestation of ideal love—and the Muse:

I saw the Virgin-mother clad in green,
Walking the sprinkled meadows at sundown;
While yet the moon's cold flame was hung between
The day and night, above the dusky town:
I saw her brighter than the Western gold,
Whereto she faced in splendour to behold.

As the mystical vision continues, a kind of trancelike state is evoked:

And o'er the treetops, scattered in mid air,
The exhausted clouds laden with crimson light
Floated or seemed to sleep.

This mystical ecstasy rises to a climax in the powerful fifth stanza:

And when I saw her, then I worshipped her,
And said.—O bounteous Spring, O beauteous Spring,
Mother of all my years, thou who dost stir
My heart to adore thee and my tongue to sing,
on my heart's blood the fire,
Of all my satisfaction the desire!

The Love Poetry. As one would expect of a major lyric poet, many of Bridges's shorter poems are devoted to the subject of love. Some are obviously addressed to a certain lady; others are about love in general.[8] There is an air of conventionality about these love lyrics; they often remind one of Elizabethan songs. Most, while paying due respect to carnal love, seem to be chiefly concerned with spiritual love and beauty. They make an interesting contrast with the love poems of Bridges's contemporary, Thomas Hardy. Hardy's attitude toward women (perhaps influenced by his reading of Schopenhauer, probably influenced by his observation of life) is often one of ironic skepticism. The women in his *Satires of Circumstance* and elsewhere are often deceivers and destroyers of men, and they are treated with a rather shallow cynicism. This treatment of women is never found in Bridges. On the other hand, Hardy wrote a series of powerful love poems addressed to his first wife, Emma Gifford, and several other equally moving poems addressed (probably) to Tryphena Sparks. They have a specificity that Bridges's poetry lacks. For example, in the admirable *"The Head above the Fog,"* which recalls Hardy's trysts with Tryphena on Egdon Heath, the reader has an immediate sense of a particular woman (who wears a plume in her hat) on particular occasions in a particular place, and the effect is one of uncontrived sincerity:

O the vision keen!—
Tripping along to me for love
As in the flesh it used to move,
Only its hat and plume above
The evening fog-fleece seen.

In Bridges's love poetry one is always conscious of the craftsman at work, and there is usually a universal quality about it rather than particularity. The poem quite frequently could be about almost any lady almost anywhere. But I do not mean these remarks to be pejorative. The following lines by Bridges are general and "literary" when compared to Hardy; yet they have become a permanent part of the Aubade tradition in English verse. The metrics are beyond praise:

Awake, my heart, to be loved, awake, awake!
The darkness silvers away, the morn doth break,
It leaps in the sky: unrisen lustres slake
The o'ertaken moon. Awake, O heart, awake!

"Thou didst delight my eyes" records a love that was intense but temporary. The lady who once inspired the poet is now moving other poets to rhyme and is rejoicing other hearts. The first two stanzas state the theme in completely abstract language. The third stanza illustrates the theme with two metaphors. The poet, although he has lost the lady, is grateful for the redeeming love she gave him, however briefly:

For what wert thou to me?
How shall I say? The moon,
That poured her midnight noon
Upon his wrecking sea:—
A sail, that for a day
Has cheered the castaway.

One of Bridges's best lyrics, **"My spirit kisseth thine"** defines a love so spiritualized that it almost seems to be a poem about love of God rather than of woman. The final stanzas, which illustrate the mystical ecstasy of the poet's love with a description of sun and a winter landscape, are breathtakingly beautiful:

Like what the shepherd sees
On late mid-winter dawns,
When thro' the branched trees,
O'er the white-frosted lawns,
The huge unclouded sun,
Surprising the world whist,

Is all uprisen thereon,
Golden with melting mist.

Bridges wrote several other successful love poems that apparently refer to experiences with an individual lady or ladies. **"Wooing"** tells of an incident in which the poet had determined to end a love affair. He says his "final" farewell, but then relents:

And should have lost that day
My life's delight for ever:
But when I saw her start
And turn aside and tremble;—
Ah! she was true, her heart
I knew did not dissemble.

"So sweet love seemed that April morn" is a comment on the superiority of mature over youthful love, which seems to refer to Bridges's own personal experience. **"I climb the mossy bank of the glade"** begins with a specific incident and ends with the comment that the kiss of his mistress combines two fires: that described by the philosopher Heraclitus as the basis of life and that described by the poet Catullus as the essence of desire. **"One grief of thine"** states that the sorrow of his mistress was a joy to the poet because it drove her into his arms. **"Since we loved"** is, evidently, a triumphant reference to Bridges's completely happy marriage:

All my joys my hope excel,
All my work hath prosper'd well,
All my songs have happy been,
O my love, my life, my queen.

"Eros,"[9] one of the most impressive poems in the entire Bridges canon, defines and communicates the power of naked sensuous sexual passion as it is incarnated in the God of Love. Bridges uses the Greek Eros rather than the Roman Cupid in order to avoid the connotations of playfulness and mischievousness sometimes associated with the Roman God. He chooses the same Greek God as his hero of ***Eros and Psyche***, and there are overtones of that famous story in **"Eros,"** particularly in the line "And wouldst in darkness come." The meaning of the poem (as I understand it) is this: sexual passion is so dominant a force that even though it subverts reason (indeed, it is completely irrational and hence incompatible with reason) its victims feel that it has a good (a "light") of its own that is superior to reason. At first glance the theme may appear to be identical with Yeats's "Leda and the Swan," but it is not. The implication of Yeats's poem is that sexual experience leads to wisdom. Bridges's poem states that the victim of Eros believes his experience to be superior to the fruits of reason, wisdom, but the word *victim* suggests that Bridges considers this belief to be in error. Yet the poem, although it adopts a critical attitude, is not an attack on Eros. It is a realization of and an evocation of his power. As Robert Beum says, "Part of the poem's charm is that Bridges' critique is put in the most charitable manner compatible with a firm moral attitude. Eros is both king of joy and tyrant; he is essential, and yet he has to be kept in his place."[10] Bridges has been frequently criticized for being too spiritual, formal, and "remote" in his love poetry, and it is true that more poems in ***The Growth of Love*** sequence are devoted to heavenly or spiritual love than to earthly love. However, **"Eros"** demonstrates that Bridges was quite capable of appreciating and depicting sensual experience. It should be noted that the poem is universalized: it is about physical love in general and it is in impersonal terms. There is no comparable poem by Bridges dealing with the poet's personal, physical love for an individual woman, a fact that makes his love poetry quite different from the poems Yeats wrote to Maud Gonne and, as previously noted, Hardy wrote to Emma Gifford and Tryphena Sparks.

Many of Bridges's best poems are meditations and are, sometimes, lacking in those qualities which the New Critics have claimed must pertain to any successful poem—immediacy and dramatic appeal. **"Eros,"** however, does have these qualities. The poem is in the form of an apostrophe to the God, or (probably) to a statue or picture of the God. The opening lines set the tone of immediacy, of dramatic urgency:

Why hast thou nothing in thy face?
Thou idol of the human race,
Thou tyrant of the human heart,

Yet, the poet answers, such is the power of **"Eros"** that his complete lack of intellectuality, of spirituality ("Surely thy body is thy mind"), is disregarded, and in his pure sensuality he becomes "An image of eternal Truth." This sensuality not only takes the place of spirit ("light") but creates a new good, a new "light" of its own as stated in four of the greatest lines in all of Bridges's poetry:

O king of joy, what is thy thought?
I dream thou knowest it is nought,
And wouldst in darkness come, but thou
Makest the light where'er thou go.

The meter of the poem is perfectly conventional octosyllabic couplets (except for the final tercet), and it is handled with a discipline and a precision that are superior to Milton. There are a very few extrametrical syllables, and those that do occur are there for special effects. As Robert Beum has pointed out[11] the light extrametrical *er* in the line "With thy exuberant flesh so fair," gives a slight yet marked feeling of freedom to the line completely appropriate to the meaning. Similarly, the extrametrical *u* in "In secret sensuous innocence" contributes an appropriately lithe gliding quality to the rhythm. **"Eros"** is an excellent example of the kind of effects that can be obtained by subtle departures from a fixed and controlled meter. These effects are simply impossible in most free verse or in loosely written metrical verse.

A poem that has grown on me during frequent rereading and after having heard it recited years ago by Robert Hillyer in a lecture is **"The evening darkens over."** Like **"Eros,"** it is a generalized comment on love, but it is much quieter in tone. It presents a single scene, but the "scenic method" is not made dramatic or immediate as in Hardy. The poem has, rather, the quality of brooding meditation. Rhythm, assonance, sound, a few visual images, and a complicated but unobtrusive rhyme scheme are employed to achieve a minor masterpiece on the theme of the indifference of the physical universe to human needs, in this instance to human love. The significance of the beautifully presented detail is not realized until the final line, which states the theme of the poem:

> The evening darkens over
> After a day so bright
> The windcapt waves discover
> That wild will be the night.
> There's sound of distant thunder.
> The latest sea-birds hover
> Along the cliff's sheer height;
> As in the memory wander
> Last flutterings of delight,
> White wings lost on the white.
> There's not a ship in sight;
> And as the sun goes under
> Thick clouds conspire to cover
> The moon that should rise yonder.
> Thou art alone, fond lover.

"The Philosopher to His Mistress" and **"The Philosopher and His Mistress"** are on the same subject—the gulf between the melancholy intellectual and the woman who loves him but cannot enter into his philosopher's world. The gulf is bridged by an act of will on the part of the philosopher, who turns his back (momentarily, it is implied) on his intellectual world to be made happy in the arms of his mistress. The first is a good example of the poem of statement in a style that is primarily though not entirely abstract. The second is a development of a single simile. The melancholy philosopher who casts a shadow over the happiness of his mistress is compared to an eclipse of the moon. The shadow is dispelled and the happiness of the mistress is restored. As for the philosopher,

> And far my sorrowing shade
> Will slip to empty space
> Invisible, but made
> Happier for that embrace.

Two elegies (which are actually love poems) make an interesting contrast. The first, entitled simply **"Elegy,"** which begins "The wood is bare," recalls the poet's love for a girl now dead. The poem begins with a description of the woods in winter:

> The wood is bare: a river-mist is steeping
> The trees that winter's chill of life bereaves:
> Only their stiffened boughs break silence, weeping
> Over their fallen leaves.

The woods are obviously sharing the grief of the poet. The pathetic fallacy is operative throughout the poem. The poet recalls these same woods in a happier mood in spring and summer when he walked in them with his love:

> Yet it was here we walked when ferns were springing,
> And through the mossy bank shot bud and blade:—
> Here found in summer, when the birds were singing,
> A green and pleasant shade.

The poet then returns to the present scene where the winter woods are haunted by the ghost of his dead love:

> So through my heart there winds a track of feeling,
> A path of memory, that is all her own:
> Whereto her phantom beauty ever stealing
> Haunts the sad spot alone.

At the end, the poet weeps and despairs of spring. The poem has been criticized for sentimentality and overwriting, with some justification perhaps. Yet the sincerity of his grief somehow survives the rhetoric. In commenting on ***The Growth of Love***, Bridges mentioned a lady whom he loved, and who died young. One may surmise that **"Elegy"** is about her, and one may further surmise that the poet was very close to his material, perhaps too close, and hence the intensity of personal feeling that borders on hysteria and sentimentality.

The other elegy has a more elaborate title—**"Elegy: On a Lady Whom Grief for the Death of Her Betrothed Killed."** The poet is completely detached from his subject: he was obviously not personally involved with the lady. The style is somewhat cold and formal. Yet the rhetoric is brilliant. The poem is one of the best of the period in the artificial, ornamental style:

> Cloke her in ermine, for the night is cold,
> And wrap her warmly, for the night is long,
> In pious hands the flaming torches hold,
> While her attendants, chosen from among
> Her faithful virgin throng,
> May lay her in her cedar litter,
> Decking her coverlet with sprigs of gold,
> Roses, and lilies white that best befit her.

The preparations for the funeral, the funeral procession, and the union of the ghostly lovers in the afterworld (more pagan than Christian) are described in language worthy of Spenser at his best.

It is difficult to say what will be Bridges's final place in the history of the love lyric. As noted above, he does not dramatize his personal love affairs in the manner of Yeats and Hardy. Yet for that very reason, those love poems of Bridges that are general and universal (such as **"Awake my heart"**) may have a lasting interest as their stylistic virtues are better understood.

Response to Beauty. There are a few poems that are responses to beauty in literature and the arts.[12] "Ye thrilled me" is a criticism of Bridges's enthusiasm for "mournful strains" when he was young. Grown older, he believes that the best of art is gay. In **"Eclogue II"** Richard and Lawrence, on the occasion of the funeral of the Florentine sculptor Giovanni Duprè[13], discuss his personality and his art. Duprè's works never deserved "The Greek or Tuscan name for beautiful." Instead of becoming a major artist like Michelangelo, he forsook his love of beauty for his love of political action. He made of his life a work of beauty and is now " number'd with the saints, not among them / Who painted saints." In theme the poem reminds us of several poems by Yeats, such as "Sailing to Byzantium," that deal with the conflict between life and art. But of course the styles of Bridges and of Yeats are entirely different. Yeats usually writes in a highly pitched, figurative, and intense style; Bridges's **"Eclogue II"** has the tone of quiet meditation. **"Emily Brontë"** by Bridges, on the other hand, which praises the novelist for her freedom, innocence, wisdom, humility, will power, and courage in the face of death and her capacity for love, is in an ecstatic lyrical style, but it is perhaps not altogether convincing because the terms of praise are so general. They might be used with reference to any person one admires; neither the individual personality of the writer nor any particular characteristic of her work is realized in the poem.

Bridges had a deep and lifelong devotion to music, and there are a number of references to music and musicians throughout his poems. The first edition of ***The Growth of Love*** was dedicated to Purcell. **"To Joseph Joachim,"** an occasional poem written for the Diamond Jubilee of Joachim, May 16, 1904, and prefixed to the program of the music, is one of Bridges's finest sonnets in the Miltonic manner. Joseph Joachim (1831-1907), a distinguished Hungarian violinist, made his first appearance at the Philharmonic Society in London in 1844 where he played Beethoven's Violin Concerto. He was only thirteen years old at the time and earned the nickname of the Hungarian Boy. At the Diamond Jubilee sixty years later he repeated his performance of the Beethoven Concerto.[14] After 1862 his appearances in London became annual events for which he was credited with raising the standards of musical taste in England. Known as the greatest master of style, repose, and tone of his day, he was famous for his interpretation of his friend Brahms. His quartet (**"The Joachim Quartet"**) gave the premiere performance of Brahms's last chamber work, the great Clarinet Quintet in B Minor. As Bridges's sonnet notes, he also excelled in the interpretation of Bach and Beethoven. **"Buch der Lieder"** records the poet's enthusiasm when he was young for love songs that now no longer appeal to him. **"To Thos. Floyd,"** another completely successful Miltonic sonnet, is an invitation to his friend to visit Boar's Hill near Oxford where the walls (still roofless) of Bridges's home, Chilswell, are being built. The poem praises the rural scene, country life, and the view of the city of Oxford:

> The lovely city, thronging tower and spire,
> The mind of the wide landscape, dreaming deep,
> Grey-silver in the vale; a shrine where keep
> Memorial hopes their pale celestial fire:
> Like man's immortal conscience of desire,
> The spirit that watcheth in me ev'n in my sleep.

This passage, completely conventional in style, makes an interesting contrast to Hopkins's more ecstatic (and mannered!) description in "Duns Scotus's Oxford":

> Towery city and branchy between towers;
> Cuckoo-echoing, bell-swarmèd, lark-charmèd, rook-racked, river-
> rounded;
> The dapple-eared lily below thee; that country and town did
> Once encounter in, here coped and poisèd powers.

When Bridges wrote his poem in 1906 the arbiters of taste would have considered his lines superior to Hopkins's; today their opinion would probably be in favor of Hopkins. As a result of excessive experimental writing in England and America during the last five decades, there may be another revolution in taste that would favor Bridges.

Philosophical Poems. Bridges wrote a number of poems on various important subjects, more complicated and more profound than those discussed above. For want of a better term I have grouped them together as *philosophical poems.*[15] **"The Affliction of Richard,"** rather widely admired by the critics in Bridges's lifetime but now not frequently anthologized,[16], deals with the religious problem of a typical late-Victorian intellectual. As shown before, Bridges as a young man was seriously considering entering the ministry, but, unlike Hopkins, he seems to have taken the discoveries and attitudes of Victorian scientists seriously, so seriously that his original Christian faith was destroyed. Instead of becoming a minister he decided to become a physician. His loss of faith was followed by a period of skepticism, and this in turn was followed by a new and more mature faith not in dogmatic Christianity but in the existence of a God of Love. This poem defines the nature of that faith based on hope and on the argument that the existence of human love demonstrates the reality of divine love. The poem is in Bridges's plain style at its best—direct, powerful, without ornament or imagery:

> Though thou, I know not why,
> Didst kill my childish trust,
> That breach with toil did I
> Repair, because I must:
> And spite of frighting schemes,
> With which the fiends of Hell
> Blaspheme thee in my dreams.
> So far I have hoped well.

Victorian skepticism has been overcome by an act of will. **"Vision,"** like **"The Affliction of Richard,"** affirms that faith in Christ is based on love and that the faith of the mature man is even stronger than the ecstasies of youth:

> So 'tis with me; the time hath clear'd
> Not dull'd my loving: I can see
> Love's passing ecstasies endear'd
> In aspects of eternity.

The impact of science on Victorian faith is squarely faced in "The sea keeps not the Sabbath day." The poet and his love, as they view the sea whose "noisy toil grindeth the shore," see little evidence of a providential God or a God of love:

> We talk of moons and cooling suns,
> Of geologic time and tide

The eternal sluggards that abide
While our fair love so swiftly runs.

They realize that they are "so fugitive a part / Of what so slowly must expire." Yet their despondency is dispelled momentarily not by a renewal of religious faith but by thoughts of happier days and of pleasures derived from music and poetry, by

Days that the thought of grief refuse,
Days that are one with human art,
Worthy of the Virgilian muse,
Fit for the gaiety of Mozart.

The attitude here is one often found in Bridges's poetry—a refined intellectual hedonism. **"Pater Filio"** appears to be addressed to the poet's son Edward, born in 1892. It is darker, more pessimistic than Bridges's other religious poems. As he speaks to the innocent child he foresees the future:

Why such beauty, to be blighted
By the swarm of foul destruction?
Why such innocence delighted,
When sin stalks to thy seduction?
All the litanies e'er chaunted
Shall not keep thy faith undaunted.

"Joy sweetest lifeborn joy" is another affirmation of faith in a beneficent Deity, an affirmation that in this instance is not an act of will but is derived instead from intuitive experience, mystical moments of spiritual illumination:

Then comes the happy moment: not a stir
In any tree, no portent in the sky:
The morn doth neither hasten nor defer,
The morrow hath no name to call it by,
But life and joy are one,—we know not why,—
As though our very blood long breathless lain
Had tasted of the breath of God again.

One of the most powerful of the temptations to skepticism is the notion that although a God of Love may exist, his love is not necessarily directed toward human beings. According to the scientific world view, comparatively new in Bridges's time, we seem to be living in a universe indifferent to human happiness or suffering. This idea (so common in Hardy's poetry) is defined and eventually rejected in this same poem:

And heaven and all the stable elements
That guard God's purpose mock us, though the mind
Be spent in searching: for his old intents
We see were never for our joy designed:
They shine as doth the bright sun on the blind,
Or like his pensioned stars, that humn above
His praise, but not toward us, that God is Love.

Even when one is fortunate enough to experience some pleasures, they are merely transitory and therefore they seem to mock us:

Sense is so tender, O and hope so high,
That common pleasures mock their hope and sense;
And swifter than doth lightning from the sky
The ecstasy they pine for flashes hence.

. . . . .

Nay even the dear occasion when we know,
We miss the joy, and on the gliding day
The special glories float and pass away.

However, all of these occasions of discontent and pessimism are overcome in moments of divine joy that can, by an act of memory, become a permanent source of strength during the rest of our ordinary earthbound existence.

Joy is a frequently expressed emotion throughout Bridges's work. Sometimes it is of divine origin; sometimes it is simply motivated by healthy animal spirits; sometimes it is an aspect of his hedonism and springs from his contented, well-regulated, domestic life in a beautiful area of rural England; sometimes it is primarily aesthetic, a response to beauty in art and nature; and sometimes it is the ecstasy of love. Of these poems **"Fortunatus Nimium"** is the best known:

To dream as I may
And awake when I will
With the song of the birds
And the sun on the hill
For a happier lot
Than God giveth me
It never hath been
Nor ever shall be.

The innocent joy of youth, changed yet reaffirmed in maturity, is the theme of **"The snow lies sprinkled on the beach."** The sea—which is literally the sea but also a symbol of the outer mysterious and potentially hostile world—when confronted by the child, is a motivation of joy that is stronger than fear:

He from his dim enchanted caves
With shuddering roar and onrush wild
Fell down in sacrificial waves
At feet of his exulting child.

The joy is in part made possible by the innocence of the child. He does not understand the implications of what he is facing. As he grows older and understands more he becomes stoical:

My heart is now too fixed to bow
Tho' all his tempests howl at me.

Yet his joy in life (fortified by memories of his youth) continues, although now the joy is more solemn than previously:

For to the gain life's summer saves,
My solemn joy's increasing store,
The tossing of his mournful waves
Makes sweetest music evermore.

It should be noted in passing that Bridges's optimism is not quite so facile and superficial as that of the earlier

Browning. It has been tempered by religious skepticism and by the hardheaded common sense of the practicing physician and by the change in intellectual climate that one associates with the fin de siècle. His joy, as Bridges says in **"Fortunatus Nimium,"** is hard earned; it is all the more convincing to the twentieth-century reader for that reason.

Notes

1. Bridges's shorter poems previous to the 1890 collection appeared in a number of small volumes: *Poems* (1873); *Poems* (1879); *Poems,* Third Series, (1880); *Poems* (1884). *The Shorter Poems* of 1890 were selected from these earlier volumes augmented with previously unpublished poems and are grouped into Books I, II, and III. Book IV of this collection consisted of previously unprinted poems. *Shorter Poems Book V* appeared in 1893. Volume II (1899) of *Poetical Works* in six volumes reprinted all five books of the shorter poems and added a section entitled *New Poems.* The one-volume *Poetical Works* (1912) reprinted the five books of shorter poems, the *New Poems,* and added a section entitled *Later Poems.* Poems Written in the Year MCMXIII appeared in 1914 and was reprinted together with a group of new poems on World War I and some miscellaneous verses in *October and Other Poems* (1920). *New Verse* (1925) reprinted the poems in neo-Miltonic syllabics from *The Tapestry* (1925) together with new poems in conventional meter. For complete details see George L. McKay, *A Bibliography of Robert Bridges* (London, 1933). For this discussion of the shorter poems I have considered all of the poems written in conventional meters that have appeared in the above volumes.

2. Percy Withers, *A Buried Life: Personal Recollections of A. E. Housman* (London, 1940), p. 58.

3. The following may be considered landscape poems: "Who has not walked," "Clear and gentle stream," "There is a hill," "The Downs" [in accentual verse], "Indolence," "The upper skies," "The clouds have left the sky," "Last Week of February," "April, 1885," "Spring goeth all in white," "The storm is over" [in accentual verse], "North Wind in October," "November," and "Dunstone Hill."

4. See particularly "The Downs," "Who has not walked," "Dunstone Hill," and "The upper skies."

5. "Last Week in February," "April, 1885," "Spring goeth all in white," "North Wind in October," "November," "The storm is over." Seasonal description also, of course, appears elsewhere, particularly in some of the poems listed in n6.

6. See "London Snow" [in accentual verse], "Gay Robin," "The summer trees," "The garden in September," "The Palm Willow," "A Robin," "Winter Nightfall," and "Idle Flowers."

7. The following poems appear to fall in this category: "Late Spring Evening," "A Water Party," "Spring Odes I and II," "Morning Hymn," "I praise the tender flower," "I love all beauteous things," "When June is come," "The pinks along my garden walks," "The birds that sing on autumn eves," "Larks," "Asian Birds," "January," "A song of my heart," "First Spring Morning," "Eclogue I," "Now all the windows," "Riding adown," "In still midsummer night," "October," "The Flowering Tree" [in neo-Miltonic syllabics], and "Cheddar Pinks" [in neo-Miltonic syllabics]. "Eclogue I" is an idealized depiction of Bridges's friendship with Canon Dixon. See chapter 5.

8. The following love poems appear to be addressed to an individual lady: "Elegy," "Dear lady," "I will not let thee go," "Cliff-Top," "I found today," "Sometimes when," "Long are the hours," "I made another song," "Wooing," "The Philosopher to His Mistress," "My bed and pillow are cold," "O thou unfaithful," "Thou didst delight my eyes," "The full moon," "Awake my heart," "Songs," "Since thou, O fondest and truest," "My spirit sang all day," "O Love, my muse," "Anniversary," "When my love was away," "My spirit kisseth thine," "Ariel," "So sweet love seemed," "I climb the mossy bank," "To my love," "My delight," "Since we loved," "When Death to either shall come,—" "Wishes," "A love Lyric," "An Anniversary," "Vivamus," "One grief of thine," and "The Philosopher and His Mistress." "Elegy on a Lady Whom Grief for the Death of Her Betrothed Killed" is addressed to the memory of an individual person, but not one loved by the poet. Poems treating the subject of love in general are: "My eyes for beauty pine," "Love on my heart," "Fire of heaven," "Since to be loved," "O Love, I Complain," "Eros," "The Duteous Heart," "In der Fremde" [in neo-Miltonic syllabics]. and "The evening darkens over."

9. See the discussion of this poem in Albert Guérard, *Robert Bridges: A Study of Traditionalism in Poetry* (Cambridge, Mass., 1942), pp. 74-75; Robert Beum, "Profundity Revisited: Bridges and His Critics," *The Dalhousie Review* 44 (1964): 172-79; M. L. Rosenthal and A. J. M. Smith, *Exploring Poetry* (New York, 1955), pp. 183-85; Yvor Winters, *Forms of Discovery* (Chicago, 1967), pp. 198-99.

10. Beum, "Bridges and His Critics," 175-76.

11. Ibid., p. 177.

12. See particularly: "Ye thrilled me," "Eclogue II," "Emily Brontë," "To Joseph Joachim," "Buch der Lieder," and "To Thos. Floyd."

13. Giovanni Duprè (1817-82), an Italian woodcarver and sculptor born in Siena, made his home in Florence where he completed his successful recumbent figure of Abel and a bas-relief, "The Triumph of the Cross," over the main door of the church of Santa Croce. Other famous works include his "Pieta" in the campo santo of Siena, "Giotto" in the Uffizi gallery, Florence, and "St. Francis" in Assisi. His last important undertaking, a monument to Cavour in Turin, is considered a failure.

14. See the *London Times,* May 17, 1904, p. 11, for an account of the program.

15. The following poems have been placed in this category: "Dejection," "I have loved flowers that fade," "O my vague desires," "Haste on, my joys!," "Joy sweetest life-born joy," "O youth whose hope

is high," "Angel spirits of sleep," "Laus Deo," "The Affiction of Richard," "The north wind came up yesternight," "Weep not to-day," "Eclogue III," "Elegy: The Summer-House on the Mound," "The south wind rose at dusk," "The sea keeps not the Sabbath day," "Pater Filio," "Recollections of Solitude," "La Gloire de Voltaire," "To Robert Burns," "Narcissus," "Our Lady," "The Curfew Tower," "Hell and Hate," "The Excellent Way," "Poor Child," "To Percy Buck," "To Harry Ellis Wooldridge," "The Great Elm," "The Sleeping Mansion," "Vision," "Low Barometer," "The idle life I lead," "Crown winter," "The snow lies sprinkled on the beach," "A Vignette," "Melancholia," "Fortunatus Nimium," "The Tramps," and "Sorrow and joy." Only the principal poems are discussed.

16. See the discussion of this poem by Yvor Winters in "Robert Bridges and Elizabeth Daryush," *The American Review* 8 (January 1937): 355-57.

FURTHER READING

Criticism

Bacon, Leonard. "The Old Lion's Voice." *The Saturday Review* VI, No. 38 (April 12, 1930): 913-14.

Reviews Bridges's *Testament of Beauty,* calling it both beautiful in itself and original in its prosody.

Bush, Douglas. "From the Nineties to the Present. I." In his *Mythology and the Romantic Tradition in English Poetry,* pp. 429-56. Cambridge: Harvard University Press, 1937. Reissued, with a new preface, 1969.

Argues that in his long poems such as *Eros and Psyche,* Bridges reveals his aptitude for experimentation in verse form as well as his continuing interest in beauty, joy, and love.

Freeman, John. "Robert Bridges." In his *The Moderns: Essays in Literary Criticism,* pp. 319-41. London: Robert Scott, 1916.

Asserts that Bridges's most effective poetry is "simple and straightforward" in its celebration of beauty and of the English countryside.

Gorman, Herbert S. "Poets Who Recall Glowing Verse of the Nineties." *The New York Times Book Review and Magazine* (August 29, 1920): 13.

Reviews *October and Other Poems,* focusing on the poet laureate's "dignified" treatment of World War I.

Grierson, Herbert J. C., and J. C. Smith. "The Nineties." In their *A Critical History of English Poetry,* pp. 512-532. New York: Oxford University Press, 1946.

Compares Bridges to other poets of his era and describes him as a writer who was part of the classical tradition but who was nevertheless interested in experimenting in verse forms.

Hutchison, Percy. "The Testament of Beauty." *The New York Times Book Review* (January 19, 1930): 1, 22.

Calls *The Testament of Beauty* a "noble experiment" influenced by the works of the poet Dante.

Squire, J. C. "Mr. Robert Bridges's Lyrical Poems." In his *Essays on Poetry,* pp. 122-39. London: Hodder and Stoughton, 1923.

Looks at Bridges's *October and Other Poems* and considers it a work that is remarkably fresh, coming as it does from an aging poet laureate.

"The Testament of Beauty." *The Times Literary Supplement,* No. 1447 (October 24, 1929): 829-30.

Reviews *The Testament of Beauty,* calling it a highly disciplined work of poetry and the best that Bridges has ever written.

Additional coverage of Bridges's life and career is contained in the following sources published by the Gale Group: *Contemporary Authors,* Vol. 104; *Concise Dictionary of Literary Biography—British, 1890-1914; Dictionary of Literary Biography,* Vol. 19,98; *DISCovering Authors Modules—Poetry; Twentieth Century Literature Criticism.*

G(ilbert) K(eith) Chesterton
1874-1936

English poet, novelist, short story writer, critic, essayist, journalist, biographer, historian, and dramatist.

INTRODUCTION

Admired for the volume and diversity of his literary endeavors during the first half of the twentieth century, Chesterton is best known today as a colorful *bon vivant* as well as the creator of the Father Brown mysteries and of the fantastical novel, *The Man Who Was Thursday* (1908). But he was also a formidable Christian polemicist and writer of such poems as *The Ballad of the White Horse* (1911) and *The Ballad of St. Barbara* (1922), both of which treat battles in England's distant and more recent past as the stuff of legend.

BIOGRAPHICAL INFORMATION

Born in London and educated at St. Paul's School, Chesterton afterward studied at the Slade School of Art. Although he never became a professional artist, Chesterton did contribute illustrations to the novels of his friend Hilaire Belloc, and his strong gift for the pictorial is reflected in the vividness of his writing. While at the Slade School, Chesterton encountered and rejected the pessimistic, fin de siècle pose that was popular during his youth, eventually embracing an optimistic attitude toward life that can be found in his light verse collection *Greybeards at Play* (1900). Chesterton regarded himself first and foremost as a journalist. Indeed, one of his first jobs upon graduating from art school was as an art reviewer for a publisher. Shortly afterward he began his journalistic career in earnest with a series of articles that he contributed to the *Speaker,* a journal formed by some of his friends. By the time he married Frances Blogg in 1901, Chesterton had already become noted in London journalistic circles for his poetry, articles, essays, and reviews.

After marriage, Chesterton settled down to write the sort of prose works for which he is most admired, including *Orthodoxy* (1908), and *The Everlasting Man* (1925). Chesterton's writings are divided in tone between comic, high-energy excursions similar to those of Charles Dickens and serious meditations on the fate of humanity and the nature of faith. In 1922 Chesterton formally embraced Catholicism. Many of his early works presage this conversion; his works afterward are devoted almost exclusively to his interest in and defense of the Church. Chesterton was a prolific writer in a variety of genres; he continued to publish until his death in 1936.

MAJOR WORKS

Chesterton's poetry has been frequently anthologized. Verses such as the ebullient "The Rolling English Road" and the patriotic, and in some cases comical, "The Englishman," "The English Graves," and "The Secret People" define and celebrate the unique personality of the English. Poems such as "Lepanto" (which describes a sea fight between European forces and the Ottoman Empire) and *The Ballad of St. Barbara* (which recalls World War I's Battle of the Marne) are rousing martial tributes. Chesterton's epic *The Ballad of the White Horse* has, in its retelling of the English King Alfred's struggle against the Danes, been compared to its successor, J. R. R. Tolkien's *Lord of the Rings.*

CRITICAL RECEPTION

Although Chesterton's poetry remains popular, it has not always been well received by critics. Some worried about the apparent frivolity of his lighter poems. One early critic described Chesterton's verse as simultaneously banal, extravagant, and devoid of any genuine feeling. Others have acknowledged the poet's skillful use of language, describing his rhetoric as "dignified" even as they suggest that his verses are flawed. Scholars tend to agree that Chesterton's work was influenced by a number of sources, including the fin de siècle, art-for-art's-sake pessimism he later rejected and the rollicking humor of Charles Dickens's early works. Chesterton's writing was also deeply affected by his Roman Catholic beliefs. This faith is reflected strongly in works written even before his conversion, such as "Lepanto" and *The Ballad of the White Horse.*

Critics often distinguish between the puckish humor of Chesterton's light verse and drinking songs on the one hand and his serious, epic poems on the other. Perhaps it is appropriate, then, that he has been called the master of irreverent paradox. Scholars have remarked that through Chesterton's paradoxes, the seemingly self-evident is turned upside-down, causing readers to view their initial beliefs in a different light. This was part of Chesterton's purpose and his "chief idea of life": the awakening of a child's sense of wonder as if experiencing things for the first time. His essay "A Defense of Nonsense" describes a method of thinking that applies equally to his prose and poetry: "Nonsense and faith (strange as the conjunction may seem) are the two supreme symbolic assertions of the truth that to draw out the soul of things with a syllogism is as impossible as to draw out Leviathan with a hook."

PRINCIPAL WORKS

Poetry

Greybeards at Play 1900
The Wild Knight and Other Poems 1900
The Ballad of the White Horse 1911
Wine, Water and Song 1915
The Ballad of St. Barbara and Other Verses 1922
Collected Poems 1933

Other Major Works

The Defendant (essays) 1901
Twelve Types (essays) 1902
Robert Browning (criticism) 1903
The Napoleon of Notting Hill (novel) 1904
Heretics (essays) 1905
Charles Dickens (criticism) 1906
The Man Who Was Thursday (novel) 1908
Orthodoxy (essays) 1908
George Bernard Shaw (criticism) 1909
The Ball and the Cross (novel) 1910
What's Wrong with the World (essays) 1910
The Innocence of Father Brown (short stories) 1911
Manalive (novel) 1912
The Victorian Age in Literature (criticism) 1913
The Flying Inn (novel) 1914
The Wisdom of Father Brown (short stories) 1914
Eugenics and Other Evils (essays) 1922
The Man Who Knew Too Much (short stories) 1922
St. Francis of Assisi (biography) 1923
The Everlasting Man (essays) 1925
The Incredulity of Father Brown (short stories) 1926
The Return of Don Quixote (novel) 1927
The Secret of Father Brown (short stories) 1927
Four Faultless Felons (short stories) 1930
St. Thomas Aquinas (biography) 1933
Autobiography (autobiography) 1936
The Paradoxes of Mr. Pond (short stories) 1936

CRITICISM

Lee Wilson Dodd (review date 1912)

SOURCE: "The Ballad of the White Horse," in *Yale Review,* Vol. 1, No. 2, January, 1912, pp. 334-35.

[*In the following review, Dodd contends that while* The Ballad of the White Horse *has an engaging story line, its quality as a poem is "rough" and at times "infelicitous."*]

A critic may well tremble who is given a book of verse to review briefly, and who opens the book to find it contains but one mighty "Ballad" in eight "Books"—a poem, however named, of almost epical sweep and proportions, dealing in a free, broadly imaginative way with certain legendary or traditional material in connection with King Alfred. There can be no doubt that Mr. Chesterton, hitherto famed as a brilliant if often perverse writer of prose, has in this ***Ballad of the White Horse*** made a serious attempt to write not merely poetry, but a nobly planned poem. He tells his tale with a purpose, choosing King Alfred for hero "because he fought for the Christian civilization against the heathen nihilism." This battle is being waged to-day in the hearts of men; there are doughty champions on both sides. As a sturdy fighter against the present-day forces of intellectual nihilism, Mr. Chesterton is never to be despised. ***The Ballad of the White Horse*** is a good sword bared in the timeless conflict.

But what is to be said of it as a poem? In a brief space very little can be said with discrimination. For ***The Ballad of the White Horse*** is not a small matter; it does not belong with the Japanese ivories of modern verse. You will search through it vainly for curious felicities of language, not vainly for some very curious infelicities of rhythm and rhyme. Much ruggedness in a manly ballad may be forgiven, but only when it is a roughness as of broken surface-water borne on by the deep-flowing under-harmony of the tide. Mr. Chesterton does not, to my ear, always make this deep-flowing under-harmony felt. But he tells his tale like one in love with the telling—in other words, like a poet, a maker. And the tale is a good tale, filled with strong sorrows and ancient wrongs; filled chiefly, none the less, with undying hope and

"The giant laughter of Christian men."

The Athenaeum (review date 1915)

SOURCE: "Poems," in *The Athenaeum,* No. 4569, May 22, 1915, pp. 460-61.

[*In the following review of Chesterton's* Poems, *the reviewer concludes that the volume contains both the "best and . . . worst" of Chesterton's works, and that Chesterton is a better poet than he is a prose writer.*]

Robustness, sometimes giving way to an affectation of the robust, has always been the leading characteristic of Mr. Chesterton's work, both in prose and verse. This preference for size and strength has led him to select exceptionally large men—Sunday, Flambeau, Innocent Smith—to be the heroes of his romances, to employ words and phrases on account of their general largeness, to use superlatives and all the tricks of emphasis, often at a heavy cost. If Mr. Chesterton's poetry at its best suggests music, as good poetry must, it degenerates at times into the sort of music we associate with a crude open-air band. Fortunately for us, however, the robustness we have mentioned has not always the peculiar brazen quality of this class of music. The large and healthy laughter of some of the 'Rhymes for the Times' has not a false note in it. The lines addressed to Mr. Walter Long and Mr. F. E. Smith are joyous commentaries on statements made in unguarded moments, and the 'Ballades' at the end of the book have the true ring. In the 'Love Poems' too, and the 'Three Dedications,' we feel that Mr. Chesterton is being truly himself. But we suspect the sincerity of some of the other pieces. The author's imagery is varied, but it consistently returns to the language of battle. It is therefore natural that he should attempt to describe battles. In previous books of verse he has made the battles of Gibeon and Ethandune the subjects of flamboyant lines. In the book before us the longest poem is **'Lepanto,'** a rough, irregular composition ringing with energetic staccato notes. But an unrestrained rhetoric robs the poem of much of the impression it was undoubtedly meant to produce. So too, in the 'Sonnet to a popular leader much to be congratulated on the avoidance of a strike at Christmas,' we feel at once that the indignation is too rhetorical:

And I say
It would be better for such men as we,
And we be nearer Bethlehem, if we lay
Shot dead on scarlet snows for liberty,
Dead in the daylight upon Christmas Day.

Instead of robustness Mr. Chesterton occasionally achieves language perilously near rodomontade. At other times the same striving after largeness of effect yields verses such as this:—

So you have gained the golden crowns and grasped the golden weather,
The kingdoms and the hemispheres that all men buy and sell;
But I will lash the leaping drum and swing the flaring feather,
For the light of seven heavens that are lost to me like hell.

One of the least satisfactory features of Mr. Chesterton's work, in prose as in verse, is the obvious rapidity of its composition. Endowed as few are with the gift of the use of words, he scatters his good things recklessly. His work nearly always conveys the impression that it awaits a final and profitable revision. This is specially to be deplored in one who, when he has chosen, has shown a remarkable succinctness and exactness of expression, and whose ideas are generally well worth careful formulation. **'The Higher Unity'**, for example, is written with a verbal neatness recalling Hood at his best. The little book before us contains a selection of Mr. Chesterton's poems written on a wide variety of subjects during several years. In it both his best and his worst work are represented, and his best in verse is very good—some way, we think, above his achievements in prose. His prose may be better known; it is his verse that deserves to survive.

George Soule (review date 1915)

SOURCE: "The Attitude of Adventure," in *The New Republic,* Vol. IV, No. 52, October 30, 1915, pp. 341-43.

[*In the following review of Chesterton's* Poems, *Soule asserts that the poet takes refuge in "religious orthodoxy," "banality and bravado" in order to avoid the discomfort of genuine feeling.*]

Anybody who fancies himself in heroic declamation will probably, if he happens to read **"Lepanto,"** read it aloud. He is likely then to be so pleased with its brave colors and insistent sonority that he will repeat it a second and perhaps a third time. After that he is sure to avoid it as he would a Sousa march, not wishing to strut always with brass and drums. But he will find no relief in this book. All the poems are not quite so loud, but all—except the humorous topical verse—are equally emphatic. Words like pomp, gorgeous, thunder, ancient, crimson, scorn, myriad, blazing, thousandfold, giant, trumpets, immortal, golden, jewelled, stars, passion, repeat themselves endlessly in walloping anapaests and staccato iambics until the only thing left with any power to stir is silence.

Perhaps it is natural that a man who cannot write prose without twisting it into paradox should proclaim his verse with such bravado. He roars out his "Strong gongs groaning as the guns boom far," and his "Torchlight crimson on the copper kettle-drums," as if they were the sort of thing he cared most about in the world. After a while one wonders why he rarely speaks of anything as if he had really seen it with his own eyes and were filled with it, so that he could not crowd it into words at all unless they were his own authentic symbols. Here is no sensitive reverence for reality. What seems to exalt Mr. Chesterton most is his rectangular way of arranging images in his mind, enabling him to speak like a journalist, comfortably, of primary colors and big noises and people all good or all bad. There is scarcely a poem in the book which does not seem an attitude.

The attitude that Mr. Chesterton least tires of emphasizing is his religious orthodoxy. Although only a small section is devoted to "religious poems," thirty-six of the fifty nine poems in the volume mention God, and all are full of churchly words. Even the "love poems" include titles like **"Love's Trappist"** and **"Confessional,"** and are sprinkled with such phrases as "my soul's anointed" and "the fires that over Sodom fell." We are likely to conclude that Mr. Chesterton is unwaveringly orthodox about the same time we conclude he is not a poet.

Mr. Chesterton's orthodoxy gives him counters of thought and emotion with which he plays a game of definite rules, protected from any real uncertainty and from any real hostility except on the part of those who may try to break up the game. This man is red, that one is black. Each thing has one name, sanctified by authority, and you can shout it as many times and as loudly as you please. There is an understandable mechanism behind the world; it gives you assurance and relieves you of the arduous necessity of knowing each thing by itself. All you have to do is to classify it. This kind of orthodoxy is not confined to people of any religious creed. It is common to Mr. Chesterton, Mr. Roosevelt, the Marxian Socialist, and the jingo in time of war. If you have accepted a mechanical orthodoxy it is easy to speak familiarly of God, believe in unconditional generalities, or write emphatic verse.

Yet true poets have been orthodox as often as not. What is the difference between the kind of orthodoxy Mr. Chesterton uses and the kind a genuine poet has? How is it that what in another man might be simplicity and courage becomes in him banality and bravado?

Let us suppose that a mind keen for paradox and alive to the mysteries of reality, begins adventurously to explore everything that may interest him in the circle of his distance. And suppose that at length he finds himself far from his starting point, a little bewildered, homesick for something sure and accustomed. He wants to go back. But long ago he has told himself that his soul is free, that he is a fearless man and self-sufficient. Therefore he does not admit that he is tired, but invents a bold reason to still his pride. Going home is the adventure! This thing that we call the distance is really nothing at all; it offers not a goal, but a beginning. Did not his ancestors come out of it to build their house? He will return within the walls, that his own garden is a microcosm of the forest, knowing that everything in the world has its symbol in his domestic kingdom. He will sit quiet, sleep long and grow fat, and still be at peace with his adventure. One can really know the distance only when it is far away.

And so Mr. Chesterton's apparent naïveté is really an inverted subtlety, his orthodoxy a defensive reaction against beterodoxy. This interest in places over the horizon, which he has pushed out of his consciousness by an effort of will, reappears disguised. He must talk vociferously about the mystery of his garden, lest the mystery of the hills overwhelm him. He must prate eternally about romance, lest the genuine romance should make him uncomfortable again. But he is so busy in protestation that all the while he never really sees even his own garden.

Does this hypothesis account for Mr. Chesterton? Try it, the next time you feel an unacknowledged insincerity in him. Remember it, when he grows orotund in verse, or defends his orthodoxy in prose with engaging contradiction and an elaborate pretense of freedom. Such a hidden conflict may go far to explain him, if it explains the diffeence between the man who believes quite simply that the universe is his garden, and the man who has deliberately chosen to assert that his garden is the universe.

The Times Literary Supplement (review date 1922)

SOURCE: "A Modern Exuberant," *The Times Literary Supplement,* No. 1089, November 30, 1922, p. 779.

[*In the following review of works by and about G. K. Chesterton, the reviewer observes that Chesterton's* The Ballad of St. Barbara and Other Verses *reveals the poet's talent as a "dignified" rhetorician as well as his flair for lively verse.*]

There was room for a critical monograph on the work of Mr. Chesterton, and after the publication of Mr. Braybrooke's little volume there is still room. One can only regret that Mr. Braybrooke has attempted a task for which he appears to possess inadequate qualification. His loosely strung series of platitudes cannot for a moment be mistaken for the critical appreciation that it sets out to be.

Yet Mr. Chesterton's writings present many problems that might be discussed with profit. There is, for example, the paradox that his prose style is at once brilliant and tedious. It has many particular merits, but its general fault is its lack of chiaroscaro: it shines with so strong a light that the eyes become dazzled and the mind fatigued. The machine-gun rattle of his verbal tricks ends by jading the attention that it has first intrigued. When Mr. Chesterton submits to the discipline of verse, these disasters do not occur; and his verse is, for this reason and for others, not the idle diversion of a busy journalist, but the sublimation of his journalism. Much of his verse succeeds in being a kind of journalism without ceasing to be poetry. He is always in contact, and generally in conflict, with the spirit of the age. Hating many of the characteristic qualities of that spirit, he began his career by leaping into "the van of the modern movement," in order to unseat the driver and turn the horse's head in the direction of the Middle Ages. In that attempt he has been engaged ever since without the slightest loss of dignity. Combined with his intellectual nimbleness is a kind of high innocence that enables him to write in the grand, heroic manner without ever becoming ridiculous. The performance of certain other poets should show how rare an achievement that has become, and what grave risks they take who attempt it. Mr. Chesterton is conscious of no risks, nor are we as we read, because he is so entirely in earnest. There is a curious irony in the popular distrust of this writer, for, though far from being himself a plain man, he is yet the plain man's apologist. Less obviously but perhaps no less truly than Whitman, he is, even in his prose, the poet of democracy: he hymns the instinctive loves and hates of ordinary people; his literary life is an untiring crusade against the major modern heresies, a crusade that threatens every moment to become a charade yet never does so. The best of his fantastic stories—"The Napoleon of Notting Hill" and "Manalive"—are expanded epigrams, and the epigrams under close scrutiny are seen to be gigantic truisms that lie under every man's nose and are therefore, like his moustache, out of sight.

If exuberance is, as we believe, Mr. Chesterton's most conspicuous quality, it is yet from his poetry, the poetry that lives in his verse and flashes intermittently through his prose, that his work derives its literary importance. The poet that lurks in him is never for long silent. And the poetry that he utters is of a kind not much in vogue: it is something very far removed from any dreamy languor or popular lyrical sentimentality. Instead of inviting us to dream on beds of asphodel, it calls upon us, in the tones of the old heroic minstrelsy, to remember ancient glories and to defend our national and spiritual heritage. In verse, it falls naturally into the singing, stirring metres that in less skilful hands so readily become mere jingles. The volume to which the fine ***Ballad of St. Barbara*** gives its name is rich in illustrations of this method:—

> For these were simple men that loved with hands and feet and eyes,
> Whose souls were humbled to the hills and narrowed to the skies,
> The hundred little lands within one little land that lie,
> Where Severn seeks the sunset isles or Sussex scales the sky.
> And what is theirs, though banners blow on Warsaw risen again,
> Or ancient laughter walks in gold through the vineyards of Lorraine,
> Their dead are marked on English stones, their loves on English trees,
> How little is the prize they win, how mean a coin for these—
> How small a shrivelled laurel-leaf lies crumpled here and curled:
> They died to save their country and they only saved the world.

In prose, this poet finds voice in imagery that is militant, but never, in the modern sense, military. The instruments of modern carnage do not appear: it is the sword and the lance, the weapons of old chivalry, that bring their brightness and vigour to his writing. The banner of Saint George, rather than the flag of Empire, flutters there. At its best there is a Biblical ring in his style. It becomes full, for a moment, of the clash of clean fighting, the splendour of tournaments: his phrases flash and ring like swords upon a shield. And the quality that enables him to write like this without incongruity is the quality that, for want of a better term, we have called high innocence. This quality—together with vigour and a remarkable verbal skill—was never more conspicuous than it is in his latest volume of verse; and it is this that wins assent even when he is betrayed, by the ecstasy of his anger, into extravagance. Here is an example. The Chief Constable had issued a statement declaring that carol singing in the streets by children was illegal, and morally and physically injurious, and had appealed to the public to discourage the practice. Mr. Chesterton's comment which begins with an ironic "God rest you, merry gentlemen," takes the form of three stanzas. We quote the last:—

> So, when the song of children ceased
> And Herod was obeyed,
> In his high hall Corinthian
> With purple and with peacock fan,
> Rested that merry gentleman;
> And nothing him dismayed.

It is not in the moment of reading, but in the moment after, that one sees the rich absurdity of suggesting a parallel between a piece of modern officiousness and the Massacre of the Innocents. We do not love Don Quixote the less because he tilts at windmills.

To emphasize Mr. Chesterton's crusading chivalry to the neglect of all other aspects of his activity would be to leave the portrait wofully out of drawing. His wit and his fancy are too remarkable to be treated as mere incidentals of literary method. His fancy, especially, is of the very essence of the matter. In his new book, as in all its predecessors, our crusader draws his sword against drab philosophies, because they affront his own philosophy of strenuous gaiety and holy mirth. For him the pursuit of righteousness is an adventure; it is even, as one can imagine himself saying, a kind of celestial lark, as merry as a schoolboy lark, and as lovely as the "blithe spirit" of Shelley's ode. To his intellectual foes life may be a sordid tale signifying only the triumph of the worm; to him it is a battle infinitely beautiful, a pageant infinitely perilous. He has the artist's delight in form and colour, and the artist's contempt for the woolly phrasing that serves to hide inexact thought. But clear hard writing, more cunningly and no less effectively than vague writing, can betray the unwary reader. One can prove almost anything by a deft choice of clever, vivid metaphors that ignore fine shades, and bruise, as all metaphors do, the truth at which they grasp. The result may be a series of minute inexactitudes, each negligible in itself, but each contributing its mite to the cumulative error. Perhaps this is why *Orthodoxy,* unquestionably a sincere book and one that bristles with cleverness, excites the very misgiving it is designed to allay. It is like a wonderful debating speech that dazzles without convincing. With one hand the author pelts us with paradoxes, while with the other he never ceases to throw gold-dust in our eyes.

But if Mr. Chesterton cannot always win us in controversy, when he indulges his talent for fantasy he is irresistible. We have all had the experience of hearing a familiar word become strange to us by repetition, of seeing a familiar object become grotesque, even elfish, while we gaze at it. Ten thousand times we look at our teapot; and then, looking once more, for the first time we see it—see it as a monstrous and unsignifying shape in matter. This ordinary faculty of seeing things, as with the eyes of a new-born child, denuded of their rational and sentimental associations, is one that Mr. Chesterton possesses in an extraordinary degree; and to it we owe some of his happiest whimsies. On every page of his essays you may find examples of this queer vision. He may exaggerate it; he may, and does, exploit it for our fun and his own; but he does not invent it. It is a fact, not a fiction, that he embellishes with fancy. In his new book—not in the machine-made mysteries of the reprinted ***Club of Queer Trades,*** but in the volume of new poems—he celebrates this happy gift in verses which, like nearly all his verses, have the best qualities of his prose without any of its defects.

> When all my days are ending
> And I have no song to sing.
> I think I shall not be too old
> To stare at everything;
> As I stared once at a nursery door
> Or a tall tree and a swing.

This poem so strikingly expresses the essential Chesterton that one is tempted to transcribe the whole of it, but two more stanzas must suffice:—

> A thrill of thunder in my hair:
> Though blackening clouds be plain,
> Still I am stung and startled
> By the first drop of the rain:
> Romance and pride and passion pass,
> And these are what remain.
> Strange crawling carpets of the grass,
> Wide windows of the sky:
> So in this perilous grace of God
> With all my sins go I:
> And things grow new though I grow old,
> Though I grow old and die.

Whatever form he writes in, Mr. Chesterton is always abundantly and exuberantly himself: this must be our excuse for dwelling on his work in general somewhat to the neglect of the particular volumes under notice. He has this in common with Dickens, the subject of his best literary criticism: that if all his writings were bound up together they would form one enormous and versatile but homogeneous book. The best of the qualities we have ascribed to him are to be found, in generous measure, in ***The Ballad of St. Barbara and other Verses***. In some of these poems he reaches the high-water mark of his literary achievement, and this is no small thing to say of a poet who had already written "*O God of Earth and Altar*." More skilfully, because more passionately, than almost any other modern author, he can use that old-fashioned weapon, rhetoric. He can write at once with pomp and with dignity. Here, for a last example, are some lines from the dedication verses **"To F. C. in Memoriam Palestine"**:—

> The mystic city many-gated,
> With monstrous columns, was your own:
> Herodian stones fell down and waited
> Two thousand years to be your throne.
> In the grey rocks the burning blossom
> Glowed terrible as the sacred blood:
> In was no stranger to your bosom
> Than bluebells of an English wood.
> Life is not void or stuff for scorners:
> We have laughed loud and kept our love,
> We have heard singers in tavern corners
> And not forgotten the birds above:
> We have known smiters and sons of thunder
> And not unworthily walked with them,
> We have grown wiser and lost not wonder;
> And we have seen Jerusalem.

H. E. P. (review date 1922)

SOURCE: "A Teutonic Minstrel," in *The New Statesman,* Vol. XX, No. 505, December 16, 1922, pp. 335-36.

[*In the following review of Chesterton's* The Ballad of St. Barbara and Other Verses, *H. E. P. describes Chesterton as a patriotic poet whose facility with words usually overcomes any flaws in his verse.*]

There are some books of verse which to criticise scrupulously seems almost a sacrilege. They may be full of eccentricities, carelessness, and distortions of metaphor and expression, laying themselves open to protest or damaging parody, but withal so full of vision, emotion, and rich music that the confounding cussedness and impish obscurity which sprawls into every third page gets very nearly obliterated when an unprejudiced reviewer pronounces a final judgment. Mr. G. K. Chesterton's ***Ballad of St. Barbara and Other Verses*** is one of these extraordinary books. The present reviewer would begin by saying that Mr. Chesterton is intensely original and individual. If you try to yoke him to one of his established English predecessors you will have a thankless task. Maybe at moments he sounds a little like Lord Macaulay, and at another time like a sort of ghostly fusion of Kit Marlowe and Blake, or of Swinburne and Blake; but the resemblance at closest is not too pronounced. Of course, Mr. Chesterton must have read all the old ballads written in the English tongue; and he may perhaps have read all the few existing epics and fragmentary poems of the Saxon scops. Add to that, if you like, everything else Teutonic, be it Danish, Icelandic, or German (though one cannot tell which particular poems); and if you have never read him at all and bear in mind that he also loves the use of amazing paradoxes, you will have some idea of his bewildering but forcible quality. A reviewer who turns over the pages of, say, three representative German anthologies containing selections from mediæval to recent times (one of them to be a student's drinking song-book) will certainly find a great deal that is remindful of Mr. Chesterton (both in this and his other verse books), particularly noticeable in their intensely racial outlook and something straightforwardly musical, resonant, and rhetorical in the language—to say nothing of their wine and beer-imbibing enthusiasm. One is tolerably certain that poets like Bürger, Schiller, and Liliencron, and probably also the divine and demoniacal Heine, would have derived pleasure from Mr. Chesterton once they had sifted away the paradoxes and the lyrics containing the most extravagant figures of speech. There is a royalist strain in the man, too. You may sing of Liberty and shout, "Down with Tyrants!" as hard as you like, but you cannot be quite so enthusiastic about mediævalism and write in the old-fashioned manner without recalling Elroy Flecker's heartening "We poets of the proud old lineage," spattering meanwhile half a hemisphere with your ancestral blue blood. Dislocate Mr. Chesterton, shake all his limbs out of joint, but at the same time preserve unbroken the great frame of the man, and then place him a little behind mediævalism or at the very door of it, and confidently assume that in remote times his disturbing voice thrilled the hearts of the thanes guarding our democratic King Alfred, and that his hand tintinnabulated on the harp while the great monarch at repose was watching his clock-candles and planning to withstand an onslaught from the Danes or other barbarians.

Of course, if in this country things go from bad to worse, Mr. Chesterton will probably be interned. Not for his mediævalism and outward Teutonic qualities (for he pretends to fearfully hate all Germans) but because he espouses the cause of the distressed and downtrodden, and smokes and blazes with uncompromising indignation when he is face to face with certain kinds of barbarians. How hard he smites at such selfish self-seekers as profiteers, land-taxers, and usurers! Take, for instance, these two stanzas culled from **"On the Downs,"** one of the best ringing songs he ever put on perishable paper:

> It has not been as the great wind spoke
> On the great green down that day:
> We have seen, wherever the wide wind spoke,
> Slavery slaying the English folk:
> The robbers of land we have seen command,
> The rulers of land obey.
> We have seen the gigantic golden worms
> In the garden of paradise:
> We have seen the great and the wise make terms
> With the peace of snakes and the pride of worms,
> And them that plant make covenant
> With the locust and the lice.

It is excellently well phrased and searingly truthful, that

> gigantic golden worms
> In the garden of paradise.

It is also typical Chestertonese, and in this instance is no example of either violence, extravagance, or bombast—three of Mr. Chesterton's most insidious pitfalls (though none of these so bad as that present-day fashionable one, the anæmic). Moreover, both stanzas are so natural and easy. A great deal of damaging nonsense has been pegged to the reviewer's condemnatory "facile." It is a good shield to push in the faces of indisputable minor poets when they do little else save smother good work beneath their own aggressive derivations; but that does not alter the essential fact that first-rate short poems (particularly those which have endured) nearly always sound "facile," and it is the conscientious poet's business to work at his stanzas until they seem as if struck from a swift and sudden pen. Often Mr. Chesterton's seemingly sudden facility under severe examination reveals very vigorous application, as in the following exceedingly moving and inspiriting lines:

> There are more windows in one house than there are eyes to see,
> There are more doors in a man's house, but God has hid the key;
> Ruin is a builder of windows; her legend witnesseth
> Barbara, the saint of gunners, and a stay in sudden death.

At any rate, it is a very good example of the facility of the artist and visionary, though, perhaps, nothing in this book for spontaneous ease and beauty will surpass the single line,

> Still as the heart of a whirlwind the heart of the world stood still.

Then take another typical stanza from a particularly musical and prophetic poem:

> His horse-hoofs go before you,
> Far beyond your bursting tyres;
> And time is bridged behind him
> And our sons are with our sires.
> A trailing meteor on the Downs he rides above the rotting towns,
> The Horseman of Apocalypse, the Rider of the Shires,
> For London Bridge is broken down, broken down, broken down;
> Blow the horn of Huntingdon from Scotland to the sea—
> . . . Only a flash of thunder light, a flying dream of thunder light,
> Had shown under the shattered sky a people that were free.

The temptation to quote a preceding stanza is not to be withstood:

I saw the kings of London town,
The kings that buy and sell,
That built it up with penny loaves
And penny lies as well:
And where the streets were paved with gold, the shrivelled paper
shone like gold,
The scorching light of promises that pave the streets of hell.
For penny loaves will melt away, melt away, melt away,
Mock the mean that haggled in the grain they did not grow;
With hungry faces in the gate, a hundred thousand in the gate,
A thunder-flash on London and the finding of the foe.

There is also a frequent note of real anguish in this book, as in the last line of **"The English Graves"**:

They died to save their country, and they only saved the world.

Another of Mr. Chesterton's distinctions is that he is one of the few good poets who have written several poems about Christmas, though the lyric included in this book is not of a very elevating character, as the first stanza of it will show:

God rest you merry, gentlemen,
Let nothing you dismay;
The Herald Angels cannot sing
The cops arrest them on the wing,
And warn them of the docketing
Of anything they say.

But it is almost a relief from the fierce tension of his passionate strains to turn to such poems and to the impish satire of his paradox oddities and the queer kaleidoscope ***Songs of Education.*** One of the best of these is***The Higher Mathematics,*** a snatch of which runs:

Half of two is one,
Half of four is two,
But half of four is forty per cent. if your name is Montagu:
For everything else is on the square
If done by the best quadratics;
And nothing is low in High Finance
Or the Higher Mathematics,

and then winds up with the exceedingly brilliant and veracious,

Where you hide in the cellar and then look down
On the poets that live in the attics;
For the whole of the house is upside down
In the Higher Mathematics.

But all this is not illustrative of everything. There are scores of questionable flashes in the book like:

Our blameless blasphemies of praise,

and

Dreams dizzy and crazy we shall know.

One could fill a page with these highly alliterative, fizzing, crackling lines that Mr. Chesterton perhaps ought not to have written; but the good and sound parts of the book are so good that much of the chaff burns with a clear steady flame, and is consumed under the heat of the good. And he is what you call a Christian poet, takes a firm stand, and plays with neither folly, vice, nor greed. His prevailing motto seems to be "He that is not with us is against us." Nor are his errors of outlook sufficiently numerous and pronounced to earn him in any way the reproach of "fanatic."

William Rose Benet (review date 1932)

SOURCE: "Round about Parnassus," in *The Saturday Review of Literature,* Vol. VIII, No. 34, March 12, 1932, p. 588.

[*In the following excerpt, Benet gives a positive review of* The Collected Poems of G. K. Chesterton*, concluding that Chesterton's poetry in particular "communicates noble emotion."*]

The Collected Poems of G. K. Chesterton (Dodd, Mead) is, to me, an event. Despite his infinite polemics, his numerous novels, his multitudinous essays, his detective stories, and his master paradoxes, Gilbert Chesterton's greatest gift from the gods was the gift of verse. If he learned his art from masters so diverse as Lord Macaulay, Algernon Charles Swinburne, and Charles Stuart Calverley, nevertheless he learned his lessons well. And from his lessons he rose to travel his own road. It turned out to be the road of the troubadour. If his paradoxes stole into his lyrics like the little dwarfs he describes that stole in and out of the black velvet tapestry on the walls of King Philip's closet, in G. K. C's great ballad of **"Lepanto,"** they attained new significance there. Frankly a militant Christian, he has sung his creed always as one of gallantry and chivalry and made of it a thrilling thing. There is a fine masculine ring and roll to his ballad stanzas. His humorous and satirical verse, on the other hand, his parody and his biting irony, have displayed a new master of light verse. There has been nothing better in the Ballade in recent times—as entirely distinguished from the Ballad—than **"A Ballade of Suicide"**—

The world will have another washing day;
The decadents decay; the pedants pall;
And H. G. Wells has found that children play,
And Bernard Shaw discovered that they squall;
Rationalists are growing rational—
And through thick woods one finds a stream astray,
So secret that the very sky seems small—
I think I will not hang myself to-day.

There is no more original drinking song in the language than **"The Rolling English Road"**:

His sins they were forgiven him; or why do flowers run
Behind him; and the hedges all strengthening in the sun?
The wild thing went from left to right and knew not which was which,
But the wild rose was above him when they found him in the ditch.
God pardon us, nor harden us; we did not see so clear
The night we went to Bannockburn by way of Brighton Pier.

Such deeply humorous things that yet preserve the essence of poetry are genuine achievements. And with what an undeniably heroic accent the remarkable ***Ballad of the White Horse*** begins! The dedication to the poet's wife gives human love a true definition in strong, compact stanzas:

And I thought, "I will go with you,
As man with God has gone,
And wander with a wandering star,
The wandering heart of things that are,
The fiery cross of love and war
That like yourself, goes on."

Such poetry accomplishes one fundamental object of poetry, it communicates noble emotion. And in that the emotion is perfectly genuine it never rings false, however rhythmically expressed. Chesterton's sense of humor, which is another way of saying his sense of proportion, controls him when he is most serious. And his poetry gains in drive because—whether one agrees with it or not—it is directed from a single point of view. This writer has always been a good antidote to a good deal of highfalutin' modernism consisting mainly of windy phrases or didacticisms accepted by the many simply because they were so positively stated. But Chesterton allows no new dictum to escape without thorough examination. One may not agree with him that the Roman Catholic Church possesses the only healthy road to life in a most peculiar world, but one must admit much sanity of vision in the man himself. And certainly he is a good workman at his song. The kind of thing he has been doing in verse all these years is, of course, as different from modern experimentation as anything could well be, but though its roots are in the great tradition, Chesterton always commands an unexpected turn of his own with which to freshen his garlands. And the argument of his ballads distinguishes them from any others. If it be said that his mysticism has a tendency toward formula I think that a closer examination of his shorter poems and of the passages of the longer where it is most in evidence, will show that his use of paradoxical statement is far more spontaneous than that. It is hard to prophesy where he will rank in contemporary English verse when the years have rolled on. But I believe that anyone who has the normal desire for poetry that sings itself will be reading ***The Ballad of the White Horse*** and others for a long time.

Thomas Curtis Clark (review date 1932)

SOURCE: "G. K. C.," in *The Christian Century,* Vol. XLIX, No. 22, June 1, 1932, p. 705.

[*In the following review of the* Collected Poems, *Clark emphasizes Chesterton's frequent use of paradox.*]

Paradoxical always, Mr. Chesterton lives up to his reputation in this new collection of his poems. He has put into the book his whole paradoxical self—newspaper rhymester, with briefs like

Mince-Pies grant wishes: let each name his prize,
But as for us, we wish for more Mince-Pies;

anti-prohibition pamphleteer; Roman Catholic champion; foe of freakish modernist poetry; playboy of literature, with takeoffs on the classic poets, Wordsworth, Byron, Swinburne; master balladist, with his masterpiece, ***The Ballad of the White Horse*** in 100 pages; biting critic of nationalism, with his **"The World State,"** beginning,

Oh, how I love Humanity,
With love so pure and pringlish,
And how I hate the horrid French,
Who never will be English!

foe of war and war-makers, with poems like "Elegy in a Country Churchyard," closing with

And they that rule in England,
In stately conclave met,
Alas, alas for England
They have no graves as yet;

true mystic, as in his poem **"A Word,"** beginning "A word came forth from Galilee, a word like to a star"; lover of beauty; battle against cranks—vegetarians, for instance.

All of Chesterton is here. Evidently this poet, unlike some others, has not looked forward to a time, a hundred years hence, when his poetic work might be weighed in the balance of critics, taking care that only his "best" is preserved. He is one poet who does not seem to take himself so very seriously. Every page of his book indicates that its author writes verse because he finds sheer delight in writing it—of all sorts, on all themes. And it is pleasant to run across just such a poet.

Chesterton can write tender poems, such as **"The Song of the Children,"** in which the little ones are grieving because

They have taken and slain our Brother,
And hanged Him on a tree.

He can write glorious, colorful poems, in ringing measures, as his **"Lepanto,"** beginning

White founts falling in the courts of the sun,
And the Soldan of Byzantium is smiling as they run.

Here is that brief poem, **"The Donkey,"** which upon its first publication was reprinted the English-speaking world over: the poem in which the despised beast of burden tells of its one glorious hour, when

> There was a shout about my ears,
> And palms before my feet.

Whether Chesterton writes as a pure poet, as a religious mystic, as a foe of war and injustice, as a champion of freedom, as a literary critic, he always writes effectively; his words go straight home. And in none of his poems is he more effective than in those in which he calls for a rebuilding of the world on the basis of justice and good will and brotherhood. If there were no poems in this new volume except those in which he attacks war and the inhumanity of our so-called civilization, it would still be one of the great books of poetry of this decade. His poem, **"The Buried City,"** belongs in our new Bible of poetry, out of these times and for these times. Here is the first stanza of this tremendous appeal:

> You that go forth upon the buried cities,
> Whose witchcraft holds the withered kings together,
> Seals up the very air of ancient seasons,
> Like secret skies walled up from the world's weather;
> You that dig up dead towns—arise and strive:
> Strike through the slums and save the towns alive!

Harold M. Petitpas (essay date 1971)

SOURCE: "Chesterton's Metapoetics," in *Renascence*, Vol. XXIII, No. 3, Spring, 1971, pp. 137-44.

[*In the following essay, Petitpas examines the philosophical, Christian, and Romantic elements that influence both Chesterton's own poetry and his ideas about poetry in general.*]

Critics of poetry may be conveniently grouped into two categories: purely poetic critics who in a rigorous scientific spirit isolate a poem from extrapoetic reality, dwelling upon its internal relationships and evaluating it primarily by the principle of coherence; and, metapoetic critics who in a more philosophic spirit relate a poem to other reality, drawing out its transcendental dimensions and evaluating it primarily by the principle of correspondence. When Bradley defends the idea of "Poetry for poetry's sake"; when MacLeish affirms that "a poem should not mean / But be"; when Auden concludes that "poetry makes nothing happen";—they are speaking in the voice of the purely poetic critic. On the other hand, when Arnold defends the idea of poetry as being "at bottom a criticism of life"; when Wordsworth affirms that "Poetry is the first and last of all knowledge"; when Shelley concludes that poetry is "at once the centre and circumference of knowledge";—they are speaking in the other voice of the metapoetic critic.

Metapoetic critics in turn may be conveniently grouped into these categories: practical critics whose primary interest is to interpret and evaluate particular poetry by standards that go beyond merely technical criteria; and, theoretical critics whose primary interest is to discover the nature of poetry itself. Within the first category of metapoetic critics may be included Arnold, Leavis, and Winters; within the second, Wordsworth, Shelley, and Chesterton. Metapoetic critics of the first category share with the purely poetic critics a primary interest in interpreting and evaluating particular poetry whereas those of the second category share with the aestheticians a primary interest in reaching the essence of the object under examination.

The purpose of this study, then, will be to identify and exemplify the metapoetic way that Gilbert Keith Chesterton (1874-1936) approaches poetry. Since Chesterton—defiantly anti-systematic as he was—did not publish a formal statement on poetics, the scholar must depend upon the numerous, scattered (and, at times, seminal) generalizations on poetry in his voluminous works to develop at least the probable contours of his metapoetics.[1] To impose some order on the discussion to follow and to interrelate Chesterton's ideas on poetry within a scheme, we shall consecutively consider how he would most probably treat in a metapoetics such central problems as these: (1) Wherein lie the origins of poetry? (2) What are its identifying elements? (3) What are its ends?

In approach alien to the puristic tendencies of much twentieth-century criticism, Chesterton would propose an ontological origin of poetry—the primal fact that things really are, that they really are there, that they are stubbornly other. The poetic urge to create is rooted in this mysterious presence of the other, of the objectively real. "That *strangeness* of things, which is the light in all poetry, and indeed in all art, is really connected with otherness; or what is called their objectivity. What is subjective must be stale; it is exactly what is objective that is in this imaginative manner strange. In this great contemplative is the complete contrary of that false contemplative, the mystic who looks only into his own soul, the selfish artist who shrinks from the world and lives only in his own mind" (*St. Thomas Aquinas,* 1933). Contrasted to the extreme romantic, to that artist who directs the imagination solipsisticly, the authentic poet—by his very psychic energies—directs it towards the other " . . . because the images that it seeks are real things. All their romance and glamour, so to speak, lies in the fact that they are real things; things *not* to be found by staring inwards at the mind" (*St. Thomas*). As the Grecian Urn teases out of thought, likewise this gratuitous nature of things, this contingency of things, stirs within the poetic mind those experiences that lie too deep for words.

The very idea of the beautiful, Chesterton would contend, is rooted in this radical otherness, this radical strangeness of things. In his words, "I believe about the universal cosmos, or for that matter about every weed or pebble in the cosmos, that men will never rightly realize that it is beautiful, until they realize that it is strange. . . . Poetry is that separation of the soul from some object, whereby we can regard it with wonder" (*Christendom in Dublin,* London, 1933). The argument here (within the Western Classical Tradition) is that the principle of identity, that of separation, is a prerequisite for all art. The implication is that the pantheistic philosopher in dissolving the artist within the cosmic stuff literally cuts the throat of poetry. In a more general way, the implication is that neither aesthetics nor poetics can be divorced from the philosophy that underpins them.

Myth which is on such easy terms with a universe intrinsically wonderful and strange Chesterton would extol as the prototype and model of all poetry. Myth is quintessentially poetical—a theme recurring in Chesterton's brilliant *The Everlasting Man.* In the seductive way that it entrances the imagination (by entrapping it to accept an image before the censorial reason can veto it), in the unexpected correspondences that it adumbrates between nature and the depths of the human soul, in the sacramental awareness that it arouses of the magic latent in material things, myth conditions man to a kind of truth that forever eludes the categories of the purely rationalist critic. In *The Everlasting Man,* poetic and mythic expression are allied in the recognition that myth belongs to the "poetical part of men," that myth evidences a distinct logic, presenting an "imaginative outline of truth," that myth is the eternal human response to the "tempting and tantalizing hints of something half-human in nature," and, that ultimately myth is an attempt to "reach the divine reality through the imagination alone." Such an alliance with myth hints at the truth that poetry is indeed ontological, nay theological.

Viewed objectively, then, poetry is rooted in ontology. Viewed subjectively, it is rooted in those subliminal stirrings within the psyche that are the wellspring of all creativity. Chesterton would state emphatically that poetry is thus rooted in the emotions. Such a primary truth eludes theorists of a scientific bent who equate poetry with rhetoric, with technical dexterity, with verbal gymnastics, with even speculative philosophy. No, poetry is not primarily a matter of technique, however ingenious, nor of theory, however subtle; rather, it is the incarnation of a vision—a vision that presents things as "they are to our emotions, not as they are to any theory . . . " (*Robert Browning,* London, 1936).

And, of the emotions that give rise to poetic expression, none, in Chesterton's judgment, rival those of joy and of praise. The poet, but primarily the Christian poet, is stirred to praise, to gratitude, to exaltation, in contemplating the gratuitous fact of existense, at the astonishing realization that things really are whereas they might not be. Such a poet "praises the passage or transition from nonentity to entity; there falls here also the shadow of that archetypal image of the bridge, which has given to the priest his archaic and mysterious name." (*St. Francis of Assisi,* 1924). Such a poet enthusiastically utters a statement of affirmation. The authentic poet, such as Chaucer, identifies himself "because he sings; because he opens his lungs and liberates his soul by a resounding and rhythmic utterance, the expression of love or admiration or passionate amazement" (*Chaucer,* London, 1932). This lyrical impulse recalls poetry's traditional association with song, in which association there lies a whole poetics.

Being rooted thus in the emotions rather than in the reason, poetry utters a distinctive truth—a truth that frequently counters that of the scientist and that of the philosopher. Not that poetry is anti-rational, but rather that is "suprarational," the voice of a higher reason. For poetry, as music, strikes a note "which expresses beyond the power of rational statement a condition of mind . . . " (*Robert Browning*). It hints at secondary meanings that are life's primary meanings.

With the authentic poet, emotion comes first, artistic expression second. Chesterton, accordingly, would agree with Maritain that poetry and art are not to be identified. For, unless the poet gives vent to a genuinely personal emotion—that is, an emotion not contrived nor manufactured, no degree of technical skill, no degree of artistic dexterity, will suffice to sound the note of true poetry. A poet's skill, his technique, subserves his creative intuition.

It is to Wordsworth that Chesterton would turn to explain the ideal conditions for poetic creation. In a somewhat modified version of the Wordsworthian dictum (poetry as emotion recollected in tranquillity), Chesterton observes that it is in escape from the hurly burly of everyday life, in seclusion, in genial isolation, that is found the ideal atmosphere for poetic creation. In his words, "For the purposes of poetic creation there is required rather a certain atmosphere of quiet, unconsciousness and carelessness; exactly that sort of soundless confusion which can be found, for instance, in a forest" (*A Handful of Authors,* 1953). The poet, in such an atmosphere, attends to those subliminal experiences to be hypostatized in his creation. To speak, to express, to utter the word, the poet must first be tranquil, submissive, passive. Paradoxically, out of such passivity arises poetic activity.

The Imagination, a power about which "there is something mysterious and perhaps more than mortal" (*The Common Man,* 1950), is the shaping spirit through which the dumb alphabet of subconsciousness is alchemized into the poetic work. It is through its incalculable workings that the chaos of experience is transformed into the order of art. It is a creative power, testifying to man's divine filiation. It is a power which through its prodigious workings, its creative movements (patterned after the prototypal creation) brings order out of chaos.

In terms of a general aesthetics, Chesterton argues that all art is thus order, that all art is form. "Every artist knows that the form is not superficial but fundamental; that the form is the foundation. Every sculptor knows that the form of the statue is not the outside of the statue, but rather the inside of the statue; even in the sense of the inside of the sculptor. Every poet knows that the sonnet-form is not only the form of the poem; but the poem" (*St. Thomas*

Aquinas). As opposed to those romantics who conceive of the Imagination as revelling in the infinite, the indefinite, Chesterton conceives of it as revelling in the finite, the definite. For, all art is limitation—and a poet is all the more creative in thus submitting to the hard limits of creation. With Patmore, Chesterton agrees that the infinite is generally alien to art: "The imagination is supposed to work towards the infinite; though in that sense the infinite is the opposite of the imagination. For the imagination deals with an image. And an image is in its nature a thing that has an outline and therefore a limit" (*The Autobiography of G. K. Chesterton,* 1936).

In such metapoetic ways would Chesterton account for the origins of poetry. Out of the elements of which poetry is made Chesterton would lay particular stress upon its rhythmical qualities—qualities that give it such a universal appeal. He denounce as another manifestation of the rationalist fallacy the tendency to denigrate as artificial and vulgar such primordial elements of poetry as rhyme and meter. Rather than being denigrated as superadded elements, both rhyme and meter should be recognized as striking chords of the eternal harmonies: rhyme in its appeal to the human love of identity; meter is in its appeal to the equally human love of similarity. Rhyme, for instance, in its appeal to the deepseated human need of identity, of absolutes, has psychological value. Rejecting the sophisticated objections to rhyme, Chesterton argues that even in its most primitive phonic aspect it is essentially poetic. "The whole history of the thing called rhyme can be found between those two things: the simple pleasure of rhyming 'diddle' to 'fiddle' and the more sophisticated pleasure of rhyming 'diddle' to 'idyl'. Now the fatal mistake about poetry, and more than half of the fatal mistake about humanity, consists in forgetting that we should have the first kind of pleasure as well as the second. It might be said that we should have the first pleasure as the basis of the second; or, yet more truly, the first pleasure inside the second" (*The Living Age,* March 13, 1920). The Chestertonian plea is this: that poetry not disown its historic, popular origins and that it not repudiate its primitive, mythic ancestry. Noting the modern antipathy towards rhyme, Chesterton tartly remarks that "in poetical criticism and creation there has also appeared the prig who insists that any new poem must avoid the sort of melody that makes the beauty of any old song" (*The Living Age*). He prophesies that when poets consent to put away childish things they will put away poetry.

Chesterton metapoetically associates meter with the psychological and even cosmological nature of things. Life itself is rhythmical: there is not a mere progress in things but a rise and a fall. In terms of such a principle, the inordinate use of free verse is questionable. As Chesterton explains, "Metre is more natural than free verse; because it has more of the movement of nature, and the curves of wind and wave" (*The Common Man*). Preferring meter to free verse, he yet concedes that "The primary case for free verse was always fair enough, so far as it went. There certainly are verbal rhythms which are not exactly those of any classical metre, but which do produce an effect which is not merely that of prose, but rather of a sort of chant or incantation" (*Avowals and Denials*). Towards all such artistic experimentation, he succinctly states his position: "With this or that particular metrical form, or unmetrical form, or unmetrical formlessness, I might be content or not, as it achieves some particular effect or not" (*Fancies Versus Fads,* 1923). Although Chesterton does not censure the entire free verse trend, he does nevertheless have serious reservations as to whether such modern practitioners of the mode as T. S. Eliot and D. H. Lawrence realized through it "any purely poetical effect that is freer or wilder or more elemental, magical, or hitherto uncaptured than Shelley or Swinburne or any good poet has produced in formal poetry. It is more conversational; it is not more primeval or even more barbaric" (*Avowals and Denials*).

Language—the very poetic matrix—Chesterton realizes is radically limited and imperfect, mirroring the finiteness of its human creator. No, language is by no means an ideal instrument even for scientific communication, yet alone for poetic expression—and the assumption that it is lies at the root of all rationalist philosophies. Because of its limitations, because of its imperfect character as an artistic medium, the poet necessarily relies upon rhythm, imagery, and symbolism to share his vision. In fact, the most serious error pervading much criticism has been to identify imagery as being merely the decoration or beautification of thought rather than as being the very poetic essence. "Poetry is not a selection of the images which will express a particular though; it is rather an analysis of thoughts which are evoked by a certain image. The metaphor, the symbol, the picture, has appeared to most critics to be a mere ornament, a piece of moulding above the gateway; but it is actually the keystone of the arch. Take away the particular image employed and the whole fabric of thought falls with a crash" (*A Handful of Authors*). Imagery is not, as neoclassical criticism appears to have thought, the decorative surface of the poem, Fancy's contribution to poetic composition; rather it is the poetic quiddity—that through which and in which and out of which a poem's "ideas" take birth.

And, the more aesthetically perfect is the imagery the more undetachable it is from the poetic content. Thus, symbolism is aesthetically superior to allegory in that "the symbol exactly fits; and there is therefore no superfluous explanation that needs to pass through ordinary language, or need be, or indeed can be, translated into other words" (*The Common Man*). Symbolism realizes that triumphant unity in that meaning and imagery are inseparable, integrally fused.

But in thus recognizing the artistic efficacy of the image, Chesterton would not have it worshipped apart from its indwelling meaning. He laments the misguided tendency in much twentieth-century creation and creation to isolate absolutely the image, to strip it of all extraneous associations: "One of the new theories about poetry is that the poet must seek to isolate an image, and even a word. He must, to use the military phrase, cut all its connections, and leave it in the air" (*A Handful of Authors*). Such a tendency counters the reality that a word, let alone a poem, cannot escape from such associations.

To illustrate what is to be considered the successful bridging between Imagination and Understanding, Chesterton offers as a model the following lines from Blake.

> Mock on, Mock on, Voltaire, Rousseau,
> Mock on, Mock on; 'tis all in vain;
> You throw the sand against the wind
> And the wind blows it back again.

In an accompanying commentary, Chesterton elevates such lines to an Arnoldian touchstone: "That is Poetry; that is a clear and direct image which does convey perfectly what is meant; the futility of the fight of what is dull and heavy against what is full of light and living energy. It is, in fact, a full and even final example of the Image; and, therefore, of the function of Imagination" (*Avowals and Denials*).

Poetry, then, should appeal not only to the ear and to the imagination, but also to the mind. In Chesterton's judgment, modern poetry—because of a lack of an integrating cosmic vision—fails to realize such an integral appeal. Twentieth-century poetry generally exemplifies the tendency of fragmentation gone wild; a poetry that isolates "not only the mind but the mood" (*Sidelights on New London and Newer York*)—a poetry that detaches the image "with or without the elucidation of its indwelling idea" (*All I Survey,* 1933). On the other hand, a poet like Dante, because he shared the certitude of a great public philosophy, realizes more effectively such an integral appeal since in him "the abstract theory still illuminates the poetry; the ideas enlighten even where the images are dark" (*The Thing*).

What are the kind of ideas with which poetry concerns itself? Are they the kind that squeeze the meaning of reality dry? Are they the kind that formulate final, definitive statements about things? Chesterton insists that poetry is indeed concerned with ideas, but with the kind of ideas that are "never new in the sense of neat, as they are never old in the sense of exhausted. They lie a little too deep to find perfect expression in any age; and great poets can give great hints of them in any" (*Chaucer*). The ideas with which poetry concerns itself are transcendental ones—those tremendous truths that a Blake intuits behind the phenomenal world.

To realize its ends, poetry must communicate. As Chesterton observes, the other name for a poet is "Pontifex, or the Builder of the Bridge. And if there is not a real bridge between his brain and ours, it is useless to argue about whether it has broken down at our end or at his. He has not got the communication" (*Avowals and Denials*). The poet is one specially gifted who can utter as contrasted to mankind's dumbness truths that are dimly felt by all.

In his metapoetics, Chesterton would have as an end of poetry its power to attune men to the essential unity and mystery of the universe. Poetry first identifies itself by corresponding to the underlying unity of all things. Thus, the poet's rhythm, his imagery, his ideas, are so inextricably one that only abstractly are they separable. Whether it be at the more rudimentary level of rhythm or at the more complex level of imagery and ideas, poetry exemplifies this universal principle of unity. At the more elemental level, sound and sense should be so interdependent that a poem "actually would not sound the same, if another meaning were expressed by the same sound. It actually would not mean as much, if other words expressed the same meaning" (*All I Survey*). At the more complex level, the poet's imagery is undetachable from his ideas. Even the images of a revered poet like Dante are "not to be worshipped, any more than any other images" (*The Thing*) apart from their indwelling ideas. The primary task of the poet is in Coleridgean terms to reconcile and unite.

As an end, poetry also should mirror the radical mystery of the universe. As opposed to rationalism, poetry attunes men to the strange music of the spheres. It is sane "because it floats easily in an infinite sea; reason seeks to cross the infinite sea, and so make it finite" (*Orthodoxy,* 1959). Poetry is sane because it suggests the kind of universe in which man really finds himself. Whether in its origins (the pre-conscious depths of the soul in which it is rooted) or in its mode of expression (the miracle of language which means more than it says) or in its effects (the veil of familiarity that it strips away from things), poetry is more than rational. Poetry realises its end when it makes men wonder at the universe, making them remember that they forgot.

As presented in this study, how may the Chestertonian approach to poetry be characterized? Chesterton's metapoetics may be characterized as being ontological, romantic, and Chsirtian. Ontological—not in that rationalist sense that identifies poetry with philosophy, but rather in that realist sense that roots its origin in being, in the mysterious otherness of things, in the gratuitous, contingent nature of existence. Romantic—not in that solipsist sense that urges the poetic mind to feed upon its own entrails, but rather in that more historic sense that recognizes that the poetic mind is elemental, mythic, barbaric. Christian—not in that narrow sectarian sense that glorifies the Divine by denigrating the human, but rather in that more liberating sense that envisions human creativity after the pattern of the prototypal creation.

It is not within the scope or purpose of this study to render a detailed assessment of the Chestertonian metapoetics. Before concluding, however, the most serious objection to the proposed Chestertonian theory should be confronted: the objection that by elevating a particular type of romantic, mystical poetry as the model and exemplar for all poetry, Chesterton relegates most metaphysical, neoclassical, and twentieth-century poetry to an inferior status. To which objection it may be answered: that if it be rediscovered that poetry, by its very nature, is indeed romantic, then, the Chestertonian metapoetics may serve to reduce the confusion so prevalent in twentieth-century criticism by which poetry is identified with impersonality, with rhetoric, with dramatic tension, with wit and irony, with mental and verbal gymnastics.

Notes

1. All references in this study are to works of Gilbert Keith Chesterton. Unless otherwise indicated, the place of publication is New York.

Christopher Clausen (essay date 1974)

SOURCE: "'Lord of the Rings' and 'The Ballad of the White Horse,'" in *South Atlantic Bulletin,* Vol. XXXIX, No. 2, May, 1974, pp. 10-16.

[*In the following essay, Clausen argues that for his own* Lord of the Rings, *J. R. R. Tolkien borrowed the narrative structure and fundamental themes of Chesterton's poem about Christianity versus the forces of evil*—The Ballad of the White Horse.]

No reasonably learned reader of J. R. R. Tolkien's *Lord of the Rings* can fail to have been struck by the extraordinary diversity of literary material that Tolkien manages to incorporate into his complicated but tightly unified narrative. Quarrying bits from Anglo-Saxon, Norse sagas, ancient Celtic poetry, Milton, Dickens, Browning, it is as if he had approached all previous literature as a mountain of uncut stones available for his own purposes—sometimes perhaps to amuse the wise and confound the unwary, but fundamentally no doubt because he felt that something in the very conception of his work required the deliberate use of literary echoes on a grand scale. Most of this source material, if one may refer so slightingly to great works of literature, is used in individual episodes and has little importance in the total structure. "The Council of Elrond" (I, 314-355),[1] for example, is strongly reminiscent of *Paradise Lost,* Book III; the arrival of Aragorn and company at Edoras (II, 143ff) is an adaptation of *Beowulf* (lines 229ff); while the characterization of Gollum owes something to Browning's "Caliban upon Setebos."

One could catalogue numerous other borrowings of this kind without, perhaps, adding much to anyone's understanding of the book. There is one case, however, which involves not only episodes and details but the basic structure and themes of Tolkien's work. In its fundamental conception, as well as in many of the significant details of its working out, *Lord of the Rings* is heavily indebted to G. K. Chesterton's now little read poem of 1911, ***The Ballad of the White Horse***.[2]

The major theme of both works is the war and eventual victory, despite all odds, of an alliance of good folk against vastly more powerful forces of evil, and the return of a king to his rightful state. Like *Lord of the Rings,* Chesterton's poem is set in a heroic society after the decay of a highly civilized imperial power—in England, that is to say, in the aftermath of the Roman Empire. (Tolkien's Minas Tirith, built on seven levels, greatly resembles a medieval idealization of Rome.) King Alfred, its hero, is fighting a losing war to save his kingdom from complete conquest by the Danes. As one would expect with Chesterton, it is a war of white against black, of Christianity against a diabolical paganism that has defeated Rome and is now trying to make all good men its slaves.

When the ends of the earth came marching in
To torch and cresset gleam.
And the roads of the world that lead to Rome
Were filled with faces that moved like foam,
Like faces in a dream.
And men rode out of the eastern lands,
Broad river and burning plain;
Trees that are Titan flowers to see,
And tiger skies, striped horribly,
With tints of tropic rain. . . .
And a Shape that moveth murkily
In mirrors of ice and night,
Hath blanched with fear all beasts and birds,
As death and a shock of evil words
Blast a man's hair with white.

(225-6)[3]

The enemy is not simply Danes, or barbarians in general, but a wholly malignant and almost irresistible force that stands behind all the enemies of Christianity: This power blights everything it touches—there are repeated references to its distorting effects even on the natural world—and the men who serve it become like Tolkien's Orcs.

Misshapen ships stood on the deep
Full of strange gold and fire,
And hairy men, as huge as sin
With hornèd heads, came wading in
Through the long, low sea-mire.
Our towns were shaken of tall kings
With scarlet beards like blood:
The world turned empty where they trod,
They took the kindly cross of God
And cut it up for wood.

(227)

To fight against this menace, Alfred, hiding in exile, summons three kindreds of free, Christian peoples as allies. Alfred himself, like Tolkien's Aragorn, is an idealized heroic figure who roams around in humble disguise and is sometimes mistreated by the ignorant. Instead of Dwarves, Elves, and Men of Numenorean descent, he leads an alliance of Saxons, Celts, and Romans. The parallels are reasonably exact. Chesterton's representative Saxon, Eldred, is a grim, laconic, dwarfish warrior with a "hand like a windy hammer-stroke" (280). The Roman, Marcus, is a proud aristocrat who looks down on lesser breeds and speaks Latin in moments of exaltation, much as the men of Minas Tirith revert to High Elven at such times. In his arrogant nobility and rather excessive pride of City he resembles Tolkien's Boromir.

Like Tolkien's Elves, Chesterton's Celt Colan is a sad singer, obsessed with the sea and with a mysterious holy land to the west.

He kept the Roman order,
He made the Christian sign;
But his eyes grew often blind and bright,
And the sea that rose in the rocks at night
Rose to his head like wine. . . .
And whether in seat or saddle,
Whether with frown or smile,
Whether at feast or fight was he,
He heard the noise of a nameless sea
On an undiscovered isle.

(242)

Memory of the sea and of their homeland beyond is one of the defining characteristics of Tolkien's Elves. They talk of it, sing of it, yearn for it; most of them return to it in the end. Their most frequently quoted song is

A! Elbereth Gilthoniel! . . .
We still remember, we who dwell
In this far land beneath the trees
The starlight on the Western Seas.

(III, 381, etc.)

Legolas, the Elf who plays the most prominent role in the story, confesses that in the midst of a battle his thoughts were turned to the sea by the sight of gulls overhead; he sings

To the Sea, to the Sea! The white gulls are crying,
The Wind is blowing, and the white foam is flying.
West, west away, the round sun is falling. . . .
Sweet are the voices in the Lost Isle calling,
In Eressëa, in Elvenholme that no man can discover.
. . .

(III, 289)

Also like the Elves, Chesterton's Celts have a special relationship with trees. One of Tolkien's most remarkable creations is the Ents, a race of ancient treelike beings, guardians of the forest, who have the ability to speak and move around. Dwarves and men are ignorant of these creatures; it is only the Elves, with their love of forests, who talk to them, or indeed know of their existence. In ***The Ballad of the White Horse*** Colan tells his Saxon and Roman companions:

The tall trees of Britain
We worshipped and were wise,
But you shall raid the whole land through
And never a tree shall talk to you,
Though every leaf is a tongue taught true
And the forest is full of eyes.
On one round hill to the seaward
The trees grow tall and grey
And the trees talk together
When all men are away.

(273)

As there are important similarities between Tolkien's and Chesterton's kindreds of "men," so there are even greater ones between their embodiments of ideal good. Chesterton's poem begins with King Alfred's vision of the Virgin, in Athelney, who counsels him to fight on against the Danes but pointedly refuses to read the future for him:

. . . But if he fail or if he win
To no good man is told. . . .
I tell you naught for your comfort,
Yea, naught for your desire,
Save that the sky grows darker yet
And the sea rises higher.
Night shall be thrice night over you,
And heaven an iron cope.
Do you have joy without a cause,
Yea, faith without a hope?

(232-233)

In *Lord of the Rings* the incarnation of goodness is the Lady Galadriel, fair and powerful Elf queen. In the sanctuary of Lothlorien she urges the eight remaining members of the company to go on with the Quest but refuses to read the future for them: "I do not foretell, for all foretelling is now vain: on the one hand lies darkness, and on the other only hope" (I, 487). Her effect on the fellowship, and indeed on all who meet her, is identical with that of the Virgin in Chesterton's poem. Later on, in desperate circumstances, Sam remembers her and the jewel she had given to Frodo: "Then as he stood, darkness about him and a blackness of despair and anger in his heart, it seemed to him that he saw a light. . . . Far off, as in a little picture drawn by elven-fingers, he saw the Lady Galadriel standing on the grass in Lorien, and gifts were in her hands" (II, 417-418). Not only in conception but verbally as well, this is an echo of the despairing Alfred's vision of Mary:

And he saw in a little picture,
Tiny and far away,
His mother sitting in Egbert's hall,
And a book she showed him, very small,
Where a sapphire Mary sat in stall
With a golden Christ at play.
It was wrought in the monk's slow manner,
From silver and sanguine shell,
Where the scenes are little and terrible,
Keyholes of heaven and hell. . . .
He looked; and there Our Lady was,
She stood and stroked the tall live grass. . . .

(229-230)

Like Aragorn, Alfread leads his army in an attack on the vastly more powerful enemy force, wins against all expectation, and is restored to power in his kingdom. Before the battle begins, however, he must suffer the scorn and laughter of an enemy leader, who sees before him only the many-times-defeated exile.

But as he [the Dane Harold] came before his line
A little space along,
His beardless face broke into mirth,
And he cried: "What broken bits of earth
Are here? For what their clothes are worth
I would sell them for a song."
Not less barbarian laughter

Choked Harold like a flood,
"And shall I fight with scarecrows
That am of Guthrum's blood?
Meeting may be of war-men,
Where the best war-man wins;
But all this carrion a man shoots
Before the fight begins."

(275-277)

Aragorn suffers similar insults from the Lieutenant of the Tower of Barad-dûr.

> Now halting a few paces before the Captains of the West he looked them up and down and laughed.
>
> "Is there any one in this rout with authority to treat with me?" he asked. "Or indeed with wit to understand me? Not thou at least!" he mocked, turning to Aragorn with scorn. "It needs more to make a king than a piece of elvish glass, or a rabble such as this. Why? any brigand of the hills can show as good a following!" (III, 202)

Once the victory is won, there is another job to be done. As the penultimate chapter of *Lord of the Rings* is called "The Scouring of the Shire," so the last section of ***The Ballad of the White Horse*** is entitled "The Scouring of the Horse." The significance of the task is the same in both cases, as indeed the normative ideas of the two works are substantially the same throughout: although good and evil are absolute terms, no victory over evil is final; life is not that simple, each generation must fight new battles, or scour the horse lest it be overgrown with weeds. As Alfred says to his people, who complain that the Danes are returning:

Will ye part with the weeds forever?
Or show daisies to the door?
Or will you bid the bold grass
Go, and return no more?

(309)

Gandalf gives the same message to the allied leaders even before the fall of Sauron:

> "Yet it is not our part to master all the tides of the world, but to do what is in us for the succour of those years wherein we are set, uprooting the evil in the fields that we know, so that those who live after may have clean earth to till." (III, 190)

One could go through the two works cataloguing other similarities and echoes of detail, but I trust I have sufficiently demonstrated that Tolkien's debt to Chesterton is more than one of echoes; it extends to basic structure and conception. I have no desire to exaggerate that debt, or to lessen anyone's regard for Tolkien as an artist. *Lord of the Rings* is a much more complex, profound, and satisfying work than ***The Ballad of the White Horse*** (which has, after all, no Hobbits and no Ring). Its author, like many writers of the Middle Ages and Renaissance, had an extraordinary ability to use substantial elements from previous literary works in a way that enhanced the power and originality of his own. With Chesterton the similarity of outlook was so close[4] that Tolkien was able to borrow a whole narrative structure and many details that took him in exactly the direction he wished to follow—superimposing both on the incredibly complicated body of mythical history and language that he had half invented, half derived from ancient and medieval literatures. He had the knack of borrowing (and often greatly elaborating)[5] exactly those things that would complement what he had invented, and what he borrowed he made his own.[6] Even the archetypal White Horse itself, in Chesterton merely a chalk figure, serves Tolkien's needs. Both as a symbol and as a convenience of plot, it is quite appropriate that Tolkien brings the preternatural animal to life and places Gandalf, the most active champion of good, on its back.

Notes

1. Citations of *Lord of the Rings* are to the three volumes of the Ballantine Books edition (New York, 1965).
2. It is surprising that Tolkien's debts to Chesterton have been so little noticed by those who have written on *Lord of the Rings.* Lin Carter (*Tolkien: A Look Behind The Lord of the Rings* [New York, 1969], p. 151) relates Tolkien vaguely to a "tradition" of modern fantasy but does not mention Chesterton. Of the authors represented in Neil D. Isaacs and Rose A. Zimbardo, eds., *Tolkien and the Critics* (Notre Dame, 1968), none mentions *The Ballad of the White Horse*, though R. J. Reilly, in making the standard (and questionable) comparison of Tolkien with Charles Williams and C. S. Lewis, says that "The historian will in turn find back of all three the face of Chesterton, and behind him one of Lewis and Chesterton's longtime favorties, George Macdonald." ("Tolkien and the Fairy Story," p. 130) The observation is not developed, however. For Tolkien, Lewis and Williams, see (*inter alia*) W. R. Irwin, "There and Back Again: The Romances of Williams, Lewis and Tolkien," *Sewanee Review,* LXIX (1961), 566-78; Roger Sale, "England's Parnassus," *Hudson Review,* XVII (1964), 203-25; Patricia Meyer Sparks, "Power and Meaning in *The Lord of the Rings"* in *Tolkien and the Critics,* 81-99; and Mariann Russell, *The Idea of the City of God* (unpublished Ph.D. dissertation, Columbia, 1965). Gloria St. Clair's *Studies in the Sources of J. R. R. Tolkien's The Lord of the Rings* (unpublished Ph.D. dissertation, University of Oklahoma, 1970) sees the trilogy as deriving mainly from the sagas and eddas. Catherine R. Stimpson's *J. R. R. Tolkien* (New York, 1969) does not mention Chesterton.
3. Citations of *The Ballad of the White Horse* are to page numbers in *The Collected Poems of G. K. Chesterton* (London, 1965).
4. Anyone who doubts this should read Tolkien's essay "On Fairy Stories" (in *The Tolkien Reader* [New York, 1966]), a varitable repository of Chestertonian opinions—indeed a recipe for the kind of story that each wrote.
5. As for example "the wizard's tower and glass" (*Ballad of the White Horse,* 284)—merely a phrase in Chesterton, but a whole subplot in Tolkien.
6. The opposite point of view is stated by Catherine R. Stimpson (*J. R. R. Tolkien,* p. 9ff).

Russell Kirk (essay date 1976)

SOURCE: "Chesterton and T. S. Eliot," in *The Chesterton Review,* Vol. II, No. 2, Spring-Summer, 1976, pp. 184-96.

[*In the following essay, Kirk compares the poetry and philosophies of T. S. Eliot and G. K. Chesterton, noting that although the two writers were both considered conservative, "Christian apologists" each approached Christianity via different, sometimes antagonistic, routes.*]

In 1917, there appeared in the pages of a rather odd little London magazine called *The Egoist* a mordant reference to G.K. Chesterton, then at the height of his influence:

> I have seen the forces of death with Mr. Chesterton at the head upon a white horse. Mr. Pound, Mr. Joyce, and Mr. Lewis write living English; one does not realise the awfulness of death until one meets with the living language.

The author of these sentences was known to a few as a poet who recently had produced a slim volume of verse, *Prufrock and Other Observations.* He was one of the new writers whom Wyndham Lewis called "the men of 1914"—Pound, Joyce, Hulme, Lewis, and Eliot—bent upon refreshing innovation in poetic form and substance. To young T.S. Eliot, Chesterton then seemed (as Bernard Bergonzi puts it) "a typical representative of English literary flaccidity," chilling poetry after the fashion of the detestable Edmund Gosse by laying his dead hand upon it.

Not many months after he had settled in London, Eliot had met nearly every well-known writer—with the exception of Chesterton. These two never would become friends, even though they had common adversaries; and the longest piece about Chesterton which Eliot ever wrote was Chesterton's obituary. It may be worth while to look into their differences and similarities.

Many find it curious that Eliot and Chesterton felt no affinity early, and not much late. Both are popularly regarded as Christian apologists—though Eliot did not so regard himself, strictly speaking. Both found their own ways, through solitary sad experience, to Christian faith. Both became Catholics, though not of the same communion. Both were champions of orthodoxy, tradition, continuity. Both were religious poets—though a gulf is fixed between the lines of **"Lepanto"** or **"The Ballad of the White Horse"** and the lines of "The Waste Land" or "Ash Wednesday." Both smote Wells, Shaw, and Russell hip and thigh. Both expressed their contempt for the existing politicians and parties of Britain, and for a society that denied the claims of imagination and beauty. The one wrote detective stories; the other relished and reviewed them—and was himself suspected, unjustly, of writing such under a pseudonym. Both edited London journals of literature and politics. Both were enthusiasts for the works of Edward Lear.

And both were centric men, not eccentric. Eliot lived by convention, even to the point of a mocking defiance of bohemianism. Chesterton, despite picturesqueness of dress, subscribed to Johnson's declaration that "orthodoxy is my doxy." Gabriel Gale, in Chesterton's book of stories "The Poet and the Lunatics," speaks for Eliot as well as for his creator:

> Genius oughtn't to be eccentric! Genius ought to be centric. It ought to be the core of the cosmos, not on the revolving edges. People seem to think it a compliment to accuse one of being an outsider, and to talk about the eccentricities of genius. What would they think if I said I only wish to God I had the centricities of genius?

Chesterton and Eliot both were eminently sane and sensible, though both, early in life, had drawn back from the brink of the most dreadful form of madness, solipsism—Eliot in "The Love Song of J. Alfred Prufrock," Chesterton in **"The Mirror of Madmen."** Both were good-natured, courteous, generous. Why, then, did they fail to find common ground?

I propose to look at their writings by way of answering that question. Eliot took up Chesterton, though somewhat glancingly, several times. Chesterton seems to have written nothing of any length about Eliot—though I do not pretend to have found my way through the whole bulk of Chesterton's journalism.

In Eliot's first collection of critical essays, *The Sacred Wood* (1920), Chesterton appears in the "Introduction," where he is coupled with H.G. Wells and compared unfavourably with Matthew Arnold—though Eliot was hard enough upon Arnold in that "Introduction." "The Temptation, to any man who is interested in ideas and primarily in literature," Eliot wrote in 1920, "to put literature into the corner until he cleaned up the whole country first, is almost irresistible. Some persons, like Mr. Wells and Mr. Chesterton, have succeeded so well in this latter profession of setting the house in order, and have attracted so much more attention than Arnold, that we must conclude that it is indeed their proper role, and that they have done well for themselves in laying literature aside."

Here Eliot reproaches Chesterton for having turned social polemicist, to the neglect of pure literature; but then, Eliot suggests, Chesterton probably is fit for nothing better. Later in the same "Introduction," Edmund Gosse, as if a kindred spirit, is pilloried similarly. And yet at the very time he wrote these mocking sentences, Eliot was preparing to edit a magazine of strong political preferences, *The Criterion,* and to do what he might to redeem the time.

In the early volumes of *The Criterion.* Chesterton is spared—by being ignored, rather as Eliot indulged a sneaking sympathy for Stanley Baldwin by never mentioning that leader of party. (Nearly every other British politician of the time was derided by Eliot—and by Chesterton.) But in a review of six political books (*The Criterion,* Volume VI, July, 1927) Eliot takes up Chesterton's *Outline of Sanity* and Belloc's *Servile State.* He is not gentle with them:

> Mr. Chesterton and Mr. Belloc sing the same tune together. I cannot admit that either of these writers 'writes well'. The former's *Outline of Sanity* is the work of the brilliant but sporadic essay writer, scoring point at the cost of lucidity and cumulative effect. Mr. Chesterton is an inheritor of the older generation of Victorian prophets, with a touch, in fact too many touches, of Arnold's irony. In essays such as *Orthodoxy, Heretics,* or *The Defendant,* his style is admirable for his purpose; he often has unique perceptions; but his mind is not equipped for sustained argument.

One may remark here that Eliot also never wrote a book-length sustained argument: *The Idea of a Christian Society, Notes towards the Definition of Culture,* and *After Strange Gods* are essays and lectures loosely joined, raising questions more than answering them. Eliot was not hostile here toward Chesterton's and Belloc's social proposals:

> One has much sympathy with the Belloc-Chesterton gospel of Distributive Property. It is a fertile idea; and in the form of exposition which they have chosen there is material for one excellent essay. But in full books we expect more than that: we expect some indication of a "way," answers to some of the objections that occur to us, and an admission that the problem is simplified for expository purposes. But there is another, perhaps more serious suspicion which lurks in our minds in reading the economics of Chesterton and Belloc. We suspect that their thorough-going Romanism—not their Romanism of religion, but their Romanism of politics and economics—sometimes blinds them to the realities of Britain and the British Empire. With their eye on the much-exploited French "peasant proprietor" (never on the problems of French industrialism or the French industrial town), they seem to neglect fundamental differences between the French State and the English State.

Aye, it is not difficult to point out a certain abstractness in the economic notions of Chesterton and Belloc; yet at this very time, Eliot himself was a devotee of the economic panacea called Social Credit, really an economic "chirping sect" of the sort which Eliot was given to ridiculing. Eliot's sympathy with Distributism did endure.

In this same lengthy review, Eliot discusses Anthony M. Ludovici's book, *A Defense of Conservatism.* Eliot did not relish or accept the label "Conservative" then; he was a true-blue Tory, little read in Burke, until about 1927. Ludovici would have had the British Tories shift from the Church of England to the Church of Rome, Eliot pointed out; and that recommendation he found mistaken in principle. Toryism is essentially Anglican, Eliot declared; Roman Catholicism, which in our time draws its greatest support from America, is more in harmony with Republicanism. . . . The problem of Toryism should be rather to make the Church of Laud survive in an age of universal suffrage, an age in which a Parliament elected by persons of every variety of religious belief or disbelief (and containing now and then a Parsee) has a certain control over the destinies of that Church.

One suspects that Eliot's criticism of Chesterton's and Belloc's lack of social realism was not unaffected by his Anglicanism; Eliot by that time having been confirmed in the Church of England, and so feeling uneasy with ultramontanists. I will touch upon this subject presently.

In the same volume of *The Criterion,* two months later (September, 1927) there appears a well-written review of Chesterton's ***Collected Poems,*** by Humbert Wolfe, an advanced poet of the "detached" school, much influenced by Eliot. (Chesterton criticises Wolfe in the essay called "Poetry—Old and New," first published in 1928 and reprinted in *A Handful of Authors:* in this essay, Chesterton remarks that revolutionary poets in fact are particularly traditional—a point to which Eliot would have assented.) Probably Wolfe's opinions of Chesterton's verse were shared by Eliot. Wolfe finds high virtue and glaring faults, from one Chesterton poem to another: "He is often a bad poet, sometimes not a poet at all, but when poetry has its way with him, he is emphatically a major poet. . . . He is, in any case, by far the greatest living satirist. He has only to add a very little to challenge the all-England title."

And in the same number of *The Criterion* appears an unsigned brief review of Chesterton's romance *The Return of Don Quixote*—reviewed, perhaps maliciously, along with H.G. Well's *Meanwhile.* "Neither of these books is worthy of its author," the reviewer finds. (Possibly the reviewer was the editor.) "As for Mr. Chesterton, his epigrams fall particularly flat, and the story is either too fantastic or not fantastic enough."

Now, although others besides the *Criterion* crowd have failed to appreciate the virtues of *The Return of Don Quixote,* that story is one of Chesterton's more significant novels, with some passages of real humour and other passages of curiously perceptive power. As Ian Boyd writes of this book, "Perceptive readers are more likely to see it as the culmination of Chesterton's fiction and to accept the judgment that it is perhaps the best and most interesting of all his novels." Myself preferring *The Ball and the Cross.* I should not praise *The Return of Don Quixote* quite so highly as that; nevertheless, the *Criterion* argument, that this story should be either more fantastic or less fantastic than it is, seems to me shallow, the product of too hasty a reading. This novel's portraits of Lord Eden and other politicians and political speculators should have struck a sympathetic nerve in Eliot, for he expresses similar views in his *Criterion* commentaries and elsewhere. Nor could the Distributist aspects of this book have been opposed by Eliot. Chesterton's rather kindly view of Syndicalism therein, however, was not shared by Eliot. Though I recall no remarks by Eliot specifically about Syndicalism, he must have looked upon that movement as an endeavour to supplant King Log by King Stork.

A year and a half later (April, 1929), *The Criterion* published Chesterton's only contribution to that magazine, a serious essay entitled, "Is Humanism a Religion?" The New Humanism, or American Humanism, then had become a major topic for discussion in the pages of *The Criterion.* Eliot, friend to Irving Babbitt and Paul Elmer More, gave those critics close attention, agreed with them in much, and disagreed in much. Chesterton's essay is virtually identical with Eliot's conclusions on this subject.

"I distrust spiritual experiments outside the central spiritual tradition," Chesterton writes here; "for the simple reason that I think they do not last, even if they manage to spread. At the most they stand for one generation; at the commonest for one fashion; at the lowest for one clique. I do not think they have the secret of continuity; certainly not of corporate continuity." Eliot would not have put that criticism very differently. Chesterton here addressed himself chiefly to Norman Foerster's recent *American Criticism;* and Foerster, rather a feeble champion for Humanism, later would be drubbed by Eliot, along lines nearly identical with Chesterton's, in "Thoughts after Lambeth" (1931). Chesterton's concluding observations in "Is Humanism a Religion?" deserve quotation; they, except for the final sentence, are Eliot's also:

> But before we call either Culture or Humanism a substitute for religion, there is a very plain question that can be asked in the form of a very homely metaphor. Humanism may try to pick up the pieces: but can it stick them together? Where is the *coment* which made religion corporate and popular, which can prevent it falling to pieces in a debris of individualistic tastes and degrees? What is to prevent one Humanist wanting chastity without humility, and another humility without chastity, and another truth or beauty without either? The problem of an enduring ethic and culture consists in finding an arrangement of the pieces by which they remain related, as do the stones arranged in an arch. And I know only one scheme that has thus proved its solidity, bestriding lands and ages with its gigantic arches, and carrying everywhere the high river of baptism upon an aqueduct of Rome.

In some degree, Eliot's and Chesterton's courses had converged. No longer did there appear in *The Criterion,* or elsewhere, Eliot barbs like this early aside: "Mr. Chesterton's brain swarms with ideas; I see no evidence that it thinks." By 1934, in a footnote to *After Strange Gods,* Eliot acknowledged some indebtedness to the political ideas of "Mr. Chesterton and his 'distributism,'" among others. In 1935, Eliot would write in *The New English Weekly,* "With Mr. Chesterton I naturally have sympathies which I did not have twenty-five years ago."

Still the two did not become close associates. Did they ever converse? London then was the most populous of cities, and in that sprawl it was quite possible for two famous men not to meet, if they had no impulse to meet. I have come upon only one exchange of letters between these two, and that concerning a blunder by Chesterton in the pages of *The Mercury.* Chesterton had confounded Eliot with quite a different reviewer who had attacked Chesterton's taste for alliteration, and in retaliation Chesterton had implied that Eliot was a snob; more, in his reply he had misquoted a line of Eliot's poetry. Eliot protested briefly, and Chesterton apologised good-naturedly—and dedicated to Eliot one of his countless books.

Yet it was to Eliot that *The Tablet* turned for Chesterton's obituary, in 1936. As Professor Ian Boyd points out, in his *Novels of G.K. Chesterton,* Eliot "writes of him as if he were writing about the leader of a religious sect or a political patry"—not about an important man of letters. Certainly Eliot had not altogether abandoned that early judgment of his concerning Chesterton, in the "Introduction" to *The Sacred Wood.* But all the same this obituary was a kind and sympathetic note, warmer than Eliot's obituary of his early friend, Virginia Woolf:

> To judge Chesterton on his "contributions to literature," then, would be to apply the wrong standards of measurement. It is in other matters that he was importantly and consistently on the side of the angels. . . . Even if Chesterton's social and economic ideas appear to be totally without effect, even if they should be demonstrated to be wrong—which would perhaps only mean that men have not the good will to carry them out—they were *the* ideas for his time that were fundamentally Christian and Catholic. He did more, I think, than any man of his time—and was able to do more than anyone else, because of his peculiar background, development, and abilities as a public performer—to maintain the existence of the important minority in the modern world.

Eliot wrote a briefer obituary for his own *Criterion* (October, 1936):

> It is not for his attainments in pure letters that he should be celebrated here: though it may be said that if he did nothing to develop the sensibility of the language, he did nothing to obstruct it. Nor are his religious convictions precisely our affair. What matters here is his lonely moral battle against his age, his courage, and his bold combination of genuine conservatism, genuine liberalism, and genuine radicalism.

The final judgment of the "Criterion crowd" concerning Chesterton was written by Eliot's friend, Montgomery Belgion, in *The Criterion* of April, 1937: his review of Chesterton's *Autobiography.* Belgion thought it shabby stuff by the side of *The Autobiography of Mark Rutherford.* His writings considered as a whole (excluding, however, his verse). Chesterton was "no more than a prolific journalist," Belgion concluded. "He could never have been a great writer, for he was incapable of deep thought as of deep feeling. Yet that does not mean that he was never right." Chesterton did affirm:

> . . . that he preferred an England partaking in the old and tested civilization of Europe to an England striving to a new problematic isolation of Empire, and that he deemed the inherited independence of the poor more precious than the prospective abolition of their poverty at the price of their certain regimentation. It was on the strength of such preferences that he chose to be a Roman Catholic. They do not justify his choice. But they cannot be shown, I fancy, to do discredit to the heart of an Englisman.

This praise is faint. Although Eliot thought somewhat better of Chesterton's mind and works than did Belgion, still even at the end there is a certain condescension in Eliot's assessment of Chesterton—rather as if the obituary of William Cobbett had been written by the Primate of All England. The heir of Laud remained uneasy with the Papist democrat.

Now for my promised examination of the causes for this seeming lack of affinity between Chesterton and Eliot. I turn first to the slighting of Chesterton as a man of letters by both Eliot and Belgion.

In their depreciation of Chesterton's writings there is a suggestion of young Miss Harriet Martineau's entreaty to Matthew Arnold (the subject of one of Max Beerbohm's caricatures): "O Uncle Matthew, why cannot you be always serious?" Eliot himself was a melancholy, witty, even humorous man, capable of comic verse; but he took his serious verse and his literary criticism and his social writings very soberly indeed, despite occasional irony or gentle mockery, including self-mockery. From a study of F.H. Bradley, as Eliot himself acknowledged, he had acquired restraint in his prose—perhaps too much restraint. Chesterton was too dashing, effervescent, and florid, at least in his polemical works, for Eliot's taste. (Eliot did like the earlier fantastic romances and some of Chesterton's critical essays.) Besides, from Irving Babbitt, Eliot had acquired a strong prejudice against Romanticism (undiminished until fairly late in life); and Chesterton was Romantic. True, Chesterton's Romanticism was far more like Walter Scott's than it was like Jean Jacques Rousseau's; but it was not easy for the Pope of Russell Square to swallow.

Maurice Reckitt touches on this point in his pamphlet "A Christian Prophet for England To-Day," and goes on to recall:

> T.S. Eliot's classic admonition—classic in two senses—"to concentrate and not to dissipate." . . . there was never, in the literary sense, so dissipated a writer as Chesterton, who was responsible for nearly a hundred books of one sort or another, besides a vast deal of what might appropriately have been called, in the case of almost any other writer, ephemeral journalism. This is ebullience, and ebullience is not now approved of, least of all by reviewers, who are wont nowadays to praise writers for publishing as little as possible.

Now Eliot's books were few and slim, for a poet and essayist of Eliot's grand reputation. A single volume contains the poems, another the plays, a third the major essays; there are four or five slim volumes of other literary and social essays. True, Eliot wrote a vast deal, recorded in Donald Gallup's bibliography of 414 pages; but he chose not to reprint most of his periodical reviews, or did not find time to gather and polish them. Chesterton wrote too much, too ephemerally, too carelessly, too rapidly, too enthusiastically—so Eliot clearly believed. Chesterton should have restrained himself; he did not do so; well, he must not expect serious critics to praise his scribbling at such a rate.

As for the poetry—why, Eliot of course was the triumphant innovator in form and style, sweeping all before him; while Chesterton, with his lyrics and narratives and ballads, lingered as the redoubtable survivor of an earlier literary order. Doubtless, Eliot preferred Chesterton's verse to Sandburg's verse, or to Lindsay's; certainly, if compelled to make the choice, he would have read Chesterton on a winter's night, rather than Whitman—Eliot appreciating Bierce's illustration of the word "incompossible . . . as, Walt Whitman's poetry and God's mercy unto man." But for Eliot, the real poets were Vergil and Dante, grave and metaphysical; Chesterton was all pulsating romantic emotion, with no philosophic grounding, in Eliot's judgment. It was Yeats, not Chesterton, whom *The Criterion* published.

In politics, Chesterton and Eliot expressed a common detestation of the men and the measures of Conservative, Liberal, and Labour parties. With Chesterton, Eliot would have liked to sustain rural life and the countryside against a devastating industrialisation. Both stood for the old concept of community—social community, spiritual community (though early, at least, Eliot thought of Chesterton as an individualist who did not understand the need for community and roots).

But Eliot never called himself a democrat, and Chesterton did. These democratic proclivities, merging with Chesterton's view of himself as a liberal of sorts, went against Eliot's grain. Continually, often expressed through the inheritance and customs of social classes, was for Eliot the means by which culture was conveyed from generation to generation. Both Chesterton and Eliot rebuffed the notion of a specialised elite: Eliot's criticisms of Karl Mannheim on that subject form perhaps Eliot's principal contribution to social thought. Yet, landed families, the "professional" aristocracy of Britain, and the whole of class structure meant far more to Eliot than to Chesterton. Despite the influence of Chesterton's Distributism upon Eliot, Eliot distrusted the levelling tendency of Chesterton's political assumptions.

Finally, I venture some remarks on the religious differences of these two—or rather, about their different communions. Both turned to Catholic dogma and doctrine after personal tribulation: Chesterton to the Roman communion, Eliot to the Anglican. Often people ask me why Eliot did not go all the way to Rome, but I do not find that question difficult to answer. As an American settling in England, Eliot (escaped from a Unitarian upbringing) encountered the wonder of Anglican churches and the beauty of the Anglican liturgy; and he was steeped in the sermons of the great English divines of the sixteenth and seventeenth centuries, and in English religious poetry. In England, the Roman Catholic Church was the church of the Irish, as in St. Louis it had been the church of the Germans, and in Boston again the church of the Irish. A Tory in his politics, a disciple of Samuel Johnson and of Richard Hooker, Eliot naturally inclined toward Anglicanism.

True, he believed that the Anglican establishment was sinking down toward dusty death; but Eliot loved lost causes. ("There are no lost causes, because there are no gained causes.") He thought that Anglicanism would trickle away to extinction ("my dog and your God") and that Rome would gain in Britain, though slowly. He lived by the Book of Common Prayer, old version.

His choice of communions was not a favourite topic of discussion with him. I never took up the matter in our conversations and I learn from Father Martin D'Arcy that he, too, never discussed John Henry Newman with Eliot, because (Father D'Arcy writes to me) "I feared he might, being Anglo-Catholic, be sensitive over Newman's conversion. I suppose I took it for granted that he relied almost entirely on his favourite Anglican divines." Eliot mentions Newman a number of times, and almost paraphrases him in several prose pasages, but apparently was not much influenced by the arguments of *Apologia pro Vita Sua* regarding the authority of the Papacy.

However that may be, Eliot seems to have regarded Chesterton as diminished by his departure from Canterbury. A strong vein of Augustinianism is obvious in Eliot's poetry and prose; Thomism is not so apparent. Eliot's saint is Thomas à Becket, not Francis or Thomas Aquinas. He implies that Chesterton has made himself less English by his conversion to Rome—that is. Chesterton has lost, in part, his roots in English continuity. Although Eliot's thought was strongly affected—particularly during and after the Second World War—by Martin D'Arcy, Christopher Dawson, and other Roman Catholic thinkers, Chesterton's enthusiastic and aggressive Romanism disturbed him.

In literary mode, then in politics, in churchly persuasion—in all these, differences impeded any close association between Chesterton and Eliot. Also, there existed strong contrasts of temperament and character: the ebullient Chesterton with his beer, the austere Eliot who preferred quiet people. Nevertheless, I think it somewhat strange that Eliot for many years spent much time with Leonard and Virginia Woolf, say, when he might have been in company with Chesterton in that handsome old inn at Beaconsfield; strange that he should be patronised by Lady Ottoline Morrell and J.M. Keynes, when Chesterton had so much more in common with him; strange even that he should be closely associated, in his early London career, with such eccentric men of talent as Wyndham Lewis, James Joyce, and Ezra Pound, when the centric Chesterton loomed large.

However that may be, Chesterton and Eliot stood up manfully and eloquently—if scarcely shoulder to shoulder—for revealed truth, old loyalties, and the moral imagination. Defying the spirit of their age, these two offer us that communication of the dead, tongued with fire, which exceeds the language of the living.

David J. Dooley (essay date 1979-80)

SOURCE: "Chesterton as Satirist," in *The Chesterton Review,* Vol. VI, No. Fall-Winter, 1979-80, pp. 233-53.

[*In the following essay, Dooley demonstrates how Chesterton used satire in his poetry and prose not simply as a gently humorous device, but also as a persuasive tool backed by moral substance.*]

In his book *The Amiable Humorist,* Stuart M. Tave describes a change in sensibility which took place in the eighteenth century and whose effects we still occasionally observe; it involved a turning away from the unsympathetic, reductive method of wit and ridicule used by Pope and Swift, and the adoption of a species of humour which drew forth tears and sympathy. How strong this emphasis became in the nineteenth century can be illustrated by the tribute Carlyle paid to Jean Paul Richter:

> in his smile itself a touching pathos may lie hidden, a pity too deep for tears. He is a man of feeling, in the noblest sense of that word; for he loves all living things with the heart of a brother; his soul rushes forth, in sympathy with gladness and sorrow, with goodness or grandeur, over all Creation.[1]

The essence of humour, therefore, is sensibility—"warm, tender fellow-feeling with all forms of existence." As Tave says, the way has obviously been cleared for Dickens—the Dickens of Pickwick, the "benevolent" old gentleman with a few human weaknesses," with his "affectionate good nature," his "amiable countenance," his "good humoured smile," his "eyes beaming cheerfulness." Dickens wrote many novels which were not particularly amiable, but the majority of nineteenth-century readers preferred the manner of *Pickwick.* When Dickens wrote astringent satire, these readers begged him to return to the "old, natural, humourous, graphic, pathetic way." In the wilderness of *Little Dorrit,* lamented a *Blackwood's* reviewer, "we sit down and weep when we remember thee, O *Pickwick!*"[2]

As you undoubtedly know, Chesterton put a high value on amiable humour; this came out in his own remarks on Dickens. George Ford sees Chesterton as the twentieth-century leader of those putting emphasis on the zestful enjoyment one receives in reading Dickens. Not for him Shaw's Dickens, indignantly exposing abuses and speaking of civilisation as a disease to be cured. Instead, as Ford puts it, Chesterton sweeps us along with a display of patter so dazzling that we have the beery and breezy feeling that we are spending Christmas at Dingley Dell with Mr. Pickwick. The popular impression of Dickens's novels, held by the general public when he died, was reinforced by Chesterton's insistence upon his healthy optimism: "Abandon hopelessness, all ye who enter here." No other critic, Ford declares, has conveyed so well the conviction that to miss the fun of Dickens is to miss the Greatest Show on Earth.[3]

In a chapter of *Heretics,* "Smart Novelists and the Smart Set," Chesterton makes precisely the kind of connection between humour and pathos which Tave is talking about. To such fashionable novelists as Robert Hichens, E.F. Benson, and Mrs. Craigie, Chesterton attaches the label of frigid; their wit is too brittle and too confined, and it mocks what it should applaud, sentimentalism:

> Everywhere the robust and uproarious humour has come from the men who were capable not merely of sentimentalism, but a very silly sentimentalism. There has been no humour so robust or uproarious as that of

> the sentimentalist Steele or the sentimentalist Sterne or the sentimentalist Dickens. These creatures who wept like women were the creatures who laughed like men.[4]

For a hearty laugh, he continues, it is necessary to have touched the heart. So he makes an extended defense of English emotionalism, culminating in warm praise of Dickens, "among whose glories it was to be a humourist, to be a sentimentalist, to be an optimist . . . "[5]

Yet Chesterton had affinities with some of those brittle, insufficiently robust contemporaries. His own style was characterised recently by John Martin in the following colourful way:

> Chesterton country is a terrain perhaps chiefly recognisable for the wild sweep of its paradoxes and epigrams, those blazes of literary colour that linger in the mind like fragments of a sunset. When we see human pride punctured in the casual paradox that man is "a beast whose superiority to other beasts consists in his having fallen," or when we see statistical bureaucracy refuted in a mere twelve words: "Because one man is a biped, fifty men are not a centipede," we know who has been at play in the fields of the Lord.[6]

Surely the style is individual and recognisable, we conclude. When we encounter something like "To draw out the soul of things with a syllogism is as impossible as to draw out Leviathan with a hook," we *do* know who has been at play in the fields of the Lord. Nevertheless, in a period which prized paradox and word play, we can find many analogues for Chestertonian epigrams. Here are some examples:

> Nothing is so dangerous as being too modern; one is apt to grow old-fashioned quite suddenly.
>
> He is one of those gifted observers who can always see through a brick wall. But the very fact that a man can see through a brick wall means that he cannot see the brick wall.
>
> Ships tossing at sea; minds firmly anchored to the commonplace . . .
>
> To want a wife . . . is better than to need one. Especially if it happens to be your neighbour's.
>
> " . . . no one can be an unbeliever nowadays. The Christian apologists have left one nothing to disbelieve."
>
> "Francesca herself, if pressed in an unguarded moment to describe her soul, would probably have described her drawing room."[7]

The first is Oscar Wilde, the second Beerbohm; the third Norman Douglas, after Wyndham Lewis, and the fourth Douglas again; the fifth and sixth are Saki. So Chesterton was carrying on, well into the twentieth century, a type of word play which we associate particularly with the 1890's. Of course, as Chesterton suggests and Martin emphasises through his title—"Some Theological Implications of Chesterton's Style"—Chesterton did not put the style to its ordinary use; it was particularly associated with urbanity, sophistication, and cynical hedonism, as in George Moore's *Confessions of a Young Man* in 1888 and Norman Douglas's *South Wind* nearly thirty years later.

Did his placing himself squarely in the tradition of amiable humourists and at an angle from the tradition of brittle *fin-de-siècle* epigrammatists mean that Chesterton did not employ the reductive wit of satire? that he was, strictly speaking, a humourist?

In his essay on humour and satire, Ronald Knox takes a paradoxical view of the relationship between these two much-disputed concepts: humour by itself preaches no gospel, except perhaps the gospel that nothing matters, so that the pure humourist is a man without a message, but satire is not necessarily a nobler thing, because the laughter which it provokes always has malice in it:

> *Facit indignatio versum;* it is seldom that the impetus to write satire comes to a man except as the result of a disappointment. . . . A pinched, warped fellow, as a rule, your satirist. It is misery that drives men to laughter.[8]

A pinched, warped fellow—is Chesterton disqualified as a satirist because of his very bulk? As a matter of fact, Knox sees Chesterton as halting between two destinies:

> he is like Johnson's friend who tried to be a philosopher, but cheerfulness would keep on coming in. The net effect of his works is serious, as it is meant to be, but his fairy-like imagination is for ever defeating its own object in matters of detail. But indeed, Mr. Chesterton is beyond our present scope; for he is rash enough to combine humour not merely with satire but with serious writing; and that, it is well known, is a thing the public will not stand.[9]

Should he have tried to be more of a satirist and less of a humourist? In his final comment, Knox evades the question; he has made clear in his previous discussion, however, that satire has an intensely remedial effect and, therefore, is an excellent discipline for the satirised, but whether it is a good thing for the satirist himself is open to question.

Virtually the same point is discussed by Belloc in his *On the Place of Gilbert Chesterton in English Letters.* He writes that Chesterton was visited at his baptism by three fairies, two good and one evil. The two good ones were the Fairy of fecundity in speech and the Fairy of wide appreciation. The bad fairy, however, was struck dead as she entered the church; consequently Chesterton "was blessed in knowing nothing of the acerbities which bite into the life of writing men." He had one leading Christian virtue, charity, and this love of his fellowmen was both a strength and a weakness to his fame. How could it have been a disability? Belloc's reply is that it prevented the presence of "bite" in what he wrote:

> You do not rise from the reading of one of Chesterton's appreciations with that feeling of being armed which you obtain from the great satirists and particularly from the masters of irony.

He wounded none, but thus also he failed to provide weapons wherewith one may wound and kill folly. Now without wounding and killing, there is no battle; and thus, in this life, no victory; but also no peril to the soul through hatred.[10]

Belloc has just previously said that the writing life is a bitter business, "unrewarded in this world and probably in the next—(seeing, that those who write well do so with their backs put up like spitting cats—witness the immortal Swift)."[11] The good satirist, therefore, is likely to be a bad Christian; on the other hand, charity is of great personal advantage to the writer, but it may be a hindrance to his literary reputation.

Belloc's judgement inevitably suggests the comparison so frequently made between Chesterton and Belloc himself. Referring to Belloc as a satirist in his political novels, Knox comments, "The very poor reception given to these last by the public proves that there is more vinegar in them than oil."[12] As Frank Swinnerton puts it, while Chesterton fought he sang lays of chivalry and in spite of all his seriousness warred against wickedness rather than a fleshly opponent, while Belloc sang only after the battle, and warred against men as well as ideas, for the love of fighting and the pleasure he took in the deployment of the intellect. Chesterton's platform manner, as Swinnerton describes it, was hardly that of the fierce and intense debater: his speech was accompanied by a curious kind of humming, and as he talked he invented amusing fancies and punctuated his works with little breathless grunts or gasps of laughter. He gave the impression of feeling nothing but sweet charity towards all those—even Jews, politicians, and sophisticates—whom he felt compelled to denounce. So, as Knox said, cheerfulness kept breaking in. Swinnerton recounts the story of the headwaiter at a Fleet Street café who described Chesterton's method of composition to Charles Masterman: "Your friend, he very clever man. He sit and laugh. And then he write. And then he laugh at what he write." "It has always been essential to Chesterton," Swinnerton adds, "that he should be amused by what he wrote, and by what he said in public. I have heard him laugh so much at a debate that he gave himself hiccups for the rest of the evening."[13]

It is very easy, then, to form an impression of Chesterton as a warm and jovial man, too kind to be an effective satirist, or at least a consistently effective one. Clifton Fadiman writes, "It is hard to think of him as a crusader, except as one of the Children's Crusade, for a certain childlike innocence clung to him all his life."[14] So Evelyn Waugh will refer to the "merrier, more droll, more whimsical, more slap-dash style of Chesterton, Belloc and Harry Graham; a style which can only be worn by the light of heart, which in a sadder and duller generation has diminished and almost run out in the no-man's-land where Grub Street and nursery meet."[15] With such an impression in mind, however, we may be surprised to read Humbert Wolfe's judgement on him in his survey of English verse satire:

Mr. Chesterton has scored so many points that he himself has tended to obscure his eminence as a satirist. Novelist, essayist, historian, publicist, playwright, and poet—in each of these capacities he fights and fills his corner. But in each of them he has competitors. Only in verse satire he is unrivalled in our age, or had he but written more, in any age save by Dryden himself. In appreciating his satire, it must be borne in mind that, like Byron, he is a great poet who boils over into anger. But, as with Byron, the anger has always the clear bitterness of genuine fire. He does not singe the objects of his indignation with little Pope-like spurts of acid prepared in a laboratory. He blasts them to Hell with its own flame.[16]

Wolfe does mention later on that the other side of Chesterton's hatred is unmeasured love, but the very emphasis he puts on indignation, on blasting to Hell, on deliberate and deserved execution, on a fiery gust which licks up shams forces us to look at Chesterton in a new light. Which view of the man as satirist, Knox's or Wolfe's, is the more reasonable one?

At the very least, Wolfe's critical verdict makes us look more closely at some of the poems than we might otherwise have done. In a poem entitled **"On Righteous Indignation,"** Chesterton declares that the sword of indignation may be perilous to him who wields it but yet may be well worth wielding:

It burns the hand that holds it
More than the skull it scores;
It doubles like a snake and stings,
Yet he in whose hand it swings,
He is the most masterful of things,
A scorner of the stars.[17]

In a few of the poems at least, he did not hesitate to grasp the sword himself. **"The Modern Manichee"** is more complaint than satire; in other words, the denunciation is unrelieved by the devices of humour:

He sayeth there is no sin, and all his sin
Swells round him into a world made merciless;
The innocent lust of the unfallen creatures
Moves him to hidden horror but no mirth;
Misplaced morality rots in the roots unconscious,
His stifled conscience stinks through the green earth.

I suppose that our initial response to this poem is that it doesn't sound like Chesterton; it is not jolly and rollicking, the lines are weighty rather than lilting, and the attitude is one of strong disgust rather than genial acceptance. However, there are other poems that are similar in tone, such as **"By a Reactionary,"** which describes smoke rolling "in stinking, suffocating wrack" on Shakespeare's land, and concludes with grim irony:

So doubtful doctors punch and prod and prick
A man thought dead; and when there's not a kick
Left in the corpse, no twitch or faint contraction,
The doctors say: "See . . . there is no Reaction."

The **"Sonnet with the Compliments of the Season,"** addressed to the popular leader "to be much congratualted on the avoidance of a strike at Christmas," is equally uncompromising. The poem begins:

> I know you. You will hail the huge release,
> Saying the sheathing of a thousand swords,
> In silence and injustice, well accords
> With Christmas bells.

As so often in Chesterton, the alliteration—*hail, huge, saying, sheathing, swords, silence*—is not really functional; it does not help to put weight where weight ought to be put. But the first brief sentence—"I know you"—is definitive; it establishes that the writer is a man of experience and sober judgement who is not easily taken in by demogogues. As the poem continues, the alliteration does sometimes effectively stress the offensive, repulsive qualities of Chesterton's target:

> vomit up the void your windy words
> To your new Christ;

These few examples will serve to establish that when Chesterton is after someone he does not always allow strong language, forceful images, and righteous indignation to be watered down by Christian charity. The open letter to Rufus Isaacs, which Chesterton wrote when the former Attorney General who had been implicated in the Marconi scandal was chosen as a delegate to the Versailles Peace Conference, is sufficient evidence that Chesterton's prose could display very strong feeling when circumstances seemed to warrant it:

> Have you ever considered, in a moment of meditation, how curiously valuable you would really have to be, that Englishmen should in comparison be careless of all the things you have corrupted, and indifferent to all the things that you may yet destroy? Are we to lose the War which we have already won? That and nothing else is involved in losing the full satisfaction of the national claim of Poland. Is there any man who doubts that the Jewish International is unsympathetic with that full national demand? And is there any man who doubts that you will be sympathetic with the Jewish International?. . . . Do you seriously imagine that those who know, that those who care, are so idolatrously infatuated with Rufus Daniel Isaacs as to tolerate such risk, let alone such ruin? Are we to set up as the standing representative of England a man who is a standing joke against England? That and nothing else is involved in setting up the chief Marconi Minister as our Foreign Minister.[18]

This is not satire, but direct and forceful condemnation, expressive of the most profound contempt for a public servant himself corrupt and the source of corruption in others. The man who could write this could be highly critical of others, sometimes uncharitably so.

Nevertheless, he did not try to blast his victims to Hell, at least not very often. His own theory and practice of satire are partially defined by Edgar Johnson in the introductory essay to his *Treasury of Satire.* Johnson puts emphasis on the breadth and pervasiveness of satire; it is not just a brandished sword or heavy bludgeon, it may be a rough jest, a laughing quip, or a sly remark. Emphasising breadth as he does. Johnson finds Chesterton's understanding of satire too narrow, especially because of its emphasis on burlesque, which, of course, involves comparison. Chesterton's definition of satire is as follows:

> The essence of satire is that it perceives some absurdity inherent in the logic of some position, and that it draws the absurdity out and isolates it, so that all can see it. Thus, for instance, when Dickens says, "Lord Coodle would go out; Sir Thomas Doodle wouldn't come in; and there being no people to speak of in England except Doodle and Coodle the country has been without a government"; when Dickens says this he suddenly pounces on and plucks out the one inherent absurdity in the English party system. . . . Dickens in substance asks, "Suppose I want somebody else who is neither Coodle nor Doodle." This is the great quality called satire; it is a kind of taunting reasonableness; and it is inseparable from a certain insane logic which is often called exaggeration.[19]

"True satire," Chesterton declares, "is always of this intellectual kind; true satire is always, so to speak, a variation or fantasia upon the air of pure logic." Applying this criterion to Chaucer, Chesterton writes, "Chaucer revelled, I might say wallowed, in the wild disproportion of making his little farmyard fowl talk like a philosopher and even a scholar."[20] Johnson agrees that satire can often be a fantasia upon the air of pure logic; but he insists that it can also be a great deal more than this. Nevertheless, as he shows, the doctrine explains Chesterton's own satiric practice in large measure; his satire is often a curious combination of satire and fantasy.

Johnson is silly enough to entitle his section on Chesterton "The Protestantism of G.K. Chesterton" and to defend this heading by saying that, in an age characterised by a uniformity of unbelief, Chesterton achieved the heresy of denying all its dogmas and calling his denial orthodoxy. Nevertheless, one can hardly quarrel with some of the remarks about technique, especially the use of paradox, the flashing of a distinctive insight:

> It does not so very much matter whether a man eats a grilled tomato or a plain tomato; it does very much matter whether he eats a plain tomato with a grilled mind.
>
> A man is angry at a libel because it is false, but at a satire because it is true.
>
> Where in earth or heaven are there any prudent marriages? One might as well talk about prudent suicides.[21]

One can sympathise with Johnson's complaint that Chesterton's great gift of paradox became a mechanical formula. He makes two points of further interest, however—one, that Chesterton assumed a role or character in his writing ("He dyed himself in motley that the world might have more abundant life.") and two, that at its best the style was a strategy as well as a splendid jest.

To the selection from *Manalive* which he quotes in his anthology Johnson gives the title "Violent Outbreak of Sanity in Beacon House." In a discussion of Chesterton's early romances, Ronald Knox explained the significance of Innocent Smith in *Manalive* in the following way:

> [Smith] represents the innocence and the fresh eyes of childhood investing with excitement and colour the drab surroundings—or so they have seemed hitherto—of half a dozen unsuccessful and disillusioned people. . . . In fact he is a spirit—the spirit of youth reborn.[22]

Knox draws a parallel between the simplicity of what Smith teaches the guests at Beacon House and the simple theme of wonder which Chesterton teaches his readers; the simple lesson is essentially that "life was after all worth living if only we would see its values from a new angle." This emphasis on innocence and simplicity provokes a retort from Father Boyd. He agrees with much of what Knox says, but contends that the stress on the simplicity of the novel is somewhat misleading: the more closely you examine it, the more clear it becomes that its air of complete ingenuousness is more apparent than real. Chesterton is trying to find a device for making the jaded and disillusioned people of his age see things in a new light, so that he is deliberately adopting a literary strategy.[23]

The reference to a taunting reasonableness also makes us think of a strategy deliberately adopted. One of the features of Chestertonian satire, as we have already seen, is the flashing of an intuitive insight. Another is a wild fancy, always susceptible of being led away by the note of jollity:

> The village green that had got mislaid
> Wound up in the Squire's backyard.

But a third quality is this taunting reasonableness, the drawing out of an absurdity so that all can see it—a drawing out often in more ways than one. It usually involves a rhetorical posture which brings in irony of inversion: what the modern world views as sanity is really madness, and what it views as madness is really sanity. Evolutionary thought, Shavianism, Socialism, vegetarianism, teetotalism—these are poor parodies of any genuine belief. When he deals with such a theme, Chesterton loves to draw out the idea in the sense of dealing with it elaborately—playing with it, tossing it about jocularly, walking around it as it were, in a leisurely and humorous way. Here, for example, is a passage from *Heretics:*

> I read yesterday a sentence which should be written in letters of gold and adamant; it is the very motto of the new philosophy of Empire. I found it (as the reader has already eagerly guessed) in *Pearson's Magazine,* while I was communing (soul to soul) with Mr. C. Arthur Pearson, whose first and suppressed name I am afraid is Chilperic. It occurred in an article on the American Presidential Election. This is the sentence, and every one should read it carefully, and roll it on the tongue, till all the honey be tasted.
>
> "A little sound common sense often goes further with an audience of working-men than much high-flown argument. A speaker who, as he brought forward his points, hammered nails into a board won hundreds of votes for his side at the last Presidential Election."

Chesterton then goes on to say that he does not wish to soil this perfect thing with comment: "the words of Mercury are harsh after the songs of Apollo." Nevertheless, he cannot refrain from conjuring up a vision of the incredible new types of appeal which are going to be made to the incredible American working-man:

> "A little common sense impresses American workingmen more than high-flown argument. A speaker who, as he made his points, pulled buttons off his waistcoat, won thousands of votes for his side." or: "Sound common sense tells better in America than high-flown argument. Thus Senator Budge, who threw his false teeth in the air every time he made an epigram, won the solid approval of American working-men." Or again: "The sound common sense of a gentleman from Earlswood, who stuck straws in his hair during the progress of his speech, assured the victory of Mr. Roosevelt."[24]

In that one sense, he says, is revealed the whole truth of what our hustlers, bustlers, and Empire builders really mean by common sense: "They mean knocking, with a deafening noise and dramatic effect, meaningless bits of iron into a useless bit of wood." So he concludes with a graphic image of senseless and futile activity; but before this he has amused himself, and satirised an idea, by working out its implications in considerable detail. And if one were looking for a model for such taunting reasonableness, one might find it in the writer who taught Shaw to stand an idea on its head and look at it comically—Samuel Butler. In her recent article Margaret Canovan quoted a passage on science from Chesterton's *Eugenics and Other Evils:*

> The thing that really is trying to tyrannise through government is Science. The thing that really does use the secular arm is Science. And the creed that really is levying tithes and capturing schools, the creed that really is enforced by fine and imprisonment, the creed that really is proclaimed not in sermons but in statutes, and spread not by pilgrims but by policemen—that creed is the great but disputed system of thought which began with Evolution and has ended in Eugenics. Materialism is really our established Church; for the Government will really help it to persecute its heretics.[25]

This probably takes its inspiration from a passage in Butler:

> Science is being daily more and more personified and anthropomorphised into a god. By and by they will say that science took our nature upon him, and sent down his only begotten son, Charles Darwin or Huxley, into the world so that those who believe in him, etc.; and they will burn people for saying that science, after all, is only an expression for our ignorance of our own ignorance.[26]

In his essay on "Pope and the Art of Satire" Chesterton indeed shows his awareness of the need for a rhetorical strategy; in fact, a comparison between satire and warfare runs through much of his discussion:

> England in the present season and spirit fails in spirit for the same simple reason that it fails in war: it despises the enemy. . . . It is impossible to vanquish an army without having a full account of its strength. It is impossible to satirise a man without having a full account of his virtues.[27]

This is part of his explanation of why Pope was the supreme practitioner of the great and civilised art of satire. "Mr. Henley and his young men," Chesterton writes, "are very fond of invective and satire; if they wish to know the reason for their failure in these things, they need only turn to the opening of Pope's superb attack upon Addison." The Henleyite's idea of satirising a man is to express a violent contempt for him; the skillful satirist salutes a whole army of virtues, and then goes beyond these to express regret at the mean compromises, the craven silences, the sullen vanities which disfigure the man's soul. "To write great satire," Chesterton says, "to attack a man so that he feels the attack and half acknowledges its justice, it is necessary to have a certain intellectual magnanimity which realises the merits of the opponent as well as his defects."[28] Without understanding a man's case and his merits, we cannot even hurt him. In this shrewd analysis of Pope's satiric practice, Chesterton disabuses us of the notion that satire is the product of a sudden rush of anger; it is a rhetorical art which involves calm appreciation of an opponent's strengths and weaknesses and rational assessment of how proper heed can be given to the one set of qualities so that the other set can be attacked in the most effective possible way.

Since, as Father Boyd shows, the novels are rather more complicated than is usually thought, perhaps a few more of the poems will serve to bring out Chesterton's qualities as a satirist more fully. The **"Ballade d'une Grande Dame"** contains the same kind of severe condemnation which we have found in some of the other satiric verse. The lady will be forgiven bridge at dawn and various other peccadilloes,

> But for the Virtuous Things you do,
> The Righteous Work, the Public Care,
> It shall not be forgiven you.

We ask how she can possibly be condemned for good works, and the second stanza provides the explanation, mincing no words as it does so:

> Because you could not even yawn
> When your Committees would prepare
> To have the teeth of paupers drawn,
> Or strip the slums of Human Hair;
> Because a Doctor Otto Maehr
> Spoke of "a segregated few"—
> And you sat smiling in your chair—
> It shall not be forgiven you.

There is plenty of exaggeration here; one can hardly believe that there was an actual proposal to strip the slums of human hair. There is more humour than the above quotations would suggest; the third stanza begins "Though your sins cried to" and, after a pause, the phrase is completed not with "heaven" but with "Father Vaughan," and the culminating sin in the envoi is not really something more serious than drawing the teeth of paupers but a descent into bathos: you trapped a mayor into meeting some people that you knew. The repeated "It shall not be forgiven you," however, illustrates that the writer is assuming a judicial attitude; evidently he possesses a sufficiently wide knowledge of the world and a sufficiently assured set of standards to enable him to make wise judgements on human behaviour. He is urbane and sophisticated—rather more sophisticated, apparently, than the Lord Mayor, whom he calls a guileless person. So the attitude which Chesterton, the satirist, takes here is not one of innocence but of superiority; he is able to see beyond shams and to examine the fads of the moment in terms of enduring human values.

A similar urbanity is to be found in the poem which earns Humbert Wolfe's special commendation (in fact, he quotes two stanzas of it): "Antichrist, or the Reunion of Christendom: an Ode." By the side of it, Wolfe writes, Dryden's attach on Shaftesbury and Pope's on Lord Hervey pale into compliment. This seems to me too strong, as does Wolfe's conviction that the poem blasts F.E. Smith to hell. It is a good-humoured poem; one can well imagine Chesterton shaking with laughter as he wrote it. He has caught a very able jurist and parliamentarian making an incautious remark—the remark that the Welsh Dis-establishment Bill has shocked the conscience of every Christian community in Europe—and he pounces with glee on the opportunity that the exaggerated statement gives him:

> Are they clining to their crosses,
> F.E. Smith,
> Where the Breton boat-fleet tosses,
> Are they, Mr. Smith?
> Do they, fasting, tramping, bleeding,
> Wait the news from this our city?
> Groaning "That's the Second Reading!"
> Hissing "There is still Committee!"
> If the voice of Cecil falters,
> If McKenna's point has pith,
> Do they tremble for their altars?
> Do they, Smith?
> Russian peasants round their pope
> Huddled, Smith,
> Hear about it all, I hope,
> Don't they, Smith?
> In the mountain hamlets clothing
> Peaks beyond Caucasian pales,
> Where Establishment means nothing
> And they never heard of Wales,
> Do they read it all in Hansard
> With a crib to read it with—
> "Welsh Tithes: Dr. Clifford Answered."
> Really, Smith?

Again, the attitude of the speaker is sophisticated and worldly-wise. The suggestion he makes is that Smith's excessive reaction to the event was hypocritical, a response not dictated by passionate concern with the state of the Anglican Church in Wales or the state of Christendom in general but by considerations of political advantage. The lapse into slang at the end of the poem—"Chuck it, Smith"—is tantamount to Chesterton saying, "Drop the pretense, Smith. You and I both know that you do not really feel the emotion you pretend to feel. Your indignation is as simulated as your language is exaggerated."

By now we have found some reason to modify our starting view of Chesterton as an amiable humourist, or Belloc's depiction of him as a man too full of the milk of human kindness to write effective satire. "He wounded none" was not literally true of him. Towards certain kinds of people, he evidently found it hard to be charitable; millionnaires were one category, but there were others: "He was a Puritan and a Prohibitionist and a Pacifist and an Internationalist; in short, everything that is in darkness and the shadow of death." To the examples of satire which we have cited, chiefly from the poems, we can add many others from the novels: on Father Quinn's authority, for example, we should be looking at the satire of the New Jerusalem in *The Napoleon of Notting Hill,* and on Father Boyd's at the satire of English social classes and political institutions in *The Flying Inn*—together with other satiric targets in many other novels.

In a discussion of Gilbert and Sullivan, Chesterton makes clear what qualities are requisite for satire and why in his own age satire flourishes more than it did in the previous one. Obviously he delights in the Savoy operas, but he sees them resulting from two men of genius consenting to dedicate their lives to playing the fool. For foolery it was. Beaumarchais's *The Marriage of Figaro* might have helped to produce the French Revolution, but Gilbert and Sullivan's *Pirates of Penzance,* though it made fun of British pride and British prejudice, would never produce even the most trivial mutiny in the most minute gun boat. These comic operas were very much of their epoch, a period in which the original forces which had sustained the hope and energy of the nineteenth century were no longer at their strongest. In fact, some of the late Victorians had arrived at a curious and half unreal detachment, in which they came at last to smile at all opinions including their own. "Hence there were not in this epoch," Chesterton writes, "any great convinced satirists, as Voltaire and Beaumarchais were on the one side, or Father Knox or Mr. Belloc are now on the other. The typical satire of this period remained what Gilbert loved to preserve it, an airy, artistic, detached and almost dehumanised thing; not unallied to the contemporary cult of art for art's sake." So the mockery had become something like a hollow mask.

The wit of Gilbert did criticise numberless things which needed to be criticised, but he lacked any particular positive philosophy to support this admirable negative criticism: "he had even less than Voltaire." "The real power of the Sophist over the Philistine," Chesterton continues, "of the pretentious person over the plain man, could hardly be better conveyed than in the limpid and flowing lines of the song about the man who had a Platonic love for a potato:

> And everyone will say
> As you walk your flowery way,
> "If he's content with a vegetable love
> Which would certainly not suit *me,*
> Why, what a singularly pure young man
> This pure young man must be."

But there is no heroic indignation behind the sarcasm, as in the great satirists; for nobody can feel a moral enthusiasm for three fatuous Gardsmen and an impossible milkmaid. There was not such prophetic satire as Aristophanes or Swift might have shown. . . . "[29]

So satire should not be a light and lambent, detached and airy thing; it should rest on a basis of moral conviction. "The moral of *The Pirates of Penzance* is in some ways exceedingly like the moral of a play by Mr. Bernard Shaw; but there is not the moral fervour behind it which really belongs to Mr. Bernard Shaw even when his moral is most immoral. For Mr. Bernard Shaw, like Mr. Belloc, belongs to a later period when the controversy has fallen back upon ultimates and reaches the end of the earth."[30]

As we have seen, Belloc described Chesterton as too kind to would or kill. We can easily find in Belloc himself the acerbity which he thought lacking in his friend:

> Here, richly, with ridiculous display,
> The Politician's corpse was laid away.
> While all of his acquaintance sneered and slanged,
> I wept: for I had longed to see him hanged.

Such a vengeful pursuit of one's antagonist even beyond the grave is bound to call to mind Dryden's question of whether satire can coexist with Christian charity. But, in his discussion of Gilbert and Sullivan, Chesterton really addresses himself to a different question, almost the reverse of Dryden's: what happens when the disposition to satirise is not accompanied by moral conviction, righteous indignation, and prophetic denunciation? His answer is that satire degenerates into something airy, detached, and almost dehumanised. He evidently thought of his own period, unlike the preceding one, as a period in which the satire had substance, since the controversy had fallen back upon ultimates. He is almost approaching the position Wyndham Lewis is going to take a few years later—that any writing of any force in the modern age has to be satire. So his own view of satire turns out to be very much more complex, more involved, and more favourable than one might have thought in approaching the topic. If he did not become the great satirist Humbert Wolfe thought he was or could be, he still had a very good understanding of the satirist's calling.

Notes

1. S.M. Tave, *The Amiable Humorist* (Chicago, 1960), p. 239.
2. *Ibid.,* p. 243.
3. George Ford, *Dickens and his Readers* (New York, 1965/*1955*/), p. 241.
4. G.K. Chesterton, *Heretics* (London, 1960/*1905*/), p. 207.
5. *Ibid.,* p. 215.
6. John Martin, "Some Theological Implications of Chesterton's Style," *C.R.,* V (1978-79), 121.
7. Leonard Russell, *English Wits* (London, 1953/*1940*/), p. 51; Richard Aldington, *Pinorman*

(London, 1954), p. 132; H.H. Munro ("Saki"), *The Unbearable Bassington* (London, 1926/*1912*/), pp. 179 and 2.

8. Ronald Knox, "Introduction: On Humour and Satire," *Essays in Satire* (London, 1955/*1928*/), p. 27.
9. *Ibid.,* p. 29.
10. Hilaire Belloc, *On the Place of Gilbert Chesterton in English Letters* (London, 1940), p. 81.
11. *Ibid.,* pp. 75-76.
12. Knox, p. 29.
13. Frank Swinnerton, *The Georgian Literary Scene,* rev. ed. (London, 1938), p. 96.
14. Quoted in Leonard Feinberg, *The Satirist* (Ames, 1963), p. 129.
15. Evelyn Waugh, *Ronald Knox* (London, 1959), p. 75.
16. Humbert Wolfe, *Notes on English Verse Satire* (London, 1929), p. 146.
17. Quotations from Chesterton's poems are taken from *The Collected Poems of G.K. Chesterton,* 12th ed. (London, 1950).
18. Maisie Ward, *G.K. Chesterton* (London, 1944), pp. 360-361.
19. Edgar Johnson, *A Treasury of Satire* (New York, 1945), p. 19.
20. *Ibid.,* p. 111.
21. *Ibid.,* p. 612.
22. Quoted in Ian Boyd, *The Novels of G.K. Chesterton* (London, 1975), p. 52.
23. *Ibid.*
24. *Heretics,* pp. 117-119.
25. Margaret Canovan, "Chesterton's Attack on the Proto-Nazis: New Light on the Black Legend," *CR,* III (1976-1977), 246.
26. *The Note-Books of Samuel Butler,* ed. Henry Festing Jones (London, 1912), p. 339.
27. G.K. Chesterton, *Five Types* (Freeport, N.Y., 1969/*1911*/), p. 22.
28. *Ibid.,* p. 21.
29. G.K. Chesterton, "Gilbert and Sullivan," in Walter de la Mare, ed., *The Eighteen-Eighties: Essays by Fellows of the Royal Society of Literature* (Cambridge, 1930), p. 155.
30. *Ibid.,* p. 156.

John D. Boyd, S. J. (essay date 1991)

SOURCE: "Christian Mythos as Theme in Chesterton's *The Ballad of the White Horse,*" in *Thought,* Vol. LXVI, No. 261, June, 1991, pp. 161-78.

[*In the following essay, Boyd argues that* The Ballad of the White Horse *conveys one of Chesterton's most important themes: that Christian faith in the creation and the redemption are crucial to the underpinnings of human culture.*]

To speak in the one breath of mythos (or myth) and poetry can easily cause confusion, for they are not the same thing; yet, if done carefully, it can help us focus on their compatibility and harmony without our losing a sense of the identity of each. This strategy can tell us a good bit about the voice of the poet in question and how this relates to his larger perspectives. These are admittedly broad-ranging interests, and, when meant to relate to ***The Ballad of the White Horse*** and to its author, G. K. Chesterton, admittedly ambitious for our limited space here. At any rate, my claim in this paper is that ***The Ballad*** is a substantive poetic statement of Chesterton's pervasive myth, which asserts the importance of the Christian life of faith and hope in the creation and the redemption as the center of truly human values and hence of a vital human culture. Let me begin, then, by clarifying some words and ideas that matter much in our discussion, and in this way try to set it in proper context.

Myth in real life is usually taken as an intuitive statement in narrative form of the values a people live by. It is something of a philosophy, in a generic and non-systematic sense, or what is sometimes called an anthropology. It was in its richest form in prehistoric primitive societies: (1) emotively intuitive in its perception, (2) social or corporate in assessing life's values, (3) cosmic in scope, (4) numinous in its pervasive reach, and (5) generating a real-life commitment to the values expressed. In all this it asserted a sense of mystery, a sense of reality's being larger and richer than we can account for.

Such myth and the consciousness that goes with it have long since passed from our scene, though they are still extant among contemporary primitive peoples in stark contrast to our dominant and merely discursive and matter-of-fact present cultures. In fact, among us today the word *myth* frequently tends to evoke the bogus, rationalistic sense of not being factually true. A further use, almost as negligible, refers to what is popularly called one's "image," in great part the product of the advertizing industry and the media. Neither of these is of direct interest to us here. Though our consciousness has significantly and quite understandably changed since primitive humanity, we still have place for a habitual intuitive assessment of our values, and we find myth in its substantive sense alive and effective at least in certain religious and patriotic forms, including their ritual expressions, where these values are genuinely appreciated. For all the mutations the centuries have witnessed, the basic instinct for genuine myth in a broad sense still survives. Two examples can be found in legend and in the heroic tale as rallying centers of a people's values and heritage. This, it seems clear, is well verified in what Chesterton accepts and develops in poetic fashion in ***The Ballad.*** While King Alfred's immediate concerns are English and for the defense of his land, by their very nature they are as broad as the Christian tradition, especially as realized in Europe, once called with vigorous meaning *Christendom.* The word signified a life, culture, and civilization growing out of the Christian faith, as historically yet mysteriously developed in the early centuries of the West, of which Alfred was a part.

An indication that the poem's theme has its source for Chesterton in the myth of Alfred as a myth of legend and heroic tale can be found in his "Prefatory Note" to ***The Ballad.***[1] *Tradition* and popular *legend,* which he sees as more vital than merely factual history, are indeed *myth* for him. The poem:

> is meant to emphasize tradition rather than history. King Alfred is not a legend in the sense that King Arthur may be [b]ut . . . in this broader and more human sense, that the legends are the most important things about him.
>
> The cult of Alfred was a popular cult, from the darkness of the ninth century to the deepening twilight of the twentieth. It is wholly as a popular legend that I deal with him here. (Crown 1)

Then the Christian dimension transforms the myth's national qualities:

> Alfred has come down to us in the best way . . . because he fought for the Christian civilization against the heathen nihilism. (Crown 2)

Chesterton's myth of Alfred in ***The Ballad,*** which is clearly Chesterton's own both here and elsewhere, is essentially and eminently Christian. It is that of a man of Christian faith and hope in the face of the challenge of life, with a mighty sense of wonder at the realities of the creation and the redemption, which make special sense of the human scene without robbing it of its native character. The author shows a Christian optimism, not edenic but hard-headedly realistic, for the all-important salvation and for the culture that derives from its concerns and is its temporal support.[2] What all this implies for a Christian humanism would take books to develop; we shall see some of this in our reading of the poem in a moment.

Specifically this myth in being Christian imitates and reflects the paschal mystery of Christ's death and resurrection, which, as I have shown elsewhere, frequently expresses the life of the Christian on earth and the pattern of the Christian imagination dealing with it (Boyd, "Christian Imaginative Patterns" 6-7). Briefly for our purposes we recall that St. Paul refers to Christ's redemptive act of death and resurrection as in no way separable, not an ordeal with a reward attached, but as a single unit. The risen Christ is not just the term of his dying but its sum and its crown, the goal that set the entire action and towards which it moved from the beginning. His wounds were glorious in his rising, because emerging victory burned in his wounds as he died. Paul stresses that the significant Christian life imitates and participates in this action, from baptism, through life's struggles, to the victory of dying in Christ. And the Christian imagination in its own order presents the same action in art. At the substantive level its action is neither comic nor tragic and hence not ironic, that is, not showing one's expectations of one reality or its issue being replaced by another. Rather the paschal action and its imitation are essentially paradoxical, revealing the coexistence of two realities, of the divine and the human, of grace and nature, of the power and wisdom of God made manifest in Christ and all his work, that incorporate the values of this world and the next in the redeeming Christ. Hence, the action is single in purpose and in form, paradoxical rather than ironic.[3]

The Ballad manifests this pattern in its structure and in local texture. Alfred does not actually die, as do many of his followers, but his victory both real and symbolic must pay its price. "'Man shall not taste of victory / Till he throws his sword away'" (V: 263-64), Alfred's words about Colan are true of himself as well. The grain of wheat must die. The conflict of good and evil, of Christian and heathen values, has issue in the same manner. At every turn the pattern of Christian paradox as the price and substance of Christian life and its values is eminently in evidence.

We may now consider *how real-life myth differs from the use of myth in poetry.* One telling way is to note how the attitude in author, participant, and audience differs in the two forms, how the poet's voice, an actor's involvement, and the audience's assent frequently diverge from their analogues in a real-life situation of myth. An author may assume one or many personae in the course of his composition, which do not necessarily or per se represent his convictions. The actor presenting Othello does not actually kill his Desdemona every night, given his respect for conscience and the law. You and I may strongly differ from Yeats's real-life personal myth of *The Vision* or from the myth of Housman's pessimism, and yet be genuinely enriched by their poetic rendering of ideas they hold. Yet what is at stake is not a matter of illusion or escape or some hollow view of the poetic art as simply entertaining. There is an important distinction between real-life and aesthetic intention, involvement, and assent; both kinds when genuine are of human value.

The basic difference lies in the new, imaginative insights into the material at stake, generated in the art structure itself, and this is because of the creative response of the poet, who is a maker, energizing his work and the themes it achieves. These themes, though analogous to his real-life myth or philosophy, offer richer vistas for contemplation of his subject matter by his creative interpretation of it. *Creative* here means not only something new in insight but something that has come about through the making or forming power given to the art structure by the poet. Philip Wheelwright puts the difference in these words—he is speaking here of philosophy, which for our purposes is the equivalent of myth:

> A poem whose meaningful utterances were confined strictly to general propositions in their abstract character would be little more than a didactic tract, and any concrete details which it might employ would function as allegory rather than as poetic symbolism. . . . Where

> a poem succeeds in conveying a specific philosophy and in being good poetry at the same time, this combination is mainly a result of its employing language in such a way as to *generate implicit insights,* adumbrated by poetic rather than logical means, so as to deepen and enliven the explicit teachings that furnish the scenario of the poem. (615, emphasis mine)

Later he cites Eliot with approval saying that, though Dante uses Aquinas's philosophical and theological vision, the *Commedia* is constructed according to a "logic of sensibility" representing "a complete scale of the depth and height of human emotion," that is, the intuitional power of poetry, working through the fresh energy of its images. The real-life myth must be thus creatively transformed into the structure of the poem, which, working on its own terms, generates its proper meaning.

If real-life myth and poetry thus differ, it is also true that they are similar, and this is especially true for an intuitive realist such as Chesterton. Though this claim may seem to be contradictory, it is really asserting the positive analogy between the two and closing in on how Chesterton's real-life beliefs can influence the central theme of his poem. His realistic grasp of his materials is essentially poetic in image, sound, and language, and hence is open to the contemplative view of all, whether or not they are in personal agreement with him. His poetic persona, though genuine, is more outward-going than those of many poets of this and the last century. At root it bespeaks a sensibility of immediacy to things and of wonder at them, what Aristotle and Aquinas thought of as the starting point, the essentially human occupation of contemplation, which Heraclitus happily described as "listening to the essence of things" (Pieper 95, 88, 33). While in real life an author may disagree with the views of a persona he presents, *he may also agree with it;* and with the realist this is usually the case.[4] The difference between one's philosophical view and one's poetic persona is essentially between ways of perceiving and expressing, not per se between the specifics or "contents" of the points of view. Chesterton's poetic voice is rooted in his deep Christian realism without in any way ceasing to be poetic, of which the poem itself is the ultimate proof. If we revert for a moment to our title, "Christian Mythos as Theme in Chesterton's ***The Ballad of the White Horse***," the intrinsic analogy of myth in the two forms, especially for a realist, should become clear. I use the Greek morpheme *mythos* deliberately (I hope not stuffily!) in the modern heightening or isolating sense to represent this analogy. To the Greeks *mythos* meant *myth* but also *theme* and *purpose,* and for Aristotle in particular it meant the *plot of a play,* based usually on real-life myth, as the artistic source of a play's theme.

At this point I would like to add that ***The Ballad*** is good and substantive poetry, a claim best tested by its epic sweep and by its local texture, to both of which we shall turn in a moment. Surely it is sustained as art, not an easy achievement for a ballad of more than a hundred pages, and especially for one that champions the point of view it does, anachronistic as it is for our time, and healthily such; yet it is very rare, even in the long battle scenes in three of its eight books, that his performance is at the expense of art. ***The Ballad*** is surely his best poetry and, more important, it is the best poetic statement of his own comprehensive view of things, of what in so many volumes he labored to say about so many matters. Then too, in that inclusive sense of the word *poet,* easily open to abuse, yet just as easily rightly understood, in all his efforts I think Chesterton was primarily a poet. These are added reasons that ***The Ballad*** stand firmly as the expression of his personal myth poetically achieved.

We now turn to the second part of our paper, to a detailed reading of the poem. So much of it is eminently quotable that it would take all day to remind ourselves of this. But we shall try to show in some detail how our theoretical claims thus far are verified.

"Dedication"

The sweep of the "Dedication" of ninety-four lines starts with a glance at the prehistoric origins of the poem's materials: "Of great limbs gone to chaos, / A great face turned to night—" (1-2). Then *via* a brief reference to "seven sunken Englands" (6) it focuses on Alfred and his struggle with the Danes to found a Christian civilization "Too English to be true" (28). The poem is dedicated to Frances Chesterton, Gilbert's wife, with whom he visited Somersetshire, the land of this Westland king: "Your face, that is a wandering home, / A flying home for me" (75-76), and who helped bring Gilbert to a serious conviction and practice of Christianity, which from then on became his ultimate perspective, the point of view pervasive of this poem.

> Lady, by one light only
> We look from Alfred's eyes,
> We know he saw athwart the wreck
> The sign that hangs about your neck,
> Where One more than Melchizedek
> Is dead and never dies.
> Therefore I bring these rhymes to you,
> Who brought the cross to me,
> Since on you flaming without flaw
> I saw the sign that Guthrum saw
> When he let break his ships of awe,
> And laid peace on the sea.
>
> (47-58)

The genuinely romantic mood of his love for Frances, and somewhat in a nineteenth-century sense of the word, Chesterton's romantic expression of his ideals, which he finds so rare these days in the welter of modern paganism: "the silent earthquake lands, / Wide as a waste is wide" (77-78), are at root intuitively realistic. His perspective, whether in myth, romance, fantasy, even in Christian apocalyptic, or sheer clowning, is never far from his Christian realism we have been speaking of, to characterize his truly ultimate assertion. This, I think, is true in all he says in this poem or elsewhere.[5]

"Book I: the Vision of the King"

The poem proper begins by drawing attention to its central symbol, the White Horse. It is the image of a horse cut out of the grass, about a football field in length, on a hillside of white stone or chalk, prehistoric in origin, from "Before the gods that made the gods" (I: 1). Chesterton is referring from among others in England to the horse at Effington in Berkshire, overlooking the battlefield of Ethandune, featured towards the end of the poem (Crown 144). Whatever its original significance and purpose, in ***The Ballad*** the White Horse stands for civilization, which needs constant human attention in order to survive, here the cutting of the grass to keep the image clear, sharp and white. Behind this is the goodness of creation in the full Christian view, as first indicated in the Book of Genesis, and the redemption with its message of salvation and its Pauline transformation of all things in Christ. The struggle to keep the horse clear thus partakes in the paschal action spoken of earlier. Alfred's love of the land blends throughout the poem with his islander's sense of being at home there—"This little land I know" (I: 193)—and being safe from the invasions from the sea, which bring in the Northmen in hordes:

> The Northmen came about our land
> A Christless chivalry:
> Who knew not of the arch or pen,
> Great, beautiful, half-witted men
> From the sunrise and the sea.
> Misshapen ships stood on the deep
> Full of strange gold and fire,
> And hairy men, as huge as sin,
> With hornèd heads, came wading in
> Through the long, low sea-mire.
>
> (I: 81-90)

In his vision of the Lady in this book he is reminded of hard times to come: "'the sky grows darker yet / And the sea rises higher'" (I: 256-57). Hence the sea in this poem is generally a symbol of hostility, yet not without exception. For example, when Alfred goes gathering his chiefs for battle, we are told:

> In the slopes away to the western bays,
> Where blows not ever a tree,
> He washed his soul in the west wind
> And his body in the sea.
>
> (II: 5-8)

Yet with a variety of nuance and emphasis throughout the poem the White Horse and the land are opposed to the sea, goodness to evil, Christian values and civilization to paganism old and new, the blind chaos of "the gods that made the gods" (I: 1) and "Pride and a little scratching pen" ("Dedication" 80) of our own day.

We then find Alfred in an "hour of panting peace" (I: 77), defeated by the invaders, a true metonym of all of Christendom in Europe of the ninth century, struggling to be born. His part in the struggle begins with a vision of Mary, the Mother of God, world-shaking in significance yet in utter simplicity:

> She stood and stroked the tall live grass
> As a man strokes his steed.
> Her face was like an open word
> When brave men speak and choose,
> The very colours of her coat
> Were better than good news.
>
> (I: 166-71)

Alfred casts at her feet an ancestral jewel from his battered armor, and she reveals to him the mysterious nature of the Christian life and, inside this, the need to struggle once again against huge odds. Alfred says he does not seek to know the secrets of heaven but only the simple future of his life on earth: "'if our hearts shall break with bliss, / Seeing the stranger go?'" (I: 195-96). Mary, who pondered the revelation in her heart (Luke 2: 19), answers:

> "The gates of heaven are lightly locked,
> We do not guard our gain,
> The heaviest hind may easily
> Come silently and suddenly
> Upon me in a lane.
> "And any little maid that walks
> In good thoughts apart,
> May break the guard of the Three Kings
> And see the dear and dreadful things
> I hid within my heart.
> "The meanest man in grey fields gone
> Behind the set of sun,
> Heareth between star and other star,
> Through the door of the darkness fallen ajar,
> The council, eldest of things that are,
> The talk of the Three in One."
>
> (I: 209-24)

Rather, man's great test in faith and hope is to accept God's providence regarding the things of earth, especially the outcome of his efforts: "'But if he fail or if he win / To no good man is told'" (I: 229-30). Eastern magic does not work; it is the complete antithesis of the Christian religion:

> "The men of the East may search the scrolls
> For sure fates and fame,
> But the men that drink the blood of God
> Go singing to their shame."
>
> (I: 235-38)[6]

Alfred's struggle will mirror the paschal mystery—in Mary's words:

> "I tell you naught for your comfort,
> Yea, naught for your desire,
> Save that the sky grows darker yet
> And the sea rises higher.
> "Night shall be thrice night over you,
> And heaven an iron cope.
> Do you have joy without a cause,
> Yea, faith without a hope?"
>
> (I: 254-61)

With this she is silent and vanishes, but the joy with its cause and the faith with its driving hope are enough for Alfred, and the venture begins.

"Book II: The Gathering of the Chiefs"

Alfred's paradoxical quest now cuts across the swath of European history and culture, and the fusion of the two is Christendom of the time and is the source of much that Chesterton prized as Christian European culture but which he regretted to see on its wane. In gathering the fictional Eldred, Mark, and Colan he was blending the Anglo-Saxon, and through it much of its Germanic origins, with the Mediterranean and the Celtic elements of this impressive tradition. All three were Christian—they "made the Christian sign" (II: 225)—yet each stood for qualitative differences in the blend.

Eldred the Franklin was massive of body and especially of hearty good nature, reminiscent of Chaucer's Franklin, the patron of English hospitality—"It snewed in his hous of mete and drynke"—and reminiscent too of the long English tradition of good feasting, so often met in literature and history, a thing Chesterton cherished no little bit, himself too so large of body and of heart.

> A mighty man was Eldred,
> A bulk for casks to fill,
> His face a dreaming furnace,
> His body a walking hill.
>
> (II: 42-45)

But, as was Alfred, Eldred was discouraged by past defeats and was unwilling to go off to battle again: "'Come not to me, King Alfred, / Save always for the ale'" (II: 52-53). It took something transcending all this to have him change his mind. Alfred's answer, which is substantially what he later says to his other chiefs, recalls his own experience already seen:

> "Out of the mouth of the Mother of God
> Like a little word come I;
> For I go gathering Christian men
> From sunken paving and ford and fen,
> To die in a battle, God knows when,
> By God, but I know why."
>
> (II: 74-79)

Eldred does change his mind and enters with Alfred into his share of the paschal mystery.

Then there is "Mark, the man from Italy" (II: 119). He reflects the rule of reason and order in life, in his soldiers, his vines, the serried ranks of his olive trees and his orchards. Even his looks are typically Roman: "A bronzed man, with a bird's bright eye, / And a strong bird's beak and brow" (II: 125-26), and deeper, "his soul remembered Rome" (II: 141). He too can see no reason to fight needlessly and fruitlessly, until Alfred speaks of his vision of Mary, and then passes on.

Finally there is Colan of the Gaels, with whom Chesterton seems to have the most fun. He finds him paradoxical at many levels, the blend of the pagan Celt and the Christian, of the boastful yet the unselfish and generous, of the warrior and the bard. He has all of Irish history and prehistory running in his blood and pulsing in his brain:

> His harp was carved and cunning,
> His sword prompt and sharp,
> And he was gay when he held the sword,
> Sad when he held the harp.
> For the great Gaels of Ireland
> Are the men that God made mad,
> For all their wars are merry,
> And all their songs are sad.
> He kept the Roman order,
> He made the Christian sign;
> But his eyes grew often blind and bright,
> And the sea that rose in the rocks at night
> Rose to his head like wine.
> He made the sign of the cross of God,
> He knew the Roman prayer,
> But he had unreason in his heart
> Because of the gods that were.
>
> (II: 216-32)

If the other two chiefs hesitated about another battle, Colan embraced the challenge heartily: "'And if the sea and sky be foes, / We will tame the sea and sky'" (II: 266-67). Nevertheless the cause he joined was beyond normal human conflict. Apart from representing three ethnic traditions, these chiefs are meant as metonyms of the empirical, the rational, and the emotive emphases, that is, significant focuses of these, not merely isolated qualities personified. And further, in Chesterton's reckoning together they signify a rich humanity, as their blood lines do the deep streams blending in the Christian cultural tradition of Europe.

"Book III: The Harp of Alfred"

With his military forces garnered as best he could, Alfred now turns in the next two books to a concern for some of the cardinal values essential to the Christian life, of which Mary spoke in her challenge to him: " 'Do you have joy without a cause, / Yea, faith without a hope?'" (I: 260-61). These values at the center of the action are laced with Christian paradox, continually fresh from the creative hand of God and his redeeming love. Though overtly contemplative in their development, they are presented indeed as part of the action. In Book III this is done as art, in song, when Alfred chances to meet his foes, known as one of the Christians, yet in personal disguise as the King; and they press him to sing of his heroes and their battles. In Book IV he is tried by the ultimate temptation, pride, and rejects it by opting for humility, prompted under grace through Christian laughter at himself.

Book III is the best known and most frequently anthologized part of the poem. After Alfred half-heartedly complies with his foes' demand that he sing of his people's prowess, they interrupt him to scoff at their failure and their faith and to sing of their own pessimism. This occasions Alfred's ringing assertion of his Christian belief in the goodness and ultimate success of creation and redemption, which amounts to his articles of war, for this ultimately is what the war means in its strong religious dimension and worth.

Three earls and their king, Guthrum, enunciate their pagan pessimism, as fashionable today as it was then, as Chesterton sees. The first to sing is Harold, "A big youth, beardless like a child" (III: 93). He mocks Christianity and craves conquest and its rewards of selfish pleasure: " 'But we, but we shall enjoy the world,/ The whole huge world a toy'" (III: 106-07).

> "Smells that a man might swill in a cup,
> Stones that a man might eat,
> And the great smooth women like ivory
> That the Turks sell in the street."
> He sang the song of the thief of the world
> And the gods that love the thief;
> And he yelled aloud at the cloister-yards,
> Where men go gathering grief.
>
> (III: 112-19)

Harold is followed by Elf, the King's nephew, who is more sensitive, yet utterly sad, reminiscent of a certain strain in Germanic and Scandinavian romanticism memorably caught in these stanzas:

> "There is always a thing forgotten
> When all the world goes well;
> A thing forgotten, as long ago,
> When the gods forgot the mistletoe;
> As soundless as an arrow of snow
> The arrow of anguish fell.
> "The thing on the blind side of the heart,
> On the wrong side of the door,
> The green plant groweth, menacing
> Almighty lovers in the spring;
> There is always a forgotten thing,
> And love is not secure."
>
> (III: 164-75)

Ogier is next, an elderly warrior, who finds nothing attractive in life save violence: "he was sad at board and bed / And savage in the fight" (III: 184-85). Whatever pleasures he knew earlier, now he can only be stern, and not the least of his reasons is "'gods behind the gods, / Gods that are best unsung'" (III: 189-90). Despite his fierce ideal, its poetic statement is a pleasure:

> "While there is one tall shrine to shake,
> Or one live man to rend;
> For the wrath of the gods behind the gods
> Who are weary to make an end.
> "There lives one moment for a man
> When the door at his shoulder shakes,
> When the taut rope parts under the pull,
> And the barest branch is beautiful
> One moment, while it breaks."
>
> (III: 201-09)

In his sophistication Guthrum the king is impatient of them all. He stands as a cultured barbarian, a man of unredeemed reason, wisdom, and common sense. His is the ultimate pessimism and frustration, that of the convinced agnostic, older, wiser, and more experienced than all his earls together, yet utterly unfulfilled in all his alertness. He speaks in several magnificent stanzas of his view of the human lot. For all the beauty of the world and the culture of life, the heart must fail at what truth one may know, must hunger yet live without hope: "'And a man may still lift up his head / But never more his heart'" (III: 264-65); for death is the end of all. And he ends thus, not very far from the modern work ethic and its despair:

> "And the heart of the locked battle
> Is the happiest place for men;
> When shrieking souls as shafts go by
> And many have died and all may die;
> Though this word be a mystery,
> Death is most distant then.
> "Death blazes bright above the cup,
> And clear above the crown;
> But in that dream of battle
> We seem to tread it down.
> "Wherefore I am a great king
> And waste the world in vain,
> Because man hath not other power,
> Save that in dealing death for dower,
> He may forget it for an hour
> To remember it again."
>
> (III: 278-93)

"'Dealing death for dower'" here should be understood in its ultimately transcending sense, the final frustration of all things and of life itself implied in the pessimism of the agnostic.

Alfred's answer is to turn the tide completely in his hymn to God's generous creation and redemption of the world. A sense of the *given* quality of all things and especially of human life reveals Chesterton's intuitive Christian realism at its best. His song, easily worth quoting in its entirety, is filled with Christian paradox, climaxed in that of our share in the paschal action. God created man, gave him freedom, through which he could and did betray him, yet Alfred "'would rather fall with Adam / Than rise with all your gods'" (III: 313-14). Further, "'Guthrum sits on a hero's throne / And asks if he is dead?'" (III: 317-18). The Danes mock Christian warriors in defeat and monks in fasting; yet Alfred replies: "'You are more tired of victory, / Than we are tired of shame'" (III: 333-34). And he asks: "'If it be not better to fast for joy / Than feast for misery'" (III: 355-56). For these and similar reasons the White Horse fades in the grass under the rule of the invaders; creation and with it all life has been neglected. Finally the book ends with these stanzas, climaxing the Christian sense of paradox, with a certain "reverse English" on the part of the Danes. The main point is not simply sociological or sectarian but utterly ontological and intuitively real:

> "Therefore your end is on you,
> Is on you and your kings,
> Not for a fire in Ely fen,
> Not that your gods are nine or ten,
> But because it is only Christian men

Guard even heathen things.
"For our God hath blessed creation,
Calling it good. I know
What spirit with whom you blindly band
Hath blessed destruction with his hand;
Yet by God's death the stars shall stand
And the small apples grow."
And the King, with harp on shoulder,
Stood up and ceased his song;
And the owls moaned from the mighty trees,
And the Danes laughed loud and long.

(III: 367-82)

"Book IV: The Woman in the Forest"

As Alfred makes his way to the gathering place of his forces, he chances upon a poor woman in the forest needing help with her work and he agrees to assist her by tending a cake she has cooking on the fire. In his meditation upon her poor and laboring lot he is immediately put in mind of the scriptural "My Father is at work until now, and I too am at work" (John 5: 17), and of Christ's identification with the poor. He sees "'God like a good giant, / That, labouring, lifts the world'" (IV: 122-23); the Creator is his gardener, his armourer, his great grey servant:

"Did not a great grey servant
Of all my sires and me,
Build this pavillion of the pines,
And herd the fowls and fill the vines,
And labour and pass and leave no signs
Save mercy and mystery?"

(IV: 97-102)

As he wept for the woman's lot, Alfred let the cake slip into the fire and it burned. In anger she caught it "And struck him suddenly on the face, / Leaving a scarlet scar" (IV: 163-64). Mindful of his status as king and of his power with his troops gathering, he momentarily thinks of revenge: "And torture stood and the evil things / That are in the childish hearts of kings / An instant in his eyes" (IV: 167-69). But had not Christ left him the ultimate example of Christian humility: "He humbled himself, becoming obedient unto death" (Phil. 2: 8)? "'Wherefore was God in Golgotha, / Slain as a serf is slain'" (IV: 124-25), and later: "'Now here is a good warrant,' / Cried Alfred, 'by my sword; / For he that is struck for an ill servant / Should be a kind lord'" (IV: 248-51).

Alfred's final preparation for entering fully into the paschal mystery is to join in this humility by way of laughter at himself: "one man laughing at himself / Under the greenwood tree—" (IV: 234-35). Included in this incident are well-known stanzas on Christian laughter, derived from a Christmas sense of the Incarnation, and telling why Alfred's scar will be a star to guide his men in battle. In fact, they are as enlightening a comment as ever was made on the meaning of the unique commodity of human laughter:

Then Alfred laughed out suddenly,
Like thunder in the spring,
Till shook aloud the lintel-beams,
And the squirrels stirred in dusty dreams,
And the startled birds went up in streams,
For the laughter of the King.
And the beasts of the earth and the birds looked down,
In a wild solemnity,
On a stranger sight than a sylph or elf,
On one man laughing at himself
Under the greenwood tree—
The giant laughter of Christian men
That roars through a thousand tales,
Where greed is an ape and pride is an ass,
And Jack's away with his master's lass,
And the miser is banged with all his brass,
The farmer with all his flails;
Tales that tumble and tales that trick,
Yet end not all in scorning—
Of kings and clowns in a merry plight,
And the clock gone wrong and the world gone right,
That the mummers sing upon Christmas night
And Christmas Day in the morning.

(IV: 225-47)

The book ends with several enthusiastic stanzas foretelling the transcendent victory that will attend this self-abandoning yet redeeming act of humility, an evident share in the final aspect of the paschal action.

"Book V: Ethandune: The First Stroke"

"Book VI: Ethandune: The Slaying of the Chiefs"

"Book VII: Ethandune: The Last Charge"

The next three books describe the battle, in which the Danes are defeated along with the culture of paganism and its attendant evil. Because of the obvious constraints of space, treatment of them will be telescoped. Actually these books would be all but impossible to paraphrase in any abbreviated way, so well told and executed are the incidents and clashes dealt with, and the values of mythos have for the most part been explicated in the earlier books. It remains mainly to test and defend them in the action that follows. The earls and thanes fight and are slain, as are many of their soldiers. Here the paschal mystery is fully and personally explored in action, and the outcome is the resurrection, the establishment of the Christian cause and its civilization, and the baptism of the Danish King, Guthrum. There will be place, however, for three observations, rounding out the epic tradition and the aspect of values in the Christian mythos.

In the first place, the thought of war is hardly welcome in any modern civilized scheme of things, Christian or otherwise. The threat of atomic devastation is too straitening for all. That Chesterton's treatment of warfare has gusto may suggest to some that he was a militarist or at least a crusader. He surely showed a romantic streak here as in other expressions of his ideals, but I think it only fair to see it as under the control of his pervasive realism. Crusader he was, when the stakes were high, and surely the values already discussed were what this war contested. Here, as in **"Lepanto"** and **"A Christmas Song for the**

Three Guilds" human freedom and full human dignity were being challenged, made all the more human for being Christian. His enthusiasm can also be more kindly appreciated, when the warfare of personal combat he envisaged here was natively more personally challenging and even more exhilarating than our modern push-button warfare can be.

Secondly, we should notice instances of the epic tradition of the warriors' boasts on the eve of battle and other forms of exhortation to their troops, poetically achieved and sprinkled through these books. And at times they are even given a Christian flavor. For example, the wild young Harold scoffs at Colan about the Gael's ragged condition: "'What broken bits of earth / Are here? For what their clothes are worth / I would sell them for a song'" (V: 194-96). The Irishman's answer is not wanting in words or in sentiment:

"Oh, truly we be broken hearts,
For that cause, it is said,
We light our candles to that Lord
That broke himself for bread.
But though we hold but bitterly
What land the Saxon leaves,
Though Ireland be but a land of saints,
And Wales a land of thieves,
I say you yet shall weary
Of the working of your word,
That striken spirits never strike
Nor lean hands hold a sword.
And if ever ye ride in Ireland,
The jest may yet be said,
There is the land of broken hearts,
And the land of broken heads."

(V: 209-24)

Finally, we find a Christian variant of this boast, really a complete transformation of it, namely, the medieval custom of soldiers confessing their sins to one another before joining in mortal conflict, when no priest was at hand to absolve them. In a similar situation, Ignatius Loyola is recorded as doing the same at Pamplona. It is a realistic way of preparing for death through a final assertion of one's faith. Here in Book V on the part of Alfred and his thanes it is especially a last acknowledgement of the gifts of creation and of their abuse. Each of these confessions offers rewarding reading; here we offer Alfred's as a warming example:

"I wronged a man to his slaying,
And a woman to her shame,
And once I looked on a sworn maid
That was wed to the Holy Name.
And once I took my neighbor's wife,
That was bound to an eastland man,
In the starkness of my evil youth,
Before my griefs began.
People, if you have any prayers,
Say prayers for me;
And lay me under a Christian stone
In that lost land I thought my own,
To wait till the holy horn is blown,
And all poor men are free."

(V: 68-81)

"Book VIII: The Scouring of the Horse"

The spirit of the last book, indeed of the entire poem, asserts that eternal vigilance is the price of freedom. This is the meaning of the pervasive symbol that gives ***The Ballad*** its name. Civilization and peace are fruits of the struggle and freedom is the motive that demanded it; and indeed for the Christian they are a foretaste of the resurrection. At the beginning of this book we find Alfred momentarily at rest in Wessex: "And Wessex lay in a patch of peace, / Like a dog in a patch of sun—" (VIII: 27-28). The works of peace are symbolized by the scouring of the Horse; they are various and energetic, constant and quite time-consuming. He made good laws, ruled his people kindly, gathered the songs of simple men, translated books, helped the poor, and received from afar legates who would partake of his wisdom. But he was not interested in building an empire, even when urged to it by his counsellors. His little island of Athelney is large enough for him to rule, large enough for his heart's desire at a very deep reach of wisdom:

And Alfred in the orchard,
Among apples green and red,
With the little book in his bosom,
Looked at green leaves and said:
"When all philosophies shall fail,
This word alone shall fit;
That a sage feels too small for life,
And a fool too large for it.
"Asia and all imperial plains
Are too little for a fool;
But for one man whose eyes can see
The little island of Athelney
Is too large a land to rule."

(VIII: 90-102)

Though he dedicates his land to the Mother of God and her protection: "'Though I give this land to Our Lady, / That helped me in Athelney'" (VIII: 236-37), he knows that the Horse must continually be scoured through human effort. Guthrum, for example, remains a threat to peace, despite his conversion; part of Alfred's plans for peace must include one more battle. Only in this way can the Horse be kept white; and the poem ends simply yet definitively with: "And the king took London town" (VIII: 371).

. . . . .

Chesterton's intuitive realism, seen here only in outline as the heart of ***The Ballad of the White Horse***, is, I think, essentially characteristic of his entire output; it continues to fascinate even our skeptical and fragmented times, for the sizeable present interest in him is not limited to his backers. Some twenty titles of his are still in print continuously since his own day—his death was more than half a century ago—with a new edition of his complete works gradually appearing; book-length studies of him continue to be written, along with articles and a scholarly journal dedicated to his work. All this is especially interesting, when one remembers that this realism was fed by his appetite for mystery, hardly a characteristic of contemporary culture. Perhaps this fascination in many quarters is dictated precisely by what can only be a dissatisfaction with such skepticism and its fragmentation. This interest signals, one hopes, some sense of the need for a new realism in philosophy, literature, aesthetics, and critical theory, currently in good part "silent earthquake lands, / Wide as a waste is wide" ("Dedication" 77-78), and, on a much larger horizon, an inkling of the satisfaction available in their far richer analogues, the theme and substance of his realistic Christian mythos.

Notes

1. References to *The Ballad* are to *The Collected Poems.* Since the "Prefatory Note" is not included in this edition, references to it are to the school text, here called the Crown Book Edition. I use this edition also for the convenience it affords of referring by numbers to the lines of each passage quoted. Though this edition is at times somewhat triumphalist in tone, it offers valuable factual and historical notes.

2. In saying that Chesterton's is a myth of Christian realism I include what is normally implied in a truly Christian sense of the creation and the redemption as richly present to one's awareness, though shrouded in mystery, with strong psychological and ontological overtones of a transcendently realistic metaphysics, but in a more intuitive than systematic sense. One thinks of Chesterton's immense admiration for St. Thomas Aquinas's characteristic realism, to be found in his book about him. "After his own 'twenty or thirty years [spent] in studying' Aquinas," the distinguished Thomist, Étienne Gilson, said in high esteem of the book: " 'I consider it as being without possible exception the best book ever written on St. Thomas' "; (quoted in Clemens 150). And again, "'How can that man, who never really studied philosophy, say the right things about St. Thomas and in just the right way?'" (quoted in Shook 218). Chesterton's aesthetic sensibility, in turn, is a part of this realism, richly intuitive in being object-centered and outward-going, without being for that reason any less personal and imaginative. See note 4 below.

3. The theology supporting my view of the paschal action as an imaginative phenomenon can be found in Durrwell (especially ch. II). He founds his statements on St. Paul: I Cor. 15; Phil. 2, 5-11; Rom. 6, 8; Col. 2, 11 ff; and on John 12, 14.

4. "Introducing Hugh Kenner's *The Paradox in Chesterton,* Marshall McLuhan observes that Chesterton was not a poet but a 'metaphysical moralist,' because his mind was outward-going. 'The artist offers us not a system but a world. An inner world is explored and developed and then projected as an object. But that was never Chesterton's way. "All my mental doors open outwards into a world I have not made," he said in a basic formulation. And this distinction must always remain between the artist who is engaged in making a world and the metaphysician who is occupied in contemplating a world.' The dichotomy is extreme and would nullify all Classical theory and practice. Chesterton's claim about his mental doors is an apt description of the needfully mimetic gesture of all art, the root of the cognitive which we have been discussing. Else's formula, which makes the poet an imitator inasmuch as he is a maker, is true of all art, but only if it is convertible: that he is a maker only by being an imitator as well." (Boyd, *Mimesis* 128-29) The priority of transcendental being in both the cognitive and the structural elements of all art, since it is primarily by nature a being, that is, a symbolic being, is forgotten here by McLuhan. (See Boyd, "A New Mimesis.")

5. It is clear that the concept of myth being developed here, both real-life and poetic, is philosophically speaking much more realistic than is often the case. John LeVay's article "The Whiteness of the Horse: Apocalypticism in *The Ballad of the White Horse*" cites *passim* a set of apocalyptic images largely from the Book of Revelation as visionary myth in elaborate analogy with the story line and characters of *The Ballad* and applicable to it. The author presents a mix of depth-psychological patterns, including Guthrum as the Dark Brother of Alfred, the one leading his three earls and the other his three thanes, forming twin sets of the Four Horsemen, each character linked in one way or another with the four colors of the horses, standing for tyranny, war, famine, and pestilence (even Alfred and his followers?), the four elements; these together with the White Goddess of Robert Graves, Eastern lore, Welsh lore, Beowulf's Grendel and his Dam; and he symbolically identifies the apocalyptic white horse with Chesterton's. The array is surely much too distracting—as well as at times contradictory—to combine poetically for an understanding of *The Ballad.* Whatever may be said of the genuine sense of the Book of Revelation and of its own apocalyptic conventions and their visionary and psychological sources, it should be remembered that this book is religious rhetoric and not poetry, and its imagery rhetorically allegorical, meant to illustrate doctrines rather than build a coherent poetic structure. For the sake of this poetic coherence in *The Ballad* it would be wise to keep to metaphor what imagery Chesterton borrows from the holy Book, unless we wish to accuse him of wide-ranging poetic inconsistency. Chesterton, it seems to me, even when—and especially when—dealing with mystery, is not a visionary in the sense of this tradition, but rather intuitively realistic. Further, there are limits in applying depth psychology to poetic imagery, so as not to render it quite generic and seemingly at times close to a priori, easily too systematic and even schematic, much as the theory of myth and symbolism, both in and out of poetry, has been too long all but exclusively in the hands of idealistic philosophers, to the genuine neglect of their obviously mimetic aspects, whatever else can be said about them.

6. There is an interesting parallel to this passage of Christian rejection of magic in Eliot's discussion of

various forms of fortune telling as escape from the conditions of time in *The Dry Salvages,* beginning with "To communicate with Mars" and ending with "on the shores of Asia, or in the Edgware Road."

Works Cited

Boyd, John D., S.J. "A New Mimesis." *Renascence* 37 (1985), 136-61.

———. "Christian Imaginative Patterns and the Poetry of Thomas Merton." *Greyfriar: Siena Studies in Literature* 13 (1972), 3-14.

———. *The Function of Mimesis and Its Decline.* Cambridge: Harvard UP, 1968.

Chesterton, Gilbert K. *The Collected Poems of G. K. Chesterton,* New York: Dodd, 1946.

———. *The Ballad of the White Horse.* Crown Book Edition. Ed. Sister Mary Bernadette, I.H.M., Brother John Totten, S.M., and Brother George Schuster, S.M. Kirkwood: Catholic Authors P, 1950.

Clemens, Cyril. *Chesterton as Seen by his Contemporaries.* Webster Groves: Mark Twain Society, 1939.

Durrwell, F. X., C.SS.R. *The Resurrection.* Trans. Rosemary Sheed. New York: Sheed, 1960.

Eliot, T. S. *The Dry Salvages. The Complete Poems and Plays.* New York: Harcourt, 1952.

LeVay, John. "The Whiteness of the Horse: Apocalypticism in *The Ballad of the White Horse.*" *The Chesterton Review* 13 (1987), 73-82.

Pieper, Josef. *Leisure the Basis of Culture.* Trans. Alexander Dru. New York: Pantheon, 1952.

Shook, Laurence K. *Étienne Gilson.* Toronto: Pontifical Institute of Mediaeval Studies, 1984.

Wheelwright, Philip. "Philosophy and Poetry." *Encyclopedia of Poetry and Poetics.* Ed. Alex Preminger. Princeton: Princeton UP, 1965.

John LeVay (essay date 1992)

SOURCE: "What Happens in 'Lepanto,'" in *The Chesterton Review,* Vol. XVIII, No. 1, February, 1992, pp. 25-29.

[*In the following essay, LeVay describes the historical events that Chesterton left out of his poem about the sixteenth-century battle between a Turkish and a Christian fleet in the Gulf of Lepanto.*]

"What doesn't happen in **'Lepanto'**." The point is, there's no way on God's green earth that one is going to find out what happened at the battle of Lepanto by reading Chesterton's pep-rally tub-thumper. That's the kind of poem it is, and it's very good of its kind. It's also a phantasmagoric slide-show with martial allegro (Beethoven) music. But some of the mundane details which Chesterton treated with such cavalier nonchalance must be considered.

The battle of Lepanto, in which Ali Pasha was crushingly defeated by Don John of Austria, took place, October 7, 1571, just south of the town of Lepanto (now Naupaktos), Greece, in the Gulf of Lepanto (Naupaktos), which adjoins the Gulf of Patras on the west and the Gulf of Corinth on the east. It is thirty miles east of Byron's Missolonghi and sixty miles east of Ulysses's Ithaca. Chesterton does not offer to locate Lepanto, which does not appear on twentieth-century maps.

A Turkish fleet of some 330 ships (273 galleys) was attacked by a Christian fleet of 320 ships including eight galeasses and 208 galleys. This force was sponsored by the Holy League[1] which was chaired by Pope St. Pius V (1504-1572) and mainly supplied by the republic of Venice and by Philip II (1527-1598) of Spain. In compliment to that great monarch, the supreme command of the Christian expedition was given to his illegitimate half-brother, Don John of Austria. Don John had four admirals under him: Andrea Doria (Genoa), Barbarigo (Venice), Colonna (Papal States), and that admirably named crusader, Santa Cruz (Spain). Ranged against him were Ali Pasha, Mahomet Scirocco, and Uluch Ali, the first two of whom were slain. Chesterton names none of these; nor does he say anything about the strategic elements of the battle, which are quite well documented.

Chesterton begins his poem, **"Lepanto"** with a flamboyantly symbolist caricature of "the Soldan of Byzantium," the Sultan of Turkey (the Ottoman empire), Selim II (1524-1574). Chesterton makes Selim a mighty figure "of all men feared," with a daunting dark forest of beard, and "blood-red crescent" of sneering lips. History tells us that this convivial Selim was content to let his grand vizier, Sokollu, do all the dirty work of government and conquest.

This impressive portrait is counterpointed with that of Philip of Spain, and not at all to the latter's benefit. It may be that Selim's sobriquet, "the drunkard," prejudiced Chesterton in his favour—our last glimpse of the Soldan is of "the Lord upon the Golden Horn [the Bay of Constantinople] laughing in the sun." The great Philip (actually a handsome man) appears as a fungus-faced necromancer skulking in a secret chamber "hung with velvet that is black and soft as sin," surrounded by lurking, obsequious "dwarfs," and toying with his sinister "crystal phial [of] death." This eclipsing denigration of His Most Catholic Majesty serves to set off the glowing account of his fiery bastard brother who figures as the rising sun ("Love-light of Spain—hurrah!/ Death-light of Africa"), to be contrasted not only with the benighted Philip but also with the setting sun of Selim, vaingloriously laughing "in the courts of the sun," unwitting of his approaching downfall.

Don John was the natural son of the great Holy Roman emperor Charles V (1500-1558) and of Barbara Blomberg of Ratisbon (then an Austrian city). He was a career soldier and Muslim-basher (and, later, a Protestant-basher in the Netherlands); but his later career was consistently insidiously undermined by the inscrutable Philip II, and this fiery one-time hero died of the fever in the Netherlands at the age of thirty-three, "heartbroken at the failure of all his soaring ambitions, and at the repeated proofs that he had received of the king his brother's jealousy and neglect."[2] Don John was an exceptionally good General-Admiral, but not otherwise a particularly admirable man. Nevertheless, Chesterton catches him at his apogee (in his brilliant twenty-seventh year), and uses him as a personification of the heroic Christian spirit fighting for the right, and laughing at his losses because he knows that his cause is just—Don John lost 8,000 men at Lepanto.

Chesterton wants Don John to stand alone as a man of unshakable faith, and of altruistic zeal for the defence of "Christendom." Philip, on the other hand, is shown communing with his own "leprous" soul in his black solipsistic chamber. We see "the cold queen of England . . . looking in the glass." The reference is to Elizabeth (1533-1603) who was Philip's narcissistic female counterpart, his eternal hater, and his almost-wife. We see Charles IX of France (1550-1574), "the shadow [the shadow-king] of the Valois . . . yawning at the Mass." This King is not interested in holy wars—though almost exactly a year later, he authorised the St. Bartholomew's Day massacre, because his mother, Catherine de Medici (1519-1589), told him to do so. None of these self-imprisoned megalomaniacs can see past the ends of their noses. "Only a crownless prince" stirs, and rises from his "doubtful seat and half attainted stall."[3] His action represents Catholic self-reliance, the outgoing giving of self, as opposed to Calvinist self-absorption, the ingoing hoarding of self. But the heroic aloneness of Don John is not how history sees the battle. The Eleventh Edition of *The Encyclopedia Britannica* closes its Lepanto article thus:

> The loss of life in the battle was enormous, being put at 20,000 [sometimes 25,000] for the Turks and 8,000 for the Christians. The battle of Lepanto was of immense political importance. It gave the naval power of the Turks a blow from which it never recovered, and put a stop to their aggression in the eastern Mediterranean. Historically the battle is interesting because it was the last example of an encounter on a great scale between fleets of galleys [oar-driven ships], and also because it was the last crusade. The Christian powers of the Mediterranean really did combine to avert the ruin of Christendom. Hardly a noble house of Spain or Italy was not represented in the fleet, and the princes headed the boarders. Volunteers came from all parts of Europe, and it is said that among them was Sir Richard Grenville. . . . Cervantes was undoubtedly present, and had his left hand shattered by a Turkish bullet.[4]

This summation is far from suggesting that Don John was quite alone in his martial zeal, but otherwise it confirms the general sense of Chesterton's version of Lepanto—especially his calling it the last "crusade" in the last line. And, of course, Chesterton cannot resist the Cervantes allusion, and he gives that great right-handed poet the all-but-last word in **"Lepanto"**:

> Cervantes on his galley sets the sword back in the sheath
> *(Don John of Austria rides homeward with a wreath.)*
> And he sees across a weary land a straggling road in Spain.
> Up which a lean and foolish knight forever rides in vain.

From a worldly perspective, Cervantes rides on in valor, but he is on the road, nevertheless, to the eternal city of light and love. The "straggling road in Spain," up which Don Quixote, Chesterton's favourite knight, is about to set out on his timeless adventure, distinctly echoes the "winding road" in Spain, up which Don John, his second-favourite knight, has just come to the last crusade.

Nevertheless, if Chesterton cannot resist the marginal Cervantes, he *can* resist all the salient material and technical elements and all but one of the major actors of the battle. He is not even interested that Ali Pasha was slain in ship-to-ship combat with Don John. He describes only an incandescent Don John "purpling all the ocean" and liberating myriads of galley-slaves, and his singular "brave beard" flying "for a flag of all the free."

The poem was originally called "The Ballad of Lepanto," and it *is* a ballad in the sense that it is meant to be popular and is meant to be sung (chanted),[5] but not in the sense that it is a narrative poem. We are given no picture of a sea battle, and nothing like a consecutive account of an action. And the happy warrior of the poem is quite divorced from the tense and driven power-quester of history. He is simply an ideal heroic personification of the Church Militant—and momentarily triumphant. In a sense, **"Lepanto"** is a ballad of signal gallantry and derring-do, like an operatic version of Scott's "Bonnie Dundee." It is also a kaleidoscopic magic lantern show (with Beethoven's *Eroica* music) of the Mediterranean world in crisis—diversified with a supernatural, but not at all surprising, leap "above the evening star," to Mohammed's ("Mahound's") epicurean "paradise," the "peacock gardens," where the vexed prophet summons up, in vain, three mighty Islamic angels and three classes of Islamic demons to confound the rising Christians and their one intrepid spirit.

This scene is balanced by a more down-to-earth visit to the Pope's chapel, in which St. Pius V[6] sees, "as in a mirror," the "cruel crescent" of the Soldan's slave-propelled ships. Mohammed had seen the cruel swords of Richard, Raymond and Godfrey, with whom Don John is identified; for in Don John's voice Mohammed hears "the voice that shook our palaces—four hundred years ago." Chesterton is not concerned with the details of a battle; he is concerned with the sound, or the reverberations, of an heroic voice.

The *sound* of **"Lepanto"** is still quite wonderful, even to jaded modern ears. In this poem which occasionally echoes Swinburne,[7] Chesterton hardly ever makes a mistake. It is probably worthwhile for the modern reader to locate Lepanto, and to identify "the shadow of the Valois"; but, having checked these facts, the reader should file them away again and forget them. He should not spoil his enjoyment of **"Lepanto"** with some craven scruple of thinking too precisely on the event. He should allow himself to revel in the *sound* of "It is Richard, it is Raymond, it is Godfrey at the gate!"[8] (the sound of the clash of arms and the surge of the sea, the sound of "the noise of the crusade," the sound of the *Eroica,* adagio and allegro and a touch of the scherzo too. Remember only "Dim drums throbbing, in the hills half heard" and "In the gloom black-purple, in the glint old-gold." Must any reader be reminded to remember and to rejoice? What happens in **"Lepanto"** is elation, if one is ready for it.

Notes

1. The Holy League was formed to prevent the Turkish fleet from gaining supremacy in the Mediterranean.
2. *Encyclopaedia Britannica,* 11th ed., s.v. "Lepanto," by David Hannay.
3. Chesterton's only allusion to Don John's bastardy.
4. *Encyclopaedia Britannica,* 11th ed.
5. John Buchan wrote to Chesterton (June 12, 1915): "The other day in the trenches we shouted your *Lepanto.*" Quoted in Maisie Ward, *Gilbert Keith Chesterton* (New York: Sheed and Ward, 1943), p. 371.
6. This sainted Pius was a stellar legislator and administrator, but apparently a less than genial personality.
7. Especially compare the rhythms of Swinburne's "The Triumph of Time." One might also compare the rhythms of Kipling's "Cold Iron."
8. Richard I, "Coeur de Lion" (1157-1199); Raymond IV. Count of Toulouse (1060-1105); Godfrey de Bouillon, Duke of lower Lorraine (1061-1100). Godfrey was elected King of Jerusalem, July 22, 1099. *The Collected Poems of G.K. Chesterton* (Newodd, Mead, 1941) misprints the end of the line as "Godfrey in the gate."

FURTHER READING

Criticism

"Bards of Passion and of Mirth." *The New York Times Book Review* (March 25, 1923): 6.

Positively reviews Chesterton's *The Ballad of St Barbara,* describing it as a poem in "which passionately lofty thought is given expression through passionately beautiful verse."

Benson, James D., and Barron Brainerd. "Chesterton's Parodies of Swinburne and Yeats: A Lexical Approach." *Literary and Linguistic Computing* 3, No. 4 (1988): 226-31.

Tabulates words from genuine poetry by Swinburne and Yeats to prove that Chesterton's parodies of these two authors works are successful imitations.

Carter, G. Emmett Cardinal. "Homily for the Mass of the Anniversary of the Death of G. K. Chesterton." *The Chesterton Review* XII, No. 4 (November 1986): 439-43.

Draws upon several of Chesterton's poems in his tribute to Chesterton, whom he describes as a "holy lay person."

Derus, David L. "Chesterton and W. B. Yeats: Vision, System and Rhetoric." *The Chesterton Review* II, No. 2 (Spring-Summer 1976): 197-214.

Compares Yeats and Chesterton in their search for a personal, more inspiring, religion

MacGregor, Geddes. "Chesterton as Satirist." *The Chesterton Review* XVI, No. 2 (May 1990): 29-36.

Examines Chesterton's attacks on political opportunism.

Mackey, Aidan. "The Poetry and the Publishers: A Review of the Collected Poems of G. K. Chesterton." *The Chesterton Review* VII, No. 4 (November 1981): 294-306.

Singles out several poems by Chesterton that are unfamiliar to most readers and argues that they should be included in anthologies as examples of his best work.

Martin, John. "Some Theological Implications of Chesterton's Style." *The Chesterton Review* V, No. 1 (Fall-Winter 1978-79): 121-37.

Examines both the morally positive and morally negative aspects of Chesterton's interpretation of his adopted religion, Catholicism.

Purves, Mary. "Some Uncollected Chesterton Poems." *The Chesterton Review* IX, No. 4 (November 1983): 308-13

Provides both typed and manuscript versions of never-before published poems by Chesterton.

Thomas, L. Garnet. "Mysticism in *The Ballad of the White Horse.*" *The Chesterton Review* VI, No. 1 (Fall-Winter 1979-80): 205-11

Describes *The Ballad of the White Horse* as visionary in terms of religion and as a "treasure-house of wisdom."

Whigham, Peter. "The Road Not Taken." *The Chesterton Review* XI, No. 3 (August 1985): 307-19.

Asserts that for Chesterton, poetry was secondary to religious faith, and was thus an instrument for expressing this faith rather than an end in itself.

White, Gertrude M. "True Words in Jest: The Light Verse of Chesterton and Belloc." *The Chesterton Review* VI, No. 1 (Fall-Winter 1979-80): 1-26

Describes Chesterton as one of the finest writers of light verse of all time, noting in particular his flair for imagery, metaphor, and parallelism.

Additional coverage of Chesterton's life and career is contained in the following sources published by the Gale Group: *Contemporary Authors,* Vols. 104, 132; *Contemporary Authors New Revision Series,* Vol. 73; *The Concise Dictionary of Literary Biography—British, 1914-1945; DISCovering Authors Modules—Novels, Poetry; Dictionary of Literary Biography,* Vols. 10, 19, 34, 70, 98, 149, 178; *Major Twentieth Century Writers; Something About the Author,* Vol. 27; *Short Story Criticism,* Vol. 1; *Twentieth Century Literary Criticism,* Vols. 1, 6, 64.

Hans Magnus Enzensberger
1929–

German poet, essayist, critic, editor, translator, and dramatist.

INTRODUCTION

Enzensberger is considered by many to be Germany's most important post-World War II poet. His clear, concise style serves to boldly state his points of contention and express his political interests, which range from the national wealth and society's materialism to more universal themes of social injustice and oppression. He rose to fame as his country's "angry young man" with the publication of his first two volumes of poetry, and his later verse and essays established him as a prominent literary figure and political thinker. His reputation is that of a poet of defiance and a voice of the oppressed—concerned, compassionate, and aware.

BIOGRAPHICAL INFORMATION

Born the eldest son of middle-class parents, Enzensberger was raised in Nuremberg, Germany. He studied literature and philosophy at universities in several cities including Freiburg, Erlangen, Hamburg, and Paris. Enzensberger's first collection of poetry, *Verteidigung der Wolfe,* was published in 1957 and *Landessprache* followed in 1960. At that time, Enzensberger began working as an editor at Suhrkamp Publishers in Frankfurt. In 1963 he was awarded the George Buchner prize for his third collection *Blindenschrift,* and became a member of the prominent literary movement *Gruppe 47,* an informal but extremely influential association of politically engaged writers. Enzensberger refers to the group as a "literary workshop . . . of 100 or so writers . . . that suddenly found that it had the power to make or break reputations." Toward the middle of the 1960s, Enzensberger founded the political journal *Kursbuch* and his emphasis shifted from verse to prose, though he maintained his focus on political, social, and historical issues. In 1976 Enzensberger published his first book of new poems in over ten years: *Mausoleum: 37 Balladen aus der Geschichte des Fortschritts* (*Mausoleum: 37 Ballads from the History of Progress*), a collection of biographical portraits of figures from the fourteenth to the twentieth century whom Enzensberger believes profoundly influenced the course of Western civilization. The 1970s also saw a broadening in Enzensberger's level of political discourse, tackling problems less specifically German, such as the material welfare of the nation after World War II, instead focusing on problems more global in scope, such as class disputes and various forms of social oppression. In 1970 Enzensberger became the publisher at Suhrkamp Publishers, a position that he held until 1975. In 1978 he published *Der Untergang der Titanic,* which he himself translated as *The Sinking of the Titanic* (1981). *Titanic,* originally written in the late 1960s during Enzensberger's year-long stay in Cuba, was lost in the mail and had to be reproduced from memory; it has become his most notable collection of verse. In the early 1980s, Enzensberger founded the periodical *TransAtlantik,* and throughout that decade and the 1990s he has published at a prolific rate, producing numerous volumes of essays and verse.

MAJOR WORKS

Beginning his literary career in post-World War II Germany, Enzensberger was concerned not only with the state of the German language, which he felt was corrupted by war and tyranny, but with the economic and spiritual state of his country as well. The aim of his work tends to be a pedagogical one, serving to arouse people's awareness of important political and social issues. In *Poems for People Who Don't Read Poems,* Enzensberger focuses on national politics and German culture. For example, the controversial poem "foam" criticizes the fabric of society and its omnipresent mores. In another highly-praised poem, "the end of the owls," Enzensberger depicts an image of animals threatened by extinction due to the destruction caused by war, an image intended to represent the masses of people who have no voice against that brutality. Enzensberger's political thought broadened with later works such as *Der Untergang der Titanic,* in which he centered on themes of oppression and social injustice. With the ocean liner as a metaphor for society, Enzensberger comments on the differences between the conditions and fates of poor and rich passengers, and describes events from several perspectives, invoking a number of historical and personal references to extend the implications of his themes.

CRITICAL RECEPTION

Critics laud Enzensberger's early works for breaking ground in German poetry at a time when artistic expression had been at a standstill. In later years, Enzensberger's work reflected his views about the writer's role and function within society, and his later disillusionment with literature's ability to effect revolutionary change. Many critics, however, consider these works to be too political, sometimes at the sacrifice of his craft. Enzensberger's more recent poetry, beginning with *Die Furie des Verschiwindens* (1980), reverts back to a more lyrical quality evident in Enzensberger's early verse, one which, the critic Peter Demetz claims is a perfect mirror of the society he attempts to portray: "open, changing, and paradoxical." Overall, Enzensberger's poetry is frequently compared to another German writer, Bertolt Brecht, for his themes and poetic precision. Enzensberger's use of language, and of modern words in particular, is notable for being concise, accessible and pertinent to the moment, both stylistically and politically.

PRINCIPAL WORKS

Poetry

Verteidigung der Wölfe [*The Wolves Defended Against the Lambs*] 1957
Landessprache [*Language of the Country*] 1960
Blindenchrift [*Braille*] 1964
Poems for People Who Don't Read Poems 1968
Gedichte: 1955-1970 [*Poems*] 1971
Mausoleum: 37 Balladen aus der Geschichte des Fortschritts [*Mausoleum: 37 Ballads from the History of Progress*] 1975
Beschreibung eines Dickichts 1979
Der Untergang der Titanic: Eine Komodie [*The Sinking of the Titanic: A Poem*] 1980
Die furie des Verschwindens 1980
Zukunftsmusik [*Future Music*] 1991
Selected Poems: German-English Bilingual Edition 1994
Kiosk 1995

Other Major Works

Einzelheiten 1962
Einzelheiten II: Poesie und Politik 1963
Bewusstseins-Industrie 1963
"In Search of the Lost Language" [in the journal *Encounter*] 1963
Politik und Verbrechen: Neun Beitraege 1964
Deutschland, Deutschland unter anderm 1967
"The Writer and Politics" [in the journal *The Times Literary Supplement*] 1967
Das Verhoer von Habana [*The Havana Inquiry*] 1970
Der kurze Sommer der Anarchie: Buenaventura Durrutis Leben und Tod 1972
Politics and Crime 1974
The Consciousness Industry: On Literature, Politics, and the Media 1974
Raids and Reconstruction: Essays on Politics, Crime, and Culture 1976
Baukasten zu einer Theorie der Medien 1981
Europe, Europe 1989
Political Crumbs 1990
Mediocrity and Delusion 1992

CRITICISM

Patrick Bridgewater (essay date 1967)

SOURCE: "The Making of a Poet: H. M. Enzensberger," in *German Life & Letters*, Vol. XXI, No. 1, October 1967, pp. 27-44.

[*In the following excerpt, Bridgewater finds that Enzensberger's first three verse collections evince the influence of such writers as Bertolt Brecht, Gottfried Benn, W. H. Auden, and others.*]

Hans Magnus Enzensberger was born in 1929. To date he has published the three books of poems that are about what we might expect from a poet of his age: ***verteidigung der wölfe***, 1957; ***landessprache***, 1960; ***blindenschrift***, 1964. In considering the work of a poet still only in his mid-thirties, it is legitimate and instructive to see what he has learnt from other poets. All young poets learn from their poetic predecessors—they would be fools, and there would be no poetic tradition, if they did not. It is, of course, what is learnt and how it works which is of interest. In the following discussion I am therefore interested *not* in the extent to which Enzensberger has been or appears to have been 'influenced' by this or that poet, but in what certain parallels between his work and that of older poets can tell us about his own work.[1]

The poets from whom Enzensberger seems to have learnt most are (in ***verteidigung der wölfe*** and ***landessprache***) Brecht, Benn and W. H. Auden, and (in ***blindenschrift***) William Carlos Williams. To a lesser extent he has benefited from the example of several other American, Latin-American, and German poets. His first collection was essentially a mixture—bound to be successful in 1957—of Brecht and Benn: these are the main sources of his characteristic combination of politics (in theme) and modernism (in expression), a combination more reminiscent of modern Latin-American, than of German, poetry. The most productive models have been Brecht and W. C. Williams. Benn and, to a lesser extent, Auden have been rather negative influences who tended to confirm Enzensberger in his own weaknesses. His earlier attitude towards his poetic models was indeed largely uncritical, though it is sometimes difficult to tell whether one is faced with uncritical or parodistic treatment of the model, that is, whether Benn, say, is being imitated or guyed. It is only with his latest collection, ***blindenschrift,*** that Enzensberger has come of age poetically; this was the first volume to be based on a mature and constructive view of poetry (as opposed to one based on the *worst* elements of Benn's and Brecht's poetics).

Enzensberger's statement that 'It was between the positions of Brecht and Benn, and in a dialogue with these poets . . . that the most recent German poetry developed' ('In Search of the Lost Language', *Encounter,* September 1963) is certainly true of his own first two collections with their mixture of artistry and social involvement, experimental techniques and social realism, collections in which Benn's cerebral smartness and concatenated imagery are combined with something of Brecht's pre-1928 public style and later political toughness. The younger poet is less vitalistic than Brecht, certainly, and the topical or fashionable element in his work is naturally a different one. Both poets, despite obvious differences of period and vocabulary, are aggressively anti-bourgeois. Like Brecht, Enzensberger insists on the *functional* value of poetry. And both poets reacted against a tragically similar situation, for both the First and Second World Wars showed the younger generation that the Germany of their parents was morally bankrupt. The post-war *nouveaux riches* described with such hatred in Enzensberger's 'socialpartner in der rüstungsindustrie' are the sons and grandsons of the bloated financiers attacked so bitterly by Brecht, George Grosz and others. But then history repeated itself.

Yet compared with Brecht's truly revolutionary attitude and temperament, the young poet's 'Wut' seemed rather suspect, seemed to rest (in the first two collections) on too negative a basis; we are faced there with more than just the 'negative' nature of satire as such ('Und wo bleibt das Positive, Herr Kästner?'). While Brecht believed to the end in a theoretical Marxist Utopia, Enzensberger—understandably—does not believe in the future. While Brecht was moved by a genuine compassion for the victims of life, Enzensberger had an almost obsessive hatred of the 'little nobody', as the poem **'die würgengel'** (in *Akzente,* 5/1958) showed. In this he was reacting not only against his own background, but against the twentieth century as such. There is frequently considerable justification for his attitude; it makes good sense to attack the (German!) lambs for their love of the wolves, for instance. But his 'angry poems' are too indiscriminate; these angry leaflets lost through being handed out at random. Brecht aimed to shock people into political action; but is Enzensberger's desire to shock justified? Though he regards himself (as Brecht did) as a 'sager der wahrheit', the desire to shock for its own sake, a perhaps irrepressible *gaminerie,* too often gained the upper hand over his concern with truth in ***verteidigung der wölfe*** and ***landessprache***. A lasting impression of his early verse is that for all its aggressive brilliance there is a persistent lack of substance. Compared with the political poets of the 1920s, their most prominent mid-century successor seemed to lack guts.

In Enzensberger's first two collections there are many direct echoes of the earlier, 'public' Brecht; it is only with ***blindenschrift*** that he comes to terms with his first master, who then becomes a productive model. Anyone reading 'option auf ein grundstück' will at once recognize the model:

meine kinder wünsche ich keineswegs zu verkaufen, sondern im setzen der segel, im harpunieren zu unterrichten. *zu unterrichten ist vom sichern endsieg der metzger, und in der herstellung von kadavern die jugend.*

The polarity here between innocent nature and butcherous humanity—emphasized typographically—is itself entirely Brechtian, as is the allegorical use of nature; there is a close parallel between harpooning whales and butchering men. Enzensberger's black humour is paralleled in the work of Brecht and Benn alike. Both the last stanza of **'an alle fernsprechteilnehmer'** with its reference to the poet's fellow-countrymen asleep in their burning shirts, and his earlier poem **'candide'** with its reference to how those same fellow-countrymen will enjoy spreading their honey while the universe explodes, are strongly reminiscent of Brecht's 'Gleichnis des Buddha vom brennenden Haus' with its attack on those who persist in asking what is to become of their money-boxes and best Sunday trousers if there is a revolution. Enzensberger has learnt from Brecht to use this bitter mockery—which has its eventual source in Heine—to try to shake his readers out of their political apathy. Another close parallel is between Brecht's anti-sermon 'Gegen Verführung', and Enzensberger's **'aschermittwoch'**, a wickedly effective gloss on the antiphons for Ash Wednesday. Both poems are informed by the same conviction, expressed in the last line: that there is no after-life. And both poems have the same aim: to make people realize that man's future—if any—is in his own hands, and that the future can only be assured in the present. Like Brecht, Enzensberger uses the language of the Church (in his case in direct quotation within a collage) to mock the teaching of the Church. The social satirist or political poet aims to make people face the facts. The title-poem of his first collection,**'verteidigung der wölfe gegen die lämmer'**, is entirely in the spirit of Brecht's 'Lob des Zweifels': both poems aim to make the reader see himself and his position for what it is.

But as I have already implied, an examination of the parallels between Enzensberger's poetry and Brecht's soon shows that as man and poet he continually falls short of his model, though he instinctively chose the best and most relevant model. Thus while Brecht's poem '1940' (= 'Mein junger Sohn fragt mich') illustrates his essential faith in life, faith in the future, Enzensberger's comparable **'ins lesebuch für die oberstufe'**shows only his cynicism; as a poem it nullifies itself. Brecht's Schweyk-like social anarchist 'Der Kirschdieb' has never had it so good as in Enzensberger's **'prozession'**, where we find him sitting like a god *in excelsis.* A comparison of **'geburtsanzeige'** with Brecht's 'Von der Freundlichkeit der Welt' shows that Enzensberger lacked in 1957 Brecht's deep humanity and compassion. That he also lacked Brecht's humility is clear if one contrasts his condemnation of his "stinking brothers" with Brecht's attitude in his famous poem "Vom armen B.B." in which he admits that he himself is no better than his fellows (whom he condemns). The crux of the matter is that while Brecht was moved by a revolutionary idealism, Enzensberger's attitude was not—in 1957-60—free from *ressentiment* and arrogance, not free from what he himself calls intellectual snobbishness. This is a fatal mistake for a would-be political poet. While both poets seek to enrage the reader, Brecht's readers really are enraged at the injustice of life and the inhumanity of man, while Enzensberger's readers are surely annoyed—if at all—by the young poet's own arrogance. If Enzensberger was hoping to change the world (in a political sense) he certainly went about it in the wrong way. His attacks on the 'Wirtschaftswunderland' which supports him also seem rather like 'Spiegelfechterei' compared with Brecht's attacks on the Third Reich. Most importantly, Enzensberger lacked, in his 'sad' and 'angry' poems, the poetic ability, the lyrical 'Grazie' of his master. But in a few personal poems and in much of ***blindenschrift*** he has developed a lyrical grace and simplicity that bears comparison with Brecht's.

Brecht's poems 'Vom armen B.B.' and 'An die Nachgeborenen' seem to have impressed Enzensberger more deeply than any others, which is hardly surprising since they contain Brecht's poetic testament in a highly memorable form. The poem **'lebenslauf'** is a direct imitation of 'Vom armen B.B.'. But while Brecht's poem is original, tough, and memorable, Enzensberger's is derivative and self-centred, and not at all memorable. In the same collection there are also several direct echoes of 'An die Nachgeborenen'. A comparison of **'lebenslauf'** with the poem **'weiterung'** in ***blindenschrift*** shows how much Enzensberger's attitude to Brecht changed between 1960 and 1964. The later poem is a deliberate review and critique of the famous final section of 'An die Nachgeborenen'; it reads:

wer soll da noch auftauchen aus der flut,
wenn wir darin untergehen?
noch ein paar fortschritte,
und wir werden weitersehen.
wer soll da unsrer gedenken
mit nachsicht?
das wird sich finden,
wenn es erst soweit ist.
und so fortan
bis auf weiteres
und ohne weiteres
so weiter und so
weiter nichts
keine nachgeborenen
keine nachsicht
nichts weiter

This is an important poem, for it shows that Enzensberger has achieved a genuinely critical attitude towards his model. Here he uses Brecht's poem critically and continues the argument where Brecht left off, a perfectly legitimate procedure. He has rewritten Brecht's poem in the new context of the thermonuclear 'flood': the world has changed out of all recognition since 1938. Previously, as in **'lebenslauf'**, he had been content to echo Brecht uncritically. Now he seems to have come to terms with the great poet on whom not a little of his early work was modelled. This impression is confirmed by another poem, **'küchenzettel'**. The sign of continuing life at the end of the poem ('links unten ganz in der ecke / seh ich einen katzenteller') parallels the equally simple but equally momentous ending of Brecht's 'Gedanken über die Dauer des Exils' ('Sieh den kleinen Kastanienbaum im Eck des Hofes, / Zu dem du die Kanne voll Wasser schlepptest!'). But this new echo of Brecht comes in a poem in which the theme is developed in a way which is at once original and genuinely Brechtian, a poem which shows a real *personal* commitment. The new simplicity of Enzensberger's style in this poem may owe much to Brecht's example; but it is original in a way in which the language of his earlier poetry was not. The theme of the poem is the acceptance of reality as it is—the main theme of the lyrical poet or 'Taoist' in Brecht. If Brecht's 'private' poetry has helped Enzensberger to his new-found acceptance of reality—necessary for the poet since poetry is about reality—this will be Brecht's most important contribution to his work. It is now that he is no longer imitating Brecht and borrowing from him, that his work has become genuinely 'Brechtian'.

Though Enzensberger has rejected Benn's aestheticism, there is no doubt at all that he has learnt a good deal from Benn in terms of poetic technique. His method of composition is surely basically what Benn described as 'prismatic infantilism', saying that it probably reminded people of children's games—shining mirrors in people's faces while themselves remaining in the shade (see Benn, *Der Ptolemäer,* 1949, 137 f.). Enzensberger's attitude in too many poems in ***verteidigung der wölfe*** and ***landessprache*** is—like Benn's own—that of the naughty child drawing attention to itself. But despite this element of exhibitionism, his attitude also tends to be an 'ohne mich' one: he sees the most manifold phenomena as part of a larger reality, but does not himself enter into this larger reality. He is all too often merely 'Anti um jeden Preis'—again like Benn. While satire may thrive on negative reactions, poetry is less prone to do so.

What Enzensberger has learnt from Benn is above all the collage technique with its concatenated images. This is clear if we compare the following lines from his **'candide'**:

> nichts ist gewaltiger als der mensch;
> d.h.
> spiralnebel, kulturkrisen, weltkriege
> sind ephemere belanglosigkeiten,
> stroh der zeit,
> kindereien.

with the passage from Benn's 'Fragmente' which they recall:

> Ausdruckskrisen und Anfälle von Erotik:
> das ist der Mensch von heute,
> das Innere ein Vakuum,
> die Kontinuität der Persönlichkeit
> wird gewahrt von den Anzügen,
> die bei gutem Stoff zehn Jahre halten.

In ***verteidigung der wölfe*** there are a number of other lines and passages which also owe a direct debt to this characteristic technique of Benn's, for instance in the poems **'erinnerung an die schrecken der jugend'**, **'anrufung des fisches'**, **'abschied von einem mittwoch'**, **'prozession'**, and **'ratschlag auf höchster ebene'**. Such parallels sometimes show Benn uncritically adopted rather than critically digested; but there are also passages in which Benn is parodied, e.g. in the last stanza of the poem **'candide'** just quoted:

> dämonie? ist gewöhnlich dilettantismus.
> katastrophen? kaffeeklatsch der geschichte,
> überdauert von tonkrügen, von profilen,
> und von deinen aprikosen, candide.

or again in the poem **'goldener schnittmusterbogen zur poetischen wiederaufrüstung'**.

The concatenated image technique is one that needs to be handled very carefully if *poetry* is to result. Disparate and diverse details only produce poetry if a significant pattern is imposed upon them. In poems such as **'schaum'** and **'gewimmer und firmament'**—which admittedly owe far more to Allen Ginsberg's 'Howl' than to anything written by Gottfried Benn—poetic self-control and self-criticism is totally lacking. An intrinsic weakness of the collage-technique as used not only by Enzensberger and Grass, but also by Benn and W. H. Auden, is that it lends itself to uncritical 'Aneinanderreihung'; all too often artistic self-discipline, the art of selection, goes by the board. In his essay 'Entstehung eines Gedichts' on the genesis of the poem **'an alle fernsprechteilnehmer'**, Enzensberger wrote of his own early drafts of the poem: 'Sein Satzbau ist brüchig und undurchsichtig, mehr eine additive Reihung als eine haltbare Konstruktion. . . . Die einzelnen Angaben sind ungenügend verzahnt.' This is very honest self-criticism, and in the final draft of the poem in question this fault has been to some extent overcome. But this same uncritical 'Aneinanderreihung' is none the less seen in too many of Enzensberger's earlier published poems; until the early 1960s his self-criticism was not sufficiently rigorous. The essay to which I have just referred is a brilliant piece of retrospective poetic self-analysis, but one which is perhaps *too* explicit; the poet's very articulateness makes **'an alle fernsprechteilnehmer'** seem contrived, too intellectual and abstract.

In using the concatenated image technique Enzensberger has also tended, like Benn, to lack the poetic tact and self-control that would prevent his work from slipping into the merely topical or into abstract slogans. A juxtaposition like 'die nike von samothrake und von cap canaveral' may be effective in its concision and width of reference, but the effectiveness depends, or depended, on its topicality. Since Enzensberger wrote the line the Nike missile has become obsolescent, and Cape Canaveral has been renamed. It is precisely the poet who is most admirably concerned to express his own age who runs most risk of expressing only his own age. Like many modern poets, for instance, both Benn and Enzensberger make considerable use of foreign words, especially Anglo-Saxonisms. But these words are often merely topical or fashionable. Examples: High Life, Sex-Appeal, Cutaway, Barvamps, Boogie-Woogie, Blues, Jitterbug (Benn); security risk, countdown, jukebox, snackbar, ban the bomb, feedback system, displaced person (Enzensberger). Some of Benn's Anglo-Saxonisms are already dated; how Enzensberger's will fare remains to be seen. But it will surely be the poems in which the Benn-like neologisms and contemporary foreign words, phrases and slogans are strung together, that will last least well. The fact that Enzensberger's use of fashionable words—like Benn's use of them—is frequently ironical, does not affect the issue. Such irony is itself topical merely: all that will remain is the dated word.

In general the extraordinary diversity, liveliness and technologically up-to-date nature of Enzensberger's vocabulary no doubt owes much to the example of Benn. Let us remember what Benn himself said:

> Diese meine Sprache . . . steht mir zur Verfügung. Diese Sprache mit ihrer Jahrhunderte alten Tradition, ihren von lyrischen Vorgängern geprägten sinn- und stimmungsgeschwängerten, seltsam geladenen Worten. Aber auch die Slang-Ausdrücke, Argots, Rotwelsch, von zwei Weltkriegen in das Sprachbewusstsein hineingehämmert, ergänzt durch Fremdworte, Zitate, Sportjargon, antike Reminiszenzen, sind in meinem Besitz. Ich von heute, der mehr aus Zeitungen lernt als aus Philosophien, der dem Journalismus nähersteht als der Bibel, dem ein Schlager von Klasse mehr Jahrhundert enthält als eine Motette. . . . (*Probleme der Lyrik,*)

This reads like a description not only of Benn's vocabulary, but of Enzensberger's too. Speaking of his own poetry and that of some of his contemporaries, Enzensberger has said:

> Fragments of everyday life, scraps of slang, words from the world of consumer goods force their way into the poetic text. The safety-pin and the Rapacki plan, the jukebox and the cough-drop appear in verse with the same right and the same naturalness as the moon, the sea, and the rose ('In Search of the Lost Language').

It can be argued that such phenomena do not always appear in Enzensberger's or any other contemporary verse with as much naturalness as he suggests. But his own poetry, whatever its quality, is nearly always about the issues that matter; and his vocabulary itself reflects our time. Where too many contemporary poets are of their time only in their self-consciousness and wilful obscurantism, Enzensberger is of his time in the intrinsic complexity of his themes and the urbanity and diversity of his vocabulary with its deliberate colloquialisms.

Benn's influence on Enzensberger's imagery, syntax and diction has in fact been considerable. He is himself a striking example of the poet as 'ein grosser Realist . . . das athenische Insekt' (*Probleme,*). There is no denying that he has 'ein hartes, massives Gehirn, ein Gehirn mit Eckzähnen' (ibid.,). And that Benn's particular form of cerebral smartness still appeals to him is shown by the recent poem **'bibliographie'**.

What must now be stressed is that in 1961 Enzensberger completely rejected Benn's poetic theory. Right from the beginning it was clear that he had implicitly rejected Benn's aestheticism. This rejection became explicit in the essay 'Scherenschleifer und Poeten' (in: *Mein Gedicht ist mein Messer,* ed. Hans Bender, 2nd ed., List-Bücher, 1961) where Enzensberger insisted that poetry is *not* about the poet himself, that 'content' is as important as 'form', and that poems are addressed to *some*one. This is a specific reversal of Benn's views. Elsewhere he implicitly condemned Benn for seeing art as a 'purpose in itself, . . . an aesthetic substitute religion beyond all social and moral responsibility' (*Encounter,* September 1963). This condemnation of Benn's egocentric formalistic aesthetic is surely justified. His view of art had led Benn to insist that works of art are historically ineffective, meaning that artists can*not* change the world in a *political* sense. Enzensberger's first two collections appeared to be based on the belief that they could; but in this respect he recently seems to have come to share Benn's view. Whether his rejection of Benn's formalism has anything to do with what is ultimately a lack of form (as opposed to style) in his own earlier poetry, is a matter for speculation. But I suggest that he went too far both in his *wholesale* rejection of Benn's poetic theory and—more especially—in his uncritical acceptance of Benn's poetic techniques.

Karl Krolow has noted Enzensberger's indebtedness to W. H. Auden:

> Enzensberger, der nicht nur Brecht, sondern vor allem die Amerikaner, Auden voran, genau kennt, bedient sich in seiner gesellschaftskritischen Sprache ihrer Errungenschaften (*Aspekte zeitgenössischer Lyrik,* Gütersloh, 1961).

W. H. Auden certainly seems to have helped Enzensberger to form his view of poetry. It is evident that he shares Auden's pragmatic view that 'Art is not enough.' Art, for him, is the means to a non-artistic end; poems have to be 'beautiful' so that people will pay attention to their moral. Like Auden, Enzensberger is in fact above all a moralist; and in him, as in Auden, there is clearly a tension between the lyric poet and the moralist, a tension which occasionally, as in 'call it love', produces an excellent poem. But in his first two collections the clever-clever moralist tends to get the better of the poet, though—again like Auden—Enzensberger can produce delightful lyrics (e.g. the 'friendly poems' in ***verteidigung der wölfe***). The poet only really gets the better of his satirical anti-self in the most impressive recent poem **'lachesis lapponica'**. His rather clinical detachment is also reminiscent of Auden; Enzensberger too trends to go in for the detached 'placing' of detail by means of successive definite articles. In his earlier poetry there is a brittle journalistic glibness, a tendency for genuine poetic exploration to be replaced by smug enumeration, e.g. in the **'goldener schnittmusterbogen'**. . . with its rejection of 'belcanto' (fair enough) and its sneers at 'trobadore' (unfortunate since it was precisely the *trobador* in Enzensberger that needed developing). As Hans Egon Holthusen has noted (in his *Kritisches Verstehen,* 1961), both poets go in for the *ironical* combination of words and phrases, often linked by alliteration or assonance. While Auden wrote, for instance:

> Nocturnal trivia, torts and dramas,
> Wrecks, arrivals, rose-bushes, armies,
> Leopards and laughs, alarming growths of
> Moulds and monsters on memories stuffed
> With dead men's doodles, dossiers written
> In lost lingos . . .
> (*The Age of Anxiety,* 1948)

we find Enzensberger using this same technique—it is a basic one in *The Age of Anxiety*—when he writes:

> wir schlafen, nett geschart
> um egel, die keine sind,
> gesalbt mit gallerte.
> aus vegetarischen villen
> streuen sie leutselig
> rosenkränze und zucker
> in den jubel der somnambulen
> wahllosen wähler.

And there are many other examples. These ironical combinations may be the work either of the poet 'playing about with words', or of the satirist. In Enzensberger's early work it is most often the latter, for in much if not most of the earlier poetry there is—as in much of Auden's work—something slick, deft, essentially journalistic; take away the satire and there is nothing much left. There was there, above all, a lack of personal emotion that made his social commitment seem rather shallow. This lack of personal emotion was deliberate; Enzensberger has said that poets' feelings are of no particular interest, and if he was thinking of feelings that remain unobjectivized, this is true; but he perhaps went *too* far in his reaction against personal feeling and the seraphic tone.

If Auden's example is reflected in Enzensberger's early work (and there is little sign of it in ***blindenschrift***), it is Auden's weaknesses, like Benn's, that are reflected there most clearly. But then in Auden's poetry it is the weaknesses that are most immediately obvious. And Auden too can be an overwhelming influence for a young poet. Naturally there are also many ways in which Enzensberger's work differs from Auden's. One obvious point concerns their imagery. If Auden tends to rely on conceptual and moral patterns rather than sensuous effects, Enzensberger at times employs a more sensuous imagery. In this he is closer to, say, Pablo Neruda. Indeed, in 1961 he said that his aim was to produce a 'highly sensuous dialectic', which is as good a definition of poetry as most (cf. J. J. Baumgarten's 'oratio sensitiva perfecta'). Though he does not often allow it to appear in his early work, he has a sensitive feeling for nature, particularly for marine life.

One of several poets translated by Enzensberger is William Carlos Williams. That he has learnt from Williams in the process seems clear. His lines in the poem **'das herz von grönland'**:

> ich will vom zerstörbaren reden,
> wo wenig lob ist
> und lob wenig, und wenig zeit,
> da haust der krebs
> in den gruben

might indeed have been written by Dr Williams in between seeing patients; one of the American poet's main themes is, as Enzensberger himself has noted, destruction and physical decay, 'the death implied'. The exciting concreteness, the elaborately assembled images in his work recall Williams's view that 'detail is all'; in his work, as in Williams's own, we see 'the juxtapositions impossible otherwise to accomplish' (W. C. Williams, *The Collected Later Poems,* N.Y., 1950). The main difference is that Enzensberger—like Auden—frequently juxtaposes slogans and ideas, while Williams normally juxtaposes images. In Williams's 'A Sort of Song' there was in fact a clear moral for Enzensberger, a moral which he now seems to have learned:

> —through metaphor to reconcile
> the people and the stones.
> Compose. (No ideas
> but in things). Invent!
> Saxifrage is my flower that splits
> the rocks

This is what he is now doing in ***blindenschrift,*** where we at last find the abstract slogans replaced by 'the particulars of poetry / that difficult art' (ibid.). In this last collection, notably in the final section ('schattenwerk') there are a number of short and short-line poems that employ a form (short 2, 3 and 4-line stanzas) used by W. C. Williams, Wallace Stevens and e. e. cummings; earlier the songs in ***verteidigung der wölfe*** appeared to be indebted to these same poets' songs: with **'lock lied'** compare Williams's 'The Fool's Song' (*The Collected Earlier Poems*, N.Y., 1951). One critic has written of Enzensberger's songs as 'zarten, fast zärtlichen Liedern . . . die wie chinesische Tuschzeichnungen anmuten' (K. G. Just, *Universitas,* May 1960), and certainly the tone and imagery of his more lyrical poems does recall Chinese and Japanese poetry. While his model here—if he had one—might have been Brecht's 'Chinesische Gedichte' and 'Buckower Elegien', it could equally well have been the Japanese-style imagism of W. C. Williams, for, as Enzensberger has said:

> Seine besten Gedichte erinnern zuweilen an ostasiatische Graphiken, besonders in ihrer genauen Ökonomie, der Kunst des Aussparens. Diese Schreibweise hat es nicht auf Deutung, sondern auf Evidenz abgesehen. Sie verzichtet konsequent auf 'Tiefen' und gibt stattdessen die Oberfläche der Erscheinungen in höchster Prägnanz; daher ihre Undurchdringlichkeit, jene Qualität, die Pound *opacity* genannt hat ('William Carlos Williams', *Einzelheiten*).

In fact Brecht and Williams have much in common as poets. Just how much can be judged from Enzensberger's translations of Williams's 'The Bare Tree', which reads exactly like a late poem by Brecht:

> Der kahle Kirschbaum
> über dem Dach
> trug reichlich Früchte?
> im letzten Jahr. Früchte?
> Dieses Gerippe da?
> Ist das denn überhaupt
> noch am Leben? Ich
> seh keine Früchte.
> Also schlagt es ab
> und braucht das Holz
> gegen die beissende Kälte.
> (W. C. Williams, *Gedichte,* tr. H. M. E., 1962)

Together Brecht and W. C. Williams have had an immensely beneficial influence on Enzensberger; it will have been their example that prevented him from becoming yet another metaphor-bound modernist. To them he owes above all his clarity and colloquial tone.

In Enzensberger's work we find several devices that are used—most notably, but not only—by Williams. In ***verteidigung der wölfe*** compound words are not only separated, but a word is sometimes split between two lines (e.g. aus-/geliefert, fest-/krallen). This word-splitting is not as startling as in the poetry of Williams who writes, for instance, grad-/ually, o-/dors; and Enzensberger seems to have decided that this device is kitschy, for he dropped it in subsequent collections. But in some of the early 'friendly poems' and in ***blindenschrift*** we find another device used by W. C. Williams, e. e. cummings, and many contemporary American poets: the discarding of punctuation (especially full-stops), and the—in ***blindenschrift*** only occasional—use of extended spaces between words and lines to replace grammatical signs and to convey the poet's personal rhythm or 'breathings' more exactly. This technique, which was used in 'friendly poems' such as **'call it love'** and—more consequentially—**'schläferung'**:

lass mich heut nacht in der gitarre schlafen
in der verwunderten gitarre der nacht
lass mich ruhn
im zerbrochenen holz
lass meine hände schlafen
auf ihren saiten
meine verwunderten hände
lass schlafen
das süsse holz
lass meine saiten
lass die nacht
auf den vergessenen griffen ruhn
meine zerbrochenen hände
lass schlafen
auf den süssen saiten
im verwunderten holz.

but was then dropped, could be partly a carrying-further of Brecht's omission of the comma at the end of the line (because there is a speech-pause there anyway). But Enzensberger is likely to have obtained the consequent typographical arrangement from recent American poetry of the 'William Carlos Williams line', perhaps even direct from Charles Olson's statement on 'Projective Verse' of 1950, which has become an *ars poetica* for many American poets of Enzensberger's generation. 'Projective Verse' stresses two things: 'composition by field' and the adoption of a 'stance toward reality outside a poem.' Enzensberger clearly agrees with Olson's view that 'Form is never more than an extension of content', and presumably (judging by his poetry) would agree with the process by which this principle is accomplished, namely that 'One perception must immediately and directly lead to a further perception' (Charles Olson, 'Projective Verse', repr. in *The New American Poetry* 1945-60, ed. Donald M. Allen, N. Y., 1960—a book which Enzensberger knows). It would therefore be natural for him to experiment in 'field composition', which would mean in practice concerning himself with the problem which was of prime importance for William Carlos Williams—the problem of colloquial speech rhythms and 'tone'. In his essay on Williams, he speaks of the American poet's 'untrüglichen Ohr für Tonfälle . . . Dieser exakte Gebrauch der Umgangssprache.' Enzensberger himself has always written mostly in irregular rhythms (regular rhythms being reserved for parodistic purposes), and has never attached much importance to the stanza as such. In ***blindenschrift*** there are few regular stanzas, and now punctuation is being dropped again too, thus making his poetry still more 'open' (Olson's synonym for 'projective'). His next collection may well continue his experiments in this field, may well go further in the direction of adopting the William Carlos Williams line of contemporary American poetry to the German language. Looking back to poems such as **'lock lied'**, **'zikade'** and **'schläferung'** in ***verteidigung der wölfe,*** one can only regret that Enzensberger did not at that time continue to allow himself to be guided by poets such as Williams instead of becoming the victim of his own publicistic success. What he needed was not only Williams's precise colloquialism, but also his poetic attitude. In ***blindenschrift*** a number of poems are concerned with the discovery of reality and the acceptance of things as they are found to be. This acceptance, unlike the derision and wholesale rejection of reality in the first two collections, has already led to some impressive poetry. Enzensberger may well have been helped to find this acceptance by the example of W. C. Williams, and of Günter Eich and (the *lyrical* poet) Brecht. It looks as though W. C. Williams has been and may continue to be a most productive and helpful model.

A few short-line poems in ***blindenschrift*** are also reminiscent of the poetry of Wallace Stevens. In particular, **'mehrere elstern'** looks like an adaptation of Stevens's famous poem 'Thirteen Ways of Looking at a Blackbird', while **'schattenreich'** too is written in the mixed 2-, 3- and 4-line stanzas, and **'trigonometrischer punkt'** (a title derived from Eich?) and **'windgriff'** in the short 3-line stanzas favoured alike by Stevens and Williams. Enzensberger also has a little in common with e. e. cummings, though—apart from his rejection of capital letters—it is more a question of tone than of anything more specific; e. e. cummings is a much more 'old-fashioned' poet than Enzensberger in the sense of being a romantic beneath his typographic disguise, but his totally irreverent attitude is shared by the young German poet. Enzensberger's early songs (**'lock lied'**, **'zikade'**, etc.) parallel some of cummings's songs in *Tulips and Chimneys* (1923) in their a-syntactical stringing-together of words, the typographical arrangement of the poems, and their general kittenish tone. Particularly in ***blindenschrift*** Enzensberger also uses the half-repetition employed by Auden, Williams and cummings, e.g. in **'schattenbild'**:

ich male den schnee
ich male beharrlich
ich male lotrecht.

But if Enzensberger's recent poems that use half-repetition and analytical progression in this way are modelled on other poets, the models are more likely to have been Erich Fried and Paul Celan—Celan, whose rhythms re-echo through ***blindenschrift***. The following lines from **'der andere'**:

einer der geld und angst und einen pass hat
einer der streitet und liebt
einer rührt sich

surely owe something to poems such as 'Traum vom Tod' or 'Taglied' by Erich Fried (see Fried, *Gedichte,* 1958), or to poems by Paul Celan which use the same technique (see his *Sprachgitter,* 1959). The most characteristic technique in Fried's earlier work, the punning word-patterns (so clearly prefigured in some of Paul Klee's poems), has naturally not commended itself to Enzensberger. In Enzensberger's first two collections one of the most obvious weaknesses was that he did not develop his themes properly; although his poems were highly articulate in one sense, in another sense they were inarticulate. This is where he now seems to have been helped by the syntactical experiments of Fried and Celan, for in ***blindenschrift*** he does articulate and co-ordinate his images, does develop his themes dialectically—from a technical point of view this is the most important development in this latest collection—and in doing so makes some use of the 'linguistic analysis' of Fried and Celan. Whether in turn Erich Fried's recent, more 'aktuell' poems owe anything to Enzensberger, is a further matter for speculation.

But so far as contemporary German poets are concerned, the most significant model has probably been Günter Eich. Enzensberger's first two collections might have been written in accordance with Eich's advice:

> Tut das Unnütze, singt die Lieder, die man aus eurem Mund nicht erwartet!
> Seid unbequem, seid Sand, nicht das Öl im Getriebe der Welt!
> (G. Eich, *Ausgewählte Gedichte,* 1950)

Whether he was consciously following this advice at any time, I do not know; if he was, he followed it too literally. Be this as it may, Enzensberger certainly seems to have learnt from Eich in his latest collection, cf. the poem **'abgelegenes haus'** dedicated to Eich. The constant theme of Günter Eich's poetry is the rediscovery of reality and therefore of self. But this is also a recurrent theme in ***blindenschrift,*** and one which has led to some very good poems (**'abgelegenes haus'**, **'küchenzettel'**, **'lachesis lapponica'**). In this latest collection Enzensberger has found himself and found a new simplicity of expression, and in this he appears to have been helped considerably by the admirable example of Günter Eich's poetry.

It is evident from his work as translator and anthologist that Enzensberger particularly admires some modern Latin-American poets, notably the Peruvian César Vallejo and the Chilean Pablo Neruda (cf. his essay on Neruda in *Einzelheiten*). That he has himself learnt from Neruda is suggested by a poem like **'an alle fernsprechteilnehmer'** which contains just such a series of approximations as we find in some of Neruda's earlier poems, e.g.:

> Etwas zwischen Lippe und Stimme stirbt dahin,
> Etwas mit Vogelschwingen, etwas aus Qual und Vergessen.
> (Pablo Neruda, *Gedichte,* tr. Erich Arendt, Bibliothek Suhrkamp, 1963)

In **'an alle fernsprechteilnehmer'** there are what seem to be verbal echoes of Neruda, cf. these lines:

> die ministerien mauscheln, nach phlox
> und erloschenen resolutionen riecht
> der august

and several others in the poem with Neruda's:

> Laast uns . . .
> in den Abgrund der Akten versinken.
> in den Zorn der gefesselten Worte,
> in hartnäckig tote Kundmachungen,
> in Systeme, eingehüllt in vergilbte Papiere.
> Kommt mit mir in die Kanzleien, in den zweifelhaften Geruch von Ministerien und Gräbern und Stempelmarken.

It will be agreed that there is at least a parallel here. Enzensberger's concatenated imagery is reminiscent of Neruda as well as of Benn and Auden, and the empty anger of his early poems is paralleled in Neruda's war-poems. But naturally there are many more differences between Enzensberger and Neruda in his various phases. A comparison of **'ehre sei der sellerie'** with Neruda's 'Oda a la cebolla' ('Ode to an Onion'), which it recalls, makes the essential difference between the poets clear. Neruda's poem is more straightforward and employs a more sensuous imagery than Enzensberger's, which is gratuitously provocative. In general, however, the mixture of politics and modernism in Enzensberger's poetry is reminiscent of Neruda and the other modern Spanish-American poets who figure largely in his *museum der modernen poesie.* There may be a strong general influence here. And certainly this is where Enzensberger's originality within German poetry lies: previously politics and modernism had tended increasingly (since the anti-Expressionist reaction of the 1920s) to be poetic opposites.

In ***verteidigung der wölfe*** there were several echoes, partly parodistic, of early Expressionist poetry, and particularly of Georg Heym. The poem **'kleiner herbst dämon'** beginning:

> nach schwefel stinkt dein gelber schopf
> die hände hast am kohlen feuer
> die augen glitzen ungeheuer
> und maus blut kocht in deinem topf

is strongly reminiscent of Heym's 'Der Gott der Stadt' and 'Die Dämonen der Städte'. Surely Enzensberger's **'kleiner herbst dämon'** (note the characteristic separation of compound words here) is a contemporary version and parody of Heym's majestic Baal, a sort of demonic equivalent of the 'kleiner niemand'. In another poem, 'larisa' there are clear echoes—in the imagery and strutting trochaic rhythms of the poem (**'nachts wird kälter'**: und sie schnarchen / fest in rauchverqualmten träumen / ist kein obdach? ach die wirte / schwenken glänzend schwer das Kinn')—of Heym's most famous poem, 'Der Krieg'. Ironical undertones of 'Der Krieg' are also found in **'die hebammen'**, where the futilely militant midwives 'springen . . . unverhofft querfeldein' (cf. Heym's poem, where *War* 'jagt das Feuer querfeldein'). More generally, lines like 'aus den dachluken zwitschern päpste' or 'springen den frauen die pelze im park auf' owe much to the satirical vision of early Expressionist poets such as Heym and Lichtenstein. Enzensberger's often brilliant inventiveness also owes much to Hans Arp.

This parodying of Heym and, as we saw earlier, Benn, is part of a general tendency by the poet to include parodistic quotations from other poets in his earlier work (another Brechtian technique). Like many other contemporary poets, he not infrequently incorporates quotations into his work, particularly in ***landessprache.*** His sources range from the Bible . . . the Ave Maria and the Proper of the Mass . . . to Karl Marx. . . . Advertisements and public inscriptions are used. But most of his quotations are from other poets, and in these cases we are usually faced with parody. It is probably a dislike of rhetoric that causes him to parody Hölderlin: 'ein gipfelkongress ist einberufen / zur verhütung des schlimmsten. bekanntlich / wächst, wo gefahr ist, das rettende auch' (V. 89, cf. Hölderlin's 'Patmos'); 'stiftet lieber, was bleibet, die dummheit' (V. 82, cf. Hölderlin's 'Andenken'); '*un*heilig herz der völker' (my italics); etc. Rilke is similarly parodied: 'hier sein ist herrlich' (L. 8, cf. 7th Elegy: the parody is in the context); 'gut sein ist nirgends' (L. 68, cf. 7th Elegy); etc. There are a number of parodistic allusions to contemporary poets, e.g. *'mohn und metaphysik'* (V. 82, cf. Paul Celan's *Mohn und Gedächtnis*); 'auf widerruf' (L. 8, cf. Ingeborg Bachmann's 'Die gestundete Zeit'); 'anrufung des fisches'(V. 40 f., cf. Bachmann's *Anrufung des Grossen Bären*); 'mystische rosen' (L. 39, where they are equated with 'schaum', cf. A. A. Scholl's 'Poesie' where poetry is called 'die mystische Rose'); 'die spieldose mit der alten sarabande' etc. The 'asphodelen' in the poem **'goldener schnittmusterbogen'**. . . no doubt contains a satirical reference to the 'Asphodelen meiner Angst' (the metaphor is from Ivan Goll's poem 'Die Hochöfen des Schmerzes') variety of post-1948 modernism, the work of those whom Enzensberger has called the belated adepts of Benn's *Ausdruckswelt.* But the poet to whom hostile allusion is most frequently made is Hans Egon Holthusen. There are several satirical echoes of his well-known poem 'Tabula rasa', cf. 'wie sind wir heruntergekommen! was für ein zustand!'; 'was soll ich hier? und was soll ich sagen? / in welcher sprache? und wem?'; 'das hört nicht auf! das stirbt, ununterbrochen . . . '. In this last case the parodistic intention is made clear both by the fact that Enzensberger here writes in Holthusen's rhetorical rhythms, and by the way in which he continues: 'das faselt geschmeichelt / von apokalypse, das frisst am nullpunkt noch kaviar / . . . / das hat keinen zweck! . . . da hilft kein rilke und kein dior!' It is a fair assumption that these hostile allusions have a political as well as an aesthetic basis. Enzensberger presumably has in mind both the neo-Rilkean *Zeitdichter* and the member of the 'literarische Regierungspartei'; but it is essentially the antagonism of the new left for the old right that we see here.

When he began writing, Enzensberger's poetry was essentially a mixture of Brecht's 'public' and Benn's private poetry. From Brecht derived the political poetry as such and some of the means of putting it across. From Benn came the basic method of composition ('prismatic infantilism'), the concatenated imagery, and much of the diction. To this topical mixture was added a type of satire that owed not a little to W. H. Auden. The poetry that resulted from this combination of models was artistically weak; the best of his early poems were the most original ones, the—very few—poems written in his *own* voice. A first major turning-point in his poetry has now come with ***blindenschrift***, where his whole attitude has changed and he has evidently learned from W. C. Williams, Brecht, and Günter Eich to concentrate his work on particulars. There is now a new sort of detailedness, a genuine articulation and elaboration of given themes, and a new lyrical grace and simplicity; Williams, Brecht, and Eich have helped Enzensberger to find himself, to rediscover his own voice.

Notes

1. Enzensberger's poetic aims and achievements are discussed in my essay "Hans Magnus Enzensberger" in *Essays on Contemporary German Literature,* ed. Brian Keith-Smith, London (Oswald Wolff), 1966.

D. J. Enright (review date 1968)

SOURCE: "Between Holderlin and Himmler," in *The New York Review of Books*, Vol. X, No. 7, April 11, 1968, pp. 21-2.

[*In the following review, Enright declares* Poems for People Who Don't Read Poems *"pure poetry" and compares it to Bertolt Brecht's poetry in its precision.*]

It is scarcely the case that we live in a time when literary conventions are so narrow and stifling that "poetry" must become, for the poet, a dirty word. Far from it. Poetically, anything goes, and the louder the faster, though perhaps not very far. So the more one considers the title of Hans Magnus Enzensberger's volume of selected poems [***Poems for People Who Don't Read Poems***]—with English translations facing the German text, except on one occasion—the more sadly irrelevant or even senseless it comes to seem. People who don't read poems don't read poems.

In the longest piece here, **"summer poem"**, the phrase *"das ist keine kunst"* keeps recurring—"that's not art." In a note the author describes the phrase as "the traditional objection of a bourgeois aesthetic against every innovation." True, such was the situation, once upon a time. But far more often today we hear the complaint "but that's *art,*" the false artist's by now traditional objection to the suggestion that art should be something more than a howl, a slash of paint, or a tangle of old iron. The genuine artist—and there is clear evidence here of Enzensberger's genuineness—oughtn't to be wasting his time and energy on this sort of shadow-boxing.

Enzensberger has set his face against Rilke, Bach, Hölderlin (*"what can we do / with everyone / who says hölderlin and means himmler"*), seemingly because their work failed to prevent the Nazi extermination camps, because indeed some camp commandants were actually connoisseurs of music and poetry. Are Rilke, Bach, and Hölderlin to blame for this? Should they have written only for good men to read? Maybe in a few score years the work of Enzensberger will be judiciously appreciated by the monsters of some new regime, whose withers are left unwrung, or are probably unwringable anyway?

Perhaps Rilke, at least, was too much the self-regarding artist, spinning literature out of his own guts, with too little concern for the guts of others. *"Hiersein ist herrlich"* ("to be here is glorious"), says Enzensberger, glancing with rather heavy irony at one of Rilke's best known and most willed announcements. The allusion comes in Enzensberger's **"man spricht deutsch"**, which plays angrily with the phraseology and appurtenances of the Economic Miracle. (A word of praise is due to the translators: here and elsewhere, thrown into a verbal blood-bath, they contrive to make on their own swings what they lose on the original roundabouts, as with "on the bonny bonny banks we play blind man's buff.") True, one expects a miracle to take place in a cowshed, on a mountain, by a lakeside, at a tomb—and not, in economic guise, in the vicinity of gas chambers, not upon the ashes of incinerated thousands. When it does, you can scream with rage and horror, but the Miracle still stands, your screams won't make it fall down like the walls of Jericho. You must also speak clearly, and say what you want instead of this Miracle. It is natural in Enzensberger that the experience of the "new Germany" should hurt all the worse because of the nearness of the old Germany:

this is a country different from any
other . . .
germany, my country, unholy heart
of the nations,
pretty notorious, more so every day,
among ordinary people elsewhere . . .
there i shall stay for a time,
till i move on to the other people
and rest, in a country quite ordinary,
elsewhere,
not here.

Is there any land left that is "*ganz gewöhnlich*" by what would seem to be Enzensberger's conception of the ordinary? If there is, what on earth would he find to do in it?

A good deal of what Enzensberger cries out against in Germany is in fact universal. Some of it is trivial. Since the artist *must* select, anyway, it is best that he *does* select. And selection appears to be this poet's weak point. Embroidered napkins, whipped creams, wage negotiators, plastic bags, chambers of commerce, murderers' dens, bonus vouchers, chamois beard hats, Coca Cola and arsenals, Rilke and Dior, branflakes and bombs—they all feature as expletives in a lengthy curse, all of equal weight apparently or, in the end, of equal weightlessness. To be angry about everything is to be angry about nothing. Enzensberger's rage declines into rant, his fierce indignation into smashing-up-the-furniture. One thinks of Brecht's poems, and of his gift for selecting the one detail, the one image, the one reference which will tell all, or as much as he set out to tell.

The last poem in this book is called **"Joy"**, and it begins,

she does not want me to speak of
her
she won't be put down on paper
she can't stand prophets . . .

It is a more hopeful poem than most of Enzensberger's, for it ends by speaking of Joy's "*siegreiche flucht*" ("her long flight to victory") but it is a little too abstract, too willed, and deficient in the urgency and the implied compassionateness of similar poems by Brecht, such as

In meinem Lied ein Reim
Käme mir fast vor wie Ubermut
(In my poetry a rhyme
Seemed to me almost like presump-
tion)

or

Der Lachende
Hat die furchtbare Nachricht
Nur noch nicht empfangen
(The man who laughs
Has not yet heard the dreadful
news)

Yet for me Enzensberger is at his best when at his nearest to Brecht, and when he eschews length, as in **"bill of fare"**, **"poem about the future"**,the grimly comic **"midwives"**, and (a very fine poem) **"the end of the owls"**:

i speak for none of your kind,
i speak of the end of the owls.
i speak for the flounder and whale
in their unlighted house . . .
i speak for those who can't speak,
for the deaf and dumb witnesses,
for otters and seals,
for the ancient owls of the earth.

These are Enzensberger's most moving, most impressive poems—and I don't mean (if indeed it means anything at all) "aesthetically." These, by implication, contain the horror and disgust of the longer pieces, but go beyond horror and disgust, not by annulling them, by selling out to "art," but by assuring us that the poet is not himself merely a destroyer with a grievance against bigger and better destroyers. Here he is not making war but speaking, soberly and lucidly, of the pity of war. In his longer poems, Enzensberger's weapon is the blunderbuss, where it should rather be the rapier. Or is that too much like "art"? In an age of nuclear weapons the rapier cannot be said to be noticeably less effective than the blunderbuss or the bludgeon, and it is certainly more discriminating. The poet, unlike the atom bomb, ought to discriminate still.

Peter Demetz (essay date 1970)

SOURCE: "Hans Magnus Enzensberger," in *Postwar German Literature*, Pegasus, 1970, pp. 92-7.

[*In this essay, Demetz surveys the themes and subjects of Enzensberger's firsth three volumes of poetry.*]

When Hans Magnus Enzensberger first published his poems he was immediately cast in the welcome role of the angry young man, but the fixed public image has tended to obfuscate the changing concerns of a highly gifted intellectual. He is more learned, cosmopolitan, and restless than any of his contemporaries; essentially unwilling to settle down in any place or way of thought, intent on radical doubt, he does not participate in collective stances for very long. . . .

Enzensberger, like Brecht, wants his reader to think, and it is difficult to isolate his poetry from his bitter polemics against the German mass media (including the August *Frankfurter Allgemeine Zeitung*), from his translations, and his editorial projects. His three volumes of poetry, ***verteidigung der wölfe,*** 1957/***in defense of the wolves***; ***landessprache***, 1960/***language of the land***; and ***blindenschrift,*** 1964/***writing for the blind***, relate chronologically and thematically to his political analyses and to the few literary essays in *Einzelheiten*, 1962/*Details; Politik und Verbrechen,* 1964/*Politics and Crime;* and *Deutschland Deutschland unter anderem,* 1967/*Germany Germany inter alia,* as well as to his anthology of modern poetry and his translations of William Carlos Williams (whom Enzensberger considers the patriarch of independent American writing). The first American anthology of Enzensberger's verse suggests in its title (taken from a subdivision of the German original) that Enzensberger offers ***poems for people who don't read poems*** (1968) and likes his writings to be used by those who want to transform a world that offends their sense of fairness.

In verbal strategies and thematic interests, Enzensberger's first two volumes of poetry differ somewhat from the more subdued tone and the lean economy of the third volume. In his ***defense of the wolves*** and ***language of the land*** Enzensberger demonstrates an impressive richness of linguistic techniques, stanzaic patterns, and modes of speech. These collections include aggressively ironic attacks against all power, property, and technology; luminous love poems in a soberly contemporary idiom; and a pensive, almost elegiac poem articulating his most intimate longing for an existence of pastoral happiness, quiet, and peace. In the well-known early poem, **"counsel at the highest level"**, he rages against the sexually impotent "makers of history," whom he advises to jump off their jets, ironically defends the "wolves" in power against the unthinking victims who blandly watch television and have given up any thought of changing the world, identifies the greedy consumers with hooked fish, dangling from the lines of cynical fishermen in the rich societies of America, Russia, and West Berlin, and coldly condemns the dead souls who live out their sham lives in the midst of red tape, accumulated files, and rustling IBM cards. In his gathering of nonpeople congregate generals, managers, consumers, functionaries, professors, mendacious researchers, rubber merchants, and "fat widows" who, all unmoved by the German past, wallow in their commercial, technological, and military "things," amassed to stifle life: bonds, telegrams, warships, tennis courts, checks, real estate (*not* on idyllic islands), cars, movies, golf, eau de cologne, barracks, department stores, and radar screens. But Enzensberger's fine sensibility is oppressed not only by industrial goods and people without memories; what he hates most is the crude force imposed upon him by the perpetual production processes of the industrial world and by media and ads that assault his eyes and ears, catching him in a net of data, sounds, commercial offers, and threatening him with the disgusting secretions of smoke, smog, soot, and foam, all anticipating the lethal radiation that some day will seep from anonymous laboratories.

To the relentless pressures of the military-industrial complex the poet (not the social critic) Enzensberger responds in a rather traditional German fashion, appealing to the quiet fortitude of animals and plants, seeking escape in the miraculous depths of the sea, and longing to merge with the elements of the earth: his "organic" refuge distinctly if paradoxically implies that he places little faith in historical progress and in definite transformations of society; his poetic utopia resides in an unchanging nature, from which all cruel struggles between strong and weak, all lethal fungi, and all poisonous growths have been carefully removed. Enzensberger likes his nature alive with rare animals that have aesthetically pleasing names (otters, seals, salmon, sables, owls, and albatrosses) and with humble, hardy plants. In many of his best poems (not all of which are included in his American anthology) he sings the glories of the white cherry blossoms which make the thunder hesitate and cause butchers to hide, fearful of "the wild yes" of innocence. He extols the lowly celery, which does not participate in the inhumanities of man; in a later volume he writes of the northern lichen that quietly survives all the vicissitudes of man. Goodness is to be found only far from people, perhaps even nowhere on the surface of the earth, and the poet eagerly follows oysters and fish into the deep or speaks as a diver who, at the bottom of the sea, finally finds happiness in solitude, in dark and undisturbed silence. Most revealingly (at least for the earlier Enzensberger), in his poem **"voices of the elements"**, the world, with its newspapers and daily social responsibilities (including unpaid bills), is of unmitigated evil, and happiness resides only in partaking of "the tender dialogue of the resins," salts, and alkalines, and in sinking "into the soundless monologue" of the substances at the dark heart of being. Sometimes the angry young man flees rather far.

Enzensberger's third collection of poems, ***writing for the blind,*** stands a little apart from his previous verse. Lines and stanzaic patterns are lean, there is less self-indulgent play with mannered paradoxes and surrealist *confiture* (or rather, secondhand Jacques Prévert), and while some of the earlier motifs recur repeatedly, a personal record emerges of Enzensberger's attempt to withdraw to a Scandinavian hideaway of water, stone, moss, and tar (and a rustic life with his family); the intellectual tries to find his haven in remote nature, and inevitably fails. In contrast to his earlier verse, too, world and counterworld are suggested less in abstract terms ingeniously polarizing nature and technology; now people and issues have individual and particular names (there are poems about Theodor W. Adorno and Karl Marx), and the alternatives of commitment and withdrawal confront each other within the pastoral experience itself. There are the simple house, the water, and the jug (one of Rilke's blessed "things"), but there are also letters, telegrams, and the "red knob on the transistor radio" blaring news about Caribbean crises and Dow-Jones averages; there is geographical distance and yet a modern conscience filled with painful knowledge ("bouvard and pécuchet . . . pontius and pilate") and, as Walter Benjamin early suggested, with reproductions of reproductions ("of images of images / of images of images of images"); gentle friends gather in the evening, alive with "light laughter and white voices," but the poet increasingly feels that there is social irresponsibility in his semblance of bliss: "fearless therefore ignorant / quiet and therefore superfluous / serene therefore without mercy." In **"lachesis lapponica"** (**"lapland lot"**) the pressures of conflicting demands turn the poem itself into a dialogue between the romantic admirer of northern plains and the ardent partisan of Fidel Castro, committed to political action: the two speakers, whose utterances are printed in different type, duly impress each other, but the discussion is left in ironic abeyance and there is little likelihood that either of them will totally prevail.

Enzensberger is at his best when he balances his erudition with his sense of quality and does not try to display his considerable bag of tricks in one poem alone. In his theoretical essays he almost makes himself out to be a late disciple of Edgar Allan Poe, and his aversion to any idea of inspiration, his scholarly awareness of the literary past as a constant challenge to the modern writer, and his philosophical and constructivist inclinations place him closer to Ezra Pound, W. H. Auden, or Gottfried Benn than the social critic Enzensberger might wish. From the work of Brentano, Enzensberger derives for his private poetics the central idea of linguistic *Entstellung* (displacement), a technique that counteracts the tendency of language to ossify in clichés and mechanical turns of phrase; I am not certain how Enzensberger's *Entstellung* differs from the "alienation device" (*priëm ostranenija*) which the Russian formalists, eager to define the de-mechanization of language, discovered in futuristic poetry. Enzensberger knows how to write romantic tetrameter and to play with the inherited techniques of the surrealists, but fundamentally he wants to shock by skillful and occasionally affected combinations of incompatible elements of rhythm, vocabulary, and idiom; while carefully exploiting, rather than negating, tradition, he avoids rhyme as well as the rules of capitalization, but secures unity of the poetic texture by means of nets of alliterations, assonances, and recurrent vowel patterns ("mokka / coma / amok / NATO"). He loves oxymora that unveil the conflicts within social reality, delights in extensive series of asyndeta that link contradictions, and handles proverbs, idioms, and quotations, made slightly disreputable by microscopic changes, with devastating meticulousness. Within the individual poem he arranges with force and determination his linguistic confrontations of the most disparate technical and professional vocabularies, and many younger poets, dissatisfied with the inherited literary idiom, have followed his lead. Few, if any, try to emulate his sober, pensive, and graceful love poetry.

Enzensberger manages to combine, with wit, urbanity, and ease, a bit of Bukharin and Lord Byron. "The blacks call me white / and the whites call me black," he says of himself; as a social critic and the editor of *Kursbuch* (1965-), the most intelligent publication of the radical German left, he may aspire to change the entire world, but as a poet he appears much more concerned with himself than with the perspiring masses anywhere; he despises the high and mighty but is equally disgusted by the little people he sees in the streets, toiling, colorless, docile, and ugly. In an illuminating essay Paul Noack has called Enzensberger a conservative anarchist, but I wonder whether this clever label quite covers the productive intellectual who loves cherry trees, old books, and a future universe free of oozing machines and terrifying sounds, inhabited by a select few who suit his egocentric, exacting, and fastidious tastes. Most intensely of all, Enzensberger does not want to suffocate in precast thoughts and cemented ideologies; and when Peter Weiss recently asked him to declare himself unequivocally for the underprivileged and to "sacrifice his doubts and his reservations," Enzensberger replied sharply that he preferred his doubts to mere sentiments and had no use for views free of internal contradictions. Fortunately, Enzensberger wants a world no less open, changing, and paradoxical than his verse.

Pamela McCallum (essay date 1979)

SOURCE: "II: Poems for People Who Don't Read Poems," in *Canadian Forum*, Vol. LVIII, No. 687, March 1979, pp. 14-7.

[*In this essay, McCallum seeks an understanding of Enzensberger's anger and cultural criticism in* Poems for People Who Don't Read Poems.]

Poems For People Who Don't Read Poems is the title given to the English publication of Hans Magnus Enzensberger's poetry. At first glance it appears to be an absurdist enterprise, perhaps the latest arrogance of an *avant-garde* deliberately courting an audience which does not exist. But nothing could be further from Enzensberger's purpose.

In reality, the impetus behind his poetic practice is a cultural theory which attempts to understand why human consciousness is distorted in advanced industrial societies. In pre-industrial periods when culture was primarily oral the relationship between master and student, priest and parish, dominator and dominated was relatively transparent: people's minds were shaped from without in a directly comprehensible manner. Advances in technological sophistication from the earliest printing presses to the latest media reversed this process, putting in its place what Enzensberger calls the "industrialization of the mind." The emancipating slogans of the first machine age—enlightenment, equality, liberty—unavoidably became twisted remnants as consciousness was warped, forced to shape its own domination. The opaque, inscrutable steps in which people willingly consent to their own domination have become even more blurred in the twentieth century urban societies where human existence is lived out under the glare of fluorescent lights, the chatter of advertising slogans, and the dim twilight cast by the TV screen. This is, Enzensberger emphasizes, no mere phenomenon of manipulation which can be remedied by simply overthrowing the manipulators. On the contrary, the depth and extent of modern domination is such that its hidden implications can barely be perceived. In his words, "the mind industry's main business and concern is not to sell its product: it is to 'sell' the existing order, to perpetuate the prevailing pattern of man's domination by man, no matter who runs the society, and by what means."[1] The monolith of modern technological society relentlessly reproduces itself in the one-dimensional lives it proffers its citizens.

How then is any entering-wedge, any perception of an alternative, to break through this barrier? The possible opening is a crucial weakness in the mind industry, a contradiction lying at the heart of its project. According to Enzensberger, the self-domination, the self-distortion of consciousness can only be achieved by granting what must be ultimately suppressed: the creative potential of human beings. As he puts it, "in order to obtain consent, you have to grant a choice, no matter how marginal and deceptive; in order to harness the faculties of the human mind, you have to develop them, no matter how narrowly and how deformed."[2] His strategic goal is to seize the measure of creative development—however small—to turn it against the very forms of manipulation it is meant to serve. Again this is no simple task. Since the mind industry cultivates its own pseudo-choices, any capacities to be won over must be snatched from the entangled confusions everyday life imposes. To be effective, intervention must take place in the murky morass of advanced technological society and for this, we need not radical innocence and purity, but determination.

Of pivotal importance to any such intervention are the new media forms—radio, television, film, videotape—all oriented toward action and activity, not contemplation. They break through mystical, reverential attitudes toward traditional art forms; they create no art objects, no authentic originals which can become the privileged possessions of collectors. Unlike traditional forms of art, they are capable of infinite reproduction without defiling authenticity. And for the first time it becomes possible to record historical material directly. While written communication structurally imposes an isolation on the reader and the text, the new media make possible collective forms of communication. With the radio transistor, everyone becomes a potential producer.

Enzensberger's championing of the new media and his insistence on their displacement of written culture superficially resembles Marshall McLuhan's theories. But Enzensberger is interested in McLuhan only for the emphasis his "undigested observations" place on the importance of the new media and substantially criticizes McLuhan's obsession with the forms of the media, his lack of any theoretical construction to understand the social and political processes in which the new media participate. Enzensberger's formulations instead bear comparison with the suggestive implications in the later work of Harold Innis. As an economic historian Innis necessarily confronts power relationships. His analysis in *The Bias of Communication* delineates the convergence of imperial expansion in societies such as Egypt and Rome, their necessity to control space, with a dependence on written culture, which in turn facilitates the monopolization of knowledge in complex script, formalized learning, the control of supplies. In contrast, an oral tradition opens up a freedom of access to information, an emancipation from the domination of space, an orientation toward the more fluid domain of time. In his phrase, "the individual became responsible for his actions and the root of authority was destroyed."[3] The achievements of Greek society—Homer's poetry, Hellenic drama, the Platonic dialogues—are examples of the creative, interactive processes generated by a substantial oral tradition. It is precisely these qualities which Enzensberger identifies as the potential points of breakthrough in the new media. *Potential* is the crucial word, for he is all too aware of the function the media play in present conditions: far from developing their possibilities for liberation they are reduced to providing another round of mindless, vacuous bombardment with only sporadic exceptions. Yet, these very exceptions are exactly what any movement for change must grasp.

Given the tenor of his cultural theory, a disturbing contradiction would seem to underlie Enzensberger's writing of poetry. Is not poetry the most formal, the most traditional, the literary form furthest removed from the new media? And isn't the worker who collapses each evening in front of the television set, or the woman mindlessly pursuing housework with the radio blaring, the person least likely to pick up a book of poetry? These objections identify a deeply felt hostility to poetry, the perception of an innate arrogance lurking behind the poet's dazzling facility with language. The courage of Enzensberger's project lies in his effort to shatter such false preconceptions. To emphasize merely these aspects of poetry, he suggests, would be to neglect the qualities which it shares with the new media, tendencies which distinguish it from other forms of written culture. The rhythms and cadence of poetry bring it close to the traditional popular modes of expression—songs, ballads, chants. In its condensation of thought, in its elliptical structures, poetry can resemble the speech patterns of oral culture, instead of the formality of prose. None of these qualities inherently ensures a politically progressive poetry: it is well to remember that the initial attempts to create a poetry based on actual speech patterns in the 1920s by Ezra Pound and T.S. Eliot resulted in a poetics compounded of allusions from traditional 'high' culture, cut off from all but an intellectual elite. Enzensberger wishes his poetry to be received like *graffiti* on the wall, open and accessible, as an act of defiance among the immobile structures of industrial societies. His poetic practice aims at reclaiming the subversive aspects in poetry which release it from the dominating elements of written culture and endow it with the liberating qualities of the oral tradition.

In this context Enzensberger's poetry must be seen as a response to a particular debate in socialist cultural theory in Europe during the 1930s. On the one side, the Hungarian critic Georg Lukacs had developed a socialist aesthetics based on the nineteenth century realist novel. In his argument the aesthetic form creates a self-contained whole, a harmonized unity, which opposes the fragmented, atomized alienation of lived experience in modern industrial societies. Because the art form embodies in its unified integration an alternative to the brutalized existence of social life, it provides an interrogation of existing conditions. Moreover, it prefigures a future when alienating conditions have been superseded. In opposition, the German critic Walter Benjamin, and the dramatist and poet Bertolt Brecht, argued that developments unique to the twentieth century—new forms of technology, the expansion of consumer-based society and the penetration of consumerism into virtually every part of human lives—had rendered Lukacs's formulations untenable. Benjamin's seminal article, "The Work of Art in the Age of Mechanical Reproduction" (the inspiration for much in Enzensberger's media theories) maintains that photography, film and modern techniques of reproduction have destroyed the authenticity and originality of art substituting in their place a plurality of copies.[4] As well as liberating art from tradition, mechanical reproduction also undermines the exalted dignity of 'high' culture. Mechanical reproduction dissociates art from the elitist aspects which made it accessible only to trained experts and opens it to the participation of a potentially wide audience. In order to do so art must abandon its disjunction from alienated existence and incorporate into itself the fractured convolutions, the distortions and fragments of lived experience. According to Benjamin, the newspaper with its juxtaposition of significant events and triviality, its pastiche format, its letters columns available to turn readers into writers, typifies the new media. Unlike Lukacs' insistence on drawing from nineteenth century models, Benjamin and Brecht immersed themselves in the degraded constituents of the contemporary world. As Brecht strikingly proposes, the maxim for the political artist must not be a nostalgic longing for the good old days, but a confrontation with the bad new ones.

Enzensberger's social commitment leads him firmly to reject any poetry based on the subjective expression of private and personal feelings. This does not imply, however, that poetry then becomes a propagandist harangue. Quite the opposite: he insists on preserving the autonomy of the poetry from the demand that it directly serve politics. In particular, he has condemned the sterile, doctrinal poetry produced when the writer has been pressed into state service. His whole poetic practice is an attempt to displace the passivity into which the readers of any didactic poetry will be thrown. Such an aesthetic commitment implies an open-ended accessible poetic form which will compel readers to become active, creative collaborators. Here his image of poetry as *graffiti* is important: like *graffiti* it invites the reader to add the next lines on the wall. The process allows the reader to escape the role of a mere consumer of a finished literary product, to become an active collaborator with the author, an active producer.

Far from forming an organic unity, each of Enzensberger's poems is designed to disrupt our conventional expectations by its discontinuity, its splintered form, its obstinate refusal to order itself into the anticipated smoothness of poetic rhythms. Part of the nightmare vision his early epic **"foam"** forces onto its readers is the shock of recognition, the clash and collision of the all too familiar images and inhabitants of advanced industrial society, now stripped of any modifying disguises. The speaking voice of **"foam"** is an ironic rage which proclaims its desire for escape, while relentlessly cataloguing the horrors of the world it is imprisoned in. Enzensberger's use of questions underlies this irony: it is at once an interrogation of the modern world and an admission of complicity, of being caught in the web. The poet is no unique genius; he has no special vantage point:

> *i'm here any day of the week a fire-eater like you*
> *like everyone else: standing on my corner from nine*
> *to five taking painful shots of my own fire*
> *for ten bucks a day kneedeep in foaming status quo*
> *between carburetors and street lights*[5]

By piling up the fragmented, discontinuous sensations of lived experience in technological societies the series of questions of **"foam"** form an unremitting montage of insidious violence. Here is Enzensberger on the brutality of an existence which is slow death:

> *who doesn't know that he's croaking? but why all the*
> *sweat*
> *if nobody dies from it?*

On the teeth and smiles of the packaged beauty queens:

> *and why not give prizes for tits? hollywood*
> *ass in the rose-colored foam: striptease*
> *of the western world from dortmund to san diego*

On the mindless leisure industry:

> *and what can we do with ourselves? and the crowds*
> *that fill up the football stadiums crying*
> *for coca colas and bloodbaths: what can we do with*
> *them?*

The succession of impressions is caught itself within the predominant image: the foam. Foam is a sticky viscous stream, murky, slippery and chaotic, the opposite of the slick chrome, plastic and vinyl face of polished modernity.

If the first great indictment of modern society, Eliot's *Waste Land,* offered the consolation of a unifying cultural tradition, **"foam"** contains no such easy promise. Nor does Enzensberger see in traditional political opposition any hope; the old organizations have been swept into the tide of foam:

moldy banners and barricades wrapped in cellophane
propped in the showcase: while from an antique juke-box
the internationale drones: a beat rock and roll

(Writing about the media, Enzensberger has even criticized the nostalgia of the new left. In May 1968 the Parisian students occupied the tradition-steeped *Odeon Theatre* while ignoring the radio and television stations.) Genuine commitment and change will not come from nostalgia but only from an intense interrogation of the present.

Far from forming an organic unity, each of Enzensberger's poems is designed to disrupt our conventional expectations by its discontinuity, its splintered form, its obstinate refusal to order itself into the anticipated smoothness of poetic rhythms.

The final lines of **"foam"** begin with a plea to transcend the insidious entanglements of technological society: "let's make out that i'm not one of you that i'm not one of us / that i'm free from all that." But any notion of transcendence is futile; complicity in the society is inescapable. The poet floats "immortal as a paper clip" into the "rose-coloured future," a virtual parody of a traditional resolution in a spiritualized transcendence. A paper clip, at once a most insignificant and a most omnipresent particle of the administered universe, is a fitting image of immortality in modern bureaucratized society.

The rage that smoulders through **"foam"** surfaces in ***the wolves defended against the lambs***, Enzensberger's indictment of those who refuse to confront the enormity of violence in advanced industrial society, retreating instead into a naive romanticism which provides no defense against the dominators of humanity. German history, specifically the refusal to oppose fascism with a hard-headed strength equal to its own, lies behind the poem, yet Enzensberger would insist on an analogous situation in the contemporary era. If the modern world has become the foaming nightmare of his darkest vision, the liberation of humanity cannot be achieved through a sentimental humanism. In **"foam"** the series of questions hurled at the reader alternated throughout the lines of the poem. ***the wolves*** polarizes this technique into two stanzas of devastating questions followed by two stanzas of assertions. "Should the vultures eat forget-me-nots?" he begins,

what do you want the jackal to do,
cut loose from his skin, or the wolf? should
he pull his own teeth out of his head?

The consciousness which hesitates in the face of evil will never be able to challenge its domination in any effective way. Just as the mentality of the lamb allowed Hitler to come to power, so in the post war world powerlessness and helplessness are implicit accessories of domination. In their refusal to see naked brutality they retreat into vacuous falsity:

you stick to your moaning lies. you'd love
to be torn limb from limb. you
won't change the world.

To characterize all Enzensberger's poetry as that of anger and rage would be to miss his genuine humour and gentleness. **"vending machine"** is predicated on the image that a cigarette machine could click out not only the cigarettes but all the associated detritus of consumer society:

he gets cancer
he gets apartheid
he gets the king of greece
federal tax state tax sales tax and excise

Ironically, the most dehumanized form of barter, the vending machine, forces the passive consumer into a moment of self-recognition. He sees himself for a fleeting instant, "and he almost looks like a man," until he disappears again "buried under all the stuff he has gotten." The humour in **"vending machine"** rests in the simplicity of its exaggeration: man is clearly already being buried by the garbage of consumer commodities. At the same time it points to the whole global network in which the simplest instruments of our technological societies are inextricably linked.

"the end of the owls," a defense of the animals who silently witness the violence of technology against nature, is the closest Enzensberger comes to a gentle romanticism. It is one of the few pieces in which Enzensberger appears to identify with the tradition of German romanticism, which saw in the forms of nature a disclosure of what unalienated existence could be. Against the lethal, death-dealing technology of man—radar screens, antennae, the military briefing table—the owls, the whale, raven and dove, the otters and seals are mute living presences. And, in a switch of voice from singular to plural ("we're as good as forgotten") he includes mankind as he waits in a world which possesses the ability to destroy itself.

One of Enzensberger's most ambitious projects is his 1964 **"summer poem."** Here he pushes his attempt to incorporate the harsh discordant sensations of speech patterns, the media and modern urban life into poetry almost to its limits. Although the occasion of the composition was autobiographical, two journeys to Finland and Prague, it opens up to contain a wide spectrum of the contemporary world, creating in its structure what Enzensberger has called "net-like constructions with which new experiences can be caught again and again." The precise texture of **"summer poem"** can be grasped in its lines:

that which does not yet exist

no great art in that
my world is as large in this night
as my errors can you help me?

The words can be read either across the page or vertically down the columns. The repetition of certain phrases throughout the poem, with each meaning emerging differently in each context, the repeated quotation from figures as varied as Marx, Wieland, Marilyn Monroe, Petrarch, are designed to force the reader into collaboration with the author, to draw him out of passivity into creativity. The reader's consciousness, caught in the web of fluctuating lines, should be forced into a creative act, his own mind constructing "that which does not exist" out of the poem.

The juxtaposition of Marilyn Monroe with Marx is no simple rhetoric, nor merely a recreation of the pastiche of modern news presentations. Rather, it also functions to release the philosophical works from their canonization as high culture, to bring them into the flux and movement of contemporary perceptions. In Enzensberger's words, the quotations provide a nexus which underlines the way systems have annulled distance:

> *This nexus is caught in flight and acceleration, in*
> *the twittering of sound tapes, in the 'parlar rotto',*
> *the broken speech of our media, in the flood of distorted*
> *information form Dante studies to the Peking People's Journal.*[6]

Enzensberger clearly intends the montage technique of **"summer poem"** to compel the reader into unsorting the entangled web of information. Yet there are problems in assessing whether **"summer poem"** actually attains its objectives. While he has retained the use of phrases from everyday speech, the convoluted syntax veers dangerously close to the stylistic exaggerations of the *avant-grade* previously condemned by Enzensberger. The rhythms of spoken language which ensured that the earlier poems would be openly accessible to "people who don't read poems" have become submerged.

The difficulties Enzensberger encounters in translating his purposes into poetic practice in **"summer poem"** suggest that he has reached an impasse. In the past decade he has published poetry only sporadically, turning instead to the explication and development of his cultural theory. His latest poetry collection, ***Mausoleum***, first published in 1975, is a shift to a different type of poetry. The "ballads from the history of progress" portray figures from the Renaissance to the present. Unlike the open accessibility Enzensberger had sought in his early poetry, ***Mausoleum*** is much more opaque, a cunning construction where the feted heroes of progress often parade while the darker voices of Goya, Flaubert, Marx, Strindberg intrude into someone else's lines. Unlike *graffiti*, ***Mausoleum*** does not ask us to write the next line, but rather draws us deeper into the network of unidentified quotations and allusions, obscure initials, cross references, in an effort to disentangle the web. "No telling the progress of swindle from the swindle of progress," Enzensberger writes, yet that is precisely what the poem challenges us to do.

The shift in Enzensberger's poetry may coincide with criticisms of his cultural theory. Just as his attempt to create a poetry accessible to people who don't read poems faltered, so his cultural theories have been assailed for an overly optimistic stance. In urging an intervention in the new media forms, he did not take into account many impediments, particularly the intransigence of the multinational corporations and bureaucracies which control television and film production. More important, Theodor Adorno's later writings have suggested some serious deficiencies in the concepts Enzensberger drew from Benjamin and Brecht.[7] The whole notion that the technical qualities of the modern media possess inherently liberating elements has proven to be an oversimplification. Far from eliminating the "aura" in traditional art, film and television have transformed it into their own concepts of the star or celebrity. And the instantly available substitute gratification and anti-enlightenment in film and television all too often pushes people deeper into passivity, abandoning them at a far remove from the active response Enzensberger sought. The deadlock his initial poetic project reached and the denser structure of ***Mausoleum*** may indicate a phase of self-evaluation and self-criticism. Still, his early work is something to be consolidated and superseded, not rejected. His latest style might offer a more complex structure, but few poems have catalogued the horrors of modern technological societies with the relentless clarity of **"foam."**

Notes

1. Enzensberger, *The Consciousness Industry* (New York: Seabury Press, 1974), 10.
2. *Ibid,* 12.
3. Innis, *The Bias of Communication* (Toronto: University of Toronto Press, 1951), 42.
4. Benjamin's essay is included in *Illuminations* (New York: Harcourt Brace, 1968); also relevant are his "The Author as Producer" *New Left Review* 62 (1970) and *Understanding Brecht* (London: New Left Books, 1973).
5. English translations of Enzensberger's poetry are available in *Hans Magnus Enzensberger: Selected Poems* (Harmondsworth: Penguin, 1968).
6. Ibid, 89.
7. Adorno, "The Culture Industry Reconsidered" *New German Critique* II (Fall 1975).

Michael Hamburger (review date 1980)

SOURCE: "The Usefulness of Poets," in *The Nation*, Vol. 230, No. 17, May 3, 1980, pp. 528-30.

[*In the following review, Hamburger analyzes the themes of* Der Untergang der Titanic (The Sinking of the Titanic) *and affirms the poem as "a celebration of bare survival."*]

How intelligent can a good poet afford to be? How knowing? How tough-minded? How well-informed? There have been times in H.M. Enzensberger's writing life when these questions troubled many of his readers and critics; and not only when Enzensberger himself posed them in his essays and statements, such as his virtual renunciation and denunciation of poetry in the later 1960s. After his three early collections, published between 1957 and 1964, it seemed for a long time that he had no more use for the spontaneous, personal lyricism that had balanced his public concerns; that the polemicist had taken over from the poet, deliberately and definitively. Apart from a few new poems added to his selection of 1971, Enzensberger remained silent as a poet until ***Mausoleum*** appeared in 1975; and, however intelligent, knowing, tough-minded, well-informed and accomplished, that sequence was not distinguished by lyricism. If those thirty-seven studies in "the history of Progress" were ballads, as he called them, they were ballads that neither sang nor danced but pinned down their subjects with a laboratory-trained efficiency.

This development remains relevant to ***The Sinking of the Titanic***, though in recent years Enzensberger has returned to more personal, even existential, preoccupations in shorter poems, and the new sequence, too, is less rigorously held down to a single purpose and manner. Behind the poetic development—or antipoetic development, some would say—lay an ideological one—from what looked like a revolutionary commitment to the "principle of hope," though it was utopian and independent enough to put no constraint on the poet, through an arduous grappling with the facts of economic, political and technological power, to a general disillusionment with every existing social system and its expectations for the future.

One important stage in that development was Enzensberger's visit to Cuba in 1969. Not only was ***The Sinking of the Titanic*** conceived and begun there but the Cuban experiences are also worked into the broken narrative of the poem, like many other seeming interpolations, digressions, leaps in space, time and even style. Like most long or longer poems written in this century, ***The Sinking of the Titanic*** is not an epic but a clustering of diverse, almost disparate, fragments around a thematic core. The main event of the poem, the shipwreck of the *Titanic* in 1912, becomes a symbol and a microcosm, with extensions, parallels, repercussions on many different levels. *The Titanic* is also Cuba, East Berlin, West Berlin (where Enzensberger lived as the editor of a magazine not primarily literary, as a writer in almost every possible medium, for every possible medium, and as the collector of the fragments assembled into this poem), an updated version of Dante's Hell and many other places besides, including any place where any reader of the poem is likely to be. Not content with that much telescoping, Enzensberger also includes historical flashbacks to the fifteenth, sixteenth and nineteenth centuries, all to do with doubts, self-doubts, about art and the relation of art to reality. Other digressions are even more explicit in their questioning of the truthfulness and usefulness of poets and poetry. These also introduce Dante by name, though he is present in the whole poem as a prototype of what poetry can and cannot achieve.

I shall not attempt to list all the many theses and subtheses ironically advanced in the poem, usually to be challenged or contradicted by others, because it is the business of poems to do that as succinctly as possible; yet one brief quotation does seem to subsume the main message:

> We are in the same boat, all of us.
> But he who is poor is the first to drown.

Characteristically for Enzensberger, that assertion is supported by statistics of the passengers—first-class, second-class, steerage and crew—drowned and saved in the *Titanic* disaster. Much other material of that kind, including a menu, has been drawn upon. The most lyrical, i.e., song-like, canto of the thirty-three in the book—not counting the unnumbered interpolations—is the twentieth, adapted from *Deep Down in the Jungle: Negro Narrative and Folklore from the Streets of Philadelphia.* Documentary collages have been one of Enzensberger's specialties in verse and prose, and they are prominent as ever here, as in the Thirteenth Canto, made up of snatches of miscellaneous hymns and popular songs. Another is the permutation of simple colloquial phrases into puzzles or tautologies, not simple at all, but devastating, as in the interpolated section "Notice of Loss."

Yet the most impressive and reassuring parts of the sequence, poetically, are those in which Enzensberger lets himself go again a little at last, relying less on his bag of tricks—a formidable one—than on the imaginative penetration of specific experience, other people's and his own. A high-spirited, often comically cynical desperation is his peculiar contribution to the range of poetry; it becomes affirmative, if not joyful, in the concluding canto of this poem, a celebration of bare survival.

As for the other side of his gifts, his sheer accomplishment, cleverness and adroitness, one instance of it is his success in translating so intricate and ambitious a sequence into a language not his own. In earlier English versions of his own poems, he allowed himself the freedom of "imitation." This one is a close rendering, with no loss of fluency or exuberance, and very little of the idiomatic rightness of his German original.

Michael Hamburger (review date 1980)

SOURCE: "Causes for Pessimism," in *The Times Literary Supplement*, No. 4045, October 10, 1980, p. 1153.

[*In this review, Hamburger considers* Die Furie des Verschwindens *an excellent example of Enzensberger's work in poetry and politics despite its pessimistic views.*]

Sixteen years have passed since Hans Magnus Enzensberger last published a collection of new short poems. Although "silence" seems quite the wrong word to use of a poet who has been active and conspicuous enough in other capacities, not least as an anti-poetic, anti-literary polemicist, but also as the author of two long sequences in which the quarrel between the poet and the anti-poet was fought out, the new collection does bridge a gap of sixteen years.

Die Furie des Verschwindens links up with the volume of 1964, ***Blindenschrift,*** by finally lifting the ban publicly imposed by Enzensberger on the kind of poetry that springs from moments of intense experience—experience inevitably subjective up to a point, however objective the correlatives; and it completes the breakthrough begun in the second of the two longer sequences into a new phase that is also a continuation of his first. Brilliant though his early poems were, and masterly as his workmanship remained even in the least lyrical of his longer sequences, ***Mausoleum***, the short poems in this new book, are as consistently excellent as any he has written.

Many of the poems are character studies which allow him to achieve an unprecedented balance between the social criticisms he had always regarded as his main function and the spontaneity with which that function tended to conflict. By getting under the skin of, for example, a thirty-three-year-old woman, an uneasy male business executive, an equally uneasy employee on holiday in Spain—each a "short history of the bourgeoisie", as another poem is called—Enzensberger is now able to present a whole complex of delicate interactions from the inside; and it no longer matters whether the social criticism is subjective or objective, whether the inside is the poet's own or another person's. The fusion is so complete, the execution so impeccable, that there is no relevant distinction to be made between poems of immediate personal experience and successful projections into fictitious characters and their situations; nor, for that matter, between "confessional" poetry and satire.

The social criticism is more incisive, more knowing, more searching than ever before; but it is so because Enzensberger has learnt to dispense with the utopian reformer's vantage point, as well as with the rhetorical bravura of his early verse. One reason for that may be that he has come to include himself among those—bourgeois or otherwise—whose prospects are summed up in the poem **"Unregierbarkeit"** (ungovernability): "on legs getting shorter and shorter/power is waddling into the future".

A first group of predominantly topical poems, concerned with this malaise, leads up to a longer, many-faceted poem, **"Die Frösche von Bikini"**, followed by a second group of short poems that have to do less with specific power structures than with larger, more existential disparities. One of them, **"Besuch bei Ingres"**, takes up the questions of the relationship between life and art—especially visual art—that were acute and persistent in Enzensberger's second long poem (published in America as ***The Sinking of the Titanic*** in the poet's own English version); but on that score, too, Enzensberger's inhibiting self-doubts seem to have been resolved. As in the long poem, extreme pessimism has neither dampened his high spirits nor detracted from the sheer skill, precision and inventiveness of the writing.

Paul West (review date 1981)

SOURCE: "Drowning as One of the Fine Arts," in *Parnassus: Poetry in Review*, Vol. 9, No. 1, Spring/Summer, 1981, pp. 91-109.

[*In the following essay about Enzensberger's* Der Untergang der Titanic (The Sinking of the Titanic) *West analyzes Enzensberger's evocation of the experience aboard the sinking ship and the passengers' final moments before death.*]

I

For whom is the *Titanic* still not going down? Not as often as the sun, but several times a year, in the furry hinterland of sleep, tweaked into mind by *A Night to Remember* (1958) or a television revival, and embellished with our own private images of airships foundering in flames, submarines rusting on the ocean bottom (remember the *Thetis*), airplanes that come apart upside down in flight long enough for photographers to snap the obscenity, and trains that race out of control to the terminal and smash clean through it. Our highly developed sense of catastrophe never goes unexploited, but there is more to the *Titanic*—to our *Titanic* ikon—than that.

Out there, among the icebergs, with the orchestra playing and the ship becoming more and more vertical, one of the last definitive frescoes of stoicism took its place in myth. Terror and technology came together in the presence of the stiff upper lip. A patrician concept drowned as the vision of bungling on the high seas came home to roost in the more local, less grave image of Alec Guinness, in *Kind Hearts and Coronets,* going down at the salute on the bridge of *his* ship. It becomes possible to make a sentence that brings it all together, although we still prefer the constituent parts of the nightmare to remain apart. *Once upon a time,* the sentence goes, *homo Icarian disregarded Mother Nature, and the rest was mere accommodation to fact.* Some people knew they were going to drown: there was just no other way, any more than there is for Dickey's freefalling stewardess, or Auden's shot unlucky dove. Others, who knew they would not drown although they might starve or freeze, also knew that hundreds would go down that night, face to face with euphemisms they'd never needed: Davy Jones's Locker, the Deep Six. And what was inexorable included the survivors' thoughts about the thinking of those who, aware that these were their last thoughts for ever and ever, went on thinking flawed, illicit, torn stuff right to the end. The mind cannot think the mind to a halt, can it? The mind of the survivor, in the extremest reach of compassion, cannot think the mind of the victim to a halt either. Perhaps, even, the survivor *hates* the victim-to-be because the victim can only suffer and die. When all hope of rescue has gone, when the bimboes have attributed the rockets to a firework display and the morse tapper has been switched off or jammed with banal Hellos From the High Seas, immutability can sink its fangs, and then the watchers in the boats and the doomed in the water or still on board have a unique encounter with the self-adjusting power of thought: to calm, to numb, to leap toward death (as some poems have it) like a bridegroom into bed. That, beyond the technology and the nitty-gritty of bungling, is what makes the *Titanic* linger in our heads: the vision of creative fatality which brings Doctor Johnson (who spoke of its power to concentrate a man's mind) in front of the firing squad, re-dooms St.-Exupéry to crash again in the desert, Admiral Byrd to be again and terminally alone, and rehearses for us all the chore of last things in the condemned mental playground.

Eschatology is the awful word we use: last things accomplished by the actual doomed, and last things guessed at—ours, theirs, anyone's—in a trance of inverted empathy. Surely the mind switches off? Or it so transmutes the immediate experience that it becomes as an after-dinner's sleep. Or, and here we shudder like De Quincey frightening himself half to death by staring at Lord Rosse's ghoulish drawing of the Great Nebula in Orion, does the mind rise to undreamed-of excesses in self-torture? Does the mind mind? It knows it minds, and what it does, perhaps, in ultimate self-defense, is to suppress the factor of fatality, rising to such control of itself as to blot death out. As Eliot says, some conditions look remarkably like one another, can flourish in the same hedgerow, and perhaps the mind, creator of categories, has final power over them, to abolish and efface. It should; otherwise, from a pragmatic point of view, it's just no good to us. The *Titanic* was full of people who'd never worried about that sort of thing, or who'd had experts do their worrying for them. Then, out of the blue, they were up against it, the ontology of the penultimate, and there was no time to think it out. What we remember, maybe in the penumbra of Captain Oates walking out into the storm to die, is the composure of all those people, many of them enacting without knowing the Latin the words of Seneca: *fatis agimur, cedite fatis.* The fates have us, so give in. And then, the myth would like to say, they all lived more richly in their last hour than in all their years before. With discipline it might be done. Some no doubt did it, but what of those who didn't? What did they say to themselves?

There must be at least two stages in this little marathon of will. The approach may be quite unrealistic, even after being dumped in the water and becoming involved in the suction down. But the ensuing moments, after the held breath fizzles out, evoke the victim in the gas chamber, who's told to fill both lungs and get it over with (whereas the person electrocuted is wholly passive). What happens, I wonder, when you willy-nilly inhale water and are become part of the ocean? If you hold your breath until you pass out, then you inhale water unknowingly. Otherwise, you do it with repugnance or, just perhaps, with Promethean relish, as a last act of defiantly collaborative drowning akin to inhaling warm saltwater to clear the sinuses. The nostrils sting. The sink beneath the pharynx feels flooded. You swallow, but this time there is far too much to swallow and the water makes its leaden way into the lung. You inhale more than you breathe out. There is no air to vent it into and all you are is a rebellious valve, dressing the water in a new suit of pulmonary tissue, the only sense of danger being that distant, heavyweight heartburn, surely someone else's, it feels so general, so vague.

That, presumably, is the good way, not fighting at all, inviting Nature in to complete an inevitable tryst. But, as Camus said, in his 1951 "Homage to André Gide," "To die is such appalling torture for some men that it seems to me as if a happy death redeems a small patch of creation." Surely the converse is true too. The torture of reluctant drowning befouls the Creation that doesn't treat us all alike, and some people have no control over how the last cupful enters their lungs before all goes still.

II

Such are my thoughts on first looking into Enzensberger's **"Poem,"** which he divides into thirty-three cantos interspersed with other poems, almost all of them, in overt or backhanded ways bearing on the *Titanic* material, sometimes usefully, sometimes not. In **"Apocalypse. Umbrian Master, about 1490,"** for instance, the question arises of how to paint Doom, and "the temple veil being rent asunder," not a far cry from the ocean liner's steel-plated hull which, in the first canto, sustains a gash two hundred yards long beneath the waterline, slit by the iceberg's knife. Yet it's in the interspersed poem that we find the following displaced apocalypse:

> the frantic sea in the background must be coated
> over and over again with a thousand layers
> of transparency, with foamy green lights,
> pierced by mastheads, by ships reeling, plunging down,
> by wrecks. . . .

In other words, what you might expect to be in the actual canto about the *Titanic* isn't there but in a neighboring poem, catching you off guard and sideswiping your response, until of course you begin to rely on that and hit on such a poem as **"Dept. of Philosophy"** (between cantos 27 and 28), which has no bearing on the disaster at all except through total speculation: "*How real is it?* Hegel is smiling,/ filled with *schadenfreude.*" There's no pattern to this, of course, only the random gravitation of elements from the interspersed poems into one's response to the overtly *Titanic* ones, somewhat in the manner of abstract expressionism when it tries to bring into play elements just outside the range of vision, nibbling at the edge of the Main Subject without ever getting in the way, yet never having utterly no effect either. As you finish ***The Sinking of the Titanic*** and begin to move about in it, skipping and flipping and reading next to each other passages from cantos far apart, the interspersed material doesn't so much fall into place as leak through, as if the cantos themselves were gashed. And the final effect—no, the most recent, anyway—is complex, with the intruded stuff functioning almost as the rumor of a background against which the calamity figures, except that sometimes the calamity—through sheer horrendousness—is the marine fresco making all other things trivial, as if death or disaster on land were a trifle compared with death by water, water in the midst and bowels of breath, the final glutted choke severing even the final trope of grace under pressure.

In my own mind, working their way through what I brought to my reading in the first place and what loosely assembles in my head after reading the thirty-three cantos, those images from elsewhere take on a monitory, oblique force, almost as if the thirty-three cantos were only a bit more about the *Titanic* than not, and the interspersed poems were only a bit less about it than they are. Soon after the rent veil comes a poem about loss which covers all the forms of loss except that which is the subject of the cantos. In its wake, as it were, come poems about an iceberg ("Look, it is breaking loose / from the glacier's face") that is two hundred and fifty feet high, a sixteenth-century *Last Supper,* a coffin-crate seen against a backdrop of "high-rolling waves / ploughed by seaworthy trunks," a volcanic eruption in Iceland which the poet watches on TV, noting an incongruous man "in braces" (= suspenders) "who held a garden hose . . . aimed at the roaring lava." You don't have to labor to feel the connections, the pertinence, the point; both sets of poems come out of the same mind-set addressed to compatible occasions over eight years. Writing about the *Titanic* on the island of Cuba, Enzensberger almost seems to feel the island going down as well, and certainly, with his heart and mind awash, relishes its fixity, its status as an *idée fixe* ("What has Cuba to do with it? It must be an *idée fixe*": Canto 15) whereas the smoke of Cuban cigars, "trademark Partagas, made by hand," in Canto 10, vanishes into the blue haze of the mid-Atlantic sky: no trace. Most tutorly of all, the story of the poem itself enacts both the major and the minor themes:

> . . . in actual fact the island of Cuba
> does not reel under our feet.
> And I was right then,
> because at that time nothing foundered
> except my poem
> about the sinking of the *Titanic.*
> It was a poem penciled
> into a notebook, wrapped up
> in black oilcloth, I had no copy,
> because on the entire island of Cuba
> there was not one sheet of carbon paper
> to be found. Do you like it? I asked
> Maria Alexandrovna, and then
> I put it into a buff Manila envelope.
> It was shipped from Havana harbor
> in a mailbag for Paris
> which never turned up again.
> We all know the rest of the story.

Yes, we do: what he'd begun in Cuba in 1969 he finished in Berlin in 1977, as page 98 says; but those matter-of-fact lines evoke the ghost of the poem lost at sea, so much so that, after one reading, a dense, prophetic marginal image begins to form: of the floating poet floated away in his lost poem, only to come back to life on the divided island of Berlin, whose one half isn't exactly a carbon copy of the other. *What* is irreplaceable in a shoddy world? What if he'd lost the second version of his elegy? Surely version 3 would have come into being. As it is, what we have is so intently underpinned and cross-echoed that it has a provisional, expendable quality: slanted for loss, as if he's remembered Beckett, who reminds us to turn away just in time from things about to disappear. Figure-ground is the leitmotif of the whole thing, from drowner-ocean to canto versus non-canto. He implies perishability; the tininess of us on the land of our planet, flailing in its seas, even walking the promenade deck of an ocean liner. Not that he deals up the overlapping twins, micro- and macrocosm (the frail bark of the self aboard the argosy that floats upon a globe floating in space); he cannily avoids routine obeisances and instead fixes on things and their vanishing points, setting up loose structures from which they can easily fall away, or through which they can drop. The "I" has no tenure in these poems, any more than the sea knows what it is. (I write this in Pittsburgh, at a window opposite the U.S. Steel skyscraper, blocked off from me this minute by a solid snow-squall which makes the building look less durable than snow; the squall will pass, but snow will outlive U.S. Steel.) It's that intuition of several brevities which he puts in the mouth of the *Titanic*'s engineer, one of many:

> Where would we be now,
> if the winged reptiles and the dinosaurs had not at some point
> met with certain problems which proved too much
> for their brains? Do you see what I mean?
> From which I conclude that it does not make sense to consider
> any old episode involving ourselves, for example our own demise,
> from an all too narrow point of view. What I, as an engineer,
> and inveterate port wine drinker, am saying, is, of course,
> not entirely new, and this is why I am about to go under.
> (Canto 8)

Notice that the engineer is about to go under not because he can't think of anything new, but because there *isn't* anything new. The point comes from Galileo who, accepting the nothing new (evolution lets us last only so long), declares our own demise useful: we make room for other life. How this cheerless clear-eyed un-"narrow" point of view bears on lives prematurely but lingeringly closed, only the individual reader can decide, choosing perhaps one of the following: 1. The deaths from the *Titanic* disaster diminished all of mankind, leaving an irremediable gash in the race. 2. It didn't matter: there are always people to replace people with. 3. Captains shouldn't be reckless, oblivious, or fatheads. 4. All such disasters instruct us in the human condition, which is lethal and full of bad luck; the longer you last (in one sense), the more bad luck you get. Would we resent the *Titanic* less if it had been full of nonagenarians all with terminal illness? I think not. We'd argue that even they, with "full lives" behind them, had paid their passage money and were entitled to a trouble-free cruise. In the end it's a matter of incongruity: you die, not because there are icebergs, but because some idiot drives his ship too fast. And then the long, pensive, utterly terminal wait until you go into the frigid water. The poem isn't, overtly, about the absurdity of things, but about the irrational quality of human behavior, at one extreme the hot rod skipper, at another utmost composure in the very teeth of death; and perhaps the core of Enzensberger's long poem is this: if we were wholly rational beings, we'd find life more intolerable than we do; but, since we often behave as weirdly as the universe itself does, we can counter its weirdness with our own, and what James called the insolence of accident unhinges us less. Maybe the wholly rational person *in extremis* can create a flawless composure, simply accepting the ways of God to Man, but it's more likely that more of us are helped by the palliative of what's irrational—not *I can't do anything about it, so I won't think about it* but *Let me come up with something that will keep me from seeing it for what it is.* Not truth but blarney. Not fact but ritual. Not so but otherwise. Ship of fools? Hardly. Every fool makes a serious final act. No fool is denied it.. . .

III

Some poets have an insufficient sense of the world's clutter. They pare down to essentials, as they're supposed to, but leave the sense of chaotic phenomena behind; the poem no longer comes out of the world, but sits on the page pristine, no longer evoking its origin in the mess. The trick, of course, is to create the artifact that's not only self-sufficient but also implies the irrelevances that have acted upon its making, so that it doesn't end up like a piece of heraldry—an amalgam of homogeneous archetypes—but perches elegantly on the brink of untidiness. Enzensberger, here producing his own English version (and a rather British English at that), does this well, seeking not so much poise or concinnity as lines that seem to have been bound together during an emergency, ready to slip and slide, to wander away. And sometimes there seems no more reason to have something in than to leave it out; behind his own mental clutter, there is the clutter of the world in 1912, sketched almost pell-mell. He drifts about, willing to repeat himself (Canto 2 observes that "there are never enough milk bottles, / shoes or lifeboats for all of us"), and the shoes—"no shoes"—crop up in the next canto too. This relaxed, almost indolent vein enables Enzensberger to juxtapose things without worrying overmuch about distracting his reader. The didacticism is more casual than in his other poetry. The persona of the poet seems unimportant, optionally selfless. And the cumulative tone—one of indignant, bemused musing in the presence of a catastrophe as much symbolic as actual—lets the reader relax, with his own mental swill allowed in: indeed, as if no kind of wrong attention, no intrusion, can damage this not-exactly amorphous but certainly loose-knit elegy. It's not a poem to get dressed up for, or even to read in the order presented. It's not a shuffle poem either, but the lines add up with sometimes minimum circumspection, not quite off the cuff, but sounding fresh from chatter with a friend while walking in the street among hubbub in Cuba or Berlin.

I write these words in Berlin, and like Berlin
I smell of old cartridge cases,
of the East, of sulfur, of disinfectant.
It is getting colder again, little by little. . . .

Repeatedly he looks back from Berlin over ten years to Cuba and through that tube of time to the *Titanic,* weaving things easily together into a human sample, in which Heberto Padilla, the Berlin Wall, Marconi, John Jacob Astor, and Mr. MacCawley, the *Titanic*'s athletics coach "always immaculate in his dapper beige flannel suit," come congruously together, all in the same boat, so to speak, while the iceberg waits offstage to be trundled in. Any sea will do:

And I looked out with an absent mind
over the quay at the Caribbean Sea,
and there I saw it, very much greater
and whiter than all things white, far away,
and I was the only one to see it out there
in the dark bay, the night was cloudless
and the sea black and smooth like mirror plate,
I saw the iceberg, looming high
and cold, like a cold fata morgana,
it drifted slowly, irrevocably,
white, nearer to me.

Using commas thus, unwilling to halt the flow merely to signal a change of sentence-subject, he backs up the *trompe l'oeil* with a hands-off, let-it-happen, rhythm. Unchecked by those commas, the iceberg can roam about in Enzensberger's mind, and his poem, like something cooked up by Artuad: an incomprehensible, enigmatic object corresponding to nothing at all and creating nothing less than awe. Featureless, it monolithically counterpoints the host of saliences which compose the ship, much as the sound of it—"'A thin jingling,' / 'a clatter of silver'"—counterpoints the *"Wigl wagl wak, my monkey"* bleated by the band—"a potpourri from *The Dollar Princess.*" If there is something eerie about a stratified mini-society floating across three thousand miles of blank, uncaring ocean, with every quirk and comfort transplanted, there is something even eerier when that society gets its death-sentence and, with only hours to live, works itself into the paroxysms or the supercharged protocols of the end of a world. It's like fin de siècle all squashed up into the span of a three-hour examination, and that pressure—akin to the pressure upon any poet to distill and foreshorten—works its way into Enzensberger's poem, attenuating it here, letting it spill there, always informing the merest allusion with suspense (whereas the tension is within the reader, wondering exactly what the interspersed poems are *for*).

No wonder the poet cannot quite believe what he's doing: paddling his palms in the dust of the dead, making them live and then watching them drown all over again, like Beckett's Watt playing with his rats.

I am playing around
with the end, the end of the *Titanic.*
I've nothing better to do.
I have time, like a God.

> I have nothing to lose. I deal
> with the menu, the radiograms, the drowning men.

No commas here. Horror makes the periods. All the sentences are death sentences and short. Not only is the poet the chef, the radio operator, the savior, the latterday Atropos; he is his own executioner too, noticing "men" in "menu" and (perhaps) "dio" in "radiogram." This, we should remember, is the poet who conjured into being, in another book, the haunting image of the "radar-spider" that overlooks us all and misses nothing we do. The moral point that emerges is not only the semi-triumphant one, vague as it is, of being determined to swim and never to give in to death until it seizes us (postlude to Camus' notion of refusal), but also that, even to set about depicting and re-enacting such a catastrophe (or an atrocity, say) involves you as an accomplice. You become the perpetrator, even if only a bit; and, where the catastrophe is "natural," the hitherto-absent culprit, a stand-in for the faceless chthonic force. This role upsets Enzensberger, who cannot separate the picking and choosing that goes into the poetic line from, here at any rate, the role of a Fate repeating a notorious past performance. Those periods in the last quotation are the dots he doesn't like to connect up, lest the Gorgon's face appear in the diagram.

Who would not, then, as he does, almost dote on the passengers, who enliven his lethal work? Not in their categories—the steerage drunks, the toffs in their tuxedos, the five Chinese stowaways—but as flotsam agonistes, individuals forced to an unthinkable extreme, given a time limit, yet surrounded more or less with the paraphernalia of social class, of shipboard leisure, and still, in spite of themselves, thinking it cannot possibly happen, not to them. Even amidst the preliminary panic there is time for usual observances: cigar ash into the ashtray, of course, opening doors for ladies, and "after you, sir." One wonders just how far etiquette can adjust a human to an act of God, or indeed if there isn't a protocol of staring death down. Yes, the British dressed for dinner in the bowels of the jungle, but the people on the *Titanic* had a chance to push correct behavior all the way to the end of the line. Could it denature death, converting its sting into a solecism? Could drowning (or freezing) be downgraded, through a final series of exquisitely willed amenities, into something like a vulgarism? Or a dull day, a walk in the wet, a Lent of the mind? The individuals are there in the poem, but we see only their iceberg tips, and it is almost like revisiting some of Eliot's crisper portrait collections, those little communities of one-line snubs ("Hakagawa bowing among the Titians"). There is "B. in the smoking lounge, an exile from Russia, / gesticulating, veiled in a blue haze / of exquisite smoke from Cuban cigars . . . perfectly happy and oblivious of himself, at the green table, not paying any attention / to icebergs, deluges, shipwrecks, / busily preaching the gospel of revolution / to a small band of barbers, gamblers / and telegraph operators." He emigrates to a more distant place, that is all, countered by a Manchester mill-owner, flushed with anger and preaching iron discipline from beneath his mustache. Someone drags a cello along the deck. "Liftboys, massage girls, bakers line up." The bandleader lifts his baton for the last tune. Disguised as a woman, with a turban on his head, the veiled millionaire gets into the last lifeboat. Countess Rothes, "witch, suffragette, depraved lesbian," dominates one lifeboat in her nightgown. No longer, in the Turkish bath, are the hermaphrodites "showing their orifices." No cabin boy is whipping a dowager under the card table. None of these mini-portraits goes very deep; after all, these people are samples and specimens, the poet isn't narrating their demise or rescue chronologically, and he soon adds to them—almost on the level of the conceit—Gordon Pym, Dante, and Bakunin, with some of the energetic dispassion of the man who painted the *Titanic*'s murals. The mode is explicit, close to the propaganda cartoon, detailed but far from penetrant:

> While down below
> the water is rising fast, on D-deck the steward
> is lacing the boots of a groaning old gentleman
> in the machine-tool and smelting trade.

That's all. Touch base and move on. You get the sense of motley. The vignettes snap out at you. There were people on that ship, that's for certain. Why, John Jacob Astor,

> . . . nail file
> in hand, rips up a lifesaver in order to show
> to his wife (nee Connaught) what is inside
> (probably cork). . . .

But what it all comes down to, not at the poem's end but here and there throughout it (as if to disregard the phases of fate were to cheat it), is the attested variety of humanity registered with the dry compassion of an incomplete-feeling heart:

> . . . Mr. Spaulding,
> last seen at 42 degrees 3 minutes North
> and 49 degrees 9 minutes West. . . .

A word to the wise is enough. Or is it? Faulkner, to take only one practitioner, would have invaded these people with ravaging speculation; he certainly would not have done it from outside, hinging the specimens into his album, but would have gotten ruffled, involved, intemperate, mixing rage with guess, tenderness with parabolical vicarious self-affliction. And none of this drypoint which, while keeping the poem terse and delineative like reeling pointillism, touches and then goes, leaving the downhill final seconds unexplored, unguessed-at, and therefore slighted. In this reportorial shipwreck, the people seem there for local color only, compatible congeners of the brightly painted iron hares which, during dog races on C-deck, "were purported / to have induced mottled greyhounds to illicit exertions." Enzensberger loves contraptions, as ***Mausoleum*** proves, and the same addiction to freakishness shows up here, numbing and starching the doomed much as it lost the inventors and thinkers of the other book in their bizarreries. Only Salomon Pollock, drawing-room artist, "decorating the walls / with an Orient made up of hot air," has plausible and lasting presence, and even he stands self-indicted. The *Titanic* going down is not *The Rape of Suleika* or *The Bedouins' Feast,* and Salomon Pollock, far from being this poem's Virgil, is only the copious guide to his own juicy fantasies: poignant, ironic, second-rate, but vivid as a bruise. Right out of ***Mausoleum***, in fact.

The poignant saliences are there of course: from **"That April night's menu"** to the first radiogram **"0015 hours Mayday CQ Position 41°46' North 50°14' West"** (did they use "Mayday" for distress even then?), and these take their place in our minds all over again as Enzensberger, with deliberately averted eye, reminds us of *A Night to Remember,* not that bad a movie, and *Titanic* ashtrays, *Titanic* T-shirts, almost as if he comes to his theme backhandedly, through its shoddiest appearances in popular lore, which puts him in the position of searching for the *Real Titanic,* hardly available at all, and raises the question I raised at the beginning of this: How can we know except through empathy? It is typical of Enzensberger that he should feel easiest with the *Titanic*'s myth, where it is most an emblem, and least easy with how the victims' consciousnesses died.

What he is really addressing himself to is Doom, Doomsday and the "Doomsday year," a terminus which, by whatever name, and "however unpunctual,"

> . . . will always be
> a tranquillizer of sorts, a sweet consolation
> for dull prospects, loss of hair, and wet feet.

But, eventually, the seagulls which have followed the *Titanic* across the ocean, and have even hovered about it during the sinking, wheel away to find another ship. I don't know about the tranquillizer and the sweet consolation. The seagulls tell the truth better, and doom as a desideratum sounds fine for Eliot's protagonist, saying he'd be glad of another death, but not so appropriate for seafarers who, although having put themselves briefly outside the timetables of the land, have certainly not volunteered for death by drowning. Of course, there is the doom of death, about which it seems the dead are not free to meditate, but there is also the doom of the survivors:

> it was one of those afternoons
> when the survivors slowly, cautiously,
> begin to realize
> that they are survivors,
> when they turn up
> in the deserted railway stations, in bunkers,
> in tabernacles and other places.

They have been spared for a different death. They have looked the ineluctable in the eyes and come home. I spent a year trying to learn that feeling from what the survivors of the 1944 bomb plot against Hitler finally made known; mostly they seemed to have earned the right to climb down from the pinnacle of matters epic and to spend the rest of their days in somnambulistic mundanity, listening to their bodies creak and gurgle: to their vital signs. In one sense these men and women, after 1944, were irrevocably linked with Hitler's survival in 1944 and his death in 1945, drenched in *his* history rather than in their own; and the *Titanic* survivors, as Enzensberger implies, were irrevocably linked with the sea, a force upon whose side he finds himself, mortifiedly thrilled by it, daunted by the winner. With what intricate relish he evokes its horrors, their gradualness, their indivisibility from paddling pools, goldfish bowls, drains, and dew:

> it is just a swelling, a steady increase,
> all over the place. Dampness is seeping in.
> Tiny pearls are forming, droplets, trickles.

A few lines later in Canto 14, he recapitulates the whole thing more grievously, with several assists from Auden (whose mineshafts and quarries are part of this wet):

> . . . its odorless smell pervades everything.
> It drips, spouts, pours, gushes forth;
> not one of these things at a time but all of them,
> blindly, coincidentally, promiscuously,
> wetting the biscuit, the felt hat, the drawers,
> lapping sweatily at the wheelchair's tires,
> stagnating brackishly in the urinals, leaking
> into the ovens; then again it is just there,
> horizontal, wet, dark, quiet, unmoving, simply rising,
> slowly, slowly lifting small objects, toys, valuables,
> bottles filled with disgusting fluids, carelessly
> carrying them until they wash away,
> rubbery things, dead, broken things; and this goes on
> until you feel it yourself, within your breastbone,
> the way it urgently, saltily, patiently interferes. . . .

The writing here is strong because, among other things, "leaking" evokes the colloquialism of "take a leak" (a preposterous enough thought when it's the sea in question), and then leaks right into the ovens; yet these double values live among the stepping-stones of such ordinary isolate words as *wet, dark, quiet, slowly, small.* The sea takes over all functions and does them in its own way. If you side with it, the logic seems to be, it will in the end do everything for you: wipe your nose, wash your feet, smooth your hair, keep you clean; and nothing of what you did in intimate, casual thinking ways is lost. It swallows you even as you swallow it. As Enzensberger writes,

> something cold and nonviolent coming up, touching first
> the hollows of your knee, then your hips, your nipples,
> your collarbones; until you are in it up to your neck,
> until you drink it, until you feel the water
> thirstily seeking your inside, your windpipe, your womb,
> your mouth; and you know what it wants to do: it wants
> to fill up everything, to swallow, and to be swallowed.

Chilling, that shows Enzensberger at his best, the poet of ebullient candor, scapegrace improvisation, and relaxed build-up. He does bodily sensations in different voices, becoming intimate not with minds but with windpipes, nipples, and so forth, an anatomist rather than one who intuits, which means of course that he stops short after he has been (as here) a long time starting, almost as if he shied away from too clammy or too conjectural an intimacy. His chemisms are disturbing because he spells out the sensations, but they are moving only if you read yourself into the interstices of his snapshots. And this means that, unless you are careful, you may end up crediting him for something he has not provided; he takes you so close to the door *into* someone, equipping you with all manner of charts and indices, sensations calibrated and auspices made plain, faces and tics and stances and tones, yet eschewing the vital imaginative intrusion which turns cut-out into character, reputation into soul. We may wish to see ourselves as others see us, but we surely don't wish to live as shallowly as others see us. Enzensberger may have a keen sense of our civil liberties vis à vis the cosmos, but his approach is anthropological, spicily generic, and in the end thwarting.

How easy it is to be taken in, as by the following passage which, with its Audenlike astringent expansiveness, its knowing itemizations, lulls you into believing anything that begins this amply must go somewhere deep:

> Sometimes, not very frequently, hunting hares in the winter,
> you will perceive in the snow, or shortly before Easter,
> peering through the half-open window of your sleeping car,
> against the dawning day, on the roof of a lonely barn,
> on a pile of coal, or on a belvedere across the valley,
> a small flock of people dressed in black coats,
> led by a prophet with steel-rimmed spectacles
> and flared nostrils, motionless, silent, waiting
> for Doom to come.

You get the sense that every clause, every phrase, could be opened out infinitely but always filled with the ore of skilled observership; the poet knows what's behind everything in view and what's behind what's behind it. He knows how to give that satisfying, almost gravid sense of deployed delineation, as if, Tiresias-like, he has been everywhere and done everything, yet somehow only as a tourist, an eager, hectoring, informal one, yes, but nimbly withholding for reasons unknown. Perhaps he has an almost voluptuous sense of outline. This is public poetry, as far from Rilke, say, or Stevens, as you can get; and, if it isn't quite on the side of the angels, it's on the side of the avenging angels, and certainly on the side of the exterminating ones, through sleight of mind coming out on top, in the last paralysis not going down with the drowned but sitting it out in a Central Europe of the heart, in those deserted railway stations, bunkers, tabernacles "and other places," *with the survivors,* who have nothing to say but mutely share with him reverence for the strong brown or green or black god who let them go. Flukes he reads hugely, as natural intermittences akin to those Proust assigned to the heart, yet without ever, in this book, rising to the level of sentient metaphor that enables Proust, in his promptu-feeling essay on Flaubert's style, to join our lack of embarrassment for having slept to the altogether more putative lack of embarrassment (or confusion) "when we come to realize, someday, that we have made the momentary passage of death." If you set Enzensberger's ***Titanic*** poem alongside, say, the "Grief and Oblivion" section of ***Albertine Disparue***, something emerges about the psychological healing-power of exact metaphors, or, if not healing-power, then power to widen the sense of human experience so much that, because life seems so much fuller and keener, death is somehow cheated.

"Dimly, hard to say why," the poet ends, "I continue to wail, and to swim." Jauntily dry-toned in the presence of sea, iceberg, and Doom, he reminds me of his earlier stanza in **"Foam"**:

> okay call me no man: say that i'm no man's kid brother
> from no man's land let me break loose so at least
> I can rest from all these live people:
> let's make out that i'm not one of you that i'm not one of us
> that i'm free from all that, from us, from this foam,
> this snivelling smirking sweet-tasting foam
> that hangs from the century's mouth that rises
> higher and higher. . . .

It's one thing to be self-less in the presence of other selves; it's quite another to be semi-self-effacing in the presence of other selves seen mainly as units of human currency. Whether they are right or wrong, it's our visions—our emblems of extruded hope—that say the most about our individuality or uniqueness, and to back away from such material into highly animated and technically adroit *vers de société* seems spiritually uncouth, as if poetry weren't allowed to be afraid, intuitive, or on the losing side. An earlier Enzensberger title, ***Poems For People Who Don't Read Poems*** (1968), has a proselytizing zeal, a rough-house poignancy, a spruced-up shamefulness, all missing here. I respond to the ikon which is the formally open poem with the tight-lipped heart (*volumes* implied), but I respond more to the idea of it, and I prefer the formally closed poem with the spilling persona within (such as Dylan Thomas' *Ballad of the Long-Legged Bait*). A formidable poetic opportunity has gone somewhat a-begging here, not that the poet lacks the equipment; it's just that the poem survives, when it might usefully have gone down, formally open as an exposed rib cage, instead of bobbing brightly and expertly about like a buoy in safe water this side of the reef. After all, the name of the deathship sank an adjective as well.

Reinhold Grimm (essay date 1982)

SOURCE: "Poetic Anarchism? The Case of Hans Magnus Enzensberger," in *MLN*, Vol. 97, No. 3, April, 1982, pp. 745-58.

[*In this essay, Grimm argues that Enzensberger is a practitioner of poetic anarchism, citing the author's fascina-*

tion with anarchic events, movements, and historical figures, as well as his extreme and sometimes conflicting statements about theoretical aspects of literature.]

> Und mit deinen Schlüssen, scheint mir, hast du mindestens insofern recht, als das Unvereinbare (und die Schwierigkeit, das Unvereinbare mit sich zu vereinbaren) den Grundstoff meiner Arbeit ausmacht, ob ich will oder nicht.[1]

In a lengthy essay published some six or seven years ago,[2] I tried to sum up Hans Magnus Enzensberger's existence as a political writer by assigning him an imaginary stance which, on the one hand, would be utopian and, on the other, anarchic, but which in truth would amount to a paradoxical coincidence of both. My argument outlining this paradox, simple as it was, ran as follows. Since, according to Enzensberger, all political systems are systems of domination, what is left to him can solely be anarchism; and if indeed he does conceive of a viable system, a system, however, that has not yet been put into practice, all he can possibly advocate is utopianism. In short, his position would have to be seen as a kind of eschatological vanishing point where anarchy and utopia intersect, as it were—or, I concluded, as a veritable point zero possessing, *verbatim,* "no place" whatsoever, either in space or in time.

Still, I had to concede—and was happy to do so—that this same man Enzensberger who expressly holds that "politics equals crime"[3] has, in effect, never ceased to fight, both as an author and a citizen, for the enlightenment and, thus, betterment of the human race and condition; that, ever so paradoxically, he has been steadfast and determined in leading an active political life, not only as an indefatigable critic but also as one of the finest and most accomplished lyrical poets in contemporary German literature. For poetic creation cannot be separated from political criticism, says Enzensberger: "poetry and politics,"[4] as will be remembered, is yet another maxim he subscribes to.

I believe, in all modesty, that my contradictory assessment is as valid today as it was in the early seventies. Enzensberger (though he may grow pale like Brecht's Herr Keuner upon reading this) has not changed. There are, granted, certain shifts of emphasis that can be discerned; but, now as then, the "essence" of Enzensberger's work—as he in turn admitted, albeit not publicly—consists of that which is "incompatible," as well as of the immense difficulty of coming to grips, somehow or other, with the experience of incompatibility. And isn't there an anarchical element involved in this very struggle? In fact it seems as if Enzensberger's entire career were imbued with a spirit of anarchy, all his concerted efforts notwithstanding. That such an anarchism must be of a special breed, however, ought to be obvious.

What, then, is this anarchism which I have chosen to label, tentatively, a "poetic" one? It behooves me at this point to confess that I am not a student of that ideology, let alone a disciple of any of its persuasions. Nonetheless, a glance cast from an oblique angle, so to speak, and coming (let us hope) from a detached and impartial eye, might have a legitimacy of its own; sometimes, at any rate, the outsider's view has brought about a salutary "alienation" of the issue at hand, and prevented even the initiated from succumbing to rash stereotyping. Isn't the outsider almost childlike in his uninhibited naïveté? If lucky, he may indeed produce effects comparable, in however limited a way, to those of poetry itself, of which we are told: its "kritisches Werk ist kein anderes als das des Kindes im Märchen [who exclaims] daß der Kaiser keine Kleider trägt."[5] Which, incidentally, constitutes one of Enzensberger's pertinent pronouncements. In the sentences immediately preceding our quote, he states categorically: "Das Gedicht ist . . . anarchisch." And: "Es überführt, solange es nur anwesend ist, Regierungser-klärung und Reklameschrei, Manifest und Transparent der Lüge."[6]

Such statements and pronouncements are numerous, manifold, and, to be sure, often quite dictatorial. But they do not exhaust the motley phenomenon of Enzensberger's anarchism in the least. Actually, there are no less than three different aspects we have to distinguish—although, needless to say, they are closely interrelated. One of them, as we just saw, derives from a concept of anarchy as a specific quality of literature and, in particular, poetry and their respective functions and usages. This brand of "poetic anarchism" appears to be rather original, all the more so since, in addition, it is defined as "durch sein bloßes Dasein subversiv."[7] Contrarily, the two remaining aspects are fairly familiar. They refer to the realm of past and present history, encompassing both historical anarchism and what I shall call, for lack of a better term, anarchic historicity. In other words, Enzensberger adopts as his subject matter the anarchistic prophets and messages, heroes and deeds, factions and developments that have manifested themselves, in varying manner and degree, since the middle of the 19th century; yet, likewise, he perceives and portrays as anarchic, indeed chaotic, processes the explosive sociopolitical, economic, and ecological events and aberrations going on around him. Their presence inevitably extending into the future, they are linked, of necessity, not only to Enzensberger's utopianism but also to its complement, his dystopian thought.

The most traditional and objective part of this elaborate triad is the one devoted to historical anarchism. In taking it up, however, Enzensberger was by no means prompted by an antiquarian interest. That he knows full well what he is dealing with is evinced, above all, by his book on the Spanish anarchists and their legendary leader, *Der kurze Sommer der Anarchie: Buenaventura Durrutis Leben und Tod* (1972). This remarkable "novel," as its subtitle claims, stemmed from a TV documentary for which Enzensberger had done extensive field work and research in archives all over Europe and beyond, as well as conducted interviews with surviving emigrants from Spain in Southern France. What seems especially noteworthy about it is its mosaic-like structure which is in itself a sort of anarchic puzzle meant to provoke the reader's historical—or, if you wish, poetic—imagination and creativeness. The author makes this quite explicit by inserting, in italics, bits and pieces of such a theory of reception, thus diversifying his vast array of most diverse fragments even further.

Less comprehensive and, surely, less innovative are other portrayals of historical anarchism. Yet they are equally telling. They include, for example, two sizable chapters on the anarchist and terrorist movements in Czarist Russia;[8] a prophetic essay on the uprising, quelled so brutally, of the sailors of Kronstadt against the newly established Soviet Republic;[9] and, last but not least, a long prose poem on Bakunin from a volume of highly unusual ballads unfolding the dialectics of progressive barbarity and barbarous progress.[10] None of these treatments, it should be stressed, is in any way unsympathetic toward the anarchists. Dating from 1964, 1967, and 1975, respectively, they may have come to register a few qualms and reservations over the years, or to show occasional flashes of irony; but, on the whole, they betray fascination and approval, admiration and nostalgia. The poet of anarchy is consistent both as a balladeer and a historian. Significantly, his novel of 1972 culminates with an expression of unabashed praise of those stern Spaniards in exile: "Die alten Männer der Revolution sind stärker als alles, was nach ihnen kam."[11]In a similar vein, and doubtless inspired by Camus[12] rather than by Marx, he glorifies that "unvergeßliche Schar gerechter Mörder" who slew, or attempted to slay, governors and generals, Grand Dukes and Czars, and whose aims and noble attitude "die Kommunisten nie verstanden."[13] As to the sailors of Kronstadt, their rebellion of 1921 is elevated to nothing short of a utopian prefiguration of the "Third [and final] Revolution"; indeed they are said to have inscribed themselves, decades ahead, in the "Annalen der Zukunft" as the true vanguard of humanity.[14] And while the poem on Bakunin does indulge in scepticism it nevertheless ends, after a seesaw battle of pros and cons, with the impassioned outcry: "Kehr wieder!" Thrice in one line, the great foe to all law and order (which he deemed oppressive by definition) as well as to their alleged abolishment under socialism, is implored by Enzensberger to return.[15]

These texts, in spite of their consistency, are hardly devoid of contradictoriness. The same holds true for those signaling what I have termed anarchic historicity. But before we consider them, let me elaborate for a moment on the concept, seemingly so new, of "poetic anarchism" proper, as it reveals itself in Enzensberger's theory. For, here as elsewhere in his writings, contradictions abound. On the one hand, according to his early utterances, poems are "anarchistic" and "subversive" and, concomitantly, utopian in nature; on the other hand, as can be inferred from his postscript to an anthology, they are like the free-wheeling fantasies of children as well.[16] Poetry, due to the mere fact that it is "überhaupt Poesie," transforms, so we learn, the wildest trapeze acts of Surrealism into *poésie engagée:* that is to say, "Widerspruch, nicht Zustimmung zum Bestehenden."[17] "Poesie tradiert Zukunft," being always anticipatory, "und sei's im Modus des Zweifels, der Absage, der Verneinung."[18] Yet, paradoxically, Enzensberger also decreed without hesitation, only some hectic years later:

> Heute liegt die politische Harmlosigkeit aller literarischen, ja aller künstlerischen Erzeugnisse überhaupt offen zutage: schon der Umstand, daß sie sich als solche definieren lassen, neutralisiert sie. Ihr aufklärerischer Anspruch, ihr utopischer Überschuß, ihr kritisches Potential ist zum bloßen Schein verkümmert.[19]

The anarchic poet went so far, at this stage, as to pronounce (or help pronounce in his *Kursbuch*) the death sentence on poetry, for little then mattered to him except plain politics. In the meantime, however, he has come full circle again, and not just readmitted poetry but reinstated it—although, to be sure, in an almost grotesque fashion. What I am referring to is, of course, his speech of 1976, "Bescheidener Vorschlag zum Schutze der Jugend vor den Erzeugnissen der Poesie," since, analogous to his previous statements, this crude satire bluntly proclaims: "Die Lektüre ist ein anarchischer Akt."[20] We are totally free, Enzensberger assures us in his **"Modest Proposal,"** to do whatever we please with a piece of verse.

Such words sound exceedingly shocking; in fact, many a dignitary felt they were a slap in the face.[21] It therefore strikes me as doubly ironical that, on closer scrutiny, neither of Enzensberger's theoretical extremisms proves to be so original as it seems at first sight. The former, extolling subversion, safely sails in the wake of Theodor W. Adorno, who held that the very autonomy of modern art, whether or not the artist wants or even knows it, is a ruthless attack on the *status quo;*[22] whereas the latter, rolling in arbitrariness, owes its gist to the flat denouncement—as put forth by Susan Sontag in *Against Interpretation*—of all exegesis as sheer allegorizing.[23] Still, what counts is not that dual influence upon Enzensberger, which was fleeting, but rather his position as a poet, which has persisted. In it, his unflinching anarcho-utopian stance, he is entirely himself.

This "poetic anarchism" in a broader sense will emerge once more when, finally, we now turn to anarchic historicity. However, we must take heed from the outset that Enzensberger spans the whole gamut from a jubilant millennialism of truly universal dimensions, right down to somber, merciless, and—quite literally—chilling visions of an impending global catastrophe; and that, worse yet, the prevailing mood in most cases is despair and pessimism, rather than any optimism or hope. Scores of lines and stanzas bespeaking this could be adduced, notably from that ominous volume, ***Der Untergang der Titanic*** of 1978, but also from the one of 1975 containing the verse on Bakunin, ***Mausoleum: Siebenunddreißig Balladen aus der Geschichte des Fortschritts.*** Moreover, an impressive number of essays could be cited as supplementary evidence, essays such as "Europäische Peripherie" (1965) or "Zur Kritik der politischen Ökologie" (1973), not to mention those apocalyptic yet, strangely enough, rigorous marginalia, "Zwei Randbemerkungen zum Weltuntergang," again of 1978.[24] It was perhaps not by chance that Enzensberger had his summary selection of 1971, ***Gedichte 1955-1970,*** begin with his ecstatic rhapsody, **"Utopia,"** which indeed performs a surrealist "trapeze act" of sorts, transmuting and transfiguring, phantasmagorially, the entire human condition;[25] nor is it, in all likelihood, a coincidence that the last poem from his latest collection, ***Die Furie des Verschwindens*** published in 1980, should be a terrifying dystopian nightmare presenting the slow, methodic, and gruesome extinction of the entire human race.[26] The joyous, exuberant anarchy of the mid-fifties has given way to gloomy chaos and anguish.

Or so it seems, at any rate. But be that as it may, the most thorough verbal embodiment of anarchic historicity is undoubtedly the penultimate poem in Enzensberger's summary of 1971, **"Das wirkliche Messer."** Space permitting, I would certainly like to discuss it in detail; and if I were a gifted translator, and sufficiently daring to boot, I might have tried my hand at rendering it into English. As things are, I shall have to content myself with quoting it in German, albeit in full, and with adding the barest commentary as well as my concluding remarks. Enzensberger's **"Real Knife"** is an uncannily terse and complex text, even in view of his own standards.

Es waren aber Abertausend in einem Zimmer
oder einer allein mit sich oder zwei
und sie kämpften gegen sich miteinander
Der eine war der der Der Mehrwert sagte
und dachte an sich nicht und wollte von uns
nichts wissen Die Lehre sagte er her
Das Proletariat und Die Revolution
Fremdwörter waren in seinem Mund wie Steine
Und auch die Steine hob er auf
Und warf sie Und er hatte recht
Das ist nicht wahr Und es war der andere
der dies sagte Ich liebe nur dich
und nicht alle Wie kalt meine Hand ist
Und der fressende Schmerz in deiner Leber
kommt nicht vor in den Losungen Wir
sterben nicht gleichzeitig Wer erst
hat wenn wir uns freuen recht? Und er hatte recht
Aber Und so fuhr der andere fort Fortan
kann ich deinen Fuß nicht zurück
setzen Wer soviel wie wir weiß
hilft sich so leicht nicht und Ich
komme nicht mehr in Betracht Also komm
in die Partei und so fort Auch wenn
wir nicht recht haben Und er hatte recht
Das wußte ich immer schon daß du das
was du selber nicht glaubst
Das sagte der andere Vor uns hin
Wie ein Messer schleppst Doch hier
steckt es schon bis zum Heft
in deinem Fleisch Das Messer
Das wirkliche Messer Und er hatte recht
Und dann starb der eine und der andere
auch Aber nicht gleichzeitig
Und sie starben alle Und dann
schrieen sie und kämpften gegeneinander
mit sich und liebten und freuten
und unterdrückten sich
Abertausend in einem Zimmer
Oder einer mit sich allein oder zwei
Und sie halfen sich Und sie hatten recht
Und sie konnten einander nicht helfen[27]

I for one cannot help pondering this poem over and over. I do think I grasp and appreciate its message and its technical subtleties, but I am not sure I completely understand every single line of it, much less its wealth of enigmatic allusions. Already its title—or, to be more precise, its central imagery of the knife and the stabbing—poses a problem. Could it be that Enzensberger took his cue from that well-known anthology of poetological tracts, *Mein Gedicht ist mein Messer,* which was first brought out in 1956, and to which the young writer was asked to contribute when, in 1961, it was reedited in an enlarged version? For here he toys, in a brief though rich account of his craft, with a real, a beautiful, a perfectly sharpened blade glittering in the sun, as opposed to the figurative knife invoked in order to intimate the latent aggressiveness of poetry.[28] On the other hand, being stabbed in the back seems to mark a lasting obsession for Enzensberger because, in the elegiac centerpiece of his most recent publication, he muses:

Utopien? Gewiß, aber wo?
Wir sehen sie nicht. Wir fühlen sie nur
wie das Messer im Rücken.[29]

Undeniably, this murderous weapon tends to become an emblem in Enzensberger's work, if only a cryptic one. Is it, for instance, suicidal as well? And is an ideology—any given ideology or *the* ideology, whichever you prefer—also but a figurative knife, much like poetry in that still popular volume, or is it "Das wirkliche Messer," as might be surmised from the verse quoted, and, specifically, the poem of the same title? None of this is altogether clear. What is clear, however, is the basic thrust of the poem: namely, its depiction of history as an anarchical process, both in terms of a world-wide entanglement and a personal strife. Equally evident is, or should be, the meaning of the "room" where this bloody turmoil rages: it no longer signifies the mythical slaughterhouse of capitalism only, but denotes the blest premises of socialism, too. In fact, this massacre is ubiquitous, engulfing all countries and societies alike, since all of them offer sites, and are means, of oppression, exploitation, and boundless carnage. The metaphorical room conjured up by Enzensberger is, in sum, the earth in its entirety—just as, at one and the same time, it stands for the torn consciousness of the individual. And there is no way out, neither for the isolated individual nor for the masses or classes. Nor is there the slightest glimpse of dawn in this utter darkness; quite to the contrary, eschatological dusk is falling, indeed an apocalyptic night has already enveloped everything. Or to put it less biblically and solemnly and to point to at least one of the many sources at work: I find it highly revealing that Enzensberger, who knows his Brecht by heart, should allude with his ending to the desperate, utterly hopeless finale of Brecht's opera from the late twenties, *Aufstieg und Fall der Stadt Mahagonny,* the punchline of which reads:

Können uns und euch und niemand helfen.[30]

Amidst an "endless" (Brecht's own word) entanglement and strife and turmoil of chaotic demonstrations milling around on the stage, the people of that doomed city (which is, naturally, as metaphorical as is Enzensberger's room) loudly confess that they cannot help themselves nor us—*i.e.,* the audience—nor anybody in the whole world. All of which bears a striking resemblance to the message and thrust of **"Das wirkliche Messer"** and, in particular, its final couplet:

> Und sie halfen sich Und sie hatten recht
> Und sie konnten einander nicht helfen

Of course, being able to help oneself is, within the context of this poem, yet another twist of bitter irony. For, unlike Brecht who wrote his verse *before* he fully committed himself to politics, though without doing away with literature, and embraced, once and for all, world revolution and the cause of Marxism, Enzensberger composed his lines *after* the days of his total commitment and ultrarevolutionary revelry. Or, more revealing still, he may well have written them right during the heyday thereof! Wasn't his ***Untergang der Titanic***, as he himself informs us,[31] conceived while he was roving the plains of Cuba, allegedly cutting sugarcane, since he too, the frail intellectual, yearned to submit his humble share to Castro's illusory "harvest of the many millions"? What Enzensberger then brandished, whether in his hands or his mind, was also a knife, after all, and might thus be regarded as a possible inspiration for his poem . . . even if a machete, admittedly, would lend itself less easily to the act of stabbing, and prove far more suitable for cutting throats.

I will be forgiven for this piece of grim humor, I trust, because my only reason for introducing it is the dire need I feel of a strong antidote. A paralyzing gloom threatens to beset any sensitive reader of such and similar outpourings. Are we not really bound to fall a prey to infinite hopelessness, to despair past help? And yet, being students of literature and history, we cannot but be aware that those insights of Enzensberger's, fearsome as they may seem, have a long and equally fearsome pre-history of their own. It was no less a literary giant than Georg Büchner who, in the spring of 1834, said in a letter concerning the events of the French Revolution:

> Ich fühlte mich wie zernichtet unter dem gräßlichen Fatalismus der Geschichte. Ich finde in der Menschennatur eine entsetzliche Gleichheit, in den menschlichen Verhältnissen eine unabwendbare Gewalt, Allen und Keinem verliehen. Der Einzelne nur Schaum auf der Welle, die Größe ein bloßer Zufall, die Herrschaft des Genies ein Puppenspiel, ein lächerliches Ringen gegen ein ehernes Gesetz, es zu erkennen das Höchste, es zu beherrschen unmöglich.[32]

These are words that truly penetrate through historical reality, laying bare to the bones what can only be termed a senseless anarchical process. Yet the young writer who put them down was, as we all know, simultaneously an active revolutionary. And none other than Enzensberger reminded us of this by publishing, along with treatises worthy of being reread, that rousing pamphlet called *Der Hessische Landbote* which provides the most telling testimony, both of Büchner's subversive activities and of his paradoxical belief in political change—a belief, by the way, that was not relinquished but, contrary to many a critic's claim, indefatigably upheld. If in German literature there is anything whose essence consists of that which is incompatible, it is the inseparable unity we associate with the name of Büchner. Even nowadays, we have not yet come to grips with this bundle of contradictions, as much as we have endeavored to do so for nearly a century and a half.

No, I do not mean to equate Enzensberger with the towering figure of him who gave us, at the age of twenty-two, the greatest and most stirring play on revolution that has even been written. Nevertheless, that there exists an elective affinity between the two men, the author of *Dantons Tod* and his modern propagator, can hardly be disputed, irrespective of the latter's own protestations.[33] Both belong to the same rare species of political writers—rare, in any case, within the confines of German letters. Their comparison, however cursory, ought to have sufficed to substantiate this kinship, especially as to their view of anarchic historicity, and to situate Enzensberger and the fundamental incompatibility pervading his life and work, the very essence of his existence, in the appropriate historical frame.

Little more remains to be added, as our quick look at Büchner has brought us back to where we began. What then, in brief, are the results we have gained in our survey of Hans Magnus Enzensberger's "poetic anarchism"? But let us never forget that they won't be definitive at all. We are dealing with an author whose career has not ended; he, in turn, deals with processes which will certainly outlast him as well as ourselves. Not even their poetic reflection can be said to have reached any finish: the fatal *bellum omnium contra omnes* unleashed in **"Das wirkliche Messer,"** a war to the knife indeed, rages on and on in its anarchical frenzy. Namely, those who have died continue, wondrous enough, to shout feverishly, fighting against each other *and,* mind you, themselves; and not only do they oppress each other and/or themselves, but they also love themselves and/or each other (compare, above all, the dual and carefully modified juxtaposition of "gegen sich miteinander" and "gegeneinander / mit sich"). In fact, somehow or other they manage to be happy ("und freuten . . . sich")! It is true, we do not perceive any development in this poem, despite its countless changes and disconcerting moves. Should we say, therefore, what prevails in it is a frantic stalemate? And are we to expand this tentative formula to cover the entire *ßuvre* and uneasy stance of Enzenberger, including his politics? Is he, the militant critic and marvelous poet, incessantly marking time, as it were?

One thing must be apparent: Enzensberger's anarchism and his utopianism (no matter how dystopian it may have become) are insolubly tied together. This is borne out by any and all manifestations of the threefold phenomenon we have investigated, as well as by their combination and mutual connections. To use the phrase "poetic anarchism" was more than justified, and my typographical provisos can henceforth be dispensed with. Clearly, the poetological notions espoused by Enzensberger are in themselves anarchical, if not always anarchistic; and though, now elated now disappointed, he did voice distrust of that innate anarchic power of poetry—or, more correctly, of those concrete political effects he once ordained—he likewise, and with an overwhelming gesture at that, empowered his readers—or, more modishly put, the subjects of his reception—to treat his poetry in as arbitrary a manner as they might choose. I dare say such are the signs of anarchic poetics or, in general, poetic anarchism . . . all the more so since, anarchically, they aren't limited to poetry, either. Really, what other label is there at hand? Isn't the treatment accorded the historical anarchists by Enzensberger also a kind of poetic anarchism? He pays both critical and near romantic homage to them and, by so doing, not just poetizes but downright poeticizes anarchy. Furthermore, these two branches of Enzensberger's work are closely intertwined, and no less with each other than with the third and most rapidly growing offshoot of his poetic anarchism, anarchic historicity. The selfsame principle that governs his poetics also rules over the huge mosaic constituted by his novel, *Der kurze Sommer der Anarchie.* Just weigh the instructions—again eminently worth reading—which accompany it! Are they not, in all seriousness, the creative reverse of his wanton (or, as some would have it, insolent) **"Modest Proposal"?** And aren't they equally applicable to the sinister, and yet so perfect, workings of his poem, **"Das wirkliche Messer"?**

I am, naturally, not unaware of the objections that could be raised. The very concept of poetic anarchism might be called a flagrant contradiction in terms. For isn't the poem—any poem—a cosmos to begin with, even when articulating chaos? Isn't poetry, like all art, as devout an *affirmation* as could be, precisely while and by *expressing negation,* indeed the most chaotic, most pessimistic nihilism? But stated in such a general way, this insight might as well be called a truism turned into a shop-worn cliché, ever since Gottfried Benn once propounded it; and I therefore shall not pursue it any further. Instead, and in conclusion, let me point to yet another jarring contrast in Hans Magnus Enzensberger's development. In 1980, side by side with his volume of gloomy poetry, ***Die Furie des Verschwindens,*** the erstwhile co-founder and co-editor of that highly political journal, *Kursbuch*—which he then abandoned, surprisingly enough—brought out, in collaboration with a close friend, the first and most impressive issue of a second such journal![34] And while, in the most furious outburst of his recent verse, he explicitly approves of Benn's poetic existence,[35] he nonetheless wants to exclude from *Transatlantik,* as his new journal is entitled, all poetry and fiction alike! He is determined, says Enzensberger,[36] to accept and publish nothing but reports based on hard facts and (his own phrase) "field work," *i.e.,* "Wirklichkeitsforschung *en détail.*" In the midst of dejection and despair, he thus seems to hark back to the very height of his political optimism and commitment when, citing the examples of Günter Wallraff, Ulrike Meinhoff, and others, he advocated precisely this kind of activistic *literatura fakta.*[37]

Art and poetry, those images of a utopian order, persist in Enzensberger's life and work; yet so do anarchy and politics and, perhaps, a paradoxical dystopian activism. Essentially, neither the man nor his production have changed over the years,[38] but both betray a chameleonic changeability within their poetic anarchism that even the motleyest triad of notions is far too fixed and orderly to contain.

Notes

1. Enzensberger in a letter to me dated June 8, 1974. The "conclusions" he is referring to are those of my essay, "Bildnis Hans Magnus Enzensberger: Struktur, Ideologie und Vorgeschichte eines Gesellschaftskritikers," *Basis,* 4 (1973 [*recte:* 1974]), pp. 131-174.
2. Cf. ibid., espec. pp. 155 f.
3. See his *Politik und Verbrechen: Neun Beiträge* (Frankfurt: Suhrkamp, 1964).
4. See his *Einzelheiten II: Poesie und Politik* (Frankfurt: Suhrkamp, 1963).
5. Ibid., p. 136.
6. Ibid.
7. Ibid.
8. *Politik und Verbrechen,* pp. 283-360.
9. Hans Magnus Enzensberger, "Kronstadt 1921 oder die Dritte Revolution," *Kursbuch,* 9 (1967), pp. 7 ff.
10. See Hans Magnus Enzensberger, *Mausoleum: Siebenunddreißig Balladen aus der Geschichte des Fortschritts* (Frankfurt: Suhrkamp, 1975), pp. 85-88.
11. Hans Magnus Enzensberger, *Der kurze Sommer der Anarchie: Buenaventura Durrutis Leben und Tod. Roman* (Frankfurt: Suhrkamp, 1972), p. 284.
12. See espec. his *L'Homme révolté* and *Les Justes.*
13. *Politik und Verbrechen,* p. 360.
14. "Kronstadt 1921," p. 32.
15. *Mausoleum,* p. 88.
16. See *Allerleirauh: Viele schöne Kinderreime,* versammelt von H.M. Enzensberger (Frankfurt: Suhrkamp, 1971), pp. 352 f. (first published in 1961).
17. Cf. *Einzelheiten II,* p. 24 (from his preface to his anthology, *Museum der modernen Poesie,* eingerichtet von Hans Magnus Enzensberger [Frankfurt: Suhrkamp, 1960]).
18. Cf. ibid., p. 136.
19. Hans Magnus Enzensberger, *Palaver: Politische Überlegungen (1967 - 1973)* (Frankfurt: Suhrkamp, 1974), pp. 49-50 (from "Gemeinplätze, die Neueste Literature betreffend," first published in 1968).
20. Hans Magnus Enzensberger, "Bescheidener Vorschlag zum Schutze der Jugend vor den Erzeugnissen der Poesie," *German Quarterly,* 49 (1976), p. 432.
21. Fully representative, in this respect, is Harald Weinrich's article, "Nicht jeder, der die Zunge herausstreckt, ist deshalb schon Einstein: Hans Magnus Enzensberger und den Deutschlehrern

zugedacht," which appeared as a rebuttal in *Frankfurter Allgemeine Zeitung,* No. 227, 9 October 1976.

22. See Adorno's *Minima moralia: Reflexionen aus dem beschädigten Leben* (Frankfurt: Suhrkamp, ^{3}1962) and *Noten zur Literatur III* (Frankfurt: Suhrkamp, 1965); in particular, compare p. 128 of the latter: "Die rücksichtslose Autonomie der Werke, die der Anpassung an den Markt und dem Verschleiß sich entzieht, wird unwillkürlich zum Angriff."
23. Cf. Susan Sontag, *Against Interpretation and Other Essays* (New York: Dell, ^{3}1970), pp. 13-23. This book was first published in 1967, the essay of the same title, in 1964. Enzensberger quotes Sontag *in extenso* on pp. 431 f. of his aforementioned diatribe.
24. See Hans Magnus Enzensberger, *Deutschland, Deutschland unter anderm: Äußerungen zur Politik* (Frankfurt: Suhrkamp, ^{2}1967), pp. 152-176; *Palaver,* pp. 169-232; "Zwei Randemerkungen zum Weltuntergang," *Kursbuch,* 52 (1978), pp. 1 ff.
25. See Hans Magnus Enzensberger, *Gedichte 1955-1970* (Frankfurt: Suhrkamp, 1971), p. 7. The poem was published in Enzensberger's first book, *verteidigung der wölfe* (Frankfurt: Suhrkamp, 1957), pp. 26 f.
26. See Hans Magnus Enzensberger, *Die Furie des Verschwindens: Gedichte* (Frankfurt: Suhrkamp, 1980), p. 86.
27. *Gedichte 1955-1970,* p. 166 f.
28. See Hans Magnus Enzensberger, "Scherenschleifer und Poeten," in *Mein Gedicht ist mein Messer: Lyriker zu ihren Gedichten,* hrsg. von Hans Bender (München: Paul List, 1969), pp. 144-48; espec. p. 148. The paperback edition I am citing is marked "31.-38. Tausend."
29. *Die Furie des Verschwindens,* p. 46.
30. Bertolt Brecht, *Gesammelte Werke in 20 Bänden* (Frankfurt: Suhrkamp, 1967), II, 564.
31. See Hans Magnus Enzensberger, *Der Untergang der Titanic: Eine Komödie* (Frankfurt: Suhrkamp, 1978), p. 115 and passim.
32. Georg Büchner, *Sämtliche Werke und Briefe,* ed. Werner R. Lehmann (Darmstadt: Wissenschaftliche Buchgesellschaft, 1971), II, 425-26.
33. See espec. Enzensberger's remark in Georg Büchner / Ludwig Weidig, *Der Hessische Landbote: Texte, Briefe, Prozeßakten,* kommentiert von Hans Magnus Enzensberger (Frankfurt: Suhrkamp, 1965, ^{2}1966), p. 168.
34. See Haug von Kuenheim's article, "Mann mit vielen Eigenschaften: Wie kommt Herr N. von *Lui* auf *Transatlantik?,*" *Die Zeit* (Overseas Edition), No. 44, 31 October 1980, p. 23, although he concentrates on the more ludicrous aspects surrounding Enzensberger's new journal.
35. Cf. *Die Furie des Verschwindens,* p. 46. However, as early as 1973, in a letter to me dated November 14, Enzensberger observed: "Benn erlebt hier ein gewisses, halb heimliches *come-back* [*sic*]. Man zitiert ihn wieder."
36. In a letter to me of May 13, 1980.
37. Cf. *Palaver,* p. 53 (again from "Gemeinplätze, die Neueste Literatur betreffend").
38. As to the shifts and waverings I indicated in the beginning, compare, among other things, Enzensberger's "Nachbemerkung zur Neuauflage," in the recent paperback edition of his *Museum der modernen Poesie* (Frankfurt: Suhrkamp, 1980), II, 786: "Der rührende Glaube an die subversiven Kräfte der Literatur ist unterdessen [*i.e.* since 1960]stark in Mitleidenschaft gezogen worden."

K. Lydia Schultz (essay date 1983)

SOURCE: "A Conversation with Hans Magnus Enzensberger," in *Northwest Review*, Vol. XXI, No. 1, 1983, pp. 142-46.

[*In the following essay, Schultz and Enzensberger discuss his poetry, its hopeful themes, and his use of language in relation to power and politics.*]

Munich, July 1982. The windows of the large upstairs apartment are open to the street noise below, to the smells of the city, the summer breeze. Hans Magnus Enzensberger is at home this afternoon, willing to respond to questions I bring from the United States. But before our conversation about reading and writing poetry gets under way, he suggests doing something practical, that is, reading together some translations I did: "Only by working on something do we get to know one another." He is interested in every word, points out allusions, explains the context. I am intrigued by his lively concern over verifying the vernacular for a particular line. "Are you *sure* people say that?" he asks while inventing several scenarios to illustrate the tone he has in mind. The guarded manner of his welcome, mixed with a sense of frailty, has given way to an infectious intensity that concentrates on the work before us. His right hand in a cast from a recent accident, Enzensberger is nonetheless efficient and energetic. He quickly pulls a volume from one of the bookshelves surrounding us, and shows me the poem by Paul van Ostaijen, to whom **"Poetry Festival"** is dedicated, and whose satirical ode to Singer sewing machines is one of Enzensberger's hidden references. Poems are made in response to other texts, he says, and translators need as much background information as possible for their work. Reading is not a question of interpreting, but of writing, of new production. To analyze and discuss what a poem "means" is useless, since too many individual and circumstantial variables come into play. According to Enzensberger, there are no misreadings, only productive and unproductive responses to a text. Translation belongs to the former: a creative response to a text in another language. I ask about his definition of reading as an anarchic act, an act that may well result in new poetry, while interpreting frustrates that impulse. What turns readers into potential poets? And other readers into critics that channel and subdue free expression? Enzensberger is as outspoken as ever in his indictment of social systems that engender institutions, and of institutions that in turn perpetuate themselves. The "official" approach to a poem consists of categorizing and labelling it, of fitting it into a slot, thus avoiding a real encounter with it. His polemic against "the bureaucrats of literature" remains unchanged. In one of his early speeches, "The Making of a Poem," he wrote that "society has created its own institutions to defuse the poetry it finds intolerable, to make it commensurate with the existing order, and thus render it harmless." Yet he is convinced that people—*all* people—still have some freedom left to think and feel for themselves, have corners and niches in their minds that are not manipulable by cultural institutions and the consciousness industry. The point is to claim and to use this freedom. He talks about children, their playfulness as they explore language. When I mention *Allerleirauh,* the anthology of children's rhymes he has edited, his eyes light up. He refers to the old magic, the bewitching quality many of these rhymes have, because they were made in the magnificent, but non-oppressive, omnipotence of play. Anarchic reading is similarly productive, for as long as no system is imposed, the text remains open. If writing implies hiding to escape social control, reading means securing a place where people can be freely social. Readers, as producers, own the means of production, and discover their own language by responding to another's.

To my question whether he considers the writing of poetry politically subversive, he responds with a careful "No." Too many false postures appear under the label "political," too much naive optimism abounds concerning the social effects of poetry. Especially alarming is the tendency to make political prescriptions, to narrow the possibilities of writing to limited forms. Yet his position does not deny his being engaged. Like everyone else, he lives in a particular political context which, he hopes, shows in every line of his poems. But there is no explicit message, no straight-jacketing "line" that demands articulation. Writing is not a political fanfare, but an affirmation of freedom. This is what the Macedonian speech ("A Speech about Making Speeches") celebrates. Enzensberger even goes so far as to say that "if someone still wants to write about flowers and can carry it off—fine. The proof is in the poem." His latest book, ***Die Furie Des Verschwindens*** [***The Fury of Disappearance***], contains a poem about the fear of always saying something wrong, a fear that flattens the voice, makes it tinny and thin

"Mark Where Applicable"

What makes your voice flat
so thin and tinny
is the fear of
saying something wrong

or always the same
or saying what all are saying
or something unimportant
or defenseless
or something that could be mistaken
or pleasing the wrong people
or something stupid
or something that's been said before
something old

Haven't you had enough of
nothing but the fear of nothing
but the fear of the fear of
saying something wrong

of always saying it wrong?

(From: Hans Magnus Enzensberger, ***Die Furie des Verschwindens***. Gedichte. Suhrkamp, Frankfurt am Main, 1980.)

I ask for the context, and he describes the dangers that fads pose for a writer, the fear of not being "in," the mistaken notion of being avant-garde while actually just being the fashion-of-the-day. Economically, of course, there are the pressures of the Frankfurt International Book Fair each fall, the pressure not to be passé, to be talked about, published, in short: marketed. He says he wrote the poem both for his colleagues and for himself. While we talk, the telephone rings and he is invited to give yet another speech, a request he eventually declines: "I simply don't feel like it."

Enzensberger is interested in a remark by Stanley Kunitz about the current "democratization of genius" in the United States, where the quantity of good poetry is unsurpassed, but no really great poems are being written. Yes, the situation is similar in Germany. Technical know-how, the fine imitation of certain "styles," does not yield the results that skilled experimentation can bring about. That people write much and well is good—but it is not good that so few take the necessary risks and strike out on their own. What does he think of the many Creative Writing Programs offered at American universities? Not much; he is sceptical of the "programming" aspect. Independent writers' groups, on the other hand, hold more promise in his opinion, generating new impulses through reading and mutual critique. Enzensberger does not sound very hopeful on the issue of writers as a social group. Referring to Germany, he states his strong aversion to writers' unions, writers' insurance, writers' pension plans, in other words, to any collective efforts that confuse the risks of writing with those of economic survival. I wonder why he considers being a writer so different from other work, whether he is simply wary of the apathy fostered by social systems that regulate away people's initiative by regulating their entire lives. (In the August issue of *Transatlantic* he argues the thesis that "The Actually Existing Socialism is the highest stage of underdevelopment.") Should there be free enterprise for the radical poet so the poet is radicallyfree? I don't ask that, but listen to his vignette of a non-capitalist utopia where poets, like bakers, can sell their products to support themselves. He admits that this analogy is tricky, since the developments in the world are such that corner bakeries hardly have a place anymore—certainly not in the United States, nor, for that matter, in any of the socialist economies.

While we talk about politics, his face reddens and his body moves. The United States completely lacks understanding for *otherness,* he says with agitation, which shows once again in its current relations with Latin America. Even if he still believed in the unity and hope implied by a "world language of poetry," he could no longer imagine any real effect of the arts on today's world. The fact that the Reagan administration has cut support for a number of programs for cultural and scientific exchange with other countries, for example, does not imply that it feels threatened; instead it proves its total indifference. If a world language of poetry existed, it would not be acknowledged. There are the far more real concerns of power, the need to exploit and imperialize, to control others by military and economic means. He scoffs at the penchant of American capitalists to adorn themselves with "high" culture and artworks, and at the generosity of the powerful private foundations. The rich in Germany are more blatant, they don't do that. I tell him that I liked his open letter to the president of Wesleyan University, protesting the United States' war against Vietnam, and the complicity of American universities with the military-industrial complex, but he is angry about his action then. He explains that he should have simply left quietly, or better: thought twice about accepting the invitation and grant in the first place. He regrets having made just a gesture—as gestures, Enzensberger says, don't make for good politics *or* good poetry.

He is pleased with the book I brought him, Adrienne Rich's *A Wild Patience Has Taken Me This Far.* We look at the passage from "Images," where she writes she will never be able to romanticize language again, having understood its relation to power. Because of this relationship, does he as a male poet perceive differences between men's and women's writing? He considers differences the necessary result of *any*one's personnal and social history, but finds feminist writing quite inaccessible and apart from him, although he is very thoughtful and unself-righteous about his position. Identification on his part would merely be false projection, an error that more politically dogmatic writers are prey to. Effective poetic language comes from one's actual experiences made conscious.

He refers again to the process of translation. Like reading, translating is a kind of text-understanding that, when it goes beyond the text, produces something new. Besides, Enzensberger says, it provides for an opportunity to build up or smooth out weak spots in the writing. The text one reads is always unfinished. His hands move, describe the work—and in a very material sense he strikes me as a maker, as someone who wants to *do.* He remarks that he has learned much through his own translations; new turns, new thoughts, new perceptions. And smilingly, a spark in his eyes, he mentions a writer's selfish motive for reading: "You always hope to find grist for your mill."

The next day, I run into Hans Magnus Enzensberger in the subway, and we say hello. From the platform I watch him disappear into the underground, his head buried in a newspaper.

Charlotte Melin (essay date 1991)

SOURCE: "Autobiography and Epic in *Der Untergang der Titanic,"* in *Germanic Notes*, Vol. 22, Nos. 1-2, 1991, pp. 14-16.

[*In the following essay, Melin considers the significance of allusions in* Der Untergang der Titanic *(*The Sinking of the Titanic*) to Enzensberger's own life and works.*]

Commenting on the problematical definition of the authorial personality in ***The Sinking of the Titanic*** (Hans Magnus Enzensberger's own English translation of his epic poem ***Der Untergang der Titanic***), an American reviewer observed, "The 'I' has no tenure in these poems . . . " The remark indicates not a response to an absence of writing in the first person, but a reaction to the nature of this text as a work of public poetry that reveals only the elusive identity for its author. Personal pronouns, in fact, abound in both the German and English versions of ***Der Untergang der Titanic*** as the *ich* or *I* of the work, a contemporary of the reader, struggles to come to terms with the conflicting details about the disaster. Nonetheless, the general biographical asides Enzensberger makes regarding the ten year composition period of the epic, the broad affinities the text shows to his earlier work, and the persona he assumes by his identification with the fictional painter Solomon Pollock constantly imperil the ontological stability of the poet's self because as a series of disparate impressions they underscore Enzensberger's preoccupation with the impossibility of perceiving the truth about events. Yet, though Enzensberger seems to call his authorial identity into question with these frequent shifts in perspective, a distinct, autobiographical element also enters ***Der Untergang der Titanic*** for the text incorporates a number of highly specific references to his earlier, lesser known works.

In the fourth canto, Enzensberger lists passengers he envisioned when writing the first version of the poem, including one Heizer Jerome (***Untergang*** 22). The name of this stoker links him to a figure the author employed earlier, Heizer Hieronymus, who at the conclusion of Enzensberger's 1967 **"Nürnberger Rede"** comes to represent persecuted individuals. With this speech, a reflection of the politically charged atmosphere of the late sixties, Enzensberger announced his intentions to use the cultural prize awarded to him by Nürnberg to open a fund that would make support available to individuals in the FRG who faced trial under political charges. Heizer Jerome, the person mentioned merely in passing in ***Der Untergang der Titanic,*** which was begun two years later in 1969, is etymologically related to Hieronymus via the French derivation of his name from the Greek *Hieronomos.* This distant, but purposeful, connection allows Enzensberger to recall a period of intense political activity in his life that must have seemed remote by 1977, when he completed the epic, ending it on a tone of resignation.

A second allusion further reveals the poet's ongoing preoccupation with his own past. Enzensberger describes a number of paintings by the aging artist figure, who is his alter ego in the epic, Solomon Pollock, including a work entitled "Heilige Anna selbdritt" in which a "Suppenschildkröte" is placed under the saint's throne. While Enzensberger's references to the history of painting are far reaching, this peculiarly incongruous detail seems to refer to an unpublished piece, **"Die Schildkröte,"** which was sharply attacked when Enzensberger read it early on in his career at a meeting of Gruppe '47. The obscure allusion adds a literary dimension to the dispute Enzensberger depicts in the poetic sequence **"Abendmahl, Venezianisch, 16. Jahrhundert"** between strict inquisition judges, who demand serious work from the creative genius, and the artist himself, who resolutely insists that art must also involve pleasure, such as this amusing detail hidden under the saint's throne. Enzensberger thus obliquely rebukes the senior literary establishment for their narrow thinking.

Somewhat later, Enzensberger makes a third reference to work from his earlier career in another poem, **"Weitere Gründe dafür, daß Dichter lügen."** Throughout the epic, attitudes, themes, and even phrasings appear that occur in Enzensberger's writings from about the time when ***Der Untergang der Titanic*** was composed. For example, the persistent skepticism about technology, especially in the eighth canto, and the references to Bakunin recall the contents of ***Mausoleum***, Enzensberger's previous volume of poetry. Further, the motif of a knife in the back, twice repeated (***Untergang*** 53 and 100), echoes a theme rehearsed in a poem of the late sixties, **"Das wirkliche Messer."** Likewise, the **"Striptease-Tänzerinnen"** of the ninth canto (***Untergang*** 36) evidently correspond to Enzensberger's collaborative effort with Hans Werner Henze on a vaudeville-inspired musical, *La Cubana,* in the early seventies.

"Weitere Gründe dafür, daß die Dichter lügen," on the other hand, adopts the cadences of Enzensberger's translation of "The Hollow Men" by T.S. Eliot from the 1960 anthology *Museum der modernen Poesie.* Freely reworking the words Goethe's Faust utters at his death, Enzensberger mimics the final section of Eliot's poem in a series of clauses, all beginning with *weil,* that meditates on the insufficiency of language to express the truth of the moment. Whereas the translation of "The Hollow Men" begins "Zwischen Idee / und Wirklichkeit . . . fällt der Schatten" (*Museum* 639), repeating the initial prepositions and the concluding line of the verse again and again over the subsequent two stanzas, **"Weitere Gründe dafür, daß die Dichter lügen"** returns ten times to the pattern established in the opening lines where Enzensberger writes, "Weil der Augenblick / in dem das Wort *glücklich* / ausgesprochen wird, / niemals der glückliche Augenblick ist" (61). Enzensberger in his epic, moreover, clearly shares the spirit of Eliot's poem by virtue of the insight that death brings a halt to living and, hence, the possibility of articulating life.

Obscure as these self-references are, they add an unexpectedly personal element to Enzensberger's complexly structured epic, which reinforces the strong autobiographical undercurrents in ***Der Untergang der Titanic***. Since few readers would be familiar with the sources of these allusions, however, Enzensberger seems to comment ironically on his own work with these asides, suggesting at once confidence in his own stature as a poet and a sense that the author today is relegated to an obscure position in the world. Indeed, when Enzensberger closes the epic with an image of himself yelling unheeded admonishments and swimming on in the midst of catastrophe, he fully acknowledges this problematical role for the writer in contemporary society today, recognizing that an artist must be both a prominent, public figure and an intensely private individual.

Philip Brady (review date 1995)

SOURCE: "Poet on a Sit-down Strike," in *The Times Literary Supplement*, No. 4816, July 21, 1995, p. 23.

[*In his review of Enzensberger's* Kiosk *and* Selected Poems, *which was translated from the German by Enzensberger and Michael Hamburger, Brady summarizes the poems in the collection and illuminates familiar aspects of Enzensberger's new poetry.*]

When Hans Magnus Enzensberger's first book appeared in 1957—it was a volume of poems whose title, ***the wolves defended against the lambs,*** promised unorthodoxy—he was hailed as Germany's angry young man. It was the first of many, often contradictory labels and it stuck for a while, even though it tells us more about what the critics wanted than about what Enzensberger was actually offering. But it was easy to be seduced by the fireworks. Here, after all, was a young poet adept at sustained tirade, bent—to quote the long title-poem of his second collection, ***Language of the Country*** (1960), which opens the poems in translation—on attacking a land "overcrowded with absent people", a "never-never-land where things are looking up but getting nowhere". But there was more to this young man than anger. Few Jimmy Porters could match his polyglot range or his store of literary cross-references, nor did they speak, as Enzensberger does in that 1960 collection, of "all that lives in the winds / and woods, and the lichen on rock . . . " And Enzensberger already had many voices, at one moment the self-disparaging throwaway mode of one who, as he puts it, grumbles but does not budge, at another the lurid imaginings of one who can make of midwives with their "taut and gleaming toolbags" a nightmare threat to more than babies.

For a time in the late 1960s, Enzensberger seemed to be making things easier for the inventors of labels. His involvements grew coherent: he founded *Kursbuch,* the most important cultural-political journal of the heady days between 1965 and 1975; he went to Cuba and found much to applaud; he wrote a documentary narrative around a Spanish Civil War anarchist, a play about the Bay of Pigs fiasco and a voluminous montage of historical material around the figures of Marx and Engels. There was no party promotion in this, not even a firm faith in the efficacy of political literature, but there was consistency. Enzensberger, whether in fiction or drama, was trying out forms of documentary and reportage, shaping the factual evidence without aestheticizing it and without raising the ideological temperature.

While the documentary-writer explored spheres of political action, Enzensberger the poet, disengaged from the nitty-gritty of politics and no longer prone to tirades, was a more negative, ironic voice, locating the symptoms of non-involvement, the smugness, the strategies for copping-out. In language that is spare, angular and short on flourishes he pinpoints the threat: "That one gets used to everything—/ one gets used to that. / The usual name for it is / a learning process." And the inactive proclaim their inactivity in chorus:

Something must be done right away
that much we know
but of course it's too soon to act
but of course it's too late in the day
oh we know

This is a poetry of close-ups, catching the *non-sequiturs* not of creeds but of people. The scale and the focus are indeed far removed from the exceptionally wide-ranging debates launched or enlivened by Enzensberger during these years. He seems to be staking out the ground for poetry in an age dominated by prose. And he seems to be assigning a special role to irony in an age inclined to overseriousness.

Even for Enzensberger, never prolific as a poet, poems could find strength in numbers, could have cumulative effect. In 1978 he published ***The Sinking of the Titanic***, a "Comedy" in thirty-three cantos (the echoes of Dante are no accident). The Bloodaxe volume offers a substantial selection from the work. With great virtuosity and in a host of voices, beautifully captured in his own translation, Enzensberger rings the changes on the themes of loss, of unheeded Doom, enacting with much self-irony the incongruous strategies of art in which "Doom is happily consummated" and words fall short "because words come always / too late or too soon". As always, Enzensberger keeps his distance, avoiding politics and avoiding high tragedy. Indeed, if there is hope amid the icebergs then it lies in the capacity of art to play unpredictably—and to survive.

The Sinking of the Titanic is poetry on a grand scale and it is exceptional in Enzensberger's work. In Enzensberger's post-Titanic world the poet has survived, but not the grand scale. In recent years—Enzensberger and Hamburger include poems published in 1991 [in the collection ***Selected Poems***]—there are few wide angles, closer attention to eloquent detail. Not that the heroic beginnings are entirely forgotten—there are few more expressive signs that the times, the poet and the poet's vision have changed than the ghostly reappearance of Fidel Castro in a poem of 1991 entitled **"Old Revolution"**. He, "a sleepwalker in front of ten microphones", scans the horizon for aggressors and finds nobody: "Even the enemy / has forgotten about him."

Forgetfulness and loss affect more than Castro. The predecessors—it is a loaded, imprecise word and it is the title of a poem—have turned away, leaving only "the smooth cushion / the empty cup, / the shirt across the chair". But all is not lost—Enzensberger finds a kind of security in the everyday and Michael Hamburger, the other half of the formidable pair of translator-poets responsible for the excellent selection, catches it finely:

A mottled quiet spreads out, tiny
and soft, into the morning, half dazed
by the sun, in an every-day trance,
and yellowly stretches, like the cat
on that bag of cement, across the road.

Such quiet moments snatched from the general din may be fleeting, but they seem to have proved durable. After an uncharacteristically short interval of only four years Enzensberger has produced another volume of poetry, ***Kiosk***—and the cat is still there. It is still in the sunshine ("tawny stripes glowed in the sun / as it trained its gaze on me") and the encounter has again about it a rare kind of quiet:

Eine Metaphysik streifte die andere,
als ich meinen Bückling mit ihr teilte
Unsere Ratschlüsse, ihre und meine,
So schein es mir, waren reziprok
unerforschlich wie die der Götter.

(One metaphysics brushed against another / as I shared my kipper with her. // Our wisdoms—hers and mine—/ were, it seemed, as reciprocally // unfathomable as the wisdom of the Gods.)

Nor is the cat alone—a bee, "living for art", perfects its assaults on the window until it collapses; a fly, its wings "Ash-grey veined, / glisteningly scaled", provokes detailed scrutiny as, not unlike the cat, it fixes the observing poet—"With the twice four thousand lenses / of his giant eyes / he looks at me."

But ***Kiosk*** is not a poetic menagerie. It is, however, a favourite strategy of Enzensberger to exploit the sometimes ironic, sometimes alarming contrast between the humdrum in sharp focus and the unfocused intractable worlds outside. In a series of cameos entitled "Old Europe"—and Europe, old and new, has become a key theme for the essayist Enzensberger in recent years—the settings are familiar enough: warm bready air outside the bakery underneath the symbol of the golden pretzel in Greyfriars Lane. But in that setting—"(who were the Grey Friars?)" is the poet's only question—there is an unexplained presence, a fat magician from Guinea selling key-rings. The essayist has waxed eloquent on a problem, the poet highlights a visible contrast.

The title-poem of this new collection expresses with particular sharpness this kind of contrast because it brings

Enzensberger's two worlds, the one tame, small-scale, observable, the other wider, more menacing, into close proximity. Even the very notion of kiosk is itself ambiguous: on the one hand the garden pavilion, three of which—white paper models set in rich greenery—give the dust-jacket a deceptively uncomplicated exotic beauty, on the other hand the newspaper kiosk on the street-corner. And it is the latter that engages the poet:

> An der nächsten Ecke
> die drei ältlichen Schwestern
> in ihrer Bretterbude.
> Zutraulich bieten sie
> Nord Gift Krieg
> einer netten Kundschaft
> zum Frühstück an.

> (At the next corner / the three elderly sisters / in their wooden stall. / Warm and friendly they are offering / murder poison war / to their nice customers / for breakfast.)

By the end of the poem the three old Ladies have become the three Fates.

Inside the kiosk, below the surface—of the skin in one poem, of a silver birch in another, of the earth, indeed of that fly—there are unsettling movements and energies. In a sense, Enzensberger is continuing where Brecht left off, not with Brecht's ideology and his certainties, but with similar acts of lyric *Verfremdung,* delimiting the observable, hedging it about with explosive understatements, with glimpses below the surface. Not that the tone of voice always has that sobriety that runs through Brecht's later poetry. There are many voices in this collection—it is one of its strengths—and among them can be heard again the angry young man when Enzensberger dedicates a hymn to stupidity or targets the rich who creep unharmed in luxuriant hordes out of the ruins after every débâcle. But matter-of-fact tone and obliqueness of angle have remained Enzensberger's most effective vehicles.

The obliqueness is two-edged because it is not an act of evasion—the poet's obliqueness locates and heightens what is inexpressible while at the same time vindicating poetry itself. Thus a poem elliptically entitled **"War, like"** is a structured display of poetic simile, yet war is not trivialized by the untoward comparisons that it seems to prompt:

> Er glitzert wie die zerbrochene Bierflasche in der Sonne
> an der Bushaltestelle vor dem Altersheim
> Er raschelt wie das Manuskript des Ghostwriters
> auf der Friedenskonferenz
> Er flackert wie der bläuliche Widerschein des Fernsehers
> auf den somnambulen Gesichtern.

> (It glistens like the broken beer bottle in the sun / at the bus-stop outside the old people's home // it rustles like the manuscript of the ghostwriter at the peace conference. // It flickers like the blue reflection of the TV-set / on somnambulist faces.)

And there is obliqueness of another, highly personal kind. Enzensberger has retained those throwaway gestures, indeed they now set the tone. Having attacked the rich he retreats into apathy: "Oh yes, you get used to everything, / till the next time." The sinister three sisters in their kiosk may be Fates, but the poet avoids histrionics: "They don't trouble me / I too like shopping at the Fates' shop." "Amazing"—thus the conclusion of a poem entitled **"Disappointed"**—"that all our lives, time and again, / we believed in the goodness of Man, that we believed in anything". His, as the title of another poem puts it, is a sit-down strike—"I'm not moving". They are familiar gestures and they are as ambiguous as ever—the unconcern looks increasingly like a feint.

Enzensberger's ironies and witty evasions are by now second nature and they create a voice that is unique in German writing. In those days when labels were thrown around he was called both a barometer and a seismograph, predicting Germany's future and recording her explosive present. They no longer fit—the state of Germany is not to be read either in these lines or between them; the issues are on the one hand broader—war, Europe, a universal unease—and on the other hand they are personal, the irony of one who playfully and seriously explores his own positions. A playful piece of self-stylization at the close of a poem entitled **"Old Medium"** sums it up. Armed with his old typewriter and a pencil the poet cultivates an image of one who is out of date and out of step, be we—and he—know better:

> Sechsundzwanzig
> dieser schwarz-weissen Tänzer,
> ganz ohne Graphik-Display
> und CD-ROM,
> als Hardware éin Bleistiftstummel—
> das ist alles.
> Entschuldigen Sie.
> Entschuldigen Sie bitte.
> Ich wollte Ihnen nicht zu nahe treten.
> Aber Sie wissen ja, wie das ist:
> Manche verlernen es nie.

> (Twenty-six / of these black-white dancers, / without graphic-display / and CD-ROM, / for hardware a pencil-stub—/ that's all. // Sorry, about this. / Really sorry. / I didn't want to cause offence. / But you know what it's like: / Some of us never unlearn things.)

FURTHER READING

Criticism

Brady, Philip. "Watermarks on the Titanic: Hans Magnus Enzensberger's Defence of Poesy." In *Papers Read before the Society, 1987-88,* pp. 3-27. England: W. S. Maney & Sons Ltd. Leeds, 1989.

Seeks the thread of "relative certainty in a poet much given to shifting his ground," comparing two of Enzensberger's works: *Der Untergang der Titanic* and *Das Wasserzeichen der Poesie.*

Koepke, Wulf. "Enzensberger and the Possibility of Political Poetry." In *Bertolt Brecht: Political Theory and Literary Practice,* edited by Betty Nance Weber and Hubert Heinen, pp. 179-89. Athens: University of Georgia Press, 1980.

Finds that Enzensberger's political poetry compares unfavorably with that of Bertolt Brecht.

Martin, Philip. "Enzensberger and the Iceberg." *Meanjin* Vol. 42, No. 2 (June 1983): 181-86.

Considers *Der Untergang der Titanic* an epic for its variety and black humor, and praises its hopeful ending.

McInnes, Neil. "The Intellectual Terrorist." *In The Times Literary Supplement* (June 3, 1977): 667.

Reviews two of Enzensberger's books, *Mausoleum,* a volume of poetry, and *Raids and Reconstructions,* a collection of essays, assessing the two as relevant political documents of the times.

Melin, Charlotte. "Williams, Enzensberger, and Recent German Poetry." *Comparative Literature Studies* Vol. 29, No. 1 (1992): 77-93.

Studies Enzensberger's poetry in relation to that of William Carlos Williams in style and form, and also compares him to other contemporary German poets.

Monroe, Jonathon. "Between Ideologies and a Hard Place: Hans Magnus Enzensberger's Utopian Pragmatist Poetics." *Studies in Twentieth Century Literature* Vol. 21, No. 1 (Winter 1997): 41-77.

Considers Enzensberger as an essayist and a poet, using his most current examples in those genres, *Civil Wars: From L. A. to Bosnia* and *Zukunftsmusik,* to emphasize the differences between the them.

Schultz, Karla Lydia. "Writing as Disappearing: Enzensberger's Negative Utopian." *Monatshefte* Vol. 78, No. 2 (Summer 1986): 195-202.

Explores two poems from different periods of Enzensberger's career, one reflecting a positive utopian view, the other reflecting a negative view.

Additional coverage of Enzensberger's life and career is contained in the following sources published by the Gale Group: *Contemporary Authors,* Vols. 116, 119; *Contemporary Literature Criticism,* Vol. 43.

William Meredith
1919-

(Full name William Morris Meredith) American poet, critic, dramatist, and editor.

INTRODUCTION

Respected for his mastery of poetic forms, including the villanelle, sestina, ballad, and sonnet, Meredith writes controlled, well-crafted poems that incorporate his observations on such topics as nature, death, love, art, daily life, and the chaotic aspects of modern existence. His unobtrusive rhyme schemes and metrical patterns evoke a sense of serenity, gentle humor, and quiet contemplation.

BIOGRAPHICAL INFORMATION

Meredith was born on January 9, 1919, in New York City and raised in Darien, Connecticut. He attended Princeton University, receiving his degree in 1940; after graduation, he became a reporter for the *New York Times.* Encouraged by the poets Allen Tate and Muriel Rukeyser, Meredith began to write poetry. He served as Navy pilot during World War II, stationed first in the Aleutians and then in the Hawaiian Islands. The verse he wrote during these years was published in his first collection, *Love Letter from an Impossible Land,* in 1944. After the war, he became an instructor at Princeton from 1946 to 1950. He accepted a position as associate professor of English at the University of Hawaii in Honolulu, but in 1952 he was called back to duty as a pilot in the Korean War. In his two years of service, he was awarded two Air Medals. Since 1955 he has held a teaching position at Connecticut College, becoming a full professor in 1964. From 1964 through 1989 he was chancellor of the Academy of American Poets, currently serving the academy as a chancellor emeritus. In 1988 Meredith received a Pulitzer Prize for his collection, *Partial Accounts: New and Selected Poems.* He received the 1980 International Vaptsarov Prize in Poetry, and in 1989 was awarded a senior fellowship from the National Endowment of the Arts.

MAJOR WORKS

Meredith's first collection, *Love Letter from an Impossible Land,* was chosen by Archibald MacLeish to be published in the Yale Series of Younger Poets. In many of his early poems, Meredith employs imagery and themes drawn from his experiences as a naval aviator during World War II and the Korean conflict. While also reflecting this background, his next three volumes, *Ships and Other Figures, The Open Sea and Other Poems,* and *The Wreck of the Thresher and Other Poems,* evince his thematic interest in nature, art, and family life. In *Earth Walk: New and Selected Poems, Hazard, the Painter,* and *The Cheer,* Meredith adopted a more colloquial and conversational tone in his observations on nature and personal experience. His 1987 collection, *Partial Accounts: New and Selected Poems,* contains pieces from Meredith's seven previous volumes of poetry along with eleven new poems, providing an overview of the poet's career. Among the new poems in the volume, several recall events Meredith witnessed in his travels. The title poem of this collection concerns the poet's heart surgery and convalescence, and "Talking Back (To W. H. Auden)" and "The American Living-Room: A Tract" reflect his continuing attention to art and ordinary life.

CRITICAL RECEPTION

Meredith is often classified with contemporary poets such as Robert Lowell, John Berryman, Randall Jarrell, Elizabeth Bishop, and Theodore Roethke. He is praised for his use of formality and restraint, and some reviewers assert that his poems are academic and meditative. His use of forms such as the villanelle, sestina, and the sonnet provoke debate amongst commentators as to the relevance and power of his work. His poems utilizing imagery from his experience as a Navy pilot in World War II are considered his most resonant and honest verse. Yet critics acknowledge that Meredith's poetry has matured throughout the years, and his contribution to twentieth-century American poetry has been influential and significant.

PRINCIPAL WORKS

Poetry

Love Letter from an Impossible Land 1944
Ships and Other Figures 1948
The Open Sea and Other Poems 1958
The Wreck of the Thresher and Other Poems 1964
Winter Verse 1964
Earth Walk: New and Selected Poems 1970
Harzard, The Painter 1975
The Cheer 1980
Partial Accounts: New and Selected Poems 1987
Effort at Speech 1997

Other Major Works

Reasons for Poetry, and The Reason for Criticism (lectures) 1982
Poems Are Hard to Read (criticism) 1991

CRITICISM

Richard M. Ludwig (essay date 1963)

SOURCE: "The Muted Lyrics of William Meredith," in *The Princeton University Library Chronicle,* Vol. XXV, No. 1, Autumn, 1963, pp. 73-85.

[*In the following essay, Ludwig offers a thematic and stylistic overview of Meredith's poetry.*]

In his third and most recent volume of verse, William Meredith devotes a deft villanelle called **"Trees in a Grove"** to "five things put in mind by sycamores." First, he thinks of "a sad bald-headed man / In a pepper-and-salt tweed suit who knew the trees." In the second verse, he recalls

> I was seven the summer that I first got hold
> Of the white pied spicy word of sycamore,
> The age when children will incant new names.
> That night I dreamt I was a flying man
> And could escape the backyard of our suburb
> By saying sycamore, rise through the trees.

It may be pushing the dream too far to say that Meredith has turned it into reality, but to anyone reading his collected poems, particularly in chronological order, the thought may well occur. For it is clear that the war years spent as a Navy pilot left him with images and memories that have helped him escape his suburb and have permeated his poetry for almost two decades: the open sea, the authority of clouds, starlight, the sky as only a pilot can know it, the Aleutians, the carrier, the battlewagon, and the ubiquitous trees.

Meredith called his first collection of verse ***Love Letter from an Impossible Land.*** The last ten poems of this 1944 volume are quite naturally war poems. But unlike the war poetry of Randall Jarrell and Karl Shapiro—or even John Ciardi, who shared some of Meredith's reactions to flying—these are seldom bitter with the injustice of war. The familiar G. I. faces are not here, nor is the language harsh, not even colloquial. Instead Meredith observes from above, as it were, or as we would expect of a pilot. His poems are landscapes, of the mind as well as of the Aleutians, and as landscapes they turn on the visual image, outward to the "unsettled mountains" of this impossible land, to "streams of snow dancing in the moon at the summits" and "the wind creaking like a green floe," inward to the mind of the airman-poet, "rootless and needing a quick home." Like the young boy of seven, the airman still marvels at the power of flight. But the pleasures now are ambiguous as he flies "just above the always-griping sea / That bitches at the bitter rock the mountains throw to it." The remoteness of these islands, their solemn beauty, their "chill and stillness" have dampened his spirits, and yet he can acknowledge "they shake and change and finally enchant." Nowhere does their presence register so deeply as in the opening lines of his poem on a naval base in the Aleutians, **"June: Dutch Harbor"**:

> In June, which is still June here, but once removed
> From other Junes, chill beardless high-voiced cousin season,
> The turf slides grow to an emerald green.
> There between the white-and-black of the snow and ash,
> Between the weak blue of the rare sky
> Or the milkwhite languid gestures of the fog,
> And the all-the-time wicked terminal sea,
> There, there, like patches of green neon,
> See it is June with the turf slides.

I have lingered over these early poems not to suggest that they are the best of his work, although **"Love Letter"** and **"Notes for an Elegy"** belong in a collected Meredith, but to note that the stance he took as early as 1944 has proven to be right and natural for a man of his talents. These talents have been praised by fellow poets for many years.

May Swenson felt that "he can occupy the sonnet so subtly that we hardly notice its familiar outline." James Merrill applauded the "intimate and urbane" tone in "poems that are elevated without arrogance or sacrifice to the sound of speech and delicate without fussiness." George Garrett admired the way in which Meredith joined toughness with the formal grace of the lyric. Dudley Fitts praised his "percipient force, [his] technical skill." What all these critics agree on is Meredith's absolute control of form, his confidence in his own taste, his wisdom in never pushing his talents to make poems out of *objets trouvés* or to generate false enthusiasms. In a dedicatory poem to an early mentor, Donald A. Stauffer, Meredith speaks of this scholar-critic's "indiscriminate delight / There in the sweet and obvious side of right." If I read him clearly (and I shall be the first to admit this poem's ambiguities could easily boomerang), Meredith himself is content to be on "the sweet and obvious side of right." From **"Love Letter"** to his most recently published poem, **"Five Accounts of a Monogamous Man"** (*Virginia Quarterly Review,* Summer, 1963), he has refused to shout, to strain, to experiment. The confines of traditional language and form are for him not obstacle but challenge. He attacks the beatnik poets who never learned discipline: "I read an impatient man / Who howls against his time, / Not angry enough to scan / Not fond enough to rhyme." He chides Léonie Adams because "she stuffs a poem full of special words, the way one does an orange encrusted with cloves." He praises Dan Hoffman for his "lucidity, which amounts to a careful and successful attention to the poem's rational exposition, . . . achieved at no expense to the intellectual or imaginative force. The diction and imagery are strong, oblique, and individual, but do not occasion any of the obscurity which we have come to allow as concomitant to those virtues." To insure himself against obscurity, he appends notes to both ***Ships and Other Figures*** (1948) and ***The Open Sea*** (1958), his second and third volumes, saying "I feel [these few notes] are valid in alleviating one quite unnecessary kind of obscurity, the kind that arises from a mere lack of special information." Meredith will be understood. In reviewing Elizabeth Drew's study of T. S. Eliot, he made his position clear: "The large body of criticism and explication which these poems have required and annexed to themselves tells against them as usable poems. In requiring such paraphernalia, Eliot's work is unlike both good art and good myth." Little wonder that his special heroes are Yeats, particularly the mature Yeats, Stephen Vincent Benét, and Robert Frost. A recent narrative poem, Poetry, January, 1962), shows clearly what he has learned from the New England poet. It has taken Meredith many years to come to this easy, colloquial diction within the pentameter line, the witty juxtaposition, the interior monologue. Needless to say, it is not typical of his work of the last decade. **"Roots"** and **"Five Accounts of a Monogamous Man"** may indicate new departures. It is too early to tell.

There are risks involved in this "calm style" as the young poet Thom Gunn warned him in a review of ***The Open Sea***: "A poem should not be an exercise in small-talk that happens to scan: there is need for the calmest poet to be fiercely committed to his subject." Meredith is scholar enough to have taken this warning from Housman or Hardy or E. A. Robinson. In fact he imbeds this awareness obliquely in **"An Account of a Visit to Hawaii."**

> Mildness can enervate as well as heat.
> The soul must labor to reach paradise.
> Many are here detained in partial grace
> Or partial penalty, for want of force.

But force and fierceness are not synonymous. When Frost tells us that "strongly spent is synonymous with kept," he is speaking not of fierceness but of "the way the will has to pitch into commitments deeper and deeper to a rounded conclusion." Meredith knows the commitments he must make to reach paradise or the rounded conclusion; and there is very little small talk along the way. When his poetry limps it is not for lack of force. Calm it may be, even mild, but it is never pallid. Reading in ***The Open Sea*** such poems as **"Miniature"** or **"Starlight," "The Fear of Beasts"** or **"Falling Asleep by Firelight,"** or the lovely villanelle, **"Notre Dame de Chartres,"** we encounter a deceptively easy surface. A re-reading reveals a poem that I can only call distilled. I do not mean rarefied. Detached, perhaps, the poetry "of a man who has put himself outside his subject so that he can comment on it calmly," as Thom Gunn suggests. But Meredith's particular achievement seems to me to lie in this very province. "There is no end to the / Deception of quiet things / And of quiet, everyday / People a lifetime brings," he writes in **"The Chinese Banyan."** His three volumes of verse are devoted to showing us "the deception of quiet things."

His subjects do not range widely, but they are deeply felt and keenly observed: a fishvendor, a dead friend, godchildren, a bachelor awakening at morning, a Korean woman seated by a wall, crows at sunrise. His people are seldom named. Like the painter, he sees them posed, or at least caught at a moment in their lives, not involved in dramatic action. And he generally uses them as catalysts to contemplation, as he does the more common trees, sea, sky, firelight. His feeling for still-life may explain his enthusiasm for opera and the Kabuki-za Theater. He prefers people in ritual, stylized, static. The bachelor "takes a long view of toes in the bath-tub / And shaves a man whose destiny is mild." The fish-vendor's "feet shift in the brine / The thick fish threshing without resignation" while he sells his carp to "wives / With boiling dishes in their eyes." The Korean woman by the wall utters no sound. "Suffering has settled like a sly disguise / On her cheerful old face" and she "shifts the crate she sits on as the March / Wind mounts from the sea." A Korean couple, "the old woman and the old man / Who came a day's journey to see the airfield," are equally mute as they "Slide down the embankment of rubble / Like frisky children." Crows at sunrise are not in flight, not flecked with sun's gold, but are "badly adjusted; at sunrise these crows, / Neither attracted nor repelled, were vaguely cawing." At the Kabuki-za,

> This lady wobbles down the flowerway
> To show: one, she is leisurely and gay,

And two, the play of all that gold brocade
Over the human form (there is a maid
To hold the weight up of her two gold sleeves),
And three, what no one really quite believes
Anymore, that she is a puppet anyway.

"Rus in Urbe" begins with a static image:

In a city garden an espaliered tree
Like Shiva, handling the brick south wall,
Or better, like a Jesse Tree, holds big
Real pears on each contrived square bough.

Even a convoy, in **"Battle Problem,"** is seen as still-life:

A company of vessels on the sea
Running in darkness, like a company
Of stars or touchless martyrs in the fields
Above, or a wan school beneath its keels,
Holds a discrete deployment.

If this urbanity is not to every reader's taste, Meredith would be the last to object. He has long ago taken sides in the split between "cooked" and "raw" verse, as Robert Lowell called it, or the poets of "the ivory tower" and the poets of "the streets," as Lawrence Ferlinghetti distinguished them. Espaliered verse, he might argue, can also bear real fruit. What is taken for catholicity in the formalist poet (detractors will point to the "contrived square bough") might only be concealing, at its worst, a fear of emotional explosions, at its best a devotion to what Coleridge called the architectonic faculty: the right details subtly organized into a coherent whole. Meredith will always sacrifice the flux of images and memories to their tight, even austere, control. If he seldom gives way to the dazzling moment (or at least seldom in his reader's presence), he develops his own kind of panache in graceful precision, immaculate diction, idea wedded exactly to form.**"Rus in Urbe,"** we might call it, taking his own lines for erudition:

And in a tub, a yew turned like a top,
Which might as easily have been a peacock
Or half of a deer, in the unnatural kingdom
Of topiary, where the will is done,
Is lovely to the point you would not ask
What would have been its genius, uncut?

All of which leaves the critic with little to do, except to register his approval or dissent. If it is the uncut yew he wants, Meredith assures him he will not find it in his muted lyrics. He has, in fact, anticipated his critics in the most beautiful sonnet he has published. He calls it **"Sonnet on Rare Animals."**

Like a deer rat-tat before we reach the clearing
I frighten what I brought you out to see,
Telling you who are tired by now of hearing
How there are five, how they take no fright of me.
I tried to point out fins inside the reef
Where the coral reef had turned the water dark;
The bathers kept the beach in half-belief
But would not swim and could not see the shark.
I have alarmed on your behalf and others'
Sauntering things galore.
It is this way with verse and animals
And love, that when you point you lose them all.
Startled or on a signal, what is rare
Is off before you have it anywhere.

Any poet who can write this well need listen only to his own voice. He knows without the help of critics what he can and cannot do. He has found his métier.

Richard Howard (essay date 1965)

SOURCE: "William Meredith: 'All of a Piece and Clever and at Some Level, True'," in *Alone with America: the Art of Poetry in the United States Since 1950,* Thames and London, 1965, pp. 318-26.

[*In the following essay, Howard praises the restraint and tone of Meredith's early verse.*]

"Art by its very nature asserts at least two kinds of good—order and delight." So William Meredith, in his introduction to a selection from Shelley, a poet who interests this decorous American for his patience with established verse forms, being "otherwise impatient of everything established." Meredith's declension of order and delight as versions of the good, a paring susceptible of a whole range of inflections, from identity to opposition, is the generating trope of his own poetry, its idiopathy or *primary affection.*

In his four books of poems, even in his translations of Apollinaire,[1] a curious restraint, a self-congratulatory withholding that is partly evasive and sly, partly loving and solicitous, testify, like so many essays in emphasis, to the war between delight and order, and yet to the necessity of divising them in each other: if order is not found in delight, the world falls apart; if delight is not taken in order, the self withers. Success, for Meredith, is provisional—he does not ask more.

In 1944, Archibald MacLeish, inheriting the editorship of the Yale Series of Younger Poets from the late Stephen Vincent Benét, commended to his predecessor's exhibited taste his first choice of poems, ***Love Letter from an Impossible Land*** by a "William Meredith, Lieutenant (jg) U.S.N.R."—so the poet signed himself on the title page—for its "quality of reticence and yet of communication, almost unwilling communication . . . after a difficult and dangerous campaign. It has an accent of its own." Dedicated to Christian Gauss of Princeton, prefaced by MacLeish, published in the Yale series, and gravely committed to military transactions, Meredith's first book certainly stands under the sign of every kind of authority: military, educational, institutional and, as an expression of them all, the formal authority of closed verse forms: strict songs, sonnets, bookish roundels worn as so many masks. If such verse has "an accent of its own," it is the accent of a young poet (Meredith was 25 when the book was published) for whom the very notion of an accent was concrescent: his success is in mastering the accent of others, so that only at odd moments, turning abrupt corners, do we hear a voice that will be, so indisputably, the poet's own:

> *This is the old, becoming grief of shepherds,*
> This is the way men have of letting go . . .

or again:

> . . . *respite from passion, real change?*
> No, we shall want again later and greatly all over.

and most characteristically:

> Only the delights of the body
> Which I am convinced are godly,
> And the brave ones, do not disappoint me now.
> *The brave ones with black hair and good eyes*
> *Come round like January and are sure;*
> For these only I resolve, wearing tokens
> And putting checks on calendars not to forget,
> Not to betray, if possible.

Against the rest, the lines printed here in roman type have a resonance that will recur, one characterized by self-doubt, submission to the evidence of the senses and an eagerness to invoke the ethical generalization; here is a final sample, from a poem called **"Altitude: 15,000"**:

> *One does not shout to end the quiet here*
> *But looks at last for a passage leading out*
> *To domesticity again and love and doubt,*
> *Where a long cloud makes a corridor to earth.*

But for the most part, these earliest poems have other echoes, or rather echo others, often with beautiful ease, but all the more evidently borrowings. Yeats is a constant aspiration:

> *Only an outward-aching soul*
> *Can hold in high disdain these ties . . .*
> *The dedicated and the dead,*
> *Themselves quite lost,*
> *Articulate at last . . .*

and Matthew Arnold a several-times invoked preceptor; the kind of phrasing Arnold developed in "Dover Beach" is splendidly engaged in the title poem here:

> *Providence occurs to me;*
> *I will salvage these parts of a loud land*
> *For symbols of war its simple wraths and duties,*
> *Against when, like . . . sailors*
> *Disbanded into chaos . . .*
> *I shall resume my several tedious parts,*
> *In an old land with people reaching backward like many curtains,*
> *Possessing a mystery beyond the mist of mountains,*
> *Ornate beyond the ritual of snow.*

Sonnets on suicide (*"Empedocles came coughing through the smoke"*) and war cleverly assimilate the Auden chime that we hear in the well-stopped lines:

> *The maps were displaced and most of the men dispersed,*
> *And worst perhaps of all, I have lost the wanderlust.*

And in the flagrantly mimicked adjectives here:

> *He was seized with an enormous remorse:*
> *The native stone was bright, the lines untrue.*

At the end of the book, though, something happens to these brevities uttered with such a stiff upper lip, these clipped phrases which embody The Good-as-order. The experience of war, the actual displacement of the poet's person to the Aleutians, provoke a mode of discourse in which the mind's response to behavior threatens order and bids, in desperation, for delight:

> *We lie in khaki rows, no two alike,*
> *Needing to be called by name*
> *And saying women's names.*

In the long title poem, in **"June: Dutch Harbor"** and in the astonishing **"Notes for an Elegy"** (where the loss of a single airman—

> *Who had not fought one public battle,*
> *Met any Fascist with his skill, but died*
> *As it were in bed, the waste conspicuous—*

is by a tone of obedient resolution reconciled with the public war, when

> *Morning came up foolish with pink clouds*
> *To say that God counts ours a cunning time,*
> *Our losses part of an old secret, somehow no loss.)—*

in these poems Meredith wrote what stand among the best poems of service in the Second World War, odes to duty that constitute a lamentable genre but a real distinction. Buttressed, as I have said, with Auden and Arnold, alienated by, say, Kodiak Island from the complacencies the word "Princeton" may be taken to represent, this Navy flyer discovered an equilibrium sufficiently endangered to be poignant, yet sufficiently realized in experience to be possessed:

> *But for your car, jeweled and appointed all for no delight,*
> *But for the strips that scar the islands that you need,*
> *But for your business, you could make a myth.*
> *Though you are drawn by a thousand remarkable horses*
> *On fat silver wings with a factor of safety of four,*
> *And are sutured with steel below and behind and before,*
> *And can know with your fingers the slightest unbalance of forces,*
> *Your mission is smaller than Siegfried's, lighter than Tristan's,*
> *And there is about it a certain undignified haste.*
> *Even with flaps there is a safe minimum;*
> *Below that the bottom is likely to drop out.*

Meredith's second book, ***Ships and Other Figures,*** published promptly in 1948, is a beating to quarters after the risks of such battle pieces. Even the tactical exercises carried over—**"Battlewagon," "Transport," "Carrier"** and **"Middle Flight"**—from the earlier experience of war are by now tamed, as another title put it, "against excess of sea or sun or reason." Various traditions are assayed: wedding song, dedicatory verses (one in a copy of Yeats' poems), an *Ubi Sunt,* an *Envoi,* even in **"Homeric Simile"** whose elaboration still affords a glimpse of the self inside:

And each man thinks of some unlikely love,
Hitherto his; and issues drop away
Like jettisoned bombs, and all is personal fog . . .

But in most of its poems, this smug little book is a retreat to modes of learning and convention. Meredith even provides several pages of notes, explaining, for example, that by **"Middle Flight"** he "would like to convey the negative of Milton's grandiose phrase," and synopsizing Sophocles as a (quite supererogatory) gloss on these last lines in the book:

We flourish now like Theban royalty
Before act one: right now Delphi seems far,
The oracle absurd. But in the wing
Is one who'll stammer later out of pity
—I know because I've seen these plays before—
To name his actions to the fatal king.

If in this collection, then, the poet has occasion to juice up his tone, to rehearse the sequestering pleasures of order perceived as a submission to the old conventions by which we cope with or understand our experience, producing such anthology-pieces as **"A Boon"** and **"Perhaps the Best Time"** with their bright and barbered lines, yet the impression given by the twenty-nine brief poems taken generally is one of constraint rather than control The excess against which the poet urges himself is not *in the poems,* and the solutions come too pat:

Everything the years do
Can be called a kindness
And what lies behind us,
Howsoever candied
By the memory,
Has for only virtue
That it lies behind.

Even so, there is a saving discontent here too, and in the **"Envoi"** to the book, with its Chaucerian echo, Meredith accounts for his activity as a poet by a covering confession of inadequacy:

. . . the comeliness I can't take in
Of ships and other figures of content
Compels me still until I give them names . . .

Awareness, then, that *figures of content* compel by their comeliness must disqualify mere decorum, though it is always easier for this poet to "give names" to what he discards than to specify what it is he keeps. At least by his third book, ***The Open Sea,*** which was published in 1958, Meredith insisted on play, on a response to selfhood as pleasure, on the morality of virtuosity. By this time, he is sure enough of his vocation to invoke it as an ethical force. Back in his first book, he had characterized a Beethoven quartet as "not tune nor harmony nor a wild sighing, but strings only . . . taught this wisdom that returns on itself with such insistence." In the second book, there had been another poem about the string quartet, dedicated to the composer Randall Thompson, in which Meredith observed that when we attribute intentions to the instruments, "these novel troubles are our own we hear." Still more determinedly, this third book insists on the autonomy of art, and with it of form. Music, for example, means only itself (the bird "holds a constant song; / He calls to what he calls") and yet is "at some level, true." Tautology is here declared a significant fiction. Everything, conversely, which does not mean only itself is, at some other level, untrue. For Meredith, all art, poetic or otherwise, is an act of self-defense against the world changing its meaning from moment to moment, against the difference, against things becoming *other,* against their loss of identity. For him, poetry is a way of asserting that things are what they are—the insight of self-reference—and that when they mean something else, order as well as delight is endangered. Hence ***The Open Sea*** contains many poems about works of art, amounting almost to a poetics—poems about Chartres, about the Brooklyn Bridge, about a Persian miniature, about Robert Frost's poems read aloud by him, as well as **"Thoughts on One's Head (in Plaster, with a Bronze Wash)"** and, in this context most important, **"To a Western Bard Still a Whoop and a Holler away from English Poetry."** Here as in a number of poems he would write subsequently, Meredith defends the very decorum that endows as well as endangers him—defends it desperately:

It is common enough to grieve
And praise is all around;
If any cry means to live
It must be an uncommon sound.
Cupped with the hands of skill,
How loud their voices ring,
Containing passion still,
Who cared enough to sing.

His meters and sentences, as Robert Lowell remarked of Meredith, "accomplish hard labors," and he will not see them jeopardized by mere exuberance, mere rebellion. Moreover, he has arrived with great certainty at his own destination now, his own tone of voice—playful, even chatty sometimes, indulgent or willful, but the movement of the lines, for all the prose syntax, is the movement of music:

A person is very self-conscious about his head.
It makes one nervous just to know it is cast
In enduring materials, and that when the real one is dead
The cast one, if nobody drops it or melts it down, will last.
We pay more attention to the front end, where the face is,
Than to the interesting and involute interior:

The Fissure of Rolando and such queer places
Are parks for the passions and fears and mild hysteria.
The things that go on there! Erotic movies are shown
To anyone not accompanied by an adult.
The marquee out front maintains a superior tone:
Documentaries on Sharks and The Japanese Tea Cult . . .
This particular head, to my certain knowledge
Has been taught to read and write, make love and money,
Operate cars and airplanes, teach in college,
And tell involved jokes, some few extremely funny . . .

The achievement of this tone, and it is a very inclusive one, brings Meredith to his final stance, which I mean to compliment when I say it is of a rueful maturity. Decorum is questioned but must be, he acknowledges, abided, and in the best-known poem of this third book, **"The Chinese Banyan,"** the heroism and "dark capacity of quiet" are celebrated with a wisdom which gives every evidence of a deepening investment in life. Meredith's adherence to reality is more powerful and complete than his—or our—acquiescence in pain and despair, though he knows, and allows, that they always win "in the end." He is not, then, an eschatological poet, for he is concerned with what is *going to happen* between now and the end:

I speak of the unremarked
Forces that split the heart
And make the pavement toss—
Forces concealed in quiet
People and plants . . .

he observes in **"The Chinese Banyan,"** and this heroism of modesty is the gravamen, too, of his latest and best book, ***The Wreck of the Thresher,*** which was published in 1964. Here the academic notes (which had persisted in ***The Open Sea***) are dropped, nor is the book dedicated (as that volume was to Professor Stauffer) to a celebrated educator "who could write / Commonplace books"; indeed the entire collection has a freshness and an amplitude of assurance which shows the poet to be in possession not only of his own voice now, but of his own vision as well. There are still the poems "about Poetry," the ritual tributes to Frost and the redeeming one to Apollinaire; there are also more charms or spells cast against chaos and change, for by opposing mutability Meredith would say that words are not a medium in which to copy or record life; their work is to restore life to order, and in doing so to enable delight. This enterprise succeeds best, I think, in the book's longest poem, **"Roots,"** which continues the impulse of **"The Chinese Banyan"** and develops the dialectic of identity and alteration, selfhood and extinction in the form of a conversation between the poet and his elderly neighbor, Mrs. Leamington, a widow wrestling with a mysterious tree-root in her garden in May, "when things tend to look allegorical." Here all of Meredith's gifts converge: the lucid, easy phrasing—easy, I mean, to read; Meredith makes no secret of the fact that "poems are hard"—the ingratiating self-deprecation, the ready sense of character:

Her face took on the aspect of quotation.
"'The Magus Zoroaster, my dead child,"
—That's Shelley, the Spirit of Earth in Shelley—
"Met his own image walking in the garden
That apparition, sole of men, he saw . . ."
—Prometheus Unbound, a long dull poem.
Please use the ashtray, not my luster saucer.'

and the recovery of the terror which resides in the usual. The poem has the rich, seemingly random detail of a novel, yet never loses its intensity as a poem: a clear presentment of life, its preoccupation with death is made normative by wit and the self-stroking charm this poet elsewhere employs a little too consciously. The other great successes in the book are the meditation on his **"Hands, on a Trip to Wisconsin"** (from **"Five Accounts of a Monogamous Man"**), the most intimate of Meredith's poems, and the Phi Beta Kappa poem read at Columbia in 1959, **"Fables about Error."** A poem in four parts, this work is a masterpiece of phrasing, image and, again, reticence, in which the poet has turned all of what had been his conventional accomplishments in the earlier volumes to his striking advantage. Consider first the management of the verse mechanics, as in this report of a dead mouse found in a trap:

His beady expressionless eyes do not speak
Of the terrible moment we sleep through.
Sometimes a little blood runs from his mouth,
Small and dry like his person.
I throw him into the laurel bush as being too small
To give the offenses that occasion burial.

The music of that concluding couplet, with its significant retard on the last word as it takes the rhyme, preceded by the rightness of "occasion" as a verb here, and the prose sensibility of that description of the mouse's mouth, could not be equalled by any poet younger than Marianne Moore except, perhaps, Richard Wilbur. Then the felicities of image as carried by phrasing, in this figure of grackles:

Like a rift of acrid smoke
A flock of grackles fling in from the river
And fight for the winter sun
Or for seed, is it, in the flailed grass.
Their speech is a mean and endless quarrel
And even in their rising
They keep a sense of strife, flat across the orchard;
Viciousness and greed
Sharpen the spaces of sky between them.

Next the control of learning—for in his intellect-despising way, Meredith is learned—the mastery of reference appropriate in this context is here conjugated with a stunning awareness of what it is like to be alive now:

Many people in Massachusetts are moved by lust,
Their hearts yearn for unseemly fittings-together
Which their minds disown. Man is aflutter
for the beautiful, Diotima told Socrates,
But the flesh is no more than an instance for the mind
to consider.

And finally, the old reverence for order, the mistrust of pleasure, the withdrawal into convention is given a new moralizing pitch, where art is seen as the mode of bringing delight and discipline needfully together:

The mind should be, like art, a gathering
Where the red heart that fumes in the chest
Saying kill, kill, kill, *or* love, love, love,
Gentled of the need to be possessed,
Can study a little the things that it dreams of.

The persistent modesty of this disarming poet makes an assessment of his achievement—its value, and in the old sense its virtue—something of a violation of his very temper. The arms of which he would strip us are self-importance and heedlessness, those devices we employ to get through life more cheaply. Meredith's voice now, submissive to his experience and the representation of a discipline at a higher frequency than itself, recalls us to a more expensive texture:

What little I attend, I know
And it argues order more than not.

Notes

1. "Readers may feel that the inaccuracy that remains in these translations stems from deliberate and humorless conviction rather than from good-natured ignorance."

John Malcolm Brinnin (review date 21 September 1975)

SOURCE: "A Poet on the Painter," in *New York Times Book Review,* September 21, 1975, p. 39.

[*In the following essay, Brinnin provides a positive assessment of* Hazard, The Painter.]

Unlike most collections of poems, this one has a named hero and an overt subject. The hero is an aging liberal, a painter called Hazard; the subject is Hazard's attempt somehow to maintain himself as one who "participates in the divinity of the world." But we meet him at a bad time, when his hopes are dashed, his guard down. While the newly victorious Nixon gang is putting it together and the kid next door with her Rolling Stones on stereo is getting it together, Hazard is trying simply to *keep* it together. Work at his easel should help, but even that has hit a bad patch—for two years now "he has been painting, in a child's palette /—not the plotted landscape that holds dim / below him, but the human figure dangling safe, / guyed to something silky, hanging there, / full of half-remembered instruction / but falling, and safe." This surrogate man in midair neither splashes down into legend like Icarus nor lands on his feet behind enemy lines. His mortal trouble is that he's "safe"—in two-car creature comforts, an enduring marriage and the restraints of his own good nature.

"The political references in the poem," says the author in a foreword, "date it like the annual rings of a weed-tree." Since his statement also suggests that all of these poems are units of one poem, we might best take him at his word and, in the absence of any conventional sort of continuity, regard each poem as a panel in a large design. Then the poem's decisive moment can be located in the panel entitled **"Nixon's the One"** and its thematic center in the lines "November 8, a cold rain. Hazard discovered / on the blacktop driveway, trying to get the McGovern- / Shriver stickers off his '65 Ford." His country has "bitterly misspoken itself," Hazard feels, but "alone in the defoliated landscape . . . the patrol he scouted with, wiped out," he is ready to face up and carry on. He can't resist making up wry little epithets—"we elect to murder, we murder to elect"—but his mood is largely one of acquiescence as he shuffles through the shades of a "late imperial decline" to his "old barn with a stove."

A thoroughly domesticated man, Hazard looks upon his material goods as "some godless benediction," and never betrays the fact that his role of paterfamilias in a household where children complain of too much pepper in the gravy is an imposture assumed out of weariness and decency. His "real" life lies in his aspiration to fix an image on canvas and in his struggle to make a kind of peace with a history of defeated possibilities. "He is in charge of morale in a morbid time," he has seen "what twenty years will do / to untended shrubbery and America," and to himself.

"Resemblances between the life and character of Hazard and those of the author are not disclaimed," says Meredith, "but are much fewer," he continues with a teasing twist, "than the author would like." Read poet for painter, and the changes that can be rung on identity quickly present themselves. The delicate social conscience of the man Meredith gives us is convincing, but his credibility as an artist is not. His one obsessive subject is more of a poet's concept than a painter's pictorial "fact," and the pictures registered in his memory are sometimes uneasily close to those of a Norman Rockwell nudged by Social Realism. In poetic terms, Meredith takes us into a region recently charted by the knuckleboned asperities of Robert Lowell and by the vaudeville turns of conscience played out in the "Dream Songs" of John Berryman. If such influences pave his way, they do so without getting in his way. Meredith's language is often as lean as Lowell's and as rhythmically adroit as Berryman's. His tone has the consistency of an achieved mode and, true to the temper of his hero, he is modestly colloquial even when imagination strains for release into the upper air of rhetoric. What has allowed Meredith to take his bearings from these other poets without being driven off his own course is perhaps his wider tolerance for human inadequacy and his ability to dramatize personal dilemma without seeming to exploit it. Whatever of "the sacred rage" remains in Hazard finds outlet not in tantrums of self-concern but in the painful, merry despair of accommodation to "things as they are."

Meredith's poem is a journey: from the dining room table to a hall of dinosaurs to the flight deck of an aircraft carrier. Since Hazard is at once our cicerone and the principal actor at every station of the cross, by the time we're back home we know what to expect of him. There, stretched out on a Rhode Island beach where a Yale *girl* is taking care of his children, he has a Yeats-like vision of sensuality in the waves which, for a moment, we think may be redeeming. But Hazard is not Yeats, and what he sees is something less than a lyrical consort of nymphs and satyrs. "Porpoise Hazard," we learn, "watches himself awhile, like a blue movie." When, finally, the last line of the book tells us that he's "back at work," we still don't hold much hope for that pesky painting. But to the words in which his author sums up his character and affirms his unfinished task we are apt to assent or, like Hazard himself, acquiesce: "Gnawed by a vision of rightness / that no one else seems to see, / what can a man do / but bear witness?"

Neva Herrington (essay date 1982)

SOURCE: "The Language of the Tribe: William Meredith's Poetry," in *Southwest Review,* Vol. 67, No. 1, Winter, 1982, pp. 1-17.

[*In the following essay, Herrington categorizes Meredith's verse as meditative poetry.*]

> *To know what is possible,*
> *and to do that.*
>
> —**"Freezing"**

From his first book, ***Love Letters from an Impossible Land***—Archibald MacLeish's 1944 choice for the Yale Younger Poets Series—to ***The Cheer*** (1980), the poetry of William Meredith has been characterized by a recognizable presence. The voice you hear is that of a poet in doubt neither about the human place in the universe nor about his privilege as a poet to strengthen that position by careful attention. Essentially classical in its celebration of the limits of human knowledge, the consolation of friendship and love, the bafflement of death, the poetry is primarily meditative in method. At his best, Meredith considers an object, a scene, or a situation and moves, in the words of his friend and mentor Robert Frost, from "delight to wisdom."

Certainly the poetry of William Meredith has those qualities of directness of language and sense of the speaker's identity which Louis Martz in his book *The Poetry of Meditation* says are the marks of the meditative poem. Martz's study of seventeenth-century religious poetry as a poetry rooted in the art of meditation includes an illuminating chapter on the nature of the meditative poem. Quoting Yeats's defense of the revision of his poems: "It is myself that I remake," Martz says. "It is the creation of the self that a meditative poem records: a self that is ideally, one with itself, with other human beings, with created nature, and with the supernatural." Martz continues: "Meditative poems, being wrought out as part of a search for the common basis of humanity, must have common speech as a basis; yet being also part of a personal quest, the language must also express that one, essential personality that is every man's unique possession."

With the exception of the supernatural, which he does not address, Meredith's best work exemplifies Martz's definition. The poet is creating a self not for himself alone but for others in a crucial relationship with others and with the world, moving outward from the subject of his attention to confirm himself in the presence of his audience, a social act. It is this awareness of the importance of the other which gives to Meredith's poems their tone of an earnestness tempered by wit and tact, the result of a control that will not permit self-pity, that insists on clarity, reflecting a considerateness toward himself and his fellows in their shared humanity. Meredith's concern for the reader is brought out in his essay **"Remembering Robert Lowell"** (1978). Speaking of Lowell's poems, he says, "I think the poems were often spoken primarily to himself, if intended for us. This accounts for some of their uncommunicativeness: things he needn't say to himself, to locate a poem, are left puzzlingly unsaid for the reader, who needs them." He describes in the essay a meeting with Lowell during which he praised the narrative and dramatic qualities and greater accessibility of Lowell's new work. Lowell made this meeting the subject of a poem, "Morning after Dining with a Friend" (1977), ending the poem with Meredith's words as he remembered them: "'If you could come a little nearer / the language of the tribe.'" Emphasizing that he intended the remark as praise, Meredith adds, "I have always felt that his poems made severer demands on their readers than they needed to, have always felt that many modern poets neglect the vulgar energy of speech for a literary language of their own." His insistence in his own poems on a nonliterary language has resulted in the creation of a voice alive with its own character, consistent in its engagement with several unchanging, central themes.

One such broad concern is the limitation of human knowledge, a limitation dignified in Meredith's view by the power of choice and by the obligation to make an affirmative response. This posture combining a recognition of evil and the refusal to despair creates the resonance of dialogue in **"A Korean Woman Seated by a Wall,"** a poem in Meredith's third book, ***The Open Sea*** (1958). Although dramatic in its unfolding, the poem is meditative in method as Martz describes the threefold process: (1) the calling to mind a scene (memory), (2) the reflecting on that scene (understanding), (3) the refining or changing of attitude (will). Here Meredith is brilliantly infusing the exchange between himself and the Korean woman with his meditation so that their gestures, his offering of the coins with guilt, her accepting them with grace, are metaphors of his insight.

> Suffering has settled like a sly disguise
> On her cheerful old face. If she dreams beyond
> Rice and a roof, now toward the end of winter,
> Is it of four sons gone, the cries she has heard,
> A square farm in the south, soured by tents?

Some alien and untranslatable loss
Is a mask she smiles through at the weak sun
That is moving north to invade the city again.
A poet penetrates a dark disguise
After his own conception, little or large.
Crossing the scaleless asia of trouble
Where it seems no one could give himself away,
He gives himself away, he sets a scale.
Hunger and pain and death, the sorts of loss,
Dispute our comforts like peninsulas
Of no particular value, places to fight.
And what it is in suffering dismays us more:
The capriciousness with which it is dispensed
Or the unflinching way we see it borne?
She may be dreaming of her wedding gift;
A celadon bowl of good dynasty
With cloud and heron cut in its green paste,
It sleeps in a hollow bed of pale blue silk.
The rice it bought was eaten the second winter.
And by what happier stove is it unwrapped
In the evening now and passed around like meat,
Making a foliage in the firelight?
She shifts the crate she sits on as the March
Wind mounts from the sea. The sun moves down the sky
Perceptibly, like the hand of a public clock,
In increments of darkness though ablaze.
Ah, now she looks at me. We are unmasked
And exchange what roles we guess at for an instant.
The questions Who comes next and Why not me
Rage at and founder my philosophy.
Guilt beyond my error and a grace past her grief
Alter the coins I tender cowardly,
Shiver the porcelain fable to green shards.

The poet is unmasked in his role of poet, his gift to himself; the image of beauty he has created for the woman is "shattered" in the human encounter by something deeper than either can account for rationally. But in that shattering, both are redeemed. The thrust of the poem is away from self-preoccupation toward an inclusive illumination, the characteristic movement of a meditative poem. Though in no way "literary," the language of the poem is nonetheless formal to a degree of elegance—its energy generated by its spareness, its many active verbs, its crucial, exact adjectives—and by the rhythm of the iambic pentameter lines, an appropriate language for this poet as speaker, in the depth of his concern, in character.

Another significant poem which builds on the tensions of inadequate knowledge is the title poem of Meredith's fourth book, ***The Wreck of the Thresher*** (1964). The poem begins with the speaker, awakened by a frightening dream, at dawn at the river's edge, considering the tragedy of the submarine lost at sea in April, 1963: "This crushing of people is something we live with." Continuing his meditation, the speaker imagines the sailors' "sunken faces set / Unsmiling, where the currents sluice to and fro / And without humor, somewhere northeast of here and below." In the next stanza, enclosed in parentheses, the speaker calls out to his *"Sea-brothers"* that he lowers them *"the ingenuity of dreams, / Strange lungs and bells to escape in"* and asks to *"stay aboard last—."* The "severe dead" answer:

(. . . *Do not be ashamed to stay alive,*
You have dreamt nothing that we do not forgive.
And gentlier, *Study something deeper than yourselves,*
As, how the heart, when it turns diver, delves and saves.)

Here as in **"A Korean Woman Seated by a Wall"** the speaker makes a gesture of reparation to the unlucky. In **"The Wreck of the Thresher,"** the irony inherent in the offer of help is greatly intensified. Whereas the coins which could not make up for the woman's suffering and loss are at least accepted by her, the rescue equipment for the drowned sailors remains an image haunting the speaker who has dreamed of "a monstrous self trapped in the black deep," saving only itself. But the heart extending itself in compassionate dreams is a "diver" and a saver of itself from self-destructive morbidity, from a willingness to "trace disaster always to [its] own acts." The final stanza with its statement that the event is beyond human understanding and guilt parallels the third stage of a traditional meditation wherein the will tries to order reflection to a meaning or resolution. In concluding the poem with the image of the ocean, the speaker places himself and the drowned within a system neither is accountable for, unfathomable even through tragedy.

Whether we give assent to this or rage
Is a question of temperament and does not matter,
Some will has been done past our understanding,
Past our guilt surely, equal to our fears.
Dullards, we are set again to the cryptic blank page
Where the sea schools us with terrible water.
The noise of a boat breaking up and its men is in our ears.
The bottom here is too far down for our sounding;
The ocean was salt before we crawled to tears.

The straightforward diction, the short simple sentences, the stark imagery with its contrast of human "dullards" facing an inscrutable void, the noise of horror in their ears, to the ancient, formidable ocean creates a somber tone. In writing about this poem in the *Hollins Critic* (February 1979), Henry Taylor calls attention to the musical qualities of these lines, to their "stateliness."

One of Meredith's most interesting poems is **"Walter Jenks' Bath,"** a meditation on the limits of knowing spoken through the persona of a black boy. This poem is included in ***Earth Walk*** (1970), his fifth book, a collection of his new work and those poems from his four earlier books which, in his words in the Foreword, "try to say things I am still trying to find ways to say, poems that engage mysteries I still pluck at the hems of, poems that are devious in ways I still like better than plainspokenness." Including this poem in a lecture he delivered in May, 1980, in Coolidge Auditorium as Consultant in Poetry to the Library of Congress, Meredith described how using the voice of the black boy had freed him to dramatize his subject. In his "own character," he says, he "could only try to explain away this mystery," a form of that plain-spokenness of which he is wary, not to be confused with a nonliterary language. He attributes his "giving the poem away to a fourteen year old black boy one third his then age," whom "he put in Beloit Wisconsin," to the advice of Robert Frost, who told him: "Some things you can say better if someone says them for you." The meditation on the physical world, focused directly on the flesh of the black boy as the poem begins and moving out to include the "far stars" in the flat, matter-of-fact voice of Walter Jenks, has the resonance of an inclusive vision:

These are my legs. I don't have to tell them, legs,
Move up and down or which leg. They are black.
They are made of atoms like everything else,
Miss Berman says. That's the green ceiling
Which on top is the Robinsons' brown floor.
This is Beloit, this is my family's bathroom on the world.
The ceiling is atoms, too, little parts running
Too fast to see. But through them running fast,
Through Audrey Robinson's floor and tub
And the roof and air, if I lived on an atom
Instead of on the world, I would see space.
Through all the little parts, I would see into space.
Outside the air it is all black.
The far apart stars run and shine, no one has to tell them,
Stars, run and shine, or the same who tells my atoms
Run and knock so Walter Jenks, me, will stay hard and real.
And when I stop the atoms go on knocking,
Even if I died the parts would go on spinning,
Alone, like the far stars, not knowing it,
Not knowing they are far apart, or running,
Or minding the black distances between.
This is me knowing, this is what I know.

In ***Hazard the Painter*** (1975), a book of sixteen poems which Meredith calls a "characterization," another persona, Hazard, attempts to reckon with the confines of his own gifts, sensibilities, and knowledge in a period of decline. Middle-aged, married with two children, Hazard is essentially a ruminating character, and the poems which explore his attitudes are a series of comic meditations on American life through the eyes of an artist, funny in his limitations, endearing in his concern. As a painter, Hazard has been occupied for two years with one subject: a human figure dangling in a parachute, "full of half-remembered instruction / but falling, and safe." In a comic extreme, Hazard himself has to jump, "—calling out to the sky, his voice / the voice of an animal that makes not words / but happy incorrigible noise, not / of this time." This physical testing of himself, the need to observe first-hand, is an integral part of Hazard's nature as painter and person. It also gives to the verse a vitality of imagery, that "felt life" on which Henry James said in *The Art of Fiction* "the 'moral' sense of a work of art" depends. As appropriate to a painter, the poetry is highly visual; action is metaphor. The diction is relatively informal. In the opening poem, Hazard laments: "We need the ceremony of one another, / meals *served,* more love," yet even the cat at the family turkey dinner "is taking notes against / his own household."

The cat will not hear of cat-food,
he waves it away. He has seen
the big thrush taken from the cold
box, dressed and put in the hot.

The cat in his animal self-preoccupation is a comic metaphor for that vice in Hazard, who in a later poem "stares at the vain, self-centered landscape / he's working on . . ." Lusting after his own wife, not wanting to dwell on the homosexuality of his painter friend Elliot, irritated by the "Yale girl without flaw," who doesn't "know the difference between lay and lie," Hazard is old-fashioned in his sensibility, contemporary in his frank response to the physical:

No matter how often you make love
in August you're always aware of genitalia,
your own and the half-naked others!
Even with the gracefulest bathers
You're aware of their kinship with porpoises,
mammals disporting themselves in a blue element,
smelling slightly of fish. Porpoise Hazard
watches himself awhile, like a blue movie.

Fundamentally Hazard is a lover of the world, a celebrator of its beauty and its conditions. Old age doesn't threaten him:

He is founding a sect for the radical old,
freaks you may call them but you're wrong,
who persist in being at home in the world,
who just naturally feel it's a good bind to be in,
let the young feel as uncanny as they like.

"Where He's Staying Now" reflects on his entrapment in his own flesh: "I have had on this funny suit for years, it's getting / baggy, but I can still move all the parts." The response to his body is positive:

I do not find it absurd—is this because
I am used to it? (trapped in it? Where are we?
This is certainly not rubber or a cheap plastic.)

Finally the exploration of himself and his world leads to a hopeful conclusion for all.

Gnawed by a vision of rightness
that no one else seems to see,
what can a man do
but bear witness?
And what has he got to tell?
Only the shaped things he's seen—
A few things made by men,
a galaxy made well.
Though more of each day is dark,
though he's awkward at the job,
he squeezes paint from a tube.
Hazard is back at work.

Limited to what he can see for himself—through his "bug-like goggles" as he drops down the sky in his parachute or through his naked eyes looking out from his suit of flesh—Hazard can choose to "bear witness."

In his new book, ***The Cheer*** (1980), Meredith continues to consider the limits of human knowledge. In the poem

"Stages," the subject of the meditation is the illusory view we take of those who are younger: "A child's contempt for his juniors: / *how can a creature endure such helplessness?*" or "the grown-up's fiction of childhood: / *time of happy reliance on trustworthy others.*" The poem—eighteen lines in six sections—proceeds in a series of statements to its ordering of response.

> iv
> The adult's acceptance of childhood as a metaphor.
> Stoically we surround ourselves with children:
> *accidents of our joy, the embarrassment joy causes,*
> *little memento mori's,*
> *our likenesses, our helpless likenesses.*
> How they laugh, how they naturally laugh.
> For a time they abide their ignorance.
> v
> For a time we abide ours.
> vi
> For the children's sake
> we must not say so.

More moving, in my view, because focused on a specific instance, **"In Loving Memory of the Late Author of the Dream Songs"** builds on the speaker's lack of adequate knowledge as he meditates on the suicide of his friend, John Berryman. He imagines the final scene:

> I watch a shaky man climb
> a cast-iron railing in my head, on
> a Mississippi bluff, though I had meant
> to dissuade him. I call out, and he doesn't hear.

Though Berryman had given warning of his death, had "told . . . how it would be underground / and how it would be for us left here," the speaker cannot accept the manner of his friend's death, asserting that "the song says . . . suicide is a crime / and that wives and children deserve better than this. / None of us deserved, of course, you." What the speaker can do is to emphasize the hopeful, to make a gesture as he did toward the Korean woman and the drowned sailors, an act of faith in surviving to praise.

> Do we wave back now, or what do we do?
> You were never reluctant to instruct.
> I do what's in character, I look for things
> to praise on the river banks and I praise them.
> We are all relicts, of some great joy, wearing black,
> but this book is full of marvelous songs.
> Don't let us contract your dread recidivism
> and start falling from our own iron railings.
> Wave from the fat book again, make us wave back.

Such optimism commands respect because it is maintained in the presence of undiminished grief, an attitude of courage. Whatever happens we can be the "bright watchers" of **"Country Stars,"** a brief but satisfying meditation:

> The nearsighted child has taken off her glasses
> and come downstairs to be kissed goodnight.
> She blows on a black windowpane until it's white.
> Over the apple trees a great bear passes
> but she puts her own construction on the night.
>
> Two cities, a chemical plant, and clotted cars
> breathe our distrust of darkness on the air,
> clouding the pane between us and the stars.
> But have no fear, or only proper fear;
> the bright watchers are still there.

Not surprisingly, it is the "bright watchers" who are chiefly responsible for the poet's hopeful outlook; the theme of friendship and love as restoratives of human equilibrium appears throughout the poetry. In ***The Cheer*** the majority of the poems are concerned with human relationships or with the thoughts and work of others. Three of the poems are meditations on the insights of Jack Gilbert, Pascal, Wendell Berry, and Wallace Stevens, respectively; two are written in homage (one to Sigmund Freud, another to Paul Mellon, I. M. Pei, Their Gallery, and Washington City); six incorporate an extensive quotation or a prose account as the beginning of Meredith's poem. The effect of these six poems is choral. We hear the resonance of voices in statement and response, a social meditation as distinguished from a solitary meditation with social significance. It is as if the reader and the poet were looking together at the work or the narration much as a student and an instructor might in a classroom, the poet answering with his poem. Several of the poems return to subjects treated in earlier poems. For example, **"Parents"** is a much less formally spoken, much more inclusive consideration of that topic than **"Ten-day Leave"** of the first book or **"For His Father"** of the fourth. Establishing a witty tone in the opening lines, "What it must be like to be an angel / or a squirrel, we can imagine sooner," the speaker moves to a serious conclusion: "Father, mother, we cry, wrinkling, / to our uncomprehending children and grandchildren." In **"Remembering Robert Lowell,"** Meredith meditates on the poets' talk of language:

> Your language moved slowly toward our language
> until we saw that we were all immigrants—
> had perhaps been shipped as convicts—
> from the land of your reluctant indictment,
> a land of our consent, if not of our doing.

The theme of human accountability in these lines echoes the attitude of a poem in ***Earth Walk,* "Reading my poems from World War II"**:

> In one of the poems the young poet himself kneels
> in the foreground, dressed as a lieutenant.
> He wears the insigna with pride, nevertheless
> you feel there is something wrong: he is rendered
> with all the compassion Velásquez reserved for his dwarfs.
> The poems are not narrative, you never find out
> how they end. Rather, they seem impelled
> by a moral purpose: we are asked not to blame the men.
> Even transformed into beasts in a stylized chase
> they seem to be hunting more than one another
> as they ride across this tapestry, one of a series.
> Certainly they have been seen by accountable eyes.
> The dwarf's eyes glitter as though in that whole scene
> he saw no one worse than himself, and he prays for us all.

Another poem in ***Earth Walk,*** **"Dalhousie Farm,"** is one of Meredith's most moving reflections on human nature. The meditation proceeds with exceptional ease and grace from its focus on the poet's life and work to the image of the farm to the conclusion that ours is a benign nature:

> *Will you live long enough to sit in the shade*
> *Of that tree, old man?* the children asked,
> And the old chinaman planting the sapling replied,
> *This world was not a desert when I came into it.*
> Now, I myself have raised some thrifty trees
> And children, entirely from words,
> But it is friends with real trees and children who will become,
> Probably, my best testimony, my best tongue.
> Between trees and children there is a resemblance
> And men and women nurture
> It by their daily commerce. I want to speak for this
> And for all such resemblances, having seen
> At this farm, in the act of sunrise
> And in certain other acts, incontrovertible evidence
> Of something too few people speak of: a benign nature,
> Ours, mirrored wherever you look, in past, in future.
> Sometimes I think trees are best, sometimes children.
> But there is no need to choose, they speak of the same thing:
> A continuing kindness in our sap and blood.
> What we admire in the green world is a benign selfhood,
> And in one another, the ability to speak of this,
> Or better, to act it out. What is
> The perverse impulse in some men and women
> To speak otherwise about themselves or their green lives?
> Well, speech is a planting, but not everything thrives.
> It would be redundant to bless trees
> Or children or anything else on a farm,
> But once I fell asleep here listening to the dawn
> Wind blessing the trees, and it came into my mind
> (Maybe no language can relinquish this pun—
> First the trees, then animals were saying it to the sun)
> To be of our own nature is what it means *to be kind.*

The poem's natural diction and persuasive, conversational tone, as if addressed to a friendly but skeptical audience, combine with its structure in a brilliantly effective meditative poem.

But even the benign nature must face its own disintegration in death, a third major theme in Meredith's work. Again the attitude is consistent throughout the work. Only what we can verify with our senses can be brought to bear on the mystery. In the war poems of his first book, Meredith sets a tone which increases in complexity in later poems on this subject. **"Notes for an Elegy,"** one of the poems in the first collection which speaks not with the restraint and academic decorum of the beginning poet but with the voice of a mastering identity, is a meditation on the death of an airman who "had not fought one public battle." Opening with a forthright statement qualifying the act of flying as one, if only indirectly, of moral choice: "The alternative to flying is cowardice, / And what is said against it excuses, excuses;" the poem moves to the "composition of place" (Martz) the scene and the event which is the immediate subject of the meditation, the woods where the airman crashed.

> He was not badly disfigured compared to some,
> But even a little stream of blood where death is
> Will whimper across a forest floor,
> Run through that whole forest shouting.

Concluding his meditation, the speaker tries to reconcile the tragedy with an ancient and inclusive order much as he does, though less arbitrarily, in the ending of **"The Wreck of the Thresher"**: "The morning came up foolish with pink clouds / To say that God counts ours a cunning time, / Our losses part of an old secret, somehow no loss."

The tone of undespairing response, established in the early poems, becomes pragmatic in **"The Fear of Death Disturbs Me"** from ***The Open Sea*** (1958).

> We will have to quit the ambient sweet air
> For dankness and stench where, mustered one by one
> By bullies, some of us they say will give
> A poor account, a worse even than here.
> With this much notice something should be done,
> Yet what is there to do but try to live?

Squire Hazard in the dinosaur section of the Natural History Museum takes hold of death in vividly physical images:

> We descend by chosen cells that are not lost
> though they wander off in streams and rivulets.
> Not everyone has issue in this creation.
> Cousins-german are everywhere in the shale
> and marshes under this dry house. In slime, in sperm,
> our living cousins flow.
> And grazers or killers, each time we must stoop low
> and enter by some thigh-lintel, gentle as rills.
> *Who consents to his own return,* Nietzche says,
> *participates in the divinity of the world.*
> Perhaps I have already eddied on, out of this backwater,
> man, on my way to the cafeteria, Hazard thinks.
> Perhaps nothing dies but husks.

Here, through Hazard's comic mask, Meredith enlarges the consideration of death to include persevering nature and man who by an act of the will "participates in the divinity of the world." Quoting the famous philosopher permits the speaker a little distance from his own conclusions. Notwithstanding, the crucial word is "consent," a significant word in Meredith's vacabulary, implying in this meditation human responsibility for every human destiny.

In ***The Cheer*** the puzzle of death is a more personal engagement of the poet with the particular dead, an extension of the impulse to wrest a response from the dead, if only in dreams, recorded in **"The Wreck of the Thresher."** The speaker of **"The Revenant"** meditates on the accomplishment of his own death in great pain from cancer of the stomach. With the perspective of a spirit, he can understand that in his stoical refusal to cry out in his agony, he "gained two stages of progress." The central image of the poem, the "hollow, life-size iron bull" contrived by the Roman Emperor Heligabalus for the torture of those dancing inside as a fire burned underneath and for the pleasure of his guests, amused by the sounds issuing from the bull's mouth, is introduced in a long quotation from Kurt Vonnegut's *Breakfast of Champions*. Using the persona of a spirit in conjunction with the work of another writer, Meredith not only "dramatizes a mystery," as he said he wished to do in **"Walter Jenks' Bath,"** he implies that the questions of cruelty, suffering, and death are too large for one voice alone. And again he suggests that momentous as these matters are, the human will can order its responses.

A meditation which draws on a dream for its imagery is **"My Mother's Life."** Here the speaker considers a scene; "a woman neither young nor old," walking on a cold, dark night "along the dark suburban street . . . expecting nothing," is suddenly illuminated by a "supernatural light" which "asks something of the face she turns upward." The speaker, who doesn't hear the question or the answer, comforts himself with thinking "she gives the right answer." This conclusion emphasizes the speaker's uncertainty, lacking sense experience, and his hope that there is a right answer, though hidden.

One of the most impressive poems in ***The Cheer,*** **"Two Masks Unearthed in Bulgaria,"** pursues the meditation on death through two works of art. Art is a significant metaphor and subject throughout Meredith's work. In **"Homeric Simile"** of his second book, for example, the successful playing of a quartet is compared in risk and difficulty to a war exercise. **"A View of the Brooklyn Bridge"** from ***The Open Sea*** celebrates the accidental discoveries, occasioning delight and grief, in the making of a work of art. In **"Two Masks,"** the speaker's position as a viewer, looking down at the masks under glass in a museum, gives him a vantage point, frees him to see himself through "the gold buttons which are their curious eyes," and to conclude his meditation with a recognition of human transitoriness yet with a sense of the necessity and importance of such momentary passage.

> When God was learning to draw the human face
> I think he may have made a few like these
> that now look up at us through museum glass
> a few miles north of where they slept
> for six thousand years, a necropolis near Varna.
> With golden staves and ornaments around them
> they lay among human bodies but had none.
> Gods themselves, or soldiers lost abroad—
> we don't know who they are.
> The gold buttons which are their curious eyes,
> the old clay which is their wrinkled skin,
> seem to have been worked by the same free hand
> that drew Adam for the Jews about that time.
> It is moving, that the eyes are still questioning
> and no sadder than they are, time being what it is—
> as though they saw nothing tragic in the faces
> looking down through glass into theirs.
> *Only clay and gold,* they seem to say,
> *passing through one condition on its way to the next.*

The acknowledgment of the relationship of the passage of time to tragedy gives to the poem a somber, elevated tone not present in the jaunty, though nonetheless serious, assurance of Hazard that "perhaps nothing dies but husks."

Discussing his respect for and care of the language of a poem in his essay "The Luck of It" (in William Heyen, ed., *American Poets in 1976*), William Meredith writes:

> A poet approaches language in the spirit of a woodman who asks pardon of the dryad in a tree before he cuts it down. Words are inhabited by the accumulated experience of the tribe. The average poet adds about as much to the language as he adds to the nitrogen content of his native soil. But he can administer the force that resides in words.

Believing in the marvelous mystery of the associative power of words, he emphasizes the necessity of being in a state of "unselfcentered attention" for that power to work. For him, he confesses: "This is apparently a rare state . . . because in the twenty-five years since the writing of **"A View of the Brooklyn Bridge"** I have averaged about six poems a year." The choice of language, if an act requiring the suspension of the self can be called a choice, involves a readiness to receive, a social if not a convivial condition. And the form of a poem as well as its words must discover itself to him: "To this day I feel surer that I'm communicating with the poem if a prosodic pattern declares itself." In support of this way of working, he quotes Thom Gunn in a letter written in 1970: "The openness of the experience is brought into relation with the structures of the mind."

By ordering a poem's discovery according to the meditative process, "a structure of the mind" fruitful in its placing of an individual in a closer relationship to himself, to others, and to a world, elusive in its revelations of meaning, William Meredith has created a body of work remarkable not only for its craftsmanship but for its individually of voice. I am not suggesting, of course, that Meredith consciously followed the practitioners of the art of meditation or those seventeenth-century poets whose work sprang from that habit of mind—though "influence hunters" might gleefully point to Meredith's poem **"Airman's Virtue,"** an imitation of Herbert's "Virtue" (see Wendell Berry's "The Specialization of Poetry," in Reginald Gibbons, ed., *The Poet's Work*). But I do suggest that this structure is especially effective in a poem that addresses a private secret in the light of its public significance. "Not yet a man given to prayer," as the poet describes himself in **"The Open Sea,"** he is nonetheless a man of religious sensibility in his abiding need to make order out of mystery and to render himself responsible for the ordering act. The wary attentiveness of this approach to himself, to circumstances, and to his art, combined with a gracious awareness of his audience, compelled the emergence of a distinctive voice from some of the earliest poems, a feat Archibald MacLeish notes admiringly in his Foreword to ***Love Letter from an Impossible Land*** as "the way in which the literary vehicle (for it is nothing else) of the

Princeton undergraduate turns into the live idiom of a poet's speech reaching for poetry."

In William Meredith's poetry there is an identifiable character, alive and informing, not that absence characteristic of the poet who speaks only of and to himself, who in Wendell Berry's words "can only describe the boundaries of an imprisoning and damning selfhood." The language of the tribe is more than "the vulgar energy of speech." It is the necessary means for the resolution of the tensions of a shared perplexity.

Guy Rotella (excerpt date 1983)

SOURCE: "'A Dark Question Answered Yes': The Poems of William Meredith," in *Three Contemporary Poets of New England: William Meredith, Philip Booth, and Peter Davison,* Twayne, 1983, pp. 6-63.

[*In the following excerpt, Rotella traces the thematic development of Meredith's verse.*]

Theme, Technique, and Development

William Meredith's major theme involves the efforts of imagination and intellect to order the chaos of the self and of the world, to overcome the resistance of life and experience to significance and form. He writes, in the phrase of Wallace Stevens, a poetry "of the mind in the act of finding / What will suffice." He seeks an art and life of meaning and value. The goal of this search does not alter appreciably as Meredith's work develops. What does alter is the degree of confidence he feels in any of the search's many methods and results, and his identification and understanding of what and where the threats to its successful completion and to the maintenance of its gains are located. This development includes recognition that the very urge to order itself may be among those threats. This can be put another way. In a recent Library of Congress lecture Meredith defined poetry as "accurate praise." The modifier is crucial. What he has always sought is affirmation, but what he has come more and more to see is that praise—to be accurate, to be true—must include what resists as well as what releases it.

In terms of technique, Meredith began his career writing in the academic manner. Many of the poems in his first two books are imitative of poetry in the metaphysical mode the academic poets favored. However, even in these early collections there are indications of the slow, relatively undramatic shifting that begins in earnest in his third volume and continues in his recent work, a shifting toward a poetry more personal in content and voice, more colloquial in diction, more straightforward—and, paradoxically, more complex—in feeling and statement, more open and organic in form, more provisional, more suspicious of the claims of the rational, and more willing to consider the claims of the non-rational. Clearly, then, although Meredith is often categorized as an unreconstructed academic, his technical development places him within the typical progression of contemporary verse. It will become clear that, at the same time and for all his technical evolution, his more or less continuous thematic commitment to accurate, affirming resistance to the chaos of self and world rather than immersed acceptance of it places him directly in the line of the academic poets and their modern ancestors.

Love Letter from an Impossible Land

Love Letter from an Impossible Land (1944) was published when William Meredith was twenty-five. A few of its poems were composed while he was still an undergraduate. Not surprisingly, much of the book is imitative, written, as Meredith himself would later say, in a "borrowed rhetoric."[1] In spite of this, ***Love Letter from an Impossible Land*** indicates what will become Meredith's continuing and developing themes and techniques.

When the book appeared, a volume in Yale University's prestigious series for younger poets, it was introduced by the poet Archibald MacLeish, dedicated to Princeton professor Christian Gauss and his wife, and bore on its title page the military rank of its author. As Richard Howard has pointed out, this extraordinary series of institutional signs is reflected in the institutional forms of the poems:[2] many sonnets and near sonnets, "strict songs," quatrains, even variations of the highly artificial French rondeau. These rigorous forms give the volume the appearance of consistency; however, that appearance is somewhat illusory. Even the commitment to traditional forms is less complete than it seems. In fact, it is possible to break the poems of ***Love Letter from an Impossible Land*** almost cleanly into two groups.

The poems of the first group (mostly early ones) are those marked by the self-conscious literary imitation noted above. The literature they imitate is very much that sanctioned by the academic establishment. Echoes of George Herbert, Allen Tate, Auden, the later Yeats, and other seventeenth- and twentieth-century metaphysical poets are everywhere in them (although there are interesting exceptions, hints of Arnold and Tennyson, for instance). At any rate, here is Meredith straining after Yeats (while imitating Herbert): "Only an outward-aching soul / Can hold in high disdain these ties" (**"Airman's Virtue"**). Impressive, no doubt, but in someone else's voice. Here is Meredith in an Auden mode:

> Sir, today is vouched for, and what is owing
> Will be paid, all that long borrowing;
> Let the day's portents and its tedious sad history
> Prompt the guarantors to no defection.[3]

The sonnet-like poem ends with these lines: "Doubting as children, they were healed at a terrible spa, / And now are eager to speak for the least stammerer," echoing Auden's own sonnet-like "Petition." Beyond such specific imitations, and there are more of them, the poems of this type are also often marked by more general and equally self-conscious adherence to other characteristics of what was becoming the academic style: allusiveness, impersonality, and intellectual contortion.

The allusiveness is self-evident. Impersonality in these poems takes the form not so much of invented, identifiable personae (such as, for instance, the speaker of T. S. Eliot's "The Love Song of J. Alfred Prufrock") as of a disembodied, unlocatable voice. Listen to the distance and indirection of the speaker of this poem:

> Who comes upon one standing in a door,
> That with a sigh tries different sorrows on,
> Thinking how best to speed a lover gone,
> Whether this leave or that becomes her more,
> Knowing him there beside her all the while;
> Or who hears lovers worry of the dawn
> Before the white of evening quite has worn
> And they not knowing dawn, and sees them smile;
> Let him not presume what thing it was
> He saw enacted in a smile or sigh
> Till he pass and the door be shut and the day be high
> And the lover wonders how his lover does.
> With such confused denouement the play ends
> That none but the spectator comprehends.
>
> (13)

Intellectual difficulty, or, rather, the appearance of it, in this volume is more often the result of syntactical contortion than of real complexity. Note, for instance, how a fairly accessible statement about desire and remorse is made momentarily puzzling by its twisted, condensed construction:

> Do not say to the gay game nay now lover
> Under cover of love enough; does puritan twinge
> Predict, against respite from passion, real change?
> No, we shall want again later and greatly all over.
>
> (19)

But it is pointless to criticize the apprentice work of a young poet imitating the received masters of his time as he learns his craft. In their proper context these poems are impressive for the skills they frequently display and, even more so, for the developments in formal, technical, and syntactical expertise they promise. They are failures not of the academic mode itself but of their own rather artificial and forced handling of its methods.

However, ***Love Letter from an Impossible Land*** also contains poems of a second type, poems more personal in voice, more colloquial in language, more straightforward in feeling, and somewhat more open in form. The orders they achieve are often convincingly earned against real threats. The last point is essential. Poems of both types are concerned with intellectual and imaginative acts of ordering; indeed, almost all of Meredith's poems are so concerned. However, while those acts in the earlier poems of ***Love Letter from an Impossible Land*** are often programmed, predictable, even smug (note, for instance, the tendency to the imperative mode), in the later poems they are often dramatic, surprising, and moving. The key to these changes seems to be Meredith's war experience. He has indirectly suggested this himself: "During the War, . . . I found myself relying on my writing to make sense of an experience and a world for which nothing in a protected and rather unobservant childhood had prepared me."[4] It may be unfair to Meredith's candor, but it is difficult not to see the earlier poems of ***Love Letter from an Impossible Land*** as issuing from protected unobservance and the later ones as gaining power from the war's challenge to what seems to have been a comfortably habitual orderliness. Perhaps Meredith needed an impossible land to challenge such habits.

Before we look at these more successful poems, however, a word about the general nature of Meredith's war poems. Although among the best to have emerged from World War II and clearly alert to war's horrors of waste and destruction, they are basically poems of duty, accepting the necessity and legitimacy of the war that is their context. As Meredith has said, "World War II was very much more plausible than any violence that the nation has been involved with since."[5] Aptly describe by Richard Howard as constituting "a lamentable genre but a real distinction," Meredith's war poems are not protest poems. Rather, they are poems that record, complain of, and then struggle to comprehend and accept the complexities of human nature, the facts of life and death.

One of the best in ***Love Letter from an Impossible Land*** is **"Notes for an Elegy,"** where the very title indicates a sense of the provisional, a lack of assurance about the efficacy of restorative institutions in the face of destruction and death. This perception is far from the comfortable stances of the earlier poems. In irregular meter and unrhymed stanzas **"Notes for an Elegy"** questions the comforting claims of pastoral elegy as it describes the death of an airman, wrecked on a training flight. With the shared fatalism of a committed fellow pilot, the speaker insists on the necessary calculus of such a death ("in practice the martyrdom has been quiet, statistical, / A fair price. This is what airmen believe"). At the same time, though, and in the same direct, factual language, he expresses a feeling that moots such mathematics:

> Note that he had not fought one public battle,
> Met any fascist with his skill, but died
> As it were in bed, the waste conspicuous;
> This is a costly wreck and costly to happen on.
>
> (36)

With faith and feeling present and not opposed, the poem proceeds to a richly inconclusive conclusion, one filled with duty and desperation: "The morning came up foolish with pink clouds / To say that God counts ours a cunning time, / Our losses part of an old secret, somehow no loss." Thus, we are left with neither easy comfort nor easy cynicism. Is the "cunning" that of skillful knowledge or knowing deceit? Does God count "our losses" "no loss" because they are a meaningless irrelevance or because they have a real, if mysteriously secret, value? In this more personal, more organic poem, with its more natural and colloquial expression and its replacement of literary allusiveness with reference to a local time and place, the possibilities are left open. In it, there is a skeptical hope for order and affirmation that fully recognizes the threats of chaos and despair.

The volume's title poem also demonstrates gains in force, feeling, and depth of conviction stemming from the war poems' shifts in modes of expression. In epistolary direct address and an easily moving blank verse **"Love Letter from an Impossible Land"** describes the islands where Meredith is stationed:

> All the charts and history you can muster
> Will not make them real as fog is real
> Or crystal as a certain hour is clear
> If you can wait.
> Write to me often, darling.
>
> (38)

In the way that final, subjectively imperative request, triggered by the idea of waiting, interrupts the objective description there is a strenuous expression of loneliness and desire. Similarly, these lines break into a catalog of pictorial detail: "Now I am convinced there is nothing to fear, / Now on these islands you are all I want." As do these, from near the poem's end: "We lie in khaki rows, no two alike, / Needing to be called by name / And saying women's names." The entire piece creates an impressive balancing of the contrasting emotions generated by war's dangers, duty's demands, and love's needs, by the conflicting claims of the tempting beauties of the alien landscape and the familiar and unaltering attractions of home.

Another of this first book's fine later poems, **"June: Dutch Harbor,"** is also set in the Aleutians of Meredith's war experience. Like **"Notes for an Elegy"** and **"Love Letter from an Impossible Land,"** it is unrhymed, colloquial, metrically and stanzaically irregular, and personal in subject and voice. Like the latter, it begins with an active and detailed description that defines place:

> In June, which is still June here, but once removed
> From other Junes, chill beardless high-voiced cousin
> season,
> The turf slides grow to an emerald green.
> There between the white-and-black of the snow and
> ash,
> Between the weak blue of the rare sky
> Or the milkwhite languid gestures of the fog,
> And the all-the-time wicked terminal sea.
>
> (41)

The island chain is a magical kingdom where the lush flowers have little regard for "precedent" ("Violets the size of pansies"). Yet if the whole chain is a bird sanctuary, it is also a military reservation where the flying is, ironically, not safe but dangerous ("above the always-griping sea / That bitches at the bitter rock the mountains throw to it"), and done only "with the permission—subject always to revoke—/ Of the proper authorities," naval and otherwise. Were it not for such facts, the life of the pilots in this miraculous land might make a beautiful, heroic myth; however, the facts will not be stilled. In lines that might be as much about poetry as flying, and that teresely suggest what separates these war poems from the earlier weak and artificial imitations, Meredith expresses a sense of order at once profoundly threatened and precariously possessed: "Even without flaps there is a safe minimum; / Below that the bottom is likely to drop out." From this colloquial recognition the poem proceeds to an ambiguous statement of affirmation and doubt: "Some of the soldiers pressed flowers in June, indicating faith, / The one who knew all about birds spun in that month. / It is hard to keep your mind on war, with all that green." Is faith rewarded or mocked, real or illusion? Did the one who knew about birds spin a mythic tale of optimistic augury or did his plane spin out and crash when his attention lapsed or shifted? Is the cyclical green of spring in even so bleak a land a sign of hope against the momentary fact of war, or a trick that distracts us from the proper concerns of the moment or from the memory of those who died in a noble cause? The answer to all these is something like a yes, a yes that adumbrates the complexities of the speaker's deeply thought and felt position.

The best poems in ***Love Letter from an Impossible Land*** are, then, stylistically quite different from the less effective earlier ones: more personal in subject and voice, more organic in meter and form, and more colloquial in diction and syntax. At the same time, though, their less complex forms embody a more complex, and so more convincing, intellectual and emotional commemoration. Indeed, their surface accessibility is the very sign of their depth. Thus, it would be an oversimplification to see all the gains of the later poems as coming from an abandonment of the earlier ones' formal and impersonal proclivities. In fact, many war poems, like the sonnet **"In Memoriam Stratton Christensen,"** successfully retain traditional forms and impersonal voices:

> Laughing young man and fiercest against sham,
> Then you have stayed at sea, at feckless sea,
> With a single angry curiosity
> Savoring fear and faith and speckled foam?
> A salt end to what was sweet begun:
> Twenty-three years and your integrity
> And already a certain number touched like me
> With a humor and a hardness from the sun.
> Without laughter we have spent your wit
> In an unwitnessed fight at sea, perhaps not won,
> And whether wisely we shall never know;
> But like Milton's friend's, to them that hear of it,
> Your death is a puzzler that will tease them on
> Reckless out on the thin, important floe.
>
> (45)

Hear, for example, how "Reckless" in the last line echoes the sounds of "feckless" and "speckled" in lines two and four, as Henry Taylor has pointed out,[6] and note how its reckless-wreckless pun picks up and extends the complexities of tone elsewhere in it, creating at once a complaint and a memorializing justification—as the reference to Milton's "Lycidas" suggests, although the comfort here is far less institutional and sure. Whether the officer's death has meaning and, if so, of what sort, remains mysterious (he was lost "In an unwitnessed fight at sea, perhaps not won, / And whether wisely we shall never know"). Yet that very mystery, at root, the question of meaning itself, is what keeps his death "important," what keeps.

Clearly, the gains in skill and power displayed by Meredith's war poems derive as much from his mastering the traditions which had earlier mastered him as from his rejection of the academic style. What really strengthens these poems is their newfound inclusiveness in technique as well as content (note, for instance, the combination of the sonnet form with colloquial and openly emotional diction in **"Ten-Day Leave"**). This inclusiveness is born of the presence of, and the poet's response to, real threats to customary models of meaning and order. Even so, it is tempting to see the at least partial shift in modes from the earlier to the later poems of ***Love Letter from an Impossible Land*** as an early example of the shifts from academic to experimental poetry characteristic of contemporary verse. In fact, one reviewer has suggested that Meredith wrote in the 1940s the way most poets would in the 1970s.[7] Such hyperbole aside, had Meredith's next book continued in the direction indicated by some of the war poems, the temptation to endorse the hypothesis might be irresistible. However, this is not the case.

Ships and Other Figures

Ships and Other Figures was published for the Princeton University Library by the Princeton University Press in 1948. By and large, its poems retreat from the freedoms gained by the war poems' openings of self, language, and form, and by their attractive weakening of self-satisfied confidence in the powers of order and good. The poems of ***Ships and Other Figures*** are generally more like the worst than the best poems of ***Love Letter from an Impossible Land.*** In spite of the "assorted Audenries" Dudley Fitts has pointed out,[8] they are somewhat less obviously imitative than previous ones. However, to an even greater degree than the earlier volume, this one is marked by studied scholarship and the use of elaborate forms and types: sonnets, quatrains, dedicatory poems, a gift poem, a wedding poem, an *ubi sunt,* an envoi, even a heroic simile. As such a list suggests, most of the poems imply confident belief in the powers of tradition, language, imagination, and mind to order and affirm the self and the world. Unfortunately, though, the poems too rarely test or demonstrate the beliefs they depend on or the claims they make. Thus, they are often merely assertive, glib, and smugly predictable, despite certain undeniable skills and intelligence. The too-assured tone is underlined by four pages of often unnecessary and condescending explanatory notes.[9] Even the many poems based in war experience which are carried over to this postwar book usually lack the forceful truths of the earlier war poems. In fact, it is difficult to resist the thought that, at this stage, Meredith requires the fairly immediate presence of evil, of violence, of some real threat if his powerful ordering consciousness is not to level all to a dull and mild neatness.

For example, the balanced octaves of **"Middle Flight,"** with their implied inversion of Milton's grander intentions ("Heavenly Muse . . . I thence / Invoke thy aid to my adventurous song / That with no middle flight intends to soar," *Paradise Lost,* I, ll. 6, 13-14), state and then all too easily escape a threat to the self:

> The loneliest place I know of nowadays
> Is a cumulo-nimbus cloud I seem to find
> As often as I fly; I went there first
> When the sky and a war were new, but memories now
> Are as heavy in its belly as a squall.
> It is a tall cloud, something gathered at the tops
> But opening to imprecision, at the base to rain,
> And the hope that it held five years ago is spilt.
> But what I mean to say about the cloud
> And its forlorn vicinity where gather
> Vapors of doubt that not our lonely day
> Shall see precipitate, is that even here
> Nobody goes alone who knows so much
> As one human love; so much I know,
> Whence hope, if any, in the covered sky,
> Choir in this uncompanionable air.
>
> (10)

The threat seems present here only to provide occasion for the affirming assertion of the saving power of human love and hope (and assertion is all it is; there is no working out, no demonstration or dramatization). This weakness is most revealed by the first, fourth, and fifth lines of the second stanza—"But what I mean to say about the cloud . . . is that even here / Nobody goes alone." The comfort offered is not in question here. What is, to repeat, is the impression created that pain was invoked solely to allow the offering of such comfort, a preconceived one at that. It this is unfair to the experiencing man behind the poem, it is not unfair to the poem. Even the penultimate line's qualifying "hope, if any," seems more compulsory than menacing. And the tendency of the poem's entire movement to recall Matthew Arnold's "Dover Beach" serves only to expose by contrast its own relative artificiality. Related flaws make many poems in ***Ships and Other Figures*** unconvincing. Several other poems, however, are quite successful. The descriptions of Navy ships are often powerful. **"Carrier,"** for instance, moves at the majestic pace of the craft it describes, creating a personification which conveys the carrier pilot's care for the caring mother ship. The precise languages of fact and strategy preserve it from false feeling. The sonnet concludes:

> The planes rise heavy from her whining deck.
> Then the bomb's luck, the gun's poise and chattering,
> The far-off dying, are her near affair;
> With her sprung creatures become weak or strong
> She watches them down the sky and disappear,
> Heart gone, sea-bound, committed all to air.
>
> (2)

Another success, **"Homeric Simile,"** makes convincing contemporary use of the unusually elaborate and extended comparison its title defines as it argues the merits of form in bringing even the most complex experiences to moments of miraculous clarity. The terms of the comparison are, of all things, a bombing raid and a string quartet, each with its moments of certainty, confusion, further certainty, confusion more disturbing still, and so on to eventual resolution. The raid is detailed at length. Troubled by cloud cover but confident of the mental and mechanical assurances of reckoning, the crew of a "heavy bomber" flies an unknown track. Their certainties of navigation are qualified by larger doubts about nations and war, about friends and foes. Then, suddenly, the clouds break; the crew finds itself sure again, in proper formation and over the target. Out of this mix of feeling and the chaos of enemy searchlights and flak comes a "penetration of the overcast": a moment when the jewelled pattern of the target town, the "lazy tracers," the certainties and doubts, the dropped bombs, even dying friends—all the complex, conflicting details of the scene—come clear and whole; they contain confusion yet are somehow unconfused. The poem then shifts to the simile's other, briefer term:

> Not otherwise the closing notes disclose,
> As the calm, intelligent strings do their duty,
> The hard objective of a quartet, reached
> After uncertain passage, through form observed,
> And at a risk no particle diminished.
>
> (19)

Like the crew on the bombing run, the quartet achieves its final clarification by accepting both dangerous uncertainty and certain form. Both clarifications contain rather than evade or ignore all that resists them. Made convincing by its detailed use of precise, dramatic language, this whole strange, metaphysical enterprise, comparing war and music, becomes an example of what it describes, of the enigmatic, inclusive ordering of the apparently antithetical.

Another convincing poem in ***Ships and Other Figures*** is **"Do Not Embrace Your Mind's New Negro Friend,"** a still pertinent critique of too-comfortable liberalism, and a similar conflation of the personal and political informs the otherwise very different **"A Figure from Politics."** Its wry wit is a minor delight:

> The gigantic sweet conspiracy of lovers
> Who had once thought to take over everything
> Will now, I am convinced, come to nothing:
> Right about race and Russia, we were wrong
> When it came to local affairs touching each other.
>
> (5)

The slightly acrid, self-deprecating humor that fuels this poem is one of the positive developments of the volume. It suggests one way in which a tendency to too-easy orders and affirmations might be resisted and even made dramatic. Although not so successfully as in **"A Figure from Politics,"** this device also appears in **"Envoi," "Dedicatory Poem," "Blues,"** and **"Two Figures from the Movies."**

The most obvious and important development of ***Ships and Other Figures*** is a related, although in some ways slight and incomplete one. Several poems indicate an awakening sense of the dangers of too much order, too much reason, too easy affirmation. **"Homeric Simile,"** for instance, returns to the complex containments of poems like **"Notes for an Elegy," "Love Letter from an Impossible Land,"** and **"June: Dutch Harbor."** In comparing the relatively exotic military dangers of a bombing raid with the relatively domestic risks of the string quarter, it begins to point toward the realization that there are powerful threats to order even in the ordinary. A similar sense of the ordinary's resistance to form appears in **"Dedicatory Poem."** In both poems the speaker is confident that clarity can be disclosed "through form observed. / And at a risk no particle diminished." However, it is not too long a step from there to the realization that such confidence can itself become a danger. Oddly enough, the clearest indication of this new direction in Meredith's work appears in the Chaucerian **"Envoi"** that opens the book:

> Go, little book. If anybody asks
> Why I add poems to a time like this,
> Tell how the comeliness I can't take in
> Of ships and other figures of content
> Compels me still until I give them names;
> And how I give them names impatiently,
> As who should pull up roses by the roots
> That keep him turning on his empty bed,
> The smell intolerable and thick with loss.
>
> (1)

These last images powerfully figure forth the orderly poet's destructive tendency to violently force the world, to falsify it in order to make it fit his own desired pattern.

Taken alone, such examples exaggerate the intensity of the glimmer of recognition in ***Ships and Other Figures*** that the drive to order itself might become a threat to sense. There are never more than indications here. And however much what they point to will eventually focus his art, this second volume is largely a backward step in Meredith's progress as a poet. The next is his breakthrough book.

The Open Sea and Other Poems

Love Letter from an Impossible Land and ***Ships and Other Figures*** appeared within four years; it was to be ten years before Alfred A. Knopf published Meredith's third collection in 1958. Like its predecessors, ***The Open Sea and Other Poems*** has pieces that are badly flawed. The ambiguities of the dedicatory poem to Donald Stauffer ("indiscriminate delight," "he could write / Commonplace books") might easily tumble into insult. The attack on Ginsberg and the Beats in **"To a Western Bard Still a Whoop and a Holler Away from English Poetry"** has its points but is narrow and more than a little self-congratulatory. **"The Alchemist"** pays tribute to Robert Frost, but suffers from sentimentality ("Laughter and tears / Can set a man apart"). **"The Rainy Season,"** along with a few other poems, has the sound of meditative seriousness, but descends to something like cuteness:

Like the reproof of that singular good man,
Unknown to you, to whom you are unknown,
Told at some length by strangers while you nod;
And not unlike the signs in rainy bars
That read themselves at the poor edge of sleep:
The lie too complicated to refute:
If you're so damn smart, why aren't you rich?

(28)

Such failures, however, are relatively rare in this volume, and most of them result from the same efforts at conversational directness and complex inclusiveness that produce its finest poems.

As Meredith's "breakthrough volume," ***The Open Sea*** breaks through on three related fronts. The first is formal. Meredith continues to enact the rage for order by which he is so often both inspired and ensnared. He extends and intensifies the formal proclivities of his earlier books, opening this one with, in sequence, a villanelle, a poem employing aspects of both villanelle and *terza rima,* a sonnet, and a sestina. And there are sonnets, quatrains, and many other, less traditional patterns throughout. However, while in the earlier books the most formal poems were often the most self-congratulatory, contrived, and unconvincing, formal control in ***The Open Sea*** is wedded to formal experiment and to a more openly meditative voice which speaks with a conversational, even colloquial, ease to produce natural and compelling art. With the less successful earlier poems in mind, look at **"Sonnet on Rare Animals":**

Like deer *rat-tat* before we reach the clearing
I frighten what I brought you out to see,
Telling you who are tired by now of hearing
How there are five, how they take no fright of me.
I tried to point out fins inside the reef
Where the coral reef had turned the water dark;
The bathers kept the beach in half-belief
But would not swim and could not see the shark.
I have alarmed on your behalf and others'
Sauntering things galore.
It is this way with verse and animals
And love, that when you point you lose them all.
Startled or on a signal, what is rare
Is off before you have it anywhere.

(3)

Although one might do better to take the poem's advice and constrain the compulsion to point, note how the sonnet's three quatrains and couplet echo in their own openings and closings the drama of possession and escape that their words describe. Related points might be made about the tensions created in the poem by its delicate hovering between Elizabethan and Italian sonnet forms, by its alternation of nearly enjambed and end-stopped lines, and by its metrical variations.

Poem after poem in this volume demonstrates an achieved grace far from the often clotted clumsiness of earlier formal efforts. Here are the opening lines of ***The Open Sea***'s title poem:

We say the sea is lonely; better say
Ourselves are lonesome creatures whom the sea
Gives neither yes nor no for company.

(2)

Such examples could easily be multiplied.

In addition to the gains in conversational ease in the formal poems of ***The Open Sea,*** there is a parallel gain in accessibility that removes these poems from the metaphysical contrivances of Meredith's earliest work. And it is not an accessibility purchased with the surrender of complexity. In fact, at their best these poems replace what was often merely syntactical intricacy with real knots of thought and feeling, and present them with brilliant clarity. Consider **"The Illiterate,"** a Petrarchan sonnet using repeated end words in place of rhyme, yet employing its virtuosity in the service of mysterious clearness:

Touching your goodness, I am like a man
Who turns a letter over in his hand
And you might think this was because the hand
Was unfamiliar but, truth is, the man
Has never had a letter from anyone;
And now he is both afraid of what it means
And ashamed because he has no other means
To find out what it says than to ask someone.
His uncle could have left the farm to him,
Or his parents died before he sent them word,
Or the dark girl changed and want him for beloved.
Afraid and letter-proud, he keeps it with him.
What would you call his feeling for the words
That keep him rich and orphaned and beloved?

(10)

Once it is noted that the entire narrative of potential knowing, losing, and having is a simile for the speaker's astonishment before the qualities of a friend, relation, or lover, its details fall into place with natural, if complicated, ease. Again, examples could be multiplied but further quotation and discussion from other angles will give sufficient evidence.

A second breakthrough in ***The Open Sea*** is thematic. In the earlier volumes the existence and efficacy of meaning, value, and order were often simply assumed; their presence was often glibly evoked. Here, however, these existences and efficacies are less certain; the human need to constantly discover, invent, and establish order against all that threatens to dissolve it becomes a more dramatic theme, in Richard Howard's descriptive phrase, "an ethical force," especially in the book's many poems about art and art objects: architecture, painting, sculpture, music, *kabuki* theater, even topiary gardening. A single example will do. The splendidly realized sestina **"Notre Dame de Chartres"** is based on the story of the building of the present great basilica after the destruction by fire of the original church in the late twelfth century. The first structure had housed a tunic supposedly worn by the Virgin at the birth of Christ, one of the major relics of medieval Christianity. When the church, and the town around it, burned to the ground, the *sancta camisa,* the "blessed shirt," was not consumed. These "miracles" were taken, respectively, as signs of dissatisfaction and continuing grace. In response, Notre Dame de Chartres was built to more fittingly enshrine the sacred tunic, which "spoke to the stone that slept in the groin of France," as the poem puts it in a fine image of spiritual and architectural engendering.

Such a tale may seem a curious way to talk about man's continuing need for meaning and order; its construal of miracle is apt to strike our largely secular time as naive, as, more than a little ruefully, the poem acknowledges. At the same time, though, it insists that if our ways of understanding destruction and salvation and of paying appeasement and thanks have changed, our impulses have not: "This is our miracle: the faith that burned / Bright and erroneous, and built that house." The word "erroneous" should be stressed. The realization that all systems for wrestling shape from chaos are threatened by being necessarily relative and wrong is the sign of what renders the searchings for order and affirmation in ***The Open Sea***—whether they succeed or fail—tentative, doubtful, and courageous.

"Notre Dame de Chartres," like many other poems in ***The Open Sea,*** admires, describes, and is committed to the creation and affirmation of artistic order, but also recognizes and includes much that resists it. This leads to consideration of the third breakthrough of ***The Open Sea,*** one which extends the hints in ***Ships and Other Figures*** of a recognition of the dangers of too much order, reason, and mild-mannered good sense. Meredith's statement that in World War II he found himself depending on his writing "to make sense of an experience and world" for which he was unprepared, and his parallel remark that it was his "two years as a carrier pilot during the Korean war that seemed to give . . . [him] another start as a writer," to initiate the discoveries of his own voice and insights recorded in ***The Open Sea,*** have already been quoted. Moreover, it was earlier suggested that Meredith's powerful ordering consciousness seems to require the resisting presence of real threat to prevent it from a leveling dullness. But if one is not to recommend lifelong warfare as a necessary condition for poetry, it seems fair to say that Meredith would have to begin to locate threats to the rationally controlled in a more ordinary, domestic world, and in himself. Of course, this is a critical rather than biographical formulation. At any rate, throughout ***The Open Sea*** (which, by the way, with the only partial exception of **"Battle Problem,"** has no war poems) precisely such acts of location occur.

In the iambic trimeter and *ababcdcd* (and so on) rhyme scheme of Yeats's "The Fisherman," Meredith's **"The Chinese Banyan"** tells the story of a calm man's heart attack and explores the extremes of power and pain in even the most ordinary things:

> There is no end to the
> Deception of quiet things
> And of quiet, everyday
> People.
>
> (26)

And later: "I speak of the unremarked / Forces that split the heart." It ends with application of this domestic lesson to speaker and reader:

> this dark capacity
> Of quiet looses a fear
> That runs by analogy
> On your page, in your house, for your dear.
>
> (27)

Personal fear of death appears in several poems, the deaths of loved ones in others. **"Bachelor"** humorously depicts the desperations bubbling beneath the most quotidian exteriors. However, the most impressive discovery of resistances to order close to home in ***The Open Sea*** is, paradoxically enough, in a poem titled **"An Account of a Visit to Hawaii."** In a nearly allegorical discussion of landscape, history, and climate Meredith demonstrates the forces of destruction and loss that underlie even the paradisal surfaces of a tropical but not too tropical island. He thereby turns to account the very mildness that often weakened his work, converting it to the kind of threat his ordering acts require to give them weight. This is the crucial passage:

> Mildness can enervate as well as heat.
> The soul must labor to reach paradise.
> Many are here detained in partial grace
> Or partial penalty, for want of force.
>
> (19)

Such precise locations of purgatorial dangers within the self and a domesticated world serve Meredith well in the poems of ***The Open Sea*** and in his later volumes.

Related to Meredith's discovery of resistances to reason within the ordinary is a new willingness to entertain the claims of the non-rational. This development is far from complete in ***The Open Sea,*** but two poems begin to indicate the shapes it will take. **"On Falling Asleep by Firelight"** occurs at the edge of consciousness. As the epigraph from Isaiah indicates, the poem describes a dream of the earthly paradise, a visionary Eden where the threatening alienness of beasts and of other men is replaced by a natural kindness, kinship, and sympathy that erases evil, otherness, and guilt. The poem insists that only by putting aside our experienced rational awareness of "ravening" and "guile" can we imagine such desirable perfection. At the same time, however, it also insists on the limitations of dreams. They strike us "dumb": speechless and, perhaps, stupid as well. They are only dreams ("We *dream* there is no ravening or guile," my italics). This qualified attention to the non-rational is condensed in the poem's last lines: "the heat / Turns softly on the hearth into that dust / Isaiah said would be the serpent's meat." Is this apparent interpenetration of the real fire and the vision a sign that the dream is coming true? Or is the dust of idle dreams what feeds the snake of evil, and the coming cold what wakes us again to fact? The poem is in delicate balance, but it does not, as Meredith's earlier poems would have done, wholly undercut the dream with reason. In fact, it even implies that reason itself is not enough and that the perfectly ordered world that reason (and, intriguingly here, imagination too) desires, even demands, is itself a visionary dream.

The claims of the non-rational are entertained in a very different way in another poem in ***The Open Sea,*** **"A View of the Brooklyn Bridge."** Writing about this poem in William Heyen's *American Poets in 1976,* Meredith describes it as a revelation which imprinted itself upon him: "I think all the poems I had written before this were primarily rational attempts to word accurately something I thought I understood. This poem . . . [and, he adds, to a lesser extent the earlier **"Love Letter from an Impossible Land"**] were irrational acts of surrender to an experience I knew very little about but which I had a sudden sense was being offered to me."[10] This is a precise description of the technical and thematic territories Meredith's poetry has so far contained and of those it now reaches out to include. Most of the poems before ***The Open Sea,*** and many in it, attempt to word accurately something fully grasped in rational form, formal language, and an impersonal voice. This commitment to reason and order persists. However, a very few earlier poems, a few more in ***The Open Sea,*** and still more in later volumes, move toward more open forms, more conversational and colloquial language, and more personal voices. They give increased attention to the less than wholly grasped, to the nonrational, the disorderly, the provisional and mysterious. Of these, **"A View of the Brooklyn Bridge"** is an example.

So far in discussing ***The Open Sea*** rather abstract categories have been used to examine Meredith's growth in it. This method is useful but also somewhat falsifying, for many poems in ***The Open Sea*** embody concurrently several of the developments separately discussed. Because of this, because ***The Open Sea*** is crucial as the volume in which Meredith discovers his characteristic voice, and because so many of its poems are so good, let us turn from categorizing and cataloging to glance at a few more of its best poems.

As noted above, several poems in ***The Open Sea*** explore the orderings of art. One of these, **"Rus in Urbe"** (the country in the city), describes a fourth-floor urban garden (containing an espaliered pear tree and a topiary yew) in order to consider the opposed claims of naturalness and artifice. The result is balance: art is lovely but often elitist and useless; for some it is what saves. The equilibrium is perfectly supported by the poem's irregular and subtly assertive placing of rhymes and by its skillful iambic variations. The related **"A Korean Woman Seated by a Wall"** is a more subtle consideration of the powers and limits of art to shape and redeem. Observing the woman of the title, the speaker invents a lovely and convincing tale to explain the suffering on the "alien and untranslatable" mask of her face. However, under the pressure of her actual presence his story and its assumptions and presumptions are shattered. Again, art's power to clarify life is asserted and qualified to produce rich truth.

Others of ***The Open Sea***'s best poems are united by imagery and metaphor rather than theme. Several continue to tap two of Meredith's richest sources of these, the sea and trees,[11] the former most impressively in the title poem. **"The Open Sea"** is a many-toned assertion of the sea's blank indifference, the reality behind our sayings, fancies, and poems about it: "The sea gives neither yes nor no for company." The speaker's response comes in the final stanza, its "not yet" and "nor yet" marking his combined resistance and recognition: "Although not yet a man given to prayer, I pray / For each creature lost since the start at sea, / And give thanks that it was not I, not yet one close to me."

Trees play a larger role in this book. In addition to pertinent poems already discussed, three more are especially fine. **"The Deciduous Trees"** presents an analogy of trees and men, of the stressed and tensioned forms they make to resist and outlast their bitter season. **"A Botanical Trope,"** like **"On Falling Asleep by Firelight,"** inverts the tendency of several poems here to expose the sentimentality of human impositions of subjective form and meaning on the world, emphasizing instead metaphor's real because properly qualified truth. Perhaps the best "tree poem" in ***The Open Sea,*** though, and one of the best poems in the book, is Meredith's inverted anti-pastoral elegy for his mother, **"In Memoriam N.K.M. (1889-1947)."** The sonnet does not complain that nature fails to reflect her death. Rather, it mourns that she did not, could not, in her dying, reflect the glory of sunset or the autumnal brightness of the trees, perhaps because her going is more "final" than such departures. The poem deserves quotation in full:

> As the day takes color twice, so youth and age
> Should glow remarkably. Or, like a maple's
> I wish her fall had been (whose quaint April
> Is still in blossom on the album's pages)
> Splendid and red, which was a sere, gray loss.
> Like a round maple, if that could just have been,
> Whose virtuous green summer went unseen
> In a mild chemistry, but at first frost
> Who stuck across herself and her slight hill
> Patterns no elm would dream of, crooked and true
> Like the serene old trees on a chinese scroll:
> This is a thing I have seen maples do.
> The sun and trees glowed fiercely at the season
> When she wandered listless forth bereft of reason.
>
> (31)

The many poems of ***The Open Sea*** examined here display increased ease of form and diction, more personal voices and contexts, and greater access combined with greater complexity. In them, the urges for order and affirmation are balanced and contained by an increasing inclusion of all that defies those urges and obstructs their satisfaction. As Richard Howard suggests, these are poems that question form, yet abide its necessity.[12] These characteristics deepen in Meredith's next volume.

The Wreck of the Thresher and Other Poems

William Meredith's fourth book, ***The Wreck of the Thresher and Other Poems,*** both consolidates and consummates previous advances, but it also moves off in new directions. In the years between ***The Open Sea*** and ***The Wreck of the Thresher*** (1964) Meredith became friendly with Robert Frost and John Berryman and translated the poems of Apollinaire. Meredith himself has spoken of Frost's influence. Asked by interviewer Gregory FitzGerald if he felt that Frost had "any effect" on his work, Meredith replied: "I think he has in making me, in my own way, strive for the kind of colloquial language that distinguishes his poems. I see a decline in the borrowed rhetoric of my first book, and gradually my poems begin to sound more and more like me. . . . I learned that from his poems. The other thing my poems aspire to do that his do is to keep a sense of humor always at the corner of the picture." Earlier in the same interview Meredith noted a more general influence, the instructiveness of Frost's "absolute solidity in the face of the twentieth century."[13] Meredith seems also to have learned something about Frost's cunning genre of the seemingly rambling narrative poem.

The influence of John Berryman is more difficult to place in even such general ways. Certainly their work is dramatically different, Berryman's extreme and pyrotechnic, Meredith's more balanced and calm. Yet, by Meredith's own account, they share an interest in "people in crisis" and a view of them that amounts to a "qualified optimism . . . about crisis as a medium of grace."[14] Meredith also seems to have learned a good deal from Berryman about more open, organic forms ("the sense of individual selection of the form for each poem")[15] and about the possibilities of a poetry that might be personal without being careless and indecorous. His beautiful prose elegy, "In Loving Memory of the Late Author of *The Dream Songs,*" as well as his poems, strongly suggest such connections.

The influence of the Apollinaire translations (five of which appear here in versions slightly different from those in *Alcools*) is in some ways even harder to pinpoint, but Meredith sheds a good deal of light on the matter himself. Commenting on the tendency of many contemporary poets to turn to translation, Meredith has said:

> "It may have to do with our needing to refresh the themes and images of our own poetry at this moment. . . . I translated Guillaume Apollinaire's *Alcools* because those poems not only had an enormous excitement for people of our moment, but they also, I think, were very useful for me. I don't believe any poet gets involved in a translation that doesn't have something to do with where he's going to. . . . Apollinaire's was one of the first really open imaginations in modern poetry, or so I think. And I have one of the up-tightest imaginations in modern poetry, or so I think. So I realized this was an affinity I had found that would be good for me to explore. I wrote some poems when I was working on Apollinaire that started me in a whole new direction."[16]

What is clear from all this is not so much who influenced Meredith to do what in any particular poem, but that Frost, Berryman, and Apollinaire each contributed something to Meredith's own already initiated and continuing development of a poetry more colloquially direct, more formally organic, more personal, more complexly accessible, and in a more relaxed and experimental line.

In spite of these changes, however, and although there are none of the sonnets, sestinas, and villanelles of earlier work in this book, Meredith does not surrender his formal tendencies. An earlier sort of allusiveness returns; references are made to Shelley's *Prometheus Unbound,* to *King Lear* and the *Inferno,* and to the classical myths of Orpheus and of the rape of Philomela by King Tereus. And there is continuing, although more experimental, exploitation of rhyme and, especially effective, of slant rhyme. There are also several poems in a verse form of which Meredith is a master, the quatrain (also, by the way, the favorite form of Frost). Recalling Meredith's statement that his earlier formal poems "were primarily rational attempts to word accurately something I thought I understood," it is not surprising that the most formal poems in this volume are best described as a poetry of statement. In *abab* quatrains, **"Orpheus"** retells the mythical musician's story in "his own" colloquial and energetic voice. As it does so, Orpheus becomes a type of the experienced artist. He has had his gifts from the gods, has won and inexplicably lost the girl, suffered through hell, won the girl back with his art, lost her again, and through it all made a music fabling order out of chaos: "The meaningless ordeals I've tuned to meaning! / The foul caprice I've zithered into just!" For all the idealizations, however, his song remains as aware of limits as of possibilities: "*Lend me Eurydice,* I sing and sing." For a living man, even at best only temporary loans of the ideal are available, no matter how potent his ordering art.

Despite its carefully distanced third-person title, **"For His Father"** makes what seems a quite personal statement—although with undeniable general application—about the conflicts and bittersweet resolutions of relations between father and son. This is not presented as drama. The statement's skeleton is more or less entire in the first of the poem's four envelope (*abba*) quatrains:

> When I was young I looked high and low for a father,
> And what blond sons you must have tried on then!
> But only your blood could give us our two men
> And in the end we settled for one another.
>
> (10)

The remaining stanzas flesh out the skeleton's form, and the poem ends on the expected, but nonetheless impressive note of reconciliation: "You use my eyes at last; I sign your name / Deliberately beneath my life and art." To say that this, like **"Orpheus,"** words accurately something understood implies no slighting of its quality. It does, though, serve to differentiate these poems and others like them from another kind that Meredith is beginning increasingly to write.

The poems of this kind are typically less final, more provisional, and more dramatic in their inclusion of what resists order, praise, and affirmation than Meredith's more statemental poems. Not surprisingly, most of them are in less formal modes. Still, examination of them can begin with one that *is* formal, with the fine quatrains of **"An Assent to Wildflowers."** With rich allusions to *King Lear,* to its complex visions of nature, and especially to Gloucester's seeing blindness, the poem considers the meaning of a large bouquet of black-eyed susans, "staring out of a bronze vase." Plucked by beloved hands, one thing the flowers mean is love, but seen from another angle, they suggest the violence and destruction that calls all love in question. While never denying the darkness of such doubts, the poem includes them in its final affirmation: "I imagine the world, I imagine the world and you in it: / There's flowering, there's a dark question answered yes." These last lines might almost be taken as a motto for the major poems of ***The Wreck of the Thresher.*** In them, as in **"An Assent to Wildflowers,"** the thematic breakthroughts claimed for ***The Open Sea*** are combined. The theme of order as a moral imperative in a less than orderly world, and an often intense awareness of the threat of chaos in the self and its domestic locales, converge in impressive dramas of the ordering consciousness. Order, affirmation, or praise still typically result, but now the results are more fully tested and qualified by their unvanquishable opposites. Unlike **"An Assent to Wildflowers,"** these poems are often open and experimental in form.

"On Falling Asleep to Birdsong" is reminiscent in title and otherwise of the earlier **"On Falling Asleep by Firelight,"** but it is even more willing than that poem to yield, at least temporarily, to the non-rational. As the speaker drifts toward sleep, he hears the native whippoorwill calling, unanswered, in dark woods. The sound creates bleak images of his own loneliness, of his parents' deaths, of his own fears of death. In an attempt to resist such thoughts, he makes a willed effort to dream of more ideal, foreign birds, of nightingales. However, will is undercut by sleep, the subconscious, and—in a stranger sense—the real. The image of nightingales triggers a dream of the story Ovid tells of Philomela (later turned into a nightingale), who was raped and had her tongue torn out by Tereus, and who, much later, took with her sister Procne horrible revenge upon him. The facts of violence, including time's violence, cannot be erased by any act of will. However, when the whippoorwill is heard again, although still unanswered by another bird, its song produces a response quite different than it had before. Given a clue by his dream of Ovid's moral tale, the speaker identifies with the whippoorwill and from its endurance takes courage for endurance of his own. He makes his own fable, inventing out of the whippoorwill's "constant song" the myth that life "indeed is one" and that, like Philomela, we therefore "will prevail." As does Ovid's tale, now also reinterpreted, his own suggests the possibility that order, meaning, and art might outlast destruction, violence, and time. This is no easy solution. The argument has qualifying flaws. It is, after all, only a dream, a fable. Nevertheless, it may be all we have, and it is something:

> I will grow old, as a man
> Will read of a transformation:
> Knowing it is a fable
> Contrived to answer a question
> Answered, if ever, in fables,
> Yet all of a piece and clever
> And at some level, true.
>
> (9)

Although far more colloquially and casually expressed, the threats of **"Roots"** are equally desperate. The affirmation won from them is equally difficult and equally qualified by the very elements of imagination that produce it (and that are now, like reason earlier, a potential source of order in Meredith's work). This extraordinary poem is a long (109-line), somewhat rambling, somewhat Frostian reminiscence of a conversation between the speaker and his elderly rural-suburban neighbor, Mrs. Leamington. The speaker discovers his neighbor struggling with a tree root that has invaded her newly spaded garden, a discovery presented in intentionally exaggerated heroic language, thus setting the stage for the strange piercings of the ordinary that mark the poem:

> Mrs. Leamington stood on a cloud,
> Quarreling with a dragon—it was May,
> When things tend to look allegorical—
> As I drove up the hill that silhouettes
> Her house against the east. In any month
> She's hard to place—scattered and sibylline.
>
> (11)

He joins her attack "like a knight in his good clothes," and they talk meanwhile about the tree root's origin and the new roots (potatoes) she wants to replace it with, all of this in the allegorical and mock-allegorical guise of questing knights taming a bedragoned wasteland to fruitfulness again. Going inside (her house is furnished in antiques; her Mercedes strains like a charger at the door), they continue their talk of roots. However, although the speaker clearly shares her near-obsession with them, Mrs. Leamington does most of the talking (like characters in many of Frost's dramatic narratives). Her conversation wanders: from what her father told her about a tree's roots' mirroring its branchings, to the painter Fragonard whose trees, she says, especially when the pictures are inverted, look like roots: "'Think of the branches tossing in the loam, / Reaching for rays of water, the way leaves / Arrange themselves for sunlight, except lacier,'" to a quotation from Shelley which asserts that there is, in addition to this world, another underground "'where do inhabit / The shadows of all forms that think and live, / Till death unite them and they part no more.'"[17] Eventually, it becomes clear that this apparently rambling discourse is focused for her by thoughts of the roots of her own past and of her coming death, her own return to the ground. She had planned to be cremated, but now wants something deeper and plans to request burial in the small graveyard on her property where some of her "mother's people" are:

'But more and more I think of the beech roots
Holding up stones like blossoms or like nests
Or like the colored stones on a jade tree—
That slope was never cleared, it's mostly stones—
And in the lower branches, a tree-house:
A box in the ground where I meet my own image sleeping,
The soft brown branches raising it aloft—
Except aloft is down or I sleep face down'.

(15)

In this fabulous place of reunion with self and ancestors, her intellectual and imaginative powers fabricate a quirky, personal, mythic heaven, and now her spirited energy lets her return to the real world of the living: "'Well, back to my spuds,' she said. 'Don't you hate that word? / Yet it's good middle English. Stop on your way home. / By then perhaps we'll both have earned a drink.'" If, as the reference to middle English adds to so many others suggesting knightly romance, we see these questers drink from a Holy Grail (compare Frost's "Directive"), the degree to which such an idea in this poem's time and place seems foolish, and the degree to which it convinces us nonetheless are the keys to the balanced affirmation Meredith achieves here. This miracle of the quotidian is called in question by its very miraculousness, and yet in spite of this, indeed because of this, is nevertheless, and somehow, saving.

"An Old Photograph of Strangers" is a relatively short poem that emphasizes the potential and the limits of art—whether photography, a pageant tableau, or poetry—to redeem the darkness of time and of loss. In one sense, the picture fails. Its held order is inevitably blurred: the people are strangers and probably all dead, and there is darkness which the light for the picture could not pierce. In another sense, though, it succeeds. We share its figures' troubled efforts at a lasting shape ("some of their faces are just like faces today"); somehow, across the years, they speak to us. Another example of how held memory might give shape in spite of the threats of time and space is the lovely "His hands, on a trip to Wisconsin," part four of **"Five Accounts of a Monogamous Man."** Lying awake in bed at night "a thousand miles from home," the speaker, perhaps Meredith himself, thinks of loneliness, aging, death, and of his hands that have sometimes countered those threats, whether in taking off from and landing on a carrier's deck, in making poems, or in knowing a woman's body. Nevertheless, the poem does not forget that death eventually prevails. His hands have ahead of them only

some years of roving
Before the white landscape of age checks them,
Your body's disaster, sure to be traced there,
Even so slight a change in a dear shape
Halting them, baffled, lascivious suddenly,
Or folded cold, or feeling your hands folded cold.

(38-39)

This careful balancing of the claims of order and chaos also appears in several less important poems in ***The Wreck of the Thresher.*** For instance, in **"The Ballet"** Meredith explores the capacities and incapacities of art in a parable-like poem reminiscent of Wallace Stevens's "Anecdote of the Jar." In **"About Poetry"** he considers the claims of exclusion and inclusion, of orderly but mild neatness and shaggy but energetic shapelessness. But Meredith's best and most important work on this theme in ***The Wreck of the Thresher*** is the title poem.

"The Wreck of the Thresher" is, in one sense, occasional, an elegy on the deaths of the crewmen crushed and drowned in the 1963 disaster of the submarine *Thresher.* Like many such elegies, however (note, by the way, in the poem's title, echoes of Hopkins's "The Wreck of the Deutschland" and Longfellow's "The Wreck of the Hesperus"), it has a more than occasional context. **"The Wreck of the Thresher"** is also a response to our accident-induced recognition of the limits of our technology—and so of our safety—a recognition that extends even to the "safe technology" of art. In this respect it is Meredith's most profound confrontation and inclusion so far of exotic and domestic, outer and inner threats. The poem opens in the speaker's private world. At dawn, he stares at an estuary of the sea. Although already "curing," it seems rabidly foul. Worse than any sound or sight of the in fact indifferent sea, however, is the nightmare of complicity that woke him and sent him there to mourn. The second stanza is more public; it locates the crew in the shockingly common context of sudden death: "Daily, by unaccountable whim / . . . Men and women break the pledge of breath." This strategy brings no comfort, however, and the personal intrudes again. Like all men, the speaker cannot "be content with the terrible facts," but is "cursed with responsible sleep." He has dreamed that his own acts, or those of some "monstrous" other self, caused the wreck and that he alone was saved. In the third stanza the poem again shifts from a private to a public voice: "The crushing of any ship has always been held / In dread, like a house burned or a great tree felled." The distance thus gained allows the speaker to consider the dead more objectively, to "judge . . . what dark compression / Astonishes them now." Coupled with the responsible and therefore saving nature of dreams, this finally permits him to join public and private voices and to offer his special version of the elegy's typical turn from tragic contemplation to principled consolation:

(Sea-brothers, I lower you the ingenuity of dreams,
Strange lungs and bells to escape in; let me stay aboard last—
We amend our dreams in half-sleep. Then it seems
Easy to talk to the severe dead and explain the past.
Now they are saying, *Do not be ashamed to stay alive,*

You have dreamt nothing that we do not forgive.
And gentlier, *Study something deeper than yourselves,*
As, how the heart, when it turns diver, delves and saves.)

(4)

However, the poem does not end here. Having found a kind of forgiveness, a kind of peace, in the thought that the sorrowing identification with the dead which the elegy enacts is itself potentially saving, the poem turns again, now to the contemplation of a principle far deeper, more constant, and less consoling. Thus, it returns to the theme that roots the entire collection: Meredith continues to affirm the powers of mind, imagination, and art to amend experience and to find in and impose on it order, meaning, and value; he does so while fully recognizing that these powers are willful and wishful, that final mysteries remain beyond their grasp. The last stanza of **"The Wreck of the Thresher"** brilliantly expresses both continuing affirmation and dark recognition. "Whether we give assent to this"—that is, to the poem's discovered and invented consolation, its redemptive order—"or rage"—to violent response to the world as unsalvageable chaos—

Is a question of temperament and does not matter.
Some will has been done past our understanding,
Past our guilt surely, equal to our fears.
Dullards, we are set again to the cryptic blank page
Where the sea schools us with terrible water.
The noise of a boat breaking up and its men is in our ears.
The bottom here is too far down for our sounding;
The ocean was salt before we crawled to tears.

(5)

Against this bleakness all we have is ourselves and "the cryptic blank page," our effort to read (and write—and right) the world, to make something of it in full knowledge of the odds against such making. In the controlled, inclusive language of this major poem Meredith enacts just this saving effort.

It should be clear that **"The Wreck of the Thresher"** and the many other fine poems of Meredith's fourth book place him—despite a few failures—in the ranks of major contemporary poets. Two important developments have, however, been left implicit in the above commentary. First, in several of these poems content and, more pervasively, tone, although hardly confessional, are closer to autobiography than anything since the war poems of ***Love Letter from an Impossible Land*** (see, for instance, **"For His Father," "Roots," "An Old Field Mowed for Appearances' Sake," "For Guillaume Apollinaire,"** and **"Consequences"**). Second, humor increases. Meredith's poems have always had wit, but now that wit (still self-deprecating) more than merely teases the intellect; it amuses, pleases, qualifies, even humanizes (see, for instance, **"Roots," "An Old Field Mowed for Appearances' Sake," "Fables About Error,"** and **"About Poetry"**). Perhaps the best example of these developments working together—although the former is harder to demonstrate in brief—is the sequence **"Five Accounts of a Monogamous Man,"** a poem wryly exploring the wildness struggling to persist in even the most domesticated middle age. Here is a representative section (*"iii: Sometimes he contemplates adultery"*):

I had no insanity to excuse this,
But for a week my heart ran with another love,
Imagined another house, down to its books and bed.
My miserable fluttered heart, you understand, chose this.
Now I am led home—cold, grave,
Contractual as a dog—by my scurrilous head.

(37)

To conclude, ***The Wreck of the Thresher*** consolidates and consummates the breakthroughs of ***The Open Sea,*** extending Meredith's movement toward more open and personal content, themes, forms, and voices, toward increasingly inclusive and qualified affirmations of threatened order. As Peter Davison rightly put it in reviewing the volume, although in ***The Wreck of the Thresher*** Meredith achieves balance, "there is no ease in it."[18]

Earth Walk: New and Selected Poems

Earth Walk, published in 1970, includes fourteen new poems and thirty-nine poems selected from previous books. It is an important volume, both because of what Meredith's own selection from his earlier work can tell us about his growth as a poet and about his sense of that growth, and because several of the new poems make distinguished additions to the body of this work. A close study of his choice is beyond the scope of this book, but a few general remarks are in order. Meredith has been severely selective. Of the thirty-three poems in ***Love Letter from an Impossible Land,*** only six are reprinted here. The same number is retained from the twenty-nine poems of ***Ships and Other Figures.*** The selections from more recent volumes are more generous: of the forty-four poems originally in ***The Open Sea,*** fifteen survive, as do twelve of the twenty-two in ***The Wreck of the Thresher.*** In a foreword to ***Earth Walk*** Meredith comments on the principles governing his choices:

In making this selection from twenty-five years of work I have represented my early books scantily, as I have come to feel they represented me. . . . The poems I've kept from ***Love Letter to an Impossible Land*** and ***Ships and Other Figures*** are not the most promising ones, maybe, but poems that engage mysteries I still pluck at the hems of, poems that are devious in ways I still like better than plainspokenness.

The latter sentence applies to the selections from ***The Open Sea*** and ***The Wreck of the Thresher*** as well. Over and over, the poems reprinted concern Meredith's central theme: the possibility of order and affirmation establishing and maintaining themselves against all that argues chaos and despair.

It should also be noted that, except for changes in the sequences of their original appearances, most of the poems reprinted in ***Earth Walk*** are without revision. More important, the fourteen new poems collected in the first section of ***Earth Walk*** continue the tendencies characteristic of ***The Wreck of the Thresher.*** The complex (sometimes "devious") conversational ease of language toward which Meredith has been moving since ***The Open Sea*** is often achieved. Personal voices and subjects, while still relatively distanced and controlled, continue to appear. There remain poems in tight forms which persist in being "primarily rational attempts to word accurately something . . . understood," while the more open poems are again more apt to explore, and to do so dramatically and provisionally and with less complete *rational* control. Nearly every poem maintains Meredith's long attention to the theme of order and affirmation tested by often domestic but rarely domesticated threat, a threat increasingly, as Meredith enters late middle age, manifested as death.

The statement that the fourteen new poems of ***Earth Walk*** appear in its first section is not quite accurate. One of them, **"Reading My Poems from World War II,"** dated 1969, is used to introduce the section of selected poems. The poem is descriptive ("The ships in these verses course through a blue meadow / like hounds, the oceans appear to be parks"), and its response to what it describes is ambiguous, at once critical and generous. It notes the tendency to mythologize and stylize, to make disaster distant and impersonal enough to seem pretty or natural:

> The seamen and the fliers in these poems
> ride their craft like so many Buffalo Bills.
> It is a pleasure to watch even the clumsy ones
> spinning earthward like sparks, or circling
> like water-bugs on the cold night sea,
> out of control, low in the water,
> or going under the water, bubbling like turtles.
>
> (25)

However, the moral position that informs the war poems, their sense of responsible purpose, their awareness of complicity, and their compassion, is also noted:

> Even transformed into beasts in a stylized chase
> they seem to be hunting more than one another
> as they ride across this tapestry, one of a series.
> Certainly they have been seen by accountable eyes.
> The dwarf's eyes glitter as though in that whole scene
> he saw no one worse than himself, and he prays for us
> all.
>
> (26)

Of the thirteen other new poems in ***Earth Walk,*** four are in strict forms, three of them in quatrains. Of these, two (each rhyming *abab,* each skillfully disposing rhymes both full and slant) are directly concerned with the human effort to give life shape. One of them, **"About Opera,"** considers a highly artificial form of that endeavor. It responds to an implied question: what is it in opera that moves us?; why do we like it? It is not the tunes and certainly not the plots. "An image of articulateness is what it is":

> What dancing is to the slightly spastic way
> Most of us teeter through our bodily life
> Are these measured cries to the clumsy things we say,
> In the heart's duresses, on the heart's behalf.
>
> (14)

The less obviously formal poems of ***Earth Walk*** treat equally familiar subjects. They are formal, if less obviously so, because, while often relatively open in stanza and line and (for the first time in Meredith) without the convention of beginning each line with a capital letter whether or not it begins a sentence, many of them are in equal or nearly equal and sometimes carefully balanced stanzas. Also, many of them, although in relatively unpatterned ways, make use of rhyme, especially for the purposes of closure. At any rate, of these more open poems, one of the best, and one of the most "free," is **"In Memory of Robert Frost."** The poem is occasional, a frankly autobiographical memorializing of a moment when Meredith met, with a story about flying, Frost's demand for "Something you had done too exactly for words, / Maybe, but too exactly to lie about either." The portrait of Frost's complex closeness and distance, his ability to give and demand, his characteristic presence ("Even his smile / He administered with some care, accurately"), is convincingly evoked. However, the poem is more than merely memorial. Like many of Meredith's apparently occasional pieces, it finds larger concerns within and behind its occasion. Here, one of these concerns is the rewards and difficulties of a relationship with someone known to be superior and whose attention and approval are wanted and needed. Another is Meredith's common interest in the mysterious way fact and fable merge when we know enough to speak the truth, to make art:

> What little I'd learned about flying
> Must have sweated my language lean. *I'd respect you*
> *For that if for nothing else,* he said not smiling
> The time I told him, thirty-two night landings
> On a carrier, or thirty-two night catapult shots—
> Whatever it was, true, something I knew.
>
> (19)

Hazard, the Painter

Hazard, the Painter is a slim sequence of sixteen poems, published in 1975. It marks a surprising, although certainly not shocking, new direction for Meredith's work. In it, all the characteristics and developments previously traced come together: the craftily conversational voice (here more like Berryman's or late Robert Lowell's than Frost's, and sometimes typified by a finely devious use of jargon and chattiness); the mixture of formal and organic modes (the latter dominating here in a dramatically loosened style); the theme of order tested by domestic, but undomesticated threat; the wry, often self-deprecating wit; and the merging of distance and indirection with autobiography. In an engaging introductory note Meredith describes his frequently topical poem as a "characterization" and goes on to say that "Resemblances between the life and character of Hazard and those of the author are not disclaimed but are much fewer than the author would like."

This at once invites us to read the painter as equivalent to the poet and also—in the manner of Berryman's rather more theatrical Henry—maintains a certain tricky distance, extending such personal-impersonal devices as the third-person titling of first-person poems in earlier collections. More important, ***Hazard, the Painter*** is a kind of fragmentary, inconsequential narrative. Inclusion of fragmentation and inconsequentiality is the newest way Meredith recognizes and attests to the existence of all that resists his impulse toward whole and highly finished statements and the order such statements imply. This inclusion is the major development of the work, again, a narrative of certain small-scale events in the life of Hazard, a middle-aged, minor American painter living in a time of decline, specifically, 1972.

Although ***Hazard*** is marked by a good deal of random casualness, it nonetheless discovers in its progression a clear image of disorder at all levels of American life: cultural, national, personal, and—for Hazard—artistic. Culturally, decline is everywhere. On one level, the Rolling Stones threaten the "frail culture of Jefferson and Adams," of painters as different as the fictional representationalist Hazard and the actual abstract expressionist Franz Kline. Hazard treats this observation, as he does the inability of a "Yale girl" to distinguish "lie" from "lay," with a combination of serious regret, crotchety annoyance, and—remembering his own excesses with **"The Land of the Sky-Blue Waters"** on the family victrola—self-amused, forgiving nostalgia. On another, more serious level, the insatiable maws of cash and consumerism replace the American ideal of the new world garden:

> Who were all those cheering on the gray glass
> screen last night, loving their violent darling,
> America, whom they had married to money?
> He couldn't tarry at that feast—when the wine
> ran out, they would change blood to money.
>
> (26)

This assessment Hazard treats with unforgiving and angry sorrow, but also with a sense of complicity: he is comfortable; he has two cars; his driveway is a *defoliated* landscape; he doesn't *do* anything about it.

The obsession with money that drives and degrades the culture also drives and degrades the nation, now in its "late imperial decline." Nixon is re-elected; a murderous war is thoughtlessly and greedily waged in Vietnam; the people, Hazard included, are snug indoors and adapt to the political weather. Things in Hazard's personal life are little better. For all his enlightened liberal awareness and no matter how hard he tries, Hazard knows he is intolerant—of women's liberationists, of homosexuals—and jealous of the success of fellow artists: "'He is strictly a one-joke painter.'" At times, he feels he is flawed by an excessive awareness of the needs of others (he has difficulty seeing like the cat, that is, "flat," without subjectivity and, therefore, responsibility) and, at other times, by an excessive selfishness:

> In his studio
> Hazard stares at the vain, self-centered landscape
> he's working on now. It is going well. It
> revels in his onanistic attention.
>
> (16)

Hazard is also troubled by his own comfortable and orderly mildness, the ease with which he makes accommodations and proceeds more or less affirmatively through bad times. Perhaps the greatest threat to Hazard, however, is age; he worries about a decline of energy and suffers from an impinging sense of his own extinction. He recalls the nausea of his fighter-pilot training; death's currency is all around him: a dead bluejay on his compost heap, the glacial boulders in his field putting him in mind of time's incomprehensible extent and of extinction. Perhaps still worse than this is the daily confrontation with his art. His painting—he is obsessed with the figure of a parachutist suspended and falling over a "plotted landscape"—does not satisfy him: "This is what for two years now / he has been painting, in a child's palette"; "He has not been to his studio / in four days"; when the outer self comes to him and "says it is looking for pictures," he tells it "it / has come to the wrong man."

These resonances with the culture's decline that he perceives in himself are only one side of things, however. As we discover a shape of disorder in the sequence, we also discover that, as bad as things are, Hazard still hopes. He still tries to affirm, to create and share in some "godless benediction," to find and / or make an order in his life and art. The pronominal circumscription of that last phrase insists that this shaping effort is narrower than the images of disorder the poem describes, and the poem's awareness that large cultural and national matters are little affected by the acts of individuals qualifies what can be said about Hazard's qualified successes in other areas as well. Nevertheless, in his personal life Hazard struggles against his own selfishness, intolerance, and jealousy by seeking a cultivated grace in his family and other relations. He puts it this way, in a lofty opening statement, interrupted and partly undercut by, among other things, his children complaining about pepper in the gravy:

> We need the ceremony of one another,
> meals *served,* more love,
> more handling of one another with love, less
> casting out of those who are not
> of our own household.
> 'This turkey is either not cooked
> enough or it's tough.'
> The culture is in late imperial decline.
> The children don't like dark meat or
> pepper. They say the mother sometimes
> deliberately puts pepper on the things
> the grown-ups like better.
> less casting out of those in our own
> household with whom we disagree.
>
> (3)

Hazard feels that he is only occasionally successful in achieving this aspiration, but even his failures include continuing efforts at willed decency, as in his attempt to accept the homosexuality of a friend and fellow painter, or in this effort to control professional jealousy:

> The fact that I don't like his pictures
> should not obscure the facts
> that he is a good man
> that many admire his work (his canvases
> threaten my existence and I hope
> mine his, the intolerant bastard)
> that we are brothers in humanity
> & the art. Often it does, though.
>
> (4)

Hazard's musings on age and death are also marked by a wary hopefulness. Some of his strategies of resistance are familiar from earlier Meredith poems. There is love and memory, as in the quasi-valentine Hazard leaves for his wife:

> What you have given me,
> in those long moments when our words
> come back, our breaths come back,
> is a whole man at last,
> and keeping me, remembers.
>
> (28)

There is his admiration for the not-always-decorous resistance of the aged: "the radical old, / freaks you may call them but you're wrong, / who persist in being at home in the world." And there is his sense of continuity in the elemental cycles of natural process, expressed more strenuously here than elsewhere in Meredith's work. Viewing the dioramas of evolution and extinction at the Museum of Natural History, Hazard (in a typical blend of formal diction and slang) considers his possible place in a life-taking, life-giving continuum:

> We descend by chosen cells that are not lost,
> though they wander off in streams and rivulets.
>
> . . . . .
>
> And grazers or killers, each time we must stoop low
> and enter by some thigh-lintel, gentle as rills.
> *Who consents to his own return,* Nietzsche says,
> *participates in the divinity of the world.*
> Perhaps I have already eddied on, out of this backwater,
> man, on my way to the cafeteria, Hazard thinks.
> Perhaps nothing dies but husks.
>
> (19, 20)

As Hazard's personal life is marked by such hopeful struggle and by limited success, so is his art. Although he feels he is in a bad patch, without energy or inspiration, he labors to overcome his inertia, even parachuting from a plane in an attempt to make his hopeful vision available to himself and, eventually, to others. Winter, the season of decline, sets in, but, with a winning mixture of confidence and wry self-deprecation, Hazard views himself as "in charge of morale in a morbid time," "Shapes up," and returns to his easel, hoping to bear witness to the "vision of rightness" that gnaws him:

> And what has he got to tell?
> Only the shaped things he's seen—
> a few things made by men,
> a galaxy made well.
> Though more of each day is dark,
> though he's awkward at the job,
> he squeezes paint from a tube.
> Hazard is back at work.
>
> (31)

On this tentative note, its mix of hope and doubt underlined by the turn to relatively formal but slant-rhymed quatrains, the poem ends.

Separating the images of disorder in ***Hazard, the Painter*** from its searchings for figures of order has somewhat falsified the nature of the poem. For its central recognition is how inseparable order and disorder are, how random, accidental, and provisional are their interpenetrations and impingements. Furthermore, commenting on the signs of decline first and those of resistance last has introduced a false indication of their relative weights. ***Hazard, the Painter*** is not a poem in which the disorderly is presented only to be straitened and put in its place by the orderly. Instead, it presents a complex man struggling to impose his own "vision of rightness" on a self and world that will never submit to it, and at the same time trying to make or keep his own recognition of that refusal a part of his vision. Thus, the image of the descending, declining but upheld, suspended parachutist is Hazard's, and the poem's, appropriate figure. However, his painting of it is never, perhaps never can be, finished; life's failings and fallings remain random, difficult, pervasive, and perverse. The systems do not always, indeed, rarely do, hold us up. Even when they do, as Meredith recognizes and accepts here more fully than ever before, they are only systems and always transient, canvases and poems the husks we leave behind. Nevertheless, at least for a time, an affirming, resisting, human spirit inhabits them and, so, "accepting and not accepting," Hazard is "back at work," as Meredith is alongside him.

The Cheer

The thirty-five poems of ***The Cheer*** (1980) are very much on Meredith's main line, meditations and richly qualified statements on such interpenetrating opposites as ignorance and knowledge, meaninglessness and meaning, chaos and order, life and art, death and life. Their goal is "accurate praise." United by a constant thematic concern with the limits and possibilities of the human effort to resist the disintegrating disorders of time, death, and chaos, and with what those limits and possibilities can teach us about our own public and private, past and future actions (and inactions), their techniques are those we would expect from the recent work that precedes them. Some poems are relatively formal, one in *abab* quatrains, another suggesting *terza rima,* several in regular stanzas—often of two or three lines, and several quite regular in line length and with iambic norms, but most are in free verse, irregular in accent and syllable count, and unrhymed. Their language and rhythms are typically colloquial and conversational, their methods intricately accessible, their material often relatively personal, their tones intelligent, informed, distressed and calm, hopeful and troubled, and their attitudes provisional and inclusive. Ironically or otherwise, they are always fully aware of all that counters or contradicts their apparent assertions of joy and despair, hope or doubt.

The paradigmatic title piece sets the tone of the volume. Printed as an "envoi," here an introductory poem addressed to the reader, it admits, not quite grudgingly, the facts of evil and poetry's obligation to attend to them:

> A great deal isn't right, as they say,
> as they are lately at some pains to tell us.
> Words have to speak about that.
> They would be the less words
> for saying *smile* when they should say *do.*
> If you ask them *do what?*
> they turn serious quick enough, but never unlovely.
> And they will tell you what to do,
> if you listen, if you want that.
>
> (ix)

Nevertheless, it finally insists that poetry—neither ignoring nor overcome by complicating context, and even in confrontation—remains an encouraging affirmation and celebration of significant, if marginal, human effort, of the effort to signify. Just such saving grace, the resistance of something to an always and awesomely present and almost overwhelming nothing, quietly lifts from these new poems to cheer us.

In the opening poems of ***The Cheer*** threat typically appears as time and change. In **"Winter on the River"** ice locks up the world, but an ice-breaker working downstream becomes an image of resistance to the season's "cold / and silence," a resistance that goes beyond mere animal endurance, if only from a particularly human vantage. In **"Two Masks Unearthed in Bulgaria"** golden-eyed clay artifacts resist decay and stretch human time into mysterious prehistory. In **"Recollections of Bellagio"** the resistances to dissolving time and change are those of imagination and memory. Immensities of astronomical and botanical time are evoked by the dance of the stars and pine trees. These expanses would seem to render the self and its transient experience irrelevant, however thoughtful. But images, the power to perceive and recreate them, and the power to do so in patterns, somehow and mysteriously persist:

> And who
> is saying these words, now that that man
> is a shade, has become his own shade?
> I see the shade rise slow and ghostly from its seat
> on the soft, grainy stone, I watch it descend
> by the gravelled paths of the promontory,
> under a net of steady stars, in April,
> from the boughs' rite and the bells'—quiet,
> my shade, and long ago, and still going on.

In **"Country Stars"** it is not the persistence of self but of future generations that resists the disintegration of time and change. A "nearsighted child" peers through a window and with her special seeing "puts her own construction on the night." The lights of contemporary life may seem to block from us the ancient patterns of the stars, but the poem reassures us that the young will make new "constructions," new meanings: "have no fear, or only proper fear: / the bright watchers are still there." Like memory and imagination, the effort for significance goes on, goes on in the context of things' refusal to submit to permanent or general significance.

References in various poems to war and politics and to the pollution of urban glow prepare for the several explicitly public and political poems to follow, poems developing themes first broached in ***Hazard, the Painter.*** Of these, the first is transitional, the best, and characteristic. **"Homage to Paul Mellon, I. M. Pei, Their Gallery, and Washington City"** has roots in William Carlos Williams's "It Is a Living Coral" and in Meredith's own **"Whorls."** It pays tribute to creativity, in particular to the construction of the new East Building of the National Gallery of Art (built with money donated by Paul Mellon and designed by architect I. M. Pei) and in general to the building of Washington, D.C., of the nation, of men, of artists, of stone. It begins by evoking expanses of geological time, seen now not as destructive but as the very locus of construction: "Granite and marble, / women and men, / took a long while to make." As time is made positive here, so is "trouble." America "took a lot of trouble" to make, "and it's not done yet," but the response to difficulty and incompleteness is (as Meredith continues the effort of ***Hazard, the Painter*** to rescue worn and cheapened language for meaningful expression) delight: "Praise be / It is so interesting, / and lucky, like crustacean deposit." With this suggestion of the making of stone, the poem turns to human making with stone, describing the solid, serene, relatively permanent structures of the past as the expression of "our guesses at un-trouble." It turns then to the contemporary addition to the National Gallery, which, by comparison, may seem "reckless," yet which in its own way has the solidity, serenity, and relative permanence of a "glacier," and which also has a cutting edge. Further, the addition was necessary, in terms of the need for increased exhibit space and in terms of the modern art it would house (Edvard Munch and Isamu Noguchi, among the "sweetest troublers" deposited by time, are the artists mentioned). It is art requiring "knives of stone," "Pink prows," and "hogans of white space"—an appropriate mix of the futuristic and the primitive. From these hints that, however "new" or unconventional, human structures continue time's glacial construction, the poem looks back and forward and accepts and insists on the combination of transience and permanence in all our human acts, a combination that places us and our brevity in time in a meaningful continuum, meaningful at least in its tendency to build or rebuild from the materials of loss, a continuum to which both our living and dying contribute.

Several poems of ***The Cheer,*** then, resist while accepting the dissolving power of time. The pattern continues in

"For Two Lovers in the Year 2075 in the Canadian Woods," which presents itself as a time-capsule relic of here-and-now lovers. Time's destruction is clearly present in the pastness of the moment the poem memorializes ("we were among your trees / in extraordinary flesh / and ecstasy now gone"), and in the fact that the lovers who speak its message to the future will surely be dead when their intended audience receives it. Concurrently, the poem transcends time by having its voices heard in the future (in this and other ways placing itself in the train of the archetypal poem of the genre, Shakespeare's Sonnet 18, which ends: "So long as men can breathe, or eyes can see, / So long lives this, and this gives life to thee"), and by placing itself in continuums of literature (E. E. Cummings, Walter Savage Landor, John Donne) and of lovers ("an Indian brave and his maiden, / a French girl and her man," and, if they "have August moonrise / and bodies to undress," future couples). As its title suggests, the next poem, **"Memoirs,"** is related to this one and considers again Meredith's familiar questions about art and life (see also **"Poem,"** 21-22).

"Memoirs" depicts Napoleon, now emperor of France and in control of virtually all Europe, recalling a supposed childhood obsession with cartography, an obsession so great that he often vexed his mother by drawing maps in chalk on the undersides of carpets. This obviously idealized story his mother, now Empress-Mother, "irritably" rebuts: "Maps? We were much too poor in Corsica to have rugs." There is little doubt that the mother's version is the true one; there is still less doubt of the deeper imaginative truth of the son's willful or invented memory, as indicated by the irony that the Empress-Mother delivers her rebuttal while resting her feet "comfortably on the Aubusson" carpet in her son's palace at Saint Cloud. Napoleon's descriptions of his child-self drawing the map of Europe geographically rather than politically, as a unit rather than as a collection of separate states, and, especially, as drawing it "after his own heart" perfectly capture both his visionary and tactical genius, and imply the achievements to which it led. The point, of course, is that autobiographical, like any creative, fictive lying can be a way of telling the truth, that the rightly imagined "fact" can tell far more than a literal one. At the same time, the poem retains the literal as a humorous and qualifying context that exposes the counter tendency of autobiography to self-dramatization and self-aggrandizement.

"Memoirs" is followed by a series of poems concerned with time and change and death in familial or generational settings. The best of these is the astonishing **"Give and Take / (Christmas, after a death in the family)."** Making unusual (for Meredith) use of experimental spacing and of refusals of punctuation, the poem develops the speaker's mixed emotions—the happiness of Christmas giving and taking and the sorrow of the remembered giving and taking of a recently dead loved one—into an extraordinary stream-of-consciousness monologue in which opposed moods meet and merge: the past and the present, innocence and the experienced recognition that death is for everyone, a Christmas wreath and a death wreath, generosity and greed. Perhaps the most impressive result of these mergings is the maturely childlike and emotionally and intellectually ambivalent imagining of the deceased's coffin as a Christmas present to God.

The Cheer's next group of poems concerns death in more public contexts. **"Dreams of Suicide"** gives the poet's response to three famous literary deaths, Ernest Hemingway's, Sylvia Plath's, and John Berryman's. His dreams demonstrate his sorrow for, interest in, and effort to identify with and understand these others, but perhaps most of all they show his difference from them, his received tendency to the ordinary rather than the extreme, to endure rather than despair. The third section, on Berryman, is the best. Its dream description is based on the facts of Berryman's death—he jumped from a bridge over the frozen Mississippi—and suggests its source in his father's suicide, committed when Berryman was a boy:

> If I hold you tight by the ankles,
> still you fly upward from the iron railing.
> Your father made these wings,
> after he made his own, and now from beyond
> he tells you *fly down,* in the voice
> my own father might say *walk, boy.*
>
> (41)

At first there seems to be a certain callousness here, as if the speaker were claiming a superior inheritance and self: *he* endures; *his* feet are on the ground. But the ordinariness of walking and the contrasting implications of flight—greater risks, greater goals—perfectly counter such claims and, with the reference to Icarus (who was also, if differently, guided by his father and who stretched for the sun, and failing, fell to his death in the sea), produce an apt mix of judgment, admiration, and compassion. A similar mixture informs the more fully developed elegy for Berryman, **"In Loving Memory of the Late Author of Dream Songs."** The poet struggles to comprehend his friend's death ("We have to understand how you got / from here to there, a hundred feet straight down") and to fit it to his own concern with "morale," with what "hopeful men and women can say and do," with what, in the language of ***Hazard the Painter,*** we can do in "a morbid time" without falsifying and thereby cheapening the facts: "'his giant faults'"; "suicide is a crime"; "wives and children deserve better." If he does not fully understand, he does discover something to affirm; the poet's "character" is to "look for things to praise," and he finds them not in Berryman's death but in his life: "None of us deserved, of course, you." His book, "full of marvelous songs," can help the living stay alive: "Don't let us contract your dread recidivism / and start falling from our own iron railings. / Wave from the fat book again, make us wave back." Another poem for Berryman, **"John and Anne,"** employs an epigraph from Berryman's study of Anne Frank and again joins judgment to tribute. He could not grow up; his "decorum" was "only parody." However, his tantrums were "tantrums of enquiry"; he maintained his search for meaning, his effort to mature. The poem's final implication is that his own flawed example can help us grow, as Anne Frank's more perfect example helped him.

The next poem, **"Dying Away / (Homage to Sigmund Freud),"** is transitional, an intriguing meditation on life and death, heroism and cowardice. Its speaker admires Freud's illuminations—for instance, his revision of death, newly defined as our calling, our heroism, "the *aim* of [our] life." In response to this, he worries about his own "love for the enduring trees and the snowfall, / for brook-noise and coins, songs, appetites"; "The love of living disturbs" him. However, in considering Freud's life, he finds another view of things. Freud, he suggests, "saw that the *aim* of life was death" only after his own "appetites, songs, orgasms," and his family "died away." Further, when his own death came he found it senseless torture and pleaded with a friend for morphine. In this context, love for the "fair world" resumes its value. The point is not to debunk Freud; the poem admires his insights and praises the genius of his effort, failed like every man's, to know the truth. At the same time, though, it returns the questions he thought to answer (did answer, for himself, for a time) to the mysteries they are: "a man cannot learn heroism from another, / he owes the world some death of his own invention."

The last group of poems in ***The Cheer,*** a series of six marked by shared use of often lengthy epigraphs on which they are often commentaries, extends this concern with the impossibility of knowing the ultimate significance of life or of knowing how to live it, and with our continuing efforts to do so nonetheless. One of the best of these is **"Crossing Over."** Its subject is love. Its epigraph, the description of the river of broken ice Eliza must try to cross in *Uncle Tom's Cabin* to reach free Ohio's paradise, is a simile for our own difficult route to paradise, for love, for its weakness and its strength: "That's what love is like. The whole river / is melting. We skim along in great peril." The course is difficult, but in the Kentucky of the constrained and real, "all we have is love, a great undulating / raft, melting steadily. We go out on it / anyhow."

Other poems in the group involve the mysteries of human death, love, knowledge, and being; the last considers those of responsible memory. The epigraph for the dramatic monologue **"Trelawny's Dream"** is provided by Meredith himself, retelling the story of Edward John Trelawny's designing the boat from which his friend Shelley was lost, of his aborted plan to "convoy" him on what became his final journey, and so on. In the poem Trelawny speaks from "late middle age." He describes a recurrent dream of his friend's death, his continuing suffering and loss, his own coming death, and, most of all, the effort of the self to maintain itself and the past in the widening seas of dream:

> All this was a long time ago, I remember.
> None of them was drowned except me
> whom a commotion of years washes over.
> They hail me from the dream, they call an old man
> to come aboard, these youths on an azure bay.
> The waters may keep the dead, as the earth may,
> and fire and air. But dream is my element.
> Though I am still a strong swimmer
> I can feel this channel widen as I swim.
>
> (60)

Once more, the image is one of constant struggle against constantly enlarging odds. It is this effort of human spirit in the always qualifying contexts of its limited condition and limiting world that cheers us, that we cheer.

The Cheer concludes appropriately with **"Examples of Created Systems,"** examples of made or discovered patterns in the world, patterns of both evil and good, of concentration camps and constellations. The poem ends in an ambiguous description of the mysterious complex of creativity, of what we make, its threatening limits and possible hope: "We flung it there, in a learned / gesture of sowing—random, lovely." In this incorrigibly dark and brightening matrix man's incorrigible making "(it is our nature)" goes on.

. . . . .

In an obvious sense, William Meredith is a New England poet. His frequent use of the native landscape, especially its sea and trees (and "its" stars), his central indebtedness to Frost (also a poet of trees and stars), and his attention to questions of morality and behavior and to the possibilities and limits of objective and subjective stances, all place his poetry in a recognizable New England tradition, as does, more particularly, his continuation of the dramas of hope and skepticism engendered by the tendency to at once read and suspect the reading of natural and human facts as types of larger, abstract truths.

It should also be clear that the usual critical description of Meredith as an unreconstructed academic formalist is, at best, imprecise. Since the later poems of his first book, and certainly since the poems of ***The Open Sea,*** Meredith has moved steadily away from the academic mode and toward the modes of the various rebellions against it. His poetry has become more experimental in language and form, more open and (if deviously so) accessible, more personal, more provisional, more suspicious of the claims of intellect and order, and more willing to consider the claims of what threatens order, including the claims of the irrational, the random, and the inconclusive. However, in addition to his continuing commitment to craft and ambivalence and his refusal to indulge in confessionalism, there is a central sense in which Meredith *is* unreconstructed. His response to the potentially chaotic nature of self and world remains one of ironic resistance rather than immersed acceptance. However chastened and chastised he is, however his confidence has weakened, however his inclusion of undeniable threat has increased, Meredith still seeks hopefully for an ordered life and art, for meaning and value, to affirm and to praise. In this, to adjust a phrase used about him by Dudley Fitts, Meredith remains a renovator and not a revolutionary.[19] Or, to apply the now fashionable terms, he remains a modern and not a post-modern. One might, however, borrow the language of **"The Wreck**

of the Thresher" to say that much of what goes to make such distinctions is "a question of temperament and does not matter."

What does matter is the poetry, which gives pleasure and satisfaction not by allegiance but by expression. There is a short poem that expresses Meredith's sense of difficult but possible miracle, of man's effort to affirm against the facts, to answer yes, to render "accurate praise." It is a minor poem, called **"A Major Work"**:

> Poems are hard to read
> Pictures are hard to see
> Music is hard to hear
> And people are hard to love
> But whether from brute need
> Or divine energy
> At last mind eye and ear
> And the great sloth heart *will* move.

(***The Open Sea,*** 56)

Notes

William Meredith, quoted in John Wakeman, ed., *World Authors, 1950-1970: A Companion Volume to Twentieth Century Authors* (New York: H. W. Wilson, 1975), p. 977. (Throughout the biographical sketch I am indebted to this work for information and to the Meredith entries in James Vinson and D. L. Kirkpatrick, eds., *Contemporary Poets,* 2d ed. (New York: St. Martin's, 1975), pp. 1035-36; Clare D. Kinsman and Mary Ann Tennenhouse, eds., *Contemporary Authors: A Bio-Bibliographical Guide to Current Authors and Their Works,* 1st rev. (Detroit: Gale Research Co., 1974), 9-12, 619; and the 1978-79 edition of *Who's Who in America.*)

Quoted in Wakeman, *World Authors,* p. 978.

1. Quoted in Gregory FitzGerald and Paul Ferguson, "The Frost Tradition: A Conversation with William Meredith," *Southwest Review* 57 (1972): 115.
2. Richard Howard, "William Meredith: 'All of a Piece and Clever and at Some Level, True,'" in *Alone with America: Essays on the Art of Poetry in the United States Since 1950* (New York: Atheneum, 1971), p. 319.
3. William Meredith, *Love Letter from an Impossible Land* (New Haven, 1944; rpt. New York, 1971), p. 32. Unless otherwise noted, the poems quoted in each section of this chapter are from the volume under discussion. The longer quotations separated from the text are referenced by page numbers in parentheses.
4. Quoted in Wakeman, *World Authors,* p. 978.
5. Quoted in FitzGerald and Ferguson, "The Frost Tradition," p. 110.
6. Henry Taylor, " In Charge of Morale in a Morbid Time. The Poetry of William Meredith," *Hollins Critic* 16 (1979): 3.
7. Thomas Landless, "New Urns for Old: A Look at Six Recent Volumes of Verse," *Sewanee Review* 81 (1973): 148.
8. Dudley Fitts, "Meredith's Second Volume," *Poetry* 73 (1948): 111.
9. This is said despite Meredith's attractive and partially convincing defense of the practice in *Ships and Other Figures, The Open Sea,* and elsewhere.
10. William Meredith, "The Luck of It," in *American Poets in 1976,* ed. William Heyen (Indianapolis, Ind.: Bobbs-Merrill, 1976), p. 193.
11. See Meredith's own comment on this matter in FitzGerald and Ferguson, "The Frost Tradition," p. 109.
12. Howard, in *Alone With America,* p. 324.
13. Quoted in FitzGerald and Ferguson, pp. 115 and 114.
14. William Meredith, "In Loving Memory of the Late Author of *The Dream Songs,*" in *John Berryman: A Checklist,* ed. Richard J. Kelley (Metuchen, N.J.: The Scarecrow Press, 1972), p. xix.
15. Ibid., p. xv.
16. Quoted in FitzGerald and Ferguson, "The Frost Tradition," pp. 111-12.
17. The quotation is from Percy Bysshe Shelley, *Prometheus Unbound,* I, ll: 192-99.
18. Peter Davison, "Madness in the New Poetry," *Atlantic,* January 1965, p. 93.
19. Dudley Fitts, "The Sweet Side of Right," *Saturday Review,* 22 March 1958, p. 23.

Edward Hirsch with William Meredith (interview date 1985)

SOURCE: An interview with William Meredith, in *Poems are Hard to Read,* The University of Michigan Press, 1991, pp. 215-38.

[*In the following interview, originally published in* Paris Review *in 1985, Meredith discusses his creative process, his opinions of other contemporary poets, and influences on his work.*]

[Hirsch]: You've said that you average about six poems per year. Why so few?

[Meredith]: Why so many? Ask any reviewer. I remember a particularly wicked review of Edna St. Vincent Millay whose new poems weren't as good as they should have been: "This Millay seems to have gone out of her way to write another book of poems." You're always afraid of that. That could be said, I believe, of certain people's poems. So I wait until the poems seem to be addressed not to "Occupant" but to "William Meredith." And it doesn't happen a lot. I think if I had a great deal more time it would happen more often because I would get immediately to the typewriter. But it might happen eight times a year instead of six—not much more than that. I'll say this because it may be interesting or important: I think it is because poetry and experience should have an exact ratio. Astonishing experience doesn't happen very often. Daily experience is astonishing on a level at which you can write a poem, but astonishing experience would be the experience which is not astonishment of reality but astonishment of insight. It is for me, as a lyric poet, to make poems only out of insights that I encounter. Robert Frost used to say, "How many things have to happen to you before something occurs to you?"

How do you usually start a poem?

It starts with an insight which gets a few words close to the ground and then the words begin to make specific the insight. Once they start growing the words are seminal—I suppose it's like the bacteria of a growth. I can hardly remember a poem in which the words are not *particular* words, often very bleak, simple words. Once they are put down they are able to focus an idea. I have, I think, only once written a poem—and it's not a very good poem—which came to me literally as a dream that was decodable. It's about an eight or ten line poem and all I could say was, "That's what it said."

Your poems tend to have a sly, angular way of going at a subject, approaching it from the side rather than directly. Would you say something about that?

If it's so, it's the nature of the work that a poem is getting at something mysterious, which no amount of staring at straight-on has ever solved, something like death or love or treachery or beauty. And we keep doing this corner-of-the-eye thing. I remember when we were in training to be night fliers in the Navy, I learned, very strangely, that the rods of the eye perceive things at night in the corner of the eye that we can't see straight ahead. That's not a bad metaphor for the vision of art. You don't stare at the mystery, but you *can* see things out of the corner of your eye that you were supposed to see.

Do you think that writing a poem is a specific engagement of a mystery?

I would say exactly that. It is the engagement of a mystery which has forced itself to the point where you feel honor-bound to see this mystery with the brilliance of a vision. Not to solve it, but to see it.

Does this relate to the statement in your poem ***"In Memory of Robert Frost,"*** *that Frost insisted on paying attention "until you at least told him an interesting lie."*

Well, he understood—and I'm afraid his biographer, Lawrence Thompson, does not understand—that at the higher reaches of our experience we don't know the things that we say, but we say that we do. That's the ultimate artistic lie. I tell you what I know today in a poem and I don't know it; in the first place it may not be true, and in the second place it may not be what I know tomorrow. Artistic truth is to declare, under torture, what the torturer does not want you to say, not what the torturer does want you to say. You try to tell the truth even though it's uncomfortable for everybody. When the hippies were talking about how the only two things you need to know about life is that you must love one another and not lie, they forgot to tell you that those are the only two really difficult things. We all know that's what we're supposed to do; it's much harder to love people than anybody ever tells you and it's much harder to tell the truth. Poets are professionally committed to telling the truth, and *how* do they tell the truth? They say something that isn't true. This is the slyness of art: if you tell enough lies, you're bound to say something true. I think my work is only as good as it is honest but as a data bank it's full of errors.

Is it fair to characterize **The Cheer** *as a work of sly survivals, a resolutely hopeful book?*

A resolutely hopeful book I think it is. The question of survival, in fact the process of survival, is something that either occurs or doesn't occur. It doesn't seem to be something that one deliberately does, but is a product of good instincts and good life. And quite right. Survival, in terms of the poems, has been such that I use them for making my way from one form of commitment to the next. I hope that the poems will lead me more directly to where I'm going and that I'll arrive directed only by instincts, social instincts.

In a memorial poem to John Berryman, ***"In Loving Memory of the Late Author of Dream Songs,"*** *you write that "Morale is what I think about all the time / now, what hopeful men and women can say and do." Why morale?*

I suppose it seems to me that the priestly function of artists in a society is to administer spiritual vision and that the obvious deficiency of a fragmented and confused society is in confidence. I use morale partly in quotation marks because I first became aware of the word in the military. Muriel Rukeyser pointed out to me that there was a certain General Euleo whose title was "Chief of Morale" and we thought that very funny. I was in the Navy so long that I have to remind myself that's a humorous title. But like General Euleo, I see the need for keeping the morale of the troops high. At one point it was in the papers that Congress had discovered large shipments of dice were being made to the troops overseas, and General Euleo explained that they were parts of a Parcheesi set they had not been able to requisition and that the whole thing would keep morale high. That's like ***The Cheer.*** My real concern is, in the first place, that we ought not to be solemn and, in the second place, the response to disaster, even cultural disaster, is an impersonal one and the personal obligation is to mental and spiritual health. Of course, it always has been.

In ***"Hazard's Optimism"*** *you also note that Hazard is "in charge of morale in a morbid time." Is that one of the poet's responsibilities?*

I would suppose so. In a happy time, like Elizabethan England, the poet is probably involved in reminding people that they're all going to come to a bad end. Nowadays, you try to keep people from precipitating their own bad ends.

Playfulness and humor also seem to be an integral part of your poetic stance.

I first learned about playfulness from W. H. Auden, who talks about it all the time. But the example of playfulness I found in Frost was the great attraction of Frost for me. I could see that he played games with words. . . . and therefore the poems were never as earnest as English teachers said they were. People who are basically humorous are constantly misunderstood in an instructive way. My social career is littered with ill-calculated humor. One doesn't want to say, "I live on the verge of despair and terror and I'm perfectly safe because I'm roped off by humor and good cheer." But sometimes, it's the only way to talk about things. Here is an example: in the Navy, when we were flying, instead of saying, "Take care of yourself," people would say, "Don't crash and burn." I don't know how funny it was, but we thought it was hilarious. Still, there were some people who forgot and didn't take care of themselves and did just that. Humorlessness is a positively morbid quality that certain people have. This is not the same as not being witty, it's not the same as not using humor in a particular instance. It's a solemnity which puts blinders on your awareness of ridicule and absurdity. I'm always suspicious of humorlessness. When you see the pictures of Hitler jumping up and down and laughing with glee over the conquest of France you see a somewhat disoriented human being whose life has had a deficiency of laughter. It's almost a snickering.

Frost has had an enormous impact both on your life and on your work. What do you think in particular that you learned from him?

When we were in Tucson on a visit once he quarreled with me about something. I guess indeed I quarreled with him on a statement of dignity, and in making up he said, "I brought you along on this trip so you could see a little how I take things." That's also his definition of style: style is how a man takes himself. I think I learned—it's not a very precise answer but it's precisely what I learned on the page and from the person—that that was the way I would like to take myself. I think one of the reasons I am so quick to rush to the defense of Frost, who after all was not any nicer than most of us, is that I wouldn't mind being as nice as he was. He took things very generously and magnanimously. His language fascinates me because he lived within his means in language, like an old man. There's never a single word that seems wanting, not a single word that seems to call attention to itself in a pretentious way.

Is this an attitude from life which applies itself to how a man takes his poems?

One time he said, in connection with his youth and his mother's life, "People used to call us riff-raff. They never knew what riff-raff I am." I take that to be his form of modesty, which is puzzling to people who think he was vain. I think it has to do with his making do with his human and verbal resources, knowing exactly what the best you could do was and doing it.

What are your favorite Frost poems?

"The Vanishing Red," "Directive," "Spring Pools," "The Birthplace."

In his poem "For John Berryman," Robert Lowell writes, "Really we had the same life, / the generic one / our generation offered." How much do you think of yourself as a poet who belongs to a particular generation?

I feel myself of that generation because I had the good luck to know those poets. As far as our experience being similar, I think the responses of people like Richard Wilbur or Elizabeth Bishop are different from the responses of Berryman and Lowell, and Randall Jarrell's was different still. So that while I'm sure we had basic encounters with history that nobody else had, we took them differently. I believe Lowell is right in associating himself so closely with Berryman. Berryman associated himself closely with Lowell, and both of them with Jarrell, although if you look at Jarrell's work, you wouldn't know that there was any relation. It's one of my theories that Jarrell is probably the most useful poet of the three.

Why?

His poems are accessible to people who are not trained readers. You have to train yourself to read Berryman, though it's very much worthwhile. I would say to somebody who wants to read Berryman what Nobokov said about Pushkin: "Learning Russian is a small price to pay for reading Pushkin." But every other poem in Jarrell's *Complete Poems* is accessible to somebody who is not a trained reader of poetry. It is just interesting, attractive, and human. Anybody who can read a short story by O. Henry can read a poem by Jarrell.

You've written about Jarrell, "The poems he left behind seem to me to speak in the most compassionate voice of any of his generation." Is compassion the virtue you most prize in Jarrell? What about his acid wit?

His wit was splendid. I think it's twice splendid because he almost never used it except when appropriate. He used it to detect falsehoods, to deflate intolerable pretension. The reason I think it's less important than compassion is that it is a more common thing in our time. Jarrell wasn't any wittier than Tom Wolfe, say. Also, I lived in mortal fear of him. Why not? He gave a talk in 1962—one of his modest talks where he was assessing fifty years of modern poetry in fifty minutes at the Library of Congress—and at the end he said, "And then there is another larger group of poets who, so to speak, came out from under Richard Wilbur's overcoat." It was a reference to Dostoyevsky's famous comment on Gogol, "We all come out from under Gogol's overcoat," and it made me feel that I was in that category of poets. I thought then that I would just like to get through life without ever attracting his attention.

When did his poems start to interest you, or influence your work?

I can date it precisely: it was when I reviewed *The Lost World* in 1964. I read his work very carefully then and with great admiration. Mary Jarrell tells me that he was very pleased with the review and when I saw him with Lowell he treated me with respect, though I can't imagine that my poems interested him very much. But really, it's the vertebra that I think mine could nearest approach. His and John Crowe Ransom's are the two works most like the works that are my mind's.

Is Ransom one of your models?

Ransom is a bad model in the sense that he wrote his book of poems and then didn't do much, didn't grow as a poet, didn't have much more to say. I just would like to have forty poems as good as that to call my own, that's what I mean. Also, I would like to have such original insights.

Lowell's poem "Morning after Dining with a Friend" describes a dinner which you had with Lowell near the end of his life. It also refers to your first meeting. How accurate is the poem, and would you talk about your relationship to Lowell both as a person and as a poet?

The poem, like everything he wrote, is terribly accurate, but the remark about the language of the tribe is changed in mode from declarative to optative. What I actually said was, reading the new batch of poems he gave me that evening, "I feel that with every book you have come a little closer to the language of the tribe." And that's what I say I said in my poem. I have it in his own handwriting that night "to move a little closer to the language of the tribe if we could." So he thought—and he may have been correct—that I was saying: "You've got a long way to go." I wouldn't have the insolence to say that then or now, but what I might have meant was, if you can write this much more accessibly every year you will eventually become as useful as Frost as well as as great as Lowell. That's what I must have had on my mind but I surely didn't urge him to do anything. It's just not my style to urge people to do things. But the account of our meeting is correct as I remember it. I was a member of the Metropolitan Opera Club in those days and we met there—it must have been in 1954—when he was a guest of his friend, Bob Giroux. I had on a uniform because you had to wear either evening clothes or a uniforms and it was easier to put on a uniform. Very soon after that he came to give a lecture at Connecticut College. He was the house guest of his friend Mackie Jarrell (Jarrell's first wife), and I spent the evening with them. In that same winter (1955-56) the Lowells invited Mackie and me to visit them at their cottage. I remember at the end of the visit he said, "I feel this has been a momentous meeting." We stayed friends through the years. Nobody had any trouble staying friends with Cal. He was an extremely loyal and generous man.

Would you gloss the last lines from your poem "Remembering Robert Lowell": "To punish the bearer of evil tidings / it is our custom to ask his blessing. / This you gave. It dawns on each of us separately now / what this entails."

To me that line is interesting because it was written under the influence of Lowell. It is not a meritorious line and I'm not sure I'm entitled to tell you what it means any more than I could tell you what it means when I paraphrase a Lowell line. He has the gift for that kind of meaningful inversion of myth. He told us these things about ourselves and we gave assent to the things that he said. And the blessing we asked was: after such knowledge, what forgiveness? And now each of us, reading Lowell, sees what is the appropriate response to that terrible lucid vision of twentieth-century America. He's a much more American poet than anyone ever probably knew. It is ultimately a very American manifestation—think of Henry James or T. S. Eliot—to look over the shoulder of the educated person to see what we can salvage from our past to regain our direction in the twentieth century.

So Lowell is particularly American because of his entanglement with American history?

Yes, he was very conscious of that. I'm very conscious of it too, but it seems to me that one doesn't talk about it. It annoys me to have been called "aristocratic" when the truth is I have a very deep sense of the commitment of eighteenth-century settlers to this country, all of my ancestors having come to this country before 1800. I don't need to talk about it, what I need to do is find out what's appropriate and do it. Also, my name isn't Lowell. My name is a considerable name: it was on a piece of paper currency in the nineteenth century, a ten-cent fractional note. But this is not the kind of bragging that Lowell did and it's certainly not the kind of bragging I would do; it's only that I'm aware of these things and not ashamed of them. I only wonder what possible usefulness they have—what sense of that kind of history can go into a modest man's modest work.

John Berryman's thirty-sixth "Dream Song" is dedicated to you. It begins, "The high ones die, die. They die. You look up and who's there?"; and it ends with a parenthetical "(Frost being still around.)" What's your attitude toward the poem? Does it set up a dialectic that's important to you: the doomed poet against the poet as survivor?

I have a version of "The high ones die" which he wrote out for me at Bread Loaf that says, "The great ones die." He was thinking specifically of the fact that Faulkner and Hemingway had died. He was thinking about mortality and not suicide. He wasn't thinking that the line means "even the high ones die"—rather that it's a bad time to be a high one. "Frost being still around" means the survival of certain high ones is to be thought of, too. The parenthesis probably means to suggest the jeopardy of age. To me the poem was a statement of praise like those other poems he wrote about Frost afterwards, when Frost died. He was saying that we live in a terrifying world where the great poets are being taken from us. It's true that we can't see anybody on the American horizon now who is quite the size of Faulkner or Frost. We are aware of all other kinds of inferiority and this is added to the hazards of the morale. It would be nice if a Robert Frost or a William Faulkner were regularly produced at twenty-year intervals.

Three of the poems in **The Cheer** *deal with Berryman,* ***"Dreams of Suicide," "In Loving Memory of the Late Author of Dream Songs,"*** *and* ***"John and Anne."*** *Berryman seems to be a key figure to you both as a person and as a poet. Would you talk about your relationship to him?*

He and I were more familiar than I ever felt myself to be with Auden, Frost, or Lowell. I was intimate with Lowell but not familiar. We were close friends and the warmth was there, but my mind is not of the size or shape of Lowell's and I was always aware of this. Berryman was wonderful: anything you didn't know that was necessary to follow his argument he would fill in. He didn't expect me to be anything but bright. I have a postcard from him, written when I was doing a piece about the sonnets at his request. I had asked him to identify a source. He wrote me back with the information and the rest of the postcard says, "Really, Meredith, what will you pretend not to know next?" I was familiar with him. You had to accept his undignified behavior in a way that was comfortable for him and you had to do that naturally. Not everybody could do it. I naturally felt that his dignity was never lost. I knew when the alcohol was taking over. I always knew that he was misspeaking himself, rather than saying something wrong. He was saying something in human need. He understood that and relied on it.

Do you think there's been too much emphasis on his tormented biography?

In the sense that John Haffenden's biography of Berryman and Ian Hamilton's biography of Lowell are not the proportions of the men's lives. Most of the time that I was with Lowell and Berryman, they were happy. They had the happiness of seriously engaged, useful people. That's the impression that I think a biography ought to give. It's our style now that a poet is taken seriously in proportion to his tortures, particularly if his tortures can be blamed on himself. I think it's inappropriate as a value judgment and inappropriate to apply to those two in life. Remember they gave of their company; they gave a great deal. This is partly what I was bitching about in the poem called **"The Cheer."** We're convinced that you shouldn't smile in public because people are being killed in El Salvador today. I am no less gravely sad about history than the solemn people are. But part of my response is to try to reverse it personally because there is dignity in our response and our response is not self-pitying or entirely angry, but a historical one. There is a historical answer to what befalls us and I think the people of good morale have better sense about how to respond.

Does Meredith's Hazard owe anything to Berryman's Henry, the protagonist of Dream Songs, beyond the fact that they're both working at a time when, in words you quote from Berryman, "The culture is in late imperial decline"?

I think it owes something in the sense of the playfulness of the character. I put three of those poems together (they may have appeared in a magazine) and sent them to Berryman and they didn't interest him at all. He was polite about them but I think that all he could see was that anything I could do he had done better. Maybe that clarified for me that I ought to distance myself more in the poem from the diction of Henry. I showed one of the poems to Mackie Jarrell and she said that she didn't like the lines. She didn't say they were from Berryman, but they were conscious attempts to fake his style. I think it does owe something to him in the freedom of colloquial speech, as in his concern about "lay" and "lie," his use of "ceremony-wise." All of which, I suppose, if the poem were to live one hundred years, would have to be glossed: "In those days there was a difference between the verb 'lie' and 'lay'; and in those days it was considered barbarous to use the suffix '-wise.'"

There is a powerful impulse in your work to move beyond the misgivings, grievances, and despair of so many of your contemporaries. Do you see your work as a dialogue or as an alternative to the work of contemporaries like Lowell and Berryman?

I see it as a dialogue because it relates me to the writers that I admire and know personally. We have different things to say in our poems, we have different visions, so that, in essence, it's a dialogue. I don't think their visions are wrong and mine is right. Mine is corrective of one thing and theirs is corrective of another. It's the distortion of art. I distort to see the truth and they distort to see the truth.

And yours is a more optimistic distortion?

It really is, and I think it comes from having been a closet Christian all my life. I believe in salvation.

Although much of your work is concerned with moral purposes, it does not strike one as being blatantly religious. In fact, the speaker in most of your poems seems to offer the consolation of a well-honed agnosticism. But in a recent poem, ***"Partial Accounts,"*** *you write, "Growing older, I have tottered into the lists / of the religious, tilt." Is this incontrovertible evidence of a conversion?*

No, I would simply say I came out of the closet. My belief is a little clearer to me now and I feel that I ought not to hide it. You know that the best Christian writers don't talk about it as though they were trying to sell you a product. I think of Gerard Manley Hopkins. All the good criticism of Hopkins is written by agnostic Jews and brainwashed nuns who understand that the poetry is true and the truth is what will prevail as a religious example. I say that I'm careful not to practice Christianity conspicuously. But I want to pay attention through the medium of religion. I'm going to give a talk in chapel this month and my theme is going to be that the greatest imaginative accomplishment of the human imagination is atheism. It's the only thing that man has thought up creatively without the help of God. It's a short course but it's a very interesting one. It's sort of like concrete poetry; after you've gotten to the bottom of atheism, you don't have very much left. It's an experiment that has run its course. It is my feeling that all the other works of the imagination are derivatives of the creative imagination of a creator. I don't believe in being very doctrinaire and when I'm among the humanists in Bulgaria, what I say is, "Indeed man isn't all the work of God. Indeed there is no reason that he need refer to God." But that's where I see it coming from.

Is it accurate to say that in recent years your work exhibits a greater willingness to speak to public subjects?

I hope so. I think this had partly to do with my having to think of myself as a public servant again after twenty-five years of not being in public service. I considered myself a public servant when I was in the Navy. Afterwards, I wondered what a public servant does in the role of a poet, when I went to Washington as the poet to the Library of Congress I had a chance to see what could be done with a large audience. Thinking about what happened at the Library of Congress, the chain of artists that one follows there, you see that Americans do have some slight sense of the public function of the poet. It's nice that the Library of Congress has that. It's the branch of Congress that has literary opinions.

In poems like ***"Politics"*** *and* ***"Nixon's the One"*** *(from* **Hazard, the Painter***) and* ***"On Jenkins' Hill"*** *and* ***"A Mild-Spoken Citizen Finally Writes to the White House"*** *(from* **The Cheer***), you develop an unusual civic stance for a contemporary poet, a kind of "poet as concerned citizen" approach to the political scene. Does that characterization seem accurate to you? And does this attitude signify a new kind of openness or political engagement in your work?*

I believe that it represents an openness that I've always felt and acted on but never found much way, before this, to talk about in poetry. The lyric poem is so often private. For example, my intention in writing **"The Wreck of the Thresher"** was to write a "public" poem about my feeling of disappointment in the hopes of the United Nations. When I was writing that poem (and I kept all the drafts of it because I wrote it as a sort of dialogue with my friend Charles Shain, who was here that summer without his wife, being the President of the College; I would leave the draft off for him in the morning and he would scribble notes on it and send it back), I remember seeing it change from a rather pretentious public statement to the very private statement it turned out to be. It occurred to me that this is simply a demonstration of what Auden said in *The Dyer's Hand,* that we don't trust a public voice in poetry today. I would say that my concern about politics is precisely the concern of a Joan Didion or a Denise Levertov but that my stance is very different, so it doesn't appear to be the same. There is a spectrum of political opinion and a spectrum of political involvement. I stand with regard to involvement where those two women stand, but in the political spectrum I'm much more Jeffersonian—I'm nearer the middle.

Your friend, the poet Muriel Rukeyser, had a great sense of the poet's social responsibility.

Yes. I was never as clear about that as she is. I suppose I'm halfway between Muriel Rukeyser, whose every breath was socially responsible, and James Merrill, who pretends not to read the newspapers. Somewhere in the middle is where most artists belong. I sign a lot of things, I send a lot of funny dollars off. Every four years I have a kind of knee-jerk political life. But I can't compare myself to Muriel in that, except insofar as I pay attention to the things that need to be done in the world. One doesn't miss Vietnam and El Salvador.

You have several poems dedicated to Rukeyser. In what way was she influential and important to you?

She was the first poet that I knew personally. I knew her when I was still an undergraduate. She was a very amazing human being and any traces of honesty in my life come from having seen how beautifully honest she was in administering her life and her poetry without any separation—you couldn't get a knife between those two things with her. And my poems are very different from my life, alas. But I understand that that's one of the things you work at when you hope to get better as a poet. The real influence was her human model of what a poet could be. Clearly, our poems have almost nothing in common. But we liked each other's poems, which is an important form of attraction to one's own insufficiency. You like people who can do things you can't do.

You mentioned James Merrill before. One of his chief poetic models is also one of yours: I'm referring to Auden.

I see more of it in my work than in Merrill's. Of course, the wandering spirit of Wystan Hugh Auden prevails in Merrill's trilogy. That spirit is charming and very genuine: it's clearly coming directly. But in my work there is a lot of Auden that nobody could see except me. I don't know how to tell you what it is. In my mind, my playfulness is a lowbrow American version of his Oxford playfulness. Two of the lines in my poem **"About Opera"**—"What dancing is to the slightly spastic way / Most of us teeter through our bodily life"—seem Audenesque to me, and I think Auden liked them. I don't know exactly what I mean by Audenesque. It's like Kafka; it's a totally subjective feeling of how you play with language until you get to something spooky.

It must have been particularly exciting to first encounter Auden's poems.

It was terribly exciting. It seemed like an appropriate way of handling a new experience of one's own and, oddly enough, what all of us sensed was the Marxism of it. And that's what Auden rejected with the style itself. It was an early mannerism, almost, with him, of such originality and so appropriate for the matter. Of course, as soon as the Marxist matter ceased to concern him the manner went with it. But at the time of my college education, the big events, the El Salvador and Vietnam, were the Scottsboro case and the Spanish War. We were very aware of right and wrong and of the correctness of Marx's diagnosis of why wrong was wrong, if not always of why right was right. The other thing—and this is pointed out very well by Edward Mendelson in his book about Auden and somewhat less well but interestingly by Humphrey Carpenter—is that Auden was trying to disguise his private life in those poems so he had to invent a code. The code language applies both to the underground camaraderie of revolutionaries and the underground camaraderie of homosexuals. I was such an underground homosexual that I didn't even talk to myself, let alone anyone else, about it. But I could see that there was something in his language that was appropriate to my intense repressions. I think I picked it up in his short line poems.

Both you and Auden share a deep passion for the opera. How is that passion related to your poetry?

Not directly at all. I think it might say something about the mystique of form, artifice and form, that we both subscribe to. The preposterous Italian opera seems just as realistic to me as Theodore Dreiser now, in the sense that it describes exactly what I see life to be like. And that's pretty peculiar. An important fact about this, which Auden points out, is that we were both fortunate enough not to know anything about opera until we were formed as poets. So it can't have been any influence, but an affinity.

Would you say something about the opera criticism that you wrote for the Hudson Review?

I would say it was lucky that I was never found out.

Did Auden's work change your sense of Yeats's poetry?

Something changed it. Auden supplanted Yeats as an influence at the time. The opposite side of me from what Frost was nourishing had been nourished by Yeats, and that was the intellectual side. I found Yeats intellectual but I found his poems cerebral. A lot of it wasn't actually sustaining with Yeats. Yeats wasn't a whole lot brighter than Tennyson, the only two poets that I feel myself equal to intellectually. It's a very interesting thing about Auden that he was able to wrestle Yeats to the mat by 1939, and pay these enormous respects to him without any animosity because he could see there was no competition.

One of the Yeats poems that crops up in your work is "The Wild Swans at Coole."

I like the early minor poems enormously. I think my favorite Yeats poem is "Upon a Dying Lady." It is a very small poem, not in length but in grasp, and it is so elegantly worded.

Is it the high rhetoric that you object to in Yeats's poetry?

I don't object to it at all. I find "Sailing to Byzantium" a wonderful piece of music, but it no longer seems to have any model value for me. As I look back, it was only an affectation to think that it ever did. I remember how odd I felt showing Frost my little poem **"To a Western Bard"** where the last paragraph starts "Or our own great poet's rage / Yeats. . . ." Frost must have wondered why the hell I didn't say Frost. And twice would he have wondered, once because he was greater than Yeats in his own mind—or maybe not, but competitive—and twice because he must have known that Yeats was no place for me to be whoring around.

Throughout your work, you continually exhibit and also prize the civic virtues of modesty and formal restraints. Why do you think these are so important?

They seem to work for me and I think they're neglected. They're a small part of the picture, but they're a part of the picture that, first of all, isn't talked about very much and, secondly, that I think I know something about.

In the fourteen new poems in **Earth Walk,** *in* **Hazard, the Painter,** *and in* **The Cheer,** *the style seems a little more casual and idiomatic, roomier and more meditative, less metrically concentrated. Do you feel that after your* **Selected Poems,** *your work has been evolving a new mode and style?*

I guess I have the poet's antennae for what's going on in the medium. I've adapted the kind of formalism that is mine with the sensibility for formalism that's abroad in the United States. I would say if you want to see how this happens you can look at the work of Berryman or Lowell and see at what point they stopped using initial capitalization and semicolons and exclamation points. My form, insofar as it's subconscious and instinctive, is responsive to the colloquial, by which I mean in this case the colloquial of the genre. What constitutes the very problematic is audibly different from what constituted my speaker's voice. I believe that I will continue to write poems that are shaped like sonnets and villanelles, I will write them in a way that sounds to me like the modern version.

It sounds like this opening up is a little unwilling.

It is the opening up of a poet who owes as much responsibility to the tradition as to the new and the novel. In that sense, I'm not willing to modify forms which seem to me very energized still. I want to use them now as they were used then, which is to say, to change them.

In a prefatory note you refer to **Hazard** *as a "characterization" and your publisher describes it as "a miniature novel in verse." Is your sequence trying to regain some of the large territory that poetry has lost to prose fiction?*

Rather, I think, an attempt to concentrate on the dramatic virtue of the lyric poem. It comes from contemplating for years Frost's remark, "Everything written is as good as it is dramatic." I felt that many of the experiences that I wanted to comment on would be more interesting if I could give them to somebody else with a different opinion. Take Hazard's problem with his friend's homosexuality: it's the reverse of my problem. I believe in equal rights for heterosexuals. I have a lot of problems with it, and this is a way of getting at them. I was thinking really about, in that relationship, what I must look like to Lowell. Mostly, I'm Hazard in the sequence, but in the poem **"Wholesome"** I'm Elliott and Lowell is Hazard. But the poet has no character in the sense that he is interchangeable.

Apollinaire, a poet you've translated particularly well, talks about the long quarrel between tradition and innovation. Is that quarrel germane to your work?

I'd rather agree with anybody than quarrel, you know. I think I would say, "Guillaume, you're perfectly right." That doesn't help me. I have no quarrel with tradition, as all of my enemies have pointed out. I think there is no point in striving to be modern or original, because I live now and I am unique. Not terribly unique, but God thinks I'm unique, and in that consists my originality. My modernity consists of the dates of birth and death. So that I don't have this battle with tradition. I feel terribly grateful for any insight that tradition gives me as to what we're about. One of the things that poets sometimes forget is that—by their job specification—they are dealing with the most conservative force in culture, that is, language. I believe that my sense of tradition is limited by my ignorance, not by my conservatism. I would like to be more indebted to Spenser but I haven't been able to get through *The Faerie Queene* yet.

What do you think you learned from Apollinaire?

I learned to lie back more fearlessly on my subconscious. I think the little poem I wrote called **"For Guillaume Apollinaire"** is an attempt to say how wonderful it was not to be held accountable for a rational organization of the poem, but simply to feel and to say in English, "Honest to God, that's what Apollinaire said." I'll stick up for him even though it would not have come to me naturally. I think I have one of the most constricted imaginations of any good poet of our time and he had the most liberty in imaginations. It was a helpful distortion. Actually, if I had known about this device I would have started to translate poets like Rilke before. Rilke may be the poet to whom I'm most completely insensitive. I can see what he's doing, but it doesn't make much sense to me. My dream life is as orderly as my waking life.

Of course, Jarrell was a great Rilkean.

Lowell was not and Berryman was not. But none of us will say a word against him. One of my favorite stories about this is the story that Charles Rosen tells about Richard Strauss. He was advisor to Mahler's widow, who had set up the notion of a foundation with her husband's money, and she gave it to composers who needed money. They wrote her and told her why they wanted it—you didn't have to explain how many boats you owned or how much booze you consumed. You just said what you wanted the money for. She consulted Strauss about Arnold Schoenberg and Strauss said, "I've heard some of his recent work and for my part, I think you would be better off in Vienna shoveling snow than giving him the money. But we never know what posterity will say, so you had better give it to him." That's the way I feel about Rilke.

Some of the poems in **The Cheer** *revolve around a single, central, and somewhat mysterious idea. I'm thinking of poems like* ***"Parents"*** *and* ***"Not Both."*** *Would you say something about how these two poems were written?*

I'd love to tell you the story about **"Parents"** because it occurred one time after I'd gone to a Thanksgiving dinner where a couple I'm very fond of had three surviving parents. The three parents seemed to me valid, charming, interesting people, about my own age, and to their children they seemed, as parents normally do, embarrassing, stupid, tedious, albeit lovable. I saw my friends suffering and I remembered such suffering. The poem says essentially, "It is in the nature of things that one's own parents are tacky, and this should give you compassion because your children will find you tacky." The poem came out of that particular experience. **"Not Both"** came from the fact that I was entrusted, unfairly, as one is often entrusted, with a secret by someone who then said, "Probably I shouldn't have told you this, because I know that you don't have the character to keep a secret." I thought, okay, that's a dare, I will. I don't have the character to keep a secret and in this one case I will keep a seret and I won't tell it to anyone. The other examples in the poem are unresolved questions about people I know. I don't know whether one is a suicide, I don't know if one was having an incestuous love affair, and not ever knowing that is almost the same as it not ever having happened. Two things can happen and one did, and I don't know which one it is. And then the final thing is Pascal's wager: Somebody knows, or nobody knows, the answer to these questions.

The final line is a comment on that: "One of those two appalling things is true too."

Some people don't see how I use the word "cheer." I'm cheerful because I'm able to say that, to see that, and live. That's all I'd lose. Those are not the rules that I myself would have chosen. But we accept this wager from God, or not from God, and we don't despair. We assent.

What does it mean to say, as Thoreau does and as you affirm, that things change, but from what they are not to what they are?

Well, any time people ask me about the difference between the poems in ***The Cheer*** formally or in content, from my earlier work, my impulse is to say that I'm more sure of what is in character for me now than when I was thirty-three, and the poems are what is in character for me. I have changed, like Thoreau's aphorism, only by sloughing off that which is not in character for me. I would have loved to write like Yeats or Matthew Arnold or Eliot at one time, but in terms of what's shown to me, I don't see in those spectrums, I don't see in that way or in those rhythms; so it was inappropriate, insofar as I imitated those people, to imitate that which is not in character. It was probably in character for me all along to imitate Wordsworth and Frost and Auden.

Theodore Roethke once said, "In spite of all the muck and welter, the dark, the dreck *of these poems, I count myself among the happy poets." Do you want to be one of the happy poets?*

I would like ***The Cheer*** to seem like someone who would say, "Yes. Without any reservations, I say yes." I speak about other things with reservations: things that I would want to change, things that I wish hadn't happened, things that we need to do and that we're not doing. But there are people who involuntarily give off an aura of "No," and those seem to be the people I quarrel with. It is inevitable to quarrel with that which you consider damaging in life.

In your introduction to a selection of Shelley's poems you wrote, "Art by its very nature asserts at least two kinds of good—order and delight." Do you still believe that?

I think I would say it more carefully.

What do you think you'll write next?

I think that at the rate that I go I will probably continue writing poems that synthesize or readdress some of the things I've seen in terms of the experience of my life. I'm not a quick study. I learn the things that are important in life very slowly and often more than once. The only thing the poet has to say is how he got an insight into what everybody already knows. I'll be trying to write poems that are generally accessible and attractive. And more and more I think happiness is the way that my poems go and the way that people take them, taking them as unpretentiously as they're offered. I am very happy about my relationships with students and friends, and I have this wonderful sense that my obligation comes from being privileged to write poems.

Henry Taylor (essay date 1992)

SOURCE: "In Charge of Morale in a Morbid Time," in *Compulsory Figures: Essays on Recent American Poets,* Louisiana State University Press, 1992, pp. 171-89.

[*In the following essay, Taylor surveys the defining qualities of Meredith's poetry.*]

The Wreck of the Thresher, published in 1964, was the book that most firmly established the nature and strength of William Meredith's poetry. It seems now to have been the culmination of a development in certain directions from which the poet has since swerved, though not unrewardingly. The poems in it reveal unobtrusive mastery of craft traditionally conceived; there are not many sonnets, villanelles, sestinas, or other insistent evidences that the poet is comfortable in formal cages; but beneath the steady, honest lines, with their sometimes unpredictable rhyme schemes, there is a sense of assurance that for Meredith, form is a method, not a barrier. In its range of subject, tone, and mode, the book consistently offers the voice of a civilized man, a man with good but not exclusive manners, engaged in encounters with matters of inexhaustible interest.

This style did not come quickly to Meredith—not that his debut was inauspicious: his first book, ***Love Letter from an Impossible Land,*** was chosen by Archibald MacLeish in his first year as editor of the Yale Series of Younger Poets. Here were a number of accomplished poems, including a few that spoke in the voice that would be firmly Meredith's by the time ***The Wreck of the Thresher*** appeared twenty years later. Much of the book is apprentice work, but in the "impossible land" of the Aleutians, of the Second World War, Meredith came to grips with strangeness for which no borrowed voice could suffice. So the book falls into two parts, whose relation MacLeish describes as "the way in which the literary vehicle (for it is nothing else) of the Princeton undergraduate turns into the live idiom of a poet's speech reaching for poetry." What is there, one wonders, to like about "the literary vehicle of the Princeton undergraduate"? A possible answer is that the earlier poems show us a young poet diligently studying his craft. In the brief lyrics that acknowledge various masters, there is little room for the voice of Meredith, but there is in them a serious and intelligent setting-forth after the tools that will give the voice, when it speaks, the distinctiveness and force of the later poems. Craft matters to the young poet: of the thirty-three poems in ***Love Letter,*** eight are traditional sonnets, and seven others are near-sonnets of twelve to fourteen lines. If some of these are predictable or flat, or if others are too insistent upon their experimentation with formal expansion (as in the packed internal rhymes and slant end-rhymes of **"War Sonnet,"** for instance), practice has made nearly perfect by the time we come to **"In Memoriam Stratton Christensen"**:

Laughing young man and fiercest against sham,
Then you have stayed at sea, at feckless sea,
With a single angry curiosity
Savoring fear and faith and speckled foam?
A salt end to what was sweet begun:
Twenty-three years and your integrity
And already a certain number touched like me
With a humor and a hardness from the sun.
Without laughter we have spent your wit
In an unwitnessed fight at sea, perhaps not won,
And whether wisely we will never know;
But like Milton's friend's, to them that hear of it

Your death is a puzzler that will tease them on
Reckless out on the thin, important floe.[1]

Here the experimentation with local sonic richness is muted, but not below the level of fruitful risk; for example, *Reckless* in the last line is right not only in itself, but because it echoes the second and fourth lines.

In **"Notes for an Elegy,"** a longer poem whose ambition and scope are larger than anything else in this book, Meredith sounds a note of modesty in the title, a note that he will sound again and again, even as his poems improve. This title, of course, means not to suggest that the poem is unfinished—it is quite brilliantly finished—but that in a time and place more distant from the war, it might have acquired more of the trappings of a formal elegy. Here, the first twenty-two lines, a meditation on flying and its relation to freedom, tyranny, and war, set the proper tone, verging toward an invocation to the muse. The death is that of an airman, but not one shot down in battle; for some mysterious reason, his plane has crashed in a wood. Having asked where the engine and the wings were at the crucial moment, the speaker concludes that

the invitation
Must have been sent to the aviator in person:
Perhaps a sly suggestion of carelessness,
A whispered invitation perhaps to death,
Death.[2]

The quietness of this passage, while it emphasizes the distance of the crash from any battle, is at odds with the noisy violence of any plane's untimely coming down; it is as if the plane and its pilot had drifted silently to rest, like so many other things that fall in the forest when no one is there to hear them. This impression is confronted in the poem's remarkable conclusion, where the phrase "as it were in bed" lifts the tone out of solemnity toward something large enough to enclose great mystery:

Note that he had not fought one public battle,
Met any fascist with his skill, but died
As it were in bed, the waste conspicuous . . .

. . . . .

The morning came up foolish with pink clouds
To say that God counts ours a cunning time,
Our losses part of an old secret, somehow no loss.

(***EW,*** 34-35)

This ability to complicate tone by the subtle use of something close to humor has been important in much of Meredith's work, though it has been only recently that many of his serious poems have contained very wide streaks of humor. But fairly early, Meredith came to an inclusive control of tone that makes for greater strength than the owlish cultivation of high seriousness.

These qualities of strength and inclusiveness, however, are not much in evidence in Meredith's second book, ***Ships and Other Figures,*** which appeared in 1948, only four years after ***Love Letter.*** A note of acknowledgement states that "most of these poems were written and all of them collected while the writer was a Woodrow Wilson Fellow of Princeton University," and one feels keenly the absence of peril in these poems, the safety of academe. Under the pressure of his credentials as a promising young poet, Meredith seems not to be the aviator inspired to struggle with his craft and its relation to puzzles of much magnitude; he seems instead to be a Wilson Fellow who would like to have enough poems for a book. Under such circumstances, he turns his hand to various exercises in tradition and occasion, and is sometimes successful with slight poems where, the pressure being momentarily off, he can indulge his excellent sense of play without fear of momentous failure. Here, for example, is the first of **"Two Figures from the Movies"**:

The papers that clear him tucked in his inside pocket
And the grip of the plucky blonde light on his bicep,
He holds the gang covered now, and backs for the door
That gives on the daylit street and the yare police.
But the regular customers know that before the end
With its kissing and money and adequate explanation,
He has still to back into the arms of the baldheaded man
With the huge signet-ring and the favorable odds of surprise,
Somehow to outface the impossible arrogant stare,
And will his luck hold, they wonder, and has he the skill?[3]

Meredith continues to be puzzled by my affection for this little poem; some years ago, when I sought to include **"Two Figures"** in an anthology, he granted his permission on the condition that my text not make fun of it or ask embarrassing study questions about it. True, its matter is more trivial than the matters that usually engage Meredith; but in its satirical arrangement of well-chosen cinematic clichés, and in its deft echo of classical heroic meters, it is a small but thorough success. The second of the **"Two Figures"** is less successful, as it lacks the particularity of the first, and is somewhat outweighed by its epigraph from Shakespeare. Even so, these two poems have intrinsic interest, and reveal an impulse that is important in much of Meredith's later work.

This is not to suggest that, in his ***New and Selected Poems*** of 1970, Meredith saved from ***Ships and Other Figures*** all the wrong things; he saved the best six poems, but would not have tarnished his reputation by carrying forward a few more. The same could be said of his selection from ***The Open Sea*** (1958), a collection of nearly fifty poems of considerable range and effectiveness. Here Meredith continues his exploration of difficult fixed forms, not merely in order to submit himself to complex rules, but also to see how some of these rules may be pushed around. Aside from the half-dozen or so sonnets that one might expect to find, there are also two sestinas and a dedicatory villanelle. The usefulness of these explorations is perhaps most apparent in the title poem, which fits the definition of none of the fixed forms mentioned above, but which clearly takes advantage of their existence:

We say the sea is lonely; better say
Our selves are lonesome creatures whom the sea
Gives neither yes nor no for company.
Oh, there are people, all right, settled in the sea—
It is as populous as Maine today—
But no one who will give you the time of day.
A man who asks there of his family
Or a friend or teacher gets a cold reply
Or finds him dead against that vast majority.
Nor does it signify, that people who stay
Very long, bereaved or not, at the edge of the sea
Hear the drowned folk call: that is mere fancy,
They are speechless. And the famous noise of sea,
Which a poet has beautifully told us in our day,
Is hardly a sound to speak comfort to the lonely.
Although not yet a man given to prayer, I pray
For each creature lost since the start at sea,
And give thanks it was not I, nor yet one close to me.

(*PA,* 23)

The poem's debt to the formal repetitions of villanelle or sestina is clear enough; what is less clear is how the poet, in suggesting a form that already exists, walks the elusive line between failure to fulfill the contract and success in making something that is complete on its own terms. Here, the success is gained through a profound awareness of the subtle tensions that arise between hypothetical form and human utterance. The first stanza, with its second line reaching just above the sound of conversation, establishes a tone that is greatly broadened, but not obliterated, by the second stanza, which stays within the metrical bounds of the poem while it introduces a much looser diction. This thoughtful changing of voices is held in suspension through the final stanza, so that the speaker earns our belief in his prayer.

Another fine example of what comes of serious play is **"The Illiterate,"** a poem whose structure is that of a Petrarchan sonnet, but repeated words appear at the ends of the lines, instead of rhymes. The octave begins by saying, "Touching your goodness, I am like a man / Who turns a letter over in his hand," and goes on to say that the man has never received a letter before, and is unable to read it, or to overcome his shame and ask someone to read it to him. The poem ends:

His uncle could have left the farm to him,
Or his parents died before he sent them word,
Or the dark girl changed and want him for beloved.
Afraid and letter-proud, he keeps it with him.
What would you call his feeling for the words
That keep him rich and orphaned and beloved?

(*PA,* 27)

The wit that chose recurring words instead of rhymes for a poem like this, and the craft that makes them work, have greatly matured since the early sonneteering experiments; this poem transcends its quite noticeable peculiarity, partly by drawing us away from the ends of the lines toward consideration of the subtle use of *your* and *you,* in the first and thirteenth lines, respectively: these words and lines are just enough to keep the simile and the form from being self-conscious studies of themselves.

Of course such forms are, in some unself-conscious way, studies of themselves. By this time Meredith has wedded technique to meditation, so that they are harder to separate, even for convenience in discussion, than they were in his earlier work. Meredith finds several occasions in ***The Open Sea*** to be explicit about the value of art; there are several poems about music, painting, sculpture, architecture, the ballet, and so on, and in all of these one finds an admiration for formal restraint, especially when it is evident that there is something beneath the form that is worth restraining, whose power is worth conserving.

To this end, Meredith joins the urge to self-consciousness and a very light touch with meter, to strike a precise balance of tones in the pleasant but complicated **"Thoughts on One's Head (In Plaster, With A Bronze Wash)."** In a delicate alternation of masculine and feminine rhymes, and in a meter of musical elasticity, these stanzas, like good heads, hold simultaneously a number of attitudes:

A person is very self-conscious about his head.
It makes one nervous just to know it is cast
In enduring materials, and that when the real one is dead
The cast one, if nobody drops it or melts it down, will last.
We pay more attention to the front end, where the face is,
Than to the interesting and involute interior:
The Fissure of Rolando and such queer places
Are parks for the passions and fears and mild hysteria.

(*PA,* 37)

The slight confusion between the cast head and the real head, introduced by the unobtrusively vague it in the second line, modulates into clarity: the head under discussion becomes the real head, with its Fissure of Rolando, its judgment, and so on; but at the end, the poem seems to shift partly back to the cast head for a moment, in the last line below:

This particular head, to my certain knowledge
Has been taught to read and write, make love and money,
Operate cars and airplanes, teach in a college,
And tell involved jokes, some few extremely funny.
It was further taught to know and to eschew
Error and sin, which it does erratically.
This is the place the soul calls home just now.
One dislikes it of course: it is the seat of Me.

(*PA,* 38)

"One dislikes it of course:" the cast head, occasion for an aesthetic judgment (however biased), has become the occasion for a meditation on its original, "the seat of Me"; and the cast head stays between the real head and the observing consciousness, a barrier against self-indulgence, a reminder that either head could be dropped or melted down.

The Wreck of the Thresher is both larger and smaller than ***The Open Sea.*** It contains fewer poems, and there is less variety of form and subject; but several of these poems are considerably more ambitious than anything preceding them. In somewhat narrowing the range of his attention, Meredith deepens his focus, producing a few poems that can stand with the best poems of his generation. (Often people write such phrases in their sleep; I am awake, and aware that I speak of the generation of Berryman, Bishop, Lowell, Nemerov, and Wilbur, among others.)

The title poem is a bold achievement, one of Meredith's rare "public" poems; its occasion was the destruction at sea of the nuclear submarine *Thresher* on April 10, 1963. Much has happened since that date to make that disaster recede from the public consciousness; one of this poem's strengths is that it has not been diminished by a fifteen-year torrent of public catastrophes. The poem deserves closer attention than it has received. Some reviewers have accused it of staginess; Richard Howard, to whose essay on Meredith I am in some ways indebted, does not mention it.[4]

The opening stanza, it is true, makes a few moves that seem suspicious; the first line arouses the fear that this may be just one more "I-am-standing" poem, a subgenre often exploited by poets who have nothing to say. And the description of the sea, with its zoömorphic similes, seems melodramatic:

> I stand on the ledge where rock runs into the river
> As the night turns brackish with morning, and mourn the drowned.
> Here the sea is diluted with river; I watch it slaver
> Like a dog curing of rabies. Its ravening over,
> Lickspittle ocean nuzzles the dry ground.
> (But the dream that woke me was worse than the sea's grey
> Slip-slap; there are no such sounds by day.)
>
> (***PA,*** 46)

But it is the dream that has imposed this animistic vision on the speaker; it is, as **"The Open Sea"** has it, "mere fancy," to which the speaker will return as the poem shifts from the present to the dream, then to meditation derived from both:

> This crushing of people is something we live with.
> Daily, by unaccountable whim
> Or caught up in some harebrained scheme of death,
> Tangled in cars, dropped from the sky, in flame,
> Men and women break the pledge of breath:
> And now under water, gone all jetsam and small
> In the pressure of oceans collected, a squad of brave men in a hull.
>
> (***PA,*** 46)

The only full rhyme in this stanza is one of the most predictable in our language, but the lines thus rhymed give the words freshness of context, and the rhyme's very obtrusiveness yokes "harebrained scheme" to "break the pledge," one of the many subtle juxtapositions that parallel the larger tensions between actuality and dream, land and sea, life and death. In dream, the speaker has met

> a monstrous self trapped in the black deep:
> *All these years,* he smiled, *I've drilled at sea*
> *For this crush of water.* Then he saved only me.
>
> (***PA,*** 46)

The phrase "a monstrous self" suggests, at the same time, an other and a version of the speaker's own self; we are reminded, more subtly here than in some other poems, of Meredith's own war experience, the losses of friends, the perils survived. The poem moves again to the question of investing the inanimate with life, as in the tradition of naming ships "for ladies and queens,"

> Although by a wise superstition these are called
> After fish, the finned boats, silent and submarine.
>
> (***PA,*** 47)

The complicated idea of a "wise superstition" carries one through the next stanza, where the sea is divested of emotion while the dead sailors, it seems, are given the capacity for it:

> I think of how sailors laugh, as if cold and wet
> And dark and lost were their private, funny derision
> And I can judge then what dark compression
> Astonishes them now, their sunken faces set
> Unsmiling, where the currents sluice to and fro
> And without humor, somewhere northeast of here and below.
>
> (***PA,*** 47)

Astonishes, of course, turns out to be completely appropriate, as it means "renders insensate"; we are forced by the syntax, and by the word's placement at the head of the line, following a breathless enjambment, to examine it before passing on to the pun in "sunken faces." This vision of the sailors leads back to the dream again, in a stanza where impossible schemes of escape and heroism give way to the voices of the drowned: "Study something deeper than yourselves, / As, how the heart, when it turns diver, delves and saves." Earlier in the poem, the speaker asks, "Why can't our dreams be content with the terrible facts?" In the light of day, no one truly hears "the drowned folk call." The poem passes from the dream to a final stanza of great stateliness; in its treatment of the terrible facts, it shifts from the nearly conversational to the nearly prophetic, its movement genuinely suggestive of a musical coda:

> Whether we give assent to this or rage
> Is a question of temperament and does not matter.
> Some will has been done past our understanding,
> Past our guilt surely, equal to our fears.
> Dullards, we are set again to the cryptic blank page
> Where the sea schools us with terrible water.
> The noise of a boat breaking up and its men is in our ears.
> The bottom here is too far down for our sounding;
> The ocean was salt before we crawled to tears.
>
> (***PA,*** 48)

In this poem, and in others in the collection, a quality of modesty asserts itself strongly; Meredith himself described it a few years later, in a foreword to ***Earth Walk: New and Selected Poems***; he selected from earlier books, he says, "poems that try to say things I am still trying to find ways to say, poems that engage mysteries I still pluck at the hems of, poems that are devious in ways I still like better than plainspokenness." **"The Wreck of the Thresher"** only seems to be plainspoken; it engages and contains deep mystery, and makes it memorable.

Plucking at the hems of old mysteries sometimes compels a poet to go over ground he has visited before. **"On Falling Asleep to Birdsong,"** the third poem in ***The Wreck of the Thresher,*** recalls the title of **"On Falling Asleep by Firelight,"** from ***The Open Sea.*** The earlier poem is perhaps too tidy to be convincing; the later poem is much better made, and goes beyond tidiness, drifting with the consciousness of a man falling asleep, who hears a whippoorwill and thinks of his parents' and his own death. Trying to dream of nightingales, he is led on to Philomela, whose story appears gracefully in the poem, not as paraded learning, but as the unwilled reverie of a man who has read some books:

> But I am in bed in the fall
> And cannot arrest the dream
> That unwinds a chase and a rape
> And ends in Thracian pain.
>
> (***PA,*** 52)

The whippoorwill calls, and is not answered; his song becomes no more than itself, and no less: "When time has gone away / He calls to what he calls." And the speaker, thinking that "life is one," accepts both the written fable and the one the whippoorwill has helped him to invent:

> I will grow old, as a man
> Will read of a transformation:
> Knowing it is a fable
> Contrived to answer a question
> Answered, if ever, in fables,
> Yet all of a piece and clever
> And at some level, true.
>
> (***PA,*** 53)

This idea, that unwilled or semiconscious rumination leads on to meditation and sometimes to fable, is taken up several times in ***The Wreck of the Thresher,*** often in sequences or in poems separated into nearly self-contained sections. **"Fables About Error," "Five Accounts of a Monogamous Man,"** and **"Consequences"** are all acts of a mind responding with attentive love to surfaces, but never being content with superficiality. The first of the **"Fables About Error"** develops the amusing notion that "The mouse in the cupboard repeats himself," being found dead every morning in the trap. On one level, then, the idea that the mouse should know better after a while is preposterous, but Meredith's conclusion is nonetheless apt:

> Surely there is always that in experience
> Which could warn us; and the worst
> That can be said of any of us is:
> He did not pay attention.
>
> (***EW,*** 82)

Meredith pays close attention, and finds even in our troubled age some vindication of his tendency to praise, as he says in "of choice," the first section of **"Consequences"**:

> More than I hoped to do, I do
> And more than I deserve I get;
> What little I attend, I know
> And it argues order more than not.
>
> (***PA,*** 64)

This attitude of hopefulness comes through these poems tentatively, free of the hectoring tone that often afflicts poems with something valuable to say. They are "all of a piece," and let themselves come gradually to those levels where they ring truest. At such levels, they are beyond cleverness.

In 1970, Meredith published ***Earth Walk: New and Selected Poems.*** I have already suggested that he was too stingy in making his selections from the four previous books, though he makes a handsome apology for this in a foreword: "In making this selection from twenty-five years of work I have represented my early books scantily, as I have come to feel they represented me. Juvenile gifts apart, it takes time to find out our real natures and purposes. But finally we have done so many things, good and bad, in character, that it is permissible to disown some of our other acts, at any rate the bad ones, as impersonations." He makes it clear in the next sentence, part of which is quoted earlier, that he is talking primarily about his first two books, and it is hard to quarrel much with his selection from those. But the slimness of the selection as a whole should have the effect, intended or not, of sending the reader back to the early work, especially to ***The Open Sea,*** where among the thirty-three "disowned" poems there are several that reward continued attention.

But one turns with greatest interest, of course, to the fourteen new poems in ***Earth Walk,*** and one is struck first by the variety of points of view. Poems spoken by fictional characters are not plentiful in Meredith's work, though on some occasions, as in **"Five Accounts of a Monogamous Man,"** he has adopted, as Yeats often did, the device of applying third-person titles to first-person poems. ***Earth Walk*** opens with such a poem, **"Winter Verse for His Sister,"** the speaker of which is not readily distinguishable from Meredith himself. Then in **"Walter Jenks' Bath"** the speaker is a young black boy thinking over what his teacher has said about the way everything is composed of atoms. The tension between the poet's level of sophistication and that of the speaker is first of all useful in setting the tone of the poem, the touching simplicity of the observations; but in the last six lines, what Walter Jenks says becomes larger in its grasp of things, so that in the final line, he seems to speak for the poet as well as for himself:

> And when I stop the atoms go on knocking,
> Even if I died the parts would go on spinning,
> Alone, like the far stars, now knowing it,
> Not knowing they are far apart, or running,

Or minding the black distances between.
This is me knowing, this is what I know.

(*PA,* 75)

That a child in the bathtub comes plausibly to thoughts like these is a tribute to the delicacy with which the tone is handled; the same delicacy sustains a tougher poem, **"Effort at Speech,"** in which the speaker relates an encounter with a mugger. The speaker and the mugger wrestle briefly, the wallet parts "like a wishbone," the mugger flees with his ill-gotten half, and the speaker comes close to guilt at having retained the other half:

Next time don't wrangle, give the boy the money,
Call across chasms what the world you know is.
Luckless and lied to, how can a child master
human decorum?
Next time a switch-blade, somewhere he is thinking,
I should have killed him and took the lousy wallet.
Reading my cards he feels a surge of anger
blind as my shame.

(*PA,* 78)

The strength of the poet's control over these lines is felt in the prosody; this narrative of violence and guilt is cast in stanzas that come as close to Sapphics as idiomatic English can come. The classical echo puts a distance between the poet and the events described, but it also recalls the actual effort that real speech requires.

Colloquial language, contractions, and exclamations fall into regular stanzas in **"Poem About Morning,"** a funny little lecture on waking up and facing the day. The suggestion of lecturing is made by casting the poem in the second person, though the "you" partakes of the speaker's experience, almost as if the speaker were addressing himself. And **"Earth Walk"** provides a final illustration of the experimentation with point of view that runs like a thread through these new poems. The title poem begins in the third person, as a man pulls off the highway and touches his seat belt. After the phrase "He thinks" the first stanza continues in the first-person plural, as it describes our habit of traveling in straps and helmets. The second stanza is in the first-person singular, but despite the stanza break, it all still follows from "He thinks." The man steps out of his car, parodying the careful steps of the men on the moon:

I pick out small white stones. This is a safe walk.
This turnpike is uninhabited. When I come back
I'll meet a trooper with a soft, wide hat
who will take away my Earth-rocks and debrief me.

(*EW,* 20)

The shift from third to first person, while it is perfectly within the bounds of narrative logic, still gives the poem a scope of observation that a single point of view might lack.

These new poems, with their restless personal pronouns, may now be seen as forerunners of Meredith's next book, ***Hazard, the Painter*** (1975). This collection of sixteen poems seems to have been designed to provoke a number of reactions, not all of them charitable, and not all of them familiar to readers of Meredith's previous books. One notices pure surface, a meticulous and beautiful job of book production in which the cover and typography seem to assert that the book amounts to more than its small bulk might suggest. Inside, there are poems composing a "characterization," as Meredith calls it in a cagey note; he adds, "Resemblances between the life and character of Hazard and those of the author are not disclaimed but are much fewer than the author would like."

It comes to mind that in the work of William Meredith and John Berryman there are several references to their friendship; furthermore, as Meredith has acknowledged in public readings, a line in the first of the ***Hazard*** poems is taken from Berryman's conversation. The uncharitable speculation arises that Hazard is too closely akin to Berryman's Henry, in strategy if not in size and style. Clearly, though, Meredith cannot have conceived this book in any competitive way, as Lowell seems to have conceived his *Notebooks*; the very brevity of ***Hazard*** indicates that it is not useful to compare it with *The Dream Songs,* even though that book continues to loom as a distant forebear.

Hazard is a middle-aged painter with a wife and two children. For two years his subject has been a parachutist, but he is at the moment stalled in his work; various pressures—family, uneasy friendships with other painters, daydreams—take up more of his time than painting does. He has a fine eye for detail, and a wry sense of the absurd; lying at the beach, where "they use the clouds over & over / again, like the rented animals in *Aïda,*" Hazard nearly dozes as things impinge at random on his consciousness, making equal claims on his curiosity:

The sand knocks like glass, struck by bare heels.
He tries to remember snow noise.
Would powder snow ping like that?
But you don't lie with your ear to powder snow.
Why doesn't the girl who takes care
of the children, a Yale girl without flaw,
know the difference between *lay* and *lie?*

(*PA,* 111)

The style of ***Hazard*** appears to be more casual, less concentrated, than anything Meredith has written before. One notices, for instance, that there is not a semicolon anywhere in these poems; instead, the independent clauses tumble along over their commas, contributing to the feeling of interior life, as in the second half of this stanza from **"Politics,"** a poem about liberals gathering to hear jazz for McGovern:

Hazard desires his wife, the way people
on the trains to the death-camps were seized
by irrational lust. She is the youngest woman
in the room, he would like to be in bed
with her now, he would like to be president.

(*PA,* 100)

Gradually, as one rereads these poems, the accumulation of anecdote and detail provides the density that is missing from the style, and there arises the illusion of a life, a way of life, made difficult by a difficult time, but still enjoyable and cherished. "The culture is in late imperial decline," Hazard thinks in the line taken from Berryman; and in **"Hazard's Optimism,"** considering his vision of the parachutist as he himself tries a parachute jump, Hazard concludes thus:

> They must have caught and spanked him
> like this when he first fell.
> He passes it along now, Hazard's vision.
> He is in charge of morale in a morbid time.
> He calls out to the sky, his voice
> the voice of an animal that makes not words
> but a happy incorrigible noise, not
> of this time.
>
> (***PA,*** 96)

The mask of Hazard gives Meredith, at least for the duration of this deceptively brief book, the freedom to work out of ways in which he might think he was becoming set. In the chattiness that contains more than it at first seems to, beneath the detailed surfaces, there is room for satire as well as for a serious, loving exploration of a peculiar world.

But Hazard was not destined to take over Meredith's voice and life. He is an interesting character met along the way, and, having met him, Meredith was usefully diverted. In more recent work, the deceptively casual tone and form in Hazard's voice have been especially useful. The title poem of ***The Cheer*** (1980) says to the reader, "Frankly, I'd like to make you smile" (*PA,* 123), and speaks up for the cheer and courage in which words are born; but **"Recollection of Bellagio"** shows how far from humor such an optimistic aim can go. The first of the poem's two strophes describes the dance of pine needles against a night sky like a ballroom floor; here is the second:

> How long has this been going on, this *allemande,*
> before a man's thoughts climbed up to sit
> on the limestone knob and watch (briefly,
> as man's thoughts' eyes watch) the needles
> keeping time to the bells which the same wind rocks
> on the water below, marking the fishermen's nets—
> thoughts he would haul in later from the lake
> of time, feeling himself drawn clumsy
> back into time's figure, hand over hand,
> by the grace of pine boughs? And who
> is saying these words, now that that man
> is a shade, has become his own shade?
> I see the shade rise slow and ghostly from its seat
> on the soft, grainy stone, I watch it descend
> by the gravelled paths of the promontory,
> under a net of steady stars, in April,
> from the boughs' rite and the bells'—quiet,
> my shade, and long ago, and still going on.
>
> (***PA,*** 129-30)

A number of the poems in this book elicit the deep and often unseen smile of pleasure at difficulty being negotiated with good cheer. Even in poems addressing a president guilty of "criminal folly," or friends—Lowell, Berryman—who have died, love of the world often matters at least as much as the world's unwitting insistence on harboring wickedness, folly, and death.

Among the best poems in ***The Cheer*** are four unusually "literary" ones; three are responses to epigraphs at least as long as the poems, and one requires a prose preface of more than 150 words. This last is **"Trelawny's Dream,"** in which Edward John Trelawny recalls—and, in dream, revises—the boating accident that took the life of his friend Shelley. A splendid poem taken alone, it also speaks to **"The Wreck of the Thresher"**; both poems are moving portrayals of our need to dream away our helplessness, and to wake to it.

Meredith's most recent book of poems, for which he received the Pulitzer Prize in Poetry, is ***Partial Accounts: New and Selected Poems*** (1987). Here, as in ***Earth Walk,*** he has represented his early work sparingly. I miss **"Fables About Error,"** and like to think it took its small revenge at being dropped: its former neighbor **"The Ballet,"** first collected in ***The Wreck of the Thresher,*** appears here among the poems selected from ***The Open Sea.***

Partial Accounts adds a translation and ten new poems to the selections from earlier books; they meditate upon violence and love about equally, and often on the human ability to separate ourselves from the rest of nature. **"The Jain Bird Hospital in Delhi"** applies to its form the nonviolent attitudes of the Jains, who see all living things as brothers and sisters; the form is based on that of a sestina, but only one end-word is varied by so slight a device as shifting between singular and plural; others are replaced with homophones, synonyms, or associates; one appears as *pigeons, bird(s), creatures, pheasants,* and *flock;* another as *beings, men, women, laymen, poultrymen, women,* and *ourselves.* Few readers will ponder the adherence to traditional word-order long enough to discover that birds are creatures and people are beings; the poem wittily exemplifies nonviolent achievement of order.

In **"Partial Accounts"** a surprising juxtaposition makes a defense of optimism; the first part, titled "surgery," humorously remarks on the appropriateness of replacing a faulty valve with a pig's valve; the second part recalls the sympathy the speaker felt as he watched, or tried not to watch, an Arab woman in Morocco having a tooth pulled in the open-air market:

> The *chirurgien dentiste* was a small man,
> authoritative, Berber I think.
> His left foot was set gently on the woman's
> shoulder, and when I last looked,
> difficult, silent progress was being made.
>
> (***PA,*** 182-83)

Meredith continues to find fresh ways of reminding us that there is joy in plucking at the hems of even the darkest mysteries; as he says in **"Among Ourselves,"** "Accountability / weighs on me, but so does happiness" (***PA,*** 181).

Notes

1. Archibald MacLeish, Foreword to *Love Letter from an Impossible Land,* by William Meredith (New Haven, 1944); William Meredith, *Partial Accounts: New and Selected Poems* (New York, 1987), 6. Hereafter cited in the text as *PA,* followed by a page number.
2. William Meredith, *Earth Walk: New and Selected Poems* (New York, 1970), 34. Hereafter cited in the text as *EW,* followed by a page number.
3. William Meredith, *Ships and Other Figures* (Princeton, 1948), 26.
4. Richard Howard, *Alone with America* (New York, 1969), 318-26.

Michael Collier (essay date 1997)

SOURCE: A foreword to *Effort at Speech: New and Selected Poems* by William Meredith, Triquarterly Books, 1997, pp. xiii-xvi.

[*In the following essay, Collier determines the major influences on Meredith's work.*]

What separates William Meredith from other poets of his generation, such as Robert Lowell, John Berryman, Howard Nemerov, and James Merrill, is his belief that "poetry and experience should have an exact ratio." For him this ratio speaks to the seriousness of the lyric. In a Spring 1985 *Paris Review* interview he says, "I wait until the poems seem addressed not to 'Occupant' but to 'William Meredith.' And it doesn't happen a lot." John Crowe Ransom and Philip Larkin are the poets Meredith invokes in praise of his parsimonious muse. Nevertheless, ***Effort at Speech*** is strong evidence that in a lifetime of writing Meredith had the luck of generous visits from his muse. His first book, ***Love Letter from an Impossible Land*** (1944), was chosen by Archibald MacLeish for the Yale Series of Younger Poets prize. In his foreword MacLeish points to an aspect of Meredith's poems that rings true throughout his oeuvre and stands as much for the man as for the work: "[The poems] give the sense of having *seen,* of having been present, which a man's face sometimes gives, returning. They have the quality of reticence and yet of communication, almost unwilling communication." What the poems have *seen* is the Second World War, which was the young Meredith's first purview as a writer. Later his poems preside over equally difficult events of human experience, such as the suicides and early deaths of his friends. More than forty years after ***Love Letter*** was published, Meredith's ***Partial Accounts: New and Selected Poems*** received the Pulitzer Prize for 1988. In between those two books, Meredith published six other volumes of poems, a highly acclaimed translation of Apollinaire's *Alcools,* a collection of essays, and an edition of Shelley's poetry. He has served as a member of the National Institute of Arts and Letters and as a chancellor of the Academy of American Poets for more than thirty years. From 1978 to 1980 he served as the poetry consultant to the Library of Congress. Meredith taught at Connecticut College for nearly thirty years.

In 1973 when I first met William Meredith at Connecticut College, where I had enrolled as an undergraduate, he was putting the finishing touches on a short, book-length poem, ***Hazard, the Painter*** (1975), and was worried the poem's "free verse was going to be the end of [him]." ***Hazard, the Painter*** is a sequence about a modest visual artist who finds his belief in manners and decorum is at odds with the fashionable and dangerous pessimism infecting the times. The urbane, witty, but earnest Hazard—a Meredith alter ego—is meant to continue the long-running argument Meredith had enjoined with his generation, the poets of suicide and confessionalism. By the late 1970s this had devolved into an argument with himself, since many of the principals were no longer around. "Friends making off ahead of time / on their own, I call that willful, John, / but that's not judgment, only argument / such as we've had before" is how he phrases it in **"In Loving Memory of the Late Author of *Dream Songs*,"** from ***The Cheer*** (1980). Although Meredith was fearful of Hazard's free verse, all of the poems are written with the unerring control that earned him a reputation for being one of his generation's most elegant metricists.

William Meredith was most influenced by Robert Frost and W. H. Auden (see **"In Memory of Robert Frost"** and **"Talking Back (To W. H. Auden)"**). In 1940, while at Princeton, Meredith wrote his senior essay on Frost and traveled to New England to meet the revered poet. Auden he met in New York City in the 1950s through a shared love of opera. When Meredith became a faculty member of the Bread Loaf School of English in the late 1950s, he enjoyed a deep friendship with Frost. In 1961 the older poet invited the younger to accompany him on a reading tour to the West Coast. Similarly, his friendship with Auden was such that when Auden died in 1973 Meredith was named an executor of his estate. Meredith discovered in Frost the metaphoric power inherent in the natural world, especially with regard to plants and trees. But from both Auden and Frost Meredith learned about wit and playfulness, and the sly ways in which poetic conventions could be renewed through colloquial language. Although Meredith enjoyed special relationships with Frost and Auden—two of the "high ones," as he likes to characterize them—the truth is that many poets of his generation were influenced by them. A more unique influence on Meredith was Muriel Rukeyser. "She was the first poet that I knew personally," he told the *Paris Review.* "I knew her when I was still an undergraduate. She was a very amazing human being and any traces of honesty in my life come from having seen how beautifully honest she was in administering her life and her poetry without any separation—you couldn't get a knife between the two things with her. The real influence was her human model of what a poet could be."

The human model of what a poet could be is what I always encounter in the work and person of William Meredith. "Character" is what Robert Lowell called it. Hazard tells us that he's "gnawed by a vision of rightness / that no one else seems to see," and he's "in charge of morale / in a morbid time." I don't think there is an American poet alive who understands, the way Meredith understands, the responsibility a poet has to "administer spiritual vision" to society. Contemporary poets in general do not see themselves as having this responsibility, and if they do it's often a loyalty to anarchy. Or their spiritualism carries the scent of snake oil and pretension. Pretension—spiritual, literary, or intellectual—is something Meredith does not abide, for it is a misrepresentation and distortion of one's self, an inaccurate response. Accuracy of response, which Meredith judges by how well we pay attention to our experience, is the litmus test for authenticity of self.

In a recent exhibition of William Meredith's papers at the Connecticut College library, the letters from his friends Robert Lowell, John Berryman, Maxine Kumin, Robert Penn Warren, and James Merrill attest to their authors' genuine regard for Meredith's work. "I have loved your poems for 40 years," Merrill wrote in 1988. What is also clear from the letters is the correspondents' trust in the fairness of his critical intelligence, which they regularly sought by sending new work to him for his opinion. The letters show that while Meredith's generation was decimated by spiritual malaise—"dread recidivism" is what he calls Berryman's affliction—they relied on his "vision of rightness" as ballast to their own difficult fathomings.

Meredith did not argue his peers away from their unremitting darkness. Instead he provided an antidote to the age's recidivistic temperament. "What can a man do / but bear witness?" Hazard asks. "And what has he got to tell? / Only the shaped things he's seen—a few things made by men, / a galaxy made well." Meredith's optimism is not facile, however. It carries with it the knowledge that "we are all relicts, of some great joy, wearing black" (**"In Loving Memory of the Late Author of *Dream Songs*").** Meredith's belief in his own vision of things is embedded in his faith that when words are used accurately to describe experience they cannot lie or bear false witness. In **"The Cheer"** he writes, "Words addressing evil won't turn evil back / but they can give heart. / The cheer is hidden in right words." Right words are born in courage, which results from our struggle to make sense of our various predicaments. Cheer is what words are "trying to tell us, / . . . It's native to the words, / and what they want us always to know, / even when it seems quite impossible to do."

In 1983, at the age of sixty-four, William Meredith suffered a stroke that left him with expressive aphasia, which means that for the past fourteen years he has not been able to use language to say or write exactly what he wants to say. "I know it!" he will utter with force, "but *I* can't say the words!" Trapped, as it were, inside his body, which has profoundly betrayed him, for the past decade and a half Meredith has remained occupied with the poet's struggle—the struggle to speak. ***Effort at Speech*** is more than an apt title for this collection of his poems. (Coincidentally, the title poem, written in the 1960s, is dedicated to Muriel Rukeyser.) It serves not only as an emblem of his present daily effort to find the "right words," but it describes what he committed himself to very early on. In the envoi to his second book, ***Ships and Other Figures*** (1948), he wrote, as a lieutenant in the Navy, "Go, little book. If anybody asks / Why I add poems to a time like this, / Tell how the comeliness I can't take in / Of ships and other figures of content / Compels me still until I give them names." The names of things are what William Meredith has been giving us in his poems for more than fifty years. It is equally true, as he said of Rukeyser, that there is no separation between Meredith's life and his poetry. You can't get a knife between the two things. "Not so! Not true at all!" Meredith will protest. But it is true. We have these poems as proof.

Additional coverage of Meredith's life and career is contained in the following sources published by the Gale Group: *Contemporary Authors,* Vols. 9-12; *Contemporary Authors Autobiography Series* Vol. 14; *Contemporary Authors New Revision Series,* Vol. 6, 40; *Contemporary Literature Criticism,* Vols. 4, 13, 22, 55; *DISCovering Authors Modules—Poetry; Dictionary of Literary Biography,* Vol. 5.

James Merrill
1926-1995

(Full name James Ingram Merrill) American poet, novelist, dramatist, and memoirist.

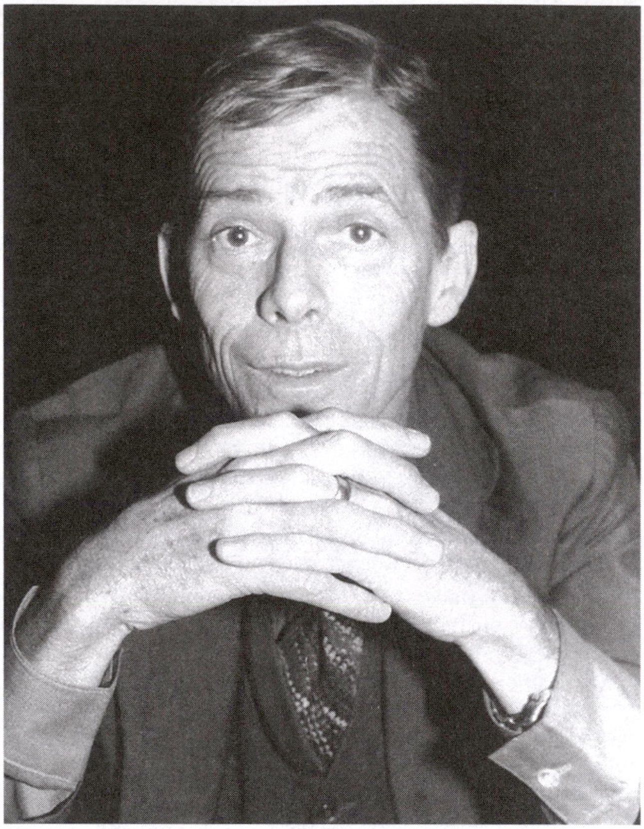

INTRODUCTION

Merrill is regarded as one of the most important poets of the twentieth century. Praised from the beginning of his fifty-year career for the formal and metrical precision of his work, he steadily developed his poetry's thematic depth, so that, in such notable works as *The Fire Screen* (1969), *Braving the Elements* (1972), and *The Changing Light at Sandover* (1982), he was able to openly address autobiographical concerns, socio-political elements, and, in J. D. McClatchy's words, "the creation of an entire cosmogony." Distinguished for his work as a whole, Merrill is principally esteemed for his epic poem *The Changing Light at Sandover,* which in the representative words of critic Robert Mazzocco is viewed as "an astonishing performance . . . as near to a masterpiece as anything else that American poetry has produced in the last two or three decades, and the capstone . . . of an extraordinary career."

BIOGRAPHICAL INFORMATION

The son of Charles Merrill, co-founder of the New York stock brokerage firm now known as Merrill Lynch, Merrill was born into great wealth and consequently did not have to rely on his writing to earn a living. He decided early in life that poetry would be his vocation and pursued his study of literature at the prestigious Lawrenceville School in New Jersey and at Amherst College. He published his first collection of poems, *Jim's Book,* in 1942, when he was sixteen. After serving in the military during World War II, he returned to graduate from Amherst and begin writing full time. In 1955, Merrill moved from New York to Connecticut, where he and David Jackson, his friend, companion, and collaborator, began experimenting with a Ouija board, transcribing "messages" from dead relatives and friends, famous literary figures, and mythological beings. Merrill edited these messages, fashioning them into poetry and publishing them in the Pulitzer Prize-winning *Divine Comedies* (1976), the National Book Award-winning *Mirabell: Books of Number* (1978), and *Scripts for the Pageant* (1980). He later collected these Ouija board poems, adding some original material, to produce *The Changing Light at Sandover.* In addition to two novels and several dramatic works, Merrill also wrote *A Different Person* (1993), a memoir in which he discusses his decisive trip to Europe in the 1950s, his relationships with his parents, and his homosexuality. Merrill died in 1995.

MAJOR WORKS

Merrill's earliest verse, collected in *The Black Swan* (1946), *First Poems* (1951), and *The Country of a Thousand Years of Peace* (1959), was written in the formal style of seventeenth-century metaphysical poetry, sometimes combined with a Romantic sensibility. In his collections *Water Street* (1962) and *Nights and Days* (1966), however, Merrill began to write of personal experiences and to combine lyrical verse with narrative. This expanding poetic sensibility is demonstrated in *The Fire Screen,* which gives voice to his deepest passions and imaginative speculations. Merrill's lengthy *The Changing Light at Sandover* is regarded as one of the most complex works of the latter half of the twentieth-century. Likened in scope to Ezra Pound's *Cantos* and T. S. Eliot's *The Waste Land,* and in theme and form to Dante's *Divine Comedy* (especially the *Inferno*), Merrill's epic poem explores the direction of morality and science in the modern world and emphasizes the importance of developing spiritual strength. In order to experience spirituality in the modern age, Merrill suggests in the work, we must acknowledge the existence of powers outside conscious control and recognize the importance of science in revealing universal patterns and processes. Throughout the poem's sections Merrill traces the decline of cultures, reflects on pain, death, the loss of close friends and relatives, and discusses reincarnation. In *The Book of Ephraim,* whose twenty-six sections correspond to the letters of the alphabet, Merrill examines the uses and abuses of language, while in the ten sections of *Mirabell: Books of Number,* which correspond to the ten digits, he explores numerology, and in *Scripts for the Pageant* he divides his concern between the Ouija board's "yes" and "no" dichotomy. Merrill places his timeless, universal themes in a modern context, and though the poems are ultimately of a serious nature, they are full of humor based on puns and incongruities.

CRITICAL RECEPTION

Most critics consider Merrill's earliest works to be meticulously crafted but occasionally lacking in emotional intensity, a flaw that, scholars agree, the poet addressed in his subsequent works. Representative of developments in his poetry of the late 1960s and early 1970s, *Braving the Elements* has been noted for the ways that its content and voice dictate the use of relatively free poetic forms, which critics suggest is the result of increased emotional honesty and willingness to reveal intimate feelings. Principal among Merrill's poetic work, *The Changing Light at Sandover* has been almost unanimously acclaimed for its evocative imagery, musical structure, narrative panache, and masterful variety of poetic styles including sonnets, ballads, villanelles, sestinas, terza rima, octava rima, and blank verse. Moreover, Merrill has been consistently recognized for the way he expands his personal quest for spiritual meaning into a poem of epic proportions confronting universal truths.

PRINCIPAL WORKS

Poetry

Jim's Book: A Collection of Poems and Short Stories (poetry and short stories) 1942
The Black Swan, and Other Poems 1946
First Poems 1951
Short Stories 1954
A Birthday Cake for David 1955
The Country of a Thousand Years of Peace, and Other Poems 1959
Selected Poems 1961
Water Street 1962
The Thousand and Second Night 1963
Violent Pastoral 1965
Nights and Days 1966
The Fire Screen 1969
Braving the Elements 1972
Two Poems: "From the Cupola" and "The Summer People" 1972
Yannina 1973
The Yellow Pages: 59 Poems 1974
Divine Comedies 1976
Metamorphosis of 741 1977
Mirabell: Books of Number 1978
Ideas, etc. 1980
Scripts for the Pageant 1980
**The Changing Light at Sandover* 1982
From the Cutting Room Floor 1982
From the First Nine: Poems 1947-1976 1982
Marbled Paper 1982
Peter 1982
Santorini: Stopping the Leak 1982
Bronze 1984
Occasions and Inscriptions 1984
Play of Light 1984
Rendezvous 1984
Souvenirs 1984
Late Settings 1985
The Inner Room 1988
Selected Poems 1993
A Scattering of Salts 1995

Other Major Works

The Bait (drama) 1953
The Immortal Husband (drama) 1955
The Seraglio (novel) 1957
The (Diblos) Notebook (novel) 1965
The Image Marker (drama) 1986
Recitative [edited by J. D. McClatchy] (prose) 1986
A Different Person: A Memoir 1993

*This work contains "The Book of Ephraim" from *Divine Comedies,* all of the poems in both *Mirabell: Books of Number* and *Scripts for the Pageant,* and an original epilogue, "Coda: The Higher Keys."

CRITICISM

David Kalstone (essay date 1977)

SOURCE: "Transparent Things," in *Modern Critical Views: James Merrill*, edited by Harold Bloom, Chelsea House Publishers, 1985, pp. 57-67.

[*In the following essay, originally published in 1977, Kalstone considers the verse of* The Fire Screen, Braving the Elements, *and* Divine Comedies.]

It would be interesting to know at what point Merrill saw a larger pattern emerging in his work—the point at which conscious shaping caught up with what unplanned or unconscious experience had thrown his way. In retrospect a reader can see that ***Braving the Elements*** (1972) gathers behind it the titles—with full metaphorical force—of Merrill's previous books. In ***The Country of a Thousand years of Peace, Water Street, Nights and Days*** and ***The Fire Screen***, he had referred to the four elements braved in the book which followed them. (***Divine Comedies*** extends it one realm further.) The books do present experience under different aspects, almost as under different zodiacal signs. And ***The Fire Screen*** is, among other things—and preeminently—the book of love. It reads like a sonnet sequence following the curve of a love affair to its close. Like important sonnet sequences, the implied narrative calls into play a range of anxieties not strictly connected to love, in Merrill's case challenging some of the balanced views of ***Nights and Days.***

"The Friend of the Fourth Decade" is the launching point for this book—the poet at forty, setting one part of himself in dialogue with another. What is being tested here is the whole commitment to memory, to personal history, to a house and settling down—the very material to which Merrill entrusted himself after ***Water Street.*** The "friend" is an alter ego who comes to visit—really to confront—his poet-host, after a long absence. In the opening scene, against the settled atmosphere of his host's house, the friend is shot through with the setting sun so that he appears to be "Any man with ears aglow, / . . . gazing inward, mute." The temptation the friend represents is crystallized in a dream at the close of the poem. "Behind a door marked DANGER . . . "

> Swaddlings of his whole civilization,
> Prayers, accounts, long priceless scroll,
> Whip, hawk, prow, queen, down to some last
> Lost comedy, all that fine writing
> Rigid with rains and suns,
> Are being gingerly unwound.
> There. Now the mirror. Feel the patient's heart
> Pounding—oh please, this once—
> Till nothing moves but to a drum.
> See his eyes darkening in bewilderment—
> No, in joy—and his lips part
> To greet the perfect stranger.

The friend has taught him a mesmerizing game in which saved-up postcards, a whole history of personal attachments, are soaked while the ink dissolves. The views remain, but the messages disappear, "rinsed of the word." When the poet tries it himself, watching his mother's "Dearest Son" unfurl in the water, the message remains legible. "The memories it stirred did not elude me."

"The Friend of the Fourth Decade" tests a dream of escape, a drama extended and detailed by the poems set in Greece which follow it in ***The Fire Screen.*** In some sense the book is like Elizabeth Bishop's *Questions of Travel,* a deepening encounter with another language and a more elemental culture, in which the speaker becomes, from poem to poem, more identified with his new world, cleansed of the assumptions of the old. In **"To My Greek,"** the Greek language, encountered as if it were a demon lover, or a siren, becomes a radiant, concrete release from the subtleties of the "mother tongue" and the burden of "Latin's rusted treasure." A newcomer to Greek, he is forced to be simple, even silly. With Merrill the experience is characteristically amplified. He treats it as a temptation to become "rinsed of the word" and to humble himself speechless in the presence of "the perfect stranger." Both the transcendental and the self-destructive overtones of that phrase from **"The Friend of the Fourth Decade,"** where the "perfect stranger" is also Death, haunt this book.

The initiation into Greece is inseparable from the exhilaration and the mystery of a love affair. It was anticipated in **"Days of 1964,"** the wonderful Cavafid conclusion to ***Nights and Days,*** and is allowed to run its course in ***The Fire Screen.*** In **"The Envoys"** Merrill finds a series of emblems for the sense of adventure and risk experienced in the lover's presence. In three narrative panels, he introduces creatures the lover momentarily traps and tames, binds and then frees: a scurrying lizard, a frightened kitten and a beetle threaded and whirled around his head:

> You knotted the frail harness, spoke,
> Revolved. Eureka! Round your head
> Whirred a living emerald satellite.

The experience is absorbed as a "modulation into a brighter key / Of terror we survive to play."

> Teach me, lizard, kitten, scarabee—
> Gemmed coffer opening on the dram
> Of everlasting life he represents,
> His brittle pharoahs in the vale of Hence
> Will hear who you are, who I am,
> And how you bound him close and set him free.

What he shares with the creatures is a moment at the gates of some other world, not insisted on, but imagined as if he were enjoying the danger. All the Greek poems, not only the love poems, benefit from that expansion of feeling. In a dramatic monologue whose tripping couplets are meant to suggest the energetic singsong of a simple Greek speaker, "Kostas Tympakianakis," Merrill seems almost literally to take up the speaker's invitation: "You'll see a different cosmos through the eyes of a Greek." He adopts the violence, the pride, the clear-eyed tone of the Greek. He accepts the welcome challenge, "Use my name," slips on the offered identity, but registers the gap between them in Kostas's final line: "Who could have imagined such a life as mine?" It is a small but telling rebuke of the poet's imagination always ticking away, its pressures momentarily relieved by taking on the voice of another. ***The Fire Screen*** contains several poems given over to the pleasures of evoking particular figures, humble like Kostas or sophisticated like Maria, the "muse of my off-days." It sees Greek peasant life through others' eyes (**"David's Night at Veliès"**) or addresses itself to shared moments of happiness, as in **"16.ix.65,"** with "evening's four and twenty candles" and the four friends who return from the beach "with honey on our drunken feet."

But at the core of the Greek section of this book are the love poems, some of them full of lyric intensity, others sharp and painful, like the dramatic soliloquy or fragment **"Part of the Vigil,"** which is, in a sense, the turning point of the affair, a surreal exploration of the images in the lover's heart:

> What
> If all you knew of me were down there, leaking
> Fluids at once abubble, pierced by fierce
> Impulsions of unfeeling, life, limb turning
> To burning cubes, to devil's dice, to ash—
> What if my effigy were down there? What,
> Dear god, if it were not!
> If it were nowhere in your heart!
> Here I turned back.

The lover's image is to "Blaze on" in the poet's own "saved skin." But the poems which follow register both the end of the affair and the folly of thinking of the Greek experience as an escape or oblivion. **"Another August," "A Fever"** and **"Flying to Byzantium"** are among the most powerful poems in the book. With **"Mornings in a New House,"** as he imagines a dwelling half way back toward cooler American landscapes, the whole experience modulates into a new key, absorbed, retrospective, fading into myth.

It is appropriate in Merrill's work that recovery should be imagined in terms of a "new house" (or a repainted one in the more comic and detached version of **"After the Fire"**). **"Mornings in a New House"** has him, "a cold man" who "hardly cares," slowly brought to life by a fire laid at dawn. Once again the new house is the available image to set against exposure. "The worst is over," the fire a tamed recall of the shattered (or spent?) affair. Against its "tamed uprush . . . Habit arranges the fire screen." The details of the screen, embroidered by his mother, place the entire lapsed passion into a withering perspective:

> Crewel-work. His mother as a child
> Stitched giant birds and flowery trees
> To dwarf a house, *her* mother's—see the chimney's
> Puff of dull yarn! Still vaguely chilled,
> Guessing how even then her eight
> Years had foreknown him, nursed him, all,
> Sewn his first dress, sung to him, let him fall,
> Howled when his face chipped like a plate,
> He stands there wondering until red
> Infraradiance, wave on wave,
> So enters each plume-petal's crazy weave,
> Each worsted brick of the homestead,
> That once more, deep indoors, blood's drawn,
> The tiny needlewoman cries,
> And to some faintest creaking shut of eyes
> His pleasure and the doll's are one.

It is hard to disentangle the impulses which contribute to this poem—harder even because the poet has added a footnote taking some of it back, imagining passion as itself a defense, not a danger, like the screen of fire that protects Brünnhilde in Wagner's opera. But, in the poem proper, the fire screen is devised against the damages of love. It bears, in a sense, the whole retrospective power of his writing, the ability of memory and art to absorb and rearrange experience. What marks this off from earlier moments in Merrill's poetry is the long perspective which the poem opens up, receding past his immediate pain, past his own childhood of **"The Broken Home,"** to his mother who stitched the screen as a device involving *her* mother.

After all the carefully noted impulses in ***The Fire Screen*** to leave the mother behind—the attempts to rinse away her handwriting in **"Friend of the Fourth Decade"**; even the efforts to be free of Latin languages, the "mother tongue"—the poet returns to her in a new way. The "new house" of this poem is interwoven with the house his mother had sewn, *her* mother's house, dwarfed by giant birds and flowery trees. The discovery of these entwined destinies "deep indoors" draws blood. There is something like the remorse of **"Childlessness"** in what happens. The resources of art are seen as self-protective, even vengeful, a miniaturization of human powers, like the moment in the earlier poem when the annihilated village—teeming generations in dwarfed versions—is loaded aboard sampans and set adrift. But in **"Mornings in a New House"** the experience is without guilt and is shared in its brittle complexity. Waves of warmth and anger carry him inward to an identification with the "tiny needlewoman" mother, to share the childish pleasure and fear which even then would shape her feelings for the child *she* would one day have. With "some faintest creaking shut of eyes" they both become toys in a larger pattern, at once foreshortened and part of their shared, terrifying but ungrudging humanity. I think what is most notable in this poem is that Merrill, however rueful and pained, has emerged from the erotic fire into a newly defined and felt natural perspective—one which becomes visible and palpable at length in many of the poems of his next book, ***Braving the Elements.***

II

I have talked about the double action we must watch in Merrill's poems, the way he twins a witty surface with the poet's power to discover the veined patterns of his life. We must pay special attention to his puns and his settings; they open alternative perspectives against which to read the time-bound and random incidents of daily life. In ***Braving the Elements*** (1972) and ***Divine Comedies*** (1976), he has become a master of this idiosyncratic method, something one might call—with apologies—symbolic autobiography, Merrill's way of making apparently ordinary detail transparent to deeper configurations.

This is quite clear in **"After the Fire"** and **"Log,"** which move us from the world of ***The Fire Screen*** to that of ***Braving the Elements.*** The brisk narrative of **"After the Fire"** brings back the Greek housekeeper Kyria Kleo, whom in **"Days of 1964"** he had seen wearing "the erotic mask / Worn the world over by illusion / To weddings of itself and simple need." Now, in the new key of **"After the Fire,"** the Athens house has been repainted after a mysterious blaze. Under its "quiet sensible light gray," the house hides his old love affairs as it hides those of Kleo and her rumpled son Noti, their erotic escapades buried and part of the past. The mood of ***Braving the Elements*** is the mood of the opening invocation, **"Log"**: banked flames of passion, burning and diminution, a life "consumed with that which it was nourished by." The muse discovered **"After the Fire"** is Kleo's mother, the half-crazed crone. In the yiayia's presence, the candles which gutter before old lovers' ghosts are replaced:

> The snuffed-out candle-ends grow tall and shine,
> Dead flames encircle us, which cannot harm,
> The table's spread, she croons, and I
> Am kneeling pressed to her old burning frame.

The comic crone turns before our eyes into a sybilline figure, mistress of the now harmless flames of passionate memory. She is, in a sense, the informing spirit of the book, for what is new about ***Braving the Elements*** is the way it opens to long—in some cases, geological—perspectives, the kind of prehistoric, penetrating wisdom which dwarfs and absorbs moments of intense present pain. The book contains, once again, love poems and poems involving the Oedipal trials of childhood. But these familiar sources of anxiety are in ***Braving the Elements*** transposed to a different key, resolved as by the all-embracing parenthesis of dream.

For example, family triangles make mysterious appearances in **"18 West 11th Street,"** but as part of a poem in which several generations are run through a New York house, almost as in a strip of film. The house is one in which Merrill spent the first years of his childhood. With one of those attempts history makes to try and rival fiction, this was also the house accidentally destroyed in 1971 by Weathermen who were using it as a center for making bombs in the absence of the owners, parents of one of the revolutionaries. Richard Sáez, in a penetrating reading of the poem, points to the unlikely and eloquent connection it makes between "Cathy Wilkerson's destruction of her paternal home and James Merrill's pained elegies for his." The parallels, Sáez asserts, "are acts of fate as well as their active wills," as poet and radicals enact in their mutually incompatibile fashions, but with equal intensity, the conflict of generations. "**'18 West 11th Street'**, like the House of Thebes, becomes an emblem for some unavoidable matrix of fate which involves both poet and revolutionary." Inexcapably linked to one another, the generations are themselves dissolved in the mirrors of the house and the long stretches of time, each generation finding its own means to suffer and to rebel. Sáez is right to single out the close of the poem as having a special new power in Merrill's work:

> Forty-odd years gone by,
> Toy blocks. Church bells. Original vacancy.
> O deepening spring.

Sáez points out—that "the 'Original vacancy' of the poem's conclusion is not merely the scene of departure from the poet's childhood. It is man's timeless exclusion from his unforgotten home." Yes, but the phrase also looks forward and seems to say "To Let." With the church bells and "toy blocks" the cityscape seems both distanced and renewed. Of course, the toy blocks are also the children's devices against their parents, whether as poems or explosives. And they are assumed into the ongoing beauty of the exclamation. "O deepening spring." Here Sáez is particularly acute: "In the concluding tercet nature itself is deflected from its amoral cyclical course to be glazed—not with the gilding, yellowing dust of earlier and lesser achieved poems but—with a patina of human destiny."

That same sense of unfolding destiny informs **"Up and Down,"** a poem whose ingredients are familiar in Merrill's work, but never in so rich a combination. In an earlier book this might well have been two separate poems: one, **"Snow King Chair Lift,"** reflecting the brief exhilarating rising arc of a love affair; the other, **"The Emerald,"** an extraordinary and sympathetic encounter with his mother. But one thing Merrill does in his work is move toward larger and larger units of composition, not only long poems, but combinations of different forms, like the free juxtapositions of prose and more or less formal verse units in **"The Thousand and Second Night"** and **"From the Cupola."** The two sections of **"Up and Down"** limn out, together, an emotional landscape which neither of them could singly suggest.

On the surface it is a poem of contrasts: rising in a ski lift with a lover, descending into a bank vault with the mother; the ostensible freedom of one experience, while in the other, "palatial bronze gates shut like jaws." Yet the exhilaration of the ski lift—it begins in dramatic present tenses—is what is relegated finally to a cherished snapshot and to the past tense: "We gazed our little fills at boundlessness." The line almost bursts with its contradictions: unslaked appetite, or appetite only fulfilled and teased by "gazing our little fills." The lovers have not quite reached the condition of the Shakespearean "pitiful thrivers in their gazing spent"; they are more buoyant, but with a redirected and only momentary pleasure. **"The Emerald,"** on the other hand, begins in brisk easy narrative pasts and moves toward a moment in the very present which the ski-lift section had forsaken. More important, whatever the surface contrasts between the two sections, there is an irresistible connection between the discoveries made by each. Or rather, the feelings of the opening poem enable the son to understand what happens to the mother in the closing poem. In the vault an unexpected secret jumps to light:

> Rustle of tissue, a sprung
> Lid. Her face gone queerly lit, fair, young,
> Like faces of our dear ones who have died.
> No rhinestone now, no dilute amethyst,
> But of the first water, linking star to pang,
> Teardrop to fire, my father's kisses hang
> In lipless concentration round her wrist.

The effect resembles the moment of thunder and lightning on the chair-lift in Part I, but here things are seen in a prolonged transforming light, the queer deathlike glow when the "mudbrown" coffin of a box is opened. It is as if the glimpse of "boundlessness" in Part I can only be extended and refined in the eternal light of underground. The poet and his mother are seen as part of a performance in the "green room" which the emerald suggests. Before his eyes she grows both youthful and like the dead. Surviving two husbands, she can still be transfixed by memory, transformed by the bracelet. "My father's kisses hang / In lipless concentration round her wrist." Contraries are reconciled: "star to pang, / Teardrop to fire." She is bride, widow and mother all at once, and something like the eternally preserved Mesopotamian consorts, "girl-bride jewelled in his grave."

Against this background mother and son have the unspoken reconciliation discussed earlier in this chapter. He slips onto her finger the emerald she had intended for his bride, the very ring his father gave her when the poet was born. All these elements compose an increasingly luminous frieze: "The world beneath the world is brightening." It is one of those moments assumed, as many are in ***Braving the Elements,*** into an ongoing process of time, and experienced not elegiacally but with a sense of promise. That deepening emotional landscape is most strongly suggested in the new physical surroundings of ***Braving the Elements.*** A series of difficult poems takes place in the Far West. Pieces like **"Under Libra"** and **"In Nine Sleep Valley"** are love poems played out against dwarfing panoramas and the geological erosions of a nonhuman world.

Geode, the troll's melon
Rind of crystals velvet smoke meat blue
Formed far away under fantastic
Pressures, then cloven in two
By the taciturn rock shop man, twins now forever
Will they hunger for each other
When one goes north and one goes east?
I expect minerals never do,
Enough for them was a feast
Of flaws, the molten start and glacial sleep,
The parting kiss.
Still face to face in halfmoonlight
Sparkling comes easy to the Gemini.
Centimeters deep yawns the abyss.

In **"Under Libra"** ancient stones are introduced into the poet's house ostensibly as doorstops and paperweights, but really as reminders of another scale of living. He goes "in the small hours from room to room / Stumbling onto their drugged stubborn sleep." These talismans overshadow desire; they place it in a perspective where past and future edge out the present. The solid human protagonists of the poem are dissolved before our eyes:

. . . Ten years from next morning, pen in hand,
Looking through saltwater, through flames,
Enkindlings of an absent *I* and *you*.
Live, spitting pronouns, sparks that flew
And were translated into windiest
Esperanto, zero tongue of powers
Diplomatic around 1 a.m.'s
Undripping centerpiece, the Swan . . .

Days were coming when the real thing
No longer shrugged a wing.

Some of the poems are pure ventriloquism. **"The Black Mesa"** speaks; so do **"Banks of a Stream Where Creatures Bathe."** They seem to embody a consensus of human voices, mythically inured to experience. History, the details of private lives—everything repeats itself in the long views these poems take. Hearing the poet take on these roles is like talking to survivors. **"The Black Mesa,"** addressing the low flatland, musters for a moment the tone of an eager roué, but finally lapses back into a weary geological view of his experience, outwaiting all competitors and invaders: "I steal past him who next reclaims you, keep / Our hushed appointments, grain by grain . . . / Dust of my dust, when will it all be plain?" The effect is to make expressions of human tenderness mere instances of the larger erosions and destinies which outlast them.

"Syrinx" is the most successful of such poems. She is, of course, an established mythological figure, brightly familiar from Marvell: "And Pan did after Syrinx speed / Not as a nymph, but for a reed." Merrill takes up her fragile link to the nature from which she was abstracted, "a thinking reed." Just who is she in this version? She addresses the poet as if she were his muse and his lover. She is sophisticated enough to know about slipware and to quote Pascal; also, to make puns about fashion and the Panpipe's traditional shape: "Among the wreckage, bent in Christian weeds, / Illiterate—X my mark—I tremble, still / A thinking reed."

"Bent in Christian weeds" makes it sound as if she were used to dresses by Chanel, and "Illiterate—X my mark" walks a tightrope of ingenuity and feeling. As unlikely as her witty denial of literacy may be, Syrinx keeps shucking off the claims of words as if they were merely garments. The most outrageous example is the incorporation of the musical scale: "Who puts his mouth to me / Draws out the scale of love and dread— / O ramify, sole antidote!" The musician's breath or the lover's kiss, and then the high tragedienne's apostrophe, which, on a second glance, taking in the enjambment ("d— / O"), we see disintegrate magically into the musical scale. This is precisely the action the poem repeats over and over: a human gesture, then the witty afflatus and effort of words which slip back before our eyes into analytic formulas, the do-re-mi of the scale, or the particles of a mathematical formula which expresses metastasis. Syrinx seems caught between human demands and ingenuity, which make her "tremble, still" and, on the other hand, her sense of being a worn part of a growing and disintegrating world:

Foxglove
Each year, cloud, hornet, fatal growths
Proliferating by metastasis
Rooted their total in the gliding stream.

Over and over the cleverness of the poem is matched by a hypnotic natural intonation, no more than in the astonishing close; as Syrinx slides back into her "scarred case,"

> Whose silvery breath-tarnished tones
> No longer rivet bone and star in place
> Or keep from shriveling, leather round a stone,
> The sunbather's precocious apricot
> Or stop the four winds racing overhead
> Nought
> Waste Eased
> Sought

Those last four words clothe the cardinal points in notions of human aspiration and loss, which we may understand in varying combinations and intensities, depending on the order in which we read them. But ultimately they slip back into the toneless ideogram of the ongoing winds. How odd human words and feelings seem, depicted in this particular way. The lozenge of four words is tinged by, but ultimately surpasses, individual feelings.

Robert von Hallberg (essay date 1980)

SOURCE: "James Merrill: Revealing by Obscuring," in *Contemporary Literature*, Vol. XXI, No. 4, Autumn, 1980, 549-71.

[*In the following essay, Hallberg maintains that Merrill's work features an ironic criticism of the conventions of confessional poetry, and instead prefers evasion and secrecy.*]

> Too much understanding petrifies.
>
> **"From the Cupola"**[1]

The term "confessional poetry" has earned widespread skepticism: as a generic term, it is mainly misleading.[2] Yet it would be hard to trace the development of recent American poetry without reference to the influence of Allen Ginsberg's *Howl* (1956), Robert Lowell's *Life Studies* (1959), W. D. Snodgrass' *Heart's Needle* (1960), and the poems collected in Sylvia Plath's *Ariel* (1966). Whatever claims may be made on behalf of "confessional poetry," it is plain that these books all contributed to the reinstatement of two closely related literary conventions: the notion that poems originate in their subject matter, and the corollary that poets mean, at least literally, what they say. These are of course not "facts" about literature (nor even about these four books) but conventions, rhetorical rules whereby poems are understood, if not often written. My point here is only the obvious one that during the sixties these conventions, which have their roots in commonsense notions about poetry, were more accessible than they had been in decades. Which is to say not only that many sixties poems invoke these conventions, but that many others deliberately flout them. My interest in this essay is James Merrill's ironic wrenching of these rules. For a number of his most important poems, as I will show, originate in calculated reticence; whereas confessional poets characteristically hold a sharp focus on subject matter, Merrill often writes around interpretable silences. More importantly, the obliqueness I am describing conforms to the attitudes and proprieties invoked by Merrill's characteristic style.

Merrill himself has insisted that confessional poetry is as conventional as any other, that it has no special claims on truth-telling (***CW,*** pp. 139-140). Confessions, however, have a special place in Merrill's writing—from Francis Tanning's confession of wealth and sexual inexperience to Xenia in *The Seraglio* (1957),[3] to Merrill's seductive invocation of his muse, Psyche, in **"From the Cupola"** (1966)—

> Tell me about him, then. Not a believer,
> I'll hold my tongue while you, my dear, dictate.
>
> (***ND***, p. 38)

—right up to the coy opening lines of **"The Book of Ephraim"** (1976): "my subject matter / Gave me pause—so intimate, so novel" (***DC,*** p. 47).[4] Full disclosure, however, is the last thing one has reason to expect of Merrill. He has admitted that one part of the subject of **"From the Cupola"** is "an unknowable situation, something I'm going to keep quiet about." Yet he invites his readers "to guess at, to triangulate . . . [that] story, the untold one" (***CW,*** p. 146). Loaded silences are a rhetorical trope for Merrill. In **"Part of the Vigil"** he imagines himself, tiny, plumbing the inner passages of his lover's heart: "What if my effigy were down there? What, / Dear god, if it were not! / If it were nowhere in your heart! / Here I turned back. Of the rest I do not speak" (***FS,*** p. 24). And near the end of **"Words for Maria"** he feigns interest in his housekeeper's buried life:

> About what went before
> Or lies beneath, how little one can glean.
> Girlhood, marriage, the war . . .
> I'd like once (not now, here comes Giulio)
> Really to hear—I mean—I didn't mean—
> You paint a smiling mouth to answer me:
> "Since when does L'Enfant care for archaeology?"
>
> (***FS***, p. 13)

Merrill's joke is that contrived obstacle to his hearing Maria's "secrets"—"here comes Giulio." Maria knows as well as Merrill's readers that what L'Enfant most enjoys is her *painted* face. These little tricks, rhetorical caresses of ignorance, have a serious tacit point to register. Speculating on the transience of glory, Merrill says: "—Might reputations be deflated there? / I wondered here, but Ephraim changed the subject / As it was in his tactful power to do" (***DC,*** p. 98). Quiet evasions like Ephraim's, like Merrill's, testify to a delicate system of human meaning whose categories, felt by people of understanding, might be compromised by express formulation. Reticence, for Merrill, is painstakingly deliberate and exact in its meaning: thus, in **"The Summer People,"** Andrew, Margaret, and Nora "dealt with Jack from then on / By never mentioning him" (***FS,*** p. 68). There is a class of people for whom silence is a badge of discretion and a measure of controlled power, the power to ignore.

There are more strictly literary ways to explain Merrill's inclination to bury certain subjects, and some of these are pertinent. Merrill himself has spoken of "buried meanings" as a kind of hedge against trivia: "Without something like them, one ends up writing light verse about love affairs."[5] But perhaps more important is his early declared allegiance to the commonplace that music and meaning rob from each other in poetry. These lines come from **"The Drowning Poet"** (1947):

To drown was the perfection of technique,
The word containing its own sense, like Time;
And turning to the sea he entered it
As one might speak of poems in a poem
Or at the crisis in the sonata quote
Five-finger exercises: a compliment
To all accomplishment.

(***FP***, p. 17)

The poet dedicated to his craft scorns referential meaning; he prefers poems which refer only to other poems (better yet, to translations of poems) and thereby honor the boundaries between Art and Life. By this understanding, allusions do not, in Eliotic fashion, deepen the resonance of themes; they gesture disdain for the bourgeois or common-sense expectation of moral wisdom from poetry. Thus the arch-poet, Apollo, "Inflicted so much music on the lyre / That no one could have told you what he sang" (1958; ***CT,*** p. 52). Music properly overpowers sense. According to this Shelleyan revision of the French Symbolists, the poet aims "at something not unlike / Meaning relieved of sense, / To plant a flag there on that needle peak / Whose diamond grates in the revolving silence" (1964; ***ND,*** p. 24).

Yet Merrill is self-critical always, and he has nicely revealed the blindness of a poetic which takes for granted the sanctified reserve of art. Here are some lines from **"Mirror"** (1958), a poem reworking the traditional art-as-mirror topos (the mirror is addressing the window):

You embrace a whole world without once caring
To set it in order. That takes thought. Out there
Something is being picked. The red-and-white bandannas
Go to my heart. A fine young man
Rides by on horseback. Now the door shuts. Hester
Confides in me her first unhappiness.
This much, you see, would never have been fitted
Together, but for me.

(11. 13-20; ***CT***, p. 36)

Constructed order characterizes the special province of art, yet the fullness and depth of this art's order is in question. For the mirror arranges surfaces on a plane, as some poets constellate images in verse. (Merrill, in a playful moment of self-parody, has referred to his own version of this poetic as "word-painting" [***DC,*** p. 48].) The three indicative sentences stretched over lines 16-18 all but iron the human drama out of the narrative: the language makes little distinction between the closing of a door and a young woman's feeling when her first romance has ended. The mirror cannot connect events: the three sentences, without conjunctions, line up like beads on a string. The mirror prides itself on the thoughtfulness of its order (1. 14), but Merrill uses his buried-subject trope to show where an art of dazzling surfaces cannot penetrate: "Out there / Something is being picked." One must guess at what is being picked, but the mirror, blindly, supplies clues. The persimmon mentioned later in the poem (1. 30) is raised chiefly in the South, and the bandannas dear to the heart of the mirror may well be worn by slaves picking cotton. What the mirror cannot penetrate is the depth of human motive in both politics and love: *why* is "something" being picked? *Why* is that "fine young man" riding away? These are questions about the human presence beyond appearances, and the mirror cannot respond to them. For the mirror, as for a poetic of artfully disposed imagery, slaves are "red-and-white bandannas," and a failed romance is a man on horseback and a shut door. On occasion, however, Merrill has obliquely honored the humaneness of this sort of poetic, for part of what it supresses is destruction. There are moments in Merrill's verse (as in the opening five lines of **"A Timepiece"** [***CT,*** p. 8], or in this clause from **"After the Fire"**: "Remembering also the gift of thumb-sized garnet / Bruises he clasped round Aleko's throat" [***BE,*** p. 6]) when his painterly style quietly indicates that below the dazzling surface lies the alternative to civilized manners: violence. But in **"Mirror"** Merrill suggests that the passing of this poetic in time is as natural and inevitable as erosion.[6]

In 1964 Merrill published **"The Thousand and Second Night,"** a wonderful poem literally about a buried subject. James, the "speaker" of the poem, likens himself to Hagia Sophia.

The building, desperate for youth, has smeared
All over its original fine bones
Acres of ochre plaster. A diagram
Indicates how deep in the mudpack
The real facade is. I want *my* face back.

(***ND***, p. 5)

C. B. Cox once noted that the subject of the poem is the anxiety of middle age,[7] but beneath that subject lies another. Merrill himself has said: "I don't know what the main subject [of **"The Thousand and Second Night"**] is—the poem is flirtatious in that sense."[8] In the third section, "Carnivals," Merrill leans rather heavily on his trope of evasion—

We had made our peace
With—everything.

(***ND***, p. 9)

Here's the dwarf back with cronies . . . oh I *say!*
Forget about it.

(***ND***, p. 11)

I spent the night rekindling with expert
Fingers—but that phase needn't be discussed. . . .

(***ND***, p. 11)

And now the long adventure
Let that wait.
I'm tired, it's late at night.

(***ND***, p. 13)

—and for good reason: this middle section bears most directly on the true subject of the poem. The opening quatrains refer to a change James has undergone: his friends accuse him of having become a "vain / Flippant unfeeling monster" (***ND,*** p. 9). Although he resents that formulation ("To hear them talk"), he does not dispute the basic diagnosis—"they were right." He has changed, and his recent meeting with M. (on whom he once had a crush) and his wife comes into the narrative as implicit evidence of that change. Their "war" is over, because James has lost feeling for all past pursuits of Eros:

A thousand and one nights! They were grotesque.
Stripping the blubber from my catch, I lit
The oil-soaked wick, then could not see by it.
Mornings, a black film lay upon the desk.
. . . Where just a week ago I thought to delve
For images of those years in a Plain Cover.
Some light verse happened as I looked them over.. . .

(***ND***, p. 10)

"The Thousand and Second Night" is a morning-after poem; James surveys his past in hung-over disgust. For James, Psyche and Eros, thought and feeling, mind and body, cannot reach each other; the right half of his face is paralyzed by that split. The witty lines on Great-Uncle Alistair's pornographic postcards enter the poem under the auspices of that colon: they describe scenes from Alistair's suppressed sexual fantasies, but James makes them serve as "images of those years in a Plain Cover"; James regards his own rendezvous with Eros as grotesque and comically pointless—much like Alistair's silly postcards. Alistair's daughter Alix wants to banish these sordid mementos: "'We'll burn them. Light the fire'" (***ND,*** p. 11)—but James knows better the consequences of fire for Psyche and Eros. The two prose passages which follow offer a rationale for re-uniting Eros and Psyche. The paragraph by "Germaine Nahman" claims that "the libertine *was* 'in search of his soul.'" (***ND,*** p. 12).[9] The extraordinary sexual ambitions of Great-Uncle Alistair and of James himself might be understood, by this analysis, not as base debauchery but as quests back toward that infantile state in which "The soul . . . could not be told from the body." The libertine (Alistair, James) sought all along to bring Eros and Psyche together again. And James's limp face is testimony that they never were entirely separated. "Natural calamities (tumor and apoplexy no less than flood and volcano) may at last be hailed as positive assurances, perverse if you like, of life in the old girl yet" (***ND,*** p. 12). Just as the earth kicks back against the abuses inflicted upon her, so the body complains of the excesses imposed upon her. And these complaints are proof that the body is more than just *physis,* that James's "precious sensibility" has not been entirely wrecked (***ND,*** p. 5), though now it may take a good "pinch . . . to recall how warmly and deeply those two [Eros and Psyche] did, in fact, love one another" (***ND,*** p. 12).

The true, and buried, subject of the poem is the difficulty one has reconciling ideas about love with erotic experience itself. Promiscuity is said to be more common, more often central to homosexual than to heterosexual experience, and that promiscuity is frequently cited as a major cause of homosexual anxiety. There is a sense, then, in which the subject of the poem has a special bearing on homosexuality. Specifically, the phrase "images of those years in a Plain Cover" may suggest that what James refers to as erotic grotesquerie dates from a period when he had not worn his homosexuality proudly, that James's "change" is related to Francis Tanning's change in *The Seraglio:* they will no longer keep their preferences under cover. Merrill's use of Great-Uncle Alistair's postcards, however, seems especially oblique, for Alistair's fantasies are plainly heterosexual and James has already indicated that his erotic inclinations have been homosexual (***ND,*** p. 9). Yet Merrill introduces those postcards in order to suggest that the split between Eros and Psyche should not be smugly dismissed or clinically "understood" as a consequence of that homosexual promiscuity which Merrill depicts as a series of whaling expeditions (***ND,*** p. 10). For in the end Merrill will make very traditional claims for his conclusions:

The heart prevails!
Affirm it! Simple decency rides the blast!—
Phrases that, quick to smell blood, lurk like sharks
Within a style's transparent lights and darks.

(***ND***, p. 12)

This section of the poem (the five sestets following the prose passages) was the most difficult for Merrill to write (***CW,*** p. 145), and for good reason. His thematic conclusion, here as elsewhere, is easily formulated in conventional, trite language, and he steps free of the inert burden of such phrases only by openly displaying, without disowning, the staleness of these truisms. This rhetorical maneuver Merrill learned in writing **"An Urban Convalescence."** In fact, he claimed that just this trope—

The sickness of our time requires
That these as well be blasted in their prime.
You would think the simple fact of having lasted
Threatened our cities like mysterious fires.
There are certain phrases which to use in a poem
Is like rubbing silver with quicksilver. Bright
But facile, the glamour deadens overnight.
For instance, how 'the sickness of our time'
Enhances, then debases, what I feel.

(1960; ***WS***, p. 5)

—was the turning point which led to ***Nights and Days.***[10] The debasement comes when Merrill sees that his analysis of experience travels the well-worn grooves of contemporary journalism. To recognize that one's ideas are as common, as vulgar, literally, as the thoughts of those who daily deal in pontifications is the challenge Merrill modestly accepts in the books following ***Water Street.*** For instance, in **"From the Cupola"** he offers Psyche the counsel of commonplaces:

Weeping? You must not.
All our pyrotechnic flights

Miss the sleeper in the pitch-dark breast.
He is love:
He is everyone's blind spot.
We see according to our lights.

(*ND*, p. 46)

To posit these sentences as conclusions is Merrill's way of mildly suggesting that there is nothing new under the sun. And much the same point is made by setting the Eros-Psyche myth on Long Island Sound, and by bringing the Tithonus story forward through the centuries, as Merrill does in ***The Immortal Husband*** (1955). Merrill is plainly skeptical of the poetic claims often made on behalf of one or another unusual subject matter. He is a poet for whom subject matter is properly subordinate to style. He has never claimed, as so many of his contemporaries have (Olson and Ammons are obvious examples) to have many ideas of his own: "In neither / The world's poem nor the poem's world have I / Learned to think for myself, much" (***DC,*** p. 129). Commonplaces, truisms, clichés may sound their notes flatly, but the sense of such formulations resonates through long experience:

take
Any poor smalltown starstruck sense of "love
That makes the world go round"—see how the phrase
Stretches from Mystic to Mount Palomar
Back to those nights before the good old days,
Before the axle jumped its socket so
That genes in shock flashed on/off head to toe
Before mill turned to maelstrom, and IBM
Wrenched from Pythagoras his diadem.

(*DC*, p. 32)

The resonance is directly due to the age-old truth (as they say) of the proposition.

Novelty and variety certainly have a place in Merrill's poetic: they are criteria of surface excellence, sheen. Likewise subject matter (though not theme) is something to be "worked up":

Hadn't—from books, from living—
The profusion dawned on us, of "languages"
Any one of which, to who could read it,
Lit up the system it conceived?—bird-flight,
Hallucinogen, chorale and horoscope:
Each its own world, hypnotic, many-sided
Facet of the universal gem.
Ephraim's revelations—we had them
For comfort, thrills and chills, "material."

(*DC*, p. 75)

Merrill's theme in the **"Book of Ephraim"** is the coming and going of love, or, as he puts it, "The incarnation and withdrawal of / A god" (***DC,*** p. 47). Ephraim's transmissions on the Ouija board are, properly speaking, his subject matter—but that hardly matters. Ephraim and the subject of ghosts (a subject that may not be there at all) are no more than a vehicle for the theme Merrill long ago took for his own. To manage that theme, he now wishes for (of all things) a plain style:

the kind of unseasoned telling found
In legends, fairy tales, a tone licked clean
Over the centuries by mild old tongues,
Grandam to cub, serene, anonymous.

(*DC*, p. 47)

Although his deepened commitment to narrative verse holds some of his mannerisms in check, he is still the last poet whose plainness can be trusted, and I will suggest below why plainness is at odds with the larger ambitions of his style.

But before turning directly to matters of style, I wish to look briefly at **"Lost in Translation"** (1974), Merrill's most recent rationale for constructed secrets. In this poem, Merrill tells how, as a young boy, he spirited away a single, palm-shaped piece of a jigsaw puzzle successfully completed with Mademoiselle in 1939. This single missing piece reminds him of his boyhood infatuation for his governess, but more importantly of his parents' divorce in 1939 (his father remarried two weeks later: hence the boy's fond imagination that "old wives who know the worst / Outsweat that virile fiction of the New . . . " [***DC,*** p. 8]). Merrill indirectly recollects feeling torn between his mother and father:

Houri and Afreet
Both claim the Page. He wonders whom to serve,
And what his duties are, and where his feet. . . .

(*DC*, p. 8)

That missing piece is a token of Merrill's lost footing, for it reminds him of his surrogate parent Mademoiselle, who kept her then dubious German ancestry a secret, and through her of the global fracture of 1939 which made her reticence prudent. And through a literary recollection of another French-German nexus, Merrill recalls "Palme," the poem Valéry wrote in 1917, one year before the threat of a German advance led him away from Paris, five years before Rilke translated the poem.[11] The tree in "Palme" manages to keep its footing in sand and, like a secret, bear its fruit in silence ("Chaque atome de silence / Est la chance d'un fruit mûr!"); it stands securely between earth and sky ("L'attirance de la terre / Et le poids du firmament!"), or mother earth and father sky/time, as Merrill imagines them in **"The Broken Home"** (***ND,*** pp. 27-28). Rilke knew, Merrill suggests, how much of Valéry's poem would be memorialized in the translation only by silent loss, absence: a phrase like "d'un fruit mûr" becomes "das Reifen genau." ("Verger" and "parfumer," incidentally, are absent from this particular Valéry poem.) And Merrill claims to know, from looking at the German text,

What Pains, what monolithic Truths
Shadow stanza to stanza's symmetrical
Rhyme-rutted pavement. Know that ground plan left
Sublime and barren, where the warm Romance
Stone by stone faded, cooled; the fluted nouns
Made taller, lonelier than life
By leaf-carved capitals in the afterglow.

(*DC*, pp. 9-10)

His secret homage to Rilke's self-deprivation is a haggard ghost of that stanzaic scheme (*ababccdeed*) buried in his own poem (11. 19-30). And Merrill's image of the prosody as a pavement reinforces the recollection of that passage in **"From the Cupola"** in which the palm-Aphrodite gradually undermines the paved sidewalk at its base, just as Psyche's fantasy of Eros obscures her grimy house-cleaning chores on Long Island Sound.[12] For the take-home message—and Merrill does choose the most inspirational passage of the Valéry/Rilke poem for his epigraph—is that even the waste and failure of misunderstanding and misstatement (on one level, his parents' divorce) harbors sustenance (on that same level, material for poems, Mnemosyne).

> Lost, is it, buried? One more missing piece?
> But nothing's lost. Or else: all is translation
> And every bit of us is lost in it
> (Or found—I wander through the ruin of S
> Now and then, wondering at the peacefulness)
> And in that loss a self-effacing tree,
> Color of context, imperceptibly
> Rustling with its angel, turns the waste
> To shade and fiber, milk and memory.
>
> (*DC*, p. 10)

Finally, the palm represents the translator himself. There are at least six translators in the poem: Rilke; Mademoiselle, who misstates her own ancestry; her nephew, the UN interpreter, who translates the misstatements known as diplomacy; Maggie Teyte, the English musical translator of French songs, who disguised her name (Tate) so that the French would pronounce it properly; Stonington, that translation of Greece on Long Island Sound; and Merrill, who brings near English the Valéry/Rilke poem and near stage-Arabic his parents' relationship (Houri and Afreet). They all suggest, diversely, that effacement, the keeping of secrets, in the translator's code is as important to communication as disclosure is. Rilke's direct translation of Valéry's stanza and his effort to make exactitude take the place of Valéry's sensuosity (fruit mûr-Reifen genau) suggest that plainness itself can be yet another version of obscurity, of shadowy self-effacement.

The patterns of thematic secrecy which I have been tracing correspond profoundly, I think, to certain of Merrill's stylistic manners. Periphrasis, talking around a subject, is the most obvious of these correspondent manners. **"Maisie,"** the poem following **"The Thousand and Second Night"** in ***Nights and Days,*** is an extended periphrasis: Merrill never mentions that the subject of the poem is a cat. These arabesques around reticence—"the mirror of the tide's / retreat" for wet sand (***CT,*** p. 59); "Great drifts of damask" for napkins (***ND,*** p. 9)—are part of the joy of Merrill's writing. Some of the wittiest moments in his verse occur when he twirls words, euphemistically, around what need not be said. For example, these lines from the postcards-section of **"The Thousand and Second Night"**—

> She strokes his handlebar who kneels
> To do for her what a dwarf does for him
>
> (*ND*, p. 10)

—twist around the contortions of double fellatio for three. For Merrill, the language of poetry is implicitly prefaced by a contractual "In other words." In fact, the more obvious the periphrasis, the purer and more apparent the playful spirit behind it—which turns out to be a grandly liberating principle.

Because Merrill wears his periphrastic motive on his sleeve, he can pursue words and phrases that are off limits to his contemporaries. From the beginning. his diction has been precious—"smilingly" (***FP,*** p. 14; ***CT,*** p. 9), "swifterly" (***FP,*** p. 23), "amberly" (***FP,*** p. 43), "lucent" (***FP,*** p. 67)—in ways that would make Robert Lowell or Charles Olson blush. Similarly, from his ***First Poems*** to his most recent, Merrill has maintained easy access to that stable of words which trail behind them the label "Poetic." In his early poems, bodies are "winsome" (***FP,*** p. 42) and, for a rhyme, can even be made to "wend" (***FP,*** p. 71). In ***The Country of a Thousand Years of Peace*** there are Miltonic "lowing beasts secure" (***CT,*** p. 11), and in **"The Thousand and Second Night"** on billboards "Loom wingèd letters" (***ND,*** p. 4). In ***The Fire Screen*** "Piebald hindquarters of another guest" identify someone vomiting in a toilet (***FS,*** p. 34). In ***Braving the Elements,*** Merrill sees his mother as "bepearled" (***BE,*** p. 14), just as in **"The Book of Ephraim"** his mirror is said to be "bespattered" (***DC,*** p. 86). And still more firmly impressed on his diction than these archaic poeticisms is that odd category of adjectives beginning with "a-" which, like tableaux, freeze actions into qualities. A few of these words are inconspicuous, ordinary: asleep (***BE,*** p. 16), awake (***WS,*** p. 27), ajar (***CT,*** p. 63; ***BE,*** p. 30), aloud (***CT,*** p. 36). Others are less so, but still familiar: askance (***FP,*** p. 36), aghast (***CT,*** p. 27; ***ND,*** p. 16), askew (***CT,*** p. 54), aloft (***CT,*** p. 6), agape (***DC,*** p. 63). But most of these adjectives are strikingly rare or novel: aspin (***CT,*** p. 6), atremble (***CT,*** p. 9), atilt (***CT,*** p. 11), aswirl (***CT,*** p. 47), atwirl (***CT,*** p. 33), ableach (***CT,*** p. 33), adrowse (***CT,*** p. 47), aflicker (***WS,*** p. 22; ***FS,*** p. 43), aswim (***ND,*** p. 30), acrackle (***ND,*** p. 52), abubble (***FS,*** p. 24), ashiver (***FS,*** p. 33), aglitter (***FS,*** p. 47), aflush (***DC,*** p. 48), awince (***DC,*** p. 77). The list, little in itself, shows Merrill's willingness to indulge his own painterly mannerisms. He would be the last poet to use such words and phrases naively; he knows that the components of his diction—precious, archaic, poetic, and mannered—have been so firmly displaced from usage that their appearance nudges his poems outside the spoken language. But that may be greater gain than loss for Merrill: his poems proudly occupy a special corner of the language where the possibilities of play are unlimited by mundane considerations of democratic usage. Likewise, syntax, which ordinarily preserves, for narration or ratiocination, the distinct categories of agent, action, object, in poems like **"Olive Grove"** and **"Thistledown"** becomes a game of suspense; questions of who did what to whom are submerged in the fluencies of syntax, as in a solvent (***CT,*** pp. 5-7).[13]

Merrill demands all the special prerogatives of poetic language: diction, syntax, and, perhaps most strikingly, metaphor. He is a master of the obviously "clever" figure. Figurative language, for him, is plainly ornamental and playful. The burden of striking figures is that they are so obviously "poetic," that they seem to display the powers of the poet more boldly than they do the facets of the subject. But this is a light burden for Merrill: he would never attempt to conceal his artfulness. His figures are almost tricks, because they rest on certain set moves. For instance, one move which often generates a figural showstopper is to liken language to objects:

> On which (to the pilgrim who forgets
> His Arabic) a wild script of gold whips . . .
>
> (***ND***, p. 4);

or the same move in the opposite direction:

> A mapmaker (attendant since Jaipur)
> Says that from San Francisco our path traces
> The Arabic for GREAT WONDER. . . .
>
> (***DC***, p. 83)

The most common move behind these witty figures (and of course it is not just Merrill's) is a mild personification: objects or animals are likened to people. Often these are just quick, deft touches, as with the "dove with Parkinson's disease" (***DC,*** p. 28) or the "snapshots old / Enough to vote" (***DC,*** p. 85). But in other instances, these figures are sustained for a line or two, as though Merrill were in no hurry to be getting anywhere. Here, for example, are two lines describing a ski-lift:

> Prey swooped up, the iron love seat shudders
> Onward into its acrophilic trance.
>
> (***BE***, p. 53)

And a few more toying with an etymological possibility:

> Moonglow starts from scratches as my oval
> Cheval-glass tilting earthward by itself
> —The rider nodding and the reins gone slack—
> Converges with lamplight ten winters back.
>
> (***DC***, p. 94)

Economy be damned: Merrill takes time to have fun. And that is a freedom sanctioned, he knows from reading Auden, by no lesser precedent than *Don Juan,* with its "air of irrelevance, of running on at the risk of never becoming terribly significant" (***CW,*** p. 151); and Merrill has lately acknowledged his debt to Byron's master, Pope (***DC,*** pp. 56, 92, 105, 116). For Merrill, energy, invention, ornamentation—not signification—are what make poetry.

These stylistic manners are mostly idiosyncratic: they are the marks by which Merrill allows his language to be identified. There is, however, a greater ambition behind his verse, one which is manifest mainly in diction and tone. He is unusual among his contemporaries, and more generally rare among American poets, in his effort to imply by his style a set of attitudes and values which is claimed by a class of American society. This is a difficult claim to substantiate, not because many other poets make the same effort (they do not: the effort itself is widely held in suspicion) but because American class boundaries are elusive; and to identify the style of an American class is doubly difficult. I will begin, therefore, by identifying the attitudes and values invoked by Merrill's writing and end by suggesting the class loyalties of those attitudes.

Some of these values have already been described: periphrasis, euphemism, and various other mannerisms—such tropes testify to Merrill's esteem for extravagance; he is a poet who, rather than unify style and content in postromantic fashion, prefers to set style at odds with content. His style often throttles content. And style, for Merrill, is a way of playing, not working, for the force behind style is energy serving no particular end but itself. The characteristic tone of his verse is ironic, but only lightly so. In **"The Book of Ephraim"** he identifies

> the tone
> We trusted most, a smiling Hellenistic
> Lightness from beyond the grave.
>
> (***DC***, p. 59)

Neither naively jubilant nor bitterly sardonic, the tone he aspires to is one of undeluded good cheer. Here are the first two lines from his elegy for his friend Hans Lodeizen:

> Here they all come to die,
> Fluent therein as in a fourth tongue.
>
> (***CT***, p. 2)

Any magazine editor might have altered the second line to conform to the canons of sixties poetic diction (the poem was actually published in the winter 1951-52 issue of *Origin,* which was militantly opposed to the reigning editorial policies of the fifties):

> Fluent in death as in a fourth tongue.

The meter and sense would be preserved and that awkward legalese ("therein") avoided, but the line would be too heavy by a tone, too naively self-absorbed by a ton.

The proper word for Merrill's tone is arch. That tone is first heard, in Merrill's oeuvre, in the opening line of **"Medusa"**:

> The head, of course, had fallen to disrepair
> If not to disrepute.
>
> (***FP***, p. 10)

This tone is often nicely tuned to syntax. Merrill strikes his note most effectively by tossing off ironic parenthetical clauses so that the irony seems casual, incidental, a result more of his temperament than of any norm or principle of judgment implied by the irony. The tone of the lines from "Medusa" is established not in the main clause but in the "of course" and "if not . . . " clauses. Rhetorically, this is a variety of understatement, for the qualifying irony of the lesser clauses in fact throws an entirely new perspective on the main clause. Here are two more examples of this archness:

Tell me, tongue of fire,
That you and I are as real
At least as the people upstairs.

(*ND*, p. 27)

From judgment, it would seem, he has refrained. (*BE,* p. 70)

The tone of the first passage, from **"The Broken Home,"** is set by two words so placed, syntactically, as to seem parenthetical: "at least." The irony of the passage can be measured not just by the apocalyptic periphrasis for a candle-flame, "tongue of fire," but by the difference between "at least as real" (which would be the ordinary syntax) and "as real / at least." Merrill's version of the phrase makes the ironic stab at his neighbors an off-hand afterthought—easy, for him. Similarly, the single line from **"The Victor Dog"** sets its tone in the throw-away clause, "it would seem." And the conditional mood turns the volume lower, as though the claims of the statement were being posited ever so hesitantly and politely. Yet politeness, in this context, has little to do with concern for others: for this archness can become, in the words of Merrill's friends, "vain / Flippant unfeeling" (*ND,* p. 9).

Merrill is his own critic in this regard:

My friend with time to kill
Asked me the price of cars in Paradise.
By which he meant my country, for in his
The stranger is a god in masquerade.
Failing to act that part, I am afraid
I was not human either—ah, who is?
He is, or was; had brothers and a wife;
Chauffeured a truck; last Friday broke his neck
Against a tree. We have no way to check
These headlong emigrations out of life.
Try, I suppose, we must, as even Valéry said,
And said more grandly than I ever shall. . . .

(*ND*, p. 8)

These lines from **"The Thousand and Second Night"** move as far toward self-criticism as Merrill has ever cared to go. He criticizes his own willingness to allow archness to become more than mischievous. On occasion, Merrill can be snotty, often when he deals with people he considers his inferiors, either in terms of class or of sensibility. Take, for instance, this quatrain from **"Days of 1971"**:

Can-can from last night's *Orphée aux Enfers*
Since daybreak you've been whistling till I wince.
Well, you were a handsome devil once.
Take the wheel. You're still a fair chauffeur.

(*BE*, p. 65)

What Merrill tries to censure in the lines quoted from **"The Thousand and Second Night"** is this sort of glib condescension.[14] But, finally, the point of the passage is that he can only try. The first sign of his effort comes in those lines "I am afraid / I was not human either—ah, who is?" No sooner is he self-critical than his all-embracing skepticism lets him off the hook—"ah, who is?"

Merrill has developed this strategy into tropes for casually universalizing chagrin:

She has brought a cake "for tomorrow"
As if tomorrows were still memorable.

(*BE*, p. 4)

Look at what's left of that young fellow strapped
Into his wheelchair. How you pity him!
The city ripples, your eyes sicken and swim.
The boy includes you in his sightseeing,
Nodding sociably as if who of us
Here below were more than half a man.

(*BE*, p. 64)

Tonight in the magician's tent
Next door a woman will be sawed in two,
But right now she's asleep, as who is not, as who . . .

(*DC*, p. 25)

I'll never know.
Who ever does?

(*DC*, p. 34)

A dirtbrown helicopter . . .
The sunniness beneath it, up and went
As much had, without saying—

(*DC*, p. 43)

For if, poor soul, he did so, he was lost.
Ah, so were we!

(*DC*, p. 99)

World-weariness, the tone of the perdu, is an attitude Merrill dons like a theatrical mask; it is purely conventional, void of genuine emotional significance—pure style without content. In these two stanzas from **"The Summer People"** Andrew and Margaret toy with the conventionality of their own cries of despair:

"Oh God, this life's so pointless,
So wearing," Margaret said.
"You're telling me," Andrew agreed.
"High time we both were dead."
"It *is.* I have pills—let's take them!"
He looked at her with wit.
"Just try. You know we'd never
Hear the end of it."

(*FS*, pp. 68-69)

Clever to the end, they know that weariness, like various small courtesies, is demanded of them; it is a code-attitude no more to be taken literally than the "love" such people express for four-hand piano, bridge, gossip, croquet, and entertaining (*FS,* pp. 58-59). Thus when James (to return to the passage from **"The Thousand and Second Night"**) says "He is, or was," he is calling into question the propriety of this programmatic skepticism. The next two and a half lines describe the death of an ordinary worker, and these lines quietly accuse James of a failure of feeling, flip callousness. But Merrill goes only so far in implicit self-accusation: at this point the suspect archness resumes control of the passage and continues with the poem—"We have no way to check / These headlong emigrations out of life." Archness is Merrill's ground-note: he cannot silence it, though he can acknowledge and regret, from time to time, its impoliteness, or, worse, insensitivity.

Archness is an apt term for describing Merrill's characteristic tone, but it does not indicate the greater aspiration of his style; for that, another term will serve better: camp. In 1929 Ezra Pound described what he called *logopoeia:* "It employs words not only for their direct meaning, but it takes count in a special way of habits of usage, of the context we *expect* to find with the word, its usual concomitants, of its known acceptances, and of ironical play. . . . It is the latest come, and perhaps most tricky and undependable mode."[15] Merrill, more than any of his American contemporaries, successfully invokes by his tone and diction patterns of usage which add up to a coherent sensibility, one whose class allegiance, or aspiration is explicit. Here are some lines from **"Words for Maria"** that display the camp tone:

> I'm calling *you* henceforth The Lunatic.
> Today at 4 a.m. in a snack bar
> You were discovered eating, if you please,
> Fried squid; alone. Aleko stood aghast.
>
> . . . . .
>
> Sappho has been to your new flat, she *says.*
> Tony, who staggered there with the Empire
> Mirror you wanted from his shop, tells how
> You had him prop it in a chair and leave
> That instant. Really now!
>
> (***FS***, p. 12)

The campiness of these lines is established largely by insistence: certain words are italicized to insist on one emphasis rather than some other, and the word "alone" is isolated by punctuation to suggest that it is full of meaning that need not, in some company, be elaborated upon. The tone suggests that there is some secret, something not being said, which would explain both the extravagance of Aleko's response and Merrill's implication that Sappho may not be telling the truth. Merrill's success with this tone is measured partly by his ability to make this voice *heard,* yet he uses it not just dramatically. He can attribute it to anyone, even "the man in the moon": "The point's to live, love, / Not shake your fist at the feast" (***FS,*** p. 30). And Ephraim, too, has his share of camp lines (***DC,*** pp. 41, 78, 94).

The camp tone is less a dialect Merrill can use for some types of characters than a norm—social as well as stylistic—which his verse erects. With that tone goes a set of attitudes and values which is boldest in its political aspect.

> Where are the chimneys, the traffic? Instead come strange
> Horizons of ink, and livid treetops massing raggedly
> Beyond the sill like poor whites in a study
> Of conditions we must one day seriously try to change.
>
> (***FS***, p. 37)
>
> THE AIR
> ABOVE LOS ALAMOS IS LIKE A BREATH
> SUCKED IN HORROR TOD MORT MUERTE DEATH
> —Meaning the nearby nuclear research
> Our instinct first is to deplore, and second
> To think no more of.
>
> (***DC***, p. 77)

Politics, with few exceptions, is a subject Merrill deliberately, and wittily, disdains:

> I rarely buy a newspaper, or vote.
> To do so, I have learned, is to invite
> The tread of a stone guest within my house.
>
> (***ND***, p. 29)

From the camp viewpoint, politics is stylelessly overladen with content; it can be ignored, because the camp sensibility is premised, as Susan Sontag has noted, on detachment.[16] Merrill—and not just in his campier moments—claims an aristocratic aloofness from political activity.[17] Yet the anachronism "aristocratic" can be taken only metaphorically, even in Merrill's case: it indicates aspiration or desire rather than actual loyalty. The camp sensibility aspires to a stable, sanctioned position from which detachment can be easily afforded, or from which engagement is impractical, uneconomical. Susan Sontag points out that the camp sensibility wants as well to take up one of the supposed burdens of the aristocracy: "Since no authentic aristocrats exist today to sponsor special tastes, who is the bearer of this taste? Answer: an improvised self-elected class, mainly homosexuals, who constitute themselves as aristocrats of taste. . . ."[18] This is not to say that Merrill's style is restrictively homosexual: often he uses phrases which are commonly upper-class without being necessarily camp: "ghastly scenes" (***CT,*** p. 28), "to launch one" (***ND,*** p. 25), "I dare say" (***ND,*** p. 54), "I'm pained" (***ND,*** p. 9), "mayn't I" (***ND,*** p. 53); and the diction of the **"The Summer People"** shows that Merrill makes no hard and fast distinction between upper-class and camp manners. The line Merrill is likely to insist upon is between upper- and lower-class diction: he typically distances himself from the language commonly understood as colloquial. For example, in **"The Locusts"** he makes a parenthetical joke of his second-hand rendering of a ruralism: "Come spring (he says) / The grubs will hatch . . ." (***CT,*** p. 78). And in **"Days of 1971"** he resorts to a vulgar expression only in a sentence which goes on to climb to high-culture:

> One self-righteous truck
> Knocked the shit out of a eucalyptus
> Whose whitewashed trunk lay twitching brokenly—
> Nijinsky in *Petrouchka*—on the quai.
>
> (***BE***, p. 68)

Street-fighting to ballet—that is the distance Merrill puts between himself and what many of his contemporaries regard as colloquial usage.[19] Which is to say that Merrill has no truck with the Whitmanesque, or Wordsworthian, dream of speaking to or for "the people." Regardless of where his poems appear, of how many copies of his books sell, or of which prizes are awarded him (so far he has received the three most prestigious American awards for poetry: the Bollingen and the National Book Award for ***Nights and Days***, and the Pulitzer Prize for ***Divine Comedies***), Merrill is a coterie poet by rhetorical choice: his diction and tone locate his poetry in a world (wished, of course) where the reigning sensibility is camp. From Merrill's point of view, to have it any other way is, frankly, disgusting:

> Must I grow broad- and dirty-minded
> Serving a community, a nation
> By now past anybody's power to shock?
>
> (***DC***, p. 12)

Ezra Pound once said that the most intense form of criticism is new composition, and Merrill's verse is critical in just this sense.[20] He has been rightly praised for making his own way during a time when gusts of literary fashion blew many of his contemporaries about. Poems such as **"The Thousand and Second Night"** and **"Lost in Translation,"** to name only two, seem from one point of view to have "confessions" to make; yet the conventions of confessional poetry are invoked only to be artfully eluded. Merrill's ironic pirouettes around these conventions are more than incidental; his unique position among recent American poets can be located by the social ambitions of his poetry. Like many of the modernist poets of the first half of the century, Merrill is a master of tone. Through his diction and syntax, he manages to situate his writing in relation to patterns of usage which confirm social relations. During the sixties, while some of his contemporaries, under the influence of W. S. Merwin, were pursuing styles that apparently disowned social relations, and others, like Lowell, were attempting to democratize with free verse, low colloquialisms and brand names the densely metaphorical styles they learned in the fifties, Merrill held by his meters and chose his phrases with a sense of class. So distinct a sense of class is implied by his style that he, at least as much as any of his contemporaries, has altered the politics of style in American poetry; which is to say that he has expanded the stylistic horizon of American poetry. Other American poets have succeeded in implying by their styles the attractions of a particular class or political camp: during the thirties there was something of a vogue in leftist literary journals for dialect poetry, and a good deal of recent black poetry is written in dialect. But, for ideological as well as artistic reasons, Merrill would rightly resist that company; the proper analogy is to British poets, and chiefly to Auden. Merrill's distinction is his skeptical view of that American *idée fixe,* the democratic or classless style.

Notes

1. James Merrill, *Nights and Days* (New York: Atheneum, 1966), p. 38; hereafter references to this volume will be abbreviated *ND.* The following abbreviations will also be used for parenthetical references to Merrill's works: *First Poems* (New York: Knopf, 1951)—*FP*; *The Country of a Thousand Years of Peace* (New York: Atheneum, 1959; enlarged edition, 1970)—*CT*; *Water Street* (New York: Atheneum, 1962)—*WS*; *The Fire Screen* (New York: Atheneum, 1969)—*FS*; *Braving the Elements* (New York: Atheneum, 1972)—*BE*; *Divine Comedies* (New York: Atheneum, 1976)—*DC*; *The Contemporary Writer*, ed. L. S. Dembo & Cyrena N. Pondrom (Madison: Univ. of Wisconsin Press, 1972)—*CW*. The quotation in my title is taken from "Little Fanfare for Felix Magowan" (*ND,* p. 31).
2. For an example of how the term has been inflated, see Robert Phillips, *The Confessional Poets* (Carbondale & Edwardsville: Southern Illinois Univ. Press, 1973), esp. pp. 16-17.
3. James Merrill, *The Seraglio* (New York: Knopf, 1957), pp. 107-108.
4. In a review of *Nights and Days* David Kalstone discusses Merrill as a master of the confessional mode (*Partisan Review,* XXXIV, 1 [Winter 1967], 146-150); however, in his recent discussion of Merrill, Mr. Kalstone prefers to emphasize the ways in which Merrill departs from "confessional" practices (David Kalstone, *Five Temperaments* [New York: Oxford Univ. Press, 1977], p. 79).
5. Ashley Brown, "An Interview with James Merrill," *Shenandoah,* XIX, 4 (Summer 1968), 10.
6. A comparable poem, thematically, is "The Friend of the Fourth Decade" (1968). In this later poem, Merrill still feels the lure of an aesthetic experience without any referential sense, a poetic of surfaces, but he is unable to slip free of human ties to the past—"Certain things die only with oneself" (*FS,* p. 7).
7. Cox actually said: "'The Thousand and Second Night' describes a breakdown in his identity in middle age, the end of purposive union between mind, soul and body or perhaps between himself and his Muse" (*The Spectator* [21 October 1966], 523).
8. Ashley Brown, "An Interview with James Merrill," p. 13.
9. "Germaine Nahman" and "A.H. Clarendon," so far as I can determine, are phantom authors, absences to which Merrill ascribes meaning.
10. Ashley Brown, "An Interview with James Merrill," pp. 12-13.
11. Henry A. Grubbs, *Paul Valéry* (New York: Twayne, 1968), p. 61.
12. Judith Moffett has discussed this connection to the Aphrodite-palm of "From the Cupola" in her review of *Divine Comedies* (*Poetry,* CXXIX, 1 [October 1976], 42-43).
13. For an excellent discussion of Merrill's syntax, see Richard Howard's essay on Merrill in *Alone with America* (New York: Atheneum, 1969), p. 329.
14. The most recent instance of Merrill's condescension is a little more comic than snide:

Another memory of Mademoiselle.
We're in a Pullman going South for Christmas,
She in the lower berth, I in the upper
As befits whatever station we pass through.

(*DC* p. 15)

15. Ezra Pound, *Literary Essays,* ed. T.S. Eliot (Norfolk, Conn.: New Directions, 1954), p. 25. Pound goes on to say that the roots of *logopoeia* lie in seventeenth- and eighteenth-century satire (p. 30); Laforgue, however, is the modern exemplar and true master of *logopoeia* (p. 33).
16. Susan Sontag, *Against Interpretation* (New York: Farrar, Straus & Giroux, 1966), p. 288. My discussion of camp style is deeply indebted to her essay "Notes on Camp"; the only other discussion of camp which I know is mentioned by Sontag: Christopher Isherwood, *The World in the Evening* (London: Methuen, 1954), pp. 125-126.
17. See, e.g., *CW,* p. 148; and *The Seraglio,* pp. 48-49 & 217.
18. *Against Interpretation,* p. 290.
19. It should be clear, though, that Merrill wants to preserve his ironic access to this level of colloquial usage; the wittiest example of his delight in that language comes in "Days of 1935" (*BE,* p. 13).
20. *Literary Essays,* p. 75.

Irvin Ehrenpreis (essay date 1981)

SOURCE: "Merrill," in *Poetries of America: Essays on the Relation of Character to Style*, edited by Daniel Albright, University Press of Virginia, 1989, pp. 192-206.

[*In the following essay, Ehrenpreis analyzes* The Book of Ephraim, Mirabell, *and* Scripts for the Pageant *as a related "three-part enterprise."*]

Anyone who wants evidence that James Merrill has held on to his formidable gifts as a poet should look at a few sections of his recent books, ***Mirabell: Books of Number*** (1978) and ***Scripts for the Pageant*** (1980). Merrill's versatility and inventiveness fill a description of the small town of Stonington, Connecticut, on Block Island Sound:

White or white-trimmed canary clapboard homes
Set in the rustling shade of monochromes;
Lighthouse and clock tower, Village Green and neat
Roseblush factory which makes, upstreet,
Exactly what, one once knew but forgets—
Something of plastic found in luncheonettes;
The Sound's quick sapphire that each day recurs
Aflock with pouter-pigeon spinnakers.

(***Mirabell*** 53-54)[1]

Here, honest observation and smiling affection make themselves known through the clever rhymes, the exact epithets, and a witty mixture of colloquial with elegant phrasing. Later in the book, the rendition of a storm in musical terms, supported by startling metaphors and (again) rhyming couplets, provides a tour de force of steady movement and shifting points of view (pp. 149-50). In ***Scripts for the Pageant*** the incantatory, expanded sestina **"Samos"** (87-88) will fill the auditory imagination of an attentive listener;[2] and the evocation of a moonlit red bedroom will delight connoisseurs of nightscapes.

Woken—a bark? Night freshness and dazzle edging
The room's pitch bright as day. Shutter flung wide,
In streams moonlight, her last quarter blazing
Inches above that wall of carbon mist
Made of the neighbors'. Whereupon the bedside
Tumbler brims and, the tallest story becoming
Swallowable, a mind-altering spansule,
This red, self-shuttered poverty and Heaven's
Glittering oxygen tent as one conspire.
Dark dark the bogs do hark . . . Instreaming, overwhelming
Even as it pulls back, the skyward undertow
Leaves, throughout city and countryside, wherever
Somebody wakes and goes to his window, a glowing
Tide-pool dram of bliss, diminuendo.

(208-9)

Normally, a critic pursues such articles of praise with the judgment that the separate bits of a long poem gain power from their relation to the whole. I am not inclined to say so much. It is true that some obscurities in the best-turned lines may be illuminated by other parts of Merrill's volumes. So also a reader may profitably recall earlier appearances (in either book) of themes, places, or characters employed in the marked passages. Still I think those passages might win strength if we read them independently.

Wallace Stevens once told Harriet Monroe that he wished to put everything else aside and amuse himself "on a large scale for a while." If he supposed the advice was good for American poets in general, I disagree. Our best poets came of age after extended narratives and lengthy works of exposition had deserted verse for prose. The so-called long poems of the last hundred twenty-five years (or since the first edition of *Leaves of Grass*) never represent a triumph of structure; the stronger the narrative, the weaker the verse.

Too many learned critics have wasted too many specious demonstrations on the effort to fit fragments together and show us a marble temple. Lowell could not make *Notebook* into one grand poem by mere fiat. As for the "long poems" of Wallace Stevens, they exhibit so many redefinitions of the same images, so many reconsiderations of the same points of view, that we should do well to call them sequences—collections of poems on related topics. They may have key words and themes in common; but they have little necessary order, little consistency of doctrine, and much material whose omission would leave no obvious gap.

In Merrill's recent books the burden of the author's ambition does not rest comfortably on the foundations of his genius. Merrill's early mature verse, collected in ***First Po-***

ems (1951), reveals a fascination with stanzaic design and with the extraction of subtle implications from a focused image or situation. The language is refined and musical; the meanings are obscure. The poet habitually works out his song in some form of aria da capo; and sometimes the observer and the image trade places.

Throughout these early poems Merrill displays the mastery of syntactic transition and verbal continuity that marks all his work. He indulges in some wordplay and in his compulsive habit of standing clichés on their heads. A pervasive feature of the poems is Merrill's avoidance of moral or social doctrine, a "chronic shyness / Vis-à-vis 'ideas'" (***Scripts*** 137). The artist in his early twenties sounds unwilling to preach on any uplifting subject. He describes a peacock in language echoing the Sermon on the Mount; but opposing "beatitude" to "beautiful," he sets the fantasy of the peacock's gorgeous feathers against the mundane defects of ordinary birds: art against normality. The peacock lacks dignity and virtue; it suggests egoism, frivolity, vanity, as well as painful effort. But the poet seems to prefer its fate to that of "merit / In body, word and deed" (**"Peacock";** 55).[3]

At the same time Merrill almost flaunts a power of fitting his expression into difficult verse forms and strict patterns of images. As compensation, perhaps, he invites the reader to fit his mind into the cryptic paradoxes which the poems convey. Merrill gives riddling human traits to objects and landscapes; he turns abstractions into evasive persons. A reader who stays with the poet must decipher stone, animal, or landscape as an emblematic center around which surprising and absorbing associations cluster themselves: secret and painful recollections of the poet, memories of innocent early experiences which become symbolic anticipations of the deceits and disappointments to be suffered in later years. **"Wreath for the Warm-Eyed"** turns on a game of hide-and-seek which the poet as a young man played with children. Instead of following the rules, the children simply ran away and left their playmate with a vivid omen of the loneliness and childlessness that were to color his adulthood.

The habit of arriving at a meaning by cross-examining an image, or by inverting the usual relation of metaphor to implication, still dominates the poems collected in ***The Country of a Thousand Years of Peace*** (1959). For instance, the pregnant sister of the poet reminds him of a pendulum as she rocks in a hammock (**"A Timepiece"**). So he works out a poem on the clocklike aspects of a pregnancy. **"The Doodler"** seems to deal with the poet's scratchings on a pad as he talks to his friends by telephone. But Merrill draws a parallel between the speaker and God.

In **"Hotel de l'Univers et Portugal,"** the poet and a lover, during their travels abroad, stay in one more bleak hotel room and find their affection deepened by the bleakness—which is of the world as well as the hotel. A lack of possessions or ties (luggage growing lighter as they travel) leaves them unfurnished and therefore open to each other. The analogy between place and person makes the poem; the lovers are a recurrent dream of the strange bed.

With no moral argument and no narrative line, the poems become static and regressive. Although autobiography underlies them, the poet blurs and masks the original experiences: we learn what they are like, what they connote, but not what they are. At last in ***Water Street*** (1962), Merrill animates his stanzas by giving us anecdotes of the poet's life. The old refinement of language remains, but it slips into and out of colloquial slackness. Although the hero of the work is memory, the present keeps springing from the past and peering into the future.

Certain motifs, familiar from earlier works, begin to seem peculiar marks of Merrill's genius: fire and water, light playing on glass; houses, rooms, and their furnishings, especially mirrors and windows. Certain themes go with them: the poet's family, erotic adventures and disillusionments, foreign travel, death. Certain devices keep challenging us: personifications that create riddles (e.g., the five senses as demanding children in **"From the Cupola"**), metaphors that expand into scenes, perceptions that dissolve into symbols; pairs of juxtaposed images which reflect or become each other.

In works like **"An Urban Convalescence"** and **"After Grace"** the poet adds psychological depth and self-knowledge to his self-exploration: these poems are permanent additions to our culture. But in **"Roger Clay's Proposal"** Merrill still rejects any involvement in public issues; he still refuses to choose among conventional social philosophies.

Instead of moral principles, what he offers in most of his poems is a form of insight which gives meaning to the present by linking and contrasting it with clues from the remote past; and this activity in turn apparently gets the poet moving ahead after a lassitude of confusing emotions. When Merrill expanded his designs into sequential poems, he mixed narrative with meditation and analysis, holding the work together on a thread of place or time: the poet's surprising travels or the evolution of his psyche. The fascination of the poems derives in part from unconventional or scandalous material: exposures of family secrets and sexual deviations, frank narcissism, an anti-Puritan indulgence in dolce far niente (jigsaw puzzles, games of patience, doodling). But the brilliance of the wordplay, the ingenuity of the conceits, the expressive skill of the versification, all keep the style from appearing self-indulgent.

"The Thousand and Second Night" stretches the snip-and-tape design as far as it will go, skipping from place to exotic place while shuttling back and forth in time. Observation yields to memory; memory to symbolism and startling self-exposure. The poem comes to a focus in the themes of physical decay and death, and the need for the artist to triumph over both by incorporating them into his art. It is as splendid a work as Merrill has produced and occupies twelve pages in ***Nights and Days*** (1966).

In the same volume Merrill also tried a full-scale verse narrative, **"From the Cupola."** But he lost the shape in allegory and personification. The story of Cupid and Psyche transplanted to a New England village became an excuse for more emblematic and cryptic fantasy than most readers, however loyal, could absorb.

Other experiments with length include **"The Summer People"** (a narrative fantasy), the openly autobiographical **"Days of 1971,"** and **"Days of 1935"** (supposed to be the nine-year-old Merrill's cinematic dream of being kidnapped by a thug and his moll).[4] Of these the weakest is the one farthest removed from experience, i.e., **"The Summer People,"** which twists and turns as the poet infuses one or another dose of allegory into it.

The strongest of the three is the mock-travel diary **"Days of 1971,"** told as an absurd sonnet sequence addressed to a former lover now serving as chauffeur. The miracle of this poem is the way the speaker conveys the most attractive side of his character through the cool sprays of analytic wit bestowed on his uncouth but inseparable companion. The paratactic, stop-and-go structure affords free expression to Merrill's verbal legerdemain; and the suggested link between irritation and the creative process is deeply characteristic of his genius.

If I have managed to sketch the features of Merrill's accomplishment as his admirers would recognize them, it was a dangerous project for the poet to undertake an enormous opus dealing with metempsychosis, theodicy, cosmogony, and (among other things!) eschatology. Yet this is what we have in ***The Book of Ephraim, Mirabell,*** and ***Scripts for the Pageant***. Each one, alas, is longer than its predecessor; and they are all to be followed by an epilogue, **"The Ballroom at Sandover,"** which closes with the poet beginning to read aloud the entire five-hundred-page text to an audience of dead authors and friends.

At the center of the three-part enterprise we find a dissatisfaction with the possibilities of human life today, a celebration of the world of the dead, and a prophecy of a better race to come. These articles naturally tempt us to wonder about the data that produced them.

The style of life evoked by Merrill's poems suggests few inhibitions upon pleasurable activities. The poet's freedom to travel as he wished, to love as he felt inclined, to accumulate possessions, and to yield to moods has set him apart from ordinary men of talent. Yet the outcome of so much accessibility to experience does not strike one as pure felicity. The poems recall love affairs that did not gratify the poet's ardor. They describe places he visited, scrutinized, and left. They can suggest a disgust with himself at the same time as a disappointment in others; "waste, self-hatred, boredom" (***Mirabell*** 93). Whether these impressions are well- or ill-founded, the doctrines elaborated in Merrill's three prophetic books do seem to spring from a profound discontent with the normal grounds of moral stability, especially with traditional religion.

The poet's attitude emerges both through innuendo and through open statement. One reason for rejecting Christianity is evidently its association with repressive morality. Another is the weakness, to the poet's mind, of its revealed theology. Yet Merrill himself is not constitutionally given to meditating on the principles of ethics, religion, or philosophy; and he has never pretended to expert knowledge in those fields of study. Like most amateurs of abstruse learning, he combines diverse materials from sources that are not naturally harmonious.

In the course of his work the poet refers to the Book of Genesis and to the version of that history which Milton supplied in *Paradise Lost.* From time to time he evokes Dante, drawing parallels between his own poems and *The Divine Comedy.* These parallels may be structural, or in the adoption of themes and images, or simply in the use of terza rima. Elsewhere, we hear echoes of Blake; and Merrill employs Blakean four-teeners for the speech of many otherworldly beings. Yeats, both as a poet and as author of *A Vision,* is another formative figure named or echoed.

The result is not unpredictable. If a poet rejects Christianity yet accepts materials from Christian texts, if he mingles these with the teachings of quasi gnostics like Blake and Yeats, he can hardly help sounding like a gnostic himself. Whether or not Merrill has studied Nietzsche, whether or not he has read the work of Hans Jonas, he presents us with inversions of biblical myth and Christian morality that suggest the tradition of gnosticism. For him, however, matter is not opposed to spirit; it is not identified with evil. Rather, it is the aspect of reality which we owe to a benevolent creator, and which an evil deity wants to dissolve. The poet's materialism and his attitude toward pleasure suggest a refined epicureanism.

On these elements Merrill imposes some principles of modern science and some narrative motifs of science fiction or quack science: DNA, the Bermuda Triangle, UFO's. He also has tastes or fantasies of his own which color and shape the eclectic materials of the poems: a passion for opera, a fascination with mirrors. As culture heroes Proust and Auden seem omnipresent. Constantly, the poet intersperses his otherworldly stuff with episodes of autobiography and images derived from the house he lives in.

So we get a revelation delivered to Merrill and his friend David Jackson by a cup which their cooperating hands move over a Ouija board, with its arched alphabet, the digits from zero to nine, and the words *Yes* and *No.* Because the board has no lower-case letters, the otherworldly messages are transcribed for us in capitals. How lightly should the reader take such a scheme of narration? Merrill's novel *The Seraglio,* published in 1957, has a section in which the hero works successfully with a Ouija board. In **"Voices from the Other World"**—a poem which appeared about the same time—Merrill again reported such success. At least once when he was asked about the trials, he said they were serious.

We have strong American precedent for such occupations. Andrew Jackson Davis, the "Poughkeepsie Seer," is known to historians of American spiritualism. While in a "magnetized" state, he delivered a course of lectures published as *The Principles of Nature, Her Divine Revelations* (1847). Here he traced the evolution of the universe and described the solar system, giving details of the planets' inhabitants. Thomas Lake Harris (1823-1906), a sometime Universalist minister, wrote volumes of "trance poetry" dictated by the spirits of Shelley and others. One assumes that Merrill would prefer a connection with Dante and Yeats. But his doctrines are not the sort one might spontaneously expect from the creator of his best poems; and the land that invented spirit-rapping may claim him for her own.

To make a poem hold together when it is five hundred pages long, the poet must keep a large design in mind as he composes his verses and stanzas. But the shape of ***Ephraim-Mirabell-Scripts*** changes obstructively during the course of our passage through it. Characters who are introduced as important figures turn out to have little or no part in the story. Doctrines promulgated in one section are casually discarded in another. Spokesmen whom we are urged to trust confess themselves to be liars. Facts laid down in one place are contradicted in another.

Merrill tries to screen himself from such complaints. He expresses doubts concerning the very principles that his poem conveys—though he soon appears persuaded of them by characters in the work itself. He often treats the rebarbative material as symbol or allegory. Yet he also condemns allegory. At points we are told that the otherworldly beings can only draw (for their revelations) on the knowledge and imagination of the poet. Or Merrill simply declares that the whole work is a fiction he is trying to believe.

In ***The Book of Ephraim*** (1976), Merrill and Jackson open communication with a person who entered the world as a Greek Jew in the time of Christ, was murdered (36 A.D.), and underwent a number of rebirths; during the reign of Louis XVI he became a French courtier.[5] His name is Ephraim, and he teaches the Ouija boarders that each living person is the "representative" or protégé of a dead one, his "patron." There are nine stages of existence in the otherworld; and to qualify for the lowest, a soul must prove itself through a course of reincarnations. Once the poet has got into the habit, other spirits converse by Ouija with him and Jackson, especially spirits of old friends who are temporarily between bodies. He discovers that higher beings exist beyond the nine stages; and these powers break off the telegraphy when patrons try to reveal celestial secrets or to intervene in human affairs. Suddenly, Ephraim declares that he has met the souls of those who lived before mankind.

In ***Mirabell*** we too meet the creatures, who are, in fact, the higher powers. They appear human but black, winged, and batlike. While essentially good-natured, they also seem to be the original fallen angels and are themselves under the government of still loftier powers or regnant archangels. Above these in turn rises the God Biology, but even he is not the ultimate, supreme authority. Outside our system are other systems with their own suns and gods—a pantheon.

One of the batmen replaces Ephraim as mentor of the poet and his comrade. About the same time, two dead friends emerge as the steadiest, most informative human connections enjoyed by Merrill and Jackson in the otherworld. These are a late Athenian friend, Maria Mitsotaki, and the poet W. H. Auden. The group of two live and two dead humans make a quadruple alliance whose education is the theme of the book.

The four pupils grow fond of their master, and he returns the affection. As a result, he undergoes a metamorphosis into the shape of a peacock, to the delight of all five. Eventually, the poet names him Mirabell. Among many other revelations he teaches that the world we know is only the latest in a series of worlds, which were destroyed by various sci-fi events commemorated in well-known myths of universal catastrophe.

Some of the doctrines thrust upon the four friends (and the reader) have peculiar significance. We hear that as men die, the elements of their souls are extracted and refined in spiritual laboratories of the otherworld, to enrich a tiny proportion of creative minds—scientists, artists, and so forth—who elevate the condition of mankind while the masses remain in an animal state. All sorts of good and evil characters are required as material for these processes; and even animals and plants have souls whose ingredients may be employed to enrich the chosen few.

Yet conflicts arise from each stage of evolution and open the way to difficulties or dangers which the "vital laboratories" of the world must labor to control. Mind keeps organizing chaos, and chaos keeps resisting mind in an almost Manichaean rhythm.

In effect, traditional morality has little place in the poem. One reason is a kind of determinism. We hear that nothing in human events is accidental; for the genes of men are altered or "cloned" in the laboratories so as to change the institutions of mankind according to the wise desires of God Biology and the governors of the otherworld. Not only are all human actions predetermined, therefore, but the direction of history is ultimately benign; and it is hardly fair to blame people for misconduct that is imposed on them.

Sin, we are told, is only pain, given and received (***Scripts for the Pageant***, p. 173). The poet certainly does not admire those who abstain from hedonistic self-indulgence. And though the recommends devotion to others, the only self-discipline clearly praised is that of the artist.

These central doctrines float above a profusion of lesser principles concerning the evolution of the human species, the organization of life after death, the uses of the imagination, and so forth. It becomes clear that many of the propositions addressed to us are wholly or partly metaphorical and that the communications with otherworldly beings are derived from the poet's own fancy. But Mirabell continues lecturing in a rather telegraphic style until at the very end of the book he makes way for an archangel, Michael.

In ***Scripts for the Pageant***, as in ***Mirabell***, the scenes of earthly life and action shrink in scope while the range given to otherworldly wisdom expands. The body of the book is a set of question-and-answer séances in which Michael and his fellow archangels (Emanuel, Raphael, and Gabriel) explain various aspects of creation and evolution to the poet and his comrades. God Biology, we now learn, has a female twin in Nature, personified as a young woman. But he is also pitted against a dark "monitor," who reverses time and annihilates matter. Among a stream of new characters two recently dead friends of the poet join the familiar foursome. They are George Cotzias, a medical research scientist, and Robert Morse, an amateur musician.

Besides the talk shows, Merrill provides scenes of preparatory dialogue leading up to them and scenes of reflective conversation commenting on them. He also affords us a number of masques in which familiar and unfamiliar characters take parts as embodiments of universal principles. Raphael, for example, is earth and wit; Gabriel is death and fire. There are performances by the nine muses and by the founders of great religions (Buddha, Christ, Mohammed). All the characters keep wavering between personality and symbolism, and the otherworldly action is heavily allegorical.

Because the doctrines set forth are numerous but fragmentary and inconsistent, it would be risky to attempt to expound them. Behind the whole assemblage, however, one detects attitudes that seem fundamentally revealing. For instance, the outcome of the process of selection and refinement that goes on in the spiritual laboratories—one that gives a benign aspect to the wars and plagues devastating mankind—is the development of a new race of men, "alpha men," about whom we are told little except that they will be healthier, longer-lived, happier, and more creative than our own lot.

Yet a third of the way through ***Scripts for the Pageant*** we hear the voice of God B singing in remote solitude to his far-off, unseen brothers of the pantheon and asking for a response from those gods. Referring to time as annihilation, he sings, "In my night I hold it back" (78). The song rings out again at the end of the poem. I cannot help relating it to the poet, who aspires to stave off annihilation by restoring lost time through art. Merrill seems to yearn to bestow immortality on his dead friends and ultimately on himself by celebrating them and grouping them with immortals of one sort or another.

But at the same time one asks whether a subtler impulse may not be at work. Ephraim and Mirabell both lose their dignity in the course of the poems. We discover, gradually, that we cannot trust their information. Although they charm and love the poet, he does not finally respect them; and at moments they become contemptible. The slide from awed fascination to condescension suggests the way a man who has many love affairs comes to feel let down by each beloved. Looking for an idealized form of himself in the other, he is eventually disappointed because of an innate self-distrust.

"Mirabell" is suspiciously close in sound to "Merrill"; and when the batman is transformed into a peacock, the poet marks the occasion with a passage in the same form of stanza that he used for the early poem, in which a peacock seemed an emblem of his own gift and burden. So also the "alpha men," whose emergence—we are advised—will not be long delayed, might reflect a disillusionment with acquaintances of the poet who have failed, over the years, to satisfy his expectations from human society.

As he appears in his works, the poet strikes one as somebody with many friends who seek him out but few (if any) warm, long-lasting intimacies that he keeps close, season after season, day after day. When friends die, during the three long poems, they become, of course, manageable. The poet can summon them and ignore them as he turns to and leaves the Ouija board. With little emotional strain, he can thus preserve a circle of trustworthy and amiable chums.

Besides (we learn), the otherworldly friends may see one another only in the poet's light, and they have no life outside his imagination. Consequently, he controls them completely; they are always, lovingly, at his service. At the close of ***Scripts for the Pageant***, Maria, Auden, and Cotzias leave the otherworld for new existences in our own, as if the poet were reluctant to let them continue together without him after he had finished his work. In a terminal ritual, Merrill and Jackson break a mirror into a bowl of water. It is through mirrors that the dead have the power to glimpse the living; so the poet is shutting them off from anyone else.

Related to this will to control one's characters is a lack of straightforward narrative. It does not seem easy for Merrill's imagination to nourish independent, self-determined persons. He seldom allows a fiction to go its own way. If the characters are not versions of figures from his childhood and youth, they take on a weight of myth that cramps them into symbolic postures. Merrill's deeply autobiographical first novel, *The Seraglio,* has a life that his second, *The (Diblos) Notebook,* lacks. In the later story the author is too busy fitting masks on his creatures to let them work through an absorbing dramatic action.

In ***Ephraim-Mirabell-Scripts*** not only does the element of narrative fail us, but the poet also relies on arbitrary schemes to give an impression of order. He divides ***The Book of Ephraim*** according to the letters of the alphabet on the Ouija board, beginning each section with the appropriate letter and sometimes finding themes that are appropriate. In ***Mirabell*** the digits from nine to zero inherit the same function, and in ***Scripts for the Pageant*** the three words *Yes, &, No.* But these arrangements seem mechanical; they want inner meaning.

Merrill's versatility as a poet constantly shines before us. Again and again he wrings a sonnet from what look like random lines; or he moves gracefully through a ballade; or he adapts the meter to the person and occasion, as when God B sings in ten lines of ten syllables each. In a passage dealing with reincarnation, Merrill rhymes the penultimate syllable of the odd lines with the final syllable of the even. Musical effects, calculated enjambments, and other expressive devices will delight the careful reader.

A specimen of the ease with which Merrill moves among stages of emotion and levels of reality is an interlude of ***Mirabell*** when the poet is about to telephone his mother (138-39). The form is peculiarly elegant, because it occurs in Book Seven and there are seven stanzas in a difficult pattern of line lengths and rhymes. Effortlessly, Merrill associates the idea of mother with nature, reality, and earth, which he contrasts for a moment with the starlit sky—emblem of mind and artifice. Yet earth herself is of course an artist, and performs acts of imagination with her seasons and landscapes. As Merrill works the telephone dial, he feels suspended between the pleasures of imagination and those of sensuous reality. Then a sudden uneasiness, when his mother does not answer at once, dissolves the symbolism and leaves us with distinct human beings.

But the most satisfying passages are the few that deal with the poet's observation of the known world and its life. In ***Scripts for the Pageant***, a detachable section called "The House in Athens" (148-52) gives us a witty record of the changes that Merrill and Jackson made in their Greek home. Puns, personifications, and brightly remembered details join to transform the ordeals of interior decoration and house repair into an affectionate comedy. The place grows into a patron goddess—cranky but maternal—of two friends' affections.

Reading such verses, one has a standard for judging the bulk of the three long poems. Surely the proportion of otherworldly business is misjudged in them, and it impedes rather than enriches the effective passages. The doctrines do not collaborate to give the poems direction; rather, they hold back the flow, and seem to fix us once more in the immobility of Merrill's first collections.

Other poets have reflected searchingly on ultimate questions. Richard Wilbur, in "Walking to Sleep," tells us, with fresh images and penetrating insight, about the darks and lights of human nature. But Wilbur was early and naturally drawn to religious and moral problems, and his poem is barely six pages long. Merrill's steady disinclination to immerse himself in "great ringing 'themes'" (***Scripts*** 109) hardly prepared him for the challenge he courageously took up in his new books.

Notes

1. *Mirabell: Books of Number* (New York: Atheneum, 1978).
2. *Scripts for the Pageant* (New York: Atheneum, 1980).
3. *First Poems* (New York: Knopf, 1951).
4. In *Braving the Elements* (New York: Atheneum, 1972).
5. Published in *Divine Comedies* (New York: Atheneum, 1976), 47-136.

J. D. McClatchy (essay date 1982)

SOURCE: "Monsters Wrapped in Silk: James Merrill's *Country of a Thousand Years of Peace*," in *Contemporary Poetry*, Vol. IV, No. 4, 1982, pp. 1-30.

[*In the following essay, McClatchy studies the elusive poems of* Country of a Thousand Years of Peace.]

Eight years elapsed between James Merrill's ***First Poems*** (1951) and the publication of ***The Country of a Thousand Years of Peace,*** the longest interval between any two of his poetry collections. During that time Merrill made two important moves. One, his change of residence from New York City to Stonington, a traditional Connecticut seacoast village, was a kind of strategic withdrawal and resettlement that had decisive repercussions on his work, though not until ***Water Street*** (1962) does a more domestic focus prevail. The other move, an elaborate and prolonged trip around the world, is more immediately apparent in ***The Country of a Thousand Years of Peace***. The literal extravagance of Merrill's travels is reflected in two ways. In an obvious sense, the volume is decked out with a good deal of local color. Without ever being merely diaristic, he takes advantage of the convention that a travel poem is to make observations. He can count on a reader's unfamiliarity with and interest in a foreign curiosity or custom. The exotic locales of many of these poems—Japan, India, Greece, Switzerland, Holland, France—are an indication not only of a more cosmopolitan viewpoint, but also of Merrill's increased respect for the genius of places. The settings of ***First Poems*** are usually the stanzas of the poems themselves, or the associations their symbols have staked out, or the compass of the poet's own imagination. These new, more varied and specific settings are a recognition of a world outside the boundaries of verse and the self, and of the poet's ability to explore it—a recognition, that is, of *history,* of events located in space and unfolding in time, of significance emerging from process rather than embodied in a product. In much the same way, this book, instead of confining itself to a limited, recurring set of self-conscious symbols and subliminal anxieties, deliberately takes up a range of experiences that lie beyond the ego recording them—hallucinations, ouija board transmissions, revenants, altered states, dreamwork and rituals, the whole welter of the preconscious life that is also a "starry land/Under the world," as the title poem describes its mythic country of death. These two impulses in ***The Country of a Thousand Years of Peace***—a recognition of history, and the cultivation of the unconscious—will, in later books, each be developed in more intricate ways, and together be combined into Merrill's attention to involuntary memories and archetypal characterizations of his past. Here, they remain impulses rather than habits.

Seeking to account for the advance this book marks over ***First Poems***, Richard Howard argued that the "patinated narcissism has been literally roughed up, and the resulting corrugation of surface corresponds, of course, to a new agitation of the depths." Howard is right to stress the connection between the book's adjusted technique and its more adventuresome subject matter, but wrong to suggest that this results from a kind of stylistic decomposition. There is less Art than in ***First Poems***, but more artfulness. It is true that the poems are projected on a smaller scale than most of his ***First Poems***, and their very concision—to say nothing of their sometimes willful obliquity—may leave some readers with the impression that the book as a whole is more thematically skittish and less formally ambitious than its predecessor. Certainly this book does specialize in that sort of poem Merrill himself calls, in a review he wrote at the time of someone else's work, "a small, perfect poem—whose subject matter may even be calculated not to engage a reader overmuch; something leanly modeled, its elements composed and juxtaposed to give a sense of much ground covered in mysterious ways." The direct proportion between smallness and perfection duly noted, it bears repeating that ***The Country of a Thousand Years of Peace*** does represent an advance. An earned mastery of technique is in charge: the mazy syntax, the more expertly fractioned rhythms, the greater variety and convincing flexibility of verse schemes. Sometimes these techniques are subtle enough to distract attention from their own ingenuity—the leisurely runs of blank verse, for instance, or a sonnet in discrete couplets, or his occasional use of apocopated schemes where the rhymes are present but never insistent. There is also more sparkle and salt in this book, the free-wheeling play of mind that comes with technical control. There is a greater ease in generalizing. This is not a question of his having created slots in a poem through which messages can be slipped, but of having learned to allow his nimble intelligence to indulge its conceptual tendencies by means of aphorism and pithy aside. In **"Midas Among Goldenrod,"** the hay-fevered hero's mouth "Shuts and opens like a ventriloquist's dummy/Eloquent with opinions it does not really believe." The "Italian Lesson" turns to Roman promenades "Where each cool eye plays moth/To flames largely its own." And in one especially sly witticism, the geography of Europe is outlined by re-enacting the rape of Europa, who is left—"The god at last indifferent," as in Yeats's sonnet—"no longer chaste but continent." The book's intellectual prowess is also noticeable in grander, more virtuosic ways. Several times, for instance—**"The Octopus"** and **"The Lovers"** are the most striking cases—a poem's overly abstract issues or too intimate *donnée* are handled by a single extended simile, the magnet of the initial comparison drawing to itself filings of phrase and detail. **"The Lovers"** begins: "They met in loving like the hands of one / Who. . . ." The rest of the poem works out the terms of the analogy and never returns to its point of departure—does not need to, the simpler image having explained the complex emotion.

But this artful control seems to bring with it, almost inevitably for a poet as mercurial as Merrill, a certain restlessness, sometimes spirited, sometimes coy. To its advantage, the book is teased, not hauled, into thought, and at the same time can entertain uncertainties, mysteries, doubts, without any irritable reaching after fact or reason. But occasionally a poem's very elegance and equanimity serve to disguise the obscurity of its subject or treatment. It is difficult to say how **"About the Phoenix"** moves from one florid or puzzling point to another; it is difficult to say what **"A View of the Burning"** is about at all. Part of the difficulty here results from a quite conscious decision by the poet to favor a chiaroscuro that dissolves a poem's structural plan into figural textures. Or, when plotting his more overtly narrative poems—**"The Day of the Eclipse"** or the waggish **"A Narrow Escape"** are convenient examples—he tends to focus on a moment before or after the action's climax, so that revelations are implied or displaced, and the emotional force of the poem depends on a reader's sense of anticipation or presumed relief. Insofar as this is a deliberate method to avoid any topical or moralizing pretensions—as, in later books, he often shies from the pitch of the sublime or from autobiography's call to candor—it is not unlike Borges's musing, in his essay "The Wall and the Books," that "music, states of happiness, mythology, faces belabored by time, certain twilights and certain places try to tell us something, or have said something we should have missed, or are about to say something; this imminence of a revelation which does not occur is, perhaps, the aesthetic phenomenon." Such a wise but wary passivity, while not exactly an abdication of the poet's responsibility to both shape and interpret his material, depends too much on what has been excluded from the poem, on what is *not* taken on or worked out.

Part of the difficulty ***The Country of a Thousand Years of Peace*** presents to a reader undoubtedly stems from the kind of material it engages—material that, despite the poetic skills used to render it, is elusive. **"The Cruise,"** an otherwise charming anecdote, can be read as an allegory of the entire book's endeavor and problem. Having passed a less than imaginary iceberg whose hidden menace reminds them of "That law of which nine-tenths is a possession/By powers we do not ourselves possess," the ship's passengers are shopping in a port of call, and shown "Monsters in crystal" that once—so they are told—were nightmares that "set aswirl the mind of China" until "belittled" by craftsmen who dealt them the "drug of Form." Purchased as souvenirs—"We took to lunch our monsters wrapped in silk"—these talismans come both to reassure and to accuse. First, the speaker wonders whether a practiced style of personality makes for a perfect social presence: "Are we less monstrous when our motive slumbers/ Drugged by a perfection of our form?" The question could as easily refer, of course, to the poetic struggle between conspicuous form and shadowy intention, or even dark inspiration. Those two readings, the personal and the literary, are together poised in the poem's final lines, in their open competition between fascination and abhorrence, between

our hungers and our dread
That, civilizing into cunning shape
Briefly appeased what it could not oppose.

Naturally it is an uneasy situation that an appeasing dread, linked with knowlege and form, substitutes for any stronger, permanent shield against the devouring . . . the devouring *what?* The monsters are never identified. Are they the wilds of the unconcious? the toils of guilt? the trials of love? the past? the future? The figure of speech is the real appeasement here. And throughout the book, in some of its best as well as in many of its weakest poems, there is a similar reticence. It is hard to say whether it is the result of a poem's ignorance of its own final purposes, or of an inadequacy of form to ambition, or of some collusion of the two. Beginning with ***Water Street***, his poems increasingly show a clear-eyed understanding and ironic appreciation of themselves. And the long poems in ***Nights and Days*** demonstrate, in ways that these earlier poems never realize, how their hybrid form and variegated tone are more than adequate to the scope and demands of the material. But ***The Country of a Thousand Years of Peace***—perhaps for the wrong reasons, his most enigmatic book until ***Braving the Elements*** (1973)—remains at once inviting and uncertain. The book's good manners seem to force the poet to hesitate before the new and surprising depths he has discovered.

2

The Country of a Thousand Years of Peace opens with an elegy for Hans Lodeizen, and closes with a dedication to him. Lodeizen (1924-1950), a Dutch poet, author of *Het innerlijk behand* (*The Inner Wallpaper*—shades of ***Mirabell***), had come to America to do graduate work at Amherst, where Merrill met him in 1946. The two young poets kept up a friendship, by occasional visits and correspondence, until Lodeizen's death four years later. Their last visit, the pretext of the title poem's elegy, was recalled once by Merrill in a paragraph introducing the poem:

In 1950, at the beginning of nearly three years abroad, I went to Lausanne for an hour with my friend the Dutch poet Hans Lodeizen. He had been reading George Sand's autobiography; there was Roussel on the phonograph and a Picasso etching of acrobats on the floor. The June sunset filled up his hospital room. He spoke with carefree relish of the injection they would give him presently. Before I left we agreed to meet in Italy sometime that fall. He had leukemia and died two weeks later, at twenty-six. It was my first deeply-felt death. I connected it with the spell of aimless living in Europe to which I was then committed and to which all those picturesque and novel sights corresponded painfully enough.

That death and the unfulfilled promise of an idealized friend so near his own age must have haunted Merrill: the meaningless death accusing, he implies, his then purposeless life. But the close, ennobling identification with Lodeizen precludes much guilt. As tutelary spirit of the book, he is apostrophized in **"Dedication."** The poem is placed last in the volume presumably to stress its sense of dedication as proclamation and resolve rather than as merely a memorial gesture. What it proclaims are privileged moments. Twice in this brief poem the equation of mind and mouth, of idea and speech, is made. These are moments of poetic inspiration—moments of which each preceding poem in the book has given evidence—that are characterized as both ecstatic and humbling, and linked by Merrill less with grief at Lodeizen's death than with gratitude for his example. In one image, his death is described as the Orphic "deep spring," the continually self-renewing source of poetic power; in another, Hans returns as a Rilkean angel. This is the heroic side of him that the title poem—less an elegy really than a tribute—emphasizes as well. There is a tone of angry bewilderment, not at his friend's eventual fate but at his treatment. Twice Merrill repeats "It was a madness" that Lodeizen be deprived of his death, so that each day was "somewhat/Less than you could bear." The final two stanzas, completing the poem's single-sentence contradiction of the "peaceful" commonplace of death, begin as a curious rebuttal of Auden. In his "Musée des Beaux Arts," Auden complacently says the Old Masters were never wrong about suffering because they realized its "human position." Merrill's "old masters of disease" are doctors, not painters, and they make him "cry aloud" at the intolerable human position in which they confine Lodeizen. They would kill him by keeping him alive; they

Would coax you still back from that starry land
Under the world, which no one sees
Without a death, its finish and sharp weight
Flashing in his own hand.

The doctor's Damoclean sword becomes the hero's emblem. Its finish and weight (the pronomial ambiguity cleverly giving those qualities to death as well as to the sword) might also be the lyre's, since the unnamed but apposite hero here is Orpheus.

Lodeizen is not Auden's falling boy, but the questing adventurer. And he signals a shift from the typical protagonist of ***First Poems***—the child, the innocent, the victim—to a more mature, though not necessarily less vulnerable persona—often a lover, an artist, a martyr, "a young man." This is a step toward autobiography, or at least toward the more naturalistic possibilities of direct address. But a poem's speaker and the poet's self are rarely merged in this book, only paralleled. "I" is used as a point of view. When more intimate or complex or troubling matters are raised, a surrogate is introduced. **"Saint"** is an example. It is a poem about the artist's practicing for eternity, with overtones that are both erotic and deadly. There are two figures: the "you" that is the speaker's own reflexive self, and the titular saint, Sebastian. These figures are set against the background of a crowd—almost a chorus and not unlike the "old masters" in the Lodeizen elegy—first of the soldier's executioners, then transformed into the saint's worshippers. And just as the two crowds, hooded archers and numbling old women, are ironic versions of each other, so too are the figures, the "young martyr" and the yearning poet, a single split personality. Sebastian has only an iconic reality, as a series of images or fantasies the speaker has of himself. The poem opens tentatively, its first word meaning both to lack and to desire, its second line equivocating:

Wanting foreknowledge of eternity
It may be you must learn
From an illumination, from an ivory triptych,
How the young martyr, stripped
And fastened to the trunk of a fruit-bearing
Tree, could in a fanfare
Of tenderness for their reluctance summon
Those hooded archers: Come!
The arrows! Come! He loves me best who nearest
To my heart hits! *In love and fear*
They let fly.

Left unanswered here is the question of *why* you want that foreknowledge. And are we to understand it to be erotic bliss or aesthetic perfection? The "illumination" is no fixed image or goal, and the excited fable is sexual but only when it is not sentimental, in the manner of T.S. Eliot's "Death of Saint Narcissus." The martyr's ecstasy or divine possession is clearly a projection of the speaker's longing for "eternity"—but for actual sublimity, or for the lifeless perfection beyond the "heart"? The reader is encouraged (or forced, according to his temper) to imply from the manifest details the poem's latent dilemma. The speaker's "you"—a reference to his distance or even alienation from himself—is no martyr, no Aeolian lyre fastened to a tree and struck by the arrows of inspiration, his efforts bear no fruit. At this point, and after such knowledge, the poem begins again:

Wanting endurance of that moment's
Music, you are afraid. Below
Your hotel window, the piazza blackens
And hisses. You do not draw back,
You hold it all in your eye's mind.

Looking up from the imaginary portrait of Sebastian that has so kindled his mind's eye, the speaker's double returns to meditate on reality—through a "hotel window" that opposes the mirroring page, the hissing a black parody of possible music. There is an evident disgust in the language he uses to describe the life before, or literally beneath him—those limping, dribbling, mumbling women. Their "hocus-pocus" and their "dyed breaths" and "human acids" are a mean inversion of the articulate energy to which the young man aspires, and with which the saint rises above them all "exuberantly" with a warning that could speak for them both: "*He kisses me who kills, who kills me kisses!* The poem then attempts a strange reconciliation. The three deaths—the romantic martyrdom, the worm-drilled baroque statue, and the poet's despair—give way to a timeless pastoral, a classic "endurance":

And what is learned? Just this:
He is the flaw through which you can glimpse meadows,
Herds, the lover piping with bent head.

The moralized scene of instruction is another piece of dreamwork, and combines the two men in a stylized innocence at once solipsistic and homoerotic: the piazza becomes a meadow, the worshippers are changed to a herd; the soldier-saint is mistaken for an idyllic text, the poet fancies himself the piping lover. But again, the figures are separated, and the poem returns to an ironic contemplation of itself, this time with a bitter, imprisoned finality:

Full of the scene, you turn back in
To serve your time. The damask bed
Creaks under you. The board groans, the stone wrinkles—
Eternity refusing to begin.

The poem seems unresolved because it cannot make up its mind, does not care to. On the one hand, it evokes the sources of pain and power, and diffidently suggests a literary solution. On the other hand, its ends or ambition refuse to begin, and the poem turns into the familiar modern fable about the impossibility of its own accomplishment.

"Saint" is followed in the book by **"The Charioteer of Delphi,"** essentially the same poem but plainer and less febrile. Merrill has taken the famous statue and reimagined its athlete as Phaeton—like Lodeizen and Sebastian another youthful victim, the memory of whose downfall still scorches. He has further conflated that sun-myth with Socrates's story in the *Phaedrus* of the winged steeds of reason and passion. The poem, then, begins with a question about its own subject—"Where are the horses of the sun?"—and continues by tracing the initial "havoc" caused by "the killing horses" from the myth of the dazzled son to actual memories shared by the inquiring speaker and the child he protectively addresses. The poem's self-conscious layering merely augments, by postponing, its conclusion:

Broken from his mild reprimand
In fire and fury hard upon the taste
Of a sweet license, even these have raced
Uncurbed in us, where fires are fanned.

Invariably, the best poems in ***The Country of a Thousand Years of Peace*** have a similar taste for sweet license, for an abandon and risk belied by their superficial self-confidence. Despite alluring or even learned trappings, they pursue resolutely what another poem calls "the inner adventure," and what **"The Charioteer of Delphi"** identifies as "fires." Several poems in the book enlarge upon that metaphor. **"Fire Poem"** is one. Like **"The Cruise"** with its encrystaled monsters, or **"Laboratory Poem"** with its chilling climb through violence into "exquisite disciplines," **"Fire Poem"** takes up the conflict between passion and intelligence, between ardor and ashes, the song of once-burned innocence and twice-shy experience.

After a theatrical introduction—the speaker and his companion seated before the hearth's stage, a scene replayed in ***The Fire Screen*** (1969)—the fire itself speaks:

> *If as I am you know me bright and warm,*
> *It is while matter bears, which I live by,*
> *For very heart the furnace of its form:*
> *By likeness and from likeness in my storm*
> *Sheltered, can all things change and changing be*
> *The rare bird bedded at the heart of harm.*

The language here is deliberately intense. Since we are first told that the fire "Built brightness in the eye already bright," it is fair to assume that the fire's italicized sermon might as well be a reverie by the speaker himself—or by the "laughing child" who, entranced by the prospect of transformation, "Reached for the fire and screamed." Like the charioteer, the child is burned. The phoenix-like possibilities of "change and changing," the escape from mere "likeness," that the fire announced are at once forgotten in the disillusioning pain and fear: "fire thereafter was the burnt child's name / For fear." Even—or, especially—the symbolic function of language, to reclaim and transform phenomena, is lost. In a sense, then, **"Fire Poem"** is a self-consuming artifact, and it is because the vision is literalized and wrongly acted upon that experience hurts and words fail. Much later, such playing with fire will earn Ephraim's rebuke: "LOOK YR FILL / BUT DO DO DO DO NOTHING."

A similar point is made, in a lighter vein and in reverse, by **"The Doodler."** It is a poem about "communing"—consciously with others over the telephone, and unconsciously with the self as the speaker idly doodles on a pad while talking. (The model of psychotherapy is clear but not stressed.) The first half of the poem draws the connection between the isolated human features obsessively figured out—kohl-daubed eyes, profiled noses, lips pursed and raised to anyone's but his—and the distant voices on the line, except that the drawings seem "more animate/ Than any new friend's voice." The regressive inner adventure then beings with his admission that "nothing I do is at all fine / Save certain abstract forms. These come unbidden." What wells up is not an involuntary memory of Merrill's own, but the apparatus of a poem—"Stars, oblongs linked, or a baroque motif"—that finally assembles the "least askew of ikons" whom **"The Doodler"** first sets out to greet. It is an image with a life of its own—or so the poet imagines—who even begins to decipher the designing poet as *"He-Who-endures-the-disembodied-Voice."*

> *Far, far behind already is that aeon Of pin-heads, bodies each a ragged weevil, Slit-mouthed and spider-leggèd, with eyes like gravel,*
>
> *Wavering under trees of purple crayon.*
>
> *Shapes never realized, were you dogs or chairs? That page is brittle now, if not long burned. This morning's little boy stands (I have learned To do feet) gazing down a flight of stairs.*

The situation here anticipates that of **"Lost in Translation,"** where the young Merrill pieces together the puzzle revealing the page-boy. The little boy brought to light by **"The Doodler"** has no immediate autobiographical significance, but is a shape of things to come in Merrill's work, a realized shape of his own past. And the image's associations are crucial. The boy's emergence as both a recognizable figure and as a resonant symbol (what he *stands* for) is linked with the poet's own ability—his having "learned / To do feet." That achievement uncovers the past and its emotional dimensions, though this little boy's loneliness—like that of Proust's Marcel at the top of the stairs—is left for now in outline. **"Lost in Translation"** concentrates retrospectively on the child's private "void." This poem goes on, in a concluding quatrain whose miniature apotheosis spans alpha to omega ("A" to "O"), to celebrate the excited power:

> *And when A. calls to tell me he enjoyed The evening, I begin again. Again Emerge, O sunbursts, garlands, creatures, men, Ever more lifelike out of the white void!*

A whole career, an evolving world of figures, emerges in a kind of triumphal pageant from out of the page's white void—an echo of *"le vide papier"* in Mallarmé's *"Brise marine."* That emptiness is not only imaginative potential or experiential loss; it is the poet's subconscious as well, both image-repertoire and word-bank. They are tapped by not trying; stylized forms, not arbitrary self-expression, yield the responsive image—not an image skimmed from the moment, but one retrieved from lost time. By having learned here to *endure* the disembodied voices from the subconscious, and then patiently to portray their lifelike images, the poet—reinforced by A.'s approval—has every reason to begin again.

3

"Your reflect and I rejoice," says the doodler of the image he has made—a line that draws attention to the fact that the white void may also be construed as a mirror. Several poems in ***The Country of a Thousand Years of Peace***—**"Mirror"** and **"In the Hall of Mirrors"** especially—introduce an object that comes to have a central importance for Merrill, as an emblematic prop in many of his best poems and as his recent trilogy's proscenium. Actually, this book abounds in "glassen surfaces," several of them related to the mirror but without its thin silver mask. In **"The Octopus,"** for example, the "vision asleep in the eye's tight translucence" is compared to an octopus behind an aquarium's plate glass—not unlike Hugo's remark that language itself is *"Tantôt comme un passant mystérieux de l'âme, tantôt comme un polype noir de l'océan pensé."* Merrill sets up a fine interplay in the poem between perception and creation, between reflecting surfaces and reflected depths, narcissistic attractions and visionary possession. The *monstre sacré* here is what rises to the surface: at one level an observor's dream of convulsive divinity, at another level the image of the octopus that the poet coaxes out by the "lusters" of his poem's associations. In another poem, **"Some Negatives: X. at the Chateau,"** the translucent eyeball is replaced by a camera lens and its "images of images." The anti-world on film—

again, a version of the subconscious—winds the speaker through a series of now paradoxical flashbacks:

Where skies are thunderous, by a cypress walk
Copied in snow, I have you: or
Sitting beside the water-jet that here
Is jet. You could be an Ethiop with hair
Powered white as chalk . . .
Your charming face not lit
But charred, as by dark beams instructing it
In all to which you were the latest heir.

As the poem continues, its tone grows more unsettling. The leap from "charming" to "charred," for instance, is even more negative than its obvious inversion. And the "ghostliness" the speaker guesses in the pictured woman comes to seem alternately more haunted and more menacing than one first suspects. As a malign, potentially monstrous dream-image, the woman may be linked with other death-dealing female figures in the book—Naomi in **"Laboratory Poem,"** Salome, and the vampire in **"A Narrow Escape."** Further, she can be traced to the myth of Medusa that pervades ***First Poems***, a myth that turns on a compelling horror overcome by having been reflected.

On the other side of the looking-glass, then, the life beneath the life is deeply ambivalent and to that extent disturbing. As in **"The Locusts,"** it can be vacantly pastoral, the imagination's paradise:

a limpid source to peer
Deep into, heaven-sent
Mirrorscope, green, wet,
All echo, orchid, and egret
In pure transports recalling you.

Or, as in the poems I have just mentioned, it can be a threatening source of psychological and emotional engulfment. These mirroring roles for the poet, Narcissus or Perseus, are ones Merrill frequently tries on in his early books. And the rivalry between them is one he must have been alert to from the start; even as an undergraduate at Amherst, he had the lead in a student production of Cocteau's *Orpheus*—a play in which a broken window and a standing mirror figure prominently, the mirror as a doorway for the hero to descend into the underworld and for Death, a glamorous woman in an evening gown, to enter the stage for her victims. By the time he came to write the trilogy's harmonic romance, he seems to have resolved the dilemma. It is his early books that are especially set upon by a Fury the poet only gradually interiorizes as a paramour.

This characterological ambivalence, the speaker's shifting attitudes and roles, and the equivocal female figure, occur within individual poems as well as between them. **"The Day of the Eclipse"** is an interesting example of this. The poem divides in two, a cause-and-effect sequence from the first nine stanzas to the concluding seven. At the outset, the poet is alone, or at least detatched, behind the summer's thin gold life mask of sun on his face. The familiar composition of place he can recall—, gull, rower, "the mirror of the tide's / Retreat"—contrasts with today's atmosphere of impending eclipse. His senses are uncertain; his spirit troubled. At this point, there is an odd vision:

There is a lone, burned child to watch
Digging so furiously for fun
As to stir up a chaos into which
They both might slip, their muscle yield
To something blinder and less skilled
Than maggots, and their boniness
Flex, fracture, effervesce,
Before the lacy vortex can be healed.

This child is, as it were, the mirror's mercury, the psychopomp leading the poet through the black field on the other side of transparent reality, conducting him through the pattern of death and resurrection Merrill's poems have favored from the start. And he is a figure who recurs, in different guises, from the ripples in the basin's "coldly wishing surface" in **"The Lovers"** on to ***Ephraim*** and *Mirabell*, whenever the mirror's hermetical associations are introduced. In this poem, the imagined downfall—half feared, half desired—is then enacted above. Like the sun, "He rises, peers up through smoked glass. / A black pupil rimmed with fire / Peers back." The burned child here becomes a black pupil—the poet's own inward gaze and futile solipsism. In the tenth stanza, the "girl of whom he has been aware all summer" abruptly appears. "He knows that she belongs to a far more / Exciting world," that she may be that "unique caryatid / Of the unthinkable" he has conjured from the sky's void and would court as his muse. But she is elusive, and remains "Companionless in a skylit shack," like the "ageless woman of the world" at the end of **"The Book of Ephraim,"** or Mother Nature in ***Scripts for the Pageant***. The poet remains curiously indifferent, paralyzed even, and instead of approaching her can only identify himself with the "mounds of matter cold and blind / She loves, how even they respond / To the least pressure of a shaping hand."

The blandness of his response here—her shaping hand so much less vital than the earlier furious digging into the chaos of the self—is paralleled by the delirium of the poem titled **"Amsterdam"** and by the stilted fervor of **"The Greenhouse."** The city and its canals are themselves seen as a vast mirror in **"Amsterdam,"** by virtue of the poem's epigraph—*"Au pays qui te ressemble,"* from *"L'Invitation au voyage"*—which adds to Baudelaire's invocation of *"Mon enfant, ma soeur"* Merrill's own implied and reflected presence. After describing the city as one where "desire is freed from the body's prison," an apparition of that desire in the imagination's labyrinth—distilled as moon, mirror, Medusa—turns the tourist into a voyeur:

Into a black impasse deep in the maze
A mirror thrusts her brilliant severed head,
Mouth red and moist, and pale curls diamonded.
A youth advances towards the wraith, delays,
Squints through the window at a rumpled bed.

The dream-encounter that follows, in four parenthetical stanzas, though it might be with absence itself or with an abstracted ideal ("the sheer gold of nobody's hair" is its only token), and is more probably the self's apprehension of the soul, is then tentatively, yet pointedly identified when the poet awakens:

Next day, is it myself whose image those
Sunning their own on the canal's far side
Are smiling to see reel . . .

This difficult poem—Merrill admits in the course of it that "a future sleuth of the oblique," more a type of the psychoanalyst than the literary critic, will be its best reader—then turns itself inside out. Macabre motifs accumulate, as if to signal the death-in-life of this particular inner adventure. In one extraordinary gesture, that links by its echo of the second stanza the poem and the mirror, the poet's own brilliant head is severed: "My head has fallen forward open-eyed." And in a kind of reverse eclipse,

By dark the world is once again intact,
Or so the mirrors, wiped clean, try to reason . . .
O little moons, misshapen but arisen
To blind with the emotions they reflect!

The balance between deflection and reflection here seems both destroyed by new knowledge and restored by the verse's closure. The Orphic overtones of the poem, used here to stress the relationship between the poet and his poem's own underworld of tangled memories and fantasies, are prominent too in **"The Greenhouse,"** which opens with "So many girls vague in the yielding orchard" who cling to the poet and "Trailingly inquire, but similingly, of the greenhouse." What seems at first to be a frieze of *jeunes filles en fleurs* gradually emerges as an animated metaphor for the poet's own green thoughts. These wilt during his allegorical descent "under glass," until he finds himself in "the least impressive room":

It was hotter here than elsewhere, being shadowed
Only by bare panes overhead
And here the seedlings had been set to breeding
Their small green tedium of need:
Each plant alike, each plaintively devouring
One form, meek sprout atremble in the glare
Of the ideal condition.

This hothouse forcing-room is both hellish and brooding. The unsteady tone—a blend of condescension ("tedium") and fear ("devouring")—in effect forces the poet to interrupt himself as he contemplates the paradoxical lost paradise: "the fiercer fading / Of as yet nobody's beauty." Once again, the terrible mother is transformed into a benevolent muse; the poet seeks to rescue what he would be devoured by. As in several poems in ***The Country of a Thousand Years of Peace,*** Merrill's latent private anxieties are manifest in familiar and recurring mythic formulas.

The whole matter of *reproduction* is raised in **"The Greenhouse"** and, naturally, in the book's other mirror-poems as well. As early as ***First Poems*** Merrill had been worrying the problem: the opposing demands of art and life. His belief in what Yeats called the perfection of the work was never in question. But the perfection of the life, insofar as that tends toward the creation of an actual and ethical family, seems to have troubled Merrill from the beginning—as it continues to in such poems as **"Childlessness"** in ***Water Street***, and **"The Emerald"** in ***Braving the Elements***, both of which seek to counter the hectoring expectations of others. Each sort of perfection claims to be an argument against time, but the generative task threatens Merrill's privileged status as only child in his own family romance, and as unique artist embodying himself in words. **"In the Hall of Mirrors"** is the most extreme and literally dazzling treatment of the problem in ***The Country of a Thousand Years of Peace*** In a nearly condescending self-appraisal, Merrill once told an interviewer of the "buried meanings" that unconsciously shape and eventually sustain his poems, and he linked this with "some kind of awful religious streak just under the surface" in himself. Among the examples he then cited is **"In the Hall of Mirrors":** it is "a fairly obvious case. It was written during the 1950s when the 'myth' poems were popular. It's about the expulsion from Eden." Such a frank interpretation is, as usual, evasive; it buries the meaning in myth. The loss of paradise, or fall from natural grace, is not this poem's "buried meaning," merely its conceptual scaffolding. The myth of the Fall, from which Merrill's account of the Broken Home draws much of its power, would more appropriately describe the plot of a later poem, **"18 West 11th Street."** This poem is at once more complex and less resolved than its plot, and more private than its analogous myth. The setting described in the opening stanzas can be seen, in the light of Merrill's own explanation, as an Edenic *locus amoenus:*

The parquet barely gleams, a lake.
The windows weaken the dark trees.
The mirrors to their bosoms take
Far glints of water, which they freeze
And wear like necklaces.
Some pause in front of others with
Glimmers of mutual admiration.
Even to draw breath is uncouth.
Steps make the silver marrow spin
Up and down every spine.

The reader may be tempted here to ignore, for the sake of the fable, the deceiving force of the figuration, its stress on the reflected glories of artifice: the mirror a mother, the floor a lake, the lake a *rivière,* the experience embossed on a spine like any book's. There is no breath of life; all complexities of mire or blood are, like mirrors, silvered. This is no country for "Anything personal or commonplace," as the reptilian guide "hisses" to the couple who next enter the hall. Lured by such pride and by the "good offices" of their guide's bad eminence, they are drawn into the room's infinity effect:

In one glass brow a tree is lit
That multiplies itself in tiers,
Tempting the pair to populate
Those vistas from which visitors
Ricochet in fours,

Eights, sixteens, till the first two gaze
At one another through the glazed crush
Of their own kind, and the man says,
'Complex but unmysterious,
This is no life for us.'

The glazed crush that nearly obscures the original pair here anticipates the "fleet blur of couples / Many of whom, by now, have reproduced" that is "inflicted" on the shatterproof glass shielding Giorgione's *Tempesta* toward the end of **"The Book of Ephraim."** In this poem, once he knows the trick, the man is bored by the repetitions. Worse, he realizes that each of the multiplying likenesses before him represents a diminishment of the self. His companion is drawn even deeper into the dilemma. She looks beyond the obvious if primal image of this *stade de miroir,* beyond the repetition compulsion. Unsatisfied by the infinity effect's parodic anti-paradise, she searches for imaginary and therefore "grander" images of the self:

The woman, making no reply,
Scans the remotest mirrors within mirrors
For grander figures,
Not just those of herself and him
Repeated soothingly, as though
Somebody's wits were growing dim—
Those! Those beyond!

The reactions, then, of those whom Merrill with a mischievous irony asks us to fancy our First Parents are not contradictory but complementary. Both conspire against the generative task: he derides it, she seeks to transcend it. When their guide—and one sees now why the Biblical spoiler is here a hermetic guide—says "'Time to go,'" there is of course no reluctance or regret in their compliance. That order comes, I think, too abruptly in the poem, so that it seems to follow as an immediate consequence of an original sin of some sort of overweening narcissism. But there is no crime here, no punishment, no "expulsion." There is, instead, a rejection of mere reproduction in favor of the poet's grander expressive figures—one of which closes the poem:

And in the solitary hall
The lobes of crystal gather dust.
From glass to glass an interval
Widens like moonrise over frost
No tracks have ever crossed.

The couple having taken their solitary way, the hall—a prototype of the trilogy's Empty Ballroom (the *Galerie des Glaces* was, after all, used as a *salon de fête*)—is empty of all but the by now familiar trope: the artistic compact, the white void, the frozen pool, the page to be written.

"In the Hall of Mirrors" begins with a refined idea of the finished book (the silvered spine), and ends by returning to the blank page of possibilities. In a sense, those are also the contrasted properties of the book's best known poem, **"Mirror":** the mirror's knowing polish and the opposite window's engaging openness. But there is no simple dialectic being proposed here. Though not inaccurate, it would be too reductive to read this poem as a debate between the reflective mind and the perceiving eye, or between the poem's surfaced depths and the novel's broad perspectives, or between a perfected, stale art and natural, generational life. The poem is too astute to deal exclusively in such standard contrasts. From its abrupt opening lines—which, with their overtone of threatened individuality, seem at first to be autobiographical—this dramatic monologue is a brooding study of frustration and transfiguration. The poem begins with a sort of moral prologue, a typifying episode of barely suppressed violence:

I grow old under an intensity
Of questioning looks. Nonsense,
I try to say, I cannot teach you children
How to live.—If not you, who will?
Cries one of them aloud, grasping my gilded
Frame till the world sways. If not you, who will?

The violence in that passage is symptomatic of the confused anger that seems to have provoked the exchange. There are strange reversals in this poem's mirror-world. Instead of taking Merrill's preferred role of vulnerable child or artist, the mirror's disembodied voice is that of a surrogate parent, his role not that of an Oedipal tyrant but of an aging father confessor. As if having given rise to it by allowing them a look at themselves, he shares the helplessness of his children. This poem is one of such redoubled and interchanged perspectives, in fact, that we do well to remind ourselves of its possibilities of address. Whenever a mirror is questioned, who is asking what of whom? Those "questioning looks" were presumably first directed at the children themselves, as introspection rather than injunction—though that is what the question becomes when repeated. The problem presented—*how to live*—is as much his as theirs, as much aesthetic as moral: how to come to life, as how rightly to live. And the reiterated question—*"If not you, who will?"*—may stress the urgency of the children's despair, or stand as an aural image of the mirror's visual reflecting, but the echo also reminds us of the stake the mirror has in the answer to it—much as a poem makes demands on the readers who presume to search it for what will suffice.

With its irregularly metered lines and pleated apocopaic rhymes, **"Mirror"** has an unstanza'd, blocky look and a conversational fluency. Even so, the poem has three distinct sections. The prologue, which nervously issues the moral and aesthetic demand and establishes the complex relationships, is balanced by an answering and resolving epilogue. Between these two sections (11. 7-32) is a compressed, novelistic chronicle of the mirror's "children." Three generations of their secret lives is what the mirror knows, much as in this description by Hawthorne a mirror holds and represents the interior life of the House of the Seven Gables: "As regards its interior life, a large, dim looking-glass used to hang in one of the rooms, and was fabled to contain within its depths all the shapes that had ever been reflected there." Merrill's mirror begins with the room's still life: "Between their visits the table, its arrangement / Of Bible, fern and Paisley, all past change, / Does very nicely." Whether that dated arrangement is incidental or is a series of metonymies for religion, domesticated nature, and decorative art, the mirror is associated with what is fixed, conventionalized, "past change." The world of change, the works and days of human beings, are the window's province. In fact, the italicized *you* specifically links the window's temper with the children's importunate *you* at the start of the poem. As in Hardy's extraordinary poem "Moments of Vision," whose mirror "makes of men a transparency," here too the window and its human traffic are, in the mirror's view, all too easily seen through. The mirror's tone, from the bemused subjunctive to the waspish irony in "takes thought," is clearly condescending:

> *If ever I feel curious*
> *As to what others endure,*
> *Across the parlor you provide examples,*
> *Wide open, sunny, of everything I am*
> *Not. You embrace a whole world without once caring*
> *To set it in order. That takes thought.*

What then follows is a montage of details from real life. And if we read into them a courtship and marriage, adultery ("her first unhappiness") and divorce, then the costume drama here is another version of Merrill's own Broken Home:

> *Out there*
> *Something is being picked. The red-and-white bandannas*
> *Go to my heart. A fine young man*
> *Rides by on horseback. Now the door shuts. Hester*
> *Confides in me her first unhappiness.*
> *This much, you see, would never have been fitted*
> *Together, but for me. Why then is it*
> *They more and more neglect me? Late one sleepless*
> *Midsummer night I strained to keep*
> *Five tapers from your breathing.* No, *the widowed*
> *Cousin said,* let them go. *I did.*
> *The room brimmed with gray sound, all the instreaming*
> *Muslin of your dream . . .*

This uncanny nocturne—the senses's five tapers extinguished, the elegaic *correspondence* of the smoke's gray sound, the window's very reality turned to dream under the force of instreaming imagination—has a forlorn quality to its modulations. Both the ellipsis and the notable shift in tenses in the scene, from continuous present to past ("strained," "said," the decisive "I did"), marks the end of one movement, and should alert us to other changes. After all, there is a submission here and an unspoken recognition on the mirror's part—as, in Merrill's family romance, his artistic vocation is linked to his parents's divorce, so that "I did" (or *made*) is a parodic consequence of "I do." The commanding "widowed / Cousin" (an antitype of Madamoiselle in ***Divine Comedies***) might as well be a *windowed* cousin, whose authority the mirror obeys—as later it is amenable to a faceless will. The ellipsis signals, then, what the mirror had hitherto resisted, a *change*—of heart, of function, of values. That change is what gives the irony in the next lines its edge. The children turn to "muse" upon the window, and looking out at its mute poesy make the remark that concludes the poem's middle section:

> *Years later now, two of the grown grandchildren*
> *Sit with novels face-down on the sill,*
> *Content to muse upon your tall transparence,*
> *Your clouds, brown fields, persimmon far*
> *And cypress near. One speaks.* How superficial
> Appearances are!

That dismissal, which on different readings of the poem may sound contemptuous or resolute or stricken, is a response but not an answer to the prologue's question: *If not you, who will?* But by concluding the historical interlude—which comprises, in a manner of speaking, the "appearances" of the poem itself—the realization frees both the mirror and the reader to return to the greater issue: *how to live.* The final third of **"Mirror"** recapitulates a familiar sequence of experiences. Of course the answer involves a transformation. The children have, in effect, turned the window into a mirror by their attitude, which frames the scene into a landscape, and in this section the mirror literally sheds its identity and becomes a window. But I think, too, that the final lines of the poem bring us back to the notion of *dedication,* a commitment that opens and closes ***The Country of a Thousand Years of Peace*** and animates it throughout. It starts with a swoon. The old order is disturbed. The mirror sinks to the pitch of a negative sublime:

> *Since then, as if a fish*
> *Had broken the perfect silver of my reflectiveness,*
> *I have lapses. I suspect*
> *Looks from behind, where nothing is, cool gazes*
> *Through the blind flaws of my mind. As days,*
> *As decades lengthen, this vision*
> *Spreads and blackens.*

In seeking to account for this new and threatening vision, the mirror utters the lines that give this poem its eerie power:

> *I do not know whose it is,*
> *But I think it watches for my last silver*
> *To blister, flake, float leaf by life, each milling-*
> *Downward dumb conceit, to a standstill*
> *From which not even you strike any brilliant*
> *Chord in me, and to a faceless will,*
> *Echo of mine, I am amenable.*

These are tricky lines. The mirror begins tentatively. And the painful process of blistering so turns on the possibilities inherent in language ("leaf by life") that the change seems a transformation, even a reincarnation. The mirror's once brilliant chords lose, with a Stevensian flourish, "each milling- / Downward dumb conceit." "In the Hall of Mirrors" trades its silver for untraced frost, or pristine contingency. Here, the dumb conceits or ineffectual tropes yield to a higher power, "a faceless will, / Echo of mine." Does this imply a rejection of narcissism—the mirror's reflecting pool of self-regard giving way to sweet Echo "that liv'st unseen / Within thy airy shell"? Or is the faceless will the tall transparence of life itself to which the poet declares himself amenable—open, responsive, dedicated? Both perhaps. It is the self and—"Echo of mine"—more than the self these lines declare, accepting determinism *and* exaltation, experience *and* language.

It is characteristic of Merrill—in this poem, and in his later, more accomplished poems—to work not with a set of opposites but with a series of dissolves. In **"Mirror,"** for instance, there is a continual exchange of perspectives, both literal and figurative. Even within the confines of a monologue, the reader is invited to watch the poem's subject through a constantly shifting framework: now mirror, now window, now picture-frame; figure to ground, contour to color, threshold to aftermath; the white oblong of the page outlining the black block of print that is the poem itself. Counterpointing these rapid, at times simultaneous variations of perspective is the slower, more decisive alternation of daybright and nightblind states of mind. The poem twice grows dark, twice moves from ferment to standstill, from perfect silver to blind flaw, from conscious order to the static chaos of the unconscious. The grasping, wide open world at the start of the poem sinks "Late one sleepless / Midsummer night" to a strained, dreamy impulse to cease, as it were, upon that midnight. At the end of the poem, the mirror again yields; the brilliant silver flakes to a blackness the mirror takes as blankness. A "faceless will" here replaces the commanding female figure in the first encounter. It is more menacing and abstract because internal—or rather, internalized. The mirror's powers of reflection are overthrown from within, and become in the end a black pane—a transfiguration of the primary pain that has suffused the poem, from the questioning looks at the start, to Heater's unhappiness and the smoking tapers. The mirror, then, amenable to this process, is another of the figures of the artist in ***The Country of a Thousand Years of Peace.*** This poem ends where the book's title-poem ends: in "that starry land / Under the world, which no one sees / Without a death."

Ross Labrie (essay date 1982)

SOURCE: *James Merrill*, Twayne Publishers, 1982, 166 p.

[*In the following excerpt, Labrie surveys the poetry of Merrill's* Water Street, Nights and Days, *and* Braving the Elements.]

Water Street

The most noticeable difference between the poems in ***Water Street*** (1962) and Merrill's earlier work is the relaxed tone. The poems show him in a bemused but absorbed conversation with himself. He wrote the poems from the settled perspective of the house he shared with David Jackson in Stonington, Connecticut, the restive years in New York and the years of foreign travel now well behind him. He divided his time in the early 1960s between Athens and Connecticut, both of which provided him with a sense of rootedness. The title of ***Water Street*** conveys a fundamental sense of stability although a symbolic dualism underlies the Heraclitean polarization of water and street. The dualism reflects Merrill's benign consciousness of change at this period in his life through which he looks both wistfully back and hopefully ahead.

Merrill's sense of being in the midstream of his life is reflected in **"The Water Hyacinth"** where he paradoxically develops paternal feelings toward his aging and forgetful grandmother. The emotional balance is righted, however, when he considers the fullness of her experience in comparison with his own incomplete life:

> Your entire honeymoon,
> A ride in a rowboat
> On the St. Johns River,
> Took up an afternoon.
> And by that time, of course,
> The water hyacinth
> Had come here from Japan,
> A mauve and rootless guest
> Thirsty for life, afloat
> With you on the broad span
> It would in sixty years
> So vividly congest.
>
> (40)[1]

As the image of the congested water flowers implies, it is the very richness of his grandmother's experience that causes her memories and anecdotes to merge and perhaps to become confused at times as she grows old.

The poems in ***Water Street*** reflect a quiet joyfulness that is based in part on self-acceptance—as can be seen in **"To a Butterfly":**

> Goodness, how tired one grows
> Just looking through a prism:
> Allegory, symbolism.
> I've tried, Lord knows,
> To keep from seeing double,
> Blushed for whenever I did,
> Prayed like a boy my cheek be hid
> By manly stubble.
>
> (43)

The high spirits of some of the poems can be seen in the ebullient puns of **"The Grand Canyon":** "This first mistake / Made by your country is also / The most sublime" (14). The play on the canyon's geological "fault" is typical of the vivacity and humor of ***Water Street***. Even in **"The Parrot Fish,"** which depicts the slow dying of the caught fish, the final shudders are partially offset by the lesson learned and by Merrill's description of the gaudiness of the fish: "Chalk-violet, olive, all veils and sequins, a / Priestess out of the next Old Testament extravaganza" (45). Similarly, in "Prism," a glass paperweight rises to life with the coming of dawn when a "toneless waltz glints through the pea-sized funhouse. / The day is breaking someone else's heart" (17). The lift created by the pun on daybreak and heartbreak keeps the emotion afloat amidst the very real pain alluded to.

In spite of the continued facelessness of Merrill's lovers, which reflects his discreet reserve at this time, the poems are rich in feeling. **"Poem of Summer's End"** portrays a shared feeling of apprehension about the coming chill of fall, which is already felt in sky and air and which causes the lovers to turn inward, confident that "love is what they are and where they go" (11). In **"Getting Through,"** the speaker's mounting frustrations at not being able to mail a love letter are warmly balanced by the underlying certainty of that love and by the thin but illuminative winter light that ends a day of strain and disappointment:

> The stationery store's brow drips, ablaze
> Where the pink sun has struck it with the hand
> Of one remembering after days and days—
> Remembering what? I am a fool, a fool!
> I hear with joy, helpless to understand
> Cries of snow-crimson children leaving school.
>
> (31)

The cries of the children and the light of the pale sun against the white background cathartically release the speaker from his own inner turmoil by showing him a picture of opposites in taut but satisfying equilibrium, an emblem of forbearance.

Some of the poems in ***Water Street*** are about the act of writing itself—or sometimes about Merrill's inability to write, as in **"Angel."** Writing represented a great deal of his experience, and so had a place in poetry that focused on daily experience. In **"From a Notebook"** the whiteness of snow falling outside merges with that of a notebook page. The oppressiveness of the scene is overcome by the writing of the first word which "stops / The blizzard" (7). After the page is filled, the blankness of Merrill's life has also, the poem implies, been filled in. Similarly, Merrill's poem **"For Proust"** celebrates the French writer's capacity to salvage fertile memories even from life's bitter disappointments, thereby transforming the flesh of the artist's face into a "thin gold mask" (19).

Merrill dwells further on the relationship between the artist and life in **"Homunculus Artifex."** The title refers to the alchemical homunculus, a legendary man-made humanoid. The "manikins" in the poem have a garden party in order to indulge their longing to be fully human:

> The kill-knit creatures, now in hues
> Of sunstroke, mulberry, white of clown,
> Yellow of bile, bruise-blacks-and-blues,
> Stumped outward, waving matchstick arms,
> Colliding, poking, hurt, in tears
> (For the wound became an eye)
> Toward the exciting, hostile greens
> And the spread cloths of Art.
>
> (25-26)

The affectiveness of the language signals the success of their brief sharing of humanity, like the artist's characters who in privileged moments manage to exceed their artificial natures.

Merrill's autobiographical gallery in ***Water Street*** includes two of his grandparents. **"The Smile"** is about his grandfather on his father's side who, according to Merrill, had a "silver plate in his skull, and died on our sleeping-porch in Palm Beach." The false teeth in the poem belong to Merrill's father, though, and recollections of his father's death as well as his grandfather's seep into the poem.[2] The simplicity of the poem's action—an old man moves slowly from his chair to his bed in order to sleep and to die—is mirrored in the unusual baldness of the language and syntax. Although the details are imagistically concrete, feeling rushes into the poem as the old man places his "round gold watch / Unwound, among / Dimes, quarters, lunatic change" on the dresser (48). The word "lunatic" releases the poem's emotion as Merrill reacts to the incongruity between the orderly chain of events that precedes the death and the death itself. The poem illustrates how firmly Merrill's poems, for all of their profusion of images, were now anchored in action. While not entirely giving up his penchant for tapestry, he had moved toward the nearer and warmer field of memory as his fundamental principle of design.

"Annie Hill's Grave" is about Merrill's grandmother on his mother's side. She had died in the early 1930s after also having lived with Merrill's family during his childhood years. The poem records Merrill's memory of her funeral and burial, events that became etched on his mind as a boy. Finally independent, the adult Merrill accompanies his grandmother to her grave in a tender reenactment of family history. Elegiac heightening can only sustain him so far, however, and he is left with the unsettling image of his grandmother in the ground where the "silence drums into her upturned face" (41). The poem's poignancy, which coexists with its unflinchingly unsentimental view of death, make it one of Merrill's most memorable poems.

Through cultivating an autobiographical art, Merrill was able to retain a narrative matrix for his poems while forsaking the fancifulness of some of his earlier work. **"Scenes of Childhood"** involves a screening of home movies by Merrill and his mother. The thirty-year-old pictures gradually reveal the young Merrill as having been at the center of an Oedipal drama. This is vividly apparent in his reaction to the shadow of his father across his mother's dress in one of the early family scenes:

> A quiet chuckle escapes
> My white-haired mother
> To see in that final light
> A man's shadow mount
> Her dress. And now she is
> Advancing, sister-
> less, but followed by
> A fair child, or fury—
> Myself at four, in tears.

I raise my fist,
Strike, she kneels down. The man's
Shadow afflicts us both.

(21)

The child's "fury" and the sexual overtones of his father's shadow constitute an emotional tinderbox whose effects reach into the present. The inflammatory nature of the filmed scene is symbolized by the film's catching fire when Merrill's mother, mesmerized by her past and by her husband once again, asks her son to slow the film down. The episode reveals Merrill's father, long after he had ceased to live with his wife and son, as a continuing emotional vortex in their lives.

In prosaic terms the portentous shadow of Merrill's father was probably caused by the fact that he took the pictures. As if in recognition of such calming realities, the poem settles toward the end. The Oedipal resonances added by the mind exhaust themselves eventually as Merrill considers his father's declining years. The later shrunken view of his father is associated with the image of the "skulls of flies," an image whose morbidness is offset by a vision of the stars as Merrill steps out under the night sky after the screening:

Immensely still
The heavens glisten. One broad
Path of vague stars is floating
Off, a shed skin
Of all whose fine cold eyes
First told us, locked in ours:
You are the heroes without name
Or origin.

(24)

The poem yokes the simplified, heroic vision of the child with the belittling viewpoint of the adult in a final unresolvable tension. More important, perhaps, Merrill shows that the adult, for all of his irony, lives his life in the shadow of determinative, childhood experiences whose lifelong effect he comes to understand too late. It is this underlying recognition that gives the poem its essential power and helps to make it one of Merrill's finest.

"The World and the Child," an accomplished example of the villanelle, recalls Merrill's experience as a sick child having been put to bed in an upstairs bedroom while his parents entertained below. Lying awake in the gray dark, the child contemplates his loneliness, his need to be comforted by parents whose attention is elsewhere. The pathos of the situation is held in check by the conspicuousness of the poem's form, especially through the recurring rhymes. The use of enclosed forms of modulate emotion is typical of the poems of Merrill's middle period.

"The Midnight Snack," one of the "Five Old Favorites" group, depicts the adult Merrill going to the refrigerator at night, wrapped in apprehensiveness because of a lingering childhood memory of his father's flaring temper. **"Childlessness"** depicts his guilt at not continuing the family line and, thereby, frustrating his parents. It is one of Merrill's most exposed poems. The dream scenario centers initially on an archetypal garden where "Nothing is planted" (28). Later, the image of the sunset evokes not only the earlier theme of unrealized possibilities, but emphasizes the fact that time had run out: "A sky stained red, a world / Clad only in rags, threadbare" (29). The depth of Merrill's guilt is shown in the derisive image of himself as a "tiny monkey" who "puzzles over fruit" (28). The diminutiveness is an important aspect of the poem's reflection of the cultural myths reviewed in the poem: children are meant to have children; only then do they themselves escape being children. The final, grisly image of Merrill's parents being eaten to the "bone" by the stigma of his childlessness marks the experience in this poem as another firing point in his autobiographical drama. Throughout the 1960s he was to chart the awesome potency of the family in determining and defining the self.

"An Urban Convalescence" is an ambitiously long autobiographical poem, one of the watermarks of Merrill's career. The poem is a retrospective look at the years in New York before he moved to Stonington. **"An Urban Convalescence"** opens ***Water Street***, just as **"A Tenancy,"** which is about the house in Stonington, closes it. The speaker, after a week in bed, strolls along New York streets, feeling dislocated by the ceaseless demolition of buildings in his neighborhood. A sculptured stone garland remembered from the lintel of a demolished doorway reminds him of an inexpensive engraving of garlands in which he had wrapped flowers given to a woman in Paris whose face he cannot quite remember. The associative sequence is a convincing portrayal of the sifting of memory and the selectivity of consciousness.

The demolished surroundings also epitomize for the speaker his own sense of failed connections. In this context he finally perceives New York itself as a failure in his experience—a false start. Gradually, the confused images of New York and the rushing images from the past yield to a deeper and more constructive need, a "dull need to make some kind of house / Out of the life lived, out of the love spent" (6). The house is a central motif in Merrill's work, usually symbolizing the totality of one's experience. The spontaneous streaming of images that characterizes the first part of the poem thus gives way in time to the sense of a cohesive purpose beneath the randomness as the speaker, initially exposed and disoriented, turns into himself for warmth and comfort.

The poem's imagery is fundamentally surrealistic. Explorative perceptions compete with each other for authenticity within the speaker as he attempts to get his footing. The contending voices are given a musical structuring, as can be seen in the division of **"An Urban Convalescence"** into an introduction, a shrill, nervous allegro, and a final series of slow, tight quatrains that stabilize the dazed poem.

By way of contrast, **"A Tenancy"** deals with Merrill's settled life in Stonington, although there are flashbacks to an earlier tenancy after the war when he had rented a furnished room in New York. In spite of Merrill's balancing of the New York and Connecticut settings, the poem leans toward Stonington as the place of arrival. Stonington is also the focus for the theme of survival that threads its way through the poem. Reflecting on the distance he has travelled since renting the furnished room in New York, Merrill writes:

> The body that lived through that day
> And the sufficient love and relative peace
> Of those short years, is now not mine.
> Would it be called a soul?
>
> (52-53)

Bewildered by the metaphysical complexities of considering a succession of selves, Merrill escapes from the recesses of memory in order to welcome visitors bearing gifts who also arrive in March, stamping themselves "free of the spring's / Last snow":

> And then, not asking why they come,
> Invite the visitors to sit.
> If I am host at last
> It is of little more than my own past.
> May others be at home in it.
>
> (53)

"A Tenancy" points up Merrill's growing sense of the psychic importance of setting. "I always find," he has confided, that "when I don't like a poem I'm writing, I don't look any more into the human components. I look more to the *setting*—a room, the objects in it. I think that objects are very subtle reflectors. When you are in an emotional state, whatever your eye lights on takes on something of the quality of a state of mind."[3] The power of setting can be felt in **"After Greece,"** which illuminated Merrill's ambivalent feelings about America. Acknowledging the dominance of American culture in the contemporary world, he nevertheless felt himself longing for the "Essentials" of Greece: "salt, wine, olive, the light, the scream" (13).

"Roger Clay's Proposal" is unusual among the poems in ***Water Street*** and is probably as close as Merrill ever came to social commentary—with the possible exception of ***Mirabell*** (1978). Clay, an extension of the Charles persona, languidly proposes a ceremonial execution of world leaders as a solution to international tensions, "say in Rome or Nice— / Towns whose economy depends on crowds" (37). Both here and in **"After Greece"** Merrill shows a satirical intolerance for heated discussion of political and social issues and a corresponding faith in the power of ordinary realities—light, memory, ocean, love—to see man through. This, more than anything else, is what the poems in ***Water Street*** have in common.

Nights and Days

The excellence of the poems in ***Nights and Days*** (1966) was recognized when the book received the National Book Award in 1967. Although ***Nights and Days*** showed Merrill at the top of his form, the award was remarkable at a time when American poets were generally committed to eye-catching, socially relevant writing. The title of the collection, which is reflected in poems like **"The Thousand and Second Night"** and **"Days of 1964,"** was drawn from the writings of the turn-of-the-century Greco-Egyptian poet Cavafy, whose focus on everyday life and candor about homosexuality Merrill had decided to emulate.

"Days of 1964," which is set in Athens, is an uninhibited celebration of love. Indeed, the speaker risks the ironic hope that his love "would climb when it needed to the heights / Even of degradation" (56).[4] The poem skirts the evanescent boundaries of love, wavering between ecstasy and a feared disillusionment: "A god breathed from my lips. / If that was illusion, I wanted it to last long" (56). Eros is "masked" in the poem not only by laughter and pain but by sexuality, causing the speaker to question whether love transcends carnality. The ambiguity of the poem's viewpoint is symbolized by Merrill's housekeeper, Kleo, who is seen alternately as whore ("*Eat me, pay me*—the erotic mask / Worn the world over by illusion") and as an aging woman faithfully trudging over the pine-covered hillside to take care of Merrill's house in Athens (55). The enigma of love, inextricably part of the "simple need" of sexuality, became in ***Nights and Days*** a touchstone for Merrill's dualistic expectations about man (55). Man is an animal driven by a sexual hunger that masquerades as love; man is also, though, somehow capable of genuine love.

"From the Cupola," which draws on the myth of Eros, is one of Merrill's major poems. This long and complex work combines narrative, autobiographical, mythic, and lyric elements into one of Merrill's densest and most elliptical poems. He described the genesis of **"From the Cupola"** to Ashley Brown:

> At first it was just a little poem in the first person. It was involved with a curious experience—receiving letters from somebody I never met, who seemed to know everything about me. I'm not paranoiac, but it was rather unsettling. After a while I became engrossed with this interior experience. I didn't want to meet the writers of the letters; I wanted to detach myself from the experience to write about it. The poem from the beginning needed "body" and I gave it this by way of landscape—what I can see from this window. And then I thought of Psyche. Psyche, you know is a Hellenistic myth. I also liked the "montage" of Hellenistic Alexandria and Stonington, which likewise has a lighthouse and a library. Well, it *is* ambitious, but the first and last parts, I think, tone it down—I frame it in "my own voice."[5]

"From the Cupola" intertwines three stories: the ancient myth of Eros and Psyche, the contemporary version of that story involving Merrill's "sister" and an anonymous admirer, and finally Merrill's own concealed story, "something I'm going to keep quiet about."[6] In the Greek myth Eros places Psyche in a dark place, warning her of dire consequences if she should ever see him. Overcome by curiosity, she does see him by lighting a lamp, and he flees. The myth underlines the traditional, allegorical role of Psyche as the soul, and thus points to the concealed theme of the poem—the speaker's love for his soul.

The relationship between Psyche and her brother ("James") is as important as her relationship with the anonymous admirer whose ardent letters so perplex her. Significantly, in terms of both the narrative and allegorical levels of the poem, the desire to know the identity of the mysterious letter writer is offset by a desire not to know: "Truth asks / Just this once to sleep with fiction, masks / Of tears and laughter on the moonstruck page" (38). To unmask Eros would risk disillusionment. Unlike the Psyche of the myth Merrill's heroine prefers the darkness. Through the sustaining of a highly charged atmosphere, which is reinforced by the heightened, often obscure speeches of the characters, Merrill wanted to create the illusion of a god's immanent presence. He regarded the motif of the stranger who knows one very well as "practically a metaphor for God," and echoed Borges's view that love is the founding of a religion "with a fallible god."[7]

Although the action of the poem, brief enough in itself, centers on the anxieties of Merrill's sister concerning her anonymous correspondent, the poem is rooted in the landscape of Stonington with its appropriate Greek architecture. There are two cupolas in the poem, the one in Stonington and the one that is the speaker's head. The anchoring of the poem in its gleaming, classical seaside setting is crucial to the design:

> Renaissance features grafted onto Greek
> Revival, glassed, hexagonal lookouts crown
> Some of the finest houses in this town.
> By day or night, cloud, sunbeam, lunatic streak.
> They alternately ravish and disown
> Earth, sky, and water.
>
> (39)

The freshness and concreteness of the setting reassure the reader's mind in its wanderings among the poem's elusive feelings whose meaning Merrill himself has said he does not fully grasp.[8]

Stonington's white pillars also prepare the reader for the encounter with Eros:

> Our town is small
> its houses built like temples
> The rare stranger I let pass with lowered
> eyes He also could be you.
>
> (39)

The figures in **"Under the Cupola"** conceal their realities from each other (mask imagery is pervasive in the poem), just as the poem artfully conceals its meaning from the reader; behind the masks, however, is the desire to protect and nurture love. For this reason the speaker confides to his mysterious soul at one point that the "mouths behind our faces kiss" (40).

The centrality of the narrator's role is underlined in the middle section, which focuses on Merrill's childhood years in Florida, a flashback that is triggered by the "dwarf Palm" in Merrill's apartment. Palm Beach had generated a sense of the ineffable in the young Merrill, an effect that parallels the emotion generated by his sister's nameless lover. Florida is presented as a timeless world "where nothing changed or died / unless to be reborn on the next tide" (40). Merrill's youthful Eden is a city that was "half desert and half dream." The sequence is dominated by the memory of a royal palm that covered the young Merrill's imagination with its shadow, that of a *"towering mother / smooth as stone and thousandbreasted"* (41). Recollection of the experience prompts the adult Merrill to talk his sister out of her terror over her anonymous correspondent, simultaneously allowing himself to grapple with his own lingering fears. While using irony to tame subconscious fears, he also talks lovingly in a hushed voice to Psyche—to his soul—in one section of the poem: "She is more strange than Iceland bathed all night / an invalid in sunshine Lava cliffs / The geyser that erupts the loon that laughs" (43).

The Stonington cupola, whose circumference of glass symbolizes the mind's multiple perception of reality, has its windows cleaned in the poem. The wiping, however, simply sharpens the ambiguity of vision by showing the self's mirrored involvement with everything it sees:

> Up here among
> spatterings and reflections wipe as I will
> these six horizons still the rain's dry ghost
> and my own features haunt the roofs the coast.
>
> (43-44)

The speaker's acceptance of these unresolvable complexities is rewarded by a dream vision "unclipped by faith or reason" of angelic Eros (44).

In the fourth section Merrill subjects the theme of love to burlesque treatment. Here, instead of the fertile, visionary darkness of dream, there is the darkness of the merely literal. The scenario is that of a drive-in movie under an evening rain. The speaker peers out at both the screen and those parked nearby:

> In the next car young Eros and his sweetheart sit
> fire and saltwater still from their embrace
> Grief plays upon his sated face
> Her mask of tears does not exactly fit
> The love goddess his mother overflows a screen
> Sixty feet wide or seems to Who can plumb
> those motes of rose and platinum
> At once they melt back into the machine.
>
> (48)

As in **"Days of 1964,"** the speaker is baffled by the dualism of love, which at times seems to be no more than lust and second-rate illusion. Although Merrill was somewhat apprehensive about the effect of the drive-in scene, aware that it might undercut the elevated mood of other sections of the poem, he felt that it was as necessary as the poem's physical surroundings, which also remind the reader of factual realities.

The final section of the poem opens on an early spring dawn which, through the newly cleaned windows of the cupola, offers a clear, fresh view of the Stonington waterfront. The speaker emerges out of his reveries into the concrete autonomy of the external world. He focuses at first on the literal scene, absorbed by a faded, red warehouse, but he also foresees the "whitewinged boats" that will scud across the bay in the summer light, an image that recalls the earlier visitation of the dream angel (51). The moment captures the interplay of conscious and subconscious images and Merill's acceptance of the plasticity and ambiguity of vision. Recalling the play of light on the Palm Beach pavement that had so aroused his youthful imagination, he now accepts the mingled contraries of light and dark which, like the interfusion of the soul and love, constitute the "dance I know / that cracks the pavement" (50).

Toward the end of the poem the image of the looming, royal palm is supplanted by harmless parsnips, which the speaker sets about gathering for his sisters, who have come to visit. Even here, though, he discovers that two of the parsnips have grown "tightly interlocked" like lovers (51). He buries them in "memory of us," he himself coming forward at this point as both Eros and Psyche (51). In preparation for the evening meal he and his sisters light the lamp, the interior lamp of the soul, which shines most brightly against the surrounding darkness.

Although the poem contains many obscrities, its delicacy of mood, undercurrent of tenderness, and visual unity allow its power to be felt. Consistent with the poem's themes, the language appeals to the ear and the subconscious rather than to the conscious mind. Through its combination of calculated reserve and spacious lyricism **"Under the Cupola"** epitomizes Merrill's fondness for buried meaning, his delaying of the mind's peremptory need to know by immersing it pleasurably in a strangeness it can be taught to trust.

The love poems in ***Nights and Days***, such as **"Between Us,"** are suffused with a happiness that runs throughout the poetry of the 1960s. Even in **"The Thousand and Second Night,"** a long, discursive poem based in part on the *Arabian Nights,* vicissitude and despair yield eventually to a vision of love. The poem's contents are heterogeneous to say the least: the tale of Scheherazade, an attack of facial palsy, a visit to the Hagia Sophia in Istanbul, a visit to a Turkish bath, a bout of depression in Athens, a cache of pornographic postcards in an old photo album. The mixture of subjects preordanied the slow emergence of the poem's structure from within, and also permitted Merrill to indulge his fondness for interruption and detour.

The title of the poem alludes to Scheherazade's survival of a sultan's cruelty through the art of storytelling. The poem in turn depicts Merrill's survival of the accumulated burden of his past through art and through love. "Rigor Vitae," the first section, recounts the effects of the awkward paralysis that froze the right side of his face in Istanbul. Taken aback, he decides to go sightseeing anyway on the first day of spring, beginning with a visit to the famous Hagia Sophia. The ancient structure, a church turned into a mosque, had in recent times thinned out to become merely a shell of its former, venerable self—a "flame- / less void" (4). Ironically, having vaguely hoped to escape introspection by entering the "transcendental" world of the Hagia, Merrill finds that he is thrown back upon himself by the resemblance between the denuded church and his own deteriorating life: "You'd let go / Learning and faith as well, you too had wrecked / Your precious sensibility" (5).

"The Hamam," the second part of the opening section, describes Merrill's visit to a Turkish bath. He goes there on the advice of a pharmacist, who recommends it for his paralyzed face. On the way to the bath, which is in the old quarter of Istanbul, Merrill is overtaken by a childhood memory. The prose jottings, which relay the immediacy of the memory, stand out against the surrounding quatrains of this section like a promise of movement amidst the stiffness of Merrill's face. The memory is about his grandmother's hand and ring. He compares his childhood view of his grandmother's hand to the "mosque of Suleiman the Magnificent, mass and minarets felt by someone fallen asleep on the deck of his moored caïque" (6). The shapes of Istanbul, mirrors of oriental mysticism, awaken a dreamlike stillness in Merrill which not only recalls pleasurable moments in childhood but also evokes images that are connected with his having become an artist. Looking through the straits of Bosporus toward Asia, he thinks of the

> "death-in-life and life-in-death" of Yeats'
> Byzantium; and, if so, by the same token,
> Alone in the sleepwalking scene, my flesh has woken
> And sailed for the fixed shore beyond the straits.
>
> (7)

Merrill's awakening to his vocation as an artist is linked ingeniously with the present, unreal paralysis of his face. The face becomes at this point a symbol of art, suspended between the empirical world and dream.

Section two, "The Cure," is set in Athens, where, although Merrill's face has been restored, part of him remains "cold and withdrawn" (7). He cannot shake a bout of accidia that drains his interest in the architectural beauty around him and saps his interest in others. In a park he puts off a Greek man who wants to make conversation, and later feels helplessly detached when he learns of the man's accidental death.

Section three, "Carnivals," sustains the poem's mood of alienation, and sends Merrill on a gloomy, retrospective search of his experience: "I wanted love, if love's the word / On the foxed spine of the long-mislaid book" (10). Looking for traces of past love, he finds only sexuality: "A thousand and one nights! They were grotesque / Stripping the blubber from my catch, I lit / The oil-soaked wick, then could not see by it" (10). He therefore comes to perceive his present alienation as continuous with a past that only superficially drew him into contact with others. Section three touches bottom with "Postcards from Hamburg, Circa 1912." The pornographic postcards, found unexpectedly in an album left by a recently deceased uncle, depict fellatio in a carnival setting. The stanzas gradually flow away from the postcards into a series of prose quotations that move the poem's center of gravity away from lust to the general relationship relationship between body and soul.

Imperceptibly, the language arrives at a vision of love against the background of Merrill's leaving his Mediterranean surroundings for the New World:

> Love. Warmth. Fist of sunlight at last
> Pounding emphatic on the gulf. High wails
> From your white ship: The heart prevails!
> Affirm it! Simple decency rides the blast!—
> Phrases that, quick to smell blood, lurk like sharks
> Within a style's transparent lights and darks.
>
> (12)

The tenuous affirmation of love is based upon Merrill's sense that his "libertine" past did, after all, portray a man "in search of his soul" (12). He tests this at once, however, by exhibiting a self-conscious wariness about the language of love.

The setting changes to a carnival in the West Indies where a macabre dancer in a "suit of bones" picks Merrill out of the crowd. The bewildering sea of masks dissolves as he awakens in his bed in Stonington. The section concludes with a grateful, redolent tribute:

> Lost friends, my long ago
> Voyages, I bless you for sore
> Limbs and mouth kissed, face bronzed and lined,
> An earth held up, a text not wholly undermined
> By fluent passages of metaphor.
>
> (14)

Merrill's "text" is that of his life, now accepted in memory and as part of the art that, flowing out of it, is finally indistinguishable from it. The poem thus arrives at that most elemental and indispensable of loves in Merrill's writings, the love of self.

The desiccated mood of section four, a waggish mini-lecture on the preceding parts, comes as a shock. The section, though, is perfectly consistent with Merrill's dialectical method and outlook, his penchant for keeping everything in a state of taut, dynamic suspension. The fifth section is a vignette of Scheherazade on the night after her serial ordeal ended, the thousand and second night. The mood is quiet and dignified, the phrasing sonorous and rounded. The imagery continues the motif of the relationship between body and soul in blissful submission now to the mystery of experience, too "late to question what the tale had meant" (15). The tight versification formalizes the reconciliation of the opposites of soul and body, fact and dream, and seals the poem's experiences and memories in a shroud of language that will paradoxically protect them from decay. In the words of the mini-lecture in section four: "Form's what affirms" (15).

Although not nearly as strenuously as **"The Thousand and Second Night,"** other poems in ***Nights and Days*** extend Merrill's autobiographical quest. **"A Carpet Not Bought,"** for example, wittily opens up a whole new area of experience by focusing on things that have *not* been done. The poem describes an occasion renounced, an impulse mastered. The speaker, who has resisted the enticement to buy an expensive Persian rug, is tormented in sleep by a vision of the rug's beauty. On awakening he is filled, though, with a compensatory vision of the woven beauty of his own marriage.

Most of the poems in ***Nights and Days*** sound a note of affirmation. This note is especially audible in sunny poems like the **"Little Fanfare for Felix MacGowan,"** which was dedicated to Merrill's grand-nephew. Even on less likely occasions, as in **"Violent Pastoral,"** a tenacious mood of ecstasy overcomes the brutality of the predatory scene:

> Against a thunderhead's
> Blue marble, the eagle
> Mounts with the lamb in his clutch:
> Two wings, four hooves,
> One pulse, pounding, pounding.
>
> (19)

In a similar mood of affirmation Charles throws off the pain and duress caused him by a boor at a cocktail party with a panache and courage that constitute a victory of the spirit (**"Charles on Fire,"** 25).

Occasions of defeat in ***Nights and Days*** are pressed into gold, as in **"The Broken Home"** in which Merrill looks back on his parents' divorce. His memory of his father's heady pursuit of wealth and wives, of his mother's desperation, and of his own Oedipal feelings coexists with his ironic recognition that he is still bound to his parents by an umbilicus of steel: "They are even so to be honored and obeyed" (29). The toy lead soldiers on the windowsill symbolize Merrill's passive isolation as a child bearing the brunt of his parents' separation. The image of the soldiers is associated with the emergence of a "heavy, silvery, pliable" feeling that prepares him stoically to face the rest of his life (29). While certainly not buoyant, the poem affirms the past by linking it through wry understatement with the survival of the cosmos: "Always that same old story— Father Time and Mother Earth, / A marriage on the rocks" (28). Similarly, the red coat of the Irish setter that Merrill makes part of the Oedipal scene in his mother's bedroom becomes centrifugally transferred to the image of the setting sun at the end of the poem.

The high energy level of ***Nights and Days*** is also reflected in the poems about music, one of Merrill's major interests. The poems **"Balanchine's"** and **"Discothèque"** are paired in an incisive musical contrast entitled **"Watching the Dance." "Balanchine's,"** which is named after the famous Russian choreographer, describes the art of classical ballet whose supernal beauty, evoked by "unseen powers twirling on their toes," induces a belief in the fresh worlds that are created on the stage ("Observe the powers. Infer the stream" [36]). By way of contrast, in **"Discothèque"** Merrill produced one of the most devastating images of popular culture to be found in contemporary writing:

> Having survived entirely your own youth,
> Last of your generation, purple gloom
> Investing you, sit, Jonah, beyond speech,
> And let towards the brute volume VOOM whale mouth
> VAM pounding viscera VAM VOOM
> A teenage plankton luminously twitch.
>
> (36)

Echoes from Puccini's opera *Tosca* appear somewhat incongruously in **"Maisie,"** which deals with the post-spaying depression of Merrill's cat. The effect is double-edged. On one level the operatic motif is simply mock-heroic, a way of reducing the emotion devoted to an animal. On another level, though, the music grandly enlarges the scale of the animal's existence. **"The Mad Scene"** originated in Merrill's memory of Joan Sutherland in *Lucia di Lammermoor.* After seeing the opera, he had a "dream called Laundry," which sprang from the picture of Sutherland, billowy and gory, moving across the stage. In the dream Merrill assumes feelings of heroic grandeur, circumventing the skepticism of his waking life. Both opera and dream transform him, permitting him to put on clothes of a "new fiber that never stains or wrinkles, never / Wears thin" (37). The image glows with an incandescence that is present in nearly all of the poems in ***Nights and Days***, a collection that is a hallmark of Merrill's art.

. . . . .

Braving the Elements

Braving the Elements (1972), which was awarded the Bollingen Prize for poetry, reflects Merrill's shift away from personal autobiography to the autobiography of the planet. The book contains a number of long poems that reveal an ambitious structuring and an increasing complexity and density in phrasing. In a sense, the collection can be seen as a culminating one since the elements of fire and water, for example, had already figured in the titles of previous collections of poetry. Nevertheless, Merrill turned toward nature with unprecedented interest in ***Braving the Elements***, particularly in the poems which grew out of his visit to the Southwest. A number of the poems have outdoor settings and show an intense awareness of the earth's geological past.

All the same, Merrill was aware of the irony of picturing himself as braving the elements: "Elizabeth Bishop, when I told her the title, remembered an old lady she used to visit in Maine who on a windless July day would take a walk with her companion, wrapped up in scarves and coats, and someone looked out of a window and said: There is Miss So-and-So braving the elements, which is pretty much the way I thought of the title, too."[9] The title of the book comes from the poem **"Dreams about Clothes"** in which Merrill somewhat skeptically questions the influence of art on life:

> Won't you help us brave the elements
> Once more, of terror, anger, love?
> Seeing there's no end to wear and tear
> Upon the lawless heart,
> Won't you as well forgive
> Whoever settles for the immaterial?
> Don't you care how we live?
>
> (61-62)[10]

Here, the elements are psychological ("terror, anger, love") and even art is of limited use in dealing with them. The poem strikes a note of resignation that is characteristic of ***Braving the Elements***, which has attrition as its principal theme.

The attrition of the heart is portrayed in **"Flèche D'or,"** which is named after the European passenger train that carries the speaker away from an extinguished love affair. The train's name, the "golden arrow," refers explicitly to the myth of Eros and the defenselessness of those who are struck down by love. The cycle of love, so overwhelming in both its coming and going, is linked to the continuum of time, which like the parallel tracks, appears to offer no break in the cycle. Alluding implicitly to the Greek philosopher, Zeno, who argued that a moving body never came to the end of a line, the speaker longs for some omnipotent cosmic observer "in whose heart of / Hearts the parallels / Meet and nothing lasts and nothing ends" (63).

The austere mood of ***Braving the Elements*** is particularly apparent in the poems about the Southwest. In these poems Merrill often places the affective qualities of human relationships against an immense non-human world. **"Nine Sleep Valley"** is a sequence of nine poems connected loosely by setting and theme, one for each of the nine days spent by two male lovers vacationing in the Southwest. The title creates a montage in which the lovers' nights merge with the sleeping eons of geologic time that surround them. In the first poem, a Shakespearean sonnet, the speaker announces his intention to interpret his surroundings, to "read in Nature's book / The pages" (30). All he gets, though, is a fleeting impression of his environment ("canyon forest landslide lake"), finding that nature's "words have wings" (30). Bewildered by the multiplicity of nature's forms, he flounders until the natural objects around him are given meaning by his companion who, "Fluent and native," interprets them (30). The second poem, composed of three quatrains, is a flashback that depicts the speaker's exit from the city to visit the Southwest. The startling allusions to the assassinations of Robert Kennedy and Martin Luther King drive the image of urban culture into the poem like a wedge, allowing the reader to experience the speaker's relief in leaving society behind in order to enter the world of nature. The third poem, a single haiku stanza, wipes out the threatening images of social turmoil in a blissful view of the lovers at dawn.

In the fourth poem the lovers set out on a hike in the heat of the day. The sky is a "high pool deep blue very hot / Illumination of the brimstone text," a smelting fire that purgatorially hovers over the aridity of the sandstone canyons around them (31). The way of the poem is up—into the heart of the cosmos: "Ice in the marrow of a star so pure / So beyond history" (31). The fifth poem, a sonnet in couplets, shows the hikers coming upon a long abandoned prospector's cabin in some trees along a river. At this point mythic images of American history enter the poem:

> Look. Out of thin air old gods (plume, hide, bead)
> Appear to weigh your offerings of seed.
> A leathery prospector god's pans fill
> With foolsgold facets of my blackbird's trill.
>
> (32)

Merrill evocatively interfuses the white man's past—including treacherous dealings with the Indians in the nineteenth-century scramble for gold—with the present treasures of the scene, the aspen's "seed" and the "blackbird's trill."

Poem six elaborates the motif of the prospector's cabin, which is now portrayed as a "flask" containing a past that the two hikers have "uncorked" so that "two rooms / Are won back to this world" (33). The hikers try to recreate the lives of the prospectors to the "last friend's guitar and stories" and finally down to the last, lonely prospector who is swallowed up by modern America. The past includes the lovers' present experience, which will eventually be someone else's past and which will inevitably invite a paradisal reading from those looking back at it: *"Here all would have been well"* (33).

The seventh poem, written in ballad-like quatrains that end in the same, rhyming sound, involves a ghostly meeting between a dead person and a speaker who ponders the past. Each perceives the radiance of the other, each convinced of the reality of a day, never his own, when "beauty, death, and love" are "coiled together in one crowning glory" (34). The central motif of the eighth poem is a geode, a nodule of stone containing a cavity lined with crystals or mineral matter. It is here that Merrill unites the beauty of his human lovers with that of their eroded surroundings. Geodes, when cracked open, reveal rich, interior waves of color that contrast with their drab, crusty exteriors ("Rind of crystals velvet smoke meat blue"), having been formed, like the lovers,

> under fantastic
> Pressures, then cloven in two
> By the taciturn rock shop man, twins now forever
> Will they hunger for each other
> When one goes north and one goes east?
>
> (34)

The geodic cavity evolves into a symbol for all of nature, including man: "Centimeters deep yawns the abyss" (34).

The final poem, which is composed of three quatrains, sums up the major themes of **"Nine Sleep Valley"** with its pronounced, unifying rhymes of "heart," "dark," and "art" (35). Nature is "dark" in that it ultimately resists man's efforts to encompass it through understanding. It has also been darkened by man, who has disfigured its ecology just as he has marred his own history—as the earlier allusions to political assassinations and Indian massacres indicate:

> Master of the ruined watercolor,
> Citizen no less of the botched country
> Where shots attain the eagle, and the grizzly
> Dies for pressing people to his heart,
> Truster, like me.
>
> (35)

In shooting the eagle, America has symbolically taken the final step towards its self-destruction. While Merrill's allusions to topical events in **"Nine Sleep Valley"** disturbed those readers who felt that they endangered the poem's integrity, the allusions indirectly imbue the image of nature with great value. Furthermore, through the symbol of the geode—and indeed through the lovers themselves—Merrill implies that paradise is still accessible within the world of the present.

"In Monument Valley," which is set amid towering, sandstone monoliths on the Arizona/Utah border, is a study in both personal and ecological attrition. The arid foreground with its wandering, starved horse—still "half in trust, half in fear of man"—is juxtaposed with an earlier, idyllic summer evening in upper New York state when Merrill rode horseback in the soft light of dusk:

> Stillnesses were swarming inward from the evening star
> Or outward from the buoyant sorrel mare
> Who moved as if not displeased by the weight upon her.
> Meadows received us, heady with unseen lilac.
> Brief, polyphonic lives abounded everywhere.
>
> (10)

While Merrill is outwardly a survivor in comparison with the "stunted, cinder-eyed" horse that approaches him as he sits in his air-conditioned car, he is nevertheless moved to consider his own aging as he drives away from the doomed horse, which is now too weak even to eat (10). Acute, tactile contrasts give the poem a well-honed vividness.

The elements themselves speak in **"The Black Mesa"** and **"Banks of a Stream Where Creatures Bathe."** The black mesa, addressing the low flatland around it, recaptures for a moment some of the grandeur of its past. The "viceroy's eagle" recalls the Spanish presence in the Southwest while the "turquoise" is a reminder of the native, Indian culture of the area (42). Both enrich the value of the mesa, which, all the same, will continue to erode until, as Merrill puts it in a final pun, "all be plain" (42).

"Under Libra: Weights and Measures" is one of the more opaque poems in ***Braving the Elements***. In a letter Merrill has sketched the background of the poem, which he described as "scenes of semi-rural life outside Santa Fe":

> I was staying with a friend who rented a house near the church and graveyard—probably I stole something of the Chimayo graveyard, too—on a ranch full of peacocks. From Santa Fe you can see the Los Alamos lights at night; a friend called them the "necklace of death." Angel Ortiz is simply the type of an old Spanish-American settler. Blanca is a dog, the Gem is a razor blade, the Swan is the constellation, though I'm also thinking of those swans of ice which cradle caviar at fancy receptions. The house where I visited had on a wall a huge white blanket woven with a black two-headed bird.[11]

The allusion to Libra places the time of the poem as mid-fall, but the opening refers to the "stones of spring," just one of many examples of balance that echo the astrological significance of the title. The poem begins with a description of some ancient stones that have been introduced into the speaker's house, where they are used as paperweights and doorstops. In spite of the pragmatic uses to which the stones are put, their effect is to remind the speaker of the vast scale of geologic time that dwarfs his own scale of living. The effect of this reminder, however, is unexpectedly positive since he "learns / To live whole days in another / Tense, avoid the bathroom scales or merely / Sing them" (44). The speaker passes from the world of the mundane ("bathroom scales") to another *scale* of things entirely, a scale in which movement is measured by the "riverbend's great horseshoe print" (44). The panorama of the New Mexican terrain dramatizes not only the wide sweep of geological time but also the cyclical return of ecological history upon itself. In this way it neatly meshes with the motif of the seasons that circulates through the poem. The associated image of the sun moving across the sky balances Santa Fe with its eastern counterpart, Stonington, the place from which Merrill had set out. Time and again images of personal significance—such as the lichen-covered stones that are souvenirs of Merrill's trip to the Southwest—are balanced against parallel images in the natural world, like the giant boulders left by receding, ice-age glaciers "Dragged south in crushing folds, / Long dirty tablecloth of ice" (43).

"Under Libra" is an elaborate, symbolistic collage of imagination, space, and time containing strands of burnt landscape, anthropological dream, and actualized nightmare (Los Alamos's "necklace of death"). On a deeper level Merrill was working toward the sort of unifying, cosmological synthesis that was to emerge in the divine comedies. Here, already, he portrays minerals flowing into plants ("Copper, silver, green / Engraved by summer's light, by spring's") which in turn flow into a relativistic matrix of space-time (44). The poem is dazzlingly modernist in both thought and execution.

The dual focus on attrition and on the massive backdrop of the inorganic in ***Braving the Elements*** underlines the transitoriness of life, as is seen in the image of the flame in **"Log"**: "Dear light along the way to nothingness" (3). Large chunks of history flash by with each click of a string of Greek worry beads in **"Komboloi."** Similarly, Merrill constructs a huge historical circuit in **"Pieces of History"** that joins the ancient Egyptians and the American astronauts. In **"Mandala"** the self spins toward extinction along with the rest of the universe, resisted only by the spiral of reincarnation, which has its own disadvantages:

> One wants, to plot the boomerang curve
> That brings one back,
> Beyond the proper coordinates of Have and Lack,
> A flair for when to swerve
> Off into utter pointlessness—
>
> (22)

The stoical mood of these poems is epitomized in the compass rose image at the end of **"Syrinx"**:

> Nought
> Waste Eased
> Sought

Ostensibly in a state of balance between negative and positive forces, the universe, with its human passenger, slopes inexorably toward disintegration with love only sporadically holding back the "great god Pain" (72-73).

The somberness of ***Braving the Elements*** hangs over the autobiographical reminiscences as well. In spite of the winsome qualities of **"Days of 1935,"** Merrill's concluding tribute in the poem to the "golden haze" of his past is deliberately hackneyed and bitter: "Those were the days" (21). The poem is based upon a contrast between his actual childhood in the 1930s and a fantasized, compensatory version which he invented as a child in order to cover his growing loneliness. The young Merrill lies awake in his room at night while his parents are out partying, and his nurse, who was "old and deaf and slow," is off in the servants' wing listening to the radio (11). Having been provoked by accounts of the Lindbergh kidnapping, he imagines himself in a semiconscious dream to have been abducted by a pair of kidnappers, Floyd and Jean. They whisk him off to their hideaway, a "hovel in the treeless / Trembling middle of nowhere" (11).

The poem's strength lies in its projection of the combined viewpoint of the emotionally charged child and the retrospective urbanity of the older Merrill. Both views converge in the description of Jean:

> A lady out of *Silver Screen*
> Her careful rosebud chewing gum,

Seems to expect us, lets us in,
Nods her platinum
Spit curls deadpan.

(12)

The passage's erotic overtones, which reflect Merrill's candor in describing his nine-year-old self, are also implicit in the description of Floyd:

The man's face
Rivets me, a lightning bolt.
Lean, sallow, lantern-jawed, he lays
Pistol and cartridge belt
Between us on the oilskin (I
Will relive some things he did
Until I die, until I die).

(12)

Sexual connotations surface more explicitly as Floyd sleeps beside the child:

Small fingers felt,
Sore point of all that wiry meat,
A nipple's tender fault.
Time stopped, His arm somnambulist
Had circled me, warm, salt as blood.

(19)

Together with the child's witnessing of the sexual play of his kidnappers, their "prone tango," the surrounding erotic language reveals the fantasy as in part a liberation from the conventional inhibitions of his upbringing (15). Hollywood B-films and movie magazines, which serve as the model for the amorous adventures of Floyd and Jean, evidently provided the young Merrill with the taste of forbidden fruit:

And one night—pure "Belshazzar's Feast"
When the slave-girl is found out—
She cowered, face a white blaze ("Beast!")
From his royal clout.

(15)

The kidnappers gradually assume a more poignant role in the fantasy as surrogate parents—as can be felt in the scene in which Jean watches as the child drops off to sleep: "I felt her watching from her chair / As no one ever had" (13). The kidnappers became alternate models by which the child can assess his actual parents, whom he imagines receiving the ransom note:

My mother gloved,
Hatted, bepearled, chin deep in fur.
Dad glowering—was it true he loved
Others beside her?

(14)

The final scenes of the dream, which depict the capture of Floyd and Jean, point not only to the child's guilty feelings about choosing new parents for himself, but show as well how even dreams become infiltrated by a stubborn, underlying sense of reality. The beginning of the end comes when Jean reveals her ingenuous sense of reality:

"Do you know any stories, Kid?
Real stories—but not real, I mean.
Not just dumb things people did . . . "
I started at her—*she* was the child!

(16)

At this point the roles reverse, and the child becomes the storytelling parent to the kidnappers, which both fits his actual role as the creator of the fantasy in which they appear and which also silhouettes his loneliness. The depth of that loneliness is revealed in the way in which by inventing and telling the story to himself he becomes the parent he never had. As in **"From the Cupola"** the self would have to comfort the self.

Following the dream, Merrill returns to the actual world in a scene in which the child, parentless for all practical purposes, watches the cook baking. Later, his father sips a bourbon in the den while leafing through the *Wall Street Journal,* and his mother quickly kisses him good night before greeting another influx of guests:

Tel & Tel executives,
Heads of Cellophane or Tin,
With their animated wives
Are due on the 6:10.

(21)

The biting puns of the quatrain underline the complex tone and mood of the poem which resist nostalgia even while evoking it in a struggle against the glib tendency of memory to sweeten and embellish the past.

"Up and Down" comprises two poems in a subtle, antithetical relationship to one another. **"Snow King Chair Lift,"** the *up* poem, is a euphoric recollection of a ride up the mountain by two lovers who gaze their "little fills at boundlessness" (55). The ride, which symbolizes the love affair, takes them to a summit that is a "cul-de-sac" from which there is nowhere to go but down. The poem thus contains a modest counter movement to the prevailing mood of uplift. Similarly, in **"The Emerald,"** the *down* poem, there is a countervailing resistance to the mood of declivity. The poem describes Merrill's visit to his mother after the death of her second husband. Together, they go down into the vault where she keeps her valuables. There, she offers her son an emerald ring that had been given her by his father when he was born, suggesting that he keep it for his future wife. He declines and slips the ring on her finger.

The poem's burgeoning ironies include the name of the bank (**"Mutual Trust"**) and the fact that Merrill survives the deaths of his mother's two husbands to—metaphorically, at any rate—become the third. The Oedipal fire of earlier poems gives way here, though, to a simple acceptance of what it is too late to alter: *"We are each other's; there will be no wife; / The little feet that patter here are* *metrical"* (57). The *"green room"* of the emerald whose light envelops both Merrill and his mother is the room of art as well as the room of age. The emerald image combines both the morbid connotations of the "vault" and those of the offsetting, heightened chamber of art, both the inertness of the hard gem and the hope symbolized in its visionary green. Hence the slight upturn at the end: "The world beneath the world is brightening" (57).

"18 West 11th Street" is the address of the New York house where Merrill spent part of his childhood, a house which was blown up in 1971 by the left-wing group the Weathermen, who had been using it as a temporary headquarters for making bombs. One of the group's members was Cathy Wilkerson, daughter of the vacationing financier who owned the house. Some of the Weathermen were killed when a bomb accidentally exploded, and the girl was seen by witnesses running from the building, naked and bleeding. She vanished into hiding.

Merrill compares his own uneventful growing up with that of the equally affluent but revolutionary girl who succeeded him in the house. He perceives the suffocating limitations of his background, limitations that in retrospect seem to merge with the decor of the house:

> Item: the carpet.
> Identical bouquets on black, rose-dusted
> Face in fifty funeral parlors,
> Scentless and shaven, wall-to-wall
> Extravagance without variety.
>
> (25)

Merrill's deepest instinct, however, is to conserve and to bridge the generational gap, as his own writings attest. It is in this respect that he most forcefully distinguishes himself from the Weathermen:

> In what at least
> Seemed anger the Aquarians in the basement
> Had been perfecting a device
> For making sense to us
> If only briefly and on pain
> Of incommunication ever after.
>
> (24)

The Edenic illusions of the Weathermen, which when punctured lead to vindictive violence, are mirrored in the name pronounced by Cathy Wilkerson on fleeing the burning house: "She stirs, she moans the name / Adam. And is *gone*" (28).

The poem does much to explain Merrill's disaffection with the 1960s. If he resented the insensitive rapacity of his parents' generation, he was outraged at the hypocrisy of activists who in the name of justice reduced to rubble what offended them and who appeared to live in a haze of mind-numbing slogans—"Rebellion . . . Pentagon . . . Black Studies" (24). The poem is noteworthy for its admixture of blunt, colloquial, angry speech and the language of elegant disdain. Also memorable is the juxtaposition of the stark scenes of urban blight—the smoking ruins, the police floodlights, the lingering pools on the street—and the faint, lyrical echoes of a lost childhood.

"Days of 1971," which consists of a series of alternating Italian and Shakespearean sonnets, recounts an automobile trip taken by Merrill and his Greek friend, Strato, through France, Italy, and Greece. Strato, with whom Merrill had been involved sexually for some years, is another of those recurring figures in the poetry. The poem's sarcastic tone sets clear limits on the relationship, which had become stale over the years. In spite of this, the mood lightens as they stop to visit old friends, and encounter some ravishing sights, particularly in Venice, where through its "vertiginous pastry / Maze we scurry through like mice" (67). The image of Venice finally deepens the mood of decay, however, and Merrill ponders the erosive effects of the sea on the baroque city, which is described as "Crumbling in the gleam of slimy knives" (67). The poem later touches bottom in a scene in which a landslide forces Merrill to interrupt his journey and to line up for overcrowded ferries: "One self-righteous truck / Knocked the shit out of a eucalyptus / Whose whitewashed trunk lay twitching brokenly" (68). As in **"18 West 11th Street,"** the language is unusually bold and raw.

The poem lifts at the end, though, as Merrill unwraps a delicate figurine which Strato had given him after visiting the famous glassmaking area of Murano near Venice:

> Two ounces of white heat
> Twirled and tweezered into shape,
> Ecco! another fanciful
> Little horse, still blushing, set to cool.
>
> (69)

The token rescues the fading affair for another day, though on the whole the poem underscores Merrill's preoccupation in ***Braving the Elements*** with attrition. **"Strato in Plaster"** sets this theme in a humorous light with a contrast between the aging Strato in a plaster cast and the image of his earlier firm attractiveness. The submerged motif of the plaster cast as a forerunner to a finished marble enters the poem through the image of the Apollo statue. The statue recalls the physical beauty that Strato once had as well as symbolizing the permanence of art as opposed to the transience of life and love.

The book's atmosphere of sinking aftermath is nowhere more visible than in the title of **"After the Fire,"** a poem that refers directly to the imagery of ***The Fire Screen*** and by implication to the vitality of Merrill's earlier poems. Rooms in Merrill's house in Athens had been repainted a "quiet sensible light gray" after a fire that occurred in his absence (5). The new sober coloring effaces the past look of the rooms and therefore to some extent the past itself including its scenes of love. Kleo, Merrill's longtime housekeeper, visits him with a cake, complaining, though, about her mother's senile rages, her daughter's looseness, and her brother's sordid homosexual adventures. Merrill visits Kleo at her house, and seeing that the brother has taken over some of his possessions, theorizes that he might also have set the fire. At this point all of Merrill's past relationships in Greece appear to sink into a melancholy gloom. Suddenly, though, the grandmother, a "little leaden oven-rosy witch" (5), returns to sanity and recognizes her guest: *"It's Tzimi! He's returned!"* And with this recognition, the speaker notes, she was restored to "human form" (7). The change alters the mood of the poem from sullenness and betrayal to dignity and a gratitude for the past as Merrill kneels before the old woman "pressed to her old burning frame" (7).

Amid the images of decay and fiery destruction in ***Braving the Elements*** are faint signs of renewal—as in **"Yam":** "Rind and resurrection, hell and seed, / Fire-folia, hotbeds of a casserole / Divinely humble" (41). The apotheosis of the humble vegetable points to a rallying energy that will in time drive the divine comedies. Paralleling the oppressiveness of loss and betrayal is the mind's fecundity, which can people the heavens and earth, though not quite as quickly or triumphantly, as decay and reversal can unpeople them.

Notes

Interview with the author, June 13, 1980.

1. James Merrill, *Water Street* (New York, 1962). Page references appear in the text.
2. Letter to the author, November 21, 1980.
3. Brown interview, p. 9.
4. James Merrill, *Nights and Days* (New York, 1966). Page references appear in the text.
5. Brown interview, p. 14.
6. Sheehan interview, p. 8.
7. Interview with the author, June 13, 1980.
8. Sheehan interview, p. 8.
9. Interview with the author, June 13, 1980.
10. James Merrill, *Braving the Elements* (New York, 1972). Page references appear in the text.
11. Letter to the author, September 27, 1980.

Judith Moffett (essay date 1984)

SOURCE: *James Merrill: An Introduction to the Poetry*, Columbia University Press, 1984, 247 p.

[*In the following excerpt, Moffett calls* The Changing Light at Sandover *"Merrill's greatest achievement" and probes the sources of composition and themes of the work.*]

Then Sky alone is left, a hundred blue
Fragments in revolution, with no clue
To where a Niche will open. Quite a task,
Putting together Heaven, yet we do.

—**"Lost in Translation"**

I have received from whom I do not know
These letters. Show me, light, if they make sense.

—**"From the Cupola"**

I

The Changing Light at Sandover is Merrill's grandest achievement. Into its more than five hundred pages has gone everything he knows about writing poetry, everything he believes about living among other people in the world, all his deepest-held values, fears, convictions, and prejudices, spread among passages of "revelation" spelled out on a Ouija board. Not everyone will wish, or know how, to approach that sort of book, and not everyone who approaches will feel welcome; the material takes getting used to. But many readers may well feel they have been waiting for this trilogy all their lives.

Beginning about 1955, when Merrill and his friend and lover David Jackson first moved to Stonington, they often diverted themselves with a Ouija board—a commercially manufactured one at first, later a larger one homemade from cardboard. A Ouija board, as described in *The Seraglio* (where Francis Tanning grew addicted to the use of one) is "a smooth wooden board on which had been printed the alphabet, the Arabic numerals, and the words YES and NO. At the top was the likeness of a female face, Oriental in spirit, lit from beneath: she peered down into a crystal ball wherein misty letters had materialized." The board is used to get in touch with the "spirit world"; the mortals below ask questions, the spirits reply by spelling out messages with a pointer on which each player allows the fingers of one hand to rest lightly. (Instead of the planchette that comes with a bought board, Merrill and Jackson preferred the handle of an inverted teacup.)

Some pairs of players, without consciously controlling the pointer, get very much livelier results than others do; and for a time JM and DJ (in the board's shorthand) made a regular parlor game of *their* extraordinary ability to summon the souls of the dead. Both the temporarily and permanently dead—for they were instructed in the rudiments of a cosmology whereby souls are reborn until advanced enough to embark upon the nine Stages of heavenly progression. The two grew ever more fascinated with the phenomenon; as to what it meant they remained in the dark. But the game had its disquieting, not to say sinister, aspects. Where in fact *were* these messages coming from? *Should* the whole affair have become so seductive that for a time DJ and JM found themselves living more within the spirit world than in their own? A poem in ***The Country of a Thousand Years of Peace,*** **"Voices from the Other World"** (written in 1955), describes how, finally, they began to call upon the spirits less often "Because, once looked at lit / By the cold reflections of the dead . . . / Our lives had never seemed more full, more real. . . . " But the board continued to play a background role in their lives, and eventually the substance of twenty years' irregular conversation with one favorite voice became the basis of "The Book of a Thousand and One Evenings Spent /

With David Jackson at the Ouija Board / In Touch with Ephraim Our Familiar Spirit."

The Book of Ephraim appeared as the greater part of ***Divine Comedies***, in 1976. ***Mirabell*** followed in 1978 and ***Scripts for the Pageant*** in 1980; these three Books, plus a Coda, make up the trilogy published in one volume in 1982 under the collective title ***The Changing Light at Sandover***. ***Ephraim*** covers the decades between 1955 and 1974. The second and third Books and the Coda document another obsessive involvement with the board lasting roughly from June 1976 into late 1978, and need to be considered separately from ***Ephraim*** for several reasons. Not reasons of style: the entire trilogy displays the same wit, formal skills, economy, and lyric power as the very best of Merrill's previous work. Nor of overt theme: all were originally undertaken as a warning against nuclear disaster. But ***Ephraim*** was composed and published, in ***Divine Comedies***, with no thought of anything to follow. In manner of composition it resembles the shorter narrative poems of that volume multiplied by ten or twelve. The varied experiences with the Ouija world have been thoroughly interpenetrated in ***Ephraim*** with the rich whole of the poet's life, and with the sea-changes of twenty years' unconscious ripening, to emerge in "timeskip and gadabout" form as a lengthier counterpart of **"Lost in Translation"** or **"Chimes for Yahya."** Time, and the material, had even allowed for a certain amount of manipulation and invention, improvements for the poem's sake on the literal truth.

Mirabell and ***Scripts***, and the Coda, were composed very differently. A routine chat with the spirits, after Ephraim's book had been completed, was abruptly intruded upon one day by dread powers bringing JM a daunting new assignment: "UNHEEDFUL ONE 3 OF YOUR YEARS MORE WE WANT WE MUST HAVE POEMS OF SCIENCE THE WEORK FINISHT IS BUT A PROLOGUE." Having impulsively accepted this charge, Merrill then found himself obliged to give up enormous amounts of time—his own and David Jackson's—to daily sessions of transcribing dictation at the board, struggling to make sense of it, and later tossing the messages lightly with details from his and DJ's ongoing lives as he drafted the POEMS OF SCIENCE he had been commissioned to create. The result is that while ***Ephraim*** reads like the rest of Merrill's work only more so, the other two Books progress by fairly (***Mirabell***) or rigidly (***Scripts***) chronological schemes to set forth material Merrill has not himself consciously chosen: a bizarre creation myth involving, among other things, Atlantan centaurs and huge radioactive bats which are at once both "life-size" earthly creatures and subatomic particles; four angels who conduct a seminar; and much gossip, often licentious, about the famous dead.

Though the assignment absorbs and enthralls the two mediums in time, Jackson initially reacts to it with fear and Merrill with dismay ("Poems of *science?* Ugh."). The poet makes an effort, a successful one, to talk himself round:

> Not for nothing had the Impressionists
> Put subject-matter in its place, a mere
> Pretext for iridescent atmosphere.
> Why couldn't Science, in the long run, serve
> As well as one's uncleared lunch-table or
> *Mme X en Culotte de Matador?*

This is no new line of thought for Merrill, who had always liked opera's emphasis on sound over sense, and that of French art songs, and who quotes Andrew Marvell in ***Scripts*** (from Heaven) as saying "THE LINE! LET IT RUN TAUT & FLEXIBLE / BETWEEN THE TWO POLES OF RHYTHM AND RHYME / & WHAT YOU HANG ON IT MAY BE AS DULL / OR AS PROVOCATIVE AS LAUNDRY." But the argument had always served *his* ends before—that is, he could cite it when he wanted to safeguard a subject with lyrical obscurity. Nowhere does ***Mirabell*** sound merely dutiful in the writing, but parts—the bat's numerology, above all—are plainly thrust upon a reluctant poet whose choice of material when writing ***Ephraim*** had been free. And both ***Mirabell*** and ***Scripts*** tax the mediums with doctrine that—at least at first—offends them: the No Accident clause, the elitism clause, the prophecy of a "thinning" to come. Two shades—W. H. Auden and Maria Mitsotáki—are permitted to assist in their instruction, which makes the project more appealing, and much of their resistance eventually evaporates. Still, when Auden blandly urges Merrill "ON WITH THE WORK! THRILLING FOR YOU JM," the younger poet retorts:

> And maddening—it's all by someone else!
> In your voice, Wystan, or in Mirabell's.
> I want it mine, but cannot spare those twenty
> Years in a cool dark place that *Ephraim* took
> In order to be palatable wine.
> This book by contrast, immature, supine,
> Still kicks against its archetypal cradle . . .
> I'd set
> My whole heart, after *Ephraim,* on returning
> To private life, to my own words. Instead,
> Here I go again, a vehicle
> In this cosmic carpool. Mirabell once said
> He taps my word banks. I'd be happier
> If *I* were tapping them. Or thought I were.

But the case is easily overstated. While ***Ephraim*** has been shaped at the center of Merrill's singular art and self in some sense that the other two Books were not, these can hardly be said to be *all* by someone else. The given subject matter determines the direction of the narrative; the daily transcriptions force a structure upon it. But in and about these Lessons is ample room for Merrill to say how he feels about it all, to talk with David, pay calls, travel between Stonington and New York, Athens, California, and one way and another—shocked, alarmed, distressed, overjoyed, stimulated by what comes across the board—to reveal a great deal about his sense of the meanings of his life. Merrill has described "the way the material came" in an interview: "Not through flashes of insight, wordplay, trains of thought" in the ordinary manner of poetic composition (and, overall, of ***Ephraim***), "More like what a friend, or stranger, might say over a telephone. DJ and I never knew until it had been spelled out letter by letter. What I felt about the material became a natural part of the poem, corresponding to those earlier poems written 'all by myself.'"[1]

It was expected that he edit the transcripts, recast the passages to be used into meters assigned to the various speakers, and polish the whole into something that would read smoothly. Sometimes this meant quite a lot of work, sometimes almost none; as DJ describes it:

> I was freer to enjoy the whole experience with the dictation than JM was. . . . great passages of it that I thought were just ravishingly beautiful, Jimmy was seeing as useless to the text, or a little too much of a good thing. And it must have been maddening for him to think that he couldn't, you know, improve upon something that was very nice; sometimes it already fitted into his syllabic scheme.[2]

But the sense of being driven to the task was unrelenting:

> They dictated it. All of the ***Scripts***—it was very much a regimen. . . . We had to do it—it started in on this cycle talking about time and the series of moon cycles. We had to get this given amount done in them, and we had to come back at this given moment. They were precise about their schedules, as they were about when the poem would be finished, when it would be published, everything.[3]

Merrill's own sense of how he "Quarried murky blocks / Of revelation" from the transcripts to build the second Book is described early in the third:

> *Mirabell*—by now more Tower of Babel
> Than Pyramid—groans upward, step by step.
> I think to make each Book's first word its number
> In a different language
> (Five is *go* in Japanese), then stop
> Sickened by these blunt stabs at "design."
> Another morning, Michael's very sun
> Glows from within the section
> I polish, whose deep grain is one with mine.

Of the three Books, ***Mirabell*** seems in one way to have been the most difficult to write. As the poet has described it:

> With ***Ephraim***, many of the transcripts I had made from Ouija board sessions had vanished, or hadn't been saved. So I mainly used whatever came to hand, except for the high points which I'd copied out over the years into a special notebook. Those years—time itself—did my winnowing for me. With ***Mirabell*** it was, to put it mildly, harder. The transcript was enormous. What you see in the poem might be half, or two-fifths, of the original. Most of the cuts were repetitions: things said a second or third time, in new ways often, to make sure we'd understood. Or further, unnecessary illustrations of a point. . . .
>
> With ***Scripts***, there was no shaping to be done. Except for the minutest changes, and deciding about line-breaks and so forth, the Lessons you see on the page appear just as we took them down. The doggerel at the fêtes, everything. In between the Lessons—our chats with Wystan or Robert [Morse] or Uni [the trilogy's resident unicorn]—I still felt free to pick and choose; but even there, the design of the book just swept me along.[4]

Increasingly the great labor grew compatible, even joyous, till Merrill could acknowledge that while writing ***Scripts*** "I woke up day after day beaming with anticipation."[5]

Though he recoiled from the word, so mammoth a poem could not be managed without "design." The Ouija board itself provided the basic frame of each Book: one section for every letter of the alphabet in ***Ephraim,*** which covers a calendar year; one (with decimal subdivisions) for each number from 0 to 9 in the book of number-happy Mirabell; and a set of Lessons for the three major divisions—YES (ten), & (five), and NO (ten)—of ***Scripts***, a fit scheme for that monument to ambiguity, corresponding to the plot's electric plusses and minuses, Whites and Blacks. A proliferation of voices from the Other World made further device imperative if the work were not to become hopelessly confusing. Merrill solved the principal problem (with help from WHA) in ***Mirabell*** 79: rough pentameter, "our virtual birthright," for the human characters living and dead; and for the bats, who think in fourteens, "WHY NOT MY BOY SYLLABICS? LET THE CASE/ REPRESENT A FALL FROM METRICAL GRACE." Five stresses by fourteen syllables, of course, borrows from the internal yardstick of the dyed-in-the-wool sonneteer. In ***Scripts*** a unicorn/centaur speaks a fair imitation of four-stress Anglo-Saxon alliterative meter. Greater powers—God, Nature, the angels—are bound to no metrical pattern and never use rhyme (apart from certain ceremonial occasions, and from Archangel Michael's clumsy couplet-making). Nor do the bats rhyme; but the humans often fall into couplets or stanzas as if for comfort. Tag phrases distingush the many upper-case human voices from one another: "MY BOYS" or "MY DEARS" for Auden, "MES ENFANTS" for Maria, "MES CHERS" for Ephraim, "LADS" (and baby talk) for Robert Morse, only George Cotzias calls DJ "DAVE," and so on. The variations of the effortlessly coalescing and dissolving lyric passages are too numerous to list; and if the middle distance of ***Mirabell*** does sometimes display what Helen Vendler tolerantly calls "a sheer willingness to bore,"[6] the verse of the trilogy's hundreds of pages consistently outdazzles everything critics can think to say about it.

2

As the foregoing should make clear, ***Mirabell*** and ***Scripts*** are the unforged record of a lived experience; for the nature of their "revelation" Merrill cannot, in the ordinary sense, be held accountable. By the terms of his commission he may—indeed must—paraphrase, condense, question, even criticize, as well as change prose to poetry. But he is not to decide which ideas to keep and which to exclude: is not to censor, embellish, nor in any way distort the *sense* of the revealed text. Thus restricted, he can take no more responsibility for its nature than John Constable could for the concepts of *cow* or *hundred-year-old oak* when he set out to paint the landscapes of East Anglia. Actually, the material revealed was such as to plague JM with skepticism (and DJ with fear) through much of the work. The first transcriptions strike them respectively as preposterous and terrifying; their harmless parlor game has changed character so drastically, in fact, that the question of *belief*—easily shrugged off in ***Ephraim***—now reasserts itself again and again. To Auden's rhapsodizing in ***Mirabell*** 2, Merrill replies in exasperated couplets:

> Dear Wystan, VERY BEAUTIFUL all this
> Warmed-up Milton, Dante, Genesis?
> This great tradition that has come to grief
> In volumes by Blavatsky and Gurdjieff?
> Von and Torro in their Star Trek capes,
> Atlantis, UFO's, God's chosen apes—?
> Nobody could transfigure stuff like that
> Without first turning down the rheostat
> To Allegory, in whose gloom the whole
> Horror of Popthink fastens on the soul,
> Harder to scrape off than bubblegum. . . .
> *I* say we very much don't merit these
> Unverifiable epiphanies.

As the experience continues, appalling and ravishing him by turns, Merrill's doubts trouble him less and less, and near the end of ***Scripts*** his assent has become all but total:

> Beneath my incredulity
> All at once is flowing
> Joy, the flash of the unbaited hook—
> *Yes, yes, it fits, it's right, it had to be!*
> Intuition weightless and ongoing
> Like stanzas in a book
> Or golden scales in the melodic brook—

Readers, of course, may more easily believe in Merrill's riveting experience than in the divine authenticity of its source, or the truth of its prophecy. "For me," Merrill has said himself (of ***Mirabell***), "the talk and the tone—along with the elements of plot—are the candy coating. The pill itself"—the poem's apocalyptic message, its insistence on determinism and elitism—"is another matter. The reader who can't swallow it has my full sympathy. I've choked on it again and again."[7] His own sense, illustrated by the quotation, of his role of Poet as distinct from his role of Scribe is a distinction readers should bear in mind. Thinking of the two roles as Mind Conscious and Unconscious is one very workable way of reading the poem—as if all of ***The Changing Light at Sandover*** were an inexhaustibly elaborate dialogue between Merrill's waking intelligence and its own unconscious sources of feeling, myth, and dream, with David Jackson as essential catalyst (and supplemental unconscious story-trove).

DJ himself reports that, to the engrossed mediums, "Whether all that dictation came out of our collective subconscious or not finally became less and less of real interest. Rather as if a flying saucer were to land on one's front lawn, would one ask, 'Where's it *from?*' as one's first question?"[8] Readers unable or unwilling to fight clear of this question of source, or the related one "What does it mean?" risk spoiling their initial plunge into the trilogy's elemental weirdness—needlessly, because its Message and its meaning are not the same. Large tracts of Message—Mirabell's mathematical formulas, kernels of concept that refuse to crack, Lessons that often seem pure pretext for extravagant spectacle, parts of the System no sooner grasped at last than made pointless by revision—will certainly frustrate an approach to the poem which is too doggedly literal. ***The Changing Light at Sandover*** is, and expects to be read as, an immensely complex Overmetaphor packed more tightly with lesser metaphors within metaphors than a plutonium atom is with atomic particles. It's best to assume that what doesn't seem to make literal sense right away makes dramatic or metaphorical sense, or none that matters intellectually. "MAKE SENSE OF IT" Merrill is told and told in ***Scripts***; but why should the sense wanted be merely verbal? As Vendler has noted, "Merrill's primary intuition is that of the absolute ravishment of the senses"[9]—those senses restored to the dead souls only at the highest heavenly Stage, and (in "YES" Lesson 7) identified one by one with the very angels. Musical and visual sense is the sort to look for in a baffling passage, like seeing a very fine operatic adaptation of *Dracula* sung in a foreign language.

Many years ago, Merrill wrote in **"To a Butterfly,"** "Goodness, how tired one grows/ Just looking through a prism: / Allegory, symbolism. / I've tried, Lord knows,// To keep from seeing double. . . . " Now in ***Mirabell*** he addresses the radioactive bats intemperately:

> How should you speak? Speak without metaphor.
> Help me to drown the double-entry book
> I've kept these fifty years. You want from me
> Science at last, instead of tapestry—
> Then tell round what brass tacks the old silk frays.
> Stop trying to have everything both ways.
> It's too much to be batwing angels *and*
> Inside the atom, don't you understand?

But truly the bats can speak no other way; "we get an effect of engines being / Gunned in frustration, blasts of sheer exhaust." (This passage is one of those exceptionally easy to read as an argument between conscious Poet, who thinks he ought not to depend so heavily on metaphor, and unconscious Scribe, who knows himself unalterably addicted to it.) Only toward the end of ***Scripts*** does Merrill gratefully allow Auden to persuade him that metaphor-making can itself be a form of freedom, that (as WHA has already asserted, late in ***Mirabell***) "FACT IS IS IS FABLE":

> But if it's all a fable
> Involving, oh, the stable and unstable
> Particles, mustn't we at last wipe clean
> The blackboard of these creatures and their talk,
> To render in a hieroglyph of chalk
> The formulas they stood for? U MY BOY
> ARE THE SCRIBE YET WHY? WHY MAKE A JOYLESS THING
> OF IT THROUGH SUCH REDUCTIVE REASONING?
> ONCE HAVING TURNED A FLITTING SHAPE OF BLACK
> TO MIRABELL, WE YOU MAKE TIME FLOW BACK?
> SUBTRACT FROM HIS OBSESSION WITH 14
> THE SHINING/DIMMING PHASES OF OUR QUEEN?
> CONDEMN POOR UNI TO THE CYCLOTRON
> AFTER THE GREENS U'VE LET HIM GALLOP ON?
> Dear Wystan, thank you for reminding me
> The rock I'm chained to is a cloud; I'm free.

Like the elements of the sonnet form, metaphor is in Merrill's marrowbone. And to speak of it thus returns us full circle to the perceptions that took shape in his Amherst honors thesis and in ***First Poems:*** that earliest perception of metaphor as ice, sheeting the black abyss, making pain bearable, and of the thin blue egg-shell of appearance with the tiny dead claw broken through. From that cracked robin's egg to "THE WHOLE FRAIL EGG-SHELL" of the Earth "SIMPLY IMPLODING AS THE MONITOR'S / BLACK FILLS THE VACUUM MOTHER N ABHORS" is but a step thirty years in length.

When it appeared as part of ***Divine Comedies***, ***The Book of Ephraim*** had seemed about ready to put masks by, as if Merrill at last had found a way to make his peace symbolically with *this* world's reality by forswearing the spirit world for good. But Poet has a way of insisting on resolutions to which Scribe has not assented. The oedipal fire supposedly extinguished by Francis Tanning in *The Seraglio* blazed on, and metaphor has cheerfully persisted in doubling Merrill's vision despite the wish voiced twenty years before ***Mirabell*** in **"To a Butterfly."** And now, with the publication of ***From the First Nine*** and ***The Changing Light at Sandover,*** in two volumes, the import of ***Ephraim*** has been shifted; we are directed to consider it not as the last and most complex work along one line of development but as the first and simplest on another. It is, of course, both—and ought rightly to be printed last in the first volume as well as first in the second.

Renounce the Other World, spiritual metaphor and twin of this "one we feel is ours, and call the real . . . "? Strip the real world, never so loved as now, of her thin gold mask at last? Not if the Powers that decide such matters have anything to say about it—and in fact They have found all this to say.

3

And so the old themes whose conflicts ***Divine Comedies*** had seemed to resolve burst forth again, their vigor all restored, in ***Mirabell*** and ***Scripts for the Pageant***. Literally, those resolutions were true enough. But some of the themes had shaped Merrill's outlook in profound psychological ways all his life, just as they had been shaped *by* his life. They are evidently not to be cast off merely because their actualizing source in life is neutralized. Now, though, the scale is grander and the mode transcendent, for none of them—masking and illusion, passion and sexuality, parents, aging, childlessness—need be life-size or earthbound any longer.

The spirits continually reaffirm that there are no appearances in Heaven; they can see JM and DJ in mirrors, and whatever their mortal "representatives" see, but never one another. The meaning of *mask* in such a realm cannot be literal, yet masking of many kinds, and the pretense of sparkling appearances, are perpetual; should this trilogy ever be adapted for the stage with skill it should play splendidly, but the costume budget would need to be generous beyond dreams. The whole poem is constructed of deceptions-for-a-purpose, successively unveiled as the mediums become able to tolerate what they will hear. Often the purpose is dramatic: quarrels between angels, rehearsed and staged to drive the Lesson home, or two characters finally revealed to be one and the same. Heavenly doctrine gets revised like drafts of a poem; Ephraim makes mistakes corrected by Mirabell, who must be corrected in his turn. The numerous pageants, fêtes, and masques overlay the revelation of "the Black" with imaginary spectacle as the schematic order of instruction overlays the revelation of Chaos—gilt or ice above the void. And much about Heaven remains permanently hidden, unfathomable.

But no secrecy now obtains between these mediums and us; and the sense of their shared life realized here forms a powerful chemical bond between reader and poem, tiding us over the "stretches of flats in the exposition of the mythology."[10] JM and DJ began together as lovers, and the "FORTUNATE CONJUNCTION" (as Ephraim calls their partnership) has withstood the stresses of Athens and Santa Fe. Passion was the keynote of Merrill's life and of his art when he and DJ first got through to Ephraim, or he to them, and continued to be its keynote for another twenty years. But, by the mid-seventies, radical social changes had affected that part of his life at the same time it was being reclaimed by trustier, less violent loves. ***The Book of Ephraim*** makes abundantly clear that their familiar shares, and rejoices in, his mediums' homosexuality. No more now of that sickness of self felt in **"After the Fire"**; nothing of the obsessive "dirt-caked" and "dirty-minded" talk New Mexico had produced. Strato himself is vividly evoked in ***Ephraim,*** in terms that recall that "animal nature" passage of **"Chimes for Yahya":**

> Strato squats within the brilliant zero,
> Craning at his bare shoulder where a spot
> Burns "like fire" invisible to me.
> Thinking what? he studies his fair skin
> So smooth, so hairless. . . .
> Strato's qualities
> All are virtues back in '64.
> Humor that breaks into an easy lope
> Of evasion my two poor legs cannot hope
> To keep up with. Devotion absolute
> Moments on end, till some besetting itch
> Galvanizes him, or a stray bitch.
> (This being seldom in my line to feel,
> I most love those for whom the world is real.)
> Shine of light green eyes, enthusiasm
> Panting and warm across the kindly chasm.
> Also, when I claim a right not written
> Into our bond, that bristling snap of fear. . . .

Some of the funniest lines in ***Mirabell*** are "spoken" by Auden's widow Chester Kallman, who complains about how Auden treats him in Heaven, about a fickle heavenly lover, about the life in Johannesburg into which he is about to be reborn—all in a style suggesting that the subject of homosexuality and the gay world, off the leash at last, went slightly mad with unconfinement:

> But you're coming back,
> It's too exciting! PLEASE TO SEE MY BLACK
> FACE IN A GLASS DARKLY? I WONT BE
> WHITE WONT BE A POET WONT BE QUEER
> CAN U CONCEIVE OF LIFE WITHOUT THOSE 3???
> Well, frankly, yes. THE MORE FOOL U MY DEAR

You shock us, Chester. After months of idle,
Useless isolation— ALL I HEAR
ARE THESE B MINOR HYMNS TO USEFULNESS:
LITTLE MISS BONAMI OOH SO GLAD
TO FIND ARCADIA IN A BRILLO PAD!
LAUGH CLONE LAUGH AH LIFE I FEEL THE LASH
OF THE NEW MASTER NOTHING NOW BUT CRASH
COURSES What does Wystan say? To PLATO?
HAVING DROPPED ME LIKE A HOT O SHIT
WHAT GOOD IS RHYME NOW

Extended passages like this one enliven ***Mirabell*** and ***Scripts,*** and the trilogy is liberally salted thoughout with witty camp chit-chat. Willing at last to exploit this source, Merrill has drawn upon it with a free hand.

But the subject of proclivity is not only a rich new wellspring of comedy; the long-stoppered avowal will swell and swell, and grant a still more deeply seated wish. "Why," wonders DJ early in the ***Mirabell*** Lessons, "did They choose *us?* / Are we more usable than Yeats or Hugo, / Doters on women . . . " An explanation ensues:

LOVE OF ONE MAN FOR ANOTHER OR LOVE BETWEEN WOMEN
IS A NEW DEVELOPMENT OF THE PAST 4000 YEARS
ENCOURAGING SUCH MIND VALUES AS PRODUCE THE BLOSSOMS
OF POETRY & MUSIC, THOSE 2 PRINCIPAL LIGHTS OF
GOD BIOLOGY. LESSER ARTS NEEDED NO EXEGETES:
ARCHITECTURE SCULPTURE THE MOSAICS & PAINTINGS THAT
FLOWERED IN GREECE & PERSIA CELEBRATED THE BODY.
POETRY MUSIC SONG INDWELL & CELEBRATE THE MIND . . .
HEART IF U WILL. . . .
NOW MIND IN ITS PURE FORM IS A NONSEXUAL PASSION
OR A UNISEXUAL ONE PRODUCING ONLY LIGHT.
FEW PAINTERS OR SCULPTORS CAN ENTER THIS LIFE OF THE
MIND.
THEY (LIKE ALL SO-CALLED NORMAL LOVERS) MUST PRODUCE
AT LAST
BODIES THEY DO NOT EXIST FOR ANY OTHER PURPOSE

"Come now," the mediums demur, "admit that certain very great/Poets and musicians have been straight." Self-despising homosexual behavior was displaced onto Panayioti in **"After the Fire"** and onto the Enfant Chic in *The (Diblos) Notebook;* in like manner this unblushing speech issues from Mirabell's mouth—or beak; Mirabell has turned, the instant before he makes it, from a bat named 741 into a peacock, in a kind of coming-out party of his own. The doctrine of homosexuals as evolution's crème-de-la-crème transforms the childlessness that once grieved JM into a trade-off beneficial, even essential, to his poetry. It also accounts for the gay-subculture ambience created in this poem by so much camp talk, and makes sense of a circumstance which would otherwise seem decidedly peculiar: that once they reach the formallesson stage, nearly all the poem's significant characters are male and gay. (The one who appears to be neither will ultimately reveal herself as both.) Two straight men added to the cast of ***Scripts*** are friends who died with ***Mirabell*** half-written and the "YES" dictations of ***Scripts*** completed; the poem fits them to a scheme whose shape is already fixed. Which cannot prevent JM from feeling, as he knows his readers must, that

A sense comes late in life of too much death,
Of standing wordless, with head bowed beneath
The buffeting of losses which we see
At once, no matter how reluctantly,
As gains. Gains to the work. Ill-gotten gains . . .
Well, Robert, we'll make room. Your elegy
Can go in *Mirabell,* Book 8, to be
Written during the hot weeks ahead;
Its only fiction, that you're not yet dead.

The dead souls most important to the entire poem are two: W. H. Auden, and Maria Mitsotáki, an Athens friend who was the subject of a **Fire Screen** poem, **"Words for Maria."** JM's peace with his own mother has been ratified. His father died in 1956. The death of DJ's aged parents is the first major event of ***Mirabell***; indeed, these impending deaths are what send them back to the Ouija board after an absence of more than a year ("As things were, / Where else to look for sense, comfort, and wit?"). Helen Vendler, wise in this as in much else, writes:

> In the usual biological cycle, parents die after their children have become parents; the internalizing of the parental role, it is believed, enables the parents to be absorbed into the filial psyche. In the childless world of ***Mirabell,*** the disappearance of parents, or parental friends, is the disappearance of the parental and therefore of the filial; JM and DJ can no longer be "boys" but must put on the mortality of the survivor.[11]

Both childless like the mediums in (this) life, WHA and MM make idealized parent-figures, their two-sided humanity masked beyond the kindly chasm of death. As Merrill has said in an interview, "In life, there are no perfect affections. . . . Yet, once dead, overnight the shrewish wife becomes 'a saint,' frustrations vanish at cockcrow, and from the once fallible human mouth come words of blessed reassurance. . . . Given the power . . . would I bring any of these figures back to earth?"[12] Vendler amplifies: Auden and Maria "are the people who call JM and DJ 'MES ENFANTS' (Maria, known as 'Maman') or 'MY BOYS' (Auden). When these voices fall silent, there will be no one to whom the poet is a child."[13] A (twinned) only child: Maria, we learn in ***Mirabell***, "Was hailed on arrival by "HORDES OF POLYGLOT / SELFSTYLED ENFANTS . . . BUT NOW A DECENT / VEIL IS DRAWN & I HAVE NONE BUT U."

These voices, even these, fall silent at poem's end—but only after the parents' and children's love has been perfected, like that of Dante and Beatrice, by its three-year ceremony of guidance, enlightenment, and farewell. Beyond this silence gleams the tantalizing hope of a rendezvous with Maria in 1991, Bombay, The World. And as the surrogate parents move inexorably toward their departures, behind them grow and fill out the personified figures of Mother Nature and God/Sultan Biology: all-powerful and capriciously destructive, even murderous, on the one hand, heartbreakingly loveable on the other, like parents as perceived by small children. By the terms of the myth, their "divorce" would destroy their third, last, human child and his green world; and the poet, struck by parallels between the broken home he grew up in and the present situation of all humanity, angry and afraid as no child of divorced parents is ever too old to be, evokes himself when young once more. "Between an often absent or abstracted/ (In mid-depression) father and still young / Mother's wronged air of commonsense the child sat," he writes, and goes on to build the metaphor, cosmic by domestic detail, which will culminate in Earth-shattering divorce. "*That* was the summer my par—YR PARALLELS / DIVERGE PRECISELY HERE," insists Maria. "HUSH ENFANT FOR NO MAN'S MIND CAN REACH / BEYOND THAT HIM & HER THEIR SEPARATION / REMAINS UNTHINKABLE." JM, if not entirely convinced, is convinced at least that Maria is right to stop this probing, terrifying line of thought. "Barbarity," he agrees, pulling himself together, "To serve uncooked one's bloody tranche de vie . . . / Later, if the hero couldn't smile, / Reader and author could; one called it style." Or called it metaphor, ever and always at work to make any new form of the oldest, most chronic pain bearable.

4

The *Prophetic Books* of William Blake and the *Vision* of Yeats come tentatively to mind when one considers all this, for ***The Changing Light at Sandover*** is a masterwork of great eccentricity. Unlike Dante's *Comedy* or *Paradise Lost,* those other major poems which purport to address man's role in the universal scheme, the value "system" given poetic expression here is not shared by an entire culture. Unlike them, it is not a morality tale. It substitutes yes-and-no ambiguities for moral absolutes. Sin is equated with the giving *and receiving* of pain, evil and good recognized on the cosmic level alone, outside the power of individual human beings (in a wholly deterministic universe) to choose, or to enact unless "cloned" to do so. Personal salvation then cannot be at issue; the issue is global survival. The poem accounts for the chief obstacles to survival—overpopulation and nuclear holocaust—in original ways, but does not propose, in the manner of science fiction, original ways of implementing the obvious solutions. Certain virtues—kindness, courtesy, devotion, affection, modesty, tolerance, tact, patience, plus intelligence, talent, and wit—are celebrated, many of these broadly shared with western religions; yet the values they embody are, lacking spiritual principles to back them up, social rather than spiritual values. ("LANGUAGE," says WHA, "IS THE POET'S CHURCH.") Neither deep religious sensibility, nor political savvy, nor philosophical inquiringness are at work in Merrill's poem, setting it off sharply in tone from Dante's and from Milton's.

The chief difficulty in viewing the trilogy as *western* religious myth is its insistence that innate class, on Earth as in Heaven, determines who can take steps to prevent the world from blowing up. Only elect "Lab souls" of sufficient "densities," preprogrammed or *cloned* in Heaven between lives, can do God's work on Earth to build an earthly Paradise; only they will read this poem's Message with comprehension:

> A MERE 2 MILLION CLONED SOULS LISTEN TO EACH OTHER WHILE OUTSIDE THEY HOWL & PRANCE SO RECENTLY OUT OF THE TREES. & SO FOR U THE HARDEST RULE: THE RULE OF THE RULERS. POLITICIANS HAVE LED MAN DOWN A ROAD WHERE HE BELIEVES ALL IS FOR ALL THIS IS THE FOOL'S PARADISE ALL WILL BE FOR ALL ONLY WHEN ALL IS UNDERSTOOD.

The absolute amount of "human soul densities" is finite, and has had to be pieced out in recent history with "animal densities" of dog and rat to cope with the glut of children. Holocaust is a present danger precisely because power has fallen into the hands of leaders with a high proportion of animal soul densities—"Rat souls"—who too easily lose control of their high-spirited but destructive impulses. And lately, therefore, accidents—slippages in the works—have infiltrated the realm of NO ACCIDENT. To restore balance, save the earth from utter destruction, and bring Paradise upon it, a thinning of the population is essential.

If the positive and negative charge within the atom is a metaphor for this global drama, the drama is in turn a metaphor for something vaster. The cosmic conflict of Good, or White, forces represented by God Biology—Earth is, so to speak, his representative, he Earth's patron, in a Galactic Pantheon—are at war with horrific forces called simply "the Black" (as in black holes), whose nature is utter nothingness: "The Black beyond black, past that eerie Wall—/ PAST MATTER BLACK OF THOUGHT UNTHINKABLE," elsewhere defined as "ATOMIC BLACK / COMPRESSED FROM TIME'S REVERSIBILITY," a phrase which resists conceptualization. Michael identifies it "IN MAN'S LIFE" with "THE DULLWITTED, THE MOB, THE IDIOT IN POWER, THE PURELY BLANK OF MIND"; perhaps these make time flow backward by reversing the evolutionary ascent of life through time toward the development of an ever larger, more convoluted brain. On his second visit Michael had stated resoundingly, "INTELLIGENCE, THAT IS THE SOURCE OF LIGHT. FEAR NOTHING WHEN YOU STAND IN IT." It follows that when the idiot rules you stand in darkness, and are afraid.

"Time's reversibility" remains a conundrum; but forward-flowing time is easy to see as Black in the context of Merrill's earlier work. "Why should Time be black?" he asks, having answered his own question through thirty years of poems wherein Time is the agent of aging, and of steadily diminishing beauty and passional capacity, and the destroyer of kindly masks and illusions. When Paradise comes upon Earth "THEN TIME WILL STOP": man will be immortal.

The poem's cryptic Message, however, is not identical with its meaning, as readers with any density of soul at all can see. Part of its meaning is its wit and style. The rest lies where the most meaning has always lain in Merrill's work: in the loves between human characters in life and beyond death, and in their losses; and especially in the evocation of twenty-five domestic years with David Jackson, which Thom Gunn has called "the most convincing description I know of a gay marriage":

> The men's life together is presented to us in detail which is almost causal: we see them choosing wallpa-

> per, keeping house, traveling, entertaining, and above all sitting at the Ouija board. It is not a minor triumph and it is not an incidental one because, after all, it is the two of them in their closeness who have evoked the whole spirit world of ***Ephraim*** and ***Mirabell*** [and ***Scripts***], or perhaps even created it.[14]

Those "genre" glimpses of JM and DJ watering on the terrace, discussing the sense of a knotty transcript, going about their days together while *not* collaborating across the Board, are the most affecting, most authentic part of the entire story unstifled here, and the most human. *Have* they created the Other World, in its infinite richness and strangeness, between them? ***The Book of Ephraim*** includes an explanation suggested by JM's former psychiatrist: "what you and David do / We call folie à deux"—a way of talking to one another from behind the mask of the Ouija board. The ex-shrink leads his ex-patient to speculate that Ephraim is an imaginary offspring produced in lieu of a real one to satisfy the biological urge to procreate, seeing that "Somewhere a Father Figure shakes his rod / At sons who have not sired a child." The explanation tidily foreshadows Mirabell's: homosexuals, being poorly suited to make children, are well-suited therefore to make poetry. ***Ephraim***—and all that follows where he led—*makes sense* as the child of JM's and DJ's love and pro/creativity, conceived through their union at the Ouija board.

"Jung says—or if he doesn't, all but does—/That God and the Unconscious are one," we read in ***Ephraim,*** Section U. To theorize that in ***The Changing Light at Sandover*** two unconsciouses, linked skillfully by long practice, have played God by creating a cosmic vision still leaves a great deal unexplained. How, for instance, did DJ and JM know that Nabokov was dead—news that reached them first via the Board? More centrally, what is it these two do that others fail to do, which yields such astonishing results? When we leave JM at the close of the Coda, nervously preparing to read the completed trilogy to the heavenly host assembled (one auditor per letter of the alphabet), his situation is both so familiar in its Proustian stance and thematic preoccupations, and so outré in its total concept, as to baffle and defy any simple explanation. Even if the two did make all of it up unconsciously, an experience has befallen them scarcely less amazing and wonderful than if, like the prophets of old, they had heard God's voice address them aloud. And if God and the Unconscious are one—? As Merrill has observed, "if it's still *yourself* that you're drawing upon, then that self is much stranger and freer and more far-seeing than the one you thought you knew."[15] Put another way, in another place: "If the spirits aren't external, how astonishing the mediums become! Victor Hugo said of *his* voices that they were like his own mental powers multiplied by five." He adds that his time among the spirits has "made me think twice about the imagination,"[16]—a reminder that Section S of ***Ephraim*** begins where this essay may properly conclude:

> Stevens imagined the imagination
> And God as one; the imagination, also,
> As that which presses back, in parlous times,
> Against "the pressure of reality."

Notes

1. Vendler, "James Merrill's Myth," p. 12.
2. J.D. McClatchy, "DJ," p. 37.
3. McClatchy, "DJ," p. 35.
4. McClatchy, "The Art of Poetry," pp. 190-91.
5. Vendler, "James Merrill's Myth," p. 13.
6. Vendler, *Part of Nature,* p. 230.
7. Vendler, "James Merrill's Myth," p. 12.
8. McClatchy, "DJ," p. 38.
9. Vendler, *Part of Nature,* p. 227.
10. Ibid., p. 230.
11. Ibid., p. 225.
12. Vendler, "James Merrill's Myth," p. 12.
13. Vendler, *Part of Nature,* p. 225.
14. Thom Gunn, "A Heroic Enterprise" [review of *Divine Comedies* and *Mirabell*], *San Francisco Review of Books* (August 1979), p. 4.
15. McClatchy, "The Art of Poetry," p. 194.
16. Vendler, "James Merrill's Myth," p. 13.

Stephen Yenser (essay date 1987)

SOURCE: *The Consuming Myth: The Works of James Merrill*, Harvard University Press, 1987, 367 p.

[*In the following excerpt, Yenser explores the themes, imagery, and structure of Merrill's* Late Settings *and his verse drama* The Image Maker.]

> Divides and rejoins, goes forward and then backward.
>
> Heraclitus (trans. Guy Davenport)

> "What next? What next?"
>
> Manuel in ***The Image Maker***

The sun sets, and songs are set, and lines of type, and precious stones. "Setting" also signifies surroundings, and scenery—and on the one hand an ambush, on the other a table laid for guests. "Late" too has its range of meanings: "toward the end," yes, but also "very recent," as in "late developments." So while ***Late Settings*** can indicate compositions done late in life, or the world's last twilights or suppers, it can also refer to recent contexts, or to newly mounted gems—or to full summer days. The phrase creeps up on the present like dawn itself and looks to the future. A setting is a placed bet, as well as the direction a current flows in. When fruit sets, it begins to develop from the flower. We might well remind ourselves, when we settle down with Merrill's first volume to be published after the completion of ***Sandover***, of such anticipatory glimmerings of his title, along with its darker shadings.

Merrill has usually constructed his volumes with an eye to the skyline that the poems create on the reader's mental horizon, and ***Late Settings*** is no exception. Its thirty-six poems are divided into three parts, each of which contains a splendid long work. The first and last poems, captivating lyrics both, give us a sense of the scale of the large efforts they abut: **"Clearing the Title,"** the second poem, which purports to discover in its course the title of ***The Changing Light at Sandover,*** and **"Santorini: Stopping the Leak,"** the penultimate poem. The book's most imposing work, **"Bronze,"** 352 lines in eight sections, comes at the end of the central part. Among these major achievements shorter poems—which include a ballade, a shaped poem, and **"Ideas,"** an exquisitely comic poem for two voices that is a study in variety of diction—form shifting alliances.

One hears throughout an elegiac tone. Like ***Sandover***, this volume faces squarely the possibility that Earth is dying. "World without end?" Merrill asks near the end of **"Radiometer,"** which plays with the notion that the solar-driven toy portends the perpetual revolution of Yin and Yang in our existence. But then he completes the couplet darkly: "Not this one. Look: the setting sun, my friend." **"Developers at Crystal River,"** which deplores the pitiless mutilation by Florida entrepreneurs of manatee cows (sweet "Muses of sheer / Indolence"), returns to the crucial problem, mind's betrayal of nature. **"Think Tank"** ingeniously interprets our covert oligarchy of experts as prolicidal fish and our faceless corporate censorship and sanitizing of information as "the Snail / Our Servant, huge and blind."

None of Merrill's incomparable technique is sacrificed to his outrage. In a poem published recently in *The New Yorker,* in much the same vein as these poems in ***Late Settings***, the twentieth-century United States is seen from the vantage point of a time after the melting of the polar ice cap, when the country has come to be a huge Venice: the "once young republic tasseled / sea to sea with golden wit," in Merrill's adaptation of **"America,"** has "tattered to a / wrack of towns, bubble / domes unpricked on the lagoon's / fogged mirror."[1] In the concluding list of items imported to this world power turned "tourist / mecca," the last is

> a fine-gauge
> 20-karat wire, from which
> our morose goldsmith
> on the Bridge of Smiles
> has already fashioned this
> shimmering, cereal wand.
> Wear it, Milady,
> in your frosted hair.

That "morose goldsmith" is behind this wiry syllabic elegy, a metaphorical hair ornament for Lady Liberty (who suddenly looks a good deal like a blighted Ceres, offered this piece of "golden wit" instead of a sheaf of wheat or an ear of corn in a fertility rite), and he is no less behind ***Late Settings***. **"Channel 13"** works out its point with touching formal precision. Even as it tracks our hard-pressed wild creatures through ever smaller arenas of activity, from "Grassland to circus to Roman floor mosaic to / TV room," and finally to that room's "snug electronic ark of / What has been," each stanza chokes its lines down three times from thirteen syllables to three. After pairing internal rhymes like Noah's animals in each stanza's first two long lines, Merrill dismisses them from the third. Like other political poems here, it is written in a chilling past tense, as though nature had already vanished down the black hole at the center of the dying tube. We hear future ghosts as well in **"Popular Demand"** (one of the coldly bitter, poignant mini-sequence entitled "Topics"), where "the worst / Has happened," and the only survivors are the politicians in their "deep strongholds." Merrill's keen ear picks up "a first, uncertain laugh": "Spirits reviving, as life's bound to do? / Not from dead land, waste water, sulphur sky."

These poems are the more affecting for the steadfast eschewal of scapegoats and simplification that we have come to expect of Merrill. **"Channel 13,"** seeming to discover the origin of "our ultimate 'breakthrough' lenses" in Adam's naming of the animals, implies that the extinguishing of other species is inextricable from our pursuit of knowledge. **"The Pier: Under Pisces,"** a poem as metrically flexible as its fisherman's "bamboo diviner . . . Vigorously nodding / Encouragement," unfolds a conceit with a Möbius twist, by virtue of which the poet—a Pisces—joins those who take the irresistible bait of their own "minced kin." After describing in flamboyant metaphor the landing of the catch, Merrill imagines certain fish left in the sea and recalls a first experience of his own:

> far and wide and deep
> Rove the great sharkskin-suited criminals
> And safe in this lit shrine
> A boy sits. He'll be eight.
> We've drunk our milk, we've eaten our stringbeans,
> But left untasted on the plate
> The fish. An eye, a broiled pearl, meeting mine,
> I lift his fork . . .
> The bite. The tug of fate.

But the boy is not "safe." As surely as the poet is the boy ("I lift his fork"), the boy and the fish are one (the "eye" meets the "I"). This is The Peer, then, too, and twice: as he and the fish peer at each other, he sees that he is the fish's peer. So it is that the boy's "bite" joins him with the fish who takes the bait, as well as with the fisherman. They are all of the fallen world, and a part of the boy's maturing is realizing his complicity with the fisherman—and thus with the "sharkskin-suited criminals." If the latter are almost more people than they are fish, as earlier the "floozy fish" have been so vivid as to seem actual streetwalkers, the point is that the natural and the human are threads in the same material.

Inspired by the discovery several years ago off Riace, Italy, of two Hellenic statues, **"Bronze"** too involves ecological themes. A "QUEENS / MAN" killed by his sons is a New York artist, but he can also be thought of, in the wake of ***Sandover,*** as QM's favorite, God B himself, and in one riveting section the statues impart certain *"cold lessons,"* the gist of which is that *"hard on the heels of God's death"* we must acknowledge that *"Nature / Is dead, or soon will be."* But **"Bronze"** fends off epitome. It is also about a stunted love affair, an Italian friend's trek through enemy territory in the closing days of World War II, his mysterious parentage, and other things. The Greek bronzes, a bust of King Umberto I, Merrill's sculpted portrait, childhood games of statues, a vivid internal "figure" of Eros: the poem's lines of force play among these and related images—as they do among shells, armatures, fortresses, and retreats. On each reading its loopings and interloopings and -lopings all become more closely knit and more diverse. Of the many things one might say about this undertaking, which like its railroad timetable is "Dense . . . with station and connection," one is that it moves away from art and toward an embracing of life—and all the while makes it clear that it is the poem that accomplishes the movement.

The relationship between art and life frames itself first in terms of a quarrel between Merrill and his traveling companion, a painter. Finding themselves in Tuscany, not long after the restored statues have gone on display in nearby Reggio Calabria, these two differ as to whether they should make the trip to the museum. The friend demurs, as he has resisted a closer relationship with the poet. As one would expect, Merrill in part sympathizes with his friend's feeling that "'Close connections . . . harm the soul.'" He has often portrayed himself as a "cold man," after all, and he is quickly "Half resigned" to his friend's recalcitrance—if "Half fuming" as well. These two halves of the self (characteristically projected in the poet's "Notebook and cigarette" and in an owl and a "twittering dither" of starlings) he figures as duelists, as he walks beneath the trees in his host's garden and wrestles with his frustration.

The poem's burden, however, is less the opposition between aesthetic detachment and affective bonds, or between the contemplative and the active lives, than the desirability of combining the two. Thus one of its heroes, his host, Umberto Morra, is at once the former confidant of Montale, Berenson, and Edith Wharton and the man who risked his life to provide the liaison at War's end between Italian anti-fascists and the Allies.[2] True, the poem superficially discounts the value of art: a seagull fouls Merrill's portrait bust, and a friend spills beer on it. Moreover, if "Umberto first intended the estate / As a 'retreat for scholars,'" in the end he has "left it intact to Mario the butler, / So long devoted and his brood so great." Time and again the poem stresses the primacy of "Close connections"—of the "social fabric" and the ecological network, rather than "the Work of Art." Yet all these details belong *to* the poem, which is an elaborate version of a friend's T-shirt, emblazoned with the motto *"Clean Air / Or Else."* No wonder that Merrill's title denotes an alloy. The Greek bronzes, *"Exultantly baring through coppery / Lips the carnivorous silver,"* are both stunning works of art and Nature's fierce spokesmen, who warn that *"the Mediterranean will in / Another few decades have perished, / And with it those human equivalents, / Memory, instinct, whatever / In you the first water so joyously / Answered to."* Since it is through the poet that we know what they have to say, it is appropriate that he too "exist in bronze," in the form of the bust, a copy of which is on the deck of the Stonington house, that one Laszlo made when Merrill was a child.

It is because his poems constitutionally resist themselves that ***Late Settings*** will not resolve into elegy. His **"Island in the Works"** claims to be "Jaded by untold blue / Subversions," and just as one sub-version of "Jaded" is something like "turned viridian," so this volume's mourning weeds have their greener side. Likewise its **"Grass":**

The river irises
Draw themselves in.
Enough to have seen
Their day. The arras
Also of evening drawn,
We light up between
Earth and Venus
On the courthouse lawn,
Kept by this cheerful
Inch of green
And ten more years—fifteen?—
From disappearing.

The ominous and the whimsical are one in this example of what the newly risen "Island" has in mind when (speaking from the vantage of a poet who has just finished an epic) it promises to "trick / Out my new 'shores' and 'bays' / With small craft, shrimpers' / Bars and rhetoric." Among *this* small craft's appointments (in addition to the tiny echo of the twenty-year-old poet's wish as reported more than two decades earlier in **"A Tenancy"**) are the delightful rhymes, not just "irises" and "arras" but their light rhyme across the stanza break with the second syllable of "Venus," which rhymes its first syllable with the middle lines in stanzas one and three (which in turn rhyme consonantally with the enveloping rhymes in stanza two). The final rhyme, hidden in "cheerful" and "disappearing," is cheerfulness itself, as it comes and goes, peering and disappearing, like the joint's glow. All flesh is grass, Isaiah teaches, but to smoke pot on the courthouse lawn is to thumb one's nose at that law too.

"Santorini" converts its valedictory drift into a paean to the dogged perseverance of things. Though it weaves in as well the various light of Marvell and Blake, it takes its fire from Yeats, and its first octave concludes with a wry revision of that earlier master's embarkation for Byzantium: "Whereupon, sporting a survivor's grin, / I've come by baby jet to Santorin." If Yeats thinks to have abandoned a country of "sensual music," Merrill imagines that in leaving a home in Greece and a lover he is also leaving a way of life. The intricacies of the reversal are formidable. But how to persuade the reader with mere excerpts that this wonderful renunciation of renunciation springs convincingly from the removal of a plantar wart? Or that the radiation treatment and the wart's return repeat perfectly the destruction and the resurgence of the volcanic island itself, the Turkish suppression and the eventual renaissance of Greek culture, the repression but persistence of a belief in vampires, the loss of the ancient *gymnopaediai* and their resurrection by Satie? The poem itself is "one throbbing multiplex," by way of which a principle in Merrill's work resurfaces. As he put it in **"Lost in Translation":** "Lost is it, buried? One more missing piece? / But nothing's lost. Or else: all is translation / And every bit of us is lost in it / (Or found . . . ." Merrill's friend and traveling companion, Nelly (or Nelláki, in the Greek diminutive), has long ago lost her twin (Plato tells us that we have all done so), but his place is taken, for the moment at least, by the poet himself.

His own attempts to achieve "an oblivion / That knew its limits" (to give up both his Greek bed and "what was done in it," for instance) can only prepare the way for a countervailing experience, a bizarre dream vision in which he is virtually possessed by a life "Utterly not my own," by the teeming memories of an "olive-skinned Iraqi" and perhaps others. It is as though the willed rift in his emotional life, the counterpart to the hole in his sole, were an opportunity for the dead or the uncreated to rush in, for Nature to prove her abhorrence of a vacuum. As he lies on his rejected bed on his last evening in Athens, vignettes run in "A cinéma-mensonge" before his mental eye, "Swifter now, churning down the optic sluice, / Faces young, old . . . all random, ravenous images / Avid for inwardness, and none but driven / To gain, like the triumphant sperm, a table / Set for one." This waking nightmare drives him from bed to mirror, where he prays to a "Queen" we will recognize as Nature/Psyche/Chaos that he *"Be made whole."* As though in response to this "petition," and heralded by "the peevish buzz" of a fly at the windowpanes, "From some remotest galaxy in the veins / A faint, familiar pulse begins," as the wart makes itself felt anew. At just this point Merrill resumes his recollection of the Santorini sojourn (which has preceded this harrowing experience in Athens)—and with good reason, since the wart is in effect his past, his memory, his very life. "Certain things die only with oneself," as the poet learned in **"Friend of the Fourth Decade."**

Against other poems in this book, **"Santorini"** asserts the possibility of continuity through renewal. (So it is, by the way, that he and Nelly are unable to meet in Santorini "three old maiden sisters," famous hostesses to whom she has hoped to gain entrée. "The ladies must be met," no doubt, as surely as the Fates must, but since that meeting is not yet to be, though "Things just aren't what they were," they are not radically different either.) One likely reason that Empedocles figures here—in the poem's most difficult passage, which summarizes by way of its legends Greek history from the beginning to this philosopher—is that he envisioned a world cycle in which the two opposing forces, Love and Strife, which produce unity and chaos respectively, alternate dominance, with Love having the last word. So this poem, after a brush with "the hole," ends with an emphasis on "a deep fault made whole"—much as Santorini's major volcanic eruption was succeeded by new islands, new vineyards, a new life. Perhaps "catastrophe" cannot "long be lulled" by our variously propitiatory creations, from the original Greek dances performed in honor of Apollo Karneios through Satie's compositions to this poem, but so far the world has endured, like the poet and Nellie at poem's end, where, after their excursion to "Prophet Elias' / Radar-crowned monastery" and other sites, they return to what is probably Kamari: "We made on sore feet, and by then *were* made, / For a black beach, a tavern in the shade."[3]

Empedocles also figures here because, in the legend that he flung himself into Mount Etna, "that primal scene / And deafening tirade," Merrill has an analogue for the consuming myth, "The mother tongue / At which his blood boiled, his brain kindled," that he confronted in ***Sandover***. The issue of renewal thus has a personal dimension, and his question as to whether Empedocles actually met his death in the volcano is also a question as to his own fate after the epic. But even the framing of the question supplies the answer, for Empedocles has become this new Oedipus (his foot swollen after the x-ray removal of the wart), just as the original "Oedipus became Empedocles" in Merrill's version of Greek history. Everything changes; nothing does—a principle consonant with Empedocles' doctrine of the elements, which taught that underlying all things are immutable elements which combine in different proportions to produce all the different phenomena. To the extent that this philosophy celebrates metamorphosis, it comports with much of Merrill's recent work. **"From the Cutting-Room Floor,"** which nonetheless salvages a few passages omitted from ***Sandover,*** characteristically concludes with Michael bidding farewell lightheartedly to the epic's cast and looking forward to a new day's revisions. His light *is* change:

> But they have had their day (& say). therefore
> change and change, o scribe! Come up to this
> instant (for you inky) at my height
> as touching the himalayas I define,
> more, refine them, fold on fold, forever
> getting at their bone of meaning. Change!
> Revise, rise, shine! Good ah my children night!

"Clearing the Title" reverses the structure of **"Santorini."** Here Merrill is at first reluctant to take up a new life, this time defined in terms of the new second residence which he and David Jackson established in Key West at the beginning of 1979 and which has come to replace the home in Athens. It seems to him that to embark on this new life is to "cast / Three decades' friendships and possessions out"—and also somehow to distance himself from ***Sandover*** (so much of which had its roots in Athens), for it is not only real estate that he has in mind when he asks "What happens next? Behind a latticework / Of deeds no one has time or patience to undo / We cultivate our little lot, meanwhile / Waiting companionably for kingdom come?" But even as he resists, he begins to like the idea of the change (to the degree that it *is* a change, for he spent much of his youth in Florida, and he sees old friends everywhere, in trumpet vine and "cracked pavement"—as will the reader of **"From the Cupola"**). After he surmises that "what at first appall precisely are the changes / That everybody is entitled to," his poem ends with a refusal to end, with the thought that "tonight we trust no real / Conclusions will be reached" and with "the changing light." **"Island in the Works"** even mocks the idea of real conclusions. The island has no sooner located itself by latitude and longitude ("This dot, securely netted / Under the starry dome") than "this page" on which the monologue has been drafted is wafted out of the poet's hand (as we learn in a parenthetical last stanza) and into his pool's "cool glares, ever / So lightly swayed, or swaying . . . / Now who did that?" To which one answer is, the eminently irreverent processive principle itself.

Being now a part of the past, an episode in the story of his life, ***Sandover*** itself changes from Merrill's point of view. Its characters now appear as background figures, diminished by distance, who can be alluded to rather than presented, and who thus contribute to the depth of the recent poems. To be sure, the new work can be admired in isolation, and there are everywhere independent felicities. In **"Days of 1941 and '44"**—a sonnet sequence that strikes notes rarely heard hitherto in Merrill's work, as the embarrassed and the vindicated, the resentful and the sorrowful jostle one another in a crowd of tones—he turns an adolescent tormentor's taunt of "Rich boy" to this dazzling advantage: "Remember, though, how untrained eyes subtract / From the coin-glint of a summer glade / The adder coiled to strike." In another poem Gertrude Stein offers Elvis Presley—in heaven, on a brief sojourn between loves—a Lethean "CUP OF NULLITY." In another a bad trip ends with the victim, fallen asleep, producing "a suite for solo pharynx / Clumsily bowed and scraped." There is perhaps no better snoring in our poetry. Merrill writes lines as abrasively witty as the bearded bronzes' self-description: *"men in their prime / With the endocrine clout so rebarbative / To the eternally boyish / Of whichever sex."* And lines as deftly lovely as "I hear the ferrous, feather-light diluvian / Lava clink at a knife-tap from our guide."

Still, many of these poems will ripen more fully in the changing light of ***Sandover.*** During the excursion on Santorini, "a toy chapel to St. Michael" helps to set the stage for the relationship between radiance and radiation, or "whole" and "hole," in the poem's antithetical rhyme. If the colorful clown of **"Clearing the Title"**—who "rides unicycle" and juggles firebrands—makes us think first of the poet, that is partly because Merrill treats ***Sandover***'s hottest issues so playfully.[4] But in his role as militant solicitor for the Salvation Army, the clown is also a genial parody of Gabriel: "'Y'all give!' our deadpan clown / Yells brandishing a hammer fit for Thor, / 'Give or Ah'll clobber yew!' and *grunt* go the trombones." **"After the Ball,"** this volume's last poem, treats the changing light itself in miniature. In what we might think of as a Merrillian remake of "In a Station of the Metro," the Muse or Sandover's chatelaine takes the form of a date dressed in "magic / Changemaking taffeta" who, by evening's end, has helped the poet to take "Such steps in dream logic / That the Turnstile at Greenwich / Chimed with laughter— / My subway token." This little poem is borne along by its own dream logic—as "taffeta," for instance, coming from a root meaning "to twist, to spin," involves itself with the "Turnstile" at the Greenwich Village station. The Turnstile in turn is a style that turns, as from epic to lyric, and that turns one thing into another, as its taffeta turns (suitably, for Rosamund Smith) from "Old rose to young spinach / And back."

Whatever its elegiac undertones, then, this closing lyric chiefly celebrates change in a "Changemaking" style—a style that finds the spin in "spinach," and the spinach's color in "Greenwich," and a crepitant rhyme for "taffeta" in "laughter." Once more "A shutter opens" (to borrow from "Trees Listening to Bach" a phrase in which Merrill lets us hear the latent paradox), and it is not surprising to discover him most recently at work anew in an old field. ***The Image Maker,*** a one-act verse play, was first produced in Los Angeles in May—the month in which the action is set—of 1986. If ***The Birthday,*** the short verse drama that Merrill wrote at Amherst in 1947, now seems a sketch for ***Sandover*** (four strange characters who look remarkably like God B, Nature, Michael, and Gabriel meet the protagonist, Raymond, in a room with red walls and inform him that "We are you"), ***The Image Maker*** rings light changes on the epic's devices and themes. Here too Merrill provides an array of verse forms, though they are comparatively simple, ranging from a basic tetrameter line through a pair of sonnets for two voices to a chain of quatrains in which Manuel, the image makre, alternately prays to God and talks to himself about his craft, which consists of carving and restoring wooden icons of household saints, or *santos.* Manuel is a *santero,* a practitioner of Santeria, the Caribbean mystery religion that syncretizes Yoruba folklore and Catholicism.[5] Santeria would be especially interesting to Merrill not just because of his acquaintance through Maya Deren with voodoo, but also because the figures venerated by its followers are essentially double: any given santo is outwardly a Christian saint but underneath an *orisha,* or pagan deity (who represents both a natural force and a human concern). Although Manuel can touch up the saint's features and repaint the costume, the much less tractable Yoruba god, the basic resisting force, is incorrigible.

In the santos Merrill has found a telling trope for humanity, with all its cross-purposes and contradictions. The most important santo in his play is Barbara, the virgin martyr, whose Yoruba self turns out (surprisingly but rightly) to be the strife-loving, philandering Changó, who most evidently resembles his Christian counterpart in that he has power over thunder, lightning, and fire—*and* likes to dress in women's clothes. St. Barbara as Changó, taking the tone of Queen Mum at her most irascible, foments a rebellion of the santos in Manuel's workroom. One of the santos, Miguel, who naturally has affinities with ***San-***

dover's Michael (and even uses the latter's signature rhyme), is closer in temperament, when the Yoruba element is awakened, to Gabriel. The "great angel" of light and balanced judgment, he becomes a wild, petulant bantam terrorist, the very wedge of chaos and anarchy, who is responsible for a minor conflagration, a reprise of the *Götterdämmerung* motif, when at the play's climax he focuses his light on a wall calender—the temporal world—and makes it catch fire. Under Changó's influence, Francisco, the gentle saint who "knows how to speak / With birds and wolves and fish," causes a pet dove's death, and the human lovers Juanita and Antonio are nearly separated. Although the santos work "to dispel / The dark within us," they also serve it. "We are you," they might as well say to Manuel—and with all the more reason since the play hints that their rebellion (which blurs into his dream) enacts the santero's own "fears and fantasies."

In the first place, however, Manuel is engaged in V work. As his name suggests to an English speaker, his task as artist is to try to make man well. He is also a rendering specifically of James Merrill, and like Merrill, he must confront the issue of having had "no time for child or wife." He calls a santo a "figure," and this *is* an apt figure, this icon represented on stage by a puppet, for this diminutive play. Manuel is at the same time a type of the deity, as Merrill makes clear when he has his woodcarver pray that God take us in hand as he himself does his errant saints. But Manuel—and here too he is like God, as well as like the author of, say, **"Island in the Works"**—cannot strictly control his creations. They unfailingly "surprise" him, and often trick him, and he can keep any one in line only "for a while." He would understand fully the Rilke who (besides appreciating puppets) saw so clearly how the world "fills us. We arrange it. It breaks down. / We rearrange it, then break down ourselves."[6] And the Heraclitus who proclaimed (in a different version of the fragment quoted in ***Ephraim***): "History is a child building a sandcastle by the sea, and that child is the whole majesty of man's power in the world."[7] And the poet who ended his first novel with children building a sandcastle.

His santo Miguel, as an orisha, goes so far as to claim that "I make the Image-Maker"—a boast that translates readily into ***Sandover***'s Delphic proposition that humankind is the god-making animal. It also reformulates Merrill's statement about his poetry: "It created me." It will have been doing so since at least as early as 1937, when he and his Mademoiselle were staging those first puppet plays—and assembling that jigsaw puzzle, whose palm-shaped piece is now the more fitting because the palm is Changó's residence. Indeed, when lightning strikes the tree it is Changó—who has remarkable affinities with St. Theodore—returning home.[8] Not that James Merrill has more in common with changeable Changó than with that dwelling place itself. The palm, in Merrill's superb rendering of Valéry's last lines, is "Like one who, thinking, spends / His inmost dividends / To grow at any cost." As Manuel—whose name (like Miguel's) shares its bounding sounds with the poet's—tells a voice that is and is not his unseen, imperious, needful mother's: "My work, Mamá. That's *my* whole life."

Notes

1. "Icecap" appeared in *The New Yorker,* 16 December 1985, 40.
2. William Weaver, in "Literary Tuscany," *Vanity Fair,* October 1984, 57-62, 119, recalls and collects other reminiscences of Count Umberto Morra's villa. The accompanying photographs by François Halard include one of "a portrait of Umberto I, second king of Italy and friend of the Morra family."
3. Background for this poem's details can be found in Stuart Rossiter, ed., *The Blue Guide to Greece* (Chicago: Rand McNally, 1973), 625-630.
4. It is partly too because the clown, with "a bright cerulean tear / On one rouged cheek," mirrors the bust of the young Merrill in "Bronze," with "a streak / Staining bluegreen my cheek."
5. See Migene Gonzalez-Wippler, *Santeria* (New York: The Julian Press, 1973). (The spell for bringing back a lover that Merrill's characters discuss at the end of the play seems to be the one described in *Santeria,* p. 157, and the Yoruba invocation to Changó that Manuel uses in his exorcism is similar to an invocation quoted on p. 43.) Merrill's first indication of his interest in this subject is his poem "Santo" in *Late Settings.*
6. *The Selected Poetry of Rainer Maria Rilke,* ed. and trans. Stephen Mitchell (New York: Random House, 1982), 195.
7. This translation is fragment 24 in Guy Davenport, *Herakleitos and Diogenes* (San Francisco: Grey Fox Press, 1979), 15.
8. See Gonzalez-Wippler, *Santeria,* 93.

Timothy Materer (essay date 1990)

SOURCE: "The Error of His Ways: James Merrill and the Fall into Myth," in *American Poetry*, Vol. 7, No. 3, Spring, 1990, pp. 64-86.

[*In the following essay, Materer probes the mythic unconscious of Merrill's poetry.*]

> You will recall that in the case of the [slip of the tongue] the man was asked how he had arrived at the wrong word *'Vorschwein'* and the first thing that occurred to him gave us the explanation. Our technique with dreams, then, is a very simple one, copied from this example . . . the dreamer knows about his dream; the only question is how to make it possible for him to discover his knowledge and communicate it to us.
>
> —Freud, Introductory Lectures on Psychoanalysis

The prosaic first lines of ***The Changing Light at Sandover,*** "Admittedly, I err by undertaking / This in its present form" (3), are a key to its poetic technique. The "error" referred to is James Merrill's decision to narrate his occult adventures in a long poem rather than in a novel of "unseasoned telling." In the first book of the trilogy, ***The Book of Ephraim***, he explains that

> my narrative
> Wanted to be limpid, unfragmented;
> My characters, conventional stock figures . . .
> The kinds of being we recall from Grimm,
> Jung, Verdi, and the commedia dell'arte.
>
> (4)

Merrill admits that "such a project was beyond me" and that he had to abandon the "mistaken enterprise." Instead he will err by describing his "Thousand and One Evenings Spent / With David Jackson at the Ouija Board" (3) in a fragmented form which now merely alludes to events and characters from the "ill-starred novel."

The sense of "error" as a "mistake," however, is qualified by its root meaning, "to wander." Merrill's decision to narrate his story as the Ouija Board dictates and according to a scheme drawn from the letters and numbers on its face limits his conscious control over its development. Despite the difference in their poetic styles, Merrill is like Pound in embarking on a poetic voyage that is a "periplum" and not a journey from one point to another. Both Pound and Merrill know how weak the structures of their long poems are in comparison to that of Dante's *Divine Comedy.* Merrill indirectly comments on this problem when his friend Robert Morse, within the poem itself, criticizes the poem in manuscript:

> Everything in Dante knew its place.
> In this guidebook of yours, how do you tell
> Up from down?
>
> (256)

The title of the volume in which part one of ***Changing Light, The Book of Ephraim,*** first appeared is ***Divine Comedies***, and the plural form of "comedy" itself acknowledges the poem's fragmentation. Merrill could only agree with Pound that the modern world gives the poet no "Aquinas-map" such as Dante's culture gave him (323). When the cup Merrill uses as a pointer begins transmitting messages through the Ouija Board, it moves "dully, incoherently" before it "swerved, clung, hesitated, / Darted off." Even when Merrill becomes more adept at both following and transcribing its movements, "THIS TOPSY-TURVY WILLOWWARE / IGLOO WALTZING WITH THE ALPHABET" (**"The Will,"** 343) delivers anything but an ordered or even rational discourse. Yet even the most "fragmentary message" the Board spells out is "Twice as entertaining, twice as wise / As either of its mediums." (6-7) The two mediums, Merrill and David Jackson (referred to throughout as JM and DJ), their hands placed together on the willowware tea cup, will follow its wanderings wherever it takes them. Despite his distrust of such a poetic method, Merrill trusts that "Wrong things in the right light are fair . . . (63)."[1]

From the sense of *error* as a "mistake" and then as a "wandering," Merrill relates the word still more widely to a "lapse" and a "fall." (In his poem **"The Grand Canyon,"** he makes a similar play on words by describing the geological "fault" of the canyon as "This mistake / Made by your country . . . [14].") The "error" of the poem is a "fall" or "lapse" into the bizarre world it explores, and many passages in the poem express Merrill's worry that his and Jackson's obsession with the Ouija Board may be *"folie à deux"* (30), or even a dangerous incursion into a demonic world (9, 73), which would be a fall in an ethical sense. And yet one only enters this world through some kind of fall, as Merrill says through a crucial play on the words *lap* and *lapse.* This passage, which occurs in section "U" (the letter highlights its concern with the Unconscious) of ***The Book of Ephraim,*** ends with an address to the "familiar spirit" who is JM's and DJ's mediator in the spirit world (the ellipsis mark in the ninth line is in the text):

> Jung says—or if he doesn't all but does—
> That God and the Unconscious are one. Hm.
> The lapse that tides us over, hither, yon;
> Tide that laps us home away from home.
> Onstage, the sudden trap about to yawn—
> Darkness impenetrable, pit wherein
> Two grapplers lock, pale skin and copper skin.
> Impenetrable brilliance, topmost panes
> Catching the sunset, of a house gone black . . .
> Ephraim, my dear, let's face it. If I fall
> from a high building, it's your name I'll call,
> OK?
>
> (74)[2]

Jung speaks of the relation of God to the Collective Unconscious in many places, but the closest he comes to equating the two is in his autobiography *Memories, Dreams, Reflections* (336-37), which Merrill cites elsewhere in the poem (229). Despite the uncertain or even dubious tone of the "Hm" in the above passage, Merrill is nevertheless making a major statement about his poetic subject. The world of Manichaean gods, black and white angels, and spirits who are desperately dependent on the living, is also the world of the Jungian Unconscious. To borrow a phrase from Merrill's poem **"Bronze,"** Merrill is using the "Jungian dreamer's / Diving bell" (51) to explore the unconscious mind. However, Merrill's point is that this exploration is no planned descent via anything so safe as a diving bell or any other rational contrivance, but is rather a "lapse" that "tides us over, hither, yon" into the other world of occult experience. The term "lapse" is drawn from psychoanalytic vocabulary. In *The Psychopathology of Everyday Life,* Freud shows how verbal mistakes, the famous "Freudian slips," can reveal the contents of the unconscious mind. Freud himself did not use the term "lapse," but his American disciple E.G. Brill introduced the terms *lapsus linguae, lapsus memoriae,* and *lapsus calami* to indicate slips of the tongue, memory, and pen. An example of such a revealing slip is described by Merrill in his poem **"The Will,"** which tells of how he lost the manuscript of the "ill-starred novel" in a taxi cab. Brooding on a slip with a carving knife which nearly cost him his thumb, he asks:

Where was my mind? Lapses like this become
Standard practice. Not all of them leave me in stitches.
In growing puzzlement I've felt things losing
Their grip on me. What's done is done, dreamlike;
Clutches itself too late to stop the oozing
Reds, the numbing inward leak
Of pressures we have effortlessly risen
Through on occasion to a brilliant
Ice blue and white sestet. . . .

(340)

The lapse into a dreamlike state as unconscious motivations control the psyche can be embarrassing or dangerous, but it may also enable the poet/dreamer, employing these psychic pressures, to create a work of art. To return to the passage from ***Changing Light,*** these slips or lapses are thus traps that lower us into the "Darkness impenetrable" of the Unconscious, where the poet can nevertheless glimpse the struggle of dark and light: "pale skin and copper skin."

The "Tide that laps us home away from home," to the unconscious level of our own minds, is related to the image of the "house gone black." The pervasive image of the house in Merrill's poetry usually signifies, as he phrases it in **"An Urban Convalescence,"** "the life lived . . . the love spent" (6). In the lines addressed to Ephraim, it is more specifically the life experience stored in the unconscious mind. Merrill uses the image in this sense in his story "Peru: The Landscape Game." A woman who is thought to be Jung's widow has the narrator play a game of "free association," in which he has to interpret the meaning of the contents of an imaginary house: "The house is your own life, your notion of it," and the "wild creature" which inhabits the house "is Yourself—the unconscious" (105-06). The light of consciousness is the "impenetrable brilliance of a house gone black," its "topmost windows," like the human mind, illumined by a dying light. A similar image is used in Merrill's **"The House,"** where the west walls of the house "take the sunset like a blow," and the house contains "wet-faced sleepers" who awaken at the poet's glance (35-36). The waking of those who are asleep or dead is ominous in this early poem, but in the ***Changing Light*** communication with the dead is more often consoling than it is frightening.

The Unconscious is thus the world of the dead, and the "fall"—say, a "fall / From a high building"—is a literal one that could cause Merrill's or anyone's death. On the point of death, it would be Ephraim's name that Merrill would call. His reason for calling on his familiar spirit as a Christian might on God is clarified in section X. Following a passage on Time as a personified ritual victim of death, the poet asks about the "Spring-tide" of his own death:

Shall I come lighter-hearted to that Spring-tide
Knowing it must be fathomed without a guide?
With no one, nothing along those lines—or these
Whose writing, if not justifies, so mirrors,
So embodies up to now some guiding force,
It can't be simply be written off.

(85)

The "guiding force" is Ephraim. If the writing of ***Ephraim*** does not justify or authenticate the experiences narrated, then it at least "mirrors" some force or other that cannot be ignored. Though his faith in a "guiding" and benevolent force will be challenged, the force is not only personified as "Ephraim" but addressed as an intimate friend: "Ephraim, my dear . . . it's your name I'll call." In the lost novel, Ephraim's name is "Eros" (47); and in the poem he mirrors and personifies the love between JM and DJ. JM fears the loss of this love, which we sense in one of the multiple meanings of the "failure" referred to in the conclusion to section U:

what vigilance will keep
Me from one emblematic, imminent,
Utterly harmless failure of recall.
Let's face it: the Unconscious, after all. . . .

(74)

The immediate meaning of the "failure of recall" refers to the difficulty of getting through to Ephraim which is described in section U. Some sinister force intervenes in the seance and pressures DJ's hand—harmlessly, but with enough force to leave it sore and to serve as a warning. The "failure of recall" is also the potential failure of JM's and DJ's love; but it is still more ominous as the "failure of recall" that comes with death. The repetition of the phrase, "Let's face it," recalls the passage about the fall from a high building and reintroduces a statement about the Unconscious, which this time ends in an ellipsis mark. The Unconscious, after all, is what . . . Merrill is even less sure than Jung about how to describe it and so fails to conclude the passage. The same technique of elision is used in the concluding lines of section X:

. . . Heaven is all peppered with black holes,
Vanishing points for the superfluous
Matter elided (just in time perhaps)
By the conclusion of a passage thus. . . .

(85-86)

The Book of Ephraim is persistently skeptical of the events it narrates, as in the above passage where the occult experience is virtually a "black hole" in Merrill's life.

Merrill readily admits that his occult world may be a projection of his own mind, although he is Jungian enough to add that "consciousness doesn't stop with human beings. There is probably a great untapped mind, if you can call it that, in the natural world itself" (Labrie, "James Merrill at Home," 24, 35). But he wisely refuses to make an issue, even to the extent that Yeats did, of the "reality" of his experience, which can be taken for whatever it's worth—particularly, of course, its poetic worth. It would therefore be pointless to argue that the poem is "really" about the Jungian Unconscious, or that the psychoanalytic "level" of the poem is the basic one. Even to Merrill the issue of whether the subject matter of the poem is merely a compulsive or neurotic personal experience devoid of the universal qualities necessary for a work of art is a crucial one. A personal mistake is bad enough, but an aesthetic one is really serious.

This issue is handled with understated humor in section "I" when JM goes to see his "ex-shrink" after an earlier incident in which they lose touch with Ephraim. The doctor's judgment on the affair is expressed in a trimeter couplet in which the simple rhyme and meter emphasize his superficiality:

> —what you and David do
> We call folie à deux.
>
> (30)

Under the shrink's prodding, JM then states an orthodox Freudian interpretation of his experiences. "Somewhere a Father Figure shakes his rod" at JM and DJ because their love is barren, and their creation Ephraim allows them "to shuffle off the blame / For how we live" . . . (30). Following the consultation, they again try to recall Ephraim, and to their surprise he answers and delivers a terse judgment of his own (in the capital letters JM uses for all transcriptions from the spirits) on the shrink: "FREUD / we learned that evening DESPAIRS / OF HIS DISCIPLES. . . . "[3] Their self-doubts have fallen away as Ephraim returns and "clouds disperse / On all sides." The issue of Ephraim as a psychological project is faced and then definitely resolved. It may be Ephraim's

> lights and darks were a projection
> Of what already burned, at some obscure
> Level or another, in our skulls.
> We, all we knew, dreamed, felt and had forgotten,
> Flesh made word, became through him a set of
> Quasi-grammatical constructions which
> Could utter some things clearly, forcibly,
> Others not.
>
> (31)

Ephraim's revelations should not be taken as in themselves "true" but as a language capable of uttering statements valid within its own "system": myself, but in his view thoughts were like animals in the forest, or people in a room. . . . It was he who taught me psychic objectivity, the reality of the psyche" (183).

Merrill's anxiety over this supernatural influence is perhaps still stronger than Jung's because he feels his autonomy as a poet is being lost as he merely transcribes the thoughts Ephraim and his successors relay to him. When a bat-like creature named 741 begins dictating, the shade of W.H. Auden (who joins the "seminar" in Book 1 of ***Mirabell*** and is always referred to as "Wystan") assures JM that "THESE CREATURES ARE / MORE LIKE INFORMATION BANKS TO TAP" (129). Yet the information begins to shape the poem, preventing Merrill from returning "To private life, to my own words" and even keeping him from shaping his narrative as carefully as he did ***Ephraim*** (261). He is not disturbed to learn that "Rimbaud ghostwrote 'The Waste Land'" (217), but later in ***Mirabell*** the idea of the author as medium makes him feel like "a vehicle / In this cosmic carpool" (262). ***The Changing Light at Sandover*** can illustrate all six of the ways poets deal with their poetic precursors that Harold Bloom identifies in *The Anxiety of Influence;* for example, Merrill's distortion of Auden's Anglo-Catholicism is the kind of misprision that Bloom calls *clinamen,* and his linking of his own poem to Yeats's occult works and Eliot's *The Waste Land* is what Bloom calls *tessera.* Moreover, Merrill's poem itself is a literal case of Bloom's "*Apophrades* or the Return of the Dead." Although Merrill's precursors return in abundance (Auden, Blake, Dante, Eliot, Hugo, Pope, Stevens, and Yeats, to name some of the major influences), there is no sense, as in Bloom, of an agonizing wrestling match with the powerful dead. Merrill's evident ambition to rival Pope's irony and descriptive powers, Auden's intellectual depth and lyricism, and Yeats's richness of imagery must weigh upon him. But he appears not to share Bloom's feeling that, "in poems as in our lives," the dead do not return "without darkening the living" (*Anxiety* 139).

Indeed, it is Auden's schooling of Merrill in the modernist doctrine of impersonality that allays his anxieties over being a mere medium. Wystan tells JM he must learn "TO SEE PAST LONE AUTONOMY" to the powers that transcend the poem and to give up his desire for "DOING YOUR OWN THING: EACH TEENY BIT / . . . MADE PERSONAL AS SHIT . . . " (262). The couplet form itself, perfected in a neo-classical age when originality meant less than it does now, illustrates the inheritance that a poet receives from beyond the self. Wystan lectures on the "MINOR / PART THE SELF PLAYS IN A WORK OF ART" in a passage on poetic language as landscape which is indeed worthy of W.H. Auden:

> FROM LATIN-LABELED HYBRIDS TO THE FAWN
> 4 LETTER FUNGI THAT ENRICH THE LAWN,
> IS NOT ARCADIA TO DWELL AMONG
> GREENWOOD PERSPECTIVES OF THE MOTHER TONGUE
> ROOTSYSTEMS UNDERFOOT WHILE OVERHEAD
> THE SUN GOD SANG & SHADES OF MEANING SPREAD
> & FAR SNOWCAPPED ABSTRACTIONS GLITTERED NEAR
> OR FAIRLY MELTED INTO ATMOSPHERE?
>
> (262)

And so JM faithfully transcribes what Ephraim and a host of spiritual beings tell him. But what are these "lessons" (as they are called in ***Mirabell***) that are so important that Merrill must efface his poetic will in order to record them?

JM himself does not readily admit the importance of the spirits' occult teachings on such matters as the nine stages of reincarnation, the three terrestrial races, or the fall of Atlantis. He complains to Wystan about the topics of his ouija lessons:

> all this
> Warmed-up Milton, Dante, Genesis?

> This great tradition that has come to grief
> In volumes by Blavatsky and Gurdjieff?
>
> (136)

The doubts in this passage are echoed by critics of the poem such as Irwin Ehrenpreis, who disapprovingly but accurately states that Merrill "presents us with inversions of Biblical myth and Christian morality that suggest the tradition of gnosticism" (48). Ehrenpreis thinks that Merrill's Gnosticism is incoherent because it does not oppose matter to the spirit; but Ehrenpreis' conclusion is based on a far too narrow (and Manichaean) understanding of the Gnostic tradition. It is true that Madame Blavatsky and the Russian mystic Gurdjieff raided Gnostic traditions and that their formulations of spiritualistic doctrines were less than coherent. It is also true that Merrill's occultism is a strange jumble of material—stranger, even, than the eclectic myths in the *Rock-Drill* or *Thrones* section of Pound's *Cantos.* But it is already clear that Merrill presents nothing as "true," as did Blavatsky, Gurdjieff, and even Pound. The reader should look through the occultism to see the issues that Merrill is trying to raise by using the Gnostic tradition.[4]

Jung's reading of Gnosticism provides a guide to Merrill's concerns because both men turn to this tradition for similar reasons. In his autobiography, Jung says that the Christian tradition of the West has been unable to explain the evil unleashed by the World Wars and the advent of nuclear weapons (*Memories,* 333). His later work was preoccupied with what he called "the still pending answer to the Gnostic question as to the origin of evil, or, to put it another way, the incompleteness of the Christian God-image" (*Memories,* 318). He considered the Christian image of God incomplete not only because it neglected the feminine but also because its conception of God as entirely good and just failed to account for the existence of evil. Although this failure is especially acute in this century, the Gnostic tradition had always struggled with the problem, and by the eleventh century:

> the belief arose that the devil, not God, had created the world. Thus the keynote was struck for the second half of the Christian aeon, after the myth of the fall of the angels had already explained that these fallen angels had taught men a dangerous knowledge of science and the arts. What would these old storytellers have to say about Hiroshima? (*Memories,* 333)

Through Merrill's poem, we can easily imagine what these old myth-makers might have said. He continues their tradition, which is the very point the spirit named "BEZELBOB" makes: "INDEED JM WE HAVE ALWAYS SPOKEN THROUGH THE POETS" (114).

Ephraim is displaced by the sinister powers JM and DJ sensed in section "P" of ***Ephraim,*** and they are disturbed by the way the "Powers . . . we've been avoiding" seem to possess them and "speed us far downstream / Through gorges echoing at the pitch of dream" (108). JM's assumption that "they're the fallen angels" (114) is correct, but every aspect of the Christian cosmology undergoes a Blakean transvaluation in this poem. These bat-creatures are indeed damned for their transgressions: "WE TRIFLED & FELL NEGATIVE ENERGY THE BLACK HOLE / WAS BORNE WE BURN" (113). But they claim not to have done evil but to have released it and, moreover, that "evil" is a negative force in the heart of matter. Having destroyed their civilization 500 million years ago, "IT IS OUR DUTY TO WARN MAN AGAINST THE CHAOS ONCE / WORSHIPT BY US":

> FOR NOW THE PHYSICIST IS DRAWN IF UN-
> WITTINGLY TO
> FIRE EXTINCTION THAT ANCIENT GLAMOR &
> COULD AGAIN
> WRECK THE LAB THE BIOLOGIST SEEKS THE
> FRUITFUL UNION
>
> (115)

The "lab" is the term the spirits use for the earthly life, in which "V" work ("V" for French *"vie"* and for the five reincarnated spirits who lead it) is meant to perfect it; and the "biologist" refers to those able to reconcile the opposites that exist in everything from the positive and negative forces in the atom to the deity.

In ***Mirabell***, the reader is faced with a theosophical system of bewildering intricacy, which becomes frankly inconsistent with the advent of a series of unreliable narrators, including major ones like Bezelbob (later spirit 741), the peacock Mirabel (a transformation of 741), the hornless unicorn Uni, the angels Michael and Gabriel, and minor ones like Jesus, Buddha, and other historical and allegorical figures. There is no need here for the kind of detailed study that critics such as Ross Labrie *(James Merrill)* and Judith Moffett have devoted to the poem. An identification of the Gnostic and Jungian features of the poem will reveal the major elements that inform the poem's structure.

One of Jung's critics has summarized three features in his Gnosticism that are related to the dynamics of the unconscious mind:

> the call—from the God beyond who has nothing to do with the established theology . . . the primacy of the feminine principle and the corresponding divine child in the constitution of the world and in its redemption. . . . (Hogenson 37)

The "call" in ***Changing Light*** occurs in one of its central and most affecting passages in which "God B" (or "Biology") calls to his "brothers" in the cosmic pantheon. The call is heard by the principal members of the "seminar," JM, DJ, Wystan and Maria Mitsotáki (1907-74), the widow of a diplomat and member of a distinguished Greek family with whom DJ and JM share a deep friendship (13, 101-02). The Call is tuned to "mortal wavelength" by the fifth principle member, Mirabel:

> IVE BROTHERS HEAR ME BROTHER SIGNAL ME
> ALONE IN MY NIGHT BROTHERS DO YOU WELL

> I AND MINE HOLD IT BACK BROTHERS I AND MINE SURVIVE BROTHERS HEAR ME SIGNAL ME
>
> IN MY NIGHT I HOLD IT BACK I AND MINE SURVIVE BROTHERS SIGNAL ME IN MY NIGHT I AND MINE HOLD IT BACK AND WE SURVIVE (360)

This "Pulse of the galactic radio" that fills the void of space comes from God B, who in Wystan's phrase, is "KEEPING UP HIS NERVE ON A LIFERAFT (362), and it performs the Jungian task of enlightening the hearer. As JM remarks to Wystan, God B seems a "Far cry from the joyous Architect" (362) that Michael, the Angel of light, had described in the last lines of ***Mirabell***. The call from God B helps to correct what Jung would call the "incompleteness" of such a "God-image." The God we learn about in ***Changing Light*** belongs to a Gnostic cosmology in which "good" or positive forces barely "SURVIVE" and "HOLD BACK" the "evil" or negative forces. In relation to our earth, "2 GODS / GOVERN BIOLOGY & CHAOS" (113). But there are many more gods in this Gnostic universe. Michael as the angel of light is balanced by Gabriel, who destroyed the first two terrestrial races when they transgressed (God B could not bear to do it) and who describes himself in a Jungian phrase as "THE SHADOW OF MY FATHER" (316). In ***Scripts,*** he tells the two mediums of

> THE PANTHEON OF GALAXIES FROM WHICH OUR
> FATHER COMES, I HAVE HEARD HIS VOICE:
> 'GABRIEL, MY DARKER SIDE, THERE ARE GALAXIES, GODS AS POWERFUL
> AS I. SON GABRIEL, WE ARE WARND. WE ARE HARD PREST.'
>
> (330)

We learn nothing about the "BROTHERS OF THE PANTHEON," except that they allowed God B, the "YOUNGEST BROTHER," to shape the world on condition that he install the "MONITOR" at its heart (392). Although it is once referred to as a god, the Monitor is not one of the pantheon but appears to represent the destructive power of time. A variety of Gnostic demiurges create life on earth. For example, a race of centaurs created the bat-creatures JM met at the beginning of ***Mirabell*** and were destroyed by them—hence the bats' punishment (or "damnation" in the Christian sense) by God B. The shaping of the earth and of mankind was the work of the four angels who narrate much of ***Scripts,*** especially the first book, Michael, Gabriel, Raphael, and Emmanuel. But it was the dark angel Gabriel who gave man the spark of consciousness that transformed him from ape to human—and made him capable of the self-destruction that now threatens the race. The Monitor seems to wait upon this destruction, but there is also a God who actively opposes God B who is called God A, the Adversary. God A is a void rather than a positive evil and is related to antimatter, black holes, and the negative charge in the atom. God Biology must press back against this "insane / Presence beyond our furthest greenhouse pane" (398), but the energy needed is enormous and may be declining.

This fear is expressed in perhaps the finest lyric passage in the poem. JM and Wystan are reflecting on the strange music ("NO MELODY BUT TONE / LEVELS") that accompanied the lyrics of God B's song. When DJ says that "Dante heard that Song," Wystan asks a question that JM answers:

> WHO WD THINK THAT THE SONG HAD HAD SUCH LYRICS?
> The lyrics may be changing. Dante saw
> The rose in rose in fullest bloom. Blake saw it sick.
> You and Maria, who have seen the bleak
> Unpetalled knob, must wonder: will it last
> Till spring? Is it still rooted in the Sun?
>
> (363)

After hearing God B's song, DJ laments that their ouija sessions now "Print out in Manichaean black and white" (362). Although Evil has been redefined as negativity or a void or a black hole, it still threatens mankind's existence. God B is assisted by his "TWIN SISTER" Nature, but her concern for the earth's survival is questionable since she is both a creative and a destructive force. This balance between good and evil, creation and destruction, and positive and negative is reflected in the title of the three sections of ***Scripts:*** "Yes," "&" and "No," which are marks on the Ouija Board. In answer to the question of the survival of mankind the cup wavers throughout between the "yes" and "no," with the "and" serving as a "bridge" (362). The hope for survival is centered in the "feminine principle," but not in the figure of Nature. With the possible exception of Wystan Auden, Maria Mitsotaki is the major character in the poem, and it is the appropriately named Maria who is the reconciling and redeeming force.

We saw that Jung considered the thoughts that arose from his Unconscious as objective as "animals in a forest, or people in a room." He had a sense of the dead crowding in on him, and he wrote his early work *Septem Sermones ad Mortuous* (1916), during a mental crisis over the World War, to answer their demands and free himself from them. Hogenson believes that the return of the dead was in Jung's case a "metaphor for the explosion of the contents of the unconscious" (144). The same may be said of Merrill's encounter with the dead. The way the supernatural beings in Merrill's "salon" or "seminar" express their strangest doctrines without our losing a sense of them as characters in a developing drama of ideas is one of the triumphs of the poem. Characters like Wystan, Maria, George Cotzias, Robert Morse, and of course DJ and JM, are indeed "people in a room" who question and modify each other's ideas. As in Jung, the dead are eager to communicate with the living. Early in the poem, a host of the dead descend on the house in Stonington (22). To Merrill's surprise, the dead "all burn / To read more of this poem" (72). The dead are demanding a poem from Merrill just as they demanded the Gnostic fantasy of *Septem Sermones* from

Jung. In both cases, the dead desire instruction by means of a visionary work. As Merrill puts it, the dead see themselves "in the mirror only / Of a live mind" (105). The figure of Maria is the key to this demand from the dead for Merrill's poem as well as to the reconciliation it offers.

Merrill began ***Ephraim*** within days of hearing that Maria had died. In his interview "The Art of Poetry," Merrill describes his friendship with her as "the perfection of intimacy, light, airy, with no confessions or possessiveness—yet one would have to be Jung or Dante to foresee her role in the poem" (189). The first hint of her special role in the poem is when she appears (mirrored in DJ's and JM's imaginations)

> TRIMMED WITH EMBROIDERIES BLUE GREEN YELLOW RED
> SO LIKE THE LOVELY TITIAN IN THE FRARI
> In Venice, of the cherub-wafted Virgin
> God waits with open arms for.
>
> (257)

It is Maria's name-day, and the vision of her as the Virgin Mary suggests her mediating role between JM and the other world. Her initial role in the poem is to explain organic nature to the seminar: "MY SOUL / SPEAKS FROM WITHIN THE GREENNESS OF A BLADE OF GRASS" (388). But Wystan suspects her larger role and tells JM that she has the "SPECIFIC GRAVITY / OF A CULT FIGURE" (422). Later Maria reminds him that he once called her "'THE MUSE OF YOUR OFF-DAYS'" in a poem (**"Words for Maria"**), and he then recalls the coincidence of her death and the beginning of the poem (465). We now learn that Maria is one of the five immortal souls who cycle through earth's history insuring the creativity of the race and protecting it from destruction. It was she as Muse who inspired JM to write the trilogy and alert mankind to the life and death issues the poem raises. In her epiphany as "ALL NINE" of the muses, she is God B's "STAR TWIN" (480)—both human and divine (467).

Maria is thus the central "cult figure" in Merrill's Gnostic cosmology. She delivers the strongest defense of mankind to Gabriel and expresses the Gnostic hope for a "divine child," or in this case a race superior to the present human race. When Gabriel complains that the present race has become too curious about nuclear power and genetics, she defends mankind's Promethean drives:

> IS IT NOT THAT WE, MANKIND, MUST DO
> IMMORTAL WORK? AND WHEN HEAVEN, LIKE A LOVELY
> MINT-SCENTED FRESHENING SETTLES & EARTH BECOMES
> PARADISE, MY LORDS, WILL NOT OUT RACE OF THIEVES
> HAVE EMERGED AS THE ELDERS IN A RACE OF GODS?
> DEFENCE RESTS.
>
> (455-56)

Early in ***Mirabell***, JM is told by 741 that "THE NEXT RACE WILL BE OF GODS" (117), and Gabriel tells the scientist George Cotzias that he will be reborn as "ONE OF THIS NEW GENERATION, AN ALPHA MAN . . . " (439). Merrill seems reluctant to use this element of the Gnostic pattern, and its presence nevertheless demonstrates its strength over his imagination. He is uncomfortable with these "Alpha men" who seem to come straight out of G.B. Shaw or H.G. Wells. Concerning this new race, he tells the spirits, "No details, please":

> lest they issue from the teller's cage
> As cheap Utopian script (blurred smile of sage
> Framed by scrollwork) promising untold
> Redemption, ages hence, in fairy gold . . .
>
> (511)

Almost unwillingly, he has thus completed a version of the Gnostic myth, including the Call, the reconciliation through the feminine, and the expectation of a perfected race. The myth includes many secondary Gnostic features such as a Manichaean pantheon, creation by demiurges, and reincarnation. Bizarre as these features are, they provide the symbolic language by which Merrill releases his fears for the human race and achieves a sense of reconciliation with our fate and a hope for its positive fulfillment. Such a release of fantasy material helped to settle Jung's mind during World War I. At the conclusion of *Septem Sermones,* "the dead were silent and ascended like the smoke above the herdsman's fire . . . " (389-90). A similar release of the dead occurs at the end of ***Changing Light***.

James Merrill began his poem with the feeling that using his ouija board fantasies was an error. It was a mistake for a poet whose "downfall was 'word painting'" (4) to begin a long narrative; a mistake for a poet who strives for a sensibility "'no idea violates'" (14) to create a "seminar" in which such "great ideas" as the existence of god and the destiny of mankind are debated; and it was a mistake, or at least a lapse in taste, to plunge into Gnostic traditions: "Raw revelation typed to maximum / Illegibility" (256), as his friend Robert Morse (before he dies and joins the seminar) describes it. Out of such mistakes, and out of the fall into the dark materials of the unconscious mind, Merrill creates an image of wholeness in the figure of Maria and in many other symbolic characters, such as Wystan and Mirabel, and emblems, such as the rose and the circle. But he never forgets the incompleteness out of which the image arises (the rose is sick, the circle is a void). At the poem's conclusion, he must let the dead leave the occult world he and DJ have formed. This farewell is expressed through the imagery of breaking, which thus joins errors, lapses, and falls in one of the poem's major image clusters.

The departure of the spirits is planned at the conclusion to the first section ("Yes") of ***Scripts.*** The spirits "see" JM and DJ through a mirror that is always present at the seance. Wystan and Maria are the spirits present at this time, and JM feels that he and DJ could well be on their side of the mirror thanks to their growing intimacy. Maria then warns him that when the "lessons" are finished, he must break the mirror and let them go. JM's and DJ's shocked reaction to this news is clear from Auden's "—IDIOTS DRY YR EYES" (364). When Maria suggests that it might be a gentler farewell if the ritual of departure used water poured out into a plant. JM disagrees because "The poem's logic . . . Calls for the shattering of a glass" (364). The glass recalls the epigraph of ***Scripts*** from Proust's *Jean Santeuil,* in which the breaking of a vase is interpreted as a good omen, like the shattering of a glass at a Jewish wedding: "'Ce sera comme au temple le symbole de l'indestructible union'" (278).[5] In a valuable study of "interruption" in ***Changing Light,*** Willard Spiegelman finds another allusion to Jewish culture in the shattering of the glass: "For Harold Bloom, reflecting on the cosmology of the Kabbalah and finding in the schemes of Isaac Luria and others a prototype for literary tradition, all acts of creation are catastrophes, broken vessels . . . " (222). The "breaking of the vessels" is not only a metaphor for what happens in Merrill's poem; it is also a final, masterly statement of the poem's Gnostic vision.

Like orthodox Christianity, the Talmudic tradition rejected Gnosticism and did not dwell on the problem of evil. As Bloom observes, however, "the true dark heart of Kabbalah [is] its vision of the problem of evil," and this is particularly true in the Kabbalism of Isaac Luria, which learned much from Gnosticism's engagement with "evil as the reality of this world" (*Kabbalah* 37). Bloom's study of the Kabbalah draws on the scholarship of Gershom Scholem, who describes the breaking of the vessels which occurred when God's light entered the ten vessels he formed to manifest His being:

> The divine light entered these vessels in order to take forms appropriate to their function in creation, but the vessels could not contain the light and thus were broken. . . . The light was dispersed. Much of it returned to its source; some portions, or "sparks," fell downward and were scattered, some rose upward. (*Messianic Ideal,* 45)

According to Scholem, Lurianic Kabbalism particularly reveals Gnostic influence in the speculation that the *"Kelipot,"* or forces of evil, existed before the breaking and were mixed with the light of God's emanations: "What really brought about the fracture of the vessels was the necessity of cleansing the elements of the Sefiroth by eliminating the *Kelipot,* in order to give a real existence and separate identity to the power of evil" (*Jewish Mysticism,* 267). Even though the vessels are reduced into fragments or "shards," the shattering is a purifying act (Bloom, *Kabbalah,* 43, 85). Still another unorthodox and Gnostic element of Kabbalism in this late tradition was the belief that the sparks of holiness which fell into human souls pass through various forms: "transmigration was not an appendage but an inextricable basic element. Transmigration, too, symbolized the state of the unamended world, the confusion of the orders of creation . . . " (*Messianic Idea,* 47).

The concepts of the breaking of the vessels, catharsis, and transmigration are all crucial to understanding the breaking of the mirror at the end of ***Scripts.*** Throughout sections two and three of ***Scripts,*** the changes of the moon bring us closer to the moment when JM and DJ must release the spirits. Maria appoints the time as three days after a new moon. At DJ's suggestion, they will break the mirror into a bowl of water and pour it over a cassia bush that Maria discovered and which still blooms on JM's terrace in Athens. The bowl, "brimming with water, / Lobs an ellipse of live brilliance" (515), which recalls the elliptical shape of the new moon and the pattern of the letters on the ouija board as well as anticipating the shapes of the fragmented glass. JM will speak the ritual words and break the mirror into the cup that DJ holds, which will then be poured into the golden branches of the cassia bush:

> Our eyes meet. DJ nods. We've risen. Shutters
> Click at dreamlike speed. Sky. Awning. Bowl.
> The stylus lifted. Giving up its whole
> Lifetime of images, the mirror utters
> A little treble shriek and rides the flood
> Or tinkling mini-waterfall through wet
> Blossoms to lie—and look the sun has set—
> In splinters apt, from now on, to draw blood,
> Each with its scimitar or bird-beak shape
> Able, days hence, aglitter in the boughs
> Or face-down, black on soil beneath, to rouse
> From its deep swoon the undestroyed heartscape
> —Then silence.
>
> (517)

The elliptical phrasing in the first three lines is appropriate to a ritual of shattering in which a virtual lifetime is lost in an instant or the snap of shutter. Much earlier, in section "V" of ***Ephraim,*** JM recalled that he was lucky when he lost his camera during a tour: "Never again / To overlook a subject for its image, / To labor images till they yield a subject . . . " (76). The implied poetics of these lines helps us understand Merrill's ambition (as it was Ezra Pound's) to write a long poem that would be more than a "batch of images" (75). But now that the poem is finished he reminds us, as Yeats did in "The Phases of the Moon," that poetry is "mere images." Although they are fragments, the pieces of the mirror assume recognizable shapes of "scimitar" or "bird-beak" that can recall their friends and reopen the wound of their loss. The shattering is thus, as JM notes, like Prospero's burying of his rod and freeing of Caliban and Ariel.

But is it a loss? Like the Kabbalistic shattering of the vessels, the shattering of the mirror is a beginning as well as an end. It signifies the "Giving up" of a "whole lifetime of images" in the creation of a poem. The marble wedge, which was merely a door stop, now becomes a "stylus" which frees images through writing. In signifying the departure of his friends, it also reminds us that the transmigration of their spirits has begun again as Maria becomes an Indian religious leader (there is more about her new life in the poem's "Coda," 526-28), George Cotzias a scientist who will be the first of a new race, Robert Morse a great composer, and Wystan (with the whimsicality that always surrounds his character) one with the kind of landscape

("A CLIFF? A BEACH?") celebrated in his poetry. The freeing of the spirits has the cathartic quality Luria gave to it in which the "shards" assume a separate existence. Using the Kabbalistic word, Maria applies it in this case to forces of good:

> SEND OUR IMAGINED SELVES
> FALLING IN SHARDS THRU THE ETERNAL WATERS
> (DJ CUPBEARER) & INTO THE GOLDEN BOUGH
> OF MYTH ON INTO LIFE
>
> (516)

The last two quatrains of the poem turn from the shards, "face-down, black on soil beneath," to thoughts of the early race of centaurs and the present one of mankind. The first of these quatrains is a conditional clause that is suspended into the first line of the second quatrain's allusion to Dante and then broken off by God B's signal, which is itself broken off.

> —Then silence. Then champagne.
> And should elsewhere
> Broad wings revolve a horselike form into
> One Creature upward-shining brief as dew,
> Swifter than bubbles in wine, through evening air
> Up, far up, O whirling point of light—:
> HERS HEAR ME I AND MINE SURVIVE SIGNAL
> ME DO YOU WELL I ALONE IN MY NIGHT
> HOLD IT BACK HEAR ME BROTHERS I AND MINE
>
> (517)

The divine order of Dante's cosmos proceeds from the "whirling point of light" that he sees in Canto XXVIII of the *Paradisio.* Merrill's universe has no such center. God B's message, which reaches us only in an elliptical form, is merely that "I AND MINE" . . . hold back the void. Nothing within the passage allows us to interpret the "HERS" that begins the signal, but we may assume that it acknowledges Maria's benign influence. Merrill's universe is like the broken vessels, fragmented and seeking wholeness.

If Rimbaud "ghostwrote" Eliot's *The Waste Land,* as we are told in ***Mirabell***, then we may say that Eliot at least co-authored ***The Changing Light at Sandover.*** Eliot later repudiated his fascination with mysticism and the occult with what he called "the reformed drunkard's abhorrence of intemperance" (261). At the time of *The Waste Land,* however, he longed for beliefs or myths that were still vital after the manifest death of a Christian civilization in World War I. The Tarot and various rituals of death and rebirth were, in the language of *The Waste Land,* a "heap of broken images"; but they were also for him "fragments I have shored against my ruins." Like Merrill, he fashioned from occultism a phantasmagoria of images that is unforgettable as poetry however suspect as orthodox belief. As we have seen, Merrill himself is suspicious of his subject matter. The poem is a "fall" or "lapse," and the images it gives us fragments of a "great tradition that has come to grief." The organizations of Eliot's and Merrill's poems seem haphazard—one structured around a Tarot pack, the other around a Ouija Board. But in both Eliot and Merrill the occult myth or counter-tradition provides a psychologically satisfying context for their images.

In length, of course, Merrill's poem seems closer to *The Cantos* than *The Waste Land.* Pound's epic is also a journey or periplum without an "Aquinas map" in search of beliefs that might vitalize a culture. But the weakness of Pound's great poem, in comparison with Eliot's and Merrill's, is that too many ideas, drawn from any number of disciplines and cultures, are presented with a bitter certainty about their truth or falsity. Eliot's relative detachment in *The Waste Land* seems preferable, even though it is a measure of his despair; and Merrill's ability to mock the weirdness of his ideas while still drawing on their imagistic power (an ability he shares with Yeats) seems better still. We can see Merrill's ironic stance toward his subject matter in Gabriel's description, late in the poem, of

> THAT DEFERENTIAL & RELIEVED AWARENESS GIVEN
> TO HIS EX-BOSS BY A FORMER EMPLOYEE
> OR BY THE POET TO A USED IDEA.
>
> (553)

The ideas in ***Changing Light*** are no less incoherent or fragmented than those in *The Waste Land* and *The Cantos.* But the charming and often humorous scenes Merrill creates of friends debating occult doctrines not only gives the poem its reassuring ironic tone but also a dramatic interest that is Merrill's unique achievement in the modern long poem.

Merrill shows how conscious he is of inheriting a challenge equal to the one that faced the Eliot/Pound generation in his foreward to a recent book of verse:

> If World War I caused, as we hear tell, the total cave-in of civilization except where it glinted in the minds of writers like Valéry and Joyce, the problem of later generations has been to create works whose resonance would last for more than a season. ("Foreword," xi)

Caught in this "cave-in," Merrill recreates out of its darkness, and from traditions that were once discredited or lost, a Gnostic myth for what he describes as a "myth starved culture" ("Art of Poetry," 32). Admittedly he has erred, but in this case one may recall Stephen Dedalus's conviction that the errors of an artist are "the portals of discovery" (Joyce, 190). Both Freud and Jung saw intimate revelations in errors. Like a dream, the error carries the message from the unconscious mind. For the dreamer or the person who errs, Freud says, "the only question is how to make it possible for him to discover his knowledge and communicate it to us" (*Introductory Lectures* 104-05). In ***The Changing Light at Sandover,*** Merrill communicates a myth that he discovers deep within his own mind through a "lapse that tides us over . . . home away from home" (74).

Notes

1. Paul de Man's *Blindness & Insight* analyzes the creativity of error, as is indicated in the book's epigraph from Proust, which is also appropriate to Merrill's work: "*Cette perpetuelle erreur, qui est precisement la 'vie'*. . . . "

2. In section "S" of "The Book of Ephraim" ("S" for Stevens in part), Merrill cites the passage in Wallace Stevens' "Final Soliloquy of the Interior Paramour" which states (or almost does) that " . . . God and the imagination are one." The reference to Stevens indicates Merrill's ambition to extend the power of his imagination into the "other world." The citation of Jung is to the passage in his autobiography in which he says that "I am aware that 'mana,' and 'God' are synonyms for the unconscious . . . (337)." Merrill may also be alluding to the temptation of Christ by the Devil (Matthew 4:6) in the reference to a "fall / from a high building." A more important biblical allusion is to story of Israel's blessing of Ephraim (the name of Merrill's familiar spirit) in Genesis 48: 13-22. Israel (mistakenly, according to his son Joseph) reverses the order in which Ephraim and Manaseh are brought to him and puts his right hand upon Ephraim—placing him above his first-born son, Manaseh. The mistake as well as the mirror-like reversal from left to right are relevant to the themes of Merrill's poem.

3. The orthodox Freudian may well disapprove of Merrill's Jungian approach to his subject, as Harold Bloom does when he refers to Merrill's use of "troublesome and in-authentic" sources "such as Dr. Carl Gustav Jung" (Bloom, *James Merrill,* 1). As Jacques Lacan has observed, the contemporary Freudian conception of the unconscious "is not at all the romantic unconscious of imaginative creation. It is not the locus of the divinities of night. This locus is no doubt not entirely unrelated to the locus towards which Freud turns his gaze—but the fact that Jung, who provides a link with the terms of the romantic unconscious, should have been repudiated by Freud, is sufficient indication that psychoanalysis is introducing something other (24)." This "something other" has little room for the strange "divinities of the night" which inhabit Merrill's poem. Lacan believes that Freudian "research into the unconscious moves, on the contrary, in the direction of a certain desiccation." We instinctively turn away from the world of "spiritist, invocatory, necromantic practice . . . of what, in the construction of the Gnostics, are called the intermediary beings—sylphs, gnomes, and even higher forms of these ambiguous mediators." But Merrill has not turned away.

4. Ehrenpreis's criticism of Merrill's Gnosticism recalls Shaun's facile dismissal of Shem in *Finnegans Wake* (170:11) as a "gnawstick." Harold Bloom calls Merrill a "curious kind of religious poet, 'curious' because the religion is a variety of Gnosticism . . . " But despite his discomfort with the poem's ideas, he readily admits the poetic genius revealed in its three books: "They *are* miracles of poetic achievement, and if I call them 'spurious' I only confess my own bewilderment or startled skepticism at being confronted by a contemporary Dante or Blake who follows Victor Hugo and Yeats by spending thousands of evenings at the Ouija Board in touch with alarmingly familiar spirits" (Bloom, *James Merrill,* 1). In *American Poetry and Culture,* Robert von Hallberg has an excellent account (113-15) of the uneasy critical reception of Merrill's trilogy and a description of his own reservations about the poem.

5. Freud refers to this custom in *The Psychopathology of Everyday Life:* "Recently we passed through a period in my house during which an unusually large amount of glass and china crockery was broken; I myself was responsible for some of the damage. But the little psychical epidemic could easily be explained; these were the days before my eldest daughter's wedding. . . . This custom may have the significance of a sacrifice and it may have another symbolic meaning as well" (173).

Works Cited

Bloom, Harold. *The Anxiety of Influence: A Theory of Poetry.* New York: Oxford U. Pr., 1973.

———, ed. *James Merrill.* New York: Chelsea House, 1985.

———. *Kabbalah and Criticism.* New York: Seabury, 1975.

de Man, Paul. *Blindness and Insight: Essays in the Rhetoric of Contemporary Criticism.* New York: Oxford, 1971.

Ehrenpreis, Irvin. "Otherworldly Goods." *The New York Review of Books* 22, January 1981: 48.

Eliot, T.S. "A.R. Orage." *The Criterion,* January 1935: 260-261.

———. "A Commentary." *The Criterion,* 14 January 1935: 260-64.

Freud, Sigmund. *Introductory Lectures on Psychoanalysis,* trans. James Strachey. New York: Norton, 1977.

———. *Psychopathology of Everyday Life.* Trans. A.A. Brill. New York: Macmillan, 1915.

Hogenson, George B. *Jung's Struggle With Freud.* Notre Dame: U of Notre Dame P, 1983.

Joyce, James. *Ulysses.* New York: Vintage, 1961.

Jung, C.J. *Memories, Dreams, Reflections,* recorded and edited by Aniela Jaffe; trans. Richard and Clara Winston. New York: Vintage, 1965.

———. "Septem Sermones ad Mortuos (1916)." Jung 378-90.

Kenner, Hugh. "Poetize or Bust." *Harper's Magazine,* September 1983: 67-70.

Labrie, Ross. *James Merrill.* Boston: Twayne, 1982.

———. "James Merrill at Home: An Interview." *Arizona Quarterly* 38 (1982): 19-36.

Lacan, Jacques. *The Four Fundemental Concepts of Psychoanalysis,* trans. Alan Sheridan. London: Hogarth Pr., 1977.

Merrill, James. "the Art of Poetry XXXI." *The Paris Review* 24, Summer 1982: 185-219.

———. *The Changing Light at Sandover, Including the Whole of The Book of Ephraim, Mirabell's Books of Number, Scripts for the Pageant and a new coda, The Higher Keys.* New York: Atheneum, 1984.

———. "Foreword." Pamela Alexander, *Navigable Waterways.* New Haven: Yale UP, 1985. ix-xiii.

———. *From the First Nine: Poems 1946-76.* New York: Atheneum, 1984.

———. "The Grand Canyon." *Water Street,* 14-15.

———. "The House." *From the First Nine,* 35-36.

———. "Peru: The Landscape Game." *Prose,* Spring 1971: 105-14.

———. *Water Street.* New York: Atheneum, 1980.

———. "An Urban Convalescence." *Water Street,* 3-6.

———. "The Will." *From the First Nine,* 339-45.

———. "Words for Maria." *From the First Nine,* 177-79.

Pound, Ezra. *Selected Letters: 1907-1941.* New York: New Directions, 1971.

Scholem, Gershom. *Major Trends in Jewish Mysticism.* New York: Schocken, 1941.

———. *The Messianic Idea in Judaism.* New York: Schocken, 1971.

Spiegelman, Willard. "Breaking the Mirror: Interruption in Merrill's Trilogy." Eds. David Lehman and Charles Berger. *James Merrill: Essays in Criticism.* Ithaca: Cornell UP, 1983. 186-210.

von Hallbereg, Robert. *American Poetry and Culture: 1945-80.* Cambridge: Harvard, 1985.

Helen Vendler (review date 1995)

SOURCE: "Chronicles of Love and Loss," in *New York Review of Books*, Vol. XLII, No. 8, May 11, 1995, pp. 46-51.

[*In the following review of Merrill's final poetry collection, Vendler investigates the retrospective verse of* A Scattering of Salts.]

James Merrill, who died on February 6 of this year, gave his last volume the title ***A Scattering of Salts***. In such a phrase there are overtones of tears, savors, and fragrances, yet with a clear implication, too, that these astringent crystals are scattered at intervals in the diffuse and oceanic medium of life. Merrill, for all the poignancy of his work, was a comic poet in the line of Pope and Byron and Auden; and from the very beginning of his long career, the poems he published combined, in sparkling ways, suffering and joy.

The son of the financier Charles E. Merrill of Merrill, Lynch, he spent his life after Lawrenceville and Amherst largely on his writing, teaching briefly now and then. Though he experimented with short plays and with novel—*The Seraglio* (1957) and *The (Diblos) Notebook* (1965)—and wrote essays (collected in *Recitative,* 1986) and a memoir (*A Different Person,* 1993), his reputation rests chiefly on his poetry. In succession he published ***First Poems*** (1951), ***The Country of a Thousand Years of Peace*** (1959), ***Water Street*** (1962), ***Nights and Days*** (1966), ***The Fire Screen*** (1969), ***Braving the Elements*** (1972), ***Divine Comedies*** (1976), ***Mirabell: Books of Number*** (1978), and ***Scripts for the Pageant*** (1980). The last three, with a coda added, were collected as a trilogy called ***The Changing Light at Sandover*** (1982). Subsequently there appeared ***Late Settings*** (1985) and ***The Inner Room*** (1988). Now, with ***A Scattering of Salts,*** twentieth-century American poetry marks the loss of a radiant and moving voice.

1.

Merrill's poems—his "chronicles of love and loss," as he called them—are often autobiographical; they tell the story of a child of divorced parents who grew up to discover himself intelligent, talented, and homosexual. "When it came to sex," he remarked in an interview, "I had to face it that the worst iniquity my parents (and many of my friends) could imagine was for me a blessed source of pleasure and security—as well as suffering, to be sure." His readers followed his life in Greece, Stonington, Connecticut, and Key West; they encountered, with some disbelief, the Ouija-board experiments with his companion, David Jackson, that gave rise to an epic trilogy; they read elegies for one dead friend after another: Hans Lodeizen, Maria Mitsotáki, David Kalstone, Howard Moss. As Merrill scattered references to family, lovers, friends, and fellow poets through the poetry—to his mother and father, David Jackson, Peter Hooten, W.H. Auden, Robert Morse, Donald Keene—it was easy for readers to assume that they knew about his life as well as his art. In fact, the apparent candor of the poems was their most disarming quality. Knowing how much of any poet's experience is altered, how much is unused, in his work, we can be sure that biography will eventually alter our perception of Merrill's life. What biography cannot alter is the poetry, which takes on an independent existence as the poet's life ends.

In the new volume, Merrill gives on almost every page the impression of looking back over the past, both as he lived it and as he wrote about it. ***A Scattering of Salts*** is an elegiac book, but one written in an ultimately comic spirit, with a Mozartian resolution into hope: Merrill's reprise of his life prompts a sense of renewal. In the moment of musical or literary reprise, one is conscious that some act or episode is returning, in life or in memory, defeating the putative uniqueness of original experience. Or, at least, one fears that with repetition the original experience may become decreasingly vivid. "After the first death," says Dylan Thomas, "there is no other." For the comic poet, however, the second and third and fourth loves, or disappointments, or even deaths are not merely the recurrences of the first; they also offer pieces of dry instruction.

What does love seem like when one takes it up (as has been said about second marriages) in the triumph of hope over experience? Or, to use another example from Merrill, what is it to see the entire *Ring* again at the Met late in life after having been transfigured by it, at twelve, in 1939? These are some of the questions that preoccupy ***A Scattering of Salts.***

The lyric tradition is full of the poetry of reprise, from the most joyous (the reunion of lovers and the repetition of their *basia mille*) to the most tragic, when exhausted memory edges toward meaninglessness. Between the joyous and the tragic lay Merrill's own sense of suffused regret, of wry irony, of mortal awareness of mistake, of reluctantly acknowledged gains, and of comically presented new adventures. As he reached an age of increasingly frequent retrospection, Merrill found himself caught, one might say, in the poetry of recall; and with his compulsion toward perfecting forms to express different nuances of feeling, he looked to tradition but also struck out on his own, writing poems of a tonal variety unmatched by almost all of his predecessors except Byron and Auden. This command of tonality takes, in ***A Scattering of Salts,*** the full measure of the oblique sadness of comic recollection.

For contrast's sake, I recall an earlier, simpler, reprise, an incomparably touching poem called **"The House Fly,"** published in ***Late Settings***. Merrill's Greek lover, hitherto known in his poems only by his first name, Strato, is in **"The House Fly"** given his inescapably absurd (in English lyric) full name, Strato Mouflouzélis. And yet (says the poem) how one cherished love, how one cherishes even the increasingly memorial quality of its anniversary; and how one rises, although wearily, to reconstruct that memory.

THE HOUSE FLY
Come October, if I close my eyes,
A self till then subliminal takes flight
Buzzing round me, settling upon the knuckle,
The lip to be explored not as in June
But with a sense verging on micromania
Of wrong, of tiny, hazy, crying wrongs
Which quite undo her—look at that zigzag totter,
Proboscis blindly tapping like a cane.
Gone? If so, only to re-alight
Or else in a stray beam resume the grand toilette
(Eggs of next year's mischief long since laid):
Unwearying strigils taken to the frayed,
Still glinting wings; the dull-red lacquer head
Lifted from its socket, turned mechanically
This way and that, like a wrist-watch being wound,
As if there would always be time . . .
Downstairs in this same house one summer night,
Founding the cult, her ancestress alit
On the bare chest of Strato Mouflouzélis
Who stirred in the lamp-glow but did not wake.
To say so brings it back on every autumn
Feebler wings, and further from that Sun,
That mist-white wafer she and I partake of
Alone this afternoon, making a rite
Distinct from both the blessing and the blight.

In this remarkable variation of the myth of Cupid and Psyche, the sleeping love god is the boy with the ridiculous name, and the cultic goddess is reduced from a butterfly to a house fly. One could say, thinking only of the transformed myth, that the poem is ironic—and so it is. Its reduction of the psychic Muse to a tottering, wronged, blind creature is hardly less than tragic; yet she is still capable of her grand toilette, and therefore no less possessed than formerly of *élan vital.*

The second myth informing the poem is that of the real presence of Jesus in the sacrament of the Lord's Supper, the rite of partaking in the body of Christ, signifying the impotence of death and the reality of transcendence. The "rite" of art—another recovery of a real presence—is, like the rite of Communion, distinct from both the "blessing" of incarnation and the "blight" of death, the blessing of love and its blighting by time. Placing his own rite somewhere between comedy and tragedy, Merrill preserves for it, in this beautiful poem, its own space, which, while painfully inflected by "real" house flies and proper names, keeps its memory impregnable.

The formal daring of the poem—evoking the memory of an affair with Strato through the Keatsian image of Psyche on the one hand, and the Christian sacrament of real presence on the other—betokens a confidence not only that the great myths, classical and Christian, apply to homosexual lovers, but also a confidence that love, as it is remembered, retains erotic and even religious grandeur in spite of its inexorable decline, as it returns "on every autumn/ Feebler wings, and further from [the] Sun."

Much more could be said about **"The House Fly,"** Merrill's ode to autumn, its house fly a direct descendant of Keats's gnats. But taking it as a model of one sort of reprise poem, I want to look at the different attitudes toward the past in ***A Scattering of Salts*** (a book dedicated to Merrill's most inspired commentator, the poet and critic Stephen Yenser). The conventional lyric image for a return welcomed without ambivalence is sunrise. Shakespeare: "For as the sun is daily new and old, /So is my love, still telling what is told"; and Stevens: "The oldest newest day is the newest alone." In the first poem of ***A Scattering of Salts,*** the poet, recollecting the love that moves the sun and the other stars, and imagining himself in a cosmic bath looked down on by that love, says,

On high, the love
That drew the bath and scattered it with salts
Still radiates new projects old as day.

The sun is the only creator without ambivalence about the daily recurrence of his daily project. The human author, addressing his reader, has considerably more mixed feelings about literary recurrence, since his new book depends on so many old themes. Never has the daily cosmological reprise—life itself—been more wryly described by an author:

To the reader

Each day, hot off the press from Moon & Son,
"Knowing of your continued interest,"
Here's a new book—well, actually the updated
Edition of their one all-time best seller—
To find last night's place in, and forge ahead.
If certain scenes and situations ("work,"
As the jacket has it, "of a blazingly
Original voice") make you look up from your page
—But this is life, is truth, is me!—*too many*
Smack of self-plagiarism. Terror and tryst,
Vow and verbena, done before, to death,
In earlier chapters, under different names . . .
You'd like to think a structure will emerge,
If only a kind of Joycean squirrel run
Returning us all neatly to page I,
But the inconsistencies of plot and style
Lead you to fear that, for this author, fiction
Aims at the cheap effect, "stranger than fiction,"
As people once thought life—no, truth *was. Strange*
. . .
Anyhow, your final thought tonight,
Before you kiss my picture and turn the light out,
Is of a more exemplary life begun
Tomorrow, truer, harder to get right.

The sweetness of the past, still evident in **"The House Fly"** has, at the beginning of **"To the Reader,"** been almost totally erased. Recurrence is now merely an "updated" edition of God's favorite fiction, life, continually erased in one set of characters and reissued in another. Or reprise, considered as a tradition, is merely a set of literary conventions ("Terror and tryst, / Vow and verbena") done to death. Or, as self-repetition, it simply has become "self-plagiarism." At best, it may participate in the "squirrel run" of the Viconian and Joycean recursions of *Finnegans Wake.*

If truth and life are not "stranger than fiction," if they are not capable of invention, then indeed "turn the light out." But in a surprising ending, Merrill's aesthetic revulsion turns into an ethical command. What is demanded of the reader, and by implication of the author, too, is not reprise but purposeful advance—toward a more exemplary life "begun tomorrow." Countering the honeyed, if weary, appeal of elegiac repetition in **"The House Fly," "To the Reader"** veers sharply from its initial cynicism to a more energetic demand, prompted by the imagined presence of the reader, for the new and the true. (The envisaged relation between reader and writer, one of affection, will strike readers of this posthumous volume with a pang, now that the light of Merrill's verse has been extinguished.)

In itself, the "once again" of late-life recall is harmless, but it is valued differently depending on its effect. When it threatens the loss of all newness, it can be dully horrifying. Yet when it evokes an episode of youth, it can be revivifying: as Merrill returns to rent the house in Athens he once lived in, he comments, "Thrilling to find oneself again on stage, /In character, at this untender age"; and he suggests, by calling his Athens poem **"Nine Lives,"** that he, like the kitten in the poem, may be less fragile than he seems.

Still, his dearest hope in the poem—to see in reincarnated form his dead friend Maria Mitsotáki—is frustrated. Though he returns, encouraged by his Ouija-board spirit Ephraim, to a familiar café ("the Bon Goût, where we always met Maria"), the poet not only finds everything in the café itself changed, but is also deprived of the longed-for encounter. The "always" of memory becomes "never again." And Strato the once-beloved is now a fearful sight: "Old troupers reemerge: / . . . from oblivion's verge/ Strato himself, whose bloodshot eyes (once green) / And immense bulk confound the dramaturge." This distanced way of describing the recent encounter with Strato is later corrected: Merrill, attempting to catch a kitten, loses it, and comments, seeing the grief of the mother cat,

From being human we grow inhumane.
We have, it seems, methodically wrecked
Her world. Analogies are rife and various
To worlds like Strato's, now disaster areas
We helped create.

By and large, the return to Greece is bleak. Merrill concedes (in a passage alluding to Elizabeth Bishop's "Over 2,000 Illustrations") that he had hoped for renewal but has been disappointed:

Like Wise Men we'd been primed to kneel in awe
At journey's end before that child whose nature
Proved Earth at one with Heaven, and past with future.
Instead, the perfect fools we still are saw
A manger full of emptiness, dust, straw . . .

It seems that perfect renewals—a reincarnation of Maria Mitsotáki or the incarnation of the new Adam in Jesus—are impossible. Yet the desire for reincarnation always persists; even the shades in Hades, says Merrill in **"Volcanic Holiday,"**

subsist
On one idea—returning.
Generation after generation
The spirit grapples, tattered butterfly,
A flower in sexual costume,
Hardon or sheath dew-fired. Our feet
At noon seek paths the evening rain degrades.

In yet another poem, **"Alabaster,"** inspection of a semi-transparent slice of skin under a microscope becomes, under the magnification of pitiless memory, only a "pious autopsy," the visual recall of painful past experiences:

And if a tissue-thin
Section of self lay on a lighted slide,

And a voice breathed in your ear,
"Yes, ah yes. That red oxide
Stain is where your iron, Lady Hera,
Entered him.
And in this corner, boldly intricate
As agate, zigzagging
Bays and salients—plans of a fortress?—date
From his twentieth spring,
When we had set the dials at First Love.
Up here's the opalescent fossil of—
Dream on. Dodo and roc
Did without your pious autopsies.
Nor will the self resist,
Broken on terror like a rack,
When waves of nightmare heat decrystallize
Her lucid molecules to chalk.

When the alabaster of Merrill's title decomposes under heat, its chemical composition degenerates: it loses its crystalline form, and turns to chalk. We are expected, I think, to recall this instance of deathly decrystallizing when we meet, in the last poem of ***A Scattering of Salts,*** the intense and satisfying "recrystallizing" of the evening star into the morning star.

In the most allusive of his reprise poems, **"Snow Jobs,"** Merrill writes a *Ballade des Hommes du Temps Jadis.* Though he is in one way glad that the snows—and snow jobs—of yesteryear are gone for good, he still has affection for his memories, even for his recollections of corrupt politics and politicians, collected in a comic list:

Where's Teapot Dome? Where's the Iran
Contra Affair? Where's Watergate—
Liddy—Magruder—Erlichman?
Their shoes squeaked down the Halls of State,
Whole networks groaned beneath their weight,
Till spinster Clotho darted near
To shroud in white a running mate.
Ah, where's the slush of yesteryear?

Even crimes have in refrain a charm they lacked in actuality.

When memories come closer to home, Merrill finds himself living in a Chirico landscape of what Hopkins called "the ruins of wrecked past purpose": "Here's a window onto a world of moonlit / Cubes and arches in ruins, populated by cats." In some moods, however, worse than recall is the incapacity for it, the forgetting of the past; in a dream retold in the poem "Novelettes," Merrill and two friends experience an episode of time travel in which the one souvenir and proof of the event—a fan kept by his companion—"falls from her sash, through cloud-shreds, past retrieval." It is art that brings us, as Whitman said, "retrievements out of the night"; without it the past is past retrieval.

And yet the image of "retrieving," Merrill thinks, is not really accurate; much of the time, the past seems rather to retrieve us. In an instant, writing can enable the leaping into the present of the irrepressible vitality of the past. In a consciously Yeatsian trimeter poem called **"My Father's Irish Setters,"** Merrill asks, calling the dogs by name,

Dead lo! these forty winters?
Not so. Tonight in perfect
Lamplit stillness begin
With updraft from the worksheet,
Leapings and tongues, far-shining
Hearths of our hinterland: . . .
Dear clan of Ginger and Finn,
As I go through your motions
(As they go through me, rather)
Love follows, pen in hand.

In such a moment, the difference between present and past is almost erased, and the resuscitated images arrive with a force that seems external to the poet's mind.

Later in the volume, the poet issues a **"Press Release,"** which tells us, in the third person, that he has been horrified by a glance at his awakened self in the mirror:

Buzzed awake, he turns
The light on—ah, how old! Who could have envisioned
Twenty years' loneliness, ill health, wrong turnings?

Yet in a book on evolution he finds encouragement to hope for a more positive reprise of the moral life on a deeper or higher level:

He opens a book, squinting to clear his vision:
"Against such dark views, Nature's best provision
Remains the tendency of certain organisms
Long on the verge of extinction to return
At depths or altitudes they had once been unfitted
To endure . . . "

The next day, Carnival arrives to plunge him once more into disgust at repetition:

this scene's
Flats and floats trundled out over the years had come
To seem less touching.

Nonetheless, taking Nature's advice, the poet decides to try a new beginning in altitudes he had once been "unfitted to endure":

So let us not
Act like children. These are the Alps. High time
For the next deep breath. My hand. Hold. Concen-
trate.

This is the heroic hope always arising to counter the staleness of life—that if there is no child in the manger, no returned Maria, there remain, in Wordsworth's Alpine words, "Effort, and expectation, and desire, /And something evermore about to be." This romantic ascent—the assent to romance—is here assumed to be conceivable till death, as when, in the poem **"Pledge,"** Merrill toasts a divorcing couple, assuring them that their future experience may contain, like his own, a lucky finding of renewed love:

"You who have drained dry
Your golden goblet are about to learn—
As in my turn
Have I—
How life, unsweetened, fizzing up again
Fills the heart.
I drink to you apart
In that champagne."

Such hope of "fizzing up again" still avoids the moment of death, in which two impersonal forces meet—one of dread at life's stopping and the other of joy at evolutionary renewal. This moment finds its epigram in Merrill in a poem entitled, after Stevens, by a serial name ("Vol. XLIV, No. 3"), suggesting a magazine that has perhaps gone on too long. To represent perfection at the moment of its extinction, Merrill juxtaposes a Christian Christmas crèche to a pagan Christmas tree:

Dread? It crows for joy in the manger.
Joy? The tree sparkles on which it will die.

In **"164 East 72nd Street,"** Merrill recounts replacing the old windows with new ones in the New York City apartment which he inherited from his grandmother. The apartment is full of the poet's memories of "things as they were." Yet "what remains/Exactly as it was except those panes?" (The play on "pains" can't be ignored.) And now the window panes are to be changed, along with the kind of life Merrill has been leading. A new monogamous regimen—one amounting to a second childhood, "once more good as gold"—is to blot out the purple past:

Our *life is turning into a whole new story:*
Juices, blue cornbread, afternoons at the gym—
Imagine who remembers how to swim!
Evenings of study, or intensive care
For one another. Early to bed. . . .

. . . . .

Things done in purple light before we met,
Uncultured things that twitched as on a slide
If thought about, fade like dreams. Two Upper East
Side
Boys again! Rereading Sir Walter Scott
Or Through the Looking Glass, it's impossible not
To feel how adult life, with its storms and follies,
Is letting up, leaving me ten years old,
Trustful, inventive, once more good as gold . . .

The distance between the Words-worthian Alpine ascent in **"Press Release"** and this willed obliteration of the troubled past in the service of a regressive innocence is the most convincing proof that the poetry of reprise gave an intense impetus to Merrill's powers of imagination. And to his literary memory as well: the last image of reprise in ***A Scattering of Salts*** is the one most conspicuously traditional—Sappho's evening star which is the morning star, Tennyson's "sweet Hesper-Phosphor" of *In Memoriam.* Wallace Stevens, from whom Merrill drew so much, internalized the star as the oldest poetic symbol of renewal:

to say of the evening star,
The most ancient light in the most ancient sky,
That it is wholly an inner light, that it shines
From the sleepy bosom of the real, re-creates,
Searches a possible for its possibleness.

Merrill, in what may now seem a consciously valedictory poem, **"An Upward Look,"** closes ***A Scattering of Salts*** with the hope that, as he watches the evening star become the morning star, he may find the clue to the mixed sadness and joy of recurrence in the cosmos:

halves of a clue
approach the earthlights Morning star
evening star salt of the sky
First the grave dissolving into dawn
then the crucial recrystallizing
from inmost depths of clear dark blue

Dissolving, the salt of life enters at death into the inorganic chemical solution that, in its recrystallized form, constitutes once again the physical basis of existence. As salt becomes star, the fear, resentment, disgust, and terror occasioned by death and the grave find a classically poised formula that is bearable to the imagination.

2.

In sketching the range of Merrill's imaginative responses to the inescapable process of looking back into the past, I have said little about his formal means, such as the recurrence of "re-" words—from "re-alight" in **"The House Fly"** to the final one, "recrystallizing." We find in ***A Scattering of Salts*** countless other words of recurrence such as "once again" or "the seasons' round" or "anew." There are also the invokings of traditional images, from the Psyche myth to the Wordsworthian mountain ascent, from the *Ring* cycle to the morning star. And Merrill also alludes to prosodic forms of recurrence, from the ballade refrain of **"Snow Jobs"** to the repetition, in **"Volcanic Holiday,"** of identical rhyme in seven seven-lined stanzas—reminiscent of George Herbert's "Sunday." Such devices show that Merrill was always conscious of the support given to a theme by form.

Two poems about Wagner's *Ring* cycle—**"Matinees,"** an eight-section sonnet sequence published in 1969, and **"The Ring Cycle,"** a six-section sequence of fifteen-line quasi sonnets in ***A Scattering of Salts***—show how brilliantly Merrill used formal means. The earlier poem is a touching narrative of the long-term effects of the *Ring* cycle on a boy who saw it for the first time when he was twelve. It is not too much to say that the operas taught the precocious adolescent the range of profane emotion; they schooled him, too, in the artificiality of art. Countering Yeats's religious sublime in "Sailing to Byzantium" ("Soul clap its hands and sing, and louder sing / For every tatter in its mortal dress"), Merrill offered in **"Matinees"** an erotic sublime learned from *La Bohème* and *La Traviata:*

Soul will cough blood and sing, and softer sing,
Drink poison, breathe her joyous last, a waltz
Rubato from his arms who sobs and stays
Behind, death after death, who fairly melts

Watching her turn from him, restored, to fling
Kisses into the furnace roaring praise.

As **"Matinees"** ends, we read, in the last sonnet, the thank-you note sent by the young James to the friend of his mother who invited him to sit in her box. Prophetically, the note contains the sentence "I play my record of the Overture / Over and over." The young opera-goer is already an addict of reprise. Eventually the poet will have the conventions down pat: "The love scene (often cut). The potion. The tableau." Where, in the first instance, one interpreted one's own emotions through those seen in art, one now begins, by way of imitation, to create emotions to order: "The point thereafter was to arrange for one's / Own chills and fever, passions and betrayals, / Chiefly in order to make song of them." By the penultimate sonnet of **"Matinees,"** set in 1969, reprise has become tatterdemalion. Addressing in double-entendre someone who is, perhaps, a former lover, Merrill says:

You and I, caro, seldom
Risk the real thing any more.
It's all too silly or too solemn.
Enough to know the score
From records or transcription
For our four hands. Old beauties, some
In advanced stages of decomposition,
Float up through the sustaining
Pedal's black and fluid medium.
Days like today
Even recur (wind whistling themes
From Lulu, *and sun shining*
On the rough Sound) when it seems
Kinder to remember than to play.

Full of puns though this is, it remains elegiac, like **"The House Fly"**; and though the circular structure of **"Matinees,"** with its closing thank-you note returning us to 1939, is a comic one, the threat of too many repetitions annihilating the originals cannot be forgotten. Still, in spite of its elegiac moments, **"Matinees"** is focused on youth, with the development of emotional understanding through art. It is concerned more with the passionate authenticity of opera than with its artificiality. "We love the good, said Plato? He was wrong. / We love as well the wicked and the weak." It hails the thrill of the fictional as the curtain goes up on *Das Rheingold,* "No one believing, everybody thrilled."

And now, in ***A Scattering of Salts,*** we find "**The Ring Cycle,**" a commentary on **"Matinees."** It begins with an offhand and rapid survey of the fifty years from 1939 to 1989:

They're doing a Ring *cycle at the Met,*
Four operas in one week, for the first time
Since 1939. I went to that one.
Then war broke out, Flagstad flew home, tastes veered
To tuneful deaths and dudgeons.

Verdi replaced Wagner, with things German proscribed during and after the war. But the poet remains devoted to the memory of how the *Ring* brought him to his senses, in the full and literal meaning of those words:

Wagner had been significance itself,
Great golden lengths of it, stitched with motifs,
A music in whose folds the mind, at twelve,
Came to its senses: Twin, Sword, Forest Bird,
Envy, Redemption through Love. . . . But left unheard
These fifty years? A fire of answered prayers
Burned round that little pitcher with big ears
Who now wakes.

It looks as if we are to be re-submerged in the twelve-year-old's mind as he sits before what Milton Cross used to call "the great gold curtain" of the Met:

Night. E-flat denotes the Rhine,
Where everything began. The world's life. Mine.

But a poetry of nostalgia is not now Merrill's aim. The rhymes are looser here than in **"Matinees,"** and this section of **"The Ring Cycle"**—like its companions—has fifteen lines, not fourteen: perfection is out of reach. And the glimpses of the opera on stage keep getting interrupted by flashes of real life. In section two, what happens after Siegried and Sieglinde have declared their love?

Young love, moon-flooded hut, and the act ends.
House lights. The matron on my left exclaims.
We gasp and kiss. Our mothers were best friends.
Now, old as mothers, here we sit. Too weird. . . .
We have long evenings to absorb together
Before the world ends . . .

Superimposed, in section three, on this overlay of the *Ring* and its real audience is an overlay of the singers, their everyday life and their art: "Fricka looks pleased with her new hairdresser. / Brünnhilde (Behrens) has abandoned hers." And superimposed on this are the troubles of the planet caused by the petroleum-rich under-writers of the Met productions: "Erda, her cobwebs beaded / With years of seeping waste, subsides unheeded /—Right, Mr. President? Right, Texaco?— / Into a gas-blue cleft." Section four, with equal matter-of-fact energy, looks at the long years required to train any *Heldentenor* or Wagnerian soprano: appended to the simple operatic moment "Brünnhilde confronts Siegfried" is Merrill's note about the singers' preparation for that moment:

Brünnhilde confronts Siegfried. That is to say,
Two singers have been patiently rehearsed
So that their tones and attitudes convey
Outrage and injured innocence. But first
Two youngsters became singers, strove to master
Every nuance of innocence and outrage
Even in the bosom of their stolid
Middleclass families who made it possible
To study voice, and languages, take lessons
In how the woman loves, the hero dies. . . .

It is no more unseemly, Merrill now believes, to mention the repetitive labor of art—lesson after lesson to master scales and German—than to mention its artifice or its passion; and a second statement about the performance—"Tonight again . . . The dire oath . . . is sworn"—is followed by a sharp juxtaposition of social reality and aesthetic reality:

Two world-class egos, painted, overweight,
Who'll joke at supper side by side, now hate
So plausibly that one old stage-hand cries.

The poet himself is an old hand at the stage, with several plays to his credit. But knowing all he knows about rehearsals, about artifice, and about the commonplace lives of the singers, he still willingly reenters the sorrows of the *Ring*.

How does **"The Ring Cycle"**—this rerun of the *Ring,* of childhood classmates, of performance, of rehearsal, of acquaintance, of love, of **"Matinees"**—come to an end? With another recurrence, of course—this time in dream, as the poet finds himself occupying at the Met the very seat bearing his name that his contribution has made possible. He takes his place, and

as I sink back,
The youth behind me, daybreak in his eyes—
A son till now undreamed of—makes to rise.

Who is this son, who has so far existed neither in life nor in dream? He is, one could say, the allegorical figure of Reprise itself. If our biological destiny as a species is self-reprise by childbearing, surely art is childbearing on another plane. Which of us, created in our emotional lives by Wagner, is not the child of Wagner? Which of us, created in our emotional lives by Merrill, is not the child of Merrill? In ***A Scattering of Salts,*** reconciled to a repetition of the past for physical and spiritual generation and regeneration, Merrill sees his return to the *Ring*—even with his adult knowledge of opera's pedestrian and everyday aspects, its artifice and emotional fickleness—as the very resurrection of the life spirit.

This conviction makes possible a far brisker poetry of reprise than we were permitted in **"Matinees"** or even in **"The House Fly."** Words that could hardly have found a place there—"world-class egos," "too weird," "hi-tech," "hairdresser," "major funding," "overweight," "Walter J. and Ortrud Fogelsong"—sit easily and ironically next to the highest elegiac memory—"The world's life. Mine." The civilizing powers—of love over human nature, of music over time—still arouse Merrill's veneration. Around them cluster the ordinary, the commercial, the repetitive, the threatening, the entropic, but none of these, the poem affirms, can undo the transfiguring powers, indubitable even in their late-life recurrence, of love and music. I would not want to give up **"Matinees"** or **"The House Fly,"** but I would grieve to have missed the mixed-diction wonders of **"The Ring Cycle."**

I should add that the polar opposite of reprise, for Merrill, is the current, the new, the non-nostalgic, the demotic, the trivial. The more a poet stretches to take in the heterogeneous without losing emotional intensity, the more ambitious lyric becames. Perhaps because of its intense focus on recollection and recurrence, no book of Merrill's has been more defiantly interested in the new, however trivial, than ***A Scattering of Salts.*** In **"Self-Portrait in Tyvek (TM) Windbreaker,"** we can see how directly reciprocal to the threat of the stale was Merrill's unregenerate delight in current fads. He visits "one of those vaguely imbecile/Emporia catering to the collective unconscious/Of our time and place":

This one featured crystals,
Cassettes of whalesong and rain-forest whistles,
Barometers, herbal cosmetics, pillows like puffins,
Recycled notebooks, mechanized lucite coffins
For sapphire waves that crest, break, and recede,
As they presumably do in nature still.

Merrill's **"Self-Portrait"** ends with a song of summation, an aria making metaphorical use of one toy seen in the shop, the "lucite coffin" for sapphire waves. The toy gives Merrill his version of Shakespeare's metaphor describing art as a "liquid prisoner pent in walls of glass." The last aria envisaged by the living poet is, of course, incomplete:

Sing our final air:
*Love, grief etc. * * * * for good reason.*
*Now only * * * * * * * STOP signs.*
*Meanwhile * * * * * if you or I've ex-*
*ceeded our [?] * * * was needed*
*To fit a text airless and * * as Tyvek*
With breathing spaces and between the lines
Days brilliantly recurring, as once we did,
To keep the blue wave dancing in its prison.

No reader of Merrill will be surprised to find that the rhyme scheme of this penultimate "final air" of his last book is a new variation on *ottava rima,* in which the last line of each stanza, in its rhyme, is a phonetic echo of the first.

The loss of Merrill, for those of us who have been reading him for twenty or thirty years, is more than the loss of future poems. It is the loss of the voice "behind" the poems, the voice that had won our confidence over many decades of our own lives. It was a voice adequate to the confusions and elations of modern experience, as most voices in verse are not. And comic voices are especially rare in lyric poetry—voices that vote, one might say, for joy in spite of the emotional and physical worst that life has to offer. Highly intellectual voices are rare, too. In his youth, Merrill had feared that his intelligence might choke his emotional life; in a poem written at twenty-one, he worried about a

voice almost of youth, yet never
pure,
As though the river of the tongue
were clogged
By an upheaval of the intellect.

He need not have worried; the balance he found between the senses and the mind became ever more finely attuned, and the quickness of his spirit and refinement of his emotion kept him from both the sentimental and the conventional.

There are said to be, roughly speaking, two kinds of artists—the kind that innovates from within tradition, and the kind that announces a break with tradition. Mozart and Beethoven are the models in music for this division, and Spenser and Shakespeare the models in our early literature. Merrill, in this crude division, stands with Mozart and Spenser; original though he was (by his instantly recognizable style), he remained visibly content to use the lyric forms he inherited from his predecessors, from Sappho onward. Yet no form that he took up remained unrevised in his hands; and in the long sifting that time will do of his work, poets, anthologists, and critics will be repeatedly struck by his technical mastery, as they will be touched by his tenderness and surprised by his wit.

Merrill once wrote of the Greek poet Cavafy words that were true of himself: "Born . . . into a world of forms and frivolities, [he] was to be anchored firmly beyond its shallows . . . by his vocation and his sexuality." He will rightly be claimed for gay studies, but his great appeal to readers male and female, gay and straight, young and old, American and European, arises from the fact that, as he said of himself, "I was drawn to both sides of things: masculine and feminine, rational and fanciful, passionate and ironic." The breadth of his sensibility, and the candor and brio of his writing about a life by no means easy, ensured that many of us have got from him what he said he got in adolescence from Rilke: help with suffering. One doesn't forget the writers from whom such help has come.

FURTHER READING

Criticism

Blasing, Mutlu Konuk. "Rethinking Models of Literary Change: The Case of James Merrill." *American Literary History* 2, No. 2 (Summer 1990): 299-317.

Considers Merrill's postmodernism despite the apparent conventionality and formalism of his verse.

Buckley, C. A. "Quantum Physics and the Ouija-Board: James Merrill's Holistic World View." *Mosaic* 26, No. 2 (Spring 1993): 39-61.

Views Merrill's *The Changing Light at Sandover* as "a blend of science and visionary lore spliced with topical issues and autobiography." Buckley suggests that Merrill's objective in the work is to confront science with a poetic vision.

Ettin, Andrew V. "On James Merrill's *Nights and Days*." *Perspective* 15, No. 1 (Spring-Summer 1967): 33-51.

Study of *Nights and Days* that sees the volume as "technically more assured, more allusive, more daring, more clearly philosophical, far more complex" than Merrill's earlier works.

Gardner, Thomas. "Imbued with Otherness: James Merrill's *The Changing Light at Sandover*." In *Discovering Ourselves in Whitman: The Contemporary American Long Poem*, pp. 170-204. Urbana: University of Illinois Press, 1989.

Analyzes *The Changing Light at Sandover* in light of the Whitmanesque poetics of awakening and embrace.

Kalaidjian, Walter. "A Poetics of Errancy: James Merrill's *The Changing Light at Sandover*." In *Languages of Liberation: The Social Text in Contemporary American Poetry*, pp. 93-119. New York: Columbia University Press, 1989.

Maintains that in *The Changing Light at Sandover* Merrill "unmasks science as fictive narration" and "dethrones the privileged status of the high modern verse epic" while traversing generic and cultural boundaries.

Lehman, David and Charles Berger, eds. *James Merrill: Essays in Criticism*. Ithaca, N. Y.: Cornell University Press, 329 p.

Collection of essays on Merrill's poetry by diverse contributors. Includes a bibliography.

Spiegelman, Willard. "The Sacred Books of James Merrill." In *The Didactic Muse: Scenes of Instruction in Contemporary American Poetry*, pp. 192-246. Princeton, N. J.: Princeton University Press, 1989.

Comprehensive analysis of *The Changing Light at Sandover,* which sees the work as a didactic, but epic, poem.

Vendler, Helen. "James Merrill." In *Part of Nature, Part of Us: Modern American Poets*, pp. 205-32. Cambridge, Mass.: Harvard University Press, 1980.

Positive, expository reviews of Merrill's *Braving the Elements, Divine Comedies,* and *Mirabell: Books of Number.*

White, Edmund. "On James Merrill." In *The Burning Library: Essays*, edited by David Bergman, pp. 43-55. New York: Alfred A. Knopf, 1994.

Comments on Merrill's "ambitious" and important work in *The Book of Ephraim* and *Mirabell.*

Yenser, Stephen. "The Fullness of Time: James Merrill's *Book of Ephraim*." Canto 3, No. 2 (May 1980): 130-59.

Observes themes of time, imagination, and the interdependence of reality and fiction in Merrill's *The Book of Ephraim.*

———. "James Merrill: His Poetry and the Age." *Southwest Review* 80, Nos. 2-3 (Spring-Summer 1995): 186-204.

Transcript of a lecture in which Yenser probes Merrill's relationship to American Romanticism.

Zimmerman, Lee. "Against Apocalypse: Politics and James Merrill's *The Changing Light at Sandover*." *Contemporary Literature* 30, No. 3 (Fall 1989): 370-86.

Investigates the political overtones of *The Changing Light at Sandover* as a warning against nuclear war.

Buckley, C. A. "Exploring *The Changing Light at Sandover*: An Interview with James Merrill." *Twentieth Century Literature* 38, No. 4 (Winter 1992): 415-35.

Buckley and Merrill discuss the method of composition and thematic significance of *The Changing Light at Sandover.*

Additional coverage of Merrill's life and career is contained in the following sources published by the Gale Group: *Contemporary Authors,* Vols. 13-16R, 147; *Contemporary Authors New Revision Series,* Vols. 10, 49, 63; *Contemporary Literary Criticism,* Vols. 2, 3, 6, 8, 13, 18, 34, 91; *Dictionary of Literary Biography,* Vols. 5, 165; *Dictionary of Literary Biography Yearbook,* Vol. 85; *DISCovering Authors Modules: Poets;* and *Major 20th-Century Writers.*

(Philip) Michael Ondaatje
1943-

Ceylonese-born Canadian poet, novelist, dramatist, editor, critic, and filmmaker.

INTRODUCTION

Ondaatje emerged during the 1960s as one of Canada's most respected young poets. In his verse, Ondaatje examines the dichotomy between rational intellect and disorderly reality and suggests that the poet's efforts to render personal experience must necessarily result in distortion. Ondaatje's style is characterized by humor, flamboyant imagery, extravagant metaphors, and sudden shifts in tone. Sam Solecki observed that in Ondaatje's poetry, "the fundamental or essential nature of experience is consistently being described and examined. The entire thrust of his vision is directed at compelling the reader to reperceive reality, to assume an unusual angle of vision from which reality appears surreal, absurd, inchoate, dynamic, and, most important, ambiguous."

BIOGRAPHICAL INFORMATION

Born into a wealthy family in Colombo, Ceylon (now Sri Lanka), Ondaatje left home after his parents' divorce in 1952 for London, where he attended Dulwich College. Shortly thereafter, Ondaatje immigrated to Montreal, Canada, to study at Bishop's University in Lennoxville, where he began writing poetry, and later at the University of Toronto, where Ondaatje met poet Raymond Souster. Souster included Ondaatje's work in his 1966 anthology of young Canadian poets titled *New Wave Canada*. After winning the university's Epstein Award for Poetry, Ondaatje was introduced by poet Wayne Clifford to Coach House press, which published his first collection, *The Dainty Monsters,* in 1967.

In 1964 Ondaatje married artist Kim Jones, who had four children from a previous marriage; the couple had two children of their own soon after. Marriage, family life, and friendships inform a number of poems in Ondaatje's first book as well as in the 1973 collection *Rat Jelly.* After completing his M.A. at Queen's University, Ondaatje began teaching English at the University of Western Ontario. In 1971, unwilling to obtain a Ph.D., Ondaatje left the university for a teaching position at Glendon College in Toronto. In 1980 Ondaatje separated from his wife and, soon after, began a relationship with another woman. The events of his life at this time, primarily the sadness of divorce and the joy of new love, are documented in Ondaatje's 1984 collection *Secular Love*. In addition to writing and teaching, Ondaatje has edited a number of important anthologies for Coach House press.

MAJOR WORKS

Ondaatje's early collections of poetry, *The Dainty Monsters* and *The man with seven toes* (1969), display a preoccupation with domestic and personal conflicts, mythical and historical figures, the often violent relationship between humans and animals, and destructive impulses among artists. Critics noted that his verse is consistently presented in musical sound-conscious language. *The Collected Works of Billy the Kid: Left Handed Poems* (1970), which won a Governor General's Award, is considered Ondaatje's most important volume of poetry to date. Combining prose, verse, photographs, and drawings, Ondaatje presents a fictionalized biography that probes the psyche of notorious American outlaw William Bonney. *There's a Trick with a Knife I'm Learning to Do* (1979), which also won a Governor General's Award, contains selections from

The Dainty Monsters and *Rat Jelly* as well as nineteen new poems centering on such topics as friendship and family history. *Secular Love* comprises four unified sequences of confessional lyrics exploring paternal love, Ondaatje's traumatic divorce, and the redemptive qualities of love. In these poems, Ondaatje is both a character and a creative observer molding his experiences into art. Ondaatje's more recent collections, *The Cinnamon Peeler* (1989) and *Handwriting* (1999), both explore Sri Lankan history and culture.

CRITICAL RECEPTION

Ondaatje's poetry has garnered popular and critical acclaim since publication of his first volume. Douglas Barbour found Ondaatje's early works "jungle-lush," noting also Ondaatje's "rhythmic control over his language." The man with seven toes has been performed as a dramatic reading and The Collected Works of Billy the Kid, Ondaatje's most acclaimed poetic work, has been adapted for the stage. While some critics have chided Ondaatje for lyrical excesses, most scholars of Ondaatje's poetry have concurred that his highly original—and occasionally dark—vision, his linguistic skill, and his manipulation of myth both established and that of his own imagination make Ondaatje one of the most important poets of his generation.

PRINCIPAL WORKS

Poetry

The Dainty Monsters 1967
the man with seven toes 1969
The Collected Works of Billy the Kid: Left Handed Poems 1970
Rat Jelly 1973
Elimination Dance 1978
There's a Trick with a Knife I'm Learning To Do: Poems, 1963-1978 1979
Secular Love 1984
All along the Mazinaw: Two Poems 1986
The Cinnamon Peeler: Selected Poems 1989
Handwriting: Poems 1999

Other Major Works

Leonard Cohen (nonfiction) 1970
The Collected Works of Billy the Kid [based on his poetry] (play) 1973
Coming Through Slaughter (novel) 1976
Running in the Family (memoir) 1982
In the Skin of a Lion (novel) 1987
In the Skin of a Lion [based on his novel] (play) 1987
The English Patient (novel) 1992

CRITICISM

Douglas Barbour (review date 1968)

SOURCE: "Controlling the Jungle," in *Canadian Literature,* No. 36, Spring, 1968, pp. 86-8.

[*In the following assessment of* Dainty Monsters, *Barbour praises Ondaatje's natural imagery, subtle narrative, and controlled language.*]

[***The Dainty Monsters***] is the finest first book of poems to appear since Margaret Avison's *Winter Sun.* Michael Ondaatje represents a healthy reaction in modern Canadian poetry. Although a completely contemporary writer, he eschews the "simple", almost barren, style of so many of the poets influenced by the Black Mountain group. He owes much of his originality to his background, I think. The exotic imagery which crowds the pages of this book appears to stem from his childhood memories of Ceylon. His poems are jungle-lush, but, unlike a jungle, they are cultivated and controlled. Their profuseness suggest a full and fertile mind always at work.

Imagery, in itself, is not enough, of course. Michael Ondaatje is also sensitive to poetic form, and he exercises a firm rhythmic control over his language. There is also, in his longer poems, his sense of plot, or story. In the poems of the second part of the book, he demonstrates a fine and subtle understanding of poetic narrative. This does not mean he longwindedly "tells the story." Rather, the story exists behind the poem, always present to focus the specific incident in a precisely imagined context. This suggestion of story context often occurs in the shorter poems, too. In **"The Moving to Griffin,"** for example, there is a gain in density from the implied context of the poet's life story.

Ondaatje's imagery is obsessively natural: the book is a kind of modern bestiary, with birds, predatory and domestic animals, and the beast, man, always present, always active. Images of birds, especially, occur again and again. Yet in the poem, **"Song to Alfred Hitchcock and Wilkinson",** he does the unexpected, and the poem fairly leaps from the page as a result:

> Flif flif flif flif very fast
> is the noise the birds make
> running over us.
> A poet would say 'fluttering',
> or
> 'see-sawing with sun on their wings'.
> But all it is
> is flif flif flif flif very fast.

Although his poems are filled with images of violence and terror, his love poems are able to stand against this vision. Life is seldom gentle in these poems, but the love lyrics salvage and savour those moments of deep gentleness which cannot last but must be accepted joyfully in their passing. **"The Diverse Causes"**, **"She Carries a 'Fat Gold Watch'"**, **"Christmas Poem, 1965"**, **"Four Eyes"**, as well as the poems of love in the Troy Town section, all present the particular moments of communion with an intensity sufficient to command belief. We accept the validity of such moments because the poems poignantly create that validity.

Yet Ondaatje's poetry never dissolves into sentimentality. His sure control, and the precision of his vision won't allow that. The ironies of his animal poems, his use of tone, the mythic vision of the Troy Town poems, the sense of the power in others, of our inability to control or protect others all preclude sentimentality. He is too tough-minded, too aware of the complexities of life, and his poetry offers no answers or escapes, as sentimentality always does.

"Troy Town", the second part of ***The Dainty Monsters,*** is concerned with myth and the creation of myth. This is a difficult term; but it should be sufficient to suggest that, in these poems, Ondaatje tells "stories" which engender responses of awe and admiration. The life of these poems is violent, for they deal with the permutations of human violence. He has used the well-known myths of Troy and Lilith for some of these poems, but he has also created new myths out of history, or, in **"Peter"**, probably the finest poem in the collection, out of his own imagination. The poem on Egypt, and the Elizabeth poems are fascinating for their sense of the person. These are monologues, and, especially in **"Elizabeth"**, he has achieved a high degree of dramatic realism. I have said that he has a clear imaginative understanding of violence, yet this violence never overwhelms the poet. The poetry is not voluptuous in its violence; it is chiseled and carefully wrought. The old idea of decorum applies perfectly to these poems. This is especially true of **"Peter"**, where the poet deals with varieties of physical and mental violence in an almost virginally pure style and manner. The result is a tremendous gain in imaginative force over most modern treatments of the theme.

This is a beautiful book. It is this in both senses of the word, as a work of poet's craft and as a work of printer's craft.

Michael Ondaatje with Jon Pearce (interview date 1978)

SOURCE: "Moving to the Clear: Michael Ondaatje," in *Twelve Voices: Interviews with Canadian Poets,* Borealis Press, 1980, pp. 129-44.

[*In the following interview, which was conducted in 1978, Ondaatje discusses his poetry, particularly the creative process.*]

[Jon Pearce]: When did you start to write? Did you write at all in England when you lived there as a teen-ager?

[Michael Ondaatje]: No. I think I did write one short story, but I didn't have much interest in writing at the time. I had read a lot, but had actually no interest in writing. I started to write in 1963 and ***The Dainty Monsters*** came out in 1967.

How do you account for such a mature, sophisticated, and well-crafted book as **The Dainty Monsters***? Most writers go through a period of apprenticeship, which seems to be necessary in order to get rid of their bad poems. But you don't seem to have had to do that.*

I don't know how to answer that question. I had no interest in poetry. I don't think, until I came to Canada and went to university here. I started writing a lot then and some of the stuff wasn't much good at first. Most of the poems in ***The Dainty Monsters*** came about from 1964 to 1967. The first couple of years they weren't there.

Who helped you? Who influenced you?

You met poets in Canada. If I'd continued to live in England, I would never have met any poets—or at least it would have been very unlikely. I met poets here like D.G. Jones and Raymond Souster. Poets in Kingston, where I was going to university, like Tom Marshall and Tom Eadie. And I think what happened was at that time there was a lot of conversation about writing among us, and I tended to ask for comments when I sent manuscripts off to magazines, and I was very lucky; I got lots of reactions to the poems. One of the persons I recall was Milton Wilson of the *Canadian Forum,* who took great trouble with the poems. Not only did he take some poems for the *Forum,* but he wrote back and made comments about them. Once he gave me good advice which I didn't take. In **"Pigeons, Sussex Avenue"**, he thought there were a couple of lines that were unnecessary; but I was convinced they were crucial and the poem was published in the magazine as it was. Later, when I was editing ***The Dainty Monsters***, I realized he was quite right and I dropped the two lines—about three years too late.

Can I interrupt for a minute? I've compared some of your poems as they have appeared in anthologies with the poem as it appears in book form. And it seems to me that there hasn't been much editing done. Is that true?

Essentially, a lot of the editing has been done *before* the poem goes out. I tend to keep a poem around for a long time—at least six months or a year—before I send it out. Before ***The Dainty Monsters*** came out, for example, two people helped me a great deal with the editing. Wayne Clifford criticized the individual poems, and George Whalley helped me with the structure of the book as a whole. I learned a great deal from both of them.

Do you find that you revise poems extensively in the six months that you keep them around?

Yes, very much so. They usually get shorter and they usually get a bit more subtle than they were in the first place. But there's a *lot* of editing going on.

How long does it take you to write a poem?

A poem like **"A House Divided"** took me about twenty seconds and I never changed that one. I was stunned: some poems get written like that but they only get written like that because you work on other poems and learn something subconsciously. I think editing comes not just in changing the words but in working with the form of the whole poem.

The matter of editing interests me a great deal—it's different for every poem. But usually the poem gets tightened in some way or gets loosened in some way. Sometimes the poem is too tight to begin with and it needs to breathe a bit more, and you go back to the poem after a couple of months and you see that it's too introverted and too tight and one has to blow some air into it somehow and start again. So, with a book, what happens usually is that there is a process of editing within the actual individual poem, and also there is a process of structuring the book which is also part of the editing.

In one of your published statements, you say, "I usually take my own aesthetics very lightly. Laws and rules and aesthetic principles I think are dangerous if you carry them over into your next poem." But then you go on to say that "there is usually a set of rules in each poem but it's organic." Do you attempt to implement the principles of organic form both within a particular poem in the book, as well as in the book as a whole? You were talking a moment ago about the structure of a book.

Well, I definitely think there has to be an organic structure in a book, and I think that's what really interests me in books like ***Billy the Kid*** and *Coming Through Slaughter* It's a case of finding that structure after you've written the book. It's a case of the poem or the book getting written as a whole and then trying to find the sharpest way of presenting that organic form—if that makes any sense.

This would involve editing, of course.

It would definitely involve editing, not just within each poem but the way in which each poem would be placed in relation to every other poem in the book. So that there would be a rhythm in the book.

Some poets don't seem to bother with the notion of a structure or a rhythm in a book; they just lump the poems together willy-nilly, with no apparent thought for the interrelationships.

That's fine for them, but it would upset me greatly.

Can I go back to **The Dainty Monsters** *for a moment? What does the epigraph from W.H. Auden refer to: "We've been watching you over the garden wall / for hours. . ."? Who are the "we?"*

I don't know.

There's a garden here with a wall that apparently divides the animal world from the human world. I'm wondering about the connection between the two worlds. Who are the "we"? The humans or the animals? And what kind of garden is this? Does it have anything to do with the Garden of Eden?

I think both things come up, but I don't know for sure who the "we" is.

What we're talking about is the poetic process. If I may, I'd like to continue along these lines and ask you a couple more questions

Sure, but you probably won't get any straight answers.

When talking about the poem **"Peter",** *you've said, "My only emotion about my own work is curiosity." This statement implies that—somehow—after the writing of the poem you've become detached from it, that you look upon it in a curious, disinterested way. As if it wasn't yours. Can you explain that: how you can dissociate yourself from something you once must have been so close to?*

I think if you still like the poem after two years or after ten years, you get a certain pleasure out of it. But it is, I think, essentially curiosity, trying to remember how you were at the time when you wrote that poem. Your state of mind, your trying to remember the sources of that poem—curiosity is what I think I'm talking about. No, once you've written the poem, the poem doesn't belong to you; once you've written the poem, it's out there—not part of you any longer. For instance, a character like Billy or Buddy Bolden: it's like having known someone very well—intensely for a certain amount of time while you were writing the book. Then there's a fantastic separation that comes when you finish the book and leave the characters or the poem behind.

In a sense, I lived with Billy when I wrote the book for three or four years and with Bolden for about six years. You know, living with those characters for all that time so intensely means they are always in the back of your mind. Your thinking will be thought by you and is thought by the character simultaneously. But when the book is finished, or when you finish the actual writing of the book, then you get the fun of shaping that person from the outside—in terms of giving the manuscript to friends and saying, "What do you think is missing here?" or "Should this be clearer there or is this too vague?". Questions like that. Then it's like a piece of sculpture more than personal expression.

I have no desire, for instance, to go back and re-write ***Billy*** or re-investigate Bolden. Just recently there's another book on Bolden that's come out in the States. I have absolutely no desire to read the thing. Even if it gives me all kinds of new material about Bolden, I'm not at all interested in it. For me, Bolden is a character who is important to me only as I knew him. He's there now and I still like him, and now and then I'll see something in the street that I will see the way he saw it.

Let me quote you again. You say that "at universities and schools teachers are preoccupied with certain aspects of content, with themes, with messages." Then you go on to say "that's only about half of poetry". If so, what's the other half?

You sound like a lawyer, a criminal lawyer.

Well, I'm not. I'm a school-teacher. But I do happen to have some notes in front of me. I've prepared a bit of a brief so I can try to get you to say what you mean.

Okay. The other half. . . style, technique, the method and movement of the poem. I think William Carlos Williams or someone said he could summarize all the main things about poetry on the back of a postage stamp. . . that's a minor part of the poem. If you read a love poem, well obviously there will be nothing new in a love poem—it's just the way it's said and it's the *way* it's said that makes it suddenly hit you.

So the question shouldn't be "What does the poem mean", but "How does a poem mean"?

Yes, the *way* the poem means.

Let me ask you something else about technique. I find the incidence of your use of figurative language more frequent than in many poets. More important, though—since figurative language is an essential element of the language of poetry—I find your use of it. . . bizarre, disturbing, arresting, sometimes shocking. It makes the reader sit up and take notice.

What do you mean by figurative language?

Figurative language is language used with a twist, as in a drink of Scotch. It's not straight Scotch; it's boosted. The girl's hair isn't honey hair, literally; it's probably browny-blonde. . . And by figurative language, I suppose I mean, most simply and conventionally, simile, metaphor, and the like.

Now, when I read that someone "drowned / in the beautiful dark orgasm of his mouth" or a young girl "burns the lake / by reflecting her red shoes in it" or a pregnant woman has inside her "another, / thrashing like a fish", I find myself getting anxious about these jagged, almost violent images. Am I getting to something that's characteristic of your poetry and that you deliberately and consciously use?

This is very difficult. Two things are very difficult for me to answer: one is, you know, why I write in a certain way, which I think is what you're asking; and the other is what I think of someone's interpretation of a poem. But, trying to answer the first question, why I use these images, I don't think I'm conscious of it when I'm writing; I'm not conscious of trying to shock someone when I'm writing with a specific image. That just happens in the process of writing, but I'm not conscious of it while I'm writing it. I don't know what more I can say about that. It's there, and it's obviously part of my style. But I don't think I'm a particularly violent poet, which some people feel I am, and I don't think I'm a grotesque poet, as some people think. You know, I think I have a vision of reality that is totally normal to me.

But a lot of the imagery tends toward the violent—

Yes, that's true—

And it's not just the material—the subject matter—that determines the nature of the imagery. In **Billy the Kid**, *for example, the image when he's riding chained to his horse and the sun reaches down through Billy's head and pulls him inside out, that—at least to my tender mind—is certainly bizarre.*

Yes, but you know, the poor guy is having some form of sunstroke. For me in ***Billy*** I can see just as much gentleness as violence; for me there's a balance. And I really tried to keep the number of deaths in *Coming Through Slaughter* to a minimum.

Maybe the elements of violence in **Billy the Kid** *and* Coming Through Slaughter *are unavoidable. But what I was interested in asking about were some of the same things in the earlier poems—in* **The Dainty Monsters** *and in* **Rat Jelly**

Well, maybe something got clarified in ***Billy*** that didn't get clarified in the earlier poems, although I think I could go back and see preparations for ***Billy*** in ***The Dainty Monsters***. . . The thing is it's a very real world to me and if people don't want to see that as part of the real world, then they're ignoring it. It's been said that violence is normal in our lifetime just as good manners were normal to the world that Jane Austen created. You know, it's a reality. It's getting a balance between the two worlds—the violent and the gentle—but both exist.

I know that you're not going to like this, but I'd like to talk about poetics once more. Poets frequently comment on poetry in the poems that they write, and the one in which you do most obviously is ***"'The gate in his head'".*** *Let me quote some of it:*

> Victor, the shy mind
> revealing the faint scars
> coloured strata of the brain,
> not clarity but the sense of shift
> a few lines, the tracks of thought
>
> . . . . .
>
> My mind is pouring chaos

in nets onto the page.
A blind lover, dont know
what I love till I write it out.
And then from Gibson's your letter
with a blurred photograph of a gull.
Caught vision. The stunning white bird
an unclear stir.
And that is all this writing should be then.
The beautiful formed things caught at the wrong moment
so they are shapeless, awkward
moving to the clear.

Now I have three questions to ask you. What do you mean by "My mind is pouring chaos / in nets onto the page"? Is that somehow a description of the poetic process for you?

Sometimes.

What does it mean?

I find it difficult answering questions that ask me specifically to interpret some lines in a poem. I'm not being evasive, but I just find it very difficult. You want me to write the poem and then to interpret the poem. But I'm not being evasive.

Let me try the second question. The poet—or let's say the speaker—is "A blind lover"; he's attached to something, but can't see or understand properly. Then: "dont know / what I love till I write it out." When I read that, I thought of that old chestnut "How do I know what I think until I see what I say?" Have you ever heard that?

No, but it sounds good to me.

The "blind lover" is "pouring chaos", which is caught "in nets" on the page; but he really doesn't know what he loves—what he's attached to, what his subject matter is—until he sees it on paper. The writing of a poem seems to be a process of discovery, knowing, seeing.

The third question is this: why are "The beautiful formed things caught at the wrong moment"? I don't understand that.

I really don't like interpreting my own poetry. I hope you can understand that.

Well, since you're reluctant to answer questions about particular lines, what is the poet's responsibility to his poetry or to his poems?

I think he has to remain silent after he's written the poem. I think it only damages a poem to have the poet try to explain it. I can't understand writers who do this. The statement that a poet makes in a poem is just as much the *way* he says it as *what* he says. To ask someone who's said something in a poem to paraphrase it or to expand that statement can only destroy a poem, for me. It's the case of a poem being looked on as a crossword puzzle; the reader wants to know *exactly* what is meant. But I don't think the reader should ask the poet *exactly* what he is saying.

What he wants to say he has *said,* and a poem is important in what it doesn't say as well as what it says. You want to reach just the right tone or mood, the point where you don't say certain things, you say certain things, you say certain things in a certain way. You have enough faith in the audience for the reader to be able to interpret what was said by *just* the amount you've said. I'm often horrified when I hear a poet talking on about a poem he's written. Often this happens at readings; people over-expand before they've read or over-expand after they've read or in a question period go on about the poem or what they wanted to do. For them to have to do this, the poem has failed in some way. I would rather try it over again when it's failed, but I think it's the duty of the poet to remain silent. I think he can talk about various things, but to say more about the poem he damages the poem in some way.

I'm not sure that I agree with you.

Maybe not; but I think it's a point of view.

I think that what a poet has to say about his own poetry or about a particular poem that he's written has a peculiar interest, and that's why I asked you those questions. I don't think that what he has to say about that poem has a peculiar authority, though. My reading of those lines might be fully as legitimate as yours.

Exactly! That's exactly the point I'm trying to make: your point of view has exactly the same validity as my point of view.

Yes, but yours might be a little more interesting. . .

But you say "peculiar" in terms of a peculiar interest—

A different interest. If a friend of mine were listening to this conversation, he might not be so interested in what I had to say about those lines as he would be in what you had to say about those lines. You'd have a peculiar interest for him because you put the lines on the page. But, nevertheless, my remarks might be just as valid as yours. Of course, if we go to the other extreme and if we say that my remarks are equally as good as yours—and so and so's are equally as good as yours and mine—don't we get into a completely relativistic view of poetry? This would allow the freshman horticulture student to read Blake's "Sick Rose" as an allegory of a certain kind of plant disease. (This is a true story, by the way.)

That's lovely.

But the reading isn't sound; it doesn't work.

I'd still be more interested in what the horticulturist had to say.

Okay, can I at this point go back to "**'The gate in his head'**" *for the last time? I still think it constitutes an important statement of Michael Ondaatje's poetics.*

First, there seems to be a catch-22 involved: though the last four lines obviously state a view of what your poetry ought to do, by their own terms they can't clearly be interpreted to state anything. "All this writing" should be, if you succeed, "beautiful formed things caught at the wrong moment / so they are shapeless, awkward"—or, as you say in the first stanza, "not clarity but the sense of shift". Therefore, even these lines that I've quoted, if they are successful, must necessarily be "blurred" themselves—"an unclear stir"—and not susceptible to a clear interpretation.

It seems to me that you're putting a radical twist on the reluctance of poets to provide questioners with the "meanings" of their poems. And this is not a bad thing; I don't disagree with you. After all, you've struggled long and hard to say with precision what you've wanted to say in the poem. So if you drop statements about the poem's meaning, you run the risk of having your poem damaged by school-teachers or critics who plaster these statements of meaning over the poetic structure you worked so hard on. I know all this—or at least you've told me all this—and I sympathize with your position.

However, it seems that your reluctance to commit yourself is extreme because of your radical view of the nature and function of poetry. You seem to be trying to write a poetry which is necessarily uninterpretable, without meaning. Yet I don't believe this is simply art for art's sake: there seems to be a fundamental seriousness of purpose here in which poetry is conceived as a necessary extension of your mind—and the world. You use the poem to create—create and discover at the same time—a freshness and vitality which can be found only midway between chaos and form: "My mind is pouring chaos / in nets onto the page." "In nets", because without form nothing is apprehensible; yet sufficiently "chaos" to be alive, not yet killed by the dead weight of absolute form—the canned, the tired, the repeatable. Thus, if you are successful, your poems must not be clear, but "moving to the clear". I don't know what you would want to call such poetic events—Truth or Reality—but I think the important point is that it is what the speaker in the poem loves.

Now, I don't know whether you want to respond to that or not. It isn't really a question, anyway.

Yes, I think that's a pretty good interpretation of it. The thing here is to remember constantly that the poem is not real life; the poem is a poem, the poem is a work of art. It's an artifice, it's a chair, it was made by somebody, and what is involved is what happens when you put the chair into a room. What is involved also is how the person made the chair, and what is important is the other chairs the person has made. I think one can look at a poem by itself and appreciate the poem as an object of pleasure or pain or whatever, but for the writer himself what is important is something else; it's not just the poem because the poem represents a certain phase he has been through or something like that which appears in the poem later on. There is some kind of continuity in a writer's work and that is what is important for the writer. A poem is a passageway, in that sense, from what he felt before to what he feels at the end of the poem. He can't go back and write poem G after having written poem H—I mean, you can't go back to the state of mind or what you believed before you wrote the poem. Basically, that's it, I think.

A poem is a process of clarifying something? A process of discovery?

Both those things. But that's not all; there is something else there, too. I'd hate to think that a poem completed was a total canning of an incident or an event. It's something more; there has to be some kind of air in the poem that comes from. . . there's got to be an open door or something at the end of the poem, so that you can step out or the writer can step out and admit that this isn't everything.

Do you ever write a poem about something you already know?

No, I don't think so. I can't think of anything I've known before I wrote the poem.

So you would never sit down and write a poem about a certain deeply-felt belief or conviction or attitude?

Well, I think all those convictions and beliefs probably come out in the poem somewhere, but I didn't necessarily have those beliefs and convictions before I sat down and wrote the poem. If I have a very definite attitude about something, I'm not going to write a poem about it—because I already know what the attitude is. The poem is the way you learn something essential about yourself or about people—or about language—all those things. What I may appreciate about a poem could be simply the way the poem moves on the page, the way the poem looks on the page, the way the language is used on the page—it could have nothing to do with these other issues.

Does what we're been talking about have anything to do with the notion of a descent into the depths of one's self, a discovery of one's self, and a final "surfacing"? Several recent essays have suggested this as an important aspect of Canadian literature. Do you think this is the case in both **Billy the Kid** *and* Coming Through Slaughter*?*

Yes, I think so, but I think that is true of all poems in a way. I think any poem has got a sense of that process of investigating something—an emotion, a problem, a feeling, a celebration.

In ***Billy*** and in *Slaughter* I think it's the same thing but on a larger scale—it's a discovery of someone. . . I could never write a formal detective novel. As much as I love

Agatha Christie, I could not plot ahead and know who the murderer was until I got to ten pages before the end. The state that I ought to be in as a writer is the state of the reader in reading an Agatha Christie novel—going into a room blind. It's that sense of finding something out in the process of the poem or a novel. When I was writing these two books, I was in the state of trying to find out something about somebody else.

It's a process of unfolding?

It's a process of unfolding. If you already *know* the last line of the poem, how can you write the poem? You can't. But you can take the last line and make it the *first* line and go on from there. Anything else is boring, you know, if you know where it is going to end.

In both books, **Billy** *and* Slaughter, *this technique of discovery leads to a pessimistic conclusion. . .*

No, I don't think so.

But Billy is dead and Buddy Bolden lives the last twenty-four years of his life in a mental asylum.

I don't think that's pessimistic.

Why not?

Because other people in the book end up in a state that's worse. I think if Billy ends up as a convict figure—this is more obnoxious to me than ending up dead. Or if Bolden ends up as a rank amateur worrying whether Perry Como is going to record his other songs—this is worse to me. I don't find *Slaughter* depressing. There's a calm in Bolden that is justified for him. If it's justified for *him,* then that's all right. Obviously the book is not *joyous,* but I don't find it depressing at all. On the physical level, it is, and in a way he's somewhat limited in vision by the end, but I don't find it a depressing book. . . The whole process of writing books like that also is not a personal one and that interests me. I *know* when I was writing both ***Billy*** and *Slaughter,* I had a sense that it wasn't just my point of view that was writing the book; it was people around me that I knew, the interests of people around me, being aware of certain things—certain questions—from the point of view of people around me as much as myself. It doesn't matter who writes the book; the book is for me a kind of funneling of various people's ideas and emotions, between the years 1968 and 1973 or 1973 to 1976, who represent your age and your group and the book comes out that way. If I'd started to write a book about Buddy Bolden in the year 1984, it would be a totally different book, obviously, because the concerns of people around me would be different and my concerns would be different. It's just as important to consider the people around you as to have your own vision, even though they don't know you're writing a book about Buddy Bolden. And I tend not to tell anyone what I'm writing about until I've finished a couple of versions of the book. So I think in that sense that the book was almost written by a community, and this is very important to me. A friend tells a joke in 1969 and I remember that, and that will somehow become part of the organic movement of the book; to me that's important. Just as in a poem, the nicest poems are the poems that kind of take in everything around you—the time, the smell of the kitchen, the taste of the wine.. Once that process is finished—the actually writing of the book into a first official draft—I give it to my wife and three or four friends who look at it and I listen to them and get their reactions to the thing, and there the conversation is on the level of "What happened to Webb?" and "Don't you think Webb should come back in a bit more?" or "What exactly is Angela's relationship?" And that I love—I love that moment. Several people are important to me when a book is finished. Dennis Lee and B.P. Nichol have been very important to me both in ***Billy the Kid*** and *Slaughter,* and friends like Ken Livingstone and my wife and Stan Dragland—these people can read something cold and can say, "This character isn't really formed here". Then you do a different kind of writing to make it clearer, which is separate from the process of investigating.

Are both Billy and Buddy artists, in a sense?

Some people have interpreted Billy as an artist, and on some level—on an instinctual level—he is an artist. But he isn't a portrait of the artist for me; I didn't intend to make a statement about the artist in ***Billy***. In *Slaughter* I probably was—so I guess that's the only reason why I hesitate to answer questions about the role of the artist in society, because in a way I spent four years writing a book about the artist. But I can't make a *general* statement about the artist in society, because you can't make a statement like that through an individual and obviously the statement about Bolden is not a statement about you or me or about John Newlove. Every artist is different, every artist begins with a different smell from the fridge. You can't generalize from one person. Obviously, Bolden is a certain individual and I wanted to keep that.

How do you yourself feel about the role of the artist? You, as an artist? You, as an artist in our society?

First of all, I try not to think of myself as an "artist". If I did, I simply wouldn't be able to continue to write. I think if people are conscious of themselves as artists *continually,* it would be a deadly situation to be in. One wants to be a real person and live in a real world, as opposed to being an artist. I certainly don't feel any kind of duty to society as an "artist" at all. God knows what the role of the poet is.

Let me ask you a further question. You've talked about some Canadian novelists and used the term "moral intent". Are your intentions "moral" in your art? Do you write poems and novels that are intended to have some "moral" effect upon the reader? Do you have some kind of "moral" view?

First of all, it's very difficult to say what is "moral" and what is *not* "moral"—we've got a whole half-hour conversation there. "Moral" unfortunately has the suggestion of being either religious or political, but for me moral is much wider; moral is everything. The word "human" is better. Morality is just one per cent of a human to me. I certainly don't intend, when I write a poem, to be moral, or to say what is the right thing one should do in a certain situation. I'm more interested in what a human being will do in a certain situation. This involves good people and bad people. I'm not too interested in bad people; I don't seem to meet characters I dislike in my writing. Take a fictional work like the Bolden book: there are very few characters I think I can say are *bad* people, even if somebody else makes this character out to be a bad person. Human beings are sometimes screwed up, sometimes not screwed up, sometimes going in the wrong direction, but I don't find any of them evil or bad. I wouldn't go out of my way to talk about a person who is bad just so I can set him up as a symbol of badness. That kind of puppetry doesn't interest me very much.

You seem to be less interested in artistic and moral beings than you are in human beings. Is that fair to say?

I suppose so. In *Slaughter,* Buddy Bolden is an artist, but he's also a barber. Obviously, the book is about art, but the artistic element is just one aspect of Bolden's being *human*. . . I hate the term "artist", I hate the term "poet", it has so many connotations of someone who is separate from the real world, someone who supposedly "deserves" more, "knows" more, than the man on the street. It suggests someone who is superior to any other craftsman that exists around us today, and I think this is a real problem of artists. It's been created by artists who go around saying they are visionaries or they're prophets or they're noble figures. To me that's a corruption. I like the term "writer" simply because it's someone who does something, who is using words.

Like an artisan.

Yes, like an artisan. I think one can be professional in the way one writes, but to put one's self forward as a "poet" is so limiting—it cuts you off essentially from the real world.

Some people look at that whole matter from the opposite end. For instance, P.K. Page would say that it's not possible for one's ego to be enhanced by writing, because writing isn't done by P.K. Page; it's done only through her, it comes from somewhere else. But let me ask you one final question: why do you write?

I'm still not sure. I enjoy it, I think.

Isn't it hard?

Oh yes, but I think there can be pleasure in certain kinds of hardness or difficulty.

Yes, but is it not difficult to do it day after day, month after month, year after year?

Well, it keeps me busy; otherwise, I might be out robbing a Mac's Milk Store.

Sam Solecki (essay date 1980)

SOURCE: "Point Blank: Narrative in Michael Ondaatje's *the man with seven toes*" in *Canadian Poetry,* No. 6, Spring/Summer, 1980, pp. 14-24.

[*In the following essay, Solecki offers an explanatory overview of Ondaatje's* the man with seven toes, *arguing that the collection is "a pivotal book in Ondaatje's development."*]

In view of the acclaim and the attention received by Michael Ondaatje's ***The Collected Works of Billy the Kid*** (1970) and *Coming Through Slaughter* (1976) it is inevitable that his first book-length work, ***the man with seven toes*** (1969), is often overlooked in most discussions either of his work or of contemporary Canadian writing. This is unfortunate because this long sequence of poems is a complex work, interesting in its own right, and a pivotal book in Ondaatje's development. It is with ***the man with seven toes*** that we first see him moving toward the longer and more experimental form that will become characteristic in his two major works. And although ***the man with seven toes*** does not go as far as they do in the direction of a temporally discontinuous form, nevertheless, aspects of its style and structure clearly anticipate the later developments. The shift toward the longer forms that is first seen with ***the man with seven toes*** is of particular importance in Ondaatje's development as a writer because not only are his longer works more experimental than his lyrics but it is in them that we find a style and form fully expressive of his vision. This is not to denigrate his very fine lyrics but only to emphasize that he seems to need the longer form or structure in order to create a world embodying and expressing his vision.

The final section in Ondaatje's first book, ***The Dainty Monsters*** (1967), showed him to be interested in writing a longer poem but neither of its two medium-length sequences, **"Paris"** and **"Peter"**, captures, in form or content, what I take to be Ondaatje's unique way of looking at reality which is already there in some of the earlier lyrics in the collection—**"Dragon," "The Republic," "Henri Rousseau and Friends,"** and **"In Another Fashion."** There is a sense in these early lyrics that material and psychological reality is fundamentally random or in a state of flux, and that poetry should communicate this particular quality of reality without, however, succumbing to either formalism or formlessness. These poems explore the borderline between form and formlessness, civilization and nature, the human and the natural, and the conscious reasoning mind and the unconscious world of instinct. They compel the reader to enter into and experience the mode of being associated with the second of the paired terms. But they do so primarily on the level of content by means of contrasted actions, settings or images. In ***the man with seven toes,*** on the other hand, it is the form as well as the content that pushes the reader into the unfamiliar ground of the work to the point that his reading of the sections of the text becomes roughly analogous to what is happening in the story, the heroine's harrowing journey through a wilderness. Beginning with this book Ondaatje turns to a variant of what Barthes terms a "scriptible"[1] (as opposed to a "lisible") text, one that demands the reader's active participation as an interpreter of a reality that is often not only ambiguous but even chaotic.

To achieve this Ondaatje attempts to "make new" both the form and content of his work so that neither will predispose the reader towards a preconceived approach to the text. I mention both form and content because at the same time that Ondaatje is creating a new form that will eventually develop into the radically discontinuous forms of his two later works, his choice of subject in ***the man with seven toes*** foreshadows as well the kinds of characters and themes to be dealt with in his later work. Where the medium-length narrative poems in his first book, ***The Dainty Monsters,*** had dealt with figures drawn from classical mythology (**"Paris"**) or who felt as if they belonged in classical myth (**"Peter"**), ***the man with seven toes*** is based on the experiences of a semi-legendary Englishwoman who, like Billy the Kid and Buddy Bolden, existed on the edge of history and about whose experiences there are contradictory accounts.[2] The life story of each of these characters provides Ondaatje with a ready-made but incomplete and ambiguous narrative straddling the border between fact and fiction, history and legend or myth. ***the man with seven toes*** shows Ondaatje turning towards myths or mythic poems based on materials not usually associated with traditional myths but rather on what we normally refer to as legends. Ondaatje's definition of myth will seem idiosyncratic to anyone nurtured on *Fables of Identity* but there is a consistency in his various references to the subject in his poems, prose works, critical writings and films. For him, a myth is any powerful story with an archetypal or universal significance; but in order for the story to become truly mythic, to have what in the article on *Tay John* he calls "the raw power of myth," it must be represented in such a way that "the original myth [story] is given to us point blank."[3] What he means is that the reader must be exposed to as direct and unmediated a representation or, better, re-enactment of the original event as art will allow; he must become or feel that he has become a participant in it, a figure in the ground of the story.

In ***the man with seven toes,*** for example, the reader enters the night-marelike world of an anomymous white woman who spends a period of time living with a group of primitives before being rescued by a white man and taken back to civilization. A brief note at the end of the book indicates that the source of Ondaatje's story lies in the experiences of a Mrs. Fraser who, in 1836, was shipwrecked off the Queensland coast of Australia, captured by aborigines, and finally rescued by a convict named Bracefell whom she betrayed once they reached civilization. Ondaatje told me that this version of the story as summarized by Colin MacInnes and painted by Sidney Nolan in his Mrs. Fraser series (1947-1957) is the only account with which he was familiar at the time of the writing of his poem.[4] In his hands the story becomes a mythic exploration, in the form of related brief and often imagistic poems, of how an unnamed white woman perceives and experiences a primitive and anarchic world totally alien to her civilized assumptions and mode of being. Like Margaret Atwood's Susanna Moodie she is compelled into a confrontation in which she must acknowledge violent and primitive aspects of life within and outside herself which she had previously either not known or ignored. This basic opposition between aspects of self, and self and land from which many of the poem's other antitheses develop is also central to Nolan's version. His first painting shows Mrs. Fraser naked and crawling on all fours with her white body placed against a setting of green jungle and blue sky; her face is covered by lank black hair, and her limbs are slightly distorted, indistinct, already on the point of becoming subtly dehumanized.[5] Both the lack of clothing and the absence of identity remove her from civilization; the effect is rather like the first collage in Atwood's *Journals* where Susanna Moodie seems to be drifting down into the middle of the forest: the human being and the landscape are contiguous but there is no connection between them.[6]

Both Ondaatje and Nolan—and later Patrick White in *A Fringe of Leaves*—use Mrs. Fraser as the basis of a myth. In Nolan's series she becomes an Australian version of Susanna Moodie, gradually developing from a situation in which she is alienated from the land to the point where she is one with it, and can be represented as an aboriginal rock painting. In contrast to Nolan, Ondaatje universalizes the meaning of her experiences by creating her in the image of an anonymous white women. He further creates the potential for her development as an archetypal or mythic figure by moving the story from the Australian historical context in which he found it to an unspecified time and place. The overall effect of these changes is to focus attention on the story's essential content, the effect upon an individual of her confrontation with a totally alien landscape and mode of being.

But this story with a potentially archetypal dimension cannot become mythic, in Ondaatje's sense of the word, unless expressed in a form and style that make the reading of the story as unmediated a confrontation with the events as is possible. To achieve this Ondaatje relies on a form made up of brief self-contained, often cinematic, lyrics each of which explodes upon the reader with a single startling revelation. To read from one to the next as the woman moves from experience to experience is to encounter a series of sensory and emotional shocks until, finally, like the character herself, the reader is numbed into accepting this surreal world as real.[7] Ondaatje has described the book's form as similar to "a kind of necklace in which each bead-poem while being related to the others on the string, was, nevertheless, self-sufficient, independent."[8] The continuity is implied rather than made explicit, and the terse almost imagistic poems are related by means of various kinds of montage (tonal, intellectual etc.) or juxtaposition as well as through the echoing of images from poem to poem. This kind of "bonding" (Hopkins' term) of essentially separate lyrics by means of recurring images is important to Ondaatje particularly as it relates to myth and mythic poems. He has written that "myth is. . . achieved by a very careful use of echoes—of phrases and images. There may be no logical connection when these are placed side by side but the variations are always there setting up parallels."[9] In ***the man with seven toes,*** for example, the woman is raped both by the natives and by the convict (32); she is "tongued" by the natives (14), Potter's fingers are "chipped tongues" (21); and he bends his "tongue down her throat / drink her throat sweat, like coconut" (35); the natives tear a fox open with their hands (16), Potter "crept up and bit open / the hot vein of a sleeping wolf" (29); the natives have "maps on the soles of their feet" (13), and at the book's end the woman lies on a bed "sensing herself like a map" (41). Ondaatje does not amplify his point to indicate how such echoes and parallels achieve a sense of the mythic but one of their effects is to create a common ground or structure—even the possibility of an unsuspected metaphysical order—underlying the separate lyrics. Contrasts and comparisons are established between individual characters, events and settings otherwise related only on the basis of a tenuous narrative line. But the structure remains deliberately indefinite and avoids becoming a constricting grid, just as the repeated images themselves stop short of shifting into a symbolic mode of meaning. It is almost as if Ondaatje is playing with the reader, undercutting his conventional notions about structure and symbolism. Most readers, for example, assume that an image, repeated often enough in a variety of contexts, will, at some point, shift in function and meaning from being simply an image and assume the status of a symbol. This is precisely the kind of expectation Ondaatje creates only in order to deny. Disoriented, the reader is compelled to reexamine the nature of his relationship to the text and to move more tentatively through it. This is as true of the individual lyrics as it is of the work as a whole.

A closer reading through the text will illustrate more clearly some of the general points I have been making up to now. The book opens with the following lyric:

> the train hummed like a low bird
> over the rails, through
> desert and pale scrub,
> air spun in the carriages.
> She moved to the doorless steps
> where wind could beat her knees.
> When they stopped for water she got off
> sat by the rails on the wrist thick stones.
> The train shuddered, then wheeled away from her.
> She was too tired even to call.
> Though, come back, she murmured to herself.
>
> (9)

Ondaatje's words describing the structure of Leonard Cohen's *The Favourite Game* also apply here: This is "a potent and enigmatic sketch rather than a full blown detailed narrative." The opening lyric has a haunting and disturbing quality because it is so brief, because so much is left unexplained. As in one of Alex Colville's enigmatic and dream-like paintings there is no explanation of why the train leaves the woman behind nor why she is too tired to call. The situation is disturbing precisely because it occurs without an overall explanatory context to give it some kind of causal perspective. The character and the scene are isolated in space—"desert and pale scrub"—and time. The reader knowing nothing about the scene's past can make no valid conjectures about the future. By itself, and then in relation to the next lyric, this poem establishes how Ondaatje wants ***the man with seven toes*** to be read.[10]

Each poem in the sequence presents a new scene or a new experience with the effect that the reader follows the woman's path, and often point of view, as she moves from one shocking and inevitably defamiliarizing experience to another. The events of each new poem are literally unexpected because Ondaatje's structuring has increased the number of narrative possibilities that each lyric creates, to the point that the reader simply does not know what to expect from poem to poem. The very form of each lyric works deliberately against a predictable narrative continuity with the effect that each poem stands out separately as a complete scene. Ondaatje has written that myth is "brief, imagistic"[11] and this certainly applies to his own poem. The revelations in ***the man with seven toes*** come in brief and enigmatic flashes which disappear and are then replaced by new ones; the effect is rather like that of a film in which the director cuts quickly and dynamically from scene to scene allowing the various kinds of montage to create the meaning. The second poem, for example, begins with a dog sitting beside her, the third with her entry into a native clearing. There is no temporal, spatial or syntactical continuity indicated between these opening lyrics.

> entered the clearing and they turned
> faces scarred with decoration
> feathers, bones, paint from clay
> pasted, skewered to their skin.
> Fanatically thin,
> black ropes of muscle.
>
> (11)

A sense of immediacy is created by the elliptical syntax of the opening line. Because the terse poem begins with the verb—"entered"—the reader's attention is focussed on the action itself. The ellipsis of the subject—either "I" or "she"—achieves an abruptness and shocking directness which would have otherwise been lacking. The effect is then reinforced by the brief catalogue of images, one piled upon the other, exotic to both character and reader. The cumulative effect of the rhetoric is to indicate the disorientation of the woman and to achieve that of the reader.

The woman has entered a physical and psychological landscape or wilderness her reaction to which is caught in the violently beautiful imagery and dismembered rhythms of successive lyrics.

goats black goats, balls bushed in the centre
cocks rising like birds flying to you reeling on you
and smiles as they ruffle you open
spill you down, jump and spill over you
white leaping like fountains in your hair
your head and mouth till it dries
and tightens your face like a scar
Then up to cook a fox or whatever, or goats
goats eating goats heaving the bodies
open like purple cunts under ribs, then tear
like to you a knife down their pit, a hand in the warm
the hot the dark boiling belly and rip
open and blood spraying out like dynamite
caught in the children's mouths on the ground
laughing collecting it in their hands
or off to a pan, holding blood like gold
and the men rip flesh tearing, the muscles
nerves green and red still jumping
stringing them out, like you

(16)

The syntax, imagery and rhythm—the entire whirling movement of the verse—re-enact her complex response to an experience which prior to leaving the train she could not have even imagined. Her confusion is registered in her simultaneously positive and negative responses to her rape. There is a moving lyricism in the natural vitality of the men's "cocks rising like birds flying to you" and in the description of their ejaculations as "white leaping like fountains in your hair." But the "fountains" suddenly dry on her "face like a scar" and the subsequent similes serve to reinforce the hinted at connection between her violation and the killing and ripping open of an animal. The cuts in the animal are "like purple cunts," the knife pushed into the animal is also the phallus forced into her, and the bleeding animal body is also hers—"like you." This kind of comparison allows her to dramatize her emotions by making them part of a response to an event outside herself—the killing of "a fox or whatever, or goats." It is almost as if she cannot articulate directly the personal violation that took place; only through her empathic response to the animal's suffering can she describe her own experience. And her recourse to similes, here and in other poems written from her point of view, is an indication of an analogous attempt to appropriate in slightly more familiar images a primal landscape and a set of experiences she finds almost indescribable. A later poem, for example, begins as follows:

evening. Sky was a wrecked black boot
a white world spilling through.
Noise like electricity in the leaves.

(32)

The metaphor ("wrecked black boot") and simile ("like electricity") are imported from the world of civilization in order to render this wilderness slightly more comprehensible, to mediate between its natural language, so to speak, and the character's mode of comprehending and describing the world. But even as these more familiar images achieve the effect of mediating between the two worlds the sense of incongruity caused by their anomalous presence serves, paradoxically, to heighten our awareness of the distance between the two.

The woman's return to the world in which these words are appropriate begins with her rescue by the convict Potter whose striped shirt, in Ondaatje as in Nolan (see the paintings "Escaped Convict," and "In the Cave"), indicates his connection, however tenuous, with civilization.[12] He rescues her from the natives—never referred to as aborigines—but not from the violent existence she had led with them. All the expectations justifiably created by the rescue are immediately thwarted.

Stripe arm caught my dress
the shirt wheeling into me,
gouging me, ankles, manacles,
cock like an ostrich, mouth
a salamander
thrashing in my throat.
Above us, birds peeing from the branches.

(32)

Unexpectedly, for both reader and character, the rescue recapitulates the events of the period of capture. Her rape by the natives is a prelude to this one, and the imagery indicates that Ondaatje wants the two scenes compared: the natives had "cocks like birds," Potter's "cock [is] like an ostrich;" the natives had previously been compared to "sticklebacks" while Potter's mouth is "a salamander." Potter has replaced the natives as her keeper but the nightmare quality of her journey through a physical and psychological chaos has not changed. Her rape, for example, is simultaneously violent, terrifying and ridiculous. The "birds peeing from the branches" put it into a grotesque perspective. Our standard shocked response to the event is suddenly qualified by a new and unanticipated context created by the absurd last line. Yet in ***the man with seven toes*** as in so much of Ondaatje's poetry the unexpected, the absurd and the surreal gradually become the normal and the familiar: a dog runs away with a knife stuck in its head (27); birds drugged on cocaine stagger across the sand (28). As Potter says, "Sometimes I don't believe what's going on" (27). The woman's attitude to these kinds of experiences is finally one of numbed and passive acceptance of events which if they had occurred earlier would have both startled and horrified her.

So we came from there to there
the sun over our shoulders and no one watching
no witness to our pain our broken mouths and bodies.
Things came at us and hit us.
Things happened and went out like matches.

(39)

Because of the reference to "broken mouths" I assume that the speaker is the woman; it is her mouth that has been pried open by the natives (14) and by Potter (35). The poem's vagueness—"from there to there," "Things"—is an effective register of her unemotional attitude at this point. The rhythmic and tonal flatness of "Things came at us and hit us / Things happened" is a fine preparation for the poem's unexpected closing simile. In poetry as in architecture, less is often more and the final image—"matches"—is a stunning close to a poem which is almost devoid of colour and metaphor.[13] The poem's texture creates a simultaneous awareness in the reader of both the essentially shocking nature of what is happening and the paradoxical fact that this no longer surprises the woman.

After her return to civilization, this violently beautiful world seems to pursue her even into the safe Royal Hotel.

> She slept in the heart of the Royal Hotel
> Her burnt arms and thighs
> soaking off the sheets.
> She moved fingers onto the rough skin,
> traced the obvious ribs, the running heart,
> sensing herself like a map, then
> lowering her hands into her body.
> In the morning she found pieces of a bird
> chopped and scattered by the fan
> blood sprayed onto the mosquito net,
> its body leaving paths on the walls
> like red snails that drifted down in lumps.
> She could imagine the feathers
> while she had slept
> falling around her
> like slow rain.
>
> (41)

The narrative itself closes with this ambiguous and densely allusive poem whose almost every image echoes some image or situation occurring earlier. Given the poem's position in the body of the text it is inevitable that we look to it to provide some kind of summarizing judgment upon the story. It does so but only through an ambiguous image or metaphor. The key to interpretation seems to lie in the image of the dead bird and the woman's attitude to it in the final stanza. I assume there is an implicit analogy between the bird's violent death and the woman's horrific and brutal experiences in the wilderness. If this is so then her response to the presence of the slaughtered bird should provide an insight into her attitude to her earlier experiences. Her reaction is either sentimental and romantic or it indicates a full acceptance of the violent natural world into which she had been thrust. I tend towards the second reading because this lyric follows a poem in which the woman's attitude toward the convict, now a memory from her past, is completely positive; and secondly, because the opening stanza seems to point to a physical and psychological awareness and acceptance of the self she has become ("sensing herself like a map, then / lowering her hands into her body"). This new attitude corresponds roughly with Nolan's later paintings of Mrs. Fraser and the land as finally indistinguishable one from another.[14] In Ondaatje, this merging of self and wilderness is reinterpreted as a rediscovery of the instinctual world within the self; the experience of the physical wilderness has led to a reperception, or even an initial awareness, of the natural world within. Here as in D. H. Lawrence's "The Woman Who Rode Away" the physical journey away from civilization is simultaneously a psychological one as well. In fact, it is safe to say that here and in his other work Ondaatje is primarily interested in landscape in so far as it can be used to reveal inner states of being.[15]

The original Mrs. Fraser returned to England, married her ship's master, a Captain Greene, and keeping her marriage a secret, "was able to exhibit herself at 6d a showing in Hyde Park." Ondaatje deals with this return to civilization in a ballad—perhaps sung by his central character—which functions as an epilogue offering another ambiguous summary. (It is worth noting that ***the man with seven toes,*** like Ondaatje's later book-length works, has more than one ending.)

> When we came into Glasgow town
> we were a lovely sight to see
> My love was all in red velvet
> and I myself in cramasie
> Three dogs came out from still grey streets
> they barked as loud as city noise,
> their tails and ears were like torn flags
> and after then came girls and boys
> The people drank the silver wine
> they ate the meals that came in pans
> And after eating watched a lady
> singing with her throat and hands
> Green wild rivers in these people
> running under ice that's calm,
> God bring you all some tender stories
> and keep you all from hurt and harm.
>
> (42)

The original Scots' ballad "Waly, Waly" from which Ondaatje borrows his opening stanza is a song of regret and disillusion in which a woman laments having given herself to her lover:

> "But had I wist before I kiss'd
> That love had been sae ill to win,
> I'd lock my heart in a case of gowd
> And pin'd it we' a siller pin."[16]

In "Waly, Waly" the apparent is not the real: a tree seems "trusty" but breaks, a lover seems true but is not. A similar duality exists in Ondaatje's version: the ostensible order and stability of Glasgow town rest upon people in whom "Green wild rivers" run "under ice that's calm." The full force of the contrast between the two images can only be felt, however, if we place them in the context of the whole text; then the ice is seen as relating to consciousness, order, civilization—everything that was left behind when the woman stepped off the train—and the "rivers" represent everything that is unconscious, chaotic and natural—the world she stepped into. The ice does not crack in the ballad but the reader, keeping in mind the action of the book, realizes how tenuous civilization really is, how at any moment the ice could crack and melt letting through everything implied by the "Green wild rivers." If the book has a theme, or what Ondaatje prefers to call a "moral", it is summarized metaphorically in the interplay of these two images.[17]

But it is also important to note that although the ballad summarizes or comprehends the book's dualities and constitutive tensions it does not resolve them. This deliberate irresolution leaves the sequence with a sense of open-endedness re-inforce by the grammar of the last sentence whose verb ("God keep you"), in the subjunctive mood, points to the future. Like the present tenses in the endings of ***The Collected Works of Billy the Kid*** ("I smell the smoke still in my shirt") and *Coming Through Slaughter* ("There are no prizes") this gives the book an ending without finality or resolution, an ending struggling against the closure inevitable in every work of art. The reader is left with a sense of the continuity of the story and its implications into present and future time. At the precise moment when the book is being finished and about to be put aside it forces itself into the reader's time. One aspect of the book's form—its various discontinuities—compelled the reader to enter the narrative as a figure in the story's ground, as a kind of character surrogate; another aspect, the lack of closure or resolution, reverses the spatial and temporal situation by having the book extend itself into the reader's world. A slight shift in the verb's mood or tense is the final aspect of a narrative form and a poetic rhetoric attempting to achieve a "point blank" and, from Ondaatje's viewpoint, mythic presentation.

Both ***The Collected Works of Billy the Kid*** and *Coming Through Slaughter* go further than ***the man with seven toes*** in bringing the reader into the text, in making his experience of its world as unmediated as possible.[18] But the more ambitious and greater achievement of these later works should not prevent us from acknowledging this minor, though by no means negligible, poem which anticipates them in so many respects.

Notes

1. Roland Barthes, *S/Z,* trans. Richard Miller (Hill and Wang, 1975), pp. 5-6.
2. For other accounts of the story see Bill Beatty, *Tales of Old Australia* (Sydney: Ure Smith, 1966); Bill Wannan, *Legendary Australians* (Adelaide: Rigby, 1974); Patrick White, *A Fringe of Leaves* (New York: Viking, 1977).
3. "O'Hagan's Rough-Edged Chronicle," *Canadian Literature,* 61 (Summer, 1974), 24.
4. Ondaatje quotes from MacInnes in a note at the end of the book. See *the man with seven toes* (Toronto: Coach House Press, 1969), p. 45. All future references will be to this edition and will be cited in the body of the essay.
5. Bryan Robertson has described this painting as follows: "This animal-like figure conveys something of the shock and horror of a white, northern European body flung down in the wild bush of a Pacific island, and forced to fend for itself: a body that has not been exposed to the ravages of strong sun before, straddles horrifically across the land, isolated and lost. Her face is hidden by her hair and this device for anonymity is also employed in all the later paintings of Mrs. Fraser." Kenneth Clark, Colin MacInnes and Bryan Robertson, *Sidney Nolan* (London: Thames and Hudson, 1961), p. 74.
6. Margaret Atwood, *The Journals of Susanna Moodie* (Toronto: Oxford University Press, 1970), p. 8.
7. Francis Bacon's comment about his paintings is relevant here: "we all need to be aware of the potential disaster which stalks us at every moment of the day." John Russell, *Francis Bacon* (London: Thames and Hudson, 1971), p. 31. Other points of comparison that could be drawn between Ondaatje and Bacon relate to their interest in the beauty of violence, in their mutual attempts to describe motion, and the sense or colour of menace that pervades their work.
8. "Interview with Michael Ondaatje," *Rune,* 2 (Spring 1975), 51.
9. *Canadian Literature, op. cit.,* 25-6.
10. Michael Ondaatje, *Leonard Cohen* (Toronto: McClelland and Stewart, 1970) p. 23.
11. *Canadian Literature, op. cit.,* 25.
12. In White's *A Fringe of Leaves* the convict's name is Jack Chance and his status as a man existing between civilization and wilderness is evident from the fact that he has almost completely forgotten the English language. White replaces the striped shirt with scars, an image that Ondaatje would probably respond to since his own work—"A Time Around Scars," *Coming Through Slaughter*—reveals a fascination with emotional and physical scars. "[She] realized that she was touching the scars she had first noticed on his first appearing at the black's camp, when their apparently motive-less welter distinguished them from the formal incisions in native backs," (p. 290).
13. Ondaatje quotes.the following sentence from *Tay John* in his article: "indeed, to tell a story is to leave most of it untold," p. 30.
14. "Woman and Billabong," "Woman in Swamp," "Woman in Mangroves."
15. In *A Fringe of Leaves,* the encounter with the wilderness is simultaneously an encounter with "secret depths with which even she, perhaps, is unacquainted, and which sooner or later must be troubled" (p. 20).
16. See Willa Muir, *Living With Ballads* (London: Hogarth Press, 1965) pp. 224-225. For the earliest treatment of Mrs. Fraser's experiences see the ballad "Wreck of the 'Stirling Castle,'" reprinted in Bill Wannan's *Legendary Australians,* pp. 47-49. As Wannan points out, "This 'Copy of Mournful Verses' was originally published in broadsheet form in 1837, by the printer of broadsides J. Catnach, of Seven Dials, London." The last two stanzas should give sufficient indication of its quality:

    The chief mate too they did despatch,
    By cutting off his head,
    And plac'd on one of their canoes
    All for a figure head.
    Also, a fine young man they bound,
    And burnt without a dread,
    With a slow fire at his feet at first
    So up unto his head.
    When you read the tortures I went thro'
    'Twill grieve your heart full sore,
    But now thank HEAVEN, I am returned

Unto my native shore.
I always shall remember,
And my prayers will ever be,
For the safety of both age and sex,
Who sail on the raging sea.

17. In *Leonard Cohen* Ondaatje writes that the world of *Let Us Compare Mythologies* is one "where the morals are imagistic, as they always are in the context of dreams," p. 14.
18. There are two other particularly important differences between *the man with seven toes* and its more famous successors: the later works are more autobiographical, if obliquely so, and self-reflexive.

Judith Owens (essay date 1983)

SOURCE: "'I Send You a Picture': Ondaatje's Portrait of Billy the Kid," in *Studies in Canadian Literature,* Vol. 8, No. 1, 1983, pp. 117-39.

[*In the essay below, Owens presents a thorough analysis of* The Collected Works of Billy the Kid, *focusing in particular on the tension between order and disorder in the collection. Owens asserts that Billy "seeks or imposes order in the external world to compensate for a disintegrating inner world."*]

I

The reader finds in Ondaatje's Billy a strong desire for order, a rage for order, one might say, if Billy's style and voice were not so deliberately flat in so many places. From his opening words, Billy reveals an inclination to order his world as he neatly lists "the killed" by himself and "by them."[1] The precision and meticulousness of Billy's list stand in contrast to the qualities of those photographs enumerated by Billy's contemporary, L. A. Huffman, on the preceding page: "bits of snow in the air—spokes well defined—some blur on top of wheel but sharp in the main" (p. 5). Imprecision marks these "daily experiements" made by Huffman, a quality to be accounted for more by Huffman's interest in motion than by any lack of sophistication in equipment or technique. Not only does he choose moving subjects—"passing horses," "men walking"—but he frequently shoots from "the saddle" when his horse is "in motion." Whereas movement strikes the keynote in Huffman's paragraph, fixity characteristizes Billy's list. And Huffman's "movement," given his paragraph's privileged position at the beginning of the volume and its lively, energetic rhythm, immediately impresses the reader as preferable to Billy's fixity.

Billy's attempt, in his opening "work," to organize his world into a clear-cut pattern fails almost immediately. J. M. Kertzer points out that the initial distinction between friend and foe breaks down in the next poem when Billy reports killing Jim Carlyle "over some mix-up, he being a friend" (p. 7).[2] In fact, in Billy's first entry itself, any distinction between adversaries seems fuzzy, at best, for Billy begins his list of those he has killed by including "Morton, Baker, early friends of mine" (p. 5).

The blurring of the lines between adversaries extends to Ondaatje's presentation of Pat Garrett as well. For, while Billy, on the one side, can kill friends, Garrett, on the other side, can "giggle" at the escapades of the men whom he pursues, imprisons, and kills (p. 28). Moreover, the relationship between Billy and Garrett, with its ambiguously sexual undertones, does not resolve simply into a question of "sheriff versus outlaw."[3] As Kertzer suggests, Ondaatje creates a world in which all categories "break apart as the imagery shifts and fuses."[4]

Despite the apparent impossibility of fixing the world, Billy remains insistent in his urge to order. He sprinkles his account of the killing of Tom O'Folliard, for example, with "thens" and "nows," words which lend the semblance of orderly progression to a narrative. The narrative mode itself presupposes some principle of order moving through time, of course.

Billy's **"Boot Hill"** poem illustrates particularly well the problematic aspect of his desire for a simple order since the poem points to natural forces which resist any imposition of order. The graveyard's path stubbornly "tangles," mocking the aspirations of a formal and imposing gate designed to maintain order:

There is an elaborate gate
but the path keeps to no main route for it tangles
like branches of a tree among the gravestones.

(p. 9)

The choice of a natural metaphor to image the garveyard's disorder betrays Billy's belief that the natural world is unmanageable and messy, if not chaotic. He quickly counters this natural disorder with another list of the killed:

300 of the dead in Boot Hill died violently
200 by guns, over 50 by knives
some were pushed under trains—a popular
and overlooked form of murder in the west.
Some from brain haemorrhages resulting from bar fights
at least 10 killed in barbed wire.

(p. 9)

That two of Billy's opening three "works" involve lists tells us something about the strength of his need for order; that both are lists of the dead suggests something about order itself: perhaps only dead things can fit tidily into a list. (And even then the result may be only a semblance of order; Billy's first list, we recall, failed to adequately contain or fix clear distinctions between adversaries.) A curious detail from the prose section preceding the **"Boot Hill"** poem—a small incident in the list of the events which follow Garrett's killing of O'Folliard—also links death and orderliness. "Mason," Billy reports, "stretched out a blanket *neat* in the corner. Garrett *placed* Tom O'Folliard down, broke open Tom's rifle, took the remaining shells and *placed* them by him" (p. 8: my italics). Again the suggestion is that only lifeless things can be so neatly placed. The association between order and death strengthens when we notice that Boot Hill's image of disorder, "the path [which] keeps to no main route," also invests the graveyard with its only signs of life when it "tangles / like branches of a tree" (p. 9). In Billy's graveyard poem, living and growing become instances of disorderly conduct.

If Billy's first three works demonstrate his compelling urge to order things, events, and people, his fourth work sketches a reason for this obsession with external order: Billy's uneasiness with the radically disordered nature of his inner world. Billy, that is, seeks or imposes order in the external world to compensate for a disintegrating inner world, a state which he projects upon the world around him. Nightmarish visions of a world in deformation constantly plague him. When he looks up, he apprehends a vast metaphysical or divine injury, seeing "wounds appearing in the sky" (p. 10). Unable to place his faith in the heavens, he cannot cling to ideals of normality in the human sphere either, because what appears to be normal may deflate at any moment: "Sometimes," Billy confesses, "a normal forehead in front of me leaked brain gasses" (p. 10). The human organism proves defective, faultily adapted to its world: "Once a nose clogged right before me, a lock of skin formed over the nostrils [he seemed] in the end to be breathing out of his eye—tiny needle jets of air reaching into the throat" (p. 10). So, "In the end," Billy turns to non-human life, seeking relief from his vision of deformation in "the only thing that never changed, never became deformed," in "animals" (p. 10).

Even as Billy is presenting his visions of deformation and disorder, however, his compulsion to order determines the development of the paragraph. His attention moves steadily downward, in orderly fashion, from sky to forehead, nose, mouth, mustache, teeth, to the body on the floor, finally coming to rest below the human level, on animals. At this lowest level, Billy finds, or imagines, that quality which, in a more traditional metaphysical view, would belong to the highest sphere—immutability. Clearly Billy desires not mere order, but unchanging, eternal order.

The notion of changelessness figures as well in the poem which follows the passage describing Billy's nightmarish perceptions, in a way which links the desire for immutability specifically to Billy's fear of mortality. Once again the disturbing fact of deformity confronts Billy, only this time it is the deformity wrought by his own hand when he shoots a man. Unwilling to consider himself at all responsible for such deformation, Billy advocates the "moral of newspapers or gun / where bodies are mindless" (p. 11). He constructs an argument that, with its "so then that is why" structure, bears at least the appearance of orderly, logical development:

> so if I had a newman's brain I'd say
> well some morals are physical
> must be clear and open
> like diagram of watch or star
> one must eliminate much
> that is one turns when the bullet leaves you
> walk off see none of the thrashing
> the very eyes welling up like bad drains
> believing then the moral of newspapers or gun
> where bodies are mindless as paper flowers you dont
> feed
> or give to drink
> that is why I can watch the stomach of clocks
> shift their wheels and pins into each other
> and emerge living, for hours.
>
> (p. 11)

But beneath the seeming straightforwardness of Billy's argument lies a confusion of semi-articulated ideas and feelings revolving around a wish to deny the very fact of human mortality. (Thus, once again, we find Billy imposing a superficial order in an attempt to compensate for inward disorder.) Since an awareness of the inexorable, forward movement of time contributes so largely to the knowledge of mortality, Billy tries to deny mortality by qualifying the movement of time, by blocking any sense of the absolute passing of time. Toward this end, he introduces the image of a "diagram of watch" which can successfully "eliminate much." What a diagram eliminates most effectively is movement, here, specifically the movement of time. When, at the end of the poem, Billy refers to his contemplation of an actual, working clock, he still has in mind a timeplace that does not tell the time. The clocks he chooses show only their inner mechanisms, their "stomachs"; they are faceless, handless, and therefore unable to register the passing of time. Billy can "watch the stomach of clocks" for hours and still "emerge living" because, despite the continual shifting of "wheels and pins," time does not appear to move. More precisely, it seems to circle endlessly round and round rather than move forward.

In an earlier "work" (pp. 7-8), and in "works" to come, we see Billy relying expressly upon narratives, upon an orderly progression through time, in an effort to fix his world. His present attempt to stop the flow of time thus introduces a seeming contradiction or inconsistency in his responses to the world. In fact, though, what strikes us here as merely contradictory really operates in a quietly ironic way throughout the volume and especially in its last quarter. Briefly, if the narrative mode involves orderly movement through time, and if movement through time contributes to the knowledge of mortality, then the narrative mode must ultimately lead to confrontation with mortality. Ironically, then, two of Billy's strongest impulses, his wish to deny the fact of mortality and his urge to order his world, prove finally incompatible. When, toward the end of the volume, Billy wins a chronologically ordered world, he pays with his life. But this is to anticipate my discussion, as well as to imply, perhaps, that Billy himself is aware of the incompatible aspects of his approach to the world. At this early stage in the book, Billy shows no such self-awareness. Nor does he reason out the implications of his reactions to events and people; he simply responds according to the demands of the moment, imposing a narrative structure in one instance, for example, and refusing to acknowledge the passage of time in another instance.

The poem presently under discussion ends with a circling motion, as we have seen a moment of stasis, really, which stands in implicit contrast to the linear, forward movement which Billy emphasizes at the start of the poem when he tells of

> moving across the world on horses
> body split at the edge of their necks
> neck sweat eating at my jeans
> moving across the world on horses.
>
> (p. 11)

These lines convey a sense of time entirely different from that suggested by diagrams or stomachs of clocks. Here, at the beginning of the poem, time presses inexorably forward. Indeed, the opening lines amount to a reworking of the conventional metaphor of "consuming time": Billy feels the sweat "eating at" the jeans of his "split" body. The poem's closing moment of stasis, from which Billy claims to "emerge living," relieves the acute physical discomfort described in the second and third lines, thereby strengthening, by contrast, the suggestion that the opening lines are playing with the idea of "consuming time."

Once the reader sees the image of all-devouring time as even faintly operative in the poem, Billy's comparison of "bodies" to "paper flowers you dont feed" assumes another dimension of meaning. One "feeds" real flowers when one is wholly consumed by time, that is, dead and buried. Billy's preference for paper flowers thus grows out of his wish to deny mortality. Logically, of course, such a notion has little to do with the strict sense of these lines. My point is that the fact of mortality and the consequent fear of consuming time determine much of this poem's imagery and on a level which runs deeper than Billy's express horror of thrashing bodies and eyes that well up like bad drains.

Any attempt to deny the fact of mortality soon proves futile, as of course it must, as we see on the next page with its startingly vivid rendering of Charlie Bowdre's death. Although Billy begins his first of two accounts of the death of Charlie in good narrative fashion with the line "When I caught Charlie Bowdre dying" (p. 12), he cannot fulfill the expectations of the narrative mode. The "when. . . while" structure remains unfinished as Billy trails off into a long silence part way down the page. Overwhelmed by Charlie's dying, Billy can only register a sense of helplessness in the face of something which he clearly feels to lie completely beyond his control: Charlie's eyes, Billy remembers, grew "*all over* his body," and his liver looked, sickeningly, like a headless hen jerking "*all over* the yard" (p. 12: my italics).

"Jesus," Billy exlaims in response to Charlie's ugly death, "I never knew" that that's what happens. The reader might easily pass over Billy's "Jesus" as simply an expletive. However, Billy's use of this word is both infrequent and select enough to warrant our reading it as something more. Billy uses "Jesus" on only three occasions throughout the volume and in each instance he is speaking about a death (p. 12, p. 22, p. 73). Since it becomes associated in this way with his abiding fear of mortality, Billy's expletive perhaps expresses an unconscious hope that there exists a Jesus who offers life after death.

As if to cleanse himself of the messy details of Charlie's dying, Billy turns to the memory of a river-crossing:

> Blurred a waist high river
> foam against the horse
> riding naked clothes and boots
> and pistol in the air.
>
> (p. 14)

The obviously phallic "pistol," an image of general potency intimates that Billy has recovered from the feelings of powerlessness which attended the death of Charlie. Certainly the river memory affords him a measure of composure, as the regularity to the poem's rhythm indicates. The choppiness of the preceding "Charlie" poem now gives way to a greater evenness. Gone, too, is the quality of unmanageableness which characterizes the scene of Charlie's death, conveyed by such awkwardly run-on lines as: "tossed 3 feet by bang bullets giggling / at me face tossed in a gaggle" (p. 12). The still more regular rhythm of the second stanza of the river poem efficiently organizes Billy's perceptions and feelings into tidy, one-line units:

> Crossed a crooked river
> loving in my head
> ambled dry on stubble
> shot a crooked bird.
>
> (p. 14)

Billy remains in control of himself in this poem, as unaffected now by the shooting of the bird as he was affected by the shooting of Charlie one page earlier. He records the distinction between these two responses imagistically, as the bird's distance from him, when he tells us that he "Held [the bird] in my fingers," and that its eyes seemed to him "small and far" (p. 14). Charlie's more immediate eyes, in contrast, "grew all over his body," and Billy's "hands," pressed against his friend, felt Charlie "pissing into his trouser legs in pain" (p. 12).

Billy distances himself from the painful knowledge of mortality still more effectively in the passage describing the shooting of Gregory. (The absence of Gregory's name from Billy's opening list of those killed by him proves just how effectively.) As Dennis Cooley observes, Billy employs various devices which amount to a "verbal narcotic," aimed at "minimizing his own responsibility and awareness."[5] Foremost among these devices stands the grimly black humour with which Billy recounts the actions of "this chicken" as it

> paddles out to [Gregory]
> and as he was falling hops on his neck

digs the beak into his throat
straightens legs and heaves
a red and blue vein out.

(p. 15)

Billy finishes his anecdote with a stroke of comic genius which not only renders Gregory's dying moment less than momentous, but which nearly absolves Billy from any blame in the matter of Gregory's death. For when we read that Gregory's "last words" were "get away from me yer stupid chicken," we almost forget that Billy has killed Gregory, that he "shot him well and careful. . . under his heart" (p. 15). Billy thus shrugs off any personal complicity, implying, as Cooley says, that "these things just happened, rather comically, and they don't have much of anything to do with me."[6]

That one can even speak of the "Gregory" passage as an anecdote gauges the extent to which Billy feels himself to be in control of circumstances once again. In the "Charlie" section, we recall, an inability to fulfill the expectations of the narrative mode signals Billy's utter helplessness in the face of his friend's death. No hiatus interrupts the narrative voice this time, however. The lines, "and the chicken walked away / still tugging. . . " promptly follow the phrase, "Meanwhile he fell," to the satisfaction of the demands of the narrative mode.

Control, order, impersonality, distance. Billy manages to achieve these goals—in defiance of the all-too-close messiness of Charlie's death—by the end of the "Gregory" passage, only to be thrust once again into the midst of turmoil when he turns his attention, in the next poem, to his sexual experiences with, presumably, Angie, The poem begins precipitously:

Tilts back to fall
black hair swivelling off her
shattering the pillow.

(p. 16)

Angie resembles a gigantic uncontrollable machine and clearly Billy perceives her as threatening. The poem's last four lines focus on a Billy who, in the aftermath of the violent love-making, feels maimed:

later my hands cracked in love juice
fingers paralyzed by it arthritic
these beautiful fingers I couldnt move
faster than a crippled witch now.

(p. 16)

Billy's extreme physical passivity forms a contrast to the violence of Angie's movements, in a way which reverses traditional notions of male and female sexual roles. Billy, we suspect, fears emasculation by Angie, feels that she has usurped his—the male's—role. His use of the word "beautiful," an adjective cutomarily reserved for the woman, to describe not Angela, but his own fingers, suggests as much, as does his likening of himself to a typically female creature, a "witch." That Billy in part images himself as female points to his feeling of helplessness in the face of Angie's onslaught.

One aspect of the poem, perhaps more than any other, exposes Billy's deeply-rooted fear that he does not have control over either Angie, or, more generally, the world he inhabits. This, the first of Billy's "love" lyrics, bears a telling relationship to the tradition of love poetry in which the beloved is identified with the world. Poems in that tradition typically image the beloved as a landscape. True to that form, we find Angie-as-landscape in the middle of Billy's poem. In keeping with his distrust of Angie and of his world, however, the landscape in Billy's version appears as a place of ambush: Angie

leans her whole body out
so breasts are thinner
stomach is a hollow
where the bright bush jumps.

(p. 16)

By this point in the volume, then, a picture emerges of a Billy who feels vulnerable, threatened by death, by the unleashed energy of sexuality, by the disorder of the natural world. Instinctively, he seeks to contain and restrain the forces ranged against him: he compiles lists, he tries to deny the passing of time, he distances himself from the knowledge of mortality. Fearing that there is no god, no divinely ordered universe, yet desperately wanting order in his world, Billy feels compelled to create order where he cannot find it. But it is not until well into the volume that Billy takes advantage of his role as the "author" of these "works" to create a more desirable world for himself, or a more favourable image of himself.

II

Billy's first clear declaration that he intends his "works" to tell his story occurs several pages into the volume. As if he has overheard Paulita Maxwell remark that a certain photograph "makes him rough and uncouth," and does not do him "justice" (p. 19), Billy asserts that he will make his own image: "Not a story about me through their eyes then" (p. 20). The making of his story offers Billy the supreme chance to assume control over his world, to order the world to his liking. And immediately after he determines to take the matter of his story into his own hands, Billy reworks two incidents from earlier in the volume, presenting himself in a new and more favourable light both in relationship to Angie and in response to the killing of Charlie Bowdre.

The second of Billy's poems about Angela (p. 21) focuses on an incident essentially similar to, if not exactly identical with, the encounter described in the first "love" poem (p. 16). Both poems present a bedroom scene, but the circumstantial parallel only underscores certain changes in Billy's position. To begin with, although each poem closes with a physically inert Billy, the second poem makes a virtue of what now appears to be a welf-willed passivity.

That is, in contrast to the first lyric's crippling paralysis, which strikes Billy independently of his will, passivity in the later poem becomes a matter of choice: "I am very still," says Billy, "I take in all the angles of the room" (p. 21). "Angles" surely refers not only to the geometry of the room but also, given Billy's status as an outlaw, to the strategems which others might use to entrap Billy. Thus, stillness becomes the means by which Billy hopes to avoid being ambushed again, as he was in the first love lyric when the "bright bush" jumped (p. 16). Billy, then, at least appears to be in a position of control and dominance.

Billy certainly exercises greater control over Angie in the second of his love lyrics, tempering, for example, the violence of her movements. Angie's great physical strength, which so frightened Billy in the first poem by shattering pillows and nearly breaking his fingers, here remains restricted to one act:

> she walks slow to the window
> lifts the sackcloth
> and jams it horizontal on a nail.
>
> (p. 21)

Even this one aggressive movement of jamming the sackcloth loses some of its force, preceded as it is by Angie's slow walk and gentle lifting of the cloth.

Above all, a general lengthening of perspective gives Billy the control over Angie and over his own responses to her which he lacked in the first love poem. That first lyric began, precipitously, with Angie tilting back to fail next to Billy on the bed (p. 16). Billy starts the second poem at an earlier point, initially focusing on Angie at a distance as she "leans against the door" and "looks at the bed" (p. 21). Not until the penultimate stanza does Angie finally fall onto the bed, and even then Billy draws out this movement with the phrase "turns toppling slow" (p. 21). His lengthening of Angie's fall towards him does not betoken a lover's desire to linger over an especially tantalizing or pleasing moment of love-making, however. Rather, it signals a wish to purge the moment of its immediacy, a desire in Billy to distance himself from the event by rendering it impersonal.

One very slight change from the first poem further reveals Billy's distance from Angie. In the first lyric, Billy remembered Angie calling him—familiarly, intimately—"Billy" (p. 16). In the second poem, Angie calls Billy by his surname, "Bonney Bonney" (p. 21). The absence of intimacy in this form of address anticipates the psychological distance from Angie which Billy maintains in the poem's closing lines. Although Angela lies next to him on the bed, (having just "toppled" on the pillows after seductively tracing Billy's bones), Billy's eyes and mind move outward from her and the bed: "I am very still / I take in all the angles of the room" (p. 21).

Despite Billy's re-presentation of this episode, his reworking of events in a way which grants him greater control, a strong sense of his vulnerability emerges nevertheless. For while Angie's movements may no longer seem so violent, Billy still unconsciously perceives her as an overwhelming presence in the room and on the bed, as his choice of verbs indicates. The heavy, ponderous motion with which the sun "hoists itself across the room" becomes associated with Angie to some degree since it is she who lifts the sackcloth to let in the sun. Angie's subsequent act of "crossing the sun" offers an image which, if taken literally just for a moment, lends a cosmic vastness to this woman. Even her action of "sweeping off the peels" strikes us as a large gesture, larger, say, than would be mere "brushing." And Angela's massiveness underlines Billy's diminutiveness. We sense this sharp contrast when Angela "traces the *thin* bones" on her lover(my italics). Perhaps we are even a little afraid that Angela, in "toppling slow back," might crush Billy beneath her. Finally, Billy still seems vulnerable to us because the reversal of traditional male and female sexual roles effected in the first love poem carries over to this poem. Billy continues to embody a feminine passivity as he "take[s] in" the angles of the room.

Although, as we have just seen, Billy cannot entirely mask his vulnerability, he does appear as a more dominant figure in the second love lyric than in the first. Similarly, the second version of Charlie's death discovers Billy equal to the circumstances, not helplessly overcome by his friend's dying, as he was in the first recounting. As in the second love poem, Billy's bid to characterize himself as calmly in control involves a lengthening of perspective. Whereas the first "Charlie" poem, directed almost accusingly at Charlie for dying, began with the fact of Charlie's death, "When I caught Charlie Bowdre dying" (p. 12), the second version approaches the shooting from a slightly earlier point in the sequence of events, and in an emotionally neutral voice:

> January, at Tivan Arroyo, called Stinking Springs
> more often. With me, Charlie, Wilson, Dave Rudabaugh.
> Snow. Charlie took my hat and went out to get wood
> and feed the horses. The shot burnt the clothes on
> his stomach off and lifted him right back into the
> room.
>
> (p. 22)

This version grants considerably more dignity to the dying Charlie: here we read that the shot "lifted" Charlie into the room while in the earlier version we read that Charlie was unceremoniously "tossed. . . by bang bullets" (p. 12). But most importantly, the Billy who, in the first version, stood by, helpless, dumbfounded, while the "eyes grew all over [Charlie's] body" (p. 12), now takes prompt and practical action: "Get up Charlie, get up, go and get one. . . I prop him to the door, put his gun in his hand" (p. 22). And he tries to do even more: "Over [Charlie's] shoulder I aimed at Pat, fired, and hit his shoulder braid" (p. 22).

That Billy misses his target tells us, of course, that, far from being calmly in control of himself, he remains as shaken by the shooting of his friend as he appeared to be in the first version. His unadmitted feelings of horror and fear also express themselves in an unwarranted emphasis on "snow," and in a curious obsession with the "straightness" of Charlie's walk towards Garrett. Billy's mind fixes on these two seemingly irrelevant details (especially the latter) with an intensity that belies his posture of emotional neutrality and control.

III

In the passages just discussed, Billy feels compelled to create (however unsuccessfully) an image of himself as strong and in complete control of circumstances. When he first writes of his visits to the Chisum ranch, however, he experiences no such compulsion. In fact, he surrenders to a sense of himself as weak and vulnerable, identifying implicity with "the tame, the half born, the wild, the wounded" animals who find sanctuary at the ranch (p. 36). Billy surrenders, lets down his guard, precisely because the ranch does seem to offer sanctuary, in that it appears to Billy as a perfectly ordered world. More accurately, Billy remembers or re-creates the ranch as just such a refuge. But just as in his role as the author of these works Billy could not entirely mask his feelings of helplessness in the face of Charlie's death or Angie's powerful presence, neither can he sustain the illusion of the ranch as refuge, as we shall see.

It is Sallie Chisum who introduces us to the ranch, in a reminiscence obviously solicited by some chronicler seeking to romanticize the "old west." "Miss Sallie Chisum," writes this historian, "later Mrs. Roberts, was living in Roswell in 1924, a sweet faced, kindly old lady of a thousand memories of frontier days" (p. 30). Sallie obliges the historian with a memory which is pat and conventional, right down to the little thrill of horror with which she mentions Billy:

> Billy the Kid would come in often
> and sometimes stayed for a week or two.
> I remember how frightened I was the first time he
> came.
>
> (p. 30)

Because of Sallie's note of casual insincerity, the depth of Billy's thoughts and feelings about the ranch impresses the reader all the more forcibly. "Forty miles ahead of us," begins Billy, "in almost a straight line, is the house" (p. 32). We might well imagine this to be a voice from the Bible—"forty" is such a biblical number, after all, especially in connection with the kind of desert landscape over which Billy is travelling. At the very least, Billy approaches the ranch with reverence. In contrast to Sallie's memory which, from far away in 1924, generalizes about life at the ranch as an impersonal round of guests and busyness, Billy's memory, "Even now, this far away," furnishes a wealth of particularities:

> It is nine in the morning. They are leaning back
> in their chairs after their slow late Saturday
> breakfast. John with the heels of his brown boots
> on the edge of the table in the space he cleared of
> his plate and cup and cutlery, the cup in his hands in
> his
> lap. The table with four plates—two large
> two small. The remnants of bacon fat and eggs on the
> larger ones, the black crumbs of toast butter and
> marmalade (Californian) on the others.
>
> (p. 32)

Billy revels in the sheer predictability of life at the Chisum ranch. It satisfies his longing for order to know that

> Across the table on the other side is Sallie, in probably her long brown and yellow dress. . . By now she would have moved the spare chair so she too could put her feet up, barefoot as always. . . Her right arm would be leaning against the table and now and then she'll scrape the bottom of her cup against the saucer and drink some of the coffee. . . On other days they would go their own ways. . . On weekdays anyway, she'd sit like that on the bed. . .
>
> (pp. 32-33)

Billy painstakingly shields his image of the ranch from disruption, weaving any changes that might have occurred into the fabric of his memory. "No I forgot, she had stopped that now," says Billy in reference to Sallie's former task of emptying the lamps (p. 33). "She left the paraffin in the lamps; instead had had John build shutters. . . all she did was close and lock them," he remembers, insisting again later "Yes. . . Yes I remember" (p. 33).

Sallie Chisum, especially, represents the immutability Billy needs so to badly. He imposes upon her the quality of unchangingness he fails to find elsewhere in the world when he sees her

> like a ghost across the room moving in white dresses, her hair knotted as always at the neck and continuing down until it splayed and withered like eternal smoke half way between the shoulder blades and the base of cobble spine.
>
> (p. 33)

Sallie's very ghostliness, her incorporeality, renders her immune to the mutability of the flesh and thus to the mortality Billy fears so much.

Temporarily released from the fears of mortality and of disorder which customarily grip it, Billy's imagination finds the time and space to expand. The slow rhythm and the long, leisurely recounting of details reflect such an imaginative expansion. So too does Billy's movement backwards in time from the present occasion to his second and first visits to the ranch. However, it is the nearly mythic quality informing much of the first "Chisum" section which best expresses this imaginative expansiveness. The following passage, with its description of cosmic forces and its subtle personification of sun and moon, approaches the level of myth; we might even hear a specific allusion to the Christian myth of regeneration in the reference to three days of deathlike stillness:

> And I sat there for three days not moving an inch, like some dead tree witnessing the tides or the sun and the moon taking over from each other as the house in front of me changed colour—the night, the early morning yellow, the gradual move to dark blue at 11 o clock, the new white 4 o clock sun let in, later the gradual growing dark again.
>
> (p. 34)

Two paragraphs later, Sallie strengthens the mythic element by seeming to repeat the movements of sun and moon. Billy witnesses Sallie

> starting from one end and disappearing down to the far end leaving black behind her as she walked into the remaining light, making it all a cold darkness. Then in other rooms not seen by me.
>
> (p. 34)

The sun tracks across the sky in a similar movement, leaving night in its wake as it goes on to light the other side of the world. Sallie then reappears, "vast in the thick blue in her long white dress," like a white moon taking over from the sun at nightfall.

The quiet, reassuringly domestic scene with which the Chisum section opens thus yields to an increasingly mythic atmosphere. And in its turn, myth gives way to mystery. A sense of the fundamental mysteriousness of reality pervades Billy's description of cages of birds

> In those dark cages the birds, there must have been 20 of them, made a steady hum all through the night—a noise you heard only if you were within five yards of them. Walking back to the house it was again sheer silence from where we had come, only now we knew they were moving and sensing the air and our departure. We knew they continued like that all night while we slept.
>
> (p. 37)

Unknown and unknowable, these birds represent an absolute "otherness," hence an absolute mystery. The sense of the inexplicableness of reality continues into the next and last paragraph, only now Billy consciously seeks to articulate this "strange" sense:

> Half way back to the house, the building we moved towards seemed to be stuffed with something yellow and wet. The night, the dark air, made it all mad. That fifteen yards away there were bright birds in cages and here John Chisum and me walked, strange bodies.
>
> (p. 37)

In his struggle to grasp the mystery confronting him, Billy turns finally to a language of pure description, deliberately eschewing the language of definition as he looks with new eyes at

> a house stuffed with yellow wet light where within the frame of a window we say a woman move carrying fire in a glass funnel and container towards the window, towards the edge of the dark where we stood.
>
> (p. 37)

Sallie's carrying of light towards Billy and the darkness exactly reverses her earlier walk "into the remaining light" which leaves "black" and a "cold darkness" behind her (p. 34). Billy represents that earlier activity of closing the shutters as "the sudden blacking out of clarity" (p. 34). As his uncharacteristic choice of so abstract a word as "clarity" indicates, he is referring to a degree of intelligibility rather than to a quality of light. And Billy, we understand, welcomes that state of darkness—of unintelligibility—because, like much else at the Chisum ranch, it releases him from the painful demands of reality, from having to make sense of the world. Perry Nodelman observes, in reference to another of Billy's works, that Billy likes to block out light because he fears "the world it allows him to see."[7]

The absence of demands in the middle section of the Chisum passage manifests itself particularly in the unobstrusiveness of Sallie's presence. Specifically, Sallie seems sexually undemanding to Billy; she wanders rather plunges (as Angie does) into love-making:

> Her shoes off, so silent, she moves a hand straying over the covers off John's books, till she comes and sits near me and puts her feet up shoeless and I reach to touch them. . . the brown tanned feet of Sallie Chisum resting on my chest, my hands rubbing them. . .
>
> (p. 35)

It is almost as if Sallie's undemanding presence returns Billy imaginatively to a world before man, a world of emergent, uncomplicated lifeforms: touching Sallie's feet, Billy imagines "some semi-shelled animal" (p. 35). At the very least, Sallie returns Billy to a simpler time in man's history, to a fresher world in which Billy feels "like a carpenter shaving wood to find new clear pulp smelling wood beneath" (p. 35).

In contrast to such a soothingly dim and inchoate world which makes few demands upon Billy's consciousness, the mystery which Billy encounters at the close of the Chisum passage will not permit a lapse into mental indolence. It demands, as we have seen, that Billy adopt a different kind of language. In short, it demands a response. The passage ends with Billy poised, momentarily and, one senses, momentously, on "the edge of dark" as a woman carrying fire moves towards this verge. The moment is one of acute self-consciousness for Billy, a moment in which the unknowableness of everything that is other than oneself forces consciousness to turn in upon itself.

The reader's sense of the precariousness of Billy's positon on "the edge" finds confirmation on the very next page when Billy suddenly prophesies his own violent death: "(To come) to where eyes will / move in head like a rat / mad since locked in a biscuit tin all day" (p. 38). The self-consciousness of the preceding page has forced upon Billy the certain knowledge of his own mortality. Characteristically, Billy images his death as a loss of control:

> sad billys body glancing out
> body going as sweating white horses go
> reeling off me wet
> scuffing down my arms
> wet horse white
> screaming wet sweat round the house.
>
> (p. 38)

On the formal level, Billy's inability to separate, either imagistically or syntactically, the vision of his death from the description of the rat mirrors the theme of loss of control. Specifically, Billy fears the loss of inner control, of control over his "eyes" which will move wildly, unable to maintain a steady vision of the world.

But, just as earlier in the volume Billy escaped from the painfulness of Charlie's ugly death to the cleansing river, so now he seeks immediate refuge from the knowledge of his own death in the memory of a pleasantly domestic scene "With the Bowdres" (p. 39). He goes on to speak, wistfully almost, of "beautiful machines" which realize his own unfulfilled desires for perfectly and effortlessly controlled energy: "The beautiful machines pivoting on themselves / sealing and fusing to others / and men throwing levers like coins at them" (p. 41). But neither evasion works completely. The Bowdres' kitchen grows suddenly "strange" when Billy feels "people / not close to me / as if their dress were against my shoulder," or when he finds his "eyes / magnifying the bones across a room / shifting a wrist" (p. 39). The panegyric to "beautiful machines" begins with Billy's fear that the cosmos might explode into chaos:

> I have seen pictures of great stars,
> drawings which show them straining to the centre
> that would explode their white
> if temperature and the speed they moved at
> shifted one degree.
>
> (p. 41)

And this fearful sense of precariousness finally overrides even the "clean speed" and beauty of machines in motion, for "there is there the same stress as with stars, / the one altered move that will make them maniac" (p. 41).

Again and again throughout the next several pages of the volume, Billy encounters an increasingly disturbing world which assaults him with its uncontained, chaotic energies. "Bloated" flowers, "bursting" their "white drop of spend," explode into entropy, anticipating the explosion of "great stars" which Billy feels to be inevitable (p. 55). This white chaos stuffs up Billy's nose so that he "can hardly breathe nothing / nothing thick sugar death" (p. 55). He recalls, for the second time in the volume, his twenty-first birthday, only now, instead of remembering it as a "celebration" (p. 7), he remembers the "angry weather in my head" (p. 58). Most significantly, each of the three passages on the Chisum ranch which punctuate the middle section of the volume centres around an unpleasant incident involving an animal. In the first, Billy must kill a rabid cat (pp. 44-45). In the second, he hears of a race of mad dogs who degenerate into

> heaps of bone and hair and sexual organs and bulging eyes and minds which were chaotic half out of hunger out of liquor out of their minds being pressed out of shape by new freakish bones that grew into their skulls.
>
> (pp. 61-62)

The last Chisum passage brings a "bloody dog" who "methodically begins to eat" Billy's vomit (p. 70). Early in the volume, we remember, Billy sought relief from his troubling vision of the world in animals, in "the only thing that never changed, never became deformed" (p. 10).

That the Chisum ranch should provide the setting in which Billy's trust in animals proves so ill-founded seems especially ironic in light of his presentation of the ranch as a pastoral world. At times, indeed, the ranch appears Edenic. For instance, the closest Billy comes to a moment of pure happiness is when he wakes at the ranch after a "bad night" into an idyllic world in which "silvery shadows roll across the ceiling" (p. 71). His sense of well-being finds its best expression in his image of Angela as a bountiful landscape:

> Angela D is golden and cool beside. . . her arm out straight over the edge of the bed like a peninsula rich with veins. . . She is so brown and lovely her hip a mountain further down the bed.
>
> (p. 71)

We remember Billy's earlier image of Angie as a landscape of ambush, of inhospital "hollows" and lurking "bushes," contours shaped by Billy's deep distrust of the world (p. 16). In the present passage, the "mountain" and especially the "peninsula rich with veins" form a landscape of wealth and untapped abundance to mirror Billy's sense of well-being and his expectations of future happiness. This is as near as Billy approaches to a paradise. It is the nearest, too, that he comes to the innocence, or unself-consciousness, belonging to the state of paradise:

> All the awkwardness of last night with the Chisums gone, like my head is empty, scoured open by acid. My head and body open to every new wind direction, every nerve new move and smell.
>
> (p. 71)

As in all paradise stories, however, the moment of happiness and unself-consciousness proves short-lived. Billy looks up, and sees "the black hoster and gun. . . coiled like a snake, glinting also in the early morning white" (p. 71).

IV

The burden of consciousness—specifically, consciousness of mortality—returns on the next page, with what is Billy's most searchingly introspective poem in this point in the volume. The poem works like a pendulum; Billy's mind moves from a belief in the vastness of human potential to a recognition of the ultimate limitedness of human nature. "I am here with the range for everything," proclaims Billy at the start of the last stanza (p. 72). But the spectre of mortality rises, and the limitless "range" dwindles to the "body's waiting rut" (p. 72).

Billy's concluding realization seems all the darker since, earlier in the poem, he achieves, for the first and only time in the volume, his ideal of perfect, effortless control. In contrast to the first stanza, with its horses whose movements are blundering and thwarted, the second stanza describes how Billy's fingers can

> control a pencil that shifts up and sideways
> mapping my thinking going its own way
> like light wet glasses drifting on polished wood.
>
> (p. 72)

"Drifting on polished wood." Not even the "beautiful machines" which Billy idolized for "pivoting on themselves / sealing and fusing" (p. 41) can match this dream of easy movement and effortless control of energy.

Billy's choice of the verb "drifting" to image his writing brings to mind his first declaration that he intends his collected works to tell his story. There Billy offers, as a beginning for his story, the image of "drifting" with Charlie Bowdre as they zigzagged across the Canadian border,

> our criss-cross like a whip in slow motion, the ridge of action rising and falling, getting narrower in radius till it ended and we drifted down to Mexico and old heat.
>
> (p. 20)

In both instances, the verb connotes a carefreeness of mind and spirit. However, in the first passage, Billy associates such carefreeness both with his movement through his story or "works" and with his passage through the world or external reality. (We can make the former assumption because the "ridge of action rising and falling. . . till it ended" not only refers to the travels of Billy and Charlie but, as well, aptly describes traditional notions of how a story should be organized around a plot whose action rises and falls to an ending.) In the later poem, Billy associates carefreeness exclusively with movement through an inner world, through his story of himself; movement through external reality has become a matter of "blunders" (p. 72). For, by this point in the volume, Billy has learned that he cannot move unimpeded through the external world. Just as the horses in this poem find it difficult to move surefootedly down their street on the "crowded" weekend, so too does Billy find it impossible to move surely and safely across the stage on which his story unfolds. A few pages earlier, for example, Billy complains about "crowdedness' in his world:

> The thing here is to explain the difference of this evening. That in fact the Chisum verandah is crowded. It could of course hold a hundred more, but that John and Sallie and I have been used to other distances. . .
>
> (p. 67)

Angie and Garret, the two newcomers, make Billy feel hemmed in. Garrett, in particular, represents a serious obstacle to Billy's progress through the world, of course, since it is Garrett who eventually imprisons and later kills Billy. In other words, the unalterable events of history close in on Billy, impeding his movement through external reality. The carefree optimism with which Billy spoke of travelling through the world with Charlie and drifting down to Mexico and "old heat" (p. 20) thus reverberates ironically against the fact that, in his movement through history, Billy ultimately meets with "old heat" in the sense of the "law," as embodied by his old adversary, Garrett.

Billy has known all along, of course, what the final outcome must be. Indeed, at the outset of the volume, he tells us that "Pat Garrett sliced off my head" (p. 6). However, the same poetic license which allows Billy to speak to us from some point beyond his death also permits him both to know from the first what must happen yet still believe that somehow he can rewrite his story in accordance with his desires. Such a belief proves groundless, though. History catches up with Billy, and immediately following the second of his two poems of self-analysis, the strictly narrative line of Billy's story gains ascendance and events press quickly and inexorably forward to Billy's death. But before that happens, Billy reaches a point of self-knowledge in the poem beginning with the line, "This nightmare by this 7 foot high doorway" (pp. 74-75).

As in the first of the self-analytical poems (p. 72), a swing from one extreme pole to another best describes the progress of Billy's introspection. Specifically, Billy moves from a belief in his own cosmic vastness, his own godlike stature and power, to a recognition of his utter impotence. Billy's self-aggrandizement begins quietly part way through the first stanza. "I am on the edge of the cold dark," writes Billy,

> watching the white landscape in its frame
> a world that's so precise
> every nail and cobweb
> has magnified itself to my presence.
>
> (p. 74)

The imperialness in the word "presence" lends Billy a godlike stature, and that the world magnifies itself not "in" but "to" Billy's presence divines Billy's sense of the world as subservient to his wishes. In the next stanza, a kind of cosmic inversion, which finds "stars" likened to "flies in their black path," contributes to Billy's godlike stature; one must be vast indeed to be able to see stars reduced to the size of flies. "[N]othing breaks my vision," Billy claims, except these inverted stars. This claim offers a more telling index to Billy's state of mind if we recall that when Billy first prophesied his death, he did so largely in the imagery of broken vision, of eyes moving wildly, uncontrollably (p. 38). Billy's vastness continues into the third stanza, only now Billy adds godlike indifference to his godlike stature:

> If I hold up my finger
> I blot out the horizon
> if I hold up my thumb
> I'd ignore a man who comes
> on a three mile trip to here.
>
> (p. 74)

Such a purely arbitrary exercise of power rather poignantly reflects Billy's apprehension of his own universe as one completely indifferent to man. Very early in the volume, we remember, Billy perceived a divine injury or death when, looking upwards, he saw "wounds appearing in the sky" (p. 10). At the same time, Billy yearns for there to be a deity in the heavens, as we have seen, for example, in his use of the expletive "Jesus." In the apparent absence of such a being, Billy now sets himself up as a godhead. In so imagining himself, Billy is making one last, supreme effort to assert himself, to place himself in complete control of his circumstances.

Given the excessive degree of this self-aggrandizement, the reader should not feel surprised that Billy proves slow to acknowledge his impotence. Forced to admit that "There is nothing in my hands," Billy qualifies this admission of weakness:

> though every move I would make
> getting up slowly walking
> on the periphery of black
> to where weapons are
> is planned by my eye.
>
> (p. 75)

Similarly, even when Billy looks at himself as if through another's eyes and plainly sees not a god, but a "boy [who] blocks out the light / in blue shirt and jeans," he still clings to his notions of power and greatness for he adds that he seems "young like some pharoah" (p. 75). The last two lines of the poem, however, undercut all postures of power and greatness: "I am unable to move / with nothing in my hands," confesses Billy, in stark recognition of his ultimate impotence.

Billy's moment of self-knowledge, this recognition of powerlessness, receives immediate and ironic validation on the next page when the statement "We moved in a batch now" (p. 76) mockingly echoes Billy's confession of being "unable to move." Bound and captured, Billy is moved by Garrett now rather than able to move himself. As if to insist indirectly upon this fact of bondage, the word "moved" occurs four times in the first paragraph of this section. Still more tellingly, Garrett and his prisoners zigzag across the desert, moving "back and forward, side to side over the county" (p. 76). Billy and Charlie, we remember, travelled in a similar style, though in perfect freedom and carefreeness, when they "criss-crossed the Canadian border" (p. 20). The repetition now of the earlier motion underscores the completeness of Billy's loss of freedom.

V

Beginning with the desert ride (p. 76), the narrative line, which has progressed only fitfully to this point in the volume, moves rapidly and fairly straightforwardly to its conclusion in Billy's death (pp. 76-95). Structurally, then, it is Billy's recognition of his powerlessness which frees the narrative line. Moreover, the strictly narrative mode reflects a world which, in one way, conforms to Billy's need for order. For a readily discernible order, specifically, chronological order, governs a substantial number of consecutive passages, and for the first time in the volume. That this group also happens to be the one sustained sequence of passages dealing exclusively with Billy's death—its details and the events immediately preceding it—draws attention once again to the relationship between "order" and "death." The volume's opening works, we recall, established just such a relationship with their neatly compiled lists of the dead. Far more clearly now, this relationship exists at Billy's expense—Billy wins an ordered world, but at the price of his life.

With a still finer irony, Ondaatje grants Billy the god he wanted. The desert ride which begins so inauspiciously with Billy's bondage and powerlessness ends with a moment of ecstasy for Billy. Having travelled hatless for four days, a sun-struck Billy claims that, on the fifth day, the sun "turned into a pair of hands" and "fucked" him (pp. 76-77). It is with jubilation that Billy relates the news to Garrett: "Ive been fucked. Ive been fuckd Ive been fucked by Christ almighty god Ive been good and fucked by Christ" (p. 78). Rhythmically, it is nearly impossible to read these "by Christs" as mere expletives. On one level, Billy believes that "Christ almighty god" has "fucked" him. And this accounts for the jubilant—ecstatic—note: to Billy's sun-maddened mind, the experience proves that a god inhabits the heavens after all. Billy thus wins a presiding deity, but at the price of his sanity, of all inner control.

Notes

1. Michael Ondaatje, *The Collected Works of Billy the Kid* (Toronto: Anansi, 1970), p. 6. Subsequent references will be indicated by page number immediately following the quotation.
2. "On Death and Dying: *The Collected Works of Billy the Kid*," *English Studies in Canada,* 1, No. 1 (Spring 1975), p. 87.
3. See, for example, p. 53 and p. 73.
4. "On Death and Dying," p. 89.
5. "'I am here on the edge': Modern Hero/Post-Modern Poetics in *The Collected Works of Billy the Kid*" (unpublished), p. 10.
6. "Modern Hero/Post-Modern Poetics," p. 10.
7. "The Collected Photographs of Billy the Kid," *Canadian Literature,* No. 87 (Winter 1980), p. 73.

Lucille King-Edwards (review date 1984)

SOURCE: "On the Brink", in *Books in Canada*, Vol. 13, No. 10, December, 1984, pp. 16-17.

[*In the following assessment of* Secular Love, *King-Edwards heralds Ondaatje's break "from reason and control" in the collection, but laments what she perceives as inconsistency in his poetry, arguing "It is jarring. . . to go from the confessional poems of anguished, passionate love to the more mundane ones of friendship and fatherly love."*]

Once again a book by Michael Ondaatje, and the expectancy is qualified by the memory of one's first encounter with ***The Collected Works of Billy the Kid,*** a book that swept one through it on an ever-cresting wave. Until *Running in the Family* and now ***Secular Love,*** the passion that Ondaatje has put into his poems and novels has been projected onto characters from the myths of his imagination: Billy of the Wild West and Buddy Bolden of Storyville. This imagination produced powerful books, but they were books that allowed their author a certain privacy removed from the scene of passion. Ondaatje questions himself in **"White Dwarfs"**

> Why do I love most
> among my heroes those
> who sail to that perfect edge
> where there is no social fuel
> Release of sandbags
> to understand their altitude—

Perhaps there is no answer to that question, or at least it is not for us to know the answer. What arouses interest in ***Secular Love*** is the opening quotation from Peter Handke, in which an actor is instructed to stop holding back and to learn to run and scream properly, without embarrassment. Although there is still the distancing of persona, as in any poetry, Ondaatje would seem to be that actor who must express his own true feelings and passions.

Running in the Family certainly opens the door for this book of poetry, for it takes Ondaatje back to his roots and the passions of his family, particularly of his father, a drunk and drowning man as he is portrayed in the book. It is almost as if ***Secular Love*** was written in order to get closer to the psyche of this father. The title comes from **"Women Like You,"** a poem set in the heart of Sri Lanka:

> Seeing you
> I want no other life
> and turn around
> to the sky
> and everywhere below
> jungle, waves of heat
> secular love

I find this passage enigmatic, but would suggest that it opens the possibilities of the passionate journey that is the book.

Secular Love opens with **"Claude Glass,"** and the poem does embody the "luscious chiaroscuro" of the concentrated night imagery, but the focus is on the man flowing drunkenly through it. This man appears in the first person. He is called to the river; a river flows through his house, and finally the people of the poem exist for him underwater. It is also the stream of the unconscious that functions here; in that river he embraces nature as he would a woman, kissing both arm and branch with equal love. **"Claude Glass"** is a romantic poem, a poem of night and darkness, and one immediately recognizes its precursors in Lowry, in John Berryman, who pops up a couple of times later in the volume, and in the romantic strain from Keats on down.

Away from reason and control seems to be the main thrust of this book:

> I wanted poetry to be walnuts
> in their green cases
> but now it is the sea
> and we let it drown us,
> and we fly to it released
> by giant catapults
> of pain loneliness deceit and vanity
>
> (**"Tin Roof"**)

If the opening poem depends on drunkeness to achieve this letting-go of emotions, in **"Tin Roof"** it is the exposure of a man on the edge of the sea. He is facing whatever is in the blue beyond the volcanic shore. Alone he contemplates the loss of self:

> How to arrive at this
> drowning
> on the edge of sea

The structure of **"Tin Roof"** is of individual poems that make up a long poem; the writing appropriately becomes spare. Dense long lines disappear. The writing has an acerbic quality, and bamboo as a talisman seems to be correct for this stripping away. Sparse as furnishings in the cabin in which he lives, the poet's pretensions are jettisoned. It is the poem of a man functioning on the brink who sees the plunge into the sea as a compelling magic. Through the poem he discovers this other, starker passion:

> which puts your feet on the ceiling
> this fist
> to smash forward
> take this silk
> somehow Ah
> out of poetry.

The third section of the book, "Rock Bottom," is divided into two sections. The first is a series of poems that plays with the idea of exposure and the confessional mode. They are primarily a prelude to the second section, a testing of the poet's willingness to, as he puts it, go "whole hog the pigs testament / what I know of passion." It has its ironic as well as its romantic moments, neatly described as

near the delicate
heart
of Billie Holiday

The second part of "Rock Bottom" is more of a mixture of styles and types of poems than the previous parts of the book. There is the passion of a love affair as theme for part of it, but we bump into the domestic Ondaatje of children, suburbs, and friends as well. The dominant theme is that of a man painfully removing himself from a known domestic environment out onto the edge of the desert with Billy the Kid.

The early part of the book has led one into expectations of continuity of tone and timbre. It is jarring now in this last section to go from the confessional poems of anguished, passionate love to the more mundane ones of friendship and fatherly love, even a clever dog poem. This is not to say that these latter poems are not well-made, but that they appear gratuitous here. In real life one does linger on friends and children when life is in upheaval, but the whole hog of passion diminishes these poems, which would thrive better in a different book.

I would like to have seen ***Secular Love*** as pure as *Coming Through Slaughter,* or ***The Collected Works of Billy the Kid,*** but there is always that other side of Ondaatje that refuses the final leap

The tug over the cliff.
What protects him
is the warmth in the sleeve.

Sam Solecki (review date 1985)

SOURCE: "Coming Through," in *The Canadian Forum,* Vol. LXIV, No. 745, January, 1985, pp. 32-4.

[*In the following laudatory evaluation of* Secular Love, *Solecki describes the collection as "the ruthless and unembarrassed engagement with the self," adding "Almost every page shows evidence of Ondaajte's brilliant visual imagination and his auditory sensitivity to the musical possibilities of free verse."*]

Although we don't usually think of it in this way, poetry, like life, has its historically significant dates: 1798, the first *Lyrical Ballads;* 1857, *Les Fleurs du Mal;* and 1922, *The Waste Land* are for us not just dates of publication but also demarcation points indicating that after that particular moment our conception of poetry changed and our view of human sensibility subtly altered. In our own time, perhaps the most significant year for many was 1959, which saw the appearance of Robert Lowell's *Life Studies,* a sequence of intensely personal poems and prose pieces dealing with Lowell's family background and his own life. Disconcertingly, even shockingly frank, the volume reveals a poet stripped of most of his defences and willingly describing the most intimate details of his life. In a later volume, savagely reviewed by Adrienne Rich, Lowell would even include parts of his estranged wife's letters in his sonnets. If Lowell inaugurated an era of what later came to be called confessional poetry, his book set a daunting standard in style and quality of experience that would be unmatched by most of his imitators. After 1959, anyone writing about the self would do so in the shadow of Lowell's intimidating example.

Because of Lowell's emphasis on his emotional and psychological problems—the whole sad history is described in detail in Ian Hamilton's recent biography—confessional came to be defined as synonymous with extreme states of being, and the most authentic poems and poetic careers were seen as those in which poetry and life most closely coincided. James Fenton's *Letter to John Fuller,* while mocking Al Alvarez's celebration of this school, notes some of its essential assumptions:

I tell you, in the sombrest notes,
If poets want to get their oats
The first step is to slit their throats.
The way to divide
The sheep of poetry from the goats
Is suicide.
Hardy and Hopkins hacked off their honkers.
Auden took laudanum in Yonkers.
Yeats ate a fatal plate of conkers.
On Margate sands
Eliot was found stark staring bonkers
Slashing his hands

* * *

For a poet to heave into view
To be emergent—
He must whine, as if he wants the loo,
"Please sir, I'm urgent."

Although Lowell died of a heart attack in the back seat of a taxi, Sylvia Plath, Anne Sexton (both sometime students of his) and John Berryman all committed suicide. Just as Mark Rothko's suicide alters our conception of the Rothko chapel in Houston, completed just before his death, the deaths of the three poets seem, in retrospect, to offer an inevitable climax authenticating the claims of the poems. The breakdowns and suicides prodded literary criticism in pathology.

On the basis of Michael Ondaatje's first seven books, few readers would claim that he has much in common with Lowell or confessional writing in general. If anything, most of his work stands opposed to the constitutive assumptions of that poetry, although *Coming Through Slaughter,* his novel about a jazz cornetist whose obsessive art leads to silence and madness, and the crucial lyrics **"Letter and Other Worlds"** and **"White Dwarfs,"** certainly reveal a compulsive fascination with an intensely subjective and directly expressive art. The speaker in most of the lyrics seems to be Ondaatje but he's rarely interested in enacting or describing his darkest and most problematic emotions and situations: the voice is too laconic, the tone too detached and the attitude to the self is ironic, even self-mocking. Often we sense, however, that the artifice and control not only shape and present the material at hand but also hint at repressed or displaced experiences and aspects of the self the writer is unwilling or unable to deal with. Ondaatje's suicidal herons and artists, his fascination with the jungle, the various hints at autobiography in ***The Collected Works of Billy the Kid*** and *Coming Through Slaughter*—both studies in pathological creativity—all point to personal events underlying the work. The publication in 1982 of the frankly autobiographical if often fictional *Running in the Family* seemed to confirm the impression that Ondaatje's work had, over the past decade, been moving towards a more direct engagement with his most intimate experiences and memories. In a manner of speaking *Running in the Family* is Ondaatje's equivalent of the early family-oriented sections of ***Life Studies: Secular Love*** is the ruthless and unembarrassed engagement with the self.

The book is made up of four chronologically arranged sequences telling the story of the break-up of a marriage and a way of life, the poet's own near breakdown and finally, after what one section calls "Rock Bottom," his recovery and return through the love of another woman. The book should be read as a seamless poetic journal rather than as a collection of discrete lyrics. Some of the poems, like the lovingly nuanced and mutedly elegiac **"To a Sad Daughter,"** can be read by themselves, yet the volume is so closely organized with so much of the overall emotional and artistic effect depending on repetitions and echoes of sound, image, situation and emotion that the poems often seem more like the chapters of a novel than parts of a collection of poems (another equally significant context is provided by Ondaatje's earlier work, and sections of ***Secular Love*** often seem like rewritings of earlier texts).

The opening epigraph from Peter Handke's *The Left-Handed Woman* simultaneously warns us about the unexpected stylistic and experiential openness, even rawness of ***Secular Love,*** and offers an implied judgment on Ondaatje's earlier work:

> Your trouble, I believe, is that you always hold back something of yourself. In my opinion you should learn how to run properly and scream properly, with your mouth wide open. I've noticed that even when you yawn you're afraid to open your mouth all the way.

In poetry, as in any art, holding back or opening up is obviously a matter of degree as well as of technique; by holding back the clutter of irrelevant detail and by compressing events and characters the writer can often create a greater impression of self-exposure and openness. ***Secular Love*** shows a writer who has found a style and a form that allows openness without sacrificing the economy and selectivity necessary for art.

A crucial aspect of that style is Ondaatje's delicate management of what I call the book's two voices or points of view: the first is that of Ondaatje the character in the story; the second of Ondaatje the poet and creative voyeur who watches his own life, reflecting and recreating it as art. This is the slightly guilty voice of the man who observes life even as he lives it always in the hope of turning "these giant scratches / of pain" into art; who when he writes that "I fear / how anything can grow from this" knows that in addition to the growing suffering and pain there is also the potential poem. This is the voice that knows that for the poet *"Il faut que tu te voies mourir / Pour savoir que tu vis encore"* (Paul Eluard). Although at one point we read that "There are those who are in / and there are those who look in" we know that this doesn't apply to Ondaatje—he's both.

The opening section is pervaded by images of merging, drowning, darkness, disappearance and drunkenness. This is the book's dark night of the soul, the son's rewriting in personal terms of the father's breakdown in **"Letters and Other Worlds"** and *Running in the Family.* At once, it's an apology, an hommage and the beginning of another story in which the central character—described here only as "he"—is shown at a party on a farm, surrounded by family and friends, and inexplicably but inexorably drinking himself into oblivion. A disturbing point of departure for the love story to follow, it sketches in a suggestive emotional landscape of unfocussed discontent and undefined anxiety and pain leaving the reader wondering why the central figure feels like an intruder, drinks so heavily and longs for the darkness of the surrounding fields. The answers can be inferred from some of the details available later in the book: a marriage and a family are breaking up.

> In the midst of love for you
> my wife's suffering
> anger in every direction
> and the children wise
> as tough shrubs
> but they are not tough
> —so I fear
> how anything can grow from this

Without self-pity, simplification or sentimentality, ***Secular Love*** follows the course of the one story of our time. It's a sign of Ondaatje's integrity as an artist (and as a human being) that he registers the impact of the break-up on everyone. The transitional lyric just quoted places the love affair within the full and necessary context, reminding us of a suffering other than the speaker's. And even in the final affirmative, celebratory section, "Skin Boat," images and words repeated from earlier poems recall what has been lived through. The gentle, genial **"Pacific Letter"** celebrates friendship—and by the way shows Ondaatje's ability to deal with the domestic emotions of the middle range—but recalls that "After separation had come to its worst / we met and travelled the Mazinaw with my sons / through all the thirty-six folds of that creature river / into the valley of bright lichen." The beautifully poignant **"To My Sad Daughter"** (which will bring to tears all fathers of all teenage daughters) offers advice about getting through while letting the images of swimming and drowning and "cuts and wounds" recall the earlier darker experiences against which the poem must be read. Telling his daughter that "If you break / break going out not in"

Ondaatje takes us back not only to the earlier lyrics but also to **"White Dwarfs,"** a poem of the early 1970s about "imploding," as well as to *Coming Through Slaughter,* whose hero "broke into" silence and madness. The book closes, although one aspect of the story is just beginning, with a tender prose piece in which a man and woman walk in and along a shallow creek in a scene recalled by him at night as he lies next to her. Walking he loses his balance, falls in, recovers and surfaces looking for her:

> He stands very still and cold in the shadow of long trees. He has gone far enough to look for a bridge and has not found it. Turns upriver. He holds onto the cedar root the way he holds her forearm.

The entire section has a quiet inevitability after the perfervid panic of much of the book, a panic recalled in the slip into the cold water. Similarly the merging of "the cedar root" and "her forearm" reminds us why in his day-to-day life he no longer feels that he is drowning, why, in D.H. Lawrence's words, he has come through. Begun in darkness, drowning and panic, the unfinished story ends with light, surfacing and tenderness.

I began with Robert Lowell partly because it seemed to me that one of the creative problems Ondaatje faced in writing ***Secular Love***—note the adjective, by the way, semantically allied with profane, phonetically with sacred—was how to stay out of the shadow of confessional poetry as well as how to be "open" without simply committing himself to nothing more than a loosely prosaic poetry dealing with intensely subjective or extreme states of being. He certainly points in that direction by telling us that "This last year I was sure / I was going to die," or, referring to another poet's suicide, that

> . . .one is able now
> in ideal situations
> to plot a stroll
> to new continents
> "doing the Berryman walk"

His problem was how to transform an intensely subjective set of experiences into an artistic whole while avoiding, on the one hand, excessive subjectivity, solipsistic self-dramatization, and sentimentality—"These are *my* feelings and therefore they're important"—or, on the other, losing the full texture of emotional immediacy through a too impersonal and objective artistry. Ondaatje solves the problem, in part, by beginning the book with a sequence narrated in the third person and following it with one shifting among "I," "you," and the implicating "we." Several poems even omit the subject, leaving us with the impression of a pure, unmediated if anonymous voice. Similarly, by omitting the names of the main characters Ondaatje generalizes the potential significance of the events so that what we read becomes something more than simply a chronological account of a particular set of experiences involving a specific group of people. The sources of the story may be as obviously autobiographical as those of Lawrence's *Look! We Have Come Through!* but the end result is a work of consummate poetry enacting a life and a love story transcending the individuals originally involved in it.

It's worth recalling that Bertrand Russell's response to Lawrence's poetic sequence about his love for Frieda was along the lines of: so they've come through; why should we care? The answer is obvious: because Lawrence transformed his love affair with Frieda into art it has become ours. As well, we no longer read it simply for the tale but also in order to linger over the telling, the sheer artistry of the thing. This is also why we reread it. The same is true of ***Secular Love,*** a book rich in human experience, carefully structured and beautifully crafted. Almost every page shows evidence of Ondaatje's brilliant visual imagination and his auditory sensitivity to the musical possibilities of free verse. Consider the following fragments:

> At certain hours of the night
> ducks are nothing but landscape
> just voices breaking as they nightmare.
> The weasel wears their blood
> home like a scarf,
> cows drain over the horizon
> and the
> dark
> vegetables hum onward
> underground
> but the mouth
> wants plum.
> We know their type of course, local heroes
> who take off their bandanas and leap naked,
> night green, seduced
> by the whispers of michelin.
> sleeping like the rumour of pearl
> in the embrace of oyster.
> a flute
> from the throat
> of a loon
> and most of all
> this
> small bamboo pipe
> not quite horizontal
> that drips
> every ten seconds
> to a shallow bowl

Those are a series of small but inimitable gestures that evoke reflective smiles and appreciative nods: "nightmare" surprisingly used as a verb; a casual surrealism recalling Mark Strand, "cows drain over the horizon"; the Getz-like sussuration of "whispers of michelin"; and the almost oriental, sculptural sense of form as something organic developing out of the relationships not only between words ("flute" / "throat" / "loon" or "small bamboo pipe" / "drips" / "seconds"/ "shallow bowl") but also between the protracting and pregnant silences of white spaces.

Few do it better.

Gillian Harding-Russell (essay date 1987)

SOURCE: "A Note on Ondaatje's 'Peter': A Creative Myth," in *Canadian Literature,* No. 112, Spring, 1987, pp. 205-11.

[*In the essay below, Harding-Russell discusses Ondaajte's handling of both myth and the artist figure in the early poem "Peter." The critic asserts that, with "Peter," Ondaajte "deftly objectifies the artist's dilemma by representing him as 'court monster' in a fairy tale setting."*]

In **"Peter"** of ***The Dainty Monsters,*** Ondaatje explores the artist's ability or inability to rise above personality and experience.[1] He creates a myth around a vindictive artist figure which recalls other implied analogues or figures for the artist in various of the "dainty monsters" that appear in this volume: the mad heron of **"Birds for Janet"** and **"In Another Fashion,"** the monstrously deformed Philoctetes of **"The Goodnight,"** the decadent Paris whose belly is an "undigested beast" or Prometheus who is "scientifically" "splayed" on a rock but fights back with ever-restored energy.[2] Although all literature borrows from mythic or story elements as its essential understructure, the creative myth typically stylizes its material and reduces it to archetypal essentials so that a speculative element surfaces within the basic structure and development of the story. Thus Ondaatje in **"Peter"** (perhaps significantly the last poem in ***The Dainty Monsters***) deftly objectifies the artist's dilemma by representing him as "court monster" in a fairy tale setting. Using images of surrealistic dislocation, Ondaatje jolts us into a psychological world where we recognize elements of ourselves through what must be considered a post-modern extension of the artist as *everyman.*

Rather than following any one borrowed mythological structure, **"Peter"** as a creative myth which is built around the tale of the beauty and the beast echoes *The Tempest,* the Golden Fleece, and Minotaur stories.[3] Here the artist as Caliban and Minotaur figure expresses his sense of persecution and personal frustration at physical handicaps (literally inflicted by society in this story) first through his art, and later by victimizing the young beauty Tara, who has been the one person to treat him with kindness. Accordingly, Tara may be seen as an Ariadne or Miranda figure.

As with Ondaatje's **"Potter"** of ***The Man With Seven Toes,*** the artist in **"Peter"** is ambivalently presented as victim and victimizer. This precludes our complete sympathy, and he finally proves himself a figure more negative than positive.[4] The convict, Potter, who gains the distinction of "seven toes" through brutalizing experience, provides a parallel for the court monster Peter, who, having been deprived of his tongue, must express himself against all odds in a particularly literal and physical manner. Since the number seven is traditional in fairy tales, it is perhaps no coincidence that the number (also notable in reference to the convict's seven toes) comes up again.[5] The series of poems entitled **"Peter"** unfolds in seven notable instalments.

In the first section of the series (71), Peter is discovered in the gruesome act of reconstructing a cow from its skeleton through ice sculpture. A significant ambiguity in the syntax surounding "freezing," and a manipulation of line-endings implies the ambivalent role of the artist as both victim and victimizer:[6]

> That spring Peter was discovered, freezing
> the maze of bones from a dead cow,
> skull and hooves glazed
> with a skin of ice.
>
> (71)

This somewhat disturbing activity tells us that Peter is a perverted individual, a suggestion that does much to undermine our sympathy, even at this early stage. Ondaatje thus links art with morbid behaviour in which the ice surface, the medium of Peter's art, is considered a "skin." On the night villagers attempt to capture him, Peter retaliates in a vicious manner. He defends himself with "three throats and a wrist." Suggestive of the artist's intensity and his need to express himself orally and manually, this symbolic evocation carries the implication of monstrosity. The villagers retreat and return at night to discover, significantly, the cow "frozen in red, and Peter / eating a meal beside it."

In the second section (72), the hunting party manage to snare Peter and subsequently torture him. A "brown bitch," a familiar symbol in Ondaatje's poetry representing a survival instinct, dispassionately "nose[s] his pain" and "stare[s] in interest." Peter is "froze[n] into consciousness," or distanced from his own pain. Here we identify a "freezing motif" which reflects an attitude necessary to the artist if he is to transcend his own pain through art.

In the third section (73), Peter in captivity expresses his resentment. Although his words, which are composed of "growls," seem "meaningless," "disgust in his tone burn[s] everyone." After the passage of a year, society retaliates by cutting out his tongue. As an analogue for the persecuted artist, Ondaatje with particularly visceral effect introduces the tableau of a baited fish which loses matter in its throat when the hook is removed:

> difficult
> to unpin a fish's mouth
> without the eventual jerk
> to empty throat of pin and matter.
>
> (73)

Having escaped being caught but maimed in this way, the fish (which carries ambivalent spiritual and phallic connotations) is thus aligned with the artist, Peter.[7] Following this cruel chastisement, Peter endures several months of silence. But eventually he overcomes his speech impediment by learning to express himself more fantastically in grunts by using the air in his body:

> There followed months of silence,
> then the eventual grunting;
> he began to speak with the air of his body,
> torturing breath into tones; it was despicable,
> they had made a dead animal of his throat.
>
> (Ibid.)

The line ending "it was despicable" jolts our sympathy by registering the villagers' point of view about this human gargoyle but, merging with the following line which establishes the extent of Peter's chastisement, returns the blame with equal force to society. Since society has "made a dead animal of his throat," the artist who is reduced to a "monster" by society's persecution of him is not entirely responsible for the cruel intensity expressed in his art. Society's restraints speak through him, and his art is autonomous. It is an "animal" whose features and size are determined not only by "genetic" (traditional genres) but also by "organic" (internal form in the individual work) necessity. Typically, Ondaatje reflects his ambivalence concerning this interesting problem of the artist's relation with society and with his art.

The spiritual connection in the fish symbol is apparent when Peter is associated with his Biblical namesake. Of course, "Peter" translates as "the rock," and this artist, Peter, is described as a "marred stone." Interestingly, Cirlot cites an instance of the stone image as a symbol for reconciliation with the self since it connotes removal from biological processes of decay.[8] The "marred stone," therefore, might imply the inner turmoil and antagonistic feelings which Ondaatje identifies in the artist. As himself an imperfect "creature," the artist must "create" to compensate for this deficiency. A complementary analogy of the "baited gargoyle" to the stone association, moreover, adds the suggestion of perverted monstrosity to this artist figure:

> He was little more than a marred stone,
> a baited gargoyle, escaped
> from the fountain in the courtyard:
> his throat swollen like an arm muscle,
> his walk stuttered with limp, his knees straight,
> his feet arcing like a compass.
>
> (Ibid.)

Peter's throat which is enlarged like "an arm muscle" and the "stuttering" metaphor convey the extent of the artist's compensation for a personal deficiency. An application of a psychological metaphor to the throat, an organ of speech for transcending the physical world to register meaning, and the unusual language metaphor that describes his physical activity effectively suggest the state of the frustrated artist and his need for expression. The fact of "his feet arcing like a compass" makes implicit a writing metaphor using mathematics (as opposed to the oral language metaphor of "stuttering"), which indicates the artist's striving for an absolute east and west direction equivalent to dialectical truth. Also, the compass's circumscribed movement suggests the artist's paralysis.

In the fourth section (74), the occupants of the castle build a "hive" or sanctuary for Peter.[9] Jason, representing a man of action and an idealist, provides the artist with "bones," or basic ideas, with which to reconstruct real-life forms. As a projection of the artist's own *psyche,* this Jason figure in Ondaatje's poem suggests MacEwen's sacred figure of the king or dancer.[10] Jason's daughter, "Tara," at once recalls the Irish home of kings and a Buddhist deity who provides essential life energy to *everyman.*[11] Appropriately, she grows fond of this artist figure, Peter:

> . . .tousling in detail
> the hair that collapsed like a nest
> over his weaving eyes.
>
> (74)

In her "bored innocence," Tara with unconscious condescension dotes on Peter, "pet[ting] him like a flower" and "plac[ing] vast kisses on his wrists." Because she is "delighted at sudden grins / that [open] his face like a dawn," she tolerantly makes allowances for his "scowls and obscenities." The artist's moments of sincerity and insight, therefore, compensate for his vulgarity and illtemper.

In this position of resentful subservience, the shackled artist remains "bouldered" at the feet of society. The stone metaphor implies his situation on an ambivalent pedestal of prospective immortality and death-in-life existence:

> He ate, bouldered at their feet,
> vast hands shaping rice,
> and he walked with them on grit drives—
> his legs dragged like a suitcase behind him.
>
> (Ibid.)

An image of Peter's "hands shaping rice" suggests the artistic process of casting amorphous reality into form.[12] Paradoxically, "grit" representing immediate circumstances of intractable reality, however, impedes his way so that his legs drag "like a suitcase behind him." As in Gwendolyn MacEwen's "Manzini: Escape Artist" or Eli Mandel's "Houdini," the artist ultimately cannot escape his own physical limitations. His art, therefore, expresses this basic deficiency over and over.

In the fifth section (75), Peter is seen as an artist of "violent beauty," first as an artisan, but later as an expressionist artist. Accordingly, we may trace the evolution of art from its function as useful craft and its part in religious ritual to its modern autonomy:

> He carved death on chalices,
> made spoons of yawning golden fishes;
> forks stemmed from the tongues of reptiles,
> candle holders bent like the ribs of men.
>
> (75)

Since death is carved on chalices, the sacred takes on a new profanity in which the absurdity of death is represented in art. Other sacred objects such as "golden fishes," and "candle holders" are also distorted and given a new function to justify their desecration for art's sake: "spoons" are made from "golden fishes," and "forks" from "tongues of reptiles." The second stanza describes a selection process implicit in producing artistic impression:

> He made fragments of people: breasts
> in the midst of a girl's stride,

a head burrowed in love,
an arm swimming—fingers heaved
to nose barricades of water.

(Ibid.)

In representing "fragments" such as "breasts / in the midst of a girl's stride" and "a head burrowed in love," Ondaatje's view of art not only becomes one of selection but of expressionistic exaggeration. The tableau in the final stanza of the section describes a figure comparable to Buddha or Coleridge's Kubla Khan. Ironically, a romantic conception combines with or provides a point of departure for Ondaatje's expressionistic and often surrealistic techniques:

His squat form, the rippled arms
of seaweeded hair,
the fingers black, bent from moulding silver,
poured all his strength
into the bare reflection of eyes.

(Ibid.)

Although "the fingers black" and "bent" suggest that the artist's expression is influenced by perverting experience and that he is "bent" in the effort of creation, the "silver" of his art concentrated in the "bare reflection" of his eyes implies a transcending of his own barren perversion through this artistic process of "moulding silver."

In the sixth section (76), Tara's development from girl to woman parallels the development of society. As an awkward girl "ungainly as trees," she is entranced by Peter's creation of "golden spiders" and "silver frogs, with opal glares," As in **"Spider Blues,"** the "golden spiders" are an image for the artist who spins his web of creation. Through a traditional association of the frog with metamorphosis, the "silver frogs with opal glares" suggest transformation in which attributes of the moon or nature are purified by the "silver" of the civilized arts.[13]

When Tara outgrows Peter's control, and as his resentment also grows, we find a parallel to the modern artist's alienation from a social reality which has grown fat and soft or shapeless with an increasing complexity that can no longer be contained in conventional or, seemingly, any other forms.[14] In a surreal description of this period of literal and figurative adolescence, Ondaatje, however, describes a splendid autonomy of the girl's body, which reflects his essentially Heraclitean attitude to a chaotic but rich and self-sufficient universe:

And as she grew, her body
burned its awkwardness.
The full bones roamed
in brown warm skin.
The ridge in her back broadened,
her dress hid seas of thighs,
arms trailed to adjust hair that paused
like a long bird at her shoulder;
and vast brown breasts
restless at each gesture
clung to her body like new sea beasts.

(76)

A dramatization of the growing process within Tara's body has a surreal effect that complicates this portrait using images of Classical simplicity and economy. Impressionistic touches such as the image of the "long bird" for her hair and her breasts "like new sea beasts" in this context establish a relation between the selectivity of romantic impression and the expressive agency of selective distortion. Ondaatje achieves a unique idiom that reflects his interesting position as a post-modernist artist who must combine the techniques of his predecessors in his own way.

In the seventh section, in which Peter mistreats his only benefactor, Tara, Ondaatje introduces Christian imagery to dramatize the vindictiveness of the artist.[15] In an implicit fishing metaphor complicated by a mention of the Cross, Peter baits Tara and ignominiously exposes her:

An arm held her, splayed
its fingers like a cross at her neck
till he could feel fear thrashing at her throat. . .

(77)

Tearing off her skirt and lifting her brutally by "buttock and neck," which suggest her physical mass and vitality, Peter places her on a table (a secular form of the sacred altar) where he proceeds to "mould" her with his "stub of tongue."[16] Accordingly, Tara takes on a third significance as the female counterpart for the sacrificial bull:[17]

while his bent hands tore the sheet of skirt,
lifted her, buttock and neck to the table.
Then laying arm above her breasts
he shaped her body like a mould. . .

(Ibid.)

As in MacEwen's vision, we identify an inherently destructive element in the creative process, which perhaps accou9nts for the suggested spitefulness of this artist prototype. Peter thereupon vents his fifteen years of resentment on Tara, the number fifteen significantly associated with the erotic and diabolic:[18]

the stub of tongue sharp as a cat, cold,
dry as a cat, rasping neck and breasts
till he poured loathing of fifteen years on her,
a vat of lush oil, staining
the large soft body like a whale.

(Ibid.)

The "stub of a tongue" which is "sharp" as a cat and "cold" again suggests the artist's distance from his work of art. Moreover a tactile metaphor of the cat's tongue "rasping" her neck and breasts together with the archetypal metaphor of the whale combine to fulfil the requirements of an experiential post-modern art that looks for and finds deep-seated psychological precedent in the human mind.

A suggestion of the crucifixion in this final scene aligns the sacrificial victim of the girl with the cow in the opening scene. Although Peter has caused the girl all this suffering, his guilt and sorrow identify him with his victim, even as the artist is identified with the subject matter of his art:

> Then he lay there breathing at her neck
> his face wet from her tears
> that glued him to her pain.
>
> (Ibid.)

Here is an almost ritual view of mourning in which the artist's "face" or identity is "glued" to the girl's neck through his tears of remorse. A certain redemption attends the artistic process even if it is not strictly therapeutic.

Because the dominant whale image (at the end of the penultimate stanza) not only connotes sexual containment but also represents the body and grave of the world, this image serves to direct meaning from the literal and allegorical levels of myth to an anagogical level. Accordingly, Ondaatje on a literal level provides us with a psychological drama of the beauty and the beast, on the allegorical level with a paradigm for the alienated artist in his society and, on an anagogical level, with a myth about the artist in his relations with reality at large.[19] Here is a series of poems having incisive imagery that works on many levels through metaphoric incongruities. With a psychological force that draws us, **"Peter"** reflects the perennial concerns of the artist.

Notes

1. *The Dainty Monsters* (Toronto, 1967), pp. 71-77; rpt. in *There's a Trick with a Knife I'm Learning to Do* (Toronto, 1979), pp. 26-32.
2. Sam Solecki in "Nets and Chaos: The Poetry of Michael Ondaatje" rpt. in *Brave New World* (Windsor, 1977) describes these analogues as a "metaphoric shorthand" to disorient the reader, pp. 25-27.
3. Stith Thompson distinguishes between the motif and the tale-type in the following manner: Whereas the motif refers to "the smallest element in a tale having power to persist in tradition" and may refer to single "actors," "items in the background of the action" or "single incidents," the tale-type is "a traditional tale that has an independent existence." *The Folktale* (New York, 1946), pp. 415-16.
4. On the whole, Ondaatje develops the convict Potter of *The Man with Seven Toes* as a more positive figure than Peter.
5. *A Dictionary of Symbols* (London, 1962), p. 223. Cirlot cites Papus' *Traité Méthodique de Science Occulte* concerning the number seven.
6. A freezing motif can be related to Ondaatje's interest in photography.
7. *Ibid.,* p. 102. Regarding the fish as spiritual and phallic symbol, Cirlot cites Marius Schneider's *El Origin.*
8. *Ibid.,* p. 229. Here Cirlot cites Marius Schneider's *La danza de espadas y la tarantela.*
9. The "hive" which implicates the bee of immortality (itself associated with the preservative honey) suggests a removal of the artist from society on a kind of glorified pedestal of dubious implication. (Cirlot cites Enel's *La Langue Sacrée* in *A Dictionary of Symbols,* pp. 22-23). In an interview with Jon Pearce, Ondaatje remarks on his dislike for this kind of artist's alienation—"it cuts you off essentially from the real world." "Moving to the Clear," *Twelve Voices* (Ottawa, 1980), p. 141.
10. The role of the "king" in MacEwen's poetry is best dramatized by "Nine Arcana of the Kings" of *The Armies of the Moon* which, in effect, provides a paradigm for her mythology.
11. Arthur Cotterell describes Tara as "the energy of [bodhisattva's] essence," and points out her democratic qualities in Buddhistic tradition: "she transcends social distinctions and offers a personal relationship to her devotees unmatched by any other single deity." *A Dictionary of World Mythology* (New York, 1979), pp. 82-84.
12. In "Elizabeth: a slight ache," we encounter a related rice image in reference to "the blood brown men" who represent raw nature.
13. Cirlot refers to Marius Schneider's *El Origin musical de los animales—simbolos on la mitologia y la escultura antiguas:* since the frog is a lunar animal and because it represents a transition from earth to water, it is a symbol of metamorphosis.
14. A likeness between the words "terra" (earth) and "Tara" perhaps becomes significant.
15. Like Peter, Theseus maltreats his benefactor, Ariadne. After taking her away from King Minos, he abandons her on the way to Athens. Paul Diel examines the story from the psychological point of view of the idealist who mistakes the meaning of life because of personal deficiencies. *Symbolism in Greek Mythology,* p. 164.
16. Peter's lifting Tara by the "buttock" has sexual implications, and his hoisting her by the "neck" implies a violent and potentially destructive tendency in the creative process.
17. The cow of the initial scene prefigures Tara's eventual sacrifice. Although in *The Man with Seven Toes* the artist becomes the sacrificial figure, the artist here "crucifies" his subject-matter as represented in Tara.
18. *A Dictionary of Symbols,* p. 244. Cirlot cites Oswald Wirth's *La Tarot des Imagiers du Moyen Age* concerning the number fifteen.
19. Hypothetically, Frye's tropological level can be identified in relation to the moral problem of creative-destructiveness. *The Great Code* (Toronto, 1982), pp. 221-33.

Ray Wilton (essay date 1993)

SOURCE: "Narrative in Michael Ondaatje's '*the man with seven toes*'," in *Canadian Literature,* No. 137, Summer, 1993, pp. 63-74.

[*In the following essay, Wilton analyzes Ondaatje's narrative technique in* the man with seven toes, *particularly the unconscious and conscious participation of the reader in the text.*]

The man with seven toes may be seen as Michael Ondaatje's first major narrative. However, reading this text as narrative presents numerous difficulties, not the least of which is the tendency of the individual poems to elicit lyric expectations that in fact resist narrative continuity. The design of the book, with its broad pages, visually emphasizes the independence of the poems, and the poems themselves tend to contain short flashes of imagery or meaning, resembling photographs or paintings hung in a series. The poem's evocation of conflicting lyric and narrative expectations disorients the reader, compelling her or him into an active awareness of the role of those expectations in the text's production of meaning.

Sam Solecki, in his essay on ***the man with seven toes,***[1] explores the form of the text concentrating primarily on imagery and texture, finding that "echoes and parallels" in phrases and images "create a common ground or structure—even the possibility of an unsuspected metaphysical order—underlying the separate lyrics." However, he notes that that order is ambiguous and "avoids becoming a constricting grid." He finds that the structure built around imagery and metaphor pulls the reader towards a static spatial apprehension of the reality depicted, but one with unresolvable ambiguities, and one that fragments when we examine the text as a whole and discover the contradictions. The resulting discomfort for the reader roughly parallels that of the heroine, the anonymous woman, in the poems:

> In ***the man with seven toes***. . . it is the form as well as the content that pushes the reader into the unfamiliar ground of the work to the point that his reading of the sections of the text becomes roughly analogous to what is happening in the story [and] demands the reader's active participation as an interpreter of a reality that is often not only ambiguous but even chaotic.[2]

However, while Solecki astutely cites ambiguities and discontinuities in the text, and also the tendency of the work to draw the reader into coming to terms with these difficulties, he says little or nothing of what the "reader's active participation" contributes to the narrative. How is our awareness of our participation significant? Perhaps answering this question requires our becoming more sensitive to what Solecki calls "the tenuous narrative line."

Roland Barthes offers a theory on the general operations of narrative which aptly applies to Ondaatje's work. He says that narrative is the working out of a "logic" that is "exposed, risked and satisfied." This working out is "a process of becoming."[3] Such a process strikes me as having important similarities to what Ondaatje refers to in the poem **"a gate in his head"** as "moving to the clear,"[4] the difference being that Barthes is referring to narrative as a recreation of the process, while Ondaatje is referring to the lyric as "exposing" the logic and freezing it in mid-process. In both cases, the end of the process, whether it be a logic "satisfied" or the achievement of intellectual clarity, implies a static apprehension of the content, or cohesion. In ***the man with seven toes*** the individual lyrics suggest a static apprehension of "a process of becoming" while the continuity developed through recognizing narrative convention draws the reader into enacting the process. Solecki, it seems to me, ignores the latter process, and thereby precludes the possibility of discovering order in the text to be, at least partially, a temporal phenomenon, which seems to me central to Ondaatje's poetics.

In the opening lyrics of the narrative Solecki finds "no temporal, spatial or syntactical continuity." Of the first poem he says, "The character and the scene are isolated in space—'desert and pale scrub'—and time."[5] Yet the content to some extent suggests an adherence to narrative convention:

> the train hummed like a low bird
> over the rails, through
> desert and pale scrub,
> air spun in the carriages.
> She moved to the doorless steps
> where wind could beat her knees.
> When they stopped for water she got off
> sat by the rails on the wrist thick stones.
> The train shuddered, then wheeled away from her.
> She was too tired even to call.
> Though come back, she murmured to herself.[6]

At the risk of stating the obvious, each time "she" is mentioned in the above poem, we assume that the pronoun refers to the same person, and that each action has a causal link with the other actions: she is on a train and when it stops she gets off, then is left behind. Convention leads us to believe in the consistency of the existents (characters, items of setting), in this case "she" in "desert and pale scrub," through a series of events.

The principles of connection and coherence assumed in the first poem at the level of 'naturalized convention,' that is convention so familiar it is no longer consciously noted, continue in the next poem. It is not too much for us to assume that the same person from the opening lyric falls asleep, and then in the second poem awakes: "She woke and there was a dog / sitting on her shoulder" (10). Despite the narrator's reticence when it comes to offering context, there is here in the first two poems sufficient cause for the assumption of "story."[7] Granted, much of that story is left out of the discourse, but in reconstructing a story from a fragmented discourse, as readers we actively participate in a narrative process, even if in making assumptions based on naturalized convention we do not participate at a conscious level.

Ondaatje jolts us into awareness of our participation when in the fourth poem he undermines narrative convention by changing the identity of the narrator without warning or seeming acknowledgement: the natives "laughed, / then threw / the red dress back at me" (12, my italics). This shift throws into doubt our previous assumptions of consistency. We are forced to reconsider those assumptions and in the process of doing that discern that the shift may actually occur between the second poem ("she woke and there was a dog. . . ") and third poem ("entered the clearing and they turned. . . "), where the identity of the missing pronoun before the verb "entered," which narrative convention initially led us to assume to be "she," becomes ambiguous. The shift in point-of-view, clearly indicated by the use of the pronoun "me" in the fourth poem, throws into doubt our assumptions maintained throughout the first three poems, and leads us into an awareness of those assumptions and the narrative process instigated by them. Clearly, such undermining of narrative convention simultaneously risks and foregrounds the narrative process. By initially allowing the possibility of conventional narrative continuity, Ondaatje lures us into expectations which he subsequently denies, compelling us into an awareness of our participation in the process of ordering.

However, more than an obvious shift in pronouns marks the transition occurring in the opening four poems. A shift from external to internal focalization also occurs. The first and second poems, where the train leaves the woman and she later follows the dog, could easily be rewritten in the first person without significantly changing the sense. The difference between the narrative in the first two poems and that which follows resides in the increasing emphasis on the woman's response to her situation. In the second poem Ondaatje provides little or no indication of how the woman thinks or feels about her situation, he simply states that situation:

She woke and there was a dog
sitting on her shoulder
doing nothing, not even looking at her
but out over the land.
She lurched and it sauntered
feet away and licked its penis
as if some red flower in the desert.
She looked away but everything around her was
empty.
Sat for an hour.
Then the dog moved and she followed,
flies prancing at her head.

(10)

Ondaatje as narrator situates the woman in proximity to the dog and in relation to the desert while a specified "hour" passes. By thus locating her in space and time he provides us as readers with a point of reference in the story. Furthermore, the narrator is essentially transparent, emphasizing the story and not his discourse. For instance, the language is more metonymic than metaphoric; of the two metaphors brightening the text, the first is introduced with the explanatory "as if," where the explicit identification of the trope suggests the narrator does not wish to confuse the story's events with their depiction. The second metaphor occurs in the last line perhaps as a hint of the change in focus about to occur. In any case, we gain an unobstructed view of the heroine's actions and her location, the story's existents and events, as well as our relation to them, without noticeable intervention from the narrator.

However, in the third poem the language becomes much more terse and metaphorical, while also providing less indication of the woman's location spatially and temporally:

entered the clearing and they turned
faces scarred with decoration
feathers, bones, paint from clay
pasted, skewered to their skin.
Fanatically thin,
black ropes of muscle.

(11)

In effect the text shifts from an emphasis on story to an emphasis on discourse, from an emphasis on what is seen to how it is seen, which results in the increased prominence of the narrator. The discourse in fact obscures the story and thereby, as readers, our point of reference. Thus, coinciding with the change in narrator, a shift that undermines the narrative process, is the growing prominence of the narrator. As we become aware of the narrative process and our role in it, we also begin to notice the presence of the narrator, and through the clouding of our view of the story as well as our point of reference, begin to identify with her disorientation.

Our participation occurs at the level of narrative act, in the act of reading, where the real action is.[8] The shift away from story induces us to seek from the increasingly discontinuous discourse the continuance of a coherent story line. This participation in the process of ordering, paralleling the woman's situation of being lost, is a temporal activity. Thus the time consumed in the narrative act parallels the implied passage of time in the story. However, as our location both temporally and spatially in the story grows more indefinite, we gain a sense of moving in time and being lost in time simultaneously; events occur with seeming randomness, without causal order.

In the next series of poems the coherent story line we saw in the earlier poems continues to fade to the point where no temporal connection exists:

not lithe, they move
like sticklebacks,
you hear toes
crack with weight,
elbows sharp as beaks
grey pads of knees.

(13)

We have here a description of an ongoing situation, given in the present tense. The use of the present tense (or in more precise narrative terms, "simultaneous" narration, wherein story and its articulation occur simultaneously) locates the narrative instance within the scope of the events narrated, but as the events are ongoing the narrative instance remains indeterminate. Although time passes, we as readers participating in the search for coherent order based on the story line, are effectively losing that sense of order.

The next two poems likewise lack temporal location. The first poem describes a rape and the second a ritualistic dance. In them, the foregrounding of the narrative process, instigated a few pages earlier by Ondaatje's undermining of convention, intensifies, while the increased discontinuity in the story threatens the narrative process altogether. A tension builds as the fragmented discourse threatens to destroy the continuity between the poems, the continuity derived from our awareness of a story line. The weakening of the connections between the poems emphasizes the structural ambiguity built into the text, the conflict between our expectation of lyric and narrative conventions. The sequence of poems threatens to fragment into individual, self-enclosed units, while we strive to link them together by providing some system of relatedness.

The impossibility of reconciling conflicting perceptions intensifies almost unbearably, and finally provokes an almost cataclysmic release. As the order offered by a continuity in story fails, and as the emphasis increasingly tips over onto the side of discourse, the discourse finally breaks free from the story line, and thereby relinquishes any temporal reference in the story. However, an alternative order offers itself, one derived spatially through imagery and metaphor.

goats black goats, balls bushed in the centre
cocks rising like birds flying to you reeling on you
and smiles as they ruffle you open
spill you down, jump and spill over you
white leaping like fountains in your hair
your head and mouth till it dries
and tightens your face like a scar
Then up to cook a fox or whatever, or goats
goats eating goats heaving the bodies
open like purple cunts under ribs, then tear
like to you a knife down their pit, a hand in the warm
the hot boiling belly and rip
open and blood spraying out like dynamite
caught in the children's mouths on the ground
laughing collecting it in their hands
or off to a pan, holding blood like gold
and the men rip flesh tearing, the muscles
nerves green and red still jumping
stringing them out, like you

(16)

The shift to spatial articulation accompanies a complex change in narrative voice. The woman, the narrator, separates herself from her environment, begins to perceive herself as a distinct entity outside the events of her story. We see this in her repeated reference to herself as "you." She, in fact, makes a conscious separation of her discourse from story, as the repeated introduction of metaphor with "like" indicates, showing her awareness of the distinction between reality and her depiction of it, and her need to distance herself from her story and rewrite it in a way that allows her some immunity. We see in her a growing disregard for the facts of the story: "[t]hen up to cook a fox or whatever, or goats. . . . " She manipulates the story to fit the pattern of discourse, attempting to give the chaos of her experience in story an order derived through imagery and metaphor.

The difficulty of sustaining a subjective position distant from the events of the story is shown in the chaotic energy of the "goats" poem, the frantic pursuit of an adequate metaphor that will capture the experience and dissipate its threat. The narrator leaps from one metaphor to the next seeking one that will hold and still that wild energy, but that energy always exceeds the attempt at its articulation. The reason for this is, of course that what the poem tries to capture at this point is its own process of ordering. To clarify this we need to note a number of processes at work.

In the "goats" poem the woman narrates an event that has already occurred in the two previous poems. At least she perceives the events as sufficiently similar to establish a sense of repetitiveness. This perception allows her to deny the difference, change, and in effect slows the narrative giving her more time to process the events. She can then begin to articulate patterns. But what becomes clear is that these patterns belong not to the events themselves but to her articulation of them. As we have already noted, the focus of the narrative shifts from story to discourse, from the action in the story to the activity of narrating. The narrative act becomes the subject of the "goats" poem as it seeks to capture that activity within lyric stasis.

Her attempt almost succeeds. Through metaphor and a distancing of herself from her story the woman as narrator develops a conceptual framework in which to articulate the violence and chaos of her experience. That articulation to some extent gives her control over the violence, the story, and she achieves a sense of order that, although uncertain and ambiguous, provides a tentative point of reference.

and put their heads in
and catch quick quick come on
COME ON! the heart still beating
shocked into death, and catch the heart still running
in their hard quiet lips and eat it alive
alive still in their mouths throats still beating Bang
still! BANG in their stomachs

(16)

The word "still" is rendered ambiguous in all its occurrences in this context, through having both temporal and spatial connotations, meaning both 'continuing' and 'not moving.' Mrs. Fraser thus expresses through the image of eating the heart alive a need to capture movement, and thereby expresses an inner reality in a constant state of flux that will not completely succumb to that need. That is, to a degree she fulfills her wish. She articulates her experience and finds within it a point of reference in the 'here and now' however ambiguous and unstable that point might be. In the poem that follows, Mrs. Fraser experiences at least partial acceptance of her situation:

at night the wind
shakes in your head

picks sweat off your body
yards away, they
buck out the night
The sky raw and wounded

(17)

She perceives herself in the second person, she perceives "they" at some distance away from herself "at night," and then there is the sky "raw and wounded," a projection of her own pained but accepting response to her environment. The important point is that she has found a tentative but temporal location: not within the story, but within her articulation of it, the discourse.

As we, as readers, participate in the woman's dislocation in the earlier poems, we also now participate in her sense of relocation in the here and now. As the discourse breaks away from the story line, the connection between where we are now and where the narrative began, beside the tracks after the train left, gives way. At the same time, the sense of certainty that such a connection offers is lost. The combination of the loss of a point of reference in the story line, with a shift to internal focalization as well as simultaneous narration,[9] evokes the sense of being in the here and now, a position relative to our location in the traversing of the foregrounded discourse. In other words, instead of relating where we are now in the narrative act to our position in the story, we are compelled into the inverse position of relating that story to our position in the narrative act. Like Mrs. Fraser we seek in the movement across the discourse, the narrative act, an order. After the order offered by story fails we seek a spatial order in terms of metaphor and imagery that will give coherence to our movement. Ordering becomes a temporal movement through space: time orders space and space orders time. We find ourselves, with Mrs. Fraser, compelled into an ontological position without a stable foundation, into accepting coherence as a movement within a fluctuating and uncertain reality.

As the woman escapes from the natives, we escape from our conventional notions of narrative and share her renewed sense of location in the present. From here, with the help of a convict escaping from civilization, she finds her way back to civilization. Meanwhile, for us a vague sense of the story line returns to the narrative: events occur from lyric to lyric which, although surprising, are both temporally and spatially located: Mrs. Fraser and the convict spend days and nights in a journey across streams, through swamp and trees, until they finally move into the plain and along a river.

Although the return of a discernible story line suggests a returning to conventional narrative, that conventionality continues to be undermined by vast ellipsis between individual lyrics, and as well by random but significant changes in the identity of the narrator:

he had tattoos on his left hand
a snake with five heads
the jaws waiting
his fingernails chipped tongues;
crossing a stream
he steadied her elbow
and she tensed body
like a tourniquet to him.

(21)

Ondaatje apparently narrates here, but unlike his narrative at the beginning of the text, now there is a different focalization. As narrator he is more prominent, registering through metaphor and imagery his reaction to the story, emphasizing the discourse while not losing sight of the story. In fact, this kind of internal focalization remains constant throughout the remainder of the text, regardless of who actually narrates. For instance, no change in focalization occurs in the next poem, although we find a change of narrator.

in grey swamp
warm as blood, thick
with moving. Flesh
round our thighs like bangles.
Teeth so sharp, it was later
he found he'd lost toes,
the stumps sheer
as from ideal knives.

(22)

It would seem the fluctuations in the identity of the narrator enact a melding of points of view, where different points of view share a common discursive reality. The effect is a sense of moving toward coherence or intellectual clarity.

Coinciding with the shifting point of view and the emergent sense of clarity are subtle but important shifts in narrative instance. In the above poem, for instance, the absence of not only the subject pronoun at the beginning of the poem, but the verb as well, renders the narrative instance indefinite. If such an ellipsis suggests anything, it is that of immediacy, a sense of present tense or simultaneous narration. Yet in the third sentence of the poem the narrative instance turns out to be an imperfect form of subsequent narration: " . . .it was later / he found he'd lost toes. . . . " In other words we have a form of interpolated narration. A clear instance of this occurs in another poem.

lost my knife. Threw the thing at a dog
and it ran away, the blade in its head.
Sometimes I don't believe what's going on.

(27)

The narrator clearly narrates the event subsequent to its occurrence, but when is not clear. The concluding comment suggests the narrative instance exists within the journey back to civilization, rather than outside that journey, thus rendering the narrative instance, like the narrator in this passage, indeterminate.

Positioned in the indeterminate here and now, having relinquished the certainty of a coherence beyond her articulation of it, the woman finds that events take on a renewed brilliance so very unlike her experience on first leaving the train. Lacking the absolute order of time or space, "Things happened and went out like matches" (38). She now sees the convict "striped and fabulous / like beast skin in greenery" (33).

> eyes were grey beetles
> toes were half gone
> chest was a rain sky
> shirt was a rainbow
> mouth a collyrium that licked my burnt eyes
>
> (40)

Those "burnt eyes" receive the salve that enables renewed vision.

In the process of moving through the text we develop a sense of continuity between the poems that is not based upon a clear story line, but upon a process of discursive ordering both spatially and temporally. We maintain throughout a sense of our participation in the process of ordering, our participation temporally in connecting a collection of disparate verses together. In the latter portion of the narrative this sense grows increasingly intense as the narrators seem to drop away; or more accurately, we merge with them, dissolving the borders between subjectivities, including the one between ourselves as readers and those depicted in the narrative. At the same time we experience a movement towards clarity. The achievement of this goal appears in sight when we arrive back in civilization and at the end of our journey:

> She slept in the heart of the Royal Hotel
> Her burnt arms and thighs
> soaking the cold off the sheets.
> She moved fingers onto the rough skin,
> traced obvious ribs, the running heart,
> sensing herself like a map, then
> lowering her hands into her body.
> In the morning she found pieces of a bird
> chopped and scattered by the fan
> blood sprayed onto the mosquito net,
> its body leaving paths on the walls
> like red snails that drifted down in lumps.
>
> (41)

Sam Solecki notes that here "the narrative closes with the ambiguous and densely allusive poem whose almost every image echoes some image or situation occurring earlier."[10] These echoes give the impression of the imagery taking on a coherent form, or of the narrative's logic "being satisfied," or as Solecki puts it a sense of "some kind of summarizing judgement upon the story." The sense of impending closure, and the reference through "echoes" back to the events of the narrative, give the illusion of arrival at the point of coherence and order in the text. A static apprehension of the narrative's content seems for the first time within reach as the narrative slows.

> She could imagine the feathers
> while she had slept
> falling around her
> like slow rain.
>
> (41)

The slowing, calming effect of this image evokes the sense of arriving or concluding. Nevertheless it is an ambiguous conclusion, as Solecki says, for however much the image of "slow rain" succeeds in taming or civilizing the violence, the violence remains within.

The last poem provides the real sense of closure, post-narrative summation, and at the same time reconfirms our awareness of static order as illusion. The cliched sentiments of the final stanza in the poem conventionalize, even trivialize, as they attempt to capture within metaphor an experience that has only been grasped temporally within the narrative act.

> Green wild rivers in these people
> running under ice that's calm,
> God bring you all some tender stories
> and keep you from hurt and harm
>
> (42)

It hardly does the story justice. Rather, it reflects ironically on our need for the illusion of static order. While it may be the end of the process of ordering, it eliminates too much to be satisfactory. The sense of cohesion it attempts fails: the narrative remains an ambiguous sequence of disparate fragments, the order of which can only be tentatively grasped in the temporal process of traversing the text. In fact, the sense of movement towards cohesion results as much from our need for order, as it does from any absolute order built into the text.

Or, an alternative reading of the conclusion offers itself, and perhaps one even more to the point. The cliched "green wild rivers" could be said to take on new meaning within the overall context of ***the man with seven toes.*** Gaining specificity, the dead metaphor is revitalized and meaning reproduced.

Notes

1. Sam Solecki, "Point Blank: Narrative in Michael Ondaatje's *The Man With Seven Toes*," *Canadian Poetry* 6 (Spring-Summer 1980): 14-20. Rpt. in *Spider Blues: Essays on Michael Ondaatje,* ed. Sam Solecki (Montreal: Véhicule, 1985); 135-49.
2. "Point Blank" 15.
3. Roland Barthes, "Introduction to the Structural Analysis of Narrative," trans. Stephen Heath, *A Barthes Reader,* ed. Susan Sontag (New York: Hill and Wang, 1982) 294-95.
4. Michael Ondaatje, "The Gate in his Head," *Rat Jelly* (Toronto: Coach House, 1973) 62. "And that is all this writing should be then. / The beautiful formed things caught at the wrong moment / so they are shapeless, awkward / moving to the clear."
5. "Point Blank" 18.

6. Michael Ondaatje, *The Man with Seven Toes* (Toronto: Coach House, 1969).
7. Seymour Chatman, *Story and Discourse: Narrative Structure in Fiction and Film* (Ithaca: Cornell UP, 1978) 19. "[E]ach narrative has two parts: a story, the content or chain of events (actions, happenings), plus what may be called the existents (characters, items of setting); and a discourse, that is, the expression, the means by which the content is communicated."
8. By "narrative act" I mean the actual event of narrating or enunciating, which by extension necessarily includes the action of both sender and receiver. See Gérard Genette, Narrative Discourse: *An Essay in Method,* trans. Jane E. Lewin (Ithaca: Cornell UP, 1980) 26-27.
9. Genette, p. 219. He points out that simultaneous narration produces an unstable situation wherein the emphasis can tip either way, onto the story or the discourse. Context determines the direction the emphasis takes.
10. "Point Blank," 21.

Douglas Barbour (essay date 1993)

SOURCE: "Poetry and Maturing Poetics," in *Michael Ondaatje,* Twayne Publishers, 1993, pp. 67-98.

[*In the following essay, Barbour traces Ondaatje's poetic development from his first collection through* There's a Trick with a Knife I'm Learning to Do. *Barbour discovers a trend in Ondaatje's writing toward more experimental and personal poetry.*]

An edition of selected poems, especially when published by major presses in a poet's own country, the United States, and the United Kingdom, signifies both achievement and recognition. For Ondaatje, the Governor General's Award-winning ***There's a Trick with a Knife I'm Learning to Do*** (1979) also provided an opportunity, again especially for the larger international audience that knew him most for ***The Collected Works of Billy the Kid*** and *Coming Through Slaughter,* to pare away some of the perceived chaff in his oeuvre and thus present a particular overview of the maturing of a poet. The poems dropped from ***The Dainty Monsters*** section appear more modernist and given to closure or too dependent upon a dictionary of mythology than his later practice allows. The selection from ***Rat Jelly***[1] is larger, as befits a more mature collection, yet the poems kept, aside from the central series of poems about art and artists, tend to foreground questions of ordinary life, friendship, and family love. If, as so many critics have pointed out, Ondaatje seems obsessed with figures who violently and often self-destructively immerse themselves in the chaotic world of the senses, the choice of poems in ***Trick with a Knife*** reveals another and equally powerful obsession: the need and desire to "deviously [think] out plots / across the character of his friends" (***RJ***, 56; ***TK***, 58). In the context of the selections from the first two books, this other obsession is best imaged in the delicate yet tough recognition of communion among friends in **"We're at the Graveyard,"** a poem I now see as central in Ondaatje's work. The "shift" of friends' "minds and bodies. . . to each other" (***RJ***, 51; ***TK***, 47), with all its implications about community, communication, and communion, is the emerging theme of Ondaatje's work as he matures from romantic young poet-hero to more complex and subtle poet-survivor. The new poems in the third part, **"Pig Glass,"** with their increased insistence on the necessary and complex intimacy with family and friends, reveal how carefully Ondaatje has selected and reordered the earlier poems in terms of this emerging theme. Not that ***Trick with a Knife*** denies the other aspects of Ondaatje's work; rather, it newly contextualizes them in an emerging order that emphasizes a greater complexity of response within its various speakers and a more profound and difficult vision than that of romantic egoism.

Ondaatje wrote the poems of ***Rat Jelly*** "before during and after two longer works—***the man with seven toes*** and ***The Collected Works of Billy the Kid***—when the right hand thought it knew what the left hand was doing" (***RJ***, [72]). Many of its poems deal with the question of art's relation to life, which is why critics continue to study them as central statements on poetics and creativity. These include **"Letters & Other Worlds," "Burning Hills," "The gate in his head," "Spider Blues,"** and **"White Dwarfs,"** often considered among his finest poems, as well as **"Dates," "Taking,"** and **"King Kong meets Wallace Stevens."** All appear in ***Trick with a Knife.*** This group makes up one-fifth of the titles in ***Rat Jelly*** and contains the only poems that stretch out to three pages in length. Although they present the best clues to his poetics at the time, I would not read them as absolutely prescriptive, except insofar as **"The gate in his head"** suggests a direction the later work might take: toward ever greater openness and exploration, "seeking the unrested form he requires, and the realization that it is in form that we present what we deem the real" (Bowering, 164).

Although Ondaatje's shorter poems seem to become more and more autobiographical as he matures as an artist, he actually "places himself directly before the reader as a *character* instead of an attitude" (Glickman, 73): the "I" who speaks in these seemingly "confessional" poems is purely inscribed, exists in each poem as a subject but alters his subjectivity from poem to poem. While it would be foolish to try to reconstruct the "real" Michael Ondaatje's life from the written ones of the poems, the writer has chosen, especially in the reordered selected poems, to shift the emphasis of his work away from the suffering and violent individual toward the communication and communion that are possible only in community, a community that begins in the small tribe of immediate family and close friends. Although this shift can best be seen in the works that follow *Coming Through Slaughter,* the poems on family and friends in ***Rat Jelly*** mark its beginning. The opening poem, **"War Machine,"** appears later in ***Trick with a Knife,*** yet, despite its explicit expression of generalized hatred of the world "out there," it points to family and friends as necessary buffers against that world: "Think I dont like people NO / like some dont like many / love wife kids dogs couple of friends" (***RJ***, 11; ***TK***, 48). The poem is a savage comic turn, a performance, in which the "I" expostulates at length about wanting "to live mute / all day long / not talk // just listen to the loathing," but only after telling us at great length how he hates art, likes certain sports, films, and scandalous gossip. Indeed, he represents himself as not too likable, definitely sexist, and willing to hurt to get attention. Perhaps he would like to escape into silence, but for now he sounds like a stand-up comedian desperate for one last laugh. The double edge of his rhetoric—cutting himself as much as his audience—should warn us to be very careful of whom we identify him with, or how we identify with him.

"Gold and Black," with its images of dreams and nightmares as "gold and black slashed bees come / [to] pluck my head away" (***RJ***, 12; ***TK,*** 37), turns to the beloved, although she, too, is presented in disturbingly ambiguous imagery: "In the black Kim is turning / a geiger counter to this pillow. / She cracks me open like a lightbulb." The lightbulb simile catches us off guard: does she break him into darkness or enter into his light? The final stanza presents an argumentative conclusion as if to a syllogism: "Love, the real, / terrifies / the dreamer in his riot cell." The turn to the third person, as it generalizes from the extremely personal imagining of the first two stanzas, suggests that this is not just "my" problem but everyone's. But is it? Some readers feel "the dream was not meant for me" (Bowering, 164). The third-person dreamer's "riot cell" implies everybody's utter lack of control in the realm of the unconscious, but the poem is not about everybody, and it has resolved nothing. That it appears to do so may be its weakness.

"Letter to Ann Landers" utterly disrupts any biographical reading we may have been constructing, as it is in the voice of a harried housewife who has found an outlet for her frustrations: "I get really / turned on by flies / crawling over my body" (***RJ,*** 13). This could be one of the stories the speaker in **"War Machine"** tells; certainly it is a casually cruel bit of black comedy: "It *is* true Ann I *do* feel worn out / it is the flies (I mean it are the flies)." As it shifts to the necessary ending of a letter to an advice columnist—Ann's reply would help the husband "feel / not so left out of things"—it perhaps suggests just how difficult dealing with "Love, the real" can be. The cruelly accurate pastiche of the awkward style of such letters somehow invokes compassion as well as superior disdain, making us oddly complicit in this contradictory lyric joke. At any rate, entering ***Rat Jelly*** in an orderly fashion leads us through a misanthropic rant, a chilling dream, and a comically outrageous image of desire. Only after these three alternate visions does the book turn to its first major poem, which explores with compassion and complexity the complications of a domestic situation, "observed with the most intimate affection, out of which the reader can reconstruct the fabric of a whole relationship" (Scobie 1985a, 50).

The title, **"Billboards,"** points to a central image in the poem, but one that emerges only after a mazelike trip through anecdotal images of "[m]y wife's problems with husbands, houses, / her children that I meet / at stations in Kingston, in Toronto, in London Ontario" (***RJ,*** 14; ***TK,*** 34). Overlapping discourses compose the language of this poem: there are seemingly traditional similes, witty metaphors, the occasionally pretentious diction of the high lyric, but they never quite mesh into a conventional lyric sensibility. Or: that sensibility is corrected, dissipated, as an effect of the overlapping. The first two stanzas establish the terms of difference between these two lovers in a tone that mixes gentle exasperation and loving humor: "All this, I was about to say, / disturbs, invades my virgin past." This image of the speaker as a youthful tabula rasa, his "mind a carefully empty diary" waiting to be written on by the experienced older woman, seems unproblematic until a sudden shift of metaphor making her a "barrier reef" opens toward subtler and more complex possibilities. As an empty diary changes into a bright fish among the coral, we realize that the fictional world of the poem is one of sudden transformations, in which nothing may be what it seems. Images associated with writing—her "anthology of kids," his "carefully empty diary"—are continually interrupted by images of raucous, chaotic life, of which the ocean is a major symbol (Cirlot, 241). In a poem essentially domestic and comic, this is not too unsettling a discovery, but it provides a sufficient reminder that the world of the shorter poems is the same as that of the longer works.

The complications increase, for "the locusts of history— / innuendoes she had missed / varied attempts at seduction (even rape)," etc. (***RJ,*** 15; ***TK,*** 35), seem to point to a naïveté on her part that almost equals his. The locusts might in some way be equivalent to the bees that invade his dreams in **"Gold and Black,"** the dark other side of this domestic comedy. Here sexual violence is quickly paralleled by the deaths of pets, and all are reduced to the same level as "[n]umerous problems I was unequal to." Although its inconsistent discourse denies it a stable lyric sensibility, the "I" asserts primacy in "a neutrality so great / I'd have nothing to think of, / just to sense / and kill it in the mind"; but that primacy cannot attain lyric superiority because of the inherent dialogism of the situation: "Nowadays I somehow get the feeling / I'm in a complex situation, / one of several billboard posters / blending in the rain." The lyric "I" is essentially selfish, an ego expressing only itself. Paradoxically, however, this "I" had nothing to express to the degree it sought to "have nothing to think of." As the only referent for "it" is "nothing," the neutrality he sought is the nothing he would have killed with his mind. Solipsism like this has nowhere to go. In fact, to write at all he must be written upon. History does that as it rains experiences, his own and others', upon him. The image of the "several billboard posters / blending" overwhelms that of the empty diary, but both depend upon the concept of writing for their effect. Writing as the marking of experience upon the self is what allows the writer to focus the final stanza on the complex feelings his engagement with other complicated lives evokes. The act of writing itself becomes a sign of the communication love both allows and is: "I am writing this with a pen my wife has used / to write a letter to her first husband." Until this stanza, the poem has concentrated on memories, bits of information gathered from other sources, historical and anecdotal, moments of generalized encounters. Now the writer writing engages the physical presence-in-absence of the other, through the sense most often associated with the erotic—smell—and does so with the generosity of spirit associated most strongly with love. He does not "attempt to reconstruct" (***TK,*** 17) and "freeze" the moment, as he did in **"Four Eyes,"** but rather imagines the possible process of the actions he did not observe: "She must have placed it down between sentences / and thought, and driven her fingers round her skull / gathered the slightest smell of her head / and brought it back to the pen." Empathetically gathering her actions out of the empty air and placing them on the page, he demonstrates an antilyric dialogism by staying out of the action. The poem ends focused on her incomplete act, which we now feel touched by.

Other poems within the "Families" section move in different directions and engage different moods. The very title of **"Notes for the legend of Salad Woman"** (***RJ,*** 18; ***TK,*** 38) suggests the direction much of the "autobiographical" writing takes here: toward a kind of comic myth-making, to be trusted, like autobiography, no more than a tall tale. I think it significant that the figure of "my wife" in these poems is never given a name: she is representative, not particular, another aspect of the performative orientation of these poems. **"Notes"** joins with **"Postcard from Piccadilly Street"** and **"The Strange Case"** to make up a delicately slapstick triptych. A line from **"Postcard"**—"We have moved to elaborate audiences now" (***RJ,*** 19; ***TK,*** 39)—provides the clue to the performative nature of these poems. In them, the poet and the wife take little vaudeville turns for the entertainment of whatever "elaborate audiences" may read them.

In **"Notes,"** the luggage "my wife" brings to the marriage expands to suggest "she must have eaten / the equivalent of two-thirds / of the original garden of Eden" (***RJ,*** 18; ***TK,*** 38). The poem elaborates this conceit at some length, moving from images of that "eradicated" garden to "flower decorations" in their house and their own small garden, now "a dust bowl." The final stanza offers them both new roles, as Adam and Eve, and turns eviction from Eden into erotic comedy. From **"Notes"** to a **"Postcard"** is not too big a step in this comic textual world. In **"Postcard,"** dogs, as "the unheralded voyeurs of this world" (***RJ,*** 19; ***TK,*** 39) assume a parodic relation to the suffering animal world of his other poems: "irate phone calls from the SPCA / . . . claim we are corrupting minors / (the dog being one and a half)." The comic timing emphasizes the light tone of this poem, especially the offhand statistic of the parenthetic line. The hint of spying, in "sparrows / with infra red eyes," the importance of performance, the slight spice of danger, all combine to turn the poem just slightly aside from mere slapstick, but the basic tone is comic—as it is in **"The Strange Case,"** where the speaker's dog is an "alter ego" displaying raw sexual desire and "nuzzling / head up skirts / while I direct my mandarin mood" (***RJ,*** 20; ***TK,*** 40). This mood could be taken as both devious and exploitative, but the domestic comedy of father and baby-sitter in the car, with the dog in the back seat suddenly licking her ear, plays off the conventional satiric comedy of "indiscretion." The final stanza again presents the stand-up comedian: "It was only the dog I said. / Oh she said. / Me interpreting her reply all the way home." Being forced to do the interpreting breaks his "mandarin mood" and alleviates any tension we might have felt about the intentions of the poem. It remains part of the domestic comedy, after all, with no real danger in it. All three poems sustain just enough ambiguity to resist any simplistic reading. So, although "[t]heir humour is not there just for its own sake, but plays a functional role in establishing the tone and credibility of the domestic image" (Scobie 1985a, 50), part of that credibility lies in the hint of darkness that is always nearby.

A suggestion of that darkness, and of the depth of empathy parenthood confers, occurs in a poem that provides another view of the domestic scene, nearly the only one in the book with children present. **"Griffin of the night"** creates a *mise-en-abyme* effect as "my son in my arms" becomes "small me / sweating after nightmares" (***RJ,*** 23; ***TK,*** 43). The poem is minimal in its gestures, which partly accounts for its power, but it is at least as much about "me" as it is about "my son": fathers and sons slip into one another's roles here, preparing the reader for the following poem, in which a son attempts to slip into the nightmare his father had come to live and die in.

"Letters & Other Worlds" has long been considered "one of Ondaatje's finest poems: the control of tone, as the poem moves from comedy to deeply moving simplicity, is breathtaking" (Scobie 1985a, 51). Ondaatje's first attempt to place and placate his father's ghost (or "his" "father's" ghost—the quotation marks signalling the essential fictionality of all autobiography, the fact that even memory is a shaping and a making, that it can never be an innocent representation), it anticipates *Running in the Family* by almost a decade.[2] Precisely because "My father's body was a globe of fear / His body was a town we never knew" (***RJ,*** 24; ***TK,*** 44), the youthful writer finds it difficult to see his life from the inside. The poem moves from a tragic chant to a frightening image of death, and then shifts into a kind of comic gossip before returning to the imagery of isolation, self-destruction, and death with which it began. The "terrifying comedy" of his father's life is represented in fragments of narrative that look forward to the full-blown novelization of *Running in the Family,* but the beginning and ending of the poem resist such carnivalization and insist on a lyric and romantic intensity of vision in which terror and despair overwhelm all other possibilities. The poem manages to juxtapose farce with despair, the two modes of discourse clashing and contradicting, acquiring a dialogic equilibrium "my father" could not maintain, finally. Its emotional power resides in the tension between the two moods.

While elsewhere in his first two volumes of verse, Ondaatje praises the painter Henri Rousseau for creating "the ideals of dreams" (***TK,*** 10), here he finds in Alfred Jarry the paradigm by which to measure his father. An infamous poet, novelist, essayist, and playwright, who seemingly devoted his final days to drinking himself to death, Jarry included among his last writings "this visionary description of the hero's approaching death: 'But soon he could drink no more, for there was no more darkness for him and, no doubt like Adam before the fall. . . he could see in the dark.'"[3] This quotation is the unacknowledged epigraph to the poem, while the comment that "Jarry's death resembled nothing so much as drowning" (Shattuck, 223) is echoed in the line, "He came to his death with his mind drowing." The discovery of such a paradigm apparently gave the poet metaphors by which to tentatively explore the meaning of his father's death.

The first two stanzas of the poem form a litany set apart from the narrative that follows. Through a series of near repetitions, the poet creates a complex keen of loss on behalf of himself and his siblings, in which the use of the first-person plural pronoun implicates us in the emotional turmoil the poem enacts. The father's body is represented as "a globe of fear," "a town we never knew," and then "a town of fear." "He hid that he had been where we were going" changes into "He hid where he had been that we might lose him," while "His letters were a room he seldom lived in" becomes "His letters were a room his body scared." The total effect is unnerving, as the father becomes a kind of incredible shrinking man, retreating from world to town until, finally, he is only an inscription in the letters that are a room he seldom lives in yet which is the only small place in which "the logic of his love could grow." In this convoluted argument, the man hid the truth about himself precisely in order that his love might free his children from the troubled inheritance he brought them. Apparently he sought to become the letters, in an attempt to erase his own early behavior and write a new figure in its place. But to do so, he had to shrink his body, his physical ability to engage the world, from "globe" to "town" to "room," a final hidden and written space in which no one else could witness his "fear dance." The "logic" of his love inevitably led to a kind of lying (a rewriting of his story that *Running in the Family* will demonstrate was a behavioral pattern for his whole generation), a loss of balance he could not maintain. His body frightened the room his letters became because the truth they sought to hide was written boldly upon it. Moreover, as the poem will demonstrate, he failed in this endeavor because gossip had inscribed him in the social history of his community, and "we" had heard all the stories already.

The narrative part of the poem leaps proleptically to the climax, as "brain blood moved / to new compartments / that never knew the wash of fluid / and he died in minutes of a new equilibrium." *Equilibrium* is a key word here; but it is ambivalent in the extreme, and the mood of isolation and loss continues the lamentation of the first two stanzas. The immediate shift into anecdotal farce suggests that the father's life was continually off balance, yet he somehow kept moving, kept going, stayed alive. The "new equilibrium" is death, a stasis he fell into when he stopped moving and hid in the small room with his bottles and the duplicitous loving writing that finally failed him.

Yet writing is the only way to bring him back. The writer takes an almost possessive delight in various scenes from the "terrifying comedy" of his father's "early life," remarking ironically that "my mother divorced him again and again." The implications of his behavior are more important than the actual stories, some of which appear in *Running in the Family.* Explanations take on an almost baroque deadpan earnestness. Of the drunken halting of a "whole procession of elephants dancers / local dignitaries," the writer adds: "As a semi-official, and semi-white at that, / the act was seen as a crucial / turning point in the Home Rule Movement / and led to Ceylon's independence in 1948" (***RJ,*** 25; ***TK,*** 45). He points out that "[m]y mother had done her share too," but the poem quickly stifles any laughter such comic stories might induce:

> And then in his last years
> he was the silent drinker,
> the man who once a week
> disappeared into his room with bottles
> and stayed there until he was drunk
> and until he was sober.
>
> (***RJ***, 25-26; ***TK***, 45-46)

Of this period there neither are nor can be any stories: the silence swallowed them up. The room and "the gentle letters [he] composed" (***RJ,*** 26; ***TK,*** 46) were the same; they were both a place of hiding, in which he could write with "the most complete empathy / . . . / while he himself edged / into the terrible acute hatred / of his own privacy." The syntactical ambiguity of that final phrase suggests the awful difficulty of actually explaining how and why he came to his death. He found the hatred in the hated privacy he could not escape precisely because he had created it. In the letters he achieved a kind of balance, as well as the "articulate emotion" (***RJ,*** 25; ***TK,*** 45) he once envied his wife, but he could not maintain it; instead, even as "his heart widen[ed] and widen[ed] and widen[ed] / to all manner of change in his children and friends" (***RJ,*** 26; ***TK,*** 46), he slowed to a stop, "balanced and fell" dead, "the blood searching in his head without metaphor." Paradoxical images, of balancing and falling as one act, and metaphors, of "blood screaming," "blood searching," an "empty reservoir" of skull, are the only means by which to argue the end of metaphor. A positive way of reading this ending suggests that, for the father "as for Jarry, the self-destruction of alcohol provided a new vision; but unlike Jarry, what he created . . . were expressions of love rather than of contempt. When Jarry died, he became completely Ubu; when Ondaatje's father died, he became completely himself" (Scobie 1985a, 58-59). We share the writer's pain because his father is, notwithstanding, dead, lost, an enigma he can never solve.

To this point, Ondaatje has seldom presented the figure of the writer in his shorter poems. In ***The Dainty Monsters,*** the writer appears only in **"Four Eyes,"** where he desires to stop time, while thus far in ***Rat Jelly,*** he reappears, altering his stance, only in **"Billboards,"** although he is also implied in the comic history of **"Dates."** There, the writer "console[s] [him]self with [his] mother's eighth month" when he lay in his mother's "significant belly" while Wallace Stevens wrote and watched "the page suddenly / becoming thought where nothing had been" (***RJ,*** 21; ***TK,*** 41). A series of present participles invokes the process of control and balance that writing should be: "his head making his hand / move where he wanted / and he saw his hand was saying / the mind is never finished, no, never." In his "speeches, head dreams, apologies, / [and] gentle letters" (***RJ,*** 26; ***TK,*** 46), his father too made "his hand / move where he wanted," but he apparently could not believe "the mind is never finished." The difficulty and the emotional power of **"Letters & Other Worlds"** derives from its inchoate recognition that the father is the kind of romantic artist Ondaatje's writing obsessively loves yet must reject in order to keep on happening. As such, he is a paradigm of all such figures one encounters in the poet's work: Peter, Billy, the "heroes" of **"White Dwarfs"** "who sail to that perfect edge / where there is no social fuel" (***RJ,*** 70; ***TK,*** 68), and Buddy Bolden, for example.[4] In the figure of the father, this romantic artist appears as a writer, but it is as a writer that his son must come to terms with what he means. The paradoxical conflict is too powerful and transgressive to be contained within the limits of a single poem; it demands the space and dialectic of a novel, where other voices can provide sufficient perspective upon it. Ondaatje had not yet found the proper "architecture of tone as well as of rhythm" (Solecki 1984, 324) by which to juxtapose document and fiction, prose and poetry, into the complex "gesture" that is *Running in the Family.* With an enigmatic and contradictory central figure who transgresses every attempt at containment, **"Letters & Other Worlds"** at least recognizes the need to mix genres as it mixes feelings. Ondaatje's first attempt at articulating the contraditions of "other people, another age" (Solecki 1984, 331), and another place probably had to be a lyric one. Yet lyric cannot do the subject justice precisely because that subject is the lyric self. The poem is emotionally successful to the very degree that it articulates its own failure to understand, and that is what the paradox of the final metaphor denying metaphor does.

"Live Bait," with an epigraph on the self-destructive power of lying,[5] is a catchall section evoking the dangers of the jungle as a "necessary complement" (Scobie 1985a, 50) to the domestic security of "Families." **"Rat Jelly,"** later paired with **"War Machine,"** brings back the nasty vaudevillian of that poem. **"Breaking Green,"** a poem about killing a snake, reveals how the destructive power of even constructive technology comes to control the actions of the human operator and influence "our" responses to them. If there is a thematic connection among the various animal poems it is only that there is no way to understand the other. The only message the "beautiful animals" (***RJ,*** 35; ***TK,*** 23) can send is a bite, which humans can interpret as love or as attack, or "a parabola of shit" (***RJ,*** 37) which puts all interpretation out of mind.

The gulf cannot be bridged—which may be why **"Loop"** returns to the writer only to have him insist that it is his "last dog poem" (***RJ,*** 46; ***TK,*** 53). This opening assumes our knowledge of past poems and their possible autobiographical intent only to suggest how they could so easily slide into sentimentality: "I leave behind all social animals / including my dog who takes / 30 seconds dismounting from a chair." Against the easy humor of this too domestic image, the poem exhorts the reader to "[t]urn to the one / who appears again on roads / one eye torn out and chasing." The antisocial animal survives; "transient as shit," he cannot be fixed—in either sense of the term—for there is "magic in his act of loss" as the "missing eye travels up / in a bird's mouth, and into the sky." Like the other animals of these poems, this dog is "Live Bait" precisely because he tempts the romantic in writer and reader to join him in "[d]eparting family." As he tears "silently into garbage" the "bird lopes into the rectangle nest of images / / and parts of him move on." Parts of the dog or parts of the bird? It doesn't matter because neither is a social animal in this poem. The temptation is to escape, even if it is into a form of fragmentation. The poems of domesticity and friendship not only stand against such poems in ***Rat Jelly,*** but remain when those are let go in ***Trick with a Knife.*** The antithematic reading of Ondaatje that I am proposing here simply acknowledges the many mood swings and changes of vision any writer can go through while exploring the possibilities of the next, new, poem.

The epigraph to "**White Dwarfs**," like the other two, is about lying and truth telling, and the dangerous border between the two.[6] Most of the poems in "**White Dwarfs**" explore the problems of art's relation to life. This is true even of the lovely and moving **"We're at the graveyard,"** which is shifted to join the other domestic poems in ***Trick with a Knife,*** but which also specifically alludes to the last and title poem in the section—for many readers a central statement on the temptations of one kind of art. In contrast to the other poems here, its title also acts as the first line: the poem is in process before we're fully aware of having entered it. Those old standbys "Birth and copulation and death"[7]—in reverse order, and with "love" substituting perhaps for "copulation"—are the basis of the poem's discourse. Beginning with the reference to the graveyard, the poem invokes the far reaches of the universe and the inner workings of mind and heart: "Stuart Sally Kim and I" are "watching still stars / or now and then sliding stars" (***RJ,*** 51; ***TK,*** 47). The stars move and do not move, they are part of "clear charts, / the systems' intricate branches / which change with hours and solstices, / the bone geometry of moving from there, to there." Clarity dissipates in motion and lack of reference, which are rooted in "the bone geometry" of the human subjects. An equilibrium between stasis and change, which the poet's father could not find, exists in the universe as perceived by "friends / whose minds and bodies / shift like acrobats to each other." The next two lines deepen the necessary equivocation of the poem: "When we leave, they move / to an altitude of silence." This seems to refer to the stars, but grammatically it refers to "friends." It could be the silence each pair enters when the two pairs are not together, an implicit silence of separation. Stars and friends, the macrocosmic and the microcosmic, are suddenly equal here, where "our minds shape / and lock the transient" in an artistic process that "parallel[s] these bats / who organize the air / with thick blinks of travel." This paradoxical metaphor, where organized motion is a momentary blindness, implies the utterly exploratory nature of the act of shaping, the act of art. Finally this poem about both friendship and art returns to the first of these, yet maintains its dedication to the latter as the final three lines point back to the opening. Here everything is held in lovely tension, an equilibrium in which stillness contains the implicit movement of growth and a single human subject contains the universe the poem evokes: "Sally is like grey snow in the grass, / Sally of the beautiful bones / pregnant below stars."

"Heron Rex" offers a supplementary vision of Ondaatje's favorite bird. While **"Birds for Janet—The Heron"** simply insists that "Heron is the true king" (***DM,*** 13; ***TK,*** 3) and tracks the path of one heron's suicide, **"Heron Rex"** sets up a series of paradoxical generalizations to create an image of a twistedly symbolic species: "Mad kings / blood lines introverted, strained pure / so the brain runs in the wrong direction // they are proud of their heritage of suicides" (***RJ,*** 52; ***TK,*** 55). This heritage of self-destruction transcends mere madness—the poem revels in its contradictions—to emerge as a kind of artistry, as the lengthy anaphora suggests. At the end of the epic list of suicidal acts, the phrase "and were led away" is repeated three times to suggest that the death sought is as much of the creative mind as of the body. Indeed, **"Heron Rex"** anticipates *Coming Through Slaughter* at least as much as **"White Dwarfs"** does, especially in its climactic fourth stanza: "There are ways of going / physically mad, physically / mad when . . . you sacrifice yourself for the race . . . celebrity a razor in the body" (***RJ,*** 53; ***TK,*** 55-6).

The sudden shift of the pronoun here expresses the implied author's own investment in the argument. Is this "you" simply "Heron Rex" or is it (also) the artist as such? For both, the act of public display is both dangerous and tempting. Celebrity is the danger here, as it is "for people who disappear" and who "hover and hover / and die in the ether peripheries" of silence in **"White Dwarfs"** (***RJ,*** 70; ***TK,*** 68), as it most certainly is for Buddy Bolden. For such people, self-destructive acts seem to be the only, if terrifyingly extreme, way out, and **"Heron Rex"** initiates a sequence of poems projecting images of the self-destructive artist who seeks to escape into an inviolable silence. If the poem ended at this point, it would leave its readers in an open space of speculation, wondering if or how the birds had disappeared into their meanings. The final stanza returns to the material objects of "small birds so precise . . . 15 year old boys could . . . break them . . . as easily as a long fingernail" (***RJ,*** 53; ***TK,*** 56). This terse brush-off grounds the metaphysical symbolism of the rest of the poem at the expense of a certain seriousness of purpose. As self-destructive artist, the heron assumes a kind of glamour that the final stanza tries to maintain and undercut at the same time. It also strives for a sense of closure that the previous stanza resists. While the poem would feel incomplete, now, if it ended after the fourth stanza, the fifth stanza's diminution of the symbol the poem has so crazily expanded is disturbing. Perhaps this is the poet's deliberate effort to distance himself from such artists, as he begins his deepest exploration of their psychology in *Coming Through Slaughter.*

"Taking," a poem on the artist as audience, insists on "the formal need / to suck blossoms out of the flesh / in those we admire / planting them private in the brain" (***RJ,*** 55; ***TK,*** 57). Taking paradoxically becomes a kind of giving, or rather they continually replace and replenish one another. "To learn to pour the exact arc / of steel still soft and crazy / before it hits the page" is an image of this process, and it is an act of the writer as reader. If having "stroked the mood and tone / of hundred year dead men and women" and "tasted their brain" smacks of taking, it is also a way to give their art its due. Although "Their idea of the immaculate moment is now" might imply that art can only "freeze this moment" (***TK,*** 17), "the rumours pass on / are planted / till they become a spine" argues the other half of the paradox. A spine is both a solid object and something that grows and changes with its body, here perhaps the body of writing itself. Such poems on the nature of the work of art resist explication precisely because they are written on the margins of their own discourse, where nothing and everything makes sense simultaneously, and where the writer cannot hold to one side of the argument only and still keep writing.

With **"Burning Hills,"** the writer turns from imagining how art works in others to registering how he works in art. A seemingly complex narrative, it continually finds ways to deny normal narrative movement by creating a palimpsest or literary archaeological dig in which to uncover remembered layers of writing that contain further "layers of civilization in his memory" (***RJ,*** 57; ***TK,*** 59). This extremely self-conscious piece of writing first sets its narrative voice apart from its "autobiographical" subject: "So he came to write again / in the burnt hill region." Paying extraordinary attention to mundane detail, the poem plots out the "schizophrenic season change, June to September, / when he deviously thought out plots / across the character of his friends." Already the adverb begins to subvert the apparent commitment to autobiographical "truth" that the realistic details imply. Although the poem expresses the fear that some "year maybe he would come and sit / for 4 months and not write a word down," it is also the writing that fear engenders.

Readers, especially male readers, are invited to identify with the protagonist as he makes a time machine of his writing room and thinks "of pieces of history" (***RJ,*** 57; ***TK,*** 59), especially his own teenage sexual history. The details have a marvelous nostalgic intensity, but what makes them work is the continual switching back and forth between them and the writer remembering. These shifts yield that sense of process that elsewhere the poems have desired and denied. The constant commentary of the mind remembering is what the poem's about, not the memories themselves, however evocative they are. Ambiguity remains the most powerful and seductive aspect of the process, as subject and object slide into one another. "The summers were layers of civilization in his memory / they were old photographs he didn't look at anymore / for girls in them were chubby not as perfect as in his mind." The summers in his memory become the old photographs he no longer looks at, but the old photographs are not as perfect as his mind even though the memory exists only in that mind. In fact, it seems that both photographs and memory are propelling the poem's narration along, as "he" assumes uncertain mastery over them. The games of sex, representing the chaotic changes of growth, haunt the protagonist, yet evade any summary comment. Memory and photography join in the "one picture that fuses 5 summers" (***RJ,*** 58; ***TK,*** 60). Here "summer and friendship will last forever," although he is "eating an apple" and "oblivious to the significance of the moment." But in photographs even more than in poems, significance is what we read into them. Photograph and poem contradict each other as "[n]ow he hungers to have that arm around the next shoulder. / The wretched apple is fresh and white." Here the layering of memory mixes a present-tense "now," which is already the past of the earlier stanzas, with the deeper past tense of the picture in which, nevertheless, the apple remains in the present tense. Such a "complex tension" can be expressed only as a process, the act of remembering discovered in the act of recording.

The final stanza again insists upon the process that writing both captures and is. Yet it also acknowledges that something of life must be lost even as the writing tries to hold on to it. Present participles in the first two sentences create a contradiction, contrasting the act of writing the poem we are reading with the action of the Shell Vapona Strip mentioned at the beginning of the poem: "Since he began burning hills / the Shell strip has taken effect." Is the poem like the insecticide? The lowercase of the title phrase implies that he has perhaps been destroying rather than making, or at least in some way razing memories to make a poem. Yet the present participle suggests that doing so is an ongoing process, which never stops, never achieves a frozen stasis, perhaps because each new reading re-creates both poem and subjects. The final lines may not even be the true confession they appear to be: "He has written slowly and carefully / with great love and great coldness. / When he finishes he will go back / hunting for the lies that are obvious." To the extent that all his poems were written this way, they may contain nonobvious lies. The greatest of these may be that confession. The "hunting" is itself a continuing process, which may or may not change the poem. Although the final line appears straightforward enough on first reading, it is as indeterminate as the whole poem: a troubling yet engaging performance that insists on having its ambivalent cake and eating it, too.

If writing must take place "in the murderer's shadow" (***RJ,*** 61; ***TK,*** 61), then it will pay that price, as **"King Kong meets Wallace Stevens"** intimates. Looking at photographs of the two figures, the writer asks, in parentheses, "(Is it significant that I eat bananas as I write this?)"—a comic aside loaded with implications of identity. While Kong wreaks destruction "in New York streets again," that "again" evoking the repetitive powers of art, "W. S. in his suit / is thinking chaos is thinking fences." This ambiguous creation-in-destruction, in which the "lack of punctuation equates the two activities," recalls the writer's activity in **"Burning Hills"** (Scobie 1985a, 56). Stevens is the exemplar here because he can write "the seeds of fresh pain . . . the bellow of locked blood" into his poems. While Kong is "at the call of Metro-Goldwyn-Mayer," "the naked brain / the thought in" Stevens exercises the control self-destructive artists repudiate.

"Spider Blues," which is moved back one to directly follow **"King Kong meets Wallace Stevens"** in ***Trick with a Knife,*** uses macabre comedy to undermine, though not utterly deny, any trust of such artists of control earlier poems might have engendered. If the writer must write and therefore cannot join his "heroes" in silence, he certainly feels too ambivalent about his art to underwrite it unequivocally. **"Spider Blues"** allows the subjects of such art their voice. The spider, "his control classic," is a "kind of writer I suppose" (***RJ,*** 63; ***TK,*** 62), says this writer, the man with a wife whose "smell spiders go for." Already black comedy and speculative poetics are merging into a tall tale of *écriture.* Spider/writer is an explorer who "thinks a path and travels . . . to new regions / where the raw of feelings exist" (***RJ,*** 63-64; ***TK,*** 62). This sounds positive, but "[s]piders like poets are obsessed with power" (***RJ,*** 64; ***TK,*** 62) does not. Such power can "kill" the subject, as the poem demonstrates in a scene of allusive black comedy where "spider comes to fly, says / Love me I can kill you," but "fly says, O no . . . you spider poets are all the same / you in your close vanity of making" (***RJ,*** 64; ***TK,*** 62-63). These contradictory voices provide a dialogical view of the writer's situation: the tautology that clarity only "comes when roads I make are being made" reveals the solipsism into which the artist may fall while working; "close" sounds enough like "close*d*" to suggest a making that process poetics would wish to transcend; the spider's desire to crucify "his victims in his spit / making them the art he cannot be" implies that the controlling artist hates the life he wants to turn into art (with the further implication that artists who turn to silence make their own lives into works of art, which yet must finish in their death?).

In this scene, the spider artists get no respect, but the poem isn't over, and in "[t]he ending we must arrive at . . . Nightmare for my wife and me" (***RJ,*** 65; ***TK,*** 63), they put on a performance, the past-tense narration of which itself suggests its success, in which "they carried her up—her whole body / into the dreaming air so gently / she did not wake or scream." The writer is lost in admiration of their art, but he is not alone, and the poem concludes on a note of certainty, which only underlines the uncertainty of the whole project: "Everybody clapped, all the flies. . . . ALL / except the working black architects / and the lady locked in their dream their theme." The flies seem to be "everybody" here, a designation of the audience that should make any reader wary. They cry and gasp, which they might also do if they were dying. The final paradox is art's central one: the artists are in process, as the present participle implies, but the firm adjectival form of "locked" equally implies the freezing of the subject of that process. It seems there is no escaping the contradiction at the heart of art, yet the essentially comic mode of this poem suggests that the paradox is, finally, acceptable—at least to the writer writing.

Artistic control is simultaneously sought and denied in **"The gate in his head,"** which is dedicated to Victor Coleman, a poet of process, whose "shy mind / reveal[s] the faint scars / coloured strata of the brain, / not clarity but the sense of shift / / a few lines, the tracks of thought" (***RJ,*** 62; ***TK,*** 64). The transformation from personal wounds to written trace occurs through a metaphoric "shift" that conflates reading and tracking. But, in a poem about the problem of netting chaos in language, the imagery undergoes continual metamorphosis. A tracker might move across a "[l]andscape of busted trees," but in a poem of transformations, that landscape melts surrealistically into "Stan's fishbowl / with a book inside . . . the typeface clarity / going slow blonde in the sun full water" erasing its bibliographicity.[8] Only after the first half of the poem has presented a series of rapid and confusing transformations does the writer argue its case for doing so, by enunciating what he always tries to do. The writing mind pours the inchoate materials of experience onto the page, but it must capture—net—them to do so. This contradiction manifests both the terror and the glory of art, but the glory is that the writing does come from love perceived as an act of exploration. Moreover, it can be communicated, as the "blurred photograph" of the "stunning white bird / an unclear stir" demonstrates. Writer-as-reader receives the other's "[c]aught vision" and understands the ideal he should seek in his own writing. The final stanza is necessarily paradoxical. Form is present in chaos even as chaos is present in form: what the writer seeks to catch is not the dead thing but the actual movement of the living, and he can do so only by allowing words their own indeterminate ambiguity. The poem desires clarity, but it also admits that too much clarity can stop the necessary movement that art seeks to illuminate. What the photograph is, and what the "writing should be," then, is a clear vision of the "beautiful formed things" in the process of escaping closure, "shapeless, awkward / moving to the clear."[9]

"White Dwarfs"[10] is central to Ondaatje's oeuvre precisely because it evokes so many themes associated with his work. "Ondaatje's most radical gesture in the direction of indicating that there are times when 'all the truth' cannot be stated, described, or re-enacted . . . [this] variation on T. W. Adorno's 'No poetry after Auschwitz' . . . is a profound meditation on both life and art. It is a tribute to those who have gone beyond 'social fuel' and language" (Solecki 1985a, 106-7). A tribute, yes, but not an uncomplicated one; if it "is for people who disappear" and "who shave their moral so raw / they can tear themselves through the eye of a needle" (***RJ,*** 70; ***TK,*** 68), it not only cannot share their silence but must speak in order to praise them. Given the reference to Jesus' parable about the rich man and heaven,[11] "moral" has a positive connotation, but the violence required to achieve "heaven"—which is perhaps simply "the ether peripheries" where they "hover and hover / and die"—savagely undercuts any sentimentalization of their behavior.

The "heroes" of silence—a silence the poet insists he fears—"sail to that perfect edge / where there is no social fuel / Release of sandbags / to understand their altitude." They join the stars of **"We're at the graveyard"** in "an altitude of silence" (***TK,*** 47) completely cut off from humanity. Beyond the ordinary connections of life, they achieve a "perfect edge," but "perfect" has the negative connotation of stasis, completion, and implies the end of living. Like the herons of **"Heron Rex,"** these heroes (note the shift of only one letter between the two) have chosen a kind of suicide, if only of their art. The poet admires them, but he does not, finally, seek to join them; he cannot, for he still believes in words. Their silence has an aura of romance about it, and it is based on real pain, but someone has to speak for them if they refuse to speak for themselves: "3rd man hung so high and lonely / we dont hear him say / say his pain, say his unbrotherhood." But perhaps it isn't they who refuse but we who "dont hear." The poem is riddled with ambiguity. Some choose not to speak, like "Dashiell Hammett [who] in success / suffered conversation and moved / to the perfect white between the words" (***RJ,*** 71; ***TK,*** 69), and that is their privilege; others are forced into silence, and perhaps need someone else to acknowledge their suffering. It may be "Ondaatje's recognition of the adolescent fatuity of the code **'White Dwarfs'** addresses, its spurious glamour, which makes him deflate it even as he continues to explore its romance" (Glickman, 79), but this is not the only contradiction at work in the poem. Of the mules with their tongues cut out, the poem asks, "after such cruelty what could they speak of anyway," and the image implies other tortures, of humans as well as animals. But mules never could speak, and always needed someone to speak on their behalf. That "perfect white" is both static, as the adjective suggests, and "can grow" into various possibilities, even into "an egg—most beautiful / when unbroken, where / what we cannot see is growing / in all the colours we cannot see." But such growth depends upon "us," who use the power of imagination to "see" the colors hidden in the white.

The whole poem maintains a delicate equilibrium, balancing silence against speech, the romantic otherness of the heroes who sail beyond society into silence against the classic responsibility of the poet as witness. There is poetry after Auschwitz because the horror had to be confronted. This poem affirms writing by denying it: that is the paradox the poems of poetics have approached over and over again. We would never "know" about "those burned out stars / who implode into silence / after parading in the sky" unless the writer told us and in telling evoked our compassion by insisting that "after such choreography what would they wish to speak of anyway." The poem honors the silenced ones by speaking. In that ambivalent balance,[12] poetry continues to explore what "writing should be then" (***RJ,*** 62; ***TK,*** 64), as it must.

The new poems in the third section of ***Trick with a Knife*** were written during and after the writing of *Coming Through Slaughter.* They present themselves as more strictly autobiographical, and the "I" who speaks them seems to have much more in common with the living writer, Michael Ondaatje, than before, while the references tend to be less mythical or literary and more seemingly "real." If, previously, "[w]hat Ondaatje d[id wa]s invite the expectations of confession and the exhilarations of parable, but leave the identity of the speaker hovering between himself and another" (Chamberlin, 38), now the speaking voices of his poems still hover "between" possibilities, but they are the various possibilities of place, stance, and attitude found under the single "name" of the implied author. Poems of Canada, mostly of rural Ontario and its history, which he comes to as an immigrant, are balanced against travel poems of Egypt, India, and Sri Lanka.[13] Because the Ceylon he returns to is a place he left too young to have truly inherited a sense of his place in its history, the poems set there are as arbitrary and float as free of/from historical referentiality as the Canadian ones. The final poems return to Toronto, children, parents, and friends, and include a re-vision of Billy the Kid from the point of view of another "actor" in the story.

The apparent refusal of history and historically grounded culture that some critics find disturbing in a postcolonial writer (see Mukherjee, 33-34)[14] may equally be a choice that reflects, and reflects upon, twentieth-century rootlessness and nomadism. Moreover, the ways these poems refuse to engage with historical and social representation paradoxically call attention to it; like much postmodern writing, they accept the past as such but suggest that, "however true [the past's] independence may be, nevertheless the past exists for us—now—only as traces on and in the present. The absent past can only be inferred from circumstantial evidence" (Hutcheon 1989, 73). Even the poems that invoke history insist that it is only the invocation that can be inscribed, not the "actual" history; this is especially apparent in **"Pig Glass"** itself.

The epigraph to **"Pig Glass,"** from Italo Calvino's *Invisible Cities,* says that, lacking the language, "Marco Polo could express himself only with gestures or with objects."[15] It thus emphasizes the difficulties of communication, and the comedy of physical expression that arises from those difficulties. A later part of the passage, not quoted by Ondaatje, adds that, "obscure or obvious as it might be, everything Marco displayed had the power of emblems, which, once seen, cannot be forgotten or confused" (Calvino, 20-21). One way of discussing many of these poems is in terms of how they either present emblems or become them. Their power often lies in the emblematic force of their images, rather than in the argumentative force of their narratives.[16] This is certainly true of **"The Agatha Christie Books by the Window"** (***TK,*** 72) and the beautifully indeterminate **"Moon Lines, after Jiménez"** (***TK,*** 74-75).

"Buying the Dog," "Moving Fred's Outhouse / Geriatrics of Pine," and **"Buck Lake Store Auction"** invoke the specific life of rural Ontario. The air of autobiography is palpable in them, and the narrative voice, studiedly realistic, "artlessly" anecdotal, seems to buttress that air of personal narrative, until the sudden illumination of poetic rhetoric just slightly undermines the apparent naturalness of the idiom. The first poem enters the world and speech of the farmer Buck McLeish only to push hard at a comic edge with the introduction of "the dog who has been / in a religious fit of silence / since birth" (***TK,*** 76). Despite the attention to detail and a somewhat grandiose attempt to make the dog symbolize this world they (the "we" of the poem—speaker and family) wish to become part of—"Towns the history of his bones"—the end comically undercuts the pretensions the poem has created, as the dog "takes off Jesus / like a dolphin / over the fields for all we know / he won't be coming back." The use of the first name in **"Moving Fred's Outhouse"** establishes a friendly intimacy, inviting us to assume it as well. The ordinariness of the events—here moving an old outhouse across a property to make it "a room thorough with flight, noise, / and pregnant with the morning's eggs /—a perch for chickens" (***TK,*** 77)—argues the autobiographical "truth" of these poems as opposed to the "mythologizing" of ***The Dainty Monsters.*** But if not mythical, these events are charged with something more than banal ordinariness, which is signaled once again through a comic gesture: "Fred the pragmatist—dragging the ancient comic / out of retirement and into a television series / among the charging democracy of rhode island reds." Unlike the previous poem, which ended in a question, this ends with an apparent summary statement—"All afternoon the silent space is turned"—that nevertheless turns interpretation aside. We are left with the images of dog or outhouse and chickens, not with an argument at all.

"Buck Lake Store Auction," the most socially conscious of these poems, maintains the autobiographical perspective, but only to provide a personal response within the poem to the scene of loss it witnesses. Beginning in minimal description, it soon puts a price on the items it lists. In the fifth stanza, the speaker finally identifies himself with either a family or everyone there in the "we" who "have the power to bid / on everything that is exposed" (***TK,*** 78). Admitting this power over others seems to clarify his vision and move him to a kind of angry sarcasm: "I expected [the old woman] to unscrew / her left arm and donate it / to the auctioneer's excitement." This excitement is responsible for whatever is being done here, and engenders both political awareness and impotence: "In certain rituals we desire / only what we cannot have" (***TK***, 79). The false logical connection of "While for her, Mrs Germain, / this is the needle's eye / where maniacs of heaven select" only underlines that impotence. Where, in **"White Dwarfs,"** that Biblical allusion implied reckless romantic courage among those who choose to "tear themselves through the eye of a needle" (***TK***, 68), the obvious lack of choice here suggests some reevaluation of the earlier vision. The tone here replaces the awe of the earlier poem with compassion, the uselessness of which is made clear by the subjunctive mood of the final three lines: the speaker "wanted to say" something useful, if only in a bid, but could and did not. Confronting an economic situation that is also political, this highly problematic poem can only offer the "liberal" act of witness in response. Even as it limns the liberal predicament, it also continues the autobiographical work of situating the writer in the country he has chosen to make home and whose life he seeks to enter. Its success in both endeavors reveals how postmodern Ondaatje's writing has become, in that it can self-reflexively balance these oppositions within the one text.

"Farre Off" (***TK***, 80) appears to be a traditionally lyric poem, with a self-conscious sense of beauty and personal engagement that fits the conventions of lyric utterance, even if the utterance is directed to, or through, other poems rather than a particular beloved person. But its deliberate intertextuality suggests something of its subversive nature. The lyric "I" represents himself specifically as a poet and a reader of poetry, speaking of a new discovery and translating the experience of the reading into his own rural setting. This is an engaged reader who desires what the poems of Campion and Wyatt, "who loved with the best," inscribe as desirable: "suddenly I want 16th century women / round me devious politic aware / of step ladders to the king." While the sudden rush of emotion and expression of personal desire are essentially lyric, the arresting encapsulation of the imagery of the earlier poetry is highly self-reflexive. Such narrative self-consciousness deepens in the deliberately ambiguous reference of the second stanza, which also links this poem to the previous poems of local place: "Tonight I am alone with dogs and lightning / aroused by Wyatt's talk of women who step / naked into his bedchamber." Ancient poetry is suddenly extraordinarily effective here, arousing not only the speaker but also the dogs and even the elements. But what is the nature of this highly contagious excitement? Rather than answering such a question, the poem presents a variety of illuminations and confounds any sense of literary or cultural inheritance by returning attention to the speaker. "I have on my thin blue parka / and walk behind the asses of the dogs / who slide under the gate / and sense cattle / deep in the fields." These lines veer wildly from Wyatt's traditional lyric vision to an antilyric naturalism and reinforce the syntactical ambiguity erasing the difference between dogs and speaker. Finally, the speaker seems to move toward an epiphany only to reverse the literary expectation of "illumination" from a text, and perhaps confess that opacity is all that poetry can offer: "I look out into the dark pasture / past where even the moonlight stops / / my eyes are against the ink of Campion." Literature, which is supposed to bring light, is inscribed in darkness, in ink, a material barrier to understanding, but one that readers understand in its physical presence: ink, poem, book connect, but do not explain. The mystery of the reader-writer relationship at the center of this poem is not new in Ondaatje's work, but seldom has it been presented in such a "natural" manner. The poem argues nothing; it simply demonstrates by a kind of handing on its complex sense of cultural inheritance.

The complexities both attract and repulse the poet, and **"Walking to Bellrock"** examines modes of escape from the responsibilities of inheritance that weigh the artist down. It presents a process, not simply a single act, over and done with. Like Depot Creek, the syntax twists and turns, pronouns slipping into each other, tenses shifting, different stories sliding over and under each other. "Two figures in deep water. / / Their frames truncated at the stomach / glide along the surface" (***TK***, 81): this is the motivating image of the poem. Two friends are taking this crazy walk, yet they are not all there; or they move along a mirror that reflects both too little and too much, and thus refutes analysis. History is present only to be ignored, yet the paradox of writing assures the affirmation and elucidation of meanings that the poem itself appears to claim are lost or tossed aside in egocentric, romantic adherence to the now of walking and talking that the poem celebrates. But even the now is lost in the welter of impressions the river, and the poem, throws up. The various images of "[l]andscapes underwater" that the "torn old Adidas tennis shoes" encounter are sharp yet indecisive, and the questions that follow cannot be answered. "Stan and I laughing joking going summer crazy / as we lived against each other" (***TK***, 82) announces the autobiographical nature of the poem and its exploration of the notion of male friendship. This companionate summer craziness might stand as an alternative to Buddy Bolden's isolated retreat into insanity, but the preposition, echoing **"Farre Off,"** suggests how opaque the communication in even the closest friendships is. Perhaps this sense of opaqueness explains why the speaker insists "there is no history or philosophy or metaphor with us," although the rest of the poem denies this assertion with complex metaphors and historical allusions that depend upon a certain degree of documentation constantly erupting into the narrative.

The poem desires to become no more than a record of immediate perception, yet in the process of ordering experience comes up short against the questions the action raises, of which "Stan, my crazy summer friend, / why are we both going crazy?" (***TK***, 83) is only the most obvious. But "in the middle of this century / following the easy fucking stupid plot to town," there are no answers beyond the crazy act of walking the river. The poem generates excitement in its representation of the "crazy" actions of the two friends, while undercutting their romantic heroism. **"Walking to Bellrock"** celebrates an act of friendship but denies it any cultural viability; its insistence on denying history consistently resists the conventional attractions of tradition while failing to erase tradition itself from the text. **"Walking to Bellrock"** denies history and tradition only to affirm their necessity; it revels in romantic escapism only to hold it up to question.

"Pig Glass," perhaps the most stringently emblematic of the new poems, suggests their problematic relation to history and inheritance. "Bonjour. This is pig glass / a piece of cloudy sea" (***TK,*** 84): while the colloquial opening addresses the reader as subject of what is said, the demonstrative pronoun points to an object that exists only in its name and in the shifting descriptions inscribed in the poem. As further transformations occur, indeterminate reference confuses "my hand," "a language," and the "pig glass" in a gesture intimating a complex intimacy, and seducing us into joining the speaker in his meditation: "the pig glass / I thought / was the buried eye of Portland Township." The line breaks imply the speaker is thinking the glass into existence as "slow faded history / waiting to be grunted up."

Only after he has allowed for such uncertainties does the speaker finally name the family who once "used this section" and describe some of the objects he has found in their "midden." Naming them places him in relation to a history, but not one he has inherited by any family right. Having said as much, he returns to the "pig glass," which the repeated demonstrative "this" self-reflexively makes identical with the text **"Pig Glass"** as both object and context. The next stanza shifts back to other objects in the land, and, more troublingly, to the letters and journals "I / disturbed in the room above the tractor shed" (***TK,*** 85). The "I" of the poem has become his own "eye" of the township through documentary invasion of a family's privacy, and, as if recognizing the impropriety of the act, the poem leaps back to the seeming objectivity of the glass. But as glass and poem are one, there can be no objectivity, and the text implodes into the present tense of the action that broke the glass: "This green fragment has behind it / the *booomm* when glass / tears free of its smoothness." Past and present are also one in the transition to subjective perception in the final stanza, where the speaker insists on his possession of an emblem of "[D]etermined histories of glass." But we possess "indeterminate histories of the poem," for it is impossible to say who or what determined those histories, only the vaguest allusions to which the poem has provided. It is "cloudy sea" (***TK,*** 84) because it allows all the possibilities of both cloud and sea to float around it: it says there is history but it cannot tell what histories there are. **"Pig Glass"** is the perfect emblem of the indeterminacy of knowledge that so many of these poems delineate.

The next five poems are from travels, but they neatly evade the usual problems of travel poems, where the lyric and romantic "I" reports back with a privileged commentary on the places and si[gh]t[e]s seen. The speaker of these poems performs a kind of perceiving and even meditation sometimes, but does not presume to report or comment on what he sees; he simply registers its presence in as imagistic a language as possible or allows it to tease his mind into other thoughts. The results are poems in which various forms of discourse slide over and continually interrupt one another, providing no easy place of rest or closure. **"The Hour of Cowdust"** opens with a "we" rather than an "I" not so much displaced as unplaced: "It is the hour we move small / in the last possibilities of light" (***TK,*** 86). Still unplaced, the "we" becomes a specific "I," thinking first of his children elsewhere and then focusing on the present moment of dusk "here by the Nile," which seems to specify place and time only to let metaphors of illusion undercut any sense of "reality" that might be building up. "Everything is reducing itself to shape" seems a generalization of sense impressions, but the impression is of loss of specificity: nothing can be named. Sliding to the second-person pronoun, the poem evokes the air and the changing color of the scene only to switch suddenly in memory to "Indian miniatures" and commentaries and stories of high romance he can allude to but "cannot quite remember." The conclusion of such fallible meditation is an offhand and oxymoronic "So many / graciously humiliated / by the distance of rivers" (***TK,*** 87). This returns the poem to the particular river at a particular hour, but only to introduce other questions and engender a series of syntactic ambiguities that reinforce the sense of illusion. Duplicitous, the scene becomes a dream, in which the final stanza's assertion that with no "depth of perception / it is now possible / for the outline of two boats / to collide silently" seems perfectly natural. But it is not natural, and the grammatical slippage from singular "outline" to implied plural verb self-reflexively reaffirms the textuality of the whole experience, in which the titular hour creates illusions of romance and of violence, only to prevent anything from actually happening. By inscribing its own imagining, the poem provides a sense of the mystery of the alien space that is Egypt, without resorting to commentary or egocentric "insight." Egypt remains as opaque as the "pig glass," and as beautiful.

A similar kind of defamiliarization occurs in **"The Palace,"** which renders an Indian dawn to match the Egyptian dusk. This time "I am alone / leaning / into flying air" and "red daylight" (***TK,*** 88), but this "I" is only one site of discourse among many, looking at the place and its animal life, and eventually its waking population. The stanza on the ancient king stands alone; lacking any personal introduction, it might be dreamed, heard, read. A kind of document inserted into the poem, it splits the singular voice of lyric meditation apart. Where history and myth once joined in story, now a startling image of international technology makes a strange mythic moment when "a beautiful wail / of a woman's voice rises / 300 street transistors / simultaneously playing / the one radio station of Udaipur." Contradictory political ironies suggest that multinational technology imposes alien knowledge on local or national culture, yet the use of such imperial gifts can be a form of resistance even as it is a sign of colonization. But the poem refuses to argue any case. It does not presume to speak for the people of Udaipur, only to register the moment of *ostranenie* they provided.

"Uswetakeiyawa" is a good introduction to Sri Lanka, for the very word is utterly alien, and as the first word of the poem it sets the tone of strangeness for "the dream journey / we travel most nights / returning from Colombo. / A landscape nightmare" (***TK,*** 90). The poem traverses illusion and paradox, as even the senses prove untrustworthy, and "lesser" senses like smell have to make up for the failure of vision (possibly implied as a pun). The sense of transformation is central, and in the final stanzas, the poem itself turns "trickster," rendering an over-whelming sensual confusion that confounds "you" as "you" encounter "something we have never been able to recognize" (***TK,*** 91). "There was then the odour we did not recognize. / The smell of a dog losing its shape" is the oxymoronic conclusion of an argument against rationality: what it recognizes as an unrecognizable odor is the final sign of a frightening transformation of something known (and in most of Ondaatje's poetry, dogs are both known and loved) into the unknown. In this night journey through a nightmare landscape, what other known shapes are lost? Although he can be read as a returning prodigal of sorts, this poem establishes the writer as outsider, a tourist lost in an alien landscape who can sense its power but never know or understand it.

"The Wars" presents a series of images of natural life and death in this mysterious place that is Sri Lanka. The title suggests the violence implicit in the natural cycle the poem perceives, yet its tone is essentially light, as the image of "hundreds of unseen bats / tuning up the auditorium / in archaic Tamil" (***TK,*** 92) reveals. That they sing a song of exile connects them to the speaker. The poem's quick shifts of attention reveal the outsider's inability to know what is and what is not "real" in this place of continual transformation; all he can do is render, in a series of typically sensuous images, the rich paradoxes of what he experiences: in "noon moonlight" (how the sun appears underwater?), "only [the Ray's] twin" (his shadow on the seabed?) "knows how to charm / the waters against him" (***TK,*** 93). This seems a conclusive gesture, but all it manages to suggest is that nothing is quite certain in these landscape nightmares.

"Sweet like a Crow," which is dedicated "for Hetti Corea, 8 years old" (***TK,*** 94) is a jeu d'esprit, all light wit and comedy, emerging from its epigraph by Paul Bowles: "'The Sinhalese are beyond a doubt one of the least musical people in the world. It would be quite impossible to have less sense of pitch, line, or rhythm.'" An increasingly bizarre set of similes shifts among images of odd auditory events, signs of pop culture, and specifically local references. Rhetorical overkill deliberately pushes the trope of simile beyond bounds to achieve a new comic decorum of delight and, finally, even beauty, as the final couplet returns to quotidian event by using the trope to undercut its tropicality: "like the sound I heard when having an afternoon sleep / and someone walked through my room in ankle bracelets" (***TK,*** 95). To suggest that the exotic range of the similes attempts to match the exotic sensual impact of Sri Lanka itself is not, I hope, to give in to an ethnocentric blindness to the culture and people that Ondaatje, too, may be ignoring (see Mukherjee, 33), for it is precisely the chaotic combination of comparisons that marks the whole "description" as culturally contextualized by the complex juxtaposition of Sri Lankan heritage and international pop iconography. Mostly, however, the poem takes pleasure in its own fertile inventiveness.

The final poems return to Canada, but only to perceive from that perspective various aspects of the world as they impinge upon a singular individual anywhere. **"Late Movies with Skyler"** is precisely domestic, but insists that even in the midst of domesticity we are connected to the larger world of personal and public dreams by the media that dominate our imaginations. It can be read against **"White Dwarfs"** only to the extent that both visions coexist in the writerly imagination. Skyler, the 21-year-old stepson visiting "home," has come back from an unromantic reality of "logging on Vancouver Island / with men who get rid of crabs with Raid" (***TK,*** 96) to watch films of romantic escapism. But he is himself romantic and is represented as being essentially alone. When the writer joins him to watch, "*The Prisoner of Zenda* / a film I saw three times in my youth / and which no doubt influenced me morally," the young man demonstrates a desire for the aesthetic purity of craft, practicing guitar during commercials. In its apparently casual articulateness, the way it slides from one small event to another, the writing seems to deny that it is a poem, yet the careful rhythms and the jumps from stanza to stanza all contribute to a specifically poetic effect. From simply describing the situation of the two men watching, the poem slips into a kind of double commentary that envelops the mood of the film within the mood of the watchers. But the "perfect world [now] over" (***TK,*** 97) cannot coexist with the mess of "the slow black rooms of the house," except in the imagination. If "Skyler is Rupert then the hero," he is also the boy-man who will shortly leave for somewhere unspecific. All the writer can realize and offer is the ironic coda that "[i]n the movies of my childhood the heroes / after skilled swordplay and moral victories / leave with absolutely nothing / to do for the rest of their lives." But the real world goes on, and although the final lines of the poem argue closure for the films, they in fact deny it for both the writer and his stepson. The writer cannot know what Skyler will do, nor even where he will go. That is an open question, as is the poem.

If **"Late Movies with Skyler"** undercuts the romantic vision of old adventure movies, **"Sallie Chisum / Last Words on Billy the Kid. 4 a.m."** does a somewhat similar job on Ondaatje's own western adventure, ***The Collected Works of Billy the Kid.*** Sallie's apparently random thoughts are based on memory engaging desire and its concomitant sense of loss, yet the whole process of remembering begins with a chance image of the moon as Billy's head. The tone throughout is dramatically precise as it shifts with the attention of its subject from comment to memory to comment again. There is a double sense of audience as both the moon-Billy and another "you" are addressed. She remembers that he taught her to smoke, shifts back to a moment of intense body awareness of "Billy's mouth . . . trying / to remove a splinter out of my foot" (***TK,*** 98), and then converses in her mind with the moon-ghost. The memories imply a strained intimacy that remains—as it was in the book—mysteriously opaque, even to one of the participants. But the degree of her intimacy with Billy is not as important as the power he still exerts over her despite her denials of it. The poem captures her contradictory feelings as she slides from memories of his presence as an object of desire to her present-day assertions that "Billy was a fool," a comment many readers of Billy's life might agree with, but which ***The Collected Works*** does not support. Like "those reversible mirrors," Billy resists both Sallie's attempts at analysis and her own continuing resistance to his charm. Thus her repetitions of key images and phrases only serve to undermine their authority even as they underline her continuing obsession with him. The poem simultaneously undercuts the romance that ***The Collected Works*** allowed but did not exploit and adds a further glamour to it. The final stanza captures all the pent-up frustration of 37 years of remembering in a gesture of complicity and denial, as she squashes her cigarette "against the window / where the moon is. / In his stupid eyes" (***TK,*** 99). The poem does not offer information so much as an opportunity to hear emotions work in memory as it works in her. Her anger reveals other, deeper, unacknowledged feelings, yet is also properly her own and completely true. Like the text it is a pendant to, **"Sallie Chisum / Last Words"** cannot determine a single view of its subject(s).

The ten prose fragments of **"Pure Memory / Chris Dewdney"** suggest that memory itself is a form of fiction making.[17] The epigraph quotes Dewdney himself, although it is not clear if it is something he wrote or something he said to the writer: "Listen, it was so savage and brutal and powerful that even though it happened out of the blue I knew there was nothing arbitrary about it" (***TK,*** 100). While there is no reference for this forceful "it," we read each fragment in terms of the unnamed catastrophe it represents even as the whole poem resists dealing with it. That is why writers tell stories, sometimes, to evade the catastrophe that cannot be written.

The poem begins in a comic mode, as the writer cannot pronounce the title of one of Dewdney's books on a radio show. This comic opening shot establishes the difficulties associated with Dewdney as writer, while part 2 represents him as full of laughter and energy. With part 3, the poem turns to concentrate upon a series of stories specifically designed to put off dealing with the core experience of Dewdney's life, as the writer perceives it. Yet, paradoxically, the stories all point to the ways in which Dewdney's behavior in every situation reveals a person whose whole life is based upon an intuitive understanding of catastrophe theory. Dewdney seems to live *ostranenie,* as the stories of his childhood, or of "[h]is most embarrassing moment" (***TK,*** 101), demonstrate. Although the various fragments build up a sense of Dewdney's resourcefulness in situations both ordinary and farcical, their humorous tone seems somewhat fragile beneath the weight of the epigraph. In part 7, the writer, seeing Dewdney after some time, notices the signs of a dark change: "Something has left his face. It is not that he is thinner but the face has lost something distinct and it seems like flesh" (***TK,*** 102). The stuttering repetitions make palpable the writer's inability to come to terms with the change he perceives, while that vague noun *something* signals what the poem will not, cannot, tell. Although he tries to turn away from these signs of pain, the writer cannot avoid returning to what he doesn't understand, his friend's face. The fragment ends with a reiteration of Dewdney's serious interest in all "important rare information like the history of rocks," and the next fragment takes another comic turn to say "[h]is favourite movie is *Earthquake*" and describe Dewdney's apartment full of beautiful fossils and other exhibits. Part 9 then describes the writer's return to Toronto with a drawing of Dewdney by another friend. Parts 7, 8, and 9 are in fact a single story of the writer's meeting Dewdney, then visiting him in London, then returning to Toronto; they suddenly bring all the memories into a single time frame in which the catastrophe, still not spoken of, looms ever closer. In a delicate metaphor, the image of the drawing on the luggage rack above the writer suddenly metamorphoses into the person, as he says, "[w]hen the bus swerves I put my arm out into the dark aisle ready to catch him if it falls" (***TK,*** 103). The "dark aisle" reinforces the disturbing undertone that the epigraph cast upon the whole poem, while the personal pronoun implies that "catching" his friend is exactly what he could not do; nor could anyone. Part 10 attempts to confront what the whole poem has evaded: "His wife's brain haemorrhage. I could not cope with that. He is 23 years old. He does. Africa Asia Australia upside down. Earthquake." What cannot be said is what turns everything upside down. As the images of previous fragments gather into a kind of litany of catastrophe, the single statement "He does" seems to suggest his ability to cope as the writer cannot. Or does it only imply the writer's hope that he can? The emotional power of the poem depends on how it both demonstrates friendship and empathy and reveals their limits.

Dedicated to the poet's mother, **"Light"** serves as a kind of prolegomenon to *Running in the Family,* where "the expanding stories" (***TK,*** 107) implied by the photographs that are the poem's subject finally get told. The "amazing light" (***TK,*** 72) of day in the first poem of **"Pig Glass"** now becomes a vaster, more complex series of night lights, including the lightning as well as the electric light that projects slides. Thus, the first image of "[t]rees walking off across the fields in fury / naked in the spark of lightning" (***TK,*** 105) suggests movement in stillness, just as the photographs do. The writer watches the midnight storm as the "past, friends and family, drift into the rain shower." The sense of "drift" is the essence of this poem; it suggests the evanescence of both the light-projected images, and the stories conjured out of them, both of which "now stand / complex ambiguous grainy on my wall."

The long second stanza points to some of the figures in the implied gossipy tales. It further establishes the tone of casual, intimate conversation that deliberately uses the indicative pronoun to include us in the small circle listening to the writer as he points out one relative after another. But a text can only point to itself; the "pictures" exist only in the words describing them, yet the verbal gesture implicates us in the implied story of the writer's telling stories. After pointing to aunts and uncles and the gossip attached to their names, he then turns to his mother and her brother, linking a picture of their childhood to the story of their deaths. Complex narrative shifts of time occur throughout these two stanzas, as when the writer recalls his mother recalling her brother's death and her earlier memories at that time. Over and over again, he speaks in precisely personal tones about his own feelings for the people in the photographs, insisting that photographs provide a way of touching the past.

When he says "[t]hese are the fragments I have of them, tonight / in this storm" (***TK,*** 106), the indicative appears to refer to the photographs, but, in the midst of the storm, it can also refer to the stories, or to the memories the photos and stories recall and create. The layers of fictional invention memory makes are implied in that single word, "these." Repeated, it emphasizes the ambiguous hold memory has on the past: "These are their fragments, all I remember, / wanting more knowledge of them" (***TK,*** 107). Memory is not knowledge, yet it is all we have, and so "[w]herever we are / they parade in my brain and the expanding stories / connect to the grey grainy pictures on the wall . . . / coming through the light, the electricity, which the storm / destroyed an hour ago." That "we" once again intimately includes us in the writer's perspective, but the passage creates images only to dissipate any sense of "reality" they might create. The pictures are no longer on the wall; even they are no more than memories, part of another expanding story now being written, and read. In fact, the passage, a single, long, winding, and complex sentence, slips and slides from images and stories to the hour-old accident, to the kids playing dominoes now, and finally to the writer meditating as he smokes, watches the lightning, and returns to the image that began the poem only to deny it: "and the trees across the fields leaving me, distinct / . . . when in truth like me they haven't moved. / Haven't moved an inch from me." The play on "light" throughout the poem complicates and undercuts any symbolic meaning it might have. Yet the slides offer a peculiarly technological "illumination" in which the silent past does communicate with the present. The slippage of syntax in the final passage signals the fusion of and the fluctuation among photographs, stories, memory, imagination, and desire that the poem invokes. Neither trees nor storied memories (or remembered stories) really move away, yet this confirmation of the deception of appearances reminds us that the whole poem *may* not be what it appears to be.

"Light" is a rich collage of moments in time laid over one another in a complex metaphoric relationship. Like many of the other poems in **"Pig Glass,"** it is deceptively anecdotal, casual in tone, and seemingly artless in narration. Here, the poet says, let me just lay out these quite ordinary random memories or impressions before you; have I told you about the time. . . . But analysis of these poems not only reveals the complicated interlocking of analepsis and prolepsis in their structures but also the subtle music of their language. Written as Ondaatje gradually involved himself in the task of writing *Running in the Family,* they provide glimpses of that larger work as well as of the other contexts of his life while he pursued it. In their more relaxed, less symbolic, approach to the idea of the lyric, itself undergoing a kind of deconstruction in both his own mind and other poets' works at the time, they also point the way toward the personal poem sequences of ***Secular Love.*** Certainly, as a summing up of where his writing had led him thus far, they provide a fitting and open-ended conclusion to ***There's a Trick with a Knife I'm Learning to Do.***

Notes

1. Michael Ondaatje, *Rat Jelly* (Toronto: Coach House Press, 1973), hereafter cited in text as *RJ.* Where the poems appear in *Trick with a Knife,* I will cite *TK* as well.
2. Ondaatje let Stephen Scobie and me have the poem to publish in *White Pelican* 1, no. 2 (Spring 1971) when we interviewed him on 3 March 1971; so it was written at the very latest in February 1971. I suspect it had been written earlier, as he usually waits a while before publicly reading or publishing his work. He began serious work on *Running in the Family* when he traveled to Sri Lanka in the spring of 1978.
3. Roger Shattuck, *The Banquet Years: The Origins of the Avant Garde in France 1885 to World War I,* rev. ed. (New York: Vintage Books, 1968), 221; hereafter cited in text.
4. Susan Glickman argues that his father "is evoked continually in Ondaatje's work" (78), and that, like Bolden, he "becomes one of those 'people who disappear'" (79), commemorated in "White Dwarfs."
5. From Howard O'Hagan, *Tay John* (New York: Clarkson N. Potter, 1960), 28, which Ondaatje would have been reading when he wrote many of these poems, as the publication of his article on the novel in the summer of 1974 indicates.
6. See *RJ,* 49; Herman Melville, *The Confidence Man: His Masquerade,* ed. Hershel Parker (New York: W. W. Norton & Co., 1971), 57-58. The ambiguous relation between "confidence" and "truth" in Melville's fiction plays across all the poems in "White Dwarfs."
7. T. S. Eliot, "Sweeney Agonistes," in *Collected Poems 1909-1962* (London: Faber and Faber, 1963), 131.
8. I could also describe this passage as "magical realist," in that there was such a fishbowl full of

book in the editorial office of Coach House Press, which was founded by Stan Bevington. The effect in the poem is definitely one of defamiliarization.

9. Solecki makes some similar points in his reading of the poem, insisting that it represents "an ideal which [Ondaatje] feels he has not yet achieved. I would suggest that it is a mark of Ondaatje's integrity as a poet that his most successful poems raise this kind of question" (Solecki 1985a, 105). Solecki's reading of the whole poem can be found on pp. 104-6.

10. "The white dwarfs comprise a group of stars [that] are of interest for several reasons, not the least of which is that they represent the last stage of stellar evolution, the last feeble glow of a dying star" (L. W. Aller, "Star," *Encyclopædia Britannica* [Chicago: Encyclopædia Britannica, 1970], 21:131).

11. See the Bible, Matt. 19:24; Mark 10:25; and Luke 18:25.

12. "The human function, which *is* here the artistic function, is as always to give form, to exercise control, to maintain equilibrium, to 'shape / and lock the transient'" (Scobie 1985a, 59-60).

13. In January 1978, Ondaatje took a sabbatical leave to travel across the Indian subcontinent to Sri Lanka, where he spent five months with his sister and other relatives. It was the first time he had returned to his birthplace, and while there he began keeping a journal, recording family stories and responding anew to the exotic qualities of what was to him an essentially new place. Many of the prose and verse entries found their way into a special issue of the *Capilano Review* 16/17 (1979): 5-43, the selection clearly intimating that a larger work was under way. He returned in 1980 to do further research on his own and his family's past in order to complete *Running in the Family,* but from this first trip he produced a number of travel poems that found their way into *Trick with a Knife* (see Mandel, 279).

14. But see Chamberlin for a different argument aligning Ondaatje with "other contemporary poets writing out of situations that define essentially colonial predicaments, where language or audience or the identity or role of the poet are indeterminate. Canada offers Ondaatje a geography, but no inheritance; Sri Lanka offers him a family history, but no tradition, no way of passing things on; the English language offers him both an inheritance and a history, but no time and place" (Chamberlin, 41).

15. Italo Calvino, *Invisible Cities,* trans. William Weaver (London: Pan Books, 1979), 20; hereafter cited in text.

16. "Indeed, in all of these poems we get the sort of arrangement of objects indicated in the epigraph from Calvino" (Marshall, 88).

17. Readers who know Dewdney's writing and his interest in geology might decide that "pure memory" can only be found in rock or "a piece of wood 120 million years old from the tar sands" (*TK,* 101). Written, therefore fictionalized, memory is never pure.

FURTHER READING

Criticism

Barbour, Douglas. *Michael Ondaatje*. New York: Twayne Publishers, 1993, 247 p.

Book-length study of Ondaatje's poetry and fiction with chapters devoted to early poetry, *The Collected Works of Billy the Kid*, and *Secular Love.*

Bök, Christian. "Destructive Creation: The Politicization of Violence in the Works of Michael Ondaatje." *Canadian Literature* No. 132 (Spring 1992): 109-24.

Analyzes the creative and destructive roles violence plays in Ondaatje's poetry and fiction, noting that while "Ondaatje's earlier texts appear to valorize violence enacted for purely idiosyncratic reasons, Ondaatje's later texts begin to reevaluate the ethics of such violence and suggest that it must ultimately serve a socially responsible end."

Clarke, George Elliott. "Michael Ondaatje and the Production of Myth." *Studies in Canadian Literature* 16, No. 1 (1991): 1-21.

Details the role of myth in Ondaatje's poetry and fiction. Clarke states that "From *Monsters* to *Love*, Ondaatje conveys the ambiguous effects of his constantly thwarted desire with metaphor which, producing myth, is obsessively dramatic."

Grace, Dominick M. "Ondaatje & Charlton Comics' 'Billy the Kid'." *Canadian Literature* No. 133 (Summer 1992): 199-203.

Discusses Ondaatje's manipulation of source materials in *The Collected Works of Billy the Kid.* Grace concludes "Ondaatje leaves incomplete a story complete in his source to underscore his own thematic concern, the impossibility of finishing Billy."

Heighton, Steven. "Approaching 'That Perfect Edge': Kinetic Techniques in the Poetry and Fiction of Michael Ondaatje." *Studies in Canadian Literature* 13, No. 2 (1988): 223-43.

Linguistic study of Ondaatje's poetry and fiction, focusing on the kinetic nature of his language.

Hornung, Rick. "Exile on Bloor Street: Michael Ondaatje's Northern Exposure." *Voice Literary Supplement* (October 1992): 29-31.

Biographical and critical overview of Ondaatje and his works through *The English Patient.*

Jones, Manina. "*The Collected Works of Billy the Kid:* Scripting the Docudrama." *Canadian Literature* No. 122-23 (Autumn-Winter 1989): 26-38

Describes Ondaatje's *The Collected Works of Billy the Kid* as a docudrama, asserting "Billy the Kid is seen as a body of texts; he becomes documentary material."

Kamboureli, Sam. "Outlawed Narrative: Michael Ondaatje's *The Collected Works of Billy the Kid.*" *Sagetrieb* 7, No. 1 (Spring 1988): 115-29.

Refutes earlier critical commentary of *The Collected Works of Billy the Kid*, arguing that it is not narrative but discourse that choreographs the poem's movement.

Kelly, Robert A. "Outlaw and Explorer: Recent Adventurers in the English-Canadian Long Poem." *The Antigonish Review* No. 79 (Autumn 1989): 27-34.

Compares Ondaatje's *The Collected Works of Billy the Kid* with similar works by poets Andy Wainwright and Paulette Jiles.

Additional coverage of Ondaatje's life and career is contained in the following sources published by the Gale Group: *Contemporary Authors,* Vols. 77-80; *Contemporary Authors New Revision Series,* Vols. 42, 74; *Contemporary Literary Criticism,* Vols. 14, 29, 51, 76; *Dictionary of Literary Biography,* Vol. 60; *DISCovering Authors: British; DISCovering Authors: Canadian; DISCovering Authors: Most-Studied Authors Module;* and *Major 20th-Century Writers,* Vol. 2

Dorothy Parker
1893–1967

American poet, essayist, and short story writer.

INTRODUCTION

As a poet, Parker is best known for three slender volumes of verse, *Enough Rope* (1926), *Sunset Gun* (1928), and *Death and Taxes* (1931). She also achieved widespread acclaim for her short stories and frequently quoted witticisms. Though she penned prose and poetry throughout her life, Parker's literary reputation rests mostly on poetry and short stories she authored prior to 1938. Mostly traditional in form, Parker's verse packs caustic sarcasm into sonnets, lyrics, ballads, Horatian odes, epigrams, and epitaphs. In her poetry, Parker most often addresses women's issues, soured love relationships, and vacuous, superficial lives of upper-crust society women who lived during the 1920s. In her characteristic burlesque style, Parker lampoons cloying women who depend too much on men for emotional and economic well-being, as well as the types of men who twist these female traits to their advantage. Following its publication in 1926, Parker's first collection of poetry, *Enough Rope,* rose to best-seller status. Nevertheless, Parker was self-deprecating when assessing her own poetry, once referring to it in an interview with the *Paris Review* as light verse that was "no damn good." In recent years, contemporary themes throughout Parker's poetry have received renewed critical acclaim. Today's readers continue to find deeper meanings in Parker's work than many of her contemporaries were able to appreciate—particularly in the poems and short stories that center on women's issues.

BIOGRAPHICAL INFORMATION

Parker was born in West End, New Jersey, in 1893 to Jewish clothier J. Henry Rothschild and Eliza Marston Rothschild. Her mother died shortly after her daughter's premature birth. Following her mother's death, Parker was raised by her father and stepmother, who Parker described as a "religious fanatic." Parker grew up ashamed of her mixed ethnic and religious background, aspiring to write an autobiographical tale entitled "Mongrel," which she never penned. Parker detested her stepmother for sending her to a convent school in New York City, an action taken to save Parker's soul from her "Jewish upbringing." While at the convent, Parker began writing poetry, but her education among the nuns was short-lived. Already showing signs of a rebellious streak, Parker described the Immaculate Conception as "spontaneous combustion" and was expelled. Parker's father and stepmother sent the young writer to an exclusive finishing school in Morristown, New Jersey, where she graduated following a year of study in 1911. During her time at the finishing school Parker began developing as a writer. Parker's persistence paid off in 1915 when one of her poems captured the attention of a *Vogue* editor, who hired her to write captions for the magazine's fashion illustrations. Two years later, an editor hired her onto *Vanity Fair* as a drama critic. Parker's acerbic wit again invoked trouble, and she was fired from this post after writing a blistering review of a play starring the wife of one of the magazine's financial backers. Parker continued writing as a literary critic for the *New Yorker*'s book review column under the pseudonym, "Constant Reader." During the 1920s, Parker became well-known in New York literary and theatrical circles as a member of the Algonquin Round Table. The round table, which included other prominent writers such as Robert Benchley, George S. Kaufman, and Franklin Pierce Adams, became famous when newspaper columnists reported the activities and discussions at the famed Algonquin Hotel debates. Many of

Parker's derisive Round Table remarks, such as "Men seldom make passes / At girls who wear glasses" were often quoted and achieved catchphrase status. In 1917, Parker married Wall Street broker Edwin Pond Parker II. While her husband was away for two years' military service, Parker's whirlwind social life led her to speakeasies and parties in uptown apartments where she became well-acquainted with Ernest Hemingway, Zelda and Scott Fitzgerald, and other literary figures. By the time her husband returned from the war, Parker's life seemed punctuated by unhappiness, which was mirrored in her poetry. By the end of the 1920s, Parker was drinking heavily, had a string of affairs, an abortion, and attempted suicide three times. After the dissolution of their marriage, Parker eventually married Alan Campbell, an actor eleven years her junior, and half-Jewish like herself. That relationship was also far from happy, and was marked by bickering, divorce, and eventual remarriage. In her later years, Parker became involved in a variety of social causes, including the Screen Writers Guild and the Anti-Nazi League. Parker's later years were marked by increasing financial instability. She died alone at the Hotel Volney in New York, where she was found dead June 7, 1967. As a final social statement, Parker willed her estate, consisting of about $20,000, to Civil Rights leader Dr. Martin Luther King Jr.

MAJOR WORKS

Parker's first poetry collection, *Enough Rope,* achieved widespread acclaim—particularly for a book of poems—shortly after its publication in 1926. Throughout the slim volume of poetry, Parker explores the threat of losing love and unveils the hypocrisy and mawkishness of romantic jargon. In "One Perfect Rose," Parker mimics the frilly language of romantic greeting card verse, rambling about a rose from a suitor. But Parker adds an unexpected twist in the last stanza: "Why is it no one ever sent me yet / One perfect limousine, do you suppose / Ah no, it's always just my luck to get / One perfect rose." In "Unfortunate Coincidence," vows exchanged between two lovers are cynically dismissed: "By the time you swear you're his, / Shivering and sighing, / And he vows his passion is / Infinite, undying— / Lady, make a note of this: / One of you is lying." Parker's second volume of poetry, *Sunset Gun,* which was published in 1928, also garnered widespread appeal. In *Sunset Gun,* Parker continued to expand on the themes of lost love and hollow promises that appeared in her first book of poetry. Also in *Sunset Gun,* Parker experimented with traditional literary forms, including a cycle of epigrams titled: "A Pig's Eye View of Literature." Parker's third book of verse, *Death and Taxes* (1931), is more morose in tone than her first two publications. Critic Franklin P. Adams called *Death and Taxes* "her saddest and her best book." In the poem, "The Flaw in Paganism," Parker encourages readers to practice hedonistic behavior. "Drink and dance and laugh and lie, / Love, the reeling midnight through, / For tomorrow we shall die!" Parker then adds dryly: "(But, alas, we never do.)"—a sardonic remark perhaps referring to her own suicide attempts. By the time Parker's collected poetry was published under the title, *Not So Deep as a Well* (1936), Parker was writing more prose than poetry. Some of Parker's poems also were published in *Life,* the *Saturday Evening Post, Everybody's,* and the *Ladies' Home Journal.* In a telling article written in 1937, Parker disagreed that "ridicule is the most effective weapon," saying that there are "things that never have been funny, and never will be . . . And I know that ridicule may be a shield, but it is not a weapon." Ridicule, however, punctuates most of Parker's poetry, allowing her to lance through the hypocrisy of social customs, vows, and the inconstancy of love ("Scratch a lover and find a foe"). Parker's poetry is mostly an attempt to use her wit as a defense—first against pain, then despair. Parker's sharp humor and skill in translating classical forms into modern idiom prompted critic Arthur Kinney to call Parker "the best epigrammatic poet in our country, in this century."

CRITICAL RECEPTION

Dismissive about the quality of her poetic output, Parker described her efforts as light verse that was "terribly dated," and was herself one of her worst and most constant critics. However, Parker's skill in packaging modern issues into classical poetic forms won the praise of many critics, noting that her lilting verse is often deceivingly airy which allows her to explore the contradictory nature of human behavior. Ogden Nash once wrote: "To say that Mrs. Parker writes well is as fatuous, I'm afraid, as proclaiming that Cellini was clever with his hands. . . . The trick about her writing is the trick about Ring Lardner's writing or Ernest Hemingway's work. It isn't a trick." In 1931, Henry Seidel Canby wrote: ". . . this belle dame sans merci has the ruthlessness of the great tragic lyricist whose work was allegorized in the fable of the nightingale singing with her breast against a thorn." Other critics have described her work as melodramatic, sentimental, and trivial because of the witticisms that thread throughout her poetry. Nevertheless, Parker's work has enjoyed a resurgence in popularity, due in part to Marion Meade's *Dorothy Parker: What Fresh Hell Is This?,* published in 1988. Writer W. Somerset Maugham once said Parker had a gift " . . . for seeing something to laugh at in the bitterest tragedies of the human animal."

PRINCIPAL WORKS

Poetry

Enough Rope 1926
Sunset Gun 1928
Death and Taxes 1931
Not So Deep as a Well [also published as *The Collected Poetry of Dorothy Parker*, 1944] 1936

Not Much Fun: Lost Poems of Dorothy Parker 1996

Other Major Works

Laments for the Living (collected short stories) 1930
After Such Pleasures (collected short stories) 1933
Here Lies (stories) 1939, reprinted as
The Collected Stories of Dorothy Parker
A Star is Born (screenplay) 1937
Poems and a Story (recording) 1962

CRITICISM

Edmund Wilson (review date 1927)

SOURCE: "Dorothy Parker's Poems," in *The New Republic,* Vol. XLIX, No. 633, January 19, 1927, p. 256.

[*Wilson compares and contrasts Parker's poetry to that of her contemporaries, noting in particular those elements which make her work distinctive.*]

Mrs. Dorothy Parker began her poetic career as a writer of humorous verse of the school of Franklin P. Adams. There are specimens of her early vein in [***Enough Rope***]: a comic roundel, a rondeau redoublé "(and scarcely worth the trouble, at that)" and a parody of some verses of Gilbert. Mrs. Parker's special invention (aside from her vers libre "hymns of hate," unrepresented here), was a kind of burlesque sentimental lyric which gave the effect, till you came to the end, of a typical magazine filler, perhaps a little more authentically felt and a little better written than the average: the last line, however, punctured the rest with incredible ferocity. Thus, to quote only a comparatively mild example included in this book, the old, old gate wreathed with lilacs where the lady waits with yearning in the gloaming turns out, at the end of the poem, to be "the gate her true love gave her."

Mrs. Parker has had scarcely a rival in the contrivance of these loaded cigars, these squirting boutonnières and these pigs-in-clover puzzles of literature; and she could have put together a most amusing book of them. Her present book is, however, quite different. During the last two or three years, Dorothy Parker—though still in the pages of *Life* and the *New Yorker*—has emerged as a distinguished and interesting poet. It is true that, in America just now, we do not lack distinguished woman poets: there are so many women who write creditable lyrics that we have come to take them more or less for granted and are no longer very much excited over the appearance of another promising apprentice of the school of Elinor Wylie or Edna Millay. But Mrs. Parker seems somehow to stand a little apart from this group. It is true that she sometimes echoes Mrs. Wylie and, more frequently, Miss Millay; yet, on the whole, her poems give the impression of differing from those of many of her sisters in being a good deal less "literary"—that is, they have the appearance of proceeding, not merely from the competent exercise of an attractive literary gift, but from a genuine necessity to write. We may be conscious that there are at least thirty women in the country who would have been incapable of spoiling an excellent epigram with such a final couplet as this,

> Inertia rides and riddles me;
> The which is called Philosophy

or who would never have commenced another as follows,

> Oh, both my shoes are shiny new
> And pristine is my hat

—we may be conscious, I say, that there are perhaps thirty expert poets who would have known why "pristine" and "the which" were impossible. But we feel, also, that a sound instinct for style has here merely been betrayed by the bad habits of humorous versifying. And, in a similar way; we are convinced that her addiction to the idiom of Miss Millay is less an evidence of imitative weakness than an accidental and probably passing phase, due to the fact that Mrs. Parker has only just begun to attempt serious poetry and that, of all the poets who are read just now, Miss Millay's temperament, in certain of its aspects, has most affinity with her own. It is on the side of bareness and sharpness that Mrs. Parker most resembles Miss Millay; but the edged and acrid style which emerges in her book is unmistakably individual.

And the personality which reveals itself in Mrs. Parker's poems is quite different from that of Miss Millay: Mrs. Parker has her own complex of emotions, her own philosophy of love. Take the sonnet of which the octet begins as follows,

> If you should sail for Trebizond, or die,
> Or cry another name in your first sleep,
> Or see me board a train, and fail to sigh,
> Appropriately, I'd clutch my breast and weep.

Here she has caught precisely the idiom of Edna Millay; yet Miss Millay would never have drawn the same moral:

> Therefore the mooning world is gratified,
> Quoting how prettily we sigh and swear;
> And you and I, correctly side by side,
> Shall live as lovers when our bones are bare;
> And though we lie forever enemies,
> Shall rank with Abélard and Héloïse.

This is not one of Mrs. Parker's most satisfactory poems; it is, on the contrary, one of her most derivative; yet at the same time, it is interesting precisely because of a certain originality of accent and of point of view. Perhaps few poems in this book are completely successful: they tend, on the one hand, as I have already suggested, to become a little cheapened in the direction of ordinary humorous verse and, on the other, to become too deeply saturated with the jargon of ordinary feminine poetry, to go in too much for plaintive Aprils, for red stains on velvet gowns and for "pretty maids" and "likely lads." But her best work is extraordinarily vivid: it has a peculiar intensity and frankness which, when they appear in poetry, seem to justify any style or method, no matter how strange to literary convention. Dorothy Parker's unprecedented feat has been to raise to the dignity of poetry to the "wise-cracking" humor of New York: She has thus almost invented a new kind of epigram: she has made the comic anti-climax tragic. With the publication of this volume, her figure becomes distinct and her voice unmistakable: in her satires, in her short stories, in her play; we had long been aware of her as somebody and something in particular; and from now on, she must command our attention. We have never before had anything quite like:

> Oh, life is a glorious song,
> A medley of extemporanea;
> And love is a thing that can never go wrong;
> And I am Marie of Roumania.

any more than anything like:

> That a heart falls tinkling down,
> Never think it ceases.
> Every likely lad in town.
> Gathers up the pieces.
> If there's one gone whistling by
> Would I let it grieve me?
> Let him wonder if I lie;
> Let him half believe me.

We have nothing quite like the hard dark crystals of Dorothy Parker's irony: they do not spark with prismatic colors and a great many of them are imperfect, but they are beginning to become valuable.

The New York Times Book Review (review date 1927)

SOURCE: A review of *Enough Rope* in *The New York Times Book Review,* March 27, 1927, p. 6.

[*The critic appraises Parker's poetry, especially her timely treatments of established forms.*]

In an earlier age Dorothy Parker's lyric effusions would have been classified as society verse. But, alas! "society" vanished long ago or has become merged with the proletariat—or so runs the complaint. In any case, it has in the male portion gone in so heavily for golf and lounge suits as to have lost all distinguishing characteristics. And the females don sport clothes instead of frocks. Miss Parker's is not society verse in the old sense; it is flapper verse. And as such it is wholesome, engaging, uncorseted and not devoid of grace.

It is at once difficult and not difficult to choose an example from ***Enough Rope***. The verses are so uniformly excellent (in their way) that to exhibit one rather than another appears invidious; on the other hand, since the degree of excellence is so uniformly high, what shall determine selection? Making a random opening of the pages, this really delicate lyric comes to light. It is called **"A Very Short Song."**

> *Once, when I was young and true,*
> *Some one left me sad—*
> *Broke my brittle heart in two;*
> *And that was very bad.*
> *Love is for unlucky folk,*
> *Love is but a curse.*
> *Once there was a heart I broke;*
> *And that, I think, is worse.*

Many of these unobtrusive versicles have not only beauty but also a turn of wit which is out of the ordinary. It would seem, to seek an explanation probably far too recondite, that Miss Parker, especially in such a poem as **"Epitaph for a Darling Lady,"** caught the spirit of Campion, rejected the conceits of that poet, or at least rejected the extravagance of Campion's conceits, and then liberated his spirit to energize anew in this very present modern day.

One would like to show Dorothy Parker's deftness with the sonnet form, which she turns to lighter use than is customary with poets. (Indeed, she is quite without veneration.) And one would like also to display her humor as distinct from her wit. . . . Those who look into this jolly yet serious little book will find these things out for themselves, for none could skip a single poem if one tried.

Marie Luhrs (review date 1927)

SOURCE: "Fashionable Poetry," in *Poetry,* Vol. XXX, No. 1, April, 1927, pp. 52-4.

[*Luhrs appreciates Parker's honest look at society and her ability to craft poetry that appeals to the general reader.*]

Enough Rope is what the well-dressed man or woman will wear inside their heads instead of brains. Here is poetry that is "smart" in the fashion designer's sense of the word. Mrs. Parker need not hide her head in shame, as the average poet must, when she admits the authorship of this book. For in its lightness, its cynicism, its pose, she has done the correct thing; she is in a class with the Prince of Wales, the Theatre Guild, Gramercy Park, and H. L. Mencken. And these somewhat facetious remarks are not intended as disparagement. It is high time that a poet with a monocle looked at the populace, instead of the populace looking at the poet through a lorgnette. It is high time that the shy, dreamy-eyed, despised creatures known as poets should received as much respect as plumbers. Edison and Ford have genius of a sort, but could either of them write a superb and piercing sonnet? As for the argument that their creations, being useful and commercial, are entitled to more prosperity than the intangible luxury of verse, what about the luxurious and useless movies? Anyone who composes a good movie is assured of a fortune; so why not anyone who composes a good narrative poem? Poetry is no more trying than a cross-word puzzle. If shop-girls spend hours fitting words into squares, why can they not spend hours fitting words into rhythms? Poetry, in spite of the stubborn notion to the contrary, is neither dull nor abstruse. As for poets—Shelley was a sheik, Sappho was a red-hot mamma, Villon swung a wicked sword, and Tennyson drank beer. Many of the present generation of women poets possess beauty and babies. If I have swung rather far from Dorothy Parker, it was only to give her little muse a great big hand.

Mrs. Parker, of course, owes much to Edna St. Vincent Millay. And I like to pass over those parts which are reminiscent or imitative of the master. For what Miss Millay did once so beautifully, can never be done again in the same manner. Mrs. Parker has her own particular field of frank American humor. She is slangy, vulgar, candid, and withal subtle, delicate and sparkling. The soul of wit distinguishes most of her pieces. **"Résumé"** a satirical rendition of Schopenhauer's expression, "the will to live":

> Razors pain you;
> Rivers are damp;
> Acids stain you;
> And drugs cause cramp;
> Guns aren't lawful;
> Nooses give;
> Gas smells awful:
> You might as well live.

And **"Indian Summer"** explains the hard-boiled woman:

> In youth, it was a way I had
> To do my best to please,
> And change, with every passing lad,
> To suit his theories.
> But now I know the things I know,
> And do the things I do;
> And if you do not like me so,
> To hell, my love, with you!

"News Item" can hardly be omitted:

> Men seldom make passes
> At girls who wear glasses.

And the final line of a poem called **"Men"** is a profound sigh from the depths of many a woman's heart:

> They make me sick, they make me tired.

The frame-work of truth is very firm in these fluttering bits. For all their pertness and bravado they mirror, in most cases, quite genuine and profound experiences. They are not so different, after all, from the hyper-sensitive and extremely refined mind of Mrs. Meynell. She said:

> I run, I run, I am gathered to thy heart,

with tender Victorian sentiment, Mrs. Parker says:

> Because your eyes are slant and slow,
> Because your hair is sweet to touch,
> My heart is high again; but oh,
> I doubt if this will get me much—

with colloquial frankness. They were both in love, their moods and diction being only the outward manner of the time and place in which they were born.

William Rose Benét (review date 1928)

SOURCE: "New Moon Madness," in *The Saturday Review of Literature,* Vol. IV, No. 46, June 9, 1928, p. 943.

[*Benét reviews* Sunset Gun, *pointing out that Parker's writing, like her personality, is difficult to categorize.*]

Is [***Sunset Gun***] as good as ***Enough Rope***? Yes. And that might constitute a review, mightn't it. A eulogium, at least. Well, there were, perhaps, one or two gems of purest ray unserene in the former book that surpass anything in this; but there were also one or two sets of verses not up to the general high level. Your microscope may be better than ours when you come to examine ***Sunset Gun***, but you will have to peer pretty intently to detect flaws.

There is a hackneyed remark made about conversationally clever people (and we are always left at the post, pawing for a rejoinder, when Mrs. Parker chooses to declare herself in a word or two,—or in danger of that old apoplexy of ours),—but they say, you know, about such people, "Oh, if she only wrote as she talks!" The most amazing thing about Dorothy Parker is that she writes precisely as she talks. Well, no, we have never heard her talk in rhyme, exactly. But, leaving that aside—.

This is a book, like the other, that you cannot put into a particular pigeonhole. It is a perfect representation of the author, who is a paradox. A moth-gray cloak of demureness hiding spangled ribaldry, a razor-keen intellect mocking a heart dark with desperation; "Ain't we got fun!" and "Weh! Weh!" rising to the lips at the same instant. And all the time, in spite of her telling you that you'll only find her in step with Trouble or Gloom, there she is off on a rainbow writing down a diamond-hard summary of the situation in a large round hand.

> The lads I've met in Cupid's deadlock
> Were—shall we say?—born out of wedlock . . .

or

> "I wouldn't have him back!"
> I hope
> Her mother washed her mouth with soap.

or

> People Who Do Things exceed my endurance;
> God, for a man that solicits insurance!

or

There and there and well and well—
Did he prick his finger!

She can contemplate the fretful porcupine with aplomb and a brilliant dexterity of rhyme, she can epigrammatize with the effectiveness of

A heart in half is chaste, archaic;
But mine resembles a mosaic.

and she can achieve a lustral and beautiful sonnet, as in **"Fair Weather."** What the devil can you do with such a girl? You can be moved to sympathy by some expression of evident distress, or to admiration for some gallantry of attitude, or to gravity at an occasional tenderness,—and then she flips a last line at you like a little carmine firecracker exploding under your nose. And it is all Dorothy Parker.

We shouldn't wonder if this ability completely and idiomatically to present the shimmering paradox of herself were not the secret of the deserved popularity of Mrs. Parker's verse. "Shouldn't wonder"? We know perfectly well it is. Long may she wave!

Garreta Busey (review date 1928)

SOURCE: "A Porcupine's View," in *The New York Herald Tribune,* Vol. 4, No. 43, July 15, 1928, p. 7.

[*Busey reviews* Sunset Gun, *discussing what she believes is Parker's appeal for readers.*]

Although Miss Parker gives us in these pages, among other charming fantasies, what she calls a **"Pig's-Eye View of Literature,"** [***Sunset Gun***] itself could never be described as a pig's-eye view of life. There is no luxurious wallowing here (except, perhaps, in misery), no sloppiness, no slothful obesity. The poems are lean and quick as a snake. One might say they represented a porcupine's-eye view of life if Miss Parker had not written that **"Parable of a Certain Virgin,"** beginning:

Oh, ponder, friend, the porcupine;
Refresh your recollection,
And sit a moment, to define
His means of self-protection.

She goes on to describe those means in swift rhythm and comic rhyme until:

Or should pursuers press him hot,
One scarcely needs to mention
His quick and cruel barbs that got
Shakespearean attention;
Or driven to his final ditch.
To his extremest thicket,
He'll fight with claws and molars which
Is not considered cricket).
How amply armored, he, to fend
The fear of chase that haunts him!
How well prepared our little friend!—
And who the devil wants him?

Well, we want Miss Parker and are willing to pursue her. As a matter of fact, I myself went through a great deal just to get the loan of ***Enough Rope*** which is no better book than this, although it is a bit thicker. We are willing to pursue Miss Parker to her extremest thicket in spite of, or rather for the sake of, her quick and cruel barbs.

One of the chief reasons why we like her is that most of us were taught in our childhood that we mustn't "sass back" or thumb our noses, and Miss Parker does these things so well for us. She sasses back at Life, or the Universe, or God, or What Have You, in nimble and absurd rhyme such as we never in the world could have thought of ourselves. And besides, we like her because she laughs at herself. We always like people to laugh at themselves. It takes their attention away from us.

The poems are not all impudent. **"Fair Weather,"** for instance, is an excellent serious sonnet. But in her milder verses there are phrases that recall Housman and rhythms that are Millaysian, as this:

The day that I was christened—
It's a hundred years, and more!
A hag came and listened
At the white church door.

We listen to her more gleefully when she is bad tempered, shocking, macabre. We like it when she makes us gasp by coming out neatly with this:

Dear dead Victoria
Rotted cosily;
In excelsts gloria.
And R. I. P.

These three letters sound so reckless and indecent! Or—but we ought not to quote any more. That would be giving away too much of what is really the property of the author and her publishers, and we don't want Miss Parker to starve to death. We hope she is not telling the truth when she says:

I'm done with this burning and giving
And reeling the rhymes of my woes.
And how I'll be making my living.
The Lord in His mystery knows.

Henry Seidel Canby (review date 1931)

SOURCE: "Belle Dame sans Merci," in *The Saturday Review of Literature,* Vol. VII, No. 47, June 13, 1931, p. 891.

[*Canby believes that the techniques Parker uses in* Death and Taxes *produce "poetry deserving high praise."*]

The times are choked and cluttered with disillusion—a sticky disillusion, an adolescent petulance, solemn and unreasonable, that pours itself out in dull, formless novels dealing with ugly people who should have been stepped upon at birth, if indeed they were really as mudgy and disagreeable as the writers make them out—which is most improbable. We are blared at and saxophoned by a tinny sophistication that means nothing, and is nothing but the restlessness of smart people who think they are not appreciated, or the shallow bawdry of children educated beyond their characters. Cynicism leaves the sincerity of a tub for the suspicious publicity of a night club, and a "hard" generation patronizes in the comic strips cruel jokes and a sentimental Tarzan using bad medieval English, without a breath's pause between.

We look for a bitterness that can still be gay, and a witty sorrow, and a disillusion that can thumb its nose at the old one who makes lives "gang agley," and find little salt of that savor in contemporary prose, but some, thank heaven! still in poetry. In verse of a Horatian lightness, with an exquisite certainty of technique, which, like the lustre on a Persian bowl, is proof that civilization is itself a philosophy, Dorothy Parker is writing poetry deserving high praise. If I compare her to Horace and Martial I do so largely, since I am no Latinist, and can better describe the perfection of her admirable lyrics by a comparison with that almost forgotten humorist, Thomas Hood, who had a gift of beauty second only to his contemporary, Keats, and yet could twist a stanza into laughter with one deft, inimitable line. Hood was a romantic, and when in his vein of sentiment was too much the slave of his mood to lift out into wit. He wrote one of Dorothy Parker's finest poems (**"Requiescat"**) in an epigram—the same figure, the same twist, but all made into farce. And in his serious poems, the last line, in which Mrs. Parker stabs sorrow with a jest, is to be found not in the verse but in the pathetic commentaries of his letters. Dorothy Parker has, it seems to me, perfected his art—

> Drink and dance and laugh and lie,
> Love, the reeling midnight through,
> For tomorrow we shall die!
> (But, alas, we never do.)

This is slight; her powers are better expressed in **"The Evening Primrose"**

> You know the bloom, unearthly white,
> That none has seen by morning light—
> The tender moon alone, may bare
> Its beauty to the secret air.
> Who'd venture past its dark retreat
> Must kneel, for holy things and sweet.
> That blossom, mystically blown,
> No man may gather for his own
> Nor touch it, lest it droop and fall. . . .
> Oh, I am not like that at all!

A lesser humorist would have overstressed the virginal beauty, a lesser poet would have failed to make the last line poignant as well as pungent.

We are easily thrown off by lightness and good humor, for pain and a burning heart may be taken, that way, in homeopathic doses. The river of criticism rolls muddy and splashing about difficult metaphysical poetry which grunts and wheezes unintelligibilities, like a Chinese poet speaking through the mouth of a hippopotamus, while we forget the perfect poems, so lucid as to seem simple, so simple in theme as to seem obvious, yet with three quarters of what matters packed in their lines—

> Ah, what avails the sceptered race!
> Ah, what the form divine!
> What every virtue, every grace!
> Rose Aylmer, all were thine.
> Rose Aylmer, whom these wakeful eyes
> May weep, but never see,
> A night of memories and sighs
> I consecrate to thee.

Or, to go back to Hood—

> I saw thee, lovely Ines,
> Descend alone the shore,
> With bands of noble gentlemen,
> And banners waved before;
> And gentle youth and maidens gay,
> And snowy plumes they wore:
> It would have been a beauteous dream—
> If it had been no more!

Yet I suspect that one should quote Latin rather than English to parallel the edged fineness of Dorothy Parker's verse. This belle dame sans merci has the ruthlessness of the great tragic lyricists whose work was allegorized in the fable of the nightingale singing with her breast against a thorn. It is disillusion recollected in tranquillity where the imagination has at last controlled the emotions. It comes out clear, and with the authentic sparkle of a great vintage. I attempt no real criticism here, but I do assert that these poems [in ***Death and Taxes***] deserve criticism and appraisal far more than many much bewritten books of more pretentious cerebration, yet with less beauty of technique and far less depth of emotion. She writes of violets—

> You are brief and frail and blue—
> Little sisters, I am, too.
> You are heaven's masterpieces—
> Little loves, the likeness ceases.

But there is no frailty in her poetry, and its brevity is in space not in time.

Percy Hutchison (review date 1931)

SOURCE: "Satire and Epigram in Dorothy Parker's Versicles," in *The New York Times Book Review,* June 14, 1931, p. 4.

[*Hutchison reads* Death and Taxes *as a "small package of literary delights," that reveals truth amid a mixture of the serious and lighthearted.*]

Since, according to the old proverb, death and taxes are the only certainties in life, we assume that Dorothy Parker means by her title that the poems of the collection were equally inevitable. But since all assumptions are likely to be fallible when dealing with the literary output of this pleasing and disconcerting lady, we discreetly withdraw from further pursuit of the subject. ***Death and Taxes*** is a thin book, housing something like half a hundred short poems—several are very short indeed. But invariably the quality is in inverse ratio to the quantity.

Dorothy Parker's function in the body literary and the body social is too well known to require more than a word. It consists for the most part in jabbing with pins, but she jabs with such contagiously impish pleasure that it is not polite to be other than pleased to be a victim. And why should one not be pleased? This spritely poet is not malicious, although she is generally satirical. Refusing to be malicious, a satirical poet perhaps sacrifices something of cutting strength. Pope, the Earl of Rochester (with his memorable quatrain on Charles II), Jonathan Swift, Matthew Prior—English satirical poets such as these slashed with a vigor one will not find in the versicles of Dorothy Parker. But the latter will be read with more genuine pleasure on the part of most. Perhaps the nearest Mrs. Parker comes to vinegar unmixed with honey is in this epitaph for a very rich man:

He'd have the best, and that was
none too good;
No barrier could hold before his terms.
terms.
He lies below, correct in cypress
wood,
And entertains the most exclusive
worms.

But even here, even if there is some slight acidity, the conception is sufficiently whimsical to draw a smile.

The most nearly humorous piece in the collection is, perhaps, one of six stanzas bearing the caption, **"The Danger of Writing Defiant Verse."** It begins with the statement, "Now I have another lad," and he is not at all an ardent wooer, a matter of great relief, as advertised in the poem up to the final stanza, which is as follows:

He's none to kiss away my mind—
A slower way is his.
Oh, Lord! On reading this I find
A silly lot he is.

As such verse should be, if it is to be at all, these epigrammatic lyrics in ***Death and Taxes*** are frequently as nearly perfect as one may hope for in this more careless age. The collection does not, as a whole, maintain the perfection of Housman, but this, **"My Own,"** could not be scorned by The Shropshire Lad himself:

Then let them point my every tear
And let them mock and moan;
Another week, another year,
And I'll be with my own
Who slumber now by night and day
In fields of level brown;
Whose hearts within their breasts
were clay
Before they laid them down.

For a last word, the reviewer will return to one of the several epitaphs in the little group labeled as a whole, **"Tombstones in the Starlight."** The lines are for an actress:

Her name, cut clear upon this mar-
ble cross,
Shines as it shone when she was
still on earth;
While tenderly the mild, agreeable
moss
Obscures the figures of her date of
birth.

Death and Taxes, besides being a small package of literary delights, is also significant in the progression of the author. The magazines and the columnists early helped Dorothy Parker to such triumph that something less than her best is so easy for her to get away with that, even in this small volume, she too often yields to temptation. This is a pity, for Dorothy Parker can at times so mingle the serious and the gay, can so pack truth into the twist of a line, that a very high place in the line of English minor poets—a line that can boast such names as Lovelace and Herrick—can be hers for the winning. Occasionally she does win.

Harold Rosenberg (essay date 1931)

SOURCE: "Nor Rosemary, Nor Rue," in *Poetry,* Vol. XXXIX, No. 3, December 1931, pp. 159-61.

[*Rosenberg focuses on* Death and Taxes *with respect to sentiment, wit, and poetic quality.*]

Since Mrs. Parker is too often satisfied with such ready-made images as "my narrow bed" for a grave, and

The weary pen that sets my sorrow down
Feeds at my heart,

it is obvious that her small lyrics can hardly be considered seriously as poetry written today. Criticism of her work, therefore, since space does not permit the more general and more interesting inquiry into the socio-psychological reasons for her popularity, must consist of an examination of those characteristics which give to it the appearance of poetry. I shall comment on three of these: its sentiment, its wit, and its trace of poetic quality.

I. The sentiment, as suggested by the title [***Death and Taxes***], varies for the most part between the death-love theme, in the "faded roses" sense, and the semi-naive smartness of the experienced female. Also, like many Broadway characters, she sometimes talks of God.

II. The wit is negligible. It operates, as in a quatrain on **"Sweet Violets,"** on the obvious mechanics of a bathetic "surprise," which occurs when the last line hangs a sophisticated conclusion on the hackneyed sentiment:

> You are brief and frail and blue—
> Little sisters, I am, too.
> You are heaven's masterpieces—
> Little loves, the likeness ceases.

But when the reader has undergone enough verse of this sort, the "surprise" no longer surprises him, since it lacks the depth of observation to keep the epigram fresh.

III. There is a trace of poetic quality in the occasional sharp ability to press an emotion into a simple description. It is on this account that one regrets her contentment with the easy rhythms, the banal feelings and phrases, by means of which she has become a social personage mentioned in newspaper notes with Amelia Earhart, Heywood Broun, Rudy Vallée, and Jack Dempsey. A bit like

> the strange new body of the dead,

the gay **"Salome's Dancing-lesson,"** an echo now and then of a Shakespeare song: these make us wish that she had chosen to go more firmly in the direction of poetry.

As for what Henry Seidel Canby calls her "exquisite certainty of technique," it is enough to note that it is easy to attain a technical glibness when the construction of verse is seen to involve none of the problems of the art of poetry.

William Rose Benét (review date 1936)

SOURCE: "Deep, At That," *The Saturday Review of Literature*, Vol. XV, No. 7, December 12,1936, p. 5.

[*In the following review, Benét studies Parker's stature as a poet dealing with the experiences of living as depicted in the poems included in her recent collection,* Not So Deep As A Well.]

Here are the collected poems of Dorothy Parker, several being stricken from the roll of those she wished to keep and several being added. In the main here are merely ***Enough Rope***, ***Sunset Gun***, and ***Death and Taxes*** all in one volume. And I should be shot for using the word "merely." Here is a lively plenty. And I am wrong too, for using the world "lively." Here is also an exquisitely distilled bitterness that improves with age. Tenderness, bravado, the arrantly colloquial inimitably made use of, and Dorothy Parker's own version of the Voice of Experience.

As I re-read poems I have already re-read a great many times, it seems to me that this notable talent has become clearer and finer through the progress of the three books. In the beginning there was more softness and affection for the word "little," and rather a clinging to stereotype, till suddenly the characteristic epigrammatic colloquialism, witty summary, or vehemently brilliant ending asserted themselves. Yet there is a quiet poem in those first pages, **"Somebody's Song,"** which has always greatly appealed to me. It is obvious that earlier influences were the earlier Miss Millay and A. E. Housman. But with **"Portrait of the Artist,"** Mrs. Parker came wholly into her own. What the average reader searches for are such pithy triumphs as

> Men seldom make passes
> At girls who wear glasses

which has been quoted from Alaska to Patagonia. And Mrs. Parker has shown that she can practise French verse-forms with the best, even to that Rondeau Redoublé subtitled "And scarcely worth the trouble, at that." Her chef d'oeuvre in the ballade, I think, is the **"Ballade of Unfortunate Mammals,"** in ***Death and Taxes***.

Death and Taxes opened with a poem so sincere and touching, yet entirely unbathetic, **"Prayer for a Prayer,"** as to demand a reconsideration of the poet's province. In fact, she has several. She still wrote the epigram brilliantly (as in **"The Flaw in Paganism"**) but with a new depth. And I would point out that in **"The Evening Primrose," "My Own," "The Sea," "Midnight,"** and that most significant and moving **"Sonnet on an Alpine Night,"** the wittiest woman of our time suddenly took on stature. For the fashioning of poetry depends upon depth of experience as well as upon extraordinary intuition. And here such emotion is conveyed clearly and directly, with a numbing truth. Many elements make up this complete and various book—of which this is by no means the least.

Louis Kronenberger (review date 1936)

SOURCE: "The Rueful, Frostbitten Laughter of Dorothy Parker," *The New York Times Book Review,* December 13, 1936, pp. 2, 28.

[*In this review, Kronenberger discussed Parker's exploration of emotion and sentimentality through her use of wit and cynicism.*]

It is just ten years since Mrs. Parker first made plain that the world is safe enough for girls who wear glasses, but reasonably precarious for most others. It is ten years or thereabouts since people began to repeat at dinner tables those bright sayings of hers which could not always have been repeated in print. She achieved, as she deserved, the title of wit; and here are her three volumes of poetry, now collected into one, to reassert her claim. Here is, I think, much the best light verse of our day which is highly personal in tone, which gains its effects through describing some one *in* a situation; and over and over again it is the same effect, one that can be vulgarly described as "The joke's on me."

If that is the formula for so much of this verse, it must yet not be dismissed as simply a device, for behind it lies a settled point of view—the immemorial, rueful, frostbitten laughter of women who, yearning for love, cry out not only because they are frustrated of the lovers they want, but also because they are bored with the lovers they have. For every door that will not open to Mrs. Parker's fluttering knock, there is another that she slams behind her. For every cadenced sob in her book, there is a rhythmical grimace. These verses are, indeed, the record of a constant shuttling between sentimentality and cynicism, of romanticism forever plucked hastily from the stalk, but never uprooted from the soil, of instinct at war with experience and at least half the time victorious.

After ten years Mrs. Parker strikes me as having achieved—as one so often puts it in the case of "weightier" writers—a kind of historical significance. These poems of hers remind us irresistibly of the era during which they were for the most part composed—the frantic Twenties, when people went gathering rosebuds with almost comic intensity and far too much self-consciousness: the frantic Twenties, when it was so imperative to be "honest" that most people became so at the cost of being insincere. No age, so shoulder-shrugging on the surface, was ever more uneasy underneath; and no age, forever denouncing the melodramatic, ever dramatized itself more constantly. The age gave birth to Hemingway, who remains the classic—indeed, the overworked—example of a man who misrepresented his emotions. As everybody now agrees, he was forever insisting that he was hardboiled to conceal the fact that he was hopelessly sentimental. Mrs. Parker played the cynic in much the same spirit of dissimulation. And no one has ever made clearer than she how inseparable from sentimentality cynicism is, just as no one has ever made sentimentality more outrageous by simply juxtaposing it to laughter.

On the serious side, therefore, there is no emotional balance in her poetry, just as there was no emotional balance in the age that produced it. There is equally no emotional relaxation: when Mrs. Parker is not ostentatiously prostrated, she is ostentatiously unmoved. Almost all her serious poems strike a false or self-conscious note: the emotion that transpires is inconsistent with the situation that determined it. Further, the high technical polish of her sentimental poems makes them artificial; there is nothing more incongruous than studied heart-break. Indeed, between emotional expression that is very simple and artless and emotion operating at white heat under the sovereign control of a deeply poetic mind, every intermediate stage is in danger of a discrepancy between meaning and manner—the two do not coincide; and Mrs. Parker seldom outwits that danger. In her case there is perhaps the additional drawback that she is sometimes derivative; the ghosts of Housman, Millay and Elinor Wylie, to name no others, too often direct her imagination.

One comes back to Mrs. Parker's light verse with the greatest pleasure; with its sharp wit, its clean bite, its perfectly conscious—and hence delightful—archness, it stands re-reading amply. Here her high technical polish has great virtue; sometimes cracking out a surprise effect with an absolute minimum of wind-up, sometimes achieving a foreseen effect by means so dexterous it is exhilarating to watch them. Mrs. Parker can extend anticlimax to irresistible bathos by altering the pitch of her language (from the high-flown to the highly colloquial) at the exact moment she alters her meaning. But what, of course, is more important is the sense of personality that converts what might otherwise be merely a witty idea into a dramatic, however cockeyed, situation; a sense of personality that gives us not cynicism in the abstract but laughter applied to an objective. There is no one else in Mrs. Parker's special field who can do half as much. I suspect that she will survive not only as the author of some first-rate light verse but also as a valuable footnote to the Twenties, out of whose slant on existence that light verse sprang.

Monica Redlich (review date 1937)

SOURCE: A review of *Not So Deep as a Well,* in *The Spectator,* Vol. 5677, April 16, 1937, p. 726.

[*In this review, Redlich supports Parker's poetry for its unembellished deceptions of "the vanity of human wishes."*]

Miss Parker's short stories are a perennial delight, and her verse is of the same calibre. No other writer can so perfectly portray not only sophistication but the obverse of sophistication—the knotted back of the canvas, the tangle of emotion and passion and fear that shall never be seen in public. **"Chant for Dark Hours"** is the title of one of her poems. It would stand as the title for three-quarters of her book—and it is a dialogue between a woman who waits for a dilatory lover and that part of her mind which utterly despises herself for doing so. Conflict, self-mockery, disillusion, regret—anything but happiness is the subject of her poems, and if by any chance she catches contentment breaking in she gives the last line a good firm twist to remind herself of the vanity of human wishes:

> Oh, gallant was the first love, and glittering and fine;
> The second love was water, in a clear white cup;
> The third love was his, and the fourth was mine;
> And after that, I always get them all mixed up.

She can get almost any story into four lines. Her **"Two-Volume Novel,"** for instance, is a model of brevity:

> The sun's gone dim, and
> The moon's turned black;
> For I loved him, and
> He didn't love back.

For advice to young women she would be hard to beat:

Lady, lady, never start
Conversation toward your heart;
Keep your pretty words serene;
Never murmur what you mean . . .
Be you wise and never sad,
You will get your lovely lad.
Never serious be, nor true,
And your wish will come to you—
And if that makes you happy, kid,
You'll be the first it ever did.

Housman and Drayton and Suckling and Donne—there are echoes in these poems of all who have concerned themselves with the follies and transience of love: but Miss Parker puts the feminine point of view as it has seldom been put before, and the divergence is exciting. Too much on one note, and not by any means all equally successful, these poems are nevertheless a real contribution to epigrammatic lore.

Edith H. Walton (review date 1928)

SOURCE: "New York Wits," in *The New Republic,* Vol. LV, No. 708, June 27, 1928, p. 155.

[*Walton examines* Sunset Gun, *noting the devices Parker uses to "puncture old illusions and then caper wickedly among the ruins."*]

A sophisticated palate, it is said, requires pungent fare. For the delight of epicures, New York has produced recently two disillusioned wits whose verse has an acrid and heady tang. Scoffers by profession, typically urban, Dorothy Parker and Samuel Hoffenstein share in common a gift of mockery which is as deadly as it is diverting. No major emotion is sacred to their venomous pens, and love, in particular, they view with a jaundiced eye. With neat, effective strokes they puncture the old illusions and then caper wickedly among the ruins. True, there are differences that separate them. Mr. Hoffenstein's gesture is a comic shrug of "fairly utter despair," while Dorothy Parker is inclined toward a gallant bravado. Both, however, appear to have taken for their motto the following lines from ***"Sunset Gun*":**

Show your quick, alarming skill in
Tidy mockeries of art;
Never, never dip your quill in
Ink that rushes from your heart.

Samuel Hoffenstein is especially indisposed to allow the sentimentalists any quarter. "Poems in Praise of Practically Nothing" crackle with hard-boiled humor and with deft, tricky rhymes. They are sour and satiric commentaries on all the phenomena of the jazz age—from radios and riveters to complexes and indigestion. They include, also, some demoniac parodies on Housman and Millay, which are, perhaps, the cream of the jest. Mr. Hoffenstein is funny at the expense of practically everything and ends, consequently, by not being so funny after all. He has ridden his formula to death, and one quickly wearies of it. The wisecracks and the ironic twist at the end of each poem arrive with such unfailing regularity that they cease to evoke a chuckle of surprise. One begins to feel that the poet's humor is not so sophisticated as it sounds—that it is tinctured, indeed, with the cheap cynicism of the adolescent.

It is this pitfall of monotony which Dorothy Parker escapes, although ***Sunset Gun*** is hardly so brave a salute as ***Enough Rope***. Again, as in her earlier book, Mrs. Parker thumbs her nose at faithless lovers and douses one with cold water at the end of a deceptively gentle lyric. Unlike Mr. Hoffenstein, however, she is able to reconcile flippancy with the exquisite and haunting phrase. The poems entitled **"A Pig's-Eye View of Literature"** are a match for his parodies—her jeers at love are more impudent and pointed. But Dorothy Parker is willing, at times, to pluck a string of genuine emotion, and in so doing she proves her superior caliber. Her fragile sonnets, her crisp and delicate ballads, have a quality of loveliness which is not evanescent. The gay defiance of **"A Whistling Girl"** and the tenderness of **"The Maid Servant at the Inn,"** alike, belong to the best tradition of lyric verse. Although a sly and jaunty irony is her especial gift—one would not wish it otherwise—it is pleasant to know that Dorothy Parker can occasionally forget to be a New York wit. Mr. Hoffenstein could profit by her example.

Arthur F. Kinney (essay date 1998)

SOURCE: "Her Apprenticeship: Essays, Light Verse, Drama," in *Dorothy Parker, Revised*, Amherst: University of Massachusetts, 1998, pp. 66-72.

[*Here, Kinney provides a discussion concerning Parker's use of meter and verbal simplicity to better satirize her view of society.*]

Light Verse: "Counting Up, Exultingly"

When the wry, regular, and apparently easy poems of Parker were selected for her first book in 1926, she had been writing and publishing short verses for more than 11 years. Parker was determined from the start to write satire from her woman's point of view—to exaggerate reality through stereotype, repetition, cataloguing, or hyperbole—rather than to write nonsense verse. She also wanted her verse to be simple, as colloquial as possible, for that way she could extend her satire to those who spoke as her lines speak—but she found, even composing longhand (later, with criticism, she would compose on the typewriter), that she continually crossed out words that were not simple enough. She was encouraged in her search for substance coupled with a simple style by F. P. A., when he was on *The Mail* and she was still at *Vogue*. Her first published poem, **"Any Porch,"** is revealing.

"I'm reading that new thing of Locke's—
So whimsical, isn't he? Yes—"

"My dear, have you seen those new smocks?
They're nightgowns—no more, and no less."
"I don't call Mrs. Brown *bad,*
She's *un*-moral, dear, not *im*moral—"
"Well, really, it makes me so mad
To think what I paid for that coral!"
"My husband says, often, 'Elsie,
You feel things too deeply, you do—"
"Yes, forty a month, if you please,
Oh, servants impose on *me,* too."

(*VF,* September 1915, 32; Silverstein, 70-71)

The poem continues for six more stanzas, a deliberate exercise in heteroglossia long before the advent of Mikhail Bakhtin, locating at once a practice that would only continue, if more subtly, throughout her career. As her reader searches for a point of entry within the superficial litany—time passing through triviality—the juxtaposition of all the comments makes each of them clichéd. Each expression judges all the others, and in turn is open to judgment. **"Any Porch"** is anyplace and about anyone including, potentially, Parker's readers.

It did not take Parker long to learn that the iamb was her most forceful foot and that strict meter had a kind of dogtrot rhythm that would reinforce the commonness of the ideas and of the people she would write about, even when lines varied in the number of feet. Clichés, too, worked better when falling into taut quatrains and full rhymes. We do not know how many unpublished starts she made after **"Any Porch,"** but her second publication, **"A Musical Comedy Thought,"** shows such a technical advance.

My heart is fairly melting at the thought of Julian Eltinge;
His vice versa, Vesta Tilley, too.
Our language is so dexterous, let us call them ambisexterous,—
Why hasn't this occurred before to you?

(*VF,* June 1916, 126; Silverstein, 86)

The poem relies too heavily on a Nash-like neologism, but her third published poem has married simple diction, iambic meter, and full rhyme without any crutches. **"The Gunman and the Debutante"** begins,

A wild and wicked gunman—one who held a gang in thrall—
A menace to the lives of me and you,
Was counting up, exultingly, the day's successful haul—
As gunmen are extremely apt to do.
A string of pearls, a watch or two, a roll of bills, a ring,
Some pocketbooks—about a dozen, say—
An emerald tiara—oh, a very pretty thing!
Yes, really, quite a gratifying day.

(*VF,* October 1916, p. 120; Silverstein, 72-73)

The trisyllabic *tiara* is a particular challenge, but even this early, Dorothy Rothschild attempted to work into regular metrics the long and unusual word, jolting the most monotonous ideas and monotonal rhythms, breaking open language and thought through dialectic.

Somewhat surprisingly—and disappointingly, from our later perspective—Dorothy Rothschild now began parodying vers libre, then especially fashionable. Beginning with the February 1917 *Vanity Fair,* she wrote a series of "hate songs" in which her compact descriptions of typed personalities resemble the captions she had written for *Vogue.* The satire is glib, the targets wide, the rhythms of stanzas (which vary in length) slack. **"Men: A Hate Song,"** the first, is subtitled "I hate men. They irritate me" and opens with the "Serious Thinkers."

There are the Serious Thinkers,—
There ought to be a law against them.
They see life, as through shell-rimmed glasses, darkly.
They are always drawing their weary hands
Across their wan brows.
They talk about Humanity
As if they had just invented it;
They have to keep helping it along.
They revel in strikes
And they are eternally getting up petitions.
They are doing a wonderful thing for the Great Unwashed,—
They are living right down among them.
They can hardly wait
For "The Masses" to appear on the newsstands,
And they read all those Russian novels,—
The sex best sellers.

(65)

The strength of such poetry lies in a distanced tone and clever observations. It is also a poetry that must always hit the bull's-eye, and so quickly grows tiresome. But such poems made her very popular then, and she went on to write more for *Vanity Fair* and a good many for *Life,* on relatives (with a stanza on husbands from a liberated woman's perspective); on actresses, actors, bohemians, slackers, and office colleagues; on bores, the drama, parties, movies, books, the younger set, summer resorts, wives, and college boys; and F. P. A. and others parodied or imitated the form.[1]

Parker's free verse can be likened to prose lists and conversational fragments she wrote for *Life,* but with another parody, called **"Oh, Look—I Can Do It, Too"** in *Vanity Fair* for December 1918 (48; Silverstein, 76-77), she began turning her attention to French forms, the ballade and rondeau, made popular by Eugene Field, Austin Dobson, and F. P. A. Once again she remained multivoiced; still she strove to look casual. **"Ballade of Big Plans"** takes its chorus from *Julia Cane:* "She loved him. He knew it. And love was a game that two could play at." The last stanza and envoy read,

Recollections can only bore us;
Now it's over, and now it's through
Our day is dead as a dinosaurus.
Other the paths that you pursue.
What is she doing to spend her day at?

Fun demands, at a minimum, two—
And love is a game that two can play at.
Prince, I'm packing away the rue:
I'll show them something to shout "Hooray" at.
I've got somebody else in view.
And love is a game that two can play at.[2]

The clichés skewer *Julia Cane*—and other popular works middle-class in taste and finally empty of meaning because of their conventionality. The residual wit available to poetry by which the last line, supplying a contrary attitude, provides a backward-looking tension dialogically, reverberates here by itself being a cliché. Thus the victory of any sort is potentially illusive and delusive. Compare the earlier **"Idyl":**

While, all forgotten, the world rolls along,
Think of us two, in a world of our own
Now that you've thought of it seriously—
Isn't it grand that it never can be?

(*Life,* July 7, 1921, 3; Silverstein, 93)

Soon this became predictable, so she tried other overriding structures, such as "moral tales" where the punch line in the final maxim both opposes the preceding lines with its more distanced tone and moves the particular into a congruent generalization.

Gracie, with her golden curls,
Took her mother's string of pearls.
Figuring—as who would not?—
It would pawn for quite a lot.
Picture, then, her indignation
When she found it imitation!
Though her grief she tries to smother,
Grace can't feel the same towards Mother!
All pretence and sham detest;
Work for nothing but the best.

(*Life,* May 4, 1922, 7; Silverstein, 124)

Like mother, like daughter (if she but knew it). Yet "the best" in the final line here—given both the prevalent situation and the inadequate moral—remains deliberately ambiguous. Another exercise in affecting overall structure is her **"Somewhat Delayed Spring Song."**

Crocuses are springing,
Birds are lightly winging,
Corydon is singing,
To his rustic lute;
Sullen winter passes,
Shepherds meet their lasses,
Tender-tinted grasses
Shoot.
All the world's a-thrilling,
Meadow larks are shrilling,
Little brooks are trilling,
You, alone, are mute;
Why do you delay it?
Love's a game—let's play it,
Go ahead and say it—
Shoot!

(*SEP,* September 30, 1922, 105; Silverstein, 137)

Last to be developed, then, was what has become the recognizable Parker persona, that of the woman who is both exploited and thick-skinned, who is put upon but can equally well put down others. **"Song"** suggests this with cynical wisdom.

Clarabelle has golden hair,
Mabel's eyes are blue,
Nancy's form is passing fair,
Mary's heart is true.
Chloë's heart has proved to be
Something else again;
Not so much on looks is she,
But she gets the men.

(*SEP,* November 18, 1922, 93; Silverstein, 144)

The rueful conclusion—what would become another Parker hallmark—combines innocence and worldliness, acceptance and condemnation. The final attitude in such dialogic writing—if there is any final attitude—rests with the reader.

"Folk Song" has the same idea, but reverses the roles.

Rafe's a fine young gentleman;
Tom's with virtue blest.
Jack, he broke my heart and ran,—
I love him the best.

(*Life,* October 16, 1924, 7; Silverstein, 163)

The earlier **"Invictus,"** built by clichés, has still more subtlety.

Black though my record as darkest jet,
Give me, I beg, my devil's due;
Only remember, I've never yet
Said, "How's the world been treating you?"

(*Life,* January 27, 1921, 161; Silverstein, 84)

So tight is her control by 1923 that she can be compared, and fruitfully, to Heinrich Heine.[3] Little wonder that by then her "little woman" persona was being widely imitated.[4] She had found, by trial and error, the subject and stance that characterize the best of her poetry.

Notes

1. See, for example, *The World,* March 19, 1922, 11:1; January 2, 1925, 9:1. The first series here lists Dorothy's "hate songs" in *VF,* the second her "hymns of hate" in *Life;* see Silverstein, 187.
2. Quoted by F. P. A. in *Innocent Merriment* (New York: McGraw-Hill, 1942), 159-60. For F. P. A.'s parodied response see his column in *The World* for September 22, 1924, 13:1. F. P. A. credits Villon with teaching him the form. An early example of Parker's rondeaus is in *SEP,* November 11, 1922, 84; see Silverstein, 142.
3. Cf., for example, "Ich trat in jene hallen" or "Es liegt der heisse Sommer," which Joseph Auslander translates:

The fervent flame of Summer
Lies in your lovely cheek;
But in your heart the Winter
Lies old and cold and bleak.
All this will change, my precious,
And sooner than you seek:
The Summer in your heart, dear,
The Winter in your cheek.

(Heinrich Heine, *Bittersweet Poems* [Mount Vernon, N.Y.: Peter Pauper Press, 1956], 19).

4. The best-known imitator of Parker is Fanny Heaslip Lea. See as an example her "Obituary" in *Harper's Bazaar,* March 1931, 156. My research has uncovered 68 poems in *Life* between 1920-1926 that Parker omitted from her volumes of published poetry, as well as 15 from *Vanity Fair* (1915-1920), 6 from *The World* (1923-1929), 5 from *New Yorker* (1925-1938), and 8 from *The Saturday Evening Post* (1922-1923). All are reprinted in Silverstein.

Arthur F. Kinney (essay date 1998)

SOURCE: "Her Accomplishment: Poetry, Fiction, Criticism," in *Dorothy Parker, Revised,* Amherst: University of Massachusetts, 1998, pp. 86-112.

[*The following is Kinney's study of Parker's maturation as a poet, offering a comparison of her with other poets of her generation and persuasion.*]

Premises: "Call Her by My Name" . . .

[Parker] learned in writing her plays, as she did in the evolution of her essays and light verse, the inherent value in imaginative application of experience, starting with a personal perspective as a handy persona and moving, more and more, toward a personal aesthetic. Voicings multiply, contradict, appear and recede, denote and imply. "The content of her verse began to change drastically, too," Meade writes, as she began to expose and analyze her own experiences, her own hopes, fears, and betrayals.

> Satin gowns turn into shrouds, decomposing corpses clinically observe the activity of worms, the living dead ghoulishly deck themselves with graveyard flowers. There were alarming glimpses, no more than a series of snapshots, of the tragedies that would be recognized by twentieth century women as peculiarly their own: the gut-searing loneliness of the women who have "careers," the women who don't marry, the women who do but divorce; the women deprived of maternal warmth and comfort who are condemned to seek love forever in the barren soil of husbands and children and even animals; women howling primitively for nourishment, flanked on one side by rejecting mothers and on the other by rejecting lovers. Her verse began to acknowledge the timeless subject of female rage. (Meade, 109).

In time she could even experience self-loathing as in the anti-Semitic **"Dark Girl's Rhyme."** Her accomplished poetry, fiction, and criticism illustrate the success of this development.

Poetry: "To Follow a Thread of Song"

Parker's maturity is clearly visible when we compare a late poem like **"War Song"** (see xiv) with an early poem from ***Enough Rope*** (1926), **"The New Love."**

If it shine or if it rain,
Little will I care or know.
Days, like drops upon a pane,
Slip, and join, and go.
At my door's another lad;
Here's his flower in my hair.
If he see me pale and sad,
Will he see me fair?
I sit looking at the floor,
Little will I think or say
If he seek another door;
Even if he stay.[1]

"The New Love" is essentially negative, its wit grounded in a rueful attitude, self-depreciation, and world-worn cynicism; the poem has a kind of half-cheerful heartlessness that echoes early Millay. **"War Song,"** on the other hand, is more positive. The later poem is also more realistic and willing to settle for less, not self-deprecating but not boasting either; instead, the persona has reconciled herself to the way of the world. **"War Song"** is essentially generous in spirit and, if it has any echoes, they are of the mature A. E. Housman.

Yet these distinctions are subordinate to the similarities: the simplicity of diction, clarity of stance, easiness of rhyme, and settledness of form and presentation; each has its own lapidary effect. Such common qualities—which distinguish all her best poems—are neoclassical and together they define all the mature work, whether they result from her Latin training at Miss Dana's or reach her by way of her contemporaries. Roman poetry lies just behind the epigrammatic poems of Dorothy Parker.

Confluences: "I Have Lived with Shades"

"Every good copy of verses is inspired by the elder poetry," John Jay Chapman wrote in *Vanity Fair* for July 1919.[2] Not one but two classical traditions merged during the period that Parker advanced from her light verse to her mature and substantial poetry; although no one has yet paid sufficient attention, these two strains caused a remarkable revival in interest in Roman poetry in the earlier part of the twentieth century. One tradition, the more learned and serious, stemming from Catullus, arose with Housman and reached Parker largely through the work of Millay and Elinor Wylie. The other, beginning with Eugene Field's imitations of Horace, reached Parker through later imitations by F. P. A. Her best poems marry both traditions, display both voicings.

One scholar has identified Catullus as the first Roman poet who shaped short lyrics by his own independent, wisecracking personality, reflecting personal sentiments rather than serving the larger community.[3] Earlier, when Parker was writing ***Enough Rope***, a popular book on Catullus held that he was "the pioneer . . . in the epigram and the lampoon," that "[h]is language is sometimes that of the nursery, sometimes that of the drawing-room, sometimes that of the street corners; [in each] he wastes no words."[4] Catullus wrote 40 songs of hate, ranging from 2 to 40 lines, his work often revealing "his open contempt for shams. . . . It was Catullus who taught Europe, and America, how to sing tender songs of love, to phrase bitter words of hate; who 'pointed the way to a more exact prosody and a richer versification' who showed us how to flash on the mental retina whole pictures in a single word" (Harrington, 62, 219). Harrington quotes Walter Pater: "'Catullus' expression of emotion: has the Greek qualities of definiteness, adequacy, point, and necessary limitation'" (Harrington, 218). Although the poetry was immediate in reference and impact, the moments chosen were eternal ones; Catullus compounded sharp wit, ingenuity, and elegance of expression from songs of beauty to poems of savage invective. His poems could be solemn or reckless in attitude, fostering an "urban consciousness"[5] the clean precision of his lines and the economy of phrase resulting from quip and cliché with a relative absence of simile and metaphor. In all these primary characteristics, "He set the pace for epigram throughout the centuries" (Harrington, 220)—and he wrote verse astonishingly similar to that of Parker. As an example, here is number 70 in a contemporary translation by Horace Gregory.

> My mother says that she would rather wear the wedding-veil for me than anyone: even if Jupiter himself came storming after her; that's what she says, but when a woman talks to a hungry, ravenous lover, her words should be written upon the wind and engraved in rapid waters.

Compare Parker's **"Prophetic Soul"** (***Enough Rope,*** 66):

> Because your eyes are slant and slow,
> Because your hair is sweet to touch,
> My heart is high again; but oh,
> I doubt if this will get me much.

with Catullus's number 85:

> I hate and love.
> And if you ask me why,
> I have no answer, but I discern,
> can feel, my senses rooted in eternal torture.[6]

Confessional yet highly disciplined, conversational yet poetically rendered, the work of both poets displays a controlled imagination grounded in irresolution. Distanced reflection and careful analysis merge problematically. And both poets are structurally similar, opening with a summary sentiment, continuing by amplification and parallelism, and concluding with a bright summary or, more often, a turn or counterturn frequently involving a change in attitude, sometimes involving a pun. Catullus and Parker share a forced (and threatened) personal integrity before failed love affairs and a disintegrating society. Catullus's misfortune with Lesbia, Parker's with many men, allow them to juxtapose a grim reality with a struggle to preserve the image of an ideal lover; for both, cynicism results.[7]

Catullus was revived in the work of A. E. Housman, a classicist known for reciting the Roman poet before his classes, even during battles at Vincy and Verdun, and who published an 11-page discussion on obscenities in Catullus and other Latin poets.[8] "The unanimous verdict of the Housman admirers," writes Cyril Connolly,

> is that he is essentially a classical poet. Master of the Latin language, he has introduced in English poetry the economy, the precision, the severity of that terse and lucid tongue. His verses are highly finished, deeply pagan; they stand outside the ordinary current of modern poetry, the inheritors, not of the romantic age, but of the poignancy and stateliness, the epigraphic quality of the poems of Catullus, Horace, and Virgil, or the flowers of the Greek Anthology.[9]

Just how closely he resembles Parker can be seen in *A Shropshire Lad,* number 18:

> Oh, when I was in love with you,
> Then I was clean and brave,
> And miles around the wonder grew
> How well did I behave.
> And now the fancy passes by,
> And nothing will remain,
> And miles around they'll say that I
> Am quite myself again.

But the cleverness of the poem is (like Parker's) misleading, because "quite myself" placed in apposition to "clean and brave" invites the reader to question the authority of the persona and, in doing so, separates the reader from (rather than fusing the reader with) the poet. As for American poets, Housman felt Millay "the best [one] living," from whom he "got more enjoyment [than] Frost or Robinson."[10]

Edna St. Vincent Millay studied Latin poetry as a child and as an adult carried with her a "tiny, shabby brown leather" copy of Catullus's poetry; in Greenwich Village, she talked about Catullus with Edmund Wilson over peach brandy. She was equally fond of Housman, once chasing him a half-mile through Cambridge "just to get a glimpse of his face, a nice face"; she was also close to Harrison Dowd, who set part of *A Shropshire Lad* to music.[11] Both poets find a place in her poetry, in her recklessness and reserve, in her devotion to learning, in her creativity and rebellion.[12] Like Parker, Millay deals with unrequited love and with sexual affairs that are "just as real and true as any other," bringing to them "a pertness, a saucy impudence—even a certain heartlessness" that reminds us of Parker's poetry (Gurko, 124-25). For our purposes, *A Few Figs from Thistles* (1922) is illustrative. The opening poems are indistinguishable from Parker's.

> First Fig
> My candle burns at both ends;
> It will not last the night;
> But ah, my foes, and oh, my friends—
> It gives a lovely light!
> Second Fig
> Safe upon the solid rock the ugly houses stand:
> Come and see my shining palace built upon the sand![13]

So is "Thursday":

> And if I loved you Wednesday,
> Well, what is that to you?
> I do not love you Thursday—
> So much is true.
> And why you come complaining
> Is more than I can see.
> I loved you Wednesday,—yes—but what
> Is that to me?[14]

And, as with Parker, death as well as love becomes an omnipresent theme in Millay's poetry.[15] Among other contemporaries, the "small, clean technique," the miniaturist art of Elinor Wylie, has also been compared to her friend Parker's.[16]

Parker learned much of her art of poetry from Catullus and the Catullan tradition in England and America, but it was the Horation tradition that taught her the inevitability of man's failings, and that led to her troubling combination of rueful and cocky tones. There is some likelihood that the *Odes of Horace* that she knew at Miss Dana's School was that translated by W. E. Gladstone (1894), which emphasized the *compression* of his verse. Warren H. Cudworth's text (1917) appeared just as she was seeking out her own form; in his preface, Cudworth stresses the tight *form* of Horatian poetry.[17] But Parker was far from alone in this interest; Louis Untermeyer's popular little book *Including Horace* pointed out ways in which he could be seen as contemporary.

> Horace in his own mood [is] light, slyly mocking, petulant, often downright flippant. In spite of his immortal literary harem, his Lydias, his Chloës, his Pyrrhas, his Lelages, there is never in all of Horace's erotic rhymes the note of genuine passion. . . . The note is always that of sophistication. . . . Over and over again he tells us to enjoy the present and distrust tomorrow.[18]

Structurally, Horace's *Satires* are like Parker's, and often begin with a hyperbole, develop by antithetical ideas, end with a surprise, a twist. Horace wrote his fashionable poetry for his own inner circle, the friends of Maecenas resembling for him what the Algonquin wits did for Parker; but as Grant Showerman wrote in 1922, Horace detached himself from the crowd so that he could see and comment on the folly of his fellow men. He is tamer and less involved than Catullus, although Horace too could use his own person as the subject or perspective for his poetry.[19]

The modern tradition of imitating Horace began with Eugene Field, who was taught classics by his father and whose managing editor on the *Chicago Daily News,* F. W. Reilly, persuaded him to try his hand. Field's methodology was a conscious one. "[Horace's] was a joyous spirit and certainly he would express himself rhythmically and with mirthful lightness if he were now on earth. So I try to interpret Horace in a way to bring his pagan poetry up to date. At least I give him the best I have in the shop."[20] Field's imitations appeared in his newspaper column *Sharps and Flats;* in the winter of 1890 he was convinced by a friend, Francis Wilson, that he should publish a whole book of such poetry. *Echoes from the Sabine Farm* appeared in 1896. Field's work was brief, colloquial, and critical—but never savage or trenchant like Parker's. He appeals frequently to Roman allusions in his originals, as in "To Chloë (II)":

> Chloë, you shun me like a hind
> That, seeking vainly for her mother,
> Hears danger in each breath of wind,
> And wildly darts this way and t'other; . . .
> But Chloë, you're no infant thing
> That should esteem a man an ogre;
> Let go your mother's apron-string,
> And pin your faith upon a toga![21]

Field perhaps gave his most serious attention to these imitations. He defended them at length in 1891, but he died before completing his ambition to write Horace's biography. His work was widely hailed and itself imitated (Dennis, 167-68).

F. P. A., who worked on Chicago newspapers during Field's last years, brought the idea of imitating Horace to New York City with him, and his own imitations became a popular feature in his "Conning Tower" column in the New York *World;* Parker herself tried her hand at them there. "The patron of the smart," as Gilbert Seldes called F. P. A. (Seldes, 246),[22] made it possible (in the words of Don Marquis) "to admit our learning and still be honorable men."[23] F. P. A.'s imitation of the same ode to Chloë (Book I, Ode xxiii) reads,

> Nay, Chloë, dear, forget your fear,
> Nor like a frightened fawn outrun me;
> No savage I to horrify—
> You shouldn't shun me.
> Come Chloë, queen, you're seventeen;
> There's many a precedent to back us.
> Why shouldn't you be Mrs. Q.
> Horatius Flaccus?[24]

His imitation of Book I, Ode v also uses a popular expression.

> What lady-like youth in his wild aberrations
> Is putting cologne on his brow?
> For whom are the puffs and the blond transformations?
> I wonder who's kissing you now.[25]

Long sections of each of F. P. A.'s early books, published during the time he was encouraging Parker, are given over to such imitations of Horace—and of Propertius, Catullus, and Martial.[26]

F. P. A. learned from imitating Horace the precision, simplicity, and compactness that distinguish his light verse as those distinguish Parker's poetry: he served her as an important model. He also turned to puns opening his verses, too, to multiplicity of meaning, as in "The Atmospheric Complex."

Give me the balmy breezes!
Give me the raging storm!
Give me the gale that freezes!
Give me the zephyrs warm!
Give me the searing tropic!
Wind on my cheek and hair!
And, while we're on the topic,
Give me the air.[27]

Like Parker, F. P. A. was fascinated by the theme of unrequited love and challenged by the difficult word, as in "The Return of the Soldier."

Lady, when I left you
Ere I sailed the sea.
Bitterly I bereft you
Told me you would be. . . .
Arguing *ex parte,*
Maybe you can tell
Why I find your heart
A. W. O. L.[28]

The legacy of Horace, summed Showerman in 1922, was "to be straightforward and rapid and omit the unessential; to be truthful to life; . . . to be appropriate in meter and diction" (Showerman, 135). Horace spawned such imitators because they, as he, were discontented with their lot (Book I, Satire i).

Still "the model and type of the epigram . . . which have not been surpassed in any literature" is Martial, and Parker may have known the Martial text by J. H. Westcott (1897). The chief characteristics of the Martial epigram are wit and point, as in **"News Item"** or **"Two-Volume Novel"** by Parker.

Men seldom make passes
At girls who wear glasses.

(***Enough Rope***, 85)

The sun's gone dim, and
The moon's turned black;
For I loved him, and
He didn't love back.

(***Sunset Gun***, 70)

Paul Nixon notes in *A Roman Wit* (1911) that Martial was an urban wit; his poetry offers as its reward an "intellectual appreciation, not an emotional reaction," and it is Westcott's text that tells us most about how Parker's generation perceived the classical epigrammatist.

> The fact that Martial's character was not a strong one, that he felt no consciousness of a moral mission, that he was neither greatly better nor worse than people about him, that he reflects so thoroughly the spirit of his age, makes him more interesting to us and more instructive in his way than many a sterner author. . . . His satire stings more than it wounds. And at his best he reveals a tenderness and pathos which prove a genuinely affectionate heart, or a refined delicacy which is hard to reconcile with coarseness of feeling. . . . Martial's versification is admirable, being clear, tasteful, and careful, without being pedantic or over precise.[29]

Nixon's 1911 translations illustrate these techniques.

Philo swears he was never known
To dine alone:
He was not.
Dine at all, when it comes about
He's not asked out,
He does n't.
Your client's applause for your poems,
Pomponious,
Would prove not your metres but menus
Euphonious.[30]

"The point, whether dependent on a pun, or an ambiguous phrase, on a new meaning given to a word, or an antithesis," writes Walter C. A. Ker in 1930, "is sharply brought out. And the words fall into their places with a fitness that suggests the solution of a puzzle: the reader feels that no other words could have been employed. He is never turgid or pompous: all he touches with a light hand."[31] The understanding the Algonquin wits had of Martial, as of Catullus and Horace, points the way to some resources of the various voicings of Parker's major poetry.

Enough Rope: "The Sweeter the Apple, the Blacker the Core"

The polyphonic, polysemous quality of Parker's major poetry was perceived at once. J. F. [John Farrar] wrote in *The Bookman* for March 1927 that "Dorothy Parker in ***Enough Rope*** . . . collects some of her fragile verses, and the effect is devastating. Singly, they are lovely. As a volume, they are terrifying; but only as they reflect what seems to be a fiery, discontented personality."[32] The *New York Times* reported that "[i]n these verses, perfected with simplicity of words and fine craftsmanship, there is more than facility—there is an outspoken manner that explodes pretense sharply and turns its sorrow into mordant wit." Other reviews described her various voicings in other ways.[33] In *Poetry* for April 1927, Marie Luhrs added: "Here is poetry that is 'smart' in the fashion designer's sense of the word. . . . Mrs. Parker has her own particular field of frank American humor. She is slangy, vulgar, candid, and withal subtle, delicate and sparkling. The soul of wit distinguishes most of her pieces. . . . For all their pertness and bravado they mirror, in most cases, quite genuine and profound experiences."[34] Summarizing the reviews, Frewin writes that "[t]he book illustrated the elliptical Dorothy Parker at her best: The droll, almost bored, prismatic author, immersed in a desire for beauty, in love with the lacerating stillness of death in life, and always sardonic in her cerebral exercises" (Frewin, 117).

Enough Rope (1926) appeared from Boni and Liveright for two dollars, in a gray dust jacket with yellow lettering—"A woman supplies enough rope to hang a hundred Egos"[35]—and a dangling rope for illustration; it went through 14 printings, a phenomenal bestseller. For the uninitiated, the plaintive, self-pitying tone of the spurned woman must have seemed obvious and trite (**"The Small Hours,"** 12) or brightly, if superficially, sophisticated

(**"Wail,"** 22). While the book's title suggests her conscious adoption of the role of satirist, one bemused by the human situation and sufficiently superior to poke fun at it, the poetry of part I, treating such commonplace themes as unrequited love, loneliness, death, and hypocrisy, makes the book appear commonplace. Attempts to be otherwise, as with **"The Immortals"** (44), strain self-consciously but are actually poor parodies of "serious" love poems.

But this is to take the worst poetry in the book as our norm. If we examine the best of it, we see already that terseness and strength whereby classical form supplies foundation and limitation to both situation and sentiment. Compare the apparently simple (because simply titled) **"Anecdote":**

So silent I when Love was by
He yawned, and turned away;
But Sorrow clings to my apron-strings,
I have so much to say.

(25)

Here is the precision and distillation characteristic of Martial at *his* succinct best, but here too she manages to combine timidity, disappointment, despair, and frustration. This is a disciplined poem like **"Threnody,"** which opens the volume.

Lilacs blossom just as sweet
Now my heart is shattered.
If I bowled it down the street,
Who's to say it mattered?
If there's one that rode away
What would I be missing?
Lips that taste of tears, they say,
Are the best for kissing.
Eyes that watch the morning star
Seem a little brighter;
Arms held out to darkness are
Usually whiter.
Shall I bar the strolling guest;
Bind my brow with willow,
When, they say, the empty breast
Is the softer pillow?
That a heart falls tinkling down,
Never think it ceases.
Every likely lad in town
Gathers up the pieces.
If there's one gone whistling by
Would I let it grieve me?
Let him wonder if I lie;
Let him half believe me.

(11)

The explosive conceit of the heart as bowling ball is at once cocky and exaggerated, although it frees the quatrains, opening them up for the drama of a defeated, undefeated spirit. Parker knows already how form can constrict when density is sought and can just as easily loosen the spirit within the form when she wishes to dramatize a willful and even reckless vitality. Consequences of recklessness within this jocular poem are precisely the point: how are we to read (and in what tone hear) "Let him half believe me"? In such a context, grief and wonder become naturally, necessarily apposite.

However different the immediate tones of **"Anecdote"** and **"Threnody,"** close reading reveals the same careful plotting of diction and sound; they are exacting as voiced feelings. Simple language, taut or loose, coiled or sprung, is economic, direct, even astringent. In **"Threnody,"** moreover, "[t]hey say" (l. 7) is not a line-filler, but an indication of the persona's naive reliance on sophistication that is assumed, not real; the victory she attempts, then, in the last lines, assuring her alliance with the code of "them," can be naive or wisely earned. Dissociated as we are from the persona's sentiment (ll. 1-2), her sudden loss of the one fine metaphor (wrenchingly changed in l. 17) shows us the ironic distance between poet and persona. The liberating metaphor (l. 3) is also misplaced and grotesque, a product of the personal. So too the authentic colloquialisms that insistently revert to clichés. In this equivocation that guarantees satire, Parker provides a wit as controlled as the Roman poets', yet in an idiom very much her own.

Enough Rope is dedicated to Elinor Wylie, whose personal copy was inscribed, "With love, gratitude, and everything." This gift to a serious poet—not one of the light versifiers who contributed doggerel to *Life* and "The Conning Tower"—anticipates some serious changes Parker made when collecting these poems from earlier publication in the magazines.[36] Some of the poems here are still early and unsuccessful (**"A Portrait"** [45], **"Chant for Dark Hours"** [50], **"Verses for a Certain Dog"** [57]), but others, like those she revised, already show her mastering her craft. The themes that run through the volume are those with which she was by now identified: unrequited love, loneliness, and death. Yet note her control in such poems as **"For a Sad Lady":**

And let her loves, when she is dead,
Write this above her bones:
"No more she lives to give us bread
Who asked her only stones."

(34)

If her imitations of Horace lack the wide-wheeling energy of F. P. A. (**"Renunciation,"** 62), when she brings her own voice to the classical form, she is unsurpassed (**"Unfortunate Coincidence,"** 51). That she manages in far briefer compass shows that she is primarily a miniaturist.

To appreciate the peculiarly successful poetic of ***Enough Rope***, we must see how Parker starts with the briefest possible situation, catches it at a split moment, and dramatizes it through a voice unaware of the clichés on which it rests.

Because your eyes are slant and slow,
Because your hair is sweet to touch,
My heart is high again; but oh,
I doubt if this will get me much.

(**"Prophetic Soul,"** 66)

The interior monologue advances amusement through its innocent self-condemnation, or its jaded, world-weary cynicism: the choice remains open. Consider the technique of **"Philosophy."**

> If I should labor through daylight and dark,
> Consecrate, valorous, serious, true,
> Then on the world I may blazon my mark;
> And what if I don't, and what if I do?
>
> (79)

Every word is measured here; the polysyllables of line 2 add variety and counterrhythm to lines 1, 3, and 4, but they are defeated by the honesty, the rueful forthrightness of the monosyllables that completely enclose them. The poem, collapsing on a line that, removed from this freshening context, is one of the tritest lines of everyday conversation, shows us how we are, for the moment, suspended between a commonplace language and sentiment and a uniquely forceful—a memorable, mnemonic—poem.

Parker's poetry appears thin partly because it is dramatic, not ruminative. But by puns, clichés, and unfortunate word choices, her poems invite us to reflect on the sharp difference between poet and persona. It is this implied contrast—one we as readers *sense*—that provides point and force. The unwinding process of thought is in us, as with **"Interview"** (106).

> The ladies men admire, I've heard,
> Would shudder at a wicked word.
> Their candle gives a single light;
> They'd rather stay at home at night.
> They do not keep awake till three,
> Nor read erotic poetry.
> They never sanction the impure,
> Nor recognize an overture.
> They shrink from powders and from paints . . .
> So far, I've had no complaints.

The controlling idea lies in the exaggerated sentiment of line 1, the allusion to Millay in line 3, the excessive catalogue of lines 4-9, all set in conflicting tonal motion, whereas the last line sharply reverses course, leaving us suspended between the last two lines, emphasizing (and placing any possible resolution on) what is missing in the ellipsis. Even more embedded is the satire of **"Pictures in the Smoke."**

> Oh, gallant was the first love, and glittering and fine;
> The second love was water, in a clear white cup;
> The third love was his, and the fourth was mine;
> And after that, I always get them all mixed up.
>
> (101)

The inability of the persona here to rescue even her first lover from romantic jargon—to award him reality—is a certain indication of the hollowness of her own self, of her own attitude toward love. But whether personal promiscuity or social practice is the subject—whether the poem is public or private—goes unanswered.

This is not to deny a rueful laughter. Parker's poems can also contain humor. In assessing both the absurdity of human behavior generally and the foolishness of her personae in particular, Parker is much like the Horace of the *Satires* and of F. P. A.'s imitations.[37] But ***Enough Rope*** remains an uneven collection throughout. Some poems are highly imitative of Housman (6, 26), Millay (11, 24, 29, 30), Eliot (32), and, even, medieval balladry (14, 49) and Herrick (89), although here too she supplies her own final signature (as in **"Portrait of the Artist"**). Her best work echoes Martial (25, 78, 83) with the forcefulness of childlike diction, masculine rhymes, and a strong reliance on nouns and active verbs. Her strange mixture of romantic and classic checks any wrong impulse or self-posturing aside from that of her persona, and supplies what Maugham calls her "many-sided humor, her irony, her sarcasm, her tenderness, her pathos" (Maugham, 15)—a stiff upper lip alongside haunting disappointment and implied recalculation (**"One Perfect Rose"**). As Genevieve Taggard has it,

> This quaint, slightly cock-eyed world where men and women go around making chest developing gestures in the direction of each other, colliding like drunken electrons, apologizing ("So sorry!"), never looked more pitifully ridiculous through the lens of any poet's microscope than it does through Dorothy Parker's. It is hard to tell how she gets her hard-bitten comedy unless by the device of always correcting the way the specimen looks by the evidence of how it feels—or vice versa. Mrs Parker has such a corrective habit in her work . . . [that next to Millay, it is] whisky straight, not champagne. (Taggard, VII, 7:2-4)

Shrewd and fastidious, in polysemous language and tight form, trenchant humor opposing clichéd love conventions surprises, engages, and amuses us, working dialogically, as in **"Words of Comfort to be Scratched on a Mirror"** in part II:

> Helen of Troy had a wandering glance;
> Sappho's restriction was only the sky;
> Ninon was ever the chatter of France;
> But oh, what a good girl am I!
>
> (83)

In the best of this book, Dorothy Parker is already the most accomplished classical epigrammatist of her time.

Sunset Gun: "Authors and Actors and Artists and Such"

The unprecedented success of ***Enough Rope*** made critics and reviewers in popular journals more knowing in reviewing Parker's second volume of poetry, published two years later, in 1928. Nearly all of them sought characteristics to praise, as if the *consensus gentium* took on inviolable authority. Therefore, the reservation of the critic for the *New York Times* is worth remembering.

> In these verses [of ***Enough Rope***] perfected with simplicity of words and fine craftsmanship—there is more than facility—there is an outspoken manner that explodes pretense sharply and turns its sorrow into mordant wit.

> *Sunset Gun* has the same exuberant vitality. And again there is the tinctured mixture of the sad and the gay, suggesting that it is better to laugh than cry. And if one may be pardoned such ungallantry—the girl grows older—a mature note of intensity is apparent in her lyric note. She does not now have to depend on the last line reverse twist for effectiveness. Happily, this is being acquired without losing the gem-like sparkle of her verse. Perhaps the most attractive thing of all is her puckish fighting spirit.[38]

"The poems are lean and quick as a snake," Garreta Busey added.[39]

The book was originally called *Songs for the Nearest Harmonica,* but upon publication it appeared with another funereal title. ***Sunset Gun***[40] was dedicated simply "To John," a current admirer (perhaps John Farrar) who, noted one friend, was replaced by another "John" (John Garrett) while the book was in press. This time there was a first printing of 10,000 copies as well as another 250 copies numbered and signed. It, too, sold for two dollars.

Sunset Gun shows Parker's attempt to expand the brief epigrammatic form by cycles of poems (**"A Pig's-Eye View of Literature"** [30-32], **"Verses in the Night"** [57-59]), but except for these, often forced, there is only one poor poem (**"For R. C. B.,"** 23), for Benchley, which she later omitted from her collected poems. Occasionally, poems here seem easy or imitative (**"There Was One"** [24], **"Frustration"** [53]), but there is a dialogic unsettledness in them, both within the verse and in dialogue with one of her sources, the work of Housman:

> New love, new love, where are you to lead me?
> *All along a narrow way that marks a crooked line.*
> How are you to slake me, and how are you to feed me?
> *With bitter yellow berries, and a sharp new wine.*
> New love, new love, shall I be forsaken?
> *One shall go a-wandering, and one of us must sigh.*
> Sweet it is to slumber, but how shall we awaken—
> Whose will be the broken heart, when dawn comes by?
>
> (**"The Last Question,"** 66)

Other Roman echoes of unreconciled wit can be found in **"The Trusting Heart"** (37), **"The Gentlest Lady"** (39), **"Afternoon"** (46), **"The Whistling Girl"** (51), **"Landscape"** (55), and the impressive **"Liebestod"** (60). Still other poems look back to Millay and capture, better than elsewhere in Parker's poetry, the gaiety of the 1920s (**"On Cheating the Fiddler"** [26], **"Pour Prendre Congé"** [71]).

But the best poems in the book still mine the epigrammatic tradition of Martial, still locate the visible grasp of tonal purity and economic wit with unreconcilable angles of vision. Here she shows considerable advance in her ability to energize a tired proverb and to pack into a quatrain level upon level of potential meanings all available to any careful reader. One such example is **"Thought for a Sunshiny Morning":**

> It costs me never a stab nor squirm
> To tread by chance upon a worm.
> "Aha, my little dear," I say,
> "Your clan will pay me back one day."
>
> (38)

A similar poem, **"Daylight Savings,"** conflates Roman form with the Elizabethan theme of the union of poetry and immortality, itself an allusion to the classical concept of art, in which small social acts become metaphorical indicators without surrendering their initial concrete signification:

> My answers are inadequate
> To those demanding day and date,
> And ever set a tiny shock
> Through strangers asking what's o'clock;
> Whose days are spent in whittling rhyme—
> What's Time to her, or she to Time?
>
> (42)

Poems such as **"Post-Graduate,"** for all their simplicity, still have this impacted quality:

> Hope it was that tutored me,
> And Love that taught me more;
> And now I learn at Sorrow's knee
> The self-same lore.
>
> (56)

"Superfluous Advice" (67) and **"But Not Forgotten"** (69) are similar achievements: "penning a tract against self-pity, cant, and affectation, and at the same time taking a kind of Pharisaical delight in putting herself on the perverse side of the text," as Henry Morton Robinson has it in *The Bookman.*[41]

Moreover, Parker varies the basis of her irony. She still relies on reversal (**"Surprise"** [43]), but more and more she employs irony of situation (**"Penelope"** [34]) and irony of condition (**"Wisdom"** [74]). In poems of dazzling simplicity, she manages to imply allusions (**"Two-Volume Novel"** [70]); even the eternal battle of the sexes is rendered as openly metaphorical (**"The Second Oldest Story"** [29], **"Mortal Enemy"** [33], **"Dilemma"** [63]). Her new ability to jam questions of philosophy, attitude, and judgment into foreshortened space, the maturing with that enables her to condense coordinates of time into reckless and yet provocative juxtapositions may be seen here in one of the best poems she ever wrote, **"Partial Comfort":**

> Whose love is given over-well
> Shall look on Helen's face in hell,
> Whilst they whose love is thin and wise
> May view John Knox in paradise,
>
> (14)

where a review of the lines shows how evenly balanced the choice is between **"Helen"** and **"Knox,"** "over-well" and "wise." Read sardonically, the poem supports paganism; read meditatively, it supports individual conscience

(Methodism). When we admit the variety of tonalities that the simple quatrain permits, it becomes almost impossibly equivocal in its twin condemnations.

Such expanding linguistic powers she appears to examine in **"For a Lady Who Must Write Verse:"**

> . . . Show your quick, alarming skill in
> Tidy mockeries of art;
> Never, never dip your quill in
> Ink that rushes from your heart. . . .
> Never print, poor child, a lay on
> Love and years and anguishing,
> Lest a cooled, benignant Phaon
> Murmur, "Silly little thing!"
>
> (72)

Such deliberate caution, such quickening critical intelligence is especially necessary in a book that attempts, for the first time in any significant way, autobiographical poetry. **"Bohemia"** works because of the wisecracking bravado of the earlier **"Resumé":**

> Authors and actors and artists and such
> Never know nothing, and never know much.
> Sculptors and singers and those of their kidney
> Tell their affairs from Seattle to Sydney.
> Playwrights and poets and such horses' necks
> Start off from anywhere, end up at sex.
> Diarists, critics, and similar roe
> Never say nothing, and never say no.
> People Who Do Things exceed my endurance;
> God, for a man that solicits insurance!
>
> (35)

The governing pun on "insurance" with its coy allusion to Eddie Parker—that which provides stability and hedges against future uncertainties, opposed to that which locks one into business so that life is here placed in opposition to "solicits," which relates selling insurance to selling sex—then falls back into a greater allusive sweep by interrogating the solicitation on which "[a]uthors and actors and artists and such" depend; patronage as well as approval. Along with this mingling series of meanings, the poem manages a kind of quick singsong rhythm that parcels out lines like a businessman, even as it frolics more for amusement than instruction. Whichever way we take the poem, we cannot be so simple about it as the persona who speaks the final line.

This kind of autobiography-as-metaphor always works for Parker. Riskier, and less often successful, is the "serious" Parker who ventures the sonnet form in **"A Dream Lies Dead."**

> A dream lies dead here. May you softly go
> Before this place, and turn away your eyes,
> Nor seek to know the look of that which dies
> Importuning Life for life. Walk not in woe,
> But, for a little, let your step be slow.
> And, of your mercy, be not sweetly wise
> With words of hope and Spring and tenderer skies.
> A dream lies dead; and this all mourners know.
>
> (47)

The new, quietly lyrical, even mournful tone is still the product of a rueful surrender to the transient, even the unreachable, quality of happiness. There remains a fundamental skepticism of love's permanence, and so a residual resistance against idealistic notions of endurance. ***Sunset Gun*** begins to reveal in Parker's poetry an unstated conflict in loyalty between the disappointing truths of love's experience, of her life, and an apprehension of, for all time, people's inherent folly, of all lives.

Death and Taxes: "Where I May Look, the Frosted Peaks Are Spun"

Death and Taxes, Parker's third volume of poetry, was named for our only certainties. Published in 1931 by a new publisher (Viking), the book is dedicated, at last, "To Mr. Benchley."

Reviewing ***Death and Taxes*** in the *Saturday Review of Literature,* Henry Seidel Canby remarked that

> one should quote Latin rather than English to parallel the edged fineness of Dorothy Parker's verse. This belle dame sans merci has the ruthlessness of the great tragic lyricists whose work was allegorized in the fable of the nightingale singing with her breast against a thorn. It is disillusion recollected in tranquillity where the imagination has at last controlled the emotions. It comes out clear, and with the authentic sparkle of a great vintage . . . there is no frailty in her poetry, and its brevity is in space not in time. (Canby, 891)

Raymond Kresensky noted in the *Christian Century* that "it is a well known fact that often the court jester is a serious philosopher beneath his cap and bells";[42] seeing the same dominance of seriousness, F. P. A. commented in "Books" that "[i]n this new collection the painful hunger for beauty and the heartbreak of its impermanence, the uncompromising idealism, are even acuter than in her previous volumes. It is her saddest and her best book."[43] Elsewhere, comments were generally favorable.[44]

Once again, Parker revised a number of poems that reappear here.[45] But she did not eliminate "wisecrack verses" that hearken back to her earlier contributions to *Life* and to the *Saturday Evening Post,* such as **"Prologue to a Saga"** (61). This poem opens with a series of classical allusions that, in the forward march of chronology, are displaced in the second quatrain by medieval references. None of them, however, prepares us especially well for the last line: here the twist is fun for its slang and abruptness, but it is only a surprise; it does not reverberate, as good poetry always does. Other examples that seem a residue of her earlier moods and practices are **"The Evening Primrose"** (17), **"Salome's Dancing-Lesson"** (20), **"Little Words"** (24), **"Purposely Ungrammatical Love Song"** (49), and **"The Danger of Writing Defiant Verse"** (14). She also enjoys an easy joke on Catullus (**"From a Letter from Lesbia"** [48]) and still experiments with French verse forms (**"Ballade of Unfortunate Mammals"** [46], **"Ballade of a Talked-off Ear"** [56]).

But she has not in the process lost her ability to write fine epigrams. **"The Flaw in Paganism,"** resembling Martial in form, borrows its theme from Horace and Juvenal, and alludes to Shakespeare's *Antony and Cleopatra* (2.7.89 ff.; 3.13.182 ff.), the mingling allusions signaling the mixed voices:

Drink and dance and laugh and lie,
Love, the reeling midnight through,
For tomorrow we shall die!
(But, alas, we never do.)

(13)

"Distance" (16) is something new—Housman's lexicon and spirit converted to the leanness characteristic of Martial—whereas **"Sanctuary"** returns again to a Horatian use of popular phrase.

My land is bare of chattering folk;
The clouds are low along the ridges,
And sweet's the air with curly smoke
From all my burning bridges.

(18)

Here our sense of plague or damnation in line 1 (a barren landscape) seems transformed by pleasant clouds (l. 2) when we learn that the clouds are not nature's doing, but the persona's; it is not really clouds but clouds of smoke, which, in turn, cause a geographical barrenness that resembles the barren love affair, the persona now left behind. When Parker so intertwines lines and vocabulary, her work is far superior to **"Prologue to a Saga."** "Cherry White" is also lapidary, adding the familiar Parker corrosiveness.

I never see that prettiest thing—
A cherry bough gone white with Spring—
But what I think, "How gay 'twould be
To hang me from a flowering tree."

(19)

The macabre humor of the final line both lifts and depresses our spirits as we read it. **"In the Meadow"** (37) is unusual for Parker because it works almost exclusively through natural symbol; idea and mood are equally well compacted in **"The Apple Tree"** (38). **"Iseult of Brittany"** realizes a deep psychological awareness of the fated medieval heroine: unlike Horace and Juvenal, who tend to portray types, Parker's poem frees the tragedy and the individuality of Iseult from the books of courtly romance. Again in ***Death and Taxes***, she displays her powers by writing a cycle of epigrams, **"Tombstones in the Starlight"** (26-31).

What is fundamentally new in ***Death and Taxes***, however, is a note of lyricism. There are faint anticipations of it in the lively and witty **"The Little Old Lady in Lavender Silk"** (32-33) if we notice how the choric line dialogically informs the spirit of the poem throughout, but it takes its newer and more characteristically solemn tones in **"Midnight"** (51) and in the satiric portrait of **"Ninon de l'Enclos, on Her Last Birthday":**

So let me have the rouge again,
And comb my hair the curly way.
The poor young men, the dear young men—
They'll all be here by noon today. . . .
So bring my scarlet slippers, then,
And fetch the powder-puff to me.
The dear young men, the poor young men—
They think I'm only seventy!

(52)

Here the dialogic intrusion of the persona's choric line invites us to the questions underlying the poem: Who here is courting whom? And who is being victimized in the process? The answers, which may seem apparent, are not, finally, clear at all.

Quiet tone is married to classical simplicity in **"Of a Woman, Dead Young: (J. H., 1905-1930)"** (54). Here the sentiment is so honest and moving that Parker returns to vers libre, relying on assonance to do the work of her normally end-stopped lines and masculine rhymes; the whole effect is one of subdued but persistent bewilderment and admiration. This hushed tone, toward which the whole volume works, is heard also in **"Prayer for a New Mother"** (the Virgin Mary [50]) and **"Sonnet on an Alpine Night"** (58), which the *China Weekly Review* of Shanghai compared to a poem of Yang I (about 1000 A.D.): "Upon this tall pagoda's peak / My hand can nigh the stars enclose."[46]

But the consummate poem, as poem, opens the book. **"Prayer for a Prayer"** uses the quiet tone to introduce a meditative moment that merges life and death, time and eternity, memory and forgetfulness, purpose and purposelessness.

Dearest one, when I am dead
Never seek to follow me.
Never mount the quiet hill
Where the copper leaves are still,
As my heart is, on the tree
Standing at my narrow bed.
Only, of your tenderness,
Pray a little prayer at night.
Say: "I have forgiven now—
I, so weak and sad; O Thou,
Wreathed in thunder, robed in light,
Surely Thou wilt do no less."

(11)

The majesty and awe that prompt the final lines, reduced suddenly to the personal level, are neither mockery nor blasphemy, but the final lines work hard to bring to some reconciliation a poem that opens with personal choice juxtaposed to the forces of nature; and **"Prayer for a Prayer"** becomes here an unaccustomed cry for mercy for mercy instead of measure for measure. Here, as elsewhere in ***Death and Taxes***, Parker breaks new ground—not new to Millay and Wylie, but new to her—while maintaining the lucidity, simplicity, and economy that distinguish her epigrammatic wit. Anguish is more openly displayed here, death closer to the surfaces of life, the laughter more hidden and more brittle. The increased seriousness really signals the end of her poetry—for her concerns will be turned over now, and more directly, to prose essay and fiction; it is as if with ***Death and Taxes*** she is already anticipating her famous statement in the years ahead of her: "There is nothing funny in the world any more."

Not So Deep as a Well: "A Terrible Sorrow Along With the Sight"

By 1936, when Parker's collected poetry was published under the title ***Not So Deep as a Well,*** she had married, moved to Hollywood, and given up most writing to devote her time to political activities. ***Not So Deep as a Well***—the title is from Mercutio's sardonic death speech in *Romeo and Juliet* (3.1.97)[47]—reprints her three volumes of poetry, omitting only the least of her poems,[48] and adds five new ones: **"Sight," "The Lady's Reward," "Prisoner," "Temps Perdu,"** and **"Autumn Valentine."** Although critics received the work well, they did so in the unwittingly reductive terms of Parker, Algonquin wit, as Louis Kronenberger remarked:

> One comes back to Mrs. Parker's light verse with the greatest pleasure; with its sharp wit, its clean bite, the perfectly conscious—and hence delightful—archness, it stands re-reading amply. Here her high technical polish has great virtue, sometimes cracking out a surprise effect with an absolute minimum of wind-up, sometimes achieving a foreseen effect by means so dexterous it is exhilarating to watch them. Mrs. Parker can extend anticlimax to irresistible bathos by altering the pitch of her language (from the high-flown to the highly colloquial) at the exact moment she alters her meaning. But what, of course, is more important is the sense of personality that converts what might otherwise be merely a witty idea into a dramatic, however cockeyed, situation; a sense of personality that gives us not cynicism in the abstract but laughter applied to an objective. There is no one else in Mrs. Parker's special field who can do half as much. I suspect that she will survive not only as the author of some first-rate light verse but also as a valuable footnote to the Twenties, out of whose slant on existence that light verse sprang.[49]

But the new poems are a product not so much of the 1920s as of Parker's late serious poetry, of the early 1930s. Rather like **"Prayer for a New Mother,"** grounded in a dramatic tension between the stated beliefs of natural motherhood and the implied countercurrent of Christianity founded in love that shocks us to new and deeper truths about humility and sacrifice, so these new works too start simply, traditionally, only to lead in new directions. Consider **"Sight":**

> Unseemly are the open eyes
> That watch the midnight sheep,
> That look upon the secret skies
> Nor close, abashed, in sleep;
> That see the dawn drag in, unbidden,
> To birth another day—
> Oh, better far their gaze were hidden
> Below the decent clay.
>
> (198)

Here the ideas of Housman take on a more subdued tone, a more regretful attitude: Housman stoicism is displaced by Parker's mordant irresolution. **"Autumn Valentine"** (202) sounds more like earlier poems, but it too ends with a sad (and unanswered) refrain. **"Prisoner"** demonstrates Parker's continuing skill as epigrammatist.

> Long I fought the driving lists,
> Plume a-stream and armor clanging;
> Link on link, between my wrists,
> Now my heavy freedom's hanging.
>
> (200)

Earlier end-stopped lines and full rhymes are reinforced by her later interests in assonance and consonance, drawing together in the wide uncertainties of "hanging." Grief and death are given lingering and beguiling memorial in the appropriately titled **"Temps Perdu"** (201), where the verse is harder than Millay's, more clipped than Wylie's, yet holds the same sad lyricism that characterizes their work.

"The wittiest woman of our time suddenly took on stature," William Rose Benêt said in response to ***Not So Deep as a Well***;[50] although she remained, as always, neither too obscure nor too erudite, Parker moves in her poetry in ***Not So Deep as a Well*** from countereffective surprise to memorable solemnity and memorably subdued tones. In the nexus of love and death that moved from the cocky response to the unrequited role women play in society to the deeper and richer awareness of death as impersonal, blind to distinctions of sex and customs of romance, she admits another kind of worldliness, reaches new audiences. We are reminded of Auden's lines—"Rummaging into his living, the poet fetches / The images out that hurt and connect." She finally sensed that, too, behind her Iseults and her Martials, behind Horace's satires and Catullus's love for Lesbia were similarities that stoutly refused connection, steadfastly resisted closure.

Notes

1. Dorothy Parker, "The New Love," in *Enough Rope,* 31. Further references will be given in the text.
2. John Jay Chapman, "The Poets of the Future," *Vanity Fair,* July 1919, 45.
3. Kenneth Quinn, *The Catullan Revolution* (Melbourne: Melbourne University Press, 1959), 26.
4. Karl Pomeroy Harrington, *Catullus and His Influence* (Boston: Marshall Jones, 1923), 46, 51-53; hereafter cited in text.
5. E. A. Havelock, *The Lyric Genius of Catullus* (Oxford: Basil Blackwell 1939), 98-100.
6. W. B. McDaniel II, ed. *The Poems of Catullus* (New York: Oxford University Press, 1931); the poems were being circulated earlier than that. Cf. Catullus, numbers 57, 69, 72.
7. Compare "One Perfect Rose" (73) and "The Choice" (96) in *Enough Rope.*
8. George L. Watson, *A. E. Housman: A Divided Life* (London: Rupert Hart-Davis, 1957), 138, 203, 219.

Reviews of *A Shropshire Lad* (161) point to qualities common to Parker's poetry; Housman too collected and published, with his brother, parodies and light verse. See Laurence Housman, *A. E. H.: Some Poems, Some Letters and a Personal Memoir by His Brother* (London: Jonathan Cape 1937), 229-47.

9. Cyril Connelly in *The New Statesman* for May 23, 1936, quoted in Grant Richards, *Housman: 1897-1936* (New York: Oxford University Press, 1942), 365.
10. A. E. Housman, letter to Sydney Cockrell, January 15, 1932, quoted in Richards, 387; Watson, 213-14.
11. Miriam Gurko, *Restless Spirit* (New York: Crowell 1962), 13, 240; hereafter cited in text; Anne Cheney, *Millay in Greenwich Village* (University: University of Alabama Press, 1975), 114; Watson, 213-14.
12. Cf. James Gray, *Edna St. Vincent Millay,* University of Minnesota Pamphlets on American Writers 64 (Minneapolis: University of Minnesota Press, 1967), 45.
13. Edna St. Vincent Millay, "First Fig," "Second Fig," *A Few Figs from Thistles* (New York: Harper and Bros., 1922), 9.
14. Millay, "Thursday," *A Few Figs,* 12. Other appropriate poems in *Figs* are on 13-15, 19-21, 23-26, 33, 34, 36, 37. Her attitude toward woman's independence as well as her tight form and classical allusions are common to Parker's work; Louise Bogan has spoken of it as Millay's influence (Louise Bogan to author, August 4, 1964). *Figs* was Millay's third book; but see also "Sonnet II" in *Renascence* (1919) and, in *Second April* (1921), 27, 37-39, 47-48, 56-57. "Vincent's first appearance on the Vassar dramatic scene was when she recited, in Latin and nestling in her hands a dead song-sparrow borrowed from the Museum of Natural History, Catullus' 'Passer Mortuus Est'" (Gurko, 62-63); the poem is in *Second April,* 29. See also Millay's fourth book, *The Harp-Weaver and Other Poems* (1923), 10, 11, 17, 19, 22, 23, 26, 27, 56.
15. Cf. Gurko, 130. There are, in fact, too many connections to be studied here. Cf. Gray, 16: "Despite the many sidelong references to the physical relationship, the enclosing interest is that of human love as a total experience of the psyche involving, on the positive side, the endless warfare of two egos that cannot effect a complete surrender into oneness."
16. A good discussion of Wylie is in Thomas A. Gray, *Elinor Wylie* (New York: Twayne, 1969), chap. 2; for their friendship, see 18-19 above. Wylie's *Collected Poems* (1932) and *Last Poems* (1943) show more interest in the soft line and enjambment and a considerably more romantic cast. A comparison can be made with "Valentine" (*Collected Poems* [New York: Knopf, 1960], 41) and the contrast seen with "Restoration Love Song" (*Last Poems* [New York: A. A. Knopf, 1943] 90).
17. Warren H. Cudworth, preface, *Odes of Horace* ([New York: Alfred A. Knopf], 1917), xi.
18. Louis Untermeyer, *Including Horace* (New York: Harcourt, Brace, and Howe, 1919), xiii-xiv.
19. These characteristics were associated then with Horace; see Showerman, *Horace and His Influence* and Tenney Frank, *Catullus and Horace* (New York: Henry Holt, 1928). Like Parker, Horace read widely but not deeply; he was especially concerned with society and manners and found it difficult, therefore, not to write satire. Housman published a number of papers on Horace and felt his *Ode IV. vii* "the most beautiful poem in ancient literature" (Tom Burns Haber, *A. E. Housman* [New York: Twayne, 1967], 96); Housman's own brief corpus of one hundred and three odes in four books may be a direct imitation of Horace. See Norman Marlow, *A. E. Housman: Scholar and Poet* (Minneapolis: University of Minnesota Press, 1958), 60. Horace was popular with the Round Table, and Broun even named his Connecticut home Sabine Farm.
20. Eugene Field, quoted in Charles H. Dennis, *Eugene Field's Creative Years* (Garden City, N.Y.: Doubleday, Page, 1924), 167; hereafter cited in text.
21. Eugene Field, "To Chloë (II)," in *Echoes from the Sabine Farm,* in *Works of Eugene Field* (New York: Charles Scribner's, 1898), 6:380.
22. Seldes recalls (245) that Adams used to quarrel about the quantitative meter in Horace.
23. Don Marquis, quoted in Yates, *The American Humorist,* 253.
24. Franklin P. Adams, *In Other Words* (Garden City, N.Y.: Doubleday, Page, 1912), 21.
25. Franklin P. Adams, *Tobogganing on Parnassus* (Garden City, N.Y.: Doubleday, Page, 1916), 12.
26. Besides *In Other Words* (9-43) and *Tobogganing on Parnassus* (6-29, 142), these also include *By and Large* (1914, 3-23), *Weights and Measures* (1917, 75-95), and *Something Else Again* (1920, 3-25), all published in Garden City, N.Y. by Doubleday, Page.
27. Franklin P. Adams, *So There!* (New York: Doubleday, Page, 1923), 38.
28. Franklin P. Adams, *Something Else Again,* 65.
29. J. H. Westcott, *One Hundred and Twenty Epigrams of Martial* (Boston: 1897), 164, vi, x.
30. Paul Nixon, *A Roman Wit* (Boston: Houghton Mifflin, 1911), 51, 52.
31. Walter C. A. Ker, introduction to Martial's *Epigrams,* Loeb ed. (Cambridge, Mass.: Harvard University Press, 1930), 1:xiii. Nixon's collection is stuffed with close analogies to Parker's work; in the more recent translation by James Mitchie, *The Epigrams of Martial* (New York: Randon House, 1972), see 25, 27, 43, 47, 121, 141, 161, 189. *Martial, the Twelve Books of Epigrams,* trans. J. A. Pott and F. A. Wright (London: G. Routledge, 1925), is dedicated to Housman.
32. John Farrar, "This Stream of Poets," *The Bookman,* March 1927, 81.
33. *New York Times,* "Three Poets Who Openly Prefer Laughter to Tears," March 27, 1927, III, 6:1-3. Other comments: *The Nation,* "Books in Brief," May 25, 1927: "a thread of traditional light verse, a wire of Edna Millay's, a hair of Elinor Wylie's . . .

and a thick strand of her own" (589); Russell Crouse, *New York Evening Post* notes a "reverberating mordancy"; *Saturday Review,* "Its laughter has a biting edge, its humors are satisfyingly terse, its wistfulness begets beautiful phrases"; Herbert Gorman, *New York World,* "The book is rich with those nuggets of gold that may be removed from their setting without losing any of their sparkle"; *Providence Journal,* "[A]ll the clarity of the finer sort of irony with no brutality. . . . Humor without scorn; wisdom without smugness"; *Milwaukee Leader,* "with a most every-day vocabulary, Miss Parker creates verses which are sometimes exquisite, sometimes comical; sometimes whimsical; but verses which are pointed and swift and earthy and vivid. She has, in short, done a new thing." See *Book Review Digest* 23 (1927): 571-72.

34. Marie Luhrs, "Fashionable Poetry," *Poetry,* April 1927, 52-54.

35. Cf. Rabelais (*Works,* chap. 62): "You shall never want rope enough."

36. Epitaph for a Darling Lady" (*The World,* August 3, 1925, 11:1) originally read "shiny sands" (l. 1), "Pretty day on pretty day" (l. 5), "Gay and scented and alarming" (l. 10), and "very charming" (l. 12). The second stanza of the original version of "Story of Mrs. W—" (*The World,* June 13, 1925, 11:1) has been omitted. It read: "Here is no aching red of rose, / Nor are there cruel fragrances, / But each untroubling thing that blows; / The spinster flowers, that live to please."

37. Cf. *Satires,* I, x.

38. *New York Times,* "Six Rhymsters in Caps and Bells," July 1, 1928, Books, 10:3-4.

39. Garreta Busey, "A Porcupine's View," *New York Herald Tribune,* July 15, 1928, XII, 7:5. She continues: "We are willing to pursue Miss Parker to her extremest thicket in spite of, or rather for the sake of, her quick and cruel barbs."

40. The title refers to a gun fired at military bases such as those Parker visited when Eddie was stationed there; James R. Gaines notes on a visit to West Point this gun especially frightened Benchley, 5.

41. Henry Morton Robinson, "Some Scrannel Pipings," *The Bookman,* September 1928, 96.

42. Raymond Kresensky, "Humor and Tragedy," *Christian Century,* October 28, 1931, 1345.

43. Franklin P. Adams, "The Parkerian Formula," *New York Herald Tribune,* Books, June 14, 1931, 7.

44. "Books in Brief," in *The Nation* for September 23, 1931: "Such clever craftsmanship is reason enough for admiration, but there is more to be said: Mrs. Parker as a light verse writer is actually a better poet than many of our very serious composers in meter" (315).

45. Originally, the last stanza of "The Danger of Writing Defiant Verse" (15) read: "He's none to come and wrench a kiss / Nor pull me in his lap . . . / Oh, Lord! I see, on reading this, / He is an awful sap!" (*The World,* March 15, 1929, 15:1). Originally line 2 of "Purposely Ungrammatical Love Song" (49) read, "Is willing to speed my woes away" (*The World,* December 25, 1928, 15:1); other changes were made in "Prayer for a Prayer" (11), "Distance" (16), "Little Words" (24), "The Crusader" (30), "Song for the End of a Sequence" (36), and "From a Letter from Lesbia" (48).

46. *China Weekly Review* (Shanghai), August 22, 1931, 479:1.

47. The reference also has the glib countermanding self-deprecation associated with Round Table wit; Mercutio's whole line (about his death wound from Tybalt) is "[t]is not so deep as a well, nor so wide as a church door; but 'tis enough, 'twill serve."

48. Omitted from *Enough Rope:* "Verse Reporting Late Arrival at a Conclusion," "Day-Dreams," "Folk Tune," "Spring Song," "Finis," "Autobiography," "Biographies," and "Song in a Minor Key." Omitted from *Sunset Gun:* "For R. C. B.," "Swan Song," "Verses in the Night," and "Directions for Finding the Road"; "To Newcastle" was retitled "The Counsellor." Omitted from *Death and Taxes:* "In the Meadow."

49. Louis Kronenberger, "The Rueful, Frostbitten Laughter of Dorothy Parker," *New York Times,* December 13, 1936, VII, 28:3-4.

50. William Rose Benêt, "Deep, at That," *Saturday Review,* December 12, 1936, 5.

Gary Soto
1952-

American poet, memoirist, short story writer, essayist, and editor.

INTRODUCTION

Soto is recognized as one of America's best Chicano writers. Incorporating his working-class background and Hispanic culture into his poetry and prose, he addresses such social issues as discrimination, violence, and poverty. Commentators maintain that Soto's ability to transcend solely personal and local concerns has established him as a major contemporary author.

BIOGRAPHICAL INFORMATION

A third-generation Mexican American, Soto was born in Fresno, California, and raised in the San Joaquin Valley where, as a child, he worked as a farm laborer. Attending Fresno City College, Soto initially majored in geography before transferring to Fresno State, now California State University, in the early 1970s. Inspired by Donald Allen and Robert Creeley's anthology *The New American Poetry, 1945-60,* Soto began taking workshops with American poet Philip Levine, whose writings often depict the harsh realities of urban life. During this time he met several other noted authors, including Ernest Trejo and Christopher Buckley. Soto graduated magna cum laude in 1974 and earned a M.F.A. from the University of California at Irvine, publishing his first poetry collection, *The Elements of San Joaquin,* in 1977. He has since received numerous awards and fellowships: the Academy of Poets Prize in 1975, the United States Award from the International Poetry Forum in 1976, and the 1985 American Book Award from the Before Columbus Foundation for *Living up the Street: Narrative Recollections.* A finalist for the Lenore Marshall Poetry Award in 1979, he was also the first Chicano writer to be nominated for a Pulitzer Prize.

MAJOR WORKS

Much of Soto's poetry documents his upbringing and experiences as a Chicano in California's Central Valley. *The Elements of San Joaquin,* for example, focuses on Fresno in the 1950s, the agricultural community of San Joaquin, and the violence associated with barrio life. Furthermore, the harsh and desolate existence of farm life and the opportunities denied many Chicanos are recurring themes in his work. His short lines, detailed descriptions, and sentimental tone are characteristic of his poetry. In *The Tale of Sunlight* he utilizes a fictional narrator named Manuel Zaragosa to illustrate the vicissitudes of life, such as death, chance, and love. *Where Sparrows Work Hard,* Soto's next collection of poetry, again focuses on the landscape of poverty and despair. His 1990 collection, *Who Will Know Us?* explores the death of Soto's father and celebrates Americana, particularly the everyday rhythms of his native California.

CRITICAL RECEPTION

Central to Soto's poetry is the importance of memory and childhood recollections. Critics often praise his incorporation of autobiographical events into his work, creating vivid and evocative images. His emphasis on topical themes important to the Chicano community—such as the frustration over discrimination and limited opportunities and the appreciation of Hispanic history and culture—is also a focus of critical commentary. Despite his ethnic consciousness, Soto has been lauded for his ability to address private concerns as well as universal issues. Commentators attribute his ability to avoid strict polemicization of Chicano concerns to the humor often present in his writing.

PRINCIPAL WORKS

Poetry

The Elements of San Joaquin 1977
The Tale of Sunlight 1978
Where Sparrows Work Hard 1981
Black Hair 1985
A Fire in My Hands 1990
Who Will Know Us? 1990
Home Course in Religion 1992
Neighborhood Odes 1992
Canto Familiar/Familiar Song 1994
New & Selected Poems 1995
Junior College: Poems 1997

Other Major Works

Living Up the Street: Narrative Recollections (memoirs) 1985
Small Faces (essays) 1986
The Cat's Meow (juvenilia) 1987
Baseball in April (short stories) 1990
Lesser Evils: Ten Quartets (essays) 1990
Taking Sides (juvenilia) 1991
Pacific Crossing (juvenilia) 1992
The Skirt (juvenilia) 1992
Too Many Tamales (juvenilia) 1993
Jesse (novel) 1994
Boys at Work (juvenilia) 1995
Chato's Kitchen (juvenilia) 1995
Off and Running (juvenilia) 1996
Buried Onions (essays) 1997
Novio Boy (drama) 1997
Big Bushy Moustache (juvenilia) 1998
Petty Crimes (juvenilia) 1998
Nerdlandia (drama) 1999
Chato and the Party Animals (juvenilia) 2000

CRITICISM

Peter Cooley (essay date 1979)

SOURCE: "I Can Hear You Now," in *Parnassus,* Vol. 8, No. 1, Fall-Winter, 1979, pp. 297-311.

[*In the following excerpt, Cooley praises the distinctive nature of Soto's verse.*]

They keep coming back: the ring of a streetcar on Grand River Avenue, the flies that hummed by a light on the screen porch, the squeak of my grandfather's huge leather chair. Under the spell of Stanley Plumly and Gary Soto, these and other sensations of my own World War II childhood in Detroit have surfaced and re-surfaced in recent weeks. Set down here in discursive prose, they can't be heard by anyone except me. But when you read *Out-of-the-Body Travel* and ***The Elements of San Joaquin,*** your past, too, will swim up out of the lost worlds into which Stanley Plumly's and Gary Soto's memory books plunge us. . . .

Gary Soto's poetry carries less life-lived-through than Plumly's. ***The Elements of San Joaquin,*** winner of the United States Award of the International Poetry Forum, is a younger man's book; it isn't patronizing to say so. The poems lay down before us a period in the speaker's life which is only recently finished, the 1950's of his childhood. But Soto's first book is no nostalgic venture into "Happy Days." Soto is a Chicano, and probably the most important voice among the young Chicano poets because his poetry comes to us through poems, not propaganda in drag:

> Young Mexicans
> Went into ovens
> Squint-eyed
> And pulled out the pipes
> Smeared black
> With tar.
> Far from home,
> He had no place
> To go. Nights
> He slept in cars
> Or behind warehouses
> Shivering
> Like the machinery
> That went on and on.
>
> (from **"San Fernando Road"**)

A former student of Philip Levine, Soto shows stylistic affinities with what has been called "The Fresno School": short lines, a denuded vocabulary, an enumeration of small objects seen not as symbols but presences which build the speaker's situation. The single line is not of great interest in itself; in fact, it may sound "anti-poetic" to some ears. Soto has learned from Levine to enjamb a flat statement with another flat but raw one, exposing the soft underbelly—and the claws.

> Because there are avenues
> Of traffic lights, a phone book
> Of brothers and lawyers,
> Why should you think your purse
> Will not be tugged from your arm
> Or the screen door
> Will remain latched
> Against the man

Who hugs and kisses
His pillow
In the corridor of loneliness?

(from **"After Tonight"**)

At times the poems talk to us by shifting from one foot to the other, as if in a hurry to be off somewhere; side by side, too, the enjambed lines may seem melodramatic or mannered. Worst of all, strong statements may assume a kind of equivalence, as in the middle of **"The Level at Which the Sky Begins."**

Through the streets
Cars fleeced in a light frost
Smoke lifting above the houses
A boy porching
The newspapers that would unfold like a towel
Over coffee over an egg
Going brown over the radio saying
It's 6:05 this is the music of America
Where the young got up hungry
Roosters cleared
What was caught in their throats
All night

Soto does not want to shut us out in protesting his condition and that of his brothers—one understands his need for a quiet insistence—but when the texture of a poem is reduced to the objects of everyday life and the poem sets image after image before us, a tremendous pressure is put on the poet to find exactly the appropriate correlative line after line. Levine and Williams (from whom Levine probably learned it) take off their gloves when they feel the reader needs a right hook with the bare hands. Think of "These things astonish me beyond words" in **"Pastoral"** or, in Levine, "Today I want to ask her / what she hoped to find / last night, I want to say, / I'm with you in this life" (**"The Sky Falling"**).

In most poems, though, Soto is convincing in giving us a situation which is some part of his lost world of San Joaquin. The speaker approaches his reconstruction with a genuine tenderness, the short lines suggesting tentative, halting evocations:

That was the '50s
And Grandma in her '50s,
A face streaked
From cutting grapes
And boxing plums.
I remember her insides
Were washed of tapeworm,
Her arms swelled into knobs
Of small growths—
Her second son
Dropped from a ladder
And was dust.
And yet I do not know
The sorrows
That sent her praying
In the dark of a closet . . .

(from **"History"**)

Though both urban and rural, there is no neat city / country topology at work in Soto's San Joaquin. The earth, in fact, is related in the title sequence to the enslavement of the speaker as a worker in the fields. This sequence implants us in the minute particulars of the worker's situation by drawing us down to the insects and plants which crawl and scratch the lines. It is a protest poem that succeeds by its gentle but willed negations, offering no salutary measures but merely insisting on our sympathy.

The wind strokes
The skulls and spines of cattle
To white dust, to nothing,
Covers the spiked tracks of beetles,
Of tumbleweed, of sparrows
That pecked the ground for insects.

(from **"Winds"**)

When autumn s flatten sycamore
leaves,
The tiny volcanos of dirt
Ants raised around their holes,
I should be out of work.

(from **"Rain")**

Gary Snyder's sheer pleasure in physical work which removes him from the life of industrial society seems tepid middle class revolt after reading Soto.

Perhaps because the poems recreate a lost world without showing how the speaker leaves it (except to go "beyond the new Freeway, searching"), Soto occasionally has difficulty ending poems. Sometimes the final words are too obvious or demand more than the situation itself:

Left of the neon glowing *Eat,*
Right of the traffic returning home,
This cold slowly deepens
The old whose bones ring with the coming weather,
The stunned face that could be your father's—
Deepens the gray space between each word
That reaches to say you are alone.

(from **"County Ward"**)

You expect your daughter
To be at the door any moment
And your husband to arrive
With the night
That is suddenly all around . . .
But remember this:
Because blood revolves from one lung to the next,
Why think it will
After tonight?

(from **"After Tonight"**)

For Plumly the past was resurrected so that he could assume his father's body and spirit; for Soto the death of the father is important but finally only one of many losses. **"Spirit"** is one of his most successful poems because the dead father is at a double remove and the catalogued objects are not stage props of the past but properties the speaker ascribes to his vision of the father's ghost:

We know you came back father
And in the doorway

Leading to your bedroom
Wanted to fog
The family's photo
With the breath
You did not have
And years later
When your wife slept
With another
You waited
At their feet
Until they turned
From one another
Eyes closed
And sighing
Leaving them
A cupboard opened
The garage light
On and burning silent
As your jealousy . . .

The more one reads ***The Elements of San Joaquin*** the sadder seems Soto's sense of absolute loss, of a world all but erased except for his poems' memorializing. He has avoided the sentimental and the strident, and his voice possesses the kind of unaffected honesty we experience only in conversations with friends.

As if himself feeling the reservations voiced above about ***The Elements of San Joaquin,*** Soto's new book attempts to answer them. Two-thirds of the poems focus on two characters, who live in separate worlds and never meet each other. Molina, the character of Part One, is a sort of Doppelgänger for the Soto-I speaker; Manuel Zaragoza, who owns the last third of the book, is a cantina owner and sad clown. The middle third of ***The Tale of Sunlight*** contains poems which generally, through third- or second-person narration, avoid the stance of the naked-I speaker. Soto's abiding theme is still loss, but his new points of view open the lyric enclosure of his earlier poems to an imaginative expansiveness in which irony can sometimes sort out the images he hurries through his fingers.

The flat warp of the earlier poems' continuous enjambments is woven richer now with more cross-stitched rhyme. The rush of enjambments still comes at us, however; one would like to slow the loom when encountering a poem like this:

The moon going orange
Through a cloud
That refuses to move,
Molina in the yard
Talking to a chicken
That blinks with eyes
Blown deep
As targets. It circles
Its droppings
And says nothing
Of the wind that passes
Through a door
Nailed shut
By its own poverty;
Or of the galaxy
Of lint tilting on its axis,
Those unmapped stars
He counted twice
And named for his country.

(from **"The Point"**)

Such enjambing reduces all the lines to the same texture; one is tempted, as in most prose, to read for an extractable idea. The first three lines are an image cluster in their own right, but we scarcely have time to remember the color of the moon before we're hurried on. As the stanza proceeds, Soto leans twice again on a phrase introduced by the pronoun "that"; further, the metaphorical appositions in "galaxy / Of lint tilting on its axis, / Those unmapped stars / He counted twice / And named for his country" seem far too complicated for the simple character.

Sometimes the cross-stitching is too tight:

When fog
Stands weed-high
And sky
Is the color
Of old bed sheets,
Molina and I . . .

(from **"The Little Ones"**)

The "high"-"sky"-"I" rhymes in the right margin along with the "when"-"stands"-"and" of the left shut down the language, making it difficult to believe amorphous objects are being compared to the vertical dimension of weeds or the potentially dynamic "old bed sheets."

Soto's earlier difficulty in ending poems has been solved, however, in poem after poem by just the right choice of images. The small fabliaux of many of his character poems are complete in themselves in ***The Tale of Sunlight*** and furnish a pleasant contrast to the naked-I poems Soto continues to write. Here is how Manuel Zaragoza stays alive:

One morning
He unearthed a salamander
Cut from bone, collared
With small holes
Where jewels shone.
He sold it
To a skinny gringo,
And in parting
With it, wept
And muttered like
A harelipped prophet—
Bird in the stupid tree,
Wink at me . . .
God above the tree,
Call me Manuel the genius—
And simply walked away.

(from **"A Few Coins"**)

Soto's tone is now so much his own and his control of it so strong in poems such as **"The Shepherd," "The Cellar,"** or the title poem that after reading the book I can hear my own Soto poems writing themselves in my head. To put it otherwise: it would be easy to create parodies of Soto's voice. And to say this is to show how much his voice belongs to him, not to any "school" at all.

Carlos Zamora (essay date 1982)

SOURCE: A review of *Where Sparrows Work So Hard* by Gary Soto, in *ABR,* Vol. 4, No. 5, July-August, 1982, p. 11.

[*In the following essay, Zamora offers a positive review of* Where Sparrows Work So Hard.]

In ***Where Sparrows Work Hard,*** the poet takes the reader on a journey of exploration through the subterranean, labyrinthine, infernal world of the human soul, where everything gives evidence of a cosmic devastation. It is not by chance that in the external world which is at once the setting of the poems and the symbolic analogue of that hell, one finds over and over again the images of ruination and perdition: the gray dusks and dark nights that succeed upon one another; the alleys and empty lots and junkyards filled with debris; the telltale dust and ash; the fallen leaves and rolling tumbleweeds; the discarded newspapers undone by the omnipresent wind, which sweeps their pages along chaotically in different directions; the flies, and sometimes the ants, which are everywhere, suggestive of vultures waiting to take possession of the carcasses of things and of people felled by violence, or disease, or old age, or death, or despair: destroyed in time and by time.

This is a profoundly elegiac poetry, in which everything appears condemned to pass away without possibility of ever achieving fruition. The fated abortion of man's being appears illustrated in the repeated depictions of his finiteness: his smallness and fragility vis-a-vis the forces of violence which pervade an essentially hostile universe; his temporal limitation, sentenced as he is to old age and death; his intellectual deficiency, in light of his inability to understand the causes of his very great misfortune; his sheer impotency to convert the ought-to-be into reality.

Given this negation of what remains only a dreamed-of fullness of being, it is not surprising that in the poems man appears typically trivialized, thingfied, reduced to the level of so many other objects of equal unimportance which clutter the world. Reified in this way, he is also shown as abandoned by god and his fellow man, as unnoticed when he walks by others, as unheard when he calls out, as faceless and nameless: a solitary wanderer amid the desolate landscape of earth.

Trapped in this terrifying world and unable to change it, man in the poems characteristically adopts an evasive behavior which takes many different forms: habitual drinking of alcohol and watching of television; reverie; fantasy; dreams; remembrances of the past, including of childhood; the longing for a reversion to still more ultimate, primeval origins: the sea; the journey; and even, in one case, suicide. In exceptional instances there does appear a flash of revolt, a defiant affirmation of the self. But the *non serviam* theme is not at all common in the poems. Neither is the stoicism which only a few characters display as a kind of irrepressible determination to go on, to endure. What one sees instead is what has been indicated: man as fugitive from a hellish world which he comes to perceive as unbearable and which he is convinced he cannot transform or "save." It is that ravaged and doomed globe that is so well described in the important poem **"Chuy"**:

Wherever his flashlight
Poked at night,
In the gutter
Or sloped weeds
Of his yard,
Chuy noted
Things that made
Him stroke his chin
And ask why

. . . . .

He bottled
A leaf, a shaving
Of bark, linked
Worms, and a trumpet
Of snail; he
Snipped a thread
From his lapel
And a lock of hair—
Gifts he buried
In a bottle
Scribbled with his name
So when the sun
Is a monocle
Pocked gray
And earth is lost
To shadow, an explorer
Far from the stars
Would know [that] where he steps
Stepped Chuy, stooping
Among the ruins.

Undoubtedly some readers will find themselves objecting to this fatalistic conception of life which the poems articulate and which, incidentally, sets them off so sharply from the affirmations of early Chicano poetry, which was more protestant rather than resignationist (e.g., Rodolfo "Corky" Gonzales, Alurista, Abelardo). The notion that man is not only imperfect but immutably so; the denial, therefore, of his historicity, and the consequent affirmation of his meaninglessness or absurdity; the vanity, accordingly, of human striving; in a word, the irrationalist view of the world which is apparent here, will be inadmissible to those who instead see man and society as imperfect but alterable, because they are historical, open and not closed, progressional, meaningful, rational. Such readers could not deny that the poems do depict more than well enough the dehumanization of man in our time. For in their own way these are, without question, songs or dirges about oppression and against oppression, which the poet illuminates and dramatizes through a sometimes brilliant imagery and symbolism (in this insightful and strikingly vivid portraiture of the oppressed, if not of the oppressor, lies the very great value of the poems). But the suggestion contained in the volume that the degradation of man has root causes which are metaphysical rather than social, the intimation that what is described is an eternal condition of man and not a transitory situation which is changeable and surmontable, present problems to which, it goes without saying, each reader will have to address himself, and which in any case are too complex to deal with in a brief review. Among other things, these problems have to do with the question of whether an ideological function can legitimately be claimed for art; whether art is a kind of knowledge; whether content supersedes form in importance; in short, whether art has an essentially contingent or autonomous character.

However different readers decide these questions, I doubt that any will come away from this collection without feeling that they have been in the presence of an extraordinary poetic talent whose evolution continues to be marked by a ceaseless experimentation with poetic diction as the primary tool with which to probe more and more deeply into the flesh and bones concreteness of fallen man.

Patricia de la Fuentes (essay date 1983)

SOURCE: "Ambiguity in the Poetry of Gary Soto," in *Revista Chicano-Riqueña,* Vol. XI, No. 2, Summer, 1983, pp. 34-9.

[*In the following essay, de la Fuentes explores Soto's use of ambiguity as a poetic device.*]

Although Aristotle was "inclined to consider all ambiguity as a perversion or failing of language instead of its natural and valuable quality,"[1] by the Seventeenth Century, the Spanish theorist and critic Baltasar Gracián firmly established, in his famous treatise "Agudeza y Arte del Ingenio,"[2] the fundamental importance of ambiguity as a poetic device. More recently, the English critic William Empson further clarified the status of this device by stating that "an ambiguity . . . is not satisfying in itself, nor is it, considered as a device on its own, a thing to be attempted; it must in each case arise from, and be justified by, the peculiar requirements of the situation."[3] In spite of Aristotelean disapproval, however, ambiguity not only became accepted as "a natural, subtle, and effective instrument for poetry and dramatic purposes"[4] in Greek literature, but is still considered a valuable rhetorical technique by modern writers.

If we understand Empson correctly, ambiguity should be something more than rhetorical ornamentation and a convenient vehicle for creative exuberance. Besides these superficial qualities, which also have their place in the creative process, ambiguity should be intrinsically functional in the sense of contributing to the internal tension of a poem; i.e., it should form part of the organic structure of the work and create, through a series of ironies, subtle contradictions and dislocations, multiple ramifications and levels of meaning, which give technical brilliance and, above all, intellectual and emotional significance to the poem.

Ambiguity acquires validity, Empson seems to suggest, in direct proportion to its function of sustaining the subtlety, delicacy and compression of poetic thought and adding suggestive, profound and complex nuances to the narrative structure of the poem. In effect, the value of ambiguity as a poetic device may be measured in terms of its organic function, manifest in unexpected or ironic repercussions, resonances or ramifications of language which, by their very dissonance, add surprising perspectives to the poetic design.

On the other hand, if such dissonant perspectives introduced through an ambiguity should distort too violently or frivolously the organic unity of the poem, such a device would lose its valid function and become an obstacle to rather than a vehicle for poetic expression. By posing a serious threat to the unity of the poem, a non-organic ambiguity not only clouds the meaning but also reveals a lack of artistic maturity.

It would seem, therefore, that the effective use of ambiguity as a poetic device requires a highly developed sensitivity to linguistic subtleties; and it is not surprising that in Chicano literature, in its newly acquired status as a legitimate branch of American Letters, no great number of poets have yet emerged as masters of the art of poetic ambiguity. Among those who have achieved this distinction, however, the Californian poet Gary Soto deserves special consideration for his exceptionally high level of linguistic sophistication.

One of the principal charactistics of Soto's poetry is the apocalyptic vision it reflects of the universe. Recurring images of loss, desintegration, decadence, demolition, solitude, terror and death create a desolate landscape in which the voice of the narrator is that of a passive, impotent observer, helplessly caught up in the inexorable destruction of human ties. Within this seemingly hopeless, profoundly grey world of Soto's poems, however, occasional affirmative images introduce muted, contrapuntual notes of something akin to hope.

In his first collection, ***The Elements of San Joaquín***,[5] for example, the presence of dust, both from the fields and from the mortal remains of the men who work them, and the action of the wind that sweeps everything before it and reduces all things to dust, are two of the most persistent images. Both dust and wind are elements of an environment that is both hostile and indifferent to human solitude and suffering. Soto often juxtaposes these two images in the same poem to suggest apocalyptic forces:

> The wind strokes
> The skulls and spines of cattle
> To white dust, to nothing.

(**"Wind,"** 16)

At first glance, this image appears to be totally negative since it depicts the slow, irreversible desintegration of the cattle skulls, and by extension those of mankind as well, into dust and then into nothingness. Faced with the terrifying indifference of the wind, which destroys everything—mountains, cattle, or the footprints of beetles, each individual existence becomes inconsequential, ephemeral, all traces of its presence obliterated as if it had never been. Upon closer examination, however, we discover an image that functions on multiple levels in this passage, one which is simultaneously harmonious and discordant. On one hand, the image "strokes" accentuates the terror and aggression implicit in the action of the wind because it denotes hitting or striking a blow which wounds or destroys, an attack; the image conjures up visions of axes, swords, fists and whips, all instruments of aggression or death. On the other hand, "strokes" also carries a denotation which is at odds with the implacable violence of the wind since it represents the diametrically opposite action of caressing, flattering, soothing. On another level, "strokes" also means the sound of a bell or clock ringing the hour, an image which inevitably recalls the passing of time, an action which brings with it the natural desintegration and wearing away of things, a universal law to which man has yet to discover an alternative.

It is clear, therefore, that the implicit ambiguities of the word "strokes" add psychological and emotional dimensions to an image that would be notably diminished had the poet chosen a word with less resonances and dissonances like "reduces" or "pulverizes." But the question still remains as to whether the inclusion of this ambiguity, which undoubtedly adds complex nuances to the narrative structure of the poem, is justified by what Empson calls "the peculiar requirements of the situation." Can we affirm, for example, that this device transcends its metaphorical function within the passage to contribute more profoundly to the organic structure by acquiring a more pervasive significance in relation to the rest of the poem? If we listen carefully, we hear the resonances of this stroking caress which the poet subtly introduces in the process of physical desintegration, and which is none other than the process of death itself, echoing in the following stanzas where they modify the image of the wind as it exercises its annihilative action on the narrator:

> Evenings, when I am in the yard weeding,
> The wind picks up the breath of my armpits
> Like dust . . .

Here, in a less obvious manner, the wind already initiates its action of reducing man to the white dust of his own bones, of reintegrating him into the elements, in a cycle which returns the human body to its beginnings in the dust, an image clearly infused with biblical echoes.

Within this apocaliptic framework, however, the same affirmative note from the previous stanza is clearly heard. In this case, what the wind carries off is the "breath" of the narrator's armpits, that is to say the sweat of a man who works his yard. On a negative level, this exhalation of sweat certainly suggests the physical desintegration of the body, a loss of vital essences which the narrator can never recuperate, a prefiguration of death, in other words. Simultaneously, on a second, affirmative level, the same action is an irrefutable sign of life, since by sweating the narrator reaffirms his existence. On the metaphorical level, this ambiguity creates a tension between life and death since the exhalation of sweat experienced by the narrator is a prefiguration of the exhalation of the spirit in the moment of death which can lead either to the defeat of total annihilation, or to the triumphant beginning of a new life. Another alternative, as the poem suggests, is an harmonic resolution between these two seemingly contradictory states.

This fundamental ambiguity of the poem, which begins as a poetic device in the style of Gracián's "agudeza simple" or simple conceit, introduced by the poet to create uncertainty regarding the precise function of the destructive wind, acquires increasingly significant dimensions and resonances as it is gradually revealed as a unifying force within the poem. By reducing all the creation to dust: the mountains, reduced grain by grain to loose earth; the cattle, whose bones become white dust; the insects, birds and plants, whose tracks are obliterated by its action, and finally man, whose exhalations are dissipated in the air, the wind acquires the personification of an anti-generative, anti-mythic force. Parallel to this negative vision, however, a regenerative force coexists within the poem which mitigates the negative indifference of the wind. Without being diverted from its destructive course, the wind pushes beyond physical desintegration, beyond chaos, beyond nothingness, to initiate a new creative cycle of existence, within which, ironically, the same demolishing wind becomes a generative force:

> The wind picks up the breath of my armpits
> Like dust, swirls it
> Miles away
> And drops it
> On the ear of a rabid dog,
> And I take on another life.
>
> (**"Wind,"** 16)

At this point it becomes evident that the ambiguity between the contradictory functions of the wind is far more profound than a simple rhetorical conceit and that, on the contrary, it constitutes the axis upon which the poem itself hinges since it establishes a dramatic tension between the disintegrative and regenerative forces operant within the poem.

The importance of this device of ambiguity in Soto's poetry becomes apparent in the consistency with which it is used to create precisely this impression of dramatic tension within the apocalyptic framework so characteristic of his artistic expression. Repeatedly one encounters similar images of desintegration and death mitigated by an ironically positive twist:

The pores of my throat and elbows
Have taken in a seed of dirt of their own.

(**"Field,"** *ESJ,* 15)

. . . Angela beaten and naked in the vineyard
Her white legs glowing.

(**"Telephoning God,"** *ESJ,* **10)**

And a sewer line tied off
Like an umbilical cord

(**"Braly Street,"** *ESJ,* **56)**

Roots cradling the skull's smile

(**"Blanco,"** *TS,* 14)

A harmonica grinning with rust

(**"Song for the Pockets,"** *TS,* 10)

Although these rhetorical ambiguities reflect the ironic vision so characteristic of this poet, Soto achieves his highest artistic brilliance and aesthetic subtlety in those poems, of which **"Wind"** is an excellent example, in which ambiguity becomes an expansive force not only by multiplying metaphorical and linguistic levels of meaning, but also by dilating the philosophical and dramatic dimensions of the fundamental theme of human existence. Such existence is revealed in Soto's poetry as a long and painful *via crucis,* a spiritual pilgrimage into a past peopled by spectres of privation, loneliness and death. Nevertheless, subtly but unequivocally, Soto manages to counterbalance this inhospitable existence by incorporating ambiguities that not only reduce the power of death to subjugate man definitively, but also substantially reduce the terror and finality of annihilation by implying a capacity in man to survive and overcome the limitations of his destiny.

This creative ability to dislocate, divert, counteract or even invert the significance of one poetic level with that of another, less obvious, though perhaps more representative of the philosophical vision implicit in the poem, is especially apparent in poems which examine different facets of death, such as **"The Starlings"** (*TS,* 34), **"The Wound"** (*TS,* 16), **"The Morning They Shot Tony Lopez"** (*ESJ,* 11), and **"Avocado Lake"** (*ESJ,* 30). This latter poem is a notable example of the artistic control Soto exercises over the different levels of a poem through judicious use of ambiguity.

It is interesting to note that although the Christian backdrop is not conspicuously negated in Soto's poetry, it does not occupy a prominent place in his philosophical vision. Therefore, when the poet speaks of death, he usually does so in worldly, physical terms related to individual existences that have been truncated or worn down by indifferent forces. His narrative control and lack of sentimentality in treating this subject confer on this narrator a rather cold, omniscient perspective. The emotional involvement of the poet himself, which gives Soto's poems their human depth and warmth, finds expression only indirectly on the metaphorical level in the ambiguities the poet introduces to offset the cold objectivity of the narrator.

In **"Avocado Lake,"** for example, this counterbalance between the narrative or literal and the metaphorical levels creates a significant dramatic tension between the action of death, that irreversible fact of a man drowned in the lake, and the reaction of the narrator, who recreates the life of the dead friend and conceptualizes his death from another perspective. On the narrative level, death undoubtedly has the upper hand, since the body floats under the water before being removed and subjected to the useless attempts at artificial revival.

On the metaphorical level, however, the scene is subtly slanted towards another reality where the power of death is subverted. Here the rigidity of the dead friend is softened, his "body moves under the dark lake," his hands "Are those of a child reaching for his mother." The very power of death is diminished by images of revival and reawakening: "The grey film peeled like tape from the eyes," and "The curled finger rubbed and kissed." The following day, at dawn, life is unequivocally reaffirmed in the presence of a young girl who plays by the same shore, skimming "pebbles across the lake, / Over what remains of him—"

The significance of this passage is that death has not been able to take everything; something of the man has remained to reintegrate itself into the elements, to initiate another cycle of existence in the physical world: "His phlegm drifts beneath the surface, / As his life did." This is another version of the dust swirled away by the wind and dropped "On the ear of a rabid dog . . . to take on another life" (*ESJ,* 16). In this latter example, however, the combination of dry wind and human heat translates into the choleric humour of the mad dog. In the case of the drowned man, his introduction into the cold humidity of the lake is no less than an extension of his own phlegmatic, sluggish, existence. Rudderless and drifting with the currents during his lifetime, the drowned man finds within the lake an existence entirely compatible with his vital essences. By suggesting this conclusion, the narrator achieves, through an astute handling of dialectic ambiguity, a reconciliation with the reality of death without sacrificing the philosophical ideal of a continued or regenerated existence.

Undoubtedly, such linguistic and metaphorical subtleties do not occur fortuitously but only as the deliberate result of a series of creative efforts and impulses. Without going into the genesis of the creative process, we can nevertheless conclude that when a poet like Gary Soto exhibits such clear control over the organic nuances of a central ambiguity in his work, he demonstrates an advanced degree of creative development and a deliberate, intelligent attempt to refine the quality of his art.

Notes

This paper was read, in a slightly different version, at the Louisiana Conference on Hispanic Languages and Literatures in Baton Rouge, February 18-20, 1982.

1. William K. Wimsatt, Jr., Cleanth Brooks, *Literary Criticism: A Short History.* (New York: Vintage Books, 1957), p. 637, note 9.

2. Baltasar Gracián, *Obras Completas* (Madrid: Aguilar, 1967), p. 231.

3. William Empson, *Seven Types of Ambiguity* (New York: New Directions, 1947), p. 235.

4. W. B. Stanford, *Ambiguity in Greek Literature* (Oxford, 1939), p. 1.

5. Gary Soto, *The Elements of San Joaquín* (Pittsburgh: University of Pittsburgh, 1977). Other collections are *The Tale of Sunlight*(University of Pittsburgh, 1978), *Father is a Pillow Tied to a Broom* (Slow Loris Press, 1980), *Como arbustos de niebla* (Mexico: Editorial Latitudes, 1980), and *Where Sparrows Work Hard* (University of Pittsburgh, 1981). These collections are abbreviated in the text as *ESJ* y *TS*.

Patricia de la Fuentes (essay date 1987)

SOURCE: "Entropy in the Poetry of Gary Soto: The Dialectics of Violence," in *Revista de Temas Hispánicos,* Vol. 5, No. 1, Autumn, 1987, pp. 111-20.

[*In the following essay, de la Fuentes examines Soto's focus on entropy and deterioration in his poetry.*]

In discussing the relationship between entropy and art, Rudolf Arnheim (1971) points out that "when the Second Law of Thermodynamics began to enter the public consciousness a century or so ago, it suggested an apocalyptic vision of the course of events on earth" by stating "that the entropy of the world strives towards a maximum, which amounted to saying that the energy of the universe, although constant in amount, was subject to more and more dissipation and degradation" (p. 9). Arnheim qualifies this definition, however, by adding that "the popular use of the notion of entropy has changed. If during the last century it served to diagnose, explain, and deplore the degradation of culture, it now provides a positive rationale for 'minimal' art and the pleasures of chaos" (pp. 11-12). If Arnheim's "positive rationale" may be taken to mean a logical and therefore organized body of principles, his definition of the entropy theory as, among other things, "a first attempt to deal with global form" (p. 21), provides a critical basis from which to explore the philosophical framework, structural dynamics, and thematic configurations in all forms of art. Hence the title of this essay, which examines the presence of entropy in the poetry of the Californian poet Gary Soto and in particular its metaphorical function as a reflection of the structural theme.[1]

Arnheim conceives of this structural theme dynamically, as "a pattern of forces" rather than "an arrangement of static shapes" (p. 33). Such forces include the anabolic, creative force, and the catabolic erosion which leads to the eventual destruction of all organized shape (p. 48). From a philosophical standpoint, Soto's choice of images in developing his seemingly antagonistic themes of corrosive social pressures and a subtle yet persistent search for a viable form of individual, social and universal order is indicative of a world view in which catabolic erosion predominates.

The catabolic destruction of shape, Arnheim speculates, is one of the two fundamentally different kinds of processes which result in the increase of entropy. The other is the principle of tension reduction or of decreasing potential energy. Arnheim describes the catabolic effect as "rather a broad, catch-all category, comprising all sorts of agents and events that act in an unpredictable, disorderly fashion and have in common the fact that they all grind things to pieces" (p. 28). Catabolism, he suggests, occurs because "we live in a sufficiently disorderly world, in which innumerable patterns of forces constantly interfere with each other" (p. 28).

If we accept Arnheim's premise that a work of art, among other things, "is intended as a portrayal of a significant type of order existing elsewhere," then it seems reasonable to say that the structural theme of, in this case, a poem "derives its value—even much of its value as a stimulant—from the human condition whose particular form of order it makes visible or audible" (p. 55). In the poetry of Gary Soto this revelation of order is articulated through images of violence, desolation, and disintegration; i.e. through the catabolic effect.

For the purpose of this discussion, Soto's poems may be divided into two principal groups, those which portray a gradual, often painful process of disintegrating structure involving a deep personal sense of disorientation, loss and desolation, and those which depict a more violent approach to changing form through suddenly unleashed disaster or the threat of it, in particular that caused by the death of the father. Although by no means absolute, these general categories will allow the identification of a consistent philosophy in a series of poems in ***The Elements of San Joaquín,*** Soto's first collection, which deal essentially with the same theme: the search for form and significance in a world which is perceived as disintegrating, degenerating and generally in the throes of catabolic forces.

Since Soto's poetic vision reveals an environment of physical and spiritual decay, it is appropriate that his recurring images are of dust, dirt, and the corrosive wind which grinds down mountains and men with equal indifference, and erodes the emotional resources that make life both bearable and meaningful. One of the most impressive examples of gradual human disintegration occurs in **"County Ward,"** a cheerless half-way house for those who are in the final stages of mental and physical dissipation. Here the catabolic force intrudes as a concrete, creeping presence of pain and cold into the world of those who have come to die in the County Ward. A distinctly threatening air accompanies its progress: "It begins in a corridor . . . It continues . . . It comes to speak in the drugged voice / That ate its tongue" (Soto, p. 6). Catabolism, the breaking down of tissue material, in this case human tissue, into simpler and more stable substances, is evident in the adverse effects of pain and cold:

There is a pain that gets up and moves, like the night attendant,
Pointing to the cough
That rises like dust and is dust
A month later . . .

(**"County Ward"** p. 6)

And towards the end of the poem, the effects of this process are treated more explicitly as inmates of the Ward approach a state of entropy or equilibrium in death:

This cold slowly deepens
The old whose bones ring with the coming weather,

. . . . .

The stunned face that could be your father's—
Deepens the gray space between each word
That reaches to say you are alone.

It is not only the old who are relentlessly ground down by hostile forces. In **"San Fernando Road,"** a young factory worker, whose energy is drained faster than he can renew it, becomes another casualty in a mechanized system when he ceased to dream of drugs and sex and thinks instead of "his body, / His weakening body, / And dawn only hours away" (p. 3).

This gradual erosion of energy is most consistently revealed on the intimate, individual level, where the very essence of the human condition is undergoing a pervasive disintegration. The wind often appears as the principal agent in this process, and dust as the concrete image of the state of equilibrium or entropy towards which the catabolic tendency aspires:

The wind sprays pale dirt into my mouth
The small, almost invisible scars
On my hands.

. . . . .

The pores in my throat and elbows
Have taken in a seed of dirt of their own.

. . . . .

A fine silt, washed by sweat,
Has settled into the lines
On my wrists and palms.

. . . . .

Already I am becoming the valley
A soil that sprouts nothing
For any of us.

(**"Field,"** p. 15)

The gradual encroachment of dirt into the mouth and pores of the field worker, while certainly suggestive of death, may also be viewed in terms of the entropy theory as the decomposition of a complex system into a simpler form. The molecular structure of the man's body appears to be breaking down, through loss of energy, into a form which is physically and symbolically closer to his own perception of himself when he says: "Already I am becoming the valley." Thus, a man who sees his existence as unproductive, assumes the metaphorically barren identity of the "soil that sprouts nothing," a physical state which reflects his inner disorientation and sense of futility. This movement towards entropy expresses the thematic structure of the poem; it gives dramatic form and substance to the narrator's barely articulated sense of worthlessness.

This action of the wind is a central catabolic image in Soto's poetic vision and embodies the essential indifference of the environment, one of Arnheim's "innumerable patterns of forces which constantly interfere with each other." Pitted against this cosmic force, Soto's narrator reveals a critical lack of energy, a physical lassitude which mirrors a pervasive spiritual weariness. His resistance has been whittled down to a minimum: he bows before the pressures of a harsh reality:

The wind pressing us close to the ground

(**"Daybreak,"** p. 22)).

The wind crossed my face, moving the dust
And a portion of my voice a step closer to a new year

(**"Harvest,"** p. 25).

Dirt lifted in the air
Entering my nostrils
And eyes
The yellow under my fingernails ("Hoeing," p. 24).
The wind picks up the breath of my armpits
Like dust

(**"Wind,"** p. 16).

Other elements provide catabolic images of grinding down, peeling or flaking away, collapsing, falling, decaying, unraveling, drowning, and graying in Soto's poems and contribute to the overall impression of a world that is winding down. The narrator at one point somberly anticipates the coming of rain in autumn, a time of unemployment, when his

. . . two good slacks
Will smother under a growth of lint
And smell of old dust
That rises
When the closet door opens and closes

(**"Rain,"** p. 20).

This scene of gradual decay, of slow, seemingly inevitable disintegration of man and his environment is echoed repeatedly. The fog, another catabolic force which appears as "a mouth nibbling everything to its origins" (**"Fog,"** p. 21), contributes to the narrator's deterioration and eventual disappearance:

Graying my hair that falls
And goes unfound, my fingerprints
Slowly growing a fur of dust

. . . . .

One hundred years from now
There should be no reason to believe
I lived.

(**"Fog,"** p. 21).

The enervating effects of this general increase in entropy are also evident in the environment of Soto's narrator. His is a world of "smashed bus window(s)" (**"Field Poem"**, p. 23), where "nothing will heal / Under the rain's broken fingers" (**"Daybreak,"** p. 22). Here the unpicked figs become "wrinkled and flattened / Like the elbows / of an old woman" (**"Summer,"** p. 26), while "the fog squatted in the vineyard / Like a stray dog" (**"Piedra,"** p. 28). It is a disintegrating world of "smashed bottles flaking back to sand" (**"Piedra,"** p. 28), where an abandoned hotel hides "A jacket forever without a shadow / And cold as the darkness it lies in" (**"Street,"** p. 32). People here "no longer / Bothered to shrug off / The flies" (**"Town,"** p. 33), and "A cane refused / The weight of the hand that carved it" (**"The Level at Which the Sky Began,"** p. 34).

The degree of physical and spiritual deterioration in the narrator's world may be judged by a comparison with the past where the energy level was noticeably higher. The vitality in the narrator's past is particularly evident in the figure of the grandmother. It is she who kept things moving in a constructive way; she "lit the stove . . . sliced papas / Pounded chiles . . . hosed down / The walk her sons paved," and later "Unearthed her / Secret cigar box / Of bright coins . . . counted them . . . And buried them elsewhere" (**"History,"** p. 40). She is putting up a fight to survive, is aggressively protective of her family and will even shoplift food from the market to feed them. Eventually, she, too, will succumb to the catabolic effect:

. . . . her insides
. . . washed of tapeworm,
Her arms swelled into knobs
Of small growths—
Her second son
Dropped from a ladder
And was dust.

(**"History,"** p. 41).

This sudden death of the father signals both an emotional crisis for the narrator and the growing intrusion of destructive forces into his life. The disintegration of home and family seem to date from this event:

. . . . the moment our father slipped
From the ladder . . .
. . . . It was the moment
I came down from the tree
And into our home
Where a leash of ants
Swarmed for the rice the cupboard the stove
Carrying off what there was to carry.

(**"The Evening of Ants,"** pp. 48-89)

Years later, the physical destruction of the family home is still associated with the father's death:

It's 16 years
Since our house
Was bulldozed and my father
Stunned into a coma . . .

(**"Braly Street,"** p. 54)

and the loss of energy is apparent in the images of encroaching catabolic forces that have reduced the past to rubble:

. . . the long caravan
Of my uncle's footprints
Has been paved
With dirt. Where my father
Cemented a pond
There is a cavern of red ants
. . . When I come
To where our house was,
And a sewer line tied off
Like an umbilical cord.

(**"Braly Street,"** pp. 55-56).

Although there is undoubtedly a prevalence of such images of destruction in Soto's poetry, a subtle, anabolic or constructive force also makes itself felt as a necessary counterbalance to establish, according to Arnheim, the "structural theme, which introduces and maintains tension" (p. 52). "The antagonistic play of forces (which) is the structural theme" (p. 32) established what Arnheim calls a "definitive order" when it comes to a standstill; i.e., "achieves the maximum of entropy attainable for the given system of constraints" (p. 33). In philosophical terms, this suggests that Soto's world view is not necessarily nihilistic, as the preponderance of negative images might indicate, but rather represents an uneven balance between an oppressively hostile environment and a personal credo of survival in such a world.

Admittedly this faint optimistic note is difficult to detect in the cacophony of a world falling to pieces around our ears. It may be heard, however, above the noise of the wind peeling "mountains, grain by grain, / To small slopes, loose dirt," and stoking "The skulls and spines of cattle / To white dust, to nothing." Caught up in this inevitable cycle of dissolution, the narrator seeks to reestablish intellectual order for himself out of physical chaos:

The wind picks up the breath of my armpits
Like dust, swirls it
Miles away
And drops it
On the ear of a rabid dog
And I take on another life.

(**"Wind,"** p. 16)

This same impulse to withstand the forces of destruction and establish an inner stronghold, a reservoir of strength and resistance, is apparent in the distinction between the unresisting creatures in the fields:

The thick caterpillars
That shriveled
Into rings
And went where the wind went

and the intellectual resistance of the narrator, who sees his sweat not as evidence of a physical drain on his energy but rather as a part of "the sea / That is still within me" (**"Hoeing,"** p. 24). This concept of the "sea" as a source of primitive energy enables the narrator to withstand, at least intellectually and momentarily, the fate of the shriveled caterpillars.

The idea of taking on another life, of establishing an anabolic force in the face of destructive catabolism, recurs in various subtle, often ambiguous images.[2] The dead body of the drowned friend in **"Avocado Lake"** (p. 30) "moves under the dark lake," its hands are like "those of a child reaching for his mother," its fingers need to be "rubbed and kissed" as if death were not an absolute, irreversible step towards physical dissolution but rather an alternative form of existence in which the drowned man can find a compatible environment:

> His phlegm drifts beneath the surface,
> As his life did.

Perhaps the most significant of these anabolic images, however, is one which is also connected to the death of the narrator's father and thus suggests a level of order that has withstood the disintegration associated with that event. Sixteen years after his father's death, the narrator returns to "Braly Street" to find the almond tree gone, the uncle's footprints "paved with dirt," the pond invaded by ants, the house bulldozed. But one thing has survived intact. The narrator comes back

> To the chinaberry
> Not pulled down
> And to its rings
> My father and uncle
> Would equal, if alive.
>
> (**"Braly Street,"** pp. 54-55)

This is the same tree the narrator "came down from" the moment his father died to witness the ant "carrying off what there was to carry" from the house (**"The Evening of Ants,"** pp. 48-49). This earlier scene foreshadows the actual destruction of sixteen years later. But something has been salvaged from the past. The chinaberry has resisted demolition and the wind has momentarily ceased its catabolic effect. Violence is held at bay and a metaphorical state of truce has been achieved. To the extent that the anabolic, constructive force survives in Soto's poetic vision in the form of the narrator's personal stronghold of intellectual resistance, symbolic perhaps of the creative energy of the poet himself, total chaos is averted and, in Arnheim's words, an uneasy "state of final equilibrium, of accomplished order and maximum entropy" is reached.[3]

Notes

1. The presence of these thematic elements in Soto's poetry places him squarely within the tradition of poets like Yeats ("Second Coming," "Sailing to Byzantium," "A Vision") and Neruda, ("Residencia en la tierra"), and the poetic prose of novelists like Gabriel García Marquez (*One Hundred years of Solitude*) who use images of apocalyptic disintegration to explore the chaotic fabric of life in our time. In *The Sense of an Ending* (1970, pp. 95-96), Frank Kermode sees this recurrence of apocalyptic imagery in literature as "a powerful eschatological element in modern thought . . . reflected in the arts . . . a pattern of anxiety [which] is a feature of our cultural tradition, if not ultimately of our physiology."9
2. For an extensive analysis of this topic, see my essay "Ambiguity in the Poetry of Gary Soto," delivered at the 1982 Louisiana Conference on Hispanic Languages and Literatures, February 18-20, 1982, and subsequently published in *Revista Chicano-Riqueña,* XI, Summer, 1983, No. 2, 34-39.
3. This essay is a revised version of a paper presented at the IXth Annual Southern Comparative Literature Association Conference, Lexington, Virginia, on February 24-26, 1983.

Patricia de la Fuentes (essay date 1989)

SOURCE: "Mutability and Stasis: Images of Time in Gary Soto's *Black Hair,*" in *The Americas Review*, Vol. 17, No. 1, Spring, 1989, pp. 100-07.

[In the following essay, de la Fuentes discusses Soto's treatment of time and his emphasis on death in Black Hair.*]*

In *Feeling and Form,* a theory of art developed from her *Philosophy in a New Key,* Susanne Langer defines the role of the poet in terms of how well he "uses discourse to create an illusion, a pure appearance, which is a non-discursive symbolic form."[1] Central to this theory is the distinction between the "actual" and the "virtual" experience:

> The appearances of events in our actual lives are fragmentary, transient and often indefinite, like most of our experiences—like the space we move in, the time we feel passing, the human and inhuman forces that challenge us. The poet's business is to create the appearance of 'experiences,' the semblance of events lived and felt, and to organize them so they constitute a purely and completely experienced reality, a piece of 'virtual life.' (202)

('Virtual' in this sense is used to mean 'being in essence or effect but not in fact' = an illusion of reality.) This "illusion of life" she believes, "is the primary illusion of all poetic art" (213). And without a doubt, any illusion of life cannot be plausible without taking into consideration the concept of *Time,* which, in one form or another, dominates and dictates the actual existence of all of us.

In the poetry of Gary Soto, whose poetic consciousness often appears to be, if not obsessed, at least profoundly concerned with the effect and passage of Time, it is interesting to note that as a 'virtual' experience in the life of the narrator, Time often exists on two levels or in two mutually exclusive dimensions. In Soto's latest collection, ***Black Hair,*** in particular, this duality of experience creates that dynamic tension within the poems which is directly responsible for their success as what Langer has called pieces of "virtual life." Soto's conflicting images of Time articulate, on the purely illusory level, those events in our actual lives which are, as Langer points out, "fragmentary, transient and . . . indefinite" (212). In many of Soto's poems, these fragmentary, transient experiences which make up the virtual world of the narrator are presented in one dimension of Time against a background of, or in juxtaposition to a second set of experiences which occur in another dimension of Time. Thus the poetic illusion seems to hinge on the intersection of two separate, though often intimately interwoven, experiential levels. The one in the foreground creates the illusion of physical mutability in the swift passing of Time, in a fleeting awareness of mortality and in a focus on the present, sensual activity of living, especially in images of eating and drinking; the impression is of a life lived in double-time, with double intensity. In the background or as a counterbalance to so much energy and vitality, Soto often imposes an experience in slow-motion, or a scene that is completely static. This illusion of simultaneous experiences, one in double-time, one in slow-motion, lends a sense urgency to the poems which heightens the primary illusion of events lived and felt, which are usually those presented in the foreground.

This superimposure or juxtaposition of time-frames occurs as a technique in Soto's poems in different degrees of intensity. In **"Black Hair,"** for example, the controlling or "lived" time in the poem is the fast-paced present of the baseball game which is being played in the foreground by men like "Hector Moreno / Quick and hard with turned muscles,"[2] whose actions are dynamic and described with food imagery, "The gloves eating balls into double plays." As a spectator, the narrator is also dynamically present in the swiftly moving foreground action—

> Waving players in and stomping my feet,
> Growing sweaty in the presence of white shirts.
> I chewed sunflower seeds. I drank water
> And bit my arm through the late innings.

—and even participates vicariously in the game itself: "in my mind I rounded the bases / With him, my face flared, my hair lifting / Beautifully." In the middle stanza, however, the static past intrudes into the momentum of the present as the narrator hovers for an instant between the two worlds:

> My black torch of hair, about to go out?
> Father was dead, his face no longer
> Hanging over the table or our sleep,

For a moment, the game is interrupted, life itself seems to be suspended as the young narrator experiences, in an instant of static self-awareness, the mutability of his own flesh, symbolized here as the black hair of youth, that "torch" which Time will inevitably dim and eventually put out. Within the poetic illusion of this fragmentary event which takes place in the narrator's mind, the presence of his dead father—whose image from another time-frame might at first seem to be an arbitrary digression in the poem—is actually essential to the articulation of the central illusion of the poem, that of directly experienced mutability (life and death). The virtual, world of the narrator thus embraces both the rushing, live time of Hector Moreno, whose gloves are described as "eating" and hence as associated with living, and the static, dead time of the father, whose passive "hanging over the table" is nonparticipatory in the act of living.

This technique of presenting one time-frame within another is characteristic of many of the poems in Soto's ***Black Hair*** collection and serves to create the illusion of philosophical or psychological depth to the virtual experiences detailed in the poems. For example, the virtual experiences of these poems often contain flashes of poetic reflections which Langer claims "are not essentially trains of logical reasoning . . . [but rather] create the 'semblance' of reasoning; of the seriousness, strain and progress, the sense of growing knowledge, growing clearness, conviction and acceptance—the whole experience of philosophical thinking" (219). One such poem is **"In August"** (4) which merges, more subtly than in **"Black Hair,"** the two levels of fast and slow time. On one level, in the vital, eating-time of the living, the narrator climbs a plum tree to pick "its dark fruit, notched and open / Where birds ate," and later joins in a ritual of eating at:

> Coleman Pickle
> Where brother, friends, tiny sister
> Were standing in barrels,
> Pickles in their hands

On another level and in another time-frame, coexisting with the first but yet removed from the realm of the activities of living and eating, lies another world, suggested in the image of the blimp, whose different nature is recognized by the narrator who, from inside the barrel, pickle in hand,

> —came up to see the blimp
> Pass quietly as a cloud,
> Its shadow dark enough to sleep
> Or dream in.

In its quietness, its dark shadows, its association with sleep and dreams, the blimp becomes the embodiment of that other, static time-frame, symbolic of the ephemeral nature of the narrator's world and everything in it, here one moment

> And then gone,
> Like all I would ever know.
> Like father with hands in my hair.
> Like uncle on the porch with his arms
> And little else.

Once again, the narrator's intuitions of his own mortality hinges on his fragmentary recollection of his dead father and uncle, both "gone, / Like all [he] would ever know," both removed from the sphere of active time, of eating plums and pickles, and imprisoned in the momentary, static vision of the blimp—now "above us / And then gone." As these two time-frames intersect briefly, the narrator experiences the fleeting moment of insight:

We watched
It, with food in our mouths,
All wondering, until it was above us
And then gone,
Like all we would ever know.

He stands with the other children, momentarily suspended in the act of living, "with food in [their] mouths," and participates briefly but vividly, through his "wondering," in that other time-frame into which his father and uncle have already passed, and into which "all [he] will ever know," and by extension all he will ever be, is in the process of passing—even in that very instant of life-sustaining, eating activity. In essence, Soto has captured, in this fleeting image of mortality, the illusion of a mutability deeply lived and felt by the narrator.

In other poems Soto uses complex variations of this same technique of intersecting time-frame to heighten the illusion of life. **"The Plum's Heart"** (5) contains several layers of action, each in its own time-frame. First there is the obvious present time in which the narrator recounts the event of picking plums with his father; "I've climbed in trees / To eat, and climbed / Down." Then there is the implied time in which this event occurred, a living-time of eating and action for both the narrator and his father. Within this fragmentary illusion of life lived in fast-time by the narrator in his plum-picking and plum-eating past there are two quite distinct intrusions of static time. One such shift in time projects forward to glimpse the familiar brief insight into the narrator's own mortality through identification with the dead father. After recalling the vitality of the past experience through food imagery:

My hands
Opened like mouths,
The juice running
Without course down
My arms, as I stabbed

For plums . . . the narrator moves forward in time to a stark glimpse of the process of mutability, not only in his father and figuratively in the fruit, but also in himself as part of the same process of change:

I called to father
To catch—father
Who would disappear
Like fruit at the end
Of summer, from a neck
Wound some say—blood
Running like the juice
Of these arms.

The plum juice running "down" the narrator's arms in one time-frame is metaphorically fused with the father's blood running, in a shift to a static time-frame in the future "at the end of summer." This brief glimpse into the immediate future provides the narrator with the insight into his own mortality, vividly implied in the poem by a smooth shift back to the plum-picking time-frame in which the narrator identifies with the doomed-but-not-yet-dead father in the image of his blood "Running like the juice / Of these arms." This last image of blood/juice is especially successful in conveying the illusion of a deeply felt event because the ambiguity of the preposition in "Of these arms" includes both the possibility of the plum juice and the father's blood which is, biologically, also that of the narrator.

The second shift in time occurs in the first few lines of the poem in which the narrator, his mouth coloured by the fruit juice, sees himself, "mouth red / From plums that were / Once clouds in March /—rain I mean," as a connecting link in the vast process of mutability in nature. This illusion of the narrator's experience of his own mortality is heightened as he re-cognizes, from the vantage point of the future, that his father

his mouth
Already red and grinning
Like the dead on their
Rack of blackness

—was already doomed, even in the same act of eating, to take his place in that inescapable sequence of universal change just as the plums, evolving from the March rains, must disappear "at the end / Of summer."

The interplay of time-frames in this complex illusion of life might be diagrammed as follows:

1. Extended past:

clouds-rain

= plums

= red juice

2. Active-past:

father-son

plum = picking

juice-running

3.Static-past:

End-of-summer

father dead

blood-running

4. Static-present:

narrator recalls

past-times

but in doing so, we destroy the "semblance of events lived and felt . . . [that] piece of virtual life" (212) which Langer defines as the creation of the poet. Just as music "spreads out time for our direct and complete apprehension, by letting our hearing monopolize it—organize, fill, and shape it" (110), so a poem spreads out time for our imaginative perception. To create the illusion of a lived and felt mutability, the poet must create the illusion of change which is, Langer maintains, "not itself something represented; it is implicitly given through the contrast of different 'states,' themselves unchanging" (112). Soto's use of contrasting states of action and meditation, of fast-time and slow-time effectively sustains the illusions of change in poems like **"Landscape in Spring"** (11), in which the speeding pickup, where

> my brother and me
> And some fat guy, are drinking from paper bags,
> Our necks blackened, our hair loose in wind.

is shown against a static background of "A woman in the yard with a hose, pointed / At a tree," and a house that "is going to stay / Where it is," while the narrator and his friends go "speeding / Through the days." Ironically, the existence of these speeding characters, so apparently full of vitality and freedom, implied in the image of "drinking," and "hair loose in wind," is merely another dimension of the static time-frame of the woman in the yard. Like the "hose pointed / At a tree," they will, "if . . . pointed / To a field, cotton or beet, . . . cut it / With a hoe." These two dimensions of time or "states" of existence, at first so different, converge towards the end of the poem into similar time-frames of slow-motion and boredom: "It's all the same if you're brown / And given hours to think about the sun."

In another poem called **"The Day After"** (10), the converging and contrasting of the two time-frames is more dramatically realized since it entails the intersecting of two normally mutually exclusive worlds:

> My brother says you came back
> And were at the foot of his bed,
> Green and telling him it was OK,
> The darkness, the place where
> You sit, waiting for this country
> To turn with flames.

The narrator immediately identifies with the static existence of the dead friend:

> I'm waiting
> Too, . . .
> I'm waiting for this day, and for you
> Frank, to show yourself, green
> Or any other way—to tell me
> It's OK

Implicit in the narrator's recognition and acceptance of the static time-frame of the waiting, presumably dead, Frank, is a rejection of the apocalyptic nature of his own living-time, that time of impending holocaust, "The bloom of smoke and the bones / Lit under running flesh." By experiencing this semblance of world destruction in his mind through the horror imagery of radioactive bones and melting flesh, the narrator vividly lives and feels a projected future time of death and chaos, while simultaneously existing, on a psychological level, in the dark place of the dead friend where things are "OK." In other words, Soto has taken fragmentary events from actual life and conflated them into a single, intense moment of virtual life. This poem is a particularly successful example of what Langer has called the "Illusion of life":

> What makes [the latter] quite different from any actual segment of life is that the events in it are simplified, and at the same time much more fully perceived and evaluated than the jumble of happenings in any person's actual history . . . The virtual experience created out of those very adroitly jumbled impressions is a full and clear vision of social tyrannies, with all of the undertones of personal dread, reluctance, half-delusion, and emotional background to hold the assorted items together in a single illusion of life. (212-13)

In terms of Langer's theory of art, therefore, Soto's often complex articulation of Time in its many psychological and physical dimensions can be seen as a creative technique for achieving that essential and primary illusion of all poetic art: the illusion of life.

Notes

1. Susanne K. Langer, *Feeling and Form: A Theory of Art Developed from 'Philosophy In A New Key'* (New York: Scribner's, 1953): 211.
2. Gary Soto, "Black Hair," *Black Hair* (Pittsburgh: University of Pittsburgh Press, 1985): 3.

Julian Olivares (essay date 1990)

SOURCE: "The Streets of Gary Soto," in *Latin American Literary Review,* Vol. XVIII, No. 35, January-June, 1990, pp. 32-49.

[*In the following essay, Olivares provides a thematic and stylistic analysis of Soto's poetry.*]

In the poem **"Chuy"** from Gary Soto's ***Where Sparrows Work Hard*** (35), the speaker describes his protagonist in a cafe:

> Chuy noted
> On a napkin
> —*a street is only so long*—
> And stared outside
> Where already the day
> Had a dog drop
> Limp as a dishtowel
> And the old staggering
> On a crutch
> Of fierce heat.
> "There is meaning
> In that bus, those kids,"
> He thought,
> And turned the dime
> In his coat pocket.

Here Chuy attempts to conceive the street solely as geographic space, a conception which he affirms by writing it down. Yet this belief is false, as apt to dissolve as the tissue he writes it on. Although he may add to the dime he has and take a bus away from the spatial barrier of his street, it will remain as a psychic barrier wherein hostile cosmic and social forces confine him to an oppressive existence.

Gary Soto is the most recognized Chicano poet in the American literary mainstream.[1] The fact that he writes exclusively in English and has published his four books of poetry in the Pitt Poetry Series has given him access to the American literary public like no other Chicano writer who relies on Chicano publishing media. Marketed for the middle-class audience which purchases his books in bookstores that do not generally include Chicano writers among their stock, Soto's poetry conveys a tone not usually found in Chicano writers who write specifically for a Chicano audience. A third-generation Mexican American, Soto is an English-dominant speaker and writer; consequently his use of English is not a matter of choice. However, if this may make his poetry at times linguistically complicitous with the object criticized, it also allows his poetry to speak "to a *you* who is part of the middle class he is attacking" (Bruce-Novoa 228).[2] Furthermore, through markers and icons that refer to his own cultural context, Soto is not only able to express himself both as an individual and member of an ethnic group, but to simultaneously redirect the Anglo American reader so as to see, for example, an existential theme in the context of a Chicano point-of-view. A case in point is the poem **"Chuy."**

The Anglo American reader, already familiar with the themes of existential bleakness and alienation, probably experiences a defamiliarization provoked by the poem's title, **"Chuy,"** which he/she may not even be able to pronounce (CHEW-y). The Spanish name, a cultural marker, redirects this reader's attention, causing him/her to now contextualize familiar themes from the unfamiliar perspective of the Chicano. That is, in addition to the expression of modern urban themes, the protagonist's name functions as an ethnic substratum that orients the reader to encompass the position of the culturally marginated. The text, therefore, gains a different resonation than would be the case if the protagonist were named "Jimmy." In this manner, then, these universal themes are redirected and intensified by the particular, Chicano point-of-view.

For the Chicano reader, on the other hand, the protagonist's name serves as the orienting device. "Chuy," the nickname for "Jesús," is frequently used by Chicano writers as a Chicano "Every man," frequently as symbolic of the oppressed, marginated, rebellious, poverty-stricken Chicano youth.[3] This type of orienting device is necessary because the Chicano reader in many of Soto's poems encounters unfamiliar poetic terrain. Soto's existential despair, his cadences, frequently terse and elliptical imagery, and models stem largely from Anglo American schools,[4] which make his poetry "strange" to various Chicano readers (and frequently disconcerting to non-Chicano readers, especially Marxist-oriented Europeans, who expect the expression of a more "ethnic" content). Soto's orienting device for the Chicano reader allows him/her to note Soto's personal vision and also to see the particular situation of the Chicano experience in the context of "universal" and "mainstream" modes of expression. Perhaps more than any other American writer, then, Gary Soto's poetry manifests the problematic of polyculturalism. For the Anglo American reader, the "strangeness" in Soto's poetry may be caused by its contextual markers, often brief but always pervasive; for the Chicano or Latino reader, the "strangeness," is often provoked by the poetry's style and form.

With regard to his personal vision, Soto often selects from his view of the streets negative signs. In the poem **"Street"** of ***The Elements of San Joaquin*** (32), the speaker declares: "What I want to remember is a street, / A wide street." The speaker does not explain why he wants to remember this street; he only affirms his volition to recall a certain wide street. Of the numerous associations conveyed by this manifold sign, such as the hustle and bustle of people, glittering neon signs, outdoor restaurants, glamorous shops—all connoting the positive semes of dynamic and joyful activities, Soto, in most instances, selects negative associations. And so the poem continues:

> And that it is cold:
> A small fire in the gutter, cats running
> (. . .) A short woman
> With a short cane, tapping
> Her way
> Past the tracks.
> Farther away
> An abandoned hotel

Gutters, sewers, cans and broken bottles, stray cats, the poor and feeble, the vagrants and criminals, the world of the outsider, industrial blight are the elements that Soto often selects from his streets.

Another indication of Soto's personal vision is noted in the poem **"Piedra"** ("Stone," ***Elements,*** 28), in which surrealistic imagery conveys a matrix of desolation where two types of elements threaten life, the elements of nature and the elemental violence of mankind:

> When the day shut like a suitcase
> And left for the horizon
> When the fog squatted in the vineyard
> Like a stray dog
> We fished there Later we
> looked for soapstone but found
> A piece of the night rising from within us
> And spreading among the cottonwoods
> The dark water wrinkling
> Like the mouth of an old woman whispering *Lord*
> I pointed out carlights fanning past the orchard
> Where the road narrows
> Toward the collapsed bridge My woman
> Showed me a card of bark
> The smashed bottles flaking back to sand
> And farther away near the road
> Someone walking toward us—
> My hand closed in my pocket

Gary Soto's poetry expresses an apocalyptic vision of the universe. As Patricia de la Fuente notes, "Recurring images of loss, disintegration, decadence, demolition, solitude, terror and death create a desolate landscape in which the voice of the narrator is that of a passive, impotent observer, helplessly caught up in the inexorable destruction of human ties." In this desolate landscape, de la Fuente perceives that "although the Christian backdrop is not conspicuously negated in Soto's poetry, it does not occupy a prominent place in his philosophical vision. Therefore, when the poet speaks of death, he usually does so in worldly, physical terms related to individual existences that have been truncated or worn down by indifferent forces" (35, 38).

The desolation and violence that Soto encounters in his streets also reflect his expression as a member of a group. Within the elements of chaos that Soto selects, there are ethnic markers which point to the Chicano experience where poverty, violence, desolation and disorientation are facts of *barrio* existence. Thus, while we are presented with an apparent realism in Soto's depictions of street life, what we encounter is a selection from a wide range of reality which underscores a personal subjectivity and social concern both molded by an apocalyptic vision.

In three of Soto's books—***The Elements of San Joaquin*** (1976). ***The Tale of Sunlight*** (1978), ***Where Sparrows Work Hard*** (1981)—the street appears as a major motif in much of his poetry and forms the title of three poems, one in each book. Although a street or road implies movement, literally through time and space, and allegorically as life's journey, in Soto's poetry the image of the street is also used as a structural component and unifying principle of his poetic vision. The street provides the realistic background for the speaker, his personae and the Chicano minority. Metaphorically, it represents their state of mind; and, allegorically, it depicts a human condition subjected by socio-economic and cosmic forces to an oppressive existence. Here, then, are Gary Soto's "mean streets."

The Elements of San Joaquin is framed at the beginning by **"San Fernando Road"** (3), near Los Angeles, and at the conclusion by **"Braly Street,"** in South Fresno. With **"San Fernando Road,"** we find the space of industry—"On this road of factories / Gray as the clouds"—and not of travel or escape. This is the "Mission Tire Factory" (***Sparrows,*** 10), where Soto worked. In **"San Fernando Road"** it is the poet's alter ego, Leonard,[5] who "was among men / Whose arms / Were bracelets / Of burns." Here Leonard "handled grinders, / Swept the dust / Of rubber / (. . . / Scrubbed the circles / From toilets / No one flushed," and with

> Young Mexicans
> Went into ovens
> Squint-eyed
> And pulled out the pipes
> Smeared black

The young Mexicans go into the ovens; realistically, this is what they do. But this laconic statement conjures up two levels of imagery. In the first, the ovens are a metaphor for a state of Hell, from which there is no escape for the blackened workers. Space here is an infernal one to which the young Mexicans are damned to suffer their socioeconomic plight. They are dehumanized and reduced to the category of machines: "Shivering / Like the machinery / That went on and on." On the second level, the poem presents allegorical imagery of genocide by which the Mexicans are removed from the mainstream of societal space.

The poem's significance stands in ironic relation to its title, **"San Fernando Road."** Instead of a road to socioeconomic salvation, a group of people are damned to the lowest level of society. Although they are enslaved by the "bracelets / Of burns" and trapped in "circles" of drudgery, the workers can withstand physical pain; but it is the mental pain that agonizes them: "whose families / Were a pain / They could not shake off." San Fernando, the saint and representative of religion, is of no real consolation to their strife. This road is an allegory of the workers' *via crucis* on which they are burdened by familial responsibilities and are concerned solely with survival. The street, then, does not lead to social and economic well-being, but is a sign of violence—industrial, social and, as indicated by other poems, criminal violence.

As Bruce-Novoa has demonstrated, ***The Elements of San Joaquin*** traces a journey to the poet's origin on **"Braly Street"** (187); it is a personal allegory of a painful peregrination that takes him through the San Joaquin Valley. Here the elements of city streets are supplanted by the elements of nature. Soto has commented on his awareness of the forces of nature upon his return to the Valley from the Ethnic Writers Workshop in Wisconsin: "When I came back from Wisconsin, I paid very much attention to forces like the wind. I was shocked—it was the power of nature which grabbed me by the throat and said, 'Wake up, sucker!' I became very conscious of these things. They later became symbols, but they also became part of my life" (Binder 194). Thus, in the poem **"Wind"** (16), we note the disintegration of the skeletal remains of cattle, wiping out all traces of their existence—and by extension those of man's: "The wind strokes / The skulls and spines of cattle / To white dust, to nothing."[6] And in the poem **"Fog"** (21), in an absurd enumeration, a heavy mist consumes and envelops organic and inorganic life, becoming a metaphor for a dark vision of nothingness:

> Not all the sweaters
> Hung in closets in summer
> Could soak up this mist. The fog:
> A mouth nibbling everything to its origin,
> Pomegranate trees, stolen bicycles,
> The string of lights at a used-car lot
> A Pontiac with scorched valves (. . .)
> One hundred years from now
> There should be no reason to believe
> I lived.

The elements of societal oppression, however, still prevail here. This agricultural San Joaquin Valley, the United States' cornucopia, is no paradise for the Chicano field worker. The poems of this section constitute an antipastoral, in which the laborers are broken physically and spiritually by agribusiness. The poem **"Field"** (15), for example, brings together two elements of destruction. It begins with an awareness of the destructive forces of nature and concludes with the realization of the exploitation and oppression waged against Chicanos:

> The wind sprays pale dirt into my mouth
> The small, almost invisible scars
> On my hands (. . .)
> Already I am becoming the valley,
> A soil that sprouts nothing
> For any of us.

"Field Poem" (23) crystallizes an image that is a metaphor of the book's fragmented vision (Bruce-Novoa 197):

> We returned to the bus
> Speaking
> In broken English, broken Spanish (. . .)
> From the smashed bus window,
> I saw the leaves of cotton plants
> Like small hands
> Waving good-bye.

There is no other Chicano poet who can achieve as condensed an expression as Soto can in depicting Mexican American life. Frequently, the references and allusions to this life are so elliptical and of such subtlety that they may not be discerned by the non-Hispanic reader (Binder 195). The above field workers may appear to be linguistically deficient, due to a lack of education, but their broken English and Spanish essentially refer to a bicultural experience in which the Mexican American is marginalized from American society, yet is not really Mexican, either. In whatever language they speak, they are "broken" by the working conditions imposed by the institutions of the majority society. The bucolic innocence of the valley's agricultural products is subverted by the institution, the "bus," against which the Chicano workers can only make a token reprisal by smashing its window. Through this dark vision the poet at once speaks for himself and his group,.

The personal, fragmented vision extends to images that the speaker encounters on the streets to home, which derive from the poet's preoccupation with death and corruption. In **"Sadako"** (27) the speaker notes "Chickens gutted and noosed on poles / In the unlit butcher shops," and in **"Town"** (33) he states: "The town smelled of tripe / pulled from an ox / and hanging." These images remind us of Pablo Neruda's "Walking Around": "Hay pájaros de azufre y horribles intestinos / colgando de las puertas de las casas que odio" (78). ["There trussed to the doors of the houses I loath / are the sulphurous birds, in a horror of tripes" 79]. This impression is confirmed in an interview where Soto states that, of the poets he was reading while writing the ***Elements,*** his favorite was Neruda (Trejo 28).[7]

In the third section of ***Elements,*** the poet returns to **"Braly Street"** (54), an archaeological site of lost artifacts, lives and memories retained in the strata of asphalt, earth and time:

> Bottle caps and glass
> Of the '40s and '50s
> Hold their breath
> Under the black earth
> Of asphalt and are silent
> Like the dead whose mouths
> Have eaten dirt and bermuda.
>
> (54)

This is the street of his childhood where tragedy struck; his father killed in an industrial accident and his uncle killed by cancer. The other cancer, the industrial blight, bulldozed his home, so that:

> Braly Street is now
> Tin ventilators
> On the warehouses, turning
> Our sweat
> Towards the yellowing sky;
> Acetylene welders
> Beading manifolds,
> Stinging the half-globes
> Of retinas. When I come
> To where our house was,
> I come to weeds
> And a sewer line tied off
> Like an umbilical cord;
> To the chinaberry
> Not pulled down
> And to its rings
> My father and uncle
> Would equal, if alive.

As in the image of "the circles / From toilets / No one flushed," of **"San Fernando Road,"** with this image of "a sewer line tied off / Like an umbilical cord," Soto equates life as birth into a world of waste, a circle of despair. These are images with which the poet retrieves the past and which reveal the causes of his experience of discontinuity. Unlike the chinaberry, the tree of poverty,[8] still there, the poet has been uprooted by personal and social tragedies which are at the source of his apocalyptic vision. Nevertheless, this vital discontinuity—as we shall note later—is challenged by the continuity the poet finds in the space of literature. ***The Elements of San Joaquin,*** then, is a book enclosed by two streets, both wielding industrial violence and images of fire. The first poem expresses the oppression of a minority; the final poem expresses a highly personal vision of loss and desolation. The book ends at the source of both an individualistic and communal point of view. There is a reckoning up of one's youth and environment: desolation, oppression, crime, death, cosmic forces—all of these are the "elements" that shape a life and an outlook which becomes exorcized but not erased in its recounting.

In his books, Soto relates two aspects of Chicano life: the urban and the rural. As we have noted in ***Elements,*** the poems of the rural space—the San Joaquin Valley—are inserted between the poems of the two urban places, Los Angeles and Fresno. This is the formal arrangement of the poetry, yet this ordering corresponds to a fact of Chicano life. Juxtaposed to the rural labor fields, only a short bus trip away, the Chicano labors in factory infernos. Most of

Soto's poetry deals with each of these activities separately, but there are poems in which the urban and rural environments are brought together. This juxtaposition and unification is accomplished through Soto's reconstruction of a street in South Fresno. The Chicano inhabits the outskirts of the town where the houses face the city and the factories, while their back doors open to animals and vegetable patches.

Soto has said that his favorite poem from ***The Tale of Sunlight*** is **"The Street":**

> To me, the writing is there, it's complex without being stupidly obscure, and the tone is haunting. But what I really enjoy about the poem is that I settled some things that were bothering me, and it had to do with remembering people from my past—childhood. What I mean is this: I grew up on a street that was slowly being torn down. I lived in a part of industrial Fresno. If I looked out my bedroom window, I saw a junkyard. If I looked across the street from the porch, I saw a printing shop. Down the streets were factories . . . Houses were being torn down, for reasons I never understood, and with each house, they were tearing down my past. Tearing it down so in a way I wouldn't know who I was . . . And, houses aside, people were dying around me. Like my uncle. He had cancer. He was on the couch, day after day, until he was gone . . . my father died very young, a neck injury while at work. And here I am, a kid, thinking, "What is going on?" And then there were people leaving, too. Other family members, like aunts and uncles, were marrying or getting the hell out. (Trejo 31)

"The Street" (18) has an epigraph taken from Elio Vittornini's *Twilight of the Elephant,* "Then we would hardly eat except to be seen," which, as Soto clarifies in the same interview, describes his life as a child. The poem deploys two points of view. One is unvoiced, that of the child Molina, the poet's alter ego, who digs in the ground, oblivious to his squalid surroundings; the second is that of the child turned speaker and adult, and who sees the street, its Chicano residents and the past through the perspective of his experience, selectivity and subjectivity of imagery. All this is presented through shifting impressions, through a montage of images which are often surrealistic and absurd, but whose ungrammaticalities are resolved on the levels of death, loneliness, poverty and violence.[9]

The poem begins with a widow who appears among her vegetables and whose realistic description is abruptly altered by an incongruous image: "Among onions and tomatos poled waist-high, / Chiles and the broken fingers of peas / That point down." The ungrammaticality of "broken fingers of peas" is the sign of fragmentation that will characterize the poem. Boredom and futility become concrete when the widow hangs the town wash on the line:

> Waving off the chickens,
> She pins the grayness to the line, and beyond
> This line, in the same boredom
> That drips from the wash[10]

These ideas of monotony, boredom and futility—expressed through the fabric of the town's wash—are now revealed in the faces of the old, who, awaiting death, "suck their tongues / And stare at each other's shoes."

As the child plays at digging and the sun begins to set, Julio, the retired butcher,

> Sits under the full skirt of a willow,
> Talking to the photo
> Of his first wife,
> Her face greased with a thumbprint
> And caught in a lean year.

Then the scene shifts on the street to Goyo's house: "Goyo at the window, and no uncle / Arrives on the porch." Here we have an ungrammaticality caused by an incongruity between an action—"Goyo at the window"—and a state of being, "and no uncle." We would expect, for example, "Goyo at the window, and no shirt on." However, the element of absence is not an article of clothing but a relative; and another one is missing two lines later: "No aunt comes, / Heavy-breasted, to bend over the sink / and gut a chicken."

In the poem's first section, the primary element is the absence caused by the death of a relative. On this street, there is a widow, a widower, the elderly who will soon die and be missed by their relatives, Goyo without an uncle or aunt, and in their midst a child. Absence, emphasized by the disappearance of the sun, is the cause of loneliness. Extratextually, this points to the poet, traumatized by the death of his father and uncle.

At night, on the rural fringe of the city, people of various occupations meet and share a silent space at the edge of a ditch. They smoke and watch the water flow beyond them, each person isolated in his own thoughts: "Barber or fieldhand, / Whore's brother, pickpocket's son / They come, shoeless, to the ditch."

Daybreak reveals additional elements in the street and in the poem: frustration, oppression and violence. Fleeing from his street but not from his condition, Cruz seeks alcohol and violence:

> When the morning is a tablet
> Of cold spit he cannot swallow,
> Cruz leaves
> For the Westside,
> The neoned juke box and the warm beer
> Sending up its last bubble,
> For the cue stick
> Swung hard against an ear, the mouth blooming.

violence and death, sniffs for the rat, both of which scavenge food and the remains of dead chickens. The grandmother is next depicted picking the fruit trees, but she is lassoed by the speaker's kid brother with a rope linked to death:

> She is Indian,
> My brother believes,
> And lassoes her

To a fence
With the rope
That pulled a cow
To its death

The brother plays at cowboys, a game by which, ironically, the *mestizo* child innocently internalizes the Whites' hatred of Indians, a racial attitude implicit in the game of Cowboys and Indians.[11] Under the guise of play, death and violence underlie the domestic scenes:

Poverty is a pair
Of boots, rain,
Twin holsters slapping
His side, and a hand
Cocked into a pistol.

The speaker then views himself as a child, himself innocently participating in a chain of violence:

I'm the child
In a chinaberry
Flicking matches
Into a jar of flies, wingless (. . .)
I shake them,
And they are a raffle
For the ants,
A small cargo
For the wind
To haul into the smeared
Ash of evening.[12]

There appears to be no escape from poverty and a condition threatened by cosmic forces. The poem concludes with a sense of inertia, as even cars stall:

A car rattles
From the drive
And stalls in
A great sigh of steam.
I see this and note
That when someone calls
No one has to go.

One other poem from this collection and worthy of note with regard to our theme is **"Mexicans Begin Jogging"** (24). The Border Patrol raids the Mission Tire Factory in search of illegal aliens; and Soto, who is American but Chicano and brown, has to run with the Mexicans:

. . . the border patrol opened
Their vans and my boss waved for us to run.
"Over the fence, Soto," he shouted,
And I shouted that I was American.
"No time for lies," he said, and pressed
A dollar in my palm, hurrying me
Through the back door.[13]

So the fleeing aliens engage in an American middle-class activity: jogging. And as they jog from the industrial area through the neighborhoods of comfortable houses, Soto is aware of the paradox of his situation, both comic and pathetic:

Since I was on his time, I ran
And became the wag to a short tail of
Mexicans—
Ran past the amazed crowds that lined
The street and blurred like photographs, in rain.
I ran from that industrial road to the soft
Houses where people paled at the turn of an
autumn sky.
What could I do but yell *vivas*
To baseball, milkshakes, and those sociologists
Who would clock me
As I jog into the next century
On the power of a great, silly grin.

Here Soto and the Mexicans engage in a *race* from the Border Patrol, and in doing so transgress the border of comfortable White America whose inhabitants grow even paler at the sight of the brown *race* on their streets. Soto, in comic desperation, tries to convince them that he, too, is American by saluting America: "What could I do but yell *vivas* / To baseball, milkshakes." Nevertheless, he is an outsider on White America's streets, only of statistical concern to sociologists who will measure into the next century his degree of assimilation into the majority society. In this poem, in which the street now becomes a metaphor of the speaker's search for a place in American society, we note another problematic of polyculturalism. On the one hand he is rejected by the dominant society because he is Brown and insists on affirming his bicultural values—being "American" means casting aside one's cultural and ethnic inheritance—; and, on the other, the Mexicans know he is not one of them, an illegal alien. The thrust of Soto's poetry, then, like all of Chicano literature, is to create a cultural space which the "alienated" Chicano can call his own. The tensions which press upon both borders of this space are, paradoxically, those which threaten to sunder it, and those which help define its cultural space and production.

The street, then, serves Soto as an organizing element of his poetic material and as a poetic figure. The street is a real place in whose houses and factories people live and work; it is the metaphorical space of the lost outsider besieged by cosmic forces; it conveys an allegory of an underprivileged minority; and it is a metaphor of the poetic voice that enunciates a cultural space.

Gary Soto's poetry is unique in American literature. Unlike many meritorious Chicano and mainland Puerto Rican poets, Soto does not—and cannot—write in Spanish or mix interlingually Spanish and English. Yet, precisely because Soto writes in English, and not because he is a better poet, he—more than any U.S. Hispanic poet—can relate to the Anglo American reader the social afflictions of his minority group. By dealing with themes and utilizing a style familiar to Anglo readers, he not only can express his personal "existential" burden but is able to overcome the criticism of some of these readers that Chicano literature is not universal. Reading his street poems, for example, is an experience akin to that of reading "The Wasteland", but stripped of its "universal" classical figures and stocked with Chicano figures and cultural icons.[14] Through his use of cultural contexts and markers, that is, by means of cultural foregrounding, he redirects the Anglo American reader to include a Chicano perspective and thrusts into their sight of universals the particular situations of Chicano society.

Notes

For the dialectic of the discontinuity of life and the continuity of literary space, see Bruce-Novoa 1982.

—"If I had any fear in my life, it would be the fear of starving. There is no reason for gathering things. Why keep a bank account, why keep a refrigerator. I was very scared. I thought that in '72, because there was a regression in the U.S., that I was certain of death. That was my greatest fear." "Is that a childhood fear?"—"It's childhood fear, absolutely." "Did you really feel hunger as a child?"—"Oh, I think we did, sure. I remember opening the refrigerator and absolutely nothing inside! Maybe there was a tomato or an apple, but it was moulding, it was not edible. That fear is always kept in my mind" (Binder 195).

1. Gary Soto has been awarded the Academy of American Poets Award, The Discovery/*Nation* Prize, The Pushcart Prize and the Bess Hokin Prize by *Poetry* magazine. Also a Guggenheim Fellow, he is an Associate Professor of Chicano Studies and English at the University of California, Berkeley. He does not reject nor find limiting the label "Chicano poet": " . . . if someone wants to label me a Chicano poet I think that's fine. I'm simply a poet, that's equally fine. I'm not concerned with those things. It doesn't bother me in the least" (Binder 197).

2. In an interview, responding to the question whether he envisages and directs himself to a certain public as he writes, Soto responds: "No. It's just writing poem after poem (. . . It's directed to an experience. That's the only thing I can do. Because I think the poems I write are pretty clear. They may be obscure here and there . . . " (Binder 197-98).

3. E.g. "So Jesse, / cuando era junior [when he was a junior], was pushed out into / dirty-brown streets of his zip-coded barrio. / He left quietly, / but on his desk he left carved his name: CHUY," Tino Villanueva, "Chicano Dropout," 65.

4. In another interview, Soto reveals that his first influence was Donald Allen's *New American Poetry,* after which came that of Philip Levine, with whom he took classes in poetry writing, as an undergraduate at Fresno State. Soto received his MFA from the Creative Writing Program at the University of California-Irvine, satisfying the thesis requirement with *The Elements of San Joaquin.* Juan Rodríguez, in his review of *The Elements of San Joaquin,* notes Soto's poetic training and how, at that time—1977, it differed from that of many Chicano poets: "Soto adheres to an Anglo-American written tradition. That is to say, his poetry lacks the strong resonance of the oral tradition, which is at the core of almost all Chicano poetry today (. . .) his poetry does not linguistically challenge the Anglo-American monolingual, as does most Chicano poetry. Neither does Soto challenge the Anglo thematically; he avoids all themes and situations which are particularly Chicano and which require, in order to understand them, more than a general knowledge of the Chicano" (269-70). The oral tradition is much less influential in the Chicano poetry of today, which may, in part, be attributable to Soto's influence. In Soto's subsequent books, as is being pointed out in the present article, Soto at times contextualizes his themes, presenting the perspective of a Chicano voice or *persona.*

5. Of "San Fernando Road," Soto says: "The poem is about me, and I ran away from home, when I was seventeen . . . It is dedicated to my uncle, because he is a factory worker. I worked in the factory at tyres, fixing tyres, and I thought I was going to die then. I was probably starving to death. I hadn't eaten in three days or something" (Binder 193).

6. For a discussion of simultaneous harmonious and discordant elements in this poem, as well as in others, that create a dramatic tension between death and life, "between the disintegrative and regenerative forces," see de la Fuente.

7. Although Soto's models and poetics are essentially Anglo American, Pablo Neruda's surrealistic imagery has had some influence on him, albeit perhaps filtered through Ben Belitt's translations.

8. "One of the plants that appear and reappear in your poetry is the chinaberry tree. Why?"—"Well, we had a chinaberry tree in the backyard. It's an ugly tree, and it smells. It has a putrid smell to it as the berries open up. But it would command a lot of attention. You'd go out and into the backyard, and it was here. Beyond that, as I look back, it is a tree of the poor. A lot of poor had chinaberries. It was not a nice tree" (Binder 196).

9. By "ungrammaticalities," I refer to those elements in a poem—deviant grammar, contradictory details, lexicon, tropes—which impede a mimetic reading but which signify through a different network of relationships on a higher level of discourse, semiosis; see Riffaterre 1-5.

10. Cf. Neruda, "Walking Around": ". . . ropas colgadas de un alambre: / calzoncillos, toallas y camisas que lloran / lentas lágrimas sucias" [" . . . laundry hung out on a wire: / the blouses and towels and the drawers . . . / slowly dribbling a slovenly tear" 79].

11. Cf. Alurista, "We've played cowboys": "We've played cowboys / not knowing / . . . /—as opposed to indians / when ancestors of mis charros abuelos / indios fueron [my cowboy grandfathers were Indians] / . . . / if we must / cowboys play /—con bigotes / y ojos negros [with black eyes and moustaches]."

12. "Another thing that surfaces frequently in your work are the ants. Why this interest in ants?"—"We had ants all over the place. Not the big red ants, but the little black ants. Beyond that, it is of symbolic value of dismantling things, of dismantling my father" (Binder 196).

13. Soto occasionally reveals different perspectives and attitudes to the same incident or situation. Note, for

example, the different perspectives and tones of the Mission Tire Factory (Valley Tire Factory, Glendale, Calif.) in "San Fernando Road," "Mexicans Begin Jogging" and in his prose recollection "Black Hair" (*Living Up The Street*).

14. Soto's most recent book of poetry, *Black Hair* (1985), marks a change in the poet's vision and attitude. His marriage and child have been instrumental in bringing him to terms with the world and instilling in him a note of optimism not found in his previous books. In this guise, see, e.g., the poems "Morning on this Street," "Under Trees" ("Even on this street / . . . / Love is a way out"), "Pepper Tree" ("Stand up, bend a little, be here tomorrow"), "When We Wake" ("But now I am awake to this life"), "These Days," "The Trees That Change Our Lives." As can be noted, trees are an important symbol/image in Soto's poetry; recall the chinaberry tree in "Braly Street" and "The Street" (Sparrows), and see in *Black Hair* "When We Wake." For the presence of a renewed spirit and optimistic tone in *Black Hair*, see also Bruce-Novoa 1985. This renewed spirit is also evident in Soto's second collection of prose reminiscences, *Small Faces,* in which his daughter is central to a changing outlook on life; e.g.: "We can say things but solve nothing. Today I've listened to a line in my head over and over: 'the past seems horrible to me, the present gray and desolate, and the future utterly appalling.' To me this bleak view is frightening. To another it's a sentence not to worry about. We believe our minds are singular and where we stand is the right place to be" ("Saying Things," 126).

I acknowledge the University of Houston for the Summer Research Grant that made this article possible.

Works Cited

Alurista, "We've Played Cowboys." *Literatura Chicana: Texto y Contexto/Chicano Literature: Text and Context.* Eds. A. Castañeda, T. Ybarra-Frausto, J. Sommers. Englewood Cliffs, N.J.: Prentice-Hall, Inc., 31.

Binder, Wolfgang. *Partial Autobiographies, Interviews With Twenty Chicano Poets.* Erlangen: Verlag Palme & Enke Erlangen, 1985.

Bruce-Novoa, Juan. *Chicano Poetry: A Response to Chaos.* Austin: The University of Texas Press, 1982.

———"La poesía de Gary Soto." *La Opinión* (22 de septiembre de 1985): 8-10.

de la Fuente, Patricia. "Ambiguity in the Poetry of Gary Soto." *Revista Chicano-Riqueña* 11.2 (Summer 1983): 34-39.

Riffaterre, Michael. *Semiotics of Poetry.* Bloomington: Indiana University Press, 1978.

Rodríguez, Juan. *The Elements of San Joaquin.* Review, *New Scholar* y6 (1977): 269-73.

Soto, Gary. *Black Hair.* Pittsburgh: University of Pittsburgh Press, 1985.

———*The Elements of San Joaquin.* Pittsburgh: University of Pittsburgh Press, 1977.

———*Living Up The Street.* San Francisco: Strawberry Hill Press, 1985.

———*Small Faces.* Houston: Arte Publico Press, 1986.

———*The Tale of Sunlight.* Pittsburgh: University of Pittsburgh Press, 1978.

———*Where Sparrows Work Hard.* Pittsburgh: University of Pittsburgh Press, 1981.

Trejo, Ernesto. "Interview of Gary Soto." *Revista Chicano-Riqueña* 11.2 (Summer 1983): 25-33.

Villanueva, Tino. *Shaking Off The Dark.* Houston: Arte Publico Press, 1984.

Gary Soto (essay date 1995)

SOURCE: "The Childhood Worries, Or Why I Became a Writer," in *The Iowa Review,* Vol. 25, No. 2, Spring-Summer, 1995, pp. 105-15.

[*In the following essay, Soto reminisces about childhood events later utilized in his verse.*]

As a boy growing up in Fresno I knew that disease lurked just beneath the skin, that it was possible to wake in the morning unable to move your legs or arms or even your head, that stone on a pillow. Your eyeballs might still swim in their own liquids as they searched the ceiling, or beyond, toward heaven and whatever savage god did this to you. Frail and whimpering, you could lie in your rickety bed. You could hear the siren blast at the Sun-Maid Raisin plant, and answer that blast with your own chirp-like cry. But that was it for you, a boy now reduced to the dull activity of blinking. In the adjoining rooms, a chair scraped against the linoleum floor, the kitchen faucet ran over frozen chicken parts, the toilet flushed, the radio sputtered something in Spanish. But you were not involved. You lay useless in bed while your family prepared for the day.

Disease startled Uncle Johnnie first, a mole on his forearm having turned cancerous and bright as a red berry. He was living in Texas when he wrote my mother about his illness. We took him in spring. He lived with us the last three months of his life, mostly lying ill on the couch, a space meant for my brother Rick and me. Before our uncle arrived, we jumped on that couch, me with a flea-like leap and my brother with the heavier bounce of a frog. Now he had the couch to himself, this uncle who was as tender as a pony.

I didn't have much memory to go on. At age six, I didn't lie in bed at night, arms folded behind my head, and savor the time when I was four and a half, a sprout of orneriness. I was too busy in my young body to consider my trail of footprints, all wiped out at the end of a day. But I recall Uncle Johnnie and the apple pie he bought me at Charlie's Market. My greed for sweetness grinned from my sticky mouth, and we devoured the pie as we strolled home, I walking backwards and looking at the market. Later I would return to that market and let my hands settle like small crabs on two candy bars. They opened and closed around them as I decided whether to take them, thus steal, thus let my mouth lather itself with the creamy taste of chocolate. Charlie was probably looking at me, wagging his large Armenian head at my stupidity. But that wasn't the point: I was deciding for myself whether I should sin and then worry about this sin, the wings of my bony shoulder blades less holy.

I recall also when our television was broken and my father pulled the tube out and took it to a repair shop. The TV was eyeless, just sprouts of wires and a smothering scent of dust. While Uncle Johnnie lay on the couch, I climbed into the back of the television set and pretended to be someone funny, one of the Three Stooges, and then someone scary, like Rodan with his monstrous roar. My uncle watched me with a weary smile but no joy. I told him that I could be funny or scary, but in such a small space I couldn't play a horse or an Indian shot by the cavalry. He died that spring, all because of a cancerous mole, died after the tube was once again fitted into the television set. Then the couch returned to us.

For one summer disease scared me. My whiskery neighbor, whose name I have forgotten, was a talker and addressed every growing plant, chicken, and dog in his dirt yard. When he got sick his talk increased, as if he needed to get out all the words that he had intended to use in his old age. He had to use them then or never. One afternoon he came into our yard and showed me his fingernails, yellow and hard. He held them out quivering, as if he were going to do a hocus-pocus magic trick, and when he said it was cancer, I flinched. When I looked up into his face, pale as a fistful of straw, I saw that his eyes were large and bluish, his face already sinking in disease. I was eating grapes, feeding them into my mouth, and I didn't know what to do about his dying except to offer him some of my grapes. He laughed at this. He walked away, straight as any other man, and returned to his yard where he talked to himself and revved up a boat engine clamped to a barrel. A scarf of smoke unfurled from the engine, and the blackish water boiled. He didn't seem to be getting anywhere.

That summer we did our rough living on the street, and our dogs did too. When my uncle Junior's collie got hit by a car on Van Ness Avenue, I watched my uncle, a teenager with a flattop haircut, gather his dog into his arms. He was the bravest person I knew, for he hugged to his chest what he loved best. A few of the kids from Braly Street milled around; the barber came out from his shop, snapped his sheet as if in surrender, and stared at the commotion for a moment, his eyes the color of twilight itself.

Uncle Junior yelled at us to get away, but I shadowed him for a while, barefoot and pagan. He walked up the alley that ran along our dusty-white house. I didn't know then that he intended to wait out the last breaths and then bury his dog. I didn't know that months later at the end of this same alley we were walking down, a car would roll, its wheels in the air, the man inside dead and his hat as flat as cardboard. I would be excited. Like my uncle's collie, I panted, except from exhilaration, when the police asked if we knew the person. I pointed and said that he lived near the man with the motorboat engine and cancer.

This was the summer I began to worry about disease. My father was in road camp with my uncle Shorty. They'd gotten drunk and stolen a car, but I was behaving. I drank my milk, ate my Graham Crackers, and dutifully picked slivers from my palm, but despite my hygiene, I was involved in disease. One morning my brother woke with his throat pinched with a clot that made it difficult for him to swallow. He opened his mouth in the backyard light and, along with my mother, I looked in, worried that I would have to wallow in the same bedroom and, in time, the same disease. His mouth was like any other mouth, wet with a push of milky air. But our mother knew better: the tonsils would have to come out. Mine would have to come out, too, no matter how many times I swallowed, cried, and said, "See, Mom, I'm OK." She figured that if you do one son you might as well do two.

That night I stood by the window in our bedroom and ate M & M candies and wondered about Father and Uncle Shorty. They were in a sort of prison camp, I knew. We had gone to see them, and father had shown me his hands, which were speckled white with paint. I rode on his knee, a camel ride of excitement because I was chewing gum and sunflower seeds at the same time. I asked him when he was coming home. Pretty soon, he answered. I didn't know that he and my uncle were painting rocks along rural Kearny Boulevard and hoisting railroad ties that became bumpers in the gravel parking lots of Kearny Park.

I thought about them as I ate my M & Ms and touched my throat when I swallowed the candy. Father wasn't there to help me. He was far away, it seemed, and I peered out the window toward the junkyard, with its silhouette of pipes, plumbing, and jagged sheet metal, the playground of my childhood. The summer wind picked up the metallic scent and whipped it about. When a sweep of headlights from the cars that turned from Van Ness onto Braly Street frisked the junkyard, the eyes of its German Shepherd watchdog glowed orange and stared at me. I ate my candy, one last taste of sweetness on the eve of blood and gagging.

When we arrived at the community hospital, I hugged my pajamas and coloring book. I glanced nervously down the corridor. I looked at the old people's yellow fingernails, clear signs of cancer, and I peeked in a lab where I knew that blood was drawn. My brother and I walked on each side of our mother. We were led to a room where there was another child sitting up in a crib-like bed, mute as a teddy bear. He spit red into a bowl, and I immediately knew this was a scary place.

After we settled into our room, I worried not about dying, but about the filthy act of baring my bottom to a bedpan. I was in a hospital gown, not my pajamas. I held out for hours, but when I couldn't stand it anymore, I told the nurse I had to use the bathroom. She wouldn't allow me to get up from bed. I started to cry, but she scolded me, and I knew better than to carry on because she had the instruments of pain. I told my brother not to laugh, but he was too scared to entertain the thought. I squatted on the bedpan and was letting my water flow when a blind, teenage girl walked past our open door, a ghost-like figure blowing down the corridor. A nurse was helping her along, step by hesitant step. I wanted to ask the nurse if she was blind forever, or would she one day peel off that bandage and smile at every bloodshot color in the precious world. I did my number and then looked over at the boy, now asleep and pale as an angel.

I don't recall my brother and me talking much at the hospital. I lay in bed, touching the plastic wrist band with my typed name. I closed my eyes. I tried to shut out the image of the "thing" they would take out of my throat, a kidney-bean sac no longer needed. I knew that my baby teeth would eventually loosen and come out, possibly when I was biting into a peach or an apple, but I was terrified that someone behind a white mask would probe my mouth.

A few hours later, my brother was wheeled away with tears brimming in his eyes. If my big brother had dime-size tears in his eyes, then I, his little brother with just baby teeth, would have silver dollars rolling down my cheeks. I considered crying and sobbing as pitifully as I could manage, but who would listen? My mother was gone, a tiny egg of memory living inside my head. Now my brother was gone. I looked over to where the other boy was, but his parents had come and rescued him. I didn't have anything to do except thumb through my animal coloring book and imagine what crayons I would use on the deer, elephant, giraffe and grinning hyena. This diversion helped. But then I was wheeled away.

This was the late '50s when almost every child's tonsils were routinely clipped from his throat. I remember the room where a nurse in a mask lowered a disc-like mask onto my nose and mouth. She lowered it three times and each time said, "breathe in" as they basted my face with ether. I did what I was told until my consciousness receded like a wave, and I was in a room full of testing patterns, something like television when it was still too early for cartoons. They operated, and I bled into a bowl all night, it seemed, but happily drank 7-Up with no ice, a treat that didn't cost me anything except hoarse speech for three days.

When Rick and I got home, we were pampered with ice cream and 7-Up, a lovely blast of carbonation which singed my nostrils. I believed that we might continue to live our remaining childhood that way with mounds of ice cream, 7-Up, and cooing words from our mother. But too soon that stopped, and we were back to the usual plates of *frijoles* and tortillas. At that time, while my father and uncle were in jail, my mother worked at Readi-Spud, peeling potatoes that scurried down troughs of icy water. She would give us over to Mrs. Molina, the mother of at least nine children and the jolliest woman in the western world. She laughed more than she spoke, and she spoke a lot. While in Mrs. Molina's care, I became even more worried about disease because I knew roaches made a princely living in her cupboards.

Mrs. Molina worked at a Chinese noodle factory and came to get Rick and me after work. One day, when we climbed into the back seat of her station wagon, her son Donald was standing in a cardboard tub of noodles. His feet pumped up and down and emitted a sucking sound with each marching step. When I asked Mrs. Molina about dinner she was laughing because the baby on the front seat was crawling toward her breast. She giggled, "You like chow mein?" I slowly lowered my gaze to Donald's bare feet and felt sick.

They ate noodles right after we arrived, slurped them so that the ends wiggled like worms into their suctioning mouths. My brother and I ate grapes and drank water. Later, all of us—eleven kids—played our version of "The Old Woman Who Lived in a Shoe." We climbed onto the roof and jumped off, a cargo of unkillable kids hitting the ground like sacks of flour. It may not have been that same evening, but I recall three babies at the end of a long, dirty hallway and some of the kids, the older ones, trying to knock them over with a real bowling ball. There was squealing and crying, but it was mostly laughter that cut through the cloistered air of a dank hallway, laughter coming even from Mrs. Molina when one of the babies went down.

One untroubled afternoon Lloyd showed me a toy rifle, the kind that you had to crack in half to cock and which shot arrows tipped with red suction cups. He took one suction cup off, cocked the rifle, and shot the arrow into the flat spatula of his palm. "It doesn't hurt," he told me, and let me shoot the arrow repeatedly into my palm, the pressure of the arrow no more than a push. He recocked the rifle and fit the arrow into one of his nostrils. I automatically stepped back even though Lloyd was smiling. He was smiling just a moment before he pulled the trigger, before blood suddenly streamed from his nose and his eyes grew huge as two white moons and full of fright. He started crying and running around the house with the arrow in his nose, and I ran after him, almost crying. When his mother caught him by the arm, I raced out of the house, not wanting to get involved, and returned home, scared as I touched my own nose. I imagined the arrow in my own nose. I imagined blood spilling on the back porch. Later, just after I had finished dinner, I returned to Lloyd's house. He was at the table, with the threads of cotton balls hanging from his nostrils. The family was eating chow mein, piled like worms and wiggling down their throats.

The house was a poor, curled shoe, and it scared me because in its carelessness lurked disease and calamity. I recall standing at their stove and asking a teenage boy who had drifted inside the house. "What's that you're making?" I looked at a large, dented kettle containing a grayish soup which Arnold was stirring with a pencil. I peeked into the soup, sipped it with a large spoon, and saw small things wheeling in the water as he stirred them—a merry-go-round of meats, I thought. When he said, "pigeons," I looked closely and could see the plucked birds bob and rise, bob and rise, and with each rise I could see the slits of their closed eyes.

The Molina place, however, was not nearly as scary as the hospital. There were no instruments of pain, unless you counted the hive of tapeworms that showed up later because I ate raw bacon, white strips we peeled like Band-Aids from the wrapper. The Molinas taught me this too; they said it was good, and I ate my share while sitting on the roof, the sunset a stain the color of bright, bright medicine. How I would need that sun! How I would need a cure for my worry, and a cure for my brother, who was sporting on the bottom of his foot a sliver the size of a chopstick.

At age six disease scared me, and so did Grandpa, who lived just down the alley from our house on Braly Street. When I went over to eat lunch—yet another pile of *frijoles* wrapped in a diaper-size tortilla—he was at the kitchen table playing solitaire with a big chunk of his head missing. I backed out of the house, bristling with fear, because the only thing left was his face. He looked like the poker-face card in front of him: Jack of Bad Luck, or King of Almighty Mistakes? While I backed out of the screen door, Uncle Junior caught me from behind and nudged me into the kitchen. He told me that Grandpa was wearing a nylon stocking on his head, trying to grow his hair black. A stinky concoction of *yerba buena* and earthly fuels smothered his crown and temples. I sat down and ate my beans while watching Grandpa eat from his plate. I asked him if his head would grow back; he was chewing a huge amount of food like a camel. I thought I would turn seven by the time he cleared his throat and heard his answer, which was, "*Mi'jo,* you got beans on your shirt. Shaddup."

Two kittens died from distemper and then Pete, our canary, was devoured by mama cat. A stray dog showed up outside our yard with a piece of wood in its watery eye. I touched my own eye, pulling at a tiny string of sleep. Everything seemed ill and ominous. Even our house began to slip on its foundation, which excited me because the bathroom was now at a slant. The water in the tub slouched now that one side was higher. With a scoop of my hands, it was easy to force a tidal wave on the line of ants scurrying along the baseboard.

I looked around at family and friends who were hurt or dying, but I didn't know that a year later my father would die, his neck broken in an industrial accident. This would be in August, when we were settled in a new house the color of cement. He didn't live in that house more than a week, and then he was gone. The funeral didn't mean much to me. It was the scent of flowers and the wash of tears; it was a sympathic squeeze of my shoulders and candies slipped into the pockets of my tweed coat, which was too small because it was borrowed. After his burial I recall eating donuts at my grandparents' house. When a doctor was called because Grandma was in hysterics, I didn't stop eating. I took what was rightly mine and devoured it in the dark, near the ugly claw-like crowns of a rose bush.

I didn't know what to think except that Father was out of prison and now in the earth forever. Because he wasn't returning, I began to play with his squeaky hand drill, boring into trees and fences. I liked the smell of the blond shavings and liked to think that maybe Father used the drill in prison. He mostly painted rocks, this much I was told, but I fantasized about how he might have used it in prison to get away. I saw him poking holes in a cement wall and then pushing over that wall to get Uncle Shorty in the adjacent cell. Uncle Johnnie was there, too, a ghost-like bundle of flesh on the cot. My father was going to save not only the both of them, but in the end himself as well.

Occasionally, we would visit my father's grave, where my mother cried and set flowers, half-shadowing the oval photo on his grave. What worried me was not his death, but the gold-painted cannon on a hill that pointed at our Chevy when we drove through the cement gates. The cannon scared me because my vision of death was that when you died an angel would pick you up, place your head in the cannon, and give your neck a little twist. I was spooked by this cannon and wanted to ask my mother about it, but she was too busy in her sorrow for a straight answer. I kept quiet on the matter. I figured there was one cannon, like one God, and all graves rolled on a hill. In time, you were asked to put your head in the cannon and die as well.

I didn't realize that I was probably ill. Neither did I realize how I used my time when my mother would send me off to school. For weeks, I didn't go there. I stayed in an alley, kicking through garbage and boredom, and returned home only after I assumed my classmates had finished with whatever the teacher had asked them to do. Sometimes I would take the drill and make holes, occasionally even into the lawn. But I had grown bored with this. I had discovered how I could make a huge noise. In the empty bedroom, the one my father and mother would have used, I spent hours with fistfuls of marbles. I bounced them off the baseboard, a ricochetting clatter that I imagined were soldiers getting their fill of death. The clatter of noise busied my mind with something like hate. If I had looked into a mirror, I would have seen this hate pleated on my forehead. If anyone, including my sister or brother, had smarted off to me, I had plans to get even. I would let them go to sleep and then blast them with marbles at close range as they inhaled a simple dream.

My mother was alone, and in her loneliness she often piled us into our Chevy and drove us over to my *nina's* house on the west side of Fresno, a place that was so scary that even the blacks were afraid. My *nina*—godmother—took in identical twin boys, same age as me but filthier. Their dirty hair was like the hair Woody Woodpecker wore. They were orphans. They were sadly nicknamed "Caca" and "Peepee," and for a while they made me feel good because I knew they were poorer than me. "Peepee, is your dad dead?" I would ask. "Caca, what grade are you in?" I would inquire. They shrugged their shoulders a lot and ran when they saw my *nina,* a woman you dared not play with. Every time we visited, I took a toy to show them—plastic plane, steel car, sock of marbles, and even my brother's glow-in-the-dark statue of Jesus. I wanted them to know that even though my father was dead, I still owned things. After a few visits I didn't have anything left to share, just a ten-foot link of rubber bands. This lack made me mad, and I began to pick on them, even beat them up, in a kind of Punch-and-Judy show in the dirt driveway. When we found out that the twins were scared of ghosts, my brother and Rachel, my *nina's* daughter, told them to sit and wait in the living room because their mother and father were going to pick them up. We gave them fistfuls of raisins. Rick and Rachel then ran outside, where they scraped a bamboo rake against the window. The twins looked at me, then the curtain that was dancing like ghosts from the blast of the window cooler. Their mouths stopped churning on those raisins and the gray light of the TV flashed briefly in their eyes. When I yelled, "*La llorona* is outside," they jumped and ran from the house, poor, terrified "Caca" and "Peepee" living up to their names that early evening.

I often attended church, a place that was scarier than the hospital or the Molinas's house or grandfather's head. Mother said that Jesus had been a good man, and he wanted peace and harmony in the hearts of all men. She said this while I looked at Jesus on his cross, poor Jesus who had nails and blood all over him. If they did that to someone who was so good I wondered what they might do to me. You see, I was turning out bad. I was so angry from having to worry all the time that I had become violent. Once I stuck a broken shaft of bottle in my brother's leg for going swimming without me. Blood ran down my knuckles, and I ran away amazed that it was so calming to hurt someone who was bigger. My mother beat me with a hanger for my violence and then made me eat dinner in the bathroom. I put my bowl first on the hamper, then moved it to my knees, because I wanted a better view of the faucet dripping water. In the bathroom, then, I began to worry about our wasting water. I counted the drips to a hundred. I swallowed and pictured in my mind a pagan baby sucking a rock for moisture. Later, after I was allowed out of the bathroom, I took a pair of pliers and tried to tighten the faucet. I managed only to scratch the chrome plating on the handles, and I went to bed worrying that my mother would conclude that it was me. I closed my eyes and let the pagan baby swallow the rock.

I asked my mother if you ever had to stop worrying, or if you had to continue until you were old. I was already tired of having to learn about Jesus and the more important apostles. She answered yes and mumbled something about life not being easy. This was when I began to look at pictures in the medical dictionary: ringworm, rickets, TB, tongues with canker sores, and elephantiasis. With elephantiasis, the scariest disease, your legs swelled fat as water balloons and, I suspected, sloshed some evil liquids. I looked down at my own legs, those reeds of bone and marrow. They were skinny, but still I worried that my legs could swell and the rest of me, arms mainly, would stay thin, possibly from rickets which had made headway at school. I would be the second deformed kid on our street, the other being an older boy with one small arm that was shaped like a banana.

I knew the face of the boy in the iron lung. His hair was black and his eyes flat. He was motherless, for who could wrap a loving hug around a machine large as a barrel. I could hardly look at this boy. He might have shared my name, or my brother's name, or been related to the kid at school who had one leg shrunken from polio. I didn't like the idea of living lying down for what might be forever. Still, I practiced what he lived by lying still on the couch until I fell asleep. When I woke I didn't know if I was at the new house or the old house, or if an angel had already picked me up and fit my head in the gold-painted cannon.

Then I worried about air and radiation and religious equations like the Trinity and, finally, the march of communists against our country. The hollowness in my face concerned my mother. She studied me when I did my homework at the kitchen table. She suspected that I might have ringworm because there were pale splotches on my face. It was only dirt, though, a film of dirt that you could rub off with spit and a thumb.

My worry lessened when I began to understand that nothing could really hurt me. It was another summer and the beginning of the '60s. On our new street, which was green with lawns and squeaky with new trikes, I discovered my invincibility when I was running with new friends, barefoot, and with no shirt. I was particularly proud because I had hooked a screwdriver in a belt loop on my pants. I tripped and fell, and as I fell I worried for a moment, wondering if the screwdriver would drive its point into my belly. The fall was slow, like the build-up to my seven years, and the result would be either yes or no to my living.

The screwdriver kicked up sparks when it cut across the sidewalk. They were wonderful, these sparks that lasted no longer than a blink. Right then with gravel pitted in my palm and my belly spanked by the fall, I rolled onto my back, cried, and knew that hurt and disease were way off, in another country, one that thanks to Jesus Almighty, I would never think to visit.

Michael Tomasek Manson (essay date 1997)

SOURCE: "Poetry and Masculinity on the Anglo/Chicano Border: Gary Soto, Robert Frost, and Robert Hass," in *The*

Calvinist Roots of the Modern Era, edited by Aliki Barnstone, Michael Tomasek Manson, and Carol J. Singley, University Press of New England, 1997, pp. 263-80.

[*In the following essay, Manson contends that Soto's poetry should be considered outside of the American poetic tradition, contrasting his work with that of Robert Hass and Robert Frost.*]

The guy who pinned
Me was named Bloodworth, a meaningful name.
That night I asked Mom what our name meant in Spanish.
She stirred crackling papas *and said it meant Mexican.*

—Gary Soto, **"The Wrestler's Heart"**

In this scene from his autobiographical sequence ***Home Course in Religion*** (1991), the adolescent Gary Soto wrestles not only with an Anglo empowered by a "meaningful name" but also with his manhood as he tries to make sense out of his defeat. He finds he must—like so many young men in U.S. literature—turn his defeat into a victory if he wants to become a man. And yet Soto's path to manhood is unfamiliar, even, we might say, un-American. As traditionally understood, U.S. literature is expected to depict a "pure American self divorced from specific social circumstances" confronting "the promise offered by the idea of America" (Baym, "Melodramas" 71). That promise, furthermore, is supposed to be threatened "with particular urgency" by "the figure of one or more women" (72). Soto, however, not only turns to his mother for succor but asks her for a heritage. He thus refuses to enter the New World naked and forge a new, self-reliant manhood. He rejects the role of Adam that so many critics have defined as the essence of the Americanness of U.S. literature. We inherited the role of Adam, of course, from the Puritans who saw the continent as an opportunity for the individual to forge an unmediated relationship with God. By turning away from this opportunity and concerning himself instead with heritage—with what different "bloods" are "worth"—Soto breaks what critics have valued as the "countinuity of American poetry" with Puritanism.[1] This break means either that Soto's poetry does not measure up to our best literature or that we will need new ways of describing our literary history.

We might begin with the notion that the term "U.S. literature" is larger and more inclusive than "*American* literature," which is centered by its writers and critics alike around a Puritan origin that posits the "American self as the embodiment of a prophetic universal design" (Bercovitch, *Puritan* 136).[2] This model of *American* literature reproduces the distinction first made by the Puritans between their City on a Hill and a surrounding wilderness populated by savages, a distinction I will call *boundary,* by which I mean to suggest both a perception of difference and a will to conquer.[3] Boundaries are created by leaps or bounds into the unknown or that which is different, and those leaps—like the Puritan leap into the Americas or the sudden jump of the U.S. boundary in 1848 across the northern half of Mexico—stretch across wilderness that must be filled in or conquered. For an alternative to boundary, we might turn to Gloria Anzaldúa, who describes the *border* as the place where "two or more cultures edge each other, . . . where the space between two individuals shrinks with intimacy" (3). Etymologically, border signifies a "cut" across a landscape, thus suggesting both difference and similarity, the difference arising from some prior, historical act of violence. To think in terms of borders, then, is to be aware of the differences that exist on either side, to know their historical causes, and to look for opportunities to cross those borders, letting difference "shrink with intimacy."

With this border model in mind, we can reread Gary Soto's wrestling scene not as a failure to produce. *American* self-reliance but as an attempt to resist it. ***Home Course in Religion,*** I will argue, tells the story of Soto's growth into manhood, describing his replacement of boundaries with borders as he gradually extricates himself from the domination of the *American* self. Empowering this reconception of the self and of masculinity is a Chicano Catholic understanding of the border as mediator rather than boundary.[4] That Soto's conception of mediation is Chicano Catholic rather than simply Catholic becomes clear when we compare it to Robert Hass's use of mediation, which is Catholic but also *American.* My desire, however, to replace an *American* literary history centered around Puritanism with a border one focused on cultural exchange also requires that we begin to see even the most *American* literature as a border product reflecting the plural origins of the United States, and toward that end, I begin by briefly considering a third California poet, Robert Frost.

I

The most popular of all the major modernists, Robert Frost is also the most *American,* frequently promoting a history of the United States based on boundaries. The most dramatic example is the poem he read at John F. Kennedy's inauguration, "The Gift Outright." Right away, the first line—"The land was ours before we were the land's"—suggests a boundary, as the British leap onto this continent is seen as manifest destiny. The settlers must only fill in the boundaries preordained for them.

There is, however, a deeper understanding of boundary here. Although the poem is explicitly concerned with the conquest of the continent in the seventeenth, eighteenth, and nineteenth centuries, its assumptions belong instead to the dawn of the twentieth century and the 1898 war with Spain. In a 1934 interview, one year before he wrote "The Gift Outright," Frost claimed that one of his ten favorite books and "surely one of the very best of our modern best-sellers" was the historical romance *The Prisoner of Zenda* (*Collected* 738), which was published in 1894, just two years after Frost graduated from high school. As Amy Kaplan explains, historical romances of the 1890s like *The Prisoner of Zenda* created a new form of masculinity more appropriate to the overseas empire gained after the Spanish-American War.

This new overseas empire required a fresh understanding of boundary both for the nation and the masculine body. During the earlier, continental expansion, U.S. writers compared the nation to a body that must expand or die, but the new overseas empire was "informal," economic rather than territorial.[5] Rejecting an older European-style colonialism, the United States concentrated on controlling trade routes and establishing military bases in former Spanish possessions like Cuba and the Philippines, while leaving these countries varying degrees of putative political independence. Because expansion was now disembodied, Kaplan argues, the united States required a "double discourse" that depicted the nation and the masculine body as "spectacles" that must be continually re-presented. Andrew Jackson, Indian-fighter, was replaced as masculine model by Teddy Roosevelt, who was seen simulating, doubling, his masculinity in photographs and in "authentic" costumes constructed in New York (Kaplan 655). While Jackson was simply vigorous, Roosevelt's spectacular masculinity was a technological feat. Roosevelt's virility was as disembodied, as "informal," as the empire he represented.

A product of this new double discourse of imperialism, "The Gift Outright" emphasizes not manly vigor but its doubling. The one reference to physical conflict takes place in a parenthesis, while the rest of the poem emphasizes the disembodied, spectacular nature of manifest destiny:

> Such as we were we gave ourselves outright (The deed of gift was many deeds of war) To the land vaguely realizing westward, But still unstoried, artless, unenhanced,

The "unstoried, artless, unenhanced" land is, of course, the Puritans' wilderness. What is new is the "land vaguely realizing westward," as if the land only became real—tangible, embodied, em-boundaried—as *Americans* took possession of it. More importantly, the conquest of the continent requires the mastery of the self, since Frost emphasizes not the hardihood of the frontiersman but his confusion and lack of self-knowledge. "We were England's," he tells us, "still colonials," and because of that, we were "weak." Ultimately, we possessed the land only when we "found salvation in surrender" and stopped "withholding . . . ourselves." Significantly, the "we" here applies specifically to white, English settlers and to any readers who can identify with their position, not to those already inhabiting the land. In fact, part of Frost's evidence that *Americans* have failed to "story" the land is that they have named their lands "Virginia" and "Massachusetts," after the English queen who sent them here and the Native Americans they conquered, not after *themselves.* Although "The Gift Outright" acknowledges as "deeds of war" the border conflicts with Mexico in 1846 and Spain in 1898, Frost's understanding of "story" represses full knowledge of these conflicts in favor of an emboundaried notion of national and racial mission. He cannot face squarely the Spanish-American War that necessitated a spectacular masculinity and informal empire. "The Gift Outright" thus represents a modern doubling of Puritan boundaries.

A border history of our literature, however, should look not only for its Puritan roots (the boundaries that have been drawn) but also for the borders that have been crossed. We might remember, first of all, that Frost was born in California because his New England father had lit out for the territories in 1873, wanting to be part of the "settlement" of the West, which of course had already been settled by Mexicans and Native Americans.[6] After his father's death, the eleven-year-old Frost moved to New England with his mother and sister, making him both foreign and native to New England. His experience moving back from the frontier thus revealed an inner border between New Englanders and Californians.

The crossing of this border, in fact, made possible his birth as a poet. John Walsh's biography has shown that the poet who, according to legend, struggled for twenty years unnoticed by an outdated literary establishment was instead a mediocre poet struggling to find his "voice." Frost only discovered his voice, Walsh tells us, when he stopped writing poetry in 1908 and started imitating the vocal mannerisms of his farmer neighbors (63). After two years, this tutelage inspired a writing process that ultimately resulted in the brilliant dialogues of *North of Boston* (1914). The origin of Frost's poetry is thus plural: he became a poet when he learned the language of his New England neighbors, letting "difference shrink with intimacy" as Anzaldúa says it must on the border.

Frost's border-crossing created not only his distinctive use of language but also the theme for much of his early work, particularly in *North of Boston* where two versions of *American* boundary frequently conflict. These dialogues have generally been seen as typical of regionalism's depiction of conflicts between rural folk and sophisticated urbanites.[7] "Mending Wall," for example, presents a confrontation between a New England farmer and the poem's speaker, who, like Frost, is knowledgeable about New England ways though perhaps not a New Englander himself. Instead of seeing a country-city conflict here, we might see the farmer as a Puritan who expresses the purity of his faith by adhering to tradition—"He will not go behind his father's saying." His father's belief that "Good fences make good neighbors" itself descends from the Puritans, who fled Europe in part because European society threatened to corrupt them. The Atlantic thus formed a "fence" between the New World and the Old, a different kind of boundary than the one we have been discussing but a boundary nonetheless. Emerson echoes and develops this distrust of neighbors when he claims in "Self-Reliance" that "Society everywhere is in conspiracy against the manhood of every one of its members" (2:49). The farmer acts on this advice when he "wall[s] out" neighbors' threats to his rootedness in tradition.

The speaker, meanwhile, rebels against tradition. Like a frontiersman, he cannot abide fences that carve up the land, robbing him of space in which to remake himself. And it is reinvention that motivates the speaker, the possibility that the "something" that "doesn't love a wall" is a mischief inherent in us that defies and goes "behind" every "father's saying." The speaker's antinomianism is an inheritance every bit as Puritan as the farmer's, but their roles in filling in *American* boundaries have put them at odds.

"Mending Wall" intends, however, to bring the two *American* perspectives together even though no simple healing is possible. The speaker may begin the poem proposing that the gaps in the wall are so large that "even two can pass abreast," but he ultimately imagines, as Puritans do, that the Other is an "old stone *savage* armed" (emphasis added). Healing thus comes not from the characters, who remain locked in conflict, but from us, the readers. Frost's note at the beginning of *North of Boston* tells us that "'Mending Wall' takes up the theme where *A Tuft of Flowers* in *A Boy's Will* laid it down," and in "The Tuft of Flowers," we learn that "Men work together . . . / Whether they work together or part" only when they focus on the work itself, letting community come in visionary moments. In "Mending Wall," that community is never realized by the speaker, but it can be there for the reader as we watch the characters work together and "mend wall" despite their disagreements. As Frost later said, we must lift such conflicts to a "higher plane of *regard*" ("Comments"). From this viewpoint, the differences between the two men "shrink with intimacy." Frost is a border poet when he crosses the division between these two different kinds of *American,* and he can do so partly because his childhood on the border has made him aware of the differences that lie within our boundaries.

On rarer occasions, as in "America Is Hard to See" (1951), Frost can step outside our boundaries and create a true border poetry. This poem revises the first one he ever wrote, "La Noche Triste," an account of Cortez's defeat of the Aztecs inspired by Frost's adolescent reading of William Hickling Prescott's famous *History of the Conquest of Mexico* (1843). In "La Noche Triste," as in Prescott's history, the defeat of the Native Americans is romanticized. The Native Americans are no longer "savage" in the Puritan sense, but the inevitability of European victory testifies to the superiority of "civilization," thus retaining the manifest destiny of Puritan historiography. Revising this poem, Frost extricates himself from its racist imperial history to understand that the destiny of the United States has never been manifest. Ending with Cortez's raid on the Aztecs, Frost spends much of the poem demythologizing Columbus's discovery of the Americas. Columbus was a bad mariner ("He wasn't off a mere degree / His reckoning was off a sea"), and his motives were suspect: "Not just for scientific news / Had the Queen backed him to a cruise."

As Frost suggests, the promise of *America* has frequently been pecuniary, but he is more disturbed by the Puritan claims for the continent as a New World, "The race's future trial place, / A fresh start for the human race." Strikingly, he admits,

> I was deceived by what he did.
> If I had had the chance when young
> I should have had Columbus sung
> As a god who had given us
> A more than Moses' exodus.
> But all he did was spread the room
> Of our enacting out the doom
> Of being in each other's way,
> And so put off the weary day
> When we would have to put our mind
> On how to crowd but still be kind.

Frost's history is still flawed—the continent was not wilderness but was already "crowded" with Native Americans and, later, with Mexicans and Mexican Americans—but he has still crossed a border. Reflecting on the history of Mexico he read as an adolescent, he realizes that the myth of American exceptionalism has prevented the United States from learning how to live on the border Anzaldúa describes, a place where peoples meet and "crowd" but can still be "kind." In his most perceptive poetry, Frost sometimes finds himself living on just such a border.

II

As a border poet, Gary Soto does not find his roots in Puritanism; he finds instead that Puritan roots threaten his growth. To thrive, he must struggle against the Puritan desire to make boundaries, and ***Home Course in Religion*** recounts his effort to create a masculinity liberated from the *American* self that dominates so much of Frost's poetry. This reconception is made possible when Soto sees the border as mediation rather than boundary. Before tracing Soto's reconstruction of a border masculinity based on mediation, however, we will need to explain how Soto's use of mediation is both Chicano and Catholic.

Unlike Calvinism, Catholicism emphasizes mediation. While Calvinism sees nothing between God and the self, Catholicism believes that the Church can both intercede with God on the self's behalf and represent God to the self (Bercovitch, *Puritan* 22). By "Church," Catholics mean not only the institutional body of priests, nuns, bishops, and so on, but the entire community of the faithful, both the living and the dead. The Church can mediate between God and the self because as the "body of Christ" it embodies the divine while remaining human. Justus Lawler uses this corollary, *analogia entis,* to distinguish between Catholicism and Protestantism: Professing *analogia entis,* Catholics believe that "the contingent self is paradoxically merged with the absolute, while . . . nevertheless remaining contingent." Protestants, however, believe that "the finite is so imprisoned . . . that it cannot become the infinite; . . . it can only be breathed upon, as one would breathe upon a piece of metal to polish it" (95). Frost represents this Protestant view when he speaks of poetry as a "momentary stay against confusion": Just for a moment, he suggests, the divine breath makes the soul's metal shine, but confusion tarnishes it quickly, requiring the soul's constant renewal.

Robert Hass, on the other hand, represents the Catholic view in "Meditation at Lagunitas" (*Praise* 1979). In this poem, Hass reflects on the continuity of recent philosophy with Plato—"All the new thinking is about loss. / In this it resembles all the old thinking"—and decides that although desire is indeed "full / of endless distances," still "There are moments when the body is as numinous / as words." Hass's "moments" differ from Frost's "momentary stays" because Hass follows the doctrine of *analogia entis* in believing that such moments occur when we experience "wonder at . . . presence," the numinous within the body, within words—in Lawler's terms, the infinite merged with the finite. Frost's work is marked by whimsy and caprice: one can never tell when God's breath will stay our confusion. For Hass, however, wonder is always available in the presence of the body, just as it is always available at the Catholic Eucharist.

Despite his Catholicism, however, Hass remains *American* (and therefore Puritan) in his attitude toward the land. This attitude can be traced back to Stevens and, behind him, to Emerson, whose vision of a "new man in a paradisiacal New World" Bercovitch has traced to Jonathan Edwards and Cotton Mather (*Puritan* 157). Stevens ends "Sunday Morning" with this promise:

> Deer walk on our mountains, and quail whistle
> About us their spontaneous cries,
> Sweet berries ripen in the wilderness

Retaining the Puritan sense of boundary, of the encircling "wilderness," Stevens points with pride to "our" mountains, the frontier again representing for *Americans* the chance to rejuvenate the self. *America,* he implies without irony, is the chosen world for supreme fictions; no place is better suited since no place is, as Frost says in "The Gift Outright," so "unstoried, artless, unenhanced." Inheriting much of Stevens's thought and imagery, Hass concludes "Meditation at Lagunitas" by remembering "Sunday Morning"'s ripening berries:

> There are moments when the body is as numinous
> as words, days that are the good flesh continuing.
> Such tenderness, those afternoons and evenings,
> saying *blackberry, blackberry, blackberry.*

If the first line is Catholic, then the rest are *American,* investing the land—as Stevens, Emerson, and the Puritans do—with redemptive promise. Only our attention to this *American* land, to its berries and bodies, Hass suggests, will help us recover our millennial mission.[8]

More even than Hass, Soto is convinced of *analogia entis,* but he looks not to an individual and visionary relation to the land as Hass, Stevens, and the Puritans do. Their repeated desire for transcendence is replaced by Soto's desire to learn how to be "nice," to build healthy relationships with others—this is what he means by "holiness." Hass's patronym is no more English than Soto's, but Hass's people belong to those Europeans who were eventually accepted economically, socially, and institutionally, racism turning into prejudice and finally acceptance. Because of that shift, Hass can be "Anglo" and his poetry *American,* despite his Catholicism. For Soto, however, people are more important than the land because they mediate between God and other humans. Living in an "occupied America," Soto lacks the classic immigrant's faith in the land's promise, knowing instead that the boundary of the United States crossed his people in 1848.[9] Soto thus places his hopes in community, expecting to find himself and God through the mediations of others.

We can see both Soto's Catholic similarity to Hass and his Chicano difference by reading **"A Sunday"** with "Meditation at Lagunitas" in mind. Soto's poem begins where Hass's leaves off: "There are moments when the body is as numinous / as words, days that are the good flesh continuing" becomes

> That the flesh should go on now seems to matter.
> And goodness in the meantime. I'm trying
> To be like others in the church. Katie
> Says it's possible, even at this corner,
> Leavenworth and Bush, drab men in three sweaters,
> Bum on his beat between a boarded-up grocery
> And hell.
>
> (70)

Soto is silent about what happened at church to make the "flesh continuing" "seem to matter," but Hass focuses precisely on that moment—the visionary transcendence achieved when the "flesh continuing" is simply "good," as the land *America* is simply good when Emerson steps onto the common to become a transparent eyeball. Soto is silent about his epiphany perhaps because Sunday Mass is supposed to remind one of the goodness of the flesh, of the miracle of the Incarnation. In fact, we might notice here that Hass functions as Matthew Arnold believed poets should, performing the role religion once did. In the United States, this understanding of the poet dovetailed nicely with Emerson's belief that the poet should create a sacred yet secular *America.* But Soto stands outside these traditions since, for him, the visions and consolations sought by Emerson, Arnold, and Hass occur at every Sunday Mass, where it "matter[s]" that "the flesh should go on now." Soto can thus turn his attention in the poem from transcendence to the kind of "goodness" that happens "in the meantime," between Sundays as we work as God's intermediaries for others. Katie reminds Soto of just that point when she explains that "God is someone who is with you, / Like now" (71). The double meaning of "someone" (God or Katie) implies that Katie mediates between God and Soto just as Soto mediates between God and Katie.

This Chicano Catholic emphasis on mediation—on the border where God and humanity meet—distinguishes Soto from the more Puritan or *American* Hass. Soto tries "To be like others in the church" while Hass transcends the "endless distances" between people in order to discover their individuality, "the way her hands dismantled bread, / the thing her father said that hurt her." Soto tries to be "nice" by finding a road or mediation between his own mean streak and others' sensibilities while Hass jumps, *bounds,* from "distance" to "tenderness." What moves **"A Sunday"** forward is not the possibility of transcendence that is so palpably in the offing in every line of Hass's "Meditation" but the many borders across which niceness must travel. Katie reminds Soto that he "should know better" than to watch her "running water / In the bathroom sink" (71), and he ends the Sunday evening by reminding himself not to look at his students' underwear when they uncross their legs (74). In between, he realizes that playing backgammon with Katie differs from playing chess with his daughter because Katie "wants my company" while "Mariko wants my money" (72), thus understanding that games require different kinds of niceness from him. With Mariko he is a "kind fool with dead bishops" (72), while he and Katie "smile at our losses / And stare out the windows" (71). Each Hass poem, like each Frost poem—like each day for the Puritan—represents a new, determined effort to achieve transcendence, bounding the distance between finite and infinite. But each Soto poem crosses—mediates between—borders, seeking the community that is found when we recognize not only the differences between us but also the commonalities.

III

"A Sunday" appears late in ***Home Course in Religion,*** representing a self that is learning how to "be like others" and be "good," to mediate "holiness." But much of the volume is devoted to describing how that growth was made possible only after Soto learned to understand masculinity outside the bounds of an *American* self. Properly understood, the masculinity Soto exhibits in the later poems is *machismo,* the masculinity of a strong and loving husband and father, not its degraded form, a violent misogyny born of poverty and oppression (Anzaldúa 83). Although Catholicism both helped and hindered Soto's growth from a degraded to a virtuous form of *machismo,* both the process and the product of his growth lie outside the bounds of *American* poetry and its corresponding Calvinism and masculinity.

The key to *machismo,* to either form of it, is that it is mediated, taught, Soto suggests, by others. He learns it first as "meanness," the invasion of the sensibilities of others. In **"Apple,"** a retelling of the Fall, Soto places his "first temptation" to steal (14) in the context of looking into the family album and remembering the mean tricks to which his family subjected him: his brother telling him that "Captain Kangaroo / Lives in that house" or that "That kid said you were black"; his uncle asking him to help start the car—"I pulled / From the front fender and was dragged up the alley, / The engine whirring warm air into my face." "I didn't catch on right away," he tells us in a characteristic understatement, "That meanness was part of the family" (12). Soto retains responsibility for his Fall (his mature *machismo* will allow nothing less), but his awareness that the Fall was a border he crossed means he also realizes the role of mediation. Falling was taught to him. Although Soto blames no single person for this culture of meanness, he does focus on his tyrannical stepfather, Jim, who liked to claim that the young Soto was having the "Best years of your life" even while he presided over a home in which "Everyone was scared . . . even Mom." Jim's claim makes the young Soto remember more meanness:

> The best years,
> He said, and I thought of my brother and David,
> How earlier they had pinned me to the ground.
> And let Pinkie, David's homing pigeon,
> Perch on my forehead, weight like a warm stone.
>
> (**"Best Years"** 19)

Although Jim is not directly responsible for this violence, he creates the conditions for it, thus mediating a degraded *machismo.*

U.S. literature is littered with abusive fathers, but ever mindful of the border, Soto implies that Jim's meanness results from *American* boundaries, the Puritan desire to conquer the wilderness. Drunk and watching a Western on TV, Jim rages about Pearl Harbor while his three stepchildren look on:

> We were scared,
> The three of us, and when he said Nips
> Should be dead, a TV Indian tumbled
> From a cliff with a fist of smoke in his back.
>
> (20)

Soto's imagery is precise and allusive: the putatively treacherous Indian is shot in the back while Jim describes Japanese treachery at Pearl Harbor, the "fist" of smoke communicating the personal hatred that belies the unreality of the TV image. Jim embraces the simplicity of TV, reproducing its emphasis on the boundaries between "white" and "red," *American* and "Nip." Crossing the border, Soto is aware of both the Anglo and Chicano origins of the meanness that dominated his youth.[10] To read Soto as a border poet thus means we must abandon quests for the continuity of U.S. poetry and articulate instead the struggle of some of our writers to forge selves out of non-Puritan origins.

Soto resisted the culture of meanness represented by Jim, not by being self-reliant as a Calvinist and *American* must, but by opening himself to mediations that represented other ways of living. First of all, Catholicism gave him pride in his difference from his Anglo neighbors ("Palm-leaf crosses withered in the kitchen window / For our Okie[11] neighbors to look at in awe"), and then in church a "good priest . . . stared holiness / Into my body," creating a new set of values:

> Now I'm quiet,
> The telephone is quiet, my family
> And the people I like best are quiet.
> The nuns would be proud of me . . .
>
> (**"Pink Hands"** 7-8)

Soto's self-presentation here may seem tame, even small in its solicitation of the nuns who taught him in grade school, to readers trained to appreciate the grand ambitions of Whitman and the ironies of Frost—the drama of the isolate self struggling to fulfill the promise of *America.* But Soto cares about a rather different drama—the question of how to build healthy communities—and thus he focuses here on how the example of particular priests and nuns provided an alternative to his own meanness, his brother's and uncle's cruelty, and his stepfather's reproduction of *American* boundaries.

Because Soto's resistance to a culture of meanness that is both Chicano and *American* originates in mediation rather than in self-reliance, the process of his transformation takes an unconventional shape. Much Anglo men's literature combines rejection of the father with some form of repatriation, some reestablishment of the patriarchy in another name. Either the son/quester experiences transcendence, thus discovering patriarchal power in the self; or he declares himself a figurative orphan and finds a new man to father him, as Robin does in "My Kinsman, Major Molineaux"; or he displaces blame onto women and seeks escape from their feminine and feminizing world, as Rip Van Winkle does (Fetterley 3).

As many feminist critics have argued, the first two forms of repatriation rely on the third in some way, but through mediation, Soto remakes masculinity without blaming women or placing them outside any bounds. For example, he experiences transcendence as a healthy response to pain but not as a satisfactory way of living. In **"Best Years,"** he tells us that

> Sometimes you don't want to get up after
> A brother has slapped you around,
> But look skyward between branches of sycamore—
> The pinpricks of stars, planes, end-of-the-world colors.
>
> (19)

Despite the efficacy of this "skyward" vision, transcendence is finally too apocalyptic, too "end-of-the-world" and dependent on extreme duress for Soto, who wants to live in a community in which people can treat each other well. For this purpose, the solitude of transcendence, even the transcendent solitude of Hass's lovers, is simply not enough. Furthermore, instead of scapegoating women or finding a mythic father, Soto discovers the father through a woman: "That night I asked Mom what our name meant in Spanish. / She stirred crackling *papas* and said it meant Mexican." In this telling phrase, which is his only use of Spanish in the volume, Soto suggests that his father—his papa—is the potato his mother fries, a cultural legacy larger and more communal, if less glamorous, than any patronym.[12] The young Anglo who pinned Soto has the "meaningful name" Bloodworth and can point to a private legacy that descends only through his father's side or "blood," but Soto can point to a culture that gives him worth (**"The Wrestler's Heart"** 36). He is repatriated into a community, not a self.

This communal legacy means that, if the father is bad, Soto can find other mediators—a central theme in ***Home Course.*** The volume portrays Soto as both resisting and participating in the culture of meanness for which his stepfather mediates. While the Church first provides Soto the motive for resistance to this culture, at adolescence Soto turns to masculinity. Again, unlike many other coming-of-age stories, the achievement of masculinity enables, not the creation of a single, isolate self, transcendent in its separation, but a place in a growing community. Soto learns about that place through his relationship with "Scott, a real friend," whose father is also dead (**"Fall and Spring"** 34).

Soto's friendship with Scott is a border meeting between the self and other selves. They share their secrets: their feelings about their dead fathers, the girl Scott "liked in seventh grade" (34), and Soto's conviction that "I have lived before" and may be "Chinese" (33). But perhaps the most important element in their friendship is their decency. Although they share a degraded *machismo*—they siphon gas, destroy abandoned houses, and flirt with self-destruction—and despite the fact that "Neither one of us / Believed in hell, and neither believed / In good grades,"

> We both agreed that Mrs. Tuttle
> Was a nice person, and, Scott first,
> Said that we were sorry for parking in front of her house
> And thinking weird thoughts about her La-Z-Boy recliner.
>
> (**"School Night"** 39)

Catholicism has lost its hold on such doctrinal issues as hell, but it impresses on the young men a respect for "nice" people. They show true *machismo* when, "Scott first," they confess their sin against Mrs. Tuttle. The moment recalls our first knowledge of Soto's Catholicism. In **"Pink Hands,"** he tells us that "I never understood / The Trinity, and still have doubts" (7), but in **"The Dictionaries,"** he says he thought the Trinity "was something like / People inside each other / And was somehow like manners" (11). We see here Soto's consistent doctrinal uncertainty as well as his consistent valorization of "manners" and "niceness," those social and cultural forms that mediate or cross borders between people. However degraded his *machismo* becomes, Soto retains this Chicano Catholic belief, building community as he resists the culture of meanness.[13]

Resistance becomes an open break with the patriarchy that underwrites this meanness when Soto learns that *machismo* goes beyond men's fraternity to a community with women. To achieve this community he must eradicate the misogyny from both his Catholicism and his early *machismo.* The volume's title poem describes Soto's frustration with studying religion in college. Quoting several books, he comments on the relative clarity of each one, stating that even the intelligible ones made him sleepy, using up "the good air in my brain" (49). After the seventh book, "I woke only when / My girlfriend came over with a bag of oranges" (52), and after she leaves, he reads the Bible's description of Doubting Thomas, who touched Jesus's wounds. The poem ends,

> I began to feel ashamed because my left hand
> Turning the pages was the hand that had snapped
> Her panties closed. I got up from the couch
> And washed that hand, stinky trout that I took to bed.
> It was then, on a night of
> More Top Ramen and a cat-and-dog storm,
> That I realized I might be in the wrong line of belief.
>
> (52)

From now on, Soto suggests, he will base both his theology and his sexuality on something other than misogyny.

The "wrong line of belief" is not only the notion that sex—particularly women's sexuality—is dirty, but also the idea that women are only sexual objects. Soto's relationship with his girlfriend is not nearly as healthy as the one he shares with Scott:

> She said that she was lonely
> When I wasn't around. I said that people feel
> Like that because they don't know themselves.
> I said just be mellow, just think of
> Yourself as a flower, etc.
> When I placed my hand on her thigh, she opened her legs
> Just a little. . . .
>
> (52)

Instead of entering her emotions as he did Scott's, Soto responds with the language of boundaries, of self-reliance (just know yourself, he tells her), and moves immediately to a formulaic attempt at seduction ("think of / Yourself as a flower, etc."), taking no heed of her reluctance as she opens her legs "just a little." There is no meeting at this border. By the end of the poem, Soto realizes that the *machismo* that brought him so close to Scott has failed to create true intimacy between the sexes.

Soto does not describe the road that led him across the border from this realization to his mature relationship with women, but the evidence of that maturity lies all about the second section of ***Home Course in Religion.*** In **"The Asking,"** displaying true *machismo,* he gives his wife and daughter respect, treats them well, and works with his wife to provide for their family and to perform household chores:

> Carolyn is tired. She went to work,
> Cooked. After dinner she'll want to be by herself.
> To smoke and run a garden hose in our pond.
> Mariko and I talk while we eat.
>
> . . . . .
>
> I do the dishes. . . .
>
> (60)

This picture contrasts sharply with Soto's stepfather, who ruled the house from his armchair and gave his wife and children no psychological space.

The maturity of Soto's new *machismo* is clearest when he addresses his failures. Returning to **"A Sunday,"** which features Soto's growing understanding that "God is someone who is with you," we also see an occasional inability to cross borders. When Soto returns from Mass, first his wife, Carolyn, jokes with him and then she shows him "where an arbor should go":

> I look at the ground and try to find
> Something to say. I want my wife to like me.
> I look up to a homing pigeon cooing
> On the neighbor's fence. We call Mariko,
> Our daughter, who comes out of the house
> With a book in her hand. That's a homing pigeon,
> I point. You see the band on its leg?
> We forget about the arbor. We go inside.
>
> (72)

Soto's response begins with a profound awareness of a failed border crossing—he has nothing to say about the arbor even though Carolyn has asked for a comment. He wants to be "nice," for her to "like" him, but apparently he cannot, at least not in the way she would like. Instead of giving up and allowing a boundary to form—what Hass calls in "Meditation" an "endless distance," or in "Heroic Simile" the "limits to imagination" found in the "silence of separate fidelities" between two people—Soto turns to another kind of mediation. By being nice to his daughter, Mariko, Soto communicates his love for Carolyn. They can now "forget about the arbor." There is loss here, a confession of his ineffectiveness that reminds us of his earlier acknowledgment that Carolyn's friends at her Japanese Methodist church "are nicer than me" and "that I would never be / As nice as they" (**"The Family in Spring"** 65). But he partially makes up for his inability to discover anything nice to say about the arbor by creating an eloquent reminder of his love. When he and Carolyn call Mariko out of the house to see the "band" on a homing pigeon, the poem picks up an important image from **"The Family in Spring"**—the wedding band, which he once never wore but now does because it "says you're married" and makes him feel like "I was in the right place" (64). Soto cannot be as nice as he wants to be, but he can still make his love felt. His love of and through his daughter brings him and Carolyn "inside." Mariko becomes Soto's pigeon, carrying him home to wife and family. The homing pigeon with which his brother had tormented him in **"Best Years"** now has a finer purpose as Soto replaces the culture of meanness with a love of border crossings.

Finally, this mature *machismo* transforms Soto's understanding of his own masculine physicality as he replaces his teenage violence and self-destructiveness with karate. He realizes that karate's physicality is an attempt to deal with the past—"Finger pokes / Can blind a stepfather" and "You admit / You're a playground kid who never had enough" (**"The History of Karate"** 57)—but he again applies masculinity to the end of building community. He teaches karate to "dirty angels in dirty *gis*" at the Boys' Club (55), giving these boys, who are growing up much as he did, a mature father figure. He understands that

They need love, Christ but not Christ,
A father with unexpected gifts in one hand,
A glove in the other.

("The Asking" 60)

These children do not need dogma; they need a mediator who can embody Christ's healing grace, like a father who can bring "unexpected gifts" as well as a constructive discipline like karate. Soto himself had no such father—unless we realize that fathers can also be found in the good father staring holiness into him and in his mother stirring crackling *papas.*

Living on the border has meant for Soto a transformation of the self as profound as any in U.S. literature, though it cannot properly be called *American:* Soto faces no wilderness either within or without; his manhood is neither "beset" nor "spectacular"; transcendence is only useful when he has been decked; and people draw the best out of him more than the land does. Soto was born only a year after Frost realized that we must learn how to "crowd but still be kind," but for Soto that is what living in the United States has always meant. Perhaps this is what our literary history can mean as well once we think of Puritanism not as the origin of our boundaries but as just one edge along our many, crowded borders. If the modern era must accomplish something, it is surely a new understanding of our world that recognizes, in the words of poet Jay Wright, that the "multi-cultural is the fundamental process of human history" (14).

Notes

I am grateful to Anne Macmaster, Marianne Noble, Carol J. Singley, Timothy Spurgin, and Kathryn Manson Tomasek for their assistance on this essay.

1. Lewis's *American Adam* and Pearce's *Continuity of American Poetry* have helped define *American* literary history around these themes. Although Bercovitch is critical of Puritanism, he too finds it central to American identity in works like *The Puritan Origins of the American Self.* In "Melodramas of Beset Manhood," Baym explains how these literary histories are masculine and therefore partial at best, and TuSmith extends Baym's argument to U.S. ethnic literatures, describing their emphasis on community. I will contrast a community similar to those TuSmith describes with Bercovitch's description of the individualistic American self instituted by Puritanism.

2. For the purposes of this essay, "Anglo," "America," and "American" will represent the hegemonic discourse of the United States that limits its history and literary criticism to Puritan and English origins. From this perspective, assimilated Germans, Italians, and other European immigrants can be seen as "Anglo" and "American" insofar as they subscribe to a specific ideology described by Bercovitch (*Puritan*), Takaki, and others: the belief that the U.S. has a special destiny, inherited through and most fully embodied by those of English descent. For a fuller explanation of this dynamic, see also Marinaccio's essay in the present volume.

3. For a history of this distinction between civilization and savagery, see Takaki 24-50. Takaki explains that settlers in the Virginia colony viewed Native Americans as ignorant but educable heathens, while the Puritans demonized them as devilish savages. Ultimately, Puritan ideology won out, setting "a course for the making of a national identity in America for centuries to come" (44). I call this construction of a difference that must be conquered "boundary."

4. Chabram notes a recent shift from studies that describe a "uniform response to mainstream practices and literary assumptions" by marginalized social groups to studies that "unearth their heterogeneous—and oftentimes contradictory—responses" (141). I hope to indicate some of this heterogeneity by describing Soto's perspective through a multiple adjective—Chicano Catholic. Many Chicano writers, for example, from Alurista to Anzaldúa, have criticized the role of Catholicism in oppressing their people. A fuller study would describe Soto's position as a middle-class writer while remaining sensitive to the changed meaning of middle-class in this context. Pérez-Torres touches on class in contrasting Soto and Ana Castillo (268), while Sánchez demonstrates what a more detailed analysis would require.

5. The term "informal empire" is LaFeber's.

6. For the Puritans and the *American* ideology they instituted, land was "wilderness" and required "settlement" if its denizens were "savages" (Takaki 39). For a description of how these attitudes carried over into the conquest of Northern Mexico in the 1830s and 1840s, see Takaki 171.

7. See, for example, Kemp's fine study.

8. Raised Catholic, Hass has rejected his childhood faith for a "mystical" one that yet shows a debt to both Puritan ideology and Catholicism. First, in essays on Lowell and Wright, Hass opposes Calvinism—the "evangelical side of American culture," with its "hatred of intelligence" (*Twentieth* 39), "stylized violence" (42), and contribution to the "annihilative rage of capitalism" (20)—to the "unborn myth which American poetry was making" (19). As his language shows, however, this *unborn* myth still participates in Puritan ideology in its jeremiad-like rhetoric. Second, although Hass wants to replace Catholic "sacramental mediation" with a "contemplative peace beyond any manifestation in the flesh," he still calls his "mystical" apprehension of God an "*embodiment* of what can't be embodied" (22, emphasis added). He thus develops a secular American mysticism through a partial rejection and refinement of a Catholic apprehension of *analogia entis.* In this sense only is he a Catholic writer.

9. See Acuña's landmark history, *Occupied America.*

10. Although racism means that "most / Of us wouldn't get good jobs, some / Would die," Soto also suggests in "The Levee" that "We deserved this life" because television has been internalized, "wreathed in dollies / And the glow-in-the-night Christ on the windowsill" (38).

11. Literally, Okies are the impoverished Oklahomans who moved West after the Dust Bowl of the 1930s.
12. In the Americas, *papa* means "potato," which in Spain is called *patata. Papa* can also refer to the Pope, thus combining the themes of religion, culture, and masculinity. *Soto,* meanwhile, means "grove" or "thicket," the wilderness Puritans hope to conquer, making very apt Soto's mother's quip that the name means "Mexican."
13. Soto reaches a low point when he imitates Jim's prejudices. In the last two poems of the first section, Soto carefully juxtaposes his teenage prejudices—"Fuckin' queers" ("Drinking in the Sixties" 43)—with his stepfather's—"He had words for blacks, / Stalin, the yellow race that could jump up and down / And destroy us all" ("Spelling Words at the Table" 45). The phrase "had words" recalls the poem that introduced Jim ("our stepfather had words / For men with long hair" ["The Music at Home" 17]), thus giving us one origin for Soto's early homophobia. Soto will become a poet when he no longer possesses or "has" words but travels across their borders.

Robin Ganz (essay date 1997)

SOURCE: "Gary Soto," in *Updating the Literary West,* Texas Christian University Press, 1997, pp. 426-33.

[*In the following essay, Ganz provides a brief overview of Soto's life and work.*]

In the early 1950s Fresno, California, was an arid and grimy city of 91,000 inhabitants. Many were caught in an economic chokehold that relegated them to a lifetime of punishing labor in the cotton field, the orchard and vineyard or the small factory. African American, "Okie," Chicano and Asian American families populated Fresno's blue-collar neighborhoods and by this time the racism of the thirties and forties had given way to a kind of mutual acceptance, born of the daily necessity of working together and by their shared "culture of poverty." Every weekday residents of Fresno's barrios and other inner-city neighborhoods would pile aboard trucks and buses that transported them to the lush and fertile farmland of the San Joaquin Valley that surrounds the city.

Against this backdrop of agricultural plenty and urban indigence, Gary Soto was born on Fresno's Braly Street on April 12, 1952. Frank Soto, Gary's paternal grandfather, had emigrated from Mexico to Fresno as a young man to escape the economic and political instability of pre-revolution Mexico. It was in Fresno that he met his future wife Paolo who sold ice cream cones on the street to support herself and her child; she'd married as a teenager in Mexico and had her first baby there before emigrating to Fresno after the Mexican Revolution. Gary's grandparents met, fell in love, married and worked in the fields, as did their children. Manuel Soto, their third son, was a charming and intelligent boy with elegant good looks and glimmering brown eyes. He and Angie Trevino, Gary's mother, met in 1947 at Edison High School. Like so many other young men and women from Fresno's working class neighborhoods, neither Angie nor Manuel finished high school. They married at eighteen and soon began having children. Gary's older brother Rick was born on June 28, 1950, Gary's birth followed two years later, and his sister Debra was born on March 6, 1953.

One August day when Gary was five years old, Manuel Soto went to work at the construction site where he was then employed. A co-worker and family friend climbed a ladder with a tray of nails on his shoulder, lost his balance and fell on top of Manuel, breaking his neck. Gary's father died two days later; he was twenty-seven years old. In a narrative recollection entitled "This Man," Soto speculates that their neighbor "must have felt guilt and shame" because he turned his back on the Sotos after the accident. Here Soto imagines what could have taken place five doors down the street:

> [S]tarting off to the store, [he] thinks of Manuel, our father, maybe sees his face whole, maybe sees his face twisted and on the ground, the blood already drying. . . . But how much? How much of our father was on his mind? Did the kids in the street distract him, the neighbors on porches, a barking dog? Did he sing inside his head, worry about bills maybe think of work? . . . He bought his butter, went home to eat with his children, who after the accident never came over to play with us. . . . We lived poor years because our father died. We suffered quietly and hurt even today. Shouldn't this mean something to him? (*Lesser Evils* 82-83)

Within the Soto family an imperturbable silence and secrecy surrounded the dead father, compounding the pain of those who mourned him. Soto writes that

> [s]omething happened in our family without us becoming aware, a quiet between mother and children settled on us like dust. We went to school, ate, watched television that wasn't funny, and because mother never said anything, father . . . became that name we never said in our house. His grave was something we saw in photographs; his remembrance those clothes hanging in the back of the closet. (*Lesser Evils* 83)

For Soto the task of resurrecting his father's spirit on the printed page is a compelling one, made more difficult by his family's continuing taciturnity. Yet for the reader who accompanies Soto on his poetic journey, fresh meanings reveal themselves with each new work. Decades pass and father is still that name never spoken within the family but it is also the name that recurs more and more frequently in the heart and poetry of his son. In **"Another Time"** from the 1990 collection ***Who Will Know Us?*** Soto writes:

> . . . Like father,
> whom we miss and don't know,
> Who would have saved us
> From those terrible years
> If that day at work he got up
> Hurt but alive. He fell
> From that ladder with an upturned palm,

> With the eyes of watery light.
> We went on with sorrow that found no tree
> To cry from. I can't go to his grave.
> I know this. I can't find my place
> Or wake up and say, Let him walk,
> Let him round the house but not come in.
> Even the sun with so much to give must fall.
>
> (97-98)

A year later in **"Fall and Spring,"** from his collection of poems entitled ***Home Course in Religion,*** Soto uses a conversation with Scott, his boyhood best friend, to diffuse the layers of time and silence that conceal the events surrounding Manuel Soto's death.

> . . . About then I began saying things like,
> Scott, I think I lived before. Or, Scotty,
> I have feelings around my eyes like I'm Chinese.
> He let me say these things and still be his friend. He told me
> That his father was dead. I ran sand through my fingers.
> I told him that when my father died
> My uncle heard gravel crunch in the path
> That ran along our house, and rock was one of
> The things God told us to look out for.

It may be that Gary Soto has only begun to write about the mystery and opacity of this profoundly important element of his experience and that we can expect to see the character and essence of Manuel Soto reanimated in his future work. Soto continues to honor his father in a fascinating pattern of discovery throughout his poetry and prose; each time he invokes his father in his writing, Soto beams new light on their unique relationship and on the damage that enforced silence inflicts on those who grieve the death of their beloved. With the apparent wealth of emotional territory that he has yet to explore, Soto may develop into a novel the theme of a child's early loss of a parent and the silence that often follows it.

Soto began to write at the age of twenty. A student at California State University at Fresno, Soto "lucked into" poet Philip Levine's creative writing class. He describes his chance meeting with Levine—and his first glimpse into his future as a writer—as pure kismet. When asked what would have happened if he hadn't ventured into Levine's class, Soto answered that he'd be mowing lawns in Fresno. Soto is an engaging conversationalist with a penchant for wry observations; his account of his own experiences is often peppered with jokes. Asked if he is serious, he assures listeners that he is.

Soto's discovery of his poetic voice coincided with a recognition of his own alienation: he realized that he was estranged not only from the culture of his heritage, but also from the Anglo world which simultaneously beckoned to him and rejected him. He experienced the epiphany of his otherness when he came upon a poem called "Unwanted" by Edward Field. Reading it, Soto saw his own aloneness described; additionally, the poem presented him with the first suggestion that he too was capable of satisfying himself and affecting others with the power of his words. What's more, in Field's poem Soto discerned that a sense of alienation was not unique to him but rather, "it was a *human* pain."

In 1974 Gary Soto graduated magna cum laude from California State University, Fresno. The next year he married Carolyn Oda, also a Fresno native, whom he'd met when he was twenty after she moved into the house next door to the apartment that Gary shared with his brother Rick. The brothers were "college poor," living on the food that Gary could take from their mother's refrigerator when Rick "called her into the backyard about a missing sock from his laundry—a ploy from the start." One day, walking home from the store, Soto saw Carolyn cracking walnuts on her front porch. During the next few weeks Gary artfully plotted, contriving numerous excuses to walk past her house, sometimes resorting to a low crouch behind a hedge until Carolyn appeared to water her geranium or sweep off her porch. So began the romance that is the mainstay of Soto's emotional life.

> a good Mexican girl—"no Okies, hijo. . . . " For her, everyone who wasn't Mexican, black or Asian were Okies. The French were Okies, the Italians in suits were Okies. When I asked about Jews, whom I had read about, she asked for a picture. I rode home on my bicycle and returned with a calendar depicting the important races of the world. "Pues, si, son Okies tambien!" she said, nodding her head. She waved the calendar away and went to the living room where she lectured me on the virtues of the Mexican girl. (*Faces* 9)

But Gary fell in love with a Japanese American girl and their romance created a furor in his family. Gary's own fears were assuaged when he'd met Carolyn's parents, Japanese American farmers who had been imprisoned in internment camps during World War II. On his terrifying first visit with them, he was relieved to discover that "these people are just like Mexicans . . . poor people" (*Faces* 13). Now he had only to reassure his family. Soto writes about their anxious response to the news of his engagement to Carolyn

> who worried my mother, who had my grandmother asking once again to see the calender of the Important Races of the World. I told her I had thrown it away years before. I took a much-glanced-at snapshot from my wallet. We looked at it together, in silence. Then Grandma reclined in her chair, lit a cigarette, and said, "Es pretty." She blew and asked with all her worry pushed up to her forehead: "Chinese?" (*Faces* 11)

Five years after the marriage Carolyn gave birth to their daughter Mariko. Fatherhood stimulated Soto's imagination in a variety of ways. Often Mariko or some aspect of their relationship is the subject of a narrative recollection, or as in the instance he writes about in "Listening Up," Soto appropriates the wisdom of her childish "turns of language" for his own use. He writes:

> One summer I heard our three-year-old daughter Mariko say, "The days are filled with air," and heard my writer self say, "That's mine. I said that. . . . "

> Little philosopher, sophist, wise-guy in a little girl's dress—she spoke a beautifully true line that suggests that the business of living (jobs, friends, love, failed love, and so on) is only air, and maybe not even blue air at that. All is transparent as air—a breeze here a strong gust there, and people and days pass from our lives. . . . I took my daughter's line and made a poem from it. (*Faces* 33-35)

In his mid-forties, his daughter Mariko off to college, Gary Soto continues to chart new literary territory, blazing untraveled paths. One of our nation's most prolific and versatile writers, Soto has in the last decade increased his audience with the publication of two children's picture books, two short story collections, four novels and three poetry collections for young readers, as well as three novels. His recently published novel, *Jesse,* chronicles the adventures of two brothers as they make the difficult transition from post-adolescence to early adulthood. By turns hilarious and thrilling, it is one of Soto's most satisfying revelations about a Catholic's relationship with God. *Buried Onions,* released in early 1997, is Soto's most recent work of prose.

Currently at work on a libretto entitled *Nerd-landia,* comissioned by the Los Angeles Opera for a 1998 production, Soto divides his time between writing and producing. Soto is a community activist who founds and supports many educational and cultural programs for Chicano/a youth. Every summer, interested young people from two small towns near Fresno take part in the Coalinga and Huron House Program, for example; they live in a Berkeley fraternity or sorority house and take accelerated high school courses at the university. Soto and others comprise the program's board of directors. Many high school drama students participate in a production of Soto's latest one-act play entitled *Novio Boy.* Introduced to Soto's work in their English classes, other students from all over the country have the opportunity to meet the author when he visits their school for a talk and a reading.

Soto renews his literary spirit and engages a growing readership as he turns his attention from the short story to the essay, from novel to film and drama, and from poetry to prose and then back again. His readers have come to expect a fresh approach with each work as it appears. In this way, Soto constantly updates his concerns and charges them with an ongoing urgency. In the twenty-second year of his career, the persistent themes of Soto's work—poverty, racism and alienation—appear in his work freshly minted with all the gleam of newly polished gold and silver. With the 1995 publication of ***New and Selected Poems***—which was nominated for the National Book Award—Soto captures the attention of an ever expanding readership. Soto encourages talented, young emerging writers as he traverses the nation spreading news of their stories—some angry and bitter, all demanding to be heard. At the same time Soto ameliorates some of the pain of his people with his boundless energy; wherever he goes he excites in his audience the promise of a dream deferred—a nationwide Chicano/a community.

Although, at present, Mexican America's literary movement lacks a geographical meeting place, its center resides in the soul of its writers. Along with other members of the Chicano/a literati Soto creates a forum and a focus for their most urgent concerns: the future of a critical discourse, how to make the transition from small ethnic presses into the mainstream, and reaching a more encompassing readership. In the hearts and minds of his colleagues and his readers of all colors, Soto is an ally, an antidote to loneliness and the embodiment of a new era for American multi-ethnic literatures. Soto's voice is the sound of many voices speaking—over the kitchen table, out on the street, in classrooms everywhere—across the borderlands and through the years.

Additional coverage of Soto's life and career is contained in the following sources published by the Gale Group: *Artists and Authors for Young Adults,* Vol. 10; *Contemporary Authors,* Vols. 19, 25; *Contemporary Authors New Revision Series,* Vols. 50, 74; *Children's Literature Review,* Vol. 38; *Contemporary Literature Criticism,* Vols. 32, 80; *DISCovering Multicultural America; Hispanic Literature Criticism,* Vol. 2; *Hispanic Writers; Junior DISCovering Authors; Major Twentieth Century Writers; Something About the Author,* Vol. 80.

How to Use This Index

The main references

Calvino, Italo 1923-1985 .... **CLC 5, 8, 11, 22, 33, 39, 73; SSC 3**

list all author entries in the following Gale Literary Criticism series:

BLC = *Black Literature Criticism*
CLC = *Contemporary Literary Criticism*
CLR = *Children's Literature Review*
CMLC = *Classical and Medieval Literature Criticism*
DA = *DISCovering Authors*
DAB = *DISCovering Authors: British*
DAC = *DISCovering Authors: Canadian*
DAM = *DISCovering Authors: Modules*
DRAM: *Dramatists Module;* ***MST:*** *Most-Studied Authors Module;*
MULT: *Multicultural Authors Module;* ***NOV:*** *Novelists Module;*
POET: *Poets Module;* ***POP:*** *Popular Fiction and Genre Authors Module*
DC = *Drama Criticism*
HLC = *Hispanic Literature Criticism*
LC = *Literature Criticism from 1400 to 1800*
NCLC = *Nineteenth-Century Literature Criticism*
PC = *Poetry Criticism*
SSC = *Short Story Criticism*
TCLC = *Twentieth-Century Literary Criticism*
WLC = *World Literature Criticism, 1500 to the Present*

The cross-references

See also CANR 23; CA 85-88; obituary CA116

list all author entries in the following Gale biographical and literary sources:

AAYA = *Authors & Artists for Young Adults*
AITN = *Authors in the News*
BEST = *Bestsellers*
BW = *Black Writers*
CA = *Contemporary Authors*
CAAS = *Contemporary Authors Autobiography Series*
CABS = *Contemporary Authors Bibliographical Series*
CANR = *Contemporary Authors New Revision Series*
CAP = *Contemporary Authors Permanent Series*
CDALB = *Concise Dictionary of American Literary Biography*
CDBLB = *Concise Dictionary of British Literary Biography*
DLB = *Dictionary of Literary Biography*
DLBD = *Dictionary of Literary Biography Documentary Series*
DLBY = *Dictionary of Literary Biography Yearbook*
HW = *Hispanic Writers*
JRDA = *Junior DISCovering Authors*
MAICYA = *Major Authors and Illustrators for Children and Young Adults*
MTCW = *Major 20th-Century Writers*
NNAL = *Native North American Literature*
SAAS = *Something about the Author Autobiography Series*
SATA = *Something about the Author*
YABC = *Yesterday's Authors of Books for Children*

Literary Criticism Series Cumulative Author Index

20/1631
See Upward, Allen
A/C Cross
See Lawrence, T(homas) E(dward)
Abasiyanik, Sait Faik 1906-1954
See Sait Faik
See CA 123
Abbey, Edward 1927-1989 . . . **CLC 36, 59**
See CA 45-48; 128; CANR 2, 41; DA3; MTCW 2
Abbott, Lee K(ittredge) 1947- .... **CLC 48**
See CA 124; CANR 51; DLB 130
Abe, Kobo 1924-1993 ..... **CLC 8, 22, 53, 81; DAM NOV**
See CA 65-68; 140; CANR 24, 60; DLB 182; MTCW 1, 2
Abelard, Peter c. 1079-c.1142 ...... **CMLC 11**
See DLB 115, 208
Abell, Kjeld 1901-1961 .... **CLC 15**
See CA 111
Abish, Walter 1931- .... **CLC 22**
See CA 101; CANR 37; DLB 130
Abrahams, Peter (Henry) 1919- .... **CLC 4**
See BW 1; CA 57-60; CANR 26; DLB 117; MTCW 1, 2
Abrams, M(eyer) H(oward) 1912- .. **CLC 24**
See CA 57-60; CANR 13, 33; DLB 67
Abse, Dannie 1923- . **CLC 7, 29; DAB;DAM POET**
See CA 53-56; CAAS 1; CANR 4, 46, 74; DLB 27; MTCW 1
Achebe, (Albert) Chinua(lumogu) 1930- ..... **CLC 1, 3, 5, 7, 11, 26, 51, 75; BLC 1; DA; DAB; DAC; DAM MST, MULT, NOV;WLC**
See AAYA 15; BW 2, 3; CA 1-4R; CANR 6, 26, 47; CLR 20; DA3; DLB 117; MAICYA; MTCW 1, 2; SATA 38, 40; SATA-Brief 38
Acker, Kathy 1948-1997 .... **CLC 45, 111**
See CA 117; 122; 162; CANR 55
Ackroyd, Peter 1949- .... **CLC 34, 52**
See CA 123; 127; CANR 51, 74; DLB 155; INT 127; MTCW 1
Acorn, Milton 1923- .... **CLC 15; DAC**
See CA 103; DLB 53; INT 103
Adamov, Arthur 1908-1970 .... **CLC 4, 25; DAM DRAM**
See CA 17-18; 25-28R; CAP 2; MTCW 1
Adams, Alice (Boyd) 1926-1999 . **CLC 6, 13, 46; SSC 24**
See CA 81-84; 179; CANR 26, 53, 75; DLBY 86; INT CANR-26; MTCW 1, 2
Adams, Andy 1859-1935 .... **TCLC 56**
See YABC 1
Adams, Brooks 1848-1927 .... **TCLC 80**
See CA 123; DLB 47
Adams, Douglas (Noel) 1952- .. **CLC 27, 60; DAM POP**
See AAYA 4; BEST 89:3; CA 106; CANR 34, 64; DA3; DLBY 83; JRDA; MTCW 1
Adams, Francis 1862-1893 .... **NCLC 33**
Adams, Henry (Brooks) 1838-1918 ... **TCLC 4, 52; DA; DAB; DAC; DAM MST**
See CA 104; 133; CANR 77; DLB 12, 47, 189; MTCW 1
Adams, Richard (George) 1920- .. **CLC 4, 5, 18; DAM NOV**
See AAYA 16; AITN 1, 2; CA 49-52; CANR 3, 35; CLR 20; JRDA; MAICYA; MTCW 1, 2; SATA 7, 69
Adamson, Joy(-Friederike Victoria) 1910-1980 .... **CLC 17**
See CA 69-72; 93-96; CANR 22; MTCW 1; SATA 11; SATA-Obit 22
Adcock, Fleur 1934- .... **CLC 41**
See CA 25-28R; CAAS 23; CANR 11, 34, 69; DLB 40
Addams, Charles (Samuel) 1912-1988 . **CLC 30**
See CA 61-64; 126; CANR 12, 79
Addams, Jane 1860-1945 .... **TCLC 76**
Addison,Joseph 1672-1719 .... **LC 18**
See CDBLB 1660-1789; DLB 101
Adler, Alfred (F.) 1870-1937 .... **TCLC 61**
See CA 119; 159
Adler, C(arole) S(chwerdtfeger) 1932- . **CLC 35**
See AAYA 4; CA 89-92; CANR 19, 40; JRDA; MAICYA; SAAS 15; SATA 26, 63, 102
Adler, Renata 1938- .... **CLC 8, 31**
See CA 49-52; CANR 5, 22, 52; MTCW 1
Ady, Endre 1877-1919 .... **TCLC 11**
See CA 107
A.E. 1867-1935 .... **TCLC 3, 10**
See Russell, George William
Aeschylus 525B.C.-456B.C. . **CMLC 11; DA; DAB; DAC; DAM DRAM, MST; DC 8; WLCS**
See DLB 176
Aesop 620(?)B.C.-564(?)B.C. .... **CMLC 24**
See CLR 14; MAICYA; SATA 64
Affable Hawk
See MacCarthy, Sir(Charles Otto) Desmond
Africa, Ben
See Bosman, Herman Charles
Afton, Effie
See Harper, Frances Ellen Watkins
Agapida, Fray Antonio
See Irving, Washington
Agee, James (Rufus) 1909-1955 .... **TCLC 1, 19; DAM NOV**
See AITN 1; CA 108; 148; CDALB 1941-1968; DLB 2, 26, 152; MTCW 1
Aghill, Gordon
See Silverberg, Robert
Agnon, S(hmuel) Y(osef Halevi) 1888-1970 .... **CLC 4, 8, 14; SSC 30**
See CA 17-18; 25-28R; CANR 60; CAP 2; MTCW 1, 2
Agrippa von Nettesheim, Henry Cornelius 1486-1535 .... **LC 27**
Aguilera Malta, Demetrio 1909-1981
See CA 111; 124; DAM MULT, NOV; DLB 145; HLCS 1; HW 1
Agustini, Delmira 1886-1914
See CA 166; HLCS 1; HW 1, 2
Aherne, Owen
See Cassill, R(onald) V(erlin)
Ai 1947- .... **CLC 4, 14, 69**
See CA 85-88; CAAS 13; CANR 70; DLB 120
Aickman, Robert (Fordyce) 1914-1981 . **CLC 57**
See CA 5-8R; CANR 3, 72
Aiken, Conrad (Potter) 1889-1973 .. **CLC 1, 3, 5, 10, 52; DAM NOV, POET; PC 26; SSC 9**
See CA 5-8R; 45-48; CANR 4, 60; CDALB 1929-1941; DLB 9, 45, 102; MTCW 1, 2; SATA 3, 30
Aiken, Joan (Delano) 1924- .... **CLC 35**
See AAYA 1, 25; CA 9-12R; CANR 4, 23, 34, 64; CLR 1, 19; DLB 161; JRDA; MAICYA; MTCW 1; SAAS 1; SATA 2, 30, 73; SATA-Essay 109
Ainsworth, William Harrison 1805-1882 ..... **NCLC 13**
See DLB 21; SATA 24
Aitmatov, Chingiz (Torekulovich) 1928- ...... **CLC 71**
See CA 103; CANR 38; MTCW 1; SATA 56
Akers, Floyd
See Baum, L(yman) Frank
Akhmadulina, Bella Akhatovna 1937- . **CLC 53; DAM POET**
See CA 65-68
Akhmatova, Anna 1888-1966 ... **CLC 11, 25, 64; DAM POET; PC 2**
See CA 19-20; 25-28R; CANR 35; CAP 1; DA3; MTCW 1, 2
Aksakov, Sergei Timofeyvich 1791-1859 ..... **NCLC 2**
See DLB 198
Aksenov, Vassily
See Aksyonov, Vassily (Pavlovich)
Akst, Daniel 1956- .... **CLC 109**
See CA 161
Aksyonov, Vassily (Pavlovich) 1932- .... **CLC 22, 37, 101**
See CA 53-56; CANR 12, 48, 77

Akutagawa, Ryunosuke 1892-1927 .... **TCLC 16**
See CA 117; 154
Alain 1868-1951 .... **TCLC 41**
See CA 163
Alain-Fournier .... **TCLC 6**
See Fournier, Henri Alban
See DLB 65
Alarcon, Pedro Antonio de 1833-1891 .... **NCLC 1**
Alas (y Urena), Leopoldo (Enrique Garcia) 1852-1901 .... **TCLC 29**
See CA 113; 131; HW 1
Albee, Edward (Franklin III) 1928- . **CLC 1, 2, 3, 5, 9, 11, 13, 25, 53, 86, 113; DA; DAB; DAC; DAM DRAM, MST; DC 11;WLC**
See AITN 1; CA 5-8R; CABS 3; CANR 8, 54, 74; CDALB 1941-1968; DA3; DLB 7; INT CANR-8; MTCW 1, 2
Alberti, Rafael 1902- .... **CLC 7**
See CA 85-88; CANR 81; DLB 108; HW 2
Albert the Great 1200(?)-1280 .... **CMLC 16**
See DLB 115
Alcala-Galiano, Juan Valera y
See Valera y Alcala-Galiano, Juan
Alcott, Amos Bronson 1799-1888 .... **NCLC 1**
See DLB 1
Alcott, Louisa May 1832-1888 . **NCLC 6, 58; DA; DAB; DAC; DAM MST, NOV; SSC 27; WLC**
See AAYA 20; CDALB 1865-1917; CLR 1, 38; DA3; DLB 1, 42, 79; DLBD 14; JRDA; MAICYA; SATA 100; YABC 1
Aldanov, M. A.
See Aldanov, Mark (Alexandrovich)
Aldanov, Mark (Alexandrovich) 1886(?)-1957 .... **TCLC 23**
See CA 118; 181
Aldington, Richard 1892-1962 .... **CLC 49**
See CA 85-88; CANR 45; DLB 20, 36, 100, 149
Aldiss, Brian W(ilson) 1925- .... **CLC 5, 14, 40; DAM NOV; SSC 36**
See CA 5-8R; CAAS 2; CANR 5, 28, 64; DLB 14; MTCW 1, 2; SATA 34
Alegria, Claribel 1924- .... **CLC 75; DAM MULT; HLCS 1; PC 26**
See CA 131; CAAS 15; CANR 66; DLB 145; HW 1; MTCW 1
Alegria, Fernando 1918- .... **CLC 57**
See CA 9-12R; CANR 5, 32, 72; HW 1, 2
Aleichem, Sholom .... **TCLC 1, 35; SSC 33**
See Rabinovitch, Sholem
Aleixandre, Vicente 1898-1984
See CANR 81; HLCS 1; HW 2
Alepoudelis, Odysseus
See Elytis, Odysseus
Aleshkovsky, Joseph 1929-
See Aleshkovsky, Yuz
See CA 121; 128
Aleshkovsky, Yuz .... **CLC 44**
See Aleshkovsky, Joseph
Alexander, Lloyd (Chudley) 1924- .. **CLC 35**
See AAYA 1, 27; CA 1-4R; CANR 1, 24, 38, 55; CLR 1, 5, 48; DLB 52; JRDA; MAICYA; MTCW 1; SAAS 19; SATA 3, 49, 81
Alexander, Meena 1951- .... **CLC 121**
See CA 115; CANR 38, 70
Alexander, Samuel 1859-1938 .... **TCLC 77**
Alexie, Sherman (Joseph, Jr.) 1966- .... **CLC 96; DAM MULT**
See AAYA 28; CA 138; CANR 65; DA3; DLB 175, 206; MTCW 1; NNAL
Alfau, Felipe 1902- .... **CLC 66**
See CA 137
Alger, Horatio, Jr. 1832-1899 .... **NCLC 8**
See DLB 42; SATA 16
Algren, Nelson 1909-1981 .... **CLC 4, 10, 33; SSC 33**
See CA 13-16R; 103; CANR 20, 61; CDALB 1941-1968; DLB 9; DLBY 81, 82; MTCW 1, 2
Ali, Ahmed 1910- .... **CLC 69**
See CA 25-28R; CANR 15, 34
Alighieri, Dante
See Dante
Allan, John B.
See Westlake, Donald E(dwin)
Allan, Sidney
See Hartmann, Sadakichi
Allan, Sydney
See Hartmann, Sadakichi
Allen, Edward 1948- .... **CLC 59**
Allen, Fred 1894-1956 .... **TCLC 87**
Allen, Paula Gunn 1939- .... **CLC 84;DAM MULT**
See CA 112; 143; CANR 63; DA3; DLB 175; MTCW 1; NNAL
Allen, Roland
See Ayckbourn, Alan
Allen, Sarah A.
See Hopkins, Pauline Elizabeth
Allen, Sidney H.
See Hartmann, Sadakichi
Allen, Woody 1935- . **CLC 16, 52;DAM POP**
See AAYA 10; CA 33-36R; CANR 27, 38, 63; DLB 44; MTCW 1
Allende, Isabel 1942- . **CLC 39, 57, 97; DAM MULT, NOV; HLC 1; WLCS**
See AAYA 18; CA 125; 130; CANR 51, 74; DA3; DLB 145; HW 1, 2; INT 130; MTCW 1, 2
Alleyn, Ellen
See Rossetti, Christina (Georgina)
Allingham, Margery (Louise) 1904-1966 .... **CLC 19**
See CA 5-8R; 25-28R; CANR 4, 58; DLB 77; MTCW 1, 2
Allingham, William 1824-1889 .... **NCLC 25**
See DLB 35
Allison, Dorothy E. 1949- .... **CLC 78**
See CA 140; CANR 66; DA3; MTCW 1
Allston, Washington 1779-1843 .... **NCLC 2**
See DLB 1
Almedingen, E. M. .... **CLC 12**
See Almedingen, Martha Edith von
See SATA 3
Almedingen, Martha Edith von 1898-1971
See Almedingen, E. M.
See CA 1-4R; CANR 1
Almodovar, Pedro 1949(?)- . **CLC 114;HLCS 1**
See CA 133; CANR 72; HW 2
Almqvist, Carl Jonas Love 1793-1866 .... **NCLC 42**
Alonso, Damaso 1898-1990 .... **CLC 14**
See CA 110; 131; 130; CANR 72; DLB 108; HW 1, 2
Alov
See Gogol, Nikolai (Vasilyevich)
Alta 1942- .... **CLC 19**
See CA 57-60
Alter, Robert B(ernard) 1935- .... **CLC 34**
See CA 49-52; CANR 1, 47
Alther, Lisa 1944- .... **CLC 7, 41**
See CA 65-68; CAAS 30; CANR 12, 30, 51; MTCW 1
Althusser, L.
See Althusser, Louis
Althusser, Louis 1918-1990 .... **CLC 106**
See CA 131; 132
Altman, Robert 1925- .... **CLC 16, 116**
See CA 73-76; CANR 43
Alurista 1949-
See Urista, Alberto H.
See DLB 82; HLCS 1
Alvarez, A(lfred) 1929- .... **CLC 5, 13**
See CA 1-4R; CANR 3, 33, 63; DLB 14, 40
Alvarez, Alejandro Rodriguez 1903-1965
See Casona, Alejandro
See CA 131; 93-96; HW 1
Alvarez, Julia 1950- .... **CLC 93;HLCS 1**
See AAYA 25; CA 147; CANR 69; DA3; MTCW 1
Alvaro, Corrado 1896-1956 .... **TCLC 60**
See CA 163
Amado, Jorge 1912- .... **CLC 13, 40, 106; DAM MULT, NOV; HLC 1**
See CA 77-80; CANR 35, 74; DLB 113; HW 2; MTCW 1, 2
Ambler, Eric 1909-1998 .... **CLC 4, 6, 9**
See CA 9-12R; 171; CANR 7, 38, 74; DLB 77; MTCW 1, 2
Amichai, Yehuda 1924- . **CLC 9, 22, 57, 116**
See CA 85-88; CANR 46, 60; MTCW 1
Amichai, Yehudah
See Amichai, Yehuda
Amiel, Henri Frederic 1821-1881 .. **NCLC 4**
Amis, Kingsley (William) 1922-1995 ... **CLC 1, 2, 3, 5, 8, 13, 40, 44; DA; DAB; DAC; DAM MST, NOV**
See AITN 2; CA 9-12R; 150; CANR 8, 28, 54; CDBLB 1945-1960; DA3; DLB 15, 27, 100, 139; DLBY 96; INT CANR-8; MTCW 1, 2
Amis, Martin (Louis) 1949- ... **CLC 4, 9, 38, 62, 101**
See BEST 90:3; CA 65-68; CANR 8, 27, 54, 73; DA3; DLB 14, 194; INT CANR-27; MTCW 1
Ammons, A(rchie) R(andolph) 1926- ... **CLC 2, 3, 5, 8, 9, 25, 57, 108; DAM POET; PC 16**
See AITN 1; CA 9-12R; CANR 6, 36, 51, 73; DLB 5, 165; MTCW 1, 2
Amo, Tauraatua i
See Adams, Henry (Brooks)
Amory, Thomas 1691(?)-1788 .... **LC 48**
Anand, Mulk Raj 1905- .. **CLC 23, 93;DAM NOV**
See CA 65-68; CANR 32, 64; MTCW 1, 2
Anatol
See Schnitzler, Arthur
Anaximander c. 610B.C.-c. 546B.C. . **CMLC 22**
Anaya, Rudolfo A(lfonso) 1937- .... **CLC 23; DAM MULT, NOV; HLC 1**
See AAYA 20; CA 45-48; CAAS 4; CANR 1, 32, 51; DLB 82, 206; HW 1; MTCW 1, 2
Andersen, Hans Christian 1805-1875 .... **NCLC 7, 79; DA; DAB; DAC; DAM MST, POP; SSC 6; WLC**
See CLR 6; DA3; MAICYA; SATA 100; YABC 1
Anderson, C. Farley
See Mencken, H(enry) L(ouis); Nathan, George Jean
Anderson, Jessica (Margaret) Queale 1916- .... **CLC 37**
See CA 9-12R; CANR 4, 62
Anderson, Jon (Victor) 1940- . **CLC 9; DAM POET**
See CA 25-28R; CANR 20
Anderson, Lindsay (Gordon) 1923-1994 .... **CLC 20**
See CA 125; 128; 146; CANR 77
Anderson, Maxwell 1888-1959 .... **TCLC 2; DAM DRAM**
See CA 105; 152; DLB 7; MTCW 2
Anderson, Poul (William) 1926- .... **CLC 15**

See AAYA 5; CA 1-4R, 181; CAAE 181; CAAS 2; CANR 2, 15, 34, 64; CLR 58; DLB 8; INT CANR-15; MTCW 1, 2; SATA 90; SATA-Brief 39; SATA-Essay 106

Anderson, Robert (Woodruff) 1917- .... **CLC 23; DAM DRAM**
See AITN 1; CA 21-24R; CANR 32; DLB 7

Anderson, Sherwood 1876-1941 .... **TCLC 1, 10, 24; DA; DAB; DAC; DAM MST, NOV; SSC 1; WLC**
See AAYA 30; CA 104; 121; CANR 61; CDALB 1917-1929; DA3; DLB 4, 9, 86; DLBD 1; MTCW 1, 2

Andier, Pierre
See Desnos, Robert

Andouard
See Giraudoux, (Hippolyte) Jean

Andrade, Carlos Drummond de ..... **CLC 18**
See Drummond de Andrade, Carlos

Andrade, Mario de 1893-1945 ...... **TCLC 43**

Andreae, Johann V(alentin) 1586-1654 .. **LC 32**
See DLB 164

Andreas-Salome, Lou 1861-1937 .. **TCLC 56**
See CA 178; DLB 66

Andress, Lesley
See Sanders, Lawrence

Andrewes, Lancelot 1555-1626 .... **LC 5**
See DLB 151, 172

Andrews, Cicily Fairfield
See West, Rebecca

Andrews, Elton V.
See Pohl, Frederik

Andreyev, Leonid (Nikolaevich) 1871-1919 . **TCLC 3**
See CA 104

Andric, Ivo 1892-1975 .... **CLC 8;SSC 36**
See CA 81-84; 57-60; CANR 43, 60; DLB 147; MTCW 1

Androvar
See Prado (Calvo), Pedro

Angelique, Pierre
See Bataille, Georges

Angell, Roger 1920- .... **CLC 26**
See CA 57-60; CANR 13, 44, 70; DLB 171, 185

Angelou, Maya 1928- ... **CLC 12, 35, 64, 77; BLC 1; DA; DAB; DAC; DAM MST, MULT, POET, POP; WLCS**
See AAYA 7, 20; BW 2, 3; CA 65-68; CANR 19, 42, 65; CDALBS; CLR 53; DA3; DLB 38; MTCW 1, 2; SATA 49

Anna Comnena 1083-1153 .... **CMLC 25**

Annensky, Innokenty (Fyodorovich) 1856-1909 .... **TCLC 14**
See CA 110; 155

Annunzio, Gabriele d'
See D'Annunzio, Gabriele

Anodos
See Coleridge, Mary E(lizabeth)

Anon, Charles Robert
See Pessoa, Fernando (Antonio Nogueira)

Anouilh, Jean (Marie Lucien Pierre) 1910-1987 .... **CLC 1, 3, 8, 13, 40, 50; DAM DRAM; DC 8**
See CA 17-20R; 123; CANR 32; MTCW 1, 2

Anthony, Florence
See Ai

Anthony, John
See Ciardi, John (Anthony)

Anthony, Peter
See Shaffer, Anthony (Joshua); Shaffer, Peter (Levin)

Anthony, Piers 1934- .... **CLC 35;DAM POP**
See AAYA 11; CA 21-24R; CANR 28, 56, 73; DLB 8; MTCW 1, 2; SAAS 22; SATA 84

Anthony, Susan B(rownell) 1916-1991 .... **TCLC 84**
See CA 89-92; 134

Antoine, Marc
See Proust, (Valentin-Louis-George-Eugene-) Marcel

Antoninus, Brother
See Everson, William (Oliver)

Antonioni, Michelangelo 1912- .... **CLC 20**
See CA 73-76; CANR 45, 77

Antschel, Paul 1920-1970
See Celan, Paul
See CA 85-88; CANR 33, 61; MTCW 1

Anwar, Chairil 1922-1949 .... **TCLC 22**
See CA 121

Anzaldua, Gloria 1942-
See CA 175; DLB 122; HLCS 1

Apess, William 1798-1839(?) .... **NCLC 73; DAM MULT**
See DLB 175; NNAL

Apollinaire, Guillaume 1880-1918 . **TCLC 3, 8, 51; DAM POET; PC 7**
See Kostrowitzki, Wilhelm Apollinaris de
See CA 152; MTCW 1

Appelfeld, Aharon 1932- .... **CLC 23, 47**
See CA 112; 133

Apple, Max (Isaac) 1941- .... **CLC 9, 33**
See CA 81-84; CANR 19, 54; DLB 130

Appleman, Philip (Dean) 1926- .... **CLC 51**
See CA 13-16R; CAAS 18; CANR 6, 29, 56

Appleton, Lawrence
See Lovecraft, H(oward) P(hillips)

Apteryx
See Eliot, T(homas) S(tearns)

Apuleius, (Lucius Madaurensis) 125(?)-175(?) .... **CMLC 1**
See DLB 211

Aquin, Hubert 1929-1977 .... **CLC 15**
See CA 105; DLB 53

Aquinas,Thomas 1224(?)-1274 ..... **CMLC 33**
See DLB 115

Aragon, Louis 1897-1982 . **CLC 3, 22; DAM NOV, POET**
See CA 69-72; 108; CANR 28, 71; DLB 72; MTCW 1, 2

Arany, Janos 1817-1882 .... **NCLC 34**

Aranyos, Kakay
See Mikszath, Kalman

Arbuthnot, John 1667-1735 .... **LC 1**
See DLB 101

Archer, Herbert Winslow
See Mencken, H(enry) L(ouis)

Archer, Jeffrey (Howard) 1940- ..... **CLC 28; DAM POP**
See AAYA 16; BEST 89:3; CA 77-80; CANR 22, 52; DA3; INT CANR-22

Archer, Jules 1915- .... **CLC 12**
See CA 9-12R; CANR 6, 69; SAAS 5; SATA 4, 85

Archer, Lee
See Ellison, Harlan (Jay)

Arden, John 1930- .... **CLC 6, 13, 15;DAM DRAM**
See CA 13-16R; CAAS 4; CANR 31, 65, 67; DLB 13; MTCW 1

Arenas, Reinaldo 1943-1990 . **CLC 41; DAM MULT; HLC 1**
See CA 124; 128; 133; CANR 73; DLB 145; HW 1; MTCW 1

Arendt, Hannah 1906-1975 .... **CLC 66,98**
See CA 17-20R; 61-64; CANR 26, 60; MTCW 1, 2

Aretino, Pietro 1492-1556 .... **LC 12**

Arghezi, Tudor 1880-1967 .... **CLC 80**
See Theodorescu, Ion N.
See CA 167

Arguedas, Jose Maria 1911-1969 ... **CLC 10, 18; HLCS 1**
See CA 89-92; CANR 73; DLB 113; HW 1

Argueta, Manlio 1936- .... **CLC 31**
See CA 131; CANR 73; DLB 145; HW 1

Arias, Ron(ald Francis) 1941-
See CA 131; CANR 81; DAM MULT; DLB 82; HLC 1; HW 1, 2; MTCW 2

Ariosto, Ludovico 1474-1533 .... **LC 6**

Aristides
See Epstein, Joseph

Aristophanes 450B.C.-385B.C. ..... **CMLC 4; DA; DAB; DAC; DAM DRAM, MST; DC 2; WLCS**
See DA3; DLB 176

Aristotle 384B.C.-322B.C. ... **CMLC 31; DA; DAB; DAC; DAM MST; WLCS**
See DA3; DLB 176

Arlt, Roberto (Godofredo Christophersen) 1900-1942 ..... **TCLC 29; DAM MULT; HLC 1**
See CA 123; 131; CANR 67; HW 1, 2

Armah, Ayi Kwei 1939- . **CLC 5, 33; BLC 1; DAM MULT, POET**
See BW 1; CA 61-64; CANR 21, 64; DLB 117; MTCW 1

Armatrading, Joan 1950- .... **CLC 17**
See CA 114

Arnette, Robert
See Silverberg, Robert

Arnim, Achim von (Ludwig Joachim von Arnim) 1781-1831 .... **NCLC 5; SSC 29**
See DLB 90

Arnim, Bettina von 1785-1859 ..... **NCLC 38**
See DLB 90

Arnold, Matthew 1822-1888 ... **NCLC 6, 29; DA; DAB; DAC; DAM MST, POET; PC 5; WLC**
See CDBLB 1832-1890; DLB 32, 57

Arnold, Thomas 1795-1842 .... **NCLC 18**
See DLB 55

Arnow, Harriette (Louisa) Simpson 1908-1986 .... **CLC 2, 7, 18**
See CA 9-12R; 118; CANR 14; DLB 6; MTCW 1, 2; SATA 42; SATA-Obit 47

Arouet, Francois-Marie
See Voltaire

Arp, Hans
See Arp, Jean

Arp, Jean 1887-1966 .... **CLC 5**
See CA 81-84; 25-28R; CANR 42, 77

Arrabal
See Arrabal, Fernando

Arrabal, Fernando 1932- .. **CLC 2, 9, 18, 58**
See CA 9-12R; CANR 15

Arreola, Juan Jose 1918-
See CA 113; 131; CANR 81; DAM MULT; DLB 113; HLC 1; HW 1, 2

Arrick, Fran .... **CLC 30**
See Gaberman, Judie Angell

Artaud, Antonin (Marie Joseph) 1896-1948 .... **TCLC 3, 36; DAM DRAM**
See CA 104; 149; DA3; MTCW 1

Arthur, Ruth M(abel) 1905-1979 .... **CLC 12**
See CA 9-12R; 85-88; CANR 4; SATA 7, 26

Artsybashev, Mikhail (Petrovich) 1878-1927 .... **TCLC 31**
See CA 170

Arundel, Honor (Morfydd) 1919-1973 . **CLC 17**
See CA 21-22; 41-44R; CAP 2; CLR 35; SATA 4; SATA-Obit 24

Arzner, Dorothy 1897-1979 .... **CLC 98**

Asch, Sholem 1880-1957 .... **TCLC 3**
See CA 105

Ash, Shalom
See Asch, Sholem
Ashbery, John (Lawrence) 1927- . **CLC 2, 3, 4, 6, 9, 13, 15, 25, 41, 77, 125; DAM POET; PC 26**
See CA 5-8R; CANR 9, 37, 66; DA3; DLB 5, 165; DLBY 81; INT CANR-9; MTCW 1, 2
Ashdown, Clifford
See Freeman, R(ichard) Austin
Ashe, Gordon
See Creasey, John
Ashton-Warner, Sylvia (Constance) 1908-1984 .... **CLC 19**
See CA 69-72; 112; CANR 29; MTCW 1, 2
Asimov, Isaac 1920-1992 .... **CLC 1, 3, 9, 19, 26, 76, 92; DAM POP**
See AAYA 13; BEST 90:2; CA 1-4R; 137; CANR 2, 19, 36, 60; CLR 12; DA3; DLB 8; DLBY 92; INT CANR-19; JRDA; MAICYA; MTCW 1, 2; SATA 1, 26, 74
Assis, Joaquim Maria Machado de
See Machado de Assis, Joaquim Maria
Astley, Thea (Beatrice May) 1925- . **CLC 41**
See CA 65-68; CANR 11, 43, 78
Aston, James
See White, T(erence) H(anbury)
Asturias, Miguel Angel 1899-1974 ... **CLC 3, 8, 13; DAM MULT, NOV; HLC 1**
See CA 25-28; 49-52; CANR 32; CAP 2; DA3; DLB 113; HW 1; MTCW 1, 2
Atares, Carlos Saura
See Saura (Atares), Carlos
Atheling, William
See Pound, Ezra (Weston Loomis)
Atheling, William, Jr.
See Blish, James (Benjamin)
Atherton, Gertrude (Franklin Horn) 1857-1948 .... **TCLC 2**
See CA 104; 155; DLB 9, 78, 186
Atherton, Lucius
See Masters, Edgar Lee
Atkins, Jack
See Harris, Mark
Atkinson, Kate .... **CLC 99**
See CA 166
Attaway, William (Alexander) 1911-1986 .... **CLC 92; BLC 1; DAM MULT**
See BW 2, 3; CA 143; CANR 82; DLB 76
Atticus
See Fleming, Ian (Lancaster); Wilson, (Thomas) Woodrow
Atwood, Margaret (Eleanor) 1939- . **CLC 2, 3, 4, 8, 13, 15, 25, 44, 84; DA; DAB; DAC; DAM MST, NOV, POET; PC 8; SSC 2; WLC**
See AAYA 12; BEST 89:2; CA 49-52; CANR 3, 24, 33, 59; DA3; DLB 53; INT CANR-24; MTCW 1, 2; SATA 50
Aubigny, Pierre d'
See Mencken, H(enry) L(ouis)
Aubin, Penelope 1685-1731(?) .... **LC 9**
See DLB 39
Auchincloss, Louis (Stanton) 1917- . **CLC 4, 6, 9, 18, 45; DAM NOV; SSC 22**
See CA 1-4R; CANR 6, 29, 55; DLB 2; DLBY 80; INT CANR-29; MTCW 1
Auden, W(ystan) H(ugh) 1907-1973 .... **CLC 1, 2, 3, 4, 6, 9, 11, 14, 43; DA; DAB; DAC; DAM DRAM, MST, POET; PC 1;WLC**
See AAYA 18; CA 9-12R; 45-48; CANR 5, 61; CDBLB 1914-1945; DA3; DLB 10, 20; MTCW 1, 2
Audiberti, Jacques 1900-1965 .... **CLC 38; DAM DRAM**
See CA 25-28R
Audubon, John James 1785-1851 . **NCLC 47**
Auel, Jean M(arie) 1936- .... **CLC 31, 107; DAM POP**
See AAYA 7; BEST 90:4; CA 103; CANR 21, 64; DA3; INT CANR-21; SATA 91
Auerbach, Erich 1892-1957 .... **TCLC 43**
See CA 118; 155
Augier, Emile 1820-1889 .... **NCLC 31**
See DLB 192
August, John
See De Voto, Bernard (Augustine)
Augustine 354-430 ...... **CMLC 6; DA; DAB; DAC; DAM MST; WLCS**
See DA3; DLB 115
Aurelius
See Bourne, Randolph S(illiman)
Aurobindo, Sri
See Ghose, Aurabinda
Austen, Jane 1775-1817 ..... **NCLC 1, 13, 19, 33, 51, 81; DA; DAB; DAC; DAM MST, NOV; WLC**
See AAYA 19; CDBLB 1789-1832; DA3; DLB 116
Auster, Paul 1947- .... **CLC 47**
See CA 69-72; CANR 23, 52, 75; DA3; MTCW 1
Austin, Frank
See Faust, Frederick (Schiller)
Austin, Mary (Hunter) 1868-1934 ..... **TCLC 25**
See CA 109; 178; DLB 9, 78, 206
Averroes 1126-1198 .... **CMLC 7**
See DLB 115
Avicenna 980-1037 .... **CMLC 16**
See DLB 115
Avison, Margaret 1918- .... **CLC 2, 4, 97; DAC; DAM POET**
See CA 17-20R; DLB 53; MTCW 1
Axton, David
See Koontz, Dean R(ay)
Ayckbourn, Alan 1939- .... **CLC 5, 8, 18, 33, 74; DAB; DAM DRAM**
See CA 21-24R; CANR 31, 59; DLB 13; MTCW 1, 2
Aydy, Catherine
See Tennant, Emma (Christina)
Ayme, Marcel (Andre) 1902-1967 ... **CLC 11**
See CA 89-92; CANR 67; CLR 25; DLB 72; SATA 91
Ayrton, Michael 1921-1975 .... **CLC 7**
See CA 5-8R; 61-64; CANR 9, 21
Azorin .... **CLC 11**
See Martinez Ruiz, Jose
Azuela, Mariano 1873-1952 . **TCLC 3; DAM MULT; HLC 1**
See CA 104; 131; CANR 81; HW 1, 2; MTCW 1, 2
Baastad, Babbis Friis
See Friis-Baastad, Babbis Ellinor
Bab
See Gilbert, W(illiam) S(chwenck)
Babbis, Eleanor
See Friis-Baastad, Babbis Ellinor
Babel, Isaac
See Babel, Isaak (Emmanuilovich)
Babel, Isaak (Emmanuilovich) 1894-1941(?) .... **TCLC 2, 13; SSC 16**
See CA 104; 155; MTCW 1
Babits, Mihaly 1883-1941 .... **TCLC 14**
See CA 114
Babur 1483-1530 .... **LC 18**
Baca, Jimmy Santiago 1952-
See CA 131; CANR 81; DAM MULT; DLB 122; HLC 1; HW 1, 2
Bacchelli, Riccardo 1891-1985 .... **CLC 19**
See CA 29-32R; 117
Bach, Richard (David) 1936- .... **CLC 14; DAM NOV, POP**
See AITN 1; BEST 89:2; CA 9-12R; CANR 18; MTCW 1; SATA 13
Bachman, Richard
See King, Stephen (Edwin)
Bachmann, Ingeborg 1926-1973 ..... **CLC 69**
See CA 93-96; 45-48; CANR 69; DLB 85
Bacon, Francis 1561-1626 .... **LC 18,32**
See CDBLB Before 1660; DLB 151
Bacon, Roger 1214(?)-1292 .... **CMLC 14**
See DLB 115
Bacovia, George .... **TCLC 24**
See Vasiliu, Gheorghe
Badanes, Jerome 1937- .... **CLC 59**
Bagehot, Walter 1826-1877 .... **NCLC 10**
See DLB 55
Bagnold, Enid 1889-1981 ...... **CLC 25;DAM DRAM**
See CA 5-8R; 103; CANR 5, 40; DLB 13, 160, 191; MAICYA; SATA 1, 25
Bagritsky, Eduard 1895-1934 .... **TCLC 60**
Bagrjana, Elisaveta
See Belcheva, Elisaveta
Bagryana, Elisaveta 1893-1991 .... **CLC 10**
See Belcheva, Elisaveta
See CA 178; DLB 147
Bailey, Paul 1937- .... **CLC 45**
See CA 21-24R; CANR 16, 62; DLB 14
Baillie, Joanna 1762-1851 .... **NCLC 71**
See DLB 93
Bainbridge, Beryl (Margaret) 1933- .... **CLC 4, 5, 8, 10, 14, 18, 22, 62; DAM NOV**
See CA 21-24R; CANR 24, 55, 75; DLB 14; MTCW 1, 2
Baker, Elliott 1922- .... **CLC 8**
See CA 45-48; CANR 2, 63
Baker, Jean H. .... **TCLC 3, 10**
See Russell, George William
Baker, Nicholson 1957- . **CLC 61;DAM POP**
See CA 135; CANR 63; DA3
Baker, Ray Stannard 1870-1946 .. **TCLC 47**
See CA 118
Baker, Russell (Wayne) 1925- .... **CLC 31**
See BEST 89:4; CA 57-60; CANR 11, 41, 59; MTCW 1, 2
Bakhtin, M.
See Bakhtin, Mikhail Mikhailovich
Bakhtin, M. M.
See Bakhtin, Mikhail Mikhailovich
Bakhtin, Mikhail
See Bakhtin, Mikhail Mikhailovich
Bakhtin, Mikhail Mikhailovich 1895-1975 .. **CLC 83**
See CA 128; 113
Bakshi, Ralph 1938(?)- .... **CLC 26**
See CA 112; 138
Bakunin, Mikhail (Alexandrovich) 1814-1876 .... **NCLC 25, 58**
Baldwin, James (Arthur) 1924-1987 .... **CLC 1, 2, 3, 4, 5, 8, 13, 15, 17, 42, 50, 67, 90; BLC 1; DA; DAB; DAC; DAM MST, MULT, NOV, POP; DC 1; SSC 10, 33; WLC**
See AAYA 4; BW 1; CA 1-4R; 124; CABS 1; CANR 3, 24; CDALB 1941-1968; DA3; DLB 2, 7, 33; DLBY 87; MTCW 1, 2; SATA 9; SATA-Obit 54
Ballard, J(ames) G(raham) 1930- .... **CLC 3, 6, 14, 36; DAM NOV, POP; SSC 1**
See AAYA 3; CA 5-8R; CANR 15, 39, 65; DA3; DLB 14, 207; MTCW 1, 2; SATA 93
Balmont, Konstantin (Dmitriyevich) 1867-1943 .... **TCLC 11**
See CA 109; 155
Baltausis, Vincas
See Mikszath, Kalman
Balzac, Honore de 1799-1850 .. **NCLC 5, 35,**

53; DA; DAB; DAC; DAM MST, NOV; SSC 5; WLC
See DA3; DLB 119
Bambara, Toni Cade 1939-1995 ..... **CLC 19, 88; BLC 1; DA; DAC; DAM MST, MULT; SSC 35; WLCS**
See AAYA 5; BW 2, 3; CA 29-32R; 150; CANR 24, 49, 81; CDALBS; DA3; DLB 38; MTCW 1, 2
Bamdad, A.
See Shamlu, Ahmad
Banat, D. R.
See Bradbury, Ray (Douglas)
Bancroft, Laura
See Baum, L(yman) Frank
Banim, John 1798-1842 .... **NCLC 13**
See DLB 116, 158, 159
Banim, Michael 1796-1874 .... **NCLC 13**
See DLB 158, 159
Banjo, The
See Paterson, A(ndrew) B(arton)
Banks, Iain
See Banks, Iain M(enzies)
Banks, Iain M(enzies) 1954- .... **CLC 34**
See CA 123; 128; CANR 61; DLB 194; INT 128
Banks, Lynne Reid .... **CLC 23**
See Reid Banks, Lynne
See AAYA 6
Banks, Russell 1940- .... **CLC 37, 72**
See CA 65-68; CAAS 15; CANR 19, 52, 73; DLB 130
Banville, John 1945- .... **CLC 46, 118**
See CA 117; 128; DLB 14; INT 128
Banville, Theodore (Faullain) de 1832-1891 .... **NCLC 9**
Baraka, Amiri 1934- . **CLC 1, 2, 3, 5, 10, 14, 33, 115; BLC 1; DA; DAC; DAM MST, MULT, POET, POP; DC 6; PC 4; WLCS**
See Jones, LeRoi
See BW 2, 3; CA 21-24R; CABS 3; CANR 27, 38, 61; CDALB 1941-1968; DA3; DLB 5, 7, 16, 38; DLBD 8; MTCW 1, 2
Barbauld, Anna Laetitia 1743-1825 .. **NCLC 50**
See DLB 107, 109, 142, 158
Barbellion, W. N. P. .... **TCLC 24**
See Cummings, Bruce F(rederick)
Barbera, Jack (Vincent) 1945- .... **CLC 44**
See CA 110; CANR 45
Barbey d'Aurevilly, Jules Amedee 1808-1889 .... **NCLC 1; SSC 17**
See DLB 119
Barbour, John c. 1316-1395 .... **CMLC 33**
See DLB 146
Barbusse, Henri 1873-1935 .... **TCLC 5**
See CA 105; 154; DLB 65
Barclay, Bill
See Moorcock, Michael (John)
Barclay, William Ewert
See Moorcock, Michael (John)
Barea, Arturo 1897-1957 .... **TCLC 14**
See CA 111
Barfoot, Joan 1946- .... **CLC 18**
See CA 105
Barham, Richard Harris 1788-1845 . **NCLC 77**
See DLB 159
Baring, Maurice 1874-1945 .... **TCLC 8**
See CA 105; 168; DLB 34
Baring-Gould, Sabine 1834-1924 . **TCLC 88**
See DLB 156, 190
Barker, Clive 1952- ...... **CLC 52;DAM POP**
See AAYA 10; BEST 90:3; CA 121; 129; CANR 71; DA3; INT 129; MTCW 1, 2
Barker, George Granville 1913-1991 ... **CLC 8, 48; DAM POET**
See CA 9-12R; 135; CANR 7, 38; DLB 20; MTCW 1
Barker, Harley Granville
See Granville-Barker, Harley
See DLB 10
Barker, Howard 1946- .... **CLC 37**
See CA 102; DLB 13
Barker, Jane 1652-1732 .... **LC 42**
Barker, Pat(ricia) 1943- .... **CLC 32, 94**
See CA 117; 122; CANR 50; INT 122
Barlach, Ernst (Heinrich) 1870-1938 . **TCLC 84**
See CA 178; DLB 56, 118
Barlow, Joel 1754-1812 .... **NCLC 23**
See DLB 37
Barnard, Mary (Ethel) 1909- .... **CLC 48**
See CA 21-22; CAP 2
Barnes, Djuna 1892-1982 ... **CLC 3, 4, 8, 11, 29; SSC 3**
See CA 9-12R; 107; CANR 16, 55; DLB 4, 9, 45; MTCW 1, 2
Barnes, Julian (Patrick) 1946- .... **CLC 42; DAB**
See CA 102; CANR 19, 54; DLB 194; DLBY 93; MTCW 1
Barnes, Peter 1931- .... **CLC 5, 56**
See CA 65-68; CAAS 12; CANR 33, 34, 64; DLB 13; MTCW 1
Barnes, William 1801-1886 .... **NCLC 75**
See DLB 32
Baroja (y Nessi), Pio 1872-1956 .... **TCLC 8; HLC 1**
See CA 104
Baron, David
See Pinter, Harold
Baron Corvo
See Rolfe, Frederick (William Serafino Austin Lewis Mary)
Barondess, Sue K(aufman) 1926-1977 . **CLC 8**
See Kaufman, Sue
See CA 1-4R; 69-72; CANR 1
Baron de Teive
See Pessoa, Fernando (Antonio Nogueira)
Baroness Von S.
See Zangwill, Israel
Barres, (Auguste-)Maurice 1862-1923 .... **TCLC 47**
See CA 164; DLB 123
Barreto, Afonso Henrique de Lima
See Lima Barreto, Afonso Henrique de
Barrett, (Roger) Syd 1946- .... **CLC 35**
Barrett, William (Christopher) 1913-1992 .. **CLC 27**
See CA 13-16R; 139; CANR 11, 67; INT CANR-11
Barrie, J(ames) M(atthew) 1860-1937 .... **TCLC 2; DAB; DAM DRAM**
See CA 104; 136; CANR 77; CDBLB 1890-1914; CLR 16; DA3; DLB 10, 141, 156; MAICYA; MTCW 1; SATA 100; YABC 1
Barrington, Michael
See Moorcock, Michael (John)
Barrol, Grady
See Bograd, Larry
Barry, Mike
See Malzberg, Barry N(athaniel)
Barry, Philip 1896-1949 .... **TCLC 11**
See CA 109; DLB 7
Bart, Andre Schwarz
See Schwarz-Bart, Andre
Barth, John (Simmons) 1930- .. **CLC 1, 2, 3, 5, 7, 9, 10, 14, 27, 51, 89; DAM NOV; SSC 10**
See AITN 1, 2; CA 1-4R; CABS 1; CANR 5, 23, 49, 64; DLB 2; MTCW 1
Barthelme, Donald 1931-1989 . **CLC 1, 2, 3, 5, 6, 8, 13, 23, 46, 59, 115; DAM NOV; SSC 2**
See CA 21-24R; 129; CANR 20, 58; DA3; DLB 2; DLBY 80, 89; MTCW 1, 2; SATA 7; SATA-Obit 62
Barthelme, Frederick 1943- .... **CLC 36, 117**
See CA 114; 122; CANR 77; DLBY 85; INT 122
Barthes, Roland (Gerard) 1915-1980 .. **CLC 24, 83**
See CA 130; 97-100; CANR 66; MTCW 1, 2
Barzun, Jacques (Martin) 1907- ..... **CLC 51**
See CA 61-64; CANR 22
Bashevis, Isaac
See Singer, Isaac Bashevis
Bashkirtseff, Marie 1859-1884 ..... **NCLC 27**
Basho
See Matsuo Basho
Basil of Caesaria c. 330-379 .... **CMLC 35**
Bass, Kingsley B., Jr.
See Bullins, Ed
Bass, Rick 1958- .... **CLC 79**
See CA 126; CANR 53; DLB 212
Bassani, Giorgio 1916- .... **CLC 9**
See CA 65-68; CANR 33; DLB 128, 177; MTCW 1
Bastos, Augusto (Antonio) Roa
See Roa Bastos, Augusto (Antonio)
Bataille, Georges 1897-1962 .... **CLC 29**
See CA 101; 89-92
Bates, H(erbert) E(rnest) 1905-1974 .... **CLC 46; DAB; DAM POP; SSC 10**
See CA 93-96; 45-48; CANR 34; DA3; DLB 162, 191; MTCW 1, 2
Bauchart
See Camus, Albert
Baudelaire, Charles 1821-1867 ...... **NCLC 6, 29, 55; DA; DAB; DAC; DAM MST, POET; PC 1; SSC 18; WLC**
See DA3
Baudrillard, Jean 1929- .... **CLC 60**
Baum, L(yman) Frank 1856-1919 .. **TCLC 7**
See CA 108; 133; CLR 15; DLB 22; JRDA; MAICYA; MTCW 1, 2; SATA 18, 100
Baum, Louis F.
See Baum, L(yman) Frank
Baumbach, Jonathan 1933- .... **CLC 6,23**
See CA 13-16R; CAAS 5; CANR 12, 66; DLBY 80; INT CANR-12; MTCW 1
Bausch, Richard (Carl) 1945- .... **CLC 51**
See CA 101; CAAS 14; CANR 43, 61; DLB 130
Baxter, Charles (Morley) 1947- ..... **CLC 45, 78; DAM POP**
See CA 57-60; CANR 40, 64; DLB 130; MTCW 2
Baxter, George Owen
See Faust, Frederick (Schiller)
Baxter, James K(eir) 1926-1972 ...... **CLC 14**
See CA 77-80
Baxter, John
See Hunt, E(verette) Howard, (Jr.)
Bayer, Sylvia
See Glassco, John
Baynton, Barbara 1857-1929 .... **TCLC 57**
Beagle, Peter S(oyer) 1939- .... **CLC 7,104**
See CA 9-12R; CANR 4, 51, 73; DA3; DLBY 80; INT CANR-4; MTCW 1; SATA 60
Bean, Normal
See Burroughs, Edgar Rice
Beard, Charles A(ustin) 1874-1948 ... **TCLC 15**
See CA 115; DLB 17; SATA 18
Beardsley, Aubrey 1872-1898 .... **NCLC 6**
Beattie, Ann 1947- .... **CLC 8, 13, 18, 40, 63; DAM NOV, POP; SSC 11**

See BEST 90:2; CA 81-84; CANR 53, 73; DA3; DLBY 82; MTCW 1, 2
Beattie, James 1735-1803 .... **NCLC 25**
See DLB 109
Beauchamp, Kathleen Mansfield 1888-1923
See Mansfield, Katherine
See CA 104; 134; DA; DAC; DAM MST; DA3; MTCW 2
Beaumarchais, Pierre-Augustin Caronde 1732-1799 .... **DC 4**
See DAM DRAM
Beaumont, Francis 1584(?)-1616 ...... **LC 33; DC 6**
See CDBLB Before 1660; DLB 58, 121
Beauvoir, Simone (Lucie Ernestine Marie Bertrand) de 1908-1986 ... **CLC 1, 2, 4, 8, 14, 31, 44, 50, 71, 124; DA; DAB; DAC; DAM MST, NOV; SSC 35; WLC**
See CA 9-12R; 118; CANR 28, 61; DA3; DLB 72; DLBY 86; MTCW 1, 2
Becker, Carl (Lotus) 1873-1945 .... **TCLC 63**
See CA 157; DLB 17
Becker, Jurek 1937-1997 .... **CLC 7, 19**
See CA 85-88; 157; CANR 60; DLB 75
Becker, Walter 1950- .... **CLC 26**
Beckett, Samuel (Barclay) 1906-1989 .. **CLC 1, 2, 3, 4, 6, 9, 10, 11, 14, 18, 29, 57, 59, 83; DA; DAB; DAC; DAM DRAM, MST, NOV; SSC 16; WLC**
See CA 5-8R; 130; CANR 33, 61; CDBLB 1945-1960; DA3; DLB 13, 15; DLBY 90; MTCW 1, 2
Beckford, William 1760-1844 .... **NCLC 16**
See DLB 39
Beckman, Gunnel 1910- .... **CLC 26**
See CA 33-36R; CANR 15; CLR 25; MAICYA; SAAS 9; SATA 6
Becque, Henri 1837-1899 .... **NCLC 3**
See DLB 192
Becquer, Gustavo Adolfo 1836-1870
See DAM MULT; HLCS 1
Beddoes, Thomas Lovell 1803-1849 .. **NCLC 3**
See DLB 96
Bede c. 673-735 .... **CMLC 20**
See DLB 146
Bedford, Donald F.
See Fearing, Kenneth (Flexner)
Beecher, Catharine Esther 1800-1878 .... **NCLC 30**
See DLB 1
Beecher, John 1904-1980 .... **CLC 6**
See AITN 1; CA 5-8R; 105; CANR 8
Beer, Johann 1655-1700 .... **LC 5**
See DLB 168
Beer, Patricia 1924- .... **CLC 58**
See CA 61-64; CANR 13, 46; DLB 40
Beerbohm, Max
See Beerbohm, (Henry) Max(imilian)
Beerbohm, (Henry) Max(imilian) 1872-1956 .... **TCLC 1, 24**
See CA 104; 154; CANR 79; DLB 34, 100
Beer-Hofmann, Richard 1866-1945 ... **TCLC 60**
See CA 160; DLB 81
Begiebing, Robert J(ohn) 1946- ...... **CLC 70**
See CA 122; CANR 40
Behan, Brendan 1923-1964 .... **CLC 1, 8, 11, 15, 79; DAM DRAM**
See CA 73-76; CANR 33; CDBLB 1945-1960; DLB 13; MTCW 1, 2
Behn, Aphra 1640(?)-1689 ...... **LC 1, 30, 42; DA; DAB; DAC; DAM DRAM, MST, NOV, POET; DC 4; PC 13; WLC**
See DA3; DLB 39, 80, 131
Behrman, S(amuel) N(athaniel) 1893-1973 . **CLC 40**
See CA 13-16; 45-48; CAP 1; DLB 7, 44
Belasco, David 1853-1931 .... **TCLC 3**
See CA 104; 168; DLB 7
Belcheva, Elisaveta 1893- .... **CLC 10**
See Bagryana, Elisaveta
Beldone, Phil "Cheech"
See Ellison, Harlan (Jay)
Beleno
See Azuela, Mariano
Belinski, VissarionGrigoryevich 1811-1848 . **NCLC 5**
See DLB 198
Belitt, Ben 1911- .... **CLC 22**
See CA 13-16R; CAAS 4; CANR 7, 77; DLB 5
Bell, Gertrude (MargaretLowthian) 1868-1926 .... **TCLC 67**
See CA 167; DLB 174
Bell, J. Freeman
See Zangwill, Israel
Bell, James Madison 1826-1902 .. **TCLC 43; BLC 1; DAM MULT**
See BW 1; CA 122; 124; DLB 50
Bell, Madison Smartt 1957- .... **CLC 41, 102**
See CA 111; CANR 28, 54, 73; MTCW 1
Bell, Marvin (Hartley) 1937- ..... **CLC 8, 31; DAM POET**
See CA 21-24R; CAAS 14; CANR 59; DLB 5; MTCW 1
Bell, W. L. D.
See Mencken, H(enry) L(ouis)
Bellamy, Atwood C.
See Mencken, H(enry) L(ouis)
Bellamy, Edward 1850-1898 .... **NCLC 4**
See DLB 12
Belli, Gioconda 1949-
See CA 152; HLCS 1
Bellin, Edward J.
See Kuttner, Henry
Belloc, (Joseph) Hilaire (Pierre Sebastien Rene Swanton) 1870-1953 ..... **TCLC 7, 18; DAM POET; PC 24**
See CA 106; 152; DLB 19, 100, 141, 174; MTCW 1; YABC 1
Belloc, Joseph Peter Rene Hilaire
See Belloc, (Joseph) Hilaire (Pierre Sebastien Rene Swanton)
Belloc, Joseph Pierre Hilaire
See Belloc, (Joseph) Hilaire (Pierre Sebastien Rene Swanton)
Belloc, M. A.
See Lowndes, Marie Adelaide (Belloc)
Bellow, Saul 1915- . **CLC 1, 2, 3, 6, 8, 10, 13, 15, 25, 33, 34, 63, 79; DA; DAB; DAC; DAM MST, NOV, POP; SSC 14; WLC**
See AITN 2; BEST 89:3; CA 5-8R; CABS 1; CANR 29, 53; CDALB 1941-1968; DA3; DLB 2, 28; DLBD 3; DLBY 82; MTCW 1, 2
Belser, Reimond Karel Maria de 1929-
See Ruyslinck, Ward
See CA 152
Bely, Andrey .... **TCLC 7; PC 11**
See Bugayev, Boris Nikolayevich
See MTCW 1
Belyi, Andrei
See Bugayev, Boris Nikolayevich
Benary, Margot
See Benary-Isbert, Margot
Benary-Isbert,Margot 1889-1979 .... **CLC 12**
See CA 5-8R; 89-92; CANR 4, 72; CLR 12; MAICYA; SATA 2; SATA-Obit 21
Benavente (y Martinez), Jacinto 1866-1954 . **TCLC 3; DAM DRAM, MULT; HLCS 1**
See CA 106; 131; CANR 81; HW 1, 2; MTCW 1, 2
Benchley, Peter (Bradford) 1940- .... **CLC 4, 8; DAM NOV, POP**
See AAYA 14; AITN 2; CA 17-20R; CANR 12, 35, 66; MTCW 1, 2; SATA 3, 89
Benchley, Robert (Charles) 1889-1945 .... **TCLC 1, 55**
See CA 105; 153; DLB 11
Benda, Julien 1867-1956 .... **TCLC 60**
See CA 120; 154
Benedict, Ruth (Fulton) 1887-1948 ... **TCLC 60**
See CA 158
Benedict, Saint c. 480-c. 547 .... **CMLC 29**
Benedikt, Michael 1935- .... **CLC 4, 14**
See CA 13-16R; CANR 7; DLB 5
Benet, Juan 1927- .... **CLC 28**
See CA 143
Benet, Stephen Vincent 1898-1943 .... **TCLC 7; DAM POET; SSC 10**
See CA 104; 152; DA3; DLB 4, 48, 102; DLBY 97; MTCW 1; YABC 1
Benet, William Rose 1886-1950 .. **TCLC 28; DAM POET**
See CA 118; 152; DLB 45
Benford, Gregory (Albert) 1941- .... **CLC 52**
See CA 69-72, 175; CAAE 175; CAAS 27; CANR 12, 24, 49; DLBY 82
Bengtsson, Frans (Gunnar) 1894-1954 .... **TCLC 48**
See CA 170
Benjamin, David
See Slavitt, David R(ytman)
Benjamin, Lois
See Gould, Lois
Benjamin, Walter 1892-1940 .... **TCLC 39**
See CA 164
Benn, Gottfried 1886-1956 .... **TCLC 3**
See CA 106; 153; DLB 56
Bennett, Alan 1934- .... **CLC 45, 77; DAB; DAM MST**
See CA 103; CANR 35, 55; MTCW 1, 2
Bennett, (Enoch) Arnold 1867-1931 .. **TCLC 5, 20**
See CA 106; 155; CDBLB 1890-1914; DLB 10, 34, 98, 135; MTCW 2
Bennett, Elizabeth
See Mitchell, Margaret (Munnerlyn)
Bennett, George Harold 1930-
See Bennett, Hal
See BW 1; CA 97-100
Bennett, Hal .... **CLC 5**
See Bennett, George Harold
See DLB 33
Bennett, Jay 1912- .... **CLC 35**
See AAYA 10; CA 69-72; CANR 11, 42, 79; JRDA; SAAS 4; SATA 41, 87; SATA-Brief 27
Bennett, Louise (Simone) 1919- ..... **CLC 28; BLC 1; DAM MULT**
See BW 2, 3; CA 151; DLB 117
Benson, E(dward) F(rederic) 1867-1940 ...... **TCLC 27**
See CA 114; 157; DLB 135, 153
Benson, Jackson J. 1930- .... **CLC 34**
See CA 25-28R; DLB 111
Benson, Sally 1900-1972 .... **CLC 17**
See CA 19-20; 37-40R; CAP 1; SATA 1, 35; SATA-Obit 27
Benson, Stella 1892-1933 .... **TCLC 17**
See CA 117; 155; DLB 36, 162
Bentham, Jeremy 1748-1832 .... **NCLC 38**
See DLB 107, 158
Bentley, E(dmund) C(lerihew) 1875-1956 ... **TCLC 12**
See CA 108; DLB 70
Bentley, Eric (Russell) 1916- .... **CLC 24**
See CA 5-8R; CANR 6, 67; INT CANR-6
Beranger, Pierre Jean de 1780-1857 . **NCLC 34**
Berdyaev, Nicolas
See Berdyaev, Nikolai (Aleksandrovich)

Berdyaev, Nikolai (Aleksandrovich) 1874-1948 .... **TCLC 67**
See CA 120; 157
Berdyayev, Nikolai (Aleksandrovich)
See Berdyaev, Nikolai (Aleksandrovich)
Berendt, John (Lawrence) 1939- .... **CLC 86**
See CA 146; CANR 75; DA3; MTCW 1
Beresford, J(ohn) D(avys) 1873-1947 . **TCLC 81**
See CA 112; 155; DLB 162, 178, 197
Bergelson, David 1884-1952 .... **TCLC 81**
Berger, Colonel
See Malraux, (Georges-)Andre
Berger, John (Peter) 1926- .... **CLC 2, 19**
See CA 81-84; CANR 51, 78; DLB 14, 207
Berger, Melvin H. 1927- .... **CLC 12**
See CA 5-8R; CANR 4; CLR 32; SAAS 2; SATA 5, 88
Berger, Thomas (Louis) 1924- . **CLC 3, 5, 8, 11, 18, 38; DAM NOV**
See CA 1-4R; CANR 5, 28, 51; DLB 2; DLBY 80; INT CANR-28; MTCW 1, 2
Bergman, (Ernst) Ingmar 1918- .... **CLC 16, 72**
See CA 81-84; CANR 33, 70; MTCW 2
Bergson,Henri(-Louis) 1859-1941 . **TCLC 32**
See CA 164
Bergstein, Eleanor 1938- .... **CLC 4**
See CA 53-56; CANR 5
Berkoff, Steven 1937- .... **CLC 56**
See CA 104; CANR 72
Bermant, Chaim (Icyk) 1929- .... **CLC 40**
See CA 57-60; CANR 6, 31, 57
Bern, Victoria
See Fisher, M(ary) F(rances) K(ennedy)
Bernanos, (Paul Louis) Georges 1888-1948 .... **TCLC 3**
See CA 104; 130; DLB 72
Bernard, April 1956- .... **CLC 59**
See CA 131
Berne, Victoria
See Fisher, M(ary) F(rances) K(ennedy)
Bernhard, Thomas 1931-1989 .... **CLC 3, 32, 61**
See CA 85-88; 127; CANR 32, 57; DLB 85, 124; MTCW 1
Bernhardt, Sarah (Henriette Rosine) 1844-1923 .... **TCLC 75**
See CA 157
Berriault, Gina 1926- . **CLC 54, 109;SSC 30**
See CA 116; 129; CANR 66; DLB 130
Berrigan, Daniel 1921- .... **CLC 4**
See CA 33-36R; CAAS 1; CANR 11, 43, 78; DLB 5
Berrigan, Edmund Joseph Michael, Jr. 1934-1983
See Berrigan, Ted
See CA 61-64; 110; CANR 14
Berrigan, Ted .... **CLC 37**
See Berrigan, Edmund Joseph Michael, Jr.
See DLB 5, 169
Berry, Charles Edward Anderson 1931-
See Berry, Chuck
See CA 115
Berry, Chuck .... **CLC 17**
See Berry, Charles Edward Anderson
Berry, Jonas
See Ashbery, John (Lawrence)
Berry, Wendell (Erdman) 1934- .. **CLC 4, 6, 8, 27, 46; DAM POET; PC 28**
See AITN 1; CA 73-76; CANR 50, 73; DLB 5, 6; MTCW 1
Berryman, John 1914-1972 . **CLC 1, 2, 3, 4, 6, 8, 10, 13, 25, 62; DAM POET**
See CA 13-16; 33-36R; CABS 2; CANR 35; CAP 1; CDALB 1941-1968; DLB 48; MTCW 1, 2
Bertolucci, Bernardo 1940- .... **CLC 16**
See CA 106
Berton, Pierre (Francis Demarigny) 1920- .. **CLC 104**
See CA 1-4R; CANR 2, 56; DLB 68; SATA 99
Bertrand, Aloysius 1807-1841 .... **NCLC 31**
Bertran de Born c. 1140-1215 .... **CMLC 5**
Besant, Annie(Wood) 1847-1933 ..... **TCLC 9**
See CA 105
Bessie, Alvah 1904-1985 .... **CLC 23**
See CA 5-8R; 116; CANR 2, 80; DLB 26
Bethlen, T. D.
See Silverberg, Robert
Beti, Mongo . **CLC 27; BLC 1; DAM MULT**
See Biyidi, Alexandre
See CANR 79
Betjeman, John 1906-1984 ..... **CLC 2, 6, 10, 34, 43; DAB; DAM MST, POET**
See CA 9-12R; 112; CANR 33, 56; CDBLB 1945-1960; DA3; DLB 20; DLBY 84; MTCW 1, 2
Bettelheim, Bruno 1903-1990 .... **CLC 79**
See CA 81-84; 131; CANR 23, 61; DA3; MTCW 1, 2
Betti, Ugo 1892-1953 .... **TCLC 5**
See CA 104; 155
Betts, Doris (Waugh) 1932- ..... **CLC 3, 6, 28**
See CA 13-16R; CANR 9, 66, 77; DLBY 82; INT CANR-9
Bevan, Alistair
See Roberts, Keith (John Kingston)
Bey, Pilaff
See Douglas, (George) Norman
Bialik, Chaim Nachman 1873-1934 ... **TCLC 25**
See CA 170
Bickerstaff, Isaac
See Swift, Jonathan
Bidart, Frank 1939- .... **CLC 33**
See CA 140
Bienek, Horst 1930- .... **CLC 7, 11**
See CA 73-76; DLB 75
Bierce, Ambrose (Gwinett) 1842-1914(?) ..... **TCLC 1, 7, 44; DA; DAC; DAM MST; SSC 9; WLC**
See CA 104; 139; CANR 78; CDALB 1865-1917; DA3; DLB 11, 12, 23, 71, 74, 186
Biggers, Earl Derr 1884-1933 .... **TCLC 65**
See CA 108; 153
Billings, Josh
See Shaw, Henry Wheeler
Billington, (Lady) Rachel (Mary) 1942- ...... **CLC 43**
See AITN 2; CA 33-36R; CANR 44
Binyon, T(imothy) J(ohn) 1936- ..... **CLC 34**
See CA 111; CANR 28
Bioy Casares, Adolfo 1914-1999 .. **CLC 4, 8, 13, 88; DAM MULT; HLC 1; SSC 17**
See CA 29-32R; 177; CANR 19, 43, 66; DLB 113; HW 1, 2; MTCW 1, 2
Bird, Cordwainer
See Ellison, Harlan (Jay)
Bird, Robert Montgomery 1806-1854 .... **NCLC 1**
See DLB 202
Birkerts, Sven 1951- .... **CLC 116**
See CA 128; 133; 176; CAAE 176; CAAS 29; INT 133
Birney, (Alfred) Earle 1904-1995 . **CLC 1, 4, 6, 11; DAC; DAM MST, POET**
See CA 1-4R; CANR 5, 20; DLB 88; MTCW 1
Biruni, al 973-1048(?) .... **CMLC 28**
Bishop, Elizabeth 1911-1979 .... **CLC 1, 4, 9, 13, 15, 32; DA; DAC; DAM MST, POET; PC 3**
See CA 5-8R; 89-92; CABS 2; CANR 26, 61; CDALB 1968-1988; DA3; DLB 5, 169; MTCW 1, 2; SATA-Obit 24
Bishop, John 1935- .... **CLC 10**
See CA 105
Bissett, Bill 1939- .... **CLC 18; PC 14**
See CA 69-72; CAAS 19; CANR 15; DLB 53; MTCW 1
Bissoondath, Neil (Devindra) 1955- ..... **CLC 120; DAC**
See CA 136
Bitov, Andrei (Georgievich) 1937- .. **CLC 57**
See CA 142
Biyidi, Alexandre 1932-
See Beti, Mongo
See BW 1, 3; CA 114; 124; CANR 81; DA3; MTCW 1, 2
Bjarme, Brynjolf
See Ibsen, Henrik (Johan)
Bjoernson, Bjoernstjerne (Martinius) 1832-1910 .... **TCLC 7, 37**
See CA 104
Black, Robert
See Holdstock, Robert P.
Blackburn, Paul 1926-1971 .... **CLC 9, 43**
See CA 81-84; 33-36R; CANR 34; DLB 16; DLBY 81
Black Elk 1863-1950 .... **TCLC 33;DAM MULT**
See CA 144; MTCW 1; NNAL
Black Hobart
See Sanders, (James) Ed(ward)
Blacklin, Malcolm
See Chambers, Aidan
Blackmore, R(ichard) D(oddridge) 1825-1900 .... **TCLC 27**
See CA 120; DLB 18
Blackmur, R(ichard) P(almer) 1904-1965 ... **CLC 2, 24**
See CA 11-12; 25-28R; CANR 71; CAP 1; DLB 63
Black Tarantula
See Acker, Kathy
Blackwood, Algernon (Henry) 1869-1951 .... **TCLC 5**
See CA 105; 150; DLB 153, 156, 178
Blackwood, Caroline 1931-1996 .. **CLC 6, 9, 100**
See CA 85-88; 151; CANR 32, 61, 65; DLB 14, 207; MTCW 1
Blade, Alexander
See Hamilton, Edmond; Silverberg, Robert
Blaga, Lucian 1895-1961 .... **CLC 75**
See CA 157
Blair, Eric (Arthur) 1903-1950
See Orwell, George
See CA 104; 132; DA; DAB; DAC; DAM MST, NOV; DA3; MTCW 1, 2; SATA 29
Blair, Hugh 1718-1800 .... **NCLC 75**
Blais, Marie-Claire 1939- ... **CLC 2, 4, 6, 13, 22; DAC; DAM MST**
See CA 21-24R; CAAS 4; CANR 38, 75; DLB 53; MTCW 1, 2
Blaise, Clark 1940- .... **CLC 29**
See AITN 2; CA 53-56; CAAS 3; CANR 5, 66; DLB 53
Blake, Fairley
See De Voto, Bernard (Augustine)
Blake, Nicholas
See Day Lewis, C(ecil)
See DLB 77
Blake, William 1757-1827 ...... **NCLC 13, 37, 57; DA; DAB; DAC; DAM MST, POET; PC 12; WLC**
See CDBLB 1789-1832; CLR 52; DA3; DLB 93, 163; MAICYA; SATA 30
Blasco Ibanez, Vicente 1867-1928 ..... **TCLC 12; DAM NOV**

See CA 110; 131; CANR 81; DA3; HW 1, 2; MTCW 1

Blatty, William Peter 1928- .... **CLC 2;DAM POP**
See CA 5-8R; CANR 9

Bleeck, Oliver
See Thomas, Ross (Elmore)

Blessing, Lee 1949- .... **CLC 54**

Blish, James (Benjamin) 1921-1975 ..... **CLC 14**
See CA 1-4R; 57-60; CANR 3; DLB 8; MTCW 1; SATA 66

Bliss, Reginald
See Wells, H(erbert) G(eorge)

Blixen, Karen (Christentze Dinesen) 1885-1962
See Dinesen, Isak
See CA 25-28; CANR 22, 50; CAP 2; DA3; MTCW 1, 2; SATA 44

Bloch, Robert (Albert) 1917-1994 ... **CLC 33**
See AAYA 29; CA 5-8R, 179; 146; CAAE 179; CAAS 20; CANR 5, 78; DA3; DLB 44; INT CANR-5; MTCW 1; SATA 12; SATA-Obit 82

Blok, Alexander (Alexandrovich) 1880-1921 .... **TCLC 5; PC 21**
See CA 104

Blom, Jan
See Breytenbach, Breyten

Bloom, Harold 1930- .... **CLC 24, 103**
See CA 13-16R; CANR 39, 75; DLB 67; MTCW 1

Bloomfield, Aurelius
See Bourne, Randolph S(illiman)

Blount, Roy (Alton), Jr. 1941- .... **CLC 38**
See CA 53-56; CANR 10, 28, 61; INT CANR-28; MTCW 1, 2

Bloy, Leon 1846-1917 .... **TCLC 22**
See CA 121; DLB 123

Blume, Judy (Sussman) 1938- . **CLC 12, 30; DAM NOV, POP**
See AAYA 3, 26; CA 29-32R; CANR 13, 37, 66; CLR 2, 15; DA3; DLB 52; JRDA; MAICYA; MTCW 1, 2; SATA 2, 31, 79

Blunden, Edmund (Charles) 1896-1974 .... **CLC 2, 56**
See CA 17-18; 45-48; CANR 54; CAP 2; DLB 20, 100, 155; MTCW 1

Bly, Robert (Elwood) 1926- ..... **CLC 1, 2, 5, 10, 15, 38; DAM POET**
See CA 5-8R; CANR 41, 73; DA3; DLB 5; MTCW 1, 2

Boas, Franz 1858-1942 .... **TCLC 56**
See CA 115; 181

Bobette
See Simenon, Georges (Jacques Christian)

Boccaccio, Giovanni 1313-1375 .. **CMLC 13; SSC 10**

Bochco, Steven 1943- .... **CLC 35**
See AAYA 11; CA 124; 138

Bodel, Jean 1167(?)-1210 .... **CMLC 28**

Bodenheim,Maxwell 1892-1954 .... **TCLC 44**
See CA 110; DLB 9, 45

Bodker, Cecil 1927- .... **CLC 21**
See CA 73-76; CANR 13, 44; CLR 23; MAICYA; SATA 14

Boell, Heinrich (Theodor) 1917-1985 .. **CLC 2, 3, 6, 9, 11, 15, 27, 32, 72; DA; DAB; DAC; DAM MST, NOV; SSC 23; WLC**
See CA 21-24R; 116; CANR 24; DA3; DLB 69; DLBY 85; MTCW 1, 2

Boerne, Alfred
See Doeblin, Alfred

Boethius 480(?)-524(?) .... **CMLC 15**
See DLB 115

Boff, Leonardo (Genezio Darci) 1938-
See CA 150; DAM MULT; HLC 1; HW 2

Bogan, Louise 1897-1970 ...... **CLC 4, 39, 46, 93; DAM POET; PC 12**
See CA 73-76; 25-28R; CANR 33, 82; DLB 45, 169; MTCW 1, 2

Bogarde, Dirk 1921-1999 .... **CLC 19**
See Van Den Bogarde, Derek Jules Gaspard Ulric Niven
See CA 179; DLB 14

Bogosian, Eric 1953- .... **CLC 45**
See CA 138

Bograd, Larry 1953- .... **CLC 35**
See CA 93-96; CANR 57; SAAS 21; SATA 33, 89

Boiardo, Matteo Maria 1441-1494 ...... **LC 6**

Boileau-Despreaux, Nicolas 1636-1711 ... **LC 3**

Bojer, Johan 1872-1959 .... **TCLC 64**

Boland, Eavan (Aisling) 1944- . **CLC 40, 67, 113; DAM POET**
See CA 143; CANR 61; DLB 40; MTCW 2

Boll, Heinrich
See Boell, Heinrich (Theodor)

Bolt, Lee
See Faust, Frederick (Schiller)

Bolt, Robert (Oxton) 1924-1995 .... **CLC 14; DAM DRAM**
See CA 17-20R; 147; CANR 35, 67; DLB 13; MTCW 1

Bombal, Maria Luisa 1910-1980 .... **SSC 37; HLCS 1**
See CA 127; CANR 72; HW 1

Bombet, Louis-Alexandre-Cesar
See Stendhal

Bomkauf
See Kaufman, Bob (Garnell)

Bonaventura .... **NCLC 35**
See DLB 90

Bond, Edward 1934- .... **CLC 4, 6, 13, 23; DAM DRAM**
See CA 25-28R; CANR 38, 67; DLB 13; MTCW 1

Bonham, Frank 1914-1989 .... **CLC 12**
See AAYA 1; CA 9-12R; CANR 4, 36; JRDA; MAICYA; SAAS 3; SATA 1, 49; SATA-Obit 62

Bonnefoy, Yves 1923- . **CLC 9, 15, 58; DAM MST, POET**
See CA 85-88; CANR 33, 75; MTCW 1, 2

Bontemps, Arna(ud Wendell) 1902-1973 ..... **CLC 1, 18; BLC 1; DAM MULT, NOV, POET**
See BW 1; CA 1-4R; 41-44R; CANR 4, 35; CLR 6; DA3; DLB 48, 51; JRDA; MAICYA; MTCW 1, 2; SATA 2, 44; SATA-Obit 24

Booth, Martin 1944- .... **CLC 13**
See CA 93-96; CAAS 2

Booth, Philip 1925- .... **CLC 23**
See CA 5-8R; CANR 5; DLBY 82

Booth, Wayne C(layson) 1921- .... **CLC 24**
See CA 1-4R; CAAS 5; CANR 3, 43; DLB 67

Borchert, Wolfgang 1921-1947 .... **TCLC 5**
See CA 104; DLB 69, 124

Borel, Petrus 1809-1859 .... **NCLC 41**

Borges, Jorge Luis 1899-1986 .. **CLC 1, 2, 3, 4, 6, 8, 9, 10, 13, 19, 44, 48, 83; DA; DAB; DAC; DAM MST, MULT; HLC 1; PC 22; SSC 4; WLC**
See AAYA 26; CA 21-24R; CANR 19, 33, 75; DA3; DLB 113; DLBY 86; HW 1, 2; MTCW 1, 2

Borowski, Tadeusz 1922-1951 .... **TCLC 9**
See CA 106; 154

Borrow, George (Henry) 1803-1881 .. **NCLC 9**
See DLB 21, 55, 166

Bosch (Gavino), Juan 1909-
See CA 151; DAM MST, MULT; DLB 145; HLCS 1; HW 1, 2

Bosman, Herman Charles 1905-1951 . **TCLC 49**
See Malan, Herman
See CA 160

Bosschere, Jeande 1878(?)-1953 ... **TCLC 19**
See CA 115

Boswell, James 1740-1795 .... **LC 4, 50; DA; DAB; DAC; DAM MST; WLC**
See CDBLB 1660-1789; DLB 104, 142

Bottoms, David 1949- .... **CLC 53**
See CA 105; CANR 22; DLB 120; DLBY 83

Boucicault, Dion 1820-1890 .... **NCLC 41**

Boucolon, Maryse 1937(?)-
See Conde, Maryse
See BW 3; CA 110; CANR 30, 53, 76

Bourget, Paul (Charles Joseph) 1852-1935 . **TCLC 12**
See CA 107; DLB 123

Bourjaily, Vance (Nye) 1922- ...... **CLC 8, 62**
See CA 1-4R; CAAS 1; CANR 2, 72; DLB 2, 143

Bourne, Randolph S(illiman) 1886-1918 ..... **TCLC 16**
See CA 117; 155; DLB 63

Bova, Ben(jamin William) 1932- .... **CLC 45**
See AAYA 16; CA 5-8R; CAAS 18; CANR 11, 56; CLR 3; DLBY 81; INT CANR-11; MAICYA; MTCW 1; SATA 6, 68

Bowen, Elizabeth (Dorothea Cole) 1899-1973 .... **CLC 1, 3, 6, 11, 15, 22, 118; DAM NOV; SSC 3, 28**
See CA 17-18; 41-44R; CANR 35; CAP 2; CDBLB 1945-1960; DA3; DLB 15, 162; MTCW 1, 2

Bowering, George 1935- .... **CLC 15, 47**
See CA 21-24R; CAAS 16; CANR 10; DLB 53

Bowering, Marilyn R(uthe) 1949- ... **CLC 32**
See CA 101; CANR 49

Bowers, Edgar 1924- .... **CLC 9**
See CA 5-8R; CANR 24; DLB 5

Bowie, David .... **CLC 17**
See Jones, David Robert

Bowles, Jane (Sydney) 1917-1973 .... **CLC 3, 68**
See CA 19-20; 41-44R; CAP 2

Bowles, Paul (Frederick) 1910- ... **CLC 1, 2, 19, 53; SSC 3**
See CA 1-4R; CAAS 1; CANR 1, 19, 50, 75; DA3; DLB 5, 6; MTCW 1, 2

Box, Edgar
See Vidal, Gore

Boyd, Nancy
See Millay, Edna St. Vincent

Boyd, William 1952- .... **CLC 28, 53, 70**
See CA 114; 120; CANR 51, 71

Boyle, Kay 1902-1992 .... **CLC 1, 5, 19, 58, 121; SSC 5**
See CA 13-16R; 140; CAAS 1; CANR 29, 61; DLB 4, 9, 48, 86; DLBY 93; MTCW 1, 2

Boyle, Mark
See Kienzle, William X(avier)

Boyle, Patrick 1905-1982 .... **CLC 19**
See CA 127

Boyle, T. C. 1948-
See Boyle, T(homas) Coraghessan

Boyle, T(homas) Coraghessan 1948- ... **CLC 36, 55, 90; DAM POP; SSC 16**
See BEST 90:4; CA 120; CANR 44, 76; DA3; DLBY 86; MTCW 2

Boz
See Dickens, Charles (John Huffam)

Brackenridge, Hugh Henry 1748-1816 .... **NCLC 7**
See DLB 11, 37

Bradbury, Edward P.
See Moorcock, Michael (John)
See MTCW 2

Bradbury, Malcolm (Stanley) 1932- .... **CLC 32, 61; DAM NOV**
See CA 1-4R; CANR 1, 33; DA3; DLB 14, 207; MTCW 1, 2

Bradbury, Ray (Douglas) 1920- ... **CLC 1, 3, 10, 15, 42, 98; DA; DAB; DAC; DAM MST, NOV, POP; SSC 29; WLC**
See AAYA 15; AITN 1, 2; CA 1-4R; CANR 2, 30, 75; CDALB 1968-1988; DA3; DLB 2, 8; MTCW 1, 2; SATA 11, 64

Bradford, Gamaliel 1863-1932 ..... **TCLC 36**
See CA 160; DLB 17

Bradley, David (Henry), Jr. 1950- . **CLC 23, 118; BLC 1; DAM MULT**
See BW 1, 3; CA 104; CANR 26, 81; DLB 33

Bradley, John Ed(mund,Jr.) 1958- . **CLC 55**
See CA 139

Bradley, Marion Zimmer 1930- ..... **CLC 30; DAM POP**
See AAYA 9; CA 57-60; CAAS 10; CANR 7, 31, 51, 75; DA3; DLB 8; MTCW 1, 2; SATA 90

Bradstreet, Anne 1612(?)-1672 ..... **LC 4, 30; DA; DAC; DAM MST, POET; PC 10**
See CDALB 1640-1865; DA3; DLB 24

Brady, Joan 1939- .... **CLC 86**
See CA 141

Bragg, Melvyn 1939- .... **CLC 10**
See BEST 89:3; CA 57-60; CANR 10, 48; DLB 14

Brahe, Tycho 1546-1601 .... **LC 45**

Braine, John (Gerard) 1922-1986 .... **CLC 1, 3, 41**
See CA 1-4R; 120; CANR 1, 33; CDBLB 1945-1960; DLB 15; DLBY 86; MTCW 1

Bramah, Ernest 1868-1942 .... **TCLC 72**
See CA 156; DLB 70

Brammer, William 1930(?)-1978 ..... **CLC 31**
See CA 77-80

Brancati, Vitaliano 1907-1954 ...... **TCLC 12**
See CA 109

Brancato, Robin F(idler) 1936- .... **CLC 35**
See AAYA 9; CA 69-72; CANR 11, 45; CLR 32; JRDA; SAAS 9; SATA 97

Brand, Max
See Faust, Frederick (Schiller)

Brand, Millen 1906-1980 .... **CLC 7**
See CA 21-24R; 97-100; CANR 72

Branden, Barbara .... **CLC 44**
See CA 148

Brandes, Georg (Morris Cohen) 1842-1927 .... **TCLC 10**
See CA 105

Brandys, Kazimierz 1916- .... **CLC 62**

Branley, Franklyn M(ansfield) 1915- ... **CLC 21**
See CA 33-36R; CANR 14, 39; CLR 13; MAICYA; SAAS 16; SATA 4, 68

Brathwaite, Edward (Kamau) 1930- ... **CLC 11; BLCS; DAM POET**
See BW 2, 3; CA 25-28R; CANR 11, 26, 47; DLB 125

Brautigan, Richard (Gary) 1935-1984 . **CLC 1, 3, 5, 9, 12, 34, 42; DAM NOV**
See CA 53-56; 113; CANR 34; DA3; DLB 2, 5, 206; DLBY 80, 84; MTCW 1; SATA 56

Brave Bird, Mary 1953-
See Crow Dog, Mary (Ellen)
See NNAL

Braverman, Kate 1950- .... **CLC 67**
See CA 89-92

Brecht, (Eugen) Bertolt (Friedrich) 1898-1956 .... **TCLC 1, 6, 13, 35; DA; DAB; DAC; DAM DRAM, MST; DC 3; WLC**
See CA 104; 133; CANR 62; DA3; DLB 56, 124; MTCW 1, 2

Brecht, Eugen Berthold Friedrich
See Brecht, (Eugen) Bertolt (Friedrich)

Bremer, Fredrika 1801-1865 .... **NCLC 11**

Brennan, ChristopherJohn 1870-1932 .... **TCLC 17**
See CA 117

Brennan, Maeve 1917-1993 .... **CLC 5**
See CA 81-84; CANR 72

Brent, Linda
See Jacobs, Harriet A(nn)

Brentano, Clemens (Maria) 1778-1842 .... **NCLC 1**
See DLB 90

Brent of Bin Bin
See Franklin, (Stella Maria Sarah) Miles (Lampe)

Brenton, Howard 1942- .... **CLC 31**
See CA 69-72; CANR 33, 67; DLB 13; MTCW 1

Breslin, James 1930-1996
See Breslin, Jimmy
See CA 73-76; CANR 31, 75; DAM NOV; MTCW 1, 2

Breslin, Jimmy .... **CLC 4, 43**
See Breslin, James
See AITN 1; DLB 185; MTCW 2

Bresson, Robert 1901- .... **CLC 16**
See CA 110; CANR 49

Breton, Andre 1896-1966 . **CLC 2, 9, 15, 54; PC 15**
See CA 19-20; 25-28R; CANR 40, 60; CAP 2; DLB 65; MTCW 1, 2

Breytenbach, Breyten 1939(?)- . **CLC 23, 37; DAM POET**
See CA 113; 129; CANR 61

Bridgers, Sue Ellen 1942- .... **CLC 26**
See AAYA 8; CA 65-68; CANR 11, 36; CLR 18; DLB 52; JRDA; MAICYA; SAAS 1; SATA 22, 90; SATA-Essay 109

Bridges, Robert (Seymour) 1844-1930 .... **TCLC 1; DAM POET; PC 28**
See CA 104; 152; CDBLB 1890-1914; DLB 19, 98

Bridie, James .... **TCLC 3**
See Mavor, Osborne Henry
See DLB 10

Brin, David 1950- .... **CLC 34**
See AAYA 21; CA 102; CANR 24, 70; INT CANR-24; SATA 65

Brink, Andre (Philippus) 1935- ...... **CLC 18, 36, 106**
See CA 104; CANR 39, 62; INT 103; MTCW 1, 2

Brinsmead, H(esba) F(ay) 1922- ..... **CLC 21**
See CA 21-24R; CANR 10; CLR 47; MAICYA; SAAS 5; SATA 18, 78

Brittain, Vera (Mary) 1893(?)-1970 . **CLC 23**
See CA 13-16; 25-28R; CANR 58; CAP 1; DLB 191; MTCW 1, 2

Broch, Hermann 1886-1951 .... **TCLC 20**
See CA 117; DLB 85, 124

Brock, Rose
See Hansen, Joseph

Brodkey, Harold (Roy) 1930-1996 .. **CLC 56**
See CA 111; 151; CANR 71; DLB 130

Brodskii, Iosif
See Brodsky, Joseph

Brodsky, Iosif Alexandrovich 1940-1996
See Brodsky, Joseph
See AITN 1; CA 41-44R; 151; CANR 37; DAM POET; DA3; MTCW 1, 2

Brodsky, Joseph 1940-1996 .... **CLC 4, 6, 13, 36, 100; PC 9**
See Brodskii, Iosif; Brodsky, Iosif Alexandrovich
See MTCW 1

Brodsky, Michael (Mark) 1948- ...... **CLC 19**
See CA 102; CANR 18, 41, 58

Bromell, Henry 1947- .... **CLC 5**
See CA 53-56; CANR 9

Bromfield, Louis (Brucker) 1896-1956 .... **TCLC 11**
See CA 107; 155; DLB 4, 9, 86

Broner, E(sther) M(asserman) 1930- ... **CLC 19**
See CA 17-20R; CANR 8, 25, 72; DLB 28

Bronk, William(M.) 1918-1999 .... **CLC 10**
See CA 89-92; 177; CANR 23; DLB 165

Bronstein, Lev Davidovich
See Trotsky, Leon

Bronte, Anne 1820-1849 .... **NCLC 71**
See DA3; DLB 21, 199

Bronte, Charlotte 1816-1855 ..... **NCLC 3, 8, 33, 58; DA; DAB; DAC; DAM MST, NOV; WLC**
See AAYA 17; CDBLB 1832-1890; DA3; DLB 21, 159, 199

Bronte, Emily (Jane) 1818-1848 .. **NCLC 16, 35; DA; DAB; DAC; DAM MST, NOV, POET; PC 8; WLC**
See AAYA 17;CDBLB 1832-1890; DA3; DLB 21, 32, 199

Brooke, Frances 1724-1789 .... **LC 6, 48**
See DLB 39, 99

Brooke, Henry 1703(?)-1783 .... **LC 1**
See DLB 39

Brooke, Rupert (Chawner) 1887-1915 .... **TCLC 2, 7; DA; DAB; DAC; DAM MST, POET; PC 24; WLC**
See CA 104; 132; CANR 61; CDBLB 1914-1945; DLB 19; MTCW 1, 2

Brooke-Haven, P.
See Wodehouse, P(elham) G(renville)

Brooke-Rose, Christine 1926(?)- ..... **CLC 40**
See CA 13-16R; CANR 58; DLB 14

Brookner, Anita 1928- .... **CLC 32, 34, 51; DAB; DAM POP**
See CA 114; 120; CANR 37, 56; DA3; DLB 194; DLBY 87; MTCW 1, 2

Brooks, Cleanth 1906-1994 ...... **CLC 24, 86, 110**
See CA 17-20R; 145; CANR 33, 35; DLB 63; DLBY 94; INT CANR-35; MTCW 1, 2

Brooks, George
See Baum, L(yman) Frank

Brooks, Gwendolyn 1917- .... **CLC 1, 2, 4, 5, 15, 49, 125; BLC 1; DA; DAC; DAM MST, MULT, POET; PC 7;WLC**
See AAYA 20; AITN 1; BW 2, 3; CA 1-4R; CANR 1, 27, 52, 75; CDALB 1941-1968; CLR 27; DA3; DLB 5, 76, 165; MTCW 1, 2; SATA 6

Brooks, Mel .... **CLC 12**
See Kaminsky, Melvin
See AAYA 13; DLB 26

Brooks, Peter 1938- .... **CLC 34**
See CA 45-48; CANR 1

Brooks, Van Wyck 1886-1963 .... **CLC 29**
See CA 1-4R; CANR 6; DLB 45, 63, 103

Brophy, Brigid (Antonia) 1929-1995 ... **CLC 6, 11, 29, 105**
See CA 5-8R; 149; CAAS 4; CANR 25, 53; DA3; DLB 14; MTCW 1, 2

Brosman, Catharine Savage 1934- ... **CLC 9**
See CA 61-64; CANR 21, 46

Brossard, Nicole 1943- .... **CLC 115**
See CA 122; CAAS 16; DLB 53

Brother Antoninus
See Everson, William (Oliver)

The Brothers Quay
See Quay, Stephen; Quay, Timothy

Broughton, T(homas) Alan 1936- ... **CLC 19**
See CA 45-48; CANR 2, 23, 48

Broumas, Olga 1949- .... **CLC 10, 73**
See CA 85-88; CANR 20, 69
Brown, Alan 1950- .... **CLC 99**
See CA 156
Brown, Charles Brockden 1771-1810 .... **NCLC 22, 74**
See CDALB 1640-1865; DLB 37, 59, 73
Brown, Christy 1932-1981 .... **CLC 63**
See CA 105; 104; CANR 72; DLB 14
Brown, Claude 1937- .... **CLC 30; BLC 1; DAM MULT**
See AAYA 7; BW 1, 3; CA 73-76; CANR 81
Brown, Dee (Alexander) 1908- . **CLC 18, 47; DAM POP**
See AAYA 30; CA 13-16R; CAAS 6; CANR 11, 45, 60; DA3; DLBY 80; MTCW 1, 2; SATA 5, 110
Brown, George
See Wertmueller, Lina
Brown, George Douglas 1869-1902 ... **TCLC 28**
See CA 162
Brown, George Mackay 1921-1996 . **CLC 5, 48, 100**
See CA 21-24R; 151; CAAS 6; CANR 12, 37, 67; DLB 14, 27, 139; MTCW 1; SATA 35
Brown, (William) Larry 1951- .... **CLC 73**
See CA 130; 134; INT 133
Brown, Moses
See Barrett, William (Christopher)
Brown, Rita Mae 1944- ...... **CLC 18, 43, 79; DAM NOV, POP**
See CA 45-48; CANR 2, 11, 35, 62; DA3; INT CANR-11; MTCW 1, 2
Brown, Roderick (Langmere) Haig-
See Haig-Brown, Roderick (Langmere)
Brown, Rosellen 1939- .... **CLC 32**
See CA 77-80; CAAS 10; CANR 14, 44
Brown, Sterling Allen 1901-1989 ..... **CLC 1, 23, 59; BLC 1; DAM MULT, POET**
See BW 1, 3; CA 85-88; 127; CANR 26; DA3; DLB 48, 51, 63; MTCW 1, 2
Brown, Will
See Ainsworth, William Harrison
Brown, William Wells 1813-1884 . **NCLC 2; BLC 1; DAM MULT; DC 1**
See DLB 3, 50
Browne, (Clyde) Jackson 1948(?)- .. **CLC 21**
See CA 120
Browning, Elizabeth Barrett 1806-1861 ...... **NCLC 1, 16, 61, 66; DA; DAB; DAC; DAM MST, POET; PC 6; WLC**
See CDBLB 1832-1890; DA3; DLB 32, 199
Browning, Robert 1812-1889 . **NCLC 19, 79; DA; DAB; DAC; DAM MST, POET; PC 2; WLCS**
See CDBLB 1832-1890; DA3; DLB 32, 163; YABC 1
Browning, Tod 1882-1962 .... **CLC 16**
See CA 141; 117
Brownson, Orestes Augustus 1803-1876 ...... **NCLC 50**
See DLB 1, 59, 73
Bruccoli, Matthew J(oseph) 1931- .. **CLC 34**
See CA 9-12R; CANR 7; DLB 103
Bruce, Lenny .... **CLC 21**
See Schneider, Leonard Alfred
Bruin, John
See Brutus, Dennis
Brulard, Henri
See Stendhal
Brulls, Christian
See Simenon, Georges (Jacques Christian)
Brunner, John (Kilian Houston) 1934-1995 .... **CLC 8, 10; DAM POP**
See CA 1-4R; 149; CAAS 8; CANR 2, 37; MTCW 1, 2
Bruno, Giordano 1548-1600 .... **LC 27**
Brutus, Dennis 1924- .... **CLC 43; BLC 1; DAM MULT, POET; PC 24**
See BW 2, 3; CA 49-52; CAAS 14; CANR 2, 27, 42, 81; DLB 117
Bryan, C(ourtlandt) D(ixon) B(arnes) 1936- .... **CLC 29**
See CA 73-76; CANR 13, 68; DLB 185; INT CANR-13
Bryan, Michael
See Moore, Brian
Bryant, William Cullen 1794-1878 .... **NCLC 6, 46; DA; DAB; DAC; DAM MST, POET; PC 20**
See CDALB 1640-1865; DLB 3, 43, 59, 189
Bryusov, Valery Yakovlevich 1873-1924 ...... **TCLC 10**
See CA 107; 155
Buchan, John 1875-1940 ... **TCLC 41; DAB; DAM POP**
See CA 108; 145; DLB 34, 70, 156; MTCW 1; YABC 2
Buchanan, George 1506-1582 .... **LC 4**
See DLB 152
Buchheim, Lothar-Guenther 1918- ... **CLC 6**
See CA 85-88
Buchner, (Karl) Georg 1813-1837 ..... **NCLC 26**
Buchwald, Art(hur) 1925- .... **CLC 33**
See AITN 1; CA 5-8R; CANR 21, 67; MTCW 1, 2; SATA 10
Buck, Pearl S(ydenstricker) 1892-1973 .... **CLC 7, 11, 18; DA; DAB; DAC; DAM MST, NOV**
See AITN 1; CA 1-4R; 41-44R; CANR 1, 34; CDALBS; DA3; DLB 9, 102; MTCW 1, 2; SATA 1, 25
Buckler, Ernest 1908-1984 .. **CLC 13; DAC; DAM MST**
See CA 11-12; 114; CAP 1; DLB 68; SATA 47
Buckley, Vincent (Thomas) 1925-1988 . **CLC 57**
See CA 101
Buckley, William F(rank), Jr. 1925- . **CLC 7, 18, 37; DAM POP**
See AITN 1; CA 1-4R; CANR 1, 24, 53; DA3; DLB 137; DLBY 80; INT CANR-24; MTCW 1, 2
Buechner, (Carl) Frederick 1926- .... **CLC 2, 4, 6, 9; DAM NOV**
See CA 13-16R; CANR 11, 39, 64; DLBY 80; INT CANR-11; MTCW 1, 2
Buell, John (Edward) 1927- .... **CLC 10**
See CA 1-4R; CANR 71; DLB 53
Buero Vallejo, Antonio 1916- .... **CLC 15, 46**
See CA 106; CANR 24, 49, 75; HW 1; MTCW 1, 2
Bufalino, Gesualdo 1920(?)- .... **CLC 74**
See DLB 196
Bugayev, Boris Nikolayevich 1880-1934 ...... **TCLC 7; PC 11**
See Bely, Andrey
See CA 104; 165; MTCW 1
Bukowski, Charles 1920-1994 .. **CLC 2, 5, 9, 41, 82, 108; DAM NOV, POET; PC 18**
See CA 17-20R; 144; CANR 40, 62; DA3; DLB 5, 130, 169; MTCW 1, 2
Bulgakov, Mikhail (Afanas'evich) 1891-1940 . **TCLC 2, 16; DAM DRAM, NOV; SSC 18**
See CA 105; 152
Bulgya, Alexander Alexandrovich 1901-1956 .... **TCLC 53**
See Fadeyev, Alexander
See CA 117; 181
Bullins, Ed 1935- .... **CLC 1, 5, 7; BLC 1; DAM DRAM, MULT; DC 6**
See BW 2, 3; CA 49-52; CAAS 16; CANR 24, 46, 73; DLB 7, 38; MTCW 1, 2
Bulwer-Lytton, Edward (George EarleLytton) 1803-1873 .... **NCLC 1, 45**
See DLB 21
Bunin, Ivan Alexeyevich 1870-1953 .. **TCLC 6; SSC 5**
See CA 104
Bunting, Basil 1900-1985 ... **CLC 10, 39, 47; DAM POET**
See CA 53-56; 115; CANR 7; DLB 20
Bunuel, Luis 1900-1983 . **CLC 16, 80; DAM MULT; HLC 1**
See CA 101; 110; CANR 32, 77; HW 1
Bunyan, John 1628-1688 .. **LC 4; DA; DAB; DAC; DAM MST; WLC**
See CDBLB 1660-1789; DLB 39
Burckhardt, Jacob (Christoph) 1818-1897 .. **NCLC 49**
Burford, Eleanor
See Hibbert, Eleanor Alice Burford
Burgess, Anthony . **CLC 1, 2, 4, 5, 8, 10, 13, 15, 22, 40, 62, 81, 94; DAB**
See Wilson, John (Anthony) Burgess
See AAYA 25; AITN 1; CDBLB 1960 to Present; DLB 14, 194; DLBY 98; MTCW 1
Burke, Edmund 1729(?)-1797 .... **LC 7, 36; DA; DAB; DAC; DAM MST; WLC**
See DA3; DLB 104
Burke, Kenneth (Duva) 1897-1993 .. **CLC 2, 24**
See CA 5-8R; 143; CANR 39, 74; DLB 45, 63; MTCW 1, 2
Burke, Leda
See Garnett, David
Burke, Ralph
See Silverberg, Robert
Burke, Thomas 1886-1945 .... **TCLC 63**
See CA 113; 155; DLB 197
Burney, Fanny 1752-1840 .... **NCLC 12, 54**
See DLB 39
Burns, Robert 1759-1796 . **LC 3, 29, 40; DA; DAB; DAC; DAM MST, POET; PC 6; WLC**
See CDBLB 1789-1832; DA3; DLB 109
Burns, Tex
See L'Amour, Louis (Dearborn)
Burnshaw, Stanley 1906- .... **CLC 3, 13,44**
See CA 9-12R; DLB 48; DLBY 97
Burr, Anne 1937- .... **CLC 6**
See CA 25-28R
Burroughs, Edgar Rice 1875-1950 . **TCLC 2, 32; DAM NOV**
See AAYA 11; CA 104; 132; DA3; DLB 8; MTCW 1, 2; SATA 41
Burroughs, William S(eward) 1914-1997 .... **CLC 1, 2, 5, 15, 22, 42, 75, 109; DA; DAB; DAC; DAM MST, NOV, POP; WLC**
See AITN 2; CA 9-12R; 160; CANR 20, 52; DA3; DLB 2, 8, 16, 152; DLBY 81, 97; MTCW 1, 2
Burton, Sir Richard F(rancis) 1821-1890 .... **NCLC 42**
See DLB 55, 166, 184
Busch, Frederick 1941- ... **CLC 7, 10, 18, 47**
See CA 33-36R; CAAS 1; CANR 45, 73; DLB 6
Bush, Ronald 1946- .... **CLC 34**
See CA 136
Bustos, F(rancisco)
See Borges, Jorge Luis
Bustos Domecq, H(onorio)
See Bioy Casares, Adolfo; Borges, Jorge Luis
Butler, Octavia E(stelle) 1947- .... **CLC 38, 121; BLCS; DAM MULT, POP**

See AAYA 18; BW 2, 3; CA 73-76; CANR 12, 24, 38, 73; DA3; DLB 33; MTCW 1, 2; SATA 84
Butler, Robert Olen (Jr.) 1945- ...... **CLC 81; DAM POP**
See CA 112; CANR 66; DLB 173; INT 112; MTCW 1
Butler, Samuel 1612-1680 .... **LC 16, 43**
See DLB 101, 126
Butler, Samuel 1835-1902 . **TCLC 1, 33; DA; DAB; DAC; DAM MST, NOV; WLC**
See CA 143; CDBLB 1890-1914; DA3; DLB 18, 57, 174
Butler, Walter C.
See Faust, Frederick (Schiller)
Butor, Michel (Marie Francois) 1926- . **CLC 1, 3, 8, 11, 15**
See CA 9-12R; CANR 33, 66; DLB 83; MTCW 1, 2
Butts, Mary 1892(?)-1937 .... **TCLC 77**
See CA 148
Buzo, Alexander(John) 1944- .... **CLC 61**
See CA 97-100; CANR 17, 39, 69
Buzzati, Dino 1906-1972 .... **CLC 36**
See CA 160; 33-36R; DLB 177
Byars, Betsy (Cromer) 1928- .... **CLC 35**
See AAYA 19; CA 33-36R; CANR 18, 36, 57; CLR 1, 16; DLB 52; INT CANR-18; JRDA; MAICYA; MTCW 1; SAAS 1; SATA 4, 46, 80; SATA-Essay 108
Byatt, A(ntonia) S(usan Drabble) 1936- ...... **CLC 19, 65; DAM NOV, POP**
See CA 13-16R; CANR 13, 33, 50, 75; DA3; DLB 14, 194; MTCW 1, 2
Byrne, David 1952- .... **CLC 26**
See CA 127
Byrne, John Keyes 1926-
See Leonard, Hugh
See CA 102; CANR 78; INT 102
Byron, George Gordon (Noel) 1788-1824 .... **NCLC 2, 12; DA; DAB; DAC; DAM MST, POET; PC 16; WLC**
See CDBLB 1789-1832; DA3; DLB 96, 110
Byron, Robert 1905-1941 .... **TCLC 67**
See CA 160; DLB 195
C. 3. 3.
See Wilde, Oscar
Caballero, Fernan 1796-1877 .... **NCLC 10**
Cabell, Branch
See Cabell, James Branch
Cabell, James Branch 1879-1958 ... **TCLC 6**
See CA 105; 152; DLB 9, 78; MTCW 1
Cable, George Washington 1844-1925 .... **TCLC 4; SSC 4**
See CA 104; 155; DLB 12, 74; DLBD 13
Cabral de Melo Neto, Joao 1920- . **CLC 76; DAM MULT**
See CA 151
Cabrera Infante, G(uillermo) 1929- . **CLC 5, 25, 45, 120; DAM MULT; HLC 1**
See CA 85-88; CANR 29, 65; DA3; DLB 113; HW 1, 2; MTCW 1, 2
Cade, Toni
See Bambara, Toni Cade
Cadmus and Harmonia
See Buchan, John
Caedmon fl. 658-680 .... **CMLC 7**
See DLB 146
Caeiro, Alberto
See Pessoa, Fernando (Antonio Nogueira)
Cage, John (Milton,Jr.) 1912-1992 . **CLC 41**
See CA 13-16R; 169; CANR 9, 78; DLB 193; INT CANR-9
Cahan, Abraham 1860-1951 .... **TCLC 71**
See CA 108; 154; DLB 9, 25, 28
Cain, G.
See Cabrera Infante, G(uillermo)
Cain, Guillermo
See Cabrera Infante, G(uillermo)
Cain, James M(allahan) 1892-1977 . **CLC 3, 11, 28**
See AITN 1; CA 17-20R; 73-76; CANR 8, 34, 61; MTCW 1
Caine, Mark
See Raphael, Frederic (Michael)
Calasso, Roberto 1941- .... **CLC 81**
See CA 143
Calderon de la Barca, Pedro 1600-1681 . **LC 23; DC 3; HLCS 1**
Caldwell, Erskine (Preston) 1903-1987 . **CLC 1, 8, 14, 50, 60; DAM NOV; SSC 19**
See AITN 1; CA 1-4R; 121; CAAS 1; CANR 2, 33; DA3; DLB 9, 86; MTCW 1, 2
Caldwell, (Janet Miriam) Taylor (Holland) 1900-1985 . **CLC 2, 28, 39; DAM NOV, POP**
See CA 5-8R; 116; CANR 5; DA3; DLBD 17
Calhoun, JohnCaldwell 1782-1850 .... **NCLC 15**
See DLB 3
Calisher, Hortense 1911- .... **CLC 2, 4, 8, 38; DAM NOV; SSC 15**
See CA 1-4R; CANR 1, 22, 67; DA3; DLB 2; INT CANR-22; MTCW 1, 2
Callaghan, Morley Edward 1903-1990 . **CLC 3, 14, 41, 65; DAC; DAM MST**
See CA 9-12R; 132; CANR 33, 73; DLB 68; MTCW 1, 2
Callimachus c. 305B.C.-c.240B.C. .... **CMLC 18**
See DLB 176
Calvin, John 1509-1564 .... **LC 37**
Calvino, Italo 1923-1985 .. **CLC 5, 8, 11, 22, 33, 39, 73; DAM NOV; SSC 3**
See CA 85-88; 116; CANR 23, 61; DLB 196; MTCW 1, 2
Cameron, Carey 1952- .... **CLC 59**
See CA 135
Cameron, Peter 1959- .... **CLC 44**
See CA 125; CANR 50
Camoens, Luis Vaz de 1524(?)-1580
See HLCS 1
Camoes, Luis de 1524(?)-1580
See HLCS 1
Campana, Dino 1885-1932 .... **TCLC 20**
See CA 117; DLB 114
Campanella, Tommaso 1568-1639 ..... **LC 32**
Campbell, John W(ood,Jr.) 1910-1971 . **CLC 32**
See CA 21-22; 29-32R; CANR 34; CAP 2; DLB 8; MTCW 1
Campbell, Joseph 1904-1987 .... **CLC 69**
See AAYA 3; BEST 89:2; CA 1-4R; 124; CANR 3, 28, 61; DA3; MTCW 1, 2
Campbell, Maria 1940- .... **CLC 85; DAC**
See CA 102; CANR 54; NNAL
Campbell, (John) Ramsey 1946- ... **CLC 42; SSC 19**
See CA 57-60; CANR 7; INT CANR-7
Campbell, (Ignatius) Roy (Dunnachie) 1901-1957 .... **TCLC 5**
See CA 104; 155; DLB 20; MTCW 2
Campbell, Thomas 1777-1844 ...... **NCLC 19**
See DLB 93; 144
Campbell, Wilfred .... **TCLC 9**
See Campbell, William
Campbell, William 1858(?)-1918
See Campbell, Wilfred
See CA 106; DLB 92
Campion, Jane .... **CLC 95**
See CA 138
Campos, Alvaro de
See Pessoa, Fernando (Antonio Nogueira)
Camus, Albert 1913-1960 ..... **CLC 1, 2, 4, 9, 11, 14, 32, 63, 69, 124; DA; DAB; DAC; DAM DRAM, MST, NOV; DC 2; SSC 9;WLC**
See CA 89-92; DA3; DLB 72; MTCW 1, 2
Canby, Vincent 1924- .... **CLC 13**
See CA 81-84
Cancale
See Desnos, Robert
Canetti, Elias 1905-1994 . **CLC 3, 14, 25, 75, 86**
See CA 21-24R; 146; CANR 23, 61, 79; DA3; DLB 85, 124; MTCW 1, 2
Canfield, Dorothea F.
See Fisher, Dorothy (Frances) Canfield
Canfield, Dorothea Frances
See Fisher, Dorothy (Frances) Canfield
Canfield, Dorothy
See Fisher, Dorothy (Frances) Canfield
Canin, Ethan 1960- .... **CLC 55**
See CA 131; 135
Cannon, Curt
See Hunter, Evan
Cao, Lan 1961- .... **CLC 109**
See CA 165
Cape, Judith
See Page, P(atricia) K(athleen)
Capek, Karel 1890-1938 .. **TCLC 6, 37; DA; DAB; DAC; DAM DRAM, MST, NOV; DC 1; SSC 36; WLC**
See CA 104; 140; DA3; MTCW 1
Capote, Truman 1924-1984 ...... **CLC 1, 3, 8, 13, 19, 34, 38, 58; DA; DAB; DAC; DAM MST, NOV, POP; SSC 2; WLC**
See CA 5-8R; 113; CANR 18, 62; CDALB 1941-1968; DA3; DLB 2, 185; DLBY 80, 84; MTCW 1, 2; SATA 91
Capra, Frank 1897-1991 .... **CLC 16**
See CA 61-64; 135
Caputo, Philip 1941- .... **CLC 32**
See CA 73-76; CANR 40
Caragiale, Ion Luca 1852-1912 .... **TCLC 76**
See CA 157
Card, Orson Scott 1951- .... **CLC 44, 47, 50; DAM POP**
See AAYA 11; CA 102; CANR 27, 47, 73; DA3; INT CANR-27; MTCW 1, 2; SATA 83
Cardenal, Ernesto 1925- ...... **CLC 31; DAM MULT, POET; HLC 1; PC 22**
See CA 49-52; CANR 2, 32, 66; HW 1, 2; MTCW 1, 2
Cardozo, Benjamin N(athan) 1870-1938 ..... **TCLC 65**
See CA 117; 164
Carducci, Giosue (Alessandro Giuseppe) 1835-1907 .... **TCLC 32**
See CA 163
Carew, Thomas 1595(?)-1640 .... **LC 13**
See DLB 126
Carey, Ernestine Gilbreth 1908- ..... **CLC 17**
See CA 5-8R; CANR 71; SATA 2
Carey, Peter 1943- .... **CLC 40, 55, 96**
See CA 123; 127; CANR 53, 76; INT 127; MTCW 1, 2; SATA 94
Carleton, William 1794-1869 .... **NCLC 3**
See DLB 159
Carlisle, Henry (Coffin) 1926- .... **CLC 33**
See CA 13-16R; CANR 15, 85
Carlsen, Chris
See Holdstock, Robert P.
Carlson, Ron(ald F.) 1947- .... **CLC 54**
See CA 105; CANR 27
Carlyle, Thomas 1795-1881 . **NCLC 70; DA; DAB; DAC; DAM MST**
See CDBLB 1789-1832; DLB 55; 144

Carman, (William) Bliss 1861-1929 .. **TCLC 7; DAC**
See CA 104; 152; DLB 92
Carnegie, Dale 1888-1955 .... **TCLC 53**
Carossa, Hans 1878-1956 .... **TCLC 48**
See CA 170; DLB 66
Carpenter, Don(ald Richard) 1931-1995 ..... **CLC 41**
See CA 45-48; 149; CANR 1, 71
Carpenter, Edward 1844-1929 ...... **TCLC 88**
See CA 163
Carpentier (y Valmont), Alejo 1904-1980 .... **CLC 8, 11, 38, 110; DAM MULT; HLC 1; SSC 35**
See CA 65-68; 97-100; CANR 11, 70; DLB 113; HW 1, 2
Carr, Caleb 1955(?)- .... **CLC 86**
See CA 147; CANR 73; DA3
Carr, Emily 1871-1945 .... **TCLC 32**
See CA 159; DLB 68
Carr, John Dickson 1906-1977 .... **CLC 3**
See Fairbairn, Roger
See CA 49-52; 69-72; CANR 3, 33, 60; MTCW 1, 2
Carr, Philippa
See Hibbert, Eleanor Alice Burford
Carr, Virginia Spencer 1929- .... **CLC 34**
See CA 61-64; DLB 111
Carrere, Emmanuel 1957- .... **CLC 89**
Carrier, Roch 1937- .... **CLC 13, 78; DAC; DAM MST**
See CA 130; CANR 61; DLB 53; SATA 105
Carroll, James P. 1943(?)- .... **CLC 38**
See CA 81-84; CANR 73; MTCW 1
Carroll, Jim 1951- .... **CLC 35**
See AAYA 17; CA 45-48; CANR 42
Carroll, Lewis ... **NCLC 2, 53; PC 18; WLC**
See Dodgson, Charles Lutwidge
See CDBLB 1832-1890; CLR 2, 18; DLB 18, 163, 178; DLBY 98; JRDA
Carroll, Paul Vincent 1900-1968 ..... **CLC 10**
See CA 9-12R; 25-28R; DLB 10
Carruth, Hayden 1921- .... **CLC 4, 7, 10, 18, 84; PC 10**
See CA 9-12R; CANR 4, 38, 59; DLB 5, 165; INT CANR-4; MTCW 1, 2; SATA 47
Carson, Rachel Louise 1907-1964 . **CLC 71; DAM POP**
See CA 77-80; CANR 35; DA3; MTCW 1, 2; SATA 23
Carter, Angela (Olive) 1940-1992 .... **CLC 5, 41, 76; SSC 13**
See CA 53-56; 136; CANR 12, 36, 61; DA3; DLB 14, 207; MTCW 1, 2; SATA 66; SATA-Obit 70
Carter, Nick
See Smith, Martin Cruz
Carver, Raymond 1938-1988 .... **CLC 22, 36, 53, 55; DAM NOV; SSC 8**
See CA 33-36R; 126; CANR 17, 34, 61; DA3; DLB 130; DLBY 84, 88; MTCW 1, 2
Cary, Elizabeth, Lady Falkland 1585-1639 . **LC 30**
Cary, (Arthur) Joyce (Lunel) 1888-1957 ..... **TCLC 1, 29**
See CA 104; 164; CDBLB 1914-1945; DLB 15, 100; MTCW 2
Casanova de Seingalt, Giovanni Jacopo 1725-1798 .... **LC 13**
Casares, Adolfo Bioy
See Bioy Casares, Adolfo
Casely-Hayford, J(oseph) E(phraim) 1866-1930 ..... **TCLC 24; BLC 1; DAM MULT**
See BW 2; CA 123; 152
Casey, John (Dudley) 1939- .... **CLC 59**
See BEST 90:2; CA 69-72; CANR 23
Casey, Michael 1947- .... **CLC 2**
See CA 65-68; DLB 5
Casey, Patrick
See Thurman, Wallace (Henry)
Casey, Warren(Peter) 1935-1988 .... **CLC 12**
See CA 101; 127; INT 101
Casona, Alejandro .... **CLC 49**
See Alvarez, Alejandro Rodriguez
Cassavetes, John 1929-1989 .... **CLC 20**
See CA 85-88; 127; CANR 82
Cassian, Nina 1924- .... **PC 17**
Cassill, R(onald) V(erlin) 1919- .. **CLC 4, 23**
See CA 9-12R; CAAS 1; CANR 7, 45; DLB 6
Cassirer, Ernst 1874-1945 .... **TCLC 61**
See CA 157
Cassity, (Allen) Turner 1929- ...... **CLC 6, 42**
See CA 17-20R; CAAS 8; CANR 11; DLB 105
Castaneda, Carlos (Cesar Aranha) 1931(?)-1998 .... **CLC 12, 119**
See CA 25-28R; CANR 32, 66; HW 1; MTCW 1
Castedo, Elena 1937- .... **CLC 65**
See CA 132
Castedo-Ellerman, Elena
See Castedo, Elena
Castellanos, Rosario 1925-1974 ..... **CLC 66; DAM MULT; HLC 1**
See CA 131; 53-56; CANR 58; DLB 113; HW 1; MTCW 1
Castelvetro, Lodovico 1505-1571 .... **LC 12**
Castiglione, Baldassare 1478-1529 ..... **LC 12**
Castle, Robert
See Hamilton, Edmond
Castro (Ruz), Fidel 1926(?)-
See CA 110; 129; CANR 81; DAM MULT; HLC 1; HW 2
Castro, Guillen de 1569-1631 .... **LC 19**
Castro, Rosalia de 1837-1885 . **NCLC 3, 78; DAM MULT**
Cather, Willa
See Cather, Willa Sibert
Cather, Willa Sibert 1873-1947 ..... **TCLC 1, 11, 31; DA; DAB; DAC; DAM MST, NOV; SSC 2; WLC**
See AAYA 24; CA 104; 128; CDALB 1865-1917; DA3; DLB 9, 54, 78; DLBD 1; MTCW 1, 2; SATA 30
Catherine, Saint 1347-1380 .... **CMLC 27**
Cato, Marcus Porcius 234B.C.-149B.C. .... **CMLC 21**
See DLB 211
Catton, (Charles) Bruce 1899-1978 . **CLC 35**
See AITN 1; CA 5-8R; 81-84; CANR 7, 74; DLB 17; SATA 2; SATA-Obit 24
Catullus c. 84B.C.-c. 54B.C. .... **CMLC 18**
See DLB 211
Cauldwell, Frank
See King, Francis (Henry)
Caunitz, WilliamJ. 1933-1996 .... **CLC 34**
See BEST 89:3; CA 125; 130; 152; CANR 73; INT 130
Causley, Charles (Stanley) 1917- ...... **CLC 7**
See CA 9-12R; CANR 5, 35; CLR 30; DLB 27; MTCW 1; SATA 3, 66
Caute, (John) David 1936- .... **CLC 29;DAM NOV**
See CA 1-4R; CAAS 4; CANR 1, 33, 64; DLB 14
Cavafy, C(onstantine) P(eter) 1863-1933 ..... **TCLC 2, 7; DAM POET**
See Kavafis, Konstantinos Petrou
See CA 148; DA3; MTCW 1
Cavallo, Evelyn
See Spark, Muriel (Sarah)
Cavanna, Betty .... **CLC 12**
See Harrison, Elizabeth Cavanna
See JRDA; MAICYA; SAAS 4; SATA 1, 30
Cavendish, MargaretLucas 1623-1673 ... **LC 30**
See DLB 131
Caxton, William 1421(?)-1491(?) .... **LC 17**
See DLB 170
Cayer, D. M.
See Duffy, Maureen
Cayrol, Jean 1911- .... **CLC 11**
See CA 89-92; DLB 83
Cela, Camilo Jose 1916- .... **CLC 4, 13, 59, 122; DAM MULT; HLC 1**
See BEST 90:2; CA 21-24R; CAAS 10; CANR 21, 32, 76; DLBY 89; HW 1; MTCW 1, 2
Celan, Paul .... **CLC 10, 19, 53, 82; PC 10**
See Antschel, Paul
See DLB 69
Celine, Louis-Ferdinand .. **CLC 1, 3, 4, 7, 9, 15, 47, 124**
See Destouches, Louis-Ferdinand
See DLB 72
Cellini, Benvenuto 1500-1571 .... **LC 7**
Cendrars, Blaise 1887-1961 ..... **CLC 18, 106**
See Sauser-Hall, Frederic
Cernuda (y Bidon), Luis 1902-1963 ..... **CLC 54; DAM POET**
See CA 131; 89-92; DLB 134; HW 1
Cervantes, Lorna Dee 1954-
See CA 131; CANR 80; DLB 82; HLCS 1; HW 1
Cervantes (Saavedra), Miguel de 1547-1616 .... **LC 6, 23; DA; DAB; DAC; DAM MST, NOV; SSC 12; WLC**
Cesaire, Aime (Fernand) 1913- . **CLC 19, 32, 112; BLC 1; DAM MULT, POET; PC 25**
See BW 2, 3; CA 65-68; CANR 24, 43, 81; DA3; MTCW 1, 2
Chabon, Michael 1963- .... **CLC 55**
See CA 139; CANR 57
Chabrol, Claude 1930- .... **CLC 16**
See CA 110
Challans, Mary 1905-1983
See Renault, Mary
See CA 81-84; 111; CANR 74; DA3; MTCW 2; SATA 23; SATA-Obit 36
Challis, George
See Faust, Frederick (Schiller)
Chambers, Aidan 1934- .... **CLC 35**
See AAYA 27; CA 25-28R; CANR 12, 31, 58; JRDA; MAICYA; SAAS 12; SATA 1, 69, 108
Chambers, James 1948-
See Cliff, Jimmy
See CA 124
Chambers, Jessie
See Lawrence, D(avid) H(erbert Richards)
Chambers, RobertW(illiam) 1865-1933 .... **TCLC 41**
See CA 165; DLB 202; SATA 107
Chandler, Raymond (Thornton) 1888-1959 .... **TCLC 1, 7; SSC 23**
See AAYA 25; CA 104; 129; CANR 60;CDALB 1929-1941; DA3; DLBD 6; MTCW 1, 2
Chang, Eileen 1920-1995 .... **SSC 28**
See CA 166
Chang, Jung 1952- .... **CLC 71**
See CA 142
Chang Ai-Ling
See Chang, Eileen
Channing, William Ellery 1780-1842 . **NCLC 17**
See DLB 1, 59
Chao, Patricia 1955- .... **CLC 119**
See CA 163
Chaplin, Charles Spencer 1889-1977 ... **CLC 16**

See Chaplin, Charlie
See CA 81-84; 73-76
Chaplin, Charlie
See Chaplin, Charles Spencer
See DLB 44
Chapman, George 1559(?)-1634 .... **LC 22; DAM DRAM**
See DLB 62, 121
Chapman, Graham 1941-1989 .... **CLC 21**
See Monty Python
See CA 116; 129; CANR 35
Chapman, John Jay 1862-1933 ...... **TCLC 7**
See CA 104
Chapman, Lee
See Bradley, Marion Zimmer
Chapman, Walker
See Silverberg, Robert
Chappell, Fred (Davis) 1936- .... **CLC 40, 78**
See CA 5-8R; CAAS 4; CANR 8, 33, 67; DLB 6, 105
Char, Rene(-Emile) 1907-1988 ... **CLC 9, 11, 14, 55; DAM POET**
See CA 13-16R; 124; CANR 32; MTCW 1, 2
Charby, Jay
See Ellison, Harlan (Jay)
Chardin, Pierre Teilhard de
See Teilhard de Chardin, (Marie Joseph) Pierre
Charles I 1600-1649 .... **LC 13**
Charriere, Isabelle de 1740-1805 . **NCLC 66**
Charyn, Jerome 1937- .... **CLC 5, 8, 18**
See CA 5-8R; CAAS 1; CANR 7, 61; DLBY 83; MTCW 1
Chase, Mary (Coyle) 1907-1981 .... **DC 1**
See CA 77-80; 105; SATA 17; SATA-Obit 29
Chase, Mary Ellen 1887-1973 .... **CLC 2**
See CA 13-16; 41-44R; CAP 1; SATA 10
Chase, Nicholas
See Hyde, Anthony
Chateaubriand, Francois Renede 1768-1848 .... **NCLC 3**
See DLB 119
Chatterje, Sarat Chandra 1876-1936(?)
See Chatterji, Saratchandra
See CA 109
Chatterji, Bankim Chandra 1838-1894 .... **NCLC 19**
Chatterji, Saratchandra .... **TCLC 13**
See Chatterje, Sarat Chandra
Chatterton, Thomas 1752-1770 .... **LC 54; DAM POET**
See DLB 109
Chatwin, (Charles) Bruce 1940-1989 ... **CLC 28, 57, 59; DAM POP**
See AAYA 4; BEST 90:1; CA 85-88; 127; DLB 194, 204
Chaucer, Daniel
See Ford, Ford Madox
Chaucer, Geoffrey 1340(?)-1400 .... **LC 17; DA; DAB; DAC; DAM MST, POET; PC 19; WLCS**
See CDBLB Before 1660; DA3; DLB 146
Chavez, Denise (Elia) 1948-
See CA 131; CANR 56, 81; DAM MULT; DLB 122; HLC 1; HW 1, 2; MTCW 2
Chaviaras, Strates 1935-
See Haviaras, Stratis
See CA 105
Chayefsky, Paddy .... **CLC 23**
See Chayefsky, Sidney
See DLB 7, 44; DLBY 81
Chayefsky, Sidney 1923-1981
See Chayefsky, Paddy
See CA 9-12R; 104; CANR 18; DAM DRAM
Chedid, Andree 1920- .... **CLC 47**
See CA 145
Cheever, John 1912-1982 ... **CLC 3, 7, 8, 11, 15, 25, 64; DA; DAB; DAC; DAM MST, NOV, POP; SSC 1; WLC**
See CA 5-8R; 106; CABS 1; CANR 5, 27, 76; CDALB 1941-1968; DA3; DLB 2, 102; DLBY 80, 82; INT CANR-5; MTCW 1, 2
Cheever, Susan 1943- .... **CLC 18, 48**
See CA 103; CANR 27, 51; DLBY 82; INT CANR-27
Chekhonte, Antosha
See Chekhov, Anton (Pavlovich)
Chekhov, Anton (Pavlovich) 1860-1904 .... **TCLC 3, 10, 31, 55, 96; DA; DAB; DAC; DAM DRAM, MST; DC 9; SSC 2, 28;WLC**
See CA 104; 124; DA3; SATA 90
Chernyshevsky, Nikolay Gavrilovich 1828-1889 .... **NCLC 1**
Cherry, Carolyn Janice 1942-
See Cherryh, C. J.
See CA 65-68; CANR 10
Cherryh, C. J. .... **CLC 35**
See Cherry, Carolyn Janice
See AAYA 24; DLBY 80; SATA 93
Chesnutt, Charles W(addell) 1858-1932 ...... **TCLC 5, 39; BLC 1; DAM MULT; SSC 7**
See BW 1, 3; CA 106; 125; CANR 76; DLB 12, 50, 78; MTCW 1, 2
Chester,Alfred 1929(?)-1971 .... **CLC 49**
See CA 33-36R; DLB 130
Chesterton, G(ilbert) K(eith) 1874-1936 ...... **TCLC 1, 6, 64; DAM NOV, POET; PC 28; SSC 1**
See CA 104; 132; CANR 73; CDBLB 1914-1945; DLB 10, 19, 34, 70, 98, 149, 178; MTCW 1, 2; SATA 27
Chiang, Pin-chin 1904-1986
See Ding Ling
See CA 118
Ch'ien Chung-shu 1910- .... **CLC 22**
See CA 130; CANR 73; MTCW 1, 2
Child, L. Maria
See Child, Lydia Maria
Child, Lydia Maria 1802-1880 . **NCLC 6, 73**
See DLB 1, 74; SATA 67
Child, Mrs.
See Child, Lydia Maria
Child, Philip 1898-1978 .... **CLC 19, 68**
See CA 13-14; CAP 1; SATA 47
Childers, (Robert) Erskine 1870-1922 .... **TCLC 65**
See CA 113; 153; DLB 70
Childress, Alice 1920-1994 . **CLC 12, 15, 86, 96; BLC 1; DAM DRAM, MULT, NOV; DC 4**
See AAYA 8; BW 2, 3; CA 45-48; 146; CANR 3, 27, 50, 74; CLR 14; DA3; DLB 7, 38; JRDA; MAICYA; MTCW 1, 2; SATA 7, 48, 81
Chin, Frank (Chew, Jr.) 1940- .... **DC 7**
See CA 33-36R; CANR 71; DAM MULT; DLB 206
Chislett, (Margaret) Anne 1943- ..... **CLC 34**
See CA 151
Chitty, Thomas Willes 1926- .... **CLC 11**
See Hinde, Thomas
See CA 5-8R
Chivers, Thomas Holley 1809-1858 .. **NCLC 49**
See DLB 3
Choi, Susan .... **CLC 119**
Chomette, Rene Lucien 1898-1981
See Clair, Rene
See CA 103
Chopin, Kate . **TCLC 5, 14; DA; DAB; SSC 8; WLCS**
See Chopin, Katherine
See CDALB 1865-1917; DLB 12, 78
Chopin, Katherine 1851-1904
See Chopin, Kate
See CA 104; 122; DAC; DAM MST, NOV; DA3
Chretien de Troyes c. 12th cent.- . **CMLC 10**
See DLB 208
Christie
See Ichikawa, Kon
Christie, Agatha (Mary Clarissa) 1890-1976 .... **CLC 1, 6, 8, 12, 39, 48, 110; DAB; DAC; DAM NOV**
See AAYA 9; AITN 1, 2; CA 17-20R; 61-64; CANR 10, 37; CDBLB 1914-1945; DA3; DLB 13, 77; MTCW 1, 2; SATA 36
Christie, (Ann) Philippa
See Pearce, Philippa
See CA 5-8R; CANR 4
Christine de Pizan 1365(?)-1431(?) ...... **LC 9**
See DLB 208
Chubb, Elmer
See Masters, Edgar Lee
Chulkov, Mikhail Dmitrievich 1743-1792 ... **LC 2**
See DLB 150
Churchill, Caryl 1938- .... **CLC 31, 55;DC 5**
See CA 102; CANR 22, 46; DLB 13; MTCW 1
Churchill, Charles 1731-1764 .... **LC 3**
See DLB 109
Chute, Carolyn 1947- .... **CLC 39**
See CA 123
Ciardi, John (Anthony) 1916-1986 . **CLC 10, 40, 44; DAM POET**
See CA 5-8R; 118; CAAS 2; CANR 5, 33; CLR 19; DLB 5; DLBY 86; INT CANR-5; MAICYA; MTCW 1, 2; SAAS 26; SATA 1, 65; SATA-Obit 46
Cicero, Marcus Tullius 106B.C.-43B.C. .... **CMLC 3**
See DLB 211
Cimino, Michael 1943- .... **CLC 16**
See CA 105
Cioran, E(mil)M. 1911-1995 .... **CLC 64**
See CA 25-28R; 149
Cisneros, Sandra 1954- . **CLC 69, 118; DAM MULT; HLC 1; SSC 32**
See AAYA 9; CA 131; CANR 64; DA3; DLB 122, 152; HW 1, 2; MTCW 2
Cixous, Helene 1937- .... **CLC 92**
See CA 126; CANR 55; DLB 83; MTCW 1, 2
Clair, Rene .... **CLC 20**
See Chomette, Rene Lucien
Clampitt, Amy 1920-1994 .... **CLC 32;PC 19**
See CA 110; 146; CANR 29, 79; DLB 105
Clancy, Thomas L., Jr. 1947-
See Clancy, Tom
See CA 125; 131; CANR 62; DA3; INT 131; MTCW 1, 2
Clancy, Tom .... **CLC 45, 112; DAM NOV, POP**
See Clancy, Thomas L., Jr.
See AAYA 9; BEST 89:1, 90:1; MTCW 2
Clare, John 1793-1864 .... **NCLC 9; DAB; DAM POET; PC 23**
See DLB 55, 96
Clarin
See Alas (y Urena), Leopoldo (Enrique Garcia)
Clark, Al C.
See Goines, Donald
Clark, (Robert) Brian 1932- .... **CLC 29**
See CA 41-44R; CANR 67
Clark, Curt
See Westlake, Donald E(dwin)
Clark, Eleanor 1913-1996 .... **CLC 5, 19**
See CA 9-12R; 151; CANR 41; DLB 6

Clark, J. P.
See Clark, John Pepper
See DLB 117
Clark, John Pepper 1935- . **CLC 38; BLC 1; DAM DRAM, MULT; DC 5**
See Clark, J. P.
See BW 1; CA 65-68; CANR 16, 72; MTCW 1
Clark, M. R.
See Clark, Mavis Thorpe
Clark, Mavis Thorpe 1909- .... **CLC 12**
See CA 57-60; CANR 8, 37; CLR 30; MAICYA; SAAS 5; SATA 8, 74
Clark, Walter Van Tilburg 1909-1971 . **CLC 28**
See CA 9-12R; 33-36R; CANR 63; DLB 9, 206; SATA 8
Clark Bekederemo, J(ohnson) P(epper)
See Clark, John Pepper
Clarke, Arthur C(harles) 1917- ... **CLC 1, 4, 13, 18, 35; DAM POP; SSC 3**
See AAYA 4; CA 1-4R; CANR 2, 28, 55, 74; DA3; JRDA; MAICYA; MTCW 1, 2; SATA 13, 70
Clarke, Austin 1896-1974 ... **CLC 6, 9;DAM POET**
See CA 29-32; 49-52; CAP 2; DLB 10, 20
Clarke, Austin C(hesterfield) 1934- . **CLC 8, 53; BLC 1; DAC; DAM MULT**
See BW 1; CA 25-28R; CAAS 16; CANR 14, 32, 68; DLB 53, 125
Clarke, Gillian 1937- .... **CLC 61**
See CA 106; DLB 40
Clarke, Marcus (Andrew Hislop) 1846-1881 .... **NCLC 19**
Clarke, Shirley 1925- .... **CLC 16**
Clash, The
See Headon, (Nicky) Topper; Jones, Mick; Simonon, Paul; Strummer, Joe
Claudel, Paul (Louis Charles Marie) 1868-1955 .... **TCLC 2, 10**
See CA 104; 165; DLB 192
Claudius, Matthias 1740-1815 ...... **NCLC 75**
See DLB 97
Clavell, James (duMaresq) 1925-1994 . **CLC 6, 25, 87; DAM NOV, POP**
See CA 25-28R; 146; CANR 26, 48; DA3; MTCW 1, 2
Cleaver, (Leroy) Eldridge 1935-1998 ... **CLC 30, 119; BLC 1; DAM MULT**
See BW 1, 3; CA 21-24R; 167; CANR 16, 75; DA3; MTCW 2
Cleese, John (Marwood) 1939- .... **CLC 21**
See Monty Python
See CA 112; 116; CANR 35; MTCW 1
Cleishbotham, Jebediah
See Scott, Walter
Cleland, John 1710-1789 .... **LC 2, 48**
See DLB 39
Clemens, Samuel Langhorne 1835-1910
See Twain, Mark
See CA 104; 135; CDALB 1865-1917; DA; DAB; DAC; DAM MST, NOV; DA3; DLB 11, 12, 23, 64, 74, 186, 189; JRDA; MAICYA; SATA 100; YABC 2
Cleophil
See Congreve, William
Clerihew, E.
See Bentley, E(dmund) C(lerihew)
Clerk, N. W.
See Lewis, C(live) S(taples)
Cliff, Jimmy .... **CLC 21**
See Chambers, James
Cliff, Michelle 1946- .... **CLC 120; BLCS**
See BW 2; CA 116; CANR 39, 72; DLB 157
Clifton, (Thelma) Lucille 1936- ...... **CLC 19, 66; BLC 1; DAM MULT, POET; PC 17**
See BW 2, 3; CA 49-52; CANR 2, 24, 42, 76; CLR 5; DA3; DLB 5, 41; MAICYA; MTCW 1, 2; SATA 20, 69
Clinton, Dirk
See Silverberg, Robert
Clough, Arthur Hugh 1819-1861 . **NCLC 27**
See DLB 32
Clutha, Janet Paterson Frame 1924-
See Frame, Janet
See CA 1-4R; CANR 2, 36, 76; MTCW 1, 2
Clyne, Terence
See Blatty, William Peter
Cobalt, Martin
See Mayne, William (James Carter)
Cobb, Irvin S(hrewsbury) 1876-1944 . **TCLC 77**
See CA 175; DLB 11, 25, 86
Cobbett, William 1763-1835 .... **NCLC 49**
See DLB 43, 107, 158
Coburn, D(onald) L(ee) 1938- .... **CLC 10**
See CA 89-92
Cocteau, Jean (Maurice Eugene Clement) 1889-1963 ... **CLC 1, 8, 15, 16, 43; DA; DAB; DAC; DAM DRAM, MST, NOV; WLC**
See CA 25-28; CANR 40; CAP 2; DA3; DLB 65; MTCW 1, 2
Codrescu, Andrei 1946- . **CLC 46, 121; DAM POET**
See CA 33-36R; CAAS 19; CANR 13, 34, 53, 76; DA3; MTCW 2
Coe, Max
See Bourne, Randolph S(illiman)
Coe, Tucker
See Westlake, Donald E(dwin)
Coen, Ethan 1958- .... **CLC 108**
See CA 126; CANR 85
Coen, Joel 1955- .... **CLC 108**
See CA 126
The Coen Brothers
See Coen, Ethan; Coen, Joel
Coetzee, J(ohn) M(ichael) 1940- .... **CLC 23, 33, 66, 117; DAM NOV**
See CA 77-80; CANR 41, 54, 74; DA3; MTCW 1, 2
Coffey, Brian
See Koontz, Dean R(ay)
Coffin, Robert P(eter) Tristram 1892-1955 . **TCLC 95**
See CA 123; 169; DLB 45
Cohan, George M(ichael) 1878-1942 . **TCLC 60**
See CA 157
Cohen, Arthur A(llen) 1928-1986 .... **CLC 7, 31**
See CA 1-4R; 120; CANR 1, 17, 42; DLB 28
Cohen, Leonard (Norman) 1934- .... **CLC 3, 38; DAC; DAM MST**
See CA 21-24R; CANR 14, 69; DLB 53; MTCW 1
Cohen, Matt 1942- .... **CLC 19; DAC**
See CA 61-64; CAAS 18; CANR 40; DLB 53
Cohen-Solal, Annie 19(?)- .... **CLC 50**
Colegate, Isabel 1931- .... **CLC 36**
See CA 17-20R; CANR 8, 22, 74; DLB 14; INT CANR-22; MTCW 1
Coleman, Emmett
See Reed, Ishmael
Coleridge, M. E.
See Coleridge, Mary E(lizabeth)
Coleridge, Mary E(lizabeth) 1861-1907 .... **TCLC 73**
See CA 116; 166; DLB 19, 98
Coleridge, Samuel Taylor 1772-1834 . **NCLC 9, 54; DA; DAB; DAC; DAM MST, POET; PC 11; WLC**
See CDBLB 1789-1832; DA3; DLB 93, 107
Coleridge, Sara 1802-1852 .... **NCLC 31**
See DLB 199
Coles, Don 1928- .... **CLC 46**
See CA 115; CANR 38
Coles, Robert (Martin) 1929- .... **CLC 108**
See CA 45-48; CANR 3, 32, 66, 70; INT CANR-32; SATA 23
Colette, (Sidonie-Gabrielle) 1873-1954 .... **TCLC 1, 5, 16; DAM NOV; SSC 10**
See CA 104; 131; DA3; DLB 65; MTCW 1, 2
Collett, (Jacobine) Camilla (Wergeland) 1813-1895 .... **NCLC 22**
Collier, Christopher 1930- .... **CLC 30**
See AAYA 13; CA 33-36R; CANR 13, 33; JRDA; MAICYA; SATA 16, 70
Collier, James L(incoln) 1928- .... **CLC 30; DAM POP**
See AAYA 13; CA 9-12R; CANR 4, 33, 60; CLR 3; JRDA; MAICYA; SAAS 21; SATA 8, 70
Collier, Jeremy 1650-1726 .... **LC 6**
Collier, John 1901-1980 .... **SSC 19**
See CA 65-68; 97-100; CANR 10; DLB 77
Collingwood, R(obin) G(eorge) 1889(?)-1943 .... **TCLC 67**
See CA 117; 155
Collins, Hunt
See Hunter, Evan
Collins, Linda 1931- .... **CLC 44**
See CA 125
Collins, (William) Wilkie 1824-1889 . **NCLC 1, 18**
See CDBLB 1832-1890; DLB 18, 70, 159
Collins, William 1721-1759 . **LC 4, 40; DAM POET**
See DLB 109
Collodi, Carlo 1826-1890 .... **NCLC 54**
See Lorenzini, Carlo
See CLR 5
Colman, George 1732-1794
See Glassco, John
Colt, Winchester Remington
See Hubbard, L(afayette) Ron(ald)
Colter, Cyrus 1910- .... **CLC 58**
See BW 1; CA 65-68; CANR 10, 66; DLB 33
Colton, James
See Hansen, Joseph
Colum, Padraic 1881-1972 .... **CLC 28**
See CA 73-76; 33-36R; CANR 35; CLR 36; MAICYA; MTCW 1; SATA 15
Colvin, James
See Moorcock, Michael (John)
Colwin, Laurie (E.) 1944-1992 ... **CLC 5, 13, 23, 84**
See CA 89-92; 139; CANR 20, 46; DLBY 80; MTCW 1
Comfort, Alex(ander) 1920- .... **CLC 7;DAM POP**
See CA 1-4R; CANR 1, 45; MTCW 1
Comfort, Montgomery
See Campbell, (John) Ramsey
Compton-Burnett, I(vy) 1884(?)-1969 . **CLC 1, 3, 10, 15, 34; DAM NOV**
See CA 1-4R; 25-28R; CANR 4; DLB 36; MTCW 1
Comstock, Anthony 1844-1915 ..... **TCLC 13**
See CA 110; 169
Comte, Auguste 1798-1857 .... **NCLC 54**
Conan Doyle, Arthur
See Doyle, Arthur Conan
Conde (Abellan), Carmen 1901-
See CA 177; DLB 108; HLCS 1; HW 2
Conde, Maryse 1937- ... **CLC 52, 92; BLCS; DAM MULT**
See Boucolon, Maryse

See BW 2; MTCW 1
Condillac, Etienne Bonnot de 1714-1780 ..... **LC 26**
Condon, Richard (Thomas) 1915-1996 . **CLC 4, 6, 8, 10, 45, 100; DAM NOV**
See BEST 90:3; CA 1-4R; 151; CAAS 1; CANR 2, 23; INT CANR-23; MTCW 1, 2
Confucius 551B.C.-479B.C. . **CMLC 19; DA; DAB; DAC; DAM MST; WLCS**
See DA3
Congreve, William 1670-1729 .... **LC 5, 21; DA; DAB; DAC; DAM DRAM, MST, POET; DC 2; WLC**
See CDBLB 1660-1789; DLB 39, 84
Connell, Evan S(helby), Jr. 1924- .... **CLC 4, 6, 45; DAM NOV**
See AAYA 7; CA 1-4R; CAAS 2; CANR 2, 39, 76; DLB 2; DLBY 81; MTCW 1, 2
Connelly, Marc(us Cook) 1890-1980 . **CLC 7**
See CA 85-88; 102; CANR 30; DLB 7; DLBY 80; SATA-Obit 25
Connor, Ralph .... **TCLC 31**
See Gordon, Charles William
See DLB 92
Conrad, Joseph 1857-1924 .. **TCLC 1, 6, 13, 25, 43, 57; DA; DAB; DAC; DAM MST, NOV; SSC 9; WLC**
See AAYA 26; CA 104; 131; CANR 60; CDBLB 1890-1914; DA3; DLB 10, 34, 98, 156; MTCW 1, 2; SATA 27
Conrad, Robert Arnold
See Hart, Moss
Conroy, Pat
See Conroy, (Donald) Pat(rick)
See MTCW 2
Conroy, (Donald) Pat(rick) 1945- .. **CLC 30, 74; DAM NOV, POP**
See Conroy, Pat
See AAYA 8; AITN 1; CA 85-88; CANR 24, 53; DA3; DLB 6; MTCW 1
Constant (de Rebecque), (Henri) Benjamin 1767-1830 .... **NCLC 6**
See DLB 119
Conybeare, Charles Augustus
See Eliot, T(homas) S(tearns)
Cook, Michael 1933- .... **CLC 58**
See CA 93-96; CANR 68; DLB 53
Cook, Robin 1940- .... **CLC 14;DAM POP**
See AAYA 32; BEST 90:2; CA 108; 111; CANR 41; DA3; INT 111
Cook, Roy
See Silverberg, Robert
Cooke, Elizabeth 1948- .... **CLC 55**
See CA 129
Cooke, John Esten 1830-1886 .... **NCLC 5**
See DLB 3
Cooke, John Estes
See Baum, L(yman) Frank
Cooke, M. E.
See Creasey, John
Cooke, Margaret
See Creasey, John
Cook-Lynn, Elizabeth 1930- . **CLC 93;DAM MULT**
See CA 133; DLB 175; NNAL
Cooney, Ray .... **CLC 62**
Cooper, Douglas 1960- .... **CLC 86**
Cooper, Henry St. John
See Creasey, John
Cooper, J(oan) California (?)- .... **CLC 56; DAM MULT**
See AAYA 12; BW 1; CA 125; CANR 55; DLB 212
Cooper, James Fenimore 1789-1851 . **NCLC 1, 27, 54**
See AAYA 22; CDALB 1640-1865; DA3; DLB 3; SATA 19
Coover, Robert (Lowell) 1932- .... **CLC 3, 7, 15, 32, 46, 87; DAM NOV; SSC 15**
See CA 45-48; CANR 3, 37, 58; DLB 2; DLBY 81; MTCW 1, 2
Copeland, Stewart (Armstrong) 1952- . **CLC 26**
Copernicus, Nicolaus 1473-1543 .... **LC 45**
Coppard, A(lfred) E(dgar) 1878-1957 .... **TCLC 5; SSC 21**
See CA 114; 167; DLB 162; YABC 1
Coppee, Francois 1842-1908 .... **TCLC 25**
See CA 170
Coppola, Francis Ford 1939- .... **CLC 16**
See CA 77-80; CANR 40, 78; DLB 44
Corbiere, Tristan 1845-1875 .... **NCLC 43**
Corcoran, Barbara 1911- .... **CLC 17**
See AAYA 14; CA 21-24R; CAAS 2; CANR 11, 28, 48; CLR 50; DLB 52; JRDA; SAAS 20; SATA 3, 77
Cordelier, Maurice
See Giraudoux, (Hippolyte) Jean
Corelli, Marie 1855-1924 .... **TCLC 51**
See Mackay, Mary
See DLB 34, 156
Corman, Cid 1924- .... **CLC 9**
See Corman, Sidney
See CAAS 2; DLB 5, 193
Corman, Sidney 1924-
See Corman, Cid
See CA 85-88; CANR 44; DAM POET
Cormier, Robert (Edmund) 1925- . **CLC 12, 30; DA; DAB; DAC; DAM MST, NOV**
See AAYA 3, 19; CA 1-4R; CANR 5, 23, 76; CDALB 1968-1988; CLR 12, 55; DLB 52; INT CANR-23; JRDA; MAICYA; MTCW 1, 2; SATA 10, 45, 83
Corn, Alfred (DeWitt III) 1943- ..... **CLC 33**
See CA 179; CAAE 179; CAAS 25; CANR 44; DLB 120; DLBY 80
Corneille, Pierre 1606-1684 ... **LC 28; DAB; DAM MST**
Cornwell, David (John Moore) 1931- .. **CLC 9, 15; DAM POP**
See le Carre, John
See CA 5-8R; CANR 13, 33, 59; DA3; MTCW 1, 2
Corso, (Nunzio) Gregory 1930- .. **CLC 1, 11**
See CA 5-8R; CANR 41, 76; DA3; DLB 5, 16; MTCW 1, 2
Cortazar, Julio 1914-1984 .. **CLC 2, 3, 5, 10, 13, 15, 33, 34, 92; DAM MULT, NOV; HLC 1; SSC 7**
See CA 21-24R; CANR 12, 32, 81; DA3; DLB 113; HW 1, 2; MTCW 1, 2
CORTES, HERNAN 1484-1547 .... **LC 31**
Corvinus, Jakob
See Raabe, Wilhelm (Karl)
Corwin, Cecil
See Kornbluth, C(yril) M.
Cosic, Dobrica 1921- .... **CLC 14**
See CA 122; 138; DLB 181
Costain, Thomas B(ertram) 1885-1965 . **CLC 30**
See CA 5-8R; 25-28R; DLB 9
Costantini, Humberto 1924(?)-1987 ..... **CLC 49**
See CA 131; 122; HW 1
Costello, Elvis 1955- .... **CLC 21**
Costenoble, Philostene
See Ghelderode, Michel de
Cotes, Cecil V.
See Duncan, Sara Jeannette
Cotter, Joseph Seamon Sr. 1861-1949 .... **TCLC 28; BLC 1; DAM MULT**
See BW 1; CA 124; DLB 50
Couch, Arthur Thomas Quiller
See Quiller-Couch, SirArthur (Thomas)
Coulton, James
See Hansen, Joseph
Couperus, Louis (Marie Anne) 1863-1923 .. **TCLC 15**
See CA 115
Coupland, Douglas 1961- .... **CLC 85; DAC; DAM POP**
See CA 142; CANR 57
Court, Wesli
See Turco, Lewis (Putnam)
Courtenay, Bryce 1933- .... **CLC 59**
See CA 138
Courtney, Robert
See Ellison, Harlan (Jay)
Cousteau,Jacques-Yves 1910-1997 .. **CLC 30**
See CA 65-68; 159; CANR 15, 67; MTCW 1; SATA 38, 98
Coventry, Francis 1725-1754 .... **LC 46**
Cowan, Peter (Walkinshaw) 1914- .. **SSC 28**
See CA 21-24R; CANR 9, 25, 50, 83
Coward, Noel (Peirce) 1899-1973 . **CLC 1, 9, 29, 51; DAM DRAM**
See AITN 1; CA 17-18; 41-44R; CANR 35; CAP 2; CDBLB 1914-1945; DA3; DLB 10; MTCW 1, 2
Cowley, Abraham 1618-1667 .... **LC 43**
See DLB 131, 151
Cowley, Malcolm 1898-1989 .... **CLC 39**
See CA 5-8R; 128; CANR 3, 55; DLB 4, 48; DLBY 81, 89; MTCW 1, 2
Cowper, William 1731-1800 . **NCLC 8;DAM POET**
See DA3; DLB 104, 109
Cox, William Trevor 1928- .. **CLC 9, 14, 71; DAM NOV**
See Trevor, William
See CA 9-12R; CANR 4, 37, 55, 76; DLB 14; INT CANR-37; MTCW 1, 2
Coyne, P. J.
See Masters, Hilary
Cozzens, James Gould 1903-1978 .... **CLC 1, 4, 11, 92**
See CA 9-12R; 81-84; CANR 19; CDALB 1941-1968; DLB 9; DLBD 2; DLBY 84, 97; MTCW 1, 2
Crabbe, George 1754-1832 .... **NCLC 26**
See DLB 93
Craddock, Charles Egbert
See Murfree, Mary Noailles
Craig, A. A.
See Anderson, Poul (William)
Craik, Dinah Maria (Mulock) 1826-1887 .... **NCLC 38**
See DLB 35, 163; MAICYA; SATA 34
Cram, Ralph Adams 1863-1942 ... **TCLC 45**
See CA 160
Crane, (Harold) Hart 1899-1932 ... **TCLC 2, 5, 80; DA; DAB; DAC; DAM MST, POET; PC 3; WLC**
See CA 104; 127; CDALB 1917-1929; DA3; DLB 4, 48; MTCW 1, 2
Crane, R(onald) S(almon) 1886-1967 .. **CLC 27**
See CA 85-88; DLB 63
Crane, Stephen (Townley) 1871-1900 . **TCLC 11, 17, 32; DA; DAB; DAC; DAM MST, NOV, POET; SSC 7; WLC**
See AAYA 21; CA 109; 140; CANR 84; CDALB 1865-1917; DA3; DLB 12, 54, 78; YABC 2
Cranshaw, Stanley
See Fisher, Dorothy (Frances) Canfield
Crase, Douglas 1944- .... **CLC 58**
See CA 106
Crashaw, Richard 1612(?)-1649 .... **LC 24**
See DLB 126
Craven, Margaret 1901-1980 . **CLC 17;DAC**
See CA 103
Crawford, F(rancis) Marion 1854-1909 .... **TCLC 10**
See CA 107; 168; DLB 71

Author Index

Crawford, Isabella Valancy 1850-1887 .... **NCLC 12**
See DLB 92
Crayon, Geoffrey
See Irving, Washington
Creasey, John 1908-1973 .... **CLC 11**
See CA 5-8R; 41-44R; CANR 8, 59; DLB 77; MTCW 1
Crebillon, Claude Prosper Jolyot de (fils) 1707-1777 .... **LC 1, 28**
Credo
See Creasey, John
Credo, Alvaro J. de
See Prado (Calvo), Pedro
Creeley, Robert (White) 1926- . **CLC 1, 2, 4, 8, 11, 15, 36, 78; DAM POET**
See CA 1-4R; CAAS 10; CANR 23, 43; DA3; DLB 5, 16, 169; DLBD 17; MTCW 1, 2
Crews, Harry (Eugene) 1935- .... **CLC 6, 23, 49**
See AITN 1; CA 25-28R; CANR 20, 57; DA3; DLB 6, 143, 185; MTCW 1, 2
Crichton, (John) Michael 1942- ... **CLC 2, 6, 54, 90; DAM NOV, POP**
See AAYA 10; AITN 2; CA 25-28R; CANR 13, 40, 54, 76; DA3; DLBY 81; INT CANR-13; JRDA; MTCW 1, 2; SATA 9, 88
Crispin, Edmund .... **CLC 22**
See Montgomery, (Robert) Bruce
See DLB 87
Cristofer, Michael 1945(?)- .. **CLC 28; DAM DRAM**
See CA 110; 152; DLB 7
Croce, Benedetto 1866-1952 .... **TCLC 37**
See CA 120; 155
Crockett, David 1786-1836 .... **NCLC 8**
See DLB 3, 11
Crockett, Davy
See Crockett, David
Crofts, Freeman Wills 1879-1957 . **TCLC 55**
See CA 115; DLB 77
Croker, John Wilson 1780-1857 ... **NCLC 10**
See DLB 110
Crommelynck, Fernand 1885-1970 . **CLC 75**
See CA 89-92
Cromwell, Oliver 1599-1658 .... **LC 43**
Cronin, A(rchibald) J(oseph) 1896-1981 ...... **CLC 32**
See CA 1-4R; 102; CANR 5; DLB 191; SATA 47; SATA-Obit 25
Cross, Amanda
See Heilbrun, Carolyn G(old)
Crothers, Rachel 1878(?)-1958 ..... **TCLC 19**
See CA 113; DLB 7
Croves, Hal
See Traven, B.
Crow Dog, Mary (Ellen) (?)- .... **CLC 93**
See Brave Bird, Mary
See CA 154
Crowfield, Christopher
See Stowe, Harriet (Elizabeth) Beecher
Crowley, Aleister .... **TCLC 7**
See Crowley, Edward Alexander
Crowley, Edward Alexander 1875-1947
See Crowley, Aleister
See CA 104
Crowley, John 1942- .... **CLC 57**
See CA 61-64; CANR 43; DLBY 82; SATA 65
Crud
See Crumb, R(obert)
Crumarums
See Crumb, R(obert)
Crumb, R(obert) 1943- .... **CLC 17**
See CA 106
Crumbum
See Crumb, R(obert)
Crumski
See Crumb, R(obert)
Crum the Bum
See Crumb, R(obert)
Crunk
See Crumb, R(obert)
Crustt
See Crumb, R(obert)
Cruz, Victor Hernandez 1949-
See BW 2; CA 65-68; CAAS 17; CANR 14, 32, 74; DAM MULT, POET; DLB 41; HLC 1; HW 1, 2; MTCW 1
Cryer, Gretchen (Kiger) 1935- .... **CLC 21**
See CA 114; 123
Csath, Geza 1887-1919 .... **TCLC 13**
See CA 111
Cudlip, David R(ockwell) 1933- ...... **CLC 34**
See CA 177
Cullen, Countee 1903-1946 ...... **TCLC 4, 37; BLC 1; DA; DAC; DAM MST, MULT, POET; PC 20; WLCS**
See BW 1; CA 108; 124; CDALB 1917-1929; DA3; DLB 4, 48, 51; MTCW 1, 2; SATA 18
Cum, R.
See Crumb, R(obert)
Cummings, Bruce F(rederick) 1889-1919
See Barbellion, W. N. P.
See CA 123
Cummings, E(dward) E(stlin) 1894-1962 .... **CLC 1, 3, 8, 12, 15, 68; DA; DAB; DAC; DAM MST, POET; PC 5; WLC**
See CA 73-76; CANR 31; CDALB 1929-1941; DA3; DLB 4, 48; MTCW 1, 2
Cunha, Euclides (Rodrigues Pimenta) da 1866-1909 .... **TCLC 24**
See CA 123
Cunningham, E. V.
See Fast, Howard (Melvin)
Cunningham, J(ames) V(incent) 1911-1985 .... **CLC 3, 31**
See CA 1-4R; 115; CANR 1, 72; DLB 5
Cunningham, Julia (Woolfolk) 1916- .. **CLC 12**
See CA 9-12R; CANR 4, 19, 36; JRDA; MAICYA; SAAS 2; SATA 1, 26
Cunningham, Michael 1952- .... **CLC 34**
See CA 136
Cunninghame Graham, R(obert)B(ontine) 1852-1936 .... **TCLC 19**
See Graham, R(obert) B(ontine) Cunninghame
See CA 119; DLB 98
Currie, Ellen 19(?)- .... **CLC 44**
Curtin, Philip
See Lowndes, Marie Adelaide (Belloc)
Curtis, Price
See Ellison, Harlan (Jay)
Cutrate, Joe
See Spiegelman, Art
Cynewulf c. 770-c. 840 .... **CMLC 23**
Czaczkes, Shmuel Yosef
See Agnon, S(hmuel) Y(osef Halevi)
Dabrowska, Maria(Szumska) 1889-1965 ..... **CLC 15**
See CA 106
Dabydeen, David 1955- .... **CLC 34**
See BW 1; CA 125; CANR 56
Dacey, Philip 1939- .... **CLC 51**
See CA 37-40R; CAAS 17; CANR 14, 32, 64; DLB 105
Dagerman, Stig (Halvard) 1923-1954 . **TCLC 17**
See CA 117; 155
Dahl, Roald 1916-1990 ..... **CLC 1, 6, 18, 79; DAB; DAC; DAM MST, NOV, POP**
See AAYA 15; CA 1-4R; 133; CANR 6, 32, 37, 62; CLR 1, 7, 41; DA3; DLB 139; JRDA; MAICYA; MTCW 1, 2; SATA 1, 26, 73; SATA-Obit 65
Dahlberg, Edward 1900-1977 . **CLC 1, 7, 14**
See CA 9-12R; 69-72; CANR 31, 62; DLB 48; MTCW 1
Daitch, Susan 1954- .... **CLC 103**
See CA 161
Dale, Colin .... **TCLC 18**
See Lawrence, T(homas) E(dward)
Dale, George E.
See Asimov, Isaac
Dalton, Roque 1935-1975
See HLCS 1; HW 2
Daly, Elizabeth 1878-1967 .... **CLC 52**
See CA 23-24; 25-28R; CANR 60; CAP 2
Daly, Maureen 1921- .... **CLC 17**
See AAYA 5; CANR 37, 83; JRDA; MAICYA; SAAS 1; SATA 2
Damas, Leon-Gontran 1912-1978 ... **CLC 84**
See BW 1; CA 125; 73-76
Dana, Richard Henry Sr. 1787-1879 . **NCLC 53**
Daniel, Samuel 1562(?)-1619 .... **LC 24**
See DLB 62
Daniels, Brett
See Adler, Renata
Dannay, Frederic 1905-1982 . **CLC 11;DAM POP**
See Queen, Ellery
See CA 1-4R; 107; CANR 1, 39; DLB 137; MTCW 1
D'Annunzio, Gabriele 1863-1938 .. **TCLC 6, 40**
See CA 104; 155
Danois, N. le
See Gourmont, Remy (-Marie-Charles) de
Dante 1265-1321 ... **CMLC 3, 18; DA; DAB; DAC; DAM MST, POET; PC 21; WLCS**
See DA3
d'Antibes, Germain
See Simenon, Georges (Jacques Christian)
Danticat, Edwidge 1969- .... **CLC 94**
See AAYA 29; CA 152; CANR 73; MTCW 1
Danvers, Dennis 1947- .... **CLC 70**
Danziger, Paula 1944- .... **CLC 21**
See AAYA 4; CA 112; 115; CANR 37; CLR 20; JRDA; MAICYA; SATA 36, 63, 102; SATA-Brief 30
Da Ponte, Lorenzo 1749-1838 ...... **NCLC 50**
Dario, Ruben 1867-1916 ..... **TCLC 4; DAM MULT; HLC 1; PC 15**
See CA 131; CANR 81; HW 1, 2; MTCW 1, 2
Darley, George 1795-1846 .... **NCLC 2**
See DLB 96
Darrow, Clarence (Seward) 1857-1938 .... **TCLC 81**
See CA 164
Darwin, Charles 1809-1882 .... **NCLC 57**
See DLB 57, 166
Daryush, Elizabeth 1887-1977 .... **CLC 6, 19**
See CA 49-52; CANR 3, 81; DLB 20
Dasgupta, Surendranath 1887-1952 .. **TCLC 81**
See CA 157
Dashwood, Edmee Elizabeth Monica de la Pasture 1890-1943
See Delafield, E. M.
See CA 119; 154
Daudet, (Louis Marie) Alphonse 1840-1897 .... **NCLC 1**
See DLB 123
Daumal, Rene 1908-1944 .... **TCLC 14**
See CA 114

Davenant, William 1606-1668 .... **LC 13**
See DLB 58, 126
Davenport, Guy (Mattison, Jr.) 1927- . **CLC 6, 14, 38; SSC 16**
See CA 33-36R; CANR 23, 73; DLB 130
Davidson, Avram (James) 1923-1993
See Queen, Ellery
See CA 101; 171; CANR 26; DLB 8
Davidson, Donald (Grady) 1893-1968 . **CLC 2, 13, 19**
See CA 5-8R; 25-28R; CANR 4, 84; DLB 45
Davidson, Hugh
See Hamilton, Edmond
Davidson, John 1857-1909 .... **TCLC 24**
See CA 118; DLB 19
Davidson, Sara 1943- .... **CLC 9**
See CA 81-84; CANR 44, 68; DLB 185
Davie, Donald (Alfred) 1922-1995 ... **CLC 5, 8, 10, 31**
See CA 1-4R; 149; CAAS 3; CANR 1, 44; DLB 27; MTCW 1
Davies, Ray(mond Douglas) 1944- .. **CLC 21**
See CA 116; 146
Davies, Rhys 1901-1978 .... **CLC 23**
See CA 9-12R; 81-84; CANR 4; DLB 139, 191
Davies, (William) Robertson 1913-1995 ...... **CLC 2, 7, 13, 25, 42, 75, 91; DA; DAB; DAC; DAM MST, NOV, POP; WLC**
See BEST 89:2; CA 33-36R; 150; CANR 17, 42; DA3; DLB 68; INT CANR-17; MTCW 1, 2
Davies, Walter C.
See Kornbluth, C(yril) M.
Davies, William Henry 1871-1940 .. **TCLC 5**
See CA 104; 179; DLB 19, 174
Davis, Angela (Yvonne) 1944- .... **CLC 77; DAM MULT**
See BW 2, 3; CA 57-60; CANR 10, 81; DA3
Davis, B. Lynch
See Bioy Casares, Adolfo; Borges, Jorge Luis
Davis, B. Lynch
See Bioy Casares, Adolfo
Davis, H(arold) L(enoir) 1894-1960 ..... **CLC 49**
See CA 178; 89-92; DLB 9, 206
Davis, Rebecca (Blaine) Harding 1831-1910 .... **TCLC 6**
See CA 104; 179; DLB 74
Davis, Richard Harding 1864-1916 ... **TCLC 24**
See CA 114; 179; DLB 12, 23, 78, 79, 189; DLBD 13
Davison, Frank Dalby 1893-1970 ... **CLC 15**
See CA 116
Davison, Lawrence H.
See Lawrence, D(avid) H(erbert Richards)
Davison, Peter (Hubert) 1928- .... **CLC 28**
See CA 9-12R; CAAS 4; CANR 3, 43, 84; DLB 5
Davys, Mary 1674-1732 .... **LC 1, 46**
See DLB 39
Dawson, Fielding 1930- .... **CLC 6**
See CA 85-88; DLB 130
Dawson, Peter
See Faust, Frederick (Schiller)
Day, Clarence (Shepard, Jr.) 1874-1935 ...... **TCLC 25**
See CA 108; DLB 11
Day, Thomas 1748-1789 .... **LC 1**
See DLB 39; YABC 1
Day Lewis, C(ecil) 1904-1972 . **CLC 1, 6, 10; DAM POET; PC 11**
See Blake, Nicholas
See CA 13-16; 33-36R; CANR 34; CAP 1; DLB 15, 20; MTCW 1, 2
Dazai Osamu 1909-1948 .... **TCLC 11**
See Tsushima, Shuji
See CA 164; DLB 182
de Andrade, Carlos Drummond 1892-1945
See Drummond de Andrade, Carlos
Deane, Norman
See Creasey, John
Deane, Seamus (Francis) 1940- ..... **CLC 122**
See CA 118; CANR 42
de Beauvoir, Simone (Lucie Ernestine Marie Bertrand)
See Beauvoir, Simone (Lucie Ernestine Marie Bertrand) de
de Beer, P.
See Bosman, Herman Charles
de Brissac, Malcolm
See Dickinson, Peter (Malcolm)
de Chardin, Pierre Teilhard
See Teilhard de Chardin, (Marie Joseph) Pierre
Dee, John 1527-1608 .... **LC 20**
Deer, Sandra 1940- .... **CLC 45**
De Ferrari, Gabriella 1941- .... **CLC 65**
See CA 146
Defoe, Daniel 1660(?)-1731 ... **LC 1, 42; DA; DAB; DAC; DAM MST, NOV; WLC**
See AAYA 27; CDBLB 1660-1789; DA3; DLB 39, 95, 101; JRDA; MAICYA; SATA 22
de Gourmont, Remy(-Marie-Charles)
See Gourmont, Remy (-Marie-Charles) de
de Hartog, Jan 1914- .... **CLC 19**
See CA 1-4R; CANR 1
de Hostos, E. M.
See Hostos (y Bonilla), Eugenio Maria de
de Hostos, Eugenio M.
See Hostos (y Bonilla), Eugenio Maria de
Deighton, Len .... **CLC 4, 7, 22, 46**
See Deighton, Leonard Cyril
See AAYA 6; BEST 89:2; CDBLB 1960 to Present; DLB 87
Deighton, Leonard Cyril 1929-
See Deighton, Len
See CA 9-12R; CANR 19, 33, 68; DAM NOV, POP; DA3; MTCW 1, 2
Dekker, Thomas 1572(?)-1632 . **LC 22;DAM DRAM**
See CDBLB Before 1660; DLB 62, 172
Delafield, E. M. 1890-1943 .... **TCLC 61**
See Dashwood, Edmee Elizabeth Monica de la Pasture
See DLB 34
de la Mare, Walter (John) 1873-1956 . **TCLC 4, 53; DAB; DAC; DAM MST, POET; SSC 14; WLC**
See CA 163; CDBLB 1914-1945; CLR 23; DA3; DLB 162; MTCW 1; SATA 16
Delaney, Franey
See O'Hara, John (Henry)
Delaney, Shelagh 1939- .... **CLC 29;DAM DRAM**
See CA 17-20R; CANR 30, 67; CDBLB 1960 to Present; DLB 13; MTCW 1
Delany, Mary (Granville Pendarves) 1700-1788 .... **LC 12**
Delany, Samuel R(ay, Jr.) 1942- . **CLC 8, 14, 38; BLC 1; DAM MULT**
See AAYA 24; BW 2, 3; CA 81-84; CANR 27, 43; DLB 8, 33; MTCW 1, 2
De La Ramee, (Marie) Louise 1839-1908
See Ouida
See SATA 20
de la Roche, Mazo 1879-1961 .... **CLC 14**
See CA 85-88; CANR 30; DLB 68; SATA 64
De La Salle, Innocent
See Hartmann, Sadakichi
Delbanco, Nicholas (Franklin) 1942- ... **CLC 6, 13**
See CA 17-20R; CAAS 2; CANR 29, 55; DLB 6
del Castillo, Michel 1933- .... **CLC 38**
See CA 109; CANR 77
Deledda, Grazia(Cosima) 1875(?)-1936 .... **TCLC 23**
See CA 123
Delgado, Abelardo B(arrientos) 1931-
See CA 131; CAAS 15; DAM MST, MULT; DLB 82; HLC 1; HW 1, 2
Delibes, Miguel .... **CLC 8, 18**
See Delibes Setien, Miguel
Delibes Setien, Miguel 1920-
See Delibes, Miguel
See CA 45-48; CANR 1, 32; HW 1; MTCW 1
DeLillo, Don 1936- ... **CLC 8, 10, 13, 27, 39, 54, 76; DAM NOV, POP**
See BEST 89:1; CA 81-84; CANR 21, 76; DA3; DLB 6, 173; MTCW 1, 2
de Lisser, H. G.
See De Lisser, H(erbert) G(eorge)
See DLB 117
De Lisser, H(erbert) G(eorge) 1878-1944 .... **TCLC 12**
See de Lisser, H. G.
See BW 2; CA 109; 152
Deloney, Thomas 1560(?)-1600 .... **LC 41**
See DLB 167
Deloria, Vine (Victor), Jr. 1933- ..... **CLC 21, 122; DAM MULT**
See CA 53-56; CANR 5, 20, 48; DLB 175; MTCW 1; NNAL; SATA 21
Del Vecchio, John M(ichael) 1947- . **CLC 29**
See CA 110; DLBD 9
de Man, Paul (Adolph Michel) 1919-1983 .. **CLC 55**
See CA 128; 111; CANR 61; DLB 67; MTCW 1, 2
De Marinis, Rick 1934- .... **CLC 54**
See CA 57-60; CAAS 24; CANR 9, 25, 50
Dembry, R. Emmet
See Murfree, Mary Noailles
Demby, William 1922- ...... **CLC 53; BLC 1; DAM MULT**
See BW 1, 3; CA 81-84; CANR 81; DLB 33
de Menton, Francisco
See Chin, Frank (Chew, Jr.)
Demetrius of Phalerum c. 307B.C.- . **CMLC 34**
Demijohn, Thom
See Disch, Thomas M(ichael)
de Molina, Tirso 1580-1648
See HLCS 2
de Montherlant, Henry (Milon)
See Montherlant, Henry (Milon) de
Demosthenes 384B.C.-322B.C. ..... **CMLC 13**
See DLB 1[0090]76
de Natale, Francine
See Malzberg, Barry N(athaniel)
Denby, Edwin (Orr) 1903-1983 .... **CLC 48**
See CA 138; 110
Denis, Julio
See Cortazar, Julio
Denmark, Harrison
See Zelazny, Roger (Joseph)
Dennis, John 1658-1734 .... **LC 11**
See DLB 101
Dennis, Nigel (Forbes) 1912-1989 ..... **CLC 8**
See CA 25-28R; 129; DLB 13, 15; MTCW 1
Dent, Lester 1904(?)-1959 .... **TCLC 72**
See CA 112; 161
De Palma, Brian (Russell) 1940- ..... **CLC 20**
See CA 109
De Quincey, Thomas 1785-1859 ..... **NCLC 4**
See CDBLB 1789-1832; DLB 110; 144

Deren, Eleanora 1908(?)-1961
See Deren, Maya
See CA 111
Deren, Maya 1917-1961 .... **CLC 16, 102**
See Deren, Eleanora
Derleth, August(William) 1909-1971 ... **CLC 31**
See CA 1-4R; 29-32R; CANR 4; DLB 9; DLBD 17; SATA 5
Der Nister 1884-1950 .... **TCLC 56**
de Routisie, Albert
See Aragon, Louis
Derrida, Jacques 1930- .... **CLC 24, 87**
See CA 124; 127; CANR 76; MTCW 1
Derry Down Derry
See Lear, Edward
Dersonnes, Jacques
See Simenon, Georges (Jacques Christian)
Desai, Anita 1937- .... **CLC 19, 37, 97; DAB; DAM NOV**
See CA 81-84; CANR 33, 53; DA3; MTCW 1, 2; SATA 63
Desai, Kiran 1971- .... **CLC 119**
See CA 171
de Saint-Luc, Jean
See Glassco, John
de Saint Roman, Arnaud
See Aragon, Louis
Descartes, Rene 1596-1650 .... **LC 20, 35**
De Sica, Vittorio 1901(?)-1974 .... **CLC 20**
See CA 117
Desnos, Robert 1900-1945 .... **TCLC 22**
See CA 121; 151
Destouches, Louis-Ferdinand 1894-1961 ..... **CLC 9, 15**
See Celine, Louis-Ferdinand
See CA 85-88; CANR 28; MTCW 1
de Tolignac, Gaston
See Griffith, D(avid Lewelyn) W(ark)
Deutsch, Babette 1895-1982 .... **CLC 18**
See CA 1-4R; 108; CANR 4, 79; DLB 45; SATA 1; SATA-Obit 33
Devenant, William 1606-1649 .... **LC 13**
Devkota, Laxmiprasad 1909-1959 ..... **TCLC 23**
See CA 123
De Voto, Bernard (Augustine) 1897-1955 .... **TCLC 29**
See CA 113; 160; DLB 9
De Vries, Peter 1910-1993 .... **CLC 1, 2, 3, 7, 10, 28, 46; DAM NOV**
See CA 17-20R; 142; CANR 41; DLB 6; DLBY 82; MTCW 1, 2
Dewey, John 1859-1952 .... **TCLC 95**
See CA 114; 170
Dexter, John
See Bradley, Marion Zimmer
Dexter, Martin
See Faust, Frederick (Schiller)
Dexter, Pete 1943- .. **CLC 34, 55;DAM POP**
See BEST 89:2; CA 127; 131; INT 131; MTCW 1
Diamano, Silmang
See Senghor, Leopold Sedar
Diamond, Neil 1941- .... **CLC 30**
See CA 108
Diaz del Castillo, Bernal 1496-1584 . **LC 31; HLCS 1**
di Bassetto, Corno
See Shaw, George Bernard
Dick, Philip K(indred) 1928-1982 .. **CLC 10, 30, 72; DAM NOV, POP**
See AAYA 24; CA 49-52; 106; CANR 2, 16; DA3; DLB 8; MTCW 1, 2
Dickens, Charles (John Huffam) 1812-1870 . **NCLC 3, 8, 18, 26, 37, 50; DA; DAB; DAC; DAM MST, NOV; SSC 17; WLC**
See AAYA 23; CDBLB 1832-1890; DA3; DLB 21, 55, 70, 159, 166; JRDA; MAICYA; SATA 15
Dickey, James (Lafayette) 1923-1997 .. **CLC 1, 2, 4, 7, 10, 15, 47, 109; DAM NOV, POET, POP**
See AITN 1, 2; CA 9-12R; 156; CABS 2; CANR 10, 48, 61; CDALB 1968-1988; DA3; DLB 5, 193; DLBD 7; DLBY 82, 93, 96, 97, 98; INT CANR-10; MTCW 1, 2
Dickey, William 1928-1994 .... **CLC 3, 28**
See CA 9-12R; 145; CANR 24, 79; DLB 5
Dickinson, Charles 1951- .... **CLC 49**
See CA 128
Dickinson, Emily (Elizabeth) 1830-1886 ...... **NCLC 21, 77; DA; DAB; DAC; DAM MST, POET; PC 1; WLC**
See AAYA 22; CDALB 1865-1917; DA3; DLB 1; SATA 29
Dickinson, Peter (Malcolm) 1927- . **CLC 12, 35**
See AAYA 9; CA 41-44R; CANR 31, 58; CLR 29; DLB 87, 161; JRDA; MAICYA; SATA 5, 62, 95
Dickson, Carr
See Carr, John Dickson
Dickson, Carter
See Carr, John Dickson
Diderot, Denis 1713-1784 .... **LC 26**
Didion, Joan 1934- .... **CLC 1, 3, 8, 14, 32; DAM NOV**
See AITN 1; CA 5-8R; CANR 14, 52, 76; CDALB 1968-1988; DA3; DLB 2, 173, 185; DLBY 81, 86; MTCW 1, 2
Dietrich, Robert
See Hunt, E(verette) Howard, (Jr.)
Difusa, Pati
See Almodovar, Pedro
Dillard, Annie 1945- . **CLC 9, 60, 115; DAM NOV**
See AAYA 6; CA 49-52; CANR 3, 43, 62; DA3; DLBY 80; MTCW 1, 2; SATA 10
Dillard, R(ichard) H(enry) W(ilde) 1937- ... **CLC 5**
See CA 21-24R; CAAS 7; CANR 10; DLB 5
Dillon, Eilis 1920-1994 .... **CLC 17**
See CA 9-12R; 147; CAAS 3; CANR 4, 38, 78; CLR 26; MAICYA; SATA 2, 74; SATA-Essay 105; SATA-Obit 83
Dimont, Penelope
See Mortimer, Penelope (Ruth)
Dinesen, Isak .... **CLC 10, 29, 95; SSC 7**
See Blixen, Karen (Christentze Dinesen)
See MTCW 1
Ding Ling .... **CLC 68**
See Chiang, Pin-chin
Diphusa, Patty
See Almodovar, Pedro
Disch, Thomas M(ichael) 1940- .. **CLC 7, 36**
See AAYA 17; CA 21-24R; CAAS 4; CANR 17, 36, 54; CLR 18; DA3; DLB 8; MAICYA; MTCW 1, 2; SAAS 15; SATA 92
Disch, Tom
See Disch, Thomas M(ichael)
d'Isly, Georges
See Simenon, Georges (Jacques Christian)
Disraeli, Benjamin 1804-1881 . **NCLC 2, 39, 79**
See DLB 21, 55
Ditcum, Steve
See Crumb, R(obert)
Dixon, Paige
See Corcoran, Barbara
Dixon, Stephen 1936- .... **CLC 52;SSC 16**
See CA 89-92; CANR 17, 40, 54; DLB 130
Doak, Annie
See Dillard, Annie
Dobell, Sydney Thompson 1824-1874 .... **NCLC 43**
See DLB 32
Doblin, Alfred .... **TCLC 13**
See Doeblin, Alfred
Dobrolyubov, Nikolai Alexandrovich 1836-1861 .... **NCLC 5**
Dobson, Austin 1840-1921 .... **TCLC 79**
See DLB 35; 144
Dobyns, Stephen 1941- .... **CLC 37**
See CA 45-48; CANR 2, 18
Doctorow, E(dgar) L(aurence) 1931- ... **CLC 6, 11, 15, 18, 37, 44, 65, 113; DAM NOV, POP**
See AAYA 22; AITN 2; BEST 89:3; CA 45-48; CANR 2, 33, 51, 76; CDALB 1968-1988; DA3; DLB 2, 28, 173; DLBY 80; MTCW 1, 2
Dodgson, Charles Lutwidge 1832-1898
See Carroll, Lewis
See CLR 2; DA; DAB; DAC; DAM MST, NOV, POET; DA3; MAICYA; SATA 100; YABC 2
Dodson, Owen (Vincent) 1914-1983 ..... **CLC 79; BLC 1; DAM MULT**
See BW 1; CA 65-68; 110; CANR 24; DLB 76
Doeblin, Alfred 1878-1957 .... **TCLC 13**
See Doblin, Alfred
See CA 110; 141; DLB 66
Doerr, Harriet 1910- .... **CLC 34**
See CA 117; 122; CANR 47; INT 122
Domecq, H(onorio Bustos)
See Bioy Casares, Adolfo
Domecq, H(onorio) Bustos
See Bioy Casares, Adolfo; Borges, Jorge Luis
Domini, Rey
See Lorde, Audre (Geraldine)
Dominique
See Proust, (Valentin-Louis-George-Eugene-) Marcel
Don, A
See Stephen, SirLeslie
Donaldson, Stephen R. 1947- .... **CLC 46; DAM POP**
See CA 89-92; CANR 13, 55; INT CANR-13
Donleavy, J(ames) P(atrick) 1926- ... **CLC 1, 4, 6, 10, 45**
See AITN 2; CA 9-12R; CANR 24, 49, 62, 80; DLB 6, 173; INT CANR-24; MTCW 1, 2
Donne, John 1572-1631 .... **LC 10, 24; DA; DAB; DAC; DAM MST, POET; PC 1; WLC**
See CDBLB Before 1660; DLB 121, 151
Donnell, David 1939(?)- .... **CLC 34**
Donoghue, P. S.
See Hunt, E(verette) Howard, (Jr.)
Donoso (Yanez), Jose 1924-1996 .. **CLC 4, 8, 11, 32, 99; DAM MULT; HLC 1; SSC 34**
See CA 81-84; 155; CANR 32, 73; DLB 113; HW 1, 2; MTCW 1, 2
Donovan, John 1928-1992 .... **CLC 35**
See AAYA 20; CA 97-100; 137; CLR 3; MAICYA; SATA 72; SATA-Brief 29
Don Roberto
See Cunninghame Graham, R(obert) B(ontine)
Doolittle, Hilda 1886-1961 ...... **CLC 3, 8, 14, 31, 34, 73; DA; DAC; DAM MST, POET; PC 5; WLC**
See H. D.
See CA 97-100; CANR 35; DLB 4, 45; MTCW 1, 2
Dorfman, Ariel 1942- ..... **CLC 48, 77; DAM MULT; HLC 1**

See CA 124; 130; CANR 67, 70; HW 1, 2; INT 130

Dorn, Edward (Merton) 1929- .. **CLC 10, 18**
See CA 93-96; CANR 42, 79; DLB 5; INT 93-96

Dorris, Michael (Anthony) 1945-1997 . **CLC 109; DAM MULT, NOV**
See AAYA 20; BEST 90:1; CA 102; 157; CANR 19, 46, 75; CLR 58; DA3; DLB 175; MTCW 2; NNAL; SATA 75; SATA-Obit 94

Dorris, Michael A.
See Dorris, Michael (Anthony)

Dorsan, Luc
See Simenon, Georges (Jacques Christian)

Dorsange, Jean
See Simenon, Georges (Jacques Christian)

Dos Passos, John (Roderigo) 1896-1970 ...... **CLC 1, 4, 8, 11, 15, 25, 34, 82; DA; DAB; DAC; DAM MST, NOV; WLC**
See CA 1-4R; 29-32R; CANR 3; CDALB 1929-1941; DA3; DLB 4, 9; DLBD 1, 15; DLBY 96; MTCW 1, 2

Dossage, Jean
See Simenon, Georges (Jacques Christian)

Dostoevsky, Fedor Mikhailovich 1821-1881 .... **NCLC 2, 7, 21, 33, 43; DA; DAB; DAC; DAM MST, NOV; SSC 2, 33; WLC**
See DA3

Doughty, Charles M(ontagu) 1843-1926 ...... **TCLC 27**
See CA 115; 178; DLB 19, 57, 174

Douglas, Ellen .... **CLC 73**
See Haxton, Josephine Ayres; Williamson, Ellen Douglas

Douglas, Gavin 1475(?)-1522 .... **LC 20**
See DLB 132

Douglas, George
See Brown, George Douglas

Douglas, Keith (Castellain) 1920-1944 .... **TCLC 40**
See CA 160; DLB 27

Douglas, Leonard
See Bradbury, Ray (Douglas)

Douglas, Michael
See Crichton, (John) Michael

Douglas, (George) Norman 1868-1952 .... **TCLC 68**
See CA 119; 157; DLB 34, 195

Douglas, William
See Brown, George Douglas

Douglass, Frederick 1817(?)-1895 . **NCLC 7, 55; BLC 1; DA; DAC; DAM MST, MULT; WLC**
See CDALB 1640-1865; DA3; DLB 1, 43, 50, 79; SATA 29

Dourado, (Waldomiro Freitas) Autran 1926- .... **CLC 23, 60**
See CA 25-28R, 179; CANR 34, 81; DLB 145; HW 2

Dourado, Waldomiro Autran 1926-
See Dourado, (Waldomiro Freitas) Autran
See CA 179

Dove, Rita (Frances) 1952- ...... **CLC 50, 81; BLCS; DAM MULT, POET; PC 6**
See BW 2; CA 109; CAAS 19; CANR 27, 42, 68, 76; CDALBS; DA3; DLB 120; MTCW 1

Doveglion
See Villa, Jose Garcia

Dowell, Coleman 1925-1985 .... **CLC 60**
See CA 25-28R; 117; CANR 10; DLB 130

Dowson, Ernest (Christopher) 1867-1900 ... **TCLC 4**
See CA 105; 150; DLB 19, 135

Doyle, A. Conan
See Doyle, Arthur Conan

Doyle, Arthur Conan 1859-1930 ... **TCLC 7; DA; DAB; DAC; DAM MST, NOV; SSC 12; WLC**
See AAYA 14; CA 104; 122; CDBLB 1890-1914; DA3; DLB 18, 70, 156, 178; MTCW 1, 2; SATA 24

Doyle, Conan
See Doyle, Arthur Conan

Doyle, John
See Graves, Robert (von Ranke)

Doyle, Roddy 1958(?)- .... **CLC 81**
See AAYA 14; CA 143; CANR 73; DA3; DLB 194

Doyle, Sir A. Conan
See Doyle, Arthur Conan

Doyle, Sir Arthur Conan
See Doyle, Arthur Conan

Dr. A
See Asimov, Isaac; Silverstein, Alvin

Drabble, Margaret 1939- ..... **CLC 2, 3, 5, 8, 10, 22, 53; DAB; DAC; DAM MST, NOV, POP**
See CA 13-16R; CANR 18, 35, 63; CDBLB 1960 to Present; DA3; DLB 14, 155; MTCW 1, 2; SATA 48

Drapier, M. B.
See Swift, Jonathan

Drayham, James
See Mencken, H(enry) L(ouis)

Drayton, Michael 1563-1631 ..... **LC 8;DAM POET**
See DLB 121

Dreadstone, Carl
See Campbell, (John) Ramsey

Dreiser, Theodore (Herman Albert) 1871-1945 ... **TCLC 10, 18, 35, 83; DA; DAC; DAM MST, NOV; SSC 30; WLC**
See CA 106; 132; CDALB 1865-1917; DA3; DLB 9, 12, 102, 137; DLBD 1; MTCW 1, 2

Drexler, Rosalyn 1926- .... **CLC 2, 6**
See CA 81-84; CANR 68

Dreyer, Carl Theodor 1889-1968 .... **CLC 16**
See CA 116

Drieu la Rochelle, Pierre(-Eugene) 1893-1945 .... **TCLC 21**
See CA 117; DLB 72

Drinkwater, John 1882-1937 .... **TCLC 57**
See CA 109; 149; DLB 10, 19, 149

Drop Shot
See Cable, George Washington

Droste-Hulshoff, Annette Freiinvon 1797-1848 .... **NCLC 3**
See DLB 133

Drummond, Walter
See Silverberg, Robert

Drummond, William Henry 1854-1907 .... **TCLC 25**
See CA 160; DLB 92

Drummond de Andrade,Carlos 1902-1987 .. **CLC 18**
See Andrade, Carlos Drummond de
See CA 132; 123

Drury, Allen (Stuart) 1918-1998 ..... **CLC 37**
See CA 57-60; 170; CANR 18, 52; INT CANR-18

Dryden, John 1631-1700 .... **LC 3, 21; DA; DAB; DAC; DAM DRAM, MST, POET; DC 3; PC 25;WLC**
See CDBLB 1660-1789; DLB 80, 101, 131

Duberman, Martin(Bauml) 1930- ..... **CLC 8**
See CA 1-4R; CANR 2, 63

Dubie, Norman (Evans) 1945- .... **CLC 36**
See CA 69-72; CANR 12; DLB 120

Du Bois, W(illiam) E(dward) B(urghardt) 1868-1963 .. **CLC 1, 2, 13, 64, 96; BLC 1; DA; DAC; DAM MST, MULT, NOV; WLC**
See BW 1, 3; CA 85-88; CANR 34, 82; CDALB 1865-1917; DA3; DLB 47, 50, 91; MTCW 1, 2; SATA 42

Dubus, Andre 1936-1999 .... **CLC 13, 36, 97; SSC 15**
See CA 21-24R; 177; CANR 17; DLB 130; INT CANR-17

Duca Minimo
See D'Annunzio, Gabriele

Ducharme, Rejean 1941- .... **CLC 74**
See CA 165; DLB 60

Duclos, Charles Pinot 1704-1772 .... **LC 1**

Dudek, Louis 1918- .... **CLC 11, 19**
See CA 45-48; CAAS 14; CANR 1; DLB 88

Duerrenmatt, Friedrich 1921-1990 .. **CLC 1, 4, 8, 11, 15, 43, 102; DAM DRAM**
See CA 17-20R; CANR 33; DLB 69, 124; MTCW 1, 2

Duffy, Bruce 1953(?)- .... **CLC 50**
See CA 172

Duffy, Maureen 1933- .... **CLC 37**
See CA 25-28R; CANR 33, 68; DLB 14; MTCW 1

Dugan, Alan 1923- .... **CLC 2, 6**
See CA 81-84; DLB 5

du Gard, Roger Martin
See Martin du Gard, Roger

Duhamel, Georges 1884-1966 .... **CLC 8**
See CA 81-84; 25-28R; CANR 35; DLB 65; MTCW 1

Dujardin, Edouard (EmileLouis) 1861-1949 .... **TCLC 13**
See CA 109; DLB 123

Dulles, John Foster 1888-1959 ..... **TCLC 72**
See CA 115; 149

Dumas, Alexandre (pere)
See Dumas, Alexandre (Davy de la Pailleterie)

Dumas, Alexandre (Davy de la Pailleterie) 1802-1870 . **NCLC 11; DA; DAB; DAC; DAM MST, NOV; WLC**
See DA3; DLB 119, 192; SATA 18

Dumas, Alexandre (fils) 1824-1895 ... **NCLC 71; DC 1**
See AAYA 22; DLB 192

Dumas, Claudine
See Malzberg, Barry N(athaniel)

Dumas, Henry L. 1934-1968 .... **CLC 6, 62**
See BW 1; CA 85-88; DLB 41

du Maurier, Daphne 1907-1989 . **CLC 6, 11, 59; DAB; DAC; DAM MST, POP; SSC 18**
See CA 5-8R; 128; CANR 6, 55; DA3; DLB 191; MTCW 1, 2; SATA 27; SATA-Obit 60

Dunbar, Paul Laurence 1872-1906 .... **TCLC 2, 12; BLC 1; DA; DAC; DAM MST, MULT, POET; PC 5; SSC 8; WLC**
See BW 1, 3; CA 104; 124; CANR 79; CDALB 1865-1917; DA3; DLB 50, 54, 78; SATA 34

Dunbar, William 1460(?)-1530(?) .... **LC 20**
See DLB 132, 146

Duncan, Dora Angela
See Duncan, Isadora

Duncan, Isadora 1877(?)-1927 ...... **TCLC 68**
See CA 118; 149

Duncan, Lois 1934- .... **CLC 26**
See AAYA 4; CA 1-4R; CANR 2, 23, 36; CLR 29; JRDA; MAICYA; SAAS 2; SATA 1, 36, 75

Duncan, Robert (Edward) 1919-1988 .. **CLC 1, 2, 4, 7, 15, 41, 55; DAM POET; PC 2**
See CA 9-12R; 124; CANR 28, 62; DLB 5, 16, 193; MTCW 1, 2

Duncan, Sara Jeannette 1861-1922 ... **TCLC 60**
See CA 157; DLB 92

Dunlap, William 1766-1839 .... **NCLC 2**
See DLB 30, 37, 59
Dunn, Douglas (Eaglesham) 1942- .. **CLC 6, 40**
See CA 45-48; CANR 2, 33; DLB 40; MTCW 1
Dunn, Katherine (Karen) 1945- ...... **CLC 71**
See CA 33-36R; CANR 72; MTCW 1
Dunn, Stephen 1939- .... **CLC 36**
See CA 33-36R; CANR 12, 48, 53; DLB 105
Dunne, Finley Peter 1867-1936 .... **TCLC 28**
See CA 108; 178; DLB 11, 23
Dunne, John Gregory 1932- .... **CLC 28**
See CA 25-28R; CANR 14, 50; DLBY 80
Dunsany, Edward John Moreton Drax Plunkett 1878-1957
See Dunsany, Lord
See CA 104; 148; DLB 10; MTCW 1
Dunsany, Lord .... **TCLC 2, 59**
See Dunsany, Edward John Moreton Drax Plunkett
See DLB 77, 153, 156
du Perry, Jean
See Simenon, Georges (Jacques Christian)
Durang, Christopher (Ferdinand) 1949- ..... **CLC 27, 38**
See CA 105; CANR 50, 76; MTCW 1
Duras, Marguerite 1914-1996 . **CLC 3, 6, 11, 20, 34, 40, 68, 100**
See CA 25-28R; 151; CANR 50; DLB 83; MTCW 1, 2
Durban, (Rosa) Pam 1947- .... **CLC 39**
See CA 123
Durcan, Paul 1944- .... **CLC 43, 70;DAM POET**
See CA 134
Durkheim, Emile 1858-1917 .... **TCLC 55**
Durrell, Lawrence (George) 1912-1990 .... **CLC 1, 4, 6, 8, 13, 27, 41; DAM NOV**
See CA 9-12R; 132; CANR 40, 77;CDBLB 1945-1960; DLB 15, 27, 204; DLBY 90; MTCW 1, 2
Durrenmatt, Friedrich
See Duerrenmatt, Friedrich
Dutt, Toru 1856-1877 .... **NCLC 29**
Dwight, Timothy 1752-1817 .... **NCLC 13**
See DLB 37
Dworkin, Andrea 1946- .... **CLC 43**
See CA 77-80; CAAS 21; CANR 16, 39, 76; INT CANR-16; MTCW 1, 2
Dwyer, Deanna
See Koontz, Dean R(ay)
Dwyer, K. R.
See Koontz, Dean R(ay)
Dwyer, Thomas A. 1923- .... **CLC 114**
See CA 115
Dye, Richard
See De Voto, Bernard (Augustine)
Dylan, Bob 1941- .... **CLC 3, 4, 6, 12, 77**
See CA 41-44R; DLB 16
E. V. L.
See Lucas, E(dward) V(errall)
Eagleton, Terence (Francis) 1943-
See Eagleton, Terry
See CA 57-60; CANR 7, 23, 68; MTCW 1, 2
Eagleton, Terry .... **CLC 63**
See Eagleton, Terence (Francis)
See MTCW 1
Early, Jack
See Scoppettone, Sandra
East, Michael
See West, Morris L(anglo)
Eastaway, Edward
See Thomas, (Philip) Edward
Eastlake, William (Derry) 1917-1997 .. **CLC 8**
See CA 5-8R; 158; CAAS 1; CANR 5, 63; DLB 6, 206; INT CANR-5
Eastman, Charles A(lexander) 1858-1939 ... **TCLC 55; DAM MULT**
See CA 179; DLB 175; NNAL; YABC 1
Eberhart, Richard (Ghormley) 1904- .. **CLC 3, 11, 19, 56; DAM POET**
See CA 1-4R; CANR 2; CDALB 1941-1968; DLB 48; MTCW 1
Eberstadt, Fernanda 1960- .... **CLC 39**
See CA 136; CANR 69
Echegaray (y Eizaguirre), Jose (Maria Waldo) 1832-1916 ... **TCLC 4; HLCS 1**
See CA 104; CANR 32; HW 1; MTCW 1
Echeverria, (Jose) Esteban (Antonino) 1805-1851 .... **NCLC 18**
Echo
See Proust, (Valentin-Louis-George-Eugene-) Marcel
Eckert, Allan W. 1931- .... **CLC 17**
See AAYA 18; CA 13-16R; CANR 14, 45; INT CANR-14; SAAS 21; SATA 29, 91; SATA-Brief 27
Eckhart, Meister 1260(?)-1328(?) .. **CMLC 9**
See DLB 115
Eckmar, F. R.
See de Hartog, Jan
Eco, Umberto 1932- .... **CLC 28, 60; DAM NOV, POP**
See BEST 90:1; CA 77-80; CANR 12, 33, 55; DA3; DLB 196; MTCW 1, 2
Eddison, E(ric) R(ucker) 1882-1945 . **TCLC 15**
See CA 109; 156
Eddy, Mary (Ann Morse) Baker 1821-1910 .... **TCLC 71**
See CA 113; 174
Edel, (Joseph) Leon 1907-1997 . **CLC 29, 34**
See CA 1-4R; 161; CANR 1, 22; DLB 103; INT CANR-22
Eden, Emily 1797-1869 .... **NCLC 10**
Edgar, David 1948- .. **CLC 42;DAM DRAM**
See CA 57-60; CANR 12, 61; DLB 13; MTCW 1
Edgerton, Clyde (Carlyle) 1944- ..... **CLC 39**
See AAYA 17; CA 118; 134; CANR 64; INT 134
Edgeworth, Maria 1768-1849 .... **NCLC 1,51**
See DLB 116, 159, 163; SATA 21
Edison, Thomas 1847-1931 .... **TCLC 96**
Edmonds, Paul
See Kuttner, Henry
Edmonds, Walter D(umaux) 1903-1998 .... **CLC 35**
See CA 5-8R; CANR 2; DLB 9; MAICYA; SAAS 4; SATA 1, 27; SATA-Obit 99
Edmondson, Wallace
See Ellison, Harlan (Jay)
Edson, Russell .... **CLC 13**
See CA 33-36R
Edwards, Bronwen Elizabeth
See Rose, Wendy
Edwards, G(erald) B(asil) 1899-1976 .. **CLC 25**
See CA 110
Edwards, Gus 1939- .... **CLC 43**
See CA 108; INT 108
Edwards, Jonathan 1703-1758 . **LC 54; DA; DAC; DAM MST**
See DLB 24
Efron, Marina Ivanovna Tsvetaeva
See Tsvetaeva (Efron), Marina (Ivanovna)
Ehle, John (Marsden,Jr.) 1925- ...... **CLC 27**
See CA 9-12R
Ehrenbourg, Ilya (Grigoryevich)
See Ehrenburg, Ilya (Grigoryevich)
Ehrenburg, Ilya (Grigoryevich) 1891-1967 . **CLC 18, 34, 62**
See CA 102; 25-28R
Ehrenburg, Ilyo (Grigoryevich)
See Ehrenburg, Ilya (Grigoryevich)
Ehrenreich, Barbara 1941- .... **CLC 110**
See BEST 90:4; CA 73-76; CANR 16, 37, 62; MTCW 1, 2
Eich, Guenter 1907-1972 .... **CLC 15**
See CA 111; 93-96; DLB 69, 124
Eichendorff, Joseph Freiherrvon 1788-1857 .... **NCLC 8**
See DLB 90
Eigner, Larry .... **CLC 9**
See Eigner, Laurence (Joel)
See CAAS 23; DLB 5
Eigner, Laurence (Joel) 1927-1996
See Eigner, Larry
See CA 9-12R; 151; CANR 6, 84; DLB 193
Einstein, Albert 1879-1955 .... **TCLC 65**
See CA 121; 133; MTCW 1, 2
Eiseley, Loren Corey 1907-1977 .... **CLC 7**
See AAYA 5; CA 1-4R; 73-76; CANR 6; DLBD 17
Eisenstadt, Jill 1963- .... **CLC 50**
See CA 140
Eisenstein, Sergei (Mikhailovich) 1898-1948 .... **TCLC 57**
See CA 114; 149
Eisner, Simon
See Kornbluth, C(yril) M.
Ekeloef, (Bengt) Gunnar 1907-1968 .... **CLC 27; DAM POET; PC 23**
See CA 123; 25-28R
Ekelof, (Bengt) Gunnar
See Ekeloef, (Bengt) Gunnar
Ekelund, Vilhelm 1880-1949 .... **TCLC 75**
Ekwensi, C. O. D.
See Ekwensi, Cyprian (Odiatu Duaka)
Ekwensi, Cyprian (Odiatu Duaka) 1921- .... **CLC 4; BLC 1; DAM MULT**
See BW 2, 3; CA 29-32R; CANR 18, 42, 74; DLB 117; MTCW 1, 2; SATA 66
Elaine .... **TCLC 18**
See Leverson, Ada
El Crummo
See Crumb, R(obert)
Elder, Lonne III 1931-1996 .... **DC 8**
See BLC 1; BW 1, 3; CA 81-84; 152; CANR 25; DAM MULT; DLB 7, 38, 44
Elia
See Lamb, Charles
Eliade, Mircea 1907-1986 .... **CLC 19**
See CA 65-68; 119; CANR 30, 62; MTCW 1
Eliot, A. D.
See Jewett, (Theodora) Sarah Orne
Eliot, Alice
See Jewett, (Theodora) Sarah Orne
Eliot, Dan
See Silverberg, Robert
Eliot, George 1819-1880 .... **NCLC 4, 13, 23, 41, 49; DA; DAB; DAC; DAM MST, NOV; PC 20; WLC**
See CDBLB 1832-1890; DA3; DLB 21, 35, 55
Eliot, John 1604-1690 .... **LC 5**
See DLB 24
Eliot, T(homas) S(tearns) 1888-1965 ... **CLC 1, 2, 3, 6, 9, 10, 13, 15, 24, 34, 41, 55, 57, 113; DA; DAB; DAC; DAM DRAM, MST, POET; PC 5; WLC**
See AAYA 28; CA 5-8R; 25-28R; CANR 41;CDALB 1929-1941; DA3; DLB 7, 10, 45, 63; DLBY 88; MTCW 1, 2
Elizabeth 1866-1941 .... **TCLC 41**
Elkin, Stanley L(awrence) 1930-1995 .. **CLC 4, 6, 9, 14, 27, 51, 91; DAM NOV, POP; SSC 12**

See CA 9-12R; 148; CANR 8, 46; DLB 2, 28; DLBY 80; INT CANR-8; MTCW 1, 2
Elledge, Scott .... **CLC 34**
Elliot, Don
See Silverberg, Robert
Elliott, Don
See Silverberg, Robert
Elliott, George P(aul) 1918-1980 .... **CLC 2**
See CA 1-4R; 97-100; CANR 2
Elliott, Janice 1931- .... **CLC 47**
See CA 13-16R; CANR 8, 29, 84; DLB 14
Elliott, Sumner Locke 1917-1991 ... **CLC 38**
See CA 5-8R; 134; CANR 2, 21
Elliott, William
See Bradbury, Ray (Douglas)
Ellis, A. E. .... **CLC 7**
Ellis, Alice Thomas .... **CLC 40**
See Haycraft, Anna
See DLB 194; MTCW 1
Ellis, Bret Easton 1964- ... **CLC 39, 71, 117; DAM POP**
See AAYA 2; CA 118; 123; CANR 51, 74; DA3; INT 123; MTCW 1
Ellis, (Henry) Havelock 1859-1939 .... **TCLC 14**
See CA 109; 169; DLB 190
Ellis, Landon
See Ellison, Harlan (Jay)
Ellis, Trey 1962- .... **CLC 55**
See CA 146
Ellison, Harlan (Jay) 1934- . **CLC 1, 13, 42; DAM POP; SSC 14**
See AAYA 29; CA 5-8R; CANR 5, 46; DLB 8; INT CANR-5; MTCW 1, 2
Ellison, Ralph (Waldo) 1914-1994 ... **CLC 1, 3, 11, 54, 86, 114; BLC 1; DA; DAB; DAC; DAM MST, MULT, NOV; SSC 26;WLC**
See AAYA 19; BW 1, 3; CA 9-12R; 145; CANR 24, 53; CDALB 1941-1968; DA3; DLB 2, 76; DLBY 94; MTCW 1, 2
Ellmann, Lucy (Elizabeth) 1956- .... **CLC 61**
See CA 128
Ellmann, Richard (David) 1918-1987 .. **CLC 50**
See BEST 89:2; CA 1-4R; 122; CANR 2, 28, 61; DLB 103; DLBY 87; MTCW 1, 2
Elman, Richard (Martin) 1934-1997 ... **CLC 19**
See CA 17-20R; 163; CAAS 3; CANR 47
Elron
See Hubbard, L(afayette) Ron(ald)
Eluard, Paul .... **TCLC 7, 41**
See Grindel, Eugene
Elyot, Sir Thomas 1490(?)-1546 .... **LC 11**
Elytis, Odysseus 1911-1996 ...... **CLC 15, 49, 100; DAM POET; PC 21**
See CA 102; 151; MTCW 1, 2
Emecheta, (Florence Onye) Buchi 1944- ..... **CLC 14, 48; BLC 2; DAM MULT**
See BW 2, 3; CA 81-84; CANR 27, 81; DA3; DLB 117; MTCW 1, 2; SATA 66
Emerson, Mary Moody 1774-1863 .... **NCLC 66**
Emerson, Ralph Waldo 1803-1882 .... **NCLC 1, 38; DA; DAB; DAC; DAM MST, POET; PC 18; WLC**
See CDALB 1640-1865; DA3; DLB 1, 59, 73
Eminescu, Mihail 1850-1889 .... **NCLC 33**
Empson, William 1906-1984 .. **CLC 3, 8, 19, 33, 34**
See CA 17-20R; 112; CANR 31, 61; DLB 20; MTCW 1, 2
Enchi, Fumiko (Ueda) 1905-1986 ... **CLC 31**
See CA 129; 121; DLB 182
Ende, Michael (Andreas Helmuth) 1929-1995 .... **CLC 31**
See CA 118; 124; 149; CANR 36; CLR 14; DLB 75; MAICYA; SATA 61; SATA-Brief 42; SATA-Obit 86
Endo, Shusaku 1923-1996 .... **CLC 7, 14, 19, 54, 99; DAM NOV**
See CA 29-32R; 153; CANR 21, 54; DA3; DLB 182; MTCW 1, 2
Engel, Marian 1933-1985 .... **CLC 36**
See CA 25-28R; CANR 12; DLB 53; INT CANR-12
Engelhardt, Frederick
See Hubbard, L(afayette) Ron(ald)
Enright, D(ennis) J(oseph) 1920- . **CLC 4, 8, 31**
See CA 1-4R; CANR 1, 42, 83; DLB 27; SATA 25
Enzensberger, Hans Magnus 1929- ...... **CLC 43; PC 28**
See CA 116; 119
Ephron, Nora 1941- .... **CLC 17, 31**
See AITN 2; CA 65-68; CANR 12, 39, 83
Epicurus 341B.C.-270B.C. .... **CMLC 21**
See DLB 176
Epsilon
See Betjeman, John
Epstein, Daniel Mark 1948- .... **CLC 7**
See CA 49-52; CANR 2, 53
Epstein, Jacob 1956- .... **CLC 19**
See CA 114
Epstein, Jean 1897-1953 .... **TCLC 92**
Epstein, Joseph 1937- .... **CLC 39**
See CA 112; 119; CANR 50, 65
Epstein, Leslie 1938- .... **CLC 27**
See CA 73-76; CAAS 12; CANR 23, 69
Equiano, Olaudah 1745(?)-1797 .... **LC 16; BLC 2; DAM MULT**
See DLB 37, 50
ER .... **TCLC 33**
See CA 160; DLB 85
Erasmus, Desiderius 1469(?)-1536 ..... **LC 16**
Erdman, Paul E(mil) 1932- .... **CLC 25**
See AITN 1; CA 61-64; CANR 13, 43, 84
Erdrich, Louise 1954- .... **CLC 39, 54, 120; DAM MULT, NOV, POP**
See AAYA 10; BEST 89:1; CA 114; CANR 41, 62; CDALBS; DA3; DLB 152, 175, 206; MTCW 1; NNAL; SATA 94
Erenburg, Ilya (Grigoryevich)
See Ehrenburg, Ilya (Grigoryevich)
Erickson, Stephen Michael 1950-
See Erickson, Steve
See CA 129
Erickson, Steve 1950- .... **CLC 64**
See Erickson, Stephen Michael
See CANR 60, 68
Ericson, Walter
See Fast, Howard (Melvin)
Eriksson, Buntel
See Bergman, (Ernst) Ingmar
Ernaux, Annie 1940- .... **CLC 88**
See CA 147
Erskine, John 1879-1951 .... **TCLC 84**
See CA 112; 159; DLB 9, 102
Eschenbach, Wolfram von
See Wolfram von Eschenbach
Eseki, Bruno
See Mphahlele, Ezekiel
Esenin, Sergei (Alexandrovich) 1895-1925 .. **TCLC 4**
See CA 104
Eshleman, Clayton 1935- .... **CLC 7**
See CA 33-36R; CAAS 6; DLB 5
Espriella, Don Manuel Alvarez
See Southey, Robert
Espriu, Salvador 1913-1985 .... **CLC 9**
See CA 154; 115; DLB 134
Espronceda, Jose de 1808-1842 .... **NCLC 39**
Esquivel, Laura 1951(?)-
See AAYA 29; CA 143; CANR 68; DA3; HLCS 1; MTCW 1
Esse, James
See Stephens, James
Esterbrook, Tom
See Hubbard, L(afayette) Ron(ald)
Estleman, Loren D. 1952- .... **CLC 48; DAM NOV, POP**
See AAYA 27; CA 85-88; CANR 27, 74; DA3; INT CANR-27; MTCW 1, 2
Euclid 306B.C.-283B.C. .... **CMLC 25**
Eugenides, Jeffrey 1960(?)- .... **CLC 81**
See CA 144
Euripides c. 485B.C.-406B.C. ..... **CMLC 23; DA; DAB; DAC; DAM DRAM, MST; DC 4; WLCS**
See DA3; DLB 176
Evan, Evin
See Faust, Frederick (Schiller)
Evans, Caradoc 1878-1945 .... **TCLC 85**
Evans, Evan
See Faust, Frederick (Schiller)
Evans, Marian
See Eliot, George
Evans, Mary Ann
See Eliot, George
Evarts, Esther
See Benson, Sally
Everett, Percival L. 1956- .... **CLC 57**
See BW 2; CA 129
Everson, R(onald) G(ilmour) 1903- ..... **CLC 27**
See CA 17-20R; DLB 88
Everson, William (Oliver) 1912-1994 .. **CLC 1, 5, 14**
See CA 9-12R; 145; CANR 20; DLB 212; MTCW 1
Evtushenko, Evgenii Aleksandrovich
See Yevtushenko, Yevgeny (Alexandrovich)
Ewart, Gavin (Buchanan) 1916-1995 .. **CLC 13, 46**
See CA 89-92; 150; CANR 17, 46; DLB 40; MTCW 1
Ewers, Hanns Heinz 1871-1943 .... **TCLC 12**
See CA 109; 149
Ewing, Frederick R.
See Sturgeon, Theodore (Hamilton)
Exley, Frederick (Earl) 1929-1992 ... **CLC 6, 11**
See AITN 2; CA 81-84; 138; DLB 143; DLBY 81
Eynhardt, Guillermo
See Quiroga, Horacio (Sylvestre)
Ezekiel, Nissim 1924- .... **CLC 61**
See CA 61-64
Ezekiel, Tish O'Dowd 1943- .... **CLC 34**
See CA 129
Fadeyev, A.
See Bulgya, Alexander Alexandrovich
Fadeyev, Alexander .... **TCLC 53**
See Bulgya, Alexander Alexandrovich
Fagen, Donald 1948- .... **CLC 26**
Fainzilberg, Ilya Arnoldovich 1897-1937
See Ilf, Ilya
See CA 120; 165
Fair, Ronald L. 1932- .... **CLC 18**
See BW 1; CA 69-72; CANR 25; DLB 33
Fairbairn, Roger
See Carr, John Dickson
Fairbairns, Zoe (Ann) 1948- .... **CLC 32**
See CA 103; CANR 21, 85
Falco, Gian
See Papini, Giovanni
Falconer, James
See Kirkup, James
Falconer, Kenneth
See Kornbluth, C(yril) M.

Falkland, Samuel
See Heijermans, Herman
Fallaci, Oriana 1930- .... **CLC 11, 110**
See CA 77-80; CANR 15, 58; MTCW 1
Faludy, George 1913- .... **CLC 42**
See CA 21-24R
Faludy, Gyoergy
See Faludy, George
Fanon, Frantz 1925-1961 . **CLC 74; BLC 2; DAM MULT**
See BW 1; CA 116; 89-92
Fanshawe, Ann 1625-1680 .... **LC 11**
Fante, John(Thomas) 1911-1983 ..... **CLC 60**
See CA 69-72; 109; CANR 23; DLB 130; DLBY 83
Farah, Nuruddin 1945- ..... **CLC 53; BLC 2; DAM MULT**
See BW 2, 3; CA 106; CANR 81; DLB 125
Fargue, Leon-Paul 1876(?)-1947 ... **TCLC 11**
See CA 109
Farigoule, Louis
See Romains, Jules
Farina, Richard 1936(?)-1966 .... **CLC 9**
See CA 81-84; 25-28R
Farley, Walter (Lorimer) 1915-1989 .... **CLC 17**
See CA 17-20R; CANR 8, 29, 84; DLB 22; JRDA; MAICYA; SATA 2, 43
Farmer, Philip Jose 1918- .... **CLC 1, 19**
See AAYA 28; CA 1-4R; CANR 4, 35; DLB 8; MTCW 1; SATA 93
Farquhar, George 1677-1707 ... **LC 21;DAM DRAM**
See DLB 84
Farrell, J(ames)G(ordon) 1935-1979 . **CLC 6**
See CA 73-76; 89-92; CANR 36; DLB 14; MTCW 1
Farrell, James T(homas) 1904-1979 . **CLC 1, 4, 8, 11, 66; SSC 28**
See CA 5-8R; 89-92; CANR 9, 61; DLB 4, 9, 86; DLBD 2; MTCW 1, 2
Farren, Richard J.
See Betjeman, John
Farren, Richard M.
See Betjeman, John
Fassbinder, Rainer Werner 1946-1982 . **CLC 20**
See CA 93-96; 106; CANR 31
Fast, Howard (Melvin) 1914- .... **CLC 23; DAM NOV**
See AAYA 16; CA 1-4R, 181; CAAE 181; CAAS 18; CANR 1, 33, 54, 75; DLB 9; INT CANR-33; MTCW 1; SATA 7; SATA-Essay 107
Faulcon, Robert
See Holdstock, Robert P.
Faulkner, William (Cuthbert) 1897-1962 .... **CLC 1, 3, 6, 8, 9, 11, 14, 18, 28, 52, 68; DA; DAB; DAC; DAM MST, NOV; SSC 1, 35; WLC**
See AAYA 7; CA 81-84; CANR 33; CDALB 1929-1941; DA3; DLB 9, 11, 44, 102; DLBD 2; DLBY 86, 97; MTCW 1, 2
Fauset, Jessie Redmon 1884(?)-1961 ... **CLC 19, 54; BLC 2; DAM MULT**
See BW 1; CA 109; CANR 83; DLB 51
Faust, Frederick (Schiller) 1892-1944(?) ..... **TCLC 49; DAM POP**
See CA 108; 152
Faust, Irvin 1924- .... **CLC 8**
See CA 33-36R; CANR 28, 67; DLB 2, 28; DLBY 80
Fawkes, Guy
See Benchley, Robert (Charles)
Fearing, Kenneth (Flexner) 1902-1961 . **CLC 51**
See CA 93-96; CANR 59; DLB 9
Fecamps, Elise
See Creasey, John
Federman, Raymond 1928- .... **CLC 6,47**
See CA 17-20R; CAAS 8; CANR 10, 43, 83; DLBY 80
Federspiel, J(uerg) F. 1931- .... **CLC 42**
See CA 146
Feiffer, Jules (Ralph) 1929- ... **CLC 2, 8, 64; DAM DRAM**
See AAYA 3; CA 17-20R; CANR 30, 59; DLB 7, 44; INT CANR-30; MTCW 1; SATA 8, 61, 111
Feige, Hermann Albert Otto Maximilian
See Traven, B.
Feinberg, David B. 1956-1994 .... **CLC 59**
See CA 135; 147
Feinstein, Elaine 1930- .... **CLC 36**
See CA 69-72; CAAS 1; CANR 31, 68; DLB 14, 40; MTCW 1
Feldman, Irving (Mordecai) 1928- ... **CLC 7**
See CA 1-4R; CANR 1; DLB 169
Felix-Tchicaya, Gerald
See Tchicaya, Gerald Felix
Fellini, Federico 1920-1993 .... **CLC 16, 85**
See CA 65-68; 143; CANR 33
Felsen, Henry Gregor 1916-1995 .... **CLC 17**
See CA 1-4R; 180; CANR 1; SAAS 2; SATA 1
Fenno, Jack
See Calisher, Hortense
Fenollosa, Ernest (Francisco) 1853-1908 ..... **TCLC 91**
Fenton, James Martin 1949- .... **CLC 32**
See CA 102; DLB 40
Ferber, Edna 1887-1968 .... **CLC 18, 93**
See AITN 1; CA 5-8R; 25-28R; CANR 68; DLB 9, 28, 86; MTCW 1, 2; SATA 7
Ferguson, Helen
See Kavan, Anna
Ferguson, Samuel 1810-1886 .... **NCLC 33**
See DLB 32
Fergusson, Robert 1750-1774 .... **LC 29**
See DLB 109
Ferling, Lawrence
See Ferlinghetti, Lawrence (Monsanto)
Ferlinghetti, Lawrence (Monsanto) 1919(?)- .... **CLC 2, 6, 10, 27, 111; DAM POET; PC 1**
See CA 5-8R; CANR 3, 41, 73; CDALB 1941-1968; DA3; DLB 5, 16; MTCW 1, 2
Fernandez, Vicente Garcia Huidobro
See Huidobro Fernandez, Vicente Garcia
Ferre, Rosario 1942- .... **SSC 36;HLCS 1**
See CA 131; CANR 55, 81; DLB 145; HW 1, 2; MTCW 1
Ferrer, Gabriel (Francisco Victor) Miro
See Miro (Ferrer), Gabriel (Francisco Victor)
Ferrier, Susan (Edmonstone) 1782-1854 ...... **NCLC 8**
See DLB 116
Ferrigno, Robert 1948(?)- .... **CLC 65**
See CA 140
Ferron, Jacques 1921-1985 .... **CLC 94;DAC**
See CA 117; 129; DLB 60
Feuchtwanger, Lion 1884-1958 .... **TCLC 3**
See CA 104; DLB 66
Feuillet, Octave 1821-1890 .... **NCLC 45**
See DLB 192
Feydeau, Georges (Leon Jules Marie) 1862-1921 ..... **TCLC 22; DAM DRAM**
See CA 113; 152; CANR 84; DLB 192
Fichte, Johann Gottlieb 1762-1814 ... **NCLC 62**
See DLB 90
Ficino, Marsilio 1433-1499 .... **LC 12**
Fiedeler, Hans
See Doeblin, Alfred
Fiedler, Leslie A(aron) 1917- . **CLC 4, 13, 24**
See CA 9-12R; CANR 7, 63; DLB 28, 67; MTCW 1, 2
Field, Andrew 1938- .... **CLC 44**
See CA 97-100; CANR 25
Field, Eugene 1850-1895 .... **NCLC 3**
See DLB 23, 42, 140; DLBD 13; MAICYA; SATA 16
Field, Gans T.
See Wellman, Manly Wade
Field, Michael 1915-1971 .... **TCLC 43**
See CA 29-32R
Field, Peter
See Hobson, Laura Z(ametkin)
Fielding, Henry 1707-1754 ... **LC 1, 46; DA; DAB; DAC; DAM DRAM, MST, NOV; WLC**
See CDBLB 1660-1789; DA3; DLB 39, 84, 101
Fielding, Sarah 1710-1768 .... **LC 1, 44**
See DLB 39
Fields, W. C. 1880-1946 .... **TCLC 80**
See DLB 44
Fierstein, Harvey (Forbes) 1954- ... **CLC 33; DAM DRAM, POP**
See CA 123; 129; DA3
Figes, Eva 1932- .... **CLC 31**
See CA 53-56; CANR 4, 44, 83; DLB 14
Finch, Anne 1661-1720 .... **LC 3; PC 21**
See DLB 95
Finch, Robert (Duer Claydon) 1900- ... **CLC 18**
See CA 57-60; CANR 9, 24, 49; DLB 88
Findley, Timothy 1930- . **CLC 27, 102; DAC; DAM MST**
See CA 25-28R; CANR 12, 42, 69; DLB 53
Fink, William
See Mencken, H(enry) L(ouis)
Firbank, Louis 1942-
See Reed, Lou
See CA 117
Firbank, (Arthur Annesley) Ronald 1886-1926 .... **TCLC 1**
See CA 104; 177; DLB 36
Fisher, Dorothy (Frances) Canfield 1879-1958 .... **TCLC 87**
See CA 114; 136; CANR 80; DLB 9, 102; MAICYA; YABC 1
Fisher, M(ary) F(rances) K(ennedy) 1908-1992 .... **CLC 76, 87**
See CA 77-80; 138; CANR 44; MTCW 1
Fisher, Roy 1930- .... **CLC 25**
See CA 81-84; CAAS 10; CANR 16; DLB 40
Fisher, Rudolph 1897-1934 . **TCLC 11; BLC 2; DAM MULT; SSC 25**
See BW 1, 3; CA 107; 124; CANR 80; DLB 51, 102
Fisher, Vardis (Alvero) 1895-1968 .... **CLC 7**
See CA 5-8R; 25-28R; CANR 68; DLB 9, 206
Fiske, Tarleton
See Bloch, Robert (Albert)
Fitch, Clarke
See Sinclair, Upton (Beall)
Fitch, John IV
See Cormier, Robert (Edmund)
Fitzgerald, Captain Hugh
See Baum, L(yman) Frank
FitzGerald, Edward 1809-1883 ...... **NCLC 9**
See DLB 32
Fitzgerald, F(rancis) Scott (Key) 1896-1940 .... **TCLC 1, 6, 14, 28, 55; DA; DAB; DAC; DAM MST, NOV; SSC 6, 31; WLC**

See AAYA 24; AITN 1; CA 110; 123; CDALB 1917-1929; DA3; DLB 4, 9, 86; DLBD 1, 15, 16; DLBY 81, 96; MTCW 1, 2

Fitzgerald, Penelope 1916- .. **CLC 19, 51, 61**
See CA 85-88; CAAS 10; CANR 56; DLB 14, 194; MTCW 2

Fitzgerald, Robert (Stuart) 1910-1985 . **CLC 39**
See CA 1-4R; 114; CANR 1; DLBY 80

FitzGerald, Robert D(avid) 1902-1987 . **CLC 19**
See CA 17-20R

Fitzgerald, Zelda (Sayre) 1900-1948 . **TCLC 52**
See CA 117; 126; DLBY 84

Flanagan, Thomas (James Bonner) 1923- ... **CLC 25, 52**
See CA 108; CANR 55; DLBY 80; INT 108; MTCW 1

Flaubert, Gustave 1821-1880 .. **NCLC 2, 10, 19, 62, 66; DA; DAB; DAC; DAM MST, NOV; SSC 11; WLC**
See DA3; DLB 119

Flecker, Herman Elroy
See Flecker, (Herman) James Elroy

Flecker, (Herman) James Elroy 1884-1915 . **TCLC 43**
See CA 109; 150; DLB 10, 19

Fleming, Ian (Lancaster) 1908-1964 .... **CLC 3, 30; DAM POP**
See AAYA 26; CA 5-8R; CANR 59;CDBLB 1945-1960; DA3; DLB 87, 201; MTCW 1, 2; SATA 9

Fleming, Thomas (James) 1927- ..... **CLC 37**
See CA 5-8R; CANR 10; INT CANR-10; SATA 8

Fletcher, John 1579-1625 .... **LC 33;DC 6**
See CDBLB Before 1660; DLB 58

Fletcher, John Gould 1886-1950 .. **TCLC 35**
See CA 107; 167; DLB 4, 45

Fleur, Paul
See Pohl, Frederik

Flooglebuckle, Al
See Spiegelman, Art

Flying Officer X
See Bates, H(erbert) E(rnest)

Fo, Dario 1926- .... **CLC 32, 109; DAM DRAM; DC 10**
See CA 116; 128; CANR 68; DA3; DLBY 97; MTCW 1, 2

Fogarty, Jonathan Titulescu Esq.
See Farrell, James T(homas)

Follett, Ken(neth Martin) 1949- .... **CLC 18; DAM NOV, POP**
See AAYA 6; BEST 89:4; CA 81-84; CANR 13, 33, 54; DA3; DLB 87; DLBY 81; INT CANR-33; MTCW 1

Fontane, Theodor 1819-1898 .... **NCLC 26**
See DLB 129

Foote, Horton 1916- .... **CLC 51, 91;DAM DRAM**
See CA 73-76; CANR 34, 51; DA3; DLB 26; INT CANR-34

Foote, Shelby 1916- ... **CLC 75; DAM NOV, POP**
See CA 5-8R; CANR 3, 45, 74; DA3; DLB 2, 17; MTCW 2

Forbes, Esther 1891-1967 .... **CLC 12**
See AAYA 17; CA 13-14; 25-28R; CAP 1; CLR 27; DLB 22; JRDA; MAICYA; SATA 2, 100

Forche, Carolyn (Louise) 1950- ..... **CLC 25, 83, 86; DAM POET; PC 10**
See CA 109; 117; CANR 50, 74; DA3; DLB 5, 193; INT 117; MTCW 1

Ford, Elbur
See Hibbert, Eleanor Alice Burford

Ford, Ford Madox 1873-1939 . **TCLC 1, 15, 39, 57; DAM NOV**
See CA 104; 132; CANR 74; CDBLB 1914-1945; DA3; DLB 162; MTCW 1, 2

Ford, Henry 1863-1947 .... **TCLC 73**
See CA 115; 148

Ford, John 1586-(?) .... **DC 8**
See CDBLB Before 1660; DAM DRAM; DA3; DLB 58

Ford, John 1895-1973 .... **CLC 16**
See CA 45-48

Ford, Richard 1944- .... **CLC 46, 99**
See CA 69-72; CANR 11, 47; MTCW 1

Ford, Webster
See Masters, Edgar Lee

Foreman, Richard 1937- .... **CLC 50**
See CA 65-68; CANR 32, 63

Forester, C(ecil) S(cott) 1899-1966 . **CLC 35**
See CA 73-76; 25-28R; CANR 83; DLB 191; SATA 13

Forez
See Mauriac, Francois (Charles)

Forman, James Douglas 1932- .... **CLC 21**
See AAYA 17; CA 9-12R; CANR 4, 19, 42; JRDA; MAICYA; SATA 8, 70

Fornes, Maria Irene 1930- . **CLC 39, 61; DC 10; HLCS 1**
See CA 25-28R; CANR 28, 81; DLB 7; HW 1, 2; INT CANR-28; MTCW 1

Forrest, Leon (Richard) 1937-1997 . **CLC 4; BLCS**
See BW 2; CA 89-92; 162; CAAS 7; CANR 25, 52; DLB 33

Forster, E(dward) M(organ) 1879-1970 .... **CLC 1, 2, 3, 4, 9, 10, 13, 15, 22, 45, 77; DA; DAB; DAC; DAM MST, NOV; SSC 27;WLC**
See AAYA 2; CA 13-14; 25-28R; CANR 45; CAP 1; CDBLB 1914-1945; DA3; DLB 34, 98, 162, 178, 195; DLBD 10; MTCW 1, 2; SATA 57

Forster, John 1812-1876 .... **NCLC 11**
See DLB 144, 184

Forsyth, Frederick 1938- .... **CLC 2, 5, 36; DAM NOV, POP**
See BEST 89:4; CA 85-88; CANR 38, 62; DLB 87; MTCW 1, 2

Forten, Charlotte L. .... **TCLC 16; BLC 2**
See Grimke, Charlotte L(ottie) Forten
See DLB 50

Foscolo, Ugo 1778-1827 .... **NCLC 8**

Fosse, Bob .... **CLC 20**
See Fosse, Robert Louis

Fosse, Robert Louis 1927-1987
See Fosse, Bob
See CA 110; 123

Foster, Stephen Collins 1826-1864 .... **NCLC 26**

Foucault, Michel 1926-1984 . **CLC 31, 34, 69**
See CA 105; 113; CANR 34; MTCW 1, 2

Fouque, Friedrich (Heinrich Karl) de la Motte 1777-1843 .... **NCLC 2**
See DLB 90

Fourier, Charles 1772-1837 .... **NCLC 51**

Fournier, Pierre 1916- .... **CLC 11**
See Gascar, Pierre
See CA 89-92; CANR 16, 40

Fowles, John (Philip) 1926- . **CLC 1, 2, 3, 4, 6, 9, 10, 15, 33, 87; DAB; DAC; DAM MST; SSC 33**
See CA 5-8R; CANR 25, 71; CDBLB 1960 to Present; DA3; DLB 14, 139, 207; MTCW 1, 2; SATA 22

Fox, Paula 1923- .... **CLC 2, 8, 121**
See AAYA 3; CA 73-76; CANR 20, 36, 62; CLR 1, 44; DLB 52; JRDA; MAICYA; MTCW 1; SATA 17, 60

Fox, William Price (Jr.) 1926- .... **CLC 22**
See CA 17-20R; CAAS 19; CANR 11; DLB 2; DLBY 81

Foxe, John 1516(?)-1587 .... **LC 14**
See DLB 132

Frame, Janet 1924- . **CLC 2, 3, 6, 22, 66, 96; SSC 29**
See Clutha, Janet Paterson Frame

France, Anatole .... **TCLC 9**
See Thibault, Jacques Anatole Francois
See DLB 123; MTCW 1

Francis, Claude 19(?)- .... **CLC 50**

Francis, Dick 1920- ...... **CLC 2, 22, 42, 102; DAM POP**
See AAYA 5, 21; BEST 89:3; CA 5-8R; CANR 9, 42, 68; CDBLB 1960 to Present; DA3; DLB 87; INT CANR-9; MTCW 1, 2

Francis, Robert (Churchill) 1901-1987 . **CLC 15**
See CA 1-4R; 123; CANR 1

Frank, Anne(lies Marie) 1929-1945 ... **TCLC 17; DA; DAB; DAC; DAM MST; WLC**
See AAYA 12; CA 113; 133; CANR 68; DA3; MTCW 1, 2; SATA 87; SATA-Brief 42

Frank, Bruno 1887-1945 .... **TCLC 81**
See DLB 118

Frank, Elizabeth 1945- .... **CLC 39**
See CA 121; 126; CANR 78; INT 126

Frankl, ViktorE(mil) 1905-1997 ...... **CLC 93**
See CA 65-68; 161

Franklin, Benjamin
See Hasek, Jaroslav (Matej Frantisek)

Franklin, Benjamin 1706-1790 . **LC 25; DA; DAB; DAC; DAM MST; WLCS**
See CDALB 1640-1865; DA3; DLB 24, 43, 73

Franklin, (Stella Maria Sarah) Miles (Lampe) 1879-1954 .... **TCLC 7**
See CA 104; 164

Fraser, (Lady) Antonia (Pakenham) 1932- .. **CLC 32, 107**
See CA 85-88; CANR 44, 65; MTCW 1, 2; SATA-Brief 32

Fraser, George MacDonald 1925- ..... **CLC 7**
See CA 45-48, 180; CAAE 180; CANR 2, 48, 74; MTCW 1

Fraser, Sylvia 1935- .... **CLC 64**
See CA 45-48; CANR 1, 16, 60

Frayn, Michael 1933- .... **CLC 3, 7, 31, 47; DAM DRAM, NOV**
See CA 5-8R; CANR 30, 69; DLB 13, 14, 194; MTCW 1, 2

Fraze, Candida (Merrill) 1945- .... **CLC 50**
See CA 126

Frazer, J(ames) G(eorge) 1854-1941 . **TCLC 32**
See CA 118

Frazer, Robert Caine
See Creasey, John

Frazer, Sir James George
See Frazer, J(ames) G(eorge)

Frazier, Charles 1950- .... **CLC 109**
See CA 161

Frazier, Ian 1951- .... **CLC 46**
See CA 130; CANR 54

Frederic, Harold 1856-1898 .... **NCLC 10**
See DLB 12, 23; DLBD 13

Frederick, John
See Faust, Frederick (Schiller)

Frederick the Great 1712-1786 .... **LC 14**

Fredro, Aleksander 1793-1876 .... **NCLC 8**

Freeling, Nicolas 1927- .... **CLC 38**
See CA 49-52; CAAS 12; CANR 1, 17, 50, 84; DLB 87

Freeman, Douglas Southall 1886-1953 .... **TCLC 11**

See CA 109; DLB 17; DLBD 17
Freeman, Judith 1946- .... **CLC 55**
See CA 148
Freeman, Mary E(leanor) Wilkins 1852-1930 .... **TCLC 9; SSC 1**
See CA 106; 177; DLB 12, 78
Freeman, R(ichard) Austin 1862-1943 .... **TCLC 21**
See CA 113; CANR 84; DLB 70
French, Albert 1943- .... **CLC 86**
See BW 3; CA 167
French, Marilyn 1929- .... **CLC 10, 18, 60; DAM DRAM, NOV, POP**
See CA 69-72; CANR 3, 31; INT CANR-31; MTCW 1, 2
French, Paul
See Asimov, Isaac
Freneau, Philip Morin 1752-1832 .. **NCLC 1**
See DLB 37, 43
Freud, Sigmund 1856-1939 .... **TCLC 52**
See CA 115; 133; CANR 69; MTCW 1, 2
Friedan, Betty (Naomi) 1921- .... **CLC 74**
See CA 65-68; CANR 18, 45, 74; MTCW 1, 2
Friedlander, Saul 1932- .... **CLC 90**
See CA 117; 130; CANR 72
Friedman, B(ernard) H(arper) 1926- .. **CLC 7**
See CA 1-4R; CANR 3, 48
Friedman, Bruce Jay 1930- .... **CLC 3, 5, 56**
See CA 9-12R; CANR 25, 52; DLB 2, 28; INT CANR-25
Friel, Brian 1929- .. **CLC 5, 42, 59, 115; DC 8**
See CA 21-24R; CANR 33, 69; DLB 13; MTCW 1
Friis-Baastad, Babbis Ellinor 1921-1970 ..... **CLC 12**
See CA 17-20R; 134; SATA 7
Frisch, Max (Rudolf) 1911-1991 .. **CLC 3, 9, 14, 18, 32, 44; DAM DRAM, NOV**
See CA 85-88; 134; CANR 32, 74; DLB 69, 124; MTCW 1, 2
Fromentin, Eugene (Samuel Auguste) 1820-1876 .... **NCLC 10**
See DLB 123
Frost, Frederick
See Faust, Frederick (Schiller)
Frost, Robert (Lee) 1874-1963 . **CLC 1, 3, 4, 9, 10, 13, 15, 26, 34, 44; DA; DAB; DAC; DAM MST, POET; PC 1; WLC**
See AAYA 21; CA 89-92; CANR 33; CDALB 1917-1929; DA3; DLB 54; DLBD 7; MTCW 1, 2; SATA 14
Froude, James Anthony 1818-1894 ... **NCLC 43**
See DLB 18, 57, 144
Froy, Herald
See Waterhouse, Keith (Spencer)
Fry, Christopher 1907- .... **CLC 2, 10, 14; DAM DRAM**
See CA 17-20R; CAAS 23; CANR 9, 30, 74; DLB 13; MTCW 1, 2; SATA 66
Frye, (Herman) Northrop 1912-1991 .. **CLC 24, 70**
See CA 5-8R; 133; CANR 8, 37; DLB 67, 68; MTCW 1, 2
Fuchs, Daniel 1909-1993 .... **CLC 8, 22**
See CA 81-84; 142; CAAS 5; CANR 40; DLB 9, 26, 28; DLBY 93
Fuchs, Daniel 1934- .... **CLC 34**
See CA 37-40R; CANR 14, 48
Fuentes, Carlos 1928- . **CLC 3, 8, 10, 13, 22, 41, 60, 113; DA; DAB; DAC; DAM MST, MULT, NOV; HLC 1; SSC 24;WLC**
See AAYA 4; AITN 2; CA 69-72; CANR 10, 32, 68; DA3; DLB 113; HW 1, 2; MTCW 1, 2
Fuentes, Gregorio Lopez y
See Lopez y Fuentes, Gregorio
Fuertes, Gloria 1918- .... **PC 27**
See CA 178, 180; DLB 108; HW 2
Fugard, (Harold) Athol 1932- . **CLC 5, 9, 14, 25, 40, 80; DAM DRAM; DC 3**
See AAYA 17; CA 85-88; CANR 32, 54; MTCW 1
Fugard, Sheila 1932- .... **CLC 48**
See CA 125
Fuller, Charles (H., Jr.) 1939- .... **CLC 25; BLC 2; DAM DRAM, MULT; DC 1**
See BW 2; CA 108; 112; DLB 38; INT 112; MTCW 1
Fuller, John (Leopold) 1937- .... **CLC 62**
See CA 21-24R; CANR 9, 44; DLB 40
Fuller, Margaret .... **NCLC 5, 50**
See Ossoli, Sarah Margaret (Fuller marchesa d')
Fuller, Roy (Broadbent) 1912-1991 . **CLC 4, 28**
See CA 5-8R; 135; CAAS 10; CANR 53, 83; DLB 15, 20; SATA 87
Fulton, Alice 1952- .... **CLC 52**
See CA 116; CANR 57; DLB 193
Furphy, Joseph 1843-1912 .... **TCLC 25**
See CA 163
Fussell, Paul 1924- .... **CLC 74**
See BEST 90:1; CA 17-20R; CANR 8, 21, 35, 69; INT CANR-21; MTCW 1, 2
Futabatei, Shimei 1864-1909 .... **TCLC 44**
See CA 162; DLB 180
Futrelle, Jacques 1875-1912 .... **TCLC 19**
See CA 113; 155
Gaboriau, Emile 1835-1873 .... **NCLC 14**
Gadda, Carlo Emilio 1893-1973 ...... **CLC 11**
See CA 89-92; DLB 177
Gaddis, William 1922-1998 .. **CLC 1, 3, 6, 8, 10, 19, 43, 86**
See CA 17-20R; 172; CANR 21, 48; DLB 2; MTCW 1, 2
Gage, Walter
See Inge, William (Motter)
Gaines, Ernest J(ames) 1933- ..... **CLC 3, 11, 18, 86; BLC 2; DAM MULT**
See AAYA 18; AITN 1; BW 2, 3; CA 9-12R; CANR 6, 24, 42, 75; CDALB 1968-1988; DA3; DLB 2, 33, 152; DLBY 80; MTCW 1, 2; SATA 86
Gaitskill, Mary 1954- .... **CLC 69**
See CA 128; CANR 61
Galdos, Benito Perez
See Perez Galdos, Benito
Gale, Zona 1874-1938 .... **TCLC 7;DAM DRAM**
See CA 105; 153; CANR 84; DLB 9, 78
Galeano, Eduardo (Hughes) 1940- . **CLC 72; HLCS 1**
See CA 29-32R; CANR 13, 32; HW 1
Galiano, Juan Valera y Alcala
See Valera y Alcala-Galiano, Juan
Galilei, Galileo 1546-1642 .... **LC 45**
Gallagher, Tess 1943- ..... **CLC 18, 63; DAM POET; PC 9**
See CA 106; DLB 212
Gallant, Mavis 1922- . **CLC 7, 18, 38; DAC; DAM MST; SSC 5**
See CA 69-72; CANR 29, 69; DLB 53; MTCW 1, 2
Gallant, Roy A(rthur) 1924- .... **CLC 17**
See CA 5-8R; CANR 4, 29, 54; CLR 30; MAICYA; SATA 4, 68, 110
Gallico, Paul (William) 1897-1976 .... **CLC 2**
See AITN 1; CA 5-8R; 69-72; CANR 23; DLB 9, 171; MAICYA; SATA 13
Gallo, Max Louis 1932- .... **CLC 95**
See CA 85-88
Gallois, Lucien
See Desnos, Robert
Gallup, Ralph
See Whitemore, Hugh (John)
Galsworthy, John 1867-1933 ... **TCLC 1, 45; DA; DAB; DAC; DAM DRAM, MST, NOV; SSC 22; WLC**
See CA 104; 141; CANR 75; CDBLB 1890-1914; DA3; DLB 10, 34, 98, 162; DLBD 16; MTCW 1
Galt, John 1779-1839 .... **NCLC 1**
See DLB 99, 116, 159
Galvin, James 1951- .... **CLC 38**
See CA 108; CANR 26
Gamboa, Federico 1864-1939 .... **TCLC 36**
See CA 167; HW 2
Gandhi, M. K.
See Gandhi, Mohandas Karamchand
Gandhi, Mahatma
See Gandhi, Mohandas Karamchand
Gandhi, Mohandas Karamchand 1869-1948 .... **TCLC 59; DAM MULT**
See CA 121; 132; DA3; MTCW 1, 2
Gann, Ernest Kellogg 1910-1991 .... **CLC 23**
See AITN 1; CA 1-4R; 136; CANR 1, 83
Garcia, Cristina 1958- .... **CLC 76**
See CA 141; CANR 73; HW 2
Garcia Lorca, Federico 1898-1936 .... **TCLC 1, 7, 49; DA; DAB; DAC; DAM DRAM, MST, MULT, POET; DC 2; HLC 2; PC 3; WLC**
See CA 104; 131; CANR 81; DA3; DLB 108; HW 1, 2; MTCW 1, 2
Garcia Marquez, Gabriel (Jose) 1928- . **CLC 2, 3, 8, 10, 15, 27, 47, 55, 68; DA; DAB; DAC; DAM MST, MULT, NOV, POP; HLC 1; SSC 8; WLC**
See AAYA 3; BEST 89:1, 90:4; CA 33-36R; CANR 10, 28, 50, 75, 82; DA3; DLB 113; HW 1, 2; MTCW 1, 2
Garcilaso de la Vega, El Inca 1503-1536
See HLCS 1
Gard, Janice
See Latham, Jean Lee
Gard, Roger Martin du
See Martin du Gard, Roger
Gardam, Jane 1928- .... **CLC 43**
See CA 49-52; CANR 2, 18, 33, 54; CLR 12; DLB 14, 161; MAICYA; MTCW 1; SAAS 9; SATA 39, 76; SATA-Brief 28
Gardner, Herb(ert) 1934- .... **CLC 44**
See CA 149
Gardner, John (Champlin), Jr. 1933-1982 .. **CLC 2, 3, 5, 7, 8, 10, 18, 28, 34; DAM NOV, POP; SSC 7**
See AITN 1; CA 65-68; 107; CANR 33, 73; CDALBS; DA3; DLB 2; DLBY 82; MTCW 1; SATA 40; SATA-Obit 31
Gardner, John (Edmund) 1926- .... **CLC 30; DAM POP**
See CA 103; CANR 15, 69; MTCW 1
Gardner, Miriam
See Bradley, Marion Zimmer
Gardner, Noel
See Kuttner, Henry
Gardons, S. S.
See Snodgrass, W(illiam) D(e Witt)
Garfield, Leon 1921-1996 .... **CLC 12**
See AAYA 8; CA 17-20R; 152; CANR 38, 41, 78; CLR 21; DLB 161; JRDA; MAICYA; SATA 1, 32, 76; SATA-Obit 90
Garland, (Hannibal) Hamlin 1860-1940 ...... **TCLC 3; SSC 18**
See CA 104; DLB 12, 71, 78, 186
Garneau, (Hector de) Saint-Denys 1912-1943 .... **TCLC 13**
See CA 111; DLB 88
Garner, Alan 1934- ..... **CLC 17; DAB;DAM POP**

See AAYA 18; CA 73-76, 178; CAAE 178; CANR 15, 64; CLR 20; DLB 161; MAICYA; MTCW 1, 2; SATA 18, 69; SATA-Essay 108
Garner, Hugh 1913-1979 .... **CLC 13**
See CA 69-72; CANR 31; DLB 68
Garnett, David 1892-1981 .... **CLC 3**
See CA 5-8R; 103; CANR 17, 79; DLB 34; MTCW 2
Garos, Stephanie
See Katz, Steve
Garrett, George (Palmer) 1929- . **CLC 3, 11, 51; SSC 30**
See CA 1-4R; CAAS 5; CANR 1, 42, 67; DLB 2, 5, 130, 152; DLBY 83
Garrick, David 1717-1779 .... **LC 15;DAM DRAM**
See DLB 84
Garrigue, Jean 1914-1972 .... **CLC 2, 8**
See CA 5-8R; 37-40R; CANR 20
Garrison, Frederick
See Sinclair, Upton (Beall)
Garro, Elena 1920(?)-1998
See CA 131; 169; DLB 145; HLCS 1; HW 1
Garth, Will
See Hamilton, Edmond; Kuttner, Henry
Garvey, Marcus (Moziah, Jr.) 1887-1940 .... **TCLC 41; BLC 2; DAM MULT**
See BW 1; CA 120; 124; CANR 79
Gary, Romain .... **CLC 25**
See Kacew, Romain
See DLB 83
Gascar, Pierre .... **CLC 11**
See Fournier, Pierre
Gascoyne, David (Emery) 1916- ..... **CLC 45**
See CA 65-68; CANR 10, 28, 54; DLB 20; MTCW 1
Gaskell, Elizabeth Cleghorn 1810-1865 .... **NCLC 70; DAB; DAM MST; SSC 25**
See CDBLB 1832-1890; DLB 21, 144, 159
Gass, William H(oward) 1924- . **CLC 1, 2, 8, 11, 15, 39; SSC 12**
See CA 17-20R; CANR 30, 71; DLB 2; MTCW 1, 2
Gassendi, Pierre 1592-1655 .... **LC 54**
Gasset, Jose Ortega y
See Ortega y Gasset, Jose
Gates, Henry Louis, Jr. 1950- .... **CLC 65; BLCS; DAM MULT**
See BW 2, 3; CA 109; CANR 25, 53, 75; DA3; DLB 67; MTCW 1
Gautier, Theophile 1811-1872 . **NCLC 1, 59; DAM POET; PC 18; SSC 20**
See DLB 119
Gawsworth, John
See Bates, H(erbert) E(rnest)
Gay, John 1685-1732 .. **LC 49;DAM DRAM**
See DLB 84, 95
Gay, Oliver
See Gogarty, Oliver St. John
Gaye, Marvin (Penze) 1939-1984 .... **CLC 26**
See CA 112
Gebler, Carlo (Ernest) 1954- .... **CLC 39**
See CA 119; 133
Gee, Maggie (Mary) 1948- .... **CLC 57**
See CA 130; DLB 207
Gee, Maurice (Gough) 1931- .... **CLC 29**
See CA 97-100; CANR 67; CLR 56; SATA 46, 101
Gelbart, Larry (Simon) 1923- ... **CLC 21, 61**
See CA 73-76; CANR 45
Gelber, Jack 1932- .... **CLC 1, 6, 14, 79**
See CA 1-4R; CANR 2; DLB 7
Gellhorn, Martha (Ellis) 1908-1998 ..... **CLC 14, 60**
See CA 77-80; 164; CANR 44; DLBY 82, 98
Genet, Jean 1910-1986 . **CLC 1, 2, 5, 10, 14, 44, 46; DAM DRAM**
See CA 13-16R; CANR 18; DA3; DLB 72; DLBY 86; MTCW 1, 2
Gent, Peter 1942- .... **CLC 29**
See AITN 1; CA 89-92; DLBY 82
Gentile, Giovanni 1875-1944 .... **TCLC 96**
See CA 119
Gentlewoman in New England, A
See Bradstreet, Anne
Gentlewoman in Those Parts, A
See Bradstreet, Anne
George, Jean Craighead 1919- .... **CLC 35**
See AAYA 8; CA 5-8R; CANR 25; CLR 1; DLB 52; JRDA; MAICYA; SATA 2, 68
George, Stefan (Anton) 1868-1933 .... **TCLC 2, 14**
See CA 104
Georges, Georges Martin
See Simenon, Georges (Jacques Christian)
Gerhardi, William Alexander
See Gerhardie, William Alexander
Gerhardie, William Alexander 1895-1977 ... **CLC 5**
See CA 25-28R; 73-76; CANR 18; DLB 36
Gerstler, Amy 1956- .... **CLC 70**
See CA 146
Gertler, T. .... **CLC 34**
See CA 116; 121; INT 121
Ghalib .... **NCLC 39, 78**
See Ghalib, Hsadullah Khan
Ghalib, Hsadullah Khan 1797-1869
See Ghalib
See DAM POET
Ghelderode, Michel de 1898-1962 ... **CLC 6, 11; DAM DRAM**
See CA 85-88; CANR 40, 77
Ghiselin, Brewster 1903- .... **CLC 23**
See CA 13-16R; CAAS 10; CANR 13
Ghose, Aurabinda 1872-1950 .... **TCLC 63**
See CA 163
Ghose, Zulfikar 1935- .... **CLC 42**
See CA 65-68; CANR 67
Ghosh, Amitav 1956- .... **CLC 44**
See CA 147; CANR 80
Giacosa, Giuseppe 1847-1906 .... **TCLC 7**
See CA 104
Gibb, Lee
See Waterhouse, Keith (Spencer)
Gibbon, Lewis Grassic .... **TCLC 4**
See Mitchell, James Leslie
Gibbons, Kaye 1960- .... **CLC 50, 88;DAM POP**
See CA 151; CANR 75; DA3; MTCW 1
Gibran, Kahlil 1883-1931 . **TCLC 1, 9; DAM POET, POP; PC 9**
See CA 104; 150; DA3; MTCW 2
Gibran, Khalil
See Gibran, Kahlil
Gibson, William 1914- . **CLC 23; DA; DAB; DAC; DAM DRAM, MST**
See CA 9-12R; CANR 9, 42, 75; DLB 7; MTCW 1; SATA 66
Gibson, William (Ford) 1948- . **CLC 39, 63; DAM POP**
See AAYA 12; CA 126; 133; CANR 52; DA3; MTCW 1
Gide, Andre (Paul Guillaume) 1869-1951 ... **TCLC 5, 12, 36; DA; DAB; DAC; DAM MST, NOV; SSC 13; WLC**
See CA 104; 124; DA3; DLB 65; MTCW 1, 2
Gifford, Barry (Colby) 1946- .... **CLC 34**
See CA 65-68; CANR 9, 30, 40
Gilbert, Frank
See De Voto, Bernard (Augustine)
Gilbert, W(illiam) S(chwenck) 1836-1911 ... **TCLC 3; DAM DRAM, POET**
See CA 104; 173; SATA 36
Gilbreth, Frank B., Jr. 1911- .... **CLC 17**
See CA 9-12R; SATA 2
Gilchrist, Ellen 1935- ..... **CLC 34, 48; DAM POP; SSC 14**
See CA 113; 116; CANR 41, 61; DLB 130; MTCW 1, 2
Giles, Molly 1942- .... **CLC 39**
See CA 126
Gill, Eric 1882-1940 .... **TCLC 85**
Gill, Patrick
See Creasey, John
Gilliam, Terry (Vance) 1940- .... **CLC 21**
See Monty Python
See AAYA 19; CA 108; 113; CANR 35; INT 113
Gillian, Jerry
See Gilliam, Terry (Vance)
Gilliatt, Penelope (Ann Douglass) 1932-1993 .... **CLC 2, 10, 13, 53**
See AITN 2; CA 13-16R; 141; CANR 49; DLB 14
Gilman, Charlotte (Anna) Perkins (Stetson) 1860-1935 .... **TCLC 9, 37; SSC 13**
See CA 106; 150; MTCW 1
Gilmour, David 1949- .... **CLC 35**
See CA 138, 147
Gilpin, William 1724-1804 .... **NCLC 30**
Gilray, J. D.
See Mencken, H(enry) L(ouis)
Gilroy, Frank D(aniel) 1925- .... **CLC 2**
See CA 81-84; CANR 32, 64; DLB 7
Gilstrap, John 1957(?)- .... **CLC 99**
See CA 160
Ginsberg, Allen 1926-1997 ... **CLC 1, 2, 3, 4, 6, 13, 36, 69, 109; DA; DAB; DAC; DAM MST, POET; PC 4; WLC**
See AITN 1; CA 1-4R; 157; CANR 2, 41, 63; CDALB 1941-1968; DA3; DLB 5, 16, 169; MTCW 1, 2
Ginzburg, Natalia 1916-1991 ..... **CLC 5, 11, 54, 70**
See CA 85-88; 135; CANR 33; DLB 177; MTCW 1, 2
Giono, Jean 1895-1970 .... **CLC 4, 11**
See CA 45-48; 29-32R; CANR 2, 35; DLB 72; MTCW 1
Giovanni, Nikki 1943- ...... **CLC 2, 4, 19, 64, 117; BLC 2; DA; DAB; DAC; DAM MST, MULT, POET; PC 19; WLCS**
See AAYA 22; AITN 1; BW 2, 3; CA 29-32R; CAAS 6; CANR 18, 41, 60; CDALBS; CLR 6; DA3; DLB 5, 41; INT CANR-18; MAICYA; MTCW 1, 2; SATA 24, 107
Giovene, Andrea 1904- .... **CLC 7**
See CA 85-88
Gippius, Zinaida (Nikolayevna) 1869-1945
See Hippius, Zinaida
See CA 106
Giraudoux, (Hippolyte) Jean 1882-1944 ...... **TCLC 2, 7; DAM DRAM**
See CA 104; DLB 65
Gironella, Jose Maria 1917- .... **CLC 11**
See CA 101
Gissing, George (Robert) 1857-1903 . **TCLC 3, 24, 47; SSC 37**
See CA 105; 167; DLB 18, 135, 184
Giurlani, Aldo
See Palazzeschi, Aldo
Gladkov, Fyodor (Vasilyevich) 1883-1958 ... **TCLC 27**
See CA 170
Glanville, Brian (Lester) 1931- .... **CLC 6**
See CA 5-8R; CAAS 9; CANR 3, 70; DLB 15, 139; SATA 42
Glasgow, Ellen (Anderson Gholson) 1873-1945 .... **TCLC 2, 7; SSC 34**
See CA 104; 164; DLB 9, 12; MTCW 2

Author Index

Glaspell, Susan 1882(?)-1948 . **TCLC 55; DC 10**
See CA 110; 154; DLB 7, 9, 78; YABC 2
Glassco, John 1909-1981 .... **CLC 9**
See CA 13-16R; 102; CANR 15; DLB 68
Glasscock, Amnesia
See Steinbeck, John (Ernst)
Glasser, Ronald J. 1940(?)- .... **CLC 37**
Glassman, Joyce
See Johnson, Joyce
Glendinning, Victoria 1937- .... **CLC 50**
See CA 120; 127; CANR 59; DLB 155
Glissant, Edouard 1928- . **CLC 10, 68; DAM MULT**
See CA 153
Gloag, Julian 1930- .... **CLC 40**
See AITN 1; CA 65-68; CANR 10, 70
Glowacki, Aleksander
See Prus, Boleslaw
Gluck, Louise (Elisabeth) 1943- . **CLC 7, 22, 44, 81; DAM POET; PC 16**
See CA 33-36R; CANR 40, 69; DA3; DLB 5; MTCW 2
Glyn, Elinor 1864-1943 .... **TCLC 72**
See DLB 153
Gobineau, Joseph Arthur (Comte) de 1816-1882 .... **NCLC 17**
See DLB 123
Godard, Jean-Luc 1930- .... **CLC 20**
See CA 93-96
Godden, (Margaret) Rumer 1907-1998 .... **CLC 53**
See AAYA 6; CA 5-8R; 172; CANR 4, 27, 36, 55, 80; CLR 20; DLB 161; MAICYA; SAAS 12; SATA 3, 36; SATA-Obit 109
Godoy Alcayaga, Lucila 1889-1957
See Mistral, Gabriela
See BW 2; CA 104; 131; CANR 81; DAM MULT; HW 1, 2; MTCW 1, 2
Godwin, Gail (Kathleen) 1937- .... **CLC 5, 8, 22, 31, 69, 125; DAM POP**
See CA 29-32R; CANR 15, 43, 69; DA3; DLB 6; INT CANR-15; MTCW 1, 2
Godwin, William 1756-1836 .... **NCLC 14**
See CDBLB 1789-1832; DLB 39, 104, 142, 158, 163
Goebbels, Josef
See Goebbels, (Paul) Joseph
Goebbels, (Paul) Joseph 1897-1945 ... **TCLC 68**
See CA 115; 148
Goebbels, Joseph Paul
See Goebbels, (Paul) Joseph
Goethe, Johann Wolfgang von 1749-1832 ... **NCLC 4, 22, 34; DA; DAB; DAC; DAM DRAM, MST, POET; PC 5; WLC**
See DA3; DLB 94
Gogarty, Oliver St.John 1878-1957 ... **TCLC 15**
See CA 109; 150; DLB 15, 19
Gogol, Nikolai (Vasilyevich) 1809-1852 .... **NCLC 5, 15, 31; DA; DAB; DAC; DAM DRAM, MST; DC 1; SSC 4, 29; WLC**
See DLB 198
Goines, Donald 1937(?)-1974 . **CLC 80; BLC 2; DAM MULT, POP**
See AITN 1; BW 1, 3; CA 124; 114; CANR 82; DA3; DLB 33
Gold, Herbert 1924- .... **CLC 4, 7, 14, 42**
See CA 9-12R; CANR 17, 45; DLB 2; DLBY 81
Goldbarth, Albert 1948- .... **CLC 5, 38**
See CA 53-56; CANR 6, 40; DLB 120
Goldberg, Anatol 1910-1982 .... **CLC 34**
See CA 131; 117
Goldemberg, Isaac 1945- .... **CLC 52**
See CA 69-72; CAAS 12; CANR 11, 32; HW 1
Golding, William (Gerald) 1911-1993 . **CLC 1, 2, 3, 8, 10, 17, 27, 58, 81; DA; DAB; DAC; DAM MST, NOV; WLC**
See AAYA 5; CA 5-8R; 141; CANR 13, 33, 54; CDBLB 1945-1960; DA3; DLB 15, 100; MTCW 1, 2
Goldman, Emma 1869-1940 .... **TCLC 13**
See CA 110; 150
Goldman, Francisco 1954- .... **CLC 76**
See CA 162
Goldman, William (W.) 1931- ...... **CLC 1,48**
See CA 9-12R; CANR 29, 69; DLB 44
Goldmann, Lucien 1913-1970 .... **CLC 24**
See CA 25-28; CAP 2
Goldoni, Carlo 1707-1793 .... **LC 4; DAM DRAM**
Goldsberry, Steven 1949- .... **CLC 34**
See CA 131
Goldsmith, Oliver 1728-1774 . **LC 2, 48; DA; DAB; DAC; DAM DRAM, MST, NOV, POET; DC 8; WLC**
See CDBLB 1660-1789; DLB 39, 89, 104, 109, 142; SATA 26
Goldsmith, Peter
See Priestley, J(ohn) B(oynton)
Gombrowicz, Witold 1904-1969 ... **CLC 4, 7, 11, 49; DAM DRAM**
See CA 19-20; 25-28R; CAP 2
Gomez de la Serna, Ramon 1888-1963 . **CLC 9**
See CA 153; 116; CANR 79; HW 1, 2
Goncharov, Ivan Alexandrovich 1812-1891 .... **NCLC 1, 63**
Goncourt, Edmond (Louis Antoine Huot) de 1822-1896 .... **NCLC 7**
See DLB 123
Goncourt, Jules (Alfred Huot) de 1830-1870 .... **NCLC 7**
See DLB 123
Gontier, Fernande 19(?)- .... **CLC 50**
Gonzalez Martinez, Enrique 1871-1952 ...... **TCLC 72**
See CA 166; CANR 81; HW 1, 2
Goodman, Paul 1911-1972 .... **CLC 1, 2, 4, 7**
See CA 19-20; 37-40R; CANR 34; CAP 2; DLB 130; MTCW 1
Gordimer, Nadine 1923- .... **CLC 3, 5, 7, 10, 18, 33, 51, 70; DA; DAB; DAC; DAM MST, NOV; SSC 17; WLCS**
See CA 5-8R; CANR 3, 28, 56; DA3; INT CANR-28; MTCW 1, 2
Gordon, Adam Lindsay 1833-1870 ... **NCLC 21**
Gordon, Caroline 1895-1981 ...... **CLC 6, 13, 29, 83; SSC 15**
See CA 11-12; 103; CANR 36; CAP 1; DLB 4, 9, 102; DLBD 17; DLBY 81; MTCW 1, 2
Gordon, Charles William 1860-1937
See Connor, Ralph
See CA 109
Gordon, Mary (Catherine) 1949- .. **CLC 13, 22**
See CA 102; CANR 44; DLB 6; DLBY 81; INT 102; MTCW 1
Gordon, N. J.
See Bosman, Herman Charles
Gordon, Sol 1923- .... **CLC 26**
See CA 53-56; CANR 4; SATA 11
Gordone, Charles 1925-1995 .... **CLC 1, 4; DAM DRAM; DC 8**
See BW 1, 3; CA 93-96, 180; 150; CAAE 180; CANR 55; DLB 7; INT 93-96; MTCW 1
Gore, Catherine 1800-1861 .... **NCLC 65**
See DLB 116
Gorenko, Anna Andreevna
See Akhmatova, Anna
Gorky, Maxim 1868-1936 ... **TCLC 8; DAB; SSC 28; WLC**
See Peshkov, Alexei Maximovich
See MTCW 2
Goryan, Sirak
See Saroyan, William
Gosse, Edmund (William) 1849-1928 . **TCLC 28**
See CA 117; DLB 57, 144, 184
Gotlieb, Phyllis Fay (Bloom) 1926- . **CLC 18**
See CA 13-16R; CANR 7; DLB 88
Gottesman, S. D.
See Kornbluth, C(yril) M.; Pohl, Frederik
Gottfried von Strassburg fl. c.1210- . **CMLC 10**
See DLB 138
Gould, Lois .... **CLC 4, 10**
See CA 77-80; CANR 29; MTCW 1
Gourmont, Remy (-Marie-Charles) de 1858-1915 .... **TCLC 17**
See CA 109; 150; MTCW 2
Govier, Katherine 1948- .... **CLC 51**
See CA 101; CANR 18, 40
Goyen, (Charles) William 1915-1983 ... **CLC 5, 8, 14, 40**
See AITN 2; CA 5-8R; 110; CANR 6, 71; DLB 2; DLBY 83; INT CANR-6
Goytisolo, Juan 1931- . **CLC 5, 10, 23; DAM MULT; HLC 1**
See CA 85-88; CANR 32, 61; HW 1, 2; MTCW 1, 2
Gozzano, Guido 1883-1916 .... **PC 10**
See CA 154; DLB 114
Gozzi, (Conte) Carlo 1720-1806 ... **NCLC 23**
Grabbe, Christian Dietrich 1801-1836 .... **NCLC 2**
See DLB 133
Grace, Patricia Frances 1937- .... **CLC 56**
See CA 176
Gracian y Morales, Baltasar 1601-1658 . **LC 15**
Gracq, Julien .... **CLC 11, 48**
See Poirier, Louis
See DLB 83
Grade, Chaim 1910-1982 .... **CLC 10**
See CA 93-96; 107
Graduate of Oxford, A
See Ruskin, John
Grafton, Garth
See Duncan, Sara Jeannette
Graham, John
See Phillips, David Graham
Graham, Jorie 1951- .... **CLC 48, 118**
See CA 111; CANR 63; DLB 120
Graham, R(obert) B(ontine) Cunninghame
See Cunninghame Graham, R(obert) B(ontine)
See DLB 98, 135, 174
Graham, Robert
See Haldeman, Joe (William)
Graham, Tom
See Lewis, (Harry) Sinclair
Graham, W(illiam) S(ydney) 1918-1986 ...... **CLC 29**
See CA 73-76; 118; DLB 20
Graham, Winston (Mawdsley) 1910- ... **CLC 23**
See CA 49-52; CANR 2, 22, 45, 66; DLB 77
Grahame, Kenneth 1859-1932 ..... **TCLC 64; DAB**
See CA 108; 136; CANR 80; CLR 5; DA3; DLB 34, 141, 178; MAICYA; MTCW 2; SATA 100; YABC 1
Granovsky, Timofei Nikolaevich 1813-1855 .... **NCLC 75**
See DLB 198

Grant, Skeeter
See Spiegelman, Art
Granville-Barker, Harley 1877-1946 . **TCLC 2; DAM DRAM**
See Barker, Harley Granville
See CA 104
Grass, Guenter (Wilhelm) 1927- . **CLC 1, 2, 4, 6, 11, 15, 22, 32, 49, 88; DA; DAB; DAC; DAM MST, NOV; WLC**
See CA 13-16R; CANR 20, 75; DA3; DLB 75, 124; MTCW 1, 2
Gratton, Thomas
See Hulme, T(homas) E(rnest)
Grau, Shirley Ann 1929- . **CLC 4, 9;SSC 15**
See CA 89-92; CANR 22, 69; DLB 2; INT CANR-22; MTCW 1
Gravel, Fern
See Hall, James Norman
Graver, Elizabeth 1964- .... **CLC 70**
See CA 135; CANR 71
Graves, Richard Perceval 1945- ..... **CLC 44**
See CA 65-68; CANR 9, 26, 51
Graves, Robert (von Ranke) 1895-1985 ...... **CLC 1, 2, 6, 11, 39, 44, 45; DAB; DAC; DAM MST, POET; PC 6**
See CA 5-8R; 117; CANR 5, 36; CDBLB 1914-1945; DA3; DLB 20, 100, 191; DLBD 18; DLBY 85; MTCW 1, 2; SATA 45
Graves, Valerie
See Bradley, Marion Zimmer
Gray, Alasdair (James) 1934- .... **CLC 41**
See CA 126; CANR 47, 69; DLB 194; INT 126; MTCW 1, 2
Gray, Amlin 1946- .... **CLC 29**
See CA 138
Gray, Francine du Plessix 1930- ... **CLC 22; DAM NOV**
See BEST 90:3; CA 61-64; CAAS 2; CANR 11, 33, 75, 81; INT CANR-11; MTCW 1, 2
Gray, John (Henry) 1866-1934 ..... **TCLC 19**
See CA 119; 162
Gray, Simon (James Holliday) 1936- ... **CLC 9, 14, 36**
See AITN 1; CA 21-24R; CAAS 3; CANR 32, 69; DLB 13; MTCW 1
Gray, Spalding 1941- ... **CLC 49, 112; DAM POP; DC 7**
See CA 128; CANR 74; MTCW 2
Gray, Thomas 1716-1771 ...... **LC 4, 40; DA; DAB; DAC; DAM MST; PC 2; WLC**
See CDBLB 1660-1789; DA3; DLB 109
Grayson, David
See Baker, Ray Stannard
Grayson, Richard (A.) 1951- .... **CLC 38**
See CA 85-88; CANR 14, 31, 57
Greeley, Andrew M(oran) 1928- .... **CLC 28; DAM POP**
See CA 5-8R; CAAS 7; CANR 7, 43, 69; DA3; MTCW 1, 2
Green, AnnaKatharine 1846-1935 ..... **TCLC 63**
See CA 112; 159; DLB 202
Green, Brian
See Card, Orson Scott
Green, Hannah
See Greenberg, Joanne (Goldenberg)
Green, Hannah 1927(?)-1996 .... **CLC 3**
See CA 73-76; CANR 59
Green, Henry 1905-1973 .... **CLC 2, 13, 97**
See Yorke, Henry Vincent
See CA 175; DLB 15
Green, Julian (Hartridge) 1900-1998
See Green, Julien
See CA 21-24R; 169; CANR 33; DLB 4, 72; MTCW 1
Green, Julien .... **CLC 3, 11, 77**
See Green, Julian (Hartridge)
See MTCW 2
Green, Paul (Eliot) 1894-1981 .... **CLC 25; DAM DRAM**
See AITN 1; CA 5-8R; 103; CANR 3; DLB 7, 9; DLBY 81
Greenberg, Ivan 1908-1973
See Rahv, Philip
See CA 85-88
Greenberg, Joanne (Goldenberg) 1932- ...... **CLC 7, 30**
See AAYA 12; CA 5-8R; CANR 14, 32, 69; SATA 25
Greenberg, Richard 1959(?)- .... **CLC 57**
See CA 138
Greene, Bette 1934- .... **CLC 30**
See AAYA 7; CA 53-56; CANR 4; CLR 2; JRDA; MAICYA; SAAS 16; SATA 8, 102
Greene, Gael .... **CLC 8**
See CA 13-16R; CANR 10
Greene, Graham (Henry) 1904-1991 ... **CLC 1, 3, 6, 9, 14, 18, 27, 37, 70, 72, 125; DA; DAB; DAC; DAM MST, NOV; SSC 29; WLC**
See AITN 2; CA 13-16R; 133; CANR 35, 61;CDBLB 1945-1960; DA3; DLB 13, 15, 77, 100, 162, 201, 204; DLBY 91; MTCW 1, 2; SATA 20
Greene, Robert 1558-1592 .... **LC 41**
See DLB 62, 167
Greer, Richard
See Silverberg, Robert
Gregor, Arthur 1923- .... **CLC 9**
See CA 25-28R; CAAS 10; CANR 11; SATA 36
Gregor, Lee
See Pohl, Frederik
Gregory, Isabella Augusta (Persse) 1852-1932 .... **TCLC 1**
See CA 104; DLB 10
Gregory, J. Dennis
See Williams, John A(lfred)
Grendon, Stephen
See Derleth, August (William)
Grenville, Kate 1950- .... **CLC 61**
See CA 118; CANR 53
Grenville, Pelham
See Wodehouse, P(elham) G(renville)
Greve, Felix Paul (Berthold Friedrich) 1879-1948
See Grove, Frederick Philip
See CA 104; 141, 175; CANR 79; DAC; DAM MST
Grey, Zane 1872-1939 . **TCLC 6;DAM POP**
See CA 104; 132; DA3; DLB 212; MTCW 1, 2
Grieg, (Johan) Nordahl(Brun) 1902-1943 ... **TCLC 10**
See CA 107
Grieve, C(hristopher) M(urray) 1892-1978 . **CLC 11, 19; DAM POET**
See MacDiarmid, Hugh; Pteleon
See CA 5-8R; 85-88; CANR 33; MTCW 1
Griffin, Gerald 1803-1840 .... **NCLC 7**
See DLB 159
Griffin, John Howard 1920-1980 .... **CLC 68**
See AITN 1; CA 1-4R; 101; CANR 2
Griffin, Peter 1942- .... **CLC 39**
See CA 136
Griffith, D(avid Lewelyn) W(ark) 1875(?)-1948 .... **TCLC 68**
See CA 119; 150; CANR 80
Griffith, Lawrence
See Griffith, D(avid Lewelyn) W(ark)
Griffiths, Trevor 1935- .... **CLC 13, 52**
See CA 97-100; CANR 45; DLB 13
Griggs, Sutton Elbert 1872-1930(?) ... **TCLC 77**
See CA 123; DLB 50
Grigson, Geoffrey (Edward Harvey) 1905-1985 .... **CLC 7, 39**
See CA 25-28R; 118; CANR 20, 33; DLB 27; MTCW 1, 2
Grillparzer, Franz 1791-1872 .... **NCLC 1; SSC 37**
See DLB 133
Grimble, Reverend Charles James
See Eliot, T(homas) S(tearns)
Grimke, Charlotte L(ottie) Forten 1837(?)-1914
See Forten, Charlotte L.
See BW 1; CA 117; 124; DAM MULT, POET
Grimm, Jacob Ludwig Karl 1785-1863 .... **NCLC 3, 77; SSC 36**
See DLB 90; MAICYA; SATA 22
Grimm, Wilhelm Karl 1786-1859 . **NCLC 3, 77; SSC 36**
See DLB 90; MAICYA; SATA 22
Grimmelshausen, Johann Jakob Christoffelvon 1621-1676 .... **LC 6**
See DLB 168
Grindel, Eugene 1895-1952
See Eluard, Paul
See CA 104
Grisham, John 1955- .... **CLC 84;DAM POP**
See AAYA 14; CA 138; CANR 47, 69; DA3; MTCW 2
Grossman, David 1954- .... **CLC 67**
See CA 138
Grossman, Vasily (Semenovich) 1905-1964 . **CLC 41**
See CA 124; 130; MTCW 1
Grove, Frederick Philip .... **TCLC 4**
See Greve, Felix Paul (Berthold Friedrich)
See DLB 92
Grubb
See Crumb, R(obert)
Grumbach, Doris (Isaac) 1918- ...... **CLC 13, 22, 64**
See CA 5-8R; CAAS 2; CANR 9, 42, 70; INT CANR-9; MTCW 2
Grundtvig, Nicolai Frederik Severin 1783-1872 .... **NCLC 1**
Grunge
See Crumb, R(obert)
Grunwald, Lisa 1959- .... **CLC 44**
See CA 120
Guare, John 1938- . **CLC 8, 14, 29, 67; DAM DRAM**
See CA 73-76; CANR 21, 69; DLB 7; MTCW 1, 2
Gudjonsson, Halldor Kiljan 1902-1998
See Laxness, Halldor
See CA 103; 164
Guenter, Erich
See Eich, Guenter
Guest, Barbara 1920- .... **CLC 34**
See CA 25-28R; CANR 11, 44, 84; DLB 5, 193
Guest, Edgar A(lbert) 1881-1959 . **TCLC 95**
See CA 112; 168
Guest, Judith (Ann) 1936- .... **CLC 8, 30; DAM NOV, POP**
See AAYA 7; CA 77-80; CANR 15, 75; DA3; INT CANR-15; MTCW 1, 2
Guevara, Che .... **CLC 87; HLC 1**
See Guevara (Serna), Ernesto
Guevara (Serna), Ernesto 1928-1967 ... **CLC 87; DAM MULT; HLC 1**
See Guevara, Che
See CA 127; 111; CANR 56; HW 1
Guicciardini, Francesco 1483-1540 ... **LC 49**
Guild, Nicholas M. 1944- .... **CLC 33**
See CA 93-96
Guillemin, Jacques
See Sartre, Jean-Paul
Guillen, Jorge 1893-1984 ..... **CLC 11; DAM**

MULT, POET; HLCS 1
See CA 89-92; 112; DLB 108; HW 1
Guillen, Nicolas (Cristobal) 1902-1989 . **CLC 48, 79; BLC 2; DAM MST, MULT, POET; HLC 1; PC 23**
See BW 2; CA 116; 125; 129; CANR 84; HW 1
Guillevic, (Eugene) 1907- .... **CLC 33**
See CA 93-96
Guillois
See Desnos, Robert
Guillois, Valentin
See Desnos, Robert
Guimaraes Rosa, Joao 1908-1967
See CA 175; HLCS 2
Guiney, LouiseImogen 1861-1920 . **TCLC 41**
See CA 160; DLB 54
Guiraldes, Ricardo (Guillermo) 1886-1927 . **TCLC 39**
See CA 131; HW 1; MTCW 1
Gumilev, Nikolai (Stepanovich) 1886-1921 . **TCLC 60**
See CA 165
Gunesekera, Romesh 1954- .... **CLC 91**
See CA 159
Gunn, Bill .... **CLC 5**
See Gunn, William Harrison
See DLB 38
Gunn, Thom(son William) 1929- . **CLC 3, 6, 18, 32, 81; DAM POET; PC 26**
See CA 17-20R; CANR 9, 33; CDBLB 1960 to Present; DLB 27; INT CANR-33; MTCW 1
Gunn, William Harrison 1934(?)-1989
See Gunn, Bill
See AITN 1; BW 1, 3; CA 13-16R; 128; CANR 12, 25, 76
Gunnars, Kristjana 1948- .... **CLC 69**
See CA 113; DLB 60
Gurdjieff, G(eorgei) I(vanovich) 1877(?)-1949 .... **TCLC 71**
See CA 157
Gurganus, Allan 1947- . **CLC 70;DAM POP**
See BEST 90:1; CA 135
Gurney, A(lbert) R(amsdell), Jr. 1930- . **CLC 32, 50, 54; DAM DRAM**
See CA 77-80; CANR 32, 64
Gurney, Ivor (Bertie) 1890-1937 .. **TCLC 33**
See CA 167
Gurney, Peter
See Gurney, A(lbert) R(amsdell), Jr.
Guro, Elena 1877-1913 .... **TCLC 56**
Gustafson, James M(oody) 1925- . **CLC 100**
See CA 25-28R; CANR 37
Gustafson, Ralph (Barker) 1909- ... **CLC 36**
See CA 21-24R; CANR 8, 45, 84; DLB 88
Gut, Gom
See Simenon, Georges (Jacques Christian)
Guterson, David 1956- .... **CLC 91**
See CA 132; CANR 73; MTCW 2
Guthrie, A(lfred) B(ertram),Jr. 1901-1991 .. **CLC 23**
See CA 57-60; 134; CANR 24; DLB 212; SATA 62; SATA-Obit 67
Guthrie, Isobel
See Grieve, C(hristopher) M(urray)
Guthrie, Woodrow Wilson 1912-1967
See Guthrie, Woody
See CA 113; 93-96
Guthrie, Woody .... **CLC 35**
See Guthrie, Woodrow Wilson
Gutierrez Najera, Manuel 1859-1895
See HLCS 2
Guy, Rosa (Cuthbert) 1928- .... **CLC 26**
See AAYA 4; BW 2; CA 17-20R; CANR 14, 34, 83; CLR 13; DLB 33; JRDA; MAICYA; SATA 14, 62
Gwendolyn
See Bennett, (Enoch) Arnold
H. D. .... **CLC 3, 8, 14, 31, 34, 73; PC 5**
See Doolittle, Hilda
H. de V.
See Buchan, John
Haavikko, Paavo Juhani 1931- . **CLC 18, 34**
See CA 106
Habbema, Koos
See Heijermans, Herman
Habermas, Juergen 1929- .... **CLC 104**
See CA 109; CANR 85
Habermas, Jurgen
See Habermas, Juergen
Hacker, Marilyn 1942- ..... **CLC 5, 9, 23, 72, 91; DAM POET**
See CA 77-80; CANR 68; DLB 120
Haeckel, Ernst Heinrich (Philipp August) 1834-1919 .... **TCLC 83**
See CA 157
Hafiz c. 1326-1389 .... **CMLC 34**
Hafiz c. 1326-1389(?) .... **CMLC 34**
Haggard, H(enry) Rider 1856-1925 .. **TCLC 11**
See CA 108; 148; DLB 70, 156, 174, 178; MTCW 2; SATA 16
Hagiosy, L.
See Larbaud, Valery (Nicolas)
Hagiwara Sakutaro 1886-1942 .... **TCLC 60; PC 18**
Haig, Fenil
See Ford, Ford Madox
Haig-Brown, Roderick (Langmere) 1908-1976 .... **CLC 21**
See CA 5-8R; 69-72; CANR 4, 38, 83; CLR 31; DLB 88; MAICYA; SATA 12
Hailey, Arthur 1920- .... **CLC 5; DAM NOV, POP**
See AITN 2; BEST 90:3; CA 1-4R; CANR 2, 36, 75; DLB 88; DLBY 82; MTCW 1, 2
Hailey, Elizabeth Forsythe 1938- .... **CLC 40**
See CA 93-96; CAAS 1; CANR 15, 48; INT CANR-15
Haines, John (Meade) 1924- .... **CLC 58**
See CA 17-20R; CANR 13, 34; DLB 212
Hakluyt, Richard 1552-1616 .... **LC 31**
Haldeman, Joe (William) 1943- ...... **CLC 61**
See Graham, Robert
See CA 53-56, 179; CAAE 179; CAAS 25; CANR 6, 70, 72; DLB 8; INT CANR-6
Hale, Sarah Josepha (Buell) 1788-1879 .... **NCLC 75**
See DLB 1, 42, 73
Haley, Alex(ander Murray Palmer) 1921-1992 . **CLC 8, 12, 76; BLC 2; DA; DAB; DAC; DAM MST, MULT, POP**
See AAYA 26; BW 2, 3; CA 77-80; 136; CANR 61; CDALBS; DA3; DLB 38; MTCW 1, 2
Haliburton, Thomas Chandler 1796-1865 ... **NCLC 15**
See DLB 11, 99
Hall, Donald (Andrew, Jr.) 1928- .... **CLC 1, 13, 37, 59; DAM POET**
See CA 5-8R; CAAS 7; CANR 2, 44, 64; DLB 5; MTCW 1; SATA 23, 97
Hall, Frederic Sauser
See Sauser-Hall, Frederic
Hall, James
See Kuttner, Henry
Hall, James Norman 1887-1951 ... **TCLC 23**
See CA 123; 173; SATA 21
Hall, Radclyffe
See Hall, (Marguerite) Radclyffe
See MTCW 2
Hall, (Marguerite) Radclyffe 1886-1943 ...... **TCLC 12**
See CA 110; 150; CANR 83; DLB 191
Hall, Rodney 1935- .... **CLC 51**
See CA 109; CANR 69
Halleck, Fitz-Greene 1790-1867 ... **NCLC 47**
See DLB 3
Halliday, Michael
See Creasey, John
Halpern, Daniel 1945- .... **CLC 14**
See CA 33-36R
Hamburger, Michael (Peter Leopold) 1924- .... **CLC 5, 14**
See CA 5-8R; CAAS 4; CANR 2, 47; DLB 27
Hamill, Pete 1935- .... **CLC 10**
See CA 25-28R; CANR 18, 71
Hamilton, Alexander 1755(?)-1804 .... **NCLC 49**
See DLB 37
Hamilton, Clive
See Lewis, C(live) S(taples)
Hamilton, Edmond 1904-1977 .... **CLC 1**
See CA 1-4R; CANR 3, 84; DLB 8
Hamilton, Eugene (Jacob) Lee
See Lee-Hamilton, Eugene (Jacob)
Hamilton, Franklin
See Silverberg, Robert
Hamilton, Gail
See Corcoran, Barbara
Hamilton, Mollie
See Kaye, M(ary) M(argaret)
Hamilton, (Anthony Walter) Patrick 1904-1962 .... **CLC 51**
See CA 176; 113; DLB 191
Hamilton, Virginia 1936- ...... **CLC 26;DAM MULT**
See AAYA 2, 21; BW 2, 3; CA 25-28R; CANR 20, 37, 73; CLR 1, 11, 40; DLB 33, 52; INT CANR-20; JRDA; MAICYA; MTCW 1, 2; SATA 4, 56, 79
Hammett, (Samuel) Dashiell 1894-1961 .... **CLC 3, 5, 10, 19, 47; SSC 17**
See AITN 1; CA 81-84; CANR 42; CDALB 1929-1941; DA3; DLBD 6; DLBY 96; MTCW 1, 2
Hammon, Jupiter 1711(?)-1800(?) . **NCLC 5; BLC 2; DAM MULT, POET; PC 16**
See DLB 31, 50
Hammond, Keith
See Kuttner, Henry
Hamner, Earl (Henry), Jr. 1923- .... **CLC 12**
See AITN 2; CA 73-76; DLB 6
Hampton, Christopher (James) 1946- . **CLC 4**
See CA 25-28R; DLB 13; MTCW 1
Hamsun, Knut .... **TCLC 2, 14, 49**
See Pedersen, Knut
Handke, Peter 1942- .. **CLC 5, 8, 10, 15, 38; DAM DRAM, NOV**
See CA 77-80; CANR 33, 75; DLB 85, 124; MTCW 1, 2
Handy, W(illiam) C(hristopher) 1873-1958 . **TCLC 97**
See BW 3; CA 121; 167
Hanley, James 1901-1985 .... **CLC 3, 5, 8, 13**
See CA 73-76; 117; CANR 36; DLB 191; MTCW 1
Hannah, Barry 1942- .... **CLC 23, 38, 90**
See CA 108; 110; CANR 43, 68; DLB 6; INT 110; MTCW 1
Hannon, Ezra
See Hunter, Evan
Hansberry, Lorraine (Vivian) 1930-1965 .... **CLC 17, 62; BLC 2; DA; DAB; DAC; DAM DRAM, MST, MULT;DC 2**
See AAYA 25; BW 1, 3; CA 109; 25-28R; CABS 3; CANR 58; CDALB 1941-1968; DA3; DLB 7, 38; MTCW 1, 2
Hansen, Joseph 1923- .... **CLC 38**

See CA 29-32R; CAAS 17; CANR 16, 44, 66; INT CANR-16
Hansen, Martin A(lfred) 1909-1955 .. **TCLC 32**
See CA 167
Hanson, Kenneth O(stlin) 1922- ..... **CLC 13**
See CA 53-56; CANR 7
Hardwick, Elizabeth (Bruce) 1916- ..... **CLC 13; DAM NOV**
See CA 5-8R; CANR 3, 32, 70; DA3; DLB 6; MTCW 1, 2
Hardy, Thomas 1840-1928 . **TCLC 4, 10, 18, 32, 48, 53, 72; DA; DAB; DAC; DAM MST, NOV, POET; PC 8; SSC 2;WLC**
See CA 104; 123; CDBLB 1890-1914; DA3; DLB 18, 19, 135; MTCW 1, 2
Hare, David 1947- .... **CLC 29, 58**
See CA 97-100; CANR 39; DLB 13; MTCW 1
Harewood, John
See Van Druten, John (William)
Harford, Henry
See Hudson, W(illiam) H(enry)
Hargrave, Leonie
See Disch, Thomas M(ichael)
Harjo, Joy 1951- ..... **CLC 83; DAM MULT; PC 27**
See CA 114; CANR 35, 67; DLB 120, 175; MTCW 2; NNAL
Harlan, Louis R(udolph) 1922- .... **CLC 34**
See CA 21-24R; CANR 25, 55, 80
Harling, Robert 1951(?)- .... **CLC 53**
See CA 147
Harmon, William (Ruth) 1938- .... **CLC 38**
See CA 33-36R; CANR 14, 32, 35; SATA 65
Harper, F. E. W.
See Harper, Frances Ellen Watkins
Harper, Frances E. W.
See Harper, Frances Ellen Watkins
Harper, Frances E. Watkins
See Harper, Frances Ellen Watkins
Harper, Frances Ellen
See Harper, Frances Ellen Watkins
Harper, Frances Ellen Watkins 1825-1911 .. **TCLC 14; BLC 2; DAM MULT, POET; PC 21**
See BW 1, 3; CA 111; 125; CANR 79; DLB 50
Harper, Michael S(teven) 1938- .. **CLC 7, 22**
See BW 1; CA 33-36R; CANR 24; DLB 41
Harper, Mrs. F. E. W.
See Harper, Frances Ellen Watkins
Harris, Christie (Lucy) Irwin 1907- .... **CLC 12**
See CA 5-8R; CANR 6, 83; CLR 47; DLB 88; JRDA; MAICYA; SAAS 10; SATA 6, 74
Harris, Frank 1856-1931 .... **TCLC 24**
See CA 109; 150; CANR 80; DLB 156, 197
Harris, George Washington 1814-1869 .... **NCLC 23**
See DLB 3, 11
Harris, Joel Chandler 1848-1908 .. **TCLC 2; SSC 19**
See CA 104; 137; CANR 80; CLR 49; DLB 11, 23, 42, 78, 91; MAICYA; SATA 100; YABC 1
Harris, John (Wyndham Parkes Lucas) Beynon 1903-1969
See Wyndham, John
See CA 102; 89-92; CANR 84
Harris, MacDonald .... **CLC 9**
See Heiney, Donald (William)
Harris, Mark 1922- .... **CLC 19**
See CA 5-8R; CAAS 3; CANR 2, 55, 83; DLB 2; DLBY 80
Harris, (Theodore) Wilson 1921- .... **CLC 25**
See BW 2, 3; CA 65-68; CAAS 16; CANR 11, 27, 69; DLB 117; MTCW 1
Harrison, Elizabeth Cavanna 1909-
See Cavanna, Betty
See CA 9-12R; CANR 6, 27, 85
Harrison, Harry (Max) 1925- .... **CLC 42**
See CA 1-4R; CANR 5, 21, 84; DLB 8; SATA 4
Harrison, James (Thomas) 1937- .... **CLC 6, 14, 33, 66; SSC 19**
See CA 13-16R; CANR 8, 51, 79; DLBY 82; INT CANR-8
Harrison, Jim
See Harrison, James (Thomas)
Harrison, Kathryn 1961- .... **CLC 70**
See CA 144; CANR 68
Harrison, Tony 1937- .... **CLC 43**
See CA 65-68; CANR 44; DLB 40; MTCW 1
Harriss, Will(ard Irvin) 1922- .... **CLC 34**
See CA 111
Harson, Sley
See Ellison, Harlan (Jay)
Hart, Ellis
See Ellison, Harlan (Jay)
Hart, Josephine 1942(?)- .... **CLC 70;DAM POP**
See CA 138; CANR 70
Hart, Moss 1904-1961 .... **CLC 66;DAM DRAM**
See CA 109; 89-92; CANR 84; DLB 7
Harte, (Francis) Bret(t) 1836(?)-1902 . **TCLC 1, 25; DA; DAC; DAM MST; SSC 8; WLC**
See CA 104; 140; CANR 80; CDALB 1865-1917; DA3; DLB 12, 64, 74, 79, 186; SATA 26
Hartley, L(eslie) P(oles) 1895-1972 .. **CLC 2, 22**
See CA 45-48; 37-40R; CANR 33; DLB 15, 139; MTCW 1, 2
Hartman, Geoffrey H. 1929- .... **CLC 27**
See CA 117; 125; CANR 79; DLB 67
Hartmann, Eduard von 1842-1906 ... **TCLC 97**
Hartmann, Sadakichi 1867-1944 .. **TCLC 73**
See CA 157; DLB 54
Hartmann von Aue c. 1160-c.1205 ... **CMLC 15**
See DLB 138
Hartmann von Aue 1170-1210 ..... **CMLC 15**
Haruf, Kent 1943- .... **CLC 34**
See CA 149
Harwood, Ronald 1934- .... **CLC 32; DAM DRAM, MST**
See CA 1-4R; CANR 4, 55; DLB 13
Hasegawa Tatsunosuke
See Futabatei, Shimei
Hasek, Jaroslav (Matej Frantisek) 1883-1923 .... **TCLC 4**
See CA 104; 129; MTCW 1, 2
Hass, Robert 1941- ... **CLC 18, 39, 99;PC 16**
See CA 111; CANR 30, 50, 71; DLB 105, 206; SATA 94
Hastings, Hudson
See Kuttner, Henry
Hastings, Selina .... **CLC 44**
Hathorne, John 1641-1717 .... **LC 38**
Hatteras, Amelia
See Mencken, H(enry) L(ouis)
Hatteras, Owen .... **TCLC 18**
See Mencken, H(enry) L(ouis); Nathan, George Jean
Hauptmann, Gerhart (Johann Robert) 1862-1946 .... **TCLC 4; DAM DRAM**
See CA 104; 153; DLB 66, 118
Havel, Vaclav 1936- . **CLC 25, 58, 65; DAM DRAM; DC 6**
See CA 104; CANR 36, 63; DA3; MTCW 1, 2
Haviaras, Stratis .... **CLC 33**
See Chaviaras, Strates
Hawes, Stephen 1475(?)-1523(?) .... **LC 17**
See DLB 132
Hawkes, John (Clendennin Burne, Jr.) 1925-1998 . **CLC 1, 2, 3, 4, 7, 9, 14, 15, 27, 49**
See CA 1-4R; 167; CANR 2, 47, 64; DLB 2, 7; DLBY 80, 98; MTCW 1, 2
Hawking, S. W.
See Hawking, Stephen W(illiam)
Hawking, Stephen W(illiam) 1942- ...... **CLC 63, 105**
See AAYA 13; BEST 89:1; CA 126; 129; CANR 48; DA3; MTCW 2
Hawkins, Anthony Hope
See Hope, Anthony
Hawthorne, Julian 1846-1934 .... **TCLC 25**
See CA 165
Hawthorne, Nathaniel 1804-1864 ...... **NCLC 39; DA; DAB; DAC; DAM MST, NOV; SSC 3, 29; WLC**
See AAYA 18;CDALB 1640-1865; DA3; DLB 1, 74; YABC 2
Haxton, Josephine Ayres 1921-
See Douglas, Ellen
See CA 115; CANR 41, 83
Hayaseca y Eizaguirre, Jorge
See Echegaray (y Eizaguirre), Jose (Maria Waldo)
Hayashi, Fumiko 1904-1951 .... **TCLC 27**
See CA 161; DLB 180
Haycraft, Anna 1932-
See Ellis, Alice Thomas
See CA 122; CANR 85; MTCW 2
Hayden, Robert E(arl) 1913-1980 .... **CLC 5, 9, 14, 37; BLC 2; DA; DAC; DAM MST, MULT, POET; PC 6**
See BW 1, 3; CA 69-72; 97-100; CABS 2; CANR 24, 75, 82; CDALB 1941-1968; DLB 5, 76; MTCW 1, 2; SATA 19; SATA-Obit 26
Hayford, J(oseph) E(phraim) Casely
See Casely-Hayford, J(oseph) E(phraim)
Hayman, Ronald 1932- .... **CLC 44**
See CA 25-28R; CANR 18, 50; DLB 155
Haywood, Eliza (Fowler) 1693(?)-1756 .. **LC 1, 44**
See DLB 39
Hazlitt, William 1778-1830 .... **NCLC 29**
See DLB 110, 158
Hazzard, Shirley 1931- .... **CLC 18**
See CA 9-12R; CANR 4, 70; DLBY 82; MTCW 1
Head, Bessie 1937-1986 ... **CLC 25, 67; BLC 2; DAM MULT**
See BW 2, 3; CA 29-32R; 119; CANR 25, 82; DA3; DLB 117; MTCW 1, 2
Headon, (Nicky) Topper 1956(?)- ... **CLC 30**
Heaney, Seamus (Justin) 1939- .... **CLC 5, 7, 14, 25, 37, 74, 91; DAB; DAM POET; PC 18; WLCS**
See CA 85-88; CANR 25, 48, 75; CDBLB 1960 to Present; DA3; DLB 40; DLBY 95; MTCW 1, 2
Hearn, (Patricio) Lafcadio (Tessima Carlos) 1850-1904 .... **TCLC 9**
See CA 105; 166; DLB 12, 78, 189
Hearne, Vicki 1946- .... **CLC 56**
See CA 139
Hearon, Shelby 1931- .... **CLC 63**
See AITN 2; CA 25-28R; CANR 18, 48
Heat-Moon, William Least .... **CLC 29**
See Trogdon, William (Lewis)
See AAYA 9
Hebbel, Friedrich 1813-1863 .... **NCLC 43; DAM DRAM**

See DLB 129
Hebert, Anne 1916- ... **CLC 4, 13, 29; DAC; DAM MST, POET**
See CA 85-88; CANR 69; DA3; DLB 68; MTCW 1, 2
Hecht, Anthony (Evan) 1923- .... **CLC 8, 13, 19; DAM POET**
See CA 9-12R; CANR 6; DLB 5, 169
Hecht, Ben 1894-1964 .... **CLC 8**
See CA 85-88; DLB 7, 9, 25, 26, 28, 86
Hedayat, Sadeq 1903-1951 .... **TCLC 21**
See CA 120
Hegel, Georg Wilhelm Friedrich 1770-1831 .... **NCLC 46**
See DLB 90
Heidegger, Martin 1889-1976 .... **CLC 24**
See CA 81-84; 65-68; CANR 34; MTCW 1, 2
Heidenstam, (Carl Gustaf) Verner von 1859-1940 .... **TCLC 5**
See CA 104
Heifner, Jack 1946- .... **CLC 11**
See CA 105; CANR 47
Heijermans, Herman 1864-1924 ... **TCLC 24**
See CA 123
Heilbrun, Carolyn G(old) 1926- ..... **CLC 25**
See CA 45-48; CANR 1, 28, 58
Heine, Heinrich 1797-1856 ...... **NCLC 4, 54; PC 25**
See DLB 90
Heinemann, Larry (Curtiss) 1944- . **CLC 50**
See CA 110; CAAS 21; CANR 31, 81; DLBD 9; INT CANR-31
Heiney, Donald (William) 1921-1993
See Harris, MacDonald
See CA 1-4R; 142; CANR 3, 58
Heinlein, Robert A(nson) 1907-1988 .... **CLC 1, 3, 8, 14, 26, 55; DAM POP**
See AAYA 17; CA 1-4R; 125; CANR 1, 20, 53; DA3; DLB 8; JRDA; MAICYA; MTCW 1, 2; SATA 9, 69; SATA-Obit 56
Helforth, John
See Doolittle, Hilda
Hellenhofferu, Vojtech Kapristian z
See Hasek, Jaroslav (Matej Frantisek)
Heller, Joseph 1923- . **CLC 1, 3, 5, 8, 11, 36, 63; DA; DAB; DAC; DAM MST, NOV, POP; WLC**
See AAYA 24; AITN 1; CA 5-8R; CABS 1; CANR 8, 42, 66; DA3; DLB 2, 28; DLBY 80; INT CANR-8; MTCW 1, 2
Hellman, Lillian (Florence) 1906-1984 . **CLC 2, 4, 8, 14, 18, 34, 44, 52; DAM DRAM; DC 1**
See AITN 1, 2; CA 13-16R; 112; CANR 33; DA3; DLB 7; DLBY 84; MTCW 1, 2
Helprin, Mark 1947- ...... **CLC 7, 10, 22, 32; DAM NOV, POP**
See CA 81-84; CANR 47, 64; CDALBS; DA3; DLBY 85; MTCW 1, 2
Helvetius, Claude-Adrien 1715-1771 . **LC 26**
Helyar, Jane Penelope Josephine 1933-
See Poole, Josephine
See CA 21-24R; CANR 10, 26; SATA 82
Hemans, Felicia 1793-1835 .... **NCLC 71**
See DLB 96
Hemingway, Ernest (Miller) 1899-1961 .... **CLC 1, 3, 6, 8, 10, 13, 19, 30, 34, 39, 41, 44, 50, 61, 80; DA; DAB; DAC; DAM MST, NOV; SSC 1, 25, 36; WLC**
See AAYA 19; CA 77-80; CANR 34; CDALB 1917-1929; DA3; DLB 4, 9, 102, 210; DLBD 1, 15, 16; DLBY 81, 87, 96, 98; MTCW 1, 2
Hempel, Amy 1951- .... **CLC 39**
See CA 118; 137; CANR 70; DA3; MTCW 2
Henderson, F. C.
See Mencken, H(enry) L(ouis)
Henderson, Sylvia
See Ashton-Warner, Sylvia (Constance)
Henderson, Zenna (Chlarson) 1917-1983 .... **SSC 29**
See CA 1-4R; 133; CANR 1, 84; DLB 8; SATA 5
Henkin, Joshua .... **CLC 119**
See CA 161
Henley, Beth .... **CLC 23; DC 6**
See Henley, Elizabeth Becker
See CABS 3; DLBY 86
Henley, Elizabeth Becker 1952-
See Henley, Beth
See CA 107; CANR 32, 73; DAM DRAM, MST; DA3; MTCW 1, 2
Henley, William Ernest 1849-1903 . **TCLC 8**
See CA 105; DLB 19
Hennissart, Martha
See Lathen, Emma
See CA 85-88; CANR 64
Henry, O. .... **TCLC 1, 19; SSC 5; WLC**
See Porter, William Sydney
Henry, Patrick 1736-1799 .... **LC 25**
Henryson, Robert 1430(?)-1506(?) ..... **LC 20**
See DLB 146
Henry VIII 1491-1547 .... **LC 10**
See DLB 132
Henschke, Alfred
See Klabund
Hentoff, Nat(han Irving) 1925- .... **CLC 26**
See AAYA 4; CA 1-4R; CAAS 6; CANR 5, 25, 77; CLR 1, 52; INT CANR-25; JRDA; MAICYA; SATA 42, 69; SATA-Brief 27
Heppenstall, (John) Rayner 1911-1981 . **CLC 10**
See CA 1-4R; 103; CANR 29
Heraclitus c. 540B.C.-c.450B.C. ... **CMLC 22**
See DLB 176
Herbert, Frank (Patrick) 1920-1986 .... **CLC 12, 23, 35, 44, 85; DAM POP**
See AAYA 21; CA 53-56; 118; CANR 5, 43; CDALBS; DLB 8; INT CANR-5; MTCW 1, 2; SATA 9, 37; SATA-Obit 47
Herbert, George 1593-1633 .... **LC 24; DAB; DAM POET; PC 4**
See CDBLB Before 1660; DLB 126
Herbert, Zbigniew 1924-1998 .... **CLC 9, 43; DAM POET**
See CA 89-92; 169; CANR 36, 74; MTCW 1
Herbst, Josephine (Frey) 1897-1969 .... **CLC 34**
See CA 5-8R; 25-28R; DLB 9
Heredia, Jose Maria 1803-1839
See HLCS 2
Hergesheimer,Joseph 1880-1954 ... **TCLC 11**
See CA 109; DLB 102, 9
Herlihy, James Leo 1927-1993 .... **CLC 6**
See CA 1-4R; 143; CANR 2
Hermogenes fl. c. 175- .... **CMLC 6**
Hernandez, Jose 1834-1886 .... **NCLC 17**
Herodotus c.484B.C.-429B.C. .... **CMLC 17**
See DLB 176
Herrick, Robert 1591-1674 .... **LC 13; DA; DAB; DAC; DAM MST, POP; PC 9**
See DLB 126
Herring, Guilles
See Somerville, Edith
Herriot, James 1916-1995 ..... **CLC 12;DAM POP**
See Wight, James Alfred
See AAYA 1; CA 148; CANR 40; MTCW 2; SATA 86
Herrmann, Dorothy 1941- .... **CLC 44**
See CA 107
Herrmann, Taffy
See Herrmann, Dorothy
Hersey, John (Richard) 1914-1993 .. **CLC 1, 2, 7, 9, 40, 81, 97; DAM POP**
See AAYA 29; CA 17-20R; 140; CANR 33; CDALBS; DLB 6, 185; MTCW 1, 2; SATA 25; SATA-Obit 76
Herzen, Aleksandr Ivanovich 1812-1870 ..... **NCLC 10, 61**
Herzl, Theodor 1860-1904 .... **TCLC 36**
See CA 168
Herzog, Werner 1942- .... **CLC 16**
See CA 89-92
Hesiod c. 8th cent. B.C.- .... **CMLC 5**
See DLB 176
Hesse, Hermann 1877-1962 . **CLC 1, 2, 3, 6, 11, 17, 25, 69; DA; DAB; DAC; DAM MST, NOV; SSC 9; WLC**
See CA 17-18; CAP 2; DA3; DLB 66; MTCW 1, 2; SATA 50
Hewes, Cady
See De Voto, Bernard (Augustine)
Heyen, William 1940- .... **CLC 13, 18**
See CA 33-36R; CAAS 9; DLB 5
Heyerdahl, Thor 1914- .... **CLC 26**
See CA 5-8R; CANR 5, 22, 66, 73; MTCW 1, 2; SATA 2, 52
Heym, Georg (Theodor Franz Arthur) 1887-1912 .... **TCLC 9**
See CA 106; 181
Heym, Stefan 1913- .... **CLC 41**
See CA 9-12R; CANR 4; DLB 69
Heyse, Paul (Johann Ludwigvon) 1830-1914 .... **TCLC 8**
See CA 104; DLB 129
Heyward, (Edwin) DuBose 1885-1940 .... **TCLC 59**
See CA 108; 157; DLB 7, 9, 45; SATA 21
Hibbert, Eleanor Alice Burford 1906-1993 . **CLC 7; DAM POP**
See BEST 90:4; CA 17-20R; 140; CANR 9, 28, 59; MTCW 2; SATA 2; SATA-Obit 74
Hichens, Robert (Smythe) 1864-1950 . **TCLC 64**
See CA 162; DLB 153
Higgins, George V(incent) 1939- . **CLC 4, 7, 10, 18**
See CA 77-80; CAAS 5; CANR 17, 51; DLB 2; DLBY 81, 98; INT CANR-17; MTCW 1
Higginson, Thomas Wentworth 1823-1911 .. **TCLC 36**
See CA 162; DLB 1, 64
Highet, Helen
See MacInnes, Helen (Clark)
Highsmith, (Mary) Patricia 1921-1995 . **CLC 2, 4, 14, 42, 102; DAM NOV, POP**
See CA 1-4R; 147; CANR 1, 20, 48, 62; DA3; MTCW 1, 2
Highwater, Jamake (Mamake) 1942(?)- ...... **CLC 12**
See AAYA 7; CA 65-68; CAAS 7; CANR 10, 34, 84; CLR 17; DLB 52; DLBY 85; JRDA; MAICYA; SATA 32, 69; SATA-Brief 30
Highway, Tomson 1951- .... **CLC 92; DAC;DAM MULT**
See CA 151; CANR 75; MTCW 2; NNAL
Higuchi, Ichiyo 1872-1896 .... **NCLC 49**
Hijuelos, Oscar 1951- .... **CLC 65; DAM MULT, POP; HLC 1**
See AAYA 25; BEST 90:1; CA 123; CANR 50, 75; DA3; DLB 145; HW 1, 2; MTCW 2
Hikmet, Nazim 1902(?)-1963 .... **CLC 40**
See CA 141; 93-96
Hildegard von Bingen 1098-1179 . **CMLC 20**
See DLB 148
Hildesheimer, Wolfgang 1916-1991 . **CLC 49**
See CA 101; 135; DLB 69, 124
Hill, Geoffrey (William) 1932- ..... **CLC 5, 8, 18, 45; DAM POET**

See CA 81-84; CANR 21; CDBLB 1960 to Present; DLB 40; MTCW 1
Hill, George Roy 1921- .... **CLC 26**
See CA 110; 122
Hill, John
See Koontz, Dean R(ay)
Hill, Susan (Elizabeth) 1942- ... **CLC 4, 113; DAB; DAM MST, NOV**
See CA 33-36R; CANR 29, 69; DLB 14, 139; MTCW 1
Hillerman, Tony 1925- . **CLC 62;DAM POP**
See AAYA 6; BEST 89:1; CA 29-32R; CANR 21, 42, 65; DA3; DLB 206; SATA 6
Hillesum, Etty 1914-1943 .... **TCLC 49**
See CA 137
Hilliard, Noel (Harvey) 1929- .... **CLC 15**
See CA 9-12R; CANR 7, 69
Hillis, Rick 1956- .... **CLC 66**
See CA 134
Hilton, James 1900-1954 .... **TCLC 21**
See CA 108; 169; DLB 34, 77; SATA 34
Himes, Chester (Bomar) 1909-1984 . **CLC 2, 4, 7, 18, 58, 108; BLC 2; DAM MULT**
See BW 2; CA 25-28R; 114; CANR 22; DLB 2, 76, 143; MTCW 1, 2
Hinde, Thomas .... **CLC 6, 11**
See Chitty, Thomas Willes
Hine, (William) Daryl 1936- .... **CLC 15**
See CA 1-4R; CAAS 15; CANR 1, 20; DLB 60
Hinkson, Katharine Tynan
See Tynan, Katharine
Hinojosa(-Smith), Rolando (R.) 1929-
See Hinojosa-Smith, Rolando
See CA 131; CAAS 16; CANR 62; DAM MULT; DLB 82; HLC 1; HW 1, 2; MTCW 2
Hinojosa-Smith, Rolando 1929-
See Hinojosa(-Smith), Rolando (R.)
See CAAS 16; HLC 1; MTCW 2
Hinton, S(usan) E(loise) 1950- . **CLC 30, 111; DA; DAB; DAC; DAM MST, NOV**
See AAYA 2; CA 81-84; CANR 32, 62; CDALBS; CLR 3, 23; DA3; JRDA; MAICYA; MTCW 1, 2; SATA 19, 58
Hippius, Zinaida .... **TCLC 9**
See Gippius, Zinaida (Nikolayevna)
Hiraoka, Kimitake 1925-1970
See Mishima, Yukio
See CA 97-100; 29-32R; DAM DRAM; DA3; MTCW 1, 2
Hirsch, E(ric) D(onald),Jr. 1928- .... **CLC 79**
See CA 25-28R; CANR 27, 51; DLB 67; INT CANR-27; MTCW 1
Hirsch, Edward 1950- .... **CLC 31, 50**
See CA 104; CANR 20, 42; DLB 120
Hitchcock, Alfred (Joseph) 1899-1980 . **CLC 16**
See AAYA 22; CA 159; 97-100; SATA 27; SATA-Obit 24
Hitler, Adolf 1889-1945 .... **TCLC 53**
See CA 117; 147
Hoagland, Edward 1932- .... **CLC 28**
See CA 1-4R; CANR 2, 31, 57; DLB 6; SATA 51
Hoban, Russell (Conwell) 1925- . **CLC 7, 25; DAM NOV**
See CA 5-8R; CANR 23, 37, 66; CLR 3; DLB 52; MAICYA; MTCW 1, 2; SATA 1, 40, 78
Hobbes, Thomas 1588-1679 .... **LC 36**
See DLB 151
Hobbs, Perry
See Blackmur, R(ichard) P(almer)
Hobson, Laura Z(ametkin) 1900-1986 . **CLC 7, 25**
See CA 17-20R; 118; CANR 55; DLB 28; SATA 52
Hochhuth, Rolf 1931- . **CLC 4, 11, 18; DAM DRAM**
See CA 5-8R; CANR 33, 75; DLB 124; MTCW 1, 2
Hochman, Sandra 1936- .... **CLC 3, 8**
See CA 5-8R; DLB 5
Hochwaelder, Fritz 1911-1986 .... **CLC 36; DAM DRAM**
See CA 29-32R; 120; CANR 42; MTCW 1
Hochwalder, Fritz
See Hochwaelder, Fritz
Hocking, Mary (Eunice) 1921- .... **CLC 13**
See CA 101; CANR 18, 40
Hodgins, Jack 1938- .... **CLC 23**
See CA 93-96; DLB 60
Hodgson, William Hope 1877(?)-1918 .... **TCLC 13**
See CA 111; 164; DLB 70, 153, 156, 178; MTCW 2
Hoeg, Peter 1957- .... **CLC 95**
See CA 151; CANR 75; DA3; MTCW 2
Hoffman, Alice 1952- ... **CLC 51;DAM NOV**
See CA 77-80; CANR 34, 66; MTCW 1, 2
Hoffman, Daniel (Gerard) 1923- ...... **CLC 6, 13, 23**
See CA 1-4R; CANR 4; DLB 5
Hoffman, Stanley 1944- .... **CLC 5**
See CA 77-80
Hoffman, William M(oses) 1939- .... **CLC 40**
See CA 57-60; CANR 11, 71
Hoffmann, E(rnst) T(heodor) A(madeus) 1776-1822 .... **NCLC 2; SSC 13**
See DLB 90; SATA 27
Hofmann, Gert 1931- .... **CLC 54**
See CA 128
Hofmannsthal, Hugo von 1874-1929 . **TCLC 11; DAM DRAM; DC 4**
See CA 106; 153; DLB 81, 118
Hogan, Linda 1947- .. **CLC 73;DAM MULT**
See CA 120; CANR 45, 73; DLB 175; NNAL
Hogarth, Charles
See Creasey, John
Hogarth, Emmett
See Polonsky, Abraham (Lincoln)
Hogg, James 1770-1835 .... **NCLC 4**
See DLB 93, 116, 159
Holbach, Paul Henri Thiry Baron 1723-1789 .... **LC 14**
Holberg, Ludvig 1684-1754 .... **LC 6**
Holden, Ursula 1921- .... **CLC 18**
See CA 101; CAAS 8; CANR 22
Holderlin, (Johann Christian) Friedrich 1770-1843 .... **NCLC 16; PC 4**
Holdstock, Robert
See Holdstock, Robert P.
Holdstock, Robert P. 1948- .... **CLC 39**
See CA 131; CANR 81
Holland, Isabelle 1920- .... **CLC 21**
See AAYA 11; CA 21-24R, 181; CAAE 181; CANR 10, 25, 47; CLR 57; JRDA; MAICYA; SATA 8, 70; SATA-Essay 103
Holland, Marcus
See Caldwell, (Janet Miriam) Taylor (Holland)
Hollander, John 1929- .... **CLC 2, 5, 8, 14**
See CA 1-4R; CANR 1, 52; DLB 5; SATA 13
Hollander, Paul
See Silverberg, Robert
Holleran, Andrew 1943(?)- .... **CLC 38**
See CA 144
Hollinghurst, Alan 1954- .... **CLC 55, 91**
See CA 114; DLB 207
Hollis, Jim
See Summers, Hollis (Spurgeon, Jr.)
Holly, Buddy 1936-1959 .... **TCLC 65**
Holmes, Gordon
See Shiel, M(atthew) P(hipps)
Holmes, John
See Souster, (Holmes) Raymond
Holmes, JohnClellon 1926-1988 ...... **CLC 56**
See CA 9-12R; 125; CANR 4; DLB 16
Holmes, Oliver Wendell,Jr. 1841-1935 .... **TCLC 77**
See CA 114
Holmes, Oliver Wendell 1809-1894 ... **NCLC 14, 81**
See CDALB 1640-1865; DLB 1, 189; SATA 34
Holmes, Raymond
See Souster, (Holmes) Raymond
Holt, Victoria
See Hibbert, Eleanor Alice Burford
Holub, Miroslav 1923-1998 .... **CLC 4**
See CA 21-24R; 169; CANR 10
Homer c. 8th cent. B.C.- . **CMLC 1, 16; DA; DAB; DAC; DAM MST, POET; PC 23; WLCS**
See DA3; DLB 176
Hongo, Garrett Kaoru 1951- .... **PC 23**
See CA 133; CAAS 22; DLB 120
Honig, Edwin 1919- .... **CLC 33**
See CA 5-8R; CAAS 8; CANR 4, 45; DLB 5
Hood, Hugh (John Blagdon) 1928- ...... **CLC 15, 28**
See CA 49-52; CAAS 17; CANR 1, 33; DLB 53
Hood, Thomas 1799-1845 .... **NCLC 16**
See DLB 96
Hooker, (Peter) Jeremy 1941- .... **CLC 43**
See CA 77-80; CANR 22; DLB 40
hooks, bell .... **CLC 94; BLCS**
See Watkins, Gloria
See MTCW 2
Hope, A(lec) D(erwent) 1907- ..... **CLC 3, 51**
See CA 21-24R; CANR 33, 74; MTCW 1, 2
Hope, Anthony 1863-1933 .... **TCLC 83**
See CA 157; DLB 153, 156
Hope, Brian
See Creasey, John
Hope, Christopher (David Tully) 1944- .... **CLC 52**
See CA 106; CANR 47; SATA 62
Hopkins, Gerard Manley 1844-1889 . **NCLC 17; DA; DAB; DAC; DAM MST, POET; PC 15; WLC**
See CDBLB 1890-1914; DA3; DLB 35, 57
Hopkins, John (Richard) 1931-1998 . **CLC 4**
See CA 85-88; 169
Hopkins, Pauline Elizabeth 1859-1930 .... **TCLC 28; BLC 2; DAM MULT**
See BW 2, 3; CA 141; CANR 82; DLB 50
Hopkinson, Francis 1737-1791 .... **LC 25**
See DLB 31
Hopley-Woolrich, Cornell George 1903-1968
See Woolrich, Cornell
See CA 13-14; CANR 58; CAP 1; MTCW 2
Horatio
See Proust, (Valentin-Louis-George-Eugene-) Marcel
Horgan, Paul (George VincentO'Shaughnessy) 1903-1995 ...... **CLC 9, 53;DAM NOV**
See CA 13-16R; 147; CANR 9, 35; DLB 212; DLBY 85; INT CANR-9; MTCW 1, 2; SATA 13; SATA-Obit 84
Horn, Peter
See Kuttner, Henry
Hornem, Horace Esq.
See Byron, George Gordon (Noel)
Horney, Karen (Clementine Theodore Danielsen) 1885-1952 .... **TCLC 71**

See CA 114; 165
Hornung, E(rnest) W(illiam) 1866-1921 ...... **TCLC 59**
See CA 108; 160; DLB 70
Horovitz, Israel (Arthur) 1939- ..... **CLC 56; DAM DRAM**
See CA 33-36R; CANR 46, 59; DLB 7
Horvath, Odon von
See Horvath, Oedoen von
See DLB 85, 124
Horvath, Oedoen von 1901-1938 .. **TCLC 45**
See Horvath, Odon von
See CA 118
Horwitz, Julius 1920-1986 .... **CLC 14**
See CA 9-12R; 119; CANR 12
Hospital, Janette Turner 1942- .... **CLC 42**
See CA 108; CANR 48
Hostos, E. M. de
See Hostos (y Bonilla), Eugenio Maria de
Hostos, Eugenio M. de
See Hostos (y Bonilla), Eugenio Maria de
Hostos, Eugenio Maria
See Hostos (y Bonilla), Eugenio Maria de
Hostos (y Bonilla), Eugenio Mariade 1839-1903 .... **TCLC 24**
See CA 123; 131; HW 1
Houdini
See Lovecraft, H(oward) P(hillips)
Hougan, Carolyn 1943- .... **CLC 34**
See CA 139
Household, Geoffrey (Edward West) 1900-1988 .... **CLC 11**
See CA 77-80; 126; CANR 58; DLB 87; SATA 14; SATA-Obit 59
Housman, A(lfred) E(dward) 1859-1936 ..... **TCLC 1, 10; DA; DAB; DAC; DAM MST, POET; PC 2; WLCS**
See CA 104; 125; DA3; DLB 19; MTCW 1, 2
Housman, Laurence 1865-1959 ...... **TCLC 7**
See CA 106; 155; DLB 10; SATA 25
Howard, Elizabeth Jane 1923- .... **CLC 7, 29**
See CA 5-8R; CANR 8, 62
Howard, Maureen 1930- .... **CLC 5, 14, 46**
See CA 53-56; CANR 31, 75; DLBY 83; INT CANR-31; MTCW 1, 2
Howard, Richard 1929- .... **CLC 7, 10, 47**
See AITN 1; CA 85-88; CANR 25, 80; DLB 5; INT CANR-25
Howard, Robert E(rvin) 1906-1936 .. **TCLC 8**
See CA 105; 157
Howard, Warren F.
See Pohl, Frederik
Howe, Fanny (Quincy) 1940- .... **CLC 47**
See CA 117; CAAS 27; CANR 70; SATA-Brief 52
Howe, Irving 1920-1993 .... **CLC 85**
See CA 9-12R; 141; CANR 21, 50; DLB 67; MTCW 1, 2
Howe, Julia Ward 1819-1910 .... **TCLC 21**
See CA 117; DLB 1, 189
Howe, Susan 1937- .... **CLC 72**
See CA 160; DLB 120
Howe, Tina 1937- .... **CLC 48**
See CA 109
Howell, James 1594(?)-1666 .... **LC 13**
See DLB 151
Howells, W. D.
See Howells, William Dean
Howells, William D.
See Howells, William Dean
Howells, William Dean 1837-1920 . **TCLC 7, 17, 41; SSC 36**
See CA 104; 134; CDALB 1865-1917; DLB 12, 64, 74, 79, 189; MTCW 2
Howes, Barbara 1914-1996 .... **CLC 15**
See CA 9-12R; 151; CAAS 3; CANR 53; SATA 5
Hrabal, Bohumil 1914-1997 ...... **CLC 13, 67**
See CA 106; 156; CAAS 12; CANR 57
Hroswitha of Gandersheim c. 935-c.1002 .... **CMLC 29**
See DLB 148
Hsun, Lu
See Lu Hsun
Hubbard, L(afayette) Ron(ald) 1911-1986 .. **CLC 43; DAM POP**
See CA 77-80; 118; CANR 52; DA3; MTCW 2
Huch, Ricarda (Octavia) 1864-1947 .. **TCLC 13**
See CA 111; DLB 66
Huddle, David 1942- .... **CLC 49**
See CA 57-60; CAAS 20; DLB 130
Hudson, Jeffrey
See Crichton, (John) Michael
Hudson, W(illiam) H(enry) 1841-1922 .... **TCLC 29**
See CA 115; DLB 98, 153, 174; SATA 35
Hueffer, Ford Madox
See Ford, Ford Madox
Hughart, Barry 1934- .... **CLC 39**
See CA 137
Hughes, Colin
See Creasey, John
Hughes, David (John) 1930- .... **CLC 48**
See CA 116; 129; DLB 14
Hughes, Edward James
See Hughes, Ted
See DAM MST, POET; DA3
Hughes, (James) Langston 1902-1967 . **CLC 1, 5, 10, 15, 35, 44, 108; BLC 2; DA; DAB; DAC; DAM DRAM, MST, MULT, POET; DC 3; PC 1; SSC 6; WLC**
See AAYA 12; BW 1, 3; CA 1-4R; 25-28R; CANR 1, 34, 82; CDALB 1929-1941; CLR 17; DA3; DLB 4, 7, 48, 51, 86; JRDA; MAICYA; MTCW 1, 2; SATA 4, 33
Hughes, Richard (Arthur Warren) 1900-1976 .... **CLC 1, 11; DAM NOV**
See CA 5-8R; 65-68; CANR 4; DLB 15, 161; MTCW 1; SATA 8; SATA-Obit 25
Hughes, Ted 1930-1998 . **CLC 2, 4, 9, 14, 37, 119; DAB; DAC; PC 7**
See Hughes, Edward James
See CA 1-4R; 171; CANR 1, 33, 66; CLR 3; DLB 40, 161; MAICYA; MTCW 1, 2; SATA 49; SATA-Brief 27; SATA-Obit 107
Hugo, Richard F(ranklin) 1923-1982 .. **CLC 6, 18, 32; DAM POET**
See CA 49-52; 108; CANR 3; DLB 5, 206
Hugo, Victor (Marie) 1802-1885 ... **NCLC 3, 10, 21; DA; DAB; DAC; DAM DRAM, MST, NOV, POET; PC 17; WLC**
See AAYA 28; DA3; DLB 119, 192; SATA 47
Huidobro, Vicente
See Huidobro Fernandez, Vicente Garcia
Huidobro Fernandez, Vicente Garcia 1893-1948 .... **TCLC 31**
See CA 131; HW 1
Hulme, Keri 1947- .... **CLC 39**
See CA 125; CANR 69; INT 125
Hulme, T(homas) E(rnest) 1883-1917 .... **TCLC 21**
See CA 117; DLB 19
Hume, David 1711-1776 .... **LC 7**
See DLB 104
Humphrey, William 1924-1997 .... **CLC 45**
See CA 77-80; 160; CANR 68; DLB 212
Humphreys, Emyr Owen 1919- ...... **CLC 47**
See CA 5-8R; CANR 3, 24; DLB 15
Humphreys, Josephine 1945- .... **CLC 34, 57**
See CA 121; 127; INT 127
Huneker, James Gibbons 1857-1921 . **TCLC 65**
See DLB 71
Hungerford, Pixie
See Brinsmead, H(esba) F(ay)
Hunt, E(verette) Howard,(Jr.) 1918- . **CLC 3**
See AITN 1; CA 45-48; CANR 2, 47
Hunt, Francesca
See Holland, Isabelle
Hunt, Kyle
See Creasey, John
Hunt, (James Henry) Leigh 1784-1859 .... **NCLC 1, 70; DAM POET**
See DLB 96, 110, 144
Hunt, Marsha 1946- .... **CLC 70**
See BW 2, 3; CA 143; CANR 79
Hunt, Violet 1866(?)-1942 .... **TCLC 53**
See DLB 162, 197
Hunter, E. Waldo
See Sturgeon, Theodore (Hamilton)
Hunter, Evan 1926- . **CLC 11, 31;DAM POP**
See CA 5-8R; CANR 5, 38, 62; DLBY 82; INT CANR-5; MTCW 1; SATA 25
Hunter, Kristin (Eggleston) 1931- .. **CLC 35**
See AITN 1; BW 1; CA 13-16R; CANR 13; CLR 3; DLB 33; INT CANR-13; MAICYA; SAAS 10; SATA 12
Hunter, Mary
See Austin, Mary (Hunter)
Hunter, Mollie 1922- .... **CLC 21**
See McIlwraith, Maureen Mollie Hunter
See AAYA 13; CANR 37, 78; CLR 25; DLB 161; JRDA; MAICYA; SAAS 7; SATA 54, 106
Hunter, Robert (?)-1734 .... **LC 7**
Hurston, Zora Neale 1903-1960 . **CLC 7, 30, 61; BLC 2; DA; DAC; DAM MST, MULT, NOV; SSC 4; WLCS**
See AAYA 15; BW 1, 3; CA 85-88; CANR 61; CDALBS; DA3; DLB 51, 86; MTCW 1, 2
Huston, John (Marcellus) 1906-1987 ... **CLC 20**
See CA 73-76; 123; CANR 34; DLB 26
Hustvedt, Siri 1955- .... **CLC 76**
See CA 137
Hutten, Ulrich von 1488-1523 .... **LC 16**
See DLB 179
Huxley, Aldous (Leonard) 1894-1963 .. **CLC 1, 3, 4, 5, 8, 11, 18, 35, 79; DA; DAB; DAC; DAM MST, NOV; WLC**
See AAYA 11; CA 85-88; CANR 44; CDBLB 1914-1945; DA3; DLB 36, 100, 162, 195; MTCW 1, 2; SATA 63
Huxley, T(homas) H(enry) 1825-1895 .... **NCLC 67**
See DLB 57
Huysmans, Joris-Karl 1848-1907 .. **TCLC 7, 69**
See CA 104; 165; DLB 123
Hwang, David Henry 1957- . **CLC 55; DAM DRAM; DC 4**
See CA 127; 132; CANR 76; DA3; DLB 212; INT 132; MTCW 2
Hyde, Anthony 1946- .... **CLC 42**
See CA 136
Hyde, Margaret O(ldroyd) 1917- .... **CLC 21**
See CA 1-4R; CANR 1, 36; CLR 23; JRDA; MAICYA; SAAS 8; SATA 1, 42, 76
Hynes, James 1956(?)- .... **CLC 65**
See CA 164
Hypatia c. 370-415 .... **CMLC 35**
Ian, Janis 1951- .... **CLC 21**
See CA 105
Ibanez, Vicente Blasco
See Blasco Ibanez, Vicente

Ibarbourou, Juana de 1895-1979
See HLCS 2; HW 1
Ibarguengoitia, Jorge 1928-1983 ..... **CLC 37**
See CA 124; 113; HW 1
Ibsen, Henrik (Johan) 1828-1906 .. **TCLC 2, 8, 16, 37, 52; DA; DAB; DAC; DAM DRAM, MST; DC 2; WLC**
See CA 104; 141; DA3
Ibuse, Masuji 1898-1993 .... **CLC 22**
See CA 127; 141; DLB 180
Ichikawa, Kon 1915- .... **CLC 20**
See CA 121
Idle, Eric 1943- .... **CLC 21**
See Monty Python
See CA 116; CANR 35
Ignatow, David 1914-1997 . **CLC 4, 7, 14, 40**
See CA 9-12R; 162; CAAS 3; CANR 31, 57; DLB 5
Ignotus
See Strachey, (Giles) Lytton
Ihimaera, Witi 1944- .... **CLC 46**
See CA 77-80
Ilf, Ilya .... **TCLC 21**
See Fainzilberg, Ilya Arnoldovich
Illyes, Gyula 1902-1983 .... **PC 16**
See CA 114; 109
Immermann, Karl (Lebrecht) 1796-1840 .... **NCLC 4, 49**
See DLB 133
Ince, Thomas H. 1882-1924 .... **TCLC 89**
Inchbald, Elizabeth 1753-1821 ..... **NCLC 62**
See DLB 39, 89
Inclan, Ramon (Maria) del Valle
See Valle-Inclan, Ramon (Maria) del
Infante, G(uillermo) Cabrera
See Cabrera Infante, G(uillermo)
Ingalls, Rachel (Holmes) 1940- .... **CLC 42**
See CA 123; 127
Ingamells, Reginald Charles
See Ingamells, Rex
Ingamells, Rex 1913-1955 .... **TCLC 35**
See CA 167
Inge, William (Motter) 1913-1973 ... **CLC 1, 8, 19; DAM DRAM**
See CA 9-12R; CDALB 1941-1968; DA3; DLB 7; MTCW 1, 2
Ingelow, Jean 1820-1897 .... **NCLC 39**
See DLB 35, 163; SATA 33
Ingram, Willis J.
See Harris, Mark
Innaurato, Albert (F.) 1948(?)- . **CLC 21, 60**
See CA 115; 122; CANR 78; INT 122
Innes, Michael
See Stewart, J(ohn) I(nnes) M(ackintosh)
Innis, Harold Adams 1894-1952 ... **TCLC 77**
See CA 181; DLB 88
Ionesco, Eugene 1909-1994 .. **CLC 1, 4, 6, 9, 11, 15, 41, 86; DA; DAB; DAC; DAM DRAM, MST; WLC**
See CA 9-12R; 144; CANR 55; DA3; MTCW 1, 2; SATA 7; SATA-Obit 79
Iqbal, Muhammad 1873-1938 .... **TCLC 28**
Ireland, Patrick
See O'Doherty, Brian
Iron, Ralph
See Schreiner, Olive (Emilie Albertina)
Irving, John (Winslow) 1942- .. **CLC 13, 23, 38, 112; DAM NOV, POP**
See AAYA 8; BEST 89:3; CA 25-28R; CANR 28, 73; DA3; DLB 6; DLBY 82; MTCW 1, 2
Irving, Washington 1783-1859 . **NCLC 2, 19; DA; DAB; DAC; DAM MST; SSC 37; WLC**
See CDALB 1640-1865; DA3; DLB 3, 11, 30, 59, 73, 74, 186; YABC 2
Irwin, P. K.
See Page, P(atricia) K(athleen)
Isaacs, Jorge Ricardo 1837-1895 . **NCLC 70**
Isaacs, Susan 1943- .... **CLC 32;DAM POP**
See BEST 89:1; CA 89-92; CANR 20, 41, 65; DA3; INT CANR-20; MTCW 1, 2
Isherwood, Christopher (William Bradshaw) 1904-1986 . **CLC 1, 9, 11, 14, 44; DAM DRAM, NOV**
See CA 13-16R; 117; CANR 35; DA3; DLB 15, 195; DLBY 86; MTCW 1, 2
Ishiguro, Kazuo 1954- . **CLC 27, 56, 59, 110; DAM NOV**
See BEST 90:2; CA 120; CANR 49; DA3; DLB 194; MTCW 1, 2
Ishikawa, Hakuhin
See Ishikawa, Takuboku
Ishikawa, Takuboku 1886(?)-1912 ..... **TCLC 15; DAM POET; PC 10**
See CA 113; 153
Iskander, Fazil 1929- .... **CLC 47**
See CA 102
Isler, Alan (David) 1934- .... **CLC 91**
See CA 156
Ivan IV 1530-1584 .... **LC 17**
Ivanov, Vyacheslav Ivanovich 1866-1949 ..... **TCLC 33**
See CA 122
Ivask, Ivar Vidrik 1927-1992 .... **CLC 14**
See CA 37-40R; 139; CANR 24
Ives, Morgan
See Bradley, Marion Zimmer
Izumi Shikibu c. 973-c. 1034 .... **CMLC 33**
J. R. S.
See Gogarty, Oliver St. John
Jabran, Kahlil
See Gibran, Kahlil
Jabran, Khalil
See Gibran, Kahlil
Jackson, Daniel
See Wingrove, David (John)
Jackson, Jesse 1908-1983 .... **CLC 12**
See BW 1; CA 25-28R; 109; CANR 27; CLR 28; MAICYA; SATA 2, 29; SATA-Obit 48
Jackson, Laura (Riding) 1901-1991
See Riding, Laura
See CA 65-68; 135; CANR 28; DLB 48
Jackson, Sam
See Trumbo, Dalton
Jackson, Sara
See Wingrove, David (John)
Jackson, Shirley 1919-1965 ...... **CLC 11, 60, 87; DA; DAC; DAM MST; SSC 9; WLC**
See AAYA 9; CA 1-4R; 25-28R; CANR 4, 52; CDALB 1941-1968; DA3; DLB 6; MTCW 2; SATA 2
Jacob, (Cyprien-)Max 1876-1944 ... **TCLC 6**
See CA 104
Jacobs, Harriet A(nn) 1813(?)-1897 .. **NCLC 67**
Jacobs, Jim 1942- .... **CLC 12**
See CA 97-100; INT 97-100
Jacobs, W(illiam) W(ymark) 1863-1943 ...... **TCLC 22**
See CA 121; 167; DLB 135
Jacobsen, Jens Peter 1847-1885 ... **NCLC 34**
Jacobsen, Josephine 1908- .... **CLC 48,102**
See CA 33-36R; CAAS 18; CANR 23, 48
Jacobson, Dan 1929- .... **CLC 4, 14**
See CA 1-4R; CANR 2, 25, 66; DLB 14, 207; MTCW 1
Jacqueline
See Carpentier (y Valmont), Alejo
Jagger, Mick 1944- .... **CLC 17**
Jahiz, al- c. 780-c. 869 .... **CMLC 25**
Jakes, John (William) 1932- . **CLC 29; DAM NOV, POP**
See AAYA 32; BEST 89:4; CA 57-60; CANR 10, 43, 66; DA3; DLBY 83; INT CANR-10; MTCW 1, 2; SATA 62
James, Andrew
See Kirkup, James
James, C(yril) L(ionel) R(obert) 1901-1989 .... **CLC 33; BLCS**
See BW 2; CA 117; 125; 128; CANR 62; DLB 125; MTCW 1
James, Daniel (Lewis) 1911-1988
See Santiago, Danny
See CA 174; 125
James, Dynely
See Mayne, William (James Carter)
James, Henry Sr. 1811-1882 .... **NCLC 53**
James, Henry 1843-1916 .... **TCLC 2, 11, 24, 40, 47, 64; DA; DAB; DAC; DAM MST, NOV; SSC 8, 32; WLC**
See CA 104; 132; CDALB 1865-1917; DA3; DLB 12, 71, 74, 189; DLBD 13; MTCW 1, 2
James, M. R.
See James, Montague (Rhodes)
See DLB 156
James, Montague (Rhodes) 1862-1936 .... **TCLC 6; SSC 16**
See CA 104; DLB 201
James, P. D. 1920- .... **CLC 18, 46, 122**
See White, Phyllis Dorothy James
See BEST 90:2; CDBLB 1960 to Present; DLB 87; DLBD 17
James, Philip
See Moorcock, Michael (John)
James, William 1842-1910 ...... **TCLC 15, 32**
See CA 109
James I 1394-1437 .... **LC 20**
Jameson, Anna 1794-1860 .... **NCLC 43**
See DLB 99, 166
Jami, Nur al-Din 'Abd al-Rahman 1414-1492 .... **LC 9**
Jammes, Francis 1868-1938 .... **TCLC 75**
Jandl, Ernst 1925- .... **CLC 34**
Janowitz, Tama 1957- .. **CLC 43;DAM POP**
See CA 106; CANR 52
Japrisot, Sebastien 1931- .... **CLC 90**
Jarrell, Randall 1914-1965 .. **CLC 1, 2, 6, 9, 13, 49; DAM POET**
See CA 5-8R; 25-28R; CABS 2; CANR 6, 34; CDALB 1941-1968; CLR 6; DLB 48, 52; MAICYA; MTCW 1, 2; SATA 7
Jarry, Alfred 1873-1907 . **TCLC 2, 14; DAM DRAM; SSC 20**
See CA 104; 153; DA3; DLB 192
Jaynes, Roderick
See Coen, Ethan
Jeake, Samuel, Jr.
See Aiken, Conrad (Potter)
Jean Paul 1763-1825 .... **NCLC 7**
Jefferies, (John) Richard 1848-1887 . **NCLC 47**
See DLB 98, 141; SATA 16
Jeffers, (John) Robinson 1887-1962 . **CLC 2, 3, 11, 15, 54; DA; DAC; DAM MST, POET; PC 17; WLC**
See CA 85-88; CANR 35; CDALB 1917-1929; DLB 45, 212; MTCW 1, 2
Jefferson, Janet
See Mencken, H(enry) L(ouis)
Jefferson,Thomas 1743-1826 .... **NCLC 11**
See CDALB 1640-1865; DA3; DLB 31
Jeffrey, Francis 1773-1850 .... **NCLC 33**
See DLB 107
Jelakowitch, Ivan
See Heijermans, Herman
Jellicoe, (Patricia) Ann 1927- .... **CLC 27**
See CA 85-88; DLB 13

Jen, Gish .... **CLC 70**
See Jen, Lillian

Jen, Lillian 1956(?)-
See Jen, Gish
See CA 135

Jenkins, (John) Robin 1912- .... **CLC 52**
See CA 1-4R; CANR 1; DLB 14

Jennings, Elizabeth (Joan) 1926- ..... **CLC 5, 14**
See CA 61-64; CAAS 5; CANR 8, 39, 66; DLB 27; MTCW 1; SATA 66

Jennings, Waylon 1937- .... **CLC 21**

Jensen, Johannes V. 1873-1950 ..... **TCLC 41**
See CA 170

Jensen, Laura (Linnea) 1948- .... **CLC 37**
See CA 103

Jerome, Jerome K(lapka) 1859-1927 . **TCLC 23**
See CA 119; 177; DLB 10, 34, 135

Jerrold, Douglas William 1803-1857 . **NCLC 2**
See DLB 158, 159

Jewett, (Theodora) Sarah Orne 1849-1909 . **TCLC 1, 22; SSC 6**
See CA 108; 127; CANR 71; DLB 12, 74; SATA 15

Jewsbury, Geraldine(Endsor) 1812-1880 ..... **NCLC 22**
See DLB 21

Jhabvala, Ruth Prawer 1927- . **CLC 4, 8, 29, 94; DAB; DAM NOV**
See CA 1-4R; CANR 2, 29, 51, 74; DLB 139, 194; INT CANR-29; MTCW 1, 2

Jibran, Kahlil
See Gibran, Kahlil

Jibran, Khalil
See Gibran, Kahlil

Jiles, Paulette 1943- .... **CLC 13, 58**
See CA 101; CANR 70

Jimenez (Mantecon), Juan Ramon 1881-1958 .... **TCLC 4; DAM MULT, POET; HLC 1; PC 7**
See CA 104; 131; CANR 74; DLB 134; HW 1; MTCW 1, 2

Jimenez, Ramon
See Jimenez (Mantecon), Juan Ramon

Jimenez Mantecon, Juan
See Jimenez (Mantecon), Juan Ramon

Jin, Ha 1956- .... **CLC 109**
See CA 152

Joel, Billy .... **CLC 26**
See Joel, William Martin

Joel, William Martin 1949-
See Joel, Billy
See CA 108

John, Saint 7th cent. - .... **CMLC 27**

John of the Cross, St. 1542-1591 .... **LC 18**

Johnson, B(ryan) S(tanley William) 1933-1973 .... **CLC 6, 9**
See CA 9-12R; 53-56; CANR 9; DLB 14, 40

Johnson, Benj. F. of Boo
See Riley, James Whitcomb

Johnson, Benjamin F. of Boo
See Riley, James Whitcomb

Johnson, Charles (Richard) 1948- ... **CLC 7, 51, 65; BLC 2; DAM MULT**
See BW 2, 3; CA 116; CAAS 18; CANR 42, 66, 82; DLB 33; MTCW 2

Johnson, Denis 1949- .... **CLC 52**
See CA 117; 121; CANR 71; DLB 120

Johnson, Diane 1934- .... **CLC 5, 13, 48**
See CA 41-44R; CANR 17, 40, 62; DLBY 80; INT CANR-17; MTCW 1

Johnson, Eyvind (Olof Verner) 1900-1976 .. **CLC 14**
See CA 73-76; 69-72; CANR 34

Johnson, J. R.
See James, C(yril) L(ionel) R(obert)

Johnson, James Weldon 1871-1938 ... **TCLC 3, 19; BLC 2; DAM MULT, POET; PC 24**
See BW 1, 3; CA 104; 125; CANR 82; CDALB 1917-1929; CLR 32; DA3; DLB 51; MTCW 1, 2; SATA 31

Johnson, Joyce 1935- .... **CLC 58**
See CA 125; 129

Johnson, Judith (Emlyn) 1936- .. **CLC 7, 15**
See Sherwin, Judith Johnson
See CA 25-28R, 153; CANR 34

Johnson, Lionel (Pigot) 1867-1902 .... **TCLC 19**
See CA 117; DLB 19

Johnson, Marguerite (Annie)
See Angelou, Maya

Johnson, Mel
See Malzberg, Barry N(athaniel)

Johnson, Pamela Hansford 1912-1981 . **CLC 1, 7, 27**
See CA 1-4R; 104; CANR 2, 28; DLB 15; MTCW 1, 2

Johnson, Robert 1911(?)-1938 ...... **TCLC 69**
See BW 3; CA 174

Johnson, Samuel 1709-1784 . **LC 15, 52; DA; DAB; DAC; DAM MST; WLC**
See CDBLB 1660-1789; DLB 39, 95, 104, 142

Johnson, Uwe 1934-1984 . **CLC 5, 10, 15, 40**
See CA 1-4R; 112; CANR 1, 39; DLB 75; MTCW 1

Johnston, George (Benson) 1913- ... **CLC 51**
See CA 1-4R; CANR 5, 20; DLB 88

Johnston, Jennifer 1930- .... **CLC 7**
See CA 85-88; DLB 14

Jolley, (Monica) Elizabeth 1923- ... **CLC 46; SSC 19**
See CA 127; CAAS 13; CANR 59

Jones, Arthur Llewellyn 1863-1947
See Machen, Arthur
See CA 104; 179

Jones, D(ouglas) G(ordon) 1929- .... **CLC 10**
See CA 29-32R; CANR 13; DLB 53

Jones, David (Michael) 1895-1974 ... **CLC 2, 4, 7, 13, 42**
See CA 9-12R; 53-56; CANR 28; CDBLB 1945-1960; DLB 20, 100; MTCW 1

Jones, David Robert 1947-
See Bowie, David
See CA 103

Jones, Diana Wynne 1934- .... **CLC 26**
See AAYA 12; CA 49-52; CANR 4, 26, 56; CLR 23; DLB 161; JRDA; MAICYA; SAAS 7; SATA 9, 70, 108

Jones, Edward P. 1950- .... **CLC 76**
See BW 2, 3; CA 142; CANR 79

Jones, Gayl 1949- . **CLC 6, 9; BLC 2; DAM MULT**
See BW 2, 3; CA 77-80; CANR 27, 66; DA3; DLB 33; MTCW 1, 2

Jones, James 1921-1977 .... **CLC 1, 3, 10, 39**
See AITN 1, 2; CA 1-4R; 69-72; CANR 6; DLB 2, 143; DLBD 17; DLBY 98; MTCW 1

Jones, John J.
See Lovecraft, H(oward) P(hillips)

Jones, LeRoi .... **CLC 1, 2, 3, 5, 10, 14**
See Baraka, Amiri
See MTCW 2

Jones, Louis B. 1953- .... **CLC 65**
See CA 141; CANR 73

Jones, Madison (Percy,Jr.) 1925- ...... **CLC 4**
See CA 13-16R; CAAS 11; CANR 7, 54, 83; DLB 152

Jones, Mervyn 1922- .... **CLC 10, 52**
See CA 45-48; CAAS 5; CANR 1; MTCW 1

Jones, Mick 1956(?)- .... **CLC 30**

Jones, Nettie (Pearl) 1941- .... **CLC 34**
See BW 2; CA 137; CAAS 20

Jones, Preston 1936-1979 .... **CLC 10**
See CA 73-76; 89-92; DLB 7

Jones, Robert F(rancis) 1934- .... **CLC 7**
See CA 49-52; CANR 2, 61

Jones, Rod 1953- .... **CLC 50**
See CA 128

Jones, Terence Graham Parry 1942- ... **CLC 21**
See Jones, Terry; Monty Python
See CA 112; 116; CANR 35; INT 116

Jones, Terry
See Jones, Terence Graham Parry
See SATA 67; SATA-Brief 51

Jones, Thom 1945(?)- .... **CLC 81**
See CA 157

Jong, Erica 1942- . **CLC 4, 6, 8, 18, 83; DAM NOV, POP**
See AITN 1; BEST 90:2; CA 73-76; CANR 26, 52, 75; DA3; DLB 2, 5, 28, 152; INT CANR-26; MTCW 1, 2

Jonson, Ben(jamin) 1572(?)-1637 . **LC 6, 33; DA; DAB; DAC; DAM DRAM, MST, POET; DC 4; PC 17; WLC**
See CDBLB Before 1660; DLB 62, 121

Jordan, June 1936- .... **CLC 5, 11, 23, 114; BLCS; DAM MULT, POET**
See AAYA 2; BW 2, 3; CA 33-36R; CANR 25, 70; CLR 10; DLB 38; MAICYA; MTCW 1; SATA 4

Jordan, Neil (Patrick) 1950- .... **CLC 110**
See CA 124; 130; CANR 54; INT 130

Jordan, Pat(rick M.) 1941- .... **CLC 37**
See CA 33-36R

Jorgensen, Ivar
See Ellison, Harlan (Jay)

Jorgenson, Ivar
See Silverberg, Robert

Josephus, Flavius c. 37-100 .... **CMLC 13**

Josipovici, Gabriel 1940- .... **CLC 6, 43**
See CA 37-40R; CAAS 8; CANR 47, 84; DLB 14

Joubert, Joseph 1754-1824 .... **NCLC 9**

Jouve, Pierre Jean 1887-1976 .... **CLC 47**
See CA 65-68

Jovine, Francesco 1902-1950 .... **TCLC 79**

Joyce, James (Augustine Aloysius) 1882-1941 . **TCLC 3, 8, 16, 35, 52; DA; DAB; DAC; DAM MST, NOV, POET; PC 22; SSC 3, 26; WLC**
See CA 104; 126; CDBLB 1914-1945; DA3; DLB 10, 19, 36, 162; MTCW 1, 2

Jozsef, Attila 1905-1937 .... **TCLC 22**
See CA 116

Juana Ines de la Cruz 1651(?)-1695 .. **LC 5; HLCS 1; PC 24**

Judd, Cyril
See Kornbluth, C(yril) M.; Pohl, Frederik

Juenger, Ernst 1895-1998 .... **CLC 125**
See CA 101; 167; CANR 21, 47; DLB 56

Julian of Norwich 1342(?)-1416(?) . **LC 6, 52**
See DLB 146

Junger, Ernst
See Juenger, Ernst

Junger, Sebastian 1962- .... **CLC 109**
See AAYA 28; CA 165

Juniper, Alex
See Hospital, Janette Turner

Junius
See Luxemburg, Rosa

Just, Ward (Swift) 1935- .... **CLC 4, 27**
See CA 25-28R; CANR 32; INT CANR-32

Justice, Donald (Rodney) 1925- . **CLC 6, 19, 102; DAM POET**
See CA 5-8R; CANR 26, 54, 74; DLBY 83; INT CANR-26; MTCW 2

Juvenal c. 60-c. 13 .... **CMLC 8**
See Juvenalis, Decimus Junius
See DLB 211
Juvenalis, Decimus Junius 55(?)-c. 127(?)
See Juvenal
Juvenis
See Bourne, Randolph S(illiman)
Kacew, Romain 1914-1980
See Gary, Romain
See CA 108; 102
Kadare, Ismail 1936- .... **CLC 52**
See CA 161
Kadohata, Cynthia .... **CLC 59, 122**
See CA 140
Kafka, Franz 1883-1924 . **TCLC 2, 6, 13, 29, 47, 53; DA; DAB; DAC; DAM MST, NOV; SSC 5, 29, 35; WLC**
See AAYA 31; CA 105; 126; DA3; DLB 81; MTCW 1, 2
Kahanovitsch, Pinkhes
See Der Nister
Kahn, Roger 1927- .... **CLC 30**
See CA 25-28R; CANR 44, 69; DLB 171; SATA 37
Kain, Saul
See Sassoon, Siegfried (Lorraine)
Kaiser, Georg 1878-1945 .... **TCLC 9**
See CA 106; DLB 124
Kaletski, Alexander 1946- .... **CLC 39**
See CA 118; 143
Kalidasa fl. c. 400- .... **CMLC 9; PC 22**
Kallman, Chester(Simon) 1921-1975 ... **CLC 2**
See CA 45-48; 53-56; CANR 3
Kaminsky, Melvin 1926-
See Brooks, Mel
See CA 65-68; CANR 16
Kaminsky, Stuart M(elvin) 1934- ... **CLC 59**
See CA 73-76; CANR 29, 53
Kandinsky, Wassily 1866-1944 ..... **TCLC 92**
See CA 118; 155
Kane, Francis
See Robbins, Harold
Kane, Paul
See Simon, Paul (Frederick)
Kanin, Garson 1912-1999 .... **CLC 22**
See AITN 1; CA 5-8R; 177; CANR 7, 78; DLB 7
Kaniuk, Yoram 1930- .... **CLC 19**
See CA 134
Kant, Immanuel 1724-1804 .... **NCLC 27, 67**
See DLB 94
Kantor, MacKinlay 1904-1977 .... **CLC 7**
See CA 61-64; 73-76; CANR 60, 63; DLB 9, 102; MTCW 2
Kaplan, David Michael 1946- .... **CLC 50**
Kaplan, James 1951- .... **CLC 59**
See CA 135
Karageorge, Michael
See Anderson, Poul (William)
Karamzin, Nikolai Mikhailovich 1766-1826 .... **NCLC 3**
See DLB 150
Karapanou, Margarita 1946- .... **CLC 13**
See CA 101
Karinthy, Frigyes 1887-1938 .... **TCLC 47**
See CA 170
Karl, Frederick R(obert) 1927- .... **CLC 34**
See CA 5-8R; CANR 3, 44
Kastel, Warren
See Silverberg, Robert
Kataev, Evgeny Petrovich 1903-1942
See Petrov, Evgeny
See CA 120
Kataphusin
See Ruskin, John
Katz, Steve 1935- .... **CLC 47**
See CA 25-28R; CAAS 14, 64; CANR 12; DLBY 83
Kauffman, Janet 1945- .... **CLC 42**
See CA 117; CANR 43, 84; DLBY 86
Kaufman, Bob(Garnell) 1925-1986 . **CLC 49**
See BW 1; CA 41-44R; 118; CANR 22; DLB 16, 41
Kaufman, George S. 1889-1961 ..... **CLC 38; DAM DRAM**
See CA 108; 93-96; DLB 7; INT 108; MTCW 2
Kaufman, Sue .... **CLC 3, 8**
See Barondess, Sue K(aufman)
Kavafis, Konstantinos Petrou 1863-1933
See Cavafy, C(onstantine) P(eter)
See CA 104
Kavan, Anna 1901-1968 .... **CLC 5, 13, 82**
See CA 5-8R; CANR 6, 57; MTCW 1
Kavanagh, Dan
See Barnes, Julian (Patrick)
Kavanagh, Julie 1952- .... **CLC 119**
See CA 163
Kavanagh, Patrick (Joseph) 1904-1967 .... **CLC 22**
See CA 123; 25-28R; DLB 15, 20; MTCW 1
Kawabata, Yasunari 1899-1972 ... **CLC 2, 5, 9, 18, 107; DAM MULT; SSC 17**
See CA 93-96; 33-36R; DLB 180; MTCW 2
Kaye, M(ary) M(argaret) 1909- ...... **CLC 28**
See CA 89-92; CANR 24, 60; MTCW 1, 2; SATA 62
Kaye, Mollie
See Kaye, M(ary) M(argaret)
Kaye-Smith, Sheila 1887-1956 ...... **TCLC 20**
See CA 118; DLB 36
Kaymor, Patrice Maguilene
See Senghor, Leopold Sedar
Kazan, Elia 1909- .... **CLC 6, 16, 63**
See CA 21-24R; CANR 32, 78
Kazantzakis, Nikos 1883(?)-1957 .. **TCLC 2, 5, 33**
See CA 105; 132; DA3; MTCW 1, 2
Kazin, Alfred 1915-1998 .... **CLC 34, 38, 119**
See CA 1-4R; CAAS 7; CANR 1, 45, 79; DLB 67
Keane, Mary Nesta (Skrine) 1904-1996
See Keane, Molly
See CA 108; 114; 151
Keane, Molly .... **CLC 31**
See Keane, Mary Nesta (Skrine)
See INT 114
Keates, Jonathan 1946(?)- .... **CLC 34**
See CA 163
Keaton, Buster 1895-1966 .... **CLC 20**
Keats, John 1795-1821 .... **NCLC 8, 73; DA; DAB; DAC; DAM MST, POET; PC 1; WLC**
See CDBLB 1789-1832; DA3; DLB 96, 110
Keene, Donald 1922- .... **CLC 34**
See CA 1-4R; CANR 5
Keillor, Garrison .... **CLC 40, 115**
See Keillor, Gary (Edward)
See AAYA 2; BEST 89:3; DLBY 87; SATA 58
Keillor, Gary (Edward) 1942-
See Keillor, Garrison
See CA 111; 117; CANR 36, 59; DAM POP; DA3; MTCW 1, 2
Keith, Michael
See Hubbard, L(afayette) Ron(ald)
Keller, Gottfried 1819-1890 .. **NCLC 2; SSC 26**
See DLB 129
Keller, Nora Okja .... **CLC 109**
Kellerman, Jonathan 1949- .. **CLC 44;DAM POP**
See BEST 90:1; CA 106; CANR 29, 51; DA3; INT CANR-29
Kelley, William Melvin 1937- .... **CLC 22**
See BW 1; CA 77-80; CANR 27, 83; DLB 33
Kellogg, Marjorie 1922- .... **CLC 2**
See CA 81-84
Kellow, Kathleen
See Hibbert, Eleanor Alice Burford
Kelly, M(ilton) T(erry) 1947- .... **CLC 55**
See CA 97-100; CAAS 22; CANR 19, 43, 84
Kelman, James 1946- .... **CLC 58, 86**
See CA 148; CANR 85; DLB 194
Kemal, Yashar 1923- .... **CLC 14, 29**
See CA 89-92; CANR 44
Kemble, Fanny 1809-1893 .... **NCLC 18**
See DLB 32
Kemelman, Harry 1908-1996 .... **CLC 2**
See AITN 1; CA 9-12R; 155; CANR 6, 71; DLB 28
Kempe, Margery 1373(?)-1440(?) .... **LC 6**
See DLB 146
Kempis, Thomas a 1380-1471 .... **LC 11**
Kendall, Henry 1839-1882 .... **NCLC 12**
Keneally, Thomas (Michael) 1935- .. **CLC 5, 8, 10, 14, 19, 27, 43, 117; DAM NOV**
See CA 85-88; CANR 10, 50, 74; DA3; MTCW 1, 2
Kennedy, Adrienne (Lita) 1931- .... **CLC 66; BLC 2; DAM MULT; DC 5**
See BW 2, 3; CA 103; CAAS 20; CABS 3; CANR 26, 53, 82; DLB 38
Kennedy, John Pendleton 1795-1870 . **NCLC 2**
See DLB 3
Kennedy, Joseph Charles 1929-
See Kennedy, X. J.
See CA 1-4R; CANR 4, 30, 40; SATA 14, 86
Kennedy, William 1928- . **CLC 6, 28, 34, 53; DAM NOV**
See AAYA 1; CA 85-88; CANR 14, 31, 76; DA3; DLB 143; DLBY 85; INT CANR-31; MTCW 1, 2; SATA 57
Kennedy, X. J. .... **CLC 8, 42**
See Kennedy, Joseph Charles
See CAAS 9; CLR 27; DLB 5; SAAS 22
Kenny, Maurice (Francis) 1929- .... **CLC 87; DAM MULT**
See CA 144; CAAS 22; DLB 175; NNAL
Kent, Kelvin
See Kuttner, Henry
Kenton, Maxwell
See Southern, Terry
Kenyon, Robert O.
See Kuttner, Henry
Kepler, Johannes 1571-1630 .... **LC 45**
Kerouac, Jack ..... **CLC 1, 2, 3, 5, 14, 29, 61**
See Kerouac, Jean-Louis Lebris de
See AAYA 25; CDALB 1941-1968; DLB 2, 16; DLBD 3; DLBY 95; MTCW 2
Kerouac, Jean-Louis Lebris de 1922-1969
See Kerouac, Jack
See AITN 1; CA 5-8R; 25-28R; CANR 26, 54; DA; DAB; DAC; DAM MST, NOV, POET, POP; DA3; MTCW 1, 2; WLC
Kerr, Jean 1923- .... **CLC 22**
See CA 5-8R; CANR 7; INT CANR-7
Kerr, M. E. .... **CLC 12, 35**
See Meaker, Marijane (Agnes)
See AAYA 2, 23; CLR 29; SAAS 1
Kerr, Robert .... **CLC 55**
Kerrigan, (Thomas) Anthony 1918- . **CLC 4, 6**
See CA 49-52; CAAS 11; CANR 4

Kerry, Lois
See Duncan, Lois
Kesey, Ken (Elton) 1935- ... **CLC 1, 3, 6, 11, 46, 64; DA; DAB; DAC; DAM MST, NOV, POP; WLC**
See AAYA 25; CA 1-4R; CANR 22, 38, 66; CDALB 1968-1988; DA3; DLB 2, 16, 206; MTCW 1, 2; SATA 66
Kesselring, Joseph (Otto) 1902-1967 ... **CLC 45; DAM DRAM, MST**
See CA 150
Kessler, Jascha(Frederick) 1929- ...... **CLC 4**
See CA 17-20R; CANR 8, 48
Kettelkamp, Larry (Dale) 1933- ..... **CLC 12**
See CA 29-32R; CANR 16; SAAS 3; SATA 2
Key, Ellen 1849-1926 .... **TCLC 65**
Keyber, Conny
See Fielding, Henry
Keyes, Daniel 1927- ..... **CLC 80; DA; DAC; DAM MST, NOV**
See AAYA 23; CA 17-20R, 181; CAAE 181; CANR 10, 26, 54, 74; DA3; MTCW 2; SATA 37
Keynes, John Maynard 1883-1946 .... **TCLC 64**
See CA 114; 162, 163; DLBD 10; MTCW 2
Khanshendel, Chiron
See Rose, Wendy
Khayyam, Omar 1048-1131 .... **CMLC 11; DAM POET; PC 8**
See DA3
Kherdian, David 1931- .... **CLC 6, 9**
See CA 21-24R; CAAS 2; CANR 39, 78; CLR 24; JRDA; MAICYA; SATA 16, 74
Khlebnikov, Velimir .... **TCLC 20**
See Khlebnikov, Viktor Vladimirovich
Khlebnikov, Viktor Vladimirovich 1885-1922
See Khlebnikov, Velimir
See CA 117
Khodasevich, Vladislav (Felitsianovich) 1886-1939 .... **TCLC 15**
See CA 115
Kielland, Alexander Lange 1849-1906 .... **TCLC 5**
See CA 104
Kiely, Benedict 1919- .... **CLC 23, 43**
See CA 1-4R; CANR 2, 84; DLB 15
Kienzle, William X(avier) 1928- .... **CLC 25; DAM POP**
See CA 93-96; CAAS 1; CANR 9, 31, 59; DA3; INT CANR-31; MTCW 1, 2
Kierkegaard, Soren 1813-1855 .... **NCLC 34, 78**
Kieslowski, Krzysztof 1941-1996 .. **CLC 120**
See CA 147; 151
Killens, John Oliver 1916-1987 .... **CLC 10**
See BW 2; CA 77-80; 123; CAAS 2; CANR 26; DLB 33
Killigrew, Anne 1660-1685 .... **LC 4**
See DLB 131
Kim
See Simenon, Georges (Jacques Christian)
Kincaid, Jamaica 1949- .. **CLC 43, 68; BLC 2; DAM MULT, NOV**
See AAYA 13; BW 2, 3; CA 125; CANR 47, 59; CDALBS; DA3; DLB 157; MTCW 2
King, Francis (Henry) 1923- ...... **CLC 8, 53; DAM NOV**
See CA 1-4R; CANR 1, 33; DLB 15, 139; MTCW 1
King, Kennedy
See Brown, George Douglas
King, Martin Luther, Jr. 1929-1968 .... **CLC 83; BLC 2; DA; DAB; DAC; DAM MST, MULT; WLCS**
See BW 2, 3; CA 25-28; CANR 27, 44; CAP 2; DA3; MTCW 1, 2; SATA 14
King, Stephen (Edwin) 1947- ... **CLC 12, 26, 37, 61, 113; DAM NOV, POP; SSC 17**
See AAYA 1, 17; BEST 90:1; CA 61-64; CANR 1, 30, 52, 76; DA3; DLB 143; DLBY 80; JRDA; MTCW 1, 2; SATA 9, 55
King, Steve
See King, Stephen (Edwin)
King, Thomas 1943- ... **CLC 89; DAC;DAM MULT**
See CA 144; DLB 175; NNAL; SATA 96
Kingman, Lee .... **CLC 17**
See Natti, (Mary) Lee
See SAAS 3; SATA 1, 67
Kingsley, Charles 1819-1875 .... **NCLC 35**
See DLB 21, 32, 163, 190; YABC 2
Kingsley, Sidney 1906-1995 .... **CLC 44**
See CA 85-88; 147; DLB 7
Kingsolver, Barbara 1955- .... **CLC 55, 81; DAM POP**
See AAYA 15; CA 129; 134; CANR 60; CDALBS; DA3; DLB 206; INT 134; MTCW 2
Kingston, Maxine (Ting Ting) Hong 1940- . **CLC 12, 19, 58, 121; DAM MULT, NOV; WLCS**
See AAYA 8; CA 69-72; CANR 13, 38, 74; CDALBS; DA3; DLB 173, 212; DLBY 80; INT CANR-13; MTCW 1, 2; SATA 53
Kinnell, Galway 1927- ... **CLC 1, 2, 3, 5, 13, 29; PC 26**
See CA 9-12R; CANR 10, 34, 66; DLB 5; DLBY 87; INT CANR-34; MTCW 1, 2
Kinsella, Thomas 1928- .... **CLC 4, 19**
See CA 17-20R; CANR 15; DLB 27; MTCW 1, 2
Kinsella, W(illiam) P(atrick) 1935- ...... **CLC 27, 43; DAC; DAM NOV, POP**
See AAYA 7; CA 97-100; CAAS 7; CANR 21, 35, 66, 75; INT CANR-21; MTCW 1, 2
Kinsey, Alfred C(harles) 1894-1956 .. **TCLC 91**
See CA 115; 170; MTCW 2
Kipling, (Joseph) Rudyard 1865-1936 .... **TCLC 8, 17; DA; DAB; DAC; DAM MST, POET; PC 3; SSC 5; WLC**
See AAYA 32; CA 105; 120; CANR 33; CDBLB 1890-1914; CLR 39; DA3; DLB 19, 34, 141, 156; MAICYA; MTCW 1, 2; SATA 100; YABC 2
Kirkup, James 1918- .... **CLC 1**
See CA 1-4R; CAAS 4; CANR 2; DLB 27; SATA 12
Kirkwood, James 1930(?)-1989 .... **CLC 9**
See AITN 2; CA 1-4R; 128; CANR 6, 40
Kirshner, Sidney
See Kingsley, Sidney
Kis, Danilo 1935-1989 .... **CLC 57**
See CA 109; 118; 129; CANR 61; DLB 181; MTCW 1
Kivi, Aleksis 1834-1872 .... **NCLC 30**
Kizer, Carolyn (Ashley) 1925- . **CLC 15, 39, 80; DAM POET**
See CA 65-68; CAAS 5; CANR 24, 70; DLB 5, 169; MTCW 2
Klabund 1890-1928 .... **TCLC 44**
See CA 162; DLB 66
Klappert, Peter 1942- .... **CLC 57**
See CA 33-36R; DLB 5
Klein, A(braham) M(oses) 1909-1972 .. **CLC 19; DAB; DAC; DAM MST**
See CA 101; 37-40R; DLB 68
Klein, Norma 1938-1989 .... **CLC 30**
See AAYA 2; CA 41-44R; 128; CANR 15, 37; CLR 2, 19; INT CANR-15; JRDA; MAICYA; SAAS 1; SATA 7, 57
Klein, T(heodore) E(ibon) D(onald) 1947- .. **CLC 34**
See CA 119; CANR 44, 75
Kleist, Heinrich von 1777-1811 ..... **NCLC 2, 37; DAM DRAM; SSC 22**
See DLB 90
Klima, Ivan 1931- .... **CLC 56;DAM NOV**
See CA 25-28R; CANR 17, 50
Klimentov, Andrei Platonovich 1899-1951
See Platonov, Andrei
See CA 108
Klinger, Friedrich Maximilianvon 1752-1831 .... **NCLC 1**
See DLB 94
Klingsor the Magician
See Hartmann, Sadakichi
Klopstock, Friedrich Gottlieb 1724-1803 .... **NCLC 11**
See DLB 97
Knapp, Caroline 1959- .... **CLC 99**
See CA 154
Knebel, Fletcher 1911-1993 .... **CLC 14**
See AITN 1; CA 1-4R; 140; CAAS 3; CANR 1, 36; SATA 36; SATA-Obit 75
Knickerbocker, Diedrich
See Irving, Washington
Knight, Etheridge 1931-1991 . **CLC 40; BLC 2; DAM POET; PC 14**
See BW 1, 3; CA 21-24R; 133; CANR 23, 82; DLB 41; MTCW 2
Knight, Sarah Kemble 1666-1727 .... **LC 7**
See DLB 24, 200
Knister, Raymond 1899-1932 .... **TCLC 56**
See DLB 68
Knowles, John 1926- . **CLC 1, 4, 10, 26; DA; DAC; DAM MST, NOV**
See AAYA 10; CA 17-20R; CANR 40, 74, 76; CDALB 1968-1988; DLB 6; MTCW 1, 2; SATA 8, 89
Knox, Calvin M.
See Silverberg, Robert
Knox, John c. 1505-1572 .... **LC 37**
See DLB 132
Knye, Cassandra
See Disch, Thomas M(ichael)
Koch, C(hristopher) J(ohn) 1932- .. **CLC 42**
See CA 127; CANR 84
Koch, Christopher
See Koch, C(hristopher) J(ohn)
Koch, Kenneth 1925- .... **CLC 5, 8, 44;DAM POET**
See CA 1-4R; CANR 6, 36, 57; DLB 5; INT CANR-36; MTCW 2; SATA 65
Kochanowski, Jan 1530-1584 .... **LC 10**
Kock, Charles Paul de 1794-1871 ..... **NCLC 16**
Koda Shigeyuki 1867-1947
See Rohan, Koda
See CA 121
Koestler, Arthur 1905-1983 . **CLC 1, 3, 6, 8, 15, 33**
See CA 1-4R; 109; CANR 1, 33; CDBLB 1945-1960; DLBY 83; MTCW 1, 2
Kogawa, Joy Nozomi 1935- . **CLC 78; DAC; DAM MST, MULT**
See CA 101; CANR 19, 62; MTCW 2; SATA 99
Kohout, Pavel 1928- .... **CLC 13**
See CA 45-48; CANR 3
Koizumi, Yakumo
See Hearn, (Patricio) Lafcadio (Tessima Carlos)
Kolmar, Gertrud 1894-1943 .... **TCLC 40**
See CA 167

Komunyakaa, Yusef 1947- .... **CLC 86, 94; BLCS**
See CA 147; CANR 83; DLB 120
Konrad, George
See Konrad, Gyoergy
Konrad, Gyoergy 1933- .... **CLC 4, 10, 73**
See CA 85-88
Konwicki, Tadeusz 1926- ...... **CLC 8, 28, 54, 117**
See CA 101; CAAS 9; CANR 39, 59; MTCW 1
Koontz, Dean R(ay) 1945- ... **CLC 78; DAM NOV, POP**
See AAYA 9, 31; BEST 89:3, 90:2; CA 108; CANR 19, 36, 52; DA3; MTCW 1; SATA 92
Kopernik, Mikolaj
See Copernicus, Nicolaus
Kopit, Arthur (Lee) 1937- ... **CLC 1, 18, 33; DAM DRAM**
See AITN 1; CA 81-84; CABS 3; DLB 7; MTCW 1
Kops, Bernard 1926- .... **CLC 4**
See CA 5-8R; CANR 84; DLB 13
Kornbluth, C(yril) M. 1923-1958 ... **TCLC 8**
See CA 105; 160; DLB 8
Korolenko, V. G.
See Korolenko, Vladimir Galaktionovich
Korolenko, Vladimir
See Korolenko, Vladimir Galaktionovich
Korolenko, Vladimir G.
See Korolenko, Vladimir Galaktionovich
Korolenko, Vladimir Galaktionovich 1853-1921 .... **TCLC 22**
See CA 121
Korzybski, Alfred (Habdank Skarbek) 1879-1950 .... **TCLC 61**
See CA 123; 160
Kosinski, Jerzy (Nikodem) 1933-1991 . **CLC 1, 2, 3, 6, 10, 15, 53, 70; DAM NOV**
See CA 17-20R; 134; CANR 9, 46; DA3; DLB 2; DLBY 82; MTCW 1, 2
Kostelanetz, Richard(Cory) 1940- .. **CLC 28**
See CA 13-16R; CAAS 8; CANR 38, 77
Kostrowitzki, Wilhelm Apollinaris de 1880-1918
See Apollinaire, Guillaume
See CA 104
Kotlowitz, Robert 1924- .... **CLC 4**
See CA 33-36R; CANR 36
Kotzebue, August (Friedrich Ferdinand) von 1761-1819 .... **NCLC 25**
See DLB 94
Kotzwinkle, William 1938- .... **CLC 5, 14, 35**
See CA 45-48; CANR 3, 44, 84; CLR 6; DLB 173; MAICYA; SATA 24, 70
Kowna, Stancy
See Szymborska, Wislawa
Kozol, Jonathan 1936- .... **CLC 17**
See CA 61-64; CANR 16, 45
Kozoll, Michael 1940(?)- .... **CLC 35**
Kramer, Kathryn 19(?)- .... **CLC 34**
Kramer, Larry 1935- . **CLC 42; DAM POP; DC 8**
See CA 124; 126; CANR 60
Krasicki, Ignacy 1735-1801 .... **NCLC 8**
Krasinski, Zygmunt 1812-1859 ...... **NCLC 4**
Kraus, Karl 1874-1936 .... **TCLC 5**
See CA 104; DLB 118
Kreve (Mickevicius),Vincas 1882-1954 .... **TCLC 27**
See CA 170
Kristeva, Julia 1941- .... **CLC 77**
See CA 154
Kristofferson, Kris 1936- .... **CLC 26**
See CA 104
Krizanc, John 1956- .... **CLC 57**
Krleza, Miroslav 1893-1981 .... **CLC 8,114**
See CA 97-100; 105; CANR 50; DLB 147
Kroetsch, Robert 1927- .... **CLC 5, 23, 57; DAC; DAM POET**
See CA 17-20R; CANR 8, 38; DLB 53; MTCW 1
Kroetz, Franz
See Kroetz, Franz Xaver
Kroetz, Franz Xaver 1946- .... **CLC 41**
See CA 130
Kroker, Arthur (W.) 1945- .... **CLC 77**
See CA 161
Kropotkin, Peter (Aleksieevich) 1842-1921 . **TCLC 36**
See CA 119
Krotkov, Yuri 1917- .... **CLC 19**
See CA 102
Krumb
See Crumb, R(obert)
Krumgold, Joseph (Quincy) 1908-1980 .... **CLC 12**
See CA 9-12R; 101; CANR 7; MAICYA; SATA 1, 48; SATA-Obit 23
Krumwitz
See Crumb, R(obert)
Krutch, JosephWood 1893-1970 ..... **CLC 24**
See CA 1-4R; 25-28R; CANR 4; DLB 63, 206
Krutzch, Gus
See Eliot, T(homas) S(tearns)
Krylov, Ivan Andreevich 1768(?)-1844 .... **NCLC 1**
See DLB 150
Kubin, Alfred (Leopold Isidor) 1877-1959 .. **TCLC 23**
See CA 112; 149; DLB 81
Kubrick, Stanley 1928-1999 .... **CLC 16**
See AAYA 30; CA 81-84; 177; CANR 33; DLB 26
Kumin, Maxine (Winokur) 1925- .... **CLC 5, 13, 28; DAM POET; PC 15**
See AITN 2; CA 1-4R; CAAS 8; CANR 1, 21, 69; DA3; DLB 5; MTCW 1, 2; SATA 12
Kundera, Milan 1929- . **CLC 4, 9, 19, 32, 68, 115; DAM NOV; SSC 24**
See AAYA 2; CA 85-88; CANR 19, 52, 74; DA3; MTCW 1, 2
Kunene, Mazisi (Raymond) 1930- .. **CLC 85**
See BW 1, 3; CA 125; CANR 81; DLB 117
Kunitz, Stanley (Jasspon) 1905- . **CLC 6, 11, 14; PC 19**
See CA 41-44R; CANR 26, 57; DA3; DLB 48; INT CANR-26; MTCW 1, 2
Kunze, Reiner 1933- .... **CLC 10**
See CA 93-96; DLB 75
Kuprin, Aleksandr Ivanovich 1870-1938 ..... **TCLC 5**
See CA 104
Kureishi, Hanif 1954(?)- .... **CLC 64**
See CA 139; DLB 194
Kurosawa, Akira 1910-1998 ... **CLC 16, 119; DAM MULT**
See AAYA 11; CA 101; 170; CANR 46
Kushner, Tony 1957(?)- .... **CLC 81; DAM DRAM; DC 10**
See CA 144; CANR 74; DA3; MTCW 2
Kuttner, Henry 1915-1958 .... **TCLC 10**
See Vance, Jack
See CA 107; 157; DLB 8
Kuzma, Greg 1944- .... **CLC 7**
See CA 33-36R; CANR 70
Kuzmin, Mikhail 1872(?)-1936 ..... **TCLC 40**
See CA 170
Kyd, Thomas 1558-1594 .... **LC 22; DAM DRAM; DC 3**
See DLB 62
Kyprianos, Iossif
See Samarakis, Antonis
La Bruyere, Jean de 1645-1696 .... **LC 17**
Lacan, Jacques (Marie Emile) 1901-1981 ... **CLC 75**
See CA 121; 104
Laclos, Pierre Ambroise Francois Choderlosde 1741-1803 .... **NCLC 4**
Lacolere, Francois
See Aragon, Louis
La Colere, Francois
See Aragon, Louis
La Deshabilleuse
See Simenon, Georges (Jacques Christian)
Lady Gregory
See Gregory, Isabella Augusta (Persse)
Lady of Quality, A
See Bagnold, Enid
La Fayette, Marie (Madelaine Pioche de la Vergne Comtes 1634-1693 .... **LC 2**
Lafayette, Rene
See Hubbard, L(afayette) Ron(ald)
Laforgue, Jules 1860-1887 . **NCLC 5, 53; PC 14; SSC 20**
Lagerkvist, Paer (Fabian) 1891-1974 .. **CLC 7, 10, 13, 54; DAM DRAM, NOV**
See Lagerkvist, Par
See CA 85-88; 49-52; DA3; MTCW 1, 2
Lagerkvist, Par .... **SSC 12**
See Lagerkvist, Paer (Fabian)
See MTCW 2
Lagerloef, Selma (Ottiliana Lovisa) 1858-1940 .... **TCLC 4, 36**
See Lagerlof, Selma (Ottiliana Lovisa)
See CA 108; MTCW 2; SATA 15
Lagerlof, Selma (Ottiliana Lovisa)
See Lagerloef, Selma (Ottiliana Lovisa)
See CLR 7; SATA 15
La Guma, (Justin) Alex(ander) 1925-1985 .. **CLC 19; BLCS; DAM NOV**
See BW 1, 3; CA 49-52; 118; CANR 25, 81; DLB 117; MTCW 1, 2
Laidlaw, A. K.
See Grieve, C(hristopher) M(urray)
Lainez, Manuel Mujica
See Mujica Lainez, Manuel
See HW 1
Laing, R(onald) D(avid) 1927-1989 . **CLC 95**
See CA 107; 129; CANR 34; MTCW 1
Lamartine, Alphonse (Marie Louis Prat) de 1790-1869 . **NCLC 11; DAM POET; PC 16**
Lamb, Charles 1775-1834 ... **NCLC 10; DA; DAB; DAC; DAM MST; WLC**
See CDBLB 1789-1832; DLB 93, 107, 163; SATA 17
Lamb, Lady Caroline 1785-1828 . **NCLC 38**
See DLB 116
Lamming, George (William) 1927- .. **CLC 2, 4, 66; BLC 2; DAM MULT**
See BW 2, 3; CA 85-88; CANR 26, 76; DLB 125; MTCW 1, 2
L'Amour, Louis (Dearborn) 1908-1988 .... **CLC 25, 55; DAM NOV, POP**
See AAYA 16; AITN 2; BEST 89:2; CA 1-4R; 125; CANR 3, 25, 40; DA3; DLB 206; DLBY 80; MTCW 1, 2
Lampedusa, Giuseppe (Tomasi)di 1896-1957 .... **TCLC 13**
See Tomasi di Lampedusa, Giuseppe
See CA 164; DLB 177; MTCW 2
Lampman, Archibald 1861-1899 .. **NCLC 25**
See DLB 92
Lancaster, Bruce 1896-1963 .... **CLC 36**
See CA 9-10; CANR 70; CAP 1; SATA 9
Lanchester, John .... **CLC 99**
Landau, Mark Alexandrovich
See Aldanov, Mark (Alexandrovich)

Author Index

Landau-Aldanov, Mark Alexandrovich
See Aldanov, Mark (Alexandrovich)
Landis, Jerry
See Simon, Paul (Frederick)
Landis, John 1950- .... **CLC 26**
See CA 112; 122
Landolfi, Tommaso 1908-1979 .. **CLC 11, 49**
See CA 127; 117; DLB 177
Landon, Letitia Elizabeth 1802-1838 . **NCLC 15**
See DLB 96
Landor, Walter Savage 1775-1864 .... **NCLC 14**
See DLB 93, 107
Landwirth, Heinz 1927-
See Lind, Jakov
See CA 9-12R; CANR 7
Lane, Patrick 1939- ... **CLC 25;DAM POET**
See CA 97-100; CANR 54; DLB 53; INT 97-100
Lang, Andrew 1844-1912 .... **TCLC 16**
See CA 114; 137; CANR 85; DLB 98, 141, 184; MAICYA; SATA 16
Lang, Fritz 1890-1976 .... **CLC 20, 103**
See CA 77-80; 69-72; CANR 30
Lange, John
See Crichton, (John) Michael
Langer, Elinor 1939- .... **CLC 34**
See CA 121
Langland, William 1330(?)-1400(?) .. **LC 19; DA; DAB; DAC; DAM MST, POET**
See DLB 146
Langstaff, Launcelot
See Irving, Washington
Lanier, Sidney 1842-1881 ..... **NCLC 6;DAM POET**
See DLB 64; DLBD 13; MAICYA; SATA 18
Lanyer, Aemilia 1569-1645 .... **LC 10, 30**
See DLB 121
Lao-Tzu
See Lao Tzu
Lao Tzu fl. 6th cent. B.C.- .... **CMLC 7**
Lapine, James (Elliot) 1949- .... **CLC 39**
See CA 123; 130; CANR 54; INT 130
Larbaud, Valery (Nicolas) 1881-1957 . **TCLC 9**
See CA 106; 152
Lardner, Ring
See Lardner, Ring(gold) W(ilmer)
Lardner, Ring W., Jr.
See Lardner, Ring(gold) W(ilmer)
Lardner, Ring(gold) W(ilmer) 1885-1933 .... **TCLC 2, 14; SSC 32**
See CA 104; 131; CDALB 1917-1929; DLB 11, 25, 86; DLBD 16; MTCW 1, 2
Laredo, Betty
See Codrescu, Andrei
Larkin, Maia
See Wojciechowska, Maia (Teresa)
Larkin, Philip (Arthur) 1922-1985 .. **CLC 3, 5, 8, 9, 13, 18, 33, 39, 64; DAB; DAM MST, POET; PC 21**
See CA 5-8R; 117; CANR 24, 62; CDBLB 1960 to Present; DA3; DLB 27; MTCW 1, 2
Larra (y Sanchez de Castro), Mariano Josede 1809-1837 .... **NCLC 17**
Larsen, Eric 1941- .... **CLC 55**
See CA 132
Larsen, Nella 1891-1964 ... **CLC 37; BLC 2; DAM MULT**
See BW 1; CA 125; CANR 83; DLB 51
Larson, Charles R(aymond) 1938- . **CLC 31**
See CA 53-56; CANR 4
Larson, Jonathan 1961-1996 .... **CLC 99**
See AAYA 28; CA 156
Las Casas, Bartolome de 1474-1566 . **LC 31**
Lasch,Christopher 1932-1994 .... **CLC 102**
See CA 73-76; 144; CANR 25; MTCW 1, 2
Lasker-Schueler, Else 1869-1945 .. **TCLC 57**
See DLB 66, 124
Laski, Harold 1893-1950 .... **TCLC 79**
Latham, Jean Lee 1902-1995 .... **CLC 12**
See AITN 1; CA 5-8R; CANR 7, 84; CLR 50; MAICYA; SATA 2, 68
Latham, Mavis
See Clark, Mavis Thorpe
Lathen, Emma .... **CLC 2**
See Hennissart, Martha; Latsis, Mary J(ane)
Lathrop, Francis
See Leiber, Fritz (Reuter, Jr.)
Latsis, Mary J(ane) 1927(?)-1997
See Lathen, Emma
See CA 85-88; 162
Lattimore, Richmond (Alexander) 1906-1984 .... **CLC 3**
See CA 1-4R; 112; CANR 1
Laughlin, James 1914-1997 .... **CLC 49**
See CA 21-24R; 162; CAAS 22; CANR 9, 47; DLB 48; DLBY 96, 97
Laurence, (Jean) Margaret (Wemyss) 1926-1987 . **CLC 3, 6, 13, 50, 62; DAC; DAM MST; SSC 7**
See CA 5-8R; 121; CANR 33; DLB 53; MTCW 1, 2; SATA-Obit 50
Laurent, Antoine 1952- .... **CLC 50**
Lauscher, Hermann
See Hesse, Hermann
Lautreamont, Comte de 1846-1870 ... **NCLC 12; SSC 14**
Laverty, Donald
See Blish, James (Benjamin)
Lavin, Mary 1912-1996 . **CLC 4, 18, 99; SSC 4**
See CA 9-12R; 151; CANR 33; DLB 15; MTCW 1
Lavond, Paul Dennis
See Kornbluth, C(yril) M.; Pohl, Frederik
Lawler, Raymond Evenor 1922- ..... **CLC 58**
See CA 103
Lawrence, D(avid) H(erbert Richards) 1885-1930 ... **TCLC 2, 9, 16, 33, 48, 61, 93; DA; DAB; DAC; DAM MST, NOV, POET; SSC 4, 19; WLC**
See CA 104; 121; CDBLB 1914-1945; DA3; DLB 10, 19, 36, 98, 162, 195; MTCW 1, 2
Lawrence, T(homas) E(dward) 1888-1935 .. **TCLC 18**
See Dale, Colin
See CA 115; 167; DLB 195
Lawrence of Arabia
See Lawrence, T(homas) E(dward)
Lawson, Henry (Archibald Hertzberg) 1867-1922 .... **TCLC 27; SSC 18**
See CA 120; 181
Lawton, Dennis
See Faust, Frederick (Schiller)
Laxness, Halldor .... **CLC 25**
See Gudjonsson, Halldor Kiljan
Layamon fl. c. 1200- .... **CMLC 10**
See DLB 146
Laye, Camara 1928-1980 .. **CLC 4, 38; BLC 2; DAM MULT**
See BW 1; CA 85-88; 97-100; CANR 25; MTCW 1, 2
Layton, Irving (Peter) 1912- ...... **CLC 2, 15; DAC; DAM MST, POET**
See CA 1-4R; CANR 2, 33, 43, 66; DLB 88; MTCW 1, 2
Lazarus, Emma 1849-1887 .... **NCLC 8**
Lazarus, Felix
See Cable, George Washington
Lazarus, Henry
See Slavitt, David R(ytman)
Lea, Joan
See Neufeld, John (Arthur)
Leacock, Stephen (Butler) 1869-1944 . **TCLC 2; DAC; DAM MST**
See CA 104; 141; CANR 80; DLB 92; MTCW 2
Lear, Edward 1812-1888 .... **NCLC 3**
See CLR 1; DLB 32, 163, 166; MAICYA; SATA 18, 100
Lear, Norman (Milton) 1922- .... **CLC 12**
See CA 73-76
Leautaud, Paul 1872-1956 .... **TCLC 83**
See DLB 65
Leavis, F(rank) R(aymond) 1895-1978 . **CLC 24**
See CA 21-24R; 77-80; CANR 44; MTCW 1, 2
Leavitt, David 1961- ..... **CLC 34;DAM POP**
See CA 116; 122; CANR 50, 62; DA3; DLB 130; INT 122; MTCW 2
Leblanc, Maurice (Marie Emile) 1864-1941 .... **TCLC 49**
See CA 110
Lebowitz, Fran(ces Ann) 1951(?)- .. **CLC 11, 36**
See CA 81-84; CANR 14, 60, 70; INT CANR-14; MTCW 1
Lebrecht, Peter
See Tieck, (Johann) Ludwig
le Carre, John .... **CLC 3, 5, 9, 15, 28**
See Cornwell, David (John Moore)
See BEST 89:4; CDBLB 1960 to Present; DLB 87; MTCW 2
Le Clezio, J(ean) M(arie) G(ustave) 1940- .. **CLC 31**
See CA 116; 128; DLB 83
Leconte de Lisle, Charles-Marie-Rene 1818-1894 .... **NCLC 29**
Le Coq, Monsieur
See Simenon, Georges (Jacques Christian)
Leduc, Violette 1907-1972 .... **CLC 22**
See CA 13-14; 33-36R; CANR 69; CAP 1
Ledwidge, Francis 1887(?)-1917 ... **TCLC 23**
See CA 123; DLB 20
Lee, Andrea 1953- .. **CLC 36; BLC 2; DAM MULT**
See BW 1, 3; CA 125; CANR 82
Lee, Andrew
See Auchincloss, Louis (Stanton)
Lee, Chang-rae 1965- .... **CLC 91**
See CA 148
Lee, Don L. .... **CLC 2**
See Madhubuti, Haki R.
Lee, George W(ashington) 1894-1976 . **CLC 52; BLC 2; DAM MULT**
See BW 1; CA 125; CANR 83; DLB 51
Lee, (Nelle) Harper 1926- . **CLC 12, 60; DA; DAB; DAC; DAM MST, NOV; WLC**
See AAYA 13; CA 13-16R; CANR 51; CDALB 1941-1968; DA3; DLB 6; MTCW 1, 2; SATA 11
Lee, Helen Elaine 1959(?)- .... **CLC 86**
See CA 148
Lee, Julian
See Latham, Jean Lee
Lee, Larry
See Lee, Lawrence
Lee, Laurie 1914-1997 . **CLC 90; DAB;DAM POP**
See CA 77-80; 158; CANR 33, 73; DLB 27; MTCW 1
Lee, Lawrence 1941-1990 .... **CLC 34**
See CA 131; CANR 43
Lee, Li-Young 1957- .... **PC 24**
See CA 153; DLB 165
Lee, Manfred B(ennington) 1905-1971 . **CLC 11**
See Queen, Ellery
See CA 1-4R; 29-32R; CANR 2; DLB 137

Lee, Shelton Jackson 1957(?)- ..... **CLC 105; BLCS; DAM MULT**
See Lee, Spike
See BW 2, 3; CA 125; CANR 42
Lee, Spike
See Lee, Shelton Jackson
See AAYA 4, 29
Lee, Stan 1922- .... **CLC 17**
See AAYA 5; CA 108; 111; INT 111
Lee, Tanith 1947- .... **CLC 46**
See AAYA 15; CA 37-40R; CANR 53; SATA 8, 88
Lee, Vernon .... **TCLC 5; SSC 33**
See Paget, Violet
See DLB 57, 153, 156, 174, 178
Lee, William
See Burroughs, William S(eward)
Lee, Willy
See Burroughs, William S(eward)
Lee-Hamilton, Eugene (Jacob) 1845-1907 ... **TCLC 22**
See CA 117
Leet, Judith 1935- .... **CLC 11**
Le Fanu, Joseph Sheridan 1814-1873 .... **NCLC 9, 58; DAM POP; SSC 14**
See DA3; DLB 21, 70, 159, 178
Leffland, Ella 1931- .... **CLC 19**
See CA 29-32R; CANR 35, 78, 82; DLBY 84; INT CANR-35; SATA 65
Leger, Alexis
See Leger, (Marie-Rene Auguste) Alexis Saint-Leger
Leger, (Marie-Rene Auguste) AlexisSaint-Leger 1887-1975 ... **CLC 4, 11, 46; DAM POET; PC 23**
See CA 13-16R; 61-64; CANR 43; MTCW 1
Leger, Saintleger
See Leger, (Marie-Rene Auguste) Alexis Saint-Leger
Le Guin, Ursula K(roeber) 1929- .... **CLC 8, 13, 22, 45, 71; DAB; DAC; DAM MST, POP; SSC 12**
See AAYA 9, 27; AITN 1; CA 21-24R; CANR 9, 32, 52, 74; CDALB 1968-1988; CLR 3, 28; DA3; DLB 8, 52; INT CANR-32; JRDA; MAICYA; MTCW 1, 2; SATA 4, 52, 99
Lehmann, Rosamond (Nina) 1901-1990 ...... **CLC 5**
See CA 77-80; 131; CANR 8, 73; DLB 15; MTCW 2
Leiber, Fritz (Reuter,Jr.) 1910-1992 ..... **CLC 25**
See CA 45-48; 139; CANR 2, 40; DLB 8; MTCW 1, 2; SATA 45; SATA-Obit 73
Leibniz, Gottfried Wilhelmvon 1646-1716 .. **LC 35**
See DLB 168
Leimbach, Martha 1963-
See Leimbach, Marti
See CA 130
Leimbach, Marti .... **CLC 65**
See Leimbach, Martha
Leino, Eino .... **TCLC 24**
See Loennbohm, Armas Eino Leopold
Leiris, Michel (Julien) 1901-1990 ... **CLC 61**
See CA 119; 128; 132
Leithauser, Brad 1953- .... **CLC 27**
See CA 107; CANR 27, 81; DLB 120
Lelchuk, Alan 1938- .... **CLC 5**
See CA 45-48; CAAS 20; CANR 1, 70
Lem, Stanislaw 1921- .... **CLC 8, 15, 40**
See CA 105; CAAS 1; CANR 32; MTCW 1
Lemann, Nancy 1956- .... **CLC 39**
See CA 118; 136
Lemonnier, (Antoine Louis) Camille 1844-1913 .... **TCLC 22**
See CA 121
Lenau, Nikolaus 1802-1850 .... **NCLC 16**
L'Engle, Madeleine (Camp Franklin) 1918- .... **CLC 12; DAM POP**
See AAYA 28; AITN 2; CA 1-4R; CANR 3, 21, 39, 66; CLR 1, 14, 57; DA3; DLB 52; JRDA; MAICYA; MTCW 1, 2; SAAS 15; SATA 1, 27, 75
Lengyel, Jozsef 1896-1975 .... **CLC 7**
See CA 85-88; 57-60; CANR 71
Lenin 1870-1924
See Lenin, V. I.
See CA 121; 168
Lenin, V. I. .... **TCLC 67**
See Lenin
Lennon, John (Ono) 1940-1980 . **CLC 12, 35**
See CA 102
Lennox, Charlotte Ramsay 1729(?)-1804 .... **NCLC 23**
See DLB 39
Lentricchia, Frank(Jr.) 1940- .... **CLC 34**
See CA 25-28R; CANR 19
Lenz, Siegfried 1926- .... **CLC 27;SSC 33**
See CA 89-92; CANR 80; DLB 75
Leonard, Elmore (John, Jr.) 1925- . **CLC 28, 34, 71, 120; DAM POP**
See AAYA 22; AITN 1; BEST 89:1, 90:4; CA 81-84; CANR 12, 28, 53, 76; DA3; DLB 173; INT CANR-28; MTCW 1, 2
Leonard, Hugh .... **CLC 19**
See Byrne, John Keyes
See DLB 13
Leonov, Leonid (Maximovich) 1899-1994 ... **CLC 92; DAM NOV**
See CA 129; CANR 74, 76; MTCW 1, 2
Leopardi, (Conte) Giacomo 1798-1837 .... **NCLC 22**
Le Reveler
See Artaud, Antonin (Marie Joseph)
Lerman, Eleanor 1952- .... **CLC 9**
See CA 85-88; CANR 69
Lerman, Rhoda 1936- .... **CLC 56**
See CA 49-52; CANR 70
Lermontov, Mikhail Yuryevich 1814-1841 .. **NCLC 47; PC 18**
See DLB 205
Leroux, Gaston 1868-1927 .... **TCLC 25**
See CA 108; 136; CANR 69; SATA 65
Lesage, Alain-Rene 1668-1747 .... **LC 2, 28**
Leskov, Nikolai (Semyonovich) 1831-1895 .. **NCLC 25; SSC 34**
Lessing, Doris (May) 1919- . **CLC 1, 2, 3, 6, 10, 15, 22, 40, 94; DA; DAB; DAC; DAM MST, NOV; SSC 6; WLCS**
See CA 9-12R; CAAS 14; CANR 33, 54, 76; CDBLB 1960 to Present; DA3; DLB 15, 139; DLBY 85; MTCW 1, 2
Lessing, Gotthold Ephraim 1729-1781 ... **LC 8**
See DLB 97
Lester, Richard 1932- .... **CLC 20**
Lever, Charles (James) 1806-1872 .... **NCLC 23**
See DLB 21
Leverson, Ada 1865(?)-1936(?) ..... **TCLC 18**
See Elaine
See CA 117; DLB 153
Levertov, Denise 1923-1997 . **CLC 1, 2, 3, 5, 8, 15, 28, 66; DAM POET; PC 11**
See CA 1-4R, 178; 163; CAAE 178; CAAS 19; CANR 3, 29, 50; CDALBS; DLB 5, 165; INT CANR-29; MTCW 1, 2
Levi, Jonathan .... **CLC 76**
Levi, Peter (Chad Tigar) 1931- .... **CLC 41**
See CA 5-8R; CANR 34, 80; DLB 40
Levi, Primo 1919-1987 . **CLC 37, 50;SSC 12**
See CA 13-16R; 122; CANR 12, 33, 61, 70; DLB 177; MTCW 1, 2
Levin, Ira 1929- .... **CLC 3, 6;DAM POP**
See CA 21-24R; CANR 17, 44, 74; DA3; MTCW 1, 2; SATA 66
Levin, Meyer 1905-1981 . **CLC 7;DAM POP**
See AITN 1; CA 9-12R; 104; CANR 15; DLB 9, 28; DLBY 81; SATA 21; SATA-Obit 27
Levine, Norman 1924- .... **CLC 54**
See CA 73-76; CAAS 23; CANR 14, 70; DLB 88
Levine, Philip 1928- . **CLC 2, 4, 5, 9, 14, 33, 118; DAM POET; PC 22**
See CA 9-12R; CANR 9, 37, 52; DLB 5
Levinson, Deirdre 1931- .... **CLC 49**
See CA 73-76; CANR 70
Levi-Strauss, Claude 1908- .... **CLC 38**
See CA 1-4R; CANR 6, 32, 57; MTCW 1, 2
Levitin, Sonia (Wolff) 1934- .... **CLC 17**
See AAYA 13; CA 29-32R; CANR 14, 32, 79; CLR 53; JRDA; MAICYA; SAAS 2; SATA 4, 68
Levon, O. U.
See Kesey, Ken (Elton)
Levy, Amy 1861-1889 .... **NCLC 59**
See DLB 156
Lewes, George Henry 1817-1878 . **NCLC 25**
See DLB 55, 144
Lewis, Alun 1915-1944 .... **TCLC 3**
See CA 104; DLB 20, 162
Lewis, C. Day
See Day Lewis, C(ecil)
Lewis, C(live) S(taples) 1898-1963 ... **CLC 1, 3, 6, 14, 27, 124; DA; DAB; DAC; DAM MST, NOV, POP; WLC**
See AAYA 3; CA 81-84; CANR 33, 71; CDBLB 1945-1960; CLR 3, 27; DA3; DLB 15, 100, 160; JRDA; MAICYA; MTCW 1, 2; SATA 13, 100
Lewis, Janet 1899-1998 .... **CLC 41**
See Winters, Janet Lewis
See CA 9-12R; 172; CANR 29, 63; CAP 1; DLBY 87
Lewis, Matthew Gregory 1775-1818 . **NCLC 11, 62**
See DLB 39, 158, 178
Lewis, (Harry) Sinclair 1885-1951 .... **TCLC 4, 13, 23, 39; DA; DAB; DAC; DAM MST, NOV; WLC**
See CA 104; 133;CDALB 1917-1929; DA3; DLB 9, 102; DLBD 1; MTCW 1, 2
Lewis, (Percy) Wyndham 1882(?)-1957 .... **TCLC 2, 9; SSC 34**
See CA 104; 157; DLB 15; MTCW 2
Lewisohn, Ludwig 1883-1955 .... **TCLC 19**
See CA 107; DLB 4, 9, 28, 102
Lewton, Val 1904-1951 .... **TCLC 76**
Leyner, Mark 1956- .... **CLC 92**
See CA 110; CANR 28, 53; DA3; MTCW 2
Lezama Lima, Jose 1910-1976 ... **CLC 4, 10, 101; DAM MULT; HLCS 2**
See CA 77-80; CANR 71; DLB 113; HW 1, 2
L'Heureux, John(Clarke) 1934- ...... **CLC 52**
See CA 13-16R; CANR 23, 45
Liddell, C. H.
See Kuttner, Henry
Lie, Jonas (Lauritz Idemil) 1833-1908(?) .... **TCLC 5**
See CA 115
Lieber, Joel 1937-1971 .... **CLC 6**
See CA 73-76; 29-32R
Lieber, Stanley Martin
See Lee, Stan
Lieberman, Laurence (James) 1935- ... **CLC 4, 36**
See CA 17-20R; CANR 8, 36

Author Index

Lieh Tzu fl. 7th cent. B.C.-5th cent. B.C. ...... **CMLC 27**
Lieksman, Anders
See Haavikko, Paavo Juhani
Li Fei-kan 1904-
See Pa Chin
See CA 105
Lifton, Robert Jay 1926- .... **CLC 67**
See CA 17-20R; CANR 27, 78; INT CANR-27; SATA 66
Lightfoot, Gordon 1938- .... **CLC 26**
See CA 109
Lightman, Alan P(aige) 1948- .... **CLC 81**
See CA 141; CANR 63
Ligotti, Thomas (Robert) 1953- ..... **CLC 44; SSC 16**
See CA 123; CANR 49
Li Ho 791-817 .... **PC 13**
Liliencron, (Friedrich Adolf Axel) Detlevvon 1844-1909 .... **TCLC 18**
See CA 117
Lilly, William 1602-1681 .... **LC 27**
Lima, Jose Lezama
See Lezama Lima, Jose
Lima Barreto, Afonso Henriquede 1881-1922 .... **TCLC 23**
See CA 117; 181
Limonov, Edward 1944- .... **CLC 67**
See CA 137
Lin, Frank
See Atherton, Gertrude (Franklin Horn)
Lincoln, Abraham 1809-1865 .... **NCLC 18**
Lind, Jakov .... **CLC 1, 2, 4, 27, 82**
See Landwirth, Heinz
See CAAS 4
Lindbergh, Anne (Spencer) Morrow 1906- . **CLC 82; DAM NOV**
See CA 17-20R; CANR 16, 73; MTCW 1, 2; SATA 33
Lindsay, David 1878-1945 .... **TCLC 15**
See CA 113
Lindsay, (Nicholas) Vachel 1879-1931 .... **TCLC 17; DA; DAC; DAM MST, POET; PC 23; WLC**
See CA 114; 135; CANR 79; CDALB 1865-1917; DA3; DLB 54; SATA 40
Linke-Poot
See Doeblin, Alfred
Linney, Romulus 1930- .... **CLC 51**
See CA 1-4R; CANR 40, 44, 79
Linton, Eliza Lynn 1822-1898 ...... **NCLC 41**
See DLB 18
Li Po 701-763 .... **CMLC 2**
Lipsius, Justus 1547-1606 .... **LC 16**
Lipsyte, Robert (Michael) 1938- .... **CLC 21; DA; DAC; DAM MST, NOV**
See AAYA 7; CA 17-20R; CANR 8, 57; CLR 23; JRDA; MAICYA; SATA 5, 68
Lish, Gordon (Jay) 1934- ... **CLC 45;SSC 18**
See CA 113; 117; CANR 79; DLB 130; INT 117
Lispector, Clarice 1925(?)-1977 ..... **CLC 43; HLCS 2; SSC 34**
See CA 139; 116; CANR 71; DLB 113; HW 2
Littell, Robert 1935(?)- .... **CLC 42**
See CA 109; 112; CANR 64
Little, Malcolm 1925-1965
See Malcolm X
See BW 1, 3; CA 125; 111; CANR 82; DA; DAB; DAC; DAM MST, MULT; DA3; MTCW 1, 2
Littlewit, Humphrey Gent.
See Lovecraft, H(oward) P(hillips)
Litwos
See Sienkiewicz, Henryk (Adam Alexander Pius)
Liu, E 1857-1909 .... **TCLC 15**
See CA 115
Lively, Penelope (Margaret) 1933- . **CLC 32, 50; DAM NOV**
See CA 41-44R; CANR 29, 67, 79; CLR 7; DLB 14, 161, 207; JRDA; MAICYA; MTCW 1, 2; SATA 7, 60, 101
Livesay, Dorothy (Kathleen) 1909- .. **CLC 4, 15, 79; DAC; DAM MST, POET**
See AITN 2; CA 25-28R; CAAS 8; CANR 36, 67; DLB 68; MTCW 1
Livy c. 59B.C.-c. 17 .... **CMLC 11**
See DLB 211
Lizardi, Jose Joaquin Fernandez de 1776-1827 .... **NCLC 30**
Llewellyn, Richard
See Llewellyn Lloyd, Richard Dafydd Vivian
See DLB 15
Llewellyn Lloyd, Richard Dafydd Vivian 1906-1983 .... **CLC 7, 80**
See Llewellyn, Richard
See CA 53-56; 111; CANR 7, 71; SATA 11; SATA-Obit 37
Llosa, (Jorge) Mario (Pedro) Vargas
See Vargas Llosa, (Jorge) Mario (Pedro)
Lloyd, Manda
See Mander, (Mary) Jane
Lloyd Webber, Andrew 1948-
See Webber, Andrew Lloyd
See AAYA 1; CA 116; 149; DAM DRAM; SATA 56
Llull, Ramon c. 1235-c. 1316 .... **CMLC 12**
Lobb, Ebenezer
See Upward, Allen
Locke, Alain (Le Roy) 1886-1954 ...... **TCLC 43; BLCS**
See BW 1, 3; CA 106; 124; CANR 79; DLB 51
Locke, John 1632-1704 .... **LC 7, 35**
See DLB 101
Locke-Elliott, Sumner
See Elliott, Sumner Locke
Lockhart, John Gibson 1794-1854 . **NCLC 6**
See DLB 110, 116, 144
Lodge, David (John) 1935- ... **CLC 36;DAM POP**
See BEST 90:1; CA 17-20R; CANR 19, 53; DLB 14, 194; INT CANR-19; MTCW 1, 2
Lodge, Thomas 1558-1625 .... **LC 41**
Lodge, Thomas 1558-1625 .... **LC 41**
See DLB 172
Loennbohm, Armas Eino Leopold 1878-1926
See Leino, Eino
See CA 123
Loewinsohn, Ron(ald William) 1937- .. **CLC 52**
See CA 25-28R; CANR 71
Logan, Jake
See Smith, Martin Cruz
Logan, John(Burton) 1923-1987 .... **CLC 5**
See CA 77-80; 124; CANR 45; DLB 5
Lo Kuan-chung 1330(?)-1400(?) .... **LC 12**
Lombard, Nap
See Johnson, Pamela Hansford
London, Jack .... **TCLC 9, 15, 39; SSC 4; WLC**
See London, John Griffith
See AAYA 13; AITN 2; CDALB 1865-1917; DLB 8, 12, 78, 212; SATA 18
London, John Griffith 1876-1916
See London, Jack
See CA 110; 119; CANR 73; DA; DAB; DAC; DAM MST, NOV; DA3; JRDA; MAICYA; MTCW 1, 2
Long, Emmett
See Leonard, Elmore (John, Jr.)
Longbaugh, Harry
See Goldman, William (W.)
Longfellow, Henry Wadsworth 1807-1882 .. **NCLC 2, 45; DA; DAB; DAC; DAM MST, POET; WLCS**
See CDALB 1640-1865; DA3; DLB 1, 59; SATA 19
Longinus c. 1st cent. - .... **CMLC 27**
See DLB 176
Longley, Michael 1939- .... **CLC 29**
See CA 102; DLB 40
Longus fl. c. 2nd cent. - .... **CMLC 7**
Longway, A. Hugh
See Lang, Andrew
Lonnrot, Elias 1802-1884 .... **NCLC 53**
Lopate, Phillip 1943- .... **CLC 29**
See CA 97-100; DLBY 80; INT 97-100
Lopez Portillo (y Pacheco),Jose 1920- . **CLC 46**
See CA 129; HW 1
Lopez y Fuentes,Gregorio 1897(?)-1966 ...... **CLC 32**
See CA 131; HW 1
Lorca, Federico Garcia
See Garcia Lorca, Federico
Lord, Bette Bao 1938- .... **CLC 23**
See BEST 90:3; CA 107; CANR 41, 79; INT 107; SATA 58
Lord Auch
See Bataille, Georges
Lord Byron
See Byron, George Gordon (Noel)
Lorde, Audre (Geraldine) 1934-1992 ... **CLC 18, 71; BLC 2; DAM MULT, POET; PC 12**
See BW 1, 3; CA 25-28R; 142; CANR 16, 26, 46, 82; DA3; DLB 41; MTCW 1, 2
Lord Houghton
See Milnes, Richard Monckton
Lord Jeffrey
See Jeffrey, Francis
Lorenzini, Carlo 1826-1890
See Collodi, Carlo
See MAICYA; SATA 29, 100
Lorenzo, Heberto Padilla
See Padilla (Lorenzo), Heberto
Loris
See Hofmannsthal, Hugo von
Loti, Pierre .... **TCLC 11**
See Viaud, (Louis Marie) Julien
See DLB 123
Lou, Henri
See Andreas-Salome, Lou
Louie, David Wong 1954- .... **CLC 70**
See CA 139
Louis, Father M.
See Merton, Thomas
Lovecraft, H(oward) P(hillips) 1890-1937 ... **TCLC 4, 22; DAM POP; SSC 3**
See AAYA 14; CA 104; 133; DA3; MTCW 1, 2
Lovelace, Earl 1935- .... **CLC 51**
See BW 2; CA 77-80; CANR 41, 72; DLB 125; MTCW 1
Lovelace, Richard 1618-1657 .... **LC 24**
See DLB 131
Lowell, Amy 1874-1925 ... **TCLC 1, 8; DAM POET; PC 13**
See CA 104; 151; DLB 54, 140; MTCW 2
Lowell, James Russell 1819-1891 ... **NCLC 2**
See CDALB 1640-1865; DLB 1, 11, 64, 79, 189
Lowell, Robert (Traill Spence, Jr.) 1917-1977 ... **CLC 1, 2, 3, 4, 5, 8, 9, 11, 15, 37, 124; DA; DAB; DAC; DAM MST, NOV; PC 3; WLC**
See CA 9-12R; 73-76; CABS 2; CANR 26, 60; CDALBS; DA3; DLB 5, 169; MTCW 1, 2

Lowenthal, Michael (Francis) 1969- .... **CLC 119**
See CA 150
Lowndes, Marie Adelaide (Belloc) 1868-1947 .... **TCLC 12**
See CA 107; DLB 70
Lowry, (Clarence) Malcolm 1909-1957 .... **TCLC 6, 40; SSC 31**
See CA 105; 131; CANR 62; CDBLB 1945-1960; DLB 15; MTCW 1, 2
Lowry, Mina Gertrude 1882-1966
See Loy, Mina
See CA 113
Loxsmith, John
See Brunner, John (Kilian Houston)
Loy, Mina ..... **CLC 28; DAM POET; PC 16**
See Lowry, Mina Gertrude
See DLB 4, 54
Loyson-Bridet
See Schwob, Marcel (Mayer Andre)
Lucan 39-65 .... **CMLC 33**
See DLB 211
Lucas, Craig 1951- .... **CLC 64**
See CA 137; CANR 71
Lucas, E(dward) V(errall) 1868-1938 .... **TCLC 73**
See CA 176; DLB 98, 149, 153; SATA 20
Lucas, George 1944- .... **CLC 16**
See AAYA 1, 23; CA 77-80; CANR 30; SATA 56
Lucas, Hans
See Godard, Jean-Luc
Lucas, Victoria
See Plath, Sylvia
Lucian c. 120-c. 180 .... **CMLC 32**
See DLB 176
Ludlam, Charles 1943-1987 .... **CLC 46,50**
See CA 85-88; 122; CANR 72
Ludlum, Robert 1927- ... **CLC 22, 43; DAM NOV, POP**
See AAYA 10; BEST 89:1, 90:3; CA 33-36R; CANR 25, 41, 68; DA3; DLBY 82; MTCW 1, 2
Ludwig, Ken .... **CLC 60**
Ludwig, Otto 1813-1865 .... **NCLC 4**
See DLB 129
Lugones, Leopoldo 1874-1938 ..... **TCLC 15; HLCS 2**
See CA 116; 131; HW 1
Lu Hsun 1881-1936 .... **TCLC 3; SSC 20**
See Shu-Jen, Chou
Lukacs, George .... **CLC 24**
See Lukacs, Gyorgy (Szegeny von)
Lukacs, Gyorgy (Szegeny von) 1885-1971
See Lukacs, George
See CA 101; 29-32R; CANR 62; MTCW 2
Luke, Peter (Ambrose Cyprian) 1919-1995 .... **CLC 38**
See CA 81-84; 147; CANR 72; DLB 13
Lunar, Dennis
See Mungo, Raymond
Lurie, Alison 1926- .... **CLC 4, 5, 18, 39**
See CA 1-4R; CANR 2, 17, 50; DLB 2; MTCW 1; SATA 46
Lustig, Arnost 1926- .... **CLC 56**
See AAYA 3; CA 69-72; CANR 47; SATA 56
Luther, Martin 1483-1546 .... **LC 9, 37**
See DLB 179
Luxemburg, Rosa 1870(?)-1919 .... **TCLC 63**
See CA 118
Luzi, Mario 1914- .... **CLC 13**
See CA 61-64; CANR 9, 70; DLB 128
Lyly, John 1554(?)-1606 .... **LC 41; DAM DRAM; DC 7**
See DLB 62, 167
L'Ymagier
See Gourmont, Remy (-Marie-Charles) de
Lynch, B. Suarez
See Bioy Casares, Adolfo; Borges, Jorge Luis
Lynch, B. Suarez
See Bioy Casares, Adolfo
Lynch, David (K.) 1946- .... **CLC 66**
See CA 124; 129
Lynch, James
See Andreyev, Leonid (Nikolaevich)
Lynch Davis, B.
See Bioy Casares, Adolfo; Borges, Jorge Luis
Lyndsay, Sir David 1490-1555 .... **LC 20**
Lynn, Kenneth S(chuyler) 1923- ..... **CLC 50**
See CA 1-4R; CANR 3, 27, 65
Lynx
See West, Rebecca
Lyons, Marcus
See Blish, James (Benjamin)
Lyre, Pinchbeck
See Sassoon, Siegfried (Lorraine)
Lytle, Andrew (Nelson) 1902-1995 .. **CLC 22**
See CA 9-12R; 150; CANR 70; DLB 6; DLBY 95
Lyttelton, George 1709-1773 .... **LC 10**
Maas, Peter 1929- .... **CLC 29**
See CA 93-96; INT 93-96; MTCW 2
Macaulay, Rose 1881-1958 .... **TCLC 7, 44**
See CA 104; DLB 36
Macaulay, Thomas Babington 1800-1859 .... **NCLC 42**
See CDBLB 1832-1890; DLB 32, 55
MacBeth, George (Mann) 1932-1992 ... **CLC 2, 5, 9**
See CA 25-28R; 136; CANR 61, 66; DLB 40; MTCW 1; SATA 4; SATA-Obit 70
MacCaig, Norman (Alexander) 1910- . **CLC 36; DAB; DAM POET**
See CA 9-12R; CANR 3, 34; DLB 27
MacCarthy, Sir (Charles Otto) Desmond 1877-1952 .... **TCLC 36**
See CA 167
MacDiarmid, Hugh .... **CLC 2, 4, 11, 19, 63; PC 9**
See Grieve, C(hristopher) M(urray)
See CDBLB 1945-1960; DLB 20
MacDonald, Anson
See Heinlein, Robert A(nson)
Macdonald, Cynthia 1928- .... **CLC 13, 19**
See CA 49-52; CANR 4, 44; DLB 105
MacDonald, George 1824-1905 ...... **TCLC 9**
See CA 106; 137; CANR 80; DLB 18, 163, 178; MAICYA; SATA 33, 100
Macdonald, John
See Millar, Kenneth
MacDonald, John D(ann) 1916-1986 ... **CLC 3, 27, 44; DAM NOV, POP**
See CA 1-4R; 121; CANR 1, 19, 60; DLB 8; DLBY 86; MTCW 1, 2
Macdonald, John Ross
See Millar, Kenneth
Macdonald, Ross ..... **CLC 1, 2, 3, 14, 34, 41**
See Millar, Kenneth
See DLBD 6
MacDougal, John
See Blish, James (Benjamin)
MacEwen, Gwendolyn (Margaret) 1941-1987 .... **CLC 13, 55**
See CA 9-12R; 124; CANR 7, 22; DLB 53; SATA 50; SATA-Obit 55
Macha, Karel Hynek 1810-1846 .. **NCLC 46**
Machado (y Ruiz),Antonio 1875-1939 .... **TCLC 3**
See CA 104; 174; DLB 108; HW 2
Machado de Assis, Joaquim Maria 1839-1908 .... **TCLC 10; BLC 2; HLCS 2; SSC 24**
See CA 107; 153
Machen, Arthur .... **TCLC 4; SSC 20**
See Jones, Arthur Llewellyn
See CA 179; DLB 36, 156, 178
Machiavelli, Niccolo 1469-1527 .... **LC 8, 36; DA; DAB; DAC; DAM MST; WLCS**
MacInnes, Colin 1914-1976 .... **CLC 4, 23**
See CA 69-72; 65-68; CANR 21; DLB 14; MTCW 1, 2
MacInnes, Helen (Clark) 1907-1985 .... **CLC 27, 39; DAM POP**
See CA 1-4R; 117; CANR 1, 28, 58; DLB 87; MTCW 1, 2; SATA 22; SATA-Obit 44
Mackenzie, Compton (Edward Montague) 1883-1972 .... **CLC 18**
See CA 21-22; 37-40R; CAP 2; DLB 34, 100
Mackenzie, Henry 1745-1831 .... **NCLC 41**
See DLB 39
Mackintosh, Elizabeth 1896(?)-1952
See Tey, Josephine
See CA 110
MacLaren, James
See Grieve, C(hristopher) M(urray)
Mac Laverty, Bernard 1942- .... **CLC 31**
See CA 116; 118; CANR 43; INT 118
MacLean, Alistair (Stuart) 1922(?)-1987 ..... **CLC 3, 13, 50, 63; DAM POP**
See CA 57-60; 121; CANR 28, 61; MTCW 1; SATA 23; SATA-Obit 50
Maclean, Norman (Fitzroy) 1902-1990 . **CLC 78; DAM POP; SSC 13**
See CA 102; 132; CANR 49; DLB 206
MacLeish, Archibald 1892-1982 .. **CLC 3, 8, 14, 68; DAM POET**
See CA 9-12R; 106; CANR 33, 63; CDALBS; DLB 4, 7, 45; DLBY 82; MTCW 1, 2
MacLennan, (John) Hugh 1907-1990 .. **CLC 2, 14, 92; DAC; DAM MST**
See CA 5-8R; 142; CANR 33; DLB 68; MTCW 1, 2
MacLeod, Alistair 1936- ...... **CLC 56; DAC; DAM MST**
See CA 123; DLB 60; MTCW 2
Macleod, Fiona
See Sharp, William
MacNeice, (Frederick) Louis 1907-1963 ...... **CLC 1, 4, 10, 53; DAB; DAM POET**
See CA 85-88; CANR 61; DLB 10, 20; MTCW 1, 2
MacNeill, Dand
See Fraser, George MacDonald
Macpherson, James 1736-1796 .... **LC 29**
See Ossian
See DLB 109
Macpherson, (Jean) Jay 1931- .... **CLC 14**
See CA 5-8R; DLB 53
MacShane, Frank 1927- .... **CLC 39**
See CA 9-12R; CANR 3, 33; DLB 111
Macumber, Mari
See Sandoz, Mari(e Susette)
Madach, Imre 1823-1864 .... **NCLC 19**
Madden, (Jerry) David 1933- ..... **CLC 5, 15**
See CA 1-4R; CAAS 3; CANR 4, 45; DLB 6; MTCW 1
Maddern, Al(an)
See Ellison, Harlan (Jay)
Madhubuti, Haki R. 1942- . **CLC 6, 73; BLC 2; DAM MULT, POET; PC 5**
See Lee, Don L.
See BW 2, 3; CA 73-76; CANR 24, 51, 73; DLB 5, 41; DLBD 8; MTCW 2
Maepenn, Hugh
See Kuttner, Henry
Maepenn, K. H.
See Kuttner, Henry
Maeterlinck, Maurice 1862-1949 .. **TCLC 3; DAM DRAM**

See CA 104; 136; CANR 80; DLB 192; SATA 66
Maginn, William 1794-1842 .... **NCLC 8**
See DLB 110, 159
Mahapatra, Jayanta 1928- .... **CLC 33;DAM MULT**
See CA 73-76; CAAS 9; CANR 15, 33, 66
Mahfouz, Naguib (Abdel Aziz Al-Sabilgi) 1911(?)-
See Mahfuz, Najib
See BEST 89:2; CA 128; CANR 55; DAM NOV; DA3; MTCW 1, 2
Mahfuz, Najib .... **CLC 52, 55**
See Mahfouz, Naguib (Abdel Aziz Al-Sabilgi)
See DLBY 88
Mahon, Derek 1941- .... **CLC 27**
See CA 113; 128; DLB 40
Mailer, Norman 1923- . **CLC 1, 2, 3, 4, 5, 8, 11, 14, 28, 39, 74, 111; DA; DAB; DAC; DAM MST, NOV, POP**
See AAYA 31; AITN 2; CA 9-12R; CABS 1; CANR 28, 74, 77; CDALB 1968-1988; DA3; DLB 2, 16, 28, 185; DLBD 3; DLBY 80, 83; MTCW 1, 2
Maillet, Antonine 1929- . **CLC 54, 118; DAC**
See CA 115; 120; CANR 46, 74, 77; DLB 60; INT 120; MTCW 2
Mais, Roger 1905-1955 .... **TCLC 8**
See BW 1, 3; CA 105; 124; CANR 82; DLB 125; MTCW 1
Maistre, Joseph de 1753-1821 ...... **NCLC 37**
Maitland, Frederic 1850-1906 ...... **TCLC 65**
Maitland, Sara (Louise) 1950- .... **CLC 49**
See CA 69-72; CANR 13, 59
Major, Clarence 1936- . **CLC 3, 19, 48; BLC 2; DAM MULT**
See BW 2, 3; CA 21-24R; CAAS 6; CANR 13, 25, 53, 82; DLB 33
Major, Kevin (Gerald) 1949- . **CLC 26; DAC**
See AAYA 16; CA 97-100; CANR 21, 38; CLR 11; DLB 60; INT CANR-21; JRDA; MAICYA; SATA 32, 82
Maki, James
See Ozu, Yasujiro
Malabaila, Damiano
See Levi, Primo
Malamud, Bernard 1914-1986 . **CLC 1, 2, 3, 5, 8, 9, 11, 18, 27, 44, 78, 85; DA; DAB; DAC; DAM MST, NOV, POP; SSC 15;WLC**
See AAYA 16; CA 5-8R; 118; CABS 1; CANR 28, 62; CDALB 1941-1968; DA3; DLB 2, 28, 152; DLBY 80, 86; MTCW 1, 2
Malan, Herman
See Bosman, Herman Charles; Bosman, Herman Charles
Malaparte, Curzio 1898-1957 .... **TCLC 52**
Malcolm, Dan
See Silverberg, Robert
Malcolm X .... **CLC 82, 117; BLC 2; WLCS**
See Little, Malcolm
Malherbe, Francois de 1555-1628 .... **LC 5**
Mallarme, Stephane 1842-1898 ..... **NCLC 4, 41; DAM POET; PC 4**
Mallet-Joris, Francoise 1930- .... **CLC 11**
See CA 65-68; CANR 17; DLB 83
Malley, Ern
See McAuley, James Phillip
Mallowan, Agatha Christie
See Christie, Agatha (Mary Clarissa)
Maloff, Saul 1922- .... **CLC 5**
See CA 33-36R
Malone, Louis
See MacNeice, (Frederick) Louis
Malone, Michael (Christopher) 1942- . **CLC 43**
See CA 77-80; CANR 14, 32, 57
Malory, (Sir) Thomas 1410(?)-1471(?) ... **LC 11; DA; DAB; DAC; DAM MST; WLCS**
See CDBLB Before 1660; DLB 146; SATA 59; SATA-Brief 33
Malouf, (George Joseph) David 1934- . **CLC 28, 86**
See CA 124; CANR 50, 76; MTCW 2
Malraux, (Georges-)Andre 1901-1976 . **CLC 1, 4, 9, 13, 15, 57; DAM NOV**
See CA 21-22; 69-72; CANR 34, 58; CAP 2; DA3; DLB 72; MTCW 1, 2
Malzberg, Barry N(athaniel) 1939- .. **CLC 7**
See CA 61-64; CAAS 4; CANR 16; DLB 8
Mamet, David (Alan) 1947- . **CLC 9, 15, 34, 46, 91; DAM DRAM; DC 4**
See AAYA 3; CA 81-84; CABS 3; CANR 15, 41, 67, 72; DA3; DLB 7; MTCW 1, 2
Mamoulian, Rouben (Zachary) 1897-1987 .. **CLC 16**
See CA 25-28R; 124; CANR 85
Mandelstam, Osip (Emilievich) 1891(?)-1938(?) .... **TCLC 2, 6; PC 14**
See CA 104; 150; MTCW 2
Mander, (Mary)Jane 1877-1949 ... **TCLC 31**
See CA 162
Mandeville, John fl. 1350- .... **CMLC 19**
See DLB 146
Mandiargues, Andre Pieyre de .... **CLC 41**
See Pieyre de Mandiargues, Andre
See DLB 83
Mandrake, Ethel Belle
See Thurman, Wallace (Henry)
Mangan, James Clarence 1803-1849 . **NCLC 27**
Maniere, J.-E.
See Giraudoux, (Hippolyte) Jean
Mankiewicz, Herman (Jacob) 1897-1953 .... **TCLC 85**
See CA 120; 169; DLB 26
Manley, (Mary) Delariviere 1672(?)-1724 ... **LC 1, 42**
See DLB 39, 80
Mann, Abel
See Creasey, John
Mann, Emily 1952- .... **DC 7**
See CA 130; CANR 55
Mann, (Luiz) Heinrich 1871-1950 .. **TCLC 9**
See CA 106; 164, 181; DLB 66, 118
Mann, (Paul) Thomas 1875-1955 .. **TCLC 2, 8, 14, 21, 35, 44, 60; DA; DAB; DAC; DAM MST, NOV; SSC 5; WLC**
See CA 104; 128; DA3; DLB 66; MTCW 1, 2
Mannheim, Karl 1893-1947 .... **TCLC 65**
Manning, David
See Faust, Frederick (Schiller)
Manning, Frederic 1887(?)-1935 .. **TCLC 25**
See CA 124
Manning, Olivia 1915-1980 .... **CLC 5, 19**
See CA 5-8R; 101; CANR 29; MTCW 1
Mano, D. Keith 1942- .... **CLC 2, 10**
See CA 25-28R; CAAS 6; CANR 26, 57; DLB 6
Mansfield, Katherine . **TCLC 2, 8, 39; DAB; SSC 9, 23; WLC**
See Beauchamp, Kathleen Mansfield
See DLB 162
Manso, Peter 1940- .... **CLC 39**
See CA 29-32R; CANR 44
Mantecon, Juan Jimenez
See Jimenez (Mantecon), Juan Ramon
Manton, Peter
See Creasey, John
Man Without a Spleen, A
See Chekhov, Anton (Pavlovich)
Manzoni, Alessandro 1785-1873 ... **NCLC 29**
Map, Walter 1140-1209 .... **CMLC 32**
Mapu, Abraham (ben Jekutiel) 1808-1867 .. **NCLC 18**
Mara, Sally
See Queneau, Raymond
Marat, Jean Paul 1743-1793 .... **LC 10**
Marcel, Gabriel Honore 1889-1973 . **CLC 15**
See CA 102; 45-48; MTCW 1, 2
March, William 1893-1954 .... **TCLC 96**
Marchbanks, Samuel
See Davies, (William) Robertson
Marchi, Giacomo
See Bassani, Giorgio
Margulies, Donald .... **CLC 76**
Marie de France c. 12th cent. - .... **CMLC 8; PC 22**
See DLB 208
Marie de l'Incarnation 1599-1672 ..... **LC 10**
Marier, Captain Victor
See Griffith, D(avid Lewelyn) W(ark)
Mariner, Scott
See Pohl, Frederik
Marinetti, Filippo Tommaso 1876-1944 .... **TCLC 10**
See CA 107; DLB 114
Marivaux, Pierre Carlet de Chamblain de 1688-1763 .... **LC 4; DC 7**
Markandaya, Kamala .... **CLC 8, 38**
See Taylor, Kamala (Purnaiya)
Markfield, Wallace 1926- .... **CLC 8**
See CA 69-72; CAAS 3; DLB 2, 28
Markham, Edwin 1852-1940 .... **TCLC 47**
See CA 160; DLB 54, 186
Markham, Robert
See Amis, Kingsley (William)
Marks, J
See Highwater, Jamake (Mamake)
Marks-Highwater, J
See Highwater, Jamake (Mamake)
Markson, David M(errill) 1927- ..... **CLC 67**
See CA 49-52; CANR 1
Marley, Bob .... **CLC 17**
See Marley, Robert Nesta
Marley, Robert Nesta 1945-1981
See Marley, Bob
See CA 107; 103
Marlowe, Christopher 1564-1593 ..... **LC 22, 47; DA; DAB; DAC; DAM DRAM, MST; DC 1; WLC**
See CDBLB Before 1660; DA3; DLB 62
Marlowe, Stephen 1928-
See Queen, Ellery
See CA 13-16R; CANR 6, 55
Marmontel, Jean-Francois 1723-1799 . **LC 2**
Marquand, John P(hillips) 1893-1960 . **CLC 2, 10**
See CA 85-88; CANR 73; DLB 9, 102; MTCW 2
Marques, Rene 1919-1979 ... **CLC 96; DAM MULT; HLC 2**
See CA 97-100; 85-88; CANR 78; DLB 113; HW 1, 2
Marquez, Gabriel (Jose) Garcia
See Garcia Marquez, Gabriel (Jose)
Marquis, Don(ald Robert Perry) 1878-1937 .... **TCLC 7**
See CA 104; 166; DLB 11, 25
Marric, J. J.
See Creasey, John
Marryat, Frederick 1792-1848 .... **NCLC 3**
See DLB 21, 163
Marsden, James
See Creasey, John
Marsh, (Edith) Ngaio 1899-1982 ...... **CLC 7, 53; DAM POP**
See CA 9-12R; CANR 6, 58; DLB 77; MTCW 1, 2
Marshall, Garry 1934- .... **CLC 17**
See AAYA 3; CA 111; SATA 60

Marshall, Paule 1929- . **CLC 27, 72; BLC 3; DAM MULT; SSC 3**
See BW 2, 3; CA 77-80; CANR 25, 73; DA3; DLB 157; MTCW 1, 2
Marshallik
See Zangwill, Israel
Marsten, Richard
See Hunter, Evan
Marston, John 1576-1634 .... **LC 33;DAM DRAM**
See DLB 58, 172
Martha, Henry
See Harris, Mark
Marti (y Perez), Jose (Julian) 1853-1895 .... **NCLC 63; DAM MULT; HLC 2**
See HW 2
Martial c. 40-c. 104 .... **CMLC 35;PC 10**
See DLB 211
Martin, Ken
See Hubbard, L(afayette) Ron(ald)
Martin, Richard
See Creasey, John
Martin, Steve 1945- .... **CLC 30**
See CA 97-100; CANR 30; MTCW 1
Martin, Valerie 1948- .... **CLC 89**
See BEST 90:2; CA 85-88; CANR 49
Martin, Violet Florence 1862-1915 .... **TCLC 51**
Martin, Webber
See Silverberg, Robert
Martindale, Patrick Victor
See White, Patrick (Victor Martindale)
Martin du Gard,Roger 1881-1958 ..... **TCLC 24**
See CA 118; DLB 65
Martineau, Harriet 1802-1876 ..... **NCLC 26**
See DLB 21, 55, 159, 163, 166, 190; YABC 2
Martines, Julia
See O'Faolain, Julia
Martinez, Enrique Gonzalez
See Gonzalez Martinez, Enrique
Martinez, Jacinto Benavente y
See Benavente (y Martinez), Jacinto
Martinez Ruiz, Jose 1873-1967
See Azorin; Ruiz, Jose Martinez
See CA 93-96; HW 1
Martinez Sierra,Gregorio 1881-1947 . **TCLC 6**
See CA 115
Martinez Sierra, Maria (de laO'LeJarraga) 1874-1974 .... **TCLC 6**
See CA 115
Martinsen, Martin
See Follett, Ken(neth Martin)
Martinson, Harry(Edmund) 1904-1978 .... **CLC 14**
See CA 77-80; CANR 34
Marut, Ret
See Traven, B.
Marut, Robert
See Traven, B.
Marvell, Andrew 1621-1678 . **LC 4, 43; DA; DAB; DAC; DAM MST, POET; PC 10; WLC**
See CDBLB 1660-1789; DLB 131
Marx, Karl (Heinrich) 1818-1883 . **NCLC 17**
See DLB 129
Masaoka Shiki .... **TCLC 18**
See Masaoka Tsunenori
Masaoka Tsunenori 1867-1902
See Masaoka Shiki
See CA 117
Masefield, John (Edward) 1878-1967 .. **CLC 11, 47; DAM POET**
See CA 19-20; 25-28R; CANR 33; CAP 2; CDBLB 1890-1914; DLB 10, 19, 153, 160; MTCW 1, 2; SATA 19
Maso, Carole 19(?)- .... **CLC 44**
See CA 170
Mason, Bobbie Ann 1940- . **CLC 28, 43, 82; SSC 4**
See AAYA 5; CA 53-56; CANR 11, 31, 58, 83; CDALBS; DA3; DLB 173; DLBY 87; INT CANR-31; MTCW 1, 2
Mason, Ernst
See Pohl, Frederik
Mason, Lee W.
See Malzberg, Barry N(athaniel)
Mason, Nick 1945- .... **CLC 35**
Mason, Tally
See Derleth, August (William)
Mass, William
See Gibson, William
Master Lao
See Lao Tzu
Masters, Edgar Lee 1868-1950 ...... **TCLC 2, 25; DA; DAC; DAM MST, POET; PC 1; WLCS**
See CA 104; 133;CDALB 1865-1917; DLB 54; MTCW 1, 2
Masters, Hilary 1928- .... **CLC 48**
See CA 25-28R; CANR 13, 47
Mastrosimone, William 19(?)- .... **CLC 36**
Mathe, Albert
See Camus, Albert
Mather,Cotton 1663-1728 .... **LC 38**
See CDALB 1640-1865; DLB 24, 30, 140
Mather, Increase 1639-1723 .... **LC 38**
See DLB 24
Matheson, RichardBurton 1926- .... **CLC 37**
See AAYA 31; CA 97-100; DLB 8, 44; INT 97-100
Mathews, Harry 1930- .... **CLC 6, 52**
See CA 21-24R; CAAS 6; CANR 18, 40
Mathews, John Joseph 1894-1979 . **CLC 84; DAM MULT**
See CA 19-20; 142; CANR 45; CAP 2; DLB 175; NNAL
Mathias, Roland (Glyn) 1915- .... **CLC 45**
See CA 97-100; CANR 19, 41; DLB 27
Matsuo Basho 1644-1694 .... **PC 3**
See DAM POET
Mattheson, Rodney
See Creasey, John
Matthews, Brander 1852-1929 ..... **TCLC 95**
See DLB 71, 78; DLBD 13
Matthews, Greg 1949- .... **CLC 45**
See CA 135
Matthews, William (Procter,III) 1942-1997 . **CLC 40**
See CA 29-32R; 162; CAAS 18; CANR 12, 57; DLB 5
Matthias, John (Edward) 1941- .... **CLC 9**
See CA 33-36R; CANR 56
Matthiessen, Peter 1927- .. **CLC 5, 7, 11, 32, 64; DAM NOV**
See AAYA 6; BEST 90:4; CA 9-12R; CANR 21, 50, 73; DA3; DLB 6, 173; MTCW 1, 2; SATA 27
Maturin, Charles Robert 1780(?)-1824 .... **NCLC 6**
See DLB 178
Matute (Ausejo), Ana Maria 1925- . **CLC 11**
See CA 89-92; MTCW 1
Maugham, W. S.
See Maugham, W(illiam) Somerset
Maugham, W(illiam) Somerset 1874-1965 .. **CLC 1, 11, 15, 67, 93; DA; DAB; DAC; DAM DRAM, MST, NOV; SSC 8; WLC**
See CA 5-8R; 25-28R; CANR 40; CDBLB 1914-1945; DA3; DLB 10, 36, 77, 100, 162, 195; MTCW 1, 2; SATA 54
Maugham, William Somerset
See Maugham, W(illiam) Somerset
Maupassant, (Henri Rene Albert) Guy de 1850-1893 ...... **NCLC 1, 42; DA; DAB; DAC; DAM MST; SSC 1; WLC**
See DA3; DLB 123
Maupin, Armistead 1944- ..... **CLC 95;DAM POP**
See CA 125; 130; CANR 58; DA3; INT 130; MTCW 2
Maurhut, Richard
See Traven, B.
Mauriac, Claude 1914-1996 .... **CLC 9**
See CA 89-92; 152; DLB 83
Mauriac, Francois (Charles) 1885-1970 ..... **CLC 4, 9, 56; SSC 24**
See CA 25-28; CAP 2; DLB 65; MTCW 1, 2
Mavor, Osborne Henry 1888-1951
See Bridie, James
See CA 104
Maxwell, William (Keepers,Jr.) 1908- . **CLC 19**
See CA 93-96; CANR 54; DLBY 80; INT 93-96
May, Elaine 1932- .... **CLC 16**
See CA 124; 142; DLB 44
Mayakovski, Vladimir (Vladimirovich) 1893-1930 .... **TCLC 4, 18**
See CA 104; 158; MTCW 2
Mayhew, Henry 1812-1887 .... **NCLC 31**
See DLB 18, 55, 190
Mayle, Peter 1939(?) .... **CLC 89**
See CA 139; CANR 64
Maynard, Joyce 1953- .... **CLC 23**
See CA 111; 129; CANR 64
Mayne, William (James Carter) 1928- . **CLC 12**
See AAYA 20; CA 9-12R; CANR 37, 80; CLR 25; JRDA; MAICYA; SAAS 11; SATA 6, 68
Mayo, Jim
See L'Amour, Louis (Dearborn)
Maysles, Albert 1926- .... **CLC 16**
See CA 29-32R
Maysles, David 1932- .... **CLC 16**
Mazer, Norma Fox 1931- .... **CLC 26**
See AAYA 5; CA 69-72; CANR 12, 32, 66; CLR 23; JRDA; MAICYA; SAAS 1; SATA 24, 67, 105
Mazzini, Guiseppe 1805-1872 .... **NCLC 34**
McAlmon, Robert (Menzies) 1895-1956 ...... **TCLC 97**
See CA 107; 168; DLB 4, 45; DLBD 15
McAuley, James Phillip 1917-1976 . **CLC 45**
See CA 97-100
McBain, Ed
See Hunter, Evan
McBrien, William Augustine 1930- . **CLC 44**
See CA 107
McCaffrey, Anne (Inez) 1926- .... **CLC 17; DAM NOV, POP**
See AAYA 6; AITN 2; BEST 89:2; CA 25-28R; CANR 15, 35, 55; CLR 49; DA3; DLB 8; JRDA; MAICYA; MTCW 1, 2; SAAS 11; SATA 8, 70
McCall, Nathan 1955(?)- .... **CLC 86**
See BW 3; CA 146
McCann, Arthur
See Campbell, John W(ood, Jr.)
McCann, Edson
See Pohl, Frederik
McCarthy, Charles, Jr. 1933-
See McCarthy, Cormac
See CANR 42, 69; DAM POP; DA3; MTCW 2
McCarthy, Cormac 1933- .... **CLC 4, 57, 59, 101**
See McCarthy, Charles, Jr.
See DLB 6, 143; MTCW 2
McCarthy, Mary (Therese) 1912-1989 . **CLC**

1, 3, 5, 14, 24, 39, 59; SSC 24
See CA 5-8R; 129; CANR 16, 50, 64; DA3; DLB 2; DLBY 81; INT CANR-16; MTCW 1, 2
McCartney, (James) Paul 1942- ..... **CLC 12, 35**
See CA 146
McCauley, Stephen (D.) 1955- .... **CLC 50**
See CA 141
McClure, Michael (Thomas) 1932- .. **CLC 6, 10**
See CA 21-24R; CANR 17, 46, 77; DLB 16
McCorkle, Jill (Collins) 1958- .... **CLC 51**
See CA 121; DLBY 87
McCourt, Frank 1930- .... **CLC 109**
See CA 157
McCourt, James 1941- .... **CLC 5**
See CA 57-60
McCourt, Malachy 1932- .... **CLC 119**
McCoy, Horace (Stanley) 1897-1955 . **TCLC 28**
See CA 108; 155; DLB 9
McCrae, John 1872-1918 .... **TCLC 12**
See CA 109; DLB 92
McCreigh, James
See Pohl, Frederik
McCullers, (Lula) Carson (Smith) 1917-1967 .. **CLC 1, 4, 10, 12, 48, 100; DA; DAB; DAC; DAM MST, NOV; SSC 9, 24;WLC**
See AAYA 21; CA 5-8R; 25-28R; CABS 1, 3; CANR 18; CDALB 1941-1968; DA3; DLB 2, 7, 173; MTCW 1, 2; SATA 27
McCulloch, John Tyler
See Burroughs, Edgar Rice
McCullough, Colleen 1938(?)- .... **CLC 27, 107; DAM NOV, POP**
See CA 81-84; CANR 17, 46, 67; DA3; MTCW 1, 2
McDermott, Alice 1953- .... **CLC 90**
See CA 109; CANR 40
McElroy, Joseph 1930- .... **CLC 5, 47**
See CA 17-20R
McEwan, Ian (Russell) 1948- .. **CLC 13, 66; DAM NOV**
See BEST 90:4; CA 61-64; CANR 14, 41, 69; DLB 14, 194; MTCW 1, 2
McFadden, David 1940- .... **CLC 48**
See CA 104; DLB 60; INT 104
McFarland, Dennis 1950- .... **CLC 65**
See CA 165
McGahern, John 1934- ... **CLC 5, 9, 48;SSC 17**
See CA 17-20R; CANR 29, 68; DLB 14; MTCW 1
McGinley, Patrick (Anthony) 1937- ..... **CLC 41**
See CA 120; 127; CANR 56; INT 127
McGinley, Phyllis 1905-1978 .... **CLC 14**
See CA 9-12R; 77-80; CANR 19; DLB 11, 48; SATA 2, 44; SATA-Obit 24
McGinniss, Joe 1942- .... **CLC 32**
See AITN 2; BEST 89:2; CA 25-28R; CANR 26, 70; DLB 185; INT CANR-26
McGivern, Maureen Daly
See Daly, Maureen
McGrath, Patrick 1950- .... **CLC 55**
See CA 136; CANR 65
McGrath, Thomas (Matthew) 1916-1990 .... **CLC 28, 59; DAM POET**
See CA 9-12R; 132; CANR 6, 33; MTCW 1; SATA 41; SATA-Obit 66
McGuane, Thomas (Francis III) 1939- . **CLC 3, 7, 18, 45**
See AITN 2; CA 49-52; CANR 5, 24, 49; DLB 2, 212; DLBY 80; INT CANR-24; MTCW 1
McGuckian, Medbh 1950- ... **CLC 48; DAM POET; PC 27**
See CA 143; DLB 40
McHale, Tom 1942(?)-1982 .... **CLC 3, 5**
See AITN 1; CA 77-80; 106
McIlvanney, William 1936- .... **CLC 42**
See CA 25-28R; CANR 61; DLB 14, 207
McIlwraith, Maureen Mollie Hunter
See Hunter, Mollie
See SATA 2
McInerney, Jay 1955- .... **CLC 34, 112;DAM POP**
See AAYA 18; CA 116; 123; CANR 45, 68; DA3; INT 123; MTCW 2
McIntyre, Vonda N(eel) 1948- .... **CLC 18**
See CA 81-84; CANR 17, 34, 69; MTCW 1
McKay, Claude .... **TCLC 7, 41; BLC 3; DAB;PC 2**
See McKay, Festus Claudius
See DLB 4, 45, 51, 117
McKay, Festus Claudius 1889-1948
See McKay, Claude
See BW 1, 3; CA 104; 124; CANR 73; DA; DAC; DAM MST, MULT, NOV, POET; MTCW 1, 2; WLC
McKuen, Rod 1933- .... **CLC 1, 3**
See AITN 1; CA 41-44R; CANR 40
McLoughlin, R. B.
See Mencken, H(enry) L(ouis)
McLuhan, (Herbert) Marshall 1911-1980 ... **CLC 37, 83**
See CA 9-12R; 102; CANR 12, 34, 61; DLB 88; INT CANR-12; MTCW 1, 2
McMillan, Terry (L.) 1951- ...... **CLC 50, 61, 112; BLCS; DAM MULT, NOV, POP**
See AAYA 21; BW 2, 3; CA 140; CANR 60; DA3; MTCW 2
McMurtry, Larry (Jeff) 1936- . **CLC 2, 3, 7, 11, 27, 44; DAM NOV, POP**
See AAYA 15; AITN 2; BEST 89:2; CA 5-8R; CANR 19, 43, 64; CDALB 1968-1988; DA3; DLB 2, 143; DLBY 80, 87; MTCW 1, 2
McNally, T. M. 1961- .... **CLC 82**
McNally, Terrence 1939- .. **CLC 4, 7, 41, 91; DAM DRAM**
See CA 45-48; CANR 2, 56; DA3; DLB 7; MTCW 2
McNamer, Deirdre 1950- .... **CLC 70**
McNeal, Tom .... **CLC 119**
McNeile, Herman Cyril 1888-1937
See Sapper
See DLB 77
McNickle, (William) D'Arcy 1904-1977 ...... **CLC 89; DAM MULT**
See CA 9-12R; 85-88; CANR 5, 45; DLB 175, 212; NNAL; SATA-Obit 22
McPhee, John (Angus) 1931- .... **CLC 36**
See BEST 90:1; CA 65-68; CANR 20, 46, 64, 69; DLB 185; MTCW 1, 2
McPherson, James Alan 1943- . **CLC 19, 77; BLCS**
See BW 1, 3; CA 25-28R; CAAS 17; CANR 24, 74; DLB 38; MTCW 1, 2
McPherson, William (Alexander) 1933- ...... **CLC 34**
See CA 69-72; CANR 28; INT CANR-28
Mead, George Herbert 1873-1958 ..... **TCLC 89**
Mead, Margaret 1901-1978 .... **CLC 37**
See AITN 1; CA 1-4R; 81-84; CANR 4; DA3; MTCW 1, 2; SATA-Obit 20
Meaker, Marijane (Agnes) 1927-
See Kerr, M. E.
See CA 107; CANR 37, 63; INT 107; JRDA; MAICYA; MTCW 1; SATA 20, 61, 99; SATA-Essay 111
Medoff, Mark (Howard) 1940- .. **CLC 6, 23; DAM DRAM**
See AITN 1; CA 53-56; CANR 5; DLB 7; INT CANR-5
Medvedev, P. N.
See Bakhtin, Mikhail Mikhailovich
Meged, Aharon
See Megged, Aharon
Meged, Aron
See Megged, Aharon
Megged, Aharon 1920- .... **CLC 9**
See CA 49-52; CAAS 13; CANR 1
Mehta, Ved (Parkash) 1934- .... **CLC 37**
See CA 1-4R; CANR 2, 23, 69; MTCW 1
Melanter
See Blackmore, R(ichard) D(oddridge)
Melies, Georges 1861-1938 .... **TCLC 81**
Melikow, Loris
See Hofmannsthal, Hugo von
Melmoth, Sebastian
See Wilde, Oscar
Meltzer, Milton 1915- .... **CLC 26**
See AAYA 8; CA 13-16R; CANR 38; CLR 13; DLB 61; JRDA; MAICYA; SAAS 1; SATA 1, 50, 80
Melville, Herman 1819-1891 ... **NCLC 3, 12, 29, 45, 49; DA; DAB; DAC; DAM MST, NOV; SSC 1, 17; WLC**
See AAYA 25; CDALB 1640-1865; DA3; DLB 3, 74; SATA 59
Menander c. 342B.C.-c. 292B.C. .. **CMLC 9; DAM DRAM; DC 3**
See DLB 176
Menchu, Rigoberta 1959-
See HLCS 2
Menchu, Rigoberta 1959-
See CA 175; HLCS 2
Mencken, H(enry) L(ouis) 1880-1956 . **TCLC 13**
See CA 105; 125; CDALB 1917-1929; DLB 11, 29, 63, 137; MTCW 1, 2
Mendelsohn, Jane 1965(?)- .... **CLC 99**
See CA 154
Mercer, David 1928-1980 .... **CLC 5;DAM DRAM**
See CA 9-12R; 102; CANR 23; DLB 13; MTCW 1
Merchant, Paul
See Ellison, Harlan (Jay)
Meredith, George 1828-1909 . **TCLC 17, 43; DAM POET**
See CA 117; 153; CANR 80; CDBLB 1832-1890; DLB 18, 35, 57, 159
Meredith, William (Morris) 1919- ... **CLC 4, 13, 22, 55; DAM POET; PC 28**
See CA 9-12R; CAAS 14; CANR 6, 40; DLB 5
Merezhkovsky, Dmitry Sergeyevich 1865-1941 .... **TCLC 29**
See CA 169
Merimee, Prosper 1803-1870 .. **NCLC 6, 65; SSC 7**
See DLB 119, 192
Merkin, Daphne 1954- .... **CLC 44**
See CA 123
Merlin, Arthur
See Blish, James (Benjamin)
Merrill, James (Ingram) 1926-1995 . **CLC 2, 3, 6, 8, 13, 18, 34, 91; DAM POET; PC 28**
See CA 13-16R; 147; CANR 10, 49, 63; DA3; DLB 5, 165; DLBY 85; INT CANR-10; MTCW 1, 2
Merriman, Alex
See Silverberg, Robert
Merriman, Brian 1747-1805 .... **NCLC 70**
Merritt, E. B.
See Waddington, Miriam
Merton, Thomas 1915-1968 ... **CLC 1, 3, 11, 34, 83; PC 10**

See CA 5-8R; 25-28R; CANR 22, 53; DA3; DLB 48; DLBY 81; MTCW 1, 2
Merwin, W(illiam) S(tanley) 1927- .. **CLC 1, 2, 3, 5, 8, 13, 18, 45, 88; DAM POET**
See CA 13-16R; CANR 15, 51; DA3; DLB 5, 169; INT CANR-15; MTCW 1, 2
Metcalf, John 1938- .... **CLC 37**
See CA 113; DLB 60
Metcalf, Suzanne
See Baum, L(yman) Frank
Mew, Charlotte (Mary) 1870-1928 . **TCLC 8**
See CA 105; DLB 19, 135
Mewshaw, Michael 1943- .... **CLC 9**
See CA 53-56; CANR 7, 47; DLBY 80
Meyer, Conrad Ferdinand 1825-1905 .... **NCLC 81**
See DLB 129
Meyer, June
See Jordan, June
Meyer, Lynn
See Slavitt, David R(ytman)
Meyer-Meyrink, Gustav 1868-1932
See Meyrink, Gustav
See CA 117
Meyers, Jeffrey 1939- .... **CLC 39**
See CA 73-76, 181; CAAE 181; CANR 54; DLB 111
Meynell, Alice (Christina Gertrude Thompson) 1847-1922 .... **TCLC 6**
See CA 104; 177; DLB 19, 98
Meyrink, Gustav .... **TCLC 21**
See Meyer-Meyrink, Gustav
See DLB 81
Michaels, Leonard 1933- .... **CLC 6, 25;SSC 16**
See CA 61-64; CANR 21, 62; DLB 130; MTCW 1
Michaux, Henri 1899-1984 .... **CLC 8, 19**
See CA 85-88; 114
Micheaux, Oscar (Devereaux) 1884-1951 .... **TCLC 76**
See BW 3; CA 174; DLB 50
Michelangelo 1475-1564 .... **LC 12**
Michelet, Jules 1798-1874 .... **NCLC 31**
Michels, Robert 1876-1936 .... **TCLC 88**
Michener, James A(lbert) 1907(?)-1997 .... **CLC 1, 5, 11, 29, 60, 109; DAM NOV, POP**
See AAYA 27; AITN 1; BEST 90:1; CA 5-8R; 161; CANR 21, 45, 68; DA3; DLB 6; MTCW 1, 2
Mickiewicz, Adam 1798-1855 .... **NCLC 3**
Middleton, Christopher 1926- .... **CLC 13**
See CA 13-16R; CANR 29, 54; DLB 40
Middleton, Richard (Barham) 1882-1911 .... **TCLC 56**
See DLB 156
Middleton, Stanley 1919- .... **CLC 7, 38**
See CA 25-28R; CAAS 23; CANR 21, 46, 81; DLB 14
Middleton, Thomas 1580-1627 .... **LC 33; DAM DRAM, MST; DC 5**
See DLB 58
Migueis, Jose Rodrigues 1901- .... **CLC 10**
Mikszath, Kalman 1847-1910 .... **TCLC 31**
See CA 170
Miles, Jack .... **CLC 100**
Miles, Josephine (Louise) 1911-1985 ... **CLC 1, 2, 14, 34, 39; DAM POET**
See CA 1-4R; 116; CANR 2, 55; DLB 48
Militant
See Sandburg, Carl (August)
Mill, John Stuart 1806-1873 ... **NCLC 11, 58**
See CDBLB 1832-1890; DLB 55, 190
Millar, Kenneth 1915-1983 ... **CLC 14;DAM POP**
See Macdonald, Ross
See CA 9-12R; 110; CANR 16, 63; DA3; DLB 2; DLBD 6; DLBY 83; MTCW 1, 2
Millay, E. Vincent
See Millay, Edna St. Vincent
Millay, Edna St. Vincent 1892-1950 .. **TCLC 4, 49; DA; DAB; DAC; DAM MST, POET; PC 6; WLCS**
See CA 104; 130; CDALB 1917-1929; DA3; DLB 45; MTCW 1, 2
Miller, Arthur 1915- ..... **CLC 1, 2, 6, 10, 15, 26, 47, 78; DA; DAB; DAC; DAM DRAM, MST; DC 1; WLC**
See AAYA 15; AITN 1; CA 1-4R; CABS 3; CANR 2, 30, 54, 76; CDALB 1941-1968; DA3; DLB 7; MTCW 1, 2
Miller, Henry (Valentine) 1891-1980 ... **CLC 1, 2, 4, 9, 14, 43, 84; DA; DAB; DAC; DAM MST, NOV; WLC**
See CA 9-12R; 97-100; CANR 33, 64; CDALB 1929-1941; DA3; DLB 4, 9; DLBY 80; MTCW 1, 2
Miller, Jason 1939(?)- .... **CLC 2**
See AITN 1; CA 73-76; DLB 7
Miller, Sue 1943- .... **CLC 44;DAM POP**
See BEST 90:3; CA 139; CANR 59; DA3; DLB 143
Miller, Walter M(ichael, Jr.) 1923- .. **CLC 4, 30**
See CA 85-88; DLB 8
Millett, Kate 1934- .... **CLC 67**
See AITN 1; CA 73-76; CANR 32, 53, 76; DA3; MTCW 1, 2
Millhauser, Steven (Lewis) 1943- ... **CLC 21, 54, 109**
See CA 110; 111; CANR 63; DA3; DLB 2; INT 111; MTCW 2
Millin, Sarah Gertrude 1889-1968 . **CLC 49**
See CA 102; 93-96
Milne, A(lan) A(lexander) 1882-1956 . **TCLC 6, 88; DAB; DAC; DAM MST**
See CA 104; 133; CLR 1, 26; DA3; DLB 10, 77, 100, 160; MAICYA; MTCW 1, 2; SATA 100; YABC 1
Milner, Ron(ald) 1938- ..... **CLC 56; BLC 3; DAM MULT**
See AITN 1; BW 1; CA 73-76; CANR 24, 81; DLB 38; MTCW 1
Milnes, Richard Monckton 1809-1885 .... **NCLC 61**
See DLB 32, 184
Milosz, Czeslaw 1911- .... **CLC 5, 11, 22, 31, 56, 82; DAM MST, POET; PC 8; WLCS**
See CA 81-84; CANR 23, 51; DA3; MTCW 1, 2
Milton, John 1608-1674 .... **LC 9, 43; DA; DAB; DAC; DAM MST, POET; PC 19; WLC**
See CDBLB 1660-1789; DA3; DLB 131, 151
Min, Anchee 1957- .... **CLC 86**
See CA 146
Minehaha, Cornelius
See Wedekind, (Benjamin) Frank(lin)
Miner, Valerie 1947- .... **CLC 40**
See CA 97-100; CANR 59
Minimo, Duca
See D'Annunzio, Gabriele
Minot, Susan 1956- .... **CLC 44**
See CA 134
Minus, Ed 1938- .... **CLC 39**
Miranda, Javier
See Bioy Casares, Adolfo
Miranda, Javier
See Bioy Casares, Adolfo
Mirbeau, Octave 1848-1917 .... **TCLC 55**
See DLB 123, 192
Miro (Ferrer), Gabriel (Francisco Victor) 1879-1930 .... **TCLC 5**
See CA 104
Mishima, Yukio 1925-1970 .. **CLC 2, 4, 6, 9, 27; DC 1; SSC 4**
See Hiraoka, Kimitake
See DLB 182; MTCW 2
Mistral, Frederic 1830-1914 .... **TCLC 51**
See CA 122
Mistral, Gabriela .... **TCLC 2; HLC 2**
See Godoy Alcayaga, Lucila
See MTCW 2
Mistry, Rohinton 1952- .... **CLC 71; DAC**
See CA 141
Mitchell, Clyde
See Ellison, Harlan (Jay); Silverberg, Robert
Mitchell, James Leslie 1901-1935
See Gibbon, Lewis Grassic
See CA 104; DLB 15
Mitchell, Joni 1943- .... **CLC 12**
See CA 112
Mitchell, Joseph (Quincy) 1908-1996 .. **CLC 98**
See CA 77-80; 152; CANR 69; DLB 185; DLBY 96
Mitchell, Margaret (Munnerlyn) 1900-1949 .... **TCLC 11; DAM NOV, POP**
See AAYA 23; CA 109; 125; CANR 55; CDALBS; DA3; DLB 9; MTCW 1, 2
Mitchell, Peggy
See Mitchell, Margaret (Munnerlyn)
Mitchell, S(ilas) Weir 1829-1914 .. **TCLC 36**
See CA 165; DLB 202
Mitchell, W(illiam) O(rmond) 1914-1998 .... **CLC 25; DAC; DAM MST**
See CA 77-80; 165; CANR 15, 43; DLB 88
Mitchell, William 1879-1936 .... **TCLC 81**
Mitford, Mary Russell 1787-1855 .. **NCLC 4**
See DLB 110, 116
Mitford, Nancy 1904-1973 .... **CLC 44**
See CA 9-12R; DLB 191
Miyamoto, (Chujo) Yuriko 1899-1951 .... **TCLC 37**
See CA 170, 174; DLB 180
Miyazawa, Kenji 1896-1933 .... **TCLC 76**
See CA 157
Mizoguchi, Kenji 1898-1956 .... **TCLC 72**
See CA 167
Mo, Timothy (Peter) 1950(?)- .... **CLC 46**
See CA 117; DLB 194; MTCW 1
Modarressi, Taghi (M.) 1931- .... **CLC 44**
See CA 121; 134; INT 134
Modiano, Patrick (Jean) 1945- .... **CLC 18**
See CA 85-88; CANR 17, 40; DLB 83
Moerck, Paal
See Roelvaag, O(le) E(dvart)
Mofolo, Thomas (Mokopu) 1875(?)-1948 .... **TCLC 22; BLC 3; DAM MULT**
See CA 121; 153; CANR 83; MTCW 2
Mohr, Nicholasa 1938- .... **CLC 12; DAM MULT; HLC 2**
See AAYA 8; CA 49-52; CANR 1, 32, 64; CLR 22; DLB 145; HW 1, 2; JRDA; SAAS 8; SATA 8, 97
Mojtabai, A(nn) G(race) 1938- .... **CLC 5, 9, 15, 29**
See CA 85-88
Moliere 1622-1673 .... **LC 10, 28; DA; DAB; DAC; DAM DRAM, MST; WLC**
See DA3
Molin, Charles
See Mayne, William (James Carter)
Molnar, Ferenc 1878-1952 .. **TCLC 20;DAM DRAM**
See CA 109; 153; CANR 83
Momaday, N(avarre) Scott 1934- .... **CLC 2, 19, 85, 95; DA; DAB; DAC; DAM MST, MULT, NOV, POP; PC 25; WLCS**

See AAYA 11; CA 25-28R; CANR 14, 34, 68; CDALBS; DA3; DLB 143, 175; INT CANR-14; MTCW 1, 2; NNAL; SATA 48; SATA-Brief 30
Monette, Paul 1945-1995 .... **CLC 82**
See CA 139; 147
Monroe, Harriet 1860-1936 .... **TCLC 12**
See CA 109; DLB 54, 91
Monroe, Lyle
See Heinlein, Robert A(nson)
Montagu, Elizabeth 1720-1800 .... **NCLC 7**
Montagu, Mary (Pierrepont) Wortley 1689-1762 .... **LC 9; PC 16**
See DLB 95, 101
Montagu, W. H.
See Coleridge, Samuel Taylor
Montague, John (Patrick) 1929- .... **CLC 13, 46**
See CA 9-12R; CANR 9, 69; DLB 40; MTCW 1
Montaigne, Michel (Eyquem) de 1533-1592 .... **LC 8; DA; DAB; DAC; DAM MST; WLC**
Montale, Eugenio 1896-1981 . **CLC 7, 9, 18; PC 13**
See CA 17-20R; 104; CANR 30; DLB 114; MTCW 1
Montesquieu, Charles-Louis de Secondat 1689-1755 .... **LC 7**
Montgomery, (Robert) Bruce 1921(?)-1978
See Crispin, Edmund
See CA 179; 104
Montgomery, L(ucy) M(aud) 1874-1942 ...... **TCLC 51; DAC; DAM MST**
See AAYA 12; CA 108; 137; CLR 8; DA3; DLB 92; DLBD 14; JRDA; MAICYA; MTCW 2; SATA 100; YABC 1
Montgomery, Marion H.,Jr. 1925- .... **CLC 7**
See AITN 1; CA 1-4R; CANR 3, 48; DLB 6
Montgomery, Max
See Davenport, Guy (Mattison, Jr.)
Montherlant, Henry (Milon) de 1896-1972 . **CLC 8, 19; DAM DRAM**
See CA 85-88; 37-40R; DLB 72; MTCW 1
Monty Python
See Chapman, Graham; Cleese, John (Marwood); Gilliam, Terry (Vance); Idle, Eric; Jones, Terence Graham Parry; Palin, Michael (Edward)
See AAYA 7
Moodie, Susanna (Strickland) 1803-1885 .... **NCLC 14**
See DLB 99
Mooney, Edward 1951-
See Mooney, Ted
See CA 130
Mooney, Ted .... **CLC 25**
See Mooney, Edward
Moorcock, Michael (John) 1939- ..... **CLC 5, 27, 58**
See Bradbury, Edward P.
See AAYA 26; CA 45-48; CAAS 5; CANR 2, 17, 38, 64; DLB 14; MTCW 1, 2; SATA 93
Moore, Brian 1921-1999 .. **CLC 1, 3, 5, 7, 8, 19, 32, 90; DAB; DAC; DAM MST**
See CA 1-4R; 174; CANR 1, 25, 42, 63; MTCW 1, 2
Moore, Edward
See Muir, Edwin
Moore, G. E. 1873-1958 .... **TCLC 89**
Moore, George Augustus 1852-1933 . **TCLC 7; SSC 19**
See CA 104; 177; DLB 10, 18, 57, 135
Moore, Lorrie .... **CLC 39, 45, 68**
See Moore, Marie Lorena
Moore, Marianne (Craig) 1887-1972 ... **CLC 1, 2, 4, 8, 10, 13, 19, 47; DA; DAB; DAC; DAM MST, POET; PC 4; WLCS**
See CA 1-4R; 33-36R; CANR 3, 61; CDALB 1929-1941; DA3; DLB 45; DLBD 7; MTCW 1, 2; SATA 20
Moore, Marie Lorena 1957-
See Moore, Lorrie
See CA 116; CANR 39, 83
Moore, Thomas 1779-1852 .... **NCLC 6**
See DLB 96, 144
Mora, Pat(ricia) 1942-
See CA 129; CANR 57, 81; CLR 58; DAM MULT; DLB 209; HLC 2; HW 1, 2; SATA 92
Morand, Paul 1888-1976 .... **CLC 41;SSC 22**
See CA 69-72; DLB 65
Morante, Elsa 1918-1985 .... **CLC 8, 47**
See CA 85-88; 117; CANR 35; DLB 177; MTCW 1, 2
Moravia, Alberto 1907-1990 .. **CLC 2, 7, 11, 27, 46; SSC 26**
See Pincherle, Alberto
See DLB 177; MTCW 2
More, Hannah 1745-1833 .... **NCLC 27**
See DLB 107, 109, 116, 158
More, Henry 1614-1687 .... **LC 9**
See DLB 126
More, Sir Thomas 1478-1535 .... **LC 10, 32**
Moreas, Jean .... **TCLC 18**
See Papadiamantopoulos, Johannes
Morgan, Berry 1919- .... **CLC 6**
See CA 49-52; DLB 6
Morgan, Claire
See Highsmith, (Mary) Patricia
Morgan, Edwin (George) 1920- ...... **CLC 31**
See CA 5-8R; CANR 3, 43; DLB 27
Morgan, (George) Frederick 1922- . **CLC 23**
See CA 17-20R; CANR 21
Morgan, Harriet
See Mencken, H(enry) L(ouis)
Morgan, Jane
See Cooper, James Fenimore
Morgan, Janet 1945- .... **CLC 39**
See CA 65-68
Morgan, Lady 1776(?)-1859 .... **NCLC 29**
See DLB 116, 158
Morgan, Robin (Evonne) 1941- .... **CLC 2**
See CA 69-72; CANR 29, 68; MTCW 1; SATA 80
Morgan, Scott
See Kuttner, Henry
Morgan, Seth 1949(?)-1990 .... **CLC 65**
See CA 132
Morgenstern, Christian 1871-1914 . **TCLC 8**
See CA 105
Morgenstern, S.
See Goldman, William (W.)
Moricz, Zsigmond 1879-1942 .... **TCLC 33**
See CA 165
Morike, Eduard (Friedrich) 1804-1875 .... **NCLC 10**
See DLB 133
Moritz, Karl Philipp 1756-1793 .... **LC 2**
See DLB 94
Morland, Peter Henry
See Faust, Frederick (Schiller)
Morley, Christopher (Darlington) 1890-1957 .... **TCLC 87**
See CA 112; DLB 9
Morren, Theophil
See Hofmannsthal, Hugo von
Morris, Bill 1952- .... **CLC 76**
Morris, Julian
See West, Morris L(anglo)
Morris, Steveland Judkins 1950(?)-
See Wonder, Stevie
See CA 111
Morris, William 1834-1896 .... **NCLC 4**
See CDBLB 1832-1890; DLB 18, 35, 57, 156, 178, 184
Morris, Wright 1910-1998 . **CLC 1, 3, 7, 18, 37**
See CA 9-12R; 167; CANR 21, 81; DLB 2, 206; DLBY 81; MTCW 1, 2
Morrison, Arthur 1863-1945 .... **TCLC 72**
See CA 120; 157; DLB 70, 135, 197
Morrison, Chloe Anthony Wofford
See Morrison, Toni
Morrison, James Douglas 1943-1971
See Morrison, Jim
See CA 73-76; CANR 40
Morrison, Jim .... **CLC 17**
See Morrison, James Douglas
Morrison, Toni 1931- ...... **CLC 4, 10, 22, 55, 81, 87; BLC 3; DA; DAB; DAC; DAM MST, MULT, NOV, POP**
See AAYA 1, 22; BW 2, 3; CA 29-32R; CANR 27, 42, 67; CDALB 1968-1988; DA3; DLB 6, 33, 143; DLBY 81; MTCW 1, 2; SATA 57
Morrison, Van 1945- .... **CLC 21**
See CA 116; 168
Morrissy, Mary 1958- .... **CLC 99**
Mortimer, John (Clifford) 1923- .... **CLC 28, 43; DAM DRAM, POP**
See CA 13-16R; CANR 21, 69; CDBLB 1960 to Present; DA3; DLB 13; INT CANR-21; MTCW 1, 2
Mortimer, Penelope(Ruth) 1918- ...... **CLC 5**
See CA 57-60; CANR 45
Morton, Anthony
See Creasey, John
Mosca, Gaetano 1858-1941 .... **TCLC 75**
Mosher, Howard Frank 1943- .... **CLC 62**
See CA 139; CANR 65
Mosley, Nicholas 1923- .... **CLC 43, 70**
See CA 69-72; CANR 41, 60; DLB 14, 207
Mosley, Walter 1952- .... **CLC 97; BLCS; DAM MULT, POP**
See AAYA 17; BW 2; CA 142; CANR 57; DA3; MTCW 2
Moss, Howard 1922-1987 ..... **CLC 7, 14, 45, 50; DAM POET**
See CA 1-4R; 123; CANR 1, 44; DLB 5
Mossgiel, Rab
See Burns, Robert
Motion, Andrew (Peter) 1952- .... **CLC 47**
See CA 146; DLB 40
Motley, Willard (Francis) 1909-1965 ... **CLC 18**
See BW 1; CA 117; 106; DLB 76, 143
Motoori, Norinaga 1730-1801 .... **NCLC 45**
Mott, Michael (Charles Alston) 1930- . **CLC 15, 34**
See CA 5-8R; CAAS 7; CANR 7, 29
Mountain Wolf Woman 1884-1960 . **CLC 92**
See CA 144; NNAL
Moure, Erin 1955- .... **CLC 88**
See CA 113; DLB 60
Mowat, Farley (McGill) 1921- .... **CLC 26; DAC; DAM MST**
See AAYA 1; CA 1-4R; CANR 4, 24, 42, 68; CLR 20; DLB 68; INT CANR-24; JRDA; MAICYA; MTCW 1, 2; SATA 3, 55
Mowatt, Anna Cora 1819-1870 .... **NCLC 74**
Moyers, Bill 1934- .... **CLC 74**
See AITN 2; CA 61-64; CANR 31, 52
Mphahlele, Es'kia
See Mphahlele, Ezekiel
See DLB 125
Mphahlele, Ezekiel 1919- . **CLC 25; BLC 3; DAM MULT**
See Mphahlele, Es'kia
See BW 2, 3; CA 81-84; CANR 26, 76; DA3; MTCW 2

Mqhayi, S(amuel) E(dward) K(runeLoliwe) 1875-1945 ...... **TCLC 25; BLC 3;DAM MULT**
See CA 153
Mrozek, Slawomir 1930- .... **CLC 3, 13**
See CA 13-16R; CAAS 10; CANR 29; MTCW 1
Mrs. Belloc-Lowndes
See Lowndes, Marie Adelaide (Belloc)
Mtwa, Percy (?)- .... **CLC 47**
Mueller, Lisel 1924- .... **CLC 13, 51**
See CA 93-96; DLB 105
Muir, Edwin 1887-1959 .... **TCLC 2, 87**
See CA 104; DLB 20, 100, 191
Muir, John 1838-1914 .... **TCLC 28**
See CA 165; DLB 186
Mujica Lainez, Manuel 1910-1984 . **CLC 31**
See Lainez, Manuel Mujica
See CA 81-84; 112; CANR 32; HW 1
Mukherjee, Bharati 1940- ...... **CLC 53, 115; DAM NOV**
See BEST 89:2; CA 107; CANR 45, 72; DLB 60; MTCW 1, 2
Muldoon, Paul 1951- .... **CLC 32, 72;DAM POET**
See CA 113; 129; CANR 52; DLB 40; INT 129
Mulisch, Harry 1927- .... **CLC 42**
See CA 9-12R; CANR 6, 26, 56
Mull, Martin 1943- .... **CLC 17**
See CA 105
Muller, Wilhelm .... **NCLC 73**
Mulock, Dinah Maria
See Craik, Dinah Maria (Mulock)
Munford, Robert 1737(?)-1783 .... **LC 5**
See DLB 31
Mungo, Raymond 1946- .... **CLC 72**
See CA 49-52; CANR 2
Munro, Alice 1931- .. **CLC 6, 10, 19, 50, 95; DAC; DAM MST, NOV; SSC 3; WLCS**
See AITN 2; CA 33-36R; CANR 33, 53, 75; DA3; DLB 53; MTCW 1, 2; SATA 29
Munro, H(ector) H(ugh) 1870-1916
See Saki
See CA 104; 130; CDBLB 1890-1914; DA; DAB; DAC; DAM MST, NOV; DA3; DLB 34, 162; MTCW 1, 2; WLC
Murdoch, (Jean) Iris 1919-1999 .. **CLC 1, 2, 3, 4, 6, 8, 11, 15, 22, 31, 51; DAB; DAC; DAM MST, NOV**
See CA 13-16R; 179; CANR 8, 43, 68; CDBLB 1960 to Present; DA3; DLB 14, 194; INT CANR-8; MTCW 1, 2
Murfree, Mary Noailles 1850-1922 .. **SSC 22**
See CA 122; 176; DLB 12, 74
Murnau, Friedrich Wilhelm
See Plumpe, Friedrich Wilhelm
Murphy, Richard 1927- .... **CLC 41**
See CA 29-32R; DLB 40
Murphy, Sylvia 1937- .... **CLC 34**
See CA 121
Murphy, Thomas (Bernard) 1935- . **CLC 51**
See CA 101
Murray, Albert L. 1916- .... **CLC 73**
See BW 2; CA 49-52; CANR 26, 52, 78; DLB 38
Murray, Judith Sargent 1751-1820 ... **NCLC 63**
See DLB 37, 200
Murray, Les(lie) A(llan) 1938- .... **CLC 40; DAM POET**
See CA 21-24R; CANR 11, 27, 56
Murry, J. Middleton
See Murry, John Middleton
Murry, John Middleton 1889-1957 ... **TCLC 16**
See CA 118; DLB 149
Musgrave, Susan 1951- .... **CLC 13, 54**
See CA 69-72; CANR 45, 84
Musil, Robert (Edler von) 1880-1942 . **TCLC 12, 68; SSC 18**
See CA 109; CANR 55, 84; DLB 81, 124; MTCW 2
Muske, Carol 1945- .... **CLC 90**
See Muske-Dukes, Carol (Anne)
Muske-Dukes, Carol (Anne) 1945-
See Muske, Carol
See CA 65-68; CANR 32, 70
Musset, (Louis Charles) Alfredde 1810-1857 .... **NCLC 7**
See DLB 192
Mussolini, Benito (Amilcare Andrea) 1883-1945 .... **TCLC 96**
See CA 116
My Brother's Brother
See Chekhov, Anton (Pavlovich)
Myers, L(eopold)H(amilton) 1881-1944 .... **TCLC 59**
See CA 157; DLB 15
Myers, Walter Dean 1937- .... **CLC 35; BLC 3; DAM MULT, NOV**
See AAYA 4, 23; BW 2; CA 33-36R; CANR 20, 42, 67; CLR 4, 16, 35; DLB 33; INT CANR-20; JRDA; MAICYA; MTCW 2; SAAS 2; SATA 41, 71, 109; SATA-Brief 27
Myers, Walter M.
See Myers, Walter Dean
Myles, Symon
See Follett, Ken(neth Martin)
Nabokov, Vladimir (Vladimirovich) 1899-1977 ..... **CLC 1, 2, 3, 6, 8, 11, 15, 23, 44, 46, 64; DA; DAB; DAC; DAM MST, NOV; SSC 11; WLC**
See CA 5-8R; 69-72; CANR 20; CDALB 1941-1968; DA3; DLB 2; DLBD 3; DLBY 80, 91; MTCW 1, 2
Nagai Kafu 1879-1959 .... **TCLC 51**
See Nagai Sokichi
See DLB 180
Nagai Sokichi 1879-1959
See Nagai Kafu
See CA 117
Nagy, Laszlo 1925-1978 .... **CLC 7**
See CA 129; 112
Naidu, Sarojini 1879-1943 .... **TCLC 80**
Naipaul, Shiva(dhar Srinivasa) 1945-1985 .. **CLC 32, 39; DAM NOV**
See CA 110; 112; 116; CANR 33; DA3; DLB 157; DLBY 85; MTCW 1, 2
Naipaul, V(idiadhar) S(urajprasad) 1932- .. **CLC 4, 7, 9, 13, 18, 37, 105; DAB; DAC; DAM MST, NOV**
See CA 1-4R; CANR 1, 33, 51; CDBLB 1960 to Present; DA3; DLB 125, 204, 206; DLBY 85; MTCW 1, 2
Nakos, Lilika 1899(?)- .... **CLC 29**
Narayan, R(asipuram) K(rishnaswami) 1906- . **CLC 7, 28, 47, 121; DAM NOV; SSC 25**
See CA 81-84; CANR 33, 61; DA3; MTCW 1, 2; SATA 62
Nash, (Frediric) Ogden 1902-1971 . **CLC 23; DAM POET; PC 21**
See CA 13-14; 29-32R; CANR 34, 61; CAP 1; DLB 11; MAICYA; MTCW 1, 2; SATA 2, 46
Nashe, Thomas 1567-1601(?) .... **LC 41**
See DLB 167
Nashe, Thomas 1567-1601 .... **LC 41**
Nathan, Daniel
See Dannay, Frederic
Nathan, George Jean 1882-1958 .. **TCLC 18**
See Hatteras, Owen
See CA 114; 169; DLB 137
Natsume, Kinnosuke 1867-1916
See Natsume, Soseki
See CA 104
Natsume, Soseki 1867-1916 ...... **TCLC 2, 10**
See Natsume, Kinnosuke
See DLB 180
Natti, (Mary) Lee 1919-
See Kingman, Lee
See CA 5-8R; CANR 2
Naylor, Gloria 1950- ... **CLC 28, 52; BLC 3; DA; DAC; DAM MST, MULT, NOV, POP; WLCS**
See AAYA 6; BW 2, 3; CA 107; CANR 27, 51, 74; DA3; DLB 173; MTCW 1, 2
Neihardt, John Gneisenau 1881-1973 .. **CLC 32**
See CA 13-14; CANR 65; CAP 1; DLB 9, 54
Nekrasov, Nikolai Alekseevich 1821-1878 ... **NCLC 11**
Nelligan, Emile 1879-1941 .... **TCLC 14**
See CA 114; DLB 92
Nelson, Willie 1933- .... **CLC 17**
See CA 107
Nemerov, Howard (Stanley) 1920-1991 .... **CLC 2, 6, 9, 36; DAM POET; PC 24**
See CA 1-4R; 134; CABS 2; CANR 1, 27, 53; DLB 5, 6; DLBY 83; INT CANR-27; MTCW 1, 2
Neruda, Pablo 1904-1973 . **CLC 1, 2, 5, 7, 9, 28, 62; DA; DAB; DAC; DAM MST, MULT, POET; HLC 2; PC 4; WLC**
See CA 19-20; 45-48; CAP 2; DA3; HW 1; MTCW 1, 2
Nerval, Gerard de 1808-1855 . **NCLC 1, 67; PC 13; SSC 18**
Nervo, (Jose) Amado (Ruiz de) 1870-1919 .. **TCLC 11; HLCS 2**
See CA 109; 131; HW 1
Nessi, Pio Baroja y
See Baroja (y Nessi), Pio
Nestroy, Johann 1801-1862 .... **NCLC 42**
See DLB 133
Netterville, Luke
See O'Grady, Standish (James)
Neufeld, John (Arthur) 1938- .... **CLC 17**
See AAYA 11; CA 25-28R; CANR 11, 37, 56; CLR 52; MAICYA; SAAS 3; SATA 6, 81
Neville, Emily Cheney 1919- .... **CLC 12**
See CA 5-8R; CANR 3, 37, 85; JRDA; MAICYA; SAAS 2; SATA 1
Newbound, Bernard Slade 1930-
See Slade, Bernard
See CA 81-84; CANR 49; DAM DRAM
Newby, P(ercy) H(oward) 1918-1997 ... **CLC 2, 13; DAM NOV**
See CA 5-8R; 161; CANR 32, 67; DLB 15; MTCW 1
Newlove, Donald 1928- .... **CLC 6**
See CA 29-32R; CANR 25
Newlove, John(Herbert) 1938- .... **CLC 14**
See CA 21-24R; CANR 9, 25
Newman, Charles 1938- .... **CLC 2, 8**
See CA 21-24R; CANR 84
Newman, Edwin (Harold) 1919- ..... **CLC 14**
See AITN 1; CA 69-72; CANR 5
Newman, John Henry 1801-1890 . **NCLC 38**
See DLB 18, 32, 55
Newton, (Sir)Isaac 1642-1727 ...... **LC 35, 52**
Newton, Suzanne 1936- .... **CLC 35**
See CA 41-44R; CANR 14; JRDA; SATA 5, 77
Nexo, Martin Andersen 1869-1954 .... **TCLC 43**
Nezval, Vitezslav 1900-1958 .... **TCLC 44**
See CA 123
Ng, Fae Myenne 1957(?)- .... **CLC 81**
See CA 146

Ngema, Mbongeni 1955- .... **CLC 57**
See BW 2; CA 143; CANR 84
Ngugi, James T(hiong'o) .... **CLC 3, 7, 13**
See Ngugi wa Thiong'o
Ngugi wa Thiong'o 1938- . **CLC 36; BLC 3; DAM MULT, NOV**
See Ngugi, James T(hiong'o)
See BW 2; CA 81-84; CANR 27, 58; DLB 125; MTCW 1, 2
Nichol, B(arrie) P(hillip) 1944-1988 ..... **CLC 18**
See CA 53-56; DLB 53; SATA 66
Nichols, John(Treadwell) 1940- .... **CLC 38**
See CA 9-12R; CAAS 2; CANR 6, 70; DLBY 82
Nichols, Leigh
See Koontz, Dean R(ay)
Nichols, Peter (Richard) 1927- .. **CLC 5, 36, 65**
See CA 104; CANR 33; DLB 13; MTCW 1
Nicolas, F. R. E.
See Freeling, Nicolas
Niedecker, Lorine 1903-1970 ... **CLC 10, 42; DAM POET**
See CA 25-28; CAP 2; DLB 48
Nietzsche, Friedrich (Wilhelm) 1844-1900 .. **TCLC 10, 18, 55**
See CA 107; 121; DLB 129
Nievo, Ippolito 1831-1861 .... **NCLC 22**
Nightingale, Anne Redmon 1943-
See Redmon, Anne
See CA 103
Nightingale, Florence 1820-1910 .. **TCLC 85**
See DLB 166
Nik. T. O.
See Annensky, Innokenty (Fyodorovich)
Nin, Anais 1903-1977 .... **CLC 1, 4, 8, 11, 14, 60; DAM NOV, POP; SSC 10**
See AITN 2; CA 13-16R; 69-72; CANR 22, 53; DLB 2, 4, 152; MTCW 1, 2
Nishida, Kitaro 1870-1945 .... **TCLC 83**
Nishiwaki, Junzaburo 1894-1982 .... **PC 15**
See CA 107
Nissenson, Hugh 1933- .... **CLC 4, 9**
See CA 17-20R; CANR 27; DLB 28
Niven, Larry .... **CLC 8**
See Niven, Laurence Van Cott
See AAYA 27; DLB 8
Niven, Laurence Van Cott 1938-
See Niven, Larry
See CA 21-24R; CAAS 12; CANR 14, 44, 66; DAM POP; MTCW 1, 2; SATA 95
Nixon, Agnes Eckhardt 1927- .... **CLC 21**
See CA 110
Nizan, Paul 1905-1940 .... **TCLC 40**
See CA 161; DLB 72
Nkosi, Lewis 1936- . **CLC 45; BLC 3; DAM MULT**
See BW 1, 3; CA 65-68; CANR 27, 81; DLB 157
Nodier, (Jean) Charles (Emmanuel) 1780-1844 .... **NCLC 19**
See DLB 119
Noguchi, Yone 1875-1947 .... **TCLC 80**
Nolan, Christopher 1965- .... **CLC 58**
See CA 111
Noon, Jeff 1957- .... **CLC 91**
See CA 148; CANR 83
Norden, Charles
See Durrell, Lawrence (George)
Nordhoff, Charles(Bernard) 1887-1947 .... **TCLC 23**
See CA 108; DLB 9; SATA 23
Norfolk, Lawrence 1963- .... **CLC 76**
See CA 144; CANR 85
Norman, Marsha 1947- .... **CLC 28; DAM DRAM; DC 8**
See CA 105; CABS 3; CANR 41; DLBY 84
Normyx
See Douglas, (George) Norman
Norris, Frank 1870-1902 .... **SSC 28**
See Norris, (Benjamin) Frank(lin, Jr.)
See CDALB 1865-1917; DLB 12, 71, 186
Norris, (Benjamin) Frank(lin,Jr.) 1870-1902 .... **TCLC 24**
See Norris, Frank
See CA 110; 160
Norris, Leslie 1921- .... **CLC 14**
See CA 11-12; CANR 14; CAP 1; DLB 27
North, Andrew
See Norton, Andre
North, Anthony
See Koontz, Dean R(ay)
North, Captain George
See Stevenson, Robert Louis (Balfour)
North, Milou
See Erdrich, Louise
Northrup, B. A.
See Hubbard, L(afayette) Ron(ald)
North Staffs
See Hulme, T(homas) E(rnest)
Norton, Alice Mary
See Norton, Andre
See MAICYA; SATA 1, 43
Norton, Andre 1912- .... **CLC 12**
See Norton, Alice Mary
See AAYA 14; CA 1-4R; CANR 68; CLR 50; DLB 8, 52; JRDA; MTCW 1; SATA 91
Norton, Caroline 1808-1877 .... **NCLC 47**
See DLB 21, 159, 199
Norway, Nevil Shute 1899-1960
See Shute, Nevil
See CA 102; 93-96; CANR 85; MTCW 2
Norwid, Cyprian Kamil 1821-1883 ... **NCLC 17**
Nosille, Nabrah
See Ellison, Harlan (Jay)
Nossack, Hans Erich 1901-1978 .... **CLC 6**
See CA 93-96; 85-88; DLB 69
Nostradamus 1503-1566 .... **LC 27**
Nosu, Chuji
See Ozu, Yasujiro
Notenburg, Eleanora (Genrikhovna) von
See Guro, Elena
Nova, Craig 1945- .... **CLC 7, 31**
See CA 45-48; CANR 2, 53
Novak, Joseph
See Kosinski, Jerzy (Nikodem)
Novalis 1772-1801 .... **NCLC 13**
See DLB 90
Novis, Emile
See Weil, Simone (Adolphine)
Nowlan, Alden (Albert) 1933-1983 . **CLC 15; DAC; DAM MST**
See CA 9-12R; CANR 5; DLB 53
Noyes, Alfred 1880-1958 ...... **TCLC 7;PC 27**
See CA 104; DLB 20
Nunn, Kem .... **CLC 34**
See CA 159
Nye, Robert 1939- . **CLC 13, 42;DAM NOV**
See CA 33-36R; CANR 29, 67; DLB 14; MTCW 1; SATA 6
Nyro, Laura 1947- .... **CLC 17**
Oates, Joyce Carol 1938- . **CLC 1, 2, 3, 6, 9, 11, 15, 19, 33, 52, 108; DA; DAB; DAC; DAM MST, NOV, POP; SSC 6;WLC**
See AAYA 15; AITN 1; BEST 89:2; CA 5-8R; CANR 25, 45, 74; CDALB 1968-1988; DA3; DLB 2, 5, 130; DLBY 81; INT CANR-25; MTCW 1, 2
O'Brien, Darcy 1939-1998 .... **CLC 11**
See CA 21-24R; 167; CANR 8, 59
O'Brien, E. G.
See Clarke, Arthur C(harles)
O'Brien, Edna 1936- .... **CLC 3, 5, 8, 13, 36, 65, 116; DAM NOV; SSC 10**
See CA 1-4R; CANR 6, 41, 65; CDBLB 1960 to Present; DA3; DLB 14; MTCW 1, 2
O'Brien, Fitz-James 1828-1862 .... **NCLC 21**
See DLB 74
O'Brien, Flann .... **CLC 1, 4, 5, 7, 10, 47**
See O Nuallain, Brian
O'Brien, Richard 1942- .... **CLC 17**
See CA 124
O'Brien, (William) Tim(othy) 1946- .... **CLC 7, 19, 40, 103; DAM POP**
See AAYA 16; CA 85-88; CANR 40, 58; CDALBS; DA3; DLB 152; DLBD 9; DLBY 80; MTCW 2
Obstfelder,Sigbjoern 1866-1900 .... **TCLC 23**
See CA 123
O'Casey, Sean 1880-1964 ... **CLC 1, 5, 9, 11, 15, 88; DAB; DAC; DAM DRAM, MST; WLCS**
See CA 89-92; CANR 62;CDBLB 1914-1945; DA3; DLB 10; MTCW 1, 2
O'Cathasaigh, Sean
See O'Casey, Sean
Ochs, Phil 1940-1976 .... **CLC 17**
See CA 65-68
O'Connor, Edwin(Greene) 1918-1968 . **CLC 14**
See CA 93-96; 25-28R
O'Connor, (Mary) Flannery 1925-1964 .... **CLC 1, 2, 3, 6, 10, 13, 15, 21, 66, 104; DA; DAB; DAC; DAM MST, NOV; SSC 1, 23;WLC**
See AAYA 7; CA 1-4R; CANR 3, 41; CDALB 1941-1968; DA3; DLB 2, 152; DLBD 12; DLBY 80; MTCW 1, 2
O'Connor, Frank .... **CLC 23; SSC 5**
See O'Donovan, Michael John
See DLB 162
O'Dell, Scott 1898-1989 .... **CLC 30**
See AAYA 3; CA 61-64; 129; CANR 12, 30; CLR 1, 16; DLB 52; JRDA; MAICYA; SATA 12, 60
Odets, Clifford 1906-1963 .... **CLC 2, 28, 98; DAM DRAM; DC 6**
See CA 85-88; CANR 62; DLB 7, 26; MTCW 1, 2
O'Doherty, Brian 1934- .... **CLC 76**
See CA 105
O'Donnell, K. M.
See Malzberg, Barry N(athaniel)
O'Donnell, Lawrence
See Kuttner, Henry
O'Donovan, Michael John 1903-1966 . **CLC 14**
See O'Connor, Frank
See CA 93-96; CANR 84
Oe, Kenzaburo 1935- .... **CLC 10, 36, 86; DAM NOV; SSC 20**
See CA 97-100; CANR 36, 50, 74; DA3; DLB 182; DLBY 94; MTCW 1, 2
O'Faolain, Julia 1932- ... **CLC 6, 19, 47, 108**
See CA 81-84; CAAS 2; CANR 12, 61; DLB 14; MTCW 1
O'Faolain, Sean 1900-1991 .... **CLC 1, 7, 14, 32, 70; SSC 13**
See CA 61-64; 134; CANR 12, 66; DLB 15, 162; MTCW 1, 2
O'Flaherty, Liam 1896-1984 ...... **CLC 5, 34; SSC 6**
See CA 101; 113; CANR 35; DLB 36, 162; DLBY 84; MTCW 1, 2
Ogilvy, Gavin
See Barrie, J(ames) M(atthew)
O'Grady, Standish (James) 1846-1928 .... **TCLC 5**

See CA 104; 157
O'Grady, Timothy 1951- .... **CLC 59**
See CA 138
O'Hara, Frank 1926-1966 ...... **CLC 2, 5, 13, 78; DAM POET**
See CA 9-12R; 25-28R; CANR 33; DA3; DLB 5, 16, 193; MTCW 1, 2
O'Hara, John (Henry) 1905-1970 .... **CLC 1, 2, 3, 6, 11, 42; DAM NOV; SSC 15**
See CA 5-8R; 25-28R; CANR 31, 60; CDALB 1929-1941; DLB 9, 86; DLBD 2; MTCW 1, 2
O Hehir, Diana 1922- .... **CLC 41**
See CA 93-96
Ohiyesa
See Eastman, Charles A(lexander)
Okigbo, Christopher (Ifenayichukwu) 1932-1967 . **CLC 25, 84; BLC 3; DAM MULT, POET; PC 7**
See BW 1, 3; CA 77-80; CANR 74; DLB 125; MTCW 1, 2
Okri, Ben 1959- .... **CLC 87**
See BW 2, 3; CA 130; 138; CANR 65; DLB 157; INT 138; MTCW 2
Olds, Sharon 1942- .. **CLC 32, 39, 85; DAM POET; PC 22**
See CA 101; CANR 18, 41, 66; DLB 120; MTCW 2
Oldstyle, Jonathan
See Irving, Washington
Olesha, Yuri(Karlovich) 1899-1960 .. **CLC 8**
See CA 85-88
Oliphant,Laurence 1829(?)-1888 .. **NCLC 47**
See DLB 18, 166
Oliphant, Margaret (Oliphant Wilson) 1828-1897 .... **NCLC 11, 61; SSC 25**
See DLB 18, 159, 190
Oliver, Mary 1935- .... **CLC 19, 34, 98**
See CA 21-24R; CANR 9, 43, 84; DLB 5, 193
Olivier, Laurence(Kerr) 1907-1989 . **CLC 20**
See CA 111; 150; 129
Olsen, Tillie 1912- .... **CLC 4, 13, 114; DA; DAB; DAC; DAM MST; SSC 11**
See CA 1-4R; CANR 1, 43, 74; CDALBS; DA3; DLB 28, 206; DLBY 80; MTCW 1, 2
Olson, Charles (John) 1910-1970 . **CLC 1, 2, 5, 6, 9, 11, 29; DAM POET; PC 19**
See CA 13-16; 25-28R; CABS 2; CANR 35, 61; CAP 1; DLB 5, 16, 193; MTCW 1, 2
Olson, Toby 1937- .... **CLC 28**
See CA 65-68; CANR 9, 31, 84
Olyesha, Yuri
See Olesha, Yuri (Karlovich)
Ondaatje, (Philip) Michael 1943- .. **CLC 14, 29, 51, 76; DAB; DAC; DAM MST; PC 28**
See CA 77-80; CANR 42, 74; DA3; DLB 60; MTCW 2
Oneal, Elizabeth 1934-
See Oneal, Zibby
See CA 106; CANR 28, 84; MAICYA; SATA 30, 82
Oneal, Zibby .... **CLC 30**
See Oneal, Elizabeth
See AAYA 5; CLR 13; JRDA
O'Neill, Eugene (Gladstone) 1888-1953 .... **TCLC 1, 6, 27, 49; DA; DAB; DAC; DAM DRAM, MST; WLC**
See AITN 1; CA 110; 132; CDALB 1929-1941; DA3; DLB 7; MTCW 1, 2
Onetti, Juan Carlos 1909-1994 .. **CLC 7, 10; DAM MULT, NOV; HLCS 2; SSC 23**
See CA 85-88; 145; CANR 32, 63; DLB 113; HW 1, 2; MTCW 1, 2
O Nuallain, Brian 1911-1966
See O'Brien, Flann
See CA 21-22; 25-28R; CAP 2
Ophuls, Max 1902-1957 .... **TCLC 79**
See CA 113
Opie, Amelia 1769-1853 .... **NCLC 65**
See DLB 116, 159
Oppen, George 1908-1984 ...... **CLC 7, 13,34**
See CA 13-16R; 113; CANR 8, 82; DLB 5, 165
Oppenheim, E(dward) Phillips 1866-1946 ... **TCLC 45**
See CA 111; DLB 70
Opuls, Max
See Ophuls, Max
Origen c. 185-c. 254 .... **CMLC 19**
Orlovitz, Gil 1918-1973 .... **CLC 22**
See CA 77-80; 45-48; DLB 2, 5
Orris
See Ingelow, Jean
Ortega y Gasset, Jose 1883-1955 .. **TCLC 9; DAM MULT; HLC 2**
See CA 106; 130; HW 1, 2; MTCW 1, 2
Ortese, Anna Maria 1914- .... **CLC 89**
See DLB 177
Ortiz, Simon J(oseph) 1941- . **CLC 45; DAM MULT, POET; PC 17**
See CA 134; CANR 69; DLB 120, 175; NNAL
Orton, Joe .... **CLC 4, 13, 43; DC 3**
See Orton, John Kingsley
See CDBLB 1960 to Present; DLB 13; MTCW 2
Orton, John Kingsley 1933-1967
See Orton, Joe
See CA 85-88; CANR 35, 66; DAM DRAM; MTCW 1, 2
Orwell, George .... **TCLC 2, 6, 15, 31, 51; DAB; WLC**
See Blair, Eric (Arthur)
See CDBLB 1945-1960; DLB 15, 98, 195
Osborne, David
See Silverberg, Robert
Osborne, George
See Silverberg, Robert
Osborne, John (James) 1929-1994 ... **CLC 1, 2, 5, 11, 45; DA; DAB; DAC; DAM DRAM, MST; WLC**
See CA 13-16R; 147; CANR 21, 56; CDBLB 1945-1960; DLB 13; MTCW 1, 2
Osborne, Lawrence 1958- .... **CLC 50**
Osbourne, Lloyd 1868-1947 .... **TCLC 93**
Oshima, Nagisa 1932- .... **CLC 20**
See CA 116; 121; CANR 78
Oskison, John Milton 1874-1947 . **TCLC 35; DAM MULT**
See CA 144; CANR 84; DLB 175; NNAL
Ossian c. 3rd cent. - .... **CMLC 28**
See Macpherson, James
Ossoli, Sarah Margaret (Fuller marchesa d') 1810-1850
See Fuller, Margaret
See SATA 25
Ostrovsky, Alexander 1823-1886 . **NCLC 30, 57**
Otero, Blas de 1916-1979 .... **CLC 11**
See CA 89-92; DLB 134
Otto, Rudolf 1869-1937 .... **TCLC 85**
Otto, Whitney 1955- .... **CLC 70**
See CA 140
Ouida .... **TCLC 43**
See De La Ramee, (Marie) Louise
See DLB 18, 156
Ousmane, Sembene 1923- ... **CLC 66;BLC 3**
See BW 1, 3; CA 117; 125; CANR 81; MTCW 1
Ovid 43B.C.-17 . **CMLC 7; DAM POET; PC 2**
See DA3; DLB 211
Owen, Hugh
See Faust, Frederick (Schiller)
Owen, Wilfred (Edward Salter) 1893-1918 **TCLC 5, 27; DA; DAB; DAC; DAM MST, POET; PC 19; WLC**
See CA 104; 141; CDBLB 1914-1945; DLB 20; MTCW 2
Owens, Rochelle 1936- .... **CLC 8**
See CA 17-20R; CAAS 2; CANR 39
Oz, Amos 1939- .... **CLC 5, 8, 11, 27, 33, 54; DAM NOV**
See CA 53-56; CANR 27, 47, 65; MTCW 1, 2
Ozick, Cynthia 1928- .... **CLC 3, 7, 28, 62; DAM NOV, POP; SSC 15**
See BEST 90:1; CA 17-20R; CANR 23, 58; DA3; DLB 28, 152; DLBY 82; INT CANR-23; MTCW 1, 2
Ozu, Yasujiro 1903-1963 .... **CLC 16**
See CA 112
Pacheco, C.
See Pessoa, Fernando (Antonio Nogueira)
Pacheco, Jose Emilio 1939-
See CA 111; 131; CANR 65; DAM MULT; HLC 2; HW 1, 2
Pa Chin .... **CLC 18**
See Li Fei-kan
Pack, Robert 1929- .... **CLC 13**
See CA 1-4R; CANR 3, 44, 82; DLB 5
Padgett, Lewis
See Kuttner, Henry
Padilla (Lorenzo), Heberto 1932- ... **CLC 38**
See AITN 1; CA 123; 131; HW 1
Page, Jimmy 1944- .... **CLC 12**
Page, Louise 1955- .... **CLC 40**
See CA 140; CANR 76
Page, P(atricia) K(athleen) 1916- .... **CLC 7, 18; DAC; DAM MST; PC 12**
See CA 53-56; CANR 4, 22, 65; DLB 68; MTCW 1
Page, Thomas Nelson 1853-1922 ...... **SSC 23**
See CA 118; 177; DLB 12, 78; DLBD 13
Pagels, Elaine Hiesey 1943- .... **CLC 104**
See CA 45-48; CANR 2, 24, 51
Paget, Violet 1856-1935
See Lee, Vernon
See CA 104; 166
Paget-Lowe, Henry
See Lovecraft, H(oward) P(hillips)
Paglia, Camille (Anna) 1947- .... **CLC 68**
See CA 140; CANR 72; MTCW 2
Paige, Richard
See Koontz, Dean R(ay)
Paine, Thomas 1737-1809 .... **NCLC 62**
See CDALB 1640-1865; DLB 31, 43, 73, 158
Pakenham, Antonia
See Fraser, (Lady) Antonia (Pakenham)
Palamas, Kostes 1859-1943 .... **TCLC 5**
See CA 105
Palazzeschi, Aldo 1885-1974 .... **CLC 11**
See CA 89-92; 53-56; DLB 114
Pales Matos, Luis 1898-1959
See HLCS 2; HW 1
Paley, Grace 1922- .... **CLC 4, 6, 37; DAM POP; SSC 8**
See CA 25-28R; CANR 13, 46, 74; DA3; DLB 28; INT CANR-13; MTCW 1, 2
Palin, Michael (Edward) 1943- .... **CLC 21**
See Monty Python
See CA 107; CANR 35; SATA 67
Palliser, Charles 1947- .... **CLC 65**
See CA 136; CANR 76
Palma, Ricardo 1833-1919 .... **TCLC 29**
See CA 168

Pancake, Breece Dexter 1952-1979
See Pancake, Breece D'J
See CA 123; 109
Pancake, Breece D'J .... **CLC 29**
See Pancake, Breece Dexter
See DLB 130
Panko, Rudy
See Gogol, Nikolai (Vasilyevich)
Papadiamantis, Alexandros 1851-1911 .... **TCLC 29**
See CA 168
Papadiamantopoulos, Johannes 1856-1910
See Moreas, Jean
See CA 117
Papini, Giovanni 1881-1956 .... **TCLC 22**
See CA 121; 180
Paracelsus 1493-1541 .... **LC 14**
See DLB 179
Parasol, Peter
See Stevens, Wallace
Pardo Bazan, Emilia 1851-1921 .... **SSC 30**
Pareto, Vilfredo 1848-1923 .... **TCLC 69**
See CA 175
Parfenie, Maria
See Codrescu, Andrei
Parini, Jay (Lee) 1948- .... **CLC 54**
See CA 97-100; CAAS 16; CANR 32
Park, Jordan
See Kornbluth, C(yril) M.; Pohl, Frederik
Park, Robert E(zra) 1864-1944 .... **TCLC 73**
See CA 122; 165
Parker, Bert
See Ellison, Harlan (Jay)
Parker, Dorothy (Rothschild) 1893-1967 ..... **CLC 15, 68; DAM POET; PC 28; SSC 2**
See CA 19-20; 25-28R; CAP 2; DA3; DLB 11, 45, 86; MTCW 1, 2
Parker, Robert B(rown) 1932- .... **CLC 27; DAM NOV, POP**
See AAYA 28; BEST 89:4; CA 49-52; CANR 1, 26, 52; INT CANR-26; MTCW 1
Parkin, Frank 1940- .... **CLC 43**
See CA 147
Parkman, Francis,Jr. 1823-1893 .. **NCLC 12**
See DLB 1, 30, 186
Parks, Gordon (Alexander Buchanan) 1912- .... **CLC 1, 16; BLC 3; DAM MULT**
See AITN 2; BW 2, 3; CA 41-44R; CANR 26, 66; DA3; DLB 33; MTCW 2; SATA 8, 108
Parmenides c. 515B.C.-c.450B.C. . **CMLC 22**
See DLB 176
Parnell, Thomas 1679-1718 .... **LC 3**
See DLB 94
Parra, Nicanor 1914- ..... **CLC 2, 102; DAM MULT; HLC 2**
See CA 85-88; CANR 32; HW 1; MTCW 1
Parra Sanojo, Ana Teresa de la 1890-1936
See HLCS 2
Parrish, Mary Frances
See Fisher, M(ary) F(rances) K(ennedy)
Parson
See Coleridge, Samuel Taylor
Parson Lot
See Kingsley, Charles
Partridge, Anthony
See Oppenheim, E(dward) Phillips
Pascal, Blaise 1623-1662 .... **LC 35**
Pascoli, Giovanni 1855-1912 .... **TCLC 45**
See CA 170
Pasolini, Pier Paolo 1922-1975 . **CLC 20, 37, 106; PC 17**
See CA 93-96; 61-64; CANR 63; DLB 128, 177; MTCW 1
Pasquini
See Silone, Ignazio
Pastan, Linda (Olenik) 1932- .... **CLC 27; DAM POET**
See CA 61-64; CANR 18, 40, 61; DLB 5
Pasternak, Boris (Leonidovich) 1890-1960 .. **CLC 7, 10, 18, 63; DA; DAB; DAC; DAM MST, NOV, POET; PC 6; SSC 31;WLC**
See CA 127; 116; DA3; MTCW 1, 2
Patchen, Kenneth 1911-1972 . **CLC 1, 2, 18; DAM POET**
See CA 1-4R; 33-36R; CANR 3, 35; DLB 16, 48; MTCW 1
Pater, Walter (Horatio) 1839-1894 . **NCLC 7**
See CDBLB 1832-1890; DLB 57, 156
Paterson, A(ndrew) B(arton) 1864-1941 ...... **TCLC 32**
See CA 155; SATA 97
Paterson, Katherine (Womeldorf) 1932- ..... **CLC 12, 30**
See AAYA 1, 31; CA 21-24R; CANR 28, 59; CLR 7, 50; DLB 52; JRDA; MAICYA; MTCW 1; SATA 13, 53, 92
Patmore, Coventry Kersey Dighton 1823-1896 .... **NCLC 9**
See DLB 35, 98
Paton, Alan (Stewart) 1903-1988 ..... **CLC 4, 10, 25, 55, 106; DA; DAB; DAC; DAM MST, NOV; WLC**
See AAYA 26; CA 13-16; 125; CANR 22; CAP 1; DA3; DLBD 17; MTCW 1, 2; SATA 11; SATA-Obit 56
Paton Walsh, Gillian 1937-
See Walsh, Jill Paton
See CANR 38, 83; JRDA; MAICYA; SAAS 3; SATA 4, 72, 109
Patton, George S. 1885-1945 .... **TCLC 79**
Paulding, James Kirke 1778-1860 . **NCLC 2**
See DLB 3, 59, 74
Paulin, Thomas Neilson 1949-
See Paulin, Tom
See CA 123; 128
Paulin, Tom .... **CLC 37**
See Paulin, Thomas Neilson
See DLB 40
Pausanias c. 1st cent. - .... **CMLC 36**
Paustovsky, Konstantin (Georgievich) 1892-1968 .... **CLC 40**
See CA 93-96; 25-28R
Pavese, Cesare 1908-1950 . **TCLC 3; PC 13; SSC 19**
See CA 104; 169; DLB 128, 177
Pavic, Milorad 1929- .... **CLC 60**
See CA 136; DLB 181
Pavlov, Ivan Petrovich 1849-1936 . **TCLC 91**
See CA 118; 180
Payne, Alan
See Jakes, John (William)
Paz, Gil
See Lugones, Leopoldo
Paz, Octavio 1914-1998 . **CLC 3, 4, 6, 10, 19, 51, 65, 119; DA; DAB; DAC; DAM MST, MULT, POET; HLC 2; PC 1;WLC**
See CA 73-76; 165; CANR 32, 65; DA3; DLBY 90, 98; HW 1, 2; MTCW 1, 2
p'Bitek, Okot 1931-1982 ... **CLC 96; BLC 3; DAM MULT**
See BW 2, 3; CA 124; 107; CANR 82; DLB 125; MTCW 1, 2
Peacock, Molly 1947- .... **CLC 60**
See CA 103; CAAS 21; CANR 52, 84; DLB 120
Peacock, ThomasLove 1785-1866 . **NCLC 22**
See DLB 96, 116
Peake, Mervyn 1911-1968 .... **CLC 7, 54**
See CA 5-8R; 25-28R; CANR 3; DLB 15, 160; MTCW 1; SATA 23
Pearce, Philippa .... **CLC 21**
See Christie, (Ann) Philippa
See CLR 9; DLB 161; MAICYA; SATA 1, 67
Pearl, Eric
See Elman, Richard (Martin)
Pearson, T(homas) R(eid) 1956- ..... **CLC 39**
See CA 120; 130; INT 130
Peck, Dale 1967- .... **CLC 81**
See CA 146; CANR 72
Peck, John 1941- .... **CLC 3**
See CA 49-52; CANR 3
Peck, Richard (Wayne) 1934- .... **CLC 21**
See AAYA 1, 24; CA 85-88; CANR 19, 38; CLR 15; INT CANR-19; JRDA; MAICYA; SAAS 2; SATA 18, 55, 97; SATA-Essay 110
Peck, Robert Newton 1928- ... **CLC 17; DA; DAC; DAM MST**
See AAYA 3; CA 81-84; CANR 31, 63; CLR 45; JRDA; MAICYA; SAAS 1; SATA 21, 62, 111; SATA-Essay 108
Peckinpah, (David) Sam(uel) 1925-1984 ...... **CLC 20**
See CA 109; 114; CANR 82
Pedersen, Knut 1859-1952
See Hamsun, Knut
See CA 104; 119; CANR 63; MTCW 1, 2
Peeslake, Gaffer
See Durrell, Lawrence (George)
Peguy, Charles Pierre 1873-1914 . **TCLC 10**
See CA 107
Peirce, Charles Sanders 1839-1914 ... **TCLC 81**
Pellicer, Carlos 1900(?)-1977
See CA 153; 69-72; HLCS 2; HW 1
Pena, Ramon del Valle y
See Valle-Inclan, Ramon (Maria) del
Pendennis, Arthur Esquir
See Thackeray, William Makepeace
Penn, William 1644-1718 .... **LC 25**
See DLB 24
PEPECE
See Prado (Calvo), Pedro
Pepys, Samuel 1633-1703 . **LC 11; DA; DAB; DAC; DAM MST; WLC**
See CDBLB 1660-1789; DA3; DLB 101
Percy, Walker 1916-1990 ..... **CLC 2, 3, 6, 8, 14, 18, 47, 65; DAM NOV, POP**
See CA 1-4R; 131; CANR 1, 23, 64; DA3; DLB 2; DLBY 80, 90; MTCW 1, 2
Percy, William Alexander 1885-1942 . **TCLC 84**
See CA 163; MTCW 2
Perec, Georges 1936-1982 .... **CLC 56, 116**
See CA 141; DLB 83
Pereda (y Sanchez de Porrua), Jose Mariade 1833-1906 .... **TCLC 16**
See CA 117
Pereda y Porrua, Jose Maria de
See Pereda (y Sanchez de Porrua), Jose Maria de
Peregoy, George Weems
See Mencken, H(enry) L(ouis)
Perelman, S(idney) J(oseph) 1904-1979 .... **CLC 3, 5, 9, 15, 23, 44, 49; DAM DRAM; SSC 32**
See AITN 1, 2; CA 73-76; 89-92; CANR 18; DLB 11, 44; MTCW 1, 2
Peret, Benjamin 1899-1959 .... **TCLC 20**
See CA 117
Peretz, Isaac Loeb 1851(?)-1915 . **TCLC 16; SSC 26**
See CA 109
Peretz, Yitzkhok Leibush
See Peretz, Isaac Loeb
Perez Galdos, Benito 1843-1920 . **TCLC 27; HLCS 2**
See CA 125; 153; HW 1

Peri Rossi, Cristina 1941-
See CA 131; CANR 59, 81; DLB 145; HLCS 2; HW 1, 2
Perrault, Charles 1628-1703 .... **LC 3, 52**
See MAICYA; SATA 25
Perry, Brighton
See Sherwood, Robert E(mmet)
Perse, St.-John
See Leger, (Marie-Rene Auguste) Alexis Saint-Leger
Perutz, Leo(pold) 1882-1957 .... **TCLC 60**
See CA 147; DLB 81
Peseenz, Tulio F.
See Lopez y Fuentes, Gregorio
Pesetsky, Bette 1932- .... **CLC 28**
See CA 133; DLB 130
Peshkov, Alexei Maximovich 1868-1936
See Gorky, Maxim
See CA 105; 141; CANR 83; DA; DAC; DAM DRAM, MST, NOV; MTCW 2
Pessoa, Fernando (Antonio Nogueira) 1888-1935 ..... **TCLC 27; DAM MULT; HLC 2; PC 20**
See CA 125
Peterkin, Julia Mood 1880-1961 ..... **CLC 31**
See CA 102; DLB 9
Peters, Joan K(aren) 1945- .... **CLC 39**
See CA 158
Peters, Robert L(ouis) 1924- .... **CLC 7**
See CA 13-16R; CAAS 8; DLB 105
Petofi, Sandor 1823-1849 .... **NCLC 21**
Petrakis, Harry Mark 1923- .... **CLC 3**
See CA 9-12R; CANR 4, 30, 85
Petrarch 1304-1374 .... **CMLC 20; DAM POET; PC 8**
See DA3
Petronius c. 20-66 .... **CMLC 34**
See DLB 211
Petrov, Evgeny .... **TCLC 21**
See Kataev, Evgeny Petrovich
Petry, Ann (Lane) 1908-1997 .. **CLC 1, 7, 18**
See BW 1, 3; CA 5-8R; 157; CAAS 6; CANR 4, 46; CLR 12; DLB 76; JRDA; MAICYA; MTCW 1; SATA 5; SATA-Obit 94
Petursson, Halligrimur 1614-1674 .... **LC 8**
Peychinovich
See Vazov, Ivan (Minchov)
Phaedrus c. 18B.C.-c. 50 .... **CMLC 25**
See DLB 211
Philips, Katherine 1632-1664 .... **LC 30**
See DLB 131
Philipson, Morris H. 1926- .... **CLC 53**
See CA 1-4R; CANR 4
Phillips, Caryl 1958- . **CLC 96; BLCS; DAM MULT**
See BW 2; CA 141; CANR 63; DA3; DLB 157; MTCW 2
Phillips, David Graham 1867-1911 ... **TCLC 44**
See CA 108; 176; DLB 9, 12
Phillips, Jack
See Sandburg, Carl (August)
Phillips, Jayne Anne 1952- .... **CLC 15, 33; SSC 16**
See CA 101; CANR 24, 50; DLBY 80; INT CANR-24; MTCW 1, 2
Phillips, Richard
See Dick, Philip K(indred)
Phillips, Robert(Schaeffer) 1938- .... **CLC 28**
See CA 17-20R; CAAS 13; CANR 8; DLB 105
Phillips, Ward
See Lovecraft, H(oward) P(hillips)
Piccolo, Lucio 1901-1969 .... **CLC 13**
See CA 97-100; DLB 114
Pickthall, Marjorie L(owry) C(hristie) 1883-1922 .... **TCLC 21**
See CA 107; DLB 92
Pico della Mirandola, Giovanni 1463-1494 . **LC 15**
Piercy, Marge 1936- ... **CLC 3, 6, 14, 18, 27, 62**
See CA 21-24R; CAAS 1; CANR 13, 43, 66; DLB 120; MTCW 1, 2
Piers, Robert
See Anthony, Piers
Pieyre de Mandiargues, Andre 1909-1991
See Mandiargues, Andre Pieyre de
See CA 103; 136; CANR 22, 82
Pilnyak, Boris .... **TCLC 23**
See Vogau, Boris Andreyevich
Pincherle, Alberto 1907-1990 ... **CLC 11, 18; DAM NOV**
See Moravia, Alberto
See CA 25-28R; 132; CANR 33, 63; MTCW 1
Pinckney, Darryl 1953- .... **CLC 76**
See BW 2, 3; CA 143; CANR 79
Pindar 518B.C.-446B.C. .... **CMLC 12;PC 19**
See DLB 176
Pineda, Cecile 1942- .... **CLC 39**
See CA 118
Pinero, Arthur Wing 1855-1934 .. **TCLC 32; DAM DRAM**
See CA 110; 153; DLB 10
Pinero, Miguel (Antonio Gomez) 1946-1988 .... **CLC 4, 55**
See CA 61-64; 125; CANR 29; HW 1
Pinget, Robert 1919-1997 ...... **CLC 7, 13, 37**
See CA 85-88; 160; DLB 83
Pink Floyd
See Barrett, (Roger) Syd; Gilmour, David; Mason, Nick; Waters, Roger; Wright, Rick
Pinkney, Edward 1802-1828 .... **NCLC 31**
Pinkwater, Daniel Manus 1941- ...... **CLC 35**
See Pinkwater, Manus
See AAYA 1; CA 29-32R; CANR 12, 38; CLR 4; JRDA; MAICYA; SAAS 3; SATA 46, 76
Pinkwater, Manus
See Pinkwater, Daniel Manus
See SATA 8
Pinsky, Robert 1940- ...... **CLC 9, 19, 38, 94, 121; DAM POET; PC 27**
See CA 29-32R; CAAS 4; CANR 58; DA3; DLBY 82, 98; MTCW 2
Pinta, Harold
See Pinter, Harold
Pinter, Harold 1930- . **CLC 1, 3, 6, 9, 11, 15, 27, 58, 73; DA; DAB; DAC; DAM DRAM, MST; WLC**
See CA 5-8R; CANR 33, 65; CDBLB 1960 to Present; DA3; DLB 13; MTCW 1, 2
Piozzi, Hester Lynch (Thrale) 1741-1821 .... **NCLC 57**
See DLB 104, 142
Pirandello, Luigi 1867-1936 .... **TCLC 4, 29; DA; DAB; DAC; DAM DRAM, MST; DC 5; SSC 22; WLC**
See CA 104; 153; DA3; MTCW 2
Pirsig, Robert M(aynard) 1928- .. **CLC 4, 6, 73; DAM POP**
See CA 53-56; CANR 42, 74; DA3; MTCW 1, 2; SATA 39
Pisarev, Dmitry Ivanovich 1840-1868 .... **NCLC 25**
Pix, Mary (Griffith) 1666-1709 .... **LC 8**
See DLB 80
Pixerecourt, (Rene Charles) Guilbert de 1773-1844 .... **NCLC 39**
See DLB 192
Plaatje, Sol(omon) T(shekisho) 1876-1932 .. **TCLC 73; BLCS**
See BW 2, 3; CA 141; CANR 79
Plaidy, Jean
See Hibbert, Eleanor Alice Burford
Planche, James Robinson 1796-1880 . **NCLC 42**
Plant, Robert 1948- .... **CLC 12**
Plante, David (Robert) 1940- ..... **CLC 7, 23, 38; DAM NOV**
See CA 37-40R; CANR 12, 36, 58, 82; DLBY 83; INT CANR-12; MTCW 1
Plath, Sylvia 1932-1963 .... **CLC 1, 2, 3, 5, 9, 11, 14, 17, 50, 51, 62, 111; DA; DAB; DAC; DAM MST, POET; PC 1; WLC**
See AAYA 13; CA 19-20; CANR 34; CAP 2; CDALB 1941-1968; DA3; DLB 5, 6, 152; MTCW 1, 2; SATA 96
Plato 428(?)B.C.-348(?)B.C. .. **CMLC 8; DA; DAB; DAC; DAM MST; WLCS**
See DA3; DLB 176
Platonov, Andrei .... **TCLC 14**
See Klimentov, Andrei Platonovich
Platt, Kin 1911- .... **CLC 26**
See AAYA 11; CA 17-20R; CANR 11; JRDA; SAAS 17; SATA 21, 86
Plautus c. 251B.C.-184B.C. .. **CMLC 24; DC 6**
See DLB 211
Plick et Plock
See Simenon, Georges (Jacques Christian)
Plimpton, George (Ames) 1927- ...... **CLC 36**
See AITN 1; CA 21-24R; CANR 32, 70; DLB 185; MTCW 1, 2; SATA 10
Pliny the Elder c. 23-79 .... **CMLC 23**
See DLB 211
Plomer, William Charles Franklin 1903-1973 .... **CLC 4, 8**
See CA 21-22; CANR 34; CAP 2; DLB 20, 162, 191; MTCW 1; SATA 24
Plowman, Piers
See Kavanagh, Patrick (Joseph)
Plum, J.
See Wodehouse, P(elham) G(renville)
Plumly, Stanley (Ross) 1939- .... **CLC 33**
See CA 108; 110; DLB 5, 193; INT 110
Plumpe, Friedrich Wilhelm 1888-1931 .... **TCLC 53**
See CA 112
Po Chu-i 772-846 .... **CMLC 24**
Poe, Edgar Allan 1809-1849 .... **NCLC 1, 16, 55, 78; DA; DAB; DAC; DAM MST, POET; PC 1; SSC 34; WLC**
See AAYA 14; CDALB 1640-1865; DA3; DLB 3, 59, 73, 74; SATA 23
Poet of Titchfield Street, The
See Pound, Ezra (Weston Loomis)
Pohl, Frederik 1919- .... **CLC 18;SSC 25**
See AAYA 24; CA 61-64; CAAS 1; CANR 11, 37, 81; DLB 8; INT CANR-11; MTCW 1, 2; SATA 24
Poirier, Louis 1910-
See Gracq, Julien
See CA 122; 126
Poitier, Sidney 1927- .... **CLC 26**
See BW 1; CA 117
Polanski, Roman 1933- .... **CLC 16**
See CA 77-80
Poliakoff, Stephen 1952- .... **CLC 38**
See CA 106; DLB 13
Police, The
See Copeland, Stewart (Armstrong); Summers, Andrew James; Sumner, Gordon Matthew
Polidori, JohnWilliam 1795-1821 . **NCLC 51**
See DLB 116
Pollitt, Katha 1949- .... **CLC 28, 122**
See CA 120; 122; CANR 66; MTCW 1, 2
Pollock, (Mary) Sharon 1936- .... **CLC 50; DAC; DAM DRAM, MST**
See CA 141; DLB 60

Polo, Marco 1254-1324 .... **CMLC 15**
Polonsky, Abraham (Lincoln) 1910- .... **CLC 92**
See CA 104; DLB 26; INT 104
Polybius c. 200B.C.-c.118B.C. ...... **CMLC 17**
See DLB 176
Pomerance, Bernard 1940- ... **CLC 13;DAM DRAM**
See CA 101; CANR 49
Ponge, Francis (Jean Gaston Alfred) 1899-1988 ..... **CLC 6, 18; DAM POET**
See CA 85-88; 126; CANR 40
Poniatowska, Elena 1933-
See CA 101; CANR 32, 66; DAM MULT; DLB 113; HLC 2; HW 1, 2
Pontoppidan, Henrik 1857-1943 ... **TCLC 29**
See CA 170
Poole, Josephine .... **CLC 17**
See Helyar, Jane Penelope Josephine
See SAAS 2; SATA 5
Popa, Vasko 1922-1991 .... **CLC 19**
See CA 112; 148; DLB 181
Pope, Alexander 1688-1744 .... **LC 3; DA; DAB; DAC; DAM MST, POET; PC 26; WLC**
See CDBLB 1660-1789; DA3; DLB 95, 101
Porter, Connie (Rose) 1959(?)- .... **CLC 70**
See BW 2, 3; CA 142; SATA 81
Porter, Gene(va Grace)Stratton 1863(?)-1924 .... **TCLC 21**
See CA 112
Porter, Katherine Anne 1890-1980 .. **CLC 1, 3, 7, 10, 13, 15, 27, 101; DA; DAB; DAC; DAM MST, NOV; SSC 4, 31**
See AITN 2; CA 1-4R; 101; CANR 1, 65; CDALBS; DA3; DLB 4, 9, 102; DLBD 12; DLBY 80; MTCW 1, 2; SATA 39; SATA-Obit 23
Porter, Peter (Neville Frederick) 1929- . **CLC 5, 13, 33**
See CA 85-88; DLB 40
Porter, William Sydney 1862-1910
See Henry, O.
See CA 104; 131; CDALB 1865-1917; DA; DAB; DAC; DAM MST; DA3; DLB 12, 78, 79; MTCW 1, 2; YABC 2
Portillo (y Pacheco), Jose Lopez
See Lopez Portillo (y Pacheco), Jose
Portillo Trambley, Estela 1927-1998
See CANR 32; DAM MULT; DLB 209; HLC 2; HW 1
Post, Melville Davisson 1869-1930 .... **TCLC 39**
See CA 110
Potok, Chaim 1929- . **CLC 2, 7, 14, 26, 112; DAM NOV**
See AAYA 15; AITN 1, 2; CA 17-20R; CANR 19, 35, 64; DA3; DLB 28, 152; INT CANR-19; MTCW 1, 2; SATA 33, 106
Potter, (Helen) Beatrix 1866-1943
See Webb, (Martha) Beatrice (Potter)
See MAICYA; MTCW 2
Potter, Dennis (Christopher George) 1935-1994 .... **CLC 58, 86**
See CA 107; 145; CANR 33, 61; MTCW 1
Pound, Ezra (Weston Loomis) 1885-1972 ... **CLC 1, 2, 3, 4, 5, 7, 10, 13, 18, 34, 48, 50, 112; DA; DAB; DAC; DAM MST, POET; PC 4; WLC**
See CA 5-8R; 37-40R; CANR 40; CDALB 1917-1929; DA3; DLB 4, 45, 63; DLBD 15; MTCW 1, 2
Povod, Reinaldo 1959-1994 .... **CLC 44**
See CA 136; 146; CANR 83
Powell, Adam Clayton, Jr. 1908-1972 .. **CLC 89; BLC 3; DAM MULT**
See BW 1, 3; CA 102; 33-36R
Powell, Anthony (Dymoke) 1905- . **CLC 1, 3, 7, 9, 10, 31**
See CA 1-4R; CANR 1, 32, 62; CDBLB 1945-1960; DLB 15; MTCW 1, 2
Powell, Dawn 1897-1965 .... **CLC 66**
See CA 5-8R; DLBY 97
Powell, Padgett 1952- .... **CLC 34**
See CA 126; CANR 63
Power, Susan 1961- .... **CLC 91**
Powers, J(ames) F(arl) 1917-1999 ... **CLC 1, 4, 8, 57; SSC 4**
See CA 1-4R; 181; CANR 2, 61; DLB 130; MTCW 1
Powers, John J(ames) 1945-
See Powers, John R.
See CA 69-72
Powers, John R. .... **CLC 66**
See Powers, John J(ames)
Powers, Richard (S.) 1957- .... **CLC 93**
See CA 148; CANR 80
Pownall, David 1938- .... **CLC 10**
See CA 89-92, 180; CAAS 18; CANR 49; DLB 14
Powys, John Cowper 1872-1963 .. **CLC 7, 9, 15, 46, 125**
See CA 85-88; DLB 15; MTCW 1, 2
Powys, T(heodore) F(rancis) 1875-1953 ...... **TCLC 9**
See CA 106; DLB 36, 162
Prado (Calvo),Pedro 1886-1952 ... **TCLC 75**
See CA 131; HW 1
Prager, Emily 1952- .... **CLC 56**
Pratt, E(dwin) J(ohn) 1883(?)-1964 ..... **CLC 19; DAC; DAM POET**
See CA 141; 93-96; CANR 77; DLB 92
Premchand .... **TCLC 21**
See Srivastava, Dhanpat Rai
Preussler, Otfried 1923- .... **CLC 17**
See CA 77-80; SATA 24
Prevert, Jacques (Henri Marie) 1900-1977 . **CLC 15**
See CA 77-80; 69-72; CANR 29, 61; MTCW 1; SATA-Obit 30
Prevost, Abbe (Antoine Francois) 1697-1763 .... **LC 1**
Price, (Edward) Reynolds 1933- .. **CLC 3, 6, 13, 43, 50, 63; DAM NOV; SSC 22**
See CA 1-4R; CANR 1, 37, 57; DLB 2; INT CANR-37
Price, Richard 1949- .... **CLC 6, 12**
See CA 49-52; CANR 3; DLBY 81
Prichard, Katharine Susannah 1883-1969 .. **CLC 46**
See CA 11-12; CANR 33; CAP 1; MTCW 1; SATA 66
Priestley, J(ohn) B(oynton) 1894-1984 . **CLC 2, 5, 9, 34; DAM DRAM, NOV**
See CA 9-12R; 113; CANR 33;CDBLB 1914-1945; DA3; DLB 10, 34, 77, 100, 139; DLBY 84; MTCW 1, 2
Prince 1958(?)- .... **CLC 35**
Prince, F(rank) T(empleton) 1912- . **CLC 22**
See CA 101; CANR 43, 79; DLB 20
Prince Kropotkin
See Kropotkin, Peter (Aleksieevich)
Prior, Matthew 1664-1721 .... **LC 4**
See DLB 95
Prishvin, Mikhail 1873-1954 .... **TCLC 75**
Pritchard, William H(arrison) 1932- ... **CLC 34**
See CA 65-68; CANR 23; DLB 111
Pritchett, V(ictor) S(awdon) 1900-1997 .... **CLC 5, 13, 15, 41; DAM NOV; SSC 14**
See CA 61-64; 157; CANR 31, 63; DA3; DLB 15, 139; MTCW 1, 2
Private 19022
See Manning, Frederic
Probst, Mark 1925- .... **CLC 59**
See CA 130
Prokosch, Frederic 1908-1989 ..... **CLC 4, 48**
See CA 73-76; 128; CANR 82; DLB 48; MTCW 2
Propertius, Sextus c. 50B.C.-c.16B.C. .... **CMLC 32**
See DLB 211
Prophet, The
See Dreiser, Theodore (Herman Albert)
Prose, Francine 1947- .... **CLC 45**
See CA 109; 112; CANR 46; SATA 101
Proudhon
See Cunha, Euclides (Rodrigues Pimenta) da
Proulx, Annie
See Proulx, E(dna) Annie
Proulx, E(dna) Annie 1935- .. **CLC 81;DAM POP**
See CA 145; CANR 65; DA3; MTCW 2
Proust, (Valentin-Louis-George-Eugene-)Marcel 1871-1922 . **TCLC 7, 13, 33; DA; DAB; DAC; DAM MST, NOV; WLC**
See CA 104; 120; DA3; DLB 65; MTCW 1, 2
Prowler, Harley
See Masters, Edgar Lee
Prus, Boleslaw 1845-1912 .... **TCLC 48**
Pryor, Richard (Franklin Lenox Thomas) 1940- .... **CLC 26**
See CA 122; 152
Przybyszewski, Stanislaw 1868-1927 . **TCLC 36**
See CA 160; DLB 66
Pteleon
See Grieve, C(hristopher) M(urray)
See DAM POET
Puckett, Lute
See Masters, Edgar Lee
Puig, Manuel 1932-1990 ... **CLC 3, 5, 10, 28, 65; DAM MULT; HLC 2**
See CA 45-48; CANR 2, 32, 63; DA3; DLB 113; HW 1, 2; MTCW 1, 2
Pulitzer, Joseph 1847-1911 .... **TCLC 76**
See CA 114; DLB 23
Purdy, A(lfred) W(ellington) 1918- .. **CLC 3, 6, 14, 50; DAC; DAM MST, POET**
See CA 81-84; CAAS 17; CANR 42, 66; DLB 88
Purdy, James (Amos) 1923- ... **CLC 2, 4, 10, 28, 52**
See CA 33-36R; CAAS 1; CANR 19, 51; DLB 2; INT CANR-19; MTCW 1
Pure, Simon
See Swinnerton, Frank Arthur
Pushkin, Alexander (Sergeyevich) 1799-1837 .. **NCLC 3, 27; DA; DAB; DAC; DAM DRAM, MST, POET; PC 10; SSC 27; WLC**
See DA3; DLB 205; SATA 61
P'u Sung-ling 1640-1715 ...... **LC 49; SSC 31**
Putnam, Arthur Lee
See Alger, Horatio, Jr.
Puzo, Mario 1920-1999 ...... **CLC 1, 2, 6, 36, 107; DAM NOV, POP**
See CA 65-68; CANR 4, 42, 65; DA3; DLB 6; MTCW 1, 2
Pygge, Edward
See Barnes, Julian (Patrick)
Pyle, Ernest Taylor 1900-1945
See Pyle, Ernie
See CA 115; 160
Pyle, Ernie 1900-1945 .... **TCLC 75**
See Pyle, Ernest Taylor
See DLB 29; MTCW 2
Pyle, Howard 1853-1911 .... **TCLC 81**
See CA 109; 137; CLR 22; DLB 42, 188; DLBD 13; MAICYA; SATA 16, 100

Pym, Barbara (Mary Crampton) 1913-1980 .... **CLC 13, 19, 37, 111**
See CA 13-14; 97-100; CANR 13, 34; CAP 1; DLB 14, 207; DLBY 87; MTCW 1, 2
Pynchon, Thomas (Ruggles, Jr.) 1937- . **CLC 2, 3, 6, 9, 11, 18, 33, 62, 72; DA; DAB; DAC; DAM MST, NOV, POP; SSC 14;WLC**
See BEST 90:2; CA 17-20R; CANR 22, 46, 73; DA3; DLB 2, 173; MTCW 1, 2
Pythagoras c. 570B.C.-c.500B.C. . **CMLC 22**
See DLB 176
Q
See Quiller-Couch, SirArthur (Thomas)
Qian Zhongshu
See Ch'ien Chung-shu
Qroll
See Dagerman, Stig (Halvard)
Quarrington, Paul (Lewis) 1953- .... **CLC 65**
See CA 129; CANR 62
Quasimodo, Salvatore 1901-1968 .... **CLC 10**
See CA 13-16; 25-28R; CAP 1; DLB 114; MTCW 1
Quay, Stephen 1947- .... **CLC 95**
Quay, Timothy 1947- .... **CLC 95**
Queen, Ellery .... **CLC 3, 11**
See Dannay, Frederic; Davidson, Avram (James); Lee, Manfred B(ennington); Marlowe, Stephen; Sturgeon, Theodore (Hamilton); Vance, John Holbrook
Queen, Ellery, Jr.
See Dannay, Frederic; Lee, Manfred B(ennington)
Queneau, Raymond 1903-1976 .... **CLC 2, 5, 10, 42**
See CA 77-80; 69-72; CANR 32; DLB 72; MTCW 1, 2
Quevedo, Francisco de 1580-1645 ..... **LC 23**
Quiller-Couch, Sir Arthur(Thomas) 1863-1944 .... **TCLC 53**
See CA 118; 166; DLB 135, 153, 190
Quin, Ann (Marie) 1936-1973 .... **CLC 6**
See CA 9-12R; 45-48; DLB 14
Quinn, Martin
See Smith, Martin Cruz
Quinn, Peter 1947- .... **CLC 91**
Quinn, Simon
See Smith, Martin Cruz
Quintana, Leroy V. 1944-
See CA 131; CANR 65; DAM MULT; DLB 82; HLC 2; HW 1, 2
Quiroga, Horacio (Sylvestre) 1878-1937 ...... **TCLC 20; DAM MULT; HLC 2**
See CA 117; 131; HW 1; MTCW 1
Quoirez, Francoise 1935- .... **CLC 9**
See Sagan, Francoise
See CA 49-52; CANR 6, 39, 73; MTCW 1, 2
Raabe, Wilhelm (Karl) 1831-1910 ..... **TCLC 45**
See CA 167; DLB 129
Rabe, David (William) 1940- . **CLC 4, 8, 33; DAM DRAM**
See CA 85-88; CABS 3; CANR 59; DLB 7
Rabelais, Francois 1483-1553 ..... **LC 5; DA; DAB; DAC; DAM MST; WLC**
Rabinovitch, Sholem 1859-1916
See Aleichem, Sholom
See CA 104
Rabinyan, Dorit 1972- .... **CLC 119**
See CA 170
Rachilde 1860-1953 .... **TCLC 67**
See DLB 123, 192
Racine, Jean 1639-1699 . **LC 28; DAB;DAM MST**
See DA3
Radcliffe, Ann (Ward) 1764-1823 . **NCLC 6, 55**
See DLB 39, 178
Radiguet, Raymond 1903-1923 ..... **TCLC 29**
See CA 162; DLB 65
Radnoti, Miklos 1909-1944 .... **TCLC 16**
See CA 118
Rado, James 1939- .... **CLC 17**
See CA 105
Radvanyi, Netty 1900-1983
See Seghers, Anna
See CA 85-88; 110; CANR 82
Rae, Ben
See Griffiths, Trevor
Raeburn, John (Hay) 1941- .... **CLC 34**
See CA 57-60
Ragni, Gerome 1942-1991 .... **CLC 17**
See CA 105; 134
Rahv, Philip 1908-1973 .... **CLC 24**
See Greenberg, Ivan
See DLB 137
Raimund, Ferdinand Jakob 1790-1836 .... **NCLC 69**
See DLB 90
Raine, Craig 1944- .... **CLC 32, 103**
See CA 108; CANR 29, 51; DLB 40
Raine, Kathleen (Jessie) 1908- .... **CLC 7, 45**
See CA 85-88; CANR 46; DLB 20; MTCW 1
Rainis, Janis 1865-1929 .... **TCLC 29**
See CA 170
Rakosi, Carl 1903- .... **CLC 47**
See Rawley, Callman
See CAAS 5; DLB 193
Raleigh, Richard
See Lovecraft, H(oward) P(hillips)
Raleigh, Sir Walter 1554(?)-1618 . **LC 31, 39**
See CDBLB Before 1660; DLB 172
Rallentando, H. P.
See Sayers, Dorothy L(eigh)
Ramal, Walter
See de la Mare, Walter (John)
Ramana Maharshi 1879-1950 .... **TCLC 84**
Ramoacn y Cajal, Santiago 1852-1934 .... **TCLC 93**
Ramon, Juan
See Jimenez (Mantecon), Juan Ramon
Ramos, Graciliano 1892-1953 .... **TCLC 32**
See CA 167; HW 2
Rampersad, Arnold 1941- .... **CLC 44**
See BW 2, 3; CA 127; 133; CANR 81; DLB 111; INT 133
Rampling, Anne
See Rice, Anne
Ramsay, Allan 1684(?)-1758 .... **LC 29**
See DLB 95
Ramuz, Charles-Ferdinand 1878-1947 .... **TCLC 33**
See CA 165
Rand, Ayn 1905-1982 ..... **CLC 3, 30, 44, 79; DA; DAC; DAM MST, NOV, POP; WLC**
See AAYA 10; CA 13-16R; 105; CANR 27, 73; CDALBS; DA3; MTCW 1, 2
Randall, Dudley (Felker) 1914- .... **CLC 1; BLC 3; DAM MULT**
See BW 1, 3; CA 25-28R; CANR 23, 82; DLB 41
Randall, Robert
See Silverberg, Robert
Ranger, Ken
See Creasey, John
Ransom, John Crowe 1888-1974 . **CLC 2, 4, 5, 11, 24; DAM POET**
See CA 5-8R; 49-52; CANR 6, 34; CDALBS; DA3; DLB 45, 63; MTCW 1, 2
Rao, Raja 1909- ..... **CLC 25, 56;DAM NOV**
See CA 73-76; CANR 51; MTCW 1, 2
Raphael, Frederic (Michael) 1931- .. **CLC 2, 14**
See CA 1-4R; CANR 1; DLB 14
Ratcliffe, James P.
See Mencken, H(enry) L(ouis)
Rathbone, Julian 1935- .... **CLC 41**
See CA 101; CANR 34, 73
Rattigan, Terence (Mervyn) 1911-1977 . **CLC 7; DAM DRAM**
See CA 85-88; 73-76; CDBLB 1945-1960; DLB 13; MTCW 1, 2
Ratushinskaya, Irina 1954- .... **CLC 54**
See CA 129; CANR 68
Raven, Simon (Arthur Noel) 1927- . **CLC 14**
See CA 81-84
Ravenna, Michael
See Welty, Eudora
Rawley, Callman 1903-
See Rakosi, Carl
See CA 21-24R; CANR 12, 32
Rawlings, Marjorie Kinnan 1896-1953 .... **TCLC 4**
See AAYA 20; CA 104; 137; CANR 74; DLB 9, 22, 102; DLBD 17; JRDA; MAICYA; MTCW 2; SATA 100; YABC 1
Ray, Satyajit 1921-1992 . **CLC 16, 76; DAM MULT**
See CA 114; 137
Read, Herbert Edward 1893-1968 .... **CLC 4**
See CA 85-88; 25-28R; DLB 20, 149
Read, Piers Paul 1941- .... **CLC 4, 10, 25**
See CA 21-24R; CANR 38; DLB 14; SATA 21
Reade, Charles 1814-1884 .... **NCLC 2, 74**
See DLB 21
Reade, Hamish
See Gray, Simon (James Holliday)
Reading, Peter 1946- .... **CLC 47**
See CA 103; CANR 46; DLB 40
Reaney, James 1926- .. **CLC 13; DAC;DAM MST**
See CA 41-44R; CAAS 15; CANR 42; DLB 68; SATA 43
Rebreanu, Liviu 1885-1944 .... **TCLC 28**
See CA 165
Rechy, John (Francisco) 1934- ..... **CLC 1, 7, 14, 18, 107; DAM MULT; HLC 2**
See CA 5-8R; CAAS 4; CANR 6, 32, 64; DLB 122; DLBY 82; HW 1, 2; INT CANR-6
Redcam, Tom 1870-1933 .... **TCLC 25**
Reddin, Keith .... **CLC 67**
Redgrove, Peter (William) 1932- . **CLC 6, 41**
See CA 1-4R; CANR 3, 39, 77; DLB 40
Redmon, Anne .... **CLC 22**
See Nightingale, Anne Redmon
See DLBY 86
Reed, Eliot
See Ambler, Eric
Reed, Ishmael 1938- . **CLC 2, 3, 5, 6, 13, 32, 60; BLC 3; DAM MULT**
See BW 2, 3; CA 21-24R; CANR 25, 48, 74; DA3; DLB 2, 5, 33, 169; DLBD 8; MTCW 1, 2
Reed, John (Silas) 1887-1920 .... **TCLC 9**
See CA 106
Reed, Lou .... **CLC 21**
See Firbank, Louis
Reeve, Clara 1729-1807 .... **NCLC 19**
See DLB 39
Reich, Wilhelm 1897-1957 .... **TCLC 57**
Reid, Christopher (John) 1949- ...... **CLC 33**
See CA 140; DLB 40
Reid, Desmond
See Moorcock, Michael (John)
Reid Banks, Lynne 1929-
See Banks, Lynne Reid

See CA 1-4R; CANR 6, 22, 38; CLR 24; JRDA; MAICYA; SATA 22, 75, 111

Reilly, William K.
See Creasey, John

Reiner, Max
See Caldwell, (Janet Miriam) Taylor (Holland)

Reis, Ricardo
See Pessoa, Fernando (Antonio Nogueira)

Remarque, Erich Maria 1898-1970 ..... **CLC 21; DA; DAB; DAC; DAM MST, NOV**
See AAYA 27; CA 77-80; 29-32R; DA3; DLB 56; MTCW 1, 2

Remington,Frederic 1861-1909 ..... **TCLC 89**
See CA 108; 169; DLB 12, 186, 188; SATA 41

Remizov, A.
See Remizov, Aleksei (Mikhailovich)

Remizov, A. M.
See Remizov, Aleksei (Mikhailovich)

Remizov, Aleksei (Mikhailovich) 1877-1957 .... **TCLC 27**
See CA 125; 133

Renan, Joseph Ernest 1823-1892 . **NCLC 26**

Renard, Jules 1864-1910 .... **TCLC 17**
See CA 117

Renault, Mary .... **CLC 3, 11, 17**
See Challans, Mary
See DLBY 83; MTCW 2

Rendell, Ruth (Barbara) 1930- ...... **CLC 28, 48; DAM POP**
See Vine, Barbara
See CA 109; CANR 32, 52, 74; DLB 87; INT CANR-32; MTCW 1, 2

Renoir, Jean 1894-1979 .... **CLC 20**
See CA 129; 85-88

Resnais, Alain 1922- .... **CLC 16**

Reverdy, Pierre 1889-1960 .... **CLC 53**
See CA 97-100; 89-92

Rexroth, Kenneth 1905-1982 ... **CLC 1, 2, 6, 11, 22, 49, 112; DAM POET; PC 20**
See CA 5-8R; 107; CANR 14, 34, 63; CDALB 1941-1968; DLB 16, 48, 165, 212; DLBY 82; INT CANR-14; MTCW 1, 2

Reyes, Alfonso 1889-1959 .. **TCLC 33;HLCS 2**
See CA 131; HW 1

Reyes y Basoalto, Ricardo Eliecer Neftali
See Neruda, Pablo

Reymont, Wladyslaw (Stanislaw) 1868(?)-1925 .... **TCLC 5**
See CA 104

Reynolds, Jonathan 1942- .... **CLC 6, 38**
See CA 65-68; CANR 28

Reynolds, Joshua 1723-1792 .... **LC 15**
See DLB 104

Reynolds, Michael Shane 1937- ...... **CLC 44**
See CA 65-68; CANR 9

Reznikoff, Charles 1894-1976 .... **CLC 9**
See CA 33-36; 61-64; CAP 2; DLB 28, 45

Rezzori (d'Arezzo), Gregorvon 1914-1998 .. **CLC 25**
See CA 122; 136; 167

Rhine, Richard
See Silverstein, Alvin

Rhodes, Eugene Manlove 1869-1934 . **TCLC 53**

Rhodius, Apollonius c. 3rd cent.B.C.- .... **CMLC 28**
See DLB 176

R'hoone
See Balzac, Honore de

Rhys, Jean 1890(?)-1979 .... **CLC 2, 4, 6, 14, 19, 51, 124; DAM NOV; SSC 21**
See CA 25-28R; 85-88; CANR 35, 62; CDBLB 1945-1960; DA3; DLB 36, 117, 162; MTCW 1, 2

Ribeiro, Darcy 1922-1997 .... **CLC 34**
See CA 33-36R; 156

Ribeiro, Joao Ubaldo (Osorio Pimentel) 1941- .... **CLC 10, 67**
See CA 81-84

Ribman, Ronald (Burt) 1932- .... **CLC 7**
See CA 21-24R; CANR 46, 80

Ricci, Nino 1959- .... **CLC 70**
See CA 137

Rice, Anne 1941- .... **CLC 41;DAM POP**
See AAYA 9; BEST 89:2; CA 65-68; CANR 12, 36, 53, 74; DA3; MTCW 2

Rice, Elmer (Leopold) 1892-1967 .... **CLC 7, 49; DAM DRAM**
See CA 21-22; 25-28R; CAP 2; DLB 4, 7; MTCW 1, 2

Rice, Tim(othy Miles Bindon) 1944- .... **CLC 21**
See CA 103; CANR 46

Rich, Adrienne (Cecile) 1929- .. **CLC 3, 6, 7, 11, 18, 36, 73, 76, 125; DAM POET; PC 5**
See CA 9-12R; CANR 20, 53, 74; CDALBS; DA3; DLB 5, 67; MTCW 1, 2

Rich, Barbara
See Graves, Robert (von Ranke)

Rich, Robert
See Trumbo, Dalton

Richard, Keith .... **CLC 17**
See Richards, Keith

Richards, David Adams 1950- .... **CLC 59; DAC**
See CA 93-96; CANR 60; DLB 53

Richards, I(vor) A(rmstrong) 1893-1979 ..... **CLC 14, 24**
See CA 41-44R; 89-92; CANR 34, 74; DLB 27; MTCW 2

Richards, Keith 1943-
See Richard, Keith
See CA 107; CANR 77

Richardson, Anne
See Roiphe, Anne (Richardson)

Richardson, Dorothy Miller 1873-1957 .... **TCLC 3**
See CA 104; DLB 36

Richardson, Ethel Florence (Lindesay) 1870-1946
See Richardson, Henry Handel
See CA 105

Richardson, Henry Handel .... **TCLC 4**
See Richardson, Ethel Florence (Lindesay)
See DLB 197

Richardson, John 1796-1852 .... **NCLC 55; DAC**
See DLB 99

Richardson, Samuel 1689-1761 .... **LC 1, 44; DA; DAB; DAC; DAM MST, NOV; WLC**
See CDBLB 1660-1789; DLB 39

Richler, Mordecai 1931- ..... **CLC 3, 5, 9, 13, 18, 46, 70; DAC; DAM MST, NOV**
See AITN 1; CA 65-68; CANR 31, 62; CLR 17; DLB 53; MAICYA; MTCW 1, 2; SATA 44, 98; SATA-Brief 27

Richter, Conrad (Michael) 1890-1968 . **CLC 30**
See AAYA 21; CA 5-8R; 25-28R; CANR 23; DLB 9, 212; MTCW 1, 2; SATA 3

Ricostranza, Tom
See Ellis, Trey

Riddell, Charlotte 1832-1906 .... **TCLC 40**
See CA 165; DLB 156

Ridgway, Keith 1965- .... **CLC 119**
See CA 172

Riding, Laura .... **CLC 3, 7**
See Jackson, Laura (Riding)

Riefenstahl, Berta Helene Amalia 1902-
See Riefenstahl, Leni
See CA 108

Riefenstahl, Leni .... **CLC 16**
See Riefenstahl, Berta Helene Amalia

Riffe, Ernest
See Bergman, (Ernst) Ingmar

Riggs, (Rolla) Lynn 1899-1954 .... **TCLC 56; DAM MULT**
See CA 144; DLB 175; NNAL

Riis, Jacob A(ugust) 1849-1914 .... **TCLC 80**
See CA 113; 168; DLB 23

Riley, James Whitcomb 1849-1916 ... **TCLC 51; DAM POET**
See CA 118; 137; MAICYA; SATA 17

Riley, Tex
See Creasey, John

Rilke, Rainer Maria 1875-1926 . **TCLC 1, 6, 19; DAM POET; PC 2**
See CA 104; 132; CANR 62; DA3; DLB 81; MTCW 1, 2

Rimbaud, (Jean Nicolas) Arthur 1854-1891 .. **NCLC 4, 35; DA; DAB; DAC; DAM MST, POET; PC 3; WLC**
See DA3

Rinehart, Mary Roberts 1876-1958 .. **TCLC 52**
See CA 108; 166

Ringmaster, The
See Mencken, H(enry) L(ouis)

Ringwood, Gwen(dolyn Margaret) Pharis 1910-1984 .... **CLC 48**
See CA 148; 112; DLB 88

Rio, Michel 19(?)- .... **CLC 43**

Ritsos, Giannes
See Ritsos, Yannis

Ritsos, Yannis 1909-1990 .... **CLC 6, 13, 31**
See CA 77-80; 133; CANR 39, 61; MTCW 1

Ritter, Erika 1948(?)- .... **CLC 52**

Rivera, Jose Eustasio 1889-1928 .. **TCLC 35**
See CA 162; HW 1, 2

Rivera, Tomas 1935-1984
See CA 49-52; CANR 32; DLB 82; HLCS 2; HW 1

Rivers, Conrad Kent 1933-1968 .... **CLC 1**
See BW 1; CA 85-88; DLB 41

Rivers, Elfrida
See Bradley, Marion Zimmer

Riverside, John
See Heinlein, Robert A(nson)

Rizal, Jose 1861-1896 .... **NCLC 27**

Roa Bastos, Augusto (Antonio) 1917- .. **CLC 45; DAM MULT; HLC 2**
See CA 131; DLB 113; HW 1

Robbe-Grillet, Alain 1922- ... **CLC 1, 2, 4, 6, 8, 10, 14, 43**
See CA 9-12R; CANR 33, 65; DLB 83; MTCW 1, 2

Robbins, Harold 1916-1997 .... **CLC 5;DAM NOV**
See CA 73-76; 162; CANR 26, 54; DA3; MTCW 1, 2

Robbins, Thomas Eugene 1936-
See Robbins, Tom
See CA 81-84; CANR 29, 59; DAM NOV, POP; DA3; MTCW 1, 2

Robbins, Tom .... **CLC 9, 32, 64**
See Robbins, Thomas Eugene
See AAYA 32; BEST 90:3; DLBY 80; MTCW 2

Robbins, Trina 1938- .... **CLC 21**
See CA 128

Roberts, Charles G(eorge) D(ouglas) 1860-1943 .... **TCLC 8**
See CA 105; CLR 33; DLB 92; SATA 88; SATA-Brief 29

Roberts, Elizabeth Madox 1886-1941 .... **TCLC 68**
See CA 111; 166; DLB 9, 54, 102; SATA 33; SATA-Brief 27

Roberts, Kate 1891-1985 .... **CLC 15**
See CA 107; 116
Roberts, Keith (John Kingston) 1935- . **CLC 14**
See CA 25-28R; CANR 46
Roberts, Kenneth (Lewis) 1885-1957 . **TCLC 23**
See CA 109; DLB 9
Roberts, Michele (B.) 1949- .... **CLC 48**
See CA 115; CANR 58
Robertson, Ellis
See Ellison, Harlan (Jay); Silverberg, Robert
Robertson, Thomas William 1829-1871 .... **NCLC 35; DAM DRAM**
Robeson, Kenneth
See Dent, Lester
Robinson, Edwin Arlington 1869-1935 .... **TCLC 5; DA; DAC; DAM MST, POET; PC 1**
See CA 104; 133; CDALB 1865-1917; DLB 54; MTCW 1, 2
Robinson, Henry Crabb 1775-1867 .. **NCLC 15**
See DLB 107
Robinson, Jill 1936- .... **CLC 10**
See CA 102; INT 102
Robinson, Kim Stanley 1952- .... **CLC 34**
See AAYA 26; CA 126; SATA 109
Robinson, Lloyd
See Silverberg, Robert
Robinson, Marilynne 1944- .... **CLC 25**
See CA 116; CANR 80; DLB 206
Robinson, Smokey .... **CLC 21**
See Robinson, William, Jr.
Robinson, William, Jr. 1940-
See Robinson, Smokey
See CA 116
Robison, Mary 1949- .... **CLC 42, 98**
See CA 113; 116; DLB 130; INT 116
Rod, Edouard 1857-1910 .... **TCLC 52**
Roddenberry, Eugene Wesley 1921-1991
See Roddenberry, Gene
See CA 110; 135; CANR 37; SATA 45; SATA-Obit 69
Roddenberry, Gene .... **CLC 17**
See Roddenberry, Eugene Wesley
See AAYA 5; SATA-Obit 69
Rodgers, Mary 1931- .... **CLC 12**
See CA 49-52; CANR 8, 55; CLR 20; INT CANR-8; JRDA; MAICYA; SATA 8
Rodgers, W(illiam) R(obert) 1909-1969 .... **CLC 7**
See CA 85-88; DLB 20
Rodman, Eric
See Silverberg, Robert
Rodman, Howard 1920(?)-1985 ...... **CLC 65**
See CA 118
Rodman, Maia
See Wojciechowska, Maia (Teresa)
Rodo, Jose Enrique 1872(?)-1917
See CA 178; HLCS 2; HW 2
Rodriguez, Claudio 1934- .... **CLC 10**
See DLB 134
Rodriguez, Richard 1944-
See CA 110; CANR 66; DAM MULT; DLB 82; HLC 2; HW 1, 2
Roelvaag, O(le) E(dvart) 1876-1931 .. **TCLC 17**
See CA 117; 171; DLB 9
Roethke, Theodore (Huebner) 1908-1963 .... **CLC 1, 3, 8, 11, 19, 46, 101; DAM POET; PC 15**
See CA 81-84; CABS 2; CDALB 1941-1968; DA3; DLB 5, 206; MTCW 1, 2
Rogers, Samuel 1763-1855 .... **NCLC 69**
See DLB 93
Rogers, Thomas Hunton 1927- .... **CLC 57**
See CA 89-92; INT 89-92
Rogers, Will(iam Penn Adair) 1879-1935 .... **TCLC 8, 71; DAM MULT**
See CA 105; 144; DA3; DLB 11; MTCW 2; NNAL
Rogin, Gilbert 1929- .... **CLC 18**
See CA 65-68; CANR 15
Rohan, Koda .... **TCLC 22**
See Koda Shigeyuki
Rohlfs, Anna Katharine Green
See Green, Anna Katharine
Rohmer, Eric .... **CLC 16**
See Scherer, Jean-Marie Maurice
Rohmer, Sax .... **TCLC 28**
See Ward, Arthur Henry Sarsfield
See DLB 70
Roiphe, Anne (Richardson) 1935- . **CLC 3, 9**
See CA 89-92; CANR 45, 73; DLBY 80; INT 89-92
Rojas, Fernando de 1465-1541 .... **LC 23; HLCS 1**
Rojas, Gonzalo 1917-
See HLCS 2; HW 2
Rojas, Gonzalo 1917-
See CA 178; HLCS 2
Rolfe, Frederick (William Serafino Austin Lewis Mary) 1860-1913 .... **TCLC 12**
See CA 107; DLB 34, 156
Rolland, Romain 1866-1944 .... **TCLC 23**
See CA 118; DLB 65
Rolle, Richard c. 1300-c.1349 ...... **CMLC 21**
See DLB 146
Rolvaag, O(le) E(dvart)
See Roelvaag, O(le) E(dvart)
Romain Arnaud, Saint
See Aragon, Louis
Romains, Jules 1885-1972 .... **CLC 7**
See CA 85-88; CANR 34; DLB 65; MTCW 1
Romero, Jose Ruben 1890-1952 ... **TCLC 14**
See CA 114; 131; HW 1
Ronsard, Pierre de 1524-1585 .... **LC 54; PC 11**
Rooke, Leon 1934- . **CLC 25, 34;DAM POP**
See CA 25-28R; CANR 23, 53
Roosevelt, Franklin Delano 1882-1945 .... **TCLC 93**
See CA 116; 173
Roosevelt, Theodore 1858-1919 .... **TCLC 69**
See CA 115; 170; DLB 47, 186
Roper, William 1498-1578 .... **LC 10**
Roquelaure, A. N.
See Rice, Anne
Rosa, Joao Guimaraes 1908-1967 . **CLC 23; HLCS 1**
See CA 89-92; DLB 113
Rose, Wendy 1948- . **CLC 85; DAM MULT; PC 13**
See CA 53-56; CANR 5, 51; DLB 175; NNAL; SATA 12
Rosen, R. D.
See Rosen, Richard (Dean)
Rosen, Richard (Dean) 1949- .... **CLC 39**
See CA 77-80; CANR 62; INT CANR-30
Rosenberg, Isaac 1890-1918 .... **TCLC 12**
See CA 107; DLB 20
Rosenblatt, Joe .... **CLC 15**
See Rosenblatt, Joseph
Rosenblatt, Joseph 1933-
See Rosenblatt, Joe
See CA 89-92; INT 89-92
Rosenfeld, Samuel
See Tzara, Tristan
Rosenstock, Sami
See Tzara, Tristan
Rosenstock, Samuel
See Tzara, Tristan
Rosenthal, M(acha) L(ouis) 1917-1996 . **CLC 28**
See CA 1-4R; 152; CAAS 6; CANR 4, 51; DLB 5; SATA 59
Ross, Barnaby
See Dannay, Frederic
Ross, Bernard L.
See Follett, Ken(neth Martin)
Ross, J. H.
See Lawrence, T(homas) E(dward)
Ross, John Hume
See Lawrence, T(homas) E(dward)
Ross, Martin
See Martin, Violet Florence
See DLB 135
Ross, (James) Sinclair 1908-1996 .. **CLC 13; DAC; DAM MST; SSC 24**
See CA 73-76; CANR 81; DLB 88
Rossetti, Christina (Georgina) 1830-1894 ... **NCLC 2, 50, 66; DA; DAB; DAC; DAM MST, POET; PC 7; WLC**
See DA3; DLB 35, 163; MAICYA; SATA 20
Rossetti, Dante Gabriel 1828-1882 .... **NCLC 4, 77; DA; DAB; DAC; DAM MST, POET; WLC**
See CDBLB 1832-1890; DLB 35
Rossner, Judith (Perelman) 1935- .... **CLC 6, 9, 29**
See AITN 2; BEST 90:3; CA 17-20R; CANR 18, 51, 73; DLB 6; INT CANR-18; MTCW 1, 2
Rostand, Edmond (Eugene Alexis) 1868-1918 ...... **TCLC 6, 37; DA; DAB; DAC; DAM DRAM, MST; DC 10**
See CA 104; 126; DA3; DLB 192; MTCW 1
Roth, Henry 1906-1995 ... **CLC 2, 6, 11, 104**
See CA 11-12; 149; CANR 38, 63; CAP 1; DA3; DLB 28; MTCW 1, 2
Roth, Philip (Milton) 1933- . **CLC 1, 2, 3, 4, 6, 9, 15, 22, 31, 47, 66, 86, 119; DA; DAB; DAC; DAM MST, NOV, POP; SSC 26; WLC**
See BEST 90:3; CA 1-4R; CANR 1, 22, 36, 55; CDALB 1968-1988; DA3; DLB 2, 28, 173; DLBY 82; MTCW 1, 2
Rothenberg, Jerome 1931- .... **CLC 6, 57**
See CA 45-48; CANR 1; DLB 5, 193
Roumain, Jacques (Jean Baptiste) 1907-1944 .... **TCLC 19; BLC 3; DAM MULT**
See BW 1; CA 117; 125
Rourke, Constance (Mayfield) 1885-1941 ... **TCLC 12**
See CA 107; YABC 1
Rousseau, Jean-Baptiste 1671-1741 ..... **LC 9**
Rousseau, Jean-Jacques 1712-1778 .. **LC 14, 36; DA; DAB; DAC; DAM MST; WLC**
See DA3
Roussel, Raymond 1877-1933 .... **TCLC 20**
See CA 117
Rovit, Earl (Herbert) 1927- .... **CLC 7**
See CA 5-8R; CANR 12
Rowe, Elizabeth Singer 1674-1737 .... **LC 44**
See DLB 39, 95
Rowe, Nicholas 1674-1718 .... **LC 8**
See DLB 84
Rowley, Ames Dorrance
See Lovecraft, H(oward) P(hillips)
Rowson, Susanna Haswell 1762(?)-1824 ...... **NCLC 5, 69**
See DLB 37, 200
Roy, Arundhati 1960(?)- .... **CLC 109**
See CA 163; DLBY 97
Roy, Gabrielle 1909-1983 .... **CLC 10, 14; DAB; DAC; DAM MST**

See CA 53-56; 110; CANR 5, 61; DLB 68; MTCW 1; SATA 104
Royko, Mike 1932-1997 .... **CLC 109**
See CA 89-92; 157; CANR 26
Rozewicz, Tadeusz 1921- .. **CLC 9, 23;DAM POET**
See CA 108; CANR 36, 66; DA3; MTCW 1, 2
Ruark, Gibbons 1941- .... **CLC 3**
See CA 33-36R; CAAS 23; CANR 14, 31, 57; DLB 120
Rubens, Bernice (Ruth) 1923- .. **CLC 19, 31**
See CA 25-28R; CANR 33, 65; DLB 14, 207; MTCW 1
Rubin, Harold
See Robbins, Harold
Rudkin, (James) David 1936- .... **CLC 14**
See CA 89-92; DLB 13
Rudnik, Raphael 1933- .... **CLC 7**
See CA 29-32R
Ruffian, M.
See Hasek, Jaroslav (Matej Frantisek)
Ruiz, Jose Martinez .... **CLC 11**
See Martinez Ruiz, Jose
Rukeyser, Muriel 1913-1980 . **CLC 6, 10, 15, 27; DAM POET; PC 12**
See CA 5-8R; 93-96; CANR 26, 60; DA3; DLB 48; MTCW 1, 2; SATA-Obit 22
Rule, Jane (Vance) 1931- .... **CLC 27**
See CA 25-28R; CAAS 18; CANR 12; DLB 60
Rulfo, Juan 1918-1986 ..... **CLC 8, 80; DAM MULT; HLC 2; SSC 25**
See CA 85-88; 118; CANR 26; DLB 113; HW 1, 2; MTCW 1, 2
Rumi, Jalal al-Din 1297-1373 ...... **CMLC 20**
Runeberg, Johan 1804-1877 .... **NCLC 41**
Runyon, (Alfred) Damon 1884(?)-1946 .... **TCLC 10**
See CA 107; 165; DLB 11, 86, 171; MTCW 2
Rush, Norman 1933- .... **CLC 44**
See CA 121; 126; INT 126
Rushdie, (Ahmed) Salman 1947- ... **CLC 23, 31, 55, 100; DAB; DAC; DAM MST, NOV, POP; WLCS**
See BEST 89:3; CA 108; 111; CANR 33, 56; DA3; DLB 194; INT 111; MTCW 1, 2
Rushforth, Peter (Scott) 1945- .... **CLC 19**
See CA 101
Ruskin, John 1819-1900 .... **TCLC 63**
See CA 114; 129; CDBLB 1832-1890; DLB 55, 163, 190; SATA 24
Russ, Joanna 1937- .... **CLC 15**
See CANR 11, 31, 65; DLB 8; MTCW 1
Russell, George William 1867-1935
See Baker, Jean H.
See CA 104; 153; CDBLB 1890-1914; DAM POET
Russell, (Henry) Ken(neth Alfred) 1927- ..... **CLC 16**
See CA 105
Russell, William Martin 1947- .... **CLC 60**
See CA 164
Rutherford, Mark .... **TCLC 25**
See White, William Hale
See DLB 18
Ruyslinck, Ward 1929- .... **CLC 14**
See Belser, Reimond Karel Maria de
Ryan, Cornelius(John) 1920-1974 ..... **CLC 7**
See CA 69-72; 53-56; CANR 38
Ryan, Michael 1946- .... **CLC 65**
See CA 49-52; DLBY 82
Ryan, Tim
See Dent, Lester
Rybakov, Anatoli (Naumovich) 1911-1998 .. **CLC 23, 53**
See CA 126; 135; 172; SATA 79; SATA-Obit 108
Ryder, Jonathan
See Ludlum, Robert
Ryga, George 1932-1987 ...... **CLC 14; DAC; DAM MST**
See CA 101; 124; CANR 43; DLB 60
S. H.
See Hartmann, Sadakichi
S. S.
See Sassoon, Siegfried (Lorraine)
Saba, Umberto 1883-1957 .... **TCLC 33**
See CA 144; CANR 79; DLB 114
Sabatini, Rafael 1875-1950 .... **TCLC 47**
See CA 162
Sabato, Ernesto (R.) 1911- .... **CLC 10, 23; DAM MULT; HLC 2**
See CA 97-100; CANR 32, 65; DLB 145; HW 1, 2; MTCW 1, 2
Sa-Carniero, Mario de 1890-1916 ..... **TCLC 83**
Sacastru, Martin
See Bioy Casares, Adolfo
Sacastru, Martin
See Bioy Casares, Adolfo
Sacher-Masoch, Leopold von 1836(?)-1895 . **NCLC 31**
Sachs, Marilyn (Stickle) 1927- .... **CLC 35**
See AAYA 2; CA 17-20R; CANR 13, 47; CLR 2; JRDA; MAICYA; SAAS 2; SATA 3, 68; SATA-Essay 110
Sachs, Nelly 1891-1970 .... **CLC 14, 98**
See CA 17-18; 25-28R; CAP 2; MTCW 2
Sackler, Howard (Oliver) 1929-1982 ... **CLC 14**
See CA 61-64; 108; CANR 30; DLB 7
Sacks, Oliver (Wolf) 1933- .... **CLC 67**
See CA 53-56; CANR 28, 50, 76; DA3; INT CANR-28; MTCW 1, 2
Sadakichi
See Hartmann, Sadakichi
Sade, Donatien Alphonse Francois, Comtede 1740-1814 .... **NCLC 47**
Sadoff, Ira 1945- .... **CLC 9**
See CA 53-56; CANR 5, 21; DLB 120
Saetone
See Camus, Albert
Safire, William 1929- .... **CLC 10**
See CA 17-20R; CANR 31, 54
Sagan, Carl (Edward) 1934-1996 .. **CLC 30, 112**
See AAYA 2; CA 25-28R; 155; CANR 11, 36, 74; DA3; MTCW 1, 2; SATA 58; SATA-Obit 94
Sagan, Francoise .... **CLC 3, 6, 9, 17, 36**
See Quoirez, Francoise
See DLB 83; MTCW 2
Sahgal, Nayantara (Pandit) 1927- .. **CLC 41**
See CA 9-12R; CANR 11
Saint, H(arry) F. 1941- .... **CLC 50**
See CA 127
St. Aubin de Teran, Lisa 1953-
See Teran, Lisa St. Aubin de
See CA 118; 126; INT 126
Saint Birgitta of Sweden c. 1303-1373 .... **CMLC 24**
Sainte-Beuve, Charles Augustin 1804-1869 . **NCLC 5**
Saint-Exupery, Antoine (Jean Baptiste Marie Roger) de 1900-1944 .. **TCLC 2, 56; DAM NOV;WLC**
See CA 108; 132; CLR 10; DA3; DLB 72; MAICYA; MTCW 1, 2; SATA 20
St. John, David
See Hunt, E(verette) Howard, (Jr.)
Saint-John Perse
See Leger, (Marie-Rene Auguste) Alexis Saint-Leger
Saintsbury, George (Edward Bateman) 1845-1933 .... **TCLC 31**
See CA 160; DLB 57, 149
Sait Faik .... **TCLC 23**
See Abasiyanik, Sait Faik
Saki .... **TCLC 3; SSC 12**
See Munro, H(ector) H(ugh)
See MTCW 2
Sala, George Augustus .... **NCLC 46**
Salama, Hannu 1936- .... **CLC 18**
Salamanca, J(ack) R(ichard) 1922- . **CLC 4, 15**
See CA 25-28R
Salas, Floyd Francis 1931-
See CA 119; CAAS 27; CANR 44, 75; DAM MULT; DLB 82; HLC 2; HW 1, 2; MTCW 2
Sale, J. Kirkpatrick
See Sale, Kirkpatrick
Sale, Kirkpatrick 1937- .... **CLC 68**
See CA 13-16R; CANR 10
Salinas, Luis Omar 1937- .... **CLC 90; DAM MULT; HLC 2**
See CA 131; CANR 81; DLB 82; HW 1, 2
Salinas (y Serrano), Pedro 1891(?)-1951 ..... **TCLC 17**
See CA 117; DLB 134
Salinger, J(erome) D(avid) 1919- . **CLC 1, 3, 8, 12, 55, 56; DA; DAB; DAC; DAM MST, NOV, POP; SSC 2, 28; WLC**
See AAYA 2; CA 5-8R; CANR 39; CDALB 1941-1968; CLR 18; DA3; DLB 2, 102, 173; MAICYA; MTCW 1, 2; SATA 67
Salisbury, John
See Caute, (John) David
Salter, James 1925- .... **CLC 7, 52, 59**
See CA 73-76; DLB 130
Saltus, Edgar (Everton) 1855-1921 . **TCLC 8**
See CA 105; DLB 202
Saltykov, Mikhail Evgrafovich 1826-1889 ... **NCLC 16**
Samarakis, Antonis 1919- .... **CLC 5**
See CA 25-28R; CAAS 16; CANR 36
Sanchez, Florencio 1875-1910 .... **TCLC 37**
See CA 153; HW 1
Sanchez, Luis Rafael 1936- .... **CLC 23**
See CA 128; DLB 145; HW 1
Sanchez, Sonia 1934- .. **CLC 5, 116; BLC 3; DAM MULT; PC 9**
See BW 2, 3; CA 33-36R; CANR 24, 49, 74; CLR 18; DA3; DLB 41; DLBD 8; MAICYA; MTCW 1, 2; SATA 22
Sand, George 1804-1876 ... **NCLC 2, 42, 57; DA; DAB; DAC; DAM MST, NOV; WLC**
See DA3; DLB 119, 192
Sandburg, Carl (August) 1878-1967 .... **CLC 1, 4, 10, 15, 35; DA; DAB; DAC; DAM MST, POET; PC 2; WLC**
See AAYA 24; CA 5-8R; 25-28R; CANR 35; CDALB 1865-1917; DA3; DLB 17, 54; MAICYA; MTCW 1, 2; SATA 8
Sandburg, Charles
See Sandburg, Carl (August)
Sandburg, Charles A.
See Sandburg, Carl (August)
Sanders, (James) Ed(ward) 1939- . **CLC 53; DAM POET**
See CA 13-16R; CAAS 21; CANR 13, 44, 78; DLB 16
Sanders, Lawrence 1920-1998 .... **CLC 41; DAM POP**
See BEST 89:4; CA 81-84; 165; CANR 33, 62; DA3; MTCW 1
Sanders, Noah
See Blount, Roy (Alton), Jr.
Sanders, Winston P.
See Anderson, Poul (William)
Sandoz, Mari(e Susette) 1896-1966 . **CLC 28**

See CA 1-4R; 25-28R; CANR 17, 64; DLB 9, 212; MTCW 1, 2; SATA 5
Saner, Reg(inald Anthony) 1931- ...... **CLC 9**
See CA 65-68
Sankara 788-820 .... **CMLC 32**
Sannazaro, Jacopo 1456(?)-1530 .... **LC 8**
Sansom, William 1912-1976 .... **CLC 2, 6; DAM NOV; SSC 21**
See CA 5-8R; 65-68; CANR 42; DLB 139; MTCW 1
Santayana, George 1863-1952 ...... **TCLC 40**
See CA 115; DLB 54, 71; DLBD 13
Santiago, Danny .... **CLC 33**
See James, Daniel (Lewis)
See DLB 122
Santmyer, Helen Hoover 1895-1986 ..... **CLC 33**
See CA 1-4R; 118; CANR 15, 33; DLBY 84; MTCW 1
Santoka, Taneda 1882-1940 .... **TCLC 72**
Santos, Bienvenido N(uqui) 1911-1996 . **CLC 22; DAM MULT**
See CA 101; 151; CANR 19, 46
Sapper .... **TCLC 44**
See McNeile, Herman Cyril
Sapphire
See Sapphire, Brenda
Sapphire, Brenda 1950- .... **CLC 99**
Sappho fl. 6th cent. B.C.- .... **CMLC 3; DAM POET; PC 5**
See DA3; DLB 176
Saramago, Jose 1922- ..... **CLC 119;HLCS 1**
See CA 153
Sarduy, Severo 1937-1993 .... **CLC 6, 97; HLCS 1**
See CA 89-92; 142; CANR 58, 81; DLB 113; HW 1, 2
Sargeson, Frank 1903-1982 .... **CLC 31**
See CA 25-28R; 106; CANR 38, 79
Sarmiento, Domingo Faustino 1811-1888
See HLCS 2
Sarmiento, Felix Ruben Garcia
See Dario, Ruben
Saro-Wiwa, Ken(ule Beeson) 1941-1995 ...... **CLC 114**
See BW 2; CA 142; 150; CANR 60; DLB 157
Saroyan, William 1908-1981 .. **CLC 1, 8, 10, 29, 34, 56; DA; DAB; DAC; DAM DRAM, MST, NOV; SSC 21; WLC**
See CA 5-8R; 103; CANR 30; CDALBS; DA3; DLB 7, 9, 86; DLBY 81; MTCW 1, 2; SATA 23; SATA-Obit 24
Sarraute, Nathalie 1900- . **CLC 1, 2, 4, 8, 10, 31, 80**
See CA 9-12R; CANR 23, 66; DLB 83; MTCW 1, 2
Sarton, (Eleanor) May 1912-1995 .... **CLC 4, 14, 49, 91; DAM POET**
See CA 1-4R; 149; CANR 1, 34, 55; DLB 48; DLBY 81; INT CANR-34; MTCW 1, 2; SATA 36; SATA-Obit 86
Sartre, Jean-Paul 1905-1980 .... **CLC 1, 4, 7, 9, 13, 18, 24, 44, 50, 52; DA; DAB; DAC; DAM DRAM, MST, NOV; DC 3; SSC 32; WLC**
See CA 9-12R; 97-100; CANR 21; DA3; DLB 72; MTCW 1, 2
Sassoon, Siegfried (Lorraine) 1886-1967 ..... **CLC 36; DAB; DAM MST, NOV, POET; PC 12**
See CA 104; 25-28R; CANR 36; DLB 20, 191; DLBD 18; MTCW 1, 2
Satterfield, Charles
See Pohl, Frederik
Saul, John (W. III) 1942- ..... **CLC 46; DAM NOV, POP**
See AAYA 10; BEST 90:4; CA 81-84; CANR 16, 40, 81; SATA 98
Saunders, Caleb
See Heinlein, Robert A(nson)
Saura (Atares), Carlos 1932- .... **CLC 20**
See CA 114; 131; CANR 79; HW 1
Sauser-Hall, Frederic 1887-1961 ..... **CLC 18**
See Cendrars, Blaise
See CA 102; 93-96; CANR 36, 62; MTCW 1
Saussure, Ferdinand de 1857-1913 ... **TCLC 49**
Savage, Catharine
See Brosman, Catharine Savage
Savage, Thomas 1915- .... **CLC 40**
See CA 126; 132; CAAS 15; INT 132
Savan, Glenn 19(?)- .... **CLC 50**
Sayers, Dorothy L(eigh) 1893-1957 ... **TCLC 2, 15; DAM POP**
See CA 104; 119; CANR 60; CDBLB 1914-1945; DLB 10, 36, 77, 100; MTCW 1, 2
Sayers, Valerie 1952- .... **CLC 50, 122**
See CA 134; CANR 61
Sayles, John (Thomas) 1950- . **CLC 7, 10, 14**
See CA 57-60; CANR 41, 84; DLB 44
Scammell, Michael 1935- .... **CLC 34**
See CA 156
Scannell, Vernon 1922- .... **CLC 49**
See CA 5-8R; CANR 8, 24, 57; DLB 27; SATA 59
Scarlett, Susan
See Streatfeild, (Mary) Noel
Scarron
See Mikszath, Kalman
Schaeffer, Susan Fromberg 1941- .... **CLC 6, 11, 22**
See CA 49-52; CANR 18, 65; DLB 28; MTCW 1, 2; SATA 22
Schary, Jill
See Robinson, Jill
Schell, Jonathan 1943- .... **CLC 35**
See CA 73-76; CANR 12
Schelling, Friedrich Wilhelm Josephvon 1775-1854 .... **NCLC 30**
See DLB 90
Schendel, Arthur van 1874-1946 .. **TCLC 56**
Scherer, Jean-Marie Maurice 1920-
See Rohmer, Eric
See CA 110
Schevill, James (Erwin) 1920- .... **CLC 7**
See CA 5-8R; CAAS 12
Schiller, Friedrich 1759-1805 . **NCLC 39, 69; DAM DRAM**
See DLB 94
Schisgal, Murray (Joseph) 1926- ...... **CLC 6**
See CA 21-24R; CANR 48
Schlee, Ann 1934- .... **CLC 35**
See CA 101; CANR 29; SATA 44; SATA-Brief 36
Schlegel, August Wilhelmvon 1767-1845 ..... **NCLC 15**
See DLB 94
Schlegel, Friedrich 1772-1829 ...... **NCLC 45**
See DLB 90
Schlegel, Johann Elias (von) 1719(?)-1749 .. **LC 5**
Schlesinger, Arthur M(eier),Jr. 1917- .. **CLC 84**
See AITN 1; CA 1-4R; CANR 1, 28, 58; DLB 17; INT CANR-28; MTCW 1, 2; SATA 61
Schmidt, Arno (Otto) 1914-1979 ..... **CLC 56**
See CA 128; 109; DLB 69
Schmitz, Aron Hector 1861-1928
See Svevo, Italo
See CA 104; 122; MTCW 1
Schnackenberg, Gjertrud 1953- ...... **CLC 40**
See CA 116; DLB 120
Schneider, Leonard Alfred 1925-1966
See Bruce, Lenny
See CA 89-92
Schnitzler, Arthur 1862-1931 . **TCLC 4; SSC 15**
See CA 104; DLB 81, 118
Schoenberg, Arnold 1874-1951 ..... **TCLC 75**
See CA 109
Schonberg, Arnold
See Schoenberg, Arnold
Schopenhauer, Arthur 1788-1860 . **NCLC 51**
See DLB 90
Schor, Sandra (M.) 1932(?)-1990 .... **CLC 65**
See CA 132
Schorer, Mark 1908-1977 .... **CLC 9**
See CA 5-8R; 73-76; CANR 7; DLB 103
Schrader, Paul (Joseph) 1946- .... **CLC 26**
See CA 37-40R; CANR 41; DLB 44
Schreiner, Olive (Emilie Albertina) 1855-1920 .... **TCLC 9**
See CA 105; 154; DLB 18, 156, 190
Schulberg, Budd (Wilson) 1914- . **CLC 7, 48**
See CA 25-28R; CANR 19; DLB 6, 26, 28; DLBY 81
Schulz, Bruno 1892-1942 . **TCLC 5, 51; SSC 13**
See CA 115; 123; MTCW 2
Schulz, Charles M(onroe) 1922- ..... **CLC 12**
See CA 9-12R; CANR 6; INT CANR-6; SATA 10
Schumacher, E(rnst) F(riedrich) 1911-1977 .... **CLC 80**
See CA 81-84; 73-76; CANR 34, 85
Schuyler, James Marcus 1923-1991 . **CLC 5, 23; DAM POET**
See CA 101; 134; DLB 5, 169; INT 101
Schwartz, Delmore (David) 1913-1966 . **CLC 2, 4, 10, 45, 87; PC 8**
See CA 17-18; 25-28R; CANR 35; CAP 2; DLB 28, 48; MTCW 1, 2
Schwartz, Ernst
See Ozu, Yasujiro
Schwartz, John Burnham 1965- ..... **CLC 59**
See CA 132
Schwartz, Lynne Sharon 1939- .... **CLC 31**
See CA 103; CANR 44; MTCW 2
Schwartz, Muriel A.
See Eliot, T(homas) S(tearns)
Schwarz-Bart, Andre 1928- .... **CLC 2, 4**
See CA 89-92
Schwarz-Bart, Simone 1938- . **CLC 7;BLCS**
See BW 2; CA 97-100
Schwitters, Kurt (Hermann Edward Karl Julius) 1887-1948 .... **TCLC 95**
See CA 158
Schwob, Marcel (Mayer Andre) 1867-1905 . **TCLC 20**
See CA 117; 168; DLB 123
Sciascia, Leonardo 1921-1989 . **CLC 8, 9, 41**
See CA 85-88; 130; CANR 35; DLB 177; MTCW 1
Scoppettone, Sandra 1936- .... **CLC 26**
See AAYA 11; CA 5-8R; CANR 41, 73; SATA 9, 92
Scorsese, Martin 1942- .... **CLC 20, 89**
See CA 110; 114; CANR 46, 85
Scotland, Jay
See Jakes, John (William)
Scott, Duncan Campbell 1862-1947 .. **TCLC 6; DAC**
See CA 104; 153; DLB 92
Scott, Evelyn 1893-1963 .... **CLC 43**
See CA 104; 112; CANR 64; DLB 9, 48
Scott, F(rancis) R(eginald) 1899-1985 . **CLC 22**
See CA 101; 114; DLB 88; INT 101

Author Index

Scott, Frank
See Scott, F(rancis) R(eginald)
Scott, Joanna 1960- .... **CLC 50**
See CA 126; CANR 53
Scott, Paul (Mark) 1920-1978 ..... **CLC 9, 60**
See CA 81-84; 77-80; CANR 33; DLB 14, 207; MTCW 1
Scott, Sarah 1723-1795 .... **LC 44**
See DLB 39
Scott, Walter 1771-1832 . **NCLC 15, 69; DA; DAB; DAC; DAM MST, NOV, POET; PC 13; SSC 32; WLC**
See AAYA 22; CDBLB 1789-1832; DLB 93, 107, 116, 144, 159; YABC 2
Scribe, (Augustin) Eugene 1791-1861 .... **NCLC 16; DAM DRAM; DC 5**
See DLB 192
Scrum, R.
See Crumb, R(obert)
Scudery, Madeleine de 1607-1701 .... **LC 2**
Scum
See Crumb, R(obert)
Scumbag, Little Bobby
See Crumb, R(obert)
Seabrook, John
See Hubbard, L(afayette) Ron(ald)
Sealy, I. Allan 1951- .... **CLC 55**
Search, Alexander
See Pessoa, Fernando (Antonio Nogueira)
Sebastian, Lee
See Silverberg, Robert
Sebastian Owl
See Thompson, Hunter S(tockton)
Sebestyen, Ouida 1924- .... **CLC 30**
See AAYA 8; CA 107; CANR 40; CLR 17; JRDA; MAICYA; SAAS 10; SATA 39
Secundus, H. Scriblerus
See Fielding, Henry
Sedges, John
See Buck, Pearl S(ydenstricker)
Sedgwick, Catharine Maria 1789-1867 .... **NCLC 19**
See DLB 1, 74
Seelye, John (Douglas) 1931- .... **CLC 7**
See CA 97-100; CANR 70; INT 97-100
Seferiades, Giorgos Stylianou 1900-1971
See Seferis, George
See CA 5-8R; 33-36R; CANR 5, 36; MTCW 1
Seferis, George .... **CLC 5, 11**
See Seferiades, Giorgos Stylianou
Segal, Erich (Wolf) 1937- . **CLC 3, 10; DAM POP**
See BEST 89:1; CA 25-28R; CANR 20, 36, 65; DLBY 86; INT CANR-20; MTCW 1
Seger, Bob 1945- .... **CLC 35**
Seghers, Anna .... **CLC 7**
See Radvanyi, Netty
See DLB 69
Seidel, Frederick (Lewis) 1936- ...... **CLC 18**
See CA 13-16R; CANR 8; DLBY 84
Seifert, Jaroslav 1901-1986 . **CLC 34, 44, 93**
See CA 127; MTCW 1, 2
Sei Shonagon c. 966-1017(?) .... **CMLC 6**
Séjour, Victor 1817-1874 .... **DC 10**
See DLB 50
Sejour Marcou et Ferrand, Juan Victor
See Séjour, Victor
Selby, Hubert, Jr. 1928- .... **CLC 1, 2, 4, 8; SSC 20**
See CA 13-16R; CANR 33, 85; DLB 2
Selzer, Richard 1928- .... **CLC 74**
See CA 65-68; CANR 14
Sembene, Ousmane
See Ousmane, Sembene
Senancour, Etienne Pivert de 1770-1846 ..... **NCLC 16**
See DLB 119
Sender, Ramon (Jose) 1902-1982 ..... **CLC 8; DAM MULT; HLC 2**
See CA 5-8R; 105; CANR 8; HW 1; MTCW 1
Seneca, Lucius Annaeus c. 1-c. 65 ... **CMLC 6; DAM DRAM; DC 5**
See DLB 211
Senghor, Leopold Sedar 1906- .... **CLC 54; BLC 3; DAM MULT, POET; PC 25**
See BW 2; CA 116; 125; CANR 47, 74; MTCW 1, 2
Senna, Danzy 1970- .... **CLC 119**
See CA 169
Serling, (Edward) Rod(man) 1924-1975 ...... **CLC 30**
See AAYA 14; AITN 1; CA 162; 57-60; DLB 26
Serna, Ramon Gomez de la
See Gomez de la Serna, Ramon
Serpieres
See Guillevic, (Eugene)
Service, Robert
See Service, Robert W(illiam)
See DAB; DLB 92
Service, Robert W(illiam) 1874(?)-1958 .... **TCLC 15; DA; DAC; DAM MST, POET; WLC**
See Service, Robert
See CA 115; 140; CANR 84; SATA 20
Seth, Vikram 1952- .... **CLC 43, 90;DAM MULT**
See CA 121; 127; CANR 50, 74; DA3; DLB 120; INT 127; MTCW 2
Seton, CynthiaPropper 1926-1982 .. **CLC 27**
See CA 5-8R; 108; CANR 7
Seton, Ernest (Evan) Thompson 1860-1946 .... **TCLC 31**
See CA 109; CLR 59; DLB 92; DLBD 13; JRDA; SATA 18
Seton-Thompson, Ernest
See Seton, Ernest (Evan) Thompson
Settle, Mary Lee 1918- .... **CLC 19, 61**
See CA 89-92; CAAS 1; CANR 44; DLB 6; INT 89-92
Seuphor, Michel
See Arp, Jean
Sevigne, Marie (de Rabutin-Chantal) Marquise de 1626-1696 .... **LC 11**
Sewall, Samuel 1652-1730 .... **LC 38**
See DLB 24
Sexton, Anne (Harvey) 1928-1974 ... **CLC 2, 4, 6, 8, 10, 15, 53; DA; DAB; DAC; DAM MST, POET; PC 2; WLC**
See CA 1-4R; 53-56; CABS 2; CANR 3, 36; CDALB 1941-1968; DA3; DLB 5, 169; MTCW 1, 2; SATA 10
Shaara, Jeff 1952- .... **CLC 119**
See CA 163
Shaara, Michael (Joseph, Jr.) 1929-1988 ..... **CLC 15; DAM POP**
See AITN 1; CA 102; 125; CANR 52, 85; DLBY 83
Shackleton, C. C.
See Aldiss, Brian W(ilson)
Shacochis, Bob .... **CLC 39**
See Shacochis, Robert G.
Shacochis, Robert G. 1951-
See Shacochis, Bob
See CA 119; 124; INT 124
Shaffer, Anthony (Joshua) 1926- ... **CLC 19; DAM DRAM**
See CA 110; 116; DLB 13
Shaffer, Peter (Levin) 1926- . **CLC 5, 14, 18, 37, 60; DAB; DAM DRAM, MST; DC 7**
See CA 25-28R; CANR 25, 47, 74; CDBLB 1960 to Present; DA3; DLB 13; MTCW 1, 2
Shakey, Bernard
See Young, Neil
Shalamov, Varlam (Tikhonovich) 1907(?)-1982 .... **CLC 18**
See CA 129; 105
Shamlu, Ahmad 1925- .... **CLC 10**
Shammas, Anton 1951- .... **CLC 55**
Shange, Ntozake 1948- ... **CLC 8, 25, 38, 74; BLC 3; DAM DRAM, MULT; DC 3**
See AAYA 9; BW 2; CA 85-88; CABS 3; CANR 27, 48, 74; DA3; DLB 38; MTCW 1, 2
Shanley, John Patrick 1950- .... **CLC 75**
See CA 128; 133; CANR 83
Shapcott, Thomas W(illiam) 1935- . **CLC 38**
See CA 69-72; CANR 49, 83
Shapiro, Jane .... **CLC 76**
Shapiro, Karl (Jay) 1913- . **CLC 4, 8, 15, 53; PC 25**
See CA 1-4R; CAAS 6; CANR 1, 36, 66; DLB 48; MTCW 1, 2
Sharp, William 1855-1905 .... **TCLC 39**
See CA 160; DLB 156
Sharpe, Thomas Ridley 1928-
See Sharpe, Tom
See CA 114; 122; CANR 85; INT 122
Sharpe, Tom .... **CLC 36**
See Sharpe, Thomas Ridley
See DLB 14
Shaw, Bernard .... **TCLC 45**
See Shaw, George Bernard
See BW 1; MTCW 2
Shaw, G. Bernard
See Shaw, George Bernard
Shaw, George Bernard 1856-1950 . **TCLC 3, 9, 21; DA; DAB; DAC; DAM DRAM, MST; WLC**
See Shaw, Bernard
See CA 104; 128; CDBLB 1914-1945; DA3; DLB 10, 57, 190; MTCW 1, 2
Shaw, Henry Wheeler 1818-1885 . **NCLC 15**
See DLB 11
Shaw, Irwin 1913-1984 .... **CLC 7, 23, 34; DAM DRAM, POP**
See AITN 1; CA 13-16R; 112; CANR 21; CDALB 1941-1968; DLB 6, 102; DLBY 84; MTCW 1, 21
Shaw, Robert 1927-1978 .... **CLC 5**
See AITN 1; CA 1-4R; 81-84; CANR 4; DLB 13, 14
Shaw, T. E.
See Lawrence, T(homas) E(dward)
Shawn, Wallace 1943- .... **CLC 41**
See CA 112
Shea, Lisa 1953- .... **CLC 86**
See CA 147
Sheed, Wilfrid (John Joseph) 1930- . **CLC 2, 4, 10, 53**
See CA 65-68; CANR 30, 66; DLB 6; MTCW 1, 2
Sheldon, Alice Hastings Bradley 1915(?)-1987
See Tiptree, James, Jr.
See CA 108; 122; CANR 34; INT 108; MTCW 1
Sheldon, John
See Bloch, Robert (Albert)
Shelley, Mary Wollstonecraft (Godwin) 1797-1851 .... **NCLC 14, 59; DA; DAB; DAC; DAM MST, NOV; WLC**
See AAYA 20; CDBLB 1789-1832; DA3; DLB 110, 116, 159, 178; SATA 29
Shelley, Percy Bysshe 1792-1822 . **NCLC 18; DA; DAB; DAC; DAM MST, POET; PC 14; WLC**
See CDBLB 1789-1832; DA3; DLB 96, 110, 158
Shepard, Jim 1956- .... **CLC 36**
See CA 137; CANR 59; SATA 90
Shepard, Lucius 1947- .... **CLC 34**
See CA 128; 141; CANR 81

Shepard, Sam 1943- ... **CLC 4, 6, 17, 34, 41, 44; DAM DRAM; DC 5**
See AAYA 1; CA 69-72; CABS 3; CANR 22; DA3; DLB 7, 212; MTCW 1, 2
Shepherd, Michael
See Ludlum, Robert
Sherburne, Zoa (Lillian Morin) 1912-1995 . **CLC 30**
See AAYA 13; CA 1-4R; 176; CANR 3, 37; MAICYA; SAAS 18; SATA 3
Sheridan, Frances 1724-1766 .... **LC 7**
See DLB 39, 84
Sheridan, Richard Brinsley 1751-1816 .... **NCLC 5; DA; DAB; DAC; DAM DRAM, MST; DC 1; WLC**
See CDBLB 1660-1789; DLB 89
Sherman, Jonathan Marc .... **CLC 55**
Sherman, Martin 1941(?)- .... **CLC 19**
See CA 116; 123
Sherwin, Judith Johnson 1936-
See Johnson, Judith (Emlyn)
See CANR 85
Sherwood, Frances 1940- .... **CLC 81**
See CA 146
Sherwood, Robert E(mmet) 1896-1955 .... **TCLC 3; DAM DRAM**
See CA 104; 153; DLB 7, 26
Shestov, Lev 1866-1938 .... **TCLC 56**
Shevchenko, Taras 1814-1861 .... **NCLC 54**
Shiel, M(atthew) P(hipps) 1865-1947 . **TCLC 8**
See Holmes, Gordon
See CA 106; 160; DLB 153; MTCW 2
Shields, Carol 1935- .... **CLC 91, 113;DAC**
See CA 81-84; CANR 51, 74; DA3; MTCW 2
Shields, David 1956- .... **CLC 97**
See CA 124; CANR 48
Shiga, Naoya 1883-1971 ..... **CLC 33;SSC 23**
See CA 101; 33-36R; DLB 180
Shikibu, Murasaki c. 978-c. 1014 . **CMLC 1**
Shilts, Randy 1951-1994 .... **CLC 85**
See AAYA 19; CA 115; 127; 144; CANR 45; DA3; INT 127; MTCW 2
Shimazaki, Haruki 1872-1943
See Shimazaki Toson
See CA 105; 134; CANR 84
Shimazaki Toson 1872-1943 .... **TCLC 5**
See Shimazaki, Haruki
See DLB 180
Sholokhov, Mikhail (Aleksandrovich) 1905-1984 .... **CLC 7, 15**
See CA 101; 112; MTCW 1, 2; SATA-Obit 36
Shone, Patric
See Hanley, James
Shreve, Susan Richards 1939- .... **CLC 23**
See CA 49-52; CAAS 5; CANR 5, 38, 69; MAICYA; SATA 46, 95; SATA-Brief 41
Shue, Larry 1946-1985 .... **CLC 52;DAM DRAM**
See CA 145; 117
Shu-Jen, Chou 1881-1936
See Lu Hsun
See CA 104
Shulman, Alix Kates 1932- .... **CLC 2,10**
See CA 29-32R; CANR 43; SATA 7
Shuster, Joe 1914- .... **CLC 21**
Shute, Nevil .... **CLC 30**
See Norway, Nevil Shute
See MTCW 2
Shuttle, Penelope (Diane) 1947- .... **CLC 7**
See CA 93-96; CANR 39, 84; DLB 14, 40
Sidney, Mary 1561-1621 .... **LC 19, 39**
Sidney, Sir Philip 1554-1586 .... **LC 19, 39; DA; DAB; DAC; DAM MST, POET**
See CDBLB Before 1660; DA3; DLB 167
Siegel, Jerome 1914-1996 .... **CLC 21**
See CA 116; 169; 151
Siegel, Jerry
See Siegel, Jerome
Sienkiewicz, Henryk (Adam Alexander Pius) 1846-1916 .... **TCLC 3**
See CA 104; 134; CANR 84
Sierra, Gregorio Martinez
See Martinez Sierra, Gregorio
Sierra, Maria (de la O'LeJarraga) Martinez
See Martinez Sierra, Maria (de la O'LeJarraga)
Sigal, Clancy 1926- .... **CLC 7**
See CA 1-4R; CANR 85
Sigourney, Lydia Howard (Huntley) 1791-1865 .... **NCLC 21**
See DLB 1, 42, 73
Siguenza y Gongora, Carlos de 1645-1700 . **LC 8; HLCS 2**
Sigurjonsson,Johann 1880-1919 ... **TCLC 27**
See CA 170
Sikelianos, Angelos 1884-1951 ...... **TCLC 39**
Silkin, Jon 1930- .... **CLC 2, 6, 43**
See CA 5-8R; CAAS 5; DLB 27
Silko, Leslie (Marmon) 1948- .. **CLC 23, 74, 114; DA; DAC; DAM MST, MULT, POP; SSC 37; WLCS**
See AAYA 14; CA 115; 122; CANR 45, 65; DA3; DLB 143, 175; MTCW 2; NNAL
Sillanpaa, Frans Eemil 1888-1964 .. **CLC 19**
See CA 129; 93-96; MTCW 1
Sillitoe, Alan 1928- .. **CLC 1, 3, 6, 10, 19, 57**
See AITN 1; CA 9-12R; CAAS 2; CANR 8, 26, 55; CDBLB 1960 to Present; DLB 14, 139; MTCW 1, 2; SATA 61
Silone, Ignazio 1900-1978 .... **CLC 4**
See CA 25-28; 81-84; CANR 34; CAP 2; MTCW 1
Silver, Joan Micklin 1935- .... **CLC 20**
See CA 114; 121; INT 121
Silver, Nicholas
See Faust, Frederick (Schiller)
Silverberg, Robert 1935- . **CLC 7;DAM POP**
See AAYA 24; CA 1-4R; CAAS 3; CANR 1, 20, 36, 85; CLR 59; DLB 8; INT CANR-20; MAICYA; MTCW 1, 2; SATA 13, 91; SATA-Essay 104
Silverstein, Alvin 1933- .... **CLC 17**
See CA 49-52; CANR 2; CLR 25; JRDA; MAICYA; SATA 8, 69
Silverstein, Virginia B(arbara Opshelor) 1937- .... **CLC 17**
See CA 49-52; CANR 2; CLR 25; JRDA; MAICYA; SATA 8, 69
Sim, Georges
See Simenon, Georges (Jacques Christian)
Simak, Clifford D(onald) 1904-1988 .... **CLC 1, 55**
See CA 1-4R; 125; CANR 1, 35; DLB 8; MTCW 1; SATA-Obit 56
Simenon, Georges (Jacques Christian) 1903-1989 .... **CLC 1, 2, 3, 8, 18, 47; DAM POP**
See CA 85-88; 129; CANR 35; DA3; DLB 72; DLBY 89; MTCW 1, 2
Simic, Charles 1938- .. **CLC 6, 9, 22, 49, 68; DAM POET**
See CA 29-32R; CAAS 4; CANR 12, 33, 52, 61; DA3; DLB 105; MTCW 2
Simmel, Georg 1858-1918 .... **TCLC 64**
See CA 157
Simmons, Charles (Paul) 1924- .... **CLC 57**
See CA 89-92; INT 89-92
Simmons, Dan 1948- .... **CLC 44;DAM POP**
See AAYA 16; CA 138; CANR 53, 81
Simmons, James (Stewart Alexander) 1933- .... **CLC 43**
See CA 105; CAAS 21; DLB 40
Simms, William Gilmore 1806-1870 . **NCLC 3**
See DLB 3, 30, 59, 73
Simon, Carly 1945- .... **CLC 26**
See CA 105
Simon, Claude 1913-1984 . **CLC 4, 9, 15, 39; DAM NOV**
See CA 89-92; CANR 33; DLB 83; MTCW 1
Simon, (Marvin) Neil 1927- . **CLC 6, 11, 31, 39, 70; DAM DRAM**
See AAYA 32; AITN 1; CA 21-24R; CANR 26, 54; DA3; DLB 7; MTCW 1, 2
Simon, Paul (Frederick) 1941(?)- ... **CLC 17**
See CA 116; 153
Simonon, Paul 1956(?)- .... **CLC 30**
Simpson, Harriette
See Arnow, Harriette (Louisa) Simpson
Simpson, Louis (Aston Marantz) 1923- .... **CLC 4, 7, 9, 32; DAM POET**
See CA 1-4R; CAAS 4; CANR 1, 61; DLB 5; MTCW 1, 2
Simpson, Mona (Elizabeth) 1957- ... **CLC 44**
See CA 122; 135; CANR 68
Simpson, N(orman) F(rederick) 1919- . **CLC 29**
See CA 13-16R; DLB 13
Sinclair, Andrew (Annandale) 1935- .... **CLC 2, 14**
See CA 9-12R; CAAS 5; CANR 14, 38; DLB 14; MTCW 1
Sinclair, Emil
See Hesse, Hermann
Sinclair, Iain 1943- .... **CLC 76**
See CA 132; CANR 81
Sinclair, Iain MacGregor
See Sinclair, Iain
Sinclair, Irene
See Griffith, D(avid Lewelyn) W(ark)
Sinclair, Mary Amelia St. Clair 1865(?)-1946
See Sinclair, May
See CA 104
Sinclair, May 1863-1946 .... **TCLC 3, 11**
See Sinclair, Mary Amelia St. Clair
See CA 166; DLB 36, 135
Sinclair, Roy
See Griffith, D(avid Lewelyn) W(ark)
Sinclair, Upton (Beall) 1878-1968 .... **CLC 1, 11, 15, 63; DA; DAB; DAC; DAM MST, NOV; WLC**
See CA 5-8R; 25-28R; CANR 7; CDALB 1929-1941; DA3; DLB 9; INT CANR-7; MTCW 1, 2; SATA 9
Singer, Isaac
See Singer, Isaac Bashevis
Singer, Isaac Bashevis 1904-1991 . **CLC 1, 3, 6, 9, 11, 15, 23, 38, 69, 111; DA; DAB; DAC; DAM MST, NOV; SSC 3; WLC**
See AAYA 32; AITN 1, 2; CA 1-4R; 134; CANR 1, 39; CDALB 1941-1968; CLR 1; DA3; DLB 6, 28, 52; DLBY 91; JRDA; MAICYA; MTCW 1, 2; SATA 3, 27; SATA-Obit 68
Singer, Israel Joshua 1893-1944 ... **TCLC 33**
See CA 169
Singh, Khushwant 1915- .... **CLC 11**
See CA 9-12R; CAAS 9; CANR 6, 84
Singleton, Ann
See Benedict, Ruth (Fulton)
Sinjohn, John
See Galsworthy, John
Sinyavsky, Andrei (Donatevich) 1925-1997 . **CLC 8**
See CA 85-88; 159
Sirin, V.
See Nabokov, Vladimir (Vladimirovich)
Sissman, L(ouis) E(dward) 1928-1976 . **CLC 9, 18**
See CA 21-24R; 65-68; CANR 13; DLB 5
Sisson, C(harles) H(ubert) 1914- ...... **CLC 8**

See CA 1-4R; CAAS 3; CANR 3, 48, 84; DLB 27
Sitwell, Dame Edith 1887-1964 .... **CLC 2, 9, 67; DAM POET; PC 3**
See CA 9-12R; CANR 35; CDBLB 1945-1960; DLB 20; MTCW 1, 2
Siwaarmill, H. P.
See Sharp, William
Sjoewall, Maj 1935- .... **CLC 7**
See CA 65-68; CANR 73
Sjowall, Maj
See Sjoewall, Maj
Skelton, John 1463-1529 .... **PC 25**
Skelton, Robin 1925-1997 .... **CLC 13**
See AITN 2; CA 5-8R; 160; CAAS 5; CANR 28; DLB 27, 53
Skolimowski, Jerzy 1938- .... **CLC 20**
See CA 128
Skram, Amalie(Bertha) 1847-1905 .... **TCLC 25**
See CA 165
Skvorecky, Josef (Vaclav) 1924- ..... **CLC 15, 39, 69; DAC; DAM NOV**
See CA 61-64; CAAS 1; CANR 10, 34, 63; DA3; MTCW 1, 2
Slade, Bernard .... **CLC 11, 46**
See Newbound, Bernard Slade
See CAAS 9; DLB 53
Slaughter, Carolyn 1946- .... **CLC 56**
See CA 85-88; CANR 85
Slaughter, Frank G(ill) 1908- .... **CLC 29**
See AITN 2; CA 5-8R; CANR 5, 85; INT CANR-5
Slavitt, David R(ytman) 1935- .... **CLC 5, 14**
See CA 21-24R; CAAS 3; CANR 41, 83; DLB 5, 6
Slesinger, Tess 1905-1945 .... **TCLC 10**
See CA 107; DLB 102
Slessor, Kenneth 1901-1971 .... **CLC 14**
See CA 102; 89-92
Slowacki, Juliusz 1809-1849 .... **NCLC 15**
Smart, Christopher 1722-1771 . **LC 3; DAM POET; PC 13**
See DLB 109
Smart, Elizabeth 1913-1986 .... **CLC 54**
See CA 81-84; 118; DLB 88
Smiley, Jane (Graves) 1949- .... **CLC 53, 76; DAM POP**
See CA 104; CANR 30, 50, 74; DA3; INT CANR-30
Smith, A(rthur) J(ames) M(arshall) 1902-1980 .... **CLC 15; DAC**
See CA 1-4R; 102; CANR 4; DLB 88
Smith, Adam 1723-1790 .... **LC 36**
See DLB 104
Smith, Alexander 1829-1867 .... **NCLC 59**
See DLB 32, 55
Smith, Anna Deavere 1950- .... **CLC 86**
See CA 133
Smith, Betty (Wehner) 1896-1972 ... **CLC 19**
See CA 5-8R; 33-36R; DLBY 82; SATA 6
Smith, Charlotte(Turner) 1749-1806 . **NCLC 23**
See DLB 39, 109
Smith, Clark Ashton 1893-1961 ...... **CLC 43**
See CA 143; CANR 81; MTCW 2
Smith, Dave .... **CLC 22, 42**
See Smith, David (Jeddie)
See CAAS 7; DLB 5
Smith, David (Jeddie) 1942-
See Smith, Dave
See CA 49-52; CANR 1, 59; DAM POET
Smith, Florence Margaret 1902-1971
See Smith, Stevie
See CA 17-18; 29-32R; CANR 35; CAP 2; DAM POET; MTCW 1, 2
Smith, Iain Crichton 1928-1998 ...... **CLC 64**
See CA 21-24R; 171; DLB 40, 139
Smith, John 1580(?)-1631 .... **LC 9**
See DLB 24, 30
Smith, Johnston
See Crane, Stephen (Townley)
Smith, Joseph, Jr. 1805-1844 .... **NCLC 53**
Smith, Lee 1944- .... **CLC 25, 73**
See CA 114; 119; CANR 46; DLB 143; DLBY 83; INT 119
Smith, Martin
See Smith, Martin Cruz
Smith, Martin Cruz 1942- ... **CLC 25; DAM MULT, POP**
See BEST 89:4; CA 85-88; CANR 6, 23, 43, 65; INT CANR-23; MTCW 2; NNAL
Smith, Mary-Ann Tirone 1944- ...... **CLC 39**
See CA 118; 136
Smith, Patti 1946- .... **CLC 12**
See CA 93-96; CANR 63
Smith, Pauline (Urmson) 1882-1959 . **TCLC 25**
Smith, Rosamond
See Oates, Joyce Carol
Smith, Sheila Kaye
See Kaye-Smith, Sheila
Smith, Stevie .... **CLC 3, 8, 25, 44; PC 12**
See Smith, Florence Margaret
See DLB 20; MTCW 2
Smith, Wilbur (Addison) 1933- .... **CLC 33**
See CA 13-16R; CANR 7, 46, 66; MTCW 1, 2
Smith, William Jay 1918- .... **CLC 6**
See CA 5-8R; CANR 44; DLB 5; MAICYA; SAAS 22; SATA 2, 68
Smith, Woodrow Wilson
See Kuttner, Henry
Smolenskin, Peretz 1842-1885 ...... **NCLC 30**
Smollett, Tobias (George) 1721-1771 .. **LC 2, 46**
See CDBLB 1660-1789; DLB 39, 104
Snodgrass, W(illiam) D(e Witt) 1926- . **CLC 2, 6, 10, 18, 68; DAM POET**
See CA 1-4R; CANR 6, 36, 65, 85; DLB 5; MTCW 1, 2
Snow, C(harles) P(ercy) 1905-1980 .. **CLC 1, 4, 6, 9, 13, 19; DAM NOV**
See CA 5-8R; 101; CANR 28; CDBLB 1945-1960; DLB 15, 77; DLBD 17; MTCW 1, 2
Snow, Frances Compton
See Adams, Henry (Brooks)
Snyder, Gary (Sherman) 1930- .... **CLC 1, 2, 5, 9, 32, 120; DAM POET; PC 21**
See CA 17-20R; CANR 30, 60; DA3; DLB 5, 16, 165, 212; MTCW 2
Snyder, Zilpha Keatley 1927- .... **CLC 17**
See AAYA 15; CA 9-12R; CANR 38; CLR 31; JRDA; MAICYA; SAAS 2; SATA 1, 28, 75, 110
Soares, Bernardo
See Pessoa, Fernando (Antonio Nogueira)
Sobh, A.
See Shamlu, Ahmad
Sobol, Joshua .... **CLC 60**
Socrates 469B.C.-399B.C. .... **CMLC 27**
Soderberg, Hjalmar 1869-1941 .... **TCLC 39**
Sodergran, Edith (Irene)
See Soedergran, Edith (Irene)
Soedergran, Edith (Irene) 1892-1923 . **TCLC 31**
Softly, Edgar
See Lovecraft, H(oward) P(hillips)
Softly, Edward
See Lovecraft, H(oward) P(hillips)
Sokolov, Raymond 1941- .... **CLC 7**
See CA 85-88
Solo, Jay
See Ellison, Harlan (Jay)
Sologub, Fyodor .... **TCLC 9**
See Teternikov, Fyodor Kuzmich
Solomons, Ikey Esquir
See Thackeray, William Makepeace
Solomos, Dionysios 1798-1857 ...... **NCLC 15**
Solwoska, Mara
See French, Marilyn
Solzhenitsyn, Aleksandr I(sayevich) 1918- .. **CLC 1, 2, 4, 7, 9, 10, 18, 26, 34, 78; DA; DAB; DAC; DAM MST, NOV; SSC 32;WLC**
See AITN 1; CA 69-72; CANR 40, 65; DA3; MTCW 1, 2
Somers, Jane
See Lessing, Doris (May)
Somerville, Edith 1858-1949 .... **TCLC 51**
See DLB 135
Somerville & Ross
See Martin, Violet Florence; Somerville, Edith
Sommer, Scott 1951- .... **CLC 25**
See CA 106
Sondheim, Stephen (Joshua) 1930- ...... **CLC 30, 39; DAM DRAM**
See AAYA 11; CA 103; CANR 47, 68
Song, Cathy 1955- .... **PC 21**
See CA 154; DLB 169
Sontag, Susan 1933- ... **CLC 1, 2, 10, 13, 31, 105; DAM POP**
See CA 17-20R; CANR 25, 51, 74; DA3; DLB 2, 67; MTCW 1, 2
Sophocles 496(?)B.C.-406(?)B.C. .. **CMLC 2; DA; DAB; DAC; DAM DRAM, MST; DC 1; WLCS**
See DA3; DLB 176
Sordello 1189-1269 .... **CMLC 15**
Sorel, Georges 1847-1922 .... **TCLC 91**
See CA 118
Sorel, Julia
See Drexler, Rosalyn
Sorrentino, Gilbert 1929- . **CLC 3, 7, 14, 22, 40**
See CA 77-80; CANR 14, 33; DLB 5, 173; DLBY 80; INT CANR-14
Soto, Gary 1952- . **CLC 32, 80; DAM MULT; HLC 2; PC 28**
See AAYA 10; CA 119; 125; CANR 50, 74; CLR 38; DLB 82; HW 1, 2; INT 125; JRDA; MTCW 2; SATA 80
Soupault, Philippe 1897-1990 .... **CLC 68**
See CA 116; 147; 131
Souster, (Holmes) Raymond 1921- .. **CLC 5, 14; DAC; DAM POET**
See CA 13-16R; CAAS 14; CANR 13, 29, 53; DA3; DLB 88; SATA 63
Southern, Terry 1924(?)-1995 .... **CLC 7**
See CA 1-4R; 150; CANR 1, 55; DLB 2
Southey, Robert 1774-1843 .... **NCLC 8**
See DLB 93, 107, 142; SATA 54
Southworth, Emma Dorothy Eliza Nevitte 1819-1899 .... **NCLC 26**
Souza, Ernest
See Scott, Evelyn
Soyinka, Wole 1934- .. **CLC 3, 5, 14, 36, 44; BLC 3; DA; DAB; DAC; DAM DRAM, MST, MULT; DC 2; WLC**
See BW 2, 3; CA 13-16R; CANR 27, 39, 82; DA3; DLB 125; MTCW 1, 2
Spackman, W(illiam) M(ode) 1905-1990 ..... **CLC 46**
See CA 81-84; 132
Spacks, Barry (Bernard) 1931- .... **CLC 14**
See CA 154; CANR 33; DLB 105
Spanidou, Irini 1946- .... **CLC 44**
Spark, Muriel (Sarah) 1918- ... **CLC 2, 3, 5, 8, 13, 18, 40, 94; DAB; DAC; DAM MST, NOV; SSC 10**
See CA 5-8R; CANR 12, 36, 76; CDBLB 1945-1960; DA3; DLB 15, 139; INT CANR-12; MTCW 1, 2

Spaulding, Douglas
See Bradbury, Ray (Douglas)
Spaulding, Leonard
See Bradbury, Ray (Douglas)
Spence, J. A. D.
See Eliot, T(homas) S(tearns)
Spencer, Elizabeth 1921- .... **CLC 22**
See CA 13-16R; CANR 32, 65; DLB 6; MTCW 1; SATA 14
Spencer, Leonard G.
See Silverberg, Robert
Spencer, Scott 1945- .... **CLC 30**
See CA 113; CANR 51; DLBY 86
Spender, Stephen (Harold) 1909-1995 . **CLC 1, 2, 5, 10, 41, 91; DAM POET**
See CA 9-12R; 149; CANR 31, 54; CDBLB 1945-1960; DA3; DLB 20; MTCW 1, 2
Spengler, Oswald (Arnold Gottfried) 1880-1936 .... **TCLC 25**
See CA 118
Spenser, Edmund 1552(?)-1599 .... **LC 5, 39; DA; DAB; DAC; DAM MST, POET; PC 8; WLC**
See CDBLB Before 1660; DA3; DLB 167
Spicer, Jack 1925-1965 .... **CLC 8, 18, 72; DAM POET**
See CA 85-88; DLB 5, 16, 193
Spiegelman, Art 1948- .... **CLC 76**
See AAYA 10; CA 125; CANR 41, 55, 74; MTCW 2; SATA 109
Spielberg, Peter 1929- .... **CLC 6**
See CA 5-8R; CANR 4, 48; DLBY 81
Spielberg, Steven 1947- .... **CLC 20**
See AAYA 8, 24; CA 77-80; CANR 32; SATA 32
Spillane, Frank Morrison 1918-
See Spillane, Mickey
See CA 25-28R; CANR 28, 63; DA3; MTCW 1, 2; SATA 66
Spillane, Mickey .... **CLC 3, 13**
See Spillane, Frank Morrison
See MTCW 2
Spinoza, Benedictus de 1632-1677 .... **LC 9**
Spinrad, Norman (Richard) 1940- . **CLC 46**
See CA 37-40R; CAAS 19; CANR 20; DLB 8; INT CANR-20
Spitteler, Carl (Friedrich Georg) 1845-1924 .... **TCLC 12**
See CA 109; DLB 129
Spivack, Kathleen (Romola Drucker) 1938- .... **CLC 6**
See CA 49-52
Spoto, Donald 1941- .... **CLC 39**
See CA 65-68; CANR 11, 57
Springsteen, Bruce (F.) 1949- .... **CLC 17**
See CA 111
Spurling, Hilary 1940- .... **CLC 34**
See CA 104; CANR 25, 52
Spyker, John Howland
See Elman, Richard (Martin)
Squires, (James) Radcliffe 1917-1993 .. **CLC 51**
See CA 1-4R; 140; CANR 6, 21
Srivastava, Dhanpat Rai 1880(?)-1936
See Premchand
See CA 118
Stacy, Donald
See Pohl, Frederik
Stael, Germaine de 1766-1817
See Stael-Holstein, Anne Louise Germaine Necker Baronn
See DLB 119
Stael-Holstein, Anne Louise Germaine Necker Baronn 1766-1817 ...... **NCLC 3**
See Stael, Germaine de
See DLB 192
Stafford, Jean 1915-1979 . **CLC 4, 7, 19, 68; SSC 26**
See CA 1-4R; 85-88; CANR 3, 65; DLB 2, 173; MTCW 1, 2; SATA-Obit 22
Stafford, William (Edgar) 1914-1993 .. **CLC 4, 7, 29; DAM POET**
See CA 5-8R; 142; CAAS 3; CANR 5, 22; DLB 5, 206; INT CANR-22
Stagnelius, Eric Johan 1793-1823 . **NCLC 61**
Staines, Trevor
See Brunner, John (Kilian Houston)
Stairs, Gordon
See Austin, Mary (Hunter)
Stairs, Gordon
See Austin, Mary (Hunter)
Stalin, Joseph 1879-1953 .... **TCLC 92**
Stannard, Martin 1947- .... **CLC 44**
See CA 142; DLB 155
Stanton, Elizabeth Cady 1815-1902 .. **TCLC 73**
See CA 171; DLB 79
Stanton, Maura 1946- .... **CLC 9**
See CA 89-92; CANR 15; DLB 120
Stanton, Schuyler
See Baum, L(yman) Frank
Stapledon, (William) Olaf 1886-1950 . **TCLC 22**
See CA 111; 162; DLB 15
Starbuck, George (Edwin) 1931-1996 . **CLC 53; DAM POET**
See CA 21-24R; 153; CANR 23
Stark, Richard
See Westlake, Donald E(dwin)
Staunton, Schuyler
See Baum, L(yman) Frank
Stead, Christina (Ellen) 1902-1983 .. **CLC 2, 5, 8, 32, 80**
See CA 13-16R; 109; CANR 33, 40; MTCW 1, 2
Stead, William Thomas 1849-1912 .... **TCLC 48**
See CA 167
Steele, Richard 1672-1729 .... **LC 18**
See CDBLB 1660-1789; DLB 84, 101
Steele, Timothy (Reid) 1948- .... **CLC 45**
See CA 93-96; CANR 16, 50; DLB 120
Steffens, (Joseph) Lincoln 1866-1936 . **TCLC 20**
See CA 117
Stegner, Wallace (Earle) 1909-1993 . **CLC 9, 49, 81; DAM NOV; SSC 27**
See AITN 1; BEST 90:3; CA 1-4R; 141; CAAS 9; CANR 1, 21, 46; DLB 9, 206; DLBY 93; MTCW 1, 2
Stein, Gertrude 1874-1946 .. **TCLC 1, 6, 28, 48; DA; DAB; DAC; DAM MST, NOV, POET; PC 18; WLC**
See CA 104; 132; CDALB 1917-1929; DA3; DLB 4, 54, 86; DLBD 15; MTCW 1, 2
Steinbeck, John (Ernst) 1902-1968 .. **CLC 1, 5, 9, 13, 21, 34, 45, 75, 124; DA; DAB; DAC; DAM DRAM, MST, NOV; SSC 37;WLC**
See AAYA 12; CA 1-4R; 25-28R; CANR 1, 35; CDALB 1929-1941; DA3; DLB 7, 9, 212; DLBD 2; MTCW 1, 2; SATA 9
Steinem, Gloria 1934- .... **CLC 63**
See CA 53-56; CANR 28, 51; MTCW 1, 2
Steiner, George 1929- .. **CLC 24;DAM NOV**
See CA 73-76; CANR 31, 67; DLB 67; MTCW 1, 2; SATA 62
Steiner, K. Leslie
See Delany, Samuel R(ay, Jr.)
Steiner, Rudolf 1861-1925 .... **TCLC 13**
See CA 107
Stendhal 1783-1842 .... **NCLC 23, 46; DA; DAB; DAC; DAM MST, NOV; SSC 27; WLC**
See DA3; DLB 119
Stephen, Adeline Virginia
See Woolf, (Adeline) Virginia
Stephen, SirLeslie 1832-1904 .... **TCLC 23**
See CA 123; DLB 57, 144, 190
Stephen, Sir Leslie
See Stephen, SirLeslie
Stephen, Virginia
See Woolf, (Adeline) Virginia
Stephens, James 1882(?)-1950 .... **TCLC 4**
See CA 104; DLB 19, 153, 162
Stephens, Reed
See Donaldson, Stephen R.
Steptoe, Lydia
See Barnes, Djuna
Sterchi, Beat 1949- .... **CLC 65**
Sterling, Brett
See Bradbury, Ray (Douglas); Hamilton, Edmond
Sterling, Bruce 1954- .... **CLC 72**
See CA 119; CANR 44
Sterling, George 1869-1926 .... **TCLC 20**
See CA 117; 165; DLB 54
Stern, Gerald 1925- .... **CLC 40, 100**
See CA 81-84; CANR 28; DLB 105
Stern, Richard (Gustave) 1928- .. **CLC 4, 39**
See CA 1-4R; CANR 1, 25, 52; DLBY 87; INT CANR-25
Sternberg, Josefvon 1894-1969 .... **CLC 20**
See CA 81-84
Sterne, Laurence 1713-1768 . **LC 2, 48; DA; DAB; DAC; DAM MST, NOV; WLC**
See CDBLB 1660-1789; DLB 39
Sternheim, (William Adolf) Carl 1878-1942 .... **TCLC 8**
See CA 105; DLB 56, 118
Stevens, Mark 1951- .... **CLC 34**
See CA 122
Stevens, Wallace 1879-1955 ..... **TCLC 3, 12, 45; DA; DAB; DAC; DAM MST, POET; PC 6; WLC**
See CA 104; 124; CDALB 1929-1941; DA3; DLB 54; MTCW 1, 2
Stevenson, Anne (Katharine) 1933- . **CLC 7, 33**
See CA 17-20R; CAAS 9; CANR 9, 33; DLB 40; MTCW 1
Stevenson, Robert Louis (Balfour) 1850-1894 . **NCLC 5, 14, 63; DA; DAB; DAC; DAM MST, NOV; SSC 11; WLC**
See AAYA 24; CDBLB 1890-1914; CLR 10, 11; DA3; DLB 18, 57, 141, 156, 174; DLBD 13; JRDA; MAICYA; SATA 100; YABC 2
Stewart, J(ohn) I(nnes) M(ackintosh) 1906-1994 .... **CLC 7, 14, 32**
See CA 85-88; 147; CAAS 3; CANR 47; MTCW 1, 2
Stewart, Mary (Florence Elinor) 1916- . **CLC 7, 35, 117; DAB**
See AAYA 29; CA 1-4R; CANR 1, 59; SATA 12
Stewart, Mary Rainbow
See Stewart, Mary (Florence Elinor)
Stifle, June
See Campbell, Maria
Stifter, Adalbert 1805-1868 . **NCLC 41; SSC 28**
See DLB 133
Still, James 1906- .... **CLC 49**
See CA 65-68; CAAS 17; CANR 10, 26; DLB 9; SATA 29
Sting 1951-
See Sumner, Gordon Matthew
See CA 167
Stirling, Arthur
See Sinclair, Upton (Beall)
Stitt, Milan 1941- .... **CLC 29**
See CA 69-72

Stockton, Francis Richard 1834-1902
See Stockton, Frank R.
See CA 108; 137; MAICYA; SATA 44
Stockton, Frank R. .... **TCLC 47**
See Stockton, Francis Richard
See DLB 42, 74; DLBD 13; SATA-Brief 32
Stoddard, Charles
See Kuttner, Henry
Stoker, Abraham 1847-1912
See Stoker, Bram
See CA 105; 150; DA; DAC; DAM MST, NOV; DA3; SATA 29
Stoker, Bram 1847-1912 ...... **TCLC 8; DAB; WLC**
See Stoker, Abraham
See AAYA 23; CDBLB 1890-1914; DLB 36, 70, 178
Stolz, Mary (Slattery) 1920- .... **CLC 12**
See AAYA 8; AITN 1; CA 5-8R; CANR 13, 41; JRDA; MAICYA; SAAS 3; SATA 10, 71
Stone, Irving 1903-1989 . **CLC 7;DAM POP**
See AITN 1; CA 1-4R; 129; CAAS 3; CANR 1, 23; DA3; INT CANR-23; MTCW 1, 2; SATA 3; SATA-Obit 64
Stone, Oliver (William) 1946- .... **CLC 73**
See AAYA 15; CA 110; CANR 55
Stone, Robert (Anthony) 1937- .. **CLC 5, 23, 42**
See CA 85-88; CANR 23, 66; DLB 152; INT CANR-23; MTCW 1
Stone, Zachary
See Follett, Ken(neth Martin)
Stoppard, Tom 1937- . **CLC 1, 3, 4, 5, 8, 15, 29, 34, 63, 91; DA; DAB; DAC; DAM DRAM, MST; DC 6; WLC**
See CA 81-84; CANR 39, 67; CDBLB 1960 to Present; DA3; DLB 13; DLBY 85; MTCW 1, 2
Storey, David (Malcolm) 1933- . **CLC 2, 4, 5, 8; DAM DRAM**
See CA 81-84; CANR 36; DLB 13, 14, 207; MTCW 1
Storm, Hyemeyohsts 1935- ..... **CLC 3;DAM MULT**
See CA 81-84; CANR 45; NNAL
Storm, Theodor 1817-1888 .... **SSC 27**
Storm, (Hans) Theodor (Woldsen) 1817-1888 .... **NCLC 1; SSC 27**
See DLB 129
Storni, Alfonsina 1892-1938 . **TCLC 5; DAM MULT; HLC 2**
See CA 104; 131; HW 1
Stoughton, William 1631-1701 .... **LC 38**
See DLB 24
Stout, Rex(Todhunter) 1886-1975 ..... **CLC 3**
See AITN 2; CA 61-64; CANR 71
Stow, (Julian) Randolph 1935- . **CLC 23, 48**
See CA 13-16R; CANR 33; MTCW 1
Stowe, Harriet (Elizabeth) Beecher 1811-1896 ...... **NCLC 3, 50; DA; DAB; DAC; DAM MST, NOV; WLC**
See CDALB 1865-1917; DA3; DLB 1, 12, 42, 74, 189; JRDA; MAICYA; YABC 1
Strachey, (Giles)Lytton 1880-1932 ..... **TCLC 12**
See CA 110; 178; DLB 149; DLBD 10; MTCW 2
Strand, Mark 1934- .... **CLC 6, 18, 41, 71; DAM POET**
See CA 21-24R; CANR 40, 65; DLB 5; SATA 41
Straub, Peter (Francis) 1943- . **CLC 28, 107; DAM POP**
See BEST 89:1; CA 85-88; CANR 28, 65; DLBY 84; MTCW 1, 2
Strauss, Botho 1944- .... **CLC 22**
See CA 157; DLB 124
Streatfeild, (Mary) Noel 1895(?)-1986 . **CLC 21**
See CA 81-84; 120; CANR 31; CLR 17; DLB 160; MAICYA; SATA 20; SATA-Obit 48
Stribling, T(homas) S(igismund) 1881-1965 .... **CLC 23**
See CA 107; DLB 9
Strindberg, (Johan) August 1849-1912 .... **TCLC 1, 8, 21, 47; DA; DAB; DAC; DAM DRAM, MST; WLC**
See CA 104; 135; DA3; MTCW 2
Stringer, Arthur 1874-1950 .... **TCLC 37**
See CA 161; DLB 92
Stringer, David
See Roberts, Keith (John Kingston)
Stroheim, Erich von 1885-1957 .... **TCLC 71**
Strugatskii, Arkadii (Natanovich) 1925-1991 .... **CLC 27**
See CA 106; 135
Strugatskii, Boris (Natanovich) 1933- . **CLC 27**
See CA 106
Strummer, Joe 1953(?)- .... **CLC 30**
Strunk, William, Jr. 1869-1946 .... **TCLC 92**
See CA 118; 164
Stryk, Lucien 1924- .... **PC 27**
See CA 13-16R; CANR 10, 28, 55
Stuart, Don A.
See Campbell, John W(ood, Jr.)
Stuart, Ian
See MacLean, Alistair (Stuart)
Stuart, Jesse (Hilton) 1906-1984 .. **CLC 1, 8, 11, 14, 34; SSC 31**
See CA 5-8R; 112; CANR 31; DLB 9, 48, 102; DLBY 84; SATA 2; SATA-Obit 36
Sturgeon, Theodore (Hamilton) 1918-1985 . **CLC 22, 39**
See Queen, Ellery
See CA 81-84; 116; CANR 32; DLB 8; DLBY 85; MTCW 1, 2
Sturges, Preston 1898-1959 .... **TCLC 48**
See CA 114; 149; DLB 26
Styron, William 1925- .. **CLC 1, 3, 5, 11, 15, 60; DAM NOV, POP; SSC 25**
See BEST 90:4; CA 5-8R; CANR 6, 33, 74; CDALB 1968-1988; DA3; DLB 2, 143; DLBY 80; INT CANR-6; MTCW 1, 2
Su, Chien 1884-1918
See Su Man-shu
See CA 123
Suarez Lynch, B.
See Bioy Casares, Adolfo; Borges, Jorge Luis
Suassuna, Ariano Vilar 1927-
See CA 178; HLCS 1; HW 2
Suckow, Ruth 1892-1960 .... **SSC 18**
See CA 113; DLB 9, 102
Sudermann, Hermann 1857-1928 . **TCLC 15**
See CA 107; DLB 118
Sue, Eugene 1804-1857 .... **NCLC 1**
See DLB 119
Sueskind, Patrick 1949- .... **CLC 44**
See Suskind, Patrick
Sukenick, Ronald 1932- ...... **CLC 3, 4, 6, 48**
See CA 25-28R; CAAS 8; CANR 32; DLB 173; DLBY 81
Suknaski, Andrew 1942- .... **CLC 19**
See CA 101; DLB 53
Sullivan, Vernon
See Vian, Boris
Sully Prudhomme 1839-1907 .... **TCLC 31**
Su Man-shu .... **TCLC 24**
See Su, Chien
Summerforest, Ivy B.
See Kirkup, James
Summers, Andrew James 1942- ...... **CLC 26**
Summers, Andy
See Summers, Andrew James
Summers, Hollis (Spurgeon,Jr.) 1916- . **CLC 10**
See CA 5-8R; CANR 3; DLB 6
Summers, (Alphonsus Joseph-Mary Augustus) Montague 1880-1948 .... **TCLC 16**
See CA 118; 163
Sumner, Gordon Matthew .... **CLC 26**
See Sting
Surtees, Robert Smith 1803-1864 . **NCLC 14**
See DLB 21
Susann, Jacqueline 1921-1974 .... **CLC 3**
See AITN 1; CA 65-68; 53-56; MTCW 1, 2
Su Shih 1036-1101 .... **CMLC 15**
Suskind, Patrick
See Sueskind, Patrick
See CA 145
Sutcliff, Rosemary 1920-1992 .... **CLC 26; DAB; DAC; DAM MST, POP**
See AAYA 10; CA 5-8R; 139; CANR 37; CLR 1, 37; JRDA; MAICYA; SATA 6, 44, 78; SATA-Obit 73
Sutro, Alfred 1863-1933 .... **TCLC 6**
See CA 105; DLB 10
Sutton, Henry
See Slavitt, David R(ytman)
Svevo, Italo 1861-1928 . **TCLC 2, 35;SSC 25**
See Schmitz, Aron Hector
Swados, Elizabeth (A.) 1951- .... **CLC 12**
See CA 97-100; CANR 49; INT 97-100
Swados, Harvey 1920-1972 .... **CLC 5**
See CA 5-8R; 37-40R; CANR 6; DLB 2
Swan, Gladys 1934- .... **CLC 69**
See CA 101; CANR 17, 39
Swarthout, Glendon (Fred) 1918-1992 . **CLC 35**
See CA 1-4R; 139; CANR 1, 47; SATA 26
Sweet, Sarah C.
See Jewett, (Theodora) Sarah Orne
Swenson, May 1919-1989 ..... **CLC 4, 14, 61, 106; DA; DAB; DAC; DAM MST, POET; PC 14**
See CA 5-8R; 130; CANR 36, 61; DLB 5; MTCW 1, 2; SATA 15
Swift, Augustus
See Lovecraft, H(oward) P(hillips)
Swift, Graham (Colin) 1949- .... **CLC 41, 88**
See CA 117; 122; CANR 46, 71; DLB 194; MTCW 2
Swift, Jonathan 1667-1745 ... **LC 1, 42; DA; DAB; DAC; DAM MST, NOV, POET; PC 9; WLC**
See CDBLB 1660-1789; CLR 53; DA3; DLB 39, 95, 101; SATA 19
Swinburne, Algernon Charles 1837-1909 .... **TCLC 8, 36; DA; DAB; DAC; DAM MST, POET; PC 24; WLC**
See CA 105; 140; CDBLB 1832-1890; DA3; DLB 35, 57
Swinfen, Ann .... **CLC 34**
Swinnerton, Frank Arthur 1884-1982 . **CLC 31**
See CA 108; DLB 34
Swithen, John
See King, Stephen (Edwin)
Sylvia
See Ashton-Warner, Sylvia (Constance)
Symmes, Robert Edward
See Duncan, Robert (Edward)
Symonds, John Addington 1840-1893 .... **NCLC 34**
See DLB 57, 144
Symons, Arthur 1865-1945 .... **TCLC 11**
See CA 107; DLB 19, 57, 149
Symons, Julian (Gustave) 1912-1994 ... **CLC 2, 14, 32**

See CA 49-52; 147; CAAS 3; CANR 3, 33, 59; DLB 87, 155; DLBY 92; MTCW 1

Synge, (Edmund) J(ohn) M(illington) 1871-1909 . **TCLC 6, 37; DAM DRAM; DC 2**
See CA 104; 141; CDBLB 1890-1914; DLB 10, 19

Syruc, J.
See Milosz, Czeslaw

Szirtes, George 1948- .... **CLC 46**
See CA 109; CANR 27, 61

Szymborska, Wislawa 1923- .... **CLC 99**
See CA 154; DA3; DLBY 96; MTCW 2

T. O., Nik
See Annensky, Innokenty (Fyodorovich)

Tabori, George 1914- .... **CLC 19**
See CA 49-52; CANR 4, 69

Tagore, Rabindranath 1861-1941 .. **TCLC 3, 53; DAM DRAM, POET; PC 8**
See CA 104; 120; DA3; MTCW 1, 2

Taine, Hippolyte Adolphe 1828-1893 . **NCLC 15**

Talese, Gay 1932- .... **CLC 37**
See AITN 1; CA 1-4R; CANR 9, 58; DLB 185; INT CANR-9; MTCW 1, 2

Tallent, Elizabeth (Ann) 1954- .... **CLC 45**
See CA 117; CANR 72; DLB 130

Tally, Ted 1952- .... **CLC 42**
See CA 120; 124; INT 124

Talvik, Heiti 1904-1947 .... **TCLC 87**

Tamayo y Baus, Manuel 1829-1898 .. **NCLC 1**

Tammsaare, A(nton) H(ansen) 1878-1940 ... **TCLC 27**
See CA 164

Tam'si, Tchicaya U
See Tchicaya, Gerald Felix

Tan, Amy (Ruth) 1952- . **CLC 59, 120; DAM MULT, NOV, POP**
See AAYA 9; BEST 89:3; CA 136; CANR 54; CDALBS; DA3; DLB 173; MTCW 2; SATA 75

Tandem, Felix
See Spitteler, Carl (Friedrich Georg)

Tanizaki, Jun'ichiro 1886-1965 .. **CLC 8, 14, 28; SSC 21**
See CA 93-96; 25-28R; DLB 180; MTCW 2

Tanner, William
See Amis, Kingsley (William)

Tao Lao
See Storni, Alfonsina

Tarantino, Quentin(Jerome) 1963- .... **CLC 125**
See CA 171

Tarassoff, Lev
See Troyat, Henri

Tarbell, Ida M(inerva) 1857-1944 . **TCLC 40**
See CA 122; 181; DLB 47

Tarkington, (Newton) Booth 1869-1946 .... **TCLC 9**
See CA 110; 143; DLB 9, 102; MTCW 2; SATA 17

Tarkovsky, Andrei (Arsenyevich) 1932-1986 .... **CLC 75**
See CA 127

Tartt, Donna 1964(?)- .... **CLC 76**
See CA 142

Tasso, Torquato 1544-1595 .... **LC 5**

Tate, (John Orley) Allen 1899-1979 . **CLC 2, 4, 6, 9, 11, 14, 24**
See CA 5-8R; 85-88; CANR 32; DLB 4, 45, 63; DLBD 17; MTCW 1, 2

Tate, Ellalice
See Hibbert, Eleanor Alice Burford

Tate, James (Vincent) 1943- .... **CLC 2, 6, 25**
See CA 21-24R; CANR 29, 57; DLB 5, 169

Tavel, Ronald 1940- .... **CLC 6**
See CA 21-24R; CANR 33

Taylor, C(ecil) P(hilip) 1929-1981 ... **CLC 27**
See CA 25-28R; 105; CANR 47

Taylor, Edward 1642(?)-1729 .... **LC 11; DA; DAB; DAC; DAM MST, POET**
See DLB 24

Taylor, Eleanor Ross 1920- .... **CLC 5**
See CA 81-84; CANR 70

Taylor, Elizabeth 1912-1975 .... **CLC 2, 4, 29**
See CA 13-16R; CANR 9, 70; DLB 139; MTCW 1; SATA 13

Taylor, Frederick Winslow 1856-1915 .... **TCLC 76**

Taylor, Henry (Splawn) 1942- .... **CLC 44**
See CA 33-36R; CAAS 7; CANR 31; DLB 5

Taylor, Kamala (Purnaiya) 1924-
See Markandaya, Kamala
See CA 77-80

Taylor, Mildred D. .... **CLC 21**
See AAYA 10; BW 1; CA 85-88; CANR 25; CLR 9, 59; DLB 52; JRDA; MAICYA; SAAS 5; SATA 15, 70

Taylor, Peter (Hillsman) 1917-1994 . **CLC 1, 4, 18, 37, 44, 50, 71; SSC 10**
See CA 13-16R; 147; CANR 9, 50; DLBY 81, 94; INT CANR-9; MTCW 1, 2

Taylor, Robert Lewis 1912-1998 ..... **CLC 14**
See CA 1-4R; 170; CANR 3, 64; SATA 10

Tchekhov, Anton
See Chekhov, Anton (Pavlovich)

Tchicaya, GeraldFelix 1931-1988 .. **CLC 101**
See CA 129; 125; CANR 81

Tchicaya U Tam'si
See Tchicaya, Gerald Felix

Teasdale, Sara 1884-1933 .... **TCLC 4**
See CA 104; 163; DLB 45; SATA 32

Tegner, Esaias 1782-1846 .... **NCLC 2**

Teilhard de Chardin, (Marie Joseph) Pierre 1881-1955 .... **TCLC 9**
See CA 105

Temple, Ann
See Mortimer, Penelope (Ruth)

Tennant, Emma (Christina) 1937- . **CLC 13, 52**
See CA 65-68; CAAS 9; CANR 10, 38, 59; DLB 14

Tenneshaw, S. M.
See Silverberg, Robert

Tennyson, Alfred 1809-1892 .. **NCLC 30, 65; DA; DAB; DAC; DAM MST, POET; PC 6; WLC**
See CDBLB 1832-1890; DA3; DLB 32

Teran, Lisa St. Aubin de .... **CLC 36**
See St. Aubin de Teran, Lisa

Terence c. 184B.C.-c. 159B.C. .... **CMLC 14; DC 7**
See DLB 211

Teresa de Jesus, St. 1515-1582 .... **LC 18**

Terkel, Louis 1912-
See Terkel, Studs
See CA 57-60; CANR 18, 45, 67; DA3; MTCW 1, 2

Terkel, Studs .... **CLC 38**
See Terkel, Louis
See AAYA 32; AITN 1; MTCW 2

Terry, C. V.
See Slaughter, Frank G(ill)

Terry, Megan 1932- .... **CLC 19**
See CA 77-80; CABS 3; CANR 43; DLB 7

Tertullian c. 155-c. 245 .... **CMLC 29**

Tertz, Abram
See Sinyavsky, Andrei (Donatevich)

Tesich, Steve 1943(?)-1996 .... **CLC 40, 69**
See CA 105; 152; DLBY 83

Tesla, Nikola 1856-1943 .... **TCLC 88**

Teternikov, Fyodor Kuzmich 1863-1927
See Sologub, Fyodor
See CA 104

Tevis, Walter 1928-1984 .... **CLC 42**
See CA 113

Tey, Josephine .... **TCLC 14**
See Mackintosh,Elizabeth
See DLB 77

Thackeray, William Makepeace 1811-1863 . **NCLC 5, 14, 22, 43; DA; DAB; DAC; DAM MST, NOV; WLC**
See CDBLB 1832-1890; DA3; DLB 21, 55, 159, 163; SATA 23

Thakura, Ravindranatha
See Tagore, Rabindranath

Tharoor, Shashi 1956- .... **CLC 70**
See CA 141

Thelwell, Michael Miles 1939- .... **CLC 22**
See BW 2; CA 101

Theobald, Lewis, Jr.
See Lovecraft, H(oward) P(hillips)

Theodorescu, Ion N. 1880-1967
See Arghezi, Tudor
See CA 116

Theriault, Yves 1915-1983 ... **CLC 79; DAC; DAM MST**
See CA 102; DLB 88

Theroux, Alexander (Louis) 1939- ... **CLC 2, 25**
See CA 85-88; CANR 20, 63

Theroux, Paul (Edward) 1941- .... **CLC 5, 8, 11, 15, 28, 46; DAM POP**
See AAYA 28; BEST 89:4; CA 33-36R; CANR 20, 45, 74; CDALBS; DA3; DLB 2; MTCW 1, 2; SATA 44, 109

Thesen, Sharon 1946- .... **CLC 56**
See CA 163

Thevenin, Denis
See Duhamel, Georges

Thibault, Jacques Anatole Francois 1844-1924
See France, Anatole
See CA 106; 127; DAM NOV; DA3; MTCW 1, 2

Thiele, Colin (Milton) 1920- .... **CLC 17**
See CA 29-32R; CANR 12, 28, 53; CLR 27; MAICYA; SAAS 2; SATA 14, 72

Thomas, Audrey (Callahan) 1935- .. **CLC 7, 13, 37, 107; SSC 20**
See AITN 2; CA 21-24R; CAAS 19; CANR 36, 58; DLB 60; MTCW 1

Thomas, Augustus 1857-1934 .... **TCLC 97**

Thomas, D(onald) M(ichael) 1935- ...... **CLC 13, 22, 31**
See CA 61-64; CAAS 11; CANR 17, 45, 75; CDBLB 1960 to Present; DA3; DLB 40, 207; INT CANR-17; MTCW 1, 2

Thomas, Dylan (Marlais) 1914-1953 . **TCLC 1, 8, 45; DA; DAB; DAC; DAM DRAM, MST, POET; PC 2; SSC 3; WLC**
See CA 104; 120; CANR 65; CDBLB 1945-1960; DA3; DLB 13, 20, 139; MTCW 1, 2; SATA 60

Thomas, (Philip) Edward 1878-1917 . **TCLC 10; DAM POET**
See CA 106; 153; DLB 98

Thomas, Joyce Carol 1938- .... **CLC 35**
See AAYA 12; BW 2, 3; CA 113; 116; CANR 48; CLR 19; DLB 33; INT 116; JRDA; MAICYA; MTCW 1, 2; SAAS 7; SATA 40, 78

Thomas, Lewis 1913-1993 .... **CLC 35**
See CA 85-88; 143; CANR 38, 60; MTCW 1, 2

Thomas, M. Carey 1857-1935 ...... **TCLC 89**

Thomas, Paul
See Mann, (Paul) Thomas

Thomas, Piri 1928- .... **CLC 17;HLCS 2**
See CA 73-76; HW 1

Thomas, R(onald) S(tuart) 1913- ..... **CLC 6, 13, 48; DAB; DAM POET**
See CA 89-92; CAAS 4; CANR 30; CDBLB 1960 to Present; DLB 27; MTCW 1

Thomas, Ross(Elmore) 1926-1995 .. **CLC 39**
See CA 33-36R; 150; CANR 22, 63

Thompson, Francis Clegg
See Mencken, H(enry) L(ouis)

Thompson, Francis Joseph 1859-1907 .... **TCLC 4**
See CA 104; CDBLB 1890-1914; DLB 19

Thompson, Hunter S(tockton) 1939- ... **CLC 9, 17, 40, 104; DAM POP**
See BEST 89:1; CA 17-20R; CANR 23, 46, 74, 77; DA3; DLB 185; MTCW 1, 2

Thompson, James Myers
See Thompson, Jim (Myers)

Thompson, Jim (Myers) 1906-1977(?) . **CLC 69**
See CA 140

Thompson, Judith .... **CLC 39**

Thomson, James 1700-1748 .. **LC 16, 29, 40; DAM POET**
See DLB 95

Thomson, James 1834-1882 .... **NCLC 18;DAM POET**
See DLB 35

Thoreau, Henry David 1817-1862 . **NCLC 7, 21, 61; DA; DAB; DAC; DAM MST; WLC**
See CDALB 1640-1865; DA3; DLB 1

Thornton, Hall
See Silverberg, Robert

Thucydides c.455B.C.-399B.C. ..... **CMLC 17**
See DLB 176

Thurber, James (Grover) 1894-1961 ... **CLC 5, 11, 25, 125; DA; DAB; DAC; DAM DRAM, MST, NOV; SSC 1**
See CA 73-76; CANR 17, 39; CDALB 1929-1941; DA3; DLB 4, 11, 22, 102; MAICYA; MTCW 1, 2; SATA 13

Thurman, Wallace (Henry) 1902-1934 .... **TCLC 6; BLC 3; DAM MULT**
See BW 1, 3; CA 104; 124; CANR 81; DLB 51

Tibullus, Albius c. 54B.C.-c. 19B.C. . **CMLC 36**
See DLB 211

Ticheburn, Cheviot
See Ainsworth, William Harrison

Tieck, (Johann) Ludwig 1773-1853 ... **NCLC 5, 46; SSC 31**
See DLB 90

Tiger, Derry
See Ellison, Harlan (Jay)

Tilghman, Christopher 1948(?)- ...... **CLC 65**
See CA 159

Tillinghast, Richard (Williford) 1940- . **CLC 29**
See CA 29-32R; CAAS 23; CANR 26, 51

Timrod, Henry 1828-1867 .... **NCLC 25**
See DLB 3

Tindall, Gillian (Elizabeth) 1938- ..... **CLC 7**
See CA 21-24R; CANR 11, 65

Tiptree, James, Jr. .... **CLC 48, 50**
See Sheldon, Alice Hastings Bradley
See DLB 8

Titmarsh, Michael Angelo
See Thackeray, William Makepeace

Tocqueville, Alexis (Charles Henri Maurice Clerel, Comte) de 1805-1859 . **NCLC 7, 63**

Tolkien, J(ohn) R(onald) R(euel) 1892-1973 .... **CLC 1, 2, 3, 8, 12, 38; DA; DAB; DAC; DAM MST, NOV, POP; WLC**
See AAYA 10; AITN 1; CA 17-18; 45-48; CANR 36; CAP 2; CDBLB 1914-1945; CLR 56; DA3; DLB 15, 160; JRDA; MAICYA; MTCW 1, 2; SATA 2, 32, 100; SATA-Obit 24

Toller, Ernst 1893-1939 .... **TCLC 10**
See CA 107; DLB 124

Tolson, M. B.
See Tolson, Melvin B(eaunorus)

Tolson, Melvin B(eaunorus) 1898(?)-1966 ... **CLC 36, 105; BLC 3; DAM MULT, POET**
See BW 1, 3; CA 124; 89-92; CANR 80; DLB 48, 76

Tolstoi, Aleksei Nikolaevich
See Tolstoy, Alexey Nikolaevich

Tolstoy, Alexey Nikolaevich 1882-1945 .... **TCLC 18**
See CA 107; 158

Tolstoy, Count Leo
See Tolstoy, Leo (Nikolaevich)

Tolstoy, Leo (Nikolaevich) 1828-1910 . **TCLC 4, 11, 17, 28, 44, 79; DA; DAB; DAC; DAM MST, NOV; SSC 9, 30; WLC**
See CA 104; 123; DA3; SATA 26

Tomasi di Lampedusa, Giuseppe 1896-1957
See Lampedusa, Giuseppe (Tomasi) di
See CA 111

Tomlin, Lily .... **CLC 17**
See Tomlin, Mary Jean

Tomlin, Mary Jean 1939(?)-
See Tomlin, Lily
See CA 117

Tomlinson, (Alfred) Charles 1927- .. **CLC 2, 4, 6, 13, 45; DAM POET; PC 17**
See CA 5-8R; CANR 33; DLB 40

Tomlinson, H(enry) M(ajor) 1873-1958 .... **TCLC 71**
See CA 118; 161; DLB 36, 100, 195

Tonson, Jacob
See Bennett, (Enoch) Arnold

Toole, John Kennedy 1937-1969 .... **CLC 19, 64**
See CA 104; DLBY 81; MTCW 2

Toomer, Jean 1894-1967 .. **CLC 1, 4, 13, 22; BLC 3; DAM MULT; PC 7; SSC 1; WLCS**
See BW 1; CA 85-88; CDALB 1917-1929; DA3; DLB 45, 51; MTCW 1, 2

Torley, Luke
See Blish, James (Benjamin)

Tornimparte, Alessandra
See Ginzburg, Natalia

Torre, Raoul della
See Mencken, H(enry) L(ouis)

Torrence, Ridgely 1874-1950 .... **TCLC 97**
See DLB 54

Torrey, E(dwin) Fuller 1937- .... **CLC 34**
See CA 119; CANR 71

Torsvan, Ben Traven
See Traven, B.

Torsvan, Benno Traven
See Traven, B.

Torsvan, Berick Traven
See Traven, B.

Torsvan, Berwick Traven
See Traven, B.

Torsvan, Bruno Traven
See Traven, B.

Torsvan, Traven
See Traven, B.

Tournier, Michel (Edouard) 1924- ... **CLC 6, 23, 36, 95**
See CA 49-52; CANR 3, 36, 74; DLB 83; MTCW 1, 2; SATA 23

Tournimparte, Alessandra
See Ginzburg, Natalia

Towers, Ivar
See Kornbluth, C(yril) M.

Towne, Robert(Burton) 1936(?)- ..... **CLC 87**
See CA 108; DLB 44

Townsend, Sue .... **CLC 61**
See Townsend, Susan Elaine
See AAYA 28; SATA 55, 93; SATA-Brief 48

Townsend, Susan Elaine 1946-
See Townsend, Sue
See CA 119; 127; CANR 65; DAB; DAC; DAM MST

Townshend, Peter (Dennis Blandford) 1945- .... **CLC 17, 42**
See CA 107

Tozzi, Federigo 1883-1920 .... **TCLC 31**
See CA 160

Traill, Catharine Parr 1802-1899 . **NCLC 31**
See DLB 99

Trakl, Georg 1887-1914 .... **TCLC 5;PC 20**
See CA 104; 165; MTCW 2

Transtroemer, Tomas (Goesta) 1931- ... **CLC 52, 65; DAM POET**
See CA 117; 129; CAAS 17

Transtromer, Tomas Gosta
See Transtroemer, Tomas (Goesta)

Traven, B. (?)-1969 .... **CLC 8, 11**
See CA 19-20; 25-28R; CAP 2; DLB 9, 56; MTCW 1

Treitel, Jonathan 1959- .... **CLC 70**

Tremain, Rose 1943- .... **CLC 42**
See CA 97-100; CANR 44; DLB 14

Tremblay, Michel 1942- .... **CLC 29, 102; DAC; DAM MST**
See CA 116; 128; DLB 60; MTCW 1, 2

Trevanian .... **CLC 29**
See Whitaker, Rod(ney)

Trevor, Glen
See Hilton, James

Trevor, William 1928- . **CLC 7, 9, 14, 25, 71, 116; SSC 21**
See Cox, William Trevor
See DLB 14, 139; MTCW 2

Trifonov, Yuri (Valentinovich) 1925-1981 .... **CLC 45**
See CA 126; 103; MTCW 1

Trilling, Lionel 1905-1975 ..... **CLC 9, 11, 24**
See CA 9-12R; 61-64; CANR 10; DLB 28, 63; INT CANR-10; MTCW 1, 2

Trimball, W. H.
See Mencken, H(enry) L(ouis)

Tristan
See Gomez de la Serna, Ramon

Tristram
See Housman, A(lfred) E(dward)

Trogdon, William (Lewis) 1939-
See Heat-Moon, William Least
See CA 115; 119; CANR 47; INT 119

Trollope, Anthony 1815-1882 .. **NCLC 6, 33; DA; DAB; DAC; DAM MST, NOV; SSC 28; WLC**
See CDBLB 1832-1890; DA3; DLB 21, 57, 159; SATA 22

Trollope, Frances 1779-1863 .... **NCLC 30**
See DLB 21, 166

Trotsky, Leon 1879-1940 .... **TCLC 22**
See CA 118; 167

Trotter (Cockburn), Catharine 1679-1749 .. **LC 8**
See DLB 84

Trout, Kilgore
See Farmer, Philip Jose

Trow, George W. S. 1943- .... **CLC 52**
See CA 126

Troyat, Henri 1911- .... **CLC 23**
See CA 45-48; CANR 2, 33, 67; MTCW 1

Trudeau, G(arretson) B(eekman) 1948-
See Trudeau, Garry B.
See CA 81-84; CANR 31; SATA 35

Trudeau, Garry B. .... **CLC 12**
See Trudeau, G(arretson) B(eekman)

See AAYA 10; AITN 2
Truffaut, Francois 1932-1984 .. **CLC 20, 101**
See CA 81-84; 113; CANR 34
Trumbo, Dalton 1905-1976 .... **CLC 19**
See CA 21-24R; 69-72; CANR 10; DLB 26
Trumbull, John 1750-1831 .... **NCLC 30**
See DLB 31
Trundlett, Helen B.
See Eliot, T(homas) S(tearns)
Tryon, Thomas 1926-1991 . **CLC 3, 11;DAM POP**
See AITN 1; CA 29-32R; 135; CANR 32, 77; DA3; MTCW 1
Tryon, Tom
See Tryon, Thomas
Ts'ao Hsueh-ch'in 1715(?)-1763 .... **LC 1**
Tsushima, Shuji 1909-1948
See Dazai Osamu
See CA 107
Tsvetaeva (Efron), Marina (Ivanovna) 1892-1941 .... **TCLC 7, 35; PC 14**
See CA 104; 128; CANR 73; MTCW 1, 2
Tuck, Lily 1938- .... **CLC 70**
See CA 139
Tu Fu 712-770 .... **PC 9**
See DAM MULT
Tunis, JohnR(oberts) 1889-1975 ..... **CLC 12**
See CA 61-64; CANR 62; DLB 22, 171; JRDA; MAICYA; SATA 37; SATA-Brief 30
Tuohy, Frank .... **CLC 37**
See Tuohy, John Francis
See DLB 14, 139
Tuohy, John Francis 1925-1999
See Tuohy, Frank
See CA 5-8R; 178; CANR 3, 47
Turco, Lewis (Putnam) 1934- .... **CLC 11, 63**
See CA 13-16R; CAAS 22; CANR 24, 51; DLBY 84
Turgenev, Ivan 1818-1883 ... **NCLC 21; DA; DAB; DAC; DAM MST, NOV; DC 7; SSC 7; WLC**
Turgot, Anne-Robert-Jacques 1727-1781 .... **LC 26**
Turner, Frederick 1943- .... **CLC 48**
See CA 73-76; CAAS 10; CANR 12, 30, 56; DLB 40
Tutu, Desmond M(pilo) 1931- .... **CLC 80; BLC 3; DAM MULT**
See BW 1, 3; CA 125; CANR 67, 81
Tutuola, Amos 1920-1997 ..... **CLC 5, 14, 29; BLC 3; DAM MULT**
See BW 2, 3; CA 9-12R; 159; CANR 27, 66; DA3; DLB 125; MTCW 1, 2
Twain, Mark .... **TCLC 6, 12, 19, 36, 48, 59; SSC 34; WLC**
See Clemens, Samuel Langhorne
See AAYA 20; CLR 58, 60; DLB 11, 12, 23, 64, 74
Tyler, Anne 1941- . **CLC 7, 11, 18, 28, 44, 59, 103; DAM NOV, POP**
See AAYA 18; BEST 89:1; CA 9-12R; CANR 11, 33, 53; CDALBS; DLB 6, 143; DLBY 82; MTCW 1, 2; SATA 7, 90
Tyler, Royall 1757-1826 .... **NCLC 3**
See DLB 37
Tynan, Katharine 1861-1931 .... **TCLC 3**
See CA 104; 167; DLB 153
Tyutchev, Fyodor 1803-1873 .... **NCLC 34**
Tzara, Tristan 1896-1963 ..... **CLC 47; DAM POET; PC 27**
See CA 153; 89-92; MTCW 2
Uhry, Alfred 1936- . **CLC 55; DAM DRAM, POP**
See CA 127; 133; DA3; INT 133
Ulf, Haerved
See Strindberg, (Johan) August
Ulf, Harved
See Strindberg, (Johan) August
Ulibarri, Sabine R(eyes) 1919- .... **CLC 83; DAM MULT; HLCS 2**
See CA 131; CANR 81; DLB 82; HW 1, 2
Unamuno (y Jugo), Miguel de 1864-1936 ... **TCLC 2, 9; DAM MULT, NOV; HLC 2; SSC 11**
See CA 104; 131; CANR 81; DLB 108; HW 1, 2; MTCW 1, 2
Undercliffe, Errol
See Campbell, (John) Ramsey
Underwood, Miles
See Glassco, John
Undset, Sigrid 1882-1949 .... **TCLC 3; DA; DAB; DAC; DAM MST, NOV; WLC**
See CA 104; 129; DA3; MTCW 1, 2
Ungaretti, Giuseppe 1888-1970 .. **CLC 7, 11, 15**
See CA 19-20; 25-28R; CAP 2; DLB 114
Unger, Douglas 1952- .... **CLC 34**
See CA 130
Unsworth, Barry (Forster) 1930- .... **CLC 76**
See CA 25-28R; CANR 30, 54; DLB 194
Updike, John (Hoyer) 1932- . **CLC 1, 2, 3, 5, 7, 9, 13, 15, 23, 34, 43, 70; DA; DAB; DAC; DAM MST, NOV, POET, POP; SSC 13, 27; WLC**
See CA 1-4R; CABS 1; CANR 4, 33, 51; CDALB 1968-1988; DA3; DLB 2, 5, 143; DLBD 3; DLBY 80, 82, 97; MTCW 1, 2
Upshaw, Margaret Mitchell
See Mitchell, Margaret (Munnerlyn)
Upton, Mark
See Sanders, Lawrence
Upward, Allen 1863-1926 .... **TCLC 85**
See CA 117; DLB 36
Urdang, Constance (Henriette) 1922- .. **CLC 47**
See CA 21-24R; CANR 9, 24
Uriel, Henry
See Faust, Frederick (Schiller)
Uris, Leon (Marcus) 1924- .... **CLC 7, 32; DAM NOV, POP**
See AITN 1, 2; BEST 89:2; CA 1-4R; CANR 1, 40, 65; DA3; MTCW 1, 2; SATA 49
Urista, Alberto H. 1947-
See Alurista
See CA 45-48; CANR 2, 32; HLCS 1; HW 1
Urmuz
See Codrescu, Andrei
Urquhart, Guy
See McAlmon, Robert (Menzies)
Urquhart, Jane 1949- .... **CLC 90; DAC**
See CA 113; CANR 32, 68
Usigli, Rodolfo 1905-1979
See CA 131; HLCS 1; HW 1
Ustinov, Peter (Alexander) 1921- ...... **CLC 1**
See AITN 1; CA 13-16R; CANR 25, 51; DLB 13; MTCW 2
U Tam'si, Gerald Felix Tchicaya
See Tchicaya, Gerald Felix
U Tam'si, Tchicaya
See Tchicaya, Gerald Felix
Vachss, Andrew (Henry) 1942- ..... **CLC 106**
See CA 118; CANR 44
Vachss, Andrew H.
See Vachss, Andrew (Henry)
Vaculik, Ludvik 1926- .... **CLC 7**
See CA 53-56; CANR 72
Vaihinger, Hans 1852-1933 .... **TCLC 71**
See CA 116; 166
Valdez, Luis (Miguel) 1940- . **CLC 84; DAM MULT; DC 10; HLC 2**
See CA 101; CANR 32, 81; DLB 122; HW 1
Valenzuela, Luisa 1938- .... **CLC 31, 104; DAM MULT; HLCS 2; SSC 14**
See CA 101; CANR 32, 65; DLB 113; HW 1, 2
Valera y Alcala-Galiano, Juan 1824-1905 ... **TCLC 10**
See CA 106
Valery, (Ambroise) Paul (Toussaint Jules) 1871-1945 .. **TCLC 4, 15; DAM POET; PC 9**
See CA 104; 122; DA3; MTCW 1, 2
Valle-Inclan, Ramon (Maria) del 1866-1936 .... **TCLC 5; DAM MULT; HLC 2**
See CA 106; 153; CANR 80; DLB 134; HW 2
Vallejo, Antonio Buero
See Buero Vallejo, Antonio
Vallejo, Cesar (Abraham) 1892-1938 . **TCLC 3, 56; DAM MULT; HLC 2**
See CA 105; 153; HW 1
Valles, Jules 1832-1885 .... **NCLC 71**
See DLB 123
Vallette, Marguerite Eymery
See Rachilde
Valle Y Pena, Ramon del
See Valle-Inclan, Ramon (Maria) del
Van Ash, Cay 1918- .... **CLC 34**
Vanbrugh, Sir John 1664-1726 .... **LC 21; DAM DRAM**
See DLB 80
Van Campen, Karl
See Campbell, John W(ood, Jr.)
Vance, Gerald
See Silverberg, Robert
Vance, Jack .... **CLC 35**
See Kuttner, Henry; Vance, John Holbrook
See DLB 8
Vance, John Holbrook 1916-
See Queen, Ellery; Vance, Jack
See CA 29-32R; CANR 17, 65; MTCW 1
Van Den Bogarde, Derek Jules Gaspard Ulric Niven 1921-1999
See Bogarde, Dirk
See CA 77-80; 179
Vandenburgh, Jane .... **CLC 59**
See CA 168
Vanderhaeghe, Guy 1951- .... **CLC 41**
See CA 113; CANR 72
van der Post, Laurens (Jan) 1906-1996 .... **CLC 5**
See CA 5-8R; 155; CANR 35; DLB 204
van de Wetering, Janwillem 1931- . **CLC 47**
See CA 49-52; CANR 4, 62
Van Dine, S. S. .... **TCLC 23**
See Wright, Willard Huntington
Van Doren, Carl(Clinton) 1885-1950 . **TCLC 18**
See CA 111; 168
Van Doren, Mark 1894-1972 .... **CLC 6, 10**
See CA 1-4R; 37-40R; CANR 3; DLB 45; MTCW 1, 2
Van Druten, John (William) 1901-1957 .... **TCLC 2**
See CA 104; 161; DLB 10
Van Duyn, Mona (Jane) 1921- ..... **CLC 3, 7, 63, 116; DAM POET**
See CA 9-12R; CANR 7, 38, 60; DLB 5
Van Dyne, Edith
See Baum, L(yman) Frank
van Itallie, Jean-Claude 1936- .... **CLC 3**
See CA 45-48; CAAS 2; CANR 1, 48; DLB 7
van Ostaijen, Paul 1896-1928 .... **TCLC 33**
See CA 163
Van Peebles, Melvin 1932- .... **CLC 2, 20; DAM MULT**
See BW 2, 3; CA 85-88; CANR 27, 67, 82
Vansittart, Peter 1920- .... **CLC 42**

See CA 1-4R; CANR 3, 49
Van Vechten, Carl 1880-1964 .... **CLC 33**
See CA 89-92; DLB 4, 9, 51
Van Vogt, A(lfred) E(lton) 1912- .... **CLC 1**
See CA 21-24R; CANR 28; DLB 8; SATA 14
Varda, Agnes 1928- .... **CLC 16**
See CA 116; 122
Vargas Llosa, (Jorge) Mario (Pedro) 1936- ..... **CLC 3, 6, 9, 10, 15, 31, 42, 85; DA; DAB; DAC; DAM MST, MULT, NOV;HLC 2**
See CA 73-76; CANR 18, 32, 42, 67; DA3; DLB 145; HW 1, 2; MTCW 1, 2
Vasiliu, Gheorghe 1881-1957
See Bacovia, George
See CA 123
Vassa, Gustavus
See Equiano, Olaudah
Vassilikos, Vassilis 1933- .... **CLC 4, 8**
See CA 81-84; CANR 75
Vaughan, Henry 1621-1695 .... **LC 27**
See DLB 131
Vaughn, Stephanie .... **CLC 62**
Vazov, Ivan (Minchov) 1850-1921 ..... **TCLC 25**
See CA 121; 167; DLB 147
Veblen, Thorstein B(unde) 1857-1929 .... **TCLC 31**
See CA 115; 165
Vega, Lope de 1562-1635 ... **LC 23; HLCS 2**
Venison, Alfred
See Pound, Ezra (Weston Loomis)
Verdi, Marie de
See Mencken, H(enry) L(ouis)
Verdu, Matilde
See Cela, Camilo Jose
Verga, Giovanni (Carmelo) 1840-1922 .... **TCLC 3; SSC 21**
See CA 104; 123
Vergil 70B.C.-19B.C. .. **CMLC 9; DA; DAB; DAC; DAM MST, POET; PC 12; WLCS**
See Virgil
See DA3
Verhaeren, Emile (Adolphe Gustave) 1855-1916 .... **TCLC 12**
See CA 109
Verlaine, Paul (Marie) 1844-1896 . **NCLC 2, 51; DAM POET; PC 2**
Verne, Jules (Gabriel) 1828-1905 .. **TCLC 6, 52**
See AAYA 16; CA 110; 131; DA3; DLB 123; JRDA; MAICYA; SATA 21
Very, Jones 1813-1880 .... **NCLC 9**
See DLB 1
Vesaas, Tarjei 1897-1970 .... **CLC 48**
See CA 29-32R
Vialis, Gaston
See Simenon, Georges (Jacques Christian)
Vian, Boris 1920-1959 .... **TCLC 9**
See CA 106; 164; DLB 72; MTCW 2
Viaud, (Louis Marie) Julien 1850-1923
See Loti, Pierre
See CA 107
Vicar, Henry
See Felsen, Henry Gregor
Vicker, Angus
See Felsen, Henry Gregor
Vidal, Gore 1925- ..... **CLC 2, 4, 6, 8, 10, 22, 33, 72; DAM NOV, POP**
See AITN 1; BEST 90:2; CA 5-8R; CANR 13, 45, 65; CDALBS; DA3; DLB 6, 152; INT CANR-13; MTCW 1, 2
Viereck, Peter (Robert Edwin) 1916- .. **CLC 4; PC 27**
See CA 1-4R; CANR 1, 47; DLB 5
Vigny, Alfred (Victor) de 1797-1863 . **NCLC 7; DAM POET; PC 26**
See DLB 119, 192
Vilakazi, Benedict Wallet 1906-1947 . **TCLC 37**
See CA 168
Villa, Jose Garcia 1904-1997 .... **PC 22**
See CA 25-28R; CANR 12
Villarreal, Jose Antonio 1924-
See CA 133; DAM MULT; DLB 82; HLC 2; HW 1
Villaurrutia, Xavier 1903-1950 ..... **TCLC 80**
See HW 1
Villiers de l'Isle Adam, Jean Marie Mathias Philippe Auguste, Comte de 1838-1889 .... **NCLC 3; SSC 14**
See DLB 123
Villon, Francois 1431-1463(?) .... **PC 13**
See DLB 208
Vinci, Leonardo da 1452-1519 .... **LC 12**
Vine, Barbara .... **CLC 50**
See Rendell, Ruth(Barbara)
See BEST 90:4
Vinge, Joan (Carol) D(ennison) 1948- . **CLC 30; SSC 24**
See AAYA 32; CA 93-96; CANR 72; SATA 36
Violis, G.
See Simenon, Georges (Jacques Christian)
Viramontes, Helena Maria 1954-
See CA 159; DLB 122; HLCS 2; HW 2
Virgil 70B.C.-19B.C.
See Vergil
See DLB 211
Visconti, Luchino 1906-1976 .... **CLC 16**
See CA 81-84; 65-68; CANR 39
Vittorini, Elio 1908-1966 .... **CLC 6, 9, 14**
See CA 133; 25-28R
Vivekananda, Swami 1863-1902 ... **TCLC 88**
Vizenor, Gerald Robert 1934- ...... **CLC 103; DAM MULT**
See CA 13-16R; CAAS 22; CANR 5, 21, 44, 67; DLB 175; MTCW 2; NNAL
Vizinczey, Stephen 1933- .... **CLC 40**
See CA 128; INT 128
Vliet, R(ussell) G(ordon) 1929-1984 .... **CLC 22**
See CA 37-40R; 112; CANR 18
Vogau, Boris Andreyevich 1894-1937(?)
See Pilnyak, Boris
See CA 123
Vogel, Paula A(nne) 1951- .... **CLC 76**
See CA 108
Voigt, Cynthia 1942- .... **CLC 30**
See AAYA 3, 30; CA 106; CANR 18, 37, 40; CLR 13, 48; INT CANR-18; JRDA; MAICYA; SATA 48, 79; SATA-Brief 33
Voigt, Ellen Bryant 1943- .... **CLC 54**
See CA 69-72; CANR 11, 29, 55; DLB 120
Voinovich, Vladimir (Nikolaevich) 1932- ..... **CLC 10, 49**
See CA 81-84; CAAS 12; CANR 33, 67; MTCW 1
Vollmann, William T. 1959- . **CLC 89; DAM NOV, POP**
See CA 134; CANR 67; DA3; MTCW 2
Voloshinov, V. N.
See Bakhtin, Mikhail Mikhailovich
Voltaire 1694-1778 .... **LC 14; DA; DAB; DAC; DAM DRAM, MST; SSC 12; WLC**
See DA3
von Aschendrof, BaronIgnatz
See Ford, Ford Madox
von Daeniken, Erich 1935- .... **CLC 30**
See AITN 1; CA 37-40R; CANR 17, 44
von Daniken, Erich
See von Daeniken, Erich
von Heidenstam, (Carl Gustaf) Verner
See Heidenstam, (Carl Gustaf) Verner von
von Heyse, Paul (Johann Ludwig)
See Heyse, Paul (Johann Ludwig von)
von Hofmannsthal, Hugo
See Hofmannsthal, Hugo von
von Horvath, Odon
See Horvath, Oedoen von
von Horvath, Oedoen
See Horvath, Oedoen von
von Liliencron, (Friedrich Adolf Axel) Detlev
See Liliencron, (Friedrich Adolf Axel) Detlev von
Vonnegut, Kurt, Jr. 1922- . **CLC 1, 2, 3, 4, 5, 8, 12, 22, 40, 60, 111; DA; DAB; DAC; DAM MST, NOV, POP; SSC 8; WLC**
See AAYA 6; AITN 1; BEST 90:4; CA 1-4R; CANR 1, 25, 49, 75; CDALB 1968-1988; DA3; DLB 2, 8, 152; DLBD 3; DLBY 80; MTCW 1, 2
Von Rachen, Kurt
See Hubbard, L(afayette) Ron(ald)
von Rezzori (d'Arezzo), Gregor
See Rezzori (d'Arezzo), Gregor von
von Sternberg, Josef
See Sternberg, Josef von
Vorster, Gordon 1924- .... **CLC 34**
See CA 133
Vosce, Trudie
See Ozick, Cynthia
Voznesensky, Andrei (Andreievich) 1933- ... **CLC 1, 15, 57; DAM POET**
See CA 89-92; CANR 37; MTCW 1
Waddington, Miriam 1917- .... **CLC 28**
See CA 21-24R; CANR 12, 30; DLB 68
Wagman, Fredrica 1937- .... **CLC 7**
See CA 97-100; INT 97-100
Wagner, Linda W.
See Wagner-Martin, Linda (C.)
Wagner, Linda Welshimer
See Wagner-Martin, Linda (C.)
Wagner, Richard 1813-1883 .... **NCLC 9**
See DLB 129
Wagner-Martin, Linda (C.) 1936- .. **CLC 50**
See CA 159
Wagoner, David (Russell) 1926- .. **CLC 3, 5, 15**
See CA 1-4R; CAAS 3; CANR 2, 71; DLB 5; SATA 14
Wah, Fred(erick James) 1939- .... **CLC 44**
See CA 107; 141; DLB 60
Wahloo, Per 1926-1975 .... **CLC 7**
See CA 61-64; CANR 73
Wahloo, Peter
See Wahloo, Per
Wain, John (Barrington) 1925-1994 .... **CLC 2, 11, 15, 46**
See CA 5-8R; 145; CAAS 4; CANR 23, 54; CDBLB 1960 to Present; DLB 15, 27, 139, 155; MTCW 1, 2
Wajda, Andrzej 1926- .... **CLC 16**
See CA 102
Wakefield, Dan 1932- .... **CLC 7**
See CA 21-24R; CAAS 7
Wakoski, Diane 1937- .... **CLC 2, 4, 7, 9, 11, 40; DAM POET; PC 15**
See CA 13-16R; CAAS 1; CANR 9, 60; DLB 5; INT CANR-9; MTCW 2
Wakoski-Sherbell, Diane
See Wakoski, Diane
Walcott, Derek (Alton) 1930- ... **CLC 2, 4, 9, 14, 25, 42, 67, 76; BLC 3; DAB; DAC; DAM MST, MULT, POET; DC 7**
See BW 2; CA 89-92; CANR 26, 47, 75, 80; DA3; DLB 117; DLBY 81; MTCW 1, 2
Waldman, Anne(Lesley) 1945- .... **CLC 7**

See CA 37-40R; CAAS 17; CANR 34, 69; DLB 16

Waldo, E. Hunter
See Sturgeon, Theodore (Hamilton)

Waldo, Edward Hamilton
See Sturgeon, Theodore (Hamilton)

Walker, Alice (Malsenior) 1944- .. **CLC 5, 6, 9, 19, 27, 46, 58, 103; BLC 3; DA; DAB; DAC; DAM MST, MULT, NOV, POET, POP; SSC 5; WLCS**
See AAYA 3; BEST 89:4; BW 2, 3; CA 37-40R; CANR 9, 27, 49, 66, 82; CDALB 1968-1988; DA3; DLB 6, 33, 143; INT CANR-27; MTCW 1, 2; SATA 31

Walker, David Harry 1911-1992 ..... **CLC 14**
See CA 1-4R; 137; CANR 1; SATA 8; SATA-Obit 71

Walker, Edward Joseph 1934-
See Walker, Ted
See CA 21-24R; CANR 12, 28, 53

Walker, George F. 1947- . **CLC 44, 61; DAB; DAC; DAM MST**
See CA 103; CANR 21, 43, 59; DLB 60

Walker, Joseph A. 1935- ...... **CLC 19; DAM DRAM, MST**
See BW 1, 3; CA 89-92; CANR 26; DLB 38

Walker, Margaret (Abigail) 1915-1998 . **CLC 1, 6; BLC; DAM MULT; PC 20**
See BW 2, 3; CA 73-76; 172; CANR 26, 54, 76; DLB 76, 152; MTCW 1, 2

Walker, Ted .... **CLC 13**
See Walker, Edward Joseph
See DLB 40

Wallace, David Foster 1962- ... **CLC 50, 114**
See CA 132; CANR 59; DA3; MTCW 2

Wallace, Dexter
See Masters, Edgar Lee

Wallace, (Richard Horatio)Edgar 1875-1932 .... **TCLC 57**
See CA 115; DLB 70

Wallace, Irving 1916-1990 .... **CLC 7, 13; DAM NOV, POP**
See AITN 1; CA 1-4R; 132; CAAS 1; CANR 1, 27; INT CANR-27; MTCW 1, 2

Wallant, Edward Lewis 1926-1962 .. **CLC 5, 10**
See CA 1-4R; CANR 22; DLB 2, 28, 143; MTCW 1, 2

Wallas, Graham 1858-1932 .... **TCLC 91**

Walley, Byron
See Card, Orson Scott

Walpole, Horace 1717-1797 .... **LC 49**
See DLB 39, 104

Walpole, Hugh (Seymour) 1884-1941 . **TCLC 5**
See CA 104; 165; DLB 34; MTCW 2

Walser, Martin 1927- .... **CLC 27**
See CA 57-60; CANR 8, 46; DLB 75, 124

Walser, Robert 1878-1956 .... **TCLC 18;SSC 20**
See CA 118; 165; DLB 66

Walsh, Jill Paton .... **CLC 35**
See Paton Walsh, Gillian
See AAYA 11; CLR 2; DLB 161; SAAS 3

Walter, Villiam Christian
See Andersen, Hans Christian

Wambaugh, Joseph (Aloysius, Jr.) 1937- .... **CLC 3, 18; DAM NOV, POP**
See AITN 1; BEST 89:3; CA 33-36R; CANR 42, 65; DA3; DLB 6; DLBY 83; MTCW 1, 2

Wang Wei 699(?)-761(?) .... **PC 18**

Ward, Arthur Henry Sarsfield 1883-1959
See Rohmer, Sax
See CA 108; 173

Ward, Douglas Turner 1930- .... **CLC 19**
See BW 1; CA 81-84; CANR 27; DLB 7, 38

Ward, E. D.
See Lucas, E(dward) V(errall)

Ward, Mary Augusta
See Ward, Mrs. Humphry

Ward, Mrs.Humphry 1851-1920 .. **TCLC 55**
See DLB 18

Ward, Peter
See Faust, Frederick (Schiller)

Warhol, Andy 1928(?)-1987 .... **CLC 20**
See AAYA 12; BEST 89:4; CA 89-92; 121; CANR 34

Warner, Francis (Robert lePlastrier) 1937- .... **CLC 14**
See CA 53-56; CANR 11

Warner, Marina 1946- .... **CLC 59**
See CA 65-68; CANR 21, 55; DLB 194

Warner, Rex(Ernest) 1905-1986 ...... **CLC 45**
See CA 89-92; 119; DLB 15

Warner, Susan (Bogert) 1819-1885 ... **NCLC 31**
See DLB 3, 42

Warner, Sylvia (Constance) Ashton
See Ashton-Warner, Sylvia (Constance)

Warner, Sylvia Townsend 1893-1978 ... **CLC 7, 19; SSC 23**
See CA 61-64; 77-80; CANR 16, 60; DLB 34, 139; MTCW 1, 2

Warren, Mercy Otis 1728-1814 .... **NCLC 13**
See DLB 31, 200

Warren, Robert Penn 1905-1989 . **CLC 1, 4, 6, 8, 10, 13, 18, 39, 53, 59; DA; DAB; DAC; DAM MST, NOV, POET; SSC 4;WLC**
See AITN 1; CA 13-16R; 129; CANR 10, 47;CDALB 1968-1988; DA3; DLB 2, 48, 152; DLBY 80, 89; INT CANR-10; MTCW 1, 2; SATA 46; SATA-Obit 63

Warshofsky, Isaac
See Singer, Isaac Bashevis

Warton, Thomas 1728-1790 ..... **LC 15;DAM POET**
See DLB 104, 109

Waruk, Kona
See Harris, (Theodore) Wilson

Warung, Price 1855-1911 .... **TCLC 45**

Warwick, Jarvis
See Garner, Hugh

Washington, Alex
See Harris, Mark

Washington, Booker T(aliaferro) 1856-1915 .... **TCLC 10; BLC 3; DAM MULT**
See BW 1; CA 114; 125; DA3; SATA 28

Washington, George 1732-1799 .... **LC 25**
See DLB 31

Wassermann, (Karl)Jakob 1873-1934 .... **TCLC 6**
See CA 104; 163; DLB 66

Wasserstein, Wendy 1950- . **CLC 32, 59, 90; DAM DRAM; DC 4**
See CA 121; 129; CABS 3; CANR 53, 75; DA3; INT 129; MTCW 2; SATA 94

Waterhouse, Keith(Spencer) 1929- . **CLC 47**
See CA 5-8R; CANR 38, 67; DLB 13, 15; MTCW 1, 2

Waters, Frank(Joseph) 1902-1995 .. **CLC 88**
See CA 5-8R; 149; CAAS 13; CANR 3, 18, 63; DLB 212; DLBY 86

Waters, Roger 1944- .... **CLC 35**

Watkins, Frances Ellen
See Harper, Frances Ellen Watkins

Watkins, Gerrold
See Malzberg, Barry N(athaniel)

Watkins, Gloria 1955(?)-
See hooks, bell
See BW 2; CA 143; MTCW 2

Watkins, Paul 1964- .... **CLC 55**
See CA 132; CANR 62

Watkins, Vernon Phillips 1906-1967 .... **CLC 43**
See CA 9-10; 25-28R; CAP 1; DLB 20

Watson, Irving S.
See Mencken, H(enry) L(ouis)

Watson, John H.
See Farmer, Philip Jose

Watson, Richard F.
See Silverberg, Robert

Waugh, Auberon (Alexander) 1939- . **CLC 7**
See CA 45-48; CANR 6, 22; DLB 14, 194

Waugh, Evelyn (Arthur St. John) 1903-1966 ... **CLC 1, 3, 8, 13, 19, 27, 44, 107; DA; DAB; DAC; DAM MST, NOV, POP; WLC**
See CA 85-88; 25-28R; CANR 22; CDBLB 1914-1945; DA3; DLB 15, 162, 195; MTCW 1, 2

Waugh, Harriet 1944- .... **CLC 6**
See CA 85-88; CANR 22

Ways, C. R.
See Blount, Roy (Alton), Jr.

Waystaff, Simon
See Swift, Jonathan

Webb, (Martha) Beatrice (Potter) 1858-1943 .... **TCLC 22**
See Potter, (Helen) Beatrix
See CA 117; DLB 190

Webb, Charles (Richard) 1939- .... **CLC 7**
See CA 25-28R

Webb, James H(enry), Jr. 1946- ..... **CLC 22**
See CA 81-84

Webb, Mary (Gladys Meredith) 1881-1927 .... **TCLC 24**
See CA 123; DLB 34

Webb, Mrs. Sidney
See Webb, (Martha) Beatrice (Potter)

Webb, Phyllis 1927- .... **CLC 18**
See CA 104; CANR 23; DLB 53

Webb, Sidney (James) 1859-1947 . **TCLC 22**
See CA 117; 163; DLB 190

Webber, Andrew Lloyd .... **CLC 21**
See Lloyd Webber, Andrew

Weber, Lenora Mattingly 1895-1971 ... **CLC 12**
See CA 19-20; 29-32R; CAP 1; SATA 2; SATA-Obit 26

Weber, Max 1864-1920 .... **TCLC 69**
See CA 109

Webster, John 1579(?)-1634(?) . **LC 33; DA; DAB; DAC; DAM DRAM, MST; DC 2; WLC**
See CDBLB Before 1660; DLB 58

Webster, Noah 1758-1843 .... **NCLC 30**
See DLB 1, 37, 42, 43, 73

Wedekind, (Benjamin) Frank(lin) 1864-1918 .... **TCLC 7; DAM DRAM**
See CA 104; 153; DLB 118

Weidman, Jerome 1913-1998 .... **CLC 7**
See AITN 2; CA 1-4R; 171; CANR 1; DLB 28

Weil, Simone (Adolphine) 1909-1943 . **TCLC 23**
See CA 117; 159; MTCW 2

Weininger, Otto 1880-1903 .... **TCLC 84**

Weinstein, Nathan
See West, Nathanael

Weinstein, Nathan von Wallenstein
See West, Nathanael

Weir, Peter (Lindsay) 1944- .... **CLC 20**
See CA 113; 123

Weiss, Peter (Ulrich) 1916-1982 . **CLC 3, 15, 51; DAM DRAM**
See CA 45-48; 106; CANR 3; DLB 69, 124

Weiss, Theodore (Russell) 1916- .. **CLC 3, 8, 14**
See CA 9-12R; CAAS 2; CANR 46; DLB 5

Welch, (Maurice) Denton 1915-1948 . **TCLC 22**
See CA 121; 148

Welch, James 1940- ... **CLC 6, 14, 52; DAM MULT, POP**
See CA 85-88; CANR 42, 66; DLB 175; NNAL

Weldon, Fay 1931- . **CLC 6, 9, 11, 19, 36, 59, 122; DAM POP**
See CA 21-24R; CANR 16, 46, 63; CDBLB 1960 to Present; DLB 14, 194; INT CANR-16; MTCW 1, 2

Wellek, Rene 1903-1995 .... **CLC 28**
See CA 5-8R; 150; CAAS 7; CANR 8; DLB 63; INT CANR-8

Weller, Michael 1942- .... **CLC 10, 53**
See CA 85-88

Weller, Paul 1958- .... **CLC 26**

Wellershoff, Dieter 1925- .... **CLC 46**
See CA 89-92; CANR 16, 37

Welles, (George) Orson 1915-1985 . **CLC 20, 80**
See CA 93-96; 117

Wellman, John McDowell 1945-
See Wellman, Mac
See CA 166

Wellman, Mac 1945- .... **CLC 65**
See Wellman, John McDowell; Wellman, John McDowell

Wellman, ManlyWade 1903-1986 ... **CLC 49**
See CA 1-4R; 118; CANR 6, 16, 44; SATA 6; SATA-Obit 47

Wells, Carolyn 1869(?)-1942 .... **TCLC 35**
See CA 113; DLB 11

Wells, H(erbert) G(eorge) 1866-1946 . **TCLC 6, 12, 19; DA; DAB; DAC; DAM MST, NOV; SSC 6; WLC**
See AAYA 18; CA 110; 121; CDBLB 1914-1945; DA3; DLB 34, 70, 156, 178; MTCW 1, 2; SATA 20

Wells, Rosemary 1943- .... **CLC 12**
See AAYA 13; CA 85-88; CANR 48; CLR 16; MAICYA; SAAS 1; SATA 18, 69

Welty, Eudora 1909- .... **CLC 1, 2, 5, 14, 22, 33, 105; DA; DAB; DAC; DAM MST, NOV; SSC 1, 27; WLC**
See CA 9-12R; CABS 1; CANR 32, 65; CDALB 1941-1968; DA3; DLB 2, 102, 143; DLBD 12; DLBY 87; MTCW 1, 2

Wen I-to 1899-1946 .... **TCLC 28**

Wentworth, Robert
See Hamilton, Edmond

Werfel, Franz (Viktor) 1890-1945 .. **TCLC 8**
See CA 104; 161; DLB 81, 124

Wergeland, Henrik Arnold 1808-1845 .... **NCLC 5**

Wersba, Barbara 1932- .... **CLC 30**
See AAYA 2, 30; CA 29-32R; CANR 16, 38; CLR 3; DLB 52; JRDA; MAICYA; SAAS 2; SATA 1, 58; SATA-Essay 103

Wertmueller, Lina 1928- .... **CLC 16**
See CA 97-100; CANR 39, 78

Wescott, Glenway 1901-1987 .. **CLC 13;SSC 35**
See CA 13-16R; 121; CANR 23, 70; DLB 4, 9, 102

Wesker, Arnold 1932- .. **CLC 3, 5, 42; DAB; DAM DRAM**
See CA 1-4R; CAAS 7; CANR 1, 33; CDBLB 1960 to Present; DLB 13; MTCW 1

Wesley, Richard (Errol) 1945- .... **CLC 7**
See BW 1; CA 57-60; CANR 27; DLB 38

Wessel, Johan Herman 1742-1785 .... **LC 7**

West, Anthony (Panther) 1914-1987 .... **CLC 50**
See CA 45-48; 124; CANR 3, 19; DLB 15

West, C. P.
See Wodehouse, P(elham) G(renville)

West, (Mary) Jessamyn 1902-1984 .. **CLC 7, 17**
See CA 9-12R; 112; CANR 27; DLB 6; DLBY 84; MTCW 1, 2; SATA-Obit 37

West, Morris L(anglo) 1916- .... **CLC 6, 33**
See CA 5-8R; CANR 24, 49, 64; MTCW 1, 2

West, Nathanael 1903-1940 ..... **TCLC 1, 14, 44; SSC 16**
See CA 104; 125; CDALB 1929-1941; DA3; DLB 4, 9, 28; MTCW 1, 2

West, Owen
See Koontz, Dean R(ay)

West, Paul 1930- .... **CLC 7, 14, 96**
See CA 13-16R; CAAS 7; CANR 22, 53, 76; DLB 14; INT CANR-22; MTCW 2

West, Rebecca 1892-1983 .. **CLC 7, 9, 31, 50**
See CA 5-8R; 109; CANR 19; DLB 36; DLBY 83; MTCW 1, 2

Westall, Robert (Atkinson) 1929-1993 . **CLC 17**
See AAYA 12; CA 69-72; 141; CANR 18, 68; CLR 13; JRDA; MAICYA; SAAS 2; SATA 23, 69; SATA-Obit 75

Westermarck, Edward 1862-1939 ..... **TCLC 87**

Westlake, Donald E(dwin) 1933- ..... **CLC 7, 33; DAM POP**
See CA 17-20R; CAAS 13; CANR 16, 44, 65; INT CANR-16; MTCW 2

Westmacott, Mary
See Christie, Agatha (Mary Clarissa)

Weston, Allen
See Norton, Andre

Wetcheek, J. L.
See Feuchtwanger, Lion

Wetering, Janwillem van de
See van de Wetering, Janwillem

Wetherald, Agnes Ethelwyn 1857-1940 .... **TCLC 81**
See DLB 99

Wetherell, Elizabeth
See Warner, Susan (Bogert)

Whale, James 1889-1957 .... **TCLC 63**

Whalen, Philip 1923- .... **CLC 6, 29**
See CA 9-12R; CANR 5, 39; DLB 16

Wharton, Edith (Newbold Jones) 1862-1937 ... **TCLC 3, 9, 27, 53; DA; DAB; DAC; DAM MST, NOV; SSC 6; WLC**
See AAYA 25; CA 104; 132; CDALB 1865-1917; DA3; DLB 4, 9, 12, 78, 189; DLBD 13; MTCW 1, 2

Wharton, James
See Mencken, H(enry) L(ouis)

Wharton, William (a pseudonym) . **CLC 18, 37**
See CA 93-96; DLBY 80; INT 93-96

Wheatley (Peters), Phillis 1754(?)-1784 .. **LC 3, 50; BLC 3; DA; DAC; DAM MST, MULT, POET; PC 3; WLC**
See CDALB 1640-1865; DA3; DLB 31, 50

Wheelock, JohnHall 1886-1978 .... **CLC 14**
See CA 13-16R; 77-80; CANR 14; DLB 45

White, E(lwyn) B(rooks) 1899-1985 ..... **CLC 10, 34, 39; DAM POP**
See AITN 2; CA 13-16R; 116; CANR 16, 37; CDALBS; CLR 1, 21; DA3; DLB 11, 22; MAICYA; MTCW 1, 2; SATA 2, 29, 100; SATA-Obit 44

White, Edmund (Valentine III) 1940- . **CLC 27, 110; DAM POP**
See AAYA 7; CA 45-48; CANR 3, 19, 36, 62; DA3; MTCW 1, 2

White, Patrick (Victor Martindale) 1912-1990 . **CLC 3, 4, 5, 7, 9, 18, 65, 69**
See CA 81-84; 132; CANR 43; MTCW 1

White, Phyllis Dorothy James 1920-
See James, P. D.
See CA 21-24R; CANR 17, 43, 65; DAM POP; DA3; MTCW 1, 2

White, T(erence) H(anbury) 1906-1964 .... **CLC 30**
See AAYA 22; CA 73-76; CANR 37; DLB 160; JRDA; MAICYA; SATA 12

White, Terence deVere 1912-1994 ... **CLC 49**
See CA 49-52; 145; CANR 3

White, Walter
See White, Walter F(rancis)
See BLC; DAM MULT

White, Walter F(rancis) 1893-1955 ... **TCLC 15**
See White, Walter
See BW 1; CA 115; 124; DLB 51

White, William Hale 1831-1913
See Rutherford, Mark
See CA 121

Whitehead, AlfredNorth 1861-1947 .. **TCLC 97**
See CA 117; 165; DLB 100

Whitehead, E(dward) A(nthony) 1933- .... **CLC 5**
See CA 65-68; CANR 58

Whitemore, Hugh (John) 1936- ...... **CLC 37**
See CA 132; CANR 77; INT 132

Whitman, Sarah Helen(Power) 1803-1878 .. **NCLC 19**
See DLB 1

Whitman, Walt(er) 1819-1892 . **NCLC 4, 31, 81; DA; DAB; DAC; DAM MST, POET; PC 3; WLC**
See CDALB 1640-1865; DA3; DLB 3, 64; SATA 20

Whitney, Phyllis A(yame) 1903- .... **CLC 42; DAM POP**
See AITN 2; BEST 90:3; CA 1-4R; CANR 3, 25, 38, 60; CLR 59; DA3; JRDA; MAICYA; MTCW 2; SATA 1, 30

Whittemore, (Edward) Reed(Jr.) 1919- .... **CLC 4**
See CA 9-12R; CAAS 8; CANR 4; DLB 5

Whittier, John Greenleaf 1807-1892 . **NCLC 8, 59**
See DLB 1

Whittlebot, Hernia
See Coward, Noel (Peirce)

Wicker, Thomas Grey 1926-
See Wicker, Tom
See CA 65-68; CANR 21, 46

Wicker, Tom .... **CLC 7**
See Wicker, Thomas Grey

Wideman, John Edgar 1941- ..... **CLC 5, 34, 36, 67, 122; BLC 3; DAM MULT**
See BW 2, 3; CA 85-88; CANR 14, 42, 67; DLB 33, 143; MTCW 2

Wiebe, Rudy (Henry) 1934- . **CLC 6, 11, 14; DAC; DAM MST**
See CA 37-40R; CANR 42, 67; DLB 60

Wieland, Christoph Martin 1733-1813 .... **NCLC 17**
See DLB 97

Wiene, Robert 1881-1938 .... **TCLC 56**

Wieners, John 1934- .... **CLC 7**
See CA 13-16R; DLB 16

Wiesel, Elie(zer) 1928- ..... **CLC 3, 5, 11, 37; DA; DAB; DAC; DAM MST, NOV; WLCS**
See AAYA 7; AITN 1; CA 5-8R; CAAS 4; CANR 8, 40, 65; CDALBS; DA3; DLB 83; DLBY 87; INT CANR-8; MTCW 1, 2; SATA 56

Wiggins, Marianne 1947- .... **CLC 57**
See BEST 89:3; CA 130; CANR 60

Wight, James Alfred 1916-1995
See Herriot, James
See CA 77-80; SATA 55; SATA-Brief 44

Wilbur, Richard (Purdy) 1921- ... **CLC 3, 6,**

9, 14, 53, 110; DA; DAB; DAC; DAM MST, POET
See CA 1-4R; CABS 2; CANR 2, 29, 76; CDALBS; DLB 5, 169; INT CANR-29; MTCW 1, 2; SATA 9, 108
Wild, Peter 1940- .... **CLC 14**
See CA 37-40R; DLB 5
Wilde, Oscar 1854(?)-1900 .. **TCLC 1, 8, 23, 41; DA; DAB; DAC; DAM DRAM, MST, NOV; SSC 11; WLC**
See CA 104; 119; CDBLB 1890-1914; DA3; DLB 10, 19, 34, 57, 141, 156, 190; SATA 24
Wilder, Billy .... **CLC 20**
See Wilder, Samuel
See DLB 26
Wilder, Samuel 1906-
See Wilder, Billy
See CA 89-92
Wilder, Thornton (Niven) 1897-1975 ... **CLC 1, 5, 6, 10, 15, 35, 82; DA; DAB; DAC; DAM DRAM, MST, NOV; DC 1; WLC**
See AAYA 29; AITN 2; CA 13-16R; 61-64; CANR 40; CDALBS; DA3; DLB 4, 7, 9; DLBY 97; MTCW 1, 2
Wilding, Michael 1942- .... **CLC 73**
See CA 104; CANR 24, 49
Wiley, Richard 1944- .... **CLC 44**
See CA 121; 129; CANR 71
Wilhelm, Kate .... **CLC 7**
See Wilhelm, KatieGertrude
See AAYA 20; CAAS 5; DLB 8; INT CANR-17
Wilhelm, Katie Gertrude 1928-
See Wilhelm, Kate
See CA 37-40R; CANR 17, 36, 60; MTCW 1
Wilkins, Mary
See Freeman, Mary E(leanor) Wilkins
Willard, Nancy 1936- .... **CLC 7, 37**
See CA 89-92; CANR 10, 39, 68; CLR 5; DLB 5, 52; MAICYA; MTCW 1; SATA 37, 71; SATA-Brief 30
William of Ockham 1285-1347 .... **CMLC 32**
Williams, BenAmes 1889-1953 ..... **TCLC 89**
See DLB 102
Williams, C(harles) K(enneth) 1936- ... **CLC 33, 56; DAM POET**
See CA 37-40R; CAAS 26; CANR 57; DLB 5
Williams, Charles
See Collier, James L(incoln)
Williams, Charles (Walter Stansby) 1886-1945 .... **TCLC 1, 11**
See CA 104; 163; DLB 100, 153
Williams, (George) Emlyn 1905-1987 .. **CLC 15; DAM DRAM**
See CA 104; 123; CANR 36; DLB 10, 77; MTCW 1
Williams, Hank 1923-1953 .... **TCLC 81**
Williams, Hugo 1942- .... **CLC 42**
See CA 17-20R; CANR 45; DLB 40
Williams, J. Walker
See Wodehouse, P(elham) G(renville)
Williams, John A(lfred) 1925- ... **CLC 5, 13; BLC 3; DAM MULT**
See BW 2, 3; CA 53-56; CAAS 3; CANR 6, 26, 51; DLB 2, 33; INT CANR-6
Williams, Jonathan (Chamberlain) 1929- ... **CLC 13**
See CA 9-12R; CAAS 12; CANR 8; DLB 5
Williams, Joy 1944- .... **CLC 31**
See CA 41-44R; CANR 22, 48
Williams, Norman 1952- .... **CLC 39**
See CA 118
Williams, Sherley Anne 1944- .... **CLC 89; BLC 3; DAM MULT, POET**
See BW 2, 3; CA 73-76; CANR 25, 82; DLB 41; INT CANR-25; SATA 78
Williams, Shirley
See Williams, Sherley Anne
Williams, Tennessee 1911-1983 . **CLC 1, 2, 5, 7, 8, 11, 15, 19, 30, 39, 45, 71, 111; DA; DAB; DAC; DAM DRAM, MST; DC 4;WLC**
See AAYA 31; AITN 1, 2; CA 5-8R; 108; CABS 3; CANR 31; CDALB 1941-1968; DA3; DLB 7; DLBD 4; DLBY 83; MTCW 1, 2
Williams, Thomas (Alonzo) 1926-1990 . **CLC 14**
See CA 1-4R; 132; CANR 2
Williams, William C.
See Williams, William Carlos
Williams, William Carlos 1883-1963 ... **CLC 1, 2, 5, 9, 13, 22, 42, 67; DA; DAB; DAC; DAM MST, POET; PC 7; SSC 31**
See CA 89-92; CANR 34; CDALB 1917-1929; DA3; DLB 4, 16, 54, 86; MTCW 1, 2
Williamson, David (Keith) 1942- .... **CLC 56**
See CA 103; CANR 41
Williamson, Ellen Douglas 1905-1984
See Douglas, Ellen
See CA 17-20R; 114; CANR 39
Williamson, Jack .... **CLC 29**
See Williamson, John Stewart
See CAAS 8; DLB 8
Williamson, John Stewart 1908-
See Williamson, Jack
See CA 17-20R; CANR 23, 70
Willie, Frederick
See Lovecraft, H(oward) P(hillips)
Willingham, Calder (Baynard, Jr.) 1922-1995 .... **CLC 5, 51**
See CA 5-8R; 147; CANR 3; DLB 2, 44; MTCW 1
Willis, Charles
See Clarke, Arthur C(harles)
Willis, Fingal O'Flahertie
See Wilde, Oscar
Willy
See Colette, (Sidonie-Gabrielle)
Willy, Colette
See Colette, (Sidonie-Gabrielle)
Wilson, A(ndrew) N(orman) 1950- . **CLC 33**
See CA 112; 122; DLB 14, 155, 194; MTCW 2
Wilson, Angus (Frank Johnstone) 1913-1991 .... **CLC 2, 3, 5, 25, 34; SSC 21**
See CA 5-8R; 134; CANR 21; DLB 15, 139, 155; MTCW 1, 2
Wilson, August 1945- . **CLC 39, 50, 63, 118; BLC 3; DA; DAB; DAC; DAM DRAM, MST, MULT; DC 2; WLCS**
See AAYA 16; BW 2, 3; CA 115; 122; CANR 42, 54, 76; DA3; MTCW 1, 2
Wilson, Brian 1942- .... **CLC 12**
Wilson, Colin 1931- .... **CLC 3, 14**
See CA 1-4R; CAAS 5; CANR 1, 22, 33, 77; DLB 14, 194; MTCW 1
Wilson, Dirk
See Pohl, Frederik
Wilson, Edmund 1895-1972 . **CLC 1, 2, 3, 8, 24**
See CA 1-4R; 37-40R; CANR 1, 46; DLB 63; MTCW 1, 2
Wilson, Ethel Davis (Bryant) 1888(?)-1980 . **CLC 13; DAC; DAM POET**
See CA 102; DLB 68; MTCW 1
Wilson, John 1785-1854 .... **NCLC 5**
Wilson, John (Anthony) Burgess 1917-1993
See Burgess, Anthony
See CA 1-4R; 143; CANR 2, 46; DAC; DAM NOV; DA3; MTCW 1, 2
Wilson, Lanford 1937- .... **CLC 7, 14, 36; DAM DRAM**
See CA 17-20R; CABS 3; CANR 45; DLB 7
Wilson, Robert M. 1944- .... **CLC 7, 9**
See CA 49-52; CANR 2, 41; MTCW 1
Wilson, Robert McLiam 1964- .... **CLC 59**
See CA 132
Wilson, Sloan 1920- .... **CLC 32**
See CA 1-4R; CANR 1, 44
Wilson, Snoo 1948- .... **CLC 33**
See CA 69-72
Wilson, William S(mith) 1932- .... **CLC 49**
See CA 81-84
Wilson, (Thomas) Woodrow 1856-1924 .... **TCLC 79**
See CA 166; DLB 47
Winchilsea, Anne (Kingsmill) Finch Counte 1661-1720
See Finch, Anne
Windham, Basil
See Wodehouse, P(elham) G(renville)
Wingrove, David (John) 1954- .... **CLC 68**
See CA 133
Winnemucca, Sarah 1844-1891 .... **NCLC 79**
Winstanley, Gerrard 1609-1676 .... **LC 52**
Wintergreen, Jane
See Duncan, Sara Jeannette
Winters, Janet Lewis .... **CLC 41**
See Lewis, Janet
See DLBY 87
Winters, (Arthur) Yvor 1900-1968 .. **CLC 4, 8, 32**
See CA 11-12; 25-28R; CAP 1; DLB 48; MTCW 1
Winterson, Jeanette 1959- .... **CLC 64;DAM POP**
See CA 136; CANR 58; DA3; DLB 207; MTCW 2
Winthrop, John 1588-1649 .... **LC 31**
See DLB 24, 30
Wirth, Louis 1897-1952 .... **TCLC 92**
Wiseman, Frederick 1930- .... **CLC 20**
See CA 159
Wister, Owen 1860-1938 .... **TCLC 21**
See CA 108; 162; DLB 9, 78, 186; SATA 62
Witkacy
See Witkiewicz, Stanislaw Ignacy
Witkiewicz, Stanislaw Ignacy 1885-1939 ..... **TCLC 8**
See CA 105; 162
Wittgenstein, Ludwig (Josef Johann) 1889-1951 .... **TCLC 59**
See CA 113; 164; MTCW 2
Wittig, Monique 1935(?)- .... **CLC 22**
See CA 116; 135; DLB 83
Wittlin, Jozef 1896-1976 .... **CLC 25**
See CA 49-52; 65-68; CANR 3
Wodehouse, P(elham) G(renville) 1881-1975 . **CLC 1, 2, 5, 10, 22; DAB; DAC; DAM NOV; SSC 2**
See AITN 2; CA 45-48; 57-60; CANR 3, 33; CDBLB 1914-1945; DA3; DLB 34, 162; MTCW 1, 2; SATA 22
Woiwode, L.
See Woiwode, Larry (Alfred)
Woiwode, Larry (Alfred) 1941- .. **CLC 6, 10**
See CA 73-76; CANR 16; DLB 6; INT CANR-16
Wojciechowska, Maia (Teresa) 1927- .. **CLC 26**
See AAYA 8; CA 9-12R; CANR 4, 41; CLR 1; JRDA; MAICYA; SAAS 1; SATA 1, 28, 83; SATA-Essay 104
Wolf, Christa 1929- .... **CLC 14, 29, 58**
See CA 85-88; CANR 45; DLB 75; MTCW 1
Wolfe, Gene (Rodman) 1931- . **CLC 25;DAM POP**

See CA 57-60; CAAS 9; CANR 6, 32, 60; DLB 8; MTCW 2
Wolfe, George C. 1954- .... **CLC 49; BLCS**
See CA 149
Wolfe, Thomas (Clayton) 1900-1938 . **TCLC 4, 13, 29, 61; DA; DAB; DAC; DAM MST, NOV; SSC 33; WLC**
See CA 104; 132; CDALB 1929-1941; DA3; DLB 9, 102; DLBD 2, 16; DLBY 85, 97; MTCW 1, 2
Wolfe, Thomas Kennerly, Jr. 1930-
See Wolfe, Tom
See CA 13-16R; CANR 9, 33, 70; DAM POP; DA3; DLB 185; INT CANR-9; MTCW 1, 2
Wolfe, Tom .... **CLC 1, 2, 9, 15, 35, 51**
See Wolfe, Thomas Kennerly, Jr.
See AAYA 8; AITN 2; BEST 89:1; DLB 152
Wolff, Geoffrey (Ansell) 1937- .... **CLC 41**
See CA 29-32R; CANR 29, 43, 78
Wolff, Sonia
See Levitin, Sonia (Wolff)
Wolff, Tobias (Jonathan Ansell) 1945- . **CLC 39, 64**
See AAYA 16; BEST 90:2; CA 114; 117; CAAS 22; CANR 54, 76; DA3; DLB 130; INT 117; MTCW 2
Wolfram von Eschenbach c. 1170-c.1220 .... **CMLC 5**
See DLB 138
Wolitzer, Hilma 1930- .... **CLC 17**
See CA 65-68; CANR 18, 40; INT CANR-18; SATA 31
Wollstonecraft, Mary 1759-1797 ... **LC 5, 50**
See CDBLB 1789-1832; DLB 39, 104, 158
Wonder, Stevie .... **CLC 12**
See Morris, Steveland Judkins
Wong, Jade Snow 1922- .... **CLC 17**
See CA 109
Woodberry, GeorgeEdward 1855-1930 .... **TCLC 73**
See CA 165; DLB 71, 103
Woodcott, Keith
See Brunner, John (Kilian Houston)
Woodruff, Robert W.
See Mencken, H(enry) L(ouis)
Woolf, (Adeline) Virginia 1882-1941 . **TCLC 1, 5, 20, 43, 56; DA; DAB; DAC; DAM MST, NOV; SSC 7; WLC**
See Woolf, Virginia Adeline
See CA 104; 130; CANR 64; CDBLB 1914-1945; DA3; DLB 36, 100, 162; DLBD 10; MTCW 1
Woolf, Virginia Adeline
See Woolf, (Adeline) Virginia
See MTCW 2
Woollcott, Alexander (Humphreys) 1887-1943 .... **TCLC 5**
See CA 105; 161; DLB 29
Woolrich,Cornell 1903-1968 .... **CLC 77**
See Hopley-Woolrich, Cornell George
Wordsworth, Dorothy 1771-1855 . **NCLC 25**
See DLB 107
Wordsworth, William 1770-1850 . **NCLC 12, 38; DA; DAB; DAC; DAM MST, POET; PC 4; WLC**
See CDBLB 1789-1832; DA3; DLB 93, 107
Wouk, Herman 1915- .. **CLC 1, 9, 38; DAM NOV, POP**
See CA 5-8R; CANR 6, 33, 67; CDALBS; DA3; DLBY 82; INT CANR-6; MTCW 1, 2
Wright, Charles (Penzel, Jr.) 1935- . **CLC 6, 13, 28, 119**
See CA 29-32R; CAAS 7; CANR 23, 36, 62; DLB 165; DLBY 82; MTCW 1, 2
Wright, Charles Stevenson 1932- .. **CLC 49; BLC 3; DAM MULT, POET**
See BW 1; CA 9-12R; CANR 26; DLB 33
Wright, Frances 1795-1852 .... **NCLC 74**
See DLB 73
Wright, Frank Lloyd 1867-1959 .. **TCLC 95**
See CA 174
Wright, Jack R.
See Harris, Mark
Wright, James (Arlington) 1927-1980 . **CLC 3, 5, 10, 28; DAM POET**
See AITN 2; CA 49-52; 97-100; CANR 4, 34, 64; CDALBS; DLB 5, 169; MTCW 1, 2
Wright, Judith (Arandell) 1915- .... **CLC 11, 53; PC 14**
See CA 13-16R; CANR 31, 76; MTCW 1, 2; SATA 14
Wright, L(aurali) R. 1939- .... **CLC 44**
See CA 138
Wright, Richard (Nathaniel) 1908-1960 ...... **CLC 1, 3, 4, 9, 14, 21, 48, 74; BLC 3; DA; DAB; DAC; DAM MST, MULT, NOV; SSC 2; WLC**
See AAYA 5; BW 1; CA 108; CANR 64;CDALB 1929-1941; DA3; DLB 76, 102; DLBD 2; MTCW 1, 2
Wright, Richard B(ruce) 1937- .... **CLC 6**
See CA 85-88; DLB 53
Wright, Rick 1945- .... **CLC 35**
Wright, Rowland
See Wells, Carolyn
Wright, Stephen 1946- .... **CLC 33**
Wright, Willard Huntington 1888-1939
See Van Dine, S. S.
See CA 115; DLBD 16
Wright, William 1930- .... **CLC 44**
See CA 53-56; CANR 7, 23
Wroth, LadyMary 1587-1653(?) .... **LC 30**
See DLB 121
Wu Ch'eng-en 1500(?)-1582(?) .... **LC 7**
Wu Ching-tzu 1701-1754 .... **LC 2**
Wurlitzer, Rudolph 1938(?)- ... **CLC 2, 4, 15**
See CA 85-88; DLB 173
Wyatt, Thomas c. 1503-1542 .... **PC 27**
See DLB 132
Wycherley, William 1641-1715 ..... **LC 8, 21; DAM DRAM**
See CDBLB 1660-1789; DLB 80
Wylie, Elinor (Morton Hoyt) 1885-1928 ...... **TCLC 8; PC 23**
See CA 105; 162; DLB 9, 45
Wylie, Philip(Gordon) 1902-1971 ... **CLC 43**
See CA 21-22; 33-36R; CAP 2; DLB 9
Wyndham, John .... **CLC 19**
See Harris, John (Wyndham Parkes Lucas) Beynon
Wyss, Johann David Von 1743-1818 . **NCLC 10**
See JRDA; MAICYA; SATA 29; SATA-Brief 27
Xenophon c. 430B.C.-c.354B.C. ... **CMLC 17**
See DLB 176
Yakumo Koizumi
See Hearn, (Patricio) Lafcadio (Tessima Carlos)
Yamamoto, Hisaye 1921- ...... **SSC 34; DAM MULT**
Yanez, Jose Donoso
See Donoso (Yanez), Jose
Yanovsky, Basile S.
See Yanovsky, V(assily) S(emenovich)
Yanovsky, V(assily) S(emenovich) 1906-1989 .... **CLC 2, 18**
See CA 97-100; 129
Yates, Richard 1926-1992 .... **CLC 7, 8, 23**
See CA 5-8R; 139; CANR 10, 43; DLB 2; DLBY 81, 92; INT CANR-10
Yeats, W. B.
See Yeats, William Butler
Yeats, William Butler 1865-1939 ... **TCLC 1, 11, 18, 31, 93; DA; DAB; DAC; DAM DRAM, MST, POET; PC 20; WLC**
See CA 104; 127; CANR 45; CDBLB 1890-1914; DA3; DLB 10, 19, 98, 156; MTCW 1, 2
Yehoshua, A(braham) B. 1936- . **CLC 13, 31**
See CA 33-36R; CANR 43
Yep, Laurence Michael 1948- .... **CLC 35**
See AAYA 5, 31; CA 49-52; CANR 1, 46; CLR 3, 17, 54; DLB 52; JRDA; MAICYA; SATA 7, 69
Yerby, Frank G(arvin) 1916-1991 .... **CLC 1, 7, 22; BLC 3; DAM MULT**
See BW 1, 3; CA 9-12R; 136; CANR 16, 52; DLB 76; INT CANR-16; MTCW 1
Yesenin, Sergei Alexandrovich
See Esenin, Sergei (Alexandrovich)
Yevtushenko, Yevgeny (Alexandrovich) 1933- .... **CLC 1, 3, 13, 26, 51; DAM POET**
See CA 81-84; CANR 33, 54; MTCW 1
Yezierska, Anzia 1885(?)-1970 .... **CLC 46**
See CA 126; 89-92; DLB 28; MTCW 1
Yglesias, Helen 1915- .... **CLC 7, 22**
See CA 37-40R; CAAS 20; CANR 15, 65; INT CANR-15; MTCW 1
Yokomitsu Riichi 1898-1947 .... **TCLC 47**
See CA 170
Yonge, Charlotte(Mary) 1823-1901 ... **TCLC 48**
See CA 109; 163; DLB 18, 163; SATA 17
York, Jeremy
See Creasey, John
York, Simon
See Heinlein, Robert A(nson)
Yorke, Henry Vincent 1905-1974 .... **CLC 13**
See Green, Henry
See CA 85-88; 49-52
Yosano Akiko 1878-1942 .... **TCLC 59;PC 11**
See CA 161
Yoshimoto, Banana .... **CLC 84**
See Yoshimoto, Mahoko
Yoshimoto, Mahoko 1964-
See Yoshimoto, Banana
See CA 144
Young, Al(bert James) 1939- . **CLC 19; BLC 3; DAM MULT**
See BW 2, 3; CA 29-32R; CANR 26, 65; DLB 33
Young, Andrew (John) 1885-1971 ..... **CLC 5**
See CA 5-8R; CANR 7, 29
Young, Collier
See Bloch, Robert (Albert)
Young, Edward 1683-1765 .... **LC 3, 40**
See DLB 95
Young, Marguerite (Vivian) 1909-1995 .... **CLC 82**
See CA 13-16; 150; CAP 1
Young, Neil 1945- .... **CLC 17**
See CA 110
Young Bear, Ray A. 1950- ..... **CLC 94;DAM MULT**
See CA 146; DLB 175; NNAL
Yourcenar, Marguerite 1903-1987 . **CLC 19, 38, 50, 87; DAM NOV**
See CA 69-72; CANR 23, 60; DLB 72; DLBY 88; MTCW 1, 2
Yuan, Chu 340(?)B.C.-278(?)B.C. ..... **CMLC 36**
Yurick, Sol 1925- .... **CLC 6**
See CA 13-16R; CANR 25
Zabolotsky, Nikolai Alekseevich 1903-1958 . **TCLC 52**
See CA 116; 164
Zagajewski, Adam .... **PC 27**

Zamiatin, Yevgenii
See Zamyatin, Evgeny Ivanovich
Zamora, Bernice (B. Ortiz) 1938- . **CLC 89; DAM MULT; HLC 2**
See CA 151; CANR 80; DLB 82; HW 1, 2
Zamyatin, Evgeny Ivanovich 1884-1937 ...... **TCLC 8, 37**
See CA 105; 166
Zangwill, Israel 1864-1926 .... **TCLC 16**
See CA 109; 167; DLB 10, 135, 197
Zappa, Francis Vincent, Jr. 1940-1993
See Zappa, Frank
See CA 108; 143; CANR 57
Zappa, Frank .... **CLC 17**
See Zappa, Francis Vincent, Jr.
Zaturenska, Marya 1902-1982 ..... **CLC 6,11**
See CA 13-16R; 105; CANR 22
Zeami 1363-1443 .... **DC 7**
Zelazny, Roger(Joseph) 1937-1995 . **CLC 21**
See AAYA 7; CA 21-24R; 148; CANR 26, 60; DLB 8; MTCW 1, 2; SATA 57; SATA-Brief 39
Zhdanov, Andrei Alexandrovich 1896-1948 .... **TCLC 18**
See CA 117; 167
Zhukovsky, Vasily (Andreevich) 1783-1852 .... **NCLC 35**
See DLB 205
Ziegenhagen, Eric .... **CLC 55**
Zimmer, Jill Schary
See Robinson, Jill
Zimmerman, Robert
See Dylan, Bob
Zindel, Paul 1936- ... **CLC 6, 26; DA; DAB; DAC; DAM DRAM, MST, NOV; DC 5**
See AAYA 2; CA 73-76; CANR 31, 65; CDALBS; CLR 3, 45; DA3; DLB 7, 52; JRDA; MAICYA; MTCW 1, 2; SATA 16, 58, 102
Zinov'Ev, A. A.
See Zinoviev, Alexander (Aleksandrovich)
Zinoviev, Alexander (Aleksandrovich) 1922- .... **CLC 19**
See CA 116; 133; CAAS 10
Zoilus
See Lovecraft, H(oward) P(hillips)
Zola, Emile (Edouard Charles Antoine) 1840-1902 .... **TCLC 1, 6, 21, 41; DA; DAB; DAC; DAM MST, NOV; WLC**
See CA 104; 138; DA3; DLB 123
Zoline, Pamela 1941- .... **CLC 62**
See CA 161
Zorrilla y Moral, Jose 1817-1893 .. **NCLC 6**
Zoshchenko, Mikhail (Mikhailovich) 1895-1958 .... **TCLC 15; SSC 15**
See CA 115; 160
Zuckmayer, Carl 1896-1977 .... **CLC 18**
See CA 69-72; DLB 56, 124
Zuk, Georges
See Skelton, Robin
Zukofsky, Louis 1904-1978 .. **CLC 1, 2, 4, 7, 11, 18; DAM POET; PC 11**
See CA 9-12R; 77-80; CANR 39; DLB 5, 165; MTCW 1
Zweig, Paul 1935-1984 .... **CLC 34, 42**
See CA 85-88; 113
Zweig, Stefan 1881-1942 .... **TCLC 17**
See CA 112; 170; DLB 81, 118
Zwingli, Huldreich 1484-1531 .... **LC 37**
See DLB 179

PC Cumulative Nationality Index

AMERICAN

Aiken, Conrad (Potter) **26**
Ammons, A(rchie) R(andolph) **16**
Ashbery, John (Lawrence) **26**
Auden, W(ystan) H(ugh) **1**
Baraka, Amiri **4**
Berry, Wendell (Erdman) **28**
Bishop, Elizabeth **3**
Bogan, Louise **12**
Bradstreet, Anne **10**
Brodsky, Joseph **9**
Brooks, Gwendolyn **7**
Bryant, William Cullen **20**
Bukowski, Charles **18**
Carruth, Hayden **10**
Clampitt, Amy **19**
Clifton, (Thelma) Lucille **17**
Crane, (Harold) Hart **3**
Cullen, Countee **20**
Cummings, E(dward) E(stlin) **5**
Dickinson, Emily (Elizabeth) **1**
Doolittle, Hilda **5**
Dove, Rita (Frances) **6**
Dunbar, Paul Laurence **5**
Duncan, Robert (Edward) **2**
Eliot, T(homas) S(tearns) **5**
Emerson, Ralph Waldo **18**
Ferlinghetti, Lawrence (Monsanto) **1**
Forche, Carolyn (Louise) **10**
Frost, Robert (Lee) **1**
Gallagher, Tess **9**
Ginsberg, Allen **4**
Giovanni, Nikki **19**
Gluck, Louise (Elisabeth) **16**
Hammon, Jupiter **16**
Harjo, Joy **27**
Harper, Frances Ellen Watkins **21**
Hass, Robert **16**
Hayden, Robert E(arl) **6**
H. D. **5**
Hongo, Garrett Kaoru **23**
Hughes, (James) Langston **1**
Jeffers, (John) Robinson **17**
Johnson, James Weldon **24**
Kinnell, Galway **26**
Knight, Etheridge **14**
Kumin, Maxine (Winokur) **15**
Kunitz, Stanley (Jasspon) **19**
Levertov, Denise **11**
Levine, Philip **22**
Lindsay, (Nicholas) Vachel **23**
Lorde, Audre (Geraldine) **12**
Lowell, Amy **13**
Lowell, Robert (Traill Spence Jr.) **3**
Loy, Mina **16**
Madhubuti, Haki R. **5**
Masters, Edgar Lee **1**
McKay, Claude **2**
Meredith, William (Morris) **28**
Merrill, James (Ingram) **28**
Merton, Thomas **10**
Millay, Edna St. Vincent **6**
Momaday, N(avarre) Scott **25**
Moore, Marianne (Craig) **4**
Nash, (Fredric) Ogden **21**
Nemerov, Howard (Stanley) **24**
Olds, Sharon **22**
Olson, Charles (John) **19**
Ortiz, Simon J(oseph) **17**
Parker, Dorothy (Rothschild) **28**
Pinsky, Robert **27**
Plath, Sylvia **1**
Poe, Edgar Allan **1**
Pound, Ezra (Weston Loomis) **4**
Rexroth, Kenneth **20**
Rich, Adrienne (Cecile) **5**
Robinson, Edwin Arlington **1**
Roethke, Theodore (Huebner) **15**
Rose, Wendy **13**
Rukeyser, Muriel **12**
Sanchez, Sonia **9**
Sandburg, Carl (August) **2**
Schwartz, Delmore (David) **8**
Sexton, Anne (Harvey) **2**
Shapiro, Karl (Jay) **25**
Snyder, Gary (Sherman) **21**
Song, Cathy **21**
Soto, Gary **28**
Stein, Gertrude **18**
Stevens, Wallace **6**
Stryk, Lucien **27**
Swenson, May **14**
Toomer, Jean **7**
Viereck, Peter (Robert Edwin) **27**
Wakoski, Diane **15**
Walker, Margaret (Abigail) **20**
Wheatley (Peters), Phillis **3**
Whitman, Walt(er) **3**
Williams, William Carlos **7**
Wylie, Elinor (Morton Hoyt) **23**
Zukofsky, Louis **11**

ARGENTINIAN

Borges, Jorge Luis **22**

AUSTRALIAN

Wright, Judith (Arandell) **14**

AUSTRIAN

Trakl, Georg **20**

CANADIAN

Atwood, Margaret (Eleanor) **8**
Bissett, Bill **14**
Ondaatje, (Philip) Michael **28**
Page, P(atricia) K(athleen) **12**

CHILEAN

Neruda, Pablo **4**

CHINESE

Li Ho **13**
Tu Fu **9**
Wang Wei **18**

CUBAN

Guillen, Nicolas (Cristobal) **23**

ENGLISH

Arnold, Matthew **5**
Auden, W(ystan) H(ugh) **1**
Behn, Aphra **13**
Belloc, (Joseph) Hilaire (Pierre Sebastien Rene Swanton) **24**
Blake, William **12**
Bradstreet, Anne **10**
Bridges, Robert (Seymour) **28**
Bronte, Emily (Jane) **8**
Brooke, Rupert (Chawner) **24**
Browning, Elizabeth Barrett **6**
Browning, Robert **2**
Byron, George Gordon (Noel) **16**
Carroll, Lewis **18**
Chaucer, Geoffrey **19**
Chesterton, G(ilbert) K(eith) **28**
Clare, John **23**
Coleridge, Samuel Taylor **11**
Day Lewis, C(ecil) **11**
Donne, John **1**
Dryden, John **25**
Eliot, George **20**
Eliot, T(homas) S(tearns) **5**
Graves, Robert (von Ranke) **6**
Gray, Thomas **2**
Gunn, Thom(son William) **26**
Hardy, Thomas **8**
Herbert, George **4**
Herrick, Robert **9**

Hopkins, Gerard Manley **15**
Housman, A(lfred) E(dward) **2**
Hughes, Ted **7**
Jonson, Ben(jamin) **17**
Keats, John **1**
Kipling, (Joseph) Rudyard **3**
Larkin, Philip (Arthur) **21**
Levertov, Denise **11**
Loy, Mina **16**
Marvell, Andrew **10**
Milton, John **19**
Montagu, Mary (Pierrepont) Wortley **16**
Noyes, Alfred **27**
Owen, Wilfred (Edward Salter) **19**
Page, P(atricia) K(athleen) **12**
Pope, Alexander **26**
Rossetti, Christina (Georgina) **7**
Sassoon, Siegfried (Lorraine) **12**
Shelley, Percy Bysshe **14**
Sitwell, Dame Edith **3**
Smart, Christopher **13**
Smith, Stevie **12**
Spenser, Edmund **8**
Swift, Jonathan **9**
Swinburne, Algernon Charles **24**
Tennyson, Alfred **6**
Tomlinson, (Alfred) Charles **17**
Wordsworth, William **4**
Wyatt, Thomas **27**

FILIPINO
Villa, Jose Garcia **22**

FRENCH
Apollinaire, Guillaume **7**
Baudelaire, Charles **1**
Breton, Andre **15**
Gautier, Theophile **18**
Hugo, Victor (Marie) **17**
Laforgue, Jules **14**
Lamartine, Alphonse (Marie Louis Prat) de **16**
Leger, (Marie-Rene Auguste) Alexis Saint-Leger **23**
Mallarme, Stephane **4**
Marie de France **22**
Merton, Thomas **10**
Nerval, Gerard de **13**
Rimbaud, (Jean Nicolas) Arthur **3**
Ronsard, Pierre de **11**
Tzara, Tristan **27**
Valery, (Ambroise) Paul (Toussaint Jules) **9**
Verlaine, Paul (Marie) **2**
Vigny, Alfred (Victor) de **26**
Villon, Francois **13**

GERMAN
Bukowski, Charles **18**
Enzensberger, Hans Magnus **28**
Goethe, Johann Wolfgang von **5**
Heine, Heinrich **25**
Holderlin, (Johann Christian) Friedrich **4**
Rilke, Rainer Maria **2**

GREEK
Elytis, Odysseus **21**
Homer **23**
Pindar **19**
Sappho **5**

HUNGARIAN
Illyes, Gyula **16**

INDIAN
Kalidasa **22**
Tagore, Rabindranath **8**

IRISH
Day Lewis, C(ecil) **11**
Heaney, Seamus (Justin) **18**
Joyce, James (Augustine Aloysius) **22**
McGuckian, Medbh **27**
Swift, Jonathan **9**
Yeats, William Butler **20**

ITALIAN
Dante **21**
Gozzano, Guido **10**
Martial **10**
Montale, Eugenio **13**
Pasolini, Pier Paolo **17**
Pavese, Cesare **13**
Petrarch **8**

JAMAICAN
McKay, Claude **2**

JAPANESE
Hagiwara Sakutaro **18**
Ishikawa, Takuboku **10**
Matsuo Basho **3**
Nishiwaki, Junzaburo **15**
Yosano Akiko **11**

LEBANESE
Gibran, Kahlil **9**

MARTINICAN
Cesaire, Aime (Fernand) **25**

MEXICAN
Juana Ines de la Cruz **24**
Paz, Octavio **1**

NICARAGUAN
Alegria, Claribel **26**
Cardenal, Ernesto **22**
Dario, Ruben **15**

NIGERIAN
Okigbo, Christopher (Ifenayichukwu) **7**

PERSIAN
Khayyam, Omar **8**

POLISH
Milosz, Czeslaw **8**
Zagajewski, Adam **27**

PORTUGUESE
Pessoa, Fernando (Antonio Nogueira) **20**

ROMAN
Ovid **2**
Vergil **12**

ROMANIAN
Cassian, Nina **17**
Celan, Paul **10**
Tzara, Tristan **27**

RUSSIAN
Akhmatova, Anna **2**
Bely, Andrey **11**
Blok, Alexander (Alexandrovich) **21**
Brodsky, Joseph **9**
Lermontov, Mikhail Yuryevich **18**
Mandelstam, Osip (Emilievich) **14**
Pasternak, Boris (Leonidovich) **6**
Pushkin, Alexander (Sergeyevich) **10**
Tsvetaeva (Efron), Marina (Ivanovna) **14**

SALVADORAN
Alegria, Claribel **26**

SCOTTISH
Burns, Robert **6**
MacDiarmid, Hugh **9**
Scott, Walter **13**

SENEGALESE
Senghor, Leopold Sedar **25**

SOUTH AFRICAN
Brutus, Dennis **24**

SPANISH
Fuertes, Gloria **27**
Garcia Lorca, Federico **3**
Jimenez (Mantecon), Juan Ramon **7**

SWEDISH
Ekeloef, (Bengt) Gunnar **23**

SYRIAN
Gibran, Kahlil **9**

WELSH
Thomas, Dylan (Marlais) **2**

PC Cumulative Title Index

"0015 hours Mayday CQ Position 41°46' North 50°14' West" (Enzensberger) **28**:155
"16.ix.65" (Merrill) **28**:220
"52 Oswald Street" (Kinnell) **26**:258
"The 151st Psalm" (Shapiro) **25**:285
"1912-1952 Full Cycle" (Viereck) **27**:264
"A" (Zukofsky) **11**:337-40, 345-46, 351, 356-58, 361-67, 369-73, 383, 385-93, 395-99
"A" 1-9 (Zukofsky) **11**:380
"A" 1-12 (Zukofsky) **11**:343-44, 367-68
"A celle qui est trop gaie" (Baudelaire) **1**:44, 60-2
"A Colón" (Dario) **15**:84, 115
"A Félix Guiliemardet" (Lamartine) **16**:284
"A Francisca" (Dario) **15**:107, 111
"A Jenn de la Peruse, poète dramatique" (Ronsard) **11**:246
"A la Forest de Gastine" (Ronsard) **11**:228
"A la musique" (Rimbaud) **3**:258, 276, 283
"A la santé" (Apollinaire) **7**:44, 46-7
"A l'Italie" (Apollinaire) **7**:22
"A lo lejos" (Jimenez) **7**:199
"A los poetas risueños" (Dario) **15**:95
"A mi alma" (Jimenez) **7**:194
"A Philippes des-Portes Chartrain" (Ronsard) **11**:269-70
"A Roosevelt" (Dario) **15**:77, 81, 90, 106, 115
"A son ame" (Ronsard) **11**:244
"A ti" (Dario) **15**:99
"A une heure du matin" (Baudelaire) **1**:59, 72
"A une Malabaraise" (Baudelaire) **1**:49
"A une passante" (Baudelaire) **1**:45, 73
"A une raison" (Rimbaud) **3**:260
"A Verlaine" (Dario) **15**:93
"Aaron" (Herbert) **4**:102, 114, 130
"Aaron Stark" (Robinson) **1**:460, 467
"The Abandoned Newborn" (Olds) **22**:329
ABC of Economics (Pound) **4**:328
"ABCs" (Olson) **19**:267, 271, 316
"The Abduction" (Kunitz) **19**:181-82
"L'abeille" (Valery) **9**:353, 387-88, 393-94
"Abel" (Stein) **18**:316
"Abel and Cain" (Baudelaire)
See "Abel et Caïn"
"Abel et Caïn" (Baudelaire) **1**:68
"Abel's Bride" (Levertov) **11**:175
"Der Abend" (Trakl) **20**:237-38, 244, 251, 258
"Abendland" (Trakl) **20**:231-32, 235, 240-44, 251, 269
"Abendländisches Lied" (Trakl) **20**:231, 236, 248-49, 251, 258, 269
"Abendlied" (Trakl) **20**:239, 269
"Abendmahl, Venezianisch, 16. Jahrhundert" (Enzensberger) **28**:165
"abgelegenes haus" (Enzensberger) **28**:140
"Abishag" (Gluck) **16**:126, 141
"Abnegation" (Rich) **5**:365
"Aboard the Santa Maria" (Illyes) **16**:248
"Abode" (Milosz) **8**:215
"The Abominable Lake" (Smith) **12**:353
"The Abortion" (Sexton) **2**:349
"About Opera" (Meredith) **28**:195, 206
"About Poetry" (Meredith) **28**:193-94
"About the House" (Auden) **1**:21, 24
"About the Phoenix" (Merrill) **28**:239
"About These Verses" (Pasternak) **6**:251
Above the Barriers (Pasternak)
See *Poverkh barierov*
"Above These Cares" (Millay) **6**:235
"Abraham and Orpheus" (Schwartz) **8**:306, 308-09
"Abraham Lincoln Walks at Midnight" (Lindsay) **23**:275, 280, 284, 288, 294-95
"Abril sus flores abría" (Guillen) **23**:125
Abrojos (Dario) **15**:94
Absalom and Achitophel (Dryden) **25**:82-3, 88, 106-08, 113-14
"abschied von einem mittwoch" (Enzensberger) **28**:136
"Absence" (Gozzano) **10**:178
"L'absence, ny l'oubly, ny la course du jour" (Ronsard) **11**:246
"Absences" (Larkin) **21**:249-51
"L'Absente" (Senghor) **25**:255, 258
"Absentia animi" (Ekeloef) **23**:59-60, 63, 76, 86
"Absent-Minded Professor" (Nemerov) **24**:266
"Absolute Clearance" (Ashbery) **26**:124
"Absolute Retreat" (Finch)
See "The Petition for an Absolute Retreat"
"Absolution" (Brooke) **24**:52
"Absolution" (Sassoon) **12**:241, 250, 252, 261, 276, 278, 280
"Abstract Old Woman in a Room" (Momaday) **25**:
"Abt Vogler" (Browning) **2**:37, 75, 80, 88, 95
"El abuelo" (Guillen) **23**:134-37
"Abur Don Pepe" (Guillen) **23**:126
"The Abyss" (Roethke) **15**:270
"The Abyss of War" (Owen) **19**:343
"Abzählreime" (Celan) **10**:124-25
"Academic" (Roethke) **15**:246
Academic Squaw: Reports to the World from the Ivory Tower (Rose) **13**:233, 238
"Acceptance" (Sassoon) **12**:259
"Accès" (Tzara) **27**:229-31
"Accidentally on Purpose" (Frost) **1**:213
"Accomplishment" (Gallagher) **9**:59
An Account of a Weatherbeaten Journey (Matsuo Basho)
See *Nozarashi kiko*
"Accountability" (Dunbar) **5**:133, 146
"Les accroupissements" (Rimbaud) **3**:284
"The Accuser" (Milosz) **8**:204
"Ach, um deine feuchten Schwingen" (Goethe) **5**:247
"The Ache of Marriage" (Levertov) **11**:169
"Achieving a Poem while Drinking Alone" (Tu Fu) **9**:327
"Achille's Song" (Duncan) **2**:115
"Acon" (H. D.) **5**:273
Aconsejo beber hilo (Fuertes) **27**:10-12
"Acquainted with the Night" (Frost) **1**:197, 205-06, 208
"Across Lamarck Col" (Snyder) **21**:288
"An Acrostic" (Poe) **1**:446
"Act of Union" (Heaney) **18**:196
"Ad Castitatem" (Bogan) **12**:117
"Ad Libitum" (Elytis) **21**:132-33
"Ad Mariam" (Hopkins) **15**:159, 164, 166
"Adam" (Tomlinson) **17**:316, 342
"Adam" (Williams) **7**:350, 354
"Adam and Eve" (Shapiro) **25**:284-85, 287, 290-91, 301, 320
Adam & Eve & the City (Williams) **7**:350, 402
"adam thinking" (Clifton) **17**:30, 36
"The Adamant" (Roethke) **15**:272, 291
"Adam's Curse" (Yeats) **20**:338
"Adam's Way" (Duncan) **2**:103
"The Addict" (Sexton) **2**:364
Additional Poems (Housman) **2**:176-77, 190
"Address for a Prize-Day" (Auden) **1**:8, 37
"Address of Beelzebub" (Burns) **6**:83-4, 88-9
"Address to a Lark" (Clare) **23**:39
"Address to a Louse" (Burns)
See "To a Louse, on Seeing One on a Lady's Bonnet at Church"
"Address to Imagination" (Wheatley) **3**:335
An Address to Miss Phillis Wheatly (Hammon) **16**:179, 187-89
"Address to My Soul" (Wylie) **23**:303, 305, 310, 313, 322, 333
"Address to the Angels" (Kumin) **15**:204
"Address to the De'il" (Burns) **6**:49, 78, 83-4, 87
"Adelaide Abner" (Smith) **12**:310, 326
"L'adieu" (Apollinaire) **7**:48
"L'adieu" (Lamartine) **16**:277, 299
"Adieu" (Rimbaud) **3**:273
"Adieu á Charlot" (Ferlinghetti) **1**:181-82, 188
"Adieu, Mlle. Veronique" (Brodsky) **9**:2, 5
"Adieux a la poesie" (Lamartine) **16**:273
"Adieux à Marie Stuart" (Swinburne) **24**:313
"The Adirondacs" (Emerson) **18**:76-77, 111, 113
"Adivinanzas" (Guillen) **23**:106
"The Admiral's Ghost" (Noyes) **27**:121, 134
"admonitions" (Clifton) **17**:31
"Adolescence" (Dove) **6**:106
"Adolescence--III" (Dove) **6**:109
"Adolescencia" (Jimenez) **7**:183, 209
"The Adolescent" (Jimenez)
See "Adolescencia"
"Adolescent" (Tsvetaeva)
See "Otrok"
"Adonais" (Arnold) **5**:7
"Adonais" (Wylie) **23**:323
Adonais: An Elegy on the Death of John Keats (Shelley) **14**:164, 171, 174, 178, 183, 186-89, 197, 211, 218, 233-34, 236-37, 239-40
"Adonis" (H. D.) **5**:269, 304, 308
"Adonis" (Ronsard) **11**:251
Adrastea (Herder) **14**:171, 173, 178, 192, 211-12, 217, 221-24, 233-37, 239
"Adult Bookstore" (Shapiro) **25**:306-307, 322
"Adulthood" (Giovanni) **19**:110, 139
"Adulto? Mai" (Pasolini) **17**:261
"An Advancement of Learning" (Heaney)

18:187, 190, 200
"Advent" (Merton) **10**:340
"Advent" (Rossetti) **7**:290, 297
Advent (Rilke) **2**:280
"Advent, 1966" (Levertov) **11**:176
"Adventures" (Pavese) **13**:205
"Adventures of Isabel" (Nash) **21**:265
Adventures While Preaching the Gospel of Beauty (Lindsay) **23**:278, 295
"Adventures While Singing These Songs" (Lindsay) **23**:282
"Adversity" (Gray)
See "Ode to Adversity"
"Advertencia" (Fuertes) **27**:26
"The Advice" (Roethke) **15**:274
"Advice about Roses" (Stein) **18**:313
"Advice to the Girls" (Harper) **21**:207, 216
"Advocates" (Graves) **6**:144
"Ae Fond Kiss" (Burns) **6**:97
"Aedh Hears the Cry ofthe Sedge" (Yeats) **20**:347
Aeginetan Odes (Pindar) **19**:406
"Aeneas and Dido" (Brodsky) **9**:7
The Aeneid (Vergil) **12**:358, 361, 364-68, 371-73, 375-78, 380-99, 401-08
"The Aeolian Harp" (Coleridge) **11**:51, 63, 73-4, 81-2, 88, 91, 97, 106-07, 109
"Aesthetic" (Tomlinson) **17**:327, 344
"The Aesthetic Point of View" (Auden) **1**:12, 15
"Aesthetics of the Shah" (Olds) **22**:314
"Aether" (Ginsberg) **4**:81
"Affliction" (Herbert) **4**:118, 131
"Affliction I" (Herbert) **4**:111-12, 128, 131-32
"Affliction IV" (Herbert) **4**:112, 120
"The Affliction of Margaret----of----" (Wordsworth) **4**:402
"The Affliction of Richard" (Bridges) **28**:88
"Afin qu'àtout jamais" (Ronsard) **11**:242
"Africa" (Giovanni) **19**:141
"Africa" (McKay) **2**:221
Africa (Blake) **12**:13
Africa (Petrarch) **8**:239-42, 246, 258, 260, 266-68, 278
"Africa and My New York" (Viereck) **27**:278, 282
"The African Chief" (Bryant) **20**:4
"An African Elegy" (Duncan) **2**:103
"After a Death" (Tomlinson) **17**:336
"After a Flight" (Montale) **13**:158
"After a Flight" (Montefiore)
See "Dopa una fuga"
"After a Journey" (Hardy) **8**:88, 93, 118, 135
"After a Long Illness" (Duncan) **2**:119
"After a Rain" (Pasternak) **6**:271
"After a Tempest" (Bryant) **20**:37-8
"After a Visit (At Padraic Colum's Where There Were Irish Poets)" (Cullen) **20**:60, 69
After and Before the Lightning (Ortiz) **17**:245
"After Apple-Picking" (Frost) **1**:193, 221-22
"After Dark" (Rich) **5**:364
"After Death" (Rossetti) **7**:269, 280, 287
"After Grace" (Merrill) **28**:234, 250
"After great stormes the cawme retornes" (Wyatt) **27**:311
"After Hearing a Waltz by Bartok" (Lowell) **13**:84
"After Keats" (Levine)
See "Having Been Asked 'What Is a Man?' I Answer"
"after Kent State" (Clifton) **17**:17, 35
"After Long Silence" (Yeats) **20**:328-29
"After Making Love We Hear Footsteps" (Kinnell) **26**:259, 292
"After Many Days" (Dunbar) **5**:137
"After Mecca" (Brooks) **7**:63, 81
"After Paradise" (Milosz) **8**:209
After Parting (Bely)
See *Posle razluki*
"After Rain" (Page) **12**:168, 178, 190
"After Reading *Mickey in the Night Kitchen* for the Third Time before Bed" (Dove) **6**:121
"After Reading Sylvia Plath" (Clampitt) **19**:99
After Russia (Tsvetaeva)
See *Posle Rossii*
"After the Agony" (Atwood) **8**:6
"After the Ball" (Merrill) **28**:270
"After the Cleansing of Bosnia" (Kumin) **15**:224
"After the Cries of the Birds" (Ferlinghetti) **1**:173-74, 176
"After the Deluge" (Rimbaud)
See "Après le déluge"
"After the Fire" (Merrill) **28**:221, 222, 225, 258, 263-64
"After the Flood, We" (Atwood) **8**:12
"After the Funeral: In Memory of Anne Jones" (Thomas) **2**:390
"After the Gentle Poet Kobayashi Issa" (Hass) **16**:196
"After the Last Dynasty" (Kunitz) **19**:179
"After the Persian" (Bogan) **12**:107, 118, 124-25, 129
"After the Sentence" (Brutus) **24**:106
"After the Storm" (Stryk) **27**:203
"After the stubbornly cheerful day" (Brutus) **24**:118
"After the Surprising Conversions" (Lowell) **3**:202-03
"After the Winter" (McKay) **2**:228
"After Tonight" (Soto) **28**:370
"After Troy" (H. D.) **5**:268
"After Twenty Years" (Rich) **5**:384
"After wards" (Stein) **18**:313
"After Work" (Snyder) **21**:288
"Afterimages" (Lorde) **12**:155
"Aftermath" (Plath) **1**:389
"Aftermath" (Sassoon) **12**:269, 289
"Afternoon" (Parker) **28**:360
Afternoon of a Faun (Mallarme)
See *L'après-midi d'un faune*
"Afternoon on a Hill" (Millay) **6**:235-36
"Afternoon Rain in State Street" (Lowell) **13**:79
"The After-thought" (Smith) **12**:329-32
"An Afterward" (Heaney) **18**:243
"Afterwards" (Hardy) **8**:101, 131
"Afterword" (Atwood) **8**:11
"Afterword" (Brodsky) **9**:25
"Afterword" (Carruth) **10**:71
"An Afterword: For Gwen Brooks" (Madhubuti) **5**:346
"Afton Water" (Burns)
See "Sweet Afton"
"Again" (Nemerov) **24**:291
"Again Again" (Viereck) **27**:265
"Again and Again and Again" (Sexton) **2**:353
"Again I Visited" (Pushkin)
See "Vnov' Ya Posetil"
"Against a comely Coistroun" (Skelton) **25**:339
"Against Botticelli" (Hass) **16**:198
"Against System Builders" (Goethe) **5**:229
"Agape" (Kinnell) **26**:287
"Agatha" (Eliot) **20**:101, 123
"Agatha" (Valery)
See "Agathe; ou, La sainte du sommeil"
"The Agatha Christie Books by the Window" (Ondaatje) **28**:335
"Agathe; ou, La sainte du sommeil" (Valery) **9**:357, 400-01
"Age" (Larkin) **21**:227, 236, 248
"The Age" (Mandelstam) **14**:121
"The Age Demanded" (Pound) **4**:320
The Age of Anxiety: A Baroque Eclogue (Auden) **1**:14, 23, 33-4, 39
"The Ages" (Bryant) **20**:4, 35
"The Ages of Man" (Bradstreet)
See "The Four Ages of Man"
The Ages of the Year (Cassian) **17**:6
"Aging Refugee from the Old Country" (Viereck) **27**:280
"An Agnostic" (Smith) **12**:352
"The Agony" (Herbert) **4**:100
"An Agony. As Now" (Baraka) **4**:16, 24
"Agora que conmigo" (Juana Ines de la Cruz) **24**:187
"Agosta the Winged Man and Rasha the Black Dove" (Dove) **6**:109
"Agrippina in the Golden House of Nero" (Lowell) **3**:222
"Agua sexual" (Neruda) **4**:306
"Ah, Are You Digging on My Grave?" (Hardy) **8**:131
"Ah! Sun-Flower" (Blake) **12**:34
"Ahasuerus" (Nemerov) **24**:257, 295
"Ahora habla Dios" (Fuertes) **27**:28
"Ahvan" (Tagore) **8**:415
"Ai critici cattolici" (Pasolini) **17**:258
"Aigeltinger" (Williams) **7**:370
"L'aigle du casque" (Hugo) **17**:56
Aika (Nishiwaki) **15**:238
"The Aim Was Song" (Frost) **1**:194
"Aimless Journey" (Tagore)
See "Niruddesh yatra"
"Air" (Toomer) **7**:333
"Air and Fire" (Berry) **28**:11
L'air de l'eau (Breton) **15**:51-2
"Air de sémiramis" (Valery) **9**:365, 391-92
"Air Liner" (Shapiro) **25**:296
"Aire and Angels" (Donne) **1**:130, 149
"Airen" (Hagiwara Sakutaro) **18**:167, 180
"Airman's Virtue" (Meredith) **28**:182-83
Airs & Tributes (Brutus) **24**:110-11, 117
"The Airy Christ" (Smith) **12**:295, 330-31, 333
"Aix-en-Provence" (Rexroth) **20**:209
"Ajanta" (Rukeyser) **12**:204, 214, 219, 224
"Ajedrez I" (Borges) **22**:83-5
"Ajedrez II" (Borges) **22**:84-5
"Akatsuki no kane" (Ishikawa) **10**:214
Akogare (Ishikawa) **10**:194, 212-16
"Al Aaraaf" (Poe) **1**:437, 449
"Al amor cualquier curioso" (Juana Ines de la Cruz) **24**:184, 234
"Al iniciar el estudio de la gramática anglosajona" (Borges) **22**:99
"Al lector" (Dario) **15**:105
"Al maragen de mis libros de estudios" (Guillen) **23**:97
"Al mio grillo" (Montale) **13**:138
"Al mismo individuo" (Guillen) **23**:126
"Al pintor Swaminathan" (Paz) **1**:354
"Al poeta español Rafael Alberti, entregándole un jamón" (Guillen) **23**:134
"Al que ingrato me deja, busco ama" (Juana Ines de la Cruz) **24**:183
Al que quiere! (Williams) **7**:344-45, 348-49, 377-79, 387-88, 398, 405-10
"Al soneto con mi alma" (Jimenez) **7**:192
"Ala bāb al-haykal" (Gibran) **9**:78
"Alaba los ojos negros de Julia" (Dario) **15**:114
"Alabama Poem" (Giovanni) **19**:140
Al-ajnihah (Gibran) **9**:78
"Alabaster" (Merrill) **28**:283
"Alas, a Prince" (Tu Fu) **9**:317
"Alas the While" (Wyatt) **27**:318
"Alaska" (Snyder) **21**:300
"Alastor; or, The Spirit of Solitude" (Shelley) **14**:171, 173, 178, 192, 211-12, 217, 221-24, 233-37, 239
Al-'awasif (Gibran) **9**:79-81
"Al-bahr" (Gibran) **9**:80
"Albaniad" (Elytis) **21**:115
"L'albatros" (Baudelaire) **1**:65
"A Albert Durer" (Hugo) **17**:94-95
Albertine Disparue (Enzensberger) **28**:156
"Albertus" (Gautier) **18**:142-43, 151-54, 160-64
Albertus, ou l'âme et le péché: légende théologique (Gautier) **18**:147, 149-51, 154
Album de vers anciens, 1890-1900 (Valery) **9**:363, 365, 386-87, 390-91, 395
"The Alchemist" (Bogan) **12**:98, 103, 114
"The Alchemist" (Meredith) **28**:187
"Alchemy of the Word" (Rimbaud)
See "Alchimie du verbe"

"Alchimie du verbe" (Rimbaud) **3**:261, 267, 274
"An Alcoholic's Death" (Hagiwara Sakutaro)
See "Death of an Alcoholic"
Alcools (Apollinaire) **7**:6, 9-10, 12, 14-15, 38-46, 48-9
"Alejamiento" (Borges) **22**:92
"Aleksandru" (Pushkin) **10**:421
"Aleluja" (Pasolini) **17**:256
"Alewives Pool" (Kinnell) **26**:238
"Alexander's Feast; or, The Power of Musique. An Ode, in Honour of St. Cecilia's Day" (Dryden) 72-5, 88
"Alexandria" (Shapiro) **25**:295
Alexis und Dora (Goethe) **5**:240
"Alfansa" (Forche) **10**:134, 169-70
"Alfonso" (McKay) **2**:205
"Alfred the Great" (Smith) **12**:296, 316
"Algernon, Who Played with a Loaded Gun, and, on Missing His Sister, Was Reprimanded by His Father" (Belloc) **24**:26
Algiers in Wartime (Viereck) **27**:265
"Al-huruf al-nāriyah" (Gibran) **9**:78
Alí dagli occhi azzurri (Pasolini) **17**:264-65
"Alice" (Graves) **6**:139
"Alice Du Clos" (Coleridge) **11**:106
"Alice Fell" (Wordsworth) **4**:404, 415
"Alive" (Harjo) **27**:56
Alive: Poems, 1971-1972 (Wright) **14**:372, 375
"Al-jamāl" (Gibran) **9**:81
"All, All Are Gone the Old Familiar Quotations" (Nash) **21**:273
"All and Some" (Ashbery) **26**:124, 127, 135
"All Clowns Are Masked and All Personae" (Schwartz) **8**:305
"an alle fernsprechteilenhmer " (Enzensberger) **28**:134, 136, 140
"All Guilt and Innocence Turned Upside Down" (Schwartz) **8**:285
"All Hallows" (Gluck) **16**:126-27, 132, 140-43, 148-49
"All I Gotta Do" (Giovanni) **19**:108, 112
"All in Green Went My Love Riding" (Cummings) **5**:87
"All Is Mine" (Guillen)
See "Tengo"
All Is Mine (Guillen)
See *Tengo*
"All Kinds of Caresses" (Ashbery) **26**:139
"All kings and all their favourites" (Donne)
See "The Anniversarie"
"All Life in a Life" (Masters) **1**:326, 328, 335-36, 342
"All Morning" (Roethke) **15**:271
"All Mountain" (H. D.) **5**:305
All My Pretty Ones (Sexton) **2**:346-47, 349-50, 353, 355, 360-61, 370
"All Nearness Pauses, While a Star Can Grow" (Cummings) **5**:109
"All of Us Always Turning Away for Solace" (Schwartz) **8**:305
"All Souls' Day" (Sassoon) **12**:258
"All Sounds Have been as Music" (Owen) **19**:336
All: The Collected Short Poems, 1923-1958 (Zukofsky) **11**:348-49, 351, 354-56, 393-94
All: The Collected Shorter Poems, 1956-64 (Zukofsky) **11**:349, 353, 356, 383, 390
"All the Dead Dears" (Plath) **1**:388, 407
"All the Earth, All the Air" (Roethke) **15**:286
"All the Fancy Things" (Williams) **7**:394
"All the Spirit Powers Went to Their Dancing Place" (Snyder) **21**:291
"All Things Conspire" (Wright) **14**:338
"All Worlds Have Halfsight, Seeing Either With" (Cummings) **5**:111
"Alla Francia" (Pasolini) **17**:295
"Allá lejos" (Dario) **15**:93
"Allá lejos" (Guillen) **23**:126
"All-destroyer" (Tagore)
See "Sarvaneshe"
"Allégorie" (Baudelaire) **1**:56
"L'Allegro" (Milton) **19**:201-02, 226, 228-34, 249, 254-56
"Alley Rats" (Sandburg) **2**:304
"Alliance of Education and Government" (Gray)
See "Essay on the Alliance of Education and Government"
"Allie" (Graves) **6**:141
"The Allies" (Lowell) **13**:76, 78
"Allons adieu messieurs tachez de revenir" (Apollinaire) **7**:22
"Alloy" (Rukeyser) **12**:210
"Almanac" (Swenson) **14**:268
"Almansor" (Heine) **25**:145, 160
"Almas de Duralex" (Fuertes) **27**:23
Almas de violeta (Jimenez) **7**:199
Al-mawakib (Gibran) **9**:79-81
"Almond" (McGuckian) **27**:92-93, 105
"The Almond of the World" (Elytis) **21**:132
"Almost a Fantasy" (Montale) **13**:151
"Alone" (Poe) **1**:442-44
"Alone I Go along the Road" (Lermontov) **18**:281, 298, 303
"Alone in a Shower" (Hongo) **23**:197
"Along History" (Rukeyser) **12**:228
"Along the Field as We Came By" (Housman) **2**:183
"The Alphabet" (Shapiro) **25**:283, 291, 298-99
"Alphabets" (Heaney) **18**:230-31, 237
"Alphonso of Castile" (Emerson) **18**:71
"Alquimia" (Borges) **22**:94
"Al-shā'ir" (Gibran) **9**:79
"The Altar" (Herbert) **4**:114, 120, 130
"The Altar of Righteousness" (Swinburne) **24**:350-54
The Altar of the Past (Gozzano)
See *L'altare del Passato*
L'altare del Passato (Gozzano) **10**:177
"Altarwise by Owl-light" (Thomas) **2**:388-89, 403, 406
"Einem alten Architekten in Rom" (Brodsky) **9**:2, 4
"Alternate Thoughts from Underground" (Atwood) **8**:40
"Altitude: 15,000" (Meredith) **28**:173
Alturas de Macchu Picchu (Neruda) **4**:282, 284-85, 292-93
"Al-umm wa wahīduha" (Gibran) **9**:78
"Always a Rose" (Lee) **24**:247-48, 251
"Always and always the amaranth astir" (Villa) **22**:346
"Always I did want more God" (Villa) **22**:352
"Always the Mob" (Sandburg) **2**:302
"Always to Love You America" (Viereck) **27**:279-80
"The Alyscamps at Arles" (Swenson) **14**:255
"Alysoun" (Snyder) **21**:288
"am or" (Bissett) **14**:14
"Am Rand Eines alten Brunes" (Trakl) **20**:265
"Am/Trak" (Baraka) **4**:39
"Am Was. Are Leaves Few This. Is This a or" (Cummings) **5**:107
"Ama tu ritmo..." (Dario) **15**:101
"Amado dueño mío" (Juana Ines de la Cruz) **24**:181
"Amam 'arsh al-jamal" (Gibran) **9**:79
"Amante dulce del alma" (Juana Ines de la Cruz) **24**:189
"Los amantes viejos" (Aleixandre) **15**:5-7
"Les Amants de Montmorency" (Vigny) **26**:391, 411-12
"Amaranth" (H. D.) **5**:305
Amaranth (Robinson) **1**:477-78, 482-83
"Ambarvalia" (Nishiwaki) **15**:238
Ambarvalia (Nishiwaki) **15**:228-29, 232-41
"The Ambassador" (Smith) **12**:330, 339
"Ambassadors of Grief" (Sandburg) **2**:308
Ambit (Aleixandre)
See *Ambito*
Ambito (Aleixandre) **15**:9, 16, 27, 29-32
Ambitus (Cassian) **17**:6
"Ambulances" (Larkin) **21**:229-30, 234
"Ame" (Nishiwaki) **15**:228
"Amen!" (Rossetti) **7**:268
"Amen" (Trakl) **20**:248
"El amenazado" (Borges) **22**:80-1
"America" (McKay) **2**:212
"America" (Merrill) **28**:267
"America" (Wheatley) **3**:363
America: A Prophecy, 1793 (Blake) **12**:13, 25-7, 63
"America, I Do Not Invoke Your Name in Vain" (Neruda)
See "América, no invoco tu nombre en vano"
"América, no invoco tu nombre en vano" (Neruda) **4**:292
"The American" (Kipling) **3**:161
"American Change" (Ginsberg) **4**:53, 84
"American Journal" (Hayden) **6**:188-89, 191-92, 195
American Journal (Hayden) **6**:194-96
"American Miscellany" (H. D.) **5**:268
American Scenes and Other Poems (Tomlinson) **17**:309, 317-18, 325-26, 333, 335, 337, 341-42, 348, 352
Americana (Viereck) **27**:263
Amers (Perse) **23**:217, 221, 223, 233, 237-47, 249-56
"Ametas and Thestylis Making Hay-Ropes" (Marvell) **10**:269, 271, 294, 304
"L'amica di nonna speranza" (Gozzano) **10**:177, 181-82
"L'amico che dorme" (Pavese) **13**:229
Les amies (Verlaine) **2**:432
L'Amitié du Prince (Perse) **23**:217, 246
Amitié d'un Prince (Perse) **23**:211, 221, 230, 249-50
"Among School Children" (Yeats) **20**:316, 326, 328, 330, 332, 336-38, 340-42
"Among the Gods" (Kunitz) **19**:149, 173
"Among the Tombs" (Kinnell) **26**:256
"Among the Trees" (Bryant) **20**:14, 47
"Among Those Killed in the Dawn Raid Was a Man Aged a Hundred" (Thomas) **2**:388
"Amor e'l cor gentil" (Dante) **21**:73
Amor humor y desamor (Fuertes) **27**:
"Amor mundi" (Rossetti) **7**:282
Amores (Ovid) **2**:234-35, 237-38, 242-43, 245, 251, 253-54, 258-59, 261
Amoretti (Spenser) **8**:329, 388-89
Amoretti and Epithalamion (Spenser) **8**:388
"Amos (Postscript 1968)" (Walker) **20**:278-79
"Amos-1963" (Walker) **20**:278-79
"Amour" (Verlaine) **2**:416-17, 425
"L'amour et le crâne" (Baudelaire) **1**:45
"Amour parcheminé" (Breton) **15**:52
"Les amours" (Laforgue) **14**:74
Amours (Ronsard) **11**:220-21, 246, 250, 254, 256, 258, 275, 277-78, 293
Amours de Cassandre (Ronsard) **11**:247-48
"Amours d'Eurymedon et de Calliree" (Ronsard) **11**:241
Amours diverses (Ronsard) **11**:270
"Amphibian" (Browning) **2**:80
Amplitude: New and Selected Poems (Gallagher) **9**:57-62
"Amravan" (Tagore) **8**:416
"Amsterdam" (Merrill) **28**:223
Amubaruwaria (Nishiwaki) **15**:232, 240
"Amy's Cruelty" (Browning) **6**:23, 28, 32
"An den Knaben Elis" (Trakl) **20**:226, 234-35, 246
"An den Wassern Babels" (Celan) **10**:127-28
"An einen Frühverstorbenen" (Trakl) **20**:230
"Ana María" (Guillen) **23**:102
Anabase (Perse) **23**:209-14, 216-18, 221-23, 225-28, 230-31, 233-34, 241-43, 246, 248, 250, 253, 256-59, 261
Anabasis (Perse)
See *Anabase*

"Anactoria" (Swinburne) **24**:308, 310-11, 322, 325-26, 343, 360-61
"Anahorish" (Heaney) **18**:201-2, 241, 251
"Ananta jivan" (Tagore) **8**:406
"Ananta maran" (Tagore) **8**:406
"Anaphora" (Bishop) **3**:37, 56
"Anasazi" (Snyder) **21**:295-96
"Anashuya and Vijaya" (Yeats) **20**:343
An Anatomie of the World (Donne)
See *The First Anniversarie. An Anatomie of the World. Wherein By Occasion of the untimely death of Mistris Elizabeth Drury, the frailtie and decay of this whole World is represented*
"An Anatomy of Migraine" (Clampitt) **19**:92
"Ancestors" (Pavese) **13**:204
"The Ancestors" (Wright) **14**:353
"Ancestral Houses" (Yeats) **20**:349
"Ancestral Photograph" (Heaney) **18**:200
"Anchar" (Pushkin) **10**:373
"Anchorage" (Harjo) **27**:55, 58, 63, 65-66
"The Anchored Angel" (Villa) **22**:348-49
The Ancient Acquaintance (Skelton) **25**:345, 351
"The Ancient Briton Lay Ynder His Rock" (Hughes) **7**:147
"Ancient discipline" (Pavese)
See "Disciplina antica"
"An Ancient Gesture" (Millay) **6**:232, 240
"The Ancient Heroes and the Bomber Pilot" (Hughes) **7**:132
"Ancient History" (Sassoon) **12**:258
"the ancient lord laydee un th univers" (Bissett) **14**:27
The Ancient Mariner (Coleridge)
See *The Rime of the Ancient Mariner: A Poet's Reverie*
"Ancient One" (Montale)
See "Antico, sono ubriacato della tua voce"
"The Ancient Sage" (Tennyson) **6**:407
"An Ancient to Ancients" (Hardy) **8**:121
"Ancient Wisdom Speaks" (H. D.) **5**:307
"Ancora ad Annecy" (Montale) **13**:138
And (Cummings)
See *&*
& (Cummings) **5**:75, 92-3, 95, 104-05
"And a Few Negroes Too" (Madhubuti)
See "A Message All Blackpeople Can Dig (& A Few Negroes Too)"
"And a Wisdom as Such" (Duncan) **2**:115
"And Another Thing" (Giovanni) **19**:118
"& Co." (Shapiro) **25**:295
"And Death Shall Have No Dominion" (Thomas) **2**:379, 385, 389-90, 397
"And Did Those Feet in Ancient Time Walk upon England's Mountains Green?" (Blake) **12**:45
"der andere" (Enzensberger) **28**:139
"And if an eye may save or slay" (Wyatt) **27**:354
"And in the Hanging Gardens" (Aiken) **26**:24
And in the Human Heart (Aiken) **26**:22
"And One for My Dame" (Sexton) **2**:363
"And Pass" (Toomer) **7**:332
"And So Goodbye to Cities" (Merton) **10**:334, 344
"And So Today" (Sandburg) **2**:307-08
"And Socializing" (Ashbery) **26**:163
"And the Children of Birmingham" (Merton) **10**:334, 341
". . .And the Clouds Return after the Rain" (Smith) **12**:331
"and the green wind is mooving thru the summr trees" (Bissett) **14**:33
"And The Land Is Just As Dry" (Ortiz) **17**:227
"And the Stars Were Shining" (Ashbery) **26**:164-166
And the Stars Were Shining (Ashbery) **26**:164-166
"And the Trains Go On" (Levine) **22**:224
"And There Was a Great Calm" (Hardy) **8**:119
"And They Call This Living!" (Stryk) **27**:203
"And Ut Pictura Poesis Is Her Name" (Ashbery) **26**:118, 123, 135
"And What About the Children" (Lorde) **12**:139
"And with What Bodies Do They Come?" (Dickinson) **1**:102
"And You as Well Must Die" (Millay) **6**:211
"El andaluz universal" (Jimenez) **7**:205
"Andenken" (Holderlin) **4**:172, 178
"Andrea del Sarto" (Browning) **2**:37, 86, 88, 95
"Andrée Rexroth" (Rexroth) **20**:206-07
"Andromeda" (Hopkins) **15**:134, 148
"Andromeda Chained to Her Rock the Great Nebula in her Heart" (Rexroth) **20**:196
"Anecdote" (Parker) **28**:360
"Anecdote for Fathers" (Wordsworth) **4**:425-28
Anecdote of Rain (Zagajewski) **27**:389, 399
"Anecdote of the Jar" (Stevens) **6**:309, 326-27
"Anecdote of the Prince of Peacocks" (Stevens) **6**:309
"Anelida and Arcite" (Chaucer) **19**:10, 74
Anew (Zukofsky) **11**:342, 347, 382-83
"L'ange du méridien" (Rilke) **2**:275
"L'ange, fragment épique" (Lamartine) **16**:266
"Das angebrochene Jahr" (Celan) **10**:124
"Angel" (Lermontov) **18**:274, 276, 279
"Angel" (Merrill) **28**:248
"Angel Boley" (Smith) **12**:352
"Angel Butcher" (Levine) **22**:222-23
The Angel of History (Forche) **10**:160, 169
"Angel smerti" (Lermontov) **18**:300
"The Angel Sons" (Lindsay) **23**:281
"Angel Surrounded by Paysans" (Stevens) **6**:304
"L'angelo nero" (Montale) **13**:134
Angels and Earthly Creatures (Wylie) **23**:303-304, 307, 309, 313-14
"Angels of the Love Affair" (Sexton) **2**:365, 367
"Angelus" (Fuertes) **27**:39
"The Anger of the Sea" (Ishikawa)
See "Umi no ikari"
"Anger's Freeing Power" (Smith) **12**:295, 311, 330
"Anglais Mort à Florence" (Stevens) **6**:311
Angle of Ascent (Hayden) **6**:188, 190, 194
Angle of Geese, and Other Poems (Momaday) **25**:187, 188-89, 193
"Angling A Day" (Kinnell) **26**:260
"Anglo-Mongrels and the Rose" (Loy) **16**:316, 322
"The Angry God" (Ferlinghetti) **1**:183
"Angry Love" (Aleixandre) **15**:19
"Angry Samson" (Graves) **6**:151
"The Anguish" (Millay) **6**:217
"Anima" (Carruth) **10**:85
"De Anima" (Nemerov) **24**:289
"Anima hominis" (Yeats) **20**:327
Animal de fondo (Jimenez) **7**:183-84, 203, 211, 214
"Animal de luz" (Neruda) **4**:289
Animal of Depth (Jimenez)
See *Animal de fondo*
Animal of Inner Depths (Jimenez)
See *Animal de fondo*
"Animal of Light" (Neruda)
See "Animal de luz"
"Animal, Vegetable, and Mineral" (Bogan) **12**:92, 99, 107, 125
"Animals Are Passing from Our Lives" (Levine) **22**:213
The Animals in That Country (Atwood) **8**:3-4, 12, 15-16, 23
Animula (Eliot) **5**:194, 197-98, 203
"Anklage" (Goethe) **5**:248
"Ankor Wat" (Ginsberg) **4**:61
"Anna" (Wyatt) **27**:345
"anna speaks of the childhood of mary her daughter" (Clifton) **17**:37
"Annabel Lee" (Poe) **1**:425, 429, 434, 438, 441, 444, 447-48
"Annandale Again" (Robinson) **1**:476
"Anne" (Valery) **9**:374, 392
"Anne Boleyn's Song" (Sitwell) **3**:315
"Anne Rutledge" (Masters) **1**:334, 348
L'année terrible (Hugo) **17**:55-56, 65, 97-99, 101
Les Années funestes (Hugo) **17**:65
"Annetta" (Montale) **13**:138
"The Anniad" (Brooks) **7**:53, 58, 61, 80, 102, 104
Annie Allen (Brooks) **7**:53-4, 56-8, 60-2, 68, 75, 78, 80-1, 85, 91, 96, 102, 104-05
"Annie Hill's Grave" (Merrill) **28**:248
"Annie's Arctic Snake" (Wakoski) **15**:334
"Annihilation" (Aiken) **26**:24
"The Anniversarie" (Donne) **1**:130
The Anniversaries (Donne) **1**:145-48, 155-56, 158
"Anniversario" (Montale) **13**:110
"Anniversary" (Elytis) **21**:118-19, 134
"An Anniversary" (Berry) **28**:12-13
"The Anniversary" (Lowell) **13**:66, 97
"Anniversary" (Marvell)
See "The First Anniversary of the Government under O. C."
"Anniversary" (Montale)
See "Anniversario"
"The Anniversary" (Stryk) **27**:204
Anno Domini MCMXXI (Akhmatova) **2**:3, 13-14, 18
"Annual" (Swenson) **14**:284
"The Annunciation" (Merton) **10**:339
"Annunciation Eve" (Tsvetaeva)
See "Kanun Blagoveshchen'ia"
Annunciations (Tomlinson) **17**:359-60
"Annus Mirabilis" (Larkin) **21**:237
"Annus Mirabilis: The Year of Wonders, 1666" (Dryden) **25**:90-1, 93, 95, 99, 115-16
"El año lírico" (Dario) **15**:95, 117
"anodetodalevy" (Bissett) **14**:31
"Another Animal" (Swenson) **14**:284
Another Animal (Swenson) **14**:246, 251-52, 260, 264, 267, 274, 277, 282-83
"Another August" (Merrill) **28**:221
"Another Letter to My Husband" (Bradstreet) **10**:28
"Another New-yeeres Gift; or song for the Circumcision" (Herrick) **9**:118, 120
"Another Poem for Me--After Recovering from an O.D." (Knight) **14**:39, 43, 53
"Another Son" (McGuckian) **27**:100
"Another Space" (Page) **12**:180, 190, 197-98
"Another Spring" (Levertov) **11**:169-70
"Another Spring" (Rexroth) **20**:207
"Another Time" (Auden) **1**:18-19, 30, 34
"Another Time" (Soto) **28**:402
"Another Word on the Scientific Aspiration" (Lindsay) **23**:269
"Another Year" (Williams) **7**:370
"anrufung des fisches" (Enzensberger) **28**:136
"Answer" (Finch)
See "Ardelia's Answer to Ephelia"
"Answer!" (Guillen)
See "Responde tú"
"The Answer" (Herbert) **4**:130
"The Answer" (Jeffers) **17**:129, 131
The Answer (Montagu) **16**:340-41, 346
"An Answer to the Rebus" (Wheatley) **3**:363
"Answering a Question in the Mountains" (Ashbery) **26**:129
"Answering Magistrate Chang" (Wang Wei) **18**:364-65
"Antaeus" (Heaney) **18**:203, 207-9
"Antaeus: A Fragment" (Owen) **19**:354
"Antaryami" (Tagore) **8**:408
"Ante Aram" (Brooke) **24**:62
"Ante Lucem" (Blok) **21**:2, 23
"Ante Mortem" (Jeffers) **17**:117, 141
"An Antebellum Sermon" (Dunbar) **5**:120, 123, 133, 147
"Antecedents" (Tomlinson) **17**:302-04, 306, 311, 323, 338
"Antenati" (Pavese) **13**:217, 220, 225-26
"Antéros" (Nerval) **13**:181, 191-92, 194, 198

"Anthem for Doomed Youth" (Owen) **19**:326, 332, 336, 346, 360-63, 365-67, 369-70
Anthology (Jimenez)
See *Antolojía poética (1898-1953)*
"Antico, sono ubriacato della tua voce" (Montale) **13**:115, 141
"Anti-Desperation" (Arnold) **5**:7
"Antigone" (Arnold) **5**:8
"Antigua casa madrileña" (Aleixandre) **15**:34, 36
"Antinous" (Pessoa) **20**:165, 169
"Antiphon" (Herbert) **4**:103
"The Antiphon" (Levertov) **11**:198
"Anti-poem" (Shapiro) **25**:316, 321
"Antipoema?" (Fuertes) **27**:48
"The Antiquity of Freedom" (Bryant) **20**:43, 47
L'Antitête (Tzara) **27**:234-37
"Anti-Vietnam War Peace Mobilization" (Ginsberg) **4**:76
Antología mayor (Guillen) **23**:142
Antología total (Aleixandre) **15**:32
Antología y poemas (Fuertes) **27**:10-1
Antología y poemas del suburbio (Fuertes) **27**:10, 18
Antologia y poemas del suburbio Aconsejo beber hilo (Fuertes) 27
Antolojía poética (1898-1953) (Jimenez) **7**:183-84
"Antrim" (Jeffers) **17**:117
"Any Human to Another" (Cullen) **20**:60
"anyone lived in a pretty how town" (Cummings) **5**:81
"Any Porch" (Parker) **28**:353-54
"Anywhere is a Street into the Night" (Momaday) **25**:202, 212
Aoneko (Hagiwara Sakutaro) **18**:170, 172-73, 175-77, 181-83
"Apache Love" (Ortiz) **17**:224
"Apache Red" (Ortiz) **17**:228
"The Apartment Is as Silent as Paper" (Mandelstam) **14**:149
"The Apennines" (Bryant) **20**:16-17
"Apes and Ivory" (Noyes) **27**:114
"Aphorisms, I" (Villa) **22**:355
"Aphorisms, II" (Villa) **22**:353, 355
"Aphorisms, III" (Villa) **22**:355
"Aphorisms on Futurism" (Loy) **16**:311-13, 316, 322, 324
"Aphrodite" (Gluck) **16**:150
"Aphrodite Ode" (Sappho)
See "Ode to Aphrodite"
"Apocalipsis" (Cardenal) **22**:112, 125, 129
"Apocalypse"
See "Apocalipsis"
"Apocalypse"
See "Apocalipsis"
"Apocalypse: Umbrian Master, abut 1490" (Enzensberger) **28**:151
"Apogee of Celery" (Neruda)
See "Apogeo del apio"
"Apogeo del apio" (Neruda) **4**:277
"Apollo at Pheræ" (Masters) **1**:329
"Apollo in New York" (Viereck) **27**:278
"Apollo of the Physiologists" (Graves) **6**:152-53
"An Apollonian Elegy" (Duncan) **2**:105
Apollonius of Tyana (Olson) **19**:282, 298
"Apollo's Edict" (Swift) **9**:252
"Apologia pro poemate meo" (Owen) **19**:329, 334-35, 344, 348, 353-55, 370
"Apologies to the Federal Bureau of Investigation" (Giovanni) **19**:108
"Apology for Bad Dreams" (Jeffers) **17**:129-30, 142, 147
"The Apology of Demetrius" (Masters) **1**:343
"Apology of Genius" (Loy) **16**:308, 321
"An Apology to the Lady Cartaret" (Swift) **9**:296
Apophoreta (Martial) **10**:230, 241
"Apostrophe to a Dead Friend" (Kumin) **15**:218-20
"The Apostrophe to Vincentine" (Stevens) **6**:309
"apoteos" (Ekeloef) **23**:75
"Apparent Failure" (Browning) **2**:68
"The Apparition" (Donne) **1**:130, 152
"The Apparition of His Mistress Calling Him to Elizium" (Herrick) **9**:93, 103, 133, 138-39
"The Apparitions" (Yeats) **20**:351
"An Appeal to the American People" (Harper) **21**:190
"Appearances" (Gluck) **16**:157, 161
Appendice (Pasolini) **17**:279
"Appendix Form in Poetry" (Viereck) **27**:287
"Appendix to the Anniad Leaves from a Loose-Leaf War Diary" (Brooks) **7**:61
"L'Appennino" (Pasolini) **17**:270
"Appetite" (Smith) **12**:310
"The Apple" (Kinnell) **26**:261
"The Apple" (Page) **12**:168, 170
"The Apple Blossom Snow Blues" (Lindsay) **23**:264
"An Apple Gathering" (Rossetti) **7**:260-1, 280
"Apple Tragedy" (Hughes) **7**:143, 159
"The Apple Tree" (Berry) **28**:5
"The Apple Trees" (Gluck) **16**:126-27, 132, 140, 142
"The Apple Woman's Complaint" (McKay) **2**:210
"Apples and Water" (Graves) **6**:141
"Appleton House" (Marvell)
See "Upon Appleton House"
"The Apple Tree" (Parker) **28**:364
The Applewood Cycles (Viereck) **27**:286, 289
"The Applicant" (Plath) **1**:394, 400-01
"The Appology" (Finch) **21**:140, 159, 162, 167, 178
"Apprehensions" (Duncan) **2**:110, 112
"An Apprentice Angel" (MacDiarmid) **9**:155
"Approach to Thebes" (Kunitz) **19**:156, 161, 168, 173-74
"The Approaching Silence" (Illyes) **16**:248
Approximate Man (Tzara)
See *L'Homme approximatif*
"Appuldurcombe Park" (Lowell) **13**:84
"Après le déluge" (Rimbaud) **3**:261
"Après une lecture de Dante" (Hugo) **17**:96-97
L'après-midi d'un faune (Mallarme) **4**:186, 188, 190, 197, 207-08
"April" (Gluck) **16**:171
"April 1885" (Bridges) **28**:83
"April Fables" (Nishiwaki) **15**:231
April Galleons (Ashbery) 162, 174
"April Is the Saddest Month" (Williams) **7**:351, 354, 400
"April was Opening its Flowers" (Guillen)
See "April was Opening its Flowers"
"Aquarelles" (Verlaine) **2**:415
"L'aquarium" (Laforgue) **14**:72
"The Aquarium" (Lowell) **13**:79
"Aquatre heures du matin" (Rimbaud) **3**:274
"Aquí estoy expuesta como todos" (Fuertes) **27**:25
"Arabel" (Masters) **1**:328
Arap Petra Velikogo (Pushkin) **10**:394
Ararat (Gluck) **16**:157-64, 168, 170
Arbre des voyageurs (Tzara) **27**:234
Arbuthnot (Pope)
See *An Epistle to Dr. Arbuthnot*
"L'Arc" (Perse) **23**:228
"The Arc Inside and Out" (Ammons) **16**:12, 61
"L'arca" (Montale) **13**:113
"La Arcadia perdida" (Cardenal) **22**:132
"Arcady Unheeding" (Sassoon) **12**:240, 275
Archaeologist of Morning (Olson) **19**:268, 282, 306, 308
"Archaic Figure" (Clampitt) **19**:92
Archaic Figure (Clampitt) **19**:91-3
The Archeology of Movies and Books (Wakoski) **15**:372-73
Archer (Viereck) **27**:285, 288-89, 291-92
Archer in the Marrow (Viereck) **27**:287-88, 292
Archer in the Marrow The Applewood Cycles 1967-1987 (Viereck) **27**:285-86
"Archibald Higbie" (Masters) **1**:333
"The Archipelago" (Holderlin)
See "Der Archipelagus"
"Der Archipelagus" (Holderlin) **4**:147-48, 164
"Architecture" (Stevens) **6**:293
"An Architecture" (Berry) **28**:4, 7
"The Architecture: Passages 9" (Duncan) **2**:107
"Ardelia to Melancholy" (Finch) **21**:146, 150, 152, 157, 165, 168, 177-80
"Ardelia's Answer to Ephelia" (Finch) **21**:148, 154-55, 163, 165
The Ardent Slingsman (Neruda)
See *El hondero entusiasta, 1923-1924*
"Ardilla de los tunes de un katu" (Cardenal) **22**:131
"La arena traicionada" (Neruda) **4**:292-93
"Arethusa" (Shelley) **14**:167
"The Argument" (Aiken) **26**:24
"The Argument of His Book" (Herrick) **9**:85, 95, 97, 101, 105, 107-10, 116, 132-34, 138-39, 141
"Ariadne" (H. D.) **5**:304
Arias tristes (Jimenez) **7**:199, 209
"Ariel" (Plath) **1**:381, 409, 413
Ariel (Plath) **1**:379-80, 383-84, 387, 389-91, 393-96, 405-07, 410-11
"Ariettes oubliées" (Verlaine) **2**:431
"Arion" (Eliot) **20**:123, 125, 134-35, 145
"Ariosto" (Mandelstam) **14**:144
"Ariosto and the Arabs" (Borges) **22**:92
"Ariso" (Ishikawa) **10**:215
Aristophanes' Apology (Browning) **2**:96
"Arizona Desert" (Tomlinson) **17**:331, 341
"The Ark" (Montale)
See "L'arca"
"The Armada" (Swinburne) **24**:312
"Armageddon" (Tennyson) **6**:407-08, 413, 415-18
"Armed with the vision of narrow wasps" (Mandelstam)
See "Vooruzhennyi zren'em uzkikh os"
"Armenia" (Mandelstam) **14**:118
"Les armes miraculeuses" (Cesaire) **25**:8, 29
Les Armes Miraculeuses (Cesaire) **25**:15, 18, 21, 29-30, 44
"Armgart" (Eliot) **20**:101, 116, 124, 131, 133-36, 144
"Armor's Undermining Modesty" (Moore) **4**:267
"Arms" (Tagore)
See "Bahu"
"Arms and the Boy" (Owen) **19**:336, 354, 358
"Army Song" (Wang Wei) **18**:367
Arogya (Tagore) **8**:424, 426
"Around Pastor Bonhoeffer" (Kunitz) **19**:158
"Arras" (Page) **12**:168, 170, 178, 180, 189-90, 197
"Arremba sulla strinata proda" (Montale) **13**:116
"Arrest of Antoñito the Camborio" (Garcia Lorca)
See "Prendimiento de Antoñito el Camborio"
"Arrival" (Guillen) **23**:105
"Arrival at Santos" (Bishop) **3**:44
"The Arrival of the Bee Box" (Plath) **1**:410-13
"Arrivals, Departures" (Larkin) **21**:236
"Arriving at the Frontier on a Mission" (Wang Wei) **18**:367, 389
"Arrow" (Dove) **6**:123
"Arrows of Flowers" (Bissett) **14**:7
Ars Amandi (Ovid)
See *Ars amatoria*
Ars amatoria (Ovid) **2**:233-34, 238-39, 241-47, 253-55, 261
"Ars poetica" (Dove) **6**:121-22
"Ars poetica?" (Milosz) **8**:197, 201
"Ars Poetica: A Found Poem" (Kumin) **15**:216
"Arsenio" (Montale) **13**:107, 120, 124-25, 147, 164
"Arsinoë" (Ekeloef) **23**:59, 61
"Art" (Emerson) **18**:98
"L'art" (Gautier) **18**:128, 156-57, 164

"An Art Called Gothonic" (Olson) **19**:305
L'Art d'être grand-père (Hugo) **17**:65, 86
Art of Love (Ovid)
See *Ars amatoria*
"Art of Poetry" (Verlaine)
See "L'Art poètique"
"The Art of Response" (Lorde) **12**:140
The Art of Worldly Wisdom (Rexroth) **20**:179, 181-83, 192, 198, 203, 211, 213
"L'Art poètique" (Verlaine) **2**:416-18, 428, 430-34
Art the Herald (Noyes) **27**:140
"Arte poética" (Guillen) **23**:128
"L'arte povera" (Montale) **13**:138
"Artémis" (Nerval) **13**:173, 179, 181, 184-87, 195-96, 198
"Artemis Prologuises" (Browning) **2**:26
"Artificer" (Milosz) **8**:191
"Artillerie" (Herbert) **4**:101, 129
"Artillery" (Herbert)
See "Artillerie"
"The Artist" (Blok) **21**:16
"An Artist" (Heaney) **18**:215
"An Artist" (Jeffers) **17**:141
"The Artist" (Kunitz) **19**:161, 168, 173-75
"The Artists' and Models' Ball" (Brooks) **7**:107
"An Arundel Tomb" (Larkin) **21**:229-30, 234, 238-39, 258
"As a Possible Lover" (Baraka) **4**:16
"As a World Would Have It" (Robinson) **1**:460
"As Any (Men's Hells Having Wrestled with)" (Cummings) **5**:108
"As Bad as a Mile" (Larkin) **21**:233-34
"As Children Together" (Forche) **10**:144, 156-57, 168-69
"As Eagles Soar" (Toomer) **7**:340
"As Envoy to the Barbarian Pass" (Wang Wei) **18**:362
As Fine As Melanctha (Stein) **18**:327
"As Flowers Are" (Kunitz) **19**:155, 162
"As for Fame I've Had It" (Ammons) **16**:44
"As Hermes Once" (Keats) **1**:279
"As I Ebb'd with the Ocean of Life" (Whitman) **3**:396-97, 421
"As I Grow Older" (Hughes) **1**:251
"As I Lay with My Head on Your Lap Camarado" (Whitman) **3**:379
"As I Sat Alone by Blue Ontario's Shore" (Whitman) **3**:377, 387
"As I Went Down to Havre de Grace" (Wylie) **23**:305, 310, 324
"As in a rose the true fire moves" (Villa) **22**:351
"As Is the Sea Marvelous" (Cummings) **5**:104
"As kingfishers catch fire" (Hopkins) **15**:169
"As Lovers Do" (MacDiarmid) **9**:156
"As Loving Hind" (Bradstreet) **10**:35-6
"As My Blood Was Drawn" (Hayden) **6**:194
"As One Does Sickness Over" (Dickinson) **1**:94
"As One Put Drunk into the Packet Boat" (Ashbery) **26**:120
"As one who hath sent forth on bold emprise" (Belloc) **24**:10
"As Seen by Disciples" (Brooks) **7**:63
As Ten, as Twenty (Page) **12**:163-64, 167, 173, 193
"As the Dead Prey upon Us" (Olson) **19**:321, 323
"As virtuous men pass mildly away" (Donne)
See "A Valediction: forbidding mourning"
"As We Desired" (Guillen)
See "Como quisimos"
"As We Know" (Ashbery) **26**:136-138, 141, 156, 172
As We Know (Ashbery) **26**:131-132, 135-137, 140
"As Weary Pilgrim" (Bradstreet) **10**:8, 15, 28, 34, 36-7
"As You Leave Me" (Knight) **14**:41, 43, 52
"Asahya bhalobasa" (Tagore) **8**:405
"Ascensão de Vasco da Gama" (Pessoa) **20**:155
"aschermittwoch" (Enzensberger) **28**:134
"Ash Snow or Moonlight" (Lee) **24**:240
"The Ash Tree" (Marie de France)
See "Le Fraisne"
"Ashar nairashya" (Tagore) **8**:405
Ashes (Bely)
See *Pepel'*
"The Ashes of Gramsci" (Pasolini) **17**:258, 284, 288-89
The Ashes of Gramsci (Pasolini)
See *Le ceneri di Gramscí*
The Ashes of Gramsci (Pasolini) **17**:286-87
"Ashes of Life" (Millay) **6**:206
Ashes: Poems New and Old (Levine) **22**:218-19, 223-24
"Ashurnatsirpal III" (Sandburg) **2**:323
Ash-Wednesday (Eliot) **5**:162-64, 170, 174, 186, 192, 194, 197-206, 209-10
"Asian Birds" (Bridges) **28**:51, 85
"Aside" (Shapiro) **25**:295
"Ask Me No More" (Tennyson) **6**:366
"Ask the Roses" (Levine) **22**:224
Ask Your Mama: 12 Moods for Jazz (Hughes) **1**:249, 251-53, 261, 268, 270
"The Asking" (Soto) **28**:400-01
"Asleep" (Owen) **19**:336, 354, 359, 368
Asolando (Browning) **2**:96
Asolando: Fancies and Facts (Browning) **2**:66-7, 88
"An Aspect of Love, Alive in the Fire and Ice" (Brooks) **7**:82, 88, 91, 94
"Aspen Tree" (Celan) **10**:112-13
Asphalt Georgics (Carruth) **10**:77, 91
"Asphodel, That Greeny Flower" (Williams) **7**:371, 375, 390-92, 402-03
"The Ass" (Smith) **12**:302-6, 319
"Assassin" (Hass) **16**:195
"The Assassin" (Sexton) **2**:365 .
"Assassin" (Tomlinson) **17**:318, 322, 325-27, 341, 345-46
"Assassination Raga" (Ferlinghetti) **1**:173
"Assault" (Millay) **6**:236, 238
"Assay of the Infinite Man" (Neruda)
See *Tentativa del hombre infinito*
"An Assent to Wildflowers" (Meredith) **28**:192
"The Assertion" (Day Lewis) **11**:146
"Assommons les pauvres" (Baudelaire) **1**:59
"The Assumption" (Noyes) **27**:136
"Astigmatism" (Lowell) **13**:84
"Astrea Redux. A Poem on the Happy Restoration and Return of His Sacred Majesty Charles the Second" (Dryden) 99-101, 103-06
"the astrologer predicts at mary's birth" (Clifton) **17**:37
"Astronauts" (Hayden) **6**:194
"The Astronomer Poems" (Wakoski) **15**:348, 365
"Astrophel" (Swinburne) **24**:313
"Astrophel: A Pastoral Elegy" (Spenser) **8**:365, 367, 387
"The Asylum" (Carruth) **10**:71, 82-4
"At a Bach Concert" (Rich) **5**:352, 387, 393
"At a Calvary near the Ancre" (Owen) **19**:334, 341, 362-63
"At a Concert of Music" (Aiken) **26**:24, 72
"At a Country Funeral" (Berry) **28**:16, 29
"At a Country Hotel" (Nemerov) **24**:260
"At a Glance" (Tomlinson) **17**:333
"At a Hasty Wedding" (Hardy) **8**:85
"At a Lunar Eclipse" (Hardy) **8**:89
"At a Party" (Bogan) **12**:106
"At a Potato Digging" (Heaney) **18**:200
"At a Solemn Music" (Milton)
See "At a Solemn Music"
"At a Solemn Musick" (Schwartz) **8**:289
"At a Wayside Shrine" (Owen) **19**:362
"At a Window" (Sandburg) **2**:300
"At Algeciras--A Meditation upon Death" (Yeats) **20**:342
"At Auden's Grave" (Shapiro) **25**:322
"At Baia" (H. D.) **5**:267
"At Barstow" (Tomlinson) **17**:353, 355
"At Candle-Lightin' Time" (Dunbar) **5**:122
"At Castle Boterel" (Hardy) **8**:118
"At Cedar Creek" (Wright) **14**:375
"At Cooloolah" (Wright) **14**:344, 371
"At Dawn" (Milosz) **8**:210
"At Daybreak" (Sassoon) **12**:247
"At Daybreak" (Zagajewski) **27**:389
"At Dusk" (Cummings) **5**:93, 106
"At Easterly" (Clampitt) **19**:100
"At First, at Last" (Swenson) **14**:262, 288
"At Grass" (Larkin) **21**:229, 238-39, 244, 251, 257
"At Hanratty's" (Tomlinson) **17**:361
"At Holwell Farm" (Tomlinson) **17**:326, 341, 349, 352, 354
"At Ithaca" (H. D.) **5**:268
"At Melville's Tomb" (Crane) **3**:90, 103
"At My Father's Grave" (MacDiarmid) **9**:156
"At My Hospital Window" (Viereck) **27**:294, 296
"At Night" (Ekeloef) **23**:85
"At North Farm" (Ashbery) **26**:159-160
"At Odd Moments" (Brutus) **24**:116
"At One O'Clock in the Morning" (Baudelaire)
See "A une heure du matin"
"At School" (Smith) **12**:330, 333
"At Sea" (Toomer) **7**:336
At Terror Street and Agony Way (Bukowski) **18**:23
"At That Hour" (Joyce)
See "III"
"At the Ball Game" (Williams) **7**:368, 385
"At the Birth of an Age" (Jeffers) **17**:111, 130,141-42, 144
"At the Caberet-Vert" (Rimbaud)
See "Au caberet-vert"
"at the cemetary walnut grove plantation south carolina 1989" (Clifton) **17**:30
"At the Centre" (Gunn) **26**:226
"At the Edge" (Tomlinson) **17**:343, 345
"At the Fall of an Age" (Jeffers) **17**:141, 144
"At the Faucet of June" (Williams) **7**:382-83, 387-89, 410
"At the feet of others I did not forget" (Lermontov)
See "At the feet of others I did not forget"
"At the Ferocious phenomenon of 5 O'clock I find Myself" (Cummings) **5**:93
"At the Fillmore" (Levine) **22**:224
"At the Fishhouses" (Bishop) **3**:42, 46, 48
"At the Gare Bruxelles-Midi" (Ferlinghetti) **1**:183
"At the Gates of the Tombs" (Sandburg) **2**:307
"At the German Writers Conference in Munich" (Dove) **6**:109
"At the Grave of Henry Vaughan" (Sassoon) **12**:246-47
"At the Hairdresser's" (Brooks) **7**:58, 68, 86, 102
"At the Head of This Street a Gasping Organ is Waving Moth-" (Cummings) **5**:93
"At the Indian Killer's Grave" (Lowell) **3**:202
"At the Lincoln Monument in Washington, August 28, 1963" (Walker) **20**:277-78
"At the Loom: Passages 2" (Duncan) **2**:107
"At the Museum of Modern Art" (Swenson) **14**:265
"At the National Black Assembly" (Baraka) **4**:28, 38
"At the Piano" (Hardy) **8**:93
"At the River Charles" (Viereck) **27**:282
"At the Tourist Centre in Boston" (Atwood) **8**:5, 23
At the Very Edge of the Sea (Akhmatova)
See *U samovo morya*
"At The-Place-of-Sadness" (Gallagher) **9**:64
"At This Point" (Montale)
See "A questo punto"
"At Waking" (Hardy) **8**:104
"At Welsh's Tomb" (Wakoski) **15**:353
Atalanta in Calydon (Swinburne) **24**:340
Atarashiki yokujo (Hagiwara Sakutaro) **18**:175
"Atavism" (Wylie) **23**:301, 307

"Atavismo" (Pavese) **13**:209, 214
Atemwende (Celan) **10**:96-7, 105, 110
"AThe Miracle" (Bukowski) **18**:5
"Atherton's Gambit" (Robinson) **1**:466
"Atlanta in Camden Town" (Carroll) **18**:46
Atlanta Offering Poems (Harper) **21**:189
"The Atlantic" (Tomlinson) **17**:333
"Atlantic City Waiter" (Cullen) **20**:52, 64
"Atlantic Oil" (Pavese) **13**:223
"Atlantis" (Crane) **3**:90, 97, 106, 110-11
"An Atlas of the Difficult World" (Rich) **5**:398
An Atlas of the Difficult World: Poems, 1988-1991 (Rich) **5**:398-99
Atta Troll: Ein Sommernachtstraum (Heine) **25**:132-34, 137-38, 164
"Attack" (Sassoon) **12**:266, 283-84, 286
"An Attempt at a Room" (Tsvetaeva)
See "Popytka komnaty"
"An Attempt at Jealousy" (Tsvetaeva)
See "Popytka revnosti"
"Attention, Attention" (Baraka) **4**:24
"The Attic Which Is Desire" (Williams) **7**:351, 399
"Attis" (Tennyson) **6**:363
"Atys, the Land of Biscay" (Housman) **2**:179, 181
"Au caberet-vert" (Rimbaud) **3**:283
"Au Clair de la lune" (MacDiarmid) **9**:191
"Au Comte d'Orsay" (Lamartine) **16**:267
"Au lecteur" (Baudelaire) **1**:46, 57, 67, 70
"Au platane" (Valery) **9**:365, 394-96
"Au Rossignol" (Lamartine) **16**:280
"Au Roy" (Ronsard)
See "Discours au Roy"
"Au Salon" (Pound) **4**:364
"Aubade" (Gluck) **16**:133
"Aubade" (Larkin) **21**:259
"Aubade" (Lowell) **13**:93
"Aubade" (Sitwell) **3**:297
"Aubade" (Smith) **12**:331
"Aubade: Harlem" (Merton) **10**:340
"Aubade: Lake Erie" (Merton) **10**:333, 340, 350
"Aubade--The Annunciation" (Merton) **10**:339
"Aube" (Rimbaud) **3**:261-62, 264
"L'aube spirituelle" (Baudelaire) **1**:56, 63
"The Auction" (Kinnell) **26**:286
"Audley Court" (Tennyson) **6**:365
"Auf dem See" (Goethe) **5**:255
"Auguries of Innocence" (Blake) **12**:35-6
"Augurios" (Paz) **1**:361
"August" (Belloc) **24**:29
"August" (Rich) **5**:371
"August" (Wylie) **23**:319, 322, 332
"August 22, 1939" (Rexroth) **20**:195
"August First" (Carruth) **10**:91
"An August Midnight" (Hardy) **8**:112
"August Night" (Swenson) **14**:266, 284
"August on Sourdough, A Visit from Dick Brewer" (Snyder) **21**:288
"August Was Foggy" (Snyder) **21**:288
Aujourd'hui (Hugo) **17**:80
"Aul Bastundzi" (Lermontov) **18**:300
"The Auld Farmer's New Year Morning Salutation" (Burns)
See "The Auld Farmer's New Year Morning Salutation"
"The Auld Farmer's New Year's Day Address to His Auld Mare Maggie" (Burns) **6**:78
"Auld Lang Syne" (Burns) **6**:59, 75, 98-9
"AÚN" (Dario) **15**:98
Aún (Neruda) **4**:289
"Aunque cegué de mirarte" (Juana Ines de la Cruz) **24**:187
"Aunt Chloe's Politics" (Harper) **21**:200, 202, 213
"Aunts" (McGuckian) **27**:95
"La aurora" (Garcia Lorca) **3**:141
"Aurora Borealis" (Dove) **6**:110
Aurora Leigh (Browning) **6**:2, 6-7, 10-13, 21-3, 25-6, 31-2, 34-8, 40, 44, 46
"The Auroras of Autumn" (Roethke) **15**:280
"The Auroras of Autumn" (Stevens) **6**:338
Auroras of Autumn (Stevens) **6**:303, 335
"Aurore" (Valery) **9**:356, 363, 365, 367-68, 371, 394, 396
"Aus der Harzreise" (Heine) **25**:139
"Aus einer Sturmnacht" (Rilke) **2**:277
"Ausencia" (Borges) **22**:94
Ausgewahlte gedichte (Celan) **10**:102
"Aussi bien que les cigales" (Apollinaire) **7**:18, 22
"Aussöhnung" (Goethe) **5**:250-51
"The Author to her Book" (Bradstreet) **10**:7, 18, 27, 34
"The Author upon Himself" (Swift) **9**:295-96, 304, 306, 308-09
"The Author's Earnest Cry and Prayer" (Burns) **6**:78-9
"The Author's Manner of Living" (Swift) **9**:295
"Author's Note on Marabouts and Planted Poets" (Viereck) **27**:259, 262
"Auto Wreck" (Shapiro) **25**:279, 288, 297, 312, 319, 325
"Autobiografía" (Fuertes) **27**:49
"Autobiography" (Ferlinghetti) **1**:177-80, 183-84, 187
"Autobiography" (Gunn) **26**:205, 208
"Autobiography" (Harjo) **27**:71
Autobiography (Zukofsky) **11**:365
"Autochthon" (Masters) **1**:333
"Automatism of Taste" (Tzara) **27**:235
"Automne" (Apollinaire) **7**:42
"L'automne" (Lamartine) **16**:277, 290, 298, 301
"Automne malade" (Apollinaire) **7**:39, 42-3
"Autoprólogo" (Fuertes) **27**:23
"Autopsicografia" (Pessoa) **20**:172
"The Autopsy" (Elytis) **21**:123
"Autopsychography" (Pessoa)
See "Autopsicografia"
"Autre complainte de Lord Pierrot" (Laforgue) **14**:81, 97
Autre complainte de Lord Pierrot (Laforgue) **14**:62, 88
"Autre complainte de l'orgue de barbarie" (Laforgue) **14**:81, 98
Autrefois (Hugo) **17**:80
"The Autumn" (Lamartine)
See "L'automne"
"Autumn" (Lowell) **13**:97
"Autumn" (Neruda)
See "Otoño"
"Autumn" (Pasternak) **6**:266
"Autumn" (Smith) **12**:345
"Autumn" (Tomlinson) **17**:339
"An Autumn Burning" (Berry) **28**:9
"Autumn Cellars" (Montale) **13**:149-50
"Autumn Equinox" (Rich) **5**:351-52, 393
"Autumn Forest" (Pasternak) **6**:267
"Autumn Gold: New England Fall" (Ginsberg) **4**:54
"Autumn in California" (Rexroth) **20**:194, 214
"Autumn Lament" (Mallarme)
See "Plainte d'automne"
"Autumn Meditation" (Wang Wei) **18**:343
"Autumn Sequence" (Rich) **5**:363, 382
"Autumn Song" (Dario)
See "Canción otoñal"
"Autumn Valentine" (Parker) **28**:365
"Autumnal" (Dario) **15**:117
Autumnal Leaves (Hugo) **17**:44
"Auvergnat" (Belloc) **24**:34
"Aux Chrétiens" (Lamartine) **16**:280
"Aux Ecluses du vide" (Cesaire) **25**:12
"Aux ruines de Montfort-L'Amaury" (Hugo) **17**:89
"Avant-dernier mot" (Laforgue) **14**:95
"Avarice" (Herbert) **4**:102, 130
"Ave atque Vale" (Swinburne) **24**:321, 330-35, 337
"Ave Imperatrix!" (Kipling) **3**:190
"Ave Maria" (Crane) **3**:84, 86
"Avenel Gray" (Robinson)
See "Mortmain"
"Avenue" (Pinsky) **27**:175
"The Avenue Bearing the Initial of Christ into the New World" (Kinnell) **26**:236-37, 239, 241, 257, 262, 264, 289
"Avenue of Limes" (Pasternak) **6**:267
"The Avenue of Poplars" (Williams) **7**:382
"Aviary" (McGuckian) **27**:81, 98
"Avis de tirs" (Cesaire) **25**:29
"Aviso a los gobernantes del mundo" (Fuertes) **27**:2
"Avisos" (Pessoa) **20**:162
"Avocado Lake" (Soto) **28**:375, 379
"Avondale" (Smith) **12**:352
"Avondall" (Smith) **12**:352
Avon's Harvest (Robinson) **1**:465-66, 468-69
"Avtobus" (Tsvetaeva) **14**:325, 327
Awake in the Red Desert (Bissett) **14**:12, 14, 18-19
"Awake, my heart, to be loved: awake, awake" (Bridges) **28**:53, 63, 87
"Awakening" (Stryk) **27**:184, 186-87, 189, 206, 213
Awakening (Stryk) **27**:181, 195-98, 202-3, 213-16
"Awakening of the Waterfall" (Tagore)
See "Nirjharer svapnabhanga"
"Away, Melancholy" (Smith) **12**:333
"Awe and Devastation of Solomos" (Elytis) **21**:135
"Awful Music" (Merton) **10**:337
The Awful Rowing Toward God (Sexton) **2**:360, 367-68, 371-73
"The Awthorn" (Clare) **23**:46-7
"Axe Handles" (Snyder) **21**:308
Axe Handles (Snyder) **21**:299-302, 307-10, 320
"The Ax-Helve" (Frost) **1**:215
The Axion Esti (Elytis) **21**:118, 120-30, 133
"Ay qué tristeza que tengo!" (Guillen) **23**:119-20, 127
"Ayer me dijeron negro" (Guillen) **23**:142
"Ayíasma" (Ekeloef) **23**:64
"Aylmer's Field" (Tennyson) **6**:362
"Aymerillot" (Hugo) **17**:58
Ázma iroikó ke pénthimo yia ton haméno anthipolohaghó tis Alvanías (Elytis) **21**:115, 120, 124, 127-29
"Azrail" (Lermontov) **18**:300
Azul (Dario) **15**:78, 86-7, 91-2, 94-6, 102-03, 105-07, 115, 117-18, 120
"L'azur" (Mallarme) **4**:199-200, 208, 213
"The Azure" (Mallarme)
See "L'azur"
"Azure and Gold" (Lowell) **13**:60
"Babbitry" (Stryk) **27**:211
"The Babe" (Olson) **19**:319-20
"Babocka" (Brodsky) **9**:29
"The Baby" (Nash) **21**:278
"Baby" (Sexton) **2**:367
"Baby Picture" (Sexton) **2**:370
"Baby song" (Gunn) **26**:210
"Baby V" (Levine)
See "Baby Villon"
"Baby Villon" (Levine) **22**:213
"Babyhood" (Swinburne) **24**:323
"Babylon Revisited" (Baraka) **4**:18
"The Bacchae" (H. D.) **5**:305
"Bacchanales" (Ronsard) **11**:230-32, 234
"Bacchanalia" (Pasternak) **6**:267
"Bacchus" (Emerson) **18**:85, 99, 103, 106
"Bacchus and the Pirates" (Noyes) **27**:121, 124-25, 133
"Bachelor" (Meredith) **28**:189
"Bachelor Uncle" (Wright) **14**:348
"Back Again, Home" (Madhubuti) **5**:324, 329, 338
The Back Country (Snyder) **21**:288, 291-92, 296, 300
"Back from a Walk" (Garcia Lorca)
See "Vuelta de paseo"
"back in th city" (Bissett) **14**:30
"The Back o' Beyond" (MacDiarmid) **9**:196
"Back to Life" (Gunn) 26;192, 212

"Backdrop Addresses Cowboy" (Atwood) **8**:4, 16, 41
"The Backlash Blues" (Hughes) **1**:251, 257
"The Backside of the Academy" (Rukeyser) **12**:236
"The Backward Look" (Nemerov) **24**:287, 301
"Backyard" (Wright) **14**:377
"The Bacterial War" (Nemerov) **24**:298
The Bad Child's Book of Beasts (Belloc) **24**:12, 23-6, 35
"Bad Dreams" (Browning) **2**:59
"Bad Dreams" (Pinsky) **27**:145
"The Bad Glazier" (Baudelaire)
See "Le mauvais vitrier"
"Bad Man" (Hughes) **1**:270
"Bad Morning" (Hughes) **1**:241
"Bad Ol' Stagolee" (Walker) **20**:287
"The Bad Old Days" (Rexroth) **20**:218
The Bad Parents' Garden of Verse (Nash) **21**:264-65
"Bad Penny" (Levine) **22**:218
"The Bad Season Makes the Poet Sad" (Herrick) **9**:89, 103, 109, 115
"Badger" (Clare) **23**:7
"The Badgers" (Heaney) **18**:219, 244
"Baha'u'llah in the Garden of Ridwan" (Hayden) **6**:185-86, 196, 198
"Bahnhofstrasse" (Joyce) **22**:137
"Bahu" (Tagore) **8**:407
"Baignée" (Valery) **9**:392
"La bailerina de los pies desnudos" (Dario) **15**:80
"Le baiser" (Char) **15**:138, 144, 171
The Bak-Chesarian fountain: A Tale of the Tauride (Pushkin)
See *Bakhchisaraiski Fontan*
The Bakhchisarai Fontan (Pushkin)
See *Bakhchisaraiski Fontan*
Bakhchisaraiski Fontan (Pushkin) **10**:358, 365, 386-88, 411, 417, 419, 421
"Le Bal" (Vigny) **26**:410-11
"Bal des pendus" (Rimbaud) **3**:281, 283
"La balada azul" (Guillen) **23**:100, 140
"Balada de los dos abuelos" (Guillen) **23**:138
Baladas de primavera (Jimenez) **7**:184
Balaka (Tagore) **8**:413-15, 418, 427
"Balakhana" (McGuckian) **27**:82, 93
"Balanchine's" (Merrill) **28**:254
"Le balcon" (Baudelaire) **1**:45, 63
"The Balcony" (Baudelaire)
See "Le balcon"
"Balcony Scene" (Shapiro) **25**:316
"Balder Dead" (Arnold) **5**:35, 37, 58-9, 62
"Balin and Balan" (Tennyson) **6**:376-77
"Ballad" (Ammons) **16**:25
"Ballad" (Pasternak) **6**:270
"Ballad Fourth: The Trogger" (Burns) **6**:78
"Ballad of Army Wagons" (Tu Fu) **9**:330
"The Ballad of Ballymote" (Gallagher) **9**:42
"The Ballad of Beautiful Words" (Nash) **21**:273
"A Ballad of Boding" (Rossetti) **7**:271
"The Ballad of Chocolate Mabbie" (Brooks) **7**:57, 68, 102, 104
"The Ballad of East and West" (Kipling) **3**:157, 182-83, 188
"Ballad of Faith" (Williams) **7**:363
"The Ballad of Father O'Hart" (Yeats) **20**:349
"A Ballad of François Villon" (Swinburne) **24**:324
"The Ballad of Jakko Hill" (Kipling) **3**:187
"The Ballad of Late Annie" (Brooks) **7**:102-04
"The Ballad of Launcelot and Elaine" (Masters) **1**:328
"The Ballad of Margie Polite" (Hughes) **1**:241, 243, 247
"Ballad of Missing Lines" (Rukeyser) **12**:228
"The Ballad of Moll Magee" (Yeats) **20**:337
"The Ballad of Nat Turner" (Hayden) **6**:176, 178-80, 186-87, 194-95, 198
"Ballad of Pearl May Lee" (Brooks) **7**:57, 68, 86, 103-04
"A Ballad of Remembrance" (Hayden) **6**:200
A Ballad of Remembrance (Hayden) **6**:183, 188, 194-95
"The Ballad of Rudolph Reed" (Brooks) **7**:62, 96
"A Ballad of Sark" (Swinburne) **24**:313
"Ballad of Simón Caraballo" (Guillen) **23**:106
The Ballad of St. Barbara and Other Verses (Chesterton) **28**:96-97
"The Ballad of Sue Ellen Westerfield" (Hayden) **6**:196
"Ballad of the Black Sorrow" (Garcia Lorca)
See "Romance de la pena negra"
"The Ballad of the *Bolivar*" (Kipling) **3**:164
"The Ballad of the Brown Girl" (Cullen) **20**:55, 64, 85-86
The Ballad of the Brown Girl: An Old Ballad Retold (Cullen) **20**:61, 77, 79, 86
"The Ballad of the Children of the Czar" (Schwartz) **8**:302, 305, 309
"Ballad of the Dark Trouble" (Garcia Lorca)
See "Romance de la pena negra"
"Ballad of the Five Senses" (MacDiarmid) **9**:157, 193
"Ballad of the Free" (Walker) **20**:276, 284, 292
"The Ballad of the Harp-Weaver" (Millay) **6**:211, 225, 233
"Ballad of the Hoppy Toad" (Walker) **20**:290-92
"Ballad of the Jollie Gleeman" (Viereck) **27**:259
"The Ballad of the King's Jest" (Kipling) **3**:182
"Ballad of The Ladies of Past Times" (Villon)
See "Ballade des Dames du Temps Jadis"
"Ballad of the Landlord" (Hughes) **1**:258, 267
"Ballad of the Little Square" (Garcia Lorca)
See "Ballada de la Placeta"
"The Ballad of the Lonely Masturbator" (Sexton) **2**:352, 370
"The Ballad of the Long-Legged Bait" (Thomas) **2**:382, 393, 402
"Ballad of the Moon, the Moon" (Garcia Lorca)
See "Romance de la luna, luna"
"The Ballad of the Red Earl" (Kipling) **3**:181-82
"Ballad of the Spanish Civil Guard" (Garcia Lorca)
See "Romance de la Guardia Civil Española"
"Ballad of the Summoned Man" (Garcia Lorca) **3**:147
"The Ballad of the True Beast" (Hayden) **6**:196-97
"Ballad of the Two Grandfathers" (Guillen) **23**:103, 132
See "Balada de los dos abuelos"
The Ballad of the White Horse (Chesterton) **28**:93, 100, 105-08, 119-28
"Ballad of the World Extinct" (Celan)
See "Ballade von der erloschenen Welt"
"The Ballad of Valès-Dunes" (Belloc) **24**:11
"Ballad Written in a Clinic" (Montale)
See "Ballata scritta in una clinica"
"Ballada de la Placeta" (Garcia Lorca) **3**:125
"Ballade" (Dunbar) **5**:139-40
"Ballade" (Gautier) **18**:348-51
"Ballade" (Stryk) **27**:191
"Ballade de bon conseil" (Villon) **13**:394-95
"Ballade de bonne doctrine" (Villon) **13**:394-95, 404-05
"Ballade de conclusion" (Villon) **13**:417
"Ballade de la Grosse Margot" (Villon) **13**:389-90, 393
"Ballade de mercy" (Villon) **13**:399, 413
"Ballade des contre verites" (Villon) **13**:414
"Ballade des Dames du Temps Jadis" (Villon) **13**:374, 405, 409-10
"Ballade des femmes de Paris" (Villon) **13**:380, 390, 413
"Ballade des Langues Envieuses" (Villon) **13**:404
"Ballade des menus propos" (Villon) **13**:409
"Ballade des Pendus" (Villon)
See "Epitaphe Villon"
"Ballade des proverbes" (Villon) **13**:404, 414
"Ballade des seigneurs du temps jadis" (Villon) **13**:410
"Ballade du concours de Blois" (Villon) **13**:392, 414
"La ballade du Mal Aimé" (Apollinaire)
See "La chanson du mal-aimé"
":Ballade d'une grande dame" (Chesterton) **28**:117
"Ballade of a Talked-off Ear" (Parker) **28**:363
"Ballade of Big Plans" (Parker) **28**:354
"Ballade of Dead Ladies" (Villon) **13**:387, 390-91
"Ballade of Fat Margot" (Villon)
See "Ballade de la Grosse Margot"
"Ballade of Hell and Mrs Roebeck" (Belloc) **24**:49
"A Ballade of Interesting News" (Belloc) **24**:42
"Ballade of the Critic" (Shapiro) **25**:281
"Ballade of the Hanged" (Villon)
See "Epitaphe Villon"
"Ballade of Suicide" (Chesterton) **28**:99
"Ballade of the Women of Paris" (Villon)
See "Ballade des femmes de Paris"
"Ballade of Unfortunate Mammals" (Parker) **28**:351, 363
"Ballade pour prier Nostre Dame" (Villon) **13**:403, 405, 413
"Ballade pour Robert d'Estouteville" (Villon) **13**:395, 415
"Ballade to Our Lady" (Villon) **13**:390-91
"Ballade vom Auszug der drei" (Celan) **10**:126
"Ballade von der erloschenen Welt" (Celan) **10**:125
Ballades en Jargon (Villon) **13**:404, 406
Ballads for Sale (Lowell) **13**:76, 84-5
Ballads of Spring (Jimenez)
See *Baladas de primavera*
"Ballata scritta in una clinica" (Montale) **13**:108, 131, 167
"The Ballet" (Meredith) **28**:193, 215
"Ballet" (Pavese)
See "Balletto"
"Balletto" (Pavese) **13**:205, 226
"Balloons" (Plath) **1**:391
"The Ballroom at Sandover" (Merrill) **28**:235
Balustion's Adventure (Browning) **2**:85-6, 95
"Bamboo" (Hagiwara Sakutaro)
See "Take"
"Bamboo Lodge" (Wang Wei) **18**:382
Banabani (Tagore) **8**:416
"Banaphul" (Tagore) **8**:405
"La Bande Noire" (Hugo) **17**:87-88
"Bandi" (Tagore) **8**:407, 412
"Bandot" (Stryk) **27**:204-5
"The Bands and the Beautiful Children" (Page) **12**:169, 177
"Banga bir" (Tagore) **8**:407
"The Bangkok Gong" (Kumin) **15**:213
"The Bangs" (Montale)
See "La frangia dei capelli"
"Banishment" (Sassoon) **12**:267, 288
"A Banjo Song" (Dunbar) **5**:146
"A Banjo Song" (Johnson) **24**:136, 141
"The Banker's Daughter" (Lowell) **3**:218, 221
"Banking Coal" (Toomer) **7**:333
"The bankrupt Peace Maker" (Lindsay) **23**:269
"Banks of a Stream Where Creatures Bathe" (Merrill) **28**:223, 255
"Banneker" (Dove) **6**:105, 109
"The Banner Bearer" (Williams) **7**:389-90
"The Banners" (Duncan) **2**:102
"Banquet" (Gozzano) **10**:183
"The Banquet" (Herbert) **4**:134
The Banquet (Dante)
See *Convivio*
"Bantams in Pine-Woods" (Stevens) **6**:293, 303, 327
"Banyan" (Swenson) **14**:273
"Baptism" (Herbert) **4**:100
"Baptism" (McKay) **2**:211
"Barbare" (Cesaire) **25**:23-25, 28, 31, 37
"Barbare" (Rimbaud) **3**:261

Barbare (Cesaire) **25**:10
"Barbecue" (Stryk) **27**:208
"The Bard" (Gray) **2**:134-35, 139, 143-44, 146, 148, 151-54
"The Bards" (Graves) **6**:140, 144
"Bards of Passion *and* of Mirth" (Keats) **1**:312
"Barefoot" (Sexton) **2**:352
"The Barefoot Dancer" (Dario)
See "La bailerina de los pies desnudos"
Barely and Widely, 1956-1958 (Zukofsky) **11**:348
Barking at the Moon (Hagiwara Sakutaro)
See *Tsuki ni hoeru*
"Barking Hall: A Year After" (Swinburne) **24**:318-19
"Barmaids Are Diviner than Mermaids" (Nash) **21**:265
"The Barn" (Heaney) **18**:194, 200
"Baroque Comment" (Bogan) **12**:90, 92, 97, 101
"A Baroque Sunburst" (Clampitt) **19**:90
"Barrabas. Eine Phantasie" (Trakl) **20**:239
Barrack Room Ballads and Other Verses (Kipling) **3**:155-56, 159-60, 163, 165, 167-69, 177, 182, 187-89
"The Barrel Organ" (Noyes) **27**:115-16, 133, 136-38
"The Barrier" (McKay) **2**:212
"Bartok" (Illyes) **16**:231
"Base Details" (Sassoon) **12**:268, 277, 280
"Baseball and Writing" (Moore) **4**:242, 256, 259-60
"Baseball Canto" (Ferlinghetti) **1**:183
"Basement Apartment" (Shapiro) **25**:316
"A Basin of Eggs" (Swenson) **14**:250
"The Basket" (Lowell) **13**:84, 95-6
"Baskets" (Gluck) **16**:152
"A Bastard Peace" (Williams) **7**:369
"The Bastille" (Brooke) **24**:66, 80, 84, 89
"Bateau ivre" (Hugo) **17**:65
Le bateau ivre (Rimbaud) **3**:249, 257-58, 268-70, 272-74, 282, 286
"The Bath" (Snyder) **21**:292, 297
"A Bather" (Lowell) **13**:93-6
"The Bathers" (Shapiro) **25**:304
"Bathos" (Pope) **26**:357
"Batjushkov" (Mandelstam) **14**:118
"Batouque" (Cesaire) **25**:29
"Battalion-Relief" (Sassoon) **12**:269
"The Battle" (Brooks) **7**:67
"The Battle of Brunanburh" (Tennyson) **6**:363, 369
The Battle of Marathon: A Poem (Browning) **6**:19
"The Battle of Osfrontalis" (Hughes) **7**:123, 142, 160-61
"The Battlefield" (Bryant) **20**:5
"Battle Problem" (Meredith) **28**:172, 189
"Battle Wagon" (Meredith) **28**:174
"Baudelaire" (Schwartz) **8**:311, 319
"Bayn al-khara'ib" (Gibran) **9**:79
"Bayonne Turnpike to Tuscarora" (Ginsberg) **4**:54
"Bayou Afternoon" (Clampitt) **19**:102
Be Angry at the Sun and Other Poems (Jeffers) **17**:123, 135
"Be Still, My Soul, Be Still" (Housman) **2**:184, 192
"Beach at Versilia" (Montale)
See "Proda di Versilia"
"Beach Glass" (Clampitt) **19**:88
"The Beach Head" (Gunn) **26**:218
"The Beach Women" (Pinsky) **27**:162
"The Beachcomber" (Stryk) **27**:185-86
"Beachy" (Sandburg) **2**:300
"The Beaks of Eagles" (Jeffers) **17**:145
"Beale Street Love" (Hughes) **1**:269
"The Bean Eaters" (Brooks) **7**:55-6, 62, 69, 100
The Bean Eaters (Brooks) **7**:56-8, 62-3, 67, 81, 86, 95-6, 98-9, 101-02, 105, 107
"Beans with Garlic" (Bukowski) **18**:23
"The Bean-Stalk" (Millay) **6**:237, 239
"The Bear" (Frost) **1**:203-04
"The Bear" (Kinnell) **26**:241-42, 244, 252, 257, 262-63, 273, 291
"The Bear" (Momaday) **25**:185-86, 188, 191, 193-95, 201-202, 209-10, 220
"The Bear and the Garden-Lover" (Moore) **4**:261
"The Bearer of Evil Tidings" (Frost) **1**:202
Beast in View (Rukeyser) **12**:231-32
"The Beast's Confession to the Priest" (Swift) **9**:281, 295
"The Beaters" (Gunn) **26**:198, 201, 220
"Le beau navire" (Baudelaire) **1**:60
"Beau sang giclé" (Cesaire) **25**:44-5
"La beauté" (Baudelaire) **1**:61, 65
"Beauté de femmes, leur faiblesse, et ces mains pâles" (Verlaine) **2**:416
"The Beautiful American Word, Sure" (Schwartz) **8**:302, 315
"Beautiful Black Men (with compliments and apologies to all not mentioned by name)" (Giovanni) **19**:106-7, 112
"Beautiful Lofty Things" (Yeats) **20**:307
"A Beautiful Young Nymph Going to Bed. Written for the Honour of the Fair Sex" (Swift) **9**:257, 262, 267-69, 279, 281, 283-84, 286, 291, 295, 298, 301-03
"The Beauty" (Pushkin) **10**:371
"Beauty" (Wylie) **23**:300, 313, 327, 333
Beauty (Jimenez)
See *Belleza*
"Beauty and Beauty" (Brooke) **24**:56, 62
"Beauty and Sadness" (Song) **21**:341, 347
"Beauty and the Beast" (Dove) **6**:108
"Beauty and the Beast" (Tomlinson) **17**:323
"Beauty and the Illiterate" (Elytis) **21**:123
"The Beauty of the Head" (Swenson) **14**:281
"Beauty Shoppe" (Brooks) **7**:59, 102
"Beauty Who Took Snuff" (Pushkin) **10**:407
"Bebop Boys" (Hughes) **1**:267
"Because I Love You (Last Night)" (Cummings) **5**:105
"Because I Was Not Able to Restrain Your Hands" (Mandelstam) **14**:114, 118
"Because One Is Always Forgotten" (Forche) **10**:138, 142, 144, 153, 155
"Because,thy,smile,is,primavera" (Villa) **22**:356, 358
Beckonings (Brooks) **7**:84, 94
"The Bed by the Window" (Jeffers) **17**:131
"The Bed in the Sky" (Snyder) **21**:289
"Bed Time" (Hughes) **1**:255
"The Bedpost" (Graves) **6**:141
"A Bedtime Story" (Hughes) **7**:159
"The Bee Meeting" (Plath) **1**:394, 410-13
Bee Time Vine (Stein) **18**:316-34, 336, 341-42, 344, 349-54
"Beech" (Frost) **1**:197
"Beech, Pine, and Sunlight" (Lowell) **13**:64
Beechen Vigil and Other Poems (Day Lewis) **11**:148
"Beehive" (Toomer) **7**:311, 320, 334
"The Beekeeper Speaks" (Nemerov) **24**:262, 274
"The Beekeeper's Daughter" (Plath) **1**:389, 410-12
"Beeny Cliff" (Hardy) **8**:136
"Bees Stopped" (Ammons) **16**:46
"Beethoven Attends the C Minor Seminar" (Tomlinson) **17**:320
"Beethoven Opus 111" (Clampitt) **19**:82, 85, 89
"Before a Blue Light" (Kumin) **15**:211
"Before a Midnight Breaks in Storm" (Kipling) **3**:183
"Before an Old Painting of the Crucifixion" (Momaday) 186, 188, 190, 197-98, 211, 219
"Before I Knocked and Flesh Let Enter" (Thomas) **2**:383, 402
"Before Knowledge" (Hardy) **8**:89
"Before the Altar" (Lowell) **13**:69, 83
"Before the Battle" (Sassoon) **12**:262
"Before the Birth of one of her Children" (Bradstreet) **10**:12, 18
"Before the Dance" (Tomlinson) **17**:319, 328, 330
"Before the Judgment" (Duncan) **2**:116
"Before the Storm" (Lowell) **13**:60-1
"Before the Trip" (Montale)
See "Prima del viaggio"
"Before We Mothernaked Fell" (Thomas) **2**:402
"Before We Sinned (Incarnate Devil)" (Thomas) **2**:402
"Begat" (Sexton) **2**:366
"The Beggar to Mab, the Fairies' Queen" (Herrick) **9**:86
"The Beggars" (Wordsworth) **4**:377
"The Beggar's Valentine" (Lindsay) **23**:286
"The Beginner" (Kipling) **3**:183
"Beginner's Guide" (Nemerov) **24**:285
"The Beginning" (Brooke) **24**:56, 82
"The Beginning" (Gluck) **16**:164, 167
"Beginning a Poem of These States" (Ginsberg) **4**:81
"The Beginning and the End" (Jeffers) **17**:128, 132, 141
The Beginning and the End and Other Poems (Jeffers) **17**:114-15, 123, 128, 136
"The Beginning of September" (Hass) **16**:199, 210
"The Beginning of the End of the World" (Clifton) **17**:29
"Beginnings" (Hayden) **6**:190
"The Beginnings" (Kipling) **3**:192
"Behind the Arras" (Dunbar) **5**:133
"Behind the Mirror" (Gunn) **26**:210-213
"Beiname" (Goethe) **5**:248
"The Being as Memory" (Carruth) **10**:71
"The Being as Moment" (Carruth) **10**:71
"The Being as Prevision" (Carruth) **10**:71
"Being Beauteous" (Rimbaud) **3**:261, 263-64
"Being of Beauty" (Rimbaud) **3**:263
"Being Young and Green" (Millay) **6**:236
"Le Bel oiseau déchiffrant l'inconnu au couple d'amoureux" (Breton) **15**:49
Belaia staia (Akhmatova)
See *Belaya staya*
Belaia staja (Akhmatova)
See *Belaya staya*
Belaya staya (Akhmatova) **2**:3, 6, 11-12, 18
"Belderg" (Heaney) **18**:203
"Belfast Tune" (Brodsky) **9**:28
"Believe History" (Jeffers) **17**:141
"La bell au bois dormant" (Valery) **9**:392
"La belle dame sans merci" (Keats) **1**:279, 282, 304-05
"La belle Dorothée" (Baudelaire) **1**:49
"La belle époque" (Milosz) **8**:211
"La Belle Hequmière aux filles de joie" (Villon) **13**:389
"Belle lecon aux enfants perdus" (Villon) **13**:394-95
Belleza (Jimenez) **7**:202
"The Bells" (Poe) **1**:430-31, 439, 441
"The Bells" (Sexton) **2**:359
Bells and Pomegrantes (Browning) **2**:27, 70
"Bells in the Rain" (Wylie) **23**:328-29
"Bells in Winter" (Milosz) **8**:189, 205
Bells in Winter (Milosz) **8**:174
Bells of Lombardy (Stryk) **27**:214-15, 218
"Bells of Winter" (Milosz)
See "Bells in Winter"
"The Bells that Signed" (Day Lewis) **11**:144
"Belly Song" (Knight) **14**:46, 48
Belly Song and Other Poems (Knight) **14**:41-2, 48, 52
"Below" (Celan) **10**:118
"Below Tintern" (Tomlinson) **17**:334, 336
"Belsazar" (Heine) **25**:140
"Belsen, Day of Liberation" (Hayden) **6**:194
"Belts" (Kipling) **3**:162
"Ben Jonson Entertains a Man from Stratford" (Robinson) **1**:462, 468, 487
"Benares" (Borges) **22**:72

"Bending the Bow" (Duncan) **2**:107
Bending the Bow (Duncan) **2**:104, 107, 113-116, 119, 125, 127
"Beneath a Cool Shade" (Behn) **13**:15
"Beneath My Hand and Eye the Distant Hills, Your Body" (Snyder) **21**:288
Beneath the Fortinaria (Bukowski) **18**:21
"Bénédiction" (Baudelaire) **1**:54, 70
"Benediction" (Kunitz) **19**:148
"Bengali Heroes" (Tagore)
See "Banga bir"
"Benjamin Pantier" (Masters) **1**:347
"Bennie's Departure" (McKay) **2**:225
"Ben's Last Fight" (Merton) **10**:345
Beowulf **22**:1-65
Beppo: A Venetian Story (Byron) **16**:83, 115-20
"Berck-Plage" (Plath) **1**:390
"Bereavement" (Smith) **12**:351
"Bereft" (Hardy) **8**:131
"Bergidylle" (Heine) **25**:145
"Berkeley Eclogue" (Hass) **16**:217
"Berlin" (Ferlinghetti) **1**:167
"Berlin in ruins" (Gunn) **26**:211-212
"Berlin Is Hard on Colored Girls" (Lorde) **12**:142
The Berlin Songbook (Bely)
See *Berlinsky pesennik*
Berlinsky pesennik (Bely) **11**:7
"Bermudas" (Marvell) **10**:268-69, 271, 275, 289, 311, 313-14
"Berry Holden" (Masters) **1**:324
"Bertha in the Lane" (Browning) **6**:17
"Los besos" (Aleixandre) **15**:38
"Bessey of the Glen" (Clare) **23**:25
"The Best of It" (Sassoon) **12**:248, 260
"Best Years" (Soto) **28**:398-99
Le bestiaire; ou, Cortège d'Orphée (Apollinaire) **7**:48
Bestiary/Bestiario (Neruda) **4**:286-87
"A Bestiary for My Daughters Mary and Katharine" (Rexroth) **20**:187, 190, 195, 218
"Bestiary U.S.A." (Sexton) **2**:367
"Besuch bei Ingres" (Enzensberger) **28**:150
"Besy" (Pushkin) **10**:413
"Betancourt" (Baraka) **4**:15
"Betraktelse" (Ekeloef) **23**:76
"Betrayal" (Pavese)
See "Tradimento"
"The Betrothal" (Apollinaire)
See "Les fiançailles"
"The Betrothal" (Millay) **6**:211
"Betrothed" (Bogan) **12**:127-28
"A Better Resurrection" (Rossetti) **7**:290
"Between Our Selves" (Lorde) **12**:139
Between Our Selves (Lorde) **12**:137, 156
"Between the Porch and the Altar" (Lowell) **3**:200, 203-04, 206
"Between Us" (Merrill) **28**:252
"Between Walls" (Williams) **7**:399, 402
"Beucolicks" (Herrick) **9**:89
"Beverly Hills, Chicago" (Brooks) **7**:81
"Beware!" (Wylie) **23**:322
"Beware, Madam!" (Graves) **6**:163
"Bewick Finzer" (Robinson) **1**:467
"Beyond Even Faithful Legends" (Bissett) **14**:6, 24, 31
Beyond Even Faithful Legends (Bissett)
See *Selected Poems: Beyond Even Faithful Legends*
"Beyond Harm" (Olds) **22**:325, 341
"Beyond Sharp Control" (Brutus) **24**:116
"Beyond the Alps" (Lowell) **3**:205, 211, 218, 221
"Beyond the Last Lamp" (Hardy) **8**:125
Beyond the Mountains (Rexroth) **20**:185-86
"Beyond the Pleasure Principle" (Nemerov) **24**:260
"Bez nazvaniya" (Pasternak) **6**:288
"Bezverie" (Pushkin) **10**:409, 411
"Bhagna mandir" (Tagore) **8**:415
"Bhairavi gan" (Tagore) **8**:407
Bhanu singha (Tagore) **8**:403
Bhanusingh Thakurer padavali (Tagore) **8**:405
"Bhar" (Tagore) **8**:412
"Biafra" (Levertov) **11**:176, 194
"Bianca among the Nightingales" (Browning) **6**:23-4, 28, 32, 38, 40
"The Bible Defense of Slavery" (Harper) **21**:190, 208, 217
"Bibliographie" (Enzensberger) **28**:137
"Bickford's Buddha" (Ferlinghetti) **1**:186-87
"Bien loin d'ici" (Baudelaire) **1**:49
"Bien que le trait de vostre belle face" (Ronsard) **11**:250
"Bifurcation" (Tzara) **27**:229-31
"The Big Baboon" (Belloc) **24**:24
"Big Bastard with a Sword" (Bukowski) **18**:13
"Big Bessie Throws Her Son into the Street" (Brooks) **7**:63, 81
"Big Elegy" (Brodsky)
See "The Great Elegy for John Donne"
"Big Fat Hairy Vision of Evil" (Ferlinghetti) **1**:167
"The Big Graveyard" (Viereck) **27**:262
"The Big Heart" (Sexton) **2**:368
"Big John Henry" (Walker) **20**:287
"Big Momma" (Madhubuti) **5**:326, 344
"Big Wind" (Roethke) **15**:276, 279
"The Bight" (Bishop) **3**:50, 52-4
"Les bijoux" (Baudelaire) **1**:61
"The Billboard Painters" (Ferlinghetti) **1**:183
"Billboards and Galleons" (Lindsay) **23**:287
"Bill of Fare" (Enzensberger) **28**:142
Billy the Kid (Ondaatje) **28**:293-94, 296-97
"Bimini" (Heine) **25**:167
"The Biographer's Mandate" (Nemerov) **24**:289
Biographical Information (Fuertes) **27**:
Biographical Information (Noyes) **27**:
"Il Biondomoro" (Pasolini) **17**:264
"Birches" (Frost) **1**:196, 221, 225, 227-28, 230
"Birches" (Wylie) **23**:326
"Bird" (Harjo) **27**:72
"The Bird and the Arras" (Finch) **21**:157, 160, 172
"The Bird Auction" (McGuckian) **27**:94
"Bird Call Valley" (Wang Wei) **18**:381-82, 391
"The Bird Frau" (Dove) **6**:108
"Bird of Air" (H. D.) **5**:287
"The Bird with the Coppery, Keen Claws" (Stevens) **6**:293, 304
"Birdbrain!" (Ginsberg) **4**:62, 76
"Birdcage Walk" (Merton) **10**:351
"Birdcries Stream" (Wang Wei)
See "Birdcries Stream"
"The Birds" (Belloc) **24**:5, 8
"Birds" (Cesaire) **25**:46
"Birds" (Jeffers) **17**:147
"Birds" (Wright) **14**:347, 349, 353, 366
Birds (Perse)
See *Oiseaux*
Birds (Wright) **14**:348-49, 354
"Birds for Janet" (Ondaatje) **28**:318, 332
"Birds in the Night" (Verlaine) **2**:415
"Birds of Prey" (McKay) **2**:212
"The birds that sing on Autumn eves" (Bridges) **28**:84
"Birds without Descent" (Aleixandre) **15**:19-21
"Bird-Singing Stream" (Wang Wei) **18**:360, 376, 380-81, 386, 390
"The Biretta" (Heaney) **18**:256
"Birmingham" (Walker) **20**:283, 287
"Birmingham Sunday" (Hughes) **1**:252
"Birth and Death" (Jeffers) **17**:141
"Birth and Death" (Swinburne) **24**:324
"The Birth in a Narrow Room" (Brooks) **7**:54, 80
"Birth of a Fascist" (Viereck) **27**:280
"Birth of a Genius among Men" (MacDiarmid) **9**:153
"Birth of a Smile" (Mandelstam)
See "Rozhdenie ulybki"
"The Birth of Christ" (Garcia Lorca)
See "Nacimiento de Cristo"
The Birth of Kumara (Kalidasa)
See *Kumarasambhava*
The Birth of the Prince (Kalidasa)
See *Kumarasambhava*
"Birth of the Virgin" (Swenson) **14**:285
The Birth of the War-God (Kalidasa)
See *Kumarasambhava*
"Birthday" (Aleixandre) **15**:16
"Birthday" (Jeffers) **17**:141
"A Birthday" (Rossetti) **7**:276, 278, 280
The Birthday (Merrill) **28**:270
"A Birthday Cake for Lionel" (Wylie) **23**:321-22
"A Birthday Kid Poem" (Ortiz) **17**:228
"Birthday on the Beach" (Nash) **21**:270
"Birthday Poem" (Shapiro) **25**:263
"Birthday Sonnet" (Wylie) **23**:315
"Birthmarks" (Song) **21**:341
"The Birthplace" (Heaney) **18**:214
"Bisclavret" (Marie de France) **22**:258, 260, 268, 272, 282-84, 286, 298-99
"Bishop Blougram" (Browning) **2**:37
"Bishop Blougram's Apology" (Browning) **2**:43, 73
"The Bishop Orders His Tomb at St. Praxed's" (Browning) **2**:37, 48, 82, 94
"The Biting Insects" (Kinnell) **26**:288
"The Bitter River" (Hughes) **1**:251
Bixby Canyon to Jessore Road (Ginsberg) **4**:89
"Black and Unknown Bards" (Johnson) **24**:137, 142
"The Black Angel" (Montale)
See "L'angelo nero"
Black Armour (Wylie) **23**:301-302, 307, 309-10, 324, 332
"Black Art" (Baraka) **4**:10, 19, 25, 40
"The Black Art" (Sexton) **2**:373
Black Arts (Baraka) **4**:18
"Black Bill's Honeymoon" (Noyes) **27**:123, 134
"Black Blood" (Blok) **21**:5
"Black Buttercups" (Clampitt) **19**:83, 86, 91
"The Black Christ" (Madhubuti) **5**:339-40
The Black Christ and Other Poems (Cullen) **20**:59, 62, 64, 68
"The Black Christ (Hopefully Dedicated to White America)" (Cullen) **20**:59, 64-66, 68, 71, 73-75, 87
"Black Cock" (Montale)
See "Gallo cedrone"
"The Black Cottage" (Frost) **1**:193, 198
"BLACK DADA NIHILISMUS" (Baraka) **4**:9, 14
"Black Dancer in the Little Savoy" (Hughes) **1**:246
"Black Eagle Returns to St. Joe" (Masters) **1**:344
"Black Earth" (Mandelstam)
See "Chernozem"
"Black Earth" (Moore) **4**:251
Black Feeling, Black Talk (Giovanni) **19**:133, 135, 139
Black Feeling, Black Talk, Black Judgement (Giovanni) **19**:107-8, 110-11, 114, 118, 120-22, 124, 128, 136
"The Black Goddess" (Graves) **6**:154
Black Hair (Soto) **28**:379-80
"Black Harmonium" (Hagiwara Sakutaro)
See "Kuroi fukin"
Black Hosts (Senghor)
See *Hosties noires*
"Black Jackets" (Gunn) **26**:201
Black Judgement (Giovanni) **19**:135, 139, 143
"Black Leather Because Bumblebees Look Like It" (Wakoski) **15**:326
"Black Love" (Madhubuti) **5**:342
"Black Magdalens" (Cullen) **20**:56, 62, 64
"Black Magic" (Sanchez) **9**:223, 234
Black Magic: Sabotage, Target Study, Black Art; Collected Poetry, 1961-1967 (Baraka) **4**:6, 8, 16-18, 24, 26
"Black Majesty" (Cullen) **20**:64
"The Black Mammy" (Johnson) **24**:142

"The Black Man Is Making New Gods" (Baraka) **4**:19
"Black March" (Smith) **12**:300-01, 308, 319, 326
"The Black Mesa" (Merrill) **28**:223, 255
"Black Money" (Gallagher) **9**:36, 53
"Black Mother Woman" (Lorde) **12**:154, 156-57
"Black Nude" (Tomlinson) **17**:311
"Black Panther" (Hughes) **1**:251-52
"Black People!" (Baraka) **4**:19, 25-6
"The Black Pit" (Hayden) **6**:187
"Black Power Chant" (Baraka) **4**:19
Black Pride (Madhubuti) **5**:321, 336, 338-41, 346
"Black Pudding" (Gallagher) **9**:64
"Black Sampson of Brandywine" (Dunbar) **5**:129, 131, 138
"Black Shroud" (Ginsberg) **4**:90
"Black Silk" (Gallagher) **9**:50, 59, 62
"Black Sketches" (Madhubuti) **5**:337
"Black Song" (Guillen)
See "Canto negro"
"Black Tambourine" (Crane) **3**:98
The Black Unicorn (Lorde) **12**:137-38, 141-42, 144, 148, 151, 153-55, 157-58, 160
"The Black Virginity" (Loy) **16**:322
"Black/White" (Wright) **14**:366
Black white (Illyes)
See *Fekete feher*
"The Black Winds" (Williams) **7**:383-85, 388-89
"Black Woman" (Senghor) **25**:224-30
"Blackberrying" (Plath) **1**:407-09
"Blackberry-Picking" (Heaney) **18**:192
The Blackbird (Zagajewski) **27**:396
"Blackgirl Learning" (Madhubuti) **5**:344
"Blackman/An Unfinished History" (Madhubuti) **5**:326, 343, 345
Blacks (Brooks) **7**:105
"Black-Shouldered Kite" (Wright) **14**:344
"The Blacksmith's Serenade" (Lindsay) **23**:264
"The Blackstone Rangers" (Brooks) **7**:88, 90-1
"Blackstudies" (Lorde) **12**:147, 158
"Blake" (Borges) **22**:97
"Blame not my lute" (Wyatt) **27**:315, 324
"Blanc" (Valery) **9**:392
"Blanco" (Soto) **28**:375
Blanco (Paz) **1**:355-56, 358, 363, 368-69, 372, 374, 376-77
"Blasting from Heaven" (Levine) **22**:223
"Blaubeuren" (Tomlinson) **17**:360
"Bleeding" (Swenson) **14**:269-70, 285
"Blessed are They that Mourn" (Bryant) **20**:6
"Blessed Sleep" (Johnson) **24**:159
"The Blessed Virgin, Compared to the Air We Breathe" (Hopkins) **15**:166
"The Blessed Virgin Mary Compared to a Window" (Merton) **10**:330, 338
"A Blessing in Disguise" (Ashbery) **26**:129, 143
Blew Ointment (Bissett) **14**:5
blew trewz (Bissett) **14**:7-8
"Blighters" (Sassoon) **12**:263, 277, 282
"Blind Curse" (Ortiz) **17**:246
"The Blind Doge at 83" (Viereck) **27**:280
"The Blind Man" (Wright) **14**:337, 369
"Blind Panorama of New York" (Garcia Lorca)
See "Panorama ceigo de Nueva York"
"Der blinde junge" (Loy) **16**:309, 316
"Der blinde Sänger" (Holderlin) **4**:147
"The Blinded Bird" (Hardy) **8**:98
Blindenschrift (Enzensberger) **28**:133-35, 138-40, 143, 150
"Bliss" (Pushkin) **10**:407
Bliznets v tuchakh (Pasternak) **6**:263, 275
"blk/chant" (Sanchez) **9**:204, 225, 234
"blk / wooooomen / chant" (Sanchez) **9**:225
"Blödigkeit" (Holderlin) **4**:148
"Blood and the Moon" (Yeats) **20**:313
"Blood Feud" (Wylie) **23**:301
"Bloodbirth" (Lorde) **12**:157
"Bloodsmiles" (Madhubuti) **5**:337
"The Bloody Sire" (Jeffers) **17**:139
The Bloomingdale Papers (Carruth) **10**:78-84
"The Blossom" (Blake) **12**:7, 23, 33
"The Blossome" (Donne) **1**:126, 130, 147
"The Blow" (Hardy) **8**:94
"The Blow" (Neruda)
See "El golpe"
"Blow and Counterblow" (Montale)
See "Botta e riposta"
"The Blow-Fly" (Graves) **6**:163
"Blowing Boy" (Page) **12**:177
Blue (Dario)
See *Azul*
"Blue and White Lines after O'Keeffe" (Song) **21**:331, 334, 336, 340-41
"The Blue Cat" (Hagiwara Sakutaro) **18**:181
Blue Cat (Hagiwara Sakutaro)
See *Aoneko*
The Blue Estuaries: Poems, 1923-1968 (Bogan) **12**:96-7, 100-03, 107, 112, 120-21
"Blue Evening" (Brooke) **24**:57-8, 76
"Blue Farm" (McGuckian) **27**:95
"The Blue from Heaven" (Smith) **12**:302, 304, 319, 331, 333
"Blue Gem Creeper" (Tagore)
See "Nilamanilata"
"Blue Lantern" (Song) **21**:331, 338-40, 343
"The Blue Meridian" (Toomer) **7**:309, 311-12, 324-26, 328-29, 336,-37, 340
"Blue Moles" (Plath) **1**:389
"Blue Monday" (Wakoski) **15**:325, 348
"A Blue Ribbon at Amesbury" (Frost) **1**:196
"The Blue She Brings with Her" (McGuckian) **27**:81-82
"Blue Sky Rain" (McGuckian) **27**:82, 93
"The Blue Swallows" (Nemerov) **24**:300
The Blue Swallows (Nemerov) **24**:260-63, 274, 277, 281, 289, 291
"The Blue Tower" (Stryk) **27**:214
"A Blue Woman with Sticking out Breasts Hanging" (Cummings) **5**:99, 103
"Bluebeard" (Millay) **6**:205
"Blueberries" (Frost) **1**:225
"The Blue-Flag in the Bog" (Millay) **6**:233
"Blues" (Meredith) **28**:187
"Blues at Dawn" (Hughes) **1**:266
A Blues Book for Blue Black Magical Women (Sanchez) **9**:207, 211-16, 218-20, 228-29, 234, 238-41, 243
"Blues for Ruby Matrix" (Aiken) **26**:29
Blues for Ruby Matrix (Aiken) **26**:24
"Boädicea" (Tennyson) **6**:360, 363
"The Boat" (Sexton) **2**:365
"The Boat of Life" (Ishikawa)
See "Inochi no fune"
"The Boat of the White Feather Bird" (Ishikawa)
See "Shiraha no toribune"
"Boat Ride" (Gallagher) **9**:50-1, 58-60
"Boats on the Marne" (Montale) **13**:146
"The Bobby to the Sneering Lady" (McKay) **2**:226
"Bobo's Metamorphosis" (Milosz) **8**:187
Le Bocage (Ronsard) **11**:246
"Boccaccio: The Plague Years" (Dove) **6**:109
"THE BODY" (Bissett) **14**:9, 34
"Body" (Tagore)
See "Tanu"
"Body and Soul: A Mediation" (Kumin) **15**:206
"Body of Summer" (Elytis) **21**:115
Body of This Death (Bogan) **12**:85-7, 103-04, 116, 119-20, 126-28
"Body of Waking" (Rukeyser) **12**:217, 220
Body of Waking (Rukeyser) **12**:217, 219-21, 224
Body Rags (Kinnell) **26**:240-42, 244, 246, 257, 261, 290-91, 293
"Bog Oak" (Heaney) **18**:201
"Bog Queen" (Heaney) **18**:188, 195, 211
"Bogland" (Heaney) **18**:188, 195, 201, 205, 209, 211
"The Bohemian" (Dunbar) **5**:125
"Le bois amical" (Valery) **9**:391
Bojarin Orsha (Lermontov) **18**:300
"Bohemia" (Parker) **28**:363
"Bokardo" (Robinson) **1**:468
"Bomba" (Fuertes) **27**:39, 45
"Bomba atómica" (Guillen) **23**:124
"Bombardment" (Lowell) **13**:78
"Une bombe aux Feuillantines" (Hugo) **17**:100
"Bombinations of a Chimera" (MacDiarmid) **9**:193
"Bonaparte" (Lamartine) **16**:277, 291
"Bone Dreams" (Heaney) **18**:188, 204
"The Bones of My Father" (Knight) **14**:43,52
Bones of the Cuttlefish (Montale)
See *Ossi di seppia*
"The Bones Speak" (Wright) **14**:337, 339
"Bonfire" (Gallagher) **9**:61-2
"Bongo Song" (Guillen)
See "La canción del bongo"
Bonheur (Verlaine) **2**:417
La bonne chanson (Verlaine) **2**:413-14, 419, 431-32
"The Bonnie Broukit Bairn" (MacDiarmid) **9**:156, 160. 187
"Les bons chiens" (Baudelaire) **1**:58-9
"Bonsal" (Guillen) **23**:126
"The Book" (Dario)
See "El libro"
"A Book" (Stein) **18**:325, 348
"Book Buying in the Tenderloin" (Hass) **16**:195
The Book of Ahania (Blake) **12**:13
"Book of Ancestors" (Atwood) **8**:28-9, 42
"The Book of Annandale" (Robinson) **1**:460-61
The Book of Earth (Noyes) **27**:130, 132-133, 135
The Book of Ephraim (Merrill) **28**:224, 225, 227, 228, 229, 230, 231, 235, 236, 237, 243, 245, 260-61, 263, 266, 271-75, 278
Book of Fame (Chaucer)
See *House of Fame*
The Book of Folly (Sexton) **2**:355-56, 360, 365, 368
Book of Gypsy Ballads (Garcia Lorca)
See *Primer romancero gitano*
"The Book of Hours of Sister Clotilde" (Lowell) **13**:84
The Book of Light (Clifton) **17**:31
The Book of Los (Blake) **12**:62-4
"The Book of Myths" (Harjo) **27**:66-67
The Book of Nightmares (Kinnell) **26**:241-45, 247-49, 252-58, 261, 264-67, 271-75, 283, 291-93
Book of Pictures (Rilke)
See *Buch der Bilder*
The Book of Purgatory (Marie de France)
See *L'Espurgatoire Saint Patrice*
Book of Questions (Neruda)
See *Libro de las preguntas*
Book of Saint Valentines Day of the Parlement of Briddes (Chaucer)
See *Parlement of Foules*
Book of Songs (Garcia Lorca)
See *Canciones*
Book of Songs (Heine) **25**:153-54
"The Book of the Dead" (Rukeyser) **12**:203, 207, 213
The Book of the Dead (Rukeyser) **12**:210
Book of the Duchess (Chaucer) **19**:6, 10, 13, 21, 23, 38, 64-9, 71-4, 76
Book of the Duchesse (Chaucer)
See *Book of the Duchess*
Book of the Five and Twenty Ladies (Chaucer)
See *Legend of Good Women*
The Book of Thel (Blake) **12**:19, 33-5, 37, 51
Book of Troilus (Chaucer)
See *Troilus and Criseyde*
The Book of Urizen (Blake) **12**:15, 19, 35, 38, 60, 62
Book of Vagaries (Neruda)
See *Extravagario*
A Book of Verses (Masters) **1**:332, 342

Cumulative Title Index

"Booker T. Washington" (Dunbar) **5**:131
"Boom!" (Nemerov) **24**:266, 278
"A Boon" (Meredith) **28**:174
"Boone" (Berry) **28**:28, 38
"Boop-Boop-Adieup Little Group!" (Nash) **21**:265
"A Boor" (Bukowski) **18**:15
"Boot Hill" (Ondaatje) **28**:304
"Boots" (Kipling) **3**:192
"Booz endormi" (Hugo) **17**:65, 85
"Bora Ring" (Wright) **14**:335, 340, 374
The Borderers (Wordsworth) **4**:416
Borderland (Tagore)
See *Prantik*
The Borderland (Tagore)
See *Prantik*
"Born in December" (Rukeyser) **12**:224
Born of a Woman: New and Selected Poems (Knight) **14**:37-9, 41-2, 46, 49, 51-2
"Borodinó" (Lermontov) **18**:278, 283, 290, 297, 304
"Boston" (Stryk) **27**:203
"A Boston Ballad" (Whitman)
See "Poem of Apparitions in Boston in the 73rd Year of These States"
"The Boston Evening Transcript" (Eliot) **5**:153
"The Boston Hymn" (Emerson) **18**:77, 113, 119-20
"The Botanic Garden" (Noyes) **27**:129
"Botanical Gardens" (Masters) **1**:330
"Botanical Gardens" (Wright) **14**:341
"A Botanical Trope" (Meredith) **28**:190
"Botta e riposta" (Montale) **13**:129, 131, 134, 147, 165
"Bottle Green" (Smith) **12**:333
"The Bottle in the Sea" (Vigny)
See "La bouteille à la mer"
"Boudaries" (Wright) **14**:374
Bouge of Court (Skelton) **25**:329, 336-37, 340, 343, 349-50, 352, 361-62, 364-65, 367
"Bound No'th Blues" (Hughes) **1**:254
"A Boundless Moment" (Frost) **1**:218
"Bouquet" (Dario) **15**:113
The Bourgeois Poet (Shapiro) **25**:287-90, 292-94, 297, 299, 301-302, 308-11, 314-17, 321-22, 325
"Bournemouth" (Verlaine) **2**:416
"La bouteille à la mer" (Vigny) **26**:367, 371, 380-83, 391-92, 397, 402-404
"Bova" (Pushkin) **10**:407
"The Bowl and the Rim" (Graves) **6**:128
"The Bowl of Blood" (Jeffers) **17**:123, 144
"Bowls" (Moore) **4**:265
"A Box" (Stein) **18**:320-31, 349-50, 353
"A Box and Its Contents" (Ashbery) **26**:133
"The Boy" (Tagore) **8**:417
"Boy Driving his Father to Confession" (Heaney) **18**:243
"Boy with a Sea Dream" (Page) **12**:168, 170
"Boy with Book of Knowledge" (Nemerov) **24**:287
"Boy with His Hair Cut Short" (Rukeyser) **12**:223
The Boyar Orsha (Lermontov) **18**:279
"Boy-Man" (Shapiro) **25**:279, 297, 319
"Boys. Black." (Brooks) **7**:84
"A Boy's Summer Song" (Dunbar) **5**:138
A Boy's Will (Frost) **1**:192, 195, 197, 207, 213-14, 223-24
"Bracken Hills in Autumn" (MacDiarmid) **9**:197
"Brahma" (Emerson) **18**:83, 85, 88
"Braid Scots: An Inventory and Appraisement" (MacDiarmid)
See "Gairmscoile"
"Braiding" (Lee) **24**:247
"Brainstorm" (Nemerov) **24**:257, 268
"Braly Street" (Soto) **28**:375, 378-79, 384-85
"A Branch from Palestine" (Lermontov) **18**:298
"La branche d'amandier" (Lamartine) **16**:278
"Branches" (McGuckian) **27**:105
"Brancusi's Golden Bird" (Loy) **16**:321
"A Brand" (Johnson) **24**:160
"Brandons Both" (Rossetti) **7**:271
"Le brasier" (Apollinaire) **7**:47
"Brass Keys" (Sandburg) **2**:329
"Brass Spittoons" (Hughes) **1**:241, 263, 265
Bratya Razboiniki (Pushkin) **10**:358, 365, 386
Braving the Elements (Merrill) **28**:220, 221, 222, 223, 228, 229, 244, 254, 256, 258-59, 281
"Brawl" (Garcia Lorca)
See "Reyerta"
"The Brazier" (Apollinaire)
See "Le brasier"
"Brazil, January 1, 1502" (Bishop) **3**:56
"Brazil-Copacabana" (Guillen) **23**:117
"Brazilian Fazenda" (Page) **12**:178, 183, 190
"Brazzaville 22 Feb 72" (Brutus) **24**:123
"Bread" (Olds) **22**:328
"Bread" (Pasternak) **6**:267
"Bread Alone" (Wylie) **23**:311, 324
"Bread and Music" (Aiken) **26**:24, 72
"Bread and Wine" (Cullen) **20**:62
"Bread and Wine" (Holderlin)
See "Brot und Wein"
Bread in the Wilderness (Merton) **10**:352
The Bread of Time (Levine) **22**:231
"The Break" (Pasternak) **6**:280-82
"The Break" (Sexton) **2**:352-53
"Break, Break, Break" (Tennyson) **6**:358
"Break of Day" (Sassoon) **12**:244, 277
"Breake of Day" (Donne) **1**:152
"Breakfast" (Stauffer) **18**:322-23
"Breaking Green" (Ondaatje) **28**:331
"The Breaking of the Rainbows" (Nemerov) **24**:288
"Breaking Open" (Rukeyser) **12**:221, 224, 230
Breaking Open (Rukeyser) **12**:220, 224-25, 230
"Breaking Out" (Ammons) **16**:45, 63
"Breaklight" (Clifton) **17**:35
"The Breast" (Sexton) **2**:352, 364
"Breasts" (Tagore)
See "Stan"
"the breath" (Bissett) **14**:19, 24, 29, 34
"The Breathing" (Levertov) **11**:171
"Breathing Landscape" (Rukeyser) **12**:209
"The Breathing, the Endless News" (Dove) **6**:122
Breathing the Water (Levertov) **11**:200, 202-05, 209-10
Breath-Turning (Celan)
See *Atemwende*
"Bredon Hill" (Housman) **2**:160, 182-83, 185
"Brennan" (Wright) **14**:375
"Brennende liebe, 1904" (Gluck) **16**:128
"Brer Rabbit, You's de Cutes' of 'Em All" (Johnson) **24**:142, 163
"Brevity" (Wright) **14**:375-76
"Brian the Still-Hunter" (Atwood) **8**:19
"Briar Rose (Sleeping Beauty)" (Sexton) **2**:354, 365, 368
"The Bridal Ballad" (Poe) **1**:428, 432, 445, 447
The Bridal of Triermain (Scott) **13**:297, 301-02, 311-12, 314, 317, 320
"Bridal Piece" (Gluck) **16**:127
"Bride and Groom Lie Hidden for Three Days" (Hughes) **7**:165, 168
"The Bride in the Country" (Montagu) **16**:338
"The Bride of Abydos: A Turkish Tale" (Byron) **16**:91, 109
"Bride Song" (Rossetti) **7**:264
"The Bridegroom" (Kipling) **3**:183
"The Bride-Night Fire" (Hardy) **8**:99
"Bridge" (Ammons) **16**:40-1,54
The Bridge (Crane) **3**:84-5, 87-90, 93-8, 100-01, 105-10
"The Bridge of Estador" (Crane) **3**:100
"Briefings" (Ammons) **16**:31
Briefings: Poems Small and Easy (Ammons) **16**:10, 21-23, 28, 45-6
The Brigand Brothers (Pushkin)
See *Bratya Razboiniki*
"Bright Star" (Keats) **1**:279
"Bright Sunlight" (Lowell) **13**:64
"The Brigs of Ayr" (Burns) **6**:78
"Brilliant Sad Sun" (Williams) **7**:396, 409
"Brindis cotidiano" (Fuertes) **27**:39
"Bring Down the Beams" (Bukowski) **18**:4
"Bring the Day" (Roethke) **15**:252, 273-74, 301-02
Bringer of Water (Berry) **28**:35
"Bringers" (Sandburg) **2**:316-17, 324
"bringing home th bacon" (Bissett) **14**:34
"Bringing in New Couples" (Hughes) **7**:166
"Bringnal Banks are Wild and Fair For a' That" (Scott) **13**:278
"Brise marine" (Mallarme) **4**:208
"The British Church" (Herbert) **4**:100
"Brittle Beauty" (Wyatt) **27**:302
"Broadcast" (Larkin) **21**:237
"The Broadstone" (Jeffers) **17**:117
"Broagh" (Heaney) **18**:202, 241
"Brod und Wein" (Holderlin)
See "Brot und Wein"
"A Broken Appointment" (Hardy) **8**:88, 110
"The Broken Balance" (Jeffers) **17**:144
"The Broken Dark" (Hayden) **6**:181, 193-95
"Broken Dreams" (Yeats) **20**:328
The Broken Ground (Berry) **28**:2-5, 14, 31
"The Broken Home" (Merrill) **28**:221, 227, 230, 253
"Broken Jar" (Paz)
See "El cántaro roto"
"The Broken Man" (Wylie) **23**:321
"The Broken Pitcher" (Paz)
See "El cántaro roto"
"The Broken Tower" (Crane) **3**:90, 103, 111
"The Broken Wings" (Gibran) **9**:75
"The Bronco That Would Not Be Broken" (Lindsay) **23**:269, 273, 286
"Bronz Trumpets and Sea Water" (Wylie) **23**:301, 315
Bronze (Merrill) **28**:267-68, 272
"A Bronze Head" (Yeats) **20**:332
The Bronze Horseman (Pushkin)
See *Medny Vsadnik*
"The Bronze Horses" (Lowell) **13**:60, 62, 64, 73, 80, 82
"Bronze Tablets" (Lowell) **13**:76, 78
"Bronzeville Man with a Belt in the Back" (Brooks) **7**:106
"A Bronzeville Mother Loiters in Mississippi. Meanwhile a Mississippi Mother Burns Bacon" (Brooks) **7**:56, 62, 81, 86, 96, 98-9
"Bronzeville Woman in a Red Hat" (Brooks) **7**:58, 62
"The Brook" (Tennyson) **6**:357, 359
"Brook Farm" (Toomer) **7**:323
"Brooklyn Bridge Nocturne" (Garcia Lorca)
See "Ciudad sin sueño"
"Brot und Wein" (Holderlin) **4**:146-51, 161, 166, 169, 171, 176
"Brother and Sister" (Eliot) **20**:102, 124
"Brother and Sisters" (Wright) **14**:336, 340, 351
"Brother, Do Not Give Your Life" (Yosano Akiko)
See "Kimi Shinitamô koto nakare"
"Brothers" (Johnson) **24**:130-31, 138, 142, 161, 170
"The Brothers" (Wordsworth) **4**:374, 380, 381, 393, 402, 414
The Brothers Highwaymen (Pushkin)
See *Bratya Razboiniki*
Brothers, I Loved You All: Poems, 1969-1977 (Carruth) **10**:69-70, 72-3, 91
"Brought from Beyond" (Clampitt) **19**:102
"A Brown" (Stein) **18**:3312
"Brown Boy to Brown Girl" (Cullen) **20**:64
"A Brown Girl Dead" (Cullen) **20**:55, 62
"The Brown Menace or Poem to the Survival of Roaches" (Lorde) **12**:154-55, 158
"Brown River, Smile" (Toomer) **7**:324
"Browning resuelve ser poeta" (Borges) **22**:98
"Brown's Descent" (Frost) **1**:195

"Bruce's Address" (Burns) **6**:55
"A Bruised Reed Shall He Not Break" (Rossetti) **7**:290; **50**:314
"Bryan, Bryan, Bryan, Bryan" (Lindsay) **23**:265, 270, 273-74, 279, 287-88, 294-95
"Bubba" (Sanchez) **9**:240
Buch der Bilder (Rilke) **2**:266-67
"Buch der Lieder" (Bridges) **28**:88
Buch der Lieder (Heine) **25**:129-131, 139-41, 143, 145-46, 157-58, 161, 164
"The Buck in the Snow" (Millay) **6**:238
The Buck in the Snow, and Other Poems (Millay) **6**:213-14
"Buck Lake Store Auction" (Ondaatje) **28**:335
Buckthorn (Akhmatova)
See *Podorozhnik*
Bucolic Comedies (Sitwell) **3**:293, 302-04, 307-08, 319, 322
"Bucolics" (Auden) **1**:23
Bucolics (Vergil)
See *Georgics*
"The Buddhist Painter Prepares to Paint" (Carruth) **10**:89
"The Buds Now Stretch" (Roethke) **15**:288
"Buenos Aires" (Lowell) **3**:214
"La bufera" (Montale) **13**:113, 131
La bufera e altro (Montale) **13**:103-04, 107, 113-14, 117-18, 122, 125, 131-33, 141, 148-49, 156, 160, 165-67
"Buffalo Bill's Defunct" (Cummings) **5**:93
"Le buffet" (Rimbaud) **3**:271, 283
"The Bugler-Boy" (Hopkins) **15**:138
"The Bugler's First Communion" (Hopkins) **15**:136, 144
"Buick" (Shapiro) **25**:288, 295, 297, 319, 322, 325
"Build Soil: A Political Pastoral" (Frost) **1**:196, 199, 203, 217
"Builder Kachina" (Rose) **13**:236-37
"The Building" (Larkin) **21**:255
"The Building of the Trophy" (Rose) **13**:235
"The Bull" (Wright) **14**:333, 359
"The Bull Moses" (Hughes) **7**:131, 140, 158
"Bull Song" (Atwood) **8**:25
"Bullfrog" (Hughes) **7**:165
"Bullocky" (Wright) **14**:336, 340, 345, 349, 351, 357, 360, 368
"Bumming" (McKay) **2**:226
"The Bunch of Grapes" (Herbert) **4**:123, 125
"The Burden" (Kipling) **3**:183
"A Burden" (Rossetti) **7**:286
"Burden" (Tagore)
See "Bhar"
"The Burghers" (Hardy) **8**:99
"The Burglar of Babylon" (Bishop) **3**:48, 56
"The Burial-place" (Bryant) **20**:3
"The Buried City" (Chesterton) **28**:101
"The Buried Life" (Arnold) **5**:37-8, 41-5, 47, 49-50, 59, 64
"The Burly Fading One" (Hayden) **6**:196
"The Burn" (Kinnell) **26**:290
"Burn and burn and burn" (Bukowski) **18**:24
"Burned" (Levine) **22**:220-21, 227-28, 232
"The Burning" (Momaday) **25**:200-201
"The Burning Child" (Clampitt) **19**:83
"Burning Hills" (Ondaatje) **28**:327, 332, 333
Burning in Water Drowning in Flame: Selected Poems 1955-1973 (Bukowski) **18**:21
"The Burning of Paper Instead of Children" (Rich) **5**:371, 393-95
"Burning Oneself Out" (Rich) **5**:360
"The Burning Passion" (MacDiarmid) **9**:153
"Burning River" (Ortiz) **17**:233
"Burning the Christmas Greens" (Williams) **7**:360
"Burning the Tomato Worms" (Forche) **10**:132, 134, 142
"Burnt Lands" (Pavese) **13**:205
"Burnt Norton" (Eliot) **5**:164, 166-68, 171, 174, 177-85, 201, 210
"The Burnt-Out Spa" (Plath) **1**:389
"Bury Me In a Free Land" (Harper) **21**:185, 187, 190, 192
"A Bus along St. Clair: December" (Atwood) **8**:40
"Búscate plata" (Guillen) **23**:142
"The Buses Headed for Scranton" (Nash) **21**:271
"The Bush Garden" (Atwood) **8**:38-9
"Busie old foole" (Donne)
See "The Sunne Rising"
"The Business Man of Alicante" (Levine) **22**:213
"Busker" (Stryk) **27**:208
"But Born" (Aleixandre) **15**:5
"But He Was Cool; or, He Even Stopped for Green Lights" (Madhubuti) **5**:329, 341
"But Not Forgotten" (Parker) **28**:362
"But We've the May" (Cummings)
See "Song"
"'Butch' Weldy" (Masters) **1**:324
"Buteo Regalis" (Momaday) **25**:186, 188, 193, 195, 199, 210, 220
Butterflies (Gozzano)
See *Le farfalle*
"The Butterfly" (Brodsky)
See "Babocka"
"The Butterfly" (Giovanni) **19**:112
"Butterfly Piece" (Hayden) **6**:194, 198
"Butterflyweed" (Ammons) **16**:4
"Buying the Dog" (Ondaatje) **28**:335
"by 3/6/51" (Olson) **19**:316
"By a Reactionary" (Chesterton) **28**:114
By Avon River (H. D.) **5**:302
"By God I Want above Fourteenth" (Cummings) **5**:94
"By Lamplight" (Kunitz) **19**:171
"By Night When Others Soundly Slept" (Bradstreet) **10**:62
"By Rugged Ways" (Dunbar) **5**:131
By the Earth's Corpse (Hardy) **8**:121
"By the Fireside" (Browning) **2**:76, 78-9, 88
"By the Hoof of the Wild Goat" (Kipling) **3**:186
"By the Lake" (Sitwell) **3**:325
"By the North Sea" (Swinburne) **24**:313-17, 319, 327, 329, 343
"By the Road" (Williams) **7**:382-83
By the Seashore (Akhmatova)
See *U samovo morya*
"By The Stream" (Dunbar) **5**:127
"By the Waters of Babylon" (Celan)
See "An den Wassern Babels"
"By Twilight" (Swinburne) **24**:317
"By Wauchopeside" (MacDiarmid) **9**:197, 199
"By-pass" (Wright) **14**:373
"Bypassing Rue Descartes" (Milosz) **8**:200
"The Byrnies" (Gunn) **26**:186
"Byzantium" (Yeats) **20**:308, 310, 316, 327, 334-35
"a C." (Montale) **13**:138
"Ça le creux" (Cesaire) **25**:33
"Ca' the Yowes to the Knowes" (Burns) **6**:76
"Cabala" (Swenson) **14**:288
"Cabaret" (Hughes) **1**:237
"Cabaret Girl Dies on Welfare Island" (Hughes) **1**:247
"A Cabin in the Clearing" (Frost) **1**:212
"A Cabin Tale" (Dunbar) **5**:120
Cables to Rage (Lorde) **12**:140
"Cables to Rage, or I've Been Talking on This Street Corner a Hell of a Long Time" (Lorde) **12**:155
"Cables to the Ace" (Merton) **10**:337
Cables to the Ace; or, Familiar Liturgies of Misunderstanding (Merton) **10**:338, 345, 348, 351, 354
"Caboose Thoughts" (Sandburg) **2**:302
"Cabra" (Joyce) **22**:149
"Le cacot" (Lamartine) **16**:284
Cadastre (Cesaire) **25**:12, 15, 17, 30-2, 35-6, 38-9
"Cadenus and Vanessa" (Swift) **9**:253-55, 296
"A Cadenza" (Clampitt) **19**:102
"Cadenza" (Hughes) **7**:159
"Caerulei Oculi" (Gautier) **18**:125
"Caesar when that the traytour of Egipt" (Wyatt) **27**:339
Caesar's Gate (Duncan) **2**:101
"Café" (Milosz) **8**:175
"Café at Rapallo" (Montale) **13**:148
"Cafe du neant" (Loy) **16**:312-13, 328
"Café Tableau" (Swenson) **14**:275
A Cage of Spines (Swenson) **14**:247-48, 252, 260, 277, 284
Cahier d'un retour au pays natal (Cesaire) **25**:2-3, 5-7, 10-11, 13-16, 18-19, 29-33, 41-4, 47-9, 51-6, 58-61, 63, 65
"Cain" (Nemerov) **24**:261
Cain (Byron) **16**:86, 88, 90, 103-05, 108, 111
"Cake" (Stein) **18**:322
"A Calder" (Shapiro) **25**:291
The Calender (Spenser)
See *The Shepheardes Calender: Conteyning Twelve Eglogues Proportionable to the Twelve Monethes*
"Calendrier lagunaire" (Cesaire) **25**:33, 45
"Caliban upon Setebos" (Browning) **2**:58-9, 88, 95
"The Calico Cat" (Lindsay) **23**:281
"The California Water Plan" (Snyder) **21**:291
Californians (Jeffers) **17**:134-35, 138
"The Call" (Brooke) **24**:57, 82
"The Call" (Herbert) **4**:130
"Call" (Lorde) **12**:139, 141
"The Call Across the Valley of Not-Knowing" (Kinnell) **26**:251, 269, 273-75
"Call It Fear" (Harjo) **27**:54, 61
"Call it Love" (Enzensberger) **28**:139
"Call Me Back Again" (Tagore)
See "Ebar phirao more"
"The Call of the Wild" (Snyder) **21**:292-93, 297
Call Yourself Alive? (Cassian) **17**:4, 6, 13
"Las Calles" (Borges) **22**:68
"Callie Ford" (Brooks) **7**:62, 69
Calligrammes (Apollinaire) **7**:3, 9-10, 12, 35-6, 42, 44, 46, 48-9
"A Calling" (Kumin) **15**:210
"Calliope" (H. D.) **5**:304
"Callow Captain" (Graves) **6**:133
"The Calls" (Owen) **19**:336
"The Calm" (Donne) **1**:122
"The Calm" (Gallagher) **9**:58
"Calming Kali" (Clifton) **17**:24
"Calmly We Walk Through This April's Day" (Schwartz) **8**:305-06
"Calverley's" (Robinson) **1**:466
"Calypso" (H. D.) **5**:306
"The Cambridge Ladies Who Live in Furnished Souls" (Cummings) **5**:94
"Cambridge, Spring 1937" (Schwartz) **8**:301
"The Camel" (Nash) **21**:278
"Camelia" (Tagore) **8**:417
"El camello (auto de los Reyes Magos)" (Fuertes) **27**:8, 15, 31
"Camilo" (Guillen) **23**:128
"Caminos" (Dario) **15**:82
"Camp" (Fuertes) **27**:23
"Camp 1940" (Senghor) **25**:235
"Camp and Cloister" (Browning) **2**:26
"Camping at Split Rock" (Wright) **14**:366
"Camps of Green" (Whitman) **3**:378
"Can Grande's Castle" (Lowell) **13**:60
Can Grande's Castle (Lowell) **13**:60, 62-3, 65-6, 72-4, 79-83, 93
"Caña" (Guillen) **23**:98
"canada" (Bissett) **14**:25, 34
Canada Gees Mate for Life (Bissett) **14**:26
"The Canadian" (Bissett) **14**:10, 25
"Canal" (Tomlinson) **17**:313, 343
"The Canal's Drowning Black" (Hughes) **7**:148
"Canción de otoño en primavera" (Dario) **15**:96, 107, 109-11
"La canción del bongo" (Guillen) **23**:106, 111-14, 136, 139

Cumulative Title Index

"Canción otoñal" (Dario) **15**:82
"Canción tonta" (Garcia Lorca) **3**:136
Canciones (Garcia Lorca) **3**:118-19, 148-49
"Candide" (Enzensberger) **28**:134, 136
"The Candle in the Cabin" (Lindsay) **23**:286
"Candle, Lamp, and Firefly" (Gallagher) **9**:59
"Candle-Lightin' Time" (Dunbar) **5**:122
"Candles at 330" (McGuckian) **27**:91
Candles in Babylon (Levertov) **11**:198-201, 209
"The Candlestick" (Brodsky) **9**:3
Cane (Toomer) **7**:309-11, 319, 323-24, 326, 330, 332-33, 335, 339-41
"El cangrejo" (Guillen) **23**:124
"The Cannery" (Stryk) **27**:211
"canoe" (Bissett) **14**:23
"The Canonization" (Bridges) **28**:73
"The Canonization" (Donne) **1**:126, 130, 132-34
"Canon's Yeoman's Prologue" (Chaucer) **19**:26
"Canon's Yeoman's Tale" (Chaucer) **19**:13, 19
"Canta el sinsonte en el Turquino" (Guillen) **23**:124
Cantares Mexicanos I (Cardenal) **22**:127-28, 129, 132
Cantares Mexicanos II (Cardenal) **22**:127-28, 129, 132
"Cantares mexicanos (II)" (Cardenal) **22**:128, 130
"Cantares mexicanos(I)" (Cardenal) **22**:127, 130
"El cántaro roto" (Paz) **1**:361
Canterburie-Tales (Chaucer)
See *Canterbury Tales*
Canterbury Tales (Chaucer) **19**:3, 6, 13, 16, 18, 20, 22, 24, 26-7, 34, 37, 43-50, 52-4, 60, 64
"Canthara" (Williams) **7**:367
"Canti Romani" (Ferlinghetti) **1**:183
"Canticle" (Berry) **28**:3-4
"Cantique des colonnes" (Valery) **9**:366, 394
"Canto I" (Pound) **4**:334, 357
"Canto VIII" (Pound) **4**:353
"Canto XIV" (Pound) **4**:328, 358
"Canto XV" (Pound) **4**:358
"Canto XVI" (Pound) **4**:328
"Canto XXVI" (Pound) **4**:324
"Canto XXVII" (Pound) **4**:325, 345
"Canto XLI" (Pound) **4**:357
"Canto XLVII" (Pound) **4**:346-47, 349
"Canto L" (Pound) **4**:360, 362
"Canto LI" (Pound) **4**:326
"Canto LXXIV" (Pound) **4**:345-49, 352, 354
"Canto LXXV" (Pound) **4**:347, 349
"Canto LXXVI" (Pound) **4**:352-53
"Canto LXXVIII" (Pound) **4**:349
"Canto LXXIX" (Pound) **4**:349
"Canto LXXX" (Pound) **4**:345, 349
"Canto LXXXI" (Pound) **4**:349, 352
"Canto LXXXII" (Pound) **4**:349, 352
"Canto LXXXIII" (Pound) **4**:345, 348
"Canto LXXXIV" (Pound) **4**:345, 348
"Canto LXXXVI" (Pound) **4**:347
"Canto XCI" (Pound) **4**:354
"Canto C" (Pound) **4**:360-62
"Canto CI" (Pound) **4**:353
"Canto CIV" (Pound) **4**:357
"Canto CX" (Pound) **4**:353
"Canto CXIII" (Pound) **4**:353-54
"Canto CXV" (Pound) **4**:354
"Canto CXVI" (Pound) **4**:353-54
"Canto CXVIII" (Pound) **4**:353
"Canto CXX" (Pound) **4**:354
"Canto a Bolivar" (Neruda) **4**:279-80
"Canto à la Argentina" (Dario) **15**:82, 115
"Canto a las madres de los milicianos muertos" (Neruda) **4**:278
"Canto a Stalingrado" (Neruda) **4**:279
"Canto de la sangre" (Dario) **15**:91-2, 96, 105
Canto general de Chile (Neruda) **4**:279-82, 291-96
"Canto nacional" (Cardenal) **22**:103
"Canto negro" (Guillen) **23**:134
"Canto notturno di un pastore errante nell'Asia" (Montale) **13**:109
"Canto popolare" (Pasolini) **17**:294
"Canto sobre unas ruinas" (Neruda) **4**:309
"Canto82" (Viereck) **27**:283
Cantos (Pound) **4**:332, 343-45, 350-54
Cantos de vida y esperanza (Dario) **15**:78, 80, 87, 89, 91-2, 96, 103-05, 107, 109, 115, 117, 120
"Cantos of Mutabilitie" (Spenser) **8**:344, 346, 375, 396
Cantos para soldados y sones para turistas (Guillen) **23**:99, 101, 131, 133, 140
"Canvas" (Zagajewski) **27**:387-88, 393, 395
Canvas (Zagajewski) **27**:389, 393, 399
"Canyon de Chelly" (Ortiz) **17**:225
"Canzone" (Mandelstam) **14**:138
"Canzone on an Old Proverb" (Stryk) **27**:198
"Canzones" (Okigbo)
See "Four Canzones (1957-1961)"
Canzoni (Pound) **4**:317
Canzoniere (Petrarch) **8**:218, 220, 224-40, 242-45, 247-49, 251-65, 268-73, 276-78
"Cape Breton" (Bishop) **3**:39, 58-9
"Cape Cod" (Brodsky)
See "A Cape Cod Lullaby"
"A Cape Cod Lullaby" (Brodsky)
See "A Cape Cod Lullaby"
"A Cape Cod Lullaby" (Brodsky) **9**:7, 19
"Cape Hatteras" (Crane) **3**:86-7, 90, 96, 106-10
"Cape Mootch" (Pasternak) **6**:251
"Capitol Air" (Ginsberg) **4**:62, 76, 83
"Cappadocian Song" (Carruth) **10**:89
"Caprice" (Cullen) **20**:55
"Captain Craig" (Robinson) **1**:460, 467, 483, 486
Captain Craig (Robinson) **1**:462-63, 470-72, 474, 490
Captain Lavender (McGuckian) **27**:104-106
The Captive of the Caucasus (Pushkin)
See *Kavkazsky plennik*
"A Captive of the Khan" (Tsvetaeva)
See "Khansky polon"
"Captured by the Khan" (Tsvetaeva)
See "Khansky polon"
"Car Wreck" (Shapiro) **25**:205
"A Carafe That Is a Blind Glass" (Stein) **18**:318, 334
"The Card Players" (Larkin) **21**:237
"Careless Water" (Stein) **18**:334
"Caribbean Sunset" (Hughes) **1**:236
"Caritas" (Cummings) **5**:94
"Carlos among the Candles" (Stevens) **6**:295
"Carmen" (Blok) **21**:26
"Carnal Knowledge" (Gunn) **26**:182, 188, 199-200, 207, 210, 218
"Carnaval" (Gautier) **18**:125
"Carnegie Hall: Rescued" (Moore) **4**:242
"Carnegie, Oklahoma, 1919" (Momaday) **25**:221
"Carnevale di Gerti" (Montale) **13**:117
"Carol" (Merton) **10**:340
"Carol" (Nemerov) **24**:258
"A Carol for Children" (Nash) **21**:275
Carolina Said Song (Ammons) **16**:19
"Carousing Students" (Pushkin) **10**:407
"The Carpenter's Son" (Housman) **2**:192
"A Carpet Not Bought" (Merrill) **28**:253
"Carrefour" (Lowell) **13**:85
"Carriers of the Dream Wheel" (Momaday) **25**:199, 217
"Carrier" (Meredith) **28**:174, 186
"A Carrion" (Baudelaire)
See "Une charogne"
"Carrion Comfort" (Hopkins) **15**:144
"Carrying Mission to the Frontier" (Wang Wei)
See "Carrying Mission to the Frontier"
"The Carrying Ring" (McGuckian) **27**:105
"Carta a Miguel Otero Silva, en Caracas, 1948" (Neruda) **4**:293
"Carta de creencia" (Paz) **1**:376
"Carta de la eme" (Fuertes) **27**:37
"Carta de la Habana" (Guillen) **23**:127
"Carta explicatoria de Gloria" (Fuertes) **27**:17, 48-9
"Cartographies of Silence" (Rich) **5**:378-79, 394-95
"Cartoons of Coming Shows Unseen Before" (Schwartz) **8**:291
"The Cartridges" (Levine) **22**:213
"La cartuja" (Dario) **15**:102
"The Caruso Poem" (Bissett) **14**:4, 19
"La casa dei doganieri" (Montale) **13**:114
La casa dei doganieri (Montale) **13**:106, 138
"Casa Elena" (Borges) **22**:92
Casa Guidi Windows: A Poem (Browning) **6**:2, 6-9, 16, 36, 38, 41, 46
"Casa in costruzione" (Pavese) **13**:226
"Casa sul mare" (Montale) **13**:137, 147, 164
"Casabianca" (Bishop) **3**:37, 56, 67
"La casada infiel" (Garcia Lorca) **3**:119, 132, 134
Case d'armons (Apollinaire) **7**:21-2
"A Case of Murder" (Hagiwara Sakutaro)
See "Satsujin jiken"
"Case-moth" (Wright) **14**:374
"Caspar Hauser Song" (Trakl) **20**:226, 259-60, 267, 269
"Cassandra" (Bogan) **12**:110
"Cassandra" (Jeffers) **17**:139
"Cassandra" (Robinson) **1**:487
"Cassinus and Peter, a Tragic Elegy" (Swift) **9**:262, 270, 274, 279, 286, 288, 298, 302-03
"Cast reci" (Brodsky) **9**:7, 19
Cast reci (Brodsky) **9**:6-8, 13-15, 26-7, 29-31
"Castástrofe en Sewell" (Neruda) **4**:294
"The Castaways" (McKay) **2**:221
"Castilian" (Wylie) **23**:310, 312
"Casting and Gathering" (Heaney) **18**:257
"The Castle" (Graves) **6**:131, 135, 142, 144
"The Castle" (Tomlinson) **17**:308, 311
"Casualty" (Heaney) **18**:198, 211, 240, 246
"The Casualty" (Hughes) **7**:114
"The Cat" (Kinnell) **26**:286
"The Cat" (Kinnell) **26**:287
"The Cat and the Moon" (Yeats) **20**:304
"The Cat and the Saxophone" (Hughes) **1**:236
"The Catalpa Tree" (Bogan) **12**:129, 131
"Catarina to Camoens" (Browning) **6**:16-17, 38
"Catastrophe at Sewell" (Neruda)
See "Castástrofe en Sewell"
"the catch" (Bukowski) **18**:25
"A Catch of Shy Fish" (Brooks) **7**:105
"Catchment" (Kumin) **15**:209, 211, 223
"Catedral" (Borges) **22**:92
"Categories" (Giovanni) **19**:110-12, 116
Cathay (Pound) **4**:317, 364, 366
"Catherine of Alexandria" (Dove) **6**:107, 109
"Catherine of Siena" (Dove) **6**:107, 109
"Cato Braden" (Masters) **1**:33, 343
"Cats" (Hagiwara Sakutaro)
See "Neko"
"Cats and a Cock" (Rukeyser) **12**:209
Cats and Bats and Things with Wings (Aiken) **26**:24, 30
"Catterskill Falls" (Bryant) **20**:14-16, 43
"Cattle Gredo" (Milosz) **8**:207
"Cattle Show" (MacDiarmid) **9**:160, 176
"Catullus" (Nishiwaki) **15**:238
The Caucasian Captive (Pushkin)
See *Kavkazsky plennik*
"Cauchemar" (Gautier) **18**:142, 164
"Caupolicán" (Dario) **15**:95
"Cause & Effect" (Swenson) **14**:264
"Causerie" (Baudelaire) **1**:45, 66
Cautionary Tales for Children (Belloc) **24**:21, 26, 49
Cautionary Verses (Belloc) **24**:13-15, 17-18, 23, 27
"Le Cavalier poursuivi" (Gautier) **18**:142-43
"Cavalier Tunes" (Browning) **2**:26, 36
Cave Birds: An Alchemical Cave Drama (Hughes) **7**:153-58, 162-65, 171
"Cave Canem" (Millay) **6**:233

Cavender's House (Robinson) **1**:471-72, 475, 479, 483
"Caves" (Wakoski) **15**:363
"Cawdor" (Jeffers) **17**:107-08, 110
Cawdor, and Other Poems (Jeffers) **17**:110,135
"Ce que dit la bouche d'ombre" (Hugo) **17**:66, 83-84, 90
"Ce qui est à moi" (Cesaire) **25**:43
"Ce qu'on entend sur la montagne" (Hugo) **17**:91
"Ce siècle est grand et fort" (Hugo) **17**:94
"Cease, Cease, Aminta to Complain" (Behn) **13**:7
"The Cedars" (Wright) **14**:339, 346
"La ceinture" (Valery) **9**:372, 374, 387, 396
"A Celebration" (Williams) **7**:345
A Celebration of Charis in Ten Lyric Pieces (Jonson) **17**:169-70, 180, 194-96, 207, 214
"Celestial Freedom" (Aleixandre) **15**:19
"Celestial Globe" (Nemerov) **24**:263, 274
Celestial Hoyden (Lowell) **3**:199
"Celestial Music" (Gluck) **16**:158
"The Celestial Poets" (Neruda)
See "Los poetas celestes"
"Celestials at the Board of Projects" (Milosz) **8**:214
"Celia's Birthday Poem" (Zukofsky) **11**:342
"Celibacy at Twenty" (Olds) **22**:338
"Célibat, célibat, tout n'est que célibat" (Laforgue) **14**:76
"Cell Song" (Knight) **14**:40, 52-3
"The Cellar" (Soto) **28**:371
"Cellar Hole in Joppa" (Kumin) **15**:190
"The Cellar of Memory" (Akhmatova) **2**:20
"Celle qui sort de l'onde" (Valery) **9**:392
"Cells" (Kipling) **3**:163
"The Celtic Fringe" (Smith) **12**:339
"Cemetery, Stratford Connecticut" (Rose) **13**:239
"La cena triste" (Pavese) **13**:205, 208
The Cenci (Shelley) **14**:165, 171-75, 182-83, 196, 202-03, 205, 208-10, 213
Ceneri (Pasolini) **17**:294-95
"Le ceneri di Gramscí" (Pasolini) **17**:263, 265, 271, 284-85, 289-92, 294-95
Le ceneri di Gramscí (Pasolini) **17**:255, 263-67, 269-70, 272, 286-87, 293
"The Census-Taker" (Frost) **1**:194
"The Centaur" (Swenson) **14**:248, 252, 255, 262-63, 281-82, 288
"El centinela" (Borges) **22**:79
"Centipede Sonnet" (Villa) **22**:351
"Central Europe" (Zagajewski) **27**:398
"Central Park" (Lowell) **3**:226
A Century of Roundels (Swinburne) **24**:313, 322-27
Cerebro y corazón (Guillen) **23**:104, 133-34
"Ceremonies for Candlemasse Eve" (Herrick) **9**:99
"Ceremonies for Christmasse" (Herrick) **9**:99, 104
"Ceremony after a Fire Raid" (Thomas) **2**:382, 388
"Certain Mercies" (Graves) **6**:152
"A Certain Morning Is" (Villa) **22**:350
"Certainty" (Paz) **1**:355
"César" (Valery) **9**:391
"Ceux qui luttent" (Smith) **12**:333
"Cezanne at Aix" (Tomlinson) **17**:304, 306, 335
"Chaadayevu" (Pushkin) **10**:408
"Chacun sa chimère" (Baudelaire) **1**:58
"La chaine a mille anneaux" (Lamartine) **16**:284
"Chains" (Apollinaire)
See "Liens"
"A Chair" (Stein) **18**:319, 349
Chaitali (Tagore) **8**:403, 409-10
"Le Chaitivel" (Marie de France) **22**:248-49, 255, 258, 260, 267-73, 295
"Chaka" (Senghor) **25**:241, 255
"The Challenge" (Graves) **6**:137
"La chambre double" (Baudelaire) **1**:54, 58
"Chameli-vitan" (Tagore) **8**:416
The Champion (Tsvetaeva)
See *Molodets*
Les Champs Magnétiques (Breton) **15**:58, 68, 73
"Chance" (H. D.) **5**:304
"Chance Meeting" (H. D.) **5**:304
"Chance Topic" (Tu Fu) **9**:324, 327
"The Chances" (Owen) **19**:334, 344, 347
"The Chances of Rhyme" (Tomlinson) **17**:333, 340
"Chanchal" (Tagore) **8**:415
"The Change" (Finch) **21**:175
"The Change" (Hardy) **8**:93
"Change" (Kunitz) **19**:147
"Change" (Pasternak)
See "Peremena"
"Change" (Wright) **14**:379
"Change Is Not Always Progress" (Madhubuti) **5**:344
"The Change: Kyoto-Tokyo Express" (Ginsberg) **4**:50, 63, 81
"Change of Season" (Lorde) **12**:154, 157
A Change of World (Rich) **5**:352-53, 358, 360, 362, 369, 375, 387-88, 392
"Change upon Change" (Browning) **6**:32
"The Changed Woman" (Bogan) **12**:94, 103
"The Changeful World" (MacDiarmid) **9**:183
"Changing Diapers" (Snyder) **21**:300
The Changing Light at Sandover (Merrill) **28**:259-60, 262-63, 265-79, 281
"Changing Mind" (Aiken) **26**:14
"Changing the Children" (Kumin) **15**:215
Ch'ang-ku (Li Ho) **13**:44
"Channel 13" (Merrill) **28**:267
"Channel Firing" (Hardy) **8**:119-21
"A Channel Passage" (Brooke) **24**:53-4, 63, 83
"A Channel Passage" (Swinburne) **24**:313, 317-18
"Chanon's Yeoman's Tale" (Chaucer)
See "Canon's Yeoman's Tale"
"Chanson" (Hugo) **17**:80
"La chanson des ingénues" (Verlaine) **2**:431
"La chanson du mal-aimé" (Apollinaire) **7**:3, 7-9, 11, 15, 22, 44, 46-9
"Chanson du petit hypertrophique" (Laforgue) **14**:66, 93
"Chanson du Présomptif" (Perse) **23**:230
"Chanson Juive" (Celan) **10**:127-28
"Chanson of a Lady in the Shade" (Celan) **10**:112
"Chanson un peu naïve" (Bogan) **12**:86, 90, 92, 101, 103
Chansons des rues et des bois (Hugo) **17**:55, 65, 67, 72
Chansons pour elle (Verlaine) **2**:417
"Chant d'amour" (Lamartine) **16**:291-92
"Chant d'automne" (Baudelaire) **1**:60, 62-3
"Chant de guerre parisien" (Rimbaud) **3**:255, 284
"Chant de l'horizon en champagne" (Apollinaire) **7**:22
"Chant de liesse" (Ronsard) **11**:262
"Chant de Printemps" (Senghor) **25**:258
Le chant du sacre (Lamartine) **16**:279
"Chant for Dark Hours" (Parker) **28**:352, 360
"A Chant for Young/Brothas and Sistuhs" (Sanchez) **9**:218, 225
"Chant to Be Used in Processions around a Site with Furnaces" (Merton) **10**:334, 337
"Chantre" (Apollinaire) **7**:48
Les chants de Crépuscule (Hugo) **17**:43, 45, 52, 63, 91-94
Chants d'ombre (Senghor) **25**:224, 227, 230-33, 236, 238, 241, 243-44, 255
"Les chants lyriques de Saül" (Lamartine) **16**:277, 290
Chants pour Naëtt (Senghor) **25**:225, 227, 232, 238-40
Chants pour signare (Senghor) **25**:239
See *Chants pour Naëtt*
"Chaos in Motion and Not in Motion" (Stevens) **6**:307-10, 313
"Chaos Poem" (Atwood) **8**:24
"Chaos Staggered" (Ammons) **16**:46
"The Chapel-Organist" (Hardy) **8**:100, 124
"Chaplinesque" (Crane) **3**:98-100
"A Character" (Montagu) **16**:338
"The Character of Holland" (Marvell) **10**:271
"The Character of the Happy Warrior" (Wordsworth) **4**:377
Characters of Women (Pope) **26**:239
"The Charge of the Light Brigade" (Tennyson) **6**:359
"The Chariot" (Dickinson) **1**:84, 86
"Charioteer" (H. D.) **5**:268
"The Charioteer of Delphi" (Merrill) **28**:241
"La charite" (Ronsard) **11**:236, 243, 263-64
"Charivari" (Atwood) **8**:38
"Charles Augustus Fortescue, Who always Did what was Right, and so accumulated an Immense Fortune" (Belloc) **24**:26
"Charles on Fire" (Merrill) **28**:253
"Charleston in the 1860s" (Rich) **5**:383
"Charlotte Corday" (Tomlinson) **17**:345-46, 350
"Charlotte's Delivery" (McGuckian) **27**:105
"A Charm" (Dickinson) **1**:112
Charmes; ou, Poèmes (Valery) **9**:355, 358, 365-67, 371, 374, 386-88, 390-96
"Charms" (Snyder) **21**:294, 297
"The Charnel Rose" (Aiken) **26**:11, 15, 37
The Charnel Rose (Aiken) **26**:6, 22, 70, 72
"Une charogne" (Baudelaire) **1**:48
"The Chase" (Toomer) **7**:338, 340
"Chase Henry" (Masters) **1**:324
"Chasing the Paper-Shaman" (Rose) **13**:238
Chast' rechi (Brodsky)
See *Cast reci*
"Le chat" (Ronsard) **11**:280, 282
"Chateau de Muzot" (Tomlinson) **17**:315, 324
"Le Château du souvenir" (Gautier) **18**:125, 129, 157
"Le châtiment de Tartuff" (Rimbaud) **3**:283
Les Châtiments (Hugo) **17**:45, 53-54, 65, 74, 78-80, 91
"Les chats blancs" (Valery) **9**:391
"The Chaunty of the Nona" (Belloc) **24**:6, 31
"Cheddar Pinks" (Bridges) **28**:80-1, 85
"Che Guevara" (Guillen) **23**:127
"The Cheer" (Meredith) **28**:205, 217
The Cheer (Meredith) **28**:177, 179-82, 197-200, 202, 205-09, 215
Cheerleader for the Funeral (Cassian) **17**:13
"Chekhov in Nice" (Stryk) **27**:187
"Chekhov on Sakhalin" (Heaney) **18**:214
"Chelyuskintsy" (Tsvetaeva) **14**:328
"Le chêne" (Lamartine) **16**:293
"Les chercheuses de poux" (Rimbaud) **3**:271, 276
"Les chères, mains qui furent miennes" (Verlaine) **2**:416
"Cherish You Then the Hope I Shall Forget" (Millay) **6**:211
"Cherkesy" (Lermontov) **18**:278, 299
"Chernozem" (Mandelstam) **14**:150-51, 154
"Cherry Blossoms" (Gallagher) **9**:65
"The Cherry Tree" (Gunn) **26**:205
"The Chestnut Casts His Flambeaux" (Housman) **2**:199
"Un cheval de race" (Baudelaire) **1**:59
"The Cheval-Glass" (Hardy) **8**:100
Les chevaliers (Lamartine) **16**:269
"La chevelure" (Baudelaire) **1**:45, 66-7, 69
"Chevelure" (Cesaire) **25**:10, 17
"Chevrefoil" (Marie de France) **22**:248, 255, 257-58, 262-64, 266-67, 269, 272, 274, 301
"Chhabi" (Tagore) **8**:414
"Chi vuol veder" (Petrarch) **8**:256
"Chiare fresche e dolci acque" (Petrarch) **8**:221, 230, 232-33, 235-36
"Chicago" (Sandburg) **2**:317, 322-23, 333, 335, 339
"The *Chicago Defender* Sends a Man to Little Rock" (Brooks) **7**:62
"The Chicago Picasso" (Brooks) **7**:82

Chicago Poems (Sandburg) **2**:300-02, 307-08, 312, 314, 316-18, 321, 333, 335-36, 338-39
"Chicago Poet" (Sandburg) **2**:339
"The Chicago Train" (Gluck) **16**:149, 153
"Chicken" (Stein) **18**:313
"Chicory and Daisies" (Williams) **7**:373, 407
"Chief Standing Water" (Tomlinson) **17**:309
"Chievrefueil" (Marie de France)
See "Chevrefoil"
"Chiffres et constellations amoureux d'une femme" (Breton) **15**:49
"The Child" (Carruth) **10**:71
"Child" (Sandburg) **2**:329
"The Child" (Wright) **14**:352
"Child and Wattle Tree" (Wright) **14**:352
"Child Harold" (Clare) **23**:46
"Child Harold" (Clare) **23**:25-6
"Child of Europe" (Milosz) **8**:191-92
"Child of the Sixtieth Century" (Viereck) **27**:259, 280
"Child Poems" (H. D.) **5**:305
"The Child Who Is Silent" (Shapiro) **25**:303
"The Child Who Saw Midas" (Sitwell) **3**:308
Childe Harold's Pilgrimage: A Romaunt (Byron) **16**:69, 72-7, 81-90, 107, 111
"Childe Roland to the Dark Tower Came" (Browning) **2**:64, 85-6, 88
"Childe Rolandine" (Smith) **12**:302, 350, 354
"Childhood" (Trakl) **20**:226
"Childhood" (Walker) **20**:276-77
"Childhood among the Ferns" (Hardy) **8**:125-26
"The Childhood of Jesus" (Pinsky) **27**:157
"A Childish Prank" (Hughes) **7**:123, 143, 161
"Childless Father" (Wordsworth) **4**:374, 428
"Childlessness" (Merrill) **28**:221, 244, 249
"Children Coming Home from School" (Gluck) **16**:159
"Children of Darkness" (Graves) **6**:137
"The Children of the Night" (Robinson) **1**:459, 467, 486
The Children of the Night (Robinson) **1**:459, 462-63, 466, 474
"The Children of the Poor" (Brooks) **7**:55, 62, 75, 78
"The Children's Song" (Kipling) **3**:171
"A Child's Grave at Florence" (Browning) **6**:6
"Child's Talk in April" (Rossetti) **7**:274
"chile" (Bissett) **14**:24
"A Chile" (Guillen) **23**:127
"Chilterns" (Brooke) **24**:56, 67
"Chimaera Sleeping" (Wylie) **23**:311, 314, 322
The Chimeras (Nerval)
See *Les Chimères*
"La Chimère" (Gautier) **18**:141-42
Les Chimères (Nerval) **13**:172, 174, 176, 179-80, 182, 184, 187, 191-92, 194-95
"The Chimney Sweeper" (Blake) **12**:7, 9, 34-5
China Poems (Brutus) **24**:117
"Chinatown" (Song) **21**:349
"The Chinese Banyan" (Meredith) **28**:171, 175, 189
Chinese Dynasty Cantos (Pound) **4**:352
"The Chinese Nightingale" (Lindsay) **23**:269, 272-73, 275-76, 278, 281-82, 286-87, 291-94
The Chinese Nightingale, and Other Poems (Lindsay) **23**:292
Chinesisch-deutsche Jahres-und Tageszeiten (Goethe) **5**:251
"Chiron" (Holderlin) **4**:148, 166
"Chitateli gazet" (Tsvetaeva) **14**:315
Chitra (Tagore) **8**:408-09, 415, 418
Cho o yumemu (Hagiwara Sakutaro) **18**:176
"Chocorua to Its Neighbour" (Stevens) **6**:335
A Choice of Kipling's Verse Made by T. S. Eliot with an Essay on Rudyard Kipling (Kipling) **3**:175
"A Choice of Weapons" (Kunitz) **19**:148
"Choir" (Hongo) **23**:199
"The Choir" (Kinnell) **26**:261
"The Choir Invisible" (Eliot)
See "O May I Join the Choir Invisible"
"Choix entre deux pations" (Hugo) **17**:101
"Cholera" (Dove) **6**:108
"Choorka" (McGuckian) **27**:110
"The Choosers" (Smith) **12**:327
"The Choral Union" (Sassoon) **12**:242
"Choriambics" (Brooke) **24**:62
"Choriambiscs II" (Brooke) **24**:57, 60
"Choros Sequence from Morpheus" (H. D.) **5**:304
"Chorus" (Lorde) **12**:159
"A Chorus of Ghosts" (Bryant) **20**:16
Chosen Defects (Neruda)
See *Defectos escogidos: 2000*
Chosen Poems: Old and New (Lorde) **12**:142, 146, 148, 154, 157
"Le Chretien Mourant" (Lamartine) **16**:277
"Chrismus on the Plantation" (Dunbar) **5**:133-34
"Christmas Poem, 1965" (Ondaatje) **28**:292
"A Christmas Song for the Three Guids" (Chesterton) **28**:125
"Le Christ aux Oliviers" (Nerval) **13**:173, 177, 181, 198
"Christ for Sale" (Lowell) **3**:203
"Christ Has Arisen" (Pushkin)
See "Khristos Voskres"
"Christ in Alabama" (Hughes) **1**:264
"Christ in Flanders" (Lowell) **3**:203
Christ is Arisen (Bely)
See *Hristos voskres*
Christ is Risen (Bely)
See *Hristos voskres*
"Christ of Pershing Square" (Stryk) **27**:190, 203
"Christ Recrucified" (Cullen) **20**:72
Christabel (Coleridge) **11**:41-2, 51-3, 84-5, 90-1, 104, 110
"The Christian Statesman" (Masters) **1**:344
"Christiane R." (Goethe) **5**:246
"Le Christianisme" (Owen) **19**:336, 341
"Christmas at Black Rock" (Lowell) **3**:201
"A Christmas Ballad" (Brodsky) **9**:2, 4
"The Christmas Cactus" (Clampitt) **19**:87
"A Christmas Card" (Merton) **10**:340
"A Christmas Card of Halley's Comet" (Nemerov) **24**:289
"Christmas Eve" (Ammons) **16**:58, 60, 65
"Christmas Eve" (Sexton) **2**:363
"Christmas Eve: Australia" (Shapiro) **25**:279, 286, 296, 300
"Christmas Eve under Hooker's Statue" (Lowell) **3**:200, 203
"Christmas Eve--Market Square" (Page) **12**:169
"Christmas in India" (Kipling) **3**:186
"Christmas in Simla" (Kipling) **3**:182
"Christmas on the Hudson" (Garcia Lorca)
See "Navidad en el Hudson"
"Christmas on the Plantation" (Dunbar)
See "Chrismus on the Plantation"
"Christmas Poem for Nancy" (Schwartz) **8**:316
"Christmas Tree" (Shapiro) **25**:269, 286
"Christmas Tree--Market Square" (Page) **12**:169
Christmas-Eve (Browning) **2**:31-2, 44, 70-1
Christmas-Eve and Easter Day (Browning) **2**:33, 36, 70, 95
"Christs Incarnation" (Herrick) **9**:119
Chronophagia (Cassian) **17**:6, 13
"Chrysallis" (Montale) **13**:151
"Chu Ming-How" (Stryk) **27**:198
"Chüeh-chü" (Tu Fu) **9**:323
"El Chulo" (Guillen) **23**:101
"Chumban" (Tagore) **8**:407
"The Church" (Herbert) **4**:103, 113
"The Church and the Hotel" (Masters) **1**:343
"Church Building" (Harper) **21**:198, 200, 213
"The Church Floore" (Herbert) **4**:109, 119
"Church Going" (Larkin) **21**:228, 230, 236-37, 247, 255, 259
"The Church Militant" (Herbert) **4**:100, 130
"Church Monuments" (Herbert) **4**:100, 119
"Church Music" (Herbert) **4**:100, 131
"The Church of Brou" (Arnold) **5**:6, 9, 12, 50
"The Church Porch" (Herbert) **4**:100-01, 103, 107, 126
"The Church-Bell" (Wylie) **23**:328
"Church-Going" (Heaney) **18**:223
"Church-lock and Key" (Herbert) **4**:127
"Churchyard" (Gray)
See "Elegy Written in a Country Churchyard"
"Churning Day" (Heaney) **18**:186
"The Chute" (Olds) **22**:319-22
La chute d'un ange (Lamartine) **16**:263, 265, 269-70, 285-87, 293-94, 296-97
"Chuva Oblíqua" (Pessoa) **20**:151, 165
"Chuy" (Soto) **28**:372, 382
"Ciant da li ciampanis" (Pasolini) **17**:256, 265
"Ciants di muart" (Pasolini) **17**:256
"The Cicadas" (Wright) **14**:346
"Cicadas" (Zagajewski) **27**:397
"Ciel brouillé" (Baudelaire) **1**:61, 66
"Cielo de tercera" (Fuertes) **27**:31
La cifra (Borges) **22**:95, 97, 99
"Un cigare allume que Fume" (Apollinaire)
See "Paysage"
"Cigola la carrucola del pozzo" (Montale) **13**:164
"Le cimetière marin" (Bishop) **3**:46
"Le cimetière marin" (Valery) **9**:348, 351-52, 355, 358, 361, 363-80, 382, 384, 387, 389-93, 395-96, 398
The Circassian (Lermontov)
See *The Circassian*
The Circassian Boy (Lermontov)
See *The Novice*
"Circe's Power" (Gluck) **16**:171
The Circle Game (Atwood) **8**:3, 12, 15, 18, 26-8
"Circles in th Sun" (Bissett) **14**:8, 19, 33
"The Circuit of Apollo" (Finch) **21**:162, 168
"Circuit total par la lune et par la couleur" (Tzara) **27**:224
"A Circular Play" (Stein) **18**:347
"Circulation of the Song" (Duncan) **2**:127
"Circumjack Cencrastus" (MacDiarmid) **9**:157
"Circumstance" (Lowell) **13**:94
"The Circus Animals' Desertion" (Yeats) **20**:307, 311, 313, 327, 332, 336
"Cirque d'hiver" (Bishop) **3**:37
"El cisne" (Dario) **15**:113
"Los cisnes" (Dario) **15**:115
"The Cited" (Garcia Lorca)
See "Romance del emplazado"
"Cities and Thrones and Powers" (Kipling) **3**:183
"Citizen Cain" (Baraka) **4**:17, 24
"Citronia" (Heine) **25**:160, 171-80
"Città in campagna" (Pavese) **13**:227
"The City" (Blok) **21**:24
"The City" (Nash) **21**:272
"The City" (Pasternak)
See "Gorod"
"The City: A Cycle" (Stryk) **27**:216
"The City Asleep" (Wright) **14**:362
"A City Dead House" (Whitman) **3**:379
"City in the Country" (Pavese)
See "Città in campagna"
"The City in the Sea" (Poe) **1**:426, 431, 434, 438, 443-45
"The City in Which I Love You" (Lee) **24**:241
The City in Which I Love You (Lee) **24**:240, 242-44
"The City Limits" (Ammons) **16**:11, 23, 37, 46
"City Midnight Junk Strains for Frank O'Hara" (Ginsberg) **4**:47
"City of Monuments" (Rukeyser) **12**:230
"The City of the Dead" (Gibran) **9**:73
"City of the Wind" (Stryk) **27**:191
"The City Planners" (Atwood) **8**:13
"City Psalm" (Rukeyser) **12**:221
"City Trees" (Millay) **6**:207
"City Walk-Up, Winter 1969" (Forche) **10**:141, 144, 147, 157-58
"City without a Name" (Milosz) **8**:194-95
"City without Walls" (Auden) **1**:20

"The City-Mouse and the Country-Mouse" (Wyatt) **27**:331
"The City's Love" (McKay) **2**:211
"Ciudad" (Borges) **22**:94
"Ciudad sin sueño" (Garcia Lorca) **3**:139-40
"Ciudad viva, ciudad muerta" (Aleixandre) **15**:35
"Ciudades" (Cardenal)
See "Las ciudades perdidas"
"Las ciudades perdidas" (Cardenal) **22**:126-28, 132
"Civil Rights Poem" (Baraka) **4**:11, 19
"Civilization and Its Discontents" (Ashbery) **26**:108, 113
"Clad All in Brown" (Swift) **9**:256-57
"The Claim" (Browning) **6**:14
"Clair de lune" (Apollinaire) **7**:45-6
"Clair de lune" (Verlaine) **2**:413, 420, 429
Claire de terre (Breton) **15**:51-2
"Claribel" (Tennyson) **6**:358-60, 365
"Claribel A Melody" (McGuckian) **27**:83
"Clasping of Hands" (Herbert) **4**:130
"Class" (Tomlinson) **17**:320
"Class Struggle" (Baraka) **4**:30, 38
"Class Struggle in Music" (Baraka) **4**:40
"The Class Will Come to Order" (Kunitz) **19**:150
"Claud Antle" (Masters) **1**:334
"Claude Glass" (Ondaatje) **28**:314
"Claus von Stuffenberg 1944" (Gunn) **26**:197
"El clavicordio de la abuela" (Dario) **15**:80
"Clay" (Baraka) **4**:30
"clay and morning star" (Clifton) **17**:29
"Cleaning Day" (Wright) **14**:356
"Cleaning the Candelabrum" (Sassoon) **12**:248, 259
"Clean,like,iodoform,between,the,tall" (Villa) **22**:356-57
"Clear and gentle stream" (Bridges) **28**:83
"Clear Autumn" (Rexroth) **20**:209
"Clear, with Light Variable Winds" (Lowell) **13**:94
"Clearances" (Heaney) **18**:228-29, 232, 238
"Cleared" (Kipling) **3**:167
"The Clearing" (Baraka) **4**:5, 15
Clearing (Berry) **28**:7-9
The Clearing (Berry) **28**:38
"Clearing the Title" (Merrill) **28**:267, 269-70
"The Cleaving" (Lee) **24**:241, 244, 248-49, 251-52
"Cleon" (Browning) **2**:36, 82, 95
"Cleopomop y Heliodemo" (Dario) **15**:81
"Clepsydra" (Ashbery) **26**:126, 157, 166
"The Clepsydras of the Unknown" (Elytis) **21**:119
"The Clerk's Journal" (Aiken) **26**:25
The Clerk's Journal: Being the Diary of a Queer Man (Aiken) **26**:46-8, 50
"Clerk's Tale" (Chaucer) **19**:13, 29, 54-60
"The Cliff" (Lermontov) **18**:297
"Cliff Klingenhagen" (Robinson) **1**:467, 486
"Clifford Ridell" (Masters) **1**:344-46
"The Cliff-Top" (Bridges) **28**:67
"The Climate of Thought" (Graves) **6**:139, 143
"Climbing a Mountain" (Hagiwara Sakutaro) 177
"Climbing Alone All Day" (Rexroth) **20**:193
"Climbing Milestone Mountain" (Rexroth) **20**:203
"Climbing Pien-chüeh Temple" (Wang Wei) **18**:371
"Climbing the Streets of Worcester, Mass." (Harjo) **27**:66
"Climbing the Streets of Worcester Mass" (Harjo) **27**:
"Climbing to the Monastery of Perception" (Wang Wei) **18**:384
"The Clinging Vine" (Robinson) **1**:468
"The Clipped Stater" (Graves) **6**:128, 137
"A Cloak" (Levertov) **11**:176, 194
"La cloche fêlée" (Baudelaire) **1**:65
"A Clock in the Square" (Rich) **5**:352
"The Clock of Tomorrow" (Apollinaire)
See "L'lorloge de demain"
"The Clock Stopped" (Dickinson) **1**:108
"The Clod and the Pebble" (Blake) **12**:7
"Clorinda and Damon" (Marvell) **10**:268, 271
"Closed for Good" (Frost) **1**:213
"Close-Up" (Ammons) **16**:24
"Clothes" (Sexton) **2**:367
"The Cloud" (Shelley) **14**:167, 171, 196, 207, 212
"Cloud" (Toomer) **7**:338
"Cloud-Catch" (Hongo) **23**:204
The Cloud-Messenger (Kalidasa)
See *Meghaduta*
"Clouds" (Ashbery) **26**:124
"Clouds" (Brooke) **24**:57-8, 73, 85
"Clouds" (Levine) **22**:214, 219, 222
"Clouds" (Tomlinson) **17**:312
The Clouds (Williams) **7**:370
"Clover" (Dario)
See "Trébol"
"The Clown Chastized" (Mallarme)
See "Le pitre châtié"
Clown's Houses (Sitwell) **3**:290, 294, 301-02
The Club of Queer Trade (Chesterton) **28**:97
Cluster of Songs (Tagore)
See *Gitali*
Cluster of Songs (Tagore)
See *Gitali*
"Coal" (Lorde) **12**:153
Coal (Lorde) **12**:142, 148
"The Coal Picker" (Lowell) **13**:84
"The Coast" (Hass) **16**:196
"The Coast Guard's Cottage" (Wylie) **23**:324
"Coast of Trees" (Ammons) **16**:45, 62
A Coast of Trees (Ammons) **16**:31, 45, 62
"The Coastwise Lights" (Kipling) **3**:162
"A Coat" (Yeats) **20**:320
"The Coats" (Gallagher) **9**:60
"Cobwebs" (Rossetti) **7**:278
"The Cock and the Fox" (Chaucer)
See "Nun's Priest's Tale"
"The Cocked Hat" (Masters) **1**:325-26, 328-29, 342
"Cockerel" (Hagiwara Sakutaro) **18**:173
"The Cocks" (Pasternak) **6**:253
"Coconut Palm" (Tagore)
See "Narikel"
"Cocotte" (Gozzano) **10**:178
"Coda" (Ekeloef) **23**:76, 86
"The Code" (Frost) **1**:195, 208, 226
"A Code of Morals" (Kipling) **3**:190
"Coeur, couronne et miroir" (Apollinaire) **7**:32-6
"La coeur volé" (Rimbaud) **3**:270
"Cogióme sin prevención" (Juana Ines de la Cruz) **24**:234
"Cohorte" (Perse) **23**:254-57
Coins and Coffins (Wakoski) **15**:338, 344, 356, 369
"Cold" (Cassian) **17**:12, 15
"Cold in the Earth" (Bronte)
See "Remembrance"
"Cold Iron" (Kipling) **3**:171
"Cold-Blooded Creatures" (Wylie) **23**:314
"La colère de Samson" (Vigny) **26**:366, 368, 371, 380-81, 391, 401, 412, 416
"Coleridge" (McGuckian) **27**:101
"Colesberg" (Brutus) **24**:105
"Colin Clout" (Spenser)
See *Colin Clouts Come Home Againe*
Colin Clouts Come Home Againe (Spenser) **8**:336, 367, 387, 396
"The Coliseum" (Poe) **1**:439
"The Collar" (Gunn) **26**:185
"The Collar" (Herbert) **4**:102-03, 112-13, 130-31
"The Collar" (Herrick) **9**:141
Collected Earlier Poems (Williams) **7**:367-69, 374-75, 378, 382, 387-88, 392-94, 406-07, 409
Collected Early Poems (Pound) **4**:355
The Collected Greed, Parts 1-13 (Wakoski) **15**:356
Collected Later Poems (Williams) **7**:370, 375
The Collected Longer Poems of Kenneth Rexroth (Rexroth) **20**:197, 202, 204, 209-10, 214
Collected Lyrics (Millay) **6**:227
Collected Poems (Aiken) **26**:21, 24, 43-5
Collected Poems (Bridges) **28**:74, 77-8
The Collected Poems (Chesterton) **28**:99, 109
Collected Poems (Cummings) **5**:82-4, 87, 107, 111
Collected Poems (Frost) **1**:203
Collected Poems (Graves) **6**:153, 165, 171
Collected Poems (Hardy) **8**:89, 95-6, 98, 101, 118, 124
Collected Poems (Larkin) **21**:256, 258
Collected Poems (Lindsay) **23**:265, 280-82, 285-86, 288, 292, 294
Collected Poems (MacDiarmid) 9;186
Collected Poems (Millay) **6**:227
Collected Poems (Milosz) **8**:190-91, 197-98, 202, 206-07, 214-15
See *Czeslaw Milosz: The Collected Poems, 1931-1987*
Collected Poems (Moore) **4**:235-36, 238, 247, 254, 271
Collected Poems (Olson) **19**:316
Collected Poems (Pinsky) **27**:168
The Collected Poems (Plath) **1**:406
Collected Poems (Robinson) **1**:467, 469, 480
Collected Poems (Rossetti)
See *The Poetical Works of Christina Georgina Rossetti*
Collected Poems (Sassoon) **12**:246-47
Collected Poems (Sitwell) **3**:299, 301, 303-05, 308, 318-21, 325
Collected Poems (Stevens) **6**:306
Collected Poems (Stryk) **27**:207, 209-10, 212-16
Collected Poems (Tomlinson) **17**:342, 351, 355, 361
Collected Poems (Yeats) **20**:307, 336-37
Collected Poems 1934 (Williams) **7**:360, 372, 402
Collected Poems, 1938 (Graves) **6**:166
Collected Poems, 1955 (Graves) **6**:138, 140-43, 145
Collected Poems, 1909-1935 (Eliot) **5**:173, 176, 179, 211
Collected Poems, 1912-1944 (H. D.) **5**:297, 305
Collected Poems, 1923-1953 (Bogan) **12**:93, 95-6, 120, 125
Collected Poems, 1929-1933 (Day Lewis) **11**:123
Collected Poems, 1940-1978 (Shapiro) **25**:313, 315
Collected Poems, 1947-1980 (Ginsberg) **4**:71-2, 76-9, 83-4, 86, 89
Collected Poems, 1951-1971 (Ammons) **16**:10, 20, 27, 40, 46, 54, 61
Collected Poems, 1957-1982 (Berry) **28**:25-29, 32, 27-29, 43-44
The Collected Poems of A. E. Housman (Housman) **2**:175-76, 180
The Collected Poems of Christopher Smart (Smart) **13**:347
Collected Poems of Elinor Wylie (Wylie) **23**:304, 306, 312, 314, 330-31
Collected Poems of H. D. (H. D.) **5**:268, 270, 276
The Collected Poems of Hart Crane (Crane) **3**:89-90
The Collected Poems of Howard Nemerov (Nemerov) **24**:298-99, 301
The Collected Poems of Jean Toomer (Toomer) **7**:340-41
The Collected Poems of Muriel Rukeyser (Rukeyser) **12**:224, 226, 235
The Collected Poems of Octavio Paz, 1957-1987 (Paz) **1**:374-76

The Collected Poems of Rupert Brooke (Brooke) **24**:52, 54, 61, 71
The Collected Poems of Stevie Smith (Smith) **12**:307, 309, 313-17, 320, 327, 346-47, 350, 352
The Collected Poems of Theodore Roethke (Roethke) **15**:281, 283-84, 288
The Collected Poems of Thomas Merton (Merton) **10**:336-337, 345, 348, 351
The Collected Poems of Wallace Stevens (Stevens) **6**:304
The Collected Poems of Wilfred Owen (Owen) **19**:351
Collected Poetry Notebook (Cesaire) **25**:48-9
Collected Shorter Poems, 1927-1957 (Auden) **1**:30
Collected Shorter Poems, 1930-1950 (Auden) **1**:30
Collected Shorter Poems, 1946-1991 (Carruth) **10**:89, 91
The Collected Shorter Poems of Kenneth Rexroth (Rexroth) **20**:197-98, 202, 204-05
Collected Sonnets (Millay) **6**:227
Collected Works (Akhmatova) **2**:19
Collected Works (Rossetti)
See *The Poetical Works of Christina Georgina Rossetti*
The Collected Works of Billy the Kid (Ondaatje) **28**:298, 303, 314-16, 327, 338-39
A Collection of Celebrated Love Poems (Hagiwara Sakutaro)
See *A Collection of Celebrated Love Poems*
Collection of Short Songs on Innocent Love (Hagiwara Sakutaro)
See *Collection of Short Songs on Innocent Love*
"Collective Dawns" (Ashbery) **26**:144, 153
"College Breakfast Party" (Eliot) **20**:125
"The College Garden" (Bridges) **28**:79-80
"Les collines" (Apollinaire) **7**:12
"The Colloquies" (Gozzano) **10**:175, 180
The Colloquies (Gozzano)
See *I Colloqui*
"Colloquy in Black Rock" (Lowell) **3**:201, 216-17, 227
"Colloquy of the Centaurs" (Dario)
See "Coloquio de los centauros"
"Collos. 3.3" (Herbert) **4**:130
Collyn Clout (Skelton) **25**:329-30, 336, 337, 341-42, 348, 356, 374
"La colombe poisnardée et le jet d'eau" (Apollinaire) **7**:18, 20-2
"A Colombia" (Guillen) **23**:127
"The Colonel" (Forche) **10**:136, 138, 140, 145, 153, 167, 169
"Colonel Fantock" (Sitwell) **3**:293, 301, 325
"Coloquio de los centauros" (Dario) **15**:88, 92, 96, 112, 114
Color (Cullen) **20**:52-54, 56-58, 62, 66-67, 72, 77, 79, 81-83, 85-86
"The Color Sergeant" (Johnson) **24**:142
"The Colored Band" (Dunbar) **5**:134, 147
"The Colored Soldiers" (Dunbar) **5**:129-31, 133-34, 140
"Colors" (Cullen) **20**:65
"The Colors of Night" (Momaday) **25**:199, 202-203, 217-18
The Colossus, and Other Poems (Plath) **1**:380-81, 84, 388-89, 391, 394, 396, 404, 407, 410, 414
"The Colour Shop" (McGuckian) **27**:106
"A Coloured Print by Shokei" (Lowell) **13**:61
"A Coltrane Poem" (Sanchez) **9**:225
"Columbian Ode" (Dunbar) **5**:128
"Combat Cultural" (Moore) **4**:259
"Come" (Smith) **12**:316
"Come Break with Time" (Bogan) **12**:87, 101, 105-06, 122
"Come, Come Now" (Aleixandre) **15**:15
"Come Death" (Smith) **12**:315
"Come Death (2)" (Smith) **12**:314, 317, 319
"Come In" (Frost) **1**:197, 213, 230
"Come on, Come back" (Smith) **12**:295
"Come Republic" (Masters) **1**:329, 343
"Come se Quando" (Bridges) **28**:76-9
"Come Thunder" (Okigbo) **7**:235
"Come to the Bower" (Heaney) **18**:197
"The Comedian as the Letter C" (Stevens) **6**:293, 295-96, 304, 306, 310, 330, 335
La Comédie de la Mort (Gautier) **18**:143-46, 155, 159, 163
La comédie de la mort (Gautier) **18**:131-32, 134-35, 141, 155
Comedy (Dante)
See *La divina commedia*
"The Comet" (Aleixandre) **15**:5
"The Comet at Yell'ham" (Hardy) **8**:89
"Comfort" (Browning) **6**:21
"Coming" (Larkin) **21**:238, 244
"Coming Close" (Levine) **22**:220
"Coming Down through Somerset" (Hughes) **7**:166
"The Coming Fall" (Levertov) **11**:185
The Coming Forth by Day of Osiris Jones (Aiken) **26**:8, 11, 57
"Coming Home" (Gallagher) **9**:36
"Coming Home from the Post Office" (Levine) **22**:221, 228
"Coming of Age in Michigan" (Levine) **22**:220, 228
"The Coming of Arthur" (Tennyson) **6**:408
"The Coming of Kali" (Clifton) **17**:24
"The Coming of the End (Moments of Vision)" (Hardy) **8**:92
"The Coming of Wisdom with Time" (Yeats) **20**:338
"Commander Lowell 1887-1950" (Lowell) **3**:219, 235
"Comme Dieu Dispense de Graces" (Stevens) **6**:294
"Comme on voit sur la branche" (Ronsard) **11**:218, 234, 236, 240
"Comme un beau pré despouillè de ses fleurs" (Ronsard) **11**:250
Commedia (Dante)
See *La divina commedia*"
"The Commemorative Mound of the Decorated Tree" (Ishikawa)
See "Nishikigizuka"
"Comment against the Lamp" (Hughes) **1**:266
"Commentary" (Milosz) **8**:212-13
"A Common Ground" (Levertov) **11**:169
"The Commonweal" (Swinburne) **24**:312
"Communication in White" (Madhubuti) **5**:340
"Communion" (Herbert) **4**:100
"A Communist to Others" (Auden) **1**:15
"The Commuted Sentence" (Smith) **12**:327
"Cómo atar" (Fuertes) **27**:27, 30
Cómo atar los bigotes al tigre (Fuertes) **27**:17-8, 25-7, 31, 49
"Como del cielo llovido" (Guillen) **23**:126
"Como quisimos" (Guillen) **23**:126
"The Compact: At Volterra" (Tomlinson) **17**:350
"The Companion of a Mile" (Noyes) **27**:134
"The Companions" (Nemerov) **24**:263
"Company" (Dove) **6**:111, 119
"Company" (Smith) **12**:325
"The Company of Lovers" (Wright) **14**:336, 340, 351, 371
"A Comparative Peace" (Brutus) **24**:116
"Comparatives" (Momaday) **25**:191, 193-194
"Comparison" (Dunbar) **5**:125
"Compass" (Borges) **22**:74
"Compensation" (Dunbar) **5**:121
"The Complaint" (Wordsworth)
See "The Complaint of the Forsaken Indian Woman"
"The Complaint of the Forsaken Indian Woman" (Wordsworth) **4**:347, 427-28
"Complaint of the Poor Knight Errant" (Laforgue) **14**:64
"Complaint of the Poor Knight Errant" (Laforgue)
See "Complainte du pauvre chevalier-errant"
"Complainte à Notre-Dame des soirs" (Laforgue) **14**:94
"Complainte de cette bonne lune" (Laforgue) **14**:93
Complainte de la bonne défunte (Laforgue) **14**:81, 98
"Complainte de la fin des journées" (Laforgue) **14**:98
"Complainte de la lune en province" (Laforgue) **14**:98
"Complainte de l'ange incurable" (Laforgue) **14**:85, 89-90, 98
"Complainte de l'automne monotone" (Laforgue) **14**:80
"Complainte de l'époux outragé" (Laforgue) **14**:81, 93
"Complainte de Lord Pierrot" (Laforgue) **14**:81, 93, 98
"Complainte de l'organiste de Nice" (Laforgue) **14**:93
"Complainte de l'orgue de barbarie" (Laforgue) **14**:95
"Complainte des blackboulés" (Laforgue) **14**:81, 96
"Complainte des complaintes" (Laforgue) **14**:95
"Complainte des consolations" (Laforgue) **14**:81
"Complainte des débats mélancoliques et littéraires" (Laforgue) **14**:64, 97
"Complainte des formalités nuptiales" (Laforgue) **14**:81, 96
"Complainte des grands pins dans une ville abandonée" (Laforgue) **14**:81, 96
"Complainte des pianos qu'on entend dans les quertiersaisés" (Laforgue) **14**:81, 93-5
"Complainte des printemps" (Laforgue) **14**:81, 98
"Complainte des voix sous le figuier bouddhique" (Laforgue) **14**:96
"Complainte du fœtus de Poète" (Laforgue) **14**:93, 96, 98
"Complainte du pauvre chevalier-errant" (Laforgue) **14**:98
"Complainte du pauvre corps humain" (Laforgue) **14**:81
"Complainte du pauvre jeune homme" (Laforgue) **14**:81, 93
"Complainte du Roi de Thulé" (Laforgue) **14**:81, 86, 89, 93, 98
"Complainte du sage de Paris" (Laforgue) **14**:95
"Complainte d'un certain dimanche" (Laforgue) **14**:96-8
"Complainte d'une convalescence en mai" (Laforgue) **14**:96, 98
"Complainte propitiatoire à l'inconscient" (Laforgue) **14**:66, 94-5
"Complainte sous le figuier boudhique" (Laforgue) **14**:81
"Complainte sur certains ennuis" (Laforgue) **14**:94, 97
"Complainte sur certains temps déplacés" (Laforgue) **14**:94
"Complainte-épitaphe" (Laforgue) **14**:95
"Complainte-Placet de Faust fils" (Laforgue) **14**:95, 98
Les complaintes (Laforgue) **14**:57, 64, 66, 68-9, 70-2, 80-1, 92, 94-5, 97-8
"Complaintes des pubertés difficiles" (Laforgue) **14**:80, 98
Complaints: Containing Sundrie Small Poemes of the Worlds Vanitie (Spenser) **8**:366
The Complete Collected Poems of William Carlos Williams, 1906-1938 (Williams) **7**:348, 355
The Complete Poems (Dickinson) **1**:102
Complete Poems (Sandburg) **2**:322-24, 328-29, 331, 333, 340
The Complete Poems, 1927-1979 (Bishop) **3**:50, 66

The Complete Poems of Frances Ellen Watkins Harper (Harper) **21**:197
The Complete Poems of Marianne Moore (Moore) **4**:251, 254, 256, 270
The Complete Poem's of Paul Laurence Dunbar (Dunbar) **5**:120, 136
The Complete Poetical Works (Lowell) **13**:95
Complete Poetical Works of Samuel Taylor Coleridge (Coleridge) **11**:44, 71
Complete Verse (Belloc) **24**:23, 36, 39
Complete Works (Aleixandre)
See *Obras completas*
Complete Works (Jeffers) **17**:125
Complete Works (Mandelstam) **14**:106
"The Complete Works of Francois Villon" (Villon) **13**:413
"Complicate" (Kunitz) **19**:156
"Complicity" (Gallagher) **9**:37
"Composed on the Cold Food Day" (Wang Wei) **18**:362
"Composition in Bhairavi" (Tagore)
See "Bhairavi gan"
"Comprehending" (Ortiz) **17**:246
"Comptine" (Cesaire) **25**:31
"Comrades Four" (McKay) **2**:225
"Con la Carta de la Habana" (Guillen) **23**:126
"Conceit of Master Gysbrecht" (Browning) **2**:38
"Conceive a Man, Should He Have Anything" (Cummings) **5**:106
"The Concert" (Millay) **6**:215
"Concert at the Railroad Station" (Mandelstam)
See "Koncert na vokzale"
"The Concert of Hyacinths" (Elytis) **21**:119
"Concerto to a Runaway" (Bissett) **14**:9
"Conch-Shell" (Wright) **14**:364
Le concile féerique (Laforgue) **14**:72, 81, 96
"Conciliator, Who Had Never Believed" (Holderlin) **4**:178
"Conclusion" (Sassoon) **12**:258
"Concord" (Swinburne) **24**:324, 326
"Concord Hymn" (Emerson) **18**:111
"Concord Ode" (Emerson) **18**:84, 88
"Concord River" (Rich) **5**:354
"The Condemned" (Page) **12**:174-75
A Coney Island of the Mind (Ferlinghetti) **1**:164-65, 167-77, 184, 187
"A Conference of the Powers" (Kipling) **3**:160
"Confession" (Baudelaire) **1**:61
"confession" (Clifton) **17**:37
"Confession" (Gluck) **16**:160
"Confession" (Heaney) **18**:243
"The Confession" (Lermontov) **18**:300
"A Confession" (Milosz) **8**:197
"The Confessional" (Browning) **2**:30
"Confessional" (Chesterton) **28**:95
"Confessions" (Browning) **6**:32
"Confessions of a Second-Rate, Sensitive Mind" (Tennyson) **6**:347
"The Confessions of Count Mowgli de Sade" (Nash) **21**:267
"Confessions of the Life Artist" (Gunn) **26**:207, 211, 226
"The Confidantes" (Kumin) **15**:215
"Confidential Instructions" (Kunitz) **19**:148
"Configurations" (Ammons) **16**:23
Configurations (Paz) **1**:355
"Confinement" (McGuckian) **27**:101
"The Confirmation" (Shapiro) **25**:286, 300
"Confiteor" (Trakl) **20**:263-64, 269
"The Conflict" (Day Lewis) **11**:126, 150
"Confusion of the Senses" (Rexroth) **20**:221
"Congo" (Lindsay) **23**:264, 266, 268, 270, 272-73, 275-76, 278, 282-84, 286-87, 289, 294, 297
The Congo and Other Poems (Lindsay) **23**:267-68, 295
"The Congo Love Song" (Johnson) **24**:151
"A Congratulatory Poem to Her Most Sacred Majesty on the Universal Hopes of All Loyal Persons for a Prince of Wales" (Behn) **13**:32
A Congratulatory Poem to . . . Queen Mary upon Her Arrival in England (Behn) **13**:9
Los conjurados (Borges) **22**:95, 99
"Conjuring in Heaven" (Hughes) **7**:159
Connecting the Dots (Kumin) **15**:224
"Connections" (Wright) **14**:376-77
"The Connoisseuse of Slugs" (Olds) **22**:312
"Connubii Flores, or the Well-Wishes at Weddings" (Herrick) **9**:86, 112
"The Conquererors" (Dunbar) **5**:131
"The Conqueror Worm" (Poe) **1**:437, 443
"Conquête de l'aube" (Cesaire) **25**:10
"A Conrado Benítez" (Guillen) **23**:128
"The Cons cientious Objector" (Shapiro) **25**:297
"Conscience" (Herbert) **4**:109, 129
"La Conscience" (Hugo) **17**:65, 85
"Conscience and Remorse" (Dunbar) **5**:115, 125
"Les Consciences atténuantes" (Tzara) **27**:235
"Conscious" (Owen) **19**:347, 361-63
"Consciousness" (Milosz)
See "Swiadomość"
The Consciousness Industry: On Literature, Politics, and the Media (Enzensberger)
See *Bewussteins-Industrie*
"Conscript" (Larkin) **21**:225
"Conscription Camp" (Shapiro) **25**:313, 324-25
"Conscripts" (Sassoon) **12**:242, 280
"The Consecrating Mother" (Sexton) **2**:374
"Consequences" (Meredith) **28**:213
"Conseil d'ami" (Valery) **9**:391
"Conserving the Magnitude of Uselessness" (Ammons) **16**:54
"Considering the Snail" (Gunn) **26**:201, 207-208, 210, 213
"Consolation" (McKay) **2**:225
"Consorting with Angels" (Sexton) **2**:363
The Conspirators (Borges)
See *Los conjurados*
Constab Ballads (McKay) **2**:208, 210, 216, 221-22, 225-27
"Constancie" (Herbert) **4**:109
"The Constant" (Ammons) **16**:6
"Constantly Risking Absurdity" (Ferlinghetti) **1**:182
"Constellation" (Stryk) **27**:208, 212
Constellations (Breton) **15**:48-9, 55, 59-60, 62
"Construction" (Shapiro) **25**:295
"Constructions" (Loy) **16**:316
"Conte" (Rimbaud) **3**:261-63
"Conte Colibri" (Cesaire) **25**:44-5
"Contemplations" (Bradstreet) **10**:7-8, 19-21, 27-30, 35, 42, 65
Les contemplations (Hugo) **17**:50, 53-54, 64, 66-67, 74, 78, 80-84, 86-87, 89-92, 95
"The Contender" (Hughes) **7**:155
"The Contention" (Sassoon) **12**:259
"Contest of the Bards" (Ginsberg) **4**:58-9
"The Continent" (Duncan) **2**:109-13
"Continent's End" (Jeffers) **17**:131
"Contingency" (Ammons) **16**:6
Continuation des amours (Ronsard) **11**:220, 230
"Continuum" (Levertov) **11**:207-09
"Contra mortem" (Carruth) **10**:83
Contra Mortem (Carruth) **10**:71
"A Contract" (Lermontov) **18**:303-4
"Contralto" (Gautier) **18**:157
"The Contraption" (Swenson) **14**:250
"The Contrariness of the Mad Farmer" (Berry) **28**:20
"The Contrast" (Harper) **21**:207, 216
"Contre les bûcherons de la forêt de Gastine" (Ronsard) **11**:236-37, 242
"Le Contrediz de Franc Gontier" (Villon) **13**:415
"Control Burn" (Snyder) **21**:292
"Contusion" (Plath) **1**:391, 394
"The Conundrum of the Workshop" (Kipling) **3**:167
"The Convalescent" (Gozzano) **10**:177
"The Convent Threshold" (Rossetti) **7**:267, 281-2, 291, 295-6, 298
"Conventionality" (Kipling) **3**:190
"The Convergence of the Twain" (Hardy) **8**:116
"Conversacíon" (Cardenal) **22**:117
"Conversation" (Giovanni) **19**:118
"The Conversation" (Masters) **1**:326
Conversation at Midnight (Millay) **6**:220, 223, 244
"Conversation in Moscow" (Levertov) **11**:197
"The Conversation of Prayer" (Thomas) **2**:390
"Conversation with a Fireman from Brooklyn" (Gallagher) **9**:44, 60
"Conversation with my Inspiration" (Tsvetaeva)
See "Razgovor s geniem"
"Conversations with Jeanne" (Milosz) **8**:213
"Conversing with Paradise" (Nemerov) **24**:285
"Conversion" (Toomer) **7**:320, 334
"The Convert" (Shapiro) **25**:286, 296, 298
"Convict" (Wordsworth) **4**:373
"Convivio!" (Williams) **7**:361
Convivio (Dante) **21**:48-53, 66, 73-4, 83, 87-92
"Cooking" (Stein) **18**:322-326
"A Cooking Egg" (Eliot) **5**:184
"Cook's Mountains" (Page) **12**:183, 190
"The Cool Web" (Graves) **6**:172
"Coole Park, 1929" (Yeats) **20**:322
"Coon Song" (Ammons) **16**:19, 41, 44, 46
"Coopérants du contingent" (Senghor) **25**:255
"Coplas americans" (Guillen) **23**:126
"Cop-Out Session" (Knight) **14**:46, 52
"Copper Red and the Seven Dachsies" (Cassian) **17**:3
Copper Sun (Cullen) **20**:56-59, 61-62, 64-65, 75, 77, 85-86
"cops" (Baraka) **4**:12
"A Coquette Conquered" (Dunbar) **5**:122
"Coquetterie posthume" (Gautier) **18**:125, 157-60, 163
"Le cor" (Vigny) **26**:369, 402-403, 410
"Cor Mio" (Rossetti) **7**:278
El corazón amarillo (Neruda) **4**:287, 289
El corazón con que vivo (Guillen) **23**:133
"El corazón de Pedro de Valdivia" (Neruda) **4**:293
"El corazón magellanico" (Neruda) **4**:281
"Corinna, Pride of Drury-Lane" (Swift) **9**:283-84
"Corinna's Going a-Maying" (Herrick) **9**:99-101, 104-05, 116, 120, 122-23, 125, 132, 137, 142, 145
"Coriolanus and His Mother" (Schwartz) **8**:282-83, 290-91, 297-98, 301, 308-09, 312
"The Corner of Night and Morning" (Lowell) **13**:64
"Cornet Solo" (Day Lewis) **11**:145
Cornhuskers (Sandburg) **2**:302, 304, 307, 309, 313-14, 316, 323, 338-39
"Cornish Heroic Song for Valda Trevlyn" (MacDiarmid) **9**:180, 183
"Corno Inglese" (Montale) **13**:105
"A Corn-Song" (Dunbar) **5**:122
La Corona (Donne) **1**:136-39, 145, 147
"A Coronal" (Williams) **7**:345, 362
"The Coronet" (Marvell) **10**:267, 271, 274, 277, 293, 313-14
"The Corporal" (Gunn) **26**:224
"Corps perdu" (Cesaire) **25**:30
Corps perdu (Cesaire) **25**:30-2, 35, 44
"The Corpse of a Cat" (Hagiwara Sakutaro)
See "Neko no shigai"
"Corpse Song" (Atwood) **8**:23, 25
"Correction: *Eve* Delved and *Adam* Span" (Nash) **21**:273
"Correspondances" (Baudelaire) **1**:55, 65, 69-70
"Correspondences" (Rukeyser) **12**:226, 233
"La Corrida" (Hayden) **6**:194
"The Corridor" (Gunn) **26**:193
"Cors de chasse" (Apollinaire) **7**:42
The Corsair (Byron) **16**:91-5, 109
The Corsair (Lermontov) **18**:299
"Corson's Inlet" (Ammons) **16**:21, 23, 29, 35-7, 54
Corson's Inlet (Ammons) **16**:4-5, 20, 28

Cumulative Title Index

"The Cortege" (Gibran) **9**:73
"Cortège for Rosenbloom" (Stevens) **6**:293
Cortege of Orpheus (Apollinaire)
See *Le bestiaire; ou, Cortège d'Orphée*
"Cosmic Comics" (Nemerov) **24**:301
"The Cossack" (Pushkin) **10**:407
"Cossack Cradlesong" (Lermontov) **18**:268, 278, 281, 304
"The Cost of Pleasure" (Bryant) **20**:46
"Costa Magic" (Loy) **16**:313
"The Costa San Giorgio" (Loy) **16**:313, 318-20, 322, 327
"The Cottage Dweller" (Tagore)
See "Kutir-vasi"
"The Cottar's Saturday Night" (Burns) **6**:50, 57, 74, 79, 96
Cotton Candy on a Rainy Day (Giovanni) **19**:114, 116-18, 123, 125, 128, 130, 134, 137, 142-43
"Cotton Song" (Toomer) **7**:319, 321
"Cottonmouth Country" (Gluck) **16**:139
"Cougar Meat" (Gallagher) **9**:59, 62
"Could Man Be Drunk for Ever" (Housman) **2**:195
"Counsel at the Highest Level" (Enzensberger) **28**:136
Count Nulin (Pushkin)
See *Graf Nulin*
"Counter Serenade" (Viereck) **27**:263
"Counter-Attack" (Sassoon) **12**:256-57, 264-65, 277-78
Counter-Attack and Other Poems (Sassoon) **12**:242, 250, 253, 257-58, 260, 263-64, 266-69, 272, 276-77
"A Counterpoint" (Aiken) **26**:4
"Counter-Walk, Reversals" (Viereck) **27**:277
Counter-Walk Reversals (Viereck) **27**:
The Countess Cathleen (Yeats) **20**:298, 302-3, 353
Counting Backward (Cassian) **17**:6
"Counting the Beats" (Graves) **6**:136-37, 155
The Country between Us (Forche) **10**:136-38, 140, 143-46, 148, 150-53, 155, 157-59, 161, 165-66, 169
"A Country Burial" (Dickinson) **1**:79
"A Country Girl" (McKay) **2**:224
"A Country Life: To His Brother, Master Thomas Herrick" (Herrick) **9**:86, 110-13, 115
"The Country Life, to the Honoured Master Endimion Porter, Groome of the Bed-Chamber to His Majesty" (Herrick) **9**:101, 139, 144
The Country of a Thousand Years of Peace and Other Poems (Merrill) **28**:220, 225, 228, 229, 231, 234, 238, 239, 240, 241, 242, 244, 246, 247, 259, 281
"Country of Marriage" (Berry) **28**:11-13, 44
The Country of Marriage (Berry) **28**:7, 13
Country Sentiment (Graves) **6**:127, 129, 132
"The Country Squire and the Mandrake" (Smart) **13**:348
"Country Stars" (Meredith) **28**:180, 198
"Country Town" (Wright) **14**:350
"The Country Whore" (Pavese)
See "La puttana contadina"
"The Countryside" (Pushkin)
See "Derevnya"
"County Ward" (Soto) **28**:370, 376-77
"Le Coup de couteau du soleil dans le dos des villes surprises" (Cesaire) **25**:30
Un coup de dés jamais n'abolira le hasard (Mallarme) **4**:192, 199, 202-03, 208-09, 217-18
"Coup d'evential..." (Apollinaire) **7**:34-5
"The Couple" (Cassian) **17**:11
"Courage" (Akhmatova)
See "Muzhestvo"
Court Poems (Montagu) **16**:338
"A Courtesy" (Wylie) **23**:322
"Courtship" (Dove) **6**:112
"Cousin Kate" (Rossetti) **7**:270, 276, 280, 289, 291
"Couteaux midi" (Cesaire) **25**:37
"The Cove" (Clampitt) **19**:83
"Coversation" (Tagore)
See "Sambhashan"
"The Cow" (Nash) **21**:278
"The Cow in Apple-Time" (Frost) **1**:195, 197
"Cowley Rider" (Masters) **1**:334
"Cowper's Grave" (Browning) **6**:6, 21
"Cows: A Vision" (Gallagher) **9**:36
"The Cows at Night" (Carruth) **10**:85
"The Coy Mistress" (Marvell)
See "To His Coy Mistress"
"Crab-Angel" (Loy) **16**:307
"The Crack" (Levertov) **11**:159
"The Cracked Bell" (Baudelaire)
See "La cloche fêlée"
"The Crack-up of American Optimism" (Viereck) **27**:284
"A Cradle Song" (Blake) **12**:7, 10, 33
"A Cradle Song" (Yeats) **20**:337
Craft (Tsvetaeva)
See *Remeslo*
Craftsmanship (Tsvetaeva)
See *Remeslo*
"Crag Jack's Apostasy" (Hughes) **7**:147
"Cramped in That Funnelled Hole" (Owen) **19**:336
"Crass Times" (Viereck) **27**:278, 281
"Crass Times Redeemed by Dignity of Souls" (Viereck) **27**:258-60, 273
"La cravate et la montre" (Apollinaire) **7**:32, 34-5
"Crazy Horse names his daughter" (Clifton) **17**:25
"Crazy Jane" (Day Lewis) **11**:151
"Crazy Jane and Jack the Journeyman" (Yeats) **20**:328
"Crazy Jane Talks with the Bishop" (Yeats) **20**:327-28
"A Crazy Spiritual" (Ginsberg) **4**:79
"Crazy Weather" (Ashbery) **26**:153
"Creating the World" (Milosz) **8**:214
"creation" (Clifton) **17**:37
"The Creation" (Gibran) **9**:73
"The Creation" (Johnson) **24**:128-29, 133, 139, 143-44, 149, 152-53, 156, 164, 166-69
Creation (Noyes) **27**:138
"The Creation, according to Coyote" (Ortiz) **17**:231
"Creation of Anguish" (Nemerov) **24**:261, 285
"Creation-Annihilation" (Wright) **14**:375
"Creation Myth" (Berry) **28**:9
"creative writing class" (Bukowski) **18**:19
"Creatures" (Kumin) **15**:182
"Creatures in the Dawn" (Aleixandre) **15**:6, 15, 38
"Crecen altas las flores" (Guillen) **23**:126
"Credat Judaeus" (Kipling) **3**:194
"Credences of Summer" (Ashbery) **26**:153
"Credences of Summer" (Stevens) **6**:306, 335, 338
"Credo" (Jeffers) **17**:117,129
"Credo" (Kumin) **15**:213, 215-16, 224
"Credo" (Robinson) **1**:485-86
"Credo" (Stryk) **27**:198
"The Cremona Violin" (Lowell) **13**:60, 77, 96
"Crepuscolo di sabbiatori" (Pavese) **13**:226
Crepúsculario (Neruda) **4**:276, 278
"Crépuscule" (Apollinaire) **7**:40
"Crépuscule" (Hugo) **17**:67, 81-82
"Le crépuscule du soir" (Baudelaire) **1**:58-9
"The Crevasse" (Tsvetaeva)
See "Rasshchelina"
"Crevasses" (Cesaire) **25**:33
"The Crew of the *Chelyuskin*" (Tsvetaeva)
See "Chelyuskintsy"
"Le cri de l'âme" (Lamartine) **16**:266
The Criminal (Lermontov) **18**:299
"The Crimson Cyclamen" (Williams) **7**:350, 354
"Cripples and Other Stories" (Sexton) **2**:363, 365
"Le Cristal automatique" (Cesaire) **25**:20
"The Critic and the Writer of Fables" (Finch) **21**:163
A Critical Fable (Lowell) **13**:65, 74-6
"Critics and Connoisseurs" (Moore) **4**:232, 257, 270
"De Critters' Dance" (Dunbar) **5**:145
"La Crocifissione" (Pasolini) **17**:265
"Croft" (Smith) **12**:333
"A la croix" (Lamartine) **16**:284
"The Crooked Stick" (Wylie) **23**:301
"Cross" (Hughes) **1**:235, 243, 263-64
"The Cross Spider" (Swenson) **14**:273
"The Crosse" (Donne) **1**:136
"The Crosse" (Herbert) **4**:111
"The Crossed Apple" (Bogan) **12**:101, 110-11
"Crossing Aguadilla" (Tomlinson) **17**:361
"Crossing Brooklyn Ferry" (Sexton) **2**:361
"Crossing Brooklyn Ferry" (Tomlinson) **17**:337
"Crossing Brooklyn Ferry" (Whitman) **3**:377, 379, 391-93, 399-400, 410, 415
"Crossing Over" (Meredith) **28**:200
"Crossing the Atlantic" (Sexton) **2**:363
"Crossing the Bar" (Tennyson) **6**:359
Crossing the Water: Transitional Poems (Plath) **1**:391, 394, 396, 404
"Crossing the Yellow River to Ch'ing-ho" (Wang Wei) **18**:362, 366-68, 373
"Crossroads" (Gunn) **26**:214
"The Cross-Roads" (Lowell) **13**:60, 76-7
"Crotchets" (Nemerov) **24**:290
"Crow Alights" (Hughes) **7**:130
"Crow and Mama" (Hughes) **7**:132
"Crow and the Birds" (Hughes) **7**:159
The Crow and the Heart (Carruth) **10**:70, 78, 89
"Crow and the Sea" (Hughes) **7**:144
"Crow Blacker Than Ever" (Hughes) **7**:138
"Crow Communes" (Hughes) **7**:143
Crow: From the Life and Songs of the Crow (Hughes) **7**:129-30, 133, 137-39, 141-43, 145, 152-53, 155-61, 163, 168-71
"Crow Frowns" (Hughes) **7**:159
"Crow Goes Hunting" (Hughes) **7**:142, 160-61
"Crow Hill" (Hughes) **7**:131, 150
"Crow Jane in High Society" (Baraka) **4**:16
"Crow on a Withered Branch" (Matsuo Basho) **3**:32
"Crow on the Beach" (Hughes) **7**:138, 144
"Crow Sickened" (Hughes) **7**:138
"Crow Song" (Atwood) **8**:25
"The Crowded Street" (Bryant) **20**:5, 36
"A Crowded Trolley Car" (Wylie) **23**:309, 328, 332
"Crowdieknowe" (MacDiarmid) **9**:156
"Crowds" (Baudelaire)
See "Les foules"
"Crowing-Hen Blues" (Hughes) **1**:256
"The Crown of Bays" (Smith) **12**:319
"The Crown of Gold" (Smith) **12**:295, 315
"Crown of Thorns" (Celan)
See "Dornenkranz"
"Crowned Out" (Celan) **10**:113
Crowned with Dreams (Rilke) **2**:280
"Crowns and Garlands" (Hughes) **1**:252
"Crow's Account of St. George" (Hughes) **7**:161, 171
"Crow's Account of the Battle" (Hughes) **7**:133, 144, 152
"Crow's Account of the Battle" (Hughes) **7**:133, 144, 152
"Crow's Battle Fury" (Hughes) **7**:143
"Crow's Elephant Totem Song" (Hughes) **7**:138, 144
"Crow's Last Stand" (Hughes) **7**:123, 144
"Crow's Nerve Fails" (Hughes) **7**:144
"Crow's Playmates" (Hughes) **7**:144
"Crow's Theology" (Hughes) **7**:159, 161
"Crow's Undersong" (Hughes) **7**:167
"Crow's Vanity" (Hughes) **7**:144

"Crucibles of Love" (Graves) **6**:172
"Le crucifix" (Lamartine) **16**:278
Crucifix in a Deathhand: New Poems, 1963-1965 (Bukowski) 21
"The Crucifix in the Filing Cabinet" (Shapiro) **25**:286, 290, 300
"The Crucifixion" (Akhmatova) **2**:15
"Crucifixión" (Garcia Lorca) **3**:140
"Crucifixion" (Garcia Lorca)
See "Crucifixión"
"The Crucifixion" (Johnson) **24**:128, 144, 156, 165, 169
"The Cruel Falcon" (Jeffers) **17**:117, 120
"The Cruell Maid" (Herrick) **9**:101
"The Cruise" (Merrill) **28**:239, 241
"Cruising 99" (Hongo) **23**:196-98
"Crumbs or the Loaf" (Jeffers) **17**:130
"Crusades of Silence" (Cesaire) **25**:18
Crusoé (Perse) **23**:231
"Crusoe in England" (Bishop) **3**:48, 63-4, 66-7, 70
"The Cry" (Levertov) **11**:198
"The Cry" (Masters) **1**:326
"Cry Ararat!" (Page) **12**:168, 190, 198
Cry Ararat! (Page) **12**:167, 179, 184, 190, 197
"Cry Faugh" (Graves) **6**:135
"The Cry of the Children" (Browning) **6**:6, 17, 21, 27, 30, 42
"The Cry of the Human" (Browning) **6**:7, 21
"Cry to Rome: From the Chrysler Building Tower" (Garcia Lorca) **3**:141
"Crying" (Kinnell) **26**:260
"The Crystal" (Aiken) **26**:29-30, 45
"The Crystal Cabinet" (Blake) **12**:36
"Crystals Like Blood" (MacDiarmid) **9**:187
Cuaderno San Martín (Borges) **22**:71, 73, 93-4
"Cualquier tiempo pasado fue peor" (Guillen) **23**:126
"Cuchualain" (Day Lewis) **11**:151
"Cuckoo Song" (H. D.) **5**:267
"Cudjoe Fresh from de Lecture" (McKay) **2**:224, 226
"Cuento de dos jardines" (Paz) **1**:361, 363
"The Cuirassiers of the Frontier" (Graves) **6**:133
"The Culprit" (Housman) **2**:162, 164, 169, 179, 186
"Cultural Exchange" (Hughes) **1**:250, 252
"Culture and Anarchy" (Rich) **5**:386
"The Culture-Hug Blues" (Viereck) **27**:279
"cum cum cum cumly witchcraft i know you care" (Bissett) **14**:34
"The Cup" (Wright) **14**:347
Cup of Blizzards (Bely)
See *Kubok metelej: Chetviortiia simfoniia*
"The Cup of Paint" (Lindsay) **23**:286
The Cup of Snowstorms (Bely)
See *Kubok metelej: Chetviortiia simfoniia*
"Cupid and Psyche" (Elytis) **21**:135
"The Cure" (Graves) **6**:155
"A Cure at Porlock" (Clampitt) **19**:87
"A Cure of Souls" (Levertov) **11**:171
"A Curfew" (Clampitt) **19**:91
"A Curious Man's Dream" (Baudelaire)
See "Le rêve d'un curieux"
"Curl Up and Diet" (Nash) **21**:265
"The Current" (Berry) **28**:14, 15
"The Curse" (Millay) **6**:211
"A Curse against Elegies" (Sexton) **2**:351
"A Curse for a Nation" (Browning) **6**:27
"The Curse of Cromwell" (Yeats) **20**:326
"Curtain" (Dunbar) **5**:119
"The Curtain" (Wright) **14**:355
"The Curve" (Levertov) **11**:176
"Custodian" (Kumin) **15**:223
"The Customs-Officer's House" (Montale)
See "La casa dei doganieri"
"Cut" (Plath) **1**:385, 392
"A Cutlet" (Stein) **18**:349
"The Cutting Edge" (Levine) **22**:215
"Cuttings" (Roethke) **15**:291, 296-98, 312
"Cuttings (Later)" (Roethke) **15**:260, 297-98, 302, 312, 314
Cuttlefish Bones (Montale)
See *Ossi di seppia*
"Cutty Sark" (Crane) **3**:84, 90, 106
"Cybernetics" (Nemerov) **24**:261, 282-83, 301
"The Cycads" (Wright) **14**:346
"The Cyclads" (Aiken) **26**:36
"The Cycle" (Jeffers) **17**:141
"The Cycle" (Roethke) **15**:265
"The Cyclical Night" (Borges) **22**:73
"Cyclops" (Shelley) **14**:227
"Le cygne" (Baudelaire) **1**:45, 66, 71
"Cyparissus" (Duncan) **2**:103
"Cyrano en España" (Dario) **15**:80
"Cyrano in Spain" (Dario)
See "Cyrano en España"
Czeslaw Milosz: The Collected Poems, 1931-1987 (Milosz) **8**:190-91, 197-98, 202, 206-07, 213-15
"D. R." (Zukofsky) **11**:351, 396
"Da, ia lezhu v zemle . . ." (Mandelstam) **14**:151
"Da una torre" (Montale) **13**:113
"Daddy" (Plath) **1**:382-83, 386-87, 392-93, 395-97, 400-02, 406-07, 414
"The Daemon" (Bogan) **12**:100, 110
"The Daemon of the World" (Shelley) **14**:185
The Daffodil Murderer (Sassoon) **12**:252, 270, 274-77
"Daffodildo" (Swenson) **14**:277, 287
"Daffy Duck in Hollywood" (Ashbery) **26**:153
"Daguerreotype Taken in Old Age" (Atwood) **8**:39
"Un dahlia" (Verlaine) **2**:431
"The Dahlia Gardens" (Clampitt) **19**:82, 90-1
"Dahomey" (Lorde) **12**:160
"The Daily Globe" (Nemerov) **24**:278
The Daily Holidays (Cassian) **17**:6
"Les daimons" (Ronsard) **11**:225, 279, 281-82
"The Dainty Monsters" (Ondaatje) **28**:292-93
The Dainty Monsters (Ondaatje) **28**:291-92, 294, 298-99, 318, 327, 331-32, 335
"Daisies Are Broken" (Williams) **7**:406
"The Daisy" (Tennyson) **6**:357, 360
"Daisy Frazer" (Masters) **1**:334
"Daisy-Cutter" (McGuckian) **27**:76, 103
"Daisy's Song" (Keats) **1**:311
"Dakar Doldrums" (Ginsberg) **4**:72
"The Dale" (Lamartine)
See "Le vallon"
"Dalhousie Farm" (Meredith) **28**:181
"The Dalliance of the Eagles" (Whitman) **3**:397
"The Dam" (Rukeyser) **12**:210
Dam 'ah wabitisamah (Gibran) **9**:73, 75, 77-8, 81
"Dämmerung" (Celan) **10**:124-25
"Damned Women" (Baudelaire)
See "Femmes damnées"
"Damon Being Asked a Reason for Loveing" (Behn) **13**:18
"Damon the Mower" (Marvell) **10**:266, 293, 295-97, 315
"The Dampe" (Donne) **1**:130
"The Dance" (Baraka) **4**:16
"Dance" (Cassian) **17**:13
"The Dance" (Crane) **3**:84, 86, 88, 90
"The Dance" (Larkin) **21**:259
"Dance" (Pavese)
See "Balletto"
"The Dance" (Roethke) **15**:266-67, 269, 273, 279
"The Dance at the Phoenix" (Hardy) **8**:99
"The Dance of Death" (Blok)
See "Danse macabre"
"Dance of Death" (Garcia Lorca)
See "Danza de la muerte"
The Dance of Death (Auden) **1**:8
"Dance of the Macabre Mice" (Stevens) **6**:296
"Dance the Orange" (Hayden) **6**:196
"The Dancer" (H. D.) **5**:305
"Dances of Death" (Blok)
See "Danse macabre"
"Dancing on the Grave of a Son of a Bitch" (Wakoski) **15**:346
Dancing on the Grave of a Son of a Bitch (Wakoski) **15**:336, 348, 365
"The Danger of Writing Defiant Verse" (Parker) **28**:350, 363
Dangling in the Tournefortia (Bukowski) **18**:15
"Daniel Bartoli" (Browning) **2**:84
"Daniel Jazz" (Lindsay) **23**:264, 270, 286
"Danny Deever" (Kipling) **3**:170-71, 179, 188-89, 191
"Dans le restaurant" (Eliot) **5**:185
"Dansa di Narcís" (Pasolini) **17**:281
"Danse macabre" (Blok) **21**:6, 14, 20
"Danse russe" (Williams) **7**:353, 367, 408
"Dante Études, Book Two" (Duncan) **2**:114-16, 127
"Danza de la muerte" (Garcia Lorca) **3**:121
"La danza del espiritu" (Cardenal) **22**:131
"Daphnaida" (Spenser) **8**:365, 367
"Daphnis and Chloe" (Marvell) **10**:265, 271, 291-92, 301
"Darest Thou Now O Soul" (Whitman) **3**:378
"Darien" (Graves) **6**:137, 144, 168
"The Dark and the Fair" (Kunitz) **19**:162, 169
"Dark Blood" (Walker) **20**:273, 282
"Dark Eye in September" (Celan) **10**:112
"Dark Gift" (Wright) **14**:338, 353, 356
"Dark Girl's Rhymne" (Parker) **28**:356
"The Dark Hills" (Robinson) **1**:468
The Dark One (Tagore)
See *Shyamali*
"The Dark Ones" (Wright) **14**:373
"Dark Prophecy: I Sing of Shine" (Knight) **14**:39
"Dark Song" (Ammons) **16**:4
"Dark Song" (Sitwell) **3**:291
Dark Summer (Bogan) **12**:87, 89, 105-06, 120-23
"Dark Waters of the Beginning" (Okigbo) **7**:231
"Dark Wild Honey" (Swenson) **14**:276
Dark World (Carruth) **10**:71, 91
"Darkling Summer, Ominous Dusk, Rumorous Rain" (Schwartz) **8**:319
"The Darkling Thrush" (Hardy) **8**:98, 105-06, 121, 131
"Darkness" (Aleixandre) **15**:5
"Darkness" (Byron) **16**:86, 89
"Darkness Chex George Whitman" (Ferlinghetti) **1**:183
"Darkness of Death" (Pasternak) **6**:253
"Darling! Because My Blood Can Sing" (Cummings) **5**:108
"Darling Daughters" (Smith) **12**:326
"Darling, It's Frightening! When a Poet Loves ..." (Pasternak) **6**:251
"Darling Room" (Tennyson) **6**:353
"Dary Tereka" (Lermontov) **18**:290
"Dat Dirty Rum" (McKay) **2**:222
"Dat ol' Mare o' Mine" (Dunbar) **5**:134
"Date Lilia" (Hugo) **17**:94
"Dates" (Ondaatje) **28**:327, 331
"Dates: Penkhull New Road" (Tomlinson) **17**:347, 352
"Dative Haruspices" (Rexroth) **20**:215
"A Daughter I" (Levertov) **11**:209
"A Daughter II" (Levertov) **11**:209
"Daughter Moon" (Wakoski) **15**:366
"The Daughter of the Forest" (Gibran)
See "Amam 'arsh al-jamal"
Daughters of Fire (Nerval)
See *Les filles du feu*
"Daughters with Curls" (Stevens) **6**:292
"David" (Pasolini) **17**:252, 281
"David and Bathsheba in the Public Garden" (Lowell) **3**:205-06, 215
"David's Lamentation for Saul and Jonathan" (Bradstreet) **10**:6
"Davy Jones' Door-Bell" (Lindsay) **23**:264
"Dawlish Fair" (Keats) **1**:311
"Dawn" (Brooke) **24**:53, 64, 82
"Dawn" (Dunbar) **5**:125, 128
"Dawn" (Garcia Lorca)
See "La aurora"

Cumulative Title Index

"Dawn Adventure" (Lowell) **13**:63
"Dawn after Storm" (Zukofsky) **11**:368
"Dawn Bombardment" (Graves) **6**:144
"Dawn Bombardment" (Graves) **6**:144
"The Dawn Wind" (Kipling) **3**:183
"Dawnbreaker" (Hayden) **6**:198
"The Dawning" (Herbert) **4**:102
"Dawn's Rose" (Hughes) **7**:138, 144, 159
"Day" (Ammons) **16**:12
"The Day After" (Soto) **28**:382
"Day and Night" (Montale)
See "Giorno e notte"
"The Day Before the Trial" (Swinburne) **24**:355
Day by Day (Lowell) **3**:231-32
"The Day Dream" (Coleridge) **11**:91, 106
"The Day Is a Poem" (Jeffers) **17**:141
"The Day is Done" (Dunbar) **5**:126
"The Day Is Gone" (Keats) **1**:279
"Daylight Savings" (Parker) **28**:362
"TH DAY MAY CUM" (Bissett) **14**:34
"The Day of Battle" (Housman) **2**:160
"The Day of the Eclipse" (Merrill) **28**:239, 243
"The Day of Judgement" (Swift) **9**:259, 265, 281, 295
"Day of Kings" (Hugo) **17**:58
"A Day on the Big Branch" (Nemerov) **24**:257, 261
"Day or Night" (Rossetti) **7**:276
"Day Six O'Hare Telephone" (Merton) **10**:336
"Day That I Have Loved" (Brooke) **24**:58, 62, 76
"The Day the Mountains Move" (Yosano Akiko)
See "Yama no ugoku hi"
"The Day They Eulogized Mahalia" (Lorde) **12**:156
"The day was five-headed" (Mandelstam)
See "Den' stoial na piati golovakh"
"A Day With Her" (McGuckian) **27**:76, 102
"The Day You Were Born" (Song) **21**:344
"Daybreak" (Hagiwara Sakutaro) **18**:178
"Daybreak" (Hughes) **1**:255
"Daybreak" (Kinnell) **26**:260-61
"Daybreak" (Soto) **28**:377-78
"A Daydream in Summer" (Clare) **23**:25
"Days" (Emerson) **18**:76, 82, 84, 88-91, 96, 102
"Days" (Larkin) **21**:235, 246
"Days of 1935" (Merrill) **28**:235, 256
"The Days of 1941 and '44" (Merrill) **28**:270
"Days of 1964" (Merrill) **28**:220, 221, 250-51
"Days of 1971" (Merrill) **28**:230, 235, 258
"The Day's Ration" (Emerson) **18**:88
The Days Run Away Like Wild Horses over the Hills (Bukowski) **18**:14, 19
"Daystar" (Dove) **6**:111
"dDionysus in Old Age" (Viereck) **27**:295
"Las de l'amer repos" (Mallarme) **4**:203
"Dea Roma" (Lowell) **3**:199-200
"Deacon Taylor" (Masters) **1**:323
"The Dead" (Brooke) **24**:63, 74
"The Dead" (Day Lewis) **11**:147
"The Dead" (Montale)
See "I morti"
The Dead and the Living (Olds) **22**:309-10, 314-16, 318-19, 321-22, 324, 326, 328, 338-39
"Dead Are My People" (Gibran) **9**:73
"The Dead Beat" (Owen) **19**:347
"Dead before Death" (Rossetti) **7**:288
"The Dead by the Side of the Road" (Snyder) **21**:292-93
"The Dead Fox Hunter" (Graves) **6**:166
"The Dead King" (Kipling) **3**:182
The Dead Lecturer (Baraka) **4**:5-6, 16-17, 23, 31, 37
"Dead Men's Love" (Brooke) **24**:53, 56
"Dead Musicians" (Sassoon) **12**:267
"The Dead Pan" (Browning) **6**:7, 19
The Dead Priestess Speaks (H. D.) **5**:305
"The Dead Princess and the Seven Heroes" (Pushkin)
See "Skazka o Mertvoy Tsarevne"
"The Dead Shall Be Raised Incorruptible" (Kinnell) **26**:245, 251, 254, 267
"The Dead II" (Brooke) **24**:59, 88
"Deaf Poem" (Gallagher) **9**:62
"Dean Dixon, Welcome Home" (Stryk) **27**:204
"The Dean of St. Patrick's to Thomas Sheridan" (Swift) **9**:295
"The Dean to Himself on St. Cecilia's Day" (Swift) **9**:295
The Dean's Provocation for Writing the "Lady's Dressing Room" (Montagu) **16**:345
"The Dean's Reasons" (Swift) **9**:295
"Dear Child of God" (Smith) **12**:335
"Dear Female Heart" (Smith) **12**:295
"Dear Judas" (Jeffers) **17**:109-10, 144
Dear Judas and Other Poems (Jeffers) **17**:109, 124, 135
"Dear Little Sirmio" (Smith) **12**:331
"Dear Muse" (Smith) **12**:335
"Dear Patron of My Virgin Muse" (Burns) **6**:84
"Dear Strager Extant in Memory by the Blue Juaniata" (Kinnell) **26**:250, 267
"Dear Toni..." (Lorde) **12**:157
"Death" (Herbert) **4**:113
"Death" (Lermontov)
See "Death"
"Death" (Olds) **22**:325
"Death" (Shelley) **14**:166
"Death and Birth" (Swinburne) **24**:324
"Death and Co." (Plath) **1**:397
"Death and Daphne" (Swift) **9**:260
"Death and Doctor Hornbook" (Burns) **6**:56, 88
"The Death and Dying Words of Poor Mailie" (Burns) **6**:52, 61, 63-4
"The Death and Last Confession of Wandering Peter" (Belloc) **24**:5
"Death and Love" (Browning) **6**:16
"Death and Morality" (Olds) **22**:323, 342
"Death and Murder" (Olds) **22**:326
Death and Taxes (Parker) **28**:349-51, 363-65
"Death and the Maiden" (Nemerov) **24**:259, 268, 270-71
"Death and the Maiden" (Wylie) **23**:317
"The Death Baby" (Sexton) **2**:373
"Death Carol" (Whitman) **3**:378
"Death, corollary to Life" (Villa) **22**:354
"The Death Dance" (Madhubuti) **5**:339
"Death Fugue" (Celan)
See "Todesfuge"
"Death, Great Smoothener" (Swenson) **14**:250, 286
"Death in Mexico" (Levertov) **11**:205-06, 209
"Death in Moonlight" (Kunitz) **19**:155
"A Death in the Desert" (Browning) **2**:36, 45, 72-73, 95
"A Death in the Desert" (Tolson) **17**:328
Death in This Garden (Bunuel)
See *La mort en ce jardin*
"Death Invited" (Swenson) **14**:266, 286
"Death Is a Woman" (Harjo) **27**:68, 70, 72-3
The Death Notebooks (Sexton) **2**:360-61, 367-68, 370-72
"Death of a Ceiling" (McGuckian) **27**:90
"Death of a Favorite Cat" (Gray)
See "Ode on the Death of a Favourite Cat, Drowned in a Tub of Gold Fishes"
"Death of a Frog" (Hagiwara Sakutaro)
See "Kaeru no shi"
"The Death of A. G. A." (Bronte) **8**:65, 74
"Death of a Naturalist" (Heaney) **18**:200, 207, 247-48, 252
Death of a Naturalist (Heaney) **18**:186, 189-90, 192, 194, 199-201, 205-8, 215, 220, 238, 247, 255
"Death of a Student" (Shapiro) **25**:309, 316
"Death of a Young Son by Drowning" (Atwood) **8**:38-9
"Death of an Alcoholic" (Hagiwara Sakutaro) **18**:167, 178
"Death of Antoñito the Camborio" (Garcia Lorca)
See "Muerte de Antoñito el Camborio"
"The Death of Artists" (Baudelaire)
See "The Death of Artists"
"Death of Autumn" (Millay) **6**:236
The Death of Blanche the Duchess (Chaucer)
See *Book of the Duchess*
"The Death of Channing" (Bryant) **20**:46
"The Death of Crazy Horse" (Clifton) **17**:25
"Death of Emma Goldman" (Shapiro) **25**:311, 324
"The Death of Fred Clifton" (Clifton) **17**:25, 27
"The Death of God" (Montale)
See "La morte di Dio"
"The Death of Lovers" (Baudelaire)
See "La mort des amants"
"The Death of Mr. Mounsel" (Smith) **12**:323
"The Death of Oenone" (Tennyson) **6**:360
"The Death of Richard Wagner" (Swinburne) **24**:323, 329
"The Death of Smet-Smet" (Brooke) **24**:56, 66
"Death of Socrates" (Lamartine)
See *La morte de Socrate*
"The Death of the Beloved" (Rilke) **2**:272-73
"The Death of the Fathers" (Sexton) **2**:356, 365-67
"The Death of the Firstborn" (Dunbar) **5**:140
"The Death of the Flowers" (Bryant) **20**:9, 12
"The Death of the Hired Man" (Frost) **1**:195, 197, 209, 216, 221, 226, 228-29
"Death of the Lord Protector" (Marvell)
See "Poem upon the Death of O. C."
"The Death of the Other Children" (Atwood) **8**:39
"Death of the Poet" (Lermontov) **18**:277, 281
"Death of the Poet" (Pasternak) **6**:268
"The Death of the Princess" (Senghor) **25**:232
"The Death of the Sheriff" (Lowell) **3**:200, 206
"The Death of the Wolf" (Vigny)
See "La mort du loup"
"A Death on Easter Day" (Swinburne) **24**:319
"Death Piece" (Roethke) **15**:272
"The Death Room" (Graves) **6**:142, 144
"Death Shall Have No Dominion" (Thomas)
See "And Death Shall Have No Dominion"
"Death, That Struck when I Was Most Confiding" (Bronte) **8**:65
"Death the Barber" (Williams) **7**:388
"Death to Van Gogh's Ear!" (Ginsberg) **4**:63, 74-5
"A Death-Day Recalled" (Hardy) **8**:136
"Deaths" (Swenson) **14**:286
"Deaths and Entrances" (Thomas) **2**:380-82, 388, 390
"The Deaths of Uncles" (Kumin) **15**:202
"Debat du cuer et du corps de Villon" (Villon) **13**:394, 396
"The Debate" (Lermontov) **18**:295, 297
"Debate with the Rabbi" (Nemerov) **24**:277
"Débauche" (Gautier) **18**:164
"Dèbris" (Cesaire) 8-9
"The Debt" (Dunbar) **5**:120, 125
"A Decade" (Lowell) **13**:97
"Decay" (Herbert) **4**:102
"The Decay of Vanity" (Hughes) **7**:113
"December" (Belloc) **24**:29
"December 1" (Milosz) **8**:215
"December 4th" (Sexton) **2**:372
"December 9th" (Sexton) **2**:352-53
"December 10th" (Sexton) **2**:364
"December 12th" (Sexton) **2**:352-53
"December 14th" (Sexton) **2**:353
"December 16th" (Sexton) **2**:352-53
"December 18th" (Sexton) **2**:352
"Deceptions" (Larkin) **21**:237
"Deciduous Branch" (Kunitz) **19**:147
"the Deciduous Trees" (Meredith) **28**:190
Declaration (Wyatt) **27**:369

"Decline" (Trakl)
See "Untergang"
"The Deconstruction of Emily Dickinson" (Kinnell) **26**:294
"Decorum and Terror Homage to Goethe and Hart Crane" (Viereck) **27**:279
"Dedica" (Pasolini) **17**:281
"The Dedication" (Herbert) **4**:125
"Dedication" (Merrill) **28**:240
"Dedication" (Milosz) **8**:193
"Dedication" (Wylie) **23**:303
Dedication (Ekeloef) **23**:75-6
"Dedication for a Plot of Ground" (Williams) **7**:362, 394
"Dedication in Time" (Schwartz)
See "Time's Dedication"
"A Dedication of Three Hats" (Gray) **6**:166
"Dedication to Hunger" (Gluck) **16**:151, 154-55
"Dedication: To William Morris" (Swinburne) **24**:313
"Dedications" (Rich) **5**:401
"Dedicatory Epistle" (Swinburne) **24**:351
"Dedicatory Ode" (Belloc) **24**:3, 6, 8, 11
"Dedicatory Poem" (Meredith) **28**:187
"Deem as ye list upon good cause" (Wyatt) **27**:354
"The Deep Sea Cables" (Kipling) **3**:162
Deep Song (Garcia Lorca)
See *Poema del cante jondo*
"Deep Woods" (Nemerov) **24**:288
"Deeply Morbid" (Smith) **12**:329, 346
"Deep-sea Fishing" (MacDiarmid) **9**:167
"Deer Dancer" (Harjo) **27**:71
"Deer Enclosure" (Wang Wei)
See "Deer Enclosure"
"Deer Park" (Wang Wei) **18**:383, 385-86, 391, 393
"Deer Walled" (Wang Wei)
See "Deer Walled"
Defectos escogidos: 2000 (Neruda) **4**:287
Defence (Wyatt) **27**:369-70
"Defending My Tongue" (Clifton) **17**:28
"definition for blk / children" (Sanchez) **9**:224, 232
"Definition in the Face of Unnamed Fury" (Dove) **6**:111
"Definition of Blue" (Ashbery) **26**:119, 123
"Definition of Creativity" (Pasternak) **6**:271
"The Definition of Love" (Marvell) **10**:264, 266, 271, 274, 277, 291, 294, 299-303, 312, 316, 319
"The Definition of Poetry" (Pasternak)
See "Opredelenyie poezii"
"The Definition of the Creative Power" (Pasternak) **6**:254
"Deher milan" (Tagore) **8**:407
"Dehorning" (Hughes) **7**:166
"Dein Schimmer" (Celan) **10**:124-25
"Dejaneira" (Arnold) **5**:8
"Dejection" (Shelley) **14**:168
"Dejection: An Ode" (Coleridge) **11**:41, 52-3, 58, 69-73, 90-2, 105-09
"Delfica" (Nerval) **13**:181, 194
"Delgusa Gardens" (Stryk) **27**:192
"Delicate Criss-Crossing Beetle Trails Left in the Sand" (Snyder) **21**:300
"Delight in Disorder" (Herrick) **9**:111-12, 115-16, 132, 135
"The Delight Song of Tsoai-talee" (Momaday) **25**:189, 196, 204, 213, 220
"The Delinquent" (Dunbar) **5**:119
"Deliverance" (Graves) **6**:157
"The Deliverance" (Harper) **21**:192, 199-201, 211
"Deliverance From a Fit of Fainting" (Bradstreet) **10**:26, 61-2
"Della primavera trasportata al morale" (Williams) **7**:408
"Delphi" (H. D.) **5**:305
"The Delphic Oracle upon Plotinus" (Yeats) **20**:312, 329, 334
"Delphine et Hippolyte" (Baudelaire)
See "Femmes damnées"
"Delta" (Montale) **13**:134, 164
"Delta" (Walker) **20**:272-73, 275, 278, 281-83
"The Deluge" (Vigny)
See "La déluge"
"La déluge" (Vigny) **26**:367, 380-81, 391, 398, 401-402, 411
"Dem aufgehenden Vollmonde" (Goethe) **5**:249
"Demain dès l'aube" (Hugo) **17**:64
"Démarrage" (Tzara) **27**:229-31
The Demesne of the Swans (Tsvetaeva)
See *Lebediny stan*
"The Demiurge's Laugh" (Frost) **1**:213
"Demobilization" (Shapiro) **25**:273, 296
"Democracy" (Hughes) **1**:241, 252, 258
"The Demon" (Pushkin) **10**:406, 412-13, 418
The Demon (Lermontov) **18**:271-72, 274, 279, 282-83, 297-98, 302
"The Demon Lover" (Rich) **5**:392
"Demonology" (Ronsard)
See "Les daimons"
"Demos and Dionysus" (Robinson) **1**:470, 487
"An den Mond" (Goethe) **5**:246-47
"Den' stoial na piati golovakh" (Mandelstam) **14**:152
"Denial" (Herbert) **4**:114, 119-20
"Denver Doldrum" (Ginsberg) **4**:74
"Deola Thinking" (Pavese) **13**:205
"Deola's Return" (Pavese)
See "Ritorno di Deola"
"Départ" (Gautier) **18**:155
Departmental Ditties (Kipling) **3**:155-56, 159, 165, 182, 190-91
"Departure" (Forche) **10**:137, 144, 156, 169
"Departure" (Gluck) **16**:142, 149-50, 172
"Departure" (Millay) **6**:211
"The Departure" (Olds) **22**:310, 312, 321-22
"Departure" (Plath) **1**:388, 407-08
"Departure" (Tomlinson) **17**:336, 346
"Departure in the Dark" (Day Lewis) **11**:145
"The Departure Song of the Divine Strings" (Li Ho) **13**:52
Depends: A Poet's Notebook (Montale)
See *Quaderno de quattro anni*
"Depression Before Spring" (Stevens) **6**:313
"Dept. of Philosophy" (Enzensberger) **28**:151
"Depth of Love" (Graves) **6**:172
"The Depths" (Apollinaire)
See "Loin du pigeonnier"
"The Derelict" (Kipling) **3**:183
"Derevnya" (Pushkin) **10**:421
"Derev'ya" (Tsvetaeva) **14**:317
Derivations: Selected Poems, 1950-1956 (Duncan) **2**:105-06
"Le dernier chant de pèlerinage de Childe Harold" (Lamartine) **16**:268, 279, 292
"Dernier jour du monde" (Hugo) **17**:87, 89
"Dernière Levée" (Breton) **15**:50
Dernières Poésies (Gautier) **18**:143
"Derniers vers" (Rimbaud) **3**:285
Les derniers vers de Jules Laforgue (Laforgue) **14**:56-7, 59-62, 68-77, 80-3, 88, 93, 95-7
Les derniers vers de Pierre de Ronsard, gentilhomme vandomois (Ronsard) **11**:244, 269, 274
"Des Beautés qui'il voudroit en s'amie" (Ronsard) **11**:247
"Des Faux" (Apollinaire) **7**:46
"Des imagistes" (Williams) **7**:345
"Desajuste en el desgaste" (Fuertes) **27**:27
"Descartes and the Stove" (Tomlinson) **17**:319
"Descending Figure" (Gluck) **16**:151
Descending Figure (Gluck) **16**:130-34, 144, 147, 150-51, 153-56, 159, 170
"The Descent" (Brooke) **24**:77
"The Descent" (Kinnell) **26**:236, 252, 280
"The Descent" (Williams) **7**:403
"The Descent from the Cross" (Rossetti) **7**:264, 285
"The Descent of Odin, an Ode" (Gray) **2**:146, 148-49, 152
The Descent of Winter (Williams) **7**:349, 352-53, 368, 400, 402
"A Descent through the Carpet" (Atwood) **8**:12, 19
"Description of a City Shower" (Swift) **9**:252, 265, 275-79
"Description of a Masque" (Ashbery) **26**:170
"A Description of the Fifteenth of November: A Portrait of T. S. Eliot" (Stein) **18**:341
"Description of the Morning" (Swift) **9**:265
"Description without Place" (Stevens) **6**:338
Descriptive Sketches (Wordsworth) **4**:372
"El Desdichado" (Nerval) **13**:174-75, 178-80, 184-87, 195
"Desecration of the Gravestone of Rose P" (Pinsky) **27**:175
Le desert (Lamartine) **16**:276, 282, 284, 286
"The Desert Music" (Williams) **7**:374
The Desert Music, and Other Poems (Williams) **7**:371, 402-03
"Desert Places" (Frost) **1**:213, 229
"The Deserted House" (Tennyson) **6**:358
"The Deserted Plantation" (Dunbar) **5**:117, 123
"The Deserter" (Smith) **12**:300, 330-31, 333
"Desertion" (Brooke) **24**:57, 63
"Le Désespéranto" (Tzara) **27**:234
"Le désespoir" (Lamartine) **16**:279, 282-83, 290-91, 293
"Design" (Frost) **1**:227-28
"Désir" (Apollinaire) **7**:3
"Desir" (Lamartine) **16**:281
"Le Désir de la Gloire" (Hugo) **17**:88
"Desire" (Hughes) **1**:240
"Desire" (Toomer) **7**:338
"Desk" (Tsvetaeva)
See "Stol"
"A Desoignated National Park" (Ortiz) **17**:227
Desolation Is a Delicate Thing (Wylie) **23**:322
"Despair" (Lamartine)
See "Le désespoir"
"Despedida" (Borges) **22**:94
"A Desperate Vitality" (Pasolini)
See "Una Disperata Vitalita"
"Despite and Still" (Graves) **6**:154
"Despondency, an Ode" (Burns) **6**:71
Les Destinees (Vigny) **26**:366-69, 371, 391-92, 394, 397, 401-404, 412-13
"Destino de la carne" (Aleixandre) **15**:38
"Destino del poeta" (Paz) **1**:358
"Destiny" (Arnold) **5**:43, 50
Destiny (Hagiwara Sakutaro)
See *Destiny*
"The Destiny of Nations" (Coleridge) **11**:49, 63-4, 80
"The Destroyer" (Graves) **6**:166
"Destroyers" (Kipling) **3**:183
La destrucción o el amor (Aleixandre) **15**:14-16, 18, 21-6, 31-4, 39-40, 42
"La destruction" (Baudelaire) **1**:63, 71
"The Destruction of Long Branch" (Pinsky) **27**:161, 163-65
Destruction or Love (Aleixandre)
See *La destrucción o el amor*
"Detail" (Williams) **7**:369
Details (Enzensberger)
See *Einzelheiten*
"Detente, sombra de mi bien esquivo" (Juana Ines de la Cruz) **24**:180, 184, 187, 238
"Detroit Conference of Unity and Art" (Giovanni) **19**:115
"Deus Amanz" (Marie de France)
See "Les Dous Amanz"
"Der Deutsche dankt" (Goethe) **5**:248
Deutschland: Ein Wintermärchen (Heine) **25**:132-38, 152, 179
Deuxième édition du cinquiesme livre des odes (Ronsard) **11**:246
"Developers at Crystal River" (Merrill) **28**:261
"Development" (Browning) **2**:96
"The Deviation" (Gluck) **16**:135-36
"The Devil and the Lady" (Tennyson) **6**:372, 408-09

"The Devil at Berry Pomery" (Graves) **6**:142, 144
"The Devils" (Pushkin)
See "Besy"
"The Devil's Advice to Story Tellers" (Graves) **6**:143
"The Devon Maid" (Keats) **1**:311
"A Devonshire Folk Song" (Noyes) **27**:136
"Devotion: That It Flow; That There Be Concentration" (Gallagher) **9**:45, 59
"Devotion to Duty" (Sassoon) **12**:257-58
"Devyatsat pyaty god" (Pasternak) **6**:265, 272
"Dezember" (Trakl) **20**:265
"Dharma prachar" (Tagore) **8**:407
"A Diagram of Life" (Swenson) **14**:262
"Diagrams" (Gunn) **26**:195-196, 198
"The Dial Tone" (Nemerov) **24**:262
"Dialectic" (Cassian) **17**:13
Diálogos del conocimiento (Aleixandre) **15**:6-7, 12-13, 16-17, 39
"A Dialogu" (Swinburne) **24**:323
"A Dialogue" (Herbert) **4**:130
"Dialogue" (Wright) **14**:343
"A Dialogue between Old England and New" (Bradstreet) **10**:5, 17, 21, 33
"A Dialogue between the Resolved Soul, and Created Pleasure" (Marvell) **10**:265, 271, 274, 277, 290-91, 294, 314
"A Dialogue between the Soul and Body" (Marvell) **10**:265, 271, 274, 290, 313, 316
"A Dialogue between the Two Horses" (Marvell) **10**:276
"A Dialogue between Thyrsis and Dorinda" (Marvell) **10**:271, 314
"A Dialogue of Self and Soul" (Yeats) **20**:313, 315-16, 327, 333, 337
"A Dialogue of Watching" (Rexroth) **20**:218
"Dialogue on Women's Rights" (Harper) **21**:198
Dialogues of Knowledge (Aleixandre)
See *Diálogos del conocimiento*
"Dialogues of the Dogs" (Burns)
See "The Twa Dogs"
"Diamant du coeur" (Gautier) **18**:130, 157
"Diamantina" (Montale) **13**:138
The Diamond Cutters, and Other Poems (Rich) **5**:350, 352-54, 358, 362-63, 368-69, 388, 392
"The Diamond Merchant" (Wakoski) **15**:348
The Diamond Merchant (Wakoski) **15**:325
Diario del '71 (Montale) **13**:138, 144, 158
Diario del '71 e del '72 (Montale) **13**:138-39, 152, 160, 168
Diario del '72 (Montale) **13**:138, 144
El diario que a diario (Guillen) **23**:111, 133
Diaro de un poeta recien casado (Jimenez) **7**:197, 201-02, 208, 212, 214
Diary of '71 and '72 (Montale)
See *Diario del '71 e del '72*
"Diary of a Change" (Rukeyser) **12**:218
"Diary of a Naturalist" (Milosz) **8**:206
Diary of a Newly-Wed Poet (Jimenez)
See *Diaro de un poeta recien casado*
"Diaspora" (Lorde) **12**:138, 140
"Il diaul cu la mari" (Pasolini) **17**:253
"Dice mía" (Dario) **15**:113
"Dices que no te acuerdas, Clori, y mientes" (Juana Ines de la Cruz) **24**:234
"La dicha" (Borges) **22**:95, 99
"Dichterberuf" (Holderlin) **4**:169
"Dichtung" (Baraka) **4**:17
"Dick, a Maggot" (Swift) **9**:296
"The Dictators" (Neruda) **4**:282
"The Dictatorship of the Proletariat" (Baraka) **4**:38-9
"Dictée en présence du glacier du Rhône" (Hugo) **17**:91
"The Dictionaries" (Soto) **28**:399
"Didactic Piece" (Bogan) **12**:122
"Dido's Farewell to Aeneas" (Smith) **12**:331
"An die Hofnung" (Holderlin) **4**:148
"An die Jungen Dichter" (Holderlin) **4**:165
"An die Natur" (Holderlin) **4**:142
"An die Verstummten" (Trakl) **20**:236
"An die Vertummten" (Trakl) **20**:232
"Died of Starvation" (Harper) **21**:191, 203, 210, 216
"Died of Wounds" (Sassoon) **12**:262
"Dieu" (Lamartine) **16**:265-66, 272, 274, 277, 285, 290-91
Dieu (Hugo) **17**:65-66, 73-74, 81, 84, 86, 91
"The Differences" (Gunn) **26**:224
"Diffugere Nives" (Noyes) **27**:136
"Digging" (Heaney) **18**:200, 206-8, 216, 243
"Dignity of Soul" (Viereck) **27**:281
"Digo que yo no soy un hombre puro" (Guillen) **23**:123-24
"Diktaren om dikten" (Ekeloef) **23**:90
"Dilemma" (Parker) **28**:362
"Dili" (Pasolini) **17**:251
"El dilitada guerra" (Neruda) **4**:295
"Dimanches" (Laforgue) **14**:72-3, 76, 78
"Dime vencedor rapaz" (Juana Ines de la Cruz) **24**:234
Dining (Nash) **21**:269
"Dining-Room Tea" (Brooke) **24**:77-8, 82, 88
"Dinner Guest: Me" (Hughes) **1**:252
"The Dinner Party" (Lowell) **13**:79
"Il Dio-Caprone" (Pavese) **13**:204, 207
"Dionysus" (Elytis) **21**:119
"Dionysus in Doubt" (Robinson) **1**:470
Dionysus in Doubt (Robinson) **1**:470
Dios deseado y deseante: Animal de fondo con numerosos poemas ineditos (Jimenez) **7**:197, 207
"Dios llama al fontanero" (Fuertes) **27**:28
"Diptych with Votive Tablet" (Paz)
See "Preparatory Exercise (Dyptych with Votive Tablet)"
Directionscore: Selected and New Poems (Madhubuti) **5**:330, 336, 346
"Directive" (Frost) **1**:213, 227
"Director of Alienation" (Ferlinghetti) **1**:187
"Dirge" (Emerson) **18**:69, 102
"Dirge" (Smith) **12**:292, 344
"A Dirge" (Tennyson) **6**:359
"Dirge for a Righteous Kitten" (Lindsay) **23**:281
"Dirge for a Town in France" (Merton) **10**:350
"Dirge for the New Sunrise (August 6, 1945)" (Sitwell) **3**:327
"A Dirge upon the Death of the Right Valiant Lord, Bernard Stuart" (Herrick) **9**:131
"Dirt and Not Copper" (Stein) **18**:319, 328
"The Dirty Word" (Shapiro) **25**:299
"Dis Aliter Visum" (Browning) **2**:68
"Disabled" (Owen) **19**:336, 354, 357
"The Disappearing Island" (Heaney) **18**:232
"Disappointed" (Enzensberger) **28**:136
"The Disappointment" (Behn) **13**:7, 10-11, 13-14, 16, 25-6, 28
"A Disaster" (Hughes) **7**:142, 160-61
"Disaster" (Valery)
See "Sinistre"
"The Discharge" (Herbert) **4**:109, 113, 120, 129
"Disciplina antica" (Pavese) **13**:226
"Discipline" (Herbert) **4**:121
"Discipline" (Herbert)
See "Throw Away Thy Rod"
The Discipline of the Harp (Cassian) **17**:6
"The Disclosure" (Levertov) **11**:169
"Discontents in Devon" (Herrick) **9**:108
"Discord" (Swinburne) **24**:324
"Discothèque" (Merrill) **28**:254
Discours (Ronsard)
See *Discours des misères de ce temps*
"Discours à Pierre Lescot" (Ronsard) **11**:266
"Discours au Roy" (Ronsard) **11**:244, 284, 291
"Discours de misères de ce temps" (Ronsard) **11**:248
Discours des misères de ce temps (Ronsard) **11**:224, 250
"Discours en forme d'élégie" (Ronsard) **11**:248
"Discovering Michael as the King of Spain" (Wakoski) **15**:329
"The Discovery" (Hardy) **8**:101
"The Discovery of the Madeiras" (Frost) **1**:196, 206
"The Discovery of the Pacific" (Gunn) **26**:207-208
Discrepancies and Apparitions (Wakoski) **15**:323-24
"Discretions of Alcibiades" (Pinsky) **27**:162
"Disembarking at Quebec" (Atwood) **8**:36, 40
"Disenchantment a Tone Poem" (Aiken) **26**:7, 29
"Disillusionment" (Hughes) **1**:246
"The Disinherited" (Nerval)
See "El Desdichado"
"The Dismal Chimes of Bells" (Lermontov) **18**:302
"The Dismissal of Tyng" (Harper) **21**:190, 218
"The Disoblig'd Love" (Behn) **13**:20
"Disorder Overtakes Us All Day Long" (Schwartz) **8**:285
"Una Disperata Vitalita" (Pasolini) **17**:257-58, 286, 288-89
"Dispersal" (Sassoon) **12**:259
"Displaced People" (Pavese) **13**:218
"Disputation" (Heine) **25**:170
"The Disquieted Muses" (Plath)
See "The Disquieting Muses"
"The Disquieting Muses" (Plath) **1**:388, 407
"Dissect This Silence" (Kunitz) **19**:148
"The Dissolution" (Donne) **1**:154
"Distance" (Kumin) **15**:223-24
"Distance" (Milosz)
See "Odlegtose"
"Distance" (Parker) **28**:364
Distances (Okigbo) **7**:228, 234-35, 240-41, 243-47, 251, 253, 255
"Distancia" (Borges) **22**:92
"The Distant Winter" (Levine) **22**:212, 216
"Distinctions" (Tomlinson) **17**:314, 328
"The Distressed Damsel" (Smart) **13**:348
"Dit d'errance" (Cesaire) **25**:31, 38, 44
"Dithyrambes" (Ronsard) **11**:230-32
"Ditty" (Hardy) **8**:90
"Diuturna enfermedad de la Esperanza" (Juana Ines de la Cruz) **24**:225
"La Diva" (Gautier) **18**:135-140
"Divagación" (Dario) **15**:96, 103-05, 119-20
Divagations (Mallarme) **4**:202, 210
"The Diver" (Hayden) **6**:187, 193, 198
"The Diverse Causes" (Ondaatje) **28**:292
Diversifications (Ammons) **16**:24, 61
La divina commedia (Dante) **21**:48-57, 59, 63, 65-6, 69, 73-7, 80-5, 87-8, 90-3, 95, 97-9, 102, 104-05, 108-11
"Divina psiquis" (Dario) **15**:101
Divine Comedies: Poems (Merrill) **28**:220, 221, 224, 225, 227, 228, 229, 230, 231, 232, 246, 260, 263, 272, 281
Divine Comedy (Dante)
See *La divina commedia*
"The Divine Image" (Blake) **12**:5, 7, 33
The Divine Pilgrim (Aiken) **26**:10, 22, 47, 53
Divine Poems (Donne) **1**:158
"Divine Psyche" (Dario)
See "Divina psiquis"
"The Diviner" (Heaney) **18**:200
"Diving into the Wreck" (Rich) **5**:371, 374, 376, 394-95
Diving into the Wreck: Poems, 1971-1972 (Rich) **5**:360, 362, 365, 367-68, 370-72, 384, 388-90, 393
"Divinità in incognito" (Montale) **13**:133
"Divinitie" (Herbert) **4**:108, 130
"Divinity" (Kinnell) **26**:286
"Division" (Bogan) **12**:98, 106, 121
"The Division" (Hardy) **8**:93
"The Division of Parts" (Sexton) **2**:351, 359-60, 367
"The Divorce Papers" (Sexton) **2**:356, 367
"Divorce, Thy Name Is Woman" (Sexton) **2**:359
"Divorcing" (Levertov) **11**:197
Diwan (Ekeloef)
See *Diwan över fursten av Emigón*

Diwan över fursten av Emigón (Ekeloef) **23**:63-5, 67-71, 77-8, 85
"Les djinns" (Hugo) **17**:63, 70, 76
"Do." (Cummings) **5**:106
"Do Jozefa Sadzika" (Milosz) **8**:190
"Do not compare: the living are incomparable" (Mandelstam)
See "Ne sravnivai: zhivushchii nesravnim"
"Do Not Embrace Your Mind's New Negro Friend" (Meredith) **28**:187
"Do Not Touch" (Pasternak) **6**:260
"Do Take Muriel Out" (Smith) **12**:331, 337
"Do the Others Speak of Me Mockingly, Maliciously?" (Schwartz) **8**:306
"Doc Hill" (Masters) **1**:327
"Dock Rats" (Moore) **4**:251
"Docker" (Heaney) **18**:200
"Dockery and Son" (Larkin) **21**:228-31, 233, 236-37, 241
"The Doctor" (Smith) **12**:330
"Doctor Mohawk" (Lindsay) **23**:285, 287
"The Doctor of the Heart" (Sexton) **2**:365
"A Document" (Wright) **14**:356, 362
"Dodger Point Lookout" (Snyder) **21**:300
"Does It Matter?" (Sassoon) **12**:267-68, 285
"Does the Road Wind Up-hill all the Way?" (Rossetti) **7**:293
"Dog" (Ferlinghetti) **1**:184
"A Dog Named Ego, the Snowflakes as Kisses" (Schwartz) **8**:307, 314
"De Dog Rose" (McKay) **2**:223
"Dog-Days" (Lowell) **13**:64
"Dogovor" (Lermontov) **18**:303-4
"Dogs Are Shakespearean, Children Are Strangers" (Schwartz) **8**:306, 312
"A Dog's Best Friend Is His Illiteracy" (Nash) **21**:273
"A Dog's Life" (MacDiarmid) **9**:155
"Dolce Ossessione" (Viereck) **27**:259
"Le dolci rime d'amor ch'io solia" (Dante) **21**:88
"The Doll" (Lowell) **13**:84-5
"The Doll" (Wylie) **23**:321
"The Dolls" (Yeats) **20**:336, 340
"A Doll's 'Arabian Nights'" (Lindsay) **23**:264, 277
"Dolly's Mistake" (Clare) **23**:40
"Dolores" (Swinburne) **24**:308-09, 360, 362-63
"Dolorida" (Vigny) **26**:401, 411
The Dolphin (Lowell) **3**:224, 229-30, 232-33, 239-41
A Dome of Many-Coloured Glass (Lowell) **13**:60, 69
"Dome of Sunday" (Shapiro) **25**:279-80, 283, 286, 295, 305, 308, 310, 315-17, 324-25
"La Domenica Uliva" (Pasolini) **17**:256
Domesday Book (Masters) **1**:330-33, 335-36, 339
"Domestic Poem for a Summer Afternoon" (Page) **12**:181
Domik v Kolomne (Pushkin) **10**:366, 381-86, 391, 400
"Domiki staroi Moskvy" (Tsvetaeva) **14**:318
"Domination of Black" (Stevens) **6**:293-94
"Le Dompteur de lions se souvient" (Tzara) **27**:224
"Don du poème" (Mallarme) **4**:196
"Don Juan" (Clare) **23**:26
Don Juan (Byron) **16**:77-88, 90-2, 95-102, 106-08, 110-13, 115-17, 120
"Don Juan aux enfers" (Baudelaire) **1**:47
"Don Juan in Hades" (Baudelaire)
See "Don Juan aux enfers"
"Done Into Verse" (Belloc) **24**:43-4
"The Donkey" (Chesterton) **28**:101
"The Donkey" (Smith) **12**:318
"Donna Clara" (Heine) **25**:145
"Donne che avete intelletto d'amore" (Dante) **21**:73, 86
"Donne perdute" (Pavese) **13**:225
"Donneycarney" (Joyce)
See "XXXI"
"Don't Be Cross Amanda" (Nash) **21**:271
Don't Cry, Scream (Madhubuti) **5**:324-25, 328, 336, 338, 340-46
Don't Go Out of the Door (Li Ho) **13**:42
"Don't Grow Old" (Ginsberg) **4**:84
"Don't Laugh at my Prophetic Anguish" (Lermontov) **18**:281
"Don't Look Now But Mary Is Everbody" (Viereck) **27**:258, 274, 278
"Don't Trust Yourself" (Lermontov) **18**:281
"Don't Wanna Be" (Sanchez) **9**:229
"The Doodler" (Merrill) **28**:234, 242
"Doom" (Dario)
See "Lo fatal"
"Doom Is the House without the Door" (Dickinson) **1**:111
"Dooms-day" (Herbert) **4**:131
The Door in the Wall (Tomlinson) **17**:360-61
Door into the Dark (Heaney) **18**:191, 194-95, 199-201, 203, 205-6, 209, 215, 220, 225-26, 238
"Doors, Doors, Doors" (Sexton) **2**:349
"Dopa una fuga" (Montale) **13**:134
"Dope" (Baraka) **4**:40
"Dora" (Tennyson) **6**:360
"Dora Markus" (Montale) **13**:106, 113-14, 119
"Dora Williams" (Masters) **1**:347
"La dormeuse" (Valery) **9**:365-66, 374, 387, 392-93, 396
"Dornenkranz" (Celan) **10**:128-30
"Dorothée" (Baudelaire)
See "La belle Dorothée"
"Las dos cartas" (Guillen) **23**:126
"Dos niños" (Guillen) **23**:139
"Dos vidas" (Aleixandre) **15**:7
"Dotage" (Herbert) **4**:130
"Dotterel" (Wright) **14**:348
The Double Axe and Other Poems (Jeffers) **17**:123-24, 130, 136, 146-47
"The Double Chamber" (Baudelaire)
See "La chambre double"
"The Double Dream of Spring" (Ashbery) **26**:115
The Double Dream of Spring (Ashbery) **26**:115, 118-119, 124-125, 128, 130, 138, 144, 148-149, 153-154, 169
"Double Feature" (Hayden) **6**:194-95
"The Double Image" (Sexton) **2**:350, 355-56, 359, 361-63, 372
"Double Image" (Wright) **14**:348
The Double Image (Levertov) **11**:163-64
"Double Monologue" (Rich) **5**:374
"Double Negative" (Nemerov) **24**:289
"Double Ode" (Rukeyser) **12**:225
Double Persephone (Atwood) **8**:21
"The Double Standard" (Harper) **21**:187, 191, 207
The Double Tree: Selected Poems, 1942-1976 (Wright) **14**:366
"The Double Voices" (Atwood) **8**:16, 32
"Doubled Mirrors" (Rexroth) **20**:217
"The Doubtful Passage" (Cardenal)
See "El estrecho dudoso"
"Doubts" (Brooke) **24**:57, 85
"The Dougtful Passage"
See "El estrecho dudoso"
"Les Dous Amanz" (Marie de France) **22**:258, 269, 271-73, 275
"The Dove Breeder" (Hughes) **7**:116
"The Dove in Spring" (Stevens) **6**:313
The Dove of Popular Flight--Elegies (Guillen)
See *La paloma de vuelo popular: Elegiás*
"Dover" (Auden) **1**:16
"Dover Beach" (Arnold) **5**:8, 13, 16-18, 35, 38, 47, 49, 53, 58, 64-5
"Dov'era il tennis" (Montale) **13**:160
"Down" (Graves) **6**:142, 144
"The Downs" (Bridges) **28**:67, 83
"Down, Wanton, Down!" (Graves) **6**:151, 153, 165
"Indentured" (Wylie) **23**:305
"Dr. Swift to Mr. Pope while He Was Writing the *Dunciad*" (Swift) **9**:295
"The Draft Horse" (Frost) **1**:213
A Draft of Eleven New Cantos (XXXI-XLI) (Pound) **4**:321-22, 353, 357-58
A Draft of Shadows (Paz)
See *Pasado en claro*
Drafts and Fragments of Cantos CX to CXVII (Pound) **4**:352-54
"Dragon" (Ondaatje) **28**:298
"The Dragon and the Undying" (Sassoon) **12**:278
"The Dragon and the Unicorn" (Rexroth) **20**:204, 221
The Dragon and the Unicorn (Rexroth) **20**:181-82, 184, 192, 205, 208, 210, 212-14
"Dragonfly" (Bogan) **12**:107-08
Drake (Noyes) **27**:114-15, 119, 123, 125, 127, 134
"A Drama of Exile" (Browning) **6**:6, 20-1, 26, 31, 34, 46
Dramatic Lyrics (Browning) **2**:26, 35, 66, 94
"Dramatic Poem: Voice of Silence" (Ishikawa)
See "Gekishi: Chimmoku no koe"
Dramatic Romances and Lyrics (Browning) **2**:94
Dramatis Personae (Browning) **2**:34, 45, 94-5
Dramatis Personae (Yeats) **20**:328
"Drawing Lessons" (Nemerov) **24**:302-03
"The Drawn-Out War" (Neruda)
See "El dilitada guerra"
"The Dream" (Berry) **28**:38
"A Dream" (Blake) **12**:7, 33-4
"The Dream" (Bogan) **12**:111
"The Dream" (Browning) **6**:19
"A Dream" (Bryant) **20**:15
"A Dream" (Burns) **6**:89
"The Dream" (Byron) **16**:73, 76
"Dream" (Heaney) **18**:201
"Dream" (Juana Ines de la Cruz)
See "Primero sueño"
"The Dream" (Roethke) 288-89
"The Dream" (Sassoon) **12**:267
"The Dream" (Stryk) **27**:204
"A Dream" (Swenson) **14**:288
"Dream" (Tagore)
See "Svapna"
"Dream" (Wright) **14**:367, 373
"The Dream, 1863" (Hayden) **6**:180, 188
"Dream and Madness" (Trakl)
See "Traum und Umnachtung"
"Dream Boogie" (Hughes) **1**:266
"A Dream Deferred" (Hughes) **1**:266
"Dream Drumming" (Rukeyser) **12**:222
"A Dream in Three Colors" (McGuckian) **27**:90
"The Dream Language of Fergus" (McGuckian) **27**:83, 88-90
"A Dream Lies Dead" (Parker) **28**:363
The Dream of a Common Language: Poems, 1974-1977 (Rich) **5**:373-76, 378, 384, 389
"The Dream of Angling the Dream of Cool Rain" (Wakoski) **15**:365
"A Dream of Comparison" (Smith) **12**:330, 332-33, 345, 352
"A Dream of Fair Women" (Tennyson) **6**:353, 359-60
"The Dream of Knowledge" (Schwartz) **8**:297, 311
"A Dream of Nourishment" (Smith) **12**:326
"A Dream of Small Children" (Song) **21**:341, 343
"Dream of the Future" (Jeffers) **17**:141
"A Dream of Whitman Paraphrased, Recognized, and Made More Vivid by Renoir" (Schwartz) **8**:318
"Dream of Youth" (Tagore)
See "Yauvan-svapna"
"A Dream or No" (Hardy) **8**:135
"A Dream (Real)" (Ekeloef) **23**:80
"Dream Variations" (Hughes) **1**:248
"A Dream within a Dream" (Poe) **1**:434
"Dreamdust" (Hughes) **1**:241

Cumulative Title Index

"The Dreame" (Donne) **1**:147, 152
"The Dreame" (Herrick) **9**:109
"The Dreamer" (Pushkin) **10**:407
"The Dreamer" (Tennyson) **6**:372
"Dreamers" (Sassoon) **12**:284, 286
"The Dreamer's Song" (Ortiz) **17**:245
"The Dream-Follower" (Hardy) **8**:108
Dreaming of Butterflies (Hagiwara Sakutaro)
See *Dreaming of Butterflies*
"Dreaming of Hair" (Lee) **24**:242, 247
"Dream-Land" (Poe) **1**:433-34, 436, 438
"Dreams" (Giovanni) **19**:110
"Dreams" (Poe) **1**:436
"Dreams about Clothes" (Merrill) **28**:254
"Dreams in War Time" (Lowell) **13**:84
"Dreams of Suicide," (Meredith) **28**:199, 205
Dreamtigers (Borges)
See *El hacedor*
"Drei Blicke in einen Opal" (Trakl) **20**:261-62
"Dressing to Wait a Table" (McKay) **2**:205
"Dried Marjoram" (Lowell) **13**:61
"The Drifter off Tarentum" (Kipling) **3**:183
Drifting into War (Bissett) **14**:10, 33
"A Driftwood Altar" (Ashbery) **26**:163
"Drink to Me Only with Thine Eyes" (Jonson) **17**:170, 180
"The Drinker" (Lowell) **3**:212
"Driving Gloves" (Wakoski) **15**:347
"Dropping Eyelids Among the Aerial Ash" (Ammons) **16**:39
"Drought" (Wright) **14**:353
"Drought Year" (Wright) **14**:366
"The Drowned Child" (Gluck) **16**:129-30, 150
"The Drowning Poet" (Merrill) **28**:225
"Drozhzhi mira dorogie" (Mandelstam) **14**:153
"Drug Store" (Shapiro) **25**:268, 295, 319, 322
"Druidic Rimes" (Nemerov) **24**:301
"A Drumlin Woodchuck" (Frost) **1**:213
"Drummer Hodge" (Hardy) **8**:121
"Drums" (Okigbo) **7**:234
Drum-Taps (Whitman) **3**:389, 414, 418
A Drunk Man Looks at the Thistle (MacDiarmid) **9**:151-52, 158, 167-70, 173, 175, 181, 186, 189-93
"The Drunkard" (Sitwell) **3**:299
"The Drunkard's Child" (Harper) **21**:191, 210, 216
"The Drunkard's Funeral" (Lindsay) **23**:269, 283-84
"The Drunkards in the Streetn" (Lindsay) **23**:284
"Drunken Americans" (Ashbery) **26**:167
The Drunken Boat (Rimbaud)
See *Le bateau ivre*
"The Drunken Fisherman" (Lowell) **3**:199-200, 202, 204, 212
"The Dry Salvages" (Eliot) **5**:164-65, 167-69, 180-81, 183, 186, 210
"Dryads" (Sassoon) **12**:240, 275
"Du coton dans les oreilles" (Apollinaire) **7**:22
"Du haut de la muraille de Paris" (Hugo) **17**:100
"Du liegst" (Celan) **10**:98
"Du sei wei du" (Celan) **10**:100-01
"Dublinesque" (Larkin) **21**:237, 244
"Dubrovnik October 14, 1980, 10:45 p. m." (Ginsberg) **4**:62
"The Duchess Potatoes" (Wakoski) **15**:330
"Duck Blind" (Hass) **16**:217
"A Duck for Dinner" (Stevens) **6**:322
"The Duckpond" (Stryk) **27**:188, 195-97, 202-03, 206
"Due donne in cima de la mente mia" (Dante) **21**:74
"Due nel crepuscolo" (Montale) **13**:107, 150
"Due sigarette" (Pavese) **13**:225-28
"Duel" (Hagiwara Sakutaro) **18**:167
"The Dug-Out" (Sassoon) **12**:281, 283
Duineser Elegien (Rilke) **2**:268-69, 279-82, 285-87, 294-95
Duino Elegies/Elegies (Rilke)
See *Duineser Elegien*
Duke of Albany (Skelton) **25**:330
"Dulce Et Decorum Est" (Owen) **19**:347, 353, 357, 359-61, 364-65, 370-71
"Dulcia Linquimus Arva" (Borges) **22**:79
"Dully Gumption's Addendum" (Hughes) **7**:120
"Dulnesse" (Herbert) **4**:112
"La dulzura del ángelus" (Dario) **15**:81, 96
"Duma" (Lermontov) **18**:268-69, 279, 281, 283, 297, 304
"Duncan" (Gunn) **26**:228
"Duncan Gray" (Burns) **6**:57, 59, 100
Dunciad (Pope) **26**:304-305, 314-17, 319, 321-22, 326-27, 334, 338-40, 357-61
Dunciad in Four Books (Pope) **26**:358-59
"Dunciad Variorum" (Pope) **26**:356-61
"Duncton Hill" (Belloc) **24**:10, 49
"The Dungeon" (Wordsworth) **4**:373
"Duns Scotus" (Lowell) **3**:201
"Duns Scotus's Oxford" (Hopkins) **15**:144
"Duranta asha" (Tagore) **8**:407
"Duration" (Paz) **1**:355
"Durham in March" (Tomlinson) **17**:361
"During a Solar Eclipse" (Nemerov) **24**:288
"During a Transatlantic Call" (Lowell) **3**:241
"During Fever" (Lowell) **3**:206, 220, 243, 245
"During the Eichmann Trial" (Levertov) **11**:169, 193
"During the Passaic Strike of 1926" (Zukofsky) **11**:351, 396
"During Wind and Rain" (Hardy) **8**:88, 113
"Dusha" (Pasternak) **6**:267, 285
"Dusha moja mrachna" (Lermontov) **18**:302
"Dust" (Brooke) **24**:57
"Dust" (Wright) **14**:379
"Dust Bowl" (Hughes) **1**:240
"Dust in the Eyes" (Frost) **1**:195
"Dust of Snow" (Frost) **1**:195, 218
"Dusting" (Dove) **6**:111, 113
"Dusty Braces" (Snyder) **21**:293
"Dutch Graves in Bucks County" (Stevens) **6**:302
"Dutch Painters" (Zagajewski) **27**:403
"Duty is my Lobster" (Smith) **12**:340
"Dva brata" (Lermontov) **18**:299
"Dva sokola" (Lermontov) **18**:288
Dvenadsat (Blok) **21**:8-12, 16-17, 21-2, 26-9, 31, 33-9, 41-3
"Dvukh stanov ne beots, a-- esli gost sluchainyi" (Tsvetaeva) **14**:325
"Dyâli" (Cesaire) **25**:40
"Dying Away" (Meredith) **28**:200
"The Dying Bondman" (Harper) **21**:187, 207
"The Dying Christian" (Harper) **21**:208, 215-16
"The Dying Mother" (Harper) **21**:197
"The Dying Queen" (Harper) **21**:198
"The Dying Swan" (Tennyson) **6**:359, 389-91
"The Dykes" (Kipling) **3**:182
The Dynasts: A Drama of the Napoleonic Wars (Hardy) **8**:79-81, 85-7, 95-6, 104, 108, 111, 121-22
The Dynasty of Raghu (Kalidasa)
See *Raghuvamsa*
"Dytiscus" (MacDiarmid) **9**:157, 183
"Dyvers Dothe Use" (Wyatt) **27**:316
"Dzhulio" (Lermontov) **18**:300
"E. P. Ode Pour L'Election de son Sepulchre" (Pound) **4**:319
"Each and All" (Emerson) **18**:84, 94-96, 98-101, 107
"Each Bird Walking" (Gallagher) **9**:44
"Each Day of Summer" (Swenson) **14**:276
"Each of You" (Lorde) **12**:154
"Eagle" (Kunitz) **19**:147
"The Eagle and the Mole" (Wylie) **23**:301, 309, 322, 327, 334
"Eagle Confin'd in a College Court" (Smart) **13**:341
Eagle or Sun? (Paz) **1**:354, 359
"Eagle Poem" (Harjo) **27**:67
"The Eagle That Is Forgotten" (Lindsay) **23**:277, 288, 294, 296
"The Eagle-Feather Fan" (Momaday) **25**:217
"Early Chronology" (Sassoon) **12**:245
"Early Evening Quarrel" (Hughes) **1**:247
"Early Lynching" (Sandburg) **2**:330
"Early March" (Sassoon) **12**:254, 259
"An Early Martyr" (Williams) **7**:353, 368
An Early Martyr, and Other Poems (Williams) **7**:350, 399, 402
"The Early Morning" (Belloc) **24**:5, 34
"Early Morning: Cape Cod" (Swenson) **14**:276
"The Early Morning Light" (Schwartz) **8**:294
"Early Poems" (Noyes) **27**:138
Early Poems (Crane) **3**:90-1
Early Poems, 1935-1955 (Paz) **1**:373, 375
Early Verse of Rudyard Kipling, 1877-99: Unpublished, Uncollected, and Rarely Collected Poems (Kipling) **3**:193
"The Earrings" (Montale)
See "Gli orecchini"
"Ears in the Turrets Hear" (Thomas) **2**:379
"Earth" (Bryant) **20**:4, 17, 19, 35, 47
"The Earth" (Noyes) **27**:129
"The Earth" (Sexton) **2**:372, 374
"Earth" (Toomer) **7**:333
"Earth Again" (Milosz) **8**:209
"Earth and Fire" (Berry) **28**:11
"Earth and I Give You Turquoise" (Momaday) **25**:188, 193, 207
The Earth Gods (Gibran) **9**:71, 75, 80
"The Earth in Snow" (Blok) **21**:4-5
"The Earth is Called Juan" (Neruda)
See "La tierra se llama Juan"
"the Earth Lantern" (Bissett) **14**:7
"Earth Psalm" (Levertov) **11**:170
"Earth Triumphant" (Aiken) **26**:7
Earth Triumphant (Aiken) **26**:21, 50
"Earth Walk" (Meredith) **28**:214
Earth Walk: New and Selected Poems (Meredith) **28**:178, 180-81, 194-95, 207, 210, 213-15
"Earth Your Dancing Place" (Swenson) **14**:283
Earthlight (Breton) **15**:73-4
"Earthly Creatures" (Wylie) **23**:311
The Earth-Owl and Other Moon-People (Hughes) **7**:120
"Earth's Answer" (Blake) **12**:7, 35, 44
"Earth's Bubbles" (Blok) **21**:14, 24, 31
"Earth's Children Cleave to Earth" (Bryant) **20**:16
"Earth-Song" (Emerson) **18**:79, 88
"Earthy Anecdote" (Stevens) **6**:294
"East Coker" (Eliot) **5**:164, 167-69, 171, 179-82, 198, 210
"East Coker" (Roethke) **15**:279
"East of Suez" (Kipling) **3**:179
"East of the Sun West of the Moon" (Wakoski) **15**:348
"East River" (Swenson) **14**:254
East Slope (Paz)
See *Ladera este*
"The East that is Now Pale, the East that is Now Silent" (Bely)
See "Vostok pobledneuskii, vostok onemesvshii"
"East, West, North, and South of a Man" (Lowell) **13**:87
East Wind (Lowell) **13**:76, 84-5
"Eastbourne" (Montale) **13**:106, 109, 120-21, 128-29, 148, 152
An East-End Coffee-Stall (Noyes) **27**:140
"An East-End Curate" (Hardy) **8**:101
"Easter" (Herbert) **4**:100, 120
"Easter" (Kinnell) **26**:238, 279
"Easter" (Studwell)
See "Easter: Wahiawa, 1959"
"Easter 1916" (Yeats) **20**:311, 313-14, 323, 325, 327, 349
Easter Day (Browning) **2**:32, 45, 71-2, 75
"Easter Eve 1945" (Rukeyser) **12**:225
"Easter Hymn" (Housman) **2**:184
"Easter Moon and Owl" (Wright) **14**:373, 375
"Easter Morning" (Ammons) **16**:30-2, 46, 63-4
"Easter: Wahiawa, 1959" (Song) **21**:331, 335, 338, 340, 342-43, 350

"Easter Wings" (Herbert) **4**:114, 120, 130
Eastern Lyrics (Hugo)
See *Les orientales*
Eastern Slope (Paz)
See *Ladera este*
"Eastern War Time" (Rich) **5**:398
"Eastport to Block Island" (Rich) **5**:352
"Eating Fire" (Atwood) **8**:27-8
"Ebar phirao more" (Tagore) **8**:409
"Ébauche d'un serpent" (Valery) **9**:352-53, 365-67, 371, 374, 384, 387, 390, 394-99
Ebb and Flow (Ishikawa) **10**:212-13, 215
"éboulis" (Cesaire) **25**:45
"Ecce Puer" (Joyce) **22**:140-41, 147-48, 151-52
"The Ecclesiast" (Ashbery) **26**:114
Ecclesiastical Sketches (Wordsworth) **4**:399
Ecclesiastical Sonnets (Wordsworth)
See *Ecclesiastical Sketches*
"Echo" (Lorde) **12**:155
"Echo" (Rossetti) **7**:280-81
"Echo" (Tagore)
See "Pratidhyani"
"Echoes" (Carroll) **18**:46
"The Echoing Green" (Blake) **12**:7
"L'eclatante victoire de Saarebrück" (Rimbaud) **3**:283
"L'eclatante victorie de Sarrebruck" (Rimbaud) **3**:283
"El eclipse" (Jimenez) **7**:200
"Eclogue" (Ronsard) **11**:262
"Eclogue" (Stevens) **6**:333
"Eclogue II" (Bridges) **28**:87 8
"Eclogue 4" (Vergil) **12**:363, 370, 372, 382-85, 392
"Eclogue 6" (Vergil) **12**:365, 371
"Eclogue 10" (Vergil) **12**:370-71
"Eclogue IV: Winter" (Brodsky) **9**:22, 28-9
"An Eclogue, or Pastorall between Endymion Porter and Lycidas Herrick" (Herrick) **9**:86
"Eclogue V: Summer" (Brodsky) **9**:21, 28
"Eclogues" (Herrick) **9**:89
Eclogues (Petrarch) **8**:246
Eclogues (Vergil) **12**:365, 370-72, 375, 383, 388
"Ecologue" (Ginsberg) **4**:54, 82, 85, 89
"Eclogue I: The Months" (Bridges) **28**:67, 84
"Economia de Tahuantinsuyo" (Cardenal) **22**:127-28, 132
"Economic Man" (Nemerov) **24**:289
"The Economy of Tahuantinsuyo"
See "Economia de Tahuantinsuyo"
"Ecoutez la chanson bien douce" (Verlaine) **2**:416
"Écrit sur la Porte" (Perse) **23**:231
"Les Écrits s'en vont" (Breton) **15**:51
"The Ecstasy" (Carruth) **10**:71
"The Ecstasy" (Donne)
See "The Exstasie"
"Eddi's Service" (Kipling) **3**:183
"Eden" (Tomlinson) **17**:342, 354
"Eden" (Wright) **14**:336, 341
"Eden Retold" (Shapiro) **25**:290
"The Edge" (Gluck) **16**:125, 153
"Edge" (Plath) **1**:391, 393, 397
"The Edge" (Stryk) **27**:198, 203
"Edge of Love" (Aleixandre) **15**:19, 23
"Edgehill Fight" (Kipling) **3**:183
"Edina, Scotia's Darling Seat!" (Burns) **6**:74
"Edinstvennye dni" (Pasternak) **6**:286
"Editorial Impressions" (Sassoon) **12**:268
"Edmonton, thy cemetery . . ." (Smith) **12**:293, 300
"Education" (Madhubuti) **5**:338
"Education a Failure" (Williams) **7**:370
"Education and Government" (Gray)
See "Essay on the Alliance of Education and Government"
"Edward Gray" (Tennyson) **6**:358
"Edward III" (Blake)
See "King Edward the Third"
"The Eel" (Montale)
See "L'anguilla"
"Eel" (Rukeyser) **12**:211
"The Eemis Stane" (MacDiarmid) **9**:158, 187
"eet me alive" (Bissett) **14**:34
"The Effect" (Sassoon) **12**:285
"The Effectual Marriage" (Loy) **16**:333
"Effort at Speech" (Meredith) **28**:214
Effort at Speech (Meredith) **28**:216-17
Efterlämnade dikter (Ekeloef) **23**:78
The Egerton Ms (Wyatt) **27**:360
"The Egg" (Gluck) **16**:125, 138-39
"The Egg and the Machine" (Frost) **1**:203
"Egg-Head" (Hughes) **7**:116, 118, 135, 140, 161
"Eggs" (Hagiwara Sakutaro) **18**:168
"Eggs" (Olds) **22**:311, 338
"Eggs and Nestlings" (Wright) **14**:348
"Ego" (Shapiro) **25**:320
"Ego Tripping" (Giovanni) **19**:118, 123, 141
"The Egoist" (Neruda)
See "El egoísta"
"El egoísta" (Neruda) **4**:290
Egorushka (Tsvetaeva) **14**:326-27
Ego-Tripping and Other Poems for Young People (Giovanni) **19**:123, 136
"Egy ev" (Illyes) **16**:239
"Ehcu Fugaces" (Belloc) **24**:10
"ehre sei der sellerie" (Enzensberger) **28**:140
"The Eichmann Trial" (Levertov)
See "During the Eichmann Trial"
"VIII" (Joyce) **22**:144-45, 153, 167, 170, 173
"8 Ahau" (Cardenal)
See "Katun 8 Ahau"
"Eight Drinking Immortals" (Tu Fu) **9**:330
"Eight Laments" (Tu Fu) **9**:333-38, 341-42
"Eight Observations on the Nature of Eternity" (Tomlinson) **17**:328
"Eight O'Clock" (Housman) **2**:162, 164, 169, 182
"XVIII" (Joyce) **22**:145, 165, 167, 169
"18 Nov 71" (Brutus) **24**:123
18 Poems (Thomas) **2**:378, 382, 384
"1887" (Housman) **2**:192, 194
"1805" (Graves) **6**:152
"Eighteen West Eleventh Street" (Merrill) **28**:222, 244, 258
"The Eighth Crusade" (Masters) **1**:330
"Eighth Duino Elegy" (Rilke) **2**:291, 293
Eighth Isthmian (Pindar)
See *Isthmian 8*
Eighth Olympian (Pindar)
See *Olympian 8*
Eighth Pythian (Pindar)
See *Pythian 8*
80 Flowers (Zukofsky) **11**:392
"84th Street, Edmonton" (Atwood) **8**:9
"Einstein Freud & Jack" (Nemerov) **24**:302
"Der Einzige" (Holderlin) **4**:150, 156, 166
"Ekloga 4-aya: Zimnyaya" (Brodsky)
See "Eclogue IV: Winter"
"Eldorado" (Poe) **1**:433, 439
"Eleanore" (Tennyson) **6**:350
"Elected Silence" (Sassoon) **12**:258
"Electra on Azalea Path" (Plath) **1**:410-11
"Electra-Orestes" (H. D.) **5**:305
"Electric Elegy" (Zagajewski) **27**:389
"The Electric Tram" (Noyes) **27**:122
"Electrical Storm" (Hayden) **6**:186, 194-95
"Elegía" (Borges) **22**:95
Elegía (Neruda) **4**:287
Elegía a Jacques Roumain (Guillen) **23**:133
"Elegía a Jesús Menéndez" (Guillen) **23**:100-101, 125
"Elegía moderna del motivo cursi" (Guillen) **23**:109-10, 128
"An Elegiac Fragment" (Duncan) **2**:101
"An Elegiac Poem on the Death of George Whitefield" (Wheatley) **3**:336, 340, 343, 348
"Elegiac Stanzas" (Wordsworth) **4**:406-07
"Elegiacs" (Tennyson) **6**:385
"Elégie" (Gautier) **18**:135
"Elegie" (Goethe) **5**:248, 251
"Elegie IV: The Perfume" (Donne) **1**:130
"Elegie VIII: The Comparison" (Donne) **1**:124
"Elegie XI: The Bracelet" (Donne) **1**:122
"Elegie XII: His parting from her" (Donne) **1**:130
"Elegie XVI: On his mistris" (Donne) **1**:130
"Elegie à Cassandre" (Ronsard) **11**:246, 248
"L'Elégie à Guillaume des Autels sur le Tumulte d'Amboise" (Ronsard) **11**:248
"Elegie à Hélène" (Ronsard) **11**:229
"l'elegie à J. Hurault, sieur de la pitardière" (Ronsard) **11**:249
"Elegie á Janet, peintre du Roi" (Ronsard) **11**:243, 247
"L'elégie à Lovs de Masures" (Ronsard) **11**:248
"Elégie à Marie Stuart" (Ronsard) **11**:224, 237
"Elegie A M. A. De Muret" (Ronsard) **11**:246, 248
"Elegie à son livre" (Ronsard) **11**:248
"Elegie au Seigneur Baillon, trésorier de l'Epargne du Roi" (Ronsard) **11**:249
"Elegie au Seigneur L'Huillier" (Ronsard) **11**:242
"Elégie de minuit" (Senghor) **25**:255
"Elégie des circoncis" (Senghor) **25**:255
"Elégie des eaux" (Senghor) **25**:255, 258
"Elégie des Saudades" (Senghor) **25**:233
"Elegie du printemps" (Ronsard) **11**:242, 250
"Elegie du Verre à Jan Brinon" (Ronsard) **11**:247
"Elegie en forme d'épitaphe d'Antoine Chateignier" (Ronsard) **11**:246, 248
"Elegie on the Lady Jane Pawlet, Marchion: of Winton" (Jonson) **17**:206
"Elégie pour Georges Pompidou" (Senghor) **25**:254-55, 257-59
"Elégie pour Jean-Marie" (Senghor) **25**:255-56, 259
"elégie pour Martin Luther King" (Senghor) **25**:258
"An Elegie upon that Honourable and renowned Knight *Sir Philip Sidney*, who was untimely slaine at the Seige of *Zutphon*, Annol586" (Bradstreet) **10**:31, 48, 54
"Elegie upon the untimely death of the incomparable Prince Henry" (Donne) **1**:122
"Elegier I" (Ekeloef) **23**:76
Elegies (Donne) **1**:129-30, 147
Elegies (Jimenez)
See *Elejías*
Elegies (Ovid)
See *Tristia*
Elegies (Rilke) **2**:280-82, 285-87, 294
Elegies (Rukeyser) **12**:207, 211-13
"Elegies And Epistles" (Wylie) **23**:311
"Elegies for Paradise Valley" (Hayden) **6**:191-92, 194-95
Elégies majeures (Senghor) **25**:254-56, 258
Elegies, Mascarades, et Bergerie (Ronsard) **11**:249-50
Elegies of Gloom (Ovid)
See *Tristia*
The Elegies of Jutting Rock (Elytis)
See *Ta eleýa tis Oxópetras*
"Elegija" (Pushkin) **10**:413-14
"Elegy" (Berry) **28**:14-17, 19, 31
"Elegy" (Bridges) **28**:67, 87
"Elegy" (Ekeloef)
See *En Mölna-elegi*
"Elegy" (Heaney) **18**:241-43
"Elegy" (Jonson) **17**:175
"Elegy" (Marvell)
See "Poem upon the Death of O. C."
"Elegy" (Pushkin)
See "Elegija"
"Elegy" (Roethke) **15**:267
"Elegy" (Walker) **20**:278-79
"Elegy" (Zagajewski) **27**:396
Elegy (Neruda)
See *Elegía*

"Elegy before Death: At Settignano" (Day Lewis) **11**:151
"Elegy for a Dead Soldier" (Shapiro) **25**:263, 269, 277, 279-80, 288-89, 295, 310, 316
"Elegy for a friend killed in the civil war" (Paz) **1**:352
"Elegy for a Long-haired Student" (Stryk) **27**:203
"Elegy for a Nature Poet" (Nemerov) **24**:293
"Elegy for Alto" (Okigbo) **7**:231, 235, 244
"An Elegy for D. H. Lawrence" (Williams) **7**:350, 354-55
"Elegy for Father Stephen" (Merton) **10**:344
"An Elegy for Five Old Ladies" (Merton) **10**:333, 343
"Elegy for Jane" (Roethke) **15**:309
"Elegy for John Donne" (Brodsky)
See "The Great Elegy for John Donne"
"Elegy for N. N." (Milosz) **8**:186, 207
"Elegy: For Robert Lowell" (Brodsky) **9**:7, 8
"Elegy for Slit-Drum" (Okigbo) **7**:233, 235, 244
"Elegy for the Monastery Barn" (Merton) **10**:331, 342, 349
"Elegy for Y. Z." (Milosz) **8**:174, 198, 203
Elegy in April and September (Owen) **19**:366
"Elegy of the Wind" (Okigbo) **7**:235
"Elegy: On a Lady Whom Grief for the Death of Her Betrothed Killed" (Bridges) **28**:87
Elegy on Dead Fashion (Sitwell) **3**:295, 300, 304
"Elegy on Poor Mailie" (Burns)
See "The Death and Dying Words of Poor Mailie"
"Elegy on the Death of King James" (Finch) **21**:169
"Elegy on the Death of Robert Ruisseaux" (Burns) **6**:67
"Elegy on the Dust" (Gunn) **26**:190-191, 193, 203
"Elegy on the Ruins of Pickworth Rutlandshire Hastily composed and written with a Pencil on the Spot'" (Clare) **23**:12
"Elegy: The Summer-House on the Mound" (Bridges) **28**:80, 84
"Elegy to the Memory of an Unfortunate Lady" (Jonson) **17**:206
"Elegy to the Memory of an Unfortunate Lady" (Pope) **26**:314, 319, 324
"Elegy Written in a Country Churchyard" (Gray) **2**:134-37, 139-43, 145, 148, 151-52, 155
"Elegy Written on a Frontporch" (Shapiro) **25**:295
"Elegy XLII" (Jonson)
See "Elegy XLII"
Elejías (Jimenez) **7**:184
"Element" (Page) **12**:168, 170
"Elemental Metamorphosis" (Kunitz) **19**:155
The Elemental Odes (Neruda)
See *Odas elementales*
Elementary Odes (Neruda)
See *Odas elementales*
"The Elements" (Bradstreet)
See "The Four Elements"
"The Elements" (Emerson) **18**:77
"Elements And Angels" (Wylie) **23**:311
The Elements of San Joaquin (Soto) **28**:369, 371, 373, 376, 383-85
"Eleonora Duse" (Lowell) **13**:91
"Elephants" (Moore) **4**:235, 260
"Elévation" (Baudelaire) **1**:46, 70
"Elevator Boy" (Hughes) **1**:263
"XI" (Joyce) **22**:136, 138, 145, 164, 169-70
"11/8" (Williams) **7**:368
"Eleventh Century Doors" (Kumin) **15**:180
"11th Floor, West 4th Street" (Swenson) **14**:261
Eleventh Nemean (Pindar)
See *Nemean 11*
Eleventh Olympian (Pindar)
See *Olympian 11*
Eleventh Pythian (Pindar)
See *Pythian 11*
"El-Hajj Malik El-Shabazz" (Hayden) **6**:176, 180-81, 187, 196
"Eliduc" (Marie de France) **22**:239, 245, 248, 258, 265, 268-75, 278, 281-82, 294
"The Elixir" (Herbert) **4**:134
"Eliza Harris" (Harper) **21**:190, 192, 194, 201, 204-05, 215
"Elizabeth" (Ondaatje) **28**:292
"Elizabeth" (Poe) **1**:446
"Elizabeth Gone" (Sexton) **2**:359
"Elm" (Plath) **1**:390, 394
"Elm" (Stryk) **27**:212
"Elms" (Gluck) **16**:152
"Eloa" (Vigny) **26**:391, 398, 411
Éloges (Perse) **23**:209-11, 217, 222, 229-32, 234, 237, 241-43, 254
"Elogio de la seguidilla" (Dario) **15**:114
Elogio de la sombra (Borges) **22**:71, 75-6
"Eloisa to Abelard" (Pope) **26**:318-19, 326, 339
Eloisa to Abelard (Pope) **26**:304
"Elsewhere" (Sassoon) **12**:252
"A Elvire" (Lamartine) **16**:290
"Elvis Presley" (Gunn) **26**:219
Emaux et camées (Gautier) **18**:127-28, 130, 138, 146, 154, 156, 159, 161, 164
Emblems of a Season of Fury (Merton) **10**:334, 343, 349-51
"Emblems of Conduct" (Crane) **3**:82
"The Embrace" (Gluck) **16**:156
"The Emerald" (Merrill) **28**:222, 244, 257
Emerald Ice: Selected Poems 1962-1987 (Wakoski) **15**:370, 372
"Emergency Haying" (Carruth) **10**:91
"TH EMERGENCY WARD" (Bissett) **14**:10-11, 17, 34
"l'emigrant de Landor Road" (Apollinaire) **7**:42, 47
"Emigranten" (Ekeloef) **23**:61
"Emilie vor ihrem Brauttag" (Holderlin) **4**:141
"Emily Before Her Wedding" (Holderlin)
See "Emilie vor ihrem Brauttag"
"Emily Brontë" (Bridges) **28**:88
"Emily Brosseau" (Masters) **1**:333
"Emily Sparks" (Masters) **1**:327, 347
Empedocles (Holderlin)
See *Empedokles*
"Empedocles on Etna" (Arnold) **5**:5, 9-10, 12, 23, 35-6, 42-3, 45, 50-1, 56-7
Empedocles on Etna, and Other Poems (Arnold) **5**:2, 25, 30, 35, 42, 50, 55, 57
Empedokles (Holderlin) **4**:146
"Empeoro y mejoro" (Fuertes) **27**:15
"The Emperor of Ice-Cream" (Stevens) **6**:293, 296
"The Emperor's New Sonnet" (Villa) **22**:351
"Employment I" (Herbert) **4**:100, 111
"Employment II" (Herbert) **4**:111, 131
"Employments" (Herbert) **4**:100
"Emporium" (Shapiro) **25**:295
Empty Chestnuts (Matsuo Basho)
See *Minashiguri*
Empty Mirror (Ginsberg) **4**:48, 73, 80, 91
"En bateau" (Verlaine) **2**:431
"En dröm" (Ekeloef) **23**:57, 76
"En la Ausencia" (Fuertes) **27**:44
"En las constelaciones" (Dario) **15**:99, 101
En natt i Oto ac (Ekeloef) **23**:63, 69, 76
En natt på horisonten (Ekeloef) **23**:77
En natt vid horisonten (Ekeloef) **23**:62, 89
"En pocas palabras" (Fuertes) **27**:49
"En que describe racionalmente los efectos irracionales del amor" (Juana Ines de la Cruz) **24**:186
En självbiografi (Ekeloef) **23**:90
"En Trinacria" (Dario) **15**:107-09
En un vasto dominio (Aleixandre) **15**:4, 7, 11-12, 17, 34, 41
"En vano tu canto suena" (Juana Ines de la Cruz) **24**:225
"En värld är varje människa" (Ekeloef) **23**:57
"En verklighet" (Ekeloef) **23**:76
Enamels and Cameos (Gautier) **18**:158
See *Emaux et camées*
"El enamorado" (Borges) **22**:95
"The Enchanted Island" (Noyes) **27**:121-23
"Enchanter's Handmaiden" (Wylie) **23**:324
"Enchantment through Fire" (Blok) **21**:20
"The Encounter" (Gluck) **16**:167
"Encounter" (Pavese) **13**:202
"Encounter" (Wright) **14**:374
"Encounter in August" (Kumin) **15**:209
Encounters (Aleixandre) **15**:4
"Encoures au Lecteur" (Ronsard) **11**:249
"End" (Hughes) **1**:240
"The End" (Owen) **19**:334
"The End" (Pasternak) **6**:268
"An End" (Rossetti) **7**:280
"The End" (Tomlinson) **17**:340
"The End of 1968" (Montale)
See "Fine del '68"
The End of a Fine Epoch (Brodsky)
See *Konets prekrasnoy epokhi*
"End of a Year" (Lowell) **3**:228
"The End of March" (Bishop) **3**:48-9, 72
"End of Play" (Graves) **6**:137
"End of Summer" (Kunitz) **19**:186
"The End of the Episode" (Hardy) **8**:91
"the end of the owls," (Enzensberger) **28**:142, 147
"The End of the Search" (Masters) **1**:344
"The End of the World" (Gluck) **16**:152
"End of the World" (Jeffers) **17**:141
"End of the World: Weekend, near Toronto" (Atwood) **8**:13
"End of the Year" (Tagore)
See "Varshashesh"
"End of the Year 1912" (Hardy) **8**:124
"The End of Your Life" (Levine) **22**:214
Endeavors of Infinite Man (Neruda)
See *Tentativa del hombre infinito*
"An Ending" (Kipling) **3**:194
"Endless Life" (Ferlinghetti) **1**:180, 182-83, 185
Endless Life: Selected Poems (Ferlinghetti) **1**:180, 182, 184-85
"Endor" (Nemerov) **24**:261
"Ends" (Frost) **1**:213
"Endurance" (Forche) **10**:141-42, 144, 147, 156
"Endymion" (Nemerov) **24**:259
Endymion (Keats)
See *Endymion: A Poetic Romance*
Endymion: A Poetic Romance (Keats) **1**:275-79, 282, 288, 290-91, 308-09, 311, 313-14
"Enemies" (Sassoon) **12**:242
"Enfance" (Rimbaud) **3**:262, 265
"L'Enfant grect" (Hugo) **17**:75
"Enfermera de pulpos" (Fuertes) **27**:8, 26
"The Engagement" (Swenson) **14**:265
"Engführung" (Celan) **10**:96, 99, 117
"The Engine Drain" (Smith) **12**:327
"England" (Moore) **4**:251
"England 1830" (Clare) **23**:37
"England: An Ode" (Swinburne) **24**:312
"England in 1819" (Shelley) **14**:210
English Bards and Scotch Reviewers (Byron) **16**:77, 82
"The English Bull Dog, Dutch Mastiff, and Quail" (Smart) **13**:348
"The English Flag" (Kipling) **3**:157, 161
"The English Graves" (Chesterton) **28**:99
"English Horn" (Montale)
See "Corno Inglese"
"English Idylls" (Tennyson) **6**:409
"English Lessons" (Pasternak) **6**:251
"An English Wood" (Graves) **6**:144, 166
The English Works of George Herbert (Herbert) **4**:103
"The Englishman in Italy" (Browning) **2**:62
"The Englishman in Sorrento" (Browning) **2**:38
"An Enigma" (Poe) **1**:446
"Enigma for an Angel" (Brodsky) **9**:2
"Enivrez-vous" (Baudelaire) **1**:58

"Ennui" (Viereck) **27**:263
Enoch Arden (Tennyson) **6**:360, 365
"Enough" (Moore) **4**:260
Enough Rope (Parker) **28**:345-48, 351, 353, 356-57, 359-61
"Enriching the Earth" (Berry) **28**:11, 43
"Enter No (Silence Is the Blood Whose Flesh)" (Cummings) **5**:111
"L'enterrement" (Verlaine) **2**:431
"L'enthousiasme" (Lamartine) **16**:276, 290
The Enthusiastic Slinger (Neruda)
See *El hondero entusiasta, 1923-1924*
The Entire Son (Guillen)
See *El son entero*
"Entrada a la madera" (Neruda) **4**:277, 306-07
"Entrance into Wood" (Neruda)
See "Entrada a la madera"
Entre la piedra y la flor (Paz) **1**:369
Entries (Berry) **28**:30-31
"Entry in an Album" (Lermontov) **18**:302
"Entwurf einer Hymne an die Madonna" (Holderlin) **4**:150
"The Envelope" (Kumin) **15**:203, 207, 221-22
"Envoi" (Meredith) **28**:174, 187
"Envoy" (Johnson) **24**:145
"The Envoys" (Merrill) **28**:220
"Envy" (H. D.) **5**:305
"The Eolian Harp" (Coleridge)
See "The Aeolian Harp"
"Ephemera" (Lowell) **13**:74
"Ephemera" (Yeats) **20**:337
"Ephemerid" (Loy) **16**:316
"Ephyphatha" (MacDiarmid) **9**:156
"Epidermal Macabre" (Roethke) **15**:272
"Epigram I" (Rexroth) **20**:180
"Epigram CI" (Jonson) **17**:158, 167, 173, 175, 182, 189-90, 208
"Epigram CII" (Jonson) **17**:157, 197
"Epigram CIII" (Jonson) **17**:197-98, 202
"Epigram CIV" (Jonson) **17**:202
"Epigram CVII" (Jonson) **17**:166
"Epigram CVIII" (Jonson) **17**:166
"Epigram CXVI" (Jonson) **17**:164
"Epigram CXXIV" (Jonson) **17**:193
"Epigram CXXXIII" (Jonson) **17**:189
"Epigram IV" (Jonson) **17**:156
"Epigram LIX" (Jonson) **17**:164
"Epigram LXV" (Jonson) **17**:157, 197
"Epigram LXXVI" (Jonson) **17**:159, 174, 192, 198, 200, 205, 214
"Epigram on Lady Elizabeth" (Jonson)
See "Epigram on Lady Elizabeth"
"Epigram: To a Friend, and Sonne" (Jonson)
See "Epigram: To a Friend, and Sonne"
"Epigram X" (Jonson) **17**:157
"Epigram XCI" (Jonson) **17**:201
"Epigram XCIV" (Jonson) **17**:159, 202
"Epigram XIV" (Jonson) **17**:166, 174
"Epigram XLIII" (Jonson) **17**:199
"Epigram XLV" (Jonson) **17**:193
"Epigram XVIII" (Jonson) **17**:179
"Epigram XXIII" (Jonson) **17**:197
"Epigram XXXV" (Jonson) **17**:156
"Epigramas" (Guillen) **23**:121
Epigramas (Cardenal) **22**:104, 117, 124-25, 131
Epigrammata (Martial) **10**:243
Epigrammaton libri (Martial)
See *Epigrammata*
Epigrams (Cardenal)
See *Epigramas*
Epigrams (Jonson) **17**:156-58, 169, 179, 196-97, 201-02, 206
Epigrams (Martial)
See *Epigrammata*
"Epilog" (Heine) **25**:162, 178
"Epilogue" (Cullen) **20**:57
"Epilogue" (Verlaine) **2**:432
"Epilogue to the Drama Founded on 'stSt. Roman's Welle'" (Scott) **13**:293
Epilogue to the Satires (Pope) **26**:319-20, 340
"Epilogue to the Tragedy of Jane Shore" (Finch) **21**:154
Epinicia (Pindar) **19**:378
Epipsychidion (Shelley) **14**:163, 171, 173-75, 178, 187, 189, 192-93, 196-97, 208, 233-37, 239-40
"Episode" (Valery) **9**:391
"Epistle" (Dario)
See "Epístola"
"Epistle" (Lee) **24**:242
"An Epistle answering one that asked to be Sealed of the Tribe of Ben" (Jonson)
See "An Epistle answering one that asked to be Sealed of the Tribe of Ben"
"Epistle Containing the Strange Medical Experiences of Karshish the Arab Physician" (Browning) **2**:36
"An Epistle from Ardelia to Mrs. Randolph in answer to her Poem upon Her Verses" (Finch) **21**:167
"Epistle from Mrs. Yonge to Her Husband" (Montagu) **16**:346
Epistle III (Pope) **26**:325-26
"An Epistle, Inviting a Friend to Supper" (Jonson)
See "An Epistle, Inviting a Friend to Supper"
Epistle IV (Pope) **26**:325
"Epistle John Hamilton to Reynolds" (Keats) **1**:289, 305
"An Epistle Mendicant" (Jonson)
See "An Epistle Mendicant"
"Epistle to a Friend" (Jonson)
See "Epistle to a Friend"
"Epistle to a Friend, to perswade him to the Warres" (Jonson)
See "Epistle to a Friend, to perswade him to the Warres"
"An Epistle to a Lady, Who Desired the Author to Make Verses on Her, in the Heroick Style" (Swift) **9**:256, 259-60, 281
"Epistle to a Young Friend" (Burns) **6**:71, 96
"Epistle to Augusta" (Byron) **16**:86
"Epistle to Augustus" (Pope) **26**:320-21
Epistle to Burlington (Pope) **26**:353, 359
"Epistle to Dr. Arbuthnot" (Pope) **26**:318, 338, 361
An Epistle to Dr. Arbuthnot (Pope) **26**:311, 320, 339-46
"Epistle to Elizabeth Countesse of Rutland" (Jonson)
See "Epistle to Elizabeth Countesse of Rutland"
"Epistle to John Rankine, Enclosing Some Poems" (Burns) **6**:65, 83
"Epistle: To Katherine, Lady Aubigny" (Jonson)
See "Epistle: To Katherine, Lady Aubigny"
"An Epistle to Master John Selden" (Jonson)
See "An Epistle to Master John Selden"
"Epistle to Sir Edward Sacvile, now Earl of Dorset" (Jonson)
See "Epistle to Sir Edward Sacvile, now Earl of Dorset"
"Epistle to the Olympians" (Nash) **21**:279-80
"Epistle to William Simpson of Ochiltree, May 1785" (Burns) **6**:69
"The Epistles" (Burns) **6**:49, 66-71, 79, 81
Epistles (Ovid)
See *Heroides*
Epistolæ Heroidum (Ovid)
See *Heroides*
"Epístola" (Dario) **15**:89-90
"Epistola a monsenor Casaldaliga" (Cardenal) **22**:103
"Epistre a ses amis" (Villon) **13**:395
"Epitáfio de B Dias" (Pessoa) **20**:155
"Epitaph: Hubert Hastings Parry" (Bridges) **28**:77
"Epitaph" (Tsvetaeva)
See "Nadgrobie"
"Epitaph" (Williams) **7**:345
"Epitaph" (Wylie) **23**:322-23
"Epitaph for a Darling Lady" (Parker) **28**:346
"Epitaph for a Poet" (Cullen) **20**:60
"Epitaph for Anton Schmidt" (Gunn) **26**:203
"Epitaph for My Father" (Walker) **20**:289, 293
"Epitaph for the Race of Man" (Millay) **6**:217, 230
"Epitaph on an Army of Mercenaries" (Housman) **2**:177
"Epitaph on Salathiel Pavy" (Jonson)
See "Epitaph on Salomon Pavy"
"Epitaph on Salomon Pavy" (Jonson) **17**:179
"Epitaph on the Politician Himself" (Belloc) **24**:31, 40
"Epitaph to Master Vincent Corbet" (Jonson) **17**:174
"An Epitaph upon a Child" (Herrick) **9**:129
"An Epitaph upon a Virgin" (Herrick) **9**:131
"Epitaphe Villon" (Villon) **13**:390, 394, 408, 410-11, 417-18
"Epitaphs of the War" (Kipling) **3**:171, 192
"Epithalamie on Sir Clipseby Crew and His Lady" (Herrick)
See "A Nuptiall Song, or Epithalamie on Sir Clipseby Crew and His Lady"
"An Epithalamie to Sir Thomas Southwell and His Ladie" (Herrick) **9**:86
"Epithalamion" (Herrick)
See "A Nuptiall Song, or Epithalamie on Sir Clipseby Crew and His Lady"
"Epithalamion" (Hopkins) **15**:124
"Epithalamion" (Spenser) **8**:336, 389
"An Epithalamion, or mariage song on the Lady Elizabeth, and Count Palatine being married on St. Valentines day" (Donne) **1**:124
"The Epithalamium" (Housman) **2**:199
"Epithalamium" (Pessoa) **20**:165, 169
"An Epitome" (Sassoon) **12**:260
"Epitre a M. de Sainte-Beuve" (Lamartine) **16**:267
"Épître à Marie d'Orléans" (Villon) **13**:399, 413
"Epîtres à la Princesse" (Senghor) **25**:258
"Epîtres à la Princesse" (Senghor) **25**:255
Epode (Jonson)
See *Epode*
"Equal Opportunity" (Lorde) **12**:140
"Equilibrist" (Swenson) **14**:274, 283
"Equinox" (Lorde) **12**:157
"Equitan" (Marie de France) **22**:239-41, 258, 265, 269, 271, 278, 296-98
"Era un aire suave" (Dario) **15**:79, 95, 107, 109, 118-19
"Ere Sleep Comes Down to Soothe the Weary Eyes" (Dunbar) **5**:121, 124
"The Eremites" (Graves) **6**:140
"Erige Cor Tuum ad Me in Coelum" (H. D.) **5**:307
"Erikönig" (Goethe) **5**:239, 254
Eril (Perse) **23**:246
"Erinna" (Eliot) **20**:137
"Erinnerung an Frankreich" (Celan) **10**:121
Erklärung (Heine) **25**:162
"Erl-King" (Goethe)
See "Erikönig"
Erlkönig (Goethe) **5**:257
"L'ermite" (Apollinaire) **7**:46-7
"Ermunterung" (Holderlin) **4**:148
"Eroded Hills" (Wright) **14**:353, 378
"Eroica" (Ginsberg) **4**:62
"L'eroismo" (Montale) **13**:156
"Eros" (Bridges) **28**:74-5, 86-7
Eros and Psyche (Bridges) **28**:47, 59, 68, 86
"Eros at Temple Stream" (Levertov) **11**:169
"Eros turannos" (Robinson) **1**:468, 490, 493-94, 497
"Erosion: Transkei" (Brutus) **24**:113
Erotic Adventures (Ovid)
See *Amores*
"erinnerung un die schrecken der jugend" (Enzensberger) **28**:136
"Erwache, Friederike" (Goethe) **5**:246
"Es así" (Neruda) **4**:311

Cumulative Title Index

"Es obligatorio" (Fuertes) **27**:12
"Es War Einmal" (Smith) **12**:312
"Escaparate" (Borges) **22**:92
"The Escape" (Levine) **22**:233
"Escape" (Wylie) **23**:301, 309, 329
"Escolares" (Guillen) **23**:127
"Escrito" (Fuertes) **27**:48
Esope (Marie de France)
See *The Fables*
Espacia (Jimenez) **7**:203, 213-14
Espadas como labios (Aleixandre) **15**:6, 18, 21, 30-1, 39-41
España (Gautier) **18**:155
España en el corazón: himno a las glorias del pueblo en la guerra (1936-1937) (Neruda) **4**:278, 283, 287, 307-09, 311
"Especially When the October Wind" (Thomas) **2**:384
"L'espoir luit comme un brin de paille dans l'étable" (Verlaine) **2**:416
"L'Esprit Pur" (Vigny) **26**:371, 374, 392, 402-404, 413
"L'esprit saint" (Lamartine) **16**:264, 277
Espurgatoire (Marie de France)
See *L'Espurgatoire Saint Patrice*
L'Espurgatoire Saint Patrice (Marie de France) **22**:287-89, 291, 293, 300
An Essay on Criticism (Pope) **26**:300, 302-303, 314-15, 318, 320-22, 340
An Essay on Man (Pope) **26**:304, 307-308, 314, 318, 326, 328-33, 335, 338-40, 351-56, 359
"Essay on Mind" (Browning) **6**:27
An Essay on Mind, with other Poems (Browning) **6**:19-20, 26
"Essay on Poetics" (Ammons) **16**:10-11, 23, 28, 47-9
"Essay on Psychiatrists" (Pinsky) **27**:144-45, 160, 162, 173, 175-76
Essay on Rime (Shapiro) **25**:264-65, 267-68, 270, 274-79, 285, 288, 290-91, 296, 310, 319, 322-23
"Essay on Stone" (Carruth) **10**:83
"Essay on the Alliance of Education and Government" (Gray) **2**:136
"An Essay on War" (Duncan) **2**:105
"Esse" (Milosz) **8**:182, 187
"Essential Beauty" (Larkin) **21**:229
The Essential Etheridge Knight (Knight) **14**:52-3
"Está bien" (Guillen) **23**:127
"Está el bisonte imperial" (Guillen) **23**:125
"Esta tarde, mi bien, cuando te hablaba" (Juana Ines de la Cruz) **24**:180
La estación violenta (Paz) **1**:353, 359-60, 362
"Estar del cuerpo" (Aleixandre) **15**:35
"Estate di San Martino" (Pavese) **13**:244
"Una estatua en el silencio" (Neruda) **4**:289
"Estatura del vino" (Neruda) **4**:277, 301
"Este libro" (Fuertes) **27**:17, 38
"Este que ves engaño colorido" (Juana Ines de la Cruz) **24**:225
Esthétique du Mal (Stevens) **6**:300, 302
"Estimable Mable" (Brooks) **7**:94
Estío (Jimenez) **7**:212
"Estival" (Dario) **15**:117
"El estrecho dudoso" (Cardenal) **22**:119-23, 125-27
El estrecho dudoso (Cardenal) **22**:
"Estudio preliminar" (Dario) **15**:80
"Et Le Sursaut Soudain" (Senghor) **25**:248
Et moi aussi je suis peintre (Apollinaire) **7**:34
Les états-généraux (Breton) **15**:50, 52, 62
"Etched Away" (Celan) **10**:97
"Été" (Valery) **9**:351, 373, 392
"Eternal Death" (Tagore)
See "Ananta maran"
"Eternal Life" (Tagore)
See "Ananta jivan"
Eternidades (Jimenez) **7**:187, 208, 212-13
"Eternite de la nature, brievete de l'homme" (Lamartine) **16**:283
"Eternity" (Crane) **3**:90
"An Eternity" (Williams) **7**:394
Eternity (Smart)
See *On the Eternity of the Supreme Being*
"The Eternity of Nature" (Clare) **23**:3-4, 26
"Ethelinda" (Smart)
See "To Ethelinda"
"Ethiopia" (Harper) **21**:189, 202, 208, 215, 217
Éthiopiques (Senghor) **25**:231-32, 238, 241, 255
"Ethnobotany" (Snyder) **21**:297
"Les étoiles" (Lamartine) **16**:291
"Eton" (Gray)
See "Ode on a Distant Prospect of Eton College"
"Eton College Ode" (Gray)
See "Ode on a Distant Prospect of Eton College"
Etroits sont les vaisseaux (Perse) **23**:244-45
"Etude" (Stryk) **27**:183, 189
"Etude de mains" (Gautier) **18**:129, 158
"The Eucalypt and the National Character" (Wright) **14**:374
"Euclid" (Millay) **6**:211
"Eugene Carman" (Masters) **1**:324
Eugene Onegin (Pushkin)
See *Yevgeny Onegin*
"Eulalie" (Poe) **1**:441
"Eulenspiegelei" (Smith) **12**:327, 342
"Eulogy for Slick" (Knight) **14**:49
"Eupheme" (Jonson) **17**:213
"Euphoria" (Ekeloef) **23**:76
"Euphrosyne" (Arnold) **5**:43
Eureka: A Prose Poem (Poe) **1**:422-24, 430-31, 437-38, 442-43, 450
"Europe" (Ashbery) **26**:113, 118, 138, 151
Europe: A Prophecy, 1794 (Blake) **12**:13, 26, 35, 57, 61
"Eurydice" (H. D.) **5**:298, 304
"Evadne" (H. D.) **5**:267
"Evanston 4 June 72" (Brutus) **24**:123
"Eva's Farewell" (Harper) **21**:201, 208, 218
"Evasion" (Tzara) **27**:230-31
"Eve" (Rossetti) **7**:264, 291
"Eve" (Williams) **7**:350, 354, 394-95
"Eve in Heaven" (Wylie) **23**:326
"The Eve of All Souls" (Clampitt) **19**:87
"The Eve of St. Agnes" (Keats) **1**:279, 282, 285-6, 288, 296, 298, 307-10
"The Eve of St. John" (Scott) **13**:269
"Eve of St. Mark" (Keats)
See "The Eve of St. Mark"
"The Eve of St. Mark" (Keats) **1**:279, 304
"Eve Scolds" (Wright) **14**:373, 375
"Eve Sings" (Wright) **14**:373
"Eve to her Daughter" (Wright) **14**:356
"Evelyn" (Stryk) **27**:208
"Evelyn Hope" (Browning) **2**:38
"Evelyn Ray" (Lowell) **13**:66, 91
"Even" (Burns) **6**:50
"Even If All Desires Things Moments Be" (Cummings) **5**:95
"The Even Sea" (Swenson) **14**:249, 263
"Even Song" (Herbert) **4**:133
"Evening" (Merton) **10**:340
"Evening" (Trakl)
See "Der Abend"
"Evening" (Wheatley)
See "An Hymn to the Evening"
Evening (Akhmatova)
See *Vecher*
Evening Album (Tsvetaeva)
See *Vecherny albom*
"The Evening Bell" (Ishikawa)
See "Yube no kane"
"Evening Dance of the Grey Flies" (Page) **12**:190
Evening Dance of the Grey Flies (Page) **12**:181, 198-99
"The evening darkens over" (Bridges) **28**:87
"Evening Fantasy" (Holderlin) **4**:140
"Evening in the Country" (Ashbery) **26**:124, 159
"Evening in the Sanitarium" (Bogan) **12**:92, 99-101, 107, 121
"The Evening of Ants" (Soto) **28**:378-79
"Evening of the Visitation" (Merton) **10**:339
"Evening on the Broads" (Swinburne) **24**:313, 322, 329, 343
"The Evening Primrose" (Parker) **28**:349, 351, 363
"The Evening Sea" (Ishikawa)
See "Yube no umi"
"Evening Song" (Toomer) **7**:320
Evening Songs (Tagore)
See *Sandhya sangit*
"Evening Star" (Bogan) **12**:98, 100
"Evening Star" (Poe) **1**:448
"The Evening That Love Enticed You Down into the Ballroom" (Ronsard)
See "Le soir qu'amour vous fist en la salle descendre"
An Evening Thought: Salvation by Christ with Penetential Cries (Hammon) **16**:176-79, 183-87
"Evening Twilight" (Baudelaire)
See "Le crépuscule du soir"
"An Evening Under Newly Cleared Skies" (Wang Wei) **18**:369
"Evening Voluntary" (Wordsworth) **4**:408
"Evensong" (Aiken) **26**:5
"The Event" (Dove) **6**:110, 112, 114
"Ever mine hap is slack" (Wyatt) **27**:357
"The Everlasting Gospel" (Blake) **12**:31
"The Everlasting Voices" (Yeats) **20**:309
"Everness" (Borges) **22**:89
"Every Blessed Day" (Levine) **22**:221
"Every Lovely Limb's a Desolation" (Smith) **12**:314
"Every Soul Is a Circus" (Lindsay) **23**:274, 280
"Every Traveler Has One Vermont Poem" (Lorde) **12**:138
Everyone Sang (Sassoon) **12**:280, 284, 289
"Everything Came True" (Pasternak) **6**:266
"eve's version" (Clifton) **17**:29, 36
Evgeni Onegin (Pushkin)
See *Yevgeny Onegin*
"Evidence" (Harjo) **27**:64
"The Evil" (Rimbaud)
See "Le mal"
"Eviradnus" (Hugo) **17**:59, 61
"Evolution" (Swenson) **14**:247, 251, 255, 275, 283-84, 286
"Evolutionary Poem No. 1" (Knight) **14**:42
"Evolutionary Poem No. 2" (Knight) **14**:42
"Evolution-Sustenance-Dissolution" (Tagore)
See "Srishti-sthiti-pralaya"
"The Evolver" (Baraka) **4**:24
"evry whun at 2 oclock" (Bissett) **14**:33
"Ex ponto" (Ekeloef) **23**:76
"Ex vermibus" (MacDiarmid) **9**:190
"Exactly what is unexact" (Villa) **22**:354
"Exageraciones divinas" (Fuertes) **27**:30
"The Exam" (Olds) **22**:324
"Examination at the Womb-Door" (Hughes) **7**:159
"Examination of the Hero in a Time of War" (Stevens) **6**:318
"The Example" (Belloc) **24**:27
"Examples of Created Systems" (Meredith) **28**:200
"An Excellent New Ballad; or, The True English Dean to Be Hang'd for a Rape" (Swift) **9**:267
"The Excesses of God" (Jeffers) **17**:132
"The Exchange" (Swenson) **14**:255, 288
"Exchanging Hats" (Bishop) **3**:64
Exclamations: Music of the Soul (Nishiwaki) **15**:237
"The Excrement Poem" (Kumin) **15**:207
"La excursión" (Fuertes) **27**:17
The Excursion, Being a Portion of "The Recluse" (Wordsworth) **4**:377-78, 383, 392, 397-99, 402-03, 405-09

"Excuse" (Arnold)
See "Urania"
"Execration upon Vulcan" (Jonson)
See "Execration upon Vulcan"
"Exhortation" (Bogan) **12**:122
Exil (Perse) **23**:209, 211, 213-14, 216-18, 221-22, 231, 234, 240-42, 246, 248-50, 252, 254, 256
Exile and Other Poems (Perse)
See *Exil*
"The Exile's Return" (Lowell) **3**:200, 202, 234
"The Exit" (Elytis) **21**:134
"Exit, Pursued by a Bear" (Nash) **21**:271
"Exmoor" (Clampitt) **19**:81, 88
"The Exorcism" (Roethke) 274, 278
"Exordium" (Noyes) **27**:127
"The Expatriate" (Forche) **10**:138, 141, 144, 156
"The Expatriates" (Sexton) **2**:359
"An Expedient-Leonardo da Vinci's-and a Query" (Moore) **4**:242
"Experience Is the Angled Road" (Dickinson) **1**:111
"L'Expiation" (Hugo) **17**:79-80
"The Expiration" (Donne) **1**:130
"Explaining a Few Things" (Neruda)
See "Explico algunas cosas"
"The Explanation" (Kipling) **3**:183
"Explanation" (Pasternak) **6**:266
"Explanation and Apology, Twenty Years After" (Carruth) **10**:78
An Explanation of America (Pinsky) **27**:143-46,153, 155-56, 162-63, 173, 176
"Explico algunas cosas" (Neruda) **4**:297, 310-11
"The Explorers" (Atwood) **8**:13
"The Explorers" (Rich) **5**:362
"Explosion" (Harjo) **27**:56
"Expostulation and Reply" (Wordsworth) **4**:419
"An Expostulation with Inigo Jones" (Jonson) **17**:181-82
"Exposure" (Heaney) **18**:194, 205
"Exposure" (Owen) **19**:327, 332, 334
"Express" (Sandburg) **2**:340
"Expression" (Clare) **23**:44
"Expression" (Gunn) **26**:217
"Expressions of Sea Level" (Ammons) **16**:29, 42, 46; **108**:22
Expressions of Sea Level (Ammons) **16**:4-5, 20, 27, 53
"The Exstasie" (Donne) **1**:126, 128, 130, 135, 147, 152
"Extase" (Hugo) **17**:91
"Extempore Effusion upon the Death of James Hogg" (Wordsworth) **4**:402
"Extracts from Addresses to the Academy of Fine Ideas" (Stevens) **6**:314
Extracts from an Opera (Keats) **1**:311
"Un extraño" (Gallagher) **9**:66
"Extraño accidente" (Fuertes) **27**:14, 27
Extravagario (Neruda) **4**:290
"Extremes and Moderations" (Ammons) **16**:10-11, 18, 23, 28, 47-9
Exultations (Pound) **4**:317
"Exvoto pour un naufrage" (Cesaire) **25**:32
"Eyasion" (Tzara) **27**:230
"Eye and Tooth" (Lowell) **3**:215
"The Eyeglasses" (Williams) **7**:381-83
"The Eye-Mote" (Plath) **1**:389
"Eyes and Tears" (Marvell) **10**:270-71
Eyes at the Back of Our Heads (Levertov)
See *With Eyes at the Back of Our Heads*
"The Eyes of the Poor" (Baudelaire)
See "Les yeux des pauvres"
"Ezekiel Saw the Wheel" (Montale) **13**:109, 129, 165
"Ezerskij" (Pushkin) **10**:391, 394
"F O Matthiessen An Anniversary" (Shapiro) **25**:320, 322, 324
"Fable" (Cassian) **17**:13
"Fable" (Emerson) **18**:103-4
"A Fable" (Gluck) **16**:161
"Fable" (Wylie) **23**:310, 316, 319
"Fable of the Cock and the Fox" (Chaucer)
See "Nun's Priest's Tale"
"The Fable of the Fragile Butterfly" (Wakoski) **15**:333
The Fables (Marie de France) **22**:287-88
Fables (Smart) **13**:341
"Fables about Error" (Meredith) **28**:175, 194, 213, 215
"Fables of the Moscow Subway" (Nemerov) **24**:268
"The Fabulists, 1914-1918" (Kipling) **3**:172
"Fabulous Ballard" (Wylie) **23**:321
Façade (Sitwell) **3**:294, 303, 306, 319, 322, 325, 328
"The Face" (Levine) **22**:224
"Face" (Toomer) **7**:310, 333
"Face and Image" (Tomlinson) **17**:348
"Face behind the Pane (An Old Man's Gaze)" (Aleixandre)
See "Rostro tras el cristal (Mirada del viejo)"
"Face Lift" (Plath) **1**:394
"The Faces" (Stryk) **27**:202
"Faces" (Whitman) **3**:397
"Facing" (Swenson) **14**:284, 286
"Facing the Oxford" (Guillen)
See "Frente al Oxford"
"Fackelzug" (Celan) **10**:127
The Fact of a Doorframe: Poems Selected and New, 1950-1984 (Rich) **5**:388-89
"Facteur Cheval" (Breton) **15**:50
"Factory Windows Are Always Broken" (Lindsay) **23**:268, 273, 276
"Facts" (Levine) **22**:221
"Facts" (Snyder) **21**:295-97
"Faded Leaves" (Arnold) **5**:13
Fadensonnen (Celan) **10**:96, 98
The Faerie Queene, Disposed into Twelve Bookes Fashioning XII Morall Vertues (Spenser) **8**:323-25, 327-28, 330, 332-34, 337, 339, 341-47, 349-50, 354, 360-61, 363, 365, 369, 371-72, 374-78, 380-82, 384-85, 388-93, 395-97
"Fafaia" (Brooke) **24**:62
"Fafnir and the Knights" (Smith) **12**:302, 329
"The Failed Spirit" (Smith) **12**:333
"Failure" (Brooke) **24**:75
"A Failure" (Day Lewis) **11**:147
"The Failure of Buffalo to Levitate" (Hass) **16**:195
"Faim" (Rimbaud) **3**:271, 282
"Faina" (Blok) **21**:20
Faina (Blok) **21**:24
"Fair Choice" (Hughes) **7**:135
"Fair Daffodils" (Herrick)
See "To Daffadills"
"Fair Elenor" (Blake) **12**:31
"The Fair in the Woods" (Gunn) **26**:219
"The Fair One in My Mind" (Tagore)
See "Manas-sundari"
"Fair Recluse" (Smart) **13**:341
"The Fair Singer" (Marvell) **10**:270-71, 294, 300
"Fair Weather" (Parker) **28**:348
"A Fairer Hope, A Brighter Morn" (Harper) **21**:190
"The Fairest One of All" (Kumin) **15**:201, 222
"The Fairie Temple: or, Oberons Chappell. Dedicated to Mr. John Merrifield, Counsellor at Law" (Herrick) **9**:86
Fairies and Fusiliers (Graves) **6**:165
"The Fairy" (Blake) **12**:34
"The Fairy Goldsmith" (Wylie) **23**:301, 318-21, 325-26, 329-30, 332
"Fairy Land" (Poe) **1**:440
"A Fairy Tale" (Lowell) **13**:96
"Fairy Tales" (Pushkin)
See "Skazki"
Fairy Tales (Pushkin)
See *Skazki*
"Fairytale" (Wright) **14**:338
A Fairy-Tale for Children (Lermontov) **18**:282, 303
"Faith" (Herbert) **4**:100, 119
"Faith" (Lamartine)
See "La foi"
"The Faith" (Nemerov) **24**:287
"Faith Healing" (Larkin) **21**:229-30, 258
"Faithfully Tinyig at Twilight Voice" (Cummings) **5**:110
"The Faithless Bride" (Garcia Lorca)
See "La casada infiel"
"The Faithless Wife" (Garcia Lorca)
See "La casada infiel"
"Fakes" (Apollinaire)
See "Des Faux"
"The Falcon" (Wylie) **23**:328
"Falcon City" (Tsvetaeva)
See "Sokolinya slobodka"
"The Falcon Woman" (Graves) **6**:156, 172
"The Fall" (Ammons) **16**:42
"Fall" (Dario)
See "Autumnal"
"Fall" (Neruda)
See "Otoño"
"Fall 1961" (Lowell) **3**:215
"Fall and Spring" (Soto) **28**:399, 403
"Fall Festival" (Holderlin) **4**:141
"Fall, Leaves, Fall" (Bronte) **8**:68-9
The Fall of America: Poems of These States 1965-1971 (Ginsberg) **4**:53-7, 59, 63-4, 66-7, 81
The Fall of an Angel (Lamartine)
See *La chute d'un ange*
"The Fall of Night" (Merton) **10**:340
"The Fall of Rome" (Auden) **1**:23
"The Fall of Zalona" (Bronte) **8**:59
"Fall, Sierra Nevada" (Rexroth) **20**:205-06
"Fall Time" (Sandburg) **2**:316
"The Fallen Angels" (Sexton) **2**:373
"Fallen Leaves" (Illyes) **16**:243
"Fallen Majesty" (Yeats) **20**:330
"Fallen Moon" (Aleixandre) **15**:18, 20, 22
"The Fallen Tower of Siloam" (Graves) **6**:137, 143
"Fallen Women" (Pavese)
See "Donne perdute"
"Falling Asleep over the 'Aeneid'" (Lowell) **3**:205
"Falling Asleep by Firelight" (Meredith) **28**:171
"Falling Leaves and Early Snow" (Rexroth) **20**:207
"The Falling of the Leaves" (Yeats) **20**:344
The Falling Star's Path (Yosano Akiko) **11**:301
"The Fallow Deer at the Lonely House" (Hardy) **8**:124
"The Falls" (Kinnell) **26**:257
"Falls Country" (Wright) **14**:378
"The False Heart" (Belloc) **24**:31
False Justice (Hagiwara Sakutaro)
See *Kyomo no seigi*
"False Prophet" (Wylie) **23**:310, 324
"A False Step" (Browning) **6**:23
"Falsetto" (Montale) **13**:115-16
Fama y obras pósthumas (Juana Ines de la Cruz) **24**:227-29, 231
"Familiar Letter to Siegfried Sassoon" (Graves) **6**:131
"Family" (Brooks) **7**:93
"The Family in Spring" (Soto) **28**:400
Family Pictures (Brooks) **7**:63-4, 66, 83, 91, 94-5
Family Reunion (Nash) **21**:267-68
"Famous Poet" (Hughes) **7**:114, 139
The Famous Tragedy of the Queen of Cornwall (Hardy) **8**:95
"The Fan" (Montale)
See "Il ventaglio"
"Fancy Etchings" (Harper) **21**:193, 197
"Fanfara" (Montale) **13**:134
"Fanfare, Coda and Finale" (Walker) **20**:294
"Fanscombe Barn" (Finch) **21**:143
"Fantaisies d'hiver" (Gautier) **18**:129

"Fantasia on 'The Nut-Brown Maid'" (Ashbery) **26**:134, 140, 156, 162
"A Fantasy" (Gluck) **16**:158, 163
"Fantoches" (Verlaine) **2**:430
"Un fantôme" (Baudelaire) **1**:64
"Fantômes" (Cesaire) **25**:10
"Far Away" (Guillen)
See "Far Away"
"Far Away and Long Ago" (Stevens) **6**:293
"The Far Field" (Roethke) **15**:280, 310, 317
The Far Field (Roethke) **15**:271, 282-83, 303, 309, 311
"Far in a Western Brookland" (Housman) **2**:180
"Far Known to Sea and Shore" (Housman) **2**:179
"Far Niente" (Gautier) **18**:172
"Far Off" (Jimenez)
See "A lo lejos"
"Far Rockaway" (Schwartz) **8**:291, 302-03, 305
"Far West" (Snyder) **21**:300
"La farandola dei fanciulli" (Montale) **13**:116
"Farewel Love and all thy lawes for ever" (Wyatt) **27**:304, 318, 340-41
"Farewell" (Kinnell) **26**:287
"Farewell" (Kipling) **3**:189
"The Farewell" (Lamartine)
See "L'adieu"
"Farewell" (Lermontov) **18**:301
"A Farewell" (Owen) **19**:336
"Farewell" (Smith) **12**:301, 339
"Farewell" (Tagore)
See "Viday"
"Farewell" (Wang Wei) **18**:387
"Farewell in the Mountains" (Wang Wei) **18**:387
"Farewell Love" (Wyatt) **27**:317
"Farewell Sweet Dust" (Wylie) **23**:322
"A Farewell to Alexandria" (Bronte) **8**:73
"A Farewell to America" (Wheatley) **3**:341
"Farewell to Arcady" (Dunbar) **5**:140
"Farewell to Barn and Stack and Tree" (Housman) **2**:161
"A Farewell to Celadon, on His Going to Ireland" (Behn) **13**:8
"Farewell to Florida" (Stevens) **6**:297, 305
"Farewell to Heaven" (Tagore)
See "Svarga ha'ite biday"
"Farewell to love" (Donne) **1**:147
"Farewell to Nancy" (Burns) **6**:58
"Farewell to Poetry" (Herrick) **9**:95, 102, 136
"Farewell to the Vertuous Gentle-woman" (Jonson)
See "To the World. A Farwell for a Gentlewoman, Vertuous and Nobel"
"Farewell to Van Gogh" (Tomlinson) **17**:301, 314
La farfalla di Dinard (Montale) **13**:161
Le farfalle (Gozzano) **10**:177-78, 184
"The Faring" (Tomlinson) **17**:349
"Farish Street" (Walker) **20**:294
Färjesång (Ekeloef) **23**:57, 62, 76
"The Farm Child's Lullaby" (Dunbar) **5**:138
"Farmer" (Stryk) **27**:203, 210
"The Farmer" (Williams) **7**:384
"Farmer's Death" (MacDiarmid) **9**:187, 191
"The Farmer's Wife" (Sexton) **2**:350
"The Farmer's Wife" (Tomlinson) **17**:311, 349, 358
Farming: A Handbook (Berry) **28**:5-7, 11-12, 35-36, 43
Farmstead of Time (Celan)
See *Zeitgehöft*
"Farre Off" (Ondaatje) **28**:336
"Farwell Frost, or Welcome the Spring" (Herrick) **9**:109
"Fast-Anchor'd Eternal O Love!" (Whitman) **3**:396
Fasti (Ovid) **2**:238, 241, 243-45, 253-55, 260-61
De Fastis (Ovid)
See *Fasti*
"Fat Lip" (Guillen)
See "Negro bembón"
"The Fat Man in the Mirror" (Lowell) **3**:205
"Fat William and the Trains" (Sitwell) **3**:301
"Fata Morgana" (Rossetti) **7**:280
Fata Morgana (Breton) **15**:51-2, 55, 62
"Fatal Interview" (Wylie) **23**:305
Fatal Interview (Millay) **6**:213, 215-16, 218, 224, 230, 235, 239, 241, 243
"Fatal Sisters" (Gray) **2**:135
"Fate" (Olds) **22**:311, 322
"The Fates" (Owen) **19**:342
The Father (Olds) **22**:319-21, 323-24, 326, 330, 332-34, 338, 340-42
"Father and Daughter" (Sanchez) **9**:220-21, 229
"Father and Daughter" (Song) **21**:337
"Father and Son" (Kunitz) **19**:152, 154, 165, 175, 177-79
"Father and Son" (Schwartz) **8**:301-03, 305, 314
"Father Ch., Many Years Later" (Milosz) **8**:181, 202, 205
"Father Explains" (Milosz) **8**:207
"Father Father Abraham" (Johnson) **24**:160
"A Father for a Fool" (Smith) **12**:333
"The Father of My Country" (Wakoski) **15**:324, 345, 354, 358
"Father, on His Unsonment" (Villa) **22**:349
"A Father out Walking on the Lawn" (Dove) **6**:109
"Fatherhood" (Pavese) **13**:203
"The Fathers" (Sassoon) **12**:168, 282
"Father's Bedroom" (Lowell) **3**:219-20
"Father's Song" (Kumin) **15**:201
"Fatigue" (Belloc) **24**:49
"Fatigue" (Lowell) **13**:60
"The Faun" (Plath) **1**:388
"The Faun Sees" (Zukofsky) **11**:368
"La fausse morte" (Valery) **9**:393, 396
"Faust" (Ashbery) **26**:118
"Faustina; or, Rock Roses" (Bishop) **3**:60
"Faustus and Helen (II)" (Crane) **3**:79, 80, 96, 98, 100
"Faustus and I" (Sexton) **2**:367, 373
"The Fawn" (Millay) **6**:214
"Faynting I folowe" (Wyatt) **27**:343
"Fe Me Sal" (McKay) **2**:225
"Fear and Fame" (Levine) **22**:228
"The Fear of Beasts" (Meredith) **28**:171
"The Fear of Bo-talee" (Momaday) **25**:189, 212-13
"The Fear of Death Disturbs Me" (Meredith) **28**:181
"Fearless" (Tagore)
See "Nirbhay"
"Fears and Scruples" (Browning) **2**:59
"Fears in Solitude" (Coleridge) **11**:92, 94, 97-104
Fears in Solitude (Coleridge) **11**:100
The Feast of the Assumption 1676 (Juana Ines de la Cruz) **24**:177
"A Feaver" (Donne) **1**:126, 130, 153
"February" (Hughes) **7**:147
"February" (Kumin) **15**:222
"february 11, 1990" (Clifton) **17**:30
"February Evening in New York" (Levertov) **11**:167
"February Seventeenth" (Hughes) **7**:162, 165
"The Fed" (Blok) **21**:11
"feed th prisoners now baby" (Bissett) **14**:32
"Feeding Out Wintery Cattle at Twilight" (Hughes) **7**:166
"Feel Me" (Swenson) **14**:267, 270, 288
"Feeling and Precision" (Moore) **4**:251
"Feeling Fucked Up" (Knight) **14**:43, 46
"The Feelings" (Olds) **22**:326
Fekete feher (Illyes) **16**:232
"Feliciano me adora y le aborrezco" (Juana Ines de la Cruz) **24**:183
"Felix Randal" (Hopkins) **15**:170
"The Felloe'd Year" (Graves) **6**:137
"Fellow Creatures" (Nash) **21**:265
"Feminist Manifesto" (Loy) **16**:329, 332, 334
"Femme a la blonde aisselle coiffant sa chevelure a la lueur des etioles" (Breton) **15**:48
"La Femme adultere" (Vigny) **26**:381, 410-11
"Femme dans la nuit" (Breton) **15**:48
"Femme et chatte" (Verlaine) **2**:431
"Femme et oiseau" (Breton) **15**:48, 55-6, 58-60
"Femme noire" (Senghor) **25**:224, 239
"Femmes au bord d'un lac a la surface irisee par le passage d'un cygne" (Breton) **15**:49
"Femmes damnées" (Baudelaire) **1**:62
"Femmes sur la plage" (Breton) **15**:48
"Fence Posts" (Snyder) **21**:307
"Les fenêtres" (Apollinaire) **7**:18, 36, 44
"Les fenêtres" (Baudelaire) **1**:59
"Les fenêtres" (Mallarme) **4**:208
"Feodosija" (Mandelstam) **14**:113
Ferishtah's Fancies (Browning) **2**:59
"Fern" (Hughes) **7**:121
"Fern Hill" (Thomas) **2**:382, 385, 392, 396-99, 405
"Fernão de Magalhães" (Pessoa) **20**:155
Ferrements (Cesaire) **25**:13, 23, 32, 44
Ferrying Across (Tagore)
See *Kheya*
Fervor de Buenos Aires (Borges) **22**:68-9, 71-2, 79, 93-4
Fervor of Buenos Aires (Borges)
See *Fervor de Buenos Aires*
"Festival of Spring" (Tagore)
See "Vasanter Kusumer mela"
Festus (Aiken) **26**:7, 29
"Fetchin' Water" (McKay) **2**:216, 223
"Fêtes de la faim" (Rimbaud) **3**:259
Fêtes galantes (Verlaine) **2**:413-15, 424-25, 430-32
"Feuer-Nacht" (Bogan) **12**:94, 121
Les feuilles d'automne (Hugo) **17**:42-45, 52, 63, 66, 68, 90-93
"A Fever" (Donne)
See "A Feaver"
"A Fever" (Merrill) **28**:221
"Fever" (Gunn) **26**:220
"Fever 103[00f8]" (Plath) **1**:382, 386, 393
"A Few Coins" (Soto) **28**:371
"A Few Figs from Thistles" (Millay) **6**:208, 211, 234
A Few Figs from Thistles (Millay) **6**:207, 211-12, 227, 230, 233-35, 237, 239
"Fiammetta Breaks Her Peace" (Dove) **6**:109
"Les fiançailles" (Apollinaire) **7**:43-4, 46, 48
"Ficha Ingreso Hospital General" (Fuertes) **27**:3
"Fiddler Jones" (Masters) **1**:333
"Fidelity" (Wordsworth) **4**:383
"Field" (Soto) **28**:375, 377-78, 384-85
Field Guide (Hass) **16**:194-95, 197, 199-201, 209, 212, 214, 216, 222, 228
"A Field of Light" (Roethke) 248, 254, 304, 307
"The Field Pansy" (Clampitt) **19**:94, 96
"Field Work" (Heaney) **18**:245
Field Work (Heaney) **18**:197-99, 211-12, 215, 238-40, 242, 245-47, 255-57
Fields of Wonder (Hughes) **1**:240-44, 247, 268
"Fiend, Dragon, Mermaid" (Graves) **6**:142, 145
"Fierce Hope" (Tagore)
See "Duranta asha"
"Fiesta" (Pasolini) **17**:253
Fifine at the Fair (Browning) **2**:42-4, 50, 72, 75, 80, 82, 96
"XV" (Joyce) **22**:138, 145, 170
"The Fifteenth Amendment" (Harper) **21**:197
"Fifteenth Farewell" (Bogan) **12**:86
Fifth Decad of Cantos (Pound) **4**:324
"Fifth Grade Autobiography" (Dove) **6**:120
Fifth Nemean (Pindar)
See *Nemean 5*
Fifty Poems (Cummings) **5**:84, 107-08
"Fifty Years" (Johnson) **24**:127, 131, 143, 145-47, 154, 157-60
Fifty Years, and Other Poems (Johnson) **24**:127, 131, 141-49, 152-55, 157, 159, 162, 166
"50-50" (Hughes) **1**:247

55 Poems (Zukofsky) **11**:341
"Fight" (Bukowski) **18**:15
Fight Back: For the Sake of the People, for the Sake of the Land (Ortiz) **17**:222-223, 233, 239, 244
"Fight Him Fair Nigger" (Knight) **14**:49
"Fight to a Finish" (Sassoon) **12**:267
Fighting Terms: A Selection (Gunn) **26**:181, 183, 188, 197, 199-200, 205-206, 210-12, 215-19, 229
"La figlia che piange" (Eliot) **5**:153, 184
"La figue l'oeillet et la pipe a opium" (Apollinaire) **7**:32
"A Figure from Politics" (Meredith) **28**:187
"The Figure in the Scene" (Hardy) **8**:137
"The Figured Wheel" (Pinsky) **27**:163, 165, 173-76
The Figured Wheel (Pinsky) **27**:175
The Figured Wheel New and Collected Poems (Pinsky) **27**:
"The Figurehead" (Shapiro) **25**:316, 325
"Figures" (Hayden) **6**:196
Figures of Thought: Speculations on the Meaning of Poetry and Other Essays (Nemerov) **24**:299, 303
"Figurine" (Hughes) **1**:245
"La fileuse" (Valery) **9**:391
"Los filibusteros" (Cardenal) **22**:110
"La Fille de Jephte" (Vigny) **26**:401, 410
Les filles du feu (Nerval) **13**:176-78, 192, 195
"Filling the Boxes of Joseph Cornell" (Wakoski) **15**:324
"La fin de la journée" (Baudelaire) **1**:54
La fin de Satan (Hugo) **17**:65, 74, 81, 84, 88, 91
"Final Call" (Hughes) **1**:252
"Final Face" (Aleixandre) **15**:4
"Final Fire" (Aleixandre) **15**:18-19
"Final Shadow" (Aleixandre) **15**:16
"The Final Slope" (Stryk) **27**:203
"the final solution" (Sanchez) **9**:224
"Finding" (Brooke) **24**:57-8
"The Finding of the Moon" (Wright) **14**:356
"Finding the One Brief Note" (Kumin) **15**:215
Findings (Berry) **28**:5
Fine Clothes to the Jew (Hughes) **1**:237-38, 244, 246, 254-55, 258, 260, 262-63, 268-71
"Fine del '68" (Montale) **13**:134
"La fine dell'infanzia" (Montale) **13**:115-16
"Finis" (Montale) **13**:139
"Finisterne" (Montale) **13**:156, 165-66
Finisterre (Montale) **13**:103, 106, 127-30
"Fins" (Sandburg) **2**:307
"The Fire" (Atwood) **8**:39
"The Fire" (Belloc) **24**:32
"The Fire" (Brodsky) **9**:2
"The Fire" (Gluck) **16**:127
"Fire" (Toomer) **7**:333
"Fire" (Zagajewski) **27**:380
"Fire and Ice" (Frost) **1**:194, 197
"Fire and Sleet and Candlelight" (Wylie) **23**:301, 307
"Fire at Murdering Hut" (Wright) **14**:339
"Fire Island" (Swenson) **14**:271, 285-86
"Fire on the Hills" (Jeffers) **17**:117, 127
"Fire Poem" (Merrill) **28**:241, 242
"Fire Practice" (McKay) **2**:225
The Fire Screen (Merrill) **28**:220, 221, 228, 230, 231, 258, 264, 281
"Fire Song" (Ekeloef) **23**:51
"Fire Station" (Bukowski) **18**:16
"'Fire Stop Thief Help Murder Save the World'" (Cummings) **5**:107
"The Firebombers" (Sexton) **2**:365
"Fired" (Hughes) **1**:247
"Fireflies" (Swenson) **14**:250
"The Firemen's Ball" (Lindsay) **23**:265, 268, 281
"Firenze" (Ferlinghetti) **1**:183
"Fireworks" (Shapiro) **25**:269
Fir-Flower Tablets (Lowell) **13**:64, 74, 93
"The 1st" (Clifton) **17**:17
"First" (Kipling) **3**:160
"First, a poem must be magical" (Villa) **22**:352
"The First American" (Toomer) **7**:337
"The First and Last Night of Love" (Cassian) **17**:4, 6
The First and Second Anniversaries (Donne)
See *The Anniversaries*
The First Anniversarie. An Anatomie of the World. Wherein By Occasion of the untimely death of Mistris Elizabeth Drury, the frailtie and decay of this whole World is represented (Donne) **1**:122, 145-50, 152, 155-57
"The First Anniversary of the Government Under His Highness the Lord Protector" (Marvell)
See "The First Anniversary of the Government under O. C."
"The First Anniversary of the Government under O. C." (Marvell) **10**:270-71, 290, 294, 305, 312, 318
First Book (Blok) **21**:2
The First Book of Urizen (Blake)
See *The Book of Urizen*
"First Calf" (Heaney) **18**:203
"First Carolina Said Song" (Ammons) **16**:5
"The First Celestial Adventure of M Antipyrine" (Tzara) **27**:249
The First Cities (Lorde) **12**:137
"First Communion" (Kinnell) **26**:239
"First Day of the Future" (Kinnell) **26**:277
The First Decade: Selected Poems (Duncan) **2**:105-06
First Dream (Juana Ines de la Cruz) **24**:207
"First Early Mornings Together" (Pinsky) **27**:144
"First Elegy" (Rilke) **2**:281, 286
"First Elegy" (Rukeyser) **12**:219
The First Encounter (Bely)
See *Pervoe svidanie*
"First Epistle of the First Book of Horace" (Pope)
See *Satires and Epistles of Horace, Imitated*
"First Fig" (Millay) **6**:227
"First Fight. Then Fiddle" (Brooks) **7**:75
"First Georgic" (Vergil) **12**:364
"The First Gloss" (Heaney) **18**:216
"First Goodbye" (Gluck) **16**:165-67
The First Half of "A"-9 (Zukofsky) **11**:339, 396-97
"First Hymn to Lenin" (MacDiarmid) **9**:177-78, 182
First Hymn to Lenin, and Other Poems (MacDiarmid) **9**:158, 162, 171, 177, 196
"First Inclined to Take What It Is Told" (Brooks) **7**:74
"First Lesson about Man" (Merton) **10**:344-45
"First Letters from a Steamer" (McGuckian) **27**:82
"The First Man" (Gunn) **26**:191
"First Meditation" (Roethke) **15**:272, 274, 279
The First Meetings (Bely)
See *Pervoe svidanie*
"First Memory" (Gluck) **16**:157
"First, Mills" (Hughes) **7**:149
The First Morning (Viereck) **27**:264-65
First Morning (Viereck) **27**:280-81, 283
First Nemean (Pindar)
See *Nemean 1*
"First News from Villafranca" (Browning) **6**:23-4
"First Night" (Olds) **22**:309
"The First Noni Daylight" (Harjo) **27**:64
"First Objectives" (MacDiarmid) **9**:154
"The First of All My Dreams Was of" (Cummings) **5**:109
"The First of January" (Lermontov) **18**:201
First Olympian (Pindar)
See *Olympian 1*
"First Page" (Stein) **18**:313
"The First Part" (Page) **12**:190
First Poems (Merrill) **28**:224, 228, 229, 233-34, 238, 239, 240, 243, 244, 262, 281
First Poems, 1946-1954 (Kinnell) **26**:279
"First Praise" (Williams) **7**:405
First Pythian (Pindar)
See *Pythian 1*
"First Song" (Akhmatova)
See "Pervaya pesenka"
"First Song" (Kinnell) **26**:253, 257
First Song (Kinnell) **26**:236-38, 253, 262
the first sufi line (Bissett) **14**:17
"The First Sunday in Lent" (Lowell) **3**:206
The First Symphony (Bely)
See *Severnaia simfoniia: Pervia geroicheskaia*
"The First Time" (Shapiro) **25**:283, 300, 302, 320
First Voronezh Notebook (Mandelstam) **14**:149, 152, 154
Firstborn (Gluck) **16**:124-25, 127, 130-32, 134, 138-40, 143-44, 147-49, 151, 153
"Der Fischer" (Goethe) **5**:239
"The Fish" (Bishop) **3**:37, 39, 42-3, 50-2, 54, 60, 66, 69, 75
"The Fish" (Brooke) **24**:58, 63, 65, 87
"The Fish" (Moore) **4**:236, 243, 252, 257
"Fish" (Stryk) **27**:209
"Fish Crier" (Sandburg) **2**:332, 338
"The Fish that Walked" (Sexton) **2**:370, 373
"Fisherman" (Kinnell) **26**:260
"The Fisherman" (Yeats) **20**:324-25
"The Fisherman and the Fish" (Pushkin)
See "Skazka o Rybake i Rybke"
The Fisherman's Art (Ovid)
See *Halieutica*
"Fishing at Dawn" (Hughes) **7**:120
"Fishing for Eel Totems" (Atwood) **8**:12
"Fishing the White Water" (Lorde) **12**:137
"Fishing with My Daughter in Miller's Meadow" (Stryk) **27**:204, 208, 214
"Fishnet" (Lowell) **3**:229
"Fist" (Levine) **22**:214, 223, 227
"Fit of Fainting" (Bradstreet)
See "Deliverance From a Fit of Fainting"
"A Fit of Rime Against Rime" (Jonson)
See "A Fit of Rime Against Rime"
"The Fitting" (Millay) **6**:230, 239
"The Fitting of the Mask" (Kunitz) **19**:154
"V" (Joyce) **22**:138, 162, 167
"Five Accounts of a Monogamous Man" (Meredith) **28**:171, 175, 193-94, 213
"Five Aspects of Fear" (Levertov) **11**:164
"The Five Day Rain" (Levertov) **11**:169
"Five Flights Up" (Bishop) **3**:48-9, 72
"5 Jan 72" (Brutus) **24**:124
The Five Nations (Kipling) **3**:192
"Five Senses" (Wright) **14**:348, 363
Five Senses: Selected Poems (Wright) **14**:348, 354, 361, 371
"Five Songs" (Rilke) **2**:273
"Five Things" (Goethe) **5**:228
Five Variations on a Theme (Sitwell) **3**:304
"Five Vignettes" (Toomer) **7**:332
"Five Walks on the Edge" (Viereck) **27**:277
Five Walks on the Edge (Viereck) **27**:
"Five-Finger Exercises" (Eliot) **5**:185
"Le flacon" (Baudelaire) **1**:45
Flagons and Apples (Jeffers) **17**:133, 138
"Le flambeau vivant" (Baudelaire) **1**:56, 61
"The Flame Tree" (Wright) **14**:347
"Flame-Heart" (McKay) **2**:216, 228
"Flammonde" (Robinson) **1**:462, 468, 476
"Flashes and Dedications" (Montale)
See "Flashes e dediche"
"Flashes e dediche" (Montale) **13**:106, 166-67
"Flat-Foot Drill" (McKay) **2**:225
"Flatted Fifth" (Hughes) **1**:267
"The Flaw" (Lowell) **3**:226-28
"The Flaw in Paganism" (Parker) **28**:351, 363
"A Flayed Crow in the Hall of Judgement" (Hughes) **7**:165
"The Flea" (Donne) **1**:134, 152

"Flèche D'or" (Merrill) **28**:254
"Fleckno" (Marvell) **10**:271, 294
"Flee on Your Donkey" (Sexton) **2**:351, 363-64
Fleeting Moments (Tagore)
See *Kshanika*
Fleeting Moments (Tagore)
See *Kshanika*
Fleeting Thoughts (Tagore)
See *Kshanika*
Fleeting Thoughts (Tagore)
See *Kshanika*
"Fleming Helphenstine" (Robinson) **1**:466
"Flesh" (Wright) **14**:347
"The Flesh and the Spirit" (Bradstreet) **10**:7-8, 13, 21, 29-30, 38
"Fletcher McGee" (Masters) **1**:345
"La Fleur qui fait le printemps" (Gautier) **18**:128-29
Les fleurs du mal (Baudelaire) **1**:44-51, 53-8, 60, 62-5, 67-71
"Flies Enter through a Closed Mouth" (Neruda)
See "Por boca cerrada entran moscas"
"Flight" (Brooke) **24**:56
"The Flight" (Roethke) **15**:302
"Flight" (Sexton) **2**:347, 361
"Flight into Egypt" (Auden) **1**:38
"The Flight into Egypt" (Merton) **10**:330
A Flight of Cranes (Tagore)
See *Balaka*
A Flight of Swans (Tagore)
See *Balaka*
A Flight of Swans (Tagore)
See *Balaka*
"Flight to the City" (Williams) **7**:385, 387-88
"The Flitting" (McGuckian) **27**:78, 97
"Floating" (Rexroth) **20**:216
"Floating of the River of Han" (Wang Wei) **18**:362
"The Flood" (Tomlinson) **17**:333
"The Flood" (Wright) **14**:337-38
The Flood (Tomlinson) **17**:332, 336, 349, 354
"The Flood of Years" (Bryant) **20**:10, 16-18
"Flooded Meadows" (Gunn) **26**:219
"Flooding" (Celan) **10**:105
"Florence" (Lowell) **3**:213, 236
"Florida" (Bishop) **3**:37
Flow Chart (Ashbery) **26**:164
"Flow Gently Sweet Afton" (Burns)
See "Sweet Afton"
"The Flower" (Herbert) **4**:104, 109, 113, 118, 127, 131-32
"The Flower and the Rock" (Page) **12**:178
Flower, Fist, and Bestial Wail (Bukowski) **18**:3, 5
Flower Herding on Mount Monadnock (Kinnell) **26**:236, 257, 290
"Flower in the Crannied Wall" (Tennyson) **6**:358
"The Flower Master" (McGuckian) **27**:78
The Flower Master (McGuckian) **27**:77-80, 84-85, 95-97, 101, 104
"Flower of Five Blossoms" (Kinnell) **26**:286
"The Flower of Old Japan" (Noyes) **27**:116-17, 139
The Flower of Old Japan (Noyes) **27**:116, 139
"Flowered Sitting Room" (McGuckian) **27**:105
"The Flower-Fed Buffaloes" (Lindsay) **23**:279
"The Flowering of the Rod" (H. D.) **5**:271-72, 274-75, 293, 296, 306, 309, 314-16
"Flowering Plum" (Gluck) **16**:128, 154
"The Flowering Tree" (Bridges) **28**:77, 80
"The Flowers" (Kipling) **3**:161, 167
Flowers from the Volcano (Alegria) **26**:
The Flowers of Evil (Baudelaire)
See *Les fleurs du mal*
"The Flume" (Bogan) **12**:95, 121
"La flûte" (Vigny) **26**:367, 392, 403, 413
"La Flute" (Vigny) **26**:367
"Flute Notes from a Reedy Pond" (Plath) **1**:389
"A Flute Overheard" (Rexroth) **20**:195
"Flute-Maker, with an Accompaniment" (Browning) **2**:88
"Flutender" (Celan) **10**:105
"FLux et reflux" (Hugo) **17**:100
"The Fly" (Blake) **12**:7, 34
"The Fly" (Brodsky) **9**:29
"The Fly" (Kinnell) **26**:255
"The Fly" (Shapiro) **25**:269, 324, 326
"Flying Above California" (Gunn) **26**:201, 219
"Flying Crooked" (Graves) **6**:149, 151
"Flying Home" (Kinnell) **26**:259, 261
"Flying Home from Utah" (Swenson) **14**:261
"Flying out of It" (Ferlinghetti) **1**:175
"Flying to Byzantium" (Merrill) **28**:221
"Flying Underground" (Giovanni) **19**:143
"Foam," (Enzensberger) **28**:146-48, 156
"Fog" (Cassian) **17**:6
"Fog" (Sandburg) **2**:301, 303
"Fog" (Soto) **28**:377, 384
"The Foggy, Foggy Blue" (Schwartz) **8**:317
"La foi" (Lamartine) **16**:277, 291
"Folie de Minuit" (Lowell) **13**:90-1
"Folk Song" (Parker) **28**:355
"Follies" (Sandburg) **2**:303
"Follow that Stagecoach" (Wakoski) **15**:323
"Follower" (Heaney) **18**:200
"Folly" (MacDiarmid) **9**:153
"The Folly of Being Comforted" (Yeats) 356
"Fonction du poète" (Hugo) **17**:77, 97
"Fontana di aga del me pais" (Pasolini) **17**:259
"The Food Chain" (Kumin) **15**:208
"Food for Fire, Food for Thought" (Duncan) **2**:120-21
"Fool Errant" (Lowell) **13**:83
"Fool o' the Moon" (Lowell) **13**:67, 83, 86
"The Foolish Heart" (Cullen) **20**:59
"Foolish Men" (Juana Ines de la Cruz)
See "Hombres necios que acusáis"
"Footnote to Howl" (Ginsberg) **4**:65, 68, 70
Footprints (Levertov) **11**:189
"The Foot-Washing" (Ammons) **16**:58
"For" (Zukofsky) **11**:349
"For a Birthday" (Gunn) **26**:206
"For a Dead Lady" (Robinson) **1**:461, 490, 492-93
"For a Dead Vole" (Smith) **12**:317
"For a Fatherless Son" (Plath) **1**:397
"For a few Hopi Ancestors" (Rose) **13**:233
"For a Good Dog" (Nash) **21**:268
"For a Lady Who Must Write Verse" (Parker) **28**:363
"For a Lovely Lady" (Cullen) **20**:52, 55
"For a Marriage" (Bogan) **12**:94
"For a Muse Meant" (Duncan) **2**:105
"For a Pastoral Family" (Wright) **14**:375, 378
"For a Picture of St. Dorothea" (Hopkins) **15**:144, 159-62
"For a Poet" (Cullen) **20**:85
"For R. C. B." (Parker) **28**:362
"For a Russian Poet" (Rich) **5**:383
"For a Sad Lady" (Parker) **28**:360
"For a' that" (Scott) **13**:293
"For A' That and A' That" (Burns)
See "Is There for Honest Poverty"
"For a Young Artist" (Hayden) **6**:187, 189-90, 196, 198
"For All Who Ever sent Lace Valentines" (Lindsay) **23**:265
"For Alva Benson and For Those Who Have Learned to Speak" (Harjo) **27**:55, 64
"For an Assyrian Frieze" (Viereck) **27**:260, 280
For an Assyrian Frieze Prince Tank (Viereck) **27**:
"For Andy Goodman, Michael Schwerner, and James Chaney" (Walker) **20**:277-78, 287
For Anna Mae Pictou Aquash Whose Spirit Is Present Here and in the Dappled Stars (1) (Harjo) **27**:
"For Anna Mae Pictou Aquash, Whose Spirit Is Present Here and in the Dappled Stars (For We Remember the Story and Tell It Again So that We May All Live)" (Harjo) **27**:71
"For Anne at Passover" (Kumin) **15**:180
"For Annie" (Poe) **1**:425, 434, 437, 444-45, 447
"For Black People" (Madhubuti) **5**:327, 345
"For Black Poets Who Think of Suicide" (Knight) **14**:42
"For Chekhov" (Hass) **16**:199, 214
"For Clarice" (Brooks) **7**:56
"For Danton" (Tomlinson) **17**:345-46, 350
"For Deliverance from a Fever" (Bradstreet) **10**:36, 60
"For Each of You" (Lorde) **12**:157
"For Eleanor and Bill Monahan" (Williams) **7**:392-93
"For Eleanor Boylan Talking with God" (Sexton) **2**:371
"For Eli Jacobsen" (Rexroth) **20**:181
"For Eric Dolphy" (Knight) **14**:39
"For Freckle-Faced Gerald" (Knight) **14**:41-2
"For George Santayana" (Lowell) **3**:219
"For God While Sleeping" (Sexton) **2**:351, 360-61, 371
"For Godsake hold your tongue, and let me love" (Donne)
See "The Canonization"
"for Guillaume Apollinaire" (Meredith) **28**:194, 208
"For Gwendolyn Brooks" (Giovanni) **19**:113
"For Helen" (Stryk) **27**:203
"For Hettie in Her Fifth Month" (Baraka) **4**:15
"For His Father" (Meredith) **28**:180, 191, 194
"For Jane Myers" (Gluck) **16**:128
"For John Clare" (Ashbery) **26**:125
"For John, Who Begs Me Not to Enquire Further" (Sexton) **2**:347, 350, 357
"For Johnny Pole on the Forgotten Beach" (Sexton) **2**:349-50, 353
"For Julia in Nebraska" (Rich) **5**:385
"For Koras and Balafons" (Senghor) **25**:231
For Lizzie and Harriet (Lowell) **3**:224, 226
"For M." (Zagajewski) **27**:396
"For Malcolm, a Year After" (Knight) **14**:38
"For marilyn m" (Bukowski) **18**:22
"For Memory" (Rich) **5**:395
"For Miriam" (Tomlinson) **17**:336-37, 349
"For Mr. Death Who Stands with His Door Open" (Sexton) **2**:367, 372
"For My Brother" (Song) **21**:331, 341
"For My Brother Reported Missing in Action, 1943" (Merton) **10**:331-32, 342, 349
"For My Daughter" (Wright) **14**:348, 355, 362
"For My Lady" (Sanchez) **9**:209, 225
"For My Lover, Returning to His Wife" (Sexton) **2**:353, 372
"For My Mothers" (Gluck) **16**:132, 138, 149
"For My People" (Walker) **20**:272, 274, 280-81, 283, 285, 289, 294
For My People (Walker) **20**:274-76, 281-83, 285-86, 289, 292-93
"For My Son on the Highways of His Mind" (Kumin) **15**:192, 201
"For New England" (Wright) **14**:340, 362
"For Precision" (Wright) **14**:342-43, 347
"For Proserpine" (Kunitz) **19**:175
"For Proust" (Merrill) **28**:248
"For Rhoda" (Schwartz) **8**:282
"For Robert Frost" (Kinnell) **26**:284
"For Sale" (Lowell) **3**:219-20
"For Saundra" (Giovanni) **19**:114-15, 139
"For Sidney Bechet" (Larkin) **21**:227
"For Signs" (Gunn) **26**:204, 214
"For the Better" (Finch) **21**:181
"for the blind" (Clifton) **17**:26
"For the Boy Who Was Dodger Point Lookout Fifteen Years Ago" (Snyder) **21**:288
"For the Children" (Snyder) **21**:298
"For the Commander of The Eliza" (Heaney) **18**:186-87, 200, 207
"For the Conjunction of Two Planets" (Rich) **5**:360

"For the Felling of a Tree in Harvard Yard" (Rich) **5**:359
For the Guitar (Borges)
See *Para las seis cuerdas*
"For the Kent State Martyrs" (Brutus) **24**:119
"For the Marriage of Faustus and Helen" (Crane) **3**:81, 83, 90, 92, 95, 97
"For the One Who Would Not Take His Life in His Hands" (Schwartz) **8**:313
"For the One Who Would Not Take Man's Life In His Hands" (Schwartz) **8**:301, 313
"For the Prisoners in South Africa" (Brutus) **24**:111
"For the Quaternary Age" (Wright) **14**:373
"For the Record" (Lorde) **12**:140
"For the Restoration of My Dear Husband from a Burning Ague" (Bradstreet) **10**:26, 62
"For the Revolutionary Outburst by Black People" (Baraka) **4**:39
"For the Stranger" (Forche) **10**:144, 157, 168
For the Time Being (Auden) **1**:17, 23, 34, 36-7
"For the Union Dead" (Lowell) **3**:211-14, 223-24, 226, 232
For the Union Dead (Lowell) **3**:211-14, 223-24, 226, 232
"For the Word is Flesh" (Kunitz) **19**:147, 152
"For the Year of the Insane" (Sexton) **2**:363
"For Those Sisters & Brothers in Gallup" (Ortiz) **17**:232
"For Tom Postell, Dead Black Poet" (Baraka) **4**:10-11, 19
"For Two Girls Setting Out in Life" (Viereck) **27**:262
"For Two Lovers in the Year 2075 in the Canadian Woods" (Meredith) **28**:199
"For Unborn Malcolms" (Sanchez) **9**:218-19, 224, 233
For You: Poems (Carruth) **10**:83
Force of Light (Celan)
See *Lichtzwang*
"The Force That through the Green Fuse Drives the Flower" (Thomas) **2**:384-84
"Forcing House" (Roethke) **15**:295
"Ford Madox Ford" (Lowell) **3**:219
"Forebears" (Pavese)
See "Antenati"
"Foreign Flower" (Tagore)
See "Videshi phul"
"Foreigner" (Page) **12**:170
The Forerunner (Gibran) **9**:69, 71, 75, 79
"Forerunners" (Emerson) **18**:79, 84
"Forest" (Swenson) **14**:268
"The Forest" (Wright) **14**:348, 361
The Forest (Jonson) **17**:158-59, 169, 180, 194
"The Forest Hymn" (Bryant) **20**:3, 14, 18, 23, 29, 33
The Forest I (Jonson) **17**:180, 194
The Forest II (Jonson) **17**:158-59, 161, 165, 169, 182, 189, 202-06, 209, 214
The Forest II (Jonson) **17**:163
The Forest III (Jonson) **17**:158-59, 161, 163, 192, 210
Forest Leaves (Harper) **21**:185
Forest Moon (Paz)
See *Luna silvestre*
"The Forest of Wild Thyme" (Noyes) **27**:116
The Forest of Wild Thyme (Noyes) **27**:139
"Forest Path" (Ishikawa)
See "Mori no michi"
"The Forest Path" (Wright) **14**:339
The Forest VII (Jonson) **17**:176
The Forest XI (Jonson) **17**:159, 172
The Forest XII (Jonson) **17**:158, 160, 214, 217
The Forest XIII (Jonson) **17**:158, 160, 163, 192
The Forest XV (Jonson) **17**:162, 171-72
"Forêt dans la Hache" (Breton) **15**:52
"La foret merveilleuse ou je vis donne un bal" (Apollinaire) **7**:3
"The Forge" (Heaney) **18**:200, 221, 223
"Le forgeron" (Rimbaud) **3**:277, 283, 285
"Forget not Yet" (Wyatt) **27**:315, 324, 357
"For-Get-Me-Not" (Stein) **18**:313
"The Forging" (Borges)
See "Forjadura"
"forgiving my father" (Clifton) **17**:18
"Forgotten Arietta" (Verlaine)
See "Ariettes oubliées"
"A Forgotten Miniature" (Hardy) **8**:137-38
"Forgotten Song" (Ashbery) **26**:162
"Forjadura" (Borges) **22**:72
"The Forlorn Sea" (Smith) **12**:326
"Form without Love" (Aleixandre) **15**:18-19, 22-3
"Forming Child" (Ortiz) **17**:225, 231
"Forms of the Earth at Abiquiu" (Momaday) **25**:201-203
"The Forsaken" (Lowell) **13**:62
"A Forsaken Garden" (Swinburne) **24**:324, 338, 344
"The Forsaken Merman" (Arnold) **5**:5-8, 12-13, 17-18, 34-5, 38-9, 42, 49
Forslin (Aiken) **26**:6-7, 27
"Forties Flick" (Ashbery) **26**:149
"The Fortress" (Sexton) **2**:362
"Fortunatus Nimium" (Bridges) **28**:73, 75, 89-90
"Fortune..." (Ferlinghetti) **1**:183
"Fortune-Telling" (Tsvetaeva)
See "Gadan'e"
"Forty Singing Seamen" (Noyes) **27**:133
Forty Singing Seamen and Other Poems (Noyes) **27**:133
45 Mercy Street (Sexton) **2**:356, 359, 367, 374
XLI Poems (Cummings) **5**:104
"Forward Observers" (Stryk) **27**:203
"Fosterling" (Heaney) **18**:259
"Les foules" (Baudelaire) **1**:59
Found Objects (Zukofsky) **11**:346
"Founders Day. A Secular Ode on the Ninth Jubilee of Eton College" (Bridges) **28**:67, 71
"The Fountain" (Bryant) **20**:4, 43, 47
"The Fountain" (Wordsworth) **4**:374, 399
"A Fountain, a Bottle, a Donkey's Ear and Some Books" (Frost) **1**:194
"The Fountain of Ammannati" (Stryk) **27**:183-84, 192
"Fountain Piece" (Swenson) **14**:263-64
"The Fountains of Aix" (Swenson) **14**:250, 255, 285-86
"IV" (Joyce) **22**:145, 163, 166, 168, 173
"The Four Ages" (Nemerov) **24**:293-24, 297
"The Four Ages of Man" (Bradstreet) **10**:4, 17, 30, 45
"Four Auguries" (Atwood) **8**:27-8
"The Four Brothers" (Sandburg) **2**:302
"Four Canzones (1957-1961)" (Okigbo) **7**:247-48
"Four Dancers at an Irish Wedding" (Gallagher) **9**:37
"4 daughters" (Clifton) **17**:25
"Four Dheetziyama Poems" (Ortiz) **17**:225
"The Four Elements" (Bradstreet) **10**:11, 17, 41
"Four Evasions" (Atwood) **8**:24, 27-8
"Four Eyes" (Ondaatje) **28**:292, 329, 331
"Four for Sir John Davies" (Roethke) **15**:263, 273-74, 286
"The Four Gospels" (Goethe) **5**:229
"Four in a Family" (Rukeyser) **12**:223
"Four Kantian Lyrics" (Tomlinson) **17**:311, 342
The Four Men (Brooke) **24**:89
"The Four Monarchies" (Bradstreet) **10**:4-5, 17-18, 20-1, 27, 31, 33-4, 40, 46-7
"Four Notions of Love and Marriage" (Momaday) **25**:189
"Four O'Clock Summer Street" (McGuckian) **27**:82, 90
"4 Other Countries" (Zukofsky) **11**:348
"Four Poems from New Zealand" (Wright) **14**:377
"Four Preludes on Playthings of the Wind" (Sandburg) **2**:316, 340
The Four Quartets (Eliot) **5**:162-65, 174, 178-80, 182, 186, 196, 198, 200, 205-06, 208, 210-11
"The Four Seasons of the Year" (Bradstreet) **10**:17, 44
"Four Sides to a House" (Lowell) **13**:61
"Four Sonnets" (Nemerov) **24**:256
"The Four Sorrows" (Marie de France)
See "Le Chaitivel"
"4/25/89 late" (Clifton) **17**:30
The Four Years' Notebook (Montale)
See *Quaderno de quattro anni*
The Four Zoas: The Torments of Love and Jealousy in the Death and Judgement of Albion the Ancient Man (Blake) **12**:13-21, 25-9, 32, 35-8, 41, 47, 49-50, 60-4, 73
"XIV" (Joyce) **22**:138, 145, 160, 163-66, 168-70
"14 Dec." (Ammons) **16**:22
Fourteenth Olympian (Pindar)
See *Olympian 14*
"Fourth Georgic" (Vergil) **12**:365, 371
"Fourth Meditation" (Roethke) **15**:272, 278
"The Fourth Month of the Landscape Architect" (Rich) **5**:384
Fourth Nemean (Pindar)
See *Nemean 4*
"Fourth of July" (Hughes) **7**:119
"Fourth of July in Maine" (Lowell) **3**:226
Fourth Pythian (Pindar)
See *Pythian 4*
Fourth Quarter and Other Poems (Wright) **14**:372-75
The Fourth Symphony (Bely)
See *Kubok metelej: Chetviortiia simfoniia*
Fowre Hymnes (Spenser) **8**:332, 334, 337, 390
"The Fox" (Tomlinson) **17**:327
"Fox" (Wright) **14**:376
"Fox Trot" (Sitwell) **3**:297, 303
"Foxes' Moon" (Tomlinson) **17**:343
"Foxhunt" (Hughes) **7**:166
"Fra Lippo Lippi" (Browning) **2**:37, 88, 95
Fra Rupert (Landor) **5**:95
"Fragment" (Ashbery) **26**:118, 125, 135, 144, 156-157
"A Fragment" (Bryant)
See "Inscription for the Entrance into a Wood"
"Fragment" (Finch) **21**:140, 172
"Fragment" (Johnson) **24**:142, 148
"Fragment: As Bronze may be much Beautified" (Owen) **19**:352
"Fragment from Correspondence" (Nemerov) **24**:298
"Fragment: I saw his Round Mouth's Crimson" (Owen) **19**:352
"Fragment of an 'Antigone'" (Arnold) **5**:48-9
"Fragment Thirty-Six" (H. D.) **5**:268, 270
"Fragments du narcisse" (Valery) **9**:348, 365-66, 372, 393, 395-96
"Fragments from a Poem to be entitled 'The Sentimental Exile'" (Brooke) **24**:68, 80, 89
"Fragments from the Deluge" (Okigbo) **7**:231, 246, 255
"Fragoletta" (Swinburne) **24**:361-62
"Frailty" (Herbert) **4**:135
"Le Fraisne" (Marie de France) **22**:241, 248, 258, 269, 271-72, 275, 277-78, 282
"Frame" (Rich) **5**:396
Frameless Windows, Squares of Light (Song) **21**:334, 344, 345-46
"Frammento alla morte" (Pasolini) **17**:295
"France" (Sassoon) **12**:276, 278
"France: An Ode" (Coleridge)
See "Ode to France"
La Franciade (Ronsard)
See *Les quatre premiers livres de la Franciade*
"Francie's Fingers" (Wylie) **23**:324
"Francis Furini" (Browning) **2**:72, 75, 84-5
"Francisco, I'll Bring You Red Carnations" (Levine) **22**:225

Cumulative Title Index

"La frangia dei capelli" (Montale) **13**:111, 128
"Franklin's Tale" (Chaucer) **19**:11-13, 15, 17, 27, 33, 47, 53, 61
"Franz Schubert A Press Conference" (Zagajewski) **27**:382, 385, 401
"Fraud" (Blok) **21**:37
"Fraulein Reads Instructive Rhymes" (Kumin) **15**:180
"Frederick Douglass" (Dunbar) **5**:131, 134, 143
"Frederick Douglass" (Hayden) **6**:176, 183, 188, 196, 199
"Free" (McKay) **2**:225
"Free Fantasia: Tiger Flowers" (Hayden) **6**:194-95
"Free Labor" (Harper) **21**:217-18
"Free Thoughts" (Blok) **21**:31
"The Freebooters" (Cardenal)
See "Los filibusteros"
"Freedman" (Heaney) **18**:205
"Freedom" (Hughes) **1**:252
"Freedom New Hampshire" (Kinnell) **26**:236, 238, 242, 284, 289
"Freedom Train" (Hughes) **1**:244
Freedom under Parole (Paz)
See *Libertad bajo palabra*
"Freedom's Plow" (Hughes) **1**:250, 258
The Freeing of the Dust (Levertov) **11**:197-98, 213
"Freeing the Boat" (Tu Fu) **9**:320
"Freezing" (Meredith) **28**:177
"La frégate 'La Sérieuse'" (Vigny) **26**:411
"A French Poem" (Merton) **10**:337
"French Poems" (Ashbery) **26**:118
The French Revolution (Blake) **12**:13, 25, 63
"A French Rooster" (Stein) **18**:313
"Frente al Oxford" (Guillen) **23**:126
"Frenzy" (Sexton) **2**:368
"Fresh Stain" (Gallagher) **9**:62, 64
Fresko-Sonett (Heine) **25**:160
"Fresne" (Marie de France)
See "Le Fraisne"
"Friar's Tale" (Chaucer) **19**:11, 13-14
"Friday the Thirteenth" (Ginsberg) **4**:75
"Friday: The Toilette: Lydia" (Montagu) **16**:338, 347-49
"The Friend" (Smith) **12**:318
"The Friend of Grandmother Speranza" (Gozzano)
See "L'amica di nonna speranza"
"The Friend of the Fourth Decade" (Merrill) **28**:220, 221, 269
"Friend Who Has Been Reading Jacques Lacan" (Hass) **16**:199
"The Friend Who Is Sleeping" (Pavese)
See "Adventures"
"Friends" (Ashbery) **26**:145
"Friends" (Sexton) **2**:365
"Friendship" (Stryk) **27**:204, 208
"Friendship Between Ephelia and Ardelia" (Finch) **21**:164
"The Frightened Man" (Bogan) **12**:86
The Frightening World (Blok) **21**:25
"Frimaire" (Lowell) **13**:97
"Friso" (Dario) **15**:112
"Frisson" (Gautier) **18**:164
"A Frivolous Conversation" (Milosz) **8**:194
"Frog Autumn" (Plath) **1**:388
"The Frog Prince" (Smith) **12**:305, 323, 341
"Froid jaune" (Tzara) **27**:227
"A Frolick" (Herrick) **9**:103
"From a Daybook" (Swenson) **14**:273
"From a Notebook" (Merrill) **28**:248
"From a Notebook, October '68--May '69" (Levertov) **11**:176, 180, 195
"From a Survivor" (Rich) **5**:360
"From a Tower" (Montale)
See "Da una torre"
"From a Train Window" (Millay) **6**:214
"From an Old House in America" (Rich) **5**:373-74, 394
"From Ancient Fangs" (Viereck) **27**:263
"From Another Sore Fit" (Bradstreet) **10**:61-2
From Feathers to Iron (Day Lewis) **11**:123-24, 128-30, 135, 138-39, 142, 148-52
"From Grants to Gallup, New Mexico" (Ortiz) **17**:233
"From House to Home" (Rossetti) **7**:260-1, 276, 282, 284, 290
"From Memory" (Forche) **10**:135
"From Memory" (Zagajewski) **27**:396
"From *Morpheus*" (H. D.) **5**:270
"From My Diary, July, 1914" (Owen) **19**:338, 343, 346
"From My Notes for a Series of Lectures on Murder" (Smith) **12**:343
From Sand Creek: Rising in This Heart Which Is Our America (Ortiz) **17**:222, 230, 234, 239-240
From Snow and Rock, from Chaos: Poems, 1965-1972 (Carruth) **10**:71, 91
"From Superstition" (Pasternak) **6**:260
"From the Bridge" (Alegria)
"From the Cave" (Lorde) **12**:143
"From the Childhood of Jesus" (Pinsky) **27**:164, 175
"From the Coptic" (Smith) **12**:313-14
"From the Corpse Woodpiles, from the Ashes" (Hayden) **6**:194-95, 198
"From the Crest" (Berry) **28**:43
"From the Cupola" (Merrill) **28**:222, 223, 226, 228, 234, 235, 250, 257, 270
From the Cutting Room Floor (Merrill) **28**:269
"From the Dark Tower" (Cullen) **20**:57-58, 63, 70, 76
"From the Dressing-Room" (McGuckian) **27**:98
"From the Eleventh Finger" (Wakoski) **15**:350
From the First Nine (Merrill) **28**:263
"From the First Underworld" (McGuckian) **27**:105
"From the Frontier of Writing" (Heaney) **18**:231-32
"From the Garden" (Sexton) **2**:351
"From the House of Yemanjá" (Lorde) **12**:151
"From the Lives of Things" (Zagajewski) **27**:389
"From the Motorway" (Tomlinson) **17**:354-55
"From the Rising of the Sun" (Milosz)
See "From Where the Sun Rises"
From the Rising of the Sun (Milosz)
See *Gdziewschodzi stonce i kedy zapada*
"From the Same" (Belloc) **24**:32
"From *The School Anthology: Albert Frolov*" (Brodsky) **9**:4
"From the Seacoast" (Tsvetaeva)
See "S morya"
From the Sick-Bed (Tagore)
See *Rogsajyae*
"From 'The Snow Lamp'" (Hayden) **6**:194-95
"From the Surface" (Pinsky) **27**:145
"From the Top of the Stairs" (Zagajewski) **27**:382
"From the Wave" (Gunn) **26**:196-197, 204, 215
"From the Wellington Museum" (Wright) **14**:377
"From the White Place" (Song) **21**:331, 340
From Threshold to Threshold (Celan)
See *Von Schwelle zu Schwelle*
"From Where the Sun Rises" (Milosz) **8**:203-05
From Where the Sun Rises to Where It Sets (Milosz)
See *Gdziewschodzi stonce i kedy zapada*
"Frondes Agrestes" (Tomlinson) **17**:315, 359
"Front Door Soliloquy" (Graves) **6**:143
"Front Lines" (Snyder) **21**:297, 319
"Front the Ages with a Smile" (Masters) **1**:335
"Frontispiece" (Swenson) **14**:249, 253
"Die Fro¨sche von Bikini" (Enzensberger) **28**:150
"Frost at Midnight" (Coleridge) **11**:51, 53, 57-8, 84, 89, 97, 100, 102-04
"The Frost of Death Was on the Pane" (Dickinson) **1**:104
"Frost-Bamboo Ranges" (Wang Wei) **18**:362
"Frosty Night" (Graves) **6**:141
"The Frozen City" (Nemerov) **24**:255
"The Frozen Greenhouse" (Hardy) **8**:92
Das Frühwerk (Celan) **10**:121
"Fruit" (Zagajewski) **27**:394
"Fruit of the Flower" (Cullen) **20**:52-53, 86
"The Fruit Shop" (Lowell) **13**:78
"Fruitlands" (Toomer) **7**:323
"Frustration" (Parker) **28**:362
"Fuga" (Pasolini) **17**:264
"The Fugitive" (Lermontov) **18**:282
"The Fugitive" (Stryk) **27**:198
Fugitive (Tagore)
See *Palataka*
"The Fugitive's Wife" (Harper) **21**:206
"El fugitivo" (Neruda) **4**:292
"Fuite d'Enfance" (Smith) **12**:325, 344
"Fulfilment" (Pasternak) **6**:267
"Full Circle" (Viereck) **27**:267-68
"Full Fathom Five" (Plath) **1**:388-89
"Full Moon" (Graves) **6**:136, 151
"Full Moon" (Hayden) **6**:187, 194-95
"Full Moon" (Wylie) **23**:322
"Full Moon and Little Frieda" (Hughes) **7**:137, 142, 168
"Full Moon New Guinea" (Shapiro) **25**:325
"Full Well Yt Maye be Sene" (Wyatt) **27**:316
"Fullness of Time" (Tomlinson) **17**:321
"Fumatori di carta" (Pavese) **13**:225, 227
"Fundamental Disagreement with Two Contemporaries" (Rexroth) **20**:196
"The Funeral" (Brooks) **7**:53, 87
"The Funeral of Bobo" (Brodsky) **9**:8
"The Funeral of Youth" (Brooke) **24**:53, 78
"Funeral Rites" (Heaney) **18**:203-4, 210-11
"The Funerall" (Donne) **1**:130
"A Funerall Elegie" (Donne) **1**:146-47, 154-58; **24**:151, 184-85, 188
"The Funerall Rites of the Rose" (Herrick) **9**:126
"Fünf Gesänge" (Rilke) **2**:265-69
"Funnel" (Sexton) **2**:345, 350
"Für die Mouche" (Heine) **25**:148
Die Furie des Verschwindens (Enzensberger) **28**:150, 159, 161, 163
"The Furies" (Masters) **1**:329, 343
"The Furies" (Sexton) **2**:367
"Furious Versions" (Lee) **24**:240, 243, 248, 251
"The Furious Voyage" (Graves) **6**:130, 143
"The Furniture of a Woman's Mind" (Swift) **9**:295
"Fürstin" (Goethe) **5**:249
"Further Arrivals" (Atwood) **8**:36, 39
A Further Range (Frost) **1**:195-97, 202
The Fury of Disappearance (Enzensberger)
See *Die Furie des Verschwindens*
"Fury Of Rain" (Harjo) **27**:66
"The Fury of Sundays" (Sexton) **2**:367, 373
"The Fury of the Cocks" (Sexton) **2**:371
"Fuscello teso" (Montale) **13**:134
"Les fusillés" (Hugo) **17**:101
"Futility" (Owen) **19**:330, 342, 347, 359, 365-68
"The Future" (Arnold) **5**:18, 43-5
"Future and Past" (Browning) **6**:16
"The Future Life" (Bryant) **20**:4, 9
"Future Present" (Shapiro) **25**:324
"Futuro" (Guillen) **23**:99
"Fuzzy-Wuzzy" (Kipling) **3**:156, 158, 167, 186-87
"Gadan'e" (Tsvetaeva) **14**:312-14
"Gaiety" (Sitwell) **3**:294
"Gairmscoile" (MacDiarmid) **9**:188-89, 193
"Gakusei" (Ishikawa) **10**:215
"Galatea Encore" (Brodsky) **9**:25, 27
"Galerías Preciadas" (Fuertes) **27**:13-4
"Galla Placidia" (Ekeloef) **23**:60
"The Gallery" (Marvell) **10**:271, 300
"The Galley" (Kipling) **3**:182
"The Galley-Slave" (Kipling) **3**:157
"Gallo cedrone" (Montale) **13**:108, 111
"The Galloping Cat" (Smith) **12**:311
"The Game" (Gluck) **16**:124

"Game after Supper" (Atwood) **8**:3
"Game Mistress" (Cassian) **17**:11
"A Game of Monopoly in Chavannes" (Kumin) **15**:211
"Gangrene" (Levine) **22**:212
"Ganymed" (Goethe) **5**:247, 254
"Ganymede" (Holderlin) **4**:148, 166
"The Gap" (Tomlinson) **17**:347
"Garage Sale" (Shapiro) **25**:322
"Garbo at the Gaumont" (McGuckian) **27**:107, 109-111
"The Garden" (Gluck) **16**:130, 150-51, 168
"Garden" (H. D.) **5**:275, 303
"The Garden" (Marvell) **10**:266, 268, 271-73, 277, 283-85, 287-92, 294, 297, 311, 313-14, 318
"The Garden" (Montale) **13**:113, 151
See "L'orto"
The Garden (Gluck) **16**:129
"Garden Abstract" (Crane) **3**:81
"Garden by Moonlight" (Lowell) **13**:64, 98
"The Garden in September" (Bridges) **28**:83
"The Garden of Boccaccio's" (Coleridge) **11**:104-09
"the garden of delight" (Clifton) **17**:36
"The Garden in September" (Bridges) **28**:67
"The Garden of Earthly Delights" (Milosz) **8**:181, 209
"The Garden of Gethsemane" (Pasternak) **6**:285
"Garden of Love" (Blake) **12**:7, 33
"Garden of Nightingales" (Blok)
See "The Nightingale Garden"
"The Garden of Proserpine" (Swinburne) **24**:345
The Garden of the Prophet (Gibran) **9**:75
"The Garden Party" (Belloc) **24**:27
"The Garden Seat" (Hardy) **8**:100
"The Garden Sees" (Elytis) **21**:132
"The Garden Wall" (Levertov) **11**:169
"Gardener" (Graves) **6**:151
Gardeners and Astronomers (Sitwell) **3**:321
"The Gardener's Daughter" (Tennyson) **6**:354
"Gare" (Tzara) **27**:223-24
"Gare au bord de la mer" (Laforgue) **14**:76
"Gareth and Lynette" (Tennyson) **6**:373, 376
The Garland of Laurel (Skelton) **25**:350-51, 353, 356, 369-75
Garland of Songs (Tagore)
See *Gitimalya*
"The Gate at the Center" (Olson) **19**:283
"The Gate in His Head" (Ondaatje) **28**:294, 296, 322, 327, 334
"The Gates" (Rukeyser) **12**:224
The Gates (Rukeyser) **12**:220, 222, 225
The Gates of Paradise (Blake) **12**:46
"The Gates of the Arsenal" (Milosz) **8**:191
The Gates of Wrath: Rhymed Poems, 1948-1952 (Ginsberg) **4**:55-7, 63, 79, 91
"The Gateway" (Wright) **14**:338, 346
The Gateway (Wright) **14**:334, 336-38, 341, 345-46, 349, 354, 374
"Gather Ye Rosebuds while Ye May" (Herrick)
See "To the Virgins, to Make Much of Time"
"Gathering Apricots" (Milosz) **8**:212, 215
"Gathering Leaves" (Frost) **1**:218
Gathering the Tribes (Forche) **10**:132-35, 137, 141-43, 145, 148, 152, 156, 158, 165-66, 168-69
"GATSBY'S THEORY OF AESTHETICS" (Baraka) **4**:19, 24
Gaudete (Hughes) **7**:154-58, 161-65, 171
Gavriiliada (Pushkin) **10**:364, 410-12
The Gavriiliada (Pushkin)
See *Gavriiliada*
"Gay Chaps at the Bar" (Brooks) **7**:70, 73, 89
"Gazing on the Great Peak" (Tu Fu) **9**:329
"Gazing on the Peak" (Tu Fu) **9**:328
"Gde, vysokaya, tvoy tsyganyonok" (Akhmatova) **2**:12
Gdziewschodzi stonce i kedy zapada (Milosz) **8**:174-75, 178, 186, 188, 195-97, 206-07
"Le géant blanc lépreux du paysage" (Tzara) **27**:226-28
"geburtsanzeige " (Enzensberger) **28**:135
"Geddondillo" (Nash) **21**:269
Gedichte (Trakl) **20**:245, 250
Gedichte, 1853 und 1854 (Heine) **25**:146, 161, 178
Gedichte 1938-1944 (Celan) **10**:121-24, 129
Gedichte: 1955-1970 (Enzensberger) **28**:159
"Geese Gone Beyond" (Snyder) **21**:308
"gegen die la¨mmer " (Enzensberger) **28**:135
"Gegen-Strophen" (Rilke) **2**:295
"Gehazi" (Kipling) **3**:171, 182
"Gekishi: Chimmoku no koe" (Ishikawa) **10**:213
"The Genealogy of My Hero" (Pushkin)
See "Rodoslovnaya Moego Geroya"
"The General" (Sassoon) **12**:268
"General Bloodstock's Lament for England" (Graves) **6**:143
"The General Elliot" (Graves) **6**:150
"General Prologue" (Chaucer) **19**:13, 15, 23-5, 34-6, 43-5, 50-2, 54, 60
General Song (Neruda)
See *Canto general de Chile*
"General William Booth Enters into Heaven" (Lindsay) **23**:267, 276-78, 289, 294, 297
General William Booth Enters into Heaven, and Other Poems (Lindsay) **23**:264, 278, 282-83, 292
"The Generals" (Ferlinghetti) **1**:183
"Generation" (Clifton) **17**:26
"Generation" (Page) **12**:177
"Generation III" (Lorde) **12**:143
Generations: A Memoir (Clifton) **17**:23, 25-27, 32
"The Generations of Men" (Frost) **1**:193
"Una generazione" (Pavese) **13**:213
"Genesis" (Knight) **14**:52
"Genesis" (Roethke) **15**:291-96
"Genesis" (Shapiro) **25**:284
Genesis: Book One (Schwartz) **8**:283-84, 301, 304, 308-10
"Genesis of After the Cries of the Birds" (Ferlinghetti) **1**:186
"Genetic Expedition" (Dove) **6**:122
"Geneva Restored" (Tomlinson) **17**:311, 359
"Genevieve" (Lorde) **12**:140
"Genevieve and Alexandra" (Robinson) **1**:470
"Génie" (Rimbaud) **3**:261-62
"Le génie dans l'obsurité" (Lamartine) **16**:290
"Genie's Prayer under the Kitchen Sink" (Dove) **6**:123
"Gente che non capisce" (Pavese) **13**:218, 227
"Gentle Lady" (Joyce)
See "XXVIII"
"The Gentleman from Shallot" (Bishop) **3**:37
"The Gentleman of Shallot" (Bishop)
See "The Gentleman from Shallot"
"Gentleman-Rankers" (Kipling) **3**:161
"Gentlemen, I Address You Publicly" (Rexroth) **20**:184
"The Gentlest Lady" (Parker) **28**:362
"Geographers" (Shapiro) **25**:270
"The Geographic Center" (Kumin) **15**:215-16
Geography III (Bishop) **3**:48-9, 63, 66, 69, 73, 75
The Geography of Lograire (Merton) **10**:334-35, 338, 348, 351
"George Washington and the Invention of Dynamite" (Wakoski) **15**:358
"George Washington and the Loss of His Teeth" (Wakoski) **15**:357
The George Washington Poems (Wakoski) **15**:324, 357-58
"George Washington: the Whole Man" (Wakoski) **15**:359
"Georgeline" (Rose) **13**:236
"Georgia Dusk" (Toomer) **7**:310, 319-20, 334
Georgics (Vergil) **12**:358-61, 364-66, 370-71, 373-77, 383, 385-86, 391-92
"Geraldine" (Bronte) **8**:67, 73-4
"Germanien" (Holderlin) **4**:149
Germany: A Winter's Tale (Heine)
See *Deutschland: Ein Wintermärchen*
Germany, Germany among Other Things (Enzensberger)
See *Deutschland, Deutschland unter anderm*
"Gerontion" (Day Lewis) **11**:151
"Gerontion" (Eliot) **5**:160-62, 165, 171, 173, 183-85, 189, 195-97, 204, 209
Gesammelte Werke (Celan) **10**:100-01, 124
"Gesang der Geister über den Wassern" (Goethe) **5**:239
"Gesang des Abgeschiedenen" (Trakl) **20**:240-41
"Gesta maximalista" (Borges) **22**:92
"Gethsemane" (Kipling) **3**:171
"Gethsemani" (Lamartine) **16**:297
Gethsemani, Ky. (Cardenal) **22**:103, 125-26
"Getting in the Wood" (Snyder) **21**:300, 302
"Getting There" (Plath) **1**:412
"Getting Through" (Merrill) **28**:248
"gewimmer und firmament" (Enzensberger) **28**:136
"Das Gewitter" (Trakl) **20**:237-38, 251, 257
"The Geysers" (Gunn) **26**:198, 204, 208, 220
"A Ghost" (Baudelaire)
See "Un fantôme"
"Ghost" (Lowell) **3**:203
"Ghost Crabs" (Hughes) **7**:137, 158-59
"The Ghost Hammer" (Pinsky) **27**:158
"A Ghost May Come" (Ginsberg) **4**:74
"Ghost of a Chance" (Rich) **5**:363, 370
"Ghosts" (Sexton) **2**:350
"Ghosts as Cocoons" (Stevens) **6**:297
"The Ghost's Leave-taking" (Plath) **1**:381, 388
"The Ghosts of James and Peirce in Harvard Yard" (Schwartz) **8**:302
"The Ghosts of the Buffaloes" (Lindsay) **23**:275, 279, 287
"The Ghost's Petition" (Rossetti) **7**:273
"Giant Toad" (Bishop) **3**:65
The Giaour: A Fragment of a Turkish Tale (Byron) **16**:91-2
"The Gibber" (Roethke) **15**:262
"Gibson" (Baraka) **4**:30
"Gic to Har" (Rexroth) **20**:193
"Gidget Agonistes" (Ashbery) **26**:137
"The Gift" (Bukowski) **18**:5
"The Gift" (Gluck) **16**:151
"The Gift" (H. D.) **5**:266, 270, 303
"The Gift" (Lee) **24**:240
"Gift" (Milosz) **8**:209
"Gift" (Tagore)
See "Upahar"
"The Gift" (Williams) **7**:371
"Gift for a Believer" (Levine) **22**:223, 225
"The Gift of a Satin Brocade" (Tu Fu) **9**:318
"The Gift of God" (Robinson) **1**:462, 467-68
"The Gift of Harun Al-Rashid" (Yeats) **20**:319
"The Gift of the Sea" (Kipling) **3**:183
"The Gift Outright" (Frost) **1**:212-13, 224
"Gift Poem" (Rukeyser) **12**:231
Gifts at Meeting (Wylie) **23**:320
"Gifts of Rain" (Heaney) **18**:201, 210
"The Gifts of the Terek" (Lermontov) **18**:268, 281, 295
See "Dary Tereka"
"Gigot Sleeves" (McGuckian) **27**:107-109
"Gin" (Levine) **22**:220
"Ginga no jo" (Matsuo Basho) **3**:13
"Ginza Samba" (Pinsky) **27**:175
"Giorno e notte" (Montale) **13**:111
"Giovanni and the Indians" (Page) **12**:168
"Giovanni Franchi" (Loy) **16**:333
Gipsies (Pushkin)
See *Tsygany*
Gipsy Ballads (Lorca)
See *Primer romancero gitano*
"Girl Drowned in a Well" (Garcia Lorca) **3**:139
A Girl in Winter (Larkin) **21**:225, 232
"The girl of live marble" (Gunn) **26**:212

"Girl Powdering Her Neck" (Song) **21**:347
"The Girl the North Wind Brought" (Elytis) **21**:123
"The Girl Who Loves to Shoot" (Smith) **12**:326
"Girls Bathing, Galway, 1965" (Heaney) **18**:224
"Girls in the Plural" (McGuckian) **27**:92-94
"Girl's Song" (Bogan) **12**:90, 100
"Girls Working in Banks" (Shapiro) **25**:306, 322
"Git Dough" (Guillen)
See "Búscate plata"
Gitali (Tagore) **8**:413, 427
Gitanjali (Tagore) **8**:402, 412-14, 416, 418
Gitimalya (Tagore) **8**:413
"Giuseppe Caponsacchi" (Browning) **2**:41
"Give All to Love" (Emerson) **18**:85, 88, 113
"Give and Take" (Meredith) **28**:199
"Give Way, Ye Gates" (Roethke) **15**:252, 261, 298-99, 301-02
Give Your Heart to the Hawks and Other Poems (Jeffers) **17**:135, 142-43, 147
"A Given Grace" (Tomlinson) **17**:309, 316, 335
"Given to Li Po" (Tu Fu) **9**:330
"Givings" (Ammons) **16**:63
Gladiolus (McGuckian) **27**:96
"Gladly Still" (Borges)
See "Jactancia de quietud"
"The Gladness of Nature" (Bryant) **20**:40
"Gladstone Street" (Tomlinson) **17**:319
"The Glance" (Herbert) **4**:132
"Glanmore Sonnets" (Heaney) **18**:198
"Glanmore Sonnets IV" (Heaney) **18**:238
"The Glass" (Olds) **22**:323, 332
"Glass" (Wakoski) **15**:325
"The Glass Air" (Page) **12**:178
The Glass Air (Page) **12**:189-90
"Glazed Glitter" (Stein) **18**:322
"Gleneden's Dream" (Bronte) **8**:67
"Glimpse" (Hughes) **7**:153
"The Global Lobal Blues" (Viereck) **27**:279
"Le gloire" (Lamartine) **16**:276, 298
"The Glory Is fallen Out of" (Cummings) **5**:105
"The Glory of the Day Was in Her Face" (Johnson) **24**:154
The Glory of the Nightingales (Robinson) **1**:472-73, 475, 479, 483
"Glory of Women" (Sassoon) **12**:267
Glossolalia Poéma o zvuke (Bely) **11**:9, 11
"The Glove" (Browning) **2**:29, 38
"Glück der Entfernung" (Goethe) **5**:246
"The Glutton" (Graves) **6**:150
"Gnat-Psalm" (Hughes) **7**:136-37, 159
Gnomes and Occasions (Nemerov) **24**:284-86, 288
"Gnothi Seauton" (Emerson) **18**:97
"Go and Look for Bread" (Guillen)
See "Búscate plata"
"Go burning sighs" (Wyatt) **27**:352
"Go Down Death" (Johnson) **24**:128-29, 139, 144, 156, 164-65, 167, 169
"Go, Fetch to Me a Pint o' Wine" (Burns) **6**:76
"Go Get Money" (Guillen)
See "Búscate plata"
"Goat Ode in Mid-Dive" (Viereck) **27**:295
"Goat's Leaf" (Marie de France)
See "Chevrefoil"
"Gobernador" (Guillen) **23**:127
The Goblet of Blizzards (Bely)
See *Kubok metelej: Chetviortiia simfoniia*
"Goblin Market" (Rossetti) **7**:259, 261, 266, 268, 272-3, 279-80, 282, 288-94, 298-304
Goblin Market, and Other Poems (Rossetti) **7**:259, 261, 279, 296-7
"Goblin Revel" (Sassoon) **12**:240
"God" (Swenson) **14**:281, 281, 286
The God (H. D.) **5**:303
"God and Devil" (Smith) **12**:331
God Desired and Desiring (Jimenez)
See *Dios deseado y deseante: Animal de fondo con numerosos poemas ineditos*
"God Is a Distant, Stately Lover" (Dickinson) **1**:93
"The God of Flowers" (Levertov) **11**:198
"The God of Youth" (Holderlin)
See "Der Gott der Jugend"
"God Speaks" (Smith) **12**:335
"God the Drinker" (Smith) **12**:326-27
"God the Eater" (Smith) **12**:326, 333
"God Works in a Mysterious Way" (Brooks) **7**:74
Godbey (Masters) **1**:339
"The Goddess" (Levertov) **11**:159, 168
"Goddess in the Wood" (Brooke) **24**:57
Godel's Proof, New Poems 1965 (Rexroth) **20**:196
"God-Forgotten" (Hardy) **8**:104, 121
"Godolphin Horne Who Was Cursed with the Sin of Pride and Became a Boot-Black" (Belloc) **24**:26
"Gods" (Cullen) **20**:53
"Gods" (Sexton) **2**:373
"The Gods Are Here" (Toomer) **7**:336
"God's Education" (Hardy) **8**:121
"God's Funeral" (Hardy) **8**:131
"God's Providence" (Herrick) **9**:91
God's Trombones: Seven Negro Sermons in Verse (Johnson) **24**:128-29, 132-33, 141, 143-44, 149, 152-56, 159, 161, 164-70
"God's World" (Millay) **6**:205, 215
"God's World" (Pasternak) **6**:268-69
Goethe's Works (Goethe) **5**:223
"Gog" (Hughes) **7**:126, 139
"The Go-goat" (Pavese)
See "Il Dio-Caprone"
"The Going" (Hardy) **8**:91, 113, 118, 133-35
"Going" (Larkin) **21**:227, 242
"Going Away" (Hagiwara Sakutaro)
See "Ryojo"
Going for the Rain (Ortiz) **17**:222, 226-227, 231-232, 238, 244
"Going from the Capital to Feng-hsien, Singing My Feelings" (Tu Fu) **9**:332
"Going To and Fro" (Lowell) **3**:215
"Going to Horse Flats" (Jeffers) **17**:141
"Going to School" (Shapiro) **25**:291, 320, 326
Going to War with All My Relations: New and Selected Poems (Rose) **13**:242
"Gold and Black" (Ondaatje) **28**:328
The Gold Cell (Olds) **22**:314-16, 318-21, 324, 326, 328
"Gold Coast Customs" (Sitwell) **3**:300, 305-06, 308-09, 314, 316, 319-20, 325-26
"Gold Hair" (Browning) **2**:95
Gold in Azure (Bely)
See *Zoloto v lazuri*
"The Gold Key" (Sexton) **2**:364
"The Gold Lily" (Gluck) **16**:170
The Gold of the Tigers: Selected Later Poems (Borges)
See *El oro de los tigres*
"The Golden Age" (Behn) **13**:8, 22, 26, 32-4, 39
"The Golden Boat" (Tagore)
See "Sonar tari"
"Golden Bough" (Wylie) **23**:314
"The Golden Cockerel" (Reisman)
See "Skazka o Zolotom Petushke"
"TH GOLDEN DAWN" (Bissett) **14**:24, 32
"The Golden Echo" (Hopkins) **15**:125, 152
"The golden gates of sleep unbar" (Shelley) **14**:177
"Golden Hair" (Owen) **19**:338
The Golden Hynde and Other Poems (Noyes) **27**:117
"The Golden Net" (Blake) **12**:36
"Golden Silences" (Rossetti) **7**:271
"The Golden Supper" (Tennyson) **6**:374
"The Golden Tortoise" (Dario)
See "La tortuga de oro..."
"Golden Venetian Light" (Olson) **19**:305
"The Golden Whales of California" (Lindsay) **23**:264, 269, 274, 288
"Goldfish" (Bukowski) **18**:5
"goldner schittmusterbogen zur poetischern wiederaufru¨stung" (Enzensberger) **28**:136-37, 141
"The Goldsmith" (Sassoon) **12**:257
"Le golfe de Baïa" (Lamartine) **16**:277, 290, 302
"Le golfe de Genes" (Lamartine) **16**:266
"Golgotha" (Sassoon) **12**:261-62
"Goliath of Gath. 1 Sam. Chap. XVII" (Wheatley) **3**:354-55, 357-61
"Golos proshlogo" (Bely) **11**:24
"El golpe" (Neruda) **4**:288
"Gone" (Heaney) **18**:201
"Gone" (Sandburg) **2**:303, 316
"Good Frend" (H. D.) **5**:297, 302
"Good Friday" (Clampitt) **19**:81, 88
"Good Friday" (Donne)
See "Goodfriday 1613: Riding Westward"
"Good Friday" (Herbert) **4**:120
"Good Friday" (Rossetti) **7**:268, 283
"Good Friday and Easter Morning" (Ammons) **16**:63
"Good Friday: Rex Tragicus, or Christ Going to His Crosse" (Herrick) **9**:109, 121
Good Intentions (Nash) **21**:266
A Good Journey (Ortiz) **17**:224-27, 229-30, 232-33, 240, 244
"The Good Life" (Hughes) **7**:119
"Good Morning, America" (Sandburg) **2**:330
Good Morning America (Sandburg) **2**:318-19, 321, 323
"Good Morning Revolution" (Hughes) **1**:268
Good News About the Earth (Clifton) **17**:16, 22-24, 26, 35
"Good Night" (Williams) **7**:348
A Good Time Was Had by All (Smith) **12**:292, 314-15, 317, 325
Good Times: Poems (Clifton) **17**:16-17, 20-21, 23-24, 26, 31, 35
Good Woman: Poems and a Memoir, 1969-1980 (Clifton) **17**:25-26, 38
"Goodbye!" (Baraka) **4**:11
"Good-bye" (Emerson) **18**:74
"Goodbye" (Kinnell) **26**:292
"Goodbye Christ" (Hughes) **1**:268
"Good-bye to the Mezzogiorno" (Auden) **1**:17
"Goodbye, Unwashed Russia" (Lermontov) **18**:281
"Goodfriday 1613: Riding Westward" (Donne) **1**:139, 158-59
"Goo-dmore-ning(en" (Cummings) **5**:107
"The good-morrow" (Donne) **1**:125, 130-34, 147, 152-54
"Goodnight" (Lee) **24**:241
"The Goodnight" (Ondaatje) **28**:318
"Goody Blake and Harry Gill" (Wordsworth) **4**:381, 414
"The Goose" (Stryk) **27**:203
"The Goose Fish" (Nemerov) **24**:261, 289-90
"Goose Pond" (Kunitz) **19**:178
"Gooseberry Fool" (Clampitt) **19**:86
"Gorbunov and Gorchakov" (Brodsky) **9**:4-6, 10-12, 26-7
"The Gorge" (Stryk) **27**:189, 203
"Gorod" (Pasternak) **6**:264
"Gorodok" (Pushkin) **10**:410
"Gospel" (Dove) **6**:117
"The Gossamers" (Tomlinson) **17**:310, 312
"Gost" (Lermontov) **18**:288
"Gothic Letter on a Hot Night" (Atwood) **8**:24
"Der Gott der Jugend" (Holderlin) **4**:142
"Gott im Mittelalter" (Rilke) **2**:275
"Die Götter Griechenlands" (Heine) **25**:145
Götterdämmerung (Heine) **25**:145
"Das Göttliche" (Goethe) **5**:239
"The Gourd Dancer" (Momaday) **25**:198-99, 214-16, 221
The Gourd Dancer (Momaday) **25**:193-97, 200-202, 205, 212, 216, 219-20
"Le goût du néant" (Baudelaire) **1**:68
"Gow's Watch" (Kipling) **3**:181
"Grabaciones" (Cardenal) **22**:131-32

"Grace" (Emerson) **18**:98
"Grace" (Herbert) **4**:111, 129
"Grace Abounding" (Ammons) **16**:63
Grace Notes (Dove) **6**:120-22
"Grace's House" (Merton) **10**:340-41, 350, 353
Gracias Haus (Merton) **10**:341
Graf Nulin (Pushkin) **10**:366, 386, 390, 400-01
"La Graine" (Perse) **23**:228
"Grainne's Sleep Song" (McGuckian) **27**:82
Grains et issues (Tzara) **27**:241-42, 251-52
"The Grammarian's Funeral" (Browning) **2**:37, 51
El gran zoo (Guillen) **23**:100
"The Grand Canyon" (Merrill) **28**:247, 272
"Grand complainte de la ville de Paris" (Laforgue) **14**:97
"Grand Galop" (Ashbery) **26**:126, 143
"Grand Marshal Kao's Dapple" (Tu Fu) **9**:330
"Le Grand Midi" (Cesaire) **25**:29-30
"The Grand Question Debated" (Swift) **9**:260
"Grand River Marshes" (Masters) **1**:330, 333
Le Grand Testament (Villon)
See *Le Testament*
"Une grande dame" (Verlaine) **2**:430-31
"The Grandfather" (Guillen)
See "El abuelo"
"Grandfather Arthur Winslow" (Lowell) **3**:200
"Grandma We Are Poets" (Clifton) **17**:29-30
"Grandmother in the Garden" (Gluck) **16**:124
"Grandmother Speranza's Friend" (Gozzano)
See "L'amica di nonna speranza"
"Grandmother's Clavichord" (Dario)
See "El clavicordio de la abuela"
"Grandparents" (Lowell) **3**:217-20
"Granite and Steel" (Moore) **4**:259, 261
"Granny and the Golden Bridge" (Alegria) **26**:
"Grant's Tomb Revisited" (Shapiro) **25**:322
"Grape Sherbet" (Dove) **6**:106, 109
"Graph for Action" (Williams) **7**:369
"Grappa in September" (Pavese) **13**:218
"Grappling in the Central Blue" (Kumin) **15**:209-10
"Grasses" (Gunn) **26**:219
"Gratitude" (Lermontov) **18**:281
"Gratitude" (Smart) **13**:361
"The Grauballe Man" (Heaney) **18**:210-11
"A Grave" (Moore) **4**:243, 251
"A Grave Illness" (Page) **12**:199
"Gravelly Run" (Ammons) **16**:29
"Graves" (Sandburg) **2**:303
"Graves Are Made to Waltz On" (Viereck) **27**:258
"Graveyard at Bolinas" (Hass) **16**:196, 209
"The Graveyard by the Sea" (Valery)
See "Le cimetière marin"
"Gray Eyes" (Gallagher) **9**:51
"The Gray Heron" (Kinnell) **26**:259
"The Great Adventure of Max Breuck" (Lowell) **13**:60, 96
"Great American Waterfront Poem" (Ferlinghetti) **1**:188
"Great Canzon" (Rexroth) **20**:190
"The Great Chinese Dragon" (Ferlinghetti) **1**:176
"The Great Elegy for John Donne" (Brodsky) **9**:2, 4, 10, 26
"The Great Explosion" (Jeffers) **17**:130
"The Great Figure" (Williams) **7**:399, 401, 410
"The Great Fillmore Street Buffalo Drive" (Momaday) **25**:221
"The Great Hunt" (Sandburg) **2**:300, 316
"The Great Lament of My Obscurity One" (Tzara) **27**:249
"The Great Lover" (Brooke) **24**:53, 56-7, 59, 65, 78, 87-8
"The Great Mother" (Snyder) **21**:297
"The Great Nebula of Andromeda" (Rexroth) **20**:190
"The Great Palace of Versailles" (Dove) **6**:111
"Great Snoring and Norwich" (Sitwell) **3**:301
"The Great Society, Mark X" (Nemerov) **24**:280
"The Great Sunset" (Jeffers) **17**:130
"Great Things" (Hardy) **8**:112
"Great Unaffected Vampires and the Moon" (Smith) **12**:330-31
The Great Valley (Masters) **1**:329, 332, 342-43
"Greater Love" (Owen) **19**:327, 332, 335, 337, 344, 347, 353-54, 358-59
Greater Testament (Villon)
See *Le Testament*
"The Greater Whiteness" (Swenson) **14**:264
"Greed" (Wakoski) **15**:325, 331, 351-52
Greed (Wakoski) **15**:325, 355-56, 372
Greed, Parts 1 & 2 (Wakoski) **15**:324
Greed, Parts 8, 9, 11 (Wakoski) **15**:345-46
Greed, Parts 5-7 (Wakoski) **15**:347
"The Greed to Be Fulfilled" (Wakoski) **15**:357
"The Greek Women" (Merton) **10**:349
"Green" (Verlaine) **2**:415
"Green Flows the River of Lethe-O" (Sitwell) **3**:309
"Green Grow the Rashes O" (Burns) **6**:67, 74
The Green Helmet (Yeats) **20**:328
"Green Lantern's Solo" (Baraka) **4**:16
"Green Linnaeus" (Zagajewski) **27**:394
"The Green Man" (Olson) **19**:283
"The Green Man: For the Boston Strangler" (Atwood) **8**:7
"Green Memory" (Hughes) **1**:267
"The Green Menagerie" (Viereck) **27**:296
"The Green Parrakeet" (Lowell) **13**:88
"Green Red Brown and White" (Swenson) **14**:261
"Green River" (Bryant) **20**:14, 16, 19, 34, 42
"Green Song" (Sitwell) **3**:312, 317
Green Song (Sitwell) **3**:308, 320
"Green Stream" (Wang Wei) **18**:378
The Green Wave (Rukeyser) **12**:204-05, 209, 213
"Green Ways" (Kunitz) **19**:162
"The Green Well" (Kumin) **15**:215
"Green Wood" (Pavese) **13**:218
"The Greenest Continent" (Stevens) **6**:317-19
"The Greenhouse" (Merrill) **28**:243, 244
"The Greeting" (Tomlinson) **17**:354
"Greetings to the Eagle" (Dario)
See "Salutación al águila"
"Greetings to the Optimist" (Dario)
See "Salutación del optimista"
"Les grenades" (Valery) **9**:387-90, 394, 396
"Grenades Are Not Free" (Sanchez) **9**:235
"Die Grenadiere" (Heine) **25**:140
"Grenouille" (Guillen) **23**:111
"Grenzen der Menschheit" (Goethe) **5**:239
"Los Grernios en el frente" (Neruda) **4**:309
"Gretel in Darkness" (Gluck) **16**:125, 140, 143-44, 149
"The Grey Monk" (Blake) **12**:35-7, 70
"Grey Sparrow" (Levertov) **11**:160
The Grid of Language (Celan)
See *Sprachgitter*
"Grief" (Browning) **6**:41
"A Grief Ago" (Thomas) **2**:405
"Grief for Dead Soldiers" (Hughes) **7**:114-15
"Grief Thief of Time" (Thomas) **2**:405
"Grifel' naja oda" (Mandelstam) **14**:121-22, 129, 148
"Griffin of the Night" (Ondaatje) **28**:329
"The Grindstone" (Frost) **1**:197
"The grocer Hudson Kearley, he" (Belloc) **24**:41
"Grodek" (Trakl) **20**:226, 229, 236-38, 244, 250-51, 253, 255-58, 260
"La Grosse Margot" (Villon)
See "Ballade de la Grosse Margot"
"Grosses Geburtstagsblaublau mit Reimzeug und Assonanz" (Celan) **10**:124
"Grotesques" (Graves) **6**:142, 144
"Grotesques" (Lowell) **13**:77
"The Ground Mist" (Levertov) **11**:160
Ground Work: Before the War (Duncan) **2**:114-17, 119, 125
Ground Work II: In the Dark (Duncan) **2**:119, 127
"Growing Old" (Arnold) **5**:13, 19, 23
"Grown-up" (Millay) **6**:234-35
"Growth" (Levine) **22**:220, 228
"The Growth of Lorraine" (Robinson) **1**:461
The Growth of Love (Bridges) **28**:49, 68, 71, 86-8
"Grub First, Then Ethics" (Auden) **1**:24
"Guadeloupe, W.I." (Guillen) **23**:99
"The Guardian Angel" (Browning) **2**:73
The Guardian of the Flock (Pessoa) **20**:167-68
"A Guerilla Handbook" (Baraka) **4**:16
"Guerre" (Breton) **15**:62
"Guerre" (Rimbaud) **3**:264
"A Guest Arrives" (Tu Fu) **9**:323
"Guía comercial" (Fuertes) **27**:12
"El guía de la abadía" (Fuertes) **27**:30
"A guichard" (Lamartine) **16**:286
"Guide" (Ammons) **16**:20, 34, 57
Guide to Kulchur (Pound) **4**:354, 359
Guide to the Ruins (Nemerov) **24**:255, 260, 264
Guide to the Underworld (Ekeloef) **23**:85
"Guigemar" (Marie de France)
See "Lay of Guigemar"
"Guildeluec and Gualadun" (Marie de France)
See "Eliduc"
Guillén Man-making Words (Guillen) **23**:102, 104, 120
"The Guilty Man" (Kunitz) **19**:160
"Guinness" (Hughes) **7**:123
"Guitar or Moon" (Aleixandre) **15**:20
"Guitare" (Laforgue) **14**:80
"The Gulf" (Levertov) **11**:194
"Gulls" (Hayden) **6**:185, 193-94
"Gulls" (Williams) **7**:378
"Gum" (Toomer) **7**:333
"Gumber" (Belloc) **24**:10
"Gum-Trees Stripping" (Wright) **14**:341-42, 347
"The Gun" (Shapiro) **25**:269, 295, 297, 312
"Gunga Din" (Kipling) **3**:157-58, 179, 187-89, 191
"The Gunman and the Debutante" (Parker) **28**:354
"Guns as Keys: And the Great Gate Swings" (Lowell) **13**:60, 64, 72, 81-2
"The Guttural Muse" (Heaney) **18**:198, 217
"Guy" (Emerson) **18**:111
"Gwin, King of Norway" (Blake) **12**:60
"The Gymnosophist" (Ekeloef) **23**:63, 86
"Gypsies" (Clare) **23**:15
The Gypsies (Pushkin)
See *Tsygany*
Gypsy Balladeer (Garcia Lorca)
See *Primer romancero gitano*
Gypsy Ballads (Garcia Lorca)
See *Primer romancero gitano*
"Gypsy Man" (Hughes) **1**:270
"The Gypsy Nun" (Garcia Lorca)
See "La monja gitana"
"The Gyres" (Yeats) **20**:314, 333
"H" (Rimbaud) **3**:261
"H. O." (Borges) **22**:80-1, 95
"Ha chi je na I Am Coming" (Forche) **10**:134
"The Habit of Perfection" (Hopkins) **15**:136
El habitante y su esperenza (Neruda) **4**:276, 281
"Habits" (Giovanni) **19**:118
"El hacedor" (Borges) **22**:76, 95
El hacedor (Borges) **22**:71
"Hacia la esclava Quisqueya" (Guillen) **23**:125
"Had I not this life decreed" (Villa) **22**:354
"Hafen" (Celan) **10**:105
"Haffār al-qubur" (Gibran) **9**:79
"The Hag Is Astride" (Herrick) **9**:86
"Hagia Sophia" (Merton) **10**:334
"Hago versos, señores" (Fuertes) **27**:49
"Haiku" (Sanchez) **9**:230
"Hailstones" (Heaney) **18**:237
"Haircut" (Shapiro) **25**:288, 318, 322
"Hairy" (Swenson) **14**:253
"Halahal" (Tagore) **8**:405
"Halcyon" (H. D.) **5**:304

"Half of Life" (Holderlin)
See "Hälfte des Lebens"
Half Sun Half Sleep (Swenson) **14**:260, 285
The Halfbreed Chronicles and Other Poems (Rose) **13**:235-36, 239-40
"Half-Caste Girl" (Wright) **14**:351
"Half-dream" (Wright) **14**:373
"The Half-moon Westers Low, My Love" (Housman) **2**:183
"Hälfte des Lebens" (Holderlin) **4**:143, 148, 167
"Halfway" (Ammons) **16**:6
Halfway (Kumin) **15**:179, 192, 198
Halieticon/On Fishing (Ovid)
See *Halieutica*
Halieutica (Ovid) **2**:232, 242, 253
"Hallowe'en" (Aiken) **26**:30, 41, 45, 53
"Hallowe'en" (Burns) **6**:50, 55, 57, 77, 91
"A Halt in the Desert" (Brodsky)
See "Ostanovka v pustyne"
"Hamatreya" (Emerson) **18**:79, 102-4, 111
"The Hambone and the Heart" (Sitwell) **3**:295
"The Ham-Bone of a Saint" (Shapiro) **25**:300
"El hambre" (Guillen) **23**:116
"Hame" (MacDiarmid) **9**:192
"The Hammers" (Lowell) **13**:60, 78
"Ha'nacker Mill" (Belloc) **24**:8, 22
"HAND" (Bissett) **14**:32
"The Hand at Callow Hill Farm" (Tomlinson) **17**:311
"The Hand That Signed the Paper" (Thomas) **2**:388
"Handed Down" (Clampitt) **19**:102
A Handful of Sand (Ishikawa)
See *Ichiaku no suna*
"The Handicapped at Risen Hotel" (Wakoski) **15**:369
"The Handing Down" (Berry) **28**:38
"Handprints" (Rose) **13**:238
"Hands" (Levertov) **11**:159
The Hands of Day (Neruda)
See *Las manos del día*
"Hands, on a Trip to Wisconsin" (Meredith) **28**:175
Handshakes (Illyes)
See *Kezfogasok*
"Hanging in Heaven" (Hagiwara Sakutaro)
See "Hanging in Heaven"
"Hangman's Oak" (Millay) **6**:217
"Hansel and Gretel" (Sexton) **2**:364, 368
"Hapax" (Rexroth) **20**:217, 220
"Happier Dead" (Baudelaire)
See "Le mort joyeux"
"The Happiest Day..." (Poe) **1**:432
"Happiness" (Borges)
See "La dicha"
"Happiness" (Gluck) **16**:131, 144, 151
"Happiness" (Owen) **19**:355
"Happiness" (Sandburg) **2**:308, 332, 334
"Happiness in Herat" (Paz) **1**:361
"The Happy Journalist" (Belloc) **24**:29
"Happy Warrior" (Wordsworth) **4**:391
"Harbor" (Celan) **10**:105
"The Harbor at Seattle" (Hass) **16**:217, 226
"Harbor Dawn" (Crane) **3**:88-9
"The Harbour" (Belloc) **24**:29
"Hard Daddy" (Hughes) **1**:270
Hard Facts: Excerpts (Baraka) **4**:29, 36-9
"Hard Fist" (Ammons) **16**:44
Hard Labor (Pavese)
See *Lavorare stanca*
A Hard Land (Illyes)
See *Nehez fold*
"Hard Lard" (Ammons) **16**:43
"Hard Lines" (Zukofsky) **11**:351
Hard Lines (Nash) **21**:263
"Hard Luck" (Hughes) **1**:255, 269
"Hard Rock Returns to Prison" (Knight) **14**:42, 52
"Hard Times" (Ashbery) **26**:154
"Hard Times" (McKay) **2**:209
"Hard Times Redeemed by Soft Discarded Values" (Viereck) **27**:258-59
"Hard Times Redeemed/By Soft $$Word$$ Values" (Viereck) **27**:
"Hardcastle Crags" (Hughes) **7**:149
"Hardcastle Crags" (Plath) **1**:388
"The Harem at Erechtheion" (Ekeloef) **23**:66
"Harem Trousers" (McGuckian) **27**:90
"Harlem Dance Hall" (Hughes) **1**:247
"The Harlem Dancer" (McKay) **2**:213-14
"Harlem Shadows" (McKay) **2**:213
Harlem Shadows (McKay) **2**:213-14, 227
"Harlem Sweeties" (Hughes) **1**:247
"Harlem Wine" (Cullen) **20**:63
"The Harm of Living" (Montale)
See "Il male di vivere"
"Harmonie du soir" (Baudelaire) **1**:46, 68-9, 71
Les harmonies (Lamartine) **16**:262-67
Harmonies poétiques et religieuses (Lamartine) **16**:279-82, 285-86, 292-93
Harmonies religieuses (Lamartine) **16**:257-62
Harmonium (Stevens) **6**:292, 294-95, 297-98, 300-01, 305, 309-11, 313-15, 329-30, 332-33, 336-37
Harold the Dauntles (Scott) **13**:269, 281, 312
Harold's Leap (Smith) **12**:335
"Harom oreg" (Illyes) **16**:239
"The Harp and the King" (Wright) **14**:343, 347
"The Harp Song of the Dane Women" (Kipling) **3**:171, 183
Harps and Violins (Blok) **21**:25-6
"The Harp-Weaver" (Millay)
See "The Ballad of the Harp-Weaver"
The Harp-Weaver, and Other Poems (Millay) **6**:211, 214-15, 224-25, 228, 230-31, 242
"Harriet Beecher Stowe" (Dunbar) **5**:128
"Harriet Tubman" (Walker) **20**:289
"Harriet's Donkey" (Lowell) **3**:241
"The Harrowing of Hell" (Rilke) **2**:275
"Harry Gill" (Wordsworth)
See "Goody Blake and Harry Gill"
"Harry Ploughman" (Hopkins) **15**:134, 160
"Harry Semen" (MacDiarmid) **9**:180, 196-97
"Hartleap Well" (Wordsworth) **4**:404, 414, 427-28
"Harvest" (Levine) **22**:218
"Harvest" (McGuckian) **27**:100
"Harvest" (Sitwell) **3**:311
"Harvest" (Soto) **28**:377
"The Harvest Bow" (Heaney) **18**:243
"Harvest Festival" (Tomlinson) **17**:328
"The Harvest Knot" (Heaney)
See "The Harvest Bow"
"Harvest Song" (Toomer) **7**:311, 317, 320, 333, 335
"Harzreise im Winter" (Goethe) **5**:247
"Has Your Soul Sipped" (Owen) **19**:346, 352
"Hassan's Journey into the World" (Thomas) **2**:402
"Hate Blows a Bubble of Despair into" (Cummings) **5**:107
"Hate whome ye list" (Wyatt) **27**:325
"Hatem--, i.e. Goethe" (Goethe) **5**:228
"Haunted" (Sassoon) **12**:240
"Haunted Country" (Jeffers) **17**:117
"Haunted House" (Graves) **6**:142
"A Haunted House" (Swenson) **14**:248
"Haunted in Old Japan" (Noyes) **27**:127
"The Haunted Oak" (Dunbar) **5**:131
"The Haunted Palace" (Poe) **1**:424, 437-38, 443
"The Haunter" (Hardy) **8**:93, 118, 135, 138
"Hauntings" (Brooke) **24**:57, 85
The Havana Inquiry (Enzensberger)
See *Das Verhör von Habana*
"Havana Rose" (Crane) **3**:90
Have Come, Am Here (Villa) **22**:346-47, 351
"Have Mercy upon Me My Soul" (Gibran) **9**:73
"Having Been Asked 'What Is a Man?' I Answer" (Levine) **22**:220
"The Haw Lantern" (Heaney) **18**:230, 233
The Haw Lantern (Heaney) **18**:226-28, 230, 232-33, 237
"The Hawk in the Rain" (Hughes) **7**:117-18, 121, 129, 165
The Hawk in the Rain (Hughes) **7**:112-13, 115-20, 123, 131, 135-36, 139-41, 150, 162-63, 165-66
"Hawk Roosting" (Hughes) **7**:113, 125, 140-41, 151, 164, 169
"The Hawks" (Montale) **13**:149
"Hawks" (Tomlinson) **17**:347
"The Hawk's Cry in Autumn" (Brodsky) **9**:27
"The Hawthorn Hedge" (Wright) **14**:336, 340
"Hawthorn Tide" (Swinburne) **24**:313, 317-18
"The Hawthorn Tree" (Gluck) **16**:171
"Hawthorne" (Lowell) **3**:212, 216
"Hay" (Tomlinson) **17**:347, 354
"Hayāt al-hubb" (Gibran) **9**:78
"The Hayswater Boat" (Arnold) **5**:50
Hazard, the Painter (Meredith) **28**:179, 195-99, 206-07, 214, 216
"Hazard's Optimism" (Meredith) **28**:202, 215
"The Hazel Grove" (Pasternak) **6**:252
"He" (Ferlinghetti) **1**:174-76
"He Abjures Love" (Hardy) **8**:90
"He Acts" (Zagajewski) **27**:385
"He Doesn't Know It" (Aleixandre) **15**:4
"He Has a Good Time There" (Duncan) **2**:101
"He hath put all things under his feet" (Bryant) **20**:7
"He Heard the Newsboy Shouting 'Europe! Europe!'" (Schwartz) **8**:293
"He Held Radical Light" (Ammons) **16**:34
"He Is Last Seen" (Atwood) **8**:10
"He is not ded that sometyme hath a fall" (Wyatt) **27**:337-338, 340, 343
"He Revisits His First School" (Hardy) **8**:102
"He Sees Through Stone" (Knight) **14**:43
"He who finds a horseshoe" (Mandelstam)
See "Nashedshij podkovu"
"He who found a Horseshoe" (Mandelstam)
See "Nashedshij podkovu"
"The Head above the Fog" (Hardy) **8**:97
"Head against White" (Atwood) **8**:27
Head and Heart (Guillen)
See *Cerebro y corazón*
"Head of a Woman" (McGuckian) **27**:101
"Headwaters" (Momaday) **25**:197
"Healing Animal" (Harjo) **27**:70
"Hear Me" (Levine) **22**:223
"Hearn in Matsue" (Stryk) **27**:187, 208
"The Heart" (Trakl)
See "Das Herz"
"Heart and Mind" (Sitwell) **3**:312, 323
"The Heart and the Lyre" (Bogan) **12**:126
"Heart, Crown and Mirror" (Apollinaire)
See "Coeur, couronne et miroir"
"The Heart of a Constab" (McKay) **2**:216, 225-26
"The Heart of Pedro de Valdivia" (Neruda)
See "El corazón de Pedro de Valdivia"
"Heart Stirrings" (McKay) **2**:223
"Heartbeat" (Harjo) **27**:56
"Heartless Rhoda" (McKay) **2**:221
"The Hearts" (Pinsky) **27**:157-58, 161, 164-65, 170
The Heart's Garden/The Garden's Heart (Rexroth) **20**:204, 209-10, 213-14
The Heart's Journey (Sassoon) **12**:258, 271, 289
"Heat" (H. D.)
See "Garden"
"HEAt MAkes TH HEARt's wINDOw" (Bissett) **14**:32
"Heatwave" (Hughes) **7**:120
"L'héautontimorouménos" (Baudelaire) **1**:63
"Heaven" (Brooke) **24**:56, 64, 73, 78
"Heaven" (Herbert) **4**:102, 114, 130
"Heaven" (Tagore)
See "Svarga"
"Heaven Alive" (Garcia Lorca) **3**:141
Heaven and Earth (Byron) **16**:88-9, 102-06, 109
"Heaven Is but the Hour" (Masters) **1**:344

"Heavenly City, Earthly City" (Duncan) **2**:105
Heavenly City, Earthly City (Duncan) **2**:100, 126
"Heavensgate" (Okigbo) **7**:250-51
Heavensgate (Okigbo) **7**:221-25, 228, 231-32, 236, 240, 242, 245, 247-48
"The Heavy Bear That Goes with Me" (Schwartz) **8**:290-91, 297, 306-09, 311, 313-14
"die hebammen" (Enzensberger) **28**:140
"Heber" (Smith) **12**:327, 354
"Hebräische Melodien" (Heine) **25**:170, 175
"Hebrew Melodies" (Heine)
See "Hebräische Melodien"
"Hector in the Garden" (Browning) **6**:16
"Hector Kane" (Robinson) **1**:476
"Hedge Island, a Retrospect and a Prophecy" (Lowell) **13**:72, 82
"A Hedge of Rubber Trees" (Clampitt) **19**:98
"The Hedgehog" (Clare) **23**:7
"Hedgerows" (Tomlinson) **17**:354
"He-goat God" (Pavese)
See "Il Dio-Caprone"
"Heidenröslein" (Goethe) **5**:254
"Height" (Ammons) **16**:6
The Heights of Macchu Picchu (Neruda)
See *Alturas de Macchu Picchu*
"Heil Heilige Nacht!" (Nash) **21**:266
"The Heiligenstadt Testament" (Shapiro) **25**:307
"Heimkehr" (Heine) **25**:130-37, 139, 141-42, 144-45, 158, 161, 163-64
Die Heimkehr (Heine) **25**:161
"Die Heimkehr No 20" (Heine) **25**:144
"Die Heimkehr No 25" (Heine) **25**:144
"Heimkunft" (Holderlin) **4**:141, 146
"Heine La Salle" (Masters) **1**:334
"Heine's Grave" (Arnold) **5**:34, 52, 63-4
Heinrich Heine's Book of Songs (Heine)
See *Buch der Lieder*
"Helen" (Elytis) **21**:131
"Helen" (H. D.) **5**:268, 300
"Helen" (Parker) **28**:362
Helen in Egypt (H. D.) **5**:276-84, 292-93, 297-301
"Helen of Troy" (Masters) **1**:325, 328, 342
Helena (Vigny) **26**:367
"Hélène" (Valery) **9**:380
"Hélène, la reine triste" (Valery) **9**:380, 391
"Helen's Rape" (Gunn) **26**:182-183
"Helian" (Trakl) **20**:239-40, 253, 259
"Helicon" (Heaney) **18**:207
"Heliodora" (H. D.) **5**:270
Heliodora, and Other Poems (H. D.) **5**:267-68, 304-05
"Helios and Athene" (H. D.) **5**:290-92, 305
"Hell" (Graves) **6**:151
Hell (Dante)
See *Inferno*
"The Hell Cantos" (Pound) **4**:328, 357, 360
"Hell Gate" (Housman) **2**:162, 165, 167, 199
Hellas (Shelley) **14**:171, 175, 188-9, 195, 197, 241
"Hellenistics" (Jeffers) **17**:117
"The Helmet" (Levine) **22**:223
"Helpstone" (Clare) **23**:11, 39
"Helter Skelter; or, The Hue and Cry after the Attorneys Going to Ride the Circuit" (Swift) **9**:271
"Hemmed-in Males" (Williams) **7**:369
"The Hen Flower" (Kinnell) **26**:243, 249-50, 252, 266, 274
"Henceforth, from the Mind" (Bogan) **12**:105, 113
"Hendecasyllabics" (Swinburne) **24**:320
"Henri Rousseau and Friends" (Ondaatje) **28**:298
"Henry and Mary" (Graves) **6**:141
"The Henry Manley Blues" (Kumin) **15**:208
"Henry Manley Living Alone Keeps Time" (Kumin) **15**:208
"Henry Purcell" (Hopkins) **15**:144, 168
"Her Becoming" (Roethke) **15**:269, 272-74
"Her Dead Brother" (Lowell) **3**:205-06
"Her Death and After" (Hardy) **8**:99
"Her Early Work" (Swenson) **14**:276-77
"Her Eyes" (Robinson) **1**:459
"Her/Flesh" (Cummings) **5**:95
"Her Garden" (Belloc) **24**:38-9
"Her Immortality" (Hardy) **8**:131
"Her Kind" (Sexton) **2**:359
"Her Lips Are Copper Wire" (Toomer) **7**:320, 332, 340
"Her Management" (Swenson) **14**:248
"Her Music" (Belloc) **24**:29
"Her Triumph" (Jonson) **17**:180
"Hera of Samos" (Clampitt) **19**:87
"Heraldos" (Dario) **15**:96
"Herbseele" (Trakl) **20**:265
Hercule Chrestien (Ronsard) **11**:273
"Hercules and Antaeus" (Heaney) **18**:203, 207-210
"The Herd of Does" (MacDiarmid) **9**:156
"Here" (Larkin) **21**:238-39, 253-55
"Here and Now" (Stryk) **27**:211
Here and Now (Levertov) **11**:159, 163, 188
"Here Come the Saints" (Gunn) **26**:206-207
"Here she lies, a pretty bud" (Herrick)
See "Upon a Child That Died"
"Heredity" (Hardy) **8**:129
"La herencia" (Guillen) **23**:118-19
"Here's to Opening and upward, to Leaf and to Sap" (Cummings) **5**:106
"Here's to the Mice" (Lindsay) **23**:269
"The Heretic's Tragedy" (Browning) **2**:37, 59, 88
"Heriot's Ford" (Kipling) **3**:181
"Heritage" (Cullen) **20**:52-54, 57, 64-65, 72, 82, 87
"Herman and Dorothea" (Goethe)
See *Hermann und Dorothea*
Hermann und Dorothea (Goethe) **5**:223, 225-26, 236, 239, 257-59, 261
"Hermaphroditus" (Swinburne) **24**:308-11, 317, 361-63
"Hermes" (H. D.) **5**:273
"Hermes of The Ways" (H. D.) **5**:303
"Hermetic Definition" (H. D.) **5**:281, 283, 285, 289, 297, 299
"Hermetic Poem" (Kunitz) **19**:172
"The Hermit" (Apollinaire)
See "L'ermite"
"The Hermit" (McKay) **2**:222
"The Hermit at Outermost House" (Plath) **1**:389
"The Hermit Goes Up Attic" (Kumin) **15**:190
The Herne's Egg (Yeats) **20**:335
"Hero" (Madhubuti) **5**:342
"The Hero" (Moore) **4**:265
"The Hero" (Sassoon) **12**:242, 263, 277, 280, 283, 285
Hérodiade (Mallarme) **4**:188, 190, 196-97, 199-203, 208, 213, 218-25
Herodias (Mallarme)
See *Hérodiade*
"Heroes Are Gang Leaders" (Baraka) **4**:10
Heroic and Elegiac Song for the Lost Second Lieutenant of the Alb nian Campaign (Elytis)
See *Ázma iroikó ke pénthimo yia ton haméno anthipolohaghó tis Alvanías*
"Heroic Poem in Praise of Wine" (Belloc) **24**:13, 20, 22, 33, 39
"Heroic Simile" (Hass) **16**:198
"Heroics" (Wylie) **23**:324
Heroides (Ovid) **2**:234, 238-39, 243-46, 253-54
Heroines (Ovid)
See *Heroides*
"Heroique Stanzas to the Glorious Memory of Cromwell" (Dryden) **25**:101
"Heroism" (Montale)
See "L'eroismo"
"Heron Rex" (Ondaatje) **28**:332, 334
"Herrin" (Goethe) **5**:249
"Hertha" (Swinburne) **24**:308, 312, 343
"Das Herz" (Trakl) **20**:235-36
"Her-zie" (Smith) **12**:339
"der herz von gro¨land" (Enzensberger) **28**:138
"Hesperia" (Swinburne) **24**:313, 316, 318, 323
"The Hesperides" (Tennyson) **6**:351
Hesperides: or, The Works Both Humane & Divine of Robert Herrick, Esq. (Herrick) **9**:85, 87, 89, 90, 92-6, 100, 102, 104-06, 108-10, 116-17, 122, 125, 127-29, 132-35, 138, 140, 143-46
"Hevyn and erth" (Wyatt) **27**:349-50
"He-Who-Came-Forth" (Levertov) **11**:177
"Hey Yu" (Bissett) **14**:7
"Hey-Hey Blues" (Hughes) **1**:240
Hi no tori (Yosano Akiko) **11**:308
"Hiawatha's Photographing" (Carroll) **18**:46
"Hibernaculum" (Ammons) **16**:10, 12, 20, 23, 29, 47-9, 60
"Hibiscus on the Sleeping Shores" (Stevens) **6**:294-95, 305
"Hidden Door" (Ferlinghetti) **1**:166
Hiding the Universe: Poems by Wang Wei (Wang Wei) **18**:382, 390
"Hieroglyphic" (Harjo) **27**:66
"the high green hill" (Bissett) **14**:20
Th High Green Hill (Bissett) **14**:14, 16, 18-21
"The High Malady" (Pasternak)
See "Vysokaya bolesn"
"High Noon" (Clampitt) **19**:97
"The High Oaks Barking Hall July 19th 1896" (Swinburne) **24**:318-20
"High Quality Information" (Snyder) **21**:326
"High Talk" (Yeats) **20**:336
"High to Low" (Hughes) **1**:258, 267
"High Windows" (Larkin) **21**:238, 259
High Windows (Larkin) **21**:250, 259
The Higher Mathematics (Chesterton) **28**:99
"The Higher Patheism in a Nutshell" (Swinburne) **24**:320
"The Higher Unity" (Chesterton) **28**:94
"Highway: Michigan" (Roethke) **15**:246, 294
"Highway Patrol" (Ferlinghetti) **1**:187
"The Highwayman" (Noyes) **27**:133, 136
"Hiking on the Coast Range" (Rexroth) **20**:215
"The Hill" (Brooke) **24**:72, 77
"The Hill" (Masters) **1**:345
"The Hill" (Tomlinson) **17**:314, 316, 337
"The Hill and Grove at Bill-Borrow" (Marvell)
See "Upon the Hill and Grove at Billborow"
"Hill at Parramatta" (Shapiro) **25**:269
"The Hill Wife" (Frost) **1**:195, 202, 229
The Hilliad (Smart) **13**:333
"Hill-Stone Was Content" (Hughes) **7**:149
"Himno del mar" (Borges) **22**:92
"Himno entre ruinas" (Paz) **1**:353, 360-61, 363
The Hind and the Panther (Dryden) **25**:81-2
"L'hinne de Bacus" (Ronsard) **11**:230, 232-33
"The Hinterland" (Clampitt) **19**:90
"Hippocrene" (Clampitt) **19**:92
"Hippolytus" (H. D.) **5**:267
"The Hippopotamus" (Carroll) **18**:31
"The Hippopotamus" (Eliot) **5**:187
"The Hippopotamus" (Nash) **21**:280
"Hippy Mo" (Smith) **12**:314, 327, 339
"Hiroshima, Watts, My Lai" (Hayden) **6**:190
"His Age, Dedicated to His Peculiar Friend, M. John Wickes, under the Name Posthumus" (Herrick) **9**:103, 107, 114-15
"His Anthem, to Christ on the Crosse" (Herrick) **9**:121
"His Bargain" (Yeats) **20**:332
"His Blindness" (Browning) **6**:16
"His Confession" (Herrick) **9**:109, 117
"His Confidence" (Yeats) **20**:314, 332-33
"His Creed" (Herrick) **9**:104
"His Death" (Browning) **6**:16
"His Embalming to Julia" (Herrick) **9**:127, 129
"His farwell unto Poetrie" (Herrick)
See "Farewell to Poetry"
"His Grange, or Private Wealth" (Herrick) **9**:89
"His Lachrimae, or Mirth, Turn'd to Mourning" (Herrick) **9**:108

"His Meditation upon Death" (Herrick) **9**:109
His Noble Numbers: or, His Pious Pieces, Wherein (amongst Other Things) He Sings the Birth of His Christ: and Sighes for His Saviours Suffering on the Crosse (Herrick) **9**:85, 87, 90-2, 94-5, 100-01, 104, 106, 109-10, 117-18, 122, 140-41
"His Own Epitaph" (Herrick) **9**:131
"His Phoenix" (Yeats) **20**:329
"His Poetry His Pillar" (Herrick) **9**:89, 106
"His Prayer for Absolution" (Herrick) **9**:94, 109, 117, 141
"His Prayer to Ben Jonson" (Herrick)
See "Prayer to Ben Jonson"
"His Returne to London" (Herrick) **9**:89, 98, 108
"His Shield" (Moore) **4**:247-48, 261
"His Shining Helmet: Its Horsehair Crest" (Gallagher) **9**:62
"His Smell" (Olds) **22**:326
"His Stillness" (Olds) **22**:321, 340
"His Tears to Thamasis" (Herrick) **9**:108
"His Terror" (Olds) **22**:324
"His Winding-Sheet" (Herrick) **9**:109
"His Words to Christ, Going to the Crosse" (Herrick) **9**:121
"Hispaniola" (Clampitt) **19**:102
"Histoire du Régent" (Perse) **23**:230
Historia de Gloria (Fuertes) **27**:20-5, 34-42, 44-7
Historia de la noche (Borges) **22**:95-6
Historia del corazón (Aleixandre) **15**:3-4, 7, 11, 15-16, 22, 41
"Histories" (Tomlinson) **17**:326, 344, 350
"History" (Berry) **28**:8
"History" (Soto) **28**:378
History (Lowell) **3**:224, 226, 228-29, 231-32
"History: 13" (Olds) **22**:319
"History is the Memory of Time" (Olson) **19**:271
"History Lesson" (Kumin) **15**:194, 202
"History of a Literary Movement" (Nemerov) **24**:258
"The History of Karate" (Soto) **28**:400
"History of My Heart" (Pinsky) **27**:176
History of My Heart (Pinsky) **27**:163-64, 173, 176
History of Peter I (Pushkin)
See *The History of Peter the Great*
The History of Peter the Great (Pushkin) **10**:394
The History of the Heart (Aleixandre)
See *Historia del corazón*
A History of the Night (Borges)
See *Historia de la noche*
"History of the Poet as a Whore" (Madhubuti) **5**:329
"The History of the Twentieth Century" (Brodsky) **9**:19
"The History of the World: A T.V. Docu-Drama" (Ferlinghetti) **1**:184
"History on Wheels" (Baraka) **4**:29
"Hitherto Uncollected" (Moore) **4**:259
"The Hitlerian Spring" (Montale)
See "La primavera Hitleriana"
"Hitoyo enishi" (Hagiwara Sakutaro) **18**:168-69
"Hits and Runs" (Sandburg) **2**:316
"L'Hiver qui vient" (Laforgue) **14**:72-4, 78, 90
"Hochbeglückt in deiner Liebe" (Goethe) **5**:247
"The Hock-Cart, or Harvest Home" (Herrick) **9**:141-42
"Hod Putt" (Masters) **1**:345
"Hoeing" (Soto) **28**:378
"Hold Me" (Levine) **22**:217
"Hölderlin" (Schwartz) **8**:316
"The Holdfast" (Herbert) **4**:123
"Holding On" (Levine) **22**:214
"Holding Out" (Rich) **5**:357
"Holding the Mirror up to Nature" (Nemerov) **24**:291
"Holiday" (Sitwell) **3**:311-12, 326
"Holiday Inn Blues" (Ferlinghetti) **1**:187
The Hollow Men (Eliot) **5**:163, 171, 174, 180, 185, 191, 193, 198, 206, 209
"Hollywood" (Shapiro) **25**:295
"Holy Baptisme I" (Herbert) **4**:120
"The Holy Child's Song" (Merton) **10**:330, 340
"Holy City of Song" (Noyes) **27**:127
"Holy Cross Day" (Browning) **2**:38, 63
"The Holy Fair" (Burns) **6**:49, 53, 57, 83-4, 86-8, 91, 94
"The Holy Grail" (Tennyson) **6**:407
"holy night" (Clifton) **17**:18, 24, 38
"Holy Satyr" (H. D.) **5**:268
"Holy Scriptures I" (Herbert) **4**:126
"Holy Scriptures 2" (Herbert) **4**:133
"Holy Sonnet XIV: Batter my heart, three-person'd God" (Donne) **1**:138
Holy Sonnets (Donne) **1**:128, 136, 138-40
"Holy Spring" (Thomas) **2**:382, 390
"Holy Thursday" (Blake) **12**:5, 7, 23-4, 34-5
"Holy Willie's Prayer" (Burns) **6**:53, 65, 83, 85-6, 88-9, 96
"Homage" (Viereck) **27**:284
"Homage and Valediction" (Tomlinson) **17**:338
Homage to Clio (Auden) **1**:17
"A Homage to John Keats" (Clampitt) **19**:91
"Homage to Literature" (Rukeyser) **12**:211
"homage to mine" (Clifton) **17**:24
"Homage to Paul Mellon, I. M. Pei, Their Gallery, and Washington City" (Meredith) **28**:198home
"Homage to Paul Robeson" (Hayden) **6**:192, 195
"Homage to Rimbaud" (Montale)
See "Omaggio a Rimbaud"
"Homage to Sextus Propertius" (Pound) **4**:317-18, 333, 363-66
"Homage to the Empress of the Blues" (Hayden) **6**:188, 196
"Homage to the Tree" (Tagore)
See "Vriksha-vandana"
"Homage to Yalta" (Brodsky) **9**:7
"Hombres necios que acusáis" (Juana Ines de la Cruz) **24**:220
"Home" (Brooke) **24**:57
"Home" (Herbert) **4**:102, 130-31
"Home" (Lorde) **12**:138-39
"Home after Three Months Away" (Lowell) **3**:206, 209, 216, 221
"Home After Three Months Away" (Sexton) **2**:350
"Home at Grasmere" (Wordsworth) **4**:414
"Home Burial" (Frost) **1**:193, 195, 229
Home Course in Religion (Soto) **28**:394, 396, 398-400, 403
"Home for the Holidays" (Nemerov) **24**:295
"Home Home Home" (Ferlinghetti) **1**:180
"Home Is So Sad" (Larkin) **21**:242
"Home, James" (Viereck) **27**:264
"Home Thoughts" (Sandburg) **2**:309
Homeage to the American Indians
See *Homenaje a los indios americanos*
"The Homecoming" (Hardy) **8**:99
"The Homecoming" (Holderlin)
See "Heimkunft"
"Homecoming" (Sanchez) **9**:207, 209, 223
"Homecoming" (Shapiro) **25**:273
"Homecoming" (Viereck) **27**:265, 280
Homecoming (Heine)
See *Die Heimkehr*
Homecoming (Sanchez) **9**:204, 206-07, 210-13, 215-16, 218-19, 222, 224, 229, 231-34, 237-38, 242
"Homecomings" (Heaney) **18**:244
Homegirls and Hand Grenades (Sanchez) **9**:228, 230-31, 234-36, 238, 244
"Homeland" (Bely)
See "Rodine"
"Homeland" (Clampitt) **19**:100, 102
Homenaje a los indios americanos (Cardenal) **22**:103, 124-26, 128, 131-32
Homenaje a Pablo Neruda de los poetas espanoles: Tres cantos materiales (Neruda) **4**:277, 306
"Homenaje y profanaciones" (Paz) **1**:356-57
"Homeric Smile" (Meredith) **28**:174, 182, 187
The Homestead Called Damascus (Rexroth) **20**:182, 209-12, 214
"Home-Thoughts" (McKay) **2**:228
"Hometown Piece for Messers Alston and Reese" (Moore) **4**:256, 259
"Homily" (Viereck) **27**:280
"Homily on the Piety of All Herd Animals" (Viereck) **27**:280
"Homily on the Piety of All Herd Animals (A Mammoth Idyll)" (Viereck) **27**:280
"L'homme" (Lamartine) **16**:275, 285, 290-91, 297-98
L'Homme approximatif (Tzara) **27**:234, 237-38, 240-42, 249
"Homuneulus Artifex" (Merrill) **28**:248
El hondero entusiasta, 1923-1924 (Neruda) **4**:276
Honey and Salt (Sandburg) **2**:336, 339
"Honey Bud" (Tagore)
See "Madhumanjari"
"The Honeysuckle" (Marie de France)
See "Chevrefoil"
"The Hooks of a Corset" (Milosz) **8**:182, 197, 210
"Hop o' My Thumb" (Ashbery) **26**:127, 160
"Hope" (Clare) **23**:44
"Hope" (Milosz) **8**:187-88, 192
"Hope Is a Subtle Glutton" (Dickinson) **1**:111
Hopes and Impediments: Selected Essays (Achebe) **6**:1015
"Hope's Despari" (Tagore)
See "Ashar nairashya"
"The Hop-Garden" (Smart) **13**:330-31, 333, 342
"Hopi Overlay" (Rose) **13**:233
"The Hopsital" (Lermontov) **18**:284-85
"La hora cero" (Cardenal)
See "La hora O"
"La hora O" (Cardenal) **22**:111
la hora 0 (Cardenal) **22**:103-4, 124-25, 131
Horace (Smart)
See *The Works of Horace, Translated into Verse*
"Horace, *Lib.* 2 *Sat.* 6. Part of It Imitated" (Swift) **9**:297
"Horace to Leuconoë" (Robinson) **1**:459
"Horae Canonicae" (Auden) **1**:17
"An Horatian Ode upon Cromwell's Return from Ireland" (Marvell) **10**:259, 261-62, 264, 267-71, 275, 277, 289, 292, 294-95, 305-09, 311, 317-18
"Horatio Alger Uses Scag" (Baraka) **4**:30
"Horizons and Rains" (Ortiz) **17**:227
"Horizons Home" (Ortiz) **17**:226
"Horizonte" (Pessoa) **20**:155
"The Horn" (Vigny)
See "Le cor"
"The Horn of Egremont Castle" (Wordsworth) **4**:377
"Horned Purple" (Williams) **7**:368
"The Horned Rampion" (Clampitt) **19**:102
"Hornpipe" (Sitwell) **3**:297, 303
"L'horreur sympathique" (Baudelaire) **1**:55
"A Horrible Religious Error" (Hughes) **7**:144
"Hors des jours étrangers" (Cesaire) **25**:31
"Horse" (Gluck) **16**:164
"Horse" (Hughes) **7**:143
"Horse" (Hugo) **17**:67
"Horse and Swan Feeding" (Swenson) **14**:246, 262, 277
"The Horse Show" (Williams) **7**:391, 394
"The Horse That Died of Shame" (Momaday) **25**:189, 213
"Horseman in Rain" (Neruda) **4**:282
"Horses" (Berry) **28**:9
"Horses" (Hughes) **7**:118
"Horses" (Sandburg) **2**:324
Horses Don't Bet on People and Neither Do I (Bukowski) **18**:15
"The Horsewoman" (Kumin) **15**:194
"Hortus" (Marvell) **10**:284, 286, 288

"Horus" (Nerval) **13**:180-81, 187-91
"Hosea" (Walker) **20**:278-79
"Hospes Comesque Corporis" (Wylie) **23**:310
"Hospital Barge at Cérisy" (Owen) **19**:342
"A Hospital named 'Hotel Universe'" (Viereck) **27**:263
"Hospital / poem (for etheridge 9/26/69)" (Sanchez) **9**:225
"The Hostage" (Smith) **12**:329-30, 333
"Hostel" (McGuckian) **27**:76, 100
Hosties noires (Senghor) **25**:231, 233, 235, 238, 248, 254-55
"The Hosting of the Sidhe" (Yeats) **20**:344, 346
"Hot" (Bukowski) **18**:24
"Hôtel" (Apollinaire) **7**:48
"Hotel" (McGuckian)
See "Hostel"
"Hotel Bed" (Graves) **6**:143-44
"Hotel Genève" (Song) **21**:335-36, 338-41
Hotel Lautreamont (Ashbery) **26**:161-164, 166
"Hotel de l'Univers et Portugal" (Merrill) **28**:234
"The Hotel of Lost Light" (Kinnell) **26**:273
"Hotel Steinplatz" (Olson) **19**:305
"The Hour and the Ghost" (Rossetti) **7**:280
"The Hour of Cowdust" (Ondaatje) **28**:337
"The Hour of Fate" (Lindsay) **23**:281
Hours of Idleness (Byron) **16**:86
Hous of Fame (Chaucer)
See *House of Fame*
"House" (Browning) **2**:59, 66
"The House" (Merrill) **28**:273
"The House" (Sexton) **2**:361-62
"The House and the Vineyard" (Lamartine)
See "La vigne et la maison"
House, Bridge, Fountain, Gate (Kumin) **15**:192, 194, 202, 208
"House by the Sea" (Montale)
See "Casa sul mare"
"A House Divided" (Ondaatje) **28**:293
"The House Fly" (Merrill) **28**:282-83, 285-87
"House Guest" (Bishop) **3**:56
"The House in Main St." (Lowell) **13**:84
The House of Dust (Aiken) **26**:4, 6, 8, 13, 22, 27, 31, 36, 50, 72
House of Fame (Chaucer) **19**:5, 10, 14, 17-18, 20-3, 73
"A House of Mercy" (Smith) **12**:326, 334-35
"The House of Over-Dew" (Smith) **12**:330, 332-33
House of the Customs Men (Montale)
See *La casa dei doganieri*
"The House of the Dead" (Apollinaire)
See "La maison des mortes"
"The House of the Heart" (Wakoski) **15**:348, 354
"The House on Bishop Street" (Dove) **6**:113
The House on Marshland (Gluck) **16**:125-30, 132-33, 136, 139-44, 147-49, 151, 153-54, 157
House on the Corner (Dove)
See *The Yellow House on the Corner*
"The House on the Hill" (Robinson) **1**:459
"House Under Construction" (Pavese)
See "Casa in costruzione"
Houseboat Days (Ashbery) **26**:140, 144-145, 153, 155, 162, 172
"Housecleaning" (Giovanni) **19**:140
"The Householder" (Browning) **2**:59
"The Housekeeper" (Frost) **1**:193
"The Houses of Old Moscow" (Tsvetaeva)
See "Domiki staroi Moskvy"
"Housewife" (Sexton) **2**:346, 370
"Houston 6 PM" (Zagajewski) **27**:402
"How" (Atwood) **8**:24
"The How and the Why" (Tennyson) **6**:347
"How Annandale Went Out" (Robinson) **1**:461
"How Cruel is the Story of Eve" (Smith) **12**:309
"How Do You See?" (Smith) **12**:325, 332-33, 352
"How Do You Tell a Story?" (Wakoski) **15**:372
"How Everything Happens (Based on a Study of the Wave)" (Swenson) **14**:271
"How Few, of All the Hearts That Loved" (Bronte) **8**:50, 74
"How I Came to Be a Graduate Student" (Rose) **13**:232
"How It Goes On" (Kumin) **15**:207
"How It Is" (Kumin) **15**:204, 218-20
"How It Strikes a Contemporary" (Browning) **2**:80
"How Lilies Came White" (Herrick) **9**:143
"How Lisa Loved the King" (Eliot) **20**:124
"How Lucy Backslid" (Dunbar) **5**:122, 146
"How Many Bards" (Keats) **1**:313
"How Many Heavens" (Sitwell) **3**:312
"How Many Nights" (Kinnell) **26**:257
"How Marigolds Came Yellow" (Herrick) **9**:102
"How Much Can It Hurt" (Levine) **22**:215
"How Much Earth" (Levine) **22**:219
"How Naked, How without a Wall" (Millay) **6**:238
"How Roses Came Red" (Herrick) **9**:143
"How Samson Bore Away the Gates of Gaza" (Lindsay) **23**:276
"How Shall I Woo Thee" (Dunbar) **5**:126
"How Sweet I roam'd" (Blake) **12**:32, 36
"How the Wallflower Came First" (Herrick) **9**:102
"How to Be Old" (Swenson) **14**:250, 288
"How to Die" (Sassoon) **12**:267, 285
"How to Enter a Big City" (Merton) **10**:337, 344
"How to Make a Good Chili Stew" (Ortiz) **17**:228, 233
"How Very Often at a Fashionable Ball" (Lermontov) **18**:297
"how we avoid prayr" (Bissett) **14**:32
"How We Danced" (Sexton) **2**:366
"How Yesterday Looked" (Sandburg) **2**:305
"Howard Lamson" (Masters) **1**:338
"Howarth Churchyard" (Arnold) **5**:33-4, 52
"Howl" (Ginsberg) **4**:44-9, 51, 57-61, 63-5, 67-70, 73-5, 79
Howl, and Other Poems (Ginsberg) **4**:73, 87
Howling at the Moon (Hagiwara Sakutaro)
See *Tsuki ni hoeru*
"The Howling of Wolves" (Hughes) **7**:137, 142, 159
Hristos voskres (Bely) **11**:7, 24, 28, 31, 33
"Hsiang Consort" (Li Ho) **13**:51-2
"Hsin-i Village" (Wang Wei) **18**:362
"The Hudsonian Curlew" (Snyder) **21**:292, 297, 308
"Hue, carcan!" (Laforgue) **14**:93
Hugh Selwyn Mauberley (Pound) **4**:318-21, 330, 338-39, 341-42, 348
"Hughie At The Inn" (Wylie) **23**:311
"Hugo at Théophile Gautier's Grave" (Lowell) **3**:224
"Huhediblu" (Celan) **10**:124
"L'Huillier, si nous perdons ceste belle Princess" (Ronsard) **11**:250
"8e vision" (Lamartine) **16**:265
"The Human Abstract" (Blake) **12**:10, 34
"Human Affection" (Smith) **12**:310
"Human Applause" (Holderlin)
See "Menschenbeitfall"
"Human Burning" (Aleixandre) **15**:19, 21
"Human Condition" (Gunn) **26**:185
"Human Cylinders" (Loy) **16**:322
"Human Grief" (Trakl)
See "Menschliche Trauer"
Human Shows, Far Phantasies, Songs, and Trifles (Hardy) **8**:89
Human Wishes (Hass) **16**:215-17, 221-22
"A Humane Materialist . . ." (Smith) **12**:331
"L'humanitè" (Lamartine) **16**:266, 281, 293
"The Humanities Building" (Shapiro) **25**:322
"Humanity I Love You" (Cummings) **5**:90
"Humble Jar" (Song) **21**:344-48
"The Humble Petition of Frances Harris" (Swift) **9**:251, 296
"The humble Petition of poore Ben: To . . . King Charles" (Jonson)
See "The humble Petition of poore Ben: To . . . King Charles"
"The Humble-Bee" (Emerson) **18**:79, 84-85, 93, 99
"Humiliation" (Blok) **21**:5, 15
"The Humming-Bird" (Dickinson) **1**:79
"The Humours" (Bradstreet)
See "Of the Four Humours in Man's Constitution"
The Humours of the Court (Bridges) 28
"Hunchback Girl: She Thinks of Heaven" (Brooks) **7**:53, 69, 80
"The Hunchback in the Park" (Thomas) **2**:394
"A Hundred Collars" (Frost) **1**:215
"Hunger" (Cullen) **20**:63, 76
"Hunger" (Rich) **5**:374
"Hunger in the South" (Neruda) **4**:282
"Hungerfield" (Jeffers) **17**:129, 136
Hungerfield and Other Poems (Jeffers) **17**:123, 136
"The Hunter" (Williams) **7**:360
"The Hunter of the Prairies" (Bryant) **20**:23
"The Hunter's Serenade" (Bryant) **20**:15
The Hunting of the Snark: An Agony in Eight Fits (Carroll) **18**:30-33, 40-49
"Hunting Watch" (Wang Wei) **18**:389
"Huntress" (H. D.) **5**:269
"The Huntress and Her Dogs" (MacDiarmid) **9**:191
Huntsman, What Quarry? (Millay) **6**:230-31, 233-34, 242
"Hurrah for Karamazov!" (Viereck) **27**:279
"Hurrah for Positive Science" (Whitman) **3**:384
"Hurrah for Thunder" (Okigbo) **7**:235, 247
"The Hurricane" (Bryant) **20**:15
"The Hurricane" (Finch)
See "A Pindarick Poem upon the Hurricane"
"Hurry Up Please It's Time" (Sexton) **2**:367-68
"Hurt Hawks" (Jeffers) **17**:117, 129
"Hurt Hawks II" (Jeffers) **17**:110
"Hush'd Be the Camps To-day" (Whitman) **3**:418
"The Hyacinth Symphony" (Elytis) **21**:131
"L'hydre Univers tordant son corps écaillé d'astres" (Hugo) **17**:90
"L'hylas" (Ronsard) **11**:235
"Hyme" (Donne)
See "Hymne to God my God, in my sicknesse"
Hymen (H. D.) **5**:266-70
"Hymme to God My God, in My Sicknesse" (Donne)
See "Hymne to God my God, in my sicknesse"
"Hymn" (Ammons) **16**:27, 40, 57-8, 60, 63-5
"Hymn" (Dunbar) **5**:137
"Hymn" (Poe) **1**:446
"Hymn among the Ruins" (Paz)
See "Himno entre ruinas"
"Hymn before Sunrise in the Vale of Chamouni" (Coleridge) **11**:48-9, 53, 55-8, 92
"Hymn from a Watermelon Pavilion" (Stevens) **6**:292
"Hymn IV" (Ammons) **16**:22
"Hymn of Apollo" (Shelley) **14**:167, 170
"Hymn of Death" (Lamartine)
See "Hymne de la mort"
"Hymn of Not Much Praise for New York City" (Merton) **10**:344
"Hymn of Pan" (Shelley) **14**:167, 177
"Hymn of the Morning" (Lamartine)
See "L'hymne du matin"
"A Hymn of the Sea" (Bryant) **20**:3, 13
"Hymn of the Waldenses" (Bryant) **20**:5
"Hymn to Adversity" (Gray)
See "Ode to Adversity"
"Hymn to Aphrodite" (Sappho)
See "Ode to Aphrodite"

"I See around Me Tombstones Grey" (Bronte) **8**:74
"I See the Boys of Summer" (Thomas) **2**:384
"I Shall Never See You Again" (Masters) **1**:333, 338
"I Sing of Olaf Glad and Big" (Cummings) **5**:88
"I Sing the Body Electric" (Whitman) **3**:385, 396
"I sing when my throat is moist . . ." (Mandelstam)
See "Poiu kngda gortan' syra . . ."
"I Sit by the Window" (Brodsky) **9**:8, 13
"I Sit in My Room" (Toomer) **7**:337
"I sonetti del ritorno" (Gozzano) **10**:188
"I Stop Writing the Poem" (Gallagher) **9**:65
"I Struck a Diminished Seventh" (Ammons) **16**:39
"I Swore to Stab the Sonnet" (Shapiro) **25**:322
"I Take Care of You: A Lantern Dashes by in the Glass" (Gallagher) **9**:50
"I Taste a Liquor Never Brewed" (Dickinson) **1**:80
"I Taste the Ashes of Your Death" (Bukowski) **18**:7
"I Tell You for Several Years of My Madness I Heard the Voice of Lilith Singing in the Trees of Chicago" (Carruth) **10**:85
"I think, yes, a leopard in Duty blue would" (Villa) **22**:355
"I Thirst" (Harper) **21**:198
"I to My Perils" (Housman) **2**:180
I Too Am a Painter (Apollinaire)
See *Et moi aussi je suis peintre*
"I, Too, Sing America" (Hughes) **1**:241, 258-59
"I Travel as a Phantom Now" (Hardy) **8**:89
"I Vecchi" (Pound) **4**:317
"I' vo pensando" (Petrarch) **8**:227
"I Wandered Lonely as a Cloud" (Wordsworth) **4**:388, 400
"I Want New York" (Nash) **21**:263
"I Wanted to be There When My Father Died" (Olds) **22**:325-26, 341-42
"I wanted to stay in September" (Cassian) **17**:5
"I Was Born in Lucerne" (Levine) **22**:226
"i was just cummin" (Bissett) **14**:34
"I was not young long; I met the soul early" (Villa) **22**:351
"I Was Reading a Scientific Article" (Atwood) **8**:13
"I Was Washing Outside in the Darkness" (Mandelstam) **14**:122
"I Went into the Maverick Bar" (Snyder) **21**:293, 296-97
"I wept for my youth" (Kunitz) **19**:175
"I Will Be" (Cummings) **5**:93
"I will break God's seamless skull" (Villa) **22**:352
"I Will Lie Down" (Swenson) **14**:286
"I Will Put Chaos into Fourteen Lines" (Millay) **6**:243, 246
"I Will Sing You One-O" (Frost) **1**:195
"I Will Wade Out" (Cummings) **5**:91
"I Wish I Had Great Knowledge or Great Art" (Schwartz) **8**:294
"I wonder by my troth" (Donne)
See "The good-morrow"
"I Would Have Been a Trumpet Player If I Hadn't Gone to College" (Baraka) **4**:36
"I Would I Were a Careless Child" (Byron) **16**:73, 86-8
"I would not be thought less than a man" (Brutus) **24**:116
"I Would Not Paint--a Picture" (Dickinson) **1**:102
"I Would Return South" (Neruda)
See "Quiero volver a sur"
I Wouldn't Have Missed It (Nash) **21**:277
"Ia dolzhen zhit', khotia ia dvazhdy umer" (Mandelstam) **14**:151
"Ia Perezhil Svoi Zhelan'ia" (Pushkin) **10**:412
"Ia zhivu na vazhnykh ogorodakh" (Mandelstam) **14**:152
"Ibadan Lagos Kano London 5 Jan 72" (Brutus) **24**:123
Ibis (Ovid) **2**:238, 242, 244
IBM (Bissett) **14**:15
"Ibo" (Hugo) **17**:83, 89
"Icarian Wings" (Cullen) **20**:67
"Ice Cream at Blaunberg" (Tomlinson) **17**:353
"The Ice Eagle" (Wakoski) **15**:324, 363
The Ice Land (Hagiwara Sakutaro)
See *Hyoto*
"Ice Storm" (Hayden) **6**:194
"Ice Storm" (Hayden) **6**:193
"The Ice-Cream Wars" (Ashbery) **26**:136
"The Ice-Storm" (Pinsky) **27**:174
Ichiaku no suna (Ishikawa) **10**:193, 200-02, 204-05, 210-11, 216
"Ichigatsu" (Nishiwaki) **15**:231-32
"Icicles" (Pinsky) **27**:158
Ici-haut. Pamyati Maksimilian Voloshin (Tsvetaeva) **14**:324
"I climb the mossy bank of the glade" (Bridges) **28**:86
Iconographs (Swenson) **14**:268-72, 274, 281, 285-86
"Idaho" (Ashbery) **26**:137
"The Idea of Ancestry" (Knight) **14**:39, 41, 43-4, 52-3
"The Idea of Order at Key West" (Stevens) **6**:305, 307, 325, 327
"The Idea of Trust" (Gunn) **26**:207, 220
"The Ideal Father" (Olds) **22**:322
"Ideal Landscape" (Rich) **5**:393
"Ideas" (Merrill) **28**:267
"L'idee de Dieu" (Lamartine) **16**:265-66, 293
"Identity" (Ammons) **16**:27, 29
"Identity: A Poem" (Stein) **18**:334
"The Idiot Boy" (Wordsworth) **4**:372, 374, 381, 416-18, 426-27
"Idoto" (Okigbo) **7**:223, 225
"Idyl" (Parker) **28**:355
"Idyll" (Roethke) **15**:246
Idylls of the Bible (Harper) **21**:185
Idylls of the Hearth (Tennyson) **6**:360
Idylls of the King (Tennyson) **6**:358, 360, 369, 374, 376, 379, 406-08
"If" (Kipling) **3**:176, 183-84, 188
"If Anyone Had Told Me" (Aleixandre)
See "If Someone Could Have Told Me"
"If Anything Will Level with You Water Will" (Ammons) **16**:54
"If Blood Were Not as Powerful as It Is" (Gallagher) **9**:59
"If Fun Is Fun Isn't That Enough?" (Nash) **21**:274
"If I Am Too Brown or Too White for You" (Rose) **13**:241
"If I Had Children" (Swenson) **14**:279
"if i have made, my lady, intricate" (Cummings) **5**:87
"If I Think About You Again It Will Be the Fifty-Third Monday of Next Year" (Harjo) **27**:70
"If I were Paris" (Johnson) **24**:144
"If I Were Tickled by the Rub of Love" (Thomas) **2**:384, 386, 401
"If in Beginning Twilight of Winter Will Stand" (Cummings) **5**:109-10
"If It Chance Your Eye Offend You" (Housman) **2**:184
"If It Were You" (Page) **12**:179
"If, My Darling" (Larkin) **21**:236, 248
"If My Head Hurt a Hair's Foot" (Thomas) **2**:386, 407
"If Only" (Rossetti) **7**:280
"If Someone Could Have Told Me" (Aleixandre) **15**:4
"If There are Any Heavens My Mother Will (All by Herself) Have" (Cummings) **5**:88
"If waker care if sudden pale colour" (Wyatt) **27**:368
"If We Must Die" (McKay) **2**:206-07, 211, 217, 220, 229
"If We Take All Gold" (Bogan) **12**:122
"If yet I have not all thy love" (Donne)
See "Lovers infinitenesse"
If You Call This Cry a Song (Carruth) **10**:77
"IFF" (Nemerov) **24**:289
Igitur (Mallarme) **4**:199, 201-03, 208
"Ignorance" (Larkin) **21**:227, 246
"I,it,was,that,saw" (Villa) **22**:355
"Ike" (Dove) **6**:109
"Ikey (Goldberg)'s Worth I'm" (Cummings) **5**:82
"Il nini muart" (Pasolini) **17**:251, 256, 281, 284
"Il penseroso" (Gray) **2**:141
"Il Penseroso" (Milton) **19**:193, 201-02, 226, 229-33, 249, 255
"Il pleut" (Apollinaire) **7**:20, 34
"Il reduce" (Gozzano) **10**:184-85, 190
"Il y a" (Apollinaire) **7**:22
Iliad (Homer) **23**:149, 151-53, 155-57, 159-63, 165-72, 175-89, 191
Iliads (Homer)
See *Iliad*
Ilias (Homer)
See *Iliad*
Ílios o prótos (Elytis) **21**:119-20, 124, 127
"I'll Run Wild in the Dark Streets Gypsy Camp" (Mandelstam) **14**:119
"I'll tell thee now (dear love) what thou shalt doe" (Donne)
See "A Valediction: of the booke"
"Illic Jacet" (Housman) **2**:184
"Illinois Farmer" (Sandburg) **2**:316
"The Illiterates" (Meredith) **28**:188
"The Illumination" (Kunitz) **19**:174-75, 178
"Illuminations" (Gluck) **16**:151
Illuminations (Rimbaud)
See *Les illuminations*
Les illuminations (Rimbaud) **3**:249, 254, 259-65, 279
The Illustrated Wilfred Funk (Ferlinghetti) **1**:186
"Illustration" (Ashbery) **26**:123, 137
"The Illustration" (Levertov) **11**:168
"I love all beauteous things" (Bridges) **28**:84
"Ilu, the Talking Drum" (Knight) **14**:39, 41, 44-6
I'm a Stranger Here Myself (Nash) **21**:264
"I'm a Whore Are You Satisfied?" (Alegria) **26**:
"Im Hafen" (Heine) **25**:157-58, 160, 163-64
"I'm Here" (Roethke) **15**:270, 272, 279
"Im Osten" (Trakl) **20**:225-26, 250, 255-56
"I'm Still Not Patriarch" (Mandelstam) **14**:122
"I'm Unwilling" (Ammons) **16**:44
"I'm Wife....I'm Woman Now" (Dickinson) **1**:93
"The Image" (Day Lewis) **11**:146
The Image and the Law (Nemerov) **24**:255, 260, 264, 285, 288-89, 298
"An Image from a Past Life" (Yeats) **20**:328
The Image Marker (Merrill) **28**:270
"The Image of God" (Browning) **6**:20
"The Images" (Rich) **5**:385, 396
Images à Crusoé (Perse) **23**:210, 217, 228, 230, 234-35, 247, 254, 256-57
"Images for Godard" (Rich) **5**:366, 391
"Images of Angels" (Page) **12**:168-69, 177, 190
"Images of Perfection" (Tomlinson) **17**:349
"Imagination" (Wheatley)
See "On Imagination"
"Imago" (Clampitt) **19**:82
L'imitation de Notre-Dame la lune (Laforgue) **14**:57, 61, 70-1, 80, 97
"Imitation of Byron" (Lermontov) **18**:302
"An Imitation of Spenser" (Blake) **12**:31
Imitations (Lowell) **3**:213, 223, 228, 232
"Imitations of Drowning" (Sexton) **2**:363
"Imitations of Horace" (Swift) **9**:265
Imitations of Horace (Pope)
See *Satires and Epistles of Horace, Imitated*
"Immature Pebbles" (Zukofsky) **11**:355
"The Immigrants" (Atwood) **8**:38

Cumulative Title Index

"The Immigration Department" (Cassian) **17**:5-6
The Immortal Husband (Merrill) **28**:227
"The Immortal Part" (Housman) **2**:179, 192
"L'immortalité" (Lamartine) **16**:275, 279, 291, 300, 302
"Immortality" (Lamartine)
See "L'immortalité"
"Immortality Ode" (Wordsworth)
See "Ode: Intimations of Immortality from Recollections of Early Childhood"
"The Immortals" (Parker) **28**:360
"The Impalpabilities" (Tomlinson) **17**:327, 357
"Impasse" (Hughes) **1**:260
"L'impenitent" (Verlaine) **2**:417
"The Impercipient" (Hardy) **8**:107-08, 112
Imperfect Thirst (Kinnell) **26**:288, 290, 293-94
"Imperia" (Gautier) **18**:125
"The Imperial Bison is" (Guillen)
See "The Imperial Bison is"
"The Impossible Indispensibility of the Ars Poetica" (Carruth) **10**:86
"Impossible to Tell" (Pinsky) **27**:174-76
"The Impossible Woman/Ideal" (Jimenez)
See "Quimérica"
"The Imprefect Lover" (Sassoon) **12**:258
"Impressionism" (Mandelstam) **14**:118
"Impressionist Picture of a Garden" (Lowell) **13**:95
"Imprint for Rio Grande" (Toomer) **7**:337
"Impromptu on Lord Holland's House" (Gray)
See "On Lord Holland's Seat near Margate, Kent"
"An Improvisation for the Stately Dwelling" (Ammons) **16**:32, 63
"Improvisations: Lights and Snow" (Aiken) **26**:50
"The Improvisatore" (Coleridge) **11**:105
"In a Boat" (Belloc) **24**:5
"In a Buggy at Dusk" (Milosz) **8**:205
"In a Caledonian Forest" (MacDiarmid) **9**:176
"In a Castle" (Lowell) **13**:70
"In a Cemetery" (Aleixandre) **15**:18
"In a Dark Time" (Roethke) **15**:268, 276, 278, 281, 306, 313
"In a Gondola" (Browning) **2**:26
In a Hotel Room in America (Zagajewski) **27**:
"In a Rosary" (Swinburne) **24**:322, 324
"In a Ship Recently Raised from the Sea" (Page) **12**:168, 184
"In a Spanish Garden" (Stryk) **27**:187
"In a Station of the Metro" (Pound) **4**:355
"In a Strange House" (Kunitz) **19**:148
"In a Time of Dearth" (Lowell) **13**:83
"In a Time of Revolution for Instance" (Ferlinghetti) **1**:188
"In a Troubled Key" (Hughes) **1**:254-55
In a Vast Dominion (Aleixandre)
See *En un vasto dominio*
"In a Waiting-Room" (Hardy) **8**:107
"In a Whispering Gallery" (Hardy) **8**:108
"In an Artist's Studio" (Rossetti) **7**:284-85
"In Another Fashion" (Ondaatje) **28**:298, 318
"In Arden" (Tomlinson) **17**:326, 343, 346-48, 353
"In August" (Soto) **28**:380
In Autumn (Ekeloef) **23**:71
"In Blood's Domaine" (Duncan) **2**:120
"In Broken Images" (Graves) **6**:134-35, 137, 151, 153
"In casa del sopravissuto" (Gozzano) **10**:180, 183, 185, 189
"In Celebration of My Uterus" (Sexton) **2**:352-53
In Cold Hell, in Thicket (Olson) **19**:284
"In Country Heaven" (Thomas) **2**:395
"In Country Sleep" (Thomas) **2**:395
"In court to serve" (Wyatt) **27**:367
"In Defense of Metaphysics" (Tomlinson) **17**:315
In Defense of the Earth (Rexroth) **20**:181, 186, 188, 190, 192, 194, 209
in defense of the wolves (Enzensberger)
See *Verteidigung der Wolfe*
"In der Fremde" (Bridges) **28**:77, 81
"In deserto" (Gautier) **18**:156
"In Distrust of Merits" (Moore) **4**:236, 238, 240, 249, 261, 267-69
In Dreams Begin Responsibilities, and Other Stories (Schwartz) **8**:281-82, 291, 294, 300-01, 305-07, 319
"In England" (Brodsky) **9**:8
"In Eternum I was ons Determed" (Wyatt) **27**:318, 324
"In Evening Air" (Roethke) **15**:275, 281
"In Examination" (Brooke) **24**:57
"In Excelsis" (Lowell) **13**:91, 97
"In Explanation of Our Times" (Hughes) **1**:258
"In Extremis: Poems about My Father" (Berry) **28**:30
"In Florida" (Swenson) **14**:272
"In Freiburg Station" (Brooke) **24**:62, 66
"In Gallarus Oratory" (Heaney) **18**:201, 223
In Gemäldegalerien (Heine) **25**:131
"In Golden Gate Park That Day" (Ferlinghetti) **1**:183
"In Gratitude to Beethoven" (Wakoski) **15**:345
"In Guernsey" (Swinburne) **24**:325-26
"In Harmony with Nature" (Arnold) **5**:31, 38, 49
"In Her Praise" (Graves) **6**:171-72
"In Honor of David Anderson Brooks, My Father" (Brooks) **7**:62
"In Honour of Du Bartas" (Bradstreet) **10**:2, 6, 52
"In Honour of that High and Mighty Princess, Queen Elizabeth, of Happy Memory" (Bradstreet) **10**:37, 56
"In Hospital" (Pasternak)
See "V bol'nitse"
"In Italy" (Brodsky) **9**:23
"In January" (Brooke) **24**:61, 82
"In Just-" (Cummings) **5**:88, 104
"In Laughter" (Hughes) **7**:159
"In Lieu of the Lyre" (Moore) **4**:259
"In limine" (Montale) **13**:114-15, 165
"In Love Made Visible" (Swenson) **14**:274, 284
"In Loving Memory of the Late Author of Dream Songs" (Meredith) **28**:180, 199, 202, 205, 216-17
In Mad Love and War (Harjo) **27**:66-67
"In Memoriam" (Brodsky) **9**:23
"In Memoriam" (Bryant) **20**:45
"In Memoriam" (Carruth) **10**:85
"In Memoriam" (Roethke) **15**:279
In Memoriam (Tennyson) **6**:354, 359-60, 362-64, 367-71, 379, 388, 392-94, 398-99, 403, 405-08, 412, 416
In Memoriam James Joyce (MacDiarmid) **9**:163-66, 173, 180, 182-84, 186
"In Memoriam Mae Noblitt" (Ammons) **16**:62
"In Memoriam N. K. M. (1889-1947)" (Meredith) **28**:190
"In Memoriam PW Jr 1921-1980" (Kumin) **15**:221
"In Memoriam Stratton Christensen" (Meredith) **28**:185, 209
"In Memoriam: Wallace Stevens" (Duncan) **2**:114
"In Memory: After a Friend's Sudden Death" (Levertov) **11**:206
"In Memory of A. I. Odoevsky" (Lermontov) **18**:268, 298
"In Memory of Ann Jones" (Thomas)
See "After the Funeral: In Memory of Anne Jones"
"In Memory of Arthur Winslow" (Lowell) **3**:218
"In Memory of Elena" (Forche)
See "The Memory of Elena"
"In Memory of Eva Gore-Booth and Con Markiewicz" (Yeats) **20**:349
"In Memory of Major Robert Gregory" (Tomlinson) **17**:307
"In Memory of Major Robert Gregory" (Yeats) **20**:321, 327
"In Memory of My Dear Grandchild Elizabeth Bradstreet" (Bradstreet) **10**:27, 45
"In Memory of Radio" (Baraka) **4**:14
"In Memory of Robert Frost," (Meredith) **28**:195, 202, 216
"In Memory of W. B. Yeats" (Auden) **1**:14
"In Memory of Walter Savage Landor" (Swinburne) **24**:335
"In Michigan" (Masters) **1**:329
"In Mind" (Levertov) **11**:211-13
"In Montgomery" (Brooks) **7**:82
"In Monument Valley" (Merrill) **28**:255
"In morte del realismo" (Pasolini) **17**:259
"In My Craft or Sullen Art" (Thomas) **2**:383
"In My Day We Used to Call It Pussy-Whipped" (Bukowski) **18**:15
"In My Dreams" (Smith) **12**:343
In My Honor (Rilke) **2**:280
"In My Solitary Hours" (Bradstreet) **10**:62-3
"In Neglect" (Frost) **1**:192
"In Nine Sleep Valley" (Merrill) **28**:223
"in nova scotia th peopul" (Bissett) **14**:32
In Other Words (Swenson) **14**:272-74, 277, 279-80, 283, 287
In Our Terribleness (Some Elements and Meaning in Black Style) (Baraka) **4**:19-21
"In Our Time" (Rukeyser) **12**:216
In Parallel (Verlaine)
See *Parallèlement*
"In Paris in a Loud Dark Winter" (Ferlinghetti) **1**:165
"In Praise of Cities" (Gunn) **26**:186, 231
"In Praise of Darkness" (Borges)
See *Elogio de la sombra*
In Praise of Darkness
See *Elogio de la sombra*
In Praise of Darkness (Borges)
See *Elogio de la sombra*
"In Praise of Johnny Appleseed" (Lindsay) **23**:280, 288
In Praise of Krishna (Levertov) **11**:181
"In Praise of Limestone" (Auden) **1**:17, 20
"In Praise of Marriages" (Wright) **14**:342, 365
"In Praise of the Fool" (Olson) **19**:283
"In Procession" (Graves) **6**:138
"In Rain" (Berry) **28**:16
In Reckless Ecstasy (Sandburg) **2**:334
"In reference to her children" (Bradstreet) **10**:13, 26-7, 34-5, 43, 59
"In Santa Maria del Popolo" (Gunn) **26**:186, 201, 219
"In Shadow" (Crane) **3**:98-9
"In Sickness" (Swift) **9**:295
"In Silence" (Merton) **10**:347, 349
"In Sleep" (Montale)
See "Nel sonno"
"In Society" (Ginsberg) **4**:71
"In Strange Cities" (Zagajewski) **27**:394
"In Strasbourg in 1349" (Ammons) **16**:39
"In Summer" (Dunbar) **5**:139
"In Tall Grass" (Sandburg) **2**:324
"In Tenebris (I)" (Hardy) **8**:94, 110
"In Thankful Remembrance for My Dear Husband's Safe Arrival" (Bradstreet) **10**:60-1, 64
"In That Time when It Was Not the Fashion" (Gallagher) **9**:60
"In the Bahamas" (Hass) **16**:217
"In the Balance" (Tomlinson) **17**:346
"In the Bamboo Hut" (Kinnell) **26**:260
"In the Beach House" (Sexton) **2**:363
"In the Beauty Created by Others" (Zagajewski) **27**:381, 383
"In the Beginning" (Sanchez) **9**:228-29
"In the Beginning" (Thomas) **2**:403
"In the Bodies of Words" (Swenson) **14**:287
In the Clearing (Frost) **1**:212-13, 224
"In the Constellations" (Dario)
See "En las constelaciones"
"In the Courtroom" (Sanchez) **9**:225

"In the Dark and Cloudy Day" (Housman) **2**:193
"In the Days of Prismatic Color" (Moore) **4**:251-52, 257-58
"In the Deep Museum" (Sexton) **2**:346, 348, 351, 360-61
"In the East" (Trakl)
See "Im Osten"
"In the Forest" (Pasternak)
See "V lesu"
"In the friendly dark" (Brutus) **24**:122
"In the Fullness of Time" (Tomlinson) **17**:312, 321, 341
"In the Glass of Fashion" (Nemerov) **24**:289, 291
"In the Greenhouse" (Montale)
See "Nella serra"
"In the Hall of Mirrors" (Merrill) **28**:242, 244
"In the Hands of a Blindman" (Gallagher) **9**:60
"In the Heart of Contemplation" (Day Lewis) **11**:144
"In the Hills" (Bely) **11**:5
"In the Hotel of Lost Night" (Kinnell) **26**:251, 267
"In the M5 Restaurant" (Hughes) **7**:162
"In the Market-Place" (Nemerov) **24**:291
"In the Mecca" (Brooks) **7**:78, 81-2, 88-91
In the Mecca (Brooks) **7**:62-3, 66, 81-3, 88, 90-1, 94, 105, 107
"In the Month of March" (Viereck) **27**:278
"In the Moonlight" (Hardy) **8**:124
"In the mountains" (Wang Wei) **18**:376, 380, 383
"In the Naked Bed, in Plato's Cave" (Schwartz) **8**:291, 297, 301-02, 308-09, 311, 316
"In the Neolithic Age" (Kipling) **3**:167
"In the Night" (Smith) **12**:345
"In the Park" (Kumin) **15**:209-11, 211
"In the Park" (Montale) **13**:151
"In the Park" (Smith) **12**:345, 352-54
"In the Past" (Zagajewski) **27**:383
"In the Pink" (Sassoon) **12**:242, 262
"In The Plaza" (Aleixandre) **15**:6, 11-12, 17
In the Presence of the Sun: A Gathering of Shields (Momaday) **25**:220-22
"In the Public Garden" (Moore) **4**:259
"In the Rain" (H. D.) **5**:304
"In the Restaurant" (Blok) **21**:3
"In the Restaurant" (Hardy) **8**:124
"In the Ruins of New York City" (Merton) **10**:344, 349
"In the Same Boat" (Kipling) **3**:183
"In the Sconset Bus" (Williams) **7**:409
"In the Secret Room" (Wakoski) **15**:348
"In the Shelter" (Day Lewis) **11**:151
"In the Square" (Aleixandre)
See "In The Plaza"
"In the Survivor's Home" (Gozzano)
See "In casa del sopravissuto"
"In the Tank" (Gunn) **26**:203
"In the Tents of Akbar" (Dunbar) **5**:138
"In the Tradition" (Baraka) **4**:40
"In the Underworld" (Rukeyser) **12**:220
"In the Waiting Room" (Bishop) **3**:59, 69-70
"In the Waxworks" (Shapiro) **25**:273
"In the White Giant's Thigh" (Thomas) **2**:395, 404
"In the Wilderness" (Graves) **6**:128-29
"In the winter in Paris" (Guillen) **23**:103
"In the Wood" (Pasternak) **6**:252-53, 259
"In This Age of Hard Trying, Nonchalance Is Good and ..." (Moore) **4**:229, 270
"In those days you were like a moter to me" (Tsvetaeva)
See "V ony dni, ty mne byla kak mat'"
"in ths forest" (Bissett) **14**:27
"In Time of Mourning" (Swinburne) **24**:319
"In Time of Plague" (Gunn) **26**:231
"In Time of 'The Breaking of Nations'" (Hardy) **8**:115, 121
"In Time of War" (Auden) **1**:18
"In vain with eye a with a nail" (Tsvetaeva)
See "Naprasno glazom kak gvozdem"
"In Valleys Green and Still" (Housman) **2**:180
"In Warm Rooms Before a Blue Light" (Kumin) **15**:211
"In Warsaw" (Milosz) **8**:192
"In Weather" (Hass) **16**:196, 200, 202-03
In What Hour (Rexroth) **20**:177, 183, 192-93, 198, 214-15, 217
"In what torne ship" (Donne)
See "A Hymne to Christ, at the authors last going into Germany"
"Inauguration Day: January 1953" (Lowell) **3**:214, 218, 222
"Incantation" (Milosz) **8**:202
"Incantation" (Pinsky) **27**:166
"Incantation at Assisi" (Viereck) **27**:267
"Incantesimo" (Montale) **13**:110
"Incarnation" (Rexroth) **20**:206, 216
"Incense of the Lucky Virgin" (Hayden) **6**:195
"Incespicare" (Montale) **13**:134
"Incident" (Cullen) **20**:61
"Incident on a Journey" (Gunn) **26**:218
Incidental Numbers (Wylie) **23**:311, 321, 325-26, 331
"Inclusions" (Browning) **6**:5-6, 15
"Incompatibilities" (Hughes) **7**:113
"Incontro" (Montale) **13**:165
"Incontro" (Pavese) **13**:217
"The Incorrigible Dirigible" (Carruth) **10**:88
"Independence Day" (Bukowski) **18**:15
"The Independent Man" (Brooks) **7**:53
"An Indian at the Burial-Ground of His Father" (Bryant) **20**:36
"Indian Bread" (Kinnell) **26**:238
"The Indian Girl's Lament" (Bryant) **20**:10, 17
Indian Journals, March 1962-May 1963 (Ginsberg) **4**:53, 56, 60
"Indian Serenade" (Montale)
See "Serenata indiana"
"Indian Summer" (Parker) **28**:347
"Indian Summer" (Pavese)
See "Estate di San Martino"
"The Indian to His Love" (Yeats) **20**:343
"Indiana" (Crane) **3**:88, 106-07
"TH INDIANS WERE WELCOMED AS BRIDGEBUILDERS" (Bissett) **14**:33
L'Indicateur des chemins de coeur (Tzara) **27**:229, 231, 234
Indicateur des chemins du coeur (Tyler) **27**:
"Indictment of Senior Officers" (Olds) **22**:307
"Indifference" (Arnold)
See "Euphrosyne"
"The Indifferent" (Donne) **1**:125
"The Indigo Glass in the Grass" (Stevens) **6**:324
"Indisciplina" (Pavese) **13**:214, 226
"Indispensability of Eyes" (Olds) **22**:307
"The Individual Man" (Duncan) **2**:118
"The Indivisible Incompatibles" (Swenson) **14**:284
"Indolence" (Bridges) **28**:48, 83
"The Indolent Monk" (Baudelaire)
See "Le mauvais moine"
"The Indweller" (Tagore)
See "Antaryami"
"Infant" (Smith) **12**:310, 326
"Infant Joy" (Blake) **12**:7, 9, 33-4
"Infant Sorrow" (Blake) **12**:7, 31, 34
"Infanta Marina" (Stevens) **6**:311
"An Inference of Mexico" (Hayden) **6**:194, 198
Inferno (Dante) **21**:53, 56, 59-67, 69-72, 75-7, 81-5, 89, 95-6, 98-9, 101, 103-08
"L'infini dans les cieux" (Lamartine) **16**:266, 280, 284-85
"Inflation Blues" (Walker) **20**:294
"El ingenuo" (Borges) **22**:97, 99
"Ingoldsby Legends" (Browning) **2**:36
The Inhabitant and His Hope (Neruda)
See *El habitante y su esperenza*
"Inheritor" (Wright)
See "Eroded Hills"
"Inhuman World" (Aleixandre) **15**:20
"The Inhumanist" (Jeffers) **17**:136
"The Iniquity of the Fathers upon the Children" (Rossetti) **7**:289-90
"Initial, Daemonic, and Celestial Love" (Emerson) **18**:93
"Initiations" (Okigbo) **7**:224-25, 232, 237
"Injudicious Gardening" (Moore) **4**:266
"The Injury" (Williams) **7**:360
"The Inlet" (Gluck) **16**:125
The Inn Album (Browning) **2**:68, 96
"The Inner Kingdom" (Dario)
See "El reino interior"
The Inner Room (Merrill) **28**:281
"Innocence" (Gunn) **26**:197, 201
"Innocence" (Levine) **22**:228
"Innocent Landscape" (Wylie) **23**:305-306, 333-34
"The Innocents" (Wylie) **23**:302-303, 310
"Inochi no fune" (Ishikawa) **10**:213, 215
"ins lesebuch fu¨r die oberstufe" (Enzensberger) **28**:135
"Inscription for the Entrance into a Wood" (Bryant) **20**:4, 17, 19, 35, 40, 47
"Insensibility" (Owen) **19**:327, 337, 340, 347-48, 355, 357, 369-70
"Inside a mountain idles an idol" (Mandelstam)
See "Vnutri gory bezdeistvuet kumir"
Inside the Blood Factory (Wakoski) **15**:324-25, 341, 348, 350-51, 362-63, 365
"The Insidious Dr. Fu Man Chu" (Baraka) **4**:15
"L'insinuant" (Valery) **9**:395
Insomnia (Tsvetaeva) **14**:299, 301
"Insomnia. Homer. Tautly Swelling Sails. . ." (Mandelstam) **14**:141
"Insomniac" (Plath) **1**:399
"Insomnio" (Borges) **22**:92
"Inspection" (Owen) **19**:335, 354, 356
"Inspiration" (Lowell) **3**:245
"Installation of the Duke of Grafton as Chancellor of Cambridge" (Gray) **2**:143
"The Instant" (Levertov) **11**:166, 168
"Instead of Camargue" (Swenson) **14**:249
"Instinct" (Pavese)
See "L'istinto"
"The Instruction Manual" (Ashbery) **26**:111, 129, 159, 164
"Instructions to the Double" (Gallagher) **9**:58, 60
Instructions to the Double (Gallagher) **9**:35-7, 43, 53-4, 58
"Instructions to the Orphic Adept" (Graves) **6**:133
"Insufficiency" (Browning) **6**:15
"Insularum Ocelle" (Swinburne) **24**:326
"The Insulted and Injured" (Viereck) **27**:279
Intact Wind (Paz)
See *Viento entero*
Intellectual Things (Kunitz) **19**:147-48, 153, 155, 159-61, 163, 185
"The Intellectuals" (Shapiro) **25**:270, 312
Inter mezzo (Heine) **25**:131
"Intercettazione telefonica" (Montale) **13**:133
"Interface" (Wright) **14**:373
"Interference" (Ammons) **16**:6
"Intérieur" (Valery) **9**:365, 396
"Interim" (Levertov) **11**:176, 195-96
"Interim" (Millay) **6**:205-07, 214
"The Interlude" (Shapiro) **25**:303, 326
"Intermezzo" (Montale) **13**:106
"Intermezzo No 1" (Heine) **25**:141
"Intermission 3" (Brooks) **7**:58, 62, 91, 104
"Interplay" (Wright) **14**:348
"Interrogaciones" (Dario) **15**:100
"The Interrogation of the Man of Many Hearts" (Sexton) **2**:352
"Interruption" (Graves) **6**:137, 143-44
"Interview" (Ekeloef) **23**:86-7
"Interview" (Parker) **28**:361
"Interview with a Tourist" (Atwood) **8**:14
"Intimation of Immortality" (Smith) **12**:313
"Intimations of Immorality" (Sappho) **5**:418

"Intimations of Immortality" (Thomas) **2**:392
"Intimations of Immortality" (Wordsworth)
See "Ode: Intimations of Immortality from Recollections of Early Childhood"
Intimité marine (Cesaire) **25**:22
"Into My Heart and Air That Kills" (Housman) **2**:192
"Into My Own" (Frost) **1**:213
"Into the Golden Vessel of Great Song" (Millay) **6**:211
"Into the Shandy Westerness" (Rexroth) **20**:196
"Into the Tree" (Milosz) **8**:198
"Into the Twilight" (Yeats) **20**:346
"Introduction" (Blake) **12**:7, 32, 34-5, 43-7
"The Introduction" (Finch) **21**:155-57, 159, 161, 181
"The Intrusion" (Graves) **6**:156
"Les Invalides" (Kinnell) **26**:260
"Invasions" (Kunitz) **19**:148
"Invective Against Swans" (Stevens) **6**:294
Invectives (Verlaine) **2**:419
"Invernal" (Dario) **15**:117
"Invictus" (Parker) **28**:355
"De invierno" (Dario) **15**:107-08, 110
"INVISIBLE" (Villa) **22**:356
"invisible presence" (Ekeloef)
See "osynlig närvaro"
Invisible Reality (Jimenez)
See *La realidad invisible*
"The Invitation" (Clare) **23**:23
"L'invitation au voyage" (Baudelaire) **1**:69
"The Invitation to Daphnis" (Finch) **21**:139, 153-54, 161
"Invitation to Miss Marianne Moore" (Bishop) **3**:44
"Invite to Eternity" (Clare) **23**:22-4, 26
"Invitation to the Country" (Bridges) **28**:66, 69
"L'invocation" (Lamartine) **16**:277, 279, 290
"Invocation" (Lamartine)
See "L'invocation"
"Invocation" (Levertov) **11**:177
"Invocation" (Sitwell) **3**:312
"An Invocation to Sleep" (Finch) **21**:143, 146, 179-80
"Io poeta delle Ceneri" (Pasolini) **17**:292
"Iola, Kansas" (Clampitt) **19**:95-6
"Ione" (Dunbar) 125
"Iork" (Brodsky)
See "York: In Memoriam W. H. Auden"
"Iride" (Montale) **13**:109, 111, 121-22, 130-31, 152, 166
"Iris" (Montale)
See "Iride"
"Irises" (Lee) **24**:240
"An Irish Airman Foresees His Death" (Yeats) **20**:304
"The Irish Cliffs of Moher" (Stevens) **6**:304
"Iron" (Zagajewski) **27**:381, 387
"the Iron Characters" (Nemerov) **24**:262, 279
"Iron Hans" (Sexton) **2**:365-68
"Iron Landscapes" (Gunn) **26**:197-198, 206, 214
"Iron Train" (Zagajewski) **27**:402
"L'irrémédiable" (Baudelaire) **1**:55
"L'Irréparable" (Baudelaire) **1**:68
is 5 (Cummings) **5**:77, 92, 95, 104
"Is it possible?" (Wyatt) **27**:353
"Is It True?" (Sexton) **2**:368, 374
"Is It Wise" (Smith) **12**:343
"Is My Team Ploughing" (Housman) **2**:180, 193, 196
I's (Pronounced Eyes) (Zukofsky) **11**:357
"Is There for Honest Poverty" (Burns) **6**:58, 83
"Is There No Way Out?" (Paz)
See "[00a8]No hay salida?"
"Isaac and Archibald" (Robinson) **1**:467, 486-87, 496
"Isabel" (Tennyson) **6**:387
"Isabella" (Keats) **1**:279, 282, 288-89, 296
"Isabella; or, The Pot of Basil" (Keats)
See "Isabella"
"Isaiah" (Walker) **20**:278
"Isaiah LXII: 1-8" (Wheatley) **3**:357
"Isba Song" (McGuckian) **27**:103
"Ischia" (Lamartine) **16**:287, 291
"Ishtar" (Wright) **14**:363
Isla ignorada (Fuertes) **27**:10, 19, 21
"Isla ignorado" (Fuertes) **27**:43
"The Island" (Forche) **10**:138, 152, 161, 166
"Island" (Hughes) **1**:244, 248
"An Island" (Robinson) **1**:465, 467
The Island (Allard) **24**:116
The Island (Byron) **16**:86, 88, 90, 109
"The Island Hawk" (Noyes) **27**:122
"Island in the Works" (Merrill) **28**:268, 270-71
"Island of Night" (Kinnell) **26**:257
"The Island of Statues" (Yeats) **20**:343, 346, 353
"The Islanders" (Kipling) **3**:179, 192
"The Islands" (H. D.) **5**:268
"The Islands" (Hayden) **6**:191, 193, 200
"Islands and Towers" (Zagajewski) **27**:389
"Ismaïl Bey" (Lermontov) **18**:278, 300
"Isolation: To Marguerite" (Arnold) **5**:13, 18
"Isolationist" (Page) **12**:170
"L'isolement" (Lamartine) **16**:265, 274-77, 290, 298-301
"Ispoved" (Lermontov) **18**:300
"Israel" (Shapiro) **25**:283, 285, 297-98, 307, 320, 325
"Israfel" (Poe) **1**:438, 447-48
"The Issues" (Olds) **22**:313
Isthm. VII (Pindar)
See *Isthmian 7*
Isthmian 3 (Pindar) **19**:426
Isthmian 4 (Pindar) **19**:426
Isthmian 6 (Pindar) **19**:398, 414, 421-22
Isthmian 7 (Pindar) **19**:425
Isthmian 8 (Pindar) **19**:398, 424
"L'istinto" (Pavese) **13**:205, 213
"Isto" (Pessoa) **20**:172
It Catches My Heart in Its Hands: New and Selected Poems, 1955-1963 (Bukowski) **18**:5, 21
"It Is a Living Coral" (Williams) **7**:369
"It Is a Spring Afternoon" (Sexton) **2**:352
"It Is Everywhere" (Toomer) **7**:337, 340
"It Is My Thoughts That Color My Soul" (Wylie) **23**:322
"It Is No Longer Possible" (Aleixandre) **15**:20
"It is over" (Guillen)
See "It is over"
"It Is So" (Neruda)
See "Es así"
"It Is the First Mild Day of March" (Wordsworth)
See "Lines on the First Mild Day of March"
"It Is Well" (Brooke) **24**:71-2
"It may be good" (Wyatt) **27**:316, 329, 341
"It Must Be Sophisticated" (Ashbery) **26**:161
"It Must Be the Milk" (Nash) **21**:278-79
"It Must Give Pleasure" (Stevens) **6**:329
"It Nods and Curtseys and Recovers" (Housman) **2**:192-93
"It Was a Face Which Darkness Could Kill" (Ferlinghetti) **1**:183
"It Was a' for Our Rightfu' King" (Burns) **6**:99
"It Was a Funky Deal" (Knight) **14**:46
"It Was a Gentle Breeze" (Dario)
See "Era un aire suave"
"It Was a Soft Air" (Dario)
See "Era un aire suave"
"It Was All Very Tidy" (Graves) **6**:142, 144
"It Was Black Black Took" (Stein) **18**:328
"It Was That Indian" (Ortiz) **17**:234
It Was When (Snyder) **21**:289
"It Was Winter" (Milosz) **8**:194
"L'Italia" (Pasolini) **17**:270, 272
"Italia mia" (Petrarch) **8**:267, 270
"Italian Morning" (Bogan) **12**:106
"An Italian Visit" (Day Lewis) **11**:150
"Italy and France" (Browning) **2**:26
"Itching Heels" (Dunbar) **5**:146
"Ite, missa est" (Dario) **15**:113
"Ithaca" (Gluck) **16**:172
"Itinerary" (Kumin) **15**:220
"Itinerary of an Obession" (Kumin) **15**:220
"It's a New Day" (Sanchez) **9**:229
It's a New Day: Poems for Young Brothas and Sistuhs (Sanchez) **9**:207, 211-12, 215, 229, 237
"It's both boring and sad" (Lermontov) **18**:268-69
"It's Dull and Dreary" (Lermontov) **18**:281
"Its Everlasting Possibility" (Pinsky) **27**:153
"Its Great Emptiness" (Pinsky) **27**:154
"Its Great Emptiness" (Pinsky) **27**:153
"It's Half an Hour Later Before" (Ammons) **16**:25
"Its Many Fragments" (Pinsky) **27**:153
"It's Nation Time" (Baraka) **4**:19, 26, 40
It's Nation Time (Baraka) **4**:19, 20, 26
"It's Not Going to Happen Again" (Brooke) **24**:84-5, 93
"It's over a (See Just" (Cummings) **5**:108
"It's Raining" (Apollinaire)
See "Il pleut"
"It's Time, My Friend, It's Time" (Pushkin)
See "Pora, Moi Drug, Pora"
"It's Unbecoming" (Pasternak) **6**:265
I've Been a Woman (Sanchez) **9**:207, 211-12, 215-16, 218-22, 227, 229, 232, 238, 242
"I've Been Asleep" (Levine) **22**:218
"The Ivory Statuette" (Wylie) **23**:321
Iz shesti knig (Akhmatova) **2**:18
"Ja k vam pishu" (Lermontov) **18**:303
"Jabberwocky" (Carroll) **18**:36, 38-40, 48-50, 52, 59-60
Jack Kelso: A Dramatic Poem (Masters) **1**:339
"Jack Straw's Castle" (Gunn) **26**:205
"Jack's Straw Castle" (Gunn) **26**:213, 228
Jack's Straw Castle, and Other Poems (Gunn) **26**:194-197, 204-206, 208, 210, 213, 219-220, 229
"Jackson, Mississippi" (Walker) **20**:283
"The Jacob's Ladder" (Gluck) **16**:171
The Jacob's Ladder (Levertov) **11**:168, 193, 206
"Jactancia de quietud" (Borges) **22**:72
Jadis et naguère (Verlaine) **2**:416
"The Jaguar" (Hughes) **7**:118, 151, 163
"The Jain Bird Hospital in Delhi" (Meredith) **28**:215
"J'ai plus de souvenirs" (Baudelaire) **1**:67
"Jam Session" (Hughes) **1**:245
"The Jam Trap" (Tomlinson) **17**:314
"Jamāl al-mawt" (Gibran) **9**:78
"James Wetherell" (Robinson) **1**:467
"The Jam-Pot" (Kipling) **3**:190
"January" (Belloc) **24**:29
"January" (Hass) **16**:216
"January" (Nishiwaki)
See "Ichigatsu"
"January" (Song) **21**:341
"January 1918" (Pasternak) **6**:261
"January 1919" (Pasternak) **6**:252
"January and May" (Chaucer)
See "Miller's Tale"
"A January Night" (Hardy) **8**:110
"Jardín de invierno" (Neruda) **4**:287, 289-90
"El jardín triste se pierde" (Jimenez) **7**:199
Jardines lejanos (Jimenez) **7**:209
"Jarrama" (Ekeloef) **23**:76
"Jasmine Arbour" (Tagore)
See "Chameli-vitan"
"Jaws" (Sandburg) **2**:330
"Jaybird" (Dunbar) **5**:144
"Jazzonia" (Hughes) **1**:246, 261
"Je plaings le temps de ma jeunesse" (Villon) **13**:388-89
"Je plante en la faveur cest arbre de Cybelle" (Ronsard) **11**:277
"Je suis bruslé, Le Gast, d'une double chaleur" (Ronsard) **11**:250

"Je suis l'empire à la fin de la décadence" (Verlaine) **2**:416
"The Jealous Man" (Graves) **6**:142, 144
"Jealousy" (Brooke) **24**:56
"Jealousy--A Confessional" (Wakoski) **15**:356
"Jeanne d'Arc" (Gluck) **16**:140
"jed bi kor benkst trik" (Bissett) **14**:34
"Jefferson" (Shapiro) **25**:270
"Jehova" (Lamartine) **16**:280, 293
"Jehuda ben Halevy" (Heine) **25**:149
"Jemez" (Tomlinson) **17**:355
"The Jerboa" (Moore) **4**:233, 236, 243
"Jeremiah" (Walker) **20**:278
"Jeronimo's House" (Bishop) **3**:37, 47
"Jerusalem" (Blake) **12**:37
"Jerusalem" (Rich) **5**:383
Jerusalem: The Emanation of the Giant Albion (Blake) **12**:13, 20, 27, 29-32, 34-40, 43-4, 51-9, 61-75, 80
"Jessie Cameron" (Rossetti) **7**:280
"Jessie Mitchell's Mother" (Brooks) **7**:58, 62, 68, 96, 99-100, 102
"The Jester" (Hughes) **1**:235
"The Jester, A Ballad" (Bely)
See "Shut, Bellada"
"Jester above It" (Bely)
See "Shut Nad ney"
"Jesu" (Herbert) **4**:100
"Jesus and Isolt" (Pinsky) **27**:157, 175
"The Jesus Papers" (Sexton) **2**:360
"Jesus Walking" (Sexton) **2**:360-61, 373
"Le jet d'eau" (Baudelaire) **1**:61
La jeune parque (Valery) **9**:346-48, 351-58, 361, 363-67, 369-74, 379-85, 387, 390-96, 401-03
"La jeune prêtre" (Valery) **9**:391
"Jeunesse" (Rimbaud) **3**:261, 263
"Jew" (Shapiro) **25**:296-97
"The Jew at Christmas Eve" (Shapiro) **25**:283, 286, 300
"Jewelled Bindings" (Wylie) **23**:320
"The Jewish Problem" (Shapiro) **25**:323
The Jig of Forslin (Aiken) **26**:5-7, 35
The Jig of Forslin: A Symphony (Aiken) **26**:16, 21-2
Jill (Larkin) **21**:225, 232
"Jim and Arabel's Sister" (Masters) **1**:328
"Jim at Sixteen" (McKay) **2**:223
"Jim Brown on the Screen" (Baraka) **4**:19
Jim Crow's Last Stand (Hughes) **1**:250, 253
Th Jinx Ship nd Othr Trips (Bissett) **14**:14
"Jitterbugs" (Baraka) **4**:12, 18
"Jivan devata" (Tagore) **8**:408
"Jivan madhyahna" (Tagore) **8**:407
"Jiving" (Dove) **6**:114, 117
"The Joachim Quartet" (Bridges) **28**:88
"Joal" (Senghor) **25**:241, 243-44, 246
"Joan and Darby" (Graves) **6**:156
"Joan of Arc" (Coleridge) **11**:80, 83, 97
"Joasaph and Fatumeh" (Ekeloef) **23**:67
"Job" (Blake) **12**:38
Jocelyn: Épisode; Journal trouvé chez un curé de village (Lamartine) **16**:257-61, 263-64, 269-70, 273-74, 286-87, 293, 297
"Jochanan Hakkadosh" (Browning) **2**:75
"Joel" (Walker) **20**:278-79
"Joggin' Erlong" (Dunbar) **5**:145
"John and Anne" (Meredith) **28**:199, 205
"John Anderson, My Jo" (Burns) **6**:78, 98
"John Barleycorn" (Burns) **6**:52
"John Brown" (Hayden) **6**:192, 195
"John Brown" (Lindsay) **23**:264-65, 275, 279, 286
"John Brown" (Robinson) **1**:468
"John Burke" (Olson) **19**:305
"John Cowper Powys" (Masters) **1**:343
John Deth: A Metaphysical Legend (Aiken) **26**:12, 53
"John Donne in California" (Clampitt) **19**:92
"John Dryden" (Carruth) **10**:74
"John Gorham" (Robinson) **1**:462, 468, 478
"John I, 14" (Borges)
See "Juan I, 14"
"John L. Sullivan, the Strong Boy of Boston" (Lindsay) **23**:265, 270, 273, 276
"John Maydew; or, The Allotment" (Tomlinson) **17**:326, 341
"John McLean (1879-1923)" (MacDiarmid) **9**:179
"Johnny Appleseed" (Masters) **1**:330
"Johnny Spain's White Heifer" (Carruth) **10**:74
"Joilet" (Sandburg) **2**:324
"Joke" (Bely)
See "Shutka"
"A Joker" (Baudelaire)
See "Un plaisant"
"La jolie rousse" (Apollinaire) **7**:3, 9, 49
"Jollie Gleeman" (Viereck) **27**:282
"The Jolly Beggars" (Burns) **6**:55-6, 58, 78, 90-6
"The Jolly Company" (Brooke) **24**:58
"Jonathan Edwards" (Lowell) **3**:212
"Jonathan Edwards in Western Massachusettes" (Lowell) **3**:216
"Jordan" (Herbert) **4**:102, 107, 113
"Jordan I" (Herbert) **4**:114, 129
"Jordan II" (Herbert) **4**:100, 114
Jorge Luis Borges: Selected Poems 1923-1969 (Borges) **22**:71
"Joseph" (Forche) **10**:144, 156-57
"Joseph's Coat" (Herbert) **4**:130
"Joshua Tree" (Ammons) **16**:5
"Le joujou du pauvre" (Baudelaire) **1**:58
"Jour et nuit" (Cesaire) **25**:30
"Journal Night Thoughts" (Ginsberg) **4**:52, 69
"Journal of an Airman" (Auden) **1**:5
"The Journalist Reader and Writer" (Lermontov) **18**:268-69, 281
Journals: Early Fifties, Early Sixties (Ginsberg) **4**:60, 69
The Journals of Susanna Moodie (Atwood) **8**:10-12, 15, 21, 29, 31, 33, 35-6, 40
"The Journey" (Kumin) **15**:198, 203
"Journey" (Millay) **6**:206
"Journey" (Olds) **22**:322
"The Journey Back" (Heaney) **18**:256
"Journey Home" (Page) **12**:178
"Journey North" (Tu Fu) **9**:332
"The Journey of Life" (Bryant) **20**:10
"Journey of the Magi" (Eliot) **5**:171, 177, 194, 197, 203, 205, 209
Journey to a Known Place (Carruth) **10**:70
Journey to Love (Williams) **7**:371, 403
"The Journey to the Interior" (Atwood) **8**:36
"Journey to the Interior" (Roethke) **15**:279, 310, 314
"Joy" (Enzensberger) **28**:142
"Joy" (Jeffers) **17**:106
"Joy" (Levertov) **11**:192
"The Joy and Agony of Improvisation" (Carruth) **10**:73
"Joy in Russia" (Bely) **11**:6
"Joyce Carol Oates Plays the Saturn Piano" (Wakoski) **15**:368
"Joyeuse Garde" (Swinburne) **24**:355
"The Joyful Black Demon of Sister Clara Flies through the Midnight Woods on Her Snowmobile" (Wakoski) **15**:332
"Joys Faces Friends" (Cummings) **5**:110
"Joy sweetest lifeborn joy" (Bridges) **28**:89
"Juan Figueroa, Casa del Yodo 'Maria Elena,' Antofagasta" (Neruda) **4**:294
"Juan Figueroa, Iodine Factory 'Maria Elena,' Antofagasta" (Neruda)
See "Juan Figueroa, Casa del Yodo 'Maria Elena,' Antofagasta"
"Juan I, 14" (Borges) **22**:75, 96
"Juan's Song" (Bogan) **12**:90, 92, 100
"Jubal" (Eliot) **20**:101, 117, 119-20, 124, 134-37, 144
"Jubilate Agno" (Smart) **13**:339-40, 342-44, 346-48, 350-52, 355, 357-58, 360-69
Jubilation (Tomlinson) **17**:361
"Judas Iscariot" (Cullen) **20**:55-56, 67, 86
"Judas Kiss" (Kinnell) **26**:286-87
Judgement Day (Johnson) **24**:128-29, 164-65, 169
Judges (Vigny) **26**:368
"The Judgment" (Akhmatova) **2**:15
"Judgment" (Herbert) **4**:129
"The Judgment of Midas" (Smart) **13**:348
"Juice Joint: Northern City" (Hughes) **1**:243
"Julia" (Wordsworth) **4**:399
"Julian and Maddalo" (Shelley) **14**:173, 175, 182, 240
"Julian M. and A. G. Rochelle" (Bronte) **8**:52
"Julia's Petticoat" (Herrick) **9**:143
"Julio" (Lermontov)
See "Julio"
"July" (Belloc) **24**:29
"July 8, 1656" (Bradstreet) **10**:60
"July, 1773" (Berry) **28**:38
"July 1968" (Levertov) **11**:194
"July, Against Hunger" (Kumin) **15**:207
"July in Vallombrosa" (Loy) **16**:313
"July in Washington" (Lowell) **3**:214
"July Midnight" (Lowell) **13**:64
"A July Night" (Ekeloef) **23**:58
"June" (Bryant) **20**:9, 14, 16, 18
"June: Dutch Harbor" (Meredith) **28**:170, 172, 185, 187
"Junge Leiden" (Heine) **25**:139
"The Jungle and the Sea" (Aleixandre) **15**:3, 14
The Jungle Book (Kipling) **3**:162, 185, 188-89
"Jungle Knot" (Ammons) **16**:4
"Das jüngste Gericht" (Rilke) **2**:277
Junjo shokyoku shu (Hagiwara Sakutaro) **18**:176, 182
"Junkman's Obbligato" (Ferlinghetti) **1**:165-66, 173
"Just Don't Never Give Up on Love" (Sanchez) **9**:234, 238, 244
"Just For Starters" (Ashbery) **26**:165
"Just Lost, When I Was Saved!" (Dickinson) **1**:97
"Just Whistle a Bit" (Dunbar) **5**:137
"Justice" (Herbert) **4**:102
"Justice" (Hughes) **1**:252
"Justice II" (Herbert) **4**:131
"Justice Denied in Massachusetts" (Millay) **6**:223
"Justice Is Reason Enough" (Wakoski) **15**:336
"The Justice of the Peace" (Belloc) **24**:28
"Juvat ire jugis" (Arnold) **5**:36
"K Liciniju" (Pushkin) **10**:408
"K Likomedu, na Skiros" (Brodsky) **9**:5
"K Muze" (Blok) **21**:6, 40
"K*** Ne dumaj chtob ja byl dostoin sozhalen'ja" (Lermontov) **18**:301, 304
"K pustoi zemle nevol'no pripadaia" (Mandelstam) **14**:155-56
K Uranii (Brodsky)
See *To Urania: Selected Poems 1965-1985*
"Ka 'Ba" (Baraka) **4**:18
"Kabi kahini" (Tagore) **8**:405
"Kaddish" (Ginsberg) **4**:49-50, 53, 59, 61, 64-5, 72, 74, 81, 83-6, 91
Kaddish, and Other Poems (Ginsberg) **4**:47
"Kaeru no shi" (Hagiwara Sakutaro) **18**:168, 179
"Kaeru yo" (Hagiwara Sakutaro) **18**:180
Kahini (Tagore) **8**:410
Kai oi (Matsuo Basho) **3**:24
"Kai, Today" (Snyder) **21**:289
"Kak svetoteni muchenik Rembrandt" (Mandelstam) **14**:154
"Kalaloch" (Forche) **10**:133-35, 168
"Kalamzoo" (Lindsay) **23**:270
"Kaleidoscopes: Baroque" (Atwood) **8**:11
"Kali" (Clifton) **17**:23
"Kalimpong" (Tagore) **8**:426
"Kally" (Lermontov) **18**:300
"The Kallyope Yell" (Lindsay) **23**:266, 272, 274-76, 280, 284, 289, 296
Kalpana (Tagore) **8**:410-11, 415

Kamen' (Mandelstam) **14**:106, 108, 112-15, 117-18, 122, 135, 142
"Kanashi Tsukio" (Hagiwara Sakutaro) **18**:168
Kanashiki gangu (Ishikawa) **10**:195-97, 200-01, 205, 210-11, 217
"Kansas" (Lindsay) **23**:273, 286
"Kansas City" (Harjo) **27**:55, 65, 72
"Kansas City to St. Louis" (Ginsberg) **4**:54, 57
"Kantian Lyrics I" (Tomlinson) **17**:346
"Kanun Blagoveshchen'ia" (Tsvetaeva) **14**:319-20, 322
"Das kapital" (Baraka) **4**:30, 38
"Das Kapitäl" (Rilke) **2**:275
"Kapuzinerberg (Saltzberg)" (Bogan) **12**:100
Kari o komal (Tagore) **8**:406-07, 415
Kashima kiko (Matsuo Basho) **3**:27
Katha (Tagore) **8**:410
"Katharinal" (Heine) **25**:135
"Käthe Kollwitz" (Rukeyser) **12**:228-30
"Die Kathedrale" (Rilke) **2**:275
"Katherine's Dream" (Lowell) **3**:201
"Katun 8 Ahau" (Cardenal) **22**:129, 131
"Katun 11 Ahau" (Cardenal) **22**:128-29
Kavkazsky plennik (Pushkin) **10**:357-58, 364-65, 371, 386-88, 395, 415-21
"Kay Rutledge" (Masters) **1**:334
"Kayanerenhkowa" (Cardenal) **22**:128-29, 131
"Kazach'ja kolybel'naja pesnja" (Lermontov) **18**:304
"Keats House" (Stryk) **27**:203
"Keen" (Millay) **6**:225
"Keep a Pluggin' Away" (Dunbar) **5**:119
"keep on th grass" (Bissett) **14**:33
"Keeper of the Flocks" (Pessoa)
See "O Guardador de Rebanhos"
"Keeping Informed in D.C." (Nemerov) **24**:262
"Keeping Their World Large" (Moore) **4**:236, 268
"Keller Gegen Dom" (Williams) **7**:378
"Kellyburn Braes" (Burns) **6**:78
"Kent and Christendome" (Wyatt) **27**:331
"*Kenyon Review*, After the Sandstorm" (Bukowski) **18**:15
"Kept" (Bogan) **12**:105, 122
"The Key to Everything" (Swenson) **14**:247
"Key West: An Island Sheaf" (Crane) **3**:90
Kezfogasok (Illyes) **16**:231, 235
"Khadji Abrek" (Lermontov) **18**:285, 300
"Khalil al-kāfir" (Gibran) **9**:78
"Khansky polon" (Tsvetaeva) **14**:314-15
Kheya (Tagore) **8**:412-13, 415
"Khristos Voskres" (Pushkin) **10**:411-12
"The Kid" (Aiken) **26**:16, 41-2
"Kid" (Hayden) **6**:196
The Kid (Aiken) **26**:24, 30, 45
"The Kids Who Die" (Hughes) **1**:243
"Kierkegaard on Hegel" (Zagajewski) **27**:383, 385
"A Kike is the Most Dangerous" (Cummings) **5**:82, 84
"Killauea" (Kinnell) **26**:286
"The Killer and the Dove" (Viereck) **27**:282
"KILLER WHALE" (Bissett) **14**:10-11, 17-18, 34
"Killiecrankie" (Burns) **6**:78
"Killing the Spring" (Sexton) **2**:365
"Kilroy" (Viereck) **27**:263
"Kilroy's Carnival" (Schwartz) **8**:311
"Kimi Shinitamô koto nakare" (Yosano Akiko) **11**:320-26, 328-29
"Kin to Sorrow" (Millay) **6**:205
"The Kind Ghosts" (Owen) **19**:343
"The Kind Master and Dutiful Servant" (Hammon) **16**:177-78, 180-82, 190
"Kind of an Ode to Duty" (Nash) **21**:272
"A Kind of Ethics" (Gunn) **26**:206
The Kind of Poetry I Want (MacDiarmid) **9**:180, 182, 184, 185-86
"Kind Sir: These Woods" (Sexton) **2**:358
Kindai no Guwa (Nishiwaki) **15**:231
"Kindliness" (Brooke) **24**:56, 77
"Kindness" (Plath) **1**:391, 393
Kindness in the Wolfpasses (Elytis)
See *I kalosíni stis likoporiés*
"The King" (Kipling) **3**:161, 166
"King Arthur's Men Have Come Again" (Lindsay) **23**:283
"King Arthur's Tomb" (Swinburne) **24**:355
"King Ban" (Swinburne) **24**:355
King Bolo (Eliot) **5**:174
"King Edward the Third" (Blake) **12**:11, 61
"King Hamlet's Ghost" (Smith) **12**:311, 353
"A King in Funeral Procession" (Smith) **12**:315
"King Kong Meets Wallace Stevens" (Ondaatje) **28**:327, 333
King Jasper (Robinson) **1**:479, 483
The King Maiden (Tsvetaeva)
See *Tsar-devitsa*
"King of Carrion" (Hughes) **7**:153
"The King of Harlem" (Garcia Lorca) **3**:139
"The King of the Ditchbacks" (Heaney) **18**:213
The King of the Great Clock Tower (Yeats) **20**:348
"King of the River" (Kunitz) **19**:157-59, 163, 168, 172-73, 175, 180
"The King of Yellow Butterflies" (Lindsay) **23**:281
"King Solomon and the Queen of Sheba" (Lindsay) **23**:264, 280
"The Kingdom of Poetry" (Schwartz) **8**:289, 308-09
"The Kingfisher" (Clampitt) **19**:82, 84
"King-fisher" (Montale) **13**:139
The Kingfisher (Clampitt) **19**:82-3, 85-91, 93
"The Kingfishers" (Olson) **19**:286, 308
"The Kings are Gone" (Bukowski) **18**:5
The King's Daughter (Bely) **11**:32
"King's Ransom" (Wylie) **23**:320
"The King's Task" (Kipling) **3**:183
"Kinship" (Heaney) **18**:195-96, 204, 210
"Kinship" (Wright) **14**:379
Kiosk (Enzensberger) **28**:166
"The Kirk's Alarm" (Burns) **6**:78
"The Kiss" (Sassoon) **12**:262
"The Kiss" (Sexton) **2**:353
"The Kiss" (Tagore)
See "Chumban"
"The kiss at Bayreuth" (Gunn) **26**:212
"Kissee Lee" (Walker) **20**:286
"Kisses" (Cassian) **17**:12-13
A Kist of Whistles: New Poems (MacDiarmid) **9**:182
"Kita no umi" (Ishikawa) **10**:213
"Kitchenette Building" (Brooks) **7**:79
"The Kite" (Elytis) **21**:131
"Kite Flying" (McKay) **2**:223
"Kitty Hawk" (Frost) **1**:213
"KKK" (Guillen) **23**:121
"Klage" (Trakl) **20**:229, 236-37, 244, 250, 255-56, 258
"Klage II" (Trakl) **20**:250-51, 253
"Klarisu yunosha lyubil" (Lermontov) **18**:288
"Kleenex" (Shapiro) **25**:324
"kleiner herbst da¨mon" (Enzensberger) **28**:140
"The Kneeling One" (Gallagher) **9**:57
"The Knight" (Hughes) **7**:126
"The Knight" (Rich) **5**:370
"The Knight Fallen on Evil Days" (Wylie) **23**:326
"Knight's" (Chaucer)
See "Knight's Tale"
"Knight's Tale" (Chaucer) **19**:13, 56, 60, 70, 75
"The Knight's to the Mountain" (Scott) **13**:305
"Knocking Around" (Ashbery) **26**:133
"Knocking Donkey Fleas off a Poet from the Southside of Chi" (Madhubuti) **5**:323, 344
"The Knot" (Kumin) **15**:202
"The Knot" (Kunitz) **19**:176
"Knotted Letter" (Gallagher) **9**:63
"The Knowing Heart" (Roethke) **15**:293
"Knowing Rubén Darío" (Aleixandre) **15**:6
"Knowledge" (Bogan) **12**:101, 103, 120
Knowledge, Acquaintance, Resort, Favour with Grace (Skelton) **25**:344-45
"Knox" (Parker) **28**:362
"Knoxville, Tennessee" (Giovanni) **19**:139-41
"Knucks" (Sandburg) **2**:308, 324
"Kodachromes of the Island" (Hayden) **6**:183, 193, 196, 198
"Kôgao no shi" (Yosano Akiko) **11**:324-26, 328
"Kogda b v pokornosti neznan'ja" (Lermontov) **18**:302
Kogda razglyaetsya (Pasternak) **6**:266-69, 284-85
"Kogda v mrachneyshey iz stolits" (Akhmatova) **2**:12
"Koi wo koi suru hito" (Hagiwara Sakutaro) **18**:168, 180
"Koide shido" (Hagiwara Sakutaro) **18**:183
Koigoromo (Yosano Akiko) **11**:306-07
"Kolbel'naya treskovogo mysa" (Brodsky)
See "A Cape Cod Lullaby"
"Komboloi" (Merrill) **28**:256
"Koncert na vokzale" (Mandelstam) **14**:115, 129
Konec prekrasnoj èpox (Brodsky)
See *Konets prekrasnoy epokhi*
Konets prekrasnoy epokhi (Brodsky) **9**:7
"the konkreet pome is on its hed" (Bissett) **14**:32
"konkreet vizual" (Bissett) **14**:33-4
Köp den blindes sång (Ekeloef) **23**:76
Kora in Hell: Improvisations (Williams) **7**:344, 349, 374-75, 377, 379-81, 383-84, 394, 400, 405, 410
"A Korean Woman Seated by a Wall" (Meredith) **28**:177-78, 190
Körper des Sommers (Elytis) **21**:116
"Korsar" (Lermontov) **18**:299
"The Kraken" (Tennyson) **6**:360, 389, 391, 406-10
"Kral Majales" (Ginsberg) **4**:82, 85
"Krasnopresnenskaya Station" (Momaday) **25**:202
"Krasnyi bychok" (Tsvetaeva) **14**:325
"Kronos; To Coachman Kronos" (Goethe)
See "An Schwager Kronos"
"Krysolov" (Tsvetaeva) **14**:325-26
Kshanika (Tagore) **8**:411
"Kubla Khan" (Coleridge) **11**:41-7, 51, 59, 73, 75-9, 84-8, 90, 104, 107, 110
Kubok metelej: Chetviortiia simfoniia (Bely) **11**:3, 6-7, 14-17, 22
"Kubota" (Hongo) **23**:197
"ku¨chenzettel" (Enzensberger) **28**:135, 140
"Kuda mne det'sia v etom Ianvare?" (Mandelstam) **14**:154
Kumarasambhava (Kalidasa) **22**:178, 180, 182, 185, 188, 191-93, 196-206
"Kung Canto" (Pound) **4**:325
"Kure no kane" (Ishikawa) **10**:214
"Kuroi fukin" (Hagiwara Sakutaro) **18**:178, 182-83
"The Kursaal at Interlaken" (Rich) **5**:359
"Kutir-vasi" (Tagore) **8**:416
"Kutoa Umoja" (Baraka) **4**:26
"Kwa Mamu Zetu Waliotuzaa (for our mothers who gave us birth)" (Sanchez) **9**:215-16, 221, 227, 229, 243
"Kyoko" (Ishikawa) **10**:213
Kyomo no seigi (Hagiwara Sakutaro) **18**:176, 182
Le La (Breton) **15**:54
"A la Ausencia" (Fuertes) **27**:44
"A la Colonne de la Place Vendôme" (Hugo) **17**:88-89
"A la muerte" (Fuertes) **27**:39, 45
"A la Petra Camara" (Gautier) **18**:125
"L.A. to Wichita" (Ginsberg) **4**:54
Laberinto (Jimenez) **7**:200-01, 211
"Labor and Management" (Baraka) **4**:13
"The Laboratory" (Browning) **2**:60
"Laboratory Poem" (Merrill) **28**:241, 243
"The Laboring Skeleton" (Baudelaire)
See "Le squelette laboureur"

Labyrinth (Jimenez)
See *Laberinto*
"The Labyrinth of Life" (Walker) **20**:294
Labyrinths, with Path of Thunder (Okigbo) **7**:231, 233-35, 241-43, 248-49, 251-52, 254-56
"Le lac" (Lamartine) **16**:265, 268, 271, 276-77, 283, 290, 298, 301-02
"Lachesis lapponica." (Enzensberger) **28**:137, 140, 144
"Lachin Y Gair" (Byron) **16**:86
"Lachrymae Christi" (Crane) **3**:82, 96-7, 102
"Lack of Discipline" (Pavese)
See "Indisciplina"
"Lack of Faith" (Pushkin)
See "Bezverie"
"Lackawanna" (Kinnell) **26**:294
"Laconic" (Elytis) **21**:116
"Lacrime" (Pasolini) **17**:265
Ladera este (Paz) **1**:354, 346, 361-63, 374, 376
"The Ladies" (Kipling) **3**:164, 166, 174
Ladies and Gentlemen (Belloc) **24**:27
"The Lads in Their Hundreds" (Housman) **2**:192
"The Lads of the Village" (Smith) **12**:330, 333
"Lady" (Carruth) **10**:74
"Lady Acheson Weary of the Dean" (Swift) **9**:295-96
"Lady Bank Dick" (Wakoski) **15**:363
"Lady Geraldine's Courtship" (Browning) **6**:10, 17-18, 26, 38-9, 42
"Lady Hsi" (Wang Wei) **18**:388-89
"The Lady in the Shingle" (Gluck) **16**:139
"Lady Lazarus" (Plath) **1**:382, 386, 391, 395-97, 400-01, 406-07, 410, 413-14
"Lady of Cowrie Palace" (Li Ho) **13**:51-4
Lady of Miracles (Cassian) **17**:13
"The Lady of Shalott" (Swinburne) **24**:357
"The Lady of Shalott" (Tennyson) **6**:350, 358-59, 378, 380, 395, 409-10
The Lady of the Lake (Scott) **13**:257-58, 261, 267-68, 270-71, 273, 276-79, 281, 283, 285, 289, 291, 293, 304, 310-11, 319-20
"The Lady of the Well-Spring" (Smith) **12**:304, 306, 329, 341
"A Lady Thinks She Is Thirty" (Nash) **21**:274
"The Lady Who Drove Me to the Airport" (Wakoski) **15**:369
"Lady's Boogie" (Hughes) **1**:266
"The Lady's Dressing Room" (Swift) **9**:257, 262, 268, 270, 273, 279, 281, 286-89, 291-92, 295, 298-99, 302-03
"Laeti et Errabundi" (Verlaine) **2**:417
"A l'Afrique" (Cesaire) **25**:5, 30, 32
"The Lag" (Rich) **5**:363
"Il lago di Annecy" (Montale) **13**:138
"Lai des Deuz Amanz" (Marie de France)
See "Les Dous Amanz"
"Lair" (Pinsky) **27**:153
"Lais" (H. D.) **5**:268
Lais (Marie de France) **22**:246, 254-55, 260-62, 264-65, 268-75, 278, 281, 283-84, 287-88, 300 -303
Les Lais (Villon) **13**:374-75, 377, 387, 396-99, 402, 404-05, 408-10, 412-13
"The Lake" (Lamartine)
See "Le lac"
"The Lake" (Wright) **14**:348, 379
"Lake Boats" (Masters) **1**:330, 333
Lake Effect Country (Ammons) **16**:63
"The Lake Isle of Innisfree" (Yeats) **20**:310
"The Lake of Gaube" (Swinburne) **24**:312-20, 322, 341, 348
"A Lake Scene" (Swenson) **14**:262
"Lake Yi" (Wang Wei) **18**:379
"Lamarck" (Mandelstam) **14**:129
"The Lamb" (Blake) **12**:7, 9, 32, 62
"The Lambs of Grasmere" (Rossetti) **7**:266
"The Lame Boy and the Fairy" (Lindsay) **23**:281
"The Lament" (Burns) **6**:53
"Lament" (Hardy) **8**:135
"Lament" (Millay) **6**:211
"Lament" (Plath) **1**:410
"Lament" (Sexton) **2**:350
"Lament" (Trakl)
See "Klage"
"Lament for Damon" (Milton) **19**:212
"Lament For Glasgerion" (Wylie) **23**:310
Lament for Ignacio Sánchez Mejías (Garcia Lorca)
See *Llanto por Ignacio Sánchez Mejías*
"Lament for Pasiphaé" (Graves) **6**:144
Lament for the Death of a Bullfighter (Garcia Lorca)
See *Llanto por Ignacio Sánchez Mejías*
"Lament for the Makers" (Pinsky) **27**:164
"Lament for the Poles of Buffalo" (Hass) **16**:195, 197
"Lament for Weldon Kees" (Stryk) **27**:204
"Lament for Yin Yao" (Wang Wei) **18**:379
"Lament of Mary Queen of Scots" (Burns) **6**:78
The Lament of Tasso (Byron) **16**:76
"Lament of the Belle Heaulmiere" (Villon) **13**:389-90
"Lament of the Drums" (Okigbo) **7**:224, 229-30, 244, 247, 254
"Lament of the Lavender Mist" (Okigbo) **7**:229, 248
"The Lament of the Masks: For W. B. Yeats: 1865-1939" (Okigbo) **7**:230, 245
"Lament of the Silent Sisters" (Okigbo)
See "Silences: Lament of the Silent Sisters"
"Lamentationen" (Heine) **25**:131
"Lamentations" (Gluck) **16**:151, 154
"Lamentations" (Sassoon) **12**:267, 286
Lamentations (Gluck) **16**:129
"The Lamentations of Jeremy, for the most part according to Tremelius" (Donne) **1**:139
Lamia, Isabella, The Eve of St. Agnes, and Other Poems (Keats) **1**:276, 279, 281, 296, 307-09, 311
"Lamium" (Gluck) **16**:132, 171
"La lampe du temple" (Lamartine) **16**:292
"Lancelot" (Swinburne) **24**:355
Lancelot (Robinson) **1**:465, 468-70, 489, 491
"Lancer" (Housman) **2**:162
"Land" (Heaney) **18**:201
"The Land" (Kipling) **3**:171
"The Land Betrayed" (Neruda)
See "La arena traicionada"
"The Land of Dreams" (Blake) **12**:35
"The Land of the Sky-Blue Waters" (Meredith) **28**:196
Land of Unlikeness (Lowell) **3**:199, 202, 213, 216-17, 232
"The Land Where All Is Gained" (Tagore)
See "Sab-peyechhir desh"
"Landcrab II" (Atwood) **8**:43
Landesprcahe (Enzensberger) **28**:133-35, 141, 143, 165
"The Landing" (Tomlinson) **17**:353
"Landing on the Moon" (Swenson) **14**:257
"Landlady, Count the Lawin" (Burns) **6**:81
Landor's Poetry (Pinsky) **27**:153
"The Landscape" (Masters) **1**:333, 344
"Landscape" (Merton) **10**:349
"Landscape" (Parker) **28**:362
"Landscape after a Battle" (Neruda)
See "Paisaje después de una batalla"
"Landscape I" (Pavese)
See "Paesaggio I"
"Landscape in Spring" (Soto) **28**:382
"Landscape of the Heart" (Jimenez)
See "Paisaje del corozon"
"Landscape of the Star" (Rich) **5**:362
"Landscape of the Urinating Multitudes (Battery Place Nocturne)" (Garcia Lorca)
See "Paisaje de la multitud que orina"
"Landscape of the Vomiting Multitudes (Coney Island Dusk)" (Garcia Lorca)
See "Paisaje de la multitud que vomita"
"Landscape VI" (Pavese)
See "Paesaggio VI"
"Landscape VII" (Pavese)
See "Paesaggio VII"
Landscape West of Eden (Aiken) **26**:24, 29-30
"Landscape with Figures" (Ammons) **16**:6
"Landscape with Serifs" (Page) **12**:183
"Landscapes" (Eliot) **5**:166, 183
"Landscapes" (Wright) **14**:339, 342-43
Landscapes of Living and Dying (Ferlinghetti) **1**:180-81, 187
"The Lang Coortin" (Carroll) **18**:46
"Language" (Ortiz) **17**:231
Language Lattice (Celan)
See *Sprachgitter*
"The Language of the Brag" (Olds) **22**:328
language of the land (Enzensberger)
See *Landesprcahe*
"Language-Mesh" (Celan)
See "Sprachgitter"
"L'anguilla" (Montale) **13**:111
"The Lantern Out of Doors" (Hopkins) **15**:145, 156
"Lanval" (Marie de France) **22**:241-45, 250-51, 254-55, 258, 260, 267-69, 271-72, 275, 282, 294, 29 7, 300-303
"Lanval Graelent Sir Landevall" (Marie de France) **22**:
"Laocoön Dream Recorded in Diary Dated 1943" (Swenson) **14**:288
"Laodamia" (Wordsworth) **4**:394, 399, 406-07
Laon and Cythna (Shelley) **14**:162, 171
"Laostic" (Marie de France)
See "Laüstic"
"Lapis Lazuli" (Yeats) **20**:314, 333
"Lapraik II" (Burns)
See "Second Epistle to John Lapraik"
"Lapse" (Dunbar) **5**:126
Lara (Byron) **16**:92, 109
"La larga busca" (Borges) **22**:95
"A Large Bad Picture" (Bishop) **3**:37, 70-1
Large Testament (Villon)
See *Le Testament*
"Larks" (Bridges) **28**:85
"Larme" (Rimbaud) **3**:271
"Last" (Kipling) **3**:160
"Last Acts" (Olds) **22**:318, 323, 326, 337
Last and Lost Poems of Delmore Schwartz (Schwartz) **8**:311, 319
"Last Canto of Childe Harold" (Lamartine)
See "Le dernier chant de pèlerinage de Childe Harold"
"The Last Chantey" (Kipling) **3**:161
"The Last Day" (Olds) **22**:33-37
"The Last Duchess" (Browning) **2**:30
The Last Epiphany (Aleixandre)
See *Nacimiento último*
The Last Harvest (Tagore)
See *Chaitali*
"The Last Hiding Places of Snow" (Kinnell) **26**:259, 271-72
"Last Hill in a Vista" (Bogan) **12**:104
"The Last Instructions to a Painter" (Marvell) **10**:275
"The Last Invocation" (Whitman) **3**:378
"Last Kiss" (Olds) **22**:321
"The Last Laugh" (Owen) **19**:366
"Last Letter" (Gluck) **16**:164-65
"Last Lines" (Bronte) **8**:59
"Last Load" (Hughes) **7**:166
"Last Looks at the Lilacs" (Stevens) **6**:292
The Last Lunar Baedeker (Loy) **16**:330, 333
"The Last Man" (Gunn) **26**:203
"The Last Meeting" (Sassoon) **12**:262
"The Last Mowing" (Frost) **1**:206
"The Last Mummer" (Heaney) **18**:201
The Last Night of the Earth Poems (Bukowski) **18**:16, 19
Last Octave (Tagore)
See *Shesh saptak*
"The Last of Saturdays" (Elytis) **21**:135

"The Last of the Flock" (Wordsworth) **4**:373, 415, 418
"The Last Oracle" (Swinburne) **24**:320, 347
"Last Poems" (Tagore)
See "Sesh lekha"
Last Poems (Browning) **6**:23-4, 38, 40
Last Poems (Celan) **10**:120
Last Poems (Housman) **2**:161-67, 173-76, 180-81, 186, 191, 196, 199-201
Last Poems (Yeats) **20**:307, 311, 314, 332
"*Last Poems:* XX--The Night Is Freezing Fast" (Housman) **2**:196
The Last Poems of Elinor Wylie (Wylie) **23**:321
"The Last Quatrain of the Ballad of Emmett Till" (Brooks) **7**:62
"The Last Question" (Parker) **28**:362
"The Last Rhyme of True Thomas" (Kipling) **3**:181-82
"The Last Ride Together" (Browning) **2**:75
"The Last River" (Kinnell) **26**:255, 257, 262, 290, 293
"The Last Signal" (Hardy) **8**:131
Last Song (Harjo) **27**:59, 64
"The Last Song of Lucifer" (Lindsay) **23**:284
"Last Supper" (Wylie) **23**:303, 308, 310
"The Last Suttee" (Kipling) **3**:183
"The Last Tournament" (Tennyson) **6**:376
"The Last Turn of the Screw" (Smith) **12**:295
Last Volume (Swift) **9**:255
The Last Voyage (Noyes) **27**:133
"The Last Word" (Tagore)
See "Shesh katha"
"Last Words" (Olds) **22**:324
"Last Words" (Plath) **1**:396, 407
"Last Words of the Dying Recruit" (McKay) **2**:226
"Lastness" (Kinnell) **26**:252, 274-75
"Late" (Bogan) **12**:122
"Late" (Olds) **22**:318
Late Arrival on Earth (Ekeloef) **23**:66, 85, 88-90
"Late August" (Atwood) **8**:28-9, 42
"Late Beethoven" (Zagajewski) **27**:384-85
"Late Echo" (Ashbery) **26**:140
"Late Feast" (Zagajewski) **27**:395
"Late Last Night" (Hughes) **1**:243
Late Lyrics and Earlier with Many Other Verses (Hardy) **8**:89, 123
"Late Movies with Skyler" (Ondaatje) **28**:338
"Late Poem to My Father" (Olds) **22**:324
Late Settings (Merrill) **28**:266-68, 281
"The Late Snow & Lumber Strike of the Summer of Fifty-four" (Snyder) **21**:322
"Late Spring" (Hass) **16**:216, 222
"Late Spring Evening" (Bridges) **28**:85
"Lately, at Night" (Kumin) **15**:200
"Later Life" (Rossetti) **7**:278
The Later Poems of John Clare 1837-1864 (Clare) **23**:46
Later Poems (Bridges) **28**:65
"Latest Face" (Larkin) **21**:236
"Lauda" (Milosz) **8**:201
"Lauda" (Paz) **1**:361
"The Laugh" (Graves) **6**:156
"Laughing Corn" (Sandburg) **2**:316
"Laughing Gas" (Ginsberg) **4**:74, 81
Laughing Lost in the Mountains: Poems of Wang Wei (Wang Wei) **18**:391
"The Laughing Song" (Blake) **12**:4, 7, 23
"Laughters" (Hughes)
See "My People"
"The Laureate" (Graves) **6**:142, 144
"Laus Veneris" (Swinburne) **24**:308, 360-61
Laus Veneris, and Other Poems and Ballads (Swinburne)
See *Poems and Ballads*
"Laüstic" (Marie de France) **22**:237, 258, 260, 264-66, 269-72, 301
"Lava" (Kinnell) **26**:260
"Lava" (Zagajewski) **27**:387
"Lavorare stanca" (Pavese) **13**:203, 213, 225-27
Lavorare stanca (Pavese) **13**:201-02, 204-05, 210-14, 216-19, 222, 224-26, 228
"Law" (Lowell) **3**:214
"The Law I Love Is Major Mover" (Duncan) **2**:124
"The Laws of God, the Laws of Man" (Housman) **2**:162, 179
"Lay le Freyne" (Marie de France)
See "Le Fraisne"
"Lay of Guigemar" (Marie de France) **22**:239-45, 258, 263-66, 268-76, 278, 293-94, 301
The Lay of the Last Minstrel (Scott) **13**:246, 248-51, 256, 258, 266, 269, 271, 273, 274-76, 279-83, 285, 303, 311-12, 315, 317-18
"The Layers" (Kunitz) **19**:180-81
"Laying the Dust" (Levertov) **11**:165
Lays (Marie de France)
See *Lais*
Lays of Twilight (Hugo) **17**:44
"Lazarillo and the Beggar" (Aleixandre) **15**:4, 6
"Lazarus" (Robinson) **1**:468
"Lead Soldiers" (Lowell) **13**:78
"The Leaden Echo and the Golden Echo" (Hopkins) **15**:130-31, 143-44, 161
"The Leaden-Eyed" (Lindsay) **23**:268, 276, 281, 296
"The Leader" (Belloc) **24**:11
"The Leaders" (Brooks) **7**:63, 90
"Leaflets" (Rich) **5**:396
Leaflets: Poems, 1965-1968 (Rich) **5**:357, 365, 370-72, 383, 388-89, 396, 399
"A Lean and Hungry Look" (Nemerov) **24**:291
"Leaping Falls" (Kinnell) **26**:238
"Lear Is Gay" (Hayden) **6**:187
"The Lea-Rig" (Burns) **6**:82
"Learning By Doing" (Nemerov) **24**:270
"Learning the Trees" (Nemerov) **24**:285
"Learning to Read" (Harper) **21**:192, 198, 200, 213
"Learning to Write" (Lorde) **12**:136
"Leather Jacket" (Page) **12**:172
"Leather Leggings" (Sandburg) **2**:302
Leaves of Grass (Whitman) **3**:370, 378-79, 382, 384, 386-87, 389, 397-99, 401, 404-08, 410-14, 416-17
"Leave-taking Near Shoku" (Pound) **4**:331
"Leaving" (Song) **21**:333, 335, 342-43
"Leaving L'Atelier-Aix-en-Provence" (Rexroth) **20**:196
"Leaving the Atocha Station" (Ashbery) **26**:113
"LEBANON VOICES" (Bissett) **14**:32
lebanon voices (Bissett) **14**:2
Lebediny stan (Tsvetaeva) **14**:313-14
"lebenslauf " (Enzensberger) **28**:135
"Lebenslauf" (Holderlin) **4**:147
"Lecture" (Milosz) **8**:200
"Lecture I" (Milosz) **8**:202
"Lecture IV" (Milosz) **8**:203
"Lecture VI" (Milosz) **8**:199
"Lecture VII" (Milosz) **8**:202
"Lecture on Mystery" (Zagajewski) **27**:400
"A Lecture upon the Shadow" (Donne) **1**:135, 145, 147
"Leda and the Swan" (Montale) **13**:150
"Leda and the Swan" (Yeats) **20**:315, 319
Lee: A Dramatic Poem (Masters) **1**:339
"Leech Gatherer" (Wordsworth) **4**:390, 394
"Leffingwell" (Robinson) **1**:466
"Left Behind" (Lowell) **13**:97
"The Leg" (Shapiro) **25**:268, 288, 297, 300-301
"Legacies" (Browning) **6**:16
"Legacies" (Giovanni) **19**:111
"Legacy" (Harjo) **27**:71
"Legend" (Crane) **3**:101
"Legend" (Wright) **14**:338
Legend (Chaucer)
See *Legend of Good Women*
Legend of Good Women (Chaucer) **19**:7, 10, 21, 23-4, 34, 60, 64, 74
The Legend of Jubal, and Other Poems (Eliot) **20**:116, 123, 125, 131-32
"A Legend of Porcelain" (Lowell) **13**:61, 65
The Legend of the Centuries (Hugo)
See *La légende des siècles*
"Legende" (Celan) **10**:126
"Lègende" (Laforgue) **14**:74
La légende des siècles (Hugo) **17**:49, 54-57, 60-61, 65, 68, 78, 80, 83-86, 89, 91
Legende of Good Women (Chaucer)
See *Legend of Good Women*
"Légende théologique" (Gautier) **18**:162
"Legender" (Ekeloef) **23**:69, 71
Legends (Lowell) **13**:60-3, 65, 74, 83, 93
"Legends and Dirges" (Ekeloef) **23**:69
"The Legion Club" (Swift) **9**:281
"The Legs" (Graves) **6**:151
"The Lemons" (Montale) **13**:149
"Lengas dai frus di sera" (Pasolini) **17**:256
"Lenore" (Poe) **1**:434, 438, 445
"Lenox Avenue: Midnight" (Hughes) **1**:265
"Lent" (Herbert) **4**:100
"The Lent Lily" (Housman) **2**:184, 192
"Leon" (Cardenal) **22**:110
"A Leone Traverso" (Montale) **13**:139
"Leonine Elegiacs" (Tennyson) **6**:385-86
"Lepanto" (Chesterton) **28**:94, 99, 100, 108, 125, 128-30
"The Leper" (Swinburne) **24**:307, 337
"Lerici" (Gunn) **26**:218
"leroy" (Baraka) **4**:19, 23
The Lesbians (Baudelaire)
See *Les fleurs du mal*
Les Lesbiennes (Baudelaire)
See *Les fleurs du mal*
"Lesbos" (Plath) **1**:394
"The Less Deceived" (Larkin) **21**:222
The Less Deceived (Larkin) **21**:224, 226-27, 230, 233, 235, 251-52, 255, 256, 259
Lesser Testament (Villon)
See *Les Lais*
"The Lesson" (Levertov) **11**:167
"The Lesson" (Lowell) **3**:211
"A Lesson in Geography" (Rexroth) **20**:215
"Lestnitsa" (Tsvetaeva)
See "Poèma lestnitsy"
"Let America Be America Again" (Hughes) **1**:250, 253
"Let Koras and Balafong Accompany Me" (Senghor)
See "Que m'accompagnent Kôras et Balafong"
"Let Me Begin Again" (Levine) **22**:219, 225
"Let Me Enjoy" (Hardy) **8**:98
"Let me go, Voronezh . . ." (Mandelstam)
See "Pusti menia, Voronezh . . ."
"let me tell yu a story of how they met" (Bissett) **14**:17
"Let My People Go" (Johnson) **24**:128-29, 139, 144, 166, 169
"Let No Charitable Hope" (Wylie) **23**:314, 323-24, 333-34
"Let not Love go to" (Noyes) **27**:134
"Let the Light Enter! The Dying Words of Goethe" (Harper) **21**:210
"Let the Rail Splitter Awake" (Alegria) **26**:
"Let Us Prepare" (Swenson) **14**:268
"Letanía de los montes de la vida" (Fuertes) **27**:39
"Letanía de nuestro Señor Don Quijote" (Dario) **15**:96
"Leter 20: not a pastoral letter" (Olson) **19**:274
"Le lethe" (Baudelaire)
See "Léthé"
"Léthé" (Baudelaire) **1**:72
"Lethe" (H. D.) **5**:287, 304
"Let's Beat Down the Poor" (Baudelaire)
See "Assommons les pauvres"
"Let's, from Some Loud Unworld's Most Rightful Wrong" (Cummings) **5**:109
"A Letter" (Berry) **28**:6
"A Letter" (Bogan) **12**:95, 127
"Letter" (Hass) **16**:196
"Letter" (Montale)
See "Lettera"

"The Letter" (Owen) **19**:347, 363-65
"Letter 2" (Olson) **19**:277, 281-82
"Letter 3" (Olson) **19**:273, 280, 282, 284
Letter 3 (Brutus) **24**:106, 115
"Letter 4" (Olson) **19**:283
"Letter 5" (Brutus) **24**:101, 106
"Letter 5" (Olson) **19**:266, 271, 282-83
"Letter 6" (Olson) **19**:280, 282-83
Letter 6 (Brutus) **24**:115
Letter 7 (Brutus) **24**:115
"Letter 8" (Olson) 280, 283
"Letter 9" (Olson) **19**:267, 281, 283-84
Letter 9 (Brutus) **24**:115
"Letter 10" (Brutus) **24**:115
"Letter 10" (Olson) **19**:267, 281, 283-84
"Letter 11" (Olson) **19**:296
Letter 13 (Brutus) **24**:99, 106, 115
"Letter 14" (Brutus) **24**:100
"Letter 14" (Olson) **19**:273
"Letter 15" (Olson) **19**:277
"Letter 16" (Brutus) **24**:101
Letter 17 (Brutus) **24**:106, 115
"Letter for Jan" (Lorde) **12**:152
"Letter for Melville" (Olson) **19**:297
"Letter from Costa Brava" (Tomlinson) **17**:315
"A Letter from Li Po" (Aiken) **26**:45, 56-7
A Letter from Li Po, and Other Poems (Aiken) **26**:24, 29-30
"Letter from Our Man in Blossomtime" (Gluck) **16**:124
"A Letter from Phillis Wheatley" (Hayden) **6**:189, 192, 195
"Letter from Prague, 1968-78" (Forche) **10**:144, 156, 168-69
"Letter from the North" (Bukowski) **18**:4
"A Letter Home" (Sassoon) **12**:262
"Letter I" (Olson) **19**:282, 284
"A Letter in a Bottle" (Brodsky) **9**:3, 4
"Letter, May 2, 1959" (Olson) **19**:306
"Letter Number Forty-One" (Olson) **19**:306
"Letter of Advice to a Young Poet" (Swift) **9**:272
"Letter to a Bourgeois Friend Whom Once I Loved (and Maybe Still Do If Love Is Valid)" (Giovanni) **19**:115
"A Letter to a Brother of the Pen in Tribulation" (Behn) **13**:7, 30
"Letter to a Friend" (Wright) **14**:
"Letter to a Friend" (Wright) **14**:336, 338
"Letter to Ann Landers" (Ondaatje) **28**:328
"Letter to a Wound" (Auden) **1**:22
"A Letter to Basil" (Brutus) **24**:106, 108
"A Letter to Dafnis April: 2nd 1685" (Finch) **21**:165
"A Letter to Dr. Martin Luther King" (Sanchez) **9**:244
"A Letter to Her Husband, Absent upon Public Employment" (Bradstreet) **10**:8, 28, 30, 34, 40, 65
"Letter to Jean-Paul Baudot, at Christmas" (Stryk) **27**:182, 196, 200, 202, 204-5, 215, 218
Letter to Lord Byron (Auden) **1**:22, 34
A Letter to Lucian and Other Poems (Noyes) **27**:135
"A Letter to Lucian the Sceptic Dated from the Island of Cos in the year AD 165" (Noyes) **27**:136
"Letter to Maxine Sullivan" (Carruth) **10**:87
"Letter to Miguel Otero Silva, in Caracas, 1948" (Neruda)
See "Carta a Miguel Otero Silva, en Caracas, 1948"
"Letter to My Father from 40,000 Feet" (Olds) **22**:324-25
"A Letter to My Friends" (Merton) **10**:346-47
"A Letter to Sara Hutchinson" (Coleridge) **11**:69-72, 91
"Letter to the Countesse of Huntingdon" (Donne) **1**:130
"Letter to the Front" (Rukeyser) **12**:228, 231-34
"A Letter to the Same Person" (Finch) **21**:160, 164
"Letter to V-" (Wylie) **23**:324
"A Letter to William Carlos Williams" (Rexroth) **20**:193
"Letter Written during a January Northeaster" (Sexton) **2**:351
"Letter Written on a Ferry Crossing Long Island Sound" (Sexton) **2**:351, 361
"Lettera" (Montale) **13**:161
"Letters" (Cassian) **17**:5
Letters (Duncan) **2**:106
Letters (Ovid)
See *Heroides*
"Letters and Other Worlds" (Ondaatje) **28**:315-16, 327, 329, 331
"Letters for the Dead" (Levine) **22**:220, 223
"Letters from a Land of Sinners" (Rich) **5**:354
Letters from a Traveller's Pannier (Matsuo Basho)
See *Oi no obumi*
Letters from Iceland (Auden) **1**:9, 13
"Letters from the Ming Dynasty" (Brodsky) **9**:29
Letters of the Heroines (Ovid)
See *Heroides*
Letters to Martha and Other Poems from a South African Prison (Brutus) **24**:99-100, 102, 104-09, 112, 114-15, 118-20
Letters to Martha II (Brutus) **24**:100
"Lettre à une femme" (Hugo) **17**:100
"Lettre-Océan" (Apollinaire) **7**:18, 25-9, 32, 34-7
"Lettres de l'Hivernage" (Senghor) **25**:232-33, 235, 247-51
"lettrs (for a passing comet)" (Bissett) **14**:20
Letzte Gedichte und Gedanken (Heine) **25**:172
"Letzter Abend" (Rilke) **2**:267
"Levedad" (Jimenez) **7**:201
"The Level at Which Sky Began" (Soto) **28**:370, 378
"Le Lever du soleil" (Breton) **15**:48
"Leviathan" (Neruda) **4**:282
"Lews estoilles envoyées à Monsieur de Pibrac en Polonne" (Ronsard) **11**:236-37, 239
"Li occi dolenti" (Dante) **21**:73
"The Liar" (Baraka) **4**:17
"The Liars" (Sandburg) **2**:304
"Libation" (Ammons) **16**:4
"Libation" (Levertov) **11**:197
Liber Spectaculorum (Martial) **10**:230
liberating skies (Bissett) **14**:7-8, 16
"Liberation" (Gluck) **16**:156
"Liberation Poem" (Sanchez) **9**:209
"The Liberators" (Neruda)
See "Los libertadores"
Libertad bajo palabra (Paz) **1**:353
"Los libertadores" (Neruda) **4**:292
"La liberte, ou une nuit a Rome" (Lamartine) **16**:278, 291
"The Libertine" (Behn) **13**:4
"Liberty" (Pushkin)
See "Vol'nost': Oda"
"Liberty and Peace" (Wheatley) **3**:337, 341, 363
Liberty behind the Words (Paz)
See *Libertad bajo palabra*
"Liberty's Twilight" (Mandelstam)
See "The Twilight of Freedom"
"Libido" (Brooke) **24**:53
"The Librarian" (Olson) **19**:280
"El libro" (Dario) **15**:99, 101-02
Libro de las preguntas (Neruda) **4**:287, 290
Libro de poemas (Garcia Lorca) **3**:117-18, 147-49
Libros inéditos de poesía (Jimenez) **7**:201
"Licentiousness" (Cassian) **17**:5
Lichee Nuts (Masters) **1**:338
Lichtzwang (Celan) **10**:96, 98, 121
"Liddy's Orange" (Olds) **22**:315
"Lidice" (Day Lewis) **11**:146
"(Liebeslied.)" (Celan) **10**:123-24
"Liebhaber in allen Gestalten" (Goethe) **5**:246, 251
"Liebestod" (Parker) **28**:362
"Lieder" (Pasolini) **17**:256
Lieder (Heine) **25**:155
"Liens" (Apollinaire) **7**:28, 49
Lieutenant Schmidt (Pasternak) **6**:265, 272
"Life" (Bryant) **20**:16
"Life" (Dunbar) **5**:121, 124-26, 130
"Life" (Herbert) **4**:100, 113
"Life and Death at Sunrise" (Hardy) **8**:124
"The Life and Genuine Character of Dr. Swift" (Swift) **9**:280, 295
"Life and Letters" (Rich) **5**:352
"Life at War" (Levertov) **11**:176, 194
"The Life Beyond" (Brooke) **24**:57
"Life Cycle of Common Man" (Nemerov) **24**:283
Life in the Forest (Levertov) **11**:205, 207-10
"Life is More True than Reason Will Decieve" (Cummings) **5**:108
"Life Is Motion" (Stevens) **6**:333
"The life of Borodin" (Bukowski) **18**:22
"Life of Life" (Shelley) **14**:181
"The Life of Lincoln West" (Brooks) **7**:85, 91-2
"The Life of My Friend" (Blok) **21**:6, 20
Life Sentence (Cassian) **17**:10-13
Life Studies (Lowell) **3**:205-09, 211-14, 216-19, 221, 223, 227, 230, 232-33, 242-43
Life Studies: Secular Love (Ondaatje) **28**:316
"The Life That Is" (Bryant) **20**:8
"Life's Noonday" (Tagore)
See "Jivan madhyahna"
"Life's Rendezvous" (Cullen) **20**:77
"Life's Work" (Kumin) **15**:202
"A Lifetime" (Bryant) **20**:8, 12, 46
"A Lifetime Later" (Ferlinghetti) **1**:183
"Lift Every Voice and Sing" (Johnson) **24**:136, 130-31, 143-44, 146, 154, 159-60, 166, 170
"The Lifting" (Olds) **22**:318, 325, 334-36, 340
"Lifting Belly" (Stein) **18**:327, 341-42
"th lifting hands" (Bissett) **14**:34
"Lifting my forehead and lowering my eyes" (Tsvetaeva)
See "Zakinuv golovu i opustiv glaza"
"The Light" (Ferlinghetti) **1**:183
"Light" (Ondaatje) **28**:339, 340
"Light" (Wakoski) **15**:369
"Light against Darkness" (Williams) **7**:385
"Light Becomes Darkness" (Williams) **7**:384, 388
"Light Becomes Where No Sun Shines" (Thomas)
See "Light Breaks Where No Sun Shines"
Light Beyond the Darkness (Harper) **21**:189
"Light Breaks Where No Sun Shines" (Thomas) **2**:304
"A Light Breather" (Roethke) **15**:268, 309
Light Compulsion (Celan)
See *Lichtzwang*
"Light in Darkness" (Harper) **21**:197
"Light Love" (Rossetti) **7**:289
"The Light on the Pewter Dish" (Rexroth) **20**:196
"Light Sleeping" (Gunn) **26**:218
"A Light Snow-Fall after Frost" (Hardy) **8**:124
"The Light Tree" (Elytis) **21**:123
The Light Tree and the Fourteenth Beauty (Elytis) **21**:123, 133
"Light Verse on a Rock" (Wang Wei) **18**:358-59
"A Lighted Cigar That Is Smoking" (Apollinaire)
See "Paysage"
"The Lighted House" (Day Lewis) **11**:145-46
"Lightenings" (Heaney) **18**:259
"Lighthouse with Dead Leaves" (McGuckian) **27**:104
"Lightness" (Jimenez)
See "Levedad"
"Lightnin' Blues" (Dove) **6**:117
"The Lightning" (Swenson) **14**:285
"Lightning Storm on Fuji" (Nemerov) **24**:295

Like a Bulwark (Moore) **4**:257
"Like a Sitting Breeze" (Viereck) **27**:267-68, 283
"Like Ankle-rings" (Ekeloef) **23**:87
"Like Decorations in a Nigger Cemetery" (Stevens) **6**:308, 318
"Like Rembrandt, martyr of chiaroscuro" (Mandelstam)
See "Kak svetoteni muchenik Rembrandt"
"Like Snow" (Graves) **6**:144, 172
"Like the Thistledown" (Aleixandre) **15**:15
"Like, This Is What I Meant" (Baraka) **4**:38
"Like This Together" (Rich) **5**:364, 382
"Like Three Fair Branches from One Root Deriv'd" (Hass) **16**:199
"Lilacs" (Lowell) **13**:64, 67, 84-5, 98-9
"Lilian" (Tennyson) **6**:359
"Lilis Park" (Goethe) **5**:246
"The Lilly" (Blake) **12**:34-5
"The Lilly in a Christal" (Herrick) **9**:112-13, 115, 137-38, 144
Les Limbes (Baudelaire)
See *Les fleurs du mal*
"Limbo" (Coleridge) **11**:52, 85
"Limbo" (Graves) **6**:166
"Lime Trees in Winter Retouched" (McGuckian) **27**:102-104
"The Limit" (Aleixandre) **15**:6
"Limitation of Perfection" (Tagore)
See "Purner abhav"
"Limitations" (Sassoon) **12**:245
"Limited" (Sandburg) **2**:312
"Límites y espejo" (Aleixandre) **15**:42-3
"Limits" (Okigbo) **7**:241-42
Limits (Okigbo) **7**:223-28, 233-34, 246-48, 250-51
"Limits and mirror" (Aleixandre)
See "Límites y espejo"
"I limoni" (Montale) **13**:114, 119, 122
"The Lincoln Relics" (Kunitz) **19**:175, 178-80
"Lindau" (Montale) **13**:146
"Lineage" (Hughes) **7**:159
"Lineage" (Walker) **20**:281
"Linen Town" (Heaney) **18**:202
"The Liner She's a Lady" (Kipling) **3**:161
"Lines" (Harper) **21**:190, 218
"Lines" (Williams) **7**:351-52
"Lines about the Unknown Soldier" (Mandelstam)
See "Stikhi o neizvestnom soldate"
"Lines Above Tintern Abbey" (Wordsworth)
See "Lines Composed a Few Miles Above Tintern Abbey"
"Lines & Circularities" (Nemerov) **24**:288, 301
"Lines Composed a Few Miles Above Tintern Abbey" (Wordsworth) **4**:373, 387, 391, 409-12, 418-19, 425-26, 428
"Lines Composed While Climbing the Left Ascent of Drockley Coomb, Somersetshire, May 1795" (Coleridge) **11**:82
"Lines for a Book" (Gunn) **26**:185, 189
"Lines for a Picture of St. Dorothea" (Hopkins) **15**:144
"Lines for an Album" (Montale)
See "Per album"
"Lines for an Ode-Threnody on England" (Brooke) **24**:89
"Lines for an Old Man" (Eliot) **5**:170
"Lines in a Country Churchyard" (Shelley) **14**:166
"Lines Left upon a Seat in a Yew-Tree, Which Stands near the Lake of Esthwaite, on a Desolate Part of the Shore, Commanding a Beautiful Prospect" (Wordsworth) **4**:373, 418
"Lines on a Young Lady's Photograph Album" (Larkin) **21**:236
"Lines on an Autumnal Evening" (Coleridge) **11**:106
"Lines on Revisiting the Country" (Bryant) **20**:37-8
"Lines on the First Mild Day of March" (Wordsworth) **4**:418
"Lines to a Don" (Belloc) **24**:11, 29, 38
"Lines to a Movement in Mozart's E-Flat Symphony" (Hardy) **8**:114
"Lines to Miles O'Reilly" (Harper) **21**:197
"Lines to Myself" (Heaney) **18**:191
"Lines to Sour-Faced Gila" (Juana Ines de la Cruz) **24**:176
"Lines Written after Detecting in Myself a Yearning toward the Large, Wise, Calm, Richly Resigned, Benignant Act Put on by a Great Many People after Having Passed the Age of Thirty Five" (Bogan) **12**:115
"Lines Written among the Euganean Hills" (Shelley) **14**:171, 177, 235
"Lines Written at a Small Distance from My House, and Sent by My Little Boy to the Person to Whom They Are Addressed" (Wordsworth) **4**:418
"Lines Written in an Asylum" (Carruth) **10**:84, 89
"Lines Written in Anticipation of a London Paper Attaining a Guaranteed Circulation of Ten Million Daily" (Sassoon) **12**:251-52
"Lines Written in Early Spring" (Wordsworth) **4**:418
"Lines Written in Kensington Gardens" (Arnold) **5**:19, 35, 49
"Lines Written in the Library of Congress after the Cleanth Brooks Lecture" (Kumin) **15**:222
"Lines Written on My Nineteenth Birthday" (Owen) **19**:371
"Lingard and the Stars" (Robinson) **1**:464
"Lingua" (Pasolini) **17**:272
"Links" (Apollinaire)
See "Liens"
"The Linnet in the Rocky Dells" (Bronte) **8**:68-9
"Linoleum" (Gallagher) **9**:44, 56, 60
"The Lion" (Belloc) **24**:24
"Lion" (Wright) **14**:346
"Lion & Honeycomb" (Nemerov) **24**:262
"The Lion and the Lamb" (Wylie) **23**:309, 324
"The Lion in Love" (Moore) **4**:261
"The Lions" (Hayden) **6**:194, 197
"Liquid Metal Fast Breeder Reactor" (Snyder) **21**:293
"Lis" (Cummings) **5**:100
"Lisa" (Eliot) **20**:102
"Lisa May" (Dunbar) **5**:137
"Lisbon Revisited, 1923" (Pessoa) **20**:158, 169
"Listen" (Nash) **21**:274
"Listen Carefully" (Levine) **22**:234
"listen children" (Clifton) **17**:26
"Listen Here Blues" (Hughes) **1**:270
"Listen, Lord" (Johnson) **24**:144, 164
"Listenen to Big Black at S.F. State" (Sanchez) **9**:225
"The Litanie" (Donne) **1**:136-39, 147, 150
"Les litanies de satan" (Baudelaire) **1**:45, 71
"The Litanies of Satan" (Baudelaire)
See "Les litanies de satan"
"Litany" (Ashbery) **26**:131-135, 140-143, 145, 156, 169-170, 172
"The Litany for Survival" (Lorde) **12**:137
"The Litany of the Dark People" (Cullen) **20**:57, 75
"The Litany of the Heroes" (Lindsay) **23**:266, 272, 285, 295
"Literary Statement On Struggle!" (Baraka) **4**:30
"The Literate Farmer and the Planet Venus" (Frost) **1**:210
"The Lithuanian" (Lermontov)
See "The Lithuanian"
"Lithuanian Dance Band" (Ashbery) **26**:145
"Lithuanian Nocturne" (Brodsky) **9**:22-4, 27
"Litovskii noktyurn" (Brodsky)
See "Lithuanian Nocturne"
"The Little Beauty That I Was Allowed" (Wylie) **23**:314
"A Little Bit of a Tumbler" (Stein) **18**:321, 334, 353
"The Little Black Boy" (Blake) **12**:7-8
"The Little Boy Found" (Blake) **12**:7
"A Little Boy Lost" (Blake) **12**:7, 23, 33-5
"Little Boy Lost" (Smith) **12**:321, 325, 332
"Little Boy Sick" (Smith) **12**:318
"Little Boy Stanton" (Garcia Lorca) **3**:143
"Little Brown Baby" (Dunbar) **5**:142
"A Little Called Pauline" (Stein) **18**:331
"A Little Child Shall Lead Them" (Harper) **21**:187
The Little Children of the Snow (Bryant)
See "The Little People of the Snow"
"A little demon in wet fur crept in" (Mandelstam)
See "Vlez besenok v mokroi sherstke"
"The Little Dog's Day" (Brooke) **24**:59
"Little Elegy" (Wylie) **23**:314-15
"Little Exercise" (Bishop) **3**:49
"Little Fanfare for Felix MacGowan" (Merrill) **28**:253
"The Little Friend" (Browning) **6**:14
"Little Fugue" (Plath) **1**:390
"The Little Ghost" (Millay) **6**:206
"Little Gidding" (Eliot) **5**:165-67, 169-70, 181-83, 185, 193, 204-05, 208, 210-11
"The Little Girl Found" (Blake) **12**:7, 33-4, 61
"A Little Girl Lost" (Blake) **12**:7, 33-4, 61
"Little Girl, My String Bean, My Lovely Woman" (Sexton) **2**:363
"Little Girls" (Page) **12**:176-77
"Little Green Sea" (Elytis) **21**:123
"Little Green Tree" (Hughes) **1**:243
"The Little Hill" (Millay) **6**:214, 233
The Little House of Kolomna (Pushkin)
See *Domik v Kolomne*
"Little Jim" (McKay) **2**:216, 222
"The Little June Book" (Stevens) **6**:332-33
"The Little Larousse" (Zagajewski) **27**:401
"Little Lion Face" (Swenson) **14**:280
"Little Lobeila's Song" (Bogan) **12**:100-01, 111
"A Little Love of Life" (Stein) **18**:313
"Little Lyric" (Hughes) **1**:240
The Little Mariner (Elytis) **21**:134-35
"Little Mattie" (Browning) **6**:24
"Little Miss Muffet Sat on a Prophet" (Nash) **21**:265
"Little Old Letter" (Hughes) **1**:243
"The Little Old Women" (Baudelaire)
See "Les petites vielles"
"The Little Ones" (Soto) **28**:371
"The Little Peasant" (Sexton) **2**:364, 368
"The Little People of the Snow" (Bryant) **20**:15-16
"De Little Pikaninny's Gone to Sleep" (Johnson) **24**:162
Little Poems in Prose (Baudelaire)
See *Petits poèmes en prose: Le spleen de Paris*
"The Little Rapids" (Swenson) **14**:262
The Little Sailor (Elytis)
See *The Little Mariner*
"A Little Scraping" (Jeffers) **17**:117
The Little Seafarer (Elytis)
See *The Little Mariner*
"The Little Serving Maid" (Belloc) **24**:5
"Little Sleep's-Head Sprouting Hair in the Moonlight" (Kinnell) **26**:251, 283, 291
"Little Songs for Gaia" (Snyder) **21**:301
"Little Sonnet" (Wylie) **23**:332
"Little T. C." (Marvell)
See "The Picture of Little T. C. in a Prospect of Flowers"
"A Little Testament" (Montale)
See "Piccolo testamento"
"Little Tree" (Cummings) **5**:93
"A Little Uncomplicated Hymn" (Sexton) **2**:363

"The Little Vagabond" (Blake) **12**:7
"The Little White Rose" (MacDiarmid) **9**:154, 176, 186
"Little Words" (Parker) **28**:363
"Littleblood" (Hughes) **7**:153, 168-69
Liturgies intimes (Verlaine) **2**:417-18
"Litvinka" (Lermontov) **18**:300
"Liubliu moroznoe dykhan'e" (Mandelstam) **14**:154
"Live" (Sexton) **2**:351, 364
"Live Niggers--Stop Bullshitting" (Baraka) **4**:18
Live or Die (Sexton) **2**.349, 351, 356, 362-65
"The lively sparks that issue from those eyes" (Wyatt) **27**:357
"Lives" (Rukeyser) **12**:207, 217, 228
"Living" (Levertov) **11**:186
"Living Earth" (Toomer) **7**:336-37
"Living in Sin" (Rich) **5**:351, 369
"Living in the Mountain on an Autumn Night" (Wang Wei) **18**:391
"Living Near the Water" (Song) **21**:345-46
"A Living Pearl" (Rexroth) **20**:186-87, 216, 218
"LIVING WITH TH VISHYUN" (Bissett) **14**:34
living with th vishyun (Bissett) **14**:16-17
Le Livre de l'Espurgatorie (Marie de France) See *L'Espurgatoire Saint Patrice*
Llanto por Ignacio Sánchez Mejías (Garcia Lorca) **3**:121-22, 124, 126, 128
"Llegada" (Guillen) **23**:99, 105-106
"Llewellyn and the Tree" (Robinson) **1**:462, 468
"Lo! A Child Is Born" (MacDiarmid) **9**:178-79
"Lo fatal" (Dario) **15**:96
"Lo lo lógico" (Fuertes) **27**:22
"El lo sabe" (Fuertes) **27**:15
"The Load of Sugar-Cane" (Stevens) **6**:293
"Loch Torridon" (Swinburne) **24**:313
"The Lockless Door" (Frost) **1**:218
"lock lied " (Enzensberger) **28**:138-39
"Locks" (Bukowski) **18**:15
"Locksley Hall" (Tennyson) **6**:354, 357, 359-60, 363
"Locus" (Hayden) **6**:189, 194, 196
"The Locust Tree in Flower" (Williams) **7**:363
"The Locusts" (Merrill) **28**:231, 243
"Locutions des Pierrots, I" (Laforgue) **14**:81
"Locutions des Pierrots XIV" (Laforgue) **14**:89
"Lofty in the Palais de Danse" (Gunn) **26**:220
"Log" (Merrill) **28**:221, 222, 256
"Logging 2" (Larkin) **21**:322
"Logos" (Hughes) **7**:120, 159
"Loi de formation du progrès" (Hugo) **17**:100
"Loin Cloth" (Sandburg) **2**:329
"Loin des oiseaux" (Rimbaud) **3**:274
"Loin du pigeonnier" (Apollinaire) **7**:18, 21, 23
"Loitering with a Vacant Eye" (Housman) **2**:193
"Lollocks" (Graves) **6**:137, 142, 144
"London" (Blake) **12**:7, 25, 34
"London" (Pinsky) **27**:150
"London Bridge" (Robinson) **1**:466, 468
"London Snow" (Bridges) **28**:51, 61, 70, 83
Loneliness (Paz) See *Soledad*
"A Lonely Character" (Hagiwara Sakutaro) See "Sabishii jinkaku"
"The Lonely Street" (Williams) **7**:362
"Lonesome" (Dunbar) **5**:119
"Long Afternoons" (Zagajewski) **27**:395
"Long Ages Past" (Owen) **19**:351
Long Ago and Not So Long Ago (Verlaine) See *Jadis et naguère*
"The Long Alley" (Roethke) **15**:248, 254
The Long Approach (Kumin) **15**:214, 221
Long Division: A Tribal History (Rose) **13**:232
"A Long Dress" (Stein) **18**:349
"The Long Hunter" (Berry) **28**:38
"Long John Brown & Little Mary Bell" (Blake) **12**:35
"Long John Nelson and Sweetie Pie" (Walker) **20**:286
"The long love" (Wyatt) **27**:340, 355
"The long love that in my thought doth harbour" (Wyatt) **27**:358
"Long Past Moncada" (Rukeyser) **12**:231-32
"Long Screams" (Hughes) **7**:150
"Long Shadow at Dulce" (Momaday) **25**:219
"The Long Shadow of Lincoln: A Litany" (Sandburg) **2**:334
"A Long Story" (Gray) **2**:143, 152-53
"Long To'ds Night" (Dunbar) **5**:147
"The Long Tunnel Ceiling" (Hughes) **7**:148
"The Long Waters" (Roethke) **15**:310, 316-17
"Longing" (Arnold) **5**.42-3
"Longing" (Brutus) **24**:114
"The Longing" (Roethke) **15**:272, 274, 310, 312-15
Longing (Ishikawa) See *Akogare*
"Longing for Heaven" (Bradstreet) **10**:27, 30, 42
A Longing for the Light: Selected Poems of Vicente Aleixandre (Aleixandre) **15**:24
"Longing Is Like the Seed" (Dickinson) **1**:111
"Long-Legged Fly" (Yeats) **20**:315
Longshot Peoms for Broke Players (Bukowski) **18**:3-4
Longshot Pomes for Brave Players (Bukowski) **18**:5
"the lonliness of literacy" (Bissett) **14**:34
"The Look" (Olds) **22**:342
"Look!" (Smith) **12**:342
"Look Back" (Snyder) **21**:300
"Look Down from the High Terrace Seeing Off Reminder Li" (Wang Wei) **18**:370
"Look for You Yesterday, Here You Come Today" (Baraka) **4**:14-15
"Look Hart That Horse You Ride Is Wood" (Viereck) **27**:284
"Look on This Picture and on This" (Rossetti) **7**:277
"Look, Stranger, on This Island Now" (Auden) **1**:7-8, 12, 22, 30
"Look What You Did, Christopher!" (Nash) **21**:275
"Look You I'll Go Pray" (Lindsay) **23**:281
"Looking at a Picture on an Anniversary" (Hardy) **8**:137-38
"Looking at My Father" (Olds) **22**:321
"Looking at Pictures to be Put Away" (Snyder) **21**:287
Looking for Luck (Kumin) **15**:213, 216, 221, 223-24
"Looking for Luck in Bangkok" (Kumin) **15**:214
"Looking for Nothing" (Snyder) **21**:310
"Looking for th Lammas" (Bissett) **14**:7
"Looking Forward" (Rossetti) **7**:277
"Looking Glass" (Gunn) **26**:206, 218
"Looking in a Mirror" (Atwood) **8**:32, 38
"Looking Up at the Top of a Blue Tree" (Hagiwara Sakutaro) **18**:177
"The Loom" (Masters) **1**:333
"The Loon's Cry" (Nemerov) **24**:295
"The Loon's Cry" (Nemerov) **24**:257, 292-93, 295, 299-300
"Loop" (Ondaatje) **28**:331
"The Loop" (Masters) **1**:329
"Loot" (Kipling) **3**:160, 163, 174, 187
"Lord Lundy" (Belloc) **24**:18
"Lord of Elbë, on Elbë Hill" (Bronte) **8**:73
The Lord of the Isles (Scott) **13**:277, 281, 288, 294, 296, 304, 311-12, 318, 321
Lord Weary's Castle (Lowell) **3**:200, 202-03, 206-07, 211-12, 216-18, 224, 230-33
"Lorelei" (Plath) **1**:388-89
"L'lorloge de demain" (Apollinaire) **7**:32
"The Los Cities" (Cardenal) See "Las ciudades perdidas"
"De los periódicos" (Fuertes) **27**:12
"The Loser" (Stryk) **27**:201
"Losing Track" (Levertov) **11**:160, 169
"Loss" (H. D.) **5**:303
"The Loss of the Eurydice" (Hopkins) **15**:147, 162
"The Loss of The Nabara" (Day Lewis) See "The Nabara"
"The Losse" (Finch) **21**:146, 179
"Lost" (Bukowski) **18**:24
"Lost" (Sandburg) **2**:303
"Lost and Found" (Levine) **22**:224
"The Lost Angel" (Levine) **22**:213
lost angel mining company (Bissett) **14**:6-7, 9, 17, 19
"The Lost Bower" (Browning) **6**:7
"Lost Child" (Wright) **14**:349, 352
"Lost Commagene" (Elytis) **21**:135
Lost Copper (Rose) **13**:235, 237-38, 240
"The Lost Dancer" (Toomer) **7**:336
"Lost Horizon" (Ashbery) **26**:127
"The Lost Ingredient" (Sexton) **2**:350, 359
"Lost in Translation" (Merrill) **28**:227, 232, 242, 260, 269
"The Lost Lilies" (Brooke) **24**:81
"Lost Love" (Graves) **6**:129
"The Lost Man" (Wright) **14**:339, 346
"The Lost Mistress" (Browning) **2**:38
"Lost Sister" (Song) **21**:331-32, 343, 350
"The Lost Son" (Roethke) **15**:248, 250, 255, 262-63, 267-68, 270, 272, 275-76, 278, 284, 298-99, 301-02
The Lost Son, and Other Poems (Roethke) **15**:246-50, 260, 282-83, 290-91, 296-97, 304, 308-09
"The Lost Wine" (Valery) See "Le vin perdu"
"The Lotos-Eaters" (Tennyson) **6**:352, 358-60, 409-12
"Lot's Wife" (Nemerov) **24**:255
"Lot's Wife 1988" (Clifton) **17**:29
Lotto-Poems (Cassian) **17**:6
"The Lotus and the Rose" (Lindsay) **23**:292
"Louenge a la court" (Villon) **13**:394-95
"A Lough Neagh Sequence" (Heaney) **18**:201
"Love" (Brooke) **24**:85
"Love" (Hagiwara Sakutaro) See "Airen"
"Love" (Herbert) **4**:100, 114
"Love III" (Herbert) **4**:121
"Love Again" (Larkin) **21**:259
"Love among the Ruins" (Browning) **2**:88
"Love & Fame & Death" (Bukowski) **18**:5
"Love and Friendship" (Bronte) **8**:51
"Love and Harmony Combine" (Blake) **12**:32
"Love and Honour" (Belloc) **24**:29
"The Love and the Hate" (Jeffers) **17**:136
Love and War, Art and God (Shapiro) **25**:318, 322
"Love Arm'd" (Behn) **13**:4, 7, 15, 23-5
"Love Despoiled" (Dunbar) **5**:125
Love Elegies (Donne) See *Elegies*
"Love Fossil" (Olds) **22**:310, 317
"Love from the North" (Rossetti) **7**:260, 278, 280, 289
"Love in Barrenness" (Graves) **6**:172
"Love in Blood Time" (Olds) **22**:316
"Love in Fantastic Triumph Sat" (Behn) See "Love Arm'd"
"Love in Moonlight" (Gluck) **16**:169
"Love in the Museum" (Rich) **5**:393
"Love Is" (Swenson) **14**:283
Love Is a Dog From Hell (Bukowski) **18**:19
"Love Is a Piece of Paper Torn to Bits" (Bukowski) **18**:6
"Love is More Thicker than Forget" (Cummings) **5**:108
"Love is the Only God" (Cummings) **5**:107
"Love Joy" (Herbert) **4**:122-23, 125
"A Love Letter" (Dunbar) **5**:147
"Love Letter" (Meredith) **28**:170-71, 185
"Love Letter from an Impossible Land" (Meredith) **28**:190
Love Letter from an Impossible Land

Cumulative Title Index

(Meredith) **28**:170, 172, 177, 182-87, 194, 209-10, 216
"Love Letter Postmarked Van Beethoven" (Wakoski) **15**:326, 331
"Love Me!" (Smith) **12**:346
"The Love Nut" (Ferlinghetti) **1**:187
"The Love of Christ which Passeth Knowledge" (Rossetti) **7**:268, 290
"A Love of Death" (Pinsky) **27**:154
"LOVE OF LIFE, the 49th parallel" (Bissett) **14**:7, 10, 18
"Love on my heart from heaven fell" (Bridges) **28**:59
"Love Passes Beyond the Incredible Hawk of Innocence" (Wakoski) **15**:351
"Love Poem" (Gluck) **16**:150
"Love Poem" (Lorde) **12**:158
"Love Poem" (Page) **12**:177
"Love Poem" (Stryk) **27**:197, 203
"Love Poem For Real" (Giovanni) **19**:126
Love Poems (Sanchez) **9**:207, 212, 216, 218-21, 227, 229, 234, 237, 242
Love Poems (Sexton) **2**:349, 351-53, 355, 364-65
The Love Poems of Marichiko (Rexroth) **20**:203, 218
The Love Poems of May Swenson (Swenson) **14**:274-75, 280, 283-84
Love Respelt (Graves) **6**:154, 156
"Love Sex and Romance" (Wakoski) **15**:357
"Love Song" (Levertov) **11**:159, 171
"Love Song" (Sexton) **2**:363
"Love Song" (Williams) **7**:345, 406-07
"Love Song" (Wylie) **23**:314
"Love Song from the Gaelic" (Yeats) **20**:345-46
"A Love Song in the Modern Taste" (Swift) **9**:252, 268
"The Love Song of J. Alfred Prufrock" (Eliot) **5**:153-54, 157, 160, 206
"Love Song of Prufrock Junior" (Viereck) **27**:264
"Love Song to Eohippus" (Viereck) **27**:280
Love Songs (Loy) **16**:310, 314-15, 320-21, 323, 325-26, 328
"Love Songs I" (Loy) **16**:306
"Love Songs in Age" (Larkin) **21**:229, 258
Love Songs to Joannes (Loy) **16**:316, 332
"Love Songs VI" (Loy) **16**:307
"A Love Story" (Graves) **6**:129, 133, 136-37, 144, 163, 172
"The Love Tree" (Cullen) **20**:85
"Love Unknown" (Herbert) **4**:109, 112, 123, 129
"Love Winter When the Plant Says Nothing" (Merton) **10**:334
"Love without Hope" (Graves) **6**:141, 144, 149-50
"Love You Right Back" (Brooks) **7**:94
"Loveliest of Trees" (Housman) **2**:184-85, 192, 194-95
"Lovely Ladies" (Tu Fu) **9**:330
"The Lovely Lady" (Tu Fu) **9**:322
"A Lovely Love" (Brooks) **7**:81, 96, 100-01
Love-Poems (Ovid)
See *Amores*
"The Lover" (Borges)
See "El enamorado"
"The Lover" (Montagu) **16**:337
"The Lover hopeth of better chance" (Wyatt) **27**:338
"The lover lamentes the death of his love" (Wyatt) **27**:340
"The Lover of Love" (Hagiwara Sakutaro)
See "Koi wo koi suru hito"
"The Lover Pleads with His Friend for Old Friends" (Yeats) **20**:330
"The Lover Seweth how He is Forsaken of Fortune who Sometime Favoured Him" (Wyatt) **27**:309
"A Lover since Childhood" (Graves) **6**:129
"The Lover Tells of the Rose in His Heart" (Yeats) **20**:338
"Lovers' Death" (Baudelaire)
See "La mort des amants"
"Lovers infinitenesse" (Donne) **1**:130, 153
"Lovers of the Poor" (Brooks) **7**:86, 88, 96
"The Lover's Song" (Yeats) **20**:308
"The Lover's Tale" (Tennyson) **6**:358, 373-74, 379-80
"The Lovers" (Merrill) **28**:239, 243
The Lovers Watch (Behn)
See *La Montre; or, The Lover's Watch*
"Loves Alchymie" (Donne) **1**:147, 159
"Love's Causes" (Browning) **6**:17
"Love's Diet" (Donne) **1**:127
"Love's Draft" (Dunbar) **5**:126
"Love's Expression" (Browning) **6**:17
"Love's Farewell" (Bronte) **8**:57
"Loves Growth" (Donne) **1**:153
"Love's Loneliness" (Yeats) **20**:333
"Love's New Creation" (Browning) **6**:17
"Love's Obstacles" (Browning) **6**:16
"The Loves of the Plants" (Noyes) **27**:129
"Love's Philosophy" (Shelley) **14**:167
"Love's Progress" (Roethke) **15**:289
"Love's Refuge" (Browning) **6**:17
"Love's Repetitions" (Browning) **6**:17
"Loves Riddles" (Donne) **1**:153
"Love's Sacrifice" (Browning) **6**:17
"Love's Trappist" (Chesterton) **28**:95
"(Lovesong.)" (Celan)
See "(Liebeslied.)"
"The Love-Song of a Leprechaun" (Noyes) **27**:136
"The Loving Shepherdess" (Jeffers) **17**:110, 131
"Loving the Killer" (Sexton) **2**:352-53
"Low Barometer" (Bridges) **28**:77
"The Low Sky" (Jeffers) **17**:117
"Low Tide" (Millay) **6**:236
"Low Tide at Schoodic" (Clampitt) **19**:86, 90
"Low to High" (Hughes) **1**:258, 267
"Lower Field--Enniscorthy" (Olson) **19**:293
"The Lowest Place" (Rossetti) **7**:274, 291
"The Lowest Room" (Rossetti)
See "The Lowest Place"
"The Lowestoft Boat" (Kipling) **3**:183
"Lub O' Mine" (McKay) **2**:221
"Lucien Létinois" (Verlaine) **2**:416
"Lucifer in the Train" (Rich) **5**:354, 362, 393
"lucifer speaks in his own voice" (Clifton) **17**:37
"lucifer understanding at last" (Clifton) **17**:30
"Lucifer's Feast" (Noyes) **27**:122
"Lucks my fair falcon and your fellows all" (Wyatt) **27**:367
The Lucky Bag (MacDiarmid) **9**:158
"Lucretius" (Tennyson) **6**:358, 360, 378, 380
"lucy and her girls" (Clifton) **17**:13
"Lucy Gray" (Coleridge) **11**:73-4
"Lucy Gray" (Wordsworth) **4**:398, 404, 428
Lueurs des tirs (Apollinaire) **7**:22
Luisa in Realityland (Alegria) **26**:
"Luke Havergal" (Robinson) **1**:467, 475, 490-94
"Lull" (Roethke) **15**:246-50, 282
"Lull (November, 1939)" (Roethke) **15**:250
"Lullaby" (Dunbar) **5**:122
"Lullaby" (Gluck) **16**:170
"Lullaby" (Sexton) **2**:359
"Lullaby" (Sitwell) **3**:309, 311, 326
"Lullaby" (Yeats) **20**:328
"Lullaby" (Zagajewski) **27**:389
"Lullaby for Jumbo" (Sitwell) **3**:303
Lullay Lullay like a Child (Skelton) **25**:345
"The Lumens" (Olds) **22**:340
"La luna" (Borges) **22**:100
Luna de enfrente (Borges) **22**:71-2, 93-4
"Luna Habitabilis" (Gray) **2**:155
Luna silvestre (Paz) **1**:367
"Lunar Baedecker" (Loy) **16**:306-08, 321
Lunar Baedecker (Loy) **16**:306, 310, 316, 321-22, 330
Lunar Baedecker and Time-tables (Loy) **16**:306, 316
"The Lunar Probe" (Kumin) **15**:180
"Lunch" (Stein) **18**:328
"Lundi rue Christine" (Apollinaire) **7**:18, 36
"Lune de miel" (Eliot) **5**:185, 191
"La lune est sterile" (Laforgue) **14**:61
Lupercal (Hughes) **7**:115, 118-20, 123, 135-38, 140-41, 150, 158, 162-63, 165, 169
"Lust" (Brooke) **24**:53, 56, 85
"Lustra" (Okigbo) **7**:221, 225, 232, 239, 250
Lustra (Pound) **4**:320, 365
"Lusts" (Verlaine)
See "Luxures"
"Lux" (Hugo) **17**:54
"Luxures" (Verlaine) **2**:416
"Lyceia" (Graves) **6**:156
"Lycidas" (Arnold) **5**:7
"Lycidas" (Milton) **19**:193, 202, 211-13, 217, 219-26, 242, 250-53
"Lycidas" (Swinburne) **24**:320
"Lyell's Hypothesis Again" (Rexroth) **20**:216, 218
"Lynch I" (Cesaire) **25**:30
"The Lynching" (McKay) **2**:205-06, 212, 217
"Lynching Song" (Hughes) **1**:241
"La Lyre" (Ronsard) **11**:266
"Lyric Intermezzo"
See *Lyrisches Intermezzo*
"The Lyric Year" (Dario)
See "El año lírico"
Lyrical Ballads (Coleridge) **11**:37, 59-60, 68, 91
Lyrical Ballads, with a Few Other Poems (Wordsworth) **4**:372-73, 375, 378, 380, 400, 412, 415-19, 425-29
"A Lyrick to Mirth" (Herrick) **9**:94, 103
Lyrics of Love and Laughter (Dunbar) **5**:119, 139
Lyrics of Lowly Life (Dunbar) **5**:117-18, 132, 136, 140
Lyrisches Intermezzo (Heine) **25**:130-31, 139, 141, 143, 161
"Lyrisches Intermezzo No 10" (Heine) **25**:142
"Lyrisches Intermezzo No 39" (Heine) **25**:144
"Lyrisches Intermezzo No.33" (Heine) **25**:142
"Lysergic Acid" (Ginsberg) **4**:74, 81
"Lyubil i ya v bylye gody" (Lermontov) **18**:293
"Lyubka" (Pasternak) **6**:253-54
"M AA l'anti-philosophe" (Tzara) **27**:235
"A M Alphonse de Lamartine" (Hugo) **17**:75, 90
"M Anti-psychologue" (Tzara) **27**:235
"M Antipyrine" (Tzara) **27**:235
"M Antitête" (Tzara) **27**:235
"A M de Chateaubriand" (Hugo) **17**:90
"Ma bohème" (Rimbaud) **3**:271, 276, 283
"Ma Man" (Hughes) **1**:270
"Macarius and the Pony" (Merton) **10**:351
"Macaw" (Bogan) **12**:86
Macchu Picchu (Neruda)
See *Alturas de Macchu Picchu*
MacFlecknoe; or, A Satire upon the Trew-Blew-Protestant Poet, T. S. (Dryden) **25**:70, 114-16, 118, 120-23
"Mackinnon's Boat" (Tomlinson) **17**:344
"Macpherson's Farewell" (Burns) **6**:55
"MacStatesman and Co." (MacDiarmid) **9**:176
"Mad As the Mist and the Snow" (Yeats) **20**:328-29
"The Mad Farmer Manifesto: The First Amendment" (Berry) **28**:13
"Mad Judy" (Hardy) **8**:102
"The Mad Maid's Song" (Herrick) **9**:87
"The Mad Monk" (Coleridge) **11**:69
"The Mad Mother" (Wordsworth) **4**:374, 380
"A Mad Negro Soldier Confined at Munich" (Lowell) **3**:205, 218, 222
"The Mad Scene" (Merrill) **28**:254
"Mad Song" (Blake) **12**:31-2
"The Mad Woman of the GRand Armee" (Alegria) **26**:
"Madam and Her Might-Have Been" (Hughes) **1**:243

"Madam and the Wrong Visitor" (Hughes) **1**:243
"Madame de Soubise" (Vigny) **26**:410-11
"Madame Decrepitude" (Cassian) **17**:13
"A Madame Sand" (Nerval) **13**:178
"Madame Withouten Many Wordes" (Wyatt) **27**:316, 328, 330
"Das Mädchen spricht" (Goethe) **5**:249
"Madeleine" (Apollinaire) **7**:32
"Mademoiselle Bistouri" (Baudelaire) **1**:58
"A Mademoiselle Louise B" (Hugo) **17**:93
"Mademoiselle Veronique" (Brodsky) **9**:10
"Madhouse Bells" (Browning) **2**:30
"Madhouse Cells" (Browning) **2**:26
"Madhumanjari" (Tagore) **8**:416
The Madman, His Parables and Poems (Gibran) **9**:69, 71, 75, 77-80, 82
"Madman's Song" (Wylie) **23**:301, 309, 326, 328
"Madness" (Baraka) **4**:27
"The Madness of King Goll" (Yeats) **20**:344, 354
"The Madonna" (Tennyson) **6**:353
"Madonna of the Evening Flowers" (Lowell) **13**:60, 64, 67, 96
"Madrid 1937" (Neruda) **4**:310
"Madrigal" (Nemerov) **24**:256
"Madrigal triste" (Baudelaire) **1**:61
"Madrigali privati" (Montale) **13**:106, 167
"Madrugada" (Fuertes) **27**:7
"Madurai" (Paz) **1**:361
"The Madwoman's Miracle" (Wylie) **23**:321
"Le maestrine" (Pavese) **13**:221
"Magadalena" (Gautier) **18**:163-64
"Magasins du Louvre" (Loy) **16**:312, 328
"The Magellanic Clouds" (Wakoski) **15**:325, 363
The Magellanic Clouds (Wakoski) **15**:350-51, 363, 365-66
"The Magellanic Heart" (Neruda)
See "El corazón magellanico"
"Les mages" (Hugo) **17**:83, 87
"Maggie, a Lady" (Rossetti) **7**:291
"The Magi" (Gluck) **16**:125, 140, 149
"Magic" (Dove) **6**:113
"Magic" (Levertov) **11**:209
"Magic Island" (Song) **21**:344
The Magic Lantern (Tsvetaeva)
See *Volshebny fonar*
"TH MAGIC LURE OF SEA SHELLS" (Bissett) **14**:34
"The Magic Morning" (Smith) **12**:331
"Magician" (Shapiro) **25**:309
The Magician's Feastletters (Wakoski) **15**:356
Magique (Cesaire) **25**:36
"Magna est Veritas" (Smith) **12**:333
The Magnetic Fields (Breton)
See *Les Champs Magnétiques*
The Magnetic Mountain (Day Lewis) **11**:123-26, 128-30, 135, 138-39, 143-45, 148, 151-52
"Magnets" (Cullen) **20**:60
"Magnitudo parvi" (Hugo) **17**:89
"Magnolia Flower" (Hughes) **1**:237
"The Magnolia Shadow" (Montale)
See "L'ombra della magnolia"
"Magnolias in Snow" (Hayden) **6**:194, 196
"Magpie's Song" (Snyder) **21**:297
"Magpiety" (Milosz)
See "Sroczość"
"Mahomets Gesang" (Goethe) **5**:247
Mahua (Tagore) **8**:415-16
"The Maid Servant at the Inn" (Parker) **28**:353
"The Maiden Marriage" (Swinburne) **24**:357
"Maiden May" (Rossetti) **7**:277
"Maiden Song" (Rossetti) **7**:264, 274-6, 289
"The Maiden without Hands" (Sexton) **2**:365
"A Maiden's Pledge" (Hardy) **8**:98
"Maiden's Sorrow" (Bryant) **20**:15
"The Maid's Thought" (Jeffers) **17**:117
"Maifest" (Goethe) **5**:251
"Mailied" (Goethe) **5**:245
"Mailie's Dying Words and Elegy" (Burns)
See "The Death and Dying Words of Poor Mailie"
"Maillol" (Tomlinson) **17**:311, 314, 335
"Maisie" (Merrill) **28**:228, 254
"La maison des mortes" (Apollinaire) **7**:47
"La maison du Berger" (Vigny) **26**:370, 377, 386-87, 391-94, 396, 402, 404, 406, 409, 413
"La Maison d'Yves" (Breton) **15**:63-7
"Maison Flake" (Tzara) **27**:233
"Maithuna" (Paz) **1**:361, 368
"The Maja and the Old Woman" (Aleixandre) **15**:5-6
"Le Majeur Ydow" (Smith) **12**:331
"Major Macroo" (Smith) **12**:309, 317
Majors and Minors (Dunbar) **5**:115, 117-18, 128, 132, 135-36, 142
"A Major Work" (Meredith) **28**:201
"Make Big Money at Home! Write Poems in Spare Time!!" (Nemerov) **24**:267
"The Maker" (Borges)
See "El hacedor"
"The Maker" (Illyes)
See "Teremteni"
The Maker (Borges)
See *El hacedor*
"The Makers" (Nemerov) **24**:289-90
"Making a Living" (Sexton) **2**:367
"Making a Sacher Torte" (Wakoski) **15**:355, 372
"the making of poems" (Clifton) **17**:27
"Making the Connection" (Kumin) **15**:208
"Le mal" (Rimbaud) **3**:283
"Malabaress" (Baudelaire)
See "A une Malabaraise"
"Malachy Deagan" (Masters) **1**:343
"Malcolm" (Sanchez) **9**:224, 231
"Malcolm" (Walker) **20**:277
"Malcolm Spoke/Who listened? (This Poem Is for My Consciousness Too)" (Madhubuti) **5**:328, 341
"Il male di vivere" (Montale) **13**:105
"Malediction Upon Myself" (Wylie) **23**:303, 310
"Le maline" (Rimbaud) **3**:283
"The Malingerer" (McKay) **2**:226
"'Mallorca,' un poema en el olvido" (Borges) **22**:92
"Malmaison" (Lowell) **13**:71, 78, 84
"Malourène" (Apollinaire) **7**:48
"Mammy Hums" (Sandburg) **2**:324
"Man" (Brooke) **24**:71, 75
"Man" (Herbert) **4**:100-01, 103
"Man" (Lamartine)
See "L'homme"
"The Man against the Sky" (Robinson) **1**:462, 471, 490, 492-94
The Man against the Sky (Robinson) **1**:462-63, 467-68, 474
"Man and Dog" (Sassoon) **12**:255
"The Man and the Echo" (Yeats) **20**:314, 335
"Man and Wife" (Lowell) **3**:206, 209, 221, 245
"Man and Wife" (Sexton) **2**:363
"The Man beneath the Tree" (Wright) **14**:343, 345, 347
"Man Bites Dog-Days" (Nash) **21**:265
"The Man Born to Farming" (Berry) **28**:26
Man Does, Woman Is (Graves) **6**:154
"Man Doesn't Exist" (Aleixandre) **15**:20, 22
"The Man He Killed" (Hardy) **8**:102-03
"A Man I Am" (Smith) **12**:295
"Man in Black" (Plath) **1**:389
A Man in the Divided Sea (Merton) **10**:338, 346-47, 350
"Man into Men" (Hughes) **1**:241, 243
"Man is a Spirit" (Smith) **12**:297, 316
"Man of Lawe's Tale" (Chaucer)
See "Man of Law's Tale"
"Man of Law's Tale" (Chaucer) **19**:13, 15, 24, 26, 45, 54-6, 59-60, 62
"A Man of the Middle Class" (Brooks) **7**:62
"Man of Words" (Ashbery) **26**:126
"The Man on His Death Bed" (Aleixandre) **15**:8
"The Man on the Dump" (Ashbery) **26**:153
"The Man on the Hotel Room Bed" (Kinnell) **26**:286
"The Man Seeking Experience Enquires His Way of a Drop of Water" (Hughes) **7**:116, 118
"Man Splitting Wood in the Daybreak" (Kinnell) **26**:293
"man spricht deutsch," (Enzensberger) **28**:142
"The Man that are Falling" (Stevens) **6**:310
"Man, the Man-Hunter" (Sandburg) **2**:308
"Man the Master" (Merton) **10**:345
"A Man Walking and Singing" (Berry) **28**:3-4, 7, 18
"Man Was Made to Mourn" (Burns) **6**:68
The Man Who Died Twice (Robinson) **1**:469, 472, 475, 477, 483, 489-90
"The Man Who Dreamed of Fairyland" (Yeats) **20**:343, 354
"A Man Who Loves Love" (Hagiwara Sakutaro)
See "Koi wo koi suru hito"
The Man Who Shook Hands (Wakoski) **15**:366
"The Man Whose Pharynx Was Bad" (Stevens) **6**:294
"The Man with a Past" (Hardy) **8**:93
Man with a Sling (Neruda)
See *El hondero entusiasta, 1923-1924*
The Man with Night Sweats (Gunn) **26**:224, 228, 230 231
"Man with One Small Hand" (Page) **12**:170
The Man with Seven Toes (Ondaatje) **28**:298-99, 300-02, 318, 322, 326-27
"The Man with the Blue Guitar" (Stevens) **6**:298, 323-24, 326, 337, 339
The Man with the Blue Guitar, and Other Poems (Stevens) **6**:304
"A Man Young and Old" (Yeats) **20**:328
"Manas-sundari" (Tagore) **8**:408
"Manciple's Tale" (Chaucer) **19**:11, 13, 48
"Mandala" (Merrill) **28**:256
"Mandalay" (Kipling) **3**:158, 160, 162, 167, 188-89, 192
"The Mandolin, the Carnation and the Bamboo" (Apollinaire)
See "La mandoline, l'oeillet et le bambou"
"La mandoline, l'oeillet et le bambou" (Apollinaire) **7**:18, 20-2, 34, 36
Manfred (Byron) **16**:68-72, 82-4, 86-90, 108, 111
"Mango Grove" (Tagore)
See "Amravan"
"Manhattan: Grace Church" (Clampitt) **19**:100
"Manhattan May Day Midnight" (Ginsberg) **4**:84
"Mania di solitudine" (Pavese) **13**:225
"Mania for solitude" (Pavese)
See "Mania di solitudine"
"Manicure" (Brooks) **7**:53
"Mankind" (Trakl)
See "Menschheit"
"The Man-Moth" (Bishop) **3**:37, 65
"The Manner of the World Nowadays" (Skelton) **25**:337
Mannerly Margery Milk and Ale (Skelton) **25**:345
"The Manor Garden" (Plath) **1**:389
Las manos del día (Neruda) **4**:288
"A Man's a Man for a' That" (Burns) **6**:60
"Man's Medley" (Herbert) **4**:101, 127
"Manscape" (Tomlinson) **17**:351-52
"Mansion" (Ammons) **16**:16, 20
"Mantis" (Zukofsky) **11**:341, 347, 356, 392-99
"'Mantis,' an Interpretation" (Zukofsky) **11**:341, 356, 394
"Manual System" (Sandburg) **2**:304
"Manuelzinho" (Bishop) **3**:59-60
"Many Farms Notes" (Ortiz) **17**:231
Many Inventions (Kipling) **3**:160
Many Long Years Ago (Nash) **21**:266

Cumulative Title Index

"The Many Mansions" (Levertov) **11**:201
"Many Swans" (Lowell) **13**:61, 64-5, 83
"Manyone Flying" (Swenson) **14**:283
"Manzanita" (Snyder) **21**:297
"The Map" (Bishop) **3**:37, 50-2
"The Map" (Stryk) **27**:203
The Map of Love (Thomas) **2**:381, 390
"A Map of the City" (Gunn) **26**:219
"Maple and Sumach" (Day Lewis) **11**:144
"El mar" (Borges) **22**:99
"Mar Portuguese" (Pessoa) **20**:170
El mar y las campanas (Neruda) **4**:287-88
"Mar y noche" (Aleixandre) **15**:16
"Mara" (Jeffers) **17**:146
"Marathon" (Gluck) **16**:152, 164, 166-67
"Marburg" (Pasternak) **6**:270-71, 281
"March" (Bryant) **20**:12
"March 21 1987" (Brutus) **24**:110
"The March of the Cameron Men" (Robinson) **1**:476
"March Twilight" (Bogan) **12**:111
Marcha triunfal (Dario) **15**:79-80, 85, 111
"Marchas pawnees" (Cardenal) **22**:131
"Marche de funèbre pour la mort de la terre" (Laforgue) **14**:95
"La marche impériale" (Valery) **9**:391
"Marchenbilder" (Ashbery) **26**:127, 150
"Marching Song" (Wang Wei) **18**:389
"Marcia funebre" (Pasolini) **17**:264
Marconi's Cottage (McGuckian) **27**:84, 91-92, 94-95, 99, 104-105, 110
"Margaret" (Sandburg) **2**:303
"Margaret" (Wordsworth) **4**:399
"Margarita Debayle" (Dario) **15**:80, 95
"Marginal Employment" (Clampitt) **19**:81, 88
"Margite, Marguerite and Margherita" (Stein) **18**:325, 334
"Margrave" (Jeffers) **17**:142
"I mari del sud" (Pavese) **13**:210, 212, 216, 220-26, 228
"Maria" (Gautier) **18**:126
Maria Neféli (Elytis) **21**:130-31
Maria Nephele (Elytis)
See *Maria Neféli*
"Maria Stuart" (Pasternak) **6**:267
"Maria Who Made Faces and a Deplorable Marriage" (Belloc) **24**:24
"The Mariachis--A Glimpse" (Wakoski) **15**:332
"Mariana" (Tennyson) **6**:359, 364, 387, 389, 391, 406-09, 411
"Mariana in the South" (Tennyson) **6**:350
"Marianne, My Mother, and Me" (Kumin) **15**:210-12
"Marichika" (Tagore) **8**:407
"Marijuana Notation" (Ginsberg) **4**:79
Marilyn Monroe and Other Poems
See *Oracion por Marilyn Monroe y otros poemas*
"Marina" (Brooke) **24**:58
"Marina" (Eliot) **5**:164, 195, 205-06, 210
"Marine" (Rimbaud) **3**:261
Mariner (Coleridge)
See *The Rime of the Ancient Mariner: A Poet's Reverie*
"Marines USA" (Guillen) **23**:126
Marino Faliero: Doge of Venice (Byron) **16**:103
"Mariposa de obsidiana" (Paz) **1**:364
"Maritime Ode" (Pessoa)
See "Ode Marítima"
"The Mark" (Bogan) **12**:87-8, 98, 106, 121
"Market" (Hayden) **6**:194, 196
"Market at Turk" (Gunn) **26**:186, 219
Marmion (Scott) **13**:249-51, 256, 258, 261, 264, 266-68, 270-71, 273, 275-76, 279, 281-85, 287-90, 304, 311-12, 317-18
"The Marmozet" (Belloc) **24**:24
"Marriage" (Moore) **4**:230-31, 233, 243, 249, 251-52, 254-55, 258, 260-61
"Le marriage d'André Salmon" (Apollinaire)
See "Poème lu au mariage d'André Salmon"
"The Marriage II" (Levertov) **11**:167
"A Marriage in the Sixties" (Rich) **5**:363
The Marriage of Heaven and Hell (Blake) **12**:12, 28, 36, 39-41, 47-51, 60-1, 64
"The Marriage of Hector and Andromache" (Sappho) **5**:414, 418
"The Marriage of Lord Fauconberg and Lady Mary Cromwell" (Marvell) **10**:270
"The Marriage Ring" (Blake) **12**:34
"The Married Man" (Kipling) **3**:192
"The Marrow" (Roethke) **15**:277, 281
"Marshall Washer" (Carruth) **10**:74
"Marsyas" (Masters) **1**:329
"The Marten" (Clare) **23**:7
"Martha" (Lorde) **12**:140, 157
"A Martial Law Carol" (Brodsky) **9**:26-7
"Martirio de Santa Olalla" (Garcia Lorca) **3**:132, 146
"The Martyr of Alabama" (Harper) **21**:190
The Martyr of Alabama, and Other Poems (Harper) **21**:189
"The Martyr Poets Did Not Tell" (Dickinson) **1**:96
"A Martyr: The Vigil of the Feast" (Rossetti) **7**:285
"The Martyrdom of Bishop Farrar" (Hughes) **7**:112
"Martyrdom of Saint Eulalia" (Garcia Lorca)
See "Martirio de Santa Olalla"
"Une martyre" (Baudelaire) **1**:45, 48, 62
The Marvelous Arithmetics of Distance (Lorde) **12**:153
"Mary" (Blake) **12**:35, 43
"Mary and Gabriel" (Brooke) **24**:59, 78, 84
"Mary and the Seasons" (Rexroth) **20**:209
"Mary at the Feet of Christ" (Harper) **21**:191
"The 'Mary Gloster'" (Kipling) **3**:161, 167, 181
"Mary Morison" (Burns)
See "Ye Are Na Mary Morison"
"Mary, Pity Women" (Kipling) **3**:161, 192
"Mary Winslow" (Lowell) **3**:206, 217-18
"mary's dream" (Clifton) **17**:19
"Marz has Ruined Nature, for the Moment" (Stevens) **6**:297
"The Mask" (Baudelaire)
See "Le masque"
"Mask" (Illyes) **16**:245, 250
"The Masked Face" (Hardy) **8**:119
"Masked Woman's Song" (Bogan) **12**:100-01
"Masks" (Stryk) **27**:191, 197
"Masks of Dawn" (Paz) **1**:359
"Le masque" (Baudelaire) **1**:45, 65, 72
"Masque nègre" (Senghor) **25**:224
The Masque of Anarchy (Shelley) **14**:171, 175, 210
A Masque of Mercy (Frost) **1**:211
"The Masque of Plenty" (Kipling) **3**:181
A Masque of Reason (Frost) **1**:203-04, 206, 217
The Masque of Snow (Blok)
See *Snezhnye maski*
"Masque of Tsars" (Viereck) **27**:280
"Masquerade in the Park" (Akhmatova) **2**:6
"Masqueraders" (Page) **12**:178
"Mass for the Day of St. Thomas Didymus" (Levertov) **11**:198, 200-01
"The Massage" (Kinnell) **26**:286
"The Master" (H. D.) **5**:306
"The Master" (Robinson) **1**:461, 465, 467
"Master and Mistress" (Kunitz) **19**:148
"Master Herrick's Farewell unto Poetry" (Herrick)
See "Farewell to Poetry"
"Master Hugues of Saxe-Gotha" (Browning) **2**:37, 61, 88
"The Masters of the Heart Touched the Unknown" (Schwartz) **8**:292
"The Matachines" (Tomlinson) **17**:328-29
"The Match" (Marvell) **10**:271, 300
"Materia humana" (Aleixandre) **15**:34
"Maternità" (Pavese) **13**:213
"Mathilde in Normady" (Rich) **5**:352, 359
"Matinée d'ivresse" (Rimbaud) **3**:261, 263, 271-73, 281-82
"Matinees" (Merrill) **28**:285-87
"Matins" (Gluck) **16**:170-71
"Matins" (Levertov) **11**:166
"Matoaka" (Clampitt) **19**:101-02
"Matrix" (Clampitt) **19**:102
"Matros v Moskve" (Pasternak) **6**:283
"Mattens" (Herbert) **4**:119
"Mattens, or Morning Prayer" (Herrick) **9**:118
"Matthew XXV: 30" (Borges) **22**:73-5
Matthias at the Door (Robinson) **1**:473-74, 479
"Mattino" (Pavese) **13**:230
"Maturity" (Ginsberg) **4**:87
Maud, and Other Poems (Tennyson) **6**:354, 356-57, 360, 363, 366, 373, 379-80, 383, 385, 387, 407
"Maude Clare" (Rossetti) **7**:260, 280, 291
"Maundy Thursday" (Owen) **19**:352, 358
"Mausfallen-Sprüchlein" (Morike) **1**:114
Mausoleum: Siebenunddreißig Balladen aus der Geschichte des Fortschritts. (Enzensberger) **28**:148-50, 154-55, 158, 165
"Le mauvais moine" (Baudelaire) **1**:59
"Le mauvais vitrier" (Baudelaire) **1**:67
"Mawu" (Lorde) **12**:143
"Maximus at the Harbor" (Olson) **19**:312-13
"Maximus From Dogtown--IV" (Olson) **19**:306
"Maximus of Gloucester" (Olson) **19**:294, 304
The Maximus Poems (Olson) **19**:266-67, 270-71, 273-75, 277, 279-83, 285-87, 294, 296-98, 304-7, 316
"Maximus, to Himself" (Olson) **19**:269
Maximus, Vol. II (Olson) **19**:306
Maximus, Vol. III (Olson) **19**:285, 287-88, 295, 305-7
"May" (Rossetti) **7**:265
"May 20, 1928" (Borges) **22**:76
"May 24, 1980" (Brodsky) **9**:24
"May 1943" (H. D.) **5**:307
"May 1968" (Olds) **22**:339
"may all thes blessings" (Bissett) **14**:30
"May Festival" (Goethe)
See "Maifest"
"May It Be" (Pasternak) **6**:261
"The May Magnificat" (Hopkins) **15**:124-25, 165
The May Queen (Tennyson) **6**:359
"Mayapán" (Cardenal) **22**:128, 131
"Mayavada" (Tagore) **8**:408
"Maybe this is a sign of madness" (Mandelstam) **14**:155
"Maybe this is the beginning of madness" (Mandelstam)
See "Mozhet byt' eto tochka bezumiia"
"May-Day" (Emerson) **18**:76, 88, 111
May-Day and Other Pieces (Emerson) **18**:75, 113
"Mayflower" (Aiken) **26**:41-2, 45
"The Mayor of Gary" (Sandburg) **2**:304, 308
"The Maypole Is Up" (Herrick) **9**:102, 145
"May's Love" (Browning) **6**:24
"A Maze of Sparks of Gold" (Rexroth) **20**:190
"Mazeppa" (Hugo) **17**:75
Mazeppa (Byron) **16**:83
"Mazurka" (McGuckian) **27**:101
"M.B." (Brodsky) **9**:10
"McAndrew's Hymn" (Kipling) **3**:161, 167, 170, 186, 192
"Me Again" (Rexroth) **20**:218
Me Again: Uncollected Writings of Stevie Smith (Smith) **12**:314, 333-34, 340, 343-44, 346-47
"Me centuplant Persée" (Cesaire) **25**:31
"Me crucé con un entierro" (Fuertes) **27**:11
"Me from Myself to Banish" (Dickinson) **1**:94
"Me Whoppin' Big-Tree Boy" (McKay) **2**:226
"Meadow Milk" (Bogan) **12**:110
Meadowlands (Gluck) **16**:171-73
"Meadowlands 3" (Gluck) **16**:171
"Meaning" (Milosz) **8**:215
"The Measure of Poetry" (Nemerov) **24**:303
"Meat without Mirth" (Herrick) **9**:98

"Mechanism" (Ammons) **16**:40
"Le médaillon toujours fermé" (Apollinaire) **7**:22
The Medall. A Satire Against Sedition (Dryden) **25**:74
The Medea, and Some Poems (Cullen) **20**:60-62, 66
Medea the Sorceress (Wakoski) **15**:372-73
Le médecin malgré lui (Williams) **7**:349
Medicamina Faciei (Ovid) **2**:238-39, 243, 251, 253, 258
"MEDICINE" (Bissett) **14**:20
MEDICINE my mouths on fire (Bissett) **14**:16, 19, 27
Medieval Scenes (Duncan) **2**:109
"Médiocriteé" (Laforgue) **14**:88
"Meditation" (Baudelaire)
See "Recueillement"
"Meditation" (Lermontov)
See "Duma"
"Meditation at Lagunitas" (Hass) **16**:200, 209, 211, 219
"Meditation at Oyster River" (Roethke) **15**:265, 276, 310, 313, 316
"A Meditation for His Mistresse" (Herrick) **9**:101
"Meditation in the Spring Rain" (Berry) **28**:6
"A Meditation in Time of War" (Yeats) **20**:314
"A Meditation in Tuscany" (Browning) **6**:16
"The Meditation of the Old Fisherman" (Yeats) **20**:337
"Meditation on a June Evening" (Aiken) **26**:7, 50
"A Meditation on John Constable" (Tomlinson) **17**:341-42
"Meditation on Saviors" (Jeffers) **17**:142, 144-45
Les meditations (Lamartine) **16**:256-62, 265, 268-69
"Meditations in Time of Civil War" (Yeats) **20**:314, 342, 349
"Meditations of an Old Woman" (Roethke) **15**:262, 264-65, 273
Méditations poétiques (Lamartine) **16**:270, 272-82, 284-85, 287, 289-93, 302
"Mediterraneo" (Montale) **13**:115
Medny Vsadnik (Pushkin) **10**:367-68, 373-74, 385, 390-400, 414
"Medusa" (Bogan) **12**:85, 104-06, 111-12, 115, 117
"Medusa" (Cullen) **20**:69
"Medusa" (Dove) **6**:123
"Medusa" (Merrill) **28**:229
"Meeting" (Arnold) **5**:42
"Meeting" (Montale)
See "Incontro"
"A Meeting" (Pasternak)
See "Vstrecha"
"The Meeting" (Rukeyser) **12**:231
"A Meeting of Minds" (Lorde) **12**:135
"Meeting-House Hill" (Lowell) **13**:67
Meghaduta (Kalidasa) **22**:177-78, 182, 185, 188-89, 192, 194-95, 204-05, 207-08
La meglio gioventù (Pasolini) **17**:250-51, 254, 262, 264-67, 275, 279, 281-83, 293
"A Mehinaku Girl in Seclusion" (Song) **21**:344
"mehrere elstern" (Enzensberger) **28**:139
"Mein Karren knarrt nicht mehr" (Celan) **10**:124
"A Mei-p'i Lake Song" (Tu Fu) **9**:330-31, 333
"Melancholia" (Gautier) **18**:135
"Melancholia en Orizba" (Neruda) **4**:281
"Melancholy" (Bely) **11**:6
"Melancholy" (Bridges) **28**:76
"Melancholy in Orizaba" (Neruda)
See "Melancholia en Orizba"
"A Melancholy Moon" (Baudelaire)
See "Les tristesses de la lune"
Melancolía (Jimenez) **7**:211
"Melancthon" (Moore) **4**:254
"Mélange adultère de tout" (Eliot) **5**:185
"Melbourne" (Shapiro) **25**:269
"Melibee" (Chaucer)
See "Tale of Melibee"
"Melinda on an Insipid Beauty in imitation of a fragment of Sapho's" (Finch) **21**:167
"Melody" (Tomlinson) **17**:341
"Memo from the Cave" (Gluck) **16**:147-48
"Memoir" (Pinsky) **27**:157
"Mémoire" (Rimbaud) **3**:262, 268
"Memoirs" (Meredith) **28**:199
"Memoirs of the World" (Gunn) **26**:203
"Memorabilia" (Masters) **1**:343
"Memorandum Confided by a Yucca to a Passion-Vine" (Lowell) **13**:61, 64
"À Memória do President Rei Sidónio" (Pessoa) **20**:154
"Memorial" (Pinsky) **27**:153
"Memorial" (Sanchez) **9**:224
"Memorial II" (Lorde) **12**:140, 157
"Memorial for the City" (Auden) **1**:23
"Memorial Tablet" (Sassoon) **12**:269
"Memories..." (Jimenez)
See "Recuerdos..."
"Memories of My Father" (Kinnell) **26**:286
"Memories of the Forest" (Ishikawa)
See "Mori no omoide"
"Memories of West Street and Lepke" (Lowell) **3**:206, 208, 220, 223, 237
"Memory" (Bogan) **12**:101, 120, 122
"A Memory" (Brooke) **24**:85-6
"A Memory" (Pavese) **13**:203
"Memory" (Roethke) **15**:275
"Memory" (Sassoon) **12**:269
"Memory" (Walker) **20**:283
"Memory" (Wright) **14**:376
"Memory I" (Rossetti) **7**:277
"The Memory of Elena" (Forche) **10**:136, 139, 152-53, 166, 169
"A Memory of the Players in a Mirror at Midnight" (Joyce) **22**:
"Memory of V. I. Ulianov" (Zukofsky) **11**:396
"A Memory Picture" (Arnold) **5**:49
"Men" (Parker) **28**:347, 354
"Men" (Toomer) **7**:336
Men and Women (Browning) **2**:66, 77, 94
"Men Improve with the Years" (Yeats) **20**:314
"Men Loved Wholly beyond Wisdom" (Bogan) **12**:104, 126
"Men of the North" (Harper) **21**:190
Men, Women, and Ghosts (Lowell) **13**:63, 71, 73, 76, 79, 85, 93
"The Menace" (Gunn) **26**:228
"El mendigo que entregaba un papel" (Fuertes) **27**:30
"Mending Wall" (Frost) **1**:225, 227, 229
"Mendocino Rose" (Hongo) **23**:199
"Menelaus and Helen" (Brooke) **24**:56, 65, 76, 79, 82
"Menons Klagen um Diotima" (Holderlin) **4**:141-42
"Menon's Lament for Diotime" (Holderlin)
See "Menons Klagen um Diotima"
"Mens Creatrix" (Kunitz) **19**:159
Mensagem (Pessoa) **20**:154-57, 159-63, 165, 168, 170
"Mensaje" (Aleixandre) **15**:6, 10
"Menschenbeitfall" (Holderlin) **4**:165
"Menschheit" (Trakl) **20**:250, 253-55
"Menschliche Trauer" (Trakl) **20**:253
"Menschliches Elend" (Trakl) **20**:253
"Menses" (Millay) **6**:233
"Menstruation at Forty" (Sexton) **2**:363 .
"Mental Cases" (Owen) **19**:330, 336, 340-41, 343, 347, 353, 355, 359, 365, 368, 370-71
"The Mental Traveller" (Blake) **12**:36, 46, 48
"The Merchantmen" (Kipling) **3**:161
"Merchant's Tale" (Chaucer) **19**:13, 15, 28, 33, 62-3
"Mercury and the Elephant" (Finch) **21**:159, 161
"Merely Statement" (Lowell) **13**:86
"Mericano" (Ortiz) **17**:228
"Meridian" (Clampitt) **19**:83
"Meriggiare pallido e assorto" (Montale) **13**:105
"Merlin" (Emerson) **18**:81-82, 88, 99, 104, 106
Merlin: A Poem (Robinson) **1**:462-63, 465, 468-71, 482-83, 488-89, 491
"Merlin and the Gleam" (Tennyson) **6**:389, 407
"Merlin in the Cave He Speculates Without a Book" (Gunn) **26**:
"The Mermaid's Children" (Lowell) **3**:241
"The Mermen" (Crane) **3**:90
Merope (Arnold) **5**:8, 12, 35, 37, 45, 47, 58-60, 62-3
"The Merry Guide" (Housman) **2**:180, 192
"Merry Margaret" (Skelton) **25**:336
"The Merry Muses" (Burns) **6**:96
"Meru" (Yeats) **20**:326
"Merveilles de la guerre" (Apollinaire) **7**:3, 22
"Mes bouguins refemés" (Mallarme) **4**:199
"Mes deux Filles" (Hugo) **17**:82
"De Mes Haras" (Cesaire) **25**:10
"Mes petites amoureuses" (Rimbaud) **3**:262, 284
"Mescaline" (Ginsberg) **4**:74, 81
"Un mese fra i bambini" (Montale) **13**:134
Les meslanges (Ronsard) **11**:247, 266
"Message" (Aleixandre)
See "Mensaje"
"Message" (Forche) **10**:139, 144, 154-55
"The Message" (Levertov) **11**:171
"The Message" (Sassoon) **12**:248
Message (Pessoa)
See *Mensagem*
"A Message All Blackpeople Can Dig (& A Few Negroes Too)" (Madhubuti) **5**:329, 341
"Message for the Sinecurist" (Gallagher) **9**:62
"Message from the NAACP" (Baraka) **4**:11
"the message of crazy horse" (Clifton) **17**:25
"Message to a Black Soldier" (Madhubuti) **5**:339
"Messages" (Senghor) **25**:255
"The Messenger" (Atwood) **8**:18
"The Messenger" (Gunn) **26**:219, 226
"The Messenger" (Merton) **10**:339
"The Messenger" (Sassoon) **12**:259
"A Messenger from the Horizon" (Merton) **10**:334
"Messengers" (Gluck) **16**:127, 133, 142
"The Messiah" (Pope) **26**:314, 319, 322
"Messianic Eclogue" (Vergil)
See "Eclogue 4"
"Messias" (Shapiro) **25**:284, 317
"The Metal and the Flower" (Page) **12**:168, 178
The Metal and the Flower (Page) **12**:167, 171, 193
Die Metamorphose der Pflanzen (Goethe) **5**:239-40
Metamorphoses (Ovid) **2**:233, 238-241, 244-45, 260
"Les métamorphoses du vampire" (Baudelaire) **1**:48, 71
"The Metamorphoses of the Vampire" (Baudelaire)
See "Les métamorphoses du vampire"
"Metamorphosis" (Gluck) **16**:163
"Metamorphosis" (Sitwell) **3**:304
Metamorphosis (Ovid)
See *Metamorphoses*
"Metaphors of a Magnifico" (Stevens) **6**:311-12
"The Metaphysical Automobile" (Nemerov) **24**:284
"Metempsicosis" (Dario) **15**:101
"Metho Drinker" (Wright) **14**:333, 341
"The Metropolis" (Clampitt) **19**:90
"Métropolitain" (Rimbaud) **3**:265
"Mexican Divertimento" (Brodsky) **9**:12
"Mexican Divertissement" (Brodsky)
See "Mexican Divertimento"
"Mexicans Begin Jogging" (Soto) **28**:387
"Mezzo Forte" (Williams) **7**:405
"Mi chiquita" (Guillen) **23**:142
"Mi suerte" (Fuertes) **27**:14, 27
"Mi vida entera" (Borges) **22**:93

Cumulative Title Index

"Mi voz" (Aleixandre) **15**:40
"Mía" (Dario) **15**:107, 113
"La mia musa" (Montale) **13**:139
"Mia vita a te non chiedo lineamenti" (Montale) **13**:139
"Miami You Are About to be Surprised" (Merton) **10**:351
"MIA's (Missing in Action and Other Atlantas)" (Sanchez) **9**:230, 235, 244
"Micah" (Walker) **20**:278
"Michael" (Wordsworth) **4**:380-81, 394, 399, 402, 412, 414, 425, 428
Michael Robartes and the Dancer (Yeats) **20**:310, 314
"Michel et Christine" (Rimbaud) **3**:264, 281
"The Microbe" (Belloc) **24**:15, 25
"Mid-August at Sourdough Mountain Lookout" (Snyder) **21**:286
"Midas among Goldenrod" (Merrill) **28**:239
"Middle Flight" (Meredith) **28**:174, 186
"Middle of a Long Poem on 'These States'" (Ginsberg) **4**:47
"The Middle of Life" (Holderlin)
See "Hälfte des Lebens"
"Middle Passage" (Hayden) **6**:176-81, 183, 187-88, 194, 196-200
"The Middle-Aged" (Rich) **5**:362-63, 367, 369
"Midnight" (Heaney) **18**:192
"Midnight" (Parker) **28**:351, 364
"Midnight" (Wright) **14**:337
"Midnight Chippie's Lament" (Hughes) **1**:255
"Midnight in Moscow" (Mandelstam) **14**:122
"A Midnight Interior" (Sassoon) **12**:246
"Midnight Nan at Leroy's" (Hughes) **1**:246
"Midnight on the Great Western" (Hardy) **8**:107
"Midnight Show" (Shapiro) **25**:295
"Midnight Snack" (Merrill) **28**:249
"Midnight Verses" (Akhmatova) **2**:16
"A Midnight Woman to the Bobby" (McKay) **2**:224
The Midsummer Cushion (Clare) **23**:45
"A Midsummer Holiday" (Swinburne) **24**:313, 329
"Mid-Term Break" (Heaney) **18**:189
"Midway" (Graves) **6**:143
"Midwinter, Presolstice" (Atwood) **8**:2
"the midwives," (Enzensberger) **28**:142
"La miej zoventút" (Pasolini) **17**:281
"Mientras dura vida, sobra el tiempo" (Forche) **10**:135
"Mientras la Gracia me excita" (Juana Ines de la Cruz) **24**:188
"Might These be Thrushes Climbing through Almost (Do They" (Cummings) **5**:108
"The Mighty Flight" (Baraka) **4**:26
"Mignonne, allons voir si la rose" (Ronsard)
See "Ode à Cassandre: 'Mignonne, allon voir'"
"Mildred's Thoughts" (Stein) **18**:346
"Mildred's Umbrella" (Stein) **18**:334
"A Mild-Spoken Citizen Finally Writes to the White House" (Meredith) **28**:206
Mileposts I (Tsvetaeva)
See *Vyorsty I*
Mileposts II (Tsvetaeva)
See *Vyorsty II*
"Milk" (Stein) **18**:323, 330
"The Milk Factory" (Heaney) **18**:237
"Milk-Wort and Bog Cotton" (MacDiarmid) **9**:160, 176, 199
"The Mill" (Robinson) **1**:468, 475, 478
"Mill Song" (Ekeloef) **23**:54
"Miller's" (Chaucer)
See "Miller's Tale"
"The Miller's Daughter" (Tennyson) **6**:350
"Miller's Tale" (Chaucer) **19**:11, 13-14, 40, 44, 54, 61
"Millibars of the Storm" (Cesaire) **25**:17
"Millibars of the Storn" (Cesaire) **25**:17
"The Millionaire" (Bukowski) **18**:13
"The Mills of the Kavanaughs" (Lowell) **3**:204, 206-07, 215, 217, 224, 226, 231
The Mills of the Kavanaughs (Lowell) **3**:204, 206-07, 215, 217, 224, 226, 231
"Milly; ou, La terre natale" (Lamartine) **16**:280, 286, 293
"Milpa" (Cardenal) **22**:131
Milton (Blake) **12**:13, 27, 30, 36-8, 42, 44-5, 50, 62-5, 73, 75-80
"Milun" (Marie de France) **22**:258, 264, 266, 268, 270-75, 295-96
"Mima: Elegía pagana" (Dario) **15**:110-11
Minashiguri (Matsuo Basho) **3**:11
Mind Breaths: Poems, 1972-1977 (Ginsberg) **4**:61, 82
"The Mind Hesitant" (Williams) **7**:390
"The Mind, Intractable Thing" (Moore) **4**:243
"The Mind is an Enchanted Thing" (Moore) **4**:261
"The Mind of the Frontispiece to a Book" (Jonson)
See "The Mind of the Frontispiece to a Book"
Mindwheel (Pinsky) **27**:157, 171
"Mine own John Poyntz" (Wyatt) **27**:333-337, 341
Mine the Harvest (Millay) **6**:226, 231-33, 237, 242
"The Mine: Yamaguchi" (Stryk) **27**:185-86, 191, 202, 214
"Mineral" (Page) **12**:170
"Miners" (Owen) **19**:342-43, 346, 348, 365, 370
"Minesweepers" (Kipling) **3**:183
"Minicursi" (Fuertes) **27**:23
"Miniature" (Meredith) **28**:171
"Miniver Cheevy" (Robinson) **1**:462, 467, 478, 487, 496
"Minnesbilder" (Ekeloef) **23**:69
"Minnie and Mattie" (Rossetti) **7**:274
"A Minor Prophet" (Eliot) **20**:123, 140-41
"Minotaur" (Wylie) **23**:302-303, 306, 323
Minstrels (Sitwell) **3**:290
"Minstrel's Song, on the Restoration of Lord Clifford the Shepherd" (Wordsworth) **4**:377
The Minstrelsy of the Scottish Border (Scott) **13**:249, 269, 278, 281, 306
"Minus 18 Street" (McGuckian) **27**:80
"The Minute" (Shapiro) **25**:306
"The Minute before Meeting" (Hardy) **8**:90
"Mirabeau Bridge" (Apollinaire)
See "Le pont Mirabeau"
Mirabell: Books of Numbers (Merrill) **28**:233, 235, 236, 237, 238, 240, 251, 260-64, 275-77, 279, 281
"The Miracle" (Gunn) **26**:220
"A Miracle for Breakfast" (Bishop) **3**:46, 57
"Miracles" (Whitman) **3**:381
"Miraculous Weapons" (Cesaire)
See "Les armes miraculeuses"
"Mirage" (Tagore)
See "Marichika"
"Mirage of the Desert" (Masters) **1**:344
"The Mirages" (Hayden) **6**:193, 197
"Miranda Dies in the Fog, 1816" (Neruda)
See "Miranda muere en la niebla, 1816"
"Miranda muere en la niebla, 1816" (Neruda) **4**:295
"Miranda's Supper" (Wylie) **23**:302, 307, 314-15, 321
"Miriam's Song" (Harper) **21**:194-95
"Miró Celi una rosa que en el prado" (Juana Ines de la Cruz) **24**:225
"Mirror" (Merrill) **28**:225, 242, 245, 246, 247
"Mirror Image" (Gluck) **16**:162-63
"The Mirror in the Roadway" (Tomlinson) **17**:334
"The Mirror in the Woods" (Rexroth) **20**:181
"The Mirror in Which Two Are Seen as One" (Rich) **5**:368
"The Mirror of Madmen" (Chesterton) **28**:108
"Mirror Sermon" (Brutus) **24**:99
"The Mirrors" (Williams) **7**:370
"Mirrors & Windows" (Nemerov) **24**:292
Mirrors and Windows (Nemerov) **24**:256, 261, 264, 295-96
"Mis queridos difuntos" (Fuertes) **27**:12
"Misanthropos" (Gunn) **26**:188-190, 192-193, 214, 223, 225-226
Misanthropos (Gunn) **26**:203
Miscellaneous Poems (Harper) **21**:185
Miscellaneous Poems (Marvell) **10**:257, 277, 311
Miscellanies (Swift) **9**:251, 253, 255, 275
A Miscellany of New Poems (Behn) **13**:7
Miscellany Poems on Several Occasions, Written by a Lady, 1713 (Finch) **21**:140, 148, 161, 163-64, 172-73
"Mise en Scene" (Lowell) **13**:96
"Miserie" (Herbert) **4**:108, 121
"Misery" (Hughes) **1**:328
"The Misfit" (Day Lewis) **11**:147
"Misgiving" (Frost) **1**:195
"Miss B--" 2 (Clare) **23**:25
"Miss Drake Proceeds to Supper" (Plath) **1**:398-99
"Miss Gee" (Auden) **1**:30
"Miss Rosie" (Clifton) **17**:32-33
"The Missing" (Gunn) **26**:224
"Mississippi Levee" (Hughes) **1**:256
"Mississippi Mother" (Brooks) **7**:96
"the missyun" (Bissett) **14**:24, 34
"Mist in the Valley" (Noyes) **27**:134
"Míster no!" (Guillen) **23**:126
"Mithridates" (Emerson) **18**:71
"Mito" (Pavese) **13**:210, 228-29
"Mixed Feelings" (Ashbery) **26**:124, 127
"Mnemonic" (Lee) **24**:243
"The Mob" (Brutus) **24**:108
Mock Beggar Hall (Graves) **6**:127-28
"Mock Confessional" (Ferlinghetti) **1**:187
"Mock Orange" (Gluck) **16**:145, 164
Mockingbird, Wish Me Luck (Bukowski) **18**:19
"Models" (Clampitt) **19**:99
"Models" (Nemerov) **24**:290
"Modern Elegy of the Motif of Affectation" (Guillen)
See "Modern Elegy of the Motif of Affectation"
Modern Fable Poems (Nishiwaki)
See *Kindai no Guwa*
"Modern Love" (Keats) **1**:311
"The Modern Manichee" (Chesterton) **28**:114
"Modern Poetry Is Prose (But It Is Saying Plenty)" (Ferlinghetti) **1**:182-83
"A Modern Sappho" (Arnold) **5**:12
The Modern Traveller (Belloc) **24**:25-7, 35
"A Modernist Ballade" (Belloc) **24**:39
"Modes of Being" (Levertov) **11**:197-98
"Modes of Pleasure" (Gunn) **26**:186, 219
"Modest Proposal" (Enzensberger) **28**:158, 161
"A Modest Proposal" (Hughes) **7**:118
"Modulations for a Solo Voice" (Levertov) **11**:209
A Moelna Elegy (Ekelof)
See *En Mölna-elegi*
"Moesta et Errabunda" (Baudelaire) **1**:70
"Mogollon Morning" (Momaday) **25**:221
"Moharram" (Stryk) **27**:214
Mohn und Gedächtnes (Celan) **10**:95
moi, Laminaire (Cesaire) **25**:33, 41, 45
"Moïse" (Vigny) **26**:369, 380-81, 384, 391, 398, 401, 410-11
"Mole" (Stryk) **27**:199-200
"Molitva" (Tsvetaeva) **14**:312
"Molitvy" (Lermontov) **18**:303
"Molly Means" (Walker) **20**:291-92
En Mölna-elegi (Ekeloef) **23**:50-8, 62-3, 77-87
Molodets (Tsvetaeva) **14**:313, 325-26
Moly (Gunn) **26**:192, 196-197, 203-204, 206-207, 209, 212, 214-215, 219, 221, 226, 228-229
"Moment" (Nemerov) **24**:264
"Moment" (Zagajewski) **27**:381, 396
"The Moment Cleary" (Kursh) **15**:179

"Moment of Eternity" (MacDiarmid) **9**:193
"Moments of Glory" (Jeffers) **17**:141
"Mon Dieu m'a dit" (Verlaine) **2**:415
"Mon Enfance" (Hugo) **17**:75
"Mon héroïsme, quelle farce" (Cesaire) **25**:56
"Monadnoc" (Emerson) **18**:71, 74, 102-3, 111
"Monarchs" (Olds) **22**:307
"Monax" (Pushkin) **10**:407
"Monday: Roxana; or The Drawing-room" (Montagu) **16**:338, 348
La moneda de hierro (Borges) **22**:96-7
"Monet's 'Waterlilies'" (Hayden) **6**:183, 195
"Money" (Nemerov) **24**:262, 281
"Money Goes Upstream" (Snyder) **21**:300
"Money, Honey, Money" (Walker) **20**:294
"Mongo" (Lermontov) **18**:281
"Mongolian Idiot" (Shapiro) **25**:300, 325
"La monja gitana" (Garcia Lorca) **3**:132
"La monja y el ruiseñor" (Dario) **15**:107-08
"The Monk" (Pushkin)
See "Monax"
"The Monkeys" (Moore) **4**:270
The Monkey's Cloak (Matsuo Basho)
See *Sarumino*
The Monkey's Raincoat (Matsuo Basho)
See *Sarumino*
"Monk's Tale" (Chaucer) **19**:13, 42, 45, 56, 63
"The Monk's Walk" (Dunbar) **5**:121, 137-38, 141
"Monna Innominata" (Rossetti) **7**:271, 275, 280-1
"Le monocle de mon oncle" (Stevens) **6**:292, 295, 303, 327
"Monody" (Zukofsky) **11**:368
"Monody on the Death of Chatterton" (Coleridge) **11**:49, 52
The Monogram (Elytis) **21**:123
"The Monoliths" (Momaday) **25**:219
"Monotone" (Sandburg) **2**:303
"Mont Blanc" (Shelley) **14**:206, 211-12, 217, 241
"Le mont des Oliviers" (Vigny) **26**:367-68, 370, 380, 383, 385, 391, 401, 412
Montage of a Dream Deferred (Hughes) **1**:244-45, 247-48, 251, 253, 258, 261, 263, 265-68, 270
"The Montain Village of Bastundzhi" (Lermontov)
See "The Montain Village of Bastundzhi"
"A Month among Children" (Montale)
See "Un mese fra i bambini"
"The Months: A Pageant" (Rossetti) **7**:280
"Montparnasse" (Apollinaire) **7**:34
La Montre; or, The Lover's Watch (Behn) **13**:3
Une montre sentimentale (Nishiwaki) **15**:237
"The Monument" (Bishop) **3**:37, 41-3, 48-9, 72
"Monument" (Pushkin)
See "Pamjatnik"
"Monument Mountain" (Bryant) **20**:14, 29, 47
"Monument of Love" (Jimenez) **7**:184
"Mood" (Cullen) **20**:63, 75
"The moon" (Borges)
See "La luna"
"The Moon" (Carruth) **10**:71
Moon Across The Way
See *Luna de enfrente*
Moon across the Way (Borges)
See *Luna de enfrente*
"Moon and Insect Panorama: Love Poem" (Garcia Lorca) **3**:141
"The Moon and the Yew Tree" (Plath) **1**:390, 409
"The Moon Being the Number 19" (Wakoski) **15**:364
Moon Crossing Bridge (Gallagher) **9**:62-5
"The Moon Explodes in Autumn as a Milkweed Pod" (Wakoski) **15**:364
"The Moon Has a Complicated Geography" (Wakoski) **15**:364
"The Moon in Your Hands" (H. D.) **5**:275
"The Moon Is the Number Eighteen" (Olson) **19**:293-94, 321
"Moon Lines, after Jimeénez" (Ondaatje) **28**:335
"Moon Poems" (Lindsay) **23**:281
"Moon Tiger" (Levertov) **11**:177
"Moonlight" (Apollinaire)
See "Clair de lune"
"Moonlight" (Harjo) **27**:56
"Moonlight" (Verlaine)
See "Clair de lune"
"Moonlight and Jellyfish" (Hagiwara Sakutaro) **18**:168
"Moonlight Night" (Tu Fu) **9**:321
"Moonlight Night: Carmel" (Hughes) **1**:240
"Moonrise" (Plath) **1**:406
"Moonrise" (Sappho) **5**:416
"The Moon's Funeral" (Belloc) **24**:49
"Moon-Set" (Carruth) **10**:85
"Moonset Glouster" (Olson) **19**:322-23
"Moonstruck" (MacDiarmid) **9**:160
The Moor of Peter the Great (Pushkin)
See *Arap Petra Velikogo*
"Moortown" (Hughes) **7**:162
Moortown (Hughes) **7**:157-58, 162-63, 165, 171
"The Moose" (Bishop) **3**:58-60, 73, 75
"The Moose Wallow" (Hayden) **6**:194-95
A Moral Alphabet (Belloc) **24**:16-18, 26
Moral Essays (Pope) **26**:320, 340
Moral Tales (Laforgue)
See *Moralités légendaires*
"Morale" (Gautier) **18**:158
Moralités légendaires (Laforgue) **14**:70
"Morality" (Arnold) **5**:42
"Un morceau en forme de poire" (Wakoski) **15**:372
Morceaux choisis (Tzara) **27**:223-4
"More" (Stein) **18**:319, 330
More Beasts--For Worse Children (Belloc) **24**:24-6, 35
"More Clues" (Rukeyser) **12**:225
"More Foreign Cities" (Tomlinson) **17**:318
More Peers (Belloc) **24**:26-7, 41, 43, 49
More Poems (Housman) **2**:167, 171-74, 176, 182-83, 188
More Poems, 1961 (Graves) **6**:154-56
More Poems to Solve (Swenson) **14**:276
"More Than a Fool's Song" (Cullen) **20**:57
"Mori no michi" (Ishikawa) **10**:213
"Mori no omoide" (Ishikawa) **10**:212-13
"Moriturus" (Millay) **6**:236
"Morning" (Gluck) **16**:152
"Morning" (Wheatley)
See "An Hymn to the Morning"
"Morning" (Williams) **7**:352
"Morning After" (Hughes) **1**:256
"The Morning Baking" (Forche) **10**:142
"The Morning Bell" (Ishikawa)
See "Akatsuki no kane"
"Morning Exercises" (Cassian) **17**:11
"Morning Express" (Sassoon) **12**:275
"A Morning Imagination of Russia" (Williams) **7**:350
"The Morning News" (Berry) **28**:11
"Morning, Noon, and Night" (Page) **12**:173
"A Morning Ride" (Kipling) **3**:194
"Morning Song" (Plath) **1**:390
"The Morning Song of Lord Zero" (Aiken) **26**:15, 24
Morning Songs (Tagore)
See *Prabhat sangit*
"The Morning Star" (Pavese)
See "Lo steddazzu"
"Morning, the Horizon" (Ortiz) **17**:245
"The Morning They Shot Tony Lopez" (Soto) **28**:375
"A Morning Wake among Dead" (Kinnell) **26**:256-57
"Morning-Land" (Sassoon) **12**:240
"Mornings in New House" (Merrill) **28**:221
"Mors" (Hugo) **17**:83
"Morskaya tsarevna" (Lermontov) **18**:292
"La Mort dans la vie" (Gautier) **18**:131, 155
"La Mort de Narcisse" (Ronsard) **11**:251
"La mort des amants" (Baudelaire) **1**:54, 73
"La mort des artistes" (Baudelaire) **1**:45
"Mort du duc de Berry" (Hugo) **17**:75
"La mort du loup" (Vigny) **26**:367, 369-70, 380-81, 401-402, 412-15
"La Mort du Soldat est près des choses naturelles (5 Mars)" (Stevens) **6**:294
La mort en ce jardin (Bunuel) **15**:207, 218
"Le mort joyeux" (Baudelaire) **1**:45
"La mort rose" (Breton) **15**:52
Mortal Acts, Mortal Words (Kinnell) **26**:257, 260-61, 271, 280, 292
"Mortal Enemy" (Parker) **28**:362
"Mortal Girl" (Rukeyser) **12**:231
"Morte d'Arthur" (Tennyson) **6**:354, 358-59, 409
La morte de Socrate (Lamartine) **16**:263, 266, 273, 278-79, 291
"La morte di Dio" (Montale) **13**:133
"I morti" (Montale) **13**:105, 112
"Mortification" (Herbert) **4**:100-01, 120, 127, 133
"Mortmain" (Robinson) **1**:470
"Morts de quatre-vingt-douze et de quatre-vingt-treize" (Rimbaud) **3**:283
Moscow Notebooks (Mandelstam) **14**:150
"Moses" (Nemerov) **24**:295
"Moses" (Shapiro) **25**:296
Moses: A Story of the Nile (Harper) **21**:185, 187-89, 191-98, 201
"Mossbawn: Sunlight" (Heaney) **18**:197, 232
"The Most of It" (Frost) **1**:205-06, 230-31
"Most Things at Second Hand through Gloves We Touch" (Schwartz) **8**:293
"Most wretched heart" (Wyatt) **27**:353
"Mostly Hospital and Old Age" (Viereck) **27**:294
"Mostru o pavea" (Pasolini) **17**:253
"Mot" (Cesaire) **25**:31
Mot (Cesaire) **25**:38
"The Motel" (Olds) **22**:341
"Motet" No. 1 (Montale) **13**:120-22
"Motet" No. 2 (Montale) **13**:120, 122
"Motet" No. 3 (Montale) **13**:118-20
"Motet" No. 4 (Montale) **13**:120
"Motet" No. 5 (Montale) **13**:118, 121-22, 125, 127
"Motet" No. 6 (Montale) **13**:121-22, 150
"Motet" No. 7 (Montale) **13**:119, 122
"Motet" No. 8 (Montale)
See "Mottetto" No. 8
"Motet" No. 9 (Montale) **13**:119, 122-24
"Motet" No. 10 (Montale) **13**:123
"Motet" No. 11 (Montale) **13**:124-25
"Motet" No. 12 (Montale) **13**:124
"Motet" No. 13 (Montale) **13**:124
"Motet" No. 14 (Montale) **13**:124
"Motet" No. 15 (Montale) **13**:125
"Motet" No. 17 (Montale) **13**:125-26
"Motet" No. 18 (Montale) **13**:125, 127
"Motet" No. 19 (Montale) **13**:126
"Motet" No. 20 (Montale) **13**:126
"Motet XX" (Montale) **13**:136
"The Mother" (Brooks) **7**:67
"The Mother" (Olds) **22**:309
"Mother" (Smith) **12**:326
The Mother (Sitwell) **3**:299
"Mother, among the Dustbins" (Smith) **12**:352
"Mother and Daughter" (Sexton) **2**:365
"Mother and Poet" (Browning) **6**:30-1
"Mother Dear" (McKay) **2**:222
"Mother Earth: Her Whales" (Snyder) **21**:293, 297
"Mother Farewell!" (Johnson) **24**:145
"Mother Goose" (Rexroth) **20**:195, 218
"Mother Hubberd's Tale" (Spenser)
See "Prosopopoia; or, Mother Hubberds Tale"
"mother i am mad" (Clifton) **17**:19
"Mother in Wartime" (Hughes) **1**:252
"Mother Marie Therese" (Lowell) **3**:205

"Mother Night" (Johnson) **24**:127, 137, 159, 166
"Mother of God I Shall Pray in Humility" (Lermontov) **18**:296
"Mother Rosarine" (Kumin) **15**:191
"Mother to Son" (Hughes) **1**:241, 248-49, 262
Mother, What is Man? (Smith) **12**:326
"Motherland" (Lermontov) **18**:281
"Mother-Right" (Rich) **5**:384
"Mothers" (Giovanni) **19**:140
"The Mother's Blessing" (Harper) **21**:197
"A Mother's Heroism" (Harper) **21**:194, 206, 217
"The Mother's Story" (Clifton) **17**:29
"The Moth-Signal" (Hardy) **8**:99
"Motion and Rest" (Toomer) **7**:338
"Motion of wish" (Kunitz) **19**:160
"The Motions" (Ammons) **16**:5
"The Motive for Metaphor" (Stevens) **6**:312-13, 340
Motivos de son (Guillen) **23**:97-98, 104-108, 110, 133, 141-45
"Motor Lights on a Hill Road" (Lowell) **13**:60
"A Motorbike" (Hughes) **7**:162
The Motorcycle Betrayal Poems (Wakoski) **15**:325-26, 331-32, 345, 350, 363, 366, 369-70
"Motoring" (Brooke) **24**:68
"Motteti" (Montale) **13**:105
"Mottetto" No. 8 (Montale) **13**:105, 113, 122, 127
"Motto" (Hughes) **1**:267
"The Motto on the Sundial" (Rexroth) **20**:192
"Motto to the Songs of Innocence and of Experience" (Blake) **12**:10
"The Mound Builders" (Kunitz) **19**:158
"Mount Chungnan" (Wang Wei) **18**:362-63
"Mount Mary" (Wright) **14**:343
"The Mount of Olives" (Vigny)
See "Le mont des Oliviers"
"Mount Zion" (Hughes) **7**:147
"th mountain" (Bissett) **14**:20
"The Mountain" (Frost) **1**:226
Mountain Interval (Frost) **1**:197, 202, 207, 215
"The Mountain Spirit" (Wang Wei) **18**:382
Mountain Talk (Ammons) **16**:14
"The Mountaineer's Ballard" (Wylie) **23**:311
"Mountains" (Auden) **1**:17
"Mountains" (Hayden) **6**:194, 196
"Mountains" (Hughes) **7**:137
Mountains and Rivers without End (Snyder) **21**:299
"A Mounted Umbrella" (Stein) **18**:334, 349
"The Mourner's Bench" (Masters) **1**:339, 343
"Mournin' for Religion" (Masters) **1**:344
"Mourning" (Marvell) **10**:271, 301, 314
"A Mourning Forbidding Valediction" (Ashbery) **26**:161
"The Mouse's Nest" (Clare) **23**:7
"The Mouth of the Hudson" (Lowell) **3**:215
"The Mouth of Truth" (Ferlinghetti) **1**:183
"Mouvement" (Tzara) **27**:227
"Move Un-noticed to be Noticed: A Nationhood Poem" (Madhubuti) **5**:345
"Movement to Establish My Identity" (Wakoski) **15**:350
"Movements" (Tomlinson) **17**:327
"Movements II" (Tomlinson) **17**:343
"Movements IV" (Tomlinson) **17**:326, 341
"Movies" (Hughes) **1**:266
"Moving Fred's Outhouse/Geriatrics of Pine" (Ondaatje) **28**:335
"The Moving Image" (Wright) **14**:337, 362
The Moving Image (Wright) **14**:334-35, 338-41, 345-51, 353, 357, 368
"Moving South" (Wright) **14**:373
"The Moving to Griffin" (Ondaatje) **28**:291
"The Mower against gardens" (Marvell) **10**:266, 293, 297
"The Mower to the Glo-Worms" (Marvell) **10**:266, 296-97, 315
"The Mower's Song" (Marvell) **10**:266, 296-97
Moya Rodoslovnaya (Pushkin) **10**:391
"Mozart, 1935" (Stevens) **6**:296
"Mozhet byt' eto tochka bezumiia" (Mandelstam) **14**:152
"Mr. Bleaney" (Larkin) **21**:228-29, 241, 247-48
"Mr. Brodsky" (Tomlinson) **17**:311, 353
"Mr. Burnshaw and the Statue" (Stevens) **6**:297, 321
"Mr. Edwards and the Spider" (Lowell) **3**:215
"Mr. Eliot's Sunday Morning Service" (Eliot) **5**:184
"Mr. Flood's Party" (Robinson) **1**:478
"Mr. Mine" (Sexton) **2**:352
"Mr. Nixon" (Pound) **4**:320
"Mr. Over" (Smith) **12**:297, 339
"Mr. Seurat's Sunday Afternoon" (Schwartz)
See "Seurat's Sunday Afternoon along the Seine"
"Mr. Sludge, 'The Medium'" (Browning) **2**:72, 82
"Mr. Styrax" (Pound) **4**:317
"Mrs. Alfred Uruguay" (Stevens) **6**:304
"Mrs Arbuthnot" (Smith) **12**:314
"Mrs. Benjamin Pantier" (Masters) **1**:347
"Mrs. Mandrill" (Nemerov) **24**:259, 268
"Mrs Simpkins" (Smith) **12**:344
"Mrs. Small" (Brooks) **7**:62, 69, 96-8
"Mrs. Walpurga" (Rukeyser) **12**:204
"Mrs. Williams" (Masters) **1**:347
"Mtsiri" (Lermontov) **18**:282-83, 298, 302
"Muchacha recién crecida" (Guillen) **23**:126
"Mud" (Cassian) **17**:4
"Mud" (Kumin) **15**:182
"The Mud Turtle" (Nemerov) **24**:274
"The Mud Vision" (Heaney) **18**:227-28, 230, 237
"Muerte de Antoñito el Camborio" (Garcia Lorca) **3**:131
"Los Muertos" (Fuertes) **27**:12
"Mugging" (Ginsberg) **4**:85
"Mugitusque Boum" (Hugo) **17**:83
"Muiopotmos; or, the Fate of the Butterflie" (Spenser) **8**:365, 367-68, 371
"La mujer desnuda" (Jimenez) **7**:213-14
La mujer desnuda (1918-1923) (Jimenez) **7**:213
"Mujer nueva" (Guillen) **23**:105
"Mulata" (Guillen) **23**:110, 142
"Mulatto" (Hughes) **1**:238, 263-64, 270
"The Mulch" (Kunitz) **19**:159
"Mulholland's Contract" (Kipling) **3**:161
Multitudes, Multitudes (Clampitt) **19**:87-8
"Mummia" (Brooke) **24**:77
Mundo a solas (Aleixandre) **15**:3, 18-24, 32-3
"The Munich Mannequins" (Plath) **1**:384, 391
"The Municipal Gallery Revisited" (Yeats) **20**:322, 324
"The Murder" (Brooks) **7**:68
"The Murder" (Page) **12**:178
The Murder of Lidice (Millay) **6**:220
"The Murder of William Remington" (Nemerov) **24**:258, 280
"Murder Poem No. 74321" (Rexroth) **20**:187
"The Murdered Traveller" (Bryant) **20**:40
"The Murderess" (Gluck) **16**:126
A Muriel Rukeyser Reader (Rukeyser) **12**:234
Museum (Dove) **6**:104-07, 109, 115-16, 118, 121
"Museum Guards (London)" (Stryk) **27**:214
"Mushrooms" (Atwood) **8**:43
"Mushrooms" (Plath) **1**:389, 404, 406, 408
"Mushrooms" (Tomlinson) **17**:334, 347, 354
"A Music" (Berry) **28**:4
"Music" (Herbert) **4**:100
"Music" (Pasternak)
See "Muzyka"
"The Music of Poetry" (Kinnell) **26**:288
"The Music of Time" (Larkin) **21**:227
"Music Swims Back to Me" (Sexton) **2**:359
"A Musical Comedy Thought" (Parker) **28**:354
"A Musical Instrument" (Browning) **6**:23
"The Musical Voice" (Ishikawa)
See "Gakusei"
"Musician" (Bogan) **12**:124
"Musicks Empire" (Marvell) **10**:313
"Musketaquid" (Emerson) **18**:88, 91, 111
"Mussel Hunter at Rock Harbour" (Plath) **1**:388, 407
"Mutabilitie Cantos" (Spenser)
See "Cantos of Mutabilitie"
"Mutability" (Brooke) **24**:56-7, 72, 85
"Mutability" (Shelley) **14**:166
"Mutation" (Bryant) **20**:34, 44
"Mutra" (Paz) **1**:369
"Mutton" (Stein) **18**:323-24
"Mutual Trust" (Merrill) **28**:257
"Muzhestvo" (Akhmatova) **2**:19
"Muzyka" (Pasternak) **6**:288
"Mwilu/or Poem for the Living" (Madhubuti) **5**:346
"My Autumn Walk" (Bryant) **20**:5, 46
My Best Poems (Aleixandre) **15**:18
"My Bohemian Life" (Rimbaud)
See "Ma bohème"
"My Cats" (Smith) **12**:339
"My City" (Johnson) **24**:144, 154
"My Comforter" (Burroughs) **8**:51
"My Corn-cob Pipe" (Dunbar) **5**:133
"My Cousin in April" (Gluck) **16**:154
"My Cousin Muriel" (Clampitt) **19**:97
"My Daughter the Junkie on a Train" (Lorde)
See "To My Daughter the Junkie on a Train"
"My Daughter's Aquarium" (Stryk) **27**:204
"My Dear and Loving Husband" (Bradstreet)
See "To My Dear and Loving Husband His Goeing into England"
"My delight and thy delight" (Bridges) **28**:70
"My Dove, My Beautiful One" (Joyce)
See "XIV"
"My Doves" (Browning) **6**:21
"my dream about being white" (Clifton) **17**:36
"My Dreams Are a Field Afar" (Housman) **2**:182
"My Dreams, My Work, Must Wait till after Hell" (Brooks) **7**:74
"My Erotic Double" (Ashbery) **26**:133
"My Fairy Godmother" (Hyde) **7**:147
"My Father Moved through Dooms of Feel" (Cummings)
See "My Father Moved through Dooms of Love"
"My Father Moved through Dooms of Love" (Cummings) **5**:81, 89
"My Father Speaks to Me from the Dead" (Olds) **22**:323, 325, 338
"My Father's Breasts" (Olds) **22**:328
"My Father's Irish Setters" (Merrill) **28**:284
"My Fathers Came from Kentucky" (Lindsay) **23**:265
"My Father's Eyes" (Olds) **22**:332
"My Father's Funeral" (Shapiro) **25**:305
"My First Weeks" (Olds) **22**:338
"My Friend" (Gibran) **9**:77
"My galley charged with forgetfulness" (Wyatt) **27**:323-324, 357-358
"My Garden" (Emerson) **18**:76, 88
My Geneology (Pushkin)
See *Moya Rodoslovnaya*
"My Gentlest Song" (Viereck) **27**:263, 278, 281
"My Grandmother's Love Letters" (Crane) **3**:98
"My Granny's Hieland Hame" (Burns) **6**:98
"My Grave" (Levine) **22**:228
"My Hat" (Smith) **12**:331
"My Heart and I" (Browning) **6**:23
"My Heart Goes Out" (Smith) **12**:318, 325
"My Heart Was Full" (Smith) **12**:333
"My Hermitage in the Bamboo Grove" (Wang Wei) **18**:358
"My Hero's Genealogy" (Pushkin)
See "Rodoslovnaya Moego Geroya"
"My Honey" (Guillen)
See "Mi chiquita"
"My House" (Giovanni) **19**:112-13, 116, 140, 142-43

My House (Giovanni) **19**:107, 110-14, 116, 118, 121-25, 136-37, 140-41, 144
"My Indigo" (Lee) **24**:240, 244
"My Kate" (Browning) **6**:23
"My Lady of the Castle Grand" (Dunbar) **5**:134, 138
"My Lady's Lamentation and Complaint against the Dean" (Swift) **9**:295-96
"My Lady's Lips Are Like de Honey" (Johnson) **24**:141
"My Last Afternoon with Uncle Devereux Winslow" (Lowell) **3**:219, 222
"My Last Duchess" (Browning) **2**:37, 94
"My Life with the Wave" (Paz) **1**:354
"My Light with Yours" (Masters) **1**:333
"My Little Lovers" (Rimbaud)
See "Mes petites amoureuses"
"My Loved Subject" (Jeffers) **17**:131
"My lute awake" (Wyatt) **27**:328, 339, 349, 357, 362
"My Luve Is Like a Red, Red Rose" (Burns) **6**:75, 77, 99
"My most. My most. O my lost!" (Villa) **22**:349
"My Mother" (McGuckian) **27**:96
"My Mother Remembers That She Was Beautiful" (Gallagher) **9**:58
"My Mother Would Be a Falconress" (Duncan) **2**:127
"My Mother's Life" (Meredith) **28**:182
My mothers maydes (Wyatt) **27**:304, 371
"My Mountain Home" (McKay) **2**:222
"My Muse" (Montale)
See "La mia musa"
"My Muse" (Smith) **12**:312, 324, 336
"My Native Land" (Lermontov) **18**:297
"My Native Land, My Home" (McKay) **2**:216, 224
"My New-Cut Ashlar" (Kipling) **3**:183
"My Own" (Parker) **28**:350-51
"My Own Sweet Good" (Brooks) **7**:55
"My pen take payn" (Wyatt) **27**:339, 341
"My People" (Hughes) **1**:270
"My Poem" (Giovanni) **19**:111
"My Poets" (Levine) **22**:212
"My Portrait" (Pushkin) **10**:407
"My Pretty Dan" (McKay) **2**:221
"My Pretty Rose Tree" (Blake) **12**:34
"My Sad Captains" (Gunn) **26**:186, 197
My Sad Captains, and Other Poems (Gunn) **26**:181, 186, 189, 194-195, 197, 201-202, 207, 209, 211, 216, 218-219, 221, 223, 225-226
"My Shy Hand" (Owen) **19**:336
"My Silks in Fine Array" (Blake) **12**:31
My Sister, Life (Pasternak)
See *Sestra moia zhizn*
"My Soldier Lad" (McKay) **2**:223
"My Song" (Brooke) **24**:62, 72, 76
"My Songs" (Yosano Akiko)
See "Waga Uta"
"My Sort of Man" (Dunbar) **5**:131
"My Soul" (Bradstreet) **10**:60-1
"My Soul Accused Me" (Dickinson) **1**:94
"My soul is dark" (Lermontov) **18**:202
"My Spectre around Me" (Blake) **12**:13
"My spirit kisseth thine" (Bridges) **28**:85
"My Spirit Will Not Haunt the Mound" (Hardy) **8**:118
"My Star" (Browning) **2**:59
"My sweet Ann Foot my bonny Ann" (Clare) **23**:25
"My Sweet Brown Gal" (Dunbar) **5**:119
"My Vegetarian Friend" (Eliot) **20**:123
"My Voice Not Being Proud" (Bogan) **12**:101, 120
"Mycerinus" (Arnold) **5**:13, 33-4, 37, 39, 48
"Mye Love toke Skorne" (Wyatt) **27**:316
"My-ness" (Milosz) **8**:179
"Myopia: A Night" (Lowell) **3**:215
"Myrtho" (Nerval) **13**:180
"Myself Was Formed--a Carpenter" (Dickinson) **1**:96
"Le mystère des trois cors" (Laforgue) **14**:73
"The Mysteries" (H. D.) **5**:305
"'Mystery Boy' Looks for Kin in Nashville" (Hayden) **6**:196
"The Mystic" (Noyes) **27**:138
"Mysticism for Beginners" (Zagajewski) **27**:
Mysticism for Beginners (Zagajewski) **27**:396, 398-401
Mystics and Zen Masters (Merton) **10**:352
"Mystique" (Rimbaud) **3**:260
"Myth" (Pavese)
See "Mito"
"Myth" (Rukeyser) **12**:228
The Myth-Making Uncles (Alegria) **26**:
"A Mythology Reflects its Region" (Stevens) **6**:306
Myths and Texts (Snyder) **21**:290-92, 297, 299, 322
N. 4 (Pindar)
See *Nemean 4*
N. 7 (Pindar)
See *Nemean 7*
N. 9 (Pindar)
See *Nemean 9*
"A na fruta" (Pasolini) **17**:274-77
"Na krasnom kone" (Tsvetaeva) **14**:315
Na rannikh poezdakh (Pasternak) **6**:282
"The Nabara" (Day Lewis) **11**:127, 130-31, 144
"Nachlied" (Trakl) **20**:259
Nachtgesänge (Holderlin) **4**:142, 146, 148, 166
"nacts wird ka¨lter" (Enzensberger) **28**:140
"Nachwort" (Heine) **25**:172-75, 177, 179
"Naci en una buhardilla" (Fuertes) **27**:49
"Nací para poeta o para muerto" (Fuertes) **27**:49
"Nacimiento de Cristo" (Garcia Lorca) **3**:141
Nacimiento último (Aleixandre) **15**:9, 16
"Nada" (Jimenez) **7**:202
"Nadezhdoi Sladostnoi" (Pushkin) **10**:412
"Nadgrobie" (Tsvetaeva) **14**:325, 327
"Nadie" (Guillen) **23**:125
"Nafsī muthqa ah bi athmāriha" (Gibran) **9**:82
"Nah, im Aortenbogen" (Celan) **10**:101
"Nähe des Todes" (Trakl) **20**:248
"La naîade" (Gautier) **18**:141
"The Nail" (Hughes) **7**:143
"Naissance du duc de Bordeaux" (Hugo) **17**:75
"The naïve person" (Borges)
See "El ingenuo"
"A Naive Poem" (Milosz)
See "The World"
Naivedya (Tagore) **8**:411-13
"Naked and Essential" (Montale) **13**:141
"Naked Girl and Mirror" (Wright) **14**:356, 362
"A Name for All" (Crane) **3**:90, 104
"Nameless" (Pasternak)
See "Bez nazvaniya"
"Nameless Flower" (Wright) **14**:347, 379
"Names" (Hayden) **6**:194
The Names of the Lost (Levine) **22**:223-24
"The Nana-Hex" (Sexton) **2**:365
"Nancy" (Wylie) **23**:301, 318-19, 324
"The Nape of the Neck" (Graves) **6**:166
"Napoleon na El'be" (Pushkin) **10**:409, 421
"Napoleon on the Elba" (Pushkin)
See "Napoleon na El'be"
"Naprasno glazom kak gvozdem" (Tsvetaeva) **14**:325
"När man kommit så långt" (Ekeloef) **23**:76
"Narcisse parle" (Valery) **9**:350, 356, 363, 365, 385, 392, 395
"Narcissus Speaks" (Valery)
See "Narcisse parle"
"Narikel" (Tagore) **8**:416
Narraciones (Garcia Lorca) **3**:148
"Narrative" (Stein) **18**:313
"A Narrow Escape" (Merrill) **28**:239, 243
The Narrow Pond (Matsuo Basho)
See *Oku no hosomichi*
The Narrow Road to the Deep North (Matsuo Basho)
See *Oku no hosomichi*
"I nascondigli" (Montale) **13**:138
"Nashedshij podkovu" (Mandelstam) **14**:121, 125, 130
"The Nation Is Like Ourselves" (Baraka) **4**:19
"Nationality in Drinks" (Browning) **2**:59
"The Native Born" (Kipling) **3**:161-62
"Native Hill" (Berry) **28**:39
Native Land (Blok) **21**:16
Native Land (Rich)
See *Your Native Land, Your Life*
"A Nativity" (Yeats) **20**:319
"A Nativity (1914-18)" (Kipling) **3**:183, 189
"Nativity Ode" (Milton)
See "On the Morning of Christ's Nativity"
"Nativity Poem" (Gluck) **16**:125, 141
"Natrabach i na cytrze" (Milosz) **8**:186, 214
"Natural Music" (Jeffers) **17**:134-35
Natural Numbers: New and Selected Poems (Rexroth) **20**:209
"Natural Resources" (Rich) **5**:374, 380, 384-85
"Naturally" (Gallagher) **9**:43
"Naturally the Foundation Will Bear Your Expenses" (Larkin) **21**:223
"Nature" (Masters) **1**:336
"Nature II" (Emerson) **18**:102
"Nature and Free Animals" (Smith) **12**:323
"Nature morte" (Brodsky) **9**:4, 12
"The Nature of an Action" (Gunn) **26**:185
"Nature Poem" (Tomlinson) **17**:345, 348
Nature: Poems Old and New (Swenson) **14**:283, 287-88
"Nature that gave the bee so feet a grace" (Wyatt) **27**:346-47
"Nature's Lineaments" (Graves) **6**:150-51
"Nature's Questioning" (Hardy) **8**:96
"Navidad en el Hudson" (Garcia Lorca) **3**:141
"Ne muchnistoi babochkoiu beloi" (Mandelstam) **14**:152, 156
"Ne Plus Ultra" (Coleridge) **11**:52
"Ne sravnivai: zhivushchii nesravnim" (Mandelstam) **14**:154
"Neap-tide" (Swinburne) **24**:313, 341, 343
"Near, as All That Is Lost" (Gallagher) **9**:64
"Near Keokuk" (Sandburg) **2**:332
"Near Lanivet, 1872" (Hardy) **8**:97, 125-26
"Near the Ocean" (Lowell) **3**:226-28, 233
Near the Ocean (Lowell) **3**:232
"Nearness of Death" (Trakl)
See "Nähe des Todes"
"Nebraska" (Shapiro) **25**:313
Necessities of Life: Poems, 1962-1965 (Rich) **5**:356, 363-64, 370-71, 382, 388-89, 397
"The Neckan" (Arnold) **5**:12
The Necklace (Tomlinson) **17**:299, 302-04, 317-18, 320-22, 327, 334-35, 341
"The Necktie and the Watch" (Apollinaire)
See "La cravate et la montre"
"Necropolis" (Shapiro) **25**:279, 297, 318
"Need: A Chorale for Black Women's Voices" (Lorde) **12**:144, 154, 156, 158
"The Need of Being Versed in Country Things" (Frost) **1**:229, 231
"A Needed Poem for My Salvation" (Sanchez) **9**:208-09
"Negro bembón" (Guillen) **23**:98, 142
"Un negro canta en Nueva York" (Guillen) **23**:127
"A Negro Cemetery Next to a White One" (Nemerov) **24**:281
"Negro Dancers" (Hughes) **1**:236
"The Negro Hero" (Brooks) **7**:86
"A Negro Love Song" (Dunbar) **5**:132, 142
"Negro Mask" (Senghor) **25**:227-30
The Negro of Peter the Great (Pushkin)
See *Arap Petra Velikogo*
"Negro Servant" (Hughes) **1**:247
"Negro Song" (Guillen) **23**:131
"A Negro Speaks of Rivers" (Hughes) **1**:241-42, 248, 258-59, 263, 268
"Negro Spiritual" (McKay) **2**:214
Nehez fold (Illyes) **16**:233, 238-39, 245
"La neige" (Vigny) **26**:401-402, 410-11
"Neige sur Paris" (Senghor) **25**:239

Cumulative Title Index

"Neiges" (Perse) **23**:213, 216-18, 220-21, 232, 234, 250, 253, 256-57
"Neither Out Far nor in Deep" (Frost) **1**:197, 218, 227-28
"Neither Sweet Pity, nor Lamentable Weeping" (Ronsard)
See "Ny la douce pitie, ny le pleur lamentable"
"Neither Wanting More" (Swenson) **14**:284
"Neko" (Hagiwara Sakutaro) **18**:181
"Neko no shigai" (Hagiwara Sakutaro) **18**:182
"Nel Mezzo del Commin di Nostra Vita" (Duncan) **2**:103
"Nel parco di Caserta" (Montague) **13**:
"Nel parco di Caserta" (Montale) **13**:127
"Nel sonno" (Montale) **13**:107, 128, 150
"Nele de Kantule" (Cardenal) **22**:127, 132
"Nella serra" (Montale) **13**:110
"Nelly Meyers" (Ammons) **16**:5, 19
Nem. IV (Pindar)
See *Nemean 4*
Nem. VIII (Pindar)
See *Nemean 8*
Nemean 1 (Pindar) **19**:398, 412
Nemean 2 (Pindar) **19**:425
Nemean 3 (Pindar) **19**:425
Nemean 4 (Pindar) **19**:387, 391
Nemean V (Pindar)
See *Nemean 5*
Nemean 5 (Pindar) **19**:388, 420, 424
Nemean 7 (Pindar) **19**:388, 413, 425
Nemean 8 (Pindar) **19**:388, 413, 420, 425
Nemean 9 (Pindar) **19**:405, 425
Nemean 10 (Pindar) **19**:398, 405, 412
Nemean 11 (Pindar) **19**:405
"Les Néréides" (Gautier) **18**:129, 141
"The Nereids of Seriphos" (Clampitt) **19**:92
"Nerve Gas part II" (Bissett) **14**:7
"Nestor's Bathtub" (Dove) **6**:109
Nets to Catch the Wind (Wylie) **23**:300-301, 306, 309, 311, 324-34
Netzahualcóyotl (Cardenal) **22**:128, 130-31
Neue Gedichte (Heine) **25**:129-132
Neue Gedichte (Rilke) **2**:266-68, 275
Der neue Pausias und sein Blumenmädchen (Goethe) **5**:239-40
Neuer Frühling (Heine) 129-131
"The Neurotic" (Day Lewis) **11**:147
"Neutral Tones" (Hardy) **8**:88, 126, 130
"Never Again Would Birds' Song Be the Same" (Frost) **1**:231
"Never Such Love" (Graves) **6**:137
"Never to Dream of Spiders" (Lorde) **12**:143
"The New Age" (Smith) **12**:313, 316
"The New America" (Blok) **21**:8, 26, 29
New and Collected Poems (Soto) **28**:404
New and Selcted Poems (Meredith) **28**:210, 215
New and Selected (Viereck) **27**:275, 279, 280-82, 284
New and Selected Poems (Nemerov) **24**:258, 260, 262, 264, 266, 268, 284, 286
New and Selected Poems (Viereck) **27**:
New and Selected Poems, 1940-1986 (Shapiro) **25**:318-22
New and Selected Things Taking Place (Swenson) **14**:274, 277, 280-81, 287
New Cautionary Tales (Belloc) **24**:27
New Collected Poems (Graves) **6**:166
The New Cultural Blues (Viereck) **27**:
"A New Day" (Levine) **22**:223-24
New Desire (Hagiwara Sakutaro)
See *New Desire*
"New Grown Girl" (Guillen)
See "New Grown Girl"
"New Hampshire" (Eliot) **5**:166, 169
New Hampshire (Frost) **1**:215, 224
"New Heavens for Old" (Lowell) **13**:85, 88
"New Koide Road" (Hagiwara Sakutaro) **18**:183
See "Koide shido"
"New Legends" (Graves) **6**:149
New Life (Dante)
See *La vita nuova*
"The New Little Larousse" (Zagajewski) **27**:401
"The New Love" (Parker) **28**:356
A New Lovesong for Stalingrad (Neruda)
See *Nuevo canto de amor a Stalingrado*
"New Morality" (Coleridge) **11**:102-03
"New Mother" (Olds) **22**:312
"New Objectives, New Cadres" (Rexroth) **20**:215
"New Orleans" (Harjo) **27**:65
"New Orleans 30 Oct 71" (Brutus) **24**:124
New Poems (Arnold) **5**:12, 43, 50
New Poems (Bridges) **28**:51, 67, 69
New Poems (Heine)
See *Neue Gedichte*
New Poems (Montale) **13**:143-46
New Poems (Rexroth) **20**:197, 204
New Poems (Rilke)
See *Neue Gedichte*
New Poems (Rilke) **2**:280-81
New Poems, 1962 (Graves) **6**:154
"A New Psalm for the Chapel of Kilmarnock" (Burns) **6**:89
"A New Reality Is Better Than a New Movie!" (Baraka) **4**:30
"A New Record" (Duncan) **2**:103
"The New Saddhus" (Pinsky) **27**:176
"New Season" (Levine) **22**:223
New Selected Poems (Levine) **22**:220-221, 223-24, 226, 228
"The New Sheriff" (Baraka) **4**:10, 15
"The New Sirens" (Arnold) **5**:5, 39
"A New Song" (Heaney) **18**:202, 241
A New Song (Hughes) **1**:242, 250, 253-54, 268
"The New Spirit" (Ashbery) **26**:108, 130, 169-170
The New Spoon River (Masters) **1**:333-34, 344-45
"New Stanzas" (Montale)
See "Nuove stanze"
"New Stanzas to Augusta" (Brodsky)
See "Novye stansy k Avguste"
"A New Story" (Ortiz) **17**:234
"New Thoughts on Old Subjects" (Coleridge) **11**:105
"The New Woman" (Guillen)
See "Mujer nueva"
"New World" (Momaday) **25**:199, 216
The New World (Masters) **1**:339
New Year Letter (Auden) **1**:16, 21, 23-24, 34
"The New Yeares Gift, or Circumcision Song" (Herrick)
See "Another New-yeeres Gift; or song for the Circumcision"
"New Year's Dawn, 1947" (Jeffers) **17**:141
"New Year's Eve" (Hardy) **8**:104, 119
"New Year's Eve 1959" (Kursh) **15**:224
"New Year's Gift" (Herrick)
See "A New-Yeares Gift Sent to Sir Simeon Steward"
"New Year's Greetings" (Tsvetaeva)
See "Novogodnee"
"New York" (Gunn) **26**:209, 220
"New York" (Senghor) **25**:255
"New York" (Viereck) **27**:274
"New York 1962: Fragment" (Lowell) **3**:215
"New York at Night" (Lowell) **13**:79
"New York City 1970" (Lorde) **12**:146, 158
The New York Head Shop and Museum (Lorde) **12**:146-47, 154
"New York: Office and Denunciation" (Garcia Lorca)
See "Nueva York: Oficina y denuncia"
"The New York Times" (Kumin) **15**:200
"The New Yorkers" (Giovanni) **19**:142
The New Youth (Pasolini)
See *La nuova gioventù*
"New Zealand Poems" (Wright) **14**:377
"Newborn Girl-Child" (Guillen) **23**:132
"Newcomer" (Okigbo) **7**:233, 240
"News for the Delphic Oracle" (Yeats) **20**:312-13, 316, 334-35
"News from Mount Amiata" (Montale)
See "Notizie dall'Amiata"
"News from the Cabin" (Swenson) **14**:253-54
"News Item" (Parker) **28**:347, 359
"Newspaper Readers" (Tsvetaeva)
See "Chitateli gazet"
"Newsreel: Man and Firing Squad" (Atwood) **8**:23
"A New-Yeares Gift Sent to Sir Simeon Steward" (Herrick) **9**:102, 145
"Next!" (Nash) **21**:270
Next: New Poems (Clifton) **17**:24, 26-28, 35-36
"Next, Please" (Larkin) **21**:226-27, 230, 235, 242, 246
The Next Room of the Dream (Nemerov) **24**:259, 262, 264, 266, 289
"Next to of Course God America I" (Cummings) **5**:89
Next-to-Last Things: New Poems and Essays (Kunitz) **19**:186
"Nezabudka" (Lermontov) **18**:188-89
"Nezdeshnii vecher" (Tsvetaeva) **14**:
Ni tiro (Fuertes) **27**:17
Ni tiro ni veneno (Fuertes) **27**:16
"Niagara" (Lindsay) **23**:275
"Nicaraguan canto" (Cardenal)
See "Canto nacional"
"A nice day" (Bukowski) **18**:23
"A Nice Shady Home" (Stevens) **6**:292
"Nick and the Candlestick" (Plath) **1**:390
"Nicodemus" (Robinson) **1**:476, 485
Die Niemandsrose (Celan) **10**:95, 98-99, 113, 117, 121
"Nieve" (Guillen) **23**:109
"Nigerian Unity/or Little Niggers Killing Little Niggers" (Madhubuti) **5**:329, 341-42
"Nigger" (Sanchez) **9**:223, 232
"Nigger" (Shapiro) **25**:270
The Nigger of Peter the Great (Pushkin)
See *Arap Petra Velikogo*
"Nigger Song: An Odyssey" (Dove) **6**:105;
"Nigger's Leap: New England" (Wright) **14**:335-36, 338, 340, 349-50, 368, 374
"Niggy the Ho" (Baraka) **4**:29, 38
"Night" (Blake) **12**:7-8, 23, 33, 61
"Night" (Bogan) **12**:96, 104
"Night" (Celan) **10**:112
"Night" (Giovanni) **19**:141
"Night" (Jeffers) **17**:107, 131, 145
"Night" (Pasternak)
See "Noch'"
"Night" (Pavese)
See "La notte"
"Night" (Rilke) **2**:275
"Night, a street, a lamp, a chemist's" (Blok)
See "Noch' ulitsa fonar' apteka'"
"Night and the Child" (Wright) **14**:352
"Night Bear Which Frightened Cattle" (Atwood) **8**:39
"The Night Before" (Robinson) **1**:460
"The Night before Great Babylon" (Sitwell) **3**:310
"The Night Dances" (Plath) **1**:388, 390
"Night, Death, Mississippi" (Hayden) **6**:194, 196
"Night, Four Songs" (Hughes) **1**:240
"The Night Game" (Pinsky) **27**:159, 176
"Night Hours" (Blok) **21**:5
"Night in Maine" (Lowell) **3**:226
"Night in the Forest" (Kinnell) **26**:240
"Night in the Old Home" (Hardy) **8**:105
"The Night Is Freezing Fast" (Housman)
See "*Last Poems:* XX--The Night Is Freezing Fast"
"The Night Journey" (Brooke) **24**:60
"Night Journey" (Roethke) **15**:246
"Night Launch" (Kumin) **15**:209
"Night Letter" (Kunitz) **19**:154, 157, 161, 169
"The Night My Father Got Me" (Housman) **2**:191
"Night of Sine" (Senghor)
See "Nuit de Sine"

"Night Operations Coastal Command RAF" (Nemerov) **24**:287
"Night Out" (Harjo) **27**:55
"Night Piece" (Heaney) **18**:201, 217
"A Night Piece" (Smart) **13**:341, 347
"Night Pleasures" (Pavese)
See "Piaceri notturni"
"Night Practice" (Swenson) **14**:266
"Night Shift" (Plath) **1**:388
"Night Song" (Gluck) **16**:145-47
"Night Song of an Asiatic Wandering Shepherd" (Montale)
See "Canto notturno di un pastore errante nell'Asia"
"Night Taxi" (Gunn) **26**:231
"Night Thoughts" (Smith) **12**:337
"Night Train" (Hagiwara Sakutaro) **18**:168, 179, 183
See "Yogisha"
"Night Transfigured" (Tomlinson) **17**:319, 342
"Night Visits with the Family" (Swenson) **14**:281
"The Night-Blooming Cereus" (Hayden) **6**:194-95, 198
The Night-Blooming Cereus (Hayden) **6**:182, 184, 187, 190, 194
"Nightbreak" (Rich) **5**:358
"Night-Flowering Cactus" (Merton) **10**:334
"The Nightingale" (Coleridge) **11**:85, 106
"The Nightingale" (Finch)
See "To the Nightingale"
"Nightingale" (Keats)
See "Ode to a Nightingale"
"The Nightingale" (Marie de France)
See "Laüstic"
"The Nightingale Garden" (Blok) **21**:20
The Nightingale of the Catholic Church (Pasolini) **17**:285, 287
See *L'usignuolo della Chiesa Cattolica*
"Nightingales" (Bridges) **28**:64, 66, 70, 75-6
"The Nightingales" (Williams) **7**:345
"The Nightingales Nest" (Clare) **23**:4-5
"Nightmare" (Kumin) **15**:198
"Nightmare" (Lowell) **13**:78
"Nightmare" (Page) **12**:168
The Nightmare Factory (Kumin) **15**:190, 200, 208
"Night-Music" (Rukeyser) **12**:209, 211
"Night-Piece" (Kunitz) **19**:148, 153
"Night-Piece" (Sassoon) **12**:240
"The Night-Piece to Julia" (Herrick) **9**:94, 132
"Nights and Days" (Rich) **5**:375
Nights and Days (Merrill) **28**:220, 225, 226, 227, 228, 230, 231, 232, 234, 240, 250, 252-54, 281
"Nightsong: City" (Brutus) **24**:113
Nightsongs (Holderlin)
See *Nachtgesänge*
"Night-Time in the Cemetery" (Smith) **12**:316
"The Nihilist as Hero" (Lowell) **3**:229
"Nikki-Rosa" (Giovanni) **19**:139
"Nilamanilata" (Tagore) **8**:416
"Nimmo" (Robinson) **1**:468
"Nimrod in September" (Sassoon) **12**:278
"Nina Replies" (Rimbaud)
See "Les reparties de Nina"
"IX" (Joyce) **22**:160, 167
"Nine Lives" (Merrill) **28**:283
"Nine Poems for the Unborn Child" (Rukeyser) **12**:228
"Nine Sleep Valley" (Merrill) **28**:254-55
"Nine Variations in a Chinese Winter Setting" (Tomlinson) **17**:299, 331
"Nine Verses of the Same Song" (Berry) **28**:5
"XIX" (Joyce) **22**:145, 169, 171
"MCMXIV" (Larkin) **21**:229, 234
"1914" (Owen) **19**:352
1914, and Other Poems (Brooke) **24**:61, 63, 80, 85, 87-8
1921-1925 (Mandelstam) **14**:151, 155
"Nineteen Hundred and Nineteen" (Yeats) **20**:314, 325, 350-51
"1909" (Apollinaire) **7**:46-7
"1963" (Dove) **6**:106
"The Nineteenth Century and After" (Yeats) **20**:314
1933 (Levine) **22**:217-18, 223
95 Poems (Cummings) **5**:109-10
"96 Tears" (Hongo) **23**:199
Ninfeas (Jimenez) **7**:197, 199
"Ninth Elegy" (Rilke) **2**:281, 286-87
"Ninth Elegy: The Antagonists" (Rukeyser) **12**:223
Ninth Nemean (Pindar)
See *Nemean 9*
"Ninth Psalm" (Sexton) **2**:367
Ninth Pythian (Pindar)
See *Pythian 9*
"The Ninth Symphony of Beethoven Understood at Last as a Sexual Message" (Rich) **5**:360, 370
"Niobe in Distress for Her Children Slain by Apollo" (Wheatley) **3**:338, 355, 357-60
Niobjeta ziemia (Milosz) **8**:179, 211
"Nipping Pussy's Feet in Fun" (Smith) **12**:339
"Nirbhay" (Tagore) **8**:415
"Nirjharer svapnabhanga" (Tagore) **8**:406
"Niruddesh yatra" (Tagore) **8**:408
"Nishikigizuka" (Ishikawa) **10**:213
"Nitrate" (Levine) **22**:224
"Niwatori" (Hagiwara Sakutaro) **18**:174, 180
"Nixon's the One" (Meredith) **28**:176, 206
"No" (Stein) **18**:327
"No Believers in the Resurrection" (Mandelstam) **14**:120
"No Buyers: A Street Scene" (Hardy) **8**:101
"No Coward Soul Is Mine" (Bronte) **8**:51, 60, 69-70
"No dejan escribir" (Fuertes) **27**:49
"[00a8]No hay salida?" (Paz) **1**:364
"No Hearing (Discovering)" (Lowell) **3**:228
"No Man's Land" (Heaney) **18**:202
"No Matter, Never Mind" (Snyder) **21**:297
"No more" (Milosz) **8**:190, 193
"No More Ghosts" (Graves) **6**:132
"No More Marching" (Madhubuti) **5**:339
"No More Sacrifices" (Ortiz) **17**:223, 234
No Nature: New and Selected Poems (Snyder) **21**:324-25
"No One Remembers" (Levine) **22**:223
"No One Sentence" (Stein) **18**:313
The No One's Rose (Celan)
See *Die Niemandsrose*
"No Possom, No Sop, No Taters" (Stevens) **6**:302
"No Resurrection" (Jeffers) **17**:141
"No Road" (Larkin) **21**:230, 235
"No Sanctuary" (Heaney) **18**:202
"No sé por qué piensas tú" (Guillen) **23**:140
"No Speech from the Scaffold" (Gunn) **26**:202
"No, Thank You, John!" (Rossetti) **7**:267, 281, 291
No Thanks (Cummings) **5**:106-07
"No Way of Knowing" (Ashbery) **26**:124, 144
"No Way of Knowing When This Song Began" (Mandelstam) **14**:118
"No Word" (Kunitz) **19**:170, 186
"No Worst, There Is None" (Hopkins) **15**:175
Noah and the Waters (Day Lewis) **11**:127-28, 144, 152-53
"Noah Built the Ark" (Johnson) **24**:128-29, 144, 155, 164-65, 169
"The Nobel Prize" (Pasternak)
See "Nobelevskaya premiya"
"Nobelevskaya premiya" (Pasternak) **6**:268, 284
"The Noble Lady's Tale" (Hardy) **8**:99
"The Noble Lord" (Belloc) **24**:41
Noble Numbers, or Pious Pieces (Herrick)
See *His Noble Numbers: or, His Pious Pieces, Wherein (amongst Other Things) He Sings the Birth of His Christ: and Sighes for His Saviours Suffering on the Crosse*
"Noble Sisters" (Rossetti) **7**:272, 274, 276, 280
"The Nobleman Orsha" (Lermontov) **18**:300
"Nobody" (Aleixandre) **15**:20, 22
"Nobody" (Guillen)
See "Nobody"
"Nobody Comes" (Hardy) **8**:101, 125
"Nobody Owns th Earth" (Bissett) **14**:10
Nobody Owns th Earth (Bissett) **14**:10-12, 18
"Nobody's Lookin' but de Owl and de Moon" (Johnson) **24**:141
The Nobody's Rose (Celan)
See *Die Niemandsrose*
Les Noces d'Hérodiade (Mallarme)
See *Hérodiade*
"Noch'" (Pasternak) **6**:285
"Noch' ulitsa fonar' apteka'" (Blok) **21**:44
"Noch'I" (Lermontov) **18**:302
"Noch'II" (Lermontov) **18**:302
"Nocturnal Pleasures" (Pavese)
See "Piaceri notturni"
"A Nocturnal Reverie" (Finch) **21**:140-41, 143, 146, 157, 160, 173-75
"A Nocturnal upon S. Lucies day, Being the shortest day" (Donne) **1**:130, 134, 149-50, 154
"Nocturne" (Pavese)
See "Notturno"
"Nocturne in a Deserted Brickyard" (Sandburg) **2**:301, 303
Nocturne of Remembered Spring and Other Poems (Aiken) **26**:50, 72
"Nocturne of the Void" (Garcia Lorca)
See "Nocturno del hueco"
"Nocturne vulgaire" (Rimbaud) **3**:264
Nocturnes (Senghor) **25**:231-33, 238-40, 255
"Nocturno de San Ildefonso" (Paz) **1**:370-72, 375
"Nocturno del hueco" (Garcia Lorca) **3**:139
"Nocturno en los muelles" (Guillen) **23**:106
"Nodier raconte" (Pound) **4**:317
"Noel: Christmas Eve, 1913" (Bridges) **28**:77, 81
"A Noiseless Patient Spider" (Whitman) **3**:390
"Un nom" (Lamartine) **16**:287
"Nomad Exquisite" (Stevens) **6**:293
No-man's Rose (Celan)
See *Die Niemandsrose*
"Le non godute" (Gozzano) **10**:184
Non Serviam (Ekeloef) **23**:51, 58-9, 63, 76
"None with Him" (Rossetti) **7**:276, 284
Nones (Auden) **1**:23
"Nonne Preestes Tale" (Chaucer)
See "Nun's Priest's Tale"
"Nonsense Rhyme" (Wylie) **23**:305
"Nonsun Blob a" (Cummings) **5**:109
"Noon" (Levine) **22**:214, 219, 222
"Noon Walk on the Asylum Lawn" (Sexton) **2**:359
"Noone' Autumnal This Great Lady's Gaze" (Cummings) **5**:107
"A Noon-Piece" (Smart) **13**:347
"Nor We of Her to Him" (Smith) **12**:326, 330
"Nora" (Toomer) **7**:317
"Die Nordsee" (Heine) **25**:139, 145, 158, 160, 162, 163
"Noria" (Cesaire) **25**:33
"Norma" (Sanchez) **9**:234
"Norma y paraíso de los negros" (Garcia Lorca) **3**:150
"North" (Heaney) **18**:203
North (Heaney) **18**:194-95, 197-99, 203, 205, 208-11, 215, 230, 238-39, 241, 246, 255
"th north aint easy to grow food in" (Bissett) **14**:25, 33
"North American Sequence" (Roethke) **15**:309-10, 312
"North American Time" (Rich) **5**:395
"North and South" (McKay) **2**:207
North & South (Bishop) **3**:37, 39, 50
"North Dakota North Light" (Momaday) **25**:219
"North Labrador" (Crane) **3**:83
North of Boston (Frost) **1**:193-95, 202, 207, 214, 217, 223-26

"The North Sea Undertaker's Complaint" (Lowell) **3**:216
The North Ship (Larkin) **21**:224-26, 230, 232-33, 235, 241, 251, 257, 259
"North Wind" (Montale)
See "Tramontana"
"North Wind in October" (Bridges) **28**:67
North Winter (Carruth) **10**:70-71
Northern Birds in Color (Bissett) **14**:25
"Northern Door" (Ortiz) **17**:234
"Northern Elegies" (Akhmatova) **2**:4, 18
"The Northern Farmer" (Tennyson) **6**:358, 360
"The Northern Farmer--Old Style" (Tennyson) **6**:406
Northern Heroic (Bely)
See *Severnaia simfoniia: Pervia geroicheskaia*
"A Northern Hoard" (Heaney) **18**:202-3
"Northern Liberal" (Hughes) **1**:252
"Northern River" (Wright) **14**:340
"The Northern Sea" (Ishikawa)
See "Kita no umi"
Northern Symphony (Bely)
See *Severnaia simfoniia: Pervia geroicheskaia*
Northfield Poems (Ammons) **16**:4-5, 28
"Northumberland House" (Smith) **12**:296
Northwest Ecolog (Ferlinghetti) **1**:187
"Northwood Path" (Gluck) **16**:126
De nos oìseaux (Tzara) **27**:233
"Nossis" (H. D.) **5**:268
"Nostalgia" (Jimenez)
See "Nostaljia"
"Nostalgia" (Shapiro) **25**:269, 288, 325
"Nostalgic Catalogue" (Hongo) **23**:198-99
"Nostalgies d'obélisques" (Gautier) **18**:158, 163
"Nostaljia" (Jimenez) **7**:201
"Not a fighter for two positions, but-- if I'm a casual guest" (Tsvetaeva)
See "Dvukh stanov ne beots, a-- esli gost sluchainyi"
"Not Both" (Meredith) **28**:208
"La not di maj" (Pasolini) **17**:252
"Not Every Day Fit for Verse" (Herrick) **9**:114
"Not Going to New York: A Letter" (Hass) **16**:198-99
"The Not Impossible Him" (Millay)
See "To the Not Impossible Him"
"Not Leaving the House" (Snyder) **21**:289
"Not like a floury white butterfly" (Mandelstam)
See "Ne muchnistoi babochkoiu beloi"
"Not Like Dante" (Ferlinghetti) **1**:182
"Not Planning a Trip Back" (Ashbery) **26**:165
Not So Deep as a Well (Parker) **28**:365
"Not So Far as the Forest" (Millay) **6**:238
"Not So, Not So" (Sexton) **2**:373
"Not That From Life, and All Its Woes" (Bryant) **20**:16
"Not There" (Gallagher) **9**:59
Not This Pig (Levine) **22**:212-13, 215-17, 220, 223, 226
"Not Waving but Drowning" (Smith) **12**:293, 300, 307, 319-21, 324, 328, 331, 333, 337, 347, 349, 354
Not Waving but Drowning (Smith) **12**:292-93
"Not with libations, but with Shouts and Laughter" (Millay) **6**:211, 244-46
"Nota biográfica" (Fuertes) **27**:18, 48-9
"note to myself" (Clifton) **17**:30
"Notebook" (Levertov)
See "From a Notebook, October '68--May '69"
Notebook 1967-68 (Lowell) **3**:223-26, 231-32, 239-40
"The Notebook in the Gate-legged Table" (Lowell) **13**:84
"Notebook of a Return to the Native Land" (Cesaire)
See *Cahier d'un retour au pays natal*
The Note-Book of William Blake (Blake) **12**:11, 34-5
"Noted in the *New York Times*" (Kumin) **15**:209
"Notes at Edge" (Wright) **14**:375, 377
Notes for a Guidbook (Stryk) **27**:181, 183, 191-94, 197, 210, 214, 216, 218
"Notes for an Elegy" (Meredith) **28**:170, 173, 181, 184-85, 187, 210
"Notes for a Guidebook" (Stryk) **27**:186, 195
"Notes for a Little Play" (Hughes) **7**:130, 152
"Notes for a Speech" (Baraka) **4**:5
"Notes for the Legend of Salad Woman" (Ondaatje) **28**:329
Notes from New York, and Other Poems (Tomlinson) **17**:333-34, 336, 353-54
"Notes From Robin Hill Cottage" (Carruth) **10**:85
"Notes From the Air" (Ashbery) **26**:163
"Notes Made in the Piazzo San Marco" (Swenson) **14**:261
"Notes on a Conspiracy" (Rose) **13**:241
"Notes toward a Poem That Can Never Be Written" (Atwood) **8**:18, 43
"Notes Toward a Supreme Fiction" (Ashbery) **26**:
Notes toward a Supreme Fiction (Stevens) **6**:310, 314, 324, 326-37, 329, 335, 337
"Nothing and Something" (Harper) **21**:187, 191
"Nothing Down" (Dove) **6**:110, 112
"Nothing Endures" (Cullen) **20**:59
Nothing for Tigers: Poems, 1959-1964 (Carruth) **10**:70
"Nothing Gold Can Stay" (Frost) **1**:194
"Nothing Makes Sense" (Giovanni) **19**:112
"Nothing Significant Was Really Said" (Larkin) **21**:259
"Nothing Stays Put" (Clampitt) **19**:94
"Nothing to Be Said" (Larkin) **21**:227
"(Nothing Whichful About" (Cummings) **5**:108
"Nothing will yield" (Nemerov) **24**:262
"Nothingness" (Jimenez)
See "La mujer desnuda"
"Notizie dall'Amiata" (Montale) **13**:106, 121, 127
"Notre-Dame" (Gautier) **18**:144-46
"Notre Dame de Chartres" (Meredith) **28**:171, 188-89
"La notte" (Pavese) **13**:230
"Notturno" (Pavese) **13**:230
"Noubousse" (Apollinaire) **7**:48
"Noun" (Shapiro) **25**:276
"nouvelle bonte" (Cesaire) **25**:45
Nouvelle confidences (Lamartine) **16**:293
Nouvelles méditations poétiques (Lamartine) **16**:266, 271, 273-74, 277-79, 287, 290-09
Nouvelles Odes (Hugo) **17**:88
"Nova" (Jeffers) **17**:130
"A Novel" (Gluck) **16**:158, 161
"November" (Belloc) **24**:34
"November" (Bryant) **20**:37, 44
"November" (Hughes) **7**:119, 132-33, 136
"November Cotton Flower" (Toomer) **7**:319, 333-34
"November Surf" (Jeffers) **17**:117, 120, 132
The Novice (Lermontov) **18**:279
"The Novices" (Levertov) **11**:169
"Novissima verba" (Lamartine) **16**:268, 280, 283, 292-93, 297
"Novogodnee" (Tsvetaeva) **14**:325
"Novye stansy k Avguste" (Brodsky) **9**:4
"Now" (Sexton) **2**:352
"Now" (Walker) **20**:276
"Now Air Is Air and Thing Is Thing: No Bliss" (Cummings) **5**:110
"Now Close the Windows" (Frost) **1**:197
"Now Does Our World Descend" (Cummings) **5**:111
"Now He Knows All There Is to Know: Now He Is Acquainted with the Day and Night" (Schwartz) **8**:319
"Now Hollow Fires" (Housman) **2**:189
Now in Wintry Delights (Bridges) **28**:76-7
"Now It Is You I Praise, Banner" (Rilke) **2**:273
"Now Pine-Needles" (Smith) **12**:318
"Now Returned Home" (Jeffers) **17**:141
"Now that Holocaust and Crucifixion are Coffee-Table Books" (Viereck) **27**:293-94, 296
Now That Holocaust and Crucifixion Are Coffee-Table Books (Viereck) **27**:
"Now That I Am Never Alone" (Gallagher) **9**:62
"Now the Record Now Record" (Duncan) **2**:103
"Now This Cold Man" (Page) **12**:168, 170, 178, 184
"Nox" (Hugo) **17**:54
Nozarashi Diary (Matsuo Basho) **3**:6
Nozarashi kiko (Matsuo Basho) **3**:11, 28
"NUCLEAR CICULAR" (Bissett) **14**:6, 24, 32
"Nude" (Cassian) **17**:4
"Nude Photograph" (Clifton) **17**:29
"The Nude Swim" (Sexton) **2**:352
"Nude Young Dancer" (Hughes) **1**:246
"La Nue" (Gautier) **18**:125, 129
"Nueva York: Oficina y denuncia" (Garcia Lorca) **3**:141, 151
Nuevo canto de amor a Stalingrado (Neruda) **4**:279-80
"La nuit blanche" (Kipling) **3**:172
"Nuit blanche" (Lowell) **13**:89-90
"La nuit d'Avril, 1915" (Apollinaire) **7**:3
"Nuit de Sine" (Senghor) **25**:224, 227, 255
"Nuits de juin" (Hugo) **17**:64
"Nullo" (Toomer) **7**:320, 330-31, 334
"Number 57" (Villa) **22**:346
"Number Man" (Sandburg) **2**:322
"Number 68" (Villa) **22**:347
"Number Three on the Docket" (Lowell) **13**:79, 84-5
"The Numbers" (Ammons) **16**:5
"Numbers" (Hughes) **1**:267
"Numbers" (Smith) **12**:317
"Numbers, Letters" (Baraka) **4**:19
"The Numerous Blood" (Guillen)
See "La sangre numerosa"
"Numpholeptos" (Browning) **2**:86, 88
"Nunc dimittis" (Brodsky) **9**:5
"Nunca se sabe" (Fuertes) **27**:17
"A Nun's Complaint" (Rilke) **2**:270
"Nuns Fret Not" (Millay) **6**:242
"Nuns in the Wind" (Rukeyser) **12**:211
"Nun's Priest's Tale" (Chaucer) **19**:6, 13-15, 26, 31-2, 48, 52, 57, 75
La nuova gioventù (Pasolini) **17**:282-83, 287
"Nuova poesia in forma di rose" (Pasolini) **17**:274, 278
"Nuove stanze" (Montale) **13**:106, 120-21
"A Nuptiall Song, or Epithalamie on Sir Clipseby Crew and His Lady" (Herrick) **9**:86, 102, 139
"Nu¨rnberge Rede " (Enzensberger) **28**:164
"Nurse Whitman" (Olds) **22**:322, 328
"A Nursery Rhyme" (Brooke) **24**:66
"Nursery Rhyme for a Seventh Son" (Wright) **14**:338
"Nursery Rhymes for Little Anglo-Indians" (Kipling) **3**:190
"Nurse's Song" (Blake) **12**:7, 21-2, 34
"Nurse's Song" (Gluck) **16**:148
"Nursing Home" (Page) **12**:176
"Nurture" (Kumin) **15**:209, 211
Nurture (Kumin) **15**:209-14, 221, 223
Nux (Ovid) **2**:244
"Ny la douce pitie, ny le pleur lamentable" (Ronsard) **11**:278
"The Nymph and the Faun" (Marvell)
See "The Nymph Complaining for the Death of Her Faun"
"The Nymph Complaining for the Death of Her Faun" (Marvell) **10**:260-62, 266-67, 271, 274, 277, 290, 294, 297, 301-02, 309-10, 315-16, 319, 325
"A Nympholept" (Swinburne) **24**:312-319, 322, 326, 341, 348
O. 1 (Pindar)
See *Olympian 1*

O. 7 (Pindar)
See *Olympian 7*
O. 8 (Pindar)
See *Olympian 8*
O. 9 (Pindar)
See *Olympian 9*
O. 14 (Pindar)
See *Olympian 14*
"O Black and Unknown Bards" (Johnson) **24**:127, 146, 152, 160, 166
"O Captain! My Captain!" (Whitman) **3**:404, 418, 422
"O Carib Isle!" (Crane) **3**:90
"O City, City" (Schwartz) **8**:302, 316
"O Daedalus, Fly Away Home" (Hayden) **6**:176, 179, 189
"O das Quinas" (Pessoa) **20**:155
"O Desejado" (Pessoa) **20**:156
"O Didn't He Ramble" (Johnson) **24**:151, 170
"O dos Castelos" (Pessoa) **20**:155
"O Dreams, O Destinations" (Day Lewis) **11**:145
"O Florida, Venereal Soil" (Stevens) **6**:305, 339
"O Glorious France" (Masters) **1**:342
"O Guardador de Rebanhos" (Pessoa) **20**:151-52
"O Happy Dogs of England" (Smith) **12**:318, 330
"O Hell" (Loy) **16**:316
"O Infante" (Pessoa) **20**:155
"O Lady, when the Tipped Cup of the Moon Blessed You" (Hughes) **7**:113
"O Lay Thy Loof in Mine, Lass" (Burns) **6**:76
"O, Let Me in This Ae Night" (Burns) **6**:81
"O Love, my muse" (Bridges) **28**:59
"O Love, Sweet Animal" (Schwartz) **8**:313
"O Love, the Interest Itself in Thoughtless Heaven..." (Auden) **1**:22
"O Lull Me, Lull Me" (Roethke) **15**:261, 273, 299, 302
"O May I Join the Choir Invisible" (Eliot) **20**:123, 131, 136, 139, 143
"O me donzel" (Pasolini) **17**:252
"O Mon Dieu, vous m'avez blessé d'amour" (Verlaine) **2**:416
"O Mostrengo" (Pessoa) **20**:155
"O muse contiens-toi! muse aux hymnes d'airain" (Hugo) **17**:97
"O my companions, O my sister Sleep" (Belloc) **24**:38
"O my joy" (Bridges) **28**:63
"O my vague desires" (Bridges) **28**:59
"O Pastor Amoroso" (Pessoa) **20**:152
"O Pug!" (Smith) **12**:301
"O saisons, ô châteaux!" (Rimbaud) **3**:275
"O Sion of my heart" (Kunitz) **19**:175
"O Southland!" (Johnson) **24**:137, 142, 147, 160
"O Sweet Spontaneous" (Cummings) **5**:105
"O Taste and See" (Levertov) **11**:169
O Taste and See (Levertov) **11**:159, 169, 171, 211
"O, Tempora! O Mores!" (Poe) **1**:449
"O, Thou Opening, O" (Roethke) **15**:284, 300, 302-03
"O to Be a Dragon" (Moore) **4**:249
"O Virtuous Light" (Wylie) **23**:311, 315
"O Wander Not So Far Away!" (Burroughs) **8**:73
"O Wha's Been Here afore Me, Lass" (MacDiarmid) **9**:155, 160
"O Word I Love to Sing" (McKay) **2**:217, 219
"O World of many Worlds" (Owen) **19**:352
"O Ye Tongues" (Sexton) **2**:367, 372-73
Oak and Ivy (Dunbar) **5**:128, 132
"The Oak Leaf" (Lermontov) **18**:281
"Oasis" (Stryk) **27**:187
"Oatmeal" (Kinnell) **26**:286
"Obedience" (Herbert) **4**:119, 125-26
"Obermann Once More" (Arnold) **5**:19, 63-4
"Oberon's Chappell" (Herrick)
See "The Fairie Temple: or, Oberons Chappell. Dedicated to Mr. John Merrifield, Counsellor at Law"
"Oberon's Feast" (Herrick) **9**:90
"Oberon's Palace" (Herrick) **9**:86, 90, 137
"Obituary for a Living Lady" (Brooks) **7**:66-7, 69
"The Objection to Being Stepped On" (Frost) **1**:215
"Objet d'Art" (Stryk) **27**:204
"Oblique Prayers" (Levertov) **11**:198, 201
Oblique Prayers (Levertov) **11**:198, 200-02, 209
"Oblivion" (Smith) **12**:317, 354
"O-Bon: Dance for The Dead" (Hongo) **23**:199
"Oboroniaet son moiu donskuiu son" (Mandelstam) **14**:154
Obra poética (Borges) **22**:95
Obra poética 1923-1967 (Borges) **22**:72, 96
Obras completas (Aleixandre) **15**:7, 18, 34
Obras completas (Juana Ines de la Cruz) **24**:202, 233
Obras incompletas (Fuertes) **27**:3-5, 19-21, 23-5, 33-47
"Observation" (Larkin) **21**:259
"Observation of Facts" (Tomlinson) **17**:299, 315, 335
Observations (Moore) **4**:229-30, 244, 249-52
"The Observatory" (Noyes) **27**:128
"The Observer" (Rich) **5**:370
"Obsessed by Her Beauty" (Viereck) **27**:263
"Obsidian Butterfly" (Paz)
See "Mariposa de obsidiana"
Obus couleur de lune (Apollinaire) **7**:22
"Occasioned by Sir William Temple's Late Illness and Recovery" (Swift) **9**:250
Le occasioni (Montale) **13**:103-05, 108-09, 113-14, 117-21, 126-28, 131-32, 136, 141 , 160, 165-66
The Occasions (Montale)
See *Le occasioni*
"L'occident" (Lamartine) **16**:266
"Ocean Waves" (Tagore)
See "Sindhu-taranga"
"Ocean-Letter" (Apollinaire)
See "Lettre-Océan"
"Oceano Nox" (Hugo) **17**:64
"Ocean's Love to Ireland" (Heaney) 18;196
Octavie: L'illusion (Nerval) **13**:177
"The Octets" (Mandelstam) **14**:152
"October" (Frost) **1**:225
"October" (Hayden) **6**:193, 195
"October" (Lorde) **12**:154
"October" (Sassoon) **12**:240
October, and Other Poems (Bridges) 28
"October Dawn" (Hughes) **7**:115
"October Journey" (Walker) **20**:284, 289
October Journey (Walker) **20**:284, 287, 289
"October Thought" (Heaney) **18**:191
"October Trees" (Sassoon) **12**:248, 254
"An Octopus" (Moore) **4**:233, 252, 254-55, 264
"The Octopus" (Merrill) **28**:239, 242
"Oda a Salvador Dali" (Garcia Lorca) **3**:136, 138, 143
"Oda a Walt Whitman" (Garcia Lorca) **3**:121, 127, 150
"Oda al edificio" (Neruda) **4**:285
"Oda al santísimo sacramento del altar: exposición y mundo" (Garcia Lorca) **3**:136, 138, 143
"Oda k nuzhniku" (Lermontov) **18**:284-85
"Oda solar al ejérito del pueblo" (Neruda) **4**:309
Odas elementales (Neruda) **4**:285, 287
Odas Mínimas (Guillen) **23**:100
Odds and Ends (Enzensberger)
See *Einzelheiten*
"Ode" (Lamartine) **16**:291
"Ode" (Marvell)
See "An Horatian Ode upon Cromwell's Return from Ireland"
"Ode" (Marvell)
See "An Horatian Ode upon Cromwell's Return from Ireland"
"Ode" (Tennyson) **6**:357
"Ode" (Wordsworth) **4**:377, 399, 403-04, 407
"Ode à Cassandre: 'Mignonne, allon voir'" (Ronsard) **11**:218-21, 234, 240
Ode à Charles Fourier (Breton) **15**:52, 61
"Ode á Joachim du Bellay" (Ronsard) **11**:280
"Ode à l'Amitié" (Hugo) **17**:87-88
"Ode à Michel de l'Hospital" (Ronsard) **11**:258, 287-91
"Ode à Victor Hugo" (Gautier) **18**:144
"Ode de la Paix" (Ronsard) **11**:283, 286, 289-91
"An Ode (Dedicated to the Under-Secretary for India in expectation of his immediate promotion to Cabinet rank through the Postmaster-General)" (Belloc) **24**:41
"Ode for All Rebels" (MacDiarmid) **9**:171, 176
"An Ode for Him" (Herrick) **9**:86
"Ode for Music" (Gray) **2**:153, 155
"Ode for St. Cecilia's Day" (Pope) **26**:315
"Ode Inscribed to W. H. Channing" (Emerson) **18**:88, 111
"Ode: Intimations of Immortality from Recollections of Early Childhood" (Wordsworth) **4**:387-88, 390, 395, 401, 403, 411
"Ode Marítima" (Pessoa) **20**:166, 169
"Ode: My Twenty-Fourth Year" (Ginsberg) **4**:73
"Ode: O Bosky Brook" (Tennyson) **6**:388-89
"Ode on a Distant Prospect of Eton College" (Gray) **2**:133-34, 137, 149-50, 153
"Ode on a Drop of Dew" (Marvell) **10**:269, 271, 277, 296, 313-14
"Ode on Indolence" (Keats) **1**:302-04, 307-08, 314
"Ode on Melancholy" (Keats) **1**:298-300, 306-07, 309, 312
"Ode on Spring" (Gray) **2**:133, 135, 143, 145, 152
"Ode on the Death of a Favourite Cat, Drowned in a Tub of Gold Fishes" (Gray) **2**:133, 146, 148, 152
"Ode on the Pleasure Arising from Vicissitude" (Gray) **2**:143, 152-53
"Ode on the Progress of Poesy" (Gray)
See "The Progress of Poesy"
"Ode on the Spring" (Gray)
See "Ode on Spring"
"Ode on Vicissitude" (Gray)
See "Ode on the Pleasure Arising from Vicissitude"
"Ode on Vicissitude" (Gray) **2**:143, 152-53
"Ode secrète" (Valery) **9**:394-96
"Ode sur la naissance du duc de Bordeaux" (Lamartine) **16**:291
"Ode to a Beloved Woman" (Sappho)
See "Ode to Anactoria"
"The Ode to a Girl" (Sappho) **5**:408
"Ode to a Grecian Urn" (Keats) **1**:281-82, 290-98, 300, 303-04, 307, 313-15
"Ode to a Nightingale" (Keats) **1**:281-83, 295-98, 301, 303, 305, 307-09, 314-15
"Ode to Adversity" (Gray) **2**:133, 135, 138-39, 141, 152
"Ode to Anactoria" (Sappho) **5**:407, 411, 413
"Ode to Aphrodite" (Sappho) **5**:408, 411, 413, 431
"Ode to Apollo" (Keats) **1**:313
"Ode to Arnold Schoenberg" (Tomlinson) **17**:308, 317, 328, 337
"Ode to Atthis" (Sappho) **5**:416
"Ode to Autumn" (Keats) **1**:282-83, 298-302, 314-15
"Ode to Beauty" (Emerson) **18**:81
"Ode to Bill" (Ashbery) **26**:135, 159
"Ode to Dr. William Sancroft" (Swift) **9**:250
"Ode to Duty" (Wordsworth) **4**:401, 406-07
"Ode to Ethiopia" (Dunbar) **5**:124, 129, 131-34, 143
"Ode to Fame" (Masters) **1**:332
"Ode to Fear" (Day Lewis) **11**:147
"Ode to France" (Coleridge) **11**:92, 94, 99-101
"ode to frank silvera" (Bissett) **14**:34

"Ode to Freedom" (Pushkin)
See "Vol'nost': Oda"
"Ode to General Draper" (Smart) **13**:342
"The Ode to Hesperus" (Sappho) **5**:418
"Ode to Himself" (Jonson) **17**:166, 174
"Ode to Liberty" (Pushkin)
See "Vol'nost': Oda"
"Ode to Liberty" (Shelley) **14**:178
"An Ode to Love" (Behn) **13**:30
"Ode to Mæcenas" (Wheatley) **3**:333, 340-41, 344-45, 348, 354, 356-57, 361-62
"Ode to Memory" (Tennyson) **6**:347, 359-60
"Ode to Neptune" (Wheatley) **3**:354, 357, 361
"Ode to Plurality" (Zagajewski) **27**:381, 383, 385, 395-96
"Ode to Psyche" (Keats) **1**:295, 301, 305, 308-09, 314
"Ode to Salvador Dali" (Garcia Lorca)
See "Oda a Salvador Dali"
"Ode to San Francisco" (Tomlinson) **17**:361
"An Ode to Sir Clipsebie Crew" (Herrick) **9**:103
"Ode: To Sir William Sydney, on his Birth-day" (Jonson) **17**:158-59
"Ode to Sir William Temple" (Swift) **9**:250
Ode to Stalin (Mandelstam) **14**:133, 148-49, 153-55
"Ode to the Athenian Society" (Swift) **9**:250
"An Ode to the Birth of Our Saviour" (Herrick) **9**:119-20
"Ode to the Departing Year" (Coleridge) **11**:49, 54, 93-4
"Ode to the Latrine" (Lermontov)
See "Ode to the Latrine"
"Ode to the Most Blessed Sacrament" (Garcia Lorca)
See "Oda al santísimo sacramento del altar: exposición y mundo"
"Ode to the Most Holy Eucharist: Exposition and World" (Garcia Lorca)
See "Oda al santísimo sacramento del altar: exposición y mundo"
"Ode to the Nightingale" (Keats)
See "Ode to a Nightingale"
"Ode to the Sacrament" (Garcia Lorca)
See "Oda al santísimo sacramento del altar: exposición y mundo"
"Ode to the Sky Lark" (Shelley) **14**:167, 171, 175, 196, 198, 207, 212
"Ode to the Spleen" (Finch) **21**:140-41, 145-46, 150, 152, 156-57, 159, 163, 165-66, 168, 172, 180-81
"Ode to the Spring" (Gray)
See "Ode on Spring"
"Ode to the West Wind" (Shelley) **14**:167-9, 171, 177, 196, 205-06, 208, 211-12, 234, 236-37, 239-40
"Ode to Venus" (Sappho)
See "Ode to Aphrodite"
"The Ode To Venus" (Sappho) **5**:408
"Ode to Walt Whitman" (Garcia Lorca)
See "Oda a Walt Whitman"
"Ode Triunfal" (Pessoa) **20**:169
Odes (Gray) **2**:135
Odes (Hugo) **17**:55, 70, 87-90
Odes (Pindar) **19**:380
Odes (Ronsard) **11**:230, 234, 280, 287, 289, 291-92
Odes (Valery) **9**:365
Odes et ballades (Hugo) **17**:45, 62, 74-75, 90-91
Odes et poésies diverses (Hugo) **17**:62
Odes to Simple Things (Neruda)
See *Odas elementales*
"Ode-Thnrenody on England" (Brooke) **24**:70
"Odious Scenery" (Hagiwara Sakutaro) **18**:177
"Odlegtose" (Milosz) **8**:189
"The Odour" (Herbert) **4**:102, 134
Odysseis (Homer)
See *Odyssey*
Odysses (Homer)
See *Odyssey*
"Odysseus to Telemachus" (Brodsky) **9**:4
Odyssey (Homer) **23**:151-53, 155-58, 161, 165-66, 176-79, 186, 188-91
"Oeconomic divina" (Milosz) **8**:186-87
"Oedipus Crow" (Hughes) **7**:138
"The Oedipus Within" (Wakoski) **15**:324
"Oenone" (Tennyson) **6**:359, 410-12
"Oeuvre" (Stryk) **27**:193, 195, 201
Oeuvres (Ronsard) **11**:247, 254, 269, 272, 276
Oeuvres complètes (Cesaire) **25**:33
Oeuvres complètes (Mallarme) **4**:198
Oeuvres completes (Perse) **23**:254
Oeuvres complètes (Tzara) **27**:232
Les Oeuvres de Francois Villon (Villon) **13**:373, 394
Oeuvres poétiques (Apollinaire) **7**:36
Oeuvres poetiques completes (Lamartine) **16**:268
"Of Beginning Light" (Tomlinson) **17**:333
"Of Being" (Levertov) **11**:199, 202
"Of De Witt Williams on His Way to Lincoln Cemetery" (Brooks) **7**:85
"Of Distress Being Humiliated by the Classical Chinese Poets" (Carruth) **10**:87-88
"Of Dying Beauty" (Zukofsky) **11**:368
"Of his love called Anna" (Wyatt) **27**:342
"Of Liberation" (Giovanni) **19**:108
"Of Modern Poetry" (Stevens) **6**:324
"Of others fained sorrow and the lovers fained mirth" (Wyatt) **27**:340
Of Pen and Ink and Paper Scraps (Stryk) **27**:214
"OF TH LAND DIVINE SERVICE" (Bissett) **14**:30
OF TH LAND DIVINE SERVICE (Bissett) **14**:2, 10
"Of the Four Humours in Man's Constitution" (Bradstreet) **10**:17, 41
Of the Progres of the Soule (Donne)
See *The Second Anniversarie. Of the Progres of the Soule. Wherein, By Occasion Of the Religious death of Mistris Elizabeth Drury, the incommodities of the Soule in this life, and her exaltation in the next, are Contemplated*
"Of the Vanity of All Worldly Creatures" (Bradstreet)
See "The Vanity of All Worldly Things"
Of the War (Duncan) **2**:104
"Of the West" (Jeffers) **17**:130
"Off from swing shift" (Hongo) **23**:196-97, 203
"Off Point Lotus" (Kunitz) **19**:171
"Off Shore" (Swinburne) **24**:313
"Off the Campus Wits" (Brutus) **24**:106, 114
"Off the Turnpike" (Lowell) **13**:78, 85
"Offering" (Tagore)
See "Utsarga"
An Offering to the Lares (Rilke) **2**:280
"Offhand Compositions" (Wang Wei) **18**:370, 374
"Offices" (Page) **12**:173
"Often I Am Permitted to Return to a Meadow" (Duncan) **2**:120, 127
"Often Rebuked, yet Always Back Returning" (Bronte) **8**:50
"The Ogre" (Williams) **7**:349, 378, 393
"Ogres and Pygmies" (Graves) **6**:139, 142, 144, 151
"Oh" (Sexton) **2**:365
"Oh Christianity, Christianity" (Smith) **12**:325, 352
"Oh, Dear! Oh Dear! A Sonnet" (Brooke) **24**:52
"Oh death shall find me" (Brooke) **24**:52, 72, 76
"Oh do not die" (Donne)
See "A Feaver"
"Oh Fair Enough Are Sky and Plain" (Housman) **2**:193
"Oh Fairest of the Rural Maids" (Bryant) **20**:35
"Oh general en tu Pentágono!" (Guillen) **23**:126
"Oh General in Your Pentagon!" (Guillen)
See "Oh General in Your Pentagon!"
"Oh, Look—I Can Do It, Too" (Parker) **28**:354
"Oh n'insultez jamais une femme qui tombe!" (Hugo) **17**:66
"Oh, See How Thick the Gold Cup Flowers" (Housman) **2**:183, 185, 196
"Oh Think Not I Am Faithful to a Vow" (Millay) **6**:211
"Oh You Sabbatarians!" (Masters) **1**:344
Oi no kobumi (Matsuo Basho) **3**:6
Oi no obumi (Matsuo Basho) **3**:12
Oiseaux (Perse) **23**:239-41, 247-48, 253-54, 256-57
Oku no hosomichi (Matsuo Basho) **3**:13, 27-30
Ol. IX (Pindar)
See *Olympian 9*
Ol. XI (Pindar)
See *Olympian 11*
"The Ol' Tunes" (Dunbar) **5**:122, 145
"The Old Adam" (Levertov) **11**:170
Old and Modern Poems (Vigny)
See *Poèmes antiques et modernes*
"Old Countryside" (Bogan) **12**:87, 94, 113
"An Old Cracked Tune" (Kunitz) **19**:158
"The Old Cumberland Beggar" (Wordsworth) **4**:411-12, 428
"Old Dogs" (Smith) **12**:331-32
"Old Dominion" (Hass) **16**:198
"Old Dwarf Heart" (Sexton) **2**:361
"Old England" (McKay) **2**:225
"Old Field Mowed for Appearance's Sake" (Meredith) **28**:194
"Old Flame" (Lowell) **3**:212, 215
"Old Florist" (Roethke) **15**:295
"Old Folks Home" (Stryk) **27**:210
"Old Folk's Home, Jerusalem" (Dove) **6**:123
"The Old Front Gate" (Dunbar) **5**:122
"Old Furniture" (Hardy) **8**:105
"Old Hills" (Ortiz) **17**:231
"The Old Horsefly" (Shapiro) **25**:324
The Old Horsefly (Shapiro) **25**:323
"Old House" (Wright) **14**:348-49, 353
"The Old Huntsman" (Sassoon) **12**:240, 242, 250, 252-53, 275-76
The Old Huntsman and Other Poems (Sassoon) **12**:249, 252, 256-57, 260, 263-64, 269, 272, 277
"The Old Italians Dying" (Ferlinghetti) **1**:182
"Old King Cole" (Robinson) **1**:468
"The Old King's New Jester" (Robinson) **1**:487
"An Old Lady's Winter Words" (Roethke) **15**:272, 278
"Old Laughter" (Brooks) **7**:61
"The Old Life" (Kinnell) **26**:277
"Old Lines" (Montale)
See "Vecchi versi"
"The Old Lovers" (Aleixandre)
See "Los amantes viejos"
"The Old Man Is Like Moses" (Aleixandre) **15**:4, 24
"The Old Man Travelling" (Wordsworth) **4**:374, 416
"The Old Man's Counsel" (Bryant) **20**:35, 41
"The Old Man's Funeral" (Bryant) **20**:10
"Old Marrieds" (Brooks) **7**:53, 69, 79
"Old Mary" (Brooks) **7**:106
"Old Medium" (Enzensberger) **28**:167
"An Old Memory" (Dunbar) **5**:140
"Old Men" (Nash) **21**:263, 274
"The Old Neighbour and the New" (Hardy) **8**:104
"Old Oak of Summer Chace" (Tennyson) **6**:356
"Old, Old, Old Andrew Jackson" (Lindsay) **23**:280, 288
"Old Paint, Old Partner" (Kumin) **15**:220
"Old Park" (Jimenez) **7**:183
"An old Photograph" (Nemerov) **24**:255
"an Old Photograph of Starngers" (Meredith) **28**:193
"Old Pictures in Florence" (Browning) **2**:37
"Old poet" (Bukowski) **18**:22
"The Old Poet" (Shapiro) **25**:304

"The Old Poet Moves to a New Apartment 14 Times" (Zukofsky) **11**:353
"The Old Pond" (Matsuo Basho) **3**:32
Old Possum's Book of Practical Cats (Eliot) **6**:174
"The Old Prison" (Wright) **14**:359
"Old Revolution" (Enzensberger) **28**:166
"The Old Sceptic" (Noyes) **27**:139
The Old sceptic (Noyes) **27**:139
"Old Song" (Crane) **3**:90
"The Old Stoic" (Bronte) **8**:60
"An Old Story" (Robinson) **1**:459
" Old Timers" (Sandburg) **2**:302
"Old Trails" (Robinson) **1**:462
"The Old Vicarage, Grantchester" (Brooke) **24**:54, 58, 63-5, 68, 78, 86, 93
"Old Walt" (Hughes) **1**:257
"Old Woman" (Pinsky) **27**:160-61
"An Old Woman" (Sitwell) **3**:312, 326
"The Old Woman and the Statue" (Stevens) **6**:297
"Old Words" (Sanchez) **9**:221
"An Old World Thicket" (Rossetti) **7**:277
The Oldest Killed Lake in North America (Carruth) **10**:91
"Olive Grove" (Merrill) **28**:228
"The Olive in Its Orchard" (Housman) **2**:189-90
"The Olive Wood Fire" (Kinnell) **26**:278
Olympian 1 (Pindar) **19**:380-81, 388-89, 396, 398, 400, 402, 407, 413-17, 420, 422
Olympian 2 (Pindar) **19**:381, 423
Olympian 3 (Pindar) **19**:425
Olympian 6 (Pindar) **19**:381, 389-90, 398, 414, 420
Olympian 7 (Pindar) **19**:396, 401, 406, 414
Olympian VII (Pindar)
See *Olympian 7*
Olympian 8 (Pindar) **19**:422-23
Olympian 9 (Pindar) **19**:390
Olympian 10 (Pindar) **19**:387-88
Olympian 11 (Pindar) **19**:389, 412
Olympian 13 (Pindar) **19**:387, 391, 398
Olympian 14 (Pindar) **19**:421-23
Olympian Odes 1 (Pindar)
See *Olympian 1*
"A Olympio" (Hugo) **17**:76
Om hösten (Ekeloef) **23**:76
"Omaggio a Rimbaud" (Montale) **13**:111, 157
"L'ombra della magnolia" (Montale) **13**:109-10, 118, 126
"Ombre Chinoise" (Lowell) **13**:94
Ommateum with Doxology (Ammons) **16**:4-5, 20, 24, 27, 39-44, 52-3
"Omnibus" (Tsvetaeva)
See "Avtobus"
Omniscience (Smart)
See *On the Omniscience of the Supreme Being*
"Omoide" (Ishikawa) **10**:213
"On a Bust" (Masters) **1**:342
"On a Certain Engagement South of Seoul" (Carruth) **10**:84, 89
"On a Child's Death" (Blok) **21**:15
"On a Clean Book" (Dunbar) **5**:125
"On a Conventicle" (Behn) **13**:7
"On a Copy of Verses Made in a Dream, and Sent to Me in a Morning before I Was Awake" (Behn) **13**:31
"On a Discovered Curl of Hair" (Hardy) **8**:137
"On a Distant Prospect of Eton College" (Gray)
See "Ode on a Distant Prospect of Eton College"
"On a Drawing by Flavio" (Levine) **22**:223
"On a Drop of Dew" (Marvell)
See "Ode on a Drop of Dew"
"On a Fine Morning" (Hardy) **8**:108
"On a Heath" (Hardy) **8**:93
"On a Juniper Tree, Cut Down to Make Busks" (Behn) **13**:7, 27-8
"On a Political Prisoner" (Yeats) **20**:314, 349
"On a Raised Beach" (MacDiarmid) **9**:157, 172, 176, 180
"On a Red Steed" (Tsvetaeva)
See "Na krasnom kone"
"On a Rocky Spur of Peoria" (Mandelstam) **14**:117
"On a Sentence by Pascal" (Schwartz) **8**:285, 292
"On a Side Street" (Zagajewski) **27**:389
"On a Singing Girl" (Wylie) **23**:324
"On a Sledge, Overlaid with Straw" (Mandelstam) **14**:119
"On a Sleeping Friend" (Belloc) **24**:9
"On a Solemn Music" (Milton) **19**:211, 253
"On a Starry Night" (Dunbar) **5**:125-27
"On a Tree Fallen Across the Road" (Frost) **1**:213
"On a winter's night long time ago" (Belloc) **24**:34
"On Affliction" (Finch) **21**:144, 146
"On an Anthology of Chinese Poems" (Jeffers) **17**:140
"On an Old Roundel" (Swinburne) **24**:324-25, 328-29
"On Anactoria" (Sappho)
See "Ode to Anactoria"
"On Angels" (Milosz) **8**:201
"On Annunciation Day" (Tsvetaeva)
See "V den' Blagoveshchen'ia"
"On Another Politician" (Belloc) **24**:36-7
"On Another's Sorrow" (Blake) **12**:7, 33
On Ballycastle Beach (McGuckian) **27**:80, 83-85, 90, 92-95, 99-102, 104
"On Barbara's Shore" (Wakoski) **15**:333
"On Beginning the Study of Anglo-Saxon Grammar" (Borges)
See "Al iniciar el estudio de la gramática anglosajona"
"On Being Asked to Write a Poem Against the War in Vietnam" (Carruth) **10**:77
"On Being Brought from Africa to America" (Wheatley) **3**:338, 340, 346, 349, 353, 362-63
"On Being Yanked from a Favorite Anthology" (Shapiro) **25**:323
"On Blake's Victory over the Spaniards" (Marvell)
See "On the Victory Obtained by Blake over the Spaniards"
"On byl v krayu svyatom" (Lermontov) **18**:289
"On Cheating the Fiddler" (Parker) **28**:362
"On Childhood" (Bradstreet) **10**:38
"On Christmas Eve" (Lowell) **13**:85
"On Court-worme" (Jonson) **17**:197
"On Death" (Clare) **23**:44
"On Desire. A Pindarick" (Behn) **13**:8, 10, 14
"On Don Surly" (Jonson) **17**:197
"On Duelling" (Graves) **6**:144
On Early Trains (Pasternak)
See *Na rannikh poezdakh*
"On Elgin Marbles" (Keats) **1**:279
"On Falling Asleep by Firelight" (Meredith) **28**:189-90, 213
"On Falling Asleep to Birdsong" (Meredith) **28**:192, 213
"On Flower Wreath Hill" (Rexroth) **20**:220-21
"On Food" (Belloc) **24**:17
"On Friendship" (Wheatley) **3**:363
"On Going Back to the Street after Viewing and Art Show" (Bukowski) **18**:5
"On Going Unnoticed" (Frost) **1**:205
"On Gut" (Jonson) **17**:174
"On Handling Some Small Shells from the Windward Islands" (Swenson) **14**:287
"On Himselfe" (Herrick) **9**:87, 89, 131
"On His Books" (Belloc) **24**:31
"On His Mistris" (Donne)
See "Elegie XVI: On his mistris"
"On Imagination" (Wheatley) **3**:336, 338, 353-55
"On Installing an American Kitchen in Lower Austria" (Auden) **1**:24
"On Jenkins' Hill" (Meredith) **28**:206
"On Julia's Clothes" (Herrick)
See "Upon Julia's Clothes"
"On Leaving Some Friends" (Keats) **1**:313;**73**:311
"On Lieutenant Shift" (Jonson) **17**:197
"On Looking at a Copy of Alice Meynell's Poems Given to Me Years Ago by a Friend" (Lowell) **13**:85, 89-90, 99-100
"On Lookout Mountain" (Hayden) **6**:180, 194
"On Lord Holland's Seat near Margate, Kent" (Gray) **2**:143
"On Lucy Countesse of Bedford" (Jonson)
See "On Lucy Countesse of Bedford"
"On Madison" (Tomlinson) **17**:353
"On Major General Lee" (Wheatley)
See "Thoughts on His Excellency Major General Lee"
"On Mr. J. H. in a Fit of Sickness" (Behn) **13**:8
"On My First Daughter" (Jonson) **17**:172, 197
"On My First Son" (Jonson) **17**:172, 177, 197
"On My Own" (Levine) **22**:226
"On My Picture Left in Scotland" (Jonson)
See "On My Picture Left in Scotland"
"On My Son's Return out of England" (Bradstreet) **10**:36, 60
"On My Way Out I Passed over You and the Verrazano Bridge" (Lorde) **12**:138-39
"On Myselfe" (Finch) **21**:146, 155, 165
"On Neal's Ashes" (Ginsberg) **4**:74
"On Not Being Listened To" (McGuckian) **27**:90
"On Obedience" (Duncan) **2**:114
"Partial Comfort" (Parker) **28**:362
"On Parting with My Wife, Jamina" (Milosz) **8**:211
"On Passing the New Menin Gate" (Sassoon) **12**:246
"On Poetry: A Rhapsody" (Swift) **9**:249
"On Police Brutality" (Walker) **20**:294
"On Portents" (Graves) **6**:149, 172-73
"On Prime Ministers" (Belloc) **24**:37
"On Reading an Old Baedeker in Schloss Leopoldskron" (Kumin) **15**:209, 212
"On Reading John Cage" (Paz) **1**:355, 363, 374
"On Reading Omar Khayyam" (Lindsay) **23**:283
"On Reading William Blake's 'The Sick Rose'" (Ginsberg) **4**:55
"On Recollection" (Wheatley) **3**:332, 340, 361
"On Returning to Detroit" (Forche) **10**:144, 156
"On Righteous Indignation" (Chesterton) **28**:114
"On San Gabriel Ridges" (Snyder) **21**:291
"On Scratchbury Camp" (Sassoon) **12**:259
"On Seeing Diana go Maddddddddd" (Madhubuti) **5**:344
"On Sir Voluptuous Beast" (Jonson) **17**:174, 212
"On Spies" (Jonson)
See "On Spies"
"On Squaw Peak" (Hass) **16**:217
"On Swimming" (Zagajewski) **27**:396
"On the Alliance of Education and Government" (Gray)
See "Essay on the Alliance of Education and Government"
"On the Author of . . . *The Way to Health* . . ." (Behn) **13**:8
"On the Battle of Kulikovo Field" (Blok) **21**:8, 26, 29
"On the Beach at Fontana" (Joyce) **22**:136
"On the Beach at Night" (Whitman) **3**:401
"On the Beach at Ostia" (Ferlinghetti) **1**:184
"On the Birth of a Black/Baby/Boy" (Knight) **14**:43
On the Boiler (Yeats) **20**:311
"On the Building of Springfield" (Lindsay) **23**:277, 281, 296
"On the Cliffs" (Swinburne) **24**:313, 315, 317, 319-20, 343
"On the Coming Victory" (Brutus) **24**:117

Cumulative Title Index

"On the Death of Mr. Grinhill, the Famous Painter" (Behn) **13**:8
On the Death of Pushkin (Lermontov) **18**:285
"On the Death of the Late Earl of Rochester" (Behn) **13**:8
"On the Death of the Noble Prince King Edward the Fourth" (Skelton) **25**:339
"On the Death of the Queen" (Finch) **21**:171-72
"On the Death of the Rev. Mr. George Whitefield" (Wheatley)
See "An Elegiac Poem on the Death of George Whitefield"
"On the Death of the Reverend Dr. Sewall" (Wheatley) **3**:342
"On The Dedication of Dorothy Hall" (Dunbar) **5**:131, 134
"On the Departure Platform" (Hardy) **8**:90
"On the Double Ninth Remembering My Brothers" (Wang Wei) **18**:365, 386
"On the Downs" (Chesterton) **28**:98
"On the Eastern Front" (Trakl)
See "Im Osten"
"On the Edge" (Levine) **22**:212
"On the Edge" (Lorde) **12**:137
On the Edge (Levine) **22**:211-12, 216
"On the Escalator" (Zagajewski) **27**:381
On the Eternity of God (Smart)
See *On the Eternity of the Supreme Being*
On the Eternity of the Supreme Being (Smart) **13**:328, 343
"On the Extinction of the Venetian Republic" (Wordsworth) **4**:377
"On the Famous Voyage" (Jonson)
See "On the Famous Voyage"
"On the Field of Kulikovo" (Blok)
See "On the Battle of Kulikovo Field"
"On the First Discovery of Falseness in Amintas. By Mrs. B." (Behn) **13**:20-1
On the Goodness of the Supreme Being (Smart) **13**:340, 359-60
"On the Hall at Stowey" (Tomlinson) **17**:341, 344
"On the Happ Life" (Martial)
See "Vitam quae faciunt beatiorem"
"On the Highest Pillar" (Montale)
See "Sulla colonna più alta"
"On the Hill and Grove at Billborow" (Marvell)
See "Upon the Hill and Grove at Billborow"
"On the Honourable Sir Francis Fane . . ." (Behn) **13**:8
"On the Idle Hill of Summer" (Housman) **2**:185
On the Immensity of the Supreme Being (Smart) **13**:343
"On the Island" (Brutus) **24**:115
"On the Lake" (Goethe)
See "Auf dem See"
"On the Last Performance of" (Hongo) **23**:197
"On the Mantelpiece" (Lowell) **13**:83
"On the Morning of Christ's Nativity" (Milton) **19**:209, 251-54
"On the Move" (Gunn) **26**:184-185, 200, 202, 207, 209
"On the Move" (Gunn) **26**:188-189, 196, 206-208
"On the Murder of Lieutenant José Del Castillo by the Falangist Bravo Martinez, July 12, 1936" (Levine) **22**:223, 225
"On the Occasion of National Mourning" (Nemerov) **24**:289
"On the Ocean Floor" (MacDiarmid) **9**:191
On the Omniscience of the Supreme Being (Smart) **13**:344
"On the Platform" (Nemerov) **24**:262
On the Power of the Supreme Being (Smart) **13**:344
"On the Republic" (Elytis) **21**:123
"On the Rhine" (Arnold) **5**:19, 43
"On the River" (Levine) **22**:228
"On the River Encountering Waters Like the Sea, I Wrote a Short Poem on the Spot" (Tu Fu) **9**:326
"On the Road" (Heaney) **18**:214
"On the Road" (McKay) **2**:205, 220
"On the Road Home" (Stevens) **6**:311-12
"On the Road to Woodlawn" (Roethke) **15**:291, 293-95
On the Scale of One to One (Cassian) **17**:6, 9
On the Sick-Bed (Tagore)
See *Rogsajyae*
"On the South Coast" (Swinburne) **24**:313, 329
"On the Spring" (Gray)
See "Ode on Spring"
"On the Spur of the Moment" (Tu Fu) **9**:323
"On the Square" (Aleixandre)
See "In The Plaza"
"On the Stage of Ghosts a Pale Gleaming" (Mandelstam) **14**:120
"On the Subway" (Olds) **22**:314
"On the Tennis Court at Night" (Kinnell) **26**:260
"On the Threshold" (Gozzano) **10**:174
"On the Threshold of His Greatness, the Poet Comes Down with a Sore Throat" (Nemerov) **24**:267
"On the Victory Obtained by Blake over the Spaniards" (Marvell) **10**:270-71
"On the Way" (Robinson) **1**:468
"On the Way to Lycomedes of Scyrus" (Brodsky)
See "K Likomedu, na Skiros"
"On the Way to School" (Aleixandre) **15**:24
"On the Wide Heath" (Millay) **6**:215, 232, 238
"On the Works of Providence" (Wheatley)
See "Thoughts on the Works of Providence"
On These I Stand: An Anthology of the Best Poems of Countee Cullen (Cullen) **20**:75-76, 79, 82-83
On This Island (Auden)
See "Look, Stranger, on This Island Now"
"On Those That Hated 'The Playboy of the Western World'" (Yeats) **20**:320
"On Torture, a Public Singer" (Belloc) **24**:34
"On Two Ministers of State" (Belloc) **24**:33, 41
"On Universalism" (Knight) **14**:37-8
"On Virtue" (Wheatley) **3**:361
"On Visiting the Tomb of Burns" (Keats) **1**:314
"On Walking Slowly After an Accident" (Smith) **12**:314, 316
"On Watching a World Series Game" (Sanchez) **9**:210, 225
"On Wenlock Edge" (Housman) **2**:180
"Once" (Celan) **10**:97
Once Again (Tagore)
See *Punascha*
"Once and Again" (Carruth) **10**:91
"the once and future dead" (Clifton) **17**:19
"Once by the Pacific" (Frost) **1**:221
"Once in May" (Levine) **22**:217-18
"Once More, the Round" (Roethke) **15**:302
"L'Ondine et le pêcheur" (Gautier) **18**:141
"I" (Joyce) **22**:138, 144, 158, 162, 164, 166, 168
"One Art" (Bishop) **3**:62-3, 66-8
"One at One with his Desire" (Ammons) **16**:50
"One by One" (Levine) **22**:218
"One Day" (Brooke) **24**:86
"One Day in Spring" (Sitwell) **3**:311
"One Day We Play a Game" (Cullen) **20**:67
One for the Rose (Levine) **22**:220, 226
"The One Girl at the Boys' Party" (Olds) **22**:311
One Handful of Sand (Ishikawa)
See *Ichiaku no suna*
One Hundred Poems from the Chinese (Rexroth) **20**:188, 204
100 Selected Poems (Cummings) **5**:86
"125th Street and Abomey" (Lorde) **12**:155, 160
"1 Jan." (Ammons) **16**:21
"1 January 1924" (Mandelstam) **14**:121, 134
"One: Many" (Ammons) **16**:6
"One More Brevity" (Frost) **1**:213
"One Morning in New Hampshire" (Swenson) **14**:249, 275
"One Need Not Be a Chamber to Be Haunted" (Dickinson) **1**:94
"One Night Stand" (Baraka) **4**:6
"One Night's Bond" (Hagiwara Sakutaro) **18**:168-69
"One O'Clock at Night" (Loy) **16**:312, 327
"One of Many" (Smith) **12**:314, 331, 333
"1.1.87" (Heaney) **18**:258
"One or Two I've Finished" (Stein) **18**:342
"One Perfect Rose" (Parker) **28**:361
"One Person" (Wylie) **23**:304-305, 311, 314, 317-18, 321-24
"One Ralph Blossom Soliloquizes" (Hardy) **8**:124
"The One Remains" (Owen) **19**:368
"One Should Not Talk to a Skilled Hunter about What is Forbidden by the Buddha" (Snyder) **21**:292
"One Sided Shoot-Out" (Madhubuti) **5**:321, 345
"164 East 72nd Street" (Merrill) **28**:285
"One Soldier" (Rukeyser) **12**:231
"The One Thing That Can Save America" (Ashbery) **26**:127, 148
"One Thousand Fearful Words for Fidel Castro" (Ferlinghetti) **1**:187
1x1 (Cummings) **5**:83, 107-08
"One Viceroy Resigns" (Kipling) **3**:181, 186
"One View of the Question" (Kipling) **3**:184
"One Volume Missing" (Dove) **6**:114
One Way Ticket (Hughes) **1**:241, 243, 247, 252, 260-61, 268
"One We Knew" (Hardy) **8**:99, 132
"One Who Used To Beat His Way" (Kinnell) **26**:240
"The One Who Was" (Aleixandre) **15**:4
"One Word More" (Browning) **2**:66, 71, 95
"One World" (Tomlinson) **17**:333
"One year" (Illyes)
See "Egy ev"
"One Year" (Olds) **22**:341
"One-Eye, Two-Eyes, Three-Eyes" (Sexton) **2**:365
"The One-Eyed King" (Levine) **22**:213
Onegin's Journey (Pushkin) **10**:400-01
"One grief of thine" (Bridges) **28**:86
"One-Legged Man" (Sassoon) **12**:242, 263
"One's-Self I Sing" (Whitman)
See "Song of Myself"
"Onirocritique" (Apollinaire) **7**:12
"Only a Curl" (Browning) **6**:24, 30
"Only a Few Left" (Madhubuti) **5**:340
"Only a Little Sleep, a Little Slumber" (Hughes) **7**:154
"Only Child" (Page) **12**:170, 175-76
"The Only One" (Holderlin)
See "Der Einzige"
"Ons As Me Thought" (Wyatt) **27**:316
"The Onset" (Frost) **1**:222
"Ontological Episode of the Asylum" (Carruth) **10**:89
"The Oon Olympian" (MacDiarmid) **9**:197
"Oonts" (Kipling) **3**:158
"The Open Boat" (Levine) **22**:223
Open Eye, Open Heart (Ferlinghetti) **1**:186-88
"Open House" (Roethke) **15**:291, 293, 302
Open House (Roethke) **15**:245-46, 248, 250, 256, 259, 282, 287, 290-91, 293-95, 298, 304
"Open It, Write" (Ekeloef) **23**:62, 64
"Open Rose" (McGuckian) **27**:105
"Open Sea" (Neruda) **4**:282
The Open Sea (Masters) **1**:333, 335
"The Open Sea" (Meredith) **28**:182, 190, 212
The Open Sea and Other Poems (Meredith) **28**:171, 174-75, 177, 181, 187-92, 194, 200-01, 210-11, 213, 215
"Open the Door to Me, O" (Burns) **6**:75
"Open the Gates" (Kunitz) **19**:155, 162, 173-74, 176-77, 186
The Opening of the Field (Duncan) **2**:103-04,

106, 113-14, 120, 122, 124-25, 127-28
Openings (Berry) **28**:5, 15-16
"An Opera House" (Lowell) **13**:79
"The Operation" (Sexton) **2**:348, 350, 353, 361, 365
"The Operation" (Tomlinson) **17**:360
"Ophélie" (Rimbaud) **3**:283
"Opiário" (Pessoa) **20**:166
"Oppositions" (Wright) **14**:379
"Oppositions debate with Mallarmé" (Tomlinson) **17**:338-39
"Opredelenyie poezii" (Pasternak) **6**:272, 285
"The Optimist's Salutation" (Dario)
See "Salutación del optimista"
Opus incertum (Ekeloef) **23**:63, 76
Opus incertum II (Ekeloef) **23**:77
Opus Posthumous (Stevens) **6**:306, 339
"Ópyt análiza chetyryokhstópnogo yàmba" (Bely) **11**:18
"Or When Your Sister Sleeps Around for Money" (Knight)
See "The Violent Space (or when your sister sleeps around for money)"
"Oración" (Fuertes) **27**:5, 11, 30
"Oracion" (Neruda) **4**:278
"Oración para altas horas de la madrugada" (Fuertes) **27**:39
Oracion por Marilyn Monroe y otros poemas (Cardenal) **22**:125
"Oracle" (Heaney) **18**:201, 203
"The Oracle" (Merton) **10**:339
"Oracle over Managua" (Cardenal)
See "Oráculo sobre Managua"
"The Oracles" (Housman) **2**:164
"Les oracles" (Vigny) **26**:369, 403, 405
"Oráculo sobre Managua" (Cardenal) **22**:103-06
"Oraculos" (Cardenal) **22**:131
"Orange In" (Stein) **18**:318, 328
"Orange of Midsummer" (Lowell) **13**:97
"The Orange Tree" (Levertov) **11**:169
"Orange-Tree" (Wright) **14**:341
"Oration on Death" (Bryant) **20**:13
The Orators (Auden) **1**:4-5, 8-11, 16, 22, 25, 30-1, 37
"Orbits" (Cassian) **17**:11
"Orchard" (H. D.)
See "Priapus"
"The Orchid House" (McGuckian) **27**:97
The Order of Nature (Bryant) **20**:5
"Orders" (Duncan) **2**:125
"The Ordinary" (Stryk) **27**:208, 214
"An Ordinary Evening in New Haven" (Stevens) **6**:338
"An Ordinary Girl" (Sirkis) **8**:417
"An Ordinary Morning" (Levine) **22**:224
An Ordinary Woman (Clifton) **17**:21, 23-24, 26, 34, 37
"Ordinary Women" (Stevens) **6**:295
"The Ordination" (Burns) **6**:83, 88
L'Ordre des Oiseaux (Perse) **23**:254, 256
"Oread" (H. D.) **5**:268, 275, 304
"Gli orecchini" (Montale) **13**:108, 128
"Orestes-Theme" (H. D.) **5**:305
"Organelle" (Swenson) **14**:247
"Organic Bloom" (Kunitz) **19**:148
"Organs" (Swenson) **14**:276
"L'orgie Parisienne; ou, Paris se Repeuple" (Rimbaud) **3**:281
"Oriana" (Tennyson) **6**:359
"The Oriental Ballerina" (Dove) **6**:113
Les orientales (Hugo) **17**:45, 50-52, 55, 62-63, 70, 74-76, 87, 90-91
Orientations (Elytis)
See *Prosanatolizmí*
"Origin" (Harjo) **27**:64
"The Origin of Cities" (Hass) **16**:199
"Original Child Bomb" (Merton) **10**:337
"Original Memory" (Harjo) **27**:68
"Original Sin" (Jeffers) **17**:132
"The Originators" (Merton) **10**:345
"Origins and History of Consciousness" (Rich) **5**:374
"Orion" (Elytis) **21**:118
"Orlovu" (Pushkin) **10**:409
"Ornières" (Rimbaud) **3**:264
El oro de los tigres (Borges) **22**:79-81, 93, 95
The Orphan Angel (Wylie) **23**:329
"The Orphan Reformed" (Smith) **12**:326
"L'Orphée" (Ronsard) **11**:251
"Orphée" (Valery) **9**:351
"L'orphelin" (Mallarme) **4**:202
"Orpheus" (Meredith) **28**:191-92
Orpheus (Rukeyser) **12**:207, 213-14, 220
"Orpheus and Eurydice" (Noyes) **27**:118, 134
"Orpheus. Eurydike. Hermes" (Rilke) **2**:295
"Orphic Scenario" (Nemerov) **24**:257, 294-97
"L'orto" (Montale) **13**:109-10, 121-22, 133
"Osgar" (Pushkin) **10**:407
"Osiris and Set" (Duncan) **2**:103
"Osiris, Come to Iris" (Thomas) **2**:402
Osiris Jones (Aiken) **26**:12, 29
"Osobny zeszyt" (Milosz) **8**:186-87, 199, 204
Osorio (Coleridge)
See *Remorse*
Ossi di seppia (Montale) **13**:103, 105-07, 109, 112-17, 119, 122, 126-27, 131, 133-34, 139, 141, 143, 160, 162-66
"Ossian's Grave" (Jeffers) **17**:117
"Ostanovka v pustyne" (Brodsky) **9**:3, 5, 7
"Ostriches & Grandmothers" (Baraka) **4**:15
"osynlig närvaro" (Ekeloef) **23**:88-92
"The Other" (Borges)
See "El otro"
"The Other" (Sexton) **2**:365
The Other Half (Wright) **14**:349, 355-56, 362, 366
"The Other Noah" (Elytis) **21**:123
"The Other One" (Borges)
See "El otro"
"The Other Side" (Heaney) **18**:205
"The Other Tiger" (Borges)
See "El otro tigre"
"Others I Am Not the First" (Housman) **2**:179, 195
"An Otherworldly Evening" (Tsvetaeva)
See "Nezdeshnii vecher"
Otho the Great (Keats) **1**:279
"Otoño" (Neruda) **4**:290
"El otro" (Borges) **22**:74
El otro, el mismo (Borges) **22**:71, 73-4, 95-6, 98, 100
"El otro tigre" (Borges) **22**:73, 96-7
"Otrok" (Tsvetaeva) **14**:315-16
"Otryvok-A Fragment" (Lermontov) **18**:302
"The Otter" (Heaney) **18**:217, 239, 245
"An Otter" (Hughes) **7**:136, 140
"Our Bodies" (Levertov) **11**:169
"Our Bog Is Dood" (Smith) **12**:331, 333
"Our Cabal" (Behn) **13**:7, 20
Our Dead Behind Us (Lorde) **12**:137-39, 141-43, 148, 154-55, 157-58
"Our English Friends" (Harper) **21**:198
"Our Forward Shadows" (Swenson) **14**:276
"Our Friends in Jail" (Bissett) **14**:7
Our Ground Time Here Will Be Brief (Kumin) **15**:214, 217, 221
"Our Lady of the Sackcloth" (Kipling) **3**:183
"Our Lord and Our Lady" (Belloc) **24**:5
"Our Mother Pocahontas" (Lindsay) **23**:288
"Our Mothers" (Rossetti) **7**:286
"Our Names" (Ortiz) **17**:245
"Our Need" (Walker) **20**:283
"Our Prayer of Thanks" (Sandburg) **2**:316
"Our Storm" (Pasternak) **6**:271
"Our Whole Life" (Rich) **5**:391
"Ourselves or Nothing" (Forche) **10**:137, 143-44, 148, 154, 158-59, 161, 168
"Ourselves We Do Inter with Sweet Derision" (Dickinson) **1**:102
"Out" (Hughes) **7**:123, 149
"Out Is Out" (Nash) **21**:268
"Out of Debt" (McKay) **2**:222
"Out of My Head" (Swenson) **14**:255, 266, 282
"Out of Superstition" (Pasternak)
See "From Superstition"
"Out of the Aegean" (Elytis) **21**:118
"Out of the Cradle Endlessly Rocking" (Whitman) **3**:378, 382, 391-92, 397, 401
"Out of the Sea, Early" (Swenson) **14**:264
"Out of the Watercolored Window, When You Look" (Schwartz) **8**:301
"Out on the Lawn I Lie in Bed..." (Auden) **1**:22
"OUT ON THE TOWN JOY RIDIN" (Bissett) **14**:31
"Out, Out--" (Frost) **1**:227
"Out to the Hard Road" (Lorde) **12**:138
"Out Walking" (Zagajewski) **27**:396
"Outcast" (McKay) **2**:213, 217, 221
The Outcasts (Sitwell) **3**:321
"The Outcome of Mr. Buck's Superstition" (Nash) **21**:267
"The Outdoor Concert" (Gunn) **26**:195, 208
Outdoor Show (Cassian) **17**:6
"The Outer Banks" (Rukeyser) **12**:224
"The Outlaw" (Heaney) **18**:200
"Outlines" (Lorde) **12**:137
"Outside a Gate" (Lowell) **13**:94
"Outside my window" (Viereck) **27**:278
"Outside the Diner" (Gunn) **26**:214
"Outside the Operating Room of the Sex-Change Doctor" (Olds) **22**:316
"The Oven Bird" (Frost) **1**:222
"Ovenstone" (Guillen) **23**:102
"Over 2,000 Illustrations" (Bishop) **3**:67
Over All the Obscene Boundaries: European Poems & Transitions (Ferlinghetti) **1**:183-85
"Over Brooklyn Bridge" (Tomlinson) **17**:359
"Over Cities" (Milosz) **8**:186
"Over Denver Again" (Ginsberg) **4**:57
"Over Sir John's Hill" (Thomas) **2**:395, 404
"Over St. John's Hill" (Thomas)
See "Over Sir John's Hill"
"Over Us If (as what Was Dusk Becomes" (Cummings) **5**:109
"The Overgrown Pasture" (Lowell) **13**:60, 78, 85
"Overheard" (Kipling) **3**:193
"Overheard" (Levertov) **11**:160
"Overland to the Islands" (Levertov) **11**:188, 192, 196
Overland to the Islands (Levertov) **11**:166, 188, 202
"Overlooking the River Stour" (Hardy) **8**:116-17
"Overpopulation" (Ferlinghetti) **1**:167, 175, 187
"Overture to a Dance of Locomotives" (Williams) **7**:345, 410
"Overtures to Death" (Day Lewis) **11**:144
Overtures to Death and Other Poems (Day Lewis) **11**:127-30, 144
"Ovid in Exile" (Graves) **6**:164
"Ovid, Old Buddy, I Would Discourse with You a While" (Carruth) **10**:88
Ovnis ' (Cardenal)
See *Los ovnis de oro*
Los ovnis de oro (Cardenal) **22**:126, 132
"Owatari Bridge" (Hagiwara Sakutaro) **18**:183
See "Owatari-bashi"
"Owatari-bashi" (Hagiwara Sakutaro) **18**:183
"Owen Ahern and His Dancers" (Yeats) **20**:328
"The Owl in the Sarcophagus" (Stevens) **6**:304
"Owl Song" (Atwood) **8**:25
Owl's Clover (Stevens) **6**:297-98, 317-20
"Owl's Song" (Hughes) **7**:160-61
"The Ox Tamer" (Whitman) **3**:377
"The Oxen" (Hardy) **8**:112, 121
"Oxen: Ploughing at Fiesole" (Tomlinson) **17**:311
"Oxford" (Auden) **1**:30
"Oysters" (Heaney) **18**:217, 239, 241
"Oysters" (Sexton) **2**:365
"Oysters" (Snyder) **21**:292
"Ozone" (Dove) **6**:121-23

Cumulative Title Index

P. 1 (Pindar)
See *Pythian 1*
P. 2 (Pindar)
See *Pythian 2*
P. 3 (Pindar)
See *Pythian 3*
P. 4 (Pindar)
See *Pythian 4*
P. 5 (Pindar)
See *Pythian 5*
P. 6 (Pindar)
See *Pythian 6*
P. 8 (Pindar)
See *Pythian 8*
Pacchiarotto (Browning) **2**:71
"A Pacific State" (Milosz) **8**:205
"A Packet of Letters" (Bogan) **12**:94
"Pacific Letter" (Ondaatje) **28**:316
Paean 8 (Pindar) **19**:396
"Paesaggio I" (Pavese) **13**:204, 212, 220, 225-26
"Paesaggio II" (Pavese) **13**:212
"Paesaggio III" (Pavese) **13**:212
"Paesaggio V" (Pavese) **13**:212
"Paesaggio VI" (Pavese) **13**:228
"Paesaggio VII" (Pavese) **13**:204, 212
"Paesaggio VIII" (Pavese) **13**:212, 230
"The Pagan Isms" (McKay) **2**:219-20
"Pagan Prayer" (Cullen) **20**:65, 72
A Pageant, and Other Poems (Rossetti) **7**:270
The Pageant of Seasons
See *Rtusamhara*
"Pagett, M. P." (Kipling) **3**:190
"La página blanca" (Dario) **15**:103-04
Paginas (Jimenez) **7**:208, 212
"The Pahty" (Dunbar) **5**:116, 119, 122-23, 146
Paid on Both Sides (Auden) **1**:5, 8, 20, 30, 34
"Pain for a Daughter" (Sexton) **2**:363
"Pain Tells You Want to Wear" (McGuckian) **27**:103
"The Pains of Sleep" (Coleridge) **11**:41, 44
"The Painted Cup" (Bryant) **20**:23
Painted Lace and Other Pieces (1914-1937) (Stein) **18**:341
"Painted Steps" (Gallagher) **9**:45
"The Painter" (Ashbery) **26**:112, 167
"The Painter Dreaming in the Scholar's House" (Nemerov) **24**:285, 300
"The Painting" (Williams) **7**:394
"Painting the North San Juan School" (Snyder) **21**:300
"Paisaje de la multitud que orina" (Garcia Lorca) **3**:140
"Paisaje de la multitud que vomita" (Garcia Lorca) **3**:140
"Paisaje del corozon" (Jimenez) **7**:199
"Paisaje después de una batalla" (Neruda) **4**:309
"Los Pájaros Anidan" (Fuertes) **27**:51
"Palabras" (Aleixandre) **15**:39
"Las palabras" (Paz) **1**:358
"Las palabras del poeta" (Aleixandre) **15**:41
"Palabras en el trópico" (Guillen) **23**:106
"Palace" (Apollinaire)
See "Palais"
"The Palace" (Ondaatje) **28**:337
"The Palace of Art" (Tennyson) **6**:353, 359-60, 370, 375, 378-80, 382, 409, 412
"The Palace of Pan" (Swinburne) **24**:313
"The Palace of the Babies" (Stevens) **6**:293
"Palais" (Apollinaire) **7**:45-6, 48
"Palais des Arts" (Gluck) **16**:130, 150
"Palamon and Arcite" (Chaucer)
See "Knight's Tale"
Palataka (Tagore) **8**:415
"A Pale Arrangement of Hands" (Song) **21**:334, 341-42
"Pale Horse" (Hagiwara Sakutaro) **18**:176-77
"Pale, Intent Noontide" (Montale)
See "Meriggiare pallido e assorto"
"Pâline" (Apollinaire) **7**:48
"Palladium" (Arnold) **5**:8
"Pallas Athene" (Masters) **1**:344
"Palm" (Valery)
See "Palme"
"Palm and Pine" (Kipling) **3**:179
"Palme" (Valery) **9**:363, 365, 367, 393-94
"Palo Alto: The Marshes" (Hass) **16**:218
La paloma de vuelo popular: Elegiás (Guillen) **23**:100, 124, 128, 133
"Pals" (Sandburg) **2**:303
"Paltry Nude" (Stevens) **6**:295
"The Paltry Nude Starts on a Spring Voyage" (Stevens) **6**:295
"Pamiatnik" (Pushkin)
See "Pamjatnik"
"Pamjatnik" (Pushkin) **10**:408, 412, 415
"Pan" (Hugo) **17**:91
"Pan and Luna" (Browning) **2**:88-9
"Pan and Thalassius" (Swinburne) **24**:315
"Pan and Thalassius" (Swinburne) **24**:315
"Panamá" (Guillen) **23**:126
"Panchishe vaisakh" (Tagore) **8**:415
"A Panegerick to Sir Lewis Pemberton" (Herrick) **9**:102
"A Panegyrick on the Dean in the Person of a Lady in the North" (Swift) **9**:262, 274, 295
"Panegyrique de la Renommée" (Ronsard) **11**:243
"The Pangolin" (Moore) **4**:235
"Panorama ceigo de Nueva York" (Garcia Lorca) **3**:141
The Panther and the Lash: Poems of Our Times (Hughes) **1**:251-52, 257-58, 260, 262, 268
"Pantomime" (Verlaine) **2**:430
"Paolo e Virginia" (Pavese) **13**:221
"The Papa and Mama Dance" (Sexton) **2**:349, 352-53
"Papà beve sempre" (Pavese) **13**:214
"Papa Love Baby" (Smith) **12**:315, 322, 325-26, 343
"The Paper Nautilus" (Moore) **4**:255
"The Paper on the Floor" (Bukowski) **18**:3
"The Paper Wind Mill" (Lowell) **13**:78
"Le papillon" (Lamartine) **16**:278
Para las seis cuerdas (Borges) **22**:71
"Parable of a Certain Virgin" (Parker) **28**:348
"Parable of the Hostages" (Gluck) **16**:171
"The Parable of the Old Man and the Young" (Owen) **19**:335, 354, 356, 359, 370
Paracelsus (Browning) **2**:26-31, 34, 42-3, 48, 65-6, 73, 82, 91-3, 96
"Parade of Painters" (Swenson) **14**:253
"Paradis Perdu" (Nishiwaki) **15**:237
"Paradise" (Gallagher) **9**:64
"Paradise" (Gluck) **16**:161
"Paradise" (Herbert) **4**:114, 130
Paradise Lost (Milton) **19**:193-200, 203-12, 219, 224, 234-36, 238, 240-49, 252, 254, 258
"Paradise of Tears" (Bryant) **20**:10
"Paradise on the Roofs" (Pavese) **13**:204
Paradise Regained (Milton) **19**:204-06, 208, 214-16, 219
Paradiso (Dante) **21**:49-50, 53-5, 57-8, 67, 69, 72, 75-7, 81-2, 92, 94, 96, 103-06, 109-11
"Paradox" (Lowell) **13**:85
The Paradox (Noyes) **27**:138
"Paragraphs" (Carruth) **10**:74-5, 83, 85
"Parajaya sangit" (Tagore) **8**:405
Parallel Destinies (Cassian) **17**:6
Parallèlement (Verlaine) **2**:414, 416-17, 419, 425-26
"Paralysis" (Brooke) **24**:56, 77
"Paralytic" (Plath) **1**:391
"Paranoid" (Page) **12**:175
"Paraphrase" (Crane) **3**:102
"The Parasceve, or Preparation" (Herrick) **9**:117, 119
"Parchiarotto" (Browning) **2**:63, 71, 75
"Pardoner's Prologue" (Chaucer) **19**:26, 46
"Pardoner's Tale" (Chaucer) **19**:13, 30, 46, 49, 51-2, 68
"Paréntesis pasional" (Borges) **22**:92
"Parents" (Meredith) **28**:180, 208
"The Parents: People Like Our Marriage, Maxie and Andrew" (Brooks) **7**:80
"Parfum exotique" (Baudelaire) **1**:45
"Paring the Apple" (Tomlinson) **17**:331
"Paris" (Ondaatje) **28**:298-99
"Paris" (Stryk) **27**:214
"Paris" (Vigny) **26**:402, 411-12
"Paris and Helen" (Schwartz) **8**:311
"Paris at Nightfall" (Baudelaire)
See "Le crépuscule du soir"
"Paris in the Snow" (Senghor) **25**:241
Paris Spleen (Baudelaire)
See *Petits poèmes en prose: Le spleen de Paris*
"A Parisian Dream" (Baudelaire)
See "Rêve parisien"
The Parisian Prowler (Baudelaire)
See *Petits poèmes en prose: Le spleen de Paris*
"Parisina" (Byron) **16**:109
"The Park" (Stryk) **27**:211
"Park Bench" (Hughes) **1**:242
"The Parklands" (Smith) **12**:317
Parlement (Chaucer)
See *Parlement of Foules*
Parlement of Foules (Chaucer) **19**:10, 12, 20-3, 38, 74
"Parleying with Charles Avison" (Browning) **2**:83
"Parleying with Gerard de Lairesse" (Browning) **2**:81, 83, 86
Parleyings with Certain People of Importance in Their Day (Browning) **2**:64, 85, 95-6
"Parlez-vous français" (Schwartz) **8**:302-03
"Parliament Hill Fields" (Plath) **1**:391
Parliament of Fowls (Chaucer)
See *Parlement of Foules*
"Parlour-Piece" (Hughes) **7**:140
"Parnell's Funeral" (Yeats) **20**:326, 348
"Parodos" (Gluck) **16**:159-62
"Le parole" (Montale) **13**:134
"La Parole aux Oricous" (Cesaire) **25**:12
"Paroles sur la dune" (Hugo) **17**:64
"Parrots" (Wright) **14**:348
"The Parrot Fish" (Merrill) **28**:247
"Parsley" (Dove) **6**:105, 110
"The Parson's Daughter and the Seminarist" (Bely) **11**:3
"Parson's Tale" (Chaucer) **19**:37, 45, 47
A Part (Berry) **28**:4, 9-10
"Part of a Bird" (Cassian) **17**:4, 12-13
"A Part of Speech" (Brodsky)
See "Cast reci"
A Part of Speech (Brodsky)
See *Cast reci*
"Part of the Doctrine" (Baraka) **4**:18
"Part of the Seventh Epistle of the First Book of Horace Imitated and Addressed to the Earl of Oxford" (Swift) **9**:296
"Part of the Vigil" (Merrill) **28**:221, 224
"Parted" (Dunbar) **5**:125, 140
"Partial Accounts" (Meredith) **28**:205, 215
Partial Accounts: New and Selected Poems (Meredith) **28**:211-16
"Parting" (Ammons) **16**:63
"Parting" (Arnold) **5**:43, 55
"The Parting" (Harper) **21**:194
"Parting Gift" (Wylie) **23**:321
Partitur (Ekeloef) **23**:68-9, 78
"Partly from the Greek" (Belloc) **24**:32
"The Partner" (Roethke) **15**:256
"The Partner's Desk" (McGuckian) **27**:105
Parts of a World (Stevens) **6**:299, 311, 318
"A Part-Sequence for Change" (Duncan) **2**:103
"Parturition" (Loy) **16**:313-14, 318, 320, 325, 329, 333
"The Party" (Dunbar)
See "The Pahty"
"Les pas" (Valery) **9**:366, 374, 396
Pasado en claro (Paz) **1**:369, 371-72, 374

"Pascuas sangrientas de 1956" (Guillen) **23**:128
Pasión de la tierra (Aleixandre) **15**:3, 10, 18, 29-32, 34, 40
"Pass on by" (Guillen)
See "Sigue"
Pass th Food Release th Spirit Book (Bissett) **14**:15-16, 24
"Passage" (Ammons) **16**:6
"Passage" (Crane) **3**:82
"Passage" (Levertov) **11**:202
"Passage" (Okigbo) **7**:223-24, 231, 236-39, 248-49, 251, 255
"Passage de l'oiseau divin" (Breton) **15**:49
"Passage to India" (Whitman) **3**:378, 394-98
"Passages 13" (Duncan) **2**:116
"Passages 21" (Duncan) **2**:116
"Passages 25" (Duncan) **2**:25
"Passages 26" (Duncan) **2**:116
"Passages 27" (Duncan) **2**:116
"Passages 29" (Duncan) **2**:116
"Passages 31" (Duncan) **2**:117
"Passages 35 (Tribunals)" (Duncan) **2**:116, 118
"Passages 36" (Duncan) **2**:115-17
The Passages of Joy (Gunn) **26**:208-209, 211-212, 214, 216-217, 220, 230-231
"Le Passe" (Hugo) **17**:64
"Passe forth my wonted cryes" (Wyatt) **27**:362
"A Passer-By" (Bridges) **28**:67, 70
"Passer mortuus est" (Millay) **6**:228
"Passing Chao-ling Again" (Tu Fu) **9**:322
"The Passing Cloud" (Smith) **12**:339
"Passing Losses On" (Frost) **1**:200
"The Passing of Arthur" (Tennyson)
See "Morte d'Arthur"
"The Passing of the Hawthorn" (Swinburne) **24**:313, 317
"Passing Through" (Kunitz) **19**:187
"Passing Through Little Rock" (Ortiz) **17**:227
Passing Through: The Later Poems New and Selected (Kunitz) **19**:186
"Passion" (Trakl) **20**:269
The Passion of Claude McKay: Selected Poetry and Prose, 1912-1948 (McKay) **2**:218
Passion of the Earth (Aleixandre)
See *Pasión de la tierra*
"La passione" (Pasolini) **17**:288
Passione e ideologia (Pasolini) **17**:250, 252, 263-64, 291, 295
Passport to the War (Kunitz) **19**:148, 154, 160-62
"The Past" (Bryant) **20**:9
"The Past" (Emerson) **18**:76
"Past" (Sanchez) **9**:219
The Past (Kinnell) **26**:277-78, 292-93
"Past and Future" (Browning) **6**:16, 41
"Past and Present" (Masters) **1**:343
"Past Days" (Swinburne) **24**:327, 329
"The Past Is the Present" (Moore) **4**:237
"Pastor hacia el puerto" (Aleixandre) **15**:35
"Pastoral" (Dove) **6**:120-21
"The Pastoral" (Soto) **28**:370
"Pastoral" (Viereck) **27**:271
"Pastoral" (Williams) **7**:367, 378
Pastoral (Williams) **7**:349
"Pastoral Dialogue" (Swift) **9**:261
"A Pastoral Pindaric . . ." (Behn) **13**:8
Pastoral Poesy (Clare) **23**:4
"A Pastoral to Mr. Stafford" (Behn) **13**:8, 32
"Pastorale" (Crane) **3**:98-9
Pastorales (Jimenez) **7**:184
"A Pastorall Song to the King" (Herrick) **9**:86
Pastorals (Pope) **26**:319, 321
Pastorals (Vergil)
See *Georgics*
"Pastorela di Narcis" (Pasolini) **17**:253, 282
"The Pasture" (Frost) **1**:197, 212, 225
"Patent Leather" (Brooks) **7**:58, 68, 79
"Pater Filio" (Bridges) **28**:89
"Paternità" (Pavese) **13**:213, 229
"Paternity" (Pavese)
See "Paternità"
"Paterson" (Ginsberg) **4**:73-5
Paterson (Williams) **7**:350, 354-60, 362, 364-65, 370-75, 377, 379, 392-95, 402-03, 408-10
Paterson I (Williams) **7**:354, 357-58, 360, 365
Paterson II (Williams) **7**:363, 391-92
Paterson IV (Williams) **7**:363, 392
Paterson V (Williams) **7**:364-65, 370-71, 393
"Paterson: Episode 17" (Williams) **7**:360
"The Path" (Dunbar) **5**:125
"The Path Among the Stones" (Kinnell) **26**:252, 269, 273, 275-76
"Path of the Chameleon" (Wylie) **23**:330
"Path of Thunder" (Okigbo) **7**:228, 246-47, 255
Path of Thunder (Okigbo)
See *Labyrinths, with Path of Thunder*
"Paths and Thingscape" (Atwood) **8**:36
"Patience" (Graves) **6**:154
"Patience" (Lowell) **13**:60
"Patmos" (Holderlin) **4**:148, 150-51, 153, 155-57, 159, 166, 172
Patria o muerte! The Great Zoo, and Other Poems by Nicolás Guillén (Guillen)
See *El gran zoo*
"Patriotic Poem" (Wakoski) **15**:358
"The Patroit" (Browning) **2**:60
"Patterns" (Lowell) **13**:60, 71, 76-7, 84-5, 89, 96
"Patterns" (Wright) **14**:376
"Paul and Virginia" (Gozzano) **10**:176, 178, 180-84
Paul Celan: Poems (Celan) **10**:95-6, 107-08, 114
"Paul Robeson" (Brooks) **7**:92-3
"Paula Becker To Clara Westhoff" (Rich) **5**:379
Pauline: A Fragment of a Confession (Browning) **2**:25-6, 42-3, 48, 66, 90-2, 94
"Paul's Wife" (Frost) **1**:194
"Paumanok" (Clampitt) **19**:102
"A Pause for Thought" (Rossetti) **7**:280, 297
"Pauvre Lélian" (Verlaine) **2**:416
"Les pauvres à l'église" (Rimbaud) **3**:255
"Les pauvres gens" (Hugo) **17**:61
"Pavitra prem" (Tagore) **8**:407
"The Pawnbroker" (Kumin) **15**:180, 192, 200
"Pax" (Dario) **15**:82, 115
"Pay Day" (Hughes) **1**:255
"Pay Day" (McKay) **2**:226
"Paying Calls" (Hardy) **8**:105
"Paysage" (Apollinaire) **7**:32, 34-5
"Paysage Moralisé" (Auden) **1**:23
"Paysages belges" (Verlaine) **2**:415
"Peace" (Brooke) **24**:59, 74, 79-80, 87-9
"Peace" (Clare) **23**:44
"Peace" (Dario)
See "Pax"
"Peace" (Herbert) **4**:101, 134
"Peace" (Hopkins) **15**:127
"Peace" (Levine) **22**:219
"Peace" (Yeats) **20**:329
"The Peace-Offering" (Hardy) **8**:93
"Peach Blossom Spring" (Wang Wei) **18**:374
"Peacock" (Merrill) **28**:234
"The Peacock Room" (Hayden) **6**:193-95, 198
"Pear Tree" (H. D.) **5**:275
"The Pearl" (Herbert) **4**:100, 128
"The Pearl Diver" (Wylie) **23**:321
"Pearl Horizons" (Sandburg) **2**:307
"The Peasant Whore" (Pavese)
See "La puttana contadina"
"The Peasant's Confession" (Hardy) **8**:124
"Pedantic Literalist" (Moore) **4**:229
"Pedro as el cuando..." (Neruda) **4**:288
"Peekaboo, I Almost See You" (Nash) **21**:269-70
"Peele Castle" (Wordsworth)
See "Stanzas on Peele Castle"
"Peers" (Toomer) **7**:336-37
Peers (Belloc) **24**:49
"Pelleas and Ettarre" (Tennyson) **6**:376
"The Pen" (Kinnell) **26**:293
"A Pencil" (Hass) **16**:196
"Penelope" (Parker) **28**:362
"Penelope's Song" (Gluck) **16**:172
"The Peninsula" (Heaney) **18**:200, 222-23
"The Penitent" (Millay) **6**:211
Penny Wheep (MacDiarmid) **9**:151, 158, 166, 179, 188
"The Pennycandystore beyond the El" (Ferlinghetti) **1**:187
"Pensar, dudar" (Hugo) **17**:92, 96-97
"Pensées des morts" (Lamartine) **16**:280
"Pensieri di Deola" (Pavese) **13**:214
"Pente" (Tzara) **27**:229-31
"La pente de la rêverie" (Hugo) **17**:48, 91, 93
"Penthesilea" (Noyes) **27**:115
"Penúltima canción de Don Simón" (Fuertes) **27**:40
"Penumbra" (Lowell) **13**:64
"People" (Toomer) **7**:336-37
"The People" (Yeats) **20**:328
"THE PEOPLE BURNING" (Baraka) **4**:12
"People Getting Divorced" (Ferlinghetti) **1**:183
"People of Unrest" (Walker) **20**:282
"People Who Don't Understand" (Pavese)
See "Gente che non capisce"
"People Who Have No Children" (Brooks) **7**:75
"People Who've Been There" (Pavese) **13**:218
The People, Yes (Sandburg) **2**:317-18, 320-23, 325-26, 328, 330, 333, 335-39, 341
A Peopled Landscape (Tomlinson) **17**:305, 309, 317-18, 327, 333, 335, 337, 341
Pepel' (Bely) **11**:3-4, 6-7, 24, 30-2
"La pequeña oda a un negro boxeador cubano" (Guillen) **23**:98
"Pequeña oda a un negro boxeador cubano" (Guillen) **23**:99, 103, 105-107
"Per album" (Montale) **13**:130
"Per quella via che la bellezza corre" (Dante) **21**:74
"Per un ritorna al paese" (Pasolini) **17**:266
"The Perch" (Kinnell) **26**:287
"Lo perdido" (Borges) **22**:80
"Perdition" (Cesaire) **25**:29
"Perdón si por mis ojos..." (Neruda) **4**:288
"Peregrinaciones" (Dario) **15**:82
"Peregrinations" (Dario)
See "Peregrinaciones"
"Peregrine" (Wylie) **23**:307, 310, 324
"Perekop" (Tsvetaeva) **14**:326-27
"Peremena" (Pasternak) **6**:285
"The Perennial Answer" (Rich) **5**:351-52
"Perennials" (Levine) **22**:228
Pereulochki (Tsvetaeva) **14**:325-26
"Perfect" (MacDiarmid) **9**:177
"The Perfect Husband" (Nash) **21**:278
"The Perfect Sky" (Gallagher) **9**:59
"Perforation, Concerning Genius" (Pinsky) **27**:144
"The Performers" (Hayden) **6**:195
"Perhaps No Poem But All I Can Say and I Cannot Be Silent" (Levertov) **11**:198
"Perhaps the Best Time" (Meredith) **28**:174
"The Permanent Tourists" (Page) **12**:178, 181-89
"Perpetuum Mobile: The City" (Williams) **7**:350
"Le Perroquet" (Perse) **23**:228, 254-56
"Persée et Andromède" (Laforgue) **14**:93
"Persephone" (Smith) **12**:331-32
"The Persian" (Smith) **12**:330
"A Persian Suite" (Stryk) **27**:186-87
"The Persian Version" (Graves) **6**:143, 152
Persimmon (Viereck) **27**:282, 284
The Persimmon Tree (Viereck) **27**:271
"Persimmons" (Lee) **24**:243, 246
Person, Place, and Thing (Shapiro) **25**:261-64, 267-69, 276, 285, 288, 295, 308, 318-19, 322, 324
Personae (Pound) **4**:317
"Personae separatae" (Montale) **13**:
"Personae Separatae" (Montale) **13**:106, 126
"Personal" (Hughes) **1**:241, 259
"Personal Helicon" (Heaney) **18**:200, 217
"Personal Landscape" (Page) **12**:178, 190

"Personal Letter No. 2" (Sanchez) **9**:224, 232-33
"Personal Letter No. 3" (Sanchez) **9**:225
"La perte de l'anio" (Lamartine) **16**:292
Pervaja simfonija (Bely) **11**:17
"Pervaya pesenka" (Akhmatova) **2**:9
Pervoe svidanie (Bely) **11**:3, 7-11, 17-21, 28-9, 31-3
"Pesnia poslednei vstrechi" (Akhmatova) **2**:11
"Peter" (Moore) **4**:257
"Peter" (Ondaatje) **28**:292-93, 298-99, 318, 321
"Peter and John" (Wylie) **23**:324
Peter Bell (Wordsworth) **4**:399, 420
Peter Bell the Third (Shelley) **14**:175
"Peter Goole" (Belloc) **24**:18
"Peter Quince at the Clavier" (Stevens) **6**:293, 295, 300-01
"Peterhot Holiday" (Lermontov) **18**:285
"Petit Paul" (Hugo) **17**:56
"Le Petit Roi de Galicie" (Hugo) **17**:61
Le Petit Testament (Villon)
See *Les Lais*
Petite prière sans prétentions (Laforgue) **14**:63
"Petite Ville" (Tzara) **27**:223
"Petite Ville en Sibérie" (Tzara) **27**:223
"Les petites vielles" (Baudelaire) **1**:45, 64
"Pétition" (Laforgue) **14**:73
"The Petition for an Absolute Retreat" (Finch) **21**:142-43, 145-48, 156-57, 164, 170, 172, 175
Petits poèmes en prose: Le spleen de Paris (Baudelaire) **1**:48-9, 58-9
"Petrificada petrificante" (Paz) **1**:367
"Pettichap's Nest" (Clare) **23**:5
"A Petticoat" (Stein) **18**:330, 341
"Pevitsa" (Tsvetaeva) **14**:325, 327
"Phaedra" (H. D.) **5**:267
"Phaius Orchid" (Wright) **14**:346, 361
"Phantasia for Elvira Shatayev" (Rich) **5**:377
Phantasmagoria (Carroll) **18**:46, 48
Phantom Dwelling (Wright) **14**:374-75, 379
"The Phantom Horsewoman" (Hardy) **8**:91, 136
"Phèdre" (Smith) **12**:331-32
"Phenomenal Survivals of Death in Nantucket" (Gluck) **16**:131, 135, 139
"The Phenomenology of Anger" (Rich) **5**:371-72, 384, 394
"Philemon and Baucis" (Gunn) **26**:214
Philip Sparrow (Skelton) **25**:330, 332-33, 335, 343-44, 346, 348, 353-54, 356-60, 367, 369, 374, 380-82, 384, 393-94, 396-400
"Phillis; or, The Progress of Love, 1716" (Swift) **9**:253
"Philomela" (Arnold) **5**:37-8, 41, 46-7
"The Philosophers" (Merton) **10**:337
"The Philosopher and His Mistress" (Bridges) **28**:87
"The Philosopher to His Mistress" (Bridges) **28**:87
"Philosophy" (Dunbar) **5**:144
"The Phoenix and the Tortoise" (Rexroth) **20**:178
The Phoenix and the Tortoise (Rexroth) **20**:180, 182-84, 192-94, 198-202, 210, 212-13, 217
"Phone Call from Mexico" (Page) **12**:198
"The Photograph" (Smith) **12**:308, 346
"Photograph of My Room" (Forche) **10**:144, 156
"Photograph of the Girl" (Olds) **22**:313
"The Photograph of the Unmade Bed" (Rich) **5**:366
"Photographs Courtesy of the Fall River Historical Society" (Olds) **22**:307
"Photomontage of the Urban Parks" (Viereck) **27**:280
"Photos of a Salt Mine" (Page) **12**:167-68, 189
"Phrases" (Rimbaud) **3**:263
"Physcial Union" (Tagore)
See "Deher milan"
"Physician's Tale" (Chaucer) **19**:15, 62
"Piaceri notturni" (Pavese) **13**:205, 226
"Piano" (Shapiro) **25**:269
"A Piano" (Stein) **18**:318, 350
"Piano after War" (Brooks) **7**:73
"The Piano Tuner's Wife" (Shapiro) **25**:303
"La pica" (Fuertes) **27**:30
"Picasso" (Pasolini) **17**:295
"Piccolo testamento" (Montale) **13**:104, 113, 165-66, 168
Pickering MS (Blake) **12**:35-7, 43
"Pickthorn Manor" (Lowell) **13**:60, 77, 84
"Pictor Ignatus" (Browning) **2**:30
"A Picture" (Nemerov) **24**:281
"The Picture" (Tagore)
See "Chhabi"
"Picture Bride" (Song) **21**:334-36, 347-48, 350
Picture Bride (Song) **21**:331-38, 340-41, 343-44, 346-50
"Picture of a Black Child with a White Doll" (Merton) **10**:341, 345
"The Picture of J. T. in a Prospect of Stone" (Tomlinson) **17**:326
"A Picture of Lee Ying" (Merton) **10**:341
"The Picture of Little J A" (Ashbery) **26**:172
"The Picture of Little T. C. in a Prospect of Flowers" (Marvell) **10**:271, 274, 277, 289, 294, 303-04
Picture Show (Sassoon) **12**:257-58, 269
"Pictures By Vuillard" (Rich) **5**:350
Pictures from Brueghel, and Other Poems (Williams) **7**:371-72, 374, 377, 392-93, 403, 408
"Pictures in Smoke" (Parker) **28**:361
Pictures of the Floating World (Lowell) **13**:73-4, 93-4, 96
Pictures of the Gone World (Ferlinghetti) **1**:167-69, 171-75, 186
"A Piece of Coffee" (Stein) **18**:333, 349
"Pieces of History" (Merrill) **28**:256
"Pied Beauty" (Hopkins) **15**:133, 158
"The Pied Piper" (Tsvetaeva)
See "Krysolov"
"Pied Piper of Hamelin" (Browning) **2**:36, 63
"Piedra" (Soto) **28**:378, 383
"Piedra de sol" (Paz) **1**:353
Piedra de sol (Paz) **1**:355-56, 358-59, 368-69, 371, 373, 375-77
"The Pier" (Hongo) **23**:201
"The Pier" (Merrill) **28**:267
"Pierce Street" (Gunn) **26**:231
"The Pier-Glass" (Graves) **6**:137, 142, 172
The Pier-Glass (Graves) **6**:128, 147, 150
Pierrot fumiste (Laforgue) **14**:81
"Pietà" (Gluck) **16**:130
"Pig Glass, 1973-1978" (Ondaatje) **28**:327, 335, 337, 339-40
"Pig Cupid" (Loy) **16**:314-15, 326
"Le pigeon" (Hugo) **17**:100
"Pigeon Woman" (Swenson) **14**:265
"Pigeons, Sussex Avenue" (Ondaatje) **28**:292
"Piggy to Joey" (Smith) **12**:321
"Pig's-Eye View of Literature" (Parker) **28**:348, 353, 362
"Pike" (Hughes) **7**:136, 158
"The Pike" (Lowell) **13**:69
"A Pilgrim" (Bradstreet)
See "As Weary Pilgrim"
"A Pilgrim Dreaming" (Levertov) **11**:209
"The Pilgrimage" (Herbert) **4**:109
"Pilgrimage" (Olds) **22**:309
"Pilgrimage" (Pinsky) **27**:158
The Pilgrimage of Festus (Aiken) **26**:13, 22
Pili's Wall (Levine) **22**:226
"The Pillar of Fame" (Herrick) **9**:106
"The pillar perished is" (Wyatt) **27**:357-58
"Le pin" (Ronsard) **11**:277
A Pindaric on the Death of Our Late Sovereign (Behn) **13**:8
A Pindaric Poem on the Happy Coronation of . . . James II (Behn) **13**:8
"Pindaric Poem to the Reverend Doctor Burnet" (Behn) **13**:32
"A Pindaric to Mr. P. Who Sings Finely" (Behn) **13**:8
"A Pindarick Poem upon the Hurricane" (Finch) **21**:163, 180
"The Pine" (Ronsard)
See "Le pin"
"The Pine Planters (Marty South's Reverie)" (Hardy) **8**:101
"The Pine Trees and the Sky" (Brooke) **24**:76
The Pink Church (Williams) **7**:370
"Pink Dog" (Bishop) **3**:65
"The Pink Dress" (Wakoski) **15**:345, 374-75
"Pink Hands" (Soto) **28**:398-99
"Pink Melon Joy" (Stein) **18**:346
"The pinks along my garden walks" (Bridges) **28**:85
"Pinoy at The Coming World" (Hongo) **23**:198
"Pioggia d'agosto" (Gozzano) **10**:184-85
"The Piper" (Blake) **12**:9
Pippa Passes (Browning) **2**:28, 30, 35, 37, 67
"Il Pirla" (Montale) **13**:138
The Pisan Cantos (Pound) **4**:320, 337, 344-48, 352, 357-58, 360
"The Pit" (Roethke) **15**:302
"The Pit" (Stryk) **27**:195, 202
The Pit and Other Poems (Stryk) **27**:181, 183, 190, 193-94, 198, 214, 216
"Pit Viper" (Momaday) **25**:188, 193-94, 199
"The Pitchfork" (Heaney) **18**:256
La Pitié suprême (Hugo) **17**:65
"Le pitre châtié" (Mallarme) **4**:202
"Pity Me" (Wylie) **23**:321, 324
"Pity Me Not" (Millay) **6**:225
"Pity the Deep in Love" (Cullen) **20**:57
"Pity 'Tis, 'Tis True" (Lowell) **13**:84
"Place; & Names" (Olson) **19**:296
"Place for a Third" (Frost) **1**:194, 221
The Place of Love (Shapiro) **25**:267, 269, 309, 311, 315
"The Place of Value" (Nemerov) **24**:255
"The Place That Is Feared I Inhabit" (Forche) **10**:143
"Place We Have Been" (Ortiz) **17**:228
"A Placeless Heaven" (Heaney) **18**:233
"Places" (Hardy) **8**:91, 104, 135-36
"Places, Loved Ones" (Larkin) **21**:246
"A Plague of Starlings" (Hayden) **6**:185, 195
"The Plaid Dress" (Millay) **6**:234
"Plainte d'automne" (Mallarme) **4**:187
"Plainview: 1" (Momaday) **25**:195, 203, 207, 213
"Plainview: 2" (Momaday) **25**:189, 195-96, 200, 213
"Plainview: 3" (Momaday) **25**:196, 213-14
"Plainview: 4" (Momaday) **25**:196, 213-14
"Un plaisant" (Baudelaire) **1**:59
"Plan for the Young English King" (Pound) **4**:364
"Plan of Future Works" (Pasolini) **17**:257
Planet News: 1961-1967 (Ginsberg) **4**:51-2, 65-6
"Planetarium" (Rich) **5**:366, 370
"Planh for the Young English King" (Pound) **4**:364
"Planning the Garden" (Lowell) **13**:64
"Planning the Perfect Evening" (Dove) **6**:106
Plantain (Akhmatova)
See *Podorozhnik*
"The Plantation" (Heaney) **18**:201, 225
"A Plantation Bacchanal" (Johnson) **24**:153
"A Plantation Portrait" (Dunbar) **5**:147
"The Planted Skull" (Viereck) **27**:265
"The Planters" (Atwood) **8**:36
Platero and I (Jimenez)
See *Platero y Yo*
Platero and I: An Andalusion Elegy (Jimenez)
See *Platero y Yo*
Platero y Yo (Jimenez) **7**:185-89, 191, 199-201, 203
"Planting Trees" (Berry) **28**:37
"Plato Elaborated" (Brodsky) **9**:19, 20
"Platypus" (Wright) **14**:372
"The Play Way" (Heaney) **18**:187
The Player Queen (Yeats) **20**:353

"Playing Cards" (Atwood) **8**:5, 7
"Playing the Inventions" (Nemerov) **24**:285-87
"Playing the Machine" (Nemerov) **24**:301
"Pleading" (McKay) **2**:223
"Please, Master" (Ginsberg) **4**:54, 90
"Pleasure Bay" (Pinsky) **27**:157-58, 161, 164-65, 169, 174, 176
"Pleasures" (Levertov) **11**:159, 164, 189
"Pleasure's Lament" (Tagore)
See "Sukher vilap"
"Pleasures of Spring" (Clare) **23**:14
"Pledge" (Merrill) **28**:284
"Plegaria" (Jimenez) **7**:198
"Plein Ciel" (Hugo) **17**:62, 87
"Pleine Mer" (Hugo) **17**:62, 89
"Plennyi rytsar" (Lermontov) **18**:291
"*Plessy vs. Ferguson*:Theme and Variations" (Merton) **10**:345
"Pleurs dans la nuit" (Hugo) **17**:89
"Ploja fòur di dut" (Pasolini) **17**:287
"Ploja tai cunfins" (Pasolini) **17**:250-52, 265, 287
"Ploughing" (Pasternak) **6**:267
"Ploughing on Sunday" (Stevens) **6**:297, 333
Pluies (Perse) **23**:211, 213-14, 221, 232, 233-34, 247, 249-51, 253
"The Plumet Basilisk" (Moore) **4**:243
"The Plum's Heart" (Soto) **28**:381
"Plus Intra" (Swinburne) **24**:324
"Plus Ultra" (Swinburne) **24**:324
Plusieurs sonnets (Mallarme) **4**:214-15
"Pluto Incognito" (Viereck) **27**:296
"Plutonian Ode" (Ginsberg) **4**:61-2
Plutonian Ode: Poems, 1977-1980 (Ginsberg) **4**:61-2
"Po' Boy Blues" (Hughes) **1**:254, 270
"Poderoso Quienseas" (Fuertes) **27**:38
"Podolie" (Apollinaire) **7**:48
Podorozhnik (Akhmatova) **2**:3, 13, 18
"Podrazhanije Bajronu" (Lermontov) **18**:302
"Poem" (Bishop) **3**:54-5, 70
"Poem" (Enzensberger) **28**:151
"Poem" (Gluck) **16**:142
"The Poem" (Kinnell) **26**:240-41
"Poem" (Kunitz) **19**:147
"The Poem" (Lowell) **13**:83
"Poem" (Meredith) **28**:199
"Poem" (Merton) **10**:349
"Poem" (Rukeyser) **12**:233
"Poem" (Sanchez) **9**:232
"A Poem" (Stein) **18**:313
"Poem" (Tomlinson) **17**:315, 323, 328, 332, 339, 342, 345
"The Poem" (Williams) **7**:399
"Poem 1" (Ferlinghetti) **1**:167
"Poem 2" (Ferlinghetti) **1**:173
"Poem 3" (Ferlinghetti) **1**:174
"Poem IV" (Auden) **1**:10
"Poem 4" (Ferlinghetti) **1**:174
"Poem 5" (Ferlinghetti) **1**:168, 172
"Poem V" (Rich) **5**:378
"Poem 6" (Ferlinghetti) **1**:168, 173-74
"Poem 7" (Ferlinghetti) **1**:187
"Poem VII" (Rich) **5**:378-79
"Poem 8" (Ferlinghetti) **1**:174
"Poem IX" (Auden) **1**:10
"Poem 10" (Ferlinghetti) **1**:172-73
"Poem 11" (Ferlinghetti) **1**:174-75
"Poem 13" (Ferlinghetti) **1**:169, 174
"Poem XIII" (Rich) **5**:379
"Poem 14" (Ferlinghetti) **1**:168, 170
"Poem 15" (Ferlinghetti) **1**:175
"Poem 16" (Ferlinghetti) **1**:175
"Poem 17" (Ferlinghetti) **1**:176
"Poem 18" (Ferlinghetti) **1**:174
"Poem 19" (Ferlinghetti) **1**:173, 175
"Poem 20" (Ferlinghetti) **1**:174, 176
"Poem XX" (Rich) **5**:379
"Poem 21" (Ferlinghetti) **1**:175
"Poem 22" (Ferlinghetti) **1**:169, 176
"Poem 23" (Ferlinghetti) **1**:172, 174
"Poem 24" (Ferlinghetti) **1**:168, 171, 175
"Poem XXV" (Auden) **1**:10
"Poem 25" (Ferlinghetti) **1**:169, 174-75
"Poem 26" (Ferlinghetti) **1**:174-75
"Poem 27" (Ferlinghetti) **1**:174
"Poem 143: The Festival Aspect" (Olson) **19**:306
"Poem about the Future" (Enzensberger) **28**:142
"Poem About People" (Pinsky) **27**:161-62, 173-74, 176
"Poem about the Imperial Family" (Tsvetaeva)
See "Poema o tsarskoi sem'e"
"The Poem as Mask: Orpheus" (Rukeyser) **12**:228
"Poem at Thirty" (Sanchez) **9**:224, 232-33, 240
"poem beginning in no and ending in yes" (Clifton) **17**:30
"Poem Beginning 'The'" (Zukofsky) **11**:366-69, 373-74, 381, 383-86, 390, 395
"A Poem Beginning with a Line by Pindar" (Duncan) **2**:121-22, 127
"Poem Catching Up with an Idea" (Carruth) **10**:88
"A Poem for 3rd World Brothers" (Knight) **14**:42
"Poem for a Birthday" (Plath) **1**:381, 390
"A Poem for a Poet" (Madhubuti) **5**:327, 344
"A Poem for Anna Russ and Fanny Jones" (Baraka) **4**:39
"Poem for Aretha" (Giovanni) **19**:110
"A Poem for Black Hearts" (Baraka) **4**:18-19
"A Poem for Black Relocation Centers" (Knight) **14**:39, 52
"Poem (For BMC No. 2)" (Giovanni) **19**:139
"A Poem for Children, with Thoughts on Death" (Hammon) **16**:177-78, 180, 183, 187-89
"Poem (for DCS 8th Graders--1966-67)" (Sanchez) **9**:224
"Poem for Etheridge" (Sanchez) **9**:225, 242
"A Poem for Max 'Nordau" (Robinson) **1**:459
"Poem for Maya" (Forche) **10**:142, 157
"A Poem for My Father" (Sanchez) **9**:220, 225, 240
"Poem for My Son" (Kumin) **15**:199, 201
"A Poem for Myself" (Knight) **14**:39
"A Poem for Negro Intellectuals (If There Bes Such a Thing)" (Madhubuti) **5**:329
"Poem (For No Name No. 2)" (Giovanni) **19**:108
"Poem for Personnel Managers" (Bukowski) **18**:4, 6
"A Poem for Sterling Brown" (Sanchez) **9**:229
"A Poem for the Birth-day of the Right HonBLE the Lady Catherine Tufton" (Finch) **21**:164
"A Poem for the End of the Century" (Milosz) **8**:213
"A Poem for Willie Best" (Baraka) **4**:10-11
A Poem Humbly Dedicated to the Great Pattern of Piety and Virtue Catherine Queen Dowager (Behn) **13**:8
"Poem (I lived in the first century of world wars. . . .)" (Rukeyser) **12**:222
"Poem in C" (Toomer) **7**:333
"Poem in October" (Thomas) **2**:382, 392, 404
"poem in praise of menstruation" (Clifton) **17**:29-30, 36
"Poem in Prose" (Bogan) **12**:100, 107, 112
"Poem in Which I Refuse Contemplation" (Dove) **6**:120
"A Poem Looking for a Reader" (Madhubuti) **5**:323
"Poem No. 2" (Sanchez) **9**:220
"Poem No. 8" (Sanchez) **9**:242
"Poem No. 13" (Sanchez) **9**:213
"Poem of Apparitions in Boston in the 73rd Year of These States" (Whitman) **3**:386
"Poem of Autumn" (Dario)
See "Poema de otoño"
Poem of Autumn, and Other Poems (Dario)
See *Poema del otoño y otros poemas*
"The Poem of Flight" (Levine) **22**:225
"Poem of Memory" (Akhmatova) **2**:16
"A Poem of Praise" (Sanchez) **9**:242
"Poem of the Air" (Tsvetaeva)
See "Poema vozdukha"
"Poem of the Body" (Whitman) **3**:385
Poem of the Cante Jondo (Garcia Lorca)
See *Poema del cante jondo*
"Poem of the Daily Work of the Workmen and Workwomen of These States" (Whitman) **3**:385
The Poem of the Deep Song (Garcia Lorca)
See *Poema del cante jondo*
"Poem of the End" (Tsvetaeva)
See "Poèma kontsa"
"Poem of the Fourth Element" (Borges)
See "Poema del cuarto elemento"
"Poem of the Hill" (Tsvetaeva)
See "Poèma gory"
"Poem of the Mountain" (Tsvetaeva)
See "Poèma gory"
"Poem of the Poet" (Whitman) **3**:386
"Poem of the Singers and of the Works of Poems" (Whitman) **3**:386
"Poem of the Staircase" (Tsvetaeva)
See "Poèma lestnitsy"
"Poem of These States" (Ginsberg) **4**:66
"A Poem of Summer's End" (Merrill) **28**:248
"A Poem of Walt Whitman, an American" (Whitman) **3**:384, 414
"A Poem Off Center" (Giovanni) **19**:116
"Poem on His Birthday" (Thomas) **2**:391
"A Poem Once Significant Now Happily Not" (Cullen) **20**:85
"Poem, or Beauty Hurts Mr. Vinal" (Cummings) **5**:96
"Poem out of Childhood" (Rukeyser) **12**:231, 235
"A POEM SOME PEOPLE WILL HAVE TO UNDERSTAND" (Baraka) **4**:16
"A Poem to Complement Other Poems" (Madhubuti) **5**:329, 342
"A Poem to Galway Kinnell" (Knight) **14**:38
"A Poem to My Daughter" (Pinsky) **27**:153
"Poem to My Husband from My Father's Daughter" (Olds) **22**:322
"A Poem to Peanut" (Brooks) **7**:90
"A Poem Upon the Death of His Late Highness the Lord Protector" (Marvell)
See "Poem upon the Death of O. C."
"Poem upon the Death of O. C." (Marvell) **10**:270-71, 305, 312
"A Poem with Children" (Guillen)
See "Poema con niños"
"A Poem with No Ending" (Levine) **22**:221, 224
"Poem With Refrains" (Pinsky) **27**:175
Poem without a Hero: Triptych (Akhmatova)
See *Poema bez geroya: Triptykh*
"Poema a la eñe" (Fuertes) **27**:37
Poema bez geroya: Triptykh (Akhmatova) **2**:4, 6-8, 16, 18-21
"Poema con niños" (Guillen) **23**:139
"Poema de otoño" (Dario) **15**:81-2, 91, 96
Poema del cante jondo (Garcia Lorca) **3**:118, 123, 127, 129, 135, 137
"Poema del cuarto elemento" (Borges) **22**:74
Poema del otoño y otros poemas (Dario) **15**:86
"Poema en ón" (Fuertes) **27**:37
"Poèma gory" (Tsvetaeva) **14**:325
"Poema komnaty" (Tsvetaeva) **14**:325
"Poèma kontsa" (Tsvetaeva) **14**:301-02, 306, 316, 325
"Poèma lestnitsy" (Tsvetaeva) **14**:325
"Poema o tsarskoi sem'e" (Tsvetaeva) **14**:326-27
"Poema vozdukha" (Tsvetaeva) **14**:325
Poemas de amor (Guillen) **23**:100, 133
Poemas de la consumación (Aleixandre) **15**:4, 6-7, 12, 16-17, 25, 39, 41-4
Poemas de transición (Guillen) **23**:108
Poeme à l'étranger (Perse) **23**:211-13, 217, 232, 234, 250, 256-57

"Poème de la femme" (Gautier) **18**:125, 129-30, 139, 157
"Le poème de la mer" (Rimbaud) **3**:272
"Poème liminaire" (Senghor) **25**:247
"Poème lu au mariage d'André Salmon" (Apollinaire) **7**:48
"Poème pour M Valery Larbaud" (Perse) **23**:223-24
Poémes (Breton) **15**:53
Poèmes (Ronsard) **11**:249
Poèmes (Senghor) **25**:232
Poëmes (Vigny) **26**:401, 410
Poèmes antiques et modernes (Vigny) **26**:367, 372, 374, 398-99, 401-402, 404, 410-12
Poemes bibliques et modernes (Vigny) **26**:391
Poemes Philosophiques (Vigny) **26**:368, 372, 412
"Philosophy" (Parker) **28**:361
Poèmes saturniens (Verlaine) **2**:413-15, 430-32
"Poemo" (Fuertes) **27**:49
"Poems" (Cooke) **6**:348, 394, 416
"Poems" (Shapiro) **25**:294, 320
"Poems" (Stein) **18**:313
Poems (Arnold) **5**:12, 43, 50
Poems (Auden) **1**:4, 8, 10
Poems (Berry) **28**:14-15
Poems (Brooke) **24**:55, 83
Poems (Browning) **6**:14, 16-17, 19, 21, 25-7, 32, 36-8, 41-2
Poems (Clare)
See *The Poems of John Clare*
Poems (Emerson) **18**:82, 84, 100
Poems (Garcia Lorca)
See *Libro de poemas*
Poems (Harper) **21**:185, 189, 193, 196-97, 209
Poems (Mandelstam) **14**:106, 135
Poems (Milton) **19**:221, 249-50
Poems (Moore) **4**:228, 239, 250-51, 264
Poems (Owen) **19**:325
Poems (Poe) **1**:428, 437, 441
Poems (Ronsard)
See *Poèmes*
Poems (Rossetti) **7**:265
Poems (Williams) **7**:367, 374, 395, 398
Poems (Wordsworth) **4**:375, 401, 415
Poems (Yeats) **20**:347
Poems 1911 (Brooke) **24**:52-4, 61, 80
Poems, 1953 (Graves) **6**:154-55
Poems, 1914-1926 (Graves) **6**:132
Poems, 1923-1954 (Cummings) **5**:85, 89
Poems, 1926-1930 (Graves) **6**:132
Poems, 1938-1945 (Graves) **6**:129
Poems, 1940-1953 (Shapiro) **25**:285, 297, 313, 317
Poems, 1943-1947 (Day Lewis) **11**:147
Poems, 1965-1975 (Heaney) **18**:206, 211
"Poems 1978-1980" (Wright) **14**:377-78
Poems about Moscow (Tsvetaeva) **14**:299
"Poems about St. Petersburg, II" (Akhmatova) **2**:12
Poems and Ballads (Swinburne) **24**:309, 314, 321, 324, 334, 337, 345, 347, 358, 362-63
Poems and Ballads, second series (Swinburne) **24**:319
Poems and Drawings (Bukowski) **18**:5
Poems and Fragments (Holderlin) **4**:171
The Poems and Letters of Andrew Marvell (Marvell) **10**:277
Poems and New Poems (Bogan) **12**:89, 91, 107, 120, 124-26
Poems and Satires (Graves) **6**:135
Poems Barbarous (Nishiwaki) **15**:237
Poems before Congress (Browning) **6**:6, 23, 27, 36
Poems by Currer, Ellis, and Acton Bell (Bronte) **8**:46
Poems by Two Brothers (Tennyson) **6**:358
Poems, Chiefly in the Scottish Dialect (Burns) **6**:49
Poems, Chiefly Lyrical (Tennyson) **6**:347, 385, 406-09
Poems Descriptive of Rural Life and Scenery (Clare) **23**:38-44
Poems for People Who Don't Read Poems (Enzensberger) **28**:141, 143-44, 156
Poems for the Times (Heine)
See *Zeitgedichte*
Poems from Algiers (Brutus) **24**:112, 115, 117
Poems from Prison (Knight) **14**:38, 41, 46, 48, 52-3
"Poems from the Margins of Thom Gunn's 'Moly'" (Duncan) **2**:127
"The Poems I Have Lost" (Ortiz) **17**:227
Poems in Classical Prosody (Bridges) **28**:65
"Poems in Imitation of the Fugue" (Schwartz) **8**:289, 305
Poems in Prose from Charles Baudelaire (Baudelaire)
See *Petits poèmes en prose: Le spleen de Paris*
Poems in the Shape of a Rose (Pasolini) **17**:286
See *Poems in the Shape of a Rose*
Poems in Wartime (Day Lewis) **11**:145
"Poems of 1912-13" (Hardy) **8**:91-4, 132, 137-8
Poems of a Jew (Shapiro) **25**:282, 285, 287, 290, 297-302, 320
Poems of Akhmatova (Akhmatova) **2**:16
Poems of André Breton: A Bilingual Anthology (Breton) **15**:54
Poems of Consummation (Aleixandre)
See *Poemas de la consumación*
Poems of Ferdinand Pessoa (Pessoa) **20**:168
The Poems of Francois Villon (Villon) **13**:412
Poems of Gerard Manley Hopkins (Hopkins) **15**:129, 133
The Poems of John Clare (Clare) **23**:3, 9, 11-14
"Poems of Night" (Kinnell) **26**:257
"The Poems of Our Climate" (Stevens) **6**:299
Poems of Paul Celan (Celan)
See *Paul Celan: Poems*
The Poems of Samuel Taylor Coleridge (Coleridge) **11**:70, 81, 83, 104
Poems of Shadow (Jimenez) **7**:183
The Poems of Stanley Kunitz, 1928-1978 (Kunitz) **19**:175-76, 186
"Poems of the Past and Present" (Hardy) **8**:121
Poems of the Past and Present (Hardy) **8**:123, 125
Poems on Affairs of State (Marvell) **10**:311
Poems on Miscellaneous Subjects (Harper) **21**:184-86, 188, 193, 196-97, 203, 206, 208-09, 215, 217-18
"poems on my fortieth birthday" (Clifton) **17**:18
Poems on Various Subjects, Religious and Moral, by Phillis Wheatley, Negro Servant to Mr. John Wheatley of Boston, in New England, 1773 (Wheatley) **3**:332-34, 336, 338, 345, 349-52, 356
Poems Selected and New (Page) **12**:180
Poems: Selected and New, 1950-1974 (Rich) **5**:384, 387
"Poems Speaking of Buddha" (Lindsay) **23**:283
Poems to Akhmatova (Tsvetaeva)
See "Stikhi K Akhmatovoi"
Poems to Blok (Tsvetaeva) **14**:299
See *Stikhi K Blok*
"Poems to Bohemia" (Tsvetaeva)
See "Stikhi k Chekhii"
"Poems to my Son" (Tsvetaeva)
See "Stikhi k synu"
"Poems to Pushkin" (Tsvetaeva)
See "Stikhi k Pushkinu"
Poems to Solve (Swenson) **14**:276
Poems upon Several Occasions, with a Voyage to the Island of Love (Behn) **13**:3, 7-8, 16, 18
Poems written before jumping out of an 8 story window (Bukowski) **18**:13
"Poesi i sak" (Ekeloef) **23**:77
"Poesía" (Jimenez) **7**:183
"La poesía" (Paz) **1**:353
Poesía (Jimenez) **7**:202
"La poesía castellana" (Dario) **15**:95
"Poesia in forma di rosa" (Pasolini) **17**:274, 276-77
Poesia in forma di rosa (Pasolini) **17**:249, 273-74, 276
La poesía juvenil (Borges) **22**:92-3
Poesía, moral, público (Aleixandre) **15**:9
Poesía superrealista (Aleixandre) **15**:3, 22, 24
Poesías completas (Dario) **15**:93, 107
Poesías últimas escojidas (1918-1958) (Jimenez) **7**:214
"Poésie" (Valery) **9**:366, 394
Poesie (Pavese) **13**:207, 210, 215, 220-21, 223-30
"Poesie a Casarsa" (Pasolini) **17**:281
Poesie a Casarsa (Pasolini) **17**:252, 254, 257, 262, 264-67, 279-82
Poesie e prose (Gozzano) **10**:184-85
Poesie edite e inedite (Pavese) **13**:208, 219, 230
"Poesie incivili" (Pasolini) **17**:273
"Poésie; ou, Le paysage dans le Golfe de Glafenes" (Lamartine) **16**:262
"Poesie, ou Paysage dans le Golfe de Genes" (Lamartine) **16**:292
"Poésie sacrée" (Lamartine) **16**:274, 290
Poèsies (Gautier) **18**:126
Poésies (Valery) **9**:399
Poésies complètes (Gautier) **18**:147
Poésies complètes (Laforgue) **14**:72
Poésies complétes (Mallarme) **4**:206
Poésies diverses (Villon) **13**:394-95, 397, 402-03, 407, 411
"The Poet" (Aleixandre)
See "El poeta"
"The Poet" (Bryant) **20**:11, 33
"The Poet" (Carruth) **10**:84
"The Poet" (Cullen) **20**:85
"The Poet" (Dario)
See "El poeta"
"The Poet" (Day Lewis) **11**:146
"The Poet" (Dunbar) **5**:121, 136
"The Poet" (Emerson) **18**:88-89
"The Poet" (H. D.) **5**:306
"A Poet" (Hardy) **8**:90
"The Poet" (Lermontov) **18**:281, 298
"The Poet" (Rilke) **2**:280
"Poet" (Shapiro) **25**:283, 286, 311
"The Poet" (Tennyson) **6**:369
"Poet" (Viereck) **27**:259, 263, 272, 282
"The Poet acquires speech from afar. . ." (Tsvetaeva)
See "Poèt--izdaleka zovodit rech'. . ."
"The Poet and His Book" (Millay) **6**:220
"The Poet and His Song" (Dunbar) **5**:118, 121, 134
"The Poet at Forty" (Nemerov) **24**:267
"Poet at Seventy" (Milosz) **8**:180, 197, 209
Poet in New York (Garcia Lorca)
See *Poeta en Nueva York*
Poet in Our Time (Montale) **13**:146
"The Poet in the Machine Age" (Viereck) **27**:284
"The Poet in the World" (Levertov) **11**:172-74
"The Poet Laments the Coming of Old Age" (Sitwell) **3**:317
"The Poet of Ignorance" (Sexton) **2**:368
"A Poet Recognizing the Echo of the Voice" (Wakoski) **15**:350
"A Poet to His Baby Son" (Johnson) **24**:144
"The Poet, to His Book" (Merton) **10**:337
"Poet to Tiger" (Swenson) **14**:280
"El poeta" (Aleixandre) **15**:3, 15, 38, 40
"El poeta" (Dario) **15**:99
Poeta de guardia (Fuertes) **27**:13, 15-8, 21, 25, 27-31, 50
Poeta en Nueva York (Garcia Lorca) **3**:120-21, 125, 136-38, 140, 143, 148-51
"El poeta pregunta por Stella" (Dario) **15**:113
"Los poetas celestes" (Neruda) **4**:293
"Le Poète" (Hugo) **17**:91
"La poéte Mourant" (Lamartine) **16**:271, 273-74, 278

"Les poètes de sept ans" (Rimbaud) **3**:258
Poetic Contemplations (Lamartine)
See *Les recueillements poétiques*
"Poetica" (Pavese) **13**:228
The Poetical Meditations of M. Alphonse de La Martine (Lamartine)
See *Méditations poétiques*
Poetical Sketches (Blake) **12**:31-2, 36, 43, 60-1
Poetical Works (Montagu) **16**:338, 341
The Poetical Works of Christina Georgina Rossetti (Rossetti) **7**:282-83
The Poetical Works of Rupert Brooke (Brooke) **24**:61, 75-6, 80-1, 89
The Poetical Works of S. T. Coleridge (Coleridge) **11**:75
"Poetics" (Ammons) **16**:21-2, 28
"Poetics" (Pavese)
See "Poetica"
"The Poetics of the Physical World" (Kinnell) **26**:289
"Poetik" (Ekeloef) **23**:77
"Poèt--izdaleka zovodit rech'. . ." (Tsvetaeva) **14**:323
"Poetry" (Arnold) **5**:41
"Poetry" (Goethe) **5**:227
"Poetry" (Moore) **4**:232, 235, 249, 251, 254, 270-71
"Poetry" (Pasternak) **6**:252, 262, 272, 279, 282
"Poetry" (Paz)
See "La poesía"
Poetry (Pavese)
See *Poesie*
"Poetry and Pleasure" (Pinsky) **27**:165
"Poetry and the World" (Pinsky) **27**:158
Poetry and the World (Pinsky) **27**:
Poetry and the World (Pinsky) **27**:156-58, 160-61, 176
"Poetry dusint have to be" (Bissett) **14**:13, 27
"Poetry Festival" (Enzensberger) **28**:136
"Poetry for the Advanced" (Baraka) **4**:39
Poetry Is (Hughes) **7**:158
"Poetry is Not a Luxury" (Lorde) **12**:143
"Poetry is the Smallest" (Ammons) **16**:43
"Poetry of Departures" (Larkin) **21**:229
"Poetry Perpetuates the Poet" (Herrick) **9**:146
"Poets" (Herrick) **9**:91, 106
"The Poets are Silent" (Smith) **12**:354
"The Poet's Death Is His Life" (Gibran) **9**:73
"The Poets of Seven Years" (Rimbaud)
See "Les poètes de sept ans"
"The Poet's Story" (Tagore)
See "Kabi kahini"
"The Poet's Vow" (Browning) **6**:38-9
"The poet's words" (Aleixandre)
See "Las palabras del poeta"
"The Point" (Hayden) **6**:193
"The Point" (Soto) **28**:371
"Point Joe" (Jeffers) **17**:130, 136
"Point Shirley" (Plath) **1**:389
"Le poison" (Baudelaire) **1**:45, 61
"Poison" (Tagore)
See "Halahal"
"A Poison Tree" (Blake) **12**:7
Poisson soluble (Breton) **15**:48, 63, 68, 70
"Poiu kngda gortan' syra . . ." (Mandelstam) **14**:150, 154
Polar Bear Hunt (Bissett) **14**:16-17, 19
"Polder" (Heaney) **18**:245
"Policía" (Guillen) **23**:101
"A Polish Dictionary" (Zagajewski) **27**:381
"Political Poem" (Baraka) **4**:10
"Political Relations" (Lorde) **12**:141
"Politics" (Meredith) **28**:206, 214
"Polonius Passing Through a Stage" (Nemerov) **24**:294-95
Poltava (Pushkin) **10**:366-69, 371, 373, 390-91, 394, 409, 411
"Pomade" (Dove) **6**:111, 113
"Pomegranate" (Gluck) **16**:126, 140-41
"Pomegranates" (Valery)
See "Les grenades"
Pomes for Yoshi (Bissett) **14**:11, 17-18
"Pompilia" (Browning) **2**:41
"The Pond" (Gluck) **16**:134
"The Pond" (Nemerov) **24**:261
"Le pont Mirabeau" (Apollinaire) **7**:11, 21
"Ponte Veneziano" (Tomlinson) **17**:342, 347, 349
"Les ponts" (Rimbaud) **3**:264
"The Pool and the Star" (Wright) **14**:346
"Poor" (Brooke) **24**:59
"Poor Art" (Montale)
See "L'arte povera"
"The Poor Child's Toy" (Baudelaire)
See "Le joujou du pauvre"
"A Poor Christian Looks at the Ghetto" (Milosz) **8**:191-92, 214
"The Poor in Church" (Rimbaud)
See "Les pauvres à l'église"
"Poor Mailie's Elegy" (Burns)
See "The Death and Dying Words of Poor Mailie"
"The Poor of London" (Belloc) **24**:28
"Poor Pierrot" (Masters) **1**:330, 333
"Poor Poll" (Bridges) **28**:77-9
"Poor Susan" (Wordsworth) **4**:374
"Poor Woman in a City Church" (Heaney) **18**:200
"The Pope" (Browning) **2**:41, 72
"Pope to Bolingbroke" (Montagu) **16**:342
"The Pope's Penis" (Olds) **22**:316
"Poppa Chicken" (Walker) **20**:273, 276, 286
"Poppies" (Sandburg) **2**:303
"Poppies in July" (Plath) **1**:381, 388
"Poppies in October" (Plath) **1**:384
Poppy and Memory (Celan)
See *Mohn und Gedächtnes*
"A Poppy" (Bridges) **28**:67
"Poppy Flower" (Hughes) **1**:240
"Popular Demand" (Merrill) **28**:267
"Popular Songs" (Ashbery) **26**:162
"Populist Manifesto" (Ferlinghetti) **1**:176, 182, 188
"Popytka komnaty" (Tsvetaeva) **14**:308, 325
"Popytka revnosti" (Tsvetaeva) **14**:306, 308
"Por boca cerrada entran moscas" (Neruda) **4**:290
"Pora, Moi Drug, Pora" (Pushkin) **10**:410
"Porcelain Bowl" (Gluck) **16**:150
"Porch Swing" (Kumin) **15**:215
"The Porcupine" (Kinnell) **26**:240-42, 244, 257, 262, 291
"Pornographer" (Hass) **16**:195
"Portail" (Gautier) **18**:143-45, 155-56
"Porter" (Hughes) **1**:242
"Pórtico" (Dario) **15**:113
"Portland, 1968" (Gluck) **16**:129, 150, 154
"Portovenere" (Montale) **13**:151
"Portrait" (Bogan) **12**:87, 101, 103
"A Portrait" (Browning) **2**:59
"The Portrait" (Graves) **6**:144
"The Portrait" (Kunitz) **19**:176-77, 179
"A Portrait" (Rossetti) **7**:296-7
"Portrait" (Wright) **14**:356, 362
"Portrait by a Neighbor" (Millay) **6**:233
"A Portrait in Greys" (Williams) **7**:409
"Portrait of a Girl" (Aiken) **26**:24, 72
"Portrait of a Lady" (Eliot) **5**:153, 161, 183, 185-86
"A Portrait of a Modern Lady" (Swift) **9**:259
"Portrait of a Women in Bed" (Williams) **7**:348, 367
"Portrait of an Old Woman on the College Tavern Wall" (Sexton) **2**:358
"Portrait of Georgia" (Toomer) **7**:310, 320, 334
"Portrait of Marina" (Page) **12**:168, 176, 189-90
"Portrait of Mrs Spaxton" (Tomlinson) **17**:311
"Portrait of the Artist" (Parker) **28**:351, 361
"Portrait of the Artist" (Tomlinson) **17**:320
"Portrait of the Artist as a Prematurely Old Man" (Nash) **21**:279
"Portrait of the Author" (Pavese) **13**:205
"Portrait of the Author as a Young Anarchist" (Rexroth) **20**:187
"Portrait of Three Conspirators" (Nemerov) **24**:292
"Portraits" (Cummings) **5**:94
Portraits with a Name (Aleixandre)
See *Retratos con nombre*
"The Portuguese Sea" (Pessoa)
See "Mar Portuguese"
"Die posaunenstelle" (Celan) **10**:98, 111
"Posesión del ayer" (Borges) **22**:95
"The Posie" (Burns) **6**:76
Positives (Gunn) **26**:202, 208. 219, 226
"Positives: For Sterling Plumpp" (Madhubuti) **5**:346
"Posle grozy" (Pasternak) **6**:267-68, 285
Posle razluki (Bely) **11**:3, 25, 32-3
Posle Rossii (Tsvetaeva) **14**:298, 306, 310-11, 315, 317, 324-25, 327
"Possessions" (Crane) **3**:83
"Possessive Case" (Stein) **18**:327
"Possom Trot" (Dunbar) **5**:133
"Possum Song" (Johnson) **24**:163
"Post aetatem nostram" (Brodsky) **9**:4
"Post mortem" (Jeffers) **17**:117, 141
"POST RESSURECTION CITY BLUES" (Bissett) **14**:31-2
"Postcard from Picadilly Street" (Ondaatje) **28**:329
"A Postcard from the Volcano" (Stevens) **6**:297
"Postcards for Bert Meyers" (Hongo) **23**:197
"A Post-Impressionist Susurration for the First of November, 1983" (Carruth) **10**:88
"Postlude" (Williams) **7**:345
"Postman Cheval" (Breton)
See "Facteur Cheval"
"Postmeridian" (Cassian) **17**:12
"A Post-Mortem" (Sassoon) **12**:248
"Postscript" (Kunitz) **19**:147
Postscripts (Tagore)
See *Punascha*
"The Posy" (Herbert) **4**:129
"The Pot of Flowers" (Williams) **7**:388
"Potato" (Viereck) **27**:279
"Potato Blossom Songs and Jigs" (Sandburg) **2**:316
"The Potatoes' Dance" (Lindsay) **23**:281
"Potter" (Ondaatje) **28**:318
"Pouir fêter des oiseaux" (Perse) **23**:254
Pour feter une enfance (3) (Perse) **23**:217, 221, 257
"Pour le livre d'amour" (Laforgue) **14**:80
"Pour Prende Congé" (Parker) **28**:362
"Pour saluer le tiers monde" (Cesaire) **25**:13
"Pouring the Milk Away" (Rukeyser) **12**:224
"Pourquoi mon âme est-elle triste?" (Lamartine) **16**:280
Poverkh barierov (Pasternak) **6**:263, 268-69
"Poverty" (Ammons) **16**:32
"Power" (Lorde) **12**:155
"Power" (Rich) **5**:377
"Power" (Rukeyser) **12**:210
"Power" (Wright) **14**:362
"The Power and the Glory" (Sassoon) **12**:246
Power Politics (Atwood) **8**:9, 12, 14-16, 21-4, 26, 31, 44
"A Portrait" (Parker) **28**:360
"Post-Graduate" (Parker) **28**:362
"Power to the People" (Walker) **20**:294
"Powers" (Milosz) **8**:202, 211
"Powhatan's Daughter" (Crane) **3**:86, 88, 105
Prabhat sangit (Tagore) **8**:405-06
"Practical People" (Jeffers) **17**:117
"A Practical Program for Monks" (Merton) **10**:334
"The Prairie" (Clampitt) **19**:93, 96-7
"Prairie" (Sandburg) **2**:303, 304, 307, 314, 316, 339
"Prairie Waters by Night" (Sandburg) **2**:316
"The Prairies" (Bryant) **20**:14, 19, 23-4, 29, 34, 40-1, 47
Praise (Hass) **16**:197-201, 210, 212, 215-16, 222, 226
"Praise II" (Herbert) **4**:121

"Praise III" (Herbert) **4**:125
"Praise Be" (Kumin) **15**:214
"Praise for an Urn" (Crane) **3**:90, 100
"Praise for Sick Women" (Snyder) **21**:325
"Praise to the End!" (Roethke) **15**:254, 272, 274, 284, 298-99, 301-02, 304, 307
Praise to the End! (Roethke) **15**:248-51, 256, 282-84, 298-99, 301-03, 309
Prantik (Tagore) **8**:422-24
"Pratidhyani" (Tagore) **8**:406
"Pravahini" (Tagore) **8**:415
"The Prayer" (Browning) **6**:19
"The Prayer" (Herbert) **4**:102, 130
"Prayer" (Hughes) **1**:240
"Prayer" (Jimenez)
See "Plegaria"
"A Prayer" (Lermontov) **18**:303
"Prayer" (Olds) **22**:316, 328
"Prayer" (Roethke) **15**:260
"Prayer" (Toomer) **7**:320-22, 334-35
"A Prayer" (Tsvetaeva)
See "Molitva"
"Prayer" (Wright) **14**:356, 366
"Prayer I" (Herbert) **4**:115
"Prayer at Sunrise" (Johnson) **24**:145, 153
"Prayer for a Prayer" (Parker) **28**:351, 364
"Prayer for a Second Flood" (MacDiarmid) **9**:155-56, 197-98
A Prayer for Marilyn Monroe and other poems (Cardenal)
See *Oracion por Marilyn Monroe y otros poemas*
"A Prayer for my Daughter" (Tomlinson) **17**:307
"A Prayer for My Daughter" (Yeats) **20**:320, 328, 336, 338-39, 342
"A Prayer for My Son" (Yeats) **20**:336, 339-40
"Prayer for Peace" (Senghor)
See "Prière de paix"
"Prayer for the Great Family" (Snyder) **21**:297
"A Prayer of Columbus" (Whitman) **3**:379, 384, 395
"The Prayer of Nature" (Byron) **16**:87
"Prayer to Ben Jonson" (Herrick) **9**:86, 96
"Prayer to Masks" (Senghor) **25**:227, 229-30
"Prayer to My Mother" (Pasolini) **17**:289
"Prayer to the Father of Heaven" (Skelton) **25**:337, 339
"Prayers of Steel" (Sandburg) **2**:302, 311
"Praying on a 707" (Sexton) **2**:373
"Prayrs for th One Habitation" (Bissett) **14**:20
"The Preacher: Ruminates behind the Sermon" (Brooks) **7**:53, 87, 94
"Preamble" (Rukeyser) **12**:209
"Prece" (Pessoa) **20**:155-56
"Precedent" (Dunbar) **5**:133
"Precession of the Equinoxes" (Rexroth) **20**:193, 196
"The Precinct. Rochester" (Lowell) **13**:83
"Preciosa and the Wind" (Garcia Lorca)
See "Preciosa y el aire"
"Preciosa y el aire" (Garcia Lorca) **3**:146
"Precious Moments" (Sandburg) **2**:331
"Precious Yeast of the World" (Mandelstam)
See "Drozhzhi mira dorogie"
"The Precipice" (Wright) **14**:354
"Préface" (Gautier) **18**:154, 156
"La préface" (Olson) **19**:318-21, 323
"Preface of the Galaxy" (Matsuo Basho)
See "Ginga no jo"
Preface to a Twenty Volume Suicide Note (Baraka) **4**:5-6, 14-17, 27, 31, 37
"The Preferred Voice" (Baudelaire)
See "La Voix"
"Preguntas Frente al lago" (Cardenal) **22**:111
"Prelenstnitse" (Lermontov) **18**:303
"Prélude" (Hugo) **17**:91-93
"Prelude" (Swinburne) **24**:313, 355, 357
"Prelude" (Tomlinson) **17**:328
"A Prelude" (Tomlinson) **17**:327, 333
The Prelude (Wordsworth)
See *The Prelude; or, Growth of a Poets Mind: Autobiographical Poem*
The Prelude; or, Growth of a Poets Mind: Autobiographical Poem (Wordsworth) **4**:397, 402-09, 412, 414, 421-27
"Prelude: The Troops" (Sassoon) **12**:264
"Prelude to a Fairy Tale" (Sitwell) **3**:295, 300, 304
"Preludes" (Eliot) **5**:153
"Les préludes" (Lamartine) **16**:278
Preludes (Aiken) **26**:23, 29-30
"Préludes autobiographiques" (Laforgue) **14**:66, 95
Preludes for Memnon; or, Preludes to Attitude (Aiken) **26**:23, 29-30, 33, 38, 52-3, 57-69, 72
Preludes to Attitude (Aiken) **26**:38-39
Preludes to Definition (Aiken) **26**:38-9
Premier livre des amours (Ronsard) **11**:246
Le premier livre des poemes (Ronsard) **11**:280
"Le premier regret" (Lamartine) **16**:293
"Premier sourire du printemps" (Gautier) **18**:128
La Première Aventure céleste de Mr Antipyrine (Tzara) **27**:227
"Première soirèe" (Rimbaud) **3**:258, 283
"Les premières communions" (Rimbaud) **3**:260
"The Premonition" (Roethke) **15**:293
"Prendimiento de Antoñito el Camborio" (Garcia Lorca) **3**:131
"Preparatory Exercise (Dyptych with Votive Tablet)" (Paz) **1**:374
"Prepare Thy Self" (Roethke) **15**:293
"The Prepositions" (Olds) **22**:320
"Pres Spoke in a Language" (Baraka) **4**:39
"Prescription of Painful Ends" (Jeffers) **17**:141-144-45
"The Prescriptive Stalls As" (Ammons) **16**:25, 44
"The Presence" (Graves) **6**:137
"The Presence" (Kumin) **15**:181
"Presence" (Zagajewski) **27**:389, 393
"Présense" (Cesaire) **25**:10
"The Presense" (Elytis) **21**:130
"Present" (Sanchez) **9**:219
"Present, Afterwards" (Aleixandre) **15**:6
"The Present Age" (Harper) **21**:190
Presented to Ch'en Shang (Li Ho) **13**:44
"Presented to Wei Pa, Gentleman in Retirement" (Tu Fu) **9**:322
"President Lincoln's Proclamation of Freedom" (Harper) **21**:197
"Prèsomptif" (Perse) **23**:230
"Press Release" (Merrill) **28**:284-85
"Pressure to Grow" (Baraka) **4**:30
"Pressures" (Wright) **14**:375
"Prestupnik" (Lermontov) **18**:289
"Pretty" (Smith) **12**:301, 318, 321, 328
"The Pretty Bar-Keeper of the Mitre" (Smart) **13**:341, 347
"The Pretty Barmaid" (Smart)
See "The Pretty Bar-Keeper of the Mitre"
"The Pretty Redhead" (Apollinaire)
See "La jolie rousse"
"Pretty Words" (Wylie) **23**:314, 324
"Priapus" (H. D.) **5**:275, 303
Priapus and the Pool and Other Poems (Aiken) **26**:46
"La prière" (Lamartine) **16**:276-77, 291, 299-301
"Prière aux Masques" (Senghor) **25**:224,241
"Prière de paix" (Senghor) **25**:231,254
"Prière du matin" (Verlaine) **2**:416
"La prière pour tous" (Hugo) **17**:45
"The Priest" (H. D.) **5**:306
"The Priest and the Matador" (Bukowski) **18**:4
"Prigovor" (Akhmatova) **2**:8-9
"Prima del viaggio" (Montale) **13**:134
"Primary Colors" (Song) **21**:333-34, 343, 350
"A Primary Ground" (Rich) **5**:361
"La primavera" (Jimenez) **7**:193-94
"La primavera Hitleriana" (Montale) **13**:104, 109, 145, 148, 165-66
"Primaveral" (Dario) **15**:117
"Prime" (Lowell) **13**:64, 67
Primer for Blacks (Brooks) **7**:83, 86
"A Primer of the Daily Round" (Nemerov) **24**:257, 283
Primer romancero gitano (Garcia Lorca) **3**:119-21, 127, 130, 133-34, 136-38, 145-49
Primeras poesias (Jimenez) **7**:209
"Primero sueño" (Juana Ines de la Cruz) **24**:182-83, 189, 191-94, 198, 209, 211, 217, 220
"The Primitive" (Madhubuti) **5**:322
"Primitive" (Olds) **22**:307
"The Primitive" (Swenson) **14**:264
"A Primitive Like an Orb" (Stevens) **6**:314, 335
"'Primitivism' Exhibit" (Kumin) **15**:209
"The Primrose" (Donne) **1**:126, 130
"Primrose" (Herrick) **9**:125
"Primrose" (Williams) **7**:345
The Primrose Path (Nash) **21**:263
"Prince Athanase" (Shelley) **14**:189, 192, 202, 234-35
Prince Hohenstiel-Schwangau (Browning) **2**:43, 47, 82, 95
"Prince Meow" (Cassian) **17**:3
"The Prince of Darkness Passing through this House" (Wakoski) **15**:363
"Prince Tank" (Viereck) **27**:260, 280
"The Prince's Progress" (Rossetti) **7**:262-4, 279-80, 287, 289, 293-4, 296-8
The Prince's Progress, and Other Poems (Rossetti) **7**:261, 263, 266, 296
The Princess: A Medley (Tennyson) **6**:354, 360, 364-65, 371, 409
The Princess and the Knights (Bely) **11**:24
De principiis (Gray)
See *De principiis cogitandi*
De principiis cogitandi (Gray) **2**:154
"Prinkin' Leddie" (Wylie) **23**:301
"Printemps" (Tzara) **27**:223
"Prioress's Tale" (Chaucer) **19**:13, 15, 54-6
"La Prison" (Vigny) **26**:380, 401-403, 410
"The Prisoner" (Bronte)
See "Julian M. and A. G. Rochelle"
"The Prisoner" (Browning) **6**:26
"The Prisoner" (Paz)
See "El prisonero"
"The Prisoner" (Tagore)
See "Bandi"
The Prisoner of Chillon, and Other Poems (Byron) **16**:87
"The Prisoner of the Caucasus" (Lermontov) **18**:278
The Prisoner of the Caucasus (Pushkin)
See *Kavkazsky plennik*
"El prisonero" (Paz) **1**:364-65
"The Prisoners" (Hayden) **6**:194-95
"The Prisoner's Complaint" (Scott) **13**:292
"The Prisoner's Dream" (Montale)
See "Il Sogno del prigioniero"
"Privacy" (Rexroth) **20**:221
The Private Dining Room (Nash) **21**:270-71
"Private Madrigals" (Montale)
See "Madrigali privati"
"Private Means is Dead" (Smith) **12**:309, 333
The Privilege (Kumin) **15**:180-81, 200, 208
"A Prize Poem submitted by Mr. Lambkin of Burford to the Examiners of the University of Oxford on the Prescribed Poetic Theme Set by Them in 1893, 'The Benefits of the Electric Light'" (Belloc) **24**:4
"The Probationer" (Page) **12**:176
"The Problem" (Emerson) **18**:74, 79, 84, 100-2
"Problemas del subdesarrollo" (Guillen) **23**:121
"Problems of Underdevelopment" (Guillen)
See "Problems of Underdevelopment"
"Procedures for Underground" (Atwood) **8**:13, 19

Procedures for Underground (Atwood) **8**:2-3, 12, 15-16, 21
"Le Procès à la Révolution" (Hugo) **17**:102
"A Process" (Tomlinson) **17**:323, 331, 339
"Processe of tyme worketh suche wounder" (Wyatt) **27**:317, 320
"Processes" (Tomlinson) **17**:322,327, 337-40
"A Procession at Candlemas" (Clampitt) **19**:82-3, 89, 98
"Procession Poem" (Wakoski) **15**:324
"Processionals, II" (Duncan) **2**:101
"Proda di Versilia" (Montale) **13**:112, 148
"The Prodigal Son" (Johnson) **24**:128-29, 133, 156, 164, 169
"The Prodigal's Return" (Harper) **21**:208
"The Produce District" (Gunn) **26**:203, 231
"Proem: To Brooklyn Bridge" (Crane) **3**:85, 88, 90, 107, 109
Profane Proses (Dario)
See *Prosas profanas, y otros poemas*
"Profezie" (Pasolini) **17**:277
"Proffitt and Batten" (Smith) **12**:339
"Les profondeurs" (Apollinaire) **7**:32, 34
"De profundis" (Browning) **6**:5, 23
"De profundis" (MacDiarmid) **9**:153
"De Profundis" (Trakl) **20**:261-62
"Profusion du soir" (Valery) **9**:391
"Progress" (Kumin) **15**:214
"The Progress of Beauty, 1720" (Swift) **9**:253, 257, 298-99
"The Progress of Faust" (Shapiro) **25**:296
"The Progress of Poesy" (Gray) **2**:133, 135, 137, 139, 143-44, 146, 148-49, 151-55
"The Progress of Poetry" (Gray)
See "The Progress of Poesy"
"The Progress of Poetry" (Swift) **9**:249
"Progress Report" (Ammons) **16**:45
"Progress Report" (Kumin) **15**:204, 208, 219
"Progression" (Smith) **12**:316
"Progressive Insanities of a Pioneer" (Atwood) **8**:4
"The Prohibition" (Donne) **1**:130
"Projected Slide of an Unknown Soldier" (Atwood) **8**:7
"Projection" (Nemerov) **24**:268
A Prolegomenon to a Theodicy (Rexroth) **20**:179, 183, 210-11
"Prolija memoria" (Juana Ines de la Cruz) **24**:180
"Prolog" (Heine) **25**:131
"Prólogo" (Borges) **22**:95
"Prólogo" (Guillen) **23**:127
"The Prologue" (Bradstreet) **10**:2, 6, 11, 52
"Prologue" (Chaucer)
See "General Prologue"
"Prologue" (Hughes) **7**:154
"Prologue" (Hugo) **17**:97
"Prologue" (Lorde) **12**:156
"Prologue" (Marie de France) **22**:246-48, 260, 264-66, 283-85, 293, 298
"Prologue" (Noyes) **27**:119, 128
"Prologue" (Verlaine) **2**:432
"Prologue: An Interim" (Levertov)
See "Interim"
"Prologue at Sixty" (Auden) **1**:20
"Prologue to a Saga" (Parker) **28**:363-64
"Prologue to King John" (Blake) **12**:31
"Prologue to the Wife of Bath's Tale" (Chaucer) **19**:26
"Promenade on Any Street" (Kunitz) **19**:147-48
"Prometheus" (Dunbar) **5**:146
"Prometheus" (Goethe) **5**:247, 254
"Prometheus" (Graves) **6**:137
"Prometheus" (Tomlinson) **17**:315, 319, 322, 325-27, 341
Prometheus Bound, and Miscellaneous Poems (Browning) **6**:16, 18
Prometheus on His Crag (Hughes) **7**:155-56
Prometheus the Firegiver (Bridges) 28
"Prometheus Unbound" (Yeats) **20**:333, 336
Prometheus Unbound (Shelley) **14**:166-67, 171-75, 177, 183, 186-91, 193, 196-97, 202, 206, 212-13, 215-16, 218-21, 224-28, 232, 240-41
"The Promise" (Toomer) **7**:338
"Promise and Fulfillment" (Dunbar) **5**:121
"Promise Me" (Kunitz) **19**:147
"The Promise of the Hawthorn" (Swinburne) **24**:313, 317
"The Promised One" (Wright) **14**:337
"The Promisers" (Owen) **19**:336, 343
"Promontoire" (Rimbaud) **3**:264
"Prooimion" (Viereck) **27**:259
"Property" (Shapiro) **25**:295
"Prophecy" (Wylie) **23**:310, 323
"Prophecy on Lethe" (Kunitz) **19**:162, 173-75
"The Prophet" (Lermontov) **18**:281
"The Prophet" (Pushkin)
See "Prorok"
The Prophet (Gibran) **9**:69-75, 80-2
"The Prophet Lost in the Hills at Evening" (Belloc) **24**:30
"Prophetic Soul" (Parker) **28**:357, 360
"Prophetie" (Cesaire) **25**:9, 19, 30
"Prophets for a New Day" (Walker) **20**:278, 288
Prophets for a New Day (Walker) **20**:275, 278-79, 283, 287-89, 292
"Propogation House" (Roethke) **15**:296
"A propos d'Horace" (Hugo) **17**:64
"Prorok" (Pushkin) **10**:409, 414
Prosanatolizmí (Elytis) **21**:118-19, 124, 127, 134
Prosas profanas, y otros poemas (Dario) **15**:78, 80, 82-4, 87-9, 91-2, 94-5, 97, 103-05, 109, 112-14, 117-20
Prosas profanos, and Other Poems (Dario)
See *Prosas profanas, y otros poemas*
"Prose Poem" (Tomlinson) **17**:338, 340
Prose Poems (Baudelaire)
See *Petits poèmes en prose: Le spleen de Paris*
"Prosopèe de Louys de Ronsard" (Ronsard) **11**:282
"Prosopopoia; or, Mother Hubberds Tale" (Spenser) **8**:335, 365, 368-71, 390
"Prospective Immigrants Please Note" (Rich) **5**:370
Prospectus to the Excursion (Wordsworth)
See *The Excursion, Being a Portion of "The Recluse"*
"Prospice" (Browning) **2**:51, 66
"Protest" (Cullen) **20**:57
Protest Against Apartheid (Brutus) **24**:100
"Protestant Easter" (Sexton) **2**:363
"Prothalamion" (Kumin) **15**:180
"Prothalamion" (Schwartz) **8**:290-91, 299, 301-02, 304-05
Prothalamion; or, A Spousall Verse (Spenser) **8**:336, 390
"The Proud Farmer" (Lindsay) **23**:287
"A Proud Lady" (Wylie) **23**:309, 321, 332
"Proud Maisie" (Scott) **13**:272, 278, 280
"Proverbs of Hell" (Blake) **12**:36, 49-50
"Provide, Provide" (Frost) **1**:227-28, 231
"Providence" (Herbert) **4**:102, 134
"La providence à l'homme" (Lamartine) **16**:276, 283, 291, 293
Provinces (Milosz) **8**:212, 214-15
"Provincia deserta" (Pound) **4**:366
"Provisional Conclusions" (Montale) **13**:131
Provisional Conclusions (Montale) **13**:135
"Provoda" (Tsvetaeva) **14**:309, 311, 315
"prozession" (Enzensberger) **28**:135-36
Prufrock and Other Observations (Eliot) **5**:152, 173, 184-85, 195, 204, 206
"The Psalm" (Bridges) **28**:80
"Psalm" (Celan) **10**:98, 101, 118, 120
"A Psalm" (Merton) **10**:332
"Psalm II" (Ginsberg) **4**:81
"Psalm 2" (Smart) **13**:330
"Psalm 94" (Smart) **13**:362
"Psalm 104" (Smart) **13**:332
"Psalm 105" (Smart) **13**:362
"Psalm 120" (Smart) **13**:363
"Psalm Concerning the Castle" (Levertov) **11**:177
"Psalm Praising the Hair of Man's Body" (Levertov) **11**:171
"Psalms" (Smart)
See *A Translation of the Psalms of David, Attempted in the Spirit of Christianity, and Adapted to the Divine Service*
Psalms of David (Smart)
See *A Translation of the Psalms of David, Attempted in the Spirit of Christianity, and Adapted to the Divine Service*
"The Psychiatrist's Song" (Bogan) **12**:101, 115
"Public Bar TV" (Hughes) **7**:120, 122
"Public Garden" (Lowell) **3**:199-200, 215
Published and Unpublished Poems (Pavese)
See *Poesie edite e inedite*
"Puck of Pook's Hill" (Kipling) **3**:192
"Puck's Song" (Kipling) **3**:183, 192
"Pueblo Pot" (Millay) **6**:215
"Puedes?" (Guillen) **23**:116, 124, 127
"Puella Mea" (Cummings) **5**:104
"Puesto del Rastro" (Fuertes) **27**:22, 45-6
"the pull" (Bissett) **14**:22
"The Pulley" (Herbert) **4**:102
"The Pulling" (Olds) **22**:318, 323, 326, 340
Punascha (Tagore) **8**:417
Punch: The Immortal Liar (Aiken) **26**:22
"Punishment" (Heaney) **18**:196, 204, 210-11, 238
"The Puppets" (Page) **12**:184
Purabi (Tagore) **8**:415
"Pure Death" (Graves) **6**:137, 151
"The Pure Fury" (Roethke) **15**:258, 272, 277, 290
"Pure Love" (Tagore)
See "Pavitra prem"
"The Pure Ones" (Hass) **16**:198
"Purely" (Villa) **22**:353
"Purely Local" (Rich) **5**:352
Purgatorio (Dante) **21**:49, 52-4, 58, 62-3, 69-82, 84-6, 91, 95-6, 104-05, 107-09
"Purgatory" (Lowell) **3**:241
Purgatory (Dante)
See *Purgatorio*
Purgatory (Marie de France)
See *L'Espurgatoire Saint Patrice*
The Purgatory of St. Patrick (Marie de France)
See *L'Espurgatoire Saint Patrice*
"The Puritan" (Shapiro) **25**:270, 286
"The Puritan's Ballard" (Wylie) **23**:310
"Purner abhav" (Tagore) **8**:414
"Purple Grackles" (Lowell) **13**:64, 67, 87, 98-9
"Les Pur-Sang" (Cesaire) **25**:8-9, 18
"The Purse of Aholibah" (Huneker) **27**:165
"The Purse Seine" (Jeffers) **17**:117
"Pursuit" (H. D.) **5**:287-88
"Pushkinskomu domu" (Blok) **21**:44
"Pusti menia, Voronezh . . ." (Mandelstam) **14**:152
"La puttana contadina" (Pavese) **13**:210, 219
"Putting to Sea" (Bogan) **12**:123
"Pygmalion" (H. D.) **5**:270, 304
"Pygmies Are Pygmies Still, Though Percht on Alps" (Brooks) **7**:55
"The Pyramids" (Brooke) **24**:66, 80
"Pyrotechnics" (Bogan) **12**:117
"Pyrotechnics" (Lowell) **13**:83
Pyth. III (Pindar)
See *Pythian 3*
Pyth. X (Pindar)
See *Pythian 10*
Pyth XI (Pindar)
See *Pythian 11*
Pythian 1 (Pindar) **19**:381, 389, 392-93, 400, 411-12, 424-25
Pythian 2 (Pindar) **19**:402, 410, 420
Pythian 3 (Pindar) **19**:390, 398, 402, 410, 412
Pythian 4 (Pindar) **19**:381, 390, 396, 398-99, 405, 413, 420, 425
Pythian 5 (Pindar) **19**:396, 408-11, 422-23, 425

Cumulative Title Index

Pythian 6 (Pindar) **19**:400, 406
Pythian 7 (Pindar) **19**:412
Pythian 8 (Pindar) **19**:381, 391, 400, 406-07, 413, 426
Pythian 9 (Pindar) **19**:391, 398, 400, 412-13
Pythian 10 (Pindar) **19**:411-12, 425-26
Pythian 11 (Pindar) **19**:413
Pythian Odes 10 (Pindar)
See *Pythian 10*
"La pythie" (Valery) **9**:353, 365-66, 369, 373, 379, 393
Quaderno de quattro anni (Montale) **13**:128, 153, 156, 160, 168
"Quaerendo Invenietis" (Nemerov) **24**:288
"Quai D'Orleans" (Bishop) **3**:37
"The Quake" (Stryk) **27**:203, 211
"Quake Theory" (Olds) **22**:309
"The Quaker Graveyard at Nantucket (for Warren Winslow, Dead at Sea)" (Lowell) **3**:200-02, 204, 212, 217, 223, 233, 235-38
"Quaker Hill" (Crane) **3**:86, 90, 106
"Qualm" (Ashbery) **26**:152
"Quand vous serez bien vieille" (Ronsard) **11**:218-21
"Quando il soave mio fido conforto" (Petrarch) **8**:235
"The Quarrel" (Aiken) **26**:24
"The Quarrel" (Kunitz) **19**:175
"Quarrel in Old Age" (Yeats) **20**:328-31
"The Quarry" (Clampitt) **19**:82, 89
"Quarry Pigeon Cove" (Kumin) **15**:181
"Quashie to Buccra" (McKay) **2**:215, 223
"Quatrains" (Emerson) **18**:77
Quatre de P. de Ronsard aux injures et calomnies (Ronsard) **11**:291
"Quatre Dols" (Marie de France)
See "Le Chaitivel"
Les quatre premiers livres de la Franciade (Ronsard) **11**:226, 234, 246, 271, 283, 286-87, 290
Les quatre vents de l'esprit (Hugo) **17**:65
"4e epoque" (Lamartine) **16**:264
Que estás en la tierra (Fuertes) **27**:44
"Que m'accompagnent Kôras et Balafong" (Senghor) **25**:255
"Que no me quiera Fabio, al verse amado" (Juana Ines de la Cruz) **24**:183
"Que nous avons le doute en nous" (Hugo) **17**:92-93
"quebec bombers" (Bissett) **14**:21-2
"The Queen and the Young Princess" (Smith) **12**:326, 352
Queen Mab (Shelley) **14**:170, 173, 178, 185-86, 212-17, 219, 222
"Queen of Bubbles" (Lindsay) **23**:277
"The Queen of Hearts" (Rossetti) **7**:272, 274
"The Queen of the Night Walks Her Thin Dog" (Wakoski) **15**:363
"Queen Worship" (Browning) **2**:26
"Queen Yseult" (Swinburne) **24**:355
"Queen-Anne's Lace" (Williams) **7**:374
"Quelques Complaintes de la vie" (Laforgue) **14**:95
"The Quest" (Noyes) **27**:130
"The Quest of the Purple-Fringed" (Frost) **1**:218
"A Question" (Arnold) **5**:38
"The Question" (Rukeyser) **12**:225
"Question" (Swenson) **14**:250, 252, 282, 286
"Question and Answer" (Browning) **6**:5
"Question au clerc du quichet" (Villon) **13**:394
"A Question of Climate" (Lorde) **12**:136
"A Question of *Essence*" (Lorde) **12**:140
"Questions Beside the Lake" (Cardenal)
See "Preguntas Frente al lago"
"Questions of Travel" (Bishop) **3**:55, 67
Questions of Travel (Bishop) **3**:48, 53, 59
"A questo punto" (Montale) **13**:158
"A qui la faute?" (Hugo) **17**:101
Quia pawper amavi (Pound) **4**:317
"Quick I the Death of Thing" (Cummings) **5**:108
"A Quickening: A Song for the Visitation" (Merton) **10**:339
"The Quickening of St. John Baptist" (Merton) **10**:339
"Quickly Delia" (Finch) **21**:178
"A quien leyere" (Borges) **22**:94
"Quiero saber" (Aleixandre) **15**:31
"Quiero volver a sur" (Neruda) **4**:281
"Quiet Evening" (Gluck) **16**:172
"Quiet Work" (Arnold) **5**:12, 36, 38, 49
"Quietness" (Williams) **7**:382
"Quilted Spreads" (Ammons) **16**:44
Quilting: Poems 1987-1990 (Clifton) **17**:28-29, 36
"Quimérica" (Jimenez) **7**:197
"Quinnapoxet" (Kunitz) **19**:175, 178-79
"The Quip" (Herbert) **4**:100, 102, 108, 119, 130
"R. A. F." (H. D.) **5**:307
"The Rabbi" (Hayden) **6**:195, 198
"Rabbi Ben Ezra" (Browning) **2**:51, 75, 95
"The Rabbi's Song" (Kipling) **3**:183
"The Rabbit" (Millay) **6**:238
"Race" (Dario)
See "Raza"
"The Race" (Olds) **22**:319, 323, 326
"The Racer's Widow" (Gluck) **16**:139
"Rack" (Ammons) **16**:39
"A radio made of seawater" (Villa) **22**:356-57
"Radiometer" (Merrill) **28**:267
"Raft" (Ammons) **16**:20, 27
"The Raft" (Lindsay) **23**:273
"The Rag Man" (Hayden) **6**:195
"Raga Malkos" (Ekeloef) **23**:87
"Rages de césars" (Rimbaud) **3**:283
"The Ragged Schools of London" (Browning)
See "A Song for the Ragged Schools of London"
"The Ragged Stocking" (Harper) **21**:191
Raghuvamsa (Kalidasa) **22**:180, 182, 185, 188-90, 198, 204-07
"Railroad Avenue" (Hughes) **1**:237
The Railway Timetable of the Heart (Tzara) **27**:250
"Rain" (Giovanni) **19**:109
"The Rain" (Levertov) **11**:176
"Rain" (Soto) **28**:370, 377
"Rain" (Stryk) **27**:201
"Rain" (Williams) **7**:349
"Rain at Bellagio" (Clampitt) **19**:87
"Rain Charm for the Duchy, a Blessed, Devout Drench for the Christening of a Prince Harry" (Hughes) **7**:171
"Rain Downriver" (Levine) **22**:224-25
"Rain Festival" (Tagore)
See "Varsha-mangal"
"The Rain, It Streams on Stone and Hillock" (Housman) **2**:162
"Rain on a Grave" (Hardy) **8**:134
"Rain on the Borders" (Pasolini) **17**:287
"Rain or Hail" (Cummings) **5**:88
"Rain Outside of Everything" (Pasolini) **17**:287
"The Rainbow" (Kinnell) **26**:259-60
"rainbow music" (Bissett) **14**:24
"Rainforest" (Wright) **14**:375, 377
"The Rainmaker" (Cassian) **17**:4
"Rain-Song" (Dunbar) **5**:125
"Rainy Mountain Cemetery" (Momaday) **25**:190, 197
"The Rainy Season" (Meredith) **28**:187
"Raise the Shade" (Cummings) **5**:89
"Raleigh" (Cardenal) **22**:107, 110
"Raleigh Was Right" (Williams) **7**:360
"La rameur" (Valery) **9**:367, 395-96
"Rank and File" (Noyes) **27**:122
"Rano Raraku" (Breton) **15**:53-4
"Rap of a Fan..." (Apollinaire)
See "Coup d'evential..."
"Rape" (Rich) **5**:361
"Rape of the Leaf" (Kunitz) **19**:147
The Rape of the Lock (Pope) **26**:303, 307-309, 314-19, 322-23, 326-27, 340, 346-51
"The Raper from Passenack" (Williams) **7**:353, 368, 399
"Rapids" (Ammons) **16**:63
"Rapids by the Luan Trees" (Wang Wei) **18**:370
"Rapunzel" (Sexton) **2**:368
"Rapunzel, Rapunzel" (Smith) **12**:341
"Rasshchelina" (Tsvetaeva) **14**:306-08
Rat Jelly (Ondaatje) **28**:294, 327-35
"Ratbert" (Hugo) **17**:59
"The Ratcatcher" (Tsvetaeva)
See "Krysolov"
"Rational Man" (Rukeyser) **12**:220, 230
"The Rats" (Levine) **22**:213
"ratschlag auf ho¨chster ebene" (Enzensberger) **28**:136
"rattle poem" (Bissett) **14**:21
"The Raven" (Poe) **1**:419-20, 424, 427, 429-34, 436, 439-40, 443-44, 447, 452-53
"The Raven: A Christmas Tale" (Coleridge) **11**:109-17
The Raven, and Other Poems (Poe) **1**:437, 449
"The Ravine" (Carruth) **10**:85, 90
"Raving Mad" (Cesaire) **25**:15
Les rayons et les ombres (Hugo) **17**:45, 50-53, 63-64, 67, 76-77, 87, 91-92, 97
"Raza" (Dario) **15**:115
"Razgovor s geniem" (Tsvetaeva) **14**:325
Rbaiyyat (Khayyam)
See *Rubáiyát*
Re:Creation (Giovanni) **19**:108-11, 114, 118, 122, 128, 136-37, 140-41
"The reaching out of warmth is never done" (Viereck) **27**:278
"Reaching Out with the Hands of the Sun" (Wakoski) **15**:363
"Re-Act for Action" (Madhubuti) **5**:338
"The Reader over My Shoulder" (Graves) **6**:143, 151
"Reading Aloud" (Gallagher) **9**:60
"Reading Apollinaire by the Rouge River" (Ferlinghetti) **1**:181, 187
"Reading Holderlin on the Patio with the Aid of a Dictionary" (Dove) **6**:109
"Reading My Poems from World War II" (Meredith) **28**:180, 195
"Reading Myself" (Lowell) **3**:229
"Reading the Japanese Poet Issa" (Milosz) **8**:189
"Reading the Will" (Kipling) **3**:190
"Reading Time: 1 Minute 26 Seconds" (Rukeyser) **12**:206
"Readings of History" (Rich) **5**:355
"Ready for Goodbye" (Cassian) **17**:3
"The Real Estate Agents Tale" (Lowell) **13**:84
"Real Life" (Baraka) **4**:30
"Real Life" (Enzensberger) **28**:159
"The Real Revolution Is Love" (Harjo) **27**:70
"The Real Work" (Snyder) **21**:324-25
The Real World (Snyder) **21**:291
La realidad invisible (Jimenez) **7**:207
"Reality" (Pasolini) **17**:258
Reality Sandwiches (Ginsberg) **4**:67, 81
"Reapers" (Toomer) **7**:319, 333-34
"Reaping" (Lowell) **13**:60
"Reaping in Heat" (Heaney) **18**:191
"The Rear-Guard" (Sassoon) **12**:266
"Rearmament" (Jeffers) **17**:117, 121-22
"Reason and Imagination" (Smart) **13**:341, 347
"Reasons for Attendance" (Larkin) **21**:223, 229, 244, 247
"Reawakening" (Pavese)
See "Risveglio"
"The Rebel" (Belloc) **24**:12, 30, 38
"Le rebelle" (Baudelaire) **1**:55
"Rebellion" (Lowell) **3**:318
"The Rebels" (Ferlinghetti) **1**:184
"Rebirth" (Pushkin) **10**:408
"A Rebus by I. B." (Wheatley) **3**:338
"Recalling War" (Graves) **6**:137, 142, 144, 165
"The Recantation: An Ode. By S. T. Coleridge" (Coleridge) **11**:94, 99

"Recapitulations" (Shapiro) **25**:272-73, 285, 296-97, 319-20, 324
"Receive Thy Sight" (Bryant) **20**:6
"The Recent Past" (Ashbery) **26**:143
"Recessional" (Masters) **1**:333
"Recipe for Happiness in Khaboronsky" (Ferlinghetti) **1**:183
"The Recital" (Ashbery) **26**:130, 149
"Rècitation à l 'Éloge d'une Reine" (Perse) **23**:230
"Recitative" (Crane) **3**:81, 83
Recklings (Hughes) **7**:120, 122-23
"The Recluse" (Smith) **12**:299, 331, 333
The Recluse; or Views on Man, Nature, and on Human Life (Wordsworth) **4**:406-07, 409
"Recollection" (Wheatley)
See "On Recollection"
"Recollections" (Swinburne) **24**:329
"Recollections of Bellagia" (Meredith) **28**:198, 215
"Recollections of Solitude" (Bridges) **28**:60
"Recollections of the Arabian Nights" (Tennyson) **6**:347, 359, 389, 406, 408-09
Recollections of Tsarskoe-Selo (Pushkin)
See "Vospominanie v Tsarskom Sele"
"The Recompense" (Tomlinson) **17**:349
"Reconciliation" (Day Lewis) **11**:147
"Reconciliation" (Milosz) **8**:213
"Reconciliation" (Sassoon) **12**:289
"Reconciliation" (Whitman) **3**:378
"The Record" (Berry) **28**:30
Records of a Weather Exposed Skeleton (Matsuo Basho)
See *Nozarashi kiko*
"Recovering" (Rukeyser) **12**:225
"Recovery" (Ammons) **16**:6
"The Recovery" (Pushkin) **10**:408
Recovery (Tagore)
See *Arogya*
Recovery (Tagore)
See *Arogya*
"Recreaciones arqueológicas" (Dario) **15**:96
"The Recruit" (Housman) **2**:196
"A Recruit on the Corpy" (McKay) **2**:226
"Recueillement" (Baudelaire) **1**:65
Les recueillements poétiques (Lamartine) **16**:263, 268, 284-85
"Recuerdo" (Millay) **6**:215
"Recuerdos..." (Jimenez) **7**:199
"Red Armchair" (McGuckian) **27**:105
"A Red Carpet for Shelley" (Wylie) **23**:322, 333
Red Dust (Levine) **22**:211, 213-15, 217-18, 222-23, 227-28
"The Red Knight" (Lowell) **13**:84
"The Red Lacquer Music Stand" (Lowell) **13**:78
"Red Maple Leaves" (Rexroth) **20**:221
"Red Poppy" (Gallagher) **9**:64
"A Red, Red Rose" (Burns)
See "My Luve Is Like a Red, Red Rose"
"Red Riding Hood" (Sexton) **2**:354, 364
Red Roses for Bronze (H. D.) **5**:270-71, 304
"Red Silk Stockings" (Hughes) **1**:269
"Red Slippers" (Lowell) **13**:79
"The Red Steer" (Tsvetaeva)
See "Krasnyi bychok"
"The Red Wheelbarrow" (Williams) **7**:378, 401-02, 409-10
"The Redbreast and the Butterfly" (Wordsworth) **4**:376
"Red-Cotton Nightcap Country" (Browning) **2**:96
"A Redeemer" (Jeffers) **17**:131, 141
"The Redeemer" (Sassoon) **12**:242, 249-51, 261-62, 276, 278, 287
"Redemption" (Herbert) **4**:119, 130
"Redeployment" (Nemerov) **24**:287, 290
"Redwing" (Gallagher) **9**:62
"The Reed" (Lermontov) **18**:304
"The Reedbeds of the Hackensack" (Clampitt) **19**:87
"The Reefy Coast" (Ishikawa)
See "Ariso"
"Reeve's Tale" (Chaucer) **19**:10, 13-14, 61
"Reference Back" (Larkin) **21**:228
"The Refiner's Gold" (Harper) **21**:189
"The Refinery" (Pinsky) **27**:158, 171-72, 176
"The Reflection: A Song" (Behn) **13**:18, 20-1
"Reflection in a Forest" (Auden) **1**:17
"Reflection in an Ironworks" (MacDiarmid) **9**:155
"Reflection on Ice-Breaking" (Nash) **21**:279
"Reflections" (Tomlinson) **17**:316, 324
"Reflections at Lake Louise" (Ginsberg) **4**:84
"Reflections by a Mailbox" (Kunitz) **19**:154
"Reflections on a Scottish Slum" (MacDiarmid) **9**:181
"Reflections on Having Left a Place of Retirement" (Coleridge) **11**:81
"Reflective" (Ammons) **16**:6
"Reflexion" (Lamartine) **16**:266, 285
"Reformation" (Finch) **21**:166
"Refrain" (Dove) **6**:117
"Refugees" (Zagajewski) **27**:402
"A Refusal to Mourn the Death, by Fire, of a Child in London" (Thomas) **2**:382-83, 386, 388, 390, 398, 400
"Regarding Wave" (Snyder) **21**:297, 304-06
Regarding Wave (Snyder) **21**:285, 288-92, 300, 304-08, 310, 317, 322
"Règle" (Tzara) **27**:230-31
"Régles de l'Ode" (Hugo) **17**:90
"Regrets of the Belle Heaumiere" (Villon)
See "Lament of the Belle Heaulmiere"
"Rehabilitation & Treatment in the Prisons of America" (Knight) **14**:53
"The Rehearsal" (Smith) **12**:330
"El reino interior" (Dario) **15**:79-80, 92, 96, 114
"Rejoice in the Lamb" (Smart)
See "Jubilate Agno"
Rekviem: Tsikl stikhotvorenii (Akhmatova) **2**:4, 7, 9, 15-16, 19-20
Relations and Contraries (Tomlinson) **17**:317, 342
"Relearning the Alphabet" (Levertov) **11**:195-98
Relearning the Alphabet (Levertov) **11**:176-78, 180, 193-94
"Religio" (Hugo) **17**:66
Religio Laici; or, A Layman's Faith (Dryden) 79-82, 97, 101
"Religion" (Dunbar) **5**:125
"The Religion of My Time" (Pasolini) **17**:257-59
The Religion of My Time (Pasolini) **17**:285
La religione del mio tempo (Pasolini) **17**:264-66, 270, 272-73, 295
"Religious Isolation" (Arnold) **5**:42
"A Religious Man" (Smith) **12**:352
"Religious Musings" (Coleridge) **11**:49-51, 53, 80-2, 93-6
"Religious Propaganda" (Tagore)
See "Dharma prachar"
"The Relique" (Donne) **1**:126, 130
"Relocation" (Ortiz) **17**:231
Remains of Elmet (Hughes) **7**:146, 149, 162
"Rembrandt to Rembrandt" (Robinson) **1**:487
"Remember" (Harjo) **27**:59
"Remember" (Rossetti) **7**:269, 280
"Rememberance" (Holderlin)
See "Andenken"
"Remembering Pearl Harbor at the Tutankhamen Exhibit" (Kumin) **15**:196, 206, 208
"Remembering Robert Lowell" (Meredith) **28**:177, 180
"Remembrance" (Bronte) **8**:52, 56, 60, 65, 68, 74-5
"Remembrance Has a Rear and Front" (Dickinson) **1**:94
"Remembrance in Tsarskoe Selo" (Pushkin)
See "Vospominanie v Tsarskom Sele"
Remeslo (Tsvetaeva) **14**:315, 318, 324-25
"Reminiscence" (Ishikawa)
See "Omoide"
"Réminiscence" (Mallarme)
See "L'orphelin"
"Reminiscences at Tsarskoe Selo" (Pushkin)
See "Vospominanie v Tsarskom Sele"
"Remittance Man" (Wright) **14**:340, 348, 368
"Remords posthume" (Baudelaire) **1**:45
"Remorse" (Sassoon) **12**:282
Remorse (Coleridge) **11**:58
"Remorse for Intemperate Speech" (Yeats) **20**:328, 333
"Remorse Is Memory Awake" (Dickinson) **1**:111
"Removing the Plate of the Pump on the Hydraulic System of the Backhoe" (Snyder) **21**:307
Ren'aimeikashu (Hagiwara Sakutaro) **18**:170, 172
"Renaming the Kings" (Levine) **22**:215
"Renascence" (Millay) 204-05, 207-08, 211, 214-15, 217, 221, 224, 226-27, 242
Renascence, and Other Poems (Millay) **6**:204-06, 225, 240
"Rendezvous" (Kumin) **15**:213, 224
"The Renewal" (Roethke) **15**:275
"Renewal of Strength" (Harper) **21**:189
"Renka" (Nishiwaki) **15**:238
"Renunciation" (Parker) **28**:360
"Les reparties de Nina" (Rimbaud) **3**:271
"Repas" (Valery) **9**:391
"Repent" (Kumin) **15**:209, 211
"Repentance" (Herbert) **4**:120
"The Repetitive Heart" (Schwartz) **8**:292-93, 302
"Repining" (Rossetti) **7**:287
"Reply" (Bridges) **28**:66, 69
"Reply to Censure" (Roethke) **15**:291
"A Replycacion" (Skelton) **25**:374, 385
"Reponse aux adieux de Sir Walter Scott" (Lamartine) **16**:283
"Report" (Harper) **21**:207, 216
"Report" (Illyes) **16**:243
"Report to the Mother" (Knight) **14**:52
"Repose of Rivers" (Crane) **3**:83, 90, 96
"Repression of War Experience" (Sassoon) **12**:264, 267, 288
"The Reproach" (Gluck) **16**:152, 156, 164
"Reproach" (Graves) **6**:140, 144
"A Reproof of Gluttony" (Belloc) **24**:17
"Republican Living Rooms" (Olds) **22**:307
"Request for Requiems" (Hughes) **1**:243
"Request to a Year" (Wright) **14**:375
"A Request to the Graces" (Herrick) **9**:88
"Requeste à Monseigneur de Bourbon" (Villon) **13**:413
"Requiem" (Berry) **28**:16-17
"Requiem" (Nash) **21**:273
Requiem (Rilke) **2**:267, 279
Requiem: A Cycle of Poems (Akhmatova)
See *Rekviem: Tsikl stikhotvorenii*
"Requiem for the Death of a Boy" (Rilke) **2**:279
"Requiem for the Spanish Dead" (Rexroth) **20**:192
"Requiescat" (Arnold) **5**:12
"Requiescat" (Parker) **28**:349
Rerum vulgarium fragmenta (Petrarch)
See *Canzoniere*
"Rescue Poem" (Wakoski) **15**:324, 361
"Rescue with Yul Brynner" (Moore) **4**:242, 256, 259
Residence on Earth (Neruda)
See *Residencia en la tierra*
Residence on Earth and Other Poems (Neruda)
See *Residencia en la tierra*
Residencia en la tierra (Neruda) **4**:277, 2809, 282-83, 285, 293, 295, 300-01, 304, 306
Residencia en la tierra, Vol. 1, 1925-31 (Neruda)
See *Residencia en la tierra*

Cumulative Title Index

Residencia en la tierra, Vol. 2, 1931-35 (Neruda)
See *Residencia en la tierra*
Residencia I (Neruda)
See *Residencia en la tierra*
Residencia II (Neruda)
See *Residencia en la tierra*
Residencia III (Neruda)
See *Residencia en la tierra*
"Resignation" (Arnold) **5**:6, 18, 32, 34, 37-41, 43, 47, 49-51, 54
"Resignation" (Dunbar) **5**:133
"Resolution and Independence" (Wordsworth) **4**:399, 404, 406, 411-12, 426
"The Resolve" (Levertov) **11**:170
"Resolve" (Plath) **1**:406
"Respectability" (Browning) **2**:95
"The Respectable Burgher on 'The Higher Criticism'" (Hardy) **8**:124
Responce aux injures (Ronsard) **11**:234
"Responde tú" (Guillen) **23**:117, 127
"Respondez!" (Whitman) **3**:405
"Response" (Dunbar) **5**:139
"Résponse à une acte d'accusation" (Hugo) **17**:64, 82
Responsibilities, and Other Poems (Yeats) **20**:311, 320, 323, 342
"Responsibilities of the Poet" (Pinsky) **27**:160, 170
"Responso a Verlaine" (Dario) **15**:98
"A Responsory, 1948" (Merton) **10**:333
"Ressouvenir du lac Leman" (Lamartine) **16**:286
"Ressurection, Imperfect" (Donne) **1**:147
"Rest" (Rossetti) **7**:277, 280
"Restless" (Tagore)
See "Chanchal"
"Restless Night" (Tu Fu) **9**:319, 323
"Résumé" (Parker) **28**:347, 363
"Resurrection" (Atwood) **8**:40
"Resurrection" (Jeffers) **17**:141
"The Resurrection of Jesus" (Harper) **21**:189
"Resurrection of the Right Side" (Rukeyser) **12**:225
"Le Rétablissement de la Statue de Henri IV" (Hugo) **17**:88
Retaliation (Blok)
See *Vozmezdie*
"Retired Ballerina, Central Park West" (Ferlinghetti) **1**:183
"The Retired Colonel" (Hughes) **7**:140
"Retort" (Dunbar) **5**:125, 127
"Le retour" (Lamartine) **16**:286
Retour au pays natal (Cesaire)
See *Cahier d'un retour au pays natal*
Retratos con nombre (Aleixandre) **15**:4, 12, 16
"Retribution" (Blok) **21**:31
"Retribution" (Harper) **21**:190
Retribution (Blok)
See *Vozmezdie*
The Retrieval System (Kumin) **15**:203-09, 217, 221
"Retrospect" (Brooke) **24**:62, 64, 86
"The Return" (Brooke) **24**:61
"Return" (Forche) **10**:136-41, 144-45, 152, 154-56, 162, 167
"The Return" (Hayden) **6**:194
"Return" (Heaney) **18**:201
"Return" (Jeffers) **17**:117, 119, 131, 141, 147
"Return" (Paz)
See "Vuelta"
"The Return" (Pound) **4**:355-56, 365
"The Return" (Roethke) **15**:274
"Return" (Wright) **14**:342
The Return (Bely)
See *Vozvrat: Tretiia simfoniia*
Return (Paz)
See *Vuelta*
"Return in Hinton" (Tomlinson) **17**:311, 327-28
"The Return of Helen" (McGuckian) **27**:77, 100
"The Return of Robinson Jeffers" (Hass) **16**:195, 203, 228
"The Return of the Birds" (Bryant) **20**:46
"The Return of the Goddess" (Graves) **6**:137, 144
"Return to DeKalb" (Stryk) **27**:214
"Return to Hiroshima" (Stryk) **27**:187, 202, 216
"Return to Kraków in 1880" (Milosz) **8**:204
"A Return to Me" (Neruda)
See "Se vuelve a yo"
Return to My Native Land (Cesaire)
See *Cahier d'un retour au pays natal*
"Return to Oneself" (Neruda)
See "Se vuelve a yo"
"Return to Wang River" (Wang Wei) **18**:392
"The Return to Work" (Williams) **7**:369
"The Return Trip" (Ekeloef) **23**:54
"Returning" (Lowell) **3**:226
"Returning a Lost Child" (Gluck) **16**:124
"Returning North of Vortex" (Ginsberg) **4**:76
"Returning to Mount Sung" (Wang Wei) **18**:371
"Returning to the Rhetoric of an Early Mode" (Duncan) **2**:109, 113
"Reuben Bright" (Robinson) **1**:467, 496
"Reuben Pantier" (Masters) **1**:347
"Reunion" (Forche) **10**:137, 142-44, 147, 157, 168
"The Reunion" (Harper) **21**:200, 214
"Le rêve d'un curieux" (Baudelaire) **1**:54
"Rêve Expérimental" (Tzara) **27**:242
"Rêve parisien" (Baudelaire) **1**:47, 54
"Reveillé" (Housman) **2**:164
"Reveille" (Hughes) **7**:123, 159
"The Reveillon" (Belloc) **24**:11
"Revenant" (Meredith) **28**:181
"Revenge Fable" (Hughes) **7**:132, 143
"Reverdure" (Berry) **28**:8-9
"Reverie" (Browning) **2**:96
"Reversibilité" (Baudelaire) **1**:56, 67
"Reversionary" (Smith) **12**:314
"Revisiting the MacDowell Colony" (Kumin) **15**:222
The Revolt of Islam (Shelley) **14**:169-70, 172-73, 177, 181, 186-87, 189, 191-93, 213, 216-17, 233-38
See *Laon and Cythna*
"The Revolution at Market Hill" (Swift) **9**:260
"Revolution in the Revolution in the Revolution" (Snyder) **21**:306
"The Revolutionary" (Stryk) **27**:208
"Revolutionary Dreams" (Giovanni) **19**:111
"Revolutionary Music" (Giovanni) **19**:110
"Revolutions" (Arnold) **5**:51
"Les revolutions" (Lamartine) **16**:280-81, 293
Le revolver á cheveux blancs (Breton) **15**:50-2
"Revolving Meditation" (Kunitz) **19**:174, 178
"Revulsion" (Hardy) **8**:91
Rewards and Fairies (Kipling) **3**:184
"Reyerta" (Garcia Lorca) **3**:131
"The Rhapsody of Life's Progress" (Browning) **6**:6
"Rhapsody on a Windy Night" (Eliot) **5**:153, 155, 171
"A Rhapsody on Poetry" (Swift) **9**:281
"Der Rhein" (Holderlin) **4**:143, 148, 153, 155, 173-74
"Rhénane d'automne" (Apollinaire) **7**:42
"The Rhine" (Holderlin)
See "Der Rhein"
"Rhododendrons" (Gallagher) **9**:60
"The Rhodora" (Emerson) **18**:74, 82, 94, 96, 98-100, 102
"A Rhyme about an Electrical Advertising Sign" (Lindsay) **23**:296
"A Rhyme for All Zionists" (Lindsay) **23**:283
"The Rhyme of Reb Nachman" (Pinsky) **27**:175
"The Rhyme of the Duchess May" (Browning) **6**:28
"The Rhyme of the Three Captains" (Kipling) **3**:181-82
"The Rhyme of the Three Sealers" (Kipling) **3**:182
"Rhymed Address to All Renegade Campbellites Exhorting Them to Return" (Lindsay) **23**:265
Rhymed Ruminations (Sassoon) **12**:252
Rhymes (Jimenez)
See *Rimas*
"Rhythm & Blues 1" (Baraka) **4**:16
"Rhythm of Autumn" (Garcia Lorca)
See "Ritmo de otoño"
"La ricchezza" (Pasolini) **17**:270, 273, 295
"Richard Bone" (Masters) **1**:324
"Richard Cory" (Robinson) **1**:467, 475, 486
"Richard Hunt's 'Arachne'" (Hayden) **6**:186
"Richard Roe and John Doe" (Graves) **6**:141
"The Riddle" (Auden) **1**:34
"The Riddle" (Heaney) **18**:229, 232, 237
"Riddles" (Guillen) **23**:131
"The Ride" (Smith) **12**:315
"Ride to Aix" (Browning) **2**:35
"The Ridge Farm" (Ammons) **16**:46-7, 50-1
"Riding the Elevator into the Sky" (Sexton) **2**:373
"Rigamarole" (Williams) **7**:383, 389
"Right in the Trail" (Snyder) **21**:327
"The Right of Way" (Williams) **7**:387, 409, 411
"The Right Thing Happens to the Happy Man" (Roethke) **15**:270
"Right's Security" (Dunbar) **5**:127
Rimas (Jimenez) **7**:197, 199
Rime (Petrarch)
See *Canzoniere*
The Rime of the Ancient Mariner: A Poet's Reverie (Coleridge) **11**:37-42, 44, 51, 53, 55, 58-69, 81, 84, 88-9, 92-7, 104, 106, 110, 117
The Rime of the Ancyent Marinere (Coleridge)
See *The Rime of the Ancient Mariner: A Poet's Reverie*
Rime sparse (Petrarch)
See *Canzoniere*
"Un rimorso" (Gozzano) **10**:188
The Ring and the Book (Browning) **2**:39-40, 42-4, 46-7, 53, 56, 63, 66-7, 73, 76-7, 82-3, 85, 88, 95
"The Ring and the Castle" (Lowell) **13**:60-1
"The Ring Cycle" (Merrill) **28**:285-87
"Ringing the Bells" (Sexton) **2**:350, 353
"Ringless" (Wakoski) **15**:324
The Rings of Saturn (Wakoski) **15**:368-69
"Los ríos del canto" (Neruda) **4**:293
"Riot" (Brooks) **7**:82, 88-9, 91
Riot (Brooks) **7**:63-4, 66, 82, 88, 91, 94
Ripostes (Pound) **4**:317, 355
"The Ripple" (Levertov) **11**:171
"A Ripple Song" (Kipling) **3**:183
"Riprap" (Snyder) **21**:284, 299, 302
Riprap (Snyder) **21**:286-87, 290-91, 297, 300, 322
"The Risen One" (Rilke) **2**:271 .
"Rising" (Berry) **28**:16, 18-19
"The Rising of the Sun" (Milosz)
See "From Where the Sun Rises"
"The Rising Out" (McGuckian) **27**:102-104
"Risks and Possibilities" (Ammons) **16**:3, 29, 40
"Risveglio" (Pavese) **13**:229
"Rite of Passage" (Olds) **22**:312
"The Rites for Cousin Vit" (Brooks) **7**:66, 78, 81
"Rites for the Extrusion of a Leper" (Merton) **10**:345
"Rites of Passage" (Gunn) **26**:204
"Rites of Passage" (Stryk) **27**:204, 210
"Ritmo de otoño" (Garcia Lorca) **3**:125
"Ritorno di Deola" (Pavese) **13**:229
"Ritratto" (Pound) **4**:317
"Ritratto d'autore" (Pavese) **13**:213
"Ritter" (Rilke) **2**:266-67
"The Ritual of Memories" (Gallagher) **9**:60
"The Ritual of Memories" (Gallagher) **9**:60
"The Rival" (Plath) **1**:390
"The Rivals" (Dunbar) **5**:122
"The Rivals" (Johnson) **24**:141
"The River" (Arnold) **5**:19, 43

"The River" (Crane) **3**:84-6, 88-90, 95
"The River" (Emerson) **18**:97
"The River" (Tagore)
See "Pravahini"
"River" (Viereck) **27**:277
The River (Hughes) **7**:163, 171
"The River, By Night" (Bryant) **20**:17
"The River God" (Smith) **12**:331, 337
The River of Heaven (Hongo) **23**:198-99, 201, 204
"River Roads" (Sandburg) **2**:316
"River Stop" (Tu Fu) **9**:319
"River Village" (Tu Fu) **9**:319
Rivers and Mountains (Ashbery) **26**:107-108, 113-114, 116, 129, 142-143, 148, 154-155, 167, 173-174
"The Rivers of Song" (Neruda)
See "Los ríos del canto"
"The River's Story" (Tagore)
See "Tatinir katha"
"Riviere" (Montale) **13**:162
"The Rivulet" (Bryant) **20**:12, 14-15
"Rizpah" (Tennyson) **6**:372-73, 377, 379, 381, 411
"Rizpah, the Daughter of Ai" (Harper) **21**:191, 209, 218
"The Road" (Aiken) **26**:24, 46
"The Road" (Pinsky) **27**:168
"The Road" (Sassoon) **12**:242
"The Road and the End" (Sandburg) **2**:300
"The Road Between Here and There" (Kinnell) **26**:292
"The Road from Delphi" (Stryk) **27**:214
"The Road Not Taken" (Frost) **1**:202, 205, 213, 221, 230
"Road to Mandalay" (Kipling) **3**:179
The Road to Ruin (Sassoon) **12**:252, 270
"The Road to Shelter" (Gozzano) **10**:177
The Road to Shelter (Gozzano)
See *La via del refugio*
"Road Up" (Smith) **12**:317
"Roads" (Dario)
See "Caminos"
"The Roads Also" (Owen) **19**:343
"Roan Stallion" (Jeffers) **17**:107, 111, 113, 116, 127, 130, 135, 146
Roan Stallion, Tamar, and Other Poems (Jeffers) **17**:106, 122, 132, 135-37
"Roarers in a Ring" (Hughes) **7**:123
"Roast Opossum" (Dove) **6**:111
"Roastbeef" (Stein) **18**:327
"Robben Island" (Brutus) **24**:120
"The Robber" (MacDiarmid) **9**:155
"Robbery" (Shapiro) **25**:312
"Robe of Love" (Yosano Akiko)
See *Koigoromo*
"Robert Frost at Bread Loaf His Hand against a Tree" (Swenson) **14**:247, 253
"Robert G. Ingersoll" (Masters) **1**:343
"Robert Gould Shaw" (Dunbar) **5**:121
"Robert Lowell" (Shapiro) **25**:323
"Robert Schumann, Or: Musical Genius Begins with Affliction" (Dove) **6**:108
"Robin Hood's Heart" (Wylie) **23**:311
"Robin Song" (Hughes) **7**:134
"A Robyn Joly Robyn" (Wyatt) **27**:315
"Rocaille" (Gautier) **18**:141
"The Rock" (Stevens) **6**:303, 313
Rock and Hawk (Jeffers) **17**:137
"The Rock Below" (Graves) **6**:128-29
"The Rock of Rubies and the Quarry of Pearls" (Herrick) **9**:146
"Rockefeller is yo vice president, & yo mamma don't wear no drawers" (Baraka) **4**:30
"Rockpool" (Wright) **14**:376
"Rocky Acres" (Graves) **6**:151
"Rodine" (Bely) **11**:24
"Rodoslovnaya Moego Geroya" (Pushkin) **10**:391, 394
"Rodrigo" (Heine) **25**:159, 161
"The Roe Deer" (Tomlinson) **17**:335, 343
"Roger Clay's Proposal" (Merrill) **28**:234, 250
Rogsajyae (Tagore) **8**:424-26
Rokeby (Scott) **13**:265, 267-68, 277-78, 281, 285, 304, 307, 311, 318
"Roland Hayes Beaten" (Hughes) **1**:241, 243, 252
"The Roll of the Ages" (Noyes) **27**:136
"Rolling in at Twilight" (Snyder) **21**:288
"Rolling, Rolling" (Toomer) **7**:337
Roma 1950 diario (Pasolini) **17**:260
"Roman" (Rimbaud) **3**:271, 276
Roman Bartholow (Robinson) **1**:483, 489
"Roman Cadences" (Viereck) **27**:278
The Roman Calendar (Ovid)
See *Fasti*
Roman Elegies (Goethe)
See *Römische Elegien*
Roman Elegies II (Brodsky) **9**:21
"Roman Fountain" (Bogan) **12**:99
"The Roman Road" (Smith) **12**:346
"Romance" (Cassian) **17**:4
"Romance" (Robinson) **1**:495
Romance 48 (Juana Ines de la Cruz) **24**:215, 217-18
"Romance de la Guardia Civil Española" (Garcia Lorca) **3**:131, 148
"Romance de la luna, luna" (Garcia Lorca) **3**:133
"Romance de la pena negra" (Garcia Lorca) **3**:133
"Romance del emplazado" (Garcia Lorca) **3**:133
"Romance moderne" (Williams) **7**:345
"A Romance of the Age" (Browning)
See "Lady Geraldine's Courtship"
"Romance of the Spanish Civil Guard" (Garcia Lorca)
See "Romance de la Guardia Civil Española"
"The Romance of the Swan's Nest" (Browning) **6**:32
"Romance sonámbulo" (Garcia Lorca) **3**:131, 133, 147
Romancero (Heine)
See *Romanzero*
Romancero (Pasolini) **17**:253-54, 279, 281
Romancero gitano (Garcia Lorca)
See *Primer romancero gitano*
Romances sans paroles (Verlaine) **2**:414-15, 418-19, 424, 431-32
"The Romantic" (Bogan) **12**:87, 100-01, 103
"The Romany Girl" (Emerson) **18**:77
Romanzen (Heine) **25**:131, 158-59
Romanzero (Heine) **25**:167
"The Romaunt of Margret" (Browning) **6**:32
"The Romaunt of the Page" (Browning) **6**:30, 37-8, 42-3, 45
Rome 1950 A Diary (Pasolini) **17**:260-61
"Rome-Sickness" (Arnold) **5**:19
Römische Elegien (Goethe) **5**:239-40, 249, 255, 257
"Römische Sarkophage" (Rilke) **2**:278
"Rondalla" (Gautier) **18**:125
"Roofers" (Hass) **16**:248
"The Roofwalker" (Rich) **5**:363, 392-93, 395
"The Room" (Aiken) **26**:24
"The Room of Mirrors" (Masters) **1**:344
"The Room of My Life" (Sexton) **2**:373
"The Room with the Tapestry Rug" (Giovanni) **19**:143
"Rooming-house, Winter" (Atwood) **8**:14
"Rooms" (Stryk) **27**:215, 218
"Roosevelt" (Lindsay) **23**:288
"Rooster" (Hagiwara Sakutaro)
See "Rooster"
"Roosters" (Bishop) **3**:37, 46-8, 56-7, 60, 66
"Root Cellar" (Roethke) **15**:260, 295
"Roots" (Heaney) **18**:202
"Roots" (Hongo) **23**:198
"Roots" (Meredith) **28**:171, 175, 192, 194
"Roots and Branches" (Duncan) **2**:103, 110
Roots and Branches (Duncan) **2**:102, 105-06, 109, 113-14, 119, 125
"Rosa divina que en gentil cultura" (Juana Ines de la Cruz) **24**:225
"Rosa Mystica" (Hopkins) **15**:148, 159, 165
La rosa profunda (Borges) **22**:97
La rosa separada: obra póstuma (Neruda) **4**:287
Rosalind and Helen (Shelley) **14**:173, 175, 192, 234
"Rosary Songs" (Trakl)
See "Rosenkranzlieder"
"Rosas de elegía" (Guillen) **23**:100
"Le Rose" (Gautier) **18**:125
"The Rose" (Roethke) **15**:310-11
"The Rose" (Williams) **7**:386, 410
"The Rose" (Yeats) **20**:310
Rose (Lee) **24**:239-44
The Rose (Yeats) **20**:326, 328, 343, 347
"The Rose and the Cross" (Blok) **21**:31
"La rose de l'infant" (Hugo) **17**:60-61, 65
"The Rose of the World" (Yeats) **20**:329
"Rose on the Heath" (Goethe)
See "Heidenröslein"
"Rose, Rose" (Bukowski) **18**:5
"rose th night nd th green flowr" (Bissett) **14**:28, 33
"The Rose Trellis" (McGuckian) **27**:94
"Roseamond" (Apollinaire)
See "Rosemonde"
"Rosemonde" (Apollinaire) **7**:45, 47-8
"Rosenkranzlieder" (Trakl) **20**:233, 248
"Rosenschimmer" (Celan) **10**:122
"Roses" (Dove) **6**:109
"Roses" (Sandburg) **2**:324
"Le rossignol" (Lamartine) **16**:293
"Röster under jorden" (Ekeloef) **23**:76
"Rostro tras el cristal (Mirada del viejo)" (Aleixandre) **15**:43
"Rosy" (Gluck) **16**:138
"Rosy-Checked Death" (Yosano Akiko)
See "Kôgao no shi"
"Rotting Clam" (Hagiwara Sakutaro) **18**:167, 177
"A Rotting Corpse" (Baudelaire)
See "Une charogne"
"A Round & A Canon" (Olson) **19**:281
"Round Dance Somewhere Around Oklahoma City/November Night" (Harjo) **27**:69
"Round the Turning" (Pasternak) **6**:267
"Round Trip" (Page) **12**:163
"The Roundel" (Swinburne) **24**:319, 322-23
A Roundhead's Rallying Song (Noyes) **27**:138
"De Route March" (McKay) **2**:225
"Route Marchin'" (Kipling) **3**:160
"A Route of Evanescence" (Dickinson) **1**:104
"Route Six" (Kunitz) **19**:175
"Rover" (Kunitz) **19**:175
"Rowing" (McGuckian) **27**:104
"Rowing" (Sexton) **2**:373
"The Rowing Endeth" (Sexton) **2**:371
"A Roxbury Garden" (Lowell) **13**:77-8, 96
"A Royal Princess" (Rossetti) **7**:272, 291
"Royauté" (Rimbaud) **3**:261-63
"Rozhdenie ulybki" (Mandelstam) **14**:152-53
Rtusamhara (Kalidasa) **22**:177, 182, 184-85, 208
Rubáiyát (Khayyam) **8**:143-45, 151-53, 157-70
Ruba'iyat (Khayyam)
See *Rubáiyát*
"Rubies" (Emerson) **18**:77
"Ruby Brown" (Hughes) **1**:249
La rueda dentada (Guillen) **23**:109, 127, 133
"Rugby Chapel" (Arnold) **5**:33
"Ruin" (Garcia Lorca)
See "Ruina"
"The Ruin" (Tomlinson) **17**:325-26, 335
"Ruina" (Garcia Lorca) **3**:139
"The Ruined Cottage" (Wordsworth) **4**:416, 418
"The Ruined Temple" (Tagore)
See "Bhagna mandir"
"The Ruines of Time" (Spenser) **8**:366-67, 371
"Ruminants" (Joyce) **22**:149
"Rumour" (Tomlinson) **17**:317

"Rumpelstiltskin" (Sexton) **2**:364
"run tonight" (Bissett) **14**:16-17
Run with the Hunted (Bukowski) **18**:4-5
"Runagate, Runagate" (Hayden) **6**:176, 178-80, 183, 185, 188, 194, 197-98
"The Runaway" (Frost) **1**:194
The Runaway, and Other Stories (Tagore)
See *Palataka*
"The Runaway Slave at Pilgrim's Point" (Browning) **6**:30, 37-8, 42-3, 45
"Runes" (Nemerov) **24**:262, 265, 268, 291
"Runes on Weland's Island" (Kipling) **3**:171
"Running on the Shore" (Swenson) **14**:288
"Running Water Music" (Snyder) **21**:306
"Rupture" (Pasternak) **6**:260
The Rural Muse (Clare) **23**:44
"Rural Objects" (Ashbery) **26**:124
"Rusalka" (Lermontov) **18**:289-90, 292
"Rus in Urbe" (Meredith) **28**:171, 190
Rush/What Fuckan Theory (Bissett) **14**:13
"Rusia en 1931" (Hass) **16**:224
Ruslan and Lyudmila (Pushkin)
See *Ruslan i Lyudmila*
Ruslan i Lyudmila (Pushkin) **10**:357-58, 363-64, 375, 381-82, 386-88, 398, 404-09
"Russia" (Williams) **7**:370
"Russia comes into Poland" (Zagajewski) **27**:389, 394
"Russian Sonia" (Masters) **1**:327
Rustic Elegies (Sitwell) **3**:294-95, 319
"Rusty Crimson (Christmas Day, 1917)" (Sandburg) **2**:331
"Ruth" (Wordsworth) **4**:380, 402
"Ruth and Naomi" (Harper) **21**:191, 194, 209, 218
"Ru'ya'" (Gibran) **9**:79
"Ryght True It is" (Wyatt) **27**:318
"Ryojo" (Hagiwara Sakutaro) **18**:178
"S morya" (Tsvetaeva) **14**:325
s th story i to (Bissett) **14**:3, 5, 7-8
"Saadi" (Emerson) **18**:81, 87-88, 98, 104, 107
"Sábados" (Borges) **22**:93
"Sabala" (Tagore) **8**:415
"Sabás" (Guillen) **23**:103
"A Sabbath Morning at Sea" (Browning) **6**:14
"Sabbath Park" (McGuckian) **27**:101
Sabbaths (Berry) **28**:34, 39, 43-44
Sabbaths: 1987-1990 (Berry) **28**:38, 43
"Sabishii jinkaku" (Hagiwara Sakutaro) **18**:177, 181
Sabotage (Baraka) **4**:38
"Sab-peyechhir desh" (Tagore) **8**:412
"El sacamuelas" (Fuertes) **27**:35
"Sacrament" (Cullen) **20**:85
"Sacred Chant for the Return of Black Spirit and Power" (Baraka) **4**:27
"The Sacrifice" (Herbert) **4**:107, 117, 120
"The Sacrifice of Er-Heb" (Kipling) **3**:181
"The Sacrilege" (Hardy) **8**:99
Sad Airs (Jimenez)
See *Arias tristes*
"A Sad Distant View" (Hagiwara Sakutaro) **18**:176
The sad field-hand (Illyes)
See *Szomoru beres*
"The Sad Garden Dissolves" (Jimenez)
See "El jardín triste se pierde"
"Sad Moments" (Gallagher) **9**:64
"Sad Moonlit Night" (Hagiwara Sakutaro)
See "Sad Moonlit Night"
"The Sad Shepherd" (Yeats) **20**:354
"Sad Song" (Kunitz) **19**:147, 155
"Sad Steps" (Larkin) **21**:229-30
"Sad Strains of a Gay Waltz" (Stevens) **6**:296-97
"The Sad Supper" (Pavese)
See "La cena triste"
Sad Toys (Ishikawa)
See *Kanashiki gangu*
"Sad Wine" (Pavese)
See "Il vino triste"
"Sadako" (Soto) **28**:383
"Sadie and Maude" (Brooks) **7**:67, 69
Sadness and Happiness An Explanation of America History of My Heart Poetry and the World (Pinsky) **27**:
Sadness and Happiness: Poems (Pinsky) **27**:143-44, 153, 156, 160-62, 173, 175-76
"The Sadness of Brothers" (Kinnell) **26**:260
"The Sadness of Lemons" (Levine) **22**:211
"Safety" (Brooke) **24**:59, 80, 88
"Saffron" (Smith) **12**:295
"Saga" (Viereck) **27**:265
Saga Diary (Matsuo Basho)
See *Saga nikki*
Saga nikki (Matsuo Basho) **3**:29
Sagan om Fatumeh (Ekeloef) **23**:60, 65, 68-9, 77-8
"Sagesse" (H. D.) **5**:275
"Sagesse" (Hugo) **17**:77-78, 97
Sagesse (H. D.) **5**:282, 285
Sagesse (Verlaine) **2**:413, 415-19, 425-26, 430
"Said Song" (Ammons) **16**:19
"Said the Poet to the Analyst" (Sexton) **2**:358-59
"The Sail" (Lermontov) **18**:297
"The Sail of Ulysses" (Stevens) **6**:326, 328
"Sailing after Lunch" (Stevens) **6**:297, 338
"Sailing Home from Rapallo" (Lowell) **3**:205, 220, 245
"Sailing of the Swallow" (Swinburne) **24**:356-57
"The Sailing of the Swan" (Swinburne) **24**:313, 349, 357
"Sailing to Byzantium" (Yeats) **20**:308, 310, 316, 329, 333, 335, 346, 349
"A Sailor in Africa" (Dove) **6**:110
"Sailor in Moscow" (Pasternak)
See "Matros v Moskve"
"The Sailor's Mother" (Wordsworth) **4**:398, 402
"Saint" (Graves) **6**:141, 144, 151
"Saint" (Merrill) **28**:240, 241
"The Saint" (Shapiro) **25**:268, 286
"A Saint about to Fall" (Thomas) **2**:408-09
"Saint Anthony and the Rose of Life" (Smith) **12**:308
"St. Augustine-by-the-Sea" (Swenson) **14**:288
"Saint Francis and Lady Clare" (Masters) **1**:325, 333
"Saint Francis and the Sow" (Kinnell) **26**:259-60, 292
"Sainte" (Mallarme) **4**:201
"Sainte-Nitouche" (Robinson) **1**:460
"Saints and Singing" (Stein) **18**:346
La Saisiaz (Browning) **2**:66, 68, 71-2, 74
Une saison en enfer (Rimbaud) **3**:249, 252-53, 260-66, 268, 270, 279, 286
"Un sajón" (Borges) **22**:98
"Sakyamuni Coming Out from the Mountain" (Ginsberg) **4**:49
"Sal" (Tagore) **8**:416
"La Salade" (Ronsard) **11**:240
The Salamander (Paz)
See *Salamandra*
Salamandra (Paz) **1**:353, 357, 360-62, 369
"Saliences" (Ammons) **16**:6, 23
Salisbury Plain (Wordsworth) **4**:429
"The Sallow Bird" (Smith) **12**:326
"Sallie Chisum/Last Words on Billy the Kid 4 a.m." (Ondaatje) **28**:338-39
"El salmo de la pluma" (Dario) **15**:93
"The Salmon Fisher to the Salmon" (Heaney) **18**:225
"The Salmon Leap" (MacDiarmid) **9**:153
"Salmon-Fishing" (Jeffers) **17**:131
Salmos (Cardenal) **22**:103, 117-19, 125, 129-31
Salmos Psalms of Struggle and Liberation (Cardenal) **22**:118
"Salomé" (Laforgue) **14**:69, 72
"Salome';s Dancing-lesson," (Parker) **28**:351, 363
"The Salt Garden" (Nemerov) **24**:261
The Salt Garden (Nemerov) **24**:260-61, 264, 288-89
"Saltimbanque Elegie" (Rilke)
See "Saltimbanques"
"Saltimbanques" (Rilke) **2**:278, 295
"Les Saltimbanques" (Tzara) **27**:224
"Salts and Oils" (Levine) **22**:224
"Salutación al águila" (Dario) **15**:77, 90, 107, 115
"Salutación del optimista" (Dario) **15**:81, 115
"Salutation to the Eagle" (Dario)
See "Salutación al águila"
"Salute to Guinea" (Cesaire) **25**:32
"Salute to Our Allies" (Brutus) **24**:119
Salutes and Censures (Brutus) **24**:118-20
"Salvador Díaz Mirón" (Dario) **15**:118
"Sambhashan" (Tagore) **8**:417
"Samos" (Merrill) **28**:233
"Samothrake" (Ekeloef) **23**:76
"Samson" (Blake) **12**:31
Samson's Anger (Vigny)
See "La colère de Samson"
Sämtliche Werke (Heine) **25**:172
"The Samuel Pie" (Belloc) **24**:42
"San Diego Poem" (Ortiz) **17**:226, 233
"San Fernando Road" (Soto) **28**:369, 377, 384-85
"San Fruttuoso: The Divers" (Tomlinson) **17**:349
"San Ildefonso Nocturne" (Paz)
See "Nocturno de San Ildefonso"
"A San Juan de la Cruz" (Fuertes) **27**:14
San Martín Copybook (Borges)
See *Cuaderno San Martín*
"San Onofre, California" (Forche) **10**:141, 152-53, 155, 158
"Sanctuary" (Wright) **14**:343
"Sanctuary" (Wylie) **23**:323, 329
"The Sand Altar" (Lowell) **13**:95
Der Sand aus den Urnen (Celan) **10**:95, 121
"Sand Dunes" (Frost) **1**:203, 218
Sand from the Urns (Celan)
See *Der Sand aus den Urnen*
"Sand Martin" (Clare) **23**:5
"The Sand-Diggrers' Twilight" (Pavese)
See "Crepuscolo di sabbiatori"
Sandhya sangit (Tagore) **8**:405-06
"Sandpiper" (Bishop) **3**:53-4
"Sands" (Cassian) **17**:11
Le sanglot de la terre (Laforgue) **14**:57, 64, 68-71, 74, 80-1, 95
"Sanglot perdu" (Laforgue) **14**:86, 88
"La sangre numerosa" (Guillen) **23**:128-29
Sangschaw (MacDiarmid) **9**:151, 158, 166, 187, 190-91, 196
"Santa" (Sexton) **2**:365
"Santa Barbara Road" (Hass) **16**:217
"Santa Claus" (Nemerov) **24**:267
"Santa Cruz Propostions" (Duncan) **2**:116
"The Santa Fé Trail" (Lindsay) **23**:264, 268, 273, 278, 286-87, 294
"Santa Lucia" (Hass) **16**:211
"Santarém" (Bishop) **3**:64-5
"Santorini: Stopping the Leak" (Merrill) **28**:267-69
Saogi (Yosano Akiko) **11**:310
"The Sap is Gone Out of the Trees" (Ammons) **16**:39
"Sapho" (Lamartine) **16**:277
"Sapphics" (Swinburne) **24**:320
"Sara" (Nishiwaki) **15**:241
"Sarajevo" (Nemerov) **24**:291
Sarashina kiko (Matsuo Basho) **3**:26
"Sarcophagi I" (Montale) **13**:116
Sardanapalus (Byron) **16**:91, 103, 109-10
Sarumino (Matsuo Basho) **3**:3, 4, 29
"Sarvaneshe" (Tagore) **8**:414
"Sashka" (Lermontov) **18**:278
"Satan Says" (Olds) **22**:319
Satan Says (Olds) **22**:307, 310, 312, 315, 317, 319-20, 322, 327-28
"Satanic Form" (Swenson) **14**:252
Satin-Legs Smith (Brooks)
See "The Sundays of Satin-Legs Smith"

"Satire III" (Wyatt) **27**:342
Satires and Epistles of Horace, Imitated (Pope) **26**:321
"Satires of Circumstance" (Hardy) **8**:124
Satires of Circumstance (Hardy) **8**:91, 97
Satires of Dr. Donne Versified (Pope) **26**:324-25
Satires of Horace (Pope) **26**:359
"A Satirical Elegy on the Death of a Late Famous General" (Swift) **9**:256, 294, 307
Satirical Poems (Sassoon) **12**:258
"The Satisfactions of the Mad Farmer" (Berry) **28**:43
"Satsujin jiken" (Hagiwara Sakutaro) **18**:177, 180
"Satturday: The Small Pox: Flavia" (Montagu) **16**:349
Satura (Montale) **13**:131-34, 138, 143, 148, 152, 161, 167
"Saturn's Rings" (Wakoski) **15**:369
"A Satyr" (Montagu) **16**:338
"The Satyr in the Periwig" (Sitwell) **3**:294
"Le satyre" (Hugo) **17**:62, 65, 85, 87, 89
"Satyre II" (Donne) **1**:144
"Satyre III" (Donne) **1**:125, 143, 147
Satyres (Donne) **1**:140-42, 145
"Saul" (Browning) **2**:36, 67-8, 72, 75
"Sausages" (Stein) **18**:353
"La sauvage" (Vigny) **26**:368-70, 372, 382, 402, 412
"Saved by Faith" (Harper) **21**:189, 208
"The Saving" (Pinsky) **27**:159
"A Saxon" (Borges)
See "Un sajón"
"Say, Lad, Have You Things to Do" (Housman) **2**:179, 192
"Saying It to Keep It from Happening" (Ashbery) **26**:136
"The Scales of the Eyes" (Nemerov) **24**:261-62
"Scapegoats and Rabies" (Hughes) **7**:137
"Scar" (Lorde) **12**:139
"Scarab" (Brutus) **24**:111
"Scarecrow" (Stryk) **27**:197
A Scattering of Salts (Merrill) **28**:281-82, 284-87
"A Scene on the Banks of the Hudson" (Bryant) **20**:14, 46
"Scenes of Childhood" (Merrill) **28**:248
"schattenbild" (Enzensberger) **28**:139
"schaum" (Enzensberger) **28**:136
"Scheherazade" (Ashbery) **26**:127, 150
"Der Scheidende" (Heine) **25**:178-80
"Die Schildkro¨te" (Enzensberger) **28**:165
"schla¨ferung" (Enzensberger) **28**:139
"Schneebett" (Celan) **10**:114
Schneepart (Celan) **10**:96, 98
"The Scholar" (Baraka) **4**:23
"The Scholar-Gipsy" (Arnold) **5**:7, 13, 18-24, 33-5, 37, 47, 51, 53, 53, 59
"The School Children" (Gluck) **16**:128, 132, 149
"School Days" (Ashbery) **26**:137
School Figures (Song) **21**:341, 347
"The School of Desire" (Swenson) **14**:276, 284
"A School of Prayer" (Baraka) **4**:10, 18
"The School-Boy" (Blake) **12**:7, 34
Schoolboy Lyrics (Kipling) **3**:190, 193
"Schoolmaster" (Larkin) **21**:234, 241
"The Schoolmistresses" (Pavese)
See "Le maestrine"
"School Night" (Soto) **28**:399
"Schopenhauer's Crying" (Zagajewski) **27**:384
"An Schwager Kronos" (Goethe) **5**:245, 247, 251
"Science" (Jeffers) **17**:113
"Science has looked" (Owen) **19**:371
"The Science of the Night" (Kunitz) **19**:153, 170, 182
"Scilla" (Gluck) **16**:169
"Scirocco" (Montale) **13**:105, 125
"Scorpion" (Smith) **12**:301, 319, 333
Scorpion and Other Poems (Smith) **12**:299, 315
Scots Unbound (MacDiarmid) **9**:158, 175-76, 196
"Scots Wha Hae wi' Wallace Bled" (Burns) **6**:78
"Scouting" (Levine) **22**:220-21, 228, 231-32
"Screaming Tarn" (Bridges) **28**:68
"Screvo meu livro à beira-mágoa" (Pessoa) **20**:155-56
"Screw: A Technical Love Poem" (Wakoski) **15**:332
"Screw Guns" (Kipling) **3**:158
"Scripts for the Pageant" (Merrill) **28**:233, 234, 235, 236, 237, 238, 243, 260-64, 276-78, 281
"Scroll" (Noyes) **27**:130
"Scrub" (Millay) **6**:235
"The Sculptor" (Plath) **1**:388-89
"Scurry" (Swenson) **14**:254
"Scyros" (Shapiro) **25**:268, 279
The Scythians (Blok)
See *Skify*
"Se acabó" (Guillen) **23**:117, 125
"Se vuelve a yo" (Neruda) **4**:287
"The Sea" (Borges)
See "El mar"
"The Sea" (Parker) **28**:351
"The Sea" (Swenson) **14**:288
"The Sea" (Williams) **7**:385, 387
"Sea and Night" (Aleixandre)
See "Mar y noche"
The Sea and the Bells (Neruda)
See *El mar y las campanas*
"The Sea and the Mirror: A Commentary on Shakespeare's *Tempest*" (Auden) **1**:22, 34
"Sea Calm" (Hughes) **1**:236
"Sea Change" (Tomlinson) **17**:321
"Sea Dirge" (Carroll) **18**:46
"Sea Dreams" (Tennyson) **6**:360
Sea Garden (H. D.) **5**:266-67, 288-90, 303
"The Sea Horse" (Graves) **6**:154
"Sea Iris" (H. D.) **5**:289
"Sea Lily" (H. D.) **5**:288
"Sea Lullaby" (Wylie) **23**:332
"Sea Poppies" (H. D.) **5**:288
"Sea Surface Full of Clouds" (Stevens) **6**:304, 332
"Sea Unicorns and Land Unicorns" (Moore) **4**:233
"Sea Violet" (H. D.) **5**:289
"The Sea Was Asleep" (Zagajewski) **27**:394
"Sea-Blue and Blood-Red" (Lowell) **13**:60, 64, 66, 72, 81, 83
"The Sea-Elephant" (Williams) **7**:360
"The Sea-Fairies" (Tennyson) **6**:348, 359
"The Seafarer" (Pound) **4**:317, 331, 364
Seamarks (Perse)
See *Amers*
"The Seamless Garment" (MacDiarmid) **9**:177
"The Seamstress" (Song) **21**:331, 333-34, 336, 341, 350
"Sea-Nymph's Prayer to Okeanos" (Zukofsky) **11**:368
"The Search" (Herbert) **4**:101
"The Search" (Masters) **1**:343-44
"Searching for the Canto Fermo" (Wakoski) **15**:362
"Searching, Not Searching" (Rukeyser) **12**:224
"Searchlight Practice" (Wright) **14**:354
"Sea-Rose" (H. D.) **5**:288, 303
"Seascape" (Bishop) **3**:37
"Sea-Serpent" (MacDiarmid) **9**:193
The Seashell Game (Matsuo Basho)
See *Kai oi*
"The Seashore" (Emerson) **18**:76, 80, 89, 91
"Seaside" (Brooke) **24**:58, 76, 84, 86, 88
"A Sea-Side Meditation" (Browning) **6**:20
A Season in Hell (Rimbaud)
See *Une saison en enfer*
The Season of Violence (Paz)
See *La estación violenta*
Season Songs (Hughes) **7**:157, 162, 171
"Seasonal" (Ashbery) **26**:166
"Seasons" (Bradstreet)
See "The Four Seasons of the Year"
"Seasons" (Tomlinson) **17**:326
The Seasons (Kalidasa)
See *Rtusamhara*
"Seated Figure" (Gluck) **16**:153
Seaton Prize Odes (Smart) **13**:329
"Seattle 7 May 72" (Brutus) **24**:123
"Sea-Wind" (Mallarme) **4**:187
Sebastian im Traum (Trakl) **20**:236, 241, 244, 250
"Sebastian in Traum" (Trakl) **20**:228, 230-31
"Sécheresse" (Perse) **23**:255, 257
"The Second Angel" (Levine) **22**:213
The Second Anniversarie. Of the Progres of the Soule. Wherein, By Occasion Of the Religious death of Mistris Elizabeth Drury, the incommodities of the Soule in this life, and her exaltation in the next, are Contemplated (Donne) **1**:122, 145-51, 155-57
"Second April" (Millay) **6**:206
Second April (Millay) **6**:211-12, 214-15, 233, 242-44
"The Second Best" (Arnold) **5**:42
"Second Best" (Brooke) **24**:76, 84
"Second Best" (Brooke) **24**:59, 60
"Second Best Bed" (Shapiro) **25**:316
The Second Birth (Pasternak) **6**:253-54, 268, 281
A Second Book (Mandelstam)
See *Vtoraya kniga*
"The Second Chambermaid's Song" (Yeats) **20**:332
"Second Chance" (Wakoski) **15**:347
"The Second Coming" (Yeats) **20**:308, 312-13, 319-20, 349
"Second Elegy" (Rilke)
See "Second Song"
"Second Epistle to John Lapraik" (Burns) **6**:68-70, 78
"Second Fig" (Millay) **6**:227
"Second Georgic" (Vergil) **12**:359, 365
"Second Glance at a Jaguar" (Hughes) **7**:136-37
"Second Hymn to Lenin" (MacDiarmid) **9**:158, 177, 180-81, 197
Second Hymn to Lenin, and Other Poems (MacDiarmid) **9**:156, 179, 196
The Second Jungle Book (Kipling) **3**:162, 185, 188-89
"Second Language" (Gallagher) **9**:60
Second livre des poemes (Ronsard) **11**:282
"Second Nun's Tale" (Chaucer) **19**:13, 15
"Second Oldest Story" (Parker) **28**:362
Second Olympian (Pindar)
See *Olympian 2*
"Second Populist Manifesto" (Ferlinghetti)
See "Adieu á Charlot"
Second Pythian (Pindar)
See *Pythian 2*
"The Second Sermon on the Warpland" (Brooks) **7**:63
"Second Song" (Bogan) **12**:90, 129
"Second Song" (Rilke) **2**:273-74, 286
"Second Song for the Worship of the Goddess at Yü Mountain: 'Bidding the Godeess Farewell'" (Wang Wei) **18**:369
The Second Symphony (Bely)
See *Vtoraia simfoniia: Dramaticheskaia*
Second Voronezh Notebook (Mandelstam) **14**:133-34, 149, 152-53
Second Year of Chang-ho (Li Ho) **13**:42
"The Second-Best Bed" (Nemerov) **24**:291
"Second-Class Constable Alston" (McKay) **2**:205
"The Secret" (Merton) **10**:348
"Secret Festival; September Moon" (Levertov) **11**:177
The Secret Meaning of Things (Ferlinghetti) **1**:173-74, 176, 186-87
"Secret Music" (Sassoon) **12**:247

"The Secret of Machu Pichhu"
See "El Secreto de Machu-Picchu"
"Secretary" (Hughes) **7**:140
"El Secreto de Machu-Picchu" (Cardenal) **22**:132
Secrets from the Center of the World (Harjo) **27**:65, 68
The Secrets of the Heart (Gibran) **9**:72
"Secrets of the Trade" (Akhmatova) **2**:5
Section: Rock-Drill, 85-95 de los cantares (Pound) **4**:352, 357
Secular Love (Ondaatje) **28**:314-17, 340
"Sed de Correr" (Clampitt) **19**:100
"Seduction" (Giovanni) **19**:111, 113, 117
"Seed and Bran" (Tzara) **27**:242
"The Seed Cutters" (Heaney) **18**:203
"Seed Pods" (Snyder) **21**:305
"The Seed-Picture" (McGuckian) **27**:79, 97
Seeds and Bran (Tzara)
See *Grains et issues*
Seeds for a Hymn (Paz)
See *Semillas para un himno*
Seeing Is Believing (Tomlinson) **17**:302, 306, 317-18, 321, 323-24, 332-33, 335, 338, 341-42, 346, 352, 359
"Seeing the Bones" (Kumin) **15**:207, 209
"Seeing Things" (Nemerov) **24**:302
Seeing Things (Heaney) **18**:254-61
"The Seekonk Woods" (Kinnell) **26**:278, 293
"Seen by the Waits" (Hardy) **8**:130
Segund antolojía poética (Jimenez) **7**:178, 201
"Le Seigneur habite en toi" (Gautier) **18**:144
"Seizure" (Sappho)
See "Ode to Anactoria"
A Seizure of Limericks (Aiken) **26**:24
"Seldom yet Now" (Graves) **6**:156
Selected Failings (Neruda)
See *Defectos escogidos: 2000*
Selected letters (Williams) **7**:374
Selected Poems (Ashbery) **26**:158
Selected Poems (Breton) **15**:57
Selected Poems (Brooks) **7**:81, 102
Selected Poems (Duncan) **2**:102
Selected Poems (Enzensberger) **28**:166
Selected Poems (Frost) **1**:195
Selected Poems (H. D.) **5**:274
Selected Poems (Hayden) **6**:176, 178-79
Selected Poems (Kinnell) **26**:261-62, 288
Selected Poems (Levine) **22**:220
Selected Poems (Lowell) **3**:226-27
Selected Poems (McKay) **2**:207, 228
Selected Poems (Meredith) **28**:207
Selected Poems (Milosz) **8**:174
Selected Poems (Montale) **13**:135
Selected Poems (Moore) **4**:240, 242, 253
Selected Poems (Pasolini) **17**:289
Selected Poems (Rukeyser) **12**:210
Selected Poems (Senghor) **25**:238, 241, 245
Selected Poems (Sexton) **2**:347-48
Selected Poems (Shapiro) **25**:315
Selected Poems (Sitwell) **3**:320
Selected Poems (Smith) **12**:293, 309, 350
Selected Poems (Stryk) **27**:185, 187-89, 191, 197-98, 201-3
Selected Poems (Tomlinson) **17**:327, 345
Selected Poems, 1928-1958 (Kunitz) **19**:148, 155, 157, 159, 161-63, 168-70, 173-76
Selected Poems (1938-1958): Summer Knowledge (Schwartz)
See *Summer Knowledge: New and Selected Poems, 1938-1958*
Selected Poems, 1950-1975 (Gunn) **26**:206
Selected Poems, 1951-1974 (Tomlinson) **17**:325
Selected Poems, 1957-1967 (Hughes) **7**:163
Selected Poems 1965-1975 (Atwood) **8**:23
Selected Poems and New (Villa) **22**:349, 351, 353-54
Selected Poems and Prose of John Clare (Clare) **23**:3-8, 11, 13-14
Selected Poems: Beyond Even Faithful Legends (Bissett) **14**:27-30, 34-5
Selected Poems, Joseph Brodsky (Brodsky) **9**:8
The Selected Poems of Langston Hughes (Hughes) **1**:248, 258
Selected Poetry of Amiri Baraka/LeRoi Jones (Baraka) **4**:31
The Selected Poetry of Hayden Carruth (Carruth) **10**:84
The Selected Poetry of Robinson Jeffers (Jeffers) **17**:111, 123, 130, 133, 136-37, 141
Selected Writings (Olson) **19**:268, 276-77, 305, 316-17
Selected Writings of Juan Ramon Jimenez (Jimenez)
See *Antolojía poética (1898-1953)*
"Selective Service" (Forche) **10**:137, 144, 146, 157, 165
"Self and Life" (Eliot) **20**:136
The Self and the Other (Borges)
See *El otro, el mismo*
"Self in 1958" (Sexton) **2**:351
"Self Portrait" (Wylie) **23**:321
"The Self Unsatisfied Runs Everywhere" (Schwartz) **8**:285
"The Self-Abuser and the Suicide" (Viereck) **27**:279
"The Self-Betrayal Which Is Nothing New" (Schwartz) **8**:294
"Self-Criticism and Answer" (Day Lewis) **11**:128, 144
"Self-Criticism in February" (Jeffers) **17**:123, 132
"Self-Dependence" (Arnold) **5**:19, 42-3, 49
"The Self-Hatred of Don L. Lee" (Madhubuti) **5**:337
"The Selfish One" (Neruda)
See "El egoísta"
"Self-Portrait" (Cassian) **17**:7
"A Self-Portrait: David" (Tomlinson) **17**:346, 348
"Self-Portrait in a Convex Mirror" (Ashbery) **26**:109, 119-21, 123-24, 126, 134, 140, 142-43, 147-50, 159, 171-72, 174
Self-Portrait in a Convex Mirror (Ashbery) **26**:115-16, 118, 124, 126-27, 130, 145, 148-50, 160, 169, 171, 174
"Self-Portrait in Tyvek (TM) Windbreaker" (Merrill) **28**:287
"Self-Praise" (Graves) **6**:139
"The Self-Unseeing" (Hardy) **8**:88, 129
"Selige Sehnsucht" (Goethe) **5**:248
"Selinda and Cloris" (Behn) **13**:30
"Sella" (Bryant) **20**:15
"A Seltzer Bottle" (Stein) **18**:334
"The Selves" (Page) **12**:198
"La semaine Sainte" (Lamartine) **16**:277, 299
"The Semblables" (Williams) **7**:360
Semillas para un himno (Paz) **1**:353, 366
"Semper eadem" (Baudelaire) **1**:61, 72
"Semplicità" (Pavese) **13**:229
"The Sence of a Letter Sent Me, Made into Verse; to a New Tune" (Behn) **13**:31
"Sence You Went Away" (Johnson) **24**:132, 141, 151, 154, 162
"Send No Money" (Larkin) **21**:234, 242, 248
"The Send-Off" (Owen) **19**:347
Senlin: A Biography (Aiken) **26**:4, 6, 12, 22, 29, 70-2
"Señor Diego Valverde" (Juana Ines de la Cruz) **24**:186
"Señor, para responderos" (Juana Ines de la Cruz) **24**:187
"Señora doña Ros" (Juana Ines de la Cruz) **24**:211
"Sensation" (Rimbaud) **3**:275, 283
"Sensation Time at the Home" (Merton)
See "A Song: Sensation Time at the Home"
"Sense and Conscience" (Tennyson) **6**:372-73
The Sense of Movement (Gunn) **26**:181, 184-185, 188-189, 200-201, 206-207, 210, 212, 218-220, 230
"Sensemayá" (Guillen) **23**:131-32, 134
"Sensibility! O La!" (Roethke) **15**:257, 278, 299, 301
The Sensitive Plant (Shelley) **14**:167, 171, 175, 193, 196, 198
"The Sensualists" (Roethke) **15**:275
sent på jorden (Ekeloef) **23**:62, 75, 77, 88
"The Sentence" (Akhmatova)
See "Prigovor"
"The Sentence" (Graves) **6**:157
"A Sentence for Tyranny" (Hass) **16**:248
"Sentences" (Milosz) **8**:189
Sentences (Nemerov) **24**:'
Sentences (Nemerov) **24**:288
"The Sententious Man" (Roethke) **15**:272, 278
"The Sentimental Surgeon" (Page) **12**:176
"The Separate Notebooks" (Milosz)
See "Osobny zeszyt"
The Separate Notebooks (Milosz) **8**:182, 195-97
The Separate Rose (Neruda)
See *La rosa separada: obra póstuma*
"Les sept epées" (Apollinaire) **7**:46
"Les sept vieillards" (Baudelaire) **1**:45, 65, 70
"September" (Belloc) **24**:29
"September" (Hughes) **7**:113, 118
"September" (Zagajewski) **27**:396
"September 1, 1939" (Auden) **1**:14, 25
"September 22nd" (Kumin) **15**:190
"September 1913" (Yeats) **20**:324-25
"September Afternoon in the Abandoned Barracks" (Zagajewski) **27**:391
"September on Jessore Road" (Ginsberg) **4**:59
"September Shooting" (Nemerov) **24**:288
"September Twilight" (Gluck) **16**:170
"Le Septiesme livre des poemes" (Ronsard) **11**:246
"Sepulchre" (Herbert) **4**:120
Sequel to Drum-Taps (Whitman) **3**:418, 422
"Sequence" (Wylie) **23**:310, 315, 322
"Sequence, Sometimes Metaphysical" (Roethke) **15**:311
Sequences (Sassoon) **12**:247-48, 255, 257-60, 271
"The Seraphim" (Browning) **6**:6, 20, 22, 26-7
The Seraphim, and Other Poems (Browning) **6**:14-15, 19, 26, 29, 31-2
"Serata romana" (Pasolini) **17**:265
"Serenade" (Viereck) **27**:263
"Serenade: Any Man to Any Woman" (Sitwell) **3**:309, 311, 314
"Serenata indiana" (Montale) **13**:107, 128
"The Sergeant's Weddin'" (Kipling) **3**:164, 192
"A Serious Step Lightly Taken" (Frost) **1**:203
"Sermon for Our Maturity" (Baraka) **4**:19
"A Sermon on the Warpland" (Brooks) **7**:63
"Le serpent" (Valery)
See "Ébauche d'un serpent"
"Le serpent qui danse" (Baudelaire) **1**:62
The Serrated Wheel (Guillen)
See *La rueda dentada*
The Serrated Wheel (Guillen)
See *La rueda dentada*
"A Servant to Servants" (Frost) **1**:193, 228
"La servante au grand coeur" (Baudelaire) **1**:67-68
"Ses purs ongles très haut dèdiant leur onyx" (Mallarme)
See "Sonnet en -yx"
"Sesenheimer Lyrik" (Goethe) **5**:245
"Sesh lekha" (Tagore) **8**:424, 426-27
Sestina (Rukeyser) **12**:232
"Sestina: Altaforte" (Pound) **4**:356
"Sestina from the Home Gardener" (Wakoski) **15**:360
"Sestina of the Tramp Royal" (Kipling) **3**:160
Sestra moia zhizn (Pasternak) **6**:250-51, 254-55, 260, 263-65, 268-69, 271-72, 278-80, 282, 285
"Set of Country Songs" (Hardy) **8**:127
"A Set of Romantic Hymns" (Duncan) **2**:103
"The Setting Sun" (Clare) **23**:40
"The Settle Bed" (Heaney) **18**:259
"The Settlers" (Atwood) **8**:12

"Le seul savant, c'est encore Moïse" (Verlaine) **2**:416
"Seurat's Sunday Afternoon along the Seine" (Schwartz) **8**:289-99, 317-18
"VII" (Joyce) **22**:136, 144, 167
"The Seven Ages" (Auden) **1**:39
"Seven Days for Eternity" (Elytis) **21**:123
"7.IV.64" (Snyder) **21**:287
"Les 7 500 000 oui Publie" (Hugo) **17**:98
"The Seven Old Men" (Baudelaire)
See "Les sept vieillards"
"Seven Poems for Marthe, My Wife" (Rexroth) **20**:181
The Seven Seas (Kipling) **3**:159-62, 164, 167, 192-93
"Seven Songs for a Journey" (Wright) **14**:369
"Seven Songs Written during the Ch'ien-yüan Era while Staying at T'ung-ku-hsien" (Tu Fu) **9**:322
The Seven Storey Mountain (Merton) **10**:
"Seven Strophes" (Brodsky) **9**:22
"The Seven Swords" (Apollinaire)
See "Les sept epées"
"Seven Years from Somewhere" (Levine) **22**:219
Seven Years from Somewhere (Levine) **22**:218-19, 234
"XVII" (Joyce) **22**:136, 144, 164, 167
"Seventeen" (Zagajewski) **27**:389
"A Seventeen Morning" (Ammons) **16**:44
"1777" (Lowell) **13**:78, 84
"Seventeen Years" (Berry) **28**:9
"A Seventeenth Century Suite" (Duncan) **2**:115-16, 127
"Seventh Birthday of the First Child" (Olds) **22**:318
"Seventh Elegy" (Rilke) **2**:281, 286
Seventh Isthmian (Pindar)
See *Isthmian 7*
Seventh Nemean (Pindar)
See *Nemean 7*
"Seventh Psalm" (Sexton) **2**:367
"The Seventh Summer" (Levine) **22**:220
73 Poems (Cummings) **5**:109-11
Several Poems Compiled with Great Variety of Wit and Learning, Full of Delight (Bradstreet) **10**:43-5, 51
"Several Voices Out of a Cloud" (Bogan) **12**:100, 107, 124
Severnaia simfoniia: Pervia geroicheskaia (Bely) **11**:3, 12-15, 21
"A Sewerplant Grows in Harlem or I'm a Stranger Here Myself When Does the Next Swan Leave?" (Lorde) **12**:158
"Sex without Love" (Olds) **22**:328-29, 339
"El sexo" (Aleixandre) **15**:34
"Sext" (Auden) **1**:23
"Sextet" (Brodsky) **9**:19, 22
"Sexual Water" (Neruda)
See "Agua sexual"
Shackles (Cesaire)
See *Ferrements*
"The Shad-Blow Tree" (Gluck) **16**:126-27, 142
"Shade of Fonvizin" (Pushkin) **10**:408
"The Shadow" (Lowell) **13**:60-1, 83
"Shadow" (Stryk) **27**:201
"Shadow: 1970" (Wright) **14**:371
The Shadow of Cain (Sitwell) **3**:320, 327
"The Shadow of Fire" (Wright) **14**:376
Shadow of Paradise (Aleixandre)
See *Sombra del paraíso*
Shadow Train: Fifty Lyrics (Ashbery) **26**:151-152, 154, 166-167
"Shadow-Maker" (Swenson) **14**:261
"Shadows of Taste" (Clare) **23**:14
"Shadows on the Wall" (Blok) **21**:14
The Shadowy Waters (Yeats) **20**:303, 353
"The Shaft" (Tomlinson) **17**:342
The Shaft (Tomlinson) **17**:325-27, 334-36, 338, 342-43, 347, 350, 353-54
"Shakespeare" (Arnold) **5**:49
"Shakespeare" (Pasternak) **6**:252
"Shakespeare in Harlem" (Hughes) **1**:239, 242, 246-47, 254-56, 268, 270
"Shakespeare Say" (Dove) **6**:109
"A Shakespearean Sonnet: To a Woman Liberationist" (Knight) **14**:46
"Shalom" (Levertov) **11**:170
"Shaman Mountain is High" (Li Ho) **13**:51
"Shantung" (Lindsay) **23**:265
"Shantung Or the Empire of China Is Crumbling Down" (Lindsay) **23**:280
"Shape of Boeotia" (Elytis) **21**:116
"The Shape of Death" (Swenson) **14**:286
"The Shape of the Fire" (Roethke) **15**:248, 254, 272, 274, 277, 282, 284-85, 287, 298
"Sharing Eve's Apple" (Keats) **1**:311
"Shark Meat" (Snyder) **21**:292, 308
"The Shark: Parents and Children" (Wakoski) **15**:356
"The Sharp Ridge" (Graves) **6**:156
"Sharpeville" (Brutus) **24**:117
Sharps and Flats (Tagore)
See *Kari o komal*
"Shatabdir surya" (Tagore) **8**:412
"Shatter Me, Music" (Rilke) **2**:275
"A Shawl" (Stein) **18**:328, 348
"She" (Roethke) **15**:275
"She Being Brand-New" (Cummings) **5**:95
"SHE CALLS ME ADONIS" (Bissett) **14**:32
"She Had Some Horses" (Harjo) **27**:64-65
She Had Some Horses (Harjo) **27**:56-8, 60, 64-65
"She of the Dancing Feet Sings" (Cullen) **20**:63
"She Remembers the Future" (Harjo) **27**:56
"She Said . . ." (Smith) **12**:326
She Steals My Heart (Li Ho) **13**:44
"She Tells Her Love while Half Asleep" (Graves) **6**:144
"She, to Him" (Hardy) **8**:90
"She Weeps over Rahoon" (Joyce) **22**:137
"She Wept, She Railed" (Kunitz) **19**:151
"She Which is Not, He Which Is" (McGuckian) **27**:
"she won't ever forgive me" (Clifton) **17**:25
"A Sheaf for Chicago" (Stryk) **27**:187, 195, 210, 214
"The Sheaves" (Robinson) **1**:478
"A Sheep Fair" (Hardy) **8**:101
"Sheep in a Fog" (Plath) **1**:408-09
"The Sheep Went On Being Dead" (Hughes) **7**:149
Sheepfold Hill: Fifteen Poems (Aiken) **26**:24
"Shell" (Zagajewski) **27**:403
"Shells" (Nemerov) **24**:299
"Sheltered Garden" (H. D.) **5**:269, 303
"Shenendoah" (Shapiro) **25**:284-85
The Shepheardes Calender: Conteyning Twelve Eglogues Proportionable to the Twelve Monethes (Spenser) **8**:326-28, 335, 385-87
"The Shepherd" (Blake) **12**:7, 32
"The Shepherd" (H. D.) **5**:305
"The Shepherd" (Soto) **28**:371
"Shepherd Bound for Mountain Pass" (Aleixandre) **15**:12, 18
"The Shepherd's Brow, Fronting Forked Lightning" (Hopkins) **15**:168
The Shepherd's Calendar, with Village Stories, and Other Poems (Clare) **23**:10, 16-21, 37-8, 40, 44
Shepherd's Home (Vigny) **26**:371
Sherwood (Noyes) **27**:123
"She's Free" (Harper) **21**:204
"Shesh katha" (Tagore) **8**:407
Shesh saptak (Tagore) **8**:417
"Shiberia no uta" (Ishikawa) **10**:213
"The Shield of Achilles" (Auden) **1**:23
"The Shih-men Monastery in the Lan-t'ien Mountains" (Wang Wei) **18**:378
"Shillin' a Day" (Kipling) **3**:191
"The Shimmer of Evil" (Roethke) **15**:278
"Shine" (Knight) **14**:49
"Shine, Perishing Republic" (Jeffers) **17**:107, 117-19, 132
"Shipbuilding Office" (Page) **12**:173, 176
"Shipman's" (Chaucer)
See "Shipman's Tale"
"Shipman's Tale" (Chaucer) **19**:13, 26
Shipovnik tsevetyot (Akhmatova) **2**:9
Ships and Other Figures (Meredith) **28**:171, 173, 186-87, 189, 210, 217
"Ships That Pass in the Night" (Dunbar) **5**:121
"Shiraha no toribune" (Ishikawa) **10**:214
"The Shirt" (Pinsky) **27**:158, 164-65, 176
"Shitsurakuen" (Nishiwaki) **15**:237, 239
"Shitsurakuen" (Nishiwaki) **15**:
"Shiv and the Grasshopper" (Kipling) **3**:183
"Shizumeru kane" (Ishikawa) **10**:214
"The Shoes of Wandering" (Kinnell) **26**:243, 249, 266, 272-73
"Shoot It Jimmy" (Williams) **7**:383
"Shoot the Buffalo" (Momaday) **25**:214
"A Shooting Incident" (Smith) **12**:318, 346
"Shooting Script" (Rich) **5**:366-67, 378, 383, 396-97
"Shootings of the Third of May" (Heaney) **18**:205
"Shop" (Browning) **2**:59
"The Shore" (Clampitt) **19**:90
"Shoreline" (Heaney) **18**:201, 203
"Shores" (Montale)
See "Riviere"
"The Shorewatchers' House" (Montale) **13**:150
"Short Poem" (Sanchez) **9**:212, 223
Short Prose Poems (Baudelaire)
See *Petits poèmes en prose: Le spleen de Paris*
"A Short Recess" (Milosz) **8**:183, 186
Short Songs of Pure Feelings (Hagiwara Sakutaro) **18**:182
See *Junjo shokyoku shu*
"Short Summary" (Bogan) **12**:101
Shorter Poems (Bridges) **28**:52-53, 67, 69, 82-83
"The Shot" (Graves) **6**:143-44
"The Shot" (Pushkin)
See "Vystrel"
"The Shovel Man" (Sandburg) **2**:332
"The Show" (Owen) **19**:327, 336-37, 341, 343-44, 347, 353, 355, 359
"Shower" (Swift)
See "Description of a City Shower"
"The Showings; Lady Julian of Norwich, 1342-1416" (Levertov) **11**:210
"The Shrine" (H. D.) **5**:270
A Shropshire Lad (Housman) **2**:159-67, 171-78, 180-81, 183-84, 186-88, 191-95, 197, 199-200
"The Shroud" (Millay) **6**:205
"The Shroud of Color" (Cullen) **20**:52, 54-55, 57, 62, 64, 67, 69, 73, 84
"Shucho" (Ishikawa) **10**:212
Shukumei (Hagiwara Sakutaro) **18**:176
Shundeishu (Yosano Akiko) **11**:305
"Shun'ya" (Hagiwara Sakutaro) **18**:181
"Shut, Bellada" (Bely) **11**:24
"Shut Nad ney" (Bely) **11**:24
"Shut Out" (Rossetti) **7**:280
"Shut: Plamen" (Bely) **11**:24
"Shutka" (Bely) **11**:24
"Shuttles" (Swenson) **14**:273
Shyamali (Tagore) **8**:417
"Shylock" (Shapiro) **25**:283
"Si acaso, Fabio mío" (Juana Ines de la Cruz) **24**:180, 184, 187
"Si daros los buenos años" (Juana Ines de la Cruz) **24**:180
"Si el desamor o el enojo" (Juana Ines de la Cruz) **24**:186, 234
"Si es amor causa productiva" (Juana Ines de la Cruz) **24**:189
"Si los riesgos del mar cpmsoderara" (Juana Ines de la Cruz) **24**:225
"Sibir" (Tsvetaeva) **14**:326
"Sibling Mysteries" (Rich) **5**:373, 384
"Sibrandus Schafnaburgensis" (Browning) **2**:59

"A Sibyl" (Atwood) **8**:25
Sibylline Leaves (Coleridge) **11**:57, 60, 97, 115
"Sic Transit" (Lowell) **3**:213
"The Sick" (Page) **12**:176
"A Sick Bed" (Bryant) **20**:17, 46
"The Sick Child" (Gluck) **16**:132, 136, 138
"The Sick King in Bokhara" (Arnold) **5**:6, 39, 49
"Sick Leave" (Sassoon) **12**:267, 288
"Sick Love" (Graves) **6**:136-37, 142, 144, 151, 169
"The Sick Rose" (Blake) **12**:7
"Sickly Face at the Bottom of the Ground" (Hagiwara Sakutaro) **18**:175
"The Sickness unto Death" (Sexton) **2**:372
Sidestreets (Tsvetaeva)
See *Pereulochki*
"Sie erlischt" (Heine) **25**:178
"Sie haben wegen der Trunkenheit" (Heine) **25**:162
"Siena mi fe'; disfecemi Maremma" (Pound) **4**:319
"Sierra Nevada" (Cardenal) **22**:125, 131
"A Sigh" (Finch) **21**:141
"The Sigh" (Hardy) **8**:104
"Sigh" (Mallarme)
See "Soupir"
"The Sigh That Heaves the Grasses" (Housman) **2**:183, 191
"Sighs and Groans" (Herbert)
See "Sighs and Grones"
"Sighs and Grones" (Herbert) **4**:120, 133-34,
"Sighs are my food drink are my tears" (Wyatt) **27**:369
"Sight" (Parker) **28**:365
"Sightseeing on a Winter Day" (Wang Wei) **18**:373
"The Sign" (Masters) **1**:333, 337
"The Sign of Saturn" (Olds) **22**:324
"The Sign of the Golden Shoe" (Noyes) **27**:124
"Signal" (Tzara) **27**:229-31
"The Signal from the House" (Kunitz) **19**:172-73
"The Signature of All Things" (Rexroth) **20**:196, 217
The Signature of All Things: Poems, Songs, Elegies, Translations, and Epigrams (Rexroth) **20**:181, 183-84, 192-94, 203
"The Significance of Veteran's Day" (Ortiz) **17**:226, 232
"The Signifying Monkey" (Knight) **14**:49
"Signing the Pledge" (Harper) **21**:191
"A Signiture. A Herold. A Span" (Brooks) **7**:90
"La Signorina Felicita" (Gozzano) **10**:176-77, 180-83
"Signpost" (Jeffers) **17**:129, 131, 145
"Signs and Tokens" (Hardy) **8**:111
"Signs of Winter" (Clare) **23**:28
"Sigue" (Guillen) **23**:142
"Die silbe schmerz" (Celan) **10**:102, 105
"Silence" (Eliot) **5**:217
"Silence" (Masters) **1**:325, 333, 342
"Silence" (Wright) **14**:342
"The Silence" (Berry) **28**:5, 7, 43
"Silence and Tears" (Smith) **12**:341
"The Silence Answered Him Accusingly" (Schwartz) **8**:293
A Silence Opens (Clampitt) **19**:100-01
"Silences: Lament of the Silent Sisters" (Okigbo) **7**:225, 228, 234, 244-47, 251
"Silent Faces at Crossroads" (Okigbo) **7**:255
"Silent in America" (Levine) **22**:212, 222
"Silent Service" (Sassoon) **12**:252
"Silent Sisters" (Okigbo)
See "Silences: Lament of the Silent Sisters"
"Silhouette of a Serpent" (Valery)
See "Ébauche d'un serpent"
"The Silken Tent" (Frost) **1**:196, 214
"Silly Song" (Garcia Lorca)
See "Canción tonta"
"Silos" (Dove) **6**:120
"Silver" (Ammons) **16**:5
"Silver Filigree" (Wylie) **23**:314, 322, 332
"The Silver Lily" (Gluck) **16**:170
"The Silver Swan" (Rexroth) **20**:221
"The Silver Tassie" (Burns) **6**:97
"Simaetha" (H. D.) **5**:266
Simfonija (1-aga) (Bely)
See *Severnaia simfoniia: Pervia geroicheskaia*
Simfonija (2-aja) (Bely)
See *Vtoraia simfoniia: Dramaticheskaia*
"Simon Lee" (Wordsworth) **4**:374, 416-17, 425-26, 428
"Simon Legree" (Lindsay) **23**:264, 269, 273, 287
"Simon Surnamed Peter" (Masters) **1**:325, 342
"Simon the Cyrenian Speaks" (Cullen) **20**:56, 65
"Simple agonie" (Laforgue) **14**:73
"Simple Autumnal" (Bogan) **12**:87-8, 106, 121
A Simple Lust: Selected Poems Including Sirens, Knuckles, Boots; Letters to Martha; Poems from Algiers, Thoughts Abroad (Brutus) **24**:113-16, 118
"Simple Sonatina" (Gallagher) **9**:60
The Simple Truth (Levine) **22**:228, 232-33
"Simplicity" (Pavese)
See "Semplicità"
"Sin" (Herbert) **4**:100
"Since we loved" (Bridges) **28**:86
"Sin I" (Herbert) **4**:130
"Since 1619" (Walker) **20**:275, 283
"Since I am comming" (Donne)
See "Hymne to God my God, in my sicknesse"
"Since ye delight to know" (Wyatt) **27**:353
"Sindhu-taranga" (Tagore) **8**:407
"Sinfonía en gris mayor" (Dario) **15**:93, 96
"The Singer" (Levertov) **11**:183
"The Singer" (Tsvetaeva)
See "Pevitsa"
"A Singer Asleep" (Hardy) **8**:125
"Singers" (Hughes) **7**:123
"Singing Nigger" (Sandburg) **2**:316
"Singing School" (Heaney) **18**:205
"Single Sonnet" (Bogan) **12**:90, 107
"Single Vision" (Kunitz) **19**:154
"Singling & Doubling Together" (Ammons) **16**:63-4
Sing-Song: A Nursery Rhyme-Book (Rossetti) **7**:291
"Sinistre" (Valery) **9**:359, 381, 399-401
The Sinking of the Titanic (Enzensberger)
See *Der Untergang der Titanic*
The Sinking of the Titanic (Enzensberger)
See "Der Untergand der Titanic"
"The Sinking Ship" (Rimbaud)
See "L'eclatante victoire de Saarebrück"
"Sinners in the Hands of an Angry God" (Lowell) **3**:203
"The Sins of Kalamazoo" (Sandburg) **2**:308
"Sin's Round" (Herbert) **4**:114
"Sion" (Herbert) **4**:100
"Sir Galahad" (Masters) **1**:330, 333
"Sir Galahad" (Tennyson) **6**:359
"Sir John Herschel Remembers" (Noyes) **27**:129
"Sir Thopas" (Chaucer) **19**:25, 33-4, 37, 47, 50-1
"Siren Limits" (Okigbo) **7**:240-46
"Siren Song" (Atwood) **8**:23, 25-6, 41
"Sirens, Knuckles, Boots" (Brutus) **24**:98-9, 112-13, 119
"The Sirens' Welcome to Cronos" (Graves) **6**:144, 146
"Sirocco" (Montale)
See "Scirocco"
"Sister Maude" (Rossetti) **7**:260, 270, 272-3, 276, 280
"The Sisters" (Lowell) **13**:67
The Sisters: A Tragedy (Swinburne) **24**:348-50, 352
"Sisters in Arms" (Lorde) **12**:141, 151-53
"Sit-Ins" (Walker) **20**:276
"The Sitting" (Day Lewis) **11**:147
"The Sitting" (McGuckian) **27**:101
"Sitting Alone on an Autumn Night" (Wang Wei) **18**:388
"The Situation in the West Followed by a Holy Proposal" (Ferlinghetti) **1**:172
The Situation of Poetry: Contemporary Poetry and Its Traditions (Pinsky) **27**:143, 153, 160, 162, 173
"S.I.W." (Owen) **19**:354, 357, 369, 371
"VI" (Joyce) **22**:136, 138, 145, 160, 167, 173
Six and One Remorses for the Sky (Elytis) **21**:118, 122, 124, 133
"Six Casually Written Poems" (Wang Wei) **18**:388
"Six Lectures in Verse" (Milosz) **8**:199-200, 202-03, 211
Six Moral Tales from Jules Laforgue (Laforgue)
See *Moralités légendaires*
"Six O'Clock in Princes Street" (Owen) **19**:342
Six Odes (Auden) **1**:8
Six Quatrains Composed in Jest (Tu Fu) **9**:327
"Six Religious Lyrics" (Shapiro) **25**:320
"Six Variations" (Levertov) **11**:183
"Six Years Later" (Brodsky) **9**:7, 8, 19, 26
"Six Young Men" (Hughes) **7**:113
"Six-Bit Blues" (Hughes) **1**:256
"XVI" (Joyce) **22**:145, 162, 170
"The Sixteenth Floor" (Lowell) **13**:97
"Sixth Elegy" (Rilke) **2**:273
"Sixth Elegy. River Elegy" (Rukeyser) **12**:231-32
Sixth Isthmian (Pindar)
See *Isthmian 6*
Sixth Olympian (Pindar)
See *Olympian 6*
Sixth Pythian (Pindar)
See *Pythian 6*
65 Poems (Celan) **10**:120
"The Size" (Herbert) **4**:100, 108
"Size and Tears" (Carroll) **18**:46
"Skateboard" (Gunn) **26**:215
"The Skaters" (Ashbery) **26**:107, 114, 129, 143, 151, 154-156
"Skazka o Mertvoy Tsarevne" (Pushkin) **10**:382
"Skazka o Pope i o Rabotnike Yego Balde" (Pushkin) **10**:382
"Skazka o Rybake i Rybke" (Pushkin) **10**:382
"Skazka o Tsare Sultane" (Pushkin) **10**:381-83
"Skazka o Zolotom Petushke" (Pushkin) **10**:382-83
"Skazki" (Pushkin) **10**:408
Skazki (Pushkin) **10**:381-86
"The Skeleton of the Future" (MacDiarmid) **9**:176, 179
"Sketch" (Sandburg) **2**:303, 335
"Sketch for a Landscape" (Swenson) **14**:246, 262
"Sketches for a Portrait" (Day Lewis) **11**:148
Sketches of Southern Life (Harper) **21**:185, 187, 189, 191-93, 197-98, 200-01, 211, 213-14
"The Skies" (Aleixandre) **15**:19-20
Skify (Blok) **21**:9, 17, 21-2, 26, 28-9, 31, 35, 41
"Skin" (Larkin) **21**:229
"Skin Canoe" (Forche) **10**:134
"the skinny voice" (Cummings) **5**:99
"Skizze zu einem Sankt Georg" (Rilke) **2**:267
"Skullshapes" (Tomlinson) **17**:340, 357
"The Skunk" (Heaney) **18**:244
"Skunk Hour" (Lowell) **3**:209-11, 213-14, 221, 223, 227, 235, 243-46
"Skunk Hour" (Sexton) **2**:350
"The Sky Falling" (Soto) **28**:370
"The Sky Lark" (Clare) **23**:6
"Sky-House" (McGuckian) **27**:78
"Skylarks" (Hughes) **7**:121-22, 136-37
"The Skylarks of Mykonos" (Clampitt) **19**:87
Skylight One: Fifteen Poems (Aiken) **26**:24
"Skylights" (Gallagher) **9**:45

"Slabs of the Sunburnt West" (Sandburg) **2**:306, 308, 310-11, 314, 323, 330
Slabs of the Sunburnt West (Sandburg) **2**:306, 308, 311, 314, 323
"The Slacker Apologizes" (Viereck) **27**:273
"The Slacker Need Not Apologize" (Viereck) **27**:263
"The Slanting Rain" (Pessoa)
See "Chuva Oblíqua"
"The Slate Ode" (Mandelstam)
See "Grifel' naja oda"
"The Slave Auction" (Harper) **21**:190, 194, 205-06, 216-17
"slave cabin sotterly plantation maryland 1989" (Clifton) **17**:30
"The Slave Mother" (Harper) **21**:192, 194, 197, 203-04, 216
"The Slave Mother, A Tale of Ohio" (Harper) **21**:197, 204-05, 210, 218
"The Sleep" (Browning) **6**:21
"Sleep" (Hughes) **1**:240
"Sleep" (Johnson) **24**:145, 159
"Sleep" (Pushkin) **10**:407
"Sleep and Poetry" (Keats) **1**:280, 289, 291-92, 313
"Sleep at Sea" (Rossetti) **7**:293, 296-7
"Sleep Brings No Joy to Me" (Bronte) **8**:74
"Sleep defends my Don drowsiness" (Mandelstam)
See "Oboroniaet son moiu donskuiu son"
"Sleep of the Valiant" (Elytis) **21**:123
"The Sleep of the Valiant (Variation)" (Elytis) **21**:116
"The Sleep Worker" (Hardy) **8**:129
"The Sleeper" (Poe) **1**:434, 443-44
"The Sleepers" (Whitman) **3**:391, 396-97, 401
"Sleeping at Last" (Rossetti) **7**:287
"Sleeping Beauty" (Clifton) **17**:29
"The Sleeping Beauty" (Owen) **19**:358
"Sleeping Beauty" (Wylie) **23**:321
The Sleeping Beauty (Carruth) **10**:75-8, 83-4, 86, 91
The Sleeping Beauty (Sitwell) **3**:292-94, 298, 300-01, 303, 307-08, 310, 316-17, 320, 324-25
"The Sleeping Fury" (Bogan) **12**:100, 104
The Sleeping Fury (Bogan) **12**:88-90, 105, 109, 111, 120, 122-25, 131
"Sleeping on the Ceiling" (Bishop) **3**:37
"Sleeping Out Full Moon" (Brooke) **24**:57
"Sleeping with Animals" (Kumin) **15**:209, 211, 215, 223
"A Sleepless Night" (Levine) **22**:214
"Sleepwalker Ballad" (Garcia Lorca)
See "Romance sonámbulo"
"The slender wire above the sea of oats" (Tsvetaeva)
See "U tonkoi pnovoloki nad volnoi ovsov"
"The Slippers of the Goddess of Beauty" (Lowell) **13**:67
"Slips" (McGuckian) **27**:97
"Slip-Shoe Lovey" (Masters) **1**:333, 336
"Slow through the Dark" (Dunbar) **5**:131
"Slug" (Roethke) **15**:274
"Sluicegates of Thought" (Tzara) **27**:235
"A Slumber Did My Spirit Steal" (Wordsworth) **4**:420
"Small Action Poem" (Tomlinson) **17**:325
"Small Comment" (Sanchez) **9**:224
"Small Garden near a Field" (Gallagher) **9**:62
"Small Hours" (Plath) **1**:391
"The Small Hours" (Parker) **28**:359
"The Small Lady" (Smith) **12**:295
"A Small Light" (Song) **21**:344
"Small Moment" (Nemerov) **24**:293
"Small Ode to a Black Cuban Boxer" (Guillen)
See "Pequeña oda a un negro boxeador cubano"
"A Small Peice of Wood" (McGuckian) **27**:107, 110-111
"Small Perfect Manhattan" (Viereck) **27**:263, 278
"Small Poems for the Winter Solstice" (Atwood) **8**:44
"Small Song for Crossing a Big River" (Cesaire) **25**:32
Small Testament (Villon)
See *Les Lais*
"A Small Will" (Montale)
See "Piccolo testamento"
"Smalltown Dance" (Wright) **14**:378-79
"Smelt Fishing" (Hayden) **6**:196
"Smert" (Lermontov) **18**:302
"The Smile" (Blake) **12**:35, 43
"The Smile" (Merrill) **28**:248
"Smile, Smile, Smile" (Owen) **19**:354, 357, 359
"Smoke" (McGuckian) **27**:97
"Smoke and Earth" (Aleixandre) **15**:18-19
"Smoke and Steel" (Sandburg) **2**:304, 316
Smoke and Steel (Sandburg) **2**:304-08, 313-14, 316, 321, 323, 338
"The Smokers" (Shapiro) **25**:323
"Smokers of Cheap Cigarettes" (Pavese)
See "Fumatori di carta"
"Smokey the Bear Sutra" (Snyder) **21**:291
"Smudging" (Wakoski) **15**:331, 364
Smudging (Wakoski) **15**:332, 345, 364
"Snail" (Hughes) **1**:241
"Snake" (Hughes) **1**:241
"Snake" (Roethke) **15**:272
"The Snake" (Berry) **28**:25
"Snake Hymn" (Hughes) **7**:159
"Snake River" (McKay) **2**:216
"Snakecharmer" (Plath) **1**:388-89
"Snakeskin on a Gate" (Wright) **14**:356
"Snapshots of a Daughter-in-Law" (Rich) **5**:370-72, 396
Snapshots of a Daughter-in-Law: Poems, 1954-1962 (Rich) **5**:354, 358, 363, 369-72, 374, 382, 388, 392
"Snarley-Yow" (Kipling) **3**:158
Snezhnye maski (Blok) **21**:20, 24
"The Snob" (Shapiro) **25**:295
"Snow" (Frost) **1**:195, 215
"Snow" (Hayden) **6**:193, 196
"Snow" (Hughes) **7**:155
"Snow" (Levine) **22**:225
"Snow" (Rich) **5**:366
"snow cummin" (Bissett) **14**:20
"The Snow Fairy" (McKay) **2**:228
"The Snow Fences" (Tomlinson) **17**:341
"Snow Jobs" (Merrill) **28**:284-85
"The Snow King" (Dove) **6**:108
"Snow King Chair Lift" (Merrill) **28**:222, 257
"The Snow Lamp" (Hayden) **6**:189, 192
"Snow Maiden" (Blok) **21**:9
The Snow Mask (Blok)
See *Snezhnye maski*
The Snow Poems (Ammons) **16**:23-6, 42-7, 49-51, 54, 61-2, 65
"Snow) Says! Says" (Cummings) **5**:106
"Snow Shower" (Bryant) **20**:15-16
"Snow Signs" (Tomlinson) **17**:342, 345
"The Snow Storm" (Emerson) **18**:79-80, 88, 98, 107
"Snow Upon Paris" (Senghor) **25**:227
"Snow White" (Sexton) **2**:368
"Snowbed" (Celan)
See "Schneebett"
"Snowdrop" (Hughes) **7**:169
"Snowfall" (Gunn) **26**:203
"Snowfall" (Vigny)
See "La neige"
"Snowflakes as Kisses" (Schwarzweller) **8**:314
"The Snow lies sprinkled on the beach" (Bridges) **28**:89
"The Snowman" (Page) **12**:167-68, 183
"Snows" (Perse)
See "Neiges"
"Snows" (Stryk) **27**:202-3
"So I Said I Am Ezra" (Ammons) **16**:39
"So Intricately Is This World Resolved" (Kunitz) **19**:170
"So Much Depends" (Williams) **7**:362
"So Old" (Snyder) **21**:307
"So, so breake off this last lamenting kisse" (Donne)
See "The Expiration"
"So To Fatness Come" (Smith) **12**:326
"So We Grew Together" (Masters) **1**:326-26, 328
Sobranie sochinenij (Mandelstam) **14**:113, 117, 123
Social Credit, An Impact (Pound) **4**:328
"Sociedad de amigos y protectores" (Fuertes) **27**:16
"Socrates' Ghost Must Haunt Me Now" (Schwartz) **8**:302, 315
"The Sofa" (McGuckian) **27**:98
"Soft Wood" (Lowell) **3**:211
"Softer-Mother's Tale" (Wordsworth) **4**:373
"Il Sogno del prigioniero" (Montale) **13**:104
"Soho Cinema" (Lorde) **12**:140
"Sohrab and Rustum" (Arnold) **5**:9, 12-13, 33, 35, 37, 45, 52, 62
"The Soil-Map" (McGuckian) **27**:97
"Un soir" (Apollinaire) **7**:46
"Le soir" (Lamartine) **16**:275-76, 298-99, 302
"Soir de carnaval" (Laforgue) **14**:92
"Le soir qu'amour vous fist en la salle descendre" (Ronsard) **11**:264-66
"Une soirée perdue" (Gautier) **18**:136-37
"Sokolinya slobodka" (Tsvetaeva) **14**:326
"El sol" (Aleixandre) **15**:25
"Sola con esperanza" (Fuertes) **27**:8, 29
Sola en la sala (Fuertes) **27**:17-8, 21, 38
"SOLACE IN WORDS" (Bissett) **14**:33
"Solar" (Larkin) **21**:250-51
"Solar Ode to the People's Army" (Neruda)
See "Oda solar al ejérito del pueblo"
"Solde" (Rimbaud) **3**:261, 264
"The Soldier" (Brooke) **24**:54, 59, 63-4, 71, 74, 80, 86-7, 89
"The Soldier" (Hopkins) **15**:144
The Soldier (Aiken) **26**:24
"Soldier, Soldier" (Kipling) **3**:163, 188-89
"The Soldiers" (Duncan) **2**:104
"Soldier's Dream" (Owen) **19**:341, 356
"Soldier's Farm" (Wright) **14**:340
"Soldier's Song" (Burns) **6**:78
"De Sole" (Tomlinson) **17**:336
"Soledad" (Hayden) **6**:194, 196
Soledad (Paz) **1**:366
Soleil Cou-Coupé (Cesaire) **25**:15, 23, 30-2, 35, 44
"Soleil et chair" (Rimbaud) **3**:251, 280, 283, 285
"Soliloquy" (Jeffers) **17**:132
"Soliloquy of a Misanthrope" (Hughes) **7**:116
"Soliloquy of the Spanish Cloister" (Browning) **2**:37
"Le solitaire" (Lamartine) **16**:281
"The Solitary Reaper" (Wordsworth) **4**:399, 404
"Solitude" (Ishikawa)
See "Kyoko"
"La solitude" (Lamartine) **16**:277
"A Solitude" (Swinburne) **24**:327
"Solitudes at Sixty" (Sassoon) **12**:259
"Solo de lune" (Laforgue) **14**:74-6
"Solominka, The Straw" (Mandelstam) **14**:111-12, 124
"Solonique" (Apollinaire) **7**:48
"Solstice" (Jeffers) **17**:111, 127, 141
"Solstice" (Lorde) **12**:153
Solstice and Other Poems (Jeffers) **17**:111, 125, 135
"Som de escalina" (Eliot) **5**:201
Sombra del paraíso (Aleixandre) **15**:6, 8, 10-11, 15-16, 18, 21, 22-5, 33-4, 37-8, 40-1
"Sombre Figuration" (Stevens) **6**:298, 318, 320
Some (Ashbery) **26**:167, 172
"Some Answers Are Cold Comfort to the Dead" (Schwartz) **8**:293

Cumulative Title Index

"Some Are Born" (Smith) **12**:316
"Some Brilliant Sky" (Wakoski) **15**:336
"Some Foreign Letters" (Sexton) **2**:350, 361, 363
"Some Foreign Wife" (Sexton) **2**:359
"Some Friends from Pascagoula" (Stevens) **6**:337
"Some Lines" (Viereck) **27**:280
"Some Lines in Three Parts" (Viereck) **27**:263, 278, 280, 282
"Some Negatives: X at the Chateau" (Merrill) **28**:242
"Some Notes on Organic Form" (Levertov) **11**:160-62
"Some Quadrangles" (Swenson) **14**:273
Some Time (Zukofsky) **11**:343
"Some Trees" (Ashbery) **26**:118
Some Trees (Ashbery) **26**:111, 113, 118, 129, 135, 137, 143, 162, 164
"Some Verses Upon the Burning of Our House, July 10th, 1666" (Bradstreet) **10**:8, 19, 21, 27, 29-30, 34, 36-7, 42
"Somebody's Song" (Parker) **28**:351
"Someone Is Harshly Coughing as Before" (Schwartz) **8**:301
"Something A Direction" (Tomlinson) **17**:312
"Something for Hope" (Frost) **1**:200
"Something to Wear" (Levertov) **11**:165-66, 168
"Something Was Happening" (Hughes) **7**:154
"Sometimes Even Now" (Brooke) **24**:62
"Sometimes I fled the fire that me brent" (Wyatt) **27**:368
"Somewhat Delayed Spring Song" (Parker) **28**:355
"Somewhere" (Nemerov) **24**:262
"Somewhere East o' Suez" (Kipling) **3**:189
"Somewhere I Have Never Travelled, Gladly Beyond" (Cummings) **5**:88
"Somewhere in Africa" (Sexton) **2**:364, 371
"Sommarnatten" (Ekeloef) **23**:76
"Sommation" (Hugo) **17**:98, 100
"Le Sommet de la tour" (Gautier) **18**:143, 146
"Somnambulent Ballad" (Garcia Lorca)
See "Romance sonámbulo"
"Somnambulist Ballad" (Garcia Lorca)
See "Romance sonámbulo"
"Son and Mother" (Blok) **21**:14
"Son del bloqueo" (Guillen) **23**:126
El son entero (Guillen) **23**:100, 108, 131, 139, 142
"Son más en una mazorca" (Guillen) **23**:125
See *Motivos de son*
"Son number 6" (Guillen)
See "Son numero 6"
"Son numero 6" (Guillen) **23**:127, 130, 132, 139
"Sonar tari" (Tagore) **8**:408
Sonar tari (Tagore) **8**:409, 418, 427
"Sonata for Methylated Prose" (Ekeloef) **23**:85
"sonatform denaturerad prosa" (Ekeloef) **23**:75
"Sonatina" (Dario) **15**:79-80, 95, 107-08, 110, 119-20
Sonetos espirituales (Jimenez) **7**:191-92, 194-96, 202, 211
Sonette (Goethe) **5**:248, 250
Sonette an Orpheus (Rilke) **2**:267-68, 277, 280-81, 283, 290, 293, 295
Die Sonette an Orpheus/Sonnets to Orpheus (Rilke)
See *Sonette an Orpheus*
"Song" (Berry) **28**:7-8
"Song" (Behn)
See "Love Arm'd"
"Song" (Blake) **12**:6
"Song" (Bogan) **12**:86, 90, 103
"Song" (Bronte) **8**:62
"Song" (Cummings) **5**:109
"Song" (Donne) **1**:125
"Song" (H. D.) **5**:304
"Song" (Nemerov) **24**:256
"Song" (Poe) **1**:432
"The Song" (Roethke) **15**:269
"Song" (Rossetti) **7**:273, 276, 289
"Song" (Sitwell) **3**:313
"Song" (Williams) **7**:408
"Song" (Wright) **14**:338, 342, 347
"The Song and Dance of" (Olson) **19**:273
"Song Coming toward Us" (Forche) **10**:132
"Song for a Colored Singer" (Bishop) **3**:37
"Song for a Dark Girl" (Hughes) **1**:238, 243
"Song for a Lady" (Sexton) **2**:352
"Song for a Lyre" (Bogan) **12**:90, 92
"Song for a Phallus" (Hughes) **7**:132, 159, 171
"Song for a Red Night Gown" (Sexton) **2**:352-53
"Song for a Slight Voice" (Bogan) **12**:90, 92
"Song for a Viola d'Amore" (Lowell) **13**:88, 97
"A Song for J. H." (Behn) **13**:19
"A Song for New-Ark" (Giovanni) **19**:143
"Song for Nobody" (Merton) **10**:349
"A Song for Occupations" (Whitman) **3**:385, 401-02
"SONG FOR OOLJAH" (Bissett) **14**:33
"Song for Our Lady of Cobre" (Merton) **10**:
"A Song for Rosemarie" (Villa) **22**:354
"A Song for Simeon" (Eliot) **5**:194, 196-97, 203, 205, 209
Song for St Cecilia's Day (Dryden) **25**:75-8
"Song for the Death of Averroës" (Merton) **10**:343
"Song for the Last Act" (Bogan) **12**:124
"Song for the Mothers of Dead Militiamen" (Neruda)
See "Canto a las madres de los milicianos muertos"
"Song for the Next River" (Gallagher) **9**:35
"Song for the Pockets" (Soto) **28**:375
"A Song for the Ragged Schools of London" (Browning) **6**:7, 23
"Song for the Rainy Season" (Bishop) **3**:67
"Song for the Saddest Ides" (Nash) **21**:263
"Song for the Squeeze Box" (Roethke) **15**:256
"A Song for the Year's End" (Zukofsky) **11**:349
"A Song from the Structures of Rime Ringing as the Poet Paul Celan Sings" (Duncan) **2**:117
"Song I" (Rilke) **2**:273
"A Song in the Front Yard" (Brooks) **7**:69
"Song in a Wine-Bar" (Wright) **14**:333
"Song in a Year of Catastrophe" (Berry) **28**:43
"Song: Lift-Boy" (Graves) **6**:142, 144
"Song of a camera" (Gunn) **26**:212
"The Song of a Rat" (Hughes) **7**:142, 155-56, 159
"Song of Another Tribe" (Rukeyser) **12**:217
"Song of Autumn in Spring" (Dario)
See "Canción de otoño en primavera"
"Song of Defeat" (Tagore)
See "Parajaya sangit"
"Song of Despair" (Neruda) **4**:301
"The Song of Diego Valdez" (Kipling) **3**:182
"The Song of God's Child" (Li Ho) **13**:52
"Song of Invisible Boundaries" (Gluck) **16**:166
"A Song of Joys" (Whitman) **3**:402
"Song of Li Ling" (Wang Wei) **18**:389
"A Song of Liberty" (Blake) **12**:33
"Song of Love" (Lamartine)
See "Chant d'amour"
"A Song of my heart" (Bridges) **28**:69
"Song of Myself" (Whitman) **3**:370, 394, 396-97, 399, 401-03, 405, 411-12, 414-17
"The Song of Nature" (Emerson) **18**:88
"Song of Opposites" (Keats) **1**:312
"Song of P'eng-ya" (Tu Fu) **9**:321, 332
"Song of Praise" (Cullen) **20**:52, 63
"A Song of Praise" (Sanchez) **9**:243
"A Song of Sherwood" (Noyes) **27**:136-137
"Song of Siberia" (Ishikawa)
See "Shiberia no uta"
"Song of the Answerer" (Whitman) **3**:386, 390
"Song of the Banjo" (Kipling) **3**:160-61
"Song of the Beasts" (Brooke) **24**:59, 82
"Song of the Beautiful Ladies" (Tu Fu) **9**:320
"Song of the Bird" (Tagore)
See "Vihanger gan"
"The Song of the Bongo" (Guillen) **23**:132
See "La canción del bongo"
"Song of the Children in Heaven" (Brooke) **24**:76
"The Song of the Cities" (Kipling) **3**:162
The Song of the Cold (Sitwell) **3**:320, 326
"Song of the Columns" (Valery)
See "Cantique des colonnes"
"Song of the Dead" (Kipling) **3**:160, 162
"A Song of the Dust" (Sitwell) **3**:327
"A Song of the English" (Kipling) **3**:160-62, 164
"The Song of the Exiles" (Kipling) **3**:194
"The Song of the Final Meeting/Song of the Last Meeting" (Akhmatova)
See "Pesnia poslednei vstrechi"
"The Song of the Galley Slaves" (Kipling) **3**:170
"The Song of the Happy Shepherd" (Yeats) **20**:354
"Song of the Highest Tower" (Rimbaud) **3**:259
"The Song of the Ill-beloved" (Apollinaire)
See "La chanson du mal-aimé"
"Song of the Little Square" (Garcia Lorca)
See "Ballada de la Placeta"
The Song of the Merchant Kaláshnikov (Lermontov)
See *The Song of Tzar Ivan Vasiljevich, His Young Life-Guardsman, and the Valiant Merchant Kaláshnikov*
"Song of the Open Road" (Whitman) **3**:387
"Song of the Peach Fountainhead" (Wang Wei) **18**:389
"The Song of the Pilgrims" (Brooke) **24**:76
"The Song of the Poorly Beloved" (Apollinaire)
See "La chanson du mal-aimé"
"The Song of the Red War-Boat" (Kipling) **3**:183
"Song of the Son" (Toomer) **7**:310, 317, 319, 334
"The Song of the Sons" (Kipling) **3**:162
"A Song of the Soul of Central" (Hughes) **1**:268
"Song of the Sower" (Bryant) **20**:14
"Song of the Stars" (Bryant) **20**:4
"Song of the Taste" (Snyder) **21**:297
"Song of the Worms" (Atwood) **8**:19, 25
The Song of Tzar Ivan Vasiljevich, His Young Life-Guardsman, and the Valiant Merchant Kaláshnikov (Lermontov) **18**:278, 281-82, 304
"Song of Women" (Masters) **1**:330, 333
Song Offerings (Tagore)
See *Gitanjali*
"A Song on Gazing at Chung-nan Mountain For Hsü of the Secretariat" (Wang Wei) **18**:369
"A Song on Greife" (Finch) **21**:150, 152, 179
"Song over Some Ruins" (Neruda)
See "Canto sobre unas ruinas"
"A Song: Sensation Time at the Home" (Merton) **10**:345
"A Song Sparrow Singing in the Fall" (Berry) **28**:7
"Song. 'Sweetest love, I do not goe'" (Donne) **1**:130
"Song: The Rev. MuBngwu Dickenson Ruminates behind the Sermon" (Brooks) **7**:94
"A Song to a Scotish Tune (Come My Phillis Let Us Improve)" (Behn) **13**:18
"Song to a Scotish Tune (When Jemmy First Began to Love)" (Behn) **13**:4, 7, 18, 32
"Song to Alfred Hitchcock and Wilkinson" (Ondaatje) **28**:291
"Song to Awaken a Little Black Child" (Guillen) **23**:132
A Song to David (Smart) **13**:328-34, 336-46, 352-54, 358, 360-65, 367-69
"Song to Ishtar" (Levertov) **11**:169

"A Song to No Music" (Brodsky) **9**:4, 9, 12
"A Song Untitled" (Hagiwara Sakutaro) **18**:173
"Song without Music" (Brodsky)
See "A Song to No Music"
"Songe D'Athalie" (Smith) **12**:331
"Songin Black Armor" (Wylie) **23**:308, 310, 332
Sóngoro cosongo: Poemas mulatos (Guillen) **23**:98-100, 105-106, 111, 114, 131, 139, 142-44
"Songs" (Hughes) **1**:241
Songs (Garcia Lorca)
See *Canciones*
"Songs:65o N" (Larkin) **21**:226
Songs and Satires (Masters) **1**:328, 335, 342
Songs and Sonets (Donne) **1**:130, 139, 145
Songs and Sonnets, second series (Masters) **1**:321, 325, 332
Songs before Sunrise (Swinburne) **24**:312
"Songs for a Colored Singer" (Bishop) **3**:37, 46-7
Songs for Naëtt (Senghor)
See *Chants pour Naëtt*
Songs for Soldiers and Tunes for Tourists (Guillen)
See *Cantos para soldados y sones para turistas*
"Songs for the People" (Harper) **21**:189
Songs for the Republic (Cassian) **17**:6
"Songs from Cyprus" (H. D.) **5**:304
"Songs in a Cornfield" (Rossetti) **7**:275
Songs of Bhanusigh Thakur (Tagore)
See *Bhanusingh Thakurer padavali*
Songs of Crow (Hughes) **7**:140
Songs of Experience (Blake) **12**:9-10, 23-5, 31, 33-5, 42-7, 61-2
Songs of Innocence (Blake) **12**:8-9, 19, 21-4, 32-4, 42, 61
Songs of Innocence and of Experience: Shewing the Two Contrary States of the Human Soul (Blake) **12**:8-11, 33-4, 42-3, 51
Songs of Jamaica (McKay) **2**:208, 210, 216, 221, 223-27
Songs of Life and Hope (Dario)
See *Cantos de vida y esperanza*
"The Songs of Maximus" (Olson) **19**:282-83
"The Song of the Children" (Chesterton) **28**:100
"Songs of Education" (Chesterton) **28**:99
"Songs of the Hen's Head" (Atwood) **8**:41
"Songs of the Ingenues" (Verlaine)
See "La chanson des ingénues"
"Songs of the Runaway Bride" (Gallagher) **9**:37
"Songs of the Shade" (Senghor)
See *Chants d'ombre*
Songs of the Springtides (Swinburne) **24**:322
"Songs of the Transformed" (Atwood) **8**:23, 25-6
Songs of Victory (Pindar)
See *Songs of Victory*
"Songs to Survive the Summer" (Hass) **16**:199, 201, 210-16
"sonik prayr" (Bissett) **14**:27
"The Sonne" (Herbert) **4**:109
"Sonnet" (Bogan) **12**:98, 110
"Sonnet II" (Thomas) **2**:388
"Sonnet III" (Thomas) **2**:388
"Sonnet 7" (Milton) **19**:214, 256
"Sonnet VIII" (Thomas) **2**:388
"Sonnet X" (Thomas) **2**:388
"Sonnet XVI" (Browning) **6**:17
"Sonnet 16 (On his blindness)" (Milton) **19**:214
"Sonnet en -yx" (Mallarme) **4**:214-15, 218
"Sonnet Entitled How to Run the World)" (Cummings) **5**:106
"Sonnet for the Seventh of August" (Belloc) **24**:43-4
"Sonnet héroïque" (Verlaine) **2**:416
"Sonnet in Polka Dots" (Villa) **22**:351
"Sonnet in time of Revolt" (Brooke) **24**:62, 82
"Sonnet on an Alpine Night" (Parker) **28**:351
"Sonnet on Rare Animals" (Meredith) **28**:172, 188
"Sonnet On Seeing a Piece of Our Artillery Brought Into Action" (Owen) **19**:336
"Sonnet Reversed" (Brooke) **24**:56, 64
"Sonnet (Suggested by some of the Proceedings of the Society for Physical Research)" (Brooke) **24**:58, 73
"Sonnet: To a Child" (Owen) **19**:343
"Sonnet--to My Mother" (Poe) **1**:439, 445-46
"Sonnet V" (Wylie) **23**:304
"Sonnet with the Compliments of the Season" (Chesterton) **28**:114
Sonnets (Carruth) **10**:91
Sonnets (Rilke) **2**:280-82
Sonnets and Verse (Belloc) **24**:11, 31-3, 36, 38, 40
Sonnets et madrigals pour astrée (Ronsard) **11**:250
Sonnets for Hélène (Ronsard)
See *Sonnets pour Hélène*
"Sonnets from an Ungrafted Tree" (Millay) **6**:224-25, 228, 230-32, 235, 239
Sonnets from the Portuguese (Browning) **6**:4-6, 15-8, 22, 32, 36-9, 41-2, 46
"Sonnets of the Twelve Months" (Belloc) **24**:29
Sonnets pour Hélène (Ronsard) **11**:218, 220-22, 239, 242, 250, 254, 275-76, 278, 283
"Sonnets That Please" (Stein) **18**:341
"Sono pronto ripeto, ma pronto a che?" (Montale) **13**:139
"sonora desert poem" (Clifton) **17**:27
"Soonest Mended" (Ashbery) **26**:125-126, 134, 138, 141, 149
"Sorapis, 40 anni fa" (Montale) **13**:138
Sordello (Browning) **2**:26-30, 34, 42, 50, 65-6, 73-6, 82, 92-6
"Sore Fit" (Bradstreet)
See "From Another Sore Fit"
Sorgen och stjärnan (Ekeloef) **23**:76
The Sorrow Dance (Levertov) **11**:175-77, 191-94
"Sorrow Home" (Walker) **20**:281-83
"Sorrowful Moonlit Night" (Hagiwara Sakutaro)
See "Sorrowful Moonlit Night"
"Sortes Vergilianae" (Ashbery) **26**:149
"SOS" (Baraka) **4**:20
"Sosedka" (Lermontov) **18**:291
"So sweet love seemed that April morn" (Bridges) **28**:86
"Sotto la pioggia" (Montale) **13**:122
"The Soul" (Pasternak)
See "Dusha"
"Soul, Be Calm" (Ishikawa)
See "Tama yo shizume"
"A Soul, Geologically" (Atwood) **8**:3, 8, 19
"The Soul Has Bandaged Moments" (Dickinson) **1**:94
"Soul in Space" (Rilke) **2**:275
"Soul's Adventure" (Kunitz) **19**:148
"Soul's Desire" (Masters) **1**:342
"The Soul's Expression" (Browning) **6**:20, 26, 30
"The Souls of the Slain" (Hardy) **8**:120-21
Souls of Violet (Jimenez)
See *Almas de violeta*
"A Soul's Tragedy" (Browning) **2**:30, 37
"The Sound of the Trees" (Frost) **1**:197, 202
"Sound of War" (Aleixandre) **15**:4-6
"Sound Poem I" (Toomer) **7**:333
"Sound Poem II" (Toomer) **7**:333
"Sound Sleep" (Rossetti) **7**:267, 280
"Sounds" (Browning) **6**:20
"The sounds begin again" (Brutus) **24**:114, 116
"Sounds of Rain" (Heaney) **18**:260
"Sounds Out of Sorrow" (Masters) **1**:333
"Soup of the evening beautiful Soup" (Carroll) **18**:49
"Soupir" (Mallarme) **4**:187
Sour Grapes (Williams) **7**:344, 349, 367, 377, 381, 399-400, 409-10
"The Source" (Olds) **22**:338
"La source dans les bois" (Lamartine) **16**:292
"Sources" (Levine) **22**:224
Sources (Rich) **5**:389-90, 397
"South" (Stryk) **27**:181, 200
"South Cottage" (Wang Wei) **18**:367
"The South Country" (Belloc) **24**:8, 10, 30
"South of My Days" (Wright) **14**:340, 349, 351, 360, 378
"Southeast Corner" (Brooks) **7**:58, 69, 80
"Souther Pacific" (Sandburg) **2**:302
"A Southern Night" (Arnold) **5**:8
"Southern Song" (Walker) **20**:272, 281-83
"The Southerner" (Shapiro) **25**:283, 296, 313
"The South Wind" (Bridges) **28**:66
"Souvenir de Monsieur Poop" (Smith) **12**:313
"Le souvenir d'enfance; ou, La vie cachée" (Lamartine) **16**:276, 300, 302
"Souvent sur la montagne" (Lamartine) **16**:302
The Sovereign Sun: Selected Poems (Elytis) **21**:118-19
"Soviet Union" (Guillen)
See "Unión Soviética"
"Sow" (Plath) **1**:388, 404
"The Sowing of Meaning" (Merton) **10**:332
"Soy como un árbol florido" (Guillen) **23**:125
"Soy Sauce" (Snyder) **21**:300
"Soy sólo una mujer" (Fuertes) **27**:7
Space (Aleixandre)
See *Ambito*
Space (Jimenez)
See *Espacia*
space travl (Bissett) **14**:34
"The Space We Live" (Levine) **22**:215
"Spaces We Leave Empty" (Song) **21**:343
Spain (Auden) **1**:22
Spain (Gautier)
See *España*
Spain at Heart (Neruda)
See *España en el corazón: himno a las glorias del pueblo en la guerra (1936-1937)*
Spain in My Heart (Neruda)
See *España en el corazón: himno a las glorias del pueblo en la guerra (1936-1937)*
Spain in the Heart (Neruda)
See *España en el corazón: himno a las glorias del pueblo en la guerra (1936-1937)*
The Spanish Gypsy (Eliot) **20**:90-100, 104-6, 111-15, 122-23, 126, 128-31, 137-39, 141-48
"The Spanish Needle" (McKay) **2**:228
"Spanish School" (Smith) **12**:316
"Spare Us from Loveliness" (H. D.) **5**:273
"spark" (Bukowski) **18**:20
"The Spark" (Cullen) **20**:58
"A Spark in the Tinder of Knowing" (Rexroth) **20**:221
"A Sparkler" (Ashbery) **26**:137
Sparrows (Soto)
See Where Sparrows Work Hard
"Sparrow Hills" (Pasternak) **6**:258
"The Sparrow's Fall" (Harper) **21**:189
The Sparrow's Fall and Other Poems (Harper) **21**:187, 189
"Spasskoye" (Pasternak) **6**:252, 259
"Spätherbst in Venedig" (Rilke) **2**:267, 277, 282, 288-90
"Speak, You Also" (Celan) **10**:99
"La Speakerine de Putney" (Smith) **12**:354
Speaking for Scotland (MacDiarmid) **9**:159
"Speaking of Love (of" (Cummings) **5**:105
"speaking speaking" (Bissett) **14**:31
"Special Starlight" (Sandburg) **2**:331
"Specimen of an Induction to a Poem" (Keats) **1**:313
Spectacula (Martial)
See *Liber Spectaculorum*
Spectaculorum Liber (Martial)
See *Liber Spectaculorum*

Cumulative Title Index

Spectrum (Nishiwaki) **15**:228, 237
"Speech to the Young. Speech to the Progress-Toward" (Brooks) **7**:91, 94
"Speeches for Doctor Frankenstein" (Atwood) **8**:11
"Speech-Grille" (Celan)
See "Sprachgitter"
Speech-Grille, and Selected Poems (Celan)
See *Sprachgitter*
The Speed of Darkness (Rukeyser) **12**:216, 222, 228, 230
Speke Parott (Skelton) **25**:329-31, 336, 341, 348, 351-52, 360, 374, 377-78, 380-85
Spektorsky (Pasternak) **6**:253, 265, 283, 285
"Spel Against Demons" (Snyder) **21**:291-92, 297
"The Spell" (Kumin) **15**:192
"Spell" (Montale)
See "Incantesimo"
"The Spell of the Rose" (Hardy) **8**:93, 136
"Spelling" (Duncan) **2**:104
"Spelt from Sibyl's Leaves" (Hopkins) **15**:128, 132-33, 138, 144
"A spending hand that alway poureth out" (Wyatt) **27**:371
"Spenser's Ireland" (Moore) **4**:258
"Sperm" (Kumin) **15**:202
"Sphere" (Ammons) **16**:31, 53
Sphere: The Form of a Motion (Ammons) **16**:23, 25, 27-30, 33, 46-7, 54, 60-1
"The Sphinx" (Emerson) **18**:71, 84, 88, 93, 102, 110
"Le Sphinx" (Gautier) **18**:141
"The Sphinx" (Hayden) **6**:186
Sphinx: A Poem Ascrib'd to Certain Anonymous Authors: By the Revd. S--t (Swift)
See "Ode to the Athenian Society"
"Le Sphynx vertébral" (Breton) **15**:51
"The Spice Tree" (Lindsay) **23**:268
"Spider Blues" (Ondaatje) **28**:320, 327, 333
"Spider's Song" (Zagajewski) **27**:389
"Spight hathe no Powre" (Wyatt) **27**:315
"Spilt Milk" (Yeats) **20**:314
Spin a Soft Black Song: Poems for Children (Giovanni) **19**:136
"Spindrift" (Kinnell) **26**:257
"The Spinner" (Valery)
See "La fileuse"
"Spinster" (Plath) **1**:388
"The Spire Cranes" (Thomas) **2**:408
"Spirit" (Soto) **28**:370
"The Spirit Medium" (Yeats) **20**:314
"Spirit of History" (Milosz) **8**:204
"The Spirit of Place" (Rich) **5**:386
The Spirit of Romance (Pound) **4**:352
Spirit Reach (Baraka) **4**:19-20, 26
"Spirit's Song" (Bogan) **12**:90, 92, 100, 124
"A Spiritual" (Dunbar) **5**:123
"Spiritual" (Pasolini) **17**:253
"Spiritual Laws" (Emerson) **18**:94
Spiritual Sonnets (Jimenez)
See *Sonetos espirituales*
"Spite" (Bukowski) **18**:5
"Spleen" (Baudelaire)
See "Le spleen"
"Le spleen" (Baudelaire) **1**:55
"The Spleen" (Finch)
See "Ode to the Spleen"
"Spleen" (Laforgue) **14**:84-5, 89
"Spleen" (Verlaine) **2**:415
Le spleen de Paris (Baudelaire)
See *Petits poèmes en prose: Le spleen de Paris*
"Splitting Wood at Six Above" (Kumin) **15**:206, 219
"Spoke Joe to Jack" (Cummings) **5**:88
"Spontaneous Me" (Whitman) **3**:387
Spoon River Anthology (Masters) **1**:321-42, 344-49
"The Spooniad" (Masters) **1**:327
"Spor" (Lermontov) **18**:291
"Sport" (Hughes) **1**:270
"Sports Field" (Wright) **14**:362
"Sprachgitter" (Celan) **10**:112, 115, 129-30
Sprachgitter (Celan) **10**:95-6, 121
"A Sprig of Rosemary" (Lowell) **13**:64
"Spring" (Blake) **12**:7, 32
"Spring" (Dario)
See "Primaveral"
"Spring" (Gray)
See "Ode on Spring"
"Spring" (Hass) **16**:209
"Spring" (Hopkins) **15**:152
"Spring" (McGuckian) **27**:96
"Spring" (Millay) **6**:236
"Spring" (Pasternak) **6**:251
"Spring" (Rexroth) **20**:209
"Spring" (Sitwell) **3**:311
"Spring" (Williams) **7**:345, 399
Spring and All (Williams) **7**:349, 351, 353, 355, 373-78, 381-83, 387-88, 400-02, 405-06, 409-11
"Spring and Fall" (Hopkins) **15**:144
"The Spring and the Fall" (Millay) **6**:225
"Spring Comes to Murray Hill" (Nash) **21**:266
"Spring Day" (Ashbery) **26**:124
"Spring Day" (Lowell) **13**:79
"Spring Drawing" (Hass) **16**:215, 221
"Spring Drawing 2" (Hass) **16**:216
"Spring Flood" (Pasternak) **6**:266
"Spring in New Hampshire" (McKay) **2**:228
Spring in New Hampshire, and Other Poems (McKay) **2**:213, 228
"Spring in the Garden" (Millay) **6**:215
"Spring Lake" (Masters) **1**:343
"Spring Night" (Hagiwara Sakutaro) **18**:181
See "Shun'ya"
"Spring Oak" (Kinnell) **26**:237-38, 257
"Spring Ode I" (Bridges) **28**:84
"Spring Ode II" (Bridges) **28**:84
"Spring Offensive" (Owen) **19**:334, 337, 341-42, 344, 347, 353-55
"Spring Pastoral" (Wylie) **23**:321-22
"Spring Poem" (Atwood) **8**:24
"Spring Pools" (Frost) **1**:206
"Spring Prospect" (Tu Fu) **9**:322
"Spring Rain" (Hass) **16**:221-22
"Spring Rain" (Pasternak) **6**:251
"Spring Season of Muddy Roads" (Brodsky) **9**:2
"Spring Song" (Baraka) **4**:39
"Spring Song" (Clifton) **17**:16
Spring Thaw (Yosano Akiko)
See *Shundeishu*
"Spring Thunder" (Rich) **5**:383
"Spring Uncovered" (Swenson) **14**:247, 250, 268
"Spring Warning" (Larkin) **21**:259
"A Spring Wooing" (Dunbar) **5**:145
"Springfield Magical" (Lindsay) **23**:284
"Spring goeth all in white" (Bridges) **28**:66-7
"Spruce Woods" (Ammons) **16**:45
"Sprüche" (Goethe) **5**:248
"The Spur of Love" (MacDiarmid) **9**:189-90
"Squarings" (Heaney) **18**:254, 257-58
"Le squelette laboureur" (Baudelaire) **1**:45
"Squieres Tale" (Chaucer)
See "Squire's Tale"
"Squire's Tale" (Chaucer) **19**:13
"The Squirrel" (Stryk) **27**:189, 203
"Srishti-sthiti-pralaya" (Tagore) **8**:406
"Sroczosć" (Milosz) **8**:187
"St. Brandan" (Arnold) **5**:12
"St. Launce's Revisited" (Hardy) **8**:136
"St. Lucies Day" (Donne)
See "A Nocturnal upon S. Lucies day, Being the shortest day"
St. Patrick's Purgatory (Marie de France)
See *L'Espurgatoire Saint Patrice*
"St. Peter Relates an Incident of the Resurrection Day" (Johnson) **24**:133, 141, 144, 153, 161, 170
St. Peter Relates an Incident: Selected Poems (Johnson) **24**:130, 159, 162
"St. Praxed's Church" (Browning) **2**:30
"St. Simeon Stylites" (Tennyson) **6**:411
"Stages" (Meredith) **28**:180
"Stagirius" (Arnold) **5**:38
"Staircase" (Tsvetaeva)
See "Poèma lestnitsy"
"Stalin" (Lowell) **3**:223
"Stalin Epigram" (Mandelstam) **14**:149, 153
"The Stalker" (Momaday) 212-13
"Stan" (Tagore) **8**:407
"Stances" (Gautier) **18**:163
"Stances de la fontaine de'Helene" (Ronsard) **11**:241
"La Standard Oil Co." (Neruda) **4**:296
"The Standard Oil Co." (Neruda)
See "La Standard Oil Co."
"Standards and Paradise of the Blacks" (Garcia Lorca)
See "Norma y paraíso de los negros"
"A Standing Ground" (Berry) **28**:43
"Standomi un giorno solo a la fenestra" (Petrarch) **8**:253-57
"The standstillness of unthought" (Villa) **22**:354
"The Stand-To" (Day Lewis) **11**:146
"Stand-to: Good Friday Morning" (Sassoon) **12**:241, 251, 262, 280
"Stanza" (Bogan) **12**:103
"Stanzas" (Brodsky) **9**:4
"Stanzas" (Mandelstam) **14**:151
"Stanzas from the Grande Chartreuse" (Arnold) **5**:18, 24, 33, 35, 52-3, 58
Stanzas in Love with Life and August Again Again (Viereck) **27**:265
"Stanzas in Meditation" (Stein) **18**:309-316, 335-37, 339-41, 343, 345-48
Stanzas in Meditation (Stein) **18**:309-316, 335-37, 339-41, 343, 345-48
"Stanzas in Memory of Edward Quillinan" (Arnold) **5**:52
"Stanzas in Memory of the Author of 'Obermann'" (Arnold) **5**:42, 50, 52
"Stanzas on Peele Castle" (Wordsworth) **4**:394, 410-11
"Stanzas to Bettine" (Browning) **6**:15
"Stanzas to Tolstoi" (Pushkin) **10**:409
"Stanzas Written at Night in Radio City" (Ginsberg) **4**:55
"Stanzas Written on Battersea Bridge during a South-Westerly Gale" (Belloc) **24**:30-1, 36
"The Star" (Masters) **1**:326, 333, 337, 342
The Star (Bely)
See *Zvezda*
"A Star in a Stone-Boat" (Frost) **1**:194, 221
stardust (Bissett) **14**:30
"The Stare of the Man from the Provinces" (Nemerov) **24**:268
"Staring at the Sea on the Day of the Death of Another" (Swenson) **14**:288
"Starlight" (Meredith) **28**:171
"Starlight like Intuition Pierced the Twelve" (Schwartz) **8**:290-91
"The Starlight Night" (Hopkins) **15**:144, 152, 160, 162
"The Starling" (Lowell) **13**:61
"The Starling" (Smith) **12**:326
"The Starling" (Soto) **28**:375
"The Starred Coverlet" (Graves) **6**:156
"The Starry Night" (Sexton) **2**:350, 371-72
"Starry Night" (Sexton) **2**:350, 371-72
"Stars" (Hayden) **6**:184-85, 190, 194, 196
"The Star-Song: A Carroll to the King; Sung at White Hall" (Herrick) **9**:118, 119
"The Star-Splitter" (Frost) **1**:194
"Start Again Somewhere" (Gallagher) **9**:58
"Star-Talk" (Graves) **6**:166
"Starting from San Francisco" (Ferlinghetti) **1**:187
Starting from San Francisco (Ferlinghetti) **1**:166, 172-76, 187

Starting Point (Day Lewis) **11**:129
Starved Rock (Masters) **1**:332, 335, 338, 342-44
"The State of World Affairs from a Third Floor Window" (Bukowski) **18**:3
"Statement on Poetics" (Hayden) **6**:198
Statements After an Arrest Under the Immorality Act (Brutus) **24**:119
"The Staten Island Ferry" (Clampitt) **19**:100
"The State's Claim" (Ortiz) **17**:233
"Station" (Olds) **22**:307, 328
"Station Island" (Heaney) **18**:220, 240
Station Island (Heaney) **18**:211-12, 214-16, 218, 226, 228, 232, 237
"Stations" (Hughes) **7**:137
"Stations" (Lorde) **12**:140
"The Statue" (Belloc) **24**:9
"La Statue" (Hugo) **17**:64
"Statue and Birds" (Bogan) **12**:94, 101, 127
"The Statue at the World's End" (Stevens)
  See "Mr. Burnshaw and the Statue"
"Statue at Tsarskoye Selo" (Akhmatova) **2**:12
The Statue Guest (Pushkin)
  See *The Stone Guest*
"The Statue in Stocks-Market" (Marvell) **10**:276
"The Statue in the Garden" (Lowell) **13**:61
"A Statue in the Silence" (Neruda)
  See "Una estatua en el silencio"
"The Statue of Liberty" (Hardy) **8**:99
"The Statues" (Yeats) **20**:324, 334
"A Statute of Wine" (Neruda)
  See "Estatura del vino"
"Stay With Me" (Hongo) **23**:203
"Staying Alive" (Levertov) **11**:178-79, 195-96
"Steak" (Snyder) **21**:292-93
"Steal Away to Jesus" (Johnson) **24**:170
"Stealing Trout on a May Morning" (Hughes) **7**:120, 170
"Steam Shovel Cut" (Masters) **1**:343
"Lo steddazzu" (Pavese) **13**:229
"Steelhead" (Jeffers) **17**:141
"Steely Silence" (Wakoski) **15**:332
Steeple Bush (Frost) **1**:200, 205-06, 217
"The Steeple-Jack" (Moore) **4**:256
"Stella's Birthday, March 13, 1718-19" (Swift) **9**:255, 297
"Stellenbosch" (Kipling) **3**:176
"The Stenographers" (Page) **12**:163, 173
"Stepchild" (Hongo) **23**:197
"Stephen A. Douglas" (Masters) **1**:334
"Stepping Backward" (Rich) **5**:352
"Stepping Outside" (Gallagher) **9**:35
Stepping Outside (Gallagher) **9**:35
"Stepping Westward" (Wordsworth) **4**:395
"The Steps of the Commander" (Blok) **21**:6
Stevie Smith: A Selection (Smith) **12**:331, 348
"Stikhi K Akhmatovoi" (Tsvetaeva) **14**:321
Stikhi K Blok (Tsvetaeva) **14**:299, 311-12
"Stikhi k Chekhii" (Tsvetaeva) **14**:325, 327
"Stikhi k Pushkinu" (Tsvetaeva) **14**:324-25
"Stikhi k synu" (Tsvetaeva) **14**:328
"Stikhi o neizvestnom soldate" (Mandelstam) **14**:145, 148-49, 152, 155
Stikhi o prekrasnoi dame (Blok) **21**:13, 18, 24, 30
Stikhotvoreniya (Bely) **11**:29
"Still at Annecy" (Montale)
  See "Ancora ad Annecy"
"Still Do I Keep My Look, My Identity" (Brooks) **7**:71
"Still Falls the Rain" (Sitwell) **3**:310, 323, 326
"Still Life" (Gluck) **16**:128, 136, 139, 142
"Still Life" (Hughes) **7**:121, 137
"Still Night" (Smith) **12**:317
"Still on Water" (Rexroth) **20**:206, 216
"The Still Time" (Kinnell) **26**:260, 281
"Stillborn" (Plath) **1**:391, 405
"Stillness" (Pasternak)
  See "Tishina"
"Stimme des Volks" (Holderlin) **4**:166
"Stinging" (Cummings)
  See "Sunset"
"Stings" (Plath) **1**:394, 410, 412-14
"Stixi na smert T. S. Èliota" (Brodsky) **9**:2, 4
"Stol" (Tsvetaeva) **14**:318
"The Stolen Child" (Yeats) **20**:337, 346
"Stond who so list" (Wyatt) **27**:331, 362, 367
"The Stone" (Carruth) **10**:71
"The Stone" (Soto)
  See "Piedra"
Stone (Mandelstam)
  See *Kamen'*
"A Stone Church Damaged by a Bomb" (Larkin) **21**:259
"The Stone from the Sea" (Celan) **10**:112
The Stone Guest (Pushkin) **10**:394
"The Stone Verdict" (Heaney) **18**:229, 233
"The Stonecarver's Poem" (Levertov) **11**:169
"The Stones" (Plath) **1**:389-90
"Stones" (Zagajewski) **27**:389
"Stony Limits" (MacDiarmid) **9**:156, 176
Stony Limits (MacDiarmid) **9**:156, 158, 172-73, 175-76, 179-80, 182-84, 196, 200
"Stopping by Woods on a Snowy Evening" (Frost) **1**:194, 197, 208, 213-14, 221, 225
"Stop-Short" (Belloc) **24**:39
"La storia" (Montale) **13**:134
"Stories of Snow" (Page) **12**:164, 167-69, 172, 190, 197
Stories of the Sioux (Chief Standing Bear) **10**:333, 341-42
"The Storm" (Montale)
  See "La bufera"
"Storm" (Owen) **19**:353-54
"Storm" (Stryk) **27**:195, 212
"Storm" (Wright) **14**:342
The Storm and Other Things (Montale)
  See *La bufera e altro*
The Storm and Other Things (Montale)
  See *La bufera e altro*
"The Storm Came" (Kipling) **3**:171, 183
"Storm Ending" (Toomer) **7**:317, 330-32
"The storm is over" (Bridges) **28**:83
"Storm of Love" (Aleixandre) **15**:19
"Storm Warnings" (Rich) **5**:392, 396
"Storm Windows" (Nemerov) **24**:264-67, 270-71
"Story" (Wakoski) **15**:365
"Story Between Two Notes" (McGuckian) **27**:91
"The Story of a Citizen" (Gallagher) **9**:60, 62
"A Story of a Cock and a Bull" (Smart) **13**:348
"The Story of a Well-Made Shield" (Momaday) **25**:189, 213
"A Story of Courage" (Ortiz) **17**:246
"A Story of How a Wall Stands" (Ortiz) **17**:225
"The Story of Richard Maxfield" (Wakoski) **15**:346, 355, 361
The Story of the Heart (Aleixandre)
  See *Historia del corazón*
"The Story of Tommy" (Kipling) **3**:194
"Story of Two Gardens" (Paz)
  See "Cuento de dos jardines"
"Strabo in Plaster" (Merrill) **28**:258
"La strada" (Pasolini) **17**:253
"Stradivarius" (Eliot) **20**:123, 125
"Straight Talk" (Giovanni) **19**:112
"Straight-Creek--Great Burn" (Snyder) **21**:297
The Straightening (Celan)
  See *Sprachgitter*
Strains (Brutus) **24**:121-22, 124
"The Strait" (Ammons) **16**:4
"The Straitening" (Celan)
  See "Engführung"
"The Strange and True Story of My Life with Billy the Kid" (Momaday) **25**:221
"Strange Fits of Passion" (Wordsworth) **4**:420
"Strange Fruit" (Harjo) **27**:71
"Strange Fruit" (Heaney) **18**:196
The Strange Islands (Merton) **10**:331, 342, 347, 349, 351
"The Strange Case" (Ondaatje) **28**:329
"Strange Meeting" (Owen) **19**:325-27, 329, 332, 335-37, 341-45, 347, 353, 355, 359, 370-71
"A Strange Song" (Wylie) **23**:324
"A Strange Story" (Wylie) **23**:307, 310
"Strangeness of Heart" (Sassoon) **12**:254
"The Stranger" (Blok) **21**:4, 24
"Stranger" (Merton) **10**:349
"The Stranger" (Rich) **5**:384
"The Strangers" (Berry) **28**:7
"Strategy" (Gallagher) **9**:59
"Straw Hat" (Dove) **6**:110, 114
"Strawberry Hill" (Hughes) **7**:119, 148
"Strawberrying" (Swenson) **14**:273
"Stray Animals" (Song) **21**:332
"The Strayed Reveller" (Arnold) **5**:5, 12, 39, 50
The Strayed Reveller, and Other Poems (Arnold) **5**:8, 31, 38-9, 42, 48
"Stream and Sun at Glendalough" (Yeats) **20**:328
"The Stream of the Golden Honey was Pouring So Slow . . ." (Mandelstam) **14**:141
"The Street" (Soto) **28**:378, 383, 386
A Street in Bronzeville (Brooks) **7**:52-4, 56-8, 60-1, 67, 70, 75, 79-80, 85-7, 95, 102, 105
"Street Song" (Sitwell) **3**:311
Street Songs (Sitwell) **3**:308, 320
"Street Window" (Sandburg) **2**:309
"Streets" (Verlaine) **2**:415
"Strephon and Chloe" (Swift) **9**:257-58, 262, 270, 274, 286, 288, 294, 298, 301
"Strephon's Song" (Belloc) **24**:6
"Stretcher Case" (Sassoon) **12**:242, 262
Strike (Viereck) **27**:280-82, 284
Strike Through the Mask! (Viereck) **27**:262-63, 278
"Stripping the vista to its depth" (Tomlinson) **17**:342
"Striptase-Ta¨nzerinnen" (Enzensberger) **28**:165
"The Stroke" (Dove) **6**:111
"The Stroke" (Smith) **12**:314
"Strong Men, Riding Horses" (Brooks) **7**:106
"A Strong New Voice Pointing the Way" (Madhubuti) **5**:346
Strountes (Ekeloef) **23**:59-61, 63, 76-8
"The Structure of Rime" (Duncan) **2**:126
The Structure of Rime (Duncan) **2**:126
"The Structure of Rime II" (Duncan) **2**:125
"The Structure of Rime XXVIII" (Duncan) **2**:114
"The Structure of the Plane" (Rukeyser) **12**:202
"Struggle" (Hughes) **7**:165-66
"The Struggle Staggers Us" (Walker) **20**:289, 294
"Strumpet Song" (Plath) **1**:388
"Stubborn Hope" (Brutus) **24**:112
Stubborn Hope: New Poems and Selections from "China Poems" and "Strains" (Brutus) **24**:112, 116, 118, 122
"The Student" (Moore) **4**:260
Studies in Song (Swinburne) **24**:322
"The Studies of Narcissus" (Schwartz) **8**:311
"A Study" (Masters) **1**:342
"The Study of History" (Rich) **5**:365
"Study to Deserve Death" (Smith) **12**:318
"Stumbling" (Montale)
  See "Incespicare"
"Stump" (Heaney) **18**:202
Stunden-Buch (Rilke) **2**:277, 282, 288-90
Stundenbuch/Das Stundenbuch/A Book for the Hours of Prayer (Rilke)
  See *Stunden-Buch*
"Stupid Piety" (Goethe) **5**:229
"Stutgard" (Holderlin) **4**:147
"Style" (Baraka) **4**:9
"Style" (Moore) **4**:259
"Styx" (Duncan) **2**:119
"La suave agonie" (Valery) **9**:391-92
"Sub Contra" (Bogan) **12**:120
Sub Specie Aeternitatis (Hayden) **6**:194
"Sub Terra" (Williams) **7**:377
"A Subaltern" (Sassoon) **12**:242
"The Subalterns" (Hardy) **8**:111, 119

"A Substance In A Cushion" (Stein) **18**:321, 328, 349
"Suburb" (Smith) **12**:317
"The Subverted Flower" (Frost) **1**:198
"Success" (Brooke) **24**:56-7
"The Succubus" (Graves) **6**:163
Such Counsels You Gave to Me and Other Poems (Jeffers) **17**:135
"Suche Happe as I ame Happed in" (Wyatt) **27**:317, 352
"Sudden Journey" (Gallagher) **9**:50
"The Sudder Bazaar" (Kipling) **3**:190, 194
El Sueño (Juana Ines de la Cruz) **24**:212-15, 224-27, 235
"Suffer the Children" (Lorde) **12**:157
"Suffering" (Page) **12**:190
Suffised not, Madam (Wyatt) **27**:317
"Suffryng in sorow in hope to attayn" (Wyatt) **27**:310
"Sugar" (Stein) **18**:320, 322-23, 328, 334
"Sugar Loaf" (Hughes) **7**:121
"Suicide" (Bukowski) **18**:5
"Suicide" (Hughes) **1**:255
"The Suicide" (Millay) **6**:206
"Suicide Blues" (Rukeyser) **12**:228
"The Suicide in the Copse" (Graves) **6**:142, 144
"Suicide in the Trenches" (Sassoon) **12**:267, 285
"Suicide off Egg Rock" (Plath) **1**:389
"Suicide's Note" (Hughes) **1**:236
"Suis-je" (Laforgue) **14**:85
"The Suit" (Levine) **22**:225
"A Suite for Augustus" (Dove) **6**:106
"Suite furlana" (Pasolini) **17**:281-82
Suite furlana (Pasolini) **17**:252, 256, 279, 281
"Sukher vilap" (Tagore) **8**:405
"Sulla colonna più alta" (Montale) **13**:109, 111
"Sulla Greve" (Montale) **13**:152
"Sultry" (Lowell) **13**:95-6
"Sultry Rain" (Pasternak) **6**:257
Summa poética 1929-1946 (Guillen) **23**:104
"Summary" (Sanchez) **9**:224, 232
"Summer" (Ashbery) **26**:124-125
"Summer" (Bryant) **20**:12
"Summer" (Dario)
See "Estival"
"Summer" (Gluck) **16**:156, 166
"Summer" (Rossetti) **7**:280
"Summer" (Stryk) **27**:196, 208
"The Summer" (Trakl) **20**:226
"Summer" (Wright) **14**:377, 379
"Summer 1961" (Levertov) **11**:165
"Summer 1969" (Heaney) **18**:205
"Summer between Terms I" (Lowell) **3**:241
"Summer Holiday" (Jeffers) **17**:132
"Summer Home" (Heaney) **18**:203
"'Summer Is Over" (Cummings) **5**:108-09
"Summer Knowledge" (Schwartz) **8**:297-98, 312-19
Summer Knowledge: New and Selected Poems, 1938-1958 (Schwartz) **8**:289-91, 296, 301-02, 305, 309, 311
"A Summer Night" (Arnold) **5**:36, 42, 49, 50
"Summer Night Piece" (Lowell) **13**:64, 67
"Summer People" (Merrill) **28**:224-25, 230-31, 235
"Summer Place" (Ammons) **16**:23, 47
"summer poem." (Enzensberger) **28**:141, 147-48
"A Summer Ramble" (Bryant) **20**:37, 39
"Summer Resort" (Page) **12**:173
"Summer Session" (Ammons) **16**:50
"Summer time T. V. (is witer than ever)" (Sanchez) **9**:210-11, 213, 225
"Summer Wind" (Bryant) **20**:40
"Summer Wish" (Bogan) **12**:94-5, 98, 100, 106, 121-22
"Summer Words of a Sistuh Addict" (Sanchez) **9**:225
"A Summer's Dream" (Bishop) **3**:47
"Summer's Elegy" (Nemerov) **24**:291
"Summertime and the Living..." (Hayden) **6**:194, 196
"Summit Beach, 1921" (Dove) **6**:121
"Summoner's Tale" (Chaucer) **19**:13
"The Summons" (Auden) **1**:38
Summonses of the Times (Bely)
See *Zovy vremen*
"The Sun" (Milosz) **8**:192, 207
"Sun" (Moore) **4**:243
"The Sun" (Nishiwaki)
See "Taiyo"
"The Sun" (Noyes) **27**:129
"The Sun" (Sexton) **2**:351, 372
"The Sun" (Trakl) **20**:226
"The Sun Does Not Move" (Bissett) **14**:5
"The Sun Is near Meridan Height" (Bronte) **8**:73
"The Sun on the Letter" (Hardy) **8**:97
"The Sun Rising" (Donne)
See "The Sunne Rising"
"The Sun Says His Prayers" (Lindsay) **23**:281
"Sun Stone" (Paz)
See "Piedra de sol"
Sun Stone (Paz)
See *Piedra de sol*
"Sun the First" (Elytis) **21**:131
Sun the First (Elytis)
See *Ílios o prótos*
"Sunbathing on a Rooftop in Berkeley" (Kumin) **15**:203
"Sunday" (Herbert) **4**:100
"Sunday" (Hughes) **1**:255
"Sunday" (Nemerov) **24**:277
"A Sunday" (Soto) **28**:397-98, 400
"Sunday" (Williams) **7**:351
"Sunday in the Country" (Swenson) **14**:247, 250, 264
"Sunday Morning" (Stevens) **6**:292, 301, 304, 306, 327, 336
"Sunday Morning" (Whitman) **3**:391
"Sunday Morning Apples" (Crane) **3**:83, 90, 100
"A Sunday Morning Tragedy" (Hardy) **8**:99
"Sunday New Guinea" (Shapiro) **25**:269, 286, 295
"A Sunday with Shepherds and Herdboys" (Clare) **23**:13
sunday work(?) (Bissett) **14**:5, 16
"Sundays before noon" (Bukowski) **18**:23
"Sundays Kill More Men than Bombs" (Bukowski) **18**:4
"The Sundays of Satin-Legs Smith" (Brooks) **7**:69, 79-80, 85
"Sunderland" (Nemerov) **24**:295
"Sundew" (Atwood) **8**:13
Sundry Phansies (Kipling) **3**:193
"Sunflower" (Breton)
See "Tournesol"
"The Sunflower" (Montale) **13**:138, 141, 149
"Sunflower Sutra" (Ginsberg) **4**:48, 50, 92
"Sung beneath the Alps" (Holderlin) **4**:142
"The Sunken Bell" (Ishikawa)
See "Shizumeru kane"
"Sunlight" (Gunn) **26**:204, 214, 219
"Sunlight" (Heaney) **18**:203
"Sunlight and Flesh" (Rimbaud)
See "Soleil et chair"
"The Sunne Rising" (Donne) **1**:125, 134, 145, 147, 152, 154
"Sunny Prestatyn" (Larkin) **21**:229
"Sunset" (Cummings) **5**:70, 94
"Sunset" (Dunbar) **5**:138-39
"Sunset" (Gluck) **16**:170
"Sunset of the Century" (Tagore)
See "Shatabdir surya"
"A Sunset of the City" (Brooks) **7**:68-9, 96
"Sunset on the Spire" (Wylie) **23**:324, 328
"Sunset Piece: After Reaching Rémy De Gourmont" (Cummings) **5**:71
Sunstone (Paz)
See *Piedra de sol*
"Superfluous Advice" (Parker) **28**:362
"The Supper after the Last" (Kinnell) **26**:238, 257, 279
"Supper Time" (Hughes) **1**:255
"A Supplication for Love" (Browning) **6**:31
"Supposed Confessions of a Second-Rate Sensitive Mind" (Tennyson) **6**:406, 409
"Supreme Fiction" (Ammons) **16**:23
"Supuesto, discurso mío" (Juana Ines de la Cruz) **24**:180, 184
"Sur l'eau" (Valery) **9**:391-92
"Sur les lagunes" (Gautier) **18**:125
"Sur l'herbe" (Verlaine) **2**:430
"The Surface" (Swenson) **14**:261, 282
"The Surfer" (Wright) **14**:345
"The Surgeons" (Kunitz) **19**:151
"Surprise" (Parker) **28**362
"Surprises" (Kumin) **15**:210, 223
Surrealist Poetry (Aleixandre)
See *Poesía superrealista*
"Surrounded by Wild Turkeys" (Snyder) **21**:326
"Survival as Tao, Beginning at 5:00 a.m." (Carruth) **10**:88
"Survival of the Fittest" (Gozzano) **10**:183
"The Survivor" (Graves) **6**:137, 142, 144
"Survivors" (Sassoon) **12**:267-68, 285
"Suspension" (Lorde) **12**:158
"Sussex" (Kipling) **3**:167, 192
"Svapna" (Tagore) **8**:410-11
"Svarga" (Tagore) **8**:414
"Svarga ha'ite biday" (Tagore) **8**:409
"Swamp Plant" (Wright) **14**:374
"The Swan" (Baudelaire)
See "Le cygne"
"The Swan" (Roethke) **15**:275, 288
"The Swans" (Dario)
See "Los cisnes"
"The Swans" (Lowell) **13**:86
The Swans' Encampment (Tsvetaeva)
See *Lebediny stan*
"The Swarm" (Plath) **1**:410, 412
"Swaziland" (Giovanni) **19**:141
"Sweeney among the Nightingales" (Eliot) **5**:184
Sweeney Astray (Heaney) **18**:215-18, 235
"Sweeney Redivivus" (Heaney) **18**:215, 228, 233
"The Sweeper of Ways" (Nemerov) **24**:282
"Sweet Afton" (Burns) **6**:77
"Sweet Boy, Give me Yr Ass" (Ginsberg) **4**:90
"A Sweet Flying Dream" (Ferlinghetti) **1**:183, 188
"Sweet Hopes" (Pushkin)
See "Nadezhdoi Sladostnoi"
"Sweet Like a Crow" (Ondaatje) **28**:338
"Sweet Mary Dove" (Clare) **23**:25
"Sweet Michel" (Browning) **2**:30
"The Sweet o' the Year" (Noyes) **27**:114
"The Sweet Primroses" (Hardy) **8**:130
"Sweet Susan" (Clare) **23**:25
"Sweet Things" (Gunn) **26**:209, 211
"Sweet Violets" (Parker) **28**:351
Sweet Will (Levine) **22**:221, 224, 226
"Sweetened Change" (Ammons) **16**:63
"Sweetest love, I do not goe" (Donne)
See "Song. 'Sweetest love, I do not goe'"
Swellfoot the Tyrant (Shelley) **14**:175, 202
"Swells" (Ammons) **16**:32, 63
"Swiadomosć" (Milosz) **8**:209
"Swiftly walk over the western wave" (Shelley) **14**:177
"The Swimmer" (Olds) **22**:323, 325
"Swimmers" (Swenson) **14**:265, 276, 287
"A Swimmer's Dream" (Swinburne) **24**:313, 325
"Swimming Chenango Lake" (Tomlinson) **17**:316, 319, 321, 328
"The Swimming Race" (Noyes) **27**:116
"Switzerland" (Arnold) **5**:12-13
Sword Blades and Poppy Seed (Lowell) **13**:69-70, 76, 93
"A Sword in a Cloud of Light" (Rexroth) **20**:190

Swords Like Lips (Aleixandre)
See *Espadas como labios*
"The Sycamore" (Berry) **28**:25
"Sydney Bridge" (Shapiro) **25**:269
"Sygil" (H. D.) **5**:306
"The Syllable Pain" (Celan) **10**:102
"Le sylphe" (Valery) **9**:387, 391, 393
Sylvae (Dryden) **25**:80
"Sylvia's Death" (Sexton) **2**:364, 370
"Symbolism in Painting" (Yeats) **20**:299
The Symbolism of Poetry (Yeats) **20**:336
"Symmetrical Companion" (Swenson) **14**:274, 284
"Sympathetic Portrait of a Child" (Williams) **7**:349
"Sympathy" (Dunbar) **5**:134
"Symphonie en blanc majeur" (Gautier) **18**:124-27, 129-30
"Symptoms of Love" (Graves) **6**:155
"The Synagogue" (Shapiro) **25**:263, 269, 283, 296, 299-300
"Syrinx" (Merrill) **28**:223, 256
"The Syrophenician Woman" (Harper) **21**:208, 215-16
"The System" (Ashbery) **26**:108, 130
Szomoru beres (Illyes) **16**:238, 247
T. V. Baby Poems (Ginsberg) **4**:47
Ta eleýa tis Oxópetras (Elytis) **21**:134-35
"Ta Lettre sur le Drap" (Senghor) **25**:233-34, 249
"Tabacaria" (Pessoa) **20**:166, 169
"Tabibito" (Nishiwaki) **15**:229
Tabibito Kaerazu (Nishiwaki) **15**:229-36
"A Table" (Stein) **18**:320-22, 324, 328, 330, 350
"Table I" (Milosz) **8**:210
"Table II" (Milosz) **8**:210
"Tableau" (Cullen) **20**:64
"Tag och skriv" (Ekeloef) **23**:51, 76, 78
"Tagore's Last Poems" (Tagore)
See "Sesh lekha"
"Tahirassawichi en Washington" (Cardenal) **22**:131
"Tahirassawichi in Washington"
See "Tahirassawichi en Washington"
"Taiyo" (Nishiwaki) **15**:240-41
"Take" (Hagiwara Sakutaro) **18**:179
"Take a whole holiday in honour of this" (Day Lewis) **11**:130
"Take from My Palms" (Mandelstam) **14**:117
"Take heed of loving mee" (Donne)
See "The Prohibition"
"Taken Aback" (McKay) **2**:221
"Taking" (Ondaatje) **28**:327, 332
"Taking In Wash" (Dove) **6**:111
"Taking Off My Clothes" (Forche) **10**:133, 135
"Taking the Lambs to Market" (Kumin) **15**:216
"Talbot Road" (Gunn) **26**:220, 229
"A Tale" (Bogan) **12**:85, 111, 127
"A Tale" (Coleridge) **11**:101
"A Tale" (Finch) **21**:166
The Tale of Balen (Swinburne) **24**:348, 350-54, 357
"The Tale of Custard the Dragon" (Nash) **21**:265
"Tale of Melibee" (Chaucer) **19**:26, 33, 47
"A Tale of Starvation" (Lowell) **13**:60, 84
The Tale of Sunlight (Soto) **28**:371
"The Tale of Sunlight" (Soto) **28**:384, 386
"The Tale of the Dead Princess and the Seven Heroes" (Pushkin)
See "Skazka o Mertvoy Tsarevne"
"The Tale of the Female Vagrant" (Wordsworth) **4**:373, 419
"The Tale of the Fisherman and the Fish" (Pushkin)
See "Skazka o Rybake i Rybke"
The Tale of the Golden Cockerel (Pushkin)
See "Skazka o Zolotom Petushke"
"The Tale of the Parson and His Man Balda" (Pushkin)
See "Skazka o Pope i o Rabotnike Yego Balde"
"A Tale of the Thirteenth Floor" (Nash) **21**:270-71
"The Tale of the Tsar Sultan" (Pushkin)
See "Skazka o Tsare Sultane"
"A Tale of Two Gardens" (Paz)
See "Cuento de dos jardines"
Tales (Chaucer)
See *Canterbury Tales*
"Tales of a Wayside Inn" (Noyes) **27**:129
Tales of Canterbury (Chaucer)
See *Canterbury Tales*
Tales of the Mermaid Tavern (Noyes) **27**:123-24, 126, 129, 134, 137
Talifer (Robinson) **1**:475, 477, 479, 483
"A Talisman" (Moore) **4**:232
"A Talk with Friedrich Nietzsche" (Zagajewski) **27**:389, 392
"Talking Back (to W. H. Auden)" (Meredith) **28**:216
"Talking in the Woods with Karl Amorelli" (Knight) **14**:43
"Talking Late with the Governor about the Budget" (Snyder) **21**:300, 326
"Ten-Day Leave" (Meredith) **28**:180, 186
"Talking Oak" (Tennyson) **6**:356
"Tam Glen" (Burns) **6**:59
"Tam o' Shanter" (Burns) **6**:55-8, 73-4, 76, 78, 81, 89, 96
"Tama yo shizume" (Ishikawa) **10**:213
"Tamar" (Jeffers) **17**:106-07, 111, 116, 130-32, 135, 138, 141, 146
Tamar and Other Poems (Jeffers) **17**:122, 124, 128, 135, 138, 146
"Tamara" (Lermontov) **18**:291-92, 298
"Tamarlane" (Poe) **1**:428, 436-38, 442, 444-45, 448
Tamarlane, and Other Poems, By a Bostonian (Poe) **1**:428, 432, 437, 449
The Tambov Treasurer's Wife (Lermontov) **18**:278, 282
"Tamer and Hawk" (Gunn) **26**:200, 221
"Tanghi-Garu Pass" (Paz) **1**:361
"Tangible Disaster" (Cesaire) **25**:18
"Tango" (Gluck) **16**:151, 154
"Tankas" (Borges) **22**:78
"Tanto e Amara" (Olson) **19**:320
"Tanu" (Tagore) **8**:407
"Die Tänzerin (D.H.)" (Sachs) **18**:162
"Tape for the Turn of the Year" (Ammons) **16**:31
Tape for the Turn of the Year (Ammons) **16**:3-4, 6, 21-4, 28, 35, 42-3, 47-50, 59-61, 64-5
"The Tapestry" (Bridges) **28**:79
The Tapestry (Bridges) **28**:76, 80-1
"Tapestry" (Cassian) **17**:5
"Taproot" (Forche) **10**:142
Taproot (Stryk) **27**:191, 197-98, 215, 218
"Tarakar atmahatya" (Tagore) **8**:405
"Tarantella" (Belloc) **24**:7, 22, 31
Target Study (Baraka) **4**:38
"Tarkington Thou Should'st Be Living in This Hour" (Nash) **21**:273
"th tarot match covr uv th lovrs" (Bissett) **14**:33
"Tarrant Moss" (Kipling) **3**:183
"Tartuffe's Punishment" (Rimbaud)
See "Le châtiment de Tartuff"
"tarzan collage" (Bissett) **14**:31
"A Task" (Milosz) **8**:206
The Tasking (Sassoon) **12**:271
"Tatinir katha" (Tagore) **8**:406
"The Tattooed Man" (Hayden) **6**:195
"Tavern" (Millay) **6**:205
"The Taxi" (Lowell) **13**:93
"Taylor Street" (Gunn) **26**:213, 231
"T-Bar" (Page) **12**:177, 183, 188
"TCB" (Sanchez) **9**:225
"Tea at the Palaz of Hoon" (Stevens) **6**:304
"Teacher" (Walker) **20**:273, 286
"Teaching a Dumb Calf" (Hughes) **7**:166
"The Teamster" (Pavese) **13**:218
"Teamsters Union" (Shapiro) **25**:316
"The Tear" (Pushkin) **10**:407
A Tear and a Smile (Gibran)
See *Dam 'ah wabitisamah*
"A Tear for Cressid" (Wylie) **23**:314
"Tear Gas" (Rich) **5**:393, 396
"Tears" (Sitwell) **3**:326
"Tears" (Whitman) **3**:379
"Tears and Laughter" (Gibran)
See *Dam 'ah wabitisamah*
"Tears of an Excavator" (Pasolini) **17**:258, 289
The Tears of the Blind Lions (Merton) **10**:339
"Teasing the Nuns" (Shapiro) **25**:286, 300
"Teatro Bambino" (Lowell) **13**:94
"The Technique of Perfection" (Graves) **6**:128
"Teddungal" (Senghor) **25**:255
"Teddy Bears" (Swenson) **14**:273
"Tehran 3 May 68" (Brutus) **24**:123
"Telegramas de urgencia escribo" (Fuertes) **27**:16
"Telephoning God" (Soto) **28**:375
"Television Is a Baby Crawling Toward That Death Chamber" (Ginsberg) **4**:51, 76
"Television Poem" (Sanchez) **9**:210
"Tell Me" (Hughes) **1**:244
"Tell Me" (Toomer) **7**:335
Tell Me Again How the White Heron Rises and Flies Across the Nacreous River at Twilight Toward the Distant Islands (Carruth) **10**:86-7
Tell Me, Tell Me: Granite, Steel, and Other Topics (Moore) **4**:242, 259
"tell me what attackd yu" (Bissett) **14**:32
"Temas candentes Agricultura" (Fuertes) **27**:28
"The Temper" (Herbert) **4**:100, 118
"The Temper I" (Herbert) **4**:101, 111
The Tempers (Williams) **7**:344, 348, 367, 378, 395, 398, 405
"Tempest and Music" (Viereck) **27**:278, 280
"Tempid: Bellosguardo" (Montale) **13**:126
"The Temple" (Herrick)
See "The Fairie Temple: or, Oberons Chappell. Dedicated to Mr. John Merrifield, Counsellor at Law"
"Le temple" (Lamartine) **16**:277
"The Temple of Fame" (Pope) **26**:318-19, 331
The Temple: Sacred Poems and Private Ejaculations (Herbert) **4**:99-102, 106, 110, 114-18, 120-21, 123, 126, 129, 132-33
"Il tempo passa" (Pavese) **13**:209, 226
"Le Temps et les Cités" (Hugo) **17**:88
"Temps Perdu" (Parker) **28**:365
"Temptation" (Cassian) **17**:4
"The Temptation of St. Joseph" (Auden) **1**:38-39
Temy i variatsi (Pasternak) **6**:252, 255, 261, 264-65, 269, 271, 275, 277-81, 283
Temy i var'iatsii (Pasternak)
See *Temy i variatsi*
"X" (Joyce) **22**:136, 138, 145, 153, 160, 162, 168
"Tenancy" (Merrill) **28**:249-50, 268
"10 April 67" (Brutus) **24**:122
"The Tenant" (Brodsky) **9**:2
Tender Buttons: Objects, Food, Rooms (Stein) **18**:316-34, 336, 341-42, 344, 349-54
Tender only To One (Smith) **12**:292, 326, 340, 343, 349
"Tenderness toward Existence" (Kinnell) **26**:251
"Tenebrae" (Celan) **10**:101-02, 118
"Tenebrae" (Levertov) **11**:176
"Tengo" (Guillen) **23**:106, 115
Tengo (Guillen) **23**:124-25, 127, 130-31, 133
"Tengo que deciros" (Fuertes) **27**:4
"Tenjo Ishi" (Hagiwara Sakutaro) **18**:178-79
"Tenki" (Nishiwaki) **15**:228
"The Tennessee Hero" (Harper) **21**:206, 218
"Tennis" (Pinsky) **27**:144, 162
"The Tennis Court Oath" (Ashbery) **26**:113
The Tennis Court Oath (Ashbery) **26**:108, 112-

Cumulative Title Index

113, 118, 129, 137-138, 143, 163
"Tenor" (Guillen) **23**:122, 124
Tentativa del hombre infinito (Neruda) **4**:276
"Tentative Description of a Dinner to Promote the Impeachment of President Eisenhower" (Ferlinghetti) **1**:167
"Tenth Elegy" (Rilke) **2**:273, 286-87
"Tenth Muse" (Lowell) **3**:213
The Tenth Muse Lately sprung up in America (Bradstreet) **10**:2-3, 6-8, 12, 18, 20-1, 25-7, 29-31, 34, 37, 40-1, 43, 46, 51-2, 59
Tenth Nemean (Pindar)
See *Nemean 10*
Tenth Olympian (Pindar)
See *Olympian 10*
"Tenth Psalm" (Sexton) **2**:372
Tenth Pythian (Pindar)
See *Pythian 10*
"Tenuous and Precarious" (Smith) **12**:312, 337
Tercera residencia, 1935-1945 (Neruda) **4**:291, 306
"Tercero antolojía poética" (Jimenez) **7**:195
"Teremteni" (Illyes) **16**:235, 249
"Terence, This Is Stupid Stuff" (Housman) **2**:193
"A Term" (Aleixandre) **15**:4
"Terminal" (Shapiro) **25**:324
"Terminal Day at Beverly Farms" (Lowell) **3**:219
"Terminal Resemblance" (Gluck) **16**:158
"Terminus" (Emerson) **18**:75-77, 113
"Terminus" (Heaney) **18**:227
"The Terrace at Berne" (Arnold) **5**:12, 19, 49
"The Terraced Valley" (Graves) **6**:135, 139, 143-44, 172
"A Terre" (Owen) **19**:327, 331, 336, 339-40, 357, 359, 368
"Territory" (Kumin) **15**:207
"Terror" (Levertov) **11**:169
"Terror and Decorum" (Viereck) **27**:267, 271
Terror and Decorum (Viereck) **27**:258-63, 277-84
Terror and $$Word$$ Poems 1940-1948 (Viereck) **27**:
"The Terror of Existing" (Montale)
See "Il terrore di esistere"
"Il terrore di esistere" (Montale) **13**:139
"Tess's Lament" (Hardy) **8**:85
"The Test" (Emerson) **18**:77
"A Testament" (Lermontov) **18**:278
"Testament" (Stryk) **27**:215
Le Testament (Villon) **13**:374-75, 377, 379, 387-90, 393-418
"Testament Coran" (Pasolini) **17**:262, 279
The Testament of Beauty (Bridges) **28**:48-50, 54-56, 59, 62, 65, 70-73, 76-78, 81
"The Testament of Love" (Bridges) **28**:65
Testament of Love (Chaucer)
See *Legend of Good Women*
"Testament of the Thief" (Kinnell) **26**:240
"The Testing Tree" (Kunitz) **19**:175, 178, 180, 183
The Testing-Tree (Kunitz) **19**:157, 161, 163, 168, 172-74, 176, 185-86
"Tête de faune" (Rimbaud) **3**:271
"Têtes du serail" (Hugo) **17**:75
"Teurer Freund" (Heine) **25**:161
"Texas" (Lowell) **13**:86
"Thalamus" (MacDiarmid) **9**:168, 176-77
"Thamár y Amnón" (Garcia Lorca) **3**:120, 131-32, 134, 146
"Thanatopsis" (Bryant) **20**:10, 12, 14, 16-19, 21-3, 26-30, 32, 34, 41, 43, 47
"Thank God for Little Children" (Harper) **21**:197
"Thank You, Fog" (Auden) **1**:31
"Thanking My Mother for Piano Lessons" (Wakoski) **15**:325, 347
"A Thanksgiving" (Auden) **1**:31
"Thanksgiving" (Gluck) **16**:124, 129, 150
"Thanksgiving for a Habitat" (Auden) **1**:24
"Thanksgiving Ode" (Wordsworth) **4**:399
"Thanksgiving's Over" (Lowell) **3**:206
"That April night's menu" (Enzensberger) **28**:155
"That Blessed Hope" (Harper) **21**:189, 208, 217
"That Bright Chimeric Beast" (Cullen) **20**:67
"That Day" (Sexton) **2**:353
"That Day That Was That Day" (Lowell) **12**:85
"That Force" (Zagajewski) **27**:385
"That Kind of Thing" (Gallagher) **9**:61
"That Moment" (Hardy) **8**:94
"That Swan's Way" (Aleixandre) **15**:5
"That the Night Come" (Yeats) **20**:351
"That which is one they shear and make it twain" (Belloc) **24**:37-8
"That Woman There" (Stryk) **27**:203
"That women are but men's shadows" (Jonson)
See "That women are but men's shadows"
"That Year" (Olds) **22**:308, 320, 322
"The Thatcher" (Heaney) **18**:200
"That's the Place Indians Talk About" (Ortiz) **17**:228, 230-31, 234
"The" (Zukofsky)
See "Poem Beginning 'The'"
"'The Annihilation of Nothing" (Gunn) **26**:
"'The Discovery of the Pacific" (Gunn) **26**:
"Thébaide" (Gautier) **18**:146
Theban Dithyramb (Pindar) **19**:423
"The,bright,Centipede" (Villa) **22**:350
"The,caprice,of,canteloupe,is,to,be" (Villa) **22**:356-57
Thee (Aiken) **26**:24, 29
"Their Behaviour" (Brutus) **24**:99
"Their Frailty" (Sassoon) **12**:267
"Thekla's Answer" (Arnold) **5**:50
"thel" (Clifton) **17**:30
"Thelassius" (Swinburne) **24**:312-315
"Theme and Variation" (Hayden) **6**:186, 197
"Theme and Variations" (Pasternak) **6**:251
Themes and Variations (Pasternak)
See *Temy i variatsi*
"Then I Saw What the Calling Was" (Rukeyser) **12**:223
"Theodore Dreiser" (Masters) **1**:343
"Theodore the Poet" (Masters) **1**:345
"Theological Cradle Songs" (Viereck) **27**:262
"Theology" (Dunbar) **5**:120, 125, 127
"Theology" (Hughes) **7**:123, 159
"Theory of Art" (Baraka) **4**:9
"Theory of Evil" (Hayden) **6**:194, 196
"Theory of Flight" (Rukeyser) **12**:207, 218, 225
Theory of Flight (Rukeyser) **12**:202-03, 206, 209-10, 226-27, 235-36
"Theory of Maya" (Tagore)
See "Mayavada"
"A Theory of Prosody" (Levine) **22**:227
"Theory of Truth" (Jeffers) **17**:131, 142, 144
"ther may have been a tunnel thru which my train rolld" (Bissett) **14**:34
"There" (Verlaine) **2**:416
"There Are Birds" (Shapiro) **25**:294
"There Are Blk/Puritans" (Sanchez) **9**:218
"There Are Orioles in Woods and Lasting Length of Vowels" (Mandelstam) **14**:141
"There Are So Many Houses and Dark Streets without Help" (Bukowski) **18**:15
"There Are Things I Tell to No One" (Kinnell) **26**:258, 260-61, 280, 292
"There Has to Be a Jail for Ladies" (Merton) **10**:341
"There is a hill beside the silver Thames" (Bridges) **28**:66-7, 83
"There Is Only One of Everything" (Atwood) **8**:23, 28
"There Once Lived a Poor Knight" (Pushkin)
See "Zhil Na Svete Rytsar' Bednyi"
"There Shines the Moon, at Noon of Night" (Bronte) **8**:75
"There Should be No Despair" (Bronte) **8**:68-9
"There Was a Child Went Forth" (Whitman) **3**:392, 396, 415
"There Was A Dance Sweetheart" (Harjo) **27**:69
"There Was a Lad Was Born in Kyle" (Burns) **6**:76
"There Was a Poor Knight" (Pushkin)
See "Zhil Na Svete Rytsar' Bednyi"
"There Was a Saviour" (Thomas) **2**:390
"There was Never Nothing" (Wyatt) **27**:318
"There Was One" (Parker) **28**:362
Therefore (Mallarme)
See *Igitur*
There's a Trick with a Knife I'm Learning to Do: Poems, 1963-1978 (Ondaatje) **28**:327-40
"These" (Williams) **7**:360, 362-63
"These Are the Young" (Lindsay) **23**:281
"These States: To Miami Presidential Convention" (Ginsberg) **4**:82
"These Streets" (Levine) **22**:224
"Theseus and Ariadne" (Graves) **6**:136-37, 144, 146
"Thetis" (H. D.) **5**:267-68
"They" (Sassoon) **12**:241, 249, 263, 275, 277-78, 286
"They Are More on a Corncob" (Guillen)
See "They Are More on a Corncob"
"They Are Not Missed" (Toomer) **7**:338-39
"They Are Not Ready" (Madhubuti) **5**:338
"They Clapped" (Giovanni) **19**:141
"They Eat Out" (Atwood) **8**:6
"They Feed They Lion" (Levine) **22**:216, 221, 227
They Feed They Lion (Levine) **22**:211, 213, 215, 217, 223
"They fle from me" (Wyatt) **27**:300, 302, 309, 314, 316, 329-31, 338, 343, 347-48, 355, 357, 362
"They Have Put Us on Hold" (Walker) **20**:294
"They Say it Snowed" (Ammons) **16**:44
"They Say This Isn't a Poem" (Rexroth) **20**:195-96
"They'd Never Know Me Now" (Masters) **1**:344
"Thick-Lipped Nigger" (Guillen)
See "Negro bembón"
"The Thief" (Kunitz) **19**:150-51, 172, 175
"Thin Air" (Hass) **16**:215, 217
"The Thin People" (Plath) **1**:388, 406
"Things of August" (Stevens) **6**:313
Things Taking Place (Swenson)
See *New and Selected Things Taking Place*
"Things That Are Worse Than Death" (Olds) **22**:313
"Think No More, Lad: Laugh, Be Jolly" (Housman) **2**:179, 183, 185
"Think of It" (Celan) **10**:98
"The Thinker" (Williams) **7**:353
"Thinking about El Salvador" (Levertov) **11**:198
"Thinking of Old Tu Fu" (Matsuo Basho) **3**:10
"Think Tank" (Merrill) **28**:267
"Third Degree" (Hughes) **1**:248
"The Third Dimension" (Levertov) **11**:159
"Third Elegy" (Rilke) **2**:271
"Third Georgic" (Vergil) **12**:361
"Third Hymn to Lenin" (MacDiarmid) **9**:180-81, 197
Third Nemean (Pindar)
See *Nemean 3*
Third Olympian (Pindar)
See *Olympian 3*
"Third Psalm" (Sexton) **2**:367
Third Pythian (Pindar)
See *Pythian 3*
The Third Residence (Neruda)
See *Tercera residencia, 1935-1945*
Third Residence (Neruda)
See *Tercera residencia, 1935-1945*
"The Third Sermon of the Warpland" (Brooks) **7**:88-9
"Third Song" (Rilke) **2**:273
The Third Symphony (Bely)
See *Vozvrat: Tretiia simfoniia*
Third Voronezh Notebook (Mandelstam) **14**:149, 152, 155

"The Third World" (Ferlinghetti) **1**:186
"Third World Calling" (Ferlinghetti) **1**:183
"XIII" (Joyce) **22**:145, 168
"Thirteen Ways of Looking at a Blackbird" (Stevens) **6**:293, 326-27
Thirteenth Olympian (Pindar)
See *Olympian 13*
"The Thirties Revisited" (Kumin) **15**:202
Thirty Poems (Merton) **10**:338-39, 350-51
"Thirty Rhymes to Hermit Chang Piao" (Tu Fu) **9**:326
"XXXV" (Joyce) **22**:138 39, 144, 154, 157, 161, 164
"XXXIV" (Joyce) **22**:139, 145, 157, 161-62, 164-65, 170
"XXXI" (Joyce) **22**:152, 164, 170
"XXXVI" (Joyce) **22**:136, 138, 144-45, 157, 161, 163-64
"XXXIII" (Joyce) **22**:145, 164, 166, 168, 173
"XXXII" (Joyce) **22**:145, 164, 167, 173
"XXXII" (Larkin) **21**:242
"This Black Rich Country" (Ammons) **16**:40
"This Bread I Break" (Thomas) **2**:379, 389
"This Cold Man" (Page)
See "Now This Cold Man"
"This Compost" (Whitman) **3**:410
"This Configuration" (Ashbery) **26**:141
"This Corruptible" (Wylie) **23**:304-305, 308, 311, 316
"This Day" (Levertov) **11**:198-99, 201
"This Do, in Remembrance of Me" (Bryant) **20**:45
"This Florida: 1924" (Williams) **7**:369
"This Frieze of Birds" (Page) **12**:168
"This Is" (Ammons) **16**:54
"This Is a Photograph of Me" (Atwood) **8**:12, 23
"This is Disgraceful and Abominable" (Smith) **12**:293, 309
"This Is Just to Say" (Williams) **7**:363, 399, 401
This Is My Century (Walker) **20**:293
"This Is Noon" (Graves) **6**:166
"This Is Not For John Lennon (And This Is Not a Poem)" (Giovanni) **19**:142
"this is the tale" (Clifton) **17**:25, 27
"This Is the Track" (Owen) **19**:342
"This Is Their Fault" (Forche) **10**:142
"This (Let's Remember) day Died Again and" (Cummings) **5**:107
"This Life" (Dove) **6**:108
"This Lime-Tree Bower My Prison" (Coleridge) **11**:51, 53, 72, 83, 88-9, 97, 104, 107
"This My Song is Made for Kerensky" (Lindsay) **23**:269
"This Near-At-Hand" (Rossetti) **7**:276
"This Occurs To Me" (Ortiz) **17**:225
"This Place Rumord to Have Been Sodom" (Duncan) **2**:127
"This Praying Fool" (Kumin) **15**:180
"This Room and Everything in It" (Lee) **24**:243
"This Side of Truth" (Thomas) **2**:390
"This sun on this rubble after rain" (Brutus) **24**:113
"This, That, and the Other" (Nemerov) **24**:298, 303
"This Urn Contains Earth from German Concentration Camps" (Lorde) **12**:136
"This Was a Poet" (Dickinson) **1**:96, 102
"This Way Is Not a Way" (Snyder) **21**:310
"Thistledown" (Merrill) **28**:228
"Thistles" (Hughes) **7**:121, 137
"Tho I cannot your crueltie constrain" (Wyatt) **27**:321
Thomas and Beulah (Dove) **6**:104, 107, 110-20, 122
"Thomas at the Wheel" (Dove) **6**:111
"Thompson's Lunch Room" (Lowell) **13**:79
"Thorkild's Song" (Kipling) **3**:183
"The Thorn" (Wordsworth) **4**:381, 402, 412, 416-17, 426, 428
"A Thorn Forever in the Breast" (Cullen) **20**:63
"Thorn Piece" (Lowell) **13**:85
"Those Dancing Days Are Gone" (Yeats) **20**:328
"Those Times" (Sexton) **2**:362-63, 370
"Those Various Scalpels" (Moore) **4**:263-64, 270
Those Who Ride the Night Winds (Giovanni) **19**:126-27, 137-38, 142-43
"Those Winter Sundays" (Hayden) **6**:194-95
"The Thou" (Montale)
See "Il tu"
"Thou Art Indeed Just, Lord" (Hopkins) **15**:171
"Thou didst delight my eyes" (Bridges) **28**:85
"Thou Famished Grave, I Will Not Fill Thee Yet" (Millay) **6**:242
"Thou Shalt Not Kill" (Rexroth) **20**:181, 187, 193, 205, 218
"Thou Unbelieving Heart" (Kunitz) **19**:155
"Though It Only Lasts a Moment" (Alegria) **26**:
"Thought for a Sunshiny Morning" (Parker) **28**:362
"A Thought of Columbus" (Whitman)
See "A Prayer of Columbus"
"The Thought-Fox" (Hughes) **7**:120, 158, 166, 168-69
"Thoughts about the Christian Doctrine of Eternal Hell" (Smith) **12**:301, 325, 333
"Thoughts about the Person from Porlock" (Smith) **12**:293, 330, 350
"Thoughts in 1932" (Sassoon) **12**:252
"Thoughts on a Breath" (Ginsberg) **4**:76
"Thoughts on His Excellency Major General Lee" (Wheatley) **3**:337
"Thoughts on One's Head" (Meredith) **28**:174, 211
"Thoughts on Saving the Manatee" (Kumin) **15**:211
"Thoughts on the Shape of the Human Body" (Brooke) **24**:56-7
"Thoughts on the Works of Providence" (Wheatley) **3**:332, 339, 358, 361, 363
"Thousand League Pool" (Tu Fu) **9**:333
"Thousand and Second Night" (Merrill) **28**:222, 225-26, 228, 230-32, 234, 250, 252-53
"A Thousand Thousand Times" (Breton) **15**:73
Thread-Suns (Celan)
See *Fadensonnen*
"Three" (Gunn) **26**:208
"III" (Joyce) **22**:144, 160, 162, 164, 166
"3 A.M. Kitchen: My Father Talking" (Gallagher) **9**:53
"Three Bushes" (Yeats) **20**:332
"The Three Captains" (Kipling) **3**:157
"The Three Conspirators" (Nemerov) **24**:293
"The Three Decker" (Kipling) **3**:161
"Three Desk Objects" (Atwood) **8**:2, 13
"Three Elegiac Poems" (Berry) **28**:15
"Three Faces" (Swinburne) **24**:329
"Three Floors" (Kunitz) **19**:178
"Three Ghosts" (Sandburg) **2**:309
"The Three Grayes" (Coleridge) **11**:117
"Three Green Windows" (Sexton) **2**:363
Three Hundred and Sixty Degrees of Blackness Comin at You (Sanchez) **9**:222
"Three Italian Pictures" (Loy) **16**:313
"The Three Kings" (Zagajewski) **27**:396
Three Material Cantos (Neruda)
See *Homenaje a Pablo Neruda de los poetas espanoles: Tres cantos materiales*
Three Material Songs (Neruda)
See *Homenaje a Pablo Neruda de los poetas espanoles: Tres cantos materiales*
"Three Meditations" (Levertov) **11**:169
"Three Modes of History and Culture" (Baraka) **4**:16
"Three Moments in Paris" (Loy) **16**:312, 327-28
"Three Movements and a Coda" (Baraka) **4**:9, 19, 24
"Three Nuns" (Rossetti) **7**:277
"3 of Swords--for dark men under the white moon" (Wakoski) **15**:362, 367
"Three old men" (Illyes)
See "Harom oreg"
"Three Palm-Trees" (Lermontov) **18**:268, 293
See "Tri palmy"
Three Poems (Ashbery) **26**:108-109, 114-116, 118, 123, 126, 130, 135, 143, 149, 167, 169-171, 173-174
Three Poems under a Flag of Convenience (Elytis) **21**:131
"Three Postcards from the Monastery" (Merton) **10**:332
"Three Songs" (Crane) **3**:106
The Three Taverns (Robinson) **1**:465-66, 468
"Three Things" (Yeats) **20**:328
"Three Times in Love" (Graves) **6**:172
"Three Times the Truth" (Elytis) **21**:123
"Three Travellers Watch a Sunrise" (Stevens) **6**:295
"Three United States Sonnets" (Cummings) **5**:94
"Three White Vases" (Swenson) **14**:273
"Threes" (Atwood) **8**:21
"Three-year-old" (Tagore)
See "Tritiya"
Threnodia Augustalis (Dryden) **25**:88-9
"Threnody" (Emerson) **18**:69, 81, 84, 86, 90, 102-3, 112-3
"Threnody" (Parker) **28**:360
"Threnody for a Brown Girl" (Cullen) **20**:57-58, 62, 66
Thrones, 96-109 de los cantares (Pound) **4**:337-38, 352, 353, 357
"Through Corralitos under Rolls of Cloud" (Rich) **5**:401
"Through Nightmare" (Graves) **6**:137, 173
"Through the Looking Glass" (Ferlinghetti) **1**:173
"Through the Round Window" (McGuckian) **27**:83
"Through the Smoke Hole" (Snyder) **21**:292
"Throughout Our Lands" (Milosz) **8**:187, 194, 214
"Throw Away Thy Rod" (Herbert) **4**:103, 121
A Throw of the Dice Never Will Abolish Chance (Mallarme)
See *Un coup de dés jamais n'abolira le hasard*
A Throw of the Dice Will Never Abolish Chance (Mallarme)
See *Un coup de dés jamais n'abolira le hasard*
"Thrushes" (Hughes) **7**:119, 169
"Thrushes" (Sassoon) **12**:253
"Thrust and Riposte" (Montale)
See "Botta e riposta"
"Thunder Can Break" (Okigbo)
See "Come Thunder"
"Thunder in Tuscany" (Tomlinson) **17**:349-50
"Thunder, Momentarily Instantaneous" (Pasternak) **6**:251
"A Thunder-Storm" (Dickinson) **1**:79
"The Thunderstorm" (Trakl)
See "Das Gewitter"
"Thursday" (Millay) **6**:208, 211
Thursday (Chesterton)
See *The Man Who Was Thursday*
"Thursday: The Bassette Table: Smilinda, Cardelia" (Montagu) **16**:338, 349
"Thurso's Landing" (Jeffers) **17**:141-42
Thurso's Landing, and Other Poems (Jeffers) **17**:122, 124-25, 135, 142
"Thyrsis" (Arnold) **5**:7-8, 18-19, 21, 23-4, 33, 36, 45, 47, 52, 55-6
"Tiare Tahiti" (Brooke) **24**:53, 64, 66, 73-4, 78, 86
Tide and Continuities (Viereck) **27**:292, 294-96
Tide and Continuities Last and First Poems 1995-1938 (Viereck) **27**:295
"The Tide at Long Point" (Swenson) **14**:247, 249

"Tierra de azules montañas" (Guillen) **23**:125
"Tierra del Fuego" (Zagajewski) **27**:396, 400
"Tierra en la sierra" (Guillen) **23**:127
"Tierra en la sierra y en el llano" (Guillen) **23**:127
"La tierra se llama Juan" (Neruda) **4**:294
"The Tiger" (Belloc) **24**:24
"The Tiger" (Blake)
See "The Tyger"
"Till de folkhemske" (Ekeloef) **23**:76
"Tilting Sail" (Hass) **16**:251
"Timbuctoo" (Tennyson) **6**:358, 389, 407-08, 413, 415-18
"Time and Life" (Swinburne) **24**:323
"The Time before You" (McGuckian) **27**:82
"Time Does Not Bring Relief" (Millay) **6**:205
"Time Goes By" (Pavese)
See "Il tempo passa"
"Time in the Rock" (Aiken) **26**:19, 57
Time in the Rock (Aiken) **26**:6, 12, 23, 29, 52
"Time Is the Mercy of Eternity" (Rexroth) **20**:181, 208-09, 216-18
"Time Lapse with Tulips" (Gallagher) **9**:37
"Time of Disturbance" (Jeffers) **17**:141
"A Timepiece" (Merrill) **28**:225, 234
"Time Spirals" (Rexroth) **20**:195, 217-18
"A Time to Dance" (Day Lewis) **11**:126
A Time to Dance and Other Poems (Day Lewis) **11**:126-27, 129
"Time to Kill in Gallup" (Ortiz) **17**:240
"Times at Bellosguardo" (Montale) **13**:147, 152
"Time's Dedication" (Schwartz) **8**:305, 307, 314
Time's Laughingstocks and Other Verses (Hardy) **8**:93, 123
"Times Passes" (Pavese)
See "Il tempo passa"
"Time's Revenges" (Browning) **2**:33
"Times Square Water Music" (Clampitt) **19**:81, 88
"The Times Table" (Frost) **1**:205
"Time-Travel" (Olds) **22**:322
"Tin Roof" (Ondaatje) **28**:314
"Tin Wedding Whistle" (Nash) **21**:268
"Tinder" (Heaney) **18**:202
"The Tingling Back" (Shapiro) **25**:317, 320
"Tintern Abbey" (Wordsworth)
See "Lines Composed a Few Miles Above Tintern Abbey"
"Tiresias" (Tennyson) **6**:361
Tiriel (Blake) **12**:61
"Tirzey Potter" (Masters) **1**:338
"Tis April and the morning love" (Clare) **23**:23
"Tishina" (Pasternak) **6**:286
"Tithonus" (Tennyson) **6**:366, 411
"Title Divine Is Mine the Wife without the Sign" (Dickinson) **1**:93
"Titmouse" (Emerson) **18**:79, 103-4, 113
"To--" (Owen) **19**:352
"To--- -- -----" (Poe) **1**:436, 445
"To a Babe Smiling in Her Sleep" (Harper) **21**:197
"To a Book" (Wylie) **23**:303
"To a Brown Boy" (Cullen) **20**:52, 62
"To a Brown Girl" (Cullen) **20**:52, 62
"To a Butterfly" (Merrill) **28**:247
"To a Captious Critic" (Dunbar) **5**:125, 127, 135
"To a Child Dancing in the Wind" (Yeats) **20**:338
"To a Child Running with Outstretched Arms in Canyon de Chelly" (Momaday) **25**:219
"To a Clergyman on the Death of His Lady" (Wheatley) **3**:357
"To a Common Prostitute" (Whitman) **3**:416
"To a Contemporary Bunkshooter" (Sandburg) **2**:317, 330
"To a Contemporary Bunk-Shooter" (Sandburg) **2**:317, 330
"To a Cuckoo at Coolanlough" (McGuckian) **27**:103
"to a dark moses" (Clifton) **17**:34
"To a Dead Child" (Bridges) **28**:57
"To a Dreamer" (Pushkin) **10**:407
"To a Fellow Scribbler" (Finch) **21**:168
"To a Fish Head Found on the Beach Near Malaga" (Levine) **22**:215
"To a Friend" (Arnold) **5**:12, 49
"To a Friend" (Herrick) **9**:90
"To a Friend" (Yeats) **20**:321
"To a Friend and Fellow-Poet" (MacDiarmid) **9**:183-84
"To a Friend in Time of Trouble" (Gunn) **26**:215
"To a Friend Whose Work Has Come to Triumph" (Sexton) **2**:370
"To a Fringed Gentian" (Bryant) **20**:12, 45
"To a Gentleman on His Voyage to Great Britain for the Recovery of His Health" (Wheatley) **3**:358
"To a Gipsy Child by the Sea-shore" (Arnold) **5**:38, 49-50
"To a Giraffe" (Moore) **4**:242-43
"To a Guinea Pig" (Shapiro) **25**:269
"To a Highland Girl" (Wordsworth) **4**:404
"To a Husband" (Lowell) **13**:74
"To a Japanese Poet" (Stryk) **27**:203-4
"To a Jealous Cat" (Sanchez) **9**:223, 232
"To a Lady and Her Children, On the Death of Her Son and Their Brother" (Wheatley) **3**:363
"To a Lady on Her Remarkable Preservation in an Hurricane in North Carolina" (Wheatley) **3**:354
"To a Lady on the Death of Three Relations" (Wheatley) **3**:343, 348
"To a Lady's Countenance" (Wylie) **23**:321
"To a Louse, on Seeing One on a Lady's Bonnet at Church" (Burns) **6**:65, 79
"To a lovely woman" (Lermontov) **18**:303
"To a Mountain Daisy, on Turning One Down with the Plough in April, 1786" (Burns) **6**:50, 74
"To a Mouse, on Turning Her Up in Her Nest with the Plough, November, 1785" (Burns) **6**:50, 65, 74, 80, 96
"To a Passing Woman" (Baudelaire)
See "A une passante"
"To a Poet" (Jimenez) **7**:183
"To a Poet" (McKay) **2**:206
"To a Poor Old Woman" (Williams) **7**:390, 399
"To a Portrait" (Lermontov) **18**:297
"To a Portrait in a Gallery" (Page) **12**:168
"To a Republican Friend" (Arnold) **5**:49
"To a Sad Daughter" (Ondaatje) **28**:316
"To a Seamew" (Swinburne) **24**:313, 328
"To a Shade" (Yeats) **20**:348
"to a Sinister Potato" (Viereck) **27**:259, 262, 279
"To a Solitary Disciple" (Williams) **7**:357, 378
"To a Strategist" (Moore) **4**:266
"To a Waterfowl" (Bryant) **20**:5-6, 14, 18, 35, 42
"To a Western Bard Still a Whoop and a Holler Away from English Poetry" (Meredith) **28**:174, 187, 207
"To a Winter Squirrel" (Brooks) **7**:82
"To a Wreath of Snow" (Bronte) **8**:67, 73
"To a Young Actress" (Pushkin) **10**:407
"To A Young Friend" (Burns)
See "Epistle to a Young Friend"
"To a Young Girl" (Millay) **6**:217
"To a Young Girl" (Yeats) **20**:330
"To Adversity" (Gray)
See "Ode to Adversity"
"To Alchymists" (Jonson) **17**:197
"To Alexander" (Pushkin)
See "Aleksandru"
"To Alexis, in Answer to His Poem against Fruition" (Behn) **13**:26
"To All Brothers" (Sanchez) **9**:224, 232
"To All Brothers: From All Sisters" (Sanchez) **9**:221
"To All Gentleness" (Williams) **7**:354
"To All Sisters" (Sanchez) **9**:224, 231-32
"To America" (Johnson) **24**:131, 142, 148, 158, 160
"To Amintas, upon Reading the Lives of Some of the Romans" (Behn) **13**:32
"To an Ancient" (Frost) **1**:200
"To an Athlete Dying Young" (Housman) **2**:180, 183, 185, 191-94, 198, 201
"To an Old Philosopher in Rome" (Stevens) **6**:304, 324, 328
"To Another Housewife" (Wright) **14**:356
"To Anthea" (Herrick) **9**:145
"To Anthea Lying in Bed" (Herrick) **9**:137
"To Anthea, Who May Command Him Any Thing" (Herrick) **9**:102
"To Any Dead Officer Who Left School for the Army in 1914" (Sassoon) **12**:268, 277
"To Aphrodite, with a Talisman" (Wylie) **23**:320, 324
"To Autumn" (Ashbery) **26**:160
"To Autumn" (Gluck) **16**:142, 149
"To Autumn" (Keats)
See "Ode to Autumn"
"To Bargain Toboggan To-Woo!" (Nash) **21**:265
To Bathurst (Pope) **26**:340
"To Be a Jew in the Twentieth Century" (Rukeyser) **12**:234
"To Be Carved on a Stone at Thoor Ballylee" (Yeats) **20**:346, 348
"To Be in Love" (Brooks) **7**:81-2
"To Be Liked by You Would Be a Calamity" (Moore) **4**:250
"To Be Quicker for Black Political Prisoners" (Madhubuti) **5**:330, 346
"To be Sung" (Viereck) **27**:265
"To Be Sung on the Water" (Bogan) **12**:90, 124
To Bedlam and Part Way Back (Sexton) **2**:345-47, 349-50, 353, 355, 357-58, 360, 363, 367
"To Bennie" (McKay) **2**:221
"To Blk/Record/Buyers" (Sanchez) **9**:209, 217
"To Blossoms" (Herrick) **9**:145
"To Bring the Dead to Life" (Graves) **6**:143
To Burlington (Pope) **26**:340
"To Camden" (Jonson)
See "To Camden"
"To Carl Sandburg" (Lowell) **13**:67
"To Carry the Child" (Smith) **12**:320
"To Cedars" (Herrick) **9**:91
"To Celia" (Jonson) **17**:170, 196
"To Certain Critics" (Cullen) **20**:66, 83
"To Chaadaev" (Pushkin)
See "Chaadayevu"
"To Change in a Good Way" (Ortiz) **17**:234
"To Charis" (Jonson)
See "To Charis"
"To Christ Our Lord" (Kinnell) **26**:239
To . . . Christopher Duke of Albemarle (Behn) **13**:8
"To Chuck" (Sanchez) **9**:224, 233
"To Cipriano, in the Wind" (Levine) **22**:225
To Circumjack Cencrastus (MacDiarmid) **9**:151-53, 158, 171, 175-77, 197
"To Clarendon Hills and H.A.H." (McKay) **2**:222
"To Claudia Homonoea" (Wylie) **23**:324
"To Clio Muse of History" (Nemerov) **24**:262
"To Cole, the Painter, Departing For Europe" (Bryant) **20**:34, 44-5
"To Columbus" (Dario)
See "A Colón"
"To Conclude" (Montale) **13**:146
"To Confirm a Thing" (Swenson) **14**:247, 252, 278
"To Constantia Singing" (Shelley) **14**:177
"To Countess Rostopchina" (Lermontov) **18**:297
"To Daddy" (Lowell) **3**:226
"To Daffadills" (Herrick) **9**:101
"To Damon. To Inquire of Him If He Cou'd Tell Me by the Style, Who Writ Me a Copy of Verses That Came to Me in an Unknown Hand" (Behn) **13**:30-1
"To Daphnie and Virginia" (Williams) **7**:360, 363, 392

"To Dean Swift" (Swift) **9**:295
"To Death" (Finch) **21**:179-80
"To Deism" (Wheatley) **3**:354
"To Delmore Schwartz" (Lowell) **3**:219, 222
"To Desire" (Behn) **13**:24
"To Dianeme" (Herrick) **9**:145
To Disembark (Brooks) **7**:84, 93
"To Dispel My Grief" (Tu Fu) **9**:326
"To *** Do not think I deserve regret" (Lermontov) **18**:301, 304
"To Doctor Alabaster" (Herrick) **9**:142
"To Don at Salaam" (Brooks) **7**:84, 92
To Dream of A Butterfly (Hagiwara Sakutaro) See *To Dream of A Butterfly*
"To Earthward" (Frost) **1**:197
"To Electra" (Herrick) **9**:94
"To Elizabeth Ward Perkins" (Lowell) **13**:90
"To Elsie" (Williams) **7**:382, 384, 411
"To E.M.E." (McKay) **2**:223
"To Endymion" (Cullen) **20**:67, 86
"To Enemies" (Bely) **11**:24
"To Enter That Rhythm Where the Self is Lost" (Rukeyser) **12**:227
"To Eros" (Owen) **19**:352
"To Ethelinda" (Smart) **13**:331, 347
"To Evalyn for Christmas" (Shapiro) **25**:286
"To Eve Man's Dream of Wifehood As Described by Milton" (Lindsay) **23**:281
"To Evoke Posterity" (Graves) **6**:143, 152
"To Fausta" (Arnold) **5**:49
"To F. C. in Memoriam Palestine" (Chesterton) **28**:97
"To Find God" (Herrick) **9**:109
"To Fine Lady Would-bee" (Jonson) **17**:197
"To Flowers" (Herrick) **9**:102
"To Flush My Dog" (Browning) **6**:6-7
"To Ford Madox Ford in Heaven" (Williams) **7**:370
"To France" (Cullen) **20**:66
"To Francis Jammes" (Bridges) **28**:76
"To Galich" (Pushkin) **10**:407
"To George Sand: A Recognition" (Browning) **6**:26
"To Gerhardt" (Olson) **19**:307
"To Go By Singing" (Berry) **28**:3-4
"To Go to Lvov" (Zagajewski) **27**:381-82, 383-85, 387
"To God" (Herrick) **9**:94-5, 109, 118
"To God, His Good Will" (Herrick) **9**:118
"To God, on His Sicknesse" (Herrick) **9**:144
"To Gurdjieff Dying" (Toomer) **7**:338
"To Hafiz of Shiraz" (Wright) **14**:356, 366
"To Have Done Nothing" (Williams) **7**:383, 389, 410
"To Heaven" (Jonson) See "To Heaven"
"To Helen" (Poe) **1**:420, 424, 426, 428, 431, 438-39, 441, 443-45, 447
"To Helen" (Stryk) **27**:204
"To Helen (of Troy NY)" (Viereck) **27**:294
"To Help" (Stein) **18**:313
"To Her" (Pushkin) **10**:408-09
"To Her Father with Some Verses" (Bradstreet) **10**:27, 35
"To Her Most Honoured Father Thomas Dudley" (Bradstreet) **10**:2
"To His Book" (Herrick) **9**:106, 109
"To His Closet-Gods" (Herrick) **9**:88
"To His Coy Mistress" (Marvell) **10**:259, 265, 269, 271, 273-74, 277-79, 281-82, 290-94, 297, 304, 310-11, 313
"To His Excellency General George Washington" (Wheatley) **3**:337, 341
"To His Father" (Jeffers) **17**:131
"To His Friend on the Untuneable Times" (Herrick) **9**:89
"To His Girles" (Herrick) **9**:107
"To His Girles Who Would Have Him Sportfull" (Herrick) **9**:107
"To His Honor the Lieutenant Governor on the Death of His Lady" (Wheatley) **3**:340
"To His Mistresses" (Herrick) **9**:128, 146
"To His Paternall Countrey" (Herrick) **9**:108
"To His Savior, a Child; a Present, by a Child" (Herrick) **9**:120, 143
"To His Saviour, the New Yeers Gift" (Herrick) **9**:95
"To His Saviours Sepulcher: His Devotion" (Herrick) **9**:122
"To His Watch" (Hopkins) **15**:167
"To Homer" (Keats) **1**:279, 314
"To Imagination" (Bronte) **8**:54
"To Imagination" (Wheatley) See "On Imagination"
"To Indianapolis 17 Nov 71" (Brutus) **24**:123
"To Insure Survival" (Ortiz) **17**:225
"To Ireland in the Coming Times" (Yeats) **20**:324, 347, 353
"To Ivor Gurney" (Tomlinson) **17**:354-55
"to joan" (Clifton) **17**:18
"To John Goldie, August 1785" (Burns) **6**:70, 78
"To John Keats, Poet: At Spring Time" (Cullen) **20**:62, 66, 86
"To Jos: Lo: Bishop of Exeter" (Herrick) **9**:146
"To Joseph Joachim" (Bridges) **28**:88
"To Joseph Sadzik" (Milosz) See "Do Jozefa Sadzika"
"To Juan at the Winter Solstice" (Graves) **6**:137, 144, 146, 168, 171-72
"To Julia" (Herrick) **9**:128, 143
"To Julia, in Her Dawne, or Day-breake" (Herrick) **9**:143
"To Julia, the Flaminica Dialis, or Queen-Priest" (Herrick) **9**:143
"To . . . K. Charles" (Jonson) See "To . . . K. Charles"
"To K. Charles . . . 1629" (Jonson) See "To K. Charles . . . 1629"
"To Keorapetse Kgositsile (Willie)" (Brooks) **7**:83, 92, 105
"To Kevin O'Leary Wherever He Is" (Levertov) **11**:189
"To King James" See "To King James"
"To Lady Crew, upon the Death of Her Child" (Herrick) See "To the Lady Crew, upon the Death of Her Child"
"To Laurels" (Herrick) **9**:127
"To Licinius" (Pushkin) See "K Liciniju"
"To Live Merrily, and to Trust to Good Verses" (Herrick) **9**:96, 103-05, 107, 114
"To Lord Byron" (Keats) **1**:313
"To Lord Harley, on His Marriage" (Swift) **9**:254
"To Lose the Earth" (Sexton) **2**:363
"To Louise" (Dunbar) **5**:121
"To Love" (Aleixandre) **15**:19, 21
"To Lu Chi" (Nemerov) **24**:257
"To Lucia at Birth" (Graves) **6**:137
"To Lucy, Countesse of Bedford, with Mr. Donnes Satyres" (Jonson) See "To Lucy, Countesse of Bedford, with Mr. Donnes Satyres"
"To Lyce" (Smart) **13**:348
"To Lycomedes on Scyros" (Brodsky) See "K Likomedu, na Skiros"
"To Lysander at the Musick-Meeting" (Behn) **13**:30
"To Lysander, on Some Verses He Writ, and Asking More for His Heart than 'Twas Worth" (Behn) **13**:30
"To Make a Poem in Prison" (Knight) **14**:48
"To Marguerite" (Arnold) **5**:19, 64
"To Marguerite--Continued" (Arnold) **5**:13, 42-5, 49, 64
"To Mark Anthony in Heaven" (Williams) **7**:367
"To Mary" (Shelley) **14**:234-36
"To Mary Lady Wroth" (Jonson) See "To Mary Lady Wroth"
"To Matilda Betham" (Coleridge) **11**:58
"To Mæcenas" (Wheatley) See "Ode to Mæcenas"
"to merle" (Clifton) **17**:18
"To Mistress Isabel Pennell" (Skelton) **25**:336
"To Mistress Margaret Hussey" (Skelton) **25**:345
To Mix with Time: New and Selected Poems (Swenson) **14**:249-50, 254-55, 257, 260, 266, 268, 274, 278, 281-82, 285
"To Mr. Congreve" (Swift) **9**:250
"To Mr. Creech (under the Name of Daphnis) on His Excellent Translation of Lucretius" (Behn) **13**:8, 31
"To Mr. Delany, Nov. 10, 1718" (Swift) **9**:255
"To Mr. F. Now Earl of W." (Finch) **21**:153, 164
"To Mr R. W. 'If as mine is'" (Donne) **1**:124
"To Mrs. Harriet Beecher Stowe" (Harper) **21**:201, 205
"To Mrs. W. on Her Excellent Verses (Writ in Praise of Some I Had Made on the Earl of Rochester)" (Behn) **13**:8, 31
"To My Brother" (Bogan) **12**:117
"To My Brother" (Sassoon) **12**:261, 278
"To My Daughter the Junkie on a Train" (Lorde) **12**:146-47, 154
"To My Dear and Loving Husband His Goeing into England" (Bradstreet) **10**:13, 36, 40, 63
"To My Fairer Brethren" (Cullen) **20**:52
"To My Father" (Olds) **22**:325
"To My Friend Jerina" (Clifton) **17**:29
"To My Friend with an Identity Disk" (Owen) **19**:334, 358
"To My Greek" (Merrill) **28**:220, 262-63
"To My Honored Friend, Dr. Charleton" (Dryden) **25**:95
"To My Ill Reader" (Herrick) **9**:89
"To My Lady Moreland at Tunbridge" (Behn) **13**:8, 29-30
"to my last period" (Clifton) **17**:29, 36
"To my lord Ignorant" (Jonson) See "To my lord Ignorant"
"To My Mother" (Montale) **13**:112, 149, 152
"To My Muse" (Jonson) See "To My Muse"
"To My Playmate" (Viereck) **27**:263, 278, 281
"To My Prince's Command" (Wang Wei) **18**:366
"To My Sister" (Roethke) **15**:275
"To Myself in an Album" (Zagajewski) **27**:389
"To Natal'ia" (Pushkin) **10**:404
"To Nature" (Holderlin) See "An die Natur"
"To Night" (Shelley) **14**:171, 177
"To One in Paradise" (Poe) **1**:432-33, 437, 444, 446
"To One Who Died Young" (Trakl) See "An einen Frühverstorbenen"
"To One Who Was With Me in the War" (Sassoon) **12**:246
"To Orlov" (Pushkin) See "Orlovu"
"To Paolo and Francesca in Purgatory" (Wylie) **23**:326
"To P'ei Ti" (Wang Wei) **18**:362-63, 373-74
"To Penshurst" (Jonson) See "To Penshurst"
"To Perenna" (Herrick) **9**:136-37
"To Perilla" (Herrick) **9**:127-28
"To Pile Like Thunder to Its Close" (Dickinson) **1**:102
"To Pliuskova" (Pushkin) **10**:409
"To R. B." (Hopkins) **15**:157
"To Raja Rao" (Milosz) **8**:195, 200
"To Remember" (Ekeloef) **23**:87
"To Rhea" (Emerson) **18**:102
"To Robert Burns" (Bridges) **28**:65
"To Robert Earle of Salisburie" (Jonson) See "To Robert Earle of Salisburie"
"To Robert Southey" (Coleridge) **11**:106
"To Robinson Jeffers" (Milosz) **8**:184, 199, 208

Cumulative Title Index

"To Roger Blin" (Stryk) **27**:203, 213
"To Roosevelt" (Dario)
See "A Roosevelt"
"To S. M., A Young African Painter, on Seeing His Works" (Wheatley) **3**:336, 338, 344, 362
"To Science" (Poe) **1**:437
"To Secretary Ling-hu" (Wang Wei) **18**:373
"To Secretary Ling-hu" (Wang Wei) **18**:373
"To See a World in a Grain of Sand" (Blake) **12**:36
"To See the Heron" (Tomlinson) **17**:348
"To Sir Horace Vere" (Jonson)
See "To Sir Horace Vere"
"To Sir Robert Wroth" (Jonson)
See "To Sir Robert Wroth"
"To Sleep" (Graves) **6**:137
"To Some Winter Is Arrack" (Mandelstam) **14**:155
"To Speak of Woe That Is in Marriage" (Lowell) **3**:221, 245
"To Stand (Alone) in Some" (Cummings) **5**:110
To Stay Alive (Levertov) **11**:178-80, 195
"To Stella, Visiting Me in My Sickness" (Swift) **9**:297
"To Stella, Who Collected and Transcribed His Poems, 1720" (Swift) **9**:255
"To Susan Countesse of Montgomerie" (Jonson)
See "To Susan Countesse of Montgomerie"
"To Sylvia" (Herrick) **9**:97
"To T. A." (Kipling) **3**:191
"To The Airport" (Rich) **5**:382
"To the American Negro Troops" (Senghor) **25**:238
"To the Balloil Men Still in Africa" (Belloc) **24**:3, 11
"To the Bitter Sweet-Heart: A Dream" (Owen) **19**:352
"To the Boy Elis" (Trakl)
See "An den Knaben Elis"
"To the Countesse of Bedford. 'Madame, reason is'" (Donne) **1**:123
"To the Countesse of Bedford. 'This twilight of'" (Donne) **1**:124
"To the Cuckoo" (Wordsworth) **4**:403
"To the Daisy" (Wordsworth) **4**:376
"To the Dean, when in England, in 1726" (Swift) **9**:255
"To the De'il" (Burns)
See "Address to the De'il"
"To the Diaspora" (Brooks) **7**:84
"To the Dog Belvoir" (Smith) **12**:317
"To the Duke of Wellington" (Arnold) **5**:49
"To the Evening Star" (Blake) **12**:31
"To the Fair Clarinda Who Made Love to Me, Imagin'd More than Woman" (Behn) **13**:10, 13-14, 20, 22-3, 29
"To The Fringed Gentian" (Bryant) **20**:10, 35, 45
"To the German Language" (Mandelstam) **14**:109
"To the Girl Who Lives in a Tree" (Lorde) **12**:154
"To the Governor and Legislature of Massachusetts" (Nemerov) **24**:262, 279
"To the Holy Ghost" (Skelton) **25**:339
"To the Honorable Edward Howard" (Behn) **13**:8
"To the Honorable the Lady Worsley at Longleat" (Finch) **21**:167, 176
"To the House" (Jeffers) **17**:131
"To the Immaculate Virgin, on a Winter Night" (Merton) **10**:339
"To the King" (Smart) **13**:342
"TO THE KING, upon His Comming with His Army into the West" (Herrick) **9**:109
"TO THE KING, upon His Welcome to Hampton-Court" (Herrick) **9**:109
"To the Lady Crew, upon the Death of Her Child" (Herrick) **9**:104, 131, 143
"To the Lark" (Herrick) **9**:98
To the Memory of . . . George Duke of Buckingham (Behn) **13**:9
"To the Memory of My Dear Daughter in Law, Mrs. Mercy Bradstreet" (Bradstreet) **10**:31
"To the Most Illustrious and Most Hopeful Prince, Charles" (Herrick) **9**:133
"To the Mothers of the Dead Militia" (Neruda)
See "Canto a las madres de los milicianos muertos"
"To the Muse" (Blok)
See "K Muze"
"To the Muses" (Blake) **12**:31
"To the Nightingale" (Finch) **21**:141, 144, 157-61, 175
"To the Not Impossible Him" (Millay) **6**:211, 235
"To the Painter of an Ill-Drawn Picture of Cleone, the Honorable Mrs. Thynne" (Finch) **21**:164
"To the Peacock of France" (Moore) **4**:261
"To the Pious Memory of the Accomplisht Young Lady Mrs. Anne Killigrew" (Dryden) **25**:69
"To the Poet Who Happens to Be Black and the Black Poet Who Happens to Be a Woman" (Lorde) **12**:136
"To the Pushkin House" (Blok)
See "Pushkinskomu domu"
"To the Queene" (Herrick) **9**:116
"To the Reader" (Baudelaire)
See "Au lecteur"
"To the Reader" (Merrill) **28**:283
"To the Right Honorable William, Earl of Dartmouth, His Majesty's Principal Secretary of State for North America" (Wheatley) **3**:337, 341, 343, 347, 350, 352
"To the Right Person" (Frost) **1**:200
"To the Road" (Dunbar) **5**:139
"To the Rose upon the Rood of Time" (Yeats) **20**:343
"To the Same" (Montagu) **16**:338
"To the Sea" (Larkin) **21**:238, 240
"To the Sea" (Pushkin) **10**:413
"To the Second Person" (Skelton) **25**:339
"To the Shore" (Swenson) **14**:263
"To the Sister" (Trakl) **20**:248
"To the Snake" (Levertov) **11**:205
"To the South: On Its New Slavery" (Dunbar) **5**:131
"To the Statue" (Swenson) **14**:264
"To the Stone-Cutters" (Jeffers) **17**:117
"To the Tune of the Coventry Carol" (Smith) **12**:316, 330
"to the unborn and waiting children" (Clifton) **17**:19
"To the Union Savers of Cleveland" (Harper) **21**:190
"To the University of Cambridge, in New England" (Wheatley) **3**:337, 340-41, 344-45, 353
"To the Unknown God" (Hardy) **8**:121
"To the Unseeable Animal" (Berry) **28**:26
"To the Virgins, to Make Much of Time" (Herrick) **9**:100, 145
"To the Vision Seekers, Remember This" (Rose) **13**:241
"To the Water Nymphs Drinking at the Fountain" (Herrick) **9**:97
"To the White Fiends" (McKay) **2**:212, 216, 218, 229
"To the Wife of a Sick Friend" (Millay) **6**:217
"To the World. A Farwell for a Gentlewoman, Vertuous and Nobel" (Jonson) **17**:172, 212
"To the Young Poets" (Holderlin)
See "An die Jungen Dichter"
"To Thee" (Dario)
See "A ti"
"To Those Grown Mute" (Trakl) **20**:258
"To Those of My Sisters Who Kept Their Naturals" (Brooks) **7**:86
"To Thos. Floyd" (Bridges) **28**:88
"To Time" (Clare) **23**:44
"To Tirzah" (Blake) **12**:7, 34-5
"To Tizengauzen" (Lermontov) **18**:284-85
To Transfigure, To Organize (Pasolini)
See *Trasumanar e organizzar*
"To Urania" (Brodsky) **9**:25, 27
To Urania: Selected Poems 1965-1985 (Brodsky) **9**:20, 23-4, 26, 29, 30
"To V. L. Davydovu" (Pushkin)
See "V. L. Davydovu"
"To Victor Hugo of My Crow Pluto" (Moore) **4**:255, 259
"To Victory" (Sassoon) **12**:261, 263, 276
"To Virgil" (Tennyson) **6**:370
"To Waken an Old Lady" (Williams) **7**:345, 353, 360, 363
"To Walk on Hills" (Graves) **6**:143
"To W.G.G." (McKay) **2**:226
"To What Listens" (Berry) **28**:9
"To What Serves Mortal Beauty" (Hopkins) **15**:144
"To William Simpson of Ochiltree, May 1785" (Burns)
See "Epistle to William Simpson of Ochiltree, May 1785"
"To William Wordsworth Composed on the Night after His Recitation of a Poem on the Growth of the Individual Mind" (Coleridge) **11**:52-3, 58, 92, 106
"To Winkey" (Lowell) **13**:64
"To Winter" (Blake) **12**:32
"To Wisshe and Want" (Wyatt) **27**:316-317, 319
"To You" (Whitman) **3**:381
"To You Who Read My Book" (Cullen) **20**:55
"Toads" (Larkin) **21**:229, 234, 238
"Toads Revisited" (Larkin) **21**:229, 234, 237-38, 244
"Tobacco Shop" (Pessoa)
See "Tabacaria"
"The Tobacconist's" (Pessoa)
See "Tabacaria"
"A Toccata of Galuppi's" (Browning) **2**:37, 88
"Todas les efes tenía la novia que yo quería" (Fuertes) **27**:37
"Today" (Baraka) **4**:30
"Today and Tomorrow" (Rossetti) **7**:275, 277
"Todesfuge" (Celan) **10**:96, 102, 115-17, 120-21
Todo asusta (Fuertes) **27**:10, 12
"Todtnauberg" (Celan) **10**:98
"Token Drunk" (Bukowski) **18**:15
"Told" (Levine) **22**:214, 224
"Tolerance" (Hardy) **8**:93
"Tolerance" (Pavese) **13**:205
"The Tollund Man" (Heaney) **18**:195, 202, 204, 210-11
"Tom May's Death" (Marvell) **10**:276
"Tom Merrit" (Masters) **1**:324
"Tom Snooks the Pundit" (Smith) **12**:333
"th tomato conspiracy aint worth a whol pome" (Bissett) **14**:23, 34
"The Tomb of Edgar Poe" (Mallarme)
See "Le tombeau d'Edgar Poe"
"The Tomb of Stuart Merrill" (Ashbery) **26**:145
"Tombeau de Charles IX" (Ronsard) **11**:243-44
"Le Tombeau de tres illustre Marquerite de France, duchesse de Savoye" (Ronsard) **11**:243-44
"Le tombeau d'Edgar Poe" (Mallarme) **4**:203, 209
"Le tombeau d'Edgard Poe" (Mallarme)
See "Le tombeau d'Edgar Poe"
"Le tombeau d'une mère" (Lamartine) **16**:264, 293
"The Tombstone-Maker" (Sassoon) **12**:242, 263
"Tombstones in the Starlight" (Parker) **28**:350
"Tom-Dobbin" (Gunn) 226
"Tomlinson" (Kipling) **3**:167, 182
"Tommy" (Kipling) **3**:187
"Tomorrow's Song" (Snyder) **21**:298
"Tom's Garland" (Hopkins) **15**:134, 138, 171
"Ton portrait" (Cesaire) **25**:31
"Ton Soir Mon Soir" (Senghor) **25**:249

"A Tone Poem" (Ashbery) **26**:132
"Tonique" (Tzara) **27**:230-31
"Too Blue" (Hughes) **1**:243
"Too Late" (Arnold) **5**:43, 56
"Toome" (Heaney) **18**:202, 204, 210, 241
"The Toome Road" (Heaney) **18**:246
"To--One word is too often profaned" (Shelley) **14**:233
Topoemas (Paz) **1**:363
The Torch Bearers (Noyes) **27**:128, 130, 133, 137-38
"Torch Procession" (Celan)
See "Fackelzug"
"The Torch-bearer's Race" (Jeffers) **17**:107
"Torero" (Stryk) **27**:187, 203, 214
"Torero nuestro de cada día" (Fuertes) **27**:38
"Torero nuestro de cada dia" (Fujiwara) **27**:
"Tornado Warning" (Shapiro) **25**:306
"Tornant al pais" (Pasolini) **17**:252, 265
"La torre" (Olson) **19**:268, 293, 309-10
The Torrent and the Night Before (Robinson) **1**:459, 474, 484-85
"Torso" (Brodsky) **9**:8
"The Tortoise in Eternity" (Wylie) **23**:301, 309
"La tortuga de oro..." (Dario) **15**:99
"The Tortured Heart" (Rimbaud)
See "La coeur volé"
"Totem" (Cesaire) **25**:21-2
"Totem" (Plath) **1**:391, 393, 399, 412
"Totem" (Senghor) **25**:224, 230
"The Totem" (Swenson) **14**:249-50
"Totò Merùmeni" (Gozzano) **10**:184-88, 190
"Tou Wan Speaks to Her Husband, Liu Sheng" (Dove) **6**:107, 109
"Touch" (Gunn) **26**:195, 202, 207, 217, 219
"The Touch" (Sexton) **2**:352
Touch (Gunn) **26**:192, 196-197, 202-203, 207-209, 211-214, 219, 223, 225-226, 231
"Touch Me" (Kunitz) **19**:187
"Toujours Miroirs" (Senghor) **25**:251
"The Tour" (Plath) **1**:399-401
"Tour" (Wakoski) **15**:359
"Tour 5" (Hayden) **6**:189, 194
"Touring for Trujillo" (Guillen) **23**:126
"The Tourist and the Town" (Rich) **5**:353, 362
"Tournesol" (Breton) **15**:61-2
"Tout Entouré de Mon Regard" (Tomlinson) **17**:321, 339
Toute la lyre (Hugo) **17**:65, 86
"Toward an Organic Philosophy" (Rexroth) **20**:215, 217, 221
"Toward Siena" (Montale)
See "Verso Siena"
Toward the Cradle of the World (Gozzano)
See *Verso la cuna del mondo*
"Toward the Empty Earth" (Mandelstam)
See "K pustoi zemle nevol'no pripadaia"
Toward the Gulf (Masters) **1**:330, 332, 335, 342-44
"Toward the Piraeus" (H. D.) **5**:268, 304
"Toward the Solstice" (Rich) **5**:374
Towards a New Poetry (Wakoski) **15**:359
"Towards a New Scotland" (MacDiarmid) **9**:176
"Towards the Slave Quisqueya" (Guillen)
See "Towards the Slave Quisqueya"
"The Tower" (Yeats) **20**:310, 318, 320, 329, 334, 342
The Tower (Yeats) **20**:307, 311, 333, 335
"The Tower beyond Tragedy" (Jeffers) **17**:106, 108, 110, 112, 135, 144-46
The Tower of Babel (Merton) **10**:344, 349
"The Tower of Pisa" (Song) **21**:344
"The Tower of Siloam" (Graves) **6**:133
"The Town" (Pushkin)
See "Gorodok"
"Town" (Soto) **28**:378, 385
"Town and Country" (Brooke) **24**:56
The Town down the River (Robinson) **1**:462-63, 467, 474, 478, 490
"The Town Dump" (Nemerov) **24**:257, 261, 291-92
"A Town Eclogue" (Swift) **9**:278
Town Eclogues (Montagu)
See *Court Poems*
"Towns in Colour" (Lowell) **13**:79
"Tract" (Williams) **7**:348, 362, 378
"Tractor" (Hughes) **7**:166
"The Trade of an Irish Poet" (Heaney) **18**:201
"Tradimento" (Pavese) **13**:202, 226
"Traditions" (Heaney) **18**:252
"Tragedy of Teeth" (Kipling) **3**:194
"The Tragedy of the Leaves" (Bukowski) **18**:6, 21
"Tragic Destiny" (Aleixandre) **15**:10
"Traigo conmigo un cuidado" (Juana Ines de la Cruz) **24**:188
"Train Time" (Bogan) **12**:107
"Training" (Owen) **19**:336
"Trainor the Druggist" (Masters) **1**:347
"Trakat poetycki" (Milosz) **8**:198-99, 204
"Tramontana" (Montale) **13**:105, 126
"Tramontana at Lerici" (Tomlinson) **17**:342
"The Tramp Transfigured" (Noyes) **27**:121, 134
"Las Trampas USA" (Tomlinson) **17**:353
"A Trampwoman's Tragedy" (Hardy) **8**:99
"Trams" (Sitwell) **3**:301
"Transaction" (Ammons) **16**:22
"Transcedental Etude" (Rich) **5**:381
The Transformation/Transformations (Ovid)
See *Metamorphoses*
"Transformations" (Hardy) **8**:113
"Transformations" (Wright) **14**:339
Transformations (Sexton) **2**:349, 354-55, 362, 364-65, 368
"The Transformed One" (Olds) **22**:326
"Transgressing the Real" (Duncan) **2**:104
"Transients and Residents" (Gunn) **26**:220
"Transitional" (Williams) **7**:392
Transitional Poem (Day Lewis) **11**:123-25, 128-31, 133-35, 137, 143-45, 148, 151
"Translating the Birds" (Tomlinson) **17**:348, 350
A Translation of the Psalms of David, Attempted in the Spirit of Christianity, and Adapted to the Divine Service (Smart) **13**:330-32, 341-42, 362
"Translations" (Rich) **5**:397
Translations, 1915-1920 (H. D.) **5**:304
The Translations of Ezra Pound (Pound) **4**:331
"Translations of the Psalms" (Wyatt) **27**:359
"Transparent Garments" (Hass) **16**:199, 210
"Transplanting" (Roethke) **15**:295
"Transport" (Meredith) **28**:174
"The Transport of Slaves from Maryland to Mississippi" (Dove) **6**:108
Transport to Summer (Stevens) **6**:301-03
"The Trap" (Wright) **14**:356
"Trapped Dingo" (Wright) **14**:345
"Le Trappist" (Vigny) **26**:401-402, 404
"The Trappist Abbey: Matins" (Merton) **10**:332
"The Trappist Cemetery, Gethsemani" (Merton) **10**:332-33, 342
"Trappists, Working" (Merton) **10**:332-33
Trasumanar e organizzar (Pasolini) **17**:273, 286
"Traum und Umnachtung" (Trakl) **20**:239, 268
"Träumerei am Abend" (Trakl) **20**:239
"Travel" (Brooke) **24**:66
"The Traveler" (Apollinaire)
See "Le voyageur"
"A Traveler at Night Writes His Thoughts" (Tu Fu) **9**:324
The Traveler Does Not Return (Nishiwaki)
See *Tabibito Kaerazu*
"Traveling on an Amtrack Train Could Humanize You" (Sanchez) **9**:234
"Traveling through Fog" (Hayden) **6**:194
"The Traveller and the Angel" (Wright) **14**:339, 346
"Traveller's Curse after Misdirection" (Graves) **6**:137
"Traveller's Palm" (Page) **12**:181
"Travelogue for Exiles" (Shapiro) **25**:269, 279, 290
"Travels in the South" (Ortiz) **17**:227, 231
"Tre donne intorno al cor mi son venute" (Dante) **21**:87
"The Treasure" (Brooke) **24**:87-9
"The Treasure" (Jeffers) **17**:117
"Treatise on Poetry" (Milosz)
See "Trakat poetycki"
"Trébol" (Dario) **15**:89
"The Tree" (Aleixandre) **15**:22
"The Tree" (Finch) **21**:149
"Tree" (Rukeyser) **12**:224
"Tree at My Window" (Frost) **1**:197, 205
"Tree Burial" (Bryant) **20**:14, 17
"Tree Disease" (Hughes) **7**:120
"Tree Planting" (Tagore)
See "Vriksha-ropan"
"A Tree Telling of Orpheus" (Levertov) **11**:177
The Tree Witch (Viereck) **27**:275-76, 278-80, 282
"The Trees" (Carruth) **10**:71
"Trees" (Hughes) **7**:120
"Trees" (Nemerov) **24**:266-67
"Trees" (Tsvetaeva)
See "Derev'ya"
"Trees" (Williams) **7**:351
"Trees in a Grove" (Meredith) **28**:170
"treez" (Bissett) **14**:24, 33
"La Trezieme" (Nerval) **13**:196; **67**:360
"Trelawny's Dream" (Meredith) **28**:215
"A Trellis for R." (Swenson) **14**:267, 280
The Trembling of the Veil (Yeats) **20**:330
"Tremor" (Zagajewski) **27**:395
Tremor (Zagajewski) **27**:380-81, 383-84, 389, 395, 397, 399
"Trench Poems" (Owen) **19**:350
"Trespass Into Spirit" (Baraka) **4**:24
The Trespasser (Stryk) **27**:191, 194, 197-98, 215-16, 218
"Tri palmy" (Lermontov) **18**:290-91
"A Triad" (Rossetti) **7**:272-3, 275, 291
"The Trial" (Sassoon) **12**:260
"Trial of a Poet" (Shapiro) **25**:277-79
Trial of a Poet (Shapiro) **25**:273-74, 285, 290, 296, 319, 322, 324
"The Trial of Dead Cleopatra" (Lindsay) **23**:280, 286
"Trial-Pieces" (Heaney) **18**:246
"Tribal Scenes" (Song) **21**:345
"Tribe" (Song) **21**:336, 343
Tribunals (Duncan) **2**:106, 116, 127
"Tribute" (Brutus) **24**:111
"The Tribute" (H. D.) **5**:298, 304
Tribute to the Angels (H. D.) **5**:272, 274-75, 283-84, 286-87, 293-97, 308-09, 313, 315
"Trickle Drops" (Whitman) **3**:406
"Tricks with Mirrors" (Atwood) **8**:21-6
"Trickster 1977" (Rose) **13**:232
"Trillium" (Gluck) **16**:171
Trilogie der Leidenschaft (Goethe) **5**:250
Trilogy (H. D.) **5**:281, 283-86, 292-93, 2960-98, 304-07, 310-15
Trilogy (Wakoski) **15**:365
"Trinchera" (Borges) **22**:92
"Trinity Churchyard" (Rukeyser) **12**:225
"Trinity Peace" (Sandburg) **2**:304
"Trio for Two Cats and a Trombone" (Sitwell) **3**:303, 306
"Triolet" (Brooke) **24**:54
Trionfi (Petrarch) **8**:224-26, 238, 240, 243, 246, 252, 254, 257, 260, 273-78
"The Triple Fool" (Donne) **1**:125
"The Triple Fool" (Millay) **6**:243
"Triple Time" (Larkin) **21**:227, 236, 242
"Triptych" (Heaney) **18**:246
"El triste" (Borges) **22**:80
"Triste, triste" (Laforgue) **14**:86, 88-9
"Tristesse" (Lamartine) **16**:293
"Tristesse d'Olympio" (Hugo) **17**:64, 76-77, 82, 97
"Tristesse d'un étoile" (Apollinaire) **7**:3
"Les tristesses de la lune" (Baudelaire) **1**:44-5
"Tristia" (Mandelstam) **14**:106

Tristia (Mandelstam)
See *Vtoraya kniga*
Tristia (Ovid) **2**:233, 240-42, 244-45, 252-53, 255-59
Tristibus (Ovid)
See *Tristia*
Tristram (Robinson) **1**:470-72, 474-75, 481, 489
"Tristram and Iseult" (Arnold) **5**:9, 12, 33-4, 42, 49, 64
Tristram of Lyonesse (Swinburne) **24**:307, 309, 310, 313-14, 316, 319, 321-23, 348-50, 352, 355-57
"Tritiya" (Tagore) **8**:415
The Triumph of Achilles (Gluck) **16**:149, 151-52, 155-57, 159, 163
"Triumph of Charis" (Jonson)
See *A Celebration of Charis in Ten Lyric Pieces*
The Triumph of Life (Shelley) **14**:174, 188, 193, 211
"The Triumph of Time" (Swinburne) **24**:308, 322, 325, 337-38, 342-43
Triumphal March (Eliot) **5**:168, 185
Triumphs (Petrarch)
See *Trionfi*
"The Triumphs of Bacchus" (Pushkin) **10**:407
"Trivial Breath" (Wylie) **23**:310
Trivial Breath (Wylie) **23**:302, 307-309, 324-25
"Trofeo" (Borges) **22**:93
Troilus (Chaucer)
See *Troilus and Criseyde*
Troilus and Criseyde (Chaucer) **19**:6-7, 11, 13, 15, 23, 36-9, 42-3, 60-1, 63, 73-5
Troilus and Cryseide (Chaucer)
See *Troilus and Criseyde*
"Trois Ans après" (Hugo) **17**:83
Les trois livres du recueil des nouvelles poesies (Ronsard) **11**:248
Troisìme livre des odes (Ronsard) **11**:283
"Trompeten" (Trakl) **20**:250, 254-55
"Troop Train" (Shapiro) **25**:263, 268, 288, 295, 297, 324
"The Tropics in New York" (McKay) **2**:228
"Trostnik" (Lermontov) **18**:304
"A troubadour I traverse all my land" (Brutus) **24**:113
"Trouble in De Kitchen" (Dunbar) **5**:146
"The Trouble is with No and Yes" (Roethke) **15**:277
"The Trouble with Women Is Men" (Nash) **21**:268, 274
"The Troubled Bay" (Cassian) **17**:11, 13
Troy Park (Sitwell) **3**:293-94, 298, 301, 303, 307-08, 320
"The Truce of the Bear" (Kipling) **3**:171, 182
"Las truchas" (Forche) **10**:134
"Truck-Garden-Market Day" (Millay) **6**:232
"The True Beatitude" (Brooke) **24**:57
"True Confessional" (Ferlinghetti) **1**:187
"The True Import of Present Dialogue, Black vs. Negro" (Giovanni) **19**:107, 114-15, 139
"True Love" (Olds) **22**:338
"True Night" (Snyder) **21**:300
"True Pearl--Belle of the Lo" (Li Ho) **13**:54
"True Recognition Often Is Refused" (Schwartz) **8**:292
"True Romance" (Kipling) **3**:161
True Stories (Atwood) **8**:43
"True Tenderness" (Akhmatova) **2**:14
"The True, the Good, and the Beautiful" (Schwartz) **8**:292
"True Vine" (Wylie) **23**:303, 305, 323
"Truganinny" (Rose) **13**:240
"Trumpet Player: 52nd Street" (Hughes) **1**:241, 247, 249
"The Trusting Heart" (Parker) **28**:362
"Truth" (Brooks) **7**:61
"The Truth" (Jimenez)
See "Paisaje del corozon"
"Truth" (McKay) **2**:215
"The Truth" (Montale) **13**:156
"Truth and Error" (Goethe) **5**:228
"Truth Is Not the Secret of a Few" (Ferlinghetti) **1**:186
"Truth Kills Everybody" (Hughes) **7**:160
"The Truth of the Matter" (Nemerov) **24**:290
"The Truth the Dead Know" (Sexton) **2**:346, 361
Tryflings (Ekeloef) **23**:63
"Tsar Sultan" (Pushkin)
See "Skazka o Tsare Sultane"
Tsar-devitsa (Tsvetaeva) **14**:313, 325-26
The Tsar-Maiden (Tsvetaeva)
See *Tsar-devitsa*
Tsuki ni hoeru (Hagiwara Sakutaro) **18**:169, 172-73, 175-82
"Tsung-wu's Birthday" (Tu Fu) **9**:324
"Tsurugai Bridge" (Ishikawa)
See "Tsurugaibashi"
"Tsurugaibashi" (Ishikawa) **10**:213
Tsygany (Pushkin) **10**:357-61, 365-66, 369, 371, 386-89, 391-92, 398, 410
"Tú" (Guillen) **23**:134-37
"Il tu" (Montale) **13**:132
"Tú no sabe inglé" (Guillen) **23**:142
"Tu Parles" (Senghor) **25**:250
"tu Te Languis" (Senghor) **25**:249-50
"Tuesday: St. James's Coffee-house: Silliander and Patch" (Montagu) **16**:348
"Tulip" (McGuckian) **27**:79-80, 102
"Tulips" (Page) **12**:176
"Tulips" (Plath) **1**:390, 395, 399-401, 405, 407, 409, 414
Tulips and Chimneys (Cummings) **5**:74-5, 77-8, 86, 91, 93-4, 104
"Tulpen" (Celan) **10**:122-23
"Tumbling-Hair" (Cummings) **5**:104
"Tumi o ami" (Tagore) **8**:414
"A Tune for Festive Dances in the Nineteen Sixties" (Merton) **10**:345
"Tunk: A Lecture of Modern Education" (Johnson) **24**:141, 163
"The Tunnel" (Crane) **3**:86, 88-90, 106-07, 110-11
The Tunnynge of Elynour Rummynge (Skelton) **25**:330, 332, 338, 342, 347-49, 361-62, 364, 367, 386-88, 390-93
"Il tuo volo" (Montale) **13**:111
"Turin" (Gozzano) **10**:177, 180
"The Turkey in the Straw" (Williams) **7**:400
"Turkeys Observed" (Heaney) **18**:189, 200
"Turkish Verses" (Montagu) **16**:338
"The Turn of the Moon" (Graves) **6**:154, 156
"The Turncoat" (Baraka) **4**:5, 14
"turning" (Clifton) **17**:21
"The Turning" (Levine) **22**:212
"Turning" (Rilke) **2**:280-81
"Turning a Moment to Say So Long" (Ammons) **16**:39
"Turning Fifty" (Wright) **14**:355
"Turning To" (Kumin) **15**:182
"A Turning Wind" (Rukeyser) **12**:213
A Turning Wind (Rukeyser) **12**:211-12
Turns and Movies and Other Tales in Verse (Aiken) **26**:21, 50, 53
Turns and Movies The Devine Pilgrim (Aiken) **26**:
"The Turtle" (Nash) **21**:278
Turtle Island (Snyder) **21**:290-300, 306-08, 310, 316-17, 320, 324-25
"Tutecotzimí" (Dario) **15**:92
"Tutto é sciolto" (Joyce) **22**:136
"The Twa Dogs" (Burns) **6**:51, 78, 83-4, 88
"The Twa Herds" (Burns) **6**:85
"Twelfth Night" (Belloc) **24**:49
"Twelfth Night, Next Year, a Weekend in Eternity" (Schwartz) **8**:294
"XII" (Joyce) **22**:136, 138, 145, 164, 169, 171
The Twelve (Blok)
See *Dvenadsat*
"Twelve Articles" (Swift) **9**:260
"The Twelve Dancing Princesses" (Sexton) **2**:365
"Twelve Months After" (Sassoon) **12**:288
Twentieth Century Harlequinade (Sitwell) **3**:299-300, 302
"20th-century Fox" (Baraka) **4**:11
"XX" (Joyce) **22**:145, 168
Twenty Love Poems and a Despairing Song (Neruda)
See *Veinte poemas de amor y una canción desesperada*
Twenty Love Poems and a Desperate Song (Neruda)
See *Veinte poemas de amor y una canción desesperada*
Twenty Love Poems and a Song of Despair (Neruda)
See *Veinte poemas de amor y una canción desesperada*
Twenty Love Poems and One Song of Despair (Neruda)
See *Veinte poemas de amor y una canción desesperada*
XX Poems (Larkin) **21**:226, 229
Twenty Poems (Neruda)
See *Veinte poemas de amor y una canción desesperada*
Twenty Poems (Trakl) **20**:227
"XXVIII" (Joyce) **22**:145, 154, 159, 162, 169, 172
"28" (Levine) **22**:224
"Twenty-fifth of Vaisakh" (Tagore)
See "Panchishe vaisakh"
"XXV" (Joyce) **22**:139, 160, 173
Twenty-Five Poems (Thomas) **2**:378, 389
"XXIV" (Joyce) **22**:136, 139, 170, 172-73
"Twenty-Four Hokku on a Modern Theme" (Lowell) **13**:66
"Twenty-four Poems" (Schwartz) **8**:302
"Twenty-Four Years" (Thomas) **2**:383
"XXIX" (Joyce) **22**:145, 167, 170, 173
"XXI" (Joyce) **22**:146, 166-68, 170
Twenty-One Love Poems (Rich) **5**:384, 395
"XXVII" (Joyce) **22**:145, 156, 170, 172-73
"XXVI" (Joyce) **22**:136, 139, 168, 171, 173
"XXIII" (Joyce) **22**:145, 170
"XXII" (Joyce) **22**:138, 145, 170-71, 173
"Twenty-two Rhymes" (Tu Fu) **9**:326
"Twice" (Rossetti) **7**:267, 275
Twice or thrice had I loved thee (Donne)
See "Aire and Angels"
"Twicknam Garden" (Donne) **1**:124, 130, 134
"Twilight" (Apollinaire)
See "Crépuscule"
"Twilight" (Clare) **23**:47
"Twilight" (Kunitz) **19**:147
"The Twilight Bell" (Ishikawa)
See "Kure no kane"
The Twilight Book (Neruda)
See *Crepúsculario*
"The Twilight of Freedom" (Mandelstam) **14**:106, 147
"Twilight of the Outward Life" (Viereck) **27**:263
"Twilight Reverie" (Hughes) **1**:255
Twilight Songs (Hugo) **17**:45
The Twin In the Clouds (Pasternak)
See *Bliznets v tuchakh*
"The Twins" (Bukowski) **18**:4, 22
"Twister" (Stryk) **27**:211
"II" (Joyce) **22**:138, 165-66
"Two Amsterdams" (Ferlinghetti) **1**:183
"The Two April Mornings" (Wordsworth) **4**:374
"The Two Brothers" (Lermontov) **18**:299
"Two Children" (Graves) **6**:156
"Two Children" (Guillen)
See "Dos niños"
"Two Cigarettes" (Pavese)
See "Due sigarette"
"Two days of fever" (Pasolini) **17**:279
"Two Deaths" (Olds) **22**:317
"Two Easter Stanzas" (Lindsay) **23**:282
"Two Egyptian Portrait Masks" (Hayden) **6**:185
"Two English Poems" (Borges) **22**:95

"Two Eskimo Songs" (Hughes) **7**:153, 159
Two Figures (Momaday) **25**:201
"The Two Fires" (Atwood) **8**:37
The Two Fires (Wright) **14**:341-49, 353-55, 369
"Two Figures from the Movies" (Meredith) **28**:187, 210
The Two Foscari (Byron) **16**:103
"Two Generations" (Wright) **14**:344, 354
"Two Girls" (Nemerov) **24**:291
"Two Gun Buster and Trigger Slim" (Walker) **20**:273
"Two Hands" (Sexton) **2**:371
"Two Hours in an Empty Tank" (Brodsky) **9**:2, 4
"Two Hymns" (Ammons) **16**:4
"Two in the Campagna" (Browning) **2**:68
"Two in the Twilight" (Montale) See "Due nel crepuscolo"
"Two Legends" (Hughes) **7**:159
"Two Little Boots" (Dunbar) **5**:122, 129
"Two Look at Two" (Frost) **1**:194, 229, 231
"Two Lovers" (Eliot) **20**:123
"The Two Lovers" (Marie de France) See "Les Dous Amanz"
"Two Masks Unearthed in Bulgaria" (Meredith) **28**:182, 198
"Two Night Pieces" (Sitwell) **3**:293
"The Two Offers" (Harper) **21**:194
"Two Old Crows" (Lindsay) **23**:281
"Two Pair" (Nemerov) **24**:302
"The Two Parents" (MacDiarmid) **9**:156, 176
"Two Parted" (Rossetti) **7**:276
"Two Pendants: For the Ears" (Williams) **7**:360, 364, 394
"Two Poems" (Madhubuti) **5**:321
"2 Poems for Black Relocation Centers" (Knight) **14**:46-8
"Two Poets" (Cullen) **20**:68
"Two Preludes" (Swinburne) **24**:323
"Two Rivers" (Emerson) **18**:76, 88-89
"The Two Roads" (Gozzano) **10**:177-78
"Two Scavengers in a Truck, Two Beautiful People in a Mercedes" (Ferlinghetti) **1**:183, 188
"Two Songs" (Rich) **5**:365
"Two Songs from a Play" (Yeats) **20**:315, 319
"Two Songs of a Fool" (Yeats) **20**:304
"Two Speak Together" (Lowell) **13**:96-7
"Two Stories" (Gallagher) **9**:36
"The Two Thieves" (Wordsworth) **4**:374, 388
"Two Tramps in Mud Time" (Frost) **1**:198, 221
"The Two Travellers" (Bryant) **20**:10, 16
"The Two Trees" (Yeats) **20**:317
"221-1424 (San Francisco suicide number)" (Sanchez) **9**:211, 224-25
"Two Views of a Cadaver Room" (Plath) **1**:389
"The Two Voices" (Tennyson) **6**:360
"Two Who Crossed a Line (He Crosses)" (Cullen) **20**:86
Two Women, Two Shores (McGuckian) **27**:95
"Two Years Later" (Yeats) **20**:338
"Two-an'-Six" (McKay) **2**:208-09
"The Two-Days-Old Baby" (Blake) See "Infant Joy"
Two-Headed Poems (Atwood) **8**:43
Two-Headed Woman (Clifton) **17**:17-18, 23-24, 26-27, 34-35
"Two-Part Pear Able" (Swenson) **14**:247
"Two-Volume Novel" (Parker) **28**:352, 359, 362
2000 (Neruda) **4**:287
"Tyaroye" (Senghor) **25**:235
"The Tyger" (Blake) **12**:6-7, 10, 25, 30, 34-5, 59-64
"The Typical American?" (Masters) **1**:343
"Typists" (Page) **12**:173
"Typists in the Phoenix Building" (Wright) **14**:348
Tyrannus Nix? (Ferlinghetti) **1**:174
"Tyrian Businesses" (Olson) **19**:280, 283
"U nog drugikh ne zabyval" (Lermontov) **18**:302
U samovo morya (Akhmatova) **2**:15
"U tonkoi pnovoloki nad volnoi ovsov" (Tsvetaeva) **14**:319, 321, 323
"Uber Das Werden im Vergehen" (Holderlin) **4**:147
"Ugolino" (Heaney) **18**:240
"Uh, Philosophy" (Ammons) **16**:6, 13, 36-7
"Ulalume" (Poe) **1**:425-26, 428, 431, 434, 436, 439-40, 442-43, 447, 453
"A Ultima Nau" (Pessoa) **20**:162
"Ultima Ratio Reagan" (Nemerov) **24**:290
"Ultimate Birth" (Aleixandre) **15**:3
"The Ultimate Infidelity" (Gozzano) **10**:180
"The Ultimate Poem Is Abstract" (Stevens) **6**:314
"Ultimatum" (Cullen) **20**:57
"Ultimatum" (Larkin) **21**:224-25
"Ultimatum" (Sassoon) **12**:259
"El último amor" (Aleixandre) **15**:38
"Ultraísmo" (Borges) **22**:93
"Ulysses" (Graves) **6**:130, 137
"Ulysses" (Tennyson) **6**:354, 359, 366, 381, 383-84, 398, 409, 411
"An Umbrella" (Stein) **18**:334
"Umi no ikari" (Ishikawa) **10**:215
"L'umile Itallia" (Pasolini) **17**:294
"Umirajushchij gladiator" (Lermontov) **18**:302
"A un poeta del siglo XIII" (Borges) **22**:82, 85
"A un riche" (Hugo) **17**:94
"Unable to Hate or Love" (Page) **12**:175
"The Unacknowledged Legislator's Dream" (Heaney) **18**:205
"Un'altra risorta" (Gozzano) **10**:185
"Un-American Investigators" (Hughes) **1**:252
Unattainable Earth (Milosz) See *Niobjeta ziemia*
"Unbelief" (Pushkin) See "Bezverie"
"The Unbeliever" (Bishop) **3**:48
"The Unborn" (Wright) **14**:352
"Unclassified Poem" (Wang Wei) **18**:387
"Unclassified Poems of Ch'in-chou" (Tu Fu) **9**:332
"Uncle Jim" (Cullen) **20**:64
"The Uncle Speaks in the Drawing Room" (Rich) **5**:359, 392
"Uncollected Poems" (Crane) **3**:90
"The Uncreation" (Pinsky) **27**:164
"Under" (Sandburg) **2**:300
Under a Soprano Sky (Sanchez) **9**:238-39, 245
"Under Ben Bulben" (Yeats) **20**:312, 324, 333
"Under Libra" (Merrill) **28**:223, 256
"Under Saturn" (Yeats) **20**:342
"Under Sirius" (Auden) **1**:23
"Under Stars" (Gallagher) **9**:37, 58, 60
Under Stars (Gallagher) **9**:37, 42, 54, 58-60
"Under the Bamboo Tree" (Johnson) **24**:151, 170
"Under the Cupola" (Merrill) **28**:251-52
"Under the Earth" (Aleixandre) **15**:20-2
"Under the L.A. Airport" (Ortiz) **17**:229
"Under the Maud Moon" (Kinnell) **26**:247-52, 255, 257, 264, 272
"Under the Mistletoe" (Cullen) **20**:85
"Under the Moon's Reign" (Tomlinson) **17**:336, 349
"Under the Olives" (Graves) **6**:155-56
"Under the Rose" (Rossetti) **7**:266
"Under the Viaduct" (Dove) **6**:110
"Under the Waterfall" (Hardy) **8**:118
"Under Willows" (Rossetti) **7**:285
Undersong: Chosen Poems Old and New (Revised) (Lorde) **12**:153-58
"Understanding but not Forgetting" (Madhubuti) **5**:337-38, 340
"The Undertaking" (Gluck) **16**:126, 128, 142
"Underwear" (Ferlinghetti) **1**:183
The Under-Wood (Jonson) **17**:191
The Under-Wood (Jonson) **17**:169, 180
The Under-Wood II (Jonson) **17**:171, 194-95, 214
The Under-Wood III (Jonson) **17**:195
The Under-Wood IV (Jonson) **17**:194
The Under-Wood LVI (Jonson) **17**:194
The Under-Wood LVIII (Jonson) **17**:194
The Under-Wood LXII (Jonson) **17**:156
The Under-Wood LXIV (Jonson) **17**:156
The Under-Wood LXIX (Jonson) **17**:153
The Under-Wood LXVIII (Jonson) **17**:156
The Under-Wood LXX (Jonson) **17**:164
The Under-Wood LXXI (Jonson) **17**:162
The Under-Wood LXXII (Jonson) **17**:193
The Under-Wood LXXVI (Jonson) **17**:156
The Under-Wood LXXXVI (Jonson) **17**:191
The Under-Wood XIII (Jonson) **17**:154, 157-59, 211
The Under-Wood XL (Jonson) **17**:194
The Under-Wood XLII (Jonson) **17**:180
The Under-Wood XLIV (Jonson) **17**:194
The Under-Wood XLV (Jonson) **17**:181, 189
The Under-Wood XLVII (Jonson) **17**:153-54, 208
The Under-Wood XV (Jonson) **17**:153, 158, 161-62, 164, 208
The Under-Wood XVI (Jonson) **17**:191
The Under-Wood XXIX (Jonson) **17**:189
The Under-Wood XXVI (Jonson) **17**:153, 172, 192
The Under-Wood XXXI (Jonson) **17**:193
The Under-Wood XXXVII (Jonson) **17**:153-54
"The Underworld" (Hongo) **23**:199
"Undraped Beauty" (Tagore) See "Vivasana"
"A une femme" (Hugo) **17**:68
"A une robe rose" (Gautier) **18**:125, 129
Unedited Books of Poetry (Jimenez) See "A Horrible Religious Error"
"The Unending Rose" (Borges) **22**:97
"Unendurable Love" (Tagore) See "Asahya bhalobasa"
"The Unequal Fetters" (Finch) **21**:154, 181
"Unequalled Days" (Pasternak) See "Edinstvennye dni"
"Unexpected Joy" (Blok) **21**:3
"The Unexplorer" (Millay) **6**:235
"The Unfaithful Married Woman" (Garcia Lorca) See "La casada infiel"
"The Unfaithful Wife" (Garcia Lorca) See "La casada infiel"
"Unfinished Ballad" (Wylie) **23**:321
"Unfinished Portrait" (Wylie) **23**:318, 322, 324
"Unfold! Unfold!" (Roethke) **15**:248, 254, 276, 300-03
"Unfortunate Coincidence" (Parker) **28**:360
"The Unfortunate Lover" (Marvell) **10**:265-66, 271, 300, 302
"The Unfortunate One" (Marie de France) See "Le Chaitivel"
Ungathered Verse (Jonson) **17**:161
"Ungratefulnesse" (Herbert) **4**:119, 133-34
"Unidentified Flying Object" (Hayden) **6**:196
"L'Union libre" (Breton) **15**:51, 62
"Unión Soviética" (Guillen) **23**:123, 127
"The Unions at the Front" (Neruda) See "Los Grernios en el frente"
"A Unison" (Williams) **7**:360
"La United Fruit Company" (Neruda) **4**:296
"The United Fruit Company" (Neruda) See "La United Fruit Company"
"U.S. 1946 King's X" (Frost) **1**:200
U.S. One (Rukeyser) **12**:203-04, 211
"The Universal Andalusia" (Jimenez) See "El andaluz universal"
Universal Prayer (Pope) **26**:311
"Universal Sorrow" (Tagore) See "Vishvashoka"
"The Universe" (Swenson) **14**:258, 268, 281
"University" (Shapiro) **25**:279, 283, 290, 297-300, 311, 313, 318
"The Unjustly Punished Child" (Olds) **22**:307
"The Unknown" (Williams) **7**:369
"Unknown Girl in the Maternity Ward" (Sexton) **2**:349, 355
"The Unknown Neighbor" (Stryk) **27**:201

"Unknown Water" (Wright) **14**:341, 353
"The Unknown Woman" (Blok) **21**:14
"Unnatural Powers" (Jeffers) **17**:118
"The Unpardonable Sin" (Lindsay) **23**:280
"Unregierbarkeit" (Enzensberger) **28**:150
The Unrepresented World (Zagajewski) **27**:
"Unresolved" (Levertov) **11**:198
"The Unreturning" (Owen) **19**:343
"Les uns et les autres" (Verlaine) **2**:416
"An Unsaid Word" (Rich) **5**:359, 393
"The Unseen" (Pinsky) **27**:163
"Unsere Marine" (Heine) **25**:134
"The Unsettled Motorcyclist's Vision of His Death" (Gunn) **26**:185, 207
"The Unsettled Motorcyclist's Vision of His Death" (Gunn) **26**:
"Unsleeping City (Brooklyn Bridge Nocturne)" (Garcia Lorca)
See "Ciudad sin sueño"
"Unsounded" (Rich) **5**:359
"The Unsung Heroes" (Dunbar) **5**:131
"Unsuspecting" (Toomer) **7**:336
"Der Untergand der Titanic" (Enzensberger) **28**:149-51, 158, 160, 164-66
"Untergang" (Trakl) **20**:234, 264-65, 267, 269
"Untitled" (Swenson) **14**:274, 285
Unto Dyvers People (Skelton) **25**:374
"Unto the Whole--How Add?" (Dickinson) **1**:103
"The Untrustworthy Speaker" (Gluck) **16**:157
"Unwilling Admission" (Wylie) **23**:310
"Unylyi kolokola zvon" (Lermontov) **18**:302
"Gli uomini che si voltano" (Montale) **13**:133
"L'uomo di pena" (Pasolini) **17**:261
"Up and Down" (Merrill) **28**:222
"Up and Down" (Smith) **12**:316
"Up at a Villa-Down in the City, as Distinguished by an Italian Person of Quality" (Browning) **2**:38
"Up at La Serra" (Tomlinson) **17**:311, 325-26, 341
"Up Branches of Duck River" (Snyder) **21**:297
Up Country: Poems of New England (Kumin) **15**:181-83, 187, 189, 194, 208
"Up Hill" (Rossetti) **7**:261, 298
"The Up Rising" (Duncan) **2**:104
"Upahar" (Tagore) **8**:407
"The Upas Tree" (Pushkin)
See "Anchar"
"An Upbraiding" (Hardy) **8**:93
"Uplands" (Ammons) **16**:31
Uplands (Ammons) **16**:22, 28, 46, 61
"Upon a Beautiful Young Nymph Going to Bed" (Swift)
See "A Beautiful Young Nymph Going to Bed. Written for the Honour of the Fair Sex"
"Upon a Child. An Epitaph" (Herrick) **9**:129-31
"Upon a Child That Died" (Herrick) **9**:130-31
"Upon a Comely and Curious Maide" (Herrick) **9**:129
Upon a Dead Man's Head (Skelton) **25**:344
"Upon a fit of Sickness, Anno 1632" (Bradstreet) **10**:20, 26, 34, 59
"Upon Appleton House" (Marvell) **10**:260, 265-67, 269, 271-73, 289-91, 294, 298, 303-04, 314-15, 318
"Upon Ben Jonson" (Herrick) **9**:86
"Upon Her Blush" (Herrick) **9**:143
"Upon Himself" (Herrick) **9**:89, 109
"Upon Himselfe Being Buried" (Herrick) **9**:128, 131
"Upon His Kinswoman Mistris Elizabeth Herrick" (Herrick) **9**:131
"Upon His Last Request to Julia" (Herrick) **9**:108
"Upon Julia's Clothes" (Herrick) **9**:135-36
"Upon Julia's Recovery" (Herrick) **9**:102
"Upon Julia's Washing Her Self in the River" (Herrick) **9**:143
"Upon Meeting Don L. Lee, in a Dream" (Dove) **6**:104-05, 108
"Upon My Daughter Hannah Wiggin Her Recovery from a Dangerous Fever" (Bradstreet) **10**:34
"Upon My Dear and Loving Husband His Goeing into England" (Bradstreet)
See "To My Dear and Loving Husband His Goeing into England"
"Upon My Lord Winchilsea's Converting the Mount in His Garden to a Terras" (Finch) **21**:176
"Upon My Son Samuel His Going to England, November 6, 1959" (Bradstreet) **10**:26, 34, 36, 63
"Upon the Annunciation and Passion" (Donne) **1**:139
"Upon the Death of King James the Second" (Finch) **21**:170
"Upon the Death of O.C." (Marvell)
See "Poem upon the Death of O. C."
"Upon the Death of Sir William Twisden" (Finch) **21**:144
"Upon the Death of the Lord Protector" (Marvell)
See "Poem upon the Death of O. C."
"Upon the Dolorous Death and Much Lamentable Chance of the Most Honourable Earl of Northumberland" (Skelton) **25**:339, 372
"Upon the Hill and Grove at Billborow" (Marvell) **10**:269
"Upon the Much Lamented, Master J. Warr" (Herrick) **9**:129
"Upon the Nipples of Julia's Breast" (Herrick) **9**:143
"Upon the Roses in Julias Bosome" (Herrick) **9**:143
"Upon Your Held-Out Hand" (Thomas) **2**:406
"Uptown" (Ginsberg) **4**:47
"An Upward Look" (Merrill) **28**:285
"The Urals" (Pasternak) **6**:268
"An Urban Convalescence" (Merrill) **28**:226, 234, 249, 273
"Urania" (Arnold) **5**:43
Urbasi (Tagore) **8**:403
"Uriel" (Emerson) **18**:69, 79, 88
"The Urn" (Olds) **22**:324
The Urn (Bely)
See *Urna*
Urna (Bely) **11**:3-4, 6-7, 24, 32-3
"Urvashi" (Tagore) **8**:409
"Us" (Sexton) **2**:352
"The Use of 'Tu'" (Montale) **13**:145
"Used Up" (Sandburg) **2**:303
"Useless" (Atwood) **8**:27
"Usignolo VI" (Pasolini) **17**:266
"Usignolo VII" (Pasolini) **17**:266
L'usignuolo della Chiesa Cattolica (Pasolini) **17**:252, 262, 264-67, 270, 272, 275, 277
"Ustica" (Paz) **1**:355, 360-61
"Uswetakiyawa" (Ondaatje) **28**:338
"Utopia" (Enzensberger) **28**:159
"Utopias" (Eliot) **20**:123
"Utopie" (Lamartine) **16**:263, 284
"Utsarga" (Tagore) **8**:409
"Uznik" (Lermontov) **18**:304
"V Al'bom" (Lermontov) **18**:302
"V bol'nitse" (Pasternak) **6**:266, 269, 286-87
"V den' Blagoveshchen'ia" (Tsvetaeva) **14**:322
"V. L. Davydovu" (Pushkin) **10**:412
"V lesu" (Pasternak) **6**:280
"V ony dni, ty mne byla kak mat'" (Tsvetaeva) **14**:321
"V starinny gody zhili-byli" (Lermontov) **18**:288
"vaalee daancers" (Bissett) **14**:33
"The Vacant Lot" (Brooks) **7**:69
"Vacation" (Shapiro) **25**:310, 316
"Vacation" (Zagajewski) **27**:389
Vacation Time: Poems for Children (Giovanni) **19**:138
"La Vache" (Hugo) **17**:76, 91
"Vacillation" (Yeats) **20**:333
"Vagabonds" (Rimbaud) **3**:261
Vägvisare till underjorden (Ekeloef) **23**:62, 68-9, 77-8
"Vain and Careless" (Graves) **6**:141, 150
"Vain Word" (Borges)
See "Vanilocuencia"
"Les vaines danseuses" (Valery) **9**:392
"Vaishnava kavita" (Tagore) **8**:408
"Vaishnava Poetry" (Tagore)
See "Vaishnava kavita"
"Vaivén" (Paz) **1**:359
Vala (Blake)
See *The Four Zoas: The Torments of Love and Jealousy in the Death and Judgement of Albion the Ancient Man*
Vala (Blake)
See *The Four Zoas: The Torments of Love and Jealousy in the Death and Judgement of Albion the Ancient Man*
Vale (Viereck) **27**:259, 278
Vale Ave (H. D.) **5**:282
"The Vale of Esthwaite" (Wordsworth) **4**:417
"Valediction" (Heaney) **18**:207
"A Valediction: forbidding mourning" (Donne) **1**:124, 126, 130, 135
"A Valediction Forbidding Mourning" (Rich) **5**:371, 395
"A Valediction: of my name, in the window" (Donne) **1**:152
"A Valediction: of the booke" (Donne) **1**:128, 130
"A Valediction: of weeping" (Donne) **1**:124, 130, 153
"Valentine" (Ashbery) **26**:145
"A Valentine" (Poe) **1**:445
"Valentine" (Wylie) **23**:332
"Valentine" (Zukofsky) **11**:349
"Valentine Delivered by a Raven" (Gallagher) **9**:63
"Valentine I" (Bishop) **3**:36
"Valerik" (Lermontov) **18**:283
"Valley Candle" (Stevens) **6**:338
"The Valley of the Shadow" (Robinson) **1**:490
"The Valley of Unrest" (Poe) **1**:438
"Le vallon" (Lamartine) **16**:268, 276, 283, 290, 298-301
"Valuable" (Smith) **12**:296
"Values in Use" (Moore) **4**:261
"Valvins" (Valery) **9**:392
"The Vampire" (Baudelaire)
See "Les métamorphoses du vampire"
"Le Vampire" (Baudelaire)
See "Les métamorphoses du vampire"
"The Vampire" (Kipling) **3**:166
"Van Winkle" (Crane) **3**:100, 109
"Vanaspati" (Tagore) **8**:415
"Vandracour" (Wordsworth) **4**:399
"Vanilocuencia" (Borges) **22**:72
"Vanishing Point: Urban Indian" (Rose) **13**:232
"Vanitie" (Herbert) **4**:120
"Vanitie I" (Herbert) **4**:132
"The Vanity of All Worldly Things" (Bradstreet) **10**:2, 6, 21
"Vanna's Twins" (Rossetti) **7**:291
"Vapor Trail Reflected in the Frog Pond" (Kinnell) **26**:263, 290
"Variation and Reflection on a Poem by Rilke" (Levertov) **11**:206
"Variation and Reflection on a Theme by Rilke (The Book of Hours Book I Poem 7)" (Levertov) **11**:203
"Variation on a Theme by Rilke" (Levertov) **11**:202
"Variations Calypso and Fugue on a Theme of Ella Wheeler Wilcox" (Ashbery) **26**:137, 155
Variations on a Sunbeam (Elytis) **21**:120
"Variations on a Theme" (Cullen) **20**:58, 85
"Variations on a Theme by Rilke (The Book of Hours Book I Poem 4)" (Levertov) **11**:203
"Variations on an Original Theme" (Ashbery) **26**:140

"Variations on Two Dicta of William Blake" (Duncan) **2**:103
"Variations sur le carnaval de Venise" (Gautier) **18**:130
Various Poems of All Periods (Valery)
  See *Poésies*
"Various Protestations from Various People" (Knight) **14**:52
"Varsha-mangal" (Tagore) **8**:411
"Varshashesh" (Tagore) **8**:411
"Vasanter Kusumer mela" (Tagore) **8**:406
"Vashti" (Harper) **21**:185, 191, 209
"Vasundhara" (Tagore) **8**:408
Vaudeville for a Princess, and Other Poems (Schwartz) **8**:285, 292-94, 318
"Vecchi versi" (Montale) **13**:108, 157
"La vecchia ubriaca" (Pavese) **13**:214
"A veces me sucede" (Fuertes) **27**:3
Vecher (Akhmatova) **2**:3, 5-6, 11, 17
Vecherny albom (Tsvetaeva) **14**:305
"Vechernyaya progulka" (Bely) **11**:22
"Vegetable Island" (Page) **12**:178
"Vegetation" (Tagore)
  See "Vanaspati"
"Vegnerà el vero Cristo" (Pasolini) **17**:254
Veinte poemas de amor y una canción desesperada (Neruda) **4**:276, 282, 284, 291, 299-305, 307
"Velvet Shoes" (Wylie) **23**:301, 305, 307, 314-15, 318-20, 322-23, 330-32
"El vendedor de papeles" (Fuertes) **27**:11
"Vendémiaire" (Apollinaire) **7**:10, 36, 44-6
"vending machine" (Enzensberger) **28**:147
Venetian Epigrams (Goethe) **5**:223
The Venetian Glass Nephew (Wylie) **23**:322, 330
"Veni vidi vixi" (Hugo) **17**:64
"Venice" (Pasternak) **6**:276
"Venice" (Tomlinson) **17**:331, 334
"The Venice Poem" (Duncan) **2**:105-06
"Il ventaglio" (Montale) **13**:108, 128-29
"Ventas" (Guillen) **23**:111
"Vento e bandiere" (Montale) **13**:164
"Vento sulla mezzaluna" (Montale) **13**:110
Vents (Perse) **23**:209, 211, 213-18, 221, 223, 232, 234-35, 238-40, 242-43, 247-53, 255, 257
Venture of the Infinite Man (Neruda)
  See *Tentativa del hombre infinito*
"Venus" (Dario) **15**:87
"Vénus anadyomène" (Rimbaud) **3**:255
"Venus and the Ark" (Sexton) **2**:355
Venus and the Rain (McGuckian) **27**:77-78, 80-81, 93, 95, 100-104
Venus and the Rain (McGuckian) **27**:
"Venus and the Sun" (McGuckian) **27**:97
"Venus Transiens" (Lowell) **13**:66, 96
"Venus Tying the Wings of Love" (McGuckian) **27**:103
"Veracruz" (Hayden) **6**:193-94
"Le Verbe Être" (Breton) **15**:51
"Le verbe marronner à René Depestre" (Cesaire) **25**:29, 33
"La verdad" (Jimenez) **7**:202
"Vermächtnis" (Goethe) **5**:248
"Vermeer" (Nemerov) **24**:262, 266, 299
"Vermont" (Carruth) **10**:73-4, 83
"Vernal Equinox" (Lowell) **13**:64
"Vernal Sentiment" (Roethke) **15**:246
"Vers dorés" (Nerval) **13**:181
Vers et prose (Mallarme) **4**:207
"Vers l'Arc en ciel" (Breton) **15**:49
"Vers nouveaux et chansons" (Rimbaud) **3**:285
Verschiedene (Heine) **25**:129-131
"Verse about a Red Officer" (Tsvetaeva) **14**:313
"Verses about Russia" (Blok) **21**:9
"Verses about the Beautiful Lady" (Blok) **21**:2-3, 23
The Verses about the Beautiful Lady (Blok)
  See *Stikhi o prekrasnoi dame*
Verses Address'd to the Imitator of the First Satire of the Second Book of Horace (Montagu) **16**:338-41
Verses and Sonnets (Belloc) **24**:28-9, 34, 38
"Verses for a Certain Dog" (Parker) **28**:360
"Verses in the Night" (Parker) **28**:362
"Verses on His Own Death" (Swift) **9**:265
"Verses on the Death of Dr. Swift" (Swift) **9**:258, 279-82, 294-95, 304, 306-08, 310
"Verses on the Death of T. S. Eliot" (Brodsky)
  See "Stixi na smert T. S. Èliota"
"Verses on the Unknown Soldier" (Mandelstam)
  See "Stikhi o neizvestnom soldate"
"Verses to Czechoslovakia" (Tsvetaeva)
  See "Stikhi k Chekhii"
Verses to the Imitator of Horace (Montagu)
  See *Verses Address'd to the Imitator of the First Satire of the Second Book of Horace*
"Verses Upon the Burning of Our House" (Bradstreet)
  See "Some Verses Upon the Burning of Our House, July 10th, 1666"
"Verses Wrote in a Lady's Ivory Table-book" (Swift)
  See "Written in a Lady's Ivory Table-book, 1698"
"Versi del testamento" (Pasolini) **17**:259
"Versilian Shore" (Montale)
  See "Proda di Versilia"
Verso la cuna del mondo (Gozzano) **10**:177, 184
"Verso la fede" (Gozzano) **10**:184
"Verso Siena" (Montale) **13**:109
Versts (Tsvetaeva)
  See *Vyorsty I*
Versty I (Tsvetaeva)
  See *Vyorsty I*
Versty II (Tsvetaeva)
  See *Vyorsty II*
Versus (Nash) **21**:267, 269
Verteidigung der Wölfe (Enzensberger) **28**:133-38, 140, 143
"Vertigo" (Rich) **5**:360
"Vertue" (Herbert) **4**:100-01, 110, 113, 132-34
"A Very Short Story" (Parker) **28**:346
"Very Tree" (Kunitz) **19**:147, 160
"Vespers" (Gluck) **16**:170
"Vespers" (Lowell) **13**:64, 67, 97
"Vestigia nulla retrorsum (In Memoriam: Rainer Maria Rilke 1875-1926)" (MacDiarmid) **9**:156, 176
"Les veuves" (Baudelaire) **1**:44, 58-9
"Via Crucis" (Noyes) **27**:136
La via del refugio (Gozzano) **10**:179, 184-85, 188
"Vibratory Description" (McGuckian) **27**:105
"Vice" (Baraka) **4**:15
"Vicissitude" (Gray)
  See "Ode on the Pleasure Arising from Vicissitude"
"The Victims" (Olds) **22**:310, 312, 319, 321, 323
"The Victor Day" (Merrill) **28**:230
"Victoria's Tears" (Browning) **6**:14, 29
"The Victorious Sun" (Aleixandre) **15**:19
Victory Odes (Pindar) **19**:378, 386, 390
"La Vida a veces es un río frío y seco" (Fuertes) **27**:16
"Viday" (Tagore) **8**:415
"Videshi phul" (Tagore) **8**:415
"La Vie dans la mort" (Gautier) **18**:131-32, 155
"Viennese Waltz" (Wylie) **23**:314, 333
Viento entero (Paz) **1**:353, 356, 362-63, 369
"El vientre" (Aleixandre) **15**:34
"Le vierge, le vivace et le bel aujourdhui" (Mallarme) **4**:202, 206
"Les Vierges de Verdun" (Hugo) **17**:62, 74
"Vies" (Rimbaud) **3**:261-62
"Vietnam Addenda" (Lorde) **12**:155
"Le vieux saltimbanque" (Baudelaire) **1**:44, 58
"The View" (Holderlin) **4**:178
"The View" (Milosz) **8**:198
"A View across the Roman Campagna" (Browning) **6**:23
"The View from an Attic Window" (Nemerov) **24**:270-71
"View from an Empty Chair" (Gallagher) **9**:50
"View from the screen" (Bukowski) **18**:22
"A View of Cracow" (Zagajewski) **27**:381, 385
"A View of Delft" (Zagajewski) **27**:385
"View of Teignmouth in Devonshire" (Lowell) **13**:67
"A View of the Brooklyn Bridge" (Meredith) **28**:182, 190
"View of the Burning" (Merrill) **28**:239
"View of the Pig" (Hughes) **7**:136, 140
"View of the Wilds" (Tu Fu) **9**:332
"View to the North" (Swenson) **14**:288
"The Vigil" (Roethke) **15**:263
"Vigil Strange I Kept on the Field One Night" (Whitman) **3**:378
"Vigilance" (Breton) **15**:50-1
Vigils (Sassoon) **12**:258-59, 271
"La vigne et la maison" (Lamartine) **16**:268
"Le vigneron champenois" (Apollinaire) **7**:22
"Vignette" (Kumin) **15**:224
"Vihanger gan" (Tagore) **8**:406
VIII (Wylie) **23**:305
"Viking Dublin: Trial Piece" (Heaney) **18**:204
"Villa Adriana" (Rich) **5**:362
"Villa on Chung-nan Mountain" (Wang Wei) **18**:368
"The Village" (Carruth) **10**:71
"The Village" (Pushkin) **10**:408-09
"The Village Atheist" (Masters) **1**:335
"A Village Edmund" (Gunn) **26**:183
The Village Minstrel, and Other Poems (Clare) **23**:25, 38, 42-4
"Village Mystery" (Wylie) **23**:301
"The Villagers and Death" (Graves) **6**:142
"A Villequier" (Hugo) **17**:64, 82-83
"Villes" (Rimbaud) **3**:261, 264-65
"Vilota" (Pasolini) **17**:252
"Le vin perdu" (Valery) **9**:388, 390, 396
"The Vindictives" (Frost) **1**:206
"Vine" (Herrick) **9**:100, 109, 137
"Vine en un barco negre" (Guillen) **23**:120, 127
"The Vineyard" (Kipling) **3**:182
Vingt-cinq poèmes (Tzara) **27**:223, 227, 233
"Vino, primero, puro" (Jimenez) **7**:187
"Il vino triste" (Pavese) **13**:224
"Vintage" (Hass) **16**:216
"Vinus sai no zenban" (Nishiwaki) **15**:238
Violent Pastoral (Merrill) **28**:253
The Violent Season (Paz)
  See *La estación violenta*
"The Violent Space (or when your sister sleeps around for money)" (Knight) **14**:39, 41, 43-4, 52
The Violet of the Night (Blok) **21**:
"Virgen de plástico" (Fuertes) **27**:23, 30
"A Virgile" (Hugo) **17**:94-95
"The Virgin Carrying a Lantern" (Stevens) **6**:310
"The Virgin Mary to the Child Jesus" (Browning) **6**:29-30
"Virginia" (Eliot) **5**:166
"Virginia" (Lindsay) **23**:280
"The Virginians Are Coming Again" (Lindsay) **23**:280, 285
"Virgins Plus Curtains Minus Dots" (Loy) **16**:333
"Virtue" (Herbert)
  See "Vertue"
"Virtue" (Wheatley)
  See "On Virtue"
"Virtuoso Literature" (Wakoski) **15**:346-47
Virtuoso Literature for Two and Four Hands (Wakoski) **15**:346, 355, 361, 365-66
"Vishvashoka" (Tagore) **8**:417
"Vision" (Bridges) **28**:63, 88
"The Vision" (Burns) **6**:50
"A Vision" (Clare) **23**:22, 25

"Vision" (Gibran)
See "Ru'ya'"
"The Vision" (Masters) **1**:342
"Vision" (Rimbaud) **3**:263
"Vision" (Sassoon) **12**:245
"A Vision" (Berry) **28**:8-9
"Vision And Prayer" (Thomas) **2**:382, 387-88, 390
"La Vision des montagnes" (Hugo) **17**:66
"Vision in the Repair Shop" (Graves) **6**:143
"A Vision of India" (Kipling) **3**:190
"Vision of Jubal" (Eliot) **20**:123
"A Vision of Poets" (Browning) **6**:7, 26, 38, 41
"The Vision of Sin" (Tennyson) **6**:359-60, 366, 378
"The Vision of the Archagels" (Brooke) **24**:62, 75-6
A Vision of the Last Judgment (Blake) **12**:40-2
"The Visionary" (Bronte) **8**:52
Les visions (Lamartine) **16**:266, 269, 287
Visions of the Daughters of Albion: The Eye Sees More Than the Heart Knows (Blake) **12**:35, 46, 57, 61, 63
"The Visions of the Maid of Orleans" (Coleridge)
See "Joan of Arc"
"Visit" (Ammons) **16**:54
"The Visit" (Baraka) **4**:17
"The Visit" (Nash) **21**:274
"Visit to Toronto, with Companions" (Atwood) **8**:40
"The Visitation" (Graves) **6**:172
"Visiting Flannery O'Connor's Grave" (Kumin) **15**:215
"Visiting Hsiang-chi Monastery" (Wang Wei) **18**:378-80
"Visiting Monk Hsüan" (Wang Wei) **18**:388
"Visiting the Ho Family Again" (Tu Fu) **9**:319
"Visiting the Temple of Gathered Fragrance" (Wang Wei) **18**:383, 386
"The Visitor" (Forche) **10**:144, 153
"Visits to St. Elizabeth" (Bishop) **3**:47, 56
"Vita Nuova" (Kunitz) **19**:148, 176, 179
La vita nuova (Dante) **21**:48-53, 55, 62, 66, 72-6, 86-92, 94
"Vitam quae faciunt beatiorem" (Martial) **10**:243
"Vitzliputzli" (Heine) **25**:167, 170
ViVa (Cummings) **5**:100, 104-07, 110-11
"Vivamus" (Bridges) **28**:59, 63
"Vivasana" (Tagore) **8**:407
V-Letter and Other Poems (Shapiro) **25**:262-67, 269, 285, 288, 292, 295, 297, 307, 309, 316, 319, 322
"Vlez besenok v mokroi sherstke" (Mandelstam) **14**:153-54
"Vnov' Ia Posetil" (Pushkin)
See "Vnov' Ya Posetil"
"Vnov' Ya Posetil" (Pushkin) **10**:384, 414-15
"Vnutri gory bezdeistvuet kumir" (Mandelstam) **14**:153
"Vocation" (Levertov) **11**:198
"Voce giunta con le folaghe" (Montale) **13**:112
"Voeu à Phebus" (Ronsard) **11**:256
"The Voice" (Arnold) **5**:49
"A Voice" (Atwood) **8**:14
"The Voice" (Brooke) **24**:56, 76
"The Voice" (Hardy) **8**:88, 117-18, 135
"The Voice" (Levine) **22**:225
"The Voice" (Roethke) **15**:275
"Voice Arriving with the Coots" (Montale) **13**:146, 149
"The Voice as a Girl" (Snyder) **21**:289
"Voice Coming with the Moorhens" (Montale)
See "Voce giunta con le folaghe"
"A Voice from a Chorus" (Blok) **21**:15
"Voice from the Tomb" (Smith) **12**:349
"The Voice of Nature" (Bridges) **28**:67
"The Voice of Rock" (Ginsberg) **4**:55
"The Voice of the Ancient Bard" (Blake) **12**:7
Voice of the Forest (Tagore)
See *Banabani*
"Voice of the Past" (Bely)
See "Golos proshlogo"
"The Voice of the People" (Belloc) **24**:42
"The Voice of the People" (Holderlin)
See "Stimme des Volks"
"Voices about the Princess Anemone" (Smith) **12**:298, 348-49
"Voices from Kansas" (Kumin) **15**:215
"Voices from the Ohter World" (Merrill) **28**:235, 259
"voices of the elements" (Enzensberger) **28**:143
"Voices under the Ground" (Ekeloef) **23**:71, 73, 75
"Voicy le temps, Hurault, qui joyeux nous convie" (Ronsard) **11**:250
"Void in Law" (Browning) **6**:28, 32
"Void Only" (Rexroth) **20**:221
"Voie" (Tzara) **27**:229-31
"La Voix" (Baudelaire) **1**:73
Les Voix intérieures (Hugo) **17**:42, 45, 52, 63, 74, 76, 80, 83, 91-92, 96-97
"Volcanic Holiday" (Merrill) **28**:283, 285
Volcano a Memoir of Hawaii (Hongo) **23**:204-206
"An vollen Büschelzweigen" (Goethe) **5**:247
"Vollmondnacht" (Goethe) **5**:247
"Vol'nost': Oda" (Pushkin) **10**:408-09
Volshebny fonar (Tsvetaeva) **14**:318
"Volt" (Tzara) **27**:229-31
Volume Two (Villa) **22**:347, 353
"Voluntaries" (Emerson) **18**:76-77, 88, 113
"La volupté" (Baudelaire) **1**:71
"Von diesen Stauden" (Celan) **10**:122
Von Schwelle zu Schwelle (Celan) **10**:95, 121
"Vooruzhennyi zren'em uzkikh os" (Mandelstam) **14**:154
"Voracities and Verities Sometimes Are Interacting" (Moore) **4**:261
"Vorobyev Hills" (Pasternak) **6**:251-54
Voronezh Notebooks (Mandelstam) **14**:123, 149-50
"Vorstadt im Föhn" (Trakl) **20**:261
"Vospominanie v Tsarskom Sele" (Pushkin) **10**:409, 421
"Vostok pobledneuskii, vostok onemesvshii" (Bely) **11**:32
"A Vow" (Ginsberg) **4**:56
"The Vow" (Kinnell) **26**:286
"The Vow" (Lowell) **13**:86-7
"Vowels 2" (Baraka) **4**:24
"vowl man" (Bissett) **14**:15
"Vox Humana" (Gunn) **26**:200
"Voy hasta Uján" (Guillen) **23**:128
"Le voyage" (Baudelaire) **1**:50, 60, 70, 73-4
"The Voyage" (Jonson) **17**:207
"Le voyage à Cythère" (Baudelaire) **1**:65, 72-3
"Le Voyage de Tours, ou les amoureus Thoinet et Perrot" (Ronsard) **11**:260-61, 264
"The Voyage of Maeldune" (Tennyson) **6**:359, 369
"Voyage to Cythera" (Baudelaire)
See "Le voyage à Cythère"
Voyage to the Island of Love (Behn)
See *Poems upon Several Occasions, with a Voyage to the Island of Love*
"Voyage to the Moon" (Pinsky) **27**:157
"Voyagers" (Page) **12**:199
"Voyages" (Clampitt) **19**:91
"Voyages" (Crane) **3**:90, 97, 104
Voyages: A Homage to John Keats (Clampitt) **19**:87
"Voyages II" (Crane) **3**:80, 83, 96, 102
"Voyages III" (Crane) **3**:83
"Voyages IV" (Crane) **3**:83
"Voyages V" (Crane) **3**:83
"Le voyageur" (Apollinaire) **7**:48
"Les Voyelles" (Rimbaud) **3**:249, 268, 274
"Vozdushnyi korabl" (Lermontov) **18**:291
Vozmezdie (Blok) **21**:10, 17, 25-6, 39, 44
Vozvrat: Tretiia simfoniia (Bely) **11**:3, 8-9, 14-17, 22
"Le vrai de la chose" (Laforgue) **14**:76
"Vriksha-ropan" (Tagore) **8**:416
"Vriksha-vandana" (Tagore) **8**:416
Vrindaban (Paz) **1**:361-63
"Vse Povtoryayv pervyi stikh" (Tsvetaeva) **14**:329
"Vstrecha" (Pasternak) **6**:280
"Vsye eto bylo bylo bylo" (Blok) **21**:15
Vtoraia simfoniia: Dramaticheskaia (Bely) **11**:3-4, 8-11, 13-16, 21, 27, 33
Vtoraya kniga (Mandelstam) **14**:106, 113-18, 121-22, 129, 135, 141, 150, 153, 155
"Vue" (Valery) **9**:392
"Vuelta" (Paz) **1**:370-72, 374
Vuelta (Paz) **1**:370-71, 374, 376
"La vuelta a America" (Cardenal) **22**:110
"La vuelta a Buenos Aires" (Borges) **22**:94
"Vuelta de paseo" (Garcia Lorca) **3**:139
VV (Cummings)
See *ViVa*
"Vykhozhu odin ja na dorogu" (Lermontov) **18**:303
Vyorsty I (Tsvetaeva) **14**:310, 318
Vyorsty II (Tsvetaeva) **14**:322
"Vysokaya bolesn" (Pasternak) **6**:265
"Vystrel" (Pushkin) **10**:414
"W. S. Landor" (Moore) **4**:242, 259
"Wadin' in de Crick" (Dunbar) **5**:144
"Wading at Wellfleet" (Bishop) **3**:49, 57
"Waga Uta" (Yosano Akiko) **11**:302, 306
"Wagner" (Brooke) **24**:53, 56, 64, 83
"The Wagoner" (Pavese) **13**:205
"Waialua" (Song)
See "Easter: Wahiawa, 1959"
"Waikiki" (Brooke) **24**:56, 67, 86
"Wail" (Parker) **28**:360
"Wait" (Kinnell) **26**:292-93
"The Waiting" (Olds) **22**:330, 332, 334, 337, 340
"Waiting" (Wright) **14**:341
"Waiting by the Gate" (Bryant) **20**:8
"Waiting for Breakfast" (Larkin) **21**:226-27
"Waiting for *It*" (Swenson) **14**:263
Waiting for the King of Spain (Wakoski) **15**:366
"The Waiting Head" (Sexton) **2**:350
"Waiting Inland" (Kumin) **15**:208
"Wake-Up Niggers" (Madhubuti) **5**:329, 338
"The Waking" (Kinnell) **26**:279
"The Waking" (Roethke) **15**:278, 286
"Waking an Angel" (Levine) **22**:213
"Waking in a Newly-Build House" (Gunn) **26**:201
"Waking in a Newly-Built House" (Gunn) **26**:211
"Waking in the Blue" (Lowell) **3**:209, 221
"Waking in the Dark" (Rich) **5**:370, 392, 395
The Waking: Poems, 1933-1953 (Roethke) **15**:249, 261, 263, 282, 284, 309
"Waking this Morning" (Rukeyser) **12**:230
"Waking Up in Streator" (Stryk) **27**:214
"Waldeinsamkeit" (Emerson) **18**:76, 88
"Wales Visitation" (Ginsberg) **4**:74, 93-4
"The Walk" (Hardy) **8**:93
"A Walk in Late Summer" (Roethke) **15**:274
"A Walk in the Country" (Kinnell) **26**:257
"A Walk on Snow" (Viereck) **27**:260, 277, 282
"Walk on the Moon" (Momaday) **25**:188
"A Walk with Tom Jefferson" (Levine) **22**:225-27
"Walking Down Park" (Giovanni) **19**:140-41, 143
"Walking in Paris" (Sexton) **2**:363
"Walking in the Blue" (Sexton) **2**:350
"The Walking Man of Rodin" (Sandburg) **2**:334
"Walking on the Prayerstick" (Rose) **13**:233
"Walking to the Bellrock" (Ondaatje) **28**:336, 337
"The Wall" (Brooks) **7**:82
"The Wall" (Montale) **13**:148
"Die Wallfahrt nach Kevlaar" (Heine) **25**:145
"Walls" (Hughes) **7**:149
The Walls Do Not Fall (H. D.) **5**:272, 274-76, 293-95, 307, 309, 312, 314-15

"The Walrus and the Carpenter" (Carroll) **18**:51-52
"Walt Whitman" (Whitman) **3**:414
"Walter Bradford" (Brooks) **7**:92
"Walter Jenks' Bath" (Meredith) **28**:178, 182, 213
"The Waltz" (Aleixandre) **15**:8, 14
"The Waltzer in the House" (Kunitz) **19**:155
"Wanda" (Vigny) **26**:369, 402
"The Wanderer" (Pushkin) **10**:409
"The Wanderer" (Smith) **12**:326, 349-50, 354
"The Wanderer" (Williams) **7**:374, 382, 394
"A Wanderer" (Zagajewski) **27**:381
"The Wanderer's Song" (Hagiwara Sakutaro) **18**:183
See "Hyohakusha no uta"
"The Wandering Jew" (Robinson) **1**:487
"The Wanderings of Cain" (Coleridge) **11**:89, 91
"The Wanderings of Oisin" (Yeats) **20**:353
The Wanderings of Oisin, and Other Poems (Yeats) **20**:298, 302, 344, 346
"Wanderschaft" (Trakl) **20**:241
"Wandrers Sturmlied" (Goethe) **5**:237-39
Wang Stream Collection (Wang Wei) **18**:367, 370, 385
"Wang-ch'uan Garland" (Wang Wei) **18**:374
"The Want" (Olds) **22**:321, 325-26, 340
The Want Bone (Pinsky) **27**:156, 160, 163-64, 169, 172, 174
"Wanting to Die" (Sexton) **2**:364
"Wants" (Larkin) **21**:227, 242, 252
"War" (Levine) **22**:218
"The War Against the Trees" (Kunitz) **19**:175
War All the Time: Poems, 1981-1984 (Bukowski) **18**:15, 18-19
"The War in the Air" (Nemerov) **24**:290
"War Machine" (Ondaatje) **28**:327-28, 331
"War Pictures" (Lowell) **13**:76
"War Song" (Parker) **28**:356
War Stories Poems about Long Ago and Now (Nemerov) **24**:287, 289-90
War Trilogy (H. D.)
See *Trilogy*
"The Ward" (Rukeyser) **12**:225
Ware the Hawk (Skelton) **25**:335, 338, 354, 377, 377-78, 380-81
"Waring" (Browning) **2**:26
"A Warm Place to Shit" (Bissett) **14**:10
"A Warm Small Rain" (Zagajewski) **27**:394
"Warning" (Hughes) **1**:252
"Warning: Children at Play" (Nemerov) **24**:255
"Warning to Children" (Graves) **6**:139, 143-44, 150
"A Warning to Those Who Live on Mountains" (Day Lewis) **11**:144
"Warnung" (Goethe) **5**:250
"The Warriors of the North" (Hughes) **7**:132, 148
"The Warrior's Prayer" (Dunbar) **5**:134
"The Wars" (Ondaatje) **28**:338
"A Warsaw Gathering" (Zagajewski) **27**:381
"Warum gabst du uns die tiefen Blicke" (Goethe) **5**:246
"Was He Married?" (Smith) **12**:333, 352
"Was I never yet" (Wyatt) **27**:356
"Washerwoman" (Sandburg) **2**:329
"Washington Cathedral" (Shapiro) **25**:286, 318
"Washyuma Motor Hotel" (Ortiz) **17**:227
"A WASP Woman Visits a Black Junkie in Prison" (Knight) **14**:42, 53
"The Wassaile" (Herrick) **9**:104
The Waste Land (Eliot) **5**:155-62, 165-67, 173-74, 176, 178-79, 183-89, 191-93, 198, 206-18
The Waste Land (Pound) **4**:353
"Waste Paper Basket" (Tagore) **8**:417
"Waste Sonata" (Olds) **22**:325
Watakushi no Oitach (Yosano Akiko) **11**:309-11
"The Watch" (Swenson) **14**:250
"Watchers of the Sky" (Noyes) **27**:128
"Watchful, A Tale of Psyche" (Smith) **12**:303-05, 337
"Watching Crow Looking South Towards the Manzano" (Harjo) **27**:64
"Watching Football on TV" (Nemerov) **24**:284
"Watching Shoah in a Hotel Room in America" (Zagajewski) **27**:388, 391
"Watching the Needleboats at San Sabra" (Joyce) **22**:137
"The Water" (Carruth) **10**:71
"Water" (Larkin) **21**:244
"Water" (Lee) **24**:247
"Water" (Lowell) **3**:212, 215
"Water" (Wright) **14**:366
"Water and Marble" (Page) **12**:178
"Water Color" (Verlaine)
See "Aquarelles"
"The Water Drop" (Elytis) **21**:130
"Water Element Song for Sylvia" (Wakoski) **15**:345
"the water falls in yr mind nd yu get wet tooo" (Bissett) **14**:16, 33
"The Water Hyacinth" (Merrill) **28**:247
Water Lilies (Jimenez)
See *Ninfeas*
"Water Music" (MacDiarmid) **9**:154, 156, 158, 171, 176
"The Water Nymph" (Lermontov)
See "Rusalka"
"Water of Life" (MacDiarmid) **9**:197-98
"Water Picture" (Swenson) **14**:261, 263; **106**:351
"Water Raining" (Stein) **18**:334, 349
"Water Sign Woman" (Clifton) **17**:29
"Water Sleep" (Wylie) **23**:301
Water Street (Merrill) **28**:220, 225,228, 234, 238, 240, 244, 247-49, 281
"Watercolor of Grantchester Meadows" (Plath) **1**:388
"Watercolors" (Rose) **13**:238
"The Watercourse" (Herbert) **4**:114
"Waterfall" (Heaney) **18**:200
"Watergate" (Baraka) **4**:30
"The Watergaw" (MacDiarmid) **9**:156, 160, 196
"Waterlily Fire" (Rukeyser) **12**:221
Waterlily Fire: Poems, 1935-1962 (Rukeyser) **12**:215-16
"Watermaid" (Okigbo) **7**:232, 239
"The Wattle-tree" (Wright) **14**:344, 353
"A Wave" (Ashbery) **26**:159
"Wave" (Snyder) **21**:304-06, 308
A Wave (Ashbery) **26**:169-170
"Wave Song" (Ekeloef) **23**:53-4
"The Wave the Flame the Cloud and the Leopard Speak to the Mind" (Swenson) **14**:247
"Waxworks" (Shapiro) **25**:308, 312
"The Way" (Lowell) **13**:60, 83
"The Way Down" (Kunitz) **19**:149, 155, 178
"Way down the Ravi River" (Kipling) **3**:194
"The Way In" (Tomlinson) **17**:319-20, 326
The Way In and Other Poems (Tomlinson) **17**:327, 336, 349, 351-52, 354
"the Way it Was" (Clifton) **17**:23
Way of All the Earth (Akhmatova) **2**:16
"The Way of Refuge" (Gozzano)
See "The Road to Shelter"
The Way of Refuge (Gozzano)
See *La via del refugio*
"The Way of the Wind" (Swinburne) **24**:329
"The Way through the Woods" (Kipling) **3**:171, 183, 186, 192
"The Way West, Underground" (Snyder) **21**:296
"The Wayfarers" (Brooke) **24**:57
"Way-Out Morgan" (Brooks) **7**:63
The Wayward and the Seeking: A Collection of Writing by Jean Toomer (Toomer) **7**:341
We a BaddDDD People (Sanchez) **9**:204, 206-08, 210-13, 216, 218-20, 224-27, 229, 234, 237-38, 240, 242
"We a BadddDDD People (for gwendolyn brooks/a fo real bad one)" (Sanchez) **9**:209, 225, 237
"We Are" (Kumin) **15**:183
"We are Alive" (Harjo) **27**:57
"We Are Muslim Women" (Sanchez) **9**:228
"We Are Seven" (Wordsworth) **4**:374, 415, 420, 428
"We Come Back" (Rexroth) **20**:217-18
"We Encounter Nat King Cole as We Invent the Future" (Harjo) **27**:65, 72
"We English" (Loy) **16**:320
"We Free Singers Be" (Knight) **14**:40, 46
"We Have Been Believers" (Walker) **20**:272-74, 283, 289
"we live in a hundrid yeer old house" (Bissett) **14**:25
"We Lying by Seasand" (Thomas) **2**:404
"We Need th Setting" (Bissett) **14**:10
"We Real Cool" (Brooks) **7**:62, 85, 90
"We Shall Gather Again in Petersburg" (Mandelstam) **14**:116, 121, 157
we sleep inside each other all (Bissett) **14**:6
"We Stood There Singing" (Kumin) **15**:213
"We Too" (H. D.) **5**:268
We Walk the Way of the New World (Madhubuti) **5**:326-27, 336, 343, 345-46
"We Wear the Mask" (Dunbar) **5**:124, 130, 132, 135, 140, 142, 144
"We Who Are Playing" (Lindsay) **23**:286
"The Weak Monk" (Smith) **12**:333
"A Wearied Pilgrim" (Herrick) **9**:108
"The Weary Blues" (Hughes) **1**:236, 246, 248, 261, 269
The Weary Blues (Hughes) **1**:236-37, 242, 244-46, 248, 258, 260, 262-64, 268-70
"Weary in Well-Doing" (Rossetti) **7**:268
"Weary of the Bitter Ease" (Mallarme)
See "Las de l'amer repos"
"The Weary Pund o' Tow" (Burns) **6**:78
"The Weather of the World" (Nemerov) **24**:287, 302
"The Weather-Cock Points South" (Lowell) **13**:96
"Weathering Out" (Dove) **6**:111
"Weathers" (Hardy) **8**:124
"Webster Ford" (Masters) **1**:344, 346,348
"The Wedding Photograph" (Smith) **12**:316, 323
"Wedding Wind" (Larkin) **21**:227, 247
The Wedge (Williams) **7**:370, 402
"Wednesday at the Waldorf" (Swenson) **14**:267, 276
"Wednesday: The Tete a Tete" (Montagu) **16**:348-49
"The Weed" (Bishop) **3**:37, 45, 75
"Weed Puller" (Roethke) **15**:278, 295, 297
"The Weeping Garden" (Pasternak) **6**:268
"The Weeping Saviour" (Browning) **6**:14
"Weggebeizt" (Celan) **10**:106, 111
"Weiß sind die Tulpen" (Celan) **10**:123
"Weight" (Tagore)
See "Bhar"
"Die Weihe" (Heine) **25**:157-61, 163-64
Die Weise von Liebe und Tod des Cornets Christoph Rilke (Rilke) **2**:266, 268
"Weitere Gru¨nde dafu¨r, dass Dichter lu¨gen" (Enzensberger) **28**:165
"weiterung" (Enzensberger) **28**:135
"Welcome Aboard the Turbojet Electra" (Swenson) **14**:268
"Welcome and Parting" (Goethe)
See "Willkommen und Abschied"
"Welcome Back, Mr. Knight: Love of My Life" (Knight) **14**:46
"Welcome Morning" (Sexton) **2**:372
"The Welcome to Sack" (Herrick) **9**:88, 94, 102
"Welcome to the Caves of Arta" (Graves) **6**:153
"The Well" (Levertov) **11**:168, 205-06
"The Well" (Tomlinson) **17**:341-42
"Well Said Old Mole" (Viereck) **27**:259
"The Well-Beloved" (Hardy) **8**:91
"The Wellspring" (Olds) **22**:338
The Wellspring (Olds) **22**:330, 338-39

"Welsh Incident" (Graves) **6**:143, 150
"The Welsh Marches" (Housman) **2**:159, 179
"wer they angels i didnt know" (Bissett) **14**:34
"We're few" (Pasternak) **6**:252
"We're Not Learnen to Be Paper Boys (for the young brothas who sell Muhammad Speaks)" (Sanchez) **9**:229
"We're at the Graveyard" (Ondaatje) **28**:327, 331, 334
"The Wereman" (Atwood) **8**:36
"The Werewolf" (Marie de France)
See "Bisclavret"
"An Werther" (Goethe) **5**:250-51
Wessex Poems, and Other Verses (Hardy) **8**:114, 123
"The West" (Housman) **2**:167, 191, 199
"West and Away the Wheels of Darkness Roll" (Housman) **2**:162
West Indies, Ltd.: Poemas (Guillen) **23**:98-99, 106-107, 114, 133, 137-39
"The West Wind" (Bryant) **20**:4, 40
"West Wind" (Wright) **14**:342, 354
"Westering" (Heaney) **18**:203
The Western Approaches: Poems, 1973-1975 (Nemerov) **24**:275, 284-86, 303
"The Western Front" (Bridges) **28**:77, 81
"Western Song" (Trakl)
See "Abendländisches Lied"
West-Östlicher Divan (Goethe) **5**:223, 225, 229, 239, 247, 250
"Westport" (Kinnell) **26**:238, 252
"West-Running Brook" (Frost) **1**:203, 218, 220
West-Running Brook (Frost) **1**:195, 203, 205, 213
"Westward" (Clampitt) **19**:95-8
Westward (Clampitt) **19**:93, 95-6
"Wet Casements" (Ashbery) **26**:155
"Wha Is That at My Bower-Door" (Burns) **6**:77
"The Whaleboat Struck" (Ammons) **16**:39
what (Bissett) **14**:15
What a Kingdom It Was (Kinnell) **26**:236, 238-39, 252-53, 255, 257, 279, 289
"What a Pretty Net" (Viereck) **27**:259, 179
"What Are Cities For?" (Jeffers) **17**:132
"What Are Years" (Moore) **4**:243
"What can I Tell My Bones?" (Roethke) **15**:264, 274
"What Did You Buy" (Wylie) **23**:330
"What God Is" (Herrick) **9**:94, 141
"What God Is Like to Him I Serve?" (Bradstreet) **10**:34
"What Happened" (Duncan) **2**:103
"What Happened Here Before" (Snyder) **21**:298, 325
What Happened When the Hopi Hit New York (Rose) **13**:239
"What Have I Learned" (Snyder) **21**:318
What I Love (Elytis) **21**:131
"What I Should Have Said" (Harjo) **27**:56
"What is Life?" (Clare) **23**:40
"What It Cost" (Forche) **10**:166
"Lo What It is to Love" (Wyatt) **27**:317, 346
"What Lips My Lips Have Kissed" (Millay) **6**:225
"What may it availl me" (Wyatt) **27**:324
"What menythe this?" (Wyatt) **27**:316, 322, 324
What Moon Drove Me To This? (Harjo) **27**:64
"What no perdy" (Wyatt) **27**:304, 328
"What of the Night?" (Kunitz) **19**:175-76, 178
what poetiks (Bissett) **14**:15
"What rage is this?" (Wyatt) **27**:304
"What Shall I Give My Children?" (Brooks) **7**:76
"What? So Soon" (Hughes) **1**:266
"What Stillness Round a God" (Rilke) **2**:275
"What the Bird with the Human Head Knew" (Sexton) **2**:372
"What the Light Was Like" (Clampitt) **19**:102
What the Light Was Like (Clampitt) **19**:85-7, 90-1, 93
"What the Moon Saw" (Lindsay) **23**:268
"What the Rattlesnake Said" (Lindsay) **23**:286
"What the Women Said" (Bogan) **12**:110
"What Then?" (Yeats) **20**:342
"What This Mode of Motion Said" (Ammons) **16**:20
"What vaileth truth" (Wyatt) **27**:366
"What Virginia Said" (Tomlinson) **17**:353
"What We Come To Know" (Ortiz) **17**:246
"what we dew if thrs anything" (Bissett) **14**:33
"What Were They Like?" (Levertov) **11**:176
"What Why When How Who" (Pinsky) **27**:164
What Work Is (Levine) **22**:220-21, 227-28, 231-32
"What Would Tennessee Williams Have Said" (Wakoski) **15**:368
"What Wourde is That" (Wyatt) **27**:314, 342
"Whatever Happened?" (Larkin) **21**:235-36
"Whatever You Say Say Nothing" (Heaney) **18**:189, 205
"Whatever You Wish, Lord" (Jimenez) **7**:184
"WHATS HAPPNING OZONE CUM BACK WE STILL LOV YU" (Bissett) **14**:32
"What's Meant by Here" (Snyder) **21**:300
What's O'Clock (Lowell) **13**:66, 76, 84-5, 91, 93-4, 97-8
"What's That" (Sexton) **2**:359
"Whe' Fe Do?" (McKay) **2**:222-23
"Wheat-in-the-Ear" (Lowell) **13**:96
"The Wheel" (Cesaire) **25**:17
"The Wheel" (Hayden) **6**:194-95
The Wheel (Berry) **28**:16
"The Wheel of Being II" (Carruth) **10**:71
"The Wheel Revolves" (Rexroth) **20**:195
"Wheesht, Wheesht, My Foolish Heart" (MacDiarmid) **9**:156, 160
"When All My Five and Country Senses See" (Thomas) **2**:392
"When Black Is a Color Because It Follows a Grey Day" (Wakoski) **15**:348
"When Coldness Wraps This Suffering Clay" (Byron) **16**:89
"When de Co'n Pone's Hot" (Dunbar) **5**:117, 122
"When Death Came April Twelve 1945" (Sandburg) **2**:333
"When First I Saw" (Burns) **6**:78
"When from Afar" (Holderlin) **4**:174, 178
"When God Lets My Body Be" (Cummings) **5**:99
"When Guilford Good" (Burns) **6**:78
"When Hair Falls Off and Eyes Blur and" (Cummings) **5**:105
"When He Would Have His Verses Read" (Herrick) **9**:87, 96, 102, 109, 139, 145
"When I Buy Pictures" (Moore) **4**:251, 266
"When I Die" (Brooks) **7**:68
"When I Die" (Giovanni) **19**:113
"When I Have Fears That I May Cease to Be" (Keats) **1**:314
"When I Nap" (Giovanni) **19**:112
"When I Roved a Young Highlander" (Byron) **16**:86
"When I Set Out for Lyonesse" (Hardy) **8**:92, 112, 115
"When I Was One-and-Twenty" (Housman) **2**:161, 192
"When I Watch the Living Meet" (Housman) **2**:184
"When in the Gloomiest of Capitals" (Akhmatova)
See "Kogda v mrachneyshey iz stolits"
"When Jemmy First Began to Love" (Behn)
See "Song to a Scotish Tune (When Jemmy First Began to Love)"
"When Lilacs Last in the Dooryard Bloom'd" (Whitman) **3**:378, 382, 396-97, 410, 418-19, 422
"When Lilacs Last in the Dooryard Bloomed" (Whitman) **3**:378, 382, 396-97, 410, 418-19, 422
"When Malindy Sings" (Dunbar) **5**:117, 119-21, 134, 146
"When Mrs. Martin's Booker T." (Brooks) **7**:67, 69
"When on my night of life the Dawn shall break" (Brooke) **24**:72
"When Once the Twilight Locks No Longer" (Thomas) **2**:402
When One Has Lived a Long Time Alone (Kinnell) **26**:285-87, 293
"When Rain Whom Fear" (Cummings) **5**:105
"When Serpents bargain for the Right to Squirm" (Cummings) **5**:90, 107
"When Sir Beelzebub" (Sitwell) **3**:303
"When Smoke Stood Up from Ludlow" (Housman) **2**:184
"When Summer's End Is Nighing" (Housman) **2**:165, 181
"When the Dead Ask My Father about Me" (Olds) **22**:323, 326
"When the Lamp Is Shattered" (Shelley) **14**:177, 207
"When the Light Falls" (Kunitz) **19**:151, 155
"When the Shy Star" (Joyce)
See "IV"
When the Skies Clear (Pasternak)
See *Kogda razglyaetsya*
"When the Yellowing Fields Billow" (Lermontov) **18**:281
"When They Have Lost" (Day Lewis) **11**:144
"When Under the Icy Eaves" (Masters) **1**:328
"When Unto Nights of Autumn Do Complain" (Cummings) **5**:104
"When We with Sappho" (Rexroth) **20**:203, 216
"When We'll Worship Jesus" (Baraka) **4**:29, 39
"When Will I Return" (Brutus) **24**:116
"When You Are Old" (Yeats) **20**:355
"When You Lie Down, the Sea Stands Up" (Swenson) **14**:261
"When You Speak to Me" (Gallagher) **9**:36
"When You've Forgotten Sunday" (Brooks) **7**:53, 68
"Where Are the War Poets?" (Day Lewis) **11**:131
"Where can I go, now it's January?" (Mandelstam)
See "Kuda mne det'sia v etom Ianvare?"
"Where Is the Real Non-Resistant?" (Lindsay) **23**:281
"Where Knock Is Open Wide" (Roethke) **15**:251, 261, 272, 275-76, 278, 298, 300
"Where, O Where?" (Wylie) **23**:324
"Where shall I have at myn owne will" (Wyatt) **27**:332, 351-352
"Where Shall the Lover Rest" (Scott) **13**:304
Where Sparrows Work Hard (Soto) **28**:372, 382-84
"Where, Tall Girl, Is Your Gypsy Babe" (Akhmatova)
See "Gde, vysokaya, tvoy tsyganyonok"
"Where the Hell Would Chopin Be?" (Bukowski) **18**:4
"Where the Picnic Was" (Hardy) **8**:136
"Where the Rainbow Ends" (Lowell) **3**:200, 207
"Where the Tennis Court Was" (Montale)
See "Dov'era il tennis"
"Where the Track Vanishes" (Kinnell) **26**:238, 252
"Wolves Defended against the Lambs" (Enzensberger) **28**:147, 165
Where the Wolves Drink (Tzara) **27**:250
"Where There's a Will There's Velleity" (Nash) **21**:265
"Where They So Fondly Go" (Bukowski) **18**:5
"Where We Live Now" (Levine) **22**:214
"Where's Agnes?" (Browning) **6**:24
"Where's the Poker" (Smart) **13**:348
"Whether on Ida's Shady Brow" (Blake) **12**:11
"Which, Being Interpreted, Is as May Be, or, Otherwise" (Lowell) **13**:91
"While Blooming Youth" (Prior) **52**:205
"While Drawing in a Churchyard" (Hardy) **8**:120-21

"While Sitting in the Tuileries and Facing the Slanting Sun" (Swenson) **14**:261, 285
"While the Record Plays" (Illyes) **16**:249, 251
"whilst waiting for" (Bissett) **14**:32
"Whip the World" (MacDiarmid) **9**:187
Whipperginny (Graves) **6**:127-28, 131
"The Whipping" (Hayden) **6**:194-96
"The Whirlwind" (Lindsay) **23**:281
"Whiskers, A Philosophical Ode" (Pushkin) **10**:407
"whispered to lucifer" (Clifton) **17**:30
"Whispers of Heavenly Death" (Whitman) **3**:378
"Whistle and I'll Come tae Ye, My Lad" (Burns) **6**:59
"Whistle and I'll Come tae Ye, My Lad" (Burns)
See "Whistle and I'll Come tae Ye, My Lad"
"The Whistle Cockade" (Burns) **6**:82
Whistles and Whistling (Ishikawa)
See *Yobuko to kuchibue*
"A Whistling Girl" (Parker) **28**:353, 362
"Whistling Sam" (Dunbar) **5**:122, 146
"White and Green" (Lowell) **13**:60, 69
"White and Violet" (Jimenez) **7**:183
"White Arrow" (Toomer) **7**:336
White Buildings (Crane) **3**:81, 84, 87, 90
"The White City" (McKay) **2**:211
The White Doe of Rylstone; or, The Fate of the Nortons (Wordsworth) **4**:394, 402, 407
"White Dwarf" (Ammons) **16**:45
"White Dwarfs" (Ondaatje) **28**:314, 317, 327, 331-32, 334, 336, 338
White Flock (Akhmatova)
See *Belaya staya*
"White Horses" (Kipling) **3**:183
"The White House" (McKay) **2**:210, 221, 229
"White Lady" (Clifton) **17**:28
"The White Lilies" (Gluck) **16**:170-71
"The White Man's Burden" (Kipling) **3**:192
"White Night" (Wright) **14**:372
"The White Porch" (Song) **21**:331-32, 334, 338, 340-41, 350
"White Shoulders" (Sandburg) **2**:303
"White Shroud" (Ginsberg) **4**:86, 90
White Shroud (Ginsberg) **4**:86-7, 89-90
"The White Snake" (Sexton) **2**:365
"The White Thought" (Smith) **12**:292, 341, 354
"The White Troops" (Brooks) **7**:73
"The White Van" (Tomlinson) **17**:333
"White Wines" (Stein) **18**:341
"The White Witch" (Johnson) **24**:127, 142, 161, 166
White-Haired Lover (Shapiro) **25**:316, 321-22
The White-Haired Revolver (Breton)
See *Le revolver á cheveux blancs*
"The White-Tailed Hornet" (Frost) **1**:221
"The Whitsun Weddings" (Larkin) **21**:228, 230, 238-39, 255
The Whitsun Weddings (Larkin) **21**:224, 227-28, 230, 233, 235, 240, 244, 253, 255, 259
"Whitsunday" (Herbert) **4**:118
"Who Among You Knows the Essence of Garlic" (Hongo) **23**:196-97
Who Are We Now? (Ferlinghetti) **1**:187-88
"Who But the Lord" (Hughes) **1**:241
"Who Cares, Long as It's B-Flat" (Carruth) **10**:85
"Who ever comes to shroud me do not harme" (Donne)
See "The Funerall"
"Who has not walked" (Bridges) **28**:83
"Who Hath Herd" (Wyatt) **27**:317
Who Is the Real Non-Resistant? (Lindsay) **23**:282
"Who is this Who Howls and Mutters?" (Smith) **12**:313, 336
"Who Knows" (Dunbar) **5**:130
"Who Know's If the Moon's" (Cummings) **5**:88
"Who list his wealth and ease retain" (Wyatt) **27**:368
"Who Made Paul Bunyan" (Sandburg) **2**:327
"Who on Earth" (Kinnell) **26**:287
"Who Said It Was Simple" (Lorde) **12**:153, 157
"Who Shot Eugenie?" (Smith) **12**:333
"Who so list to hount" (Wyatt) **27**:300-01, 303, 309-10, 323, 329-30, 342-44, 348, 356, 358, 360, 363, 367
Who Will Know Us? (Soto) **28**:402
"Who Will Survive America?/Few Americans/Very Few Negroes/No Crackers at All" (Baraka) **4**:14, 19
"Whoever Finds a Horseshoe" (Mandelstam)
See "Nashedshij podkovu"
"Wholesome" (Meredith) **28**:208
"Whorls" (Meredith) **28**:198
"Whuchulls" (MacDiarmid) **9**:197-98
"Why Can't I Live Forever?" (Viereck) **27**:258, 276
Why Can't I Live Forever? (Viereck) **27**:
"Why Come Ye Nat to Courte?" (Skelton) **25**:336-37, 342, 348, 350, 356, 374, 379
"why dew magazines lie" (Bissett) **14**:32
"Why Did I Laugh Tonight" (Keats) **1**:279, 305
"'Why Did I Sketch'" (Hardy) **8**:137
"Why do I" (Smith) **12**:337
"Why Do You Sing My Bird" (Ekeloef) **23**:87
"Why East Wind Chills" (Thomas) **2**:379
"Why I Am a Liberal" (Browning) **2**:66
"Why I Voted the Socialist Ticket" (Lindsay) **23**:267, 282, 296
"Why I write not of love" (Jonson)
See "Why I write not of love"
"Why Some Look Up to Planets and Heroes" (Merton) **10**:334
"Why We Die" (Swenson) **14**:247
"Whys/Wise" (Baraka) **4**:40
"Wichita Vortex Sutra" (Ginsberg) **4**:50, 53, 66, 82, 85
"The Wide Mouth" (Snyder) **21**:292
"The Widow at Windsor" (Kipling) **3**:161, 186-87, 191
"Widow La Rue" (Masters) **1**:330, 333
"The Widow o' Windsor" (Kipling)
See "The Widow at Windsor"
"The Widow of Windsor" (Kipling)
See "The Widow at Windsor"
"Widower's Tango" (Neruda) **4**:306
"Widowhood or the Home-Coming of Lady Ross" (Smith) **12**:351-52
"Widows" (Baudelaire)
See "Les veuves"
"The Widow's Lament in Springtime" (Williams) **7**:345, 353, 360, 363
"The Widow's Party" (Kipling) **3**:160
"The Widow's Resolution" (Smart) **13**:347
"Wie wenn am Feiertage ..." (Holderlin) **4**:162, 165-66, 169
"A Wife at Daybreak I Shall Be" (Dickinson) **1**:93
"Wife of Bath's Prologue" (Chaucer)
See "Prologue to the Wife of Bath's Tale"
"Wife of Bath's Tale" (Chaucer) **19**:13, 15, 29, 33, 60, 63
"Wife to Husband" (Rossetti) **7**:267
"Wife's Tale" (Chaucer)
See "Wife of Bath's Tale"
"The Wild" (Berry) **28**:14, 37
"Wild Blessings" (Clifton) **17**:29
"Wild Boys of the Road" (Ashbery) **26**:163
"Wild Cherries" (Zagajewski) **27**:389
Wild Dreams of a New Beginning (Ferlinghetti) **1**:188
"Wild Flower" (Tagore)
See "Banaphul"
"WILD FLOWRS ABOVE TH TREE LINE" (Bissett) **14**:20
"Wild Grapes" (Frost) **1**:215
The Wild Iris (Gluck) **16**:168, 170-71
"Wild Life Cameo, Early Morn" (Ferlinghetti) **1**:182-83, 188
"Wild Oats" (Larkin) **21**:230, 234, 244, 247
"Wild Orchard" (Williams) **7**:345
A Wild Patience Has Taken Me This Far: Poems, 1978-1981 (Rich) **5**:385, 389
"Wild Peaches" (Wylie) **23**:301, 305, 314, 329, 333-34
The Wild Rose Flowers (Akhmatova)
See *Shipovnik tsevetyot*
"The Wild Sky" (Rich) **5**:362
"The Wild Swans at Coole" (Yeats) **20**:303, 327
The Wild Swans at Coole (Yeats) **20**:304, 310-11, 314, 326, 328
"Wild Water" (Swenson) **14**:283
"Wild Without Love" (McGuckian) **27**:83
"The Wilderness" (Robinson) **1**:459
"Wilderness" (Sandburg) **2**:302
"The Wildflower" (Williams) **7**:382, 386
"Wildflower Plain" (Wright) **14**:342
"Wilfred Owen's Photographs" (Hughes) **7**:133
"The Will" (Donne) **1**:126
"The Will" (Merrill) **28**:272
"Will Be" (Pasternak) **6**:252
"Will Boyden Lectures" (Masters) **1**:343
"Will Not Come Back" (Lowell) **3**:226-27
"Will Out of Kindness of Their Hearts a Few Philosophers Tell Me" (Cummings) **5**:93
"Will They Cry When You're Gone, You Bet" (Baraka) **4**:18
The Will to Change: Poems, 1968-1970 (Rich) **5**:365-67, 370-72, 383, 387-89, 391, 399
"Will Waterproof's Lyrical Monologue" (Tennyson) **6**:360
"Will You Perhaps Consent to Be" (Schwartz) **8**:305
"Willful Homing" (Frost) **1**:197
William Blake's Prophetic Writing (Blake) **12**:25
"William Bond" (Blake) **12**:35, 43
William Carlos Williams: Selected Poems (Williams) **7**:357
"William H. Herndon" (Masters) **1**:334
"William Marion Reedy" (Masters) **1**:325, 333, 342
"Willie" (Brooks)
See "To Keorapetse Kgositsile (Willie)"
"Willie Brew'd a Peck o' Maut" (Burns) **6**:76
"Willie Wastle" (Burns) **6**:78, 81; **40**:97
"The Willing Mistress" (Behn) **13**:4, 14-16, 18-20, 29
"Willingly" (Gallagher) **9**:58
Willingly (Gallagher) **9**:42-4, 50-1, 53, 56, 58-62
"Willkommen und Abschied" (Goethe) **5**:247, 251
"Willow Waves" (Wang Wei) **18**:364
"Willows" (Stryk) **27**:212-13
"Wilt thou forgive" (Donne)
See "A Hymne to God the Father"
"Wind" (Hughes) **7**:118, 165
"Wind" (Soto) **28**:370, 373-75, 377-78, 384
"Wind" (Tomlinson) **17**:328
The Wind among the Reeds (Yeats) **20**:303, 330
"Wind and Flags" (Montale)
See "Vento e bandiere"
"Wind and Glacier Voices" (Ortiz) **17**:232
"Wind and Silver" (Lowell) **13**:94-5
"The Wind and Stream" (Bryant) **20**:15
"The Wind and the Rain" (Frost) **1**:196
"Wind at Night" (Zagajewski) **27**:394
"The Wind Bloweth Where It Listeth" (Cullen) **20**:58
"The Wind Coming Down From" (Ammons) **16**:5
"Wind in Florence" (Brodsky) **9**:14
"The Windmill" (Bridges) **28**:67
"Wind on the Crescent" (Lewis) **13**:
See "Vento sulla mezzaluna"
"The Windhover" (Hopkins) **15**:125, 127, 132-33, 144, 160, 168, 169, 171
The Winding Stair (Yeats) **20**:307, 311, 326-28, 330, 333, 335
"Window" (Hass) **16**:222

"A Window" (Merton)
See "The Blessed Virgin Mary Compared to a Window"
"Window" (Pinsky) **27**:157, 164, 172
"Window Poems" (Berry) **28**:5, 39
"The Windows" (Apollinaire) **7**:36
"The Windows" (Herbert) **4**:119, 131
"The Windows" (Mallarme)
See "Les fenêtres"
"Windows in th Straw" (Bissett) **14**:8
"Windows to the Fifth Season" (Elytis) **21**:118
"Windröschen" (Celan) **10**:122
"Winds" (Auden) **1**:23
"The Winds" (Williams) **7**:369
Winds (Perse) **23**:215-16, 247
See *Vents*
"The Winds of Orisha" (Lorde) **12**:155
"The Wind's Prophecy" (Hardy) **8**:115-17
"the Wind's Way" (Swinburne) **24**:327
Windsor Forest (Pope) **26**:315, 319, 321
"The Windy City" (Sandburg) **2**:306, 308, 314
"The Wine" (Ashbery) **26**:135-136
Wine from These Grapes (Millay) **6**:214, 217, 232
"The Wine Menagerie" (Crane) **3**:81, 90
"Wine: Passages 12" (Duncan) **2**:108
"The Winged Horse" (Belloc) **24**:11
"Wingfoot Lake" (Dove) **6**:112
"Wings" (Hughes) **7**:132, 137
"Wings of a God" (Levertov) **11**:176
"Winiter's gone the summer breezes" (Clare) **23**:23
"Winkel im Wald" (Trakl) **20**:232
"Der Winkel von Hahrdt" (Holderlin) **4**:148
"Winning His Way" (Stein) **18**:312-14, 316
"The Winnowers" (Bridges) **28**:66-7
"Wino" (Hughes) **7**:123, 132, 137
"Winston Prairie" (Masters) **1**:343
"Winter" (Celan) **10**:129
"Winter" (Clare) **23**:44-5
"Winter" (Dario)
See "Invernal"
"Winter" (Giovanni) **19**:116
"Winter" (Hagiwara Sakutaro) **18**:168
"Winter" (Milosz) **8**:210
"Winter" (Wright) **14**:376
"Winter, a Dirge" (Burns) **6**:52
"Winter Encounters" (Tomlinson) **17**:333, 344, 352
"Winter Evening" (Pushkin)
See "Zimniy Vecher"
"Winter Event" (Cassian) **17**:5
"Winter Festivities" (Pasternak) **6**:266
"Winter Fields" (Clare) **23**:45
"Winter Garden" (Neruda)
See "Jardín de invierno"
"Winter Holding off the Coast of North America" (Momaday) **25**:219
"Winter in Dunbarton" (Lowell) **3**:218-19
Winter Love (H. D.) **5**:299-300
"Winter on the River" (Meredith) **28**:198
"Winter: My Secret" (Rossetti) **7**:281
"A Winter Piece" (Bryant) **20**:18, 35-7, 39
"Winter Piece" (Tomlinson) **17**:325
"A Winter Poem For Tony Weinberger Written on the Occasion of Feeling Very Happy" (Wakoski) **15**:331
"A Winter Scene" (Bryant) **20**:15
"The Winter Ship" (Plath) **1**:389
"Winter Sleep" (Wylie) **23**:309, 329, 332
"Winter Sleepers" (Atwood) **8**:12
"Winter Song" (Owen) **19**:336, 343
"Winter Swan" (Bogan) **12**:95, 106, 122
Winter Trees (Plath) **1**:396
"The Winter Twilight Glowing Black and Gold" (Schwartz) **8**:295
"Winter Verse for His Sister" (Meredith) **28**:213
"Words for Maria" (Merrill) **28**:224, 231, 264, 277
"Words of Comfort to be Scratched on a Mirror" (Parker) **28**:361
Winter Words: Various Moods and Metres (Hardy) **8**:89, 96, 124
"Wintering" (Plath) **1**:410, 412-13
Wintering Out (Heaney) **18**:188, 192-95, 199, 202-5, 209-11, 215, 238, 241, 252
Wintermarchen (Heine)
See *Deutschland: Ein Wintermärchen*
"Winternacht" (Trakl) **20**:229
"A Winter's Day" (Dunbar) **5**:126
"The Winter's Night" (Merton) **10**:340, 351
"A Winter's Tale" (Thomas) **2**:382, 385, 402
Winter's Tale (Heine)
See *Deutschland: Ein Wintermärchen*
"Wintry" (Gozzano)
See "A Wintry Scene"
"A Wintry Scene" (Gozzano) **10**:177-78, 180
"Wintry Sky" (Pasternak) **6**:250
"Wirers" (Sassoon) **12**:267, 285
"Wires" (Tsvetaeva)
See "Provoda"
"Wiretapping" (Montale)
See "Intercettazione telefonica"
"Das wirkliche Messer" (Enzensberger) **28**:159-61
"Wisdom" (Parker) **28**:362
"Wisdom Cometh with the Years" (Cullen) **20**:52, 62
"The Wise" (Cullen) **20**:54-55
"Wise Men in Their Bad Hours" (Jeffers) **17**:129
"The Wish" (Lermontov) **18**:277, 295
"Wish: Metamorphosis to Hearldic Emblem" (Atwood) **8**:32, 39
"The Wish to Be Generous" (Berry) **28**:43
"The Wish to Escape into Inner Space" (Swenson) **14**:250
"Wishbones" (Wakoski) **15**:332
"Wishes" (Wright) **14**:355
"wishes for sons" (Clifton) **17**:29, 36
"The Wishing Tree" (Heaney) **18**:229, 232
"Witch Burning" (Plath) **1**:394
"Witch Doctor" (Hayden) **6**:186, 196
"The Witch of Atlas" (Shelley) **14**:174, 193, 196, 198
"The Witch of Coös" (Frost) **1**:197, 209, 220
"Witches are Flying" (Shapiro) **25**:316
"The Witch's Life" (Sexton) **2**:373
"Witch-Woman" (Lowell) **13**:61, 64
"With a Guitar, to Jane" (Shelley) **14**:177, 189
"With a Rose to Brunhilde" (Lindsay) **23**:286
"With All Deliberate Speed" (Madhubuti) **5**:346
"With Eyes At The Back of Our Heads" (Levertov) **11**:168
With Eyes at the Back of Our Heads (Levertov) **11**:168, 205
"With Garments Flowinig" (Clare) **23**:23
"With Happiness Stretch's across the Hills" (Blake) **12**:36
"With Her Lips Only" (Graves) **6**:151
"With Mercy for the Greedy" (Sexton) **2**:346, 348, 351, 370
"With Official Lu Hsiang Passing Hermit Hsiu-Chung's Bower" (Wang Wei) **18**:358
"With Rue My Heart Is Laden" (Housman) **2**:180, 184, 192
"With Scindia to Delhi" (Kipling) **3**:182
"With Seed the Sowers Scatter" (Housman) **2**:180
"With the Caribou" (Kumin) **15**:212, 223
"With the World in My Bloodstream" (Merton) **10**:345
"With Trumpets and Zithers" (Milosz)
See "Natrabach i na cytrze"
"With Vengeance Like a Tiger Crawls" (Bukowski) **18**:5
"Without" (Snyder) **21**:297
"Without a Counterpart" (Gunn) **26**:218
"Without Benefit of Declaration" (Hughes) **1**:252
"Without Ceremony" (Hardy) **8**:134-35
"Without End" (Zagajewski) **27**:383
"Without Faith" (Aleixandre) **15**:5
"The Witness" (Tomlinson) **17**:344
A Witness Tree (Frost) **1**:196-97, 203, 205-06
"The Witnesses" (Auden) **1**:22
"Wives in the Sere" (Hardy) **8**:90
"Wizards" (Noyes) **27**:135
"Wm. Brazier" (Graves) **6**:143
"Wodwo" (Hughes) **7**:127-28, 155
Wodwo (Hughes) **7**:120-23, 133-34, 136-38, 140-42, 150, 157-60, 163, 171-72
"Woefully arrayed" (Skelton) **25**:330
"Wolf" (Mandelstam) **14**:149
"Wolfe Tone" (Heaney) **18**:228, 232
"The Woman" (Carruth) **10**:71
"The Woman" (Levertov) **11**:213-14
"A Woman" (Pinsky) **27**:176
"A Woman Alone" (Levertov) **11**:210
"Woman and Tree" (Graves) **6**:149
"A Woman Dead in Her Forties" (Rich) **5**:379-80, 394
"The Woman Hanging From the Thirteenth Floor" (Harjo) **27**:64-65
"A Woman Homer Sung" (Yeats) **20**:329
"A Woman in Heat Wiping Herself" (Olds) **22**:316
"Woman in Orchard" (Wright) **14**:373
"Woman Like You" (Ondaatje) **28**:314
"Woman of Strength" (Tagore)
See "Sabala"
"The Woman of the Sumpul River" (Alegria) **26**:
"Woman Poem" (Giovanni) **19**:108
"A Woman Resurrected" (Gozzano) **10**:177-78
"A Woman Speaks" (Lorde) **12**:160
"Woman to Child" (Wright) **14**:337, 341, 349, 352, 360, 362, 364
"Woman to Man" (Wright) **14**:333, 336-39, 349, 358-60, 363
Woman to Man (Wright) **14**:334, 336-38, 341, 345-47, 349, 352, 358, 363, 365-66, 369
"A Woman Waits for Me" (Whitman) **3**:372, 387
"The Woman Who Lived in a Crate" (Stryk) **27**:187
"The Woman Who Raised Goats" (Gallagher) **9**:35-6, 59
"Woman with Girdle" (Sexton) **2**:346, 350
"Woman With the Blue-Ringed Bowl" (McGuckian) **27**:102
"A Woman Young and Old" (Yeats) **20**:327
"The Womanhood" (Brooks) **7**:54
"Woman's Constancy" (Donne) **1**:125
"Woman's Song" (Wright) **14**:349, 352, 364
"Women" (Bogan) **12**:101
"Women" (Rich) **5**:370
"Women" (Swenson) **14**:279
The Women and the Men (Giovanni) **19**:114, 124, 128, 130, 137
"The Women at Point Sur" (Jeffers) **17**:130
The Women at Point Sur (Jeffers) **17**:107, 109-11, 116, 124, 135, 144-46
"The Women of Dan Dance With Swords in Their Hands to Mark the Time When They Were Warriors" (Lorde) **12**:159-60
"the women you are accustomed to" (Clifton) **17**:30
"Women's Tug of War at Lough Arrow" (Gallagher) **9**:37
"The Wonder Castle" (Illyes) **16**:234, 250
"The Wonder Woman" (Giovanni) **19**:107, 110, 112
"The Wonderful Musician" (Sexton) **2**:365
"Wonga Vine" (Wright) **14**:348
"Woodcutting on Lost Mountain" (Gallagher) **9**:60
The Wooden Pegasus (Sitwell) **3**:301-02
"The Woodlot" (Clampitt) **19**:89
"The Woodman" (Clare) **23**:13
"Woodnotes" (Emerson) **18**:79, 87-88, 99, 102-3, 108-10
"The Woodpile" (Frost) **1**:220, 222, 226, 228
"Woodrow Wilson (February, 1924)" (Jeffers) **17**:107

"Woods" (Berry) **28**:43
"Wooing" (Bridges) **28**:63, 86
"A Word" (Chesterton) **28**:100
"The Word" (Smith) **12**:354
"Word Basket Woman" (Snyder) **21**:326
"The Word 'Beautiful'" (Swenson) **14**:250
"The Word Crys Out" (Ammons) **16**:25
"A Word on the Quick and Modern Poem-Makers" (Bukowski) **18**:5
Word over All (Day Lewis) **11**:144, 148
"Words" (Gunn) **26**:212
"Words" (Levine) **22**:219
"The Words" (Montale)
See "Le parole"
"Words" (Plath) **1**:409
"Words" (Sexton) **2**:372-73
"Words" (Yeats) **20**:329, 331
"Words for a Wall-Painting" (Shapiro) **25**:304
"Words for Hart Crane" (Lowell) **3**:219, 222
"Words for Music Perhaps" (Yeats) **20**:326-29, 331, 333
Words for Music Perhaps, and Other Poems (Yeats) **20**:328, 334
"Words for the Hour" (Harper) **21**:190
"Words for the Wind" (Roethke) **15**:263
Words for the Wind: The Collected Verse of Theodore Roethke (Roethke) **15**:257, 262-64, 267, 282, 284, 286, 288, 309
Words in th Fire (Bissett) **14**:13-14
"Words in the Mourning Time" (Hayden) **6**:197-98
Words in the Mourning Time (Hayden) **6**:179, 181-83, 193, 195
"Words of Comfort" (Ammons) **16**:25, 43
"The Words of the Poet" (Aleixandre) **15**:6
"The Words of the Preacher" (Kunitz) **19**:149, 170
"Words on a Windy Day" (Stryk) **27**:212
"Words, Roses, Stars" (Wright) **14**:378-79
"Work" (Hass) **16**:249
"Work Gangs" (Sandburg) **2**:304, 308
"Work in Progress" (MacDiarmid) **9**:199
"Work Song" (Berry) **28**:8-9
Work Is Tiresome (Pavese)
See *Lavorare stanca*
"Work Wearies" (Pavese)
See "Lavorare stanca"
Work Wearies (Pavese)
See *Lavorare stanca*
"A Worker Reads History" (MacDiarmid) **9**:181
"Working on the '58 Willys Pickup" (Snyder) **21**:300
"A Working Party" (Sassoon) **12**:257, 261-62, 277-78, 284
"The Workingman's Drink" (Baudelaire) **1**:47
Works (Pope) **26**:359-60
Works, 1735--Poems on Several Occasions (Swift) **9**:256
"The Works and Wonders of Almighty Power" (Thomson) **23**:
Works II (Pope) **26**:360
The Works of Aphra Behn (Behn) **13**:16, 18
The Works of George Herbert (Herbert) **4**:107
The Works of Horace, Translated into Verse (Smart) **13**:361-62
The Works of William Blake (Blake) **12**:51
"The World" (Herbert) **4**:100
"The World" (Milosz) **8**:187, 192, 194, 207, 209
"The World" (Rossetti) **7**:277
"The World" (Smith) **12**:328
"The World" (Tagore)
See "Vasundhara"
World Alone (Aleixandre)
See *Mundo a solas*
"The World and the Child" (Merrill) **28**:249
"The World and the Child" (Wright) **14**:352
"The World and the Quietist" (Arnold) **5**:38, 49
"A World in Crystal" (Illyes) **16**:249
"The World Is a Beautiful Place" (Ferlinghetti) **1**:180, 182-83
"The World Is a Wedding" (Schwartz) **8**:303
"A World Is Everyone" (Ekeloef) **23**:80
"The World Is Full of Remarkable Things" (Baraka) **4**:23-4
"The World of Fantasy the Buddha Saw" (Hagiwara Sakutaro) **18**:178
The World of Gwendolyn Brooks (Brooks) **7**:64, 66, 105
World of the Buddha (Stryk) **27**:181, 194, 198
"The World Outside" (Levertov) **11**:168, 193
"World Soul" (Bely) **11**:24
"The World State" (Chesterton) **28**:100
Worldly Hopes (Ammons) **16**:45-6
"Worlds" (Masters) **1**:333
"Worlds Back of Worlds" (Masters) **1**:343
"The World's Desire" (Masters) **1**:333
"World's End" (Ashbery) **26**:166
"The World's Wonders" (Jeffers) **17**:141
"The World-Soul" (Emerson) **18**:86
"The Worms of History" (Graves) **6**:137, 142, 144
"The Wormwood Star" (Milosz) **8**:201, 204
"Worsening Situation" (Ashbery) **26**:124
"The Worst Of It" (Sassoon) **12**:248
Worthy It Is (Elytis)
See *The Axion Esti*
"Would Jacob Wrestle with a Flabby Angel?" (Viereck) **27**:286
"The Wound" (Gluck) **16**:124, 138, 154
"The Wound" (Gunn) **26**:199, 206-207
"The Wound" (Hardy) **8**:93
"The Wound" (Soto) **28**:375
The Wound (Hughes) **7**:155
"The Wounded Wilderness of Morris Graves" (Ferlinghetti) **1**:165
Woven Stone (Ortiz) **17**:244
"The Wraith" (Roethke) **15**:256, 272
"The Wrath of Samson" (Vigny)
See "La colère de Samson"
"A Wreath" (Herbert) **4**:127, 130
"Wreath" (Illyes) **16**:250
"The Wreck of the Deutschland" (Hopkins) 129, 131-32, 134, 136-38, 144, 146, 151-52, 156, 170, 172-73
"The Wreck of the Thresher" (Meredith) **28**:178, 181, 193-94, 200, 206, 213, 215
The Wreck of the Thresher (Meredith) **28**:175, 178, 191-95, 209, 211, 213, 215
"Wreckage" (Momaday) **25**:221
"The Wrestler's Heart" (Soto) **28**:394, 399
"The Wretched One" (Marie de France) See "Le Chaitivel"
"Write It Down" (Ekeloef) **23**:86
"The Writhing Imperfect Earth" (Lindsay) **23**:281
"Writing" (Nemerov) **24**:259
writing for the blind (Enzensberger)
See *Blindenchrift*
"Writing in the Dark" (Levertov) **11**:199
"Writing to Aaron" (Levertov) **11**:208
Writing Writing (Duncan) **2**:106
"The Writings Depart" (Breton) **15**:73
"Written aboard a Boat on the Day of Little Cold Food" (Tu Fu) **9**:320
"Written after Long Rains at My Villa by Wang Stream" (Wang Wei) **18**:392
"Written by Dr. Swift on His Own Deafness" (Swift) **9**:295
"Written in a Lady's Ivory Table-book, 1698" (Swift) **9**:251, 295
"Written in Emerson's Essays" (Arnold) **5**:38, 49
"Written in the Mountains in Early Autumn" (Wang Wei) **18**:392
"Written on The Door" (Perse) **23**:229
Written on Water (Tomlinson) **17**:321-23, 327, 333
Written on Water (Tomlinson) **17**:321-23, 327, 333
"The Wrong Kind of Insurance" (Ashbery) **26**:134
"Wrong Number" (Bukowski) **18**:4
"die wu¨rgengel" (Enzensberger) **28**:134
Xaipe: Seventy-One Poems (Cummings) **5**:82-3, 86, 107-08
Xenia (Martial) **10**:230
Xenia (Montale) **13**:132-33, 135-36, 138, 165, 167
"Xenia I" (Montale) **13**:144
"Xenia II" (Montale) **13**:144
"Xenion" (Montale) **13**:133-34
"Xenion" No. 7 (Montale) **13**:134
Xénophiles (Breton) **15**:53-4
"Xoanon" (Ekeloef) **23**:67
"XVI" (Shapiro) **25**:285
"XXX" (Joyce) **22**:138, 144-45, 164, 173
Y and X (Olson) **19**:318
"Ya que para despedirme" (Juana Ines de la Cruz) **24**:180
"The Yachts" (Williams) **7**:360, 368
"Yalluh Hammer" (Walker) **20**:273, 275-76, 286, 292
"Yam" (Merrill) **28**:259
"Yama no ugoku hi" (Yosano Akiko) **11**:321
"Yamanote Sen" (Hongo) **23**:197
"Los yaruros" (Cardenal) **22**:132
"Yauvan-svapna" (Tagore) **8**:407
"Yawm mawlidi" (Gibran) **9**:78
"Ye Are Na Mary Morison" (Burns) **6**:99
"Ye Know My Herte" (Wyatt) **27**:314-15
"Ye old mule" (Wyatt) **27**:362
"yeah man?" (Bukowski) **18**:14
"The Year 1905" (Pasternak)
See "Devyatsat pyaty god"
"Year at Mudstraw" (Forche) **10**:133
"The Year of Mourning" (Jeffers) **17**:141
"The Year of the Double Spring" (Swenson) **14**:267, 275
"The Years" (Aleixandre) **15**:4
The Years as Catches (Duncan) **2**:104, 109
"The Year's Awakening" (Hardy) **8**:105
"Years of Indiscretion" (Ashbery) **26**:115, 124
"A Year's Spinning" (Browning) **6**:32
"A Year's Windfalls" (Rossetti) **7**:262
"Yee Bow" (Masters) **1**:327
"Yell'ham Wood's Story" (Hardy) **8**:91
The Yellow Heart (Neruda)
See *El corazón amarillo*
The Yellow House on the Corner (Dove) **6**:104-09, 116, 118, 122
"Yellow Light" (Hongo) **23**:203
Yellow Light (Hongo) **23**:195, 197, 202-204
"Yellow Ribbons, Baghdad 1991" (Rose) **13**:241
"The Yellow Violet" (Bryant) **20**:4, 35, 40
"Yellowhammer's Nest" (Clare) **23**:5
"Yes" (Ferlinghetti) **1**:187
"Yes" (Gallagher) **9**:64-5
"Yes and It's Hopeless" (Ginsberg) **4**:76, 85
"Yes, I am lying in the earth, moving my lips" (Mandelstam)
See "Da, ia lezhu v zemle . . ."
"Yesterday" (Aleixandre) **15**:5
"Yesterday" (Sitwell) **3**:293
"Yesterday I Was Called Nigger" (Guillen)
See "Ayer me dijeron negro"
"Yestreen I Had a Pint o' Wine" (Burns) **6**:75
"Yet Do I Marvel" (Cullen) **20**:63, 76
"the yeti poet returns to his village to tell his story" (Clifton) **17**:30
"Les yeux des pauvres" (Baudelaire) **1**:58
"Yeux Glauques" (Pound) **4**:319
Yevgeny Onegin (Pushkin) **10**:357-62, 366, 368-69, 371, 374-83, 386, 391, 400-04, 406, 409
"YgUDuh" (Cummings) **5**:98
"Ylang-Ylang" (McGuckian) **27**:83
"Yo" (Fuertes) **27**:26, 49-50
"Yo persigo una forma" (Dario) **15**:103-04, 119
"Yo soy aqué1" (Dario) **15**:97
Yobuko to kuchibue (Ishikawa) **10**:211
"Yogisha" (Hagiwara Sakutaro) **18**:168, 179, 183
"Yonder See the Morning Blink" (Housman) **2**:179
"Yonec" (Marie de France) **22**:241-45, 258,

260-66, 269-72, 274-75, 299-300, 302-03
"York: In Memoriam W. H. Auden" (Brodsky) **9**:12
"You" (Cummings) **5**:105
"You All Are State I Alone Am Moving" (Viereck) **27**:258
You All Are Static I Alone Am Moving (Viereck) **27**:
"You All Know the Story of the Other Woman" (Sexton) **2**:352-53
"You and Me" (Tagore)
See "Tumi o ami"
"You Are" (Swenson) **14**:274, 283-84
"You Are Happy" (Atwood) **8**:25, 27
You Are Happy (Atwood) **8**:20-4, 29, 31, 33, 41-2
"You are old Father William" (Carroll) **18**:49
"You Are Waiting" (Aleixandre) **15**:6
"You Asked About My Life; I Send You, Pei Di, These Lines" (Wang Wei) **18**:391
"You Be Like You" (Celan)
See "Du sei wei du"
"You Bet Travel Is Broadening" (Nash) **21**:273
"You Can Have It" (Levine) **22**:223
You Can't Get There from Here (Nash) **21**:274
"You, Dr. Martin" (Sexton) **2**:359, 365
"You Drive in a Circle" (Hughes) **7**:137
"You Frog!" (Hagiwara Sakutaro)
See "You Frog!"
"You Have a Name" (Aleixandre) **15**:5
"You may not see the Nazis" (Brutus) **24**:118
"You Speak No English" (Guillen)
See "Tú no sabe inglé"
"You Talk on Your Telephone; I Talk on Mine" (Gallagher) **9**:59
"You Think of the Sun That It" (Ammons) **16**:43
"The Young" (Aleixandre) **15**:5
"Young" (Sexton) **2**:350
"Young Africans" (Brooks) **7**:65, 91, 93
"A Young Birch" (Frost) **1**:200
"The Young British Soldier" (Kipling) **3**:158
Young Cherry Trees Secured Against Hares (Breton) **15**:47
"A Young Child and His Pregnant Mother" (Schwartz) **8**:282, 302, 304
"The Young Cordwainer" (Graves) **6**:144
The Young Fate (Valery)
See *La jeune parque*
"Young Girls" (Page) **12**:176
"Young Heroes" (Brooks) **7**:92-3, 105
"The Young Housewife" (Williams) **7**:348, 363, 378, 409
"Young Love" (Marvell) **10**:303-04
"Young Love" (Williams) **7**:382, 410
"The Young Lovers" (Aleixandre) **15**:4-6
"The Young Mage" (Bogan) **12**:100
"Young Man with Letter" (Ashbery) **26**:125
"A Young Man's Exhortation" (Hardy) **8**:108
"Young Man's Song" (Yeats) **20**:331, 333
"Young Mothers" (Olds) **22**:328
"Young Mothers I" (Olds) **22**:308
"Young Singer" (Hughes) **1**:236, 246
"Young Sorrows"
See "Junge Leiden"
"Young Soul" (Baraka) **4**:9
"Young Sycamore" (Williams) **7**:372-77
"The Young Warrior" (Johnson) **24**:127, 166
"The Youngest Daughter" (Song) **21**:331-32, 350
"Your Birthday in the California Mountains" (Rexroth) **20**:204
"Your Face on the Dog's Neck" (Sexton) **2**:363
"Your Flight" (Montale)
See "Il tuo volo"
"Your Last Drive" (Hardy) **8**:134
"Your Lead Partner I Hope We've Read the Same Book" (Nash) **21**:
Your Native Land, Your Life (Rich) **5**:387-89
"You're" (Plath) **1**:389-90
"You's Sweet to Yo' Mammy jes de Same" (Johnson) **24**:141
"Youth" (Akhmatova) **2**:8
"Youth" (Zukofsky) **11**:368
"Youth and Calm" (Arnold) **5**:42, 51
"Youth in Heaven" (Harper) **21**:209
"The Youth of Man" (Arnold) **5**:19, 49
"The Youth of Nature" (Arnold) **5**:19, 42, 49, 51, 59
"The Youth's Magic Horn" (Ashbery) **26**:162
"Ys It Possyble" (Wyatt) **27**:317, 324
Ysopet (Marie de France) **22**:258-59
yu can eat it at th opening (Bissett) **14**:17
"yu know th creaturs ar ourselvs" (Bissett) **14**:34
"yu sing" (Bissett) **14**:30
"yu want th music" (Bissett) **14**:34
"Yube no kane" (Ishikawa) **10**:214
"Yube no umi" (Ishikawa) **10**:213, 215
"Yugel'skii baron" (Lermontov) **18**:288
"Za Ki Tan Ke Parlay Lot" (Lorde) **12**:155
Zahme Xenien (Goethe) **5**:223
"Zakinuv golovu i opustiv glaza" (Tsvetaeva) **14**:319, 322-23
"Zambesi and Ranee" (Swenson) **14**:277
"Zaporogue" (Apollinaire) **7**:48
"Ein zärtlich jugendlicher Kummer" (Goethe) **5**:247
"Zauberspruch" (Celan) **10**:124-25
"Zaveshchanije" (Lermontov) **18**:303
"Zaydee" (Levine) **22**:223
"Zeitgedichte" (Heine) **25**:131, 134
Zeitgedichte (Heine) **25**:129
Zeitgehöft (Celan) **10**:96, 111
"Der Zeitgeist" (Holderlin) **4**:166
"Zen Poems of China and Japan: The Crane's Bill" (Stryk) **27**:181
"Zen Poetry" (Stryk) **27**:188
"The Zeppelin Factory" (Dove) **6**:110
"Zero" (Gallagher) **9**:58
"Zero" (Berry) **28**:6
"Zero Hour" (Cardenal)
See "La hora O"
Zero Hour and Other Documentary Poems (Cardenal) **22**:117
"Zeroing In" (Levertov) **11**:205
"Zeus over Redeye" (Hayden) **6**:183, 194
"Zhil Na Svete Rytsar' Bednyi" (Pushkin) **10**:411
"Zikade" (Enzensberger) **28**:139
"Zimniy Vecher" (Pushkin) **10**:381
"Zim-Zizimi" (Hugo) **17**:59
"Znayu" (Bely) **11**:32
Zoloto v lazuri (Bely) **11**:3-6, 22, 26, 31-2
"Zone" (Ammons) **16**:6, 28
"Zone" (Apollinaire) **7**:6, 10-12, 14-15, 21, 41, 44-8
"Zone" (Bogan) **12**:126
"Zoo de verbena" (Fuertes) **27**:16
"Zoo Keeper's Wife" (Plath) **1**:399
Zovy vremen (Bely) **11**:31-2
"Zueignung" (Goethe) **5**:257
"Zuleika" (Goethe) **5**:228
Zvezda (Bely) **11**:7, 24, 30, 32